STUDENT'S ENGLISH DICTIONARY

MARTIN MANSER AND

NIGEL TURTON

Acknowledgements

The editors acknowledge their indebtedness to the following: Rod Neilsen; Paul R. Manser; Gwyn Johnson; Dr J. M. Hill of the School of English, University of Leeds; Professor David Crystal of University College of North Wales; Donald McFarlan; Rosalind Desmond; Lynn Elias; and Rosalind Fergusson.

Printed in China

Tribute to Nigel Turton

Nigel died in January 2007 while this edition was being prepared for publication. We gratefully recognize his considerable inspiration, dedication and enthusiasm, which have been vital to the success of this dictionary. He is warmly remembered as a trusted colleague and good friend.

CONTENTS

PREFACE

I think there are few people (apart from lexicographers) who would describe a dictionary as leisure reading. Dictionaries are traditionally meant to solve your lexical problems—to check on a spelling, or a meaning, or (if you're a Scrabbler) to establish whether a word exists at all. It is a close encounter of the briefest kind: you open the book, find the word, check the point, and close the book. Most of a dictionary, therefore, remains forever unread—which is a shame, for there is nothing more fascinating than the biography of the words of your language. But the average dictionary is not for browsing.

This dictionary, however, is no average dictionary. It has all the usual features of a work of this size, of course; but it also contains elements from other kinds of word-book, such as the thesaurus, the usage guide, the teaching lexicon, and the historical survey. It is difficult to know what to call it. 'Dictionary' comes closest, but that leaves out half of what is going on.

What makes this book so different is the way the editors have used expository panels throughout the work—panels which present a point of usage, the history of a word, an area of vocabulary, or the nuances of a definition. When you look a word up, you get a bonus, in the form of a panel. It makes you stop and read on, learning more than you bargained for. It's a novel and interesting idea, and one which is bound to prove attractive both to mother-tongue users and to foreign students of English.

The home user will surely be fascinated by the panels on the origins of words. Why on earth do we say that something is a *shambles*? What's the origin of *barmy*, *pantechnicon*, *quiz*, and *white elephant*? Why do we say *between the devil and the deep blue sea* (it's nothing to do with Satan)? Most dictionaries give only a brief and dry reference to the shape of a word in an earlier state of the language: this one goes further, into the meaning and social background as well. These etymologies have blood in their veins.

The foreign student will find the panel lists of words and idioms particularly helpful. Look at the various uses of *hang* and *hell,* for example, or the collections of phrases based on a single theme, such as parts of the body (see the panel at *toe*) or clothing (see the panel at *sock*). I can imagine these lists being much appreciated in classroom discussions of English idioms, especially as a great deal of care has been taken to make the examples of usage contemporary and convincing.

This is a dictionary to be read, as well as used. The test, quite simply, is to open it, at any page, and see if you can stop yourself browsing. I couldn't.

David Crystal

HOW TO USE THE DICTIONARY

☐ ORDER OF ENTRIES. All main entries in the dictionary are in alphabetical order. Where words have the same spelling but a different history, they are shown as separate entries, with small raised numbers.

tear[1] (tɪə) *n* one of the drops of salty liquid that lubricate the eye and which are shed during times of grief, etc. **in tears** weeping: I found her in tears. **tear-drop** *n* a tear. **tearful** *adj* shedding, about to shed, or accompanied by tears: a tearful goodbye. **tear-gas** *n* any substance which causes the eyes to be blinded with floods of tears. **tear-jerker** *n* a sentimental story, film, etc., that is intended to provoke tears or sadness. < Old English *tēar.*

tear[2] (tɛə) *vb* **tore; torn; tearing 1** pull violently apart or into pieces: She tore the letter up. **2** seize or remove violently: He tore the book from my grasp. **3** make (a hole or opening in) by tearing: Its claws tore holes in his sleeve. **4** be easily torn: The advantage of this fabric is it won't tear. **5** rush or hurry. **tearaway** *n* (*informal*) a wild or reckless young person. < Old English *teran.*

☐ IRREGULAR PARTS. Plurals of nouns, comparatives (-*er*) and superlatives (-*est*) of adjectives and adverbs, and inflected forms of verbs are shown if they are irregular or where there might be doubt about the spelling. With verbs, where two parts are shown, the first is the past tense and past participle, the second is the present participle. Where three parts are shown, the first is the past tense, the second is the past participle and the third is the present participle.

shelf (ʃɛlf) *n, pl* **shelves 1** a thin, flat, long, narrow board fastened horizontally to the wall, in a cupboard, etc., to display or store things on. **2** something resembling this; ledge. **on the shelf** no longer of use or sought after; esp. of an

send (sɛnd) *vb* **sent; sending 1** cause to be conveyed by a means of communication: send a letter. **2** bring to a particular condition: It sent him crazy. **3** pass on (a message or request) for delivery. **4** direct; request: send out for groceries.

fat (fæt) *adj* **fatter; fattest 1** containing much fat. **2** too plump. **3** thick: a fat book **4** substantial: fat profits.
• *n* an oily substance in animal tissue and plant seeds; this substance used in cooking. **fatness** *n* < Old English *fæt*

run (rʌn) *vb* **ran; run; running 1** (of a person or animal) move quickly. **2** cover (a distance) by running: I ran two miles this morning. **3** move on or as if on wheels, castors, or runners. **4** (of water) flow. **5** (of a machine) operate or function:

☐ DEFINITIONS AND EXAMPLES. Definitions are numbered; examples are included to reflect natural English usage.

> **delicate** (ˈdɛlɪkət) *adj* **1** subtle or fine in quality or structure. **2** subtly pleasant in effect on the senses: delicate colours; delicate taste. **3** extremely frail or sensitive: delicate plants; delicate health. **4** calling for careful treatment: a delicate situation. **5** precise; sensitive to the touch: delicate mechanism.

☐ PRONUNCIATIONS. Pronunciations are given in the internationally recognized phonetic alphabet of the International Phonetic Association, and represent the standard speech of British English.

p	as in	*p*an	æ	as in	b*a*d
b	as in	*b*ed	ɑː	as in	f*a*ther
t	as in	*t*ea	ã	as in	vol-au-v*ent*
d	as in	*d*ig	iː	as in	s*ee*
k	as in	*k*eep	ɪ	as in	*i*t
x	as in	lo*ch*	ɛ	as in	g*e*t
g	as in	*g*o	ɒ	as in	h*o*t
tʃ	as in	*ch*eese	ɔː	as in	s*aw*
dʒ	as in	*j*am	ʊ	as in	p*u*sh
f	as in	*f*or	uː	as in	z*oo*
v	as in	*v*an	ʌ	as in	*u*p
θ	as in	*th*in	ɜː	as in	b*ir*d
ð	as in	*th*ese	ə	as in	driv*er*
s	as in	*s*it	aɪ	as in	tr*y*
z	as in	*z*ero	aʊ	as in	n*ow*
ʃ	as in	*sh*ip	eɪ	as in	m*ay*
ʒ	as in	trea*s*ure	ɛə	as in	d*are*
h	as in	*h*at	ɪə	as in	h*ere*
m	as in	*m*an	əʊ	as in	n*o*
n	as in	*n*o	ɔɪ	as in	b*oy*
ŋ	as in	si*ng*	ʊə	as in	c*ure*
l	as in	*l*ie			
r	as in	*r*ed	ˈ		before a syllable with main stress as in *sis*ter
j	as in	*y*es			
w	as in	*w*in	ˌ		before a syllable with secondary stress as in cele*brate*
			̩		under *l, m, n, r* to show that the sound is pronounced as a syllable as in bott*le*

☐ STYLE MARKERS. Some of the words and definitions are marked to show that their use is restricted to particular situations or that they are used only by certain people.

adduce (ə'djuːs) *vb* (*formal*) offer as evidence, a reason, etc. < Latin *adducere* to lead to.

into ('ɪntə; *stressed* 'ɪntuː) *prep* **1** to the inside of: get into the car. **2** to a condition, state, or occupation that is mentioned: grow into a man; translate into Spanish; go into banking. **3** against: He drove into a wall. **4** advancing to the middle of: far into the night. **5** used to show division: 4 into 12 goes 3. **6** (*informal*) interested in; involved with: He's heavily into jazz. < Old English. SEE PANEL.

☐ UNDEFINED WORDS. Words whose meaning can easily be worked out, because they are made up of the base word and an ending, are not defined. Such words follow the definition of the base word.

racy ('reɪsɪ) *adj* **1** spirited or vigorous. **2** suggestive or risqué. **racily** *adv* **raciness** *n* < *race*^{2}.

☐ ETYMOLOGIES. A concise history of each word is shown at the end of its entry after the symbol <.

ferrous ('fɛrəs) *adj* of or containing iron. < Latin *ferrum* iron.

☐ CROSS-REFERENCES. At the end of many entries are cross-references to where further information may be found or to a panel.

abode^1 (ə'bəʊd) *n* (*formal*) a home; dwelling-place. < SEE **ABIDE.**

acrobat ('ækrəˌbæt) *n* a person who performs gymnastic feats. **acrobatic** *adj* **acrobatics** *pl n* **1** acrobatic feats. **2** any activity requiring agility and skill: verbal acrobatics. SEE PANEL.

acronym ('ækrəˌnɪm) *n* a word formed from the initial letters of other words. < Greek *akros* extreme + *onyma* name. SEE PANEL AT **RADAR.**

□ FEATURE PANELS. Most pages feature one or more panels. These focus on a particular word, commenting on its usage, history, etc.

salary

Salary, 'the monthly sum received by an employee for his or her services', derives from the Latin word *salarium,* the part of a Roman soldier's pay that he was given for the purchase of salt (Latin *sal*). This provides an explanation of the expression not worth one's salt. A worker who is not worth his salt is one who doesn't deserve the salary he receives.

ABBREVIATIONS AND SYMBOLS

abbrev	abbreviation	*interj*	interjection
adj	adjective	*n*	noun
adv	adverb	*NZ*	New Zealand English
Brit	British English	*pl*	plural
c.	circa	*prep*	preposition
conj	conjunction	*pron*	pronoun
def.	definition	*US*	American English
defs.	definitions	*vb*	verb
esp.	especially	•	introduces a new part of speech
fem.	feminine	<	introduces an etymology

ENGLISH THROUGH THE AGES

Estimates as to the number of English users in the world today vary considerably. The figures range from a conservative 700 million up to as many as 2 billion, almost two-fifths of the world's population. The problem of calculation is fraught with difficulties. For example, are those who have learned English as a second or foreign language to be counted? If so, how fluent must they be before they are included in the reckoning?

Whatever the figure that we settle on, and one billion plus would seem to be a reasonable approximation, one thing is certain. English today is the international language *par excellence,* and fluency in English provides a passport to the ever-expanding anglophone world.

Old English

Behind the rise of English to become the world's first global tongue is a story of unparalleled fascination. The tale begins in the middle of the 5th century with the invasion of England by three Germanic tribes, the Angles, Saxons, and Jutes, rowing across from what is today northern Germany and southern Denmark. Setting the stage for the invasion was the withdrawal in 410 AD of the occupying Roman forces, who were now needed closer to home. No sooner had their country been returned to them than the native Celts again found themselves under attack. Having lived in subjection for the previous four hundred years, they were able to offer the new enemy little resistance. Most were either killed or driven back into Cornwall, Wales, Cumberland, Scotland, and Ireland. In the 7th century some managed to escape to Brittany where Breton, a descendant variety of Celtic, may still be heard.

Linguistic fossils of the pre-Anglo-Saxon period are encountered mostly in place-names. For example, the Latin word for 'camp', castra, is perpetuated in names such as *Doncaster, Winchester,* and *Cirencester,* while the Celtic word for 'water' is echoed in the names of the *Esk, Usk, Axe,* and *Exe.* However, most of the place-names we use today are of Anglo-Saxon origin.

The language spoken by the English, as the country's new wave of settlers began to call themselves, was a variety of Germanic. Like most of the languages spoken in

Europe and as far east as India, this had evolved from Indo-European, a tongue spoken some five to six thousand years ago by peoples living in the region of the Black Sea. Where Indo-European came from and, for that matter, how language itself began, remain a mystery.

Severed from their European counterparts, the newcomers gradually acquired a new, basically agrarian identity. More to the point, their language slowly developed features which made it quite distinct from other Germanic varieties. Within two hundred years of the first landings, English—nowadays referred to as Old English or Anglo-Saxon—had begun to emerge.

Old English bears very little resemblance to the English of today. Grammatically, it was akin to Modern German. Nouns and adjectives, for example, had a number of different declensions, as well as gender and case inflections. As for its vocabulary, this was almost exclusively Germanic. Unlike Modern English, Old English was a highly homogeneous tongue, with just a handful of Latin words that had been absorbed before the westward migration.

The relative purity of Old English was short-lived. From the end of the 8th century the country found itself yet again under attack, this time from marauding Danes and Norwegians. The initial raids were a precursor to armed hosts set upon conquest. Successive victories led to widespread settlement, culminating in 1016 with the enthronement of Canute as the English king. Predictably, a number of Old Norse words and expressions entered the language during this stormy period.

However, since Old Norse and Old English were ultimately of the same Germanic family, the overall effect of these Scandinavian introductions was unremarkable. Of greater influence was the reintroduction of Christianity to England in 597 AD and the conversion of the English in the decades that followed. The language of the church was Latin and a great number of Latin words, ecclesiastical and secular alike, were absorbed into English at this time.

With Latin came the Roman alphabet, a writing system that, with slight adaptations, was successfully applied to the vernacular. At the beginning of the 8th century the first texts written in Old English began to appear. Nowadays these documents are intelligible only to scholars. As an example, here is a short extract from a prose piece written under the auspices of King Alfred (849-899) and based upon West Saxon, the prestigious dialect of the day. It comes from an account of a voyage by a Scandinavian explorer named Ohthere.

> Hē sǣde ðæt Norðmanna land wǣre swȳþe lang ond swȳðe smæl. Eal þæt his man āþeroððe ettan oððe erian mæg, þæt līð wið ðā sǣ; ond þæt is þēah on sumum stōwum swȳðe clūdig; ond licgað wilde mōras wiðēastan ond wiðuppon emnlange þǣm bȳnum lande.

> He said that the land of the Norsemen was very long and very narrow. All of it that a man can either graze (cattle on) or plough, that part lies next to the sea; and that is nevertheless in some parts very rocky; and wild moors lie to the east, above and alongside the cultivated land.

Middle English

Had their own country been more hospitable, the Norsemen might well have been less tempted by the rich farming lands to be won abroad. One such prize was Normandy, to which they gave their name. Following their invasion and settlement of this region in the 9th century, the Norsemen or 'Normans' adopted many Gallic ways, including the local language. The result of the assimilation was that when their descendants invaded England in 1066, they brought with them a predominantly French culture and tongue.

More than any previous event, it was the Norman Conquest that splintered the homogeneity of English. For the next two hundred years, Norman French (Old French with a strong Germanic element) was the language of England's ruling classes. It was used for administrative and business purposes, and until as late as 1362 remained the language of the law. During these centuries the various regional dialects of English continued to be spoken, but chiefly by the peasant masses in their wattle-and-daub huts. As a medium of written expression English fell into disuse.

The re-emergence of English at the beginning of the 14th century was the outcome of sweeping changes both at home and abroad. Neither William nor his successors had regarded England as their true home. However, in the year 1204 Normandy was won back by France. Suddenly the Anglo-Normans were forced to stop looking upon England as a sort of backward colony and their attitudes towards the English became adjusted accordingly. At the same time the social gulf between lord and villein had begun to close with the disintegration of the feudal manor and the ascendancy of a predominantly English yeoman-farmer and commercial class. Many of the latter were attracted to London, the cultural, political, industrial, and commercial centre, which drew its population from all over the country. Within the educated sector of this linguistic melting-pot there developed a new form of English, an offshoot of the East Midland dialect. The prestige enjoyed by this new variety grew in leaps and bounds. Before long it had asserted itself as England's standard language and formed the basis of English as we know it today.

As a result of these developments and the integration of the two races that ensued, French was gradually displaced. However, the influence of French on Middle English was profound. Not only were vast numbers of French words absorbed into the language, but the process of grammatical simplification, already apparent towards the end of the Old English period, showed increased acceleration. Additionally, the Norman scribes made considerable orthographic changes.

All this meant that the English used by Chaucer was very different from that of King Alfred's day, as was the culture that it expressed. Unlike Old English, the language of this period is recognizably English. Its relative modernity can be glimpsed in the following extract from Chaucer's 'General Prologue' to *The Canterbury Tales,* written about 1387.

A Knyght ther was, and that a worthy man,
That fro the tyme that he first bigan
To riden out, he loved chivalrie,
Trouthe and honour, fredom and curteisie.
Ful worthy was he in his lordes werre,
And therto hadde he riden, no man ferre,
As wel in cristendom as in hethenesse,
And evere honoured for his worthynesse.

Early Modern English

The period of Middle English stretches approximately

from 1150, when the Norman influence first took a hold on the language, to the time when it had let go, about 1450. The advent of Modern English is generally associated with the arrival in Britain of the Renaissance at the beginning of the 16th century. The Renaissance or 'rebirth of learning' brought about a revival of interest in the cultures and languages of ancient Greece and Rome. As a result, English received a whole storehouse of words from Latin and a sizable number from Greek. So strong was the Latin penetration that existing English words were on occasion refashioned in accordance with their Latin roots. Such was the case with, for example, *receipt* and *debt*. In Middle English these had been written *receite* and *dette*. Suddenly, under the influence of the Latin *recipere* and *debitum*, a *p* and *b* were added.

Increased contact with the countries of Europe during the 16th and 17th centuries helped to further increase the vocabulary. Sources worthy of mention include Italy and France, and to a lesser degree, Spain, Portugal, and the Netherlands. However, in comparison with the all-pervading influence of Latin, these contributions were relatively small.

In addition to the widening of vocabulary, the English of this period is marked grammatically by a further reduction of inflections and in pronunciation by the culmination of the 'Great Vowel Shift'. The effect of the latter was to provide the long vowels of Middle English with their modern pronunciations. For example, Middle English *hous* and *mice*, pronounced (hu:s) and (mi:s), received the diphthongs with which they are pronounced today. It was an unfortunate coincidence that printing was introduced into England in 1476 while this shift in pronunciation was still under way. As a result, late Middle English spellings became fossilized in print at the very time when their equivalent pronunciations were marching on.

By the turn of the 18th century English had become, to all intents and purposes, the English we use today, so that writers of the time present the modern reader with very few difficulties. The following example is from one of Jonathan Swift's letters to Stella (Esther Johnson), dated 9 September 1710.

> I got here last Thursday, after five days traveling, weary the first, almost dead the second, tolerable the third, and well enough the rest; and am now glad of

> the fatigue, which has served for exercise; and I am at present well enough. The Whigs were ravished to see me, and would lay hold on me as a twig while they are drowning, and the great men making me their clumsy apologies, &c. But my lord treasurer received me with a great deal of coldness, which has enraged me so, I am almost vowing revenge.

English today

Over the last three hundred years the vocabulary has continued to expand. On the one hand, many new words have been fashioned from existing words and word elements. The major word-formation processes by which the language has fed upon itself include compounding (e.g. *greenhouse, teacup*), affixation (e.g. *multinational, privatize, deprivatize*), conversion (e.g. *film, audition* used as verbs), shortening (e.g. *taxi, phone*), and back formation (e.g. *burgle* from *burglar, edit* from *editor*).

The area of vocabulary that has undergone by far the most rapid expansion—virtually an explosion—is that of science and technology. Vast numbers of new words have been needed for the names of new disciplines, concepts, objects, substances, qualities, processes, and units, and

the classics have again provided an invaluable source. While some of the new words are direct borrowings, most have been produced by word-formation processes operating on Latin and Greek roots. Meanwhile the core of the vocabulary has continued to increase through world-wide borrowing and assimilation.

By far the most important chapter in the recent history of English, however, has been its establishment overseas. Beginning in the 17th century, relatively small boatloads of native speakers left British shores in search of a new life in a new land. As a consequence there are today well over 300 million people in various parts of the world using English as their mother tongue. However, the geographical distribution of native speakers does not by itself explain why English today has more users than any other language. There are many involved reasons for this, but only one that stands out as crucial, namely, the role of English as the international language of science and technology, and the influence of science and technology upon a country's economic fate.

Nigel Turton

LANDMARKS IN THE HISTORY OF ENGLISH

Roman invasion 43 AD

Roman withdrawal 410 AD

Invasion by Angles, Saxons, and Jutes in the 5th century AD

Arrival of St Augustine 597 AD

OLD ENGLISH
700–1100

First Old English written texts appear at the beginning of the 8th century

Viking raids commence towards the end of the 8th century

Canute enthroned 1016

Norman Conquest 1066

MIDDLE ENGLISH
1150–1450

Normandy won back by France 1204

Re-emergence of English at the beginning of the 14th century

Introduction of printing 1476

EARLY MODERN ENGLISH
1500–1700

Arrival of the Renaissance at the beginning of the 16th century

Landing of the first permanent English settlers in America in the 17th century

MODERN ENGLISH
1700–today

Boom in world trade and travel in the 18th century and the establishment of British colonies

Rapid growth of science and technology since the 19th century

English in the 21st century becomes the most widely spoken language in the world

ENGLISH TODAY

Two things must strike any contemporary observer of the English language at the beginning of the 21st century. First, there is its remarkable range and variety, which in recent decades has increased in ways that were totally unpredictable a century ago. And secondly, there is the equally remarkable increase in the number of people who have become aware of this fact, and wish to study it. Their reasons vary greatly. Some are concerned to safeguard the language from the effects of too rapid change. Some are worried about their ability to keep pace with changing standards in their own usage. Some are concerned to develop their awareness of new language varieties because they frequently encounter them —at home (television talk), at work (computer jargon), or while travelling (dialect words). Some are, quite simply, fascinated by the language, and wish to learn more about it. But all, as a first step, need to have access to the facts of linguistic history, structure, and use.

Regional diversity

The modern situation is largely a consequence of the growth in the number of English-language speakers in all parts of the world, especially in areas where English is not a mother tongue. Statistics about English speakers are notoriously difficult to obtain and evaluate, but there is no doubt that, in most countries, we are more likely to encounter English than any other foreign language—whether in school, in the media, or through the use of scientific or technological loan-words.

The chief result of the spread of English has been the growth of regional dialects on a world-wide scale. All languages develop dialects, of course, based on the geographical, social, ethnic, occupational, and other divisions within society; and when a language spreads across the world, the same thing happens. The *intranational* dialects of English which have existed for hundreds of years—even in Anglo-Saxon times—continue to develop (though these days within cities, rather than within country areas); and they are now supplemented by the existence of major *international* dialects. Most notably, we find the thousands of variations in spelling, pronunciation, grammar, and vocabulary which distinguish

American and British English: *color* (*colour*), *center* (*centre*), *snuck* (*sneaked*), *gotten* (*got*), *in back of* (*behind*), *fall* (*autumn*), *faucet* (*tap*), and so on. But there are many other major English-using parts of the world where standard regional varieties have developed: Wales, Scotland, Ireland, South Africa, Australia, New Zealand, Canada, India, Pakistan, Bangladesh, Sri Lanka, several countries in West and East Africa—and not forgetting the dozens of pidgin and creole Englishes used in the West Indies, Africa, South America, and the Far East.

Standard and standards

At the same time as regional differentiation takes place, there is also increasing social differentiation, reflecting the various social roles which language users perform. In older times, the *class* background of the speaker was the main reason for distinctive language—upper-class vs lower-class, in particular—and this factor continues to be important in the guise of 'educated' vs 'uneducated' language use. The modern concept of 'standard English' primarily reflects a level of language use which is the result of schooling—instilling norms of spelling, punctuation, grammatical usage, and vocabulary. But standard English is difficult to define, for several reasons. The language continues to change, as it always has, and what is the nonstandard usage of one generation can become the standard usage of the next (or vice versa). The growth of regional dialects makes it more difficult to see a universal standard in use around the world. And standard English is itself composed of hundreds of varieties which differ in sometimes quite basic ways—notably occupational differences (such as the English of science, religion, the law, and the press) and the major contrast between formal and informal English.

This last point is central to an appreciation of the nature of English today. Many of the arguments about the nature of correct usage result from a failure to appreciate that, within the domain of standard English, there are systematic variations in formality. At one extreme there is formal English, appropriate for careful, 'proper' occasions (such as job interviews); at the other extreme there is informal English for casual, everyday occasions (such as family conversation). It is sometimes thought that the formal style is somehow more 'correct' than the other, and should be used at all times—but this is no more reasonable than to assert that formal clothing should be used at all times. A varied wardrobe is usually considered to be an asset—and so it is, or should be, with our linguistic habits.

On the other hand, it has to be recognized that there are such things as our 'best clothes', for special occasions—and the same applies to language. For a mixture of historical and social reasons, certain accents, words, and grammatical usages of English are considered special by the community. All languages have *prestige* forms, which act as an important index of a person's social identity and role. In the case of English, the ability to spell, to speak carefully, to use formal grammar and vocabulary, and to follow the rules of grammatical usage as taught in schools over the past 200 years, is the most distinctive and widely-accepted sign that a person is educated. That is why there is always a concern, within a literate community, to maintain a tradition of formal mother-tongue language-teaching.

Language awareness

When formal grammar-teaching went out of fashion (notably in the UK and USA) in the 1950s and 1960s, the anxiety which many people felt was expressed as a concern over lost standards. As a result, grammar teaching is now resurfacing in several schools and syllabuses, but in a more dynamic and interesting form. In modern *language awareness* programmes, rules are not taught in isolation, to be learned off by heart as unchanging absolutes; rather, children are taught to discover the rules of language for themselves, and to develop a sense of language variation, so that they are in a better position to control and evaluate the use of linguistic forms. Just as they learn to develop their 'clothes sense', so, it is argued, they need to develop their 'language sense'.

The new approach, it is hoped, will help children to cope much more confidently with the varied and changing facts of their language. Instead of being told 'You must speak/write like this because I say so' (where 'I' might be a teacher, a grammar book, or a usage guide), they are told, in effect, 'Here are the ways different kinds of people speak/write; if you identify the differences and grasp what their function is, you'll then be in a better position to make up your mind about how you yourself should speak/write, and to see why society expects you to speak/write in a certain way'. There is no abrogation of standards in this approach; rather it is a way of giving children a sharper sense of standards—a rationale for why standards are there at all. It also helps to develop a greater tolerance of language diversity—which in turn may help to promote tolerance in a broader social context.

The need for information

But the first, essential step in this process is to become aware of the differences—to realize that English does contain many variations, and that one's own way of using English is not always the same as that of others. It is then a moot point whether one should be tolerant of these differences or rail at them. But there is no gainsaying the fact that a rational approach to the English language requires, in the first instance, that one finds out what the differences are, and why they are there. And this, in turn, requires that one appreciates the fundamental role of language change.

There is only one way I know to develop an understanding of language change, and that is to reflect on the way it has taken place, and how it continues to take place. That is why the panels in this dictionary have the form they do. About a third of them draw attention to variations in usage, the result of language change; the remainder illustrate language change in action, by giving a sketch of the history of words and phrases. The focus is critical, especially for those who never received any kind of formal training in grammatical analysis or language awareness in school. For only by knowing about the factors which have influenced the language in the past can we appreciate what is happening to the language of the present, and, thus, be in a position to make useful recommendations about what should happen to it in the future.

David Crystal

A

a (ə; *stressed* eɪ), **an** *determiner* **1** used before a noun that is not known or has not been previously mentioned: A man came into the shop. **2** any; every: A spider has eight legs. **3** used before a proper noun to show similarity or membership: I see we have a budding Rembrandt in our midst! **4** a container or one of: a tea please. **5** used before a noun, etc., showing quantity: a dozen eggs. < Old English *ān* one. SEE PANEL.

aback (əˈbæk) *adv* **taken aback** surprised and disconcerted. < Old English *on bæc* on, to the back.

abacus (ˈæbəkəs) *n* a frame that holds parallel rods with movable beads, used for counting. < Latin, from Greek *abax* board, slab covered with dust for calculations, from Hebrew *ābhāq* dust.

abandon (əˈbændən) *vb* **1** give up completely: Attempts to rescue the missing child were finally abandoned. **2** leave behind; forsake: abandon one's family; abandon ship. **3** give (oneself) freely and completely to an emotion.

• *n* freedom from inhibitions, restraints, etc. **abandonment** *n* **abandoned** *adj* free from inhibitions, restraints, etc. <Middle French *a bandon* in one's power.

abase (əˈbeɪs) *vb* bring lower in esteem, rank, etc. **abasement** *n* < Middle French *abaissier* to make low.

abashed (əˈbæʃt) *adj* embarrassed or disconcerted. < Middle French *es-* out + *baer* to yawn.

abate (əˈbeɪt) *vb* decrease in intensity, amount, etc.: The storm gradually abated. **abatement** *n* < Old French *abattre* to beat down.

abattoir (ˈæbəˌtwɑː) *n* a slaughterhouse. <French *abattre* to fell.

abbey (ˈæbɪ) *n* **1** a building in which a community of monks or nuns live, governed by an abbot or abbess; church associated with such a building. **2** such a community of monks or nuns. **abbess** *n* the superior of a community of nuns. **abbot** *n* the superior of a community of monks. < Old French *abaïe*, from Late Latin *abbatia*.

abbreviate (əˈbriːvɪˌeɪt) *vb* shorten (esp. a word, phrase, or title). **abbreviation** *n* a shortened form of a word, etc. < Late Latin *abbreviare*, from Latin *ad-* to + *brevis* short. SEE PANEL.

abdicate (ˈæbdɪˌkeɪt) *vb* renounce (a throne, responsibility, power, etc.), esp. formally. **abdication** *n* < Latin *abdicare*, from *ab-* off + *dicare* to proclaim.

abdomen (ˈæbdəmən, æbˈdəʊmən) *n* **1** (in mammals) the part of the body between the thorax and the pelvis, containing the intestines, liver, etc. **2** the rear part of the body behind the thorax in an insect, spider, etc. **abdominal** *adj* < Latin.

abduct (æbˈdʌkt) *vb* carry off (a person) secretly or by force. **abduction** *n* **abductor** *n* < Latin *abducere* to lead away.

aberration (ˌæbəˈreɪʃən) *n* **1** a deviation from what is normal or usual. **2** a lapse in the soundness of the mind: a mental aberration. **3** a defect in a lens or mirror that causes distortion of an image. **aberrant** *adj* deviating from what is normal or usual: aberrant behaviour. < Latin *aberrare*, from *ab-* away + *errare* to wander.

abet (əˈbɛt) *vb* **abetted; abetting** encourage or assist, esp. in committing a crime or doing something foolish. **abetter** or (*law*) **abettor** *n* < Old French *a-* + *beter* to bait.

---

a hotel or **an hotel**?

The general rule regarding the use of a or an is that a is used before consonants and an before vowels: *a* book, *a* pen; *an* elephant, *an* opportunity. The significant point to note is that consonant and vowel here refer to sounds, not letters. So since the *h* is silent in words such as heir, honour, and hour, an is used.

In words like hotel that begin with *h* in an unstressed syllable, the *h* is nowadays sounded and is therefore used with a: *a* hotel. The use of *an* hotel, with the *h* not pronounced, is becoming increasingly rare.

Note too, that words which have an initial *y*-sound also take a: *a* uniform, *a* European. Similarly, where there is an initial *w*-sound, a is used: *a* one-man band.

---

abeyance (əˈbeɪəns) *n* **in abeyance** suspended or laid aside temporarily. < Middle French *a-* + *baer* to yawn, gape.

abhor (əbˈhɔː) *vb* **abhorred; abhorring** detest very strongly; loathe. **abhorrent** *adj* **1** causing horror; repugnant. **2** conflicting (with). **abhorrence** *n* < Latin *ab* away from + *horrēre* to shudder.

abide (əˈbaɪd) *vb* **abided,** except def. **2, abode; abiding 1** tolerate: I can't abide such disturbances any longer. **2** (*archaic*) dwell; remain. **abide by** accept (a decision); obey (a rule, etc.). **abiding** *adj* enduring; permanent: an abiding dislike of anything new. < Old English *ā-* + *bīdan* to wait.

ability (əˈbɪlɪtɪ) *n* **1** the physical, mental, etc., power to do something. **2** great proficiency. **3** natural or acquired talents; skill. < SEE **ABLE.**

abject (ˈæbdʒɛkt) *adj* **1** wretched; hopeless: living in abject poverty. **2** contemptible; despicable. **3** extremely humble; servile: an abject apology. **abjectly** *adv* < Latin *abicere* to cast off, from *ab-* away + *jacere* to throw.

ablaze (əˈbleɪz) *adj, adv* on fire; brightly lit.

able (ˈeɪbl) *adj* **1** having the necessary knowledge, skill, power, etc., (to do something). **2** showing competence, intelligence, skill, etc.: the most able pupils. **ably** *adv* **able-bodied** *adj* physically strong and fit. < Latin *habilis* apt, from *habēre* to have, hold.

ablution (əˈbluː ʃən) n (*formal*) the washing of one's body. < Latin *abluere* to wash away.

abnegation (ˌæbnɪˈgeɪʃən) *n* renunciation; self-denial. < Latin *abnegare* to deny.

abnormal (æbˈnɔːməl) *adj* different from the normal or typical; irregular or strange. **abnormality** *n* **abnormally** *adv*

aboard (əˈbɔːd) *adv, prep* on, onto, or in a ship, aircraft, train, etc.

abode[1] (əˈbəʊd) n (*formal*) a home; dwelling-place. < SEE **ABIDE.**

abode[2] SEE **ABIDE.**

abolish (əˈbɒlɪʃ) *vb* do away with; put an end to: Should the House of Lords be abolished? **abolition** *n* **abolitionist** *n* a person who supports the abolition of something, such as slavery or capital punishment. < ultimately Latin *abolēre.*

abominate (əˈbɒmɪˌneɪt) *vb* detest; loathe. **abominable** *adj* **1** (*informal*)

abbreviations

☐ **Full stops in abbreviations**. Should you write BBC or B.B.C.? U.S.A. or USA? Increasingly, full stops are omitted from abbreviations. In particular, the full stop is now commonly omitted when the abbreviation ends with the last letter of the full, unabbreviated word, for example Mr (from *Mister*), Dr (from *Doctor*), St (from *Street* or *Saint*).

In contrast, the full stop tends to be retained when the final letter of the abbreviation is not the last letter of the full, unabbreviated word, for example Capt. (from *Captain*), Rev. (from *Reverend*), anon. (from anonymous).

Abbreviations consisting of initial letters, such as NATO or Nato (*North Atlantic Treaty Organization*) and SALT (*Strategic Arms Limitation Talks*), are written without full stops. Such words are called *acronyms*. (See also panel at **radar**.)

☐ **The pronunciation of abbreviations**. The letters are spelt out: B-B-C, U-S-A or the word is pronounced in full: Mister (*Mr*) Doctor (*Dr*). With acronyms, the initial letters are pronounced as a word: NATO (to rhyme with Plato), SALT (like salt). Some acronyms are pronounced either by spelling out the letters or by pronouncing the initial letters as a word. For example VAT (value-added tax) is pronounced either as V-A-T or as a word, to rhyme with bat, UFO (unidentified flying object) is pronounced either as U-F-O or you-foe.

☐ **The use of** a **or** an **with abbreviations**. We say *an* MA, not *a* MA, but *a* BA, not *an* BA. Why? Abbreviations that begin with a vowel sound, such as MA, take an; abbreviations that begin with a consonant sound, such as BA, take a. This is an example of the general rule regarding the use of a and an: see also panel at **a**.

very unpleasant. **2** detestable; offensive. **abomination** *n* **abominable snowman** yeti. < Latin *abominari* to consider as an ill omen.

aborigine (ˌæbəˈrɪdʒɪnɪ) *n* an original inhabitant, esp. in contrast to an invader or colonizer. **aboriginal** *adj* existing in a land from earliest known times. < back formation from Latin plural *aborigines*.

abort (əˈbɔːt) *vb* **1** cause or suffer an abortion. **2** end or fail prematurely and unsuccessfully; not develop completely. **abortion** *n* the expulsion or removal of a foetus from the womb, esp. before the 28th week of pregnancy. **abortive** *adj* **1** unsuccessful: an abortive attempt. **2** imperfectly developed. **abortively** *adv* < Latin *aboriri* to miscarry, from *ab-* wrongly + *oriri* to appear.

abound (əˈbaʊnd) *vb* **1** exist in large numbers. **2** be well supplied (with). < Latin *abundare* to overflow, from *ab-* + *unda* wave.

about (əˈbaʊt) *prep* **1** concerning: an argument about money. **2** in or near: He must be somewhere about here! **3** around: papers scattered about the room. **4** from place to place in. **5** on (one's person). **6 about to** on the point of: We're about to have tea.
• *adv* **1** approximately: about 100 people. **2** nearby. **3** here and there: We wandered about for a few minutes. **4** on every side: flowers all about. **5** in the opposite direction: turn about.
• *adj* active; out of bed: He's up and about again. **about-turn** *n* a complete change or reversal of direction, attitude, etc. **how** or **what about?** (*informal*) used to introduce a suggestion: How about going to the cinema? < Old English *abūtan*, from *a-* + *būtan* outside.

above (əˈbʌv) *prep* **1** higher, greater, or more than: 1000 metres above sea-level. **2** too honourable for: She's not above gossiping. **3** beyond the level or understanding of: The lecture was quite above me. **4** louder than: Above the noise, I could just hear the bell. **5** upstream from.
• *adv* **1** to or in a higher place. **2** earlier in a book, etc.: See above. **3** higher in status, etc. **4** upstream.
• *adj* already mentioned.
• *n* something above, esp. written above. **above all** most of all; especially. **above-board** *adv, adj* with no indications of deception or dishonesty. < Old English *abufan*, from *a-* + *bufan* above.

abrade (əˈbreɪd) *vb* scrape or wear away by rubbing. **abrasion** *n* abrading. < Latin *abradere* to scrape away, from *ab-* + *radere* to scrape.

abrasive (əˈbreɪsɪv) *n* a substance used for grinding, polishing, or smoothing.
• *adj* **1** causing abrasion. **2** irritating in manner; harsh. < SEE **ABRADE.**

abreast (əˈbrɛst) *adj, adv* **1** alongside and facing in the same way. **2** up to date (with): He tries to keep abreast of the latest scientific developments.

abridge (əˈbrɪdʒ) *vb* shorten by using fewer words; condense. **abridgment** *n* < Late Latin *abbreviare*.

abroad (əˈbrɔːd) *adv, adj* **1** to or in a foreign country. **2** (*formal or literary*) away from home; out of doors; widely. **3** in general circulation: The rumour of his resignation was noised abroad. < Middle English *a-* + *brood* broad.

abrogate (ˈæbrəˌgeɪt) *vb* cancel formally; repeal; annul. **abrogation** *n* < Latin *ab-* away + *rogare* to propose a law.

abrupt (əˈbrʌpt) *adj* **1** sudden; unexpected. **2** curt in manner or speech. **3** having sudden transitions from one subject to another: abrupt, disconnected sentences. **abruptly** *adv* **abruptness** *n* < Latin *abrumpere* to break off, from *ab-* off + *rumpere* to break.

abscess (ˈæbsɛs, ˈæbsɪs) *n* a collection of pus surrounded by inflamed tissue. < Latin *abscedere* to go away.

abscond (əbˈskɒnd) *vb* run away secretly, esp. to avoid punishment after doing wrong. **absconder** *n* < Latin *abscondere* to hide away.

absent (ˈæbsənt) *adj* **1** not present; away. **2** not existing. **3** inattentive; absent-minded. **absently** *adv* **absence** *n* **1** the state or period of time of being absent. **2** a lack: in the absence of any agreement. **absentee** *n* a person who is absent. **absenteeism** *n* frequent, deliberate absence from work or school. **absent-minded** *adj* preoccupied with other things; forgetful. **absent-mindedly** *adv* **absent-mindedness** *n*
• *vb* (æbˈsɛnt) take or keep (oneself) away (from). < Latin *abesse* to be away.

absolute (ˈæbsəˌluːt) *adj* **1** complete; perfect: absolute silence. **2** having no restrictions: absolute ownership; absolute power. **3** outright. **4** certain: the absolute truth. **5** independent; self-sufficient: absolute standards. **6** pure; not mixed. **absolutely** *adv* **1** in an absolute manner. **2** completely; often used to express agreement. < SEE **ABSOLVE.**

absolve (əbˈzɒlv) *vb* **1** set free from blame, guilt, obligation, etc. **2** give religious absolution to. **absolution** *n* a priest's declaration of forgiveness of sins. < Latin *absolvere*, from *ab-* from

+ *solvere* to loosen.
absorb (əbˈzɔːb, əbˈsɔːb) *vb* **1** suck or take up. **2** take in and incorporate. **3** take in and not reflect or transmit (light, sound, etc.). **4** occupy the attention of; engross. **absorption** *n* **absorbed** *adj* engrossed. **absorbent** *adj, n* (a substance that is) able to absorb moisture, gas, etc. < Latin *absorbēre*, from *ab-* from + *sorbēre* to suck up.
abstain (əbˈsteɪn) *vb* **1** refrain deliberately, as from drinking alcohol. **2** refrain from voting. **abstention** *n* abstaining, esp. from voting. **abstinence** *n* abstaining, esp. from drinking alcohol or eating certain foods. < Latin *abstinēre*, from *ab-* from + *tenēre* to hold.
abstemious (əbˈstiːmɪəs) *adj* sparing in eating and drinking. **abstemiously** *adv* < Latin *abs-* from + *temetum* strong drink.
abstract (ˈæbstrækt) *adj* **1** not having a material existence. **2** theoretical rather than practical. **3** marked by non-representational qualities: abstract art.
• *n* **1** a summary. **2** an abstract quality or concept. **3** an abstract composition.
• *vb* (æbˈstrækt) **1** consider theoretically. **2** summarize. **3** remove, separate, or extract. **abstractly** *adv* **abstractness** *n* **abstractor** *n* **abstraction** *n* **1** an abstract idea, etc. **2** absent-mindedness. < Latin *abstractus* drawn off, from *ab-* from + *trahere* to draw.
abstruse (əbˈstruːs) *adj* difficult to understand. **abstrusely** *adv* **abstruseness** *n* < Latin *abstrudere* to hide, from *ab-* away + *trudere* to thrust, push.
absurd (əbˈsɜːd) *adj* not in accordance with reason; ridiculous or incongruous; silly. **absurdity** *n* **absurdly** *adv* < ultimately Latin *absurdus*, from *ab-* + *surdus* deaf, dull-sounding.
abundance (əˈbʌndəns) *n* a quantity that is more than enough; profusion. **abundant** *adj* existing in or marked by plentiful supply. **abundantly** *adv* < ultimately Latin *abundare* to abound.
abuse (əˈbjuːz) *vb* **1** use wrongly, badly, or improperly. **2** attack with insults.
• *n* (əˈbjuːs) **1** a wrong, bad, or improper use. **2** a corrupt practice. **3** strong, insulting language. **abusive** *adj* marked by strong, insulting language. **abusively** *adv* **abusiveness** *n* < ultimately Latin *ab-* away + *uti* to use. SEE PANEL.
abut (əˈbʌt) *vb* **abutted; abutting** border (on); touch; lean against. **abutment** *n* < Old French *abouter*.
abysmal (əˈbɪzməl) *adj* **1** very great; immeasurable. **2** (*informal*) extremely bad. **abysmally** *adv* < SEE **ABYSS.**
abyss (əˈbɪs) *n* **1** a very deep or unfathomable hole. **2** anything that appears immeasurably deep. < ultimately Greek *abyssos* bottomless, from *a-* without + *byssos* depth.
AC *abbrev* alternating current.
academic (ˌækəˈdɛmɪk) *adj* **1** of a school, college, or university; scholarly. **2** theoretical, rather than practical: a purely academic question. **3** learned but lacking experience in practical or technical matters.
• *n* a member, esp. a teacher, of a college or university.
academy (əˈkædəmɪ) *n* **1** a school that gives training in a particular field: a military academy. **2** an association of learned people organized to promote literature, art, or science. **3** (in Scotland) a secondary school. < ultimately Greek *akademeia* the place where Plato taught.
accede (ækˈsiːd) *vb* **1** take up an important office or position, esp. become monarch: William the Conqueror acceded to the throne in 1066. **2** approve or consent (to); become party (to a formal agreement). **accession** *n* **1** the taking up of an important office or position: the Queen's accession to the throne. **2** being added; something added, esp. a book added to a library. **3** approval or agreement; acceptance of a formal agreement. < ultimately Latin *accedere* to go to, agree, from *ad-* to + *cedere* to go.
accelerate (ækˈsɛləˌreɪt) *vb* **1** move, occur, or cause to move or occur faster. **2** cause to happen earlier. **acceleration** *n* **accelerator** *n* a device in a motor vehicle that controls the speed of the motor; pedal for this. < Latin *accelerare* to go faster, from *ad-* to + *celer* swift.

abuse or **misuse?**

These two words are sometimes confused.

Abuse means 'to use or treat wrongly, badly, or improperly' as in to *abuse* one's official position or 'to attack with words; revile': She constantly *abuses* her ex-husband.

Misuse means 'to use something incorrectly or for a purpose for which it was not intended': to *misuse* the association's funds.

So to misuse such words is to abuse the language.

accent (ˈæksɛnt) *n* **1** emphasis or prominence of a syllable or word. **2** a written mark used to show the stress, pronunciation, etc., of a syllable or vowel. **3** a distinctive local, regional, or national pronunciation: a Yorkshire accent. **4** special emphasis.
• *vb* (ækˈsɛnt) **1** pronounce with an accent; mark with a written accent. **2** emphasize. **accentuate** *vb* draw attention to; emphasize. **accentuation** *n* < ultimately Latin *ad-* to + *cantus* chant.

accept (əkˈsɛpt) *vb* **1** receive or take. **2** give an affirmative reply to: I accept your kind invitation. **3** recognize as true: The police accepted his alibi. **4** be willing to agree to: We reluctantly accept the suggested changes. **5** bear; tolerate: You must accept the responsibility. **6** admit and approve of: My mother-in-law has never accepted me as one of the family. **7** take on (duties). **8** be able to take (something inserted): The slot-machine accepts only 50p and £1 coins. **acceptance** *n* **acceptable** *adj* **1** capable of being accepted; satisfactory. **2** welcome. **3** tolerable. **acceptably** *adv* **accepted** *adj* commonly recognized or approved; usual: the accepted standards of morality. < ultimately Latin *accipere* to receive, from *ad-* to + *capere* to take.

access (ˈæksɛs) *n* **1** the right or opportunity to approach or make use of something: His job gives him free access to military intelligence reports. **2** a means of entering; state of being easily entered, etc.: ease of access.
• *vb* gain access to (information stored on a computer); obtain or retrieve. **accessible** *adj* able to be reached, found, or used. **accessibility** *n* **accessibly** *adv* < SEE **ACCEDE.**

accessory (əkˈsɛsərɪ) *n* **1** a supplementary attachment or fitting: car accessories. **2** also **accessary** (*law*) a person who incites another to commit a crime: an accessory before the fact.

accident (ˈæksɪdənt) *n* **1** an event that occurs by chance, esp. one causing injury or damage. **2** chance: We met by accident. **accidental** *adj* happening by accident: accidental damage. **accidentally** *adv* < ultimately Latin *accidere* to befall, happen, from *ad-* to + *cadere* to fall.

acclaim (əˈkleɪm) *vb* **1** greet or welcome with strong approval. **2** proclaim with great praise: They acclaimed him king.
• *n* also **acclamation** an enthusiastic expression of great praise and strong approval. < Latin *acclamare* to shout at, from *ad-* to + *clamare* to shout.

acclimatize (əˈklaɪməˌtaɪz) *vb* adapt or become used to a new climate or conditions. **acclimatization** *n*

accolade (ˈækəˌleɪd) *n* **1** a touch with a sword when conferring a knighthood. **2** an award; expression of great praise. < ultimately Latin *ad-* to + *collum* neck.

accommodate (əˈkɒməˌdeɪt) *vb* **1** provide with lodging or food and lodging. **2** have room for; hold: A new church was built to accommodate a larger congregation. **3** be able to cope with; allow for. **4** (*formal*) do a favour for; fulfil or oblige: We shall do our best to accommodate your wishes. **5** adjust or adapt (to). **accommodating** *adj* willing to help; obliging. **accommodation** *n* **1** lodging. **2** premises: office accommodation. **3** accommodating. < Latin *ad-* to + *commodare* to make fit. SEE PANEL AT **EMBARRASS.**

accompany (əˈkʌmpənɪ) *vb* **1** go along with as a companion or escort. **2** be present with: the accompanying problems. **3** supplement. **4** play a musical accompaniment to or for. **accompaniment** *n* **1** a subsidiary instrumental or vocal part. **2** an accompanying thing. **accompanist** *n* a person who plays a musical accompaniment. < Middle French *accompaignier*, from *compaing* companion.

accomplice (əˈkʌmplɪs, əˈkɒmplɪs) *n* a person who helps another in doing wrong. < ultimately Latin *complex* partner, associate.

accomplish (əˈkʌmplɪʃ, əˈkɒmplɪʃ) *vb* succeed in doing; fulfil or complete. **accomplished** *adj* **1** skilled: an accomplished performer. **2** already done or established: an accomplished fact. **accomplishment** *n* **1** fulfilment or completion. **2** an achievement. **3** a skill. **4** grace. < ultimately Latin *complēre to* fill up.

accord (əˈkɔːd) *n* agreement; consent.
• *vb* **1** be in harmony (with): His statement does not accord with the facts. **2** grant or award. **of one's own accord** willingly; without interference: The machine seems to have stopped of its own accord. **with one accord** unanimously. < ultimately Latin *ad-* to + *cor* heart.

according (əˈkɔːdɪŋ) *adv* **according to** **1** also **in accordance with** in relation to; consistent with: The boxes are stored according to their size. **2** as expressed or indicated by: according to the report. **accordingly** *adv* **1** appropriately. **2** consequently.

accordion (əˈkɔːdɪən) *n* a portable,

keyboard musical instrument incorporating hand-operated bellows which force air through reeds. < German *Akkordion,* from Italian *accordare* to be in tune.

accost (əˈkɒst) *vb* approach and speak to, esp. boldly. < ultimately Latin *ad-* to + *costa* rib, side.

account (əˈkaʊnt) *n* **1** a statement of money received or paid. **2** a business arrangement with a bank, firm, etc. **3** significance; value: a man of no account. **4** a statement or description: He gave the director a full account of his business trip. **5** consideration: I'll take your suggestions into account.
• *vb* consider. **accountable** *adj* **1** responsible. **2** able to be explained. **accountability** *n* **accountancy** *n* the profession of preparing, verifying, and interpreting business accounts. **accountant** *n* a person whose profession is accountancy. **account for 1** give an explanation of. **2** be the source of. **3** cause the death or destruction of. **by all accounts** according to the information generally available. **on account of** because of. < Middle French *compter* to count.

accoutrements (əˈku:trəmənts) *pl n* equipment, such as a soldier's outfit other than weapons and clothes. < Middle French *accoutrer* to equip.

accredit (əˈkrɛdɪt) *vb* **1** approve or recognize officially. **2** attribute or ascribe (to). < French *accréditer,* from *ad-* + *crédit* credit.

accrue (əˈkru:) *vb* occur as a natural increase or development: Interest accrues twice yearly. **accrual** *n* **accretion** *n* **1** a gradual increase in size. **2** something added. **3** the growing of separate things into one. < ultimately Latin *accrescere* to increase.

accumulate (əˈkju:mjʊˌleɪt) *vb* **1** collect together gradually. **2** increase in quantity or amount. **accumulation** *n* **accumulator** *n* a storage cell or group of storage cells. < Latin *ad-* to + *cumulare* to heap up.

accurate (ˈækjərət) *adj* **1** free from error. **2** conforming exactly to a standard or truth. **accuracy** *n* **accurately** *adv* < Latin *accurate* to perform with care.

accursed (əˈkɜ:st, əˈkɜ:sɪd) *adj* **1** under a curse. **2** (*informal*) hateful; detestable. < Old English *acursian* to put under a curse.

accusative (əˈkju:zətɪv) *adj, n* (of or in) the grammatical case used to express the direct object of a verb or of some prepositions. < SEE ACCUSE.

accuse (əˈkju:z) *vb* charge (a person) with a particular fault, crime, etc. **accuser** *n* **accusation** *n* **1** accusing; being accused. **2** a charge accusing a person of a particular fault, crime, etc. **the accused** *n* the defendant in a legal case. < ultimately Latin *accusare* to call to account, from *ad-* to + *causa* lawsuit.

accustom (əˈkʌstəm) *vb* make used (to) or familiar (with). **accustomed** *adj* usual. < Middle French *acostumer,* from *costume* custom.

ace (eɪs) *n* **1** a playing-card with one spot. **2** an expert in a field that is mentioned: a speedway ace. **3** (*tennis*) a service that one's opponent fails to return.
• *adj* (*informal*) excellent. < ultimately Latin *as* a unit.

acetylene (əˈsɛtɪˌli:n) *n* a colourless, toxic, flammable gas used esp. in cutting and welding metals. < Latin *acetum* vinegar.

ache (eɪk) *vb* **1** suffer a continuous, dull pain. **2** yearn (for).
• *n* a continuous, dull pain. **achy** *adj* < Old English *acan.*

achieve (əˈtʃi:v) *vb* succeed in doing, gaining, or reaching by effort; accomplish. **achievable** *adj* **achievement** *n* < Middle French *achever* to bring to an end.

acid (ˈæsɪd) *adj* **1** sharp to the taste; sour. **2** sharp or sarcastic in speech, manner, etc. **3** of or like an acid.
• *n* **1** a chemical compound containing hydrogen that can be replaced by a metal to form a salt. **2** a sour-tasting substance. **3** (*slang*) LSD. **acidity** *n* **acidic** *adj* acid-forming; acid. **acidify** *vb* **acidified; acidifying** change into or become an acid. < Latin *acēre* to be sour or sharp. SEE PANEL.

acknowledge (əkˈnɒlɪdʒ) *vb* **1** admit that something is true or valid. **2** show recognition of, by greeting, smiling, etc.

the acid test

The acid test of something is a crucial or thorough examination of its truth, value, suitability, etc.: The *acid test* is not whether people are interested in the new product but whether they will buy it. The expression derives from the chemical test of using nitric acid to establish whether a metal is gold or not.

3 express appreciation or thanks for. **4** confirm receipt of: We acknowledge your order of 22 July. **acknowledgment** *n* **acknowledged** *adv* generally accepted or admitted. < SEE **KNOWLEDGE.**

acme (ˈækmɪ) *n* the highest point of achievement, excellence, etc. < Greek *akmē*.

acne (ˈæknɪ) *n* a skin condition, common amongst adolescents, characterized by pimples and blackheads. < Greek *akmē* eruption on the face.

acorn (ˈeɪkɔːn) *n* the fruit of the oak tree; smooth nut set in a hard, woody, cup-like base. < Old English *æcern*.

acoustic (əˈkuːstɪk) *adj* of sound, hearing, or acoustics. **acoustically** *adv* **acoustics** *n* **1** the scientific study of sound. **2** *pl* the qualities of a hall, etc., that determine how clearly sounds are heard in it. < Greek *akouein* to hear. SEE PANEL.

acquaint (əˈkweɪnt) *vb* make familiar (with) or informed (about). **acquaintance** *n* **1** being acquainted. **2** a person whom one knows slightly, as distinct from a friend. < ultimately Latin *accognoscere* to know perfectly.

acquiesce (ˌækwɪˈɛs) *vb* agree to quietly without protest. **acquiescence** *n* **acquiescent** *adj* < ultimately Latin *ad-* to + *quiescere* to be quiet.

acquire (əˈkwaɪə) *vb* gain possession of. **acquired taste** a liking for something as a result of much exposure to it. **acquisition** *n* acquiring; something acquired. **acquisitive** *adj* eager to acquire things. < ultimately Latin *ad-* to + *quaerere* to seek, obtain.

acquit (əˈkwɪt) *vb* **acquitted; acquitting** **1** declare not guilty. **2** free from responsibility. **3** (*formal*) conduct (oneself) in a manner that is mentioned: He acquitted himself well in the examinations. **acquittal** *n* the release of a person who is declared not guilty. < Old French *quite* released.

acre (ˈeɪkə) *n* **1** a unit of area equal to 4840 square yards (4046.86 square metres). **2** *pl* (*informal*) a large amount. **acreage** *n* area in acres. < Old English *æcer*. SEE PANEL.

acrid (ˈækrɪd) *adj* **1** unpleasantly sharp and strong in taste or smell. **2** very bitter in manner or temper; caustic. **acridity** *n* < Latin *acer* sharp.

acrimony (ˈækrɪmənɪ) *n* sharpness and bitterness in manner or language, esp. as a result of anger. **acrimonious** *adj* **acrimoniously** *adv* < Latin *acer* sharp.

acrobat (ˈækrəˌbæt) *n* a person who performs gymnastic feats. **acrobatic** *adj* **acrobatics** *pl n* **1** acrobatic feats. **2** any activity requiring agility and skill: verbal acrobatics. SEE PANEL.

acronym (ˈækrəˌnɪm) *n* a word formed from the initial letters of other words. < Greek *akros* extreme + *onyma* name. SEE PANEL AT **RADAR.**

across (əˈkrɒs) *prep* **1** from one side to the other side of. **2** on the opposite side of.

• *adv* **1** from one side to the other; crossed. **2** on or to the opposite side.

acrostic (əˈkrɒstɪk) *n* a verse or arrangement of words in which certain letters, esp. the first of each line, form a word or

acoustics is ... or acoustics are ...?

Nouns ending in -ics such as acoustics, economics, athletics, and politics, are sometimes treated as singular and sometimes as plural. When used as the name of an art or subject, they take a singular verb: Mathematics *is* a very difficult subject. Politics *is* the art of government. Otherwise, they are plural: The acoustics of this hall *are* very poor. What *are* his politics?

acres and furlongs

In one of its modern uses acre provides an exact unit of measurement: 4046.86 square metres. This narrow meaning came about only after social organization had advanced to such an extent that such precision became essential. In the days before the countryside was criss-crossed with fences, acre, Old English *æcer,* simply meant 'a field', which is still what the equivalent German word Acker means today.

Furlong, formerly 'the length of a furrow', and gallon, 'the capacity of a pail', provide similar examples of words which were once no more than rough approximations. A furlong is equal to 220 yards (201.168 metres) and a gallon equal to four quarts (in the UK 4.546 litres, USA 3.785 litres).

phrase. < ultimately Greek *akros* topmost + *stichos* line of verse.

acrylic fibre (əˈkrɪlɪk) *n* a strong, synthetic textile fibre. < Latin *acer* sharp + *olēre* to smell.

act (ækt) *n* **1** something done; deed. **2** a decree or law made by parliament; statute. **3** the process of doing something: He was caught in the act! **4** one of the main divisions of a play or opera. **5** one of a series of short performances: a circus act. **6** a display of affected behaviour.
• *vb* **1** do something; take action. **2** function or behave in a way that is mentioned: You acted very foolishly. **3** perform (a part) in a play, etc. **4** perform a function that is mentioned; serve (as). **5** pretend to be; simulate. **6** behave insincerely. **act on 1** affect. **2** take action on. < Latin *agere* to do.

acting (ˈæktɪŋ) *adj* taking on duties temporarily: the acting manager.
• *n* the art or profession of representing a character, esp. on a stage or for a film.

action (ˈækʃən) *n* **1** the process of doing something. **2** the process of producing an effect on something. **3** movement, as of the body. **4** something done. **5** the state of working properly: The machine is temporarily out of action. **6** practical, esp. bold activity: a man of action. **7** military combat: We first saw action in the South Atlantic. **8** the events in a story or play; series of these. **9** the mechanism of an instrument; manner in which it operates. **10** a lawsuit. **11** (*informal*) exciting activity: Go where the action is! < SEE **ACT.**

active (ˈæktɪv) *adj* **1** acting, working, or functioning. **2** marked by lively activity: He leads an active life. **3** marked by practical action not just thought. **4** (of a volcano) liable to erupt. **5** capable of producing an effect: active ingredients. **6** also *n (grammar)* (of) a verb form that has the person or thing doing the action as the subject. **7** engaged in full-time service in the armed services: on active service. **actively** *adv* **activeness** *n* **activate** *vb* make active. < SEE **ACT.** SEE PANEL AT **PASSIVE.**

activity (ækˈtɪvɪtɪ) *n* **1** the state of being active. **2** lively, energetic action. **3** *pl* actions; pursuits: social activities. **activist** *n* a person who emphasizes the taking of strong, esp. public action: political activists. **activism** *n*

actor (ˈæktə) fem. **actress** *n* a performer in a play, film, etc.

actual (ˈæktʃʊəl) *adj* existing in fact; real, genuine, or current. **actually** *adv* < ultimately Latin *actus* act.

actuality (ˌæktʃʊˈælɪtɪ) *n* **1** a real fact or condition. **2** the state of being real.

actuary (ˈæktʃʊərɪ) *n* a statistician employed by an insurance company to calculate the premiums payable on policies. **actuarial** *adj* < Latin *actuarius* accountant, from *actum* record.

actuate (ˈæktʃʊˌeɪt) *vb* put or stir into action. **actuation** *n* < Latin *actus* act.

acumen (ˈækjʊˌmɛn) *n* the ability to discern well; keen judgment or insight. < Latin: sharpness, point.

acupuncture (ˈækjʊˌpʌŋktʃə) *n* the insertion of thin, metal needles into selected points on the body to cure disease, relieve pain, etc. < Latin *acus* needle + English *puncture*.

acute (əˈkjuːt) *adj* **1** serious or severe: acute problems. **2** having a sharp mind. **3** very sensitive to stimulation. **4** strongly felt: acute pain. **5** (of an illness) quickly coming to a crisis. **6** (of an angle) less than 90°. **acutely** *adv*

acrobats and **gymnasts**

A type of gymnast who performs feats both on and off the ground for the entertainment of the public is known as an acrobat. This word derives ultimately from the Greek *akrobatos* ‘walking on tiptoe’, from *akro* ‘at the top or tip’ and *bainein* ‘to go’.

Gymnast is also of Greek origin. It comes from *gymnazein* ‘to exercise naked’, from *gymnos* ‘naked’.

acute and **sharp**

Someone with a keen sense of perception might be informally described as sharp or acute. These usages are figurative extensions of words of very different origins.

Sharp, like many *sh-* words, is of Teutonic descent. It comes from the Old English *scearp*. Acute, on the other hand, derives from *acus,* the Latin word for ‘needle’. *Acus* also provides the root of acumen ‘the ability to discern well’ and acupuncture ‘the use of needles to treat bodily disorders’.

acuteness *n* SEE PANEL.
ad (æd) *n* (*informal*) an advertisement.
AD *abbrev* (*Latin*) anno Domini (in the year of our Lord).
adage (ˈædɪdʒ) *n* a traditional saying that incorporates a commonly recognized truth. < ultimately Latin *adagium*.
adamant (ˈædəmənt) *adj* not yielding; determined. **adamantly** *adv* SEE PANEL.
adapt (əˈdæpt) *vb* make or become suitable, esp. by adjusting and modifying. **adaptable** *adj* **adaptability** *n* **adaptation** *n* **adaptor** *n* a device that enables different parts to be fitted together. < Latin *ad-* to + *aptare* to fit.
add (æd) *vb* **1** combine (numbers) into a total. **2** join to something to increase its size, quantity, etc., or improve its quality. **3** say or write further. **addition** *n* **1** (esp. of numbers) adding; being added. **2** the thing that is added. **in addition** as well. **additional** *adj* supplementary; extra. **additionally** *adv* **add up** seem logical; make sense: His behaviour just doesn't add up! **add up to** mean or indicate; amount to. < ultimately Latin *ad-* to + *-dere* to put.
addendum (əˈdɛndəm) *n, pl* **addenda** something added at the end of a book, etc.; supplement or appendix. < SEE ADD.
adder (ˈædə) *n* a greyish viper with a black, zigzag pattern along the back. < Old English *nǣdre*. SEE PANEL AT APRON.
addict (əˈdɪkt) *vb* **1** cause to become dependent on a drug. **2** devote (oneself) habitually or compulsively to.
• *n* (ˈædɪkt) a person who is addicted to something, esp. a drug. **addiction** *n* **addictive** *adj* of or causing addiction. < Latin *ad-* to + *dicere* to say.
additive (ˈædɪtɪv) *n* a substance added in small amounts to another to improve or preserve it, etc.
• *adj* of or marked by addition.
addle (ˈædl̩) *vb* **1** (of an egg) become rotten. **2** confuse: to addle the brain. < Old English *adela* filth.
address (əˈdrɛs) *n* **1** the written description of the location of a building where a person lives or works; form of this on an envelope, etc. **2** a speech delivered to an audience. **3** a particular style of writing or speaking: modes of address.
• *vb* **1** write an address on (an envelope, parcel, etc.). **2** deliver a speech to. **3** direct words to. **4** direct one's energy or attention to. **5** use a particular style when writing or speaking to. **addressee** *n* a person, etc., to whom a letter or parcel is addressed. < ultimately Latin *ad-* to + *directus* direct.
adduce (əˈdjuːs) *vb* (*formal*) offer as evidence, a reason, etc. < Latin *adducere* to lead to.
adenoids (ˈædəˌnɔɪdz) *pl n* the mass of lymphatic tissue at the back of the nose. < Greek *adēn* gland.
adept (əˈdɛpt) *adj* very skilled at. < Latin *ad-* to + *apisci* to reach.
adequate (ˈædɪkwət) *adj* **1** fulfilling a requirement. **2** barely satisfactory. **adequacy** *n* **adequately** *adv* < Latin *ad-* to + *aequare* to equal.
adhere (ədˈhɪə) *vb* **1** stick or hold fast by or as if by gluing, sucking, etc. **2** continue to support or act according to a rule, etc.: He adhered strictly to the original plans. **adherence** *n* **adherent** *n* a supporter or follower. **adhesion** *n* adhering. **adhesive** *adj, n* (a substance) that is able to adhere or cause things to adhere. **adhesiveness** *n* < ultimately Latin *ad-* to + *haerēre* to stick.
ad hoc (ˌæd ˈhɒk) *adj, adv* for a particular purpose: an ad hoc committee. < Latin: for this.
adieu (əˈdjuː, æˈdʒɜː) *interj, n, pl* **adieus, adieux** (*literary*) farewell. < Old French, from *a* to + *dieu* God.
ad infinitum (æd ˌɪnfɪˈnaɪtəm) *adv* without end; to infinity. < Latin.
adjacent (əˈdʒeɪsn̩t) *adj* having a common boundary; near. < Latin *ad-* near + *jacēre* to lie.
adjective (ˈædʒɪktɪv) *n* a word that describes a quality of a noun. **adjectival** *adj* **adjectivally** *adv* < Latin *ad-* to +

adamant and **diamond**

Behaviour which displays stubborn or unyielding determination is sometimes described as adamant: 'He remained adamant in his refusal to help.' Adamant comes ultimately from the Greek *adamas*, meaning 'invincible' or 'unconquerable'. This was originally used to describe a legendary mineral of impenetrable hardness but in time came to be applied to the diamond.

The similarity in form of adamant and diamond is not accidental—both come from *adamas*.

jacere to throw.
adjoin (əˈdʒɔɪn) *vb* be next to. < ultimately Latin *ad-* to + *jungere* to join.
adjourn (əˈdʒɜːn) *vb* **1** (of a court, etc.) close a session temporarily. **2** postpone or be postponed. **adjournment** *n* < ultimately Latin *ad-* to + *diurnus* daily.
adjudge (əˈdʒʌdʒ) *vb* declare or pronounce formally. < ultimately Latin *ad-* to + *judicare* to judge.
adjudicate (əˈdʒuːdɪˌkeɪt) *vb* **1** decide (a legal case). **2** serve as a judge in a competition. **adjudication** *n* **adjudicator** *n* < SEE ADJUDGE.
adjunct (ˈædʒʌŋkt) *n* something added that is secondary. < SEE ADJOIN.
adjure (əˈdʒʊə) *vb* (*formal*) charge, command, or appeal to solemnly and earnestly. < ultimately Latin *ad-* to + *jurare* to swear.
adjust (əˈdʒʌst) *vb* **1** change slightly so as to make more accurate, satisfactory, or suitable. **2** adapt, as to new conditions. **adjustment** *n* **adjustable** *adj* able to be adjusted. < Old French *adjuster,* from *a-* to + *juste* right, exact.
adjutant (ˈædʒətənt) *n* an officer who assists a superior officer by carrying out administrative work. < Latin *adjutare* to help.
ad-lib (ædˈlɪb) *vb* **ad-libbed; ad-libbing** speak or sing spontaneously and without preparation.
• *adj* spoken, performed, etc., without preparation. < short for Latin *ad libitum* according to pleasure.
admin (ˈædmɪn) *n* (*informal*) administration.
administer (ədˈmɪnɪstə) *vb* **1** direct, control, supervise, or manage. **2** dispense or give: The court administers justice. **3** supervise the taking of (an oath). **administrate** *vb* act as administrator (for). **administration** *n* **1** administering. **2** the management of affairs, esp. public or business affairs or government policy. **3** the group of people who manage or govern. **administrative** *adj* of or concerned with administration. **administrator** *n* a person who administers. < ultimately Latin *ad-* to + *ministrare* to serve.
admiral (ˈædmərəl) *n* the chief commander of a navy. < ultimately Arabic *amīr-al-* commander.
admire (ədˈmaɪə) *vb* regard with respect or approval; express such a feeling. **admiration** *n* **admirer** *n* **admirable** *adj* worthy of admiration. **admirably** *adv* < ultimately Latin *ad-* at + *mirari* to wonder.
admit (ədˈmɪt) *vb* **admitted; admitting** **1** allow to enter. **2** acknowledge or confess (a mistake, crime, etc.). **3** concede or grant (the truth of something). **4** allow (of). **5** give access or entrance. **admissible** *adj* capable of being allowed: That document is not admissible as evidence. **admissibility** *n* **admissibly** *adv* **admission** *n* **1** admitting; being admitted. **2** the charge for this. **3** an acknowledgment that something is true; confession. **admittance** *n* the right to enter. **admittedly** *adv* as must be admitted. < Latin *ad-* to + *mittere* to send.
admixture (ədˈmɪkstʃə) *n* a mixture; something added as an ingredient. < Latin *ad-* to + *miscēre* to mix.
admonish (ədˈmɒnɪʃ) *vb* **1** warn or reprove firmly, but mildly. **2** advise earnestly. **admonition** *n* < ultimately Latin *ad-* to + *monēre* to warn.
ad nauseam (ˌæd ˈnɔːzɪˌæm) *adv* to a tedious extent. < Latin: to the point of nausea.
ado (əˈduː) *n* fussy, bustling activity. < Middle English *at do* to do.
adolescence (ˌædəˈlɛsəns) *n* the period between puberty and maturity. **adolescent** *n, adj* < ultimately Latin *adolescere* to grow up.
adopt (əˈdɒpt) *vb* **1** take (a child) into one's family as one's own child for whom one is legally responsible. **2** take and use as one's own: He urged them to adopt a more positive attitude. **3** agree on (a report, etc.), esp. by voting. **4** choose as a candidate. **adoption** *n* **adoptive** *adj* made or gained by adoption. < Latin *ad-* to + *optare* to choose.
adore (əˈdɔː) *vb* **1** love intensely. **2** worship or honour as God. **3** (*informal*) like very much. **adoration** *n* **adorer** *n* **adorable** *adj* lovable; charming. < ultimately Latin *ad-* to + *orare* to speak, pray.
adorn (əˈdɔːn) *vb* **1** decorate. **2** add to the pleasantness of. **adornment** *n* < ultimately Latin *ad-* to + *ornare* to furnish.
adrenalin (əˈdrɛnəlɪn) *n* a hormone secreted by the adrenal glands, which increases the heart rate and raises blood pressure. < *ad-* near + *renal,* from Latin *renes* kidneys.
adrift (əˈdrɪft) *adj, adv* **1** drifting. **2** loose. **3** (*informal*) astray.
adroit (əˈdrɔɪt) *adj* **1** skilful. **2** shrewd and resourceful. **adroitly** *adv* **adroitness** *n* < French *à* at + *droit* right.
adulation (ˌædjʊˈleɪʃən) *n* excessive

flattery or admiration. < ultimately Latin *adulari* to flatter.

adult (ˈædʌlt, əˈdʌlt) *adj* **1** fully developed and mature. **2** of or for adults. **3** (*euphemistic*) pornographic: adult films. • *n* an adult person. **adulthood** *n* < Latin *ad-* + *alescere* to grow.

adulterate (əˈdʌltəˌreɪt) *vb* make impure, esp. by adding an inferior substance. **adulteration** *n* < Latin *ad-* to + *alter* other.

adultery (əˈdʌltərɪ) *n* voluntary sexual intercourse between a married person and someone other than his or her spouse. **adulterous** *adj* **adulterer** fem. **adulteress** *n* a person who commits adultery. < SEE **ADULTERATE.**

advance (ədˈvɑːns) *vb* **1** go or bring forward. **2** further or promote; help: to advance the cause of science. **3** move (an event) to an earlier time. **4** bring (an opinion) forward for notice. **5** lend (money); pay before the date due. **6** raise or rise in rank, position, etc. • *n* **1** a forward movement. **2** progress or development: significant advances in treating cancer. **3** a loan; payment before it is due. **4** *pl* friendly, esp. amorous, approaches. • *adj* **1** made or provided beforehand: an advance warning. **2** going before others: the advance party. **advanced** *adj* **1** old: an advanced age. **2** developed; not elementary: advanced studies. **Advanced level** an examination at the higher level in the General Certificate of Education. **advancement** *n* **1** promotion in rank, etc. **2** furtherance. **in advance** beforehand. < ultimately Latin *ab-* away from + *ante* before.

advantage (ədˈvɑːntɪdʒ) *n* something that gives a more favourable position; benefit. **advantageous** *adj* providing an advantage; beneficial. **advantageously** *adv* **take advantage of** make good use of; use to one's own ends; exploit. **to advantage** so as to produce a favourable impression. < SEE **ADVANCE.**

adventure (ədˈventʃə) *n* **1** an exciting or risky experience or undertaking. **2** the excitement characteristic of such experiences: a sense of adventure. • *vb* risk. **adventurous** *adj* **adventurously** *adv* **adventurer** *n* a person who takes risks, esp. hoping to make money. < ultimately Latin *ad-* to + *venire* to come.

adverb (ˈædˌvɜːb) *n* a word that modifies a sentence, verb, adjective, another adverb, etc., and expresses how, when, where, etc. **adverbial** *adj* **adverbially** *adv* < Latin *ad-* to + *verbum* word.

adversary (ˈædvəsərɪ) *n* an enemy or opponent. < SEE **ADVERSE.**

adverse (ˈædvɜːs, ædˈvɜːs) *adj* unfavourable; antagonistic. **adversely** *adv* **adversity** *n* trouble; hardship. < ultimately Latin *ad-* to + *vertere* to turn. SEE PANEL.

advert (ˈædvɜːt) *n* (*informal*) an advertisement.

advertise (ˈædvəˌtaɪz) *vb* **1** present (a product) to the public in order to promote sales. **2** make known to possible applicants: to advertise a job. **3** make a public request (for): They're advertising for a cleaner. **advertiser** *n* **advertisement** *n* advertising; public notice that is displayed or broadcast to advertise a product, etc. **advertising** *n* the action, practice, or profession of making advertisements; advertisements collectively. < ultimately Latin *advertere* to turn one's attention to.

advice (ədˈvaɪs) *n* **1** a recommendation given about a course of action or behaviour: If the symptoms persist, seek medical advice. **2** an official business communication: a remittance advice. < Latin *ad-* to + *visum* view.

advise (ədˈvaɪz) *vb* **1** offer advice (to). **2** notify; inform. **adviser, advisor** *n* **advisable** *adj* sensible; prudent. **advisability** *n* **advisory** *adj* giving advice: an advisory council. < ultimately Latin *ad-* to + *vidēre* to view.

advocate (ˈædvəkət) *n* **1** a person who pleads on behalf of another in a lawcourt. **2** a person who defends or supports a cause or policy. • *vb* (ˈædvəˌkeɪt) recommend; plead for. **advocacy** *n* active support. < ultimately Latin *ad-* to + *vocare* to call. SEE PANEL.

aegis (ˈiːdʒɪs) *n* protection or sponsor-

> **adverse** or **averse?**
>
> These two words are sometimes confused.
>
> Adverse means 'unfavourable; antagonistic': the *adverse* effects of the drug, *adverse* comments about their behaviour.
>
> Averse refers to an attitude of strong dislike (aversion) of something. It is followed by to: He was in principle not *averse* to the suggestion. Public institutions are usually *averse* to change.

ship: under the aegis of the government. < ultimately Greek *aigis* shield of Zeus.

aeon (ˈiːən, ˈiːɒn) *n* an immeasurably long period of time. < Greek *aiōn*.

aerate (ˈɛəreɪt) *vb* **1** charge or supply with a gas, esp. air, oxygen, or carbon dioxide. **2** expose to air in order to purify. **aeration** *n* **aerator** *n* < ultimately Greek *aēr* air.

aerial (ˈɛərɪəl) *adj* **1** of, occurring in, or consisting of air. **2** of, by, or from aircraft: aerial photography.
● *n* a wire or rod or set of these designed to transmit or receive radio waves. < ultimately Greek *aēr* air.

aerobatics (ˌɛərəʊˈbætɪks) *pl n* spectacular manoeuvres of flying aircraft. < *aero-*, ultimately from Greek *aēr* air + English acro*batics*.

aerodrome (ˈɛərəˌdrəʊm) *n* an airfield.

aerodynamics (ˌɛərəʊdaɪˈnæmɪks) *n* the study of the flow of air and its relation to the motion of solid bodies. **aerodynamic** *adj*

aerofoil (ˈɛərəʊˌfɔɪl) *n* a surface, such as a wing, that is designed to produce lift in an aircraft.

aeronautics (ˌɛərəˈnɔːtɪks) *n* the scientific study and history of flight. **aeronautical** *adj*

aeroplane (ˈɛərəˌpleɪn) *n* a mechanically propelled aircraft that has fixed wings. < French *aéro*, ultimately from Greek *aēr* air + *planos* wandering.

aerosol (ˈɛərəˌsɒl) *n* **1** a suspension of fine particles of liquid or solid in a gas. **2** the substance dispensed from a pressurized container; such a pressurized container. < *aero-*, ultimately from *Greek aēr* air + English *sol*ution.

aerospace (ˈɛərəˌspeɪs) *n* the earth's atmosphere and the space beyond it; branch of science dealing with this.
● *adj* of or relating to aerospace, or vehicles, etc., used in aerospace.

the devil's advocate

A devil's advocate is a person who supports an opposing or unpopular view, especially for the sake of argument. The phrase is a translation of Latin *advocatus diaboli*, and comes from the popular name of an official of the Roman Catholic Church appointed to raise objections against a proposed canonization.

aesthetic (iːsˈθɛtɪk) *adj* **1** of or relating to aesthetics. **2** characterized by a tasteful sense of beauty; artistic. **aesthetically** *adv* **aesthetics** *n* a branch of philosophy dealing with art, critical judgments about art, and general principles about the nature of beauty. < ultimately Greek *aisthanesthai* to perceive.

afar (əˈfɑː) *adv, n* (*literary*) (at, from, or to) a great distance. < Middle English *on fer* and *of fer*.

affable (ˈæfəbl̩) *adj* approachable and easy to talk to; friendly and kind. **affability** *n* **affably** *adv* < ultimately Latin *ad-* to + *fari* to speak.

affair (əˈfɛə) *n* **1** something to be done; matter or concern. **2** *pl* public, professional, or business matters. **3** a sexual relationship outside marriage. **4** a matter that causes public scandal or controversy: the Profumo affair. **5** (*informal*) an object or thing that is vaguely described. < Middle French a *faire* to do.

affect¹ (əˈfɛkt) *vb* **1** have an effect on; influence. **2** move emotionally or mentally. < ultimately Latin *ad-* to + *facere* to do. SEE PANEL.

affect² *vb* pretend to have, feel, etc. **affectation** *n* **affected** *adj* pretended. < Latin *affectare* to pretend to have.

affection (əˈfɛkʃən) *n* a feeling of fondness. **affectionate** *adj* showing affection; loving. **affectionately** *adv* < SEE AFFECT¹.

affidavit (ˌæfɪˌdeɪvɪt) *n* a written statement made on oath, intended to be produced as evidence in a law-court. < Medieval Latin: he has made an oath.

affiliate (əˈfɪlɪˌeɪt) *vb* connect, esp. in a dependent position such as a member or branch: The trade union is affiliated to the TUC.

affect or **effect?**

To affect something is to have an effect on it: Smoking *affects* your health—Smoking has an *effect* on your health. The strike is bound to *affect* the economy—The strike is bound to have an *effect* on the economy.

When used as a verb (which is relatively seldom) effect has a completely different meaning and sounds rather formal: The lowering of prices *effected* (brought about) an increase in sales.

• *n* (ə'fɪlɪɪt, ə'fɪlɪˌeɪt) an affiliated person or organization. **affiliation** *n* < ultimately Latin *ad-* to + *filius* son.

affinity (ə'fɪnɪtɪ) *n* **1** a natural liking or attraction. **2** a close similarity based on relationship. < ultimately Latin *ad-* to + *finis* border.

affirm (ə'fɜːm) *vb* **1** declare or assert positively. **2** confirm or ratify. **3** declare by affirmation. **affirmation** *n* **1** affirming; positive assertion. **2** (*law*) a solemn declaration made by someone who conscientiously objects to taking an oath. < ultimately Latin *ad-* to + *firmare* to make firm.

affirmative (ə'fɜːmətɪv) *adj* showing agreement or that something is true: an affirmative answer.
• *n* an affirmative statement, word, etc. **affirmatively** *adv*

affix (ə'fɪks) *vb* **1** attach or stick. **2** add in writing.
• *n* ('æfɪks) (*grammar*) a prefix or suffix. < Latin *ad-* to + *figere* to fasten.

afflict (ə'flɪkt) *vb* cause suffering to; distress severely. **affliction** *n* great pain or suffering; cause of this. < ultimately Latin *ad-* to + *fligere* to strike.

affluent ('æfluənt) *adj* amply provided with material possessions; wealthy: the affluent society. **affluence** *n* **affluently** *adv* < ultimately Latin *ad-* to + *fluere* to flow.

afford (ə'fɔːd) *vb* **1** have enough (esp. money) to be able to do or spare something: We can't afford to buy a new car. **2** (*formal*) provide; yield: He seized the opportunity afforded by the financial schemes. < Old English *geforthian* to promote.

affray (ə'freɪ) *n* a public brawl or quarrel. < Middle French *affreer* to frighten.

affront (ə'frʌnt) *n* a deliberate insult or disrespectful behaviour.
• *vb* insult openly; offend. < ultimately Latin *ad-* to + *frons* forehead.

afield (ə'fiːld) *adv, adj* **1** away from home. **2** astray.

aflame (ə'fleɪm) *adj*, adv on fire; passionate.

afloat (ə'fləʊt) *adj, adv* **1** carried on the water. **2** at sea; on ship. **3** flooded. **4** rumoured. **5** free from debt.

afoot (ə'fʊt) *adj, adv* in progress: Plans are afoot to start a new training scheme.

aforesaid (ə'fɔːˌsɛd) *adj* referred to previously.

aforethought (ə'fɔːˌθɔːt) *adj* premeditated: with malice aforethought.

afraid (ə'freɪd) *adj* **1** feeling fear; frightened. **2** sorry (to have to say that): I'm afraid I can't go. < SEE **AFFRAY.**

afresh (ə'frɛʃ) *adv* once more; again.

aft (ɑːft) *adj, adv* (situated) in, to, or at the rear or stern. < Old English *æftan* behind.

after ('ɑːftə) *prep* **1** following in time. **2** behind in place or order. **3** in pursuit or search of: They ran after the thief. **4** concerning: He asked after you. **5** resembling, in imitation of: She takes after her mother. **6** in view of; in spite of: After all our hard work, we still failed. **7** directly following: one complaint after the other.
• *adv* **1** behind. **2** afterwards.
• *conj* at a time later than.
• *adj* **1** later. **2** towards the stern of a ship, etc. **after-effect** *n* a result that occurs some time after a cause. **afterlife** *n* life after death. **aftermath** *n* a result; period immediately after a disaster. **afternoon** *n* the time between noon and evening. **afters** *pl n* (*informal*) a dessert. **afterthought** *n* something thought of, said, or added later. **afterwards** *adv* after that. < Old English *æfter.* SEE PANEL.

again (ə'geɪn, ə'gɛn) *adv* **1** another time; once more: I'll try again in an hour. **2** back to where or how one was before: She was soon well again. **3** further; besides. **4** on the other hand: But then again, it may not be true. < Old English *ongegn* opposite to.

against (ə'geɪnst, ə'gɛnst) *prep* **1** in opposition to. **2** in contrast to. **3** in preparation for: We keep a cash reserve against the possibility of breakdowns. **4** in contact with: leaning against a wall. **5** in exchange for. < SEE **AGAIN.**

agape (ə'geɪp) *adj* (of the mouth) wide open, as with wonder.

aftermath

A situation that follows as the immediate outcome of a disaster such as a war, fire, or flood, is known as an aftermath: In its aftermath the earthquake left a thousand families homeless. Originally this word had a very different meaning. A *math* was a 'mowing' or 'crop' and *aftermath* was the name given to the second mowing of a field of grass (the one coming 'after' the hay harvest). The figurative sense in which the word is used today dates back to the mid-17th century.

age (eɪdʒ) *n* **1** the period of time that a person or thing has existed. **2** a point in life; period or state of life: the voting age. **3** the later part of life; old age. **4** a period of time marked by a person or feature that is mentioned: the golden age of steam; the television age. **5** (*informal*) a very long time: It takes ages to do the shopping.
• *vb* **1** grow old or cause to grow old; show signs of old age. **2** become or cause to become mature. **aged** *adj* **1** grown old. **2** of the age of: aged 60. **ageless** *adj* **1** never growing or appearing old. **2** timeless; eternal. **age-old** *adj* very old; ancient. < ultimately Latin *aevum* lifetime.

agenda (əˈdʒɛndə) *n* a list of items to be dealt with at a meeting. < Latin: things to be done, from *agere* to do.

agent (ˈeɪdʒənt) *n* **1** a person who acts on behalf of another; representative. **2** a person or thing that produces an effect. **3** a spy. **agency** *n* **1** a business or organization that provides a service: a news agency. **2** the means by which something is done. < ultimately Latin *agere* to act.

agglutinate (əˈgluːtɪˌneɪt) *vb* cause to stick. **agglutination** *n* < Latin *ad-* to + *glutinare* to glue, from *gluten* glue.

aggrandize (əˈgrændaɪz) *vb* increase the power, wealth, etc., of, esp. falsely. **aggrandizement** *n* < ultimately Latin *ad-* to + *grandir* to increase.

aggravate (ˈægrəˌveɪt) *vb* **1** make worse or more severe. **2** (*informal*) annoy. **aggravation** *n* < Latin *ad-* to + *gravare* to burden, from *gravis* heavy. SEE PANEL.

aggregate (ˈægrɪgət) *adj* formed of separate units combined into a whole.
• *vb* (ˈægrɪˌgeɪt) combine to form (a whole, total, etc.).
• *n* (ˈægrɪgət) **1** a sum or mass of many separate parts. **2** sand, gravel, etc., mixed with cement and water to make concrete. < ultimately Latin *ad-* to + *grex* herd.

aggression (əˈgrɛʃən) *n* **1** an unprovoked attack. **2** hostile behaviour or attitudes. **aggressor** *n* < Latin *ad-* to + *gradi* to step.

aggressive (əˈgrɛsɪv) *adj* **1** inclined towards or showing aggression. **2** forceful; self-assertive. **aggressively** *adv* **aggressiveness** *n*

aggrieve (əˈgriːv) *vb* distress; injure, esp. unfairly. < SEE **AGGRAVATE.**

aggro (ˈægrəʊ) *n* (*slang*) **1** trouble. **2** aggressive behaviour; provocation. < *aggravation.*

aghast (əˈgɑːst) *adj* struck with amazement or horror. < Old English *gæstan* to frighten.

agile (ˈædʒaɪl) *adj* quick, esp. in movement; nimble. **agilely** *adv* **agility** *n* < Latin *agere* to act.

agitate (ˈædʒɪˌteɪt) *vb* **1** excite or trouble emotionally or mentally. **2** cause to move briskly; shake. **3** stir up public opinion. **agitation** *n* **agitator** *n* < Latin *agere* to act.

aglow (əˈgləʊ) *adj* glowing.

AGM *abbrev* annual general meeting.

agnostic (ægˈnɒstɪk) *n* **1** a person who holds that it is impossible to know whether or not God exists. **2** (*informal*) a person who doubts the existence of God.
• *adj* of an agnostic. **agnosticism** *n* < Greek *a-* not + *gignōskein* to know.

ago (əˈgəʊ) *adv* in the past. < Old English *āgān* to pass away.

agog (əˈgɒg) *adj* full of strong, excited anticipation; eager and curious. < perhaps Middle French *en gogues* in mirth.

agony (ˈægənɪ) *n* extreme mental or physical pain. **agonize** *vb* suffer great anxiety; worry intensely: agonize over a decision. **agonizingly** *adv* < ultimately Greek *agōn* contest.

agoraphobia (ˌægrəˈfəʊbɪə) *n* an abnormal fear of open spaces. < Greek *agora* market-place + *-phobia,* from *phobos* fear.

agree (əˈgriː) *vb* **agreed; agreeing 1** be of the same opinion. **2** give assent (to). **3** admit or concede. **4** arrive at an understanding (on). **5** be in or bring into harmony (with). **6** suit the health, etc., of: Shrimps don't agree with me. **7** (*grammar*) correspond in gender, number, case, or person. **agreeable** *adj* **1** pleasing. **2** willing to agree. **agreement** *n* **1** agreeing. **2** harmony. **3** an arrangement stating terms, conditions, etc.;

that aggravating word

Careful speakers and writers of English avoid using aggravate to mean 'to annoy or exasperate', considering such usage to be incorrect. Aggravate is widely used in this sense in informal English, however, where it has become firmly established: 'Stop *aggravating* the child!'

contract. < ultimately Latin *ad-* to + *gratus* pleasing.

agriculture (ˈægrɪˌkʌltʃə) *n* the science and practice of cultivating land and raising livestock. **agricultural** *adj* **agriculturally** *adv* < Latin *ager* field + *cultura* cultivation.

aground (əˈgraʊnd) *adv, adj* on or onto the shore or the bottom of shallow water.

ahead (əˈhɛd) *adv, adj* **1** in front; in a forward direction. **2** in or for the future. **3** in or to a more advanced position.

aid (eɪd) *vb* give support to; help or facilitate.
• *n* **1** assistance, esp. money or food: aid to Third World countries. **2** a person or device that helps or assists: a hearing-aid; a visual aid. < ultimately Latin *ad-* to + *juvare* to help. SEE PANEL.

AIDS *abbrev* acquired immune deficiency syndrome.

ail (eɪl) *vb* be unwell; give pain to. **ailment** *n* an illness, esp. a mild one. < Old English *eglan*.

aim (eɪm) *vb* **1** point or direct (a weapon, blow, etc.) at a target. **2** intend or propose; mean. **3** aspire; strive (towards). **4** direct towards a goal that is mentioned: an advertisement aimed at housewives.
• *n* **1** the aiming of a weapon, etc., at a target. **2** a purpose. **aimless** *adj* without a purpose. **aimlessly** *adv* **aimlessness** *n* < ultimately Latin *aestimare* to estimate.

air (ɛə) *n* **1** the mixture of gases that surrounds the earth and forms its atmosphere. **2** the earth's atmosphere thought of as the region in which aircraft travel; transportation by aircraft. **3** a light wind; breeze. **4** a special, esp. outward quality. **5** a person's manner or bearing. **6** *pl* affected, haughty manners. **7** a song; melody.
• *adj* of aircraft, the air force, etc.
• *vb* **1** expose to the air for drying, etc.; ventilate. **2** expose (clothes, etc.) to warm air so as to dry. **3** express publicly: air one's views. **air-conditioning** *n* equipment that controls the humidity and temperature in a room, etc. **air force** the branch of a country's armed services for air warfare and defence. **air hostess** a stewardess on an aeroplane. **air letter** a sheet of light paper that can be folded and sealed and may be sent cheaply by airmail. **air raid** an attack by armed aircraft. **air-strip** *n* a cleared area of ground on which aircraft can land and take off. **airy** *adj* **1** having lots of fresh air. **2** spacious: light, airy classrooms. **3** illusory; vague. **4** flippant; casual. **airily** *adv* **airiness** *n* **airy-fairy** *adj* fanciful and unrealistic. < ultimately Greek *aēr*. SEE PANEL.

airborne (ˈɛəˌbɔːn) *adj* carried or transported by air.

aircraft (ˈɛəˌkrɑːft) *n* any machine capable of flying, such as an aeroplane, helicopter, or glider. **aircraft-carrier** *n* a warship with a large, flat deck for the take-off and landing of aircraft.

airer (ˈɛərə) *n* a framework on which clothes may be aired.

airfield (ˈɛəˌfiːld) *n* an area of land equipped for the take-off and landing

What's all this in aid of?

What's ... in aid of? is an informal expression used to mean 'What is the purpose of (something)?' It often expresses surprise, indignation, etc.: 'What's all this noise in aid of?'

The phrase dates from the street collections of the First World War, when people asked for information about the cause for which money was wanted.

in the air

Air features in a number of idiomatic expressions, including:

clear the air to talk openly about doubts, worries, suspicions, etc., so reducing tension: Their frank discussion did a great deal to clear the air.
hot air impressive, but empty and worthless promises, boasts, etc.
in the air in circulation; being rumoured: talk of a merger in the air.
on/off the air (of radio or television) broadcasting/not broadcasting: We'll be back on the air at 6 o'clock tomorrow morning.
walk or **tread on air** to be very happy: She's been walking on air ever since she heard she'd passed the exam.

of aeroplanes.

airgun (ˈɛəˌgʌn) *n* **1** a gun from which a projectile is propelled by compressed air. **2** a hand-tool that works by compressed air.

airless (ˈɛələs) *adj* **1** stuffy. **2** still; windless. **airlessness** *n*

airlift (ˈɛəˌlɪft) *n* the transportation by air of supplies or troops.
• *vb* transport in this way.

airline (ˈɛəˌlaɪn) *n* an organization that provides regular, public air-transport services. **airliner** *n* a large, passenger aircraft.

airlock (ˈɛəˌlɒk) *n* **1** an airtight compartment that allows movement between two areas of different pressures. **2** a blockage in the flow of a liquid in a pipe, etc., caused by trapped air.

airmail (ˈɛəˌmeɪl) *n* mail carried by air; postal system performing this.
• *vb* send by airmail.

airman (ˈɛəmən) *n, pl* **airmen** an aviator, esp. one in the armed forces.

airport (ˈɛəˌpɔːt) *n* an airfield that has full facilities for transporting passengers and cargo by air and for receiving them.

airship (ˈɛəˌʃɪp) *n* a self-propelled aircraft that is lighter than air and has a steering-system.

airspace (ˈɛəˌspeɪs) *n* the area of sky above a country and coming under its jurisdiction.

airtight (ˈɛəˌtaɪt) *adj* not allowing air to enter or escape: an airtight container.

aisle (aɪl) *n* a passageway between areas of seating in a theatre, church, etc. < Latin *ala* wing.

ajar (əˈdʒɑː) *adj, adv* (esp. of a door or window) slightly open. < Old English *cierran* to turn.

akimbo (əˈkɪmbəʊ) *adj, adv* with hands on the hips and elbows turned outwards. < Middle English *in kenebowe*.

akin (əˈkɪn) *adj* similar; related (to).

alabaster (ˈæləˌbæstə, ˈæləˌbɑːstə) *n* a pure, fine-grained, usually white and translucent, chalky stone, often carved into ornaments. < ultimately Greek *alabastros*.

à la carte (ˌɑː lɑː ˈkɑːt) ordered as separate items from a menu. < French.

alacrity (əˈlækrɪtɪ) *n* briskness; liveliness. < Latin *alacer* lively.

alarm (əˈlɑːm) *n* **1** fear caused by awareness of danger. **2** a warning signal or noise; device that gives this. **3** an alarm-clock.
• *vb* **1** frighten. **2** warn about danger. **alarm-clock** *n* a clock with a device that rings at a particular time. < ultimately Old Italian *all'arme* to arms.

alas (əˈlæs) *interj* an exclamation of sorrow, compassion, or disappointment. < Old French *a* ah + *las* weary.

albatross (ˈælbəˌtrɒs) *n* a large sea-bird with a stout, hooked bill and long, narrow wings. < Portuguese *alcatraz* pelican.

albeit (ɔːlˈbiːɪt) *conj* (*formal*) even though; although. < Middle English *al be it* although it be (that).

albino (ælˈbiːnəʊ) *n, pl* **albinos** a person or animal with a lack of pigment that results in a pale skin, fair hair, and pink irises. < ultimately Latin *albus* white.

album (ˈælbəm) *n* **1** a book in which a collection of stamps, photographs, etc., may be kept. **2** a long-playing record or cassette. < Latin: blank tablet.

albumen (ˈælbjʊmən) *n* the white of an egg. < Latin *albus* white.

alchemy (ˈælkəmɪ) *n* a medieval philosophy that combined practical chemistry with mystical cosmology and esp. sought to change base metals into gold. **alchemist** *n* < Arabic *al* the + *kīmiyā'*.

alcohol (ˈælkəˌhɒl) *n* **1** a colourless, flammable liquid that is present in intoxicating drinks such as wine or beer. **2** a drink or drinks containing this. **3** (*chemistry*) one of a group of organic compounds. < ultimately Arabic *al-kuḥul* powdered antimony.

alcoholic (ˌælkəˈhɒlɪk) *adj* of, containing, or resulting from alcohol.
• *n* a person suffering from alcoholism. **alcoholism** *n* a disease caused by the continual, heavy drinking of alcohol.

alcove (ˈælkəʊv) *n* a recess in the wall of a room or off a room. < ultimately Arabic *al-qubbah* the arch.

alder (ˈɔːldə) *n* a shrub or tree of the birch family. < Old English *alor*.

alderman (ˈɔːldəmən) *n, pl* **aldermen** (formerly) a senior member of a local council, elected by the other councillors. < Old English *eald* old + *man*.

ale (eɪl) *n* beer. < Old English *ealu*.

alert (əˈlɜːt) *adj* watchful; aware.
• *n* an alarm or warning of a danger.
• *vb* warn; cause to be aware of. **alertly** *adv* **alertness** *n* **on the alert** looking out for danger or opportunity. < Italian *all'erta* on the watch.

algae (ˈældʒiː) *pl n* simple water-plants that have no stems, roots, or leaves. < Latin, plural of *alga* seaweed.

algebra (ˈældʒɪbrə) *n* a branch of mathematics in which symbols represent unknown quantities. **algebraic** *adj*

algebraically *adv* < Arabic *al-jabr* the reunion of broken parts. SEE PANEL.

alias (ˈeɪlɪəs) *adv* otherwise called, esp. falsely: Stibbs, alias Smith.
• *n* an assumed name. < Latin: otherwise.

alibi (ˈælɪˌbaɪ) *n* **1** evidence that an accused person was elsewhere when the crime was committed. **2** (*informal*) an excuse offered esp. to avoid punishment. < Latin: elsewhere. SEE PANEL.

alien (ˈeɪljən, ˈeɪlɪən) *adj* **1** belonging to a different person, place, etc.; unfamiliar or foreign. **2** different or opposite in nature: utterly alien to the British way of life.
• *n* a person from a different family, country, or world. **alienate** *vb* cause to become indifferent or hostile. **alienation** *n* < Latin *alius* other.

alight¹ (əˈlaɪt) *vb* **1** get down from a vehicle. **2** come down from the air and settle. < Old English *ā* + *līhtan* to dismount.

alight² *adj, adv* **1** on fire. **2** excited.

align (əˈlaɪn) *vb* **1** place or be placed in a line. **2** bring into agreement. **alignment** *n* < Old French *a-* to + *ligne* line.

alike (əˈlaɪk) *adj* having similar features.
• *adv* in the same way or degree. < Old English *gelīc*.

alimentary canal (ˌælɪˈmɛntərɪ) the tubular passage from the mouth to the anus through which food is digested. < Latin *alere* to nourish.

alimony (ˈælɪmənɪ) *n* an allowance of money that a court may order a man to pay to his wife or former wife. < Latin *alere* to nourish.

alive (əˈlaɪv) *adj* **1** living. **2** in existence; active. **3** aware of; alert. **4** teeming with living or moving things. < Old English *on* + *līf* life. SEE PANEL. SEE PANEL AT **DEAD**.

alkali (ˈælkeˌlaɪ) *n, pl* **alkalis** a chemical base that dissolves in water. **alkaline** *adj* < Arabic *al-qili* the ashes of saltwort.

alkaloid (ˈælkəˌlɔɪd) *n* any of a group of nitrogenous compounds derived from plants.

all (ɔːl) *determiner* **1** the whole quantity, extent, etc., of. **2** every part together.
• *adv* **1** totally; altogether. **2** (in scores)

algebra

Algebra and zero are two of the mathematical terms that have come into English from Arabic.

As well as being the mathematicians of the Middle Ages, the Arabians were also celebrated astronomers, without whom English would today also lack words such as almanac and zenith. As if mathematics and astronomy were not enough, the Arabians also occupied themselves with chemistry. Evidence of this is provided by alcohol and alkali, also Arabic in origin.

What's your alibi?

Evidence that a person charged with a crime was in another place at the time and therefore could not have done it is known as an alibi. This word, like many legal terms, is a direct borrowing from Latin. In Latin it means 'elsewhere'.

alive and dead

Dead is a typical adjective: it can occur both before a noun (a *dead* parrot) and after a verb like be or look (the parrot looks *dead*). Although closely related to dead in meaning, alive cannot occur in the same places as dead in a sentence. A more technical way of expressing this is to say that the syntactic behaviour of dead is different from that of alive: although we can say a dead parrot, we can't say an alive parrot, only The parrot looks alive.

Adjectives like alive which do not occur before a noun are known as *predicative* adjectives. Others in the group include:

afraid	**awake**
ajar	**unwell**
asleep	

to each side: 2 all.
• *pron* everything; everyone.
• *n* one's whole interest, resources, etc. < Old English *eall.* SEE PANEL.
allay (ə'leɪ) *vb* **1** lessen (fears, etc.). **2** relieve (pain, sorrow, etc.). < Old English *ālecgan* to put down.
allege (ə'lɛdʒ) *vb* state without proof or before proving. **allegation** *n* a statement made without proof. **allegedly** *adv* according to allegation. < ultimately Latin *allegare* to send on a mission.
allegiance (ə'li:dʒəns) *n* loyal support given to one's country, a cause, etc. < Old French *lige* liege, from Late Latin *laetus* serf.
allegory ('ælɪgərɪ) *n* a story in verse or prose in which the characters and events have a symbolic, esp. moral meaning. **allegorical** *adj* **allegorically** *adv* < ultimately Greek *allos* other + *agoreuein* to speak publicly.
allergy ('ælədʒɪ) *n* an abnormal reaction by the body caused by substances such as pollen or certain foods. **allergic** *adj* **1** of or causing allergy. **2** (*informal*) having a strong dislike for: allergic to work. < ultimately Greek *allos* other + *ergon* work.
alleviate (ə'li:vɪˌeɪt) *vb* make easier to bear; relieve. **alleviation** *n* < Latin *ad-* to + *levis* light.
alley ('ælɪ) *n, pl* **alleys 1** a narrow street behind or between buildings. **2** a path in a garden or park. **3** the long, narrow lane along which balls are rolled in ten-pin bowling, etc. < ultimately Latin *ambulare* to walk.
alliance (ə'laɪəns) *n* a formal association or union, for example of countries by a treaty, or of families by marriage. **allied** *adj* **1** joined in alliance; united. **2** related; similar. < SEE **ALLY.**
alligator ('ælɪˌgeɪtə) *n* a large reptile with a broad snout, strong jaws, and sharp teeth. < Spanish *el lagarto* the lizard, from Latin *lacerta* lizard. SEE PANEL.
alliteration (əˌlɪtə'reɪʃən) *n* a figure of

all in all

All features in a number of common expressions, many of them informal, including:

all at once 1 at the same time: 'Now, children, don't speak all at once.' **2** unexpectedly; suddenly: All at once he remembered what happened before the crash.
all being well if nothing goes wrong: All being well I'll be with you at 6 o'clock.
all but almost; nearly: He had all but solved the problem.
all-clear *n* a signal that danger is over. See also panel at **clear**.
all important extremely important, urgent, etc.
all in exhausted.
all-in *adj* including everything: an all-in price.
all in all taking everything into consideration; generally.
all out with the greatest possible speed, strength, etc.
all over 1 on every part of: all over the world. **2** in every respect; typically: That's Jane all over!
all right 1 happy, safe, etc.: Will you be all right while I'm away? **2** operating properly: I've mended the radio now. It should work all right for you. **3** just acceptable; satisfactory: The food's all right but not as good as Mum's! **4** used to express agreement: 'Let's go to town this evening, shall we?'—'All right, let's.' Note that the spelling alright, although very common, has not yet been fully accepted as standard English.
all-round *adj* general; comprehensive: an all-round education.
all there mentally normal: He's not quite all there.
all the same 1 nevertheless: All the same, I wish you'd told me earlier. **2** not making any difference at all: It's all the same to them.
all-time *adj* unsurpassed: an all-time record.
all told taking everyone or everything into consideration.

The expression **the be-all and end-all** is used in contemporary English to mean 'the ultimate purpose': Why do you spend all your time going to football matches. After all, football isn't the be-all and end-all of life, is it? It comes originally from Shakespeare's 'Macbeth', Act 1, Scene 7:

... that but this blow
Might be the be-all and the end-all here,
But here, upon this back and shoal of time,
We'd jump the life to come.

speech in which consonants, esp. at the beginning of words, are repeated. **alliterative** *adj* < Latin *ad-* to + *littera* letter. SEE PANEL AT **BUSY.**

allocate (ˈæləˌkeɪt) *vb* assign or designate for a particular purpose. **allocation** *n* < Latin *ad-* to + *locare* to place.

allot (əˈlɒt) *vb* **allotted; allotting** distribute or designate for a particular purpose. **allotment** *n* a small plot of land let out for cultivation. < Middle French *aloter*, from *a-* to + *lot* portion.

allow (əˈlaʊ) *vb* **1** permit or let; agree to. **2** enable. **3** afford or make possible: Having a car allows us more freedom. **4** allocate or grant. **5** take into consideration; set aside. **6** admit as true or possible; concede. **7** accept (a claim, etc.). **allowable** *adj* permissible. **allowably** *adv* **allowance** *n* **1** an amount, esp. of money, given for a particular purpose: a clothing allowance. **2** a stated amount of income granted free of tax to a tax-payer: a personal allowance. **3** the taking into account of certain factors in an assessment: make allowance for his age. < ultimately Latin *ad-* to + *laudare* to praise.

alloy (ˈælɔɪ) *n* a blend of a metal with one or more other metals or non-metals. < ultimately Latin *alligare* to bind.

allude (əˈluːd) *vb* refer indirectly (to). **allusion** *n* **allusive** *adj* **allusively** *adv* < Latin *ad-* to + *ludere* to play. SEE PANEL.

allure (əˈlʊə) *vb* entice or tempt; attract or charm. **allurement** *n* < Old French *a-* + *loire* lure.

ally (əˈlaɪ) *vb* **1** join or unite formally. **2** connect or associate.
• *n* (ˈælaɪ) **1** a country or ruler in alliance with another. **2** a helper or co-operator. < ultimately Latin *ad-* to + *ligare* to bind.

almanac (ˈɔːlməˌnæk) *n* a yearly publication containing statistical, astronomical, and general information. < ultimately Medieval Latin *almanachus*.

almighty (ɔːlˈmaɪtɪ) *adj* **1** all-powerful. **2** (*informal*) great in extent, force, etc.: It dropped to earth with an almighty bump!

almond (ˈɑːmənd) *n* **1** a small tree with pink flowers and a green fruit containing an edible kernel. **2** this edible, oval kernel. < ultimately Greek *amygdalē*.

almost (ˈɔːlməʊst) *adv* very nearly.

alms (ɑːmz) *pl n* money or goods given to the poor. **almshouse** *n* a house endowed by charity for the elderly or poor. < ultimately Greek *eleos* pity.

aloft (əˈlɒft) *adv, adj* in, at, or to a great height. < Old Norse *ā on*, in + *lopt* air.

alone (əˈləʊn) *adj, adv* **1** separated; isolated. **2** without the help of others. **3** without interference. < Middle English *al* all + *one* one.

along (əˈlɒŋ) *adv* **1** in a line. **2** onwards. **3** in accompaniment: Can my brother come along as well? **4** there: I'll be along soon.
• *prep* **1** parallel or close to the length of. **2** in the direction of. **alongside** *adv, prep* along or at the side (of). < Old English *and-* against + *lang* long.

aloof (əˈluːf) *adj, adv* **1** at a distance; apart. **2** distant in feeling; unfriendly. **aloofly** *adv* **aloofness** *n* < *a-* + *loof*, from *luff* weather side of a ship.

aloud (əˈlaʊd) *adv, adj* with a voice loud enough to be heard.

alp (ælp) *n* a high mountain. **alpine** *adj* < back formation from *Alps*, mountain range in Europe.

alpha (ˈælfə) *n* the first letter of the Greek alphabet.

alphabet (ˈælfəˌbɛt) *n* **1** the set of letters

alligator

The Spanish name for a lizard is *lagarto*. When the Spaniards first came across the alligator during their travels in the New World, they called it *el lagarto* or 'the lizard' because of its lizard-like features. To English ears the two words *el lagarto* sounded like a single word. Hence the English name alligator.

allusion, illusion, or **delusion**?

An allusion is an indirect reference: During the speech he made several *allusions* to the former prime minister.

An illusion is a wrong impression or opinion: They are under no *illusions* about the enormity of the task. An illusion is also a misleading appearance that seems real to the senses: an optical *illusion*.

A delusion is a false belief, often strongly held but which has no factual basis: *delusions* of grandeur; He is suffering from the *delusion* that he is Julius Caesar.

used in writing a language. **2** a system of signs or symbols used to represent sounds. **alphabetical** *adj* in the order of the letters of the alphabet. **alphabetically** *adv* < Greek *alphabētos,* from *alpha* + *bēta.*

already (ɔːlˈrɛdɪ) *adv* **1** by or before a particular time. **2** earlier than expected. **3** previously; before.

alright (ɔːlˈraɪt) *adv* all right. SEE PANEL AT ALL.

also (ˈɔːlsəʊ) *adv* in addition; besides. **also-ran** *n* a horse, etc., not among the first three to finish in a race; unsuccessful person. < Old English *eallswā,* from *eall* all + *swā* so.

altar (ˈɔːltə) *n* **1** a place where sacrifices are offered to a god. **2** the table on which the bread and wine are consecrated in Communion services. < Latin *altare.*

alter (ˈɔːltə) *vb* make or become different; change. **alterable** *adj* **alteration** *n* < ultimately Latin *alter* other.

altercation (ˌɔːltəˈkeɪʃən) *n* a noisy, angry quarrel. < ultimately Latin *altercari* to quarrel.

alternate (ɔːlˌtɜːnət) *adj* **1** happening in turns. **2** every other: He works alternate weekends.

• *vb* (ˈɔːltəˌneɪt) **1** occur or cause to occur in turns. **2** move from one condition to another. **alternately** *adv* **alternation** *n* **alternating current** electric current that reverses its direction regularly. < Latin *alter* other.

alternative (ɔːlˈtɜːnətɪv) *adj* giving a choice between two or more possibilities.

• *n* one of two or more possibilities to be chosen; opportunity to make such a choice. **alternatively** *adv*

alternator (ˈɔːltəˌneɪtə) *n* an electric generator that produces alternating current.

although (ɔːlˈðəʊ) *conj* despite the fact or possibility that; though.

altimeter (ˈæltɪˌmiːtə) *n* an instrument that measures altitude.

altitude (ˈæltɪˌtjuːd) *n* the height above sea-level. < Latin *altus* high.

alto (ˈæltəʊ) *n, pl* **altos** the highest adult male voice in singing; singer with such a voice; part for such a voice. < Italian: high, from Latin *altus* high.

altogether (ˌɔːltəˈgɛðə, ˈɔːltəˌgɛðə) *adv* **1** with everything considered. **2** completely. **3** mainly.

altruism (ˈæltruːˌɪzəm) *n* unselfish concern for others' welfare. **altruist** *n* **altruistic** *adj* **altruistically** *adv* < Latin *alter* other.

aluminium (ˌæljʊˈmɪnɪəm) *n* a light, silvery-white, malleable metal that resists corrosion. < Latin *alumen* alum, kind of mineral salt.

always (ˈɔːlweɪz) *adv* **1** at all times. **2** repeatedly. **3** as a last resort. < Old English *ealne weg* all the way.

am (əm; *stressed* æm) SEE BE.

a.m. *abbrev* (*Latin)* ante meridiem (before noon).

amalgam (əˈmælgəm) *n* **1** an alloy of mercury and another metal. **2** a combination or mixture. < Medieval Latin *amalgama.*

amalgamate (əˈmælgəˌmeɪt) *vb* combine into one; unite. **amalgamation** *n*

amass (əˈmæs) *vb* heap up; accumulate or collect. < Old French *masse* mass.

amateur (ˈæmətə, ˈæmətʃə) *n* a person who does something as a pastime rather than as a profession. **amateurish** *adj* showing a lack of professional skill; inexpert. **amateurishly** *adv* **amateurishness** *n* < ultimately Latin *amare* to love.

amaze (æˈmeɪz) *vb* fill with wonder or surprise. **amazement** *n* < Old English *āmasian* SEE MAZE.

ambassador (æmˈbæsədə) *n* **1** a diplomatic minister sent by a country as a permanent representative or on a special, esp. temporary, assignment. **2** an official representative. **ambassadorial** *adj* < SEE EMBASSY.

amber (ˈæmbə) *n* **1** a brownish-yellow fossil resin used in making ornaments; colour of this. **2** a yellowish traffic-light indicating caution.

• *adj* made of or of the colour of amber. < Arabic *'ambar* ambergris, waxy substance.

ambidextrous (ˌæmbɪˈdɛkstrəs) *adj* able to use either hand equally well. < Latin *ambi-* both + *dexter* right-handed.

ambience (ˈæmbɪəns) *n* the atmosphere or surroundings of a place. < French *ambiance,* ultimately Latina *ambi-* round + *ire* to go.

ambiguous (æmˈbɪgjʊəs) *adj* **1** having two or more possible meanings. **2** obscure or doubtful; uncertain. **ambiguity** *n* **ambiguously** *adv* < Latin *ambi-* round + *ire* to go. SEE PANEL AT TIP[1].

ambition (æmˈbɪʃən) *n* **1** a strong desire for success, riches, power, etc. **2** a strong desire to achieve something. **3** the object of ambition. **ambitious** *adj* full of ambition. **ambitiously** *adv* < Latin *ambitio* going round.

ambivalent (æmˈbɪvələnt) *adj* having two different and opposing attitudes

towards a thing, person, etc. **ambivalence** *n* **ambivalently** *adv* < Latin *ambi-* both + *valēre* to be strong.
amble (ˈæmbl̩) *vb* walk at a leisurely pace.
• *n* a leisurely pace. < ultimately Latin *ambulare* to walk.
ambulance (ˈæmbjʊləns) *n* a motor vehicle designed to transport injured or sick people. < ultimately Latin *ambulare* to walk.
ambush (ˈæmbʊʃ) *n* the hiding of soldiers, etc., to make a surprise attack on an approaching enemy or victim; such an attack.
• *vb* attack in an ambush; lie in wait (for). < Old French *en* in + *busche* piece of firewood.
ameliorate (əˈmiːljəˌreɪt) *vb* (*formal*) make or become better; improve. **amelioration** *n* < alteration of *meliorate*, ultimately from Latin *melior* better.
amenable (əˈmiːnəbl̩) *adj* **1** likely to agree, respond favourably, etc. **2** responsible or answerable. **amenability** *n* **amenably** *adv* < ultimately Latin *minari* to threaten.
amend (əˈmɛnd) *vb* **1** improve or put right. **2** change (a document such as a constitution) formally. **amendment** *n* **amends** *pl n* compensation or recompense: make amends for past failures. < ultimately Latin *emendare* to emend.
amenity (əˈmiːnɪtɪ) *n* a useful, convenient, or pleasant facility. < ultimately Latin *amoenus* pleasant.
americanism (əˈmɛrɪkəˌnɪzəm) *n* a distinctive feature of American culture, such as a custom or linguistic usage. **americanize** *vb* cause to gain American characteristics.
amethyst (ˈæmɪθɪst) *n* a semi-precious stone of purple or violet quartz. < Greek *amethystos* not drunken.
amiable (ˈeɪmɪəbl̩) *adj* appearing pleasant, agreeable, and friendly. **amiability** *n* **amiably** *adv* < Latin *amicus* friend. SEE PANEL.
amicable (ˈæmikəbl̩) *adj* showing friendly goodwill. **amicability** *n* **amicably** *adv* < SEE **AMIABLE.** SEE PANEL AT **AMIABLE.**
amid (əˈmɪd) or **amidst** (əˈmɪdst) *prep* in the middle of. < Old English *on* at + *middan* middle.
amiss (əˈmɪs) *adv* in a wrong or inappropriate way.
• *adj* wrong; out of order. < Middle English *a mis*, from *mis* mistake.
ammeter (ˈæmˌmiːtə) *n* an instrument for measuring electric current in amperes. < *ampere* + *-meter*. SEE **METER**[1].
ammo (ˈæməʊ) *n* (*informal*) ammunition.
ammonia (əˈməʊnjə) *n* a colourless, toxic, highly soluble gas used in making fertilizers, explosives, etc. < Greek *Ammōn*, name of temple, near which a related substance was found.
ammunition (ˌæmjʊˈnɪʃən) *n* **1** missiles that can be fired from a weapon. **2** a means of defence or attack in an argument. < SEE **MUNITIONS.**
amnesia (æmˈniːzɪə) *n* loss of memory. < Greek *amnēsia* forgetfulness.
amnesty (ˈæmnəstɪ) *n* a general pardon, for example for political offences. < Greek *amnēstia* forgetfulness.
amoeba (əˈmiːbə) *n* one of a group of free-living, microscopic, single-cell animals. < Greek *ameibein* to change.
amok (əˈmʌk) *adv* in a murderous frenzy. < Malay.
among (əˈmʌŋ) or **amongst** (əˈmʌŋkst) *prep* **1** in the middle of. **2** to each of. **3** in the number or group of. **4** with one another. **5** through the joint action of. < Old English *on* in + *gemong* crowd.
amoral (eɪˈmɒrəl) *adj* not related to morality; neither moral nor immoral. SEE PANEL.
amorous (ˈæmərəs) *adj* of, showing, or tending towards love or desire. **amorously** *adv* **amorousness** *n* < Latin *amare* to love.
amorphous (əˈmɔːfəs) *adj* having no definite shape, form, or nature. < Greek *a-* without + *morphē* form.
amount (əˈmaʊnt) *n* **1** a total quantity. **2** a quantity: a small amount of water.
• *vb* **1** be equal in number or quantity. **2** be equivalent in significance: The concessions amount to a betrayal of basic principles. < Old French *amonter*, from *a-* to + *mont* mountain.

amiable or **amicable**?

These two words should be carefully distinguished.

Amiable is used to describe people or expressions and means 'appearing pleasant, agreeable, and friendly': an *amiable* mood, an *amiable* smile.

Amicable is used to describe arrangements or agreements and means 'showing friendly goodwill': The two sides reached an *amicable* agreement. They settled their *differences* in an *amicable* manner.

amp (æmp) *n* (*informal*) an ampere.
ampere (ˈæmpɛə) *n* the SI unit of electric current. SEE PANEL AT **VOLT.**
ampersand (ˈæmpəˌsænd) *n* the sign & = and. < shortened from *and* (&) *per se and* & by itself (represents) *and.*
amphetamine (æmˈfɛtəˌmiːn) *n* a drug that stimulates the nervous system but has unpleasant or dangerous side-effects. < alpha + *m*ethyl + *ph*enyl + *e*thyl + *amine.*
amphibian (æmˈfɪbɪən) *n* **1** an animal that can live both on land and in water such as a frog or newt. **2** a vehicle that can operate on both land and water. **amphibious** *adj* **1** able to live both on land and in water. **2** of or for a military operation from the sea to the shore. < Greek *amphi-* on both sides + *bios* life.
amphitheatre (ˈæmfɪˌθɪətə) *n* an oval or circular building with tiers of seats around a central, open space. < Greek *amphi-* around + *theatron* theatre.
ample (ˈæmpl̩) *adj* **1** abundant; plentiful: ample supplies. **2** large in size, extent, etc. **amply** *adv* < Latin *amplus* large.
amplify (ˈæmplɪˌfaɪ) *vb* **amplified; amplifying 1** increase the strength of an electrical signal. **2** expand on (a statement) by giving further details. **amplification** *n* **amplifier** *n* a device that increases the strength of an electrical signal. < ultimately Latin *amplus* large + *facere* to make.
amputate (ˈæmpjʊˌteɪt) *vb* cut off (part of the body) by surgical operation. **amputation** *n* < Latin *am-* around + *putare* to cut.
amulet (ˈæmjʊlət) *n* a small object worn as a protection against evil. < Latin *amuletum.*
amuse (əˈmjuːz) *vb* **1** cause to laugh or smile. **2** occupy in a pleasant way. **amusement** *n* < Old French *a-* + *muser* to muse. SEE PANEL.
an (ən; *stressed* æn) SEE **A.** SEE PANEL AT **A.**
anachronism (əˈnækrəˌnɪzəm) *n* **1** the placing of people, events, etc., in an incongruous historical period. **2** a person or thing that is considered to belong to an earlier period. **anachronistic** *adj* < ultimately Greek *ana-* backward + *chronos* time.
anaemia (əˈniːmɪə) *n* a deficiency in the number of red cells or the quantity of red pigment in the blood. **anaemic** *adj* **1** of or suffering from anaemia. **2** lacking strength and vitality. < Greek *an-* without + *haima* blood.
anaesthetic (ˌænɪsˈθɛtɪk) *n* a substance that produces loss of sensation, esp. of pain.
• *adj* causing or marked by such a loss of sensation. **anaesthetist** *n* a person who administers anaesthetics. **anaesthetize** *vb* administer an anaesthetic to. < ultimately Greek *an-* without + *aisthēsis* feeling.
anagram (ˈænəˌgræm) *n* a word or phrase formed by rearranging the letters of another. < ultimately Greek *ana-* back + *gramma* letter.
anal (ˈeɪnl̩) *adj* of the anus. < SEE **ANUS.**
analgesic (ˌænl̩ˈdʒiːzɪk) *adj* relieving pain without losing consciousness.
• *n* an analgesic drug. < ultimately Greek *an-* without + *algos* pain.
analogue (ˈænəˌlɒg) *n* something analogous to something else. **analogue computer** a computer that deals with numbers represented by measurable quantities as of current or voltage.
analogy (əˈnælədʒɪ) *n* **1** likeness or

amoral or **immoral?**

These words are sometimes confused.

Amoral is used of something which is not concerned with matters of morality or ethics or to describe a lack of acceptance that there are moral standards by which actions may be judged: an *amoral* attitude.

Immoral, a much more common word, refers to something that goes against the accepted rules of morality: obscene or *immoral* behaviour.

We are not amused

Queen Victoria's famous snub, 'We are not amused' comes from her 'Notebooks of a Spinster Lady', 2 January 1900. It was originally her comment on being imitated by her groom-in-waiting, the Hon. Alexander Grantham Yorke. It is now used as a wry expression of coldness towards something that has been said or done. See also panel at **stupid**.

similarity, esp. in some respects. **2** a comparison or inference drawn to show such a similarity. **analogous** *adj* like or similar, esp. in some respects. **analogously** *adv* < Greek *ana-* up, again + *logos* speech, ratio.

analyse (ˈænəˌlaɪz) *vb* **1** examine in detail, esp. to identify the essential features, structure, etc. **2** separate into components. **analysis** *n, pl* **analyses** analysing; statement of the result of this. **analytic** or **analytical** *adj* **analytically** *adv* **analyst** *n* a person who analyses or who is skilled at analysis. < ultimately Greek *ana-* up + *lyein* to loosen.

anarchism (ˈænəˌkɪzəm) *n* **1** a political theory that advocates the abolition of the state and all authority by the government. **2** rebellious attacking of the established social order. **anarchist** *n* **anarchistic** *adj* **anarchy** *n* **1** absence of government. **2** lawlessness; disorder. **anarchic** or **anarchical** *adj* < Greek *an-* without + *archos* ruler.

anathema (əˈnæθəmə) *n* a person or thing that is detested or despised. < ultimately Greek *anatithenai* to dedicate.

anatomy (aˈnætəmɪ) *n* the study of the structure of organisms. **anatomical** *adj* **anatomically** *adv* < ultimately Greek *ana-* up + *temnein* to cut.

ancestor (ˈænsɛstə) *n* **1** a person from whom one is descended, esp. further removed than grandparents. **2** an earlier, more primitive form of a machine or device. **ancestral** *adj* **ancestry** *n* a line of descent; lineage. < SEE ANTECEDENT.

anchor (ˈæŋkə) *n* a device, esp. made of metal, that is dropped overboard from a vessel to moor it in a particular place.
• *vb* moor (a vessel) in a particular place with an anchor. **anchorage** *n* a place where vessels may anchor safely. < ultimately Greek *ankyra*.

anchovy (ˈæntʃəvɪ) *n* a small, salty-tasting fish like a herring, used to make a paste. < Spanish *anchova*.

ancient (ˈeɪnʃənt) *adj* of times long ago; very old; old-fashioned. < ultimately Latin *ante* before.

ancillary (ænˈsɪlərɪ) *adj* subsidiary or auxiliary. < Latin *ancilla* maid-servant.

and (ənd, ən; *stressed* ænd) *conj* **1** in addition to: fish and chips. **2** plus: 3 and 3 equals 6. **3** as a result; afterwards. **4** used with words that are repeated to show steady progression: worse and worse. < Old English.

anecdote (ˈænɪkˌdəut) *n* a short, entertaining story about a person or event. **anecdotal** *adj* < Greek *anekdotos* unpublished.

anemone (əˈnɛmənɪ) *n* any of a group of plants of the buttercup family, with brightly coloured flowers. < Greek *anemōnē*.

anew (əˈnjuː) *adv* once more; afresh.

angel (ˈeɪndʒəl) *n* **1** a spiritual being that is a worshipper and messenger of God. **2** a very kind, loving, or beautiful person, esp. a woman or girl. **angelic** *adj* **angelically** *adv* < ultimately Greek *angelos* messenger.

anger (ˈæŋgə) *n* a strong feeling of displeasure and annoyance.
• *vb* make or become angry. < Old Norse *angr* grief.

angle[1] (ˈæŋgḷ) *n* **1** a measure of the extent to which two lines or surfaces diverge. **2** a divergent line; corner. **3** a point of view.
• *vb* place at an angle. < ultimately from Latin *angulus*.

angle[2] *vb* **1** fish with a hook and line. **2** try to obtain in an indirect way: angling for compliments. **angler** *n* < Old English *angul* fish-hook.

anglicize (ˈæŋglɪˌsaɪz) *vb* make or become English in character. < Medieval Latin *anglicus* English. SEE PANEL.

angry (ˈæŋgrɪ) *adj* feeling or showing anger. **angrily** *adv*

anguish (ˈæŋgwɪʃ) *n* extreme pain or distress. **anguished** *adj* feeling or showing anguish. < ultimately Latin *angustus* narrow.

angular (ˈæŋgjʊlə) *adj* **1** having angles. **2** measured by an angle. **3** thin and bony: a gaunt, angular body. **4** stiff and awkward in movement. **angularity** *n*

animal (ˈænɪməl) *n* **1** any living creature which has sense organs and can move freely. **2** any such creature other than a human being. **3** a brutal person.
• *adj* **1** of or from animals. **2** of the body as distinct from the mind or spirit: animal instincts. < Latin *anima* breath, soul.

animate (ˈænɪˌmeɪt) *vb* **1** give life, energy, or strength to; make lively. **2** give encouragement to; motivate.
• *adj* (ˈænɪmət) **1** having life. **2** lively. **animator** *n* **animated cartoon** a film made from drawings that give an illusion of movement. **animation** *n* **1** liveliness. **2** the production of an animated cartoon. < Latin *animare* to fill with life: SEE ANIMAL.

animosity (ˌænɪˈmɒsɪtɪ) *n* powerful and often aggressive dislike or hostility.

< ultimately Latin *animus* passion.
aniseed (ˈænɪˌsiːd) *n* the liquorice-flavoured seed of the anise plant, used for flavouring. < Middle English *anis seed*, ultimately Greek *annēson*.
ankle (ˈæŋkl̩) *n* the joint connecting the leg and the foot. < Old English *anclēow*.
annals (ˈænəlz) *pl n* **1** a written account of historical events year by year. **2** historical records. < Latin *annus* year.
annex (æˈnɛks) *vb* **1** join to something larger. **2** take possession of (a country). **annexation** *n* **annexe** *n* a subordinate building that provides additional accommodation, etc. < ultimately Latin *ad-* to + *nectere* to bind.
annihilate (əˈnaɪəˌleɪt) *vb* **1** destroy completely. **2** defeat decisively. **annihilation** *n* < Latin *ad-* to + *nihil* nothing.
anniversary (ˌænɪˈvɜːsərɪ) *n* the date each year when a special day is remembered; celebration of this. < Latin *annus* year + *vertere* to turn.
annotate (ˈænəˌteɪt) *vb* provide with notes, esp. as an explanation. **annotation** *n* < Latin *ad-* to + *notare* to mark.
announce (əˈnaʊns) *vb* **1** make known publicly. **2** proclaim the arrival of. **3** foretell. **announcement** *n* **announcer** *n* a person who announces, esp. one who introduces broadcasts. < Latin *ad-* to + *nuntiare* to report.
annoy (əˈnɔɪ) *vb* **1** cause slight irritation to. **2** harass. **annoyance** *n* < ultimately Latin *in* + *odium* hatred.
annual (ˈænjʊəl) *adj* **1** occurring or coming once every year: an annual report. **2** lasting for one year. **3** (of a plant) completing its life cycle in one year. • *n* **1** an annual plant. **2** a book, etc., that is published yearly. **annually** *adv* < Latin *annus* year.
annuity (əˈnjuːɪtɪ) *n* a fixed sum of money received yearly in return for paying an insurance premium.
annul (əˈnʌl) *vb* **annulled**; **annulling** declare invalid; cancel: Their marriage was annulled. **annulment** *n* < ultimately Latin *ad-* to + *nullus* not any.
anoint (əˈnɔɪnt) *vb* **1** apply oil to as a sign of consecration; consecrate. **2** smear or rub with oil, grease, etc. < ultimately Latin *in-* on + *unguere* to smear.
anomaly (əˈnɒməlɪ) *n* something that deviates from what is normal or common; irregularity. **anomalous** *adj* < Greek *an-* not + *homos* same.
anon (əˈnɒn) *adv* (*archaic*) soon; later. < Old English *on an* in one.
anonymous (əˈnɒnɪməs) *adj* by or from an unknown or unnamed author or origin. **anonymity** *n* **anonymously** *adv* < Greek *an-* without + *onyma* name.
anorak (ˈænəˌræk) *n* a hip-length, waterproof jacket with a hood attached. < Eskimo *ánorâq*.
anorexia nervosa (ænɒˌrɛksɪə nɜːˈvəʊzə) a psychological illness in which a person refuses to eat for a long period. < New Latin: nervous anorexia; *anorexia* ultimately from Greek *an-* without + *orexis* appetite.
another (əˈnʌðə) *determiner* **1** different. **2** some other. **3** additional. • *pron* another person or thing. < Middle English *an other*.
answer (ˈɑːnsə) *n* **1** something said or written in reply to a question, comment, etc. **2** a solution to a problem. • *vb* **1** make an answer to; act in response to. **2** take responsibility (for). **3** correspond (to): a man answering to his description. **answerable** *adj* **1** responsible. **2** capable of being answered. **answer back** reply rudely. < Old English *andswaru*.
ant (ænt) *n* one of a large group of very small insects that live in highly organized, social groups. < Old English *æmette*.
antacid (æntˈæsɪd) *n, adj* (a medicine)

---

anglicize or **anglicise**?

Whether to spell certain verbs -ize or -ise is essentially a matter of choice. Anglicize or anglicise, organize or organise, realize or realise, etc., are equally acceptable. It is, however, desirable to use one spelling or the other consistently. The present trend in Britain is increasingly to use -ize.

Note, however, that in certain words the -s- spelling is obligatory:

advertise	**compromise**	**improvise**
advise	**despise**	**revise**
analyse	**devise**	**supervise**
arise	**enterprise**	**surprise**
comprise	**exercise**	**televise**

---

neutralizing or preventing acid conditions, esp. in the stomach.

antagonism (æn'tægəˌnɪzəm) *n* opposition or hostility that is actively shown. **antagonist** *n* an opponent. **antagonistic** *adj* feeling or showing antagonism. **antagonistically** *adv* **antagonize** *vb* arouse the hostility of. < Greek *anti-* against + *agōn* contest.

antecedent (ˌæntɪ'siːdənt) *n* **1** something that goes before something else. **2** *pl* a person's ancestry.
● *adj* preceding in time or cause.
< ultimately Latin *ante-* before + *cedere* to go. SEE PANEL.

antelope ('æntɪˌləʊp) *n* a fast-running, graceful, hoofed mammal, such as a gazelle. < ultimately Late Greek *antholops*.

antenatal (ˌæntɪ'neɪtḷ) *adj* of or relating to an unborn child or pregnancy: an antenatal clinic.

antenna (æn'tɛnə) *n* **1** *pl* **antennae** either of the movable feelers attached to the head of insects, etc. **2** *pl* **antennas** an aerial. < Latin: sail-yard.

ante-room ('æntɪrʊm) *n* an outer room that leads to a larger, more important room.

anthem ('ænθəm) *n* a short piece of music for a church choir, often set to words from the Bible. < ultimately Greek *anti-* against + *phonē* sound.

anther ('ænθə) *n* the pollen-bearing part at the end of the stamen on a flower. < ultimately Greek *anthos* flower.

anthology (æn'θɒlədʒɪ) *n* a collection of literary texts, esp. poems. < Greek *anthos* flower + *legein* to collect.

anthracite ('ænθrəˌsaɪt) *n* a hard coal that burns slowly with a little flame. < Greek *anthrax* coal.

ante- or **anti-**?

These prefixes are sometimes confused.
Ante- comes from Latin and means 'before'. Examples of its use are antenatal (before birth) and antepenultimate (before the penultimate).
Anti- comes from Greek and means 'against; opposing'. It is a very common prefix and occurs in words such as anti-aircraft, anti-apartheid, anti-European, anti-intellectual, anti-theft device, anti-vivisectionist.

anthrax ('ænθræks) *n* a contagious disease of many animals, esp. cattle and sheep, that can be transmitted to man. < ultimately Greek: coal, carbuncle.

anthropoid ('ænθrəˌpɔɪd) *adj* resembling man.
● *n* an anthropoid ape. < Greek *anthropo-* human.

anthropology (ˌænθrə'pɒlədʒɪ) *n* the scientific study of man, esp. his origin, development, customs, and beliefs. **anthropological** *adj* **anthropologically** *adv* **anthropologist** *n* an expert in anthropology. < Greek *anthropo-* human + *logy*, ultimately *logos* word.

anthropomorphism (ˌænθrəpə'mɔːfɪzəm) *n* the attribution of human motives, feelings, etc., to non-human beings such as an animal or god. **anthropomorphic** *adj* < Greek *anthro-* human + *morphē* form.

antibiotic (ˌæntɪbaɪ'ɒtɪk) *n* a drug derived from living matter, used to treat infections caused by bacteria. < Greek *anti-* against + *bios* life.

antibody ('æntɪˌbɒdɪ) *n* a protein that is produced by the body and which counteracts the effects of a foreign protein.

anticipate (æn'tɪsɪˌpeɪt) *vb* **1** see in advance and prepare for; forestall. **2** consider likely; expect. **3** do before someone else. **4** use or act on prematurely. **anticipation** *n* **anticipatory** *adj* < Latin *ante-* before + *capere* to take. SEE PANEL.

anticlimax (ˌæntɪ'klaɪmæks) *n* an ending or event that is disappointing or less important than expected.

anticlockwise (ˌæntɪ'klɒkwaɪz) *adv*, *adj* in the opposite direction to that in which the hands of a clock move.

antics ('æntɪks) *pl n* absurd or peculiar behaviour. < ultimately Latin *antiquus* ancient.

anticipating correctly

Some careful users of English object to the use of anticipate to mean 'to consider likely; expect'. This usage is nowadays so common, however, that it must be considered acceptable: He *anticipated* that the total cost of the materials would be £1000; The police are not *anticipating* any trouble at the demonstration.

anticyclone (ˌæntɪˈsaɪkləʊn) *n* an area of high atmospheric pressure, often leading to calm, settled weather.

antidote (ˈæntɪˌdəʊt) *n* **1** a substance that counteracts the effects of a poison. **2** something that counteracts harmful effects. < ultimately Greek *anti-* against + *didonai* to give.

antifreeze (ˈæntɪˌfriːz) *n* a liquid that is added to water to lower its freezing-point, used in car radiators, etc.

antipathy (ænˈtɪpəθɪ) *n* a strong, settled dislike. < ultimately Greek *anti-* against + *pathos* experience.

antipodes (ænˈtɪpəˌdiːz) *pl n* places diametrically opposite; Australasia. **antipodean** *adj* < ultimately Greek *anti-* opposite + *pous* foot.

antiquary (ˈæntɪˌkwərɪ) *n* a person who collects or studies antiques or antiquities. **antiquarian** *adj* of antiques or antiquities. < Latin *antiquarius.*

antiquated (ˈæntɪˌkweɪtɪd) *adj* old-fashioned; obsolete; ancient.

antique (ænˈtiːk) *adj* **1** made in an earlier period; having the style of an earlier period. **2** of an earlier, esp. remote period.
• *n* an antique object, such as a piece of furniture or work of art, that is sought by collectors. < Latin *ante* before.

antiquity (ænˈtɪkwɪtɪ) *n* **1** being ancient. **2** the distant past, esp. before the Middle Ages. **3** an object dating from ancient times.

antirrhinum (ˌæntɪˈraɪnəm) *n* one of a group of plants with brightly coloured, two-lipped flowers, esp. the snapdragon. < ultimately Greek *anti-* like, against + *rhis* nose.

antiseptic (ˌæntɪˈsɛptɪk) *n* a substance that stops the growth of micro-organisms, esp. bacteria.
• *adj* **1** stopping the growth of micro-organisms, etc. **2** scrupulously clean and free from contamination.

antisocial (ˌæntɪˈsəʊʃəl) *adj* **1** avoiding the company of others; unsociable. **2** harmful to the interests of society.

antithesis (ænˈtɪθəsɪs) *n, pl* **antitheses** a contrast or direct opposite in words or ideas. < ultimately Greek: opposition, from *anti-* against + *tithenai* to set.

antler (ˈæntlə) *n* one of a pair of bony outgrowths on the head of an animal of the deer family. < Old French *antoillier.*

antonym (ˈæntənɪm) *n* a word that means the opposite of another word. < Greek *anti-* against + *onyma* name. SEE PANEL AT BIG.

anus (ˈeɪnəs) *n* the opening at the end of the alimentary canal, through which waste matter is discharged from the body. < Latin.

anvil (ˈænvɪl) *n* a heavy block of iron on which metals are hammered into shape. < Old English *anfilt.*

anxious (ˈæŋkʃəs) *adj* **1** worried and troubled. **2** causing worry. **3** eager or keen: anxious to avoid any embarrassment. **anxiously** *adv* **anxiousness** or **anxiety** *n* < Latin *anxius.*

any (ˈɛnɪ) *determiner* **1** some; used in negative sentences and questions: Do you have any money? **2** one or some (no matter which or what): You can choose any colour you like. **3** every: Any idiot knows that! **4** unlimited in size, amount, etc.: any number of explanations. **5** (*informal*) a or an: You don't mean there isn't any fire escape! **6** whatever: in any case.
• *pron* any person, thing, number, or amount.
• *adv* to any degree or extent: Are you feeling any better now? **anybody** *pron* any person: Does anybody want a cup of tea? **anyhow** *adv* **1** in any case; anyway. **2** in a careless, haphazard manner. **any more** any longer. **anyone** *pron* anybody: Is anyone there? **anyway** *adv* in any case. **anywhere** *adv* in, to, or at any place. < Old English *ǣnig.* SEE PANEL.

anything (ˈɛnɪˌθɪŋ) *pron* any thing, event, etc.
• *adv* in any degree: The picture isn't anything like her!

apace (əˈpeɪs) *adv* quickly. < Middle English.

apart (əˈpɑːt) *adv* **1** so as to separate. **2** at or to a distance. **3** not taking into account: joking apart. **apart from** besides; except for: fine, apart from a cold. < Middle

anyone or **any one?**

When anyone is used as an indefinite pronoun to mean 'anybody', it is written as one word: *Anyone* could tell you the answer. Do you know *anyone* else who could help? Otherwise, it is written as two words: *Any* one of us could have scored a high mark. A maximum of six people are allowed in this lift at *any one* time.

Anything and anywhere are written as one word; any time as two words.

French *a part* to the side.
apartheid (əˈpɑːtaɪd, əˈpɑːteɪt) *n* the policy of racial segregation in South Africa. < Afrikaans: separateness.
apartment (əˈpɑːtmənt) *n* **1** a single room in a building. **2** a set of rooms. **3** (*chiefly US*) a flat. < ultimately Italian *appartamento*.
apathy (ˈæpəθɪ) *n* a lack of interest, concern, or feeling. **apathetic** *adj* **apathetically** *adv* < ultimately Greek *a-* without + *pathos* feeling.
ape (eɪp) *n* an intelligent primate such as the gorilla or chimpanzee.
• *vb* imitate; mimic. < Old English *apa*.
aperitif (əˌperɪˈtiːf) *n* an alcoholic drink served before a meal to stimulate the appetite. < French, ultimately from Latin *aperire* to open.
aperture (ˈæpətʃə) *n* **1** an opening, hole, or gap. **2** (the size of) the adjustable diaphragm in a camera. < ultimately Latin *aperire* to open.
apex (ˈeɪpeks) *n, pl* **apexes** the highest point; tip. < Latin: summit, point.
aphorism (ˈæfəˌrɪzəm) *n* a short, wise saying expressing a truth; maxim. < ultimately Greek *apo-* from + *horizein* to bound.
aphrodisiac (ˌæfrəˈdɪzɪæk) *adj, n* (a substance) that arouses sexual desire. < *Aphrodite*, Greek goddess of love.
apiary (ˈeɪpɪərɪ) *n* a place where bees are kept. < Latin *apis* bee.
apiece (ˈəˈpiːs) *adv* to, for, or from each one.
aplomb (əˈplɒm) *n* calm and dignified poise or composure. < French: uprightness, from *a plomb* according to the plumb-line, vertically.
apocalyptic (əˌpɒkəˈlɪptɪk) *adj* **1** of or like the end of the world. **2** great in revelation, meaning, etc. < Greek *apokalyptein* to uncover.
apocryphal (əˈpɒkrɪfəl) *adj* **1** of doubtful authenticity. **2** of the Apocrypha. < Greek *apokryptein* to hide away.
apology (əˈpɒlədʒɪ) *n* **1** an expression of regret; admission of error. **2** a poor substitute (for). **apologetic** *adj* expressing an apology. **apologetically** *adv* **apologize** *vb* make an apology. < ultimately Greek *apo-* from + *logos* speech.
apoplexy (ˈæpəˌpleksɪ) *n* a sudden loss of consciousness, usually followed by varying degrees of paralysis, caused by the rupture or blocking of a blood-vessel in the brain; stroke. < ultimately Greek *apo-* down + *plēssein* to strike.
apostle (əˈpɒsl̩) *n* **1** one of the 12 disciples sent by Christ to preach the Gospel. **2** a strong supporter, esp. of a new movement. **apostolic** *adj* < ultimately Greek *apostellein* to send forth.
apostrophe (əˈpɒstrəfɪ) *n* the punctuation mark ’ used to show the omission of a letter or number and to show the possessive case. < ultimately Greek *apo-* away + *strephein* to turn.
appal (əˈpɔːl) *vb* **appalled; appalling** fill with horror, dismay, or shock. < Old French *apalir* grow pale.
apparatus (ˌæpəˈreɪtəs) *n* **1** (a piece of) the equipment used for a particular task: scientific apparatus. **2** a group of bodily organs that work as a system: the breathing apparatus. **3** a machine or appliance used for a particular purpose: a heating apparatus. **4** an organization or system: the apparatus of government. < Latin *ad-* to + *parare* to prepare.
apparel (əˈpærəl) *n* (*formal*) clothing. < SEE **APPARATUS.**
apparent (əˈpærənt) *adj* **1** readily seen or understood. **2** seeming as distinct from actual or real. **apparently** *adv* < ultimately Latin *apparēre* to appear.
appeal (əˈpiːl) *vb* **1** make an earnest request. **2** ask another person for confirmation, justification, or decision. **3** be attractive (to): Hang-gliding doesn't appeal to me. **4** take (a case) to a higher court.
• *n* **1** the act of appealing. **2** the power of attraction. < ultimately Latin *ad-* to + *pellere* to drive.
appear (əˈpɪə) *vb* **1** come into sight. **2** give the impression; seem. **3** seem true or clear. **4** come or perform before the public. **5** present oneself in court. **6** be noticed or discovered. **apparition** *n* a remarkable or unexpected sight; ghost. **appearance** *n* **1** appearing. **2** outward view; look; semblance. **to all appearances** as far as one can tell. < ultimately Latin *ad-* to + *parēre* to show oneself.
appease (əˈpiːz) *vb* pacify or conciliate by making concessions to meet the demands of. **appeasement** *n* < ultimately Latin *pax* peace.
append (əˈpend) *vb* add as a supplement. **appendage** *n* something appended, esp. to something larger. < Latin *ad-* to + *pendere* to weigh.
appendix (əˈpendɪks) *n, pl* **appendices, appendixes 1** a supplement at the end of a book, etc. **2** a short, closed tube extending from the large intestine. **appendicitis** *n* inflammation of the appendix. < SEE **APPEND.** SEE PANEL.
appertain (ˌæpəˈteɪn) *vb* belong or relate

(to). < ultimately Latin *ad-* to + *pertinēre* to belong.

appetite (ˈæpəˌtaɪt) *n* **1** a desire, esp. for food. **2** a desire or liking: an unhealthy appetite for gossip. **appetizer** *n* food or drink served before a meal to stimulate the appetite. **appetizing** *adj* stimulating the appetite. < ultimately Latin *appetere* to desire strongly.

applaud (əˈplɔːd) *vb* show approval of, esp. by clapping the hands. **applause** *n* praise or approval; clapping of the hands. < Latin *plaudere* to applaud.

apple (ˈæpl̩) *n* a round, edible fruit with crisp, whitish flesh. < Old English *æppel.* SEE PANEL.

appliqué (æˈpliːkeɪ) *n* a piece of cut-out material sewn or fixed onto a larger piece of material. < French, from Latin *applicare*: SEE **APPLY.**

apply (əˈplaɪ) *vb* **applied; applying 1** put into contact with; spread on a surface. **2** put to use: apply one's knowledge. **3** devote (oneself) attentively (to). **4** have relevance: The rule doesn't apply in this case. **5** make a request: apply for a job. **appliance** *n* an instrument or device: domestic appliances. **applicable** *adj* able to be applied; appropriate. **applicant** *n* a person who applies. **application** *n* **1** applying. **2** a formal request. **3** the use to which something is put; relevance. **4** close attention; concentration. **applied** *adj* put to practical use; not theoretical: applied science. < ultimately Latin *ad-* to + *plicare* to fold.

appendices or appendixes?

Usage varies regarding the plural of appendix. Some use either appendixes or appendices both for the supplement at the end of a book and also the part extending from the intestine. Others prefer to use appendixes to refer to the anatomical part and appendices to refer to the part of the book.

Usage is similarly varied regarding index. Both indexes and indices are acceptable, but some reserve indices for technical contexts and use indexes for alphabetical lists.

apples

The protrusion at the front of the neck formed by the thyroid cartilage is commonly known as the **Adam's apple.** More pronounced in men than in women, the bulge gets its name from the story of the Garden of Eden and the piece of the forbidden fruit which is supposed to have got stuck in Adam's throat.

For centuries it has been supposed that the fruit that Eve handed to Adam was an apple, and yet there is no mention of this in the Bible. All we learn from the book of Genesis is that the tree was in the middle of the garden and that it had a pleasant appearance.

A person of whom one is especially fond is sometimes referred to as **the apple of one's eye**. But why? The apple of one's eye was originally a metaphor for the pupil of the eye—apple and pupil having roundness in common. But eyes are something that we all care very much about and it is the association of the eye with something treasured that lies behind the extended application of the expression. The apple of one's eye is a person whom one cherishes as much as the power of sight—a very precious loved one indeed.

Apple has been used in the past to refer to various objects of roundish shape, although nowadays they do not strike us as particularly apple-like at all. For example, there is the oak-apple, a phrase still used for 'oak gall', and the now obsolete golden apple, an old name for the 'orange', and earth-apple, better known today as the 'potato'. In French the name pomme de terre—'earth-apple'—still persists but is losing ground to the more colloquial patate.

An **apple-pie bed** is a bed made in such a way that its would-be occupant is unable to enter it. While most people are familiar with this practical joke, the origin of the phrase is somewhat uncertain. Some suggest that it is an approximation of the French *nappe pliée* —'a folded sheet'. Others contend that the -pie in question is a loose synonym for -turnover, on the grounds that a turnover is made by folding pastry in half just as an apple-pie bed is made by folding a sheet in half.

appoint (əˈpɔɪnt) *vb* **1** choose for an office or task. **2** fix or decide officially. **appointee** *n* a person appointed. **appointment** *n* **1** appointing. **2** a position, etc., to which a person is appointed. **3** an arrangement for a meeting at a particular time. < Middle French *apointier* to arrange.

apportion (əˈpɔːʃən) *vb* divide and share out. **apportionment** *n*

apposite (ˈæpəzɪt) *adj* appropriate. **appositely** *adv* < Latin *ad-* to + *ponere* to put.

apposition (ˌæpəˈzɪʃən) *n* a grammatical relationship in which a word or expression, esp. a noun or noun phrase, is placed beside another which it describes.

appraise (əˈpreɪz) *vb* assess the worth, quality, etc., of. **appraisal** *n* < Old French *aprisier*.

appreciable (əˈpriːʃɪəbl̩) *adj* capable of being seen or measured; fairly large. **appreciably** *adv*

appreciate (əˈpriːʃɪˌeɪt, əˈpriːsɪˌeɪt) *vb* **1** be grateful for. **2** understand or recognize, esp. sympathetically: I fully appreciate your reluctance to disclose the source of your information. **3** enjoy or value greatly: appreciate beautiful poetry. **4** increase in value. **appreciation** *n* **appreciative** *adj* showing appreciation, esp. gratitude. **appreciatively** *adv* < Latin *ad-* to + *pretium* price.

apprehend (ˌæprɪˈhɛnd) *vb* **1** grasp the meaning of; understand. **2** arrest or seize. **apprehension** *n* **1** apprehending. **2** anxious fear about what may happen. **apprehensive** *adj* feeling apprehension. **apprehensively** *adv* < ultimately Latin *ad-* to + *prehendere* to seize.

apprentice (əˈprɛntɪs) *n* **1** a person who works for a skilled, experienced person in order to be taught his or her trade, etc. **2** a novice.
• *vb* place as an apprentice. **apprenticeship** *n* < ultimately Latin *apprehendere* to apprehend.

approach (əˈprəʊtʃ) *vb* **1** come near or nearer. **2** begin to deal with; set about. **3** make advances to; go to with an offer, suggestion, etc.
• *n* **1** approaching. **2** a means of access. **3** a way of doing something: different approaches to solving the problem. **4** the final part of an aircraft's flight before landing. **5** an attempt to establish a personal or business relationship: friendly approaches. **6** a close approximation. **approachable** *adj* (of a person) easy to approach and talk to; friendly. < ultimately Latin *ad-* to + *prope* near.

appropriate (əˈprəʊprɪət) *adj* suitable; fitting.
• *vb* (əˈprəʊprɪˌeɪt) **1** take and use as one's own. **2** take illegally or without authority and use as one's own. **3** set aside for a particular person. **appropriately** *adv* **appropriation** *n* < ultimately Latin *ad-* to + *proprius* own.

approve (əˈpruːv) *vb* **1** think favourably about; commend (a person or thing). **2** agree to; authorize. **approval** *n* **1** a favourable opinion; commendation. **2** a formal agreement; authorization. **on approval** (of goods) kept and paid for only if found satisfactory. < ultimately Latin *ad-* to + *probare* to prove.

approx. *abbrev* approximate; approximately.

approximate (əˈprɒksɪmət) *adj* nearly accurate, exact, or correct.
• *vb* (əˈprɒksɪˌmeɪt) bring or come near or close (to); be nearly the same (as). **approximately** *adv* **approximation** *n* < Latin *ad-* to + *proximus* nearest.

apricot (ˈeɪprɪˌkɒt) *n* a round, soft, orange-yellow fruit with sweet, juicy flesh and a smooth stone. < ultimately Latin *praecoquus* early ripened.

apron (ˈeɪprən) *n* **1** a garment worn over the front part of the body to protect clothing. **2** something like this in shape, function, or position. **3** the large, hard-surfaced area near an airport terminal or in front of hangars. **one's mother's apron-strings** a mother's dominating influence: Even at the age of 50 he's still tied to his mother's apron-strings. < Middle English *a napron*, ultimately from Latin *mappa* napkin. SEE PANEL.

apropos (ˌæprəˈpəʊ) *adv* also **apropos of** concerning. < French *à propos* to the purpose.

apt (æpt) *adj* **1** likely (to): apt to be late. **2** relevant; suitable: apt quotations. **3** quick at learning: an apt pupil. **aptly** *adv* **aptness** *n* **aptitude** *n* a natural ability; talent or skill. < Latin *apere* to fasten.

aqualung (ˈækwəˌlʌŋ) *n* the breathing-apparatus of a diver consisting of a cylinder of compressed air, oxygen, etc., connected to a face-mask. < Latin *aqua* water + English *lung*.

aquarium (əˈkwɛərɪəm) *n, pl* **aquariums, aquaria 1** a glass tank or artificial pond in which fish and other water-animals are kept. **2** a building housing such tanks or ponds. < Latin *aquarius* of water. SEE PANEL.

aquatic (əˈkwætɪk) *adj* **1** growing, living, or found near or in water: aquatic plants. **2** performed in or on water: aquatic sports.

aqueduct (ˈækwɪˌdʌkt) *n* a man-made channel that carries water, esp. one supported on a bridge across a valley. < Latin *aqua* water + *ducere* to convey.

aquiline (ˈækwɪˌlaɪn) *adj* (of a nose) curved or hooked like an eagle's beak. < Latin *aquila* eagle.

arable (ˈærəbl̩) *adj* **1** (of land) suitable for growing crops. **2** of or using such land: arable farming.
• *n* arable land. < Latin *arare* to plough.

arbiter (ˈɑːbɪtə) *n* a person who has the full authority to judge and determine. < Latin.

arbitrary (ˈɑːbɪtrərɪ) *adj* **1** chosen randomly and without reason; based on personal whims: an arbitrary decision. **2** unrestrained; despotic or tyrannical. **arbitrarily** *adv* **arbitrariness** *n*

arbitrate (ˈɑːbɪˌtreɪt) *vb* act as an arbitrator. **arbitration** *n* **arbitrator** *n* a person who is chosen to settle a dispute between two people, groups, etc.

arboreal (ɑːˈbɔːrɪəl) *adj* of, like, or living in or near trees. < Latin *arbor* tree.

arboretum (ˌɑbəˈriːtəm) *n, pl* **arboreta**, **arboretums** a place where trees or shrubs are grown for study and display. < Latin *arbor* tree.

a wrong apron?

When we speak, the words in a sentence tend to run together. There are no obvious divisions between them as there are in writing. In the past this running together has actually resulted in words changing their original form. For example, in Middle French the word for apron was *naperon.* So in Middle English speech one would have heard people talk of a napron. However, by the time this came to be written down it was heard not as a napron but as an apron: the first sound of the original word was mistakenly accredited to the preceding indefinite article.

Other examples of such 'wrong' shortening include an adder, which in Middle English was *a naddre,* and an umpire, originally *a noumpere.*

Conversely, the reverse procedure of lengthening has also occurred. Historically, newt should be shorter than it is: a newt is a mistaken version of *an ewt.*

arbour (ˈɑːbə) *n* a place shaded by trees, shrubs, climbing plants, etc. < ultimately Latin *herba* grass.

arc (ɑːk) *n* **1** something curved or arched; part of a curve. **2** a luminous, electrical discharge across a gap between two electrodes.
• *vb* form an arc. < ultimately Latin *arcus* arch, bow.

arcade (ɑːˈkeɪd) *n* **1** a covered passage, esp. with shops on both sides. **2** a line of arches and their columns. < SEE **ARC.**

arch[1] (ɑːtʃ) *n* **1** a curved structure, esp. one that acts as a support and spans an opening. **2** also **archway** a passage under an arch. **3** something like this, esp. the raised bony part at the base of the foot.
• *vb* **1** span or provide with an arch. **2** form (into) an arch. < Latin *arcus.*

arch[2] *adj* **1** chief; leading: his arch enemy. **2** mischievous; sly. **archly** *adv* **archness** *n* < ultimately Greek *archein* to rule.

archaeology (ˌɑːkɪˈɒlədʒɪ) *n* the scientific study of the material remains of man's past. **archaeological** *adj* **archaeologist** *n* an expert in archaeology. < ultimately Greek *archē* beginning + *-logy,* ultimately *logos* word.

archaic (ɑːˈkeɪɪk) *adj* **1** of a remote period; ancient. **2** old-fashioned; antiquated. **3** (of a word, etc.) of an earlier period of the language and no

aquaria and aquariums

Aquarium is an example of a noun derived from Latin which has retained its original plural form, aquaria, but which has over the years acquired a regular plural form as well, aquariums. Generally speaking, the use of the vernacular (-s) plural tends to be less formal than the imported one. Other nouns which belong to this -um group include:

colloquium colloquiums—colloquia
memorandum memorandums—memoranda
millennium millenniums—millennia
moratorium moratoriums—moratoria
referendum referendums—referenda
symposium symposiums—symposia
ultimatum ultimatums—ultimata

longer in use. < ultimately Greek *archaios* ancient.

archbishop (ˌɑːtʃˈbɪʃəp) *n* a chief bishop with some jurisdiction over the other bishops in an ecclesiastical province.

archer (ˈɑːtʃə) *n* a person who is skilled at archery. **archery** *n* the sport of shooting with bows and arrows. < ultimately Latin *arcus* bow.

archetype (ˈɑːkɪˌtaɪp) *n* **1** a perfect or typical example. **2** an original pattern or model; prototype. **archetypal** *adj* < Greek *archein* to begin + *typos* model.

archipelago (ˌɑːkɪˈpɛlɪˌgəʊ) *n, pl* **archipelagos** a group of islands. < ultimately Greek *archi-* chief + *pelagos* sea.

architect (ˈɑːkɪˌtɛkt) *n* a person who designs buildings and supervises their construction. **architecture** *n* 1 the art or science of designing buildings. **2** a style of building construction: a good example of modern architecture. **architectural** *adj* **architecturally** *adv* < ultimately Greek *archi-* chief + *tektōn* builder, carpenter.

archives (ˈɑːkaɪvz) *pl n* a collection of documents or tapes which record the history of an institution, etc.; place where these are kept. **archivist** *n* a person in charge of archives. < ultimately Greek *archeion* government house for official records, from *archē* government, rule.

archway (ˈɑːtʃˌweɪ) SEE **ARCH**[1] (def. **2**).

ardent (ˈɑːdn̩t) *adj* strongly felt; enthusiastic. **ardently** *adv* **ardour** *n* intense feeling; enthusiasm and zeal. < ultimately Latin *ardēre* to burn.

arduous (ˈɑːdjuːəs) *adj* needing great effort; laborious or strenuous. **arduously** *adv* < Latin *arduus* steep, difficult.

are (ə; *stressed* ɑː) SEE **BE**.

area (ˈɛərɪə) *n* **1** the expanse or extent of a surface: an area of 100 square metres. **2** a particular expanse: the area behind the radiator. **3** a region or district: the London postal area. **4** the extent of an activity, etc.: her areas of responsibility. **5** a subject or specialist field. < Latin: level ground; threshing-floor.

arena (əˈriːnə) *n* **1** an enclosed area used for sports events, entertainments, etc. **2** a sphere of activity, interest, etc. < Latin *harena* sand.

argue (ˈɑːgjuː) *vb* **1** quarrel. **2** put forward reasons for or against something; try to prove in this way. **3** persuade: We argued her into coming. **arguable** *adj* **1** not certain; doubtful. **2** able to be stated. **arguably** *adv* **argument** *n* **1** a quarrel. **2** a reason or series of reasons for or against something: I can't follow his line of argument. **3** a summary of a book, etc. **argumentative** *adj* fond of arguing. **argumentatively** *adv* < ultimately Latin *arguere* to make clear.

aria (ˈɑːrɪə) *n* a song for solo voice, esp. in an opera. < Italian: tune, air.

arid (ˈærɪd) *adj* **1** parched with heat; dry. **2** lacking interest and vitality. **aridity** *n* **aridly** *adv* < Latin *arere* to be dry.

arise (əˈraɪz) *vb* **arose; arisen; arising** **1** come into being or to one's notice. **2** (*old-fashioned*) stand up. < Old English *ārisan*. SEE PANEL.

aristocracy (ˌærɪˈstɒkrəsɪ) *n* **1** the privileged class; nobility. **2** a superior or outstanding group of people. **3** government by the aristocracy; state or country so governed. **aristocrat** *n* a member of the aristocracy. **aristocratic** *adj* of or like an aristocrat. < ultimately Greek *aristos* best + *kratos* power.

arithmetic (əˈrɪθmətɪk) *n* **1** the branch of mathematics that deals with numbers and numerical calculations. **2** (skill in) numerical calculations.
• *adj* (ˌærɪθˈmɛtɪk) also **arithmetical** of or using arithmetic. **arithmetically** *adv* < ultimately Greek *arithmos* number.

ark (ɑːk) *n* the covered boat in which Noah lived during the Flood. < ultimately Latin *arca* chest.

arm[1] (ɑːm) *n* **1** either of the two upper, human limbs; part between the shoulder and the wrist. **2** something resembling an arm in form or function: the arms of a chair. **3** a sleeve. **4** authority: the arm of the law. **5** a section of a group that serves a particular purpose. **armchair** *n* a chair with supports for the arms. **armful** *n* the

Arise, Sir ...

'Arise, Sir ...' is supposedly the expression used by the monarch of the United Kingdom when knighting someone: 'Arise, Sir Walter!'

However, contrary to popular belief, the act of knighting is performed in silence. The monarch touches the new knight on the shoulders with the flat of a sword and invests him with the insignia.

The phrase 'Arise, Sir ...' nevertheless continues to be used in films, etc., depicting the scene.

amount that can be held by an arm. **armhole** *n* an opening for an arm in a garment. **armpit** *n* the hollow beneath the arm where it joins the shoulder. < Old English *earm*.

arm² *vb* **1** equip or provide with weapons. **2** equip or provide with, esp. in preparation for a conflict. **3** prepare (esp. a bomb) for operation.
• *n* **1** a branch (of an army, etc.): the Fleet Air Arm. **2** *pl* weapons. **3** *pl* a coat of arms. **armament** *n* **1** the military equipment of a ship, aircraft, etc. **2** the process of preparation for war. **armed forces** the military forces of a country. < ultimately Latin *arma* weapons. SEE PANEL.

armada (ɑːˈmɑːdə) *n* a fleet of warships. < Spanish, from Latin *armare* to provide with arms. SEE PANEL.

armadillo (ˌɑːməˈdɪləʊ) *n, pl* **armadillos** a burrowing mammal with a covering of jointed bands or horny plates. < Spanish, ultimately from Latin *armatus* armed.

armistice (ˈɑːmɪstɪs) *n* an agreement during war to suspend hostilities temporarily. < Latin *arma* arms + *sistere* to stop.

armour (ˈɑːmə) *n* **1** defensive covering for the body. **2** protective, metal covering for a tank, warship, etc. **armoured** *adj* of or fitted with armour: an armoured car. **armoury** *n* a place where weapons are stored. < ultimately Latin *armatura*.

army (ˈɑːmɪ) *n* **1** a country's organized force for fighting on land. **2** a large group. **3** a group of people organized for a purpose. < Medieval Latin *armata*.

aroma (əˈrəʊmə) *n* a distinctive, usually pleasant smell. **aromatic** *adj* < ultimately Greek *arōma* spice.

arose (əˈrəʊz) SEE **ARISE**.

around (əˈraʊnd) *prep* **1** surrounding or enveloping. **2** on all sides of. **3** on the perimeter of. **4** on every side of. **5** in several different places in.
• *adv* **1** on every side. **2** in rotation; in every direction. **3** here and there; in no particular place. **4** nearby. **5** to all members of a group. < Middle English *a-* on + *round*.

arouse (əˈraʊz) *vb* **1** call forth or stimulate (a response). **2** wake (a person) from sleep.

arrange (əˈreɪndʒ) *vb* **1** put in order. **2** prepare for; settle the details of; plan. **3** adapt (a musical composition) for different voices or instruments. **arrangement** *n* < Old French *a-* + *rengier* to put in a row.

arrant (ˈærənt) *adj* utter or extreme; notorious. SEE PANEL.

array (əˈreɪ) *vb* **1** put in order. **2** decorate or dress, esp. magnificently.
• *n* **1** an impressive group or show. **2** a military arrangement. < Old French *arayer* to arrange.

arrears (əˈrɪəz) *pl n* **1** money owed that ought to have been paid earlier. **2** a duty that has not yet been dealt with. **in arrears** late in paying money owed or in fulfilling an obligation. < ultimately Latin *ad* to + *retro* behind.

arrest (əˈrɛst) *vb* **1** place (a person) in custody by legal authority. **2** stop: arrest the growth of the cancer. **3** hold: This new line of argument arrested his attention.
• *n* **1** the act of arresting. **2** the stopping of something: cardiac arrest. < ultimately Latin *ad-* to + *restare* to remain.

Present arms!

The military senses of arm and arms form the basis of several idiomatic expressions, including:

armed to the teeth fully equipped with guns, etc.; fully supplied with things that are necessary for a particular task.
up in arms protesting angrily: Local parents are up in arms about the closure of the school.

the Spanish armada

One need know very little about history to be able to guess the origin of the word armada. The word comes from the Spanish *armada* and has remained in the language ever since the threat to British sovereignty posed by the Spanish fleet in 1588. Other words which have come into English from Spanish include:

albino	**eldorado**	**parade**
alligator	**embargo**	**peccadillo**
armadillo	**flotilla**	**quinine**
barricade	**grenade**	**savanna**
bravado	**guerrilla**	**sherry**
cargo	**merino**	**stampede**
cigar	**mosquito**	**tornado**
cochineal	**mulatto**	**vanilla**
creole	**negro**	**veranda**

arrive (əˈraɪv) *vb* **1** come to or reach a destination. **2** reach: arrive at a decision. **3** happen or come: Their great day finally arrived! **4** (of a baby) to be born. **5** achieve fame or success: Don't think that you've arrived! **arrival** *n* arriving; person or thing that has arrived. < ultimately Latin *ad-* to + *ripa* shore.

arrogant (ˈærəgənt) *adj* displaying a proud, exaggerated opinion of one's own importance. **arrogance** *n* **arrogantly** *adv* < ultimately Latin *ad-* to + *rogare* to ask.

arrow (ˈærəʊ) *n* **1** a long, slender, pointed shaft that is shot from a bow. **2** a sign resembling this, esp. used to show direction. < Old English *arwe.*

arsenal (ˈɑːsənl̩) *n* a place where weapons and ammunition are stored or produced. < ultimately Arabic *dār ṣinā'ah* house of manufacture.

arsenic (ˈɑːsnɪk) *n* a brittle, steel-grey, semi-metallic, poisonous element. < ultimately Syriac *zarnīg.*

arson (ˈɑːsn̩) *n* the act of maliciously setting fire to property. **arsonist** *n* < ultimately Latin *ardēre* to burn.

art (ɑːt) *n* **1** the use of creative abilities and imagination to produce aesthetic works. **2** paintings, sculptures, etc., produced in this way. **3** a skill: the art of writing poetry. **4** *pl* non-scientific subjects such as languages. < ultimately Latin *ars* skill, craftsmanship.

artefact (ˈɑːtɪˌfækt) *n* a man-made object, esp. a simple one. < Latin *ars* skill + *facere* to make.

artery (ˈɑːtərɪ) *n* **1** a thick-walled blood vessel that carries blood away from the heart to all parts of the body. **2** a major road or transport route. **arterial** *adj* < ultimately Greek *artēria.*

artful (ˈɑːtfʊl) *adj* cunning; clever at achieving what one wants. **artfully** *adv* **artfulness** *n*

arthritis (ɑːˈθraɪtəs) *n* inflammation of one or more joints, causing pain and stiffness. **arthritic** *adj, n* < Greek *arthron* joint + *itis,* feminine of *itēs* belonging to.

artichoke (ˈɑːtɪˌtʃəʊk) *n* also **globe artichoke** a thistle-like plant grown for its edible flower head. < ultimately Arabic *al-khurshūf.*

article (ˈɑːtɪkl̩) *n* **1** a particular or separate object, esp. one of many: articles of clothing. **2** a piece of non-fictional writing in a newspaper, etc. **3** a separate clause or point in a formal agreement, etc. **4** one of the words a, an, or the.
• *vb* bind by a written contract: an articled clerk. < ultimately Latin *artus* joint.

articulate (ɑːˈtɪkjʊlət) *adj* **1** able to express oneself clearly. **2** able to speak.
• *vb* (ɑːˈtɪkjʊˌleɪt) speak clearly. **articulation** *n* **articulated** *adj* with two sections flexibly joined but operating together: articulated lorries. < SEE **ARTICLE.**

artifice (ˈɑːtɪfɪs) *n* **1** a trick. **2** cleverness; crafty deception. < ultimately Latin *ars* skill + *facere* to make.

artificial (ˈɑːtɪˈfɪʃəl) *adj* **1** not occurring naturally; made by man, esp. in imitation of something natural. **2** pretended; affected. **artificiality** *n* **artificially** *adv* **artificial insemination** the introduction of sperm into the uterus by non-natural means. **artificial respiration** the forcing of air into and out of the lungs when a person's own breathing has stopped. < SEE **ARTIFICE.**

artillery (ɑːˈtɪlərɪ) *n* **1** large, heavy, mounted firearms. **2** the branch of an army using artillery. < Middle French *artillier* to equip with weapons.

artisan (ˈɑːtɪˌzæn, ˌɑːtɪˈzæn) *n* a skilled manual worker or craftsman. < ultimately Latin *ars* skill.

artist (ˈɑːtɪst) *n* **1** a person who produces works of art, esp. paintings. **2** a person who is skilled in something. **artistic** *adj* **1** of art or artists. **2** showing creative skill. **artistically** *adv* **artistry** *n* artistic skill, ability, or quality. < SEE **ART.**

artiste (ɑːˈtiːst) *n* a public entertainer such as a singer. < French.

artless (ˈɑːtləs) *adj* **1** free from deceit;

---

arrant nonsense

It may come as a surprise to know that arrant, as in an *arrant* liar, and errant, as in a knight *errant,* were originally the same word, errant. Errant, derived ultimately from the Latin *iter,* 'a journey', literally means 'wandering'—a knight errant was one sent forth from the castle to wander through the countryside in search of chivalrous deeds. However, the notion of wandering also conjured up pictures of people roaming around being a nuisance —hence, an *arrant* thief.

In the course of time the word arrant lost the meaning of 'wandering' altogether and became just another adjective of degree like utter or absolute, and so came to be applied not only to thieves and liars but to anything vaguely undesirable.

---

simple or innocent. **2** free from artificiality; natural. **artlessly** *adv* **artlessness** *n*

as (əz; *stressed* æz) *adv* **1** to the same degree or amount: as deaf as a post. **2** when considered in the way that is mentioned.
• *conj* **1** in or to the same degree in which. **2** in the way that. **3** while. **4** for the reason that.
• *pron* according to what or the way in which.
• *prep* **1** like. **2** in the state, role, etc., of: He works as a writer. < Old English *eallswā* likewise. SEE PANEL.

asbestos (æzˈbɛstəs) *n* a fibrous, non-combustible, chemically resistant mineral. < ultimately Greek: inextinguishable.

ascend (əˈsɛnd) *vb* **1** move upwards. **2** rise to a higher point, etc. **3** succeed to: ascend the throne. **ascendancy** *n* dominating influence. **ascent** *n* ascending; upward slope. < ultimately Latin *ad-* to + *scandere* to climb.

ascertain (ˌæsəˈteɪn) *vb* discover with certainty. **ascertainable** *adj* able to be ascertained. < Middle French *acertener* to make certain.

ascetic (əˈsɛtɪk) *adj* self-denying, esp. for religious reasons.
• *n* an ascetic person. **ascetically** *adv* **asceticism** *n* < Greek *askein* to exercise.

ascribe (əˈskraɪb) *vb* attribute or assign. **ascription** *n* < Latin *ad-* to + *scribere* to write.

asexual (eɪˈsɛksjʊəl) *adj* having no sex or sex organs.

ash[1] (æʃ) *n* the powder that is left after matter has been burnt. **ashtray** *n* a container for tobacco ash. < Old English *æsce*.

ash[2] *n* a tree of the olive family with small flowers and winged seeds. < Old English *æsc*.

ashamed (əˈʃeɪmd) *adj* feeling shame. **ashamedly** *adv* < SEE SHAME.

ashen (ˈæʃən) *adj* **1** of or like ashes. **2** extremely pale.

ashore (əˈʃɔː) *adv* to or on the shore.

aside (əˈsaɪd) *adv, adj* **1** to the side. **2** out of the way. **3** not being thought about. **4** in reserve.
• *n* a remark made in a low voice so that not everyone will hear it.

ask (ɑːsk) *vb* **1** put (a question) (to). **2** make a request: ask for help. **3** invite: They've asked us over for coffee. **4** set as a price: He's asking £1000! **5** attract (something unpleasant) by one's behaviour: ask for trouble. **ask after** enquire about the welfare of. < Old English *āscian*.

askance (əˈskæns, əˈskɑːns) *adv* with distrust or disapproval. < origin uncertain.

askew (əˈskjuː) *adv, adj* at an oblique angle; awry.

asleep (əˈsliːp) *adj* **1** in or into a state of sleep. **2** numbed.

asparagus (əˈspærəgəs) *n* one of a group of tall plants grown for its edible shoots; these shoots. < ultimately Greek *asparagos*. SEE PANEL.

aspect (ˈæspɛkt) *n* **1** a feature or way of looking: consider every aspect of the problem. **2** the appearance of a person or thing. **3** the direction in which something faces. < Latin *ad-* to + *specere* to look.

aspersion (əˈspɜːʃən) *n* an unkind or harmful remark that expresses doubt: He cast aspersions on her sincerity. < Latin *ad-* to + *spargere* to scatter.

asphalt (ˈæsfælt) *n* a black, sticky substance used in surfacing roads. < ultimately Greek *asphaltos*.

---

as it were

As features in a number of expressions, including:

as for concerning: As for the rest of my holiday, I spent the time rather aimlessly.
as from from the date that is mentioned: The new rule applies as from 1 January.
as if 1 in a way that would be right or suitable if: They treated him as if he were still a baby. **2** in a way that suggests: He hesitated as if he were about to change his mind.
as it were if it may be expressed in this way; speaking figuratively: Language is, as it were, a reflection of society.
as to with regard to; according to.
as well 1 in addition; too: Think not only of yourself but of other people as well. **2** fortunate: Perhaps it was just as well that I failed my exams.
as well as in addition to: polytechnics as well as universities.
as yet up to this or that time.
as you were used as an instruction to return to a previous position or to withdraw a previous comment.

asphyxia (æs'fɪksɪə) *n* lack of oxygen in the body; suffocation. **asphyxiate** *vb* suffocate. **asphyxiation** *n* < ultimately Greek *a*- not + *sphyzein* to throb.
aspic ('æspɪk) *n* a savoury jelly used as a relish or as a mould for meat, eggs, etc. < French: asp, snake.
aspidistra (ˌæspɪ'dɪstrə) *n* a plant with long, dark-green leaves. < ultimately Greek *aspis* shield.
aspire (ə'spaɪə) *vb* try to reach or achieve an aim. **aspirant** *n* a person who aspires to something. **aspirate** *n* an h sound as at the beginning of home. **aspiration** *n* aspiring; great ambition. < Latin *ad*- to + *spirare* to breathe.
aspirin ('æsprɪn) *n* a drug used to treat mild pain such as headaches; tablet of this; acetylsalicylic acid. < *a*cetyl + *spir*aeic acid, its former name.
ass (æs) *n* **1** a hardy mammal related to the horse; donkey. **2** (*informal*) a foolish or obstinate person. < Old English *assa.*
assail (ə'seɪl) *vb* attack violently. **assailant** *n* an attacker. < ultimately Latin *ad*- to + *salire* to leap.
assassinate (ə'sæsɪˌneɪt) *vb* murder (a prominent person), esp. for political reasons. **assassination** *n* **assassin** *n* a person who assassinates someone. SEE PANEL.
assault (ə'sɔːlt) *n* a violent attack.
• *vb* make an assault on. < SEE **ASSAIL.**
assemble (ə'sɛmbḷ) *vb* **1** bring or come together. **2** fit together. **assembly** *n* **1** assembling. **2** a group of people gathered for a specific purpose. **3** a legislative body. **assembly line** a series of machines and workers through which work passes to be assembled in successive operations. < ultimately Latin *ad*- to + *simul* same.
assent (ə'sɛnt) *n* agreement or acceptance.
• *vb* agree or accept. < ultimately Latin *ad*- to + *sentire* to feel.
assert (ə'sɜːt) *vb* **1** declare, esp. forcefully. **2** put (oneself) forward or express (oneself) positively. **assertion** *n* asserting; declaration. **assertive** *adj* marked by forceful assertion. **assertively** *adv* **assertiveness** *n* < Latin *ad*- to + *serere* to join.
assess (ə'sɛs) *vb* **1** estimate the importance, value, or likelihood of. **2** determine the amount or value of; levy (a tax, etc.). **assessment** *n* **assessor** *n* < ultimately Latin *assidēre* to sit beside.
asset ('æsɛt) *n* **1** *pl* everything that is owned by a person, firm, etc., and has money value, esp. that which can be used to pay debts. **2** (*informal*) a person or thing that is helpful; advantage. < back formation from *assets,* ultimately from Latin *ad* to + *satis* enough.
assiduous (ə'sɪdjʊəs) *adj* hard-working; diligent. **assiduity** *n* **assiduously** *adv* < SEE **ASSESS.**
assign (ə'saɪn) *vb* **1** choose for a particular task; allot to. **2** designate for a particular function; specify or ascribe. **assignation** *n* **1** assigning. **2** a secret meeting, as between lovers. **assignment** *n* **1** assigning. **2** a task assigned to a person. < ultimately Latin *ad*- to + *signare* to mark.
assimilate (ə'sɪmɪˌleɪt) *vb* **1** take into the mind, understanding it fully. **2** absorb (food) into the body. **3** become incorporated. **assimilation** *n* < ultimately Latin *ad*- to + *simulare* to make similar.
assist (ə'sɪst) *vb* give help or support (to). **assistance** *n* **assistant** *n* < ultimately Latin *ad*- to + *sistere* to cause to

asparagus

Unfamiliar words of foreign or classical origin have over the centuries been particularly susceptible to the influence of *folk etymology.* This basically refers to the process whereby an unfamiliar word acquires a recognizable form. A good example of such linguistic metamorphosis is the word asparagus which, though derived from the Greek *asparagos,* developed the dialectal variant sparrow-grass.

assassin

The word assassin derives ultimately from the Arabic *hashshāshīn,* meaning 'hashish users'. This was the name given to a fanatical Muslim sect operating in Persia and Syria in the 11th and 12th centuries, which is remembered for the campaign of terror by which it sought to gain control of the Muslim world. Newcomers to the sect were given hashish to brainwash them into accepting terrorist murder as part of their religious duty, as well as to help them carry out their bloody deeds.

stand. SEE PANEL.
assizes (əˈsaɪzɪz) *pl n* (formerly) the sessions held periodically of the superior court in a county. < ultimately Latin *assidēre* to sit beside.
Assoc. *abbrev* Association; Associate.
associate (əˈsəʊʃɪˌeɪt) *vb* **1** join as colleague, partner, etc. **2** link in the mind, etc.: I associate the smell of cabbage with school dinners. **3** keep company (with).
● *n* (əˈsəʊʃɪət) **1** a colleague or partner. **2** a person admitted to a lower degree of membership.
● *adj* (əˈsəʊʃɪət) **1** associated. **2** with a lower status, degree of membership, etc. **association** *n* **1** associated; being associated. **2** a group of people organized for a common purpose. **3** a mental connection of ideas. **association football** soccer. < Latin *socius* companion.
assonance (ˈæsənəns) *n* **1** the repetition of similar vowel sounds. **2** similarity of sound in words or syllables. < ultimately Latin *ad-* to + *sonare* to sound.
assorted (əˈsɔːtɪd) *adj* **1** made up of different kinds put together. **2** suited.

assist

When a person starts to learn a foreign language, it doesn't take long before he discovers the existence of *false friends*, words which *appear* to be exactly the same as words in the learner's language, but which actually have different meanings.

For example, in French the verb *assister* means 'to attend'. However, an English learner of French tends to associate *assister* with the English verb assist and ends up asking in his beginner's French if he can 'attend' when what he means to ask is 'help'.

assortment *n* a collection of different sorts. < Middle French *a-* + *sorte* sort.
asst. *abbrev* assistant.
assuage (əˈsweɪdʒ) *vb* moderate or relieve. < ultimately Latin *ad-* to + *suavis* sweet.
assume (əˈsjuːm) *vb* **1** consider as true or certain to happen. **2** undertake; take up (an office): assume responsibilities. **3** pretend: He assumed an air of resignation. **4** take on; adopt: The problem then assumed even greater proportions. **assuming** *adj* presumptuous. **assumption** *n* assuming; something assumed. < ultimately Latin *ad-* to + *sumere* to take.
assure (əˈʃʊə, əˈʃɔː) *vb* **1** cause to feel confident. **2** promise; guarantee or make certain. **3** insure by an assurance policy. **assurance** *n* **1** something that inspires confidence. **2** a guarantee. **3** confidence; quality of being sure. **4** a kind of life insurance. **assured** *adj* **1** certain; convinced. **2** confident; self-confident. **3** payable under an assurance policy. **assuredly** *adv* < ultimately Latin *ad-* to + *securus* secure. SEE PANEL.
aster (ˈæstə) *n* one of a group of garden plants with daisy-like flowers of different colours. < ultimately Greek *astēr* star.
asterisk (ˈæstərɪsk) *n* a star-shaped symbol * used to draw attention to something.
● *vb* mark with an asterisk. < SEE **ASTER**.
astern (əˈstɜːn) *adv, adj* **1** in or to the rear; behind the stern. **2** backwards.
asteroid (ˈæstəˌrɔɪd) *n* a small planet that orbits the sun, esp. between Mars and Jupiter. < SEE **ASTER**.
asthma (ˈæsmə) *n* a respiratory disorder with breathlessness and wheezing due to muscular spasm of the tubes of the windpipe. **asthmatic** *adj, n* **asthmatically** *adv* < ultimately Greek: laborious breathing. SEE PANEL.
astigmatism (əˈstɪgməˌtɪzəm) *n* a defect

assure, ensure, or **insure?**

These words are sometimes confused.

Assure means 'to cause (a person) to feel confident by stating firmly': I can *assure* you that your suitcase will be safe with me.

Ensure (in American English insure) means 'to make (an action or event) certain or inevitable': Measures have been taken to *ensure* that the machine will not fail again.

In insurance, assure and insure, and assurance and insurance, have distinct meanings. Assure and assurance are used of things that are certain to happen, especially death. So you assure your life and take out life assurance. You insure or take out insurance against things that may or may not happen, such as theft or fire. The distinction between insure and assure and insurance and assurance is, however, not always made in non-technical usage.

in an eye or lens that results in a blurred image. **astigmatic** *adj* < Greek *a-* without + *stigma* mark.

astir (əˈstɜː) *adj* moving; excited.

astonish (əˈstɒnɪʃ) *vb* surprise greatly. **astonishment** *n* < ultimately Latin *tonare* to thunder.

astound (əˈstaʊnd) *vb* shock with surprise and wonder. < SEE **ASTONISH.**

astray (əˈstreɪ) *adv, adj* **1** away from the right path, way, etc. **2** in error; out of the right or proper way.

astride (əˈstraɪd) *adv, adj* with the legs far apart.
• *prep* **1** with a leg on either side of. **2** with a part on both sides of; extending across.

astringent (əˈstrɪndʒənt) *adj* **1** very severe; harsh. **2** causing contraction of organic tissues.
• *n* an astringent substance. **astringency** *n* **astringently** *adv* < ultimately Latin *ad-* to + *stringere* to bind tight.

astrology (əˈstrɒlədʒɪ) *n* the study of the supposed influence of heavenly bodies on human affairs. **astrological** *adj* **astrologically** *adv* **astrologer** *n* an expert in astrology. < ultimately Greek *astron* star + *-logy*, from *logos* word.

astronaut (ˈæstrəˌnɔːt) *n* a person who travels beyond the atmosphere of the earth. < ultimately Greek *astron* star + *nautēs* sailor.

astronomy (əˈstrɒnəmɪ) *n* the scientific study of stars and planets. **astronomer** *n* an expert in astronomy. **astronomical** *adj* **1** of astronomy. **2** enormously large. **astronomically** *adv* < ultimately Greek *astron* star + *nemein* to distribute.

astute (əˈstjuːt) *adj* shrewd and perceptive. **astutely** *adv* **astuteness** *n* < Latin *astus* craft.

asunder (əˈsʌndə) *adv, adj* into parts: split asunder. < Old English *sundor*.

asylum (əˈsaɪləm) *n* **1** a place of refuge; refuge and safety. **2** (formerly) a place for the care of the mentally ill. < ultimately Greek *a-* without + *sylon* right of seizure.

asymmetric (ˌeɪsɪˈmɛtrɪk) or **asymmetrical** (ˌeɪsɪˈmɛtrɪkəl) *adj* not symmetrical. **asymmetrically** *adv* **asymmetry** *n*

at (ət; *stressed* æt) *prep* **1** used to show a place: at the airport. **2** used to show a point in time: at 6 o'clock. **3** used to show a state or condition: at ease. **4** used to show an aim or target: He was jailed for shooting at a policeman. **5** engaged in: at play. **6** used to show circumstances, manner, or reason: I was angry at such injustices. **7** used to show a rate or charge: at 120 kilometres per hour. < Old English *æt*.

ate (ɛt, eɪt) SEE **EAT.**

atheist (ˈeɪθɪˌɪst) *n* a person who does not believe in the existence of God or divine beings. **atheism** *n* **atheistic** *adj* < ultimately Greek *a-* without + *theos* god.

athlete (ˈæθliːt) *n* a person who is trained in exercises or games needing physical strength, agility, etc. **athletic** *adj* **1** of athletes or athletics. **2** physically strong and active. **athletically** *adv* **athletics** *n* competitive track and field events; running, walking, throwing, and jumping contests. < ultimately Greek *athlon* prize, contest.

atlas (ˈætləs) *n* a collection of maps in a book. < Greek *Atlas*, from drawings of Atlas supporting the heavens. SEE PANEL.

atmosphere (ˈætməsˌfɪə) *n* **1** the air surrounding the earth; mixture of gases surrounding any heavenly body such as a planet. **2** the air in a place. **3** a general environment; dominant influence, feeling, or mood. **atmospheric** *adj* < ultimately Greek *atmos* vapour + *sphaira* sphere.

atom (ˈætəm) *n* **1** the smallest particle of an element that takes part in chemical reactions. **2** this as a source of atomic energy. **3** a tiny amount or quantity.

---

asthma and **fuchsia**

Spellings such as asthma and fuchsia present considerable pronunciation problems. In words of this type we have not just a single silent letter, but combinations of silent letters: the th in asthma and the ch in fuchsia. Fortunately, th and ch are the only two silent pairs. The single silent letter, on the other hand, occurs across a whole range of letters, including:

- b **debt, lamb, plumber**
- c **acquaint, indict**
- d **handsome, handkerchief, Wednesday**
- g **sign, gnaw**
- h **heir, khaki, exhibit**
- k **knee**
- l **calm, would**
- n **autumn**
- p **pneumonia, cupboard**
- s **island, debris**
- t **listen, whistle, mortgage**
- w **write, who, answer**

---

atom bomb also **atomic bomb** a bomb that derives its power from the sudden release of atomic energy. **atomic** *adj* of atoms, atom bombs, or atomic energy. **atomic energy** nuclear energy. < ultimately Greek *a-* not + *temnein* to cut.

atone (ə'təʊn) *vb* make amends for or take away (sin, etc.); reconcile. **atonement** *n* < *atonement*: from Middle English *at onement* in harmony.

atrocious (ə'trəʊʃəs) *adj* **1** extremely wicked or cruel. **2** (*informal*) very unpleasant. **atrociously** *adv* **atrocity** *n* < Latin *atrox* gloomy, dreadful.

attach (ə'tætʃ) *vb* **1** join or fasten. **2** join or become associated with. **3** attribute or ascribe: I wouldn't attach much importance to your exclusion from the list. **4** be attributed or ascribed. **attached** *adj* feeling affection. **attachment** *n* **1** attaching; being attached. **2** something attached. **3** affection. < Old French *estachier*. SEE PANEL.

attaché (ə'tæʃeɪ) *n* an expert or specialist attached to a diplomatic staff: a military attaché. **attaché case** a small, flat case, used esp. for carrying documents.

atlas

According to Greek mythology, *Atlas* was a giant Titan who, as a punishment for his part in the war to overthrow Zeus, was made to support the heavens on his shoulders. A book of maps came to be known as an atlas after the early map-maker Rumold Mercator put a drawing of Atlas supporting the world on his back on the title page of a collection of maps published in 1595.

< French: SEE **ATTACH.**

attack (ə'tæk) *vb* **1** act forcefully against in order to harm, injure, etc. **2** speak or write hostile or bitter words to. **3** set to work on or begin to deal with, esp. vigorously. **4** take the initiative in a game or sport.
• *n* **1** the act of attacking. **2** strong, hostile criticism. **3** a sudden onset of a disease, etc.: a heart attack. **attacker** *n* < ultimately Old Italian *stacca* stake.

attain (ə'teɪn) *vb* achieve or fulfil by effort; reach. **attainable** *adj* able to be attained. **attainment** *n* attaining; something attained; achievement or accomplishment. < ultimately Latin *ad-* to + *tangere* to touch.

attempt (ə'tɛmpt) *vb* make an effort (to do something) or achieve, solve, etc., (something), esp. unsuccessfully.
• *n* **1** the act of attempting something. **2** an attack, esp. with the intention of killing: an attempt on the President's life. < ultimately Latin *ad-* to + *temptare* to try.

attend (ə'tɛnd) *vb* **1** be present at (a meeting, event, etc.). **2** take care of; stay with as a companion, etc. **3** pay attention or apply oneself (to); deal with. **attendance** *n* the number of people attending; number of times a person attends as considered against a possible maximum. < ultimately Latin *ad-* to + *tendere* to stretch.

attendant (ə'tɛndənt) *n* a person who is present as a companion or who provides a service for the general public: a car-park attendant.
• *adj* associated or connected: the attendant problems.

attention (ə'tɛnʃən) *n* **1** concentrated application of the mind. **2** thought, esp.

attachable

A word segment which is added to the end of a word to turn, say, an adjective into an adverb or a noun into a verb is known as a *suffix*. One of the hardest working suffixes in English is -able with its variant form -ible. On the one hand it can be appended to virtually any transitive verb to make an adjective. For example, from transform, recover, read, and wash we get transform*able*, recover*able*, read*able*, and wash*able*. And if a transitive verb such as vean existed, the derived form vean*able* would also be possible. In addition to this highly productive pattern, -able also combines with a number of intransitive verbs, as in laughable and variable and even with certain nouns, as in pleasurable and fashionable.

Problems of comprehension arise more with -ible forms than -able forms because very often the -ible form derives from a Latin verb—one that was either not imported or that exists in an unrecognizable form. Examples include plausible, dirigible, compatible, and audible, the roots of which are obvious only to Latin scholars. See also panel at **lament.**

with a view to action. **3** awareness or notice. **4** an act of courtesy, sometimes showing love. **5** also *interj* (a call to) a soldier's formal position of readiness. **attentive** *adj* **1** paying attention. **2** observant; mindful. **attentively** *adv* **attentiveness** *n*

attenuate (əˈtɛnjʊˌeɪt) *vb* make thin or weaker. **attenuation** *n* < Latin *ad-* to + *tenuis* thin.

attest (əˈtɛst) *vb* **1** declare to be true. **2** bear witness to (an act, event, etc.). **3** be evidence for; demonstrate. **attestation** *n* < Latin *ad-* to + *testis* witness.

attic (ˈætɪk) *n* a room in the space immediately below the roof of a house. < *Attica*, state of ancient Greece. SEE PANEL.

attire (əˈtaɪə) *vb* dress, esp. in splendid clothes.
● *n* clothes, esp. splendid ones. < Old French *a* + *tire* order, row.

attitude (ˈætɪˌtjuːd) *n* **1** a mental position or feeling regarding something. **2** a position of the body. < Latin *aptus* fit, apt.

attorney (əˈtɜːnɪ) *n, pl* **attorneys** **1** a person who has legal authority to act for another person. **2** (*US*) a lawyer. **attorney-general** *n* the chief legal officer of a country. < Old French *a-* + *torner* to turn.

attract (əˈtrækt) *vb* **1** draw to oneself (attention, notice, etc.). **2** arouse the feelings, senses, etc., of. **3** pull towards oneself. **attraction** *n* **1** attracting. **2** a person or thing that attracts. **3** the quality or power of attracting. **attractive** *adj* pleasing to the senses, one's interests, etc. **attractively** *adv* **attractiveness** *n* < ultimately Latin *ad-* to + *trahere* to draw.

attribute (əˈtrɪbjuːt) *vb* regard or reckon as belonging to or originated by.
● *n* (ˈætrɪˌbjuːt) **1** a characteristic or inherent feature or quality. **2** something associated with a person or thing. **attributable** *adj* **attribution** *n* < ultimately Latin *ad-* to + *tribuere* to bestow.

attributive (əˈtrɪbjʊtɪv) *adj* (of an adjective) preceding the noun that is modified. **attributively** *adv*

attrition (əˈtrɪʃən) *n* **1** wearing away, as by friction. **2** a gradual weakening by constant harassment, etc.: a war of attrition. < Latin *ad-* to + *terere* to rub.

atypical (eɪˈtɪpɪkl̩) *adj* not typical. **atypically** *adv* SEE PANEL.

aubergine (ˈəʊbəˌʒiːn) *n* **1** also **egg-plant** a type of plant with a large, purple fruit that is cooked and eaten as a vegetable; fruit of this plant. **2** a dark purple colour. < ultimately Persian *bādingān*.

aubrietia (ɔːˈbriːʃə) *n* a trailing, perennial plant with small, purple or reddish

the noble attic

The empty space immediately beneath the roof of a house is known as an attic. Rather surprisingly, this word has connections with the architectural splendours of ancient Greece.

Attic entered the language in the late 17th century in the heyday of neoclassicism as part of the name of the top floor or *Attic storey* of a building constructed after the classical style. Unlike the modern-day attic, the Attic storey was an essentially decorative feature, built in imitation of the original *Attic order* which was a purely decorative device.

Attic derives ultimately from the Latin *Atticus* meaning 'of Attica' or 'Athenian'.

atypical words

The negative prefix a- is pronounced either as a diphthong as in asexual, atheist, and atypical or as a short vowel as in agnostic, anarchy, and anomalous. The general rule is that the former pronunciation is used when the prefix occurs in a word having a positive opposite (asexual—sexual, atheist—theist, atypical—typical). When no such positive form exists, however, the short vowel is used. Apathetic follows the latter pattern since pathetic—although it exists—does not have the opposite meaning.

aubrietia

It is very rare for an artist to be honoured by having his name given to the subject of his paintings. However, this happened in the case of the French painter of flowers and animals, Claude *Aubriet;* 1665–1742, after whom aubrietia takes its name.

flowers. < Claude *Aubriet*, died 1742, French painter of flowers and animals. SEE PANEL.

auburn (ˈɔːbn̩) *adj, n* (of hair) reddish-brown. < ultimately Latin *albus* white.

auction (ˈɔːkʃən) *n* a public sale in which the goods, property, etc., are sold to the person who bids the highest price. • *vb* sell by auction. **auctioneer** *n* a person who conducts an auction. < Latin *augēre* to increase.

audacious (ɔːˈdeɪʃəs) *adj* **1** bold and daring, esp. recklessly. **2** insolent or impudent. **audaciously** *adv* **audacity** *n* < Latin *audēre* to dare.

audible (ˈɔːdɪbl̩) *adj* loud enough to be heard. **audibility** *n* **audibly** *adv* < Latin *audire* to hear.

audience (ˈɔːdɪəns) *n* **1** a group of people who are viewing or listening to a public event such as a play or concert. **2** the people reached by a broadcast programme. **3** a formal interview with a ruler or other important person. < SEE **AUDIO**.

audio (ˈɔːdɪˌəʊ) *adj* **1** of or relating to sound or hearing. **2** of or used in the transmission, reception, or reproduction of sound. **audio typist** a typist who is trained to type from a sound recording. **audio-visual** *adj* for both hearing and sight: audio-visual aids. < Latin *audire* to hear.

audit (ˈɔːdɪt) *n* an official, esp. independent examination and verification of the annual accounts of an organization. • *vb* carry out an audit on. **auditor** *n* a person who is authorized to carry out audits. < SEE **AUDIO**.

audition (ɔːˈdɪʃən) *n* a test in which a performer shows his or her abilities for a prospective role, etc. • *vb* **1** test in an audition. **2** give a performance in an audition. < SEE **AUDIO**.

auditorium (ɔːdɪˈtɔːrɪəm) *n* the part of a concert hall, etc., where the public sits.

augment (ɔːgˈmɛnt) *vb* make or become greater or more numerous; increase. **augmentation** *n* < ultimately Latin *augēre* to increase.

augur (ˈɔːgə) *vb* be an omen of: This augurs well for the future. < Latin: diviner, soothsayer.

august (ɔːˈgʌst) *adj* dignified or grand: an august occasion. < Latin *augustus*. SEE PANEL.

aunt (ɑːnt) *n* **1** a sister of one's father or mother. **2** the wife of one's uncle. **3** an affectionate term for a woman who is a close friend of a child or his or her parents. **aunty, auntie** *n* (*informal*) an aunt. < Latin *amita*. SEE PANEL.

au pair (ˌəʊ ˈpɛə) *n* a foreign girl who undertakes domestic work for a family in return for board and lodging, esp. in order to learn the language of the family. < French: on an equal footing.

aura (ˈɔːrə) *n* a distinctive quality thought to be characteristic of a person or thing. < ultimately Greek: breeze.

aural (ˈɔːrəl) *adj* of the ear or hearing.

Aunt Sally

Originally, an Aunt Sally was a fair-ground effigy of an old woman at which objects were thrown. This sense has broadened over the years and the expression may now be applied to any easy target for insults, criticism, etc.

august Augustus

The names of the months September through to December derive from Latin numerals that indicate their position in the Roman calendar (see panel at **month**). In accordance with this pattern, the month preceding September—'the seventh month'—had been known by the Romans as *Sextilis* —'the sixth month'. In 8 BC, however, this name was changed to *Augustus* in celebration of Augustus Caesar, the first Roman Emperor, just as *Quintilis* —'the fifth month'—had been changed by Mark Anthony to *Julius*, after Julius Caesar.

The naming of a month after Augustus was not the first but the second great honour to be bestowed upon him. The first was the change of his name. Augustus had previously been known as *Octavianus* but this was replaced by a more noble title derived from the adjective *augustus* meaning 'majestic' or 'showing grandeur'. Without the granting of this new name, the calendar might have had two months beginning with *Oct:* October and Octavian!

< Latin *auris* ear.
au revoir (ˌəʊ rəˈvwɑː) *interj* goodbye. < French: to the seeing again.
auspices (ˈɔːspɪsɪz) *pl n* patronage or guidance, **auspicious** *adj* favourable; being right for a future success: an auspicious occasion. < Latin *auspex* diviner by birds.
austere (ɒˈstɪə) *adj* **1** forbidding or stern in appearance or manner. **2** self-denying. **3** very simple and without ornament or comfort, **austerely** *adv* **austerity** *n* **1** being austere. **2** enforced economy; shortage of goods. < Greek *austēros* harsh.
authentic (ɔːˈθɛntɪk) *adj* genuine; reliable; corresponding to the truth or facts, **authentically** *adv* **authenticity** *n* **authenticate** *vb* prove the authenticity of. **authentication** *n* < ultimately Greek *aut-* same, self + *hentēs* doer.
author (ˈɔːθə) fem, **authoress** *n* **1** the writer of a book, play, etc. **2** the originator or creator (of a plan, etc.). **authorship** *n* < ultimately Latin *augēre* to increase.
authority (ɔːˈθɒrɪtɪ) *n* **1** the power or right to influence, command, or take action and to expect and receive submission. **2** a person or group with this. **3** an expert: a great authority on butterflies. **4** convincing force, weight, or influence. **5** a definitive book, etc., used as a source. **authoritarian** *adj* of or favouring submission to authority, **authoritative** *adj* having authority; official or definitive; despotic, **authoritatively** *adv* **authorize** *vb* give authority to; sanction. **authorization** *n* < SEE AUTHOR.
autism (ˈɔːtɪzəm) *n* a severe mental illness in which a child cannot develop normal, personal relationships, **autistic** *adj* < ultimately Greek *autos* self.
autobiography (ˌɔːtəˈbaɪˈɒgrəfɪ) *n* the biography of a person written by himself or herself. **autobiographer** *n* **autobiographical** *adj*
autocrat (ˈɔːtəˌkræt) *n* a ruler with absolute, unlimited power. **autocracy** *n* **autocratic** *adj* < ultimately Greek *aut-* self + *kratos* strength.
autograph (ˈɔːtəˌgrɑːf) *n* a person's signature or handwriting.
• *vb* write one's signature in; sign. < ultimately Greek *autos* self + *graphein* to write.
automate (ˈɔːtəˌmeɪt) *vb* convert to or work by automatic operation, **automation** *n* the use of automatic methods and equipment, esp. to save manpower.
automatic (ˌɔːtəˈmætɪk) *adj* **1** working by itself without direct, human intervention: an automatic control system. **2** (of a firearm) replacing an empty shell with a new one and firing continuously until pressure on the trigger is released. **3** done spontaneously; mechanical; involuntary: automatic reflex actions.
• *n* an automatic machine, such as a firearm or vehicle, **automatically** *adv* < Greek *automatos* self-acting.
automaton (ɔːˈtɒməˌtən) *n* **1** a mechanical device that operates from its own source of power; robot. **2** a person who acts mechanically.
automobile (ˈɔːtəməˌbiːl) *n* (*US*) a car.
autonomous (ɔːˈtɒnəməs) *adj* self-governing. **autonomy** *n* self-government; degree of independence. < Greek *aut-* self + *nomos* law.
autopsy (ˈɔːtɒpsɪ) *n* a post-mortem examination. < Greek *autopsia* seeing with one's own eyes.
autumn (ˈɔːtəm) *n* the season between summer and winter. **autumnal** *adj* < ultimately Latin *autumnus*.
auxiliary (ɔːgˈzɪljərɪ) *adj* **1** subsidiary or additional; providing support. **2** (of a verb) used to express tense, voice, or mood.
• *n* **1** an auxiliary person or thing. **2** *pl* foreign troops serving a country at war. < Latin *auxilium* help.
avail (əˈveɪl) *vb* be of use or advantage (to). **avail oneself of** make use of.
• *n* use or advantage: They shouted, but to no avail. < ultimately Latin *valere* to be strong.
available (əˈveɪləbḷ) *adj* able to be used, obtained, or reached, **availability** *n*
avalanche (ˈævəˌlɑːntʃ) *n* **1** a large mass of snow, rock, etc., falling quickly down a mountain. **2** a sudden or overwhelming onrush. < French dialect *lavantse*.
avant-garde (ˌævɒŋˈgɑːd) *n* the group of people in artistic or intellectual fields with creatively radical or experimental ideas.
• *adj* of the work of the avant-garde. < French: vanguard.
avarice (ˈævərɪs) *n* greed for wealth. **avaricious** *adj* < ultimately Latin *avēre* to covet.
Ave. *abbrev* avenue.
avenge (əˈvɛndʒ) *vb* take vengeance for. **avenger** *n* < Old French *vengier*.
avenue (ˈævɪˌnjuː) *n* **1** a road or street, esp. broad and lined with trees. **2** a way of approach: We must explore every avenue. < ultimately Latin *ad-* to + *venire* to come.
average (ˈævərɪdʒ, ˈævrɪdʒ) *n* **1** the

result of adding several quantities together and dividing the total by the number of quantities. **2** the typical or usual quality, amount, etc.
• *adj* **1** found by taking an average: the average salary. **2** ordinary; usual.
• *vb* **1** work out the average of. **2** amount to or perform as an average. < ultimately Arabic *awār* damage.

averse (əˈvɜːs) *adj* actively disinclined (to). **aversion** *n* a strong dislike; object of this. < SEE **AVERT.** SEE PANEL AT **ADVERSE.**

avert (əˈvɜːt) *vb* **1** turn away: avert one's eyes. **2** prevent: avert a disaster. < Latin *a-* from + *vertere* to turn.

aviary (ˈeɪvjərɪ) *n* a large enclosure in which birds are kept. < Latin *avis* bird.

aviation (ˌeɪvɪˈeɪʃən) *n* **1** the art or science of flying aircraft. **2** the design, manufacture, and maintenance of aircraft. **aviator** *n* the pilot of an aircraft. < ultimately Latin *avis* bird.

avid (ˈævɪd) *adj* keen; greedy. **avidity** *n* **avidly** *adv* < SEE **AVARICE.**

avocado (ˌævəˈkɑːdəʊ) *n, pl* **avocados** also **avocado pear** the pear-shaped fruit of the avocado tree, with a green to dark-purple skin, a rich, fatty flesh, and a large, hard seed. < Aztec *ahuacatl* testicle. SEE PANEL.

avoid (əˈvɔɪd) *vb* **1** keep away from. **2** refrain from. **3** not allow to happen. **avoidance** *n* **avoidable** *adj* able to be avoided. < Old French *esvuidier.* SEE PANEL.

avow (əˈvaʊ) *vb* declare certainly; admit openly and shamelessly. **avowal** *n* **avowedly** *adv* < ultimately Latin *advocare* to call upon.

await (əˈweɪt) *vb* **1** wait for; expect. **2** be in store for.

awake (əˈweɪk) *vb* **awoke, awaked; awoken, awaked; awaking 1** emerge or rouse from sleep. **2** become aware of. **3** arouse (feelings, memories, etc.).
• *adj* not sleeping. < Old English *awacian.*

awaken (əˈweɪkən) *vb* awake. **awakening** *n* < Old English *awæcnian.*

award (əˈwɔːd) *vb* **1** give officially, esp. for merit. **2** grant legally.
• *n* something awarded, esp. as a prize. < Old Northern French *eswarder.*

aware (əˈwɛə) *adj* having knowledge (of): aware of the dangers. **awareness** *n* < Old English *gewær.*

awash (əˈwɒʃ) *adv, adj* covered with water.

away (əˈweɪ) *adv* **1** from one place; to another place; in another direction: Go away! **2** in a secure place: lock all valuables away. **3** to an end: The sound died away in the distance. **4** from one's possession: He gave away all his money. **5** continuously. **6** so as to remove: I've cut away all the dead pieces. **far and away** by far; easily. **right away** immediately. **well away** started and making good progress.
• *adj* (of a sports match) played on an opponent's ground.
• *n* an away match. < Old English *aweg.*

awe (ɔː) *n* great wonder, reverence, or dread.
• *vb* fill with awe. **awesome** *adj* filled with or showing awe. **awestruck** *adj* filled with awe. < Old Norse *agi.*

awful (ˈɔːfʊl) *adj* **1** unpleasant or

avocado

Avocado comes from the Aztec word *ahuacatl*, a shortened form of *ahuacacuahuitl* or 'testicle tree'. The Aztecs, who invented amongst other things a pictorial writing system, were anything but unimaginative and the name they chose for the tree alludes to the shape of its fruit. The Spanish came upon this delicacy whilst conquering Central America, whereupon the native name was corrupted into *avocado*. This was the nearest phonetic equivalent in Spanish, meaning 'advocate'. Just as *ahuacatl* was corrupted by the Spanish, so *avocado* underwent further corruption by the British so that the fruit also came to be known as the alligator pear.

tax avoidance or **tax evasion?**

Avoid means 'to keep away or refrain from; not allow to happen': Much drudgery can be *avoided* by installing labour-saving devices. His accountant advised him on how to *avoid* paying too much tax.

Evade means 'to avoid by artfulness or deception': He *evaded* paying any tax for several years. The nouns from these words are avoidance and evasion: tax evasion is illegal; tax avoidance is not.

disagreeable; nasty. **2** (*informal*) very great: an awful lot of people. **awfully** *adv* (*informal*) very; very much: awfully tired. < SEE **AWE.** SEE PANEL AT **TERRIBLE.**

awhile (əˈwaɪl) *adv* for a short time.

awkward (ˈɔːkwəd) *adj* **1** clumsy in using the hands; not skilful. **2** not showing grace or ease of movement. **3** difficult to handle, use, or tackle: awkward questions. **4** embarrassing or embarrassed: an awkward silence **awkwardly** *adv* **awkwardness** *n* < Old Norse *öfugr* turned the wrong way.

awl (ɔːl) *n* a small, pointed tool used for making small holes in wood, leather, etc. < Old Norse *alr.*

awning (ˈɔːnɪŋ) *n* a roof-like cover of canvas, etc., on a frame; used as a protection from the sun or rain. < origin unknown.

awoke (əˈwəʊk) SEE **AWAKE. awoken** SEE **AWAKE.**

awry (əˈraɪ) *adv, adj* **1** turned or twisted. **2** away from the suitable or desired course: All our plans have gone awry. < Middle English *on wry.*

axe (æks) *n* **1** a tool for felling trees, chopping wood, etc. **2** (*informal*) a great reduction or removal.
• *vb* **1** cut with an axe. **2** (*informal*) dismiss, restrict, or stop abruptly: The council was forced to axe plans for the by-pass. < Old English *æx.*

axiom (ˈæksɪəm) *n* a generally accepted statement. **axiomatic** *adj* self-evident. < Greek *axios* worthy.

axis (ˈæksɪs) *n, pl* **axes** a straight line, etc., about which a body rotates or is supposed to rotate. < Latin: axis, axle.

axle (ˈæksəl) *n* a bar or shaft on which a wheel or wheels turn. < Old Norse *öxull.*

aye (aɪ) *adv* yes: Aye, aye sir.
• *n* an affirmative vote. < origin uncertain.

azalea (əˈzeɪljə) *n* a shrub with showy, fragrant, funnel-shaped flowers. < ultimately Greek *azaleos* dry.

azure (ˈæʒʊə, ˈæʒə) *adj, n* (of) the colour of a clear, blue sky. < ultimately Persian *lāzhuward.*

B

BA *abbrev* Bachelor of Arts.
babble (ˈbæbl̩) *vb* **1** utter continuously (sounds or words) in an incoherent or unintelligible manner. **2** chatter in a foolish way.
• *n* babbling talk or sounds. < probably like the sound.
babe (beɪb) *n* **1** (*chiefly poetic*) a baby. **2** an inexperienced person. **3** (*slang*) a girl or young woman.
baboon (bəˈbuːn) *n* a large monkey with a long, dog-like face and big teeth. < Middle French *baboue* grimace.
baby (ˈbeɪbɪ) *n* **1** a very young child or animal. **2** the youngest of a group. **3** an immature, inexperienced person. **4** something that is one's responsibility; obsession: That's your baby. **5** (*slang*) a person, esp. a girl or woman.
• *vb* **babied; babying** treat like a baby.
• *adj* very small. **babyhood** *n* **babyish** *adj* **baby buggy** a light, foldable pram. **baby-sit** *vb* **baby-sat; baby-sitting** act as a baby-sitter. **baby-sitter** *n* a person who looks after a child or children while the parents are out. < Middle English *babe, babi.*
bachelor (ˈbætʃələ) *n* **1** an unmarried man. **2** a person with an academic degree below a master's. **bachelor girl** an unmarried girl or woman who lives independently. < Celtic.
back (bæk) *n* **1** the rear part of the human body, from the neck to the hips; corresponding part of an animal's body. **2** the rear part of something. **3** the part of something that gives support. **4** the part of a garment covering the back. **5** a defensive player in soccer, etc.

back to back

The word back features in a number of expressions, many of them idiomatic, including:

back down to withdraw a claim, argument, etc.: The union is not prepared to back down in the dispute.
back of beyond a remote, isolated place.
back off to move backwards, as in fear.
back out to withdraw from an agreement: Once you've paid the money, it's too late to back out.
back seat a position of little importance or responsibility: Having managed the firm for 30 years, it's now time for me to take a back seat and make way for a younger man.
back-seat driver 1 a passenger in a car who offers unwanted advice to the driver on how to drive. **2** a person who criticizes or gives advice on matters that do not concern him or her.
back to back (of houses) built with an adjoining back wall.
back to front having the back placed where the front should be: He's put his sweater on back to front.
back up to support or help: Thank you for backing me up—I don't think Jeff would have been persuaded if you'd not agreed with me.
back-up *n* **1** support: with the back-up of a multi-million dollar corporation. **2** a substitute or reserve.
behind someone's back without someone's knowledge or agreement, in secret, and deceitfully: Why did you go behind my back and never ask my permission?
get off someone's back to stop bothering or annoying someone.
have one's back to the wall to be in a very difficult situation: We've really got our backs to the wall. Unless we get some more orders, the firm will go bust in three months.
know something backwards to know something very thoroughly: He's been revising for weeks so he should know everything backwards by now.
put one's back into something to use the greatest effort to do something: They put their backs into the decorating and finished it by 10 o'clock.
put someone's back up to annoy, offend, or antagonize someone: Her continual nagging really gets my back up!
turn one's back on to reject or abandon: The unions have decisively turned their backs on the management's latest pay offer.

• *adv* **1** at or to the rear; away. **2** in or to a previous position, time, state, etc. **3** in reply or return.
• *adj* **1** at or to the back. **2** distant; remote; less important: in the back streets. **3** being in arrears: back pay.
• *vb* **1** cause to go back. **2** support or help, esp. financially. **3** place a bet on (a horse, etc.). **4** cover the back of. **5** (of the wind) move anticlockwise. **backer** *n* **back-bencher** *n* a Member of Parliament who does not hold office in the government or opposition. **back boiler** a boiler fitted behind a domestic coal or gas fire. < Old English *bæc*. SEE PANEL.

backbiting (ˈbækˌbaɪtɪŋ) *n* spiteful talk about someone, esp. in his or her absence.

backbone (ˈbækˌbəʊn) *n* **1** a series of bony segments surrounding and protecting the spinal cord; spine. **2** courage and determination.

backdate (ˌbækˈdeɪt) *vb* make valid or effective from an earlier date.

backdrop (ˈbækˌdrɒp) *n* also **backcloth** **1** a painted curtain hung at the back of a stage. **2** background; circumstances.

backfire (ˌbækˈfaɪə) *vb* **1** (in an internal-combustion engine) explode prematurely in the cylinder. **2** have the reverse of the intended effect.

backgammon (ˈbækˌgæmən) *n* a board game for two people, played with dice. < *back* + Middle English *gammon* game.

background (ˈbækˌgraʊnd) *n* **1** the ground or scenery furthest from the viewer. **2** an inconspicuous position: stay in the background. **3** the circumstances and conditions in which an event or experience takes place. **4** the sum of a person's education, experience, etc.

backhand (ˈbækˌhænd) *n* a stroke in tennis, squash, etc., made with the back of the hand facing the direction of the stroke.
• *adv* with a backhand stroke. **backhanded** *adj* **1** using or made with a backhand. **2** indirect and sarcastic: a backhanded compliment.

backing (ˈbækɪŋ) *n* **1** support; help. **2** something that forms a back. **3** a musical accompaniment, esp. for a pop singer.

backlash (ˈbækˌlæʃ) *n* **1** a sudden, violent reaction or recoil. **2** a sudden, violent, and adverse reaction to an event.

backlog (ˈbækˌlɒg) *n* an accumulation of work not dealt with.

back-pedal (ˈbækˌpɛdl̩) *vb* **back-pedalled; back-pedalling** **1** pedal backwards. **2** withdraw or reverse a previous opinion or position.

backside (ˈbæksaɪd) *n* (*informal*) the buttocks.

backslide (ˈbækˌslaɪd) *vb* **backslid; backslidden; backsliding** lapse from good behaviour or in the practice of religion. **backslider** *n*

backstage (ˌbækˈsteɪdʒ) *adj, adv* **1** (situated or taking place) in the parts of a theatre that cannot be seen by the audience. **2** away from public view; privately.

backstroke (ˈbækˌstrəʊk) *n* a swimming stroke swum on the back.

backtrack (ˈbækˌtræk) *vb* **1** go back by the same route by which one has come. **2** withdraw or reverse one's opinion, policy, etc.

backward (ˈbækwəd) *adj* **1** directed towards the back: a backward glance. **2** retarded in development.
• *adv* backwards. **backwards** *adv* **1** away from the front; towards the back. **2** with the back foremost. **3** in a reverse sequence.

backwash (ˈbækˌwɒʃ) *n* the backward movement of water caused by the movement of oars, etc., or by retreating waves.

backwater (ˈbækˌwɔːtə) *n* **1** a body of stagnant water. **2** a place or state that is isolated or not progressive, esp. intellectually.

bacon (ˈbeɪkən) *n* meat from the back and sides of a pig, dried, salted, and often smoked. < Old High German *bahho*.

bacteriology (bækˌtɪərɪˈɒlədʒɪ) *n* the scientific study of bacteria. **bacteriological** *adj* **bacteriologist** *n*

bacterium (bækˈtɪərɪəm) *n, pl* **bacteria** a microscopic organism incapable of photosynthesis, usually single-celled. **bacterial** *adj* < ultimately Greek *baktērion* staff.

bad (bæd) *adj* **worse; worst** **1** having unpleasant or unfavourable qualities: bad news. **2** wicked; evil. **3** disobedient; mischievous. **4** not reaching an accepted standard. **5** severe; serious: a bad accident. **6** decayed or spoiled; rotten: bad eggs. **7** incompetent: bad at speaking French. **8** harmful: Too much sugar is bad for you. **9** inopportune: a bad time to ask for a pay rise. **10** in poor health; sick. **11** guilty or regretful: I feel bad about not helping. **12** invalid; damaged. **13** (of a debt) not recoverable.
• *adv* (*not standard*) badly.
• *n* something bad; bad state.

badness *n* **baddy** *n* (*informal*) a villain. **badly** *adv* **1** in a bad manner. **2** (*informal*) very much; greatly. < Middle English. SEE PANEL.

bade (bæd, beɪd) SEE **BID.**

badge (bædʒ) *n* a distinguishing emblem to show membership, achievement, etc. < Middle English *bage.*

badger (ˈbædʒə) *n* a nocturnal, burrowing mammal of the weasel family, with a black and white striped head.
• *vb* pester. < probably *badge,* from the white mark on its forehead.

badminton (ˈbædmɪntən) *n* a game played with rackets and a shuttlecock, which is hit backwards and forwards over a high net. < probably *Badminton,* estate in Avon, England. SEE PANEL.

baffle (ˈbæfl) *vb* **1** perplex or confuse. **2** block or hinder; frustrate. < origin uncertain.

bag (bæg) *n* **1** a container, esp. a flexible one, with an opening at the top, used for holding, carrying, or storing things. **2** this with its contents; amount it contains. **3** something like a bag. **4** (*derogatory*) an ugly woman: silly, old bag.
• *vb* **bagged; bagging 1** put into a bag. **2** capture or kill. **3** (*informal*) take possession of; secure a right to: I bag that chair! **bagful** *n* **bag and baggage** all one's belongings. **baggage** *n* luggage. **baggy** *adj* loose; hanging in wide folds: baggy trousers. **bags** *pl n* (*informal*) **1** a lot: bags of money. **2** trousers. **in the bag** (*informal*) certain to be accomplished or achieved. < Old Norse *baggi.*

bagpipes (ˈbægˌpaɪps) *pl n* a reed-pipe instrument in which air that is forced into a windbag is pushed out into sounding pipes.

bail[1] (beɪl) *n* **1** the security deposited as a guarantee for the appearance of a prisoner. **2** the temporary release on bail.
• *vb* **1** release on bail; gain the release of by giving bail. **2** also **bale out** help out of a predicament, esp. by paying money. < ultimately Latin *bajulus* porter. SEE PANEL.

bail[2] *n* either of the two cross-pieces over the stumps in cricket. < Old French *baile* stake.

bail[3], **bale** *vb* scoop (water) out of (a boat). **bail** or **bale out** escape from an aircraft in an emergency by using a parachute. < Middle French *baille* bucket, from Latin *bajulus* carrier.

bailiff (ˈbeɪlɪf) *n* **1** an official who helps a sheriff by serving writs, making arrests, etc. **2** the manager of an estate or farm. < SEE **BAIL**[1].

bad language

The word bad features in a number of expressions, many of them idiomatic, including:

bad language swear-words.
feel bad about to feel unhappy or guilty about: 'You know, I feel really bad about not visiting her in hospital.'
go from bad to worse to continue to deteriorate.
in someone's bad books out of favour with someone.
make the best of a bad job to manage as well as possible in unfavourable circumstances.
not bad quite good; very good: Not bad considering she's over 80.
too bad regrettable, but nothing can be done about it: It's too bad that you've got to go now.

badminton

The popular indoor racket game in which a shuttlecock is sent back and forth over a high net is known as badminton. The name of the game derives from *Badminton* estate in Avon, England. It was here that the game was devised in 1870, reputedly in order to while away a wet weekend.

bail or **bale?**

For the sense 'to release on bail; gain the release by giving money as surety', use bail. (Thinking of the spelling of jail may help.) For the sense 'to make (straw, hay, etc.) into a compact mass', use bale.

For the senses 'to help out of a predicament', 'to escape from an aircraft in an emergency by using a parachute', and 'to scoop water out of a boat', both bail out and bale out are acceptable in British English.

bait (beɪt) *n* **1** food, etc., placed on a hook or trap to lure prey. **2** any enticement.
• *vb* **1** provoke or exasperate persistently. **2** put food, etc., on (a hook or trap) for prey. < Old Norse *beita* to hunt.

baize (beɪz) *n* a woollen fabric like felt, used to cover tables, etc. < Middle French *bai* bay-coloured.

bake (beɪk) *vb* **1** cook by dry heat, esp. in an oven. **2** make or become hard by heat. **3** (*informal*) become extremely hot: I'm baking in this sun! **baker** *n* a person who bakes and sells bread, cakes, etc. **bakery** *n* a place where bread, cakes, etc., are baked or sold. **baking-powder** *n* a mixture of powders used in baking to make the dough rise. < Old English *bacan*.

balaclava (ˌbælə'klɑːvə) *n* a tight-fitting woollen hood that covers the head, ears, and neck. SEE PANEL AT **CARDIGAN.**

balance ('bæləns) *n* **1** a device for weighing, esp. one consisting of two pans or scales suspended from a cross-piece. **2** a state of equal adjustment in weight, importance, etc. **3** stability in the body or mind. **4** a weight or force that counteracts another. **5** the pleasing harmony of various parts in a painting, etc. **6** the difference between credits and debits. **7** the amount still owed after payment of a debt. **8** a remainder: I'll give you £50 now, and I'll send the balance later.
• *vb* **1** weigh in a balance. **2** bring or come into a state of equilibrium. **3** compare the relative values, etc., of. **4** offset; make equal in weight, force, etc. < ultimately Latin *bi-* two + *lanx* plate, scale. SEE PANEL.

balcony ('bælkənɪ) *n* **1** a platform extending from the wall of a building, with a rail or low wall. **2** an upper gallery in a theatre, etc. < Italian *balcone*.

bald (bɔːld) *adj* **1** lacking hair on the scalp. **2** (of tyres) with a worn tread. **3** plain or blunt; simple. **baldly** *adv* **baldness** *n* **balding** *adj* becoming bald. < Middle English *balled*.

bale[1] (beɪl) *n* **1** a large bundle of pressed straw, hay, etc., bound with rope or wire. **2** a large package or bundle of goods.
• *vb* make into a bale. < Old French. SEE PANEL AT **BAIL**[1].

bale[2] SEE **BAIL**[3].

balk, baulk (bɔːk, bɔːlk) *vb* **1** stop short and not proceed further. **2** turn away suddenly: He balked at the very thought of bribery. **3** thwart or frustrate. < Old English *balca* ridge between furrows.

ball[1] (bɔːl) *n* **1** a round or approximately round sphere or mass. **2** such a sphere used in a game or sport. **3** the rounded, slightly raised part at the base of a thumb or big toe.
• *vb* make or gather into a ball. **ball-bearing** *n* a bearing with small, hardened, steel balls; one of these balls. **ball-cock** *n* an automatic valve with a floating ball that controls the level of water in a cistern. **ball-point** *n* also **ball-point pen** a pen with a small, metal ball as its writing-point. < Old Norse *böllr*. SEE PANEL.

ball[2] *n* a large, formal, social gathering for dancing. **ballroom** *n* a large hall for dancing. **have a ball** (*informal*) enjoy

---

in the balance

Balance features in a number of expressions including:

balance of payments the difference between a country's overseas income and overseas expenditure in a given period.
balance of power the principle of trying to ensure that no one country or group of countries gains too prominent a position.
balance of trade the difference in value between a country's exports and imports.
in the balance in a critical, undecided state: The future of the school is still in the balance.
on balance everything considered: I'm not sure whether to take the job—but on balance I think I will.

---

spot the ball

Those who are on the ball when it comes to idioms will be familiar with the following expressions:
on the ball alert and informed: Jake's really on the ball as far as computer technology is concerned.
play ball to co-operate (with others): Some unions have decided not to play ball with the management in their efforts to streamline production.
set the ball rolling to start an activity, discussion, etc.

---

oneself. < ultimately Greek *ballizein* to dance.

ballad (ˈbæləd) *n* a simple song or poem, esp. one that narrates a story. < Middle English *balade* song sung while dancing, ultimately from Late Latin *ballare* to dance.

ballast (ˈbæləst) *n* **1** heavy material used to improve stability in a ship, etc. **2** crushed rock used as a foundation for roads, railway lines, etc. < probably Scandinavian.

ballerina (ˌbæləˈriːnə) *n* a female ballet dancer. < Italian, ultimately Late Latin *ballare* to dance.

ballet (ˈbæleɪ) *n* artistic dancing and mime to music; esp. to convey a story or mood. < French, from Italian *balletto*.

ballistics (bəˈlɪstɪks) *pl n* the study of the motion and flight of projectiles. **ballistic missile** a missile that is propelled to a desired height and then falls unpowered. < ultimately Greek *ballein* to throw.

balloon (bəˈluːn) *n* **1** a large bag that is inflated with a gas that is lighter than air, so that it can rise in the atmosphere. **2** a brightly coloured, inflatable, rubber bag used as a decoration or toy. **3** an approximately circular line enclosing the words or thoughts of a person in a cartoon.
• *vb* **1** travel in a balloon. **2** swell or puff out like a balloon. **balloonist** *n* a person who travels by balloon. < Italian *balla*, of Germanic origin.

ballot (ˈbælət) *n* **1** secret voting. **2** paper used in secret voting. **3** the number of votes cast.
• *vb* vote by ballot; cause to do this. < Italian *ballotta* a little ball, originally used in voting.

ballyhoo (ˈbælɪˌhuː) *n* (*informal*) noisy, showy talk; showy advertising. < origin uncertain.

balm (bɑːm) *n* **1** something that soothes or relieves. **2** a plant with fragrant leaves used for flavouring foods and for scenting perfumes. **balmy** *adj* **1** like balm; soothing. **2** mild. < ultimately Latin *balsamum* balsam.

balsa (ˈbɔːlsə) *n* a very light, pale-coloured wood from a tropical American tree. < Spanish: raft.

balustrade (ˈbæləˌstreɪd) *n* a row of short pillars topped by a rail; low parapet round a balcony, etc. < ultimately Greek *balaustion* wild pomegranate flower, from its shape.

bamboo (bæmˈbuː) *n* a tropical, tree-like plant with tall, hollow, woody, jointed stems used in building, making furniture, etc. < Malay *bambu*.

bamboozle (bæmˈbuːzl̩) *vb* (*informal*) confuse or trick. < origin unknown.

ban (bæn) *vb* **banned; banning** prohibit officially.
• *n* an official prohibition. < Old English *bannan* to proclaim.

banal (bəˈnɑːl) *adj* trite; common; not original or fresh. **banality** *n* **banally** *adv* < Middle French: compulsory, common.

banana (bəˈnɑːnə) *n* **1** a slightly curved fruit with a soft, pulpy flesh and a yellow skin. **2** the tropical plant on which large clusters of these grow. **go bananas** (*informal*) go crazy. < Spanish or Portuguese, of African origin.

band[1] (bænd) *n* **1** a group of people with a common purpose. **2** a group of musicians.
• *vb* join; unite. < French *bande*.

band[2] *n* **1** a thin strip of material used to hold things together or as a ring or decoration. **2** a range of values, wavelengths, etc., in a series.
• *vb* fasten or tie with a band. < of Germanic origin.

bandage (ˈbændɪdʒ) *n* a piece of material used to dress and bind up a wound.
• *vb* bind, dress, or cover with a bandage. < SEE **BAND**[2].

b. and b. *abbrev* bed and breakfast.

bandit (ˈbændɪt) *n* a member of an armed gang; robber. < Italian *bandito*.

bandstand (ˈbændˌstænd) *n* a covered, outdoor platform for a band.

bandwagon (ˈbændˌwægən) *n* a successful movement that attracts attention. **climb** or **jump on the bandwagon** (*informal*) join a movement, etc., that seems bound to be successful.

bandy (ˈbændɪ) *adj* (of legs) curving outward at the knees.
• *vb* **bandied; bandying** pass about in a casual and careless manner. < probably Middle French *bander* to hit to and fro.

bane (beɪn) *n* a person or thing that causes misery or trouble. < Old English *bana*.

bang (bæŋ) *vb* **1** make a sudden, loud noise, like an explosion. **2** strike or shut, esp. with a loud noise.
• *n* **1** a sudden, loud noise like an explosion. **2** a sharp blow. **3** a sudden rush of energy.
• *adv* **1** with a bang. **2** (*informal*) right; exactly: bang on 1 o'clock. **banger** *n* **1** a firework that explodes noisily. **2** (*informal*) a sausage. **3** (*informal*) a noisy, old car. < Old Norse *banga* hammer.

bangle (ˈbæŋgl̩) *n* a rigid bracelet. < Hindi *banglī*.

banish (ˈbænɪʃ) *vb* **1** expel officially from

a country. **2** drive away; dismiss or dispel: banish all one's fears. **banishment** *n* < of Germanic origin.

banisters (ˈbænɪstəz) *pl n* the pillars supporting the handrail of a stairway; this handrail. < SEE **BALUSTRADE.**

banjo (ˈbændʒəʊ) *n, pl* **banjos** a plucked string instrument with a drum-like body. < probably of African origin.

bank[1] (bæŋk) *n* **1** a mound or ridge of earth, snow, etc. **2** a slope at the side of a river.
• *vb* **1** form into a bank. **2** cover (a fire) with ashes, etc., so that it will burn slowly. **3** build (a road, etc.) so that the outer edge of a curve is higher than the inner. **4** (of an aircraft) incline or be inclined sideways when turning. < Scandinavian.

bank[2] *n* **1** an establishment for the keeping, lending, issuing, etc., of money. **2** a supply of something held in reserve or for use when needed: a data bank.
• *vb* put money in or have an account with (a bank). **banker** *n* a person who engages in the business of banking. **bank holiday** a public holiday on which banks and most businesses are closed by law. **banking** *n* the business of a bank. **banknote** *n* a printed paper issued by a country's central bank; promissory note. **bank on** rely on. < of Germanic origin.

bank[3] *n* a row or series of lights, switches, keys, etc. < Old French *banc* bench, of Germanic origin.

bankrupt (ˈbænkrʌpt) *n* a person whom a court has declared unable to pay his or her debts in full and whose affairs are administered for the benefit of creditors.
• *adj* **1** declared to be bankrupt. **2** financially ruined; broken.
• *vb* make bankrupt. **bankruptcy** *n* < Old Italian *banca* bank + *rotta* broken.

banner (ˈbænə) *n* **1** a flag. **2** a long strip of cloth displaying a slogan, etc., hung between two poles in a procession. **3** also **banner headline** a headline printed in large type and extending across the width of a page. < of Germanic origin.

banns (bænz) *pl n* the public announcement, esp. in a church, of a forthcoming marriage. < SEE **BAN.**

banquet (ˈbæŋkwɪt) *n* an elaborate, ceremonial meal for many people; feast. < Old Italian *banca* bench.

banter (ˈbæntə) *vb* speak or behave in a light-hearted, teasing manner.
• *n* light-hearted teasing. < origin unknown.

bap (bæp) *n* a soft, bread roll. < origin unknown.

baptism (ˈbæptɪzəm) *n* the Christian ordinance of sprinkling with or immersing in water as a sign of the person's cleansing from sin and of admission into the church. **baptismal** *adj* **baptize** *vb* administer baptism to. < ultimately Greek *baptein* to dip.

bar[1] (bɑː) *n* **1** a long, straight piece of metal, wood, etc. **2** a solid, esp. rectangular block of any material: a bar of chocolate; a bar of soap. **3** a straight band or stripe: a bar of colour. **4** a barrier or obstruction: the colour bar. **5 the Bar** barristers; profession of barristers: called to the Bar. **6** a counter or room where alcohol is served. **7** a counter at which food or drink is served; room with this: a coffee bar. **8** a series of musical notes and rests that make up a particular group.
• *vb* **barred; barring 1** fasten with a bar. **2** shut in or out with or as if with a barrier; obstruct. **3** forbid.
• *prep* except. **bar code** a series of dark bars and light spaces for use with a computer to identify a product. < Old French *barre.*

bar[2] *n* a unit of pressure. < Greek *baros* weight.

barb (bɑːb) *n* **1** the sharp, backward pointing part of an arrow, fish-hook, etc. **2** a penetrating, critical comment. **barbed** *adj* **1** having barbs. **2** penetrating and critical. **barbed wire** twisted wire with sharp points at intervals. < ultimately Latin *barba* beard.

barbarian (bɑːˈbɛərɪən) *adj* **1** uncivilized and primitive. **2** uncouth, rude, and uncultured.
• *n* a barbarian person. **barbaric** *adj* **1** uncultured; unsophisticated. **2** barbarous; cruel. **barbarically** *adv* **barbarism** *n* **1** a word or expression considered wrong by contemporary standards. **2** a barbarian condition. **barbarity** *n* an instance of barbarous behaviour or treatment. **barbarous** *adj* extremely cruel and harsh; inhuman. **barbarously** *adv* **barbarousness** *n* < ultimately Greek *barbaros* like the sound of incomprehensible speech.

barbecue (ˈbɑːbɪˌkjuː) *n* **1** a gathering at which a meal is cooked out of doors over an open fire. **2** the metal frame for grilling food, esp. one over an open fire of hot coals. **3** the food cooked at a barbecue.
• *vb* cook on a barbecue. < American Spanish *barbacoa.*

barbel (ˈbɑːbl̩) *n* **1** a spine or bristle that

hangs from the jaws of certain fish. **2** any of several European freshwater fish. < ultimately Latin *barba* beard.

barber (ˈbɑːbə) *n* a person whose business is cutting men's hair and shaving. < ultimately Latin *barba* beard.

barbiturate (bɑːˈbɪtjʊːrət) *n* a kind of hypnotic or sedative drug. < *barbituric acid:* partial translation of German *Barbitursäure.*

bard (bɑːd) *n* **1** a Celtic poet-singer. **2** a poet. **3 the Bard** William Shakespeare. < Scottish Gaelic.

bare (bɛə) *adj* **1** without clothing; naked. **2** without the usual covering, furnishings, etc. **3** exposed: lay bare the meaning. **4** empty (of). **5** just sufficient; mere: the bare necessities of life. **6** simple; unadorned: the bare facts.
• *vb* make bare. **bareness** *n* **bareback** *adv, adj* on a horse without a saddle. **barefaced** *adj* shameless. **barefoot** or **barefooted** *adv, adj* with the feet uncovered. **bare-handed** *adj* **1** without weapons, etc. **2** without gloves. **barely** *adv* **1** hardly: barely conscious. **2** scantily. < Old English *bær.*

bargain (ˈbɑːgən) *n* **1** an agreement between parties on a transaction or course of action. **2** something gained as a result of this. **3** something bought cheaply.
• *vb* negotiate in a bargain. **bargain for** or **on** expect and be prepared for: He got more than he'd bargained for! **into the bargain** also. < Middle French *bargaignier,* of Germanic origin.

barge (bɑːdʒ) *n* a flat-bottomed vessel, traditionally used for carrying freight on canals or rivers.
• *vb* move in an awkward, heavy manner. **bargee** *n* a person who works on a barge. **barge in** interrupt; intrude. **barge-pole** *n* a long pole used to propel a barge. < Late Latin *barca* small boat.

baritone (ˈbærɪˌtəʊn) *n* a male singer with a voice between a bass and a tenor; such a voice; part for this. < Italian, ultimately from Greek *barys* heavy + *tonos* tone.

bark[1] (bɑːk) *vb* **1** (of a dog, etc.) make its characteristic short, loud cry. **2** utter in a loud, abrupt manner.
• *n* the sound made by a barking dog; sound like this. **bark up the wrong tree** be mistaken. < Old English *beorcan.* SEE PANEL AT **WOOF**[2].

bark[2] *n* the protective, outer layer of tree trunks and branches. < Old Norse *börkr.*

barley (ˈbɑːlɪ) *n* a cereal grass, the seed of which is used in making beer and foods. < Old English *bærlic* of barley.

barman (ˈbɑːmən) fem. **barmaid** *n* a person who serves drinks in a bar.

barmy (ˈbɑːmɪ) *adj* (*slang*) crazy. < Old English *beorma* froth, yeast. SEE PANEL.

barn (bɑːn) *n* a simple, large farm building, esp. used for storing hay, grain, etc. < Old English *bere* barley + *ærn* place. SEE PANEL.

barnacle (ˈbɑːnəkl̩) *n* a sea-animal with a hard shell, esp. one that lives attached to rocks, the hulls of ships, etc. < ultimately Medieval Latin *bernaca* European goose.

barometer (bəˈrɒmɪtə) *n* **1** an instrument for measuring atmospheric pressure, esp. to forecast changes in the weather. **2** something that measures changes. **barometric** *adj* < Greek *baros* weight + *metron* measure.

baron (ˈbærən) *n* a member of the lowest rank of nobility in Britain. **2** a

You must be barmy!

A person considered to be slightly mad or foolish is sometimes referred to informally as barmy: If you think I'm going to work for nothing, you must be *barmy*! The word barmy derives from the Old English *beorma,* the name given to the yeasty froth that gathers on the top of beer while it is fermenting. Since the time of Shakespeare, any person who behaves as if full of barm is in danger of being called barmy.

barn

A large farm outbuilding used for storing harvested crops or sheltering livestock is known as a barn. However, the original barns were simply storage places for barley. The word barn comes from the Old English compound *bereærn,* from *bere* 'barley' and *ærn* 'place'.

The long association of barns with barley helps to explain the now obsolete expression bitten by a barn mouse, meaning 'slightly intoxicated' or 'tipsy'.

very powerful man in an activity that is mentioned: a press baron. **baronial** *adj* **baroness** *n* **1** the wife or widow of a baron. **2** a woman holding the rank of baron in her own right. < of Germanic origin.

baronet (ˌbærəˈnɛt) *n* a commoner having a rank below a baron and above a knight. **baronetcy** *n* the rank of a baronet.

baroque (bəˈrɒk) *adj, n* (of) a style of architecture, art, and music of the 17th and 18th centuries marked by extravagant ornamentation. < Portuguese *barroco* or Spanish *barrueco* imperfect pearl.

barracks (ˈbærəks) *pl n* **1** a large building or group of buildings used for soldiers to live in. **2** a large, very plain building. < Catalan *barraca*.

barrage (ˈbærɑːʒ) *n* **1** heavy artillery fire. **2** a rapid, continuous series: a barrage of questions. **3** an artificial construction across a river, etc. < SEE **BAR**[1].

barrel (ˈbærəl) *n* **1** a roughly cylindrical container with bulging sides and flat ends. **2** a cylindrical part, for example the tube of a gun or the part of a fountain-pen that contains the ink. **3** a measure of capacity of oil: 35 gallons (42 US gallons).
• *vb* **barrelled; barrelling** put in a barrel or barrels. < Middle French *baril*.

barrel-organ (ˈbærəl ˌɔːgən) *n* a musical instrument consisting of a revolving cylinder that is set with brass pins which open pipe valves.

barren (ˈbærən) *adj* **1** not able to produce crops. **2** not able to produce offspring or fruit. **3** lacking interest or stimulation. **barrenness** *n* < Old French *baraine*.

barricade (ˌbærɪˈkeɪd) *n* a barrier, esp. one erected quickly as a defence.
• *vb* block or defend by a barricade. < ultimately Spanish *barrica* cask.

barrier (ˈbærɪə) *n* an obstruction or means of separation that prevents access or advance: a crash barrier. **barrier reef** a reef that lies roughly parallel to the coast and is separated from it by a lagoon. < SEE **BAR**[1].

barrister (ˈbærɪstə) *n* a lawyer who has the right to plead in the higher law-courts. < SEE **BAR**[1].

barrow (ˈbærəʊ) *n* **1** a wheelbarrow. **2** a hand-cart with two wheels that is pushed or pulled and is used for selling goods in the street. < Old English *bearwe*.

barter (ˈbɑːtə) *vb* trade (goods, etc.) in exchange for other goods, etc., not money.
• *n* trading by bartering. < Middle French *barater*.

base[1] (beɪs) *n* **1** the thing or part on which something rests or is supported. **2** a main or essential ingredient; fundamental part. **3** the starting-point of an activity, operation, or in certain games. **4** the central point of an organization or enterprise, where supplies are stored. **5** one of the four stations in baseball to which a batter must run. **6** (*chemistry*) a substance that reacts with an acid to form a salt and water only.
• *vb* make, use, or serve as a base for; establish. < Latin *basis*.

base[2] *adj* **1** (of a metal) having comparatively inferior value. **2** degrading; dishonourable. **basely** *adv* **baseness** *n* < Late Latin *bassus* low.

baseball (ˈbeɪsˌbɔːl) *n* a nine-a-side ball-game in which runs are scored by hitting the ball and completing a circuit of four bases.

baseless (ˈbeɪsləs) *adj* having no foundation: a baseless charge.

basement (ˈbeɪsmənt) *n* the part of a building that is totally or partly below ground-level.

bash (bæʃ) *vb* (*informal*) strike violently; attack.
• *n* (*informal*) a forceful blow. **have a bash** make an attempt. < origin uncertain.

bashful (ˈbæʃfʊl) *adj* shy, timid, and self-conscious. **bashfully** *adv* **bashfulness** *n* < SEE **ABASHED**.

basic (ˈbeɪsɪk) *adj* **1** of or forming a base or basis; fundamental: the basic issue at stake. **2** without additions: basic pay. **basically** *adv* **basics** *pl n* basic facts, principles, etc.

basil (ˈbæzl̩) *n* a plant with leaves that are used as a herb for seasoning foods. < ultimately Greek *basilikos* royal.

basin (ˈbeɪsn̩) *n* **1** a round, open vessel used for holding water for washing; wash-basin. **2** a bowl for preparing or cooking food: a pudding-basin. **3** a dock in a river or harbour; partly enclosed area of water: a yacht basin. **4** an area of land drained by a river: a river basin. **basinful** *n* < Late Latin *bacchinon*.

basis (ˈbeɪsɪs) *n, pl* **bases** **1** a foundation or base. **2** a main constituent or fundamental principle. < ultimately Greek: step.

bask (bɑːsk) *vb* **1** be exposed to or lie in a pleasant warmth. **2** take comfort in someone's approval, etc. < Old Norse *bathask* to bathe.

basket (ˈbɑːskɪt) *n* **1** a container for carrying or holding things, made of interwoven material; contents of this. **2** something like a basket in shape or use. **3** (*basketball*) the round, open net hanging from a metal ring; goal. **basketful** *n* < probably Old Northern French *baskot.*

basketball (ˈbɑːskɪtˌbɔːl) *n* a five-a-side ball-game, the aim of which is to toss the ball through a raised basket.

basketwork (ˈbɑːskɪtˌwɜːk) *n* also **basketry** the art of making baskets or similar objects.

bass[1] (beɪs) *n* the lowest adult male voice; singer with this; part for this. • *adj* **1** of or denoting the bass; deep-sounding. **2** of the lowest-pitched member of a group of similar instruments: a bass clarinet. < Middle English *bas* base.

bass[2] (bæs) *n* a bony food and game fish like a perch. < ultimately Old English *bærs.*

bassoon (bəˈsuːn) *n* a double-reeded, deep-toned, woodwind instrument. **bassoonist** *n* < Italian *basso* deep.

bastard (ˈbɑːstəd) *n* **1** an illegitimate child. **2** (*slang*) an awkward or despicable person; person. • *adj* **1** illegitimate. **2** false; spurious. < Old French *bastart.*

baste (beɪst) *vb* moisten (meat) with fat during cooking. < origin uncertain.

bastion (ˈbæstɪən) *n* **1** a projecting part of a fortification; any fortification. **2** a thing or person considered as a defence. < Old Provençal *bastir* to build, of Germanic origin.

bat[1] (bæt) *n* **1** wooden implement used to hit the ball in games such as cricket. **2** a turn at batting. • *vb* **batted; batting** strike with a bat; use a bat. **batsman** *n, pl* **batsmen** a cricketer who uses a bat to score runs and prevent the bowler from breaking his wicket. **off one's own bat** (*informal*) on one's own initiative. < Old English *batt,* probably of Celtic origin.

bat[2] *n* a nocturnal, flying mammal. < probably of Scandinavian origin.

bat[3] *vb* **batted; batting** wink or flutter. **not bat an eyelid** show no signs of surprise, fear, etc. < probably alteration of *bate,* from Middle French *batre* to beat.

batch (bætʃ) *n* **1** a group or set of similar objects or people. **2** a group of loaves, cakes, etc., baked together. < Middle English *bache.*

bated (ˈbeɪtɪd) *adj* **with bated breath** tense with excitement or anxiety: They listened to the results with bated breath. < Middle English *baten* to abate.

bath (bɑːθ) *n* **1** a large container in which one sits to wash the body. **2** washing of one's body in such a container. **3** water for such a container. **4** *pl* a building with baths or a swimming-pool for public use. • *vb* wash in a bath. **bathroom** *n* a room with a bath or shower and usually a wash-basin and toilet. < Old English *bæth.*

bathe (beɪð) *vb* **1** swim for pleasure. **2** apply liquid to (a wound, etc.). **3** immerse or be immersed in. • *n* a swim. **bather** *n* **bathing-suit** *n* a swimming-costume. < Old English *bathian.*

batik (bæˈtiːk) *n* **1** a method of dyeing patterns on cloth, esp. cotton, by waxing the areas not to be coloured. **2** cloth treated in this way. < Javanese: painted.

batman (ˈbætmən) *n, pl* **batmen** an officer's personal servant. < Middle French *bat* pack-saddle.

baton (ˈbætɒn) *n* **1** a stick that a conductor uses to direct an orchestra. **2** a short stick or tube carried in relay races. < French *bâton,* from Late Latin *bastum* rod.

battalion (bəˈtæljən) *n* **1** a large group of soldiers. **2** a military unit composed of three or more companies. < Old Italian *battaglione.*

batten (ˈbætn̩) *n* a narrow strip of sawn timber. • *vb* fasten with battens. < French *bâton* stick.

batter[1] (ˈbætə) *vb* **1** hit (a person or thing) repeatedly and violently: battered babies. **2** wear by heavy use. **battering-ram** *n* a large, wooden beam with an iron head formerly used to break down walls. < Middle English *bateren.*

batter[2] *n* a mixture of flour, eggs, and milk or water, used in cooking. < Middle English *bater.*

battery (ˈbætərɪ) *n* **1** an electric cell or cells that provide current. **2** the unlawful use of physical force on someone else: assault and battery. **3** a group of guns, etc., operated together. **4** a small artillery unit. **5** a set or series, as of small cages for the intensive rearing of poultry: battery hens. < ultimately Latin *battuere* to beat.

battle (ˈbætl̩) *n* **1** a fight, esp. one between large, organized armed forces. **2** a conflict or struggle: a battle of wits.

• *vb* engage in battle; fight. **battleaxe** *n* (*informal*) a tempestuous, domineering woman. **battle-cry** *n* a shout cried when going into battle; slogan. **battlefield** *n* also **battleground** a place where a battle is fought. **battlements** *pl n* a parapet with open spaces at intervals, originally for shooting from. **battleship** *n* the largest, most heavily armoured kind of warship. < Latin *battuere* to beat, of Celtic origin.

batty (ˈbætɪ) *adj* (*informal*) crazy. < SEE BAT².

bauble (ˈbɔːbl̩) *n* a showy ornament of little value. < Middle French *baubel* plaything.

baulk (bɔːk, bɔːlk) SEE BALK.

bawdy (ˈbɔːdɪ) *adj* humorously coarse or indecent. **bawdily** *adv* **bawdiness** *n* < Middle French *baud* merry.

bawl (bɔːl) *vb* utter with a loud cry or shout. < Middle English *baulen*.

bay¹ (beɪ) *n* a wide inlet of a sea or lake. <Middle French *baie*.

bay² *n* **1** a recess in a wall. **2** a partly enclosed compartment. **bay window** a window that projects from an outside wall of a house. < Old French *baer* to gape.

bay³ *n* a long, deep cry of a hound, esp. when chasing an animal. **at bay** a position of being kept away.
• *vb* make this sound. < Old French *abaiier* like the sound.

bay⁴ *n* **1** also *adj* (of) a reddish-brown colour. **2** a bay horse. < ultimately Latin *badius*.

bay⁵ *n* a Mediterranean, evergreen tree with dark green leaves that are used for seasoning. < ultimately Latin *baca*.

bayonet (ˈbeɪənət) *n* a blade fixed to the muzzle of a firearm.
• *vb* stab with a bayonet. < *Bayonne*, city in France.

bazaar (bəˈzɑː) *n* **1** an Oriental market area with small stalls. **2** a sale of miscellaneous goods in aid of charity. < Persian *bāzār*.

bazooka (bəˈzuːkə) *n* a portable, anti-tank rocket launcher. < originally coined for a comic musical horn.

BBC *abbrev* British Broadcasting Corporation.

BC *abbrev* **1** before Christ. **2** British Columbia.

be (bɪ; *stressed* biː) *vb* **am, are, is; was, were; been; being 1** exist or remain. **2** have a particular physical or mental state: I am cold. **3** have a particular age: I'll be 35 next year. **4** used to show cost: That'll be £20.95. **5** used to show possession: It's your brother's. **6** used to show situation: Bromley is in south London. **7** visit: I've been to Bath. **8** used to point something out: Here's a cup of tea for you. **9** become: She wants to be a banker.
• *auxiliary vb* **1** used to form the continuous tense of verbs: I'm eating my breakfast. **2** used to form the passive of verbs: The president was shot. **3** used to express what should or must happen: You are to come now, children! **4** used to express plans or intentions: They are to be married next year. < Old English *bēon*.

beach (biːtʃ) *n* an area by a sea or lake covered by sand or pebbles.
• *vb* run or pull onto a beach. **beach-head** *n* an area on an enemy shore that is established to enable further landing of troops, etc. < origin unknown.

beacon (ˈbiːkən) *n* **1** a signal-fire on a hill. **2** a light used as a warning, as in a lighthouse. **3** a Belisha beacon. < Old English *bēacen* sign. SEE PANEL.

bead (biːd) *n* **1** a small ball of hard material pierced for threading on a string or wire. **2** something small shaped like a ball: beads of sweat. **3** *pl a* necklace of beads. **beady** *adj* small, round, and bright: beady eyes. < Old English *bed* prayer.

beagle (ˈbiːgl̩) *n* a breed of short, smooth-coated dog used as a hunting hound. < Middle English *begle*.

beak (biːk) *n* **1** the projecting jaws of a bird. **2** (*slang*) a nose. **3** (*slang*) a schoolmaster, judge, or magistrate. **beaked** *adj* < Latin *beccus*, of Gaulish origin.

beaker (ˈbiːkə) *n* **1** a wide-mouthed drinking-cup, often without a handle. **2** a cylindrical, glass container with a pouring lip, used in laboratories. < Old Norse *bikarr*.

beam (biːm) *n* **1** a long, thick piece of wood, etc., used in building. **2** the cross-piece of a balance. **3** a narrow shaft

Belisha beacon

A flashing amber globe mounted on a black and white striped pole at a zebra crossing is known as a Belisha beacon. The name belongs to its innovator, Sir Leslie Hore-*Belisha*, 1893–1957, an English politician who from 1934 to 1937 was Minister of Transport.

of light, etc.; ray. **4** a radiant look or smile.
• *vb* **1** emit (beams of light, etc.); transmit (a radio signal). **2** shine brightly; smile warmly. < Old English *bēam* tree, beam. SEE PANEL.

bean (biːn) *n* the seed or fruit of certain plants, eaten as a vegetable; plant bearing such seeds. < Old English *bēan*.

bear[1] (bɛə) *vb* **bore; borne, born; bearing 1** carry. **2** have or show: He still bears the scars of the accident. **3** have in one's heart or mind: bear a grudge. **4** support or sustain: The evidence does not bear close examination. **5** weigh: The responsibilities bore heavily on him. **6** move or go in a direction that is mentioned: Bear right where the road forks. **7** tolerate; put up with: It's so awful that I can't bear to look. **8** allow: His language doesn't bear repeating. **9** produce or yield: bear fruit. **10** give birth to. **11** bring or supply. **12** conduct (oneself). **bearable** *adj* tolerable. **bearably** *adv* **bear down** approach in a determined manner. **bearer** *n* **1** a person who holds a cheque, banknote, etc., for payment. **2** a person who carries something. **bear on** affect or be relevant to. **bear out** confirm or support. **bear up** not despair. < Old English *beran*. SEE PANEL AT **BORN.**

bear[2] *n* **1** a large, heavy mammal with a shaggy coat and a short tail. **2** a rough, rude person. **3** (*Stock Exchange*) someone who sells shares expecting a fall in price. **bearskin** *n* a tall, black, fur, military head-dress worn by certain guards. < Old English *bera*.

beard (bɪəd) *n* **1** the hair that grows on the lower part of a man's face. **2** a hairy or bristly growth on an animal or plant, for example on a goat's chin.
• *vb* confront boldly. **bearded** *adj* < Old English.

bearing (ˈbɛərɪŋ) *n* **1** a relation; relevance or significance. **2** behaviour or conduct. **3** grasp of one's position: lose one's bearings. **4** a support or supporting mechanical part.

beast (biːst) *n* **1** a large, wild, four-footed animal. **2** a brutal person. **3** a person or thing that is disliked. **beastly** *adj* **1** like a beast. **2** (*informal*) very unpleasant. < ultimately Latin *bestia*.

beat (biːt) *vb* **beat; beaten; beating 1** hit repeatedly. **2** strike repeatedly (against): waves beating against the shore. **3** punish by hitting repeatedly. **4** defeat in a game or competition. **5** surpass; be or come before. **6** (of the heart, etc.) throb repeatedly. **7** shape with blows. **8** mix vigorously: Beat the eggs and sugar together. **9** (*informal*) be too difficult for; puzzle: It beats me! **10** (of drums, etc.) sound by being struck.
• *n* **1** one in a series of blows or strokes. **2** a pulsating, throbbing sound. **3** a unit of musical rhythm or the stress in a verse. **4** the regular course of a policeman, etc.
• *adj* (*informal*) exhausted: I'm dead beat! **beater** *n* **1** a person who beats or hammers: a panel beater. **2** a blade or tool for beating or whisking. **beating** *n* **1** the process of striking or being struck with a stick, etc. **2** a defeat. **3** a pulsating. < Old English *bēatan*. SEE PANEL.

beautician (bjuːˈtɪʃən) *n* a person who gives beautifying treatments to

---

beam-ends

A person who is virtually penniless and out of just about everything else as well, including luck, is said to be on his or her beam-ends.

The phrase comes from old nautical times when the sides of a ship were joined by horizontal timbers or beams, which also supported the deck. A ship that found itself on its side or on its beam-ends was indeed in desperate straits.

Can you beat that?

Beat features in a number of idiomatic expressions, including:

beat about the bush to avoid talking about the main point of an issue: It's no use beating about the bush; come to the point.
beat down to cause to reduce the price of something in bargaining: He wanted £1000 for the car but I eventually beat him down to £650.
beat off to repel or repulse: beat off an attack.
beat one's breast to express remorse and guilt publicly.
beat the drum to try to win interest or support for something: The prime minister was beating the drum for British goods on a recent trip abroad.
beat up to attack severely, by punching, kicking, etc.
off the beaten track in a remote place.

---

the face or body.
beauty (ˈbjuːtɪ) *n* **1** the qualities of a person or thing that delight the senses. **2** a person with such qualities, esp. a beautiful woman. **3** (*informal*) an outstanding example: The second goal was a real beauty! **4** (*informal*) an advantageous quality: The beauty of the idea is that it is so simple! **beautiful** *adj* **1** having beauty. **2** very pleasant. **beautifully** *adv* **beautify** *vb* **beautified; beautifying** make beautiful. **beauty sleep** sleep thought to enhance a person's beauty. **beauty spot 1** a place that has beautiful scenery. **2** a natural mark on the skin. < ultimately Latin *bellus* pretty.

Become what?

Verbs which cannot stand alone but have to be followed by one or more words are usually transitive. However, this is not always the case. Become, for example, has to be followed by something—we can't say just She became or They'll become. These need to be completed by a word or phrase: She became *a famous actress*. They'll become *ill*.

Yet become is not a transitive verb. On the one hand a transitive verb does not have an adjective (ill) as an object. Furthermore, if become were transitive, the sentences in which it occurs could be made passive and A famous actress was become would make sense. (See also panel at **bring.**)

Become is in fact a special type of intransitive verb known as a *linking verb*. Unlike the majority of intransitive verbs, linking verbs require a *complement* to round them off. This is a word or phrase which stands in some sort of adjectival relationship with the subject. Some of the most common linking verbs are shown in the sentences below.

They *are* stinking rich.
She *seems* a lot more cheerful.
He wants to *remain* a bachelor.
How do you *stay* so fit?
The meat *smells* off.
The wine *tasted* wonderful.
Your chest *sounds* fine.
It suddenly *grew* dark.
Her help *proved* invaluable.
Your garden *looks* a picture.

beaver (ˈbiːvə) *n* a large aquatic rodent with soft brown hair, a broad flat tail, and webbed hind feet.
• *vb* **beaver away** work hard and steadily. < Old English *beofor.*
became (bɪˈkeɪm) SEE **BECOME.**
because (bɪˈkɒz) *conj* for the reason that; since. **because of** as a result of. < Middle English *bi* by + *cause.*
beckon (ˈbɛkən) *vb* summon or signal by a gesture. < Old English *bēacen* sign.
become (bɪˈkʌm) *vb* **became; become; becoming 1** come to be. **2** be attractive and suitable for. **become of** happen to: Whatever became of that girl you were friendly with at school? **becoming** *adj* (of clothes, etc.) attractive and suitable. < Old English *becuman.* SEE PANEL.
bed (bɛd) *n* **1** a piece of furniture, esp. with mattress and coverings, to sleep or rest on. **2** sleep; place for sleeping. **3** (*informal*) a place for sexual intercourse. **4** a plot of ground for plants: a flower bed. **5** the bottom of a river, lake, etc.: the sea bed. **6** a supporting surface; foundation.
• *vb* **bedded; bedding 1** put to bed; provide with a bed. **2** put into a foundation; establish. **3** arrange (plants, etc.) in beds. **bedclothes** *pl n* also **bedding** the coverings such as sheets and blankets on a bed. **bedfellow** *n* **1** a person who shares a bed. **2** an unexpected associate: strange bedfellows. **bedpan** *n* a shallow vessel used as a toilet by a person confined to bed. **bedridden** *adj* confined, esp. by illness, to bed. **bedrock** *n* **1** the solid rock below loose soil, etc. **2** basic principles, etc. **bedroom** *n* a room for sleeping in. **bedside** *n* the space by the side of a bed. **bed-sitter** *n* a single room used for both living and sleeping in. **bedsore** *n* a sore caused by lying in bed for a long time. **bedspread** *n* a cloth cover for a bed. **bedstead** *n* the frame of a bed. < Old English *bedd.*
bedlam (ˈbɛdləm) *n* a place or state of uproar. < Hospital of St Mary of *Bethlehem,* mental hospital in London.
bedraggled (bɪˈdræɡl̩d) *adj* wet, limp, untidy, or dirty, as with rain or mud.
bee (biː) *n* a social, four-winged insect which feeds on nectar from flowers and produces honey. **beehive** *n* a hive. **beeswax** *n* a yellowish substance produced by bees to build honeycombs, used as a wood-polish. **have a bee in one's bonnet** be obsessed with a particular idea, etc. **make a beeline for** move directly and straight towards.

< Old English *bēo*.

beech (biːtʃ) *n* a tree with smooth, grey bark and oval, pointed, glossy leaves; wood of this tree. < Old English *bēce*.

beef (biːf) *n* **1** the flesh of a cow, bull, etc., used as meat. **2** muscular flesh or strength; brawn. **3** (*informal*) a grumble.
• *vb* **1** (*informal*) grumble. **2** add strength or weight to. **beefburger** *n* a flat cake of minced beef. **beefsteak** *n* a piece of beef for grilling or frying. **beefy** *adj* **1** full of beef. **2** strong; brawny.
< Old French *buef* ox, beef, from Latin *bos* ox.

beefeater (ˈbiːfˌiːtə) *n* a yeoman of the guard at the Tower of London. SEE PANEL.

been (bɪn; *stressed* biːn) SEE **BE.**

beer (bɪə) *n* an alcoholic drink made from fermented malt flavoured with hops. **beery** *adj* of or like beer; smelling of beer. < Old English *bēor*.

beet (biːt) *n* a plant with a thick, fleshy, white or red root. < ultimately Latin *beta*.

beetle (ˈbiːtḷ) *n* an insect with hard, front wings that cover the hind wings when these are not in use.
• *vb* **beetle off** go quickly; scurry.
< Old English *bitela*.

beetroot (ˈbiːtˌruːt) *n* a beet with a red, fleshy, bulbous root, often eaten in salads.

befall (bɪˈfɔːl) *vb* **befell; befallen; befalling** (*formal*) happen (to).
< Old English *befeallan*.

befit (bɪˈfɪt) *vb* **befitted; befitting** be proper or suitable for.

before (bɪˈfɔː) *adv* at an earlier time; already: I think we've met before.
• *prep* **1** earlier in time than: before 1945. **2** in a higher or more important position than. **3** in front of: right before her very eyes. **4** in the presence of: brought before the judge.
• *conj* **1** earlier than the time when. **2** rather than. **beforehand** *adj, adv* in advance; in anticipation. < Old English *beforan*.

befriend (bɪˈfrɛnd) *vb* become a friend of; act in a kindly way towards.

beg (bɛg) *vb* **begged; begging 1** ask for as charity. **2** ask earnestly, humbly, or formally: We begged him to reconsider his decision. **3** (of a dog) sit up and hold out its front paws. < probably Old English *bedecian*. SEE PANEL.

began (bɪˈgæn) SEE **BEGIN.**

beget (bɪˈgɛt) *vb* **begot; begotten; begetting 1** be the father of. **2** cause or create. < Old English *bigietan*.

beggar (ˈbɛgə) *n* **1** a person who begs, esp. who lives by begging. **2** (*informal*) a person; fellow: You lucky beggar!
• *vb* impoverish. **beggary** *n* **beggar description** be extremely difficult to describe.

Why **beefeater?**

The yeoman warders of the Tower of London are commonly known by the colloquial name beefeaters. Although this might seem to be a straightforward combination of beef and eater, neither of the two components should be interpreted literally. In Tudor times when the royal bodyguard was instituted, the word eater still retained the meaning of 'servant'. Beef, on the other hand, was used as an indicator of advanced status, ease of duty, and enviable living standard. Compared with more menial servants—referred to in earlier days as 'loaf-eaters'—the *beef* servants or beefeaters indeed enjoyed a life-style of relative comfort and prosperity.

An alternative theory suggests that the word is a corruption of *buffetier,* a privileged servant whose job was to stand near the *buffet* or 'sideboard'.

I beg your pardon

'I beg your pardon—what did you say?' 'I beg your pardon! That's my place you've parked your car in!' 'I beg your pardon—I didn't realize you were busy.'

The phrase I beg your pardon has a number of different meanings. I beg your pardon can be:

☐ **used as a polite request** to someone to repeat what he or she has just said: 'I beg your pardon, Dr Smith—what did you say?' This is usually shortened in informal usage to Pardon: 'Pardon? I didn't quite catch that.'

☐ **used as an expression of disagreement or indignation:** 'I beg your pardon! The person you're being so rude about happens to be my wife!'

☐ **used as a polite expression of apology** for what the speaker has just said or done: 'I beg your pardon. I didn't mean to interrupt you two.'

begin (bɪˈgɪn) *vb* **began; begun; beginning 1** perform the earliest or first part of an activity; start. **2** bring or come into existence. **3** be or come first in. **beginner** *n* a person who has just begun to learn a skill. **beginning** *n* the first part; starting-point or source. **to begin with** in the first place. < Old English *beginnan.*

begonia (bɪˈgəʊnjə) *n* an ornamental plant with showy, wax-like flowers. < Michel *Bégon,* died 1710, French promoter of botany.

begot (bɪˈgɒt) SEE BEGET. **begotten** SEE BEGET.

begrudge (bɪˈgrʌdʒ) *vb* grudge.

beguile (bɪˈgaɪl) *vb* **1** deceive; cheat. **2** charm; fascinate. **beguilement** *n* **beguiler** *n*

begun (bɪˈgʌn) SEE BEGIN.

behalf (bɪˈhɑːf) *n* **on behalf of** representing or supporting. < Old English *be* by + *halfe* side.

behave (bɪˈheɪv) *vb* act, function, or conduct (oneself) in a specified or proper way. **behaviour** *n* a way of behaving. **behavioural** *adj* < Middle English *be-* + *haven* to have, hold.

behead (bɪˈhɛd) *vb* cut off the head of.

beheld (bɪˈhɛld) SEE BEHOLD.

behind (bɪˈhaɪnd) *adv* **1** in or to a position further back. **2** in a former time, place, etc. **3** in a secondary or less important position. **4** in arrears.
• *prep* **1** in or to a position further back than. **2** in the past relative to. **3** later than: behind schedule. **4** remaining after. **5** hidden by. **6** supporting. **7** having made less progress than.
• *n* (*slang*) the buttocks. **behindhand** *adj, adv* **1** in arrears. **2** late; behind time. < Old English *behindan.*

behold (bɪˈhəʊld) *vb* **beheld; beholding** (*chiefly archaic*) look (at); observe. **beholder** *n* < Old English *bihealdan.*

beige (beɪʒ) *n, adj* (of) a yellowish grey colour. < French.

being (ˈbiːɪŋ) SEE BE.
• *n* **1** existence. **2** the essential qualities. **3** a living thing: human beings.

belated (bɪˈleɪtɪd) *adj* coming, happening, etc., later than the proper time. **belatedly** *adv*

belch (bɛltʃ) *vb* **1** expel (gas) through the mouth from the stomach. **2** send out forcefully.
• *n* an act or sound of belching. < Old English *bealcian.*

belfry (ˈbɛlfrɪ) *n* a steeple or tower, esp. one in which bells are hung, and associated with a church. < Middle French *berfrei* movable siege-tower.

belief (bɪˈliːf) *n* **1** a principle or set of principles accepted as true. **2** an opinion. **3** trust or confidence. **believable** *adj* able to be believed. **believe** *vb* **1** accept as true or real. **2** have as an opinion; think. **3** have a religious faith. **4** be convinced concerning the rightness of: He believes in having a cold shower every morning. **believer** *n* < Old English *beliefan.*

belittle (bɪˈlɪtl̩) *vb* cause to seem unimportant, worthless, etc.

bell (bɛl) *n* **1** a device that makes a ringing sound: a bicycle bell. **2** a hollow, cup-shaped device that makes a ringing sound when struck by a hammer-like object which hangs inside it: church bells. **3** something with this shape. **bell-bottoms** *pl n* trousers with wide, flaring bottoms. **bell-push** *n* a button that is pressed to operate an electric bell. < Old English *belle.*

belligerent (bɪˈlɪdʒərənt) *adj* **1** engaged in war. **2** aggressive. **belligerence** *n* **belligerently** *adv* < Latin *bellum* war + *gerere* to wage.

bellow (ˈbɛləʊ) *vb* **1** make the loud, deep, rough sound like that of a bull; roar. **2** shout in a loud, deep voice; bawl.
• *n* a bellowing sound or noise. < Old English *bylgian.*

bellows (ˈbɛləʊz) *pl n* a device that produces a current of air when operated. < SEE BELLY.

belly (ˈbɛlɪ) *n* **1** the abdomen. **2** the stomach. **3** a bulging or rounded surface. **4** an inside part.
• vb **bellied; bellying** swell. **belly-ache** *n* pain in the belly. **belly-button** *n* (*informal*) the navel. **belly-dance** *n* a dance marked by emphatic, erotic movements of the hips and abdomen. **belly-dancer** *n* **belly-flop** *n* an awkward dive in which the belly strikes flat against the water. **bellyful** *n* (*informal*) more than one can bear. < Old English *belg* bag, skin.

belong (bɪˈlɒŋ) *vb* **1** be the property or possession (of): That book belongs to me. **2** be a member of (a club, etc.). **3** have a correct or normal place. **4** be properly classified. **belongings** *pl n* one's possessions. < Middle English *belongen.*

beloved (bɪˈlʌvɪd, bɪˈlʌvd) *adj, n* (a person) dearly loved.

below (bɪˈləʊ) *adv* **1** in a lower place. **2** in, at, or to a lower rank or position. **3** later in a book, etc.: see below. **4** downstream.

• *prep* **1** in a lower place than. **2** lower in amount, number, rank, etc., than. **3** downstream from.
• *adj* mentioned later.
• *n* something below, esp. written below. < Old English *bi* by + *looghe* low.

belt (bɛlt) *n* **1** a band of leather, etc., worn around the waist. **2** an endless band of flexible material between pulleys, shafts, etc.: a fan-belt. **3** an area marked by a particular feature: a belt of rain.
• *vb* **1** put a belt around. **2** beat with a belt. **3** (*informal*) hit. **4** (*informal*) move fast: They belted along the motorway. **belt out** (*informal*) play or sing loudly. **belt up 1** (*slang*) shut up. **2** (*informal*) fasten a seat-belt. **under one's belt** as part of one's experience; in one's possession. < Old English. SEE PANEL.

bemused (bɪˈmjuːzd) *adj* confused; bewildered.

bench (bɛntʃ) *n* **1** a long seat, esp. without a back, for two or more people. **2** a long work-table. **the Bench 1** the office of a judge. **2** judges or magistrates. **3** a law-court. < Old English *benc*.

bend (bɛnd) *vb* **bent; bending 1** form or cause to form a curve; force or be forced out of straightness. **2** incline the body; stoop. **3** turn or cause to turn in a direction: The road bends sharply at the bottom of the hill. **4** direct (one's steps, efforts, etc.). **5** submit or subdue.
• *n* a curve or turn: a hairpin bend. **bend over backwards** make very great efforts. **bend the rules** change rules, esp. so that they suit oneself. **round the bend** (*informal*) crazy. < Old English *bendan*.

beneath (bɪˈniːθ) *prep* **1** in or to a lower position than; below. **2** not worthy of: beneath one's dignity.
• *adv* **1** in or to a lower position. **2** directly underneath. < Old English *be-* + *neothan* below.

benefactor (ˈbɛnɪˌfæktə) fem. **benefactress** *n* a person who helps, esp. by making a gift or bequest to a person, institution, etc. < Latin *bene* well + *facere* to do.

beneficiary (ˌbɛnɪˈfɪʃərɪ) *n* **1** a person who benefits from something. **2** a person who is entitled to receive money or property from a will, insurance policy, etc.

benefit (ˈbɛnɪfɪt) *n* **1** something that helps, improves, or promotes; advantage. **2** a payment provided under an insurance policy, pension scheme, etc.: sickness benefit. **3** a public entertainment, the proceeds of which go to a particular person or cause: a benefit match.
• *vb* be useful, advantageous, or profitable to. **give someone the benefit of the doubt** believe the best about someone, assuming his or her innocence, as long as there is no clear evidence of guilt, etc. **beneficial** *adj* causing a helpful, useful, or advantageous result: beneficial effects. **beneficially** *adv* < SEE BENEFACTOR.

benevolent (bɪˈnɛvələnt) *adj* inclined to do good; kindly. **benevolence** *n* **benevolently** *adv* < Latin *bene* well + *velle* to wish.

benign (bɪˈnaɪn) *adj* **1** gentle; kindly. **2** (of a climate) mild. **3** (of a tumour) not malignant. **benignly** *adv* < ultimately Latin *bene* well + *gignere* to beget.

bent (bɛnt) SEE BEND.
• *n* a strong liking; special ability: He has a natural bent for art.
• *adj* **1** (*slang*) corrupt. **2** determined; set (on): bent on wrecking all our arrangements.

benzene (ˈbɛnziːn) *n* a colourless, flammable liquid that is obtained from oil and coal tar and used as a solvent. < *benzoin*, ultimately from Arabic

below the belt

Below the belt is commonly used in colloquial English to mean 'unfair': That last remark was really a bit *below the belt*. This is one of several idioms that have entered the vocabulary from *boxing;* a blow dealt to an opponent below the belt of his shorts is considered foul play. Other expressions that carry a similar 'punch' include:

out for the count sound asleep; unwakable: 'If you drink any more of that whisky you'll be out for the count.'

throw in the sponge or **towel** to give up or admit defeat: 'After staying out for almost a year, the strikers decided to throw in the towel and return to work.'

straight from the shoulder frankly and bluntly: 'She told me straight from the shoulder she had no intention of marrying me.'

down and out destitute: 'That old suit makes you look really down and out!'

lubān jāwi incense of Java.
benzine (ˈbɛnziːn) *n* a colourless, flammable liquid obtained from the distillation of petroleum and used as a motor fuel. < SEE **BENZENE.**
bequeath (bɪˈkwiːð) *vb* leave as a legacy. **bequest** *n* bequeathing; legacy. < Old English *be-* + *cwethan* to say.
berate (bɪˈreɪt) *vb* scold harshly. < *be-* + *rate,* from Middle English *raten.*
bereave (bɪˈriːv) *vb* deprive of (a person), as by death: the bereaved parents. **bereavement** *n* **bereft** *adj* deprived (of): bereft of all hope. < Old English *be-* + *rēafian* to rob.
beret (ˈbɛreɪ) *n* a soft, round, flat cap with no peak. < French *berret,* ultimately Late Latin *birrus* hooded cape.
berry (ˈbɛrɪ) *n* a small, edible fruit such as a strawberry or raspberry. < Old English *berie.*
berserk (bəˈzɜːk) *adj* frenzied in anger: go berserk, SEE PANEL.
berth (bɜːθ) *n* **1** a bed or bunk on a ship or train. **2** a place for a ship to anchor at a wharf.
• *vb* moor at a berth. **give a wide berth** to keep at a safe distance. < SEE **BEAR**[1].
beseech (bɪˈsiːtʃ) *vb* **besought, beseeched; beseeching** beg or implore. < Middle English *be-* + *sechen* to seek.
beset (bɪˈsɛt) *vb* **beset; besetting** **1** trouble or attack constantly. **2** surround. **besetting** *adj* constantly troubling or worrying. < Old English *be-* + *settan* to set.
beside (bɪˈsaɪd) *prep* **1** at or near the side of. **2** in comparison with.
• *adv* at or near the side of a person or thing. **beside oneself** overwhelmed (by a strong emotion): almost beside himself with joy. **beside the point** irrelevant. < Old English *be* by + *sīdan* side.
besides (bɪˈsaɪdz) *adv* in addition; moreover.
• *prep* in addition to.
besiege (bɪˈsiːdʒ) *vb* **1** lay siege to (a fortified city, etc.). **2** overwhelm. **besieger** *n*
besmirch (bɪˈsmɜːtʃ) *vb* make dirty; sully.
besom (ˈbiːzəm) *n* a broom, esp. one made of twigs. < Old English *besma.*
besotted (bɪˈsɒtɪd) *adj* **1** infatuated. **2** drunk; intoxicated. < *be-* + *sot* to make a fool of.
besought (bɪˈsɔːt) SEE **BESEECH.**
best (bɛst) *adj* SEE **GOOD. 1** of the most excellent, suitable, attractive, etc., kind. **2** largest: We've spent the best part of the money already!
• *adv* SEE **WELL**[1]. **1** in the best way. **2** to the greatest degree. **3** most suitably, usefully, or wisely: I'd best go soon.
• *n* **1** the best person, thing, or condition. **2** one's utmost effort: We did our best! **Sunday best** one's best clothes. < Old English *betst.* SEE PANEL.
bestial (ˈbɛstɪəl) *adj* of or like beasts; cruel or savage. **bestiality** *n* < ultimately Latin *bestia* beast.
bestow (bɪˈstəʊ) *vb* present (a gift); confer (an award, honour, etc.). **bestowal** *n* < Middle English *be-* + *stowe* place.
bet (bɛt) *n* **1** an agreement that a sum of money or other stake will be forfeited if a forecast of an event such as a race proves wrong. **2** the stake risked in this way. **3** the forecast of the result of a race, etc., on which a stake is risked. **4** (*informal*) an opinion or prediction: It's a safe bet that she won't turn up. **5** (*informal*) a course of action.

going berserk

To go berserk is to enter a state of violent frenzy: 'He'll go *berserk* when he sees what you've done to his new car!' The word comes from the Old Norse *berserkr,* from *bjorn* 'bear' and *serkr* 'shirt'. A *berserkr* was an extraordinarily ferocious warrior, so possessed by battle fever that he would rush at his opponents without armour and clad only in a bearskin.

All the best!

Best features in a number of expressions including:

all the best used when saying goodbye to someone or at the end of a letter to a friend, wishing him or her well.
at best taking the most favourable view: At best, our profit will be £9000 by July.
best man the main attendant of the bridegroom at a wedding.
best-seller *n* a product, especially a book, that is very popular and sells in great numbers.

• *vb* **bet, betted; betting 1** stake as a bet; make a bet (with). **2** (*informal*) think very likely: I bet it'll rain today. **better** *n* a person who bets. **betting-shop** *n* a bookmaker's shop. < origin unknown.

bête noire (ˌbɛt ˈnwɑː) *n* a person or thing that one dislikes very much. < French: black beast.

betide (bɪˈtaɪd) *vb* happen or befall: Woe betide him if he forgets to come! < Middle English *be-* + *tiden* to happen.

betray (bɪˈtreɪ) *vb* **1** deliver into the hands of an enemy. **2** be a traitor to (one's country, a friend, etc.). **3** be disloyal to. **4** reveal (a secret, etc.). **betrayal** *n* **betrayer** *n* < ultimately Latin *tradere.*

betroth (bɪˈtrəʊð) *vb* promise to marry or give in marriage. **betrothal** *n* **betrothed** *n* the person to whom one is betrothed. < Middle English *be-* + *trouthe* truth.

> **getting better**
>
> Better features in a number of expressions, some of them idiomatic, including:
>
> **better half** used as a humorous way of referring to one's wife or husband.
> **better late than never** used as an excuse for someone's lateness.
> **better luck next time** used to express regret that someone did not succeed this time and as a wish for success at the next attempt.
> **better safe than sorry** it is wiser to be very cautious than to act rashly.
> **get the better of** to overcome or defeat: In the end, her curiosity got the better of her, and she had to ask what the surprise was.
> **go one better** to improve on the efforts or achievement of another person; outdo.
> **had better** ought to; should: I think we'd better go now.
> **think better of** to consider doing something and decide not to do it: He realized that the situation was already very tense and so thought better of intervening.
>
> When better is used in expressions such as Are you feeling better now?, the meaning is ambiguous. It can mean either 'fully recovered; completely well': He soon felt better and went back to work or 'partly recovered; improved': She's feeling better but hasn't got out of bed yet.

better (ˈbɛtə) *adj* SEE **GOOD. 1** of a more excellent, suitable, attractive, etc., kind. **2** larger: He spent the better part of his life in London. **3** partly or fully recovered from an illness.
• *adv* SEE **WELL**[1]. **1** in a better way. **2** to a greater degree. **had better** ought to; should: You'd better mind your step.
• *n* **1** something better. **2** a superior: one's betters.
• *vb* be, make, or become better (than). < Old English *betera.* SEE PANEL.

between (bɪˈtwiːn) *prep* **1** connecting two things in space or time. **2** used to show division: Divide the cake equally between the two children. **3** intermediate to: a colour between red and pink. **4** used to show joint effort or activity: Between them, they did the washing-up very quickly.
• *adv* between two things that are mentioned. < Old English *betwēonum.*

betwixt (bɪˈtwɪkst) *adv, prep* (*archaic*) between. **betwixt and between** midway. < Old English *betwux.*

bevel (ˈbɛvl̩) *n* **1** the angle or slope of a surface that is not a right angle. **2** a tool for making such a slope.
• *vb* **bevelled; bevelling** shape to a bevel; slope. < Old French *baer* to yawn.

beverage (ˈbɛvərɪdʒ) *n* any drink other than water. < ultimately Latin *bibere* to drink.

bevy (ˈbɛvɪ) *n* a large group. < Middle English *bevey.*

bewail (bɪˈweɪl) *vb* express deep sorrow for.

beware (bɪˈwɛə) *vb* be cautious (of): Beware of the dog! < Middle English *been* to be + *war* wary.

bewilder (bɪˈwɪldə) *vb* puzzle or confuse. **bewilderment** *n* < *be* + archaic *wilder* to lose one's way.

bewitch (bɪˈwɪtʃ) *vb* **1** cast a spell over. **2** attract in a fascinating way; charm.

beyond (bɪˈjɒnd) *prep* **1** on or to the further side of. **2** outside the reach or range of. **3** in a degree greater than. **4** later than. **5** not within the understanding of. **6** later than. **7** besides.
• *adv* **1** on to the further side. **2** besides. < Old English *be-* + *geond* yonder.

b.f. *abbrev* brought forward.

biannual (baɪˈænjʊəl) *adj* occurring twice a year. **biannually** *adv* SEE PANEL.

bias (ˈbaɪəs) *n* **1** a tendency or inclination, esp. a personal, irrational prejudice. **2** a diagonal line across the grain of a fabric. **3** (*bowls*) the tendency of a bowl to curve when rolled; quality of shape or weight that causes this.

• *vb* give a bias to; influence or prejudice. < Middle French *biais,* from Old Provençal. SEE PANEL AT **BUS.**

bib (bɪb) *n* **1** a piece of cloth or plastic worn esp. by children to protect their clothes while eating. **2** the upper part of an apron, etc. **best bib and tucker** finest clothes. < perhaps ultimately Latin *bibere* to drink.

bible (ˈbaɪbl̩) *n* **1 Bible** the sacred book of Christians; Old and New Testament. **2** a book of the sacred writings of a religion. **3** an authoritative book. **biblical** *adj* of, in, or like the Bible. < Greek *byblos* papyrus, book.

bibliography (ˌbɪblɪˈɒgrəfɪ) *n* **1** a list of writings on a particular subject or on a particular author. **2** the study of the history, description, etc., of books. **bibliographical** *adj* < Greek *biblio*- book + *graphein* to write.

bicentenary (ˌbaɪsɛnˈtiːnərɪ) *n* a 200th anniversary.

biceps (ˈbaɪsɛps) *n* the large muscle at the front of the upper arm that bends the elbow. < ultimately Latin *bi*- two + *caput* head.

bicker (ˈbɪkə) *vb* argue constantly about petty matters. < Middle English *bikeren.*

bicycle (ˈbaɪsɪkl̩) *n* a light, two-wheeled vehicle driven by pedals.
• *vb* ride on a bicycle. **bicyclist** *n*

bid (bɪd) *vb* **bid, bade; bidden, bid; bidding 1** offer (a price) when trying to buy something, esp. at an auction. **2** (*bridge, etc.*) announce the number of tricks to be won. **3** order, tell, or invite. **4** express.
• *n* **1** an offer of a price when trying to buy somethings esp. at an auction. **2** (*bridge, etc.*) an announcement of the number of tricks to be won. **3** an attempt to gain something: a take-over bid. **bidder** *n* < Old English *biddan.*

bide (baɪd) *vb* **bide one's time** wait patiently for an opportunity. < Old English *bīdan* to stay. SEE PANEL.

bidet (ˈbiːdeɪ) *n* a low, bowl-shaped, bathroom fixture for washing the genital area. < French: small horse.

biennial (baɪˈɛnɪəl) *adj* **1** occurring every two years. **2** (of a plant) growing during its first year and flowering and dying in its second.
• *n* a biennial plant. **biennially** *adv* SEE PANEL AT **BIANNUAL.**

bier (bɪə) *n* a stand on which a coffin or dead body is placed before burial. < Old English *bǣr.*

bifocals (baɪˈfəʊkl̩s) *pl n* a pair of spectacles with lenses that have one part suitable for near vision and another part for distant vision.

big (bɪg) *adj* **bigger; biggest 1** large in size, amount, extent, etc. **2** large relative to others of the same kind. **3** elder; more grown up: my big brother.

bide one's time

Bide is an example of a word whose usage has become highly restricted. It occurs only within the phrase bide one's time ('to wait patiently for an opportunity'). Similarly umbrage, is rarely encountered other than with give or take. Other words which have become similarly restricted include:

foregone a foregone conclusion
snoot cock a snoot
duress under duress
trice in a trice
betide woe betide
amok run amok

biannual or **biennial?**

Is a biannual periodical published every six months or every two years? Does a biennial conference meet every six months or every two years?

The meanings of biannual and biennial are sometimes confused. Biannual means 'occurring, published, etc., twice a year'; biennial means 'occurring, published, etc., every two years'.

Similar problems sometimes occur with other words beginning with the prefix bi-: bi-monthly means 'occurring, published, etc., every two months or twice a month'; bi-weekly means 'occurring, published, etc., every two weeks or twice a week'.

In the interests of clarity it is probably better to write the intended meaning in full: every two months, once every two years, fortnightly, etc.

big and **small**

Pairs of words like young and old, big and small, and hot and cold are commonly known as 'opposites'. Pairs like dead and alive, legal and illegal, and male and female are called 'opposites' too. However, it is quite easy to show that, say, big and small and legal and illegal belong to different groups.

A basic grammatical difference is that big and small have comparative (bigger, smaller) and superlative (biggest, smallest) forms, whereas legal and illegal do not. There is also a fundamental semantic difference: the meaning of a word like big or small changes according to what is described, a *big* mouse being big in comparison with or relative to the average size of a mouse, but smaller than, say, a *small* elephant. In contrast, words like legal and dead have absolute values.

Gradable pairs such as big and small are known as *antonyms.* One of the tests of an *antonym* is that you can usually attach an -ish suffix to it, as in tallish, sottish, darkish, etc. Similarly, pairs of antonyms will often fit a neither ... nor ... pattern, as in neither heavy nor light.

Big features in a number of expressions, including:

big-bang theory a theory in cosmology that the universe originated from the explosion of a very dense mass of material.
big deal! used to suggest that someone is not impressed: 'I'm off to Africa for a year.'—'Big deal! I've lived there half my life!'
big gun, noise, or **shot** an important person.
big head a conceited person.
big-headed *adj* conceited.
big stick force or the threat of force, from a speech made by the US President Theodore Roosevelt (1858–1919) in 1901: 'Speak softly and carry a big stick'.
big talk or **words** boastful claims.
big time *adj, n* (of) the highest or most important level, for example in the world of entertainment: big-time performers.
big top the large, main tent of a circus.
(**get**) **too big for one's boots** (to become) too conceited.
what's the big idea? why are you acting in such a way?, used chiefly as a complaint or objection: 'What's the big idea? Walking into my office without even knocking?'

4 important or significant: big improvements; a big decision. **5** boastful; conceited: big talk. **6** (*informal*) magnanimous: That's very big of you!
• *adv* (*informal*) **1** on a large scale: Think big! **2** pretentiously: talk big. **big-hearted** *adj* generous and kind. < perhaps of Scandinavian origin. SEE PANEL.

bigamy (ˈbɪgəmɪ) *n* the crime of marrying a person while being married to another. **bigamist** *n* **bigamous** *adj* < Latin *bi-* two + Greek *gamos* marriage.

bigot (ˈbɪgət) *n* a person who obstinately holds a belief and is intolerant of those who do not. **bigoted** *adj* **bigotry** *n* < Middle French.

bigwig (ˈbɪgˌwɪg) *n* (*informal*) an important person.

bike (baɪk) *n* (*informal*) a bicycle or motor cycle.
• *vb* (*informal*) ride a bike.

bikini (bɪˈkiːnɪ) *n* a woman's brief, two-piece, swimming-costume. SEE PANEL.

bilateral (baɪˈlætərəl) *adj* **1** of or having two sides. **2** affecting two parties; mutual: a bilateral agreement. **bilaterally** *adv*

bilberry (ˈbɪlbərɪ) *n* the small, edible, bluish fruit of a shrub found on moors. < probably of Scandinavian origin.

bile (baɪl) *n* a bitter, greenish-yellow to brown liquid secreted by the liver and stored in the gall-bladder. < Latin *bilis.*

bilingual (baɪˈlɪŋgwəl) *adj* **1** able to speak two languages fluently. **2** written in two languages. **bilingualism** *n*

a teeny bikini

Bikini derives from *Bikini,* an atoll in the Marshall Islands in the Pacific Ocean and the site of atomic-bomb tests in 1946. The main reason for choosing this particular name for the bathing-suit was to highlight the effect of wearing a bikini—it was thought to be as powerful as that of an atomic blast! However, the ee sound in the middle of bikini inevitably also played some part in the decision, being a sound that is universally associated with the idea of 'smallness' and therefore a suitable sound representation of the bikini's minimal size. (See also panel at **teeny.**)

Who likes bills?

The British are much less fond of bills than are their American cousins—in British English the word bill means 'a statement of an amount that is owing' but in American English it means 'banknote'. Vocabulary differences of this type are not hard to find. Below is a list of common American English words together with their British English counterparts:

American	British
antenna	aerial
egg-plant	aubergine
fall	autumn
check	bill
cookie	biscuit
suspenders	braces
trailer	caravan
janitor	caretaker
drugstore	chemist's
the movies	the cinema
patrolman	constable
potato chips	crisps
drapes	curtains
thumbtack	drawing-pin
checkers	draughts
narcotic	drug
garbage can	dustbin
motor	engine
movie	film
apartment	flat
sneakers	gymshoes
vacation	holiday
shot	injection
attorney	lawyer
elevator	lift
truck	lorry
math	maths
freeway	motorway
diaper	nappy
kerosene	paraffin
sidewalk	pavement
gas	petrol
mailman	postman
railroad	railway
store	shop
wrench	spanner
candy	sweets
hobo	tramp
pants	trousers
shorts	underpants
vest	waistcoat
rubbers	wellingtons

< Latin *bi-* two + *lingua* tongue.

bilious (ˈbɪlɪəs) *adj* **1** of or suffering from biliousness. **2** (*informal*) (of colours) sickly: He turned a bilious green. **biliousness** *n* a condition caused by too much secretion of bile.

bill[1] (bɪl) *n* **1** a document listing charges for goods or services supplied. **2** a notice or advertisement: Stick no bills! **3** (*US*) a banknote: a dollar bill. **4** the draft of a proposed new law. **5** a certificate.
• *vb* **1** send a note of charges for goods or services supplied. **2** advertise. **bill of lading** a document giving full details of goods shipped or to be shipped. **fit** or **fill the bill** be suitable for what is required. < alteration of Late Latin *bulla* document. SEE PANEL.

bill[2] *n* a bird's beak.
• *vb* caress lovingly: bill and coo. < Old English *bile*.

billet (ˈbɪlɪt) *n* **1** a lodging, esp. for a soldier, in a private home. **2** (*informal*) a position or job.
• *vb* assign a billet to. < SEE BILL[1].

billet-doux (ˌbɪleɪˈduː) *n* a love-letter. < French: sweet letter.

billiards (ˈbɪljədz) *n* any of various games played using cues and balls on an oblong, cloth-covered table. < Middle French *billard* billiard-cue.

billion (ˈbɪljən) *n* **1** a thousand million. **2** a million million. < French *bi-* + *-llion* as in *million*. SEE PANEL.

billow (ˈbɪləʊ) *n* a large wave.
• *vb* rise or swell or cause to do this. < Old Norse *bylgja*.

billy (ˈbɪlɪ) *n* a can or pot of metal or enamel, used for cooking by campers. < Scottish *billypot* cooking vessel.

billy goat a male goat. < *Billy*, nickname for *William*.

bin (bɪn) *n* **1** a large container or enclosed space for storing something such as coal or grain. **2** a container for rubbish.

billions and billions

In British English, one billion used to be one million million. Now, in accordance with European and American practice, it is one thousand million.

However, it is probably best to state in full which is meant: rather than writing The scheme will cost £6 billion, it is preferable to write The scheme will cost £6 thousand million or £6 000 000 000.

< Old English *binne* basket.
binary (ˈbaɪnərɪ) *adj* **1** made up of two parts. **2** (of a number system) using only the two digits 0 and 1. < Late Latin *binarius*.
bind (baɪnd) *vb* **bound; binding 1** tie or fasten together, as with a rope, etc. **2** restrain or hold. **3** encircle with a band, belt, etc. **4** bandage. **5** fasten the pages of (a book, etc.) between a cover. **6** provide with a covering in order to strengthen or decorate. **7** oblige, esp. legally. **8** stick together.
• *n* (*informal*) a bore or nuisance. **binder** *n* **1** a folder or cover for holding sheets of paper. **2** a person who binds books. **3** something such as tar that binds things together. < Old English *bindan*.
binding (ˈbaɪndɪŋ) *n* **1** the covering that fastens the pages of a book. **2** the fabric used in binding edges.
• *adj* making a legal obligation.
binge (bɪndʒ) *n* (*informal*) a bout of unrestrained indulgence, esp. in eating and drinking. < probably English dialect *binge* to soak.
bingo (ˈbɪŋgəʊ) *n* a gambling game played with cards having numbered squares that are covered as the corresponding numbers are called out at random.
• *interj* an exclamation of surprise or joy at a sudden event. < perhaps *bing* like the sound of a bell ringing.
binoculars (bɪˈnɒkjʊləz) *pl n* an optical instrument held to the eyes to make distant objects appear nearer. < *bi-* + Latin *oculus* eye.
biochemistry (ˌbaɪəʊˈkɛmɪstrɪ) *n* the scientific study of the chemistry of living organisms. **biochemical** *adj* **biochemist** *n*
biography (baɪˈɒgrəfɪ) *n* an account of a person's life. **biographical** *adj* **biographer** *n* a person who writes a biography. < *bio-*, from Greek *bios* life + *graphein* to write.
biology (baɪˈɒlədʒɪ) *n* the scientific study of the life, structure, function, etc., of living organisms. **biological** *adj* **biologically** *adv* **biological warfare** the use of micro-organisms as weapons to cause disease. < Greek *bios* life + *logos* word.
bionics (baɪˈɒnɪks) *n* the study of the application of living systems to the development of man-made systems. < Greek *bios* English *-onics*, as in *electronics*.
biopsy (ˈbaɪɒpsɪ) *n* the removal and examination of a sample of living tissue from the body. < Greek *bios* + *opsis* appearance, sight.
bipartisan (baɪˈpɑːtɪˌzæn) *adj* of or involving two parties.
bipartite (baɪˈpɑːtaɪt) *adj* **1** having two parts. **2** affecting or undertaken by two parties.
biped (ˈbaɪpɛd) *n* an animal with two feet. < Latin *bi-* two + *pes* foot.
biplane (ˈbaɪˌpleɪn) *n* an aeroplane with two sets of wings, one above the other.
birch (bɜːtʃ) *n* **1** a tree with smooth, thin, peeling bark and glossy leaves. **2** a bundle of twigs or a stick of this tree used, esp. formerly, for flogging. < Old English *beorc*.
bird (bɜːd) *n* **1** a warm-blooded, feathered animal with fore limbs adapted as wings. **2** (*informal*) a person; fellow. **3** (*informal*) a girl. **bird's-eye view** a view from above; summary. < Old English *bridd*.
SEE PANEL.
Biro (ˈbaɪrəʊ) *n, pl* **Biros** (*Trademark*) a ball-point pen. < Lászlo Jozsef *Biró*, died 1985, Hungarian inventor.
birth (bɜːθ) *n* **1** the emergence of a new being from its parent. **2** origin; beginning: It's 20 years since the birth of the company. **birth certificate** an official document giving details of a person's parents, date and place of birth, etc. **birth-control** *n* control of the number of children born; contraception. **birthday** *n* the anniversary of the day of a person's birth. **birthmark** *n* a blemish on the skin at birth. **birth rate** the number of live births in a given area or group, usually expressed as per 1000 people in one year. **birthright** *n* a privilege or possession that a person is entitled to by birth. < Old Norse *byrth*.
biscuit (ˈbɪskɪt) *n* a small, thin, dry piece of pastry baked crisp. < Middle French (*pain*) *bescuit* twice-cooked (bread), ultimately from Latin *bis* twice + *coquere* to cook.
bisect (baɪˈsɛkt) *vb* cut or divide into two. **bisection** n **bisector** n < Latin *bi-* two + *secare* to cut.
bisexual (baɪˈsɛksjʊəl) *adj* **1** having the characteristics of two sexes. **2** attracted to people of both sexes. **bisexuality** *n*
bishop (ˈbɪʃəp) *n* **1** a clergyman above a priest in rank and having spiritual and administrative authority over a diocese. **2** (*chess*) either of two pieces which can move diagonally over any number of vacant squares. < ultimately Greek *episkopos* overseer, from *epi-* upon + *skeptesthai* to look.
bison (ˈbaɪsn̩) *n, pl* **bison 1** a very large, hoofed mammal with a shaggy mane,

formerly widespread in Europe. **2** a buffalo. < of Germanic origin.

bistro (ˈbiːstrəʊ) *n, pl* **bistros** a small restaurant. < French.

bit[1] (bɪt) *n* **1** a small piece, share, or quantity. **2** a short time or distance. **a bit** (*informal*) rather: I'm feeling a bit tired. **bitty** *adj* containing bits; disjointed. < Old English *bita*.

birds of a feather...

English contains a large number of words and expressions featuring birds:

☐ **proverbs:**

a bird in the hand is worth two in the bush it is better to be satisfied with what one already has or is certain to receive than to lose it in the hope of getting something better.
birds of a feather flock together people of the same character tend to be attracted to one another and associate with each other closely.
the early bird catches the worm the person who rises early for work will be successful.

☐ **idioms:**

a little bird told me used to refer to an undisclosable or unofficial source of information: A little bird told me you were changing your job!
give someone the bird to send someone away in a rude manner; jeer rudely at a performer, disapproving of his or her performance.
kill two birds with one stone to achieve two purposes by means of a single action: While I was shopping in Oxford, I popped in to see my sister and killed two birds with one stone.
the birds and the bees a euphemistic reference to the sexual relations between men and women: Stephen's getting a big boy now. I think it's about time you told him about the birds and the bees.

☐ **other words and expressions** featuring birds or words associated with birds:

a nest egg
birdbrain
birdbrained
egghead
feather one's nest
keep an eagle eye on someone
take someone under one's wing
the beak

bit[2] *n* **1** a metal mouthpiece on a bridle, used to control a horse. **2** the part of a tool that bores. < Old English *bite*.

bit[3] SEE **BITE.**

bit[4] *n* (*computers*) the basic unit of information storage, representing a choice between two possibilities. < *bi*nary + digi*t*.

bitch (bɪtʃ) *n* **1** a female dog or similar animal. **2** (*informal*) a malicious and spiteful woman. **3** an unpleasant or difficult thing. **bitchy** *adj* malicious and spiteful. **bitchiness** *n* < Old English *bicce*.

bite (baɪt) *vb* **bit; bitten; biting 1** cut, crush, or seize with the teeth. **2** cut into, as with something sharp. **3** (of an insect) sting. **4** take hold of; grip. **5** have a deep and sharp effect (on): The strike is beginning to bite.
• *n* **1** an act of biting. **2** a wound made by this. **3** the amount of food taken by one bite. **4** a snack: I'll snatch a quick bite before I go out. **5** a firm hold or grip. **biter** *n* **biting** *adj* **1** piercing; keen and penetrating: a biting wind. **2** sarcastic and sharp. < Old English *bītan*.

bitter (ˈbɪtə) *adj* **1** having a sharp, unpleasant taste. **2** marked by strong enmity or resentment. **3** difficult to accept; distressing. **4** sharp and sarcastic: bitter comments. **5** very cold: a bitter wind.
• *n* draught beer with a slightly bitter taste. **bitterly** *adv* **bitterness** *n* **bittersweet** *adj* pleasant but with traces of sadness or suffering. < Old English *biter*. SEE PANEL.

bitumen (ˈbɪtjʊmɪn) *n* a black, sticky substance used esp. in road-making and waterproofing. **bituminous** *adj* < Latin.

bivouac (ˈbɪvuːˌæk) *n* a temporary camp

bittersweet

Bittersweet is a rare example of a word containing an *oxymoron,* a figure of speech whose effect results from the juxtaposition of two contradictory senses. Such juxtapositions are usually found not within single words but within phrases, as in Lamb's 'I like a smuggler. He is the only *honest thief*' or Milton's 'No light, but rather *darkness visible.*'

The word oxymoron derives from the Greek *oxymōros* meaning 'pointedly foolish', from *oxys* 'sharp' and *mōros* 'foolish'.

with little or no shelter.
• *vb* **bivouacked; bivouacking** camp in a bivouac. < French, probably from Low German *bi* at + *wake* guard.

bizarre (bɪˈzɑː) *adj* odd or unusual; strange. < Italian *bizzarro.*

blab (blæb) *vb* **blabbed; blabbing** **1** reveal (secrets, etc.) indiscreetly. **2** talk away thoughtlessly. < of Germanic origin.

black (blæk) *adj* **1** of the colour of coal; completely dark; with no light. **2** very dirty. **3** (of coffee, etc.) served without milk or cream. **4** evil: black deeds. **5** without hope: The prospects look black. **6** **Black** having dark pigmentation. **7** marked by grotesque humour: black comedy.
• *n* **1** a black colour. **2** black clothing, worn esp. in mourning. **3** **Black** a Black person.
• *vb* **1** make black. **2** (of trade-union members) boycott. **blackly** *adv* **blackness** *n* **blackberry** *n* **1** the bramble. **2** the small, edible fruit of this shrub. **blackbird** *n* a songbird, the male of which is black. **blackboard** *n* a hard, smooth, esp. black surface for writing on with chalk. **black box** an electronic device in an aircraft that records details of its flight. **blacken** *vb* **1** make or become black. **2** defame or besmirch. **black eye** an area of bruising and swelling round the eye, esp. caused by a blow. **blackfly** *n* a small, black insect that sucks the juices of plants. **blackhead** *n* a small, black-tipped, hard lump blocking a pore of the skin. **black hole** a celestial body that has collapsed under such gravitational forces that no light can escape from it. **black ice** a thin, transparent layer of ice on a road. **black out** **1** lose consciousness temporarily. **2** stop light from being seen. **3** stop television or radio programmes from being broadcast; prevent the release of information. **blackout** *n* **black pudding** a dark sausage made from suet, pig's blood, etc. **blacksmith** *n* a person who works iron at a forge. **in black and white** in writing or in print; explicitly. < Old English *blæc.* SEE PANEL.

> **black**
>
> The absence of light has since time began injected fear into the hearts of men. As a consequence, darkness occurs in various cultures as a symbol of death, evil, treachery, and foreboding. In English such associations are reflected in a cluster of words and phrases that have formed around the word black. All of them contain amongst their senses something less than desirable. They include:
>
> **blackball** *vb* to ostracize or vote against.
> **black cap** the head-covering worn by a British judge while passing the death sentence.
> **blacken** *vb* to defame or besmirch: blacken someone's character.
> **blackleg** *n* a derogatory term for someone who flouts or opposes trade-union policies.
> **black list** a list of individuals or groups that have been proscribed.
> **black looks** looks of hostility or disapproval: John's answer met with the teacher's black looks.
> **black magic** magic performed supposedly with the help of the devil or evil spirits.
> **blackmail** *vb* to obtain something by extortion.
> **blackmail** *n* extortion or money extorted.
> **black mark** a note in an official record that a person has done something wrong.
> **black market** or **economy** unlawful or proscribed trading.
> **black sheep** a member of a group who has somehow failed.
> **black spot** a stretch of road particularly prone to accidents.
> **in someone's black books** out of favour with someone: He's been in the headmaster's black books from the day he was caught stealing.

bladder (ˈblædə) *n* the bag-like structure that stores urine until it is discharged from the body. < Old English *blǣdre.*

blade (bleɪd) *n* **1** the cutting-part of a knife, tool, or weapon. **2** the flat, wide part of an oar, propeller, etc. **3** a flat, narrow leaf of grass, etc. < Old English *blǣd.*

blame (bleɪm) *n* **1** responsibility for a fault. **2** an expression of disapproval, etc.
• *vb* hold (a person) responsible for (a fault). **blameless** *adj* < ultimately Late Latin *blasphemare* to blaspheme.

blanch (blɑːntʃ) *vb* make or become white or pale. < Old French *blanc* white.

blancmange (bləˈmɒnʒ) *n* a flavoured, jelly-like dessert made with milk. < Middle French *blanc manger* white food.

bland (blænd) *adj* without any stimulating or special features; mild in a dull or uninteresting way: bland foods. **blandly** *adv* **blandness** *n* < Latin *blandus*.

blank (blæŋk) *adj* **1** not written or printed on: blank paper. **2** without interest or expression: a blank look. **3** complete; utter. **4** without decoration or opening: a blank wall.
• *n* **1** a blank space; blank paper. **2** an empty space. **3** a piece of metal or other material prepared for finishing, stamping, etc., in a later operation. **4** a cartridge filled with powder but with no bullet. **blankly** *adv* **blankness** *n* **blank cheque 1** a signed cheque with the amount not filled in. **2** complete freedom to do something. **draw a blank** be unsuccessful. < Middle French *blanc* white, of Germanic origin.

blanket (ˈblæŋkɪt) *n* **1** a large, thick covering, used esp. on a bed. **2** a thick covering: a blanket of snow.
• *vb* cover with or as if with a blanket.
• *adj* applying to all instances, people, etc.: blanket condemnation. < Old French *blanc* white.

blare (blɛə) *vb* sound loudly and harshly.
• *n* a loud, harsh sound: the blare of trumpets. < Middle English *bleren*.

blasé (ˈblɑːzeɪ) *adj* indifferent to something, esp. because of familiarity or indulgence. < French *blaser* to cloy.

blaspheme (blæsˈfiːm) *vb* utter blasphemies. **blasphemer** *n* **blasphemous** *adj* **blasphemously** *adv* **blasphemy** *n* (an expression of) contempt or irreverence for God or something considered sacred. < ultimately Greek *blasphēmein* to speak evil.

blast (blɑːst) *n* **1** an explosion; rush of air from an explosion. **2** a charge of explosive. **3** a sudden, strong rush of wind or air. **4** a sudden, loud sound. **5** a violent outburst. **6** speed; capacity: They went off at full blast down the road.

> **blatant** or **flagrant?**
>
> These two words are sometimes confused.
> Blatant means 'very obvious or obtrusive; conspicuous': a *blatant* lie or, less commonly, 'offensively noisy': *blatant* showmanship.
> Flagrant is used to refer to actions, especially violations, undertaken in an open and unashamed manner: a *flagrant* breach of justice.

• *vb* **1** blow up with explosives. **2** make or remove by explosives. **3** make a loud, harsh sound. **4** (*informal*) criticize sharply. **5** destroy.
• *interj* an expression of annoyance, impatience, etc. **blast-furnace** *n* a furnace in which a forced blast of air is used to smelt iron ore. **blast off** (of a rocket) be launched. **blast-off** *n* < Old English *blǣst*.

blatant (ˈbleɪtn̩t) *adj* **1** very obvious or obtrusive; conspicuous. **2** offensively noisy. **blatancy** *n* **blatantly** *adv* < perhaps Latin *blatire* to chatter. SEE PANEL.

blaze (bleɪz) *n* **1** a strongly burning flame or fire. **2** intense light or glare. **3** a brightly coloured display; brilliance. **4** an outburst. **5** *pl* hell: What the blazes is going on?
• *vb* **1** burn strongly. **2** shine intensely. **3** have an outburst of strong feeling, esp. anger. **4** (of guns) fire rapidly. < Old English *blæse*.

blazer (ˈbleɪzə) *n* a jacket, often in the colours of a sports club or worn as part of a school uniform.

blazon (ˈbleɪzn̩) *n* a coat of arms.
• *vb* **1** proclaim widely. **2** describe (a coat of arms) in heraldic terms. < Middle French *blason*.

bleach (bliːtʃ) *vb* make or become white by the action of sunlight or chemicals.
• *n* a substance used in bleaching. < Old English *blǣcean*.

bleak (bliːk) *adj* **1** cold, harsh, and cheerless. **2** offering little hope or encouragement; gloomy: bleak prospects for the future. **bleakly** *adv* **bleakness** *n* < Middle English *bleke* pale.

bleary (ˈblɪərɪ) *adj* **1** dimmed by tears, tiredness, etc. **2** blurred. < Middle English *bleren* to make the eyes bleary.

bleat (bliːt) *vb* **1** make the characteristic sound of a sheep, goat, etc., or a sound like this. **2** utter complaints; whine.
• *n* the characteristic sound of a sheep, goat, etc. < Old English *blǣtan*.

bleed (bliːd) *vb* **bled; bleeding 1** lose or discharge blood. **2** draw blood or a liquid from. **3** (*informal*) extort money from. < Old English *blēdan*.

bleep (bliːp) *n* a short, high-pitched sound, esp. one produced electronically, used as a signal.
• *vb* make this sound. < like the sound.

blemish (ˈblɛmɪʃ) *n* a flaw or defect; clear imperfection.
• *vb* spoil with a blemish. < Middle French *blesmir* to make pale.

blend (blɛnd) *vb* **1** mix thoroughly;

combine into a whole. **2** have no strong contrasts; harmonize.
• *n* **1** a mixture made by blending. **2** a word derived from the combination of the sounds and meanings of two words. **blender** *n* an electric appliance that liquidizes foods. < Middle English *blenden*. SEE PANEL AT **MOPED**.

bless (blɛs) *vb* **1** make holy or consecrate. **2** give honour or praise to (God or a person). **3** grant happiness, health, etc., to; ask God's favour on. **4** endow with a talent, etc. **blessed** *adj* **1** holy. **2** (*old-fashioned*) fortunate. **3** (*euphemistic*) damned: I couldn't remember a blessed thing! **blessedly** *adv* **blessedness** *n* **blessing** *n* **1** God's favour; prayer asking for this. **2** a short prayer of thanksgiving said at a meal. **3** approval: The council gave their blessing to the scheme. **4** a happy event: a blessing in disguise. < Old English *blētsian* consecrate with blood.

blew (bluː) SEE **BLOW**[1].

blight (blaɪt) *n* **1** a plant disease caused by pests, fungi, etc. **2** an organism that causes this disease. **3** something that prevents growth, improvement, etc.: planning blight.
• *vb* affect with blight; suffer from blight. **blighter** *n* (*informal*) a fellow, esp. someone annoying. < origin uncertain.

blind (blaɪnd) *adj* **1** unable to see. **2** of or for people who cannot see. **3** not willing or able to understand. **4** (of the flying of an aircraft) performed by instruments only. **5** hidden: a blind entrance. **6** having only one opening: a blind alley. **7** not based on reason or evidence: blind faith. **8** without adequate information or understanding.
• *vb* **1** make blind. **2** dazzle. **3** deprive of understanding: Don't blind me with science!
• *n* **1** a screen for a window; cover. **2** a pretext.
• *adv* blindly. **blindly** *adv* **blindness** *n* **blind drunk** very drunk. < Old English. SEE PANEL.

blindfold (ˈblaɪndˌfəʊld) *vb* cover (the eyes) of (a person) with a piece of cloth.
• *n* a cloth used for this.
• *adj, adv* with the eyes blindfolded. < Middle English *blindfellen* to strike blind.

blink (blɪŋk) *vb* **1** close and open (the eyes) involuntarily. **2** shine intermittently or unsteadily.
• *n* **1** an act of blinking. **2** a glance or glimpse. **on the blink** (*informal*) not functioning properly. < Middle English *blinken* to open one's eyes.

blinker (ˈblɪŋkə) *n* **1** a flashing light serving as a signal or warning. **2** *pl* leather pieces attached to a horse's bridle to prevent it from seeing sideways. **3** *pl* obstruction to sight or understanding.

bliss (blɪs) *n* perfect happiness: marital bliss. **blissful** *adj* **blissfully** *adv* < Old English.

blister (ˈblɪstə) *n* **1** a small swelling on the skin, containing an accumulation of fluid. **2** a raised swelling, as on paintwork.
• *vb* **1** have or cause to have blisters. **2** criticize strongly. **blistering** *adj* severe. < probably Middle Dutch *bluyster*.

blitz (blɪts) *n* also **blitzkrieg** a violent attack, esp. from aircraft.
• *vb* attack suddenly and violently. < German *Blitzkrieg* lightning war.

blizzard (ˈblɪzəd) *n* a severe snowstorm. < origin unknown.

bloated (ˈbləʊtɪd) *adj* swollen, as with a liquid or air. < *bloat* to swell, from Middle English *blout*.

blind spots

The word blind features in a number of expressions, some of them idiomatic, including:

blind date an informal, often social meeting between a man and a woman who have not previously met.
blind spot 1 an area on the retina of the eye that is insensitive to light. **2** a part of an area of vision that cannot be seen by a motorist. **3** an area where understanding or knowledge is lacking: He's got a bit of a blind spot when it comes to geometry.
not a blind bit of not the slightest: It won't make a blind bit of difference.
turn a blind eye to to pretend not to notice: The authorities are turning a blind eye to a number of minor offences.

The expression **the blind leading the blind** refers to a situation in which those directing, teaching, etc., others know as little as those they are trying to help. The expression comes from the Authorized (King James) Version of the Bible, Matthew 15:14: Let them alone: they be blind leaders of the blind. And if the blind lead the blind, both shall fall into the ditch.

bloater (ˈbləʊtə) *n* a salted, smoked herring or mackerel. < obsolete *bloat* to cure.

blob (blɒb) *n* **1** a drop of liquid, etc. **2** a spot of colour, ink, etc. < Middle English.

bloc (blɒk) *n* a group of individuals, countries, etc., with a common purpose: a power bloc. < French: block.

block (blɒk) *n* **1** a large, solid piece of wood, metal, etc. **2** an obstacle, obstruction, or hindrance: a mental block. **3** a large building of separate flats or offices. **4** a group of buildings enclosed by streets: I'll just drive round the block. **5** a group of things considered as a unit. **6** a pad of paper. **7** (*slang*) the head. **8** a case enclosing pulleys. **9** a building brick for children.
• *vb* obstruct; prevent the movement of. **block in** fill in. **block letters** capital letters. < Middle Dutch *blok*.

blockade (blɒˈkeɪd) *n* the blocking of access to an area to prevent the supply of goods, etc.
• *vb* impose a blockade on.

blockage (ˈblɒkɪdʒ) *n* blocking or being blocked; obstruction.

blockhead (ˈblɒkˌhɛd) *n* (*derogatory*) a stupid person.

bloke (bləʊk) *n* (*informal*) a man. < perhaps Shelta.

blond (blɒnd) *adj* **1** (esp. of hair) light; fair. **2** having fair hair, a light complexion, and blue or grey eyes.
• *n* a blond person.

blonde (blɒnd) *n, adj* (a girl or woman who is) blond. < French.

blood (blʌd) *n* **1** the red, oxygen-bearing fluid in the arteries and veins that is pumped round the body by the heart. **2** bloodshed. **3** guilt for injuring or killing: have blood on one's hands. **4** lifeblood; life. **5** lineage; kinship: royal blood. **blood-bath** *n* a massacre. **blood-curdling** *adj* horrific. **blood group** one of various types into which human blood is classified. **bloodhound** *n* a dog with a keen sense of smell used in tracking. **bloodless** *adj* **1** without blood. **2** without bloodshed: a bloodless coup. **blood poisoning** the presence of bacteria or poisonous, bacterial proteins in the blood. **blood pressure** the pressure that blood exerts on the arteries; abnormally high pressure of this kind. **blood-red** *adj* having the colour of blood. **bloodshed** *n* the shedding of blood; slaughter or killing. **bloodshot** *adj* (of eyes) having the white parts tinged with red because the small blood vessels are swollen or broken. **blood sports** sports in which an animal is hunted and killed. **bloodstain** *n* a stain made by blood. **bloodstained** *adj* **bloodstream** *n* the flow of blood around the body. **bloodsucker** *n* **1** a leech. **2** a person who extorts money from others. **blood test** an analysis of a sample of blood. **bloodthirsty** *adj* eager for bloodshed. **blood-vessel** *n* an artery, capillary, or vein. < Old English *blōd*.

bloody (ˈblʌdɪ) *adj* **1** covered or stained with blood. **2** marked by much bloodshed. **3** murderous; cruel. **4** also *adv* (*slang*) very great; very. **bloodily** *adv* **bloodiness** *n* **bloody-minded** *adj* (*informal*) deliberately awkward and uncooperative. **bloody-mindedness** *n* < Old English *blōdig*.

bloom (blu:m) *n* **1** a flower. **2** a state of flowering: in full bloom. **3** a period of beauty, health, and strength: the bloom of youth.
• *vb* **1** bear or produce flowers; be in bloom. **2** reach maturity; prosper, flourish, or blossom. < Old Norse *blom*.

bloomer (ˈblu:mə) *n* (*informal*) a stupid mistake; blunder.

bloomers (ˈblu:məz) *pl n* a variety of women's close-fitting knickers that reach just above the knee. SEE PANEL.

blossom (ˈblɒsəm) *n* **1** the flower of a plant, esp. one that produces fruit. **2** a

bloomers

The word bloomers owes its origin to a certain Mrs Amelia Jenks *Bloomer*, 1818–94, a New York feminist and women's magazine editor. Mrs Bloomer channelled much of her support for the cause of women's rights into dress reform. The original bloomers made their first appearance in about the middle of the 19th century. These were essentially 'trousers for women' which had long, baggy legs gathered by elastic at the ankle and were to be worn beneath a skirt that came down to the calf. Despite her advocacy of the fashion in her magazine, it found little favour.

Towards the end of the 19th century bloomers enjoyed a revival when it was used as the name of knee-length knickerbockers, worn without a skirt, which found a very warm welcome amongst lady cyclists. Nowadays, it refers to yet a different garment—a variety of women's knickers.

mass of such flowers.
• *vb* **1** open into blossoms. **2** develop; flourish. < Old English *blōstm.*

blot (blɒt) *n* **1** a stain or spot of ink, etc. **2** something that disfigures; blemish.
• *vb* **blotted; blotting 1** make a blot (on). **2** dry or remove with a paper that absorbs blots. **blot one's copybook** spoil one's good record. **blot out 1** hide from view. **2** destroy or annihilate. **blotting-paper** *n* also **blotter** a soft, absorbent paper for soaking up surplus ink. < Middle English.

blotch (blɒtʃ) *n* a large, irregular mark: red blotches on his face. **blotched** *adj* **blotchy** *adj* < probably *botch,* influenced by *blot.*

blotto (ˈblɒtəʊ) *adj* (*slang*) very drunk. < probably *blot.*

blouse (blaʊz) *n* a woman's loose, shirt-like garment. < French.

blow[1] (bləʊ) *vb* **blew; blown; blowing 1** (of the wind) move or flow with force. **2** force a current of air out, into, etc. **3** shape or produce by blowing. **4** puff and pant. **5** sound by blowing. **6** melt (a fuse), when overloaded. **7** burst by an explosion, puncture, or excessive pressure. **8** (*informal*) reveal: His cover was blown. **9** (*informal*) disregard: Blow the expense! **10** (*informal*) spend recklessly; waste. **blower** *n* **1** a person or thing that blows. **2** (*old-fashioned informal*) a telephone. < Old English *blāwan.* SEE PANEL.

blow[2] *n* **1** a powerful stroke with one's hand, fist, etc., or a weapon. **2** a shock; unfortunate event. **blow-by-blow** *adj* detailed. < Middle English *blaw.*

blowlamp (ˈbləʊˌlæmp) *n* a small, portable burner that produces a very hot flame, used to remove old paint, etc.

blown (bləʊn) SEE BLOW[1].

blubber (ˈblʌbə) *n* whale fat.
• *vb* sob noisily; utter while sobbing. < Middle English *bluber* bubble.

bludgeon (ˈblʌdʒən) *n* a short, heavy stick with one end thicker than the other, used as a weapon.
• *vb* **1** strike with a bludgeon. **2** persuade by using force; bully. < origin uncertain.

blue (bluː) *adj* **1** having the colour of a clear sky. **2** (of the skin) tinged with a bluish-purple colour through cold or anger. **3** sad and depressed. **4** obscene or indecent; pornographic.
• *n* **1** a blue colour. **2** blue clothing. **3** the sky or sea; far distance: into the blue.
• *vb* turn blue. **blueness** *n* **bluish** *adj* **bluebell** *n* a plant with blue, bell-shaped flowers. **blueberry** *n* a shrub with edible, blue berries; its fruit. **bluebottle** *n* a large fly that deposits its eggs in food, dung, or wounds. **blueprint** *n* **1** a blue photographic print of technical plans. **2** a detailed plan of action: a blueprint for the future of the railways. **bluestocking** *n* a woman with intellectual or scholarly interests. **bluetit** *n* a tit with a blue crown and wings. < Old French *blou,* of Germanic origin. SEE PANEL.

bluff[1] (blʌf) *vb* deceive by pretence or a show of confidence, strength, etc.
• *n* bluffing. **bluffer** *n* < probably Dutch *bluffen* to boast.

bluff[2] *n* a high, steep headland. < obsolete Dutch *blaf* flat.

blunder (ˈblʌndə) *n* a stupid or clumsy error or mistake.
• *vb* **1** move clumsily and uncertainly. **2** make a blunder. **blunderer** *n* < probably of Scandinavian origin.

blunderbuss (ˈblʌndəˌbʌs) *n* a short-range gun with a large bore and flared muzzle. < Dutch *donderbus* thunder gun.

blunt (blʌnt) *adj* **1** not having a sharp edge or point. **2** straightforward and direct; not refined.

blowing up

The word blow features in a number of idiomatic expressions, including:

blow in to arrive suddenly or casually.

blow one's own trumpet to boast or praise oneself.

blow one's top to lose one's temper.

blow out 1 to extinguish or be extinguished. **2** to fill with food: I feel blown out after that heavy meal. **blow-out** *n* **3** (of a tyre) to burst. **blow-out** *n* **4** (of an oil- or gas-well) to produce oil or gas uncontrollably. **blow-out** *n*

blow over (especially of a storm or quarrel) to subside or cease.

blow someone's mind to cause someone to have hallucinations.

blow the gaff to reveal or disclose a secret.

blow up 1 to explode; destroy by the use of explosives. **2** to arise; become a crisis. **3** to lose one's temper. **4** to reprimand severely. **5** to enlarge (a photograph). **blow-up** *n*

• *vb* make or become blunt. **bluntly** *adv* **bluntness** *n* < Middle English.

blur (blɜ:) *vb* **blurred; blurring** make or become less sharp or clear.
• *n* **1** something vague or unclear. **2** a smear. < origin uncertain.

blurb (blɜ:b) *n* a short, promotional description of something, esp. on the cover of a book. < coined by Gelett Burgess, died 1951, US humorist.
SEE PANEL.

blurt (blɜ:t) *vb* **blurt out** utter suddenly and impulsively. < probably like the sound.

blush (blʌʃ) *vb* **1** become red in the face from embarrassment, shame, etc. **2** feel embarrassment, shame, etc.
• *n* **1** a reddening of the face from embarrassment, shame, etc. **2** a red tinge. < Old English *blȳsa* flame.

bluster ('blʌstə) *vb* **1** speak or act in a loud, assertive manner. **2** (of the wind) blow in gusts.
• *n* loud, assertive talk. **blustery** *adj* < Middle English *blustren*.

boa ('bəʊə) *n* a snake that kills its prey by biting and then crushing it. < Latin: water-snake.

boar (bɔ:) *n* **1** an uncastrated male pig. **2** a male wild pig. < Old English *bār*.

board (bɔ:d) *n* **1** a long, flat piece of wood; plank. **2** a flat piece of wood or other stiff material for a particular purpose: a notice-board; a chess-board. **3** thick, stiff paper used in book covers. **4** a wood pulp or construction material in stiff, flat, rectangular sheets: cardboard. **5** food provided regularly for money: board and lodging. **6** a group of people with supervisory, etc., functions: the board of directors; a board of examiners. **7** an official organization: the water board.
• *vb* **1** get on; go aboard (a ship, bus, etc.). **2** provide or be provided with meals and often lodging for pay. **3** cover with boards. **boarder** *n* **1** a lodger. **2** a resident pupil at a boarding-school. **boarding-house** *n* a place that provides board and lodging. **boarding-school** *n* a school at which pupils receive board and lodging. **boardroom** *n* a room in which meetings of company directors

---

the blues

Blue features in a number of expressions, many of them idiomatic, including:

blue chip *adj, n* (considered) a reliable investment.
blue-collar worker a worker engaged in manual work.
blue-eyed boy a favourite.
blue fit intense annoyance.
bolt from the blue something sudden, unexpected, and often unpleasant: His resignation came as a bolt from the blue. The expression refers to a thunderbolt coming from the sky.
once in a blue moon very rarely: He visits his parents only once in a blue moon.
out of the blue unexpectedly: I'd not heard from my sister in Australia for years and then out of the blue she turned up on my doorstep!
shout, scream, cry, etc., **blue murder** to shout or protest very noisily, because one strongly disagrees with what is happening.
talk, argue, etc., **till one is blue in the face** to talk, argue, etc., for a long time, but without achieving one's desired purpose: We all know we could discuss pay and working conditions till we're blue in the face, but until the management compromise a bit, we won't get anywhere.
the blues 1 a song or form of music marked by a slow, sad melody. **2** a state of depression.

---

blurb

The promotional description of a book that appears on its dustjacket or back cover is known as a blurb. This word was coined in 1907 by Gelett Burgess, 1866–1951, an American humorist and illustrator. In the early years of the 20th century virtually every novel published in the United States came with the picture of an alluring young woman on its dustjacket. Burgess's decision to parody this convention produced the grotesquely enhanced beauty 'Miss Belinda *Blurb*', whose portrait (adapted from a tooth-powder advertisement) adorned the jacket of his book 'Are You a Bromide?'.

are held. **go by the board** be neglected or ignored. **on board** on or in a ship, aircraft, etc. **sweep the board** win every prize in a competition. < Old English *bord.*

boast (bəʊst) *vb* **1** speak about or state with excessive pride. **2** possess as something to be proud of.
• *n* **1** boasting. **2** something that one is proud of. **boastful** *adj* **boastfully** *adv* **boastfulness** *n* < Middle English *boost.*

boat (bəʊt) *n* **1** a small, open vessel for travelling on water. **2** a boat-shaped dish: a gravy boat. **boatman** *n, pl* **boatmen** a man who works with or rents out boats. **boat people** refugees who left their country in small boats, as from Vietnam. **boat-train** *n* a train that takes people to or from a ship. **in the same boat** experiencing the same difficulties. **miss the boat** or **bus** lose an opportunity. < Old English *bāt.*

boater (ˈbəʊtə) *n* a stiff, straw hat with a flat crown and a straight brim.

boatswain (ˈbəʊsn̩) *n* a ship's officer who is responsible for the maintenance of the ship. < Middle English *boot* boat + *swein* servant.

bob[1] (bɒb) *vb* **bobbed; bobbing 1** move quickly up and down. **2** move jerkily. **3** make (a bow or curtsy). **4 bob up** appear or arise suddenly.
• *n* a bobbing movement. < Middle English *boben.*

bob[2] *n* **1** a haircut in which the hair is cut short and hangs loosely just above the shoulders. **2** a knot of hair.
• *vb* **bobbed; bobbing** cut (the hair) in a bob. < Middle English *bobbe* bunch.

bob[3] *n, pl* **bob** (*informal*) a shilling; 5p. < origin unknown.

bobbin (ˈbɒbɪn) *n* a small spool holding yarn, thread, etc. < French *bobine.*

bob-sleigh (ˈbɒbˌsleɪ) *n* a large, usually metal racing-sledge for two or four people.
• *vb* ride on a bob-sleigh. < perhaps BOB[2].

bode (bəʊd) *vb* be an omen of. < Old English *bodian.*

bodice (ˈbɒdɪs) *n* the part of a woman's dress above the waist. < ultimately Scottish *bodies,* plural of *body.*

bodily (ˈbɒdɪlɪ) *adj* of the body: bodily injuries.
• *adv* **1** in person. **2** as a whole; altogether.

bodkin (ˈbɒdkɪn) *n* a large, blunt needle, used for drawing tape, etc., through a loop or hem. < Middle English.

body (ˈbɒdɪ) *n* **1** the whole physical substance of an animal, person, or plant. **2** the main part of a person, animal, or plant; trunk or torso. **3** a corpse. **4** the main part of something: in the body of the hall. **5** a mass of matter: a body of water. **6** a material object in space: heavenly bodies. **7** a group considered as a unit: an advisory body; the student body. **8** a collection: the body of evidence. **9** density; rich concentration of flavour: This wine hasn't enough body. **10** (*informal*) a person. **body-blow** *n* a severe setback. **bodyguard** *n* an escort who protects an important person. **bodywork** *n* the shell of a motor vehicle. < Old English *bodig.*

boffin (ˈbɒfɪn) *n* (*informal*) a scientist, esp. one engaged in technical research. < origin unknown.

bog (bɒg) *n* **1** wet, spongy ground, formed of decomposing vegetation. **2** (*slang*) a toilet.
• *vb* **bogged; bogging** meet with difficulties that prevent progress: Try not to get bogged down in all the details. **boggy** *adj* < of Celtic origin.

boggle (ˈbɒgl̩) *vb* be surprised or overwhelmed; hesitate: The mind boggles at the expense involved! < perhaps English dialect *bogle* spectre.

bogie (ˈbəʊgɪ) *n* a wheeled, swivelling undercarriage fitted below one end of a railway vehicle. < origin unknown.

bogus (ˈbəʊgəs) *adj* not genuine; spurious. < apparatus for making counterfeit money.

bogy, bogey (ˈbəʊgɪ) *n* **1** an evil spirit; spectre or ghost. **2** something that causes fear. **bogyman, bogeyman** *n* an imaginary figure used in threatening children. < probably alteration of *bogle* spectre.

Bohemian (bəʊˈhiːmɪən) *adj, n* (a person who is) unconventional in conduct, appearance, etc. < *Bohemia,* region of Czechoslovakia. SEE PANEL.

boil[1] (bɔɪl) *vb* **1** change into a vapour when heated. **2** heat or be heated to boiling-point. **3** cook or be cooked by the action of a boiling liquid. **4** bubble or foam strongly. **5** make excited with anger; seethe.
• *n* boiling; boiling-point. **boil down 1** reduce by boiling. **2** condense. **3** amount (to). **boiled sweet** a sweet of boiled sugar. **boiler** *n* **1** a container used for boiling. **2** a tank in which water is heated or stored. **3** a tank in which water is turned into steam under pressure for power. **boiler suit** a one-piece, outer garment combining shirt and trousers,

worn for dirty work. **boiling** *adj, adv (informal)* very (hot). **boiling-point** *n* **1** the temperature at which a liquid boils. **2** the point at which a person's anger, etc., overcomes his or her self-control. **boil over 1** overflow when boiling. **2** lose one's temper. < ultimately Latin *bulla* bubble.

boil[2] *n* an inflamed swelling on the skin, filled with pus. < Old English *bȳl.*

boisterous (ˈbɔɪstərəs) *adj* **1** exuberant, noisy, and rough: boisterous children. **2** windy or rough; stormy. **boisterously** *adv* < Middle English *boistous* rough.

bold (bəʊld) *adj* **1** marked by confidence and courage. **2** impudent. **3** conspicuous; imaginative: bold, new designs. **boldly** *adv* **boldness** *n* < Old English *beald.*

bollard (ˈbɒlɑːd, ˈbɒləd) *n* **1** a strong post on a wharf around which mooring lines may be fastened. **2** a short post to guide vehicles or to prevent access. < perhaps *bole* trunk of a tree.

bolshie (ˈbɒlʃɪ) *adj (informal)* rebellious; uncooperative and stubborn. < *Bolshevik,* ultimately from Russian *bol'she* larger.

bolster (ˈbəʊlstə) *n* a long pillow at the head of a bed, esp. under other pillows. • *vb* support; reinforce: bolster up ailing parts of the economy. < Old English.

bolt (bəʊlt) *n* **1** a sliding bar or rod for fastening a door. **2** the part of a lock that is moved by a key. **3** a flash of lightning. **4** a sudden movement: They made a bolt for the door. • *vb* **1** fasten with a bolt or bolts. **2** move quickly; flee or escape. **3** (of plants) to produce flowers and seeds too soon. **4** swallow (food) very quickly. **a bolt from the blue** an unexpected, esp. unpleasant event. **bolt upright** stiffly erect. < Old English.

bomb (bɒm) *n* **1** a container filled with explosive or incendiary substance that is set off by impact or a timing device. **2 the bomb** an atom or hydrogen bomb. **3** *(slang)* a large amount of money: He earns a bomb. • *vb* **1** attack with bombs. **2** move very fast. **bomber** *n* **1** an aircraft that carries and drops bombs. **2** a person who throws or places bombs. **bombshell** *n* something that has a surprising, shocking effect. **(like) a bomb** *(informal)* very successfully. < Italian *bomba,* probably ultimately Greek *bombos,* like the sound.

bombard (bɒmˈbɑːd) *vb* **1** attack with artillery or bombs. **2** direct electrons or other particles towards. **3** attack with (questions, etc.). **bombardment** *n* < Middle French *bombarde* cannon.

bombastic (bɒmˈbæstɪk) *adj* using grand, pompous words. < Latin *bombax* cotton.

bona fide (ˌbəʊnə ˈfaɪdɪ) *adj* genuine: This car-park is for the use of bona fide customers only. < Latin: in good faith.

bonanza (bəˈnænzə) *n* a source of esp. sudden great wealth. < Spanish: calm sea, ultimately Greek *malakos* soft.

bond (bɒnd) *n* **1** something that binds or fastens. **2** something that unites: the bonds of friendship. **3** an adhesive material; adhesive quality. **4** a binding agreement. **5** a security issued by a government, local authority, or public company as a means of raising money. **6** the status of imported goods in a warehouse, etc., until duties are paid. **7** a strong, white paper used for writing and typing. • *vb* **1** bind, fasten, or unite with a bond. **2** place (goods) in bond. < Old Norse *band.*

bondage (ˈbɒndɪdʒ) *n* slavery; captivity.

bone (bəʊn) *n* **1** one of the parts of hard tissue that makes up the skeleton of an animal; this tissue. **2** a piece of bone with meat on it. **3** *pl* the skeleton or body. **4** *pl* the essential part of something: the bare bones. **5** a strip of whalebone or material used to stiffen a corset, etc. • *vb* remove the bones from. **bone china** fine china made from bone ash and kaolin. **bone-dry** *adj* completely dry. **bonehead** *n* a stupid person. **bone idle** very lazy. **bonemeal** *n* fertilizer, etc., made from crushed, powdered bones. **bone-shaker** *n* an early bicycle with wooden wheels. **bone up on** *(informal)* learn by studying intensively. **bony** *adj* **1** of or like bone. **2** full of

pity the Bohemians

It is unfortunate for the Czechoslovakian population of Bohemia that the name derived from their former province and present region has long had rather undesirable overtones in English. They may not feel so slighted, however, if they realize that originally the adoption of the word had nothing to do with the manners of their forefathers. The name was first applied to gypsies who, according to one of several schools of thought, were believed to come from Bohemia. (See panel at **gypsy**.)

bones; with large or prominent bones. **3** skinny. < Old English *bān.* SEE PANEL.

bonfire (ˈbɒnˌfaɪə) *n* a large outdoor fire. < Middle English *bonefire* bone-fire.

bongo (ˈbɒŋgəʊ) *n, pl* **bongos** one of a pair of small drums played with the fingers. < American Spanish *bongó.*

bonkers (ˈbɒŋkəz) *adj* (*slang*) crazy. < origin unknown.

bonnet (ˈbɒnɪt) *n* **1** a hat with ribbons that are tied under the chin. **2** the hinged cover over the engine, etc., of a motor vehicle. < Middle French *bonet,* from Medieval Latin *abonnis.* SEE PANEL.

bonny (ˈbɒnɪ) *adj* **1** attractive. **2** looking healthy. < Old French *bon* good, from Latin *bonus.*

bonsai (ˈbɒnsaɪ) *n* **1** a shrub or tree that is specially developed as a miniature in an earthenware pot. **2** the art of growing shrubs or trees in this way. < Japanese: plant grown in a pot.

bonus (ˈbəʊnəs) *n* something given or paid in addition to what is usual or expected. < Latin: good.

bon voyage (ˌbɒn vɔɪˈɑːdʒ, ˌbɒn vwaɪˈɑːdʒ) *n, interj* (a) farewell; used to wish a traveller well on his or her journey. < French: good journey.

boo (buː) *interj* **1** used to express disapproval or contempt. **2** used to startle or frighten someone.
• *vb* shout boo at. < Middle English *bo.*

boob (buːb) *n* **1** (*informal*) a stupid mistake. **2** (*slang*) a woman's breast.
• *vb* (*informal*) make a stupid mistake.

the bones of the matter

Bone features in a number of expressions, including:

a bone of contention the cause of a disagreement or dispute. This was originally a reference to a fight by two dogs over a bone.

have a bone to pick with someone to have a reason for a quarrel or complaint. This was originally a reference to the fact that two dogs would in all probability fight over the same bone.

make no bones about to have no doubt at all about (something); used to add emphasis to a statement or promise: Make no bones about it, lad, I'm going to make sure you're really punished this time! An older version of this idiom was find no bones in and referred originally to finding no bones in one's soup.

< SEE **BOOBY.**

booby (ˈbuːbɪ) *n* a foolish person. **booby prize** a mock award given to the competitor who has come last. **booby trap 1** a hidden trap for the unsuspecting. **2** a hidden bomb so placed that it is detonated by an unsuspecting victim. **booby-trap** *vb* **booby-trapped; booby-trapping** place a booby trap in or on. < Spanish *bobo,* from Latin *balbus* stammering.

book (bʊk) *n* **1** a series of esp. printed sheets of paper fastened between covers. **2** a long, literary work. **3** a major division of a written work. **4** *pl* a record of business transactions. **5** a number of things such as cheques or stamps, bound together.
• *vb* **1** reserve, buy, or engage in advance. **2** take the name of, in order to prosecute. **3** register in a hotel: Have you booked in yet? **bookcase** *n* a piece of furniture that consists of shelves for books. **book club** a club that sells books at a reduced price to members. **bookend** *n* a support placed at the end of a row of books to keep them upright. **bookie** *n* (*informal*) a bookmaker. **booking-office** *n* an office where tickets are sold, for railway journeys, etc. **bookish** *adj* **1** fond of reading. **2** dependent on academic knowledge. **bookkeeping** *n* the recording of the accounts and transactions of a business. **bookkeeper** *n* **booklet** *n* a small, thin book, esp. one with paper covers. **bookmaker** *n* a person whose business is to take bets on horse-races, etc. **bookmark** *n* something, esp. a strip of paper, etc.,

bonnet and hood

One area of vocabulary in which British and American English show a remarkable degree of variation is the language of cars. Even the most common components like 'the hinged sheet of metal that covers the engine' are described by different names: bonnet in British English and hood in American English. Other examples include:

American English	British English
gas pedal	**accelerator**
energizer	**battery**
trunk	**boot**
gasoline	**petrol**
muffler	**silencer**
fender	**wing**

used to mark a place in a book. **bookseller** *n* a person whose business is selling books. **bookshop** *n* a shop that sells books. **bookstall** *n* a stall where books, newspapers, and magazines are sold. **bookworm** *n* **1** an insect that damages books by feeding on the binding, etc. **2** a person who is very fond of reading. < Old English *bōc*.

boom¹ (buːm) *vb* **1** make a deep, hollow sound. **2** prosper greatly; grow quickly; increase in economic activity: Business is booming!
• *n* **1** a booming sound. **2** a period of increasing, esp. economic activity: a boom in house building. < like the sound.

boom² *n* **1** a pole extending from a mast to hold the bottom of a sail stretched. **2** a long pole carrying a microphone, etc. < Dutch: tree, beam.

boomerang (ˈbuːməˌræŋ) *n* **1** a bent piece of wood so shaped that it returns to the thrower, used by Australian aborigines. **2** something that has an unexpected, harmful effect on its originator. < native Australian name.

boon¹ (buːn) *n* a blessing or favour; benefit. < Old Norse *bōn* request.

boon² *adj* close and intimate: a boon companion. < Middle French *bon* good.

boor (bʊə) *n* a rude or insensitive person. **boorish** *adj* < Dutch *boer* peasant.

boost (buːst) *vb* **1** push upwards. **2** raise or increase; promote: to boost production.
• *n* **1** an upward push. **2** an increase or encouragement: a tremendous boost to our morale. **booster** *n* **1** a device which increases power or thrust. **2** a supplementary injection of a vaccine to maintain the level of an earlier immunization. **3** an amplifier of radio, television, etc., signals. < origin unknown.

boot (buːt) *n* **1** a strong shoe or outer covering for the foot, extending above the ankle. **2** the compartment for luggage in a car. **3 the boot** (*slang*) dismissal.
• *vb* kick. **put the boot in** kick or act cruelly, **the boot is on the other foot** the situation has been reversed. < Middle French *bote*. SEE PANEL.

bootee (ˈbuːtiː) *n* a soft, knitted shoe for a baby.

booth (buːð) *n* **1** a stall for selling or displaying goods. **2** a small enclosure, esp. a cubicle, giving privacy: a telephone booth. < Scandinavian.

bootleg (ˈbuːtˌlɛg) *vb* **bootlegged; bootlegging** manufacture, sell, or carry (illicit goods, esp. alcohol).
• *adj* manufactured, sold, or smuggled illegally. **bootlegger** *n* < practice of carrying illicit goods in the legs of boots.

booty (ˈbuːtɪ) *n* valuable goods, esp. obtained as plunder. < ultimately Middle Low German *būte* exchange.

booze (buːz) *n* (*informal*) **1** alcoholic drink. **2** a drinking spree.
• *vb* (*informal*) drink alcohol, esp. to excess. **boozy** *adj* **boozer** *n* (*slang*) a public house. < Middle Dutch *būsen*.

border (ˈbɔːdə) *n* **1** a dividing line between countries, regions, etc.; area near this: the border between England and Scotland. **2** a margin along the edge of something; decorative strip around something. **3** a narrow strip of planted ground: herbaceous borders.
• *vb* **1** be or put a border on. **2 border on** be close to; verge (on): bordering on hysteria. **borderland** *n* the area near a border. **borderline** *adj, n* (classified as being on) a dividing line between categories: a borderline case. < Old French *border* to border, of Germanic origin.

bore¹ (bɔː) SEE **BEAR¹**.

bore² *vb* **1** make (a hole) in (wood, etc.), using a tool such as a drill. **2** make by boring.
• *n* **1** a hole made by boring. **2** the hollow part of a gun barrel, cylinder, etc.; diameter of this. < Old English *borian*.

bore³ *vb* make tired by being dull or monotonous. **boredom** *n* **boring** *adj*
• *n* a boring person or thing. < origin uncertain.

born (bɔːn) SEE **BEAR¹**.
• *adj* **1** brought into existence by birth. **2** by birth: British born. **3** possessing certain qualities from birth: a born leader. SEE PANEL.

to boot

The phrase to boot means 'as well' or 'in addition'; He's a greedy man, and dishonest *to boot*. The word boot in to boot has no connection with the boot of boots and shoes. Rather, it comes from the Old English noun *bōt* meaning 'advantage' or 'avail'. In this meaning it was formerly used both as a verb (What *boots* it to be rich in gold and poor in health?) and adjective, as in Shakespeare's bootless errands. Nowadays it survives only in to boot.

borne (bɔːn) SEE **BEAR**[1]. SEE PANEL AT **BORN.**
borough (ˈbʌrə) *n* a British urban constituency or administrative area. < Old English *burg* fortified town.
borrow (ˈbɒrəʊ) *vb* **1** take or receive (something) temporarily, intending to return it. **2** adopt (words, ideas, methods, etc.). **borrower** *n* < Old English *borgian.*
Borstal (ˈbɔːstəl) *n* a penal institution where young offenders are detained for rehabilitation and training. < *Borstal,* village in Kent, England, site of first such institution.
bosom (ˈbʊzəm) *n* **1** the chest or breast of a person; part of a garment covering this. **2** the centre of one's private thoughts and feelings. **3** a protective, inmost part: He returned to the bosom of the family.
• *adj* close; intimate; dear: bosom friends. < Old English *bōsm.*
boss[1] (bɒs) *n* (*informal*) a person who directs and supervises workers.
• *vb* (*informal*) **1** be the boss of. **2** act in a domineering way towards; order about: Stop bossing me about! **bossy** *adj* (*informal*) domineering. **bossily** *adv* **bossiness** *n* < Dutch *baas* master.
boss[2] *n* a round, projecting knob, stud, etc., often for ornamentation. < Old French *boce.*
botany (ˈbɒtənɪ) *n* the scientific study of plants. **botanical** *adj* of botany. **botanic gardens** a place in which plants are grown, often for scientific research. **botanist** *n* an expert in botany. < ultimately Greek *botanē* plant, pasture.
botch (bɒtʃ) *vb* **1** spoil hopelessly; mess up or bungle. **2** repair badly or clumsily.
• *n* something botched. < Middle English *bocchen.*
both (bəʊθ) *determiner* being the two: with both hands.
• *pron* the one as well as the other: both of them.
• *conj* used to show that two or more things are included: People are both body and soul. < Old Norse *bāthir.*
bother (ˈbɒðə) *vb* **1** cause annoyance or trouble to; irritate. **2** take the trouble.
• *interj* an exclamation of annoyance.
• *n* **1** a cause of annoyance or minor trouble. **2** a disturbance: There was a spot of bother here last night. **botheration** *interj, n* bother. **bothersome** *adj* causing bother. < perhaps Irish Gaelic *bodhar* deaf, bothered.
bottle (ˈbɒtl̩) *n* **1** a container of glass or plastic with a narrow neck, used for storing liquids. **2** the amount contained in this. **3** milk in a bottle, for babies. **4 the bottle** (*slang*) alcoholic drinks. **5** (*slang*) courage; boldness.
• *vb* put in or store in bottles. **bottleneck** *n* **1** place where the free flow of traffic is hindered. **2** something that delays progress: bottlenecks in production. **bottle up** hold back (expressions of strong feeling). < ultimately Late Latin *buttis* cask. SEE PANEL.
bottom (ˈbɒtəm) *n* **1** the lowest, deepest,

born or borne?

Bear in the sense 'to give birth to' is most commonly used in the passive, the past participle being spelt born: She was *born* in London. This is also the spelling of the adjective: German-*born,* a *born* leader.

The spelling borne is used in active sentences: She has *borne* six children, and in passive sentences followed by by: Of the six children *borne* by her, only two lived for more than a year.

Borne is also the spelling for all other senses of the verb bear: The following points should be *borne* in mind. Your theory is simply not *borne* out by the facts, and other adjectival uses: *airborne* troops.

hit the bottle

Far from being confined to poetry and prose, figures of speech occur all the time in even the most commonplace varieties of English. In fact, it's exactly because everyday conversation is so full of them that they tend not to be noticed. Take, for example, the slang expression hit the bottle. Here the word bottle means more than it literally says. The meaning—'intoxicating drink'—is figurative. This type of usage is known as *metonymy,* which comes ultimately from the Greek word metōnymia, 'a change of name'.

As its name suggests, metonymy is a figure of speech by which a noun or phrase is represented by some other noun closely associated with it. Thus to read Dickens is to read 'the novels of Dickens', to boil the kettle is to boil 'the water in the kettle', and to earn a living from one's pen is to earn a living from 'writing'.

or farthest part of something. **2** the surface of something on which it rests. **3** the part of the hull of a vessel under water. **4** the buttocks. **5** the lowest place in order of importance. **6** the ground under a body of water. **7** the lower part of a two-piece garment: pyjama bottoms.
• *adj* of or at the bottom.
• *vb* reach or touch the bottom: When will the recession bottom out? **bottomless** *adj* extremely deep; unlimited. **bottom-most** *adj* lowest. < Old English *botm.* SEE PANEL.

boudoir (ˈbuːdwɑː) *n* a woman's private room. < French: a room in which to pout or sulk.

bough (baʊ) *n* a large branch of a tree. < Old English *bōg.*

bought (bɔːt) SEE **BUY.**

boulder (ˈbəʊldə) *n* a large stone or rock, esp. one worn smooth by weather and water. < Scandinavian.

boulevard (ˈbuːləvɑːd, ˈbuːlvɑːd) *n* a wide road, often lined with trees. < modified from Middle Dutch *bolwerc* bulwark.

bounce (baʊns) *vb* **1** spring back after striking a surface; cause to do this. **2** move in a lively, noisy manner. **3** (*informal*) (of a worthless cheque) be returned by a bank,
• *n* **1** bouncing; leap. **2** vitality. **bouncer** *n* a man employed at a public place to restrain or expel troublesome people. **bouncing** *adj* healthy and strong. **bouncy** *adj* **1** lively. **2** bouncing well: a bouncy ball. < probably like the sound.

bound^1 (baʊnd) SEE **BIND.**
• *adj* **1** certain or sure: It's bound to happen one day. **2** obstructed or confined by: fog-bound. **3** under an obligation: I'm bound to inform you of your rights. **bound up** closely involved or linked (with).

bound^2 *vb* move forward with jumping movements.
• *n* bounding movements. **by leaps and bounds** very rapidly. < ultimately Latin *bombus* booming sound.

bound^3 *vb* limit, have or form a boundary of: The district is bounded by three lakes.
• *n* usually **bounds** a limit: out of bounds. **boundless** *adj* without limits. < ultimately Medieval Latin *bodina.*

bound^4 *adj* going or heading towards: bound for Calais; homeward-bound. < ultimately Old Norse *būa* to live, prepare.

boundary (ˈbaʊndərɪ) *n* **1** a line that marks a division, as between counties, parishes, etc. **2** the marked limit of a cricket field.

bounty (ˈbaʊntɪ) *n* **1** generosity. **2** a generous gift. **3** a payment or reward offered as an inducement. **bountiful** *adj* generous; abundant. < ultimately Latin *bonus* good.

bouquet (bəʊˈkeɪ, ˈbəʊkeɪ, ˈbuːkeɪ) *n* **1** a bunch of flowers, esp. a large one. **2** the perfume of wine. **3** a compliment. **bouquet garni** a small bunch of herbs used for flavouring. < Old French *bosc* forest.

bourgeois (ˈbʊəʒwɑː) *adj* (*derogatory*) of the middle class; having conventional values, interests, etc. **bourgeoisie** *n* (*derogatory*) the bourgeois class. < Middie French: citizen, ultimately of Germanic origin.

bout (baʊt) *n* **1** a period or spell of activity: a drinking bout. **2** a contest or fight, as of boxing or wrestling. < Middle English *bought* bend.

boutique (buːˈtiːk) *n* a small shop selling fashionable goods. < French: shop.

bovine (ˈbəʊvaɪn) *adj* of or like oxen or cows. < Latin *bos* ox, cow.

bow^1 (baʊ) *vb* **1** lower (one's head, etc.) in respect, greeting, submission, or shame. **2** submit or yield. **3** bend downwards, as under a heavy weight.
• *n* a bending of the head or trunk in

---

the bottom line

Bottom features in a number of idiomatic expressions, including;

be at the bottom of to be the underlying cause or instigator of: His thirst for power is at the bottom of all his troubles.

bottom drawer a young woman's collection of clothes, linen, etc., stored in preparation for her marriage.

bottom line the significant conclusion, etc.; most important fact: The bottom line is that his job is more important to him than his wife and children. The phrase comes from financial statements: the bottom line gives a summary of a company's profit or loss.

from the bottom of one's heart with deep, genuine feeling: I want to say thank you from the bottom of my heart for all the help you've given me over the years.

get to the bottom of to find the cause of: Police are still trying to get to the bottom of the mystery.

---

respect, greeting, etc. < Old English *būgan*.

bow² (bəʊ) *n* **1** a strip of wood or other flexible material bent by a tight string between its ends, used to shoot an arrow. **2** a knot of ribbon, etc., made with loops. **3** a rod with horse-hair stretched between its ends, used to play a violin, etc. **bow-legged** *adj* having bandy legs. **bow-tie** *n* a man's short necktie tied in a bow. **bow-window** *n* a curved bay window. < Old English *boga*.

bow³ (baʊ) *n* the forward part of a boat or ship. < origin uncertain.

bowdlerize (ˈbaʊdləˌraɪz) *vb* remove passages considered vulgar from (a book, etc.). SEE PANEL.

bowel (ˈbaʊəl) *n* the intestine. **bowels** *pl n* **1** the intestines. **2** the innermost parts: the bowels of the earth. < ultimately Latin *botulus* sausage.

bower (ˈbaʊə) *n* (*literary*) a leafy shelter. < Old English *būr* dwelling.

bowl¹ (bəʊl) *n* **1** a round, hollow vessel for holding a liquid or food. **2** this with its contents; amount it contains. **3** the hollow of a spoon, tobacco pipe, etc. **4** something shaped like a bowl such as the receptacle of a toilet. < Old English *bolla*.

bowl² *n* **1** a wooden ball used in the game of bowls. **2** a ball used in tenpin bowling, etc.

bowdlerize

To bowdlerize a play or book is to expurgate it of words considered by its expurgator to be vulgar. The word owes its origin to Thomas *Bowdler*, 1754–1825, a medical doctor who in his retirement published in 1818 a ten-volume edition of Shakespeare. Prompted by the prudery of the age, Bowdler omitted from the volumes all the words which, in his own words, 'could not with propriety be read aloud in a family'. The family edition of Shakespeare was followed in 1825 by a similarly cleaned-up version of Gibbon's 'Decline and Fall of the Roman Empire'. Even in his own day, however, much of Bowdler's censorship was regarded as excessive and the word bowdlerize soon acquired the pejorative sense that it has today.

• *vb* **1** roll smoothly. **2** travel fast and smoothly: bowling along the motorway. **3** play the game of bowling or bowls. **4** (*cricket*) deliver (a ball) to a batsman; dismiss (a batsman) by knocking down the wicket with a delivery. **bowling** *n* any of various games in which balls are rolled at a number of objects, such as tenpin bowling or skittles. **bowling-alley** *n* a long, narrow enclosure for bowling. **bowling-green** *n* a smooth, close-cut lawn for playing bowls. **bowl over 1** knock down. **2** overwhelm with surprise or other strong feeling. **bowls** *pl n* a game in which biased bowls are rolled towards a target bowl. < ultimately Latin *bulla* bubble.

bowler¹ (ˈbəʊlə) *n* **1** a person who bowls in cricket. **2** a person who plays at bowls.

bowler² *n* also **bowler hat** a man's round, hard hat, usually black. < J. *Bowler*, 19th-century London hatter.

box¹ (bɒks) *n* **1** a rigid container with a flat base and usually a lid. **2** the contents of a box. **3** any of various box-like containers for a particular purpose: money-box; pillar-box. **4** a compartment with seats for a group of people, esp. in a theatre. **5** a protective housing for machinery. **6** a rectangular or square area marked with lines. **7** a building, esp. a simple enclosure, for a particular purpose: signal-box; sentry-box; phone-box. **8 the box** (*informal*) television. **9** a gift given to tradespeople: a Christmas box. • *vb* **1** put in a box. **2** supply with a box. **box-junction** *n* an intersection with yellow lines painted on the road surface to warn drivers not to enter the area until their exit is clear. **box-kite** *n* a kite with an open, box-like frame. **box number** a number given to newspaper advertisements to which replies may be sent. **box-office** *n* an office in a theatre, etc., where tickets may be bought. **box-room** *n* a small, storage room. < ultimately Greek *pyxos*.

box² *vb* fight with fists; engage in boxing. • *n* a punch with the fist: a box on the ear. **boxer** *n* **1** a person who boxes. **2** a medium-sized, smooth-haired breed of dog. **boxing** *n* the sport of fighting with the fists. **boxing-glove** *n* one of a pair of thickly padded, leather mittens worn in boxing. < Middle English.

box³ *n* a small, evergreen tree, esp. grown as hedges. < ultimately Greek *pyxos*.

Boxing Day the first weekday after Christmas Day.

boy (bɔɪ) *n* **1** a male child. **2** a young man. **3** (*informal*) a fellow; friend.

• *interj* an exclamation of surprise, excitement, etc. **boyhood** *n* **boyish** *adj* **boyfriend** *n* a male friend, esp. a girl or woman's regular companion. < Middle English.

boycott (ˈbɔɪkɒt) *vb* refuse to deal with (a person, organization, etc.) or buy (certain goods), esp. as a protest.
• *n* an instance of boycotting. SEE PANEL.

BR *abbrev* British Rail.

bra (brɑː) *n* a woman's undergarment for supporting the breasts; brassière. < short for *brassière,* from Old French *braciere* arm-protector, ultimately Latin *bracchium* arm.

brace (breɪs) *n* **1** a crank-shaped tool: a wheel-brace; brace and bit. **2** a device that clasps or clamps. **3** a piece of wood, metal, etc., that gives extra support. **4** a fitting worn to correct the position of irregular teeth. **5** a pair: a brace of pheasants. **6** *pl* straps worn over the shoulders to hold the trousers up.
• *vb* **1** support or fit with a brace. **2** prepare (oneself) for a shock, impact, etc. < ultimately Latin *bracchium* arm.

bracelet (ˈbreɪslɪt) *n* an ornamental band worn round the wrist. < SEE **BRACE.**

bracing (ˈbreɪsɪŋ) *adj* refreshing; invigorating: a bracing walk along the beach.

bracken (ˈbrækən) *n* a large, coarse fern that grows on moorland; dense mass of such ferns. < Middle English *braken.*

bracket (ˈbrækɪt) *n* **1** a support projecting from an upright surface. **2** either of a pair of marks ( ) or [ ] used to enclose a separate section of writing or printing. **3** a category that falls within certain limits: the highest tax bracket.
• *vb* **1** put in or as if in brackets. **2** provide or fit with brackets. **3** put in the same category; link: Their names are usually bracketed together. < Latin *braca* breeches, of Germanic origin.

brackish (ˈbrækɪʃ) *adj* (of water) slightly salty. < Dutch *brac* salty.

bradawl (ˈbrædɔːl) *n* an awl. < *brad:* from Old Norse *broddr* spike + *awl.*

brag (bræg) *vb* **bragged; bragging** boast. **braggart** *n* a person who brags. < origin uncertain.

braid (breɪd) *n* **1** decorative ribbon used as a trimming. **2** a plait of hair.
• *vb* **1** decorate with braid. **2** plait. < Old English *bregdan* to weave together.

Braille (breɪl) *n* a system of writing and printing for the blind, in which characters are represented by raised

---

boycott

The original meaning of this word was 'to ostracize' or 'socially isolate'. It dates from the 1880s and the troubles between landlords and tenant-farmers in Ireland. In order to protect the latter the Irish Land League was formed in 1879. Under the presidency of Charles Stewart Parnell, 1846–91, it was decided that anyone judged to be a 'land-grabber'—a person who took over a farm following the eviction of its tenant—should be shown how much his action was detested by 'isolating him from his kind as if he were a leper of old'.

This manner of dealing with oppressors of the tenant-farmer found a name when a certain Charles Cunningham *Boycott,* a land agent for Lord Erne and a farmer in his own right, came under fire from the Land League. Boycott made himself unpopular by refusing to grant rent reductions to a number of Lord Erne's tenants and as a consequence was systematically ostracized to the extent that he finally fled the country.

Braille

Braille is the name of a writing system for the blind in which letters are represented by arrangements of raised dots that can be interpreted by touch. The word comes from the name of its inventor, Louis *Braille,* 1809-52, for most of his life a teacher at the Institute for the Blind in Paris. He himself was left blind at the age of three after an accident with an awl.

Braille's invention was a progression of the work of an army captain called Charles Barbier. Barbier had developed a primitive type of Braille based on dots and dashes, which allowed messages to be written and read by touch in the dark. Braille seized upon the principle behind Barbier's work and proceeded to design a system that would allow longer messages to be read with greater efficiency.

dots. < Louis *Braille,* died 1852, French teacher of the blind. SEE PANEL.

brain (breɪn) *n* **1** the mass of nervous tissue in the skull that is the organ of the mind, directing and co-ordinating many bodily functions. **2** the mind or intellect; intelligence: She has a good brain. **3** a very intelligent person; chief planner: the brains behind the plan.
• *vb* **1** hit on the head. **2** knock out the brains of. **brain-child** *n* an idea or invention. **brain drain** the emigration of professionals or intellectuals to countries that offer better job opportunities. **brainless** *adj* stupid. **brainstorming** *n* intensive discussion by members of a group in order to solve a problem. **brainwash** *vb* systematically indoctrinate (a person) with new beliefs, esp. by subjecting him or her to intense mental pressure. **brainwave** *n* a sudden, good idea. **brainy** *adj* intelligent; clever. **on the brain** (*informal*) constantly in one's mind. < Old English *brǣgen.*

braise (breɪz) *vb* cook slowly with a little liquid in a closed container. < Old French *brese* live coals.

brake (breɪk) *n* **1** a device for slowing down or stopping something; pedal, etc., operating this. **2** something that slows down or stops a movement.
• *vb* **1** slow or stop by a brake. **2** operate or apply a brake. < probably Middle English: bridle, curb.

bramble (ˈbræmbḷ) *n* a prickly, scrambling shrub; blackberry. < Old English *brēmel.*

bran (bræn) *n* the husks of cereal grain sifted from the flour. < Old French.

branch (brɑːntʃ) *n* **1** a limb of a tree or shrub. **2** a subdivision of something such as a river or railway: a branch line. **3** a subdivision of a whole; local shop, etc., as part of a large organization: Speak to the manager of your local branch.
• *vb* send out branches. **branch out** expand by extending one's activities. < ultimately Latin *branca* paw.

brand (brænd) *n* **1** a trademark; particular make of goods. **2** an identifying mark made with a hot iron, esp. on cattle.
• *vb* **1** mark with a hot iron. **2** give (someone) a bad reputation: He was branded a coward. **brand new** absolutely new. < Middle English: torch, sword. SEE PANEL.

brandish (ˈbrændɪʃ) *vb* wave (something) in display or as a threat.

brandy (ˈbrændɪ) *n* a strong alcoholic drink made from distilled wine. **brandysnap** *n* a thin, crisp, rolled biscuit. < Dutch *brandewijn* burnt wine.

brash (bræʃ) *adj* **1** tastelessly loud or showy. **2** reckless. **brashly** *adv* **brashness** *n* < origin unknown.

brass (brɑːs) *n* **1** an alloy of copper and zinc. **2** musical wind instruments made of brass: brass band. **3** (*slang*) officials of high rank: top brass.
• *adj* made of brass; brass-coloured. **brassy** *adj* showy. **get down to brass tacks** start to consider practical details. < Old English *bræs.*

brassière (ˈbræzɪə) *n* (*formal*) a bra.

brat (bræt) *n* (*derogatory*) a child. < perhaps English dialect *brat* ragamuffin.

bravado (brəˈvɑːdəʊ) *n* a display of showy self-confidence. < Spanish, from Old Italian *bravare* to challenge.

brave (breɪv) *adj* showing courage.
• *vb* face courageously; defy: brave the storm. **bravely** *adv* **bravery** *n* < Italian *bravo* wild. SEE PANEL.

brand new

Nowadays, almost any new item which has never been used may be referred to as brand new. Originally, however, the phrase applied only to those metal objects which had just left the *brand* or 'fire' of the forge. In modern German, where Brand continues to mean 'fire', the same phrase is used (brandneu) but there is also the cognate expression nagelneu, 'nail new' or 'as new as a nail'.

brave new world

Brave new world has become a catch-phrase denoting a future era brought about by great, dehumanizing changes in society. The expression was coined originally by Shakespeare, in 'The Tempest', Act 5, Scene 1:

How many goodly creatures are there here!
How beauteous mankind is!
O brave new world,
That has such people in't.

The contemporary, usually derogatory, application of the expression derives from the title of the novel 'Brave New World' by the English novelist Aldous Huxley (1894–1964), published in 1932.

bravo (brɑːˈvəʊ) *interj* well done!

brawl (brɔːl) *n* a noisy fight.
• *vb* fight or quarrel loudly. < Middle English *brawlen.*

brawn (brɔːn) *n* **1** physical strength, esp. muscular. **2** a jellied loaf made from the head of a pig or calf. **brawny** *adj* muscular. < Middle French *braon* muscle.

bray (breɪ) *n* a donkey's cry; similar sound.
• *vb* make this sound. < Old French *braire.*

brazen (ˈbreɪzn̩) *adj* shameless.
• *vb* face shamelessly: brazen it out. < Old English *bræs* brass.

brazier (ˈbreɪzɪə) *n* a metal stand for burning coal, used for cooking or heating. < French *brasier.*

breach (briːtʃ) *n* **1** a gap. **2** the breaking of a rule or arrangement: a breach of the peace; in breach of contract.
• *vb* make an opening in. < Old High German *brechan* to break.

bread (brɛd) *n* **1** a food made from flour and water, raised with yeast then baked. **2** (*slang*) money. **bread-winner** *n* the person who supports a family with his or her earnings. **on the breadline** in poverty. < Old English *brēad.*

break (breɪk) *vb* **broke; broken; breaking 1** fall into pieces; make this happen. **2** make or become useless by damaging. **3** stop for a while: They broke for lunch. **4** transgress: break the law. **5** surpass: break a record. **6** overwhelm the spirit of: a broken man. **7** reduce the force of: break someone's fall. **8** make known: break the news. **9** come into being: The storm broke. **10** (of weather) change suddenly, esp. after a period of hot weather. **11** (of a voice) change sharply from one register to another: His voice broke at the age of 13. **12** (of waves) curl and disintegrate into foam. **13** (*cricket*) knock down a bail from (a wicket).
• *n* **1** a fracture. **2** a gap. **3** an interval of time; rest: have a break. **4** the action of breaking out: a jailbreak. **5** (*informal*) a piece of luck; good opportunity.
breakage *n* the result of breaking.
breakneck *adj* dangerously fast: at breakneck speed. < Old English *brecan.* SEE PANEL.

breaker (ˈbreɪkə) *n* a large wave that breaks on the sea-shore.

breakfast (ˈbrɛkfəst) *vb, n* (eat) the first meal of the day. < *break* + *fast:* SEE FAST[2].

breakwater (ˈbreɪkˌwɔːtə) *n* a sea-wall built to protect the coast against waves.

bream (briːm) *n* a type of freshwater fish, related to the carp. < Middle English *breme.*

breast (brɛst) *n* **1** one of two milk-producing organs on a woman's body: breast-fed. **2** the front of the body between

---

breaking away

Break features in a number of idiomatic expressions, including:

break away to end an association.
breakaway *adj, n* (a political group) that has broken away.
break down 1 to develop a mechanical or electrical fault and stop working. **2** to fail to make progress: Talks between the union and management broke down last night. **3** to separate into different parts, etc.; analyse. **4** to suppress or overcome (opposition, suspicion, etc.). **5** to be overwhelmed by intense feeling.
breakdown *n* **1** a failure to work; result of a mechanical or electrical fault. **2** a failure to make progress. **3** a physical, nervous, or mental collapse: suffer a nervous breakdown. **4** an analysis: a breakdown of the statistics.
break even to make neither a profit nor loss.
break in 1 to force one's way into a building, etc., especially criminally. **break-in** *n* **2** also **break in on** to interrupt. **3** to accustom (someone) to a new job, etc.
break off 1 to bring to an end, often unexpectedly: She broke off the engagement. **2** to stop speaking. **3** to stop work.
break out 1 to start suddenly: Fire broke out on the first floor and quickly spread throughout the whole building. **2** to escape: Two prisoners broke out of the local prison last night. **3** to become covered with a rash, etc.: to break out in little red spots.
break the ice to overcome social awkwardness.
breakthrough *n* a significant advance in knowledge, technology, etc.
break up 1 to bring or come to an end.
breakup *n* **2** to separate or end a relationship. **3** to reach the end of a school term and begin the holidays.
break with to end one's relationship or friendship with.

the neck and the stomach. **breastbone** *n* the vertical bone connected to the ribs. **breast-feed** *vb* **breast-fed; breast-feeding** feed (a baby) milk from the breast; suckle. **breast-stroke** *n* a swimming style in which the arms are thrust forwards and the legs backwards and outwards. **make a clean breast of** confess. < Old English *brēost.*

breath (brεθ) *n* **1** air circulated through the lungs. **2** a single intake of air: take a deep breath. **3** a suggestion: a breath of scandal. **breathless** *adj* out of breath. **breathtaking** *adj* very exciting: a breathtaking view. **breathy** *adj* with a breathing sound. **out of breath** panting after exertion. < Old English *brǣth.*

breathalyse (ˈbrεθəˌlaɪz) *vb* measure the amount of alcohol in the breath of (someone). **Breathalyser** *n* (*Trademark*) a device used by police to do this.

breathe (bri:ð) *vb* **1** take in and expel (air) from the lungs. **2** utter: Don't breathe a sound! **breather** *n* **1** a short rest. **2** exercise in the fresh air: I'm going out for a breather. **breathing-space** *n* a short time for rest. SEE PANEL.

bred (brεd) SEE **BREED.**

breech (bri:tʃ) *n* the part of a gun behind the barrel. **breech birth** a birth where the baby appears bottom first. **breeches** *pl n* trousers which reach just below the knee. < Old English *brēc* leg coverings.

breed (bri:d) *vb* **bred; breeding 1** give birth to. **2** keep (animals) for producing young. **3** cause to happen: Unemployment may breed trouble in our inner cities.
• *n* **1** one type of animal within a species. **2** a kind (of something). **breeder** *n* a person who keeps animals for breeding. < Old English *brēdan.*

breeding (ˈbri:dɪŋ) *n* **1** the reproduction of animals. **2** good behaviour as a result of upbringing.

breeze (bri:z) *n* a gentle wind.
• *vb* (*informal*) move in a lively way: He breezed in. **breezy** *adj* **breezily** *adv* < Middle French *brise* north-east wind.

breeze-blocks (ˈbri:zˌblɒks) *pl n* light bricks made from ash, etc., and used in building.

brethren (ˈbrεðrən) *pl n* (*chiefly archaic*) brothers.

breve (bri:v) *n* the longest note in music. < SEE **BRIEF.**

brevity (ˈbrεvɪtɪ) *n* shortness. < Latin *brevitas.*

brew (bru:) *vb* **1** make (beer) by boiling and fermentation. **2** prepare (tea) by infusion. **3** develop: There's trouble brewing.
• *n* a liquid which is brewed. **brewer** *n* someone who brews beer professionally. **brewery** *n* < Old English *brēowan.*

bribe (braɪb) *n* a reward offered to persuade someone to act in a way beneficial to the giver.
• *vb* persuade by a bribe. **bribery** *n* < Middle French: bread given to a beggar.

bric-à-brac (ˈbrɪkəˌbræk) *n* an assortment of ornaments, furniture, etc., of small value. < French.

brick (brɪk) *n* a rectangular building-block usually made of clay.
• *adj* made of brick. **bricklayer** *n* a workman skilled in building with bricks. **brickwork** *n* a brick structure. **drop a brick** (*informal*) speak tactlessly. < Middle Dutch *bricke.*

bride (braɪd) *n* a woman at her wedding or just married. **bridal** *adj* < Old English *brȳd.*

bridegroom (ˈbraɪdˌgru:m) *n* a man at his wedding or just married. < Old English *brȳd guma* man.

bridesmaid (ˈbraɪdzˌmeɪd) *n* a young, unmarried woman attending a bride at her wedding.

bridge[1] (brɪdʒ) *n* **1** a construction allowing a passage over a road, railway, river, etc. **2** the control room of a ship. **3** the top of the nose. **4** something connecting two items.
• *vb* link two things: bridge the gap. < Old English *brycg.*

bridge[2] *n* a card-game based on whist. < origin uncertain.

---

breathing normally

Breathe, dream, sleep, and die are examples of verbs which are essentially intransitive (He's breathing normally again—I've been dreaming—He's still sleeping—She died last night). There is, however, one pattern in which such verbs are used transitively: when they are followed by what is called a *cognate object,* a noun that is closely related to the verb in sense and which may even come from the same root. Common examples include:

She's *breathed* her last *breath.*
He *died* a slow *death.*
I *dreamt* the strangest *dream* last night.
She's *sleeping* the *sleep* of the just.
Fight the good *fight.*

---

bridle (ˈbraɪdl̩) *n* the headgear of the harness on a horse.
• *vb* **1** put a bridle on (a horse). **2** keep control of (anger, etc.). **3** show resentment. **bridle-path** *n* a path for the use of horse-riders. < Old English *brīdel.*

brief (bri:f) *adj* short in duration or length. **briefly** *adv* **briefness** *n* **in brief** in a few words.
• *n* **1** a set of advance instructions. **2** a summary of a court case prepared for a barrister.
• *vb* instruct in advance. < Latin *brevis.*

briefcase (ˈbri:fˌkeɪs) *n* a thin case for official papers, books, etc.

briefs (bri:fs) *pl n* short knickers worn by men or women.

brier (ˈbraɪə) *n* **1** a type of prickly bush. **2** a bush with a strong, woody root; tobacco pipe made of this. < ultimately Latin *brucus* heather.

brigade (brɪˈgeɪd) *n* **1** an army unit. **2** an organized group of people: boy's brigade. **brigadier** *n* an army officer ranking above a colonel and below a major-general. < French, from Italian *brigata.*

bright (braɪt) *adj* **1** giving out much light. **2** clever. **3** in good spirits. **brightly** *adv* **brightness** *n* **brighten** *vb* make or become brighter. < Old English *beorht.*

brilliant (ˈbrɪljənt) *adj* **1** shining brightly. **2** extremely intelligent.
• *n* a finely-cut diamond. **brilliance** *n* **brilliantly** *adv* < Italian *brillare* to shine.

brim (brɪm) *n* **1** the upper edge of a vessel or hollow. **2** the edge of a hat which projects.
• *vb* **brimmed; brimming** make or become full to the top. **brim over** overflow. < Middle English *brimme.*

brine (braɪn) *n* salt water. < Old English *brȳne.*

bring (brɪŋ) *vb* **brought; bringing** **1** carry (something) to someone or somewhere. **2** cause to happen or arrive at a particular state. **3** initiate (a legal process): bring charges. **bring-and-buy sale** an informal sale where people bring things to sell and buy things which others bring. **bring home** to convince. **bring oneself to** (**do something**) act with reluctance. **bring to light** uncover. **bring to mind** cause to remember. **bring up the rear** come last in a group. < Old English *bringan.* SEE PANEL.

brink (brɪŋk) *n* **1** the edge of something steep. **2** the verge of an event: on the brink of a major discovery. < Middle English.

Always bring something!

Sentences such as She brought or They use are ungrammatical. The reason for this is that the verbs bring and use are *transitive,* meaning that they must be followed by an object (She brought *her friend* to the party and They use *computers*). Verbs which do not require an object such as sleep and arrive are *intransitive.* She slept and The taxi has arrived contain no objects but are grammatical because the action expressed by each verb is confined to the subject alone. The word transitive comes ultimately from the Latin verb *transire* 'to go across'.

A test for transitivity is to try to make the active sentence in which the verb occurs passive (see panel at **passive**). If the verb is transitive its object can usually be brought to the front of the sentence, as in *Her friend* was brought to the party and *Computers* are used.

The word bring itself features in a number of idiomatic expressions, including:

bring about to cause to happen; produce.
bring back to restore (a law, etc.): bring back capital punishment.
bring down to cause the defeat or fall of: to bring down the government.
bring forward **1** to arrange for (a meeting, etc.) to happen in advance of an intended time. **2** to raise (a matter) for attention or discussion. **3** to transfer from one page, account, etc., to the top of the next page, etc.
bring in **1** to introduce: bring in reforms. **2** to yield: bring in £1000 profit.
bring off to achieve successfully: The deal will be very profitable if he can bring it off.
bring on to cause; cause to develop: The cold weather brought on his fever.
bring out **1** to show or express clearly. **2** to publish; release. **3** to cause to go on strike. **4** to cause to become less shy.
bring round to cause to regain consciousness.
bring through to lead safely through a crisis, etc.
bring up **1** to care for and educate (a child). **2** to raise (a topic) for discussion. **3** to vomit.

brinkmanship (ˈbrɪŋkmənˌʃɪp) *n* the art of following a dangerous course of action to the last possible moment before stopping, esp. in politics.

briny (ˈbraɪnɪ) *adj* of or like brine.
• *n* the sea. SEE PANEL.

brisk (brɪsk) *adj* quick-moving: a brisk walk. **briskly** *adv* **briskness** *n* < probably Middle French *brusque*.

brisket (ˈbrɪskɪt) *n* the meat cut from the breast of a cow. < Middle English *brusket*.

bristle (ˈbrɪsl̩) *n* a short, stiff hair used in a brush; something like this.
• *vb* **1** (of an animal) stiffen the hair in fear or anger. **2** be indignant. **bristly** *adj* < Old English *byrst*.

brittle (ˈbrɪtl̩) *adj* **1** easily broken. **2** irritable: a brittle mood. < Middle English *britil*.

broach (brəʊtʃ) *vb* **1** make a hole in (a vessel) and extract liquid. **2** open a discussion on: He broached the subject. < Latin *broccus* projecting.

broad (brɔːd) *adj* **1** wide or spacious. **2** strongly obvious: a broad northern accent. **3** full and clear: in broad daylight. **4** general: a broad outline. **broadly** *adv* **broadness** *n* **broaden** *vb* make or become broader. **broad-minded** *adj* tolerant in opinions. < Old English *brād*.

broadcast (ˈbrɔːdˌkɑːst) *vb* **broadcast; broadcasting** send out by radio or television.
• *n* a broadcast programme. **broadcaster** *n*

broadside (ˈbrɔːdˌsaɪd) *n* **1** the simultaneous firing of guns on one side of a warship. **2** a strong attack in words or in writing. **broadside on** sideways on.

over the briny

There is a tendency in colloquial usage to drop a noun when the preceding adjective makes it so predictable as to be unnecessary. An example is over the *briny* (*sea*). By this process an adjective becomes a surrogate noun. Nouns like briny which over the years have been formed in this way include:

landing 'I met her on the *landing* (*place*) as I was going upstairs.'
kindling 'We've run out of *kindling* (*wood*).
peregrine 'A *peregrine* (*falcon*) was flying overhead.'

brocade (brəʊˈkeɪd) *n* a fabric with a raised design woven into it. < Latin *broccus* projecting.

broccoli (ˈbrɒkəlɪ) *n* a hardy, green vegetable related to the cauliflower. < Italian *brocco* sprout.

brochure (ˈbrəʊʃə) *n* a pamphlet containing a summary of information or advertising. < Old French *brochier* to prick.

brogue (brəʊg) *n* **1** a regional accent of English, esp. spoken in Ireland. **2** a strong shoe with perforations on the uppers. < Old Norse *brōk* leg covering.

broil (brɔɪl) *vb* cook (meat) over a fire. < Middle French *bruler* to burn.

broiler (ˈbrɔɪlə) *n* a young chicken suitable for roasting.

broke (brəʊk) SEE **BREAK.**
• *adj* (*slang*) having no money.

broken (ˈbrəʊkən) SEE **BREAK.**
• *adj* **1** violently separated into pieces. **2** fractured: a broken leg. **broken English** English spoken inaccurately (by foreigners). **broken-hearted** *adj* overcome with grief. **broken home** a family in which the parents are divorced or separated.

broker (ˈbrəʊkə) *n* an agent who acts on someone's behalf, esp. in business deals, for commission. **brokerage** *n* a broker's fee. < Anglo-French *brocour*.

brolly (ˈbrɒlɪ) *n* (*informal*) an umbrella.

bronchial (ˈbrɒŋkɪəl) *adj* of the bronchi, or tubes branching from the lungs. < Greek *bronchos* windpipe.

bronchitis (brɒŋˈkaɪtɪs) *n* an inflammation of the bronchial tubes causing coughing and catarrh.

brontosaurus (ˌbrɒntəˈsɔːrəs) *n* a large, plant-eating dinosaur with a long neck and tail. < Greek *brontē* thunder + *sauros* lizard.

bronze (brɒnz) *n* a brown-coloured alloy of copper and tin.
• *adj* made of bronze; bronze-coloured.
• *vb* make or become sun-tanned. **bronze medal** a medal (of bronze) awarded to someone who comes third in a competition or race. < Italian *bronzo*.

brooch (brəʊtʃ) *n* an ornament fastened with a pin, worn on clothing. < Middle English *broche* pointed tool.

brood (bruːd) *n* **1** young animals, esp. birds, born of the same parent at the same time. **2** (*humorous*) the children of one family.
• *vb* **1** (of a bird) hatch eggs by sitting on them: a brooding hen. **2** think for a long time and gloomily. **broody** *adj* **1** wanting to give birth. **2** moody. < Old

English *brōd.*

brook (brʊk) *n* a small, freshwater stream. < Old English *brōc.*

broom (bruːm, brʊm) *n* **1** a brush with a long handle, used for sweeping. **2** a shrub with long, thin branches and yellow flowers. **a new broom** a newly appointed official keen to make major changes. **broomstick** *n* the handle of a broom. < Old English *brōm.*

Bros *abbrev* brothers, used esp. in the name of a company.

broth (brɒθ) *n* a soup made from water in which meat, fish, or vegetables have been boiled. < Old English.

brothel (ˈbrɒθəl) *n* a house where men pay for sexual intercourse with prostitutes. < Middle English: worthless person.

brother (ˈbrʌðə) *n* **1** a son of the same parents as another person. **2** a male fellow member of a group or sect. **3** a male member of a religious order who is not a priest. **brotherly** *adj* **brotherhood** *n* **1** the relationship between brothers. **2** a society of men doing religious or charitable work. **brother-in-law** *n, pl* **brothers-in-law** the brother of one's husband or wife; husband of one's sister. < Old English *brōthor.* SEE PANEL.

brought (brɔːt) SEE **BRING.**

brow (braʊ) *n* **1** an eyebrow. **2** the forehead. **3** a part (of something) which overhangs: the brow of a hill. **browbeat** *vb* **browbeat; browbeaten; browbeating** bully or intimidate. < Old English *brū.*

brown (braʊn) adj **1** of a dark colour between orange and black. **2** having skin of this colour.
• *n* **1** brown colour. **2** a brown material or substance; brown clothes.
• *vb* make or become brown. **brown bread** bread of this colour, esp. made with wheatmeal or wholemeal flour. **browned off** (*slang*) annoyed. **brown sugar** partly refined sugar. < Old English *brūn.*

browse (braʊz) *vb* **1** look through books, etc., in a casual way. **2** (of animals) feed on leaves, grass, etc., by nibbling. < Old French *brost.*

bruise (bruːz) *n* a bodily injury which discolours but does not break the skin.
• *vb* **1** cause a bruise or bruises on. **2** hurt the feelings of: a bruised ego. < Middle French *bruisier* to break.

brunette (bruːˈnɛt) *n* a woman with dark hair and complexion. < ultimately Latin *brunus* brown.

brunt (brʌnt) *n* the main stress or force: bear the brunt of the attack. < Middle English.

brush (brʌʃ) *n* **1** a device used for cleaning or sweeping, made of filaments of hair, wire, etc., set in a solid base. **2** an electrical contact between static and moving parts. **3** a brief encounter: a brush with the law. **4** the act of brushing: The rug needs a good brush.
• *vb* **1** apply a brush to; remove (something) from a surface by brushing. **2** touch gently in passing. **brush aside** dismiss casually. **brush off** reject in an offhand way. **brush up 1** tidy one's appearance: wash and brush up. **2** refresh one's knowledge of: She brushed up her French. < Old French *broce.*

brusque (bruːsk) *adj* offhand to the point of rudeness. **brusquely** *adv* **brusqueness** *n* < Medieval Latin *bruscus* butcher's broom.

Brussels sprout (ˌbrʌsl̩z ˈspraʊt) *n* a type of wild cabbage grown for its large, green, edible buds.

brutal (ˈbruːtl̩) *adj* mercilessly cruel. **brutality** *n* **brutally** *adv* **brutalize** *vb* make brutal. < Latin *brutus* stupid, heavy.

brute (bruːt) *n* **1** a beast. **2** a cruel person. **3** (*informal*) an unpleasant person. **brutish** *adj* **brute force** unthinking, physical power: They persuaded him to give in by sheer brute force.

B.Sc. *abbrev* Bachelor of Science.

BST *abbrev* British Summer Time.

bubble (ˈbʌbl̩) *n* **1** a thin, liquid ball containing gas. **2** a dome, esp. of glass or plastic.
• *vb* **1** make bubbles; make the sound of these. **2** be lively or excited: bubbling over with happiness. **bubble-and-squeak** *n* a hot dish of mixed cabbage and potato. **bubble gum** chewing gum which can be blown into bubbles. **bubbly** *adj* **1** full of

big brother

Big brother is the title of the all-powerful head of state in the novel '1984' by the English novelist and essayist George Orwell (1903–50), published in 1949.

The phrase has passed into the language to refer to a ruthless and dictatorial person, organization, or state. It occurs most commonly in the expression Big brother is watching you. This expression is quoted sardonically for example when people think that officialdom's modern computer technology is encroaching on their private lives.

bubbles. **2** lively. < Middle English *bublen,* probably like the sound.

buccaneer (ˌbʌkəˈnɪə) *n* a pirate; adventurer without scruples, esp. in politics or business. < French *boucaner* to smoke meat over a fire.

buck[1] (bʌk) *n* a male deer, rabbit, etc. • *vb* **1** (of a horse) jump with the legs stiff and the back bent. **2** oppose: buck the system. **buck rarebit** melted cheese on toast topped with a poached egg. **buck up** (*slang*) **1** hurry. **2** make or become more cheerful. < Old English *bucca* stag.

buck[2] *n* an object used to mark the next dealer in a game of poker. **pass the buck** (*slang*) shift the blame or responsibility onto someone else. < short for *buckhorn knife.* SEE PANEL.

buck[3] *n* (*US slang*) a dollar. < origin uncertain.

bucked (bʌkt) *adj* encouraged.

bucket (ˈbʌkɪt) *n* a round, open-topped container with a handle, used mostly for carrying liquids; this and its contents. • *vb* (*informal*) rain heavily: It's bucketing down. **bucketful** *n* **bucket seat** a round-backed seat for one person, esp. in cars or aircraft. < Old English *būc* belly.

buckle (ˈbʌkḷ) *n* a device with a hinged pin, used for fastening. • *vb* **1** fasten with a buckle. **2** bend or collapse under pressure. **buckle down** to start work on something in a determined way. < ultimately Latin *bucca* cheek.

bucolic (bjuːˈkɒlɪk) *adj* characteristic of rural life. < Greek *boukolos* herdsman.

bud (bʌd) *n* **1** a small swelling on a tree, plant, etc., that will develop into a flower or leaf: in bud. **2** anything of a similar shape: taste buds. • *vb* **budded; budding** produce buds. **budding** *adj* starting to develop: a budding musician. **nip in the bud** stop (something) in the early stages. < Middle English *budde.*

Buddha (ˈbʊdə) *n* the title of the 5th-century Indian prince Gautama Siddhartha. **Buddhism** *n* the religion and philosophy based on the teachings of the Buddha and his followers. **Buddhist** *adj, n* < Sanskrit: the Awakened One.

buddleia (ˈbʌdlɪə) *n* one of a group of shrubs or trees, with lilac or yellow flowers. < Adam *Buddle,* died 1715, British botanist, SEE PANEL AT **DAHLIA.**

buddy (ˈbʌdɪ) *n* (*chiefly US informal*) a friend. < probably baby language *brother.*

budge (bʌdʒ) *vb* **1** move or shift. **2** change one's or someone's opinion or position: He won't budge on the issue. < ultimately Latin *bullire* to bubble, boil.

budgerigar (ˈbʌdʒərɪˌgɑː) *n* an Australian bird of the parrot family, often kept as a cage-bird. < native Australian name.

budget (ˈbʌdʒɪt) *n* **1** a yearly financial plan for a nation, usually made by the Chancellor of the Exchequer. **2** an amount of money planned for a purpose. • *vb* plan for in a budget. < ultimately Latin *bulga* leather bag.

budgie (ˈbʌdʒɪ) *n* (*informal*) a budgerigar.

buff (bʌf) *n* a strong, supple, yellowish leather; colour of this. **2** (*informal*) an enthusiast: a jazz buff. • *adj* dull yellow. • *vb* polish. < SEE **BUFFALO.**

buffalo (ˈbʌfəˌləʊ) *n* a kind of wild ox found chiefly in North America. < ultimately Greek *boubalos* African gazelle.

buffer (ˈbʌfə) *n* **1** a device, used to reduce the effect of a shock, esp. on a railway engine. **2** a fellow: old buffer. **buffer state** a small country lying between two rival powers, which may reduce the chances of aggression between them. < *buff* to reduce the force of: SEE **BUFFET**[2].

buffet[1] (ˈbʊfeɪ) *n* **1** a counter where food and drink are served. **2** food set out (on tables, etc.), for guests to help themselves. **buffet car** a railway carriage which serves refreshments. < French.

passing the buck

To evade an unwanted task or responsibility by passing it to someone else is known informally as passing the buck. This expression derives from the game of poker and the former practice of using a *buckhorn knife* as a marker to indicate the player whose turn it was to deal. This was a typically unwanted task because the dealer was also usually responsible for putting up the initial stake.

The expression gained popularity from the sign on the desk of President Harry S. Truman—The Buck Stops Here.

buffet[2] (ˈbʌfɪt) *vb* knock against sharply. < Old French *buffe* light blow.

buffoon (bəˈfuːn) *n* someone who acts the fool; ridiculous figure. **buffoonery** *n* < Latin *bufo* toad.

bug (bʌg) *n* **1** any of a group of insects, esp. which infest dirty places: bedbugs. **2** a germ causing disease; disease caused by this. **3** a hidden listening device. **4** a defect: iron out all the bugs.
• *vb* **bugged; bugging 1** install a secret listening device in, in order to eavesdrop. **2** (*slang*) irritate: What's bugging her? < Middle English: goblin.

buggy (ˈbʌgɪ) *n* **1** a baby buggy. **2** (*archaic*) a light, horse-drawn vehicle. **beach buggy** a small, open car, used mostly at the seaside. < origin unknown.

bugle (ˈbjuːgl̩) *n* a brass musical instrument, like a trumpet but without valves, used esp. for military ceremony.
• *vb* sound a bugle. **bugler** *n* < Latin *buculus* young bullock.

build (bɪld) *vb* **built; building 1** make (a structure) by joining parts together. **2** create or establish.
• *n* physical shape: of light build. **builder** *n* someone who builds houses, etc., professionally. **building** *n* a permanent structure with a roof and walls; constructing of this. **building society** an organization in which people invest money and borrow it to buy a house. **build up 1** increase in size or number. **2** flatter with praise or publicity. **build-up** *n* < Old English *byldan*.

built (bɪlt) SEE **BUILD.**
• *adj* formed in a specific way: well-built. **built-in** *adj* forming part of a structure: built-in wardrobe. **built-up** *adj* covered with buildings: a built-up area.

bulb (bʌlb) n **1** a round base of a plant, with overlapping leaves, and producing a stem and roots; plant grown from this. **2** anything bulb-shaped: a light bulb. **bulbous** *adj* < Greek *bolbos* bulbous plant.

bulge (bʌldʒ) *n* a swelling or curve projecting from a surface.
• *vb* form a swelling. < Middle French *bouge* leather bag.

bulk (bʌlk) *n* **1** a large amount: bulk buying. **2** the larger part (of something). **3** a large body, esp. of a person.
• *vb* make or become larger. **bulky** *adj* < Old Norse *bulki* cargo.

bull[1] (bʊl) *n* **1** an adult male ox. **2** the male of large animals such as the elephant or whale. **3** (*Stock Exchange*) someone who buys shares expecting a rise in price. **bullfight** *n* the Spanish sport of baiting and killing bulls. **bullring** *n* the arena for bullfights. **bull's-eye** *n* the centre of a target. < Old English *bula*.

bull[2] *n* (*slang*) obvious nonsense: a load of bull < short for *bullshit*.

bulldog (ˈbʊlˌdɒg) *n* a strong breed of dog with a short, thick neck. **bulldog clip** a strongly-closing spring fastener.

bulldoze (ˈbʊlˌdəʊz) *vb* **1** flatten (an area of land) with a bulldozer. **2** force (someone to do something): He bulldozed them into accepting it. **bulldozer** *n* a powerful vehicle used for clearing land.
< perhaps *bull*: SEE **BULL**[1] + *dose*.

bullet (ˈbʊlɪt) n a small, round missile, used in a gun. **bullet-proof** *adj* able to keep out bullets. < French *boulette* small ball.

bulletin (ˈbʊlɪtɪn) *n* a short, official news statement. < ultimately Latin *bulla* papal edict.

bullion (ˈbʊljən) *n* gold or silver, before it is melted down for coining or manufacture. < Latin *bullire* to boil.

bullock (ˈbʊlək) *n* a castrated bull. < SEE **BULL**[1].

bully (ˈbʊlɪ) *n* someone who uses his or her strength to frighten others.
• *vb* **bullied; bullying** intimidate. **bully for you!** well done. < Middle High German *buole* lover.

bum[1] (bʌm) *n* (*slang*) the buttocks. < Middle English *bom*.

bum[2] *n* (*US slang*) an idle person; beggar. **bum around** (*slang*) spend time uselessly. < probably German *bummeln* to loaf.

bumble-bee (ˈbʌmbl̩ˌbiː) *n* a large bee with a loud hum. < Middle English *bomblen* to buzz + *bee*.

bumf (bʌmf) *n* (*derogatory*) official papers. SEE PANEL.

bump (bʌmp) *vb* **1** knock with a jolt: things that go bump in the night. **2** hurt by knocking.

wading through bumf

A number of slang and informal words have more vulgar origins than those who use them sometimes realize. This is especially true in the case of words that are mildly derogatory, such as bumf—'paperwork'—which is a shortened form of *bum fodder* or 'toilet-paper'.

• n **1** a dull sound. **2** a swelling caused by a blow. **3** a lump on a surface. **bumpy** *adj* **bump into** (*informal*) meet by chance. **bump off** (*slang*) kill. **bump up** (*informal*) increase or raise: bump up prices. < like the sound.
bumper (ˈbʌmpə) *n* a bar fixed to the front and back of a motor vehicle in order to lessen the shock of a collision.
• *adj* extraordinarily large: a bumper crop.
bumpkin (ˈbʌmpkɪn) *n* a country person with clumsy manners. < perhaps Middle Dutch *boomekijn* small barrel.
bumptious (ˈbʌmpʃəs) *adj* offensively self-important. < *bump* + frac*tious*.
bun (bʌn) *n* **1** a small, round, sweet cake: a hot cross bun. **2** hair in a bun shape at the back of the head. < Middle English *bunne*.
bunch (bʌntʃ) *n* **1** a number of things growing or fastened together: a bunch of grapes; a bunch of keys. **2** a group of people.
• *vb* come or bring together in a bunch: The runners bunched together. < Middle English *banche*.
bundle (ˈbʌndl̩) *n* **1** a number of things loosely held together. **2** (*slang*) a large amount (of money).
• *vb* **1** make into a bundle. **2** push hurriedly: They bundled him into the car. **go a bundle on** (*slang*) like a great deal. < Middle English *bundel*.
bung (bʌŋ) *n* a stopper, used to block an opening in a jar or barrel.
• *vb* **1** plug (a hole) with a bung. **2** (*slang*) toss; throw: Bung it over. **bunged up** blocked. < Middle Dutch *bonghe*.
bungalow (ˈbʌŋgəˌləʊ) *n* a one-storey house. SEE PANEL.
bungle (ˈbʌŋgl̩) *vb* spoil (a task) through clumsiness.
• *n* a mishandled attempt. **bungler** *n* < perhaps Scandinavian.
bunion (ˈbʌnjən) *n* an inflamed lump at the first joint of the big toe. < probably Middle French *bugne* swelling on the head.
bunk[1] (bʌŋk) *n* a built-in bed, in a home or on a ship. **bunk beds** two single beds placed one above the other as a unit. < probably short for *bunker*.
bunk[2] *vb* (*slang*) run away. **do a bunk** run away. < origin unknown.
bunk[3] *n* (*slang*) nonsense. < short for *bunkum*.
bunker (ˈbʌŋkə) *n* **1** a storage tank (on a ship), esp. for fuel. **2** a fortified underground shelter. **3** a sand-pit on a golf-course which constitutes a hazard. **bunkered** *adj* (of a ball) stuck in a bunker. < Scottish *bonker* chest, box.
bunkum (ˈbʌŋkəm) *n* nonsense. < *Buncombe* County, North Carolina USA. SEE PANEL.
bunny (ˈbʌnɪ) *n* (*children's informal*) a rabbit. < English dialect *bun* rabbit.
bunting (ˈbʌntɪŋ) *n* **1** decorative flags and streamers, esp. for buildings and

bungalow

Of the many languages of India that have provided English with loan-words, Hindi has been a significant source. An example is bungalow, which comes from the Hindi *banglā*, meaning '(a house) in the Bengal style'. Other words that derive from Hindi include:

bangle	**dinghy**	**puttee**
buckshee	**juggernaut**	**pyjamas**
chutney	**khaki**	**shampoo**
cushy	**loot**	**thug**
dungaree	**pundit**	

bunkum

To talk a lot of bunkum or buncombe is to talk foolish nonsense or twaddle. This highly expressive word derives from *Buncombe*, a county in North Carolina, USA. It came into being as a result of a speech made in 1820 by Buncombe's congressional representative, Felix Walker. The speech was exceedingly long and completely irrelevant to the debate which it interrupted. When asked to explain the purpose of his oration, Walker replied that the people of Buncombe expected him to make a speech in the Congress and so he had made one. His defence of its seeming irrelevance was that 'he was only talking for Buncombe'.

Following this bizarre event the word and its shortened form bunk entered the language in the narrow sense of political claptrap. However, as Walker and his speech faded from living memory, the meaning broadened.

streets. **2** a loosely-woven cotton fabric, used for making these. < perhaps English dialect *bunt* to sift.

buoy (bɔɪ) *n* a float, anchored to the sea-bed, used as a navigational aid or a hazard warning (for ships).
• *vb* **1** mark with a buoy. **2** raise the spirits of: buoyed up by hope. **buoyant** *adj* **1** capable of floating. **2** in good spirits. **buoyancy** *n* **buoyantly** *adv* SEE PANEL.

burble (ˈbɜːbl̩) *vb* **1** make a gentle bubbling sound. **2** speak at length or excitedly: He burbled on about nothing. < Middle English *burblen*, probably like the sound.

burden (ˈbɜːdn̩) *n* **1** a load; anything carried. **2** something which is difficult to bear; duty: the burden of responsibility.
• *vb* load; oppress. **beast of burden** an animal, used for carrying a load. **burden of proof** the obligation, as in law, to prove the truth of what is said. **burdensome** *adj* tedious; troublesome. < Old English *byrthen*.

bureau (ˈbjʊərəʊ) *n, pl* **bureaus 1** a writing desk, usually with drawers and a hinged top. **2** a department or office: travel bureau. < ultimately Latin *burra* shaggy cloth.

bureaucracy (bjʊəˈrɒkrəsɪ) a **1** an administrative system based on division of functions, fixed rules, and hierarchy of authority; government on these lines. **2** unnecessarily excessive official routine, esp. which hinders action. **bureaucrat** *n* an official in government or public service who abides unthinkingly by departmental rules and regulations. **bureaucratic** *adj*

burger (ˈbɜːgə) *n* a grilled meat cake in a bread roll, eaten in various combinations: hamburger, cheeseburger.

Dutch buoys

Throughout their history the Dutch have been renowned as a seafaring nation. Testimony of this is provided in the number of English nautical terms which are of Dutch descent. These include:

boom	**deck**	**smuggle**
bulwark	**dock**	**splice**
buoy	**skipper**	**yacht**
cruise	**sloop**	

burgh (ˈbʌrə) *n* a borough in Scotland. < SEE **BOROUGH.**

burglar (ˈbɜːglə) *n* someone who breaks into a house or building to steal. **burglary** *n* **burgle** *vb* steal things from (a house). < ultimately Latin *burgus* fortified place.

burgundy (ˈbɜːgəndɪ) *n* **1** a red or white table wine from Burgundy in France. **2** a dark, purplish-red colour. SEE PANEL AT **CHAMPAGNE.**

burial (ˈbɛrɪəl) *n* the act of burying; being buried: burial at sea. < Old English *byrgels*.

burlesque (bɜːˈlɛsk) *n* a satirical imitation, esp. of a literary or dramatic work; caricature. < Spanish *burla* joke.

burly (ˈbɜːlɪ) *adj* of a strong, heavy build; sturdy. **burliness** *n* < Middle English: well-built.

burn (bɜːn) *vb* **burned, burnt; burning 1** consume fuel; give off heat and light by this. **2** destroy or damage by fire, heat, chemical action, electricity, or radiation; be damaged or injured by this. **3** produce (a mark) by burning. **4** make or become red or uncomfortably hot: His ears are burning. **5** make or become brown from heat or light: sunburnt. **6** kill or be killed by burning: burnt to death. **7** be filled (with an intense emotion). **burn one's boats** or **bridges** act so as to make retreat impossible. **burn the candle at both ends** use up one's energies by being active day and night. **burn the midnight oil** study late into the night. **have money to burn** have such an amount of money that one is careless with it.
• *n* **1** injury or damage made by burning; burnt area. **2** a burning sensation: an antiseptic burn. **3** the firing of a spacecraft rocket engine. **burner** *n* a part (of a lamp or cooker) which produces a flame. **burning** *adj* **1** on fire. **2** emotionally intense: burning anger. **3** urgent: a burning question. < Old English *byrnan, bærnan*.

burnish (ˈbɜːnɪʃ) *vb* make shiny by rubbing; polish. < Middle French *brunir* to make brown.

burnt (bɜːnt) SEE **BURN.**
• *adj* deep in hue: burnt umber; burnt sienna.

burp (bɜːp) *n* (*informal*) a belch.
• *vb* **1** belch. **2** cause (a baby) to get rid of stomach wind. < like the sound.

burr (bɜː) *n* **1** a whirring noise. **2** the pronunciation of r in rural accents, esp. Somerset. **3** a small drill. **4** a rough covering on a seed or fruit. **5** a rough edge left after cutting metal, etc.
• *vb* make a whirring noise. < Middle

English *burre.*
burrow (ˈbʌrəʊ) *n* a hole or tunnel in the ground made by a fox, rabbit, etc., for shelter and dwelling-space.
• *vb* **1** dig by tunnelling; make a burrow. **2** delve deeply; investigate. < Middle English *borow.*
bursar (ˈbɜːsə) n **1** an official, on a ship or in a school, who manages funds. **2** (*Scottish*) a student holding a bursary. < Medieval Latin *bursa* grant.
bursary (ˈbɜːsərɪ) *n* a financial grant given to a student.
burst (bɜːst) *vb* **burst; bursting 1** break or cause to break open or into pieces from impact or internal pressure: a burst pipe. **2** appear suddenly. **3** express strong feelings suddenly and forcefully: burst into tears; burst out laughing; burst into song. **burst at the seams** be uncomfortably full.
• *n* **1** a split. **2** an outbreak; eruption: a burst of applause; burst of gunfire. **3** a sudden increase of effort, speed, etc.: put on a burst. **bursting** *adj* full to the point of breaking: bursting with life; bursting to tell. < Old English *berstan.*
bury (ˈbɛrɪ) *vb* **buried; burying 1** put (a corpse) in a grave, in the earth or at sea. **2** hide (something) underground; conceal: bury the past. **3** devote oneself to: She buried herself in her work. **bury the hatchet** settle an argument and be on good terms. < Old English *byrgan.*
bus (bʌs) *n* a large passenger vehicle, esp. which operates along a fixed route at certain times.

bused or **bussed?**

Do you write biassed or biased? Bused or bussed? Focussed or focused? Usage varies regarding the spelling of several verbs ending in *-s.*

The general rule is that the consonant is doubled with words of one syllable ending in *-s:* gassed, gassing, from the verb gas, and with words of more than one syllable when the final syllable is stressed: nonplussed, from the verb nonplus.

For the following words, however, both single *-s-* and double *-ss-* are commonly acceptable, though the single *-s-* spelling is gaining wider popularity:

biased or **biassed**
focused or **focussed**
bused or **bussed**

• *vb* travel or transport by bus. **bus lane** a strip of road for the exclusive use of buses. **bus station** a terminus for buses with facilities for passengers. **bus-stop** *n* one of several regular stopping-points for a bus. < short for *omnibus.*
SEE PANEL.
bush (bʊʃ) *n* **1** a shrub or group of shrubs. **2** a thick mass: a bush of hair. **3** wild, sparsely settled land, esp. in Africa and Australia. **bushy** *adj* **1** overgrown with bushes. **2** growing thickly: bushy eyebrows. < Middle English.
bushel (ˈbʊʃl̩) *n* a measure of volume (in the UK 0.036 cubic metres, USA 0.035 cubic metres). < Old French *boissel.*
business (ˈbɪznɪs) *n* **1** a particular task or function: What business do you have here? **2** one's profession or trade. **3** a commercial firm; shop: a small bakery business. **4** the agenda at a meeting; matters for consideration: get down to business. **5** financial dealings: do business with. **6** an affair; event. **7** personal concern: That's none of your business! **business-like** *adj* practical; efficient. **business man** someone engaged in commerce; someone with commercial flair. < Middle English *bisy* busy.
busker (ˈbʌskə) *n* someone who performs (music) in the street for money. < origin unknown.
bust[1] (bʌst) *n* **1** a sculpture of the head, neck, and shoulders of a human figure. **2** the breasts of a woman; their size. < ultimately Latin *bustum* tomb.
bust[2] *vb* **busted, bust; busting 1** (*informal*) break or collapse, physically or financially. **2** (*slang*) arrest or raid (by the police): He was busted for drugs.
• *n* (*slang*) an arrest or raid by the police.
• *adj* **1** (*slang*) broken: My watch is bust. **2** (*informal*) bankrupt. < alteration of *burst.*
bustle (ˈbʌsl̩) *vb* make a show of moving busily; cause to hurry: He was bustled off to school.
• a noisy, lively activity: the hustle and bustle of city life. **bustling** *adj* < probably *buskle* to prepare.
busy (ˈbɪzɪ) *adj* **1** working; fully occupied. **2** with much activity: a busy morning. **3** (of a telephone) engaged: The line's busy. **4** (of music or pictures) with too much detail.
• *vb* make (oneself) busy: He busied himself with the housework. **busily** *adv* **busybody** *n* a nosey person. < Old English *bisig.*
SEE PANEL.
but (bət; *stressed* bʌt) *conj, prep* **1** on the other hand; however. **2** only: I can but try.

3 except: There's no one here but me. **4** not counting: the next but one.
• *n* an objection: no buts about it; ifs and buts. < Old English *būtan* outside, without.

butane (ˈbjuːteɪn) *n* a flammable gas refined from petroleum, used esp. as a fuel (in cigarette lighters). < ultimately Latin *butyrum* butter.

butch (bʊtʃ) *adj* (of a woman or homosexual man) tough or masculine in appearance. < probably short for *butcher.*

butcher (ˈbʊtʃə) *n* **1** someone who slaughters animals by trade; someone who cuts up and sells meat. **2** a brutal killer.
• *vb* kill brutally. **butcher's** *n* (*slang*) a look. **butchery** *n* **1** a butcher's trade. **2** brutal killing. < Old French *bouc* male goat.

butler (ˈbʌtlə) *n* the head manservant in a household, esp. one in charge of the wines and spirits. < Old French *bouteille* bottle.

butt[1] (bʌt) *n* a large barrel or cask. < ultimately Latin *buttis.*

butt[2] *n* **1** the thicker, blunt end of a weapon or tool: a rifle butt. **2** a remnant: a cigarette butt. < Middle English.

butt[3] *n* **1** someone who is the object of ridicule: the butt of his jokes. **2** an earthen mound behind a target on a shooting range which stops bullets.
• *vb* strike with the head, as a goat does.

busy as a bee

The repetition of the same initial sound in two or more words, as in *busy* as a *bee,* is known as *alliteration.* This device is usually associated with poetry and such lines as found in Coleridge's 'Kubla Khan':

Five miles meandering with a mazy motion

and with tongue-twisters such as:

Peter Piper picked a peck of pickled peppers.

However, as seen in busy as a bee, it also features in everyday usage. Bold as brass, dead as a doornail, part and parcel, rack and ruin, are just a few more of the many stock phrases which also show alliteration. Also, many book, play, and film titles owe more than a little of their memorability to this device, including 'Of Mice and Men', 'Pilgrim's Progress', 'Love's Labours Lost', 'A School for Scandal', and 'The Great Gatsby'.

butt in interrupt; interfere. < Middle English *but* target, end.

butter (ˈbʌtə) *n* **1** a yellow, fatty food made by churning milk or cream. **2** a similar substance made from other (vegetable) materials: peanut butter; cocoa butter.
• *vb* spread butter on. **butter-cream** *n* flavoured butter, used for filling or topping cakes. **buttered** *adj* cooked or spread with butter: buttered toast. **butter-fingers** *n* someone who lets fall through the fingers; careless person. **butter up** (*informal*) flatter. < ultimately Greek *bous* cow + *tyros* cheese.

buttercup (ˈbʌtəˌkʌp) *n* one of a group of plants with bright yellow, cup-shaped flowers, commonly found in fields.

butterfly (ˈbʌtəˌflaɪ) *n* **1** one of a group of flying insects with broad, often brightly coloured wings. **2** a swimming stroke in which the arms are moved at the same time. **3** a pleasure-seeking or frivolous person. **have butterflies in one's stomach** feel nervous. < Old English *butere* butter + *flēoge* fly.

buttermilk (ˈbʌtəˌmɪlk) *n* the liquid which remains after butter has been churned from milk.

butterscotch (ˈbʌtəˌskɒtʃ) *n* (the flavour of) a hard toffee made from brown sugar, butter, syrup, and water.

buttock (ˈbʌtək) *n* one of the two round, fleshy parts at the human rear, on which someone sits; similar part of an animal. < Middle English *buttok.*

button (ˈbʌtn̩) *n* **1** a small, round knob attached to a garment, used as a fastener. **2** a small, round object (on a machine), pressed to set a process in motion.
• *vb* secure with a button or buttons. **button mushroom** a small, immature mushroom. **button-through** *adj* (of a garment) fastened by buttons down the complete length: a button-through skirt. < Old French *boter* to thrust.

buttonhole (ˈbʌtn̩ˌhəʊl) *n* **1** a slit in a garment through which a button is passed. **2** a flower to be put into a buttonhole.
• *vb* accost and engage (someone) in conversation.

buttress (ˈbʌtrɪs) *n* **1** a supporting structure built against a wall. **2** anything which supports or reinforces.
• *vb* support: buttress the economy. < Old French *boter* to thrust.

buxom (ˈbʌksəm) *adj* (of a woman) attractively plump; full-bosomed. < Old English *būgan* to bend. SEE PANEL.

buy (baɪ) *vb* **bought; buying 1** obtain (something) by payment, esp. of money. **2** bribe; hire: He can be bought. **3** (*slang*) believe: She won't buy that old story.
• *n* a purchase: a good buy. **buyer** *n* **1** someone who buys. **2** an agent who chooses and buys stock (for a shop or company). **buy off** get rid of (someone) by paying him or her. **buy out** get full control of (a company) by paying another for his or her share. **buy up** buy as much as one can of. < Old English *bycgan.*

buzz (bʌz) *n* **1** a low, humming sound like that of a bee; murmur of conversation. **2** a rumour. **3** (*slang*) a telephone call.
• *vb* **1** make a buzzing sound; fill (a room) with this sound. **2** act busily: buzz around. **3** threaten (an aircraft) by flying very close to it. **buzzer** *n* an electric signalling device that makes a buzzing sound. **buzz off** (*slang*) go away. < Middle English *bussen,* like the sound. SEE PANEL.

buzzard (ˈbʌzəd) *n* a large European hawk with broad wings and a soaring flight. < Latin *buteo.*

by (baɪ) *adv, prep* **1** near; beside: stand by the door. **2** during: by day. **3** not later than: by 10 o'clock. **4** through the means of: by airmail. **5** through the creation of: a play by Shakespeare. **6** (of measurements or numbers) taken together with: 10 foot by 4 foot. **7** according to: judge by appearances. **8** in succession: one by one. **9** to the extent of: taller by a few inches. **10** with respect to: German by birth. **11** in the belief of: swear by almighty God. **by and by** before long. **by and large** all things considered. **by oneself** alone; unaided. < Old English *be, bī.*

bye-bye (ˈbaɪˌbaɪ) *interj* (*informal*) goodbye.

by-election (ˈbaɪɪˌlɛkʃən) *n* a special election to fill one seat in the House of Commons, vacant due to the resignation or death of a member.

bygone (ˈbaɪˌgɒn) *adj* of the past: a bygone age. **let bygones be bygones** forgive and forget past disputes.

by-law (ˈbaɪˌlɔː) *n* a local law; company regulation. < Old Norse *bȳr* town + *lög* law. SEE PANEL.

bypass (ˈbaɪˌpɑːs) *n* **1** a road which takes traffic away from a town centre. **2** a means of rerouting (a liquid or electrical current) round an appliance and back into the main flow.
• *vb* **1** avoid by means of a bypass. **2** neglect or omit (rules and regulations) on purpose.

by-product (ˈbaɪˌprɒdʌkt) *n* something made (in a manufacturing process) in

buxom

Nowadays the word buxom conjures up the picture of a woman with a healthily well-rounded figure, in particular a full bosom. This may be regarded as no more than the most recent stage in a series of extensions of the word's original meaning. Buxom derives ultimately from the Old English *būgan* 'to bend'. A person who bends may be described as 'submissive' or 'obedient' and this was the meaning of *būhsum* when the word first appeared in the 12th century. It applied equally to men as to women.

Much to the amused bewilderment of schoolchildren who come across the word in Chaucer, it retained this sense for several centuries. Gradually, however, the sense shifted from 'submissive' to 'easy-going' and 'jolly' and then from 'jolly' to the 16th-century meaning, 'plump'. From this time on the application became restricted to women.

Why do bees buzz?

The fact that we call a dog dog and a cat cat is purely arbitrary. As long as we are all agreed, the labels could be reversed: a cat could be called dog and a dog cat. The reason why this is so is that speech sounds do not have intrinsic meaning.

There are one or two exceptions to this rule, however. The major exception involves words that seem to imitate the sound or the source of the sound that they refer to. Clang, crash, buzz, moo, whisper, zoom, for instance, are all like the sounds they refer to; the sound reflects the sense. Words of this type are examples of *onomatopoeia.*

by-laws and **Whitby**

Place-names can tell us a great deal about our history. Take, for example, the host of names ending in -by like Whitby or Grimsby. The -by ending of such names reveals that they were once Scandinavian settlements, bȳr being the Old Norse word for 'farmstead' or 'village'. The same word lies behind our modern-day by-law, 'a local law', from Old Norse *bȳlög* 'a town law'.

addition to the main product.

byre (baɪə) *n* a cowshed. < Old English *bȳre*.

bystander (ˈbaɪˌstændə) *n* someone who is present in a situation but not involved in it.

byte (baɪt) *n* a sequence of bits in a computer, processed as one unit of information. < perhaps alteration of *bite*.

byway (ˈbaɪˌweɪ) *n* a secondary road.

byword (ˈbaɪˌwɜːd) *n* **1** someone or something spoken of as a notable example: Their name is a byword for efficiency. **2** a proverb.

C

C *abbrev* Celsius; centigrade.
cab (kæb) *n* **1** a taxi. **2** a compartment in a train, lorry, crane, etc., where the driver sits. < short for *cabriolet,* from French: little skip.
cabaret (ˈkæbəˌreɪ) *n* a floor show in a restaurant or night-club, usually consisting of a series of acts. < French: tavern.
cabbage (ˈkæbɪdʒ) *n* **1** one of a group of vegetables with green or purple leaves forming a round head. **2** (*informal*) someone who has lost his or her mental faculties through injury or accident. < Old Northern French *caboche* head.
caber (ˈkeɪbə) *n* a heavy wooden pole, usually a tree trunk, thrown for distance in the Scottish sport of tossing the caber. < Scottish Gaelic *cabar.*
cabin (ˈkæbɪn) *n* **1** a compartment in a ship, aircraft, etc., for crew or passengers. **2** a small, simple dwelling, often made of wood. **cabin cruiser** a large motor boat equipped with cabins. < Medieval Latin *capanna* hut.
cabinet (ˈkæbɪnɪt) *n* **1** a piece of furniture with shelves, cupboards, or drawers, used for display or storing: a filing cabinet. **2 the Cabinet** a body of ministers, chosen by the Prime Minister, who shape government policy. **cabinet-maker** *n* a craftsman who makes wooden furniture. < Old Northern French *cabine* small gambling house.
cable (ˈkeɪbl̩) *n* **1** a strong, thick rope, often of twisted wire or fibre; anchor chain. **2** insulated wires which carry electricity or an electrical signal: cable TV. **3** a nautical measure of length (in the UK 185 metres, USA 219 metres). • *vb* send (someone) a telegram abroad; send money or information like this. **cable-car** *n* one of several carriages in a cable railway in which cars move round a looped cable driven by a static engine. **cable stitch** a knitting pattern resembling a cable. < Medieval Latin *capulum* lasso, from *capere* to take.
cacao (kəˈkɑːəʊ) *n* one of a group of tropical trees which produces seeds, used for making cocoa and chocolate; fatty seed of this. < Nahuatl *cacahuatl.*
cache (kæʃ) *n* a hiding place as for weapons or stocks of food; anything hidden in this. < Latin *cogere* to compel.
cackle (ˈkækl̩) *n* the loud, sharp cry of a hen after laying; laughing noise like this. • *vb* make a cackling sound. < Middle English *cakelen* like the sound.
cacophony (kəˈkɒfənɪ) *n* a harsh, discordant sound; dissonance. **cacophonous** *adj* < ultimately Greek *kak,* from *kakos* bad + *phōnē* sound.
cactus (ˈkæktəs) *n, pl* **cacti** one of a family of plants with fleshy stems and spines but no leaves, usually found in a hot, dry climate. < Greek *kaktos.*
cad (kæd) *n* (*derogatory old-fashioned*) an unscrupulous man; rogue. **caddish** *adj* < English dialect: unskilled assistant.
caddie (ˈkædɪ) *n* someone who carries a golfer's clubs during a game. • *vb* **caddied; caddying** act as a caddie. **caddie car** or **cart** a light, two-wheeled trolley for carrying golf-clubs around a course. < French *cadet* military cadet.
caddy (ˈkædɪ) *n* a small tin or box (for tea). < Malay *kati* unit of weight.
cadence (ˈkeɪdn̩s) *n* **1** rhythm and intonation in speech or sound. **2** a fall in pitch at the end of an utterance. **3** a concluding musical phrase. < ultimately Latin *cadere* to fall.
cadet (kəˈdɛt) *n* someone training to be an officer in the police or armed forces. < ultimately Latin *caput* head.
cadge (kædʒ) *vb* get (food or money) by begging: cadge cigarettes. **cadger** *n* < back formation from Middle English *caggen* to tie.
cadre (ˈkɑːdə) *n* the nucleus of a (military) organization, which can be expanded when necessary. < ultimately Latin *quadrum* square.
caecum (ˈsiːkəm) *n* the pouch that marks the beginning of the large intestine. < Latin *intestinum caecum* blind intestine.
caesarean (sɪˈzɛərɪən) *n* also **caesarean section** a surgical operation for the delivery of a baby by cutting through the wall of the mother's abdomen and into the womb. < probably Julius *Caesar,* supposedly born by this method. SEE PANEL.
caesura (sɪˈzjʊərə) *n, pl* **caesuras, caesurae** a break or pause in, esp. the middle of a line of verse. < Latin: cutting, from *caedere* to cut.
café (ˈkæfeɪ) *n* a small restaurant selling refreshments. < Turkish *kahve* coffee.

cafeteria (ˌkæfɪˈtɪərɪə) *n* a small, self-service restaurant. < Spanish *café* coffee.
caffeine (ˈkæfiːn) *n* an alkaloid (in tea or coffee) which acts as a stimulant. < French *café* coffee.
caftan (ˈkæftæn) *n* also **kaftan** an ankle-length, long-sleeved garment, traditionally worn in the Near East. < Persian *qaftān*.
cage (keɪdʒ) *n* a (metal) framework structure for keeping birds or animals; similar structure for carrying people.
• *vb* confine in a cage. **cage-bird** *n* a type of bird usually kept in a cage. < Latin *cavus* hollow.
cagey (ˈkeɪdʒɪ) *adj* **cagier; cagiest** (*informal*) secretive; shrewd. **cagily** *adv* **caginess** *n* < origin unknown.
cajole (kəˈdʒəʊl) *vb* persuade (someone) with flattery. **cajolery** *n* < ultimately Latin *cavea* cage.
cake (keɪk) *n* **1** a sweet food like bread. **2** a food mixture cooked in a round, flat shape: fish cake. **3** a shaped, hard block or mass: a cake of soap.
• *vb* **1** form a hard mass. **2** cover with a hard crust. < Old Norse *kaka*.
calamine (ˈkæləˌmaɪn) *n* a pink powder of zinc oxide and ferric oxide, used in soothing lotions for the skin. < ultimately Greek *Kadmos* Cadmus, legendary founder of Thebes.
calamity (kəˈlæmɪtɪ) *n* a great misfortune. **calamitous** *adj* < Latin *calamitas*.
calcify (ˈkælsɪˌfaɪ) *vb* **calcified; calcifying** make or become hard by a deposit of calcium salts. **calcification** *n*
calcium (ˈkælsɪəm) *n* a silvery-white, alkaline metal, occurring naturally only in combinations such as limestone, marble, and chalk; present in bones and teeth. < Latin *calx* lime.
calculate (ˈkælkjʊˌleɪt) *vb* **1** solve (problems) by mathematics; compute. **2** plan deliberately. **3** determine by judgment; estimate. **calculation** *n* **calculated risk** a risk taken with full awareness of the dangers. **calculating** *adj* (of people) scheming. **calculator** *n* a device, esp. electronic, for making mathematical calculations. < ultimately Latin *calx* (lime) stone used in gambling.
calculus (ˈkælkjʊləs) *n* **1** a method of mathematical calculation dealing with rates of variation. **2** an abnormal stony mass formed inside the body. < Latin: pebble, stone used in counting.
calendar (ˈkælɪndə) *n* **1** a display chart showing time divisions of the year. **2** a system for dividing this: the Gregorian calendar. **3** a list of events or activities: social calendar. < ultimately Latin *kalendarium* money-lender's account book.
calf[1] (kɑːf) *n, pl* **calves** **1** the young of cattle; young of the elephant, seal, whale, and other large animals. **2** calfskin leather. < Old English *cealf*.
calf[2] *n, pl* **calves** the fleshy, hind part of the leg between the knee and the ankle. < Old Norse *kālfi*.
calibrate (ˈkælɪˌbreɪt) *vb* **1** determine units of measurement on (a scale or gauge). **2** determine the calibre of. **calibration** *n* **calibre** *n* **1** the internal diameter of a cylinder, esp. a gun-barrel or bullet. **2** degree of capability or excellence: We need someone of her calibre. < Arabic *qālib* shoemaker's last.
calico (ˈkælɪˌkəʊ) *n, pl* **calicoes, calicos** a plain, white, cotton cloth, originally imported from India. < *Calicut*, city in India. SEE PANEL AT **TULLE**.
call (kɔːl) *n* **1** a cry (of a human or animal). **2** an order to assemble; summons: band call. **3** an attraction: the call of the wild. **4** a signal on a musical instrument: bugle call. **5** a need: There's no call for that kind of behaviour. **6** a demand: many calls on my time. **7** a short visit: courtesy call. **8** a telephone conversation; telephoning: I'll give you a call later.
• *vb* **1** cry out, esp. to attract attention. **2** make a short visit. **3** describe; refer to as: I call it a waste of time. **4** declare (trumps) in card-games. **5** wake (someone) up.

caesarean

A caesarean or caesarean section is the delivery of a foetus by a surgical incision through the mother's abdominal wall and uterus. One school of thought has it that the name of the operation derives from Caius Julius *Caesar*, 101–44 BC, the Roman statesman, general, and historian, who is believed to have been born by this method. If this were the case, it would be the second word to enter the language from his name, since July is derived from *Julius*.

A second theory is that caesarean comes ultimately from the Latin verb *caedere* 'to cut', as does caesura—'a pause, break, or interruption'.

6 summon: Call the police! **7** order; urge: call a strike. **8** telephone. **caller** *n* **call-box** *n* a telephone box. **call-girl** *n* a prostitute who accepts business by telephone. **call it a day** decide to stop work for that day. **call-sign** *n* an identification signal for a radio transmitter. **call someone's bluff** challenge in order to expose an empty threat. **call the tune** or **shots** be in charge of procedure. **on call** (of a doctor, etc.) available for duty. < probably Old Norse *kalla.* SEE PANEL.

calligraphy (kəˈlɪgrəfɪ) *n* (the art of producing) beautiful handwriting. **calligrapher** *n* **calligraphic** *adj* < ultimately Greek *kallos* beauty + *graphia* writing.

calling (ˈkɔːlɪŋ) *n* a vocation; occupation.

calliper (ˈkælɪpə) *n* a metal support for the (injured) human leg, extending from the knee or thigh to the foot. **callipers** *pl n* a device for measuring thickness or diameter. < alteration of *calibre.*

> **call up**
>
> Call features in a number of idiomatic expressions, including:
>
> **call away** to summon to carry out another activity.
> **call by** to stop somewhere, especially on one's way to another place: If I have time, I'll call by and see you again this evening.
> **call for 1** to go and collect: I'll call for your cleaning on my way home. **2** to require or deserve: I think your exam results call for a celebration!
> **call in 1** to stop somewhere, especially on one's way to another place. **2** to ask (someone, such as a doctor) to come to one's house, etc., to give advice or help. **3** to order the return of: The manufacturers are calling in all the X971 models, because a fault has been discovered.
> **call off** to cancel or abandon.
> **call on 1** to visit. **2** also **call upon** to request; invite or appeal to.
> **call out 1** to summon, especially in an emergency. **2** to order to go on strike.
> **call up 1** to telephone. **2** to summon to join the army, navy, etc. **call-up** *n* **3** to recall; evoke: The photographs called up happy memories of our visit to France.

callous (ˈkæləs) *adj* **1** thickened; hardened. **2** uncaring. **callously** *adv* **callousness** *n* < Latin *callus* callous skin.

callow (ˈkæləʊ) *adj* immature: callow youth. **callowly** *adv* **callowness** *n* < Old English *calu* bald.

calm (kɑːm) *adj* **1** (of weather) not windy; tranquil. **2** under control; not excited: Keep calm!
• *n* a calm condition: the calm before the storm.
• *vb* make or become calm: calm down. **calmly** *adv* **calmness** *n* < ultimately Greek *kaiein* to burn.

calorie (ˈkælərɪ) *n* **1** a unit of measurement for heat quantity. **2** a unit for measuring the energy value of food. < Latin *calēre* to be warm.

calumny (ˈkæləmnɪ) *n* slander; slanderous utterance. < Latin *calvi* to deceive.

calve (kɑːv) *vb* give birth to a calf.

calypso (kəˈlɪpsəʊ) *n, pl* **calypsos** a syncopated ballad, esp. of West Indian origin. < perhaps *Calypso,* sea-nymph in Homer's 'Odyssey'.

cam (kæm) *n* a mechanical device (on a wheel) that by its circular motion causes a back-and-forth motion in another moving part. **camshaft** *n* < Old High German *kamb* comb.

camaraderie (ˌkæməˈrɑːdərɪ) *n* friendly good humour. < French *camarade* comrade.

camber (ˈkæmbə) *n* a slight rising curve made in a surface, esp. of a road. **cambered** *adj* < Latin *camur* curved.

came (keɪm) SEE **COME.**

camel (ˈkæməl) *n* **1** an animal with a long neck and one or two humps, used as a means of transport in desert countries. **2** a fawn colour. **camel-hair** *n* soft, fine hair, used in an artist's brush; cloth made from the hair of a camel, sometimes mixed with wool. < Greek *kamēlos.*

camellia (kəˈmiːlɪə) *n* one of a group of evergreen, flowering shrubs of the tea family; its rose-like flower. < Georg Josef *Kamel,* died 1706, Moravian Jesuit missionary.

cameo (ˈkæmɪˌəʊ) *n, pl* **cameos 1** a small (gem) carving, consisting of a raised design on a background layer, often of a different colour: cameo brooch. **2** a brief part (in a play) that highlights plot or character. < Italian.

camera (ˈkæmərə, ˈkæmrə) *n* a device for taking photographs, TV or moving pictures. **cameraman** *n* a camera operator. < Latin *camera* room.

camouflage (ˈkæməˌflɑːʒ) *n* the hiding of (military) objects by disguising them so that they blend in with their surroundings.
• *vb* conceal by camouflage. < French, from Italian *camuffare* to disguise.

camp[1] (kæmp) *n* **1** an area of land where people stay in temporary shelters, esp. tents or huts: holiday camp. **2** a group of people sharing a theory or ideal.
• *vb* live outdoors temporarily; make or occupy a camp. **camper** *n* **camp-bed** *n* a portable bed which folds. **camp out** sleep outdoors (in a tent). < Latin *campus* field.

camp[2] *adj* **1** homosexual; effeminate. **2** outrageously affected in style.
• *n* a camp manner. **camp it up** act outrageously for humorous effect. < origin unknown.

campaign (kæmˈpeɪn) *n* **1** a series of military operations with a set purpose (in a war). **2** a series of activities planned to achieve a definite result: sales campaign.
• *vb* take part in a campaign. **campaigner** *n* < ultimately Latin *campania* level country.

camphor (ˈkæmfə) *n* a white, aromatic substance from tree-bark, used in plastics, insect repellent, etc. **camphorated** *adj* < Malay *kāpūr*.

campus (ˈkæmpəs) *n* the buildings and grounds of a (self-contained) college or university. < Latin: plain.

can[1] (kæn) *n* **1** a container of metal or plastic for liquids. **2** a sealed tin for preserved food or drink; its contents.
• *vb* preserve (food) in a tin. **canful** *adj* **canner** *n* **carry the can** (*slang*) bear responsibility. **in the can** (of films) ready for release. < Old English *canne*.

can[2] (kən; *stressed* kæn) *auxiliary vb* **could 1** be able to; know how to: He can speak Dutch. **2** be allowed to (do something): You can stay. < Old English.

canal (kəˈnæl) *n* **1** a man-made watercourse for irrigation or transport by boat. **2** a channel in the body (of a plant or animal) for the passage of food or air: the alimentary canal. < Latin *canna* reed.

canary (kəˈnɛərɪ) *n* a small, yellow cage-bird of the finch family. < Spanish *Islas Canarias* Canary Islands.

canasta (kəˈnæstə) *n* a card-game for four, played with two full packs and two jokers, similar to rummy. < Spanish: basket.

cancel (ˈkænsḷ) *vb* **cancelled; cancelling 1** make void (an arrangement); call off (a meeting). **2** discontinue (a subscription). **3** neutralize; cross out: cancel the first digit. **4** put a mark on (a stamp) so it cannot be reused. **cancellation** *n* **cancel out** counterbalance. < ultimately Latin *carcer* prison.

cancer (ˈkænsə) *n* **1** (a disease shown by) a malignant tumour. **2** something evil and likely to spread: a cancer on society. **cancerous** *adj* < Latin: crab.

candelabrum (ˌkændɪˈlɑːbrəm) *n, pl* **candelabra** a large, branched holder for candles or lights. < Latin *candela* candle.

candid (ˈkændɪd) *adj* frank and open. **candidly** *adv* **candidness** *n* < Latin *candēre* to shine.

candidate (ˈkændɪˌdeɪt) *n* **1** someone seeking or nominated for office, reward, or membership of a society. **2** someone taking an examination. **candidature** *n* < Latin *candidus* white. SEE PANEL.

candle (ˈkændḷ) *n* a piece of wax in a stick shape, enclosing a wick and providing light when set alight. **candle-light** *n* **candlepower** *n* a unit for measuring light. **candlestick** *n* a candle-holder. **candlewick** *n* a soft, thick, cotton yarn, often spun into a material for bedspreads with a raised, tufted pattern. **cannot hold a candle to** is extremely inferior

---

candidate

A person who solicits or is nominated for a particular office is known as a candidate. This word derives ultimately from the Latin *candidus* or 'white'. In ancient Rome a candidate for public office would parade in a white toga, white being a symbol of purity. A candidate or *candidatus* was literally 'one dressed in white'.

---

not worth the candle

Not worth the candle harks back to the early days of Newmarket's Jockey Club when anybody wishing to participate in a card-game was obliged to pay for the privilege. The entry fee was one shilling (5p), the price of a candle. While the lucky winners would naturally have no regrets about this outlay, to the losers the game was not worth the candle.

---

to. **not worth the candle** not worth the effort. < Latin *candēre* to shine.
SEE PANEL.

candour (ˈkændə) *n* frankness and openness. < Latin *candere* to shine.

candy (ˈkændɪ) *n* (*US*) sweets; one sweet. **candy-floss** *n* fluffy, spun sugar wound onto a stick as a sweet. **candy-stripes** *pl n* alternating white and coloured stripes. **candy-striped** *adj* < Arabic *qand* sugar.

cane (keɪn) *n* **1** any of several kinds of reeds or grasses: sugar cane. **2** the hollow, jointed stem of plants such as bamboo; this material, used in making furniture. **3** a length of wood, etc., used as a walking-stick, support for a plant, or as a rod for flogging.
• *vb* **1** flog with a cane. **2** weave (furniture) with cane. **cane-sugar** *n* sugar obtained from sugar-cane juice. < Greek *kanna.*

canine (ˈkeɪnaɪn) *adj* of dogs or the dog family. **canine tooth** a strong, pointed tooth between the incisor and the first premolar. < Latin *canis* dog.

canister(ˈkænɪstə) *n* **1** a metal container, used for keeping something dry. **2** a cylinder (of shot or gas) designed to burst and release its contents when fired or thrown: tear-gas canister. < Greek *kanna* reed.

canker (ˈkæŋkə) *n* **1** a disease which destroys areas of plant tissue or causes sores on animal skin. **2** a source of corruption. < Latin *cancer* crab.

cannabis (ˈkænəbɪs) *n* a hemp plant; preparation of its leaves or resin, smoked or eaten for its euphoric effect. < Greek *kannabis.*

cannibal (ˈkænɪbl̩) *n* someone who eats human flesh; animal which eats its own kind. **cannibalism** *n* < Arawakan *Caniba* Carib.

cannon (ˈkænən) *n* **1** an old-fashioned type of heavy gun firing large, solid, metal balls. **2** an automatic gun which fires shells from an aircraft. **3** a shot in billiards in which two balls are hit consecutively by the cue ball.
• *vb* **1** collide with. **2** make a cannon shot in billiards. **cannon-fodder** *n* people regarded as expendable in war. < Latin *canna* cane.

canny (ˈkænɪ) *adj* shrewd; cautious. **cannily** *adv* **canniness** *n* < *can*[2] + *-y.*

canoe (kəˈnuː) *n* a long, light, narrow boat propelled by paddling.
• *vb* travel in or paddle a canoe. **canoeist** *n* < Arawakan *canoa.*

canon (ˈkænən) *n* **1** a general standard (of morals). **2** a writer's authentic work, such as the divinely inspired writings of the Bible. **3** a clergyman with duties in a cathedral. **4** a musical piece in which the melody is repeated by successively entering voices or instruments. **canonical** *adj* **1** as commanded by canon law. **2** accepted; standard. **canonically** *adv* **canonize** *vb* officially declare the sainthood of. **canon law** church law. < Latin: rule.

canopy (ˈkænəpɪ) *n* **1** cloth covering hanging over a bed, throne, etc., (as a shelter); any similar covering: a canopy of stars. **2** the part of a parachute which unfolds in the air. **canopied** *adj* < ultimately Greek *kōnōps* mosquito.

cant (kænt) *n* jargon; stock phrases. < Latin *cantare* sing.

cantankerous (kænˈtæŋkərəs) *adj* ill-tempered. **cantankerously** *adv* < perhaps obsolete *contack* contention.

cantata (kænˈtɑːtə) *n* a usually religious musical composition; form of short oratorio. < ultimately Latin *cantare* to sing.

canteen (kænˈtiːn) *n* **1** a restaurant in a factory, college, etc., for employees or students. **2** a box for cutlery. **3** a cask, as for water, carried by a soldier or traveller. < ultimately Latin *canthus* iron hoop.

canter (ˈkæntə) *n* a pace of a horse slower than a gallop.
• *vb* ride at a canter. < *Canter*bury, England the assumed pace of pilgrims to Canterbury. SEE PANEL.

canticle (ˈkæntɪkl̩) *n* words from the Bible set to music, such as the Magnificat. < ultimately Latin *canere* to sing.

cantilever (ˈkæntɪˌliːvə) *n* a projecting beam supported only at one end, used to prop a balcony or similar structure: cantilever bridge. < perhaps *cant* slanting surface + *lever.*

canton (ˈkæntɒn) *n* a division or department of a country, esp. Switzerland.

canter

A horse can be thought of as having four gaits: walk, trot, canter, and gallop. Canter, the name of the gait which is faster than a trot but slower and smoother than a gallop, comes ultimately from *Canterbury* in England. It was coined reputedly to describe the steady pace at which mounted pilgrims made their way to Canterbury and the shrine of St Thomas à Becket in Canterbury Cathedral.

< ultimately Latin *canthus* iron hoop.

canvas (ˈkænvəs) *n* a sturdy, woven, cotton cloth, used in sails, tents, etc., and by artists to paint on with oils. < ultimately Latin *cannabis* hemp.

canvass (ˈkænvəs) *vb* visit (voters) in order to gain (support) for political parties or find out opinions. **canvasser** *n* < obsolete *canvas* toss in a canvas sheet.

canyon (ˈkænjən) *n* a very large, deep valley or gorge, usually with a river flowing at the bottom. < ultimately Latin *canna* cane.

cap (kæp) *n* **1** a soft head-covering, with a peak but no brim. **2** an academic head-covering; mortar-board. **3** a natural covering: snowcap. **4** a small, explosive charge, used in toy guns.
• *vb* **capped; capping 1** cover the top of (something). **2** outdo (someone or something): Cap that if you can! < Latin *cappa* head-covering.

capable (ˈkeɪpəbḷ) *adj* **1** able or competent: in capable hands. **2** having the capacity to (do something): capable of murder. **capability** *n* **capably** *adv* < ultimately Latin *capere* to take.

capacity (kəˈpæsɪtɪ) *n* **1** the ability to hold or deal with something; amount held: full to capacity. **2** potential: working at full capacity. **3** an assigned role: signed in his official capacity.

cape[1] (keɪp) *n* a sleeveless, outer garment; cloak. < Latin *cappa* head-covering.

cape[2] *n* a peninsula; land projecting at the coast: Cape Horn. < Latin *caput* head.

caper (ˈkeɪpə) *vb* run or leap about playfully.
• *n* **1** capering. **2** (*slang*) an escapade; prank. < probably Middle French *capriole*.

capillary (kəˈpɪlərɪ) *n* a very fine tube such as one of the smaller blood-vessels.
• *adj* of or like a capillary. < Latin *capillus* hair.

capital (ˈkæpɪtḷ) *adj* **1** chief; most important. **2** punishable by death: a capital crime. **3** (of letters) of the form used to begin proper nouns or sentences: capital A.
• *n* **1** a city with the centre of national government. **2** a capital letter. **3** money or stock invested to create income; money used to start a business: capital gain: capital assets. **capital goods** goods such as ships or railways not sold but used to produce other goods. **capitalism** *n* an economic system based on private ownership and the profit motive. **capitalist** *n* someone who believes in capitalism, esp. a rich person. **capitalize** *vb* **1** print or write in capitals. **2** turn into or provide with capital. **capitalization** *n* **capitalize on** take advantage of; profit by. **make capital out of** take advantage of (a situation). < Latin *caput* head.

capitulate (kəˈpɪtjʊˌleɪt) *vb* surrender; acquiesce. **capitulation** *n* < Latin *capitulum* chapter.

caprice (kəˈpriːs) *n* **1** a whim; sudden change of mind; tendency to this. **2** a lively, whimsical piece of music. **capricious** *adj* < Italian *capo* head + *riccio* hedgehog.

capsize (kæpˈsaɪz) *vb* overturn: The boat capsized. < origin unknown.

capstan (ˈkæpstən) *n* **1** a rotating drum, used on a ship to wind in heavy weights by rope or cable. **2** a rotating shaft that drives magnetic tape at a constant speed in a tape-recorder. < Middle English.

capsule (ˈkæpsjʊl) *n* **1** the casing of a seed which bursts, releasing spores. **2** a casing usually of gelatin containing a dose of medicine to be swallowed. **3** a detachable compartment in a spacecraft for instruments and crew. < Latin *capsula* small box.

captain (ˈkæptɪn) *n* **1** an army officer ranking above a lieutenant and below a major. **2** a naval officer ranking above a commander and below a commodore. **3** the officer commanding a ship; pilot in charge of a civil aircraft. **4** the leader of a (sports) team.
• *vb* be captain of. **captaincy** *n* < ultimately Latin *caput* head.

caption (ˈkæpʃən) *n* **1** a title or heading of a newspaper article. **2** a comment or description printed with a picture, cartoon, etc. **3** a subtitle on a television screen or film. < ultimately Latin *capere* to take.

captivate (ˈkæptɪˌveɪt) *vb* hold (someone's) attention by fascinating; charm. **captivating** *adj* **captivation** *n*

captive (ˈkæptɪv) *adj* taken or kept as a prisoner (in war).
• *n* someone who is captured. **captive audience** people in a situation where it is difficult to escape. **captivity** *n* < ultimately Latin *capere* to take.

captor (ˈkæptə) *n* someone who captures (a human or animal).

capture (ˈkæptʃə) *vb* **1** take as a prisoner; gain: They captured the city. **2** preserve in a lasting form: The artist captured her likeness.
• *n* capturing; being captured. < Latin *captus*.

car (kɑː) *n* **1** a motor car. **2** a type of wheeled carriage, esp. on a railway: buffet car. **car coat** a short top coat worn by car drivers. **car-ferry** *n* a boat used for conveying cars. **car-park** *n* a place for parking cars. **carport** *n* an open-sided shelter, esp. beside a house, for cars. < Latin *carrus.*

carafe (kəˈræf, ˈkærəf) *n* a glass container for serving wine or water (at a table). < Arabic *gharrāfah.*

caramel (ˈkærəməl) *n* a brown substance for colouring and flavouring food, made from heated sugar; type of toffee with this taste. < Latin *calamellus* small reed.

carat (ˈkærət) *n* **1** a unit of weight for precious stones, esp. diamonds (200 milligrams). **2** a measure for the purity of gold, with pure gold taken as 24 carat. < ultimately Greek *keration* small weight.

caravan (ˈkærəˌvæn) *n* **1** a covered vehicle designed for towing, esp. by a car, and used as a dwelling. **2** a group of people travelling together, esp. merchants across desert or wild country. **caravanning** *n* going (on holiday) by caravan. < Persian *kārwān.*

carbine (ˈkɑːbaɪn) *n* a light, short-range, automatic rifle. < Middle French *carabin* carabineer.

carbohydrate (ˌkɑːbəʊˈhaɪdreɪt) *n* any of the organic compounds (such as sugar or starch) which contain carbon, hydrogen and oxygen. < *carbon* + *hydrate.*

carbon (ˈkɑːbn̩) *n* **1** a chemical element present in all organic substances, occurring as diamond, graphite, charcoal, etc., and present in coal or petroleum. **2** a sheet of carbon paper: carbon copy. **carbon dating** fixing a date (of ancient artefacts) by recording the decay of a radioactive form of carbon. **carbon dioxide** a gas without smell or colour, breathed out by animals. **carbon monoxide** a poisonous gas occurring in engine exhausts. **carbon paper** thin, carbon-coated paper, used for making copies of typed or written material. < Latin *carbo* ember.

carbuncle (ˈkɑːˌbʌŋkl̩) *n* **1** a painful inflammation of the skin. **2** a bright-red gemstone cut in a knob-like shape without facets. < Latin *carbunculus* small coal.

carburettor (ˌkɑːbjʊˈrɛtə) *n* a device for supplying an internal-combustion engine with an explosive mixture of fuel and air. < obsolete *carburet* carbide.

carcass (ˈkɑːkəs) *n* **1** a dead body, esp. of an animal, prepared to be cut up for meat. **2** a framework (of a tyre). < Old French *carcois.*

card[1] (kɑːd) *n* **1** a small, stiff piece of usually rectangular paper or thin cardboard, often used for sending messages, greetings, or to record information: visiting-card; greetings-card. **2** a playing-card: game of cards. **3** a programme for a sporting event: race card. **4** (*old-fashioned*) a funny fellow. **be on the cards** be likely to happen. **card-carrying member** a registered member (of a political party). **card index** an index with a separate entry on each card for every item. **cards** *pl n* National Insurance and other papers of an employee, held by the employer: get one's cards when one is sacked. **have a card up one's sleeve** have something hidden for an emergency. **put one's cards on the table** be open about one's plans. < ultimately Greek *chartēs* leaf of papyrus.

card[2] *n* (part of) a machine for cleaning or combing fibres, consisting of a wire brush or comb-like tool.
• *vb* comb or clean with a carding machine. < ultimately Latin *carduus* thistle.

cardboard (ˈkɑːdˌbɔːd) *n* a thick, stiff material similar to paper, used esp. for making boxes.

cardiac (ˈkɑːdɪˌæk) *adj* of, near, or affecting the heart. < Greek *kardia* heart.

cardigan (ˈkɑːdɪgən) *n* a knitted jacket, fastened by buttons down the front. SEE PANEL.

balaclava and **cardigan**

The hood-like, woollen head-covering known as a balaclava helmet takes its name from the Crimean village of *Balaclava,* in whose vicinity the most famous battle of the Crimean War was fought on 25 October 1854. The balaclava helmet was one of two additional garments issued to British soldiers to afford protection against the chill of the Crimean winter. The other was the cardigan, a knitted, woollen jacket with buttons down the front, named after James Thomas Brudenell, the 7th Earl of *Cardigan,* 1797–1868. It was the Earl of Cardigan who led the ill-fated charge of the Light Brigade.

cardinal (ˈkɑːdɪnl̩) *adj* **1** most important; fundamental: cardinal virtues. **2** deep red in colour.
• *n* a member of the Sacred College of the Roman Catholic Church, with powers to elect the pope. **cardinal numbers** whole numbers: 1, 2, 3, etc. **cardinal points** the four main compass points: north, south, east, west. < ultimately Latin *cardo* hinge.

care (kɛə) *n* **1** serious thought or effort: He did his work with care. **2** protective supervision: under the care of a doctor. **3** a worry; trouble: the cares of the world.
• *vb* **1** feel concerned (about). **2** like; feel affection for. **3** wish: Would you care for some tea? **care for** have in one's charge. **carefree** *adj* free from worry; elated. **care of** also **c/o** to an address for forwarding mail, etc. **in care** under the charge of the Social Services. **take care** look after (oneself). **take care of** take charge of; deal with or provide for. < Old English *caru.*

career (kəˈrɪə) *n* **1** an occupation in which one may remain and advance. **2** the course of someone's life; progress of an organization.
• *vb* move quickly in an uncontrolled way: The lorry careered off the road. **career woman** a woman who chooses to work in a trained, paid occupation. < ultimately Latin *carrus* car.

careful (ˈkɛəfʊl) *adj* **1** painstaking. **2** done with close attention: careful handwriting. **3** prudent; cautious: be careful of fire. **carefully** *adv* **carefulness** *n*

careless (ˈkɛəlɪs) *adj* not careful; negligent. **carelessly** *adv* **carelessness** *n*

caress (kəˈrɛs) *n* a loving touch or stroke; kiss.
• *vb* kiss; touch lovingly or gently: The waves caressed his body. < Latin *carus* dear.

caretaker (ˈkɛəˌteɪkə) *n* someone whose job is to look after a house or building. **caretaker government** a temporary government, pending an election.

cargo (ˈkɑːgəʊ) *n, pl* **cargoes** goods carried by ship, aircraft, or in a vehicle. < ultimately Latin *carricare* to load.

caricature (ˈkærɪkəˌtjʊə) *n* a ludicrous exaggeration of features or characteristics (in literature or art) for comic effect.
• *vb* make or draw a caricature of. < Italian, from Latin *carricare* to load.

caries (ˈkɛəriːz) *n* tooth or bone decay: dental caries. < Latin.

carnage (ˈkɑːnɪdʒ) *n* killing, esp. in battle on a large scale. < Medieval Latin *carnaticum,* from Latin *caro* flesh.

carnal (ˈkɑːnl̩) *adj* worldly; of the physical body, esp. sexually. **carnally** *adv* < ultimately Latin *caro* flesh.

carnation (kɑːˈneɪʃən) *n* any of a group of cultivated, double-headed, pink flowers; colour of these. < ultimately Latin *caro* flesh.

carnival (ˈkɑːnɪvl̩) *n* a festive occasion for public merry-making, often with street processions. < Italian *carnevale,* from *carne* meat + *levare* to remove.

carnivore (ˈkɑːnɪˌvɔː) *n* a meat-eating animal. **carnivorous** *adj* < Latin *carnivorus.*

carol (ˈkærəl) *n* a religious song of rejoicing, sung esp. at Christmas.
• *vb* sing carols; sing joyfully. **caroller** *n* < ultimately Greek *choros* chorus + *aulos* reed instrument.

carouse (kəˈraʊz) *vb* have an enjoyable bout of drinking. **carousal** *n* < German (*trinken*) *garaus* (to drink) all out.

carousel (ˌkærəˈsɛl) *n* **1** (*US*) a merry-go-round (at a fun-fair). **2** a rotating delivery system: luggage carousel. < Italian *carosello* tournament for horsemen.

carp[1] (kɑːp) *n, pl* **carp** a large, edible, freshwater fish that lives in ponds. < Latin *carpa.*

carp[2] *vb* find fault (unnecessarily); make petty complaints. < Middle English *carpen.*

carpel (ˈkɑːpl̩) *n* the seed-bearing part of a flower consisting of a stigma, style, and ovary. < ultimately Greek *karpos* fruit.

carpenter (ˈkɑːpɪntə) *n* someone who makes or mends wooden structures, furniture, etc. **carpentry** *n* < Latin *carpentum* carriage.

carpet (ˈkɑːpɪt) *n* a heavy, woven material, used for covering floors; layer on the ground like this: a carpet of leaves.
• *vb* **1** cover with or as if with a carpet. **2** (*informal*) reprimand. **carpeting** *n* material for carpets. **carpet slippers** slippers with uppers of cloth. **carpet-sweeper** *n* a manual device with rotating brushes for cleaning. **on the carpet** (*informal*) reprimanded (by an authority). < ultimately Latin *carpere* to pluck.

carriage (ˈkærɪdʒ) *n* **1** a wheeled passenger vehicle, esp. horse-drawn. **2** a railway car. **3** the act of conveying goods; its cost: carriage paid. **4** a moving part in a machine which supports another part: typewriter carriage. **5** body posture, esp. when walking. **carriage clock** a small, portable clock. **carriage forward** the charge for sending goods is paid by the receiver. **carriageway** *n* the part of a road used by vehicles: dual carriageway. < Old Northern French *carier* to transport in a vehicle.

carrier (ˈkærɪə) *n* **1** someone or something that carries something. **2** an individual or company under contract to transport people or goods. **3** a device for carrying: luggage carrier. **4** an animal or human that transmits disease, but is immune to it. **5** an aircraft-carrier. **carrier-bag** *n* a bag of paper or plastic used for holding shopping. **carrier pigeon** a homing pigeon, used to send messages.

carrion (ˈkærɪən) *n* dead, rotting flesh. **carrion crow** a common, black crow that feeds on carrion and small animals. < ultimately Latin *caro* flesh.

carrot (ˈkærət) *n* **1** an orange, tapering, root vegetable. **2** a promised reward: the carrot and the stick. < ultimately Greek *karōton*.

carry (ˈkærɪ) *vb* **carried; carrying 1** hold and move (a load); transport. **2** bear the weight of: This bridge carries 20 tons. **3** have on the body: He never carries any cash. **4** involve as a consequence: Murder carries a life sentence. **5** continue; extend: That's carrying it too far. **6** transfer to another column in sums. **7** behave or bear oneself in a certain way: She carries herself well. **8** capture; win: He carried the day. **9** (of newspapers or television) communicate: They carried the same story. **10** (of sound) be clearly transmitted. **11** be pregnant: carrying a child. **12** maintain through personal effort: He carries the team. **carry conviction** sound convincing. **carry-cot** *n* a portable, box-like bed for a baby. **carry weight** be influential. < ultimately Latin *carrus* carriage, SEE PANEL.

cart (kɑːt) n **1** a two or four-wheeled vehicle, used for transporting bulky loads, often pulled by a horse. **2** a small, hand-drawn vehicle with a shaft.
• *vb* (*slang*) carry (as if) by hard work: He carted the children off to school. **carter** *n* someone who drives carts or carries goods by trade. **cart-horse** *n* a strong horse, used for heavy labour. **cart-load** *n* as much as a cart can hold. **cart-track** *n* a rough dirt-track. **put the cart before the horse** reverse the logical order of things. < probably Old Norse *kartr*.

carte blanche (ˌkɑːt ˈblɑːntʃ) authority to act at one's own discretion. < French: blank document.

cartel (kɑːˈtɛl) *n* a group of companies, etc., which combine their interests to limit competition between them. < ultimately Latin *carta* leaf of paper.

cartilage (ˈkɑːtɪlɪdʒ) *n* a tough, elastic tissue in animals that mostly develops into bone or is attached to it; structure made of this. **cartilaginous** *adj* < Latin *cartilago*.

cartography (kɑːˈtɒgrəfɪ) *n* the art of making maps. **cartographer** *n* **cartographic** *adj* < French *carte* map.

carton (ˈkɑːtn̩) *n* a container, usually of cardboard; amount contained in this. < Italian *cartone* pasteboard.

cartoon (kɑːˈtuːn̩) *n* **1** a comical, often satirical drawing (in a newspaper); sequence of these telling a story: strip cartoon. **2** an animated sequence of drawings (on film). **3** a first sketch made by an artist before painting.
• *vb* draw cartoons. **cartoonist** *n* < Italian *cartone* pasteboard.

cartridge (ˈkɑːtrɪdʒ) *n* **1** a (tubular) casing for a bullet or explosive charge for blasting. **2** a sealed casing for film or magnetic tape. **3** the detachable part of the arm on a record-player that turns the vibrations of the stylus into an electrical signal. **cartridge paper** stiff, strong paper for drawing. < Middle French *cartouche*.

cartwheel (ˈkɑːtˌwiːl) *n* a sideways handspring with arms and legs extended

carrying out

Carry features in a number of idiomatic expressions, including:

carry away to fill (someone) with great emotion so that he or she can no longer control his or her thoughts, actions, etc.: She always gets carried away listening to records by Elvis.
carry forward to transfer from one page, account, etc., to the next one.
carry off 1 to win (a prize) in a competition. **2** to seize and take away. **3** to perform (a demanding task) successfully: It was a brave attempt, but she didn't quite carry it off.
carry on 1 to continue. **2** to hold or conduct (a conversation, discussion, etc.). **3** to pursue or conduct (a business or trade): It was in these premises that my father carried on his car-repair business. **4** to complain or fuss constantly. **5** to have an affair (with).
carry out to put into practice; fulfil, perform, or accomplish.

like the spokes of a wheel.

carve (kɑːv) *vb* **1** shape (wood, metal, or stone) by cutting. **2** cut (meat) into slices. **3** make by one's own efforts: She carved out a career for herself. **carver** *n* a sharp knife for carving meat. **carve up** divide into parts. **carving** *n* an article or design carved by a sculptor or engraver. < Old English *ceorfan.*

casanova (ˌkæsəˈnəʊvə) *n* a man who indulges in amorous adventures. < G. J. *Casanova,* died 1798, Italian libertine. SEE PANEL.

cascade (kæsˈkeɪd) *n* a waterfall; anything similar.
• *vb* fall in or as if in a cascade. < ultimately Latin *cadere* to fall.

case[1] (keɪs) *n* **1** an example of something happening: a case in point. **2** a diseased or injured condition; someone suffering from this: a bad case of fever. **3** a legal action. **4** a police investigation: a murder case. **5** evidence supporting something. **6** an (inflectional) form of a noun, pronoun, etc., showing grammatical relationship. **case-book** *n* legal or medical records. **case history** the record of one patient or offender. **in any case** whatever happens. **in case** as a precaution. **in case of** in the event of: in case of fire. < ultimately Latin *cadere* to fall.

case[2] *n* **1** a container; amount it contains. **2** a suitcase.
• *vb* **1** put in a case. **2** (*slang*) examine (a building) with the intention of stealing. < ultimately Latin *capere* to take.

casement (ˈkeɪsmənt) *n* a window-frame; hinged window-frame that opens outwards. < Old French *encassement* frame.

cash (kæʃ) *n* **1** money in notes or coins; wealth: short of cash. **2** money paid (in full) immediately for goods.
• *vb* give or receive cash for: cash a cheque. **cash-and-carry** *adj* (of goods) sold for cash and taken immediately by the purchaser. **cash crop** a crop produced for selling, not for the grower's use. **cash desk** the payment counter in a shop, etc. **cash flow** money moving into and out of a business in the course of trading. **cash in on** exploit. **cash on delivery** also **COD** payment on receipt. **cash register** a device which records the amount of every purchase. < ultimately Latin *capsa* chest.

cashew (ˈkæʃuː) *n* a tropical tree; small, edible nut it produces. < Tupi *acajú.*

cashier[1] (kæˈʃɪə) *n* someone responsible for receiving and paying out money in a bank; someone employed to take payment in a shop. < Middle French *casse* money-box.

cashier[2] *vb* dismiss from service in disgrace, esp. in the armed forces. < Middle French *casser.*

cashmere (ˈkæʃmɪə) *n* (fabric made from) the fine wool of the Kashmir goat. < *Kashmir,* region of Asia. SEE PANEL AT TULLE.

casing (ˈkeɪsɪŋ) *n* a (protective) covering; material this is made from.

casino (kəˈsiːnəʊ) *n, pl* **casinos** a room or building for gambling. < Latin *casa* cabin.

cask (kɑːsk) *n* a barrel, usually for keeping alcoholic drinks; amount contained in this. < Spanish *cascar* to break.

casket (ˈkɑːskɪt) *n* a small, ornamental box for jewellery. < Middle French *cassette.*

cassava (kəˈsɑːvə) *n* a tropical plant with edible, starchy roots; these roots. < Spanish *cazabe* cassava bread, from Taino *caçábi.*

casserole (ˈkæsəˌrəʊl) *n* a covered, heatproof dish for cooking and serving food; food served in this.
• *vb* cook (meat) in a casserole. < ultimately Greek *kyathos* ladle.

cassette (kæˈsɛt) *n* **1** a small, sealed container for magnetic tape. **2** a small, lightproof container holding photographic film. < Middle French: small case.

cassock (ˈkæsək) *n* an ankle-length garment worn by clergymen and

casanova

A man with the reputation of being a casanova is regarded as someone who indulges in amorous adventures. The name derives from Giovanni Jacopo *Casanova,* 1725–98, an Italian libertine and sexual athlete who regarded marriage as 'the tomb of love'. A great deal has been written about Casanova's exploits. He himself recorded them in graphic detail in his memoirs, entitled 'Histoire de ma vie'. Since he boasted some 130 different conquests, it is hardly surprising that the memoirs ran to 12 volumes.

choristers during church services. < Persian *kazh* raw silk + *āghand* padded.

cast (kɑːst) *vb* **cast; casting 1** throw: cast a fishing line. **2** shed; get rid of: cast doubt aside. **3** give (a vote). **4** shape (an object) by pouring metal or plastic into a mould and letting it harden. **5** select actors for; give out roles in (a play).
• *n* **1** throwing. **2** an object made from soft material hardened in a mould: plaster cast. **3** a set of performers (in a show). **4** a slight squint. **cast about for** look around for. **castaway** *n* someone who is shipwrecked. **casting vote** a vote deciding an issue if there is a tie. **cast iron** a hard alloy of iron, carbon, and silicon, cast in a mould. **cast-iron** *adj* of or like cast iron: a cast-iron stomach. **cast off** *vb* **1** untie a ship from its moorings. **2** loop stitches off a knitting-needle. **cast-offs** *pl n* clothes discarded by their owner. **cast on** loop stitches on a knitting-needle. < Old Norse *kasta.*

castanets (ˌkæstəˈnɛts) *pl n* a pair of wooden pieces clicked together rhythmically by the fingers, used esp. to accompany a Spanish dance. < Latin *castanea* chestnut.

caste (kɑːst) *n* **1** any of the restrictive, hereditary, social groups in Hinduism. **2** a social class. < ultimately Latin *castus* pure, chaste.

castle (ˈkɑːsl̩) *n* **1** a large, fortified building or set of buildings. **2** (*chess*) a rook. **castles in the air** fantasies. < Latin *castellum.* SEE PANEL.

castor (ˈkɑːstə) *n* **1** a small, swivelling wheel set on the base of a chair, etc., allowing motion. **2** a small container with holes in the top for sprinkling (salt or sugar). **castor sugar** white, finely granulated sugar. SEE PANEL.

castor oil (ˌkɑːstərˈɔɪl) *n* medicinal or lubricating oil made from the beans of a tropical plant. < Greek *kastōr* beaver. SEE PANEL AT **CASTOR.**

castrate (kæˈstreɪt) *vb* take away the testicles of; geld. **castration** *n* < Latin *castrare.*

casual (ˈkæʒjʊəl) *adj* **1** resulting from chance: a casual meeting. **2** with little concern or forethought: a casual comment. **3** occasional; irregular: casual work. **4** informal: casual clothes. **casually** *adv* **casualness** *n* **casuals** *pl n* casual clothes or shoes. < ultimately Latin *casus* fall, chance.

casualty (ˈkæʒjʊəltɪ) *n* **1** someone injured or killed in an accident or war. **2** something damaged, lost, or destroyed. < Latin *casualis* mischance, loss.

cat (kæt) *n* **1** a small, domestic animal with fur, kept as a household pet. **2** a wild animal, for example a lion or tiger, of the same family. **3** (*informal*) a spiteful woman. **4** a whip formerly used for flogging: cat-o'-nine-tails. **cat-and-mouse game** repeated bouts of near escapes and near captures. **cat burglar** a burglar who climbs up walls and drain-pipes to enter buildings. **cat's-eye** (*Trademark*) *n* a small reflector set in a road to mark the centre. **catty** *adj* spiteful. **catwalk** *n* a narrow gangway. **let the cat out of the bag** reveal a secret. **put the cat among the pigeons** say or do something controversial. < Old English *catt.*

cataclysm (ˈkætəˌklɪzəm) *n* **1** a sudden, violent, esp. destructive change. **2** a great flood. **cataclysmic** *adj* < Greek *kata-* down + *klyzein* to wash.

catacombs (ˈkætəˌkuːmz) *pl n* an underground cemetery of galleries with recessed tombs. < Latin *catacumbae.*

---

an Englishman's home is his castle

The expression an Englishman's home is his castle is a metaphorical reference to the fact that an Englishman thinks of his own home as an inviolable and impregnable sanctuary from which he can exclude the outside world.

The expression comes from the 'Third Institute' by the English lawyer and politician Sir Edward Coke, 1552–1634: For a man's house is his castle, *et domus sua cuique est tutissimum refugium* (and his own home is to each person the safest refuge).

---

castor or **caster?**

The meanings 'a small, swivelling wheel on furniture', 'a small container for sprinkling sugar, etc' may be spelt either castor or caster, as in armchair castors (or casters), castor (or caster) sugar.

Castor oil is, however, always spelt with an *-o-*, so a way of remembering the difference is to think of o for oil.

catalogue (ˈkætəˌlɒg) *n* a systematic list of items with a description of each; classification, register, or prospectus. • *vb* list in a catalogue. **cataloguer** *n* < ultimately Greek *katalegein* to list.

catalyst (ˈkætəˌlɪst) *n* a chemical which aids a chemical reaction but remains unchanged itself; someone or something whose action causes change. < Greek *katalyein* to dissolve.

catamaran (ˌkætəməˈræn) *n* a sailing vessel with twin hulls. < Tamil *kaṭṭu* to tie + *maram* tree.

catapult (ˈkætəˌpʌlt) *n* **1** a Y-shaped device with elastic, used for firing small stones. **2** a device for launching gliders or aircraft from a carrier. • *vb* **1** throw or launch from a catapult. **2** move suddenly: She was catapulted to stardom overnight. < ultimately Greek *kata* down + *pallein* to hurl.

cataract (ˈkætəˌrækt) *n* **1** a large waterfall; steep rapids. **2** a clouding over of the lens of the eye; area of this. < Medieval Latin *cataracta*.

catarrh (kəˈtɑː) *n* a watery discharge caused by an inflamed, mucous membrane, esp. of the nose or throat. **catarrhal** *adj* < ultimately Greek *kata* down + *rhein* to flow.

catastrophe (kəˈtæstrəfɪ) *n* a great and sudden disaster. **catastrophic** *adj* **catastrophically** *adv* < Greek *kata* + *strephein* to turn.

catch (kætʃ) *vb* **caught; catching** **1** capture after a chase. **2** discover; take by surprise: caught in the act. **3** stop the motion of (an object) and hold it. **4** be in time for: catch a bus; catch the late news. **5** briefly hear or see: I didn't catch what you said. **6** hit: The blow caught him on the head. **7** contract (an infection). **8** ignite: catch fire. **9** attract notice: catch her eye. • *n* **1** something caught: a large catch of fish. **2** a hidden difficulty: catch question. **3** a fastener. **4** a humorous round for voices. **catch-as-catch-can** *n* wrestling with all holds allowed. **catching** *adj* infectious. **catch it** (*informal*) be told off or punished. **catchment area** **1** an area from which a river, lake, or reservoir collects rainwater. **2** an area from which a hospital takes its patients or a school its pupils. **catch on** **1** become popular. **2** understand. **catch out** discover (someone) doing wrong or making a mistake. **catch-phrase** *n* also **catch-word** a current saying; slogan. **catch up** **1** draw level (with someone). **2** deal with work in arrears. **catchy** *adj* agreeable and easily remembered: a catchy tune. < ultimately Latin *capere* to take. SEE PANEL.

> **a catch-22 situation**
>
> A catch-22 or a catch-22 situation is an absurd dilemma from which the victim cannot escape, because the very means of escape is prohibited by the nature of the dilemma. The expression comes from the title of the novel 'Catch-22' by the US novelist Joseph Heller (1923–), published in 1961.

catechism (ˈkætɪˌkɪzəm) *n* a summary of (religious) principles in question and answer form; set of questions. < Greek *katēchein* to teach.

categorical (ˌkætəˈgɒrɪkl̩) *adj* positive; unqualified: a categorical denial. **categorically** *adv* **categorize** *vb* classify. **category** *n* a class of people or things. < Greek *katēgoria*.

cater (ˈkeɪtə) *vb* supply what is required, esp. food (for): They catered for 100 at the reception. **caterer** *n* someone whose trade is to provide food. < Old Northern French *acater* to buy.

caterpillar (ˈkætəˌpɪlə) *n* **1** the larva of a moth or butterfly. **2** **Caterpillar** (*Trademark*) a metal belt looped round the wheels of a tank or tractor, so that it can travel over rough ground. < Old Northern French *catepelose* hairy cat.

catfish (ˈkætˌfɪʃ) *n* a large-headed, freshwater fish with whisker-like barbels.

catgut (ˈkætˌgʌt) *n* a tough cord made from dried animal intestines, used in tennis rackets, strings for musical instruments, and surgical stitching.

catharsis (kəˈθɑːsɪs) *n* emotional relief gained by expressing feelings through art, drama, psychoanalysis, etc. **cathartic** *adj* < Greek *katharos* pure.

cathedral (kəˈθiːdrəl) *n* the principal church in a bishop's diocese. < Latin *cathedralis*, from *cathedra* bishop's chair.

cathode (ˈkæθəʊd) *n* a negative electrode, from which current enters a device from an electrical circuit. **cathode-ray tube** a vacuum tube in which a beam of electrons bombard a fluorescent screen and produce a picture, as in a television set. < Greek *kathodos* way down.

catholic (ˈkæθəlɪk) *adj* **1** universal;

comprehensive: catholic tastes. **2 Catholic** of Christians or Churches; Roman Catholic.
• *n* Roman Catholic. **Catholicism** *n* < ultimately Greek *kata* down + *holos* whole.

cation (ˈkætaɪən) *n* a positively-charged ion. < Greek *kata* down + *ienai* to go.

catkin (ˈkætkɪn) *n* a group of spiky, soft flowers hanging from a tree such as the willow or hazel. < obsolete Dutch *katteken* kitten.

cattle (ˈkætl̩) *pl n* bovine animals bred for meat or dairy produce. **cattle-grid** *n* a set of parallel bars over a shallow road-ditch, which stop cattle passing but allow vehicles to pass over. < ultimately Latin *capitalis* of the head.

caught (kɔːt) SEE **CATCH.**

cauldron (ˈkɔːldrən) *n* a large, deep pot for boiling, esp. over an open fire. < ultimately Latin *calēre* to be warm.

cauliflower (ˈkɒlɪˌflaʊə) *n* a vegetable related to the cabbage, with a white, compact flower-head. **cauliflower ear** a thickened, deformed ear, esp. from many blows received in boxing. < ultimately Latin *caulis* stem + *fiore* flower.

cause (kɔːz) *n* **1** someone or something that makes an event occur. **2** a reason: There's no cause to worry. **3** a principle or organization such as a charity, worthy of support. **4** (ground for) a lawsuit.
• *vb* bring about. **causal** *adj* **causality** *n* (the relationship of) cause and effect. **causative** *adj* effecting or expressing a cause. **cause célébre** a legal case or an issue attracting widespread interest. < Latin *causa.*

causeway (ˈkɔːzˌweɪ) *n* a raised path or road, esp. above land often covered by water. < Middle English *cauci* raised path + *wey* way.

caustic (ˈkɔːstɪk) *adj* **1** capable of corroding by chemical action. **2** biting; sarcastic: caustic wit. **caustically** *adv* < ultimately Greek *kaiein* to burn.

cauterize (ˈkɔːtəˌraɪz) *vb* destroy (skin tissue) by burning with caustic material, to prevent the spread of infection or remove it. **cauterization** *n*

caution (ˈkɔːʃən) *n* **1** care; regard for safety. **2** a warning of danger. **3** an (official) reprimand: let off with a caution. **4** (*informal*) someone or something that creates amusement or surprise.
• *vb* **1** advise care. **2** (of the police) warn someone that what he or she says will be recorded for possible evidence; reprimand. **cautionary** *adj* containing a warning: a cautionary tale. **cautious** *adj* wary. **cautiously** *adv* < Latin *cavēre* to be on guard.

cavalcade (ˌkævəlˈkeɪd) *n* a procession of horse-riders or cars. < Latin *caballus* horse.

cavalier (ˌkævəˈlɪə) *n* **1 Cavalier** a supporter of King Charles I during the English Civil War. **2** (*humorous*) a gallant gentleman, esp. in manners towards women.
• *adj* dismissive; haughty. < ultimately Latin *caballarius* horseman.

cavalry(ˈkævəlrɪ) *n* **1** (esp. formerly) a branch of the army consisting of troops on horseback. **2** troops in armoured vehicles in the modern army. < Italian *cavaliere.*

cave (keɪv) *n* a natural, underground chamber, often in the side of a cliff or hill. **cave in 1** collapse; make this happen. **2** (*informal*) submit. **caveman** *n* **1** someone who lived in a cave in prehistoric times. **2** a man treating a woman coarsely or primitively. < Latin *cavus* hollow.

caveat (ˈkævɪˌæt) *n* a caution; warning. < Latin: let him beware, from *cavēre.*

cavern (ˈkævn̩) *n* a large (underground) chamber or cave. **cavernous** *adj* < ultimately Latin *cavus.*

caviare (ˈkævɪˌɑː) *n* the salted roe of the sturgeon, eaten as a delicacy. < Turkish *havyar.*

cavil (ˈkævɪl) *vb* **cavilled; cavilling** make trivial objections. < Latin *cavilla* teasing.

cavity (ˈkævɪtɪ) *n* a hollow space within a mass: dental cavity. **cavity wall** a double wall with space between for insulation. < Latin *cavus* cave.

cavort (kəˈvɔːt) *vb* leap about excitedly; behave extravagantly. < origin uncertain.

CBI *abbrev* Confederation of British Industry.

cc *abbrev* **1** cubic centimetre(s). **2** carbon copy.

CD *abbrev* compact disc.

cease (siːs) *vb* end or stop. **ceasing** *n* **cease-fire** *n* (in war) an order to stop fighting. **ceaseless** *adj* never-ending. **ceaselessly** *adv* < ultimately Latin *cedere* to go, withdraw.

cedar (ˈsiːdə) *n* (the fragrant wood of) one of a group of tall, evergreen trees of the pine family. **cedarwood** *n* < Greek *kedros.*

cede (siːd) *vb* surrender (land), often by treaty. < Latin *cedere.*

ceiling (ˈsiːlɪŋ) *n* **1** the part of a room over one's head. **2** the maximum height an aircraft can fly at. **3** a (fixed) upper limit: price ceiling. < ultimately probably Latin *caedere* to cut. SEE PANEL.

celebrate (ˈsɛlɪˌbreɪt) *vb* **1** observe (a special occasion) by making festivities. **2** extol: His music celebrates the glories of nature. **3** take part (officially) in (a religious ceremony): celebrate mass. **celebration** *n* **celebrated** *adj* well-known. **celebrity** *n* renown; someone who is famous. < Latin *celeber* famous.

celerity (sɪˈlɛrɪtɪ) *n* swiftness of action or motion. < Latin *celer* swift.

celery (ˈsɛlərɪ) *n* a plant of the carrot family with a crisp stem, eaten in salads or cooked. < modified from Latin *selinon*.

celestial (sɪˈlɛstɪəl) *adj* **1** of or in the sky: celestial body. **2** divine; spiritual. < ultimately Latin *caelum* sky.

celibate (ˈsɛlɪbət) *adj* unmarried; not having a sexual relationship, esp. for reasons of religion. **celibacy** *n* < Latin *caelebs* unmarried.

cell (sɛl) *n* **1** a small room for a prisoner, religious recluse, etc. **2** one of many small compartments making up a honeycomb. **3** a unit of organic matter, containing a nucleus. **4** a device for generating electricity by chemical action. **5** a group of people forming a unit for political activity. **cellular** *adj* **1** of or like a cell. **2** with an open weave: cellular blanket. < Latin *cella* small room.

cellar (ˈsɛlə) *n* **1** an underground storage room. **2** a storage space for a stock of wine. < Latin *cella*. SEE PANEL.

cello (ˈtʃɛləʊ) *n, pl* **cellos** a violoncello; large musical instrument of the violin family, played in a seated position and held between the knees. **cellist** *n* a cello-player. < short for *violoncello*, from Italian *violone* small double-bass.

Cellophane (ˈsɛləˌfeɪn) *n* (*Trademark*) thin, transparent material, used esp. for wrapping goods. < French *cell*ulose + *-phane*, from Greek *phainein* to appear.

celluloid (ˈsɛljʊˌlɔɪd) *n* a tough plastic made from camphor and cellulose nitrate, used in cinema film. < *Celluloid*, trademark.

cellulose (ˈsɛljʊˌləʊs, ˈsɛljʊˌləʊz) *n* an organic substance present in plant tissue, used in the making of paper, plastics, and paints. < Latin *cellula*.

Celsius (ˈsɛlsɪəs) *adj* denoting a temperature scale of 100 degrees, with 0° as the freezing-point of water and 100° as the boiling-point of water. SEE PANEL.

Watch the ceiling!

Care should be taken when using ceiling in the sense 'an upper limit; fixed upper limit'. It is all too easy to evoke, unintentionally, the literal sense of the word, as in Carpet prices have reached a new ceiling, and so produce a humorous effect.

Headline writers tend to exploit the word's humorous potential, as for example: Oil ministers want to stick to ceiling, a headline in the 'Daily Gulf Times'.

cellar door

Pronounced slowly and carefully, many words and phrases can acquire a certain musical quality. However, unlike Shangri-La, those that are most pleasing to the ear sometimes have far from lyrical meanings. For James Joyce, for example, the word with the most pleasing sound was cuspidor, 'a spittoon'. Cellar door and Cellophane are equally musical but, again, hardly the stuff of poetry!

Celsius or centigrade?

Centigrade is the former name of the temperature scale for which 0° is the freezing-point of water and 100° is the boiling-point. The name was officially changed to Celsius in 1948, to avoid confusion with centigrade meaning 'a hundredth part of a grade'. Centigrade continues, however, to be used in some non-technical contexts, the name Celsius now commonly being used in meteorological and other scientific contexts. The scale is named after the Swedish astronomer Anders *Celsius*, 1701–44, who devised it in 1742. He originally designated 0° as the boiling-point of water and 100° as the freezing-point; the designations were later reversed.

cement (sɪˈmɛnt) *n* a binding material for building, consisting of a grey, lime-based powder that hardens when mixed with water; any similar binding material.
• *vb* **1** bind with cement. **2** unite strongly: They cemented their relationship by marrying. < Latin *caementum* rough stone.

cemetery (ˈsɛmətrɪ) *n* a burial ground not in a churchyard. < ultimately Greek *koimētērion* sleeping-chamber.

cenotaph (ˈsɛnəˌtɑːf) *n* a monument built to the memory of someone who is buried elsewhere. < ultimately Greek *kenos* empty + *taphos* tomb.

censor (ˈsɛnsə) *n* someone who examines letters, films, books, etc., with the authority to remove or delete anything considered objectionable.
• *vb* subject to this kind of examination. **censorship** *n* < Latin *censēre* to assess. SEE PANEL.

censure (ˈsɛnʃə) *n* strong condemnation; blaming.
• *vb* criticize strongly; blame. < Latin *censēre*. SEE PANEL AT **CENSOR.**

census (ˈsɛnsəs) *n* an official count or gathering of statistics, population, etc. < Latin *censēre*.

cent (sɛnt) *n* (a coin worth) one 100th of the standard currency unit of various countries, for example the US dollar; very small amount: not worth a cent. < Latin *centum* hundred.

centaur (ˈsɛntɔː) *n* a mythological creature, human from the waist up and with the lower body and legs of a horse. < Greek *kentauros*.

centenarian (ˌsɛntɪˈnɛərɪən) *n* someone who is 100 or more years old. < Latin *centum* hundred.

centenary (sɛnˈtiːnərɪ) *n* a 100th anniversary; celebration of this. **centennial** *adj* < Latin *centum* hundred.

center (ˈsɛntə) *vb, n* (*US*) (a) centre.

> **censor** or **censure?**
>
> These two words are sometimes confused.
> To censor means 'to examine letters, films, books, etc., with the authority to remove or delete anything considered objectionable or conflicting with official policy'.
> To censure is 'to criticize strongly or blame': They *censured* him for his unsatisfactory work.

centigrade (ˈsɛntɪˌgreɪd) *adj* **Celsius.** SEE PANEL AT **CELSIUS.**

centimetre (ˈsɛntɪˌmiːtə) *n* one 100th of a metre.

centipede (ˈsɛntɪˌpiːd) *n* an insect resembling a millipede with one pair of legs on each segment of its body. < Latin *centi-* hundred + *pes* foot.

central (ˈsɛntrəl) *adj* **1** of or being the centre. **2** principal; most important: the central figure of the drama. **centrality** *n* **centrally** *adv* **central heating** a heating system in which water, air, etc., is heated (by a boiler) and circulated via radiators or air vents through a building. **centralize** *vb* bring under central control, esp. of the State. **centralization** *n* **central processor** the main co-ordinating unit in a computer.

centre (ˈsɛntə) *n* **1** the exact middle. **2** someone or something that generates interest; gathering point: the centre of a controversy. **3** a concentration of buildings, etc., for a specific purpose: sports centre. **4** a moderate group or political party. **5** a centre-forward in soccer.
• *vb* **1** put at the centre. **2** concentrate (attention): All hopes are centred on him. **3** hit (a football) towards the middle. **centre-board** *n* a retractable keel on a small yacht. **centre-forward** *n* a player in hockey or soccer positioned in the middle of the forward line. **centre-half** *n* the player in the middle of the half-back line. < ultimately Greek *kentron* sharp point. SEE PANEL.

centrifugal (ˌsɛntrɪˈfjuːgl̩) *adj* **1** moving away from a centre or axis. **2** acting by centrifugal force, which pushes an object travelling round a centre away and outwards from its path. < Latin *centri* centre + *fugere* to flee.

century (ˈsɛntʃərɪ) *n* **1** a time-period of 100 years, esp. one reckoned in each direction from the birth of Christ. **2** 100 runs in one innings made by one cricketer. < Latin *centum* hundred.

ceramic (sɪˈræmɪk) *adj* of ceramics; of or

> **centre on** or **centre round?**
>
> Some careful users consider centre round, centre around and centre about to be nonstandard, preferring to use centre on instead: A new development, *centred on* the motorway intersection is planned.

being a pottery product.
• *n* **1** *pl* the art or work of making objects of baked clay. **2** such an object. < Greek *keramos* potter's clay.

cereal (ˈsɪərɪəl) *n* **1** a grass plant such as barley, wheat, or rice which produces grain for food; its seed. **2** breakfast food made from grain. < Greek *Ceres* goddess of agriculture.

cerebral (ˈsɛrɪbrəl) *adj* of or appealing to the brain or intellect. **cerebrally** *adv* < Latin *cerebrum* brain.

ceremony (ˈsɛrɪmənɪ) *n* **1** a formal occasion, esp. public or religious: the marriage ceremony. **2** formal politeness or civility. **ceremonial** *adj* of or used in ceremonies. **ceremonially** *adv* **ceremonious** *adj* elaborate; excessively formal. **ceremoniously** *adv* < ultimately Latin *caerimonia*. SEE PANEL.

certain (ˈsɜːtn̩) *adj* **1** beyond doubt; determined. **2** feeling sure: I'm certain this is the place. **3** dependable; accurate. **4** having a real, but unnamed quality: The road has a certain charm. **5** named but not actually known: a certain Mrs Jones. **6** some: to a certain extent. **certainly** *adv* **1** surely. **2** yes, emphatically. **certainty** *n* the state of being certain; something certain to happen. **certitude** *n* the feeling of being certain. **for certain** without a doubt. **make certain** make sure. < Latin *cernere* to decide.

certificate (səˈtɪfɪkət) *n* an official document declaring certain facts, esp. about the holder: birth certificate. < Latin *certificare* to certify.

certify (ˈsɜːtɪˌfaɪ) *vb* **certified; certifying** declare formally, esp. by displaying on a certificate. **certifiable** *adj* **certifiably** *adv* < ultimately Latin *certus* certain.

cervix (ˈsɜːvɪks) *n, pl* **cervices** **1** (the back of) the neck. **2** the narrow, outer end of the womb. < Latin.

cessation (sɛˈseɪʃn̩) *n* a temporary or final ending. < Latin *cessare* to delay.

cesspit (ˈsɛsˌpɪt) *n* also **cesspool** an underground, covered basin for the disposing of refuse or sewage. < ultimately Latin *suspirare* to breathe deeply.

cf *abbrev* compare. < Latin *conferre*.

c.f. *abbrev* carried forward.

chafe (tʃeɪf) *vb* **1** warm (the hands) by rubbing; make or become sore like this. **2** become impatient or irritated: chafing at the bit. < ultimately Latin *calefacere* to make warm.

chaff[1] (tʃɑːf, tʃæf) *n* **1** husks separated from seeds when grain is threshed. **2** chopped hay or straw, used as cattle fodder. **3** useless people or things. < Old English *ceaf*.

chaff[2] (tʃɑːf) *vb* banter; tease good-naturedly. < probably *chafe*.

chaffinch (ˈtʃæfɪntʃ) *n* a common European finch with a reddish chest and a bluish head. < Old English *ceaffinc*.

chagrin (ˈʃægrɪn) *n* a feeling of mixed irritation and disappointment. **chagrined** *adj* < French: sad.

chain (tʃeɪn) *n* **1** a length of interconnected metal loops, used for pulling, linking, or restraining objects or in jewellery. **2** a series of connected things: a mountain chain; chain of events. **3** a series of shops or hotels under the same ownership. **4** a unit of length (about 20.12 metres).
• *vb* restrict or secure with a chain or chains. **chain-letter** *n* a letter asking the receiver to make copies and send to others, sometimes with money, who will continue the process. **chain reaction** **1** a chemical or nuclear reaction making products that cause further changes. **2** a sequence of events, each one caused by the one before. **chain-saw** *n* a power saw with teeth on a revolving chain. **chain-smoke** *vb* smoke cigarettes continuously. **chain-smoker** *n* **chain-stitch** *n* a looped pattern in crochet or embroidery like a chain. **chain store** one of a group of similar shops under the same ownership. < ultimately Latin *catena*.

chair (tʃɛə) *n* **1** a seat for one person, with a back and sometimes arms. **2** an official position of authority at a meeting; chairmanship. **3** a professorship: a university chair.
• *vb* **1** install (someone) in a position of honour or office. **2** act as chairman of. **chair-lift** *n* a set of chairs on a looped cable, used for taking people up a mountain; ski-lift. **chairman** fem. **chairwoman** *n* someone who officiates

---

ceremonial or **ceremonious?**

These two words are sometimes confused.

Ceremonial means 'of or used in ceremonies' and is used in objective descriptions: a *ceremonial* occasion, *ceremonial* dress.

Ceremonious means 'elaborate; punctilious; excessively formal' and is used in giving subjective opinions or evaluations: *ceremonious* attention to detail.

---

at a meeting; someone who presides over a board of company directors. **chairmanship** *n* < ultimately Greek *kathedra,* from *kata* down + *hedra* seat. SEE PANEL.

chaise longue (ˌʃeɪz ˈlɒŋ) *n* a long, low seat for stretching out on, with a back and one arm rest. < French: long chair.

chalet (ˈʃæleɪ) *n* **1** a wooden hut or cottage in the mountains, common in Switzerland. **2** a small hut for staying in temporarily: holiday chalet. < French.

chalice (ˈtʃælɪs) *n* a large drinking cup or goblet, used esp. for holding the wine for the Holy Communion. < Latin *calix.*

chalk (tʃɔːk) *n* a soft, whitish, limestone; piece of this or a like substance, used for writing or drawing.
• *vb* mark or write with chalk. **chalky** *adj* **by a long chalk** by a long way. **chalk up** make a note of (a debt); achieve. < ultimately Greek *chalix* pebble.

challenge (ˈtʃælɪndʒ) *n* **1** an objection; calling into question. **2** a demand for an answer, esp. the demand to identify oneself made by a sentry. **3** a demanding or stimulating task or duty.
• *vb* **1** make a challenge: challenge to a duel. **2** object formally to (in a court of law). **3** question the rightness or validity of. **challenger** *n* **challenging** *adj* stimulating; demanding. < ultimately Latin *calumnia* calumny.

chamber (ˈtʃeɪmbə) *n* **1** a hall for formal purposes, esp. parliamentary meetings. **2** the part of a gun holding the cartridge or explosive charge. **3** *pl* rooms used by a firm of barristers. **4** (*archaic*) a room or bedroom. **chamber-maid** *n* a woman who works in a hotel, cleaning and servicing bedrooms. **chamber music** music composed for a small group of instruments. **chamber-pot** *n* a bowl for urine, used in the bedroom. < ultimately Greek *kamara* room.

chamberlain (ˈtʃeɪmbəlɪn) *n* the chief official of a noble or royal household. < Old French *chamberlayn.*

chameleon (kəˈmiːlɪən) *n* **1** a small lizard which changes the colour of its skin to blend in with its environment for protection. **2** someone who changes his or her mind according to a whim or circumstance. < ultimately Greek *chamai* on the ground + *leōn* lion.

chamois *n* **1** (ˈʃæmwɑː) a type of small, mountain antelope. **2** (ˈʃæmɪ) also **chamois leather** a soft, buff-coloured leather made from goat or sheepskin, used for polishing. < Latin *camox.*

champ (tʃæmp) *vb* **1** chew noisily. **2** be impatient or restless. < perhaps from the sound.

champagne (ʃæmˈpeɪn) *n* a sparkling white wine, made esp. in Champagne,

---

chairman, chairwoman, or ... ?

Traditional use of the word chairman has been attacked by those who wish to avoid language that reflects a male-dominated society. Various alternatives have been suggested:

☐ Use chairman when the person referred to is a man and chairwoman when the person is a woman.
☐ Use chairperson throughout.
☐ Use chair: Mrs Carter is in the chair tonight. (Chair is used as a verb, especially in spoken usage: Mrs Carter is chairing the meeting tonight.)

Other words that have been considered suitable for similar changes include the following (alternatives are shown in brackets):

spokesman (spokeswoman; spokesperson)
salesman (saleswoman; salesperson)
statesman (stateswoman; statesperson)

---

champagne

The name of a wine or spirit often borrows the name of the region where it was developed. Such is the case with champagne, the celebrated, sparkling white wine that was named after the former French province of *Champagne.* Also of French origin are burgundy, the red or white table wine from the *Burgundy* region, and the wine-based cognac, from the town of *Cognac* in Charente in western France.

Such a list would not be complete without mention of the two most popular fortified wines, port and sherry. Port takes its name from *Oporto,* a seaport in Portugal, and sherry, from *Xeres* (now Jerez) in southern Spain, where it was first produced.

France. < *Champagne*, France.
SEE PANEL.

champion (ˈtʃæmpɪən) *n* **1** the winner of a race or competition. **2** someone who fights or pleads for a cause: a champion of women's rights.
• *adj* (*chiefly Northern England informal*) wonderful.
• *vb* support; speak for. **championship** *n* < Medieval Latin *campio*.

chance (tʃɑːns) *n* **1** fate or luck; way things happen without explanation: We met totally by chance. **2** the possibility of (something) happening: There's a chance you might get the job. **3** an opportunity.
• *vb* **1** take a risk. **2** happen.
• *adj* occurring by chance: a chance meeting. **by chance** unintentionally. **chance on** meet or find accidentally. **chancy** *adj* uncertain; risky. **take one's chances** trust in luck or fate. < ultimately Latin *cadere* to fall.

chancel (ˈtʃɑːnsl̩) *n* a part of a church with seats for clergy and choir, near the altar. < ultimately Latin *cancelli* latticework.

chancellor (ˈtʃɑːnsələ) *n* **1** an official of the State or of an Anglican diocese. **2** the head of State in some European nations, such as Germany. **3** the head of a university. **chancellorship** *n* **chancellery** *n* **1** the department or position of a chancellor. **2** the office of an embassy or consulate. **Chancellor of the Exchequer** the minister in charge of Britain's finances. < ultimately Latin *cancellarius* porter, secretary.

chancery (ˈtʃɑːnsərɪ) *n* a division of the High Court. < Old French *chancelier*.

chandelier (ˌʃændɪˈlɪə) *n* an ornamental fixture for many lights, suspended from a ceiling. < ultimately Latin *candelabrum*.

change (tʃeɪndʒ) *vb* **1** make or become different; alter. **2** move from one state to another. **3** replace one thing by another: change the subject. **4** exchange (money) for foreign currency or for smaller coins or notes. **5** put different clothes on: change the baby. **6** get off a bus, train, etc., and get on another.
• *n* **1** changing; modification. **2** a substitution; alternative: a change of clothes. **3** a new job or environment: a change of air. **4** money in small denominations; money given back when the purchase price is lower than what is given. **changeable** *adj* **1** capable of changing. **2** frequently changing: changeable weather. **change down** put a car into a lower gear. **change hands** change ownership. **change of heart** a major shift in attitude or feelings. **change of life** the menopause. **change over** move to a different position or attitude. **change-over** *n* **change up** put a car into a higher gear. **for a change** in order to depart from routine. **get no change out of** (*slang*) be unsuccessful in trying to exploit or get information from (someone). **ring the changes 1** ring church bells in various set patterns. **2** herald a new era or situation. < ultimately Latin *cambiare* to exchange.

channel (ˈtʃænl̩) *n* **1** the bed of a stream or river; navigable part of a waterway. **2** a narrow stretch of sea between two land masses: the English Channel. **3** a course for directing enquiries or information: You'll have to go through the proper channels. **4** a passage or groove along which liquids can flow. **5** a band of frequencies on which programmes can be broadcast; television station. **6** a path for the flow of data, as in a computer. **7** a path for an electrical signal to flow.
• *vb* **channelled; channelling 1** create a channel or channels in. **2** direct along a particular route: channel one's energies. < ultimately Latin *canalis*.

chant (tʃɑːnt) *n* **1** a repetitive melody, esp. for a liturgical song, in which several syllables are sung on one note. **2** a monotonous song or shout, with a rhythm.
• *vb* **1** sing (a chant). **2** utter or shout rhythmically. **chanter** *n* < ultimately Latin *canere* to sing.

chaos (ˈkeɪɒs) *n* a state of great confusion. **chaotic** *adj* **chaotically** *adv* < Greek.

chap¹ (tʃæp) *vb* **chapped; chapping** make or become cracked; split.
• *n* a crack in the skin, caused by being exposed to cold or wind. < Middle English *chappen*.

chap² *n* (*informal*) a man. < Old English *cēapman* merchant.

chapel (ˈtʃæpl̩) *n* **1** a place for worship in a residence, school, etc. **2** a service in a chapel. **3** a room within a church or cathedral with an altar, often for private prayer. < Medieval Latin *cappella* small cloak.

chaperon (ˈʃæpəˌrəʊn) *n* an older woman who accompanies a young woman or girl on social occasions to ensure proper behaviour.
• *vb* escort; act as a chaperon to. < Middle French: head covering.

chaplain (ˈtʃæplɪn) *n* a clergyman attached to a private chapel or to a branch of the armed forces, etc. **chaplaincy** *n* < Medieval Latin *cappella* small cloak.

chapter (ˈtʃæptə) *n* **1** a numbered division of a book; something like this: a new chapter in her life. **2** (a meeting of) the canons of a cathedral or members of a religious order. **chapter and verse** exact specification of a piece of information. **chapter-house** *n* a building used for the gatherings of a cathedral chapter. < ultimately Latin *caput* head.

char[1] (tʃɑː) *vb* **charred; charring** blacken by burning; scorch. < back formation from *charcoal*.

char[2] *n* (*slang*) tea. < Chinese *chá* tea. SEE PANEL.

charabanc (ˈʃærəˌbæŋ) *n* an early form of motor coach, used for outings. < French *char à bancs* wagon with benches.

character (ˈkærɪktə) *n* **1** the qualities which distinguish people or things from others. **2** the essence of something: The city has a unique character. **3** integrity; moral strength: a woman of character. **4** someone who is noticeable or odd: He's quite a character. **5** a letter or sign which is part of an alphabet or other writing system. **6** a personage in a novel, play, film, etc. **characteristic** *adj, n* (being) part of the character of. **characterize** *vb* **1** describe the character of. **2** be typical of. **characterization** *n* **in/out of character** conforming/not conforming to someone's general behaviour. < ultimately Greek *charassein* to engrave.

charade (ʃəˈrɑːd) *n* **1** a ridiculous pretence. **2** an episode in the game of charades, in which the clue to a word is mimed. < Provençal *charrado* conversation.

charcoal (ˈtʃɑːˌkəʊl) *n* a form of carbon, produced by partly burning wood, and used as fuel or for drawing. **charcoal grey** dark grey. < Middle English *charcole*.

charge (tʃɑːdʒ) *n* **1** the payment asked for an item or service. **2** the amount an apparatus can hold at one time, esp. a gun or bomb: explosive charge. **3** an amount of electricity, as stored in a battery. **4** a duty or responsibility. **5** someone or something to be supervised. **6** an accusation, esp. by the police. **7** an attack made by violently rushing forwards.
• *vb* **1** ask for as payment; record (an item) as an expense: Charge it to my account. **2** load (a gun) with a charge. **3** store electricity in (a battery). **4** entrust (someone) with a duty. **5** indict formally. **6** attack in a sudden rush. **charge in** act with little forethought. **in charge** in command. **take charge** take command of. < ultimately Latin *carricare*, from *carrus* vehicle.

chariot (ˈtʃærɪət) *n* a horse-drawn carriage with two wheels, used in ancient times for racing and warfare. < ultimately Latin *carrus*.

charisma (kəˈrɪzmə) *n* the quality of leadership or charm of someone who can inspire loyalty and enthusiasm in others. **charismatic** *adj* < Greek: gift.

charity (ˈtʃærɪtɪ) *n* **1** kindness to others; kindness in judgment of people or actions. **2** generosity to the poor. **3** an organization which helps those in need. **charitable** *adj* **charitably** *adv* < ultimately Latin *carus* dear.

charlady (ˈtʃɑːˌleɪdɪ) *n* a charwoman.

charlatan (ˈʃɑːlətn̩) *n* someone who claims falsely to have special knowledge, esp. about medicine; fraud. < Italian *ciarlatano*.

charm (tʃɑːm) *n* **1** the power to fascinate or attract others. **2** a magical chant or object. **3** a small ornament worn round the neck on a chain.
• *vb* **1** fascinate; attract. **2** influence (as if) by magic; bewitch. **charmer** *n* **charming** *adj* extremely agreeable; fascinating. < Latin *canere* to sing.

chart (tʃɑːt) *n* **1** a navigation map. **2** an outline map for displaying geographical information: a weather chart. **3** a sheet or graph showing information in tabulated form. **the charts** *pl n* a list of currently popular songs.
• *vb* make a plan or chart of; map. < ultimately Latin *charta* papyrus.

charter (ˈtʃɑːtə) *n* **1** a formal document granting certain privileges; contract: royal charter. **2** the (group) hiring of a vehicle, ship, or aircraft.

a cup of char

The word char as used in a cup of char ('a cup of tea') is popularly thought to derive from char, a curtailed form of charwoman. However, this is not the case. Char, formerly spelt tcha, comes ultimately from the Chinese word for tea: chá. British servicemen encountered the word in its Hindi form cā while serving in India during the days of the British Empire.

• *vb* **1** grant by charter. **2** hire or lease (a vehicle, ship, or aircraft). **chartered** *adj* certified as professionally qualified according to the regulations of an organization which has a royal charter: chartered accountant; chartered surveyor. < Latin *chartula* small document.

charwoman (ˈtʃɑːˌwʊmən) *n, pl* **charwomen** also **charlady** a woman employed to clean a house, etc. < *chare* chore.

chary (ˈtʃɛərɪ) *adj* **1** cautious. 2 reluctant to grant or accept: chary of compliments. < Old English *caru* sorrow.

chase (tʃeɪs) *vb* **1** go after rapidly with the purpose of capturing; cause to flee. **2** rush around: I chased all over town for it.
• *n* **1** pursuing. **2** hunting as a sport. **3** a steeplechase. **4** unenclosed land, often where animals are bred for hunting. **chase up** (*informal*) contact (someone) in order to get results quickly; investigate. < Middle French *chasser.*

chasm (ˈkæzəm) *n* **1** a deep gap in the earth. **2** a seemingly unbridgeable difference of opinion or position. < Greek *chasma.*

chassis (ˈʃæsɪ) *n, pl* **chassis** a supporting framework for the body of a vehicle; frame for mounting parts of a radio, TV, etc. < ultimately Latin *capsa* box.

chaste (tʃeɪst) *adj* **1** not having sexual intercourse outside marriage, or at all; celibate. **2** modest in behaviour. **3** plain or austere in design. **chastely** *adv* **chastity** *n* < Latin *castus* pure.

chasten (ˈtʃeɪsn̩) *vb* **1** subdue or restrain. **2** discipline by punishing. < Latin *castigare.*

chastise (tʃæsˈtaɪz) *vb* **1** criticize or reprimand severely. **2** punish, esp. by beating. **chastisement** *n* < Middle English *chastisen.*

chat (tʃæt) *n* a friendly, informal talk.
• *vb* **chatted; chatting** have a chat. **chat show** a radio or television programme in which well-known people are interviewed. **chat someone up** (*informal*) flirt with someone; talk persuasively to someone with a hidden motive. < Middle English *chatten.*

château (ˈʃætəʊ) *n, pl* **châteaux** a French castle or large, country house. < French, from Latin *castellum* castle.

chattel (ˈtʃætl̩) *n* a personal possession, esp. movable: goods and chattels. < Medieval Latin *capitale.*

chatter (ˈtʃætə) *vb* **1** talk idly and rapidly. **2** (of animals) make fast, repeated sounds like this. **3** click uncontrollably and repeatedly, from cold: His teeth chattered.
• *n* chattering talk or sound. **chatterer** *n* **chatterbox** *n* someone fond of talking, esp. trivially. **chatty** *adj* **1** fond of chatting. **2** similar to a chat: a chatty letter. **chattily** *adv* **chattiness** *n* < like the sound.

chauffeur (ˈʃəʊfə, ʃəʊˈfɜː) *n* someone who is employed to drive a car for someone else.
• *vb* work as a chauffeur; drive someone around like this. < Middle French *chauffer* to heat. SEE PANEL.

chauvinism (ˈʃəʊvɪˌnɪzəm) *n* excessive patriotism; prejudiced belief of superiority by one group over another: male chauvinism. **chauvinist** *n* **chauvinistic** *adj* < Nicolas *Chauvin,* patriotic French soldier devoted to Napoleon. SEE PANEL.

cheap (tʃiːp) *adj* **1** with a (relatively) low price; below the real value of (an article). **2** gained by little effort: a cheap victory. **3** showy but poor in quality; tawdry. **4** contemptible. **cheaply** *adv* **cheapness** *n* **cheapen** *vb* make or become cheap; lower in value or esteem. < Old English *cēap* trade.

cheat (tʃiːt) *vb* **1** behave unfairly for

the French chauffeur

The origin of words which have come into English from other languages is often recognizable from their spelling and pronunciation. This is especially true of words that have entered the language in recent centuries from French. Words ending in *-eur* for example, such as chauffeur, connoisseur, raconteur, and masseur, have retained their French spelling, and despite a certain assimilation still sound more French than English. Other French loan-words which are equally recognizable include:

-vue revue, venue
-et ballet, valet, chalet, cabaret, bouquet
-ette brunette, coquette, cigarette
-que clique, critique
-age sabotage, camouflage, fuselage, barrage
-oir abattoir, boudoir
-ge prestige, rouge
-ade promenade, brigade
-eau tableau, bureau
-é risqué, communiqué, cliché, résumé
-re macabre, manoeuvre
-lle vaudeville

one's own benefit; deprive (someone) by trickery. **2** avoid; defeat the effects of.
● *n* **1** someone who cheats (at a game). **2** deceit by fraud. < Middle English *chet* escheat, reversion of property to the lord, etc.

check[1] (tʃɛk) *vb* **1** inspect (goods, etc.) for good condition, safety, or performance. **2** slow or stop (a moving object); stop suddenly. **3** threaten (the king of one's opponent) in chess. **4** (*chiefly US*) also **check out** correspond.
● *n* **1** an inspection. **2** a sudden stop; slowing down. **3** a position in which the king of one's opponent is threatened in chess: in check. **4** a receipt. **5** a restaurant bill. **6** (*US*) a cheque. **checker** *n* **checkers** *pl n* (*US*) the game of draughts. **check in** register one's arrival at a hotel, etc. **check-in** *n* **check-list** *n* an itemized list for reference. **checkmate** *n, vb* (cause) the complete defeat of one's opponent in chess; defeat in any other situation. **check on** or **up** verify or investigate. **check out** register at one's departure from a hotel, etc. **check-out** *n* the till-counter where goods are paid for, for example in a supermarket. **check-point** *n* an inspection area for vehicles or documents. **check-up** *n* a (medical) examination. < Persian *shāh* king.

check[2] *n* a pattern of crossed lines or squares, like a chess-board. **checked** *adj* < Persian *shāh* king.

cheek (tʃi:k) *n* **1** either side of the face above and beside the mouth and below the eye. **2** insolent speech or actions.
● *vb* speak rudely to (someone). **cheek by jowl** close together. **cheeky** *adj* rude; insolent. **cheekily** *adv* **cheekiness** *n* < Old English *cēace*. SEE PANEL.

cheep (tʃi:p) *n* a faint, shrill cry of or like a young bird.
● *vb* make this sound. < like the sound.

cheer (tʃɪə) *n* **1** applause or encouragement by shouting: Three cheers! **2** good spirits: be of good cheer.
● *vb* **1** applaud or encourage with cheers. **2** also **cheer up** give hope or courage to; gladden. **cheerful** *adj* in good spirits; agreeably bright: a cheerful tune. **cheerfully** *adv* **cheerfulness** *n* **cheerio** *interj* (*informal*) goodbye. **cheerless** *adj* dreary; miserable. **cheers** *interj* used as a toast. < Old French *chere* face.

cheese (tʃi:z) *n* **1** food made from ripened, compressed, milk curds; this in a cylinder-shaped mass. **2** fruit preserves of a similar consistency: lemon cheese. **cheesy** *adj* **cheesecake** *n* a dessert with a soft, sweet cheese filling on a biscuit or pastry base. **cheesecloth** *n* a fine type of loosely-woven cotton. **cheesed** *adj* (*slang*) also **cheesed off** bored; peeved. **cheese-paring** *adj* miserly. < Old English *cēse*.

cheetah (ˈtʃi:tə) *n* an African animal of the cat family, the swiftest mammal, with long legs and a black-spotted, yellowish coat. < Sanskrit *citrakāya* tiger, from *citra* bright + *kāya* body.

chef (ʃɛf) *n* a skilled cook, esp. the head cook in a restaurant or hotel. < French, short for *chef de cuisine* head of kitchen.

chemical (ˈkɛmɪkḷ) *adj* of or produced by chemistry.
● *n* a substance occurring as a result of a process of chemistry. **chemically** *adv*

chemistry (ˈkɛmɪstrɪ) *n* the science dealing with the nature of substances and how they react with or relate to one another; chemical structure. **chemist** *n* **1** someone trained in chemistry. **2** someone working in a pharmacy; pharmacy. < SEE **ALCHEMY.**

cheque (tʃɛk) *n* a written order instructing a bank to pay out money from an

chauvinism

In recent years the phrase male chauvinism has become a stock phrase in feminist literature. Chauvinism is a derogatory term signifying an irrational or prejudiced belief in the superiority of one's group or cause and a male chauvinist therefore denotes a man who believes in or advocates male supremacy. The word derives from the name of Nicolas *Chauvin,* a veteran of the Napoleonic wars who in his day was widely ridiculed for his excessive patriotism and fanatical allegiance to Napoleon.

turn the other cheek

The expression to turn the other cheek means 'to respond to a blow not by retaliating but by being prepared to accept further blows'. The expression comes from the Authorized (King James) Version of the Bible, Matthew 5:39: But I say unto you, That ye resist not evil: but whosoever shall smite thee on thy right cheek, turn to him the other also.

account; paper issued by banks for this. **cheque-book** *n* a book of unused cheques. **cheque card** a card issued by a bank, which guarantees the carrier's cheques up to a specified amount. < modified from *check*.

chequer (ˈtʃɛkə) *n* a pattern of squares of two different colours. **chequer-board** *n* a board of this pattern. **chequered** *adj* **1** marked with a pattern of chequers. **2** varied; irregular. < Old French *eschec* check (in chess). SEE PANEL.

cherish (ˈtʃɛrɪʃ) *vb* **1** feel or show tenderness towards. **2** hold deeply and affectionately in the heart: I cherish the memory. < ultimately Latin *carus* dear.

cheroot (ʃəˈruːt) *n* a cigar with both ends squarely cut off. < Tamil *curuṭṭu* roll.

cherry (ˈtʃɛrɪ) *n* **1** one of a group of trees and shrubs of the rose family, grown for its fruit or ornamental flowers; its wood or small, soft, round fruit. **2** bright-red. • *adj* bright-red. **cherry brandy** a cherry-flavoured, brandy liqueur. < Greek *kerasos*.

cherub (ˈtʃɛrəb) *n, pl* **cherubs, cherubim 1** a kind of angel, often represented in art as a beautiful child with wings. **2** a sweet, angelic child. < Hebrew *kĕrūbh*.

chess (tʃɛs) *n* a game for two players with sixteen pieces each to be moved across a chess-board, the object being to capture the opponent's king. < Old French *eschec* check at chess.

chest (tʃɛst) *n* **1** a large, sturdy, lidded case for storage or shipping. **2** the upper, front part of the body from the neck to the abdomen. **chest of drawers** a piece of furniture with drawers, used for keeping clothes in. **chesty** *adj* tending to or symptomatic of bronchial disorders: a chesty cough. **get off one's chest** (*informal*) get relief from (worries or troubles) by talking about them. **play it close to one's chest** act secretly. < Old English *cest*.

chestnut (ˈtʃɛsˌnʌt) *n* **1** one of a group of trees of the beech family which produces hard, brown nuts, edible in some varieties; its nut or wood. **2** reddish-brown; horse of this colour. **3** a well-worn story or joke. • *adj* reddish-brown. < ultimately Greek *kastanea*.

chew (tʃuː) *vb* crush or grind (food) with the teeth; make a movement like this. • *n* chewing; something chewed. **chewing-gum** *n* a sweet, sticky substance that can be chewed for a long time. **chew over** (*informal*) think lengthily about. < Old English *cēowan*.

chic (ʃiːk) *adj, n* (displaying) style or sophistication. < French.

chicanery (ʃɪˈkeɪnərɪ) *n* verbal trickery, esp. legal; sharp practice. **chicane** *n* a movable barrier placed at tight bends on a motor-racing course. **chicane** *vb* trick; deceive. < Middle French *chicaner* to quibble.

chick (tʃɪk) *n* **1** a newly-hatched, young bird; chicken. **2** (*slang*) a young woman.

chicken (ˈtʃɪkɪn) *n* **1** a young, domestic fowl; meat from this. **2** (*slang*) a coward. **3** (*slang*) a game testing bravery by setting up dangerous situations. **4** (*slang*) a young person: You're no spring chicken! • *adj* (*slang*) scared; cowardly. **chicken-feed** *n* **1** poultry food. **2** (*informal*) an insignificant amount. **chicken out** (*slang*) fail to do something through fear. **chicken-pox** *n* a disease, esp. of children, causing spots on the skin. **chicken wire** light, wire netting with a hexagonal mesh. < Old English *cicen* young chicken. SEE PANEL.

chicory (ˈtʃɪkərɪ) *n* a blue-flowered plant grown for its roots and salad leaves; its ground, roasted root, sometimes used with coffee. < Greek *kichoreia*.

chide (tʃaɪd) *vb* **chided, chid; chidden; chiding** scold; tell off angrily. < Old English *cīd* strife.

chief (tʃiːf) *n* the head of a group of

Chinese chequers

Of the many national adjectives in the vocabulary, relatively few have found their way into commonly used expressions. Chinese, as in Chinese chequers and Chinese lantern, is an example of one which has. Far more productive, however, is Dutch, which features in:

Dutch auction
Dutch barn
Dutch cap
Dutch courage
Dutch oven
Dutch treat
Dutch uncle

Other adjectives used in this way include:

African violet
French kiss
French leave
German measles
Indian summer
Irish stew
Scotch whisky
Spanish omelette
Spanish onion
Swiss roll
Welsh rarebit

people or organization; leader.
• *adj* **1** of the highest rank. **2** most important. **chiefly** *adv* < ultimately Latin *caput* head.

chieftain (ˈtʃiːftən) *n* the leader of a tribe, clan, etc.

chiffon (ˈʃɪfɒn, ʃɪˈfɒn) *n* a very fine, semi-transparent silk or nylon fabric. < Middle English *chip* chip.

chilblain (ˈtʃɪlˌbleɪn) *n* an inflamed sore, esp. on the hands or feet, caused by over-exposure to cold. < *chill* + *blain* swelling.

child (tʃaɪld) *n, pl* **children 1** a young human, esp. between infancy and adolescence; boy or girl. **2** a son or daughter. **childbirth** *n* the act of giving birth. **childhood** *n* the period or condition of life before adolescence. **childish** *adj* immature in behaviour. **childishly** *adv* **childishness** *n* **childless** *adj* without children. **childlike** *adj* innocent; trusting. **child-minder** *n* someone paid to look after children. < Old English *cild.* SEE PANEL. SEE PANEL AT **OX.**

chill (tʃɪl) *n* **1** a disagreeable sensation of cold. **2** a slight fever with shivers; the common cold. **3** coldness of manner.
• *vb* **1** make or become disagreeably cold. **2** keep (wine or food) cool without freezing. **chilly** *adj* **1** disagreeably cold. **2** unfriendly: a chilly reception. **chilliness** *n* < Old English *cele.*

chilli (ˈtʃɪlɪ) *n, pl* **chillies** the dried pod of a hot pepper, eaten whole or ground as seasoning. **chilli con carne** a minced beef stew, spiced with chillies. < Nahuatl *chilli.*

chime (tʃaɪm) *n* a percussion instrument consisting of a set of tuned, metal tubes; sound of these when struck.
• *vb* ring (bells); (of a clock) signal (the hour) by chiming. **chime in** interrupt. < ultimately Latin *cymbalum* cymbal.

chimney (ˈtʃɪmnɪ) *n* a vertical structure (on the roof of a building) that carries away smoke or gases from a fire. **chimney-pot** *n* a pipe on top of a chimney. **chimney-stack** *n* a group of chimneys close together. **chimney-sweep** *n* someone who cleans soot from chimneys for a living. < ultimately Greek *kaminos* fireplace.

chimpanzee (ˌtʃɪmpænˈziː) *n* an African ape that lives in trees, smaller than a gorilla. < Kongo dialect *chimpenzi.*

chin (tʃɪn) *n* the front part of the lower jaw. **chin-wag** *n* (*informal*) a chat. **keep one's chin up** keep in good spirits. < Old English *cinn.*

china (ˈtʃaɪnə) *n* fine porcelain; household crockery: bone china. < Persian *chīnī* Chinese porcelain.

chink¹ (tʃɪŋk) *n* a small slit or opening: a chink in his armour. < probably modified from Middle English *chin, chine.*

chink² *n* a short, sharp sound, like that of glasses being struck together.
• *vb* make or cause to make this sound. < like the sound.

chip (tʃɪp) *n* **1** a small piece cut or struck off from a hard substance; flaw left from this. **2** a strip of potato fried in fat. **3** (*US*) a potato crisp. **4** a counter used as a gambling token. **5** a computer microchip.
• *vb* **chipped; chipping** cut or break off a small piece (of something); carve or shape in this way. **chipboard** *n* an artificial board made from compressed wood chips and resin. **chip in 1** interrupt with a comment. **2** contribute money. < Middle English. SEE PANEL.

chiropody (kɪˈrɒpədɪ, ʃɪˈrɒpədɪ) *n* the treatment of human feet (for corns, etc.). **chiropodist** *n* < Greek *chir-* hand

chicken

The chicken is neither a particularly affectionate nor attractive bird and yet, in informal usage, the word chicken is sometimes used as a term of endearment: 'Come on, chicken. Let's be going.' Interestingly, in the language of the playground, the word has a very different meaning: 'I bet he won't do it. He's too chicken!' Here the sense is 'cowardly' or 'lacking courage'.

childish or childlike?

The basic difference between childish and childlike is that, unlike childlike, childish expresses the negative, pejorative aspects of a child's behaviour. Childlike is used in neutral and positive descriptions. So childish means 'marked by an unpleasant immaturity in behaviour': *childish* displays of temper; Don't be so *childish!* And childlike means 'marked by an innocence or simplicity characteristic of a child': *childlike* credulity.

+ *pod-* foot.
chirp (tʃɜːp) *vb, n* (make) the short, shrill sound of a small bird or grasshopper. **chirpy** *adj* bright and cheerful. < like the sound.
chirrup (ˈtʃɪrəp) *vb, n* (make) a repeated chirping sound. < like the sound.
chisel (ˈtʃɪzl̩) *n* a metal tool, used for working or shaping wood, metal, etc.
• *vb* **chiselled; chiselling** work or shape with a chisel. **chiseller** *n* < ultimately Latin *caedere* to cut.
chit (tʃɪt) *n* a brief, written note, esp. a goods order or statement of money owed. < Hindi *ciṭṭhī.*
chit-chat (ˈtʃɪtˌtʃæt) *n* small talk; gossip. < SEE **CHAT.**
chivalry (ˈʃɪvəlrɪ) *n* courtesy and consideration, esp. towards women. **chivalrous** *adj* < Middle French *chevalier* horseman.
chive (tʃaɪv) *n* a small, purple-flowered herb related to the onion, used for flavouring. < Latin *cepa* onion.
chivvy (ˈtʃɪvɪ) *vb* **chivvied; chivvying** (*informal*) also **chivvy up** annoy (someone) by constant urging; harass. < probably English dialect *Chevy Chase,* title of a ballad.
chlorine (ˈklɔːriːn) *n* a chemical element of the halogen group, a poisonous greenish-yellow gas, used in purifying water and cleaning agents. **chlorinate** *vb* treat with chlorine. **chlorination** *n* < Greek *chlōros* greenish-yellow.
chloroform (ˈklɒrəˌfɔːm) *n* a colourless liquid, formerly used as an anaesthetic, giving off a vapour causing unconsciousness when breathed.
• *vb* apply chloroform to. < French *chloroforme,* from *chlor-* + *formyle* formyl.
chlorophyll (ˈklɒrəfɪl) *n* the green pigment that colours plants. < Greek *chlor-* + *phyllon* leaf.
chock (tʃɒk) *n* a block or wedge (of wood), used to prevent an object from moving.
• *vb* wedge or secure with chocks.
chock-a-block *adv, adj* crammed together tightly. < origin unknown.
chocolate (ˈtʃɒklət, ˈtʃɒkələt) *n* **1** (a block of) food prepared with ground, roasted cacao seeds; sweet made of or coated with this. **2** a drink made from chocolate and hot water or milk. **3** dark-brown.
• *adj* **1** chocolate-flavoured or covered. **2** dark-brown. < Nahuatl *xocoatl.*
choice (tʃɔɪs) *n* **1** choosing; power to choose. **2** a selection to choose from: a wide choice of goods. **3** someone or something chosen.
• *adj* of high quality: choice vegetables. < Old French *choisir* to choose.
choir (kwaɪə) *n* **1** an organized group of singers, esp. in a church. **2** the part of a church where the singers and clergy sit. **choirboy** *n* a boy who sings in a (church) choir. < ultimately Latin *chorus* chorus.
choke (tʃəʊk) *vb* **1** have or cause difficulty in breathing normally by blocking the windpipe or breathing poisonous gas or smoke. **2** also **choke up** obstruct by clogging: Weeds are choking the garden. **3** make or become speechless from strong emotion; silence.
• *n* **1** (the sound of) choking. **2** a valve for controlling the amount of air mixed with fuel in a petrol engine. < Old English *acēocian.*
cholera (ˈkɒlərə) *n* an infectious, often fatal, disease, the symptoms of which include severe diarrhoea. < Latin: bile.
cholesterol (kəˈlɛstəˌrɒl) *n* a fatty substance found in animal and plant cells. < French *cholésterine,* from Latin *chol* bile + Greek *stereos* solid.
choose (tʃuːz) *vb* **chose; chosen; choosing 1** select from a range (of people or things). **2** decide; prefer: He chose to do it this way. **chooser** *n* **choosy** *adj* particular in choosing; difficult to satisfy. < Old English *cēosan.*
chop (tʃɒp) *vb* **chopped; chopping** hit

---

when the chips are down

Gambling and betting have given the language a number of idiomatic expressions:

bet one's bottom dollar to bet everything one has (used to express certainty).
cash in one's chips to die.
have had one's chips to suffer a serious loss or failure.
hedge one's bets to do something in order to protect oneself from possible loss, failure, or criticism.
when the chips are down when a situation has reached a critical point.

See also panel at **sweep.**

---

or cut with a blow or sharp instrument; sever: chop down a tree.
• *n* **1** a cutting stroke (made by an axe or knife); chopping movement: karate chop. **2** a thick cut of meat, usually with part of a rib. **chop and change** change continually. **chopper** *n* **1** a tool for chopping; axe. **2** (*slang*) a helicopter. **choppy** *adj* (of the sea) rough with small, broken waves. **chop up** cut into small pieces. **get the chop** (*slang*) **1** lose one's job. **2** be killed. < Middle English *choppen.*

chopstick (ˈtʃɒpstɪk) *n* one of two thin sticks, used in oriental countries to raise food to the mouth. < Pidgin English *chop* fast + English *stick.*

choral (ˈkɔːrəl) *adj* written for singing by a choir. **chorally** *adv* **choral society** a society formed for singing choral music. < Latin *chorus* chorus.

chord (kɔːd) *n* a group of musical notes sounded together in combination. < SEE ACCORD.

chore (tʃɔː) *n* **1** a routine (domestic) task. **2** a tedious task. < Old English *cierr* piece of work.

choreography (ˌkɒrɪˈɒgrəfɪ) *n* the arrangement of steps and movements in ballet, dancing, etc. **choreographer** *n* < Greek *choreia* dance + French *-graphie* writing.

chorister (ˈkɒrɪstə) *n* a choir member.

chortle (ˈtʃɔːtḷ) *vb, n* (utter) a laugh of gleeful satisfaction. < *chuckle* + *snort.*

chorus (ˈkɔːrəs) *n* **1** a company of singers; piece of music written for these. **2** a part of a song or hymn sung at repeated intervals; refrain. **3** something uttered at the same time by a group of people or animals: the dawn chorus; a chorus of groans. **4** a group of singing dancers in a stage musical: chorus line; chorus girl.
• *vb* utter or sing at the same time. < Latin, from Greek *choros.*

chose (tʃəʊz) SEE CHOOSE. **chosen** SEE CHOOSE.

christen (ˈkrɪsṇ) *vb* **1** baptize in the Christian faith. **2** name (someone or something) for the first time. < Latin *christianus* Christian.

Christian (ˈkrɪstʃən) *adj* **1** of Christians or the Christian faith. **2** humane; kind and generous in spirit.
• *n* someone who believes in and follows Jesus Christ. **Christianity** *n* the religion based on the life and teachings of Jesus Christ. **Christian name** someone's first name. < Greek *Christos* anointed.

Christmas (ˈkrɪsməs) *n* the festival of the Christian Church commemorating the birth of Christ, celebrated on Christmas Day: 25 December; period around this time. **Christmas-box** *n* a small Christmas present given to employees, tradesmen, etc. **Christmas Eve** 24 December. **Christmas pudding** a rich, plum pudding. **Christmas rose** a white-flowered plant of the buttercup family that flowers in winter. **Christmas tree** an evergreen or artificial tree decorated with lights or tinsel at Christmas. < Old English *Cristes mæsse* Christ's mass.

chrome (krəʊm) *n* chromium; chromium-plated. **chromium** *n* a hard, metallic element, used in alloys and for coating other materials. < Greek *chrōma.*

chromosome (ˈkrəʊməˌsəʊm) *n* any of the microscopic, thread-like structures containing genes, found in the nucleus of plant or animal cells. < Greek *chrōma* colour + *sōma* body.

chronic (ˈkrɒnɪk) *adj* **1** (of an illness) long-lasting and recurrent: chronic bronchitis. **2** habitual: a chronic gambler. **3** (*slang*) bad; unpleasant: chronic weather. < Greek *chronos* time.

chronicle (ˈkrɒnɪkḷ) *vb, n* (make) a record of events in the order in which they happened. **chronicler** *n* < ultimately Greek *chronikos.*

chronology (krəˈnɒlədʒɪ) *n* a list or arrangement of dates or events in the order in which they happened; determination of this. **chronological** *adj* **chronologically** *adv* < Greek *chron-* time + *-logy,* ultimately from *logo* word.

chrysalis (ˈkrɪsəlɪs) *n* (the stage of forming) a casing for a pupa, esp. of a butterfly or moth, in which it changes from a grub to its full-grown form. < Greek *chrysos* gold.

chrysanthemum (krɪˈsænθəməm) *n* any of a group of cultivated plants with brightly-coloured flowers. < Greek *chrys-* gold + *anthemon* flower.

chubby (ˈtʃʌbɪ) *adj* plump and rounded. **chubbiness** *n* < Middle English *chubbe* chub, a type of fish.

chuck[1] (tʃʌk) *vb* **1** (*informal*) toss; throw. **2** (*informal*) also **chuck in** give up: He chucked in his job. **3** tap affectionately (under the chin).
• *n* a playful tap. **chuck out** throw out (a trouble-maker). < perhaps Middle French *choquer* to knock.

chuck[2] *n* **1** a cut of beef including the neck and shoulder-blade. **2** a device in a lathe for holding the drill; part of a drill holding the bit. < probably modified from *chock*.

chuckle (ˈtʃʌkl̩) *vb* **1** laugh quietly (to oneself). **2** make a clucking sound like hens.
• *n* the sound of chuckling. < probably *chuck* to make a clucking noise.

chuffed (tʃʌft) *adj* (*slang*) pleased. < English dialect *chuff* fat.

chug (tʃʌg) *vb* **chugged; chugging** make a short, heavy, repeated sound, like a slow-moving, steam train.
• *n* the sound of this. < like the sound.

chum (tʃʌm) *n* (*informal*) a close friend; pal. **chummy** *adj* intimate; friendly. < perhaps short for *chamber fellow* room-mate.

chump (tʃʌmp) *n* **1** (*slang*) a fool. **2** a cut of meat from the thick end of a loin of mutton or pork: chump chop. < perhaps *chunk* + *lump*.

chunk (tʃʌŋk) *n* a lump (of a substance); fairly large amount (of something). **chunky** *adj* **1** thick and short. **2** consisting of chunks. < perhaps English dialect *chuck* lump, log.

church (tʃɜːtʃ) *n* **1** a building for public, esp. Christian, worship; service held in this: I saw her after church. **2 the Church** a body of (Christian) believers; one branch of this: the Anglican Church. **3 the Church** the clerical profession: He went into the Church. **churching** *n* a thanksgiving service for a woman after giving birth. **churchwarden** *n* a lay churchman who looks after parish property and performs other parish duties. **churchyard** *n* an enclosed piece of land round a church, often also a burial ground. < Old English *cirice*.

churn (tʃɜːn) *n* **1** a vessel in which milk is beaten to make butter. **2** a large, metal container, used for transporting milk.
• *vb* **1** beat (milk or cream) to make butter. **2** stir violently: His stomach churned at the thought of it. **3 churn out** produce in quantity without much regard for quality. < Old English *cyrin*.

chute (ʃuːt) *n* **1** a sloping channel or passage for dropping things down: laundry chute. **2** (*informal*) a parachute. < ultimately Latin *cadere* to fall.

chutney (ˈtʃʌtnɪ) *n* a spicy relish of Indian origin, made with fruit, sugar, and vinegar. < Hindi *catnī*.

CIA *abbrev* Central Intelligence Agency.

CID *abbrev* Criminal Investigation Department.

cider (ˈsaɪdə) *n* an alcoholic drink made from fermented apple juice. < Hebrew *shēkhār* strong drink.

cigar (sɪˈgɑː) *n* a roll of cured tobacco leaves for smoking. < Spanish *cigarro*.

cigarette (ˌsɪgəˈrɛt) *n* a thin tube of paper filled with shredded tobacco or herbs for smoking. < French: small cigar.

cinch (sɪntʃ) *n* (*informal*) something done with ease; certainty. < Latin *cingula* girdle, girth.

cinder (ˈsɪndə) *n* a fragment of ash or partly burnt coal or wood. **cinders** *pl n* ashes. < Old English *sinder*.

cine- (ˈsɪnɪ) *prefix* of or relating to the cinema: cine-film; cine-camera.

cinema (ˈsɪnɪmə) *n* **1** films as art, industry, or entertainment. **2** a theatre where cinema films are shown. < ultimately Greek *kinēma* movement.

cinnamon (ˈsɪnəmən) *n* **1** a spice taken from the aromatic bark of a south-east Asian tree of the laurel family. **2** its yellowish-brown colour. < Greek *kinnamon*.

cipher (ˈsaɪfə) *n* **1** zero represented by the symbol 0. **2** someone or something of no value or importance. **3** any Arabic numeral: 1,2,3, etc. **4** a secret code; message in this. < Arabic *ṣifr* zero.

circa (ˈsɜːkə) *prep* at, in, approximately (with dates): born circa 1800. < Latin *circum* round.

circle (ˈsɜːkl̩) *n* **1** a closed plane curve, every point on which is the same distance from its centre; figure enclosed by this. **2** anything with this shape. **3** a balcony or upper tier of seats in a theatre or cinema. **4** a group of people with interests in common.
• *vb* move round a fixed point; form a circle around (something). < Latin *circulus* small ring. SEE PANEL.

circuit (ˈsɜːkɪt) *n* **1** a route or course round an object or area. **2** a race-track. **3** a regular tour (by a judge) round an area; route travelled. **4** a group of Methodist churches in one area. **5** a series of sporting tournaments: the international golf circuit. **6** the closed path of an electrical current, including its source and linked components. **7** a chain of theatres or cinemas. **circuit-breaker** *n* a switch for automatically breaking an electric current under certain conditions. **circuitous** *adj* indirect: a circuitous route. < Latin *circumire* to go round.

circular (ˈsɜkjʊlə) *adj* **1** circle-shaped. **2** describing a circle; circuitous. **3** (of arguments) futile because the conclusions are based on initial assumptions. **4** intended for distribution: a circular letter.
• *n* a circular letter or leaflet. **circularity**

n **circularize** *vb* send circular letters to; publicize. < Latin *circulus* circle.
circulate (ˈsɜːkjʊˌleɪt) *vb* **1** move in a circular path. **2** move from one place or person to another. **3** distribute (information). **4** make or become widely known: Rumours are circulating. **circulation** *n* **1** movement in a circular path. **2** the flow of blood round the body, pumped by the heart. **3** the number of copies (of magazines or newspapers) distributed or sold. < Latin *circulus* circle.
circumcise (ˈsɜːkəmˌsaɪz) *vb* remove the male foreskin or female clitoris by surgery. **circumcision** *n* < Latin *circum* round + *caedere* to cut.
circumference (səˈkʌmfərəns) *n* (the distance round) the edge of a circle. < Latin *circum* + *ferre* to bear.
circumlocution (ˌsɜːkəmləˈkjuːʃən) *n* **1** the use of too many unnecessary words to express something. **2** indirect or evasive speech. < Latin *circum* + *locutio* speech.
circumnavigate (ˌsɜːkəmˈnævɪˌgeɪt) *vb* go completely round, esp. by sea. **circumnavigation** *n* < Latin *circum* + *navigare* to navigate.
circumscribe (ˈsɜːkəmˌskraɪb) *vb* **1** draw a real or imaginary line round (something). **2** set limits; restrict. **circumscription** *n* < Latin *circum* + *scribere* to write.
circumspect (ˈsɜːkəmˌspɛkt) *adj* considering all possibilities; cautious. < Latin *circum* + *specere* to look.
circumstance (ˈsɜːkəmstɑːns) *n* **1** a factor connected with a situation; sum of these factors. **2** a state of affairs; event: a rare circumstance. **3** one's financial state: in good circumstances. **4** ceremony. **circumstantial** *adj* **1** relating to circumstances. **2** relevant but not conclusive: circumstantial evidence. **circumstantially** *adv* **in** or **under the circumstances** allowing for the situation. **under no circumstances** in whatever case not. < Latin *circum* + *stare* to stand.
circumvent (ˌsɜːkəmˈvɛnt) *vb* go around; evade. < Latin *circum* + *venire* to come.
circus (ˈsɜːkəs) *n* **1** a travelling show with a variety of acts such as clowns, acrobats, and performing animals; something suggestive of this; noise and activity. **2** a large oval or circular sports arena. **3** a (circular) open space in a town where several streets meet: Piccadilly Circus. < Latin: ring.
cissy (ˈsɪsɪ) *n* (*informal*) a cowardly or effeminate man or boy. < *sis*, short for *sister*.
cistern (ˈsɪstən) *n* a water storage tank, esp. at the top of a house or above a lavatory. < ultimately Latin *cista* box.
citadel (ˈsɪtəˌdɛl) *n* a stronghold in or overlooking a city. < Old Italian *cittadella* small city.
cite (saɪt) *vb* **1** refer to (a book, quotation, etc.) as evidence or as an example. **2** (of the military) commend in dispatches. **citation** *n* < ultimately Latin *ciēre* to stir.
citizen (ˈsɪtɪzn̩) *n* **1** anyone living in a town or city. **2** someone native to or a naturalized member of a state. **citizenship** *n* **Citizens' Band** radio frequencies used by drivers or other private individuals for local communication. < Old French *citeien*, from *cité* city.
citrus (ˈsɪtrəs) *n* any of a group of trees grown for their fruit, such as lemon or orange: citrus fruit. < Latin: citron tree.
city (ˈsɪtɪ) *n* a large town, esp. one with a cathedral. **the City** the commercial and financial centre of London; oldest part of it. < ultimately Latin *civis* citizen.
civic (ˈsɪvɪk) *adj* of or relating to a city, citizens, or citizenship. **civics** *pl n* the study of the rights and duties of citizenship. < Latin *civis* citizen.
civil (ˈsɪvl̩) *adj* **1** of citizens: civil rights. **2** of the general public; non-military;

going round in circles

The geometric figures circle, square, and triangle feature in a number of idioms, including:

a vicious circle a situation in which an effect leads back to the original cause, making the process endless: Price increases lead to wage increases which in turn lead to further price increases—it's a vicious circle.
come full circle to arrive at the starting-point again: With more and more people looking to nature for cures, we seem to have come full circle.
go round in circles **1** also **run round in circles** to rush around, but not achieve one's purpose. **2** to mention the same points in a discussion, making no progress.
a square peg in a round hole a person whose character, skills, etc., are not suited to his or her job or position.
the eternal triangle the conflict that arises from the sexual attraction between a man and two women or a woman and two men.

non-religious. **3** relating to civil, not criminal law. **4** polite; courteous. **civility** *n* **civilly** *adv* **civil engineering** the design and construction of roads, bridges, etc. **civilian** *n* someone non-military. **civil law** law protecting the rights of private citizens. **civil list** money allocated by parliament for the expenses of the royal family. **Civil Servant** someone working in the Civil Service. **Civil Service** all non-military government departments. < Latin *civis* citizen.

civilize (ˈsɪvɪˌlaɪz) *vb* **1** cause to develop from a primitive stage to a higher cultural or technological one. **2** educate or refine. **civilization** *n* **1** the process of bringing or reaching a higher level of development. **2** (conditions of) life in the modern world: miles from civilization. **3** a culture of a particular time and place: ancient Greek civilization.

cl *abbrev* centilitre(s).

clack (klæk) *vb, n* (make) a short, striking sound like two pieces of wood hitting each other; clatter. < Middle English *clacken,* like the sound.

clad (klæd) *adj* covered or clothed: clad all in white; iron-clad < *clothe.*

cladding (ˈklædiŋ) *n* a thin, protective overlay (of metal or stone).

claim (kleɪm) *vb* **1** request or demand as a right: She claimed her inheritance. **2** take; account for: The bombing claimed many lives. **3** assert without being able to prove.
• *n* **1** a demand or request for something held to be a right; right or title to something: insurance claim. **2** an assertion that something is a fact: a claim to fame. 3 an area of land staked out. **claimant** *n* someone who makes a claim, esp. in law. < Latin *clamare* to shout.

clairvoyance (klɛəˈvɔɪəns) *n* the alleged power of being aware of things beyond the normal range of the senses. **clairvoyant** *adj, n* < French, from Latin *clarus* clear + *vidēre* to see.

clam (klæm) *n* any of various marine molluscs with a hinged shell such as a scallop.
• *vb* **clammed; clamming** also **clam up** keep silent; refuse to talk. < Old English *clamm* fetter.

clamber (ˈklæmbə) *vb* climb (as if) over obstacles or obstructions. < Middle English *clambren.*

clammy (ˈklæmɪ) *adj* (disagreeably) damp and sticky. **clamminess** *n* < Old English *clæman* to smear.

clamour (ˈklæmə) *n* loud, persistent noise, esp. of shouting. **2** a loud demand or protest.
• *vb* demand or protest loudly. **clamorous** *adj* < ultimately Latin *clamare* to cry out.

clamp (klæmp) *n* a device for keeping things tightly pressed together.
• *vb* press together (as if) with a clamp. **clamp down on** restrict; suppress (something undesirable). < probably Middle Dutch *klampe.*

clan (klæn) *n* **1** a (Celtic) group of people with a common ancestor. **2** any group of closely related people. < ultimately Latin *planta* plant.

clandestine (klænˈdɛstɪn) *adj* done or held in secrecy. **clandestinely** *adv* < Latin *clandestinus.*

clang (klæŋ) *vb, n* (make) a loud, metallic, ringing sound. **clanger** *n* (*slang*) a gross blunder: drop a clanger. < Latin *clangere.*

clank (klæŋk) *vb, n* (make) a short, sharp, metallic sound. < probably like the sound.

clap (klæp) *vb* **clapped; clapping** **1** applaud by striking the hands together repeatedly; strike any two flat surfaces together. **2** place hurriedly: They clapped him in irons.
• *n* **1** the sound of clapping hands. **2** a loud, percussive noise: thunderclap. **clap eyes on** (*informal*) catch sight of. **clapped out** (*slang*) old and worn out, esp. of machinery. < Old English *clæppan.*

clapper (ˈklæpə) *n* the tongue of a bell. **go like the clappers** (*slang*) go extremely fast.

claptrap (ˈklæpˌtræp) *n* spoken, pretentious rubbish. < *clap* + *trap.*

claret (ˈklærət) *n* **1** a dry, red wine. **2** dark purplish-red. < Middle French *cler* clear.

clarify (ˈklærɪˌfaɪ) *vb* **clarified; clarifying** **1** make or become more understandable. **2** make (liquid or fat) pure, often by heating: clarified butter. **clarification** *n* < Latin *clarificare.*

clarinet (ˌklærɪˈnɛt) *n* a keyed, woodwind musical instrument with a single reed. **clarinettist** *n* a clarinet player. < Latin *clarus* clear.

clarity (ˈklærɪtɪ) *n* the condition of being clear. < Latin *clarus* clear.

clash (klæʃ) *vb* **1** make a harsh, metallic sound (like cymbals striking). **2** be incompatible; disagree. **3** (of arrangements) coincide. **4** make a disharmonious combination; mismatch.
• *n* **1** a clashing sound. **2** a disagreement: personality clash. **3** an ugly combina-

tion (of colours). < like the sound.

clasp (klɑːsp) *n* **1** a fastening device such as a catch or hook. **2** a grip (of the hand or arm); handshake.
• *vb* **1** fasten with a clasp. **2** grasp or hold closely. **clasp-knife** *n* a large, folding knife with a catch for keeping the blade open. < Middle English *claspe*.

class (klɑːs) *n* **1** a group of people sharing the same social or economic status: the middle classes. **2** any group of people, animals, or things with common characteristics. **3** a group of students studying together; one teaching session for these. **4** a rating based on quality: first class; economy class. **5** excellence; high quality: a singer with class.
• *vb* put in a class; classify. **classless** *adj* without social class distinctions. **classroom** *n* a room for teaching a class of students. **in a class of its own** unequalled; superior. < Latin *classis* class, fleet.

classic (ˈklæsɪk) *adj* **1** having a recognized degree of excellence; exemplary or distinguished. **2** definitive; archetypal: a classic case of schizophrenia. **3** enduringly traditional: a classic suit.
• *n* **1** (the author of) a lasting work of excellence, esp. a novel. **2** a typical example. **3** an established sporting event, such as the Epsom or Derby races. **classics** *n* the study of ancient Greek and Roman literature and culture. < Latin *classicus* of the first rank. SEE PANEL.

classic or **classical?**

Classic and classical are seldom interchangeable although their meanings do overlap.

One way of getting to the heart of the meaning of classic is to relate it to class. From class comes first-class, and something which is first-class or excellent often comes to serve as a standard or model. Hence a *classic* example, or a *classic* novel. As a noun, classic has a similar meaning; if a play is a classic it is of the highest quality or sets a new standard and is of lasting importance.

Classical should *not* be used in this evaluative way; a *classical* reference book is not a quality standard text but one that deals with the classics, 'the languages and literatures of ancient Greece and Rome'.

classical (ˈklæsɪkl̩) *adj* **1** standard; exemplary. **2** of ancient Greek and Roman culture. **3** plain in style. **4** (of music) traditional; in the style of the late 18th and early 19th centuries. **classically** *adv* SEE PANEL AT CLASSIC.

classify (ˈklæsɪˌfaɪ) *vb* **classified; classifying** arrange in classes; categorize. **classification** *n* **classified** *adj* **1** (of advertisements) listed in subject order. **2** (of information) kept secret from the general public for reasons of national security.

clatter (ˈklætə) *n* **1** a rattling sound such as pots and pans hitting together. **2** a noisy commotion (of talk).
• *vb* make or cause to make a clatter. < Middle English *clatrian* like the sound.

clause (klɔːz) *n* **1** an article or condition in a law, treaty, or contract. **2** a self-contained phrase within a complex sentence: relative clause. < Latin *claudere* to close.

claustrophobia (ˌklɒstrəˈfəʊbɪə) *n* the abnormal fear of being in a confined space. **claustrophobic** *adj* < Latin *claustrum* bolt + *phobia* fear.

claw (klɔː) *n* **1** the sharp nail on the toe of an animal. **2** a pincer on the end of some limbs of a lobster, scorpion, etc. **3** a device for gripping like a claw: claw-hammer.
• *vb* seize, pull, or scratch with or as if with claws. **claw back** take back (in taxation). **claw-back** *n* < Old English *clawu*.

clay (kleɪ) *n* soft, earthy material that hardens when baked, used in brick and pottery-making. **clay pigeon** a (clay) disc thrown into the air as a target for shooting at. < Old English *clǣg*.

clean (kliːn) *adj* **1** free of dirt. **2** as yet unused: a clean sheet of paper. **3** (of an atomic explosion) with (relatively) little fall-out. **4** free of contamination or infection: a clean wound. **5** morally pure; free from obscenity: Keep your language clean. **6** clean by habit. **7** smooth and even: a clean cut. **8** (of sports) played fairly: a clean fight. **9** with no record of offences: a clean driving-licence.
• *adv* thoroughly: He clean forgot.
• *vb* **1** also **clean up** make clean. **2** remove the insides of (fish) before cooking. **cleanly** *adv* **cleanness** *n* **clean-cut** *adj* with a well-defined outline: clean-cut features. **cleaner** *n* **1** a machine or substance for cleaning. **2** someone who cleans (rooms or

clothes) for a living. **cleaners** *pl n* a dry-cleaners. **take someone to the cleaners** (*slang*) defraud or criticize (someone). **cleanliness** *n* cleanness by habit. **clean out** empty, so as to make clean. **clean-shaven** *adj* with all facial hair shaved off. < Old English *clæne*.

cleanse (klɛnz) *vb* clean thoroughly; purify. **cleanser** *n* a cleansing material (for the skin); cleansing cream. < Old English *clæne* clean.

clear (klɪə) *adj* **1** bright; not cloudy: a clear sky. **2** transparent: clear glass. **3** easily heard, seen, or comprehended: Her voice was very clear. **4** sure; obvious: a clear case of fraud. **5** free from blemishes or guilt: My conscience is clear. **6** unobstructed: The roads are clear. **7** complete; net: a clear profit.
• *adv* **1** clearly. **2** absolutely. **3** away (from): stand clear of the doors.
• *vb* **1** make or become clear. **2** remove blame from: He cleared his name. **3** authorize: The consignment was cleared through customs. **4** pass (a cheque) through a bank. **5** gain in total: They cleared £5000 on the deal. **6** finish; remove: He cleared the table. **7** go or reach past, esp. without touching. **clearly** *adv* **clearness** *n* **clear away** remove (crockery) after a meal. **clear-cut** *adj* distinct. **clear off** (*slang*) go away. **clear the decks** get everything ready (for action). **clear up 1** make tidy. **2** (of weather) become brighter. **in the clear** without being suspected or hindered. < Latin *clarus*, SEE PANEL.

clearance (ˈklɪərəns) *n* **1** an authorization. **2** a sale of old stock: a clearance sale. **3** the removal of people or buildings from an area: slum clearance. **4** the clear space between two (moving) objects.

clearing (ˈklɪərɪŋ) *n* an area of land free of trees and bushes. **clearing-house** *n* an office for settling mutual bank claims and accounts.

cleave (kliːv) *vb* **cleft, cleaved, clove; cleft, cleaved, cloven; cleaving 1** split by chopping or cutting. **2** clear a way through. **cleavage** *n* **1** splitting. **2** (the hollow between) a woman's breasts. **cleaver** *n* a butcher's heavy knife or hatchet. < Old English *clēofan*.

clef (klɛf) *n* a sign at the beginning of a musical stave, showing the pitch of the notes which follow: bass clef; treble clef. < Latin *clavis* key.

cleft (klɛft) SEE **CLEAVE**.
• *adj* split; divided.
• *n* a split; division. **cleft chin** a chin with a V-shaped indentation. **cleft palate** a congenital crack in the roof of the mouth.

clematis (ˈklɛmətɪs, klɪˈmeɪtəs) *n* a climbing plant of the buttercup family with white or purple flowers. < Greek *klēma* twig.

clemency (ˈklɛmənsɪ) *n* leniency; mercy. **clement** *adj* < Latin *clemens* mild.

clementine (ˈklɛmən,tiːn) *n* a citrus fruit with few seeds, a hybrid between an orange and a tangerine. < French *clémentine*.

clench (klɛntʃ) *vb* **1** squeeze (the fingers or teeth) together tightly. **2** clutch or hold tightly. < Old English *clencan*.

clergy (ˈklɜːdʒɪ) *n* a group of men ordained as ministers of the Christian Church. **clergyman** *n* also **cleric** a member of the clergy. **clerical** *adj* **clerical collar** a stiff, white collar, fastening at the back, worn by clergymen. < Old French *clerc* clergyman.

clerk (klɑːk) *n* **1** an office-worker with general duties including filing and keeping records and accounts. **2** an official who keeps records in a court or town council. **clerical** *adj* **clerk of the works** someone in charge of local building works. < ultimately Greek *klēros* lot, heritage.

clever (ˈklɛvə) *adj* **1** intelligent; skilful. **2** showing wit or ingenuity: a clever idea. **cleverly** *adv* **cleverness** *n* **clever dick** (*informal*) someone with a (mistakenly) high opinion of his or her cleverness. < Middle English *cliver*.

The coast's clear!

The coast is clear means that (an action may proceed as) there are no sources of danger or interference around: 'Come on! The coast's clear! All the teachers have gone to a staff meeting.' The expression was originally used by smugglers, at which time its meaning was interpreted literally: 'the coast is clear of coastguards'.

The shorter phrase all clear has a very similar meaning to the coast is clear: Once the nightwatchman had been disposed of and it was all clear, they started work on the safe. However, its derivation is more modern. All clear was originally a military expression used to signal that enemy aircraft had left an area and that there was no more danger.

cliché (ˈkliːʃeɪ) *n* a well-worn idea or expression. < French *clicher* to stereotype. SEE PANEL AT **STONE.**

click (klɪk) n a brief, sharp sound like a switch being flicked.
• *vb* **1** make or cause to make a click: He clicked his heels. **2** (*informal*) quickly become friendly: They clicked straight away. **3** bring or reach sudden understanding: At last his name clicked. < probably like the sound.

client (ˈklaɪənt) *n* someone who seeks the services of a professional person or organization. **clientele** *n* clients or customers collectively. < Latin *cliens.*

cliff (klɪf) *n* a steep, high rock-face, esp. found at a coast. **cliff-hanger** *n* a situation in a story, etc., in which the outcome is kept in suspense. **cliff-hanging** *adj* < Old English *clif.*

climate (ˈklaɪmət) *n* **1** the normal conditions of weather in a region. **2** a region with particular weather conditions. **3** a particular state of affairs or feelings: a climate of opinion. **climatic** *adj* < ultimately Greek *klinein* to lean.

climax (ˈklaɪmæks) *n* **1** the most intense point, for example of an experience: The film was the climax of her career. **2** an orgasm. **climactic** *adj* < Greek *klimax* ladder.

climb (klaɪm) *vb* **1** go upwards or over using the hands and feet. **2** go gradually higher.
• *n* an ascent made by climbing; place climbed. **climb down** retreat from a stated position. **climb-down** *n* **climber** *n* **1** someone who climbs. **2** a climbing plant. **climbing-frame** *n* a framework of bars for children to climb on. < Old English *climban.*

clinch (klɪntʃ) *vb* **1** fasten tightly, esp. with a nail, rivet, or bolt. **2** hold an opponent closely, for example in boxing. **3** (*informal*) finalize (a matter, such as a deal).
• *n* **1** clinching in boxing. **2** (*slang*) a lover's embrace. < probably alteration of *clench.*

cling (klɪŋ) *vb* **clung; clinging 1** hold on tightly (to); stick (to). **2** depend on emotionally. < Old English *clingan.*

clinic (ˈklɪnɪk) *n* **1** a session where visitors are given aid or advice by an expert or authority: ante-natal clinic. **2** a private or specialized hospital. **clinical** *adj* **1** of a clinic or the treatment given there. **2** based on direct observation: clinical psychology. **3** emotionally detached. **4** clean and bare in appearance. **clinically** *adv* < ultimately Greek *klinein* to lean.

clink[1] (klɪŋk) *vb, n* (cause) a short, sharp ringing sound like glasses struck together. < Middle English *clinken,* like the sound.

clink[2] *n* (*slang*) prison, SEE PANEL.

clinker (ˈklɪŋkə) *n* stony matter left after burning coal; slag. < obsolete Dutch *klinkaard* thing that clinks.

clip[1] (klɪp) *n* **1** a device for fastening or gripping: paper-clip, **2** a set of attached cartridges for a firearm. **3** a piece of jewellery fastened with a spring clip.
• *vb* **clipped; clipping** fasten with a clip. **clip-board** *n* a portable writing board with a clip, used for holding papers. **clip-on** *adj* fastened by a clip. < Old English *clyppan.*

clip[2] *vb* **clipped; clipping 1** cut or trim with or as if with scissors or shears. **2** punch (a ticket) to stop it being used again. **3** (*informal*) hit with a sharp, glancing blow.
• *n* **1** the act of clipping. **2** the product of one sheep-shearing. **3** an extract from a film or newspaper. **4** (*informal*) a sharp, glancing blow. **5** (*informal*) speed. **clippers** *pl n* an instrument for cutting hair or nails. **clipping** *n* something cut out or off, for example, a newspaper cutting. < Old Norse *Klippa.*

clique (kliːk) *n* an exclusive group of people with common interests. **cliquish** *adj* **cliquy** *adj* < French.

cloak (kləʊk) *n* **1** a sleeveless outer garment that hangs from the shoulders. **2** something that covers or conceals: a cloak of secrecy.
• *vb* cover or conceal (as if) with a cloak. **cloak-and-dagger** *adj* involving intrigue or spying in a melodramatic fashion. **cloakroom** *n* **1** a room for leaving clothing or luggage temporarily. **2** (*euphemistic*) a room with a toilet. < Medieval Latin *clocca* bell.

clobber[1] (ˈklɒbə) *n* (*informal*) clothing

clink

One of several synonyms for 'prison' is the slang expression clink: If you can't keep your nose clean you'll end up back in *clink.* Clink is so called after the prison of the same name that used to stand in *Clink* Street in Southwark, London. The Clink was destroyed in the 1780 Gordon Riots.

and accessories; belongings. < probably alteration of *clothes.*

clobber[2] *vb* **1** (*informal*) hit with force repeatedly. **2** (*informal*) defeat completely. < origin unknown.

cloche (klɒʃ) *n* a bell-shaped cover, often of glass or plastic, for protecting young plants. < Medieval Latin *clocca* bell.

clock (klɒk) *n* **1** a device other than a watch which measures and shows time. **2** a measuring device with a dial and indicator, such as a speedometer.
• *vb* **1** time with a stop-watch or similar device. **2** attain as a time or speed; achieve. **3** (*informal*) hit. **clock in** or **on** record one's arrival time at work. **clock out** or **off** record one's leaving time from work. **clock-watcher** *n* someone who watches the time closely in order to stop or leave work as soon as possible. **clockwise** *adv, adj* moving in the same direction as the hands of a clock. **clockwork** *n* machinery operating like a clock, with wheels and springs. **like clockwork** smoothly and without problems. < Medieval Latin *clocca* bell.

clod (klɒd) *n* **1** a lump of clay or earth. **2** (*informal*) a stupid person. < Middle English, alteration of *clot.*

clog (klɒg) *n* a shoe with a thick, wooden sole.
• *vb* **clogged; clogging** make or become blocked. < Middle English *clogge* block of wood.

cloister (ˈklɔɪstə) *n* **1** a covered passage with a wall on one side and a courtyard on the other, usually adjoining a church. **2** a monastery or convent; style of life in this. **cloistered** *adj* shut off from the world; sheltered. < ultimately Latin *claudere* to close.

clone (kləʊn) *n* an individual produced asexually from its parent; all the progeny produced in this way.
• *vb* produce or cause to produce a clone. < Greek *klōn* twig.

close[1] (kləʊs) *adj* **1** near in time or space. **2** near in relationship; intimate: close friends. **3** very much alike: a close resemblance. **4** restricted; confined: close quarters. **5** secretive; quiet: He's very close about what he does. **6** rigorously strict: a close watch. **7** dense; compact: a close texture, **8** with a nearly even result: a close game. **9** lacking fresh air; stuffy.
• *adv* nearby; closely: They live close to the church.
• *n* **1** a road with only one opening. **2** the grounds and buildings next to a cathedral or abbey. **closely** *adv* **closeness** *n* **close-up** *n* a photograph or film that is taken at close range. < ultimately Latin *claudere* to close.

close[2] (kləʊz) *vb* **1** shut. **2** finish: The matter is closed. **3** draw or cause to draw nearer: close ranks.
• *n* an end; conclusion: The evening drew to a close. SEE PANEL.

closet (ˈklɒzɪt) *n* **1** a small room, often for storage. **2** (*US*) a cupboard.
• *vb* shut up in a small room, esp. for private discussion or study. < Middle French: small enclosure.

closure (ˈkləʊʒə) *n* **1** the condition of being closed; closing. **2** the closing of a debate, esp. in parliament, by calling for a vote.

clot (klɒt) *n* **1** a small lump formed in a thickening liquid, such as blood. **2** (*informal*) a fool.
• *vb* **clotted; clotting** form clots; coagulate, **clotted cream** thick cream made from scalded milk. < Old English *clott.*

cloth (klɒθ) *n* **1** material made from natural or synthetic fibre by weaving, knitting, or felting; piece of this for a particular use: dishcloth; table-cloth. **2** (the distinctive dress of) the clergy: a man of the cloth. < Old English *clāth.*

clothe (kləʊð) *vb* **clothed, clad; clothing** cover (as if) with clothing; provide with clothing.

clothes (kləʊðz) *pl n* **1** items of material worn on the body for warmth, protection, or decoration; garments. **2** bedclothes. **clothes-horse** *n* a frame

---

closing in

Close features in a number of expressions, including:

behind closed doors in secret.

closed book something that is unknown or cannot be understood: Trigonometry's a completely closed book to me.

closed-circuit television a television system in which the signal is transmitted by wire to a number of receivers.

close down 1 to stop working or operating. **2** to stop broadcasting for the day.

closedown *n*

closed shop an industrial establishment in which all employees have to be members of one or more specified trade unions.

close in (**on**) to approach or surround: The enemy were gradually closing in on us.

---

for hanging clothes on to dry or air. **clothes-line** *n* a line of nylon, cord, etc., used for hanging clothes on to dry, esp. outside. **clothes-peg** *n* a clip or forked device of wood or plastic, used for hanging and securing clothes on a clothes-line. < Old English *clāthas.*

clothing (ˈkləʊðɪŋ) *n* clothes.

cloud (klaʊd) *n* **1** a visible mass of water vapour floating in the sky. **2** a mass of insects, etc., suggesting this. **3** something that threatens or brings gloom: living under a cloud.
• *vb* **1 cloud over** become overcast with clouds. **2** become gloomy. **3** become unclear or opaque: clouded liquid. **4** make or become confused. **cloudburst** *n* a sudden, heavy fall of rain. **cloudless** *adj* free of clouds. **cloudy** *adj* **1** (of the sky) overcast with clouds. **2** not clear or transparent: cloudy beer. **cloudiness** *n* **on cloud nine** feeling extremely elated. **under a cloud** under suspicion; disgraced. **with one's head in the clouds** day-dreaming. < Old English *clūd.*

clout (klaʊt) *n* **1** a blow. **2** (*informal*) influence, esp. political: The unions have plenty of clout.
• *vb* (*informal*) hit. < Old English *clūt.*

clove[1] (kləʊv) SEE **CLEAVE.**

clove[2] *n* any of the small bulbs which make up a larger bulb such as garlic. < Old English *clufu.*

clove[3] *n* a flower bud from a tree of the myrtle family, dried and used as a spice. < ultimately Latin *clavus* nail.

cloven (ˈkləʊvn̩) SEE **CLEAVE. cloven hoof** a divided hoof, like that of a sheep or ox.

clover (ˈkləʊvə) *n* any of a group of plants with small leaves in three parts. **clover-leaf** *n* a road junction, the pattern of which resembles a four-leaf clover. **in clover** in pleasant circumstances, esp. financially. < Old English *clāfre.*

clown (klaʊn) *n* **1** a comic performer, usually in a circus, dressed and made up grotesquely. **2** someone who behaves comically as a habit; joker.
• *vb* **1** perform as a clown. 2 act comically or foolishly. < perhaps Low German.

cloy (klɔɪ) *vb* sicken by an excess of pleasure or sweetness: cloy the appetite. < Middle English *acloien,* ultimately from Latin *in* + *clavus* nail.

club (klʌb) *n* **1** a heavy stick with one thick end, often used as a weapon. **2** one of several sticks with various heads, used to hit a ball in golf. **3** a playing-card marked with the pattern of a black clover-leaf of the suit (**clubs**) marked with these. **4** a group of people who meet to pursue common interests; premises used by them: sports club. **5** a group of people who make payments to gain certain benefits: a book club. **6** a night-club.
• *vb* **clubbed; clubbing 1** hit with a club. **2** join (together) to subscribe or share an interest: They clubbed together to buy a present. **club-foot** *n* a foot deformed from birth. **club-root** *n* a disease of cabbages, etc., which distorts the root. < Old Norse *klubba.*

cluck (klʌk) *vb, n* (make) a throaty sound of or like a hen. < like the sound.

clue (kiu:) *n* something that gives a guide to how to solve a problem: a crossword clue.
• *vb* **clue in** or **up** inform. **clueless** *adj* useless; stupid. < Middle English *clewe* ball of thread.

clump (klʌmp) *n* **1** a compact mass or cluster of similar objects: a clump of trees. **2** a dull, heavy treading sound.
• *vb* **1** form or organize in clumps. **2** tread heavily. **3** (*informal*) punch (someone). < probably Low German *klump.*

clumsy (ˈklʌmzɪ) *adj* **1** awkward in shape or movement; unsubtle. **2** awkwardly made; unwieldy: a clumsy piece of furniture. **clumsily** *adv* **clumsiness** *n* < probably Middle English *clumse* numb with cold.

clung (klʌŋ) SEE **CLING.**

clunk (klʌŋk) *vb, n* (make) a short, dull, metallic sound. < like the sound.

cluster (ˈklʌstə) *vb, n* (bring or come together in) a compact group of similar people or things: star cluster. < Old English *clyster.*

clutch[1] (klʌtʃ) *vb* seize tightly, esp. with the hands.
• *n* **1** gripping tightly. **2** (a pedal which operates) a device which connects or disconnects moving machine parts, esp. in a vehicle. **in someone's clutches** in someone's power or possession. < Old English *clyccan.*

clutch[2] *n* a nest of eggs for hatching; chickens hatched from these. < alteration of English dialect *cletch.*

clutter (ˈklʌtə) *n* a disordered state; mass of objects lying about untidily.
• *vb* also **clutter up** fill with clutter. < Middle English *clotteren* to clot.

cm *abbrev* centimetre(s).

Co. *abbrev* **1 Company:** Smith and Co. Ltd. **2** County: Co. Down; Co. Durham

c/o *abbrev* care of.

co- *prefix* with; joint: coexist; co-driver. < Latin *com-*.

coach (kəʊtʃ) *n* **1** a large, usually closed,

horse-drawn carriage with four wheels. **2** a railway carriage. **3** a single-decker bus, esp. one used for long-distance travel. **4** a sports instructor or private specialized tutor.
• *vb* train; instruct. **coachwork** *n* the bodywork of a rail or road vehicle.
< probably *Kocs,* village in Hungary. SEE PANEL.

coagulate (kəʊˈægjʊˌleɪt) *vb* (of a liquid) thicken; clot. **coagulation** *n*
< Latin *cogere* to drive together.

coal (kəʊl) n a hard, black, carbon-based material, burnt as fuel or to provide heat; piece of this: live coals. **coal-face** *n* an exposed surface in a coal-mine. **coalfield** *n* an area where coal is found naturally. **coal gas** gas produced by heating coal in the absence of air, used for lighting and heating. **coal-mine** *n* underground works from where coal is dug. **coal tar** tar produced from coal gas, used in dyes and drugs. < Old English *col.* SEE PANEL.

coalesce (ˌkəʊəˈlɛs) *vb* combine into a whole; fuse. < Latin *co-* + *alescere* to increase.

coalition (ˌkəʊəˈlɪʃən) *n* **1** uniting. **2** a temporary alliance of political parties, esp. to form a government. < SEE COALESCE.

coarse (kɔːs) *adj* **1** consisting of large particles: coarse sand. **2** with a rough tone or texture: coarse paper. **3** crude or unrefined in speech or manner: coarse language. **coarsely** *adv* **coarseness** *n*
coarse fish common freshwater fish other than the salmon family. < origin uncertain.

coast (kəʊst) *n* the line where the land meets the sea; sea-shore.
• *vb* **1** sail along a shore. **2** move without using power, esp. downhill. **3** proceed without much effort: coasting through life. **coastal** *adj* **coaster** *n* **1** a ship trading from port to port on a coast. **2** a tray for a decanter; small mat used under a drinking-glass. **coastguard** *n* (a member of) an organization which maintains a watch on the coast to protect shipping, detect smuggling, etc. **coastline** *n* the shape or outline of a coast. < Latin *costa* rib, side. SEE PANEL AT **CLEAR.**

coat (kəʊt) *n* **1** an outer garment with sleeves, opening down the middle of its front. **2** the hair or fur covering of an animal. **3** an outer or protective layer: a coat of paint.
• *vb* cover with an outer layer. **coating** *n* a covering; layer. **coat of arms** a design serving as the emblem of a family, city, etc., usually on a shield.
< Old French *cote.*

coax (kəʊks) *vb* persuade or urge gently; gain in this way: She coaxed a smile from him.
< obsolete *cokes* fool.

cob (kɒb) *n* **1** a male swan. **2** the core of an ear of maize: corn on the cob. **3** one of a breed of sturdy horses with short legs. **4** a small, round, crusty loaf. < Middle English *cobbe* leader.

cobalt (ˈkəʊbɔːlt) *n* **1** a tough, whitish, metallic element, used widely in alloys; pigment made from this. **2** a deep blue colour. < Middle High German *kobolt* goblin. SEE PANEL.

coach

Not many people today think of Hungary when they hear the word coach. However, the latter probably derives ultimately from *Kocs,* the name of the village in Hungary where it was first made. The original name was *kocsi szekér* meaning 'wagon from Kocs'. This was taken over into German as simply *Kutsche* before passing into French as *coche,* the form from which the English word derived.

The original application of coach was to the horse-drawn carriage. However, with the advent of the railway the language of coaching was taken over wholesale so that words like coach and carriage became part of the machine age.

carrying coals to Newcastle

To carry or take coals to Newcastle means to take something to a place where it is already plentiful or, more generally, to do something which is ludicrously superfluous. The allusion is to *Newcastle upon Tyne,* an English port 13km up the River Tyne, which has shipped locally mined coal since the 13th century. The equivalent French expression is less cryptic: *porter de l'eau à la rivière* or 'to carry water to the river'.

cobble[1] (ˈkɒbl̩) *n* also **cobble-stone** a naturally rounded stone used for paving.
• *vb* pave with cobble-stones. < probably *cob* roundish lump.

cobble[2] *vb* **1** make or repair shoes. **2** put together or repair in a rough fashion. **cobbler** *n* **1** a shoe-maker or shoe-mender. **2** *pl* (*slang*) nonsense. < Middle English *coblen*.

cobra (ˈkɒbrə, ˈkəʊbrə) *n* a venomous snake from Asia or Africa with grooved fangs; it expands the skin round the neck into a hood when agitated. < Portuguese *cobra* (*de capello*) hooded snake, from Latin *colubra* snake.

cobweb (ˈkɒbˌwɛb) *n* a network of threads spun by a spider; single thread of this. < Old English (*ātor*) *coppe* spider + *web*.

cocaine (kəʊˈkɪn, kəˈkeɪn) *n* a drug prepared from coca leaves, used as a stimulant or medicinally as a local anaesthetic. < Quechua *kúka* coca.

cochineal (ˌkɒtʃɪˈniːl) *n* a red dye-substance made from dried bodies of certain female insects. < Old Spanish *cochinilla*.

cock (kɒk) *n* **1** the male of various birds, esp. the domestic fowl. **2** a tap or valve for regulating the flow of a liquid: stopcock. **3** the hammer of a gun when raised before firing.
• *vb* **1** set the hammer of (a gun) ready for firing. **2** turn or tilt upwards or to one side: The dog cocked its ears. **at half cock** unprepared. **cock-a-doodle doo** the sound of a cock crowing. **cock-a-hoop** *adj* (*informal*) very pleased; exultant or boasting. **cock-and-bull story** a long, foolish story that is unlikely to be believed. **cock up** (*informal*) make a mess of. **cock-up** *n* < Old English *cocc*.

cockatoo (ˌkɒkəˈtuː) *n, pl* **cockatoos** a type of large, noisy, crested parrot found chiefly in Australasia. < Malay *kakatua*.

cockerel (ˈkɒkrəl) *n* a young domestic cock. < Old French dialect *kokerel*.

cock-eyed (ˈkɒkˌaɪd) *adj* (*informal*) **1** not properly aligned; askew. **2** foolish; impractical: a cock-eyed idea.

cockle (ˈkɒkl̩) *n* **1** (the shell of) a common edible shellfish. **2** a wrinkle, in cloth, paper, etc.
• *vb* bulge or wrinkle or cause to bulge or wrinkle. **warm the cockles of one's heart** make one really happy. < ultimately Greek *konchē* conch.

cockney (ˈkɒknɪ) *n, pl* **cockneys 1** a native of London's East End. **2** the dialect of this area.
• *adj* of cockneys or the cockney dialect. < Middle English *cokeney* cock's egg, townsman.

cockpit (ˈkɒkˌpɪt) *n* **1** an enclosure for cockfighting. **2** the space in an aircraft for the pilot and crew. **3** the driver's seat in a sports or racing car. **4** a recess below deck level in a small boat, for the steersman, etc.

cockroach (ˈkɒkˌrəʊtʃ) *n* a dark brown insect similar to a beetle; household pest. < Spanish *cucaracha*.

cocksure (ˌkɒkˈʃʊə) *adj* (*informal*) positive to the point of overconfidence.

cocktail (ˈkɒkˌteɪl) *n* **1** a mixed alcoholic drink with a spirit base. **2** any mixture of diverse elements: fruit cocktail; prawn cocktail. **cocktail stick** a small, pointed stick for serving an olive, piece of cheese, small sausage, etc.

cocky (ˈkɒkɪ) *adj* overconfident; arrogant. **cockily** *adv* **cockiness** *n*

cocoa (ˈkəʊkəʊ) *n* roasted cacao seeds ground into powder; drink made from this, usually served hot. < ultimately Spanish *cacao*.

coconut (ˈkəʊkˌənʌt) *n* the large oval fruit of the tropical coconut palm which contains a thick, sweet, milky juice; its thick, white, edible lining. SEE PANEL.

cocoon (kəˈkuːn) *n* **1** a silky wrapping in which insect larvae change into the next stage of their life cycle. **2** any protective wrapping.
• *vb* envelop (as if) in a cocoon. < ultimately Greek *kokkos* grain, seed.

cobalt and **goblins**

The name of the metallic element known as cobalt derives ultimately from the Middle High German *kobolt* meaning 'gnome' or 'goblin'. But what is the connection between cobalt and goblins?

Cobalt occurs in silver ore. According to one school of thought the name derives from the belief that it was deposited there by goblins.

On the other hand the mining of cobalt exposed workers to arsenic and sulphur. Such exposure took a toll on their health and, seeking an explanation for this, they attributed it to the ill will of the goblin who dwelt in the mine.

cod (kɒd) *n, pl* **cod** (the flesh of) a large edible sea-fish with soft fins. **cod-liver oil** oil from the liver of the cod, rich in vitamins A and D. < Middle English.
COD *abbrev* cash on delivery.
coddle (ˈkɒdl̩) *vb* **1** treat protectively; pamper. **2** cook (esp. eggs) in water just below boiling-point. < perhaps obsolete *caudle*.
code (kəʊd) *n* **1** a body of laws, rules, or principles: a moral code **2** a system of letters, words, or symbols used to represent others, used for sending messages in secret, etc.
• *vb* set into code. < ultimately Latin *codex* book.
codify (ˈkəʊdɪˌfaɪ) *vb* **codified; codifying** set out in a systematic form; reduce to a code. **codification** *n*
codswallop (ˈkɒdzˌwɒləp) *n* (*informal*) foolish talk or nonsense; rubbish. < origin unknown.
coeducation (ˌkəʊɛdjʊˈkeɪʃən) *n* the education of girls and boys together in the same school and classes. **coeducational** *adj*
coefficient (ˌkəʊɪˈfɪʃənt) n a specified constant numerical factor in mathematics or physics. < Latin *co-* + *efficiens* efficient.
coerce (kəʊˈɜːs) *vb* restrain or compel by force. **coercion** *n* **coercive** *adj* < Latin *co-* + *arcēre* to enclose.
coexist (ˌkəʊɪgˈzɪst) *vb* exist at the same time or together; mutually tolerate: The two countries coexisted peacefully. **coexistence** *n* **coexistent** *adj*
C. of E. *abbrev* Church of England.
coffee (ˈkɒfɪ) *n* **1** (a drink made from) the ground roasted seeds of the coffee tree. **2** a light brown colour. **coffee bar** a place which serves coffee and light refreshments. **coffee-cup** *n* a small cup for serving coffee. **coffee morning** a morning where people meet to drink coffee, often to raise money for a good cause. **coffee shop** a coffee bar, esp. in a hotel or large store. **coffee-table** *n* a small, low table, usually put in a living-room. < ultimately Arabic *qahwa*.

> **Beware of the coconut!**
>
> Not many people nowadays would be frightened by seeing a coconut. However, the name of this fruit derives ultimately from the Portuguese word *côco* meaning 'bogeyman'. Those Portuguese who gave the coconut its name saw in the base of the nut, which has three black marks, a likeness to a rather gruesome face.

coffer (ˈkɒfə) *n* **1** a strong chest or box for keeping money or valuables in. **2** funds; wealth: the coffers of the treasury. **coffer-dam** *n* a watertight structure from which water can be pumped out so that repairs or construction can be carried out. < ultimately Greek *kophinos* basket.
coffin (ˈkɒfɪn) *n* a box in which a corpse is buried or cremated. < Latin *cophinus* basket.
cog (kɒg) *n* a tooth on the edge of a wheel or gear which fits into and drives another wheel. **cog-wheel** *n* a wheel with teeth or cogs. < Middle English *cogge*.
cogent (ˈkəʊdʒənt) *adj* appealing strongly to reason; convincing: cogent evidence. < Latin *cogere* to drive together.
cogitate (ˈkɒdʒɪˌteɪt) *vb* think intently or meditate (on), **cogitation** *n* < Latin *cogitare* to think about.
cognac (ˈkɒnjæk) *n* a high-quality brandy made in Cognac. < *Cognac*, town in western France. SEE PANEL AT CHAMPAGNE.
cognate (ˈkɒgneɪt) *adj* related; from the same source. < ultimately Latin *co-* + *nasci* to be born.
cognition (kɒgˈnɪʃən) *n* the mental act or process of knowing, including perception, judgment, and intuition. **cognitive** *adj* < Latin *cognoscere* to know.
cognizant (ˈkɒgnɪzənt) *adj* having special knowledge or awareness. **cognizance** *n* < ultimately Latin *cognoscere* to know.
cohabit (kəʊˈhæbɪt) *vb* live together as husband and wife without being married. **cohabitation** *n* < Latin *co-* + *habitare* to inhabit.
cohere (kəʊˈhɪə) *vb* hold or stick together firmly in a mass. **cohesion** *n* **cohesive** *adj* < Latin *co-* + *haerēre* to stick.
coherent (kəʊˈhɪərənt) *adj* **1** sticking together. **2** logically connected; consistent. **coherence** *n* **coherently** *adv*
coiffure (kwɒˈfjʊə) *n* a hair-style. **coiffured** *adj* < French *coiffer* to arrange hair.
coil (kɔɪl) *vb* wind into loops or a spiral.
• *n* **1** something wound into a coil; loop of this. **2** wire wound round something in a spiral as an electrical conductor. **3** a contraceptive device fitted inside the

womb. < Middle French *coillir* to collect.

coin (kɔɪn) *n* (a round piece of) metal money.
• *vb* **1** make metal money by stamping; mint. **2** (*informal*) make or earn money rapidly in quantity: He's coining it in. **3** create (a word or phrase). < Latin *cuneus* wedge.

coincide (ˌkəʊɪnˈsaɪd) *vb* **1** happen at the same place or time. **2** be the same; agree: Their wishes coincided. **coincidence** *n* **1** coinciding. **2** a remarkable chance happening of similar or related events at the same time. **coincident** *adj* occupying the same time or space. **coincidental** *adj* taking place by chance at the same time as a similar or related event. **coincidentally** *adv* < Latin *co-* + *incidere* to fall on.

coke (kəʊk) *n* a fuel remaining after gases and coal tar have been extracted from coal. < Middle English.

colander (ˈkɒləndə, ˈkʌləndə) *n* a bowl-shaped utensil with holes, used for washing or straining water from cooked food. < ultimately Latin *colum* sieve.

cold (kəʊld) *adj* **1** having a low temperature, esp. below the level of human comfort. **2** (of food) unheated or cooked and cooled before serving: cold meats. **3** unfriendly; impersonal: a cold reception. **4** depressing; gloomy: cold colours. **5** dead or unconscious: He's out cold. **6** (of hunting) with only faint traces: a cold trail. **7** (of games) far from a solution or object looked for.
• *adv* **1** in a cold condition. **2** in an unprepared way: You'll have to do it cold.
• *n* **1** a low temperature; lack of heat. **2** an infection causing catarrh, sneezing, etc.: the common cold. **coldly** *adv* **coldness** *n* **cold-blooded** *adj* **1** (of animals) with a body temperature that alters with the environment. **2** ruthless: cold-blooded murder. **cold cream** a soothing, cleansing ointment for the skin, esp. of the face. **cold storage** a refrigerated place for storing things. < Old English *ceald*. SEE PANEL.

coleslaw (ˈkəʊlˌslɔː) *n* a salad of shredded raw white cabbage in dressing. < Dutch *kool* cabbage + *sla* salad.

colic (ˈkɒlɪk) *n* (a spasm of) severe abdominal pain. **colicky** *adj* < ultimately Greek *kolon* colon.

collaborate (kəˈlæbəˌreɪt) *vb* **1** work together as partners; co-operate. **2** co-operate with the enemy of one's country. **collaboration** *n* **collaborator** *n* < Latin *com-* together + *laborare* to labour.

collage (kɒˈlɑːʒ) *n* artwork made by sticking pieces of paper, cloth, etc., to a surface. < ultimately Greek *kolla* glue.

collapse (kəˈlæps) *vb* **1** break or fall down completely. **2** give way or lose strength suddenly: The enemy collapsed. **3** fold into a more compact shape.
• *n* **1** the act of collapsing. **2** a breakdown of health or self-control. **collapsible** *adj* constructed so as to fold into a compact shape. < ultimately Latin *com-* + *labi* to fall.

collar (ˈkɒlə) *n* **1** a band around the neckline of a garment, often turned over. **2** a band put round the neck of an animal. **3** a ring resembling a collar that holds a machine part in place. **4** a cut of bacon from the pig's neck.
• *vb* (*informal*) seize; apprehend: The police collared him. **collar-bone** *n* the bone which joins the shoulder-blade and breastbone; clavicle. < Latin *collum* neck.

collate (kəˈleɪt) *vb* **1** collect and compare, esp. for authentication. **2** assemble systematically: collate information. **collation** *n* **collator** *n* < ultimately Latin *com-* + *latus*, from *ferre* to carry.

cold thoughts

Cold features in a number of idiomatic phrases, including:

cold comfort (of) little or no consolation: Telling her that he had a spare key at home was cold comfort. There they were—locked out of the car and 200 miles from home!

cold war a conflict between countries conducted by means of propaganda, etc., rather than by fighting.

get cold feet to feel afraid or reluctant, especially just before an event takes place.

get the cold shoulder to be rejected.

in cold blood calmly and ruthlessly: murdered in cold blood.

leave cold to fail to interest (someone): All this talk of holidays leaves Jack cold—he's quite happy with two weeks at home.

collateral (kəˈlætərəl) *adj* **1** parallel. **2** secondary; subordinate: collateral evidence.
• *n* property pledged as security by a borrower to a lender. **collaterally** *adv* < Latin *com-* + *lateralis* lateral.

colleague (ˈkɒliːg) *n* a fellow worker, esp. in a business or profession. < ultimately Latin *com-* + *legare* to choose.

collect (kəˈlɛkt) *vb* **1** bring or come together in a group or mass. **2** gather or receive (payment or contributions) from various sources. **3** get samples or specimens of, esp. as a hobby: collect stamps. **4** fetch: She collected the children from school. **5** gather and arrange in order: He collected his thoughts. **6** bring (oneself) under control. **collection** *n* **1** the act of collecting. **2** contributions of money taken for charity, for example. **3** objects or specimens gathered and arranged for study, comparison, or display. **4** a number of things brought together. **collective** *adj* of a number of individual items considered as a whole: a collective impression. **collectively** *adv* **collective bargaining** negotiation between employers and unions, usually on wages and conditions. **collector** *n* someone who collects. **collector's item** something worth obtaining because of its beauty or rarity. < Latin *com-* + *legere* to gather.

college (ˈkɒlɪdʒ) *n* **1** an institution for higher, professional, or specialized education: art college; business college. **2** an independent section of a university with its own students and lecturers. **3** the buildings of these. **4** an organization of people with special privileges or duties: the Royal College of Surgeons. **5** a public school; (private) secondary school. **collegiate** *adj* of a college or college student. < Latin *collega* colleague.

collide (kəˈlaɪd) *vb* **1** meet and hit against each other violently while in motion. **2** come into conflict. **collision** *n* **collision course** a course that results in collision unless altered. < Latin *com-* + *laedere* to strike. SEE PANEL.

collier (ˈkɒlɪə) *n* **1** a coal-miner. **2** a cargo ship that carries coal. **colliery** *n* a coal-mine and its adjacent buildings. < Middle English *col* coal.

colloquial (kəˈləʊkwɪəl) *adj* characteristic of informal speech; conversational. **colloquially** *adv* **colloquialism** *n* an informal expression. < Latin *com-* + *loqui* to speak.

colloquium (kəˈləʊkwɪəm) *n, pl* **colloquiums, colloquia** an organized conference or seminar. < SEE **COLLOQUIAL.**

collusion (kəˈluːʒən) *n* co-operation in secret for an illegal or fraudulent purpose. **collusive** *adj* < Latin *com-* + *ludere* to play.

cologne (kəˈləʊn) *n* a cooling scented liquid for the skin; eau-de-cologne. < *Cologne,* city in Germany. SEE PANEL.

colon[1] (ˈkəʊlən) *n* the part of the large intestine extending from the caecum to the rectum. < Greek *kolon.*

colon[2] *n* **1** the punctuation mark : used to show that what follows is an example, list, or summary of what is before it, or to show contrast. **2** the sign : used in a mathematical ratio: 5:1. < Greek *kōlon.*

Who collided with whom?

The way that words are arranged in a sentence provides a layer of meaning over and above the meanings of the individual words. This can be illustrated by producing a sentence in which the words themselves have no meanings: The bloobies snoogled the gogglies. The grammatical meaning provided by this arrangement tells us that it was the bloobies who did the snoogling, not the gogglies, and that it was the gogglies who were snoogled.

The above example shows how the subject of a sentence is interpreted as the 'doer' or instigator of the action. Consider now the following sentences:

(1) The Datsun collided with the Volvo.
(2) The Volvo collided with the Datsun.
(3) The Datsun and the Volvo collided.

The arrangement of words in the first sentence leads us to assume that it was the Datsun that was moving, not the Volvo. In the second sentence we assume that it was the Volvo that was moving. Finally, the third arrangement tells us that both cars were moving.

So we see that grammar isn't just a matter of putting a singular verb with a singular noun. It is an integral part of our ability to say exactly what we mean.

---

colonel (ˈkɜːnḷ) *n* an army officer ranking above a lieutenant-colonel and below a brigadier. < ultimately Latin *columna* column of soldiers.
colonnade (ˌkɒləˈneɪd) *n* a row of columns. < Italian *colonna* column.
colony (ˈkɒlənɪ) *n* **1** a new territory under the control of a remote parent state; group of settlers in such a territory. **2** a group of people with common interests or nationality living together in an area; area in which they live: an artist's colony. **3** a group of similar plants, animals, etc., living or growing together: a colony of bees. **colonial** *adj* **colonialism** *n* a State policy of control over a dependent territory. **colonist** *n* a settler in a colony. **colonize** *vb* make or establish a colony in; settle. **colonization** *n* < ultimately Latin *colere* to cultivate.
colossal (kəˈlɒsḷ) *adj* of great size or degree. **colossally** *adv* < Greek *kolossus* colossus, enormous statue.
colour (ˈkʌlə) *n* **1** the visual sensation produced by light rays of different wavelengths; one example of this, such as red or green. **2** colours with hue as opposed to black or white; using all colours: colour television. **3** a ruddy tint of the complexion characterizing good health: He looks off colour. **4** skin pigmentation, esp. dark. **5** the set of points of interest or vitality: local colour. **6** a paint or dye. **7** an identifying badge or flag, for example of a ship or regiment.
• *vb* **1** give colour to; paint or dye. **2** take on colour; blush. **3** influence or bias: It coloured his judgment. **colour bar** discrimination between White people and those of a different colour. **colour-blind** *adj* unable to distinguish certain colours. **coloured** *adj* **1** having colour. **2** biased. **3** also *n* (a person) of a non-White or mixed race. **colourful** *adj* **1** full of striking colour. **2** vividly detailed or interesting: a colourful tale. **colourfully** *adv* **colouring** *n* **1** the manner in which something is coloured. **2** a colouring substance. **colours** *pl n* an award made to a regular member of a sports team. **colour scheme** colours planned systematically, for example, in a room. **in its true colours** showing its real nature. < Latin *color*.

eau-de-cologne

A perfume or toilet water tends to sound much more exotic and desirable when it has a foreign name. Take for example eau-de-cologne. This is a straight adoption of a French phrase meaning 'Cologne water', Cologne being the German city where it was first manufactured in 1709. Compared with eau-de-cologne, Cologne water has a certain lack of appeal.

colt (kəʊlt) *n* a young, male horse. < Old English.
column (ˈkɒləm) *n* **1** a rounded pillar; something suggesting this: a column of water. **2** a vertical printed section on a page of, for example, a newspaper; regular feature in a newspaper: sports column. **3** a long, narrow formation of troops or vehicles in rows. **columnist** *n* someone who writes a column for a newspaper or magazine. < ultimately Latin *columen* top.
coma (ˈkəʊmə) *n* a condition of deep unconsciousness caused by injury or disease. **comatose** *adj* **1** in a coma. **2** lethargic. < Greek *kōma*.
comb (kəʊm) *n* **1** a device with teeth for tidying the hair or keeping it in place; structure like this, esp. used in handling textile fibres. **2** the fleshy crest on the head of the domestic fowl. **3** a honeycomb.
• *vb* **1** tidy with a comb. **2** examine or search thoroughly: Police combed the area for clues. **comb out** (*informal*) eliminate (unwanted people or things) from a group; separate for removal. < Old English *camb*.
combat (ˈkɒmbæt) *n* a struggle or contest between groups or individuals: in single combat.
• *vb* struggle against, esp. in order to reduce: combat inflation. < Latin *com-* + *battuere* to beat.
combatant (ˈkɒmbətṇt) *n* someone prepared for or involved in active fighting.
• *adj* involved in fighting.
combine (kəmˈbaɪn) *vb* join together; merge. **combination** *n* **1** the result of combining. **2** a number of people or things combined. **combination lock** a lock that can only be opened by setting numbers or letters on a dial at certain positions. **combinations** *pl n* a single undergarment covering the legs and body.
• *n* (ˈkɒmbaɪn) a combination of people or organizations, often in industry or commerce, acting together to further their interests. **combine harvester** a

machine that reaps, threshes, and cleans grain while moving across a field of crops. < ultimately Latin *com-* + *bini* two by two.

combustion (kəmˈbʌstʃən) *n* a chemical process producing heat and light when substances are oxidized. **combustible** *adj, n* (a substance that is) capable of or used for burning. **combustibility** *n*
< Latin *com-* + *urere* to burn.

come (kʌm) *vb* **came; come; coming** **1** move towards a nearer point or the speaker: Come here! **2** arrive; appear: Summer has come. **3** reach a certain condition or point in a sequence: Now we come to Chapter 2. **4** extend: The coal comes to his knees. **5** happen: How did he come to do that? **6** amount: That comes to £5 exactly. **7** happen

come, come

Come features in a large number of idiomatic expressions, including:

come about to happen.
come across 1 to find or meet by chance. **2** to be understood.
come along 1 to make progress; improve. **2** to make a greater effort; hurry.
come back to to talk again to (someone) (on a particular matter): I'll come back to you on that question shortly.
come between to interfere in a relationship between.
come by to obtain (something).
come clean to confess fully.
come down 1 to collapse or fall. **2** to lose one's social position, prestige, etc.: come down in the world. **3** to reach a decision: to come down in favour of the scheme.
come-down *n* a fall in social position, prestige, etc.; anticlimax.
come down on to criticize severely.
come forward to present oneself, especially in order to give information: The police are asking any member of the public who saw the accident to come forward.
come in 1 to arrive. **2** to be received as income: They have £200 coming in each week. **3** to be introduced; become fashionable or available. **4** to take a position that is mentioned in a race: His horse came in second. **5** to take part; serve a purpose: Where do I come in?
come in for to be the target of (criticism, etc.).
come into to inherit or receive.
come of to result from; happen to: I'm sure nothing but good can come of all your efforts.
come off 1 to become detached. **2** to take place as planned: The wedding didn't come off after all. **3** to be successful: It was a clever idea but it didn't come off. **4** to fare in a way that is mentioned: From all his cuts and bruises, it was clear who had come off worse in the fight.
come on 1 to make progress; improve. **2** to appear on stage, etc., in order to perform. **3** to begin.
come out 1 (of the sun, moon, etc.) to appear. **2** to be published. **3** to be removed from: These ink stains won't come out. **4** to become known; be announced: Eventually the truth came out. **5** to go on strike. **6** to become clear or evident. **7** to be seen clearly: Jean always comes out well in photographs. **8** to declare one's opinion: The commission came out against the plan. **9** to develop (a rash, etc.). **10** to bloom.
come out with to utter (something surprising or shocking).
come over to affect; be affected by: I suddenly came over very dizzy.
come round 1 to make a casual, informal visit. **2** to regain consciousness. **3** to change one's opinion, etc., to agree with (the opinion of someone else). **4** to recur.
come through to survive (a crisis, serious illness, etc.).
come to 1 to make a total of; amount to. **2** to concern: When it comes to computers, David's the expert!
come up 1 to arise, especially unexpectedly: Something has just come up and I will be late home. **2** to be raised for discussion or consideration.
come up against to be faced with (a problem).
come upon to find or meet by chance.
come up to to equal or reach (a particular standard).
come up with to discover, produce, or contribute: to come up with an interesting idea.
how come? why is it that?; what is the explanation of?: If he's ill, how come I saw him in town at lunchtime?

as a result of; originate: Milk comes from cows. **8** be descended from: He comes from a noble family. **9** (*informal*) behave as: Don't come the poor victim with me.
• *interj* also **come on** wait; think again. **come-back** *n* **1** a return to an earlier successful condition: making a come-back. **2** a reply. **come-hither** *adj* seductive: a come-hither look. **come-uppance** *n* a deserved punishment or rebuke. < Old English *cuman.* SEE PANEL.

comedy (ˈkɒmɪdɪ) *n* **1** a light, humorous film or play; genre of drama characterized by this. **2** a humorous or farcical incident. **3** humour. **comedian** *n* **1** an actor playing comic roles. **2** an amusing entertainer. **3** someone who behaves in an amusing way. **comedienne** *n* a female comedian. < ultimately Greek *kōmos* festival + *aeidein* to sing.

comely (ˈkʌmlɪ) *adj* (*old-fashioned*) attractive; good-looking. < Old English *cӯme.*

comestibles (kəˈmɛstɪbl̩z) *pl n* (*formal*) food. < ultimately Latin *com-* + *edere* to eat.

comet (ˈkɒmɪt) *n* a body of ice and dust particles with a gaseous tail that travels round the sun in an elliptical orbit. < ultimately Greek *komē* hair.

comfort (ˈkʌmfət) *n* **1** contentment; well-being. **2** encouragement or relief in suffering; giver of this.
• *vb* console; cheer up. **comforter** *n* **comfortable** *adj* **1** giving or enjoying ease or security: a comfortable home. **2** free from stress or restriction: a comfortable life **comfortably** *adv* < ultimately Latin *com-* + *fortis* strong.

comic (ˈkɒmɪk) *adj* **1** of comedy. **2** intending to cause amusement.
• *n* **1** a comedian. **2** a children's paper, mostly with strip cartoons. **comical** *adj* **comically** *adv* < Greek *kōmikos.*

coming (ˈkʌmɪŋ) *adj* **1** due; approaching: the coming year. **2** increasing in importance: up and coming.
• *n* arriving: comings and goings.

comma (ˈkɒmə) *n* the punctuation mark, used to show a pause or break within a sentence, or to separate words or figures in a list. < ultimately Greek *koptein* to cut.

command (kəˈmɑ:nd) *n* **1** a direction or order given with authority; right to give this: He's in command. **2** an electrical signal, esp. to instruct a computer. **3** knowledge or mastery: She has a good command of Spanish. **4** a military unit: Bomber Command.
• *vb* **1** direct or order; have control or authority over. **2** have within reach: He commands a wide audience. **3** ask for and receive: She commands a high fee. **4** gain through deserving: a woman who commands respect. **5** look over from a height or strategic position: The castle commands a fine view of the city. **commander** *n* **1** someone in command. **2** a naval officer ranking above a lieutenant-commander and below a captain. **commander-in-chief** *n* someone in supreme command, esp. of a military force. < Latin *commendare.*

commandant (ˈkɒmənˌdænt) *n* a commanding officer, esp. military.

commandeer (ˌkɒmənˈdɪə) *vb* **1** take possession of for military purposes. **2** take for one's own purposes. < Old French *comander.*

commandment (kəˈmɑ:ndmənt) *n* an order, esp. one of the ten given by God to Moses.

commando (kəˈmɑ:ndəʊ) *n, pl* **commandos** a member of a small military unit trained for surprise raids. < French *commander.*

commemorate (kəˈmɛməˌreɪt) *vb* **1** keep remembrance of by a ceremony. **2** serve as a memorial to. **commemoration** *n* **commemorative** *adj* < Latin *com-* + *memorare* to remind.

commence (kəˈmɛns) *vb* start. **commencement** *n* < Latin *com-* + *initiare* to begin.

commend (kəˈmɛnd) *vb* **1** praise; recommend: He was commended for his bravery. **2** give into the care of; entrust: She commended her soul to God. **commendable** *adj* praiseworthy. **commendably** *adv* **commendation** *n* < Latin *com-* + *mandare* to entrust.

commensurate (kəˈmɛnsərət) *adj* equal in size or extent; proportionate: a job commensurate with her experience. **commensurable** *adj* < Latin *com-* + *mensura* measure.

comment (ˈkɒmɛnt) *n* **1** a short note explaining or criticizing a piece of writing. **2** a remark or observation expressing an opinion: The play is a comment on modern society.
• *vb* make a comment. < Latin *comminisci* to contrive.

commentary (ˈkɒməntərɪ) *n* **1** a systematic series of comments, for example, on a written or performed work. **2** a continuous spoken description of a sporting event, esp. broadcast on radio or television: a running commentary. **commentate** *vb* act as a commentator. **commentator** *n* someone who writes or broadcasts a commentary.

commerce (ˈkɒmɜːs) *n* all aspects of business and trading on a large scale. < Latin *com-* + *merx* merchandise.

commercial (kəˈmɜːʃəl) *adj* **1** of or used for commerce: commercial vehicles. **2** profit-making, or something seen as such: commercial success. **3** produced for the market rather than for any artistic value. **4** financed by sponsors or advertisers: commercial television.
• *n* an advertisement broadcast on radio or television. **commercially** *adv* **commercialese** *n* the special style of language used in business. **commercialism** *n* commercial methods or attitudes. **commercialize** *vb* make commercial or profitable. **commercial traveller** a sales representative. SEE PANEL.

commiserate (kəˈmɪzəˌreɪt) *vb* express sympathy (with). **commiseration** *n* < Latin *com-* + *miserari* to pity.

commission (kəˈmɪʃən) *n* **1** a duty or task given to an individual or group. **2** the authority, esp. a formal document, given for this. **3** a group of people instructed to perform a task, usually by the government. **4** (a certificate conferring) rank in the armed forces. **5** the act of committing something. **6** a percentage paid to an agent for his or her services: commission-agent.
• *vb* **1** formally assign a task to: The poem was specially commissioned for the occasion. **2** confer a commission on: a commissioned officer. **commissioner** *n* **1** a member or head of a commission. **2** the government representative in charge of a district overseas. **commissioner for oaths** someone empowered to authenticate the swearing of an oath on affidavits, etc. **in/out of commission** in/not in service. < Latin *committere* to commit.

commissionaire (kəˈmɪʃəˌnɛə) *n* an attendant in uniform at the entrance to a theatre, department store, or large office. < French *commission.*

> **commercialese**
>
> The ending -ese refers to a language or place of origin: Japanese, Burmese, Maltese, Vietnamese, Cantonese.
>
> It also refers to a distinctive style of language: commercialese, journalese, officialese. In this sense it is usually pejorative in tone.

commit (kəˈmɪt) *vb* **committed; committing 1** do; carry out: commit murder. **2** entrust. **3** place in a prison or mental hospital. **4** obligate; pledge: They were committed to a peaceful solution. **commitment** *n* **1** committing. **2** an obligation or agreed duty. **3** loyalty to a cause or idea. **committal** *n* **1** an act of consigning, for example, to prison. **2** committing a body for cremation or burial. **committed** *adj* dedicated, esp. to a cause. < Latin *committere.*

committee (kəˈmɪtɪ) *n* a group of people appointed to investigate or report on a matter or organize an event or society. < Middle English *committen.* SEE PANEL AT **EMBARRASS.**

commode (kəˈməʊd) *n* **1** a chest of drawers. **2** a chair with a removable seat covering a chamber-pot. < Latin *com-* + *modus* measure.

commodity (kəˈmɒdɪtɪ) *n* something which can be bought and sold; useful article. < Latin *commodus.*

commodore (ˈkɒməˌdɔː) *n* **1** a naval officer ranking above a captain and below a rear-admiral. **2** the senior captain of a line of merchant ships. **3** the chief officer of a yacht club. < French *comander.*

common (ˈkɒmən) *adj* **1** of the general public or community: acting for the common good. **2** belonging to or shared by two or more individuals: a common factor. **3** frequent in occurrence; familiar: a common sight. **4** ordinary: the common people. **5** basic: common decency. **6** unrefined; vulgar.
• *n* an open piece of land for public use. **commonly** *adv* **commonness** *n* **commoner** *n* one who is not of noble birth. **common law** law based on custom. **common-law husband** or **wife** a man or woman living with a partner as if married, recognized by common law. **Common Market** the European Economic Community. **common or garden** ordinary. **commonplace** *adj, n* (something) ordinary or usual: Computers are now a commonplace. **common-room** *n* a room in a school, college, etc., shared by staff or students for recreation. **common sense** practical sense based on experience of life. **common-sense** *adj* **commoner** *n* one who is not of noble birth. **commonwealth** *n* **1** a politically independent state or unit. **2** an association of independent states; federation of states: the Commonwealth of Australia. (**House of**) **Commons** the lower assembly in Parliament. **in common** shared by or characteristic of two or more people or

things. < Latin *communis*. SEE PANEL.

commotion (kəˈməʊʃən) *n* a loud confusion of noises. < Latin *com-* + *movēre* to move.

commune¹ (ˈkɒmjuːn) *n* **1** a group of people or families who live together, sharing possessions and responsibilities. **2** a small administrative district in various European countries. **communal** *adj* shared between individuals in a community. **communally** *adv* < Latin *communis*.

commune² (kəˈmjuːn) *vb* communicate intimately; feel in harmony (with): commune with nature. < Latin *communicare*.

communicate (kəˈmjuːnɪˌkeɪt) *vb* **1** convey (messages, information, etc.). **2** transmit (ideas and feelings) so that they are understood: I can't communicate with my parents. **3** transmit (a disease). **4** be connected, as by a door. **communicable** *adj* **communicant** *n* **1** someone receiving Holy Communion. **2** someone conveying information. **communication** *n* **1** communicating. **2** information transmitted; message. **3** *pl* means for communicating such as the radio or telephone. **communication cord** a chain or cord in a railway carriage, pulled by passengers to stop the train in an emergency. **communicative** *adj* willing to give information; talkative. < ultimately Latin *communis* common.

communion (kəˈmjuːnjən) *n* sharing of ideas or feeling; fellowship. **Holy Communion** the Christian service in which bread and wine are blessed and consumed; the Eucharist.

communiqué (kəˈmjuːnɪˌkeɪ) *n* an official message; bulletin. < French.

communism (ˈkɒmjʊˌnɪzəm) *n* **1** a social system in which possessions are held in common. **2 Communism** a doctrine based on the writings of Karl Marx in which the state controls and owns the means of production, as practised in the USSR and other countries. < French *commun* common.

communist (ˈkɒmjʊnɪst) *n* often **Communist 1** someone who believes in Communism. **2** a member of the Communist Party.
• *adj* often **Communist** of Communism or communism.

community (kəˈmjuːnɪtɪ) *n* **1** a body of people living in a particular area. **2** a group of people with common interests or origins: an immigrant community. **3** likeness; fellowship: a community of interests. **community centre** a place providing education and recreation for a community. **community home** a centre for young offenders and deprived children.

commute (kəˈmjuːt) *vb* **1** convert: commute metal into gold. **2** (in law) exchange (a punishment) for one less severe: commuted to life imprisonment. **3** travel regularly to and from work, esp. in a city. **commuter** *n* < Latin *com-* + *mutare* to change.

compact¹ (kəmˈpækt) *adj* **1** packed closely together. **2** concise; succinct: a compact statement. **compactly** *adv* **compactness** *n* **compact disc** a digitally-recorded disc that is read by a laser beam.
• *n* (ˈkɒmpækt) a small, flat case for face powder. < Latin *com-* + *pangere* to fasten.

compact² (ˈkɒmpækt) *n* a contract or agreement. < Latin *com-* + *pacisci* to contract.

companion (kəmˈpænjən) *n* **1** someone who accompanies another; comrade. **2** someone employed to live with another. **3** one of a matching pair: a companion volume. **companionable** *adj* sociable. **companionship** *n* friendly feeling between people. **companionway** *n* stairs from the deck of a ship to its cabins. < ultimately Latin *com-* + *panis* bread. SEE PANEL.

company (ˈkʌmpənɪ) *n* **1** the state of being with others: Come along for company. **2** guests: They've got company. **3** associates: the company he keeps. **4** an organization for business purposes formed under the

---

commoner or **more common** adjectives?

The general rule for forming comparative and superlative forms of adjectives is to add -er and -est to very short adjectives—those of one syllable—and to two-syllable adjectives ending in -y: high—higher—highest, happy—happier—happiest. Other adjectives tend to take more and most: beautiful—more beautiful—most beautiful.

Both kinds of comparative and superlative forms are possible, however, with a few two-syllable adjectives, for instance you can say either commoner or more common. Other examples are: handsome, polite, quiet, and adjectives ending in -er or -ure (for example, clever, mature), -le (for example, gentle), and -ow (for example, shallow).

Companies Acts; people working for this. **5** the officers and crew of a ship: ship's company. < SEE **COMPANION.**

compare (kəmˈpɛə) *vb* **1** assess the similarities and differences of. **2** be worthy of comparison; be considered similar. **3** modify (an adjective or adverb) according to the degree of comparison.
● *n* comparison: an intellect beyond compare. **comparable** *adj* suitable or capable of being compared; similar. **comparability** *n* **comparably** *adv* **comparative** *adj* **1** relative: a comparative study. **2** also *n* (a word) showing the degree of grammatical comparison generally expressing more, such as better, worse, larger. **comparatively** *adv* **compare notes** exchange ideas or information. **comparison** *n* **1** comparing. **2** the listing of the positive, comparative, and superlative forms of an adjective or adverb. < ultimately Latin *com-* + *par* equal. SEE PANEL.

compartment (kəmˈpɑːtmənt) *n* **1** a divided section of something. **2** a section of a railway carriage. **compartmentalize** *vb* divide into sections. < ultimately Latin *com-* + *partiri* to share.

compass (ˈkʌmpəs) *n* **1** an instrument which shows direction with a needle pointing to the magnetic north. **2** a boundary; range: the compass of a voice. **compasses** *pl n* an instrument with two legs on a pivot, used for drawing circles. < ultimately Latin *com-* + *passus* pace.

compassion (kəmˈpæʃən) *n* sympathy or pity for others that makes one want to help. **compassionate** *adj* **compassionately** *adv* < ultimately Latin *com-* + *pati* to bear, suffer.

compatible (kəmˈpætəbḷ) *adj* **1** capable of living together in harmony. **2** capable of being used together: a compatible stereo system. **compatibility** *n* **compatibly** *adv* < Latin *compati* sympathetic.

hungry companions

Another word for an associate or comrade is a companion. The latter first appears in English in the 13th century as *compainoun*, a modification of the Old French *compagnon*. This derives from the Late Latin *companio*, literally 'a person with whom one eats bread', which is a combination of the Latin *com-* 'with' and *panis* 'bread'.

compatriot (kəmˈpætrɪət) *n* a fellow countryman or countrywoman. < Late Latin *com-* + *patriota* fellow countryman.

compel (kəmˈpɛl) *vb* **compelled; compelling 1** force to do something. **2** arouse forcibly; exact: The scene compels wonder. < ultimately Latin *com-* + *pellere* to drive.

compendium (kəmˈpɛndɪəm) *n, pl* **compendiums, compendia 1** a brief, comprehensive summary. **2** a collection of indoor puzzles and games. **compendious** *adj* < Latin *com-* + *pendere* to weigh.

compensate (ˈkɒmpənˌseɪt) *vb* **1** make amends for (loss or damage) by a suitable payment. **2** counterbalance. **compensation** *n* **compensatory** *adj* < Latin *compendere* to weigh together.

compère (ˈkɒmpɛə) *vb, n* (act as) someone who presents a variety programme, esp. on radio or television. < French: godfather, from Latin *com-* + *pater* father.

compete (kəmˈpiːt) *vb* take part (in a contest or competition); contend or strive (for). **competition** *n* **1** a usually friendly contest in which the skill or performance of those taking part is compared. **2** competing or rivalry; those who compete with oneself. **competitive** *adj* **1** competing. **2** (of prices, etc.) favourable. **competitively** *adj* **competitiveness** *n* **competitor** *n* someone who competes. < ultimately Latin *com-* + *petere* to seek. SEE PANEL AT **CONTEST.**

competent (ˈkɒmpɪtənt) *adj* **1** with adequate knowledge or ability to do something. **2** legally qualified. **competence** *n* **competently** *adv* < Latin *competere* to be competent.

compare to or compare with?

Compare to and compare with are sometimes used interchangeably but careful users distinguish them. Compare to is reserved for stating similarities: The poet *compared* life *to* an adventure, and compare with for stating similarities and differences, especially differences: Prices have risen by only 2% this year, *compared with* 5% two years ago.

In intransitive uses compare with is correct and compare to wrong: The salary he earns at home does not *compare with* (not to) what he might earn abroad.

compile (kəmˈpaɪl) *vb* collect (information, etc.) into a single work; make (a book) like this. **compilation** *n* **compiler** *n* someone who compiles. < Latin *compilare* to plunder.

complacent (kəmˈpleɪsn̩t) *adj* self-satisfied; smug. **complacency** *n* **complacently** *adv* < Latin *com-* + *placēre* to please.

complain (kəmˈpleɪn) *vb* express discontent or discomfort; protest: He complained about the poor service. **complaint** *n* **1** an expression of dissatisfaction. **2** a formal accusation or protest. **3** an ailment: kidney complaint. < ultimately Latin *com-* + *plangere* to bewail.

complement (ˈkɒmplɪmənt) *n* something which completes another thing; quantity needed for this: a full complement of passengers. • *vb* be or act as a complement to; make more complete. **complementary** *adj* < ultimately Latin *complēre* to complete. SEE PANEL. SEE PANEL AT **SUPPLEMENT.**

complete (kəmˈpliːt) *adj* **1** having all necessary parts. **2** finished. **3** absolute: a complete stranger.
• *vb* **1** make (something) whole. **2** finish: He completed his homework. **3** fulfil: complete a contract. **4** fill in: complete the form. **completely** *adv* **completeness** *n* being complete. **completion** *n* being completed. < ultimately Latin *com-* + *plēre* to fill.

complex (ˈkɒmplɛks) *adj* made up of two or more parts; difficult to analyse or understand.

complement or **compliment?**

Words that look and sound alike are commonly confused. Such is the case with complement and compliment, although their meanings are quite different.

To compl*i*ment someone or pay someone a compl*i*ment means 'to express one's praise or admiration to': She was *complimented* on her fine performance.

To complement something or act as a complement to something means 'to enhance' or 'to make something more complete (and often more satisfying as a result)': Nothing *complements* steak better than a good red wine.

On the difference between complement and supplement, see panel at **supplement.**

• *n* **1** a whole made up of parts. **2** a group of feelings and ideas that affect someone's personality: inferiority complex. **3** a group of related buildings or structures: sports complex. **complexity** *n* < Latin *com-* + *plectere* to braid. SEE PANEL.

complexion (kəmˈplɛkʃən) *n* **1** the colouring and general appearance of the facial skin. **2** the overall character of something: That puts a different complexion on things. SEE PANEL.

complicate (ˈkɒmplɪˌkeɪt) *vb* cause to combine in an involved way; make difficult. **complicated** *adj* not straightforward; difficult to analyse or understand: a complicated issue. **complication** *n* **1** complexity. **2** something which creates difficulties. **3** a secondary ailment that develops during a prior illness. < ultimately Latin *com-* + *plicare* to fold. SEE PANEL AT **COMPLEX.**

complicity (kəmˈplɪsɪtɪ) *n* participation in doing wrong. < Late Latin *complex* confederate.

compliment (ˈkɒmplɪmənt) *n* **1** an expression of esteem or admiration; flattering remark. **2** *pl* regards; best wishes: the compliments of the season.
• *vb* pay a compliment to; express one's praise or admiration to. **complimentary** *adj* **1** expressing admiration. **2** given without charge: complimentary tickets. < Spanish *cumplir* to be polite. SEE PANEL AT **COMPLEMENT.**

comply (kəmˈplaɪ) *vb* **complied; complying** do what another asks; obey: comply with house rules. **compliance** *n* **compliant** *adj* < Latin *complēre* to complete.

component (kəmˈpəʊnənt) *adj, n* (being) one of the parts of which

complex or **complicated?**

Complex is used to describe things that are made up of several or many parts: a *complex* piece of machinery, a *complex* system.

Complicated means 'not straightforward; hard to understand': a *complicated* task, a *complicated* question.

However, things that are complex (structurally intricate) by nature tend to be complicated (not straightforward), and so there is considerable overlap in usage.

something is made. < Latin *componere* to put together.

compose (kəm'pəʊz) *vb* **1** put together to make (something): Bronze is composed of copper and tin. **2** create (a piece of music or literature). **3** put into order. **4** settle; calm: compose oneself. **composed** *adj* with control of one's feelings. **composedly** *adv* **composer** *n* someone who creates music. < Latin *componere* to put together.

composite ('kɒmpəzɪt) *n, adj* (something) made up of distinct parts.

composition (ˌkɒmpə'zɪʃən) *n* **1** making into a whole. **2** something created with the mind, such as a piece of music or a poem. **3** a short essay set as an exercise in school. **4** the harmonious way elements are arranged, for example in a picture. **5** a product of mixed ingredients.

compositor (kəm'pɒzɪtə) *n* a typesetter in printing.

compost ('kɒmpɒst) *n* a mixture of decaying organic substances, used as a fertilizer.
• *vb* convert into or treat with compost. < SEE **COMPONENT**.

composure ('kəm'pəʊʒə) *n* calmness of mind or appearance.

compote ('kɒmpəʊt) *n* a fruit dessert stewed in syrup and served cold. < Latin *composta*.

compound[1] ('kɒmpaʊnd) *adj* made up of two or more parts.
• *n* **1** a compound substance or thing. **2** a word made up of combined words or forms, such as lifeboat. **compound fracture** a bone fracture which also pierces the skin. **compound interest** interest paid on an original amount plus the accumulated interest.
• *vb* (kəm'paʊnd) **1** combine to make a whole. **2** add to; augment. **3** (in law) agree, for payment, not to prosecute or reveal (an offence): compound a felony. < Latin *componere* to put together.

compound[2] ('kɒmpaʊnd) *n* a fenced-in area containing buildings, esp. dwellings. < Malay *kampong* village, enclosure.

comprehend (ˌkɒmprɪ'hɛnd) *vb* **1** grasp the meaning of; understand. **2** include. **comprehensible** *adj* intelligible. **comprehensibly** *adv* **comprehension** *n* **comprehensive** *adj* all-inclusive. **comprehensively** *adv* **comprehensiveness** *n* **comprehensive school** also **comprehensive** a secondary school for children of mixed abilities. < Latin *comprehendere*.

compress[1] (kəm'prɛs) *vb* press together; squeeze (something) into a smaller space. **compression** *n* **compressor** *n* something that compresses. < Latin *com-* + *premere* to press.

compress[2] ('kɒmprɛs) *n* a usually cold pad pressed on to a part of the body to ease pain or stop bleeding. < Late Latin *compressare* to compress.

comprise (kəm'praɪz) *vb* **1** include; contain. **2** make up of or be made up of: The organization comprises three departments. < ultimately Latin *comprehendere*. SEE PANEL.

compromise ('kɒmprəˌmaɪz) *n* **1** the settling of differences by concessions made on both sides. **2** a half-way position between opposing actions or attitudes.
• *vb* **1** settle differences by making

---

complexion

Nowadays the word complexion refers to the colouring and appearance of the facial skin. The sense with which it entered English in the 14th century, however, was 'character' or 'temperament'.

According to the ancients, a person's disposition was determined by the exact proportions in which four fluids were combined in the body. These four fluids or 'humours' were blood, phlegm, choler (yellow bile), and melancholy (black bile). The Latin word for their all-important combination within an individual was *complexio* 'combination', from the verb *complectere* 'to braid, plait, or combine'. It was in this sense that complexion, derived from *complexio*, was first used.

---

comprise of?

Speakers and writers of English sometimes mistake comprise for consist or compose and follow it by of: The board *is comprised of* three layers of different thicknesses. The verb comprise, however, itself means 'to consist *of*; be composed *of*' so comprise of is wrong. The above sentence should therefore be: The board *comprises* three layers of different thicknesses.

concessions. **2** expose to scandal or embarrassment. < ultimately Latin *com-* + *promittere* to promise.

compulsion (kəmˈpʌlʃən) *n* **1** compelling or being compelled. **2** a powerful urge to do something, often irrational. **compulsive** *adj* **1** compelling. **2** caused by or suffering from an obsessive urge: a compulsive gambler. **compulsively** *adv* **compulsory** *adj* required by law or regulation: compulsory education. **compulsorily** *adv* < ultimately Latin *compellere* to compel.

compunction (kəmˈpʌŋkʃən) *n* a feeling of guilt or remorse: He stole without compunction. < ultimately Latin *com-* + *pungere* to prick. SEE PANEL.

compute (kəmˈpjuːt) *vb* calculate mathematically. **computation** *n* **computer** *n* an electronic machine which is programmed to store and process information or instructions. **computerize** *vb* **1** perform or operate by means of a computer. **2** equip with computers. < Latin *computare,* from *com-* + *putare* to reckon.

comrade (ˈkɒmreɪd) *n* **1** a friend or companion. **2** a fellow Communist or socialist. **comradely** *adv* **comradeship** *n* < ultimately Latin *camera* room.

con (kɒn) *vb* **conned; conning** (*informal*) persuade or trick.
• *n* (*informal*) a confidence trick. **con man** (*informal*) a confidence trickster. < short for *confidence* (*trick*).

concave (ˈkɒnkeɪv) *adj* curved inwards like the inside of a bowl. **concavity** *n* < ultimately Latin *com-* + *cavus* hollow.

conceal (kənˈsiːl) *vb* keep secret; hide. **concealment** *n* < ultimately Latin *com-* + *celare* to hide.

concede (kənˈsiːd) *vb* **1** accept the truth of (something). **2** grant or allow: The government conceded the right to demonstrate. **3** yield; admit defeat, esp. in sports. < Latin *com-* + *cedere* to yield.

conceit (kənˈsiːt) *n* excessive pride in oneself. **conceited** *adj* **conceitedly** *adv* < Middle English: opinion.

conceive (kənˈsiːv) *vb* **1** become pregnant (with). **2** mentally form (a plan, etc.). **conceivable** *adj* imaginable; believable. **conceivably** *adv* **conception** *n* **1** becoming pregnant. **2** an idea. < ultimately Latin *com-* + *capere* to take.

concentrate (ˈkɒnsənˌtreɪt) *vb* **1** direct (all one's thought or effort) towards something. **2** gather in one mass, body, or place. **3** make less dilute; condense.
• *n* a concentrated liquid solution. **concentrated** *adj* **concentration** *n* **concentration camp** a prison camp for political prisoners, etc. < Latin *com-* + *centrum* centre.

concentric (kənˈsɛntrɪk) *adj* with a common centre: concentric circles.

concept (ˈkɒnsɛpt) *n* a general idea or notion: the concept of democracy.

concern (kənˈsɜːn) *vb* **1** relate to; deal with: The play concerns good and evil. **2** influence; affect: The election concerns us all. **3** worry; distress: Her absence concerns me. **4** take up the time of; occupy: She concerned herself with the new project.
• *n* **1** something that relates to someone; responsibility: It's no concern of yours. **2** a worry. **3** a share, in a business for example. **4** a business: a large concern. **concerned** *adj* worried. **concerning** *prep* related to; about. < ultimately Latin *com-* + *cernere* to sift.

concert (ˈkɒnsət) *n* a public performance of music by two or more musicians. **concerted** *adj* planned or executed together: a concerted effort. **in concert** **1** performing music. **2** working together. < ultimately Latin *com-* + *certus* decided.

concertina (ˌkɒnsəˈtiːnə) *n* a small portable musical instrument of the accordion family with hexagonal ends and bellows, which produces notes when it is squeezed and buttons are pressed. < *concert* + *-ina.*

concerto (kənˈtʃɛətəʊ, kənˈtʃɜːtəʊ) *n, pl* **concertos** a piece of music for one or more soloists and an orchestra. < Italian: concert.

concession (kənˈsɛʃən) *n* **1** conceding; something which is conceded. **2** a grant of land or a right given by the owners to use it for mining, selling goods, etc.: mineral concession. **concessional** *adj* **concessionally** *adv* < Latin *concedere*

compunction and **puncture**

The similarity in form of compunction and puncture is not coincidental—they both derive ultimately from the Latin verb *pungere* 'to prick or sting'. Compunction is literally 'the pricking of the conscience'. The words pungent ('sharp-tasting or piquant') and poignant ('sharply-distressing; cutting or penetrating') are of the same origin.

to concede.
conch (kɒntʃ) *n* (the spiral shell of) a large shellfish. < Greek *konchē*.
conciliate (kən'sɪlɪˌeɪt) *vb* **1** win (someone) over; placate. **2** reconcile. **conciliation** *n* **conciliatory** *adj* **conciliator** *n* someone who conciliates. < ultimately Latin *concilium* council.
concise (kən'saɪs) *adj* brief in expression. **concisely** *adv* **conciseness** *n* < Latin *com-* + *caedere* to cut, strike.
conclude (kən'klu:d) *vb* **1** finish. **2** reach (an agreement); settle: conclude a sale. **3** arrive at through logic. **conclusion** *n* **1** an end; ending. **2** a settlement. **3** a judgment based on logic. **conclusive** *adj* absolutely convincing: conclusive proof. **conclusively** *adv* **in conclusion** finally. < ultimately Latin *com-* + *claudere* to close.
concoct (kən'kɒkt) *vb* **1** prepare (food, etc.) by combining different ingredients. **2** invent: concoct a story. **concoction** *n* < Latin *com-* + *coquere* to cook.
concomitant (kən'kɒmɪtənt) *adj* accompanying, esp. incidentally.
● *n* something accompanying another thing. < Latin *com-* + *comitari* to accompany.
concord ('kɒŋkɔ:d) *n* a state of harmony or agreement. **concordant** *adj* < Latin *com-* + *cor* heart.
concordance (kən'kɔ:dn̩s) *n* an index of the main words in a book or the works of an author: a concordance to the Bible. < Latin *concordans*.
concourse ('kɒŋkɔ:s) *n* **1** a gathering of people. **2** an open space where people pass through, such as in a railway station. < Latin *concurrere* to run together.
concrete ('kɒnkri:t) *n* a building material which binds other materials, made of cement, sand, and gravel mixed with water to harden it.
● *vb* **1** cover with or set in concrete. **2** solidify.
● *adj* **1** physically existing; tangible. **2** real; positive: concrete proof. < Latin *com-* + *crescere* to grow.
concubine ('kɒŋkjʊˌbaɪn) *n* a woman living with a man as his wife, esp. in addition to his lawful wife. < Latin *com-* + *cubare* to lie.
concur (kən'kɜ:) *vb* **concurred; concurring 1** act or happen together. **2** agree. **concurrence** *n* **1** events happening at the same time. **2** agreement. **concurrent** *adj* happening or existing at the same time. **concurrently** *adv* < Latin *com-* + *currere* to run.
concussion (kən'kʌʃən) *n* **1** a brain injury caused by a hard blow or fall. **2** a violent jarring. **concussed** *adj* < Latin *com-* + *quatere* to shake.
condemn (kən'dɛm) *vb* **1** declare (something) to be extremely wrong or evil. **2** prescribe punishment upon; sentence: condemned to death. **3** pronounce unsuitable for use or habitation: condemned buildings. **4** force into a particular state: His work condemned him to loneliness. **condemnation** *n* **condemnatory** *adj* < Latin *com-* + *damnare* to damn, condemn.
condense (kən'dɛns) *vb* **1** make denser; compress. **2** change to a denser form, as from a gas into a liquid. **3** express in a shorter form: a condensed volume. **condensation** *n* **condensed milk** evaporated, sweetened milk. **condenser** *n* an apparatus for condensing gas. < Latin *com-* + *densus* dense.
condescend (ˌkɒndɪ'sɛnd) *vb* behave in a superior manner; do something as if beneath one's dignity: He condescended to sit with us. **condescension** *n* < Latin *com-* + *descendere* to descend.
condiment ('kɒndɪmənt) *n* a spice or seasoning for food, such as salt or pepper. < Latin *condire* to pickle.
condition (kən'dɪʃən) *n* **1** the state or circumstances of someone or something: weather conditions. **2** a state of health or physical fitness: out of condition. **3** something required before something else can take place; terms: under certain conditions. **4** a physical defect: a heart condition.
● *vb* **1** bring to a state of fitness or readiness for use. **2** adapt to a different environment; accustom: conditioned response. **conditioner** *n* **on condition that** on the understanding that. < Latin *com-* + *dicere* to say.
conditional (kən'dɪʃənl̩) *adj* **1** subject to a condition: conditional discharge. **2** also *n* (*grammar*) (a verb, clause, etc.) expressing a condition on which something else is dependent: the conditional clause 'if you try'. **conditionally** *adv*
condolence (kən'dəʊləns) *n* usually **condolences** an expression of sympathy with someone in grief or pain. **condole** *vb* express condolences. < Latin *com-* + *dolēre* to feel pain.
condone (kən'dəʊn) *vb* overlook (a wrongful action, etc.); accept without condemning. < Latin *com-* + *donare* to give.
conducive (kən'dju:sɪv) *adj* helping towards a usually desired result: an

atmosphere conducive to relaxation. < Latin *com-* + *ducere* to lead.

conduct (kən'dʌkt) *vb* **1** accompany by leading or guiding: a conducted tour. **2** carry out; direct: conduct an experiment; conduct business. **3** act as a means of transmitting sound, heat, or electricity. **4** direct (a musical performance) by beating time. **conduction** *n* **conduct oneself** behave. **conductor** *n* **1** someone who conducts a musical performance. **2** a material which allows sound, light, etc., to be transmitted. **3** someone employed to collect bus fares. **conductress** *n* a female bus-conductor.
• *n* ('kɒndʌkt) **1** the way something is carried out; management. **2** someone's personal behaviour. < Latin *com-* + *ducere* to lead.

conduit ('kɒndɪt, 'kɒndjuɪt) *n* **1** a channel for conveying a fluid. **2** a pipe or tube which protects electric cable or wire. < Middle French: leading.

cone (kəʊn) *n* **1** a solid figure with a flat, circular base that narrows to a point at the other end; anything with this shape. **2** the dry fruit that is made up of woody scales in a cone shape, esp. on trees of the pine family. < Greek *kōnos.*

confection (kən'fɛkʃən) *n* a rich, sweet dish or cake prepared with fruit, cream or nuts, etc. **confectioner** *n* someone who makes or sells these by trade. **confectionery** *n* sweets, pastries, and cakes; confectioner's shop. < Latin *conficere* to prepare.

confederate (kən'fɛdərət) *adj* united by treaty; allied.
• *n* **1** a member of a league. **2** an accomplice or ally. **confederacy** *n* a union of states. **confederated** *adj* joined by treaty or agreement. **confederation** *n* **1** uniting in an alliance. **2** a league; confederacy. < ultimately Latin *com-* + *foedus* treaty.

confer (kən'fɜː) *vb* **conferred; conferring 1** bestow (an honour, gift, etc.). **2** discuss together; consult. **conference** *n* a meeting for exchanging information and consultation. < Latin *com-* + *ferre* to bear.

confess (kən'fɛs) *vb* **1** admit that one has acted wrongly: confess to a crime. **2** admit (one's sins) to God or a priest. **3** declare (one's attitude) with reluctance: I must confess I'm surprised. **confessedly** *adv* admittedly. **confession** *n* **1** confessing. **2** something confessed, esp. in a formal statement. **3** a formal declaration of religious belief: a confession of faith. **confessional** *n* an enclosed booth in a church where a priest hears confessions. **confessor** *n* a priest who listens to confessions and gives spiritual advice. < Latin *com-* + *fatēri* to confess.

confetti (kən'fɛtɪ) *n* small bits of coloured paper thrown over a bride and groom at their wedding. < Italian *confetto* bonbon, from Latin *conficere* to prepare.

confide (kən'faɪd) *vb* reveal (a secret, etc.) in private; trust (in) by sharing a secret, etc. **confidant** fem. **confidante** *n* someone entrusted with a secret. **confidence** *n* **1** faith; trust: a vote of confidence. **2** belief in one's own powers; self-assurance. **3** something confided. **confidence man** or **trickster** a man who pretends to be or have something in order to defraud. **confidence trick** a swindle by a confidence man. **confident** *adj* self-assured. **confidently** *adv* **confidential** *adj* **1** secret; private. **2** suggestive of confiding: a confidential tone. **confidentiality** *n* **confidentially** *adv* **in confidence** in secret. **in someone's confidence** trusted with someone's secrets. < Latin *com-* + *fidere* to trust.
SEE PANEL.

configuration (kənˌfɪgjʊ'reɪʃən) *n* an arrangement of parts in a pattern or outline, etc. < Latin *com-* + *fgurare* to shape.

confine (kən'faɪn) *vb* **1** keep within certain limits; restrict. **2** keep indoors, esp. through sickness: confined to bed. **3** imprison. **confined** *adj* restricted; limited. **confinement** *n* confining or being confined. **confines** *pl n* boundaries; limits. < Latin *com-* + *finis* end, limit.

confirm (kən'fɜːm) *vb* **1** prove to be true or correct. **2** make more certain or

confidant or **confident?**

The spelling of confident, confidence, and confidant are sometimes confused. As a simple way of avoiding such mistakes, just remember the phrases feel confident and feel confidence. The spelling of feel will remind you to use an e when it is necessary.

Confidant (feminine confidante) is by comparison a much less common word. It refers to the person in whom one confides, who could be an aunt or an attorney.

definite: My suspicions were confirmed. **3** formally validate: confirm bookings. **4** administer the rite of confirmation to. **confirmation** *n* **1** confirming; proof. **2** a religious rite admitting someone fully into a church. **confirmatory** *adj* confirming: confirmatory evidence. **confirmed** *adj* fixed in one's habits or life-style: a confirmed bachelor. < Latin *com-* + *firmus* firm.

confiscate (ˈkɒnfɪˌskeɪt) *vb* take or seize (as if) by authority. **confiscation** *n* < Latin *com-* + *fiscus* treasury.

conflagration (ˌkɒnfləˈgreɪʃən) *n* a great and disastrous fire. < Latin *com-* + *flagrare* to burn.

conflict (ˈkɒnflɪkt) *n* **1** a disagreement between people; clash of interests. **2** a fight; battle.
• *vb* (kənˈflɪkt) come into opposition; disagree. < Latin *com-* + *fligere* to strike.

conform (kənˈfɔːm) *vb* **1** adapt to or comply with rules or general custom; harmonize. **2** resemble. **conformist** *n* someone who conforms to accepted standards of behaviour. **conformity** *n* conforming; correspondence: in conformity with his principles. < Latin *com-* + *formare* to form.

confound (kənˈfaʊnd) *vb* **1** confuse or perplex. **2** put to shame; defeat: She confounded her critics. **3** damn: Confound it! **confounded** *adj* damned: a confounded nuisance. < ultimately Latin *com-* + *fundere* to pour.

confront (kənˈfrʌnt) *vb* **1** bring face to face with; be faced with. **2** face defiantly; oppose: confront the enemy. **confrontation** *n* < ultimately Latin *com-* + *frons* forehead.

confuse (kənˈfjuːz) *vb* **1** mix up: a confused pile of papers. **2** fail to recognize the differences between: confusing business with pleasure. **3** make indistinct; blur: confuse the issue. **4** cause the feelings of to be disordered; embarrass. **confused** *adj* **confusion** *n* < ultimately Latin *confundere* to confound.

confute (kənˈfjuːt) *vb* prove (someone or something) to be mistaken; refute. < Latin *confutare*.

conga (ˈkɒŋgə) *n* **1** a dance with three steps and a kick performed by a group of people in a long, winding line. **2** a tall drum played with the hands. < Spanish *congo* of the Congo, region in Africa.

congeal (kənˈdʒiːl) *vb* change from a liquid into a solid state, esp. by cold. **congelation** *n* < Latin *com-* + *gelare* to freeze.

congenial (kənˈdʒiːnjəl) *adj* **1** friendly; pleasant: a congenial atmosphere. **2** agreeably similar in tastes or attitudes; compatible: a congenial companion. < Latin *com-* + *genius* kind.

congenital (kənˈdʒɛnɪtl̩) *adj* **1** in a certain condition from birth: congenital deformity. **2** being a certain way by nature: a congenital liar. **congenitally** *adv* < ultimately Latin *com-* + *gignere* to produce, beget.

conger (ˈkɒŋgə) *n* a large, edible sea-eel. < Greek *gongros*.

congestion (kənˈdʒɛstʃən) *n* a crowded or clogged condition: traffic congestion. **congested** *adj* **1** overcrowded. **2** (of a bodily organ) excessively full of blood. < ultimately Latin *com-* + *gerere* to bear.

conglomerate (kənˈglɒməˌrət) *adj* made up of various different parts.
• *n* **1** a composite mass, esp. of rock. **2** a group of firms with widely varied interests. < ultimately Latin *com-* + *glomus* ball.

congratulate (kənˈgrætjʊˌleɪt) *vb* **1** express praise or approval to (a person) because of his or her success or good fortune. **2** think (oneself) clever or fortunate: He congratulated himself on his narrow escape. **congratulatory** *adj* **congratulations** *interj* well done! < ultimately Latin *com-* + *gratus* pleasing.

congregate (ˈkɒŋgrɪˌgeɪt) *vb* assemble in a crowd. **congregation** *n* a gathering of people, esp. for a religious service; group of believers. **congregational** *adj* < ultimately Latin *com-* + *grex* flock.

congress (ˈkɒŋgrɛs) *n* **1** a formal meeting, esp. of delegates of various nations. **2 Congress** the supreme law-making body of a nation, esp. of the USA. **congressional** *adj* < ultimately Latin *com-* + *gradi* to go.

conical (ˈkɒnɪkl̩) *adj* shaped like a cone. **conically** *adv*

conifer (ˈkɒnɪfə) *n* any of a group of cone-bearing, mostly evergreen trees or shrubs including pines, yews, and cypresses. **coniferous** *adj* < ultimately Latin *conus* cone + *ferre* to bear.

conjecture (kənˈdʒɛktʃə) *vb, n* (make) a guess. **conjectural** *adj* based on guesswork. < ultimately Latin *com-* + *jacere* to throw.

conjugal (ˈkɒndʒʊgl̩) *adj* of marriage or the relationships within it. < Latin *conjungere* to join in marriage.

conjugate (ˈkɒndʒʊˌgeɪt) *vb* give the various inflected forms of (a verb). **conjugation** *n* < ultimately Latin *com-* + *jugum* yoke.

conjunction (kən'dʒʌŋkʃən) *n* **1** a word that links other words, phrases, etc., such as and or although. **2** joining together; union: He works in close conjunction with a government department. **3** events happening at the same time. < Latin *conjungere* to join together.

conjunctivitis (kənˌdʒʌŋktɪ'vaɪtɪs) *n* an inflammation of the mucous membrane lining the inner eyelid and part of the eyeball. < ultimately Latin *conjunctus* conjoined.

conjure ('kʌndʒə) *vb* **1** perform seemingly magical tricks. **2** summon (a spirit, etc.) by a spell or incantation. **3** cause to appear (as if) from nowhere: He conjured up cup-final tickets. **4** imagine: The poem conjures up a feeling of loneliness. **conjuror** *n* someone who performs conjuring tricks. < ultimately Latin *com-* + *jurare* to swear.

conk (kɒŋk) *n* (*informal*) the head or nose.
• *vb* (*informal*) hit on the head or nose. **conk out** (*informal*) break down; become exhausted; die: The machine suddenly conked out. < probably alteration of *conch*.

conker ('kɒŋkə) *n* the seed of the horse-chestnut tree, used in conkers. **conkers** *n* a children's game in which each player tries to break the other's conker with his own, both being tied to a string. SEE PANEL.

connect (kə'nɛkt) *vb* **1** join or fasten together. **2** associate (ideas, people, or things) in the mind: He can't be connected with the crime. **3** (of a bus, train, etc.) be timed to arrive so that passengers can change from one to another to continue travelling. **4** enable telephone communication between. **connection** *n* **1** connecting; being connected. **2** something which connects; somewhere things are connected. **3** a relationship of ideas, things, or people: family connections. **4** a bus, train, or aeroplane that passengers transfer to in order to continue a journey: They missed their connection. **connective** *adj* **connector** *n* something which connects. < ultimately Latin *com-* + *nectere* to bind.

connive (kə'naɪv) *vb* **connive at** seem to ignore (wrongful actions) so appearing to approve of them; conspire. **connivance** *n* < Latin *connivēre.*

connoisseur (ˌkɒnə'sɜː) *n* someone with expert knowledge in matters of art, taste, etc. < ultimately Latin *cognoscere* to know.

connote (kə'nəʊt) *vb* imply (associations or overtones) beyond the literal meaning. **connotation** *n* < Latin *com-* + *notare* to note.

conquer ('kɒŋkə) *vb* gain or overcome by force or effort: Hillary conquered Everest. **conqueror** *n* someone who conquers. **conquest** *n* conquering; something conquered, esp. in war. < ultimately Latin *com-* + *quaerere* to seek.

conscience ('kɒnʃəns) *n* **1** an awareness of right and wrong in one's own behaviour: My conscience is clear. **2** remorse: He had no conscience about cheating. **conscience clause** a clause in a law exempting people who object on moral grounds. **conscience money** money paid by someone with a guilty conscience, in the hope of making amends. **conscience-stricken** *adj* full of remorse. **on one's conscience** making one feel guilty or full of remorse. < ultimately Latin *com-* + *scire* to know.

conscientious (ˌkɒnʃɪ'ɛnʃəs) *adj* scrupulous; hard-working. **conscientiously** *adv* **conscientiousness** *n* **conscientious objector** someone who refuses to fight, in a war for example, on moral or religious grounds. < Latin *conscientia* conscience.

conscious ('kɒnʃəs) *adj* **1** fully awake. **2** aware: She was conscious of a slight irritation. **3** intended: a conscious insult. **consciously** *adv* **consciousness** *n* < ultimately Latin *com-* + *scire* to know.

conscript (kən'skrɪpt) *vb* call up for compulsory military service.
• *n* ('kɒnskrɪpt) someone who is conscripted. **conscription** *n* < ultimately Latin *com-* + *scribere* to write.

consecrate ('kɒnsɪˌkreɪt) *vb* make or declare to be sacred by religious ceremony. **consecration** *n* < ultimately Latin *com-* + *sacrare* to consecrate.

consecutive (kən'sɛkjʊtɪv) *adj* following one after another without a break.

conker

Why do snails like horse-chestnuts? The answer is that the game of conkers was originally played not with horse-chestnut seeds but with snail shells. To find evidence of this one has to look no further than the name of the game. The root of conkers is *conch* or 'shell'.

consecutively *adv* < ultimately Latin *consequi* to follow.

consensus (kən'sɛnsəs) *n* general agreement, esp. of opinion. < Latin *consentire* to agree. SEE PANEL.

consent (kən'sɛnt) *vb* agree (to); approve.
• *n* agreement or permission. < ultimately Latin *com-* + *sentire* to feel.

consequence ('kɒnsɪkwəns) *n* **1** the result of a set of conditions or actions; logical result. **2** importance: a woman of consequence. **3** *pl* a game in which a story is constructed by each player writing one part. **consequent** *adj* resulting. **consequential** *adj* **1** resulting. **2** important. **consequently** *adv* as a result. **in consequence** as a result. < ultimately Latin *com-* + *sequi* to follow.

conservancy (kən'sɜːvənsɪ) *n* **1** an organization authorized to protect an environment; such an environment. **2** a board which controls a river or port: the Thames Conservancy. < Latin *conservatus.*

conservative (kən'sɜːvətɪv) *adj* **1** opposed to change; traditional. **2 Conservative** of the Conservative Party. **3** cautious; moderate: a conservative guess.
• *n* **1** a moderate or traditional person. **2 Conservative** a member of the Conservative Party. **conservatively** *adv* **conservatism** *n* conservative attitudes or principles. **Conservative Party** a political party in favour of private enterprise and traditional institutions.

conservatory (kən'sɜːvətrɪ) *n* a greenhouse for keeping ornamental plants, usually built onto a house.

conserve (kən'sɜːv) *vb* keep safe or whole, esp. for later use: conserve energy. **conservation** *n* conserving; being conserved, esp. of the natural environment: wildlife conservation. **conservationist** *n.*
• *n* ('kɒnsɜːv) a jam made from sugar and fruit. < Latin *conservare.*

consider (kən'sɪdə) *vb* **1** give careful thought to; deliberate. **2** regard specifically: Patience is considered a virtue. **3** take into account: all things considered. **considerable** *adj* large in extent or degree; significant: a considerable sum. **considerate** *adj* taking the rights and feelings of others into account. **consideration** *n* **1** careful thought: The matter is under consideration. **2** sympathetic regard; kindness. **3** something to be taken into account: Money is a major consideration. **4** payment: for a small consideration. **considering** *prep* with allowances made: She's very lively considering her age. **in consideration of** in return for; because of. **take into consideration** make allowances for. < ultimately Latin *considerare* to observe the stars.

consign (kən'saɪn) *vb* **1** give over into someone's charge. **2** transfer or deliver formally. **consignee** *n* someone to whom something is consigned. **consignment** *n* **1** consigning. **2** something consigned, esp. a shipment of goods. **consignor** *n* < ultimately Latin *com-* + *signum* sign, mark.

consist (kən'sɪst) *vb* **1** be composed (of). **2 consist in** have as a basis or essence. < ultimately Latin *com-* + *sistere* to stand. SEE PANEL.

consistent (kən'sɪstənt) *adj* **1** unvarying; regular. **2** in accordance with; not self-contradictory: His behaviour is consistent with his general attitude. **consistently** *adv* **consistency** *n* **1** being consistent. **2** the degree of firmness of a soft substance or liquid.

console[1] (kən'səʊl) *vb* give comfort to (someone in distress). **consolable** *adj* **consolation** *n* **consolation prize** a prize given to someone who narrowly misses winning a contest. < ultimately Latin *com-* + *solari* to console.

console[2] ('kɒnsəʊl) *n* **1** a bracket supporting a shelf or other wall fixture.

consensus

Careful users of English use the word consensus precisely. Since consensus itself means 'a general agreement, especially of opinion', expressions such as a general consensus or a consensus of opinion are considered tautological. However, these usages are nowadays so common that they are often considered acceptable.

consist of or **consist in?**

Consist of means 'to be made up of': Water *consists of* hydrogen and oxygen. His whole stock of cattle *consisted of* twenty cows.

Consist in is less common and means 'to have as a basis or essence'. It often applies to abstract matters: Her entire happiness *consists in* working hard. The appeal of the book *consists in* its imaginative plot.

2 a control panel on a computer or other electrical equipment. **3** the part of an organ containing the stops and keys. **4** a floor cabinet for a radio or television set. < Middle French *consolateur* supporting bracket, from Latin *consolari*.

consolidate (kənˈsɒlɪˌdeɪt) *vb* **1** secure; strengthen: He consolidated his position on the board. **2** unite; merge. **consolidation** *n* < Latin *com-* + *solidus* solid.

consommé (kənˈsɒmeɪ) *n* a thin, clear, meat soup. < French, from Latin *consummare* to complete.

consonant (ˈkɒnsənənt) *n* a speech-sound made by friction or obstruction in the vocal tract; letter or letters representing such a sound, such as b, d.
• *adj* in agreement; consistent. < ultimately Latin *com-* + *sonare* to sound.

consort (ˈkɒnsɔːt) *n* a wife or husband of a monarch: Prince consort.
• *vb* (kənˈsɔːt) keep company with. < ultimately Latin *com-* + *sors* share, portion.

consortium (kənˈsɔːtɪəm) *n* a combined organization of business firms, banks, etc. < Latin: fellowship.

conspicuous (kənˈspɪkjʊəs) *adj* clearly visible; attracting attention. **conspicuously** *adv* **conspicuousness** *n* < ultimately Latin *com-* + *specere* to look.

conspire (kənˈspaɪə) *vb* **1** plot secretly with others. **2** act together as if on purpose: Events conspired to keep him away. **conspiracy** *n* **1** conspiring. **2** a plot. **conspirator** *n* someone who conspires. **conspiratorial** *adj* **conspiratorially** *adv* < ultimately Latin *com-* + *spirare* to breathe.

constable (ˈkʌnstəbl̩) *n* a policeman or policewoman of the lowest rank, below a sergeant. **constabulary** *n* a police force in a particular area. < Late Latin *comes stabuli* officer of the stable. SEE PANEL.

constant (ˈkɒnstənt) *adj* **1** continually happening. **2** steadfast; loyal: a constant companion.
• *n* something which never changes. **constantly** *adv* **constancy** *n* **1** being constant. **2** loyalty. < Latin *com-* + *stare* to stand.

constellation (ˌkɒnstəˈleɪʃən) *n* a pattern of stars in an arbitrarily fixed group. < ultimately Latin *com-* + *stella* star.

consternation (ˌkɒnstəˈneɪʃən) *n* a state of worried confusion; dismay. < Latin *com-* + *sternere* to throw down.

constipation (ˌkɒnstɪˈpeɪʃən) *n* a blockage that hinders bowel movements. **constipated** *adj* < Latin *com-* + *stipare* to press together.

constituency (kənˈstɪtjʊənsɪ) *n* an area which elects one Member of Parliament, etc.; resident voters of such an area. **constituent** *n* **1** a member of a constituency. **2** also *adj* (something that is) essential; component. < Latin *constituere* to constitute.

constitute (ˈkɒnstɪˌtjuːt) *vb* **1** make; form: His actions constituted a breach of the peace. **2** appoint to office. < ultimately Latin *com-* + *statuere* to place.

constitution (ˌkɒnstɪˈtjuːʃən) *n* **1** forming or establishing. **2** the way something is structured. **3** someone's general physical condition and character: a strong constitution. **4** the system of principles on which a society is run.

constitutional (ˌkɒnstɪˈtjuːʃənl̩) *adj* **1** of the constitution of a society: constitutional crisis. **2** of someone's physical or mental structure.
• *n* a walk taken for reasons of health.

constrain (kənˈstreɪn) *vb* force; oblige. **constraint** *n* **1** an obligation. **2** a repression of one's natural feelings. < ultimately Latin *com-* + *stringere* to bind.

constrict (kənˈstrɪkt) *vb* squeeze; tighten. **constriction** *n* **constrictor** *n* < Latin *constringere*.

construct (kənˈstrʌkt) *vb* make by putting parts together; build. **construction** *n* **1** the manner or process of constructing. **2** something which is

---

constable

The level of rank designated by the word constable has not always been as low as it is today. The word comes from the Late Latin *comes stabuli* meaning 'officer or attendant of the stable'. This sense underwent a dramatic upgrading and by the time constable entered English in the 13th century it designated a very high-ranking official indeed, known formally at court and in noble households as 'Master of the Horse'.

The association of constable with law enforcement first appeared in Tudor times when it became the name of a parish officer responsible for keeping the peace.

---

constructed. **3** an arrangement of words forming a phrase, clause, or sentence. **4** an explanation or interpretation. **constructional** *adj* **constructive** *adj* suggesting improvement: constructive criticism. **constructively** *adv* < ultimately Latin *com-* + *struere* to build.

construe (kənˈstruː) *vb* understand; interpret. < Latin *construere* to construct.

consul (ˈkɒnsəl) *n* a government official living in a foreign city who looks after the interests of his fellow countrymen and countrywomen. **consulate** *n* the residence, office, or position of a consul. < Latin *consulere* to consult.

consult (kənˈsʌlt) *vb* **1** ask (someone) for advice or information: She consulted a doctor. **2** refer to for information: He consulted a dictionary. **3** confer: Workers consulted with management. **consultancy** *n* **consultant** *n* someone qualified to give professional advice or services: a consultant engineer. **consultation** *n* **1** consulting. **2** a conference. **consultative** *adj* < Latin *consulere.*

consume (kənˈsjuːm) *vb* **1** use up: The engine consumes a lot of oil. **2** eat or drink up, esp. in quantity. **3** destroy totally: The building was consumed by fire. **consumer** *n* someone who uses goods or services; customer. **consumer goods** goods such as food or clothing, bought by individuals. **consumerism** *n* the furtherance and protection of consumer interests. **consuming** *adj* extreme; overpowering: a consuming passion. < Latin *com-* + *sumere* to take.

consummate (ˈkɒnsəˌmeɪt) *vb* complete; fulfil (esp. a marriage), by having sexual intercourse.
• *adj* (kənˈsʌmət, ˈkɒnsəmət) of the highest degree; highly skilled: a consummate musician. < ultimately Latin *com-* + *summa* sum.

consumption (kənˈsʌmpʃən) *n* **1** using up; amount used up: fuel consumption. **2** (*archaic*) tuberculosis of the lungs.

contact (ˈkɒntækt) *n* **1** the state of physically touching. **2** association; communication: in contact. **3** an electrical connection. **4** someone who has been exposed to a contagious illness. **5** someone who may be useful for information or introductions: business contacts.
• *vb* communicate with (someone). **contact lens** a thin lens that fits over the cornea of the eye to improve eyesight. < ultimately Latin *contingere* to touch.

contagion (kənˈteɪdʒən) *n* the spreading of disease by contact with others; disease spread like this. **contagious** *adj* **1** (of a disease) capable of being passed on by contact. **2** quickly spreading to others. < Latin *contingere* to touch, pollute. SEE PANEL.

contain (kənˈteɪn) *vb* **1** have inside; include: This book contains 100 illustrations. **2** limit; control: He couldn't contain his joy. **3** prevent (an enemy, etc.) from making progress. **container** *n* **1** anything which contains things. **2** a very large, often metal case for transporting goods. **containerize** *vb* transport by container; change to this method of transportation. **containerization** *n* **containment** *n* the prevention of something's expansion. < ultimately Latin *com-* + *tenēre* to hold.

contaminate (kənˈtæmɪˌneɪt) *vb* make impure; pollute. **contamination** *n* < Latin *contaminare.*

contemplate (ˈkɒntəmˌpleɪt) *vb* **1** gaze attentively at. **2** view as a possibility; consider. **3** meditate. **contemplation** *n* **contemplative** *adj* < ultimately Latin *com-* + *templum* temple.

contemporary (kənˈtɛmpərərɪ, kənˈtɛmpərɪ) *adj* **1** living or happening in the same period of time: Gladstone was contemporary with Disraeli. **2** up-to-date; modern: contemporary trends.
• *n* someone living at the same time as another; someone about the same age as another. < Latin *com-* + *tempus* time.

contempt (kənˈtɛmpt) *n* **1** despising. **2** being despised: held in contempt. **3** disrespect of a court of justice: contempt of court. **contemptible** *adj* deserving or provoking contempt. **contemptibility** *n*

contagious or **infectious?**

In medical usage, contagious and infectious are not synonymous. Contagious means 'capable of being passed on by contact'; infectious means 'capable of being passed on by micro-organisms such as bacteria or viruses'. Contagious diseases include syphilis and gonorrhoea. Examples of infectious diseases are diphtheria, measles, and malaria. Popular usage, however, often ignores this distinction and the words tend to be used interchangeably.

In their extended, figurative uses, the meaning of the two words is the same—'quickly spreading to others': contagious (or infectious) laughter.

contemptibly *adv* **contemptuous** *adj* expressing contempt. **contemptuously** *adv* **contemptuousness** *n* < Latin *contemnere* to despise. SEE PANEL.
contend (kən'tɛnd) *vb* **1** struggle in a contest or argument. **2** maintain; argue: The plaintiff contends he has rights. **contender** *n* < ultimately Latin *com-* + *tendere* to stretch.
content[1] (kən'tɛnt) *adj* happy with the state of things; satisfied.
• *n* satisfaction.
• *vb* **1** satisfy. **2** settle for: Hs contented himself with what he could find. **contented** *adj* happy. **contentedly** *adv* **contentment** *n* **to one's heart's content** as much as one wants. < ultimately Latin *continēre* to contain.
content[2] ('kɒntɛnt) *n* **1** something which is contained: the contents of a house. **2** meaning or substance as opposed to form: The picture is all technique and no content.
contention (kən'tɛnʃən) *n* arguing or contending; point made in an argument or debate. **contentious** *adj* argumentative; likely to cause argument. **contentiously** *adv* < SEE **CONTEND.**
contest ('kɒntɛst) *n* **1** a fight for superiority. **2** a test of skill between two or more people.
• *vb* (kən'tɛst) **1** contend; compete in or for. **2** argue against; challenge: contest a will. **contestable** *adj* **contestant** *n* a competitor. < ultimately Latin *com-* + *testis* witness. SEE PANEL.
context ('kɒnˌtɛkst) *n* **1** the setting of a word, phrase, or passage within language which gives it a specific meaning: in context; out of context. **2** the conditions surrounding an event. **contextual** *adj* **contextually** *adv* < Latin *com-* + *texere* to weave.
contiguous (kən'tɪgjʊəs) *adj* **1** touching, esp. along a boundary or at a point. **2** near in a sequence of time. **contiguity** *n* **contiguously** *adv* < Latin *contingere* to touch.
continent ('kɒntɪnənt) *n* **1** any of the great land masses on the earth's surface, such as Africa or Asia. **2 the Continent** mainland Europe as distinguished from the British Isles. **continental** *adj* of mainland Europe. **continental breakfast** a light breakfast, esp. of bread rolls and coffee. **continental quilt** a duvet. < Latin *continēre* to contain.
contingency (kən'tɪndʒənsɪ) *n* an unforeseen event; future possibility: contingency plans.
contingent (kən'tɪndʒənt) *adj* **1** occurring by chance. **2** dependent on the occurrence of something else. **3** possible; uncertain.
• *n* a group of people who make up part of a group or military force. < ultimately Latin *com-* + *tangere* to touch.
continue (kən'tɪnju:) *vb* **1** carry on (a course of action) without stopping. **2** remain or cause to remain in a certain place or condition: He continued as leader. **3** extend: The road continues to the hills. **4** resume after a break: continued next week. **5** say in addition: '... and I did,' he continued. **continual** *adj* repeated regularly; repeated so often as to appear to be happening all the time. **continually** *adv* **continuance** *n* continuing. **continuation** *n* continuing; something which continues. **continuity** *n* **1** the continuing of certain conditions. **2** the details of a complete scenario, of a film, for example. **continuous** *adj* not interrupted in space, time, or order. **continuously** *adv* **continuous assessment** taking into account all of a student's coursework in giving a final mark. **continuum** *n* a continuous succession of identical elements. < Latin *continuus* continuous. SEE PANEL.
contort (kən'tɔ:t) *vb* twist (something)

contemptible or **contemptuous?**

These two words are sometimes confused.
Contemptible means 'deserving or provoking contempt': His uncouth behaviour was *contemptible;* a *contemptible* crime.
Contemptuous means 'expressing contempt': a *contemptuous* disregard of his critics; Bagster remained *contemptuous* of public opinion.

contest or **competition?**

Contest normally involves the pitting of skill against an opponent: the *contest* for the world heavyweight title, the *contest* for the party leadership.
Competition involves general rivalry: We face strong *competition* from overseas; the *competition* for promotion to the First Division; We need to keep one step ahead of the *competition*.

forcibly out of the usual shape. **contortion** *n* **contortionist** *n* an acrobat who moulds his or her body into unnatural postures. < ultimately Latin *com-* + *torquēre* to twist.

contour (ˈkɒntʊə) *n* **1** the outline of a shape or figure: body contours. **2** a line on a map which connects points of equal height.
• *vb* shape the outline of. < ultimately Latin *com-* + *tornus* lathe.

contra- *prefix* against. < Latin.

contraband (ˈkɒntrəˌbænd) *n* smuggled merchandise; smuggling. < ultimately Latin *contra-* + *bannum* ban.

contraception (ˌkɒntrəˈsɛpʃən) *n* (methods for) the prevention of pregnancy. **contraceptive** *n, adj* (a device or drug) preventing pregnancy. < *contra-* + *conception.*

contract (ˈkɒntrækt) *n* a formal agreement between two or more people or parties; document describing this.
• *vb* (kənˈtrækt) **1** undertake by contract. **2** reduce in size or length. **3** catch (an infection); acquire (a habit). **contraction** *n* **contractual** *adj* **contract bridge** a form of bridge in which only the number of tricks bid for and won count in the score. **contractor** *n* someone who contracts to perform work, esp. building, or supply materials. **contract out** agree not to participate in a particular scheme. < ultimately Latin *com-* + *trahere* to draw.

contradict (ˌkɒntrəˈdɪkt) *vb* **1** state something opposite to (a statement, etc.). **2** declare that (something) is untrue. **contradiction** *n* **1** something logically inconsistent: a contradiction in terms. **2** going against; denying. **contradictory** *adj* < ultimately Latin *contra-* + *dicere* to say.

contralto (kənˈtræltəʊ) *n, pl* **contraltos** (a singer with) the lowest female singing voice; part written for this. < Italian *contra-* + *alto* high.

contraption (kənˈtræpʃən) *n* (*informal*) a complicated device or gadget. < perhaps blend of *con*(*trivance*), *trap,* and (*inven*)*tion.*

contrariwise (ˈkɒntrɛərɪˌwaɪz) *adv* on the other hand; conversely.

contrary (ˈkɒntrərɪ) *adj* **1** different or opposed in nature. **2** opposite in position or direction: contrary winds. **3** stubbornly inclined to oppose others' wishes.
• *n* the opposite: on the contrary; to the contrary.
• *adv* against: acting contrary to orders. **contrariness** *n* < Latin *contra.*

contrast (ˈkɒntrɑːst) *n* **1** a difference made obvious when two things are looked at together. **2** something showing this difference. **3** putting different elements together, for example, tone or colour in a work of art, for their effect.
• *vb* (kənˈtrɑːst) distinguish or be distinguished by a comparison of the differences; provide or show a contrast. **contrastive** *adj* **contrastively** *adv* < ultimately Latin *contra-* + *stare* to stand.

contravene (ˌkɒntrəˈviːn) *vb* conflict with; go against: contravene a law. **contravention** *n* < ultimately Latin *contra-* + *venire* to come.

contretemps (ˈkɔntrəˌtɑ̃) *n* a setback or confrontation, usually minor. < French, from Latin *contra-* + *tempus* time.

contribute (kənˈtrɪbjuːt) *vb* **1** give (money or things) with others for a common cause. **2** submit (an article, etc.) for publication. **3** aid (an end result): Drinking contributed to his downfall. **contributor** *n* **contributory** *adj* **1** helping towards an end result. **2** financed by contributions: a contributory pension scheme. < ultimately Latin *com-* + *tribuere* to grant.

contrite (kənˈtraɪt) *adj* feeling deep sorrow for having done wrong. **contritely** *adv* **contrition** *n* < ultimately Latin *com-* + *terere* to rub.

contrive (kənˈtraɪv) *vb* plan or bring about in a creative way; manage. **contrivance** *n* **1** (making) an inventive

continual or **continuous?**

Continual and continuous and their derived forms continually and continuously are often confused with each other because of similarity in form. Their meanings, however, are quite different.

A continu*al* action is one that is regularly repeated, or repeated so often that it seems to be happening all the time: 'I'm tired of these *continual* interruptions.' 'She is *continually* asking me for money.'

Continu*ous*, on the other hand, applies to something that is without any break or interruption whatsoever: *continuous* computer stationery; The canals join to form one *continuous* waterway. He ran *continuously* for half an hour.

plan. **2** a mechanical device. **contrived** *adj* obviously artificial; unnatural. < Late Latin *contropare* to compare.

control (kənˈtrəʊl) *n* **1** the power to command, direct, or restrain. **2** the ability to operate, for example, a vehicle or oneself: self-control. **3** *pl* the means of operating an instrument or vehicle. **4** something used as a standard of comparison in an experiment. **5** an entity believed to direct the actions of a medium in a séance.
• *vb* **controlled; controlling 1** command; rule. **2** exercise restraint over. **3** verify; test. **controller** *n* **controlling interest** the power to influence the running of a business concern by owning enough shares. **out of/in** or **under control** unable/able to control or be controlled. < Middle French *contrerolle* duplicate of an account, from *contre-* counter + *rolle* roll.

controversy (ˈkɒntrəˌvɜːsɪ, kɒnˈtrɒvəsɪ) *n* a matter for dispute, esp. public. **controversial** *adj* of or arousing controversy. < ultimately Latin *contra-* + *vertere* to turn. SEE PANEL.

controvert (ˈkɒntrəˌvɜːt, ˌkɒntrəˈvɜːt) *vb* contradict; dispute. **controvertible** *adj* < back formation from *controversy*.

conundrum (kəˈnʌndrəm) *n* an intricate problem or riddle, esp. with a punning answer. < origin unknown.

conurbation (ˌkɒnɜːˈbeɪʃən) *n* a large, densely populated, urban area. < Latin *com-* + *urbs* city.

convalesce (ˌkɒnvəˈlɛs) *vb* recover health after illness. **convalescence** *n* **convalescent** *adj, n* < Latin *com-* + *valescere* to grow strong.

convection (kənˈvɛkʃən) *n* the transfer of heat through a fluid by a circulation of the warmer parts: convection current. **convector** *n* a heating unit that warms and circulates air. < ultimately Latin *com-* + *vehere* to carry.

convene (kənˈviːn) *vb* come or bring together in a group; gather. < Latin *convenire* to come together.

convenient (kənˈviːnɪənt) *adj* **1** easy to use. **2** suitable or opportune. **3** easily accessible: convenient shops. **conveniently** *adv* **convenience** *n* **1** being convenient; something that is convenient. **2** a public toilet. **convenience foods** packaged foods that can be quickly prepared. < ultimately Latin *convenire* to come together.

convent (ˈkɒnʌənt) *n* (the buildings housing) a religious community, esp. of nuns. **convent school** a school run by nuns.

convention (kənˈvɛnʃən) *n* **1** a formal gathering of people. **2** an agreement or contract, esp. between nations: the Geneva Convention. **3** a generally accepted principle or custom: the conventions of the novel. **conventional** *adj* **1** conforming to custom; traditional. **2** unoriginal. **conventionally** *adv* **conventional weapons** non-nuclear weapons.

converge (kənˈvɜːdʒ) *vb* move towards or arrive at a common point. **convergence** *n* **convergent** *adj* < Latin *com-* + *vergere* to incline.

conversant (kənˈvɜːsn̩t) *adj* **conversant with** familiar with; experienced: He quickly became conversant with the principles involved.
< Latin *conversari* to associate with.

converse[1] (kənˈvɜːs) *vb* exchange thoughts and opinions (with others); talk. **conversation** *n* informal talk. **conversational** *adj* **conversationalist** *n* someone who makes interesting conversation. < ultimately Latin *convertere* to turn round.

converse[2] (ˈkɒnvɜːs) *adj* reversed; opposite.
• *n* an idea or proposition which is contrary to another. **conversely** *adv*

convert (kənˈvɜːt) *vb* **1** alter the nature or use of (something). **2** exchange for an equivalent: convert foreign currency. **3** be capable of changing: The table converts into a desk. **4** cause to change one's beliefs or

---

controversy

Should you say *con*troversy or con*tro*versy? Traditional usage in British English favours the first pronunciation, with the stress on the first syllable (*con*troversy), but stressing on the second syllable (con*tro*versy) is becoming increasingly common.

Other four-syllable words that in British English have traditionally been stressed on the first syllable but are often stressed on the second syllable include:

adversary
applicable
formidable
kilometre
participle
primarily

attitudes: converted to Christianity. **5** complete (a try) in rugby by scoring a goal. **conversion** *n*
• *n* (ˈkɒnvɜːt) someone who has experienced a conversion, esp. religious. < ultimately Latin *com-* + *vertere* to turn.

convertible (kənˈvɜːtəbl) *adj* capable of being converted.
• *n* a car with a top that may be folded or removed. **convertibility** *n*

convex (ˈkɒnvɛks) *adj* curving outwards like the outside of a bowl. **convexity** *n* **convexly** *adv* < Latin *convexus* vaulted.

convey (kənˈveɪ) *vb* **1** carry, take, or send from one place to another. **2** transfer (rights or ownership rights to property). **3** communicate (meaning). **conveyable** *adj* **conveyor** *n* **conveyance** *n* (a means of) conveying; vehicle. **conveyancing** *n* the act or business of conveying property. **conveyor belt** a continuous moving belt that conveys objects, esp. on an assembly line in a factory. < Latin *com-* + *via* way.

convict (kənˈvɪkt) *vb* pronounce (someone) to be guilty of a crime.
• *n* (ˈkɒnvɪkt) someone serving a sentence in prison for a crime. **conviction** *n* **1** convicting; being convicted. **2** a strong belief. < ultimately Latin *convincere* to refute.

convince (kənˈvins) *vb* make (someone) believe; persuade: I am convinced it was him. < ultimately Latin *com-* + *vincere* to conquer.

convivial (kənˈvɪvɪəl) *adj* lively; sociable: convivial surroundings. **conviviality** *n* **convivially** *adv* < Latin *convivium* banquet, from *com-* + *vivere* to live.

convoke (kənˈvəʊk) *vb* summon to a formal meeting. **convocation** *n* < ultimately Latin *com-* + *vocare* to call.

convoy (ˈkɒnvɔɪ) *vb* escort for protection.
• *n* a group of ships or vehicles, esp. military, travelling together, often under a protective escort. < Middle French *convoier.*

convulse (kənˈvʌls) *vb* **1** shake violently, often with spasms. **2** cause to laugh helplessly. **convulsion** *n* **1** a muscular spasm. **2** a violent disturbance. **convulsive** *adj* producing or affected by convulsion. **convulsively** *adv* < Latin *com-* + *vellere* to pluck.

coo (kuː) *vb* **1** make a low, soft sound like that of a dove. **2** talk lovingly.
• *n* cooing sound.
• *interj* (*informal*) an expression of surprise. < like the sound.

cook (kʊk) *vb* **1** heat (food) in order to eat. **2** undergo this process: The meat's still cooking.
• *n* someone who cooks, esp. professionally, **cooker** *n* **1** an apparatus for cooking. **2** a variety of fruit suitable for cooking, such as a cooking apple. **cookery** *n* the art or practice of cooking. **cookery book** a book of recipes. **cook the books** deliberately falsify financial records. **cook up** (*informal*) invent. **what's cooking?** (*informal*) what's happening? < Old English *cōc.*
SEE PANEL.

cookie (ˈkʊkɪ) *n* **1** (*US*) a biscuit. **2** (*Scottish*) a plain bun. < Dutch *koekje* small cake.

cool (kuːl) *adj* **1** moderately cold: a cool breeze. **2** calm and self-controlled: He kept a cool head. **3** producing a refreshing coldness: cool clothes. **4** unenthusiastic: a

Too many cooks...

A short, pithy saying which conveys a general truth such as Too many cooks spoil the broth is known as *a proverb.* Many of the proverbs in current use are centuries old. Common examples include:

Enough is as good as a feast.
There's no smoke without fire.
One good turn deserves another.
Birds of a feather flock together.
A fool and his money are soon parted.
Every cloud has a silver lining.
Do as you would be done by.
Familiarity breeds contempt.
It takes a thief to catch a thief.
Nothing succeeds like success.
A bird in the hand is worth two in the bush.
It never rains but it pours.

It is not difficult to find pairs of proverbs which contradict each other. For example, while Too many cooks spoil the broth, who would deny that Many hands make light work? Similarly, which maxim does one follow: More haste less speed or He who hesitates is lost?

cool reception. **5** producing an impression of coldness: cool colours. **6** confident, often to the point of impudence: a cool customer. **7** (used to intensify): He paid a cool million for it. **8** (*slang*) excellent.
• *n* **1** a moderately cold temperature. **2** composure: Don't lose your cool!
• *vb* **1** also **cool off** make or become cool. **2 cool it** (*slang*) calm down. **coolant** *n* a fluid used to cool for example, machinery. < Old English cōl.

coolie (ˈkuːlɪ) *n* an unskilled, low-paid porter or labourer, esp. in the Far East. < Hindi *kulī*.

coop (kuːp) *n* a cage or enclosure for poultry.
• *vb* also **coop up** confine in a small space: cooped up in her room. < Middle English *cupe*.

cooper (ˈkuːpə) *n* someone who makes or repairs barrels and casks for a living. < ultimately Latin *cupa* cask. SEE PANEL.

co-operate (kəʊˈɒpəˌreɪt) *vb* work or act with others for a common purpose. **co-operation** *n* **co-operative** *adj* **1** willing to work or act with others. **2** also *n* (an enterprise) owned and run jointly by a group of people. **co-operatively** *adv* **co-operator** *n* < Latin *co-* + *operari* to work.

co-ordinate (kəʊˈɔːdɪˌneɪt) *vb* bring together so as to act as an efficient whole.
• *n* (kəʊˈɔːdɪnət) **1** one of a set of numbers used to specify the position of a point on a line or surface or in space. **2** *pl* matching outer garments, usually for women.
• *adj* (kəʊˈɔːdɪnət) equal in significance. **co-ordinately** *adv* **co-ordination** *n* **co-ordinator** *n* < Latin *co-* + *ordinare* to arrange.

coot (kuːt) *n* a kind of black water-bird, often with a horny white plate on the forehead. < Middle English *coote*.

cop (kɒp) *vb* copped; copping **1** (*informal*) get hold of; catch. **2** arrest.
• *n* (*informal*) **1** arrest; capture: a fair cop. **2** a policeman. **cop it** be in trouble. **cop out** (*informal*) avoid a responsibility or commitment. **cop-out** *n* **not much cop** of low quality; worthless. < origin uncertain.

cope (kəʊp) *vb* also **cope with** deal effectively with (a problem, task, etc.). < Old French *coup* blow.

coping (ˈkəʊpɪŋ) *n* the final, usually sloping course of masonry on top of a wall: coping-stone. < Late Latin *cappa* head covering.

copious (ˈkəʊpɪəs) *adj* abundant; plentiful. **copiously** *adv* < Latin *co-* + *ops* wealth.

copper[1] (ˈkɒpə) *n* **1** a reddish-brown metallic element. **2** a coin made of copper or bronze. **3** a reddish-brown colour.
• *adj* **1** made of copper. **2** reddish-brown in colour. < Latin *Cyprium*, Cyprian metal. -

copper[2] *n* (*informal*) a policeman. SEE PANEL.

copperplate (ˈkɒpəˌpleɪt) *n* a clear, ornate handwriting style.

coppice (ˈkɒpɪs) *n* also **copse** a thicket of small trees and shrubs. < Middle French *couper* to cut.

copulate (ˈkɒpjʊˌleɪt) *vb* have sexual intercourse. **copulation** *n* < Latin

---

Cooper and **Smith**

In the days before keg beer and the motor car, the cooper or 'barrel-maker' and the smith or 'blacksmith' were in great demand. Nowadays the words are encountered not so much as the names of trades than as surnames. Other surnames derived from trades or callings include:

Archer	**Fuller**
Baker	**Hunter**
Butcher	**Mason**
Butler	**Potter**
Carpenter	**Tailor** or **Taylor**
Carter	**Tanner**
Chandler	**Thatcher**
Cook	**Turner**
Farmer	**Wheeler**
Fletcher	

---

copper

Among the most common informal expressions for a policeman are cop and copper, the person whose job is to cop (catch or arrest) criminals. This usage dates from the 1840s. Pig, a more offensive term, is popularly believed to be of 20th-century import from the United States. However, this is far from the case. Pig and the parallel term grunter actually predate cop—instances of their usage were recorded as early as the beginning of the 19th century.

copula bond.

copy (ˈkɒpɪ) *n* **1** an imitation of an original. **2** one reproduction of a book, newspaper, etc. **3** material to be included in a newspaper.
• *vb* **copied; copying 1** imitate. **2** make a copy or copies of. **copy-cat** *n* (*informal*) someone who imitates the actions of another. **copyright** *vb, n* (secure) the exclusive right to publish, perform, film, or record a work of art, literature, or music. **copywriter** *n* someone who writes advertising or publicity material. < Latin *copia* abundance.

coquette (kɒˈkɛt) *n* a woman who is inclined to flirt. **coquetry** *n* **coquettish** *adj* < French *coquet* small cock.

coral (ˈkɒrəl) *n* **1** a hard, usually pink or white deposit formed by the skeletons of minute sea-creatures: coral reef; coral necklace. **2** an orange-pink colour.
• *adj* orange-pink. < ultimately Greek *korallion*.

cord (kɔːd) *n* **1** (a length of) thin, flexible material made from several strands twisted together. **2** something like this, for example in the body: umbilical cord. **3** corduroy.
• *vb* supply or bind with cord. < ultimately Greek *chordē*.

cordial (ˈkɔːdɪəl) *n* a sweet, soft drink made from fruit essence diluted with water.
• *adj* friendly; genial: a cordial invitation. **cordiality** *n* **cordially** *adv* < ultimately Latin *cor* heart. SEE PANEL.

cordon (ˈkɔːdn̩) *n* **1** a ring of police or troops, for example surrounding an area; ring of people or things. **2** a fruit tree trained to grow as a single stem by pruning. **3** a ribbon worn as an honour or ornament.
• *vb* also **cordon off** surround with a cordon. < French: small cord.

cordon bleu (ˌkɔːdɒn ˈblə) highly skilled and qualified in the art of French cookery. < French: blue cordon.

corduroy (ˈkɔːdəˌrɔɪ) *n* a cotton fabric with a velvety, ribbed pattern. **corduroys** *pl n* also **cords** trousers made of this. < origin uncertain.

core (kɔː) *n* **1** the hard, inedible centre of various fruit such as the apple. **2** the central or essential part of something: He's rotten to the core. **3** the part of a nuclear reactor where the reaction takes place.
• *vb* remove the core from. **corer** *n* < Middle English.

corgi (ˈkɔːgɪ) *n* a breed of short-legged dog with a fox-like head. SEE PANEL.

cork (kɔːk) *n* **1** a tough, elastic tissue, the bark of cork oak. **2** a piece of this, used as a float. **3** a stopper for a bottle, often made of cork.
• *vb* fit or stop up with a cork. **corkage** *n* a charge made for serving alcohol in a restaurant. **corked** *adj* (of wine) spoiled by a decayed cork. **corker** *n* (*old-fashioned informal*) someone or something astonishingly good. **corkscrew** *n* a device for removing corks from bottles; something shaped in a spiral. < probably Latin *cortex*.

corm (kɔːm) *n* a thick, round underground plant stem base, from which buds sprout. < ultimately Greek *keirein* to cut.

corn[1] (kɔːn) *n* **1** a small, hard grain or seed: peppercorn. **2** a cereal crop, esp. wheat or barley. **3** (*US*) maize. **4** something trite or sentimental. **cornflour** *n* fine flour made from rice or maize, used to thicken sauces. **cornflower** *n* a blue-flowered plant cultivated or growing wild in cornfields. < Old English.

corn[2] *n* a small hardened area of skin, esp. on the foot. < Latin *cornu* horn.

cordial

To give someone a *cordial* welcome is to welcome him or her in a warm and friendly way. Strictly speaking, however, the feelings demonstrated should always be deeply felt, since cordial derives ultimately from *cor,* the Latin word for 'heart'. This explains why at one stage in its history cordial was also the name of a drink or medicine that was supposed to stimulate the heart. Today's lime cordial is derived from this.

corgi

A sturdily-built dog with short legs, a long back, and a fox-like head is known as a corgi. Both the breed and the name by which it is known are of Welsh origin. Corgi is a combination of *cor* meaning 'dwarf' and *ci* 'dog'.

Other words of Welsh origin include:

coracle	**eisteddfod**
cwm	**penguin**

cornea (ˈkɔːnɪə) *n* the hard, transparent protective covering on the front, outer surface of the eye. **corneal** *adj* < Latin *cornu* horn.

corner (ˈkɔːnə) *n* **1** the point at which two lines, edges, or sides meet, or two streets intersect. **2** a remote or private place: a quiet corner. **3** a kick or hit from the corner of a field in soccer or hockey. **4** a perilous situation: a tight corner. **5** a near-monopoly of a commodity, giving the owner control of prices.
• *vb* **1** drive into a corner; force into a situation offering no escape. **2** grab the attention of (a person), esp. to talk to him or her. **3** get the larger part of; monopolize: corner the market. **4** turn a corner: The new car corners well. **cornerstone** *n* **1** the stone laid in the corner of a building. **2** the foundation or basis of something. < Old French *corne.*

cornet (ˈkɔːnɪt) *n* **1** a brass musical instrument with valves, similar to a trumpet. **2** something shaped like a cone; wafer like this for ice-cream. < Latin *cornu* horn.

cornice (ˈkɔːnɪs) *n* an ornamental course of often plaster moulding at the top of a building or pillar, or between a wall and ceiling. **corniced** ad; < Italian.

corny (ˈkɔːnɪ) *adj* hackneyed.

corollary (kəˈrɒlərɪ) *n* something that follows naturally or logically from a proved proposition. < Latin *corollarium* money paid for a garland.

corona (kəˈrəʊnə) *n* a circle of glowing light seen round something, such as the sun or moon. < Latin: crown.

coronary (ˈkɒrənərɪ) *adj* of the arteries or veins of the heart.
• *n* also **coronary thrombosis** blood-clotting in a coronary artery.

coronation (ˌkɒrəˈneɪʃən) *n* the ceremony of crowning a monarch. < Middle French *coroner* to crown.

coroner (ˈkɒrənə) *n* a public official appointed to lead an enquiry into the cause of any death thought to be from unnatural causes. < Anglo-French *corouner* officer of the crown.

coronet (ˈkɒrənɛt, ˌkɒrəˈnɛt) *n* **1** a small crown. **2** an ornamental band worn round the head.

corporal[1] (ˈkɔːpərəl, ˈkɔːprəl) *adj* of or affecting the human body: corporal punishment. < Latin *corpus* body.

corporal[2] *n* a non-commissioned officer in the army ranking above a lance-corporal and below a sergeant. < ultimately Latin *caput* head.

corporation (ˌkɔːpəˈreɪʃən) *n* **1** the local authorities of a city or town. **2** any group of people with sometimes legal authority to act as an individual, esp. in business. **3** (*humorous*) a pot-belly. **corporate** *adj* **1** shared by a group of individuals: corporate responsibility. **2** formed into a united body. < ultimately Latin *corpus* body.

corps (kɔː) *n, pl* **corps** (kɔːz) **1** a military unit comprising two or more divisions: Royal Marine corps. **2** a body of associated individuals: diplomatic corps.

corpse (kɔːps) *n* a dead human body.

corpulent (ˈkɔːpjʊlənt) *adj* with a bulky body; fat. **corpulence** *n*

corpus (ˈkɔːpəs) *n* a body of writings or works, usually on one topic or by one author.

corpuscle (ˈkɔːpʌsl) *n* a white or red blood cell. < Latin *corpusculum* small body.

correct (kəˈrɛkt) *adj* **1** conforming to an approved standard, of behaviour for example. **2** accurate; right.
• *vb* **1** put right by adjusting. **2** mark the mistakes in (a piece of work). **3** point out or punish (someone's faults). **correctly** *adv* **correctness** *n* **correction** *n* **1** correcting or being corrected. **2** an amendment made to something not correct. **corrective** *n, adj* (something) which tends to correct: corrective measures. < ultimately Latin *com-* + *regere* to rule.

correlate (ˈkɒrəˌleɪt) *vb* have or connect in a mutual or reciprocal relationship. **correlation** *n* **correlative** *adj* < Latin *com-* + *relatio* relation.

correspond (ˌkɒrɪˈspɒnd) *vb* **1** conform or be equal to; match. **2** communicate by writing letters. **correspondence** *n* **1** agreement; similarity. **2** letter-writing; letters. **correspondence course** a study course which is carried on by post. < Latin *com-* + *respondēre* to respond.

correspondent (ˌkɒrɪˈspɒndənt) *n* **1** someone who writes letters. **2** someone who contributes news reports to a newspaper or radio or television station.
• *adj* corresponding; matching.

corridor (ˈkɒrɪˌdɔː) *n* **1** a narrow passage-way, from which doors open onto rooms or compartments. **2** a strip of land through a foreign-held country; path for air traffic: air corridor. < ultimately Latin *currere* to run.

corroborate (kəˈrɒbəˌreɪt) *vb* support with evidence; confirm. **corroboratlon** *n* **corroborative** *adj* **corroboratory** *adj*

< Latin *com-* + *robur* strength.
corrode (kəˈrəʊd) *vb* wear away gradually, esp. by chemical action. **corrosion** *n* **corrosive** *adj* < ultimately Latin *com-* + *rodere* to gnaw.
corrugated (ˈkɒrʊˌgeɪtɪd) *adj* folded into alternating ridges and furrows: corrugated iron; corrugated cardboard. < Latin *com-* + *ruga* wrinkle.
corrupt (kəˈrʌpt) *adj* **1** dishonest, esp. open to bribery: corrupt practices. **2** immoral; perverted. **3** rotting.
• *vb* **1** make or become dishonest. **2** pervert the morals of (someone): corrupting a minor. **3** spoil by altering. **corruptibility** *n* **corruptible** *adj* < ultimately Latin *com-* + *rumpere* to break.
corset (ˈkɔːsɪt) *n* an undergarment, esp. of a woman, that fits closely to give shape to the figure. < Old French: small bodice.
cortège (kɔːˈteɪʒ) *n* a procession, esp. at a funeral. < French, ultimately from Latin *cohors* throng.
cortex (ˈkɔːtɛks) *n* **1** the outer layer of a plant stem; tree bark. **2** the outer layer of bodily tissue, such as the kidney or the grey matter of the brain. **cortical** *adj* < Latin: bark.
cosh (kɒʃ) *vb, n* (hit with) a short, heavy hand weapon, often of hard rubber. < perhaps Romany: stick.
cosmetic (kɒzˈmɛtɪk) *n* a prepared substance, applied to the skin, esp. of the face, to beautify it.
• *adj* for improving outward appearances: cosmetic surgery. < ultimately Greek *kosmos* order, universe, world.
cosmic (ˈkɒzmɪk) *adj* **1** of the entire universe. **2** vast in extent. **cosmic rays** streams of high-energy radiation reaching earth from outer space. < Greek *kosmos*.
cosmopolitan (ˌkɒzməˈpɒlɪtn̩) *adj* **1** made up of people or influences from many parts of the world: London is a cosmopolitan city. **2** international in scope; sophisticated: a cosmopolitan life-style.
• *n* someone who is cosmopolitan in outlook or experience. < Greek *kosmos* + *politēs* citizen.
cosmos (ˈkɒzmɒs) *n* the universe. **cosmonaut** *n* a Soviet astronaut.
cost (kɒst) *n* **1** an amount of money charged or given as payment. **2** an effort made or loss suffered in order to achieve something: The cost in human life was high.
• *vb* **cost,** except def. **3**, **costed; costing 1** be available at (a certain price). **2** require (a certain loss, effort, or sacrifice): The mistake cost him his job. **3** fix or estimate the cost of. **at all costs** whatever sacrifice is necessary. **cost-effective** *adj* economically practical and worthwhile. **costly** *adj* expensive. **costliness** *n* **cost of living** the general price level of consumer goods. **costs** *pl n* expenses incurred, as in a legal case. **to one's cost** to one's disadvantage. < ultimately Latin *constare* to stand firm.
costume (ˈkɒstjuːm) *n* **1** the distinctive style in clothes of a particular place, time, or group of people: national costume. **2** special clothes worn by an actor or actress for a particular role: costume drama. **costume jewellery** inexpensive jewellery. < ultimately Latin *consuetudo* custom.
cosy (ˈkəʊzɪ) *adj* comfortably warm; intimate.
• *n* a covering for a teapot to keep the tea warm. **cosily** *adv* **cosiness** *n* < Scottish.
cot (kɒt) *n* a small bed with high sides for a baby. **cot-death** *n* the sudden death of a sleeping baby from an unknown cause. < Sanskrit *khaṭvā*.
coterie (ˈkəʊtərɪ) *n* an exclusive group of people with common interests; clique. < Medieval Latin *cotarius* peasant occupying a cottage.
cottage (ˈkɒtɪdʒ) *n* a small house, esp. in a country area. **cottage cheese** soft, white cheese made from the curds of skimmed milk. **cottage industry** a craft carried on in the home, such as knitting. **cottage loaf** a round loaf with a smaller round mass on top. **cottage pie** a pie made with minced meat and topped with mashed potato. < Middle English *cot*.
cotton (ˈkɒtn̩) *n* **1** a plant which produces a soft, white, fibrous substance round the seeds; this substance. **2** the thread or fabric spun or made from this.
• *vb* **cotton on** come to understand. **cotton wool** raw cotton pressed for cleaning or surgical dressing. < Arabic *quṭn*.
couch (kaʊtʃ) *n* **1** a sofa; similar piece of furniture with only one raised end. **2** a long, reclining seat for psychiatric or medical patients to lie on when examined.
• *vb* express using particular language: couched in polite words. < ultimately Latin *collocare* to set in place.
couchette (kuːˈʃɛt) *n* a seat in a railway compartment that converts into a sleeping berth for overnight passengers. < French: small couch.

cough (kɒf) *vb* expel air from the lungs with a short, sharp sound.
• *n* **1** coughing. **2** an ailment marked by frequent coughing. **cough up** (*informal*) hand over (information or money) reluctantly. < Old English *cohhian*.

could (kəd; *stressed* kʊd) *auxiliary vb* SEE CAN[2]. **1** used in polite requests: Could you tell me the time, please? **2** used to express possibility: You could be right. **3** feel like: I could eat a horse. < Old English *cūthe*.

council (ˈkaʊnsəl) *n* **1** an assembly of people; meeting. **2** the elected body with authority over a town, county, parish, etc. **council estate** an area of council houses. **council house** or **flat** a dwelling let by a local council. **councillor** *n* a council member. < ultimately Latin *com-* + *calare* to call. SEE PANEL.

counsel (ˈkaʊnsəl) *n* **1** advice; consultation: give good counsel. **2** a barrister or barristers involved in a legal case.
• *vb* **counselled; counselling** advise, esp. professionally. **counsellor** *n* **keep one's own counsel** keep one's thoughts or plans secret. **take counsel with** consult. < ultimately Latin *consuiere* to Consult. SEE PANEL AT **COUNCIL.**

count[1] (kaʊnt) *vb* **1** also **count up** reckon in order to find a total. **2** say numbers out loud and in order. **3** take or be taken into account: His past counted against him. **4** consider: She counted herself lucky. **5** have worth or importance: Honesty counts in this job.
• *n* **1** a calculation; reckoning. **2** a total number. **3** an allegation in a court of law: guilty on all counts. **countable** *adj* **count-down** *n* numbers called in reverse order, for example in the launching procedure of a rocket. **count in** include. **countless** *adj* too many to be counted. **count on 1** depend on. **2** expect. **count out 1** exclude. **2** declare (a boxer) as having lost when he fails to rise from the canvas within ten seconds. **out for the count** unconscious, as when a boxer is counted out. < ultimately Latin *com-* + *putare* to consider. SEE PANEL.

count[2] *n* a European nobleman equivalent in rank to an earl. < Latin *comes* companion.

countenance (ˈkaʊntənəns) *n* **1** facial

---

council or counsel?

Because these two words have the same pronunciation, they are sometimes confused.

A council is an elected body or organizing committee with authority over a town, group of people, etc.: the County *Council,* the *Council for* National Academic Awards.

Counsel means 'advice or consultation' and is often used in expressions such as take or hold counsel: The ministers took *counsel* with their advisers. In a legal sense, counsel means 'barristers': the defending *counsel* in the case, Queen's *Counsel.* Counsel is also used as a verb, meaning 'to advise': He *counselled* me against acting hastily.

A member of a council is a councillor; a person who counsels is a counsellor, for example a marriage-guidance *counsellor.*

Don't count your chickens!

Don't count your chickens before they're hatched! is a warning given to someone who is confidently making plans on the basis that something is bound to happen when it may not: 'I'm sure to get the job in Paris, so I've already begun to look for a flat there.'—'Don't count your chickens before they're hatched!' The idiom comes originally from Aesop's fable of 'The Milkmaid and her Pail'.

This idiom is very well-known, and is often shortened to Don't count your chickens! or is phrased in variant forms, for example He had been counting his chickens, expecting to make a profit from selling his car. In fact, he made a loss, so now he's really got problems.

Other idiomatic expressions, proverbs, and sayings that are shortened include:

a bird in the hand (is worth two in the bush)
a fool and his money (are soon parted)
a jack of all trades (and master of none)
a rolling stone (gathers no moss)
a stitch in time (saves nine)
better the devil you know (than the devil you don't know)
birds of a feather (flock together)
fools rush in (where angels fear to tread)
if at first you don't succeed (try, try again)
if the cap fits (wear it)
swings and roundabouts (from: what one gains on the swings one loses on the roundabouts)
the early bird (catches the worm)
talk of the devil (and he appears)
the last straw (breaks the camel's back)

expression: a cheerful countenance. **2** approval; moral support.
• *vb* approve: I can't countenance your staying out late. < ultimately Latin *continēre* to hold together.

counter[1] (ˈkaʊntə) *n* **1** a flat, level surface in shops, banks, etc., over which goods are sold or business is transacted. **2** a small metal, wooden, or plastic disc, used in board-games; token. **3** an asset: bargaining counter. **4** a device for counting. **under the counter** sold or done in an illicit way. < Latin *computare* to count.

counter[2] *adv* in an opposite direction.
• *adj* contrary; opposed.
• *vb* **1** oppose. **2** offset. < Latin *contra* against, opposite.

counter[3] *prefix* **1** in the opposite direction: counter-clockwise. **2** opposing: counteract. **3** corresponding: counterpart. **4** substitute: counterfeit. < Middle French *contre*.

counteract (ˌkaʊntəˈrækt) *vb* to lessen or nullify the effects of. **counteraction** *n*

counter-attack (ˈkaʊntərəˌtæk) *vb, n* (make) an attack in retaliation for a previous attack by an enemy.

counterbalance (ˈkaʊntəˌbæləns) *vb, n* (act as) an influence, force, or weight that balances another.

counter-espionage (ˌkaʊntəˈrɛspɪəˌnɑːʒ) *n* activities directed towards uncovering and thwarting enemy spying.

counterfeit (ˈkaʊntəfɪt) *adj* artificial; forged: counterfeit money.
• *n* a forgery. < Middle French *contre-* counter + *faire* to make.

counterfoil (ˈkaʊntəˌfɔɪl) *n* a detachable part of a cheque, ticket, etc., kept as a receipt.

countermeasure (ˈkaʊntəˌmɛʒə) *n* an action designed to offset a particular state of affairs.

counter-offensive (ˈkaʊntərəˌfɛnsɪv) *n* a military counter-attack on a large scale.

counterpane (ˈkaʊntəˌpeɪn) *n* a bedspread. < Middle French *coute pointe* quilt.

counterpart (ˈkaʊntəˌpɑːt) *n* **1** someone or something with a similar function or characteristic to another. **2** something which completes a pair.

counterpoint (ˈkaʊntəˌpɔɪnt) *n* **1** an independent melody accompanying another, musical system of melodic combination. **2** contrast or interplay of elements in an artistic work. < Latin *contra-* + *punctus* musical note.

counterpoise (ˈkaʊntəˌpɔɪz) *vb, n* (maintain) a state of equilibrium.

counter-productive (ˌkaʊntəprəˈdʌktɪv) *adj* tending to hinder the achievement of a desired result.

countersign (ˈkaʊntəˌsaɪn) *vb* add the signature of a witness to the signing of (a document, etc.).

countersink (ˈkaʊntəˌsɪŋk) *vb* **countersunk; countersinking** enlarge (a hole) so that the head of (a screw or bolt) fits level with or below a surface.

countess (ˈkaʊntɪs) *n* **1** the wife or widow of a count or earl. **2** a woman of the rank of a count or earl.

country (ˈkʌntrɪ) *n* **1** a political state or nation; its territory. **2** a region with specific features: bandit country. **3** land with open fields and woods as opposed to urban areas. **countrified** *adj* characteristic of the countryside or country life; rustic. **country-and-western** *n* folk music originating from the southern and western USA. **country dance** any of various traditional dances for pairs of dancers in rows, circles, or squares. **countryman** fem. **countrywoman** *n* **1** someone living in a rural area. **2** someone who lives in one's own country. **countryside** *n* rural areas. **go to the country** hold a general election. < ultimately Latin *contra* against.

county (ˈkaʊntɪ) *n* an administrative division of a country; people living in this.
• *adj* **1** of a county: county court. **2** characteristic of the established upper classes in a county. **county town** a town which is the seat of county administration. < ultimately Latin *comes* count.

coup (kuː) *n* **1** a sudden, brilliant action, usually successful. **2** a coup d'état. < French: blow.

coup d'état (ˌkuː deɪˈtɑː) *n* the overthrow of an existing government by violence or unconstitutional means. < French: stroke of state.

coupé (ˈkuːpeɪ) *n* a two-door car with a fixed roof and sloping back. < French *couper* to cut.

couple (ˈkʌpḷ) *n* **1** two people considered as a pair, esp. a man and a woman. **2** two things taken together; pair. **3** a few: I'll be a couple of minutes.
• *vb* **1** fasten or join together. **2** copulate. **couplet** *n* two consecutive lines of verse with the same metre that rhyme. **coupling** *n* a device connecting the ends of objects next to each other, esp. on railway carriages. < Old French *cople*.

coupon (ˈkuːpɒn) *n* **1** a form, ticket, etc., that entitles the holder to something; voucher. **2** a printed entry form for the football pools or similar competition. < Old French *couper* to cut.

courage (ˈkʌrɪdʒ) *n* the strength of will to face danger or pain fearlessly; bravery. **courageous** *adj* **courageously** *adv* **have the courage of one's convictions** have the confidence to do as one thinks right. < ultimately Latin *cor* heart.

courgette (kʊəˈʒɛt) *n* a small variety of vegetable marrow which is cooked and eaten. < French *courge* gourd.

courier (ˈkʊrɪə) *n* **1** a messenger carrying papers or news. **2** someone employed by a travel company as a tourist guide. < Latin *currere* to run.

course (kɔːs) *n* **1** the movement from point to point in time or space: in the course of time. **2** a direction travelled: the course of a river. **3** a procedure: Your best course is to retreat. **4** a series of education classes or medical treatment: a typing course; a course of injections. **5** an area of land or water for sports or races: a golf-course. **6** an unbroken layer of stone or brick in a wall. **7** one dish in a meal: a three-course meal.
• *vb* **1** run or flow freely. **2** follow a course; pursue. **in course of** in the process of. **in the course of** during. **of course** naturally; without a doubt. **on/off course** in/not in the right direction. < ultimately Latin *currere* to run.

court (kɔːt) *n* **1** an open space surrounded by buildings or the walls of one building; courtyard. **2** the establishment of a sovereign; his or her attendants, advisers, etc. **3** a court of law. **4** an enclosed space, often rectangular, for various games: tennis court; squash court.
• *vb* **1** behave as if to invite or provoke: courting disaster. **2** seek favour from; woo: a courting couple. **3** (of animals) try to attract (a mate). **court-card** *n* a jack, queen, or king in a playing-card suit. **courtier** *n* a companion or attendant on a sovereign in a royal court. **courtly** *adj* dignified; refined. **court martial** *n, pl* **courts martial** a trial by a military court. **court-martial** *vb* **court-martialled; court-martialling** try at a court martial. **courtship** *n* the act or period of courting. **pay court to** give (someone) special attention in order to win favour. < ultimately Latin *cohors* enclosure, throng. SEE PANEL.

courteous (ˈkɜːtɪəs) *adj* polite; respectful. **courteously** *adv* **courtesy** *n* **(by) courtesy of** by permission or favour of. < Old French *corteis*.

cousin (ˈkʌzn̩) *n* also **first cousin** a child of one's aunt or uncle. **second cousin** a child of a first cousin of one's mother or father. < ultimately Latin *com-* + *sobrinus* cousin on the mother's side.

cove (kəʊv) *n* a small, sheltered inlet or bay. < Old English *cofa*.

coven (ˈkʌvn̩) *n* a gathering of witches. < ultimately Latin *convenire* to agree.

covenant (ˈkʌvənənt) *n* a binding agreement or promise; contract.
• *vb* make a solemn promise by covenant.

cover (ˈkʌvə) *vb* **1** lie or extend over: Frost covered the ground. **2** lay or spread something over, esp. in order to protect. **3** also **cover up** hide (something) from sight or knowledge: He covered up his mistake cleverly. **4** travel (a certain distance). **5** guard, esp. with a gun. **6** protect by guarantee or insurance: covered against fire and theft. **7** consider; include. **8** report (esp. news): All the papers covered the story. **9** have as one's area of operations: Two salesmen covered the north-west. **10** **cover for** act as a substitute for (someone who is absent). **11** be enough money for: Will £10 cover it?

---

court martials or courts martial?

What is the plural of court martial? Court martials or courts martial? It is sometimes difficult to decide how to form the plural of a compound noun.

□ **Compounds made up of a noun followed by an adjective.** Careful users follow the basic rule that the first element, the noun, is made plural:
court martial—courts martial
poet laureate—poets laureate
In less formal usage, however, -s is often added to the second element: court martials.
There are exceptions to this general rule: sergeant-majors, brigadier-generals, lieutenant-colonels.

□ **Compounds made up of a noun and a prepositional phrase or adverb.** The first element, the noun, is made plural:
mother-in-law—mothers-in-law
man-of-war—men-of-war
hanger-on—hangers-on

□ **Compounds containing no noun, nouns derived from verbal expressions, and words ending in** -ful usually add -s at the end:
forget-me-nots
go-betweens
grown-ups
spoonfuls (occasionally spoonsful)

• *n* **1** something that covers or conceals: under cover of darkness. **2** the binding of a book. **3** a bedspread. **4** a position safe from attack: The jungle affords good cover. **5** a military supporting force. **6** a pretext: The mob used a betting-shop as a cover. **7** an envelope or wrapper: under separate cover. **8** insurance protection. **9** also **cover version** a new recording of a well-known song. **coverage** *n* covering; amount or area covered. **cover charge** an extra amount charged per person, for example, in a restaurant or club. **cover-up** *n* concealment, esp. of information. < Latin *co-* + *operire* to cover over.

covert (ˈkʌvət) *n* **1** a shelter, esp. of thick undergrowth for game. **2** a bird's feather which covers the base of the wing or tail feathers.
• *adj* (ˈkəʊvɜːt) hidden; secret: a covert glance. **covertly** *adv* < Old French *covrir* to cover.

covet (ˈkʌvət) *vb* wish eagerly for (something that belongs to another). **covetous** *adj* **covetously** *adv* **covetousness** *n* < ultimately Latin *cupere* to desire.

cow[1] (kaʊ) *n* **1** the adult female of cattle or other large animals including the whale and the elephant. **2** (*derogatory*) an unpleasant woman. **cowboy** *n* **1** a man who tends and drives cattle in the western USA. **2** (*informal*) someone who uses unscrupulous methods, in business for example. **cowshed** n a shed for cattle. < Old English *cū.*

cow[2] *vb* frighten with threats. < probably Scandinavian.

coward (ˈkaʊəd) *n* someone without courage or determination. **cowardice** *n* < ultimately Latin *cauda* tail. SEE PANEL.

cower (ˈkaʊə) *vb* crouch down or cringe with fear. < Scandinavian.

cowl (kaʊl) *n* **1** a hood or hooded robe, for example worn by a monk. **2** a covering on a chimney for ventilation. **cowled** *adj* < ultimately Latin *cucullus* hood.

coward

Coward, 'a person who lacks courage or shrinks from danger', ultimately derives from *cauda,* the Latin word for 'tail'. The allusion is to an animal which, when frightened, 'turns tail' and runs away.

coxswain (ˈkɒksən) *n* also **cox 1** a sailor in charge of a ship's boat. **2** someone who steers the boat and directs the crew in a rowing race. **cox** *vb* act as coxswain. < Middle English *cok* small boat + *swain* servant.

coy (kɔɪ) *adj* **1** affectedly modest or shy. **2** evasive; reticent. **coyly** *adv* **coyness** *n* < ultimately Latin *quietus* quiet.

crab (kræb) *n, pl* **crabs, crab** a shellfish with a broad, flat shell and front limbs modified as pincers; its flesh cooked and eaten for food.
• *vb* **crabbed; crabbing** carp; grumble. **crabbed** *adj* **1** irritable. **2** difficult to read. **crabby** *adj* irritable. < Old English *crabba.*

crack (kræk) *n* **1** a sudden, sharp noise: the crack of a whip. **2** a sharp blow: a crack on the head. **3** a line marking a break in something; fracture. **4** a chink. **5** a break in the tone of the voice. **6** (*informal*) a quip or joke. **7** (*informal*) an attempt: Let's have a crack at it.
• *vb* **1** make or cause to make a sudden, sharp noise. **2** develop a break; fracture. **3** (of the voice) break in tone or fail, esp. with emotion. **4** find an answer or solution to: crack a code. **5** break into (a safe, etc.). **6** also **crack up** lose effectiveness or collapse under strain. **7** tell (a joke). **8** break (something) open with a sharp sound: crack nuts. **crack down on** (*informal*) take serious action against (something). **cracked** *adj* (*slang*) insane. **cracker** *n* **1** a firework that makes a sharp crack when exploded. **2** a coloured paper tube that makes a cracking sound when pulled apart. **3** a thin, dry, savoury biscuit. **cracking** *adj* (*old-fashioned*) excellent. **crackling** *n* the crisp, brown skin on roasted pork. **crackpot** *n* (*informal*) someone with crazy or eccentric ideas. < Old English *cracian.*

crackle (ˈkrækl̩) *vb, n* (make) a series of slight, cracking sounds.

cradle (ˈkreɪdl̩) *n* **1** a baby's cot or bed, often on rockers. **2** a framework which supports something. **3** the place of origin of something: the cradle of civilization. **4** one's early life: I've known him from the cradle.
• *vb* hold as if in a cradle; support: He cradled her in his arms. < Old English *cradol.*

craft (krɑːft) *n* **1** an activity needing skill or dexterity; skill or technique used. **2** skill at deception; cunning. **3** a boat, aircraft, or spacecraft.
• *vb* make with skill or dexterity. **craftsman** fem. **craftswoman** *n* a worker skilled in a particular craft.

craftsmanship *n* **crafty** *adj* using subtle methods; cunning. **craftily** *adv* **craftiness** *n* < Old English *cræft*. SEE PANEL AT VILLAIN.

crag (kræg) *n* a steep, rugged mountain peak or rock. **craggy** *adj* rugged; rough: a craggy face. **cragginess** *n* < Middle English.

cram (kræm) *vb* **crammed; cramming** **1** pack (things) tightly into too small a space: He crammed everything into his suitcase. **2** eat too much too quickly: Don't cram your food. **3** revise intensively for an examination. < Old English *crammian*, of Germanic origin.

cramp (kræmp) *n* **1** a painful, involuntary muscle contraction. **2** a strip of metal bent at the ends, used to bind masonry.
• *vb* restrain or hamper. **cramped** *adj* **1** restricted. **2** (of handwriting) with letters too close together, making it hard to read. **cramp someone's style** restrict someone's free expression. < Middle French *crampe*.

cranberry (ˈkrænbərɪ) *n* a small red acid berry, used in making jellies and sauces; shrub bearing this. < Low German *kraan* crane + *bere* berry.

crane (kreɪn) *n* **1** a tall wading-bird with a long neck and legs. **2** a device for moving heavy weights, either with a swinging arm or with lifting apparatus on an overhead track.
• *vb* stretch (the neck) esp. in order to see something. **crane fly** a two-winged fly with very long legs. < Old English *cran*.

cranium (ˈkreɪnɪəm) *n* the part of the skull covering the brain; skull. **cranial** *adj* < Greek *kranion*.

crank (kræŋk) *n* **1** a device, usually an L-shaped shaft, which converts a back-and-forth motion into a circular one. **2** an eccentric person.
• *vb* turn or cause movement with a crank. **cranky** *adj* eccentric. **crankiness** *n* < Old English *cranc*.

cranny (ˈkrænɪ) *n* a small crack; crevice. < Middle French *cran* notch.

crash (kræʃ) *n* **1** a sudden, loud noise like that of objects smashing. **2** a collision or fall that causes breaking: a car crash. **3** a sudden decline or failure, as in business or finance: the Wall Street Crash.
• *vb* **1** make a crashing sound. **2** collide or cause to collide; smash: He crashed the car into a lamppost. **3** enter uninvited; gatecrash. **4** (of a business, etc.) collapse suddenly. **5** (*slang*) spend the night: Can I crash here tonight? **crash barrier** a fence erected to prevent vehicles colliding or going off the road accidentally. **crash-dive** *n* a sudden, steep dive by an aircraft or submarine in an emergency. **crash-helmet** *n* a padded protective helmet worn by motor-cyclists. **crashing** *adj* (*informal*) absolute: a crashing bore. **crash-land** *vb* make an emergency landing in an aircraft, usually causing damage. **crash-landing** *n* < Middle English *crasschen*.

crass (kræs) *adj* **1** absolute; utter: crass stupidity. **2** coarse; stupid: crass behaviour. **crassly** *adv* **crassness** *n* < Latin *crassus* gross.

crate (kreɪt) *n* **1** a usually wooden framework or box, often used for transporting goods or possessions; its contents. **2** (*derogatory*) an old car, aircraft, etc.
• *vb* pack in a crate. < Latin *cratis* wickerwork.

crater (ˈkreɪtə) *n* a depression shaped like a bowl, esp. at the top of a volcano or left by the impact of a meteorite. < Greek *kratēr*.

cravat (krəˈvæt) *n* a short scarf worn around the neck. < French *cravate*. SEE PANEL.

crave (kreɪv) *vb* **1** desire strongly. **2** beg: I crave your indulgence. **craving** *n* a longing: a craving for a cigarette. < Old English *crafian*.

craven (ˈkreɪvn̩) *adj* cowardly. < probably Old French *crevant*.

crawl (krɔːl) *vb* **1** move slowly with the body close to the ground. **2** move on one's hands and knees. **3** progress slowly and laboriously. **4** be swarming (with crawling things): The room is crawling with bugs. **5** have the sensation of things crawling over one: The sound made her skin crawl. **6** act in a servile manner to gain favour.

cravat

A type of short, lightweight scarf that is worn loosely folded round the neck and tucked inside an open-necked shirt is known as a cravat. This word is a 17th-century borrowing of the French *cravate*. The French came by the word at the time of the Thirty Years War when it was worn by Croats or *Cravates* who had been enrolled in the French army to guard the Turkish borders of the Hapsburg territories.

• *n* **1** a crawling movement or pace: The traffic moved at a crawl. **2** a swimming stroke executed by alternating overarm movements and kicking the legs. **crawler** *n* a servile person. < Old Norse *krafla.*

crayfish (ˈkreɪˌfɪʃ) *n, pl* **crayfish** a small, lobster-shaped, freshwater shellfish. < Middle French *crevice* crab.

crayon (ˈkreɪən) *n* a stick of coloured wax or chalk, used for drawing. < ultimately Latin *creta* chalk.

craze (kreɪz) *n* an exaggerated but short-lived enthusiasm for something; fad: the latest dance craze. **crazed** *adj* driven mad: crazed with fear. **crazy** *adj* **1** insane; mad. **2** impractical; foolish: a crazy scheme. **3** very enthusiastic: He's crazy about her. **crazily** *adv* **craziness** *n* **crazy paving** a paved surface made up of irregular pieces of stone. **like crazy** (*informal*) to an extreme degree: dancing like crazy. < Middle English *crasen* to crush.

creak (kriːk) *vb, n* (make) a squeaking or rasping sound. < Middle English *creken* to croak, like the sound.

cream (kriːm) *n* **1** the fatty part of milk; its yellowish-white colour. **2** a food prepared with or like cream: cream cakes. **3** something resembling thick cream, such as a medicine or cosmetic: face cream. **4** the choicest part of something: the cream of society.
• *vb* **1** also **cream off** take the cream away from; take the best part from. **2** form into a creamy substance: cream butter and sugar. **3** put cream on (something). **cream cheese** soft, white cheese made from unskimmed milk and cream. **cream of tartar** a compound of potassium; white powder used in baking-powder. **creamy** *adj* **1** rich in cream. **2** resembling cream. < Late Latin *cramum.*

crease (kriːs) *n* **1** a mark or line made by folding or pressing. **2** (in cricket) the line marking the position of the batsman or bowler.
• *vb* **1** make a crease or creases in. **2** become creased. **crease up** (*informal*) amuse greatly. < SEE **CREST.**

create (kriːˈeɪt) *vb* **1** cause to exist: God created heaven and earth. **2** cause; produce: create a disturbance. **3** give a new office or title to: He was created a life peer. **4** (*informal*) make a fuss; complain. **creation** *n* **creative** *adj* **1** requiring or having the power to create. **2** imaginative. **creatively** *adv* **creativity** *n* **creator** *n* someone who creates. **the Creator** God. < Latin *creare.*

creature (ˈkriːtʃə) *n* **1** something created: a creature of his imagination. **2** a living being, esp. non-human. **3** a human being: a miserable creature.

crèche (krɛʃ) *n* a day nursery for young children. < Old French *creche* manger, crib.

credence (ˈkriːdn̩s) *n* acceptance of something as authentic; belief: Don't give credence to gossip. < ultimately Latin *credere* to believe.

credentials (krɪˈdɛnʃəlz) *pl n* letters or papers giving proof of identity or authority.

credible (ˈkrɛdɪbl̩) *adj* that can be believed. **credibility** *n* **credibly** *adv* **credibility gap** doubt arising from the difference between what is claimed and what is seen to be true. SEE PANEL.

credit (ˈkrɛdɪt) *n* **1** the positive balance in someone's bank account. **2** a trading system in which payment is made on trust at a later date; buying like this; sum of money lent by a bank. **3** belief. **4** approval; acknowledgment: He was given credit for the idea. **5** someone giving honour to: She's a credit to the school. **6** good reputation; honour.
• *vb* **1** believe. **2** enter in an account as a credit. **3** attribute: They credited him with the invention. **creditable** *adj* praiseworthy. **credit card** a card giving someone authority to buy on credit. **credit note** a form crediting a customer with an amount of money. **creditor** *n* someone to whom a debt is owed. **credits** *pl n* also **credit titles** a list of acknowledgments in a film or television programme. **creditworthy** *adj* qualifying for financial credit. < ultimately Latin *credere* to believe.

credulous (ˈkrɛdjʊləs) *adj* tending to believe too readily. **credulity** *n* SEE PANEL AT **CREDIBLE.**

creed (kriːd) *n* **1** a statement summariz-

---

credible or **credulous?**

These two words are sometimes confused.

Credible means 'believable': a *credible* story; His account seems too unlikely to be *credible*.

Credulous means 'believing too readily': Only someone as *credulous* as Helen would believe that pigs could fly! He's *credulous* enough to believe anything.

---

ing the beliefs of the Christian faith. **2** any set of principles or beliefs.

creek (kri:k) *n* **1** a narrow inlet of a lake or sea. **2** (*US and Australia*) a brook. **up the creek** (*informal*) in trouble. < Old Norse *kriki* bend.

creep (kri:p) *vb* **crept; creeping 1** move with the body close to the ground; crawl. **2** move carefully or timidly, esp. to escape attention. **3** move slowly or gradually: The days crept by. **4** (of plants) grow along a surface. **5** have the sensation of things crawling over one.
• *n* **1** a creeping movement. **2** (*informal*) a servile or unpleasant person. **creeper** *n* a creeping plant. **creepy** *adj* arousing fear or disgust. **creepy-crawly** *n* (*informal*) a small creature that creeps. < Old English *crēopan*.

cremate (krɪˈmeɪt) *vb* reduce (a corpse) to ashes by burning. **cremation** *n* **crematorium** *n, pl* **crematoria** a place where bodies are cremated. < Latin *cremare*.

creosote (ˈkri:əˌsəʊt) *n* **1** a brown, oily liquid derived from coal tar, used for preserving wood. **2** a clear liquid derived from wood tar, used as an antiseptic.
• *vb* apply creosote to. < Greek *kreas* flesh + *sōs* safe.

crêpe (kreɪp) *n* **1** a type of light, wrinkled fabric. **2** a type of wrinkled rubber, used in the soles of shoes. **3** also **crêpe suzette** a small, thin pancake. **crêpe paper** thin paper with a wrinkled texture. < French, ultimately from Latin *crispus* curled.

crept (krɛpt) SEE **CREEP**.

crescendo (krɪˈʃɛndəʊ) *adj, adv* (*music*) gradually becoming louder.
• *n, pl* **crescendos** a gradual increase in volume. < Italian *crescere* to grow.

crescent (ˈkrɛznt) *n* a curved, tapering shape, like that of the moon in its first and last quarters. < Latin *crescere* to grow.

cress (krɛs) *n* one of a variety of plants of the mustard family with mildly hot-tasting leaves used in salads. < Old English *cressa*.

crest (krɛst) *n* **1** a showy tuft or outgrowth on the head of some animals and birds. **2** the plume on a knight's helmet. **3** the top or ridge of a hill, wave, or roof. **4** the symbol of a family or office appearing on a coat of arms or on printed notepaper. **crested** *adj* **crestfallen** *adj* dejected; downcast. < Latin *crista*.

cretin (ˈkrɛtɪn) *n* **1** someone born mentally retarded due to thyroid gland deficiency. **2** an idiot. **cretinous** *adj* < French dialect *cretin* Christian, human being.

crevasse (krəˈvæs) *n* a deep fissure, esp. in ice on a glacier. < Old French *crevace*.

crevice (ˈkrɛvɪs) *n* a narrow opening caused by a crack, in a rock, wall, etc. < ultimately Latin *crepare* to crack, break with a crash.

crew[1] (kru:) *n* **1** a group of people working together on one task or under one foreman: camera crew. **2** the people working on a ship or aircraft, excluding the officers. **3** a gang.
• *vb* serve as a crew member (on). **crew-cut** *n* a hair-style in which the hair is cropped close. < Middle French *creistre* to increase.

crew[2] SEE **CROW**[2].

crib (krɪb) *n* **1** a wooden framework from which animals are fed. **2** a cot or cradle for a baby. **3** cribbage; cards given by each player to the dealer in this game. **4** a literal translation for students of material in a foreign language. **5** something copied from work done by another.
• *vb* **cribbed; cribbing 1** steal. **2** copy without acknowledgment; plagiarize. < Old English *cribb*.

cribbage (ˈkrɪbɪdʒ) *n* a card-game in which players try to gain a set number of points before others do.

crick (krɪk) *vb, n* (cause) a stiff, painful feeling in the muscles of the back of the neck. < Middle English *cryk*.

cricket[1] (ˈkrɪkɪt) *n* an outdoor sport played on a large field with a bat, ball, and wickets, between two teams of eleven players each. **cricketer** *n* **not cricket** (*old-fashioned informal*) unfair. < Middle French *criquet* goal.

cricket[2] *n* a leaping, chirping insect like a grasshopper. < Middle French *criquet* like its sound.

crime (kraɪm) *n* **1** a severe offence which is punishable by law. **2** offences like these considered together: crime prevention. **3** (*informal*) something foolish or shameful: It's a crime to waste food.

criminal (ˈkrɪmɪnḷ) *n* someone guilty of a crime.
• *adj* **1** being or involving a crime: criminal negligence. **2** relating to crime or its punishment: criminal lawyer. **criminology** *n* the study of crime and its punishment. **criminologist** *n* < Latin *crimen*.

crimp (krɪmp) *vb* **1** curl or wave (hair). **2** press together in order to link or seal. < Old English *crympan*.

crimson (ˈkrɪmzən) *n, adj* (of) a deep red colour. < Arabic *qirmiz* kermes.

cringe (krɪndʒ) *vb* flinch or cower with fear. < Middle English *crengen.*

crinkle (ˈkrɪŋkl̩) *vb* form or cause to form small folds or wrinkles.
• *n* a wrinkle or fold. **crinkly** *adj* < Middle English *crynkelen.*

crinoline (ˈkrɪnəlɪn) *n* a petticoat framework, formerly worn under a skirt to make it stand out; skirt supported like this. < ultimately Latin *crinis* hair + *lino* flax.

cripple (ˈkrɪpl̩) *n* someone who is partly disabled or lame.
• *vb* **1** make (someone) lame or crippled. **2** seriously weaken or harm: The economy was crippled by war. < Old English *crypel.*

crisis (ˈkraɪsɪs) *n, pl* **crises** (ˈkraɪsiːz) **1** a turning-point, for example in a fever. **2** a time of extreme trouble or danger; instability: a political crisis. < ultimately Greek *krinein* to decide. SEE PANEL.

crisp (krɪsp) *adj* **1** brittle and dry. **2** fresh and firm: a crisp lettuce. **3** fresh and cold: a crisp morning. **4** decisive; terse: a crisp manner,
• *n* a thin, fried potato slice, sold in packets.

---

crisis

Nouns like crisis which end in -is are of Greek derivation and have an unusual plural form. We talk about not crisises but crises. The majority of the members of this group are fairly common but are typically used in their singular forms. It is only now and again when the plural forms are required that problems occur. A familiar example of incorrect usage is the person who advertises to type thesises instead of theses.

Other nouns that have this irregular plural include:

analysis—analyses
basis—bases
ellipsis—ellipses
hypothesis—hypotheses
oasis—oases
parenthesis—parentheses
synopsis—synopses

A notable exception is metropolis, whose plural metropolises is regular.

• *vb* make, become, or keep crisp. **crisply** *adv* **crispness** *n* **burnt to a crisp** badly burnt. < Latin *crispus.*

criss-cross (ˈkrɪsˌkrɒs) *adj, n* (with) a pattern of intersecting lines.
• *vb* **1** mark with a criss-cross pattern. **2** go or pass something back and forth.

criterion (kraɪˈtɪərɪən) *n, pl* **criteria** a standard on which to base a decision or judgment. < Greek *krinein* to decide. SEE PANEL.

critic (ˈkrɪtɪk) *n* **1** someone who judges or finds fault with something. **2** someone who evaluates artistic works, esp. professionally. **critical** *adj* **1** fault-finding. **2** involving criticism: a critical analysis. **3** crucial; of or involving a crisis: the critical moment; a critical condition. **critically** *adv* **criticism** *n* **1** a remark demonstrating a fault or faults. **2** a critic's work; evaluation of artistic works. **criticize** *vb* **1** analyse critically. **2** find fault with. **critique** *n* an essay or article containing a critical judgment. < ultimately Greek *krinein* to decide.

croak (krəʊk) *vb, n* (utter) a hoarse, throaty sound, like that made by a frog. < Middle English *croken,* like the sound.

crochet (ˈkrəʊʃeɪ) *n* a handicraft in which continuous thread is looped in an interlocking pattern with a hooked needle.
• *vb* be engaged in crochet work; make using crochet. < Middle French: small hook.

crock[1] (krɒk) *n* (a broken piece of) a thick, earthenware pot or jar. < Old English *crocc.*

---

criterion or **criteria?**

Criterion is singular; criteria is plural: if the chairman should resign, then by the same *criterion,* so should his deputy. By what *criteria* have you drawn this conclusion? These are the *criteria* by which we have reached our decision.

Criteria and a singular verb is often used but is nonstandard. Criteria is one of a group of words of foreign origin ending in -a that are not singular nouns. Other words in this group include: media, with singular medium (see also panel at **media**); phenomena, with singular phenomenon; strata, with singular stratum. The usage of data has changed: for details, see panel at **data**.

---

crock[2] *n* (*informal*) **1** an old, worn-out vehicle. **2** someone who is old and disabled.
• *vb* also **crock up** make or become like a crock. < Scottish.

crockery (ˈkrɒkərɪ) *n* household china; tableware.

crocodile (ˈkrɒkəˌdaɪl) *n* **1** a large tropical reptile with a broad head, massive jaws, and a thick skin; leather prepared from this: crocodile boots. **2** a line of schoolchildren walking two by two. **crocodile tears** false or hypocritical sorrow. < ultimately Greek *krokē* pebble + *drilos* worm. SEE PANEL.

crocus (ˈkrəʊkəs) *n* one of a group of plants of the iris family, growing from a corm and with purple, white, or yellow long-tubed flowers. < Greek *krokos* saffron.

croft (krɒft) *n* **1** a small enclosed field next to a house. **2** a small rented farm, esp. in Scotland. **crofter** *n* a usually Scottish tenant farmer. < Old English.

croissant (ˈkwʌsɒn) *n* a flaky, crescent-shaped roll of bread or pastry. < Middle French *creissant* crescent.

crony (ˈkrəʊnɪ) *n* a close friend, esp. of long standing. < ultimately Greek *chronos* time.

crook (krʊk) *n* **1** a shepherd's hooked staff. **2** a curve or bend: held in the crook of his arm. **3** (*informal*) someone who is dishonest; thief or swindler.
• *vb* bend; curve. **crooked** *adj* **1** with curves or twists; not straight. **2** dishonest. **crookedly** *adv* **crookedness** *n* < Old Norse *krōkr* hook. SEE PANEL.

croon (kruːn) *vb* sing usually sentimental songs in a low, soft voice. < Middle Dutch *cronen*.

crop (krɒp) *n* **1** an agricultural plant that is grown and harvested: cereal crops. **2** a harvest of these: a large crop of fruit. **3** a group or amount appearing at any one time: this year's crop of recruits. **4** a riding whip; handle of this. **5** a short haircut. **6** a pouch in the throat of some birds where food is broken down for digestion.
• *vb* **cropped; cropping 1** grow as a crop. **2** (of land) bear a crop. **3** cut or trim: crop hair. **crop up** happen unexpectedly. < Old English *cropp*.

croquet (ˈkrəʊkeɪ) *n* a lawn game in which wooden balls are driven through a series of hoops by mallets. < SEE **CROCHET**.

croquette (krəʊˈkɛt) *n* a small ball of meat, fish, etc., coated with egg and breadcrumbs then fried. < French *croquer* to crunch, like the sound.

cross (krɒs) *n* **1** an upright post with a beam across, used by the ancient Romans for crucifixion. **2 the Cross** a cross like this on which Jesus died. **3** a model of this used as an emblem by Christians. **4** any emblem, medal, etc., with this shape: the George Cross. **5** a monument topped with or shaped like a cross: market cross. **6** a burden; trial: It's a cross I have to bear. **7** the cross-breeding of two different plants or animals; resulting hybrid. **8** any mixture of two different elements. **9** a mark made by two lines crossing each other: + or ×.
• *vb* **1** lie or go across; intersect: The river crosses the plain; cross the road. **2** draw a line or lines through: cross a cheque; cross the 't's. **3** make the sign of the cross over, for blessing or protection. **4** frustrate; oppose: Don't cross me. **5** breed (an animal) from two different parents; hybridize (a plant). **6** fold or place crosswise: He crossed his fingers. **7** (of each of two letters) be posted before receipt of the other.
• *adj* **1** lying or going across: cross winds. **2** grumpy; vexed. **crossbar** *n* a horizontal bar, for example on a bicycle or between goal-posts. **crossbow** *n* a short, powerful bow fixed on a wooden stock, used esp. in medieval times.

crocodile tears

A person who feigns sorrow or sympathy is sometimes said to shed crocodile tears. This expression derives from an ancient folk legend. According to the legend the cunning crocodile would utter loud moans and shed bountiful tears as a ploy to allure the curious passer-by. Once the victim came within reach, he or she would be promptly seized and devoured.

by hook or by crook

To do something by hook or by crook means to accomplish it by one means or another: By hook or by crook he was determined to finish the essay before midnight. The expression dates back to feudal times and refers to the restraints imposed upon peasants when collecting firewood. They were entitled to any wood that could be reached either by hook (by a sickle) or by crook (a shepherd's staff).

cross-bred *n* also **cross-breed** the result of cross-breeding. **cross-breed** *vb* **cross-bred; cross-breeding** produce (a hybrid animal) by mating two different types. **cross-check** *vb* check by consulting more than one source. **cross-country** *adj, adv* across fields rather than along roads. **cross-examine** *vb* question thoroughly, esp. in a law-court. **cross-eyed** *adj* with one or both eyes turned inwards to the nose. **crossfire** *n* gunfire from two or more sources intersecting. **crossing** *n* **1** a place where people or vehicles cross: pedestrian crossing. **2** a place where a railway track crosses a road: level crossing. **3** a voyage across water: a rough crossing. **cross-legged** *adj, adv* **1** with legs crossed and knees apart. **2** with one leg over and across the other. **crossly** *adv* angrily. **crossness** *n* anger; vexation. **cross-patch** *n* a bad-tempered person. **cross-ply** *adj* (of tyres) with crosswise cords to strengthen the tread. **cross-question** *vb* cross-examine. **cross-reference** *n* a note indicating that further information can be found elsewhere, in a book, etc. **crossroads** *n* **1** a place where roads intersect. **2** a crucial or decisive point: He'd reached a crossroads in his life. **cross-section** *n* **1** a diagram showing the inside of something, made by cutting across it at right angles to its length. **2** a representative selection: a cross-section of society. **crossways** or **crosswise** *adj, adv* so as to cross; diagonally. **crossword** *n* a puzzle in which words are guessed from clues and fitted into corresponding boxes in a grid of a horizontal and vertical pattern. < Latin *crux*. SEE PANEL.

crotch (krɒtʃ) *n* **1** also **crutch** the angle formed where the thighs meet the lower body; corresponding part on a pair of trousers, pants, etc. **2** an angle formed by any two things forking. < probably alteration of *crutch*.

crotchet (ˈkrɒtʃɪt) *n* a musical note equal to the length of half a minim. **crotchety** *adj* bad-tempered. < Old French *croche* hook, SEE PANEL.

crouch (krautʃ) *vb* lower the body by bending the legs; be in this position < perhaps Middle French *croche* hook.

croupier (ˈkru:pɪə) *n* someone employed to collect and pay out bets at a gambling table. < French *croupe* rump of a horse.

crow[1] (krəʊ) *n* a large, black bird. **as the crow flies** in a direct line. **crow's-feet** *pl n* wrinkles in the skin at the corner of the eyes, esp. from age. **crow's nest** a look-out at the top of a ship's mast. < Old English *crāwe*.

crow[2] *vb* **crowed, crew; crowed; crowing 1** make the loud, shrill cry of a

crotchet

A musical note that is half the length of a minim is called a crotchet. This derives from the Old French *crochet*, 'a little hook', from *croche*, 'a hook'. To those familiar with musical notation this makes little sense, since the note used to represent a crotchet does not have a hook. Earlier in its history, however, crotchet was the name of the note now called a minim, which at that time was represented with a hooked tail.

cross words

Cross features in a number of expressions, many of them idiomatic, including:

at cross purposes misunderstanding each other; having conflicting aims, etc.

cross off or **out** to draw a line through (something), to show a cancellation, mistake, etc.

cross one's bridges when one comes to them to worry about a problem when it arises, and not before.

cross one's mind to occur to one briefly: It never crossed my mind that he might be lying.

cross someone's path to come into contact with someone, especially casually or accidentally: Old Barny's such an awkward person to deal with—I hope he'll never cross my path again!

get one's lines or **wires crossed** to think that one is communicating effectively with someone, whereas in reality one is not: We must have got our lines crossed somewhere—he thought he was coming today but I thought he would be here tomorrow. This idiom comes from the making of a wrong telephone connection, because of a technical fault.

cock. **2** (of a baby) make sounds of happiness. **3** gloat triumphantly; brag.
• *n* **1** the cry of a cock. **2** a triumphant cry. < Old English *crāwan*.

crowbar (ˈkrəʊˌbɑː) *n* a heavy, metal bar with one often forked, wedge-shaped end, used as a lever.

crowd (kraʊd) *n* **1** a large gathering of people or things in no particular order; throng. **2** a specific social group: the in crowd.
• *vb* **1** assemble in a crowd. **2** cram or fill with people or objects. **crowded** *adj* **crowd out** exclude by crowding. < Old English *crūdan*.

crown (kraʊn) *n* **1** an ornamental head-dress worn by a monarch. **2** the sovereign as head of State; his or her authority. **3 the Crown** the supreme authority of government under a constitutional monarchy. **4** a mark of honour or victory, such as the championship title in a sport; head-dress worn as an honour. **5** the top part of the head; part of a hat covering it. **6** an artificial covering for a tooth. **7** the top part of something, for example a hill or tree.
• *vb* **1** place a crown on the head of, esp. to invest as monarch: She was crowned queen. **2** bestow something as an honour or reward. **3** cover or form the topmost part of. **4** put an artificial crown on (a tooth). **5** cause to conclude successfully: her crowning achievement. **6** (*informal*) hit on the head. **Crown Court** a criminal court in England and Wales. **Crown jewels** jewels, such as the crown and sceptre, of a sovereign, worn at a coronation. **Crown Prince or Princess** the heir to a throne. < ultimately Greek *korōnē*.

crucial (ˈkruːʃəl) *adj* very important; decisive. **crucially** *adv* < Latin *crux* cross.

crucible (ˈkruːsɪbl̩) *n* **1** a vessel in which substances are melted. **2** a severe trial. < Medieval Latin *crucibulum*.

crucifix (ˈkruːsɪfɪks) *n* a model of the cross or Christ on the cross. **crucifixion** *n* the act of crucifying. **the Crucifixion** the crucifying of Christ. **crucify** *vb* **crucified; crucifying 1** put to death by binding or nailing the hands and feet to a cross and leaving. **2** cause pain or anguish to. < Latin *crux* + *figere* to fasten.

crude (kruːd) *adj* **1** unrefined; natural: crude petroleum. **2** rough; unfinished: a crude sketch. **3** coarse; vulgar: crude jokes.
• *n* crude oil. **crudely** *adv* **crudity** *n* < Latin *crudus* raw.

cruel (ˈkruːəl) *adj* **1** taking pleasure in causing suffering; merciless. **2** causing suffering: cruel laws. **cruelly** *adv* **cruelty** *n* < ultimately Latin *crudus*.

cruet (ˈkruːɪt) *n* a small container for holding salt, pepper, oil, or vinegar, used at the table; set of these on a stand. < Anglo-French.

cruise (kruːz) *vb* **1** sail for pleasure. **2** travel or patrol with no destination: a cruising taxi. **3** travel at a moderate, economical speed.
• *n* **1** cruising. **2** a pleasure voyage by sea. **cruise missile** a subsonic missile, esp. one carrying a nuclear warhead, that is guided throughout its flight. **cruiser** *n* **1** a large, fast ship of war. **2** a pleasure yacht: cabin cruiser. < ultimately Latin *crux* cross.

crumb (krʌm) *n* a fragment of bread, cake, or similar food. < Old English *cruma*.

crumble (ˈkrʌmbl̩) *vb* fall or break into fragments; disintegrate.
• *n* a dessert of stewed fruit topped with a crumbly mixture: rhubarb crumble. **crumbly** *adj* easily crumbled or crumbling.

crummy (ˈkrʌmɪ) *adj* (*slang*) **1** contemptible; inferior. **2** dirty or filthy. < SEE **CRUMB.**

crumpet (ˈkrʌmpɪt) *n* **1** a round, soft yeast cake, eaten toasted and buttered. **2** (*slang*) sexually desirable women. < origin uncertain.

crumple (ˈkrʌmpl̩) *vb* **1** bend or crush (something) so that it loses its shape: a crumpled newspaper. **2** collapse: The enemy's defence crumpled. < Middle English *crumpen*.

crunch (krʌntʃ) *vb* **1** chew or bite with a noisy, crushing sound. **2** make a crushing sound.
• *n* **1** crushing noise. **2** a crucial moment: When it comes to the crunch, run! < alteration of *craunch*, probably like the sound.

crusade (kruːˈseɪd) *n* **1** one of several Christian military expeditions made to recapture the Holy Land from Islam during the Middle Ages. **2** an enthusiastic campaign taken up for a particular cause.
• *vb* be involved in a crusade. **crusader** *n* < ultimately Latin *crux* cross.

crush (krʌʃ) *vb* **1** destroy or alter by pressing or squeezing. **2** pound or ground into fragments. **3** subdue; defeat: The rebellion was crushed.
• *n* **1** a large number of people crowding together. **2** a drink prepared with

crushed fruit. **3** an infatuation: He had a crush on her < Middle French *cruisir.*

crust (krʌst) *n* **1** the hard outer layer of bread, pastry, or similar food. **2** the rocky outer layer of the earth. **crusty** *adj* **1** with a hard crust. **2** with a harsh manner; surly. **crustiness** *n* < Latin *crusta.*

crustacean (krʌˈsteɪʃən) *n* a usually aquatic animal with a hard shell, such as a lobster or crab. < Latin *crusra* shell.

crutch (krʌtʃ) *n* **1** a wooden or metal support to assist a disabled person in walking. **2** the crotch of the body or corresponding part of a garment. < Old English *crycc.*

crux (krʌks) *n, pl* **cruxes, cruces** a vital or decisive point. < Latin: cross.

cry (kraɪ) *n* **1** a wordless utterance expressing pain, anger, joy, etc. **2** a shout. **3** the characteristic call of a bird or animal. **4** a public appeal or complaint. **5** a fit of weeping: a good cry. **6** a war-cry. **7** pursuit: in full cry.
• *vb* **cried; crying 1** shout in fear or pain, for example. **2** weep: She cried her heart out. **3** (of an animal) make its characteristic sound. **4** advertise: Stallholders were crying their wares. **5** appeal; require: The schools are crying out for more teachers. **cry-baby** *n* someone who weeps too easily without much reason. **cry off** cancel an arrangement. < ultimately Latin *quiritare* to call help, wail. SEE PANEL.

crypt (krɪpt) *n* an underground chamber, esp. in a church. < ultimately Greek *kryptein* to hide. SEE PANEL.

cryptic (ˈkrɪptɪk) *adj* **1** hidden; occult. **2** obscure in meaning; mysterious: a cryptic crossword. **cryptically** *adv*

crystal (ˈkrɪstl̩) *n* **1** (a piece of) a transparent, colourless mineral. **2** (an object made of) clear, colourless glass of high quality. **3** a piece of a substance, with a regular shape because of its internal structure: ice-crystals. **crystal ball** a glass ball used by fortune-tellers. **crystal-gazing** *n* **1** looking into a crystal ball to attempt to see the future. **2** attempting to predict, without supporting information. **crystalline** *adj* composed of or like crystals. **crystallize** *vb* **1** form crystals. **2** take on a definite form: His ideas crystallized. **crystallization** *n* < ultimately Greek *krystallos* ice, crystal.

CSE *abbrev* Certificate of Secondary Education.

cub (kʌb) *n* **1** the young of various mammals such as the lion or bear. **2** an inexperienced journalist. **3 Cub** also **Cub scout** a junior member of the Scout movement. < origin unknown.

cubby-hole (ˈkʌbɪˌhəʊl) *n* a cramped space; small compartment. < dialect *cub* little shed.

cube (kjuːb) *n* **1** a regular solid body with six equal square faces. **2** a block with this form: an ice cube. **3** the result obtained by multiplying a number by itself twice, for example the cube of 2 is 8.
• *vb* **1** cut into cubes. **2** find the cube of (a number). < Greek *kybos.*

cubic (ˈkjuːbɪk) *adj* three-dimensional: cubic centimetre. **cubical** *adj* shaped like a cube.

cubicle (ˈkjuːbɪkl̩) *n* a space partitioned off a large room; compartment screened off for privacy. < Latin *cubare* to recline.

cuckoo (ˈkʊkuː) *n* **1** one of a family of European birds that lays its eggs in other birds' nests. **2** the characteristic call of

crying wolf

To cry wolf is to give a false alarm of danger, especially as a practical joke. I'd be careful about crying wolf if I were you, in case the joke backfires. The expression comes from the fable about a shepherd boy who used to call out wolf in jest, to try to make the villagers come running and beat off attacks from the supposed wolves. The boy did this so often that when one day a wolf actually attacked his sheep, and he gave a genuine cry, no one believed him and all his sheep were killed.

cryptic—the hidden meaning

A remark or clue whose meaning or reference is obscure is sometimes described as cryptic: At the end of the letter was a cryptic message that no one but George could understand. Cryptic derives ultimately from the Greek verb *kryptein* meaning 'to hide'. The same source provides crypt, a vault or chamber beneath a church, often used in the past as a secret hiding place, and cryptography, the science or study of writing and deciphering codes.

the cuckoo. **cuckoo-clock** *n* a clock that strikes the hour by sounds like the cuckoo's call.
• *adj* (*informal*) mentally deficient; silly. < Middle English *cuccu,* like the sound.

cucumber (ˈkjuːˌkʌmbə) *n* (a plant producing) a long, green fruit which is pickled or eaten in a salad. < Latin *cucumis.*

cud (kʌd) *n* food brought back to the mouth from the first stomach of cattle etc., to be chewed again. < Old English *cwudu.*

cuddle (ˈkʌdl̩) *vb* **1** hold closely in one's arms for warmth or affection. **2** snuggle.
• *n* a loving hug. **cuddlesome** or **cuddly** *adj* pleasant to cuddle; lovable. < origin unknown.

cudgel (ˈkʌdʒəl) *n* a short, heavy stick, used as a weapon.
• *vb* **cudgelled; cudgelling** hit with a cudgel. **take up the cudgels for** defend (a person or argument) vigorously. < Old English *cycgel.*

cue[1] (kjuː) *n* a signal to prompt someone to do something, such as for an actor to speak a line in a play.
• *vb* **cued; cueing** give a cue to. < ultimately Latin *quando* when.

cue[2] n a long, tapering rod for hitting the ball in billiards or snooker. < Latin *cauda* tail.

cuff[1] (kʌf) *n* **1** a fold of cloth or band at the end of a sleeve which encircles the wrist. **2** *pl* handcuffs. **cuff-links** *pl n* a pair of fasteners for shirt cuffs, in place of buttons. **off the cuff** without preparation; spontaneously. < Middle English: glove.

cuff[2] *vb, n* (strike) a blow with the palm of the hand. < perhaps obsolete *cuff* glove.

cuisine (kwɪˈziːn) *n* a style of cooking or preparing food; food prepared. < French, from Late Latin *coquina* kitchen.

cul-de-sac (ˈkʌldəˌsæk) *n, pl* **culs-de-sac** a street closed at one end. < French: bottom of the bag.

culinary (ˈkʌlɪnərɪ) *adj* of or used in cooking or a kitchen. < Latin *culina* kitchen.

cull (kʌl) *vb* **1** choose; select. **2** take out (inferior animals) from a herd or flock for slaughter.
• *n* **1** culling. **2** a culled animal. < ultimately Latin *colligere* to bind together.

culminate (ˈkʌlmɪˌneɪt) *vb* reach the highest or most decisive point: The dispute culminated in violence. **culmination** *n* < Latin *culmen* top.

culottes (kjuːˈlɒts) *pl n* short trousers resembling a skirt, worn by women. < French *culotte* breeches.

culpable (ˈkʌlpəbl̩) *adj* blameworthy. **culpability** *n* **culpably** *adv* < Latin *culpa* guilt.

culprit (ˈkʌlprɪt) *n* someone who is guilty of a fault or offence. < Anglo-French *culpable* + *prit* ready.

cult (kʌlt) *n* **1** a system of religious belief and ritual. **2** devotion to someone or something; group of people devoted to this: a personality cult. < ultimately Latin *colere* to cultivate.

cultivate (ˈkʌltɪˌveɪt) *vb* **1** prepare or use (land) for crop-growing. **2** grow (plants or crops) with regular tending. **3** develop by study or labour. **4** spend time on furthering or encouraging: cultivate a friendship. **cultivation** *n* **cultivator** *n* < ultimately Latin *colere* to cultivate.

culture (ˈkʌltʃə) *n* **1** the shared customs, traditions, and beliefs of a particular group of people: African culture. **2** a knowledge and appreciation of the arts: a man of culture. **3** cultivation of land or plants. **cultured** *adj* **1** cultivated. **2** educated to value and appreciate the arts.

culvert (ˈkʌlvət) *n* a drain or covered channel crossing under an obstacle such as a road, canal, or railway line. < origin unknown.

cumbersome (ˈkʌmbəsəm) *adj* bulky and heavy; unwieldy. < Middle English *cumbren* to hamper.

cumin (ˈkʌmɪn) *n* a plant of the carrot family with aromatic seeds used for flavouring. < Greek *kyminon.*

cumulative (ˈkjuːmjʊlətɪv) *adj* increasing in amount by successive additions: Pollution has a cumulative effect. < Latin *cumulus* mass.

cunning (ˈkʌnɪŋ) *adj* **1** skilled in deceit; sly. **2** ingenious: a cunning plan. **3** (*US*) attractive; cute.
• *n* slyness. < Middle English *cunnen* to know.

cup (kʌp) *n* **1** a small, open vessel for drinking from, usually bowl-shaped with one handle. **2** the contents of this; amount contained: a cup of tea. **3** something with the shape of a cup, such as one of the two parts of a bra which fit over the breast. **4** an ornamental metal vessel awarded as a prize in a competition; the competition: the World Cup. **5** an alcoholic drink with mixed ingredients: cider cup.
• *vb* **cupped; cupping 1** form into the shape of a cup: She cupped her hands. **2** put or hold (as if) in a cup: She cupped her chin

in her hands. **not my cup of tea** not what suits me. < Old English *cuppe.*

cupboard (ˈkʌbəd) *n* a recess with shelves or a piece of furniture with doors, used for storage. **cupboard love** a show of affection made in the hope of gaining something.

cupidity (kjuːˈpɪdɪtɪ) *n* greed for wealth; avarice. < Latin *cupiditas.*

cupola (ˈkjuːpələ) *n* a small domed structure built onto a roof. < Latin *cupula* small tub.

curate (ˈkjʊərət) *n a* clergyman who assists a parish rector, etc., in his duties. < Latin *cura* care. SEE PANEL.

curator (kjʊəˈreɪtə) *n* someone in charge of a museum or other place of exhibition, such as a zoo.

curb (kɜːb) *n* **1** something that checks or restrains. **2** a strap or chain for restraining a horse, passing under its lower jaw. **3** (*US*) a kerb.
• *vb* check; restrain: You'll have to curb your spending. < ultimately Latin *curvus* curved.

curd (kɜːd) *n* also **curds 1** the thick part of coagulated milk, used in making cheese. **2** a rich fruit preserve prepared with sugar, butter, and eggs: lemon curd. < Middle English.

curdle (ˈkɜːdl̩) *vb* **1** form curds. **2** sour; spoil. **curdle one's blood** fill one with terror.

cure (kjʊə) *vb* **1** restore to health or normality. **2** cause to recover from an ailment or disease. **3** correct (a fault or difficult situation); remedy. **4** preserve (substances such as meat, fish, or tobacco) by salting, drying, or smoking.
• *n* **1** something causing recovery from illness. **2** a remedy. **curative** *adj* of or helping to cure illness. < Latin *cura* care.

curfew (ˈkɜːfjuː) *n* an order, esp. in times of civil unrest, confining people to their homes, esp. from a specific time until the next morning. < Middle French *covrefeu* cover the fire.

curio (ˈkjʊərɪˌəʊ) *n, pl* **curios** an object considered rare or bizarre, and therefore interesting. < short for *curiosity.*

curious (ˈkjəʊrɪəs) *adj* **1** eager to learn; inquisitive. **2** novel or unusual: a curious coincidence. **curiously** *adv* **curiosity** *n* **1** eagerness to learn. **2** a curio. < Latin cura cure.

curl (kɜːl) *vb* **1** bend or form into a spiral or wave. **2** move in coils or spirals.
• *n* **1** something spiral or winding in form. **2** a curled lock of hair. **3** the act of curling. **curler** *n* a small tube for curling the hair. **curl up** (*informal*) get comfortable, esp. by lying with the knees drawn up. **curly** *adj* tending to curl; full of curls. < probably Middle Dutch *crul* curly.

curlew (ˈkɜːljuː) *n* a large wading-bird with long legs and a long, slender, downward-curving bill. < Middle French *corlieu.*

curling (ˈkɜːlɪŋ) *n* a game played on ice in which heavy, round, flat stones are slid towards a target circle.

currant (ˈkʌrənt) *n* **1** a type of small, seedless dried grape, used in cooking. **2** a small berry such as a blackcurrant; shrub bearing this. SEE PANEL.

currency (ˈkʌrənsɪ) *n* **1** the coins and notes used as money in a country. **2** the state of being generally accepted or in common use. < ultimately Latin

---

like the curate's egg

The expression like the curate's egg, referring to something that has both good and bad parts, comes from a cartoon in 'Punch' (9 November 1895). This shows a nervous curate who has been served a bad boiled egg while at table with his bishop. In reply to the bishop's comment, 'I'm afraid your egg is bad,' the curate declared, 'Oh no, my lord, I assure you! Parts of it are excellent!'

---

currants and **raisins**

A small, dried, seedless grape commonly used in baking is known as a currant. The currant takes its name from *Corinth,* the region in Greece where it originated. In Middle English it was referred to as the *raison of Coraunte,* 'raisin of Corinth', which was shortened in the 16th century to its modern-day form.

Raisin, a partially dried grape which is larger than the currant, comes from the Middle French word for grape *raisin,* which derives from the Latin word *racemus* or 'cluster of grapes'.

In modern French *raisin* continues to be the equivalent of the English word grape, while the English raisin is expressed in French by *raisin sec* or 'dried grape'.

currere to run.

current (ˈkʌrənt) *adj* **1** of the present time; contemporary: current affairs. **2** in general use or circulation: That phrase is no longer current.
• *n* **1** a body such as air or water which moves continuously in a particular direction. **2** a flow of electricity; rate of such a flow. **currently** *adv* **current account** a bank account from which money can be drawn on demand.

curriculum (kəˈrɪkjʊləm) *n, pl* **curricula** a study course or courses. **curriculum vitae** a brief summary of one's career to date. < Latin: course.

curry[1] (ˈkʌrɪ) *n* a dish flavoured with a mixture of hot-tasting spices. < Tamil *kari*.

curry[2] *vb* **curried; currying curry favour** ingratiate oneself by flattery, etc. SEE PANEL AT **FAVOUR**.

curse (kɜːs) *n* **1** a call to invoke evil or harm; evil which comes from this. **2** the cause of an evil or misfortune. **3** a profane expression of anger. **the curse** (*informal*) menstruation.
• *vb* **1** call up misfortune on. **2** utter profane language in anger; swear at. **3** burden: He was cursed with a bad memory. < Old English *curs*.

cursor (ˈkɜːsə) *n* **1** a transparent slide with a reference line on, for example, a slide rule. **2** a position indicator on a visual display unit. < ultimately Latin *currere* to run.

cursory (ˈkɜːsərɪ) *adj* hasty; superficial: a cursory examination.

curt (kɜːt) *adj* brief in an uncivil manner; brusque. **curtly** *adv* **curtness** *n* < Latin *curtus* shortened.

curtail (kɜːˈteɪl) *vb* limit; cut short. **curtailment** *n* < obsolete *curtal* to dock.

curtain (ˈkɜːtn̩) *n* **1** a piece of fabric hung up as a screen, at a window, etc. **2** the opening or closing of a stage-curtain at the beginning or end of an act or scene. **3** a curtain-call.
• *vb* provide or veil with or as if with a curtain. **curtain-call** *n* a performer's appearance after the final curtain of a play in answer to sustained applause. < ultimately Latin *cohors* court.

curtsy (ˈkɜːtsɪ) *n* also **curtsey** an act of respect of a girl or woman, made by bending the knees with one foot forward.
• *vb* **curtsied; curtsying** make a curtsy. < alteration of *courtesy*.

curvaceous (kɜːˈveɪʃəs) *adj* (*informal*) (of a woman) with an attractive shapely figure.

curve (kɜːv) *n* **1** a continuously bending line or surface with no straight or flat parts. **2** something curved or represented by a curve: the inflation curve.
• *vb* shape or bend into a curve. **curvy** *adj* **curvature** *n* curving: the curvature of the earth. < Latin *curvus* curved.

cushion (ˈkʊʃən) *n* **1** a bag made of cloth or other fabric filled with springy material, used to make sitting or reclining more comfortable; anything like this to protect against jarring. **2** the springy border round a billiard table. **3** anything which reduces the effect of a mental or physical shock.
• *vb* **1** furnish with a cushion. **2** reduce the impact of; protect against the effects of. < ultimately Latin *coxa* hip.

cushy (ˈkʊʃɪ) *adj* (*informal*) agreeable and easy: a cushy job. < Hindi, from Persian *khūsh* pleasant.

custard (ˈkʌstəd) *n* **1** a sweetened mixture made with eggs and milk and baked. **2** a sweet sauce made from milk and coloured cornflour. < probably Old French *crouste* crust.

custody (ˈkʌstədɪ) *n* **1** the state of being cared for or guarded; imprisonment: in police custody; in safe custody. **2** the right to the guardianship of a minor, usually granted in a court of law: The mother was awarded custody. **custodian** *n* someone who guards or maintains a public building, etc. < ultimately Latin *custos* guardian.

custom (ˈkʌʃtəm) *n* **1** an established practice or way of behaving. **2** patronage of a business by customers. **customary** *adj* in accordance with usual practice. **customarily** *adv* **custom-built** *adj* made according to individual specifications. **custom car** a car built or altered according to the owner's design. **customer** *n* **1** someone who buys goods or services. **2** someone with a particular trait: a tricky customer. < ultimately Latin *com-* + *suescere* to accustom.

customs (ˈkʌstəmz) *n* **1** payment of duty on imported goods. **2 Customs** the government agency or procedure dealing with the collection of duty; area at a port or airport where this takes place.

cut (kʌt) *vb* **cut; cutting 1** penetrate (something) with a sharp instrument in order to divide, wound, or detach. **2** trim, shape, or shorten with or as if with a sharp instrument: cut the grass. **3** be capable of being cut: Butter cuts easily. **4** hurt the feelings of: His remarks cut her deeply. **5** lessen (an amount): cut costs. **6** dilute; adulterate: This whisky is cut with water. **7** feel (a tooth) emerging through a gum. **8** go across or through: We cut through the woods. **9** turn off: cut power; cut the engine. **10** divide into two parts: cut the cards. **11** stay away from: cut classes. **12** ignore on purpose. **13** stop (something): cut the nonsense. **14** record sounds on: cut a record. **15** hit (a ball) in a chopping fashion in cricket. **16** present: cut a fine figure. • *n* **1** a wound made by cutting; gash. **2** the division or opening of an object made (as if) by cutting: a cut of meat. **3** a sharp, downward stroke, such as that made by a sword or whip. **4** an attacking stroke in cricket. **5** a remark or gesture that hurts one's feelings. **6** the style in which something is made or cut: a suit of a good cut; a short haircut. **7** a sudden move from one sound or image to another on radio, television, or film; something removed from any of these. **8** a reduction or stoppage: public spending cuts; a power cut. **9** a share of profit; commission. **cutter** *n* **1** someone or something that cuts. **2** a small sailing boat with a single mast. < Middle English *cutten*. SEE PANEL.

cute (kjuːt) *adj* **1** attractive; pretty. **2** ingenious; shrewd. **cutely** *adv* **cuteness** *n* < short for *acute*.

cuticle (ˈkjuːtɪkl̩) *n* skin, esp. at the base of a finger-nail or toe-nail. < Latin *cuticula* small skin.

cutlass (ˈkʌtləs) *n* a short sword with a curved blade, often used formerly by sailors. < ultimately Latin *cultellus* small knife.

cutlery (ˈkʌtlərɪ) *n* knives, forks, and spoons used in serving or eating food.

cutlet (ˈkʌtlɪt) *n* a small cut of meat from the neck of veal, mutton, or lamb; other food of this shape: nut cutlet. < Old French *costelette* small rib.

cut-throat (ˈkʌtˌθrəʊt) *n* a murderer. • *adj* **1** murderous. **2** intense; ruthless: cut-throat competition.

cutting (ˈkʌtɪŋ) *adj* **1** sharp. **2** hurtful or sarcastic: a cutting remark. • *n* **1** something cut out or off: newspaper cutting. **2** a digging through high ground for a road, railway, canal, etc. **3** a part of a plant which when removed and replanted will form a new plant.

cuttlefish (ˈkʌtl̩ˌfɪʃ) *n* a marine creature with a hard, internal shell. < Middle English *cotul* + *fish*.

cv *abbrev* curriculum vitae.

cwt *abbrev* hundredweight.

cyanide (ˈsaɪəˌnaɪd) *n* an extremely poisonous chemical; salt of hydrocyanic acid.

cyclamen (ˈsɪkləmən) *n* a plant of the primrose family with white, pink, or purple flowers that droop. < Greek *kyklaminos*.

cycle (ˈsaɪkl̩) *n* **1** (the time taken to complete) a series of events which occur regularly in the same order: life cycle. **2** one complete instance of a continually repeated process, such as sound vibration or electrical oscillation. **3** a set of songs, poems, novels, or plays with

to cut a long story short ...

Cut features in a number of idiomatic expressions, including:

a cut above superior to.

cut-and-dried *adj* definite; fixed: cut-and-dried religious views. The expression alludes to seasoned timber that is ready for use.

cut and thrust fierce, competitive methods in business, etc.; lively exchange of opinions. The expression derives from sword-fighting.

cut back to reduce: cut back on government expenditure. **cutback** *n*

cut in 1 to move suddenly in front (of another vehicle). **2** to interrupt.

cut it fine to allow a very small margin, especially of time: You're cutting it a bit fine, aren't you? The train is due to leave in half a minute!

cut no ice to have no influence.

cut off 1 to disconnect (a telephone line or a supply of gas, etc.). **2** to isolate or separate. **3** to block the passage of, in order to prevent escape. **4** to disinherit.

cut one's losses to close a business or abandon a scheme, etc., before incurring further losses or worse difficulties.

cut out 1 to shape by cutting. **cut-out** *n* **2** to stop consuming: cut out sugar. **3** to stop talking or doing something: Cut it out! **4** to fail to operate: The engine cut out.

cut out for to have the abilities, etc., suitable for: I don't think I'm cut out for teaching.

cut up 1 to cut into pieces. **2** to be emotionally very distressed: He was very cut up at not getting the job.

to cut a long story short to be brief.

a central theme. **4** a bicycle, tricycle, or motor cycle.
● *vb* ride a bicycle. **cyclic** *adj* forming or belonging to a cycle. **cyclist** *n* someone who rides a cycle. < Greek *kyklos* circle.

cyclone (ˈsaɪkləʊn) *n* a stormy wind system rotating round an area of low atmospheric pressure; destructive storm of this type; tornado. **cyclonic** *adj*

cyclostyle (ˈsaɪkləˌstaɪl) *vb*, *n* (use) a machine that makes multiple copies from a stencil. < *Cyclostyle*, trademark.

cygnet (ˈsɪgnɪt) *n* a young swan.< Greek *kyknos* swan.

cylinder (ˈsɪlɪndə) *n* **1** a hollow or solid object with straight sides and a circular cross-section. **2** a machine part with this shape, such as the piston chamber in an engine. **cylindrical** *adj* < ultimately Greek *kylindein* to roll.

cymbal (ˈsɪmbl̩) *n* a concave brass plate that makes a clashing sound when struck by another or by a drumstick, used as a percussion instrument. < ultimately Greek *kymbē* bowl.

cynic (ˈsɪnɪk) *n* someone who doubts people's sincerity and often shows this with sarcasm. **cynical** *adj* **cynically** *adv* **cynicism** *n* < Greek *kynikos* like a dog, from *kyōn* dog.

cypress (ˈsaɪprəs) *n* a type of coniferous evergreen tree with dark, scale-like leaves. < ultimately Greek *kyparissos*.

cyst (sɪst) *n* a sac which develops abnormally in the body, containing a watery liquid. < Greek *kystis* pouch.

cytology (saɪˈtɒlədʒɪ) *n* the biology of cells; scientific study of this. < Greek *kytos* vessel + *logos* word.

czar (zɑː) *n* a tsar.

D

d *abbrev* (formerly) penny or pence. < short for Latin *denarius*.

dab (dæb) *n* **1** a feeble blow; poke. **2** a quick, gentle touch with something soft, such as a sponge; pat. **3** a small amount of something applied: a dab of paint. **4** *pl* (*slang*) fingerprints. **5** (*informal*) an expert: a dab hand at cooking.
• *vb* **dabbed; dabbing 1** strike a feeble blow. **2** touch or apply lightly.
< Middle English *dabbe*, probably like the sound.

dabble (ˈdæbl̩) *vb* **1** wet slightly by dipping in water or another liquid. **2** play or paddle in water or mud. **3 dabble in** concern oneself with casually: He dabbles in antiques. **dabbler** *n* < perhaps *dab*.

dachshund (ˈdæksˌhʊnd) *n* one of a breed of dogs with a long body and short legs. < German, from *Dachs* badger + *Hund* dog.

dad (dæd) *n* (*informal*) father. **daddy** *n* (*informal*) father. **daddy-long-legs** *n* a crane fly. < probably baby language.

daffodil (ˈdæfədɪl) *n* a plant with a large, yellow, trumpet-shaped flower, grown from a bulb. < ultimately Greek *asphodelos* asphodel. SEE PANEL.

daft (dɑːft) *adj* (*informal*) **1** stupid; silly. **2** extremely keen on: He's daft about pop music. < Middle English *defte* gentle, meek.

dagger (ˈdægə) *n* a short, double-edged, pointed weapon, used for stabbing. **at daggers drawn** on the point of conflict. **look daggers at** glare at angrily.
< Middle English.

dahlia (ˈdeɪljə) *n* any of a group of garden plants with brightly-coloured flower heads and roots that form tubers.
< Anders *Dahl*, died 1789, Swedish botanist. SEE PANEL.

daily (ˈdeɪlɪ) *adj* made or occurring every day or weekday.
• *adv* every day or weekday.
• *n* **1** a newspaper issued every day or weekday. **2** (*informal*) a charwoman.
< Old English *dæglīc*.

dainty (ˈdeɪntɪ) *adj* **1** beautifully small and delicate. **2** fastidious. **daintily** *adv* **daintiness** *n* < ultimately Latin *dignitas* dignity.

dairy (ˈdɛərɪ) *n* **1** a building or room where milk is processed and cheese or butter is made. **2** a place where these are sold or distributed. **dairy farm** a farm concerned chiefly with the production of milk, butter, and cheese. **dairyman** *n*, *pl* **dairymen** someone whose work is concerned with dairy produce. < Old English *dǣge* kneader of bread.

dais (ˈdeɪəs) *n* a slightly-raised platform, usually at the end of a hall. < ultimately Latin *discus* discus.

daisy (ˈdeɪzɪ) *n* a common European plant with usually white, petal-like rays round a centre. **daisywheel** *n* a flat, wheel-like device that carries the characters in some electric typewriters and printers. **pushing up the daisies** (*informal*) dead and buried. < Old English *dæg* day + *ēage* eye. SEE PANEL.

dale (deɪl) *n* a vale or valley, esp. in the north of England. < Old English *dæl*.

dally (ˈdælɪ) *vb* **dallied; dallying 1** waste time; dawdle. **2** flirt. **dalliance** *n* < Anglo-French *dalier*.

daffodil

Holland has long been admired as the European capital of bulb-growing. So it comes as no surprise to know that the name of our most popular bulb-forming plant, the daffodil, is of Dutch derivation. What is unusual about the name is that it is based upon a mistake, a sandwiching of the two Dutch words *de affodil* 'the asphodel' (from the Greek word for the flower, *asphodelos*).

dahlia

Several of the plants and shrubs found in nearly every garden take their names from *botanists*. The dahlia, for example, is named after the Swedish botanist, Anders *Dahl*, died 1789, who introduced it into Europe from Mexico. Lobelia, on the other hand, is so called after the Flemish botanist, Matthias de *Lobel*, 1538–1616. Fuchsia perpetuates the name of the German botanist, Leonhard *Fuchs*, 1501–66 and buddleia that of the British botanist, Adam *Buddle*, died 1715.

dam[1] (dæm) *n* a barrier across a river which restricts its flow or forms a reservoir.
• *vb* **dammed; damming 1** supply or restrict with a dam. **2** block the flow of. < Middle English.

dam[2] *n* a mother, esp. of domestic animals. < SEE **DAME.**

damage (ˈdæmɪdʒ) *n* **1** loss or harm caused by something done to a person, object, reputation, etc. **2** (*informal*) cost: What's the damage? **3** *pl* financial compensation for loss or injury, awarded in a court of law.
• *vb* suffer or cause damage to. < ultimately Latin *damnum.*

damask (ˈdæməsk) *n* a plain fabric of, for example, linen, cotton, or silk with a pattern visible on both sides. **damask rose** a large, pink, sweet-scented rose. < Medieval Latin *damascus,* of *Damascus,* city in Syria. SEE PANEL AT **TULLE.**

dame (deɪm) *n* **1** a woman of status or authority. **2 Dame** a title awarded to a woman, conferring membership of an order of knighthood, corresponding to *Sir* for a man. **3** a comic, usually elderly, female figure in a pantomime, played by a man. **4** (*archaic or US slang*) a woman. < ultimately Latin *domina* mistress of a household.

damn (dæm) *vb* **1** condemn to a punishment, esp. in hell. **2** condemn publicly as a failure. **3** bring ruin on; doom. **4** swear at.
• *interj* also **damnation!** an expression of anger or irritation: Damn it!
• *n* **1** a curse using the word *damn.* **2** the slightest bit: I don't give a damn. **damnable** *adj* hateful; irritating. **damnably** *adv* **damn all** (*slang*) nothing whatsoever. **damnation** *n* condemnation to hell; being damned. **damned** *adj, adv* (*slang*) outrageous(ly); extremely: It's damned cold. **do one's damnedest** do one's utmost. < ultimately Latin *damnum* loss.

damp (dæmp) *n* **1** humidity; moisture. **2** a foul gas in a coal-mine.
• *adj* slightly wet.
• *vb* **1** make damp; dampen. **2** lessen the activity, intensity, or vibration of: damp down a fire; damp a guitar string. **3** also **dampen** discourage: The news damped her spirits. **damp course** a damp-resistant layer built into a wall near the ground. < Middle Low German: vapour.

damper (ˈdæmpə) *n* **1** a device that damps, such as a plate in the flue of a furnace to restrict airflow. **2** someone or something that discourages: He put a damper on the proceedings. **3** a small pad used to stop a piano string vibrating.

damsel (ˈdæmzl̩) *n* (*archaic*) a young woman; girl. < ultimately Latin *domina* lady.

damson (ˈdæmzən) *n* **1** a type of Asiatic tree bearing a small, plum-like fruit; this fruit. **2** a deep-purple colour. < ultimately Latin *prunum damascenum* plum of Damascus.

dance (dɑːns) *vb* **1** move the body in a rhythmical pattern, usually in time to music. **2** move up and down in a lively manner.
• *n* **1** a pattern of movements performed to music. **2** a piece of music which is danced to, for example a waltz. **3** a social occasion where people dance. **dancer** *n* < Old French *dancier.*

dandelion (ˈdændɪˌlaɪən) *n* a type of common weed with bright-yellow flowers. < Middle French *dent de lion* lion's tooth. SEE PANEL.

dandruff (ˈdændrʌf) *n* flakes of dead

daisy

That the Saxons were obviously keen observers of nature is suggested by the name they chose for the most common wild flower, the daisy. The daisy opens when the sun comes up and closes when it goes down. It was this habit that gave rise to its Old English name, *dægesēage,* 'day's eye', from *dæg* 'day' and *ēage* 'eye'.

dandelion

The name of the dandelion is more poetic than appearances would reveal. Imported from France at the beginning of the 16th century, the word first appeared in its original form as *dent de lion* or 'lion's tooth', so called probably on account of the shape of the leaf. Dent de lion proceeded to become increasingly anglicized until by the end of the 17th century it had acquired its modern-day form.

In French the plant continues to be known as *dent-de-lion* (echoed in German as *Löwenzahn*); in other words the poetry of the name is still visible.

skin which come off the scalp; scurf. < probably *dand-*, origin unknown + Scandinavian *-ruff.*

dandy (ˈdændɪ) *n* a man who takes excessive care in his dress and appearance.
● *adj (US or old-fashioned informal)* excellent. < perhaps *Dandy*, nickname for *Andrew*.

danger (ˈdeɪndʒə) *n* **1** the state of being exposed to harm or death; peril. **2** something causing this. **danger money** wages higher than usual for people whose work is dangerous. **dangerous** *adj* causing or involving danger. **dangerously** *adv* < ultimately Latin *dominium* ownership.

dangle (ˈdæŋɡl̩) *vb* **1** hang or swing or cause to hang or swing freely. **2** show enticingly: The promise of wealth was dangled before her. < probably Scandinavian.

dank (dæŋk) *adj* disagreeably wet and cold. < Middle English *danke*.

dapper (ˈdæpə) *adj* neat and trim in dress and appearance: a dapper young man. < Middle Dutch: quick.

dapple (ˈdæpl̩) *vb* mark with rounded spots or patches of a varying shade or colour. < Middle English *dappel-grey*.

dare (dɛə) *vb* **1** be brave or impudent enough to (do something): He didn't dare speak. **2** confront; defy: They dared the storm. **3** challenge someone (to do something bold or dangerous).
● *n* a challenge to do something bold or dangerous: She did it for a dare. **daredevil** *n, adj* (a person who is) recklessly bold. **daring** *adj* bold; risk-taking. **daringly** *adv* **I dare say** quite likely; I suppose. < Old English *dear*. SEE PANEL.

dark (dɑːk) *adj* **1** with hardly any light, or none at all. **2** of a colour closer to black than white: dark hair, dark skin. **3** suggestive of evil or malice: dark desires. **4** sad; gloomy: dark moods. **5** secret; mysterious: She kept her intentions dark.
● *n* **1** lack of light. **2** a period of darkness; night: They got home before dark. **3** a deep colour. **darkly** *adv* **darkness** *n* **darken** *vb* make or become dark or darker. **dark-room** *n* a room in which photographs are processed in darkness or in a safe light. < Old English *deorc*. SEE PANEL.

dare and **need**

The verbs dare and need have some grammatical features that native speakers are scarcely aware of but which pose problems for foreign learners of English.

Dare can be used as in the following constructions: He *dare* not risk the possibility of dividing the party. I'd be surprised if he *dares* to show his face. In the first sentence, dare functions as a modal auxiliary verb (like may, will, or must) and therefore has no -s with he, she, or it: he dare. It is followed by an infinitive without to: He dare not risk. But dare also functions as an ordinary verb, as in the second sentence: it takes an -s inflection with he, she, or it: he dares, and is followed by an infinitive with to. He dares to show his face.

Need functions in the same way: He *need* not ask my permission before leaving (no -s, no to); It *needs* to be made clear to him that he can't behave like that (with -s, with to).

Interestingly, the modal auxiliary form is mostly restricted to negative and interrogative sentences: I *daren't* ask him for more money. *Dare* she tell her parents? He *needn't* ask my permission before leaving. *Need* I wait here any longer?

in the dark

Dark features in a number of idiomatic expressions, including:

a dark horse a person who does not make his or her actions, abilities, or intentions widely known: You're a dark horse. I didn't know you'd even applied for the job let alone got it! The expression originally referred to a horse whose ability to win races was unknown.

a leap in the dark an action that has unpredictable consequences.

a shot in the dark a guess that is based on little information, and so is unlikely to be correct.

in the dark in a state of ignorance.

keep something dark to keep something secret: We've won the contract but have got to keep it dark until the press conference tomorrow.

darling (ˈdɑːlɪŋ) *n* **1** someone well-loved. **2** a favourite: the critics' darling.
• *adj* **1** beloved. **2** (*informal*) charming. < Old English *dēore* dear.

darn (dɑːn) *vb* mend (socks, etc.) by weaving stitches across a hole or worn area.
• *n* a place which has been darned. < probably French dialect *darner.*

dart (dɑːt) *n* **1** a small, pointed missile with a flight of usually feather or plastic, used for throwing in the game of darts. **2** a tapering fold in dressmaking. **3** a sudden movement.
• *vb* **1** move suddenly and quickly in a particular direction: He darted across the street. **2** throw or send out quickly: a darting glance. **dartboard** *n* a circular board with marked score areas, used as a target in darts. **darts** *n* an indoor competitive game in which darts are thrown at a dartboard. < Middle French.

dash (dæʃ) *vb* **1** move or run quickly. **2** throw or knock an object violently (against); smash or break in this way. **3** draw or write hurriedly: She dashed off an essay. **4** ruin; destroy: His hopes were dashed.
• *n* **1** a hurried action; rush: a mad dash to work. **2** a small amount of something added: a dash of sauce. **3** energy or liveliness of style. **4** the punctuation mark — used to show a break in sentence structure. **5** a symbol representing the longer of the two signals used in the Morse Code. **dashboard** *n* a panel for the controls and instruments of a motor vehicle, placed below the windscreen. **dashing** *adj* **1** lively; spirited: a dashing young man. **2** stylish. < Middle English *dasshen.*

data (ˈdeɪtə, ˈdɑːtə) *pl n* observations, facts, or information used as a basis for discussion or calculation. **data bank** a large store of data such as that organized for rapid processing by a computer. **database** *n* data accessible to a computer for processing. **data processing** the conversion of information into a usable form, esp. by computer. < SEE **DATUM.** SEE PANEL.

date¹ (deɪt) *n* **1** the time (of a particular event) referred to in terms of the day, month, and year: date of birth. **2** the time period to which something belongs: relics of an earlier date. **3** (*informal*) a social appointment, esp. between two people of opposite sexes. **4** (*chiefly US informal*) the person of the opposite sex one has a social appointment with.
• *vb* **1** mark or record the date of. **2** determine the date of origin or occurrence of. **3** originate from a particular date or period: a custom dating from the Middle Ages. **4** show up the date of; show to be old-fashioned: His style in clothes dates him. **5** (*informal*) meet (someone of the opposite sex) socially. **dated** *adj* old-fashioned. **dateline** *n* also **the international dateline** a north-south line along the meridian 180° from Greenwich, the date being one day earlier east of this. **to date** up until this time. < ultimately Latin *dare* to give.

date² *n* a brown, oblong, edible fruit from the date-palm, a tree found in warm regions. < ultimately Greek *daktylos* finger.

datum (ˈdeɪtəm, ˈdɑːtəm) *n* **1** *pl* **data** one piece of information. **2** *pl* **datums** something taken as given as the basis for measurement or calculation. < ultimately Latin *dare* to give. SEE PANEL AT **DATA.**

daub (dɔːb) *vb* **1** coat or smear roughly with a soft, sticky substance; plaster. **2** apply (paint, etc.) roughly.
• *n* **1** material used in daubing walls: wattle and daub. **2** a rough picture. **3** daubing; something daubed on. < ultimately Latin *de-* + *albus* white.

daughter (ˈdɔːtə) *n* **1** a human female child in relation to her parents. **2** a female who descends from or is affiliated to a particular group: a daughter of the Revolution. **daughter-in-law** *n, pl* **daughters-in-law** the wife of one's son. < Old English *dohtor.*

daunt (dɔːnt) *vb* dishearten; discourage.

the data is ... or the data are ...?

Once a plural noun in English, data has in recent years entered general usage as a collective noun, indeed to such an extent that it is now possible to say that its grammatical status has changed.

Typically, data is now used with a singular not a plural verb, and with this, not these. So This data is incomplete is preferred by many people to These data are incomplete which, unless used in a technical context, can sound forced and stilted. Moreover, the plural usage goes against our modern-day sense of the word as 'a body of data'.

dauntless *adj* brave; fearless. **dauntlessly** *adv* < ultimately Latin *domitare* to tame.

dawdle (ˈdɔːdl̩) *vb* **1** walk idly; lag behind. **2** waste time in idle actions. **dawdler** *n* < origin unknown.

dawn (dɔːn) *n* **1** the first appearance of daylight. **2** a beginning.
• *vb* **1** start to grow light as the sun rises. **2** start to appear to be understood. < Old English *dagian* to dawn.

day (deɪ) *n* **1** the time of light when the sun is above the horizon. **2** the time taken for the earth to make one complete rotation; 24 hours. **3** a particular day set aside for something: workday; washing-day. **4** a specified period of time: in Wellington's day. **5** an established time for work, school, etc.: an eight-hour day. **day-break** *n* the first daylight; dawn. **day centre** a place providing daytime facilities for the elderly and handicapped. **day-dream** *vb, n* (have) idle, pleasant fantasies. **daylight** *n* **1** the light of the daytime. **2** dawn. **daylight robbery** a shameless swindle. **day nursery** a place caring for young children when their parents are working. **day release** a system allowing employees time off for further training or education. **day-return** *n* a reduced-rate ticket for a journey and a return on the same day. **daytime** *n* the time of light during the day. < Old English *dæg*. SEE PANEL.

daze (deɪz) *vb* stun with a blow, etc.; bewilder.
• *n* a confused or stunned state. < Old Norse *dasask* to become exhausted.

dazzle (ˈdæzl̩) *vb* **1** cause a temporary loss of clear vision in, through exposure to excessively bright light. **2** amaze by an impressive display: a dazzling performance.
• *n* **1** a blinding light. **2** confusion caused by brilliance, glamour, etc. < *daze*.

DC *abbrev* direct current.

de- *prefix* **1** used to show motion away or

---

day by day

A day which is remembered as being particularly happy, important, or rewarding is sometimes referred to as a red-letter day: 'The day Mary won the premium bonds was a real *red-letter day!*' The expression derives from the practice in olden days of printing church calendars with the festivals and saints' days printed in red.

Day features in a number of other idiomatic expressions, including:

call it a day to decide to stop doing something, esp. work: 'I've been hard at this job since 9 o'clock this morning—I think I'll call it a day and go and have some tea.'
day by day as each day passes.
day in, day out every day; continuously.
have had its day to be too old, worn out, etc., to be useful, important, or successful any more.
make someone's day (of an event or experience) to make someone very happy: 'It really made her day when someone actually told her how grateful they were for all her hard work.'
one of these days sometime in the future.
one of those days a day on which many things go wrong: It was one of those days! The washing-machine flooded, I lost my temper with the children, and the dinner got burnt!
save the day to turn a certain defeat or failure into a victory or success: Johnson saved the day for United with a last-minute equalizer.

The names of the days of the week are of Germanic origin, which explains why their modern German equivalents are so similar. Each is a compound whose first element honours either a planet or a god or goddess:

Sunday Old English *sunnandæg,* from *sunne* 'sun' + *dæg* 'day'
Monday Old English *mōnandæg,* from *mōna* 'moon' + *dæg* 'day'
Tuesday Old English *tīwesdæg,* from *Tiw* the Germanic god of war + *dæg* 'day'
Wednesday Old English *wōdnesdæg,* from *Wōden* 'Odin', the chief of the Germanic gods + *dæg* 'day'
Thursday Old English *thursdæg,* from Old High German *Donar* 'Thor', the Germanic god of the sky (and of thunder) + Old English *dæg* 'day'
Friday Old English *frīgedæg,* from Old High German *Frīa* the Germanic goddess of love + Old English *dæg* 'day'
Saturday Old English *sæterndæg,* from Latin *Saturnus* 'Saturn' + Old English *dæg* 'day'

removal: decapitate; dethrone; deduct. **2** used to show a reversal: desegregate; depopulate. **3** used to show a downward action: depress; descend. **4** used to show a reduction: devalue. **5** used as an intensifier: declare; denude. < Latin.

---

dead or **alive**

A person who is dead is not alive. Conversely, a person who is not alive must be dead. Pairs of words like dead and alive or male and female, which pass this two-way *not* test, are known as *complementaries*.

By way of contrast, consider a pair of words like hot and cold. If water is hot, it is certainly not cold, but if it's not cold, it need not be hot. It could be anything on a scale from lukewarm to hottish. Pairs of words of this type which occupy the opposite ends of a scale belong to a much larger group known as *antonyms* (see panel at **big**).

Dead features in a number of expressions, including:

be dead right to be absolutely correct.
cut someone dead to refuse to greet or recognize someone one knows, so showing one's dislike, scorn, etc.
dead beat exhausted.
dead duck something, esp. a plan, that is unlikely to succeed.
dead-end *adj* **1** describing a path or road that is closed at one end. **2** having no opportunities for advancement: a dead-end job.
dead heat a contest in which two or more competitors tie for first place.
dead-pan *adj, adv* with an expressionless face.
dead wood useless people or things: get rid of all the dead wood.
drop dead 1 to die, esp. suddenly. **2** to shut up; stop bothering: 'Drop dead, unless you want a punch-up!'
flog a dead horse to pursue vigorously something that is unlikely to result in success.
over my dead body used to show opposition to something that has just been mentioned: 'Can you lend me £50, Dad?'—'Over my dead body! You've already had £100 from me this week!'
not be seen dead with someone or **in something** to refuse to go with someone or wear something: 'You expect me to wear that old blouse! I wouldn't be seen dead in it!'

---

deacon ('di:kən) *n* **1** a clergyman who ranks below a priest in the Anglican and Roman Catholic Churches. **2** a layman with usually administrative duties in various Protestant Churches. **deaconess** *n* a woman with these duties. < ultimately Greek *diakonos* servant.

dead (dɛd) *adj* **1** no longer having life. **2** lacking sensation; numb. **3** no longer in existence or used: a dead language. **4** no longer having power or effect: The engine's dead. **5** lacking warmth or energy. **6** without interest or activity: a dead town. **7** exact; complete: the dead centre.
• *adv* **1** exactly; completely: dead certain. **2** (*informal*) extremely: dead good.
• *n* **1** dead people or animals. **2** the condition of being dead: risen from the dead. **3** the quietest time: the dead of night. **deaden** *vb* cause to lose energy, feeling, volume, etc. **deadline** *n* a time by which something must be done. **deadlock** *vb, n* (reach) a complete standstill. **deadly** *adj* **1** capable of causing death: a deadly blow. **2** (*informal*) very boring: deadly conversation. **3** death-like in appearance: deadly pale. **4** extremely. **deadliness** *n* **dead-pan** *adj* with no expression on the face. < Old English *dēad*. SEE PANEL. SEE PANEL AT **ALIVE.**

deaf (dɛf) *adj* **1** partially or totally lacking a sense of hearing. **2** unwilling to listen: She turned a deaf ear. **deafness** *n* **deaf-aid** *n* a hearing aid. **deafen** *vb* make deaf, esp. by a very loud noise. **deaf mute** someone who is deaf and dumb. < Old English *dēaf*.

deal[1] (di:l) *n* timber from fir or pine trees. < Middle Dutch *dele* plank.

deal[2] *vb* **dealt; dealing 1** hand out as a portion or portions. **2** hand out (playing-cards) to players in a game of cards. **3** give out; administer: The business was dealt a severe blow. **4** be concerned with: The book deals with wide issues. **5** trade as a business: They deal in antiques.
• *n* **1** someone's turn to deal in a card-game. **2** a business transaction or agreement: They made a deal. **3** treatment given: a rough deal. **4** (*informal*) a lot: a great deal. **dealer** *n* < Old English *dǣl*.

dean (di:n) *n* **1** the head clergyman of a cathedral chapter. **2** the head of a faculty or division within a university. **deanery** *n* < ultimately Latin *decem* ten.

dear (dɪə) *adj* **1** well-loved; precious. **2** esteemed, as in the beginning of a letter: Dear Sir. **3** expensive.
• *n* someone much loved or respected.
• *adv* expensively: It will cost him dear.
• *interj* a mild expression of surprise or

dismay. **dearly** *adv* **dearness** *n* < Old English *dēore.*

dearth (dɜːθ) *n* a lack or scarcity. < Middle English *dere* dear.

death (dɛθ) *n* **1** the ending of life. **2** the condition of being dead. **3** the cause of dying: Alcohol was the death of him. **4** the extinction or disappearance of something: the death of hope. **at death's door** near to death. **death-bed** *n* the bed on which someone dies. **death certificate** an official document stating the time, place, and cause of death. **death duty** a property tax imposed after the death of the owner. **deathly** *adj, adv* like death: a deathly silence. **death penalty** punishment by execution for a crime. **death rate** the number of deaths per 1000 people, recorded annually. **death-trap** *n* a lethal place or situation. **death-watch beetle** a type of beetle whose larvae bore holes in wood, found in old buildings. **to death** utterly: scared to death. < Old English *dēath.*

debar (dɪˈbɑː) *vb* **debarred; debarring** exclude or prohibit from doing or undergoing. < Middle French *des* de- + *barrer* to bar.

debase (dɪˈbeɪs) *vb* lower in value, quality, or character. **debasement** *n* < Latin *de-* + *base:* SEE **BASE²**.

debate (dɪˈbeɪt) *n* a formal discussion based on two opposing points of view. • *vb* **1** hold or participate in a debate. **2** discuss; argue. **debatable** *adj* **debatably** *adv* < Old French *de-* + *batre* to beat.

debauch (dɪˈbɔːtʃ) *vb* lead into self-indulgence or depraved sensuality.

debauchery *n* over-indulgence in carnal or immoral pleasures. < Old French *des-* de- + *bauch* beam.

debilitate (dɪˈbɪlɪˌteɪt) *vb* weaken. **debility** *n* weakness; feebleness. < Latin *debilis* weak.

debit (ˈdɛbɪt) *n* a statement of money owed, esp. recorded in an account book. • *vb* enter as a debit; charge payment to (someone). < Latin *debitum* debt.

debonair (ˌdɛbəˈnɛə) *adj* suave; carefree in manner. < Old French *de bonne aire* of good nature. SEE PANEL.

debrief (diːˈbriːf) *vb* interrogate to gain information about a mission just accomplished. < Latin *de-* + *brevis* short.

debris (ˈdɛbrɪ) *n* loose, scattered fragments; rubble. < Old French *de-* + *brisier* to break.

debt (dɛt) *n* **1** a state of owing esp. money: deep in debt. **2** something owed. **debtor** *n* someone who owes something.

debonair

A person who is pleasantly suave in manner and of elegant appearance is sometimes described as debonair. This word comes from the Old French *debonaire,* which is a stringing together in a single word of the phrase *de bonne aire* meaning 'of good stock' or 'of good nature'.

debt

A regular complaint about English spelling concerns its large number of silent letters, as illustrated by the b in debt. Ironically, many of the silent letters which trouble us today were introduced as 'improvements'.

At the time of the Renaissance the languages of ancient Greece and Rome enjoyed great prestige. English scholars believed that some of this prestige could be transferred to their own language if the link between English words and their classical counterparts were visibly restored.

Consequently, the Middle English word *dette,* (from the Old French *dette,* from the Latin *debitum* 'a debt') was respelt debte, the b being introduced to show its Latin roots. For the same reason a p suddenly appeared in receite (today's receipt) and a c in enditer, (today's indict).

The spellings which had over the centuries come into line with pronunciation were transfigured overnight, although the old ways of pronouncing the words naturally remained unchanged. It was at about this time that the booming invention of printing brought about the fossilization of spellings, so the silent letters inspired by the Renaissance have stayed with us ever since.

See also panel at **asthma.**

< Latin *debēre* to owe. SEE PANEL.
debunk (diːˈbʌŋk) *vb* (*informal*) expose as false. < Latin *de-* + *bunk*: SEE **BUNK**[3].
début (ˈdeɪbjuː) *n* a first public appearance. **débutante** a (*old-fashioned*) a young woman making her formal entrance into society. < French *débuter* to begin.
decade (ˈdɛkeɪd) *n* a ten-year period. < ultimately Greek *deka* ten.
decadent (ˈdɛkədənt) *adj* in decline, esp. in moral or cultural standards. **decadence** *n* **decadently** *adv* < Latin *decadere* to fall.
decaffeinated (dɪˈkæfɪˌneɪtɪd) *adj* (of coffee) with the caffeine content reduced or removed.
decamp (dɪˈkæmp) *vb* **1** dismantle a camp. **2** leave suddenly or secretly.
decant (dɪˈkænt) *vb* pour (liquid) from one vessel to another without disturbing the sediment. **decanter** *n* a glass container with a stopper, in which liquids such as wine are decanted before serving. < Medieval Latin *de-* + *cantus* side.
decapitate (dɪˈkæpɪˌteɪt) *vb* cut off the head of. **decapitation** *n* < Latin *de-* + *caput* head.
decathlon (dɪˈkæθlɒn) *n* an athletic competition consisting of ten events in which each competitor takes part. < French *déca-* ten + Greek *athlon* contest.
decay (dɪˈkeɪ) *vb* **1** decline from a good condition; waste away. **2** decompose or cause to decompose.
• *n* **1** declining. **2** decomposing. < ultimately Latin *decadere* to fall.
decease (dɪˈsiːs) *n* (*formal*) death. **deceased** *adj* dead. **the deceased** someone who has died recently. < Latin *de-* + *cedere* to go.
deceit (dɪˈsiːt) *n* cheating; deceiving. **deceitful** *adj* tending to cheat; dishonest. **deceitfully** *adv* **deceive** *vb* cause to accept or believe something untrue or invalid. **deceiver** *n* < ultimately Latin *de-* + *capere* to take.
decelerate (diːˈsɛləˌreɪt) *vb* cause to reduce or reduce speed. **deceleration** *n* < *de-* + *accelerate*.
decent (ˈdiːsn̩t) *adj* **1** in accordance with accepted standards of propriety; respectable. **2** reasonable; adequate: He earns a decent salary. **3** considerate; obliging: He's a decent fellow. **decency** *n* **decently** *adv* < ultimately Latin *decēre* to be fitting.
decentralize (diːˈsɛntrəˌlaɪz) *vb* distribute (functions and powers) from a central authority to regional, etc., ones. **decentralization** *n*
deception (dɪˈsɛpʃən) *n* **1** deceiving or being deceived. **2** something that deceives; trick. **deceptive** *adj* deceiving; misleading. **deceptively** *adv* < Latin *decipere* to deceive.
decibel (ˈdɛsɪˌbɛl) *n* a unit for measuring the relative intensity of sound. < *dec-* tenth + *bel* from Alexander Graham *Bell*, died 1922, US scientist.
decide (dɪˈsaɪd) *vb* **1** make a choice or judgment about, after consideration. **2** settle; determine: His exam results decided his future. **decider** *n* **decided** *adj* **1** untroubled; clear. **2** determined. **decidedly** *adv* < ultimately Latin *de-* + *caedere* to cut.
deciduous (dɪˈsɪdjʊəs) *adj* **1** (of a tree) with leaves which fall off every year. **2** being shed at the end of a growing period: deciduous antlers. < ultimately Latin *de-* + *cadere* to fall.
decimal (ˈdɛsɪməl) *n* a fraction expressed with a power of ten as a denominator, written as a dot followed by digits representing tenths, hundredths, etc., for example 0.25.
• *adj* reckoned in tenths or multiples of ten. **decimal currency** currency in which each monetary unit is one tenth or one hundredth the value of the one above it. **decimalize** *vb* **1** express in decimal form. **2** convert (measurements, weights, etc.) into a decimal system. **decimalization** *n* < Latin *decima* tithe.
decimate (ˈdɛsɪˌmeɪt) *vb* kill or destroy one tenth of (an army, etc.); kill or destroy a large part of. < ultimately Latin *decem* ten. SEE PANEL.
decipher (dɪˈsaɪfə) *vb* uncover the meaning of (something difficult to read or interpret, such as a message in code or untidy handwriting). **decipherable** *adj* **decipherment** *n* < Latin *de-* + *cipher* from Arabic *ṣifr* empty, zero.
decision (dɪˈsɪʒən) *n* **1** reaching a judgment; making up one's mind. **2** a

decimate

In its broad, everyday application, decimate means 'to kill or destroy a large part of' as in The earthquake *decimated* the population. Some careful users of English, however, prefer to restrict the usage of the verb to the original meaning 'to kill or destroy one tenth of'.

judgment made or conclusion reached. **3** clarity and firmness in deciding. **decisive** *adj* **1** showing firmness in making up one's mind; resolute. **2** settling something unquestionably: a decisive move. < Latin *decidere* to decide.

deck[1] (dɛk) *n* **1** one of the horizontal floor levels on a ship. **2** something like this, such as a floor on a bus with more than one level. **3** a record-player turntable. **4** a device for playing or recording on magnetic tape, usually part of a stereo system; tape deck. **5** (*informal*) a pack of cards. **deck-chair** *n* an adjustable, folding chair of canvas stretched over a frame of wood or metal. < Middle Low German *vordecken* to cover.

deck[2] *vb* dress; decorate: decked out in his Sunday best. < Dutch *dekken* to cover.

declaim (dɪˈkleɪm) *vb* speak or deliver rhetorically or dramatically. **declamation** *n* **declamatory** *adj* < Latin *de-* + *clamare* to cry out.

declare (dɪˈklɛə) *vb* **1** make known in an explicit or formal manner. **2** state emphatically: He declared his love for her. **3** make a statement to customs officials concerning (goods on which duty may be charged). **4** (*cricket*) decide to end the innings of one's side before all the batsmen are out. **declaration** *n* **declare war** announce formally the start of hostilities. < ultimately Latin *de-* + *clarus* clear.

decline (dɪˈklaɪn) *vb* **1** descend; slope downwards. **2** refuse: She declined the offer. **3** lose power; wane. **4** give the grammatical forms of (a noun, pronoun, etc.) in a specific order.
• *n* a decrease in power or strength: The decline of the Roman Empire. < Latin *de-* + *clinare* to incline.

decode (diːˈkəʊd) *vb* convert (a coded message) into ordinary language. **decoder** *n* **1** someone or something that decodes messages, etc. **2** a device forming part of a stereo system which separates the sounds into channels.

decompose (ˌdiːkəmˈpəʊz) *vb* **1** (of a substance) break down into its constituent parts. **2** decay; rot. **decomposition** *n*

decompress (ˌdiːkəmˈprɛs) *vb* release from pressure. **decompression** *n* **1** decompressing. **2** the slow reduction of air pressure on, for example a diver who has been in compressed air.

decontaminate (ˌdiːkənˈtæmɪˌneɪt) *vb* remove contamination, esp. radioactivity from. **decontamination** *n*

décor (ˈdeɪkɔː) *n* the style in which a room, etc., is decorated and furnished. < Latin *decorare* to decorate.

decorate (ˈdɛkəˌreɪt) *vb* **1** add ornamental details to in order to make more appealing or striking. **2** put new coverings of paint, wallpaper, etc., on (an interior wall). **3** award an honour to: He was decorated for bravery. **decoration** *n* **1** the process of decorating. **2** *pl* things that decorate, such as flags or streamers, on festive occasions. **3** a medal, etc., conferred as a mark of honour. **decorative** *adj* ornamental; pleasant in appearance. **decorator** *n* someone who decorates, esp. professionally. < ultimately Latin *decus* ornament.

decorous (ˈdɛkərəs) *adj* correct in behaviour; decent. **decorum** *n* correctness in behaviour; dignity. < Latin *decor* grace.

decoy (ˈdiːkɔɪ) *n* something used to lead an animal or person into a trap.
• *vb* (dɪˈkɔɪ) lure into danger with a decoy. < probably Dutch *de kooi* the cage.

decrease (dɪˈkriːs) *vb* make or become smaller or less in size, amount, number, or intensity.
• *n* (ˈdiːkriːs) **1** the process of decreasing. **2** the amount of decrease of something. **decreasingly** *adv* < Latin *de-* + *crescere* to grow.

decree (dɪˈkriː) *n* **1** an order backed by force of law made by a governing body. **2** a judicial decision, as made in an equity or divorce court.
• *vb* order by decree. **decree nisi** a divorce order which becomes absolute after a fixed time. < ultimately Latin *de-* + *cernere* to judge.

decrepit (dɪˈkrɛpɪt) *adj* weakened by age or use; ruined. **decrepitude** *n* < ultimately Latin *de-* + *crepare* to creak.

decry (dɪˈkraɪ) *vb* **decried; decrying** express disapproval of; disparage. < Old French *des-* dé- + *crier* to cry.

dedicate (ˈdɛdɪˌkeɪt) *vb* **1** consecrate. **2** give all one's time and attention to: He dedicated himself to his work. **3** address (something such as a book or song) to someone, as a sign of esteem or affection. **dedication** *n* **dedicatory** *adj* < ultimately Latin *de-* + *dicare* to proclaim.

deduce (dɪˈdjuːs) *vb* reach (a conclusion) by weighing up evidence. **deducible** *adj* **deduction** *n* < ultimately Latin *de-* + *ducere* to lead.

deduct (dɪˈdʌkt) *vb* take away or subtract (a certain amount) from a total. **deduction** *n* < ultimately Latin *deducere* to lead away.

deed (di:d) *n* **1** something that is done: good deeds. **2** a signed, written or printed document containing a legal agreement, dealing with property transfer, etc. **deed of covenant** an agreement to pay a yearly amount to a charity, etc., which may also claim the tax due on this amount. **deed poll** a deed executed by one party, for example, for the purpose of changing one's name. < Old English *dǣd.*

deem (di:m) *vb* (*formal*) consider; judge. < Old English *dēman.*

deep (di:p) *adj* **1** placed or extending far from a surface: a deep well; deep wardrobe. **2** near the boundaries in a sports field, esp. far from the batsman in cricket. **3** profound or obscure: deep thoughts. **4** intense or extreme: deep blue; deep sleep. **5** (of a voice) low-pitched and full-bodied. **6** strongly felt: deep feelings. **7** engrossed: She was deep in her books.
• *adv* to a specified or great depth: They waded knee-deep in water.
• *n* **1** a vast, deep place. **2 the deep** the sea. **deeply** *adv* **deepen** *vb* make or become deeper. **deep-freeze** *vb, n* (store or freeze in) a freezer. **deep-fry** *vb* fry (food) by completely immersing in fat or hot oil. **deep-seated** *adj* strongly-rooted: a deep-seated hatred. **go off the deep end** (*informal*) lose one's temper. < Old English *dēop.*

deer (dɪə) *n, pl* **deer** a swift-footed, ruminant mammal, the male of which usually bears antlers. **deerstalker** *n* a soft, close-fitting cap with peaks at the back and front and sometimes ear-flaps. < Old English *dēor* beast. SEE PANEL.

deface (dɪˈfeɪs) *vb* ruin or damage the surface appearance of. **defacement** *n* < Middle French *desfacier.*

deer

Nowadays the word deer conjures up a picture of a particular type of hoofed animal. Until the 16th century, however, the word meant any kind of animal. It derives from the Old English *dēor* or 'beast'.

Interestingly, while the Old English word has undergone a narrowing of meaning over the centuries, its Old High German equivalent, *tior,* has retained its original broad sense. In modern German *Tier* still means 'beast'.

de facto (deɪ ˈfæktəʊ) *adv* in actuality.
• *adj* actually existing, whether by legal right or not. < Latin.

defame (dɪˈfeɪm) *vb* injure the reputation of by speaking maliciously; libel or slander. **defamation** *n* **defamatory** *adj* < ultimately Latin *de-* + *fama* fame.

default (dɪˈfɔ:lt) *vb* fail to do what one is supposed to: default on payments.
• *n* a failure to complete, appear, pay, etc.: The other team won by default. **in default of** in absence of. **defaulter** *n* < ultimately Latin *de-* + *fallere* to deceive.

defeat (dɪˈfi:t) *vb* **1** gain victory over. **2** frustrate; thwart.
• *n* the loss of a battle, competition, etc. **defeatist** *n* someone who accepts or expects defeat too readily; pessimist. **defeatism** *n* < ultimately Latin *dis-* + *facere* to do.

defecate (ˈdɛfəˌkeɪt) *vb* discharge waste via the bowels. **defecation** *n* < Latin *de-* + *faex* dregs.

defect (dɪˈfɛkt) *vb* desert one's cause, party, or country; switch allegiances. **defection** *n* **defector** *n*
• *n* (ˈdi:fɛkt) a flaw or irregularity. **defective** *adj* flawed or incomplete. **defectively** *adv* **defectiveness** *n* < Latin *deficere* to desert. SEE PANEL.

defence (dɪˈfɛns) *n* **1** resisting attack; defending. **2** a method or structure which defends. **3** a supportive argument or justification against an accusation. **4** (*law*) the defendant's case and the legal counsel who act for him or her. **defenceless** *adj* unprotected. < Latin *defendere* to defend.

defend (dɪˈfɛnd) *vb* **1** protect against attack. **2** maintain (a point of view, etc.) by argument; justify. **3** (in a law-court) represent an accused person. **defendant** *n* someone who is accused or sued in a court of law. **defender** *n* **defensible** *adj* capable of being defended. **defensibly** *adv* **defensibility** *n* **defensive** *adj* protective. **defensively** *adv* **on the defensive** prepared to react against

defective or **deficient?**

Defective means 'flawed or incomplete; not operating properly': His eyesight is *defective.* Each *defective* component has been replaced.

Deficient means 'lacking a sufficient or adequate supply': *deficient* in vitamins; mentally *deficient.*

expected criticism or aggression. < Latin *defendere*.

defer[1] (dɪˈfɜː) *vb* **deferred; deferring** put off until later; postpone. **deferment** or **deferral** *n* < ultimately Latin *differe*.

defer[2] *vb* **deferred; deferring** submit to the wishes or authority of another, often through respect. **deference** *n* respect. **deferential** *adj* **deferentially** *adv* **in deference to** out of respect for. < ultimately Latin *deferre* to bear down.

defiance (dɪˈfaɪəns) *n* a disposition to resist or disobey. **defiant** *adj* **defiantly** *adv* < SEE **DEFY.**

deficient (dɪˈfɪʃənt) *adj* with an insufficient or inadequate supply. **deficiency** *n* **1** lacking something. **2** a shortage or lack. **deficiency disease** a disease caused by a lack of vitamins, etc., in one's diet. < ultimately Latin *deficere* to be wanting; SEE PANEL AT **DEFECT.**

deficit (ˈdɛfɪsɪt) *n* **1** the amount of a shortage. **2** an excess of spending over income. < Latin *deficere*.

defile (dɪˈfaɪl) *vb* make unclean; pollute. **defilement** *n* < Old French *de-* + *fouler* to trample.

define (dɪˈfaɪn) *vb* **1** state the meaning of (a word, phrase, etc.). **2** make clear or exact: My duties aren't well-defined. **3** be the essence of; identify. **definable** *adj* **definition** *n* **1** a precise explanation of a word or phrase, or of the essence of something. **2** distinctness or clarity of outline. **definitive** *adj* **1** final and decisive. **2** authoritative and comprehensive: a definitive work. < ultimately Latin *de-* + *finis* boundary. SEE PANEL AT **DEFINITE.**

definite (ˈdɛfɪnət) *adj* **1** with precise boundaries. **2** clear and unambiguous. **3** certain; decided. **definitely** *adv* **definite article** the word the. < Latin *definire* to define. SEE PANEL.

> **definite** or **definitive?**
>
> These two words are sometimes confused. Definite, the commoner word, means 'clear and unambiguous; certain and decided': *definite* proof; a *definite* answer.
>
> Definitive means 'final and decisive': a *definitive* victory and 'authoritative and comprehensive': the *definitive* reference work on Greek mythology.

deflate (diːˈfleɪt) *vb* **1** let air or gas escape from (a balloon, inflated tyre, etc.). **2** cause to lose self-confidence or esteem. **3** reduce (the availability of money in a country), esp. to combat inflation. **deflation** *n* < Latin *de-* + *-flate*, as in *inflate*.

deflect (dɪˈflɛkt) *vb* turn away from a fixed direction. **deflector** *n* **deflexion** *n* < Latin *de-* + *flectere* to bend.

deform (dɪˈfɔːm) *vb* ruin the shape or form of. **deformation** *n* **deformed** *adj* misshapen. **deformity** *n* **1** the condition of being deformed. **2** a physical blemish; disfigurement. < Latin *de-* + *forma* form.

defraud (dɪˈfrɔːd) *vb* trick (someone) out of something; cheat. < Latin *de-* + *fraus* fraud.

defrost (diːˈfrɒst) *vb* free from ice or frost; thaw: defrost the fridge.

deft (dɛft) *adj* nimble; dexterous. **deftly** *adv* **deftness** *n* < Middle English *defte*.

defunct (dɪˈfʌŋkt) *adj* **1** no longer existing, valid, or functioning. **2** dead. < Latin *de-* + *fungi* to perform.

defuse (diːˈfjuːz) *vb* **1** remove the fuse from (a bomb, etc.) in order to make it safe. **2** make (a situation) less tense or dangerous: The crisis was defused.

defy (dɪˈfaɪ) *vb* **defied; defying 1** disobey or confront without fear; resist. **2** dare (someone) to do something considered to be impossible: I defy you to try. **3** resist or elude, often in a confusing way: The code defied all attempts to break it. < ultimately Latin *de-* + *fidere* to trust.

degenerate (dɪˈdʒɛnəˌreɪt) *vb* go from a higher to a lower level of quality or condition.
• *adj* (dɪˈdʒɛnərət) having sunk or declined to a lower level. **degeneration** *n* < ultimately Latin *de-* + *genus* race.

degrade (dɪˈgreɪd) *vb* **1** lower in status or rank; demote. **2** lower the dignity or self-esteem of. **degradation** *n* **degrading** *adj* debasing; humiliating. < ultimately Latin *de-* + *gradus* step.

degree (dɪˈgriː) *n* **1** a stage in a process or series. **2** an extent or level of intensity: a high degree of excellence. **3** an academic title awarded to successful students on a course, or to anyone as an honour. **4** a unit of the measurement of temperature or angles, represented by the symbol °. **by degrees** gradually. **to a degree 1** to a great extent. **2** rather; quite. < ultimately Latin *de-* + *gradus* step.

dehydrate (diːˈhaɪdreɪt) *vb* take away the water content from; lose water content. **dehydration** *n*

de-ice (diːˈaɪs) *vb* take away ice or prevent it forming on a surface such as a windscreen. **de-icer** *n*

deify (ˈdiːɪˌfaɪ, ˈdeɪɪˌfaɪ) *vb* **deified; deifying** treat as a god; glorify. **deification** *n* < ultimately Latin *deus* god.

deign (deɪn) *vb* (*formal*) consider worthy of doing; condescend. < ultimately Latin *dignus* worthy.

deity (ˈdiːɪtɪ, ˈdeɪɪtɪ) *n* a divine being; god or goddess; essential nature of being divine. < ultimately Greek *dios* heavenly.

déjà vu (ˌdeɪʒɑː ˈvuː) the sensation that one has experienced a current event or situation in the past. < French: already seen.

dejected (dɪˈdʒektɪd) *adj* miserable; depressed. **dejectedly** *adv* **dejection** *n* < ultimately Latin *de-* + *jacere* to throw.

delay (dɪˈleɪ) *vb* **1** put off; postpone. **2** detain; make late.
• *n* **1** delaying or being delayed. **2** the amount of time something is delayed. **delayed-action** *adj* functioning after a usually fixed interval of time. < ultimately Latin *de-* + *laxare* to slacken.

delectable (dɪˈlɛktəbl̩) *adj* extremely pleasant; delicious. < ultimately Latin *delectare* to delight.

delegate (ˈdɛlɪgət) *n* someone representing and acting on behalf of others.
• *vb* (ˈdɛlɪˌgeɪt) **1** entrust (authority or responsibility) to another. **2** appoint as a delegate. **delegation** *n* **1** delegating. **2** a group of people representing and acting for others. < Latin *de-* + *legare* to send.

delete (dɪˈliːt) *vb* cut, blot, or strike out, for example on a written or printed page. **deletion** *n* < Latin *delēre* to wipe out.

deleterious (ˌdɛlɪˈtɪərɪəs) *adj* physically or mentally harmful. < ultimately Greek *dēleisthai* to hurt.

deliberate (dɪˈlɪbərət) *adj* **1** spoken or done with intent. **2** carefully considered; definite: deliberate movements.
• *vb* (dɪˈlɪbəˌreɪt) consider and often discuss carefully before deciding. **deliberately** *adv* **deliberation** *n* **1** considering or discussing carefully. **2** careful unhurriedness in movement or speech. **deliberative** *adj* < Latin *de-* + *libra* scales.

delicate (ˈdɛlɪkət) *adj* **1** subtle or fine in quality or structure. **2** subtly pleasant in effect on the senses: delicate colours; delicate taste. **3** extremely frail or sensitive: delicate plants; delicate health. **4** calling for careful treatment: a delicate situation. **5** precise; sensitive to the touch: delicate mechanism. **delicately** *adv* **delicateness** *n* **delicacy** *n* **1** being subtle or delicate. **2** showing tact. **3** a rare or choice food. < Latin *delicatus* giving pleasure.

delicatessen (ˌdɛlɪkəˈtɛsn̩) *n* a shop selling choice prepared foods. < ultimately Latin *delicatus.*

delicious (dɪˈlɪʃəs) *adj* extremely pleasant to the senses, esp. of taste and smell. < ultimately Latin *delicere* to allure.

delight (dɪˈlaɪt) *vb* **1** give great pleasure (to). **2** take great pleasure in: He delights in listening to Bach.
• *n* great pleasure; something giving this. **delighted** *adj* **delightful** *adj* giving great pleasure; charming. **delightfully** *adv* < ultimately Latin *de-* + *lacere* to allure.

delimit (diːˈlɪmɪt) *vb* establish the boundaries of. **delimitation** *n*

delineate (dɪˈlɪnɪˌeɪt) *vb* **1** show by drawing an outline of. **2** describe in a detailed manner. **delineation** *n* < Latin *de-* + *linea* line.

delinquent (dɪˈlɪŋkwənt) *adj* guilty of committing an offence or neglecting a duty.
• *n* someone who is delinquent, esp. someone young who commits an offence: juvenile delinquent. **delinquency** *n* < Latin *de-* + *linquere* to leave.

delirium (dɪˈlɪərɪəm) *n, pl* **deliriums, deliria 1** a confused state of mind, during fever, etc., often accompanied by hallucinations. **2** extreme excitement; frenzy. **delirious** *adj* **deliriously** *adv* **delirium tremens** a state of shaking and often frightening hallucinations caused by chronic drinking of alcohol. < ultimately Latin *de-* + *lira* furrow.

deliver (dɪˈlɪvə) *vb* **1** take to or hand over to someone: deliver letters; deliver goods. **2** aim at an intended goal: He delivered a fast ball; deliver a blow. **3** utter: She delivered a stirring speech. **4** set free; rescue. **5** help to bring to birth or give birth to. **deliverer** *n* **deliverance** *n* rescue; liberation. **delivery** *n* **1** delivering or being delivered. **2** an often regular conveyance of, for example goods or letters. **3** the way in which something is performed, such as bowling in cricket. **4** the way in which a speech is made. **delivery note** a check-list of items sent with goods from a seller to the buyer. < ultimately Latin *de-* + *liberare* to liberate.

delphinium (dɛlˈfɪnɪəm) *n* one of a group of plants of the buttercup family with often blue flowers in spikes. < ultimately Greek *delphis* dolphin.

delta (ˈdɛltə) *n* **1** a triangle of land formed between branches of a river at its mouth: the Mekong Delta. **2** the fourth letter of the Greek alphabet. < Greek.

delude (dɪˈluːd) *vb* mislead; deceive. **delusion** *n* **1** a false idea. **2** a persistent state of believing false notions, to the point of madness. **delusive** *adj* < ultimately Latin *de-* + *ludere* to play. SEE PANEL AT **ALLUDE.**

deluge (ˈdɛljuːdʒ) *n* **1** a disastrous flood. **2** heavy rainfall. **3** something which comes quickly in large quantities: a deluge of letters.
• *vb* flood; overwhelm. < ultimately Latin *dis-* + *lavere* to wash.

de luxe (də ˈlʌks) *adj* of superior quality; luxurious: a de luxe hotel. < French: of luxury.

delve (dɛlv) *vb* **1** look very carefully for information. **2** dig or act in a way similar to digging: He delved into his pockets. < Old English *delfan.*

demagogue (ˈdɛməˌgɒg) *n* someone who gains the support of people by arousing their prejudices and emotions rather than by reasoning. < ultimately Greek *dēmos* people + *agein* to lead.

demand (dɪˈmɑːnd) *n* **1** the act of asking with or as if with authority or right. **2** the desire by consumers for particular goods or services: There's a great demand for computers these days. **3** a pressing need or claim: demands on someone's time.
• *vb* **1** ask (as if) by right. **2** require: The work demands great patience. **demanding** *adj* making demands; exacting. **demand note** a payment request. **in demand** sought eagerly. **on demand** immediately something is demanded: to be shown on demand < ultimately Latin *de-* + *mandare* to entrust.

demarcation (ˌdiːmɑːˈkeɪʃən) *n* the fixing or marking of boundaries, for example between areas of duties at work: demarcation dispute. < Spanish *demarcar* to delimit.

demean (dɪˈmiːn) *vb* lessen the dignity of; degrade. **demeaning** *adj* < *de-* + *mean*[2].

demeanour (dɪˈmiːnə) *n* someone's general behaviour towards others. < ultimately Latin *de-* + *minari* to threaten.

demented (dɪˈmɛntɪd) *adj* driven insane; crazy. < Latin *demens.*

demerara (ˌdɛməˈrɛərə) *n* unrefined, brown sugar from the West Indies. < *Demerara,* region of Guyana.

demilitarized (diːˈmɪlɪtəˌraɪzd) *adj* with no military personnel or installations: a demilitarized zone.

demise (dɪˈmaɪz) *n* **1** ending; collapse. **2** (*formal or euphemistic*) death. < Latin *de-* + *mittere* to send.

demist (diːˈmɪst) *vb* clear mist from. **demister** *n*

demo (ˈdɛməʊ) *n, pl* **demos** (*informal*) a demonstration.

demob (diːˈmɒb) *vb* **demobbed; demobbing** (*informal*) demobilize.
• *n* (*informal*) demobilization.

demobilize (diːˈməʊbɪˌlaɪz) *vb* discharge from service in the military. **demobilization** *n*

democracy (dɪˈmɒkrəsɪ) *n* **1** government by the people, esp. through elected representatives. **2** a nation governed like this. **democrat** *n* **1** someone who favours social equality. **2 Democrat** a member of the US Democratic party. **democratic** *adj* **1** relating to or favouring democracy or equal rights. **2 Democratic** of the US Democratic party. **democratically** *adv* **democratize** *vb* make democratic. **democratization** *n* < ultimately Greek *dēmos* people + *kratos* power.

demolish (dɪˈmɒlɪʃ) *vb* **1** destroy or pull down (a building, etc.). **2** break down or refute (an argument, etc.). **3** (*informal*) eat up. **demolition** *n* < ultimately Latin *de-* + *moliri* to construct.

demon (ˈdiːmən) *n* **1** a spirit of evil; cruel person. **2** someone with very strong drive or determination: He's a demon for work. **demoniacal** or **demonic** *adj* like or influenced by a demon. < Greek *daimōn.*

demonstrate (ˈdɛmənˌstreɪt) *vb* **1** show or explain clearly with evidence. **2** show the function, value, or use of, to a prospective buyer. **3** participate in a demonstration. **demonstration** *n* **1** showing; displaying. **2** an explanation and display of an item to a prospective buyer. **3** a mass gathering or procession to express the feelings of a group about, for example, political issues. **4** a show of military force. **demonstrator** *n* **demonstrative** *adj* **1** showing or explaining with proof. **2** openly showing one's emotions. **demonstratively** *adv* **demonstrativeness** *n* **demonstrative pronoun** a pronoun that refers to the person, thing, etc., named by the noun it represents, such as this in This is my house. < Latin *de-* + *monstrare* to show.

demoralize (dɪˈmɒrəˌlaɪz) *vb* discourage; dishearten. **demoralization** *n*

demote (dɪˈməʊt) *vb* reduce in grade or rank. < *de-* + *-mote,* as in pro*mote.*

demure (dɪˈmjʊə) *adj* quietly serious or modest, or seemingly like this. **demurely** *adv* **demureness** *n* < Middle French *demourer* to linger.

den (dɛn) *n* **1** the lair of a wild animal. **2** a place where secret or illegal activity is carried on: an opium den. **3** a secluded room, for someone to work or relax in private. < Old English *denn.*

denationalize (diːˈnæʃənəˌlaɪz) *vb* transfer from state control or ownership to private interests. **denationalization** *n*

denial (dɪˈnaɪəl) *n* **1** a statement that something is false. **2** a refusal to comply with a wish or request: a denial of freedom.

denier (ˈdɛnɪə) *n* a unit of weight, used in measuring the fineness of textiles such as silk or nylon. < ultimately Latin *decem* ten.

denigrate (ˈdɛnɪˌgreɪt) *vb* belittle the reputation of; defame. < ultimately Latin *de-* + *niger* black.

denim (ˈdɛnɪm) *n* a durable, twilled, cotton fabric, usually blue, used in making clothes. **denims** *pl n* denim trousers; jeans. < French (*serge*) *de Nîmes,* town in France. SEE PANEL.

denomination (dɪˌnɒmɪˈneɪʃən) *n* **1** a title or name, for example, of a category. **2** a particular branch of a church: the Anglican denomination. **3** a unit of value or size, esp. of money. **denominational** *adj* of a specified religious denomination. **denominationalism** *n* < Latin *de-* + *nominare* to name.

denominator (dɪˈnɒmɪˌneɪtə) *n* the part of a fraction written below the line, for example, 2 in ½, showing how many parts a unit is divided into.

denote (dɪˈnəʊt) *vb* **1** be a symbol or sign for; indicate. **2** (esp. of words or phrases) mean. **denotation** *n* < Latin *de-* + *notare* to note.

denouement (deɪˈnuːmã) *n* the resolution of a plot, at the end of a play, story, etc. < ultimately Latin *de-* + *nodus* knot.

denounce (dɪˈnaʊns) *vb* **1** condemn publicly or strongly. **2** formally announce the termination of (a treaty, etc.). < Latin *de-* + *nuntiare* to report, make known.

dense (dɛns) *adj* **1** closely packed together; thick: dense forest; dense fog. **2** difficult to understand; complicated: dense writing. **3** stupid. **densely** *adv* **denseness** *n* **density** *n* **1** a state of being packed closely together. **2** stupidity. **3** the relationship of mass to volume of a substance. < Latin *densus.*

dent (dɛnt) *n* **1** a depression in a surface made by pressure or a blow. **2** a noticeable lessening: The holiday made a dent in our funds.

• *vb* make a dent on or in; become dented. < Middle English: blow, alteration of *dint.*

dental (ˈdɛntl̩) *adj* concerning the teeth or their treatment. **dental floss** a strong, waxed thread, used to clean between the teeth. **dentifrice** *n* a liquid, paste, or powder for cleaning the teeth. **dentist** *n* someone qualified to treat and fill teeth or replace teeth with artificial ones. **dentistry** *n* the dental profession. **denture** *n* often **dentures** a set of artificial teeth. < Latin *dens* tooth.

denude (dɪˈnjuːd) *vb* **1** take away all covering from; strip. **2** take something important from. **denudation** *n* < Latin *de-* + *nudus* bare.

denunciation (dɪˌnʌnsɪˈeɪʃən) *n* condemnation, esp. in public.

deny (dɪˈnaɪ) *vb* **denied; denying 1** assert to be untrue; reject as untrue. **2** refuse to recognize; disown. **3** refuse to grant; prevent from having: The prisoner was denied all visitors. **deny oneself** restrain oneself from indulgence in pleasures, esp. of the senses. < Latin *de-* + *negare* to deny. SEE PANEL AT **REFUTE.**

deodorant (diːˈəʊdərənt) *n* a prepared substance that takes away or masks unwanted smells. **deodorize** *vb* take away or mask the odour of. **deodorization** *n*

depart (dɪˈpɑːt) *vb* **1** leave; go away. **2** turn away from: She departed from her routine. **3** (esp. of buses or trains) begin a journey. **departed** *adj* **1** gone; past. **2** recently dead. **departure** *n* **1** the act of leaving. **2** the act of setting out on a new course of action. < ultimately Latin *de-* + *pars* part.

department (dɪˈpɑːtmənt) *n* **1** a specialized unit or division of an organi-

denim jeans

Both denim and jeans derive from place-names. Denim has come into English from the French expression (*serge*) *de Nîmes,* '(serge) made in Nîmes', a town in France. Jeans, on the other hand, is a plural form of *jean,* a 16th-century reduction of *jean fustian,* in which jean is a transformation of the Middle English name for Genoa, *Gene,* a city in Italy.

zation, shop, or business. **2** an area of activity. **3** an administrative district in France. **departmental** *adj* **department store** a large shop divided into areas, each selling a separate type of goods. < Middle French *departir* to divide.

depend (dɪˈpɛnd) *vb* **1** be decided by a particular condition: Where we go depends on how much time we have. **2** be reliant on: She depends on her pension. **dependable** *adj* reliable. **dependability** *n* **dependably** *adv* **dependant** *n* someone who relies on another for support, esp. financial. **dependence** *n* **1** being subject to something. **2** reliance; trust. **3** a strong need or addiction: drug dependence. **dependency** *n* a country governed by another state. **dependent** *adj* **1** subject to: Play is dependent on the weather. **2** addicted to; needing strongly. **3** under the control of another. < ultimately Latin *de-* + *pendēre* to hang. SEE PANEL.

depict (dɪˈpɪkt) *vb* **1** show by drawing or painting. **2** describe. **depiction** *n* < Latin *de-* + *pingere* to paint.

depilatory (dɪˈpɪlətərɪ) *n* a chemical which removes unwanted hair from the body.
• *adj* able to or used for removing hair. < Latin *de-* + *pilus* hair.

deplete (dɪˈpliːt) *vb* lessen the amount of by using up; exhaust: depleted resources. **depletion** *n* < Latin *de-* + *plēre* to fill.

deplore (dɪˈplɔː) *vb* **1** strongly disapprove of. **2** grieve for. **deplorable** *adj* **1** regrettable. **2** very bad: deplorable behaviour. **deplorably** *adv* < Latin *de-* + *plorare* to wail.

deploy (dɪˈplɔɪ) *vb* **1** (of ships, troops, etc.) spread out in battle formation. **2** put or be put ready for action systematically: deployed resources. **deployment** *n* < Latin *displicare* to scatter, unfold, display.

depopulate (dɪˈpɒpjʊˌleɪt) *vb* decrease the size of the population of (an area). **depopulation** *n* < Latin *de-* + *populari* to ravage.

deport (dɪˈpɔːt) *vb* expel (an unwanted alien, etc.) from a country by court order. **deportation** *n* expulsion. < Latin *de-* + *portare* to carry.

deportment (dɪˈpɔːtmənt) *n* someone's behaviour or posture.

depose (dɪˈpəʊz) *vb* **1** remove from power or authority. **2** bear witness or testify under oath. **deposition** *n* **1** removal from power. **2** a usually written and sworn statement, used in court as evidence. **3** depositing. < ultimately Latin *deponere* to put down, deposit.

deposit (dɪˈpɒzɪt) *n* **1** an amount of money paid into a bank. **2** a down payment or guarantee of payment on a purchase. **3** something accumulated or laid down, such as natural layers of matter: mineral deposits.
• *vb* **1** put away (esp. money or valuables) for safe keeping, in a bank. **2** lay or put down. **3** make an initial payment; pay a sum of money as a guarantee. **4** lay down naturally as a covering: Rivers deposit mud. **deposit account** a bank account on which interest is paid on money deposited. **depositor** *n* someone who deposits, esp. money. **depository** *n* a place for storage or safe keeping. < Latin *deponere*.

depot (ˈdɛpəʊ) *n* **1** a place for storing military supplies. **2** a regimental headquarters; place for accepting and training new recruits. **3** a place for storing goods, and from where they are sent out. **4** a place or garage for maintenance work on buses or trains. < Latin *depositus*, from *deponere*.

deprave (dɪˈpreɪv) *vb* corrupt the morals of; pervert. **depravation** *n* **depraved** *adj* immoral; perverted. **depravity** *n* < ultimately Latin *de-* + *pravus* crooked.

deprecate (ˈdɛprɪˌkeɪt) *vb* **1** regretfully show disapproval of; belittle. **2** ward off (praise, blame, etc.) in a polite way. **deprecation** *n* **deprecatory** *adj* < Latin

---

dependant or **dependent?**

Care needs to be taken over the spelling of the words dependant and dependent. Dependant is a noun meaning 'someone who relies on another person for financial support': Do you have any *dependants* apart from your wife?

Dependent is an adjective meaning 'relying on; subject to': They are increasingly *dependent* on our support; *dependent* territories.

Of all the words that derive from depend, only the noun dependant is spelt with an a. All the others such as independent, dependency, and dependence are spelt with an e.

---

de- + *precari* to pray. SEE PANEL.
depreciate (dɪˈpriːʃɪˌeɪt) *vb* **1** lower in value or price. **2** belittle or disparage. **depreciation** *n* **depreciatory** *adj* < Latin *de-* + *pretium* price. SEE PANEL AT **DEPRECATE.**
depress (dɪˈprɛs) *vb* **1** sadden; dishearten. **2** press down: depress a button. **3** decrease the activity of (esp. something financial): a depressed market. **depressant** *n* a drug or chemical which slows down the activity of the nervous system; sedative. **depression** *n* **1** a condition of extreme sadness and loss of vitality. **2** a period of high unemployment and low economic activity. **3** a hollow or sunken area. **4** an area of low atmospheric pressure often accompanied by rain. **5** lowering or pressing down. **depressive** *adj* **1** depressing. **2** also *n* (a person) liable to mental depression. < ultimately Latin *de-* + *premere* to press.
deprive (dɪˈpraɪv) *vb* withhold or take something away from. **deprivation** *n* **1** being deprived. **2** depriving; loss. **deprived child** a child who has not been able to have a normal home life. < Latin *de-* + *privare* to deprive.
depth (dɛpθ) *n* **1** a deep place; part of a place far from the outside or surface: the depths of the forest. **2** the distance measured between the top and bottom or front and back of something. **3** intensity of for example colour. **4** lowness of pitch in a sound or voice. **5** intensity of thought or feeling; profundity. **depth-charge** *n* an anti-submarine explosive that functions under water. **in depth** thoroughly; comprehensively: I've studied this in depth. **out of one's depth 1** in water too deep to stand up in. **2** involved in something beyond one's capability. < probably Middle English *dep* deep, of Germanic origin.
depute (dɪˈpjuːt) *vb* **1** delegate. **2** appoint as one's representative. **deputation** *n* a group of people acting as representatives for others. **deputize** *vb* function as a deputy; represent. **deputization** *n*
deputy *n* **1** someone appointed to act on behalf of another. **2** (in some countries) a member of parliament: The Chamber of Deputies. < ultimately Latin *de-* + *putare* to consider.
derail (ˌdiːˈreɪl) *vb* cause (a train) to come off the rails. **derailment** *n*
derange (dɪˈreɪndʒ) *vb* **1** disturb the operation of; cause confusion in. **2** drive insane. **derangement** *n* < Old French *de-* + *reng* place.
derelict (ˈdɛrɪlɪkt) *adj* abandoned; neglected: a derelict house.
• *n* a social outcast; down-and-out. **dereliction** *n* < Latin *de-* + *relinquere* to leave.
derestrict (ˌdiːrɪˈstrɪkt) *vb* take away restrictions, esp. speed limits, from. **derestriction** *n*
deride (dɪˈraɪd) *vb* scorn; mock. **derision** *n* ridicule. **derisive** *adj* mocking. **derisory** *adj* deserving derision; ridiculous. < Latin *de-* + *ridēre* to laugh. SEE PANEL.
de rigueur (də riˈgɜː) *adj* necessary through etiquette or custom: Dark suits are de rigueur. < French: of strictness, compulsory.
derive (dɪˈraɪv) *vb* **1** obtain from a particular source: She derives great pleasure

derisive or derisory?

Something is derisive if it mocks or scorns: He made *derisive* grunts during the roll-call; *derisive* laughter.

Derisory means 'deserving derision; ridiculous': The management made a *derisory* pay offer. A derisory offer may well prompt a derisive response.

deprecate or depreciate?

The similarity of deprecate and depreciate sometimes leads to incorrect usage. Deprecate means 'to express disapproval of' as in The British Standards Institution deprecates the use of *infllammable* on warning labels.

The basic meaning of depreciate is 'to become less in value': A car stops depreciating once it becomes a collector's item. The meaning of depreciate that is sometimes confused with deprecate is 'to belittle or make light of': It's wrong to depreciate his efforts just because he happened to fail.

from books. **2** trace the source of: Most French words are derived from Latin. **3** deduce. **derivation** *n* **1** deriving. **2** a source; origin. **derivative** *n* something derived from something else. < Latin *de-* + *rivus* stream, brook.

dermatitis (ˌdɜːməˈtaɪtɪs) *n* a skin disease or inflammation. < Greek *derma* skin + *itis,* feminine of *itēs* belonging to.

dermatology (ˌdɜːməˈtɒlədʒɪ) *n* an area of medicine involving study of the skin and its diseases. **dermatologist** *n* a specialist in this.

derogatory (dɪˈrɒgətərɪ) *adj* belittling; disparaging. < Latin *de-* + *rogare* to ask.

derrick (ˈdɛrɪk) *n* **1** a type of crane with a fixed base and a pivotal arm. **2** a framework supporting drilling tackle over an oil-well or bore-hole. < obsolete *derrick* gallows, from *Derrick,* surname of 17th-century English hangman.

derv (dɜːv) *n* fuel oil for a diesel engine. < *d*iesel-*e*ngined *r*oad *v*ehicle.

descale (ˌdiːˈskeɪl) *vb* remove or scrape encrusted scale from (a kettle or boiler).

descant (ˈdɛskænt) *n* a subordinate melody usually higher than the main melody which is sung or played along with it. < Latin *dis-* apart + *cantus* song.

descend (dɪˈsɛnd) *vb* **1** move or pass down. **2** fall in pitch. **3** lead or slope downwards: stairs descending to the basement. **4** attack suddenly or make a disconcerting appearance: Relatives descended on us last week. **5** fall in dignity or status; stoop. **6** pass to by inheritance. **be descended from** come from (a particular family or ancestor). **descendant** *n* someone descended by birth from another. **descent** *n* **1** the act of moving downwards. **2** a means of descending something, such as a hill or staircase. **3** a fall in value, status, etc. **4** a sudden raid or invasion. **5** ancestral origin; lineage: of German descent. < ultimately Latin *de-* + *scandere* to climb.

describe (dɪˈskraɪb) *vb* **1** give the characteristics of, esp. in words. **2** trace an outline of: The aircraft described a complete circle. **description** *n* **1** describing. **2** something described. **3** kind; type: people of every description. **descriptive** *adj* < Latin *de-* + *scribere* to write.

desecrate (ˈdɛsɪˌkreɪt) *vb* deal disrespectfully with (something sacred); profane. **desecration** *n* **desecrator** *n* < *de-* + *-secrate,* as in con*secrate.*

desert[1] (ˈdɛzət) *n* a dry, infertile expanse of land, often covered with sand. • *adj* **1** (of land) infertile. **2** unpopulated: a desert island. < Latin *deserere* to desert. SEE PANEL.

desert[2] (dɪˈzɜːt) *vb* **1** abandon or forsake. **2** abandon (military service) without permission. **deserter** *n* **desertion** *n* < ultimately Latin *de-* + *serere* to join together. SEE PANEL AT **DESERT**[1].

deserts (dɪˈzɜːts) *pl n* something deserved; just reward or punishment. < SEE **DESERVE.** SEE PANEL AT **DESERT**[1].

deserve (dɪˈzɜːv) *vb* be fitted for or worthy of through one's actions; merit. **deservedly** *adv* **deserving** *adj* worth reward or support: a deserving cause. < ultimately Latin *de-* + *servire* to serve.

desiccate (ˈdɛsɪˌkeɪt) *vb* dry out or preserve (food) by drying: desiccated coconut. **desiccation** *n* < Latin *de-* + *siccus* dry.

design (dɪˈzaɪn) *n* **1** a drawing made as a plan for the construction of an object, building, etc. **2** the art or study of construction planning. **3** the arrangement of parts or elements in something. **4** an ornamental pattern. **5** a plan formed in the mind; intention. • *vb* **1** draw up a plan for. **2** plan for a specific function. **designer** *n* **designing** *adj* scheming; sly. **have designs on** plan to seize for oneself. < Latin *de-* + *signare* to mark.

designate (ˈdɛzɪgnət, ˈdɛzɪgˌneɪt) *adj* appointed to an office but not yet taking up duties: Prime Minister designate. • *vb* (ˈdɛzɪgˌneɪt) **1** specify; indicate. **2** give a title to; style. **3** appoint to an office. **designation** *n*

desire (dɪˈzaɪə) *n* **1** a compulsion to have or experience something that promises pleasure or satisfaction; object of this. **2** an expressed wish, often formal; request. **3** a sexual impulse; lust.

---

desert or **dessert?**

The spelling of the words desert and dessert sometimes causes confusion. Dessert, with double -ss-, is the sweet course eaten at a meal.

In all other cases, the spelling is with a single -s-; as a noun: the Sahara *desert,* He got his just *deserts* and as a verb: He *deserted* his wife and four children.

• *vb* **1** long for. **2** request. **desirable** *adj* **1** attractive. **2** worth doing; beneficial. **desirability** *n* **desirably** *adv* **desirous** *adj* desiring; longing for. **leave much to be desired** be lacking or imperfect. < ultimately Latin *de-* + *sidus* star.

desist (dɪˈzɪst) *vb* (*formal*) stop doing something. < Latin *de-* + *sistere* to stand.

desk (dɛsk) *n* **1** a table with a level or sloping top and often drawers, used for reading and writing. **2** a table or counter at which people such as clerks or cashiers work: reception desk. **3** a section of an organization such as a newspaper specializing in one activity: sports desk. < ultimately Latin *discus* dish, disc.

desolate (ˈdɛsələt) *adj* **1** deserted; barren: desolate regions. **2** sad and forlorn; lonely. **desolated** *adj* lonely; miserable. **desolation** *n* **1** a deserted state. **2** devastation; waste. **3** loneliness; misery. < Latin *de-* + *solus* alone.

despair (dɪˈspɛə) *n* total loss or lack of hope; something causing this.
• *vb* lose all hope. < Latin *de-* + *sperare* to hope.

despatch (dɪˈspætʃ) SEE **DISPATCH.**

desperate (ˈdɛspərət) *adj* **1** serious; with little or no hope: a desperate state of affairs. **2** reckless, esp. because of dire need: desperate for money. **3** applied through despair when there is little hope left: desperate measures. **desperately** *adv* **desperation** *n*

despicable (dɪˈspɪkəbl̩) *adj* deserving of contempt; mean. **despicably** *adv* < Latin *despicari* to despise.

despise (dɪˈspaɪz) *vb* consider to be worthless or contemptible; hate. < ultimately Latin *de-* + *specere* to look at.

despite (dɪˈspaɪt) *prep* in spite of; notwithstanding. < Latin *despicere* to defy.

despoil (dɪˈspɔɪl) *vb* rob; plunder. < Latin *de-* + *spoliare* to plunder.

despondent (dɪˈspɒndənt) *adj* depressed; dejected. **despondency** *n* **despondently** *adv* < ultimately Latin *de-* + *spondēre* to promise.

despot (ˈdɛspɒt) *n* a ruler who exercises absolute power. **despotic** *adj* **despotically** *adv* **despotism** *n* rule by a despot; tyranny; country governed in this way. < Greek *despotēs*.

dessert (dɪˈzɜːt) *n* a sweet course served usually at the end of dinner. **dessertspoon** *n* a spoon of medium size for eating sweet courses. **dessertspoonful** *n, pl* **dessertspoonfuls** as much as a dessert-spoon holds. < ultimately Latin *de-* + *servire* to serve. SEE PANEL AT **DESERT[1].**

destination (ˌdɛstɪˈneɪʃən) *n* somewhere a thing is sent or a journey ends.

destine (ˈdɛstɪn) *vb* allot a particular purpose to; determine in advance: He was destined to become famous. **destiny** *n* **1** fate; fortune. **2** events considered to be predetermined. < Latin *destinare*.

destitute (ˈdɛstɪˌtjuːt) *adj* **1** lacking in means; extremely poor. **2** deprived of: destitute of feeling. **destitution** *n* < Latin *de-* + *statuere* to set up.

destroy (dɪˈstrɔɪ) *vb* **1** totally ruin or break. **2** kill; put an end to: destroy all hope. **destroyer** *n* **1** a fast warship smaller than a cruiser, designed to protect other ships. **2** someone or something which destroys. **destructible** *adj* **destructibility** *n* **destruction** *n* **destructive** *adj* **1** causing destruction. **2** liable to destroy often: destructive behaviour. < ultimately Latin *de-* + *struere* to build.

detach (dɪˈtætʃ) *vb* **1** separate (one thing) from another without damage. **2** send (troops, etc.) on a special mission. **detachable** *adj* **detached** *adj* **1** unconnected: a detached house. **2** unbiased; aloof. **detachment** *n* **1** separation. **2** impartiality; aloofness. **3** a group of troops or ships, for example, separated from a main body for a special mission. < Old French *destachier*.

detail (ˈdiːteɪl) *n* **1** an individual part, esp. small and subordinate to a whole; parts like this collectively. **2** a part or parts of an artistic work seen in isolation: His work shows fine attention to detail. **3** a small military detachment which is given a special task; this task.
• *vb* **1** describe or report fully. **2** give a particular task to. **detailed** *adj* with many details; thorough. **go into details** explain all particulars. **in detail** with all particulars; thoroughly. < Old French *de-* + *taillier* to cut.

detain (dɪˈteɪn) *vb* **1** keep confined; restrain: detained in custody. **2** delay; stop. **detainee** *n* someone detained, esp. by the authorities. **detention** *n* **1** being confined; confining. **2** (of a school pupil) being kept in after school as a punishment. **detention centre** an establishment for detaining young offenders for a short period. < ultimately Latin *de-* + *tenēre* to hold.

detect (dɪˈtɛkt) *vb* **1** discover or notice. **2** find (someone committing an offence): They were detected shoplifting. **detection** *n* **detective** *n* someone who investigates

crimes, esp. a member of the police force. **detector** *n* an apparatus which shows up the presence of something: lie-detector. < Latin *de-* + *tegere* to cover.
détente (deɪ'tɒnt) *n* the relaxing of tension between nations. < French.
deter (dɪ'tɜː) *vb* **deterred; deterring** discourage or prevent from acting or happening, esp. through fear or doubt. **determent** *n* < Latin *de-* + *terrēre* to frighten.
detergent (dɪ'tɜːdʒənt) *n* a chemical substance other than soap, used as a cleansing agent.
• *adj* with the power to cleanse. < Latin *de-* + *tergēre* to wipe off.
deteriorate (dɪ'tɪərɪəˌreɪt) *vb* make or become worse. **deterioration** *n* < Latin *deterior* worse.
determine (dɪ'tɜːmɪn) *vb* **1** settle conclusively; decide: determine whether he is innocent or guilty. **2** calculate with precision. **3** influence; regulate: Availability determines the price. **determinable** *adj* **determinate** *adj* fixed; definitive. **determination** *n* **1** firm intent. **2** calculating or deciding. **determined** *adj* with firm intent; resolute. **determiner** *n* a word that restricts the meaning of a noun such as her in her new dress. < Latin *de-* + *terminare* to limit.
deterrent (dɪ'tɛrənt) *n* something that deters, such as a nuclear weapon that stops other countries from attacking one that possesses it. < Latin *deterrēre* to deter.
detest (dɪ'tɛst) *vb* hate; loathe. **detestable** *adj* **detestably** *adv* **detestation** *n* < Latin *de-* + *testari* to bear witness, call to witness.
dethrone (ˌdiː'θrəʊn) *vb* depose (a monarch, etc.). **dethronement** *n*
detonate ('dɛtəˌneɪt) *vb* explode or cause to explode violently. **detonation** *n* **detonator** *n* a device used to detonate explosives. < Latin *de-* + *tonare* to thunder.
detour ('diːtʊə) *n* a deviation from a planned route or course: make a detour. < Old French *des-* de- + *torner* to turn.
detract (dɪ'trækt) *vb* remove something desirable from; diminish. **detraction** *n* **detractor** *n* someone who criticizes or belittles someone or something. < ultimately Latin *de-* + *trahere* to draw.
detriment ('dɛtrɪmənt) *n* damage; injury. **detrimental** *adj* harmful; damaging: Smoking can be detrimental to one's health. **detrimentally** *adv* < ultimately Latin *de-* + *terere* to rub.
detritus (dɪ'traɪtəs) *n* debris; rubble. < Latin *deterere* to rub away.
deuce (djuːs) *n* **1** a playing-card with two pips. **2** (*tennis*) having a score of forty points each. < ultimately Latin *duo* two. SEE PANEL.
devalue (diː'væljuː) *vb* **1** reduce the exchange value of (a currency): devalue the pound. **2** reduce the worth or reputation of. **devaluation** *n*
devastate ('dɛvəˌsteɪt) *vb* **1** utterly ruin; lay waste: The city was devastated. **2** shatter; overwhelm: The news devastated her. **devastating** *adj* **devastation** *n* < Latin *de-* + *vastare* to lay waste.
develop (dɪ'vɛləp) *vb* **1** grow or mature or cause to grow or mature. **2** bring out the potential of. **3** appear or cause to appear gradually: A row developed over rates of pay. **4** acquire gradually: She developed bad habits. **5** treat (photographic materials) with chemicals in order to make a visible image: develop a film. **6** build on (land, etc.) to use its resources for industry or living space. **developer** *n* **1** someone or a firm that develops land. **2** a chemical used in developing photographic film. **developing country** a country that is lacking in economic and social development. **development** *n* **1** developing or being developed. **2** an event that has developed. **development area** an area in which the government encourages new industries to offset high unemployment there. < Old French *des-* de- + *voloper* to wrap.

Why **deuce?**

The system of scoring in tennis is for the uninitiated rather less than straightforward. Also obscure is some of the language that it uses. For example, when each player or side has reached 40 the score goes not to '40 all' but to deuce. Why deuce? Those familiar with French will notice a similarity between this word and the French deux meaning 'two'. This explains why a playing-card with two spots is sometimes called a deuce. The tennis expression derives from the Old French equivalent of deux 'two to go', signifying that the player or side that proceeds to win two consecutive points will win the game.

deviate (ˈdiːvɪˌeɪt) *vb* turn away (from a subject, course of action, etc.). **deviant** *adj, n* (someone) deviating from the norm. **deviation** *n* < Latin *de-* + *via* way.

device (dɪˈvaɪs) *n* **1** something planned or made for a specific application or purpose: a labour-saving device. **2** a scheme with a specific aim, such as tricking someone. **3** a design used as an emblem, esp. in heraldry. **leave someone to his** or **her own devices** leave someone alone to do as he or she pleases. < Old French *deviser* to divide.

devil (ˈdɛvl̩) *n* **1 the Devil** the supreme evil spirit in Christian and Jewish belief. **2** an evil spirit; demon. **3** someone who is cruel or merciless. **4** (*informal*) chap; soul: lucky devil; poor devil. **5** someone who is reckless or highly energetic. **6** (*informal*) something trying or difficult to handle: We had the devil of a job to do it. **7** (*informal*) used to express irritation or surprise: 'What the devil is that?'
• *vb* **devilled; devilling** season (food), esp. with hot spices: devilled kidneys. **devilish** *adj* **devil-may-care** *adj* cheerfully flouting convention or authority. **devilment** or **devilry** *n* mischievous behaviour. < ultimately Greek *diabolos* slanderer, from *dia-* + *ballein* to throw. SEE PANEL.

devious (ˈdiːvɪəs) *adj* **1** turning; winding: a devious route. **2** scheming; insincere. **deviously** *adv* **deviousness** *n* < Latin *de-* + *via* way.

devise (dɪˈvaɪz) *vb* mentally formulate; plan. < ultimately Latin *dividere* to divide.

devoid (dɪˈvɔɪd) *adj* completely lacking: devoid of humour. < Old French *des-* de- + *vuidier* to empty.

devolve (dɪˈvɒlv) *vb* transfer or hand down or cause to transfer or hand down (duties, tasks, etc.) to a successor. **devolution** *n* **1** the transfer of rights or property to a successor. **2** the transference of power from a central authority to a regional one. < Latin *de-* + *volvere* to roll.

devote (dɪˈvəʊt) *vb* set apart for a particular purpose; dedicate: She devoted herself to her career. **devoted** *adj* dedicated; loyal or loving. **devotedly** *adv* **devotee** *n* someone who keenly supports something: football devotees. **devotion** *n* **1** great affection, love, or loyalty. **2** religious worship. **devotions** *pl n* acts of prayer. < Latin *de-* + *vovēre* to vow.

devour (dɪˈvaʊə) *vb* **1** eat up in a greedy or hungry manner. **2** totally destroy or consume. **3** take in through the senses with great enthusiasm. **4** engross; absorb: devoured by envy. < Latin *de-* + *vorare* to devour.

devout (dɪˈvaʊt) *adj* **1** very religious; pious. **2** genuine; earnest: a devout wish. **devoutly** *adv* **devoutness** *n* < Latin *devovēre* to vow.

dew (djuː) *n* moisture from water vapour in the atmosphere that condenses on cool surfaces during the night. < Old English *dēaw*.

talk of the devil

Devil features in a number of idiomatic and proverbial expressions, including:

between the devil and the deep (blue sea) faced with a choice of two equally undesirable alternatives. This expression is of nautical origin; the devil is not Satan but a large seam on the hull of a sailing-ship. Since the seam was near the water-line, a seaman who found himself between the devil and the deep was in a very awkward predicament.

give the devil his due to be fair in one's assessment of even an unworthy person.

like the devil very energetically.

talk of the devil (and he appears) used on the unexpected arrival of a person who has just been mentioned.

the devil looks after his own bad or evil people seem to be fortunate and successful.

the devil one knows is better than the devil one doesn't it is better to endure someone or something unpleasant that one knows than to risk experiencing someone or something unknown that might be even worse.

the devil to pay trouble is to be expected as a result of some action: There'll be the devil to pay if they find out who's taken the money.
The expression derives not from legendary bargains made with the devil, as is commonly supposed, but from the expression there's the devil to pay and no hot pitch. Here, the devil is the seam on the hull of a sailing-ship, as in between the devil and the deep blue sea. To pay comes from Old French *peier* 'to cover with hot pitch'. So, the devil to pay and no hot pitch meant that there was a task to be undertaken, but no material was available for it, hence one was in a difficult or troublesome situation.

dexterity (dɛkˈstɛrɪtɪ) *n* skill or ability in doing things with the hands. **dextrous** *adj* < Latin *dexter* skilful.

diabetes (ˌdaɪəˈbiːtiːz) *n* a disorder caused by the underactivity of the hormone insulin resulting in too high a level of glucose in the body. **diabetic** *adj, n* (someone) suffering from diabetes. < ultimately Greek *dia-* + *bainein* to go.

diabolical (ˌdaɪəˈbɒlɪkl̩) *adj* **1** of or like a devil; fiendish. **2** awful; dreadful. **diabolically** *adv* < Greek *diabolos* devil.

diadem (ˈdaɪəˌdɛm) *n* a crown or headband worn as a symbol of royalty. < ultimately Greek *dia-* + *dein* to bind.

diagnose (ˈdaɪəgˌnəʊz) *vb* recognize and state the nature of (a disease, condition, etc.) after assessing its symptoms. **diagnosis** *n* **diagnostic** *adj* < Greek *dia-* + *gignōskein* to know.

diagonal (daɪˈægənl̩) *adj* running from one corner to another; oblique. **diagonally** *adv* < Greek *dia-* + *gōnia* angle.

diagram (ˈdaɪəˌgræm) *n* a drawn plan or design which shows the arrangements of parts or the workings of something. < Greek *dia-* + *graphein* to write.

dial (ˈdaɪəl) *n* **1** a clock or watch face. **2** a flat face on which something is measured, usually by a movable pointer and fixed numerals. **3** a movable, disc-shaped control on an electrical or mechanical apparatus such as a television or telephone.
• *vb* **dialled; dialling 1** connect with by using a telephone dial; try to do this. **2** select, indicate, or operate with a dial. < Latin *dies* day.

dialect (ˈdaɪəˌlɛkt) *n* a variety of a language spoken in a particular region and differing from the standard in words and pronunciation. < ultimately Greek *dialegesthai* to converse.

dialectic (ˌdaɪəˈlɛktɪk) *n* a process of trying to resolve a usually philosophical issue by juxtaposing contradictory ideas. < Greek *dialektos.*

dialogue (ˈdaɪəˌlɒg) *n* **1** an exchange of ideas or opinions; conversation. **2** the lines spoken by characters in a play, story, etc. < ultimately Greek *dia-* + *legein* to speak.

dialysis (daɪˈælɪsɪs) *n* the separation of substances in a solution by making them flow through a semipermeable membrane; purifying blood in this way. < Greek *dia-* + *lyein* to loosen.

diameter (daɪˈæmɪtə) *n* a line which runs through the centre of a circle or sphere from one side to another. **diametrical** *adj* **1** of or being a diameter. **2** exactly opposite. **diametrically** *adv* < Greek *dia-* + *metron* measure.

diamond (ˈdaɪəmənd) *n* **1** a precious stone of very hard, crystallized carbon. **2** a figure with four equal sides, two acute and two obtuse angles; rhombus. **3** something with this shape. **4** a red figure with this shape, used as a symbol of the playing-card suit **diamonds.**
• *adj* of or set with diamonds. **diamond wedding** a 60th wedding anniversary.
SEE PANEL AT **ADAMANT.**

diaphragm (ˈdaɪəˌfræm) *n* **1** the muscular partition which separates the chest from the abdomen, used in breathing. **2** a thin, dividing membrane or partition. **3** a vibrating disc, used in an earphone, microphone, etc. **4** a device which limits the lens aperture in a camera. **5** a contraceptive cap which is fitted over the neck of the womb. < ultimately Greek *dia-* + *phrassein* to close.

diarrhoea (ˌdaɪəˈrɪə) *n* a condition of abnormally frequent and fluid bowel movements. < ultimately Greek *dia-* + *rhein* to flow.

diary (ˈdaɪərɪ) *n* a daily record of events, appointments, or observations, usually contained in a notebook for this purpose; this notebook. < Latin *dies* day.

diatribe (ˈdaɪəˌtraɪb) *n* a verbal attack; bitter and abusive criticism. < Greek *dia-* + *tribein* to rub.

dice (daɪs) *n, pl* **dice 1** a small cube marked with spots numbering 1–6 on each face, used in various games of chance. **2** a gambling game played with these.
• *vb* **1** play games or gamble with dice. **2** take a great risk: dicing with death. **3** chop or cut into small cubes: diced carrots. **dicey** *adj* (*informal*) unpredictable; risky. **no dice** (*informal*) an expression of refusal or uselessness. < Middle French *dé*.
SEE PANEL.

dichotomy (daɪˈkɒtəmɪ) *n* a division into

> **dice**
>
> Originally, dice was the plural of die. Now, dice is used as both the singular and plural form.
>
> The singular die remains only in the idiom the die is cast 'a step has been taken from which there is no turning back'.

two sharply contrasting groups. < Greek *dichotomos.*

dicky ('dɪkɪ) *adj* (*informal*) weak or unsound: a dicky heart. < origin unknown.

dictate (dɪk'teɪt) *vb* **1** speak or read out loud (to someone) to write down or (to a machine) to record. **2** state or declare with authority: dictate terms. **3** order around imperiously. **dictation** *n* **dictates** *pl n* commands or guiding principles: the dictates of conscience. **dictator** *n* **1** someone who has taken power by force and rules (a country) absolutely and oppressively. **2** someone who is arrogant and domineering. **dictatorial** *adj* **dictatorially** *adv* **dictatorship** *n* absolute rule; state governed in this way. < ultimately Latin *dicere* to say.

diction ('dɪkʃən) *n* someone's choice of words or way of pronouncing them in speaking or singing. < Latin *dicere* to say.

dictionary ('dɪkʃənərɪ) *n* a reference book that lists and explains the words of a language or subject, usually in alphabetical order, or giving equivalents of words in another language. < Latin *dictio* speaking.

dictum ('dɪktəm) *n, pl* **dicta** a pronouncement or statement about a particular topic; maxim.

did (dɪd) SEE **DO.**

didactic (dɪ'dæktɪk) *adj* **1** instructive, esp. morally. **2** with a lecturing or preaching manner. **didactically** *adv* < Greek *didaskein* to teach.

diddle ('dɪdl̩) *vb* (*informal*) swindle or cheat. < probably Jeremy *Diddler,* character in a play 'Raising the Wind' by James Kenny, died 1849, English dramatist.

die[1] (daɪ) *vb* **died; dying 1** cease to live. **2** cease to be. **3** stop working: The motor died. **4** long for intensely; crave: dying for a drink. **5** be overwhelmed: dying of boredom. < Middle English *dien.* SEE PANEL.

die[2] *n* a device or tool which moulds and shapes material or impresses designs on coins, medals, etc. **die-cast** *adj* formed by pouring material into a mould. < Middle French *dé.*

diesel ('diːzl̩) *n* **1** a diesel engine or a vehicle driven by this. **2** diesel engine fuel. **diesel-electric** *adj* driven by a combination of a diesel engine and an electric generator. **diesel engine** a combustion engine in which fuel is ignited by highly compressed air. < Rudolf *Diesel,* died 1913, German engineer. SEE PANEL.

diet ('daɪət) *n* **1** the types of food and drink taken habitually by an individual, group, or animal. **2** a restricted range of food prescribed to someone for health reasons, etc.
• *vb* keep to a special range or amount of

never say die

The English language is full of words and phrases considered by many to be either too coarse or too blunt to mention. For each of them there is a milder or indirect equivalent, a sort of verbal palliative. For example, in the context of bereavement the word die is rarely heard. To avoid aggravating a person's grief as far as possible, expressions such as the following are used: 'When did he *pass away?*' 'He's been *gone* three years now.' Such expressions are known as *euphemisms,* from the Greek word *euphēmos* 'sounding good'.

Euphemisms tend to cluster around topics which are considered by a culture to be taboo, such as sexual intercourse, certain parts of the anatomy, and certain bodily functions.

The word die does, however, feature in a number of idiomatic expressions, including:

die away to become weaker or fainter: The noise of the plane gradually died away.
die down to become less violent or intense: The forecast is that the gales will soon begin to die down.
die-hard *n* a person who persistently refuses to change his or her views, methods, etc.
die out to cease to exist: Many species of wild animals are dying out.

diesel and **petrol**

The word petrol comes from *petroleum,* a combination of *petra,* the word for 'rock' in ancient Greece which was taken over into Latin, and *oleum,* the Latin word for 'oil'.

Diesel has very different and considerably shorter roots. It comes from the name of its inventor, Rudolf Diesel, 1858–1913, a German mechanical engineer who, following up the ideas of the French scientist, Carnot, developed not only the diesel engine but also the relatively cheap fuel that would power it.

food, esp. in order to lose weight. **dietary** *adj* **dieter** *n* **dietetic** *adj* of diet or nutrition. **dietetics** *pl n* the scientific study of this. **dietitian** *n* someone qualified in the study of diet and nutrition. < ultimately Greek *diaita* manner of living.

differ (ˈdɪfə) *vb* **1** be unlike or distinct (from). **2** hold an alternative view. **difference** *n* **1** unlikeness; distinctness; example of this. **2** distinguishing feature or change in something. **3** a disagreement; quarrel. **4** the result of subtracting one number or quantity from another. **different** *adj* **1** dissimilar; varying. **2** various; distinct. **3** extraordinary; unusual. **differently** *adv* **differential** *n* the amount of variance between things which are compared, as the difference in workers' wages for distinct jobs. **differential gear** an arrangement of gears which allows a drive wheel to rotate faster than the others while cornering, etc. **differentiate** *vb* **1** make or show a difference; distinguish. **2** show bias; discriminate. **3** become different or distinct in nature. **differentiation** *n* **make all the difference** make an important difference. < ultimately Latin *dis-* + *ferre* to carry. SEE PANEL.

difficult (ˈdɪfɪkḷt) *adj* **1** needing skill or effort to do, make, or understand. **2** puzzling; troubling: a difficult childhood. **3** hard to please or deal with: a difficult man. **difficulty** *n* **1** being difficult. **2** a hindrance or problem. **3** trial; trouble: in financial difficulty. < ultimately Latin *dis-* not + *facilis* easy.

diffident (ˈdɪfɪdənt) *adj* without much self-confidence; reserved. **diffidence** *n* **diffidently** *adv* < Latin *dis-* + *fidere* to trust.

diffraction (dɪˈfrækʃən) *n* the breaking up of a light beam into light and dark or coloured bands by passing it through a small opening. < Latin *dis-* + *frangere* to break.

diffuse (dɪˈfjuːs) *adj* **1** scattered; spread out: diffuse light. **2** verbose; wordy.
• *vb* (dɪˈfjuːz) **1** spread out or distribute freely and widely. **2** intermingle (esp. gases or liquids). **diffusely** *adv* **diffuseness** *n* **diffuser** *n* **diffusion** *n* < Latin *dis-* + *fundere* to pour.

dig (dɪg) *vb* **dug; digging 1** break up or take away (earth); make (a hole or passage) like this: dig the garden; dig a tunnel. **2** get by digging; unearth. **3** drive down into; plunge. **4** poke, prod, or nudge: She dug him in the ribs. **5** search and find: They dug up some evidence. **6** (*informal*) appreciate; understand.
• *n* **1** the act of digging, esp. for archaeological purposes; site of this. **2** a disparaging or cutting remark. **3** a prod, poke, or nudge. **dig in** or **into** (*informal*) **1** mix with earth by digging. **2** start to eat or work eagerly. **3** defend a position or argument stubbornly. **dig one's heels** or **toes in** resist stubbornly. < Middle English *diggen*.

digest (daɪˈdʒɛst) *vb* **1** (of food) convert or be converted in the stomach so that the body can absorb and use it. **2** absorb mentally; consider. **digestible** *adj* able to be digested. **digestibility** *n* **digestion** *n* the process or power of digesting, esp. food. **digestive** *adj* concerning or helping the digestion of food: the digestive tract.
• *n* (ˈdaɪdʒɛst) **1** a systematic summary. **2** a compilation of news, articles, stories, etc., often abridged. < ultimately Latin *dis-* + *gerere* to carry.

digit (ˈdɪdʒɪt) *n* **1** any of the Arabic numerals from 0 to 9; figure. **2** a finger or toe. **digital** *adj* **digital clock** a clock that displays the time as a row of figures. **digital computer** a computer that functions and processes data represented by digits. **digital recording** sound

different from, to, or **than?**

Would you put from, to, or than in this sentence? This shape is different ___ that one. Careful users of British English favour different from, have reservations about different to, and have a strong dislike of different than.

Different to is becoming increasingly common, especially in informal English, perhaps under the influence of phrases such as opposed to and similar to: His car is different to his brother's, but similar to his sister's.

Different than is avoided by careful users of British English, for example in This book is different than yours. But it is not uncommon as a way of avoiding longwindedness when a clause follows. So This is a different sort of book than most people would have expected is tending to replace the longer, awkward This is a different sort of book from that which most people would have expected.

turned into electrical pulses which represent binary digits in recording. < Latin *digitus* finger, toe.

dignity (ˈdɪgnɪtɪ) *n* **1** being worthy or honoured: the dignity of office. **2** seriousness or gravity of manner. **3** high status or office. **beneath one's dignity** too lowly for one to do. **dignify** *vb* **dignified; dignifying 1** invest with dignity. **2** make appear more significant than in reality. **dignitary** *n* someone who holds a high office or rank. < Latin *dignus* worthy.

digress (daɪˈgrɛs) *vb* turn away from the main subject in speaking or writing. **digression** *n* **digressive** *adj* < Latin *dis-* + *gradi* to step.

digs (dɪgz) *pl n* (*informal*) lodgings. < *diggings,* perhaps referring to where one works.

dike (daɪk) SEE **DYKE.**

dilapidated (dɪˈlæpɪˌdeɪtɪd) *adj* falling into ruin or disrepair, esp. through neglect. **dilapidation** *n* < Latin *dis-* + *lapis* stone.

dilate (daɪˈleɪt) *vb* **1** widen or enlarge. **2** comment lengthily on. **dilation** *n* **dilator** *n* < Latin *dis-* + *latus* wide.

dilatory (ˈdɪlətərɪ) *adj* **1** inclined to cause delay. **2** slow; tardy. **dilatoriness** *n* < Latin *dis-* + *ferre* to carry.

dilemma (dɪˈlɛmə, daɪˈlɛmə) *n* **1** a situation which demands a choice between two or more equally undesirable alternatives. **2** a problem which seemingly cannot be solved. < Greek *di-* + *lēmma* assumption. SEE PANEL.

dilettante (ˌdɪlɪˈtæntɪ) *n* someone who takes a superficial interest in something for pleasure. < Latin *delectare* to delight.

diligent (ˈdɪlɪdʒənt) *adj* involving care and effort; hard-working. **diligence** *n* **diligently** *adv* < Latin *di-* + *legere* to select.

dill (dɪl) *n* an aromatic plant with yellow flowers, the spicy seeds of which are used to flavour pickles. < Old English *dile.*

dilly-dally (ˈdɪlɪˌdælɪ) *vb* (*informal*) waste time in indecision; dawdle. < *dally.*

dilute (daɪˈluːt) *vb* **1** add water or another liquid to make it less concentrated. **2** cause to lose force or effect; weaken.
• *adj* diluted. **dilution** *n* < Latin *di-* + *lavere* to wash.

dim (dɪm) *adj* **dimmer; dimmest 1** emitting a faint light. **2** vague or indistinct: a dim outline. **3** with impaired vision: His eyes were dim with tears. **4** slow; stupid.
• *vb* **dimmed; dimming** make or become dim or dimmer. **dimmer** *n* a device for regulating the brightness of a light. < Old English.

dimension (dɪˈmɛnʃən, daɪˈmɛnʃən) *n* **1** a measurement in a particular direction; length, breadth, thickness, etc. **2** size; extent. **3** an aspect; scope: This gives things a new dimension. **dimensional** *adj* < ultimately Latin *dis-* + *metiri* to measure.

diminish (dɪˈmɪnɪʃ) *vb* reduce in size or value; lessen in quantity. **diminution** *n* **diminutive** *n* a word denoting a smaller version of something such as duckling, or an affectionate name such as Jimmy. < Latin *de-* + *minuere* to lessen.

dimple (ˈdɪmpl̩) *n* a small crease or hollow in a surface, esp. a natural one on the skin of the cheek or chin.
• *vb* display dimples. < Middle English *dympull.*

din (dɪn) *n* a loud, discordant and irritating noise.
• *vb* **dinned; dinning 1** make a din. **2 din into** force (information) into (someone) by constant repetition. < Old English *dyne.*

dine (daɪn) *vb* **1** eat dinner. **2** have or entertain to dinner: He wined and dined her. **diner** *n* **1** someone eating dinner. **2** a dining-room. **3** a dining-car on a train. **dining-car** *n* a railway carriage where meals are served. **dining-room** *n* a room where meals are eaten. < ultimately Latin *dis-* + *jejunus* fasting.

ding-dong (ˈdɪŋˌdɒŋ) *n* **1** the ringing sound of repeated strokes on a bell or bells. **2** (*informal*) a heated argument or fight.
• *adj* **1** of or like the sound of a bell. **2** strongly contested. < like the sound.

on the horns of a dilemma

The expression on the horns of a dilemma means 'faced with the choice between two equally undesirable alternatives'. In medieval logic and rhetoric, a dilemma was an argument in which a person had to choose between two alternatives, both of which were unfavourable to him. The alternatives in the argument were likened to the two horns of an animal, so a person on the horns of a dilemma would be tossed by the animal, whichever horn was grasped.

dinghy (ˈdɪŋɪ) *n* **1** a small, open boat. **2** an inflatable life raft. < Hindi *dingī*.

dingy (ˈdɪndʒɪ) *adj* shabby; dirty. **dingily** *adv* **dinginess** *n* < origin unknown.

dinky (ˈdɪŋkɪ) *adj* attractively small; dainty. < Scottish *dink* neat.

dinner (ˈdɪnə) *n* **1** the main meal of the day, taken at midday or in the evening. **2** a formal evening meal or banquet. **dinner-jacket** *n* a short, usually black evening jacket worn by men. < Old French *diner* to dine.

dinosaur (ˈdaɪnəˌsɔː) *n* one of a group of usually very large reptiles which used to live on land and are now long extinct. < Greek *deinos* terrible + *sauros* lizard.

dint (dɪnt) *n* (*archaic*) a blow. **by dint of** by means of. < Old English *dynt*.

diocese (ˈdaɪəsɪs) *n* a district under the jurisdiction of a bishop. **diocesan** *adj* < ultimately Greek *dia-* + *oikos* house.

dip (dɪp) *vb* **dipped; dipping 1** lower or plunge (something) into a liquid in order to wet, dye, etc. **2** plunge into and quickly draw out from a liquid. **3** drop down gradually or suddenly. **4** lower or drop momentarily: The car dipped its headlights. **5** slope or incline downwards. **6 dip into** go or put into in order to withdraw something: She dipped into her savings. **7 dip into** read superficially or at random.

• *n* **1** dipping. **2** a short bathe for sport or exercise. **3** a downward slope; slight hollow. **4** a sauce or something similar into which food is dipped before being eaten. **5** a liquid for dipping things into: sheep-dip. **dip-stick** *n* a rod used for measuring the level of a liquid such as oil in an engine. **dip-switch** *n* a switch for dipping the headlights of a vehicle. < Old English *dyppan*.

diphtheria (dɪfˈθɪərɪə, dɪpˈθɪərɪə) *n* an acute, infectious disease, characterized by severe inflammation of a membrane, esp. in the throat. < Greek *diphthera* leather.

diphthong (ˈdɪfθɒŋ, ˈdɪpθɒŋ) *n* a combined sound made up of two vowels, one of which glides into the other, for example oy in boy. < ultimately Greek *di-* two + *phthongos* sound.

diploma (dɪˈpləʊmə) *n* a certificate of qualification in a usually specialized subject, conferred on a student who has successfully completed a course or passed examinations. < Greek *diplōma* folded paper.

diplomacy (dɪˈpləʊməsɪ) *n* **1** the conducting of international relations; skill involved in this. **2** tact. **diplomat** *n* **1** someone employed in the diplomatic service, such as a consul or ambassador. **2** someone who deals with people tactfully. **diplomatic** *adj* **diplomatically** *adv* < SEE **DIPLOMA.**

dire (daɪə) *adj* **1** awful; terrible: His acting was dire. **2** predicting disaster; ominous: a dire warning. **3** extremely urgent: in dire need; dire straits. < Latin *dirus*.

direct (dɪˈrɛkt, daɪˈrɛkt) *adj* **1** going from one point to another in a straight line: the direct route. **2** in an uninterrupted sequence: a direct result. **3** frank and straightforward: He speaks in a very direct manner. **4** exact or diametrical: a direct contradiction. **5** (of a tax such as income tax) levied on individuals and companies.

• *adv* by the shortest route: You can fly direct.

• *vb* **1** cause to have a particular aim or move in a particular direction: Direct all complaints to the management. **2** address (a letter, parcel, etc.). **3** point out the way to; instruct (someone) how to do something. **4** be in charge of; supervise. **5** command with authority; order. **directness** *n* **direct current** electric current which flows one way only. **direction** *n* **1** the point towards which something moves; way to somewhere. **2** aiming; targeting. **3** supervising or managing. **4** *pl* instructions. **directional** *adj* **1** of direction or guidance. **2** capable of sending or receiving, for example radio signals in one direction only. **directive** *n* an instruction issued with authority, esp. at a high level. **directly** *adv* **1** in a direct route or manner. **2** also *conj* immediately. **3** soon; shortly. **director** *n* **1** a member of the board of a business firm. **2** someone who supervises the making of a play, film, etc. **directorship** *n* **directory** *n* a reference book which contains a usually alphabetical list of names, addresses, and telephone numbers of people, businesses, etc. **sense of direction** the ability to guide oneself without help. < Latin *dirigere* to guide.

dirge (dɜːdʒ) *n* **1** a lament for the dead; slow, mournful hymn or song. **2** a slow, mournful piece of music. < Latin *dirige*, from *dirigere* to direct.

dirt (dɜːt) *n* **1** a substance which soils; filth or grime. **2** soil; earth. **3** something to be scorned. **4** slanderous gossip; obscenity. **dirt cheap** (*informal*) extremely cheap. < Old Norse *drit*.

dirty (ˈdɜːtɪ) *adj* **1** unclean; impure. **2** causing the doer to become

unclean: a dirty job. **3** with unclean or unhygienic habits. **4** unfair; contemptible: a dirty trick. **5** obscene; indecent: a dirty joke. **6** (of weather) stormy and rough.
• *vb* **dirtied; dirtying** make or become dirty. **dirty look** a look of disapproval. **dirty word** an obscenity or word which has become discredited. **do the dirty on** behave meanly to; cheat.

dis- *prefix* **1** used to show an opposite or reversal: disappear; disembark; discomfort. **2** used to show a removal or release: disarm; discharge. **3** used to show negation: disloyal. < Latin: apart.

disable (dɪsˈeɪbl̩) *vb* deprive of some capacity or ability; make ineffective. **disability** *n* something that disables; handicap. **disabled** *adj* with a physical disability. **disablement** *n*

disadvantage (ˌdɪsədˈvɑːntɪdʒ) *n* **1** an unfavourable or inferior situation. **2** damage or loss to finances, reputation, etc.
• *vb* place at a disadvantage. **disadvantaged** *adj* underprivileged. **disadvantageous** *adj* unfavourable.

disaffected (ˌdɪsəˈfɛktɪd) *adj* discontented; alienated, esp. from authority or government.

disagree (ˌdɪsəˈgriː) *vb* **1** differ in point of view. **2** vary from; contradict. **3** have unpleasant effects: Spicy food disagrees with me. **disagreement** *n* **disagreeable** *adj* **1** unpleasant. **2** ill-tempered. **disagreeably** *adv* < Middle French *des-* + *agreer* to agree.

disallow (ˌdɪsəˈlaʊ) *vb* refuse to accept as valid or recognize.

disappear (ˌdɪsəˈpɪə) *vb* **1** cease to be seen. **2** cease to exist. **3** leave; go. **disappearance** *n*

disappoint (ˌdɪsəˈpɔɪnt) *vb* fail to come up to the hopes or expectations of; sadden by this. **disappointed** *adj* **disappointment** *n* < Middle French *des-* dis- + *apointier* to arrange.

disapprove (ˌdɪsəˈpruːv) *vb* consider to be wrong or unacceptable; reject. **disapproval** *n*

disarm (dɪsˈɑːm) *vb* **1** take away weapons or means of defence from. **2** reduce or get rid of armed forces. **3** remove the fuse from (a bomb). **4** win the trust or confidence of. **disarmament** *n* the reduction of weapons or fighting capability, esp. of a country.

disarrange (ˌdɪsəˈreɪndʒ) *vb* disturb the organization of; make untidy. **disarrangement** *n*

disarray (ˌdɪsəˈreɪ) *n* untidiness; disorder.
• *vb* make untidy; confuse. < Middle French *des-* + *areer* to array.

disassociate (ˌdɪsəˈsəʊʃɪˌeɪt) *vb* dissociate.

disaster (dɪˈzɑːstə) *n* **1** an event causing great destruction or misfortune. **2** a failure. **disastrous** *adj* **disastrously** *adv* **disaster area** an area in which a great disaster such as a flood or earthquake has taken place. SEE PANEL.

disband (dɪsˈbænd) *vb* stop existing as a group, unit, etc.; break up. **disbandment** *n*

disbelieve (ˌdɪsbɪˈliːv) *vb* reject as untrue; refuse to believe. **disbelief** *n* **disbeliever** *n*

disburse (dɪsˈbɜːs) *vb* pay out (money). **disbursement** *n* < Old French *desborser*.

disc (dɪsk) *n* **1** a thin, flat, circular plate; something with this shape or appearance. **2** a round, flat, cartilaginous structure in the body between the spinal vertebrae: a slipped disc. **3** a gramophone record. **disc brake** a brake operated by a flat plate pressing against a rotating disc on a wheel. **disc jockey** someone who introduces and plays popular records on the radio or at a discothèque, party, etc. < Latin *discus*.

discard (dɪsˈkɑːd) *vb* throw away; get rid of as unnecessary or unwanted.

discern (dɪˈsɜːn) *vb* recognize or detect clearly with the mind or the senses. **discernible** *adj* **discernment** *n* **discerning** *adj* discriminating; perceptive. < Latin *dis-* apart + *cernere* to sift.

discharge (dɪsˈtʃɑːdʒ) *vb* **1** give out; emit. **2** fire (a gun, missile, etc.). **3** give out or cause to give out (an electric charge). **4** dismiss from service or employment. **5** release from care or custody: discharged from hospital. **6** fulfil (an

space disasters

An event which causes great ruin or misfortune is commonly referred to as a disaster. This word has not always had such a broad meaning. It derives from the Italian word *disastro*, 'a malevolent astral influence'. It was in this astrological sense that disaster was used when it entered English in the 16th century. At that time one's fate was still considered to be determined by one's star.

The root of disaster is ultimately the Greek word for 'star' *astron*, from which derived the Latin *astrum*.

obligation): discharge a debt.
• *n* (ˈdɪstʃɑːdʒ) the process of discharging; something discharged. < ultimately Latin *dis-* + Late Latin *carricare* to load.

disciple (dɪˈsaɪpl̩) *n* **1** one of the original followers of Christ, esp. one of the 12 apostles. **2** someone who accepts the leadership and teachings of another. < Latin *discipulus* pupil.

discipline (ˈdɪsɪplɪn) *n* **1** training of the mind and character that produces self-control and obedience. **2** order produced by enforced obedience, for example in the army. **3** punishment. **4** an area of study.
• *vb* **1** train to be obedient and self-controlled. **2** punish. **disciplinary** *adj* **disciplinarian** *n* a person who enforces strict discipline. < Latin *discipulus* pupil.

disclaim (dɪsˈkleɪm) *vb* deny; disown. **disclaimer** *n* a denial of responsibility.

disclose (dɪsˈkləʊz) *vb* make known; reveal. **disclosure** *n* < Latin *dis-* + *claudere* to close.

disco (ˈdɪskəʊ) *n, pl* **discos** (*informal*) a discothèque.

discolour (dɪsˈkʌlə) *vb* change colour; stain or fade. **discoloration** *n* < Latin *dis-* + *color* colour.

discomfit (dɪsˈkʌmfət) *vb* embarrass; disconcert. **discomfiture** *n* < Old French *des-* + *confire* to make.

discomfort (dɪsˈkʌmfət) *n* a lack of comfort; uneasiness.

discompose (ˌdɪskəmˈpəʊz) *vb* disturb or destroy the composure of. **discomposure** *n*

disconcert (ˌdɪskənˈsɜːt) *vb* upset the composure of; fluster. < Middle French *des-* + *concerter* to concert.

disconnect (ˈdɪskəˈnɛkt) *vb* cut or break the connection of or between, esp. so as to put out of action. **disconnection** *n* **disconnected** *adj* confused; disjointed.

disconsolate (dɪsˈkɑnsələt) *adj* disappointed; downcast. **disconsolately** *adv* < Latin *dis-* + *consolari* to console.

discontent (ˌdɪskənˈtɛnt) *n* dissatisfaction. **discontented** *adj*

discontinue (ˌdɪskənˈtɪnjuː) *vb* bring or come to an end. **discontinuance** *n* **discontinuity** *n* **discontinuous** *adj*

discord (ˈdɪskɔːd) *n* **1** disagreement; conflict. **2** a disagreeably harsh combination of musical notes sounded together. **discordant** *adj* **discordantly** *adv* < ultimately Latin *dis* + *cor* heart.

discothèque (ˈdɪskəˌtɛk) *n* **1** a night-club where people dance to recorded music. **2** the equipment used for playing records at a night-club, party, etc. < French *disque* disc + *-o-* + *thèque*, as in biblio*thèque* library.

discount (ˈdɪskaʊnt) *n* a financial reduction made from a full price or amount. **at a discount** below the regular price or value. **discount shop** a shop which sells goods at prices below the norm.
• *vb* (dɪsˈkaʊnt) consider to be unimportant or unreliable; disregard. < Latin *dis-* + *computare* to count.

discourage (dɪsˈkʌrɪdʒ) *vb* **1** dishearten; depress. **2** inhibit; hinder. **discouragement** *n*

discourse (ˈdɪskɔːs) *n* **1** a formal speech or piece of writing. **2** a conversation.
• *vb* (dɪsˈkɔːs) **1** express ideas, thoughts, etc., in speech or writing. **2** converse. < Latin *dis-* + *currere* to run.

discourteous (dɪsˈkɜːtɪəs) *adj* impolite. **discourteously** *adv* **discourtesy** *n*

discover (dɪˈskʌvə) *vb* notice or learn about by searching, esp. for the first time. **discoverer** *n* **discovery** *n* discovering; something discovered. < ultimately Latin *dis-* + *cooperire* to cover.

discredit (dɪsˈkrɛdɪt) *vb* **1** harm the reputation of; defame. **2** doubt; distrust.
• *n* **1** harm to a reputation; disrepute. **2** the cause of this. **3** lack of belief; doubt. **discreditable** *adj* bringing disgrace. **discreditably** *adv*

discreet (dɪˈskriːt) *adj* **1** cautious, esp. in speech; tactful. **2** unostentatious; modest. **discreetly** *adv* **discretion** *n* **1** being discreet in what one says; keeping secrets. **2** good sense or judgment: I leave it to your discretion. **3** freedom of choice: the age of discretion. **discretionary**

discreet or **discrete?**

These two words are sometimes confused. Discreet, the more common of the two, means 'cautious, especially in speech; tactful, not saying or doing anything that might cause trouble or embarrassment': She made some *discreet* enquiries concerning his background. Remember to be *discreet*. Don't mention the mistakes you've found.

Discrete is a rarer, more technical word and means 'unconnected, distinct, or indivisible': *discrete* units of energy, *discrete* molecules of gas.

adj left to someone's discretion: discretionary powers. < ultimately Latin *discernere* to discern, separate. SEE PANEL.

discrepancy (dɪˈskrɛpənsɪ) *n* a difference or conflict between facts, figures, etc. **discrepant** *adj* < Latin *dis-* + *crepare* to be noisy.

discrete (dɪˈskriːt) *adj* unconnected; distinct. **discretely** *adv* **discreteness** *n* < Latin *discretus.* SEE PANEL AT **DISCREET.**

discriminate (dɪˈskrɪmɪˌneɪt) *vb* **1** treat someone as different or inferior, esp. because of prejudice. **2** show good taste or judgment; discern. **discrimination** *n* < ultimately Latin *discernere* to discern.

discursive (dɪˈskɜːsɪv) *adj* rambling or digressive in speech. < Latin *discurrere* to run about.

discus (ˈdɪskəs) *n, pl* **discuses** a solid, heavy disc, thrown in an athletic competition. < Latin.

discuss (dɪˈskʌs) *vb* examine by speaking or writing about; debate. **discussion** *n* < ultimately Latin *dis-* + *quatere* to shake.

disdain (dɪsˈdeɪn) *n* arrogance; contempt.
• *vb* **1** regard as insignificant; sneer at. **2** refuse haughtily: He disdained to answer. **disdainful** *adj* **disdainfully** *adv* < Latin *dis-* + *dignare* to deign.

disease (dɪˈziːz) *n* **1** an impaired condition of the body caused by infection or malfunction; sickness. **2** harmful conditions; disorder: the disease of ignorance. **diseased** *adj* < Middle French *desdis-* + *aise* ease.

disembark (ˌdɪsɪmˈbɑːk) *vb* step down from a ship, plane, etc., onto land. **disembarkation** *n*

disembodied (ˌdɪsɪmˈbɒdɪd) *adj* (of a spirit, voice, etc.) separated from the body.

disembowel (ˌdɪsɪmˈbaʊəl) *vb* **disembowelled; disembowelling** take out the entrails of; gut.

disenchant (ˌdɪsɪnˈtʃɑːnt) *vb* destroy the illusions of. **disenchantment** *n*

disengage (ˌdɪsɪnˈgeɪdʒ) *vb* withdraw; detach. **disengagement** *n*

disentangle (ˌdɪsɪnˈtæŋgl) *vb* free from complication; sort out. **disentanglement** *n*

disestablish (ˌdɪsɪˈstæblɪʃ) *vb* sever an established connection, esp. of a Church with the State. **disestablishment** *n*

disfavour (dɪsˈfeɪvə) *n* disapproval; displeasure.

disfigure (dɪsˈfɪgə) *vb* damage the appearance of; mutilate. **disfigurement** *n*

disgrace (dɪsˈgreɪs) *n* **1** shame; dishonour. **2** someone or something that is shameful.
• *vb* bring shame upon; discredit. **disgraceful** *adj* **disgracefully** *adv* < ultimately Latin *dis-* + *gratia* grace.

disgruntled (dɪsˈgrʌntl̩d) *adj* dissatisfied; vexed. < *dis-* + Middle English *gruntlen* to grumble.

disguise (dɪsˈgaɪz) *vb* **1** hide the identity of by making changes in appearance. **2** hide or falsify (facts, information, etc.).
• *n* something which hides the nature or identity of a person or thing; use of this. < Old French *des-* + *guise.*

disgust (dɪsˈgʌst) *n* loathing or aversion.
• *vb* put off; nauseate. **disgusted** *adj* < Middle French *des-* + *goust* taste.

dish (dɪʃ) *n* **1** a shallow, open vessel for serving food or eating from; amount it contains. **2** a type of specially prepared food. **3** something with the shape of a dish: radar dish. **4** (*informal*) someone who is attractive.
• *vb* (*informal*) spoil. **dishcloth** *n* a cloth for washing dishes. **dish out** (*informal*) give out; distribute. **dish up** serve up (food, facts, etc.). **dishwasher** *n* a machine that washes dishes automatically. **dish-water** *n* water in which dishes have been washed. < Old English *disc* plate.

disharmony (dɪsˈhɑːmənɪ) *n* discord; friction.

dishearten (dɪsˈhɑːtn̩) *vb* depress; dispirit. **disheartenment** *n*

dishevelled (dɪˈʃɛvl̩d) *adj* untidy; messy. **dishevelment** *n* < Middle French *descheveler* to disarrange the hair. SEE PANEL AT **INADVERTENT.**

dishonest (dɪsˈɒnɪst) *adj* unfair; untrustworthy. **dishonestly** *adv* **dishonesty** *n*

dishonour (dɪsˈɒnə) *n* shame or disgrace; something causing this.
• *vb* shame; discredit. **dishonourable** *adj* contemptible. **dishonourably** *adv*

dishy (ˈdɪʃɪ) *adj* (*informal*) attractive.

disillusion (ˌdɪsɪˈluːʒən) *vb* shatter the false beliefs or ideals of; disenchant.
• *n* the condition of being disillusioned. **disillusionment** *n*

disincentive (ˌdɪsɪnˈsɛntɪv) *n* a discouragement or deterrent to action or effort.

disincline (ˌdɪsɪnˌklaɪn) *vb* make reluctant or unwilling. **disinclination** *n* reluctance; mild aversion.

disinfect (ˌdɪsɪnˈfɛkt) *vb* cleanse or

purify by destroying possibly harmful bacteria. **disinfectant** *n* a chemical substance used for cleansing or purifying.

disinherit (ˌdɪsɪnˈhɛrɪt) *vb* take away the right of inheritance from.

disintegrate (dɪsˈɪntɪˌgreɪt) *vb* break into fragments. **disintegration** *n*

disinter (ˌdɪsɪnˈtɜː) *vb* **disinterred; disinterring 1** dig up (a body). **2** bring to light.

disinterested (dɪsˈɪntrəstɪd) *adj* neutral; impartial. **disinterestedly** *adv* SEE PANEL.

disjointed (dɪsˈdʒɔɪntɪd) *adj* aimless or incoherent, esp. in speech.

disk (dɪsk) *n* (*computers*) a thin plate of plastic, etc., with a magnetized, etc., coating on which data are stored. **disk drive** an apparatus for turning a disk. < SEE **DISC.**

dislike (dɪsˈlaɪk) *n* disapproval; aversion. • *vb* consider to be unpleasant; object to.

dislocate (ˈdɪsləˌkeɪt) *vb* **1** displace or disconnect (esp. a bone) from its usual position. **2** disturb; disrupt. **dislocation** *n* < Latin *dis-* + *locare* to locate.

dislodge (dɪsˈlɒdʒ) *vb* force out from a fixed position; uproot. < Middle French *des-* + *loge* lodge.

disloyal (dɪsˈlɔɪəl) *adj* unfaithful; treacherous or traitorous. **disloyally** *adv* **disloyalty** *n* < Old French *des-* + *loial* loyal.

dismal (ˈdɪzməl) *adj* depressing; gloomy. **dismally** *adv* < Middle English *dismal* days marked as unlucky in medieval calendars. SEE PANEL.

dismantle (dɪsˈmæntḷ) *vb* take away furnishings, etc., from; take apart. < Middle French *des-* + *mantel* mantle.

dismay (dɪsˈmeɪ) *n* a feeling of anxiety or disappointment.
• *vb* alarm or disappoint. < Old French *desmaiier.*

disinterested or **uninterested?**

Disinterested means 'neutral; impartial': a *disinterested* evaluation of the facts

Uninterested means 'having no interest (in) or concern (for); bored or indifferent': Those who are *uninterested* can do something else.

A judge, referee, or umpire must always remain disinterested but should not be uninterested.

dismember (dɪsˈmɛmbə) *vb* **1** cut off or take away the limbs of. **2** partition (a country, empire, etc.). < Old French *des-* + *membre* member.

dismiss (dɪsˈmɪs) *vb* **1** send away or allow to leave from employment, service, etc. **2** put out of mind; reject as unimportant. **3** reject from a court of law: The case was dismissed. **4** (*cricket*) put out (a batsman or side). **dismissal** *n* < Latin *dis-* apart + *mittere* to send.

dismount (dɪsˈmaʊnt) *vb* get down from a horse, bicycle, etc.

disobey (ˌdɪsəˈbeɪ) *vb* refuse to obey; rebel. **disobedience** *n* **disobedient** *adj* defiant. **disobediently** *adv*

disorder (dɪsˈɔːdə) *n* **1** chaos; disorganization. **2** public unrest; riot. **3** a mental or physical affliction.
• *vb* disturb; upset. **disorderly** *adj*

disorganize (dɪsˈɔːgəˌnaɪz) *vb* disturb the arrangement of; disrupt. **disorganization** *n* **disorganized** *adj* confused.

disorientate (dɪsˈɔːrɪənˌteɪt) *vb* cause to lose one's sense of position or identity; confuse.

disown (dɪsˈəʊn) *vb* refuse to recognize or acknowledge.

disparage (dɪˈspærɪdʒ) *vb* speak scornfully of; belittle. **disparagement** *n* **disparagingly** *adv* < Old French *des-* dis- + *per* peer.

disparate (ˈdɪspərət) *adj* markedly different in type; contrasting. **disparity** *n* imbalance; dissimilarity. < Latin *dis-* + *parare* to prepare.

dispassionate (dɪsˈpæʃənət) *adj* calm; objective. **dispassionately** *adv*

dispatch (dɪˈspætʃ) *vb* **1** send away, usually for a specific purpose. **2** finish off; kill. **3** complete or conclude quickly. • *n* **1** sending away. **2** a message, esp.

dismal

Something that triggers feelings of gloom, despondency, or depression might be described as dismal: United gave yet another *dismal* performance, going down 4–0 to City. The modern meaning derives from a Middle English noun (*dismal*) meaning 'a list of 24 days marked on medieval calendars as unlucky'. This in turn comes via Anglo-French from the Medieval Latin phrase *dies mali* or 'evil days', from the Latin *dies* 'day' and *malus* 'bad'.

diplomatic or official. **3** speed; efficiency. **4** an item of news sent to a newspaper or news agency. **dispatch-rider** *n* a motor-cycle messenger. < Old French *des-* + *-peechier.*

dispel (dɪˈspɛl) *vb* **dispelled; dispelling** scatter; chase away. < Latin *dis-* + *pellere* to drive. SEE PANEL.

dispense (dɪˈspɛns) *vb* **1** give out; distribute. **2** carry out; administer: dispense justice. **3** prepare and give out (esp. medicine on prescription). **4 dispense with** do without; omit. **dispensable** *adj* unnecessary. **dispensary** *n* a place, for example in a hospital, from where drugs and medicines are distributed. **dispensation** *n* **1** distribution. **2** the arrangement of the world according to Nature or Providence. **3** exemption from a law, vow, duty, etc. **dispenser** *n* a machine that gives out specific items such as food or drink. < ultimately Latin *dis-* + *pendere* to weigh.

disperse (dɪˈspɜːs) *vb* **1** break up and scatter. **2** spread or be spread over a wide area. **3** distribute (particles) evenly through a liquid. **dispersal** *n* **dispersion** *n* < ultimately Latin *dis-* + *spargere* to scatter. SEE PANEL AT **DISPEL.**

dispirited (dɪˈspɪrɪtɪd) *adj* gloomy; dejected.

displace (dɪsˈpleɪs) *vb* **1** move from a usual place; dislodge. **2** replace; supersede. **displacement** *n*

display (dɪˈspleɪ) *vb* **1** present for viewing; show. **2** parade; show off. • *n* **1** an exhibition. **2** showing or something shown. < ultimately Latin *dis-* + *plicare* to fold.

displease (dɪsˈpliːz) *vb* annoy; upset. **displeasure** *n*

dispel or **disperse?**

Dispel means 'to scatter; chase away' and tends to be used of things that are intangible such as doubts, fears, or rumours: The Secretary made an official statement in order to *dispel* rumours about the resignation.

Disperse means 'to break up or cause to break up and scatter': The police asked the crowd to *disperse* as quickly as possible and also 'to spread or be spread over a wide area': The seeds were *dispersed* by the wind.

disport (dɪˈspɔːt) *vb* (*formal*) indulge in pleasure; play. < Middle French *des-* + *porter* to carry.

dispose (dɪˈspəʊz) *vb* **1** place in order; arrange. **2** cause to have a certain attitude: He's well-disposed to the idea. **3 dispose of** get rid of; deal with. **disposable** *adj* **1** available for use. **2** made to be thrown away after use. **disposal** *n* **1** throwing away. **2** arrangement; position. **3** the authority to use. **disposition** *n* **1** placement; organization. **2** character; nature: a cheerful disposition. **3** a habit or tendency. < ultimately Latin *dis-* + *ponere* to put.

dispossess (ˌdɪspəˈzɛs) *vb* take away from; deprive. **dispossession** *n*

disproportion (ˌdɪsprəˈpɔːʃən) *n* imbalance; inequality. **disproportionate** *adj* **disproportionately** *adv*

disprove (dɪsˈpruːv) *vb* prove to be wrong; discredit.

dispute (dɪsˈpjuːt) *vb* **1** discuss or argue. **2** call into question; challenge. • *n* (ˈdɪspjuːt) **1** a debate or controversy. **2** an argument. **disputant** *n* **disputable** *adj* arguable. < Latin *dis-* + *putare* to think.

disqualify (dɪsˈkwɒlɪˌfaɪ) *vb* **disqualified; disqualifying 1** rule out of a competition, exam, etc., for violating rules. **2** make or be unfit or unsuitable for. **disqualification** *n*

disquiet (dɪsˈkwaɪət) *vb, n* (cause) concern or anxiety. **disquieting** *adj* troubling.

disregard (ˌdɪsrɪˈgɑːd) *vb* treat as unimportant; ignore. • *n* indifference; neglect.

disrepair (ˌdɪsrɪˈpɛə) *n* a state of being out of order or needing repair.

disrepute (ˌdɪsrɪˈpjuːt) *n* lack of respectability; disgrace: The club fell info disrepute. **disreputable** *adj* **disreputably** *adv*

disrespect (ˌdɪsrɪˈspɛkt) *n* lack of respect; incivility. **disrespectful** *adj*

disrobe (dɪsˈrəʊb) *vb* take off clothing, esp. official or ceremonial; undress.

disrupt (dɪsˈrʌpt) *vb* **1** throw into a disorganized state; upset: Traffic was disrupted. **2** break up; interrupt. **disruption** *n* **disruptive** < Latin *dis-* + *rumpere* to break.

dissatisfied (dɪˈsætɪsˌfaɪd) *adj* discontented; fed up. **dissatisfaction** *n*

dissect (dɪˈsɛkt, daɪˈsɛkt) *vb* **1** cut up for scientific study. **2** break down; analyse. **dissection** *n* **dissector** *n* < Latin *dis-* + *secare* to cut.

disseminate (dɪˈsɛmɪˌneɪt) *vb* circulate; distribute (ideas, information, etc.).

dissemination *n* < Latin *dis-* + *semen* seed.

dissent (dɪˈsɛnt) *vb* differ in opinion; disagree.
• *n* a difference in opinion, esp. political. **dissension** *n* **dissenter** *n* < Latin *dis-* + *sentire* to feel.

dissertation (ˌdɪsəˈteɪʃən) *n* a long essay on a specific subject. < Latin *dis-* + *serere* to arrange.

disservice (dɪˈsɜːvɪs) *n* a bad turn or unkindness.

dissident (ˈdɪsɪdənt) *n* someone who disagrees with or protests against established opinion or the government. **dissidence** *n* **dissident** *adj* < Latin *dis-* + *sedēre* to sit.

dissimilar (dɪˈsɪmɪlə) *adj* different; unlike. **dissimilarity** *n*

dissipate (ˈdɪsɪˌpeɪt) *vb* **1** scatter or vanish or cause to scatter or vanish. **2** use up wastefully; squander. **dissipation** *n* **dissipated** *adj* self-indulgent; wasted. < Latin *dis-* + *supare* to throw.

dissociate (dɪˈsəʊʃɪˌeɪt) *vb* break off connections with; separate. **dissociation** *n* < Latin *dis-* + *socius* companion.

dissolute (ˈdɪsəˌluːt) *adj* immoral; corrupt. < Latin *dissolvere* to dissolve.

dissolve (dɪˈzɒlv) *vb* **1** make, become, or be dispersed in a fluid. **2** bring to an end officially: dissolve parliament; dissolve a marriage. **3** fade or disappear. **4** be emotionally overcome: He dissolved into tears. **dissolution** *n* < Latin *dis-* + *solvere* to loosen.

dissuade (dɪˈsweɪd) *vb* advise against doing something. **dissuasion** *n* **dissuasive** *adj* < Latin *dis-* + *suadēre* to urge.

distance (ˈdɪstəns) *n* **1** the length of space or time between two points, events, etc. **2** a far-off place: in the distance. **3** reserve; aloofness: She kept her distance.
• *vb* **1** separate (oneself) from, mentally or physically. **2** outdo or outrun. **distant** *adj* **1** at a specified distance. **2** remote in space, time, relationship, etc.: a distant cousin. **3** aloof; withdrawn. **distantly** *adv* < Latin *dis-* + *stare* to stand.

distaste (dɪsˈteɪst) *n* dislike; revulsion. **distasteful** *adj* offensive. **distastefully** *adv*

distemper (dɪˈstɛmpə) *n* **1** an animal disease, esp. of dogs, causing breathing difficulties. **2** a paint of mixed pigments and glue or size.
• *vb* paint with distemper. < Latin *dis-* + *temperare* to mingle.

distend (dɪˈstɛnd) *vb* swell or become swollen from internal pressure. **distension** *n* < Latin *dis-* + *tendere* to stretch.

distil (dɪˈstɪl) *vb* **distilled; distilling** **1** condense or purify. **2** subject to or undergo distillation. **3** produce (spirits, etc.) in this way. **distillation** *n* **1** a process in which substances are vaporized by heating, then new or purified substances are formed from the condensed gases. **2** something produced by this process. **distiller** *n* someone who distils alcoholic liquors. **distillery** *n* a place where alcoholic liquors are distilled. < ultimately Latin *de-* + *stillare* to drip.

distinct (dɪˈstɪŋkt) *adj* **1** clearly noticeable; definite. **2** different; unconnected. **distinctly** *adv* **distinctness** *n* **distinction** *n* **1** separation or differentiation; something differentiated. **2** a feature or characteristic. **3** outstanding quality; excellence: a man of distinction. **distinctive** *adj* distinguishing; characteristic.
SEE PANEL.

distinguish (dɪˈstɪŋgwɪʃ) *vb* **1** make or recognize a difference between. **2** set apart; characterize. **3** make out; discern. **4** bring honour to: He distinguished himself in battle. **distinguished** *adj* **1** renowned; celebrated. **2** striking; conspicuous. < Latin *distinguere* to separate.

distort (dɪˈstɔːt) *vb* **1** alter the normal shape of by bending, twisting, etc. **2** change the true meaning of; misrepresent. **distortion** *n* < Latin *dis-* + *torquēre* to twist.

---

distinct or **distinctive?**

These two words are sometimes confused. Distinct means ‘definite; clearly noticeable’ as in a *distinct* smell of burning; a *distinct* possibility of redundancies; The patient’s condition has shown a *distinct* improvement today; I had the *distinct* feeling that something awful was going to happen.

Distinctive means ‘distinguishing one person or thing from another; characteristic’: the *distinctive* call of the cuckoo; the *distinctive* smell of leather; *distinctive* military uniforms; His car has been sprayed a *distinctive* shade of blue.

distract (dɪˈstrækt) *vb* **1** draw attention away from. **2** divert; entertain. **distracted** *adj* agitated. **distraction** *n* **1** something that disturbs concentration. **2** an amusement or diversion. **3** distress; derangement: driven to distraction. < Latin *dis-* + *trahere* to draw.

distraught (dɪˈstrɔːt) *adj* frantic with grief or worry; agitated. < Latin *distractus.*

distress (dɪˈstrɛs) *n* **1** anguish or suffering, whether mental or physical. **2** a condition of desperate need.
• *vb* cause suffering to. < Latin *distringere* to impede.

distribute (dɪˈstrɪbjuːt) *vb* **1** divide up and share out; allocate. **2** pass round; circulate. **distribution** *n* **distributive** *adj* **distributor** *n* **1** someone who distributes, esp. goods. **2** an apparatus for passing electric current to the spark-plugs in an internal-combustion engine. < Latin *dis-* + *tribuere* to allot.

district (ˈdɪstrɪkt) *n* a division of land regarded as a unit for administrative purposes, or with distinguishing features: the Peak District; a postal district. < Latin *distringere.*

distrust (dɪsˈtrʌst) *vb, n* (regard with) wariness or suspicion. **distrustful** *adj*

disturb (dɪˈstɜːb) *vb* **1** interrupt or intrude on; make uneasy. **2** change the order or position of. **disturbance** *n* **1** interruption; something that interrupts. **2** a disorder or commotion, esp. public. **disturbed** *adj* mentally or emotionally unbalanced. < ultimately Latin *dis-* + *turbare* to confuse.

disuse (dɪsˈjuːs) *n* the condition of being no longer in use. **disused** *adj*

ditch (dɪtʃ) *n* a long, narrow channel of dug earth for irrigation, defence, etc.
• *vb* **1** dig or enclose with a ditch. **2** (of an aircraft) make a forced landing on water. **3** (*informal*) discard; get rid of. **dull as ditch-water** extremely dull. < Old English *dīc.*

dither (ˈdɪðə) *vb* behave indecisively; hesitate.
• *n* a state of nervous agitation: all of a dither. < Middle English *didderen.*

ditto (ˈdɪtəʊ) *n, pl* **dittos** the same; the above, denoted by the marks to avoid repeating a word. < ultimately Latin *dicere* to say. SEE PANEL.

ditty (ˈdɪtɪ) *n* a short, simple poem or song. < Latin *dictare* to dictate.

divan (dɪˈvæn) *n* a long, low couch, often without back or arms; bed like this. < Persian *dīwān* account book.

dive (daɪv) *vb* **1** jump into water, head first. **2** (of a submarine, diver, etc.) submerge. **3** (of an aircraft) descend steeply and rapidly. **4** dash or leap out of sight: dive for cover. **5** dip (the hand) into.
• *n* **1** diving. **2** a sudden, sharp descent or decline. **3** (*informal*) a sleazy or disreputable club, bar, etc. **diver** *n* someone who dives underwater, esp. professionally. **diving-board** *n* a board at a swimming-pool, beach, etc., for diving from. **diving-suit** *n* a watertight suit with helmet and air supply for underwater work. < Old English *dyfan.*

diverge (daɪˈvɜːdʒ) *vb* **1** split or move in different directions from a common point. **2** turn aside from. **divergence** *n* **divergent** *adj* < Latin *dis-* + *vergere* to incline.

diversify (daɪˈvɜːsɪˌfaɪ) *vb* **diversified; diversifying** branch out; vary. **diverse** *adj* **1** of different kinds; assorted. **2** differing; dissimilar. **diversity** *n* **1** being different. **2** variety. < ultimately Latin *divertere* to turn in opposite directions.

divert (daɪˈvɜːt) *vb* **1** turn from one direction to another; distract. **2** amuse; entertain. **diversion** *n* **1** turning away from a course, activity, etc. **2** an alternative route for traffic when the main route is temporarily closed. **3** an amusement or entertainment. **4** something that takes away attention: create a diversion. **diversionary** *adj* **diverting** *adj* entertaining. < ultimately Latin *dis-* + *vertere* to turn.

divest (daɪˈvɛst) *vb* **1** take (property, rights, etc.) away from. **2** strip (of clothing or equipment). < Latin *dis-* + *vestire* to clothe.

divide (dɪˈvaɪd) *vb* **1** separate into two or more parts. **2** exist as a boundary between; separate. **3** classify; categorize. **4** also **divide out** allocate; distribute. **5** cause to disagree; alienate: The hanging question divided the Party. **6** determine how many times one number contains another.
• *n* **1** a watershed. **2** a split or division.

ditto

The word ditto meaning 'the same again' or 'aforementioned' derives via Italian dialect from the Latin *dictum* meaning 'that which has been said before', from *dicere* 'to say'.

dividend *n* **1** a number or amount to be divided. **2** a share of the profits of a company, or a football-pool win. **3** a benefit or reward: Hard work pays dividends.
divider *n* **1** a screen or partition. **2** *pl* measuring-compasses with two pointed arms. **divisible** *adj* capable of being divided. **division** *n* **1** dividing or being divided; divided part. **2** a partition or boundary. **3** a major unit of an organization such as a firm or army. **4** a class or category. **5** a difference of opinion. **6** the separating of members of parliament into lobbies for voting. **7** the process of dividing in mathematics, denoted by the sign ÷. **divisional** *adj* **divisive** *adj* tending to cause disunity; disruptive. < Latin *dis-* + *-videre* to separate.

divine (dɪˈvaɪn) *adj* **1** of, concerning, or like a god or God; sacred. **2** (*informal*) beautiful; delightful.
• *vb* foretell intuitively by or as if by magic; guess. **diviner** *n* **divining-rod** *n* a forked rod, used for detecting the presence of water or minerals. **divinity** *n* **1** being divine. **2** God or a god. **3** the study of the Christian faith. < Latin *divus* god.

divorce (dɪˈvɔːs) *n* **1** the ending of a marriage, recognized in law. **2** a split or separation.
• *vb* **1** end a marriage with (one's wife or husband) by divorce. **2** separate, esp. completely. **divorcee** *n* someone who is divorced. < Latin *divortere* to divert.

divulge (daɪˈvʌldʒ) *vb* disclose; reveal (information). < Latin *dis-* + *vulgare* to make known, from *vulgus* common people

DIY *abbrev* do-it-yourself.

dizzy (ˈdɪzɪ) *adj* **1** giddy; light-headed. **2** causing giddiness or confusion: dizzy heights. **dizzily** *adv* **dizziness** *n* < Old English *dysig* stupid.

DJ *abbrev* disc jockey.

do (dʊ, də; *stressed* duː) *vb* **did; done; doing 1** carry out; achieve. **2** be adequate or useful: These will do. **3** work out; solve: do a puzzle. **4** produce or provide: They do good meals here. **5** arrange; fix: do the beds. **6** perform or put on (a play, show, etc.). **7** complete or cover (a distance): This car does 30 miles to the gallon. **8** carry on; behave. **9** visit; explore: We did Europe last year. **10** (*informal*) swindle: He did me out of £5. **11** make out; manage: She did quite well out of it. **12** serve as a prison sentence: He did five years. **13** (*informal*) attack or arrest. **14** attend to or serve professionally.
• *auxiliary vb* **1** used to express present and past tense in negative statements and questions. **2** used for emphasis: I do like ice-cream. **3** used to avoid the repetition of a verb just mentioned: I know as much as you do.
• *n* (*informal*) a function, party, or gathering. < Old English *dōn*. SEE PANEL.

docile (ˈdəʊsaɪl) *adj* willing; compliant. **docilely** *adv* **docility** *n* < Latin *docēre* to teach.

dock[1] (dɒk) *vb* **1** cut off part of (the tail of

That will do!

Do features in a number of idiomatic expressions, including:

do away with 1 to abolish: do away with restrictions on Sunday trading. **2 to kill:** do away with oneself.
do down to talk about (someone) unkindly.
do for 1 to destroy or ruin: We'll be done for if we don't get back to base camp. **2** to do housework for. **3** also **do as** to serve as a substitute for: This saucer will do as an ashtray.
do-gooder *n* a well-intentioned but naïve person.
do in to murder.
do-it-yourself *n* the skill of doing practical jobs around the house oneself, rather than employing a tradesman.
do or die to make a desperate, especially final, attempt to achieve something.
do out to tidy or clean; decorate.
do out of to stop (someone) from having.
do over to attack severely and beat up.
do up 1 to fasten; wrap up. **2** to modernize; repair or decorate. **3** to make (oneself) look attractive: Sally did herself up for the party.
do with to need or want: I could just do with a nice cup of tea!
do without to manage without: You can borrow my car for a day or two. I can do without it.
how do you do? a polite, conventional greeting used when people meet each other for the first time.
that will do! that is enough; stop it: That will do, children! You've made enough noise for one morning!

an animal). **2** deduct an amount from (fees, wages, etc.). < Old English *-docca.*

dock[2] *n* an area of a port or harbour which is artificially enclosed for ships to moor or be repaired.
• *vb* **1** go or come into dock. **2** (of spacecraft) join together in space. **docker** *n* someone who loads and unloads ships. **dockland** *n* the area surrounding a dockyard. **docks** or **dockyard** *n* an area where ships are built, repaired, loaded, or unloaded. < ultimately Latin *ductio* leading.

dock[3] *n* an enclosure in a criminal court where the accused sits or stands. < Flemish *docke* cage.

docket (ˈdɒkɪt) *n* a document recording goods delivered, the contents of a parcel, or an amount of customs duty payable.
• *vb* mark with an identifying label; register. < Middle English *doggette.*

doctor (ˈdɒktə) *n* **1** someone qualified to practise medicine. **2** someone who holds a doctorate from a university.
• *vb* **1** apply medication to; treat. **2** modify or tamper with: doctored evidence. **3** castrate; spay. < ultimately Latin *docēre* to teach.

doctorate (ˈdɒktərət) *n* the highest academic degree awarded by a university, conferring the title of *doctor.*

doctrine (ˈdɒktrɪn) *n* a principle or body of principles held in a system of belief, esp. political or religious. **doctrinaire** *n, adj* (someone) concerned with theory rather than practical considerations. **doctrinal** *adj* of doctrine.

document (ˈdɒkjʊmənt) *n* a paper, esp. official, that gives information or proof about something.
• *vb* (ˈdɒkjʊˌmɛnt) provide with factual support, references, etc.; authenticate. **documentation** *n* < Latin *docēre* to teach.

documentary (ˌdɒkjʊˈmɛntərɪ) *adj* **1** contained in written documents; certified: documentary evidence. **2** based on factual information or material.
• *n* a documentary film.

dodder (ˈdɒdə) *vb* shake or tremble from age or weakness. **dodderer** *n* **doddery** *adj* < Middle English *dadiren.*

doddle (ˈdɒdḷ) *n* an extremely easy task. < probably *dodder.*

dodge (dɒdʒ) *vb* **1** shift position suddenly in order to avoid something. **2** evade (a task, duty, etc.) by trickery.
• *n* **1** a sudden, rapid movement to avoid something. **2** an ingenious way of evading or tricking: tax dodge. **dodger** *n* < origin unknown.

dodgy (ˈdɒdʒɪ) *adj* (*informal*) **1** unreliable; shady: a dodgy character. **2** risky; dangerous.

doe (dəʊ) *n* the adult female of various animals including the rabbit and deer. < Old English *dā.*

doff (dɒf) *vb* take off (a hat), esp. in greeting or to show respect. < Middle English *don* to do + *of* off.

dog (dɒg) *n* **1** one of a family of four-legged, flesh-eating mammals, kept as a pet or for racing, hunting, etc. **2** the male of this and related animals such as the fox or wolf. **3** a mechanical device for holding or fastening. **4 the dogs** greyhound racing.
• *vb* **dogged; dogging** follow closely and persistently: dog someone's footsteps. **dogfish** *n* any of various small sharks. **doghouse** *n* a dog kennel. **dog-paddle** *n* an elementary swimming stroke performed by kicking the legs and paddling the arms quickly. **dogsbody** *n* (*informal*) someone who does menial labour. < Old English *docga.* SEE PANEL.

dogged (ˈdɒgɪd) *adj* persevering; stubborn. **doggedly** *adv*

doggerel (ˈdɒgərəl) *n* comic and usually irregular verse. < Middle English *dogerel.*

dogma (ˈdɒgmə) *n* a belief or teaching put forward as unquestionable, esp. by a church; article of faith. **dogmatic** *adj* **1** of dogma. **2** assertive; arrogant. **dogmatism** *n* < ultimately Greek *dokein* to seem.

doily (ˈdɔɪlɪ) *n* a small, decorative mat laid on or under plates, dishes, etc. < *Doily,* 18th-century London draper.

doing (ˈduːɪŋ) SEE **DO.**
• *n* **1** an action: It was none of my doing. **2** effort: It took a lot of doing. **3** *pl* actions or activities.

doldrums (ˈdɒldrəmz) *pl n* **1** a region of the ocean near the equator where calm persists for long periods. **2** a state of depression or boredom. < probably Old English *dol* foolish.

dole (dəʊl) *vb* also **dole out** hand or share out; apportion.
• *n* (*informal*) unemployment benefit paid by the State: on the dole. < Old English *dāl* portion.

doleful (ˈdəʊlfʊl) *adj* gloomy; mournful. **dolefully** *adv* < Latin *dolus* grief.

doll (dɒl) *n* **1** a small-scale model of a human, used esp. as a child's toy. **2** (*informal*) an attractive but silly woman or girl.

• *vb* **doll up** dress up. < probably *Doll*, nickname for *Dorothy*.
dollar (ˈdɒlə) *n* the basic monetary unit in the USA, Canada, etc. < German *Taler*, from Sankt Joachimsthal, town in Bohemia. SEE PANEL.
dollop (ˈdɒləp) *n* (*informal*) a shapeless mass, esp. of a soft, mushy food or substance. < perhaps Scandinavian.
dolly (ˈdɒlɪ) *n* **1** (*children's informal*) a doll. **2** a wheeled platform for moving a film or television camera. **dolly-bird** *n* (*informal*) a pretty young woman.
dolphin (ˈdɒlfɪn) *n* a sea-mammal, smaller than a whale, with a beak-like snout. < ultimately Greek *delphis*.
domain (dəˈmeɪn) *n* **1** a controlled area or territory; sphere of influence. **2** a field of knowledge, study, etc. < ultimately Latin *dominus* master.
dome (dəʊm) *n* a roof shaped like a hemisphere; any structure like this. **domed** *adj* < ultimately Latin *domus* house.
domestic (dəˈmɛstɪk) *adj* **1** of a household or family. **2** of one's own or a particular country; not foreign. **3** (of animals) kept or bred by man; tame. • *n* a household servant. **domestically** *adv* **domesticated** *adj* **1** (of animals) trained or tamed. **2** home-loving. **domesticity** *n* home or family life; fondness for this. **domestic science** instruction in household skills such as cooking, cleaning, etc. < ultimately Latin *domus* home.
domicile (ˈdɒmɪˌsaɪl) *n* a legal residence; home. **domiciliary** *adj* **domiciled** *adj* dwelling in.
dominate (ˈdɒmɪˌneɪt) *vb* **1** have control or influence over. **2** have an influential position in. **3** overlook from a higher position: Skyscrapers dominate the city. **dominance** *n* **domination** *n* **dominant** *adj* prevailing. **domineer** *vb* behave overbearingly; boss around. < Latin *dominus* master.
dominion (dəˈmɪnjən) *n* **1** the power to govern or control. **2** a self-governing territory, esp. a Commonwealth country other than the United Kingdom.

dogs and **hounds**

Hound, at one time meaning 'any breed of dog', is an example of a word whose meaning has *narrowed* during the course of time (see also panel at **meat**). Dog, on the other hand, has ironically undergone the reverse process. In Middle English a dogge was one particular breed of man's best friend, a meaning which has since *broadened*.

Butcher is another word whose meaning was once highly restricted in comparison with its modern sense. In the days when dogs were 'hounds' a bocher was 'a slaughterer of goats'.

One of the causes of broadening has to do with technological development. For instance, following the arrival of the combustion engine, the verb drive has been extended so that it now embraces not just the horse-drawn cart, but the motor vehicle as well. It is only when your car refuses to start on a wet winter morning and you are tempted to beat it with a stick that the original, narrow meaning of drive comes to mind!

Dog features in a number of expressions, including:

dog-eared *adj* (of a corner of a page) turned down; shabby.
dog eat dog ruthless competition.
dog-end *n* a cigarette end.
dog in the manger someone who selfishly refuses to give to others the things that he himself or she herself cannot use, from Aesop's fable of a dog living in a manger who prevented an ox from eating the hay, despite the fact that the dog couldn't eat it himself.
dog's life a dull, miserable existence.
dog-tired *adj* very tired.
go to the dogs to go to ruin: 'This country's going to the dogs!'

dollar

The basic unit of currency in a number of countries including the USA, Canada, and Australia is the dollar. The word dollar derives ultimately from *Sankt Joachimsthal*, the name of the town in Bohemia where they were first minted at the end of the 15th century. *Joachimsthal* is a combination of *Joachim* and *Thal* or 'valley'.

For some time the coin went by the German name of *Joachimstaler*. Gradually this was replaced by the shortened form *Taler* or *Thaler*, which entered Dutch and Low German as *daler*. It is uncertain from which of these sources the word dollar derives.

domino (ˈdɒmɪˌnəʊ) *n, pl* **dominoes** a flat, oblong block with up to six pips on each half of one face, used in the game of dominoes. **domino effect** the effect of one event triggering off a series of similar events, esp. political. < ultimately Latin *dominus* master.

don[1] (dɒn) *vb* **donned; donning** put on (a disguise, clothes, etc.). < *do* + *on*.

don[2] *n* a tutor, fellow, or head in a college of Oxford or Cambridge university; university teacher. < Latin *dominus* master.

donate (dəʊˈneɪt) *vb* make a gift or donation. **donation** *n* a gift of money, property, etc., esp. to a worthy cause. < ultimately Latin *donum* gift.

done (dʌn) SEE **DO.**
• *adj* **1** acceptable; proper: It's not the done thing. **2** also **done in** exhausted. **3** sufficiently cooked: done to a turn. **4** also **done with** completed; over.
• *interj* used to express agreement in a business deal, bet, etc.

donkey (ˈdɒŋkɪ) *n, pl* **donkeys** a domesticated member of the horse family with long ears; ass. **donkey jacket** a thick, mid-length, workman's jacket. **donkey's years** (*informal*) an extremely long time. **donkey-work** *n* hard, monotonous labour; drudgery. < perhaps *dun* + *-key*, as in mon*key*.

donor (ˈdəʊnə) *n* **1** someone who makes a gift or donation. **2** somebody who provides blood, body organs, etc., for the use of another. < Latin *donare* to present.

doodle (ˈduːdl̩) *vb, n* (make) an aimless sketch or drawing while the mind is on something else. < perhaps: simpleton, from Low German *dudeltopf*.

doom (duːm) *vb, n* (destine to) an unhappy fate, esp. death or destruction. **doomsday** *n* the judgment day; day of reckoning. < Old English *dōm*.

door (dɔː) *n* **1** a barrier that closes a way in or out of a place, usually hinged or sliding. **2** a doorway. **3** a means of getting or reaching something. **doorkeeper** *n* also **doorman** someone on duty at the entrance to a hotel, theatre, etc. **doormat** *n* **1** a mat near a door for wiping dirt off shoes. **2** (*informal*) someone who meekly submits to ill-treatment. **doorstep** *n* **1** a step on the outside of a door. **2** (*informal*) a thick slice of bread. **doorstop** *n* a device for keeping an open door from moving. **door-to-door** *adj* (of selling or canvassing) calling at every house in an area in turn. **doorway** *n* an entrance or exit filled by a door. < Old English *duru*.

dope (dəʊp) *n* **1** a thick, liquid preparation for coating, lubricating, etc. **2** (*informal*) medicines, narcotics, or drugs. **3** (*informal*) facts; information. **4** (*informal*) an idiot; fool.
• *vb* **1** apply dope to. **2** treat with a medicine or drug. **dopey** *adj* (*informal*) **1** sleepy or drugged. **2** stupid. **dopiness** *n* < Dutch *dopen* to dip.

dormant (ˈdɔːmənt) *adj* **1** sleeping or appearing like this. **2** with growth or activity suspended: a dormant volcano; dormant plants. **dormancy** *n* < Latin *dormire* to sleep.

dormitory (ˈdɔːmɪtrɪ) *n* a room equipped with a number of beds in a school, institution, etc. **dormitory town** a town where the inhabitants commute to work elsewhere.

dormouse (ˈdɔːˌmaʊs) *n, pl* **dormice** a small, mouse-like rodent, with a bushy tail, that hibernates in winter. < perhaps Middle French *dormir* to sleep + Middle English *mous* mouse.

dorsal (ˈdɔːsl̩) *adj* relating to the spine or back of, for example an animal or plant: dorsal fin. < Latin *dorsum* back.

dose (dəʊs) *n* **1** a measured amount of medicine taken at one time or at intervals. **2** an amount of radiation absorbed. **3** something experienced, esp. something unpleasant: a dose of flu.
• *vb* give a dose, esp. of medicine, to. **dosage** *n* the giving of a dose of medicine; amount given. < ultimately Greek *didonai* to give.

doss (dɒs) *vb* (*slang*) also **doss down** sleep, esp. in a makeshift bed or in a doss-house. **dosser** *n* **doss-house** *n* a cheap hostel, esp. for down-and-outs. < origin uncertain.

dossier (ˈdɒsjeɪ) *n* a file of papers or documents containing detailed reports, information, etc. < ultimately Latin *dorsum*.

dot (dɒt) *n* **1** a small spot, point, or speck. **2** one of the two signals used in the Morse Code, shorter than the dash.
• *vb* **dotted; dotting 1** mark with a dot; set a dot above a letter. **2** scatter at random: Various people were dotted around. **dotted line** a line of dots for entering a signature on a form, document, etc. **on the dot** exactly on time. **the year dot** (*informal*) the distant past. < Old English *dott* head of a boil.

dotage (ˈdəʊtɪdʒ) *n* feeble-mindedness caused by old age; senility. < Middle English *doten* to dote.

dote (dəʊt) *vb* **dote on** lavish affection

on; adore. < Middle English *doten.*

dotty (ˈdɒtɪ) *adj* (*informal*) peculiar; eccentric.

double (ˈdʌbḷ) *adj* **1** composed of two similar parts or things forming a pair. **2** twice as great or as many. **3** designed for two people or things: a double room. **4** combining two aspects or qualities. **5** (of flowers) having more than the usual quantity of petals. **6** with two layers; folded in two.
• *adv* **1** twice as much or as far. **2** two together.
• *n* **1** a twofold amount. **2** someone who looks very much like another. **3** (in darts) a throw within the outermost ring of a dartboard, scoring double. **4** a bet in which the stake and winnings from one race are used to bet in another.
• *vb* **1** increase by an equal number or amount. **2** fold or bend in two. **3 double back** turn back on a particular course. **4 double up** join; couple. **5** play two parts; serve two purposes: The sofa doubles as a bed. **at the double** quickly; in a hurry. **double agent** a spy pretending to work for one country while working for another. **double-barrelled** *adj* **1** (of a gun) with two barrels. **2** (of a surname) with two parts. **double-bass** *n* the largest instrument of the violin family with the lowest pitch. **double-breasted** *adj* (of a jacket, coat, etc.) with one half of the front overlapping the other when fastened. **double-check** *vb* check again. **double chin** a chin with a large fold of skin under it. **double cream** a thick, heavy cream, suitable for whipping. **double-cross** *vb* cheat or betray. **double-dealing** *n* underhand actions, esp. in business. **double-decker** *n* a bus with two passenger decks. **double Dutch** incomprehensible talk; gibberish. **double entendre** a word or expression with a second meaning, often slightly obscene. **double entry** a book-keeping system in which transactions are entered as a debit in one account and as a credit in another. **double glazing** windows of two layers of glass with a space between, to keep out noise or keep in heat. **double-jointed** *adj* with very flexible joints of the fingers, arms, etc. **double or quits** (in dice, cards, etc.) a throw or play deciding whether a player pays nothing or twice the amount owed. **double-park** *vb* park a car at the side of another parked car in a street. **doubles** *pl n* a game played by two pairs of players. **double-take** *n* a delayed or secondary reaction to a remark or situation. **double-talk** *n* deceptive or ambiguous talk. **double time 1** (of troops) marching at twice the normal rate. **2** payment to a worker at twice the normal rate. < ultimately Latin *duo* two + *-plus* multiplied by.

doublet (ˈdʌblɪt) *n* **1** a close-fitting, often sleeveless jacket worn by men in the 15th-17th centuries. **2** either of a pair of related things. < SEE **DOUBLE.**

doubt (daʊt) *n* **1** a state of uncertainty. **2** distrust; disbelief.
• *vb* **1** lack faith in. **2** be uncertain about. **doubter** *n* **doubtful** *adj* **1** questionable. **2** hesitant; unsettled. **doubtfully** *adv* **doubtless** *adv* **1** without doubt. **2** probably. **doubtlessly** *adv* **no doubt** probably. < Latin *dubitare.*

douche (du:ʃ) *n* a jet of liquid directed towards a part of the body to cleanse it; device for this.
• *vb* apply a douche to. < ultimately Latin *ducere* to lead.

dough (dəʊ) *n* **1** a mixture of usually flour and water or another liquid, used for baking as bread, pastry, etc. **2** (*slang*) money. **doughnut** *n* a small, sweet, deep-fried roll or ring of dough, **doughy** *adj* < Old English *dāg.*

dour (dʊə) *adj* **1** rigid; austere. **2** sullen; unfriendly. **dourly** *adv* **dourness** *n* < perhaps Latin *durus* hard.

douse (daʊs) *vb* **1** submerge or soak in water. **2** put out (a light). < probably obsolete *douse* to smite.

dove (dʌv) *n* **1** a kind of pigeon, commonly regarded as a symbol of peace. **2** someone who prefers political negotiation to war: doves and hawks. **dovecote** *n* a shed or box with compartments for domestic pigeons. < Old English *dūfe.*

dovetail (ˈdʌvˌteɪl) *n* a wedge-shaped joint.
• *vb* **1** interlock by means of a dovetail joint. **2** fit closely or neatly together.

dowager (ˈdaʊədʒə) *n* **1** a widow holding a title or property derived from her late husband: dowager duchess. **2** a dignified elderly woman. < Middle French *douer* to endow.

dowdy (ˈdaʊdɪ) *adj* **1** (of clothes) old-fashioned or drab. **2** dressed shabbily. **dowdily** *adv* **dowdiness** *n* < Middle English *doude* ugly woman.

dowel (ˈdaʊəl) *n* a pin of wood, metal, etc., for fixing the position of something by fitting into adjacent holes; rods of wood for cutting into pins.
• *vb* fasten with dowels. < Middle

English *dowle*.

down[1] (daʊn) *n* a region of gently rolling, often treeless uplands, esp. in S. England. < Old English *dūn* hill.

down[2] *n* a covering of soft feathers or hairs. < Old Norse *dūnn*.

down[3] *adv* **1** from a higher to a lower position. **2** towards, in, or at a relatively low place, condition, or level. **3** so as to be less intense or active: calm down. **4** on paper: Write this down. **5** away from a more important place or centre: He's down from the city. **6** (esp. of payment) immediate. **7** to the origin or moment of discovery: He tracked it down. **8** planned; scheduled: She's down for a meeting on Thursday. **9** in a particular area of a country, esp. towards the south. **10** incapacitated by illness: down with flu.
• *prep* **1** downwards through, on, or into. **2** down to or into: going down town.
• *adj* **1** going downwards: the down lift. **2** travelling away from a large place or centre. **3** in low spirits: feel down.
• *n* **1** a depression: ups and downs. **2** a grudge: He has a real down on them.
• *vb* **1** come or bring down. **2** swallow quickly. **down and out** a destitute person. **down-and-out** *adj* **downcast** *adj* **1** directed downwards: downcast eyes. **2** unhappy. **downfall** *n* a sudden fall from power or wealth; cause of this. **downgrade** *vb* reduce in rank or value. **down-hearted** *adj* dejected. **downpour** *n* a heavy rainfall. **downstream** *adj, adv* in the direction a stream flows. **down-to-earth** *adj* practical; sensible. **downtrodden** *adj* oppressed; exploited. **downturn** *n* a decline, esp. in business or activity. **down under** the antipodes; Australia and New Zealand. **down with** an expression of strong disapproval or hatred towards (a person or thing). < Old English *dūn* hill. SEE PANEL.

downhill (ˌdaʊnˈhɪl) *adv* **1** in a direction sloping downwards. **2** towards a lower or inferior state: go downhill.
• *adj* sloping downwards.

downright (ˈdaʊnˌraɪt) *adj* **1** absolute; thorough: a downright lie. **2** blunt; straightforward.
• *adv* thoroughly.

downstairs (ˌdaʊnˈstɛəz) *adv* on or to a lower floor; down the stairs.
• *adj* located on a lower floor.

downward (ˈdaʊnwəd) *adj* moving towards a lower level or state.
• *adv* also **downwards** towards a lower level, etc.

dowry (ˈdaʊrɪ) *n* a gift of money, goods, or property that a bride brings to her husband on their marriage. < ultimately Latin *dos* gift.

doyen (ˈdɔɪən) fem. **doyenne** (dɔɪˈɛn) *n* a senior or very experienced member of a group, staff, etc. < Late Latin *decanus* dean.

doze (dəʊz) *vb* **1** sleep lightly. **2 doze off** fall into a light sleep.
• *n* a short sleep; nap. < probably Scandinavian.

dozen (ˈdʌzn̩) *determiner, n* a group of 12. < ultimately Latin *duo* two + *decem* ten.

Dr *abbrev* **1** Doctor. **2** (in road names) Drive.

drab (dræb) *adj* **1** dull, greyish-brown. **2** dull; dreary. **drably** *adv* **drabness** *n* < alteration of *drap* cloth, from Late Latin *drappus*.

Draconian (drəˈkəʊnɪən) *adj* harsh; drastic, esp. of laws. < Greek *Drakōn*, 7th-century BC Athenian law-giver.

draft (drɑːft) *n* **1** a rough, preliminary sketch or outline. **2** a written order for a bank to pay out a sum of money; withdrawing money like this. **3** a group of individuals chosen for special duty; choosing of these. **4** (*US*) conscription.
• *vb* **1** prepare a preliminary sketch or

---

downpour

There are many nouns in English that are derived from two-part verbs. Kick-off comes from to kick off, setback from to set back, etc. (See also panel at **show.**) Within this larger group of nouns there is a much smaller group of the downpour type. Members of this minor group also derive from two-part verbs. Their difference lies in the fact that the verb's parts are reversed. To pour down gives rise not to pourdown, which conforms to the regular pattern, but downpour. Other examples of this phenomenon include:

onlooker from to look on + -er
outcast from to cast out
outfit from to fit out
outlay from to lay out
outlook from to look out
output from to put out
upbringing from to bring up + -ing
upkeep from to keep up

---

outline of. **2** single out for special duty. **3** (*US*) conscript. < SEE **DRAUGHT.**
SEE PANEL.

drag (dræg) *vb* **dragged; dragging** **1** pull or draw slowly with difficulty. **2** trail or cause to trail along the ground. **3** search the bottom of (a river, lake, etc.) with a drag-net. **4** carry on tediously: The lesson dragged on. **5** take or bring by compelling: She dragged me into the lecture. • *n* **1** a device for underwater searches; drag-net. **2** something that slows motion or action; hindrance. **3** (*slang*) something boring or depressing. **4** (*slang*) women's clothing worn by men. **5** an intake of tobacco smoke. **drag in** introduce (a point or topic) in a contrived way. **drag-net** *n* a net pulled along the ground or bottom of a lake or river to catch game or fish. **drag one's heels** or **feet** act slowly on purpose; stall. **drag out** prolong without reason. **drag race** a contest of acceleration for cars or motor cycles. **drag up** (*informal*) **1** bring up (a child) without proper training. **2** revive (an unpleasant incident, story, etc.). < Old English *dragan*.

dragon (ˈdrægən) *n* **1** a mythical, fire-breathing reptile with wings and claws. **2** someone who is very fierce or strict. **dragonfly** *n* a brightly-coloured, winged insect with a long, slender body. < ultimately Greek *drakōn* serpent.

dragoon (drəˈguːn) *vb* compel to do something; browbeat. < Middle French *dragon* dragon.

drain (dreɪn) *vb* **1** remove liquid from by drawing off through pipes, channels, etc. **2** flow out or away. **3** use up; exhaust. **4** finish a drink. • *n* **1** a means of drawing off liquid such as a pipe or conduit. **2** something that uses up or saps: a drain on resources. **down the drain** (*informal*) gone for ever; wasted. **drainage** *n* **1** draining or something drained. **2** a system of drains. **draining-board** *n* a sloping, often grooved surface beside a sink for draining dishes, etc., after washing-up. **drain-pipe** *n* a pipe carrying liquid waste or excess water away from a building. < Old English *drēahnian*.

drake (dreɪk) *n* a male duck. < Middle English.

dram (dræm) *n* **1** (*chiefly Scottish*) a small drink of spirits, esp. whisky. **2** a unit of mass; one sixteenth of an ounce (about 1.77 grams). < ultimately Greek *drachmē* handful.

drama (ˈdrɑːmə) *n* **1** a play performed in a theatre, or on radio or television. **2** the art of writing or acting in plays. **3** a situation with the qualities of drama. **dramatic** *adj* **1** concerning drama. **2** thrilling; startling. **dramatically** *adv* **dramatics** *pl n* **1** the study or practice of drama. **2** theatrical behaviour. **dramatist** *n* someone who writes dramas. **dramatize** *vb* **1** make (a novel, etc.) into a play. **2** express in an exaggerated way. < ultimately Greek *dran* to do.

drank (dræŋk) SEE **DRINK.**

drape (dreɪp) *vb* **1** cover with folds of cloth. **2** arrange or hang loosely. • *n* the way in which a piece of cloth hangs; piece of drapery. **draper** *n* someone who retails cloth and sometimes clothing, **drapery** *n* **1** the trade or goods of a draper. **2** cloth or fabric hung gracefully in loose folds. < Middle French *drap* cloth.

drastic (ˈdræstɪk) *adj* extreme or severe in effect. **drastically** *adv* < Greek *dran* to do.

draught (drɑːft) *n* **1** a flow of air in a closed-in place. **2** pulling a load, by a vehicle or animal. **3** drawing a fishing-net; fish caught. **4** drinking; amount drunk. **5** the depth of water needed to float a ship. **6** drawing (liquor) from a cask, barrel, etc.: draught beer. **draughtboard** *n* a chequered board used in draughts. **draughts** *pl n* a game for two players using twelve round pieces each. **draughtsman** *n, pl* **draughtsmen** **1** someone who draws plans and sketches, esp. of machinery and buildings. **2** a round piece used in draughts. **draughty** *adj* with cold air blowing

draft or **draught?**

These two words are often confused. A draft is a preliminary sketch, a rough version of a document, a written order of money, or a group of soldiers. Draught is the spelling for *draught* beer, *draught* animals, a *draught* caused by an open door, and the game of *draughts*.

The confusion between the spelling of the two words arises partly because the American spelling of draught is draft. And to make matters more confusing, a person who draws plans is a draughtsman, and a person who drafts documents is either a draftsman or draughtsman.

through. **feel the draught** experience a sense of loss or hardship. < Middle English *draght.* SEE PANEL AT **DRAFT.**

draw (drɔː) *vb* **drew; drawn; drawing** **1** pull, tow, or haul. **2** take out; extract: draw water; draw a salary. **3** make (a picture, plan, etc.) by sketching marks on a surface. **4** move in a particular direction: The car drew alongside. **5** take (air or smoke) into the lungs. **6** bring in; attract: The concert drew people for miles around. **7** arrive at by reasoning: draw a conclusion. **8** receive or take at random: draw lots; draw a card. **9** write, making a demand for cash: draw a cheque. **10** take or get from a particular source: Authors draw ideas from real life. **11** (of tea) infuse. **12** (of contestants) finish with an equal score; tie.
• *n* **1** drawing. **2** an intake of air or smoke. **3** taking a gun out to shoot: quick on the draw. **4** a pull; attraction. **5** a lottery or raffle. **6** a game or contest ending in a tie. **drawback** *n* an obstacle; snag. **drawbridge** *n* a platform made to be raised or lowered to obstruct or allow passage. **drawer** *n* **1** someone who draws, esp. money from a bank. **2** an open-topped compartment which slides in and out of a piece of furniture. **3** *pl* underpants or knickers. **draw in 1** (of the hours of daylight) become fewer. **2** (of a train or vehicle) slow down and stop. **drawing** *n* **1** sketching; delineating. **2** a picture formed by drawing lines. **drawing-board** *n* **1** a board for attaching drawing paper to. **2** a planning stage: back to the drawing-board. **drawing-pin** *n* a flat-headed pin for attaching paper to boards. **drawing-room** *n* a formal room for receiving guests in a private house. **draw out 1** extend or prolong. **2** (of the hours of daylight) increase. **3** move away from. **4** encourage (someone) to talk. **draw up 1** (of a train or vehicle) come to a stop. **2** prepare in a formal way: draw up a report. < Old English *dragan.* SEE PANEL.

drawl (drɔːl) *vb* speak slowly, with drawn-out vowel sounds.
• *n* a drawling way of speaking. < probably *draw.*

drawn (drɔːn) SEE **DRAW.**
• *adj* looking strained or tired.

dray (dreɪ) *n* a strong, low, flat cart without sides, often used by brewers. < Old English *dræge* drag-net.

dread (drɛd) *vb, n* (feel) terror or awe.
• *adj* (*archaic*) greatly feared. **dreadful** *adj* **1** inspiring terror. **2** extremely disagreeable or bad. **dreadfully** *adv* < Old English *drǣdan.*

dream (drɪːm) *n* **1** a sequence of thoughts, images, or events happening in the mind during sleep. **2** a state of reverie or day-dreaming. **3** a wish or ambition.

drawing

Drawing is an example of a noun that has been formed by adding -ing to a verb. Nowadays this pattern of formation is so common that we take it for granted. In fact, there are very few verbs indeed from which nouns cannot be derived in this way; (the modal verbs may, should, must, etc., are notable exceptions). However, this was not always the case. At one time the root of a derived -ing form could not be a verb at all—it had to be a noun. In modern-day terms, this meant that -ing could be appended to school to give schooling, or wench to give wenching, but not to, say, draw, swim, or jump. A great increase in -ing forms came about as people gradually forgot whether the root of, say, schooling was the noun school or its verb counterpart to school. In time it was the verb that came to be regarded as the root, whereupon the floodgates were open. Even so, it was not until the very end of the Old English period that irregular verbs started to be used in this way.

I wouldn't dream of it!

The great majority of verbs can be used in either positive or negative sentences. For example, you can say either 'I want to go' or 'I don't want to go.' 'I like Harry' or 'I don't like Harry.' There is a small group of verbs, however, which do not share this grammatical flexibility. Take, for example, the verb dream of when used with the meaning 'to consider'. Although you can say 'I wouldn't dream of buying a used teapot', you cannot say 'I would dream of buying a used teapot'. The verb occurs in negative sentences only. Similarly, you can say 'I can't abide strong tea' but not 'I can abide strong tea.'

4 someone or something marvellous, beautiful, or excellent.
• *vb* **dreamt, dreamed; dreaming** **1** have dreams while asleep. **2** fantasize; imagine. **3** consider as possible: I wouldn't dream of disturbing you. **4 dream up** invent. **dreamer** *n* **dreamless** *adj* **dreamy** *adj* **1** far away in one's thoughts. **2** (*informal*) marvellous. **dreamily** *adv* **dreaminess** *n* < Old English *drēam* song. SEE PANEL.

dreary (ˈdrɪərɪ) *adj* bleak; boring. **drearily** *adv* **dreariness** *n* < Old English *drēor* gore.

dredge (drɛdʒ) *n* a machine for removing things from the bottom of the sea or a river.
• *vb* also **dredge up 1** remove with a dredge. **2** uncover by a thorough search. **dredger** *n* a boat with dredging apparatus. < perhaps Scottish *dreg.*

dregs (drɛgz) *pl n* **1** sediment in a liquid. **2** the most worthless part: the dregs of society. < Old Norse *dregg.*

drench (drɛntʃ) *vb* make thoroughly wet; soak. < Old English *drencan.*

dress (drɛs) *n* **1** clothing, often for a particular purpose or occasion: evening dress. **2** a one-piece, outer garment for women.
• *vb* **1** put on or supply with clothes; put on clothes for a formal occasion. **2** decorate. **3** apply bandages and medicine to (a wound). **4** arrange (hair); groom. **5** finish the surface of (stone, leather, etc.). **6** prepare for cooking or eating; apply salad dressing to. **7** (of troops) align in straight rows. **8 dress up** put on special clothes or costume. **9 dress up** cause to appear more interesting; embellish. **dress circle** the lowest gallery in a theatre. **dresser** *n* **1** a piece of kitchen furniture like a sideboard, for holding dishes and kitchenware. **2** someone who dresses; someone who helps actors into costume. **dressing** *n* **1** a sauce, stuffing, or seasoning for food. **2** a plaster, bandage, or medicine applied to a wound. **3** manure or compost spread over land as a fertilizer. **4** a size, used for stiffening textiles or fabrics. **dressing-down** *n* a telling off. **dressing-gown** *n* a loose robe worn when not properly dressed. **dressing-room** *n* a room for dressing or changing clothes, esp. for actors. **dressing-table** *n* a table with a mirror, used for dressing or grooming at. **dressmaker** *n* a woman who makes clothes for women. **dressmaking** *n* **dress rehearsal** a full costume rehearsal. **dressy** *adj* **1** stylish in dress. **2** (of clothes) smart; elegant. < ultimately Latin *dirigere* to direct.

dressage (ˈdrɛsɑːʒ) *n* the training of a horse to make it responsive to the rider's movements. < French: preparation.

drew (druː) SEE **DRAW.**

drey (dreɪ) *n, pl* **dreys** the nest of a squirrel. < origin unknown.

dribble (ˈdrɪbl̩) *vb* **1** allow saliva to trickle from the mouth. **2** fall or flow in drops; trickle. **3** (in football, etc.) run with the ball, esp. past an opposing player, keeping it carefully under control.
• *n* **1** a trickle. **2** a tiny or unimportant amount. < probably alteration of *drip.*

driblet (ˈdrɪblɪt) *n* a tiny amount.

dribs and drabs (drɪbz) tiny, often scattered amounts. < obsolete *drib,* from *drip.*

drier (ˈdraɪə) *n* something that dries, esp. a machine for drying hair or laundry.

drift (drɪft) *vb* **1** float along a current of water or air. **2** move or wander aimlessly. **3** pile up, esp. because of the action of wind or water.
• *n* **1** drifting. **2** a mass of sand, snow, etc., piled up through the action of wind or water. **3** a movement away from a fixed course. **4** the trend of what is said; gist: I get your drift. **drifter** *n* **1** a fishing-boat that uses a drift-net. **2** someone who wanders through life aimlessly. **drift-net** *n* a fishing-net which drifts with the tide or current. **driftwood** *n* wood washed up on a shore. < Middle English.

drill[1] (drɪl) *n* **1** (a machine with) a pointed tool for boring holes. **2** military training in marching and handling weapons. **3** exercise designed to improve skill, esp. with repeated practice. **4** a set procedure.
• *vb* **1** use a drill; make a hole with this. **2** train or exercise through repeated practice. < Dutch *drillen.*

drill[2] *n* **1** a shallow furrow for sowing seeds in; row of seeds sown in this. **2** a machine for making or sowing seeds in furrows.
• *vb* sow in furrows. < perhaps archaic *drill* rill.

drink (drɪŋk) *vb* **drank; drunk; drinking** **1** swallow (a liquid). **2** also **drink in** take in; absorb: He drank in every word she said. **3** take in alcohol, esp. to excess. **4** also **drink to** join in a toast for.
• *n* **1** a liquid which can be drunk; measure of this. **2** alcoholic beverages. **3** (*slang*) the sea. **drinker** *n* < Old English *drincan.*

drip (drɪp) *vb* **dripped; dripping** fall or allow to fall in drops.

• *n* **1** the falling of drops of liquid; one drop of this. **2** the sound this makes. **3** (*informal*) a dull person; nonentity. **drip-dry** *adj, vb* (of clothes) (able to) become dry easily without wringing or ironing. **dripping wet** soaked; drenched. < Old English *dryppan.*

dripping (ˈdrɪpɪŋ) *n* the fat that runs out of roast meat.

drive (draɪv) *vb* **drove; driven; driving** **1** cause to move in a particular direction by force. **2** force into with blows: He drove a nail into the wall. **3** direct the course of (an animal or vehicle); steer. **4** operate, travel, or convey in a private vehicle. **5** cause (machinery) to keep going: driven by electricity. **6** force; compel: She was driven to drink. **7** propel by striking (a ball, etc.). **8** rush or dash rapidly and forcefully: driving rain.

• *n* **1** an excursion in a motor vehicle. **2** a road, esp. scenic or private. **3** a driving stroke in golf, cricket, etc. **4** a means of transmitting power to the moving parts of a machine: front-wheel drive. **5** a systematic effort; campaign: a sales drive. **6** energy; motivation. **7** a gathering of people to play bridge, whist, etc. **driver** *n* **drive a hard bargain** make a deal without conceding anything. **drive at** mean; intend. **drive-in** *n, adj* (being) a place such as a bank or cinema that people can use while remaining in a car. < Old English *drīfan.*

drivel (ˈdrɪvl̩) *n* nonsense. < Old English *dreflian.*

driven (ˈdrɪvn) SEE **DRIVE.**

drizzle (ˈdrɪzl̩) *n* light rain.

• *vb* rain lightly in small drops. **drizzly** *adj* < perhaps Old English *drysnian* to disappear.

droll (drəʊl) *adj* amusing in a strange way; whimsical. **drollness** *n* **drolly** *adv* < Middle Dutch *drolle* imp.

drone (drəʊn) *n* **1** the male of the honey-bee. **2** someone who lives off others; scrounger. **3** a low, humming sound.

• *vb* **1** make a low, humming sound. **2** also **drone on** talk in a monotonous manner. < Old English *drān.*

drool (druːl) *vb* **1** water at the mouth, esp. in expectation of food; salivate. **2** make an excessive show of fondness or appreciation. < perhaps alteration of *drivel.*

droop (druːp) *vb* **1** hang down or sag. **2** weaken; lose heart.

• *n* the state or appearance of drooping. **droopy** *adj* < Old Norse *drūpa.*

drop (drɒp) *n* **1** a small amount of a liquid that falls in a rounded mass. **2** something shaped like this, for example a bead of jewellery or a sweet. **3** a tiny amount of something, esp. alcohol. **4** (the distance of) a vertical descent: a 20-foot drop. **5** the act of dropping; fall. **6** a sudden decline or decrease. **7** something that drops, falls, or hangs. **8** a piece of cloth stage scenery. **9** a hinged platform on a gallows.

• *vb* **dropped; dropping** **1** fall in drops; trickle. **2** fall or let fall suddenly or unexpectedly. **3** set down from a vehicle, ship, etc.; unload. **4** fall or collapse from exhaustion. **5** decline or descend sharply. **6** bring down with a blow, shot, etc. **7** make or become lower or weaker: Her voice dropped. **8** discontinue or give up: drop the subject. **9** leave out; omit: drop one's h's. **10** score with a drop-kick. **drop by** or **in** pay someone a short, casual visit. **drop-kick** *n* a kick, esp. in rugby, made by dropping a ball and kicking it on the rebound. **droplet** *n* a small drop. **drop off** **1** fall asleep. **2** deliver. **drop out** leave a college, etc., prematurely; leave conventional society. **drop-out** *n* **droppings** *pl n* animal or bird dung. **drops** *pl n* liquid medicine taken in drops. < Old English *dropa.* SEE PANEL.

dropsy (ˈdrɒpsɪ) *n* a diseased condition in which watery fluid accumulates in the body. < ultimately Greek *hydōr* water.

dross (drɒs) *n* **1** scum forming on molten metal. **2** impurities; dregs. < Old English *drōs* dregs.

drought (draʊt) *n* a prolonged spell of dry weather. < Old English *drūgian* to dry up.

drove (drəʊv) SEE **DRIVE.**

• *n* **1** a group of animals moving together. **2** a moving crowd of people.

a drop in the ocean

The idiom a drop-in the bucket, with its variant a drop in the ocean, means 'something very small or insignificant compared with something larger': Government aid of £50 000 to help the victims of the disaster is just *a drop in the ocean* compared with what is needed.

The origin of the expression is Isaiah 40:15 in the Authorized (King James) Version of the Bible: Behold, the nations are as a drop of a bucket, and are counted as the small dust of the balance.

drover *n* someone who herds cattle or sheep. < Old English *drīfan* to drive.

drown (draʊn) *vb* **1** suffocate by submerging in liquid, esp. water. **2** wet through; flood. **3** make inaudible with a louder noise; muffle. **4** wipe out (an unpleasant sensation), esp. by drinking alcohol: drown one's sorrows. < Middle English *drounen*.

drowse (draʊz) *vb* be sleepy; doze. **drowsy** *adj* sleepy. **drowsily** *adv* **drowsiness** *n* < probably Old English *drūsian* to sink.

drudge (drʌdʒ) *n* someone who does tedious or menial work.
• *vb* perform menial work. **drudgery** *n* < Middle English *druggen*.

drug (drʌg) *n* **1** a medicinal substance. **2** a substance such as a narcotic or stimulant that causes physical or psychological addiction.
• *vb* **drugged; drugging 1** mix a drug into (food, drink, etc.). **2** administer a drug to; dope. **3** numb or stupefy (as if) with a drug. **druggist** *n* a pharmacist. **drugstore** *n* (*US*) a chemist's shop that also sells refreshments, magazines, etc. < Old French *drogue*.

drum (drʌm) *n* **1** a percussion instrument sounded by beating a skin stretched over a hollow cylinder; the sound this makes. **2** an object or container with this shape: oil drum. **3** the ear-drum.
• *vb* **drummed; drumming 1** beat a drum or drums. **2** make a drumlike sound; tap or throb rhythmically. **3 drum into** instil by constant repetition. **drum brake** a type of brake which operates by pads pressing against the inner part of a wheel. **drum major** the leader of a marching band. **drummer** *n* someone who plays a drum or drums. **drumstick** *n* **1** a stick for hitting a drum. **2** the lower part of a fowl's leg when cooked. **drum up 1** bring about by enthusiastic effort. **2** invent: drum up an excuse. < probably Dutch *trom*.

drunk (drʌŋk) SEE **DRINK.**
• *adj* **1** affected by alcoholic drink. **2** affected by intense feeling: drunk with power.
• *n* someone who is drunk with alcohol. **drunkard** *n* someone who is habitually drunk. **drunken** *adj* **1** tending to drink alcohol frequently; drunk. **2** relating to a drunken state. **drunkenly** *adv* **drunkenness** *n* < Middle English *drunke*.

dry (draɪ) *adj* **1** without moisture; without liquid, esp. water: a dry climate. **2** with an exhausted supply of liquid or water: a dry well; dry cows. **3** thirsty. **4** with the sale of alcohol prohibited. **5** dull; boring. **6** (of wine) lacking sweetness. **7** terse or ironic: a dry sense of humour.
• *vb* **dried; drying** also **dry out** make or become dry. **drily** *adv* **dryness** *n* **dry-clean** *vb* clean (clothes) with organic solvents, not water. **dry dock** a dock, from which water can be removed, used for repairing ships. **dry-fly** *adj* (of fishing) using an artificial fly that floats on water. **dry rot** wood decay; fungus causing this. **dry run** (*informal*) a practice run. **drystone** *adj* made of stone without using mortar. **dry up 1** wipe dishes after washing. **2** (of a source or supply) become exhausted. **3** stop talking; shut up. < Old English *drȳge*.

dual (ˈdjuːəl) *adj* made up of two elements; double. **duality** *n* **dual carriageway** a road with a central strip that divides traffic travelling in opposite directions. **dual-purpose** *adj* having two functions. < Latin *duo* two.

dub[1] (dʌb) *vb* **dubbed; dubbing 1** knight by touching on the shoulder with a sword. **2** create a nickname for. < Old English *dubbian*.

dub[2] *vb* **dubbed; dubbing** add to or alter a film soundtrack. < *double*.

dubbin (ˈdʌbɪn) *n* a dressing of oil and tallow for softening and waterproofing leather. < *dub* to dress leather.

dubious (ˈdjuːbɪəs) *adj* doubtful; suspicious. **dubiously** *adv* < Latin *dubare* to vacillate.

duchess (ˈdʌtʃɪs) *n* **1** the wife or widow of a duke. **2** a woman ranking equally with a duke. < Middle French *duc* duke.

duchy (ˈdʌtʃɪ) *n* the land and estates of a duke or duchess.

duck[1] (dʌk) *n* **1** one of several kinds of

What is the plural of **duck?**

What is the plural of duck? Ducks or duck? The answer is: it depends. In general usage, the plural form is ducks, but duck, without -s, is the plural often used by hunters, butchers, and other specialists.

Other animal names with two plural forms include: crab (crabs, crab), herring (herrings, herring), and reindeer (reindeers, reindeer).

Some animal names always have the plural without -s: sheep, deer, grouse, cod, plaice, and salmon.

---

swimming-birds with webbed feet and short neck and legs; flesh of this as food. **2** the female of this. **3** (*informal*) dear. **4** a batsman's score of nought in cricket. **duckling** *n* a young duck. < Middle English *doke.* SEE PANEL.

duck² *vb* **1** lower (the head) quickly, esp. to avoid being hit or seen. **2** plunge (the head) briefly under water. **3** dodge or evade (a task, responsibility, etc.). < Middle English *douken.*

duct (dʌkt) *n* **1** a pipe, tube, or channel that conveys air, gas, liquid, cables, etc. **2** a tube in the body that carries gland secretions: tear ducts.
• *vb* convey by means of a duct. < ultimately Latin *ducere* to lead.

dud (dʌd) *n* (*informal*) something artificial, ineffective, or useless.
• *adj* (*informal*) not working; worthless. < perhaps *duds* clothes, rags.

due (dju:) *adj* **1** owed as a debt. **2** payable immediately. **3** deserved; appropriate. **4** expected to arrive; scheduled.
• *adv* directly: They sailed due west.
• *n* **1** something deserved by or owed to someone: Give him his due. **2** *pl* a fee or charge. **due to** caused by. **in due course** at the proper time. < ultimately Latin *debēre* to owe. SEE PANEL.

duel (ˈdju:əl) *n* **1** a combat with weapons fought by two opponents. **2** a conflict or contest between two people or forces.
• *vb* **duelled; duelling** fight a duel. **duellist** *n* < Old Latin *duellum* war.

duet (dju:ˈɛt) *n* a piece of music for two performers or voices. < Latin *duo* two.

duffel (ˈdʌfl̩) *n* a heavy, woollen material with a thick nap. **duffel bag** a cylindrical bag of canvas for personal belongings, closed by a string. **duffel coat** a hooded coat made of duffel and fastened with toggles. < *Duffel,* town in Belgium. SEE PANEL.

dug (dʌg) SEE **DIG. dug-out** *n* **1** an underground shelter, esp. for troops. **2** a boat made by hollowing out a tree trunk.

duke (dju:k) *n* **1** a nobleman of the highest hereditary rank. **2** the male ruler of a European duchy. **dukedom** *n* **ducal** *adj* of a duke or duchy. < ultimately Latin *ducere* to lead.

dull (dʌl) *adj* **1** overcast; cloudy. **2** (of a colour) lacking brightness; dim. **3** slow-witted; stupid. **4** tedious; boring. **5** blunt: a dull blade. **6** (of sound) not sharp or resonant.
• *vb* make or become dull. **dullness** *n* **dully** *adv* < Old English *dol* foolish.

duly (ˈdju:lɪ) *adv in* an appropriate way; at the proper time.

dumb (dʌm) *adj* **1** lacking the power of speech. **2** temporarily unable to speak: struck dumb with terror. **3** (*informal*) stupid. **dumbly** *adv* **dumbness** *n* **dumb-bell** *n* a short bar with weights at either end, used in weight-training. **dumbfound** *vb* startle; astonish. **dumb waiter 1** a movable stand from which food is served. **2** a lift for conveying food, dishes, etc. < Old English.

dummy (ˈdʌmɪ) *n* **1** a model of the human body, used for displaying clothes. **2** a rubber teat given to babies to suck. **3** an imitation; copy. **4** in card-games, an exposed hand; player whose hand this is. **5** a fool.
• *adj* fake. **dummy run** a practice run. < *dumb* + *-y.*

dump (dʌmp) *vb* **1** drop or put down without care. **2** get rid of; throw away. **3** sell (goods) abroad for less than the price at home.
• *n* **1** a place for depositing rubbish. **2** a place for storing supplies, esp. military: ammunition dump. **3** (*informal*) an untidy or unattractive place. **dumpling** *n* **1** a ball of dough, usually boiled or steamed in a stew. **2** (*humorous*) someone who is short and fat. **dumps** *pl n* (*informal*)

due to or owing to?

Careful users of English distinguish between due to and owing to. On the basis that due is an adjective, it is argued that due to should be used only adjectivally, as in His absence was *due to* illness. The use of due to in a sentence such as *Due to* illness he was unable to attend, in which it functions as a compound preposition, is considered incorrect. To serve the latter function, owing to is preferred. Nevertheless, the use of due to as a substitute for owing to is becoming increasingly common, especially in informal contexts.

duffel coat

A warm coat made of heavy woollen cloth, usually having a hood and fastened with toggles is called a duffel coat. It takes its name from *Duffel,* a town close to Antwerp in Belgium and the home of the cloth.

gloom; depression: down in the dumps. **dumpy** *adj* short and thickly-built. **dumpiness** *n* < perhaps Scandinavian.

dun (dʌn) *adj, n* greyish-brown. < Old English *dunn*.

dunce (dʌns) *n* someone who is stupid or slow at learning. < John *Duns* Scotus, died 1308, Scottish theologian. SEE PANEL.

dune (djuːn) *n* a pile of sand formed by the action of the wind. < Middle Dutch.

dung (dʌŋ) *n* the excrement of animals and birds. **dunghill** *n* a heap of dung. < Old English.

dungarees (ˌdʌŋgəˈriːz) *pl n* a one-piece, outer garment of heavy, cotton cloth; overalls. < Hindi *dūngrī*. SEE PANEL.

dungeon (ˈdʌndʒən) *n* an underground cell or prison, esp. in a castle. < Middle English *donjon*.

dunk (dʌŋk) *vb* dip into a liquid. < Old High German *dunkōn*.

duo (ˈdjuːəʊ) *n, pl* **duos 1** a pair of performers. **2** a duet. < Latin: two.

duodecimal (ˌdjuːəʊˈdɛsɪməl) *adj* using 12 as a base number. < Latin *duodecim* 12.

duodenum (ˌdjuːəˈdiːnəm) *n* the first part of the small intestine, immediately below the stomach. **duodenal** *adj* < Latin *duodecim* 12, from its length of 12 fingers.

dupe (djuːp) *n* someone who is easily deceived.
• *vb* trick; deceive. < probably alteration of Middle French *huppe* hoopoe.

duplicate (ˈdjuːplɪkət) *n* **1** one of two identical things. **2** a copy.
• *adj* (ˈdjuːplɪkət) matching; identical.
• *vb* (ˈdjuːplɪˌkeɪt) **1** make or consist of an exact copy. **2** repeat. **duplicator** *n* a copying machine. < ultimately Latin *duplex* double.

duplicity (djuːˈplɪsɪtɪ) *n* deception; dishonesty.

durable (ˈdjʊərəbl̩) *adj* long-lasting; not likely to decay. **durability** *n* **durably** *adv* **duration** *n* the amount of time something lasts. < Latin *durare* to last.

duress (djʊˈrɛs) *n* persuasion by force or threats. < ultimately Latin *durus* hard.

during (ˈdjʊərɪŋ) *prep* throughout or at one point within a period of time of. < ultimately Latin *durus* hard.

dusk (dʌsk) *n* the darker part of twilight. **dusky** *adj* **1** shady; dim. **2** dark-complexioned. **duskiness** *n* < alteration of Old English *dox*.

dust (dʌst) *n* fine, dry particles of matter, esp. earth.
• *vb* **1** make free of dust by wiping, sweeping, or brushing. **2** cover lightly with dust or powder. **dustbin** *n* a container for household rubbish. **dust cover** or **jacket** a detachable paper cover on a book. **duster** *n* a cloth for removing dust, esp. from furniture. **dustman** *n, pl* **dustmen** someone employed to take away household rubbish. **dustpan** *n* a hooded shovel with a handle, for sweeping dust into. **dust-sheet** *n* a sheet for covering furniture to prevent dust from collecting, **dusty** *adj* **1** like, full of, or covered with dust. **2** pale-greyish in colour. < Old English *dūst*.

duty (ˈdjuːtɪ) *n* **1** moral or legal obligation or responsibility. **2** tasks or expected behaviour arising from one's job or position. **3** loyalty and respect, esp. towards elders or superiors. **4** a tax or charge on imported goods. **dutiable** *adj* (of goods) on which an import tax must be paid. **dutiful** *adj* with or showing a sense of duty. **duty-bound** *adj* morally obliged. **on/off duty** occupied/not occupied in one's normal work. < Old French *deu* due.

dunce

An unusually dim-witted or stupid person is sometimes referred to as a dunce. This word derives from the name of John *Duns* Scotus, 1256-1308, a Scottish theologian. The followers of Duns were known as *Dunses* or *Dunsmen*. These nicknames were to become terms of ridicule amongst 16th-century humanists who mocked the Dunses for their theological hair-splitting and hostile resistance to new ideas.

dungarees

Work trousers or overalls made of a coarse cotton fabric are known as dungarees after the cloth—dungaree—from which they were originally made. Dungaree—a strong type of calico—takes its name ultimately from *Dungrī*, the Hindi name of the district of Bombay where the cloth (*dungrī*) was first produced.

> **dyed-in-the-wool**
>
> One of the many expressions to emerge from the textile industry is dyed-in-the-wool: She's a *dyed-in-the-wool* Conservative if ever I saw one. This usage came about following the discovery that yarn that was dyed before being woven into cloth held its colour better than yarn that was dyed 'in the piece' (after undergoing the weaving process).

duvet ('du:veɪ) *n* a continental quilt; thick, soft quilt used in place of bedclothes. < French: down.

dwarf (dwɔ:f) *n, pl* **dwarfs, dwarves** **1** someone who is abnormally short; plant or animal well below normal size. **2** a mythical, small, man-like creature with magic powers.
• *adj* abnormally small.
• *vb* **1** retard the growth of. **2** cause to seem smaller. < Old English *dweorg*. SEE PANEL AT **SHELF**.

dwell (dwɛl) *vb* **dwelt, dwelled; dwelling** inhabit. **dweller** *n* **dwelling** *n* a house; residence. **dwell on** write, speak, or think about at length. < Old English *dwellan* to go astray.

dwindle ('dwɪndl̩) *vb* shrink or diminish gradually. < Old English *dwīnan* to waste away.

dye (daɪ) *vb* **dyed; dyeing** alter the colour of by dipping in liquid colouring matter.
• *n* **1** a substance for colouring or tinting. **2** a colour produced by dyeing. **dyer** *n* < Old English *dēag*. SEE PANEL.

dyke, dike (daɪk) *n* **1** a bank constructed to keep out water, esp. from the sea. **2** a watercourse or ditch. < Old English *dīc*.

dynamic (daɪ'næmɪk) *adj* **1** of a motive force. **2** marked by activity, energy, and drive. **dynamically** *adv* **dynamics** *n* **1** a branch of mechanics dealing with matter in motion. **2** a pattern of changes in a relationship. **3** variation; contrast, esp. in music. < ultimately Greek *dynasthai* to be able.

dynamite ('daɪnəˌmaɪt) *n* **1** an explosive made of nitro-glycerine, used for blasting. **2** someone or something that is spectacular or potentially dangerous.
• *vb* blow up with dynamite.

dynamo ('daɪnəˌməʊ) *n, pl* **dynamos** a device which converts mechanical energy into electrical energy, esp. in a motor vehicle. < short for *dynamo*electric machine.

dynasty ('dɪnəstɪ) *n* a series of hereditary rulers. **dynastic** *adj* < SEE **DYNAMIC**.

dysentery ('dɪsn̩trɪ) *n* an infection marked by inflamed intestines and severe diarrhoea. < Greek *dys-* bad + *enteron* intestine.

dyslexia (dɪs'lɛksɪə) *n* an abnormal development in reading ability caused by a neurological disorder. < New Latin, from *dys-* + Greek *lexis* word.

dyspepsia (dɪs'pɛpsɪə) *n* indigestion. **dyspeptic** *adj* **1** suffering from indigestion. **2** bad-tempered. < ultimately Greek *dys-* + *peptein* to cook.

E

E. *abbrev* east; eastern.

each (iːtʃ) *determiner* every one of two or more people or things.
• *pron, adv* (for or to) every one: That'll be 50p each. **each other** used in reciprocal actions or relations: They loved each other. **each way** (of a bet) backing a horse, dog, etc., to win or be placed. < Old English *ǣlc*. SEE PANEL.

eager (ˈiːgə) *adj* keen; enthusiastic. **eagerly** *adv* **eagerness** *n* < ultimately Latin *acer* sharp.

eagle (ˈiːgl̩) *n* **1** a large bird of prey; representation of this used as an emblem. **2** in golf, a score two strokes under par for a hole. **eagle eye** keen eyes or watchfulness. **eagle-eyed** *adj* < Latin *aquila*.

ear[1] (ɪə) *n* **1** the organ of hearing and balance in man and various animals; outer part of this. **2** something shaped like an ear. **3** sensitivity to tone and pitch of sound: an ear for music. **4** attention; notice. **be all ears** (*informal*) listen keenly. **earache** *n* a pain in the ear. **ear-drum** *n* the membrane in the ear which is vibrated by sound waves. **earful** *n* **1** a large amount of talk or gossip. **2** a strong rebuke. **earmark** *vb* **1** put a mark of identification on. **2** designate for a specific purpose. **earphone** *n* a headphone. **ear-plug** *n* a plug fitted in the ear to keep out water or noise. **ear-ring** *n* an ornament attached to the ear-lobe. **earshot** *n* the range within which something can be heard. **ear-splitting** *adj* painfully loud. < Old English *ēare*. SEE PANEL.

ear[2] *n* the fruiting spike of a cereal. < Old English *ēar*.

earl (ɜːl) *n* a British nobleman who ranks above a viscount and below a marquess. **earldom** *n* < Old English *eorl*.

early (ˈɜːlɪ) *adj, adv* **1** at or near the start of a period, series, or development. **2** before the regular or proper time. **earliness** *n* **early bird** someone who gets up or arrives early. **early closing** the shutting of shops on a specified afternoon every week. < Old English *ǣr*.

earn (ɜːn) *vb* **1** receive (money) in return for working. **2** deserve in return for one's qualities or conduct. **3** bring in as income: His shares earned a lot of interest last year. **earnings** *pl n* payment earned. < Old English *earnien*.

earnest (ˈɜːnɪst) *adj* serious; resolute. **earnestly** *adv* **earnestness** *n* **in earnest** seriously; determinedly. < Old English *eornost*.

earth (ɜːθ) *n* **1 Earth** the planet on which we live; world. **2** the land as opposed to the sea or air. **3** soil or clay. **4** the lair of a badger or fox. **5** an electrical connection to earth which completes a circuit. **6** (*informal*) a lot of money.
• *vb* **1** heap earth over. **2** make an electrical connection with earth.

---

each other or **one another?**

A few careful users of English prefer to use each other when referring to two people and one another when referring to more than two. However, common usage tends to ignore this preference: The six children chased *each other* round the swimming-pool is widely acceptable.

---

all ears

Ear features in a number of idiomatic expressions including:

all ears listening closely: As soon as the teacher mentioned a Christmas party, the children were all ears.
fall on deaf ears to be disregarded: The complaints about the lack of cleanliness in the kitchen seem to have fallen on deaf ears.
go in one ear and out the other to fail to make an impression on someone; be forgotten as soon as heard.
keep or **have one's ear to the ground** to be closely attentive to rumours, current trends, etc. The expression may refer to an alleged tracking technique used by American Indians.
turn a deaf ear to to refuse to listen to; pretend not to hear.
up to one's ears involved in a great quantity of work, etc.
walls have ears a saying advising care in what one is saying, as someone may be listening to the conversation.

earthen *adj* made of earth or baked clay. **earthenware** *n* pottery made of clay baked at a low temperature. **earthly** *adj* of this world or human life on it. **earthquake** *n* a violent upheaval of a section of the earth's crust. **earthwork** *n* an embankment of earth for defence, etc. **earthworm** *n* a common worm that burrows in the soil. **earthy** *adj* **1** being or like earth. **2** lusty; crude. < Old English *eorthe.*

earwig (ˈɪəˌwɪg) *n* a small insect with limbs like forceps at the end of its body. < Old English *ēare* ear + *wicga* beetle. SEE PANEL.

ease (iːz) *n* **1** freedom or relief from pain or worry; comfort. **2** absence of effort, difficulty, or awkwardness.
• *vb* **1** relieve from pain, worry, or burdens. **2** reduce tension or pressure on (something). **3** move (something) slowly and carefully: He eased the lorry into the opening. **4 ease off** decline in activity or intensity: The rain eased off. **at ease 1** relaxed. **2** a military command to stand relaxed with feet apart. < ultimately Latin *adjacēre* to lie near.

easel (ˈiːzl̩) *n* a frame which supports for example a blackboard or artist's canvas. < Dutch *ezel* ass. SEE PANEL.

east (iːst) *n* the point or direction to the right of a person facing north; general direction of sunrise.
• *adj, adv* **1** towards, in, or from the east. **2** (of the wind) from the east. **the east** often also **the East** land lying in or towards the east. **the East** the regions lying east of Europe or the Communist countries of eastern Europe. **easterly** *adj* **1** in or towards the east. **2** (of the wind) from the east. **eastern** *adj* of or in the east. **easterner** *n* a native or inhabitant of the east. **easternmost** *adj* furthest east. **eastward, eastwards** *adj, adv* towards the east. < Old English *ēast.* SEE PANEL AT **EASTER.**

Easter (ˈiːstə) *n* a festival commemorating the resurrection of Christ, observed on the first Sunday after the full moon following 21 March; period about this time. **Easter egg** a chocolate egg given as a gift at this time. < Old English *ēastre.* SEE PANEL.

earwig

In bygone days one of the insects most feared by human beings was the earwig. This name derives from the Old English *ēarwicga,* from *ēare* 'ear' and *wicga* 'beetle'. According to folk superstition the insect's favourite pastime was to creep into the ear of a sleeping victim and then drill a passage into the brain. The same belief gave rise to the insect's French and German names: *perce-oreille* ('ear-driller') and *Ohrwurm* ('ear-worm').

It seems likely that it was not only the unlearned who harboured the superstition. Included in Pliny's 37-volume 'Natural History' is the'advice: 'If an earwig be gotten into the eare ... spit into the same, and it will come forth anon.'

easel

The stand that an artist uses for supporting his canvas while painting is known as an easel. This word comes from the Dutch *ezel,* meaning 'ass' or 'donkey', which in turn comes from the Latin word for the same creature, *asinus.* To make sense of the name it has to be interpreted metaphorically. Like the trusty old clothes-horse, both easel and ass serve a basic, load-bearing function.

Easter and **east**

The close similarity of Easter and east is not accidental. Predating by some considerable margin the Christian festival with which it is nowadays connected, Easter is derived from the Old English *ēastre.* This was the name of an ancient spring festival commemorating *Eostre,* a goddess of dawn and symbol of regeneration. The name of the pagan goddess approximates *ēast* ('east'), a name which in one form or another has been attached since prehistoric days to the place where the sun was each day miraculously reborn.

As well as in the name, the pre-Christian roots of the festival are also evident in the continuing practice of giving eggs at Easter. The egg has long been a symbol of fertility and rebirth and decorated eggs were eaten at each spring festival.

easy (ˈiːzɪ) *adj* **1** involving little or no effort, difficulty, or discomfort. **2** free from pain, worry, or constraint. **3** readily persuaded; compliant: He's easy game. **4** natural; friendly: easy manners.
● *adv* **1** with ease. **2** carefully: take it easy **easiness** *n* **easily** *adv* **1** with ease. **2** without a doubt. **easy chair** a large, comfortable armchair. **easy-going** *adj* relaxed; tolerant. **easy on the eye** attractive to look at. **easy street** (*informal*) a condition of affluence. **go easy with** be careful or prudent with. **stand easy** stand at ease. **take it easy** **1** be careful. **2** relax. < Old French *aisé*.

eat (iːt) *vb* **ate; eaten; eating** **1** take in (food) through the mouth and swallow it; have a meal. **2** consume gradually; corrode: The metal has been eaten away. **eatable** *adj* fit to be eaten; palatable. **eatables** *pl n* food. **eater** *n* **1** someone who eats. **2** an eating-apple. **eat one's heart out** suffer with longing for something out of reach. **eat one's words** take back what one has said. **eats** *pl n* (*informal*) food. < Old English *etan*.

eau-de-cologne (ˌəʊ də kəˈləʊn) *n* a perfumed toilet water. < *Cologne*, city in Germany.

eaves (iːvz) *pl n* the lower edge of a roof that overhangs. **eavesdrop** *vb* **eavesdropped; eavesdropping** listen secretly to things said in private. **eavesdropper** *n* < Old English *efes*. SEE PANEL.

ebb (ɛb) *n* **1** the moving back of the tide out to sea. **2** a declining or decreased condition: Things are at a low ebb.
● *vb* **1** (of the tide) flow out to sea. **2** weaken; deteriorate. < Old English *ebba*.

ebony (ˈɛbənɪ) *n* a hard, heavy, black wood from a tree found in the tropics.
● *adj* very dark; black. < Egyptian *hbnj*.

ebullient (ɪˈbʌljənt) *adj* in high spirits; vivacious. **ebullience** *n* < Latin *e-* + *bullire* to boil.

eccentric (ɪkˈsɛntrɪk) *adj* **1** odd or strange in behaviour. **2** having different centres or an off-centre pivot; not following a circular path.
● *n* someone who is strange or unconventional. **eccentrically** *adv* **eccentricity** *n* < Greek *ex* out of + *kentron* centre.

ecclesiastical (ɪˌkliːzɪˈæstɪkl̩) *adj* of a church or its clergy. < Greek *ekklēsia* assembly.

echelon (ˈɛʃəˌlɒn) *n* **1** an arrangement (of troops, aircraft, etc.) in or like a series of steps. **2** a grade or level of rank, authority, etc. < French: small ladder.

echo (ˈɛkəʊ) *n, pl* **echoes** **1** the reflection of sound waves causing repetition of sounds; one sound repeated like this. **2** someone that imitates or something imitated.
● *vb* **1** produce or resound with echoes. **2** repeat; copy. < Greek *ēchō*.

éclair (ɪˈklɛə) *n* a light, finger-shaped cake of pastry with cream filling and often chocolate topping. < French: lightning.

eclectic (ɪˈklɛktɪk) *adj* using or choosing from various sources. < ultimately Greek *ex* out + *legein* to gather.

eclipse (ɪˈklɪps) *n* **1** the complete or partial obscuring of one heavenly body by another. **2** a loss or decline in power, reputation, etc.
● *vb* **1** obscure; darken. **2** outshine; surpass. < ultimately Greek *ex-* + *leipein* to leave.

ecology (ɪˈkɒlədʒɪ) *n* the scientific study of living things and how they relate to their environment. **ecological** *adj* **ecologist** *n* < ultimately Greek *oikos* house + *logos* word.

economic (ˌiːkəˈnɒmɪk) *adj* **1** of or relating to commerce or finance: economic policies. **2** profitable. **3** inexpensive; reasonable. **economical** *adj* saving time, work, energy, or money. **economics** *n* **1** a social science dealing with the production and consumption of goods and services. **2** *pl n* the economic

Eavesdroppers exposed!

An eavesdropper is a person who furtively listens in to private conversations, often from a place of concealment. Since eaves refers to a part of a roof (the part that projects beyond the walls), it might well be imagined that the eavesdropper conducted his malicious practice from the roof-top. This, however, was not the case. The eavesdropper kept his feet firmly on the ground, on the *eavesdrop* or *eavesdrip* to be precise, which was the strip of ground adjoining the walls of a house that received the drips from the eaves. In this position, preferably near a window, the eavesdropper was ideally situated to overhear conversations taking place within.

aspects of something. **economist** *n*
economize *vb* save; cut back (on wastage, etc.); be economical. **economy** *n* **1** efficiency in using things; thriftiness. **2** the system of making goods and using resources in a community or country: an industrial economy. < ultimately Greek *oikos* house + *nemein* to manage.
SEE PANEL.

ecstasy (ˈɛkstəsɪ) *n* a state of intense joy; bliss. **ecstatic** *adj* **ecstatically** *adv* < ultimately Greek *ex* out + *histanai* to cause to stand.

eczema (ˈɛksmə, ˈɛksɪmə) *n* a skin condition marked by inflamed, itchy patches. < Greek *ex* out + *zein* to boil.

eddy (ˈɛdɪ) *n* a current of air, water, smoke, etc., which swirls against the main current.
• *vb* **eddied; eddying** swirl around. < probably Old Norse *itha*.

edelweiss (ˈeɪdḷˌvaɪs) *n* a perennial plant with white flowers and downy leaves, found high in the Alps. < German *edel* noble + *weiss* white.

edge (ɛdʒ) *n* **1** the sharp side of a blade; its degree of sharpness. **2** the line where two plane faces meet at an angle. **3** the border or limit of an area; threshold of a state: the edge of madness. **4** keenness or bite: Her voice had an edge of sarcasm. **5** advantage: He had the edge on his opponent.
• *vb* **1** give or provide with an edge. **2** move or force gradually: He edged the car out of the way. **be on edge** be nervous or irritable. **edgeways** *adv* sideways. **edging** *n* something which forms an edge. **edgy** *adj* nervous. **get a word in edgeways** manage to interrupt a lengthy monologue. **set someone's teeth on edge** annoy someone. **take the edge off** make blunt or dull. < Old English *ecg*.

edible (ˈɛdɪbḷ) *adj* fit to be eaten as food. **edibility** *n* < Latin *edere* to eat.

edict (ˈiːdɪkt) *n* an official command; public decree. < Latin *e-* + *dicere* to say.

edifice (ˈɛdɪfɪs) *n* a large structure or building. < ultimately Latin *aedificare* to build.

edify (ˈɛdɪˌfaɪ) *vb* **edified; edifying** influence and improve, esp. morally or spiritually. < ultimately Latin *aedes* temple + *facere* to make.

edit (ˈɛdɪt) *vb* **1** be the editor of (a newspaper, magazine, etc.). **2** prepare (something) for publication. **3** put together (a film or recording) by arranging individual sequences. **4** alter the words of for a specific purpose. **5 edit out** delete. **edition** *n* **1** the published form of a text: hardback edition. **2** the total number of copies of a book, etc., published at one time. **3** a version or copy. **editor** *n* **1** someone who is responsible for the contents of a book, newspaper, or periodical, or of one section of this: fashion editor. **2** someone who edits written, filmed, or recorded material, esp. as a job. < ultimately Latin *e-* + *dare* to give.

editorial (ˌɛdɪˈtɔːrɪəl) *adj* of or written by an editor.
• *n* a newspaper article giving the opinions of the editors or publishers.

educate (ˈɛdjʊˌkeɪt) *vb* instruct in or develop the skills, morals, judgment, etc., of; train. **education** *n* a system of instruction or training. **educational** *adj* **educationist** or **educationalist** *n* an educational expert. < Latin *educare*.

EEC *abbrev* European Economic Community.

eel (iːl) *n* one of a group of long, snake-like fish. < Old English *ǣl*.

eerie (ˈɪərɪ) *adj* strange and frightening; weird. < Old English *earg* cowardly.

eff (ɛf) SEE PANEL.

efface (ɪˈfeɪs) *vb* **1** make indistinct;

economic or **economical?**

Economic*al* is nowadays most commonly found in the language of advertising. It is applied to a whole range of things that are somehow 'thrifty' or 'saving', from the economical little motor car that uses less petrol, to the economical family size with its lower unit cost. It is related to the verb economize.

Economic has mostly to do with the science of economics and with a country's economy: a government makes economic decisions in its country's economic interests but may end up facing an economic crisis.

There is a certain area of overlap between the two words. Economic is being increasingly used as a variant of economical: 'You'll find the larger packet much more economic.' However, to avoid confusing the words it is probably best if this meaning is reserved for economical.

obliterate. **2 efface oneself** make oneself humble or inconspicuous. < Latin *ex* + Middle French *face*.

effect (ɪˈfɛkt) *n* **1** a change produced by a cause; result: an adverse effect. **2** a particular impression on the senses: a striking effect. **3** the state of being in operation: The new schedule comes into effect next week.
• *vb* bring about; accomplish. **effective** *adj* **1** producing a desired effect; impressive; striking. **2** actual; not theoretical. **effectively** *adv* **effectiveness** *n* **effects** *pl n* **1** personal belongings. **2** sounds, lighting, etc., that accompany a broadcast or film: special effects. **effectual** *adj* able to produce or be successful in producing a desired effect. **in effect** for all practical purposes; actually, though not appearing to be: The suggestion is, in effect, a compromise. **take effect** come into operation; produce an intended effect. **with effect from** coming into operation at (a time that is mentioned). < Latin *ex-* out + *facere* to do. SEE PANEL. SEE PANEL AT **AFFECT**[1].

effeminate (ɪˈfɛmɪnət) *adj* (of a man) having qualities usually associated with women. < Latin *ex-* out + *femina* woman.

effervesce (ˌɛfəˈvɛs) *vb* **1** (of a liquid) produce a large quantity of small bubbles of gas. **2** show liveliness or great excitement. **effervescence** *n* **effervescent** *adj* < Latin *ex-* out + *fervēre* to boil.

efficacious (ˌɛfɪˈkeɪʃəs) *adj* capable of producing a desired effect. **efficacy** *n* < SEE **EFFECT.**

efficient (ɪˈfɪʃənt) *adj* **1** able to produce the desired effects, esp. with the least waste: the most efficient method. **2** (of a person) able to work in an organized way, to do things competently and quickly. **efficiency** *n* **efficiently** *adv* < SEE **EFFECT.**

effigy (ˈɛfɪdʒɪ) *n* a sculpture or model of a person. < Latin *ex-* out + *fingere* to form.

effluent (ˈɛflʊənt) *n* something that flows out; industrial waste. < Latin *ex-* out + *fluere* to flow.

effort (ˈɛfət) *n* **1** the use of physical or mental power; energy exerted: a determined effort to reach an agreement. **2** an attempt; try. **3** a result of trying; achievement. **effortless** *adj* **effortlessly** *adv* < ultimately Latin *fortis* strong.

effusive (ɪˈfjuːsɪv) *adj* showing emotions in an unrestrained way. **effusively** *adv* < Latin *ex-* out + *fundere* to pour.

e.g. *abbrev* (*Latin*) exempli gratia (for example). SEE PANEL.

egalitarian (ɪˌgælɪˈtɛərɪən) *adj* marked by or showing support of social, political, and economic equality for all people. < French *égalité* equality.

egg[1] (ɛg) *n* **1** the reproductive body produced by the female of birds, reptiles, etc. **2** the hard-shelled egg of a domestic hen used as food. **egg-cup** *n* a small cup without a handle for holding a boiled egg. **egg-timer** *n* a device for timing the boiling of eggs. < Old Norse.

egg[2] *vb* encourage or urge (someone) to

effective or **effectual?**

These words are often confused. Effective means 'producing a desired effect' as in What will be the most *effective* way of selling our new product?

Effectual is a less common word. It means 'able to produce or be successful in producing a desired effect' as in Attempts to lower the unemployment rate have so far not proved *effectual*.

eff and **em**

A small number of compound words contain a letter of the alphabet as their first element. These include S-bend, V-neck, U-turn, Y-fronts, and T-bone (steak). In such cases the letter usually serves an iconic function: the V of V-neck provides a pictorial representation of the shape in question.

Letters of the alphabet also occur in idiomatic expressions such as mind one's *p's* and *q's* and dot one's *i's* and cross one's *t's*.

Finally, the vocabulary contains odd instances of words like eff as in the phrase effing and blinding which are formed by spelling a letter out. Long-established examples are em and en, the units of measurement used in printing equal to one-sixth and one-twelfth of an inch respectively.

do something. < Old Norse *eggja.*
egghead (ˈɛgˌhɛd) *n* (*informal*) an intellectual person.
egg-plant (ˈɛgˌplɑːnt) *n* an aubergine.
eggshell (ˈɛgˌʃɛl) *n* the shell of an egg.
• *adj* **1** (of china) thin and fragile. **2** (of paint) having a slightly glossy finish.
ego (ˈiːgəʊ, ˈɛgəʊ) *n, pl* **egos 1** the self. **2** self-esteem; self-respect. **egocentric** *adj* self-centred. **egoism** *n* self-centredness. **egotism** *n* the practice of talking about oneself too much. **egotist** *n* **egotistic** or **egotistical** *adj* **ego trip** (*informal*) an act that selfishly indulges one's own interests or self-expression. < Latin: I.
eiderdown (ˈaɪdəˌdaʊn) *n* a thick, warm quilt stuffed with a soft filling. < Old Norse *æthr* eider duck + *dūnn* down.
eight (eɪt) *n* **1** the number 8. **2** an eight-person racing boat; its crew.
• *determiner, pron* 8 in number. **one over the eight** (*informal*) too much to drink. < Old English *eahta.*
eighteen (ˌeɪˈtiːn) *determiner, pron* 18 in number.
• *n* the number 18. **eighteenth** *determiner, pron, n, adv* < Old English *eahtatīene.*
eighth (eɪtθ) *determiner, pron, adv* next after seventh.
• *n* **1** something that is eighth. **2** one of eight equal parts of a thing. **eighthly** *adv*
eighty (ˈeɪtɪ) *determiner, pron* 80 in number.
• *n* the number 80. **eightieth** *determiner, pron, n, adv* **eighties** *pl n* the numbers, range of temperatures, ages, or dates in a century from 80-89. < Old English *eahtatig.*
either (ˈaɪðə, ˈiːðə) *determiner, pron* **1** one or the other of two: You can follow either path. **2** each of two: trees on either side of the road.
• *conj* used before two or more alternatives: You can have either soup or fruit juice.
• *adv* for that matter; likewise: 'I can't drive.'—'I can't, either.' < Old English *ǣghwæther.* SEE PANEL.
ejaculate (ɪˈdʒækjʊˌleɪt) *vb* **1** eject (semen) from the body. **2** (*formal*) utter suddenly and briefly. < Latin *e-* out + *jacere* to throw.
eject (ɪˈdʒɛkt) *vb* **1** drive or throw out; expel or discharge. **2** evict from property. **3** escape from an aeroplane by using an ejector seat. **ejection** *n* **ejector** *n* **ejector seat** a seat that propels an occupant out of an aeroplane in an emergency. < Latin *e-* out + *jacere* to throw.
eke (iːk) *vb* **eke out 1** make (a supply) last by using it very carefully. **2** make (a living) with difficulty. **3** supplement: He ekes out his income with an evening job. < Old English *ēcan* to increase. SEE PANEL.
elaborate (ɪˈlæbərət) *adj* **1** devised or developed with great care. **2** complicated; intricate.
• *vb* (ɪˈlæbəˌreɪt) work out or describe in detail; develop. **elaborately** *adv* **elaboration** *n* < Latin e- out + *laborare* to work.
elapse (ɪˈlæps) *vb* (of time) pass by. < Latin *e-* out + *labi* to slide.
elastic (ɪˈlæstɪk) *adj* **1** capable of being stretched or expanded and going back to its former shape. **2** able to be changed

e.g. or **i.e.?**

E.g. is short for Latin *exempli gratia* and means 'for example'. It is used to introduce one or more examples of what has gone before: The holiday will include visits to some of the local attractions, *e.g.* the caves and the pottery.

I. e. is short for Latin *id est* and means 'that is'. It is used to explain, define, or amplify what has gone before: Before you travel abroad, ensure that you have all the relevant details of your insurance, *i.e.* the name of your insurance company, the policy number, and the name of your insurance broker. I.e. should not be used to introduce an example.

either is ... or **either are ...?**

The general rule is that the number of the verb depends on whether the immediately preceding noun is singular or plural: Either my mother or my sister *is* coming—sister is singular, and so the verb is singular. Either my mother or my sisters *are* coming—sisters is plural and so the verb is plural. According to this rule, it should be possible to say: Either my sisters or my mother *is* coming. However, to avoid awkwardness, the plural noun is generally put next to the verb: Either my mother or my sisters *are* coming or the sentence can be slightly rephrased: Either my mother or my sisters *may* come.

readily; flexible: The rules are fairly elastic.
• *n* a fabric containing interwoven strands of flexible rubber. **elasticity** *n* **elasticated** *adj* (of a fabric) made elastic by interweaving strands of flexible rubber. < Greek *elaunein* to drive.

elated (ɪˈleɪtɪd) *adj* feeling very pleased or proud. **elation** *n* < Latin *ex-* out + *ferre* to bear.

elbow (ˈɛlbəʊ) *n* **1** the joint between the forearm and upper arm. **2** the part of a garment covering this. **3** a sharp bend in a pipe, etc.
• *vb* push or force with or as if with the elbow. **elbow grease** (*informal*) hard, physical effort. **elbow-room** *n* sufficient space or scope for movement or operation. < Old English *elboga.*

elder¹ (ˈɛldə) *adj* older: his elder sister.
• *n* **1** a person who is older: Respect your elders. **2** a leader in some churches. **elder statesman** an influential, senior or retired person whose opinions are valued. < Old English *eald* old.
SEE PANEL.

elder² *n* also **elderberry** any of several shrubs or trees with small white flowers and dark berries. **elderberry** *n* its berry. < Old English *ellærn.*

eke out

Many verbs in English consist of two or three separate parts: come off, pick up, look forward to, etc. These *phrasal verbs* form a large group, of which eke out is a member. Unlike most of the others in the group, however, eke, the first part of eke out, does not occur in the language without the second part, out. **Mete out** is another example.

elder or **older?**

Elder is used in connection with family relationships: I have an *elder* sister. Roger is the *elder* of the two brothers.

Older is used in other contexts: *older* pupils, the *older* generation.

You cannot say elder than; use older than instead: Rosalind is *older than* Martin.

elderly (ˈɛldəlɪ) *adj* rather old.

eldest (ˈɛldɪst) *adj* oldest, esp. first-born or oldest surviving.

eldorado (ˌɛldəˈrɑːdəʊ) *n a* place of very great wealth or opportunity. < Spanish: the gilded (place).

elect (ɪˈlɛkt) *vb* **1** choose by vote: elect a chairman. **2** (*formal*) choose; decide. **3** (of God) choose (someone) to receive salvation.
• *adj* chosen but not yet in office: the President elect. **election** *n* **elector** *n* a person qualified to vote in an election. **electorate** *n* the whole body of electors. < Latin *e-* out + *legere* to choose.

electric (ɪˈlɛktrɪk) *adj* **1** of, supplying, or producing electricity. **2** worked by electricity. **3** producing an intensely stimulating effect: Her performance was electric! **electrical** *adj* of or concerned with electricity. **electric chair** a chair in which criminals are executed by electricity. **electric eel** a large, eel-shaped fish that can give a severe electric shock. **electrics** *pl n* electrical parts. **electric shock** the effect of the sudden passage of electricity through the body, stimulating the nerves and contracting the muscles. SEE PANEL.

electrician (ɪlɛkˈtrɪʃən, ˌiːlɛkˈtrɪʃən) *n* a person whose job is to maintain, install, or operate electrical equipment.

electricity (ɪlɛkˈtrɪsɪtɪ, ˌiːlɛkˈtrɪsɪtɪ) *n* **1** the phenomena that arise from the existence of positively and negatively charged particles. **2** a supply of electric current.

electrify (ɪˈlɛktrɪˌfaɪ) *vb* **electrified; electrifying 1** charge with electricity. **2** equip for the use of electric power. **3** stimulate intensely. **electrification** *n*

electrocute (ɪˈlɛktrəˌkjuːt) *vb* kill by electricity. **electrocution** *n* < *electro-* electric + *-cute* as in *execute.*

electrode (ɪˈlɛktrəʊd) *n* a conductor

electric shocks

Like many things, electricity was first discovered by the Greeks. Static electricity in the form of a spark or slight shock was produced by rubbing a piece of amber, and the Greek word for amber is *elektron.* It is from this word that the 17th-century coinage electricity came into being. The same Greek word also gives us electron and electrode.

through which electric current enters or leaves a device. < *electro-* electric + Greek *hodos* way.

electrolysis (ɪlɛkˈtrɒlɪsɪs) *n* **1** the passage of an electric current through an electrolyte causing the decomposition of the electrolyte. **2** the destruction of hair roots or other living tissue by an electric current.

electrolyte (ɪˈlɛktrəˌlaɪt) *n* a solution or molten substance that conducts electricity.

electromagnet (ɪˌlɛktrəʊˈmægnɪt) *n* a magnet consisting of a metal core with a coil of wire wound round it, through which an electric current is passed. **electromagnetic** *adj*

electron (ɪˈlɛktrɒn) *n* a very small particle with the smallest known negative electric charge. **electronic** *adj* **1** of electrons. **2** of, using, or operated by devices which work by the principles of electronics. **electronics** *n* the science and technology dealing with the development and behaviour of electrons in electronic devices such as transistors. < *electro-* electric + *-on* from *ion.*

electroplate (ɪˈlɛktrəʊˌpleɪt) *vb* plate with a metallic coat by electrolysis.

elegant (ˈɛlɪgənt) *adj* graceful, refined, and dignified in appearance or style. **elegance** *n* **elegantly** *adv* < Latin *elegans,* from *e-* out + *legere* to choose.

elegy (ˈɛlɪdʒɪ) *n* a sorrowful poem or song lamenting a person's death. < Greek *elegos.*

element (ˈɛlɪmənt) *n* **1** a part that makes up a whole: the basic elements of economics. **2** any of about 100 fundamental substances that cannot be decomposed by chemical reaction into simpler substances. **3** the state or sphere that is natural or suited to someone or something: He is in his element when he is telling jokes. **4** a trace: an element of doubt. **5** a wire conductor that gives out heat in an electric kettle, cooker, etc. **6** *pl* forces of nature; severe weather. **7** *pl* the bread and wine at Communion. **elemental** *adj* **elementary** *adj* of or dealing with the simplest facts about something; basic. < Latin *elementum.* SEE PANEL.

elephant (ˈɛlɪfənt) *n* a very large mammal with a trunk and two long ivory tusks. **elephantine** *adj* of or like elephants; huge or clumsy. < Greek *elephas.* SEE PANEL AT **WHITE.**

elevate (ˈɛlɪˌveɪt) *vb* **1** raise in position, rank, or status. **2** raise to a higher intellectual or moral level. **elevation** *n* **1** elevating or being elevated. **2** the height to which something is raised; elevated place. **3** a drawing of a building on a vertical plane. **elevator** *n* **1** a device that raises or lifts things up: a grain elevator. **1** (*US*) a lift. < Latin *e-* out + *levare* to lift. SEE PANEL.

eleven (ɪˈlɛvn̩) *n* **1** the number 11. **2** a team of 11 players at football, cricket, etc.
• *determiner, pron* 11 in number. **eleven-plus** *n* (esp. formerly) an examination taken at the age of about 11 to determine which type of secondary school a child should attend. **elevenses** *pl n* mid-morning light refreshments. < Old English *endleofan.*

eleventh (ɪˈlɛvn̩θ) *determiner, pron, adv* next after tenth.
• *n* **1** something that is eleventh. **2** one of eleven equal parts of a thing. **at the eleventh hour** at the latest possible time.

elf (ɛlf) *n, pl* **elves** a mischievous fairy. **elfish** *adj* < Old English *ælf.*

elicit (ɪˈlɪsɪt) *vb* draw out (a response, information, etc.). < Latin *elicere.* SEE PANEL.

eligible (ˈɛlɪdʒəbl̩) *adj* **1** qualified to be chosen; entitled: eligible for promotion.

elemental or **elementary?**

These two words should not be confused.

Elemental means 'of the elements—earth, air, fire, or water; concerned with the forces of nature' as in *elemental* spirits, *elemental* passions.

Elementary is a commoner word and refers to the simplest or basic facts about something as in an *elementary* guide to French grammar, *elementary* education.

elevator and **lift**

Imagine that an American friend has come over to the United Kingdom to visit you and that while out shopping one day you arrange to meet 'next to the elevator' on the 'first floor' of a large department store. There is a good possibility that the pair of you will fail to meet up. In American English elevator means 'lift' and first floor is the name for what British English speakers call the 'ground floor'!

2 considered suitable or desirable, esp. for marriage. **eligibility** *n* < SEE **ELECT.**

eliminate (ɪˈlɪmɪˌneɪt) *vb* **1** get rid of (something unwanted) completely. **2** leave out of consideration; ignore. **3** exclude from a further stage in a competition. **4** kill in a cold-blooded way. **elimination** *n* < Latin *e-* out + *limen* threshold.

elision (ɪˈlɪʒən) *n* omission of a vowel or syllable in pronunciation, for example I'm = I am. < Latin *elidere* to strike out.

élite (ɪˈliːt, eɪˈliːt) *n* **1** a small, superior group, esp. a powerful one. **2** a typewriter typesize having 12 characters per inch. **élitism** *n* belief in leadership by an élite. **élitist** *n* < French: SEE **ELECT.**

elixir (ɪˈlɪksə) *n* **1** a substance thought to be capable of prolonging life indefinitely or of changing base metals into gold: elixir of life. **2** a cure-all. **3** a sweetened liquid containing a medicinal drug. < Arabic.

elk (ɛlk) *n* the largest existing deer of northern Europe and Asia. < Old English *eolh.*

ellipse (ɪˈlɪps) *n* a closed plane curve produced by a point that moves so that the sum of its distance from two fixed points is constant. < SEE **ELLIPSIS.**

ellipsis (ɪˈlɪpsɪs) *n, pl* **ellipses** the omission of one or more words needed to complete a meaning or grammatical construction. **elliptical** *adj* **1** shaped like an ellipse. **2** containing ellipses; extremely or too concise. < Greek *ellepein* to leave out.

elm (ɛlm) *n* any of a group of very tall, deciduous trees with rough, serrated leaves; its wood. < Old English.

elocution (ˌɛləˈkjuːʃən) *n* the art of good, clear, and effective public speaking. < SEE **ELOQUENCE.**

elongate (ˈiːlɒŋgeɪt) *vb* make or become longer. < Latin *e-* out + *longus* long.

elope (ɪˈləʊp) *vb* run away secretly with a lover, esp. in order to get married. **elopement** *n* < Anglo-French *aloper.*

eloquent (ˈɛləkwənt) *adj* **1** characterized by an ability to speak fluently and powerfully. **2** vividly or movingly expressive: an eloquent performance. **eloquence** *n* **eloquently** *adv* < Latin *e-* out + *loqui* to speak.

else (ɛls) *adv* **1** besides: Who else is coming? **2** apart from what is mentioned or understood: Let's go somewhere else. **3** otherwise; if not: Run or else you'll miss the bus. **elsewhere** *adv* in or to another place. < Old English *elles.*

elucidate (ɪˈluːsɪˌdeɪt) *vb* make clear (something difficult); clarify. **elucidation** *n* < Latin *e-* out + *lucidus* clear.

elude (ɪˈluːd) *vb* **1** avoid or escape from by quickness, cunning, etc. **2** escape the memory, understanding, or attention of. **elusive** *adj* **elusiveness** *n* < Latin *e-* out + *ludere* to play.

elver (ˈɛlvə) *n* a young eel. < alteration of *eelfare* migration of eels.

emaciated (ɪˈmeɪsɪˌeɪtɪd) *adj* excessively thin or feeble from illness or starvation. < Latin *e-* out + *macies* leanness.

emanate (ˈɛməˌneɪt) *vb* issue or arise from: A foul smell emanated from the sewer. **emanation** *n* < Latin *e-* out + *manare* to flow.

emancipate (ɪˈmænsɪˌpeɪt) *vb* free from slavery, restraint, or other control. **emancipation** *n* **emancipator** *n* < Latin *e-* out + *manus* hand + *capere* to take.

emasculate (ɪˈmæskjʊˌleɪt) *vb* **1** castrate. **2** deprive of masculinity or vigour; weaken. **emasculation** *n* < Latin *e-* out + *masculus* masculine.

embalm (ɪmˈbɑːm) *vb* treat (a dead body) with preservatives to protect against decay. < Old French *embaumer,* from *en-* + *baume* balm: SEE **BALM.**

embankment (ɪmˈbæŋkmənt) *n* a long, raised mound of earth or stone that keeps back a river or carries a road or railway.

embargo (ɛmˈbɑːgəʊ) *n, pl* **embargoes** an order forbidding commerce or other activity. < ultimately Latin *in-* on + *barra* bar.

embark (ɛmˈbɑːk) *vb* **1** put or go on board a boat or aircraft. **2** begin: embark on an undertaking. **embarkation** *n* < Latin *in-* in + *barca* small boat.

embarrass (ɪmˈbærəs) *vb* make (someone) feel self-conscious, awkward, or ashamed. **embarrassment** *n* SEE PANEL.

embassy (ˈɛmbəsɪ) *n* **1** the official headquarters of an ambassador. **2** an

---

elicit or **illicit?**

Elicit is a verb and means 'to draw out (a response, information, etc.); evoke' as in All his attempts to *elicit* the truth were unsuccessful.

Illicit is an adjective meaning 'contrary to the law; not allowed' such as the *illicit* sales of rum, *illicit* relationships.

---

ambassador and his or her associated staff. < Middle French *ambassee,* ultimately of Germanic origin.

embattled (ɪmˈbætḷd) *adj* prepared for or engaged in a battle.

embed (ɪmˈbɛd) *vb* **embedded; embedding** place or fix firmly in or as if in a surrounding solid mass.

embellish (ɪmˈbɛlɪʃ) *vb* **1** make beautiful by adding ornaments. **2** improve (a story, etc.) by adding fictitious or exaggerated details. < Middle French *em-* in + *bel* beautiful.

ember (ˈɛmbə) *n* a glowing, smouldering piece of coal or wood in a dying fire. < Middle English *eymere.*

embezzle (ɪmˈbɛzḷ) *vb* take (money or property that has been placed in one's care) fraudulently for one's own use. **embezzler** *n* < Middle French *en-* + *besillier* to destroy.

embitter (ɪmˈbɪtə) *vb* excite bitter feelings in.

emblazon (ɪmˈbleɪzṇ) *vb* **1** decorate with heraldic or other devices. **2** exhibit conspicuously. **3** make splendid, with bright colours. < *en-* in + Old French *blason* shield.

emblem (ˈɛmbləm) *n* an object, symbol, or device that represents or symbolizes something. < Greek *emblēma* insertion, from *en-* in + *ballein* to throw.

embody (ɪmˈbɒdɪ) *vb* **embodied; embodying 1** incorporate; include. **2** give bodily or definite form to. **embodiment** *n*

emboss (ɪmˈbɒs) *vb* decorate with raised designs; raise (a design, etc.) in relief. < Middle French *embocer,* from *en-* + *boce* boss.

embrace (ɪmˈbreɪs) *vb* **1** clasp in the arms to show affection; hug. **2** take up; adopt and use. **3** include as a part of a whole.
• *n* the act of embracing; hug. < Latin *im-* in + *brachium* arm.

embrocation (ˌɛmbrəˈkeɪʃən) *n* a liquid that is applied to the skin to relieve pain or irritation. < Greek *embroche* lotion, from *en-* in + *breichein* to wet.

embroider (ɪmˈbrɔɪdə) *vb* **1** do decorative needlework on (cloth, etc.). **2** elaborate on (a story). **embroidery** *n* < Middle French *embroder.*

embroil (ɪmˈbrɔɪl) *vb* involve in conflict, confusion, or difficulties. < Middle French *en-* + *brouiller* to broil.

embryo (ˈɛmbrɪˌəʊ) *n, pl* **embryos 1** an animal in the earliest stages of its development, before birth or hatching. **2** the developing human being in the first eight weeks after conception. **3** something undeveloped; state of being undeveloped. **embryonic** *adj* < Greek *en-* in + *bryein* to swell.

emend (ɪˈmɛnd) *vb* correct, esp. by changing the written text. **emendation** *n* < Latin *e-* out + *mendum* mistake.

emerald (ˈɛmərəld, ˈɛmrəld) *n* a transparent, bright-green precious stone.
• *adj* having this colour. < Greek *smaragdos.*

emerge (ɪˈmɜːdʒ) *vb* **1** come out or up into view. **2** become clear or known; rise from an obscure or subordinate position. **emergence** *n* **emergent** *adj* < Latin *e-* out + *mergere* to plunge.

emergency (ɪˈmɜːdʒənsɪ) *n* a serious, unexpected event or set of circumstances needing action immediately. **state of emergency** a condition, declared by a government, in which the law is administered by military forces.

emery (ˈɛmərɪ) *n* a hard, dark mineral,

---

embarrass

The word emba*rrass* is misspelt not only by non-native speakers of English, but by native speakers too. Other words which have pairs of double consonants and provide similar spelling difficulty include accommodate and committee.

One way to avoid misspelling these words is to remember their distinctive feature (double consonants) and to make up a sentence that includes them, such as: We can Accommodate the Committee without Embarrassment. (This also gives us the acronym: ACE.) The use of grouping and mnemonics means that the load on the memory is very slight, and you need never be embarrassed by embarrass, embarrassing, embarrassment again!

Embarrass comes into English from the French *embarrasser,* which comes from the Spanish *embarazar,* which in turn derives from the Portuguese *embaracar.* So without such memory aids the etymologist would be completely at a loss when it came to spelling the word.

---

used for grinding and polishing. **emery paper** paper coated with emery powder for use as an abrasive. < Greek *smyris.*

emetic (ɪˈmɛtɪk) *adj, n* (something) that causes vomiting. < Greek *emein* to vomit.

emigrate (ˈɛmɪˌgreɪt) *vb* leave one's country and settle elsewhere. **emigration** *n* **emigrant** *n* a person who emigrates. < Latin *e-* out + *migrare* to move. SEE PANEL.

eminent (ˈɛmɪnənt) *adj* **1** famous and having a high rank in science, the arts, etc. **2** conspicuous; notable. **eminently** *adv* **eminence** *n* **1** an eminent position or state. **2** the title for a cardinal: His Eminence. < Latin *eminēre* to stand out. SEE PANEL.

emir (ˈɛmɪə) *n* a ruler of any of several Muslim states. **emirate** *n* the authority or territory of an emir. < Arabic *amīr* commander.

emissary (ˈɛmɪsərɪ) *n* a person sent on a mission; representative. < SEE **EMIT.**

emit (ɪˈmɪt) *vb* **emitted; emitting 1** send out (light, heat, etc.). **2** utter. **emission** *n* **emitter** *n* < Latin *e-* out + *mittere* to send.

emolument (ɪˈmɒljʊmənt) *n* (*formal*) a gain from professional employment; fee or salary. < Latin *e-* out + *molere* to grind.

emotion (ɪˈməʊʃən) *n* any strong feeling such as joy, fear, or anger. **emotional** *adj* **1** of the emotions. **2** inclined to show excessive emotion. **emotionalism** *n* **emotionally** *adv* **emotive** *adj* arousing emotion, not reason: an emotive issue. < Latin *e-* out + *movere* to move. SEE PANEL.

empathy (ˈɛmpəθɪ) *n* the ability to understand and imaginatively participate in the feelings or ideas of another person. < Greek *en-* in + *pathos* feeling.

emperor (ˈɛmpərə) *n* the supreme ruler of an empire. < Latin *imperator,* from *imperare* to command.

emphasis (ˈɛmfəsɪs) *n, pl* **emphases 1** special importance or consideration given to something. **2** strong or forceful expression or action. **3** the particular prominence given to a word or part of a word in speaking. **emphasize** *vb* place emphasis on. **emphatic** *adj* **1** tending to express oneself in forceful speech or action. **2** spoken or expressed with emphasis. **emphatically** *adv* < Greek *en-* in + *phainein* to show.

empire (ˈɛmpaɪə) *n* **1** a large group of countries ruled by one supreme authority; territory of such countries. **2** a large commercial enterprise controlled by one person or group. **empire-building** *n* (*informal*) the seeking of extra power, esp. for its own sake. < SEE **EMPEROR.**

empirical (ɛmˈpɪrɪkl̩) *adj* based on or relating to experiment or observation rather than theory. < Greek *en-* in + *peira* trial.

emplacement (ɪmˈpleɪsmənt) *n* **1** the prepared position from which guns are fired. **2** a position or place.

employ (ɪmˈplɔɪ) *vb* **1** provide with a paid job; use the services of. **2** (*formal*)

emigrant or **immigrant?**

These words are confused sometimes. A helpful way of remembering which is which is to remember the meaning of the prefixes: an *im*migrant (from the Latin *in* 'in or into') is a person who comes into and settles in a foreign country; an emigrant (from the Latin *ex* 'out of') goes out of one country to settle in another.

eminent or **imminent?**

The main meaning of eminent is 'famous and having a high rank in science, the arts, etc.' as in an *eminent* professor, an *eminent* lawyer.

Imminent means 'liable to occur soon; impending or threatening' as in an *imminent* disaster, no warning that changes are *imminent*.

emotional or **emotive?**

Careful users of English distinguish these two words. Emotional is the more common of the two and means 'of the emotions; inclined to show excessive emotions' as in an *emotional* reaction, sex without *emotional* involvement, an *emotional* child.

Emotive means 'arousing emotion, not reason' as in *emotive* issues like abortion and capital punishment.

use for a particular purpose; spend (time).
• *n* (*formal*) the state of being employed: in the employ of. **employee** *n* a person employed by a person or firm, esp. one below executive level. **employer** *n* a person or firm that employs people. **employment** *n* the state of being employed; form of work on which a person can be employed. < Latin *implicare* to enfold. SEE PANEL.

empower (ɪmˈpaʊə) *vb* give official authority or power to.

empress (ˈɛmprɪs) *n* **1** the wife or widow of an emperor. **2** the female ruler of an empire.

empty (ˈɛmptɪ) *adj* **1** having nothing or no one in it. **2** not occupied or inhabited. **3** lacking effectiveness, value, or substance; insincere: empty threats. **4** lacking sense: empty ideas. **5** (*informal*) hungry.
• *vb* **emptied; emptying 1** make or become empty. **2** transfer by emptying.
• *n* a bottle, box, etc., that has been emptied. **emptiness** *n* **empty-handed** *adj* bringing or taking away nothing. < Old English *ǣmettig* unoccupied.

emu (ˈiːmjuː) *n* a large, flightless Australian bird. < modified from Portuguese *ema* ostrich.

emulate (ˈɛmjʊˌleɪt) *vb* imitate closely, esp. to try to equal or do better than. < Latin *aemulus* rivalling.

emulsion (ɪˈmʌlʃən) *n* **1** a substance consisting of one liquid dispersed in particles through another liquid; paint or medicine in this form. **2** a light-sensitive coating on a photographic film. **emulsify** *vb* **emulsified; emulsifying** convert into an emulsion. < Latin *e-* out + *mulgere* to milk.

enable (ɪˈneɪbl̩) *vb* make possible or practical; provide with an opportunity or means.

enact (ɪˈnækt) *vb* **1** make into a law. **2** perform in or as in (a play); act out. **enactment** *n*

enamel (ɪˈnæməl) *n* **1** a usually opaque, glassy substance used for coating the surface of metal, glass, or pottery. **2** something decorated with enamel. **3** a paint that gives a hard, glossy surface when it dries. **4** the hard, white, smooth outer covering of teeth.
• *vb* **enamelled; enamelling** cover or decorate with enamel. < Middle French *en* + *esmail* enamel.

enamoured (ɪˈnæməd) *adj* fond. < Middle French *en-* in + *amour* love.

en bloc (ˌɒn ˈblɒk) *adv, adj* (*French*) as a whole; all together.

encamp (ɪnˈkæmp) *vb* set up or put in a camp. **encampment** *n*

encase (ɪnˈkeɪs) *vb* enclose in a case.

enchant (ɪnˈtʃɑːnt) *vb* **1** charm greatly; delight. **2** cast a spell on; bewitch. **enchantment** *n* < Latin *incantare,* from *in-* + *cantare* to sing.

encircle (ɪnˈsɜːkl̩) *vb* **1** form a circle round; surround. **2** move in a circle round. **encirclement** *n*

encl. *abbrev* **1** enclosed. **2** enclosure.

enclave (ˈɛnkleɪv) *n* a small territory surrounded by a foreign territory. < Latin *in-* + *clavis* key.

enclose (ɪnˈkləʊz) *vb* **1** close or shut in completely; surround. **2** shut up in a container; hold in; confine. **3** insert in an envelope or wrapping, esp. with something else. **enclosure** *n* **1** enclosing. **2** an enclosed place, for example at a sports ground. **3** something included in the same envelope or wrapping.

encode (ɪnˈkəʊd) *vb* **1** convert (a message) into code. **2** convert (information) into a different communication system.

encompass (ɪnˈkʌmpəs) *vb* surround; include.

encore (ˈɒŋkɔː) *n* (an audience's appreciative call for) an additional performance. < French: again. SEE PANEL.

encounter (ɪnˈkaʊntə) *vb* **1** meet, esp. unexpectedly. **2** be faced with: to encounter difficulties. **3** come into conflict with (an enemy).
• *n* **1** an unexpected meeting. **2** a hostile

---

employer or **employee?**

The endings -er and -ee are sometimes confused. The ending -er means 'a person or thing that performs the action expressed by the root verb', for example employ*er* (a person who employs others) and interview*er* (a person who interviews people).

The suffix -ee refers to the 'recipient' of the action expressed by the root verb, for example employee (a person who is employed) and interviewee (a person who is interviewed).

The suffix -er is more productive than -ee, and many words that may be used with the suffix -er may not be used with -ee, for example murderer, but not murderee, thriller, but not thrillee. For an interesting application of the suffix -er, see panel at **prison.**

---

meeting or clash. < Latin *in-* + *contra* against.

encourage (ɪn'kʌrɪdʒ) *vb* **1** give courage, confidence, or hope to. **2** spur on; urge. **3** give support to; stimulate or promote: encourage small businesses. **encouragement** *n* < Old French *en-* + *corage* courage.

encroach (ɪn'krəʊtʃ) *vb* **1** intrude upon someone's rights, property, etc. **2** advance beyond the usual or proper limits. **encroachment** *n* < Old French *en-* + *croc* hook.

encrust (ɪn'krʌst) *vb* **1** cover with a crust. **2** decorate lavishly with a layer of jewels. **encrustation** *n*

encumber (ɪn'kʌmbə) *vb* burden; hinder the operation or activity of. **encumbrance** *n* < Old French *encombrer,* from *en-* + *combre* barrier.

encyclopaedia, encyclopedia (ɪnˌsaɪklə'piːdɪə) *n* a book or set of books containing information on all branches of knowledge or one subject, usually arranged alphabetically. **encyclopaedic**, **encyclopedic** *adj* of or like an encyclopaedia; comprehensive. < Greek *enkyklios* general + *paideia* education.

end (ɛnd) *n* **1** the extreme limit of something; furthest point from where one is. **2** the point that concludes something in time; events just preceding this. **3** the point when something stops existing. **4** the final condition of something. **5** something remaining; remnant: odds and ends. **6** an aim or purpose: means and ends. **7** either half of a football pitch, etc.: change ends at half-time.
• *vb* **1** bring or come to an end. **2** reach a certain state, place, or condition eventually: They ended up getting married. **endless** *adj* **1** (seeming to be) without end. **2** very numerous. **3** (of a belt, etc.) that is without ends. **end-product** *n* the final product of a process; outcome.

< Old English *ende.* SEE PANEL.

endanger (ɪn'deɪndʒə) *vb* bring into or expose to danger, loss, or extinction.

endear (ɪn'dɪə) *vb* cause to be loved. **endearment** *n*

endeavour (ɪn'dɛvə) *vb* attempt; try.
• *n* an attempt. < Middle English *en-* + *dever* duty, from Old French *deveir* to owe.

endemic (ɛn'dɛmɪk) *adj* native to a particular people or area; not introduced. < Greek *en-* in + *dēmos* people.

ending ('ɛndɪŋ) *n* the last part.

endorse (ɪn'dɔːs) *vb* **1** express approval of; support. **2** sign (a document); sign the back of (a cheque). **3** officially record on (a driving licence) details of an offence by the holder. **endorsement** *n* < Latin *in* on + *dorsum* back.

endow (ɪn'daʊ) *vb* **1** give money or property so as to provide with a continuing income. **2** provide with a talent or quality. **endowment** *n* **1** something endowed, esp. an endowed income. **2** a natural ability or quality. **endowment assurance** a form of life insurance in which a fixed sum is paid to the policyholder at a particular date or to his or her beneficiaries if death occurs before this date. < Middle French *en-* + *douer,* from Latin *dotare* to endow, from *dos* dowry.

endue (ɪn'djuː) *vb* provide; endow or invest (with). < Middle French *enduire,* ultimately from Latin *ducere* to lead.

endure (ɪn'djʊə) *vb* **1** bear (suffering or a

Encore!

An audience which has enjoyed a particular performance will often call for an encore. This is a French word meaning, amongst other things, 'again' and 'more'. Interestingly enough, however, French audiences do not use it. Instead of Encore!, the cry that triggers in French soloists a sigh of relief is Bis!

the end

End features in a number of idiomatic expressions, including:

be the end to reach the limit of one's patience: The children really are the end! I can't stand them any longer!
in the end ultimately.
keep one's end up to (continue to) fulfil one's share of responsibilities or duties.
make ends meet to keep one's expenditure within the amount of money earned.
no end a huge number or amount of: no end of problems.
not the end of the world not as bad as it seems: 'Cheer up! It's not the end of the world!'
on end without stopping: raining for days on end.

hardship), esp. without giving in. **2** tolerate; put up with. **3** continue in existence; last. **endurable** *adj* **endurance** *n* the ability to withstand hardship, pain, or stress. < Latin *in-* in + *durus* hard.

enemy ('ɛnəmɪ) *n* **1** a person, group, etc., that is hostile to another and seeks to harm or remove the other. **2** a member of a hostile army, nation, etc.; opposing military force. **3** something harmful or deadly. < Latin *in-* not + *amicus* friend.

energy ('ɛnədʒɪ) *n* **1** the capacity for much activity. **2** effective power. **3** the capacity for doing work: solar energy. **energetic** *adj* of, having, or showing energy; very active and strong; forceful. **energize** *vb* give energy to; activate. < Greek *en-* in + *ergon* work.

enervate ('ɛnəˌveɪt) *vb* lessen the strength or vitality of; weaken. < Latin *e-* out + *nervus* nerve. SEE PANEL.

enfeeble (ɪn'fi:bḷ) *vb* make feeble.

enfold (ɪn'fəʊld) *vb* **1** wrap up; envelop. **2** embrace.

enforce (ɪn'fɔ:s) *vb* **1** compel observance of (a law, rule, etc.). **2** impose by force. **enforceable** *adj* **enforcement** *n*

engage (ɪn'geɪdʒ) *vb* **1** gain the services of; employ. **2** order (a room, etc.); reserve. **3** hold (the attention) of (a person); engross. **4** enter into conflict with: to engage the enemy. **5** interlock or cause to interlock. **engaged** *adj* **1** having promised to marry. **2** involved in an activity. **3** (of a telephone line) already in use. **engagement** *n* **1** an agreement to marry. **2** an appointment made with another person. **3** a battle between military forces. < Old French *en-* + *gage* pledge.

engender (ɪn'dʒɛndə) *vb* cause to develop; produce. < Latin *in-* in + *generare* to generate.

enervate or **invigorate?**

These words are sometimes confused. Careful users of English use enervate to mean 'to lessen the strength or vitality of; weaken' as in He returned home, jaded by the *enervating* tropical climate.

Invigorate means 'to give vitality and energy to; refresh' as in He found an early morning dip most *invigorating*.

engine ('ɛndʒɪn) *n* **1** any machine that converts energy into work. **2** a railway locomotive. < Latin *ingenium* natural quality or disposition, from *in-* + *gignere* to beget.

engineer (ˌɛndʒɪ'nɪə) *n* **1** a person skilled in a branch of engineering. **2** a person who runs or supervises machines or engines, for example on a ship. **3** a person who devises or manages a plan, esp. in a clever and subtle way.
• *vb* **1** plan or work as an engineer. **2** devise or manage, esp. in a clever and subtle way.

engineering (ˌɛndʒɪ'nɪərɪŋ) *n* the application of scientific knowledge to designing, constructing, and using structures and machines: mechanical engineering.

engrave (ɪn'greɪv) *vb* **1** cut (a design) on a (hard surface). **2** impress deeply on the mind or memory. **engraving** *n* a print made from an engraved printing surface. < Middle French *en-* in + *graver* to cut.

engross (ɪn'grʊəs) *vb* **1** fully occupy the attention of. **2** prepare the final text of (a legal document) so that it is ready to be made effective. < ultimately Latin *in-* + *grossus* thick.

engulf (ɪn'gʌlf) *vb* flow over and overwhelm.

enhance (ɪn'hɑ:ns) *vb* improve, esp. in value or attractiveness; heighten. **enhancement** *n* < ultimately Latin *in* in + *altus* high.

enigma (ɪ'nɪgmə) *n* someone or something that is mysterious and hard to understand. **enigmatic** *adj* < Greek *ainigma*.

enjoy (ɪn'dʒɔɪ) *vb* **1** experience pleasure or satisfaction in. **2** have the benefit of: This room enjoys excellent views of the hills. **3** experience: to enjoy good health. **enjoyable** *adj* **enjoyment** *n* **enjoy oneself** take pleasure and satisfaction in what one is doing. < Middle French *enjoir* to rejoice.

enlarge (ɪn'lɑ'dʒ) *vb* **1** make or become larger. **2** reproduce (a photograph) in a larger form. **3** speak or write more about something. **enlarger** *n* **enlargement** *n* **1** enlarging or being enlarged. **2** a photographic print larger than its negative.

enlighten (ɪn'laɪtṇ) *vb* cause to understand; inform. **enlightenment** *n*

enlist (ɪn'lɪst) *vb* **1** take into or enter the armed forces. **2** secure (a person's help or support) for an action or undertaking. **enlistment** *n*

enliven (ɪnˈlaɪvn̩) *vb* make more active, interesting, or happy.

en masse (ˌɒn ˈmæs) *adv* (*French*) in a group; as a whole.

enmesh (ɪnˈmɛʃ) *vb* catch in or as if in a net.

enmity (ˈɛnmɪtɪ) *n* the state or feeling of being an enemy or enemies: bitter enmity. < SEE **ENEMY.**

ennoble (ɪˈnəʊbl̩) *vb* **1** make noble or more dignified; exalt. **2** raise (a person) to a noble rank. **ennoblement** *n*

enormous (ɪˈnɔːməs) *adj* extraordinarily great in size, number, or degree: enormous sums of money. **enormously** *adv* **enormousness** *n* **enormity** *n* **1** the quality or state of being enormous. **2** the quality or state of being outrageous: the enormity of the crime. < Latin *e-* out + *norma* rule. SEE PANEL.

enough (ɪˈnʌf) *determiner* sufficient in quantity, number, or degree: not enough butter.

● *adv* **1** sufficiently: not hot enough. **2** just adequately: He scored well enough to pass the test.

● *pron* a sufficient quantity or number. < Old English *genōg.*

enquire (ɪnˈkwaɪə) *vb* ask about; seek information by questioning. **enquirer** *n* **enquiry** *n* < SEE **INQUIRE.** SEE PANEL.

enrage (ɪnˈreɪdʒ) *vb* make very angry.

enrapture (ɪnˈræptʃə) *vb* fill with great delight.

enrich (ɪnˈrɪtʃ) *vb* **1** make richer. **2** improve (a food) by adding nutrients. **3** make (soil) more fertile. **enrichment** *n*

enrol (ɪnˈrəʊl) *vb* **enrolled; enrolling** **1** record on a list. **2** become or cause to become a member; register. **enrolment** *n*

en route (ˌɒn ˈruːt) *adv* (*French*) on or along the way.

ensconce (ɪnˈskɒns) *vb* establish or settle firmly or comfortably. < *en* + ultimately Dutch *schans* wickerwork.

ensemble (ɒnˈsɒmbl̩) *n* **1** a group of musicians performing together. **2** a complete outfit of matching garments. **3** all the parts of something considered together. < French: together, from Latin *in-* in + *simul* at the same time.

enshrine (ɪnˈʃraɪn) *vb* **1** enclose in or as if in a shrine. **2** preserve as sacred; treasure.

enshroud (ɪnˈʃraʊd) *vb* cover or hide with or as if with a shroud; obscure; veil.

ensign (ˈɛnsaɪn) *n* **1** (also ˈɛnsən) a flag flown, for example by a ship, to show nationality. **2** any flag, standard, or banner. < Middle French *enseigne,* from Latin *insignia* insignia.

enslave (ɪnˈsleɪv) *vb* make a slave of; dominate. **enslavement** *n*

ensue (ɪnˈsjuː) *vb* occur or happen afterwards or as a consequence: in the ensuing months. < Latin *in-* in + *sequi* to follow.

ensure (ɛnˈʃʊə, ɛnˈʃɔː) *vb* make certain or safe; guarantee. SEE PANEL AT **ASSURE.**

ENT *abbrev* (*medical*) ear, nose, and throat.

entail (ɪnˈteɪl) *vb* involve or incur as a necessary consequence or accompaniment. < Middle English *en-* in + *taile* agreement.

entangle (ɪnˈtæŋgl̩) *vb* **1** catch in something that is difficult to escape from: entangled in the branches. **2** become a confused, twisted mass. **3** involve in a complicated or confused affair: get entangled with the criminal underworld. **entanglement** *n*

entente (ɒnˈtɒnt) *n* a friendly relationship between countries. < French: understanding.

enter (ˈɛntə) *vb* **1** go or come in or into.

enormity or **enormousness?**

Some careful users of English avoid using enormity to refer to something of great size as in the sheer *enormity* of their achievement. Such users prefer to use enormousness or their synonyms such as magnitude or greatness in these contexts, reserving enormity for 'the quality of state of being outrageous or wicked' as in the *enormity* of the crime.

enquiry or **inquiry?**

In British English personal preference will probably dictate which of these you use. However, the general tendency is that enquiry is used for more informal requests for information: *Enquiries* about the travel arrangements should be made at the office in the High Street. Inquiry is used to refer to more formal investigations: A public *inquiry* will be held into the cause of the accident.

American English has a general preference for *inquiry.*

2 write down (a name, details, etc.) on a list; register as a competitor. **3** put in; insert. **4** become a member of; actively take part in: to enter the navy; enter politics. **5** record formally: enter a plea of guilty. **enter into 1** take part in (a discussion or agreement). **2** be included in (a plan, etc.). **enter on** or **upon** (*formal*) begin (a new stage of life or work). < Latin *intrare*.

enterprise (ˈɛntəˌpraɪz) *n* **1** a project or undertaking, esp. a difficult or courageous one. **2** initiative: a lack of enterprise. **3** an economic system that allows freedom to private businessmen; business organization: private enterprise. **enterprising** *adj* showing initiative. < Middle French *entreprendre* to undertake.

entertain (ˌɛntəˈteɪn) *vb* **1** hold the attention of (a person or audience) with enjoyment. **2** receive (a guest) into one's home. **3** have in the mind: entertain an idea. **entertainer** *n* **entertainment** *n* **1** something entertaining. **2** a public performance. < ultimately Latin *inter* between + *tenere* to hold.

enthral (ɪnˈθrɔːl) *vb* **enthralled; enthralling** hold the complete attention of; captivate. < Middle English *enthrallen*, from *en-* + *thrall* thrall, slave.

enthrone (ɛnˈθrəʊn) *vb* place on or as if on a throne, esp. at a special ceremony. **enthronement** *n*

enthusiasm (ɪnˈθjuːzɪˌæzəm) *n* **1** eager liking and interest: great enthusiasm for good literature. **2** an object of enthusiasm. **enthuse** *vb* show enthusiasm; make enthusiastic. **enthusiast** *n* someone who has great enthusiasm for a particular interest: a railway enthusiast. **enthusiastic** *adj* full of enthusiasm. **enthusiastically** *adv* < Greek *enthous* inspired by a god.

entice (ɪnˈtaɪs) *vb* attract or tempt by exciting hope or desire. **enticement** *n* < probably ultimately Latin *in-* in + *titio* firebrand.

entire (ɪnˈtaɪə) *adj* complete; total. **entirely** *adv* wholly or completely; only. **entirety** *n* the state of being entire; whole or total: in its entirety. < Latin *integer* untouched, whole.

entitle (ɪnˈtaɪtl̩) *vb* **1** give a title to (a book, etc.). **2** give the right: I'm entitled to know all the facts. **entitlement** *n*

entity (ˈɛntɪtɪ) *n* something that has a separate existence. < ultimately Latin *esse* to be.

entomb (ɪnˈtuːm) *vb* put in or as if in a tomb; bury.

entomology (ˌɛntəˈmɒlədʒɪ) *n* the scientific study of insects. **entomological** *adj* **entomologist** *n* < Greek *entomon* insect + *-logy*, ultimately *logos* word.

entourage (ˈɒntʊrɑːʒ) *n* a group of people that accompany a person, esp. an important person. < French *entourer* to surround.

entrails (ˈɛntreɪlz) *pl n* the intestines. < Latin *interaneus* internal.

entrance[1] (ˈɛntrəns) *n* **1** the act of entering. **2** the place or means of entering. **3** the right of admission: The entrance fee is £20.

entrance[2] (ɪnˈtrɑːns) *vb* fill with great delight; put into a trance.

entrant (ˈɛntrənt) *n* someone who enters a contest; competitor.

entreat (ɪnˈtriːt) *vb* ask (someone) earnestly for (something); beg or plead. **entreaty** *n* < Middle French *entraitier*, from *en-* + *traitier* to treat.

entrench (ɪnˈtrɛntʃ) *vb* **1** surround or fortify with a trench. **2** establish strongly, so as to prevent removal or change: firmly entrenched ideas. **entrenchment** *n*

entrepreneur (ˌɒntrəprəˈnɜː) *n* a person who organizes and assumes the risks of a commercial undertaking. **entrepreneurial** *adj* < SEE **ENTERPRISE**.

entrust (ɪnˈtrʌst) *vb* **1** place something in trust to. **2** put into the care and protection of someone.

entry (ˈɛntrɪ) *n* **1** the act of entering. **2** the right of entering: conditions of entry. **3** the place of entering. **4** an item recorded in a list, diary, etc. **5** an entrant. < SEE **ENTER**.

entwine (ɪnˈtwaɪn) *vb* twine round or together.

enumerate (ɪˈnjuːməˌreɪt) *vb* count; list one after another. **enumeration** *n* < Latin *e-* out + *numerare* to count.

enunciate (ɪˈnʌnsɪˌeɪt) *vb* **1** articulate or pronounce (words). **2** state clearly or definitely. **enunciation** *n* < Latin *e-* out + *nuntiare* to report.

envelop (ɪnˈvɛləp) *vb* wrap or enclose in or as if in a covering; conceal or obscure: enveloped in mist. < Old French *envoloper*, from *en-* + *voloper* to wrap.

envelope (ˈɛnvəˌləʊp, ˈɒnvəˌləʊp) *n* a folded paper covering, usually rectangular, with a flap that can be folded over and sealed, used to enclose a letter, etc. < SEE **ENVELOP**.

environment (ɪnˈvaɪrənmənt) *n* **1** the external conditions and circumstances that affect people's life and work. **2** the conditions, influences, etc., affecting the development of an organism.

environmental *adj* **environmentalist** *n* someone who seeks to protect the quality of the environment. < SEE **ENVIRONS.**

environs (ɪnˈvaɪrənz) *pl n* the surrounding areas, esp. of a town or city. < Middle French *environ* surroundings, from *en-* in + *viron* circuit.

envisage (ɪnˈvɪzɪdʒ) *vb* visualize or imagine, esp. in advance; foresee. < French *envisager,* from *en-* + *visage* face. SEE PANEL.

envoy (ˈɛnvɔɪ) *n* **1** a messenger or representative. **2** a diplomatic agent below an ambassador in rank. < French *envoyé,* from *envoyer* to send.

envy (ˈɛnvɪ) *n* **1** a feeling of grudging or admiring discontent at a possession or state enjoyed by another person. **2** the object of such a feeling.
• *vb* **envied; envying** feel envy towards or because of. **enviable** *adj* sufficiently desirable to arouse envy. **enviably** *adv* **envious** *adj* feeling or showing envy. **enviously** *adv* < Latin *invidia,* from *in-* upon + *vidēre* to look. SEE PANEL.

enzyme (ˈɛnzaɪm) *n* any one of a number of organic substances produced by cells; protein that acts as a catalyst in biochemical reactions. < ultimately Greek *en-* in + *zymē* leaven.

ephemeral (ɪˈfɛmərəl) *adj* lasting a very short time: ephemeral pleasures. < Greek *epi-* upon + *hēmera* day.

epic (ˈɛpɪk) *n* **1** a long, narrative poem describing the deeds of a legendary or historical hero. **2** a book, film, etc., like this. **3** a series of episodes fit to be described in an epic.
• *adj* **1** of or like an epic. **2** extraordinary, esp. in size or scope: of epic proportions. < Greek *epos* word, poem.

epicentre (ˈɛpɪˌsɛntə) *n* the point on the earth's surface directly above the point of origin of an earthquake. < Greek *epi-* at + Latin *centrum* centre.

epicure (ˈɛpɪˌkjʊə) *n* someone with refined and discriminating tastes, esp. in food and wine. **epicurean** *adj* fond of luxury and sensuous pleasure. < *Epicurus,* died 270 BC, Greek philosopher. SEE PANEL.

epidemic (ˌɛpɪˈdɛmɪk) *n* an outbreak of a disease that spreads rapidly through a community: a cholera epidemic. < Greek *epi-* among + *dēmos* people.

envisage or **envision?**

American writers tend to use envision rather than envisage. Both words mean 'to visualize or imagine; foresee': The plan *envisages* a substantial expansion of the motorway network. Until that moment I hadn't *envisaged* the possibility that I might actually succeed!

Careful users of English avoid using a that-clause after either word as in The government *envisages* that the strike will be settled soon, or where a mental image is not involved and the word is merely used as an alternative to expect or think: No further price increases are *envisaged*.

epicure

A person with refinement of taste in food or wine is known as an epicure. This word comes from the name of the Greek philosopher, *Epicurus*, 341–270 BC.

Epicurus regarded pleasure as the highest good. However, the pleasure in question was attainable not through sensual indulgence but through achieving emotional and intellectual calm. This was often misunderstood and his teachings were sometimes seen as defending the pursuit of bodily pleasure.

envy or **jealousy?**

Careful users of English distinguish the words envy and jealousy. With envy, the emphasis is on a desire for something that someone else has. You may look with envy at your neighbour's new car; you may be envious of your friends who travel widely while you're stuck at home; yet you may not envy them having to work so hard.

With jealousy, the emphasis is on what you consider to be or desire for your own. A husband will be jealous if his wife is seeing another man; there may be jealousy at work as rivals fight for promotion; and a company will jealously guard its secrets.

epidermis (ˌɛpɪˈdɜːmɪs) *n* the outside layer of cells of a plant or animal; skin. < Greek *epi-* upon + *derma* skin.
epigram (ˈɛpɪˌɡræm) *n* a short, witty, often paradoxical comment. < Greek *epi-* upon + *graphein* to write.
epilepsy (ˈɛpɪˌlɛpsɪ) *n* a disorder of the nervous system, characterized by fits or sudden loss of consciousness. **epileptic** *adj, n* < Greek *epi-* upon + *lambanein* to seize.
epilogue (ˈɛpɪˌlɒɡ) *n* a short, concluding section of a literary work, etc. < Greek *epi-* upon + *legein* to say.
episcopal (ɪˈpɪskəpḷ) *adj* of a bishop or bishops; having government by bishops. < Latin *episcopalis,* from *episcopus* bishop: SEE **BISHOP.**
episode (ˈɛpɪˌsəʊd) *n* **1** an event or incident that is complete in itself and is part of a play, etc. **2** a separate event that forms part of a sequence. < Greek *epi-* upon + *eis* into + *hodos* way, passage.
epistle (ɪˈpɪsḷ) *n* **1** (a reading from) one of the letters of the New Testament: the Epistle to the Romans. **2** (*humorous or formal*) a letter. < Greek *epi-* to + *stellein* to send.
epitaph (ˈɛpɪˌtɑːf) *n* the words inscribed on a tomb or monument that commemorate a dead person or past event. < Greek *epi- upon* + *taphos* tomb.
epithet (ˈɛpɪˌθɛt) *n* a word or phrase that describes a person or thing. < Greek *epi-* on + *tithenai* to put.
epitome (ɪˈpɪtəmɪ) *n* an ideal or typical example; embodiment. < Greek *epi-* upon + *temnein* to cut.
EPNS *abbrev* electroplated nickel silver.
epoch (ˈiːpɒk) *n* **1** a period of time characterized by a distinctive feature or series of events. **2** a memorable event. < Greek *epochē* pause, fixed point.
equable (ˈɛkwəbḷ) *adj* even, unchanging, and moderate: an equable climate. < Latin *aequabilis,* from *aequare* to make even. SEE PANEL.
equal (ˈiːkwəl) *adj* **1** having the same quantity, amount, number, or value as another. **2** having the same nature, quality, or importance: equal rights. **3** evenly matched or balanced. **4** able to meet the requirements of: equal to the task.
• *n* somebody or something equal: mix with one's equals.
• *vb* **equalled; equalling 1** be equal to; be identical in value to. **2** achieve or produce something equal to. **equality** *n* **equally** *adv* **equalize** *vb* make or become equal, esp. bring the scores level in a sports match. **equalizer** *n* < Latin *aequus* even.
equanimity (ˈɛkwəˌnɪmɪtɪ) *n* calmness in mind or temper. < Latin *aequus* even + *animus* mind.
equate (ɪˈkweɪt) *vb* **1** make equal. **2** consider or represent as equal, equivalent, or comparable. **equation** *n* **1** equating or being equated. **2** a mathematical statement that two expressions are equal.
equator (ɪˈkweɪtə) *n* an imaginary line round the earth through points that are an equal distance from the North and South Poles. **equatorial** *adj* **1** of or near the equator. **2** (of a climate) having high temperatures and rainfall throughout the year. < Medieval Latin *aequator* equalizer.
equerry (ˈɛkwərɪ, ɪˈkwɛrɪ) *n* an officer of the British royal household who is a personal attendant on a member of the royal family. < Middle French *escuirie* status of a squire.
equestrian (ɪˈkwɛstrɪən) *adj* of or featuring horses, horse-riding, or horsemanship.
• *n* a person who rides on horseback. < Latin *equus* horse.
equidistant (ˌiːkwɪˈdɪstənt) *adj* equally distant.
equilateral (ˌiːkwɪˈlætərəl) *adj* having all sides equal: an equilateral triangle. < Latin *aequus* equal + *latus* side.
equilibrium (ˌiːkwɪˈlɪbrɪəm) *n* a state of balance between opposing or different forces, reactions, etc. < Latin *aequus* equal + *libra* weight, balance.
equine (ˈɛkwaɪn) *adj* of or like a horse. < Latin *equus* horse.
equinox (ˈɛkwɪˌnɒks) *n* either of the two times each year when the sun crosses the

equable or **equitable?**

These two words are sometimes confused.

Equable means 'free from extremes or sudden changes; even, unchanging, and moderate' as in an *equable* climate or an *equable* temperament.

Equitable means 'fair and just' as in The party manifesto advocates a more *equitable* distribution of wealth. The two sides in the dispute eventually reached an *equitable* agreement.

equator and day and night are of equal duration everywhere on the earth, about 21 March and 23 September. **equinoctial** *adj* < Latin *aequus* equal + *nox* night.

equip (ɪˈkwɪp) *vb* **equipped; equipping** provide with what is needed. **equipment** *n* the things needed to equip someone or something; articles, apparatus, or physical resources. < Old French *eschiper,* of Germanic origin.

equipoise (ˈɛkwɪˌpɔɪz) *n* **1** a state of equilibrium. **2** a counterbalance.

equity (ˈɛkwɪtɪ) *n* **1** fairness; justice. **2** (*law*) the set of rules applied to achieve a fair result where ordinary law would fail to do so. **equitable** *adj* fair and just. **equitably** *adv* **equities** *pl n* shares that do not bear fixed interest. < Latin *aequus* equal. SEE PANEL AT **EQUABLE.**

equivalent (ɪˈkwɪvələnt) *adj* equal or corresponding in value, function, effect, etc.
• *n* something that is equivalent. **equivalence** *n* < Latin *aequus* equal + *valere* to be strong.

equivocal (ɪˈkwɪvəkl̩) *adj* **1** able to be interpreted in two or more ways. **2** suspicious or mysterious. **equivocally** *adv* **equivocate** *vb* use equivocal language to hide the truth or avoid committing oneself. **equivocation** *n* < Latin *aequi-* equi- + *vox* voice.

ER *abbrev* (*Latin*) Elizabeth Regina (Queen Elizabeth).

era (ˈɪərə) *n* a period, esp. in history, that is characterized by a distinctive feature: mark the end of an era. < Late Latin *aera.*

eradicate (ɪˈrædɪˌkeɪt) *vb* eliminate; put an end to. **eradicable** *adj* **eradication** *n* < ultimately Latin *e-* out + *radix* root.

erase (ɪˈreɪz) *vb* **1** rub or scrape out (writing, marks, etc.). **2** remove (recorded matter) from (a magnetic tape, etc.). **3** remove from one's memory. **eraser** *n* a thing that erases marks, esp. a piece of rubber to rub out pencil marks. < ultimately Latin *e-* out + *radere* to scratch, scrape.

erect (ɪˈrɛkt) *adj* **1** vertical in position; upright; firm or rigid in posture. **2** (of a part of the body) enlarged and rigid from sexual stimulation.
• *vb* put up or build; set up. **erection** *n* **erectly** *adv* < Latin *erectus,* from *e-* up + *regere* to make straight.

ermine (ˈɜːmɪn) *n* a stoat with a white winter coat; this white fur. < Old French.

erode (ɪˈrəʊd) *vb* **1** wear away by the action of water, etc.; eat into or away; become worn away or eaten into or away. **2** deteriorate or cause to deteriorate. **erosion** *n* < Latin *e-* out + *rodere* to gnaw. SEE PANEL.

erogenous (ɪˈrɒdʒənəs) *adj* of or producing sexual excitement when stimulated: erogenous zones. < Greek *erōs* love + *-genous,* from Greek *genēs* born.

erotic (ɪˈrɒtɪk) *adj* of or tending to arouse sexual desire; strongly sensitive to sexual desire. **erotically** *adv* **erotica** *pl n* erotic books, pictures, etc. < Greek *erōs* love.

err (ɜː) *vb* **1** make a mistake; do wrong. **2** be inaccurate: err on the safe side. < Latin *errare* to wander.

errand (ˈɛrənd) *n* **1** a short journey taken to do something, esp. for another person. **2** the object or purpose of such a journey. < Old English *ǣrend.*

errant (ˈɛrənt) *adj* **1** going astray; doing wrong. **2** (*archaic or literary*) wandering in search of adventure. < ultimately Latin *iter* journey. SEE PANEL AT **ARRANT.**

erratic (ɪˈrætɪk) *adj* irregular, uneven, or inconsistent in behaviour, movement, etc. **erratically** *adv* < Latin *errare* to wander.

erratum (ɪˈrɑːtəm) *n, pl* **errata** an error in printing or writing. < Latin *errare* to wander.

error (ˈɛrə) *n* **1** a mistake or inaccuracy: an error of judgment. **2** the state of being wrong in behaviour or belief. **3** the amount of inaccuracy in a calculation or measuring instrument: an error of 3%. **erroneous** *adj* containing or marked by error; incorrect. **erroneously** *adv* **in error** by mistake; mistakenly. < Latin *errare* to wander.

erstwhile (ˈɜːstˌwaɪl) *adj* former. < Old English *ǣrest* earliest + *while.*

erudite (ˈɛrʊˌdaɪt) *adj* having or showing wide or deep knowledge; learned. **erudition** *n* < Latin *erudire* to instruct.

erupt (ɪˈrʌpt) *vb* **1** (of a volcano) shoot out lava, steam, etc., suddenly. **2** burst out suddenly; become active suddenly.

erode and **rodent**

Mammals with teeth designed for gnawing, such as rats and mice, are commonly referred to as rodents. This word comes from the Latin verb *rodere* 'to gnaw', which is also the root of erode, literally 'to gnaw away'.

3 break out in a rash. **eruption** *n* **eruptive** *adj* < ultimately Latin *e-* out + *rumpere* to break.

escalate (ˈɛskəˌleɪt) *vb* make or become greater in size, extent, number, etc. **escalation** *n* **escalator** *n* a staircase consisting of an endless belt that is driven upwards and downwards continuously. < back formation from *Escalator,* originally a trademark.

escalope (ˈɛskələʊp) *n* a thin, boneless slice of meat, esp. veal. < Middle French: shell.

escapade (ˈɛskəpeɪd) *n* a reckless, often mischievous adventure.

escape (ɪˈskeɪp) *vb* **1** get free from confinement or limits. **2** (of gases, liquids, etc.) leak out gradually. **3** succeed in avoiding (punishment, capture, etc.). **4** fail to be noticed or remembered by: His name escapes me. • *n* **1** an act or instance of escaping: a lucky escape. **2** a means of escaping. • *adj* **1** providing a means of escape: an escape route. **2** giving a basis for evading a rule, claim, etc.: an escape clause. **escaper** *n* **escapee** *n* a person who has escaped; escaped prisoner. **escapism** *n* escape from the reality or routines of life by absorbing the mind in entertainment or fantasy. **escapist** *adj, n* < ultimately Latin *ex-* out of + *cappa* head covering, cloak.

escargot (ɛˈskɑːgəʊ) *n* a snail that has been prepared as food. < French.

escarpment (ɪˈskɑːpmənt) *n* a long, steep slope. < Italian *scarpa.*

eschew (ɪsˈtʃuː) *vb* (*formal*) avoid, esp. for moral or practical reasons; shun. < Middle French *eschiuver,* of Germanic origin.

escort (ˈɛskɔːt) *n* **1** a person, group of people, ship, etc., that accompanies a person or thing to give protection or to show respect: an armed escort. **2** a person who accompanies someone, esp. of the opposite sex, socially. • *vb* (ɪˈskɔːt) act as an escort to. < Latin *ex-* out + *corrigere* to make straight, correct.

ESN *abbrev* educationally subnormal.

esoteric (ˌɛsəʊˈtɛrɪk, ˌiːsəˈtɛrɪk) *adj* intended for, understood by, or limited to a small group of people with special knowledge. < Greek *esōteros* inner.

ESP *abbrev* extra-sensory perception.

especial (ɪˈspɛʃəl) *adj* (*formal*) **1** unusual or exceptional; notable. **2** applying to one person or thing in particular. **especially** *adv* < SEE **SPECIAL.** SEE PANEL AT **SPECIAL.**

espionage (ˈɛspɪəˌnɑːʒ) *n* spying or the use of spies to obtain secret information: industrial espionage. < French *espion* spy.

esplanade (ˈɛspləneɪd) *n* level, open ground, esp. by a shore, where people may walk or ride for pleasure. < ultimately Latin *explanare* to level.

espouse (ɪˈspaʊz) *vb* **1** take up and support (a theory, cause, etc.). **2** (*archaic*) marry. < SEE **SPOUSE.**

espresso (ɛˈsprɛsəʊ) *n, pl* **espressos** the apparatus for making coffee by forcing steam through finely ground coffee beans; coffee produced in this way. < Italian, short for *caffè espresso* pressed-out coffee.

espy (ɪˈspaɪ) *vb* **espied; espying** catch sight of.

Esq. *abbrev* Esquire; used instead of Mr as a formal title in correspondence and placed after a man's surname: M.H. Duckworth, Esq. < *esquire:* from Latin *scutum* shield.

essay (ˈɛseɪ) *n* **1** a short, literary composition on a particular topic. **2** (ɛˈseɪ) (*formal*) an attempt or effort. • *vb* (ɛˈseɪ) (*formal*) attempt. **essayist** *n* < Latin *ex-* out of + *agere* to do.

essence (ˈɛsn̩s) *n* **1** the basic nature of something. **2** the most distinctive part or quality of something. **3** an extract of something, containing the special qualities of a plant or drug, etc., in concentrated form. **of the essence** of the greatest importance: Good management is of the essence. < Latin esse to be.

essential (ɪˈsɛnʃəl) *adj* **1** necessary; indispensable. **2** of the essence of a thing; inherent: all the essential details. • *n* something basic or indispensable: grasp the essentials of French. **essentially** *adv*

establish (ɪˈstæblɪʃ) *vb* **1** bring into existence; set up: establish a new company. **2** make firm or stable. **3** settle (a person or oneself) in a permanent, esp, favourable position: He has firmly established himself as an expert. **4** prove (a fact, someone's innocence, etc.) to be true. **5** cause to be widely accepted. **6** bring about: establish contact. **7** make (a church or religion) officially the Church of a country. **establishment** *n* **1** something established, such as a country or a large organization or its premises. **2** an organized group of people working for a purpose. **3** the well-established, conservative leaders who exercise power and authority in public life: the Establishment. < Latin *stabilis* firm.

estate (ɪˈsteɪt) *n* **1** landed property with

a large house on it. **2** a district planned as a unit, used for housing or industry: a trading estate. **3** the whole of somebody's property, esp. that left at death. **4** (*formal or archaic*) a condition: of low estate. **estate agent** a person who acts as an agent in the buying and selling of land and property. **estate car** a car with esp. folding back seats and a rear door for loading and unloading bulky luggage. < Middle French *estat.*

esteem (ɪˈsti:m) *n* favourable opinion: He is held in high esteem.
• *vb* (*formal*) **1** think highly of. **2** consider or regard. **estimable** *adj* worthy of esteem. < Latin *aestimare* to value, estimate.

ester (ˈɛstə) *n* any of a class of organic compounds formed by reaction between alcohols and acids. < German, probably a shortening of *Essigäther* acetic ether.

estimate (ˈɛstɪˌmeɪt) *vb* **1** calculate approximately (a number, distance, size, cost, etc.). **2** form an opinion about the value or significance of. **3** produce a statement of the approximate cost of.
• *n* (ˈɛstɪmət) **1** an approximate calculation. **2** a statement of the approximate cost of. **3** a judgment or opinion. **estimation** *n* **estimator** *n* < Latin *aestimare* to value.

estrange (ɪˈstreɪndʒ) *vb* cause enmity or indifference in (someone), in place of friendship. **estrangement** *n* < Latin *extraneus* strange.

estuary (ˈɛstjʊərɪ) *n* the wide sea inlet at the mouth of a river, where the tide meets the river. < Latin *aestus* tide, swell.

etc. *abbrev* (*Latin*) et cetera (and other things of the same sort).

etch (ɛtʃ) *vb* **1** make (a picture, pattern, etc.) on a plate of metal or glass, by the corrosive action of an acid; subject (metal, glass, etc.) to such etching. **2** mark or impress deeply: etched on our minds. **etcher** *n* **etching** *n* an impression from an etched plate. < Dutch *etsen,* from Old High German *azzen* to feed.

eternal (ɪˈtɜ:nl) *adj* **1** lasting for ever, without beginning or end: the eternal God. **2** unchanging; not affected by time: eternal truths. **3** (*informal*) seemingly unceasing; occurring again and again: eternal bickering. **eternally** *adv* **eternity** *n* **1** infinite time. **2** eternal life after death. **3** (*informal*) a very long time: We waited what seemed an eternity. < Latin *aeternus.*

ether (ˈi:θə) *n* **1** a colourless, volatile, highly flammable liquid used as a solvent. **2** a hypothetical medium formerly believed to transmit electromagnetic waves. **3** the upper regions of the atmosphere; clear sky. **ethereal** *adj* **1** of the upper regions of the atmosphere. **2** lacking material substance; looking light and delicate. < Greek *aithēr,* from *aithein* to burn.

ethics (ˈɛθɪks) *n* **1** the science of morality. **2** *pl* moral principles: business ethics. **ethical** *adj* **1** of ethics. **2** conforming to accepted moral principles of behaviour. **ethically** *adv* < Greek *ēthos* character, usage.

ethnic (ˈɛθnɪk) *adj* **1** of human races or peoples grouped according to common features: ethnic minorities. **2** of an exotic, esp. peasant, culture. **ethnically** *adv* < Greek *ethnos* nation.

ethnology (ɛθˈnɒlədʒɪ) *n* the study of cultures, esp. considering social relationships and in preliterate cultures. **ethnologist** *n* < Greek *ethnos* nation + *-logy,* ultimately *logos* word.

ethos (ˈi:θɒs) *n* the distinctive character and attitudes of a people, culture, etc. < Greek *ēthos* character.

etiquette (ˈɛtɪˌkɛt, ˈɛtɪˌkət) *n* the conventionally accepted principles of correct social or professional behaviour. < French *étiquette* ticket. SEE PANEL.

étude (ˈeɪtju:d) *n* a musical composition designed for the practice of a particular technique. < French: study.

etymology (ˌɛtɪˈmɒlədʒɪ) *n* **1** an account of the origin and development of a word, etc. **2** a branch of linguistics dealing with etymologies. < Greek *etymos* true + *-logy,* ultimately *logos* word.

eucalyptus (ˌju:kəˌlɪptəs) *n* any of a group of tropical and subtropical trees of the myrtle family, grown for their gums, oils, and wood. < Greek *eu-* well + *kalyptos* covered.

eulogy (ˈju:ləˌdʒɪ) *n* a formal speech or piece of writing in praise of a person

etiquette

The accepted principles of correct social behaviour are sometimes referred to as etiquette. This word was originally used in a much narrower sense. It entered English in the 18th century from the French *étiquette,* literally 'ticket'. This was the name of the card issued to those attending court, on which were written formal instructions concerning dress and conduct.

or thing. **eulogistic** *adj* **eulogize** *vb* praise in a eulogy. < Greek *eulogia* praise.

eunuch (ˈjuːnək) *n* a man who has been castrated, esp. (formerly) for an office such as a guard in a harem. < Latin *eunuchus*, from Greek *eunē* bed + *echein* to keep.

euphemism (ˈjuːfəmɪzəm) *n* (the use of) a mild, vague, or indirect expression to substitute for a blunt or matter-of-fact one. **euphemistic** *adj* **euphemistically** *adv* < Greek *eu-* good + *phēmē* voice. SEE PANEL AT **DIE**[1].

euphonium (juːˈfəʊnɪəm) *n* a brass instrument resembling but smaller than a tuba; tenor tuba. < Greek *euphōnos* + English *-ium*, as in *harmonium*.

euphony (ˈjuːfənɪ) *n* pleasantness of sounds, esp. in speech. < Greek *eu-* well + *phōnē* voice.

euphoria (juˈfɔːrɪə) *n* a feeling of well-being and great happiness. **euphoric** *adj* < Greek *eu-* well + *pherein* to bear.

euthanasia (ˌjuːθəˈneɪzɪə) *n* the act or practice of bringing about the painless death of a person with an incurable disease. < Greek: easy death, from *eu-* well + *thanatos* death.

evacuate (ɪˈvækjʊˌeɪt) *vb* **1** withdraw or cause to withdraw from (a place of danger). **2** make empty by removing the contents of. **evacuation** *n* **evacuee** *n* an evacuated person. < Latin *e-* out + *vacuare* to make empty.

evade (ɪˈveɪd) *vb* **1** avoid, by artfulness or deception. **2** avoid facing up to. **evasion** *n* **evasive** *adj* **evasively** *adv* < Latin *e-* out + *vadere* to go. SEE PANEL AT **AVOID**.

evaluate (ɪˈvæljʊˌeɪt) *vb* determine the amount, value, or importance of, by careful assessment. **evaluation** *n* < SEE **VALUE**.

evangelical (ˌiːvænˈdʒɛlɪkl̩) *adj* **1** of the Christian group that emphasizes salvation by faith in the death of Christ, personal conversion, and the authority of the Bible. **2** zealous: evangelical fervour.
• *n* a person who follows evangelical teachings. **evangelism** *n* the preaching and telling of the gospel. **evangelist** *n* **1** any of the authors of the four Gospels. **2** a person who evangelizes. **evangelize** *vb* preach and tell the gospel to. < ultimately Greek *eu-* good + *angelos* messenger.

evaporate (ɪˈvæpəˌreɪt) *vb* **1** turn or be turned into vapour. **2** disappear or fade: Her fears soon evaporated. **3** expel moisture, esp. water, from. **evaporation** *n* **evaporated milk** milk thickened by evaporation and tinned. < Latin *e-* out + *vapor* vapour.

eve (iːv) *n* **1** the evening or day before a special day: Christmas Eve. **2** the period immediately before an event: on the eve of an election. **3** (*archaic or poetic*) an evening. < Middle English *eve, even*.

even (ˈiːvn̩) *adj* **1** flat; level; free from irregularities. **2** uniform; unchanging. **3** calm; not easily upset: an even temper. **4** equal; balanced: After six games the scores were even. **5** (of a number) exactly divisible by two.
• *vb* make or become even.
• *adv* **1** at the very time: Even as we are talking .... **2** used to contrast with something less strong: She was happy, even joyful. **3** still; yet: It was even easier than I thought! **evenly** *adv* **evenness** *n* **be** or **get even with** take revenge on. **even if** or **though** in spite of the fact that. **even so** nevertheless. < Old English *efen*.

evening (ˈiːvnɪŋ) *n* the last part of the day and early part of the night. **evening dress** the clothes worn at a formal evening occasion. < Old English *ǣfnung*.

Evensong (ˈiːvn̩ˌsɒŋ) *n* also **Evening Prayer** the daily evening service of the Anglican Church.

event (ɪˈvɛnt) *n* **1** something that happens, esp. something important. **2** a social occasion or activity. **3** any of the individual contests in a sports programme. **eventful** *adj* full of incidents: an eventful holiday. **in the event** as actually happened. **in the event of** if something that is mentioned happens or is done: in the event of his death. < Latin *e-* out + *venire* to come.

eventual (ɪˈvɛntʃʊəl) *adj* happening in the course of time; ultimate. **eventually** *adv*

eventuality (ɪˌvɛntʃʊˈælɪtɪ) *n* a possible event, esp. an unpleasant one.

ever (ˈɛvə) *adv* **1** always: ever-increasing. **2** at any time: Come and see us if you are ever in Leeds. **3** used for emphasis: He looks ever so angry. **ever so** (*informal*) very much: Thanks ever so! < Old English *ǣfre*. SEE PANEL.

evergreen (ˈɛvəˌgriːn) *adj* **1** having leaves that remain green throughout the year. **2** staying fresh and interesting.
• *n* an evergreen tree or shrub.

everlasting (ˌɛvəˈlɑːstɪŋ) *adj* **1** lasting for ever. **2** continuing for a very long time. **3** (of a plant) keeping its form or colour for a long time when dried.

4 (*informal*) seemingly unceasing. **everlastingly** *adv*

evermore (ˌɛvəˈmɔː) *adv* always; for ever.

every (ˈɛvrɪ) *determiner* **1** each (of a group of three or more). **2** each or all possible: take every opportunity. **everybody** *pron* every person. **everyday** *adj* worn or used routinely; ordinary: everyday clothes. **everyone** *pron* everybody. **every other** each alternate: every other day. **everything** *pron* **1** all that exists or is necessary. **2** all that is important or of value to someone: He was everything to her. **everywhere** *adv* in every place. < Old English *ǣfre ǣlc,* from *ǣfre* ever + *ǣlc* each. SEE PANEL.

evict (ɪˈvɪkt) *vb* remove (a tenant) from property by a legal process. **eviction** *n* < SEE **EVINCE.**

evidence (ˈɛvɪdəns) *n* **1** anything which provides a basis for believing or disbelieving something. **2** information or objects used in a court to establish the truth.
• *vb* show or offer evidence of. **evident** *adj* clear; obvious; plain: It quickly became evident that the difficulties were insurmountable. **evidently** *adv* < Latin *e-* from + *videre* to see.

evil (ˈiːvl̩) *adj* **1** morally bad; wicked. **2** causing discomfort; offensive: an evil smell. **3** very unpleasant: an evil temper.
• *n* something evil; fact of wrong or suffering; sin. < Old English *yfel.*

evince (ɪˈvɪns) *vb* (*formal*) show clearly. < Latin *evincere* to conquer utterly.

evoke (ɪˈvəʊk) *vb* call up or bring (a feeling, memory, etc.) to the mind. **evocation** *n* **evocative** *adj* < Latin *e-* out + *vocare* to call.

evolve (ɪˈvɒlv) *vb* **1** work out; develop. **2** produce or be produced by evolution. **evolution** *n* **1** the process of gradual change and development, esp. to a more advanced or complex state. **2** the historical development of a biological group; theory that living things developed from earlier forms as opposed to the belief in special creation. **evolutionary** *adj* < Latin *e-* out + *volvere* to roll.

ewe (juː) *n* a female sheep. < Old English *ēowu.*

ex (ɛks) *prep* **1** from a place that is mentioned: the ex-works price. **2** without; exclusive of: ex interest.
• *n* (*informal*) a former husband, wife, boyfriend, or girlfriend. < Latin.

ex- *prefix* former: ex-president; ex-serviceman < Latin. SEE PANEL.

exacerbate (ɪgˈzæsəbeɪt, ɛkˈsæsəbeɪt) *vb* make worse; aggravate. **exacerbation** *n* < Latin *ex-* + *acerbus* harsh.

exact (ɪgˈzækt) *adj* **1** completely accurate; free from error. **2** precise; not approximate: the exact time. **3** giving all the details: exact instructions.
• *vb* demand or require: exact the highest

---

how ever or **however, what ever** or **whatever?**

Whether to write however, whatever, etc., or how ever, what ever, etc., is sometimes a problem. If ever is used to intensify how, what, etc., two words are used: How ever ('on earth') did you find out? What ever did she say?

If ever means 'no matter how, what, etc.', however, whatever, etc., are written as one word: Whatever you decide to do ('no matter what'), it will be difficult. I'll follow you wherever ('no matter where') you go.

---

every word counts

Do you say everyone *is*… or everyone *are*…? Everybody, everyone, and everything are used with singular verbs: Everyone *has* come. Everything *is* now ready for the party.

Do you write everyday or every day, everyone or every one? Everyday is an adjective meaning 'worn or used routinely, on typical days; ordinary' as in clothes for *everyday* wear, in *everyday* conversation, *everyday* life. In other senses, it is two words: I come here *every day.*

Everyone means the same as everybody and is used to refer to people: *Everyone* knows where you've hidden the Easter eggs! When the meaning is 'every single one' and for things, two words are used: They gave *every one* of us a present. *Every one* of the investments has yielded a great profit.

price. **exactness** *n* **exacting** *adj* making rigorous demands. < Latin *ex*- out + *agere* to drive.

exactly (ɪgˈzæktlɪ) *adv* **1** in an exact manner. **2** in every respect: exactly what I want. **3** quite so; used to express agreement.

exaggerate (ɪgˈzædʒəˌreɪt) *vb* **1** consider or represent as larger, greater, more important, etc., than is true. **2** make greater, more noticeable, etc., than usual. **exaggeration** *n* < Latin *ex*- out + *agger* heap.

exalt (ɪgˈzɔːlt) *vb* **1** raise high in rank, dignity, etc. **2** praise highly. **exaltation** *n* < Latin *ex*- out + *altus* high.

exam (ɪgˈzæm) *n* an examination.

examine (ɪgˈzæmɪn) *vb* **1** look at closely; inspect or investigate. **2** put questions or exercises to, in order to test knowledge or ability. **3** investigate the health of (a patient). **4** interrogate closely: examine a witness. **examination** *n* **examiner** *n* **examinee** *n* a person being tested in an examination. < Latin *examen* tongue of a balance.

example (ɪgˈzɑːmpl̩) *n* **1** something that is typical of others in the same group or set. **2** someone or something that is worthy of imitation: set an example. **3** a punishment given as a warning to others; recipient of such a punishment: make an example of someone. **for example** as an example. < Latin *exemplum,* from *eximere* to take out.

exasperate (ɪgˈzɑːspəˌreɪt) *vb* annoy greatly. **exasperation** *n* < Latin *ex*- out + *asper* rough.

excavate (ˈɛkskəˌveɪt) *vb* **1** form a hole in; form by hollowing. **2** dig out and remove; reveal by digging and removing a covering. **excavation** *n* **excavator** *n* < ultimately Latin *ex*- out + *cavus* hollow.

ex-

Ex- is an example of a prefix (ex-president, ex-police chief) that over the years has also come to be used as a word in its own right. It is used as a noun to mean 'one's former wife, husband, girlfriend, or boyfriend': Does your *ex* still work at Harrods?

Other prefixes that are words in their own right include: anti, used as a noun to mean 'an opponent of a policy, etc.', pro, used as a noun to mean 'an argument in favour of' in the phrase pros and cons, and semi, used as a noun to mean 'a semi-detached house'.

exceed (ɪkˈsiːd) *vb* **1** be greater than or superior to. **2** act or go beyond the bounds of. **exceedingly** *adv* extremely: exceedingly well done. < ultimately Latin *ex*- out + *cedere* to go.

excel (ɪkˈsɛl) *vb* **excelled; excelling** be superior (to); be better than (others) at doing something. < Latin *excellere* to rise.

Excellency (ˈɛksələnsɪ) *n* the title for a high-ranking official such as an ambassador or governor.

excellent (ˈɛksələnt) *adj* extremely good: excellent results. **excellence** *n* **excellently** *adv*

except (ɪkˈsɛpt) *prep* not including: Everyone understood except me.

• *conj* **1** apart from. **2** (*informal*) but for the fact that.

• *vb* take or leave out; exclude. **excepting** *prep* except. < Latin *ex*- out + *capere* to take.

exception (ɪkˈsɛpʃən) *n* **1** excepting or being excepted. **2** something to which a general rule does not apply. **take exception to** be offended by.

exceptional (ɪkˈsɛpʃənl̩) *adj* **1** unusual: in exceptional circumstances. **2** not average, esp. extremely good. **exceptionally** *adv*

excerpt (ɛkˈsɜːpt) *vb* select (a passage) from a book, play, etc.

• *n* (ˈɛksɜːpt) an extract from a book, play, etc. < Latin *ex*- out + *carpere* to pick.

excess (ɪkˈsɛs, ˈɛksɛs) *n* **1** the exceeding of normal, reasonable, or permitted limits. **2** the amount, extent, etc., by which one thing exceeds another: in excess of 10%. **3** an immoderate amount, extent, etc.: drinking to excess. **4** an agreed amount that the insured will bear each time a claim is made on an insurance policy.

• *adj* (ˈɛksɛs) more than the normal, proper, or permitted limits: excess baggage. **excessive** *adj* **excessively** *adv* < SEE **EXCEED**.

exchange (ɪksˈtʃeɪndʒ) *vb* **1** give or transfer (one thing) for an equivalent. **2** give to and receive from another person: The two men exchanged blows; to exchange gifts.

• *n* **1** the act of exchanging one thing for another; something offered or received in exchange: an exchange of information. **2** a trading place where things such as commodities or services are exchanged. **3** an argument or quarrel. **4** a centre that controls the connection of telephone lines. **exchangeable** *adj* **exchange rate** the amount which one currency will buy of another currency at a particular time. < Latin *ex-* + *cambire* to barter.

exchequer (ɪks'tʃɛkə) *n* **1** often **Exchequer** the government department in charge of the country's revenue. **2** the national treasury. < Old French *eschequier* chess-board.

excise[1] ('ɛksaɪz) *n* a duty or tax charged on certain goods and services: excise duty. < ultimately Latin *assidēre* to assist in the office of.

excise[2] (ɛk'saɪz) *vb* remove by or as if by cutting out. **excision** *n* < Latin *ex-* out + *caedere* to cut.

excite (ɪk'saɪt) *vb* **1** arouse the feelings of. **2** arouse (a feeling or response): He excited a lot of curiosity. **3** stir up (action). **excitement** *n* **excitable** *adj* (of a person) easily excited. **excitability** *n* **exciting** *adj* causing excitement. < Latin *ex-* out + *citare* to rouse.

exclaim (ɪk'skleɪm) *vb* cry out or speak suddenly and with strong emotion. **exclamatory** *adj* **exclamation** *n* exclaiming; the words exclaimed. **exclamation mark** the punctuation mark ! used after an exclamation. < Latin *ex-* out + *clamare* to cry out.

exclude (ɪk'sklu:d) *vb* **1** shut out from a place, etc. **2** not consider; omit or ignore as irrelevant. **3** make impossible; prevent. **exclusion** *n* **exclusive** *adj* **1** excluding or having the right to exclude. **2** restricting or restricted to use, control, etc., by one person or group: exclusive rights. **3** excluding others, thought of as inferior, from membership, etc.: an exclusive club. **4** fashionable and expensive. **5** single; unique. **6** not including: £50 exclusive of fitting charges. **exclusively** *adv* **exclusiveness** *n* < Latin *ex-* out + *claudere* to close.

excommunicate (ˌɛkskə'mju:nɪˌkeɪt) *vb* exclude (a person) from membership of or participation in a group, esp. a church. **excommunication** *n* < Latin *ex-* + *communicare* to communicate.

excrete (ɪk'skri:t) *vb* discharge (waste matter) from the body. **excretory** *adj* **excrement** *n* waste matter discharged from the body. **excreta** *pl n* excrement. < Latin *ex-* out of + *cernere* to sift, separate.

excruciating (ɪk'skru:ʃɪˌeɪtɪŋ) *adj* **1** very painful. **2** very intense; extreme. < Latin *ex-* + *cruciare* to crucify. SEE PANEL.

exculpate ('ɛkskʌlˌpeɪt) *vb* free from alleged blame or guilt. < Latin *ex-* out + *culpa* fault.

excursion (ɪk'skɜ:ʃən) *n* **1** a short trip; outing: a half-day excursion. **2** a digression. < Latin *ex-* out + *currere* to run.

excuse (ɪk'skju:z) *vb* **1** pardon; free from blame. **2** ignore as unimportant: Please excuse my bad handwriting. **3** be an acceptable reason for; justify: Such rudeness cannot be excused. **4** release (from an obligation).
● *n* (ɪk'skju:s) a reason offered as a ground for excusing a fault, etc. **excuse me** used to attract attention or apologize. **excuse oneself** ask permission to be absent. < Latin *ex-* from + *causa* charge.

ex-directory (ˌɛksdɪ'rɛktərɪ) *adj* intentionally not listed in a telephone directory.

execrable ('ɛksɪkrəbl̩) *adj* detestable; abominable. < Latin *execrabilis.*

execute ('ɛksɪˌkju:t) *vb* **1** carry out fully: execute a plan. **2** put to death as a legal punishment. **3** produce (a work of art). **4** perform (a piece of music, etc.). **5** make (a legal deed, etc.) valid. **execution** *n* **executioner** *n* a person who executes a condemned person. **executor** *n* a person appointed to carry out the provisions of a will. < ultimately Latin *exsequi* to execute, from *ex-* + *sequi* to follow.

executive (ɪg'zɛkjʊtɪv) *n* **1** a branch of government empowered to administer the laws and affairs of a country. **2** a person or group that has administrative or managerial powers in an organization.
● *adj* **1** concerned with the application of policies, laws, etc. **2** of an executive.

exemplary (ɪg'zɛmplərɪ) *adj* **1** worthy of imitation: exemplary patience. **2** serving as a warning: exemplary punishment.

exemplify (ɪg'zɛmplɪˌfaɪ) *vb* **exemplified; exemplifying 1** be an example of. **2** show or illustrate by example.

excruciating

Something which is unbearably painful is often described as excruciating. According to the derivation of this word, the person who is suffering such pain is virtually undergoing crucifixion. Excruciating comes from the Latin *excruciare* 'to torture or torment'. This is a derivative of *cruciare* 'to crucify', from *crux* 'cross'.

exemplification *n* < Latin *exemplum* example + *facere* to make.

exempt (ɪg'zɛmpt) *adj* freed from an obligation or requirement which others are subject to.
• *vb* make exempt. **exemption** *n* < Latin *eximere* to take out, deliver, free.

exercise ('ɛksə,saɪz) *n* **1** the use of a power or authority that is mentioned: the exercise of one's rights. **2** activity for developing the body or mind; exertion of the body to develop physical fitness: You must get more exercise. **3** a set of movements, questions, tasks, etc., performed to develop a skill: piano exercises. **4** a manoeuvre or drill undertaken for training and discipline: military exercises.
• *vb* **1** make use of or employ: exercise all one's powers. **2** use regularly to strengthen and develop; train. **3** occupy the attention of. < Latin *exercere* to put to work.

exert (ɪg'zɜːt) *vb* **1** bring (a quality, esp. strength or influence) to bear. **2** apply (oneself) energetically. **exertion** *n* < Latin *exserere* to thrust out.

ex gratia (,ɛks 'greɪʃə) *adj, adv* (*Latin*) done or given as a favour, not by legal right: an ex gratia payment.

exhale (ɛks'heɪl) *vb* breathe out. **exhalation** *n* < Latin *ex-* out + *halare* to breathe.

exhaust (ɪg'zɔːst) *vb* **1** draw out the contents of; empty. **2** use up completely: exhaust all the supplies. **3** tire out: completely exhausted. **4** deal with (a subject) to the fullest extent.
• *n* the escape of waste gas or vapour from an engine; such gas, etc. **exhaustion** *n* **exhaustive** *adj* thorough; comprehensive: an exhaustive analysis. **exhaustively** *adv* **exhaust pipe** the pipe through which waste gases escape. < Latin *ex-* out + *haurire* to draw.

exhibit (ɪg'zɪbɪt) *vb* **1** show outwardly by visible signs or actions: They exhibited no emotion. **2** display (something) to the public for interest, in a competition, etc.
• *n* **1** something exhibited. **2** something produced as evidence in a law-court. **exhibitor** *n* < Latin *ex-* out + *habēre* to have, hold.

exhibition (,ɛksɪ'bɪʃən) *n* **1** exhibiting; being exhibited. **2** a public showing or display of skills, works of art, industrial products, etc. **make an exhibition of oneself** draw attention to oneself by showy, vulgar behaviour.

exhibitionism (,ɛksɪ'bɪʃənɪzəm) *n* a desire to attract attention to oneself. **exhibitionist** *n*

exhilarate (ɪg'zɪlə,reɪt) *vb* make lively or happy. **exhilaration** *n* < Latin *ex-* + *hilarus* cheerful.

exhort (ɪg'zɔːt) *vb* urge strongly and earnestly. **exhortation** *n* < Latin *ex-* out + *hortari* to urge.

exhume (ɛks'hjuːm) *vb* dig up (a corpse); disinter. **exhumation** *n* < Latin ex out of + *humus* ground.

exigency (ɪg'zɪdʒənsɪ, 'ɛksɪdʒənsɪ) *n* (*formal*) **1** an urgent need or requirement. **2** an emergency. < SEE **EXACT.**

exile ('ɛksaɪl) *n* a long, usually enforced absence from one's country or home. **2** an exiled person.
• *vb* send (a person) into exile. < Latin *exilium* banishment.

exist (ɪg'zɪst) *vb* **1** have being or reality. **2** have being under certain conditions or in a certain place. **3** continue to live: We need water to exist. **existence** *n* **existent** *adj* < Latin *ex-* forth + *sistere* to take up a position.

existentialism (,ɛgzɪ'stɛnʃəlɪzəm) *n* a philosophical movement that sees man as isolated in an apparently meaningless universe, in which he is free to choose and is solely responsible for his actions. **existentialist** *n*

exit ('ɛksɪt) *n* **1** the act of going out or away. **2** a way out; door, passage, etc., by which people may leave. < Latin *ex-* out + *ire* go.

exodus ('ɛksədəs) *n* the act or an instance of going out by many people. < Greek *ex-* out + *hodos* way.

ex officio (,ɛks ə'fɪʃɪəʊ) *adj, adv* (*Latin*) because of his or her official position: an ex officio member of the committee.

exonerate (ɪg'zɒnə,reɪt) *vb* free from blame or a criminal charge. **exoneration** *n* < Latin *ex-* out + *onus* burden.

exorbitant (ɪg'zɔːbɪtn̩t) *adj* (of a price or demand) much greater than what is thought reasonable; excessive. < Latin *ex-* out + *orbita* track.

exorcise ('ɛksɔː,saɪz) *vb* expel an evil spirit from (a person or place). **exorcism** *n* < Greek *ex-* out + *horkos* oath.

exotic (ɪg'zɒtɪk) *adj* **1** introduced from another country; not native: an exotic plant. **2** very different or unusual and striking: an exotic dish. **exotically** *adv* < Greek *exō* outside.

expand (ɪk'spænd) *vb* **1** make or become larger in size, extent, scope, etc.: Metals expand when heated; The economy expanded rapidly. **2** express in more detail: Let me expand on my reasons. **expanse** *n* something spread out; extent to which something is spread out. **expansion** *n* expanding or being expanded; something expanded. **expansive** *adj* **1** able or tending to expand. **2** communicating freely. **expansively** *adv* **expansiveness** *n* < Latin *ex-* out + *pandere* to spread.

expatiate (ɪkˈspeɪʃɪˌeɪt) *vb* (*formal*) speak or write at length or in detail about a subject. < Latin *ex-* out + *spatiari* to walk about.

expatriate (ɛkˈspætrɪˌeɪt, ɛkˈspeɪtrɪˌeɪt) *vb* **1** exile or banish. **2** withdraw (oneself) from one's native country.
• *adj* (ɛkˈspætrɪət) living in a country other than one's native country.
• *n* (ɛkˈspætrɪət, ɛkˈspeɪtrɪˌət) an expatriate person. < Latin *ex-* out of + *patria* fatherland.

expect (ɪkˈspɛkt) *vb* **1** consider probable or likely. **2** look forward to with anticipation. **3** decide that (something) is necessary; require: He expects obedience from his children. **4** suppose: I expect you're tired after your long journey. **be expecting** (*informal*) be pregnant. **expectant** *adj* **1** marked by expectation. **2** (of a pregnant woman) expecting the birth of a child. **expectancy** *n* **expectantly** *adv* **expectation** *n* expecting; looking forward with hope; something expected. < Latin *ex-* out + *spectare* to look at.

expectorant (ɪkˈspɛktərənt) *n* a medicine that causes or helps a person to bring up phlegm, mucus, etc., from the throat or lungs. < Latin *ex-* out + *pectus* breast.

expedient (ɪkˈspiːdɪənt) *adi* **1** useful for achieving a desired result. **2** advantageous and of interest to oneself rather than fair or just.
• *n* a means of achieving a purpose, esp. an urgent one. **expediency** *n* **expediently** *adv* < SEE **EXPEDITE.**

expedite (ˈɛkspɪˌdaɪt) *vb* (*formal*) **1** carry out promptly. **2** speed the progress of; facilitate. < Latin *expedire* free the feet, liberate.

expedition (ˌɛkspɪˈdɪʃən) *n* **1** a journey undertaken for a purpose such as exploration or war; people or ships that make such a journey. **2** (*formal*) speed and efficiency. **expeditionary** *adj* of an expedition: an expeditionary force. **expeditious** *adj* done promptly, speedily, and efficiently. **expeditiously** *adv* < SEE **EXPEDITE.**

expel (ɪkˈspɛl) *vb* **expelled; expelling** **1** drive, send, or force out. **2** compel (a person) to leave a school, country, etc. < Latin *ex-* out + *pellere* to thrust.

expend (ɪkˈspɛnd) *vb* **1** spend (money). **2** consume (time, energy, effort, etc.); use up. **expendable** *adj* **1** that may be used up; not essential; not worth keeping. **2** thought of as able to be sacrificed to achieve a purpose, esp. a military one. **expenditure** *n* **1** the act or process of expending. **2** the amount of money, etc., expended. < Latin *ex-* out + *pendere* to weigh.

expense (ɪkˈspɛns) *n* **1** something expended to gain a benefit; spending of money. **2** *pl* money spent in the performance of one's job; reimbursement of these by an employer, etc. **3** something on which a lot of money is spent. **at someone's expense** involving the ridicule of someone. **at the expense of** to the detriment of: He succeeded, but at the expense of his marriage. **expensive** *adj* costing or charging a lot of money. **expensively** *adv* **expensiveness** *n* < SEE **EXPEND.**

experience (ɪkˈspɪərɪəns) *n* **1** the awareness or apprehension of reality or an event; facts or events perceived. **2** direct participation or observation; knowledge, skill, etc., gained in this way. **3** a particular incident, feeling, etc., that a person has undergone.
• *vb* have experience of. **experienced** *adj* having knowledge or skill gained as a result of experience: an experienced climber. < Latin *experiri* to try.

experiment (ɪkˈspɛrɪmənt) *n* **1** an operation or investigation carried out to establish a hypothesis or to demonstrate a known fact. **2** a tentative, trial arrangement or policy.
• *vb* conduct an experiment or experiments. **experimental** *adj* **experimentally** *adv* **experimentation** *n* < SEE **EXPERIENCE.**

expert (ˈɛkspɜːt) *n* a person with great skill in or knowledge of a particular field.
• *adj* skilful or knowledgeable. **expertly** *adv* **expertise** *n* special skill in or knowledge of a particular field. < SEE **EXPERIENCE.**

expiate (ˈɛkspɪˌeɪt) *vb* **1** remove (the guilt) incurred by (a sin); pay the penalty for (a crime). **2** make amends for. **expiation** *n* < Latin *ex-* out + *piare* to appease.

expire (ɪkˈspaɪə) *vb* **1** breathe out (air). **2** come to an end: The lease expires after 99 years. **3** (*formal*) die. **expiration** *n* **expiry** *n* the coming to an end, esp. of a period fixed in a formal agreement. < Latin *ex-* out + *spirare* to breathe.

explain (ɪkˈspleɪn) *vb* **1** make (something) plain, clear, and understandable;

show the meaning of. **2** be the reason for or cause of. **3** try to justify (oneself) by giving reasons for one's behaviour. **explain away** remove an objection, criticism, etc., by offering excuses or reasons. **explanation** *n* explaining; statement, etc., that explains. **explanatory** *adj* serving to explain: explanatory notes. **explicable** *adj* able to be explained. < Latin *ex-* out + *planus* plain, level.

expletive (ɛkˈspliːtɪv) *n* a word, often a meaningless one, used to express very strong feeling. < Latin *ex-* out + *plēre* to fill.

explicate (ˈɛksplɪˌkeɪt) *vb* (*formal*) explain in detail; analyse logically to bring out the implicit meaning of. < Latin *ex-* out + *plicare* to fold.

explicit (ɪkˈsplɪsɪt) *adj* clear and unambiguous, with nothing implied: explicit instructions. **explicitly** *adv* **explicitness** *n* < SEE **EXPLICATE.**

explode (ɪkˈspləʊd) *vb* **1** burst or cause to burst noisily, esp. by the detonation of an explosive. **2** react suddenly with a violent emotion: explode with anger. **3** (of a population, supply of goods, etc.) increase suddenly and rapidly. **4** destroy (a belief or theory) by showing it to be false. **exploded** *adj* (of a diagram) showing the individual parts separately in their relative positions. < Latin *explodere* to drive out by clapping, hiss off the stage.

exploit (ˈɛksplɔɪt) *n* a notable deed.
• *vb* (ɪkˈsplɔɪt) **1** make the best use of: exploit natural resources. **2** take unfair advantage of, for one's personal gain. **exploitation** *n* < SEE **EXPLICATE.**

explore (ɪkˈsplɔː) *vb* **1** travel into or through (unfamiliar or unknown areas), esp. for geographical discovery. **2** examine thoroughly: explore all the possibilities. **3** examine by touch. **exploration** *n* **exploratory** *adj* **explorer** *n* < Latin *ex-* + *plorare* to cry out.

explosion (ɪkˈspləʊʒən) *n* **1** the act or an instance of exploding; loud noise caused by this. **2** a sudden outburst of violent emotion. **3** a sudden and rapid increase: the population explosion.

explosive (ɪkˈspləʊsɪv) *adj* **1** tending or threatening to explode. **2** threatening to cause violent reactions: an explosive situation.
• *n* an explosive substance.

exponent (ɪkˈspəʊnənt) *n* **1** a person who explains or interprets something. **2** a person who favours or supports an idea or policy. **3** (*mathematics*) a number or symbol written above and to the right of another number or expression indicating the number of times that this is to be multiplied by itself. < SEE **EXPOUND.**

export (ɪkˈspɔːt, ˈɛkspɔːt) *vb* sell (goods or services) or ship (goods) abroad as trade.
• *n* (ˈɛkspɔːt) something exported; act of exporting. **exportation** *n* **exporter** *n* < Latin *ex-* out + *portare* to carry.

expose (ɪkˈspəʊz) *vb* **1** lay open to view; reveal or display. **2** subject to an influence. **3** lay open to attack, ridicule, or danger. **4** make known (something shameful). **5** subject (a photographic film or plate) to light, etc. **exposed** *adj* not sheltered or protected. **expose oneself** display one's sexual organs in public. **exposure** *n* **1** exposing or being exposed. **2** exposing to air, cold, danger, etc. **3** the disclosure of shameful actions. **4** presentation to the public by the mass media; publicity. **5** exposing of photographic film or plate to light, etc.; length of time for which this is done; section of a film for one picture. < SEE **EXPOUND.**

expound (ɪkˈspaʊnd) *vb* set forth or explain in careful detail. **exposition** *n* **1** a careful, detailed explanation of something. **2** a large, usually international, public exhibition. < Latin *ex-* out + *ponere* to put.

express (ɪkˈsprɛs) *adj* **1** definitely and explicitly stated; specific. **2** (suitable for) travelling at high speed: an express train. **3** to be delivered quickly by special service: an express letter.
• *adv* by express.
• *n* **1** an express train. **2** express mail.
• *vb* **1** show or represent; state, esp. in words. **2** make known one's feelings, opinions, etc. **3** press or squeeze out. **expressly** *adv* **expression** *n* **1** expressing or being expressed. **2** an outward sign or representation. **3** a word or phrase. **4** a way of performing, looking, or speaking, esp. one that shows feeling. **expressive** *adj* **expressively** *adv* **expressiveness** *n* **expressionless** *adj* < Latin *ex-* out + *premere* to press.

expulsion (ɪkˈspʌlʃən) *n* expelling or being expelled.

expunge (ɪkˈspʌndʒ) *vb* (*formal*) delete or erase; wipe out or destroy. < Latin *ex-* out + *pungere* to prick.

expurgate (ˈɛkspəˌgeɪt) *vb* remove (parts considered objectionable) from (a book, etc.). **expurgation** *n* < Latin *ex-* out + *purgare* to cleanse.

exquisite (ɪkˈskwɪzɪt, ˈɛkskwɪzɪt) *adj* **1** very beautiful, esp. also delicate:

exquisite lace fabric. **2** keenly discriminating. **exquisitely** *adv* < Latin *ex-* out + *quaerere* to seek.

extant (ɛk'stænt) *adj* still or currently existing or surviving: the oldest extant manuscripts. < Latin *ex-* out + *stare* to stand.

extempore (ɪk'stɛmpərɪ) *adj, adv* with little or no preparation. **extemporize** *vb* speak, perform, etc., extempore. **extemporization** *n* < Latin *ex-* out of + *tempus* time. SEE PANEL.

extend (ɪk'stɛnd) *vb* **1** reach in distance, space, time, or scope. **2** make longer in space or time. **3** spread or stretch out: extend one's arms. **4** make larger in scope, application, or meaning. **5** give or offer, esp. in response to a need: extend a welcome, extend one's sympathies to the bereaved. **extendible** or **extensible** *adj* able to be extended. **extension** *n* **1** extending or being extended. **2** an additional period. **3** a part added to a building. **4** an extra telephone line connected to a main one. **5** instruction for non-resident students and non-members of a college: extension courses. **extensive** *adj* large or great in area or scope: extensive damage. **extensively** *adv* **extensiveness** *n* **extent** *n* **1** the length, range, or scope over which something extends. **2** a degree that is mentioned: I agree with you to some extent. < Latin *ex-* out + *tendere* to stretch.

extenuate (ɪk'stɛnjʊˌeɪt) *vb* make (a person's crime or guilt) seem less by giving excuses: extenuating circumstances. < Latin *ex-* out + *tenuis* thin.

exterior (ɪk'stɪərɪə) *adj* on the outside; for use on the outside.
• *n* an exterior surface, part, or appearance. < Latin *exterus* on the outside.

exterminate (ɪk'stɜːmɪˌneɪt) *vb* destroy completely. **extermination** *n* < Latin *ex-* out + *terminus* boundary.

external (ɪk'stɜːnl̩) *adj* **1** of or suitable for the outside. **2** coming from an independent source: external evidence. **3** of or involving foreign countries: external affairs. **4** (of a medicine) to be applied to the outside of the body. **externally** *adv* **externals** *pl n* external aspects or appearances. < Latin *externus.*

extinct (ɪk'stɪŋkt) *adj* **1** (of a species) no longer existing. **2** (of a volcano) no longer liable to erupt. **extinction** *n* **1** making or being extinct. **2** extinguishing or being extinguished. < SEE EXTINGUISH.

extinguish (ɪk'stɪŋgwɪʃ) *vb* **1** put out (a fire, light, etc.). **2** bring (a hope, feeling, etc.) to an end. **extinguisher** *n* < Latin *ex-* + *stinguere* to extinguish.

extirpate ('ɛkstəˌpeɪt) *vb* destroy completely. **extirpation** *n* < Latin *ex-* out + *stirps* root.

extol (ɪk'stəʊl) *vb* **extolled; extolling** praise highly. < Latin *ex-* + *tollere* to raise.

extort (ɪk'stɔːt) *vb* obtain from someone by force or threats. **extortion** *n* **extortionate** *adj* (of a price or demand) excessive. **extortionately** *adv* < Latin *ex-* out + *torquere* to twist.

extra ('ɛkstrə) *adj* more than what is usual or expected; additional.
• *n* something or somebody that is additional, such as a run in cricket not scored by a stroke of the bat or an additional person temporarily hired to act in a film.
• *adv* more than the usual size, amount, extent, etc. < probably short for *extraordinary.*

extra- *prefix* outside; beyond: extraterrestrial. < Latin *extra,* from *exter* on the outside: SEE EXTERIOR.

extract (ɪk'strækt) *vb* **1** draw, pull out, or obtain with effort: extract a tooth. **2** separate (metal) from ore; obtain (juice, etc.) by pressing, distilling, etc. **3** obtain (information, etc.) from a source; take passages from (a book, etc.). **4** derive (a benefit, pleasure, etc.) from a situation.
• *n* ('ɛkstrækt) **1** a passage from a book, etc. **2** a substance containing the concentrated essence of a material: beef extract. **extractor** *n* **extraction** *n* **1** extracting or being extracted. **2** ancestry; origin: of Chinese extraction. < Latin *ex-* out + *trahere* to draw.

extradite ('ɛkstrəˌdaɪt) *vb* **1** hand over (an alleged criminal) to the state that has the authority to try the charge. **2** obtain (such a person) for trial or punishment. **extradition** *n* < Latin *ex-* out + *traditio* surrender.

extramarital (ˌɛkstrə'mærɪtl̩) *adj* (of sexual relationships) occurring outside marriage.

extempore or **impromptu?**

An extempore speech is one that may have been prepared, but has not been memorized, or, usually, written down.

An impromptu speech is one that is made spontaneously by a speaker, who has been given no notice that he or she is to make it.

extramural (ˌɛkstrəˈmjʊərəl) *adj* for non-resident students and non-members of a college: extramural studies.

extraneous (ɪkˈstreɪnɪəs) *adj* **1** coming from the outside. **2** not essential; irrelevant. < Latin *extraneus* foreign.

extraordinary (ɪkˈstrɔːdnrɪ) *adj* **1** very unusual or remarkable. **2** for a special event or purpose: an extraordinary general meeting. **extraordinarily** *adv* < Latin *extra ordinem* out of the usual order.

extrapolate (ɪkˈstræpəˌleɪt) *vb* estimate (something unknown) by using and extending the results of (data and experience). **extrapolation** *n* < Latin *extra* + *-polate*: SEE **INTERPOLATE.**

extra-sensory (ˌɛkstrəˈsɛnsərɪ) *adj* (of perception) beyond or outside normal physical senses.

extraterrestrial (ˌɛkstrətəˈrɛstrɪəl) *adj* occurring or existing outside the earth or its atmosphere. < Latin *extra* outside + *terra* earth.

extravagant (ɪkˈstrævɪgənt) *adj* **1** not moderate or restrained; excessive. **2** wasteful, esp. of money; costing too much. **3** too elaborate or ornate. **extravagance** *n* **extravagantly** *adv* **extravaganza** *n* **1** a literary, musical, or dramatic fantasy. **2** a lavish, spectacular film, show, etc. < Latin *extra* beyond + *vagari* to wander.

extreme (ɪkˈstriːm) *adj* **1** existing in a very high degree: extreme cold. **2** very strict or severe: extreme measures. **3** at the end; furthest: the extreme north. **4** not moderate in actions or views: extreme left-wing.
• *n* **1** either extreme point of a range: extremes of hot and cold. **2** an extreme degree or act: go to extremes. **extremely** *adv* **extremism** *n* the holding of extreme views, esp. in politics. **extremist** *n* **extremity** *n* **1** an extreme point or end of something. **2** a (human) hand, foot, or other limb. **3** a moment of great misfortune or danger. < Latin *exterus* outer.

extricate (ˈɛkstrɪˌkeɪt) *vb* remove or free from hindrances, complications, etc.; disentangle. **extricable** *adj* **extrication** *n* < Latin *ex-* out + *tricae* hindrances, perplexities.

extrovert (ˈɛkstrəˌvɜːt) *n* a person whose attention and interests are directed outside his or her own self.
• *adj* having such characteristics.
< Latin *extra-* + *vertere* to turn.

exuberant (ɪgˈzjuːbərənt) *adj* **1** very lively and joyful. **2** lavish and effusive. **3** growing abundantly. **exuberance** *n* **exuberantly** *adv* < Latin *ex-* + *uberare* to bear abundantly.

exude (ɪgˈzjuːd) *vb* **1** release or be released through pores, etc., as sweat or sap. **2** make apparent by mood or behaviour: exude confidence. < Latin *ex-* out + *sudare* to sweat.

exult (ɪgˈzʌlt) *vb* be very joyful. **exultant** *adj* **exultation** *n* < Latin *ex-* + *salire* to leap.

eye (aɪ) *n* **1** the organ of sight of animals. **2** the visible part of this and the region around it: She has blue eyes. **3** the faculty of seeing: a discerning eye. **4** a look, expression, or gaze. **5** attention or view: in the public eye. **6** the faculty of aesthetic appreciation: an eye for good design. **7** the hole at the end of a needle. **8** the bud on a potato tuber. **9** the calm at the centre of a cyclone.
• *vb* watch closely. < Old English *ēage*. SEE PANEL.

eyeball (ˈaɪˌbɔːl) *n* the ball-shaped part of the eye.

eyebrow (ˈaɪˌbraʊ) *n* the ridge above the eye; hair growing on this.

eyeful (ˈaɪˌfʊl) *n* (*informal*) **1** a look, view, or glance: Get an eyeful of this! **2** an attractive sight, esp. a woman.

eyeglass (ˈaɪˌglɑːs) *n* a lens worn or held in front of an eye with defective vision; monocle. **eyeglasses** *pl n* spectacles.

eyelash (ˈaɪˌlæʃ) *n* any one of the short hairs that grow from the edge of each eyelid.

eyelet (ˈaɪlɪt) *n* a small hole designed for a cord, shoelace, etc., to be passed through or for a hook to be inserted into. < Middle French *oillet* little eye.

eyelid (ˈaɪlɪd) *n* either of the two folds of skin that can be moved to cover the

an eye for an eye

The expression an eye for an eye means 'retaliation, especially in the same form as the injury inflicted': For the people in favour of capital punishment, it's a case of *an eye for an eye*. If a man murders someone, then he also should forfeit his right to live.

The longer form of the expression is an eye for an eye and a tooth for a tooth. This comes from the Authorized (King James) Version of the Bible: If men strive, and hurt a woman with child ... and if any mischief follow, then thou shalt give life for life, eye for eye, tooth for tooth (Exodus 21:22-24) and Ye have heard that it hath been said, An eye for an eye, and a tooth for a tooth (Matthew 5:38).

exposed part of the eyeball.
eye-opener (ˈaɪˌəʊpənə) *n* (*informal*) something surprising and revealing: a real eye-opener.
eyesight (ˈaɪˌsaɪt) *n* **1** the ability to see. **2** the range of vision: within eyesight.
eyesore (ˈaɪˌsɔː) *n* something that is very ugly to look at.
eyewash (ˈaɪˌwɒʃ) *n* **1** a mild lotion applied to the eye to relieve irritation. **2** (*informal*) nonsense; rubbish.
eyewitness (ˈaɪˌwɪtnɪs) *n* a person actually present at an event and who saw what happened.
eyrie (ˈɪərɪ, ˈaɪərɪ) *n* the nest of an eagle or other bird of prey on a cliff or mountain top. < Medieval Latin *airea,* from Latin *area* open field, nest.

F

FA *abbrev* Football Association.
fable (ˈfeɪbl̩) *n* **1** a story, esp. one about animals, that teaches a moral lesson: Aesop's fables. **2** a myth or legend. **3** a false story; lie. < Latin *fabula* story.
fabric (ˈfæbrɪk) *n* **1** material made by weaving, knitting, or felting natural or man-made fibres; cloth. **2** the basic structure of a building. **3** the underlying structure: the fabric of society. **fabricate** *vb* **1** make by putting many parts together. **2** make or create, esp. in order to deceive: fabricate a story. **fabrication** *n* < Latin *fabrica* workshop, from *faber* workman.
fabulous (ˈfæbjʊləs) *adj* **1** (*informal*) very good; wonderful: a fabulous party. **2** incredible; extraordinary: a fabulous sum of money. **fabulously** *adv* < SEE **FABLE.**
façade (fəˈsɑːd) *n* **1** the front of a building, esp. when this has distinctive architectural features. **2** a false or superficial appearance: a façade of optimism. < French, from Italian *facciata,* from *faccia* face.
face (feɪs) *n* **1** the front part of the (human) head from the chin to the forehead. **2** an expression on the face: a happy face. **3** the front, upper, or outer surface of something: a clock face. **4** the surface of a rock from which coal, etc., is dug: He works at the coal face.
• *vb* **1** have the face or front turned towards or in a certain direction; be opposite: The house faces south. **2** meet, esp. without trying to avoid: He faced defeat bravely. **3** make (someone) meet a difficulty; confront: The workers are faced with redundancy. **4** (*informal*) bear; endure: I can't face going to work today. **5** cover the front or surface of with a different material. **face to face** (**with**) facing; confronted by: face to face with danger. **face up to** accept (something difficult and painful) honestly and boldly. **in the face of** despite. **on the face of it** considering the (insufficient) evidence available; judging by appearances. **to someone's face** openly in someone's presence. < Latin *facies.* SEE PANEL.
face-cloth (ˈfeɪsklɒθ) *n* also **face flannel** a small cloth used for washing the face, hands, etc.
faceless (ˈfeɪslɪs) *adj* without identity; anonymous: faceless bureaucrats.
face-lift (ˈfeɪsˌlɪft) *n* **1** a medical operation that removes imperfections on the face, performed esp. to make someone look younger. **2** a change that is intended to improve the appearance or usefulness: undergo a complete face-lift.
facet (ˈfæsɪt) *n* **1** a small, flat surface on a cut jewel or other precious stone. **2** any of the ways in which something mentioned may be considered: different facets of the problem. < French *facette* little face.
facetious (fəˈsiːʃəs) *adj* joking or jocular, esp. at an unsuitable time; flippant: facetious remarks. **facetiously** *adv* **facetiousness** *n* < Latin *facetus* witty.
facia (ˈfeɪʃɪə) *n* **1** the dashboard of a motor car. **2** the name-plate over the front of a shop. < SEE **FASCIA.**
facial (ˈfeɪʃəl) *adj* of or concerning the face.

face value

Face features in a number of expressions, many of them idiomatic, including:

a long face a sad, disappointed expression.
a red face an expression or feeling of embarrassment or shame.
face the music to be confronted with the unpleasant consequences of one's action.
face value 1 the value printed on money, etc. **2** the apparent value or meaning: take the statement at face value.
fly in the lace of to be contrary to: The decision flies in the face of all the evidence.
keep a straight face not to laugh or smile when one wants to, especially in a humorous situation.
laugh in someone's face to show a mocking disrespect for someone.
make or **pull a face** or **faces** to adopt an expression of pain, dislike, etc.
one's face falls one shows one's disappointment in one's expression.
put on a brave or **bold face** to appear brave or bold when faced with difficulties, failure, etc.
save/lose face to keep/lose one's dignity, reputation, etc.

• *n* a facial beauty treatment. **facially** *adv*

facile (ˈfæsaɪl) *adj* **1** too easy; superficial; glib: a facile answer. **2** done, used, or understood easily. < Latin *facere* to do.

facility (ˈfəsɪlɪtɪ) *n* **1** something, esp. equipment, that makes it easier or more convenient to do things: facilities for disabled people; cooking facilities. **2** the ability to do something easily and well: to play the piano with great facility **3** (*informal*) a building or room used for a particular purpose. **facilitate** *vb (formal)* make easier. **facilitative** *adj* **facilitation** *n*

facing (ˈfeɪsɪŋ) *n* **1** an outer covering for a surface such as a wall, for protection or decoration. **2** material that is put at the edge of a garment for stiffening or decoration.

facsimile (fækˈsɪmɪlɪ) *n* an exact copy, esp. of something printed. < Latin *facere* to make + *simile* like.

fact (fækt) *n* **1** something that has been done, that exists, or is true: Space travel is now a fact. **2** a piece of information that is presented as real and true: Statistics consists of more than just facts and figures. **3** the state of actually existing; truth: Is the story fact or fiction? **fact of life** something, esp. something unpleasant or harsh, that exists and must be considered: Unemployment is a fact of life. **facts of life** the details of human sexual activity and reproduction. **in fact** used to explain further what has already been stated. < Latin *factum* something done, from *facere* to do.

faction (ˈfækʃən) *n* a small group or party within a larger party; splinter group. < Latin *factio* making, from *facere* to make.

factor (ˈfæktə) *n* **1** a condition, fact, etc., that, with others, causes a result. **2** a whole number (except 1) by which a larger whole number can be divided exactly: 2, 4, 5, and 10 are factors of 20. **3** (*formal*) a person who acts on behalf of another; agent. **4** a gene. < Latin: one who acts, from *facere* to do.

factory (ˈfæktərɪ) *n* a building or group of buildings where goods are made or assembled, esp. in large quantities. **factory farm** a farm in which animals are bred and fattened using modern industrial methods. < Late Latin *factorium:* SEE **FACTOR**.

factual (ˈfæktʃʊəl) *adj* of, based on, or restricted to facts: a factual description. **factually** *adv*

faculty (ˈfækl̩tɪ) *n* **1** a natural ability of the mind or body: in full possession of all one's faculties; the faculty of hearing. **2** an ability to do something. **3** a group of related departments at a university, etc.: the Faculty of Medicine. < Medieval Latin *facultas* branch of learning, from Latin: ability, from *facilis* easy.

fad (fæd) *n* an interest or practice that is enthusiastically followed, but lasts only a short time; craze. < origin unknown.

fade (feɪd) *vb* **1** lose or cause to lose freshness or intensity of colour: The shirts have faded. **2** lose strength: Resistance to the idea soon faded. **3** disappear gradually: The roar of the motor cycles faded into the distance. **4** (of sound or vision) gradually decrease. < Middle French *fade* feeble, pale.

faeces (ˈfiːsiːz) *pl n* the solid waste passed from the bowels. **faecal** *adj* < Latin: dregs.

fag[1] (fæg) *n* **1** (*informal*) a boring or tiring task. **2** (esp. formerly) a junior pupil who performs services for a senior pupil.
• *vb* **fagged; fagging 1** also **fag out** (*informal*) tire (esp. oneself) by hard work; exhaust. **2** act as a fag. < origin unknown.

fag[2] *n* (*informal*) a cigarette. **fag end** (*informal*) **1** a poor or worthless remnant. **2** the stub of a cigarette. < origin unknown.

faggot (ˈfægət) *n* **1** a round mass of chopped, seasoned meat. **2** a bundle of small sticks for burning. **3** (*informal*) an unpleasant person. **4** (*chiefly US*) a homosexual. < Greek *phakelos* bundle.

fail (feɪl) *vb* **1** be unsuccessful in an attempt to do something, pass a test, etc.; grade (a student) as not passing. **2** stop working: The engine suddenly failed. **3** prove disappointing to. **4** leave undone; neglect. **5** prove insufficient in strength, intensity, etc.: His health gradually failed. **6** go bankrupt.
• *n* a failure in an examination. **failure** *n* **without fail** with absolute certainty: I'll be back at 11 o'clock without fail. < Latin *fallere* to deceive.

failing (ˈfeɪlɪŋ) *n* a weakness or fault.
• *prep* in the absence of.

faint (feɪnt) *adj* **1** not clear or bright; not strong in colour, sound, or smell. **2** weak or vague: faint hopes. **3** dizzy and weak: I feel faint.
• *vb* lose consciousness temporarily. **faintly** *adv* **faintness** *n* **faint-hearted** *adj* timid; feeble. < Old French *faindre* to be idle.

fair[1] (fɛə) *adj* **1** light in colour: fair hair. **2** (of the weather) fine; (of winds or tide) favourable. **3** just, free from prejudice, and in accordance with rules.

4 moderately good or large. **5** clean; clear: a fair copy.
• *adv* in a fair manner. **fairness** *n* **fair and square** honestly; directly. **fair play** justice. < Old English *fæger*.

fair² *n* **1** a travelling entertainment with side-shows, etc., esp. one that comes to a place at the same time each year; fun fair. **2** an exhibition of commercial or industrial products. **3** a sale of articles, esp. for a charity. **fairground** *n* an outdoor area where a fair is held. < Latin *feriae* holidays.

fairly (ˈfɛəlɪ) *adv* **1** in a fair manner. **2** moderately; quite: fairly small.

fairway (ˈfɛəˌweɪ) *n* **1** the navigable part of a river, harbour, etc. **2** the area of mown grass on a golf-course between a tee and a green.

fairy (ˈfɛərɪ) *n* **1** an imaginary small being with magic powers. **2** (*informal*) a male homosexual. **fairyland** *n* the imaginary land where fairies live; enchanted, wonderful place. **fairy story** also **fairy-tale 1** a children's story concerned with supernatural events. **2** a false account or description; lie. < Old French *faerie*.

fait accompli (ˌfeɪt əˈkɒmpliː) *n* (*French*) something already done and not reversible.

faith (feɪθ) *n* **1** belief and trust in and commitment to God or the teachings of a religion; strong belief and confidence in something or someone. **2** a system of religious beliefs: the Christian faith. **3** loyalty and faithfulness. **faith healing** the practice of trying to cure illnesses by prayer and religious faith rather than medical skill. **in good/bad faith** with sincere/insincere motives or aims. < Latin *fides* trust.

faithful (ˈfeɪθfʊl) *adj* **1** loyal. **2** loyal to one's marriage partner. **3** trustworthy and conscientious. **4** true to the facts; accurate. **faithfully** *adv* **faithfulness** *n* **the faithful** believers in and loyal adherents to a religion, political party, etc.

fake (feɪk) *vb* **1** change or treat so as to give a false appearance or character. **2** pretend to have (an illness); feign.
• *n* an object or person that is not genuine; counterfeit.
• *adj* not genuine; counterfeit. < origin uncertain.

falcon (ˈfɔːlkən) *n* any of several different kinds of bird of prey having pointed wings and a notched, hooked bill. **falconry** *n* **1** the art of training falcons to hunt game. **2** the sport of hunting with falcons. < ultimately Late Latin *falco* hawk.

fall (fɔːl) *vb* **fell; fallen; falling 1** drop down, as from an upright position. **2** come as if by falling: Silence fell. **3** become less or lower in number, quality, etc. **4** lose one's position or office. **5** (of the face) show dismay: His face fell at the news. **6** hang down freely: Her hair falls over her shoulders. **7** come into an undesirable state; stray; yield to temptation. **8** die in battle. **9** suffer military capture: The city fell. **10** slope downwards: The land falls away to the east. **11** happen at a time that is mentioned: Christmas falls on a Tuesday this year. **12** pass into a state that is mentioned: fall asleep.
• *n* **1** the act of falling; amount, distance, etc., which something falls. **2** the loss of power, reputation, etc. **3** the capture of a city, etc. **4** Adam's sin of disobedience: the Fall. **5** a downward slope; waterfall. **6** (*US*) autumn. **fall back on** go to as a reliable source of help. **fall down** be unsatisfactory. **fall flat** fail in its intended effect: The joke fell flat. **fall for 1** fall in love with. **2** be deceived by. **fall foul of** clash with. **fall in 1** (of a roof, etc.) collapse inwards. **2** take one's place in a military formation. **falling star** a meteor. **fall in with** agree with. **fall off** decline in quantity, etc. **fall out** quarrel. **fall-out** *n* radioactive material after a nuclear explosion. **fall short of** be less than (a required standard). **fall through** (of a plan) fail. < Old English *feallan*. SEE PANEL.

fallacy (ˈfæləsɪ) *n* **1** a false idea or belief. **2** an argument having an invalid form of reasoning. **fallacious** *adj* < Latin *fallere* to deceive.

fallible (ˈfælɪbl̩) *adj* capable of being

> **fall between two stools**
>
> A person or thing that suffers from a failure either to choose between or reconcile two alternative courses or principles is sometimes said to fall between two stools. At the heart of the expression is the meaning 'to fail through indecisiveness'. The allusion is to the person who, unable to decide which of the two stools at his back he is to sit on, ends up falling on the floor.
>
> The French equivalent is *être assis entre deux chaises* 'to be seated between two chairs'.

wrong. **fallibility** *n* < Latin *fallere* to deceive.

fallow (ˈfæləʊ) *adj* **1** (of land) left unsown after being ploughed in order to restore its fertility. **2** inactive; dormant. < Old English *fealh* fallow land.

false (fɔːls) *adj* **1** not true; wrong; untruthful. **2** not loyal; unfaithful. **3** not real; artificial: false teeth; a suitcase with a false bottom. **4** unwise: a false move. **falsely** *adv* **falseness** *n* **falsehood** *n* **1** an untrue statement; lie. **2** the quality of being untrue. **3** the act of deceiving. **falsify** *vb* **falsified; falsifying 1** make false by changing fraudulently. **2** misrepresent (facts). **falsification** *n* **falsity** *n* < Latin *fallere* to deceive.

falsetto (fɔːlˈsɛtəʊ) *n, pl* **falsettos** an artificially high singing range.
• *adv* in a falsetto voice. < SEE **FALSE.**

falter (ˈfɔːltə) *vb* **1** move unsteadily. **2** waver in purpose or action. **3** become weaker in strength or effectiveness. **4** speak with hesitation; stammer. < Middle English *falteren.*

fame (feɪm) *n* **1** the state of being known to many people. **2** a good reputation. **famed** *adj* well-known; famous. < Latin *fama.*

familiar (fəˈmɪlɪə) *adj* **1** frequently seen or experienced; common. **2** informal: on familiar terms. **3** too informal and intimate. **4** closely acquainted: familiar with legal terms. **familiarity** *n* **familiarly** *adv* **familiarize** *vb* **1** make commonly known. **2** make well acquainted. **familiarization** *n* < SEE **FAMILY.**

family (ˈfæməlɪ) *n* **1** a social unit of parents and their children; children of the same parents. **2** a group of people related by ancestry or marriage. **3** a group of things that are alike; group of related animals or plants. SEE PANEL.

famine (ˈfæmɪn) *n* **1** an extreme scarcity of food. **2** any very great shortage. < Latin *fames* hunger.

famished (ˈfæmɪʃt) *adj* very hungry: I'm famished! < SEE **FAMINE.**

famous (ˈfeɪməs) *adj* known and talked about by a great many people: a famous film star. **famously** *adv* excellently: We got on famously! < Latin *fama* fame.

fan[1] (fæn) *n* a device, such as a piece of paper, cloth, etc., waved in the hand, used to produce a current of air.
• *vb* **fanned; fanning 1** move (air) with a fan. **2** drive a current of air on with or as if with a fan. **3** stimulate (a great activity, enthusiasm, etc.). **4** spread out from a central point. **fan belt** the belt that drives the cooling fan for a radiator in a motor vehicle. < Latin *vannus* basket for winnowing grain.

fan[2] *n* an enthusiastic supporter or admirer. < short for *fanatic.*

fanatic (fəˈnætɪk) *n* a person who is excessively enthusiastic about something. **fanatical** *adj* **fanatically** *adv* **fanaticism** *n* < ultimately Latin *fanum* temple.

fancier (ˈfænsɪə) *n* **1** a person who breeds animals or grows plants: a pigeon fancier. **2** a person with a special interest in and knowledge of something.

fancy (ˈfænsɪ) *n* **1** a liking that is based on whim rather than reason; notion or whim: He only works when the fancy takes him. **2** imagination; thing imagined.
• *vb* **fancied; fancying 1** believe without certain evidence: I rather fancy we've met before. **2** (*informal*) be attracted by; like. **3** (*informal*) have too high an opinion of (oneself). **4** (*informal*), imagine; used in exclamations: Why, fancy you remembering that!
• *adj* **1** not ordinary; elaborate: a fancy hair-do. **2** ornamental: fancy goods. **fanciful** *adj* **1** guided by or using fancy or imagination, not reason. **2** not real; imaginary: fanciful tales. **fancifully** *adv* **fancy dress** an unusual or fancy costume, esp. one representing a historical character, animal, etc., worn at a party or other special occasion. **fancy-free** *adj* free to do what one wants, esp. because not committed in a relationship. < Middle English *fantsy,*

in the family

Family features in a number of expressions including:

family name a surname.
family planning methods of controlling the number of children born to parents, especially by contraception; birth-control.
family tree a genealogy.
in the family way pregnant.
run in the family to be a characteristic that a person shares with his or her parents and others in the family: I'm not surprised he's so obstinate—it runs in the family.

It is interesting to note that the origin of family, Latin *familia,* meant 'household' and so included servants as well as relatives.

shortened from *fantasie* fantasy.

fandango (fæn'dæŋgəʊ) *n, pl* **fandangoes** a lively Spanish dance performed by a couple. < Spanish.

fanfare ('fænfεə) *n* a sounding of trumpets. < French, back formation from *fanfarer* to play a flourish on trumpets.

fang (fæŋ) *n* **1** the long, pointed tooth of a snake, through which it injects venom. **2** any large, pointed tooth, esp. of dogs or wolves. < Old English: what is caught, prey.

fanlight ('fænˌlaɪt) *n* a semicircular window above a door, esp. one having bars like the ribs of a fan.

fantasia (fæn'teɪzɪə) *n* **1** a musical composition of no fixed form. **2** a medley of popular tunes. < SEE **FANTASY.**

fantasy ('fæntəsɪ) *n* **1** creative imagination. **2** a wild or strange product of the imagination. **3** an extravagant mental image; day-dream. **fantasize** *vb* form imaginative ideas (about). **fantastic** *adj* **1** unreal; imaginary. **2** extravagant and very imaginative. **3** very great: fantastic sums of money. **4** (*informal*) excellent. **fantastically** *adv* < Greek *phantazein* to make visible.

far (fɑː) *adv* **farther, further; farthest, furthest 1** to or at a great distance in space or time. **2** very much: He is far better than me. **3** to an extent or degree: as far as I know.

• *adj* distant in space, time, or degree. **a far cry from** very different from. **by far** by a great amount. **far-away** *adj* **1** remote. **2** dreamy: a far-away look. **far-fetched** *adj* improbable. **far-flung** *adj* **1** widely distributed. **2** remote. **far-reaching** *adj* having a wide range or influence: far-reaching implications. < Old English *feorr.*

farce (fɑːs) *n* **1** a comedy based on improbable situations; this type of drama. **2** a ludicrous or meaningless situation. **farcical** *adj* < Latin *farcire* to stuff.

fare (fεə) *n* **1** the money paid for a journey in a train, bus, etc. **2** a passenger who pays a fare. **3** food provided.

• *vb* get along: The party fared badly in the election. < Old English *faran* to go.

farewell (fεə'wεl) *interj* goodbye.

• *n* act of leave-taking; parting wish.

farm (fɑːm) *n* **1** an area of land and its buildings used for growing crops or raising animals. **2** a farmhouse.

• *vb* **1** grow crops or raise animals. **2** manage and cultivate (land) for this purpose. **3** pass to someone else; delegate: farm out work to others. **farmer** *n* a person who owns or manages a farm. **farmhouse** *n* the dwelling from which a farm is managed. **farmyard** *n* the area surrounded by or adjacent to farm buildings. < ultimately Latin *firmare* to make firm.

farrier ('færɪə) *n* a person who shoes horses. < Old French *ferrier,* from Latin *ferrarius* smith, from *ferrum* iron.

farther ('fɑːðə) *adv, adj* at or to a greater distance in space or time; more distant. **farthest** *adv, adj* at or to the greatest distance in space or time; most distant. SEE PANEL.

farthing ('fɑːðɪŋ) *n* a former British coin worth a quarter of an old penny. < Old English *feorthing* fourth part.

fascia ('feiʃə) *n, pl* **fasciae 1** a long, flat surface under eaves or a cornice. **2** a facia. < Latin: band.

fascinate ('fæsɪˌnεɪt) *vb* arouse and hold the interest of. **fascination** *n* < Latin *fascinare* to bewitch.

fascism ('fæʃɪzəm) *n* a system of extreme right-wing, nationalist, dictatorial government. **fascist** *adj, n* < Italian *fascismo,* from *fascio* political group, from Latin *fascis* bundle.

fashion ('fæʃən) *n* **1** a way or manner of doing something. **2** a current, popular style, esp. of dress.

• *vb* make into a particular form; mould. **after a fashion** in a rudimentary way; not very skilfully. **fashionable** *adj* **1** in or having a style that is currently popular. **2** used or frequented by people of fashion. **fashionably** *adv* < ultimately Latin *facere* to make.

fast[1] (fɑːst) *adj* **1** moving or able to move quickly. **2** producing or allowing quick movement: a fast road. **3** (of a clock, etc.) showing a time ahead of what is correct.

farther or **further?**

Use further when the meaning is 'additional' as in *further* information, *further* details, *further* education or 'in addition; moreover': *Further,* the report elaborates the need for improved safety precautions. Further is also used for the verb sense 'to help; promote': to *further* one's children's welfare.

As an adjective or adverb referring to distance, either can be used; though further is more common: There is another garage a mile or two *further* on. Aberdeen is *farther* north than Dundee.

4 (of a photographic film) very sensitive to light. **5** firmly fixed or attached. **6** (of colours) not liable to fade or run.
• *adv* **1** quickly. **2** ahead of a correct time or schedule. **3** in a firm or fixed manner. **4** soundly: fast asleep. **fast food** quickly prepared food served in a restaurant. < Old English *fæst*.

fast[2] *vb* go without all or some food or meals, esp. as a religious observance.
• *n* an act or period of fasting. < Old English *fæstan*.

fastback (ˈfɑːstˌbæk) *n* a car with a back that forms one continuous slope from the roof to the rear.

fasten (ˈfɑːsn̩) *vb* **1** fix firmly, esp. by pinning or tying; make secure. **2** direct (one's attention) steadily. **3** become fast or fixed. **4** lay hold of: fasten onto an idea. **fastener** *n* **fastening** *n* < Old English *fæstnian*.

fastidious (fæˈstɪdɪəs) *adj* **1** excessively difficult to please. **2** excessively fussy about details. **3** exceedingly delicate. **fastidiously** *adv* **fastidiousness** *n* < Latin *fastidium* loathing.

fat (fæt) *adj* **fatter; fattest 1** containing much fat. **2** too plump. **3** thick: a fat book **4** substantial: fat profits.
• *n* an oily substance in animal tissue and plant seeds; this substance used in cooking. **fatness** *n* < Old English *fæt* fatted.

fatal (ˈfeɪtl̩) *adj* **1** causing or ending in death: a fatal accident. **2** bringing ruin: fatal consequences. **fatally** *adv* **fatality** *n* death caused by a disaster. SEE PANEL.

fatalism (ˈfeɪtəˌlɪzəm) *n* the belief that all events are predetermined, inevitable, and completely outside the control of human beings. **fatalist** *n* **fatalistic** *adj*

fate (feɪt) *n* **1** the power that is supposed to determine the outcome of all events and is impossible to resist. **2** a person's destiny. **3** the final outcome. **fated** *adj* destined; doomed. **fateful** *adj* having important and often unpleasant consequences. < Latin *fatum* what has been spoken. SEE PANEL AT **FATAL.**

fatal or **fateful?**

The basic meaning of fatal is 'causing or ending in death' as in a *fatal* accident or 'bringing ruin or disaster' as in a *fatal* move, *fatal* consequences.

Fateful means 'decisive; momentous; having important and often unpleasant consequences; directed or marked by the power of fate' as in That *fateful* occasion when they met each other for the first time.

But in loose, popular usage fatal can also mean 'decisive; momentous' as in That *fatal* day I left home.

father (ˈfɑːðə) *n* **1** a male parent. **2** a male ancestor; forefather. **3** an originator; inventor: the father of modern communications. **4** any of the leaders of a city, assembly, etc. **5** the title of certain Christian priests.
• *vb* **1** beget; give rise to. **2** accept responsibility for. **fatherhood** *n* **fatherly** *adj* **father-figure** *n* an older man who is respected and trusted like a father. **father-in-law** *n, pl* **fathers-in-law** the father of one's husband or wife. **fatherland** *n* one's native land. < Old English *fæder*.

fathom (ˈfæðəm) *n* a unit of length equal to six feet (about 1.83 metres), used to measure depths of water.
• *vb* **1** measure the depth of. **2** understand completely. **fathomless** *adj* incapable of being understood. < Old English *fæthm*.

fatigue (fəˈtiːg) *n* **1** physical or nervous tiredness. **2** the tendency of a material to break or weaken under repeated stress: metal fatigue. **3** domestic duties performed by soldiers.
• *vb* weary; tire. < Latin *fatigare* to weary.

fatten (ˈfætn̩) *vb* make or become fat.

fatty (ˈfætɪ) *adj* containing, derived from, or like fat.
• *n (informal)* a fat person.

fatuous (ˈfætjʊəs) *adj* complacently or inanely foolish. **fatuously** *adv* **fatuousness** *n* < Latin *fatuus* foolish.

fault (fɔːlt) *n* **1** an imperfection or defect. **2** a mistake or error. **3** something wrongly done; offence. **4** the responsibility for wrongdoing or failure. **5** a fracture and displacement of rock strata.
• *vb* **1** find a fault in. **2** make imperfect. **faultless** *adj* **faultlessly** *adv* **faulty** *adj* **at fault** guilty of error. **find fault with** criticize; complain about. **to a fault** excessively. < Old French *faute*.

fauna (ˈfɔːnə) *n* the animals of an area or period. < Late Latin *Fauna*, Roman goddess.

faux pas (ˌfəʊ ˈpɑː) *n, pl* **faux pas** an embarrassing social blunder. < French: false step.

favour (ˈfeɪvə) *n* **1** friendly liking or goodwill. **2** a kind or helpful act. **3** unfair support or preference.

• *vb* **1** like or approve. **2** do a kindness for. **3** show unfair preference towards. **4** support or confirm. **5** make easier or possible. **in favour of 1** in agreement with. **2** to the advantage of. **3** out of preference for. **in/out of favour** having/not having someone's goodwill. < Latin *favēre* to protect. SEE PANEL.

favourable (ˈfeɪvrəbl̩) *adj* **1** approving. **2** helpful; advantageous: favourable weather. **favourably** *adv*

favourite (ˈfeɪvrɪt) *adj* preferred above others.
• *n* **1** a favoured person or thing. **2** the competitor, horse, etc., that is expected to win. **favouritism** *n* the showing of unfair favour.

fawn¹ (fɔːn) *n* **1** a young deer less than one year old. **2** a light-greyish brown colour.
• *adj* of this colour. < Latin *fetus* offspring.

fawn² *vb* **1** seek affection by cringing and flattering. **2** (of a dog, etc.) show affection. < Old English *fagnian* to rejoice.

FBI *abbrev* Federal Bureau of Investigation.

FC *abbrev* Football Club.

fear (fɪə) *n* **1** a strong emotion caused by expectation or awareness of danger, pain, etc. **2** deep reverence and awe, esp. of God.
• *vb* **1** be afraid (of). **2** have a deep reverence and awe of. **fearless** *adj* **fearlessly** *adv* **fearful** *adj* **1** causing fear. **2** feeling fear. **3** *(informal)* very great: a fearful price. **fearfully** *adv* **fearsome** *adj* causing fear. **for fear of** in case of. < Old English *fǣr* danger.

feasible (ˈfiːzəbl̩) *adj* **1** capable of being carried out, used, or dealt with successfully: a feasible plan. **2** likely; plausible: a feasible explanation. **feasibility** *n* **feasibly** *adv* < Latin *facere* to do. SEE PANEL.

feast (fiːst) *n* **1** large, elaborate meal. **2** something that gives delight. **3** a religious festival.
• *vb* **1** take part in a feast. **2** give a feast to. **3** delight. < Latin *festus* joyful.

feat (fiːt) *n* a remarkable, skilful, or daring achievement. < Latin *factum* deed.

feather (ˈfɛðə) *n* **1** any of the light structures that grow from a bird's body, with a central staff and soft, hair-like material growing on either side. **2** the vane of an arrow.
• *vb* provide or cover with feathers. **feathery** *adj* **feather bed** a bed with a mattress stuffed with feathers. **featherbrained** *adj* foolish; scatter-brained. < Old English *fether*. SEE PANEL.

feature (ˈfiːtʃə) *n* **1** a part of the face; appearance of the face. **2** a prominent or special part or characteristic of something. **3** a special article in a newspaper, etc. **4** a full-length cinema film.
• *vb* **1** give special prominence to. **2** be a feature of. **3** have an important part. **featureless** *adj* < Latin *facere* to do.

fed (fɛd) SEE **FEED**. **fed up** bored; discontented.

federal (ˈfɛdərəl) *adj* **1** of a union of separate states joined together to serve their common interests while retaining some self-government. **2** of the central government of such a union: federal laws. **federally** *adv* **federate** *vb* join a federation. **federation** *n* **1** the formation of a federal union; country formed by the

currying favour

To seek to ingratiate oneself by flattery, especially with one's superiors, is sometimes referred to as to curry favour. The expression comes from the Middle English *curry favel.* The curry in question derives from the Old French *correer* 'to groom (a horse)'. Favel is a corruption of the Old French *Fauvel,* the name of a chestnut horse in a popular 14th-century satirical romance called 'Roman de Fauvel'. The horse served to symbolize duplicity and cunning. Hence to *curry favel* was to seek to ingratiate oneself through insincere means.

During the 15th century *favel* slowly became favour as a result of sound association and semantic fit.

feasible suggestions

The basic meaning of feasible is 'capable of being carried out, used, or dealt with successfully; practicable' as in a *feasible* plan; The suggestion certainly is *feasible,* even though it might prove very expensive.

Some careful users of English object to feasible being used to mean 'likely; plausible' as in a *feasible* theory; The explanation is *feasible,* though improbable.

federation of separate states. **2** a union of organizations. < Latin *foedus* league.

fee (fi:) *n* a payment made for something such as professional services, admission to a society, education, or transfer of a footballer. < Old English *fie*.

feeble (ˈfi:bl̩) *adj* **1** lacking strength; weak. **2** lacking force or authority. **feebleness** *n* **feebly** *adv* **feeble-minded** *adj* mentally deficient; stupid. < Latin *flēre* to weep.

feed (fi:d) *vb* **fed; feeding 1** give food to; provide as food (to animals). **2** supply with what maintains or develops growth, etc.
• *n* **1** food for animals or a baby. **2** the part of a machine that carries material into the machine. < Old English *fēdan*.

feedback (ˈfi:dˌbæk) *n* **1** the return of a part of the output of a machine or process to the input. **2** reaction or response to an action, product, etc.

feeder (ˈfi:də) *n* **1** an instrument that feeds material into a machine. **2** a road, railway, etc., that links outlying areas into the main transport system.

feel (fi:l) *vb* **felt; feeling 1** examine by touch or handling. **2** be aware of (being); experience (an emotion). **3** be able to receive the sensation of touch; search for something by touch. **4** think or believe: I feel you're making a mistake.
• *n* **1** the act of feeling; sense of touch. **2** the quality of something as experienced through touch; atmosphere: a velvety feel. **3** intuitive appreciation or skill: a feel for good design. **feeler** *n* **1** a long, thin part or organ of touch of some animals. **2** a proposal offered to test people's reactions, **feel for** sympathize with. **feeling** *n* **1** the sense of touch; ability to experience sensation. **2** an emotional state; sense: hurt someone's feelings. **3** opinion or belief, esp. one not wholly based on reason. **4** sympathy. **5** a premonition. **feel like** want: I feel like a cold drink. < Old English *fēlan*.

feet (fi:t) SEE **FOOT.**

feign (feɪn) *vb* deliberately give a false impression or appearance; pretend or simulate. < Latin *fingere* to shape, feign.

feint[1] (feɪnt) *n* a mock attack or movement to distract an opponent.
• *vb* make a feint. < SEE **FEIGN.**

feint[2] *adj* (of ruled lines) faint. < alteration of *faint*.

felicity (fɪˈlɪsɪtɪ) *n* (*formal*) **1** happiness; joy. **2** a suitable, pleasing expression or style. **felicitous** *adj* < Latin *felix* happy.

feline (ˈfi:laɪn) *adj* of or like a cat. < Latin *feles* cat.

fell[1] (fɛl) SEE **FALL.**

fell[2] *vb* cut or knock down: fell trees. < Old English *fellan*.

fell[3] *n* a steep, rugged expanse of high moorland. < Old Norse *fjall*.

fellow (ˈfɛləʊ) *n* **1** a comrade or associate. **2** a person of the same rank, power, etc. **3** a member of a learned society. **4** (*informal*) a man or boy.
• *adj* belonging to the same group: fellow countrymen. **fellow-traveller** *n* a person who sympathizes with the cause of a party without being a member. < Old English *fēolaga* partner.

fellowship (ˈfɛləʊˌʃɪp) *n* **1** friendly relations between people; companionship. **2** mutual sharing. **3** a group of people with the same interests. **4** an endowment for the support of a person doing advanced research.

felon (ˈfɛlən) *n* a person who has committed a felony. **felony** *n* (formerly) a serious crime, such as murder or arson. < Medieval Latin *fello* villain.

felt[1] (fɛlt) SEE **FEEL.**

felt[2] *n* a kind of cloth made by compressing wool or fur and other fibres.
• *vb* **1** make into or cover with felt.

---

feathers

Feather features in a number of idiomatic expressions, including:

a feather in one's cap an achievement of which one can deservedly feel proud: Being promoted to manager so soon was quite a feather in Rod's cap.

feather one's nest to take care of one's own financial interests, especially when being greedy or dishonest: He's not in the least concerned about paying his workers a fair wage—he's just out to exploit them so that he can feather his own nest.

ruffle someone's feathers to cause to lose one's composure and show disquiet, impatience, etc.

you could have knocked someone down with a feather someone was extremely surprised.

---

2 become matted like felt. < Old English.

female (ˈfiːmeɪl) *adj* **1** of the sex that bears offspring or produces eggs. **2** (of a plant) with an ovary but no stamens. **3** with a hollow into which a corresponding male part fits.
• *n* a female animal or plant. < Latin *femina* woman. SEE PANEL.

feminine (ˈfɛmɪnɪn) *adj* **1** of women or the qualities thought typical of or suitable for women. **2** of a particular grammatical gender.
• *n* a feminine word, etc. **femininity** *n* < Latin *femina* woman. SEE PANEL AT **FEMALE.**

feminism (ˈfɛmɪˌnɪzəm) *n* the movement to gain political, economic, and social equality for women. **feminist** *adj, n*

femur (ˈfiːmə) *n* the thigh-bone.< Latin. < Latin.

fen (fɛn) *n* an area of low, marshy or flooded land. < Old English *fenn.*

fence (fɛns) *n* **1** a barrier designed to prevent escape or entrance or to mark a boundary. **2** a raised structure for a horse to jump. **3** (*slang*) a dealer in stolen goods.
• *vb* **1** surround with a fence; close (in) or separate (off) with or as with a fence. **2** engage in the sport of fencing. **3** (*slang*) deal in stolen goods. **fencer** *n* < Middle English *defens* defence.

fencing (ˈfɛnsɪŋ) *n* **1** fences; material used in building fences. **2** the sport of fighting with a foil or other sword.

fend (fɛnd) *vb* **fend for** provide for; support. **fend off** ward off. < Middle English *defenden* to defend.

fender (ˈfɛndə) *n* anything that protects something else, such as a low, metal guard in front of a fireplace to confine falling coal.

ferment (ˈfɜːmɛnt) *n* **1** a substance such as yeast that causes fermentation. **2** excitement; agitation.
• *vb* (fəˈmɛnt) **1** cause fermentation in; undergo fermentation. **2** arouse or seethe with excitement. **fermentation** *n* a chemical change brought about in organic substances by living organisms, for example yeast and bacteria, as a result of their enzyme action. < Latin *fervēre* to boil.

fern (fɜːn) *n* a non-flowering plant with feathery, green leaves. < Old English *fearn.*

ferocious (fəˈrəʊʃəs) *adj* extremely fierce or violent. **ferociously** *adv* **ferocity** *n* < Latin *ferox* fierce.

ferret (ˈfɛrɪt) *n* a small animal like a weasel, tamed for hunting rabbits, rats, etc.
• *vb* **1** hunt with ferrets. **2** search. **ferret out** discover by searching. < Latin *fur* thief.

ferrous (ˈfɛrəs) *adj* of or containing iron. < Latin *ferrum* iron.

ferry (ˈfɛrɪ) *vb* **ferried; ferrying 1** carry by boat over water; cross water in a boat. **2** transport regularly from one place to another.
• *n* a boat used for ferrying; place where a ferry operates. < Old English *ferian* to carry.

fertile (ˈfɜːtaɪl) *adj* **1** (of soil) capable of sustaining the abundant growth of plants; productive. **2** able to undergo development and reproduction. **3** (of the mind) having great resourcefulness and activity; inventive: a fertile imagination. **fertility** *n* < Latin *ferre* to bear.

fertilize (ˈfɜːtɪˌlaɪz) *vb* make fertile. **fertilization** *n* **fertilizer** *n* material that is added to soil to make it more fertile.

fervent (ˈfɜːvənt) *adj* showing strong and sincere feeling: a fervent supporter. **fervently** *adv* **fervour** *n* < Latin *fervēre* to boil.

fester (ˈfɛstə) *vb* **1** form pus. **2** cause continuing anger and irritation. **3** decay or rot. < Latin *fistula* ulcer.

festival (ˈfɛstɪvl̩) *n* **1** a day or time of religious or other celebration. **2** a programme or season of cultural events: music festival. **festive** *adj* of or like a feast or festival; merry. **festivity** *n* festive activity. < Latin *festus* of a feast.

festoon (fɛˈstuːn) *n* a garland of flowers, etc., hanging in a curve or loop.
• *vb* decorate with hanging ornaments. < Italian *festa* festival.

fetch (fɛtʃ) *vb* **1** go or come after (something) and bring or take (it) back.

---

female or **feminine?**

These two words are sometimes confused. Female refers to the sex of the animal or to a physical part of such an animal, as in A vixen is a *female* fox.
Feminine means 'of women or the qualities thought typical of or suitable for women' as in *feminine* charms, *feminine* intuitions. It is also used to refer to a gender of words in some languages: La porte is a *feminine* noun in French (see also panel at **host**[1]).

---

2 cause to come. **3** sell for: The vase fetched £1000. **fetch up** (*informal*) **1** arrive (at); end up (in). **2** vomit (food). < Old English *feccan.*

fetching (ˈfɛtʃɪŋ) *adj* attractive; becoming.

fête (feɪt) *n* **1** a festival. **2** an outdoor entertainment with stalls, etc., to raise money: a garden fête.
• *vb* honour with a fête. or other ceremony. < SEE **FEAST.**

fetish (ˈfɛtɪʃ) *n* **1** an object believed to have magical power. **2** anything to which one is irrationally devoted.
< Portuguese *feitiço.* sorcery.

fetter (ˈfɛtə) *n* **1** a chain or shackle for the feet. **2** anything that confines; restraint.
• *vb* **1** put fetters on. **2** bind with or as if with fetters; restrain. < Old English *fetor.*

fettle (ˈfɛtl̩) *n* a state of body and mind: in fine fettle. < Middle English *fetlen* to shape.

feud (fju:d) *n* a long-lasting hostility, esp. between families or clans.
• *vb* carry on a feud. < Middle French *feide.*

feudal (ˈfju:dl̩) *adj* of or like feudalism: the feudal system. **feudalism** *n* the system in medieval Europe in which land was held by a vassal of a lord in exchange for military and other services. **feudalistic** *adj* < Medieval Latin *feodum* feudal land.

fever (ˈfi:və) *n* **1** an abnormally high body temperature; disease marked by this. **2** a state of nervous excitement: fever pitch. **feverish** *adj* **1** having (a slight) fever. **2** of, like, caused by, or causing fever. **3** intensely excited. **feverishly** *adv* < Latin *febris.*

few (fju:) *determiner, pron, n* not many; a small number: a few years ago. **a good few; quite a few** (*informal*) a rather large number. **the few** a small, exclusive group. < Old English *fēawa.* SEE PANEL AT **LESS.**

fez (fɛz) *n, pl* **fezzes**, **fezes** an originally Turkish, conical, felt hat, usually red and with a tassel. < *Fez,* city in Morocco.

fiancé (fɪˈɒnseɪ) fem. **fiancée** *n* a person engaged to be married. < French.

fiasco (fɪˈæskəʊ) *n, pl* **fiascos** a complete, ridiculous failure. < Italian: bottle.

fib (fɪb) *n* a trivial lie.
• *vb* **fibbed; fibbing** tell a fib. **fibber** *n* < perhaps from *fable.*

fibre (ˈfaɪbə) *n* **1** a filament that may be spun into yarn; material made from such yarn. **2** essential substance or character; strength of character: moral fibre. **fibrous** *adj* < Latin *fibra.*

fibreglass (ˈfaɪbəˌglɑ:s) *n* a material made of filaments of glass, used in textiles, insulation, etc.

fibula (ˈfɪbjʊlə) *n* the long, thin, outer bone of the lower part of the leg.
< Latin: clasp.

fiche (fi:ʃ) *n, pl* **fiche, fiches** microfiche.

fickle (ˈfɪkl̩) *adj* changeable in purpose, affections, loyalties, etc. < Old English *ficol* deceitful.

fiction (ˈfɪkʃən) *n* **1** something invented by the imagination. **2** an invented story; class of literature consisting of books containing such stories. **fictional** *adj* **fictitious** *adj* not real; imaginary; pretended: a fictitious name. < Latin *fingere* to shape. SEE PANEL.

fiddle (ˈfɪdl̩) *n* **1** (*informal*) a violin. **2** (*informal*) a dishonest arrangement.
• *vb* **1** (*informal*) play the fiddle.

---

fictional or **fictitious?**

Fictional means 'of or concerned with fiction' as in a *fictional* characterization of actual historical events.

Fictitious means 'imaginary; unreal; false' as in a *fictitious* account; He assumed a *fictitious* name. Careful users distinguish between these two words.

---

fiddling

Fiddle features in a number of expressions, including:

as fit as a fiddle in good health; fully fit: She feels as fit as a fiddle again after her convalescence.

fiddle while Rome burns to behave in a frivolous or lazy manner when urgent action is required. The expression comes from a story that the Roman emperor, Nero, continued playing a lute while he watched Rome being devastated by fire.

play second fiddle (**to someone**) to have a subordinate role (to another person). The expression comes from the roles of first and second violins (fiddles) in an orchestra.

---

2 move the hands or fingers restlessly; fidget. **3** (*informal*) cheat; falsify (accounts, etc.). **fiddler** *n* **fiddling** *adj* trivial; petty. **fiddly** *adj* (*informal*) requiring very close attention to detail. < Old English *fithele.* SEE PANEL.

fiddlesticks (ˈfɪdlˌstɪks) *interj* nonsense.

fidelity (fɪˈdɛlɪtɪ) *n* **1** faithfulness; loyalty. **2** accuracy; exactness. **3** the degree of similarity between reproduced sound and the original. < Latin *fides* faith.

fidget (ˈfɪdʒɪt) *n* **1** restlessness shown by nervous movements. **2** a person who fidgets.
• *vb* move about in a restless, nervous way. **fidgety** *adj* < probably Old Norse *fíkja.*

field (fiːld) *n* **1** a wide stretch of open land, esp. one used for crops or pasture. **2** a piece of land for some particular purpose or producing a natural product: an oilfield. **3** a sports ground. **4** a battlefield. **5** a sphere of knowledge or work: an expert in his field. **6** a sphere of work, for example away from an office or laboratory, where practical work is done. **7** all the competitors in a contest.
• *vb* **1** stop or catch and return (a ball) in cricket. **2** deal successfully with (questions). **fielder** *n* **field events** athletic events, such as jumping and throwing, that do not take place on the track. **field glasses** small, portable binoculars for outdoor use. **field marshal** an army officer of the highest rank. **field sports** outdoor sports such as hunting or racing. < Old English *feld.*

fieldwork (ˈfiːldˌwɜːk) *n* practical work done away from an office or laboratory, by a scientist, social worker, etc. **fieldworker** *n*

fiend (fiːnd) *n* **1** an evil spirit. **2** an extremely wicked person. **3** *(informal)* an addict: a fresh-air fiend. **fiendish** *adj* **fiendishly** *adv* < Old English *feond.*

fierce (fɪəs) *adj* **1** violently cruel; uncontrolled. **2** intense: fierce heat; fierce competition. **fiercely** *adv* **fierceness** *n* < Latin *ferus* wild.

fiery (ˈfaɪərɪ) *adj* **1** consisting of fire; burning; of the colour of fire. **2** full of intense emotion; passionate. **3** easily provoked.

fifteen (ˌfɪfˈtiːn) *n* **1** the number 15. **2** a rugby union football team.
• *determiner, pron* 15 in number. **fifteenth** *determiner, pron, n, adv* < Old English *fiftēne.*

fifth (fɪθ, fɪfθ) *determiner, pron, adv* next after fourth.
• *n* **1** something that is fifth. **2** one of five equal parts of a thing. **fifthly** *adv* < Old English *fīfta.*

fifty (ˈfɪftɪ) *n* the number 50.
• *determiner, pron* 50 in number. **fiftieth** *determiner, pron, n, adv* **fifties** *pl n* the numbers, range of temperatures, ages, or dates in a century from 50–59. **fifty-fifty** *adj, adv* shared or sharing equally. < Old English *fiftig.*

fig (fɪg) *n* one of a group of trees that bear fleshy, pear-shaped fruits; this fruit. < Latin *ficus.*

fight (faɪt) *vb* **fought; fighting 1** struggle against (a person or country) in physical combat or battle. **2** carry on (a war). **3** struggle to endure or overcome: fight an illness. **4** engage in a boxing-match with (a person). **5** strive to obtain or accomplish something.
• *n* **1** an act of fighting; battle; struggle: the fight for freedom. **2** a boxing-match. **3** a verbal disagreement. **fight back** recover, esp. with a struggle; resist. **fighter** *n* **1** a person who fights. **2** a fast military aircraft designed to destroy other aircraft. **fight off** struggle to overcome (an attack, illness, etc.). **fight out** settle (an argument) by fighting: fight it out. < Old English *feohtan.*

figment (ˈfɪgmənt) *n* something that exists only in the imagination. < Latin *fingere* to shape.

figurative (ˈfɪgərətɪv) *adj* using a figure of speech, esp. a metaphor; not literal. **figuratively** *adv*

figure (ˈfɪgə) *n* **1** the symbol of a number. **2** the bodily shape or external form, esp. of a person. **3** a diagram or pictorial illustration in a text. **4** a geometrical shape. **5** a person, esp. with some special qualities.
• *vb* **1** represent in a figure. **2** imagine. **3** take a conspicuous part. **4** (*chiefly US*) consider. **figure-head** *n* **1** an ornamental, carved figure on a ship's bow. **2** a head or chief in name but with no real power. **figure of speech** an expression, such as a simile or metaphor, containing a departure from the literal use of words. **figure out 1** calculate the answer to. **2** understand: I just can't figure him out. **figures** *pl n* arithmetic: good at figures. < Latin *fingere* to form.

filament (ˈfɪləmənt) *n* a single, very thin thread or thread-like strand, such as the fine wire in a light bulb. < Latin *filum* thread.

filch (fɪltʃ) *vb* steal (something of small value); pilfer. < Middle English *filchen,* of unknown origin.

file[1] (faɪl) *n* **1** a folder, box, etc., used to keep papers in order and for reference; contents of this. **2** a line of people, esp. one behind the other. **3** a set of related data in a computer.
• *vb* **1** place in a file. **2** submit or record officially: file an application. **3** march or go in file. < Latin *filum* thread.

file[2] *n* a steel tool with a rough, ridged surface, used for shaping or smoothing.
• *vb* shape or smooth with a file. **filings** *pl n* shavings, etc., removed by a file: iron filings. < Old English *fēol.*

filial (ˈfɪlɪəl) *adj* of or due from a son or daughter, esp. in his or her relationship to a parent: filial duty. < Latin *filius* son.

filibuster (ˈfɪlɪˌbʌstə) *n, vb* (engage in) the use of delaying tactics in a legislative assembly. < Spanish *filibustero* freebooter, pirate.

fill (fɪl) *vb* **1** make or become full. **2** stop up (a hole, crack, etc.). **3** spread through or occupy the whole of: Smoke filled the room. **4** occupy (a position); place a person in (a vacant job). **5** feed; satisfy. **6** occupy (vacant time).
• *n* **1** all that is needed to fill something. **2** all that is needed to satisfy a person's appetite: eat one's fill. **filler** *n* an object or substance used to fill a hole or increase the bulk or strength of something. **fill in 1** complete (the details) in a form. **2** act as a substitute. **filling** *n* **1** something used to fill a hole: a filling for a tooth. **2** a food mixture used to fill sandwiches or cakes. **filling station** a place where petrol, oil, etc., are sold to motorists. **fill in on** inform (someone) about (something). **fill out** make or become bulkier or plumper. < Old English *fyllan.*

fillet (ˈfɪlɪt) *n* a piece of fleshy, boneless meat cut from near the loin or rib; long slice of boneless fish.
• *vb* remove the bones from (a fish). < Latin *filum* thread.

fillip (ˈfɪlɪp) *n* something that stimulates or boosts.
• *vb* stimulate. < movement made with the finger, like the sound.

filly (ˈfɪlɪ) *n* **1** a young female horse, usually of less than four years. **2** (*informal*) a woman or girl. < Old Norse *fylja.*

film (fɪlm) *n* **1** a flexible, cellulose material coated with a light-sensitive substance, used in photography; length of this. **2** a sequence of photographs projected quickly onto a screen so as to create the illusion of movement; story, play, etc., photographed as a film. **3** a thin layer, skin, or covering.
• *vb* make a film (of something). **filmstrip** *n* a strip of film containing still photographs for projection separately. < Old English *filmen* membrane.

filter (ˈfɪltə) *n* **1** a device that allows one substance to pass through it, but not others. **2** an arrangement for filtering traffic.
• *vb* **1** pass through a filter; remove impurities in this way. **2** make a way in or out gradually. **3** (of a line of traffic) be allowed to pass while other traffic is stopped. **filter-tip** *n* a cigarette with a filter at the mouth that absorbs the impurities. < Medieval Latin *filtrum* piece of felt used as a filter.

filth (fɪlθ) *n* **1** foul or disgusting dirt; refuse or uncleanliness. **2** vulgarity or obscenity. **filthy** *adj* **filthily** *adv* **filthiness** *n* < Old English *fylth.*

filtrate (ˈfɪltreɪt) *n* a liquid or gas that has been filtered.
• *vb* filter. **filtration** *n*

fin (fɪn) *n* **1** any of several wing-like organs of a fish, etc., used to propel or guide the body. **2** a part of an aircraft wing that gives stability. **3** a flipper. < Old English *finn.*

final (ˈfaɪnl̩) *adj* **1** coming at the end; last. **2** that cannot be altered; conclusive.
• *n* the last in a series of competitions. **finality** *n* **finally** *adv* **finalist** *n* a competitor in a final. **finalize** *vb* put in a final or complete form; bring to an end. **finals** *pl n* the last examinations in a course. < Latin *finis* end.

finale (fɪˈnɑːlɪ) *n* the last part of a performance or musical composition. < Italian.

finance (ˈfaɪnæns) *n* **1** the management of money. **2** funds or the provision of funds. **3** *pl* resources of money.
• *vb* provide money for. **financial** *adj* **financially** *adv* **financier** *n* a person who arranges finance for businesses. < Middle French *finer* to end, pay.

finch (fɪntʃ) *n* any of a group of songbirds with a hard, conical bill. < Old English *finc.*

find (faɪnd) *vb* **found; finding 1** discover by searching or by chance; obtain. **2** obtain by effort: find the time. **3** perceive or learn. **4** feel or experience: find pleasure. **5** consider to be: find it difficult to believe. **6** supply or provide: find the funds. **7** reach: Water finds its own level. **8** declare (a decision): find him guilty.
• *n* an act of finding something; someone or something, esp. valuable or pleasing, that is found. **finder** *n* **findings** *pl n* the result of an enquiry. **find oneself** discover one's abilities or calling. **find**

out 1 discover (something). **2** detect (a person) who has done wrong. < Old English *findan*.

fine[1] (faɪn) *adj* **1** of very good quality; excellent. **2** (of weather) bright and sunny. **3** very thin or small. **4** with no impurities; refined. **5** not heavy or coarse: fine texture. **6** sharp: a fine edge. **7** subtle: a fine distinction. **8** delicate: fine china. **9** performed with great skill: fine workmanship. **10** (*informal*) awful: a fine mess! **11** in good health and spirits.
• *adv* **1** finely. **2** (*informal*) very well. **finely** *adv* **fineness** *n* **fine arts** painting, sculpture, architecture, etc. < Latin *finis* end.

fine[2] *n* a sum of money paid as a punishment for an offence.
• *vb* punish by a fine. < Latin *finis* end.

finery (ˈfaɪnərɪ) *n* elaborate or showy clothes, jewellery, etc.

finesse (fɪˈnɛs) *n* skilfulness, esp. in handling difficult situations. < Middle French *fin* fine.

finger (ˈfɪŋgə) *n* **1** one of the five parts extending from the hand, esp. one other than the thumb. **2** something like a finger; part of a glove that covers a finger.
• *vb* touch or feel with the fingers.

a finger on the pulse

Finger features in a number of idiomatic expressions, including:

get one's fingers burnt to cause harm, trouble, financial loss, etc., by miscalculation or stupidity.
have a finger in every pie to be involved in a number of different projects.
keep one's finger on the pulse to remain fully aware of the current activities of an organization, etc.
not lift or **raise a finger** not bother to make the slightest effort to help someone.
pull one's finger out to apply oneself with increased vigour.
put one's finger on to identify precisely: I can't quite put my finger on what's wrong.
twist or **wind round one's little finger** to manipulate (someone) easily: Laura is her dad's darling daughter. She can twist him round her little finger and get whatever she wants.

finger-bowl *n* a small bowl of water for rinsing one's fingers at the table. **fingering** *n* the use of one's fingers to play a musical instrument; notation for this. **finger-nail** *n* a nail at the end of a finger. **fingerprint** *n* the trace made by the pattern of the ridges of the fingertip, used as a means of identification. **fingertip** *n* the tip of a finger. < Old English. SEE PANEL.

finicky (ˈfɪnɪkɪ) *adj* **1** too exacting or meticulous; fussy. **2** requiring precise attention to detail. < SEE **FINE[1]**.

finish (ˈfɪnɪʃ) *vb* **1** bring or come to an end. **2** use up. **3** cause the defeat, death, etc., of. **4** give (wood, cloth, etc.) the final, surface effects. **5 finish with** end a relationship with.
• *n* **1** the last part of something. **2** the point at which a race, etc., ends. **3** the texture or appearance of a surface; material used for finishing woodwork, etc. **finishing school** a private school that prepares girls for society by teaching social graces. < Latin *finis* end.

finite (ˈfaɪnaɪt) *adj* limited; not infinite. < Latin *finire* to finish.

fiord (fiːɔːd, fjɔːd) *n* a long, narrow sea inlet between high, steep cliffs, as in Norway. < Old Norse *fjörthr*.

fir (fɜː) *n* any of a group of evergreen trees with needle-like leaves and erect, stout cones; its wood. < Old English *fyrh*.

fire (faɪə) *n* **1** the state of combustion shown in light, flames, heat, and often smoke. **2** a mass of burning material. **3** destructive burning. **4** a domestic gas or electric heater. **5** the firing of guns. **6** intense emotion or passion.
• *vb* **1** propel a bullet or shell from (a gun); detonate. **2** set fire to; ignite. **3** supply with fuel. **4** bake (bricks, pottery, etc.) in a kiln. **5** inspire or excite. **6** (*informal*) dismiss (an employee). **fire-alarm** *n* a bell, siren, etc., that gives warning of a fire. **firearm** *n* a gun, esp. one that is easy to carry. **firebrand** *n* a trouble-maker. **fire-brick** *n* a brick that is resistant to high temperatures, used in furnaces, etc. **fire brigade** an organized group of firemen employed to extinguish fires. **fire-drill** *n* a practice of the procedure to be used in case of fire. **fire-eater** *n* a performer who appears to eat fire. **fire-engine** *n* a vehicle fitted with equipment for fighting fires. **fire-escape** *n* a way of escape from a building in a fire, esp. an outside staircase. **firefly** *n* a kind of night-flying beetle that gives off a bright

light. **fire-irons** *pl n* tools for looking after a domestic fire. **fire-lighter** *n* a piece of flammable material used to help light a domestic fire. **fireman** *n, pl* **firemen 1** a member of a fire brigade. **2** a person who tends a furnace, etc. **fireplace** *n* an open recess in a wall at the base of a chimney for a fire; surrounding structure of this. **fireproof** *adj* capable of resisting damage by fire. **fireside** *n* a place near the fireplace; home. **fire station** a building housing fire-fighting equipment and where firemen stay while on duty. **firewood** *n* wood cut for use as fuel. **firework** *n* **1** a device containing chemicals that burn or explode and produce a spectacular display of light or noise. **2** *pl* a display of fireworks. **3** *pl* an outburst of anger. **firing-line** *n* **1** the position at which troops are sufficiently close to fire on the enemy. **2** the vulnerable, front position in an activity. **firing-squad** *n* a small military group ordered to shoot a condemned person. < Old English *fȳr*. SEE PANEL.

firm[1] (fɜːm) *adj* **1** not yielding when touched or pressed; hard. **2** steady. **3** securely fixed in place. **4** not easily changed; settled. **5** having determination; resolute.
• *adv* firmly.
• *vb* make or become firm. **firmly** *adv* **firmness** *n* < Latin *firmus*.

firm[2] *n* a business unit or enterprise; partnership. < Latin *firmus*.

firmament (ˈfɜːməmənt) *n* the extent of the sky; heavens. < Latin *firmus* firm.

first (fɜːst) *determiner, pron* coming before all others in place, sequence, number, time, or rank.
• *adv* **1** before any other. **2** before doing anything else. **3** for the first time. **4** sooner; preferably: I'll see him dead first!
• *n* **1** the first time, person, thing, etc. **2** the first and lowest forward gear. **3** the highest level of an honours degree. **firstly** *adv* **at first** at or in the beginning. **first aid** immediate medical help given in an emergency. **first-class** *adj* **1** very good; excellent: a first-class performance. **2** (of accommodation, etc.) the most expensive. **3** (of letters) of a delivery service that is faster than second-class. **firsthand** *adj* coming directly from the original source. **first name** a personal or Christian name. **first-rate** *adj* of the best class. < Old English *fyrst*. SEE PANEL.

fiscal (ˈfɪskḷ) *adj* of or relating to government finance, taxes, debts, etc. < Latin *fiscus* money basket.

fish (fɪʃ) *n, pl* **fish, fishes** a cold-blooded animal living in water; its flesh as food.
• *vb* **1** try to catch fish (in). **2** search for something under water or by groping. **fish cake** a small cake of shredded fish and mashed potato. **fisherman** *n, pl* **fishermen** a man who fishes as an occupation or for pleasure. **fishery** *n* the

Fire away!

Fire features in a number of idiomatic expressions, including:

fire away to begin to ask questions: I've not got a lot of time to answer your questions, so fire away!
hang fire to wait. The expression derives from the delay in firing the charge of a gun.
have many irons in the fire to be involved in many activities at the same time.
play with fire to take great risks: Anyone who takes drugs regularly is really playing with fire.

first things first

First features in a number of expressions, including:

first come, first served people who arrive or apply first will be served or dealt with first.
first-footing *n* the Scottish tradition of being the first to enter a household in the New Year.
first-fruits *pl n* the first of a season's agricultural produce; first results of an undertaking.
First Lady the wife or hostess of a president or state governor of the USA.
first night the first public performance of a play.
first refusal the option to buy something before it is offered to others.
first thing early in the morning.
first things first priorities must be attended to first.
get to first base to reach the first important stage in a series: The plan was so badly thought out that it didn't even get to first base. The expression derives from the completion of the first of four sections in scoring a run in baseball.

business of catching fish; part of the sea where fish are caught. **fish finger** a small oblong-shaped portion of fish coated with breadcrumbs or batter. **fish for** try to obtain (compliments, etc.). **fishing** *n* the occupation or sport of catching fish. **fishing-rod** *n* a long, thin pole to which a line, hook, and usually a reel are attached, used in fishing. **fishmonger** *n* a shopkeeper who sells fish. **fishy** *adj* **1** of or like fish, esp. in smell or taste. **2** (*informal*) causing doubt or suspicion. < Old English *fisc*. SEE PANEL.

fission (ˈfɪʃən) *n* **1** the splitting of an atomic nucleus, with a release of energy. **2** (*biology*) reproduction in which an organism splits into two or more equal parts, each part becoming a new organism. < Latin *findere* to split.

fist (fɪst) *n* the hand with the fingers tightly closed into the palm. < Old English *fyst*.

fisticuffs (ˈfɪstɪˌkʌfs) *pl n* (*humorous*) fighting with the fists.

fit[1] (fɪt) *adj* **fitter; fittest 1** adapted or suitable for a purpose. **2** in a suitable state; ready. **3** healthy. **4** right and proper.
• *vb* **fitted; fitting 1** be or make suitable for. **2** be or make the right size or shape for (a person). **3** move or adjust until in the right place. **4** agree or correspond with; match: The theory fits all the facts.
• *n* the way in which something, esp. clothing, fits. **fitly** *adv* **fitness** *n* **fit in 1** be in agreement or harmony with. **2** find or make space or time for. **fit out** or **up** provide with necessary equipment. **fitter** *n* **1** a person who fits clothes. **2** a person skilled in the assembly and adjustment of machinery. < Middle English *fitten*.

fit[2] *n* **1** a sudden, physical seizure with convulsions. **2** a brief spell of an illness or particular symptoms. **3** a sudden outburst of emotion or activity: a fit of rage. **fitful** *adj* occurring in short, irregular periods. **fitfully** *adv* **in fits and starts** in a jerky, irregular manner. < Old English *fitt* conflict.

fitment (ˈfɪtmənt) *n* a piece of equipment such as an item of built-in furniture.

fitting (ˈfɪtɪŋ) *adj* appropriate or suitable; proper.
• *n* **1** the act of having clothes, etc., fitted. **2** an accessory or part: a light fitting.

five (faɪv) *n* the number 5.
• *determiner, pron* 5 in number. **fiver** *n* (*informal*) £5; a five-pound note. **fives** *n* a game in which players hit a ball with their gloved hands against certain areas of a three- or four-walled court. < Old English *fīf*.

fix (fɪks) *vb* **1** make or become firm or stable. **2** direct or hold (the eyes or attention) firmly. **3** specify or establish; arrange: fix a date. **4** repair or mend. **5** (*informal*) get even with. **6** (*informal*) influence unfairly, as by bribery.
• *n* **1** (*informal*) a position of difficulty or embarrassment. **2** the finding of the position (of a ship or aircraft) by radio, etc. **3** (*informal*) something influenced unfairly. **4** (*informal*) an addict's dose of a narcotic drug. **fixation** *n* an attachment or preoccupation, esp. an obsessive one. **fixative** *n* something that fixes, hardens, or sets. **fixture** *n* **1** something fixed to a building as a permanent part: fixtures and fittings. **2** a date or time for a sporting event; this event. < Latin *figere* to fasten.

fizz (fɪz) *vb* make a hissing, bubbling sound.
• *n* **1** this sound. **2** excitement; liveliness. **3** (*informal*) a fizzy drink. **fizzy** *adj* **fizziness** *n* < probably like the sound.

fizzle (ˈfɪzl̩) *vb* make a spluttering, bubbling sound. **fizzle out** (*informal*) end in a disappointing way. < probably alteration of *fist* to break wind.

fjord (fjɔːd) SEE **FIORD**.

flab (flæb) *n* (*informal*) soft, flabby fat on the body. **flabby** *adj* not strong or firm. **flabbily** *adv* **flabbiness** *n* < alteration of *flappy*.

flabbergast (ˈflæbəˌgɑːst) *vb* (*informal*)

---

fish or **ghoti?**

One of the most vigorous advocates of spelling reform was the Irish dramatist, George Bernard Shaw, 1856–1950. Following in the wake of other notable critics such as Charles Darwin and Alfred Lord Tennyson, Shaw pointed to the shortcomings of the existing system by his spelling of fish as ghoti, where the gh sounds like that in enough, the o like that in women, and the ti like that in nation.

Shaw felt that little could be done to reduce the discrepancies between sounds and spellings unless a new, extended alphabet were produced with at least 40 characters. He left it as a provision in his will that such an alphabet be designed and published.

overwhelm with great shock or surprise. < perhaps from *flabby* + *aghast.*

flag[1] (flæg) *n* a usually rectangular piece of cloth with a special design, often attached to a staff or rope and used as the symbol of a country, organization, etc., or as a signal.
• *vb* **flagged; flagging 1** put a flag on. **2** signal with or as if with a flag; esp. to stop: flag a vehicle down. < origin uncertain.

flag[2] *vb* **flagged; flagging** lose strength; become feeble or weak. < origin unknown.

flagon (ˈflægən) *n* **1** a large bottle or container, used esp. for wine or cider. **2** a large vessel with a handle, spout, and narrow neck. < Late Latin *flasco* flask.

flagrant (ˈfleɪgrənt) *adj* undertaken in an open, unashamed manner; outrageous. **flagrantly** *adv* < Latin *flagrare* to burn. SEE PANEL AT **BLATANT.**

flagship (ˈflægˌʃɪp) *n* **1** a ship that carries the commander of a fleet. **2** a firm's best or most important product.

flagstone (ˈflægˌstəʊn) *n* a flat piece of hard stone used for paving. < *flag:* turf, from Old Norse *flaga* slab of stone.

flail (fleɪl) *n* a tool consisting of a wooden handle and a free-swinging stick, used for threshing grain.
• *vb* **1** strike with or as if with a flail. **2** wave or swing about. < Latin *flagellum* whip.

flair (flɛə) *n* **1** natural ability to do or perceive something. **2** (*informal*) smartness and sophistication; stylishness. < Latin *fragrare* to smell. SEE PANEL.

flak (flæk) *n* **1** the fire from anti-aircraft guns. **2** (*informal*) strong criticism or opposition. SEE PANEL.

flake (fleɪk) *n* **1** a small, loose piece: a snow-flake. **2** a flat, thin layer; chip.
• *vb* **1** come off in flakes. **2** form or separate into flakes. **flaky** *adj* **flake out** (*informal*) collapse or faint. < Scandinavian.

flamboyant (flæmˈbɔɪənt) *adj* **1** very decorative and showy. **2** (of a person) having a very showy manner and appearance. **flamboyance** *n* **flamboyantly** *adv* < French *flamboyer* to flame.

flame (fleɪm) *n* **1** the tongue-shaped part of a fire. **2** a reddish-orange colour; brightness. **3** intense passion or love.
• *vb* **1** burn with flames. **2** break out very suddenly or passionately. < Latin *flamma* flame.

flamenco (fləˈmɛŋkəʊ) *n, pl* **flamencos** a type of gypsy song or dance from Andalusia in southern Spain. < Spanish: like a gypsy.

flamingo (fləˈmɪŋgəʊ) *n, pl* **flamingos** a large, web-footed, wading bird with pink-and-red feathers and a long neck. < Portuguese, from Latin *flamma* flame.

flammable (ˈflæməbḷ) *adj* liable to catch fire easily and rapidly. **flammability** *n* SEE PANEL.

flan (flæn) *n* an open pastry or sponge tart containing a sweet or savoury filling. < Late Latin *flado* flat cake.

flange (flændʒ) *n* a projecting rim or collar. < origin uncertain.

flank (flæŋk) *n* **1** the fleshy side of an animal between the ribs and the hip. **2** the side of a building or mountain. **3** the side of a navy or military formation.
• *vb* be situated at the side of. < Old French *flanc.*

---

flair or **flare?**

Flair is 'a natural ability to do or perceive something' as in She has a real *flair* for writing.

Flare is a noun or verb. As a noun it means 'a sudden burst of flame; blaze of light' as in solar *flares,* landing *flares.* As a verb flare means 'to burst into flame; burst into a sudden activity or intensity' as in Violent quarrels *flared* up again.

Both can be used in the context of fashions: flair meaning 'stylishness; sophistication' and flare referring to a widening towards the lower edge of something, as in *flared* trousers.

---

flak

Flak or 'anti-aircraft fire' is an acronym formed upon the German phrase *Fl*ieger *A*bwehr *K*anonen, literally 'aircraft defence guns'.

The word is also used in an informal, metaphorical way to mean 'heavy criticism': 'The government's plan to withdraw aid has come under a lot of flak from the opposition.' Although flak has developed a figurative sense, the derived phrase flak jacket has undergone no such extension of meaning.

flannel (ˈflænl̩) *n* **1** a soft, light, woollen fabric. **2** a small piece of cloth used for washing the face, etc. **3** (*informal*) flattery; nonsense. **flannelette** *n* a cotton imitation of flannel. **flannels** *pl n* clothes made of flannel, esp. men's trousers. < probably Welsh *gwlanen* woollen fabric.

flap (flæp) *vb* **flapped; flapping 1** move up and down or from side to side: The curtains were flapping in the wind. **2** (*informal*) become flustered; panic. **3** give a light blow to, with a flat object.
• *n* **1** the action or noise made by flapping. **2** a light blow with a flat object. **3** a wide piece hinged or fixed at one side, for example the surface fixed to the edge of an aircraft wing. **4** (*informal*) a state of panic. < probably like the sound.

flapjack (ˈflæpˌdʒæk) *n* a chewy biscuit made with oats and syrup.

flare (flɛə) *vb* **1** burn with an unsteady or sudden bright flame. **2** burst into sudden and intense excitement, activity, etc. **3** widen towards the lower edge.
• *n* **1** a sudden burst of flame. **2** a device producing a blaze of light, used as an illumination, signal, etc. **3** a flared shape. < origin unknown. SEE PANEL AT **FLAIR.**

flash (flæʃ) *vb* **1** give out a sudden, brief, or intermittent bright light. **2** move very quickly. **3** come very quickly (into one's sight or mind). **4** signal or communicate with light. **5** (*informal*) show suddenly and briefly. **6** (*informal*) display in a showy way. **7** (*slang*) expose oneself indecently.
• *n* **1** a sudden burst of light. **2** a sudden display of perception, feeling, etc. **3** a very brief time. **4** a brief news report on radio or television. **5** an emblem, etc., worn on a military uniform.
• *adj* flashy. **flasher** *n* **flashback** *n* a return in a story, film, etc., to an earlier time. **flashbulb** *n* a bulb used to produce a flash of light in photography. **flashcube** *n* a small cube housing four flashbulbs. **flashlight** *n* **1** the sudden, brief light emitted artificially for taking photographs. **2** (*chiefly US*) an electric torch. **flashpoint** *n* **1** the temperature at which vapour from a volatile liquid will ignite. **2** the point at which violent action breaks out. **flashy** *adj* showy; superficially attractive. < origin uncertain. SEE PANEL.

flask (flɑːsk) *n* **1** a bottle with a narrow neck. **2** a vacuum flask. < Late Latin *flasco*.

flat[1] (flæt) *adj* **flatter; flattest 1** having a smooth, level surface. **2** lying at full length; spread out. **3** having a broad, smooth surface and little depth. **4** (of a tyre) lacking air; deflated. **5** (of a battery) discharged. **6** (of a musical note) lower in pitch by a semitone. **7** absolute: a flat denial. **8** fixed: charge a flat rate. **9** lacking excitement; dull. **10** (of a drink) having lost its effervescence.
• *adv* **1** in a flat manner: He fell flat on the ground. **2** exactly: She ran there in ten seconds flat. **3** completely: That goes flat against all the rules. **4** lower than the correct musical pitch.
• *n* **1** level ground; flat part or surface.

flammable or **inflammable?**

When used to describe materials, flammable and inflammable share the same meaning. A night-dress which is either flammable or inflammable is liable to catch fire easily. However, the prefix in-often combines with a word to mean 'not', as in inefficient and inedible. There is therefore a potential danger that inflammable may be misunderstood to mean 'not flammable'. For this reason the use of inflammable on warning labels is discouraged by the British Standards Institution which, to avoid the risk of what could prove to be tragic misunderstandings, advocates the use of flammable. The word which means *'not* liable to catch fire easily' is non-flammable.

a flash in the pan

Someone or something whose sudden success turns out to be short-lived and unrepeated is sometimes referred to as a flash in the pan: 'Her first record actually made the charts, but it was just a flash in the pan; within a year she'd stopped recording.'

The expression derives from the days of the less than totally reliable flintlock musket. A flash in the pan occurred when the priming (in the pan of the gun) fired (with a flash), but nevertheless failed to explode the charge. What seemed to be a promising start came to nothing.

2 a musical note one semitone lower than the corresponding note of natural pitch, shown by the sign ♭. **3** the season of races over flat ground for horses. **flatly** *adv* **flatness** *n* **flatten** *vb* make or become flat. < Old Norse *flatr*.

flat[2] *n* a self-contained set of rooms on one floor used for living in. **flatlet** *n* a small flat. < alteration of Scottish *flet* inner part of a house.

flat-fish (ˈflætˌfɪʃ) *n, pl* **flat-fish, flat-fishes** any of a number of fish with a flat body, including the flounder, plaice, halibut, and sole.

flatter (ˈflætə) *vb* **1** praise (a person) too much, esp. in order to win favour. **2** gratify by honouring: We were flattered to be invited. **3** represent too favourably **4** deceive (oneself). **flatterer** *n* **flattery** *n* < Old French *flater* to lick.

flaunt (flɔːnt) *vb* **1** display proudly or ostentatiously; show off. **2** wave freely; flutter. < perhaps Scandinavian. SEE PANEL.

flautist (ˈflɔːtɪst) *n* a flute-player. < Italian *flauto* flute.

flavour (ˈfleɪvə) *n* **1** the combination of taste and smell brought about by a substance in the mouth; special taste. **2** a special quality or characteristic. • *vb* give a flavour to; season. **flavouring** *n* a substance used to give a special flavour to food. < Old French *flaour*.

flaw (flɔː) *n* **1** an imperfection; blemish. **2** a weakness: a flaw in an argument. • *vb* spoil with a flaw. **flawless** *adj* **flawlessly** *adv* **flawlessness** *n* < probably Scandinavian.

flax (flæks) *n* a plant with narrow leaves and blue flowers, grown for its fibre and oily seeds; its fibre. < Old English *fleax*.

flea (fliː) *n* a small, wingless, jumping, blood-sucking insect. **fleabite** *n* the bite of a flea; slight annoyance or expense. **flea market** an open-air market selling second-hand goods. < Old English *flēa*.

flaunt or **flout?**

Flaunt means 'to display in a showy way; show off' as in *flaunting* one's wealth. Flout means 'to show scorn or contempt for'. The two words are sometimes confused, flaunt on occasion being used instead of flout, as in He delights in *flaunting* the law of the land. Flout is correct here.

fleck (flɛk) *n* **1** a small mark of colour. **2** a grain; particle. **flecked** *adj* marked or covered with flecks. < probably Old Norse *flekkr*.

fled (flɛd) SEE **FLEE**.

fledge (flɛdʒ) *vb* **1** rear until ready to fly or act independently. **2** grow the feathers needed for flying. **fledgeling** *n* **1** a young bird that is just fledged. **2** a young, inexperienced person. < Old English *-flycge*.

flee (fliː) *vb* **fled; fleeing 1** run away from danger, etc. **2** run away from: flee the country. **3** disappear quickly. < Old English *flēon*.

fleece (fliːs) *n* **1** the wool of a sheep, etc. **2** a soft, woolly covering or lining. • *vb* (*informal*) deprive of money, etc., by fraud; overcharge. **fleecy** *adj* < Old English *flēos*.

fleet[1] (fliːt) *n* **1** a number of warships under one command. **2** a country's naval force. **3** a number of aircraft, ships, buses, etc., operating under the same owner. < Old English *flēot* ship.

fleet[2] *adj* swift; rapid. **fleeting** *adj* moving quickly; brief: a fleeting view. < probably Old English *flēotan* to float, glide quickly.

flesh (flɛʃ) *n* **1** the soft substance of the body, esp. muscular parts. **2** (*informal*) excess weight; fat. **3** the edible part of an

in the flesh

Flesh features in a number of idiomatic expressions, including:

flesh and blood 1 one's family: help one's own flesh and blood. **2** human nature, especially considered in terms of its frailty.
in the flesh in person; actually present: It was Paul McCartney in the flesh!
make one's flesh creep or **crawl** to cause one to feel a great loathing.
one's pound of flesh the full amount of something owed to a person, even though great suffering may be experienced in paying it back. The origin of the expression is Shakespeare's 'The Merchant of Venice', Act 4, Scene 1, in which the usurer Shylock tries to enforce an agreement that would allow him to remove a pound of the merchant Antonio's flesh.

animal. **4** the pulpy part of fruits and vegetables. **5** a pinkish-white colour. **6** the body, esp. as distinguished from the soul. **7** human nature, esp. its sensual aspects. **8** all mankind. **fleshy** *adj* **1** of or like flesh. **2** having much flesh. **3** pulpy. **fleshiness** *n* < Old English *flæsc*. SEE PANEL.

flew (fluː) SEE FLY[2].

flex (flɛks) *n* a flexible, insulated electric cable.
• *vb* **1** bend or be bent. **2** move (a muscle) so as to bend a limb or joint. **flexible** *adj* **1** able to be bent easily without breaking. **2** adaptable. **flexibility** *n* **flexibly** *adv* < Latin *flectere* to bend.

flick (flɪk) *vb* **1** hit lightly with a quick, sharp movement; make such a movement. **2** remove with flicks.
• *n* a quick, light movement. **flick-knife** *n* a pocket knife with a blade that springs out when a button is pressed. **flick through** look at (a magazine, etc.) quickly or idly. < like the sound.

flicker (ˈflɪkə) *vb* **1** burn or shine unsteadily or irregularly. **2** move unsteadily or irregularly.
• *n* a flickering movement or light. < Old English *flicorian*.

flight[1] (flaɪt) *n* **1** movement through the air, esp. using wings. **2** a journey through air or space. **3** a group of flying birds. **4** a set of stairs. **5** a mental rising above the ordinary: a flight of imagination. < Old English *flyht*.

flight[2] *n* fleeing; running away. < Middle English *fliht*.

flighty (ˈflaɪtɪ) *adj* irresponsible or frivolous. **flightily** *adv* **flightiness** *n*

flimsy (ˈflɪmzɪ) *adj* **1** not strong or substantial. **2** of poor quality or workmanship. **3** not convincing: a flimsy excuse. **flimsily** *adv* **flimsiness** *n* < origin uncertain.

flinch (flɪntʃ) *vb* draw back suddenly as from fear. < Middle French *flenchir*.

fling (flɪŋ) *vb* **flung; flinging 1** throw, esp. with force. **2** put suddenly or violently. **3** direct (oneself or one's energies) strongly.
• *n* **1** the act of flinging. **2** a period of self-indulgence: a final fling. **3** a kind of vigorous dance: a Highland fling. < Scandinavian.

flint (flɪnt) *n* **1** a very hard kind of rock that makes sparks when struck with steel; piece of this. **2** a material such as an alloy used to produce a spark. < Old English.

flip (flɪp) *vb* **flipped; flipping 1** toss (something) with a sharp movement so that it turns over in the air. **2** flick. **3** (*informal*) lose one's self-control or sanity.
• *n* the action of flipping something. **flip side** the less popular side of a gramophone record. < probably like the sound.

flippant (ˈflɪpənt) *adj* not showing proper respect or seriousness. **flippancy** *n* **flippantly** *adv* < SEE **FLIP.**

flipper (ˈflɪpə) *n* **1** the flat, broad limb of certain sea-animals such as seals, used for swimming. **2** one of a pair of flat, rubber, paddle-like attachments worn on the feet in underwater swimming.

flirt (flɜːt) *vb* **1** act amorously but without serious intentions. **2 flirt with** show a casual interest in.
• *n* a person who flirts. **flirtation** *n* **flirtatious** *adj* **flirtatiously** *adv* < origin uncertain.

flit (flɪt) *vb* **flitted; flitting 1** move or fly lightly and quickly. **2** leave hurriedly and secretly.
• *n* the act of flitting. < Old Norse *flytja* to carry.

float (fləʊt) *vb* **1** rest or cause to rest on the surface of a liquid. **2** drift gently. **3** move about aimlessly. **4** start (a business). **5** allow the rate of exchange of (a currency) to vary.
• *n* **1** a thing designed to float on a liquid, such as a cork. **2** a very low, flat lorry: a milk float. **3** a sum of money used to provide change or for small expenses. < Old English *flēotan*.

flock[1] (flɒk) *n* **1** a group of animals or birds of one kind, esp. sheep. **2** the congregation of a church. **3** a large group.
• *vb* gather or move in a crowd. < Old English *flocc* crowd. SEE PANEL.

flock[2] *n* **1** a tuft of wool or cotton fibre. **2** wool or cotton waste. < Latin *floccus*.

floe (fləʊ) *n* a sheet of floating ice. < probably Norwegian *flo* layer.

flog (flɒg) *vb* **flogged; flogging 1** beat severely with a rod, etc. **2** (*informal*) sell. < probably Latin *flagellare* to whip.

flood (flʌd) *n* **1** an overflowing of water, esp. onto normally dry land. **2** an overwhelming quantity. **3** the flowing in of the tide: the flood-tide. **4 the Flood** the flood described in Genesis which destroyed all living things except Noah, his family, and the creatures on his ark.
• *vb* **1** cover with a flood. **2** pour forth in a flood; become flooded. **3** come in overwhelming quantities: Applications

flooded in. **flood out** force to leave (one's house, etc.) because of a flood. < Old English *flōd.*

floodgate (ˈflʌdˌgeɪt) *n* **1** a gate for shutting out or allowing in water. **2** a control of an outburst.

floodlight (ˈflʌdˌlaɪt) *n* a broad beam of artificial light to illuminate a stage, building, etc.; source producing such light.
• *vb* **floodlit; floodlighting** illuminate with such a light.

floor (flɔː) *n* **1** the surface of a room on which one stands. **2** the bottom of the sea or a cave, etc. **3** a storey of a building. **4** the part of a legislative assembly where members sit; members themselves or their right to speak.
• *vb* **1** cover with a floor. **2** knock down. **3** (*informal*) baffle, confuse, or overwhelm. < Old English *flōr.*

flop (flɒp) *vb* **flopped; flopping 1** hang or sway loosely and heavily. **2** fall or move in a heavy or awkward manner. **3** (*informal*) fail completely.
• *n* **1** a flopping movement or sound. **2** (*informal*) a complete failure.
• *adv* with a flop. **floppy** *adj* hanging loosely; not hard and rigid. **floppy disk** a flexible disk with a magnetic coating, used to store data for a computer. < alteration of *flap.*

flora (ˈflɔːrə) *n* all the plants of an area or period of time. **floral** *adj* of flowers. **florist** *n* a person who sells or grows flowers. < Latin *flōs* flower.

florid (ˈflɒrɪd) *adj* **1** (of the complexion) ruddy. **2** flowery or ornate. < Latin *floridus* blooming.

floss (flɒs) *n* fine silk thread. **flossy** *adj* < origin unknown.

flotation (fləʊˈteɪʃən) *n* the starting, esp. financing, of a new business.

flotilla (fləˈtɪlə) *n* a small fleet of ships; fleet of small ships. < Spanish.

flotsam (ˈflɒtsəm) *n* floating wreckage, esp. of a ship. **flotsam and jetsam** odds and ends; vagrants. < Old French *floter* to float.

flounce[1] (flaʊns) *vb* move in an exaggerated or posturing way. < probably Scandinavian.

flounce[2] *n* a wide, ornamental frill, as on a skirt. < Old French *froncir* to wrinkle.

flounder[1] (ˈflaʊndə) *vb* **1** move with difficulty; struggle. **2** speak or act in an awkward, ineffectual way. < probably blend of *founder* + *blunder.*

flounder[2] *n* a kind of small, edible flat-fish. < Scandinavian.

flour (flaʊə) *n* **1** the powdered grain of wheat or other cereal, used in baking. **2** any finely powdered substance.
• *vb* put flour on or in. **floury** *adj* < Middle English *flur* finer portion of meal, flower.

flourish (ˈflʌrɪʃ) *vb* **1** grow strongly; thrive. **2** achieve success; prosper. **3** make showy, waving motions; brandish.
• *n* **1** a showy or dramatic action. **2** a flowery decoration, as in writing. **3** a fanfare. < Latin *flos* flower.

flout (flaʊt) *vb* show scorn or contempt for. < probably Middle English *flouten* to play the flute. SEE PANEL AT **FLAUNT.**

flow (fləʊ) *vb* **1** move as a stream. **2** circulate. **3** proceed smoothly and evenly. **4** hang loosely and freely: flowing hair. **5** (of the tide) to rise. **6** be derived; come.
• *n* **1** a flowing; amount that flows. **2** the flowing in of the tide towards the land. **3** a steady movement: the flow of ideas. **flow chart** a diagram that shows the progress of something through a series of operations. < Old English *flōwan.*

flower (flaʊə) *n* **1** the part of many plants that produces seeds; blossom. **2** a plant grown for its blossom. **3** the best part of something.
• *vb* **1** (of a plant) produce flowers. **2** cause to bear flowers. **3** decorate with a floral design. **4** reach the best period or

---

a flock of sheep

A word that refers to a group of people, creatures, or things as in a flock of sheep, is a kind of collective noun called a *group collective.*

Further examples of group collective nouns are:

a gaggle of geese
a gang of thieves
a herd of cattle
a litter of puppies
a pack of wolves
a peal of bells
a plague of locusts
a pride of lions
a school of porpoises
a swarm of bees

On whether to say a herd of cattle *is* ... or a herd of cattle *are* ..., see panel at **govern.**

---

condition. **flowerpot** *n* a pot, esp. one shaped like a small bucket, in which a plant may be grown. **flowery** *adj* **1** covered with flowers. **2** (of language) very ornate. < Latin *flos*.

flown (fləʊn) SEE **FLY**[2].

flu (flu:) *n* (*informal*) influenza.

fluctuate (ˈflʌktjʊˌeɪt) *vb* vary irregularly; move up and down. **fluctuation** *n* < Latin *fluctus* wave.

flue (flu:) *n* **1** a channel in a chimney for smoke. **2** a channel for conveying heat. < origin unknown.

fluent (ˈflu:ənt) *adj* **1** (of a person) able to speak or write (a particular language) easily and smoothly. **2** flowing easily and smoothly. **fluency** *n* **fluently** *adv* < Latin *fluere* to flow.

fluff (flʌf) *n* soft, light, downy substance.
• *vb* **1** make or become fluffy. **2** (*informal*) make a mistake (in); bungle. **fluffy** *adj* **1** having or covered with fluff. **2** light and soft. < perhaps alteration of *flue* down, from Flemish *vluwe*.

fluid (ˈflu:ɪd) *n* any material that flows; liquid or gas.
• *adj* **1** able to flow; not solid or fixed. **2** flowing easily and smoothly. **fluidity** *n* **fluid ounce** a liquid measure (in the UK equal to one-twentieth of a pint, 0.0284 litre, USA, one-sixteenth of a pint, 0.0295 litre). < Latin *fluere* to flow.

fluke (flu:k) *n* an accidental stroke of good luck. < origin unknown.

flummox (ˈflʌməks) *vb* bewilder or perplex. < origin unknown.

flung (flʌŋ) SEE **FLING**.

flunk (flʌŋk) *vb* (*chiefly US informal*) fail, esp. in an examination. < perhaps blend of *flinch* + *funk* fear.

fluorescence (ˌflʊəˈrɛsəns) *n* the emission of light by a substance while it is exposed to light or other radiation of a shorter wavelength. **fluorescent** *adj* **1** of or having fluorescence. **2** glowing, because of fluorescence. < ultimately Latin *fluor* flux.

fluoride (ˈflʊəˌraɪd) *n* a compound of fluorine, esp. one that combats tooth decay.

fluorine (ˈflʊəri:n) *n* a chemical element that is usually a pale yellow toxic gas.

flurry (ˈflʌrɪ) *n* **1** a light gust of wind; brief fall of snow or rain. **2** a commotion; brief burst of activity.
• *vb* **flurried; flurrying** make or become excited or nervous. < origin uncertain.

flush[1] (flʌʃ) *vb* **1** glow or blush. **2** flow and spread suddenly. **3** send water quickly through (a channel) or into (a toilet) in order to cleanse or empty it. **4** excite: flushed with confidence.
• *n* **1** flushing of the face; blush. **2** a sudden flow of water. **3** a surge of feeling; fresh and strong state.
• *adj* **1** level or even (with). **2** (*informal*) well supplied with money. < Middle English *flusschen* to fly up suddenly.

flush[2] *n* a hand of playing-cards all of the same suit. < Latin *fluxus* flow.

fluster (ˈflʌstə) *vb* make confused or nervous.
• *n* a flustered state. < probably Scandinavian.

flute (flu:t) *n* **1** a high-pitched, keyed wind instrument that consists of a long pipe stopped at one end and is played by blowing air across a side hole. **2** an ornamental groove. **fluted** *adj* decorated with grooves. < Middle French *flahute*.

fluting (ˈflu:tɪŋ) *n* a series of ornamental grooves.

flutter (ˈflʌtə) *vb* **1** move the wings quickly and lightly. **2** move or wave quickly and lightly.
• *n* **1** a fluttering movement. **2** an excited state. **3** (*informal*) a bet. < Old English *flotian* to float.

flux (flʌks) *n* **1** a state of continual change. **2** a substance used to assist in soldering. **3** a flow or flowing. < ultimately Latin *fluere* to flow.

fly[1] (flaɪ) *n* **1** a two-winged insect. **2** a natural or artificial fly used as a bait in fishing. < Old English *flēoge*.

fly[2] *vb* **flew; flown; flying 1** move through

flying colours

Fly features in a number of idiomatic expressions, including:
fly-by-night *adj* unreliable, especially in financial matters.
flying saucer an unidentified, disc-shaped flying object, alleged to come from space.
flying start a good, vigorous beginning that gives an advantage: get off to a flying start.
fly off the handle to lose one's temper.
with flying colours with great success: He passed the exam with flying colours. The phrase comes from victorious fighting ships leaving a battle with their flags still flying at the mast-heads.

the air by using wings. **2** travel through the air or space. **3** travel in an aircraft. **4** operate an aircraft. **5** wave or float in the air. **6** move, go, or pass quickly: Time flies! **7** pass suddenly into a state that is mentioned: fly into a rage. **fly at** attack suddenly.
• *n* a flap of material with buttons or a zip, esp. at the front of trousers. < Old English *flēogan.* SEE PANEL.

flyer (ˈflaɪə) *n* **1** a person or thing that flies or moves very fast. **2** an airman.

flying (ˈflaɪɪŋ) *adj* **1** very brief; hasty: a flying visit. **2** prepared for movement: flying pickets.

flyover (ˈflaɪˌəʊvə) *n* a bridge that carries a road or railway over another.

flywheel (ˈflaɪˌwiːl) *n* a heavy wheel that is used to even out fluctuations in the speed of an engine or to store energy.

foal (fəʊl) *n* the young of a horse or related animal.
• *vb* give birth to (a foal). < Old English *fola.*

foam (fəʊm) *n* **1** a mass of small bubbles on the surface of a liquid. **2** a frothy mass, as in saliva or perspiration. **3** a light, cellular mass made from liquid rubber, plastic, etc.
• *vb* **1** produce or form foam. **2** froth at the mouth, esp. in anger. **foamy** *adj* < Old English *fām.*

fob off (fɒb) *vb* **fobbed; fobbing** get someone to buy, accept, etc., something of little or no value. < Middle English *fobben* to cheat.

focus (ˈfəʊkəs) *n, pl* **focuses, foci 1** the point at which rays of light, etc., meet or from which they appear to diverge. **2** the point at which an object is most clearly seen through a lens, etc. **3** adjustment on a lens to produce a clear image. **4** the state into which something becomes clearly understood. **5** a centre of interest or activity.
• *vb* **1** bring or come into focus. **2** adjust the focus of. **3** cause to be directed or concentrated on. **focal** *adj* of or at a focus. < Latin: fireplace, hearth. SEE PANEL AT **BUS.**

fodder (ˈfɒdə) *n* coarse food for cattle, horses, etc.; for example, hay and straw. < Old English *fōdor.*

foe (fəʊ) *n* an enemy. < Old English *fāh* hostile.

foetus (ˈfiːtəs) *n, pl* **foetuses** the embryo of a mammal, esp. a human being from eight weeks after conception to birth. **foetal** *adj* of a foetus. < Latin *fetus* offspring.

fog (fɒg) *n* **1** a thick mist that is difficult to see through. **2** a state of confusion or perplexity. **3** something that obscures or confuses.
• *vb* **fogged; fogging 1** cover or become covered with fog. **2** perplex or confuse. **foggy** *adj* **fogginess** *n* **foghorn** *n* a horn, esp. on a ship, sounded as a warning in fog. < probably Scandinavian.

foible (ˈfɔɪbl̩) *n* a small, unimportant weakness in character or behaviour. < Old French *feble* feeble.

foil[1] (fɔɪl) *vb* baffle or frustrate. < Middle English *foilen* to trample.

foil[2] *n* **1** a paper-thin sheet of metal. **2** someone or something that contrasts strongly with another. < Latin *folium* leaf.

foil[3] *n* a long, thin, blunted sword used in fencing. < origin unknown.

foist (fɔɪst) *vb* get someone to accept, tolerate, etc., something inferior or untrue. < probably Dutch *vuisten* to hide in one's hand.

fold[1] (fəʊld) *vb* **1** bend or be bent double so that one part lies on another. **2** be or become folded. **3** clasp together and entwine: fold one's arms. **4** wrap or envelop. **5** (*informal*) fail completely: The business folded.
• *n* **1** a folded part. **2** a crease or line made by folding. **3** a bend in rock strata produced by compression. **fold in** or **into** mix gently with other ingredients, without stirring or beating. **fold up 1** collapse with pain or laughter. **2** collapse; cease business: The company folded up when orders stopped coming in. < Old English *fealdan.*

fold[2] *n* **1** an enclosure for sheep. **2** a group of people with the same faith, beliefs, or aims. < Old English *falod.*

folder (ˈfəʊldə) *n* **1** a folded cover for holding loose papers. **2** a folded leaflet.

foliage (ˈfəʊlɪɪdʒ) *n* the leaves of a plant or group of plants. < Latin *folium* leaf.

folio (ˈfəʊlɪəʊ) *n, pl* **folios 1** a leaf of a manuscript or book. **2** the size of each of the two leaves formed from a sheet of paper folded once; such a sheet. **3** a folder or case for loose papers. < Latin *folium* leaf.

folk (fəʊk) *n* **1** people generally. **2** people of a particular group or class. **3** (*informal*) members of a family.
• *adj* traditional to the people of a country: a folk dance. **folklore** *n* the traditional beliefs, customs, etc., of a people. < Old English *folc.*

follicle (ˈfɒlɪkl̩) *n* a small sac or cavity in the body, for example one that protects:

a hair follicle. < Latin *follis* bag.

follow (ˈfɒləʊ) *vb* **1** go or come after. **2** walk or go along: follow a path. **3** pursue (a course of action). **4** listen to or observe closely; understand. **5** obey; conform to. **6** result from. **follower** *n* **1** a person who follows. **2** a person who accepts the teachings of another; disciple. **3** an enthusiast. **follow up** follow with something similar or additional; undertake further investigation or work. **follow-up** *n* < Old English *folgian*. SEE PANEL.

following (ˈfɒləʊɪŋ) *n* a group of followers.
• *adj* **1** next after: the following day. **2** to be stated now.
• *prep* after.

folly (ˈfɒlɪ) *n* **1** foolishness; foolish act or idea. **2** a costly, fanciful building. < SEE FOOL.

fond (fɒnd) *adj* **1** having a liking or affection for: fond of cakes. **2** very affectionate: fond parents. **3** cherished, but unlikely to be fulfilled: fond ambitions. **fondly** *adv* **fondness** *n* < Middle English *fonne* fool.

fondant (ˈfɒndənt) *n* a soft sweet made from a preparation of flavoured sugar and water. < French *fondre* to melt.

fondle (ˈfɒndl̩) *vb* touch or stroke lovingly; caress. < obsolete *fond*.

fondue (ˈfɒndu:) *n* **1** a dish consisting of cheese melted in white wine into which small pieces of bread, etc., are dipped. **2** a dish cooked by placing forked cubes of meat, mushrooms, etc., into a pan of hot oil. < French *fondre* to melt.

font (fɒnt) *n* a large bowl for holding water, esp. used in baptism. < Latin *fons* fountain.

food (fu:d) *n* **1** any substance taken into the body of an animal or absorbed by a plant and used to provide energy and maintain life and growth. **2** such solid substances: food and drink. **foodstuff** *n* a substance made into or used as food. < Old English *fōda*.

fool (fu:l) *n* **1** a person who lacks good sense, judgment, or understanding. **2** a jester. **3** a cold, creamy dessert of fruit purée mixed with cream or custard: rhubarb fool.
• *vb* **1** behave or spend time idly, playfully, or irresponsibly. **2** deceive. **foolhardy** *adj* foolishly rash or adventurous. **foolish** *adj* **1** lacking good sense, judgment, or understanding; silly. **2** (of an action) unwise. **3** absurd or ridiculous. **foolishly** *adv* **foolishness** *n* **foolproof** *adj* so simple or dependable that error, failure, etc., is not possible. < ultimately Latin *follis* bellows, inflated ball.

foolscap (ˈfu:lzˌkæp) *n* a large size of paper, esp. 17 × 13½ inches (432 × 343 millimetres).

foot (fʊt) *n, pl* **feet** **1** the lowermost part of the leg. **2** the part of a stocking, etc., covering the foot. **3** the bottom or base; lowest part of something. **4** the last in a series. **5** a unit of length equal to ⅓ yard (30.48 centimetres). **6** the basic unit of metre in poetry.
• *vb* travel on foot; not ride: have to foot it. **foot-and-mouth disease** an infectious virus disease affecting cattle, etc., marked by ulcers of the mouth and feet. **football** *n* **1** a large round or oval inflated ball. **2** a game played with such a ball between two teams. **footballer** *n* **football pools** a system of gambling, with postal betting on the results of football matches. **footbridge** *n* a bridge for pedestrians. **foothill** *n* a hill at the bottom of a mountain. **foothold** *n* **1** a place that offers a secure grip for the foot when climbing. **2** a secure position from which further progress can be made: gain

---

following on

Follow features in a number of idiomatic expressions, including:

follow in someone's footsteps to continue the tradition adopted by a predecessor: Their father was a top banker in the city and he wanted all his sons to follow in his footsteps.

follow on (of a side in cricket) to have to bat again immediately, as a result of accumulating an insufficient score in the first innings. **follow-on** *n*

follow one's nose **1** to go straight forward. **2** to act according to instinct.

follow suit to do what another has just done: Two of the major oil companies raised the price of petrol last night and the others are expected to follow suit. The phrase comes from playing the same suit (hearts, clubs, etc.) as the previous player.

---

a foothold. **footing** *n* **1** a place that offers a secure grip for the foot. **2** a position, status, or set of conditions: on war footing. **footlights** *pl n* a row of lights across the front of a stage floor. **footnote** *n* a reference, explanation, etc., esp. printed at the bottom of a page. **footpath** *n* a path for pedestrians; pavement. **footprint** *n* an impression left by a foot. **footstep** *n* a distance covered by a step; sound of a step. **footwear** *n* shoes, boots, etc., worn on the feet. **footwork** *n* the control and use of the feet, esp. in sport. < Old English *fōt*. SEE PANEL.

for (fə; *stressed* fɔː) *prep* **1** used to show purpose, aim, or direction: to leave for home. **2** intended to be given to, belong to, or used in: a present for you. **3** considering the nature of; considering that he, she, or it is: tall for her age. **4** because of: famous for its cheese. **5** in spite of: For all her friends, she is not happy. **6** in place of; also used to show payment: I bought it for £100. **7** on behalf of; representing: act for one's clients. **8** in favour of: Are you for the idea? **9** used to show extent of time or space. **10** on the occasion of: at home for Christmas.

• *conj* for the following reason; because. < Old English.

forage (ˈfɒrɪdʒ) *n* **1** food for animals.

My foot!

Foot and feet occur frequently in informal spoken English in expressions like My foot!, get a foot in the door, put one's best foot forward, put one's foot down, sweep someone off his feet, stand on one's own two feet, get cold feet, and put one's foot in it. Such expressions are known as *idioms*. An idiom is an utterance whose meaning cannot be arrived at simply by adding together the literal meanings of its parts. Indeed, to take the component meanings literally can produce the most amazing contortions: Whenever she opens her mouth, she puts her foot in it.

One of the interesting aspects of idioms has to do with flexibility. On the one hand, many seem to be completely fixed, such as My foot!, How do you do?, and hand over fist. We cannot say, for example, My feet!, How does he do?, or hand over palm. In contrast the majority of idioms do show some degree of flexibility, but there are always restrictions on their behaviour. For example, we can say She put her foot in it but we cannot say Her foot was put in it. Even when referring to more than one person we have to say They put their foot in it (not *feet*).

The meanings of these idioms, and others with the word foot or feet, are:

drag one's feet to proceed very slowly, especially because one is unwilling.
feet of clay a basic, but usually concealed weakness in a person or thing that is honoured. The phrase comes from the Authorized (King James) Version of the Bible, Daniel 2:33, describing the feet of a statue.
find one's feet to gain experience and become able to make full use of one's knowledge, etc.: She soon found her feet in her new job.
get a foot in the door to secure an initial appointment, etc., with a business or organization, where this is difficult to obtain.
get cold feet to feel apprehension before an activity.
get off on the wrong/right foot to make a bad/good start.
have a foot in both camps to be involved with two opposing groups or activities.
have one foot in the grave to be near death; be very old.
my foot! an expression showing strong disagreement or disbelief.
not put a foot wrong to make no mistakes.
put one's best foot forward to start doing something vigorously and with determination.
put one's feet up to relax or rest, as by sitting down.
put one's foot down to assert one's authority firmly.
put one's foot in it to do or say something unintentionally that causes offence, distress, or embarrassment.
sit at the feet of to receive instruction from (an authority).
stand on one's own two feet to act or live independently.
sweep someone off his or **her feet** to influence greatly, especially make a person fall in love with one.
under foot on the ground.
under one's feet causing inconvenience and annoyance by getting in the way.

2 searching.
• *vb* **1** search for food, provisions, etc. **2** get or take provisions from. **3** rummage. < Old French.

foray (ˈfɒreɪ) *n* a short, sudden attack or raid. < Middle French *forre* fodder.

forbade (fəˈbæd, fəˈbeɪd) SEE **FORBID.**

forbear (fɔːˈbɛə) *vb* **forbore; forborne; forbearing** (*formal*) hold (oneself) back (from). **forbearance** *n* leniency; patience. < Old English *forberan.*
SEE PANEL.

forbid (fəˈbɪd) *vb* **forbade; forbidden; forbidding 1** order not to do something; refuse to allow. **2** prevent. **forbidding** *adj* threatening or dangerous; unfriendly. < Old English *forbēodan.*

force (fɔːs) *n* **1** strength, power, or energy. **2** violence or intense physical effort: use force. **3** (*science*) a measurable influence that produces a change. **4** a body of troops or police. **5** *pl* the armed services of a country. **6** the body of people performing a task: a work-force. **7** legal validity: The law comes into force on 1 May. **8** great influence or strength: the force of an argument.
• *vb* **1** cause to do something by force. **2** break into or open using force: force a door. **3** produce unnaturally or unwillingly: force a smile. **4** cause to grow more quickly. **forceful** *adj* having or filled with force. **forcefully** *adv* **forcefulness** *n* **forcible** *adj* performed with force; powerful. **forcibly** *adv* < Latin *fortis* strong. SEE PANEL.

forceps (ˈfɔːsɛps) *n, pl* **forceps** an instrument used for example by surgeons, for grasping firmly or pulling things. < Latin *formus* warm + *capere* to take.

ford (fɔːd) *n* a shallow place in a river that can be crossed by a vehicle, etc.
• *vb* cross (a river) in this way. < Old English.

fore (fɔː) *adj, adv* (situated) in, to, or at the front.
• *n* something that is in a forward or prominent position. < Old English.

forearm[1] (ˈfɔːrˌɑːm) *n* the part of the arm from the elbow to the wrist.

forearm[2] (fɔːrˈɑːm) *vb* arm or prepare in advance.

forebear (ˈfɔːˌbɛə) *n* an ancestor.
SEE PANEL AT **FORBEAR.**

foreboding (fɔːˈbəʊdɪŋ) *n* a feeling that evil, a disaster, etc., is approaching.

forecast (ˈfɔːˌkɑːst) *vb* **forecast; forecasting** predict (a future event or condition).
• *n* a statement that forecasts. < Middle English *fore-* fore + *caster* to cast.

forecastle (ˈfəʊksl̩) *n* the front part of a ship. < *fore* + *castle.*

forecourt (ˈfɔːˌkɔːt) *n* an open area in front of a building, esp. the part of a filling station where petrol is sold.

forefather (ˈfɔːˌfɑːðə) *n* an ancestor.

forefinger (ˈfɔːˌfɪŋgə) *n* the finger next to the thumb.

forego (fɔːˈgəʊ) *vb* go before. **foregoing** *adj* immediately preceding. **foregone conclusion** an inevitable result.
SEE PANEL.

foreground (ˈfɔːˌgraʊnd) *n* **1** the part of a picture or view that is nearest to the observer. **2** a prominent position.

forehand (ˈfɔːˌhænd) *adj, adv* (of a stroke in tennis, etc.) (played) with the palm of the hand turned in the direction ofmovement.
• *n* a forehand stroke.

forehead (ˈfɒrɪd, ˈfɔːˌhɛd) *n* the part of the face above the eyes.

forbear or forebear?

These two words are sometimes confused.

Forbear (with the stress on the second syllable for*bear*) is a verb used in formal contexts that means 'to hold oneself back from' as in I could not *forbear* remarking on his behaviour. It is perhaps more commonly used in the noun form forbearance meaning 'leniency; patience'.

Forebear (with the stress on the first syllable *fore*bear) is a noun meaning 'an ancestor' and is usually used in the plural: his Teutonic *forebears.*

forceful or forcible?

Forceful means 'having force; filled with force' and is used of a person or thing that acts with or has great power, sometimes great potential power, as in a *forceful* personality, a *forceful* argument.

Forcible means 'performed or carried out with force' as in a *forcible* expulsion. Forcible tends to be used in the derived adverb forcibly: They imposed their prejudices rather too *forcibly.*

foreign (ˈfɒrən) *adj* **1** of, in, or from another country or other countries, esp. not one's own country. **2** of a place or country other than one being considered. **3** of another person or material than the one being considered. **4** alien in character. **foreigner** *n* a person born in or coming from a foreign country. < Latin *foris* outside.

foreknowledge (fɔːˈnɒlɪdʒ) *n* knowledge of something before it occurs.

foreleg (ˈfɔːˌlɛg) *n* an animal's front leg.

foreman (ˈfɔːmən) fem. **forewoman** *n* **1** a person, esp. a chief worker, who supervises other workers. **2** the chairman and spokesman of a jury.

foremost (ˈfɔːˌməʊst) *adj, adv* first in a series, position, or importance.

forename (ˈfɔːˌneɪm) *n* a person's first name.

forensic (fəˈrɛnsɪk, fəˈrɛnzɪk) *adj* of or relating to law-courts. **forensic medicine** the application of medical knowledge to legal matters, etc. < Latin *forum* market-place.

forerunner (ˈfɔːˌrʌnə) *n* a person or thing that prepares the way for or is a sign of the coming of someone or something else more important.

foresee (fɔːˈsiː) *vb* **foresaw; foreseen; foreseeing** be aware of beforehand. **foreseeable** *adj* **foresight** *n* careful consideration and provision for future needs or difficulties.

foreshadow (fɔːˈʃædəʊ) *vb* represent or suggest beforehand.

forest (ˈfɒrɪst) *n* a large wooded area with a dense growth of trees and plants.
• *vb* cover with trees or forest. **forester** *n* a person trained in forestry. **forestry** *n* the planting and tending of forests. < Latin *foris* outside.

forestall (fɔːˈstɔːl) *vb* hinder or exclude by taking action first; anticipate. < Middle English *forstallen* to waylay.

foretaste (ˈfɔːˌteɪst) *n* a small, limited experience of something to come.

foretell (fɔːˈtɛl) *vb* **foretold; foretelling** tell beforehand; predict.

forethought (ˈfɔːˌθɔːt) *n* careful thought and planning in advance.

forever (fəˈrɛvə) *adv* **1** for all time in the future. **2** continually. SEE PANEL.

forewarn (fɔːˈwɔːn) *vb* warn beforehand.

foreword (ˈfɔːˌwɜːd) *n* an introductory statement to a book, esp. written by someone other than the author.

forfeit (ˈfɔːfɪt) *n* something lost or taken away, as a penalty.
• *vb* **1** lose the right to by an error, crime, etc. **2** confiscate as a punishment. **forfeiture** *n* < Latin *foris* outside + *facere* to do.

forgave (fəˈgeɪv) SEE **FORGIVE**.

forge[1] (fɔːdʒ) *n* a workshop with an open furnace in which metal, esp. iron, is heated and shaped; such a furnace.
• *vb* **1** shape (metal) by heating in fire and hammering. **2** form or bring into being, esp. by making an effort: forge an agreement. **3** counterfeit (something such as a document). **forger** *n* **forgery** *n* **1** forging or the crime of forging. **2** a forged document, etc. < Latin *faber* craftsman.

forge[2] *vb* move forward at a steady pace: forge ahead. < probably alteration of *force*.

forget (fəˈgɛt) *vb* **forgot; forgotten; forgetting 1** fail to remember or lose remembrance of (something). **2** disregard; overlook: forget our differences. **forgetful** *adj* tending to forget things. **forgetfulness** *n* **forget oneself** behave in a thoughtless, unseemly way. < Old English *forgietan*.

forget-me-not (fəˈgɛtmɪˌnɒt) *n* a plant with small blue flowers.

forgive (fəˈgɪv) *vb* **forgave; forgiven; forgiving 1** stop blaming or holding resentment against (someone or some-

forego or **forgo?**

These two words are quite often confused. Forego means 'to go before; precede' and is usually used in the forms foregoing or foregone: the *foregoing* provisions of the act, a *foregone* conclusion.

Forgo means 'to give up; do without; relinquish' as in The workers may be willing to *forgo* a pay increase this year if it means their jobs will remain secure.

forever or **for ever?**

Some careful writers of British English prefer to write for ever (two words) to mean 'for all time in the future; for always' as in I will love you *for ever*. Do you want to live *for ever* and ever?

Such users write forever (one word) when the meaning is 'continually; persistently' as in Some people are *forever* complaining!

thing). **2** grant pardon for (a mistake, etc.) to (someone). **forgiveness** *n* < Old English *forgifan*.

forgo (fɔːˈgəʊ) *vb* **forwent; forgone; forgoing** give up or do without. < Old English *forgān*. SEE PANEL AT **FOREGO.**

forgot (fəˈgɒt) SEE **FORGET. forgotten** SEE **FORGET.**

fork (fɔːk) *n* **1** an implement with two or more prongs used in eating. **2** a tool with two or more prongs used in agriculture. **3** something shaped like a fork. **4** a place where a road, etc., separates into two or more parts; one of these parts. • *vb* **1** pick up or dig with a fork. **2** divide into two or more branches; follow one of these branches. **fork-lift truck** a vehicle for lifting and moving heavy objects. **fork out** (*informal*) pay for something, esp. unwillingly. < Latin *furca*.

forlorn (fəˈlɔːn) *adj* **1** sad, lonely, and isolated. **2** desperate: a forlorn attempt. **forlornly** *adv* < Old English *forloren*.

form (fɔːm) *n* **1** the shape, structure, or appearance of something. **2** a kind or type; way in which something exists. **3** a paper with printed questions and space for writing answers. **4** the usual or correct method of acting or behaving. **5** a class in a school. **6** a long seat. **7** the nest of a hare. **8** the condition of performing, for example in sports: in good form. • *vb* **1** shape, mould, or arrange. **2** develop or acquire: form a habit. **3** organize. **4** become formed or shaped. **formless** *adj* **formation** *n* **1** forming or being formed. **2** something formed: a rock formation. **3** a particular arrangement. **formative** *adj* **1** helping to form: a formative influence. **2** of formation or development: formative years. < Latin *forma*.

formal (ˈfɔːməl) *adj* **1** of the outward form of something. **2** following or according to the usual customs; conventional. **3** marked by strict observance of correct procedures. **4** designed for wear at ceremonies, etc.: formal dress. **formally** *adv* **formality** *n* **1** strict observance of correct procedures. **2** a formal act: legal formalities. **formalize** *vb* **1** make formal. **2** give formal status to.

format (ˈfɔːmæt) *n* **1** the size, shape, and general appearance of a book, etc. **2** a general plan of arrangement or organization. < Latin *formare* to form.

former (ˈfɔːmə) *adj* **1** of or happening in the past. **2** the first of two mentioned: the former. **formerly** *adv* in former times. < Old English *forma*. SEE PANEL.

formidable (ˈfɔːmɪdəbl̩) *adj* **1** causing fear or apprehension. **2** difficult to do or overcome. **formidably** *adv* < Latin *formidare* to fear.

formula (ˈfɔːmjʊlə) *n, pl* **formulas, formulae 1** a fixed set of words, as used in a ceremony. **2** a scientific relationship, principle, or rule stated in the form of symbols. **3** a statement that expresses a truth, principle, etc.: a peace formula; the formula for a happy marriage. **formulate** *vb* express clearly in a formula or in a precise way. **formulation** *n* < Latin *forma*.

fornicate (ˈfɔːnɪˌkeɪt) *vb* have sexual intercourse voluntarily outside marriage. **fornication** *n* < Latin *fornix* brothel.

forsake (fəˈseɪk) *vb* **forsook; forsaken; forsaking 1** give up (something valued). **2** abandon. < Old English *forsacan*.

forswear (fɔːˈswɛə) *vb* **forswore; forsworn; forswearing 1** give up with determination or as on oath. **2** deny earnestly or on oath. < Old English *forswerian*.

fort (fɔːt) *n* a fortified building or position. < Latin *fortis* strong.

the former ... the latter

The former refers to the first of two previously mentioned people, things, etc. The latter refers to the last of two previously mentioned people, things, etc., as in Mrs Bruce and Mrs Chapman arrived, *the former* wearing a red dress, *the latter* a blue one.

If you want to refer to the first of more than two people or things, use *first,* not former: They visited Belgium, France, and Switzerland on holiday, spending most of their time in the *first* (not former) country.

If you want to refer to the last of more than two people or things, often *last* or *last-mentioned* can be used: Forms for new equipment, notification of holidays, and personal matters are available from the Secretary; the *last-mentioned* (not latter) only by special request.

forte (ˈfɔːteɪ) *n* something at which a person excels; strong point. < Middle French *fort* strong.

forth (fɔːθ) *adv* **1** onwards; forwards. **2** out. **and so forth** and so on. **back and forth** to and fro. < Old English.

forthcoming (ˌfɔːθˈkʌmɪŋ) *adj* **1** approaching in time. **2** available or ready. **3** willing to give information; responsive.

forthright (ˈfɔːθˌraɪt) *adj* direct and outspoken.

forthwith (ˌfɔːθˈwɪð) *adv* immediately.

fortify (ˈfɔːtɪˌfaɪ) *vb* **fortified; fortifying** **1** make (a place) stronger by adding military defences. **2** strengthen physically, mentally, etc. **3** add material to for strengthening or enriching. **fortification** *n* **1** fortifying. **2** something, such as a fort or wall, built to defend a place. < Latin *fortis* strong + *facere* to make.

fortitude (ˈfɔːtɪˌtjuːd) *n* strong, patient courage in pain or difficulty. < Latin *fortis* strong.

fortnight (ˈfɔːtˌnaɪt) *n* two weeks. **fortnightly** *adj, adv* (happening or appearing) once a fortnight. < Old English *fēowertȳne niht* fourteen nights.

fortress (ˈfɔːtrɪs) *n* a large, fortified building or town. < Latin *fortis* strong.

fortuitous (fɔːˈtjuːɪtəs) *adj* happening by chance. **fortuitously** *adv* < Latin *fors* chance. SEE PANEL.

fortune (ˈfɔːtʃən) *n* **1** (*informal*) a large sum of money: We've won a fortune! **2** a supposed power or force that is thought responsible for human affairs. **3** luck, esp. good luck. **4** the events that accompany the progress of a person or thing. **5** a person's destiny: tell someone's fortune. **fortunate** *adj* having, bringing, or happening by good luck or fortune. **fortunately** *adv* < Latin *fors* luck. SEE PANEL AT **FORTUITOUS.**

forty (ˈfɔːtɪ) *determiner, pron* 40 in number.
- *n* the number 40. **fortieth** *determiner, pron, adv, n* **forties** *pl n* the numbers, range of temperatures, ages, or dates in a century from 40–49. **forty winks** (*informal*) a nap. < Old English *fēowertig.*

> **fortuitous** or **fortunate?**
>
> The meaning of fortuitous is 'happening by chance, as opposed to by design': Finding himself sitting next to her in the plane was purely *fortuitous.*
>
> Fortunate means 'having, bringing, or happening by good luck or fortune': You are *fortunate* in having a chance to travel.
>
> If something is fortuitous it may or may not be fortunate or lucky as well.

forum (ˈfɔːrəm) *n* a public place or meeting for discussion. < Latin: public place.

forward (ˈfɔːwəd) *adj* **1** situated at, directed, or moving towards the front. **2** of or preparing for the future: forward planning. **3** advanced in development. **4** very eager; not modest or reserved.
- *adv* **1** to or towards the front; ahead in space or time. **2** into a prominent position.
- *n* a mainly attacking player in hockey, soccer, etc., near the front of the team.
- *vb* **1** send or pass on to a new address. **2** send (goods) to a customer. **3** further, help, or promote. **forwardness** *n* **forwards** *adv* forward, esp. in space. < Old English *foreweard.*

forwent (fɔːˈwɛnt) SEE **FORGO.**

fossil (ˈfɒsl̩) *n* the remains or traces of a plant or animal that lived in a past geological age, preserved in rock. **fossilize** *vb* **1** turn or be turned into a fossil. **2** make or become antiquated or rigid. < Latin *fossilis* dug up, from *fodere* to dig.

foster (ˈfɒstə) *vb* **1** promote the development or growth of. **2** bring up (a child that is not one's own).
- *adj* of or involved in the upbringing of a child by parents who are not the natural or adopted parents: a foster child. < Old English *fostrian* to nourish.

fought (fɔːt) SEE **FIGHT.**

foul (faʊl) *adj* **1** offensive to the senses, esp. smell or taste; revolting. **2** obscene: foul language. **3** (esp. of weather) very unpleasant; stormy.
- *n* a breaking of the rules in a game.
- *vb* **1** become entangled (with); obstruct. **2** commit a foul in a game. **foully** *adv* **foulness** *n* **foul-mouthed** *adj* using foul language. **foul play** a violent crime, esp. murder. < Old English *fūl.*

found[1] (faʊnd) SEE **FIND.**

found[2] *vb* **1** establish (an institution, society, etc.). **2** base on something solid. **founder** *n* < Latin *fundus* bottom.

found[3] *vb* melt (metal) and pour into a mould. < Latin *fundere* to pour.

foundation (faʊnˈdeɪʃən) *n* **1** the act of founding. **2** the strong base on which something stands or is built or supported. **3** an endowment or fund for the continual support of an institution; institution so endowed. **4** a cosmetic applied as a base for other make-up. **foundational** *adj* **foundation-stone** *n* a stone laid at a ceremony to mark the foundation of a building.

founder (ˈfaʊndə) *vb* **1** (of a ship, etc.) sink. **2** break down or fail. **3** stumble or fall. < Latin *fundus* bottom.

foundry (ˈfaʊndrɪ) *n* a place where metal is cast.

fount[1] (faʊnt) *n* a fountain or source. < Latin *fons* fountain.

fount[2] (faʊnt, fɒnt) *n* a set of printing type in one size and style. < Latin *fondere* to pour.

fountain (ˈfaʊntɪn) *n* **1** a natural spring of water. **2** a decorative, artificial jet of water; structure where this flows. **3** a source. **fountain-pen** *n* a pen with a supply of ink that is automatically fed to the nib. < Latin *fons* spring.

four (fɔː) *determiner, pron* 4 in number.
• *n* the number 4. **four-letter word** any of several short vulgar or obscene English words. **four-poster bed** a bed with a post at each corner to support a canopy. **foursome** *n* a group of four people. < Old English *fēower.*

fourteen (ˌfɔːˈtiːn) *determiner, pron* 14 in number.
• *n* the number 14. **fourteenth** *determiner, pron, adv, n* < Old English *fēowertiēne.*

fourth (fɔːθ) *determiner, pron, adv* next after third.
• *n* **1** something that is fourth. **2** one of four equal parts of a thing. **3** the fourth gear of a motor vehicle. **fourthly** *adv*

fowl (faʊl) *n* **1** any bird. **2** any domestic bird, such as a chicken or duck, used as food; flesh of such birds used as food. < Old English *fugel.*

fox (fɒks) *n* **1** a small, wild, flesh-eating animal of the dog family, with a bushy tail. **2** a sly, crafty person.
• *vb* (*informal*) perplex or baffle. **foxy** *adj* **1** crafty and sly. **2** reddish-brown. < Old English.

foxglove (ˈfɒksˌglʌv) *n* a tall, herbal plant with showy purple, yellow, or white bell-shaped flowers.

fox-hunting (ˈfɒksˌhʌntɪŋ) *n* an outdoor activity in which huntsmen on horseback chase a fox with a pack of hounds.

foxtrot (ˈfɒksˌtrɒt) *n* a ballroom dance with slow and quick steps.
• *vb* **foxtrotted; foxtrotting** perform this dance.

foyer (ˈfɔɪeɪ) *n* the entrance room, lobby, or hallway of a theatre, etc. < Latin *focus* hearth.

fracas (ˈfrækɑː) *n* a noisy quarrel or fight; brawl. < French, from Italian *fracassare* to shatter.

fraction (ˈfrækʃən) *n* **1** a part of a whole number, for example ¼. **2** a very small part, amount, or bit. **fractional** *adj* **fractionally** *adv* < Latin *frangere* to break.

fracture (ˈfræktʃə) *n* a break or breaking, esp. of a bone.
• *vb* cause a fracture in; suffer a fracture. < Latin *frangere* to break.

fragile (ˈfrædʒaɪl) *adj* **1** easily broken. **2** physically weak; delicate. < Latin *frangere* to break.

fragment (ˈfrægmənt) *n* a part or piece broken off or detached; incomplete piece.
• *vb* (frægˈmɛnt) break or be broken into fragments. **fragmentation** *n* **fragmentary** *adj* consisting of fragments. < Latin *frangere* to break.

fragrant (ˈfreɪgrənt) *adj* having a pleasant or sweet smell. **fragrance** *n* < Latin *fragrare* to be fragrant.

frail (freɪl) *adj* physically weak. **frailty** *n* **1** physical weakness. **2** moral weakness; fault arising from such a weakness. < Latin *fragilis* fragile.

frame (freɪm) *n* **1** a structure that gives shape, strength, or support to something such as a building. **2** the physical structure of the human body. **3** an open structure that encloses or supports something: a picture frame. **4** the outer structure of a pair of glasses that holds the lenses. **5** a state: a frame of mind. **6** a single exposure on a strip of film.
• *vb* **1** put a frame round. **2** construct. **3** form according to a pattern. **4** put into words; compose. **5** (*informal*) make (someone) appear to be guilty of a crime. **framework** *n* the structure, outline, or shape of something. < Old English *framian* to benefit.

franchise (ˈfræntʃaɪz) *n* **1** the right to vote in elections. **2** the right to sell a company's goods or services in a particular area. < Old French *franc* free.

frank (fræŋk) *adj* free, direct, and honest in speech or attitude.
• *vb* put a mark on (a letter, etc.) to cancel a postage stamp or in place of a stamp. **frankly** *adj* **frankness** *n* < Old French *franc* free.

frankfurter (ˈfræŋkˌfɜːtə) *n* a light-brown, smoked sausage, made of beef and pork. < *Frankfurt,* city in Germany.

frantic (ˈfræntɪk) *adj* wildly excited or anxious. **frantically** *adv* < Latin *phreneticus.*

fraternal (frəˈtɜːnḷ) *adj* **1** of a brother or brothers. **2** of a fraternity or society. **fraternity** *n* **1** a group of people with a common purpose or pleasure. **2** brotherliness. **fraternize** *vb* associate on friendly terms. < Latin *frater* brother.

fraud (frɔːd) *n* **1** the gaining of a material advantage dishonestly. **2** a person or thing that deceives or is false; impostor. **fraudulent** *adj* acting with or obtained by fraud. **fraudulence** *n* **fraudulently** *adv* < Latin *fraus.*

fraught (frɔːt) *adj* **1** filled with (something mentioned): fraught with danger. **2** marked by anxieties. < Middle Dutch *vracht* freight.

fray[1] (freɪ) *n* a noisy quarrel or fight. < short for *affray.*

fray[2] *vb* **1** wear or cause to wear away into loose threads at the edge. **2** make strained or upset. < Latin *fricare* to rub.

freak (friːk) *n* **1** a person or thing that is abnormal. **2** (*informal*) a person who acts or dresses in a very unconventional way. **3** (*informal*) a great enthusiast for something mentioned: a computer freak. **4** something extremely unusual. **freakish** *adj* like a freak.
• *vb* **freak out** (*informal*) behave in a highly excited or uncontrolled way. < origin uncertain.

freckle (ˈfrɛkḷ) *n* a small, brownish spot on the skin.
• *vb* mark or become marked with freckles. < Scandinavian.

free (friː) *adj* **freer; freest 1** not under the control or power of another. **2** not confined, restricted, or detained. **3** not subject to (an influence): free from worry. **4** costing or charging nothing. **5** (of a room, etc.) not occupied. **6** (of a person) without engagements or things to do. **7** generous or lavish: free with one's praises. **8** improper or licentious: free behaviour. **9** having no trade restrictions. **10** not

Free gifts going cheap!

A gift is by definition 'free' or it is not a gift. Similarly, if a certainty is not 'sure' it is hardly a certainty, and an innovation that is not 'new' is anything but an innovation. The words free, sure, and new in the expressions free gift, sure certainty and new innovation are therefore quite superfluous. Such use of unnecessary words is known as *pleonasm,* which derives ultimately from the Greek verb *pleonazein* 'to be excessive'.

In the above examples the superfluous words free, sure, and new have been deliberately added for emphasis. However, the use of unnecessary words is often unconscious, as in 'Would you mind *repeating* what you said *again*.' 'Her eyes are *blue* in *colour*.' 'Why not split the orange into *two halves*?' and 'Edwards *continued* to *remain* at the back of the pack until the last lap.' Careful users of English regard even the rhetorical use of pleonasm as undesirable.

Free features in a number of expressions, including:

free enterprise an economic system in which private businesses operate competitively for profit, without government control.

free fall 1 the unrestrained fall of a body under the force of gravity. **2** the part of a parachute jump before the parachute opens.

free-for-all *n* **1** a noisy fight in which anyone may join. **2** a discussion or competition in which anyone may join.

free hand the right to make one's own decisions and arrangements: He was given a free hand in organizing the exhibition.

free-hand *adj, adv* not using special drawing instruments, etc.

free house a public house that may stock more than one brand of beer, etc.

free kick a kick in football, rugby, etc., that is allowed to be taken without interference, because of a breach of the rules by the opponents.

free-range *adj* of or produced by poultry reared in the open air, not in a battery: free-range eggs.

free-wheel *vb* **1** to ride without power from the pedals or engine. **2** to act freely or irresponsibly.

free will the power of choosing one's own course of actions.

A person who earns a living without being contracted to a single employer is known as a **freelance** or **freelancer**. The word originally denoted a type of medieval mercenary or 'lance-for-hire', one whose 'lance' was 'free' of any particular long-term allegiance.

exact or literal: a free translation.
• *vb* **1** release; make or help free. **2** relieve: free from worry. **3** disentangle or disengage; clear. **freely** *adv* **freedom** *n* **1** the condition of being free. **2** frankness and openness. **3** unrestricted use. **freehand** *adj* done without drawing or measuring instruments. **freehold** *n* the legal right to hold land as the absolute owner. **freelance** *n* a person who pursues a profession without a long-term commitment to one employer. **Freemason** *n* a member of a secret order, sworn to brotherliness and helping other members. **freestyle** *n* a competition or race, for example in swimming, in which a contestant may use a style of his or her own choice. < Old English *frēo*. SEE PANEL.

freeze (fri:z) *vb* **froze; frozen; freezing** **1** change or be changed from a liquid into a solid as a result of a reduction in temperature. **2** make or become extremely cold. **3** become blocked by ice: The pipes froze. **4** be made speechless and motionless by fright, etc. **5** fix (prices, wages, etc.) at a particular level. **6** make (funds, etc.) unavailable. **7** preserve (food) by refrigeration.
• *n* **1** a period of freezing cold weather. **2** the freezing of prices, wages, etc. **freeze-dry** *vb* **freeze-dried; freeze-drying** preserve by fast freezing and then drying in a vacuum. **freezer** *n* a container that stores frozen food or freezes food very quickly. **freezing-point** *n* the temperature below which a liquid turns into a solid. < Old English *frēosan*.

freight (freɪt) *n* **1** the transport of goods, esp. by water or air. **2** the goods transported. **3** the charge for transporting goods. **freighter** *n* a ship or aircraft that carries mainly freight. < Middle Dutch *vracht*.

frenzy (ˈfrɛnzɪ) *n* a wild outburst; brief spell of madness. **frenzied** *adj* in a state of frenzy. < Greek *phrenitis* madness.

frequent (ˈfri:kwənt) *adj* occurring or appearing often.
• *vb* (frɪˈkwɛnt) visit often or regularly.
frequently *adv* **frequency** *n* **1** frequent occurrence. **2** the rate of repetition of a regular event. **3** (*physics*) the number of cycles completed by a vibrating system per unit of time. < Latin *frequens* numerous.

fresco (ˈfrɛskəʊ) *n, pl* **frescoes** a water-colour picture painted on damp plaster. < Italian: fresh.

fresh (frɛʃ) *adj* **1** recently grown, made, etc.; not stale. **2** not preserved: fresh fruit. **3** free from taint; clean. **4** (of the wind) rather strong. **5** (of the weather) cool. **6** not weary; refreshed. **7** new or different: make a fresh start. **8** having just arrived. **9** (*informal*) cheeky; impudent; too forward, esp. with someone of the opposite sex: Don't get fresh with me! **10** not salt: fresh water. **11** bright in colour, not dull or faded. **freshly** *adv* **freshness** *n* **freshen** *vb* make or become fresh. **freshwater** *adj* of or living in fresh water. < Old English *farsc*.

fret[1] (frɛt) *vb* **fretted; fretting** irritate or become irritated; worry. **fretful** *adj* constantly worrying. **fretfulness** *n* < Old English *fretan* to devour.

fret[2] *n* any of a series of ridges on the finger-board of a guitar, lute, etc., which determine the notes produced. < origin uncertain.

fretsaw (ˈfrɛtˌsɔ:) *n* a saw with a long, thin, narrow blade, used for cutting patterns in thin wood.

friable (ˈfraɪəbl̩) *adj* easily broken up; crumbly. < Latin *friare* to crumble.

friar (ˈfraɪə) *n* a member of certain Roman Catholic orders that combine monastic life with outside activity. **friary** *n* a monastery of friars. < Old French *frere* brother.

friction (ˈfrɪkʃən) *n* **1** the rubbing of one thing against another. **2** the resistance to motion between two surfaces moving over each other. **3** conflict between people, groups, etc., having different ideas. < Latin *fricare* to rub.

fridge (frɪdʒ) *n* (*informal*) a refrigerator.

friend (frɛnd) *n* **1** a person whom one knows well and considers with affection and loyalty. **2** an ally; supporter or sympathizer. **3 Friend** a Quaker. **friendship** *n* **friendless** *adj* without a friend. **friendly** *adj* **1** of or like a friend; kind. **2** not hostile: friendly nations. **3** undertaken only for pleasure, not in a competition: a friendly game. **friendliness** *n* **friendly society** a voluntary mutual-aid association, whose members contribute money regularly to provide for times of need. < Old English *frēond*.

frieze (fri:z) *n* **1** a band of decoration or sculpture below the ceiling or top of a building. **2** a picture on a long strip of paper, esp. when displayed on a wall. < Middle French *frise*.

frigate (ˈfrɪgət) *n* a naval vessel, smaller than a destroyer. < Old Italian *fregata*.

fright (fraɪt) *n* fear caused by an unexpected danger, etc. **frighten** *vb* **1** make suddenly afraid; scare. **2** force by frightening. **3** become frightened.

frightful *adj* **1** causing very strong fear, horror, or shock. 2 (*informal*) very great; very unpleasant. **frightfully** *adv* < Old English *fryhto.*

frigid (ˈfrɪdʒɪd) *adj* **1** extremely cold. **2** cold, formal, and unfeeling in manner. **3** (of a woman) sexually unresponsive. **frigidity** *n* frigidly *adv* < Latin *frigēre* to be cold.

frill (frɪl) *n* **1** a gathered or pleated decorative strip of cloth, etc., at the edge of something. **2** (*informal*) something decorative but not essential.
• *vb* decorate with frills. **frilly** *adj* < origin uncertain.

fringe (frɪndʒ) *n* **1** a decorative border of hanging threads or tassels. **2** the front hair cut short over the forehead. **3** an outer edge. **4** a group with unconventional or extreme styles or views.
• *vb* **1** provide with a fringe. **2** serve as a fringe for. **fringe benefit** an employee's benefit in addition to wages or a salary. < Latin *frimbria.*

frippery (ˈfrɪpərɪ) *n* showy or tawdry decoration or finery. < Old French *frepe* frill, rag.

frisk (frɪsk) *vb* **1** leap or skip in a playful way. **2** pass the hands over (a person) to search for hidden weapons, etc. **frisky** *adj* playful or lively. **friskiness** *n* < Middle French *frisque.*

fritter[1] (ˈfrɪtə) *vb* waste or squander gradually: fritter away hard-earned money. < alteration of *fitters* rags.

fritter[2] *n* a piece of fried batter containing fruit, meat, etc. < Latin *frigere* to fry.

frivolous (ˈfrɪvələs) *adj* **1** not serious; unimportant. **2** irresponsibly pleasure-loving. **frivolity** *n* **frivolously** *adv* < Latin *frivolus.*

frizz (frɪz) also **frizzle** (frɪzl̩) *vb* to form into tight, wiry curls or crisp tufts.
• *n* hair that has been frizzed. **frizzy** or **frizzly** *adj* < French *friser.*

frizzle (ˈfrɪzl̩) *vb* **1** fry (bacon, etc.) until crisp and curled. **2** burn or scorch. < blend of fry and *sizzle.*

fro (frəʊ) *adv* back or from: to and fro. < Old Norse *frā.*

frock (frɒk) *n* a dress. < Middle French *froc.*

frog (frɒg) *n* a small, tail-less, jumping amphibian. **frogman** *n, pl* **frogmen** a swimmer equipped with flippers, rubber suit, etc., and an air supply for swimming under water. **frogmarch** *vb* force (a person) to move forward against his or her will. < Old English *frogga.*

frolic (ˈfrɒlɪk) *vb* **frolicked; frolicking** play about in a happy, lively way.
• *n* lively, happy playing or entertainment. < Middle Dutch *vro* happy.

from (frəm; *stressed* frɒm) *prep* **1** showing the starting-point in space or time or in reckoning: travelling from Leeds; from midnight. **2** showing a movement away, prevention, etc.: released from prison. **3** showing a source or origin: take money from one's account. **4** showing a change or difference: go from bad to worse. **5** showing a cause or reason: weak from hunger. **6** showing a material from which something is made. < Old English.

front (frʌnt) *n* **1** the part or side that is forward or more important. **2** the area of conflict between armies; forwardmost line of an army. **3** an outward appearance, esp. a feigned one in the face of danger, etc.: put on a brave front. **4** the boundary between two different air masses. **5** the promenade of a seaside resort. **6** a field of activity that is mentioned. **7** (*informal*) a cover for secret activities. **8** a movement linking different groups: a united front.
• *vb* have the front towards; face.
• *adj, adv* of, towards, or situated at the front: the front door. **frontage** *n* the front of a building; land at the front. **frontal** *adj* of, at, or showing the front. **front-bencher** *n* a Member of Parliament who holds office in the government or opposition. **front-runner** *n* a person who is leading in a race or contest. **in front of** directly ahead of; in the presence of. < Latin *frons* forehead.

frontier (ˈfrʌntɪə, frʌnˈtɪə) *n* **1** the border between two countries. **2** the limit of knowledge in a particular subject. < SEE **FRONT.**

frontispiece (ˈfrʌntɪsˌpiːs) *n* an illustration facing the title-page of a book. < Latin *frons* front + *specere* to look at.

frost (frɒst) *n* a weather condition when the temperature falls below the freezing-point of water; icy deposit formed in such a condition.
• *vb* **1** cover with or as if with frost. **2** injure (plants, etc.) by frost. **3** make the surface of (glass, etc.) slightly rough and opaque. **frostbite** *n* injury to the tissues of part of the body, because of exposure to extreme cold. **frostbitten** *adj* affected with frostbite. **frosty** *adj* **1** covered with, marked by, or producing frost. **2** very cold and unfriendly. **frostily** *adv* **frostiness** *n* < Old English.

froth (frɒθ) *n* **1** a mass of small bubbles of air or gas in a liquid. **2** a foamy saliva formed at the lips in certain diseases.

3 trivial, unimportant matters.
• *vb* produce or form froth. **frothy** *adj* < Old Norse *frotha.*

frown (fraʊn) *vb* **1** wrinkle the brows, as in deep thought or disapproval. **2** disapprove: frown on spending so much.
• *n* a frowning look or movement. < Middle English *frounen.*

froze (frəʊz) SEE **FREEZE. frozen** SEE **FREEZE.**

frugal (ˈfruːgl̩) *adj* **1** not wasteful in using resources; sparing. **2** inexpensive or meagre: a frugal meal. **frugality** *n* **frugally** *adv* < Latin *frugalis.*

fruit (fruːt) *n* **1** the part of a plant containing the seed; this as food. **2** any plant product such as grain or vegetables: the fruits of the field. **3** a result or product, esp. a favourable one: the fruits of our labours. **fruiterer** *n* a person who deals in fruit. **fruitful** *adj* **1** very productive. **2** producing good results. **fruitfully** *adv* **fruitfulness** *n* **fruition** *n* realization or fulfilment: come to fruition. **fruitless** *adj* unsuccessful. **fruitlessly** *adv* **fruitlessness** *n* **fruit machine** a kind of coin-operated gambling machine. **fruity** *adj* **1** like fruit in taste or smell. **2** (of a voice) rich. **3** (*informal*) full of coarse humour. < Latin *fructus.*

frump (frʌmp) *n* a dowdy, unattractive woman. **frumpish** *adj* < Middle Dutch *verrompelen* to rumple.

frustrate (frʌˈstreɪt) *vb* **1** hinder or prevent (efforts, desires, etc.) from being fulfilled. **2** discourage, agitate, or upset. **frustration** *n* < Latin *frustra* in vain.

fry[1] (fraɪ) *vb* **fried; frying** cook or be cooked in hot fat, oil, etc.
• *n* a dish of something fried, esp. offal: pig's fry. **frying-pan** *n* a shallow pan with a long handle, used for frying. < Latin *frigere.*

fry[2] *n* the young of various fish or other animals. **small fry** (*informal*) children; people or organizations thought unimportant. < Old French *frier* to rub, spawn.

ft. *abbrev* foot; feet.

fuchsia (ˈfjuːʃə) *n* a decorative shrub with showy, drooping pink, red, or purple flowers. < Leonhard *Fuchs,* died 1566, German botanist. SEE PANELS AT **ASTHMA; DAHLIA.**

fuddy-duddy (ˈfʌdɪˌdʌdɪ) *adj* (*informal*) old-fashioned, dull, and unimaginative.
• *n* (*informal*) a fuddy-duddy person. < origin uncertain.

fudge[1] (fʌdʒ) *n* a soft, flavoured sweet made from sugar, butter, and milk. < origin unknown.

fudge[2] *vb* **1** avoid commitment (on); dodge. **2** devise in a false or clumsy way; fake. < probably alteration of *fadge* to fit.

fuel (ˈfjʊəl) *n* **1** material burnt to produce heat, light, or energy. **2** a source of strength or strong emotion.
• *vb* **fuelled; fuelling 1** provide with fuel. **2** stimulate. < ultimately Latin *focus* hearth.

fugitive(ˈfjuːdʒɪtɪv) *n* a person who flees.
• *adj* **1** fleeing, esp. from arrest or justice. **2** passing quickly; transient. < Latin *fugere* to flee.

fugue (fjuːg) *n* a musical composition in which the main theme is repeated and developed. < Latin *fuga* flight.

fulcrum (ˈfʊlkrəm) *n, pl* **fulcra** the point about which a lever moves. < Latin *fulcire* to prop.

fulfil (fʊlˈfɪl) *vb* **fulfilled; fulfilling 1** bring about the realization of (a promise, etc.). **2** carry out (a task, etc.). **3** satisfy (a requirement, etc.). **4** develop one's potential fully. **fulfilment** *n* < Old English *fullfyllan.*

full (fʊl) *adj* **1** holding or containing as much as possible or usual. **2** complete in number, development, etc.: full details; in full bloom; We waited a full hour. **3** having eaten or drunk to satisfaction. **4** rich in experience: a full life. **5** not restrained or qualified: full support. **6** having clearness, depth, and mellowness: a full tone. **7** round and plump. **8** rounded: full lips. **9** with much material hanging loose in folds: a full skirt. **10** with the attention centred on: full of himself.
• *adv* exactly. **fullness** or **fulness** *n* **fully** *adv* < Old English. SEE PANEL.

fulminate (ˈfʌlmɪˌneɪt) *vb* utter violent criticism and denunciation. **fulmination** *n* < Latin *fulminare* to flash with lightning.

fulsome (ˈfʊlsəm) *adj* exaggerated or insincere, esp. in a distasteful way: fulsome praise.

fumble (ˈfʌmbl̩) *vb* **1** grope about awkwardly or clumsily, as in searching. **2** deal with hesitantly or awkwardly. < probably Scandinavian.

fume (fjuːm) *n* smoke, vapour, or gas, esp. if offensive: exhaust fumes.
• *vb* **1** treat with fumes. **2** emit fumes. **3** be extremely angry. < Latin *fumus.*

fumigate (ˈfjuːmɪˌgeɪt) *vb* treat with fumes, esp. in order to disinfect. **fumigation** *n* < Latin *fumus* smoke + *agere* to make.

fun (fʌŋ) *n* light-hearted pleasure; source of this. **fun-fair** *n* an outdoor fair consisting of side-shows and other amusements. **make fun of** ridicule. < Middle English *fonne* fool.

function (ˈfʌŋkʃən) *n* **1** the natural or intended purpose of a person or thing. **2** a special ceremony or social gathering. **3** an action that is related to another action.
• *vb* serve or operate. **functional** *adj* **1** of a function. **2** designed for practical use without being decorative. **functionally** *adv* < Latin *fungi* to perform.

fund (fʌnd) *n* **1** a supply of money, esp. for a particular purpose. **2** an available quantity of resources: a fund of information.
• *vb* provide with money. < Latin *fundus* bottom.

fundamental (ˌfʌndəˈmɛntl̩) *adj* **1** acting as or forming a foundation or basis. **2** of the essential structure or function. **3** most important.
• *n* a fundamental principle, fact, etc. **fundamentally** *adv* < Latin *fundus* bottom.

funeral (ˈfjuːnərəl) *n* a formal ceremony at which a dead person is buried; procession to this. **funereal** *adj* **1** of a funeral. **2** gloomy; dismal. < Latin *funus*.

fungus (ˈfʌŋgəs) *n*, *pl* **fungi** any of a group of plants, such as moulds and mushrooms, that lack chlorophyll and leaves and grow on other plants or decaying matter. fungicide *n* a substance that destroys fungi. < Latin.

funicular (fjuːˈnɪkjʊlə) *n* a cable railway in which an ascending carriage counterbalances a descending carriage. < Latin *funis* rope.

funnel (ˈfʌnl̩) *n* **1** a utensil shaped like a hollow cone with a tube extending from the narrow end, used for pouring liquids, etc., into small openings. **2** a shaft or flue for the escape of smoke or steam.
• *vb* **funnelled; funnelling** pass through a funnel or narrow space. < Latin *in-* in + *fundere* to pour.

funny (ˈfʌnɪ) *adj* **1** causing amusement. **2** odd; peculiar. **3** (*informal*) slightly unwell or mad. **funnily** *adv* **funniness** *n*
SEE PANEL.

fur (fɜː) *n* **1** the soft, short, thick hair covering many mammals. **2** a skin bearing such hair, used for making clothes; garment made of this. **3** the

---

full marks

Full features in a number of expressions, including:

full-back *n* one of the defensive players in soccer, hockey, etc., positioned near the goal.
full-blooded *adj* vigorous: The prime minister delivered a full-blooded defence of the government's record.
full-blown *adj* fully developed.
full board provision of a bed and all meals in a hotel, etc.
full-length *adj* **1** extending the entire length of the human figure. **2** unabridged.
full marks the maximum marks possible in an examination; great praise or credit.
full moon the moon visible as a fully illuminated disc.
full-scale *adj* **1** of the actual size. **2** very thorough.
full speed or **steam ahead** an order to move forward with maximum speed.
full stop 1 the punctuation mark . used at the end of a sentence and in some abbreviations. **2** the point of cessation or completion: The work came to a full stop.
full time 1 the end of a football, etc., match. **2** the whole of a working day or week.
full-time *adj* working or employed full time.
in full with nothing omitted: publish the diaries in full.
to the full as completely as possible: enjoy life to the full.

---

funny peculiar or funny ha-ha?

The funny-bone is the area at the back of the elbow where the ulnar nerve is close to the surface of the skin; knocking this area causes a tingling sensation in the forearm. The name funny-bone is a pun on *humerus,* Latin for the arm-bone.

The expression funny peculiar or funny ha-ha? means 'when you say funny, do you mean something strange or something amusing?' It comes from 'The Housemaster' by the Scottish novelist and dramatist Ian Hay (1876–1952): 'What do you mean, funny? Funny peculiar or funny ha-ha?'

coating formed in kettles, etc., by the depositing of scale from hard water.
• *vb* **furred; furring** make or become covered or blocked with fur. **furry** *adj* < Old French *fuerre* sheath.

furious (ˈfjʊərɪəs) *adj* **1** extremely angry. **2** appearing very stormy. **3** marked by intense noise, speed, or excitement. **furiously** *adv* < Latin *furiosus.*

furlong (ˈfɜːlɒŋ) *n* a unit of length equal to 220 yards (201.168 metres). < Old English *furh* furrow + *lang* long. SEE PANEL AT **ACRE.**

furnace (ˈfɜːnɪs) *n* an enclosed structure in which heat is produced, for example to refine ores. < Latin *fornax.*

furnish (ˈfɜːnɪʃ) *vb* **1** provide (a house, room, etc.) with furniture. **2** provide or supply. **furnishings** *pl n* furniture and accessories such as curtains and carpets for a room or house. **furniture** *n* the movable articles, such as chairs and beds, needed in a room or house. < Middle French *fournir.*

furore (ˈfjʊərɔː, fjʊˈrɔːrɪ) *n* an outburst of public protest or excitement. < Latin *furor.*

furrow (ˈfʌrəʊ) *n* **1** a long, narrow trench made by a plough. **2** a groove like this; wrinkle.
• *vb* make furrows in. < Old English *furh.*

further (ˈfɜːðə) *adv* **1** farther. **2** in addition; moreover. **3** to a greater extent.
• *adj* **1** farther; more distant. **2** additional.
• *vb* help; promote. **furtherance** *n* **further education** formal education for people who have left school. **furthermore** *adv* in addition; moreover. **furthest** *adv, adj* at or to the greatest distance in space or time; most distant. < Old English *furthor.* SEE PANEL AT **FARTHER.**

furtive (ˈfɜːtɪv) *adj* showing or done by stealth. **furtively** *adv* **furtiveness** *n* < Latin *fur* thief.

fury (ˈfjʊərɪ) *n* **1** intense and violent anger. **2** intense and wild force or activity. < Latin *furere* to rage.

fuse[1] (fjuːz) *vb* **1** unite or become united, by or as if by melting together. **2** fail or cause to fail because a fuse has blown: The lights have fused.
• *n* a length of wire designed to melt and break the circuit when the electric current exceeds a certain safe level. < Latin *fundere* to pour.

fuse[2] *n* a length of easily burnt material for setting off an explosive charge. < Latin *fusus.*

fuselage (ˈfjuːzəˌlɒːʒ) *n* the main body of an aeroplane. < Middle French *fus* spindle.

fusion (ˈfjuːʒən) *n* **1** the act of fusing or melting together. **2** the union of two nuclei into a nucleus of heavier mass, with a release of energy.

fuss (fʌs) *n* **1** excessive or unnecessary excitement or activity. **2** agitation, esp. about something unimportant. **3** a display of great affection: They made a fuss of the new baby. **4** a complaint or protest.
• *vb* **1** be restlessly excited or busy. **2** display great affection. **3** give too much attention to unimportant details. **4** make or become worried or upset. **fussy** *adj* **1** nervous and excitable. **2** showing too much concern for unimportant details. **3** very particular: fussy about food. **4** too decorative. **fussily** *adv* **fussiness** *n* < origin uncertain.

fusty (ˈfʌstɪ) *adj* **1** smelling of damp or mould. **2** stuffy. **3** old-fashioned. < Latin *fustis* club.

futile (ˈfjuːtaɪl) *adj* having no effective result; worthless. **futility** *n* < Latin *futilis* that pours out easily, worthless.

future (ˈfjuːtʃə) *adj* **1** that is to be or come. **2** showing time that is to come: the future tense.
• *n* **1** the time that is to come. **2** prospect of success: no future in it. **futuristic** *adj* of or relating to the design, technology, etc., thought to belong to the future, esp. where different from traditional forms. < Latin *futurus* about to be.

fuzz (fʌz) *n* **1** a mass or covering of fine, light particles or fibres. **2** (*slang*) the police. **fuzzy** *adj* **1** like fuzz. **2** blurred and unclear: a fuzzy picture. **fuzzily** *adv* **fuzziness** *n* < origin uncertain.

G

g *abbrev* **1** gram; grams, **2** acceleration of free fall due to gravity.

gab (gæb) *vb* **gabbed**; **gabbing** (*informal*) talk idly.
• *n* idle talk. **the gift of the gab** (*informal*) ability to talk fluently and for a long time. < probably Irish Gaelic *gob* mouth.

gabble (ˈgæbl̩) *vb* talk or utter rapidly and indistinctly.
• *n* gabbled talk. **gabbler** *n* < probably like the sound.

gaberdine (ˈgæbəˌdiːn) *n* **1** a strong, twilled cloth of wool, cotton, etc., with a diagonal weave. **2** a waterproof coat made of this. < Middle French *gaverdine.*

gable (ˈgeɪbl̩) *n* the triangular upper section of an outside wall between the sloping roofs. **gabled** *adj* < probably Old Norse *gafl* gable.

gad (gæd) *vb* **gadded; gadding** go or travel about, esp. in an aimless way for pleasure. < probably back formation from obsolete *gadling* companion.

gadget (ˈgædʒɪt) *n* a small mechanical device or appliance. **gadgetry** *n* gadgets. < origin uncertain.

gaffe (gæf) *n* a social blunder; tactless remark. < French.

gag (gæg) *n* **1** something thrust into or tied across a person's mouth. **2** something said or done to provoke laughter; joke.
• *vb* **gagged; gagging 1** put a gag in or across the mouth of. **2** prevent from having free speech. **3** tell jokes. **4** retch; cause to retch. < origin uncertain.

gaggle (ˈgægl̩) *n* **1** a flock of geese. **2** (*informal*) a noisy or very talkative group.
• *vb* (of geese) to cackle. < Middle English *gagelen* to cackle.

gaiety (ˈgeɪətɪ) *n* **1** a cheerful, light-hearted manner. **2** happy, festive activity; merrymaking. **gaily** *adv* **1** in a cheerful, light-hearted manner. **2** brightly.

gain (geɪn) *n* an increase, as in an advantage, profit, degree, etc.
• *vb* **1** obtain possession of; acquire. **2** win an advantage; profit. **3** acquire by natural development: gain strength. **4** increase in: gain speed. **5** get further ahead (than); catch up: gain ground on one's rivals. **6** (of a clock, etc.) run fast (by an amount of). **gainer** *n* < Old French *gaaignier* to earn.

gainsay (geɪnˈseɪ) *vb* **gainsaid; gainsaying** (*formal*) dispute; oppose. < Middle English *gain-* against + *sayen* to say.

gait (geɪt) *n* **1** a manner of walking. **2** any of the various leg movements of a horse, such as trotting. < Middle English *gait, gate* gate.

gala (ˈgɑːlə) *n* **1** a festive occasion. **2** a sporting competition: a swimming gala. < Middle French *gale* merrymaking.

galaxy (ˈgæləksɪ) *n* **1** any of the many huge systems of stars, gas, and dust. **2 the Galaxy** the Milky Way. **3** an assembly of famous people: a galaxy of stars. **galactic** *adj* < Greek *gala* milk.

gale (geɪl) *n* **1** a strong wind. **2** a noisy outburst. < origin unknown.

gall (gɔːl) *n* **1** (*informal*) impudence. **2** something bitter. **3** bile. **gall-bladder** *n* a sac-like organ near the liver that stores bile. **gallstone** *n* a stone in the gall-bladder formed from cholesterol and bile pigments. < Old English *gealla.*

gallant (ˈgælənt) *adj* **1** brave and high-spirited. **2** (also gəˈlænt) courteously attentive to ladies. **3** fine; splendid. **gallantly** *adv* **gallantry** *n* < SEE **GALA.**

galleon (ˈgælɪən) *n* a large, square-rigged sailing ship, esp. one used by the Spanish in the 16th–17th centuries. < SEE **GALLEY.**

gallery (ˈgælərɪ) *n* **1** a covered passage for walking. **2** a balcony projecting from one or more inside walls of a hall, church, etc. **3** (in a theatre) an upper floor projecting over the main floor. **4** a long, narrow room, esp. one used for a particular purpose. **5** a building or room for displaying works of art. < Medieval Latin *galeria.*

galley (ˈgælɪ) *n, pl* **galleys 1** (in ancient and medieval times) a long, low ship propelled by oars and sails. **2** a kitchen on a ship or aircraft. < Old French *galie.*

galling (ˈgɔːlɪŋ) *adj* annoying or exasperating; humiliating. < *gall* sore caused by chafing, from Latin *galla* gallnut.

gallivant (ˈgælɪˌvænt) *vb* gad about. < perhaps from *gallant.*

gallon (ˈgælən) *n* a measure of liquids equal to four quarts (in the UK 4.546 litres, USA 3.785 litres). < Medieval Latin *galeta* pail.

gallop (ˈgæləp) *n* **1** a horse's fastest pace, with all feet off the ground simultaneously. **2** a ride at this pace; very rapid movement.
• *vb* ride or progress or cause to ride or progress at a gallop. < Old French *galoper* to gallop.

gallows (ˈgæləʊz) *n* **1** a frame of two upright posts and a crosspiece from which a rope is suspended, used for hanging criminals. **2** the hanging of criminals: the gallows. < Old English *gealga*.

galore (gəˈlɔː) *adj* in plenty: whisky galore!; bargains galore! < Irish Gaelic *go leōr* to sufficiency. SEE PANEL.

galosh (gəˈlɒʃ) *n* a waterproof rubber shoe worn over an ordinary shoe for protection in wet weather. < Middle French *galoche*.

galvanize (ˈgælvəˌnaɪz) *vb* **1** cover (iron or steel) with zinc for protection from rust. **2** stimulate into sudden activity: The threat of redundancy galvanized the workers into action. **galvanization** *n* SEE PANEL.

gambit (ˈgæmbɪt) *n* an opening move in chess or any action or remark by which one hopes to gain an advantage. < Italian *gambetto* tripping-up.

gamble (ˈgæmbl̩) *vb* **1** risk money on the occurrence of an event. **2** play games of chance for money. **3** act, with the expectation of the occurrence of an event: I wouldn't gamble on it being a fine day.
• *n* **1** a bet or other risk taken in the hope of monetary gain. **2** a risky act or undertaking. **gambler** *n* < probably Middle English *gamen* to play.

gambol (ˈgæmbl̩) *vb* **gambolled; gambolling** skip or jump about playfully.
• *n* a gambolling movement. < French *gambade*.

game (geɪm) *n* **1** a form of amusement or sport, esp. one with rules. **2** a single scoring unit in some games. **3** a style of playing: off one's game. **4** *pl* sports, esp. athletics: the Olympic Games. **5** a type of activity, esp. one involving rivalry. **6** a scheme or plan: So that's your little game! **7** wild animals hunted for sport or food; flesh of such animals.
• *vb* gamble.
• *adj* **1** brave and determined. **2** (*informal*) ready: game for anything! **gamekeeper** *n* a person employed to breed and protect game on an estate. < Old English *gamen*.

gamesmanship (ˈgeɪmzmənˌʃɪp) *n* the art of winning games by clever or cunning actions without actually breaking the rules. SEE PANEL.

gamete (ˈgæmiːt) *n* either of two cells, one male and one female, that combine

---

galore

Galore is an example of an adjective that follows the noun referred to. This is different from the normal pattern of the adjective coming before the word being modified.

Other examples of adjectives like galore are:

elect 'soon to take office': the president elect
proper 'as strictly defined': the City of London proper
regent 'governing during the minority, incapacity, etc., of the rightful monarch': a prince regent.

---

galvanize

Galvanize owes its origin to Luigi *Galvani*, 1737–98, a physician and physicist of Bologna. The word is an example of an *eponym*, that is, a word that derives from the name of a person.

Galvani observed that the twitching of muscles in the legs of a frog, when brought into contact with certain metals, was due to a kind of animal electricity—hence galvanize 'to stimulate into sudden action'.

Other eponyms include:
Biro from Lászlo *Biró* (1900–85)
cardigan from James Thomas Brudenell, seventh Earl of *Cardigan* (1797–1868)
Heath Robinson (used to describe absurdly complicated machines) from William *Heath Robinson* (1872–1944)
Hoover from W.H.*Hoover* (1849–1932)
mackintosh from Charles M. *Macintosh* (1766–1843)
sandwich from John Montagu, fourth Earl of *Sandwich* (1718–92)
silhouette from Étienne de *Silhouette* (1709–67)
wellington from Arthur Wellesley, first Duke of *Wellington* (1769–1852)

in sexual reproduction. < ultimately Greek *gamos* marriage.

gamma (ˈgæmə) *n* the third letter of the Greek alphabet.

gammon (ˈgæmən) *n* the quick-cured hind leg of a bacon pig, bought boned and uncooked and then boiled or grilled. < Old Northern French *gambon,* from *gambe* leg.

gammy (ˈgæmɪ) *adj* (*informal*) lame: a gammy leg. < origin uncertain.

gamut (ˈgæmət) *n* an entire range. SEE PANEL.

gander (ˈgændə) *n* a male goose. < Old English *gandra.*

gang (gæŋ) *n* **1** a group of people working together: a road gang. **2** a group of people associating together: a gang of crooks.
• *vb* form or act as a gang. **gangster** *n* a member of a criminal gang. **gang up on** join together against. < Old English.

gangling (ˈgæŋglɪŋ) *adj* tall, thin, and awkward in movement. < origin uncertain.

gangplank (ˈgæŋˌplæŋk) *n* a movable plank used for boarding and leaving a ship at the quay.

gangrene (ˈgæŋgriːn) *n* death of body tissues, esp. those of a limb, due to loss of blood supply. **gangrenous** *adj* < Greek *gangraina.*

gangway (ˈgæŋˌweɪ) *n* **1** a passageway such as an opening in the side of a ship; gangplank. **2** a passageway between rows of seats.
• *interj* clear a passage; make way!

gannet (ˈgænɪt) *n* a large, fish-eating sea-bird. < Old English *ganot.*

gantry (ˈgæntrɪ) *n* a bridge-like, overhead structure used for example to support motorway signs or a travelling crane. < Latin *cantherius* trellis, pack ass.

gaol (dʒeɪl) SEE **JAIL**. SEE PANEL AT **JAIL**.

gap (gæp) *n* **1** a break or empty space, as in a barrier or between two objects or amounts. **2** an interruption of continuity. **3** a mountain pass or ravine. **4** a difference between natures, ideas, attitudes, etc.: the generation gap. < Old Norse: chasm.

gape (geɪp) *vb* **1** open the mouth wide. **2** stare with one's mouth open, as in surprise or wonder. **3** open, esp. widely: a gaping cavity.
• *n* an open-mouthed stare. < Old Norse *gapa.*

garage (ˈgærɑːʒ, ˈgærɪdʒ) *n* **1** a building used to house a motor vehicle. **2** a commercial establishment in which motor vehicles are serviced, repaired, bought, and sold. **3** a commercial establishment that sells petrol, oil, etc.
• *vb* to keep or put in a garage. < Middle French *garer* to take care.

garb (gɑːb) *n* a distinctive style of clothing.
• *vb* clothe. < Old Italian *garbo* grace.

garbage (ˈgɑːbɪdʒ) *n* **1** useless or unwanted matter; nonsense. **2** (*chiefly US*) rubbish. < Middle English: animal entrails.

garble (ˈgɑːbl̩) *vb* distort or confuse a message or story, so giving a false impression: a garbled account. < Old Italian, from Arabic *gharbala* to sift.

garden (ˈgɑːdn̩) *n* **1** an area of land, esp. planted with grass, flowers, vegetables, etc., adjoining a house. **2** a public recreation area or park, esp. with plants: botanical gardens.
• *vb* work in or cultivate a garden. **garden centre** an establishment where plants, seeds, garden tools, etc., are sold. **gardener** *n* a person who works in or looks after a garden, as an occupation or hobby. **garden party** a social gathering, usually formal, on the lawn of a

gamesmanship

'Gamesmanship' is the title of a book, published in 1947, by the English writer Stephen Potter (1900–69). Under the influence of gamesmanship, the suffix -manship, used to indicate a skill or art (horsemanship, craftsmanship), sometimes implies a cunning, sly activity in an effort to disconcert one's rival, for example oneupmanship.

gamut

Gamut was originally the lowest note in the medieval musical scale. It comes from *gamma* and *ut. Gamma* was the lowest note in the 'great scale' established by Guido d'Arezzo, the 11th-century Italian monk and musical theorist. *Ut* was the first of the notes *ut, re, mi, fa, sol, la, si,* coming from the Latin hymn to St John the Baptist. *Doh,* the first note in the modern major scale, probably comes from *ut,* the sounds *ut* being reversed and modified.

garden. < Old Northern French *gardin*.

gargantuan (gɑːˈgæntjʊən) *adj* colossal; huge. < *Gargantua*, giant king in 'Gargantua', satire by Rabelais.

gargle (ˈgɑːgl̩) *vb* rinse the throat and mouth with (a liquid) by forcing air from the lungs through the liquid.
• *n* a liquid used in gargling. < Middle French *gargouiller*, like the sound.

gargoyle (ˈgɑːgɔɪl) *n* a carved water-spout in the form of a grotesque person or animal that projects from a gutter. < Middle French *gargouille*.

garish (ˈgɛərɪʃ) *adj* excessively bright, colourful, or showy; gaudy. **garishly** *adv* < origin unknown.

garland (ˈgɑːlənd) *n* a wreath of flowers, etc., worn as a decoration.
• *vb* decorate with a garland or garlands. < Old French *garlande*.

garlic (ˈgɑːlɪk) *n* **1** an onion-like plant. **2** the bulbous root of this plant with a strong aroma and taste, used for flavouring. **garlicky** *adj* < Old English *gār* spear + *lēac* leek.

garment (ˈgɑːmənt) *n* an article of clothing. < Old French *garnir* to equip.

garnet (ˈgɑːnɪt) *n* a semi-precious stone, esp. red in colour. < Medieval Latin *grenat* red, from *pome grenate* pomegranate.

garnish (ˈgɑːnɪʃ) *vb* decorate (esp. food) with something that improves its appearance or flavour.
• *n* something used to garnish. < Middle French *garnir* to equip.

garret (ˈgærət) *n* the space or room within the sloping roof of a house; attic. < Middle French *garite*.

garrison (ˈgærɪsn̩) *n* a base or fortified place; troops who maintain or guard it.
• *vb* place (troops) in (a town, etc.). < Old French *garir* to protect.

garrulous (ˈgærʊləs) *adj* too talkative, esp. about unimportant matters. **garrulously** *adv* **garrulousness** or **garrulity** *n* < Latin *garrire* to chatter.

garter (ˈgɑːtə) *n* a band, esp. of elastic, worn round the leg to keep a sock or stocking up. < Old Northern French *gartier*, from *garet* bend of the knee.

gas (gæs) *n* **1** a substance with molecules that are free to move about, with no forces holding them together. **2** a gas or mixture of gases used for lighting, heating, etc. **3** a substance that can be used to produce something poisonous, suffocating, or irritating: tear gas. **4** also **gasoline** (*US*) petrol. **5** (*informal*) empty talk.
• *vb* **gassed; gassing 1** treat with a gas. **2** poison or affect by a gas. **3** (*informal*) talk idly. **gasbag** *n* (*informal*) a person who talks too much. **gaseous** *adj* of or like gas. **gaslight** *n* a light in which the flame comes from a jet of burning gas. **gasmask** *n* SEE **MASK** (def. **4**). **gasometer** *n* a large, cylindrical storage container for gas. **gasworks** *pl n* a place where gas is manufactured. **gassy** *adj* of or like gas. < coined by J.B. van Helmont, died 1644, Flemish chemist, alteration of Latin *chaos* space, chaos.

gash (gæʃ) *n* a long, deep cut or wound.
• *vb* make a gash in. < Old Northern French *garser*, ultimately from Greek *charassein* to scratch.

gasket (ˈgæskɪt) *n* a piece of material inserted between two surfaces to seal a joint so that a liquid or gas does not escape. < probably Old French *garcette* thin rope.

gasp (gɑːsp) *vb* **1** catch one's breath suddenly, as in surprise. **2** breathe with much effort. **3** utter with gasps.
• *n* a gasping. < Middle English *gaspen*.

gastric (ˈgæstrɪk) *adj* of the stomach. **gastro-enteritis** *n* infection of the stomach and intestines. < Greek *gastēr*.

gastronomy (gæsˈtrɒnəmɪ) *n* the art of good eating. **gastronomical** *adj*

gate (geɪt) *n* **1** a movable barrier, usually hinged, for closing an opening in a wall or fence; such an opening. **2** the entrance to a city or castle, esp. with fortifications. **3** a means of entrance or exit. **4** either of a pair of barriers, for example for regulating the flow of water in a lock. **5** the total number of spectators at an event; total amount of admission money paid. **gatecrash** *vb* go to (a private party, etc.) without an invitation. **gatecrasher** *n* **gatehouse** *n* a house built beside or over a gate. **gatekeeper** *n* a person who guards or looks after a gate. **gateway** *n* **1** an entrance that may be closed by a gate. **2** a means of access. < Old English gear.

gâteau (ˈgætəʊ) *n, pl* **gâteaux** a large, rich, cream cake. < French: cake.

gather (ˈgæðə) *vb* **1** bring or come together. **2** pick or harvest: gather corn. **3** increase gradually: gather momentum. **4** bring together the parts of. **5** pull (fabric) together to create small tucks. **6** prepare (oneself) for an effort. **7** reach a conclusion: From what's been said, I gather you're not very keen on the idea.
• *n* a tuck in cloth made by gathering. **gathering** *n* a meeting; assembly.

< Old English *gaderian.*

gauche (gəʊʃ) *adj* lacking social grace; awkward. < French: awkward, left, from Old French *gauchir* to turn aside.

gaudy (ˈgɔːdɪ) *adj* decorated in a showy or tastelessly bright way. **gaudily** *adv* **gaudiness** *n* < Middle English *gaude* trick, toy.

gauge (geɪdʒ) *n* **1** a measurement according to a standard or system. **2** an instrument for measuring or testing something: a pressure gauge. **3** the distance between the rails of a railway or wheels on an axle. **4** the thickness or diameter of something such as wire.
• *vb* **1** measure the size, capacity, etc., of. **2** judge or estimate. < Old Northern French.

gaunt (gɔːnt) *adj* **1** very thin and haggard. **2** grim or desolate. < origin uncertain.

gauntlet (ˈgɔːntlɪt) *n* a heavy glove with a long cuff. < Middle French *gant* glove.

gauze (gɔːz) *n* **1** a thin, transparent fabric used for clothing. **2** a loosely woven cotton fabric used as a surgical dressing. **3** a fine wire mesh. **gauzy** *adj* < Middle French *gaze.*

gave (geɪv) SEE **GIVE.**

gavel (ˈgævl̩) *n* a small hammer used by a chairman or auctioneer to command attention, confirm a sale, etc. < origin unknown.

gawky (ˈgɔːkɪ) *adj* clumsy or awkward; ungainly. **gawkily** *adv* < probably English dialect *gawk* left-handed.

gawp (gɔːp) *vb* (*informal*) stare stupidly. < alteration of Middle English *galpen* to gape.

gay (geɪ) *adj* **1** light-hearted and cheerful; fun-loving. **2** bright and attractive: gay colours. **3** (*informal*) homosexual.
• *n* (*informal*) a homosexual. < Middle French *gai.*

gaze (geɪz) *vb* fix the eyes in a long, steady look.
• *n* such a look. < Middle English *gazen,* from Scandinavian.

gazelle (gəˈzɛl) *n* a small, slender, fawn-coloured African or Asian antelope. < Arabic *ghazāl.*

gazette (gəˈzɛt) *n* a newspaper or official journal; title of this, SEE PANEL.

gazetteer (ˌgæzɪˈtɪə) *n* a book or section of a book dealing with geographical names.

gazump (gəˈzʌmp) *vb* thwart (a would-be house-buyer) by raising the price after a price has previously been agreed. < origin uncertain.

GB *abbrev* Great Britain.

GCE *abbrev* General Certificate of Education.

GCSE *abbrev* General Certificate of Secondary Education.

Gdn(s) *abbrev* Garden(s).

gear (gɪə) *n* **1** a toothed wheel that engages with another toothed wheel or rack, in order to change the speed or direction. **2** a mechanism performing a specific function: landing gear. **3** clothing; garments. **4** equipment: fishing gear.
• *vb* **1** provide with or connect by gears. **2** put into gear. **3** adapt (to suit a purpose). **gearbox** *n* a set of gears and its housing. **in/out of gear** in/not in a working relation or position. < probably Old Norse *gervi.*

gee-gee (ˈdʒiːˌdʒiː) *n* a horse; used

gazette

The origin of gazette is uncertain. On the one hand it is believed to derive from *gazeta,* the Venetian word for the small copper coin similar to the farthing that was paid by Venetians in the 16th century as the price of the government newspaper. An alternative theory is that the word is a diminutive of *gazza* 'a magpie', on the basis that the newspaper was filled with the chatter that is associated with the bird.

gee-gee

An interesting feature of language usage is the way new parents suddenly find a whole new vocabulary available for addressing their gurgling offspring. For example, within the field of animal names a considerable number of different words occur. A horse is rarely referred to as a horse. It tends to become a more cuddly creature—a gee-gee or horsie. Similarly a cat becomes a pussy or pussy cat. Other animal names that are adapted for baby's ears include:

bunny rabbit or **bunny** a rabbit
quack quack a duck
moo cow a cow
baa lamb a lamb
dickie bird or **birdie** a bird
doggie a dog

mostly by or to small children. SEE PANEL.

geese (giːs) SEE **GOOSE**.

geezer (ˈgiːzə) *n* (*informal*) a man, esp. an old or eccentric one. < probably alteration of Scottish *guiser* a person in disguise.

gel (dʒɛl) SEE **JELL**.

gelatin (ˈdʒɛlətɪn) or **gelatine** (ˈdʒɛləˌtiːn) *n* a colourless, jelly-like substance formed by boiling animal tissues, used in foods and photography. **gelatinous** *adj* < Latin *gelare* to freeze.

geld (gɛld) *vb* castrate (a horse or other animal). **gelding** *n* a castrated male horse. < Old Norse *gelda*.

gelignite (ˈdʒɛlɪgˌnaɪt) *n* an explosive containing nitro-glycerine. < *gel*atin + Latin *ignis* fire + *-ite*.

gem (dʒɛm) *n* **1** a precious stone, esp. when cut and polished and used as jewellery. **2** something highly valued and prized. < Latin *gemma*.

gen (dʒɛn) *n* (*informal*) information. < short for *general* (*information*).

gender (ˈdʒɛndə) *n* **1** the grammatical classification of words, esp. into masculine, feminine, and neuter; such a class. **2** sex. < Latin *genus* kind.

gene (dʒiːn) *n* a unit of the hereditary material of an organism that is carried on a chromosome. < ultimately Greek *-genēs* born.

genealogy (ˌdʒiːnɪˈælədʒɪ) *n* **1** an account of the descendants of a person from an ancestor. **2** the study of family descents. **genealogical** *adj* **genealogist** *n* < Greek *genea* race, family + *-logy*, ultimately *logos* word.

general (ˈdʒɛnərəl, ˈdʒɛnrəl) *adj* **1** of or for the whole. **2** of or for every member of a group. **3** for or characteristic of most of the individuals; widespread: general unrest. **4** of universal rather than particular or detailed aspects: in general terms. **5** not specialized or limited: general knowledge. **6** holding a superior rank: the General Secretary, the Director-General. • *n* an army officer below a field marshal. **generality** *n* **1** being general. **2** a vague or indefinite statement. **generalize** *vb* **1** form (a general principle) from (a detailed fact). **2** speak in generalities. **3** bring into general use. **generalization** *n* **generally** *adv* **1** usually: Generally the trains arrive punctually. **2** widely or commonly: generally accepted standards. **3** without referring to details; broadly: generally speaking. **4** considered with reference to all its parts; collectively. **general election** a nationwide election in which representatives are chosen for parliament. **general practitioner** a doctor who treats cases of all kinds, not specializing in any particular branch of medicine. **general-purpose** *adj* having a wide variety of uses. **in general** generally; mostly or usually. < Latin *genus* class.

generate (ˈdʒɛnəˌreɪt) *vb* bring into existence; produce. **generation** *n* **1** generating or being generated. **2** a single stage in the descent from an ancestor. **3** a group of people born and living at the same time. **4** the average time between the birth of parents and that of their children. **5** a stage in the development of machinery: a new generation of computers. **generation gap** a lack of understanding and difference in outlook between different generations. **generator** *n* **1** a device which converts mechanical energy into electrical energy. **2** an apparatus for producing a gas. < Latin *genus* race, kind.

generic (dʒəˈnɛrik) *adj* **1** applying to a whole group or genus. **2** (of a drug) not having a trademark. < Latin *genus* kind, class.

generous (ˈdʒɛnərəs, ˈdʒɛnrəs) *adj* **1** ready and liberal in giving one's time, money, help, etc. **2** big-hearted; kind: a generous nature. **3** marked by abundance or greatness: a generous gift. **generosity** *n* **generously** *adv* < Latin *generosus* nobly born, from *genus* birth.

genetic (dʒəˈnɛtɪk) *adj* of genes or genetics. **genetically** *adv* **genetics** *n* the study of heredity and variation in living organisms.

genial (ˈdʒiːnjəl) *adj* **1** warm, friendly, and cheerful. **2** mild: a genial climate. **geniality** *n* **genially** *adv* < SEE **GENIUS**.

genie (ˈdʒiːnɪ) *n* (in fairy-tales, etc.) a spirit, esp. in human form, who fulfils a person's wishes. < Arabic *jinnīy*.

genital (ˈdʒɛnɪtḷ) *adj* of the sexual organs or reproduction. **genitals** *pl n* also **genitalia** the external reproductive and sexual organs. < Latin *gignere* to beget. SEE PANEL.

genitive (ˈdʒɛnɪtɪv) *adj, n* (of or in) the grammatical case showing possession or source. < Latin *genitivus* of birth.

genius (ˈdʒiːnɪəs, ˈdʒiːnjəs) *n* **1** an exceptionally intelligent or able person. **2** exceptional intelligence or ability. **3** the special spirit or creative nature of a country, period, etc. < Latin *gignere* to beget.

genocide (ˈdʒɛnəˌsaɪd) *n* the murder of a race of people. < Greek *genos* race + *-cide*, from Latin *caedere* to kill.

genre (ˈʒɒnrə) *n* a particular type of musical, literary, etc., composition. < Middle French, from Latin *genus* kind.

gent (dʒɛnt) *n* (*informal*) a gentleman; man. **the Gents** (*informal*) a men's public lavatory.

genteel (dʒɛnˈtiːl) *adj* **1** of or relating to the gentry or upper class. **2** affectedly proper or refined. **genteelly** *adv* < Middle French *gentil* gentle.

gentility (dʒɛnˈtɪlɪtɪ) *n* **1** the upper class. **2** genteel status, attitudes, or actions. < Latin *gentilitas* belonging to the same clan.

gentle (ˈdʒɛntḷ) *adj* **1** not harsh, stern, or severe; mild or moderate: a gentle breeze. **2** (*old-fashioned*) of honourable birth. **gentleness** *n* **gently** *adv* **gentleman** *n, pl* **gentlemen 1** (*chiefly polite*) a man: Ladies and gentlemen .... **2** a man of noble birth. **3** an honourable, well-mannered man: He's a real gentleman! **gentlemanly** *adj* **gentleman's** or **gentlemen's agreement** an informal agreement based on honour and trust as opposed to a formal written contract. < Latin *gentilis* of the same clan.

gentry (ˈdʒɛntrɪ) *pl n* **1** people of high birth or social status. **2** the people just below the nobility in social rank. < SEE **GENTLE.**

genuine (ˈdʒɛnjʊɪn) *adj* **1** not false or pretended; sincere: a genuine interest in his welfare. **2** real; authentic: a genuine antique. **genuinely** *adv* **genuineness** *n* < Latin *gignere* to beget.

gen up (dʒɛn) *vb* **genned; genning** give full information (about something) to. < SEE **GEN.**

genus (ˈdʒiːnəs) *n, pl* **genera 1** a category in the classification of living things, containing one or more species. **2** a group with common characteristics. < Latin: race.

geography (dʒɪˈɔgrəfɪ) *n* **1** the scientific study of the natural features of the earth's surface, considered as man's environment. **2** the natural features of a region. **geographer** *n* **geographical** *adj* **geographically** *adv* < Greek *geographein* to describe the earth's surface.

geology (dʒɪˈɒlədʒɪ) *n* **1** the scientific study of the history, structure, and composition of the earth. **2** the geological features of a region. **geological** *adj* **geologically** *adv* **geologist** *n* < Greek *gē* earth + *-logy,* ultimately *logos* word.

geometry (dʒɪˈɒmətrɪ) *n* the branch of mathematics concerned with the measurements, properties, and relations of angles, lines, surfaces, and solids. **geometric** or **geometrical** *adj* **geometrically** *adv* < Greek *gē* earth + *metrein* to measure.

geranium (dʒəˈreɪnɪəm) *n* a plant with roundish leaves and ball-like clusters of showy red, pink, or white flowers. < Greek *geranos* crane.

gerbil (ˈdʒɜːbəl) *n* a small, burrowing rodent with long hind legs that inhabits dry, open country. < New Latin *jerboa.*

geriatrics (ˌdʒɛrɪˈætrɪks) *n* the branch of medicine that deals with the diseases and problems of old age. **geriatric** *adj* < Greek *gēras* old age.

germ (dʒɜːm) *n* **1** a micro-organism, esp. one that can cause disease. **2** a simple structure that is capable of developing into a new organism; embryo of a seed. **3** the source or beginning of something. **germinate** *vb* **1** sprout or cause to sprout. **2** grow or cause to grow; develop. **3** originate. **germination** *n* < Latin *germen* bud, seed.

germane (dʒɜːˈmeɪn) *adj* relevant. < variant of *german,* from Latin *germanus* having the same parents.

gestation (dʒɛˈsteɪʃən) *n* **1** the carrying of young in the womb during pregnancy; duration of this. **2** the development of an idea in the mind. < Latin *gerere* to bear.

gesticulate (dʒeˈstɪkjʊˌleɪt) *vb* express by gestures. **gesticulation** *n* < Latin *gesticulari,* ultimately from *gerere* to bear.

---

hiding one's genitals

Language can provide a highly revealing mirror of social attitudes. One of the best illustrations of this is in the wealth of 'genteel' words (or *euphemisms*) to be found in Victorian literature, which provide telling evidence of the prudery of the age. The word belly, for example, could under no circumstances be mentioned in polite society. Instead, delicacy demanded that names such as abdomen, stomach, or tummy be used. Buttocks was similarly considered far too coarse and seat, sit-upon, posterior or the lyrical-sounding derrière were used instead. Bosom, chest, and bust were much less likely to cause outrage than breasts, and the genitals remained safely hidden behind private parts or parts.

---

gesture (ˈdʒestʃə) *n* **1** a movement, esp. of the hands or arms, to express or emphasize an idea or attitude. **2** something done as a formality or to convey a feeling: a gesture of goodwill.
• *vb* make a gesture. < Latin *gestus*, past participle of *gerere* to bear.

get (gɛt) *vb* **got; getting 1** gain possession of; receive, obtain, or fetch: Did you get my letter? **2** become affected by; contract (an illness). **3** change or become or cause to change or become: get old; get one's hair cut.

get

In British English the past participle of get is got: 'Somehow she had *got* lost'. At one time, however, the past participle was formed by adding -en: gott*en*, like fall*en*, *eaten*, or ris*en*. The original form, gotten, continues to be used in American English: 'I wish I hadn't *gotten* ill'.

Although the -en ending has disappeared from get in British English, it has been retained in forget—past participle forgotten—and also appears in the phrase ill-gotten: They're still living it up on their *ill-gotten* gains.

Get features in a large number of idiomatic expressions, including:

get across to communicate.
get ahead to make progress; succeed.
get along or **on 1** to be on friendly terms. **2** to make progress; manage or advance.
get at 1 to reach. **2** to suggest; imply: What are you getting at? **3** to criticize. **4** to influence; bribe.
get-at-able *adj* accessible.
get away 1 to escape or leave. **getaway** *adj*, *n* **2** to go on a holiday.
get away with to escape with little or no blame or punishment.
get back at to take revenge on.
get by to pass; just manage to do something: We'll get by somehow.
get down 1 to swallow. **2** to record in writing. **3** to make (someone) depressed. **4** (of children) to leave the table: Can I get down?
get down to to start working on.
get going 1 to begin moving or walking. **2** to organize (something).
get in 1 to gather or collect. **2** to ask (a doctor, builder, etc.) to provide a specialist service at one's home, office, etc. **3** also **get into** be elected to (a committee, etc.).
get in on to take part in or cause to take part in.
get into 1 to preoccupy or take control of: What's got into him? **2** to become interested in and familiar with: In any new job it always takes a few days to get into things. **3** to interfere with: Our toddler gets into everything!
get in with to become on friendly terms with.
get off 1 to begin a journey; leave; alight from. **2** to escape with little or no blame or punishment. **3** to save from blame or punishment.
get off with to begin a friendly or sexual relationship with.
get on 1 to board (a bus, etc.). **2** to become late; become old. **3** to be nearly (a time, age, etc., that is mentioned): It's getting on for 1 o'clock. **4** to get along.
get on at to criticize or nag.
get one's own back to take revenge.
get on to 1 to contact. **2** to discover: The police soon got on to the suspect's whereabouts.
get out 1 to become known. **2** to publish.
get-out *n* a means of escape or evasion.
get out of to avoid: He always gets out of thewashing-up.
get over 1 to recover from (an illness, intense experience, etc.). **2** to overcome. **3** to accept or appreciate fully and calmly: I just can't get over your beard!
get round 1 to influence by flattery. **2** to overcome (a problem). **3** to evade (a rule, etc.).
get round to to succeed in finding time to (do something).
get there to achieve one's aim.
get through 1 to pass (an examination, etc.). **2** to consume, spend, or finish. **3** to contact by telephone.
get through to 1 to reach. **2** to make (a person) understand; communicate.
get-together *n* an informal meeting.
get up 1 to rise from bed. **2** to stand up. **3** to organize: get up a petition. **4** to increase in force: The wind is suddenly getting up. **5** to dress in a showy way. **get-up** *n*
get up to to become involved in (mischief, etc.).

4 make ready; prepare (a meal). **5** catch; take vengeance on; kill: I'll get you for that! **6** send, take, or move: We'll get you to hospital somehow. **7** persuade: I'll get her to come and see you. **8** have: I've got no money. **9** used to express obligation: You've got to go and see the headmaster! **10** (*informal*) irritate: His constant bickering really gets me! **11** (*informal*) understand: Don't get me wrong! < Old Norse *geta*. SEE **PANEL**.

geyser (ˈgi:zə) *n* **1** a natural spring that sends up jets of heated water and steam at intervals. **2** a gas water-heater. < Old Norse *geysa* to rush forth.

ghastly (ˈgɑ:stlɪ) *adj* **1** causing horror: a ghastly accident. **2** (*informal*) extremely unpleasant; awful. **3** pale and looking ill. **ghastliness** *n* < Middle English *gasten* to terrify.

gherkin (ˈgɜ:kɪn) *n* a small cucumber used for pickling. < Low German *augurke*. SEE PANEL.

ghetto (ˈgetəʊ) *n, pl* **ghettos** a part of a city, esp. a slum area, in which a minority group lives; area with chiefly one type of resident. < Italian.

ghost (gəʊst) *n* **1** a disembodied soul, esp. of a dead person. **2** a trace; least bit. • *vb* write as a ghost-writer. **ghostly** *adj* **ghostliness** *n* **ghost-writer** *n* a person who writes for another person who is credited as the author. < Old English *gāst*.

ghoul (gu:l) *n* **1** (in Arabic legends) an evil being that robs graves and feeds on the dead. **2** a person who enjoys morbid or macabre things. **ghoulish** *adj* **ghoulishly** *adv* < Arabic *ghāla* to seize.

giant (ˈdʒaɪənt) fem. **giantess** (ˈdʒaɪəntɛs) *n* **1** a legendary being of human form but of superhuman size and strength. **2** a person or thing that is extremely large. **3** a person of extraordinary powers. • *adj* very large in size: a giant packet of washing-powder. < Greek *gigas*.

gherkin

The history of gherkin is as long as the baby cucumber to which it refers is short. Gherkin comes from the Dutch *gurken*, the plural of *gurk*, 'a cucumber'. Gurk is a development of an earlier Dutch word, *augurk*, derived from the Low German *augurke*, which was the form inherited from Middle Low German. This in turn is traceable to the Polish *ogurek*, which comes from the Middle Greek word *agouros*, 'a water-melon or cucumber'. The Greeks are believed to have adopted the word from Persian.

gibber (ˈdʒɪbə) *vb* utter very quickly and unintelligibly. **gibberish** *n* unintelligible or meaningless talk. < like the sound.

gibbet (ˈdʒɪbɪt) *n* (formerly) an upright post with an arm from which the bodies of executed criminals were hung. < Middle French *gibet* gallows.

gibbon (ˈgɪbn̩) *n* a small, long-armed, tree-dwelling, Asian ape. < French.

gibe (dʒaɪb) *vb* jeer (at). • *n* a jeer. < perhaps Middle French *giber* to handle roughly.

giblets (ˈdʒɪblɪts) *pl n* the edible internal organs of a bird, such as the heart and liver. < Middle French *gibelet* stew of game birds.

giddy (ˈgɪdɪ) *adj* **1** feeling unsteady and unbalanced as if everything is spinning round; causing such a feeling. **2** not serious; frivolous. **giddily** *adv* **giddiness** *n* < Old English *gydig* mad.

gift (gɪft) *n* **1** something freely given. **2** a natural ability or talent. **gifted** *adj* having great natural ability. **giftwrap** *vb* **giftwrapped; giftwrapping** wrap (goods intended as a gift) decoratively. < Old English, from Old Norse: something given.

gig (gɪg) *n* (*informal*) a musician's engagement, esp. for one performance. < origin unknown.

gigantic (dʒaɪˈgæntɪk) *adj* extremely large. **gigantically** *adv* < SEE **GIANT**.

giggle (ˈgɪgl̩) *vb* laugh with rapid catches of the breath, esp. in a foolish way. • *n* **1** this kind of laugh. **2** something amusing. **giggly** *adj* < like the sound.

gild (gɪld) *vb* **gilded, gilt; gilding** overlay with or as if with a thin covering of gold. < Old English *gyldan*.

gill[1] (gɪl) *n* the respiratory organ of aquatic animals, esp. fish. < probably Scandinavian.

gill[2] (dʒɪl) *n* a unit for measuring liquids, equal to ¼ pint (about 0.142 litres). < Late Latin *gillo* cooling-vessel.

gilt (gɪlt) SEE **GILD**. • *adj* covered with gold or gilt; gold. • *n* **1** gold leaf; substance like this. **2** a gilt-edged security.

gimlet (ˈgɪmlɪt) *n* a small tool with a pointed spiral tip for boring holes. < Middle French *guimbelet*.

gimmick (ˈgɪmɪk) *n* a scheme, trick, or device for attracting attention or publicity. **gimmicky** *adj* < origin unknown.

gin (dʒɪn) *n* a spirit distilled from grain flavoured with juniper berries. < ultimately Latin *juniperus* juniper.

ginger (ˈdʒɪndʒə) *n* **1** a tropical plant with a pungent underground stem used as a spice or food or in medicine; such a stem. **2** a strong reddish-brown or yellowish-brown colour.
• *adj* ginger-coloured: ginger hair.
• *vb* **ginger up** make more lively or interesting. **gingerly** *adj, adv* (in a way that is) very cautious. < probably ultimately Sanskrit *śṛngavera.*

gingham (ˈgɪŋəm) *n* a striped or checked cotton fabric. < modified from Malay *genggang* checkered cloth.

gipsy (ˈdʒɪpsɪ) SEE **GYPSY**.

giraffe (dʒɪˈrɑːf) *n* a long-necked African animal with a buff-coloured coat marked with reddish-brown blotches. < Arabic *zirāfah.*

gird (gɜːd) *vb* **1** encircle or fasten with a belt. **2** prepare (oneself) for action. **girder** *n* a main supporting beam in a building, etc. < Old English *gyrdan.*

girdle (ˈgɜːdḷ) *n* **1** a belt or cord round the body, esp. at the waist. **2** a woman's tightly-fitting undergarment from the waist to below the hips.
• *vb* encircle with or as if with a girdle. < Old English *gyrdel.*

girl (gɜːl) *n* **1** a female child. **2** a young unmarried woman. **3** (*informal*) a woman. **4** a girlfriend. **girlhood** *n* **girlish** *adj* **girlfriend** *n* a female friend, esp. a boy's or man's regular companion. < Middle English *girle* youngster.
SEE PANEL.

giro (ˈdʒaɪrəʊ) *n* a system for settling payments in which money is transferred between accounts or by cheque; operated by post offices or banks. < German, from Italian: transfer, ultimately from Greek *gyros* circuit.

girth (gɜːθ) *n* **1** the distance around something. **2** a strap that passes under a horse's belly to fasten the saddle. < Old Norse *gjörth.*

gist (dʒɪst) *n* the essential point of a speech, argument, etc. < ultimately Latin *jacēre* to lie.

give (gɪv) *vb* **gave; given; giving 1** make a present of. **2** hand over formally; supply or bestow. **3** convey or express: Give her my best wishes. **4** pay: How much will you give me for my car? **5** present for consideration: to give full details. **6** provide (a meal or party) as a host. **7** utter; perform in public: give a speech. **8** yield as a product or result: Cows give milk. **9** allow: I was given a

---

Who's **a girl?**

Girl is an example of one of the words which in previous stages of the language applied equally to members of either sex. In Middle English a girle or gurle was simply 'a young person', derived perhaps from the Old Low German word gre, 'a child'.

Shrew is another word which has become sexually marked during the course of time. A shrewe in Middle English was used to refer to any evil or scolding person, male and female alike.

---

giving it away

Give features in a number of idiomatic expressions, including:

give and take (of discussions, etc., between two sides) to make concessions. **give-and-take** *n*

give away 1 to give as a present or without charge. **2** to reveal (a secret); betray. **3** to present (a bride) to the groom at a wedding. **give-away** *n* **1** something unintentionally revealed. **2** something given without charge.

give in 1 to hand in or submit (a document, etc.). **2** to acknowledge defeat; yield or surrender.

give off to emit or produce: give off fumes.

give or take allowing for a smaller or larger amount: 1000, give or take 5%.

give out 1 to distribute. **2** to announce or broadcast. **3** to become used or consumed: After three days, the rations gave out. **4** to emit.

give over 1 to devote: A large part of the induction programme is given over to informal discussion between staff and students. **2** to stop doing something annoying: Give over, will you!

give rise to to cause.

give up 1 to abandon: give up an attempt; give up all hope. **2** to stop (doing something): give up smoking. **3** to acknowledge defeat; stop trying. **4** to surrender, as a prisoner: He gave himself up. **5** to declare as being beyond help: The doctors gave him up for dead.

give way 1 to collapse. **2** to yield to pressure. **3** to allow other traffic to proceed first.

week to do the work. **10** make or deliver, as by a bodily action: gave her a push. **11** cause to undergo or contract: Work gives me a headache! **12** devote: give one's time to helping others. **13** yield in response to pressure: The bridge gave under the weight of the lorries.
• *n* the capacity to yield to pressure, **giver** *n* < Middle English *given.*
SEE PANEL.

given (ˈgɪvn̩) SEE **GIVE**.
• *adj* **1** specified: at a given time. **2** prone, disposed. **3** assumed. **given name** a first name; Christian name.

glacé (ˈglæseɪ) *adj* candied or glazed: glacé cherries. < French: iced.

glacier (ˈglæsɪə, ˈgleɪsɪə) *n* a mass of ice and snow that moves down a slope on a land surface. **glacial** *adj* **1** icy. **2** of or formed by glaciers. < Latin *glacies* ice.

glad (glæd) *adj* **gladder; gladdest**
1 showing, feeling, or causing pleasure or happiness. **2** very willing: glad to help. **gladly** *adv* **gladness** *n* **gladden** *vb* make glad. < Old English *glæd.*

gladiator (ˈglædɪˌeɪtə) *n* a man who fought in public shows in ancient Rome. < Latin *gladius* sword.

gladiolus (ˌglædɪˈəʊləs) *n, pl* **gladioli** a plant with sword-shaped leaves and spikes of very brightly coloured flowers. < Latin *gladius* sword.

glamour (ˈglæmə) *n* an alluring, romantic attractiveness, esp. one that is unreal: the glamour of working in television. **glamorous** *adj* **glamorize** *vb* make glamorous. < Scottish, alteration of *grammar.*

glance (glɑːns) *vb* **1** (of the eyes) move quickly from one thing to another; look (at) quickly. **2** strike (a surface) lightly at an angle.
• *n* a quick movement of the eyes; quick look. < Middle English *glenchen.*

gland (glænd) *n* an organ or group of cells that takes substances from blood and makes a particular chemical substance that is needed. **glandular** *adj* < Latin *glans* acorn.

glare (glɛə) *vb* **1** shine with a harsh, dazzling light. **2** stare angrily or fiercely.
• *n* **1** a harsh, dazzling light. **2** an angry or fierce stare. **glaring** *adj* unpleasantly conspicuous: a glaring omission. **glaringly** *adv* < Middle English *glaren.*

glass (glɑːs) *n* **1** a hard, brittle, usually transparent substance. **2** something made of glass such as a mirror. **3** a container made from glass, for drinking from; contents of this. **glasses** *pl n* a pair of lenses held in a frame, esp. used to correct faulty vision. **glasshouse** *n* a greenhouse. **glass-paper** *n* paper coated with powdered glass, used as an abrasive. **glassy** *adj* **1** like glass, esp. in smoothness or transparency. **2** not having expression; dull or lifeless. **glassily** *adv* < Old English *glæs.*

glaze (gleɪz) *vb* **1** fit or cover with glass. **2** cover (pottery) with a substance that gives a glassy, non-porous finish. **3** cover (foods) with a shiny coating of beaten egg, etc. **4** become glazed or glassy.
• *n* a glassy finish, as on pottery; substance used to produce this. **glazier** *n* a person whose work is to fit glass, esp. into windows. < Middle English *glas* glass.

gleam (gliːm) *n* **1** a small beam or ray of soft light. **2** a brief or faint trace: a gleam of triumph.
• *vb* shine with soft, steady light. < Old English *glǣm.*

glean (gliːn) *vb* **1** gather (material) gradually: glean information. **2** pick up (grain, etc.) left by reapers. **gleaner** *n* **gleanings** *pl n* things obtained by gleaning. < Late Latin *glennare.*

glee (gliː) *n* great joy or delight. **gleeful** *adj* full of glee. **gleefully** *adv* < Old English *glēo* entertainment.

glen (glɛn) *n* a deep, narrow, secluded valley. < Scottish Gaelic *glenn.*

glib (glɪb) *adj* **1** not having depth; superficial: a glib answer. **2** showing great ease and fluency, esp. insincerely. **glibly** *adv* **glibness** *n* < probably modified from Low German *glibberig* slippery.

glide (glaɪd) *vb* **1** move along smoothly. **2** (of an aircraft) fly without the use of engines.
• *n* a gliding movement. **glider** *n* a light, fixed-wing aircraft without an engine. < Old English *glīdan.*

glimmer (ˈglɪmə) *vb* **1** shine faintly or unsteadily. **2** appear faintly.
• *n* a glimmering light, appearance, or trace: a glimmer of hope. < probably Scandinavian.

glimpse (glɪmps) *n* a brief view or look.
• *vb* look at briefly. < Middle English *glimsen.*

glint (glɪnt) *n* **1** a tiny, brief, bright flash of light: a glint in his eye. **2** a brief or faint appearance.
• *vb* send out a glint of light. < probably Scandinavian.

glisten (ˈglɪsn̩) *vb* shine with reflected light; sparkle. < Old English *glisnian.*

glitter (ˈglɪtə) *vb* **1** reflect light in bright flashes. **2** be showy, attractive, and brilliant.
• *n* **1** a bright, sparkling light. **2** showy

brilliance. < Old Norse *glitra.*

gloat (gləʊt) *vb* think or observe with malicious delight. < probably Scandinavian.

globe (gləʊb) *n* **1** a sphere with a map of the world on it. **2** the world. **3** an object shaped like a sphere such as a glass lampshade. **global** *adj* **1** of or relating to the whole world. **2** comprehensive. **globally** *adv* **globe-trotter** *n* a person who travels all over the world. **globular** *adj* shaped like a globe or globule. **globule** *n* a tiny ball. < Latin *globus.*

gloom (glu:m) *n* **1** partial or total darkness. **2** a feeling of sadness and depression. **gloomy** *adj* **1** partially or totally dark. **2** depressed and sad. **3** causing gloom; depressing. **gloomily** *adv* **gloominess** *n* < Middle English *gloumen.*

glory (ˈglɔ:rɪ) *n* **1** fame or praise. **2** worshipful praise and adoration: give glory to God. **3** something worthy of praise: a crowning glory. **4** splendour or beauty.
• *vb* **gloried; glorying** rejoice greatly. **glorify** *vb* **glorified; glorifying 1** make glorious by praising and honouring. **2** give glory to, in worship. **3** cause to appear more splendid or important than in reality. **glorification** *n* **glorious** *adj* **1** having, deserving, or bringing glory. **2** very beautiful; splendid; wonderful: a glorious view. **gloriously** *adv* < Latin *gloria.*

gloss¹ (glɒs) *n* **1** the lustre of a polished surface. **2** also **gloss paint** a paint which produces a glossy finish.
• *vb* put a gloss on. **gloss over** try to hide or ignore (a fault, etc.). **glossy** *adj* **1** having a surface lustre or brightness. **2** attractive, esp. in a showy, superficial way. **3** (of a magazine) printed on shiny paper and with many colour illustrations. < probably Scandinavian.

gloss² *n* a short explanatory comment.
• *vb* add a gloss to; annotate. **glossary** *n* a list of technical or special words with their meanings. < Latin *glossa* unusual word requiring explanation, from Greek *glōssa* tongue.

glove (glʌv) *n* a covering for the hand with separate parts for each finger and the thumb. **glove-compartment** *n* a small compartment in the dashboard of a car for storing small articles. **gloved** *adj* covered with a glove or gloves. < Old English *glōf.*

glow (gləʊ) *vb* **1** send out a steady, bright light and heat, esp. without a flame. **2** feel hot; show a ruddy colour, as from being too warm. **3** show delight or satisfaction.
• *n* **1** a steady light and heat sent out, esp. without a flame. **2** warm, brilliant colour. **3** a feeling of warmth, happiness, and well-being. < Old English *glōwan.*

glower (ˈglaʊə) *vb* stare with sullen annoyance; scowl. < probably Scandinavian.

glucose (ˈglu:kəʊz, ˈglu:kəʊs) *n* a soluble, crystalline form of sugar, used for energy in the body. < Greek *gleukos* sweet wine.

glue (glu:) *n* a strong adhesive, esp. a sticky substance obtained by boiling hides, bones, etc.
• *vb* fasten with or as if with glue. **gluey** *adj* < Late Latin *glus.* SEE PANEL.

glum (glʌm) *adj* **glummer; glummest** sad or silent, as from gloom. **glumly** *adv* **glumness** *n* < probably variant of *gloom.*

glut (glʌt) *n* a great excess.
• *vb* **glutted; glutting 1** supply more than is needed. **2** fill with too much food. < Middle French *gloutir* to swallow.

glutton (ˈglʌtn̩) *n* **1** a person who regularly eats and drinks too much. **2** a person with a great capacity for something: a glutton for hard work. **gluttonous** *adj* **gluttony** *n* < Latin *gluttire* swallow.

glycerine (ˈglɪsərɪn, ˌglɪsəˈri:n) *n* a colourless, sweet-tasting, syrupy liquid, esp. made from fats and used in explosives, cosmetics, and antifreeze.

glued to the set

When we say that a person sits glued to the television, we probably don't mean to convey that that person has had an accident with a bottle of glue. We are more likely to be using language *metaphorically*. A *metaphor* is a figure of speech which contains an implicit or suggested comparison (a comparison that does not use the words like or as). In the above expression the intensity of the viewer's concentration is conveyed by comparing it, by suggestion, to the bonding quality of glue.

The language is full of meanings which have metaphorical roots. For example, a problem does not come fitted with a lock, but we nonetheless seek a key to it. We cannot go for a cruise on a campaign, but we may certainly launch one.

< ultimately Greek *glykeros* sweet.

GMT *abbrev* Greenwich Mean Time.

gnarled (nɑːld) *adj* **1** covered with knots or protuberances. **2** rough, twisted, and misshapen. < probably from *knurled,* from Middle English *knorre* knot.

gnash (næʃ) *vb* grind (the teeth) together. < probably Scandinavian.

gnat (næt) *n* a small, two-winged fly. < Old English *gnætt.*

gnaw (nɔː) *vb* **1** bite constantly (at something) with the teeth, esp. to wear away. **2** make by gnawing. **3** erode or cause to erode. **4** cause constant anxiety (to). < Old English *gnagan.*

gnome (nəʊm) *n* **1** (in fairy-tales) a dwarf who lives underground, guarding the earth's treasure. **2** the statue of a gnome, as in a garden. < French, from New Latin *gnomus,* coined by Philipp von Hohenheim, dated 1541, Swiss scientist and alchemist.

gnu (nuː) *n* a large, horned antelope with an ox-like head and a long tail. < Kaffir *nqu.*

go (gəʊ) *vb* **went; gone; going 1** move along; travel; depart. **2** move towards an activity: go shopping. **3** extend; reach: The boundary goes as far as the river. **4** operate; work. **5** happen in a way that is mentioned: All our plans went wrong. **6** be or become in a state that is mentioned: go hungry; go mad. **7** (of time) pass. **8** (of a distance) be travelled. **9** be in harmony; fit in: Does the carpet go with the wallpaper? **10** attend; participate in: go to school. **11** have as a regular place or position: Tins go in the cupboard. **12** make a sound that is mentioned: go bang. **13** be given or allotted to: All the money went to her son. **14** be sold: The vase went for £100. **15** (of supplies or money) be spent or used up. **16** fail: His eyesight is going. **17** disappear: The spot has gone. **18** be removed. **19** die. **20** (of music, poetry, etc.) be expressed or sounded: How does that song go? **21** be contained in; fit: The book is too big to go in the envelope. **22** be allowable or acceptable: Anything goes these days. **23** have authority: What he says, goes. **24** be available: Several new jobs are going at the factory.
• *n, pl* **goes 1** the act of going. **2** energy: full of go. **3** a turn in an activity. **4** an attempt: have a go. **5** a period of activity.
• *adj* operating properly: All systems go.
goer *n* **1** a regular attender: a church-goer. **2** a person or thing that goes, esp. very fast. < Old English *gan.* SEE PANEL.

goad (gəʊd) *n* **1** a pointed stick used to urge an animal to move onwards. **2** something that urges or stimulates into action.
• *vb* urge with or as if with a goad; spur. < Old English *gād.*

goal (gəʊl) *n* **1** an aim or objective. **2** (in various sports) a structure or area into which players attempt to put a ball, etc., to score. **3** a successful attempt at scoring in such a sport; point scored in this way. **goalkeeper** *n* a player who defends the goal. **goal-post** *n* either of the two posts that mark the limits of the goal. < Middle English *gol* boundary.

goat (gəʊt) *n* a long-legged, cud-chewing mammal with hollow horns, related to the sheep. **get someone's goat** (*informal*) annoy someone. < Old English *gāt.*

goatee (gəʊˈtiː) *n* a short, pointed beard. < like the tufted beard of a he-goat.

gob (gɒb) *n* (*slang*) the mouth. < perhaps from Gaelic.

gobble (ˈgɒbl̩) *vb* **1** eat greedily or noisily. **2** accept or read eagerly. < probably from *gob* lump, from Middle French *gobe* chunk of meat.

gobbledegook (ˈgɒbl̩dɪˌguːk) *n* (*informal*) wordy, obscure, and generally unintelligible language, esp. as used by officials. < *gobble.*

goblet (ˈgɒblɪt) *n* a drinking-glass with a rounded bowl, foot, and stem, used esp. for wine. < Middle French *gobel.*

goblin (ˈgɒblɪn) *n* an ugly, mischievous elf. < Medieval Latin *gobelinus.* SEE PANEL AT **COBALT.**

god (gɒd) *n* **1 God** (in various religions) the supreme being; creator and ruler of all. **2** a being believed to have supernatural powers. **3** an image, idol, etc., of such a being. **4** a person or thing to which excessive devotion is given: Football is his god. **godchild** *n* a person, esp. a child, who is sponsored by adults at baptism. **god-daughter** *n* a female godchild. **goddess** *n* a female god. **godfather** *n* a male godparent, **godly** *adj* devout. **godliness** *n* **godmother** *n* a female godparent. **godparent** *n* a sponsor at baptism. **godsend** *n* a person or thing that comes unexpectedly but is greatly needed or desired. **godson** *n* a male godchild. < Old English. SEE PANEL.

goggle (ˈgɒgl̩) *vb* stare with wide-open eyes. **goggles** *pl n* glasses for protecting the eyes from water, dust, etc. < Middle English *gogelen* to look aside.

going (ˈgəʊɪŋ) SEE **GO.**
• *n* **1** the act of going. **2** progress or speed: make good going. **3** the condition of the ground for walking or riding on.

● *adj* **1** current: the going rate. **2** prosperous: a going concern.

goitre (ˈgɔɪtə) *n* a swelling in the front of the neck caused by enlargement of the thyroid gland. < ultimately Latin *guttur* throat.

go-kart (ˈgəʊkɑːt) *n* a miniature racing-car with small wheels.

gold (gəʊld) *n* **1** a very valuable, soft, dense, yellow metal; its colour. **2** coins or other articles made of gold. **3** something very valuable: She has a heart of gold.

It's all go!

Go features in a large number of idiomatic expressions, including:

be going to to intend to; also used to describe things that are certain or have already been decided: I'm going to buy a new car next month. Look out—we're going to crash!
go about to tackle or deal with (a task): He'd no idea how to go about mending the tap.
go ahead to proceed.
go-ahead *adj* progressive.
go-ahead *n* a signal to proceed.
go along to proceed.
go a long way 1 to make a lot of progress. **2** to make a major contribution to: Their gift goes a long way towards reaching our target.
go along with 1 to accompany. **2** to agree with.
go and used to express dismay, surprise, disbelief, etc.: Then she had to go and spoil everything! To cap it all, he went and won first prize!
go around to be passed from person to person; circulate: There are some vicious rumours going around.
go at to attack.
go back on to fail to keep (a promise).
go back to to be known to have existed since: This custom goes back to the 12th century.
go-between *n* a mediator or negotiator.
go by 1 to pass: Many years went by. **2** to be guided or directed by.
go down 1 (of a ship) to sink. **2** (of the sun) to disappear below the horizon. **3** to be swallowed. **4** to decrease in size, level, value, etc. **5** to be recorded in writing. **6** to be received: The suggestion didn't go down very well with the others.
go down with to become ill with.
go far 1 to last a long time: £10 doesn't go far these days. **2** to become successful. **3** to make a major contribution (to).
go for 1 to attack. **2** to be attracted by; prefer: I don't really go for jazz. **3** to go to fetch. **4** to apply to.
go-getter *n* a person who is successful by being self-assertive.
go in to be concealed by cloud: The sun's gone in.
go in for 1 to compete in. **2** to have as a hobby or regular activity.
go into 1 to investigate carefully. **2** to start (a career): go into the army.
go it alone to pursue an undertaking, career, etc., without the support or assistance of others.
go off 1 to explode. **2** go bad or stale: The milk's gone off. **3** to fall asleep. **4** to stop liking. **5** to stop working. **6** to proceed: The party went off well.
go on 1 to continue. **2** to happen. **3** to behave, especially in an unusual way.
goings-on *pl n* **4** to continue speaking. **5** to proceed: He went on to win the whole tournament. **6** to talk a lot (about). **7** to keep complaining: Stop going on at me the whole time!
go out 1 to go to social functions. **2** to stop burning or giving light. **3** to be broadcast. **4** to be no longer fashionable.
go out with to spend time regularly with (a person of esp. the opposite sex).
go over 1 to examine or check. **2** to clean or repair. **going-over** *n* **3** to rehearse: Let's go over your lines once more.
go round to be enough for everyone.
go slow to reduce the rate of work, especially as a form of protest. **go-slow** *n*
go through 1 to be officially approved; be completed: Has Jack's divorce gone through yet? **2** to examine or search: The police went through the whole house to try to find the drugs. **3** to experience or suffer. **4** to review or discuss. **5** to rehearse.
go up 1 to rise or increase: Prices are always going up. **2** to be destroyed by explosion; burn rapidly. **3** to be built.
go without to be deprived of; not have.
on the go constantly active or busy.

4 a gold medal. **goldfish** *n, pl* **goldfish** a freshwater fish widely kept in aquariums. **gold leaf** gold beaten into paper-thin sheets. **gold medal** a medal (of gold) awarded to the winner of a competition or race. **gold-mine** *n* a rich source of wealth or other desirable things. **gold-rush** *n* a rush to a newly discovered goldfield. **goldsmith** *n* a person who works in gold or who deals in articles made of gold. **gold standard** a monetary system in which the value of a country's unit of currency equals a fixed weight of gold of a stated fineness. < Old English.

golden (ˈgəʊldən) *adj* **1** made of, relating to, or containing gold. **2** of the colour of gold. **3** prosperous and happy: a golden age. **4** favourable: a golden opportunity. **5** marking a 50th anniversary: a golden jubilee.

golf (gɒlf) *n* a game in which a ball is hit into each of the 9 or 18 successive holes on a course with as few strokes as possible. **golf ball 1** a ball used in golf. **2** a small, detachable sphere that carries the characters in some electric typewriters. **golf-course** also **golf-links** *n* an area of land on which golf is played. **golfer** *n* a person who plays golf. < perhaps from Middle Dutch *colf* club.

golliwog (ˈgɒlɪˌwɒg) *n* a soft doll that is dressed as a man and has a black face and black fuzzy hair. < *Golliwog,* name of animated doll in children's stories by Bertha Upton, died 1912, US writer.

gollop (ˈgɒləp) *vb* eat or drink quickly and greedily. < SEE **GULP.**

gondola (ˈgɒndələ) *n* **1** a long, narrow, flat-bottomed boat, used on the canals in Venice. **2** a cabin suspended from a balloon; moving cabin suspended from a cable on a ski-slope, etc. **gondolier** *n* a boatman who propels a gondola. < Italian, from Medieval Latin *gondula.*

gone (gɒn) SEE **GO.**
• *adj* (*informal*) **1** enthusiastic. **2** pregnant for a time that is mentioned: six months gone.
• *adv* turned: It's gone 3 o'clock. **goner** *n* (*informal*) a person who is doomed or is about to die

gong (gɒŋ) *n* **1** a metal, plate-like percussion instrument that produces a resounding tone when struck. **2** a rimmed, metal disc that produces a note when struck or operated electrically. < Malay, like the sound.

gonorrhoea (ˈgɒnəˌrɪə) *n* a venereal disease marked by inflammation of the genital organs. < Greek *gonos* semen + *rheein* to flow.

goo (guː) *n* (*informal*) **1** a sticky substance. **2** sentimental language, events, etc. **gooey** *adj* < origin uncertain.

good (gʊd) *adj* **better; best 1** having pleasing or favourable qualities: good news. **2** morally fine or excellent. **3** kind and generous. **4** well-behaved: Have the children been good? **5** having a fine appearance: good looks. **6** reliable; hard-working: a good secretary. **7** enjoyable; refreshing; comfortable: have a good rest. **8** not depressed: in good spirits. **9** of a higher quality than average: good results. **10** rich or fertile: good soil. **11** valid; genuine: a good reason. **12** strong: a pair of good shoes. **13** beneficial for health or character: Vegetables are good for you. **14** competent: good at swimming. **15** opportune: a good time to ask for more money. **16** suitable for a particular medium: good television. **17** rather more than: It must be a good five years since I saw them. **18** considerable: a good deal of money. **19** thorough: a good thrashing. **20** (of birth, one's family, etc.) not lowly or humble. **21** (*informal*) well; happy: I feel good.
• *interj* used to show pleasure, satisfaction, etc.
• *n* **1** that which is morally right, kind, or generous. **2** material or moral benefit: for the good of others; It's no good crying! **goodness** *n* **1** the state or quality of being good. **2** kindness or generosity. **3** moral excellence. **4** the nutritious part

God knows

God features in a number of expressions, including:

God bless an expression used when saying goodbye, used to convey good wishes.
God-fearing *adj* devout.
God forbid I hope (something mentioned) will not happen.
God-forsaken *adj* remote; dismal.
God knows 1 I do not know; it is impossible to say. **2** certainly: God knows we've tried to bring him up in the right way.
God willing if circumstances allow.
good God also **ye gods** an expression of surprise, disbelief, etc.
the gods the highest gallery in a theatre.

Some speakers use expressions with God carefully, to avoid showing disrespect.

of something. **goodwill** *n* **1** a feeling of kind interest and concern. **2** willingness or consent. **3** the benefits that belong to a business from, for example, being well known to customers, considered as an asset. < Old English *gōd.* SEE PANEL.

goodbye (ˌgʊdˈbaɪ) *interj* used to express farewell.
• *n* a farewell. < alteration of *God be with you.*

goods (gʊdz) *pl n* **1** movable possessions. **2** manufactured articles. **3** heavy articles that are carried by train, etc.; freight. **deliver the goods** (*informal*) do what is expected of one.

goody (ˈgʊdɪ) *interj* a child's exclamation of delight.
• *n* (*informal*) **1** something good to eat. **2** a hero. **goody-goody** *adj, n* (*informal*) (a person who is) smugly virtuous.

goof (gu:f) *n* (*informal*) **1** a foolish mistake. **2** a stupid person.
• *vb* (*informal*) bungle (something). **goofy** *adj* (*informal*) **1** very stupid. **2** (of teeth) sticking out. < probably English dialect *goff* foolish person.

goose (gu:s) *n, pl* **geese** **1** a large, long-necked, web-footed bird, valued for its meat. **2** the female of such a bird. **3** its flesh as food. **4** a foolish person.

for good

Good features in a number of expressions, many of them idiomatic, including:

as good as almost; practically: as good as dead.
for good permanently: I'm going away for good.
good for able to be depended on to provide: My dad's always good for some money till we get paid.
good-for-nothing *adj, n* (someone who is) worthless.
good for you an expression of congratulations or approval.
Good Friday the Friday before Easter, observed by Christians as the commemoration of the crucifixion of Jesus. In this expression good means 'holy'.
good-looking *adj* attractive.
in good time early: Although we left in good time, we got held up by road-works on the motorway.
too good to be true extremely good.

goose-pimples *pl n a* roughened condition of the skin, caused by cold or fear. < Old English *gōs.* SEE PANEL AT **MONGOOSE.**

gooseberry (ˈgʊzbərɪ, ˈgʊzbrɪ) *n* **1** a thorny shrub, grown for its green, edible berries; such a berry. **2** a single person accompanying two lovers: play gooseberry.

gore (gɔ:) *n* blood shed from a wound; clotted blood. < Old English *gor* filth.

gorge (gɔ:dʒ) *n* a narrow, steep-sided valley.
• *vb* stuff (oneself) with food. < Latin *gurges* whirlpool.

gorgeous (ˈgɔ:dʒəs) *adj* **1** magnificent and beautiful. **2** (*informal*) extremely pleasant. **gorgeously** *adv* **gorgeousness** *n* < Middle French *gorgias* fine, stylish.

gorilla (gəˈrɪlə) *n* the largest man-like ape of Africa, with a short muzzle and coarse, dark hair. < ultimately Greek *Gorillai,* hirsute African tribe.

gormless (ˈgɔ:mləs) *adj* (*informal*) stupid. < ultimately Old Norse *gaumr* understanding + *-less.*

gorse (gɔ:s) *n* a very spiny, thickly branched, evergreen shrub with yellow flowers. < Old English *gorst.*

gory (ˈgɔ:rɪ) *adj* **1** full of violence; horrific. **2** covered in gore.

gosling (ˈgɒzlɪŋ) *n* a young goose. < Old Norse *gæslingr.*

gospel (ˈgɒspl̩) *n* **1** the teachings of Jesus Christ and the apostles; message of salvation in Jesus. **2** **Gospel** one of the first four books of the New Testament; reading from this. **3** something accepted as true: You may take it as the gospel truth. **4** a set of teachings believed to be very important. SEE PANEL.

The gospel—and now the good news...

When, according to legend, the chief librarian at the ancient city of Alexandria was sent a copy of one of the four Gospels, he didn't know which section of the library to put it in.

Having discounted fiction, history, and biography, he finally decided that it should go in a new category—*bonus nuntius.* This was translated directly into Old English as *gōdspel,* meaning 'a good message' from *gōd* 'good' and *spel* 'a message'.

gossamer (ˈgɒsəmə) *n* **1** a film of cobwebs on bushes, etc. **2** any fine, filmy, delicate material. < Middle English *gosesomer* goose summer.

gossip (ˈgɒsɪp) *n* **1** a person who talks casually about other people's affairs, often maliciously. **2** such talk. **3** any casual talk; chat.
• *vb* tell gossip. **gossiper** *n* **gossipy** *adj* < Old English *godsibbe* godparent. SEE PANEL.

got (gɒt) SEE **GET.** SEE PANEL.

gouge (gaʊdʒ) *n* a chisel with a concave blade for cutting grooves in wood.
• *vb* **1** scoop out with or as if with a gouge. **2** force out (an eye) with one's thumb. < Late Latin *gulbia.*

goulash (ˈgu:læʃ) *n* a stew made of beef, lamb, or veal, seasoned with paprika. < Hungarian *gulyás hus* herdsman's meat.

gourd (gʊəd) *n* **1** any of several trailing or climbing plants, such as the melon. **2** any of several hard-rinded, inedible fruits used for decoration, as a drinking-cup, etc. < Latin *cucurbita.*

gourmand (ˈgʊəmənd) *n* a person who is devoted to eating and drinking, esp. to excess. < Middle French *gourmant.* SEE PANEL.

gourmet (ˈgʊəmeɪ) *n* a person with a discriminating taste for good food and drink. < Middle French *gromet* boy-servant. SEE PANEL AT **GOURMAND.**

gout (gaʊt) *n* a disease marked by painful inflammation of the joints, esp. in the big toe. < Latin *gutta* drop.

govern (ˈgʌvn̩) *vb* **1** exercise authority (over). **2** determine, influence, or decide. **3** keep under control. **governess** *n* a woman employed in a private household to teach the children. **government** *n* **1** governing; system, method, or function of governing. **2** the group or organization governing a country. **3** the state and its administration. **governor** *n* **1** a person who governs. **2** the head or a member of a group that controls an institution such as a school or prison. **3** (*slang*) used by men to address other men, esp. employers. < Greek *kybernan* to steer. SEE PANEL.

gown (gaʊn) *n* **1** an outer garment such as a woman's long, formal dress or a dressing robe. **2** a loose, outer garment worn esp. by an academic or professional person. **gowned** *adj* wearing a gown. < Late Latin *gunna* fur or leather garment.

gossip

A person who makes a point of talking about other people's business behind their backs is often referred to as a gossip. This derives from the Old English equivalent for godparent—*godsibb,* a compound of *god* 'god' and *sibb* 'a kinsman'. In time the name came to be applied to any of the women who were attendant at the birth of a child, an occasion when there were many conversation topics of common interest. Still later the meaning became generalized—a *godsib* was simply a friend or acquaintance.

The evolution of meaning from 'godparent' to 'birth attendant' to 'acquaintance' had followed a fairly steady course. The next stage, however, saw a departure. This was the arrival by the end of the 16th century of the word's modern form and derogatory meaning.

What's wrong with **have got?**

Some careful users of British English object to the use of have got in formal contexts, for example It was claimed by the head of the languages department that his students *had got* less opportunity to use the language laboratory than previously. Here, got would be omitted in formal usage.

In informal usage, however, have got is used frequently, often being shortened: I'*ve got* a bit of a headache. He *had*n't *got* the guts to say no.

gourmand or gourmet?

These words are sometimes confused. A gourmand is a person who is devoted to eating and drinking, especially to excess. The word tends to be used in derogatory descriptions of someone who is not very discriminating in what he or she eats or drinks. In contrast, a gourmet is a connoisseur of food and drink.

GP *abbrev* general practitioner.

grab (græb) *vb* **grabbed; grabbing** **1** grasp suddenly or hastily. **2** seize unscrupulously or illegally. **3** (*informal*) catch the attention of.
• *n* **1** a sudden, hasty snatch. **2** an illegal or unscrupulous snatching. **3** a mechanical device for grasping an object. **up for grabs** (*informal*) available for anyone to take. < Low German or Dutch *grabben*.

grace (greɪs) *n* **1** charm or elegance in movement, expression, or design. **2** sense of decency. **3** goodwill or favour. **4** a temporary exemption: 14 days' grace. **5** the free and undeserved kindness of God towards mankind. **6** a short prayer of thanksgiving at a meal. **7** the title for a duke, duchess, or archbishop.
• *vb* **1** add elegance to. **2** honour. **graceful** *adj* showing grace in form, movement, or expression. **gracefully** *adv* **gracefulness** *n* **gracious** *adj* **1** showing kindness and courtesy. **2** compassionate and merciful. **3** marked by or suitable for a life of elegance, comfort, and ease. **graciously** *adv* **graciousness** *n* **with good grace** cheerfully and willingly, without anger or resentment. < Latin *gratus* pleasing. SEE PANEL.

grade (greɪd) *n* **1** a position in a scale of ranks, qualities, or values. **2** a stage in a process. **3** a group of the same rank, etc. **4** a mark given to a student for the standard of his or her work.
• *vb* **1** arrange in grades. **2** give a grade to. **gradation** *n* a series or process made up of different stages; stage in this. < Latin *gradus* step, degree.

gradient (ˈgreɪdɪənt) *n* **1** the degree of slope of a road, etc. **2** a sloping road or railway. < Latin *gradi* to go.

gradual (ˈgrædjʊəl) *adj* proceeding or occurring by steps or degrees; not sudden or abrupt. **gradually** *adv* < Latin *gradus* step.

graduate (ˈgrædjʊət) *n* a person who has been awarded a degree from a university or college.
• *vb* (ˈgrædjʊˌeɪt) **1** receive an academic degree. **2** mark with degrees for measurement; divide into sections or stages. **3** move to a higher level of experience, etc. **graduation** *n* < SEE **GRADE.**

graffiti (græˈfiːtɪ) *pl n* words or drawings, esp. of an obscene or political nature, on a wall, poster, etc. < Italian: scribblings. SEE PANEL.

the government is ...
or **the government are ...?**

Singular words that refer to groups of people such as government, army, family, and committee can sometimes be used as if they were plural. They are called *collective nouns.*

When we want to draw particular attention to the individual members of the group, a plural verb is used and the group is referred to with the pronouns they and their: The team *are* very optimistic about winning the match. The committee discussed the suggestion, but *they* rejected it by one vote. The audience are requested to be in *their* seats by 7.20 p.m.

When the group is thought of as a unit, singular verbs and pronouns are used: The committee *is* made up of distinguished local citizens. The government *has* made it clear *it* will play no part in the matter.

graceful or **gracious?**

Graceful and gracious and their derivatives gracefully and graciously are sometimes confused. Graceful means 'showing grace in form, movement, or expression' as in a *graceful* gesture; She danced *gracefully.*

Gracious means 'showing kindness and courtesy; compassionate' as in God's *gracious* blessing, a *gracious* act, or 'marked by a life of elegance and comfort' as in *gracious* living. Gracious may also imply a patronizing or condescending manner as in We were honoured by his *gracious* presence. It is also used in exclamations such as Goodness *gracious* me! and Good *gracious!*

graffiti

Graffiti comes from Italian and means 'the words or drawings on a wall, poster, etc.' Strictly speaking, the word graffiti is plural, but since the singular graffito is rarely used, graffiti is increasingly becoming thought of as a singular noun.

graft[1] (grɑ:ft) *n* **1** a small piece of a plant or tree that is united with another, with which it grows permanently; plant formed by this; point of union between the two pieces. **2** living tissue transplanted surgically.
• *vb* **1** insert as a graft. **2** join by grafting. **3** transplant (living tissue) surgically. < Greek *graphein* to write.

graft[2] *n* **1** (*informal*) work: hard graft. **2** unfair use of one's position to gain a financial or other advantage; something obtained in this way.
• *vb* (*informal*) work. < origin uncertain.

grain (greɪn) *n* **1** a small, hard seed or fruit of a cereal grass, such as wheat. **2** the seeds of such plants considered collectively. **3** such plants themselves. **4** a small, hard particle: grains of sand. **5** the smallest amount possible. **6** the general direction or pattern of fibres in wood, etc. **7** a unit of weight (0.0648 grams). **grainy** *adj* < Latin *granum.*

gram (græm) *n* a unit of mass; one 1000th of a kilogram. < Greek *gramma* small weight.

grammar (ˈgræmə) *n* **1** the study of the rules governing the structure of sentences. **2** the system of such rules; description of these. **3** a textbook on grammar. **4** the use of language in conformity with grammatical rules. **grammar school** a secondary school providing an academic type of education. **grammatical** *adj* of grammar; conforming to the rules of grammar. **grammatically** *adv* < Greek *gramma* writing.

gramophone (ˈgræməˌfəʊn) *n* a record-player. < inversion of first and last syllables of *phonogram.*

granary (ˈgrænərɪ) *n* a storehouse for grain. < Latin *granum* grain.

grand (grænd) *adj* **1** large and impressive in size, extent, etc. **2** magnificent; splendid. **3** intended to impress. **4** (*informal*) wonderful. **5** complete: a grand total. **6** of the highest rank. **7** important.
• *n* **1** a grand piano. **2** (*slang*) a thousand pounds or dollars. **grandly** *adv* **grandness** *n* **grandchild** *n* a child of one's son or daughter. **granddad** *n* (*informal*) a grandfather. **granddaughter** *n* a daughter of one's son or daughter. **grandeur** *n* magnificence; grandness. **grandfather** *n* the father of one's father or mother. **grandma** *n* (*informal*) a grandmother. **grandmother** *n* the mother of one's father or mother. **grandpa** *n* (*informal*) a grandfather. **grandparent** *n* a grandfather or grandmother. **grand piano** a large piano with the strings arranged horizontally. **grandson** *n* a son of one's son or daughter. **grandstand** *n* a roofed stand for spectators that gives the best view of a racecourse, football match, etc. < Latin *grandis.*

grandiloquent (grænˈdɪləkwənt) *adj* using pompous language. **grandiloquence** *n* **grandiloquently** *adv* < Latin *grandis* great + *loqui* to speak.

grandiose (ˈgrændɪˌəʊs) *adj* **1** very large or impressive. **2** marked by pretence of grandeur: grandiose ideas. < Latin *grandis* great.

granite (ˈgrænɪt) *n* a very hard, coarse-grained, igneous rock used for building. < Italian, from Latin *granum* grain.

granny (ˈgrænɪ) *n* (*informal*) a grandmother.

grant (grɑ:nt) *vb* **1** agree to perform or fulfil. **2** allow as a right or favour. **3** bestow or hand over formally. **4** be willing to concede.
• *n* something granted, esp. money for a particular purpose: students' grants. < Latin *credere* to believe.

granule (ˈgrænju:l) *n* a small grain. **granular** *adj* **1** of, like, or containing grains or granules. **2** having a grainy surface. **granulate** *vb* make into grains or granules: granulated sugar. < Late Latin *granulum* a small grain.

grape (greɪp) *n* **1** a juicy, smooth-skinned, green or purple berry eaten as a fruit or used for making wine. **2** a vine that bears such berries. **grapevine** *n* **1** a vine on which grapes grow. **2** an unofficial or secret way of passing on information. < Old French *grape* bunch of grapes.

grapefruit (ˈgreɪpˌfru:t) *n, pl* **grapefruit** a large, round, yellow, citrus fruit with a juicy, usually bitter pulp; tree on which such fruits grow.

graph (grɑ:f, græf) *n* a diagram showing the relationships between quantities or variables.
• *vb* draw a graph of. **graphic** *adj* **1** of writing, drawing, and engraving: the graphic arts. **2** of or relating to graphics: graphic design. **3** marked by a vivid description. **graphically** *adv* **graphics** *n* **1** the art of drawing in accordance with mathematical principles. **2** *pl* designs containing typography and pictures. **graph paper** paper ruled into small squares for drawing graphs. < Greek *graphein* to write.

graphite (ˈgræfaɪt) *n* a soft, dark form of carbon that conducts electricity and is used as a lubricant and in lead pencils. < Greek *graphein* to write.

graphology (græˈfɒlədʒɪ) *n* the study of handwriting, esp. to analyse a person's character. **graphologist** *n* < Greek *graphein* to write + *-logy*, ultimately *logos* word.

grapple (ˈgræpl̩) *vb* **1** grip or seize firmly. **2** contend or cope; wrestle.
• *n* **1** the act of grappling. **2** something which grips, seizes, or holds fast. < Middle French *grape* hook.

grasp (grɑːsp) *vb* **1** seize or clasp firmly with or as if with the fingers or arms. **2** understand.
• *n* **1** a firm hold. **2** power of control or accomplishment. **3** understanding. **grasping** *adj* greedy for material possessions. < perhaps Low German *grapsen*.

grass (grɑːs) *n* **1** any of a family of plants with long, narrow leaves and flowers, esp. green, in small clusters or spikes; such leaves. **2** ground covered with grass: Keep off the grass! **3** land covered with grass for grazing animals. **4** (*slang*) marijuana. **5** (*slang*) a police informer.
• *vb* **1** cover with grass. **2** (*slang*) inform the police, esp. in betraying someone. **grassy** *adj* **grasshopper** *n* a jumping insect that produces a ticking sound by rubbing the hind legs against the front wings. **grassland** *n* **1** land on which grass predominates. **2** farmland used for grazing. < Old English *græs*.

grate[1] (greɪt) *vb* **1** reduce to small pieces by rubbing against a rough surface. **2** rub, grind, or sound noisily or harshly. **grater** *n* < Middle French *grater* to scratch.

grate[2] *n* a metal frame that holds the fuel in a fireplace; fireplace. < Latin *cratis* hurdle.

grateful (ˈgreɪtfʊl) *adj* feeling or showing thanks for a kindness or something received. **gratefully** *adv* **gratefulness** *n* < obsolete *grate*, from Latin *gratus* pleasing.

gratify (ˈgrætɪˌfaɪ) *vb* **gratified; gratifying** **1** be a source of pleasure. **2** satisfy. **gratification** *n* < Latin *gratus* pleasing + *facere* to make.

grating (ˈgreɪtɪŋ) *n* a framework of bars placed across an opening.

gratis (ˈgrætɪs, ˈgrɑːtɪs, ˈgreɪtɪs) *adv, adj* free. < Latin *gratia* favour.

gratitude (ˈgrætɪˌtjuːd) *n* gratefulness. < SEE **GRATEFUL.**

gratuitous (grəˈtjuːɪtəs) *adj* **1** free. **2** not justified. **gratuitously** *adv* < Latin *gratia* favour.

gratuity (grəˈtjuːɪ) *n* a gift of money for services rendered; tip.

grave[1] (greɪv) *n* a place for burying a corpse, esp. beneath the ground. **gravestone** *n* a stone monument over or at one end of a grave. **graveyard** *n* a burial ground. < Old English *græf*.

grave[2] *adj* **1** serious; causing worry: grave doubts; in grave danger. **2** solemn; earnest. **gravely** *adv* < Latin *gravis* heavy, important.

gravel (ˈgrævl̩) *n* a mixture of small, loose fragments of rock and sand, used for example on paths.
• *vb* **gravelled; gravelling** cover with gravel. **gravelly** *adj* **1** of or covered with gravel. **2** (of a voice) harsh and grating. < Old French *grave*.

gravity (ˈgrævɪtɪ) *n* **1** seriousness or importance. **2** solemnity of manner or actions. **3** the natural force that moves or tends to move objects towards the centre of the earth, moon, etc. **gravitate** *vb* **1** move or cause to move by gravity. **2** move or be strongly attracted (towards). **gravitation** *n* **gravitational** *adj* < Latin *gravis* heavy.

gravy (ˈgreɪvɪ) *n* the juices and fat from meat while it is cooking; sauce made from this. < Middle French *gravē*.

graze[1] (greɪz) *vb* **1** feed on (growing grass, etc.). **2** put (animals) to feed on growing grass, etc. **grazing** *n* the grass, etc., suitable for animals to graze on. < Old English *græs* grass.

graze[2] *vb* **1** touch (something) lightly in passing. **2** scrape the skin from.
• *n* a grazing or slight injury caused by it. < probably **GRAZE**[1].

grease (griːs) *n* **1** soft or melted animal fat. **2** any oily substance.
• *vb* put grease on or in. **greasy** *adj* **1** covered with grease. **2** containing much grease: greasy food. **3** slippery. **4** (*informal*) having an ingratiating smoothness and false sincerity. **greasily** *adv* **greasiness** *n* < Latin *crassus* fat.

great (greɪt) *adj* **1** relatively large in size, number, etc.: a great many people. **2** extreme in amount, extent, etc.: in great pain. **3** eminent: a great writer. **4** notably superior in quality; noble. **5** main: the great hall. **6** elaborate: told the story in great detail. **7** significant: a great day for democracy. **8** enthusiastic: He's a great one for fell-walking. **9** (*informal*) very good or enjoyable: We had a great time! **10** of a family relationship one generation removed: great-grandfather.
• *n* a person or thing that is great: the

all-time greats. **greatly** *adv* **greatness** *n* < Old English *grēat.* SEE PANEL.

greedy (ˈgriːdɪ) *adj* **1** having a very great desire for something, esp. food. **2** very eager (for). **greed** *n* **greedily** *adv* **greediness** *n* < Old English *grædig.*

green (griːn) *adj* **1** of the colour between blue and yellow or of fresh, growing grass. **2** covered by green growth. **3** youthful and strong. **4** fresh and new. **5** immature and inexperienced; naïve. **6** not ripe or seasoned. **7** pale and looking sickly. **8** (*informal*) affected by jealousy or envy.
• *n* **1** green colour. **2** a green material; green clothes. **3** *pl* edible leaves of certain green vegetables such as cabbage. **4** grassy public land: a village green. **5** a grassy area: a bowling-green. **greenly** *adv* **greenness** *n* **greenery** *n* green foliage or plants. **greenfly** *n* a small, green plant pest. **greengage** *n* a small, roundish, green plum. **greengrocer** *n* a shopkeeper selling fresh vegetables and fruit. **greengrocery** *n* **greenhouse** *n* a building with glass sides and roof, for growing and protecting plants. < Old English *grēne.* SEE PANEL.

greet (griːt) *vb* **1** address with expressions of welcome, respect, etc. **2** receive or acknowledge in a way that is mentioned: The first issue was greeted with great enthusiasm. **3** appear to: An awful sight greeted our eyes. **greeting** *n* **1** words or gestures used in greeting. **2** an expression of good wishes: birthday greetings. < Old English *grētan.*

gregarious (grɪˈgɛərɪəs) *adj* **1** fond of the company of other people. **2** (of animals) living together in herds or flocks. **gregariously** *adv* **gregariousness** *n* < Latin *grex* flock.

gremlin (ˈgrɛmlɪn) *n* a mischievous spirit said to cause mechanical troubles. < origin unknown. SEE PANEL.

grenade (grəˈneɪd) *n* a small container filled with explosive, gas, etc., thrown by hand or fired from a rifle. SEE PANEL.

grew (gruː) SEE **GROW.**

grey (greɪ) *adj* **1** of the neutral colour between black and white. **2** dull in colour; darkish. **3** having grey hair. **4** lacking brightness: a grey day.
• *n* **1** grey colour. **2** something grey, such as clothes. **3** a grey horse. **greyly** *adv* **greyness** *n* **greyhound** *n* a tall, slender, long-legged, smooth-coated dog noted for its speed, used in hare-coursing and racing. < Old English *grǣg.*

grid (grɪd) *n* **1** a grating. **2** a network of horizontal and vertical lines for locating points on a map. **3** a network for transmitting or distributing electricity, gas, etc., over a large area. **4** a grill. < back formation from *gridiron,* from

great heat

People whose mother tongue is English seldom appreciate the intricacy of the language. To gain an insight into the nature of its complexity, we need look no further than the relationship between spelling and pronunciation. The correct pronunciation of a phrase like great heat presents no problems for a native speaker, and yet the ea in each of the two words is pronounced very differently. In fact, the ea combination has no fewer than 11 different pronunciations! The other ways of pronouncing it are as in head, dreary, hearth, create, cornea, wear, meander, guinea, and yearn.

surrounded by green

Green features in a number of expressions, including:

green belt an area of open or farming land, parks, etc., around a town or city that is subject to restrictions on development.
green card an insurance document that covers motorists against accidents abroad.
green cross code a safety code for children crossing roads.
green fingers an ability to grow plants.
green light authority to proceed with a project, from the green traffic-light that signals permission to go.
Green Paper a set of proposals of government policy, for public comment and discussion.
green pound the agreed value of the pound in which EEC farm prices are expressed.

The name of the type of plum known as the **greengage** is of a rather curious construction. The first element is the adjective green, added to which is the surname of Sir William *Gage,* 1777–1864, a Suffolk botanist who introduced the fruit into England from France.

Middle English *gredire.*

grief (gri:f) *n* deep sorrow or distress; something causing this. **grievance** *n* a cause for complaint. **grieve** *vb* suffer or cause to suffer grief. **grievous** *adj* **1** causing or marked by grief. **2** serious: a grievous error. **grievously** *adv* < Latin *gravis* heavy.

grill (grɪl) *n* **1** a framework of metal bars for cooking on. **2** an apparatus on a cooker that radiates heat downwards. **3** grilled food: a mixed grill. **4** also **grill-room** a restaurant or dining-room where grilled meats are served.
• *vb* **1** cook on or under a grill. **2** torment with or as if with great heat. **3** (*informal*) question intensely, esp. for a long period. < Latin *cratis* wickerwork.

grille (grɪl) *n* a grating, for example the chromium-plated grating at the front of a motor vehicle. < SEE **GRILL.**

grim (grɪm) *adj* **grimmer; grimmest** **1** severe or forbidding in appearance. **2** unrelenting; resolute: grim determination. **3** (*informal*) unpleasant. **4** sinister: grim news. **grimly** *adv* **grimness** *n* < Old English *grimm.*

grimace (ˈgrɪməs, grɪˈmeɪs) *n* a distortion of the face, expressing pain, disgust, or wry humour.
• *vb* make a grimace. < Middle French *grimache.*

grime (graɪm) *n* dirt or soot, esp. when thick or ingrained in a surface. **grimy** *adj* **griminess** *n* < Middle Dutch.

grin (grɪn) *vb* **grinned; grinning** smile broadly, so as to show the teeth.
• *n* a broad smile. < Old English *grennian.*

grind (graɪnd) *vb* **ground; grinding** **1** crush or be crushed into fine particles; produce in this way. **2** sharpen or polish by friction. **3** rub or press harshly: grind one's teeth. **4** oppress cruelly. **5** (*informal*) work hard in a monotonous way.
• *n* **1** the art of grinding. **2** (*informal*) monotonous, hard work. **grind out** produce in a routine way. **grindstone** *n* a thick, flat, revolving stone for grinding tools. **grind to a halt** come slowly or noisily to a stop. < Old English *grindan.*

grip (grɪp) *vb* **gripped; gripping** **1** hold or seize firmly. **2** hold the attention of.
• *n* **1** a firm grasp; manner or power of gripping. **2** control or understanding. **3** a part that grips. **4** a travelling-bag. < Old English *grippan.*

gripe (graɪp) *vb* **1** cause or feel sudden, intense pains in the intestines. **2** (*informal*) complain.
• *n* (*informal*) a complaint. < Old English *grīpan.*

grisly (ˈgrɪzlɪ) *adj* causing fear, horror, or dread. < Old English *grislic.*

gristle (ˈgrɪsl̩) *n* cartilage, esp. in cooked meat. **gristly** *adj* < Old English.

grit (grɪt) *n* **1** a substance consisting of hard, sharp particles, as of sand or stone. **2** (*informal*) firm courage.
• *vb* **gritted; gritting** **1** apply grit to. **2** clench or grind (one's teeth) together. **3** make a grating sound. **gritty** *adj* **grittiness** *n* < Old English *grēot.*

grizzle (ˈgrɪzl̩) *vb* (*informal*) **1** (of a child) cry fretfully; whine. **2** complain. **grizzler** *n* < origin uncertain.

grizzly (ˈgrɪzlɪ) *adj* grey; grey-haired.
• *n* also **grizzly bear** a very large, greyish-brown bear of North America.

grenade

The explosive missile known as a grenade takes its name from the French *grenade* from the same word in Spanish, meaning 'pomegranate'. Early grenades obviously must have borne a close resemblance to the fruit, which over the years has become less obvious. Grenadiers, the soldiers to whom was entrusted the throwing of grenades, were chosen for their stature and muscle.

Watch out for gremlins!

When a machine unaccountably breaks down or develops a fault, it is often wryly claimed that the gremlins are to blame. The name of these mischievous little creatures is of appropriately elusive origin. Indeed, despite a good deal of conjecture and research, very little is known about them outside the trail of malfunctions they leave behind them. What we do know is that the aircraft is a favourite target for gremlin attack. During the Second World War a number of RAF stations were to claim evidence of their presence. It was at this time that the word became popularized, since when it has entered common usage.

< Old French *gris* grey.

groan (grəʊn) *vb* **1** utter a deep sound showing pain, disapproval, etc. **2** creak under a strain: The tables groaned under the weight of all the food.
• *n* a groaning sound. < Old English *grānian*.

grocer (ˈgrəʊsə) *n* a shopkeeper who sells food and household goods. **groceries** *pl n* goods sold by a grocer. **grocery** *n* a grocer's shop. < Middle French *gros* large.

grog (grɒg) *n* an alcoholic drink, esp. diluted rum. **groggy** *adj* weak or shaky, as from illness. SEE PANEL.

groin (grɔɪn) *n* **1** the fold where the thighs join the abdomen. **2** (*euphemistic*) the male genitals. < Old English *grynde* abyss. SEE PANEL.

groom (gruːm) *n* **1** a person who is employed to look after horses. **2** a bridegroom.
• *vb* **1** clean and look after (a horse, etc.). **2** make neat and attractive. **3** prepare for a particular career or task. < Middle English *grom* manservant.

groove (gruːv) *n* **1** a long, narrow channel. **2** the spiral channel of a gramophone record. **3** a monotonous routine; rut.
• *vb* make or form a groove in. **groovy** *adj* (*informal*) exciting; excellent. < Dutch *groeve*.

grope (grəʊp) *vb* **1** feel about uncertainly with the hands. **2** search uncertainly (for words, a solution, etc.). < Old English *grāpian*.

gross (grəʊs) *adj* **1** extremely bad and obvious; outrageous: gross injustices. **2** very fat and bulky. **3** consisting of a total without deductions for tax, etc. **4** vulgar; coarse.
• *n, pl* **gross** a unit of quantity of 12 dozen.
• *vb* earn or produce as a total income, before deductions for tax, etc. **grossly** *adv* < Latin *grossus* thick.

grotesque (grəʊˈtɛsk) *adj* very odd; looking very strange or ugly. **grotesquely** *adv* **grotesqueness** *n* SEE PANEL.

grotto (ˈgrɒtəʊ) *n, pl* **grottoes 1** a picturesque cave. **2** a structure made to look like a natural, attractive cave: Let's visit Santa in the Christmas grotto! < Italian, from Latin *crypta* cavern.

grotty (ˈgrɒtɪ) *adj* (*informal*) unattractive or unpleasant. < alteration of *grotesque*.

ground[1] (graʊnd) *n* **1** the surface of the earth. **2** soil; earth. **3** an area used for a particular purpose: a training-ground. **4** an area to be gained, defended, etc., in or as if in a battle: lose ground to one's opponents. **5** an area of knowledge or enquiry: The report covered a lot of ground. **6** a basis or justification for a belief, action, or complaint: on the grounds of adultery.
• *vb* **1** put or place on the ground. **2** run aground. **3** prevent (a pilot or aircraft) from flying. **4** teach the fundamentals to. **5** provide a basis or justification for. **get off the ground** make a successful start. **ground floor** the floor of a

grog

Until recently naval officers and ratings received issues of grog, originally a quarter of a pint of rum added to a pint of water. The word derives from Old *Grog,* which was the nickname given to the British admiral, Edward Vernon, 1684–1757. Vernon's nickname alludes to a certain part of his attire—a cloak that was made from grogram, a coarse fabric of silk or with a silk base.

Not another kick in the groin!

In many cultures mention of certain parts of the human anatomy is often taboo, especially in polite or formal situations. When mention is made, it is very often by way of a *euphemism* —a polite synonym or 'genteel' paraphrase (see panel at **die**[1]). For example, if you examined all the sports commentaries that have ever been recorded since the beginning of broadcasting, it would be discovered that not a single player had ever received injury to the genitals! It is not that such injuries have never been received. Rather, the explanation is to be found in the commentator's use of euphemism—'Jones is down again—this time with a bit of a nasty *groin* injury.'

building that is level with the ground. **grounding** *n* basic, thorough training in a subject. **groundless** *adj* without basis: Your fears are groundless. **groundlessly** *adv* **grounds** *pl n* **1** the land attached to a house or other building. **2** the matter that settles to the bottom of a liquid: coffee grounds. **groundsheet** *n* a waterproof sheet for placing on the ground. **groundsman** *n, pl* **groundsmen** a person who looks after a sports ground. **groundwork** *n* the work that provides a foundation or basis. < Old English *grund.*

ground[2] SEE **GRIND.**

group (gruːp) *n* **1** a number of people or things gathered together or having a common feature, purpose, relationship, etc. **2** a pop group. **3** a combination of companies under single ownership consisting of a holding company and subsidiary companies.
• *vb* form or gather into one or more groups. **group practice** a medical practice run by a group of associated general practitioners. < Italian *gruppo.*

grouse[1] (graʊs) *n, pl* **grouse** a game-bird with a stocky body, a short, strong bill, and feathered legs. < origin unknown.

grouse[2] *vb, n* (*informal*) (a) grumble. **grouser** *n* < origin unknown.

grove (grəʊv) *n* a small wood. < Old English *grāf.*

grovel (ˈgrɒvl̩) *vb* **grovelled; grovelling** **1** lie or crawl face downwards as a sign of submission or humility. **2** humble oneself abjectly. < back formation from obsolete *groveling,* from Old Norse *ā grūfu* face down + *-ling.*

grow (grəʊ) *vb* **grew; grown; growing** **1** increase in size, quantity, degree, etc. **2** come into being and become mature. **3** become gradually: to grow dark. **4** produce by cultivation: grow tomatoes. **5** allow to grow: grow a beard. **grower** *n* **growing pains** **1** aches and pains felt by growing children. **2** difficulties encountered by a new enterprise, etc. **grow on** become more appealing to. **grow out** (esp. of children) become too old or big for (clothes, etc.). **growth** *n* **1** the process or result of growing; development. **2** an abnormal growth of tissue; tumour. **grow up** become older or more mature or sensible; develop. < Old English *grōwan.*

growl (graʊl) *vb* **1** make a low, rumbling sound. **2** utter in a growling way; grumble.
• *n* the act or sound of growling. **growler** *n* < probably like the sound.

grown (grəʊn) SEE **GROW.**
• *adj* **1** fully developed; mature: grown men. **2** overgrown (with). **grown-up** *adj, n* (an) adult.

grub (grʌb) *vb* **grubbed; grubbing** **1** dig in the ground. **2** uproot. **3** search about; rummage.
• *n* **1** the short, soft, legless larva of certain insects. **2** (*informal*) food. < Middle English *grubben.*

grubby (ˈgrʌbɪ) *adj* dirty.

grudge (grʌdʒ) *n* a persistent feeling of resentment or ill will.
• *vb* accept, give, or admit unwillingly. **grudgingly** *adv* < Old French *groucier.*

gruelling (ˈgrʊəlɪŋ) *adj* very tiring; exhausting. < obsolete *gruel* to punish.

gruesome (ˈgruːsəm) *adj* inspiring horror or loathing. < English dialect *grue* to shudder.

gruff (grʌf) *adj* **1** (of a voice, etc.) deep and harsh. **2** surly in manner. **gruffly** *adv* **gruffness** *n* < Dutch *grof.*

grumble (ˈgrʌmbl̩) *vb* **1** complain in a nagging, discontented way. **2** rumble.
• *n* **1** a complaint. **2** a rumbling sound. **grumbler** *n* **grumbling** *adj* causing pain intermittently: a grumbling appendix. < probably Middle Dutch *grommen.*

grumpy (ˈgrʌmpɪ) *adj* moody and bad-tempered. **grumpily** *adv* **grumpiness** *n* < probably English dialect *grump* surly remark.

grunt (grʌnt) *vb* make or utter with the short, low, snorting sound of a pig or a

---

grotesque

A 70-year-old grandmother who goes to the supermarket wearing a bathing-costume, crash helmet, and wellington boots might be said to look grotesque. This word derives from the Old Italian (*pittura*) *grotesca,* literally 'a cave painting'. The paintings in question were those that adorned the walls of ancient caves excavated in medieval times. The digging revealed highly fantastic depictions of sundry monsters combining human and animal forms. Later on, in the 18th century, artificial caves or grottoes were to be constructed and decorated in imitation of the original ones.

---

sound like this.
• *n* a grunting sound. < Old English *grunnettan.*

guarantee (ˌgærənˈtiː) *n* **1** a formal promise of the good quality of an article and that faults that develop within a specified period will be made good. **2** a formal promise that a particular agreement will be kept. **3** a formal promise to be responsible for the debt, default, etc., of another. **4** something given as a security; pledge. **5** a guarantor.
• *vb* **guaranteed; guaranteeing 1** take responsibility for (the debts, defaults of another person). **2** give security for. **3** promise; ensure: I cannot guarantee good results. **guarantor** *n* a person who gives or makes a guarantee. < Old French *garant* warrant.

guard (gɑːd) *vb* **1** watch over and protect from danger. **2** supervise, to prevent escape, theft, etc. **3** hold in check; control. **4** take precautions: guard against possible difficulties.
• *n* **1** a person or group that guards, such as a sentry. **2** the state of keeping watch for danger, etc.: be on one's guard. **3** a defensive position in boxing, fencing, etc. **4** the person in charge of a railway train. **5** a protective device on a machine. **guarded** *adj* cautious. **guardedness** *n* **guardsman** *n, pl* **guardsmen** a member of a military guard. < Old French *garder.*

guardian (ˈgɑːdɪən) *n* **1** a person who is legally entrusted with the care of someone who cannot act for himself or herself, such as an infant. **2** a person who guards or protects. **guardianship** *n*

guava (ˈgwɑːvə) *n* a tropical American tree with yellow, pear-shaped, pulpy fruits; such a fruit. < Spanish *guayaba,* from South American Indian.

guerrilla warfare

Guerrilla is noteworthy for three reasons.

□ **its spelling:** in Spanish the word is spelt guerrilla, but in English the spelling with one r (guerilla) is also found.

□ **its meaning:** in Spanish the meaning of guerrilla is 'a small war'—the word being first used to refer to the Spanish resistance movement against the French conquest in the Peninsular War.

□ **its pronunciation:** guerrilla is now usually indistinguishable from the pronunciation of gorilla.

guerrilla (gəˈrɪlə) *n* a member of a small, independent, armed force that engages in surprise attacks, sabotage, etc. **guerrilla warfare** such military action. < Spanish: *small war.* SEE PANEL.

guess (gɛs) *vb* **1** form or express an estimate, opinion, answer, etc., without exact calculation or definite knowledge. **2** arrive at the correct answer by chance or estimating. **3** (*chiefly US*) believe; suppose.
• *n* an estimate, opinion, answer, etc., made by guessing. **guesswork** *n* the act of guessing; result of this. < probably Scandinavian.

guest (gɛst) *n* **1** a person who is entertained at the home of another. **2** a person who is taken out, entertained, etc., at the expense of another. **3** a person who pays for accommodation and meals at a hotel, etc. **4** a performer who is invited to participate in an entertainment: a guest artist. **guest-house** *n* a private house that offers accommodation to paying guests. < Old Norse *gestr.*

guffaw (gʌˈfɔː) *n* a crude, boisterous laugh.
• *vb* laugh in this way. < like the sound.

guide (gaɪd) *n* **1** a person who leads the way for others. **2** a person employed to show places of interest to visitors. **3** a supervisor or advisor. **4** a person or thing that directs or influences a person's way of life. **5** also **guidebook** a book that provides information on a place or subject. **6 Guide** a member of a worldwide movement of girls and young women that teaches character, responsibility, and good citizenship. **7** a device that directs the motion of a moving part.
• *vb* act as a guide to. **guidance** *n* **1** the act of guiding. **2** advice or counselling: marriage guidance. **guide-dog** *n* a dog trained to guide a blind person. **guidelines** *pl n* principles that set out standards or courses of action. < Old French *guider.*

guild (gɪld) *n* (in medieval Europe) an association formed to further members' interests or aims. < Scandinavian.

guile (gaɪl) *n* deceitful cunning. **guileless** *adj* without guile. < Old French.

guillotine (ˈgɪləˌtiːn) *n* **1** a device for beheading people consisting of a heavy blade that slides down two upright posts. **2** a device with a long blade used for cutting paper, etc.
• *vb* cut, using a guillotine. SEE PANEL.

guilt (gɪlt) *n* **1** the fact of having committed an offence. **2** a feeling that one is to blame for something or is at fault. **guiltless** *adj* without guilt. **guilty** *adj* **1** legally judged as having committed an offence. **2** of, showing, or feeling guilt: a guilty conscience. **guiltily** *adv* **guiltiness** *n* < Old English *gylt.*

guinea (ˈgɪnɪ) *n* a former British gold coin of 21 shillings; this sum (£1.05). **guinea-pig** *n* **1** a small, short-eared rodent, commonly kept as a pet. **2** a person or thing used as a subject for experiments. SEE PANEL.

guise (gaɪz) *n* an outward appearance, esp. in pretence. < Old French, from Germanic.

guitar (gɪˈtɑː) *n* a string instrument having a fretted finger-board and usually six strings which are plucked with a plectrum or the fingers. **guitarist** *n* < Spanish *guitarra,* ultimately from Greek *kithara* cithara, lyre.

gulf (gʌlf) *n* **1** a large, deep bay. **2** a deep chasm. **3** a very wide gap, in opinions, etc. < Old French *golfe,* ultimately from Greek *kolpos* bosom.

gull (gʌl) *n* a long-winged, short-legged sea-bird, with grey and white plumage. < Celtic.

gullet (ˈgʌlɪt) *n* the oesophagus; throat. < Middle French *goulet,* ultimately from Latin *gula.*

gullible (ˈgʌləbl) *adj* easily deceived or tricked. **gullibility** *n* < *gull* to cheat, from Middle French *goule.*

gully (ˈgʌlɪ) *n* a channel cut into the earth by running water; deep gutter. < SEE GULLET.

gulp (gʌlp) *vb* **1** swallow quickly and greedily, esp. in large mouthfuls. **2** catch one's breath, as in swallowing. • *n* the act of gulping; quantity taken in a gulp. **gulp back** suppress, as if by swallowing. < probably Middle Dutch *gulpen.*

gum[1] (gʌm) *n* **1** a sticky substance exuded by certain plants; product made from this. **2** any sticky substance. **3** also **gum-drop** a small, jelly-like sweet made of gelatine or gum arabic. • *vb* **gummed; gumming** cover or stick with gum or as if with gum. **gum arabic** a widely used, water-soluble gum obtained from acacia trees. **gumboot** *n* a strong waterproof rubber boot. **gummy** *adj* sticky with gum. < Latin *gummi,* from Egyptian *kemai.*

gum[2] *n* the fleshy tissue that covers the base of the teeth. **gumboil** *n* an abscess on the gum. < Old English *gōma* palate.

gumption (ˈgʌmpʃən) *n* (*informal*) practical common sense and initiative. < origin unknown.

gun (gʌn) *n* **1** a firearm that discharges shells or bullets through a metal tube by force of an explosion. **2** a discharge of a gun. **3** a device that forces out a substance through a tube: a spray gun. • *vb* **gunned; gunning** fire on; shoot with a gun: The terrorists gunned him down. **gunboat** *n* a small, armed ship used to patrol coasts, etc. **gunfire** *n* the firing of

guillotine

Not many people would be proud of having an instrument of death named after them. The French physician, Dr Joseph Ignace *Guillotin,* 1738–1814, was no exception, yet despite his loud protests it was his name that was given to the guillotine. Ironically, Guillotin neither invented the device, nor did he introduce it to France. It so happened that, at the height of the Reign of Terror in 1792, it was Guillotin who strongly recommended its use, not on account of some blood lust but because he considered it the most humane means of execution. With the acceptance of his proposal, the machine and the name of its major advocate became inextricably linked.

guinea

A guinea was originally a British gold coin worth 21 shillings (£1.05). It was last struck in 1813 and finally removed from circulation in 1817. The name guinea comes from *Guinea* in West Africa, the reputed home of the gold from which the coin was made.

Despite the disappearance of the coin, the word guinea continued to be used and was commonly encountered in the pricing of professional fees and luxury goods, where it signified the money unit of £1.05. Since the advent of decimal currency, this usage has steadily fallen from favour. Today the word is fossilized in the names of certain horse-races.

guns. **gunman** *n, pl* **gunmen** a man armed with a gun, esp. illegally. **gunner** *n* **1** a serviceman who works with guns. **2** a private in the Royal Artillery. **gunpoint** *n* **at gunpoint** under the threat of being shot. **gunpowder** *n* an explosive mixture of potassium nitrate, charcoal, and sulphur. **gun-running** *n* the smuggling of guns and ammunition into a country. **gun-runner** *n* **gunshot** *n* **1** a shot fired from a gun. **2** the range of a gun. **gunsmith** *n* a person who makes or repairs firearms. < Middle English *gonne*. SEE PANEL.

gunwale (ˈgʌnḷ) *n* the top edge of the side of a ship or boat. < *gun* + *wale*, from Old English *walu*.

gurgle (ˈgɜːgḷ) *vb* make a low, bubbling noise.
• *n* such a noise. < probably like the sound.

guru (ˈgʊruː, ˈguːruː) *n* **1** a personal religious teacher, for example in Hinduism. **2** (*informal*) an influential or acknowledged teacher. < Hindi *gurū*, from Sanskrit *guru* heavy.

gush (gʌʃ) *vb* **1** pour out profusely or suddenly. **2** show one's emotions very enthusiastically, often in an affected manner.
• *n* **1** a sudden or profuse outpouring. **2** a demonstration of great emotion; effusiveness. < Middle English *guschen*.

gusset (ˈgʌsɪt) *n* a piece of cloth put into a garment to strengthen or enlarge it.
• *vb* fit with a gusset. < Middle French *gousset* piece of armour.

gust (gʌst) *n* **1** a sudden, brief rush of wind, rain, smoke, etc. **2** a sudden outburst of emotion.
• *vb* blow in gusts. **gusty** *adj* < Old Norse *gustr*.

gusto (ˈgʌstəʊ) *n* great, lively enjoyment. < Spanish, from Latin *gustus* tasting.

gut (gʌt) *n* **1** the alimentary canal; lower part of this. **2** the belly or abdomen. **3** catgut. **4** *pl* (*informal*) courage and determination.
• *vb* **gutted; gutting 1** remove the guts from (an animal). **2** destroy the inside of: The hotel was completely gutted by fire.
• *adj* **1** of or based on instinct as opposed to reason: a gut feeling. **2** of or from what is basic or essential. **gutless** *adj* (*informal*) lacking courage. **gutsy** *adj* (*informal*) **1** courageous. **2** gluttonous. **hate someone's guts** (*informal*) dislike someone intensely. < Old English *gutt*.

gutter (ˈgʌtə) *n* **1** a channel at the side of a street or under the eaves of a roof to carry off rain-water. **2** the poorest and lowest level or condition of human life. **guttering** *n* a length of gutter. < Latin *gutta* drop.

guttural (ˈgʌtərəl) *adj* **1** of the throat; pronounced in the throat. **2** harsh or strident. **gutturally** *adv* < Latin *guttur* throat.

guy[1] (gaɪ) *n* **1** (*informal*) a man. **2** a crude effigy of Guy Fawkes, burnt on top of a bonfire on or about 5 November. < *Guy* Fawkes, died 1606, English conspirator.

guy[2] *n* a rope, chain, etc., used to secure, steady, or guide an object. < origin uncertain.

guzzle (ˈgʌzḷ) *vb* consume (food or drink) greedily. **guzzler** *n* < origin unknown.

gym (dʒɪm) *n* (*informal*) **1** a gymnasium. **2** conditioning of the body by exercises, etc., esp. at school. **gymnasium** *n, pl* **gymnasiums** a large room or building used for gymnastics and physical exercises. **gymnast** *n* a person trained in gymnastics. **gymnastic** *adj* of gymnastics. **gymnastics** *pl n* exercises to develop bodily strength and agility. SEE PANEL AT **ACROBAT**.

Stuck with our guns!

Gun features in a number of idiomatic expressions, including:

gun for to seek in order to attack or get revenge on.

jump the gun to be too hasty in doing or saying something, especially in drawing a conclusion: 'Now don't jump the gun. I only said that Sue might be coming, not that it was definite.'

one's big guns one's most important arguments, witnesses, etc.: 'I'm still waiting for them to bring on their big guns.'

spike someone's guns to spoil someone's plans: 'Publishing this report before they publish theirs will really spike their guns.' This derives from the practice of disabling early cannon and firearms by driving a spike into the hole through which the charge was ignited (the touch-hole).

stick to one's guns to be persistent in defending one's opinion, supporting a case, etc.: 'If I were you, I'd stick to my guns and demand my money back.'

gymkhana (dʒɪmˈkɑːnə) *n* a meeting with competitions in which horses and riders show their skills. < Hindi *gend-khāna* ball-house.

gynaecology (ˌgaɪnəˈkɒlədʒɪ) *n* the branch of medicine dealing with diseases of women, esp. those affecting the reproductive system. **gynaecological** *adj* **gynaecologist** *n* < Greek *gynaik-* woman + *-logy*, ultimately *logos* word.

gypsy, gipsy (ˈdʒɪpsɪ) *n* a person who moves from one place to another; wanderer. SEE PANEL.

gyrate (dʒaɪˈreɪt) *vb* move in circles or spirals; rotate or revolve. **gyration** *n* **gyratory** *adj* < Latin *gȳrus* circle, from Greek *gyros*.

gyroscope (ˈdʒaɪrəˌskəʊp) *n* a spinning wheel which is mounted so that it is free to turn about any axis and tends to maintain the same orientation in space; used in ships and aircraft.

Call me Gypsy

The highly elusive and enigmatic aura surrounding gypsies is reflected in their name. Originally the gypsy came from north-west India, migrating first to what was then Persia and later on to Europe. Gypsies are so-called, however, because it was thought in the 16th century that they came from Egypt and so were called Egyptians. In time Egyptians became shortened to Gyptians, from which developed the present form.

H

habeas corpus (ˈheɪbɪəs ˈkɔːpəs) *n* an order requiring that a detained person be brought before a court so that legality of his or her detention may be established. < Latin: you may have the body.

haberdasher (ˈhæbəˌdæʃə) *n* a dealer in small articles used in sewing such as buttons and threads. **haberdashery** *n* such goods. < probably Anglo-French *hapertas.*

habit (ˈhæbɪt) *n* **1** a usual or customary way of behaving. **2** addiction. **3** a mental disposition. **4** a costume worn by a monk or nun. **habitual** *adj* **1** of the nature of a habit; usual. **2** by habit: a habitual smoker. **habitually** *adv* **habituate** *vb* accustom to. < Latin *habitus* custom, from *habēre* to have, hold.

habitable (ˈhæbɪtəbl̩) *adj* fit for living in.

habitat (ˈhæbɪˌtæt) *n* the natural environment of an animal or plant. < Latin: it inhabits.

habitation (ˌhæbɪˈteɪʃən) *n* a dwelling-place or occupation of this.

habitué (həˈbɪtjʊˌeɪ) *n* a frequent visitor to a place. < French, from *habituer* to frequent.

hack[1] (hæk) *vb* **1** cut or chop (at) roughly. **2** clear by cutting away undergrowth. **3** deal a rough blow to. **4** cough in a harsh, dry manner. **hack-saw** *n* a saw for cutting metal. < Old English *haccian.*

hack[2] *n* **1** a horse kept for riding; one kept for hire. **2** a person who does uninteresting or mediocre work, esp. writing.
• *vb* ride (a horse) at an ordinary pace, esp. along roads. < *Hackney,* borough of London.

hackle (ˈhækl̩) *n* **1** the long, slender, neck feathers on a pheasant, turkey, etc. **2** *pl* the hairs on the neck and back of a dog, etc., that rise when it is afraid. **raise someone's hackles** cause someone to feel and show anger or resentment. < Middle English *hakell.*

hackneyed (ˈhæknɪd) *adj* (of a phrase, etc.) having lost its original freshness through over-use. < *Hackney,* borough of London.

had (həd, əd, d; *stressed* hæd) SEE **HAVE.**

haddock (ˈhædək) *n, pl* **haddock** a North Atlantic food fish related to cod; eaten fresh or smoked. < origin uncertain.

haemoglobin (ˌhiːməˈgləʊbɪn) *n* the substance within the red blood cells that is responsible for the colour of blood and carries oxygen through the body. < originally short for *haematoglobulin,* from Greek *haemato-* blood + *globulin,* from Latin *globus* ball.

haemophilia (ˌhiːməʊˈfɪlɪə) *n* a hereditary disease in which the blood does not clot normally. **haemophiliac** *n* a person suffering from this. < Greek *haimo-* blood + *-philia* abnormal appetite, from *philos* dear.

haemorrhage (ˈhɛmərɪdʒ) *n* a great loss of blood from the blood vessels.
• *vb* have a haemorrhage. < Greek *haimo-* blood + *rhēgnynai* to break.

haemorrhoids (ˈhɛməˌrɔɪdz) *pl n* swollen veins round or near the anus. < Greek *haimo-* blood + *rhein* to flow.

haft (hɑːft) *n* the handle of an axe, knife, or other cutting-tool. < Old English *hæft.*

hag (hæg) *n* **1** an unpleasant or ugly, old woman. **2** a witch. < Old English *hægtesse* witch.

haggard (ˈhægəd) *adj* looking worn or thin, as from worry or lack of sleep. < Middle French *hagard* untamed.

haggis (ˈhægɪs) *n* a traditional Scottish meat dish made from sheep's heart, liver, and lungs, minced with oatmeal, suet, and seasonings and boiled in the stomach of the animal. < origin uncertain.

haggle (ˈhægl̩) *vb* argue about the terms, price, etc., in bargaining. < Scandinavian.

hail[1] (heɪl) *n* **1** small pellets of ice that fall in showers or storms; such a shower or storm. **2** a large group of things directed with force: a hail of bullets.
• *vb* **1** (of hail) fall. **2** pour down or hit like hail. **hailstone** *n* a pellet of hail. < Old English *hægl.*

hail[2] *vb* **1** greet enthusiastically; acclaim (as). **2** summon: hail a taxi. **3** have come: Where do you hail from originally? < Old Norse *heill* whole.

hair (hɛə) *n* **1** a thread-like structure that grows from the skin of mammals. **2** the coating of hairs, esp. on the human head. **hairbrush** *n* a brush for the hair. **haircut** *n* cutting the hair; style in which it is cut. **hair-do** *n, pl* **hair-dos** a hair-style. **hairdresser** *n* a person whose business is cutting and styling hair. **hairdressing** *n* **haired** *adj* having hair of a colour, etc., that is mentioned: dark-haired. **hair-grip** *n* a small clip for keeping the hair in place. **hairless** *adj* without hair. **hair-line** *n* **1** the natural edge formed by hair on the face. **2** a very thin crack or line. **hair-piece** *n* a section of false hair worn to increase the length or bulk of one's real hair; toupee.

hair-raising

The word hair features in a number of idiomatic expressions, including:

hair-raising *adj* terrifying: a hair-raising experience.
hair's breadth a very short distance or margin: He escaped death by a hair's breadth.
let one's hair down to relax completely and enjoy oneself: Go on! Let your hair down! You don't win the pools every day!
make one's hair stand on end to cause extreme fear or horror.
not turn a hair not to show any signs of losing composure. The expression alludes to a horse that is hot after racing, yet is not sweaty; its hairs are therefore unruffled.
split hairs to argue about tiny, insignificant points.
tear one's hair (out) to be very troubled or worried: Don't tear your hair out trying to finish all the work today!

hairpin *n* a small U-shaped pin for keeping the hair in place. **hairpin bend** a bend on a road that curves very sharply. **hair-slide** *n* a hinged fastener for keeping the hair in place. **hairspring** *n* a fine, spiral spring that regulates the balance-wheel in a clock, etc. **hair-style** *n* a way of cutting, shaping, and setting the hair. **hairy** *adj* **1** having much hair. **2** (*informal*) scaring or exciting; difficult. < Old English *hær*. SEE PANEL.

hake (heɪk) *n, pl* **hake** a food fish related to cod. < perhaps Old Norse *haki* hook.

hale (heɪl) *adj* healthy and strong: hale and hearty. < Old English *hāl*.

half (hɑːf) *n, pl* **halves** **1** either of two equal, approximately equal, or corresponding parts that together make a whole. **2** something of half or approximately half the value or quantity such as half a pint or a child's ticket. **3** (*informal*) half past: half nine.
• *determiner, pron* being a half or approximately a half.
• *adv* **1** to an equal part or extent. **2** partly. **go halves** share (something such as expenses) equally. **half-and-half** *adj, n* (something) that is approximately half one thing and half another. **half-back** *n* a player between the forwards and full backs in football, hockey, etc. **half-brother** *n* a brother related through one parent only. **half-caste** *n* a person of mixed race. **half-hearted** *adj* lacking enthusiasm and determination. **half-mast** *n* the position of a flag lowered half-way down a mast, as a mark of respect for a dead person. **half past** half an hour after (an hour that is

half

Half features in many expressions, including the following:

and a half unusually big, good, important, etc.: 'My goodness! That was a meal and a half!'
by half excessively: too clever by half.
by halves not thoroughly: He does nothing by halves.
go off at half-cock to fail because of inadequate preparation.
half-baked *adj* showing a lack of careful planning.
half board provision of bed, breakfast, and one main meal at a hotel, etc.
half-breed *n* a person whose parents are of different races.
half holiday a holiday of half a day, especially an afternoon.
half measures something inadequate; compromise.
half-truth *n* a partially true statement, especially one intended to deceive.
half-wit *n* a foolish or stupid person.
half-witted *adj*

Do you say half *is* ... or half *are* ...? The rule here is to use a singular verb when the following noun is singular: Half of the field *is* being sold off, and a plural when the following noun is plural: Half of the places *are* reserved for guests.

mentioned); used in telling the time. **halfpenny** *n* a former British coin worth a half of a penny. **half-term** *n* a short holiday midway through a school term. **half-time** *n* the interval for rest between the two halves of a sports game. **half-tone** *n* **1** any of the shades between the darkest and lightest tones. **2** a reproductive process of photographing an image through a screen to break it up into dots; etched plate obtained in this way. **half-way** *adj, adv* midway between two points; partially. < Old English *healf*. SEE PANEL.

halibut (ˈhælɪbət) *n, pl* **halibut** a large, North Atlantic flat-fish used as food. < Middle English *hali* holy + *butt* flounder.

hall (hɔ:l) *n* **1** the room or passage at the entrance of a house or building. **2** a building for public meetings, concerts, etc. **3** a large country house, esp. with much land attached to it. **4** a residential building in a college, etc.: a hall of residence. < Old English *heall*.

hallmark (ˈhɔ:lˌmɑ:k) *n* **1** an official mark stamped on articles of gold or silver after their purity has been tested. **2** a distinguishing feature.
• *vb* stamp with a hallmark.

hallo (həˈləʊ) *interj, n, pl* **hallos** an exclamation used in greeting, answering the telephone, expressing surprise, or to attract attention. < alteration of *hollo, holla* cry for attention. SEE PANEL.

hallow (ˈhæləʊ) *vb* **1** make holy or set apart as being holy. **2** respect greatly. < Old English *hālgian*.

hallucination (həˈlu:sɪˈneɪʃən) *n* a vivid perception of something that does not really exist; image, thing, etc., perceived in this way. **hallucinatory** *adj* tending to cause hallucinations. < Latin *hallucinari* to dream.

halo (ˈheɪləʊ) *n, pl* **haloes** **1** a ring of light around the head of a sacred figure in a painting. **2** a circle of light appearing around the sun or moon, caused by diffraction by particles in the earth's atmosphere. **haloed** *adj* < Greek *halōs* threshing-floor.

halogen (ˈhæləˌdʒən) *n* (*chemistry*) any of the non-metal elements fluorine, chlorine, bromine, iodine, and astatine. < Swedish, from Greek *hals* salt + *-gen*.

halt (hɔ:lt) *n* **1** an interruption or cessation of movement, operation, etc. **2** a minor railway station without normal facilities.
• *vb* come or bring to a halt. < German *halten* to hold, stop.

halting (ˈhɔ:ltɪŋ) *adj* hesitant. < archaic *halt* lame, from Old English *healt*.

halve (hɑ:v) *vb* **1** divide into two equal parts. **2** reduce by half.

ham (hæm) *n* **1** the hind end of a bacon pig, esp. the thigh; meat of this part, dried and salted or smoked. **2** a buttock and thigh; back of the thigh. **3** (*informal*) the operator of an amateur radio station: a radio ham. **4** (*informal*) a poor actor or performer.
• *vb* **hammed; hamming** (*informal*) overact. **ham-fisted** *adj* (*informal*) clumsy. < Old English *hamm*.

hamburger (ˈhæmˌbɜ:gə) *n* a round, flat cake of minced beef; such a cake in a bread roll. < *Hamburg*, city in Germany.

hamlet (ˈhæmlɪt) *n* a small village. < Middle French *hamelet*.

hammer (ˈhæmə) *n* **1** a hand tool with a heavy, metal head, used for driving in nails, beating metal, etc. **2** something with a similar shape, action, or function to this, such as an auctioneer's gavel or the lever for striking a bell. **3** a metal ball weighing about 7.3 kilograms attached by a chain to a handle and thrown in an athletic contest; such a contest.
• *vb* **1** beat or strike (a nail, wood, etc.) with or as if with a hammer. **2** shape with or as if with a hammer. **3** (*informal*) defeat. **come** or **go under the hammer** be sold by auction. **hammer and tongs** with great energy or violence. **hammer**

hallo

The one part of speech that receives relatively little attention is the *interjection*. The name derives from the Latin verb *intericere*, from *inter-* 'among or in the midst' and *jacere* 'to throw'. In other words, an interjection is something that is 'thrown into' a sentence as opposed to being integrated within its grammatical structure like, say, a noun or verb. The major types of interjection include words used to draw a person's attention: Hey! Hoy!, words used to express pain: Ouch! Ow!, words used to express sudden emotion: Oh, dear! Hurray!, obscene or profane expletives: Damn!, and words used for greetings and farewells: Hallo! Cheerio!

in or **into** teach or force understanding of by constant repetition. **hammer out** produce as a result of long, concentrated discussion: hammer out an agreement. < Old English *hamor*.

hammock (ˈhæmək) *n* a hanging bed of canvas or netting. < Spanish *hamaca*, from Taino.

hamper[1] (ˈhæmpə) *vb* prevent the progress or restrict the movement of. < Middle English *hamperen*.

hamper[2] *n* a large, covered basket and its contents, esp. food. < Middle French *hanap* cup, goblet.

hamster (ˈhæmstə) *n* a small rodent with very large cheek pouches. < Old High German *hamustro*, from Slavonic.

hamstring (ˈhæmˌstrɪŋ) *n* **1** any of the tendons at the back of the knee. **2** a large tendon at the back of an animal's hock. • *vb* **hamstrung; hamstringing** **1** cripple by cutting the hamstrings. **2** cripple the activity or effectiveness of. < *ham* + *string*.

hand (hænd) *n* **1** the part of the arm below the wrist. **2** a direction or position; side: on my right hand. **3** control or possession. **4** help, esp. using physical effort: Can you give me a hand? **5** an active part. **6** a pledge of marriage. **7** skill;

Can you give me a hand?

A request for someone to give a *hand* is neither made nor interpreted literally. If it were, one would come across answers such as 'Certainly. Which one? The right or the left?' The expression contains one of the many figures of speech found in the language which enable users to mean more than they say. The hand in question stands for the whole person. Face is used in exactly the same way in a sentence like 'Don't let me see your *face* in here again!' Here we have another example of *synecdoche*, a figure of speech in which a part is used to stand for the whole. Under the same heading, however, are included expressions which reverse the pattern—a part is understood by mention of the whole. For example, in *Leeds* won the match 3-0 it is not the *whole* city of Leeds that is referred to but just a *part* of it, namely its football team.

The word hand features in a large number of idiomatic phrases, including:

at hand 1 very near. **2** very close in time.

by hand 1 delivered by personal messenger rather than through the postal service. **2** performed by a person rather than by a machine.

eat out of someone's hand to comply readily with someone's wishes: He'll do anything I ask him to do. I've got him eating out of my hand.

hand down to pass or be passed from one generation to the next.

hand in to submit: Please hand in your scripts before leaving the examination hall.

hand in hand with hands linked; closely associated.

hand it to to give praise when this is due: I've got to hand it to you Mark! You've really done very well this time.

hand on to pass to the next person, group, or generation.

hand out to distribute. **hand-out** *n*

hand over 1 to transfer (control, power, etc.). **2** to pass or present. **hand-over** *n*

hand over fist constantly and rapidly: making profits hand over fist.

hand-picked *adj* chosen very carefully.

hands off an order not to touch or interfere with something.

hands up an order to raise one's hands, as in agreement or surrender.

hand-to-hand *adj* involving close physical contact: hand-to-hand fighting.

in hand being dealt with: The arrangements are in hand.

live from hand to mouth to meet only one's basic needs from one's income, without being able to save anything.

on hand available.

on one's hands 1 having as a responsibility, especially an unwanted one. **2** with little to do: He has a lot of time on his hands.

out of hand 1 uncontrolled. **2** immediately, without even considering (something): They rejected the proposal out of hand.

play into someone's hands to do something that enables someone to gain an advantage over one.

win hands down to win easily. The expression comes from racing, referring to a jockey who relaxes his grip on the reins when he knows he is winning easily.

ability. **8** handwriting. **9** a manual worker on a farm, in a factory, etc. **10** a member of a ship's crew: All hands on deck! **11** a person skilled at an activity: He's an old hand at parachuting. **12** an indicator on a dial, etc. **13** used to introduce either of two reasons, arguments, points, etc.: On the one hand.... **14** a unit equal to four inches (about 102 millimetres), used to measure a horse's height. **15** a round of applause: Give her a big hand! **16** the cards dealt to a player in a card-game; single round in a game. **17** one's negotiating position: Don't show your hand. **18** a shoulder of pork.
• *vb* **1** give or pass with the hand. **2** help or lead with the hand. **handbag** *n* a bag for carrying small personal articles, carried esp. by women. **handbook** *n* a short reference book. **handcuff** *vb* put handcuffs on. **handcuffs** *pl n* a pair of linked metal rings for locking round a prisoner's wrists. **handful** *n* **1** a quantity that can fill the hands. **2** a small number of people or things. **3** (*informal*) a person or thing that is difficult to control or troublesome: Looking after two young children is quite a handful! **handrail** *n* a narrow rail, for example by stairs, for people to grasp for support. **handshake** *n* grasping and shaking of a person's hand in greeting or agreement. **handstand** *n* balancing one's body on only the hands, with the feet in the air. **handwriting** *n* writing done by hand; style of this. < Old English. SEE PANEL.

handicap (ˈhændɪˌkæp) *n* **1** a disability or disadvantage that hinders progress or reduces one's chances of success. **2** a contest in which competitors are given advantages or disadvantages to equalize their chances of winning; such advantages or disadvantages.
• *vb* **handicapped; handicapping** **1** give handicaps to. **2** put at a disadvantage. < *hand in cap,* former lottery game.

handicraft (ˈhændɪˌkrɑːft) *n* skilled work done by the hands such as needlework or pottery. < alteration of *handcraft* through the influence of *handiwork.*

handiwork (ˈhændɪˌwɜːk) *n* **1** work done by the hands. **2** the result of the action of a person. < Old English *handgeweorc.*

handkerchief (ˈhæŋkətʃiːf) *n, pl* **handkerchiefs, handkerchieves** a small piece of cloth used for wiping the nose, eyes, etc. SEE PANEL.

handle (ˈhændl̩) *n* the part of an object that is designed to be held, in order to move, lift, or use the object.
• *vb* **1** examine with the hands. **2** manage or control. **3** deal with (a subject, etc.). **4** respond to being operated in a manner that is mentioned: This car handles well. **5** deal in (goods). **handlebars** *pl n* the steering-bar on a bicycle, etc. **handler** *n* a person in charge of an animal: a dog handler. < Old English.

handsome (ˈhænsəm) *adj* **1** (esp. of a man) good-looking. **2** generous: a handsome salary. **3** (of a price) considerable. **handsomely** *adv* **handsomeness** *n* < Middle English *handsom* easily handled.

handy (ˈhændɪ) *adj* **1** conveniently near. **2** easy to use: a handy reference book. **3** skilful at using one's hands to do practical tasks. **4** convenient; useful: come in handy. **handily** *adv* **handyman** *n, pl* **handymen** **1** a person who is employed to do odd jobs. **2** a person who is skilful at doing practical repairs, etc.

hang (hæŋ) *vb* **hung,** except def. **5,** **hanged; hanging** **1** attach to a high point by the top so that the lower part is free; be attached in this way. **2** attach (a door or gate) to hinges so that it swings freely; be attached in this way. **3** fasten (wallpaper) to a wall with paste. **4** decorate with material, etc., that hangs: hang

hand kerchief or **handkerchief?**

A word like dropout, (or should it be drop-out?) provides a small, daily reminder of the fact that English, like all languages, is in a constant state of flux. Nothing better illustrates change at work in language than the hyphen.

The typical pattern of evolution falls into three stages: courtship, engagement, and marriage. In the courtship stage we find that two words start to appear together regularly, but nevertheless remain separate words (hand kerchief). In due course the association is formally recognized through hyphenation (hand-kerchief). This usually continues until, after a long engagement, the final union takes place: the hyphen drops out and the two words become one (handkerchief).

Other words that have successfully completed this evolutionary process include landlord, seaside, doorkeeper, waistcoat, and loophole.

a room with tapestries. **5** put to death by suspending from a rope around the neck; die in this way. **6** hold in an inclined position: He hung his head in shame. **7** remain or persist: The threat of redundancy still hangs over the factory.
• *n* the way something hangs. **hanger** *n* **1** a loop or hook by which something is hung. **2** a shaped piece of wood or plastic for hanging a garment on. **hang-glider** *n* an unpowered aircraft consisting of a large, bat-shaped, cloth wing over a light, metal frame from which the pilot hangs in a harness. **hang-gliding** *n* **hangman** *n* a man who carries out the sentence of hanging on condemned criminals. **hangover** *n* **1** a severe headache, etc., that occurs as the after-effect of too much drinking. **2** something that remains from an earlier time. < Old English *hangian.* SEE PANEL.

hangar (ˈhæŋə) *n* a large shed for housing aircraft. < French.

hanging (ˈhæŋɪŋ) *n* **1** putting to death by hanging. **2** something hung, such as a tapestry.
• *adj* **1** situated on a steep slope. **2** overhanging.

hanker (ˈhæŋkə) *vb* have a strong wish or desire; yearn: hanker for the past. < probably Flemish *hankeren.*

hanky-panky (ˌhæŋkɪˈpæŋkɪ) *n* (*informal*) mildly improper behaviour. < probably *hocus-pocus.*

haphazard (hæpˈhæzəd) *adj* showing a lack of order, care, or plan.
• *adj, adv* by chance. **haphazardly** *adv* **haphazardness** *n* < archaic *hap* chance + *hazard.*

hapless (ˈhæpləs) *adj* unfortunate. < archaic *hap* chance + *less.*

happen (ˈhæpn̩) *vb* **1** be or occur by chance: I happened to meet David this morning. **2** occur as an event. **3** have the good or bad fortune to do something. **happening** *n* something that happens; event. **happen on** or **upon** find or meet by chance. **happen to** cause damage, loss, etc., to: What happened to your leg? < archaic *hap* chance.

happy (ˈhæpɪ) *adj* **1** having, showing, or causing pleasure. **2** well suited or expressed. **3** fortunate. **happily** *adv* **happiness** *n* **happy-go-lucky** *adj* carefree. < archaic *hap* chance.

hara-kiri (ˌhærəˈkɪrɪ) *n* (in Japan) suicide by ritual disembowelment, esp. when disgraced or under sentence of death. < Japanese.

harangue (həˈræŋ) *n* a lengthy, esp. critical speech.
• *vb* speak or address in a harangue. < Old Italian *aringa* public speech.

harass (ˈhærəs) *vb* **1** trouble or worry persistently. **2** attack (an enemy) repeatedly. **harassment** *n* < Middle French *harer* to set a dog on.

harbinger (ˈhɑːbɪndʒə) *n* a person or thing that announces or shows the approach of another. < Old French *herberge* shelter.

harbour (ˈhɑːbə) *n* a place of protection and anchorage for ships.
• *vb* **1** provide protection for. **2** keep in the mind: harbour a grudge. **3** conceal or contain. < Old English *here* army + *beorg* shelter.

hard (hɑːd) *adj* **1** not yielding to pressure; firm or tough. **2** difficult to do, understand, or explain. **3** using or demanding great energy: hard work. **4** harsh or severe. **5** unfeeling or resentful: a hard heart. **6** searching or close: take a hard look.

Hang on!

Hang features in a number of idiomatic expressions, including:

get the hang of to understand or master the technique of: She could never get the hang of using a sewing-machine.
hang about or around to wait; spend time idly.
hang back to be slow or reluctant to do something.
hanger-on *n* a person who associates himself or herself with a person or group, especially for personal gain.
hang in there a slang expression used as an exhortation not to give up, especially when under great pressure.
hang on 1 to depend on. **2** to pay close attention to: She hung on his every word. **3** to remain. **4** to wait.
hang out to visit frequently: The kids hang out in coffee bars. **hang-out** *n*
hang together to fit well together; be consistent.
hang up to end a telephone conversation.
hang-up *n* a source of mental, nervous, or emotional difficulty.

7 having difficulty in doing something: hard of hearing. **8** (of water) containing salts that prevent soap from lathering freely. **9** (of a drug) highly addictive.
• *adv* **1** with great energy: work hard. **2** in a concentrated way. **3** close: hard by the motorway. **4** in or with difficulty: I'd be hard put to find £100. **hardness** *n* **hardboard** *n* a thin, stiff board made of compressed sawdust and woodchips. **hardware** *n* **1** tools, implements, and utensils; ironmongery. **2** the physical equipment of a computer system. **hardwood** *n* the wood of a broad-leaved tree such as the oak or beech; such a tree. < Old English *heard.* SEE PANEL.

harden (ˈhɑːdn̩) *vb* **1** make or become hard or harder. **2** make or become stronger or more determined. **hardener** *n*

hardly (ˈhɑːdlɪ) *adv* **1** scarcely; barely: I could hardly believe the news! **2** in a harsh manner. SEE PANEL.

hardship (ˈhɑːdʃɪp) *n* a state of suffering or severe need; something that causes such suffering.

hardy (ˈhɑːdɪ) *adj* **1** able to withstand tiredness, cold, and other difficulties. **2** (of plants) able to withstand the weather conditions of winter. **hardiness** *n* < Old French *hardi.*

hare (hɛə) *n* a fast, long-eared mammal resembling but larger than a rabbit and living in the open.
• *vb* (*informal*) run fast. **harelip** *n* an upper lip with a vertical slit, like that of a hare, occurring as a congenital deformity. < Old English *hara.*

harem (ˈhɛərəm, hɑːˈriːm) *n* the women in a Muslim household living in a separate part of the house; the part of the house where they live. < Arabic *ḥarīm* something prohibited.

hark (hɑːk) *vb* listen closely. **hark back to** return to or recall (an earlier action, time, etc.). < Middle English *herken.*

harlequin (ˈhɑːlɪkwɪn) *adj* having bright or varied colours. < Middle French *Herlequin* demon.

harlot (ˈhɑːlət) *n* (*archaic*) a prostitute. < Old French *herlot* rogue.

harm (hɑːm) *n* **1** damage or injury. **2** mischief or wrong.
• *vb* cause harm to. **harmful** *adj* causing or likely to cause harm. **harmfully** *adv* **harmless** *adj* not likely to cause harm; inoffensive. **harmlessly** *adv* < Old English *hearm.*

harmony (ˈhɑːmənɪ) *n* **1** the combination of parts into a pleasing, ordered unity. **2** agreement in action, opinions, etc. **3** a pleasant sound. **4** the combining of musical notes into chords. **harmonic** *adj*

hard lines

Hard features in a number of expressions, many of them idiomatic, including:

hard-and-fast *adj* that cannot be changed; fixed: hard-and-fast rules. The expression was used originally to describe a ship that had run aground.
hard-boiled *adj* **1** (of eggs) boiled until the yolk and white are solid. **2** (of people) tough; callous.
hard copy printed material produced by a computer, etc., that can be read without the aid of a special device; print-out.
hard core the firmly committed members of a group.
hard-headed *adj* realistic and tough; shrewd.
hard line a firm, uncompromising pursuit of a particular course of action: a hard line on motorists who drink and drive. **hard-line** *adj* **hard-liner** *n*
hard lines or **luck** an expression of sympathy at someone's bad luck or failure.
hard sell an aggressive selling technique.
hard shoulder the surfaced strip at the side of a motorway, for use in emergencies.
hard up short of money.
hard-wearing *adj* durable.

hardly ... than or hardly ... when?

Hardly is followed by when, not than: She had *hardly* recovered from glandular fever *when* (not than) she developed laryngitis. Alternative ways of expressing this are scarcely (also followed by when) and no sooner (followed by than, not when): I had scarcely begun my speech *when* the fire-alarm rang. The duke had *no sooner* left the palace *than* the princess arrived.

In formal or literary styles, the word-order is sometimes inverted: *No sooner* were the orders issued *than* they were put into effect.

of a harmony. **harmonica** *n* a mouth-organ. **harmonious** *adj* **1** making a pleasant sound. **2** agreeing in action, opinions, etc. **3** having the parts combined in a pleasing, ordered unity. **harmoniously** *adv* **harmonium** *n* a keyboard instrument in which pedals operate a bellows that causes reeds to vibrate. **harmonize** *vb* **1** make or become harmonious. **2** provide a musical harmony for. **3** sing or play in harmony. < Greek *harmos* joint.

harness (ˈhɑ:nɪs) *n* **1** the straps and fittings by which a horse is attached to a cart. **2** something similar to this, esp. attached to the human body: a safety harness.
• *vb* **1** put a harness on. **2** control so as to use the power of. < Old French *herneis* baggage.

harp (hɑ:p) *n* a musical instrument with strings stretched across an open, triangular frame, plucked with the fingers.
• *vb* **harp on** (**about**) mention repeatedly, esp. critically. **harpist** *n* a person who plays the harp. < Old English *hearpe*.

harpoon (hɑ:ˈpu:n) *n* a barbed spear with a rope attached, used for hunting whales, etc.
• *vb* strike with a harpoon. < probably Old French *harper* to grapple.

harpsichord (ˈhɑ:psɪˌkɔ:d) *n* a keyboard instrument with a horizontal frame and strings that are plucked by quills. < Italian *arpicordo*, from Late Latin *harpa* harp + *chorda* chord.

harrow (ˈhærəʊ) *n* a heavy frame with spikes or discs for breaking up or levelling the soil.
• *vb* **1** draw a harrow over (land). **2** distress greatly. < Scandinavian.

harry (ˈhærɪ) *vb* **harried; harrying** harass or ravage. < Old English *hergian*.

harsh (hɑ:ʃ) *adj* **1** rough to the senses: a harsh voice. **2** severe or cruel: a harsh judgment. **harshly** *adv* **harshness** *n* < Scandinavian.

hart (hɑ:t) *n* a male deer, esp. an adult red deer. < Old English *heort*.

harvest (ˈhɑ:vɪst) *n* **1** the gathering of ripened crops. **2** the crop itself. **3** the season when this is done. **4** the result of effort.
• *vb* gather (a crop); reap. **harvester** *n* < Old English *hærfest*.

has (həz, əz, z, s; *stressed* hæz) SEE **HAVE**. **has-been** *n* (*informal*) a person or thing that has passed its most effective or popular point.

hash (hæʃ) *n* **1** a meal of cut, cooked meat, vegetables, etc., reheated. **2** (*informal*) a mess: make a hash of things.
• *vb* make (meat, etc.) into a hash. < Old French *hachier* to chop.

hashish (ˈhæʃi:ʃ, ˈhæʃɪʃ) *n* the resin obtained from certain species of hemp, used as a drug. < Arabic *hashīsh*.

hasp (hɑ:sp) *n* (on a door) a hinged metal piece with a slot that fits over a staple and is secured by a padlock or pin. < Old English *hæpse*.

hassle (ˈhæsl̩) *n* (*informal*) a struggle or quarrel; troublesome situation.
• *vb* (*informal*) **1** fight or argue. **2** harass; jostle. < origin uncertain.

hassock (ˈhæsək) *n* a firm cushion for kneeling on in a church. < Old English *hassuc*.

haste (heɪst) *n* **1** speed of movement. **2** rash action. **hasten** *vb* **1** hurry. **2** add quickly: I hasten to assure you that.... **3** cause to occur earlier. **hasty** *adj* **1** made or done in a hurry. **2** rash. **hastily** *adv* **make haste** hurry. < Old French.

hat (hæt) *n* **1** a covering for the head, esp. one with a brim and a shaped crown. **2** (*informal*) a role or capacity. **hatband** *n* a band of fabric, etc., around the hat just above the brim. < Old English *hæt*. SEE PANEL.

hatch[1] (hætʃ) *vb* **1** bring forth (young) from (an egg or eggs). **2** come forth from an egg. **3** devise (a plan), esp. secretly.
• *n* **1** the process of hatching. **2** the brood hatched. **hatchery** *n* a place for

hat trick

Contrary to popular belief the phrase hat trick comes not from the stage of the magician but from the world of cricket. A cricketer who succeeded in taking three wickets in three successive balls was at one time awarded a new cap by his club. It is from this former method of honouring a player that hat trick derives.

As the origin of the expression has steadily sunk into obscurity, its application has become increasingly generalized. Today it is used to refer to anything from a stunning triple achievement in sports to the less laudable feat of a driver who has somehow managed to wreck three new cars in the same number of days.

hatching fish eggs. < Middle English *hacchen.*

hatch[2] *n* **1** a small opening or door, as in a wall or aircraft. **2** also **hatchway** an opening in a ship's deck; covering for this. **hatchback** *n* a car with a rear sloping door that opens upwards; such a door. < Old English *hæc.*

hatch[3] *vb* mark with fine parallel lines. **hatching** *n* < Middle French *hacher* chop up.

hatchet (ˈhætʃɪt) *n* a short axe used for chopping wood, etc. < Middle French *hache* axe.

hate (heɪt) *n* **1** extreme dislike or hostility. **2** a hated person or thing.
• *vb* **1** feel extreme hostility or dislike towards. **2** be unwilling: I hate having to disturb you, but... **hater** *n* **hateful** *adj* provoking hate. **hatred** *n* hate. < Old English *hete.*

haughty (ˈhɔːtɪ) *adj* looking on others with arrogance; proud. **haughtily** *adv* **haughtiness** *n* < Middle French *haut* high.

haul (hɔːl) *vb* **1** pull with effort; drag. **2** transport in a vehicle or cart. **3** (*informal*) call to account: hauled up before the judge.
• *n* **1** hauling. **2** an amount gathered or caught. **3** the transportation of goods by hauling; goods transported. **4** the distance over which goods are transported: a long haul. **haulage** *n* hauling; charge for this. **haulier** *n* a person or business that transports goods by lorry. < Old French *haler.* SEE PANEL.

haunch (hɔːntʃ) *n* **1** the fleshy part of the hip. **2** leg and loin of an animal, used as food. < Old French *hanche.*

haunt (hɔːnt) *vb* **1** (of ghosts) inhabit or frequent (a place). **2** visit (a place) often. **3** recur to the mind of (a person) constantly.
• *n* a place frequently visited: his favourite haunt. **haunted** *adj* frequented by ghosts. < Old French *hanter.*

have (həv, əv, v; *stressed* hæv) *vb* **had; having 1** hold in one's possession. **2** contain. **3** obtain or receive. **4** experience; undergo: have a cold. **5** hold in the mind: have doubts. **6** put into a condition that is mentioned; cause to be done: have the house painted. **7** hold: He had him by the throat. **8** give birth to: have a child. **9** have as a relation: How many brothers have you? **10** engage in: have a talk with her. **11** arrange: have a party. **12** eat or drink: have a meal. **13** feel and show: have compassion. **14** allow: I won't have such nonsense! **15** (*informal*) fool or cheat: I've been had! **16** perplex: You have me there!
• *auxiliary vb* **1** used to form tenses expressing completion: Have you heard the news?; I expect to have finished the work by Friday. **2** used to express obligation or necessity: I have to go now. < Old English *habban.* SEE PANEL.

haven (ˈheɪvn̩) *n* **1** a port or harbour. **2** a sanctuary; refuge. < Old English *hæfen.*

haversack (ˈhævəˌsæk) *n* a canvas bag carried on the back or shoulder. SEE PANEL.

havoc (ˈhævək) *n* **1** widespread destruction. **2** great chaos or disorder. < Old

haul over the coals

To haul (someone) over the coals is to give a person a severe reprimand: The Prime Minister threatened that any minister found guilty of divulging Cabinet secrets would be hauled over the coals. The idiom alludes to the torture dealt out in previous centuries to heretics.

A similar expression exists in to give (someone) a good roasting.

having it out

Have features in a number of idiomatic expressions, including:

have had it 1 to have missed one's opportunity. **2** to have come to the end of one's life or career. **3** to become exhausted, obsolete, or ruined.

have it coming to be about to experience something unpleasant, especially punishment.

have it in for to intend harm towards.

have it off to have sexual intercourse (with).

have it out to settle a matter by frank discussion.

have on 1 to try to make (someone) believe something untrue or strange; kid: You're having me on, aren't you? **2** to have (evidence) against (someone): We've nothing on him at all, I'm afraid.

have up to bring (someone) to court for an offence.

the haves and the have-nots people with wealth and those without.

French *havot* pillage.

hawk[1] (hɔːk) *n* **1** a bird of prey with rounded wings and a long tail. **2** a person who prefers aggressive politics to political negotiation. < Old English *hafoc.*

hawk[2] *vb* offer (goods) for sale in the street. **hawker** *n* < ultimately Middle Low German *hōken* to peddle.

hawthorn (ˈhɔːˌθɔːn) *n* a thorny shrub or tree with white flowers and red berries. < Old English *haga* hedge + *thorn.*

hay (heɪ) *n* grass, clover, etc., cut and dried for fodder. **haystack** *n* a large, regularly shaped, outdoor pile of firm hay. **haywire** *adj* (*informal*) out of control; disorganized. < Old English *hīeg.* SEE PANEL.

hazard (ˈhæzəd) *n* **1** a risk or danger; source of this. **2** an obstacle on a golf-course.
• *vb* **1** guess; venture: hazard a guess. **2** risk. **hazardous** *adj* risky. **hazardously** *adv* < ultimately Arabic *az-zahr* the die.

haze (heɪz) *n* **1** a thin mist of fog, smoke, etc. **2** mental confusion or vagueness. **hazy** *adj* **1** misty. **2** unclear; vague. **hazily** *adv* **haziness** *n* < origin unknown.

hazel (ˈheɪzl) *n* **1** a hardy shrub or tree grown for its small, edible nuts. **2** a light, yellowish-brown colour. < Old English *hæsel.*

he (iː; *stressed* hiː) *pron* **1** the male person or animal mentioned. **2** a person, male or female.
• *n* a male animal or person. < Old English *hē.* SEE PANEL.

head (hɛd) *n* **1** the part of the body containing the eyes, ears, nose, mouth, and brain. **2** intelligence or aptitude: a good head for figures. **3** mental or emotional control: lose one's head. **4** (*informal*) a headache. **5** the obverse of a coin. **6** a person or individual: Tickets are £15 a head. **7** a number of animals: 300 head of cattle. **8** the upper, higher, or front part of

haversack

A haversack tends to be used by soldiers or hikers for carrying provisions or equipment. According to the word's etymology, however, it should be used for oats. Haversack derives via the French *havresac* from the German *Habersack* 'a bag for oats', from the Old High German *habero* 'oats' and *Sack* 'bag'.

haywire

The phrase go haywire means 'to go wrong; behave or operate in an uncontrolled or disorganized manner': Because of the unexpected torrential rain, the original programme for the athletics contest *went haywire*. The expression derives from the wire used in binding and baling hay which often became twisted. So haywire came to refer to something disorganized or confused.

he, he or she, or they?

Which word would you put in the gap: Anyone can learn a foreign language if____ wants to? Traditionally, he is used here, even when women are included, but this usage has been attacked by feminists as showing a male bias.

The problem is that English doesn't have a pronoun which everyone is happy with that can be used to refer to one person when you don't want to say whether the person is male or female. Various alternatives are used, notably he or she or they.

He or she can be a bit long-winded and awkward: Anyone can learn a language if *he or she* wants to. No child will be refused the help that *he or she* requires. They is often used in informal, conversational style, the verb changing from the singular to the plural: Anyone can learn a language if *they* want to. But some careful users object to this usage, insisting that they is plural and cannot therefore be used to refer to a singular pronoun.

A similar problem exists with him and her: Each student must see *his* (or *his or her* or *their*) tutor immediately. Again, his has conventionally been used here, but the alternatives, particularly their in informal, conversational style, are becoming more common.

A further solution that is sometimes possible is to avoid singular pronouns and to turn the singular subject into a plural one: *All students* must see *their* tutors immediately.

something: at the head of the queue. **9** a leader or director; such a position. **10** a headmaster. **11** a crisis: Matters came to a head.
• *adj* **1** main; principal: head office. **2** situated at the head.
• *vb* **1** be or put at the head of. **2** be in charge of; lead. **3** propel (a ball) with the head in soccer. **4** move or point in a direction that is mentioned: heading for a breakdown. **headache** *n* **1** a pain in the head. **2** (*informal*) a problem that causes worry. **headboard** *n* a board at the head of a bed. **head-dress** *n* a decorative covering for the head. **header** *n* a heading of the ball in soccer. **headgear** *n* something worn on the head. **heading** *n* a title for a chapter, page, paragraph, etc. **headland** *n* a narrow area of land jutting out into the sea. **headlight** *n* also **headlamp** the main light on the front of a motor vehicle. **headlong** *adv* **1** with the head first. **2** in a hasty way. **headmaster** *fem.* **headmistress** *n* the principal of a school. **head off 1** get in front of and force to change direction. **2** avoid or prevent. **head-on** *adv, adj* with the head or heads pointing towards the front: a head-on collision. **headphones** *pl n* two earphones held in position by a band fitting over the head. **headquarters** *pl n* the place from which a military or other organization is administered and controlled. **headroom** *n* the amount of space or clearance that allows passage, for example below a bridge. **headstone** *n* a memorial stone at the head of a grave. **headstrong** *adj* determined; obstinate. **headway** *n* movement forwards; progress. **heady** *adj* **1** intoxicating. **2** strongly affecting the senses; exciting. **3** rash. < Old English *hēafod.* SEE PANEL.

headline ('hɛdˌlaɪn) *n* **1** the title of a story or article in a newspaper. **2** *pl* a broadcast summary of the main news items. SEE PANEL.

heal (hiːl) *vb* make or become healthy, well, or sound again. **healer** *n* < Old English *hǣlan.*

health (hɛlθ) *n* **1** the state of being well in body, mind, or spirit. **2** a condition: in poor health. **3** a toast to a person, wishing him or her well. **health foods** natural, untreated foods, thought to be good for one's health. **healthful** *adj* healthy. **health visitor** a nurse who visits old people, nursing mothers, etc., in their homes. **healthy** *adj* **1** enjoying, showing, or tending to produce good health. **2** thriving. **healthily** *adv* **healthiness** *n* < Old English *hǣlth.*

heap (hiːp) *n* **1** a collection of things lying on top of one another; pile. **2** *pl* (*informal*) a great number; plenty.
• *vb* **1** put in a heap. **2** load abundantly

going to your head

Head features in a number of idiomatic expressions, including:

bite someone's head off to shout angrily at someone, especially without good reason.
bury one's head in the sand to refuse to notice a difficulty or problem; avoid facing realities. The expression alludes to the belief that ostriches bury their heads in the sand when being hunted, thinking that by being unable to see their enemy they themselves cannot be seen.
come to a head to reach a crisis: Matters came to a head at the meeting and the chairman resigned. The expression alludes to the maturing of a boil on the body.
go to someone's head 1 to make someone slightly drunk, etc. **2** to make someone conceited: Don't let success go to your head!
head and shoulders far superior to.
head over heels completely; utterly: She fell head over heels in love with him.
heads will roll some people will be punished or made to lose their position: Heads are bound to roll over the latest leak of cabinet secrets. The expression alludes to the use of the guillotine in executions.
keep one's head above water 1 to manage to cope. **2** to just remain solvent.
make head or tail of to understand: I can't make head or tail of these statistics.
off one's head crazy; mad.
over someone's head 1 without taking into account someone who has a right to be consulted or considered: He was promoted over the heads of two people senior to him. **2** too difficult for someone to understand.
put our, your, or **their heads together** to share ideas in an attempt to solve a problem or make a decision.
two heads are better than one a proverb advising the benefit of discussion with someone else.

with. < Old English *hēap*.

hear (hɪə) *vb* **heard; hearing 1** perceive (a sound) with the ear. **2** pay attention to; listen. **3** give a hearing to (a legal case). **4** receive information (about). **hearer** *n* **hear from** receive a communication from. **hear! hear!** used to express agreement or approval, esp. at a public meeting. **hearing** *n* **1** the ability to hear. **2** the distance within which a sound can be heard; earshot. **3** an opportunity of being heard. **4** the trial of a case in a law-court. **hearing-aid** *n* a device worn by a partially deaf person that amplifies sound. **hear out** listen to the whole or end of. **hearsay** *n* rumour or gossip. **not hear of** refuse to allow: I wouldn't hear of it! < Old English *hīeran*.

hearse (hɜːs) *n* a vehicle used to carry a coffin at a funeral. < ultimately Latin *hirpex* harrow.

heart (hɑːt) *n* **1** the hollow, muscular organ that pumps blood round the body. **2** the centre of a person's feelings, thoughts, or character: know in one's heart. **3** love or sympathy. **4** the ability to feel emotion. **5** courage or enthusiasm. **6** the central or innermost part of something: the heart of the matter. **7** a figure shaped like a heart; playing-card of the suit (**hearts**) marked with such figures. **heartache** *n* mental pain; sorrow. **heart attack** a sudden, severe instance of abnormal functioning of the heart. **heart-break** *n* intense sorrow. **heart-breaking** *adj* also **heart-rending** causing intense sorrow.

hitting the headlines

Imagine what a strange picture might be drawn of English grammar were, say, a foreign learner asked to draw it on the basis of newspaper headlines alone. The grammar of headlines contains a number of idiosyncrasies, mostly the predictable result of space restrictions. Examples of the most common non-standard features include:

Dollar plunges (omission of article)
Missing wife alive and well (omission of be as main verb)
Four men accused (omission of be in passive constructions)
Pope to visit Leeds (omission of be in constructions expressing a plan or intention)
Explosion kills 52 (use of present tense for past events to provide a dramatic sense of immediacy)
City fire death probe shock (long strings of nouns used as modifiers)

See also panel at **probe.**

heart-to-heart

The word heart features in a number of idiomatic expressions, including:

after one's own heart appealing to one's own liking or disposition.
at heart fundamentally.
by heart memorized perfectly.
change of heart a significant change in feelings towards a person, group, etc.
have a heart used as an appeal asking someone to be more considerate, sympathetic, etc.
have the heart to be willing (to do something that causes distress): I hadn't the heart to turn him away on such a cold night.
heart-strings *pl n* deep feelings.
heart-throb *n* someone with whom a person is infatuated.
heart-to-heart *adj, n* (a conversation that is) open, frank, and personal.
in one's heart of hearts in the deepest realm of one's conscience or emotions: In your heart of hearts you know she's right.
one's heart goes out to or **bleeds for someone** one feels great sympathy towards someone; sometimes used ironically.
set one's heart on to desire with great longing: He'd set his heart on a new, red bicycle.
take to heart to be deeply affected by.
to one's heart's content as long as one wants: sing away to one's heart's content.
with all one's heart sincerely; very willingly.

A man who lets his innermost thoughts and feelings be known to all is said to **wear his heart on his sleeve.** The expression is thought to derive from the days when a Roman soldier would apparently wear the name of his sweetheart embroidered on his sleeve for all to see. The custom re-emerged in the age of chivalry when, instead of an embroidered name, a ribbon, kerchief, or other favour presented by one's lady was worn as the tell-tale decoration.

heart-broken *adj* overwhelmed by intense sorrow. **heartburn** *n* a burning pain felt behind the breastbone. **hearten** *vb* encourage. **heartfelt** *adj* deeply felt; sincere. **heartily** *adv* **1** in a hearty way. **2** thoroughly: heartily sick of hearing such nonsense. **heartless** *adj* not feeling pity or sympathy; cruel. **heart-searching** *n* intense examination of one's feelings, motives, etc. **heart-warming** *adj* causing happy feelings. **hearty** *adj* **1** very friendly; jovial. **2** vigorous and unrestrained: a hearty laugh. **3** healthy and strong: hale and hearty. **4** substantial. **heartiness** *n* < Old English *heorte*.

SEE PANEL.

hearth (hɑːθ) *n* **1** the floor of a fireplace; area in front of this. **2** fireside; home < Old English *heorth*.

heat (hiːt) *n* **1** the condition of being hot. **2** the form of energy associated with the movement of molecules, etc. **3** hot weather. **4** a very strong feeling; tension. **5** the most intense part: in the heat of battle. **6** (in female mammals) a state of readiness for mating. **7** a preliminary contest, the winners of which take part in further contests or a final.
• *vb* make or become warm or hot. **heated** *adj* angry. **heatedly** *adv* **heater** *n* a device that emits heat. **heat-stroke** *n* collapse caused by prolonged exposure to very high temperatures. **heat wave** a period of very hot weather. < Old English *hǣtu*.

heath (hiːθ) *n* a large area of open, level, uncultivated land with low shrubs, esp. heather. < Old English *hǣth*.

heathen (ˈhiːðən) *n* **1** a person who does not believe in the God of Christianity, Judaism, or Islam. **2** a person regarded as uncivilized or irreligious. < Old English *hǣthen*.

heather (ˈhɛðə) *n* a low-growing evergreen shrub, commonly found on moors. < probably *heath*.

Heath Robinson (hiːθ ˈrɒbɪnsn̩) (of a mechanical device) absurdly complicated. < William *Heath Robinson*, died 1944, English cartoonist.

heave (hiːv) *vb* **1** lift, esp. with great effort. **2** throw. **3** rise and fall heavily or cause this to happen. **4** utter with effort and noise: heave a sigh of relief.
• *n* an act of heaving. < Old English *hebban*.

heaven (ˈhɛvn̩) *n* **1** the dwelling-place of God, his angels, and the souls of those who have received salvation. **2** a place or state of supreme happiness. **3 the heavens** the space surrounding the earth. **heavenly** *adj* **1** of heaven or the heavens; divine or celestial. **2** (*informal*) wonderful. **heaven-sent** *adj* providential. < Old English *heofon*.

heavy (ˈhɛvɪ) *adj* **1** having great weight. **2** greater or more intense than usual: heavy traffic. **3** difficult, esp. because involving much physical work. **4** oppressed or burdened: with a heavy heart. **5** hard to endure or fulfil: heavy responsibilities. **6** slow and clumsy: make heavy going. **7** not having liveliness: a heavy book. **8** digested with difficulty: a heavy meal. **9** overcast: heavy skies. **10** (of soil) containing much clay. **11** (of an industry) producing heavy, bulky materials. **12** deep and loud: heavy thunder. **13** sleepy. **14** (*slang*) unpleasant; tedious. **15** (*slang*) wonderful. **heavily** *adv* **heaviness** *n* **heavy-duty** *adj* designed to withstand hard wear, etc. **heavy-handed** *adj* **1** awkward. **2** harsh. **heavyweight** *n* **1** a person or thing above average weight. **2** a person in the heaviest boxing or wrestling weight. **3** (*informal*) a person with great importance. < Old English *hefig*.

heck (hɛk) *n* (*informal*) hell. < euphemism.

heckle (ˈhɛkl̩) *vb* harass (a public speaker) with interruptions, taunts, etc. **heckler** *n* < Middle English *heckele*.

hectare (ˈhɛktɑː) *n* a unit of area equal to 100 ares; 10 000 square metres. < French *hect-* hundred, from Greek *hekaton* + *are*, from Latin *area*.

hectic (ˈhɛktɪk) *adj* marked by great activity or excitement. **hectically** *adv* < Greek *hektikos* habitual.

hedge (hɛdʒ) *n* **1** a row of densely growing shrubs or bushes marking a boundary. **2** a means of protection, for example against losing money.
• *vb* **1** protect or surround with or as if with a hedge. **2** protect oneself against losing (a bet, etc.) by making a further bet. **3** avoid answering directly or committing oneself fully. **hedgehog** *n* a small, spine-covered, nocturnal mammal that eats insects. < Old English *hecg*.

hedonism (ˈhɛdəˌnɪzəm) *n* the belief that pleasure is the greatest good in life. **hedonist** *n* **hedonistic** *adj* < Greek *hēdonē* pleasure.

heed (hiːd) *vb* pay careful attention to.
• *n* careful attention; notice: take heed. **heedless** *adj* taking no notice; careless or thoughtless. **heedlessly** *adv* < Old English *hēdan*.

heel[1] (hiːl) *n* **1** the back part of the foot below the ankle and behind the arch.

2 the part of a garment, shoe, etc., that covers or supports this.
● *vb* **1** provide or fit with a heel, esp. a new one. **2** kick the ball with the heel in rugby. **bring/come to heel** bring/come into a state of submission. **down at heel** (of a person) shabby. **on the heels of** closely following. **take to one's heels** run away. **well-heeled** *adj* wealthy.
< Old English *hēla.* SEE PANEL.

heel[2] *vb* (of a ship) lean over. < Old English *hieldan.*

hefty (ˈhɛftɪ) *adj* **1** large and strong. **2** marked by great force. < SEE **HEAVE.**

heifer (ˈhefə) *n* a young cow, esp. one that has not given birth to a calf. < Old English *hēahfore.*

height (haɪt) *n* **1** the distance from the base to the top of a person or thing. **2** the distance above a level. **3** a high area of land. **4** the highest or most extreme point or extent of something. **heighten** *vb* make or become higher or more intense. < Old English *hīehthu.*

heinous (ˈheɪnəs, ˈhiːnəs) *adj* very evil. < Middle French *hair* to hate.

heir (ɛə) *n* **1** a person who inherits or is entitled to inherit property or rank. **2** a person that continues a tradition, characteristic, etc., from a predecessor. **heiress** *n* a female heir, esp. to great wealth. **heirloom** *n* a piece of valuable personal property that is handed down within a family for generations. < Latin *heres.*

held (hɛld) SEE **HOLD**[1].

Achilles' heel

To mention a person's Achilles' heel is to refer to the spot where he or she is most vulnerable to attack. The metaphor derives from Greek mythology, in which Achilles appears as one of the most formidable heroes. The reason why he came through so many battles unscathed was largely because of his mother, Thetis, who had dipped him as a baby into the magic waters of the river Styx. This made Achilles virtually invulnerable. His one weak spot remained the heel by which Thetis had held him during the dipping and which had not entered the water.

It was during the siege of Troy that Achilles' luck ran out when, after slaying Hector, he was mortally wounded in the heel by an arrow from Paris.

helicopter (ˈhɛlɪˌkɒptə) *n* an aircraft with horizontally rotating rotors or vanes that can take off and land vertically. **heliport** *n* a place where helicopters can take off and land. < Greek *helix* spiral + *pteron* wing.

helium (ˈhiːlɪəm) *n* a very light, non-flammable, colourless gas, used for filling balloons. < Greek *hēlios* sun.

hell (hɛl) *n* **1** the dwelling-place of the devil, demons, and of the damned, suffering punishment. **2** a place or state of torment or extreme misery. **hellish** *adj* of or like hell; extremely unpleasant. < Old English. SEE PANEL.

hello (hɛˈləʊ, həˈləʊ) SEE **HALLO.**

helm (hɛlm) *n* **1** the wheel, tiller, or whole apparatus used to control the steering of a ship. **2** a position of control or leadership: at the helm. **helmsman** *n, pl* **helmsmen** the person at the helm. < Old English *helma.*

helmet (ˈhɛlmɪt) *n* a protective or defensive head-covering worn by policemen, firemen, motor cyclists, etc. < Middle French *helme.*

help (hɛlp) *vb* **1** give aid or support to. **2** further or contribute to. **3** relieve: Take some medicine to help your cough. **4** be beneficial for (a situation or person). **5** serve (a customer or oneself). **6** take something for (oneself), esp. dishonestly. **7** stop: She can't help crying.
● *n* **1** the action of helping. **2** a person or thing that helps. **3** a person, esp. a woman, employed to do housework: a daily help. **helpful** *adj* giving help. **helpfully** *adv* **helpfulness** *n* **helping** *n* a portion of food served. **helpless** *adj* **1** not able to manage independently. **2** powerless. **helplessly** *adv* **helplessness** *n* < Old English *helpan.*

helter-skelter (ˌhɛltəˈskɛltə) *adj, adv* in disorderly haste.
● *n* a high, spiral slide at a fair.
< probably like the sound.

hem (hɛm) *n* the edge of a cloth article, esp. at the bottom, when turned back and sewn down.
● *vb* **hemmed; hemming 1** finish (a cloth article) with a hem. **2** surround and confine. < Old English.

hemisphere (ˈhɛmɪˌsfɪə) *n* half of the globe of the earth, divided by the equator or a meridian: the Northern hemisphere. < Greek *hēmi* half + *sphairion* small sphere.

hemp (hɛmp) *n* **1** a tall plant from which a tough, coarse fibre is prepared, used for making rope, sacking, and cloth. **2** a narcotic drug obtained from the flowers of this plant. < Old English *hænep.*

hen (hɛn) *n* the female of any bird, esp. the chicken. **hen party** a party for women only. **henpecked** *adj* (of a man) nagged or dominated by a woman. < Old English *henn.*

like hell

The word hell features in a number of expressions, many of them idiomatic, including:

a hell of a a very impressive or remarkable (person or thing): She's one hell of a girl! This is sometimes spelt helluva.
come hell or high water whatever difficulties may occur.
for the hell of it merely for the sake of the experience of doing it: They used to beat up old ladies just for the hell of it.
go to hell a strong expression used to tell someone to go away, stop talking, etc.
hell-bent *adj* determined, especially in a reckless way: hell-bent on getting revenge.
hell's angels members of motor-cycle gangs who wear black leather clothing and who are noted for their reckless, sometimes violent behaviour.
like hell 1 very much; very fast: They ran like hell to get away from the police. **2** used to express strong denial or refusal: 'You can work late tonight, can't you George?'—'Like hell I can!'
not have a cat in hell's chance to have not the slightest chance (of doing something).
to hell with an expression of dismissal: To hell with exams!

Hell is also used in expressions such as **Who the hell told you? How the hell should I know?** to express a strong feeling such as annoyance or surprise. Alternative expressions include: the devil, the heck, the blazes, the dickens, and on earth or in the world: Where *the blazes* are my keys? Why *the dickens* did you come, then? What on *earth's* going on?
The expression **all hell broke loose,** meaning 'there was great uproar and disorder', comes from Milton's 'Paradise Lost':

> But wherefore thou alone? Wherefore with thee
> Came not all hell broke loose?

hence (hɛns) *adv* **1** from this time. **2** for this reason. **3** (*formal*) from here. **henceforth** also **henceforward** *adv* from this time forward. < Old English *heonan.*

henchman (ˈhɛntʃmən) *n, pl* **henchmen** a trusted supporter. < Old English *hengest* male horse + *man.*

henna (ˈhɛnə) *n* **1** a tropical shrub with fragrant, white flowers. **2** a reddish dye obtained from the leaves of this plant, used for tinting the hairs and nails. < Arabic *hinnā'.*

hepatitis (ˌhɛpəˈtaɪtəs) *n* inflammation of the liver. < Greek *hēpar* liver + *itis,* feminine of *itēs* belonging to.

her (hə, ə; *stressed* hɜː) *pron* **1** the objective case of *she.* **2** she: It's her.
• *n* something suitable for her: That dress really isn't her.
• *determiner* **1** of or belonging to her. **2** used in titles for women: Her Majesty. **hers** *possessive pron* (the one or ones) belonging to or associated with her. **herself** *pron* the form of *she* and *her* used reflexively or for emphasis: She washed herself; She did it herself. **be herself** behave in a normal way: She isn't quite herself today. **by herself 1** without help. **2** alone. < Old English *hiere.* SEE PANEL.

herald (ˈhɛrəld) *n* **1** a person who announces important news. **2** a forerunner.
• *vb* announce the approach of. **heraldic** *adj* of heralds or heraldry. **heraldry** *n* the study and use of coats of arms. < Middle French *hiraut.*

herb (hɜːb) *n* a seed-bearing plant that dies down to the ground after flowering and does not have woody parts, commonly used in cooking and medicine. **herbaceous** *adj* of or like herbs. **herbal** *adj* of or using herbs. < Latin *herba.*

herculean (ˌhɜːkjʊˈliːən, hɜːˈkjuːlɪən) *adj* requiring very great strength or effort: a herculean task. < *Hercules,* hero in classical mythology.

herd (hɜːd) *n* **1** a group of animals feeding or living together. **2** (*sometimes derogatory*) a large group of people.
• *vb* collect or move in or as if in a herd. < Old English *heord.*

here (hɪə) *adv* **1** in, to, or at this place. **2** in or at this point in speech, action, etc. **hereabouts** *adv* near this place. **hereafter** *adv, n* (in) the future; (in) the life after death. **hereby** *adv* by means of this; as a result of this. **herewith** *adv* with this. < Old English *hēr.* SEE PANEL.

heredity (həˈrɛdətɪ) *n* the genetic transmission of characteristics from parents to the next generation; sum of characteristics transmitted. **hereditary** *adj* **1** genetically transmitted or transmissible from one generation to the next. **2** having a position or title by inheritance. < Latin *heres* heir.

heresy (ˈhɛrəsɪ) *n* **1** an opinion or teaching that is contrary to the orthodox beliefs of a church. **2** an opinion or teaching that is contrary to generally accepted beliefs. **heretic** *n* a person who professes a heresy. **heretical** *adj* < Greek *hairein* to take.

heritage (ˈherɪtɪdʒ) *n* something transmitted or gained by inheritance. < Latin *heres* heir.

hermaphrodite (hɜːˈmæfrəˌdaɪt) *n* an animal or plant with both male and female reproductive organs. < Greek *Hemaphroditos*, son of Hermes and Aphrodite, united in body with a nymph.

Why **her?**

Pronouns form a very mixed bag. Of the various classes, the largest is that of *personal pronouns*—I, me, my, mine, you, your, yours, he, him, his, etc. If this group of words did not exist, one would encounter sentences like: I stopped the driver and asked the driver if the driver had the driver's licence on the driver (I stopped the driver and asked *her* if *she* had *her* licence on *her*).

Sentences such as this are often referred to as 'awkward', with the implication that the job of the personal pronoun is to make such sentences less 'awkward'.

This is true, but what exactly does 'reducing awkwardness' mean? The answer is that the personal pronoun enables the user to avoid the repetition of content words. The advantage of this is not just a matter of style. Rather, the absence of such repetition means that prominence is given to the content words bearing the load of new information (ask, licence). In other words, personal pronouns enable a user to assemble a sentence in such a way that it may be decoded with maximum efficiency.

here and there

'Here comes John' and 'There goes Alice' are both statements. The order of the words in these sentences, however, is different from the usual order in statements. Normally, the subject precedes the verb: John (subject) is coming (verb). But in 'Here comes John' and 'There goes Alice' the normal sequence of subject and verb is inverted: John and Alice, the subjects, *follow* their respective verbs.

The point is that while such sentences beginning with here and there are very common in everyday English, the grammatical pattern that each displays is highly restricted and is generally found only in literary varieties, as epitomized, say, in 'Into the valley of death rode the 600' (in everyday English 'The 600 rode into the valley of death').

One of the interesting features of this pattern is that the normal substitution of a noun with a pronoun is not possible. We can't say 'Here comes he' or 'There goes she'. If a pronoun is used, the normal sequence of subject and verb is restored: 'Here he comes'. 'There she goes'.

Here features in a number of expressions, including:

here and now immediately.
here and there in various places: scattered here and there throughout the room.
here goes used to show determination before starting something: 'Here goes then—I'll see you in an hour after the dentist's finished with me!'
here's to an expression used when drinking a toast: 'Here's to you liking your new house!'
here, there, and everywhere in many different places.
here we go again the same events, esp. unpleasant ones, are happening again.
here you are an expression used when giving something to a person.
neither here nor there irrelevant: 'What time you come to the office is neither here nor there. As long as you do your eight hours' work, that's all that matters to me.

hermetic (hɜːˈmɛtɪk) or **hermetical** (hɜːˈmɛtɪkl̩) *adj* airtight. **hermetically** *adv* < Greek *Hermēs*, legendary founder of alchemy.

hermit (ˈhɜːmɪt) *n* a person who has withdrawn from society and lives in solitude, sometimes for religious reasons. **hermitage** *n* the dwelling-place of a hermit. < Greek *erēmos* solitary.

hernia (ˈhɛːnɪə) *n* the protrusion of an organ or tissue of the body through a weak spot in the wall that normally encloses it. < Latin.

hero (ˈhɪərəʊ) *n, pl* **heroes 1** a person, esp. a man, who is admired for his courage and noble acts. **2** the main, male person in a play, novel, etc. **heroic** *adj* **1** of or like heroes. **2** showing great courage. **heroically** *adv* **heroics** *pl n* grand, showy behaviour or language. **heroine** *n* a female hero. **heroism** *n* heroic behaviour. < Greek *hērōs.*

heroin (ˈhɛrəʊɪn) *n* a pain-killing, addictive drug made from but stronger than morphine. < originally a trademark.

heron (ˈhɛrən) *n* a long-necked, slim-bodied wading-bird living near rivers and lakes. < Middle French *hairon.*

herpes (ˈhɛːpiːz) *n* a virus that causes chicken-pox, shingles, and cold sores. < Greek *herpein* to creep.

herring (ˈhɛrɪŋ) *n, pl* **herrings, herring** a North Atlantic food fish. **herring-bone** *n* a pattern of rows of short, parallel lines slanting in alternate, zigzag directions, esp. a textile woven in this pattern. < Old English *hæring.* SEE PANEL.

hertz (hɜːts) *n, pl* **hertz** a unit of frequency equal to one cycle per second. < Heinrich *Hertz,* died 1894, German physicist.

hesitate (ˈhɛzɪˌteɪt) *vb* **1** be slow to act or speak because of uncertainty or doubt; hold back. **2** be unwilling (to do something). **hesitancy** *n* **hesitation** *n* **hesitant** *adj* hesitating. **hesitantly** *adv* < Latin *haerēre* to stick.

hessian (ˈhɛsɪən) *n* a strong, coarse cloth of jute or hemp used for upholstery, bags, etc. < *Hesse,* state in Germany.

het (hɛt) *adj* **het up** (*informal*) angry or excited. < dialect past form of *heat.*

heterodox (ˈhɛtərəˌdɒks) *adj* opposed to the usual or established beliefs or teachings. < Greek *heter-,* from *heteros* other + *doxa* opinion.

heterogeneous (ˌhɛtərəˈdʒiːnɪəs) *adj* consisting of various parts that are unlike one another. < Greek *heter-,* from *heteros* other + *genos* kind.

heterosexual (ˌhɛtərəˈsɛksjʊl) *adj, n* (of) a person who is sexually attracted to people of the opposite sex.

hew (hjuː) *vb* **hewed; hewed, hewn; hewing 1** chop or cause to fall with cutting blows of an axe, etc. **2** shape with or as if with cutting blows. < Old English *hēawan.*

hexagon (ˈhɛksəgən) *n* a closed plane figure with six sides. **hexagonal** *adj* < Greek *hex* six + *gōnia* angle.

heyday (ˈheɪˌdeɪ) *n* the time of greatest popularity, success, etc.

HGV *abbrev* heavy goods vehicle.

hiatus (haɪˈeɪtəs) *n* **1** a break or gap in a sequence or continuity. **2** a disruption or quarrel. < Latin *hiare* gape.

hibernate (ˈhaɪbəˌneɪt) *vb* spend the winter in a dormant state. **hibernation** *n* < Latin *hibernus* of winter.

hiccup (ˈhɪkʌp) *n* **1** a sudden, involuntary intake of breath interrupted by a closure of the space between the vocal cords, accompanied by a sharp sound.
2 hiccups an attack of hiccuping.
3 (*informal*) a minor difficulty or problem; hitch.
• *vb* make a hiccup. < like the sound.

hide[1] (haɪd) *vb* **hid; hidden, hid; hiding**
1 put or keep (something or oneself) out of sight; conceal. **2** keep secret.
3 obscure.
• *n* a place of concealment, esp. disguised, to observe animals or birds. **hide-out** *n* a hiding-place. **hiding** *n* a state or place of hiding. < Old English *hȳdan.*

hide[2] *n* the skin of an animal, either tanned or raw. **hidebound** *adj* obstinately holding fixed opinions; narrow-minded. **hiding** *n* (*informal*) a thrashing or beating. < Old English *hȳd.*

hideous (ˈhɪdɪəs) *adj* very ugly; revolt-

red herring

A red herring—a herring that had been dried, smoked, and salted—had a very powerful aroma. In fact it was so strong that by drawing a red herring across the trail of a fox, hounds could be thrown off the scent and led in the wrong direction. Nowadays the red herring has given way to the kipper, but the phrase red herring survives as an idiomatic expression for something that is introduced in order to distract attention or mislead: 'That's just another red herring to try to get the voters to forget about the real issue of unemployment.'

ing. **hideously** *adv* < Old French *hide* terror.

hierarchy (ˈhaɪəˌrɑːkɪ) *n* a series of people or things arranged in grades or ranks. **hierarchical** *adj* < Greek *hierarchēs* high priest.

hieroglyphics (ˌhaɪərəˈglɪfɪks) *n* **1** a form of pictorial writing, esp. as used in ancient Egypt. **2** writing that is very difficult to read. **hieroglyphic** *adj* < Greek *hiero-* holy + *glyphein* to carve.

hi-fi (ˈhaɪˌfaɪ) *n* **1** high fidelity. **2** equipment for high-quality sound reproduction.

high (haɪ) *adj* **1** extending a long way from the base to the top. **2** situated a long way above the ground. **3** lying above the normal level. **4** measuring a distance that is mentioned: The tower is 100 metres high. **5** raised in pitch. **6** noble in character. **7** favourable; approving: a high opinion of him. **8** above normal in size, amount, value, etc.: high prices. **9** above others in rank, importance, etc.: a high official. **10** at the time of more advanced or fullest development: the high season. **11** (*informal*) excited or elated; intoxicated, under the influence of drugs. **12** intended for fast speeds.
• *adv* in, at, or to a high level, degree, or position.
• *n* **1** a high level: Production is now at an all-time high. **2** a region of high atmospheric pressure. **highbrow** *adj, n* (a person) having an interest in the arts and intellectual things. **higher education** education beyond the level of schools, at college or university. **high fidelity** highly accurate reproduction of sound with little or no distortion. **highland** *adj, n* (of) high or mountainous land. **highlight** *vb, n* (draw attention to) a feature that has special significance. **highly** *adv* **1** to a high degree; extremely: highly significant. **2** very favourably: I think highly of him. **Highness** *n* the title used to address a prince or princess. **high-rise** *adj* (of a building) having many storeys: high-rise flats. **high-spirited** *adj* happy and lively; excited. **high tide** (the time of) the tide at its highest level. **highway** *n* a public way; main road. < Old English *hēah*. SEE PANEL.

hijack (ˈhaɪˌdʒæk) *vb* seize control of (a vehicle or aircraft in transit) to steal goods, take passengers hostage, or divert to a new destination.
• *n* a hijacking. **hijacker** *n* < origin unknown.

hike (haɪk) *vb* walk a long way in the country, esp. for pleasure.
• *n* such a walk. **hiker** *n* < origin uncertain.

a high-powered word

High features in a number of expressions, including:

high and dry 1 out of the water. **2** abandoned and isolated.
high and low everywhere: We searched high and low to try to find the key.
high and mighty arrogant; self-important.
high finance large, complicated financial dealings.
high-flyer *n* a person with great abilities, ambitions, etc.
high jinks lively fun.
high jump 1 an athletic event in which competitors jump over a high horizontal bar. **2** a severe punishment or reprimand.
high-level *adj* of great importance or rank.
high-powered *adj* having great energy; dynamic: high-powered executives.
high road a main road.
high school a secondary school, especially a grammar school.
high seas the open seas of the world, not under the jurisdiction of any country.
high spot the most exciting or memorable feature of something.
high tea a fairly substantial meal eaten in the early evening, usually accompanied by tea.
high time a time that is long overdue: It's high time you started taking your studies more seriously, isn't it?'
in high places in important, i nfluential positions, as in government: friends in high places.

Since high and highly can both be used as adverbs, they are sometimes confused. High is used to refer to altitude or position as in The kite soared *high* into the air. Don't set your hopes too high; *high*–heeled shoes; *high*–pitched music

Highly means 'to a high degree; extremely' and is followed by adjectives such as complex, significant, or successful, or participles such as developed, mechanized, paid or qualified. Highly also means 'very favourably' in the idiom think *highly* of.

hilarious (hɪˈlɛərɪəs) *adj* very funny; merry in a noisy way. **hilariously** *adv* **hilarity** *n* < Greek *hilaros* cheerful.

hill (hɪl) *n* **1** a usually rounded, natural rise of land that is lower than a mountain. **2** a heap or mound of earth: an ant-hill. **3** a steep slope in a road, etc. **hilly** *adj* **hillock** *n* a small hill; mound.< Old English *hyll.*

hilt (hɪlt) *n* the handle of a sword or dagger. **to the hilt** completely. < Old English.

him (ɪm; *stressed* hɪm) *pron* **1** the objective case of *he*. **2** he: It's him again! **himself** *pron* the form of *he* and *him* used reflexively or for emphasis: He shot himself. He told me himself. **be himself** behave in a normal way: He's not quite himself today. **by himself 1** without help. **2** alone. < Old English. SEE PANEL.

hind[1] (haɪnd) *adj* also **hinder** (of parts of the body) at the back. **hindmost** *adj* furthest to the back. **hindquarters** *pl n* the hind part of a four-legged animal. **hindsight** *n* wise understanding of a situation after it has occurred. < Old English *hinder.*

hind[2] *n* a female deer, esp. a red deer. < Old English.

hinder (ˈhɪndə) *vb* **1** slow or obstruct the movement or progress of. **2** prevent. **hindrance** *n* **1** hindering. **2** something that hinders. < Old English *hindrian.*

Hindu (ˈhɪnduː) *adj* of Hindus or Hinduism.

• *n* a person who adheres to Hinduism.

Hinduism *n* the dominant religious and philosophical system of India. < Persian *Hindu* inhabitant of India, from *Hind* India.

hinge (hɪndʒ) *n* **1** a device on which a door, gate, etc., can turn or swing. **2** a small piece of gummed paper used to fasten a stamp in an album.

• *vb* **1** fit with hinges. **2** turn or swing on a hinge. **3** depend (on). < Middle English *heng.*

hint (hɪnt) *n* **1** a brief piece of practical information. **2** a suggestion made indirectly; insinuation. **3** a slight indication: a hint of defiance.

• *vb* suggest or imply indirectly. < probably Old English *hentan* to seize.

hinterland (ˈhɪntəˌlænd) *n* a district lying inland from a coast. < German, from *hinter* behind + *land* land.

hip[1] (hɪp) *n* the part of the body surrounding the joint formed by the upper part of the thigh and pelvis. < Old English *hype.*

hip[2] *n* the fruit of the wild rose. < Old English *hēope.*

hip[3] *adj* (*informal*) very fashionable; trendy. < probably earlier *hep,* origin unknown.

hippie, hippy (ˈhɪpɪ) *n* a young person with an unconventional attitude to life, often expressed in his or her habits and mode of dress. < SEE **HIP**[3].

hippo (ˈhɪpəʊ) *n, pl* **hippos** (*informal*) a hippopotamus.

hippopotamus (ˌhɪpəˈpɒtəməs) *n, pl* **hippopotamuses, hippopotami** a very heavy, plant-eating mammal with a large head and mouth, short legs, and thick, hairless skin. < Greek *hippos* horse + *potamus* river. SEE PANEL.

hipster (ˈhɪpstə) *adj* (of trousers) worn from the hips rather than the waist.

hire (ˈhaɪə) *vb* **1** pay for the use of (something), or the services of (a

---

I don't mind him coming or **I don't mind his coming?**

Should you say I don't mind *him* coming or I don't mind *his* coming? Here, him functions as the object of the sentence, whereas his is a possessive. Careful users of English prefer to use a possessive in more formal contexts: I don't mind *his* coming, since, so it is thought, it is not him that is minded but *his* coming.

In informal English, however, it is more common to use the objective form: I don't mind *him* coming.

Other examples:

Do you mind *me* giving you some advice? (*my* in formal English).

There is little possibility of *the train* coming punctually (*the train's* in formal English).

---

hippopotamus

Hippopotamus is one of the many words that the Romans took from the Greeks and, by a long route, transported to our shores. To the Greeks hippopotamus meant 'river horse', from *hippos* 'a horse' and *potamos* 'a river'. The name reflects the animal's two primary features: its size and aquatic habit. The first element, hippos, is also found in hippodrome, originally a course for horse and chariot races.

person) esp. temporarily: hire a car. **2** sell the use of (something), esp. temporarily.
• *n* **1** hiring. **2** the payment for hiring. **hirer** *n* **hire-purchase** *n* a form of paying for an article in instalments, at the end of which the article belongs to the buyer. < Old English *hȳrian*.

hirsute (ˈhɜːsjuːt) *adj* covered with hair; hairy or shaggy. < Latin *hirsutus*.

his (ɪz; *stressed* hɪz) *determiner* **1** of or belonging to him. **2** used in titles for men: His Majesty.
• *possessive pron* (the one or ones) belonging to or associated with him. < Old English.

hiss (hɪs) *vb* **1** make a sound like that of a prolonged *s*, esp. in disapproval. **2** show disapproval in this way.
• *n* a hissing sound. < like the sound.

history (ˈhɪstərɪ) *n* **1** significant past events, esp. when recorded chronologically. **2** the study of past events, esp. relating to human affairs. **3** an ordered presentation of the development of something: the history of medicine. **4** an ordered presentation of a person's medical, etc., background: a case history. **5** the sum of past events, esp. when no longer relevant: That's all ancient history now. **6** an interesting past: That palace has a long history. **historian** *n* a writer of or expert in history. **historic** *adj* **1** famous or significant in history. **2** having a long history. **historical** *adj* **1** of or relating to history. **2** based on facts, not legend, etc. **3** based on or inspired by history: a historical novel. **historicity** *n* historical existence or authenticity. < Greek *historia* enquiry, from *histōr* knowing. SEE PANEL.

> **historic** or **historical?**
>
> Historic and historical are not interchangeable.
>
> Historic means 'having a long history': a *historic* tradition, a *historic* building or 'important in history': a *historic* voyage, a *historic* decision.
>
> Historic*al* usually means either 'based upon people who actually lived or events that actually happened': *historical* characters or 'concerned with history': a *historical* account.
>
> To keep the words apart, remember that it is only historic that carries the idea of 'importance'.

histrionic (ˌhɪstrɪˈɒnɪk) *adj* dramatically exaggerated and insincere. **histrionics** *pl n* dramatically exaggerated behaviour. < Latin *histrio* actor.

hit (hɪt) *vb* **hit; hitting 1** deal (a stroke or blow) to (a person or thing); strike. **2** make or cause to make violent contact with (something). **3** have a bad effect on: be hit hard by depression. **4** meet or encounter: hit a snag. **5** reach (a level): Unemployment has hit a new high. **6** score (runs, etc.). **7** (*informal*) occur to: Then suddenly it hit me.
• *n* **1** a blow or stroke, esp. one that strikes a target. **2** a piece of music, play, etc., that has become successful: a big hit. **hit and run** *adj* (of a motorist) not stopping after having an accident. **hit back** retaliate. **hit it off** (*informal*) get on well (with a person). **hit on** discover unexpectedly. **hit out at** attack verbally. **hit the bottle** (*informal*) (start to) drink too much alcohol. **hit the nail on the head** say something that is exactly right. **hit the road** (*informal*) begin a journey; leave. **hit the roof** (*informal*) show or express great anger. **hit the sack** or **hay** (*informal*) go to bed. < Old Norse *hitta*.

hitch (hɪtʃ) *vb* **1** fasten with a hook, loop, etc. **2** lift with a jerk. **3** hitch-hike; obtain (a lift) in this way.
• *n* **1** a slight jerk. **2** a stoppage, esp. a temporary or insignificant one. **3** a knot for fastening temporarily. **hitch-hike** *vb* travel by obtaining free lifts in passing vehicles. **hitch-hiker** *n* < Middle English *hytchen*.

hither (ˈhɪðə) *adv* (*formal*) to or towards this place. **hither and thither** aimlessly; in different directions. **hitherto** (*formal*) until this time. < Old English *hider*.

hive (haɪv) *n* **1** a shelter for a colony of bees; bees living in this. **2** a busy place: a hive of industry.
• *vb* **hive off** transfer to a subsidiary company, etc. < Old English *hȳf*.

HM *abbrev* His (or Her) Majesty. **HMS** *abbrev* His (or Her) Majesty's Ship. **HMSO** *abbrev* His (or Her) Majesty's Stationery Office.

hoar (hɔː) *n* also **hoar-frost** a deposit of tiny crystals of ice on a cold surface. < Old English *hār*.

hoard (hɔːd) *n* a hidden store, esp. of food or treasure, that is carefully preserved or kept for future use.
• *vb* gather a hoard (of). < Old English *hord*. SEE PANEL.

hoarding (ˈhɔːdɪŋ) *n* a large board by a

road, etc., for displaying advertisements. < *hoard* fence, probably from Old French *hourt* platform.

hoarse (hɔːs) *adj* **1** (of the voice) sounding harsh and rough. **2** with a hoarse voice. **hoarsely** *adv* **hoarseness** *n* < Old English *hās.*

hoary (ˈhɔːrɪ) *adj* **1** having grey or white hair from old age. **2** white or grey. **3** impressively old. **4** (of a joke, etc.) hackneyed. < SEE **HOAR.**

hoax (həʊks) *n* an act of joking deception; trick.
• *vb* deceive or play a joke on. **hoaxer** *n* < probably from *hocus.*

hob (hɒb) *n* the flat surface on a cooker or a separate unit that contains hotplates or burners. < origin unknown.

hobble (ˈhɒbl̩) *vb* walk lamely and awkwardly.
• *n* a hobbling movement. < Middle English *hoblen.*

hobby (ˈhɒbɪ) *n* an activity pursued in one's spare time, for pleasure or interest. **hobbyhorse** *n* **1** a toy consisting of a horse's head on a stick. **2** a rocking-horse. **3** a favourite topic for discussion. < Middle English *hoby,* probably from name *Robin.*

hobgoblin (hɒbˈgɒblɪn) *n* an evil or mischievous spirit. < *hob* elf + *goblin.*

hobnail (ˈhɒbˌneɪl) *n* a short nail with a large head, used in the soles of heavy boots. **hobnailed** *adj* < archaic *hob* peg + *nail.*

hobnob (ˈhɒbˌnɒb) *vb* **hobnobbed; hobnobbing** (*informal*) associate together or talk informally: hobnobbing with royalty. < *hob or nob* to drink to one another alternately.

hock¹ (hɒk) *n* the middle joint of an animal's back leg. < Old English *hōh* heel.

hock² *n* a white wine produced in the Rhine Valley in Germany. < *Hochheim,* town in Germany.

hockey (ˈhɒkɪ) *n* a field game between two teams of 11 players who try to hit a small, hard ball into the opponent's goal, using a long stick that is curved at the end. < perhaps Middle French *hoquet* shepherd's crook.

hocus-pocus (ˌhəʊkəsˈpəʊkəs) *n* **1** deception; trickery. **2** pointless words or activity. < probably imitation of a Latin phrase used by jugglers.

hod (hɒd) *n* **1** an open, wooden box on a pole, used for carrying bricks, etc. **2** a tall coal scuttle. < probably Middle Dutch *hodde.*

hoe (həʊ) *n* a long-handled tool with a light, flat blade used for weeding, tilling, etc.
• *vb* **hoed; hoeing** scrape, weed, or till (soil) with a hoe. < Middle French *houe.*

hog (hɒg) *n* **1** a castrated, male pig reared for meat. **2** (*informal*) a greedy or selfish person.
• *vb* **hogged; hogging** (*informal*) take more than one's fair share of. < Old English *hogg.*

Hogmanay (ˈhɒgmənei, ˌhɒgməˈneɪ) *n* New Year's Eve in Scotland. < origin unknown.

hoick (hɔɪk) *vb* lift abruptly and sharply. < origin uncertain.

hoi polloi (hɔɪ pəˈlɔɪ) the common people; masses. < Greek: the many.

hoist (hɔɪst) *vb* raise, esp. by using pulleys, ropes, etc.
• *n* an apparatus for hoisting. < alteration of *hoise.*

hold¹ (həʊld) *vb* **held; holding 1** have or keep in the hands, arms, etc. **2** control or restrain; keep back. **3** attract and keep: He held their attention. **4** defend from an enemy. **5** conduct (a conversation, etc.). **6** have capacity or room for; contain: The hall holds 200 people. **7** consider; believe: I hold you responsible. **8** rule: The court held that he was guilty. **9** keep in a position, state, or condition that is mentioned. **10** occupy (a position or title). **11** carry (oneself): Hold yourself upright. **12** retain or keep: The house will hold its value. **13** remain unchanged, unbroken, etc.: Will the weather hold?; The rope held fast. **14** remain valid: The rule still holds.
• *n* **1** the act or manner of holding something. **2** control or influence: a firm hold on the market. **holder** *n* **holdall** *n* a

hoard or **horde?**

These two words are sometimes confused.

A hoard is 'a store, usually hidden, that is carefully preserved or kept for future use' as in *hoards* of gold. Hoard is also used as a verb: People caught *hoarding* foodstuffs during the shortage will be fined.

Horde, on the other hand, means 'a great crowd or throng, usually of people or animals', as in *hordes* of angry football supporters. It tends to be used in a derogatory sense.

large, strong bag. **holding** *n* property, esp. land, owned. < Old English *healdan.* SEE PANEL.

hold² *n* the space below a ship's deck or in an aircraft where cargo is stored. < alteration of *hole.*

hole (həʊl) *n* **1** a hollow place; cavity. **2** an opening in or through something. **3** an animal's burrow. **4** (*informal*) a small, dark, and unpleasant place. **5** (*informal*) a difficult situation. **6** a cavity into which a ball must be played in golf. **7** a unit of play from the tee to the hole in golf.
• *vb* **1** make a hole or holes in (something). **2** put into a hole. < Old English *hol.*

holiday (ˈhɒləˌdeɪ, ˈhɒlɪdɪ) *n* **1** a period during which one rests from work. **2** a day, such as a bank holiday, on which, by law or custom, work is not generally carried out.
• *vb* spend or take a holiday. **holiday-maker** *n* a person who is on holiday. < Old English *hālig* holy + *dæg* day.

hollow (ˈhɒləʊ) *adj* **1** having a hole or space within. **2** sunken. **3** (of a sound) as if echoing in a hollow space. **4** lacking truth, sincerity, or real significance: hollow promises.
• *n* a hollow place or area.
• *vb* make or become hollow.
• *adv* **1** in a hollow way. **2** (*informal*) decisively: We beat them hollow. < Old English *holh.*

holly (ˈhɒlɪ) *n* an evergreen shrub or tree with shiny, prickly-edged leaves and bright red berries; branches of these shrubs or trees used for Christmas decorations. < Old English *holegn.*

hollyhock (ˈhɒlɪˌhɒk) *n* a plant with tall spikes of showy flowers. < *holy* + *hock,* from Old English *hoc* mallow, plant with downy leaves.

holocaust (ˈhɒləˌkɔːst) *n* **1** great destruction or loss of life; the cause of this, esp. fire. **2 Holocaust** the mass murder of Jews by Nazis in 1939-45. < Greek *holos* whole + *kaustos* burnt.

hologram (ˈhɒləˌgræm) *n* the pattern caused by one part of a beam of light from a laser and the other part of the same beam reflected off an object. < Greek *holos* whole + English *-gram* record, from Greek *gramma* writing.

holster (ˈhəʊlstə) *n* a leather holder for a pistol. < Dutch.

holy (ˈhəʊlɪ) *adj* **1** of or associated with God or a god, esp. set apart for the service of God. **2** spiritually pure; godly or devout. **3** deserving reverence. **holiness** *n* < Old English *hālig.*

homage (ˈhɒmɪdʒ) *n* a show of respect or honour. < Latin *homo* man.

home (həʊm) *n* **1** the place where one lives; residence, esp. of a family. **2** a house or other dwelling-place. **3** the country, district, etc., where one was born or brought up or to which one feels one belongs. **4** an establishment for the care of old people, or children, etc.
• *adj* **1** of or associated with one's home

---

no holds barred

Hold features in a number of idiomatic expressions, including:

get hold of 1 to obtain or acquire. **2** to make contact with.
hold back to restrain or withhold.
hold down to manage to keep (a job).
hold forth to speak for a long time.
hold good to remain valid or true.
hold off 1 not to begin: Fortunately the rain held off. **2** to cause to remain at a distance.
hold on 1 to wait or stop. **2** (in telephone conversations) to wait: 'The line's engaged. Will you hold on?'
hold one's ground to maintain one's position, when under attack or pressure.
hold one's peace to remain silent.
hold out 1 to last; be sufficient. **2** to continue to resist.
hold over to postpone.
hold the fort to look after something in the temporary absence of someone: The foreman is off sick so I've been asked to hold the fort while he's away.
hold up 1 to delay, obstruct, or stop. **2** to steal money from a bank, etc., with the use of guns. **hold-up** *n*
hold water (of a theory, etc.) to be sound or valid.
hold with to approve of.
no holds barred with all restrictions removed; any methods may be freely used. **no-holds-barred** *adj*: a no-holds-barred competition. The expression comes from wrestling, meaning that any method of gripping or handling is allowed.

---

or country. **2** (*sports*) of, at, etc., one's own ground: a home game.
• *adv* **1** to or at home. **2** to the mark aimed at; to the fullest extent: hammer a nail home.
• *vb* **1** go home. **2** (of birds or animals) return home from a distance. **homeless** *adj* **homelessness** *n* **homebird** *n* a person who enjoys staying at home. **home in on** detect and move towards (a target). **homeland** *n* **1** one's native land. **2** an area in the Republic of South Africa for the Black populations, with limited self-government. **homely** *adj* **1** simple; unpretentious. **2** sympathetic; kind. **3** (*US*) plain or ugly. **homesick** *adj* depressed because one is away from one's home and family. **homestead** *n* a house and the adjacent land or buildings, esp. a farm. **homeward** *adj, adv* going home. **homewards** *adv* towards home. **homework** *n* **1** work given to a pupil to be completed esp. away from school. **2** paid work done in one's own home. **3** (*informal*) preparatory study. < Old English *hām* village. SEE PANEL.

homicide (ˈhɒmɪˌsaɪd) *n* the killing of one person by another. **homicidal** *adj* < Latin *homo* man + *caedere* to kill.

homily (ˈhɒmɪlɪ) *n* a sermon or moralizing talk. < Greek *homilia* discourse, from *homilos* crowd.

homing (ˈhəʊmɪŋ) *adj* (of a pigeon) trained to return home from a distance.

homoeopathy (ˌhɒmɪˈɒpəθɪ) *n* the method of treating illness by prescribing small doses of a drug that, in larger quantities in a healthy person, would cause the symptoms similar to those of the disease being treated. **homoeopathic** *adj* < Greek *homos* same + *-path,* from *pathēs* suffering.

homogeneous (ˌhɒməˈdʒiːnɪəs) or **homogenous** (həˈmɒdʒɪnəs) *adj* having the same kind or nature; made up of parts of the same kind. **homogeneity** *n* < Greek *homos* same + *-genous,* from *genēs* born.

homogenize (həˈmɒdʒəˌnaɪz) *vb* process (milk) so that the particles of fat are broken down and the cream does not separate and rise to the surface.

homonym (ˈhɒmənɪm) *n* one of a group of words with the same spelling or pronunciation but different meanings, for example sail and sale. < Greek *homos* same + *onyma* name.

homosexual (ˌhɒməˈsɛksjʊəl) *adj, n* (of) a person who is sexually attracted to people of the same sex. **homosexuality** *n*

Hon. *abbrev* **1** Honourable. **2** Honorary.

hone (həʊn) *vb* sharpen or polish with or as if with a fine-grained stone. < Old English *hān* stone.

honest (ˈɒnɪst) *adj* **1** not lying, cheating, or stealing; truthful or trustworthy; respectable. **2** fair. **3** frank and sincere. **honestly** *adv* **1** in an honest manner. **2** (*informal*) really. **honesty** *n* **1** being honest. **2** a plant with round, papery seed-heads. < Latin *honor* honour.

honey (ˈhʌnɪ) *n* **1** a thick, sweet, yellow syrup made by bees from nectar. **2** something sweet or pleasant. **3** (*informal*) darling. **honeycomb** *n* a bees' wax structure of six-sided cells in a hive, in which honey is stored and eggs are laid.

home sweet home

The word home features in a number of expressions, many of them idiomatic, including:

at home 1 in one's own dwelling-place or one's own country. **2** relaxed, as if in one's own home: Make yourself at home.
at-home *n* a reception for visitors.
bring/come home to to make/become clear to someone: The full scale of the disaster came home to them.
home and dry having successfully achieved one's purpose.
home from home a place where one feels as comfortable, welcome, etc., as in one's own home: The hotel was a real home from home.
home help a person who is paid to do housework for the sick, elderly, etc.
home rule self-government, especially to a limited degree and in a dependency.
home straight or **stretch** the final part of a racecourse.
home truth an outspoken, unpleasant, but valid criticism: And let me tell you a few home truths, young man!
The expressions **Home sweet home** and **There's no place like home** come originally from the song 'Home, Sweet Home' in the opera 'Clari, the Maid of Milan', the words of which were written by the American actor and dramatist John Howard Payne (1791–1852).

honeycombed *adj* having holes like the cells in a honeycomb. < Old English *hunig.*

honeymoon (ˈhʌnɪˌmuːn) *n* **1** a holiday taken by a newly married couple. **2** a period of calm and harmony following the beginning of a new relationship or position.
• *vb* spend a honeymoon. < origin uncertain.

honeysuckle (ˈhʌnɪˌsʌkl̩) *n* a climbing shrub with clusters of sweet-smelling, tube-like, yellow, pink, or white flowers.

honk (hɒŋk) *n* a short, harsh, loud sound like that made by a goose.
• *vb* make or cause to make such a sound; sound (a horn). < like the sound.

honky-tonk (ˈhɒŋkɪˌtɒŋk) *n* a form of ragtime music played on a piano. < origin uncertain.

honorarium (ˌɒnəˈrɛərɪəm) *n* a payment for professional services, such as those of a lawyer.

honorary (ˈɒnərərɪ) *adj* **1** conferred as an honour, and without the usual responsibilities: an honorary degree. **2** unpaid: the honorary treasurer. < Latin *honorarius* of or giving honour. SEE PANEL.

honour (ˈɒnə) *n* **1** a good reputation or great public respect. **2** respect for truth, honesty, etc.; personal integrity: a man of honour. **3** a privilege: I had the great honour of representing my school at the games. **4** fame or glory. **5** a person who brings respect and fame: an honour to her country. **6** the recognition given for special achievements: buried with full military honours. **7** *pl* a degree of the highest academic standard. **8** a title of respect for a holder of a high-ranking office such as a judge: Your Honour.
• *vb* **1** consider or treat with honour. **2** confer honour on. **3** fulfil completely: honour all one's commitments. **4** accept and pay: honour a cheque. **honourable** *adj* **1** worthy of honour. **2** having or showing honour. **3** a title of respect placed before the name of certain people. **honourably** *adv* < Latin *honor.*
SEE PANEL AT **HONORARY.**

> **honorary** or **honourable?**
>
> Honorary has two basic meanings: first 'conferred as an honour; not with the usual responsibilities': The Home Secretary was awarded an *honorary* degree in law, and secondly 'holding a position but not receiving pay for it' as in an *honorary* treasurer or an *honorary* secretary.
>
> Honourable (note the u in British English) means 'worthy of honour; having or showing honour' as in an *honourable* deed. It is also used as a title of respect before the name of certain people and this is when the confusion with honorary occurs, because both honourable and honorary are abbreviated to Hon.
>
> Hon. (standing for Honourable) is the title given to the children of viscounts and barons and the younger sons of earls. It is also used in Parliament by one member speaking of another ('The *Honourable* member for Hitchin') and for certain officials such as members of the Privy Council, who are designated The Right *Honourable*.

hood (hʊd) *n* **1** a loose covering for the top and back of the head and neck, esp. attached to a garment. **2** anything which protects like this, such as a waterproof cover for a pram or car. **3** (*US*) the bonnet of a car. **hooded** *adj* having a hood. < Old English *hōd.* SEE PANEL AT **BONNET.**

hoodlum (ˈhuːdləm) *n* **1** a thug, esp. a violent one. **2** a lawless young person. < origin uncertain.

hoodwink (ˈhʊdˌwɪŋk) *vb* deceive or trick. < *hood* + *wink.*

hoof (huːf) *n, pl* **hoofs, hooves** the horny end of the foot of a horse, deer, etc. < Old English *hōf.* SEE PANEL AT **SHELF.**

hoo-ha (ˈhuːˌhɑː) *n* (*informal*) a noisy fuss. < origin uncertain.

hook (hʊk) *n* **1** a curved or bent piece of metal, etc., used for holding, catching, or pulling. **2** something shaped like this, such as a curved tool for cutting grain. **3** a curving stroke in golf, cricket, etc. **4** a short, swinging blow in boxing, delivered with the arm bent.
• *vb* **1** grasp, pull, catch, or fasten with a hook. **2** cause (a ball) to move in a curving path. **hooked** *adj* **1** shaped like a hook. **2** (*informal*) very enthusiastic (about); obsessed (with). **3** (*informal*) addicted to drugs. < Old English *hōc.*

hooky, hookey (ˈhʊkɪ) *n* (*chiefly US informal*) truant: play hooky. < perhaps *hook it* to escape.

hooligan (ˈhuːlɪgən) *n* a rough, lawless, young person. **hooliganism** *n* < perhaps *Hooligan,* family name.

hoop (huːp) *n* a large, thin ring of metal, etc., used to hold the staves of a barrel together, or as a child's toy.

• *vb* bind or surround with hoops. < Old English *hōp.*

hoot (huːt) *n* **1** the cry of an owl. **2** the sound of a vehicle's horn or steam whistle. **3** a shout of scorn or laughter: hoots of derision. **4** (*informal*) an amusing person or thing: it's a real hoot!
• *vb* **1** make the sound of an owl. **2** sound the horn, whistle, etc., of a vehicle. **3** yell (something) contemptuously at (a person). **hooter** *n* **1** a device, esp. a car horn, that produces a hooting noise. **2** (*informal*) the nose. < Middle English *hoten,* like the sound.

Hoover (ˈhuːvə) *n* (*Trademark*) a vacuum cleaner.
• *vb* clean (a carpet, etc.) with a vacuum cleaner.

hop[1] (hɒp) *vb* **hopped; hopping 1** (of a person) jump forwards on one foot. **2** (of animals such as rabbits) move in quick leaps. **3** (*informal*) make a quick trip: We're hopping across to France for the day. **4** (*informal*) move quickly (in, out of, etc.): hop on a bus.
• *n* **1** a hopping movement. **2** (*informal*) a dance. **hop it** (*informal*) go away. **on the hop 1** unprepared: We were caught on the hop. **2** busy or active. < Middle English *hoppen.*

hop[2] *n* a climbing herb grown for its pale green flowers that are used to give a bitter flavour to beer. < Middle English *hoppe.*

hope (həʊp) *n* **1** desire for something and expectancy of its fulfilment; reason, person, or thing causing this: He came to London in the hope of getting a job. **2** the object of one's hope.
• *vb* wish for (something) with some expectancy of its fulfilment or being obtained: Since they've already got a baby girl, they're hoping for a boy. < Old English *hopian.*

hopeful (ˈhəʊpfʊl) *adj* feeling or giving hope.
• *n* a person who hopes or is considered as likely to be successful: young hopefuls. **hopefully** *adv* **1** in a hopeful manner. **2** (*informal*) it is to be hoped that. SEE PANEL.

hopeless (ˈhəʊpləs) *adj* **1** having or offering no hope. **2** impossible to solve, control, or undertake successfully. **3** (*informal*) incompetent: hopeless at speaking foreign languages. **hopelessly** *adv* **hopelessness** *n*

hopper (ˈhɒpə) *n* **1** a hopping person or thing; hopping insect. **2** a container shaped like a funnel to store or discharge grain, etc.

horde (hɔːd) *n* a great crowd or throng. < Polish *horda.* SEE PANEL AT **HOARD**.

horizon (həˈraɪzn̩) *n* **1** the line at which the earth and sky appear to meet. **2** the range or limit of knowledge, experience, etc.: broaden one's horizons. < Greek *horizein* to bound.

horizontal (ˌhɒrɪˈzɒntl̩) *adj* **1** parallel to the horizon. **2** of or relating to people or things at the same level or status. **horizontally** *adv*

hormone (ˈhɔːməʊn) *n* a substance secreted into the blood that causes a specific response in a particular part of the body. < Greek *horman* to stir up, from *hormē* impulse.

horn (hɔːn) *n* **1** a pointed bony projection on the head of some animals such as deer; hard, smooth substance of which this is made. **2** a projection like a horn, such as a tentacle on a snail. **3** a wind instrument with a pipe or tube of brass and a mouthpiece. **4** a device for sounding loud warning signals: a fog horn. **horned** *adj* having horns. **horny** *adj* hard like horn. < Old English. SEE PANEL.

hopefully

Careful users of English prefer not to use hopefully to mean 'I hope' or 'we hope' as in *Hopefully,* we'll be back by 6 o'clock. They prefer to reserve hopefully to mean 'in a hopeful manner' as in 'Can I have a drink?' she asked *hopefully.* The first usage is nowadays, however, commonly acceptable.

The similar use of words such as thankfully, mercifully, and regrettably (*Thankfully,* they all arrived home safely) is generally not considered controversial.

draw in one's horns

To check oneself and suddenly become cautious or defensive is sometimes referred to by the informal expression to draw in one's horns. The allusion is to the snail. When the latter's tentacles encounter a strange and potentially dangerous object, they are immediately retracted.

hornet (ˈhɔːnɪt) *n* a large, brown-and-orange wasp that can give a severe sting. < Old English *hyrnet.*

hornpipe (ˈhɔːnˌpaɪp) *n* a lively folk dance for one person, traditionally associated with sailors.

horoscope (ˈhɒrəˌskəʊp) *n* a chart foretelling events in a person's life, based on the relative positions of planets and signs of the zodiac at the time of someone's birth. < Greek *hōra* hour + *skopein* to look at.

horrendous (hɒˈrɛndəs) *adj* horrible. < Latin *horrēre* to bristle, shudder.

horrible (ˈhɒrəbl̩) *adj* **1** marked by or causing horror. **2** very unpleasant. **3** (*informal*) unkind; cruel. **horribly** *adv*

horrid (ˈhɒrɪd) *adj* **1** unpleasant. **2** frightening. **3** (*informal*) unkind; cruel. **horridly** *adv*

horror (ˈhɒrə) *n* **1** extreme terror. **2** extreme hatred. **3** a person or thing that causes horror: the horrors of war.
• *adj* (of a film, etc.) containing much violence which is presented in a sensational manner. **horrific** *adj* causing horror. **horrifically** *adv* **horrify** *vb* **horrified; horrifying** causing horror in; terrify. < Latin *horrēre* to tremble.

hors-d' œuvre (ɔː ˈdɜːv) *n* food served as an appetizer at the beginning of a meal. < French.

horse (hɔːs) *n* **1** a four-footed mammal with a flowing mane and tail, used for carrying loads, pulling carts, or riding. **2** an adult, male horse; stallion or gelding. **3** a frame for hanging clothes on to dry; clothes-horse. **4** a padded apparatus for vaulting over in a gymnasium.
• *vb* **horse around** engage in horseplay: Stop horsing around! **horse-box** *n* a closed vehicle for transporting horses. **horse-chestnut** *n* **1** a large tree that produces clusters of white flowers and green, spiny fruits which release large, brown, shiny seeds. **2** such a seed; conker. **horsehair** *n* hair from the tail or mane of a horse, used in upholstery, etc. **horse-laugh** *n* a loud, harsh laugh. **horseman** fem. **horsewoman** *n* a rider on horseback. **horsemanship** *n* **horseplay** *n* wild, noisy play. **horsepower** *n* a unit of power (about 746 watts). **horse-radish** *n* a herb with white flowers and thick, pungent roots; sauce made from these roots. **horseshoe** *n* an iron U-shaped plate nailed to the rim of a horse's hoof. **horsy** *adj* **1** of or like a horse. **2** very interested in horses and horse-racing. < Old English *hors.* SEE PANEL.

horticulture (ˈhɔːtɪˌkʌltʃə) *n* the growing of vegetables, fruit and trees, shrubs, etc. **horticultural** *adj* **horticulturist** *n* < Latin *hortus* garden + *culture,* as in *agriculture.*

hose (həʊz) *n* also **hose-pipe** a flexible pipe for conveying water.
• *vb* water or wash with a hose. < Old English *hosa.*

hosier (ˈhəʊzɪə) *n* a person who sells stockings, etc. **hosiery** *n* stockings, socks, and knitted underwear.

hospice (ˈhɒspɪs) *n* **1** a nursing home, esp. for people who are terminally ill. **2** a lodging-place for travellers, esp. one run by a religious order. < Latin *hospes* guest, host.

hospitable (ˈhɒspɪtəbl̩, hɒˈspɪtəbl̩) *adj* given to hospitality. **hospitably** *adv* **hospitality** *n* friendly and generous reception and entertainment of guests.

hospital (ˈhɒspɪtl̩) *n* an institution providing medical care for the sick, injured, etc. **hospitalize** *vb* send as a

horses for courses

The word horse features in a number of idiomatic expressions, including:

a horse of another colour a very different matter.

a Trojan horse something intended to undermine, subvert, or infiltrate: The new factory could be a Trojan horse—destroying more jobs than it creates. The expression comes from the Greek legend of the large, hollow wooden horse that the Trojans dragged into their city, only to allow the Greek soldiers hidden inside the horse to emerge and launch their final assault on Troy.

flog a dead horse to try to arouse interest in something that is already rejected or fully accepted.

get on/off one's high horse to speak/stop speaking in an offended, haughty manner.

hold one's horses to wait; be more patient; proceed more slowly: Hold your horses! I'm not ready yet!

horses for courses particular people or things are best used for the purpose for which they are suited. The expression comes from horse-racing: a racehorse is likely to perform best when it has the conditions it prefers.

patient to a hospital. **hospitalization** *n* < Latin *hospes* guest, host.

host[1] (həʊst) *n* **1** a person who receives or entertains guests, esp. in his or her home. **2** a compère on a television or radio show. **3** an animal or plant on which a parasite lives.
• *vb* act as a host to (a person or event). **hostess** *n* **1** a woman who receives or entertains guests, esp. in her home. **2** a stewardess on an aeroplane, etc. < Latin *hospes*. SEE PANEL.

host[2] *n* a great number. < Latin *hostis* stranger, enemy.

hostage (ˈhɒstɪdʒ) *n* a person held by an individual, organization, etc., as a security that promises will be kept or terms fulfilled by another party. < Old French *hoste* host, guest.

hostel (ˈhɒstl̩) *n* **1** a residential home for nurses, students, etc. **2** an institution for young offenders, etc. < Latin *hospes* guest, host.

hostile (ˈhɒstaɪl) *adj* **1** of or relating to an enemy. **2** antagonistic or opposed; unfriendly. **hostilely** *adv* **hostility** *n* **1** opposition; enmity. **2** *pl* warfare or fighting. < Latin *hostis* enemy.

host and **hostess**

Many languages have what is known as *gender*. For example, in French door is feminine, in Spanish sun is masculine, in Italian moon is feminine, and in German window is neuter. Unlike languages such as these, in which every noun is either masculine, feminine, or (when there are three genders) neuter, English does not have gender at all.

Commonly mistaken for gender are the ways in which sex distinctions are expressed, sometimes called *natural gender*. On the one hand this can take the form of different words for male and female creatures, such as bull/cow, dog/bitch, or the use of related words such as man/woman, male/female. (See panel at **chair.**) Another way is by means of the suffix -ess: actor/actress, waiter/waitress, host/hostess. Finally there is the use of she-, lady, or woman as modifiers: she-goat, lady doctor, woman politician. There are devices, then, which allow us to distinguish between the sexes when it is necessary to do so, but English nouns do not fall into vast masculine, feminine (and neuter) classes, as do those of a language which does have gender.

hot (hɒt) *adj* **hotter; hottest 1** having a high temperature; giving off or feeling heat. **2** causing a burning sensation to the taste: a hot curry. **3** fiery or angry; excitable: a hot temper. **4** passionate. **5** (*informal*) enthusiastic or eager. **6** strict or severe: The new boss is hot on punctuality. **7** (of news) recent; fresh. **8** (*informal*) competent or able: He's not so hot at French. **9** (*slang*) recently stolen: hot goods. **10** strong and clear: a hot scent.
• *adv* hotly. **hotly** *adv* **hotness** *n* **hotbed** *n* **1** a place that encourages the rapid growth of something bad: a hotbed of vice. **2** a bed of soil heated by fermenting manure. **hot dog** a heated sausage, especially a frankfurter, served in a bread roll. **hotfoot** *adv*, *vb* (go) quickly. **hothead** *n* an excitable, impetuous person. **hot-headed** *adj* excitable; impetuous. **hothouse** *n* a heated greenhouse for plants. **hot line** a special, direct telephone line, especially that between the leaders of superpowers. **hotplate** *n* a metal surface, esp. on a cooker, on which food is cooked or kept hot. **hot-pot** *n* a stew containing mutton, lamb, etc., with potatoes and other vegetables. **hot potato** a controversial topic. **hot seat** a position in which one has great responsibilities. **hot under the collar** angry and excited; agitated. **hot up** (*informal*) make or become hot, more lively or active, etc. < Old English *hāt*.

hotchpotch (ˈhɒtʃˌpɒtʃ) *n* a jumbled mixture. < Old French *hochier* to shake + *pot*.

hotel (həʊˈtɛl) *n* an establishment providing accommodation and meals for travellers. **hotelier** *n* an owner or manager of a hotel. < French *hôtel*, from Old French *hostel*.

hound (haʊnd) *n* **1** a breed of dog used for hunting. **2** a despicable person.
• *vb* **1** chase with or as if with hounds. **2** harass relentlessly. < Old English *hund*. SEE PANEL AT **DOG.**

hour (aʊə) *n* **1** a 24th part of a day; 60 minutes. **2** the time of day. **3** the beginning of an hour: Trains for London leave on the hour. **4** *pl* the time on a 24-hour clock: 18.00 hours. **5** a period of time for an activity that is mentioned: a lunch hour; office hours. **6** a particular time, esp. for action; present time: Our finest hour; the question of the hour. **hourglass** *n* an instrument for measuring time that consists of two clear bulbs linked by a narrow channel, containing fine sand that takes one hour to run from the upper section to the lower. **hourly** *adv* **1** at or done every hour. **2** frequent. **3** by the hour: hourly paid workers. < Greek *hōra* hour.

house (haʊs) *n* **1** a building for people, esp. one family, to live in. **2** the people living in a house. **3** a building used for purposes or occupants that are mentioned: a chicken-house. **4** one of the groups into which a school's pupils may be divided for sports contests, etc. **5** a law-making body; one assembly of this: the House of Commons. **6** a business organization: a publishing house. **7** a theatre or concert hall; audience in this: a full house. **8** a family, including ancestors: the House of York. **9** the people gathered for debate: the motion before the house.
• *vb* (haʊz) **1** provide accommodation for. **2** contain; store. **houseboat** *n* a boat that is fitted out as a home, esp. one moored permanently. **housebreaker** *n* a burglar. **household** *n* the people who live in one house, esp. a family. **householder** *n* a person who owns or pays the rent for a house. **housekeeper** *n* a woman employed to look after a house. **housekeeping** *n* the everyday running of a house; money for this. **house party** a party, recreation, etc., for a group of guests, esp. at a house in the country. **housewife** *n* a woman, esp. married, who runs a house. **housework** *n* work, such as cleaning, done in looking after a house. **housing** *n* **1** accommodation. **2** a protective cover for machinery. < Old English *hūs*. SEE PANEL.

hovel (ˈhɒvl̩) *n* a small, unpleasant dwelling. < Middle English.

hover (ˈhɒvə) *vb* **1** remain in the air in one place. **2** linger with uncertainty, as in doubt. **hovercraft** *n* a vehicle supported on a cushion of air that travels over land and water. **hoverport** *n* a port used for hovercraft. < Middle English *hoven*.

how (haʊ) *adv* **1** in what manner, way, or condition: How could I have known?; How are you? **2** to what extent: How many people were there? **3** for what reason. < Old English *hū*.

however (haʊˈɛvə) *adv* **1** to whatever extent: however large. **2** nevertheless, still; on the other hand: It sounds a good idea; in practice, however, it wouldn't work.
• *conj* in whatever way. SEE PANEL AT **EVER.**

howl (haʊl) *n* **1** the long, loud cry of a wolf or hound. **2** a cry like this of pain or amusement.
• *vb* **1** make or utter with a howl. **2** weep loudly. **howl down** prevent (a speaker) from being heard by howling disapproval. **howler** *n* (*informal*) an obvious mistake. < Middle English *houlen*.

HP *abbrev* **1** hire-purchase. **2** also **h.p.** horsepower.

HRH *abbrev* His (or Her) Royal Highness.

hub (hʌb) *n* **1** the central part of a wheel, etc., through which the axle passes. **2** the centre of activity. < probably alteration of *hob*.

hubbub (ˈhʌbʌb) *n* a confused sound of many voices; uproar. < Celtic.

huddle (ˈhʌdl̩) *vb* **1** crowd or gather

---

house

Asked how the plural of house is formed, you would probably say simply by adding an s. In the written language, the answer is correct: house—houses is perfectly regular.
However, in the spoken language the way in which house forms its plural is irregular. Nouns ending in an s sound like horse and hearse normally just add the sounds of the word is to form their plurals. House is unique in that before this ending is added, the s changes to a z sound.

House features in a number of idiomatic expressions, including:

bring the house down to win great applause or laughter from an audience: 'What really brought the house down was his imitation of the Prime Minister.'

household name a very well-known name: Within months she had rocketed from obscurity to become a household name.

house-trained *adj* (of a pet) trained to urinate and defecate outside.

house-warming *n* a party given to celebrate a move into a new home.

like a house on fire very well: 'Sarah and Dave are getting on like a house on fire—it's as if they've known each other for years.'

on the house at the expense of the management (of a hotel, restaurant, etc.): have a drink on the house.

put one's (own) house in order to settle or organize one's own affairs: 'You'd better put your own house in order before you come telling me how to run my business.'

closely together. **2** draw or curl one's body up, as in cold.
● *n* **1** a closely packed group. **2** (*informal*) a private discussion. < origin uncertain.

hue[1] (hju:) *n* **1** a shade or tint of a colour; colour. **2** complexion; aspect. < Old English *hīw*.

hue[2] *n* **hue and cry** a loud, general outcry of protest, demands, etc. < Old French *hu* warning cry. SEE PANEL.

huff (hʌf) *n* a mood of anger: in a huff.
● *vb* give out puffs loudly. **huffish** *adj* **huffy** *adj* < like the sound.

hug (hʌg) *vb* **hugged; hugging 1** hold or clasp tightly in one's arms. **2** keep or stay close to. **3** be delighted with (oneself).
● *n* a strong clasp with the arms. < probably Scandinavian.

huge (hju:dʒ) *adj* extremely large in size, extent, etc.; enormous: a huge wave. **hugely** *adv* < Old French *ahuge*.

hulk (hʌlk) *n* **1** the body of an old, abandoned ship. **2** a bulky, awkward person or thing. **hulking** *adj* bulky; massive. < Old English *hulc*.

hull (hʌl) *n* the main body of a ship or boat.
● *vb* pierce the hull of (a ship, etc.). < Old English *hulu*.

hullabaloo (ˌhʌləbə'lu:) *n* commotion; uproar. < perhaps *hallo* + Scottish *baloo* lullaby.

hullo (hʌ'ləʊ, hə'ləʊ) SEE **HALLO**.

hum (hʌm) *vb* **hummed; humming 1** make a continuous, low sound like that of a long *m*. **2** sing with the lips closed. **3** be active or lively.
● *n* a humming sound. < Middle English *hummen*.

human ('hju:mən) *adj* **1** of, relating to, or consisting of human beings. **2** of or like human beings, as opposed to animals, gods, or machines: After all, we're only human; human weaknesses.
● *n* also **human being** a man, woman, or child. **humane** *adj* **1** marked by kindness, mercy, etc. **2** causing as little suffering as possible: humane killings. **humanely** *adv* **humanism** *n* a belief in human efforts, skills, etc., rather than religion. **humanist** *n* **humanitarian** *adj* relating to human welfare and the lessening of suffering. **humanity** *n* **1** the human race; people. **2** being human. **3** *pl* literature, philosophy, and the arts. **humanize** *vb* make human. **humanization** *n* **humanly** *adv* **1** in a human way. **2** within the extent of human abilities. **3** with human limitations. **humanoid** *adj, n* (a being) with a human appearance or human characteristics. < Latin *humanus*. SEE PANEL AT **URBAN**.

humble ('hʌmbl̩) *adj* **1** having a modest opinion of oneself; meek; not proud. **2** marked by lowliness or submission: a humble apology. **3** of low social, etc., rank. **4** not showy; unpretentious: my humble cottage.
● *vb* make humble; lower in status. **humbleness** *n* **humbly** *adv* < Latin *humilis* low, from *humus* ground.

humbug ('hʌmˌbʌg) *n* **1** empty or misleading talk; nonsense or deception. **2** an impostor; sham. **3** a hard, peppermint, boiled sweet. < origin unknown.

humdrum ('hʌmˌdrʌm) *adj* dull, ordinary, and monotonous.
● *n* humdrum routine. < SEE **HUM**.

humid ('hju:mɪd) *adj* (of air, etc.) moist or damp. **humidity** *n* < Latin *humēre* to be moist.

humility (hju:'mɪlətɪ) *n* the state or quality of being humble. **humiliate** *vb* cause to feel humble; hurt the pride of. **humiliation** *n* < SEE **HUMBLE**.

humming-bird ('hʌmɪŋˌbɜ:d) *n* a brightly coloured bird with a slender bill and narrow wings that produce a humming sound in flight.

humour ('hju:mə) *n* **1** the quality of being funny. **2** the ability to appreciate and enjoy amusement: a sense of humour. **3** a temper or mood: in good humour.
● *vb* try to please (someone), esp. by giving in to his or her wishes. **humorist** *n* a person noted for humour in speech, writing, etc. **humorous** *adj* marked by or showing humour. **humorously** *adv* < Latin *humor* moisture, SEE PANEL.

hump (hʌmp) *n* **1** a rounded projection or protuberance. **2** a rounded protuberance on the back of a camel, etc.
● *vb* **1** form or rise into a hump. **2** (*informal*) carry (a heavy load) with difficulty. < probably Low German *humpe*.

humus ('hju:məs) *n* the dark, organic material in soil formed from the decom-

hue and cry

A loud or raucous clamour is sometimes referred to as a hue and cry. This expression derives from Elizabethan times when a person was legally bound to join in the pursuit of a suspected criminal, and at the same time shout out so as to raise the alarm.

position of dead plants, etc. < Latin: earth.

hunch (hʌntʃ) *n* **1** an intuitive feeling or guess. **2** a hump.
• *vb* bend into a hump. **hunchback** *n* a person with a humped back. < origin unknown.

hundred (ˈhʌndrəd) *determiner, pron* 100 in number.
• *n* **1** the number 100. **2** *pl* (*informal*) a very large number: There were hundreds of people there. **hundredth** *determiner, pron, n, adv* **hundred per cent** totally; completely. **hundreds** *pl n* **1** the numbers 100–109, 100–199, or 100–999. **2** the dates in a century that is mentioned: in the 1800s. **hundredweight** *n* **1** a unit of weight (in the UK 112 pounds, 50.802 kilograms; USA 100 pounds, 45.359 kilograms). **2** also **metric hundredweight** a metric unit of weight equal to 50 kilograms. < Old English.

hung (hʌŋ) SEE **HANG.**

hunger (ˈhʌŋgə) *n* **1** a desire for food; strong, unpleasant feeling caused by lack of food. **2** a strong desire for something.
• *vb* feel hunger. **hunger-strike** *n* refusal to eat, esp. by a prisoner as a protest. **hungry** *adj* feeling hunger. **hungrily** *adv* < Old English *hungor.*

hunk (hʌŋk) *n* a large piece: a hunk of bread. < Flemish *hunke.*

hunt (hʌnt) *vb* **1** pursue and kill or capture (wild animals) for food or sport. **2** use (hounds, etc.) to pursue wild animals. **3** search (for); search (an area) for something: I've hunted everywhere for my keys. **4** track, in order to capture: hunt down a criminal.
• *n* **1** hunting; instance of this. **2** a group of hunters and hounds; area hunted. **hunter** *n* **1** also **huntsman** a person who hunts wild animals. **2** a horse used in hunting. **3** a person who enthusiastically seeks something mentioned: a fortune-hunter. < Old English *huntian.*

hurdle (ˈhɜːdl̩) *n* **1** a light, upright frame which is jumped over in certain races. **2** *pl* a hurdle-race. **3** an obstacle or difficulty.
• *vb* jump over, esp. while running. < Old English *hyrdel.*

hurl (hɜːl) *vb* **1** throw or thrust forcefully. **2** utter forcefully: hurl insults.
• *n* an instance of hurling. < Middle English *hurlen,* probably like the sound.

hurly-burly (ˌhɜːlɪˈbɜːlɪ) *n* rough confusion or commotion. < SEE **HURL.**

hurricane (ˈhʌrɪkən) *n* **1** a violent storm, esp. a tropical cyclone. **2** a wind of great velocity, force 12 on the Beaufort scale; over 117 kilometres per hour (73 miles per hour). < Spanish *huracán,* from Taino *hurakán.*

hurry (ˈhʌrɪ) *vb* **hurried; hurrying** go or cause to go with great or greater haste.
• *n* **1** great haste. **2** urgency. **hurried** *adj* done with great haste. **hurriedly** *adv* < Middle English *horyen.*

hurt (hɜːt) *vb* **hurt; hurting 1** cause physical injury to (a person or thing). **2** cause emotional or mental pain to (a person). **3** feel pain: My arm hurts.
• *n* **1** a physical injury. **2** emotional or mental distress; cause of this. **3** harm. **hurtful** *adj* < Old French *hurter* to push.

hurtle (ˈhɜːtl̩) *vb* **1** move very quickly. **2** throw with great force; fling. < Middle English *hurtlen.*

husband (ˈhʌzbənd) *n* a married man, in relation to his wife.
• *vb* manage or use (resources) economically; try to save. **husbandry** *n* **1** the good management of resources. **2** farming. < Old Norse *hūs* house + *bōndi* freeholder.

hush (hʌʃ) *vb* make or become quiet or silent.
• *n* quietness; silence. < Middle English *huscht* quiet.

husk (hʌsk) *n* the dry, outer covering of certain seeds or fruits.

---

humour and **humorous**

Humour is one of a group of words spelt -our in British English and -or in American English. Other examples are: colour, favour, honour, rigour, and vapour. The u is dropped in the derived forms of these words before the suffixes -ous, -ation, -ize, -ific, -iferous, for example humorous, rigorous, vigorous, discoloration, vaporize, honorific, odoriferous.

In British English the u is retained, however, in the derived forms with the suffixes -able, -ful, -ite, -ism, -ist, -er, -less, for example honourable, colourful, favourite, behaviourism, behaviourist, labourer, odourless. An exception is humorist.

• *vb* remove the husk from. < Middle English.

husky[1] (ˈhʌskɪ) *adj* **1** (of a voice) hoarse; dry in the throat. **2** of, like, or containing husks. **3** (*informal*) big and strong; hefty. **huskily** *adv* **huskiness** *n*

husky[2] *n* an Eskimo dog, used for pulling sleds. < perhaps Eskimo.

hussy (ˈhʌsɪ) *n* a cheeky or promiscuous woman or girl. < alteration of *housewife.*

hustings (ˈhʌstɪŋz) *n* the proceedings of an election campaign. < Old Norse *hūs* house + *thing* assembly.

hustle (ˈhʌsḷ) *vb* **1** push roughly or very quickly. **2** hurry or force.
• *n* hustling, instance of this: hustle and bustle. **hustler** *n* < Middle Dutch *hutsen.*

hut (hʌt) *n* a small, simply and roughly made house or shelter. < Middle French *hutte.*

hutch (hʌtʃ) *n* a small cage, made of wood and wire mesh, for animals, esp. rabbits. < Old French *huche.*

hyacinth (ˈhaɪəsɪnθ) *n* a plant, which grows from a bulb, having a dense head of bell-shaped flowers. < Greek *hyakinthos.*

hybrid (ˈhaɪbrɪd) *n* **1** the offspring of two unrelated species, varieties, etc., of animal or plant. **2** something made of elements of different origins.
• *adj* of or being a hybrid. **hybridize** *vb* produce or cause to produce hybrids. < Latin *hybrida.*

hydrangea (haɪˈdreɪndʒə) *n* a shrub with showy clusters of white, pink, or blue flowers. < Greek *hȳdor* water + *angeion* vessel.

hydrant (ˈhaɪdrənt) *n* a pipe from a water-main, with a valve and nozzle, to which a hose may be attached for fire-fighting, etc. < Greek *hydōr* water.

hydraulic (haɪˈdrɒlɪk) *adj* **1** operated by means of a liquid being transmitted through pipes under pressure: a hydraulic press. **2** concerned with the use of water in this way: a hydraulic engineer. **hydraulically** *adv* **hydraulics** *n* the branch of physics dealing with the applications of the mechanical and flow properties of liquids. < Greek *hȳdor* water + *aulos* tube.

hydrocarbon (ˌhaɪdrəʊˈkɑːbṇ) *n* an organic compound containing only carbon and hydrogen.

hydroelectric (ˌhaɪdrəʊɪˈlɛktrɪk) *adj* of or concerning the generation of electricity by water pressure: hydroelectric power. **hydroelectricity** *n*

hydrofoil (ˈhaɪdrəˌfɔɪl) *n* a ship with a device like an aerofoil that raises the hull out of the water as the speed increases.

hydrogen (ˈhaɪdrədʒən) *n* a colourless, flammable gas that is the simplest, lightest, and most abundant element in the universe. **hydrogen bomb** a violently destructive bomb in which energy is released by fusion of hydrogen nuclei.

hydrophobia (ˌhaɪdrəˈfəʊbɪə) *n* **1** abnormal fear of water. **2** rabies. < Greek *hydōr* water + *phobos* fear.

hyena (haɪˈiːnə) *n* a strong, flesh-eating, dog-like mammal. < Greek *hyaina,* from *hys* hog.

hygiene (ˈhaɪdʒiːn) *n* **1** the maintenance of good health. **2** the conditions, esp. cleanliness, that tend to lead to this. **hygienic** *adj* **hygienically** *adv* < Greek *hygiēs* healthy.

hymen (ˈhaɪmən) *n* a fold of mucous membrane that partly covers the opening of the vagina in a girl or woman who has not had sexual intercourse. < Greek *hymēn* membrane.

hymn (hɪm) *n* a song of praise to God, esp. as part of a religious service. **hymn-book** *n* also **hymnal** a book of hymns. < Greek *hymnos.*

hyperactive (ˌhaɪpərˈæktɪv) *adj* excessively active. SEE PANEL.

hyperbole (haɪˈpɜːbəlɪ) *n* deliberately extravagant exaggeration, for emphasis. < Greek *hyper-* over + *ballein* to throw. SEE PANEL AT **THOUSAND**.

hypermarket (ˈhaɪpəˌmɑːkɪt) *n* an enormous self-service store, larger than a supermarket, selling a wide range of goods and usually situated outside a town or city centre.

hyphen (ˈhaɪfṇ) *n* the sign - used to join or divide words. **hyphenate** *vb* join or divide with a hyphen. **hyphenation** *n* < Greek *hypo-* under + *heis* one.

hypnosis (hɪpˈnəʊsɪs) *n* the production of a state of trance in a person, marked by a susceptibility to suggestions of the hypnotist; condition produced by this. < SEE **HYPNOTIC**.

hyper- and **hypo-**

The prefixes hyper- and hypo- should not be confused.

Hyper- means 'above, over, or beyond; in excess': hyperactive, hypersensitive.

Hypo- means 'under or beneath': a hypodermic syringe is one that is used to give injections *beneath* the skin.

hypnotic (hɪpˈnɒtɪk) *adj* **1** of hypnosis or hypnotism. **2** (of a drug) tending to produce sleep.
• *n* a hypnotic drug. **hypnotically** *adv* **hypnotism** *n* the production of hypnosis; hypnosis. **hypnotist** *n* a person skilled at producing hypnosis in another person. **hypnotize** *vb* **1** produce hypnosis in. **2** fascinate; mesmerize. < Greek *hypnos* sleep.

hypochondria (ˌhaɪpəˈkɒndrɪə) *n* great anxiety about one's health. **hypochondriac** *n, adj*

hypocrisy (hɪˈpɒkrəsɪ) *n* the pretence of standards, beliefs, etc., esp. in morals or religion. **hypocrite** *n* a person who practises hypocrisy. **hypocritical** *adj* **hypocritically** *adv* < Greek *hypo-* under + *krinesthai* to dispute.

hypodermic (ˌhaɪpəˈdɜːmɪk) *adj* of the parts beneath the skin; used in or given by injection beneath the skin: a hypodermic syringe. < Greek *hypo-* under + *derma* skin.

hypotenuse (haɪˈpɒtəˌnjuːz) *n* the side in a right-angled triangle that is opposite the right angle. < Greek *hypo-* under + *teinein* to stretch.

hypothermia (ˌhaɪpəʊˈθɜːmɪə) *n* a lowering of the body temperature, esp. in old people. < Greek *hypo-* under + *thermē* heat.

hypothesis (haɪˈpɒθəsɪs) *n, pl* **hypotheses** a provisional explanation for a set of facts, etc., used as a basis for further investigation. **hypothetical** *adj* **hypothetically** *adv* < Greek *hypo-* under + *tithenai* to place.

hysterectomy (ˌhɪstəˈrɛktəmɪ) *n* surgical removal of the womb. < Greek *hystera* womb + *-ectomy,* from Greek *ektemnein* to cut out.

hysteria (hɪˈstɪərɪə) *n* **1** a mental disorder marked by emotional instability and often physical symptoms such as paralysis. **2** intense, uncontrolled emotion or excitement. **hysterical** *adj* **hysterically** *adv* **hysterics** *pl n* **1** an attack of hysteria. **2** intense, uncontrolled emotion or excitement, esp. crying or laughter. < Greek *hystera* womb, from the belief that hysteria was caused by disorders of the womb.

I

I (aɪ) *pron* the person who is speaking or writing. < Old English *ic.*

iambic (aɪˈæmbɪk) *adj* of a metrical foot with one unstressed or short syllable followed by a stressed or long syllable. < Greek *iambos* iambic foot.

IBA *abbrev* Independent Broadcasting Authority.

ice (aɪs) *n* **1** frozen water; mass or sheet of this. **2** a portion of ice-cream or water-ice.
• *vb* **1** cover with or change into ice. **2** provide, make, or become cold with ice. **3** cover with icing. **4** become covered or blocked with ice. **iceberg** *n* a huge mass of ice in the sea, coming esp. from a glacier. **ice-blue** *adj, n* very pale blue. **ice-cap** *n* the permanent covering of ice in the polar regions. **ice-cream** *n* a sweet, creamy flavoured frozen food. **ice hockey** a game played on an ice rink by players who try to propel a flat puck into the opponent's goal with a long stick. **ice lolly** a flavoured piece of ice on a small stick. **icicle** *n* a hanging, pointed mass of ice formed by the freezing of water as it drips. **icing** *n* a sweet coating for cakes and biscuits. **icing sugar** finely powdered sugar used to make icing. **icy** *adj* **1** extremely cold. **2** covered with ice: icy roads. **3** very unfriendly in manner: an icy stare. **icily** *adv* **iciness** *n* < Old English *īs.*

icon (ˈaɪkɒn) *n* (in the Byzantine and Orthodox churches) a painted or mosaic image of Christ or a saint, which is itself revered. **iconic** *adj* < Greek *eikōn* image. SEE PANEL AT **EFF**.

idea (aɪˈdɪə) *n* **1** a mental conception, impression, or image. **2** a plan, etc., formed in the mind. **3** an opinion: That's not my idea of a pleasant evening! **4** a vague notion. **5** the main aim: The idea of the game is to score points. **6** knowledge: You've no idea how much we worried about you! < Greek: pattern, notion.

ideal (aɪˈdɪəl) *adj* **1** considered as perfect: ideal conditions for sailing. **2** existing as an idea or only in the mind; imaginary.
• *n* **1** a conception of something perfect. **2** a perfect model, aim, principle, etc.: high ideals. **ideally** *adv* **idealism** *n* belief in or the practice of living according to ideals, esp. when considered before practical matters. **idealist** *n* **idealistic** *adj* **idealize** *vb* represent or portray as ideal.

identical (aɪˈdɛntɪkl̩) *adj* **1** being the same. **2** exactly alike or very similar. **3** (of twins, etc.) developed from a single, fertilized ovum, and so of the same sex and very alike.

identify (aɪˈdɛntɪˌfaɪ) *vb* **identified; identifying 1** determine the identity of. **2** consider (oneself) as similar to another. **3** consider as identical; equate. **4** associate closely in feeling or interest. **5** consider oneself as sharing the characteristics, etc., of. **identifiable** *adj* **identification** *n* **Identikit** *n* (*Trademark*) a set of different facial characteristics drawn by artists and put together to make up a composite picture of a police suspect. **identity** *n* **1** the state of being identical. **2** the state of being a particular person or thing. **3** the set of distinguishing features of someone's character and personality: establish one's identity. < Latin *idem* the same.

ideogram (ˈɪdɪəʊˌɡræm) *n* a sign or symbol (rather than a word) that is used to represent a thing or idea, for example numbers, road signs, or Chinese characters. < Greek *idea* pattern + *gram,* from *gramma* writing.

ideology (ˌaɪdɪˈɒlədʒɪ) *n* a set of ideas, esp. those of a political or economic system. **ideological** *adj* < Greek *ideo-,* from *idea* pattern + *-logy,* ultimately *logos* word.

idiom (ˈɪdɪəm) *n* **1** an expression in a language that cannot be understood from putting together the meanings of the individual words. **2** the grammatical use of a language that is natural to its native speakers. **3** the characteristic language of a particular community, area, etc. **4** a characteristic artistic or musical style. **idiomatic** *adj* **idiomatically** *adv* < Greek *idios* one's own. SEE PANEL AT **FOOT**.

idiosyncrasy (ˌɪdɪəʊˈsɪŋkrəsɪ) *n* a characteristic, esp. eccentric way of behaving; mannerism, etc., of a particular person. **idiosyncratic** *adj* < Greek *idio-* personal + *syn* with + *kerannynai* to mix.

idiot (ˈɪdɪət) *n* **1** a very stupid person. **2** a severely mentally deficient person. **idiocy** *n* **idiotic** *adj* **idiotically** *adv* < ultimately Greek *idiōtēs* private person.

idle (ˈaɪdl̩) *adj* **1** lazy. **2** not employed or

used. **3** having no value or purpose: idle gossip.
• *vb* **1** spend (time) inactively or fruitlessly. **2** (of an engine) run at low speed but not be connected to the driving parts. **idleness** *n* **idler** *n* **idly** *adv* < Old English *īdel.*

idol (ˈaɪdl̩) *n* **1** an image of a god used as an object of worship. **2** an object of extreme devotion. **idolater** *n* a worshipper of idols. **idolatry** *n* **1** worship of idols. **2** extreme devotion. **idolatrous** *adj* **idolize** *vb* feel extreme devotion towards. < Greek *eidōlon.*

idyll (ˈɪdɪl) *n* a short poem or prose work describing a peaceful, rural life, pastoral scenes, etc.; such a scene. **idyllic** *adj* as depicted in an idyll, esp. peaceful and happy. **idyllically** *adv* < Greek *eidos* form.

i.e. *abbrev* (*Latin*) id est (that is). SEE PANEL AT **E.G.**

if (ɪf) *conj* **1** in the event that: If I had enough money, I would emigrate. **2** even though: a distinct, if remote possibility. **3** whether: Ask him if he knows the way.
• *n* a condition or supposition: ifs and buts. < Old English *gif.* SEE PANEL.

igloo (ˈɪɡlu:) *n* a dome-shaped, Eskimo dwelling, built of blocks of snow. < Eskimo *iglu* house.

igneous (ˈɪɡnɪəs) *adj* (of rock) consisting mainly of crystalline rocks cooled from the molten rock deep in the earth. < Latin *ignis* fire.

ignite (ɪɡˈnaɪt) *vb* catch fire or set fire to. **ignition** *n* **1** igniting. **2** the means used to ignite a fuel in an internal-combustion engine. < Latin *ignis* fire.

if I were ... or if I was ...?

It is sometimes difficult to decide whether to say If I *were* ... or If I *was* ....

If I *were* you is a common way of introducing advice: If I *were* you, I wouldn't marry him. If I were is also used to introduce something that is improbable or obviously unreal or untrue: If I *were* 30 years younger, I would emigrate. If I *were* king, then I'd give everyone £1000. In colloquial speech If I *was* is used, especially for this second meaning.

If I *was* is also used to introduce something that is true, factual, or that actually happened: If I *was* wrong, then I apologize.

ignoble (ɪɡˈnəʊbl̩) *adj* **1** dishonourable; base. **2** of lowly birth or origins. **ignobly** *adv* < Latin *in-* not + *nobilis* noble.

ignominy (ˈɪɡnəmɪnɪ) *n* disgrace or deep humiliation; cause of this. **ignominious** *adj* marked by or causing ignominy. **ignominiously** *adv* < Latin *in-* not + *nomen* name.

ignoramus (ˌɪɡnəˈreɪməs) *n, pl* **ignoramuses** an ignorant person. < Latin: we do not know.

ignorant (ˈɪɡnərənt) *adj* **1** lacking in knowledge, education, or awareness of (something mentioned): ignorant of the law. **2** marked by or caused by a lack of knowledge or awareness. **3** rude, because of a lack of knowledge of good manners. **ignorance** *n* **ignorantly** *adv*

ignore (ɪɡˈnɔ:) *vb* fail or refuse to notice; disregard. < Latin *in-* not + *gnarus* knowing.

iguana (ɪˈɡwɑ:nə) *n* a large, tree-climbing, amphibious, tropical American lizard. < Spanish, from Arawak *iwana.*

ilk (ɪlk) *n* a sort: people of that ilk. < Old English *ilca* the same family.

ill (ɪl) *adj* **worse; worst 1** unwell: seriously ill. **2** (of health) not good. **3** harmful; bad: ill effects; ill repute. **4** unfavourable: no ill feelings. **5** unkind: ill will.
• *adv* **1** badly, unfavourably, or imperfectly: ill-equipped; ill-informed. **2** scarcely: We can ill afford such luxuries.
• *n* evil; harm. **illness** *n* a sickness or disease; state of bad health. < Old Norse *illr* bad.

illegal (ɪˈli:gl) *adj* forbidden or not authorized by law. **illegality** *n* **illegally** *adv* SEE PANEL.

illegible (ɪˈlɛdʒəbl̩) *adj* not legible. **illegibility** *n* **illegibly** *adv*

illegitimate (ˌɪləˈdʒɪtəmət) *adj* **1** born of parents who are not married to each other. **2** contrary to the law or rules: illegitimate uses of drugs. **3** (of a conclusion) wrongly inferred. **illegitimacy** *n* **illegitimately** *adv* SEE PANEL AT **ILLEGAL.**

illicit (ɪˈlɪsɪt) *adj* contrary to the law; not allowed. **illicitly** *adv* < Latin *in-* not + *licēre* to be permitted. SEE PANELS AT **ELICIT; ILLEGAL.**

illiterate (ɪˈlɪtərət) *adj* **1** unable to read or write. **2** uneducated or uncultured.
• *n* an illiterate person. **illiteracy** *n*

illogical (ɪˈlɒdʒɪkl̩) *adj* not logical. **illogicality** *n* **illogically** *adv*

illuminate (ɪˈlu:mɪˌneɪt) *vb* **1** cast light on; light up: an illuminated sign. **2** make clear or understandable; explain. **3** decorate with lights. **4** decorate (a manuscript) with elaborate letters or designs. **illumination** *n* < Latin *in-* in + *luminare* to light up.

illusion (ɪˈlu:ʒən) *n* **1** a wrong impression or opinion. **2** a misleading image or appearance: perception causing this: an optical illusion. **illusory** *adj* also **illusive** unreal; misleading. < Latin *illudere* to mock at. SEE PANEL AT **ALLUDE.**

illustrate (ˈɪləˌstreɪt) *vb* **1** provide (a book, etc.) with pictures or drawings. **2** make clear or explain by examples, etc. **3** be an example or explanation of. **illustrative** *adj* **illustrator** *n* **illustration** *n* **1** illustrating. **2** a picture or drawing in a book, etc. **3** an example or explanation. < Latin *in-* in + *lustrare* to make bright.

illustrious (ɪˈlʌstrɪəs) *adj* famous and distinguished. < SEE **ILLUSTRATE.**

image (ˈɪmɪdʒ) *n* **1** a representation of a person or thing; statue. **2** the optical appearance of something produced by a mirror, lens, etc. **3** exact likeness; person very much like another person mentioned: the image of her mother. **4** a mental conception. **5** a conception or impression of a particular person, product, etc., in the minds of the public. **imagery** *n* **1** images; art of making images. **2** mental images. **3** descriptive or figurative language. < Latin *imago.*

imagine (ɪˈmædʒən) *vb* **1** make a mental image of. **2** suppose; think. **imaginable** *adj* capable of being imagined. **imaginary** *adj* existing only in the imagination; not real. **imagination** *n* **1** the act, power, or ability to imagine things. **2** creative ability; resourcefulness. **imaginative** *adj* having or showing imagination. **imaginatively** *adv* < Latin *imago* image.

imbalance (ɪmˈbæləns) *n* a lack of balance; disproportion.

imbecile (ˈɪmbɪˌsi:l) *n* **1** a very stupid person. **2** a person who is mentally deficient. **imbecility** *n* < Latin *imbecillus* weak-minded.

imbibe (ɪmˈbaɪb) *vb* **1** drink. **2** absorb or assimilate. < Latin *imbibere.*

imbue (ɪmˈbju:) *vb* fill (with qualities, ideals, etc.). < Latin *imbuere.*

IMF *abbrev* International Monetary Fund.

imitate (ˈɪmɪˌteɪt) *vb* **1** follow the example of. **2** mimic. **3** copy or reproduce. **4** resemble. **imitative** *adj* **imitator** *n* **imitation** *n* **1** imitating; act of imitating. **2** something produced as a copy or reproduction. < Latin *imitari.*

immaculate (ɪˈmækjʊlət) *adj* **1** spotlessly clean. **2** without flaw or error. **3** without blemish; pure. **immaculately** *adv* < Latin *in-* not + *macula* spot.

immaterial (ɪməˈtɪərɪəl) *adj* **1** not made of matter; having no physical substance. **2** not important or relevant.

immature (ˌɪməˈtjʊə) *adj* not mature. **immaturity** *n*

immeasurable (ɪˈmɛʒərəbl̩) *adj* incapable of being measured, esp. because of great size. **immeasurably** *adv*

immediate (ɪˈmi:dɪət) *adj* **1** occurring or done without delay: take immediate action. **2** the closest or most direct in effect, relationship, etc.: our immediate family. **immediacy** *n* < Latin *in-* not + *mediare* to be in the middle.

immediately (ɪˈmi:dɪətlɪ) *adv* **1** without delay. **2** directly.
• *conj* as soon as.

immemorial (ˌɪməˈmɔ:rɪəl) *adj* existing before what can be remembered or what was recorded; extremely old.

immense (ɪˈmɛns) *adj* extremely great in size or degree. **immensity** *n* **immensely** *adv* extremely. < Latin *in-* not + *metiri* to measure.

immerse (ɪˈmɜ:s) *vb* **1** put completely into a liquid, esp. water. **2** absorb deeply in thought, etc. **immersion** *n* **immersion heater** an electric heating-element fixed inside a hot-water tank. < Latin *immergere.*

immigrate (ˈɪmɪgreɪt) *vb* come into and settle in a foreign country. **immigration** *n* **immigrant** *n* a person who has immigrated. < Latin *in-* + *migrare* to

---

illegal, illegitimate, or **illicit?**

The meanings of these words overlap, but some differences may be noted. Illegal means 'forbidden or not authorized by law': The new law made it *illegal* not to wear a seat-belt.

Illegitimate is most commonly used to refer to children born of parents who are not married to each other, but it can also mean 'contrary to the law or rules' as in *illegitimate* uses of drugs.

Illicit means 'contrary to the law; not allowed' and is used to refer to activities that the law allows under certain conditions which are being pursued in a secretive way, as in the *illicit* sales of vodka. It is also used of secret relationships: an *illicit* love affair.

---

migrate. SEE PANEL AT **EMIGRANT**.

imminent (ˈɪmɪnənt) *adj* liable to occur soon; impending. **imminence** *n* < Latin *in-* in + *-minēre* to project. SEE PANEL AT **EMINENT.**

immobile (ɪˈməʊbaɪl) *adj* incapable of being moved; not moving. **immobility** *n* **immobilize** *vb* make immobile.

immolate (ˈɪməˌleɪt) *vb* **1** offer as a sacrifice. **2** kill or destroy. < Latin *immolare* to sprinkle an offering with sacrificial meal.

immoral (ɪˈmɒrəl) *adj* going against the accepted rules of morality, esp. in sexual matters. **immorality** *n* **immorally** *adv* SEE PANEL AT **AMORAL.**

immortal (ɪˈmɔːtl̩) *adj* **1** living for ever. **2** famous for ever.
• *n* an immortal person. **immortality** *n* **immortalize** *vb* make immortal.

immune (ɪˈmjuːn) *adj* **1** free (from) or not susceptible (to): immune to criticism. **2** having resistance to infection, esp. due to antibodies. **immunity** *n* **immunize** *vb* make immune, esp. against infection. **immunization** *n* < Latin *in-* without + *munia* duties.

immutable (ɪˈmjuːtəbl̩) *adj* unchangeable. **immutability** *n* **immutably** *adv*

imp (ɪmp) *n* **1** a small demon. **2** a mischievous child. **impish** *adj* < Old English *impa* young shoot, offspring. SEE PANEL AT **VILLAIN.**

impact (ˈɪmpækt) *n* **1** the striking of one thing against another; collision. **2** a powerful effect or impression: Computers have made a great impact on contemporary life.
• *vb* (ɪmˈpækt) fix firmly by packing or wedging. < Latin *impingere* press firmly together.

impair (ɪmˈpɛə) *vb* reduce in strength or quality; weaken or damage. **impairment** *n* < Late Latin *pejorare* to make worse.

impala (ɪmˈpɑːlə) *n* an African antelope, known for its great leaps. < Zulu.

impale (ɪmˈpeɪl) *vb* pierce with something pointed. **impalement** *n* < Latin *in-* + *palus* stake.

impalpable (ɪmˈpælpəbl̩) *adj* **1** not capable of being touched or felt. **2** too difficult to be easily grasped with the mind.

impart (ɪmˈpɑːt) *vb* communicate (information); give or convey. < Latin *in-* + *partire* to divide.

impartial (ɪmˈpɑːʃəl) *adj* not biased. **impartiality** *n* **impartially** *adv*

impasse (ˈæmˌpæs) *n* a situation from which there is no obvious escape; deadlock. < French.

impassioned (ɪmˈpæʃənd) *adj* filled with deep feeling: an impassioned plea.

impassive (ɪmˈpæsɪv) *adj* not showing or affected by emotion. **impassively** *adv* **impassiveness** or **impassivity** *n*

impatient (ɪmˈpeɪʃənt) *adj* **1** quickly annoyed; intolerant. **2** showing or marked by a lack of patience: an impatient glance. **3** restless and eager (to do something). **impatience** *n* **impatiently** *adv*

impeach (ɪmˈpiːtʃ) *vb* **1** accuse of a serious crime such as treason. **2** (*chiefly US*) charge (a public official) with misconduct committed during office. **3** challenge (someone's character, testimony, etc.). **impeachment** *n* < Latin *in-* in + *pedica* fetter.

impeccable (ɪmˈpɛkəbl̩) *adj* faultless: impeccable behaviour. **impeccably** *adv* < Latin *in-* not + *peccare* to sin.

impecunious (ˌɪmpɪˈkjuːnɪəs) *adj* having little or no money. < Latin *in-* not + *pecunia* money.

impedance (ɪmˈpiːdn̩s) *n* a measure of the resistance in an electrical circuit to the flow of an alternating current. < SEE **IMPEDE.**

impede (ɪmˈpiːd) *vb* restrict or slow down the movement or progress of; hinder. **impediment** *n* something that impedes, esp. a speech defect. **impedimenta** *pl n* things that hinder progress; large amount of baggage or equipment. < Latin *in-* + *pes* foot.

impel (ɪmˈpɛl) *vb* **impelled; impelling** **1** urge or force to do something; constrain. **2** send or drive forward. < Latin *in-* + *pellere* to drive.

impending (ɪmˈpɛndɪŋ) *adj* imminent: the impending visit of the President. < Latin *in-* + *pendēre* to hang.

imperative (ɪmˈpɛrətɪv) *adj* **1** essential: It is imperative that you leave at once. **2** expressing a command.
• *n* **1** a command; verb form expressing this. **2** something essential. < Latin *imperare* to command. SEE PANEL.

imperceptible (ˌɪmpəˈsɛptəbl̩) *adj* too slight, gradual, etc., to be perceived. **imperceptibly** *adv*

imperfect (ɪmˈpɜːfɪkt) *adj* not perfect. **imperfectly** *adv* **imperfection** *n* state of being imperfect; flaw or blemish.

imperial (ɪmˈpɪərɪəl) *adj* **1** of an empire, emperor, or empress. **2** sovereign or majestic. **3** (of weights and measures) conforming to legal, British, non-metric standards. **imperialism** *n* the extension of a country's rule over other countries by conquest, colonization, and the imposition of economic and political ideologies. **imperialist** *adj, n* < Latin

imperium command, empire. SEE PANEL.
imperil (ɪm'pɛrəl) *vb* **imperilled; imperilling** place in danger.
imperious (ɪm'pɪərɪəs) *adj* dominant; commanding. **imperiously** *adv* < Latin *imperium* power, command. SEE PANEL AT **IMPERIAL.**
impersonal (ɪm'pɜːsənḷ) *adj* **1** not showing human personality or feelings: a cold, impersonal stare. **2** not referring to any particular person: impersonal justice. **3** not having human features or characteristics. **4** (of verbs) having the subject it, as in It is snowing. **impersonality** *n* **impersonally** *adv*
impersonate (ɪm'pɜːsəˌneɪt) *vb* **1** act the part of. **2** pretend to be (another person), for entertainment or fraud. **impersonation** *n* **impersonator** *n*
impertinent (ɪm'pɜːtɪnənt) *adj* impudent and rude; insolent. **impertinence** *n* **impertinently** *adv*
imperturbable (ˌɪmpə'tɜːbəbḷ) *adj* not easily excited; very calm and composed. **imperturbability** *n* **imperturbably** *adv*
impervious (ɪm'pɜːvɪəs) *adj* **1** not able to be penetrated: impervious to rain. **2** not able to be influenced: impervious to reason. < Latin *in-* not + *pervius* pervious, permeable.
impetuous (ɪm'pɛtjʊəs) *adj* marked by violent or hasty action not accompanied by thought; rash. **impetuously** *adv* **impetuousness** or **impetuosity** *n* < SEE **IMPETUS.**
impetus ('ɪmpətəs) *n* a driving force; stimulus or incentive: The report's findings gave a fresh impetus to the strikers' demands. < Latin: onset, from *in-* + *petere* to go to.
impinge (ɪm'pɪndʒ) *vb* **1** encroach or infringe: impinge on someone's rights. **2** touch or collide with. < Latin *in-* + *pangere* to fasten.
implacable (ɪm'plækəbḷ) *adj* incapable of being placated or pacified. **implacably** *adv*
implant (ɪm'plɑːnt) *vb* **1** fix (ideas, etc.) deeply and securely in the mind. **2** insert (tissue, etc.) into a living organism.
• *n* ('ɪmˌplɑːnt) anything implanted, esp. tissue, etc.
implement ('ɪmplɪmənt) *n* a tool or instrument to work with: garden implements.
• *vb* ('ɪmplɪˌmɛnt) put into action; carry out: It will cost £10 million to implement all the report's findings. **implementation** *n* < Latin *in-* in + *plēre* to fill.
implicate ('ɪmplɪˌkeɪt) *vb* involve or show to be involved in a crime. **implication** *n* **1** implicating or being implicated. **2** implying or being implied. **3** a necessary consequence or effect: The new proposals have far-reaching implications. < Latin *implicare* to involve.
implicit (ɪm'plɪsɪt) *adj* **1** implied, though not expressed plainly: implicit assumptions. **2** unquestioning and complete: He expects implicit obedience. **implicitly** *adv* < SEE **IMPLICATE.**
implore (ɪm'plɔː) *vb* beg earnestly; entreat. < Latin *in-* + *plorare* to cry out.
imply (ɪm'plaɪ) *vb* **implied; implying** **1** show or indicate without stating directly; hint at. **2** suggest as a necessary consequence or effect. < SEE **IMPLICATE.** SEE PANEL.
impolite (ˌɪmpə'laɪt) *adj* not polite; rude.

imperative

The imperative form of a verb, the so-called 'bare' infinitive, has long been characterized as the form used to issue commands, as in *Shut* the door! or *Come* here immediately! However, the issuing of commands is a language function that in most social situations is relatively rare. While it is true that the imperative may be used to express a command, it serves to perform many other types of speech act as well. These include giving instructions: *Bake* the pie in a slow oven, issuing invitations: *Come* round for a meal tomorrow night, making suggestions: *Try* adding a little salt, giving advice: *Take* up his offer— I would, and, in sharp contrast with giving commands, the issuing of pleas: Please *forgive* me!

imperial or **imperious?**

The basic meaning of imperial is 'of or concerned with an empire, emperor, or empress' as in an *imperial* decree. It can also mean 'sovereign or majestic' and is further used to refer to the British, non-metric system of weights and measures. (In fact in the United Kingdom, standards such as the yard are now officially defined in metric terms.)

Imperious means 'dominant or commanding' and implies an overbearing, dictatorial manner: a proud, *imperious* attitude.

impolitely *adv* **impoliteness** *n*
impolitic (ɪmˈpɒlɪtɪk) *adj* not politic; unwise.
imponderable (ɪmˈpɒndərəbl̩) *adj, n* (something) that cannot be assessed or evaluated.
import (ɪmˈpɔːt, ˈɪmpɔːt) *vb* buy (goods or services) from abroad.
• *n* (ˈɪmpɔːt) **1** something imported; act of importing. **2** (*formal*) meaning, significance, or importance. **importation** *n* **importer** *n* < Latin *in-* in + *portare* to carry.
important (ɪmˈpɔːtn̩t) *adj* **1** of great significance, effect, or consequence. **2** (of a person) having great authority or influence. **importance** *n* **importantly** *adv* < SEE **IMPORT.**
importunate (ɪmˈpɔːtjʊnət) *adj* making persistent requests. **importunately** *adv* **importunity** *n* < Latin *importunatus* troublesome.
impose (ɪmˈpəʊz) *vb* **1** place (a burden, tax, etc.). **2** force (oneself) on the attention of: impose oneself on others. **3** take unfair advantage: I don't want to impose on your hospitality any longer. **imposing** *adj* impressive. **imposition** *n* imposing or something imposed. < Latin *in-* + *ponere* to place.
impossible (ɪmˈpɒsəbl̩) *adj* **1** not possible. **2** extremely difficult to put up with. **impossibility** *n* **impossibly** *adv*
impostor (ɪmˈpɒstə) *n* a person who fraudulently pretends to be another person. < SEE **IMPOSE.**
impotent (ˈɪmpətənt) *adj* **1** lacking strength or power. **2** (of a man) unable to engage in sexual intercourse. **impotence** *n* **impotently** *adv*
impound (ɪmˈpaʊnd) *vb* take and keep in a pound or in legal custody.
impoverish (ɪmˈpɒvərɪʃ) *vb* **1** make poor. **2** reduce the quality, richness, etc., of. **impoverishment** *n* < Middle French *empovrir*, from *povre* poor.
impracticable (ɪmˈpræktɪkəbl̩) *adj* incapable of being put into practice or accomplished. **impracticability** *n* SEE PANEL.
impractical (ɪmˈpræktɪkl̩) *adj* **1** not practical or workable. **2** unskilled in practical matters. SEE PANEL AT **IMPRACTICABLE.**
imprecation (ˌɪmprɪˈkeɪʃən) *n* invocation of evil; curse. < Latin *in-* + *precari* to pray.
impregnable (ɪmˈprɛgnəbl̩) *adj* incapable of being captured or entered into by force. **impregnability** *n* < Middle French *in-* not + *prenable* able to be captured, from *prendre* to take.
impregnate (ɪmˈprɛgneɪt) *vb* **1** fertilize or make pregnant. **2** fill or saturate. **impregnation** *n* < Latin *in-* in + *praegnans* pregnant.
impresario (ˌɪmprəˈsɑːrɪəʊ) *n, pl* **impresarios** the manager or conductor of an operatic or concert company. < Italian: one who undertakes.
impress (ɪmˈprɛs) *vb* **1** produce a deep, esp. favourable effect (on): The trade delegation were greatly impressed by the wide range of our products. **2** fix deeply or firmly in the mind. **3** produce (an imprint, etc.) by pressure on (something). **4** emphasize: He impressed on them the risks they were taking. **impression** *n* **1** an effect impressed on the mind or senses. **2** an imprecise notion: vague impressions. **3** an impressing; mark or imprint. **4** an entertaining and amusing impersonation. **5** the set of copies of a book, etc., printed in one operation from the same type, plates,

imply or **infer?**

These two words are often confused.

Imply means 'to show or indicate without stating directly; hint at or suggest' as in The contract is so worded as to *imply* a statement of priorities. (It wasn't explicitly stated.)

Infer means 'to conclude from facts or assumptions; deduce' as in What can be *inferred* from the results of the election? Thus a speaker, writer, or report implies, while a listener or reader infers.

impracticable or **impractical?**

Careful users of English distinguish these words. Impracticable means 'incapable of being put into practice or accomplished'. A scheme or plan may be said to be impracticable if it can't be done at all.

Impractical refers to things that are not practical or workable, though possible. An *impractical* suggestion is one that isn't worth putting into practice because it would require too much time or effort, although it could be carried out.

etc. **impressionable** *adj* easily influenced. **impressionism** *n* the late 19th-century French art movement that aimed to capture the effects of light with dabs of bright colour without drawing firm details. **impressionist** *adj, n* **impressive** *adj* making a strong, deep impression on the senses; striking. **impressively** *adv* < Latin *in-* + *premere* to press.

imprint (ˈɪmprɪnt) *n* **1** a mark produced by pressing or stamping. **2** a distinguishing mark or feature. **3** the name of the publisher and place and date of publication printed at the foot of a book's title page.
• *vb* (ɪmˈprɪnt) **1** mark by pressing or stamping. **2** fix in a deep lasting way on the mind. < SEE **IMPRESS.**

imprison (ɪmˈprɪzən) *vb* confine in or as if in a prison. **imprisonment** *n*

improbable (ɪmˈprɒbəbḷ) *adj* not probable or likely. **improbability** *n* **improbably** *adv*

impromptu (ɪmˈprɒmptjuː) *adj, adv* done, composed, or performed in a spontaneous, improvised way.
• *n* **1** something impromptu. **2** a musical composition that suggests that it has been composed impromptu. < French, from Latin *in promptu* in readiness. SEE PANEL AT **EXTEMPORE.**

improper (ɪmˈprɒpə) *adj* **1** wrong; incorrect. **2** not suitable or appropriate. **3** indecent. **improperly** *adv* **impropriety** *n* being improper; improper act, comment, etc.

improve (ɪmˈpruːv) *vb* **1** make or become better or more valuable. **2** produce something better than: improve on last month's output. **improvement** *n* **1** improving or being improved. **2** something that improves: improvements in working conditions; home improvements. < Latin *in-* in + *prodesse* to be advantageous.

improvident (ɪmˈprɒvɪdənt) *adj* not providing for the future; carelessly wasting one's resources. **improvidence** *n* **improvidently** *adv*

improvise (ˈɪmprəˌvaɪz) *vb* **1** make quickly with materials readily available, with no previous planning. **2** compose and perform impromptu. **improvisation** *n* < Latin *in-* not + *providēre* to foresee.

imprudent (ɪmˈpruːdṇt) *adj* not prudent; indiscreet or rash. **imprudence** *n* **imprudently** *adv*

impudent (ˈɪmpjʊdənt) *adj* disrespectful and cheeky. **impudence** *n* **impudently** *adv* < Latin *in-* not + *pudēre* to feel shame.

impugn (ɪmˈpjuːn) *vb* attack as false. < Latin *in-* + *pugnare* to fight.

impulse (ˈɪmpʌls) *n* **1** an impelling force; motion caused by this. **2** stimulus to act; inspiration. **3** a spontaneous inclination to do something: We bought the books on impulse. **impulsive** *adj* marked by actions done on impulse. **impulsively** *adv* **impulsiveness** *n* < SEE **IMPEL.**

impunity (ɪmˈpjuːnɪtɪ) *n* exemption or freedom from punishment or injury. < Latin *in-* without + *poena* pain.

impure (ɪmˈpjʊə) *adj* not pure. **impurity** *n*

impute (ɪmˈpjuːt) *vb* attribute (esp. a fault) to another person. **imputation** *n* < Latin *in-* + *putare* to think, consider.

in (ɪn) *prep* **1** used to show a position where something is: in the road. **2** used to show when something happens: in winter; in 2000. **3** contained by; inside: in the house **4** into: come in the office. **5** during: He wrote the poem in a morning. **6** at the end of: I'll be back in an hour. **7** used to show a means, manner, or condition: speak in German; cry in pain; lacking in ability. **8** used to show an activity or occupation: He is in the navy. **9** used to show a material: write in ink. **10** wearing: in pink. **11** out of a group; used in proportions: 1 in 10 people. **12** (of an animal) pregnant with: in calf.
• *adv* **1** towards the centre or inside, home, or one's destination: I'll be in tonight; The train came in. **2** into a place where it cannot be seen: The sun went in. **3** so as to

in a word

The word in features in a number of idiomatic expressions, including:

be in for to be about to experience: If she thinks she's going to have an easy time once the baby's born, she's in for a shock.
be in on to join; participate in: Many members of the public wanted to be in on the share issue.
be in with to be on good terms with: They say that it was only because he was in with the managing director that he got the contract.
ins and outs the detailed points of something: We don't need to go into all the ins and outs of the scheme just yet—let me explain the basic outline for now.

enclose: cover in the hole. **4** having a position of power: 1964 saw Labour voted in. **5** (in cricket, etc.) taking a turn at batting. **6** (of tides) high.
• *adj* **1** situated inside. **2** enjoyed by a small group: an in joke. **3** ingoing: the in-tray. **4** (*informal*) very fashionable and popular: the in place to eat. < Old English. SEE PANEL. SEE PANEL AT **INTO.**

in. *abbrev* inch; inches.

in- *prefix* SEE PANEL.

inadequate (ɪnˈædɪkwət) *adj* **1** not adequate; insufficient. **2** unable to cope: feel inadequate. **inadequacy** *n* **inadequately** *adv*

in- words

The list below includes many of the more common words formed with the prefix in-, meaning 'not' or 'lack of'.

inability	**indiscernible**
inaccessible	**indiscipline**
inaccuracy	**indiscreet**
inaccurate	**indisputable**
inaction	**indistinct**
inactive	**indivisible**
inactivity	**inedible**
inadmissible	**ineffective**
inadvisable	**ineffectual**
inapplicable	**inefficiency**
inappropriate	**inefficient**
inattentive	**inelegant**
inaudible	**ineligible**
inauspicious	**inequitable**
incapable	**inessential**
incommensurable	**inexact**
incommensurate	**inexplicable**
incompetence	**infertile**
incompetent	**infrequent**
incomplete	**ingratitude**
incomprehensible	**inhumane**
inconsistency	**injudicious**
inconsistent	**inopportune**
inconspicuous	**insalubrious**
inconstant	**insensitive**
incontestable	**inseparable**
incontrovertible	**insincere**
incorrect	**instability**
incorruptible	**insufficiency**
incurable	**insufficient**
indefensible	**insurmountable**
indefinable	**insusceptible**
indestructible	**intangible**
indigestible	**invulnerable**

inadvertent (ˌɪnədˈvɜːtn̩t) *adj* **1** unintentional. **2** (of a person) negligent. **inadvertency** *n* **inadvertently** *adv* < Latin *in-* not -+- *advertere* to turn attention to. SEE PANEL.

inalienable (ɪnˈeɪljənəbl̩) *adj* incapable of being taken away: inalienable rights.

inane (ɪˈneɪn) *adj* lacking sense; silly or meaningless: an inane comment. **inanely** *adv* **inanity** *n* < Latin *inanis* empty.

inanimate (ɪnˈænɪmət) *adj* **1** without life. **2** showing no signs of life; not animated.

inarticulate (ˌɪnɑːˈtɪkjʊlət) *adj* **1** not comprehensible as spoken words: inarticulate cries for help. **2** incapable of speaking or being expressed coherently, esp. because of great emotion. **3** not able to express oneself clearly: an exceptionally brilliant, but inarticulate inventor. **4** marked by incoherent, unclear expression: an inarticulate speech.

inasmuch as (ˌɪnəzˈmʌtʃ) **1** seeing that; since. **2** (*chiefly archaic*) to the extent that. SEE PANEL.

inaugural (ɪnˈɔːgjʊrəl) *adj* marking a beginning: an inaugural speech. **inaugurate** *vb* **1** admit (a person) into office in a special ceremony. **2** bring about the formal beginning of. **3** celebrate the opening of. **inauguration** *n* < Latin *inaugurare* to practise augury.

inborn (ˌɪnˈbɔːn) *adj* existing from birth; inherited; natural.

inbreeding (ˈɪnˌbriːdɪŋ) *n* breeding of closely related individuals. **inbred** *adj* **1** produced from inbreeding. **2** deeply rooted in one's nature.

inbuilt (ˌɪnˈbɪlt) *adj* built-in; integral; inherent.

incalculable (ɪnˈkælkjʊləbl̩) *adj* unable to be calculated because too large.

incandescent (ˌɪnkænˈdesn̩t) *adj* glowing with light as a result of being heated. **incandescence** *n* < Latin *in-* + *candescere* to become hot.

inadvertent

Most adjectives beginning with a negative prefix have a positive equivalent: dishonourable—honourable; inadequate—adequate; irrelevant—relevant; unnecessary—necessary; etc. Inadvertent, meaning 'unintentional', is one of a small number of exceptions: there is no such word as advertent. Other examples include uncouth, unwitting, dishevelled, and unkempt.

incantation (ˌɪnkænˈteɪʃən) *n* the words or sounds spoken or sung in a magical spell; uttering of these. < Latin *incantare* to enchant.

incapacitate (ˌɪnkəˈpæsɪˌteɪt) *vb* **1** deprive of natural abilities or power; disable. **2** deprive of legal eligibility; disqualify. **incapacitation** *n* **incapacity** *n* a lack of natural abilities or power.

incarcerate (ɪnˈkɑːsəˌreɪt) *vb* imprison. **incarceration** *n* < Latin *in-* + *carcer* prison.

incarnate (ɪnˈkɑːnət) *adj* **1** having human bodily form. **2** typified: folly incarnate. **incarnation** *n* embodiment, esp. in human bodily form; embodiment of God in human form as Jesus Christ. < Latin *in-* + *caro* flesh.

incendiary (ɪnˈsɛndɪərɪ) *adj* intended for setting buildings, etc., on fire: an incendiary bomb. < Latin *incendere* to kindle.

incense[1] (ˈɪnsɛns) *n* an aromatic substance burnt for its sweet smell, esp. in religious ceremonies; smoke of this. < Latin *incendere* to kindle.

incense[2] (ɪnˈsɛns) *vb* make very angry. < SEE **INCENSE**[1].

incentive (ɪnˈsɛntɪv) *n* something that urges or motivates one on to action, greater effort, etc. < Latin *in-* + *canere* to sing.

inception (ɪnˈsɛpʃən) *n* the beginning of a project, etc. < Latin *incipere* to begin.

incessant (ɪnˈsɛsn̩t) *adj* not ceasing; continuing uninterruptedly. **incessantly** *adv* < Latin *in-* + *cessare* to delay.

incest (ˈɪnsɛst) *n* sexual intercourse between people so closely related that they are legally forbidden to marry. **incestuous** *adj* **1** of or involving incest. **2** too intimate and closed to outside influences. < Latin *in-* not + *castus* chaste, pure.

inch (ɪntʃ) *n* **1** a unit of length equal to one twelfth of a foot (2.54 centimetres). **2** an amount of rain, snow, etc., that covers a surface to the depth of one inch. • *vb* move slowly in very small steps. **every inch** in all respects: every inch a leader. **within an inch of** very close to: within an inch of losing his life. < Old English *ynce*, from Latin *uncia* twelfth part.

inchoate (ɪnˈkəʊət) *adj* (*formal*) just begun; not yet perfectly developed. < Latin *inchoare* to begin.

incidence (ˈɪnsɪdəns) *n* **1** a degree, extent, or rate of occurrence: a high incidence of burglaries. **2** the meeting of a ray of light with a surface. **incident** *n* **1** an event, esp. a minor one. **2** a public disturbance or a cause of conflict. **incidental** *adj* occurring by chance or as a consequence of something more important. **incidentally** *adv* **1** in an incidental way. **2** by the way. **incidental music** background music to a play, film, etc. < Latin *incidere* to fall upon, happen to.

incinerate (ɪnˈsɪnəˌreɪt) *vb* burn to ashes. **incineration** *n* **incinerator** *n* a furnace or container for incinerating waste. < Latin *in-* + *cinis* ashes.

incipient (ɪnˈsɪpɪənt) *adj* just beginning. < SEE **INCEPTION**.

incise (ɪnˈsaɪz) *vb* cut into; engrave by cutting. **incised** *adj* (of a wound) cleanly cut, as with a sharp knife. **incision** *n* incising; cut, esp. one made surgically. **incisive** *adj* very clear, direct, and decisive. **incisively** *adv* **incisiveness** *n* **incisor** *n* one of the sharp, cutting teeth at the front of the mouth. < Latin *in-* + *caedere* to cut.

incite (ɪnˈsaɪt) *vb* stir or provoke to action. **incitement** *n* < Latin *in-* + *citare* to put in motion.

inclement (ɪnˈklɛmənt) *adj* (of weather) bad, esp. cold, wet, or stormy. **inclemency** *n* **inclemently** *adv*

incline (ɪnˈklaɪn) *vb* **1** lean or slope or cause to lean or slope. **2** draw or become drawn towards an opinion or course of action: I'm inclined to agree with you. **3** bend (the head or body) forward. • *n* (ˈɪnklaɪn) a slope. **inclination** *n* **1** a leaning, sloping, or bending. **2** a tendency; liking: I have no inclination to see her again. < Latin *in-* + *clinare* to lean.

include (ɪnˈkluːd) *vb* **1** put in as part of a larger group, set, etc. **2** contain. **inclusion** *n* **inclusive** *adj* **1** including the

inasmuch or **in as much?**

Inasmuch is usually written as one word. It is used with as and has two meanings. The more common meaning is 'seeing that; since; in view of the fact that' as in He was at a disadvantage *inasmuch as* he had less money than her.

The older, now chiefly archaic meaning of inasmuch as is 'to the extent that'; in so far (three words rather than one) as is usually used in this sense today.

limits mentioned: from January to April inclusive. **2** covering all the items, esp. charges. **inclusively** *adv* < Latin *in-* + *claudere* to close.

incognito (ˌɪnkɒgˈniːtəʊ) *adj, adv* with one's identity kept secret.
• *n, pl* **incognitos** the disguise of a person who is incognito. < Italian, from Latin *in-* + *cognoscere* to know.

incognizant (ɪnˈkɒgnɪzənt) *adj* unaware (of).

incoherent (ˌɪnkəʊˈhɪərənt) *adj* lacking in organization or clarity of expression. **incoherence** *n* **incoherently** *adv*

income (ˈɪnkʌm, ˈɪnkəm) *n* the amount of money gained from work, investment, etc., during a certain period, esp. one year. **income tax** a tax on income.

incoming (ˈɪnˌkʌmɪŋ) *adj* **1** coming in: incoming mail. **2** new or next: the incoming tenant.

incommunicado (ˌɪnkəˌmjuːnɪˈkɑːdəʊ) *adj, adv* not being allowed to communicate with other people, as during solitary confinement. < Spanish *incomunicar* to deprive of communication.

incomparable (ɪnˈkɒmpərəbl̩) *adj* **1** without an equal; matchless. **2** beyond comparison. **incomparably** *adv*

incompatible (ˌɪnkəmˈpætəbl̩) *adj* **1** not compatible. **2** logically contradictory; inconsistent. **3** not suitable for use together. **incompatibility** *n*

inconceivable (ˌɪnkənˈsiːvəbl̩) *adj* beyond understanding; unbelievable. **inconceivably** *adv*

inconclusive (ˌɪnkənˈkluːsɪv) *adj* not leading to a definite conclusion or result: inconclusive evidence. **inconclusively** *adv* **inconclusiveness** *n*

incongruous (ɪnˈkɒŋgrʊəs) *adj* out of place; not harmonious. **incongruity** *n* < Latin *in-* + *congruere* to come together, agree.

inconsequential (ɪnˌkɒnsɪˈkwɛnʃəl) *adj* not following logically; irrelevant or insignificant. **inconsequentially** *adv*

inconsiderable (ˌɪnkənˈsɪdərəbl̩) *adj* small and insignificant; trivial. **inconsiderably** *adv*

inconsiderate (ˌɪnkənˈsɪdərət) *adj* not caring for or thinking of others; thoughtless. **inconsiderately** *adv* **inconsiderateness** *n*

incontinent (ɪnˈkɒntɪnənt) *adj* unable to control the discharging of the bladder and bowels. **incontinence** *n* < Latin *in-* not + *continere* to hold, restrain.

inconvenience (ˌɪnkənˈviːnjəns) *n* being inconvenient; something that is inconvenient.
• *vb* cause inconvenience to. **inconvenient** *adj* not convenient; causing slight difficulty or discomfort. **inconveniently** *adv*

incorporate (ɪnˈkɔːpəˌreɪt) *vb* **1** include as a part to form a whole. **2** form into a legal corporation. **incorporation** *n* < Latin *in-* + *corpus* body.

incorrigible (ɪnˈkɒrɪdʒəbl̩) *adj* (of a person or his or her faults, etc.) incapable of correction or improvement: an incorrigible gossip. **incorrigibly** *adv* < Latin *in-* not + *corrigere* to correct.

increase (ɪnˈkriːs) *vb* make or become greater in size, intensity, etc.
• *n* (ˈɪnkriːs) act of increasing; addition or expansion in size, intensity, etc.: a dramatic increase in the number of crimes. **increasingly** *adv* < Latin *in-* + *crescere* to grow.

incredible (ɪnˈkrɛdəbl̩) *adj* **1** unbelievable. **2** (*informal*) amazing. **incredibly** *adv* SEE PANEL.

incredulous (ɪnˈkrɛdʒʊləs) *adj* not willing to believe (something); disbelieving. **incredulity** *n* **incredulously** *adv*

increment (ˈɪnkrɪmənt) *n* an increase, esp. in pay because of a further year's work: annual increments. **incremental** *adj* < SEE **INCREASE.**

incriminate (ɪnˈkrɪmɪˌneɪt) *vb* involve or suggest involvement in a crime or wrongdoing. **incrimination** *n* **incriminatory** *adj* < Latin *in-* + *crimen* accusation, crime.

incubate (ˈɪnkjʊˌbeɪt) *vb* **1** sit on and hatch (eggs). **2** keep in an environment that is favourable for development, hatching, etc. **incubation** *n* incubating; period between the exposure to a disease and the first appearance of its symptoms. **incubator** *n* **1** an apparatus in which eggs are hatched artificially. **2** an apparatus for keeping premature babies in controlled conditions. < Latin *in-* + *cubare* to lie.

inculcate (ˈɪnkʌlˌkeɪt) *vb* instil by persistent, strong teaching. **inculcation** *n* < Latin *in-* + *calcare* to trample.

incumbent (ɪnˈkʌmbənt) *adj* **1** imposed as a duty; obligatory: It is incumbent on him to resign. **2** occupying a position that is mentioned: the incumbent mayor.
• *n* a person who holds a particular office, esp. in the Anglican Church; rector or vicar. < Latin *incumbere* to lie down.

incur (ɪnˈkɜː) *vb* **incurred; incurring** bring upon oneself: Any expenses incurred in your work will be reimbursed. < Latin *in-* + *currere* to run.

incursion (ɪn'kɜːʃən) *n* a sudden, esp. brief attack or raid into another's territory. < SEE **INCUR.**

indebted (ɪn'dɛtɪd) *adj* owing gratitude or money. **indebtedness** *n*

indecent (ɪn'diːsn̩t) *adj* **1** offensive to standards of decency. **2** unseemly. **indecency** *n* **indecently** *adv*

indecipherable (ˌɪndɪ'saɪfərəbl̩) *adj* unable to be deciphered; illegible.

indecisive (ˌɪndɪ'saɪsɪv) *adj* not decisive. **indecision** *n* an inability to make up one's mind.

indeed (ɪn'diːd) *adv* **1** really; in fact: I think, indeed I know, he's right. **2** used to intensify: very old indeed. **3** used to agree with what has just been said: 'Are you going?'—'Indeed I am!' **4** used to express surprise, disbelief, irony, etc.: 'He's been promoted.'—'Oh, has he, indeed?' < Middle English *in* + *dede* deed.

indefatigable (ˌɪndɪ'fætɪgəbl̩) *adj* unable to be tired out. < Latin *in-* + *defatigare* to fatigue.

indefinite (ɪn'dɛfənət) *adj* **1** not clearly defined or decided; vague. **2** with no exact limits. **indefinite article** a word such as a or some. **indefinitely** *adv* **1** in an indefinite way. **2** for an unlimited length of time.

indelible (ɪn'dɛləbl̩) *adj* **1** incapable of being erased or removed. **2** (of a pencil) making indelible marks. **indelibly** *adv* < Latin *in-* not + *delēre* to delete.

indelicate (ɪn'dɛləkət) *adj* **1** slightly indecent; crude or rough. **2** offensive or embarrassing to good manners or taste. **indelicacy** *n* **indelicately** *adv*

indemnify (ɪn'dɛmnɪˌfaɪ) *vb* **indemnified; indemnifying 1** secure against harm, loss, or damage. **2** compensate for an injury suffered. **indemnity** *n* security against harm, loss, or damage. < Latin *in-* + *damnum* damage.

indent (ɪn'dɛnt) *vb* **1** position (a line of written or printed matter) in from the margin. **2** order by indent.
• *n* ('ɪnˌdɛnt) an official order for goods or stores. **indentation** *n* **1** a notched or cut place as on an edge or coastline. **2** indenting on a paper, etc. < Latin *in-* + *dens* tooth.

indenture (ɪn'dɛntʃə) *n* **1** a written contract or agreement. **2** a written agreement between a master and apprentice.

independent (ˌɪndɪ'pɛndənt) *adj* **1** self-governing: independent states. **2** objective and unbiased: an independent report. **3** self-confident and able to act for oneself: He likes to be independent. **4** marked by a lack of dependence on others for financial support: independent means. **5** not belonging to a larger unit. **6** not committed to a political party. **7** (of broadcasting) not financed by fees from licences. **8** unrelated or unconnected: The two attacks were entirely independent. **independence** *n* **independently** *adv*

in-depth (ˌɪn'dɛpθ) *adj* thorough and detailed: an in-depth report.

indescribable (ˌɪndɪ'skraɪbəbl̩) *adj* too extreme to be described. **indescribably** *adv*

indeterminable (ˌɪndɪ'tɜːmɪnəbl̩) *adj* incapable of being determined or

---

How incredible!

The negative prefix in- has provided a great number of antonyms, such as *in*decent, *in*conspicuous, and *in*valid. What is interesting about this prefix is the way it changes according to the first sound of the word or *stem* to which it is attached. For example, we say *im*possible not *in*possible, *im*proper not *in*proper, *im*movable not *in*movable, and *im*pure not *in*pure. The reason for the change in such instances from in- to im- becomes immediately obvious upon trying to pronounce, say, *in*proper or *in*movable. The effort involved in pronouncing in- before stems beginning with p or m is simply too much. With im- the lips are already in the right position for pronouncing the stem and the articulation is therefore relatively effortless.

The same principle of avoiding unnecessary effort lies behind the two other variants of in-. Before stems beginning with l, it changes to il- as in *il*legible, *il*liberal, and *il*legal, and before stems beginning with r, it becomes ir- as in *ir*responsible and *ir*relevant.

Further examples of such words beginning with im- and ir- include:

immoderate
immodest
impassable
impenetrable
imprecise

irrational
irreplaceable
irretrievable
irreverent

settled. **indeterminably** *adv* SEE PANEL.

indeterminate (ˌɪndɪˈtɜːmənət) *adj* not fixed or definite in extent, amount, etc.; vague. SEE PANEL AT **INDETERMINABLE.**

index (ˈɪndɛks) *n, pl* **indexes, indices** **1** a list, esp. arranged alphabetically at the back of a book, of names, subjects, etc., with page numbers showing where each appears in the text. **2** a catalogue: a card index; a library index. **3** a pointer or indication. **4** a number used to indicate relative changes in value when compared with an earlier time: the retail-price index. • *vb* **1** make an index to (a book, etc.). **2** make (wages, pensions, etc.) index-linked. **indexer** *n* **indexation** *n* making (pensions, etc.) index-linked. **index finger** the forefinger. **index-linked** *adj* (of wages, pensions, etc.) rising or falling in value according to changes in the cost-of-living index. < Latin *indicare* to indicate. SEE PANEL AT **APPENDIX.**

indicate (ˈɪndɪˌkeɪt) *vb* **1** point to or show; be a sign of. **2** suggest the need for. **3** state briefly. **indication** *n* **indicator** *n* **1** something that indicates, esp. a pointer or needle on an instrument. **2** a device such as a flashing light used to show that a vehicle is about to change direction. < Latin *in-* + *dicare* to proclaim.

indicative (ɪnˈdɪkətɪv) *adj* **1** serving to indicate. **2** (of a form of a verb) used chiefly to make statements. • *n* an indicative verb.

indict (ɪnˈdaɪt) *vb* charge with an offence or crime. **indictable** *adj* (of an offence) making a person liable to be indicted. **indictment** *n* **1** a formal, written statement of charges against an accused person. **2** a serious condemnation. < alteration of *indite,* ultimately from Latin *in-* + *dicere* to say.

indifferent (ɪnˈdɪfrənt) *adj* **1** showing no concern or interest: He was completely indifferent to the dangers involved. **2** neither good nor bad. **3** not very good. **indifference** *n* **indifferently** *adv*

indigenous (ɪnˈdɪdʒənəs) *adj* **1** originating or occurring naturally (in a country, area, etc.); native (to). **2** made or grown locally; not foreign. < Old Latin *indu* in + Latin *gignere* to beget.

indigent (ˈɪndɪdʒənt) *adj* (*formal*) poor and needy. < Old Latin *indu* in + Latin *egēre* to need.

indigestion (ˌɪndɪˈdʒɛstʃən) *n* difficulty in digesting food; pain caused by this.

indignant (ɪnˈdɪgnənt) *adj* feeling or marked by indignation. **indignantly** *adv* **indignation** *n* anger aroused by something unjust, wrong, etc. < Latin *in-* not + *dignus* worthy.

indignity (ɪnˈdɪgnɪtɪ) *n* treatment that offends a person's dignity or self-respect; humiliation.

indigo (ˈɪndɪˌgəʊ) *n* a dark, greyish-blue colour or dye. < Spanish, ultimately Greek *Indos,* India.

indirect (ˌɪndɪˈrɛkt) *adj* not direct. **indirectly** *adv* **indirect tax** a tax not paid directly by the tax-payer to the government, but collected by suppliers, etc., for example value-added tax.

indiscretion (ˌɪndɪˈskrɛʃən) *n* lack of discretion; act or remark showing this.

indiscriminate (ˌɪndɪˈskrɪmənət) *adj* showing no discrimination or careful choice; random; reckless. **indiscriminately** *adv* SEE PANEL.

indispensable (ˌɪndɪˈspɛnsəbl̩) *adj* essential; necessary. **indispensability** *n*

indisposed (ˌɪndɪˈspəʊzd) *adj* **1** slightly unwell. **2** unwilling; disinclined. **indisposition** *n*

indissoluble (ˌɪndɪˈsɒljʊbl̩) *adj* incapable of being dissolved or destroyed; firm and permanent.

indistinguishable (ˌɪndɪˈstɪŋgwɪʃəbl̩) *adj* not able to be distinguished. **indistinguishably** *adv*

individual (ˌɪndɪˈvɪdjʊəl) *adj* **1** separate:

---

indeterminable or **indeterminate?**

These two words are sometimes confused. Indeterminable means 'incapable of being determined or settled' as in The demand for the new product is still *indeterminable* at this stage; an *indeterminable* response.

Indeterminate means 'not fixed or definite in extent, amount, etc.; vague': of *indeterminate* length, a programme of *indeterminate* duration.

---

indiscriminate or **undiscriminating?**

These two words are sometimes confused. A person who lacks an ability to distinguish between different things may be described as undiscriminating: He tends to be *undiscriminating* in his choice of wine.

Indiscriminate means 'random; reckless': the *indiscriminate* killing of innocent citizens.

---

the individual parts of a machine. **2** of or for one person: individual portions. **3** having great individuality; distinctive.
• *n* **1** one person, being, or thing, in contrast to a group. **2** (*informal*) a person. **individually** *adv* **individualist** *n* a person who shows great individuality and independence in thought and action. **individualism** *n* **individualistic** *adj* **individuality** *n* **1** unique character. **2** the qualities that distinguish one person from another, esp. concerning independence and self-reliance. < Latin *in-* not + *dividuus* divisible.

indoctrinate (ɪn'dɒktrɪˌneɪt) *vb* fill (the mind of a person) with a teaching or set of beliefs. **indoctrination** *n*

indolent ('ɪndələnt) *adj* avoiding work; lazy. **indolence** *n* **indolently** *adv* < Latin *in-* not + *dolēre* to feel pain.

indomitable (ɪn'dɒmɪtəbl̩) *adj* not capable of being subdued or overcome: indomitable courage. **indomitably** *adv* < Latin *in-* not + *domitare* to tame.

indoor (ˌɪn'dɔː) *adj* belonging to or done in the inside of a building. **indoors** *adv* in or into a building.

indubitable (ɪn'djuːbɪtəbl̩) *adj* incapable of being doubted. **indubitably** *adv* < Latin *in-* + *dubitare* to doubt.

induce (ɪn'djuːs) *vb* **1** bring on; cause or produce. **2** persuade or influence. **3** cause labour to begin, as by the use of drugs. **4** draw (a conclusion) from facts or examples. **inducement** *n* something that induces, esp. a means of persuasion. < Latin *in-* + *ducere* to lead.

induct (ɪn'dʌkt) *vb* bring formally into an office. **induction** *n* **1** inducting. **2** the method or an instance of reasoning by which a general principle is inferred from facts. **3** (*physics*) a change in the state of a body produced by an electric or magnetic field. **inductive** *adj* < SEE INDUCE.

industrial action

The expression industrial action refers to disruptive activities such as strikes, go-slows, work-to-rules, and overtime bans, which seek to put pressure on an employer or management to gain concessions from them. Despite its name, however, industrial action can be staged outside industry proper, for example in the Civil Service.

indulge (ɪn'dʌldʒ) *vb* **1** satisfy; give free rein to. **2** allow (oneself) to have what one wishes. **3** pander to the wishes of. **indulgence** *n* **1** indulging. **2** something indulged in. **indulgent** *adj* showing indulgence. **indulgently** *adv* < Latin *indulgēre* to be kind to.

industry ('ɪndəstrɪ) *n* **1** a branch of organized activity, esp. manufacturing a particular product or group of products: the motor industry. **2** manufacturing activity considered generally: Industry is getting back to work after the Christmas break. **3** persistent hard work and diligence. **industrial** *adj* **1** of or concerned with industry. **2** having many highly-developed industries: the industrial countries. **industrially** *adv* **industrialist** *n* a person who controls or runs a large, industrial business. **industrialized** *adj* made industrial. **industrious** *adj* persistently hard-working and diligent. **industriously** *adv* < Latin *industrius* active. SEE PANEL.

inebriate (ɪn'iːbrɪˌeɪt) *vb* make drunk; intoxicate. **inebriation** *n* < Latin *in-* + *ebriare* to intoxicate.

ineffable (ɪn'ɛfəbl̩) *adj* too great to be uttered or described. **ineffably** *adv* < Latin *in-* not + *effabilis* capable of being expressed.

inept (ɪn'ɛpt) *adj* **1** not suitable. **2** awkward and generally incompetent. **ineptitude** *n* **ineptly** *adv* < Latin *in-* + *aptus* apt.

inequality (ˌɪnɪ'kwɒlɪtɪ) *n* lack of equality in size, social and economic opportunity, standard, etc.

inert (ɪn'ɜːt) *adj* **1** not having the power to move. **2** (of a gas) unreactive. **3** slow to move; inactive. **inertly** *adv* **inertness** *n* **inertia** *n* **1** the state of being inert; unwillingness to move, change, etc. **2** a property of matter that causes it to resist any change in its motion. < Latin *in-* not + *ars* art, skill.

inescapable (ˌɪnɪ'skeɪpəbl̩) *adj* that cannot be avoided. **inescapably** *adv*

inestimable (ɪn'ɛstɪməbl̩) *adj* too great, precious, etc., to be estimated or measured. **inestimably** *adv*

inevitable (ɪn'ɛvɪtəbl̩) *adj* that cannot be avoided; certain. **inevitability** *n* **inevitably** *adv* < Latin *in-* + *evitabilis* avoidable.

inexcusable (ˌɪnɪk'skjuːzəbl̩) *adj* unable to be excused or justified.

inexhaustible (ˌɪnɪg'zɔːstəbl̩) *adj* incapable of being used up completely.

inexorable (ɪn'ɛksərəbl̩) *adj* **1** relentless. **2** unable to be moved by persuasion.

inexorably *adv* < Latin *in-* + *ex-* + *orare* to speak.

inexpensive (ˌɪnɪkˈspɛnsɪv) *adj* good value for the price; cheap. **inexpensively** *adv*

inexperience (ˌɪn ɪkˈspɪərɪəns) *n* lack of experience. **inexperienced** *adj*

inexpert (ɪnˈɛkspɜːt) *adj* not expert or skilled. **inexpertly** *adv*

inexplicable (ˌɪnɪkˈsplɪkəbl̩) *adj* incapable of being explained or accounted for. **inexplicably** *adv*

in extremis (ɪn ɪkˈstriːmɪs) *adv* (*Latin*) in great difficulties, esp. at the point of death.

inextricable (ˌɪnɪkˈstrɪkəbl̩) *adj* **1** that one cannot extricate oneself from. **2** that cannot be disentangled. **inextricably** *adv*

infallible (ɪnˈfæləbl̩) *adj* **1** incapable of error. **2** not liable to fail. **infallibility** *n* **infallibly** *adv*

infamous (ˈɪnfəməs) *adj* having a very bad reputation; notorious or disgraceful. **infamy** *n*

infant (ˈɪnfənt) *n* a child in the first period of its life. **infancy** *n* **1** early childhood. **2** an early stage of development: The project is still in its infancy. **infanticide** *n* the killing of a newly born child. **infantile** *adj* of or like infants; very childish. SEE PANEL.

infantry (ˈɪnfəntrɪ) *n* soldiers who fight on foot. **infantryman** *n, pl* **infantrymen** an infantry soldier. < Italian *infante* boy, foot soldier.

infatuated (ɪnˈfætjʊˌeɪtɪd) *adj* filled with a very strong, but superficial or temporary love or desire for a person or thing.

infant

The word infant means different things to different people. In strict medical usage it usually designates a young child that has not yet assumed an erect posture. This is in contrast with the British educational usage which refers to a child between the ages of five and seven or eight. Further, in legal usage the word embraces anyone below the age of majority.

According to its roots, however, infant describes a child who is still too young to speak. The word derives via the Middle French *enfant* from the Latin *infans* 'incapable of speech', from the negative prefix *in-* and *fari* 'to speak'.

infatuation *n* < Latin *in-* + *fatuus* fatuous.

infect (ɪnˈfɛkt) *vb* **1** contaminate or affect with a disease by bringing into contact with micro-organisms such as bacteria or viruses. **2** pass on (a feeling). **infection** *n* **1** infecting. **2** the spreading of a disease by infection; disease spread in this way. **infectious** *adj* **1** capable of causing infection. **2** communicable by infection. **3** quickly spread to others: infectious laughter. < Latin *in-* + *facere* to make. SEE PANEL AT **CONTAGION.**

infer (ɪnˈfɜː) *vb* **inferred; inferring** conclude from facts or assumptions. **inference** *n* < Latin *in-* + *ferre* to carry. SEE PANEL AT **IMPLY.**

inferior (ɪnˈfɪərɪə) *adj* lower in rank, importance, quality, etc.
• *n* a person inferior to another in rank, etc. **inferiority** *n* < Latin: lower, from *inferus* low.

infernal (ɪnˈfɜːnl̩) *adj* **1** of hell; hellish. **2** (*informal*) outrageous or detestable: What infernal cheek! **infernally** *adv* < Late Latin *infernus* hell, from Latin: lower, hellish.

inferno (ɪnˈfɜːnəʊ) *n, pl* **infernos** a place resembling hell, esp. an intensely hot fire. < Italian, from Late Latin *infernus* hell.

infest (ɪnˈfɛst) *vb* spread in or over in large numbers, esp. producing a harmful effect. **infestation** *n* < Latin *infestus* hostile.

infidel (ˈɪnfɪdl̩) *n* a person who does not believe in a particular religion such as Christianity or Islam or in any religion. **infidelity** *n* **1** lack of belief in a religion. **2** unfaithfulness, esp. in marriage. < Latin *in-* + *fides* faith.

infighting (ˈɪnˌfaɪtɪŋ) *n* **1** intense, often bitter conflict in a group or organization. **2** fighting or boxing at close range.

infiltrate (ˈɪnfɪlˌtreɪt) *vb* **1** cause to permeate. **2** enter unobtrusively and gradually: The soldiers infiltrated enemy lines. **infiltration** *n*

infinite (ˈɪnfɪnət) *adj* **1** having no limits; endless. **2** immeasurably great or numerous. **infinitely** *adv* **infinitude** *n* being infinite; infinity. **infinity** *n* **1** being infinite. **2** an infinite number or extent. < Latin *in-* + *finitus* finite.

infinitesimal (ˌɪnfɪnɪˈtɛsɪməl) *adj* extremely or infinitely small. **infinitesimally** *adv* < SEE **INFINITE.**

infinitive (ɪnˈfɪnɪtɪv) *n* a form of the verb that does not indicate a particular person or tense. < Latin *infinitus.* SEE PANEL AT **TO.**

infirm (ɪnˈfɜːm) *adj* **1** weak in health, esp. from old age. **2** weak in mind or character. **infirmary** *n* a hospital. **infirmity** *n* **1** being infirm. **2** a disease. < Latin *in-* + *firmus* firm.

inflame (ɪnˈfleɪm) *vb* **1** excite intense feeling, such as anger, in. **2** set on fire. **3** cause inflammation in. **inflammable** *adj* capable of burning easily. **inflammation** *n* redness, heat, and painful swelling in the body, caused by injury or infection, etc. **inflammatory** *adj* tending to arouse intense feeling: inflammatory remarks. < Latin *in-* + *flamma* flame. SEE PANEL AT **FLAMMABLE.**

inflatable (ɪnˈfleɪtəbḷ) *adj* capable of being filled with air.

• *n* an inflatable dinghy, toy, etc.

inflate (ɪnˈfleɪt) *vb* **1** fill or become filled with air or gas. **2** cause (prices or the level of economic activity) to rise. **inflation** *n* **1** inflating; being inflated. **2** a general rise in prices. **3** (*informal*) the rate of increase of prices: Inflation is 10% again. **inflationary** *adj* causing inflation. < Latin *in-* + *flare* to blow.

inflect (ɪnˈflɛkt) *vb* **1** change (a word) by inflection. **2** change the pitch of (the voice). **inflection, inflexion** *n* **1** a change in the pitch or loudness of the voice. **2** a change in the ending or form of a word to show its gender, number, tense, etc. < Latin *in-* + *flectere* to bend.

inflexible (ɪnˈflɛksəbḷ) *adj* **1** not flexible; rigid. **2** obstinate; unyielding. **3** not able to be changed; fixed. **inflexibility** *n* **inflexibly** *adv*

inflict (ɪnˈflɪkt) *vb* impose (a blow, pain, a penalty, etc.) on someone. **infliction** *n* < Latin *in-* + *fligere* to strike.

in-flight (ˈɪnˌflaɪt) *adj* made or provided during flight.

inflow (ˈɪnˌfləʊ) *n* a flowing in: an inflow of funds.

influence (ˈɪnflʊəns) *n* **1** the act, power, or ability to produce an effect, esp. in an indirect or intangible way; such an effect. **2** power resulting from position, wealth, etc. **3** a person or thing that has influence, esp. to produce a good or bad effect on another.

• *vb* exert influence on. **influential** *adj* having great influence. < Latin *in-* + *fluere* to flow.

influenza (ˌɪnflʊˈɛnzə) *n* a virus disease marked by chills, fever, aches and pains, and catarrh. < Medieval Latin *influentia.* SEE PANEL.

influx (ˈɪnˌflʌks) *n* a flowing in, esp. in large numbers or amounts.

inform (ɪnˈfɔːm) *vb* **1** communicate information to. **2** give information to the police, etc., about criminal activities; betray to the police, etc. **informant** *n* a person who gives information. **information** *n* **1** facts, ideas, or data; news. **2** knowledge derived from study or instruction. **3** informing. **informative** *adj* giving information. **informer** *n* a person who gives information about criminal activities to the police, etc. < Latin *informare* to give shape to.

informal (ɪnˈfɔːməl) *adj* lacking formality or ceremony. **informality** *n* **informally** *adv*

infra-red (ˌɪnfrəˈrɛd) *adj* (of radiation) having a wavelength in the electromagnetic spectrum between the red end of visible light and microwaves. < Latin *infra-* below, beneath + *red.*

infrastructure (ˈɪnfrəˌstrʌktʃə) *n* **1** a basic, underlying framework. **2** the extensive public services such as power supplies and communication systems that are needed to support a country's industry. < Latin *infra-* below + *structure.*

infringe (ɪnˈfrɪndʒ) *vb* break (an agreement, etc.); violate; encroach (on). **infringement** *n* < Latin *infringere* to break off, from *frangere* to break.

infuriate (ɪnˈfjʊərɪˌeɪt) *vb* anger; enrage. < Latin *infuriare,* from *in-* + *furia* fury.

infuse (ɪnˈfjuːz) *vb* **1** fill or inspire; imbue. **2** steep in a liquid, without boiling, in order to extract the soluble constituents. **infusion** *n* **1** infusing. **2** a continuous introduction of something, as a liquid into a vein. **3** an extract obtained from infusing. < Latin *infundere* to pour in.

ingenious (ɪnˈdʒiːnjəs) *adj* original,

---

influenza

The origin of influenza tells us a great deal about people's attitudes to illness in days gone by. The word derives via Italian from the Latin word *influentia*, meaning 'influence'. Nowadays when influence is mentioned in the context of illness, it usually refers to the influence of drink. However, in medieval times a person with influenza was suffering not from the influence of drink but, as superstition had it, from the influence of the stars.

---

inventive, and clever: an ingenious suggestion. **ingeniously** *adv* **ingenuity** *n* < Latin *ingenium* natural capacity. SEE PANEL.

ingenuous (ɪnˈdʒɛnjʊəs) *adj* simple, innocent, and childlike; frank; unsophisticated; naïve. **ingenuously** *adv* **ingenuousness** *n* < Latin *ingenuus* free-born, from *in-* + *gignere* to beget. SEE PANEL AT **INGENIOUS.**

inglorious (ɪnˈglɔːrɪəs) *adj* **1** shameful; dishonourable. **2** not bringing glory; obscure. < Latin *in-* + *gloria* glory.

ingot (ˈɪŋgət) *n* a bar-shaped mass of cast metal. < probably Old English in + *goten,* from *gēotan* to pour, cast.

ingrained (ɪnˈgreɪnd) *adj* **1** firmly and deeply fixed: ingrained habits. **2** (of dirt) worked into a surface deeply.

ingratiate (ɪnˈgreɪʃɪˌeɪt) *vb* put (oneself) into a person's favour deliberately, esp. to gain an advantage. < Latin *in-* + *gratia* grace.

ingredient (ɪnˈgriːdɪənt) *n* one of the parts of a combination or mixture, esp. in cooking. < Latin *ingredi* to go into.

ingrowing (ˈɪnˌgrəʊɪŋ) *adj* (of a toe-nail) growing abnormally into the flesh.

inhabit (ɪnˈhæbɪt) *vb* live or be present in; occupy. **inhabitable** *adj* able to be inhabited. **inhabitant** *n* a person or animal that inhabits a place. < Latin *in-* + *habitare* to dwell.

inhale (ɪnˈheɪl) *vb* breathe in. **inhalation** *n* **inhaler** *n* a device for inhaling medicinal vapours, esp. to relieve congestion in the nose. < Latin *in-* in + *halare* to breathe.

inherent (ɪnˈhɪərənt, ɪnˈhɛrənt) *adj* belonging to the essential nature or constitution of something. **inherently** *adv* < Latin *inhaerēre,* from *in-* + *haerēre* to adhere.

inherit (ɪnˈhɛrɪt) *vb* **1** receive by legal right from an ancestor after his or her death. **2** receive from a predecessor. **3** receive by genetic transmission. **inheritance** *n* **inheritor** *n* < Latin *in-* + *hereditas* inheritance.

inhibit (ɪnˈhɪbɪt) *vb* **1** restrain or hinder from an activity. **2** restrain or prohibit. **inhibition** *n* **1** inhibiting or being inhibited. **2** something that restrains or prohibits. **3** a psychological restraint on an activity. < Latin *in-* + *habēre* to have.

inhospitable (ˌɪnhɒˈspɪtəbl̩) *adj* **1** not given to hospitality. **2** (of a place) providing no shelter or favourable climate.

in-house (ˈɪnˌhaʊs) *adj* being or done within an organization, company, etc.

inhuman (ɪnˈhjuːmən) *adj* lacking normal qualities such as kindness or compassion; cruel. **inhumanity** *n*

inimical (ɪˈnɪmɪkl̩) *adj* unfriendly or unfavourable. < Latin *inimicus* enemy.

inimitable (ɪˈnɪmɪtəbl̩) *adj* that cannot be imitated.

iniquity (ɪˈnɪkwɪtɪ) *n* great injustice; wickedness. **iniquitous** *adj* < Latin *in* + *aequus* even, level.

initial (ɪˈnɪʃəl) *adj* of or concerning the beginning: the initial stages of a project.
• *n* the first letter of a word, esp. of each of a person's names.
• *vb* **initialled; initialling** put initials on, as a signature or authorization. **initially** *adv* < Latin *initium* beginning, from *inire* to go into.

initiate (ɪˈnɪʃɪˌeɪt) *vb* **1** cause the beginning of; start. **2** give (a person) the basic information about something unfamiliar. **3** admit (a person) into membership of a society, etc., esp. with special ceremonies.
• *n* (ɪˈnɪʃɪət) an initiated person. **initiation** *n* **initiator** *n* **initiatory** *adj* < SEE **INITIAL.**

initiative (ɪˈnɪʃətɪv) *n* **1** the ability to initiate things; resourcefulness and enterprise. **2** the first step or action in something: a new peace initiative. **3** the power or right to begin something. **on one's own initiative** without being prompted. **take the initiative** be the first to act.

inject (ɪnˈdʒɛkt) *vb* **1** force or drive (a liquid, etc.) into something, esp. using a syringe. **2** introduce: Let's hope the new chairman will inject some fresh ideas into the club! **injection** *n* < Latin *in-* + *jacere* to throw.

---

ingenious or **ingenuous?**

Ingenious means 'original, inventive, and clever' and can refer to things or people: an *ingenious* suggestion, an *ingenious,* creative film director, an *ingenious* toy.

Ingenuous is a rarer word and means 'simple, innocent, and childlike': an *ingenuous* look on his face.

The noun derived from ingenious is ingenuity: The sheer *ingenuity* of his productions is striking, and from ingenuous, ingenuousness.

---

injunction (ɪnˈdʒʌŋkʃən) *n* a legal instruction or order issued by a court, stating that something must or must not be done. < Latin *injungere* to enjoin.

injure (ˈɪndʒə) *vb* **1** cause physical hurt to. **2** do injustice to; wrong. **3** offend, esp. by an injustice. **injurious** *adj* causing or likely to cause injury. **injury** *n* **1** harm or damage. **2** a wrong; injustice. < *injury*: from Latin *in-* + *jus* right.

injustice (ɪnˈdʒʌstɪs) *n* lack of justice; unjust act.

ink (ɪŋk) *n* a coloured liquid used for writing and printing.
• *vb* put ink on. **inky** *adj* **1** stained with ink. **2** like the colour of ink, esp. dark. < Greek *enkaiein* to burn in.

inkling (ˈɪŋklɪŋ) *n* a slight suggestion; hint or suspicion. < probably Middle English *inclen* to hint at.

inlaid (ɪnˈleɪd) SEE **INLAY.**

inland (ˈɪnlənd) *adj* (also *adv* ˈɪnˌlænd) concerning, in, or towards the interior of a country.

in-law (ˈɪnˌlɔː) *n* a relative by marriage: We'll be visiting my in-laws for the New Year.

inlay (ɪnˈleɪ) *vb* **inlaid; inlaying 1** set (pieces of wood, ivory, etc.) into a surface for decoration or strengthening. **2** decorate with such materials.
• *n* (ˈɪnˌleɪ) **1** inlaid material or pattern. **2** a dental filling that fits into a cavity.

inlet (ˈɪnˌlɛt) *n* **1** a narrow strip of water extending into a coastline or between two land areas. **2** an entrance, esp. for a liquid to enter a device.

inmate (ˈɪnˌmeɪt) *n* a person who is confined to a prison or other institution.

inmost (ˈɪnˌməʊst) *adj* furthest in; deepest: my inmost thoughts.

inn (ɪn) *n* a pub or small hotel that provides lodging and food. **innkeeper** *n* the landlord of an inn. < Old English. SEE PANEL.

innards (ˈɪnədz) *pl n* (*informal*) **1** the internal organs of the body, esp. the viscera. **2** the inner parts of a machine, computer, etc. < alteration of *inwards*.

innate (ɪˈneɪt) *adj* inborn; inherent. **innately** *adv* < Latin *in-* + *nasci* to be born.

inner (ˈɪnə) *adj* **1** situated within or nearer to the centre: the inner door; an inner ring road. **2** of the mind, soul, or feelings: one's inner life; inner excitement. **innermost** *adj* furthest inward; deepest: one's innermost feelings.

innings (ˈɪnɪŋz) *n, pl* **innings** one of the divisions of a cricket match in which one side bats and the other bowls; batsman's turn at batting.

innocent (ˈɪnəsənt) *adj* **1** declared free from guilt or sin, esp. not guilty of a particular crime. **2** harmless: an innocent remark. **3** simple; naïve; foolishly trustful. **4** ignorant.
• *n* an innocent person, esp. a child or a foolishly trustful adult. **innocence** *n* **innocently** *adv* < Latin *in-* not + *nocēre* to harm.

innocuous (ɪˈnɒkjʊəs) *adj* harmless; inoffensive. **innocuously** *adv* < SEE **INNOCENT.**

innovate (ˈɪnəˌveɪt) *vb* introduce something new. **innovation** *n* **innovative** *adj* **innovator** *n* < Latin *in-* + *novus* new.

innuendo (ˌɪnjʊˈəndəʊ) *n, pl* **innuendoes** an indirect reference or allusion, esp. one made with harmful intention. < Latin *innuere* to nod to.

innumerable (ɪˈnjuːmərəbḷ) *adj* too many to be counted; countless. **innumerably** *adv*

inoculate (ɪˈnɒkjʊˌleɪt) *vb* inject an immunizing vaccine into; vaccinate. **inoculation** *n* < Latin *in-* + *oculus* eye.

inoffensive (ˌɪnəˈfɛnsɪv) *adj* harmless; not unpleasant.

inoperable (ɪnˈɒpərəbḷ) *adj* unsuitable for surgical operation without risk; incurable.

inoperative (ɪnˈɒpərətɪv) *adj* not functioning; ineffective.

inordinate (ɪnˈɔːdɪnət) *adj* excessive. **inordinately** *adv*

inorganic (ˌɪnɔːˈgænɪk) *adj* **1** of mineral sources; not organic. **2** of a branch of chemistry concerned with inorganic substances.

input (ˈɪnˌpʊt) *n* **1** putting in; amount put in. **2** something supplied to a machine, computer, etc.; place where this enters a

Inns of Court

Apart from being 'a public house or small hotel', an inn used to be a residence for students, especially those studying law. This usage now only survives in the name Inns of Court. The Inns of Court are the four associations in the United Kingdom that have the exclusive right of conferring the degree of barrister-at-law, known as calling to the Bar. The four Inns of Court are: Lincoln's Inn, Inner Temple, Middle Temple, and Gray's Inn.

system. **3** a factor of production such as land, labour, or materials.

inquest (ˈɪnˌkwɛst) *n* **1** an investigation, esp. by a coroner, into the cause of a death. **2** (*informal*) an investigation into something that has failed. < Latin *inquaerere* to inquire.

inquire (ɪnˈkwaɪə) *vb* ask about; seek information by questioning. **inquirer** *n* **inquiry** *n* < Latin *in-* + *quaerere* to seek. SEE PANEL AT **ENQUIRE.**

inquisition (ˌɪnkwɪˈzɪʃən) *n* a detailed, esp. ruthless investigation. **inquisitor** *n* a person who inquires deeply or ruthlessly. < SEE **INQUIRE.**

inquisitive (ɪnˈkwɪzɪtɪv) *adj* **1** eager to learn. **2** too curious about other people's affairs; prying. **inquisitively** *adv* **inquisitiveness** *n*

inroad (ˈɪnˌrəʊd) *n* **1** a raid or incursion. **2** a significant advance: The Germans have made great inroads into the British market.

insane (ɪnˈseɪn) *adj* **1** not sane; mentally disordered. **2** very foolish. **insanely** *adv* **insanity** *n*

insanitary (ɪnˈsænɪtərɪ) *adj* sufficiently unclean to endanger health.

insatiable (ɪnˈseɪʃəbl̩) *adj* not able to be satisfied: insatiable curiosity. **insatiably** *adv* < Latin *in-* + *satiare* to satisfy.

inscribe (ɪnˈskraɪb) *vb* **1** write, cut, or mark (words, a design, etc.) on (a surface). **2** record on a list. **3** dedicate (a book, etc.) to someone by signing one's name on it. **inscription** *n* < Latin *in-* + *scribere* to write.

inscrutable (ɪnˈskruːtəbl̩) *adj* very difficult to understand or interpret; enigmatic. < Latin *in-* + *scrutari* to search.

insect (ˈɪnsəkt) *n* a small, invertebrate animal, with a head, a thorax of three segments, and an abdomen. **insecticide** *n* a substance for killing insects by chemical action. < Latin *insectum* notched.

insecure (ˌɪnsɪˈkjʊə) *adj* **1** not secure, safe, or stable. **2** not confident. **insecurely** *adv* **insecurity** *n*

inseminate (ɪnˈsɛmɪˌneɪt) *vb* impregnate with semen. **insemination** *n* < Latin *in-* + *semen* seed.

insensible (ɪnˈsɛnsəbl̩) *adj* **1** not capable of feeling; unconscious. **2** not capable of being felt. **3** unconcerned; callous. **insensibility** *n*

insert (ɪnˈsɜːt) *vb* put in or between.
• *n* (ˈɪnsɜːt) a thing inserted. **insertion** *n* < Latin *in-* + *serere* to join.

in-service (ˌɪnˈsɜːvɪs) *adj* undertaken during one's career: in-service training.

inset (ɪnˈsɛt) *vb* **inset; insetting** put or set in.
• *n* (ˈɪnˌsɛt) **1** something inserted. **2** a small illustration set within a larger one. **3** a piece of fabric set into a garment for decoration, shaping, etc.

inshore (ˌɪnˈʃɔː) *adj, adv* near or towards the shore.

inside (ˌɪnˈsaɪd, ˈɪnsaɪd) *n* **1** the inner part or surface. **2** often **insides** (*informal*) the internal organs of the body, esp. the stomach and bowels.
• *adj* (ˈɪnsaɪd) on, near, or towards the inside.
• *adv* (ɪnˈsaɪd) on, in, or to the inside.
• *prep* (ˌɪnˈsaɪd) in or to the inside of; within: inside the house; I'll be back inside half an hour! **inside information** confidential information provided by someone within an organization, esp. illicitly. **inside job** a crime committed against an organization by one of its members. **inside out 1** with the inner and outer sides reversed. **2** very thoroughly: She knows her job inside out. **insider** *n* a person who is recognized as a member of a particular group or one with access to confidential information.

insidious (ɪnˈsɪdɪəs) *adj* acting in a subtle, but harmful way. **insidiously** *adv* **insidiousness** *n* < Latin *insidiae* ambush.

insight (ˈɪnˌsaɪt) *n* the ability to perceive the true nature of something complex or difficult; knowledge obtained by this.

insignia (ɪnˈsɪgnɪə) *pl n* symbols of authority, office, or honour. < Latin *in-* + *signum* mark, sign.

insignificant (ˌɪnsɪgˈnɪfɪkənt) *adj* **1** not having meaning or importance. **2** very small in value, size, etc. **insignificance** *n* **insignificantly** *adv*

insinuate (ɪnˈsɪnjʊˌeɪt) *vb* **1** introduce or suggest (something unpleasant) indirectly. **2** cause (someone, esp. oneself) to be accepted by cunning. **insinuation** *n* < Latin *in-* + *sinuare* to bend.

insipid (ɪnˈsɪpɪd) *adj* lacking in flavour or lively qualities. **insipidity** *n* **insipidly** *adv* < Latin *in-* + *sapidus* savoury, from *sapere* to taste.

insist (ɪnˈsɪst) *vb* maintain a demand, course of action, etc., strongly, in spite of objections from others: They insisted on paying for the meal. **insistent** *adj* **1** insisting strongly. **2** demanding attention. **insistence** *n* **insistently** *adv* < Latin *in-* + *sistere* to stand.

in situ (ɪn ˈsɪtjuː) *adj, adv* (*Latin*) in the natural, original, or suitable position.

insobriety (ˌɪnsəˈbraɪətɪ) *n* intemper-

ance; drunkenness.
in so far *conj* to the extent (that).
insolent (ˈɪnsələnt) *adj* disrespectfully rude; impudent. **insolence** *n* **insolently** *adv* < Latin *in-* + *solere* to be accustomed.
insoluble (ɪnˈsɒljʊbl) *adj* **1** incapable of being solved or explained: insoluble problems. **2** incapable of being dissolved.
insolvent (ɪnˈsɒlvənt) *adj* unable to pay one's debts. **insolvency** *n*
insomnia (ɪnˈsɒmnɪə) *n* inability to sleep adequately. **insomniac** *n* a person who suffers from insomnia. < Latin *in-* + *somnus* sleep.
insomuch (ˌɪnsəʊˈmʌtʃ) *conj* to such a degree (that).
inspect (ɪnˈspɛkt) *vb* **1** examine carefully and critically. **2** examine officially. **inspection** *n* **inspector** *n* **1** a person who inspects, esp. officially. **2** a police officer ranking immediately above a sergeant. < Latin *in-* + *specere* to look.
inspire (ɪnˈspaɪə) *vb* **1** arouse (respect, trust, confidence, etc.) in (a person). **2** act as a stimulus for (a person), esp. to think or work creatively. **3** guide by divine communication. **inspiration** *n* **1** inspiring or being inspired. **2** an inspired idea. **3** an inspiring influence. < Latin *in-* + *spirare* to breathe.
inst. *abbrev* instant (this month). SEE PANEL.
install (ɪnˈstɔːl) *vb* **1** place in position and connect, ready for use: to install central heating. **2** place (a person) in office, esp. with formal ceremonies. **3** establish in a place, status, etc., that is mentioned. **installation** *n* **1** installing; being installed. **2** the device, machinery, etc., that is installed. < Medieval Latin *in-* + *stallum* stall. SEE PANEL.
instalment (ɪnˈstɔːlmənt) *n* **1** any of the parts into which a debt is divided when repayment is to be made over a period of time. **2** any of the parts into which something such as a magazine or broadcast story is presented over a period of time. < probably Old French *estaler* to place.
instance (ˈɪnstəns) *n* a case or particular example.
instant (ˈɪnstənt) *adj* **1** immediate: The film was an instant success. **2** (of food) designed to be prepared quickly and easily.
• *n* the briefest space of time; point in time between two states: He hesitated for an instant. **instantaneous** *adj* immediate. **instantaneously** *adv* immediately. **instantly** *adv* immediately. < Latin *instare* to stand upon.
instead (ɪnˈstɛd) *adv* as a substitute or alternative. < Middle English *in stead* in place.
instep (ˈɪnˌstɛp) *n* **1** the upper surface of the middle part of the foot; arched section between the toes and ankle. **2** the part of a shoe, etc., covering this. < probably *in* + *step*.
instigate (ˈɪnstɪˌgeɪt) *vb* **1** set up or begin (an investigation, course of action, etc.). **2** urge or incite; provoke. **instigation** *n* **instigator** *n* < Latin *instigare* to urge on.
instil (ɪnˈstɪl) *vb* **instilled; instilling** introduce into a person's mind gradually. < Latin *in-* + *stillare* to drip.
instinct (ˈɪnstɪŋkt) *n* **1** the inborn capacity to respond in certain ways, esp. not using reason; such a response: to trust one's instinct. **2** a natural impulse or ability. **instinctive** *adj* **instinctively** *adv* < Latin *instinguere* to incite.
institute (ˈɪnstɪˌtjuːt) *vb* **1** establish; organize. **2** initiate; begin: institute an inquiry.
• *n* an organization for an educational,

instant dates

The expressions inst. or instant ('this month'), ult. or ultimo ('last month'), and prox. or proximo ('next month') are now considered old-fashioned commercial jargon. It is best to avoid these Latin abbreviations and instead state the name of the month. Thus, Thank you for your letter of the *12th inst* ... could become Thank you for your letter of *12 May* ....

install or **instal?**

Two l's are preferred in the spelling of install: It has become necessary to *install* a new air-conditioning system. The spelling with one l is, however, also found. Note that if the spelling with one l is used, then it follows the general rule of doubling the l before suffixes beginning with a vowel letter. Hence installing, installed, installation, installer. In British English instalment has one l, while the usual American spelling has two l's: installment.

social, etc., activity: the Commonwealth Institute. **institution** *n* **1** instituting; being instituted. **2** an established custom or practice: the institution of the monarchy. **3** an established organization: a mental institution. **institutional** *adj* **institutionalize** *vb* **1** make into an institution. **2** place or confine in an institution; subject to the harmful effects of an institution. < Latin *in-* + *statuere* to set up.

instruct (ɪnˈstrʌkt) *vb* **1** direct (someone) authoritatively; order. **2** teach. **3** inform. **4** authorize (a barrister, etc.) to act on one's behalf. **instructor** *n* **instruction** *n* **1** an authoritative order. **2** teaching. **3** *pl* guidelines on the use, operation, etc., of something: Have you read the maker's instructions? **instructional** *adj* **instructive** *adj* giving information or instructions; enlightening. < Latin *in-* + *struere* to build. SEE PANEL.

instrument (ˈɪnstrəmənt) *n* **1** a device or tool used for delicate or scientific work. **2** a device designed to produce music. **3** a means of achieving something; factor or agency. **4** a device for use in navigating or controlling an aircraft, etc. **5** a formal, legal document. **instrumental** *adj* **1** serving as an instrument, means, etc., for doing something. **2** performed on musical instruments. **instrumentalist** *n* a player of a musical instrument. **instrumentation** *n* **1** the arrangement or composition of music for instruments. **2** the use of instruments. **3** a means; agency. < SEE INSTRUCT.

insubordinate (ˌɪnsəˈbɔːdɪnət) *adj* not submissive to authority. **insubordination** *n*

insubstantial (ˌɪnsəbˈstænʃəl) *adj* **1** not substantial; not real; slight. **2** not well founded; weak; flimsy.

insufferable (ɪnˈsʌfərəbl̩) *adj* intolerable or unbearable: insufferable noise.

> **instructional** or **instructive?**
>
> Instructional is a fairly rare word and means 'having the character of instruction; educational' as in a series of *instructional* programmes on the art of ceramics.
>
> Instructive is a commoner word and means 'giving information or instructions; enlightening or informative' as in I thought the exhibition was most *instructive*.

insular (ˈɪnsjʊlə) *adj* **1** of or like an island or islanders. **2** narrow-minded. **insularity** *n* < Latin *insula* island.

insulate (ˈɪnsjʊˌleɪt) *vb* **1** separate, cover, or provide with a material that prevents or reduces the transmission of electricity, heat, or sound. **2** isolate or separate. **insulation** *n* **insulator** *n* < Late Latin *insulatus* made into an island.

insulin (ˈɪnsjʊlɪn) *n* a protein hormone secreted in the pancreas in response to much glucose in the blood. < Latin *insula* island (of tissue in the pancreas).

insult (ɪnˈsʌlt) *vb* treat or talk to rudely and offensively.
• *n* (ˈɪnsʌlt) an insulting remark, action, etc. < Latin *insultare* to spring upon.

insuperable (ɪnˈsjuːpərəbl̩) *adj* incapable of being overcome: insuperable problems. < Latin *in-* not + *superare* to surmount.

insupportable (ˌɪnsəˈpɔːtəbl̩) *adj* **1** intolerable. **2** incapable of being supported or sustained.

insure (ɪnˈʃɔː) *vb* give or obtain an insurance policy for. **insurer** *n* **insurance** *n* **1** the business or practice of insuring lives or property against specified harm, damage, etc., in return for the payment of money; protection so offered. **2** a contract undertaking to provide compensation if a specified event should happen, in return for payment of money; policy. **3** the amount payable to the company, etc., providing such a contract; premium. **4** the amount payable by the company, etc., as compensation. < Middle English *insuren*. SEE PANEL AT ASSURE.

insurgent (ɪnˈsɜːdʒənt) *adj* rebellious.
• *n* a rebel; insurrectionist. **insurgence** or **insurgency** *n* < Latin *in-* + *surgere* to rise.

insurrection (ˌɪnsəˈrɛkʃən) *n* a rebelling against government or civil authorities. **insurrectionist** *n, adj* < SEE INSURGENT.

intact (ɪnˈtækt) *adj* undamaged and complete. < Latin *in-* not + *tangere* to touch.

intake (ˈɪnˌteɪk) *n* **1** the people, things, quantity, etc., taken in: a new intake of students. **2** a taking in. **3** an opening through which air, a liquid, etc., passes into a system.

integer (ˈɪntɪdʒə) *n* a whole number such as 3, 0, or −17, not a fraction. < Latin: untouched, whole.

integral (ˈɪntɪgrəl) *adj* **1** essential to the completeness of the whole: an integral part. **2** formed of integral parts. **3** entire;

whole. < SEE **INTEGER.**

integrate (ˈɪntɪˌgreɪt) *vb* **1** make or form into a whole. **2** bring or come into equal rights and treatment in a community; desegregate. **integration** *n* **integrated circuit** a miniature electronic circuit comprising a number of components formed within a single chip of silicon or other semiconducting material. < SEE **INTEGER.**

integrity (ɪnˈtɛgrɪtɪ) *n* strong adherence to moral standards; honesty.

intellect (ˈɪntəˌlɛkt) *n* the ability to think, reason, and understand, esp. when highly developed and in contrast to feeling or wishing. < SEE **INTELLIGENCE.**

intellectual (ˌɪntəˈlɛktʃʊəl) *adj* **1** of the intellect. **2** appealing to or of people with a highly developed intellect and advanced tastes in literature, art, etc. • *n* an intellectual person. **intellectually** *adv* < SEE **INTELLIGENCE.**

intelligence (ɪnˈtɛlədʒəns) *n* **1** the ability to think, reason, understand, and learn from experience. **2** information about an enemy; group of people or department collecting such information: military intelligence. **intelligent** *adj* having or showing great intelligence. **intelligently** *adv* **intelligentsia** *n* the intellectual group of people in a society. < Latin *intellegere* to choose between.

intense or **intensive?**

Careful users of English distinguish these two words. Intense means 'very strong in quality or degree' as in *intense* heat, *intense* competition, an *intense* desire to succeed.

Intensive means 'thorough; directed to one area, subject, etc.': *intensive* studies, *intensive* care and implies a concentration on something: an *intensive* search.

intelligible (ɪnˈtɛlɪdʒəbl) *adj* able to be understood. **intelligibility** *n* **intelligibly** *adv* < SEE **INTELLIGENCE.**

intemperate (ɪnˈtɛmpərət) *adj* not temperate; unrestrained. **intemperance** *n*

intend (ɪnˈtɛnd) *vb* **1** propose; have in mind as an aim. **2** design for a use or purpose that is mentioned: The meeting was intended to provide an opportunity for everyone to air their views. **intention** *n* **1** what one intends to do; goal or purpose. **2** determination; resolve. **3** *pl* purposes concerning marriage. **intentional** *adj* intended; deliberate; not accidental. **intentionally** *adv* < Latin *intendere* to stretch out, give one's attention to, from *in-* + *tendere* to stretch.

intense (ɪnˈtɛns) *adj* **1** very strong in quality or degree: intense heat. **2** (of a person) marked by strong, deep feelings. **intensely** *adv* **intensity** *n* **intensify** *vb* **intensified; intensifying** make or become more intense. **intensification** *n* **intensive** *adj* thorough; concentrated. **intensively** *adv* < SEE **INTEND**. SEE PANEL.

intent (ɪnˈtənt) *n* **1** something that is intended. **2** the purpose with which one does something. **3** criminal intention. • *adj* **1** having one's mind fixed on a purpose that is mentioned: He was intent on speaking to her. **2** concentrated: an intent expression. **intently** *adv* **intentness** *n* < SEE **INTEND.**

inter (ɪnˈtɜː) *vb* **interred; interring** place (a dead body) in the earth or a tomb. **interment** *n* < Latin *in-* in + *terra* earth. SEE PANEL.

interact (ˌɪntəˈrækt) *vb* act on each other. **interaction** *n* **interactive** *adj*

inter alia (ˌɪntə ˈreɪlɪə) *adv* (*Latin*) among other things.

intercede (ˌntəˈsiːd) *vb* **1** plead on behalf of another. **2** intervene in order to produce a peaceful agreement between two sides. **intercession** *n* interceding, esp. by prayer or entreaty. < Latin *inter-* between + *cedere* to go.

intercept (ˌɪntəˈsɛpt) *vb* **1** seize, stop, or

inter or **intern?**

Inter is a formal word and means 'to place (a corpse) in the earth or a tomb'. The noun interment is derived from it.

Intern (with the stress on the second syllable) means 'to confine or detain, esp. during war'. The noun internment is derived from it; and an internee is a person who is interned.

In American English an intern (with the stress on the first syllable) is someone who has nearly or recently finished advanced professional training, for example in medicine.

interrupt in progress, movement, transmission, etc.: The message was intercepted by the police. **2** intersect. < Latin *inter-* between + *capere* to take.

interchange (ˌɪntəˈtʃeɪndʒ) *vb* put (each of two things) in the place of the other; alternate or exchange.
• *n* (ˈɪntəˌtʃeɪndʒ) **1** interchanging. **2** a road junction with different levels designed so that streams of traffic do not cross at the same level. **interchangeable** *adj* able to be interchanged. **interchangeability** *n*

intercom (ˈɪntəˌkɒm) *n* a local communication system with a microphone and loudspeaker at each location. < short for *intercommunication*.

intercontinental (ˌɪntəˌkɒntɪˈnəntl̩) *adj* connecting, carried on, or designed to travel between continents: intercontinental flights; intercontinental ballistic missile.

intercourse (ˈɪntəˌkɔːs) *n* **1** communication, exchange, or dealings between two people or groups. **2** sexual intercourse. < Latin *intercurrere* to run between.

interest (ˈɪntrəst) *n* **1** a sense of curiosity or concern about something or someone. **2** the power to arouse such a sense. **3** something in which one is interested. **4** advantage or benefit: in the interests of scholarship. **5** a legal right or share in business, etc. **6** money paid by a borrower of cash for its use; percentage of the amount borrowed. **7** something added beyond what is due.
• *vb* arouse the interest of. **interested** *adj* **1** feeling or showing interest. **2** personally involved: all the interested parties. **interesting** *adj* arousing interest. < probably Latin: it concerns, from *inter-* + *esse* to be.

interface (ˈɪntəˌfeɪs) *n* **1** a surface that forms a common boundary between two parts, areas, etc. **2** a point of communication between two different systems. SEE PANEL.

interfere (ˌɪntəˈfɪə) *vb* **1** become involved in matters which do not concern one; meddle. **2** hinder; obstruct. **interference** *n* **1** interfering. **2** unwanted signals that hinder the reception of radio waves. < Latin *inter-* between + *ferire* to strike.

interim (ˈɪntərɪm) *n* an intervening period.
• *adj* provisional: an interim report. < Latin: meanwhile.

interior (ɪnˈtɪərɪə) *adj* on the inside; for use on the inside: interior decorations.
• *n* **1** an interior surface, part, or area. **2** the inside of a building or room. **3** domestic or internal affairs: the Minister of the Interior. < Latin: comparative of *interus* on the inside.

interject (ˌɪntəˈdʒɛkt) *vb* utter or interpose suddenly and sharply. **interjection** *n* an exclamatory word or phrase, esp. one expressing feeling. < Latin *inter-* between + *jacere* to throw. SEE PANEL AT **HALLO**.

interlock (ˌɪntəˈlɒk) *vb* join or be joined together, as by parts that connect with one another.

interloper (ˈɪntəˌləʊpə) *n* a person who interferes; intruder. < *inter-* + *loper*, from Middle Dutch *loopen* to leap.

interlude (ˈɪntəluːd) *n* a period of time or different activity that comes between parts of a play, etc.; interval. < Latin *inter-* + *ludus* play.

intermediary (ˌɪntəˈmiːdɪərɪ) *n* a person who acts as a mediator between two opposing people or groups. **intermediate** *adj* coming between two things or extremes, in position, time, degree, etc. < Latin *inter-* + *medius* middle.

interminable (ɪnˈtɜːmɪnəbl̩) *adj* endless or appearing to be endless because very boring. **interminably** *adv*

intermingle (ˌɪntəˈmɪŋgl̩) *vb* mingle or mix together.

intermission (ˌɪntəˈmɪʃən) *n* an interval, as between two parts of a film; pause in an activity. < SEE **INTERMITTEMT**.

intermittent (ˌɪntəˈmɪtn̩t) *adj* occurring at intervals; not continuous: intermittent bursts of gunfire. **intermittently** *adv* < Latin

interface

In technical contexts, interface means 'a point of communication between two different systems' as in the fields of electronics or computers.

Interface also means 'a surface that forms a common boundary between two parts, areas, etc.'. Careful users of English prefer to limit this use to literal applications, as in the *interface* between liquid and gas in a jar containing water and water vapour, and to avoid its extended meaning when referring to a point or area of interaction between two disciplines, groups, etc., as in the *interface* between design and technology. Such users prefer to use words such as boundary, interaction, or link in such contexts.

inter- + *mittere* to send.

intern (ɪnˈtɜːn) *vb* confine or detain, esp. during war. **internment** *n* **internee** *n* a person who is interned. < Latin *internus* internal. SEE PANEL AT **INTER**.

internal (ɪnˈtɜːnl̩) *adj* **1** of or suitable for the inside. **2** (of a medicine) to be swallowed or applied within the body. **3** relating to the interior of the body: internal injuries. **4** of the domestic affairs of a country, etc. **5** based on what is under consideration, not on matters outside it: internal evidence. **internally** *adv* **internal-combustion engine** an engine with one or more cylinders within which combustion takes place. < Latin *internus*.

international (ˌɪntəˈnæʃənl) *adj* **1** of or involving two or more countries: international trade; an international conference. **2** known or famous in many countries: an international star.

• *n* **1** a person who has represented his or her country in a sports contest between different nations. **2** such a contest. **internationally** *adv*

internecine (ˌɪntəˈniːsaɪn) *adj* mutually destructive: internecine war. < Latin *inter-* between + *necare* to kill.

interplay (ˈɪntəˌpleɪ) *n* interaction.

interpolate (ɪnˈtɜːpəˌleɪt) *vb* **1** insert between others. **2** insert (new material) into (a text, etc.), esp. to give a false impression. **3** interject. **interpolation** *n* < Latin *interpolare* give a new appearance to, from *inter-* + *polire* to polish.

interpose (ˌɪntəˈpəʊz) *vb* **1** place or come between. **2** interrupt (with); interject. **3** intervene. < Latin *inter-* + *ponere* to put.

interpret (ɪnˈtɜːprɪt) *vb* **1** explain the meaning of. **2** understand in a particular way: How else can I interpret what he said? **3** represent in an artistic performance. **4** act as an interpreter. **interpretation** *n* **interpretative** *adj* **interpreter** *n* a person who translates the speech of a foreign language. < Latin *interpres* negotiator.

interregnum (ˌɪntəˈrɛgnəm) *n* an interval between two reigns, governments, or holders of other offices. < Latin *inter-* between + *regnum* reign.

interrelate (ˌɪntərɪˈleɪt) *vb* bring or come into a relationship where each one is related to the other.

interrogate (ɪnˈtɛrəˌgeɪt) *vb* question closely or formally. **interrogation** *n* **interrogator** *n* **interrogative** *adj, n* (a word, phrase, etc.) having the form of or expressing a question. **interrogatively** *adv* < Latin *inter-* + *rogare* to ask.

interrupt (ˌɪntəˈrʌpt) *vb* **1** break the continuity or flow of. **2** break in on (someone) while he or she is speaking. **interrupter** *n* **interruption** *n* < Latin *inter-* between + *rumpere* to break.

intersect (ˌɪntəˈsɛkt) *vb* **1** divide by passing through or across. **2** (of roads, lines, etc.) cross each other. **intersection** *n* < Latin *inter-* between + *secare* to cut.

intersperse (ˌɪntəˈspɜːs) *vb* distribute (contrasting material) among or on. < Latin *inter-* among + *spargere* to scatter.

interstice (ɪnˈtɜːstɪs) *n* a tiny space between two things next to each other. < Latin *inter-* between + *sistere* to stand.

intertwine (ˌɪntəˈtwaɪn) *vb* twine together.

interval (ˈɪntəvəl) *n* **1** a space that comes between two events or things. **2** a pause between parts of a performance. **3** the difference in musical pitch between two notes. < Latin *inter-* between + *vallum* wall.

intervene (ˌɪntəˈviːn) *vb* **1** occur or come between events in time. **2** enter a disagreement, discussion, etc., in order to change its course or settle it. **3** (of an event) prevent a course of action. **4** interfere in the internal affairs of another country. **intervention** *n* < Latin *inter-* between + *venire* to come. SEE PANEL.

interview (ˈɪntəˌvjuː) *n* **1** a formal meeting in which an employer, etc., assesses a candidate for a job, etc. **2** a questioning of a person on radio or television or for a newspaper, etc.

• *vb* conduct an interview with. **interviewee** *n* **interviewer** *n* < Middle French *entrevue*, from *entre-* inter- + *voir* to see.

inter- or **intra-?**

Confusion sometimes arises in the use of these prefixes. Inter- is used in the sense 'between or among': inter-city, interplanetary, and also to show a reciprocal relationship: intermarry, interdependent, inter-connected.

Intra- is less common than inter- and means 'on the inside; into or within' as in intravenous 'within or into a vein', intra-uterine, used of a device inserted into the uterus to prevent conception.

interweave (ˌɪntəˈwiːv) *vb* **interwove; interwoven; interweaving** weave, mix, or twine together.

intestate (ɪnˈtɛsteɪt) *adj* (of a person) not having made a will. **intestacy** *n* < Latin *in-* not + *testari* make a will.

intestine (ɪnˈtɛstɪn) *n* the long, tubular part of the alimentary canal between the stomach and the anus. **intestinal** *adj* < Latin *intus* within.

intimate[1] (ˈɪntɪmət) *adj* **1** marked by close or warm association or friendship. **2** very personal and private. **3** having a sexual relationship with. **4** (of knowledge) deep.
• *n* an intimate friend. **intimacy** *n* **intimately** *adv* < Latin *intus* within.

intimate[2] (ˈɪntɪˌmeɪt) *vb* hint or suggest. **intimation** *n* < Latin *intimus* innermost.

intimidate (ɪnˈtɪmɪˌdeɪt) *vb* make afraid by threatening or force. **intimidation** *n* < Latin *in-* in + *timidus* afraid.

into (ˈɪntə; *stressed* ˈɪntuː) *prep* **1** to the inside of: get into the car. **2** to a condition, state, or occupation that is mentioned: grow into a man; translate into Spanish; go into banking. **3** against: He drove into a wall. **4** advancing to the middle of: far into the night. **5** used to show division: 4 into 12 goes 3. **6** (*informal*) interested in; involved with: He's heavily into jazz. < Old English. SEE PANEL.

intolerable (ɪnˈtɒlərəbl̩) *adj* unbearable. **intolerably** *adv*

intolerant (ɪnˈtɒlərənt) *adj* unwilling to respect or tolerate other people's behaviour or beliefs; bigoted. **intolerance** *n* **intolerantly** *adv*

intone (ɪnˈtəʊn) *vb* recite or utter in a singing tone. **intonation** *n* **1** intoning. **2** the pitch of the voice when speaking. < Latin *in-* + *tonus* tone.

intoxicate (ɪnˈtɒksɪˌkeɪt) *vb* **1** make drunk. **2** stimulate or excite to the point of losing self-control. **intoxicant** *n* **intoxication** *n* < Latin *in-* + *toxicum* poison.

into or **in to?**

Into and in to are often confused. In to must be written as two words when in is an adverb that is part of the preceding verb and to introduces a phrase or an infinitive: I looked *in* to (not into) see him while I was passing. She turned him *in* to (not into) the authorities.

intractable (ɪnˈtræktəbl̩) *adj* **1** not easily influenced; stubborn. **2** not easily solved or cured. **intractability** *n*

intransigent (ɪnˈtrænsɪdʒənt) *adj* refusing to compromise; stubborn. **intransigence** *n* < Latin *in-* + *transigere* to settle.

intransitive (ɪnˈtrænsɪtɪv) *adj* (of a verb) not having a direct object. **intransitively** *adv*

intravenous (ˌɪntrəˈviːnəs) *adj* within or into a vein. **intravenously** *adv* < Latin *intra-* inside + *venous,* from *vena* vein. SEE PANEL AT **INTERVENE.**

intrepid (ɪnˈtrɛpɪd) *adj* fearless, courageous, and determined: intrepid explorers. **intrepidity** *n* **intrepidly** *adv* < Latin *in-* not + *trepidus* alarmed.

intricate (ˈɪntrɪkət) *adj* very complicated; difficult to understand or analyse. **intricacy** *n* **intricately** *adv* < Latin *in-* in + *tricae* trifles, perplexities.

intrigue (ɪnˈtriːg) *vb* **1** arouse the interest or curiosity of. **2** fascinate or puzzle. **3** plot or scheme.
• *n* (ˈɪntriːg) **1** a secret scheme or plot. **2** secret plotting. **3** a secret love affair. < SEE **INTRICATE.**

intrinsic (ɪnˈtrɪnsɪk) *adj* belonging to the essential nature of something. **intrinsically** *adv* < Latin *intrinsecus* inwardly.

introduce (ˌɪntrəˈdjuːs) *vb* **1** bring into use: The factory has introduced a new shift system. **2** make (oneself or a person) known to a person or people by name. **3** make known to a person for the first time: He was introduced to the club by a friend. **4** put into: He introduced a new clause into the contract. **5** bring (a bill) before a legislative body. **6** present (a radio or television programme, etc.). **introduction** *n* **1** introducing; being introduced. **2** the formal presentation of one person to another or others. **3** a preliminary part of a book, etc. **4** a preliminary study. **introductory** *adj* serving as an introduction; preliminary. < Latin *intro-* within + *ducere* to lead.

introspection (ˌɪntrəˈspɛkʃən) *n* examination of one's thoughts and feelings. **introspective** *adj* < Latin *intro-* within + *specere* to look.

introvert (ˈɪntrəˌvɜːt) *n* a person whose attention and interests are directed upon his or her own self.
• *adj* also **introverted** having such characteristics. < Latin *intro* within + *vertere* to turn.

intrude (ɪnˈtruːd) *vb* push or force (something); force (oneself) upon others. **intruder** *n* **intrusion** *n* **intrusive**

adj < Latin *in-* in + *trudere* to thrust.
intuition (ˌɪntjʊˈɪʃən) *n* **1** immediate apprehension; knowledge derived from this. **2** the power of knowing something directly without evident reasoning. **3** direct or quick insight. **intuitive** *adj* **intuitively** *adv* < Latin *in-* + *tueri* to look at.
inundate (ˈɪnʌnˌdeɪt) *vb* overwhelm with or as if with a flood. **inundation** *n* < Latin *in-* + *unda* wave.
inure (ɪˈnjʊə) *vb* accustom, esp. to something unpleasant. < Middle English *en-* + *ure* use, work.
invade (ɪnˈveɪd) *vb* **1** enter (a country, etc.) with military force, in order to conquer. **2** encroach upon (privacy, etc.). **3** occupy in large numbers. **4** spread throughout harmfully. **invader** *n* < Latin *in-* in + *vadere* to go.
invalid[1] (ˈɪnvəˌlɪd) *n* a person who is disabled or who suffers bad health for a long time.
• *vb* (ˈɪnvəˌlɪd, ˈɪnvəˌliːd) **1** cause to become an invalid. **2** remove from active service because of bad health or injury. < Latin *in-* not + *validus* strong.
invalid[2] (ɪnˈvælɪd) *adj* not valid. **invalidity** *n* **invalidate** *vb* make invalid.
invaluable (ɪnˈvæljʊəbḷ) *adj* having a great value that cannot be measured. **invaluably** *adv*
invariable (ɪnˈvɛərɪəbḷ) *adj* unchanging. **invariably** *adv*
invasion (ɪnˈveɪʒən) *n* invading; being invaded. **invasive** *adj*
invective (ɪnˈvɛktɪv) *n* a very strong, abusive attack in words; denunciation. < SEE **INVEIGH.**
inveigh (ɪnˈveɪ) *vb* make a very strong attack in words. < Latin *in-* + *vehere* to carry.
inveigle (ɪnˈveɪgḷ) *vb* persuade or trick (into doing something). < ultimately Medieval Latin *ab oculis* without eyes.
invent (ɪnˈvɛnt) *n* **1** think of and produce (something that has not existed before). **2** make up (an excuse, lie, etc.). **inventor** *n* **invention** *n* something invented; inventing. **inventive** *adj* creative; resourceful. **inventively** *adv* **inventiveness** *n* < Latin *in-* on + *venire* to come.
inventory (ˈɪnvəntrɪ) *n* a detailed list of individual items, for example of property.
inverse (ɪnˈvɜːs, ˈɪnvɜːs) *adj* opposite in order, direction, effect, etc.
• *n* a thing that is inverse to another. **inversely** *adv* < SEE **INVERT.**
invert (ɪnˈvɜːt) *vb* turn upside down; reverse in order, position, relationship, etc. **inversion** *n* **inverted commas** quotation marks. < Latin *in-* to + *vertere* to turn.
invertebrate (ɪnˈvɜːtɪbrət, ɪnˈvɜːtɪbreɪt) *adj* (of an animal) not having a backbone.
• *n* an invertebrate animal.
invest (ɪnˈvɛst) *vb* **1** commit (money) to a business, as by buying shares, in order to make a profit. **2** devote (time, effort, etc.) to a project. **3** install in an office with a formal ceremony, by presenting a title or robes and insignia. **4** endow with a quality. **5** (*informal*) spend money on a useful article. **investiture** *n* a formal ceremony for the presentation of a title or robes and insignia of an office or rank. **investment** *n* **1** investing money. **2** an amount of money invested. **3** something in which money is invested. **investor** *n* a person who invests money. < Latin *in-* in + *vestis* clothing.
investigate (ɪnˈvɛstɪˌgeɪt) *vb* **1** examine or study closely. **2** conduct an official enquiry. **investigation** *n* **investigative** *adj* **investigator** *n* **investigatory** *adj* < Latin *investigare.*
inveterate (ɪnˈvɛtərət) *adj* **1** firmly established: inveterate hatred. **2** habitual: an inveterate liar. < Latin *in-* in + *vetus* old.
invidious (ɪnˈvɪdɪəs) *adj* likely to cause resentment, unpopularity, or harm. **invidiously** *adv* **invidiousness** *n* < Latin *invidia* envy.
invigilate (ɪnˈvɪdʒɪleɪt) *vb* supervise candidates at an examination. **invigilation** *n* **invigilator** *n* < Latin *in-* + *vigilare* to keep watch.
invigorate (ɪnˈvɪgəˌreɪt) *vb* give vitality and energy to; refresh. < *in-* + *vigour.* SEE PANEL AT **ENERVATE.**
invincible (ɪnˈvɪnsəbḷ) *adj* incapable of being conquered. **invincibility** *n* **invincibly** *adv* < Latin *in-* + *vincere* to conquer.
inviolable (ɪnˈvaɪələbḷ) *adj* not to be violated. **inviolate** *adj* not violated.
invisible (ɪnˈvɪzɪbḷ) *adj* incapable of being seen. **invisibility** *n* **invisibly** *adv*
invite (ɪnˈvaɪt) *vb* **1** ask politely to come to one's house, a meeting, etc., or to do something. **2** ask for (questions, comments, etc.). **3** make more likely, esp. unintentionally: To suggest a better method now will only invite criticism.
• *n* (ˈɪnvaɪt) (*informal*) an invitation. **invitation** *n* a polite, written or spoken request for a person to come to one's house, attend a meeting, etc. **inviting** *adj* attractive; enticing. **invitingly** *adv* < Latin *invitare.*

invoice (ˈɪnvɔɪs) *n* a document issued by a seller to a buyer giving details of the goods or services supplied and stating the sum of money due.
• *vb* send an invoice of (goods or services) to (a person, company, etc.). < probably Middle French *envoi* message.

invoke (ɪnˈvəʊk) *vb* **1** call upon (God) for help. **2** appeal to as an authority, for confirmation, etc. **3** call forth (a spirit) with words. **4** implore (help). **invocation** *n* < Latin *in-* on + *vocare* to call.

involuntary (ɪnˈvɒləntərɪ, ɪnˈvɒləntrɪ) *adj* performed without conscious effort of the will or intention. **involuntarily** *adv*

involve (ɪnˈvɒlv) *vb* **1** include as a necessary part; entail. **2** associate or concern. **3** make complicated. **4** commit (oneself) emotionally. **5** have a part (in a quarrel, crime, etc.). **involvement** *n* **involved** *adj* **1** complicated. **2** concerned (in something). < Latin *in-* in + *volvere* to roll. SEE PANEL.

inward (ˈɪnwəd) *adj* **1** situated on or going towards the inside. **2** in the mind or spirit. **inwardly** *adj* **1** of the inside. **2** in one's mind or spirit; to oneself. **inwards** *adv* towards the inside; in the mind or spirit. < Old English *inweard.*

iodine (ˈaɪəˌdiːn) *n* a purple-black, non-metallic element that evaporates to give a purple gas. < Greek *ion* violet + *eidos* form.

ion (ˈaɪən) *n* an electrically charged atom or group of atoms formed by the loss or gain of one or more electrons. **ionize** *vb* convert or be converted into ions. < Greek: going, from *ienai* to go.

iota (aɪˈəʊtə) *n* **1** the ninth letter of the Greek alphabet. **2** a tiny amount.

IOU *n* a written promise to repay a debt. < pronunciation of *I owe you.*

ipso facto (ˌɪpsəʊ ˈfæktəʊ) *adv* (*Latin*) by that very fact or act.

IQ *abbrev* intelligence quotient.

IRA *abbrev* Irish Republican Army.

irascible (ɪˈræsɪbḷ) *adj* easily angered. **irascibility** *n* **irascibly** *adv* < SEE IRATE.

irate (aɪˈreɪt) *adj* very angry. **irately** *adv* **irateness** *n* **ire** *n* anger. < Latin *ira* anger.

iridescent (ˌɪrɪˈdɛsṇt) *adj* having or showing an interplay of rainbow-like colours. **iridescence** *n* < Latin *irido-* rainbow + *-escent* reflecting or giving off light.

iris (ˈaɪrɪs) *n* **1** the muscular tissue in the eye that surrounds the pupil. **2** a plant with long, straight leaves and showy flowers. < Greek *iris* rainbow.

irk (ɜːk) *vb* irritate or annoy. **irksome** *adj* causing annoyance. < Middle English *irken.*

iron (ˈaɪən) *n* **1** a common, hard, grey, metallic element that can be magnetized. **2** something made of iron, esp. a metal implement with a flat base that is heated to smooth or press clothes. **3** any of a numbered series of golf-clubs with an iron or steel head. **4** a metal splint or support for a leg. **5** *pl* fetters or chains: in irons. **6** great strength of character; determination.
• *adj* **1** made of iron. **2** like iron in strength, appearance, etc. **3** cruel; without mercy.

involved in words

Careful users of English avoid overworking the verb involve. Often, another word can be substituted for it, as the following examples show:

Any transfer of power would *involve* considerable work (*mean* or *lead to*).
The problems *involved* in the use of the vaccine (*caused* or *entailed*).
The additional expenses *involved* (*incurred*).
Agreements *involving* goods worth £1000 or more (*concerning*).
He's *involved* in many of my business activities (*active*).
A collision *involving* two cars and a bus (*between*).

Watch your ironing!

Careful users of English take care over which sort of object is chosen for the verb iron out in its figurative sense of 'to solve (a problem); correct and remove'. Objects that might evoke the literal sense of smoothing or pressing clothes with an iron, in order to remove creases are avoided. Otherwise, unfortunate or ridiculous clashes may result, such as *ironing out* bottlenecks, stumbling-blocks, or thorny problems.

• *vb* **1** smooth or press clothes with an iron. **2 iron out** solve (a problem); correct and remove. **iron-grey** *adj, n* dark, grey colour. **ironing-board** *n* a board on legs with a suitable covering for ironing clothes on. **ironmonger** *n* a dealer in household hardware. **ironwork** *n* decorative work done in iron. **ironworks** *n* a building in which iron is smelted or heavy, iron goods are made. < Old English *īren*. SEE PANEL.

irony (ˈaɪrənɪ) *n* **1** the use of words to express a meaning opposite to the literal meaning, to add force to one's remarks. **2** incongruity between what actually is and what is expected or normal; event, situation, etc., showing such incongruity. **ironic** or **ironical** *adj* of, marked by, or using irony. < Greek *eirōn* dissembler in speech.

irradiate (ɪˈreɪdɪˌəɪt) *vb* **1** shine upon. **2** enlighten. **3** radiate. **4** subject to radiation. **irradiation** *n*

irreconcilable (ɪˈrɛkn̩ˌsaɪləbl̩) *adj* unable to be reconciled. **irreconcilably** *adv*

irrecoverable (ˌɪrɪˈkʌvrəbl̩) *adj* not capable of being recovered. **irrecoverably** *adv*

irredeemable (ˌɪrɪˈdiːməbl̩) *adj* unable to be redeemed; hopeless. **irredeemably** *adv*

irreducible (ˌɪrɪˈdjuːsəbl̩) *adj* unable to be reduced or simplified.

irrefutable (ɪˈrɛfjʊtəbl̩, ˌɪrɪˈfjuːtəbl̩) *adj* unable to be refuted. **irrefutably** *adv*

irregular (ɪˈrɛgjʊlə) *adj* **1** lacking uniformity or evenness. **2** lacking continuity or regularity of occurrence. **3** contrary to established conventions or rules. **4** (of troops) not belonging to the regular armed forces.
• *n* an irregular soldier. **irregularity** *n* **irregularly** *adv*

irreligion (ˌɪrɪˈlɪdʒən) *n* lack of or hostility to religious faith. **irreligious** *adj*

irreparable (ɪˈrɛpərəbl̩) *adj* unable to be repaired, remedied, etc. **irreparably** *adv*

irrepressible (ˌɪrɪˈprɛsəbl̩) *adj* unable to be restrained or controlled.

irreproachable (ˌɪrɪˈprəʊtʃəbl̩) *adj* blameless; faultless.

irresistible (ˌɪrɪˈzɪstəbl̩) *adj* too attractive, enticing, or terrible to resist. **irresistibly** *adv*

irresolute (ɪˈrɛzəˌluːt) *adj* hesitating; wavering. **irresolution** *n*

irrespective (ˌɪrɪˈspɛktɪv) *adj* **irrespective of** without taking account of.

irresponsible (ˌɪrɪˈspɒnsəbl̩) *adj* not showing a proper sense of responsibility. **irresponsibility** *n* **irresponsibly** *adv*

irreversible (ˌɪrɪˈvɜːsəbl̩) *adj* not able to be reversed, changed, or revoked. **irreversibility** *n* **irreversibly** *adv*

irrevocable (ɪˈrɛvəkəbl̩) *adj* not able to be revoked or changed. **irrevocably** *adv*

irrigate (ˈɪrɪˌgeɪt) *vb* supply (land) with water by artificial channels, etc., in order to further the growth of food crops. **irrigation** *n* < Latin *in-* in + *rigare* to water.

irritate (ˈɪrɪˌteɪt) *vb* **1** arouse impatience and slight anger in. **2** make (a part of the body) inflamed or sore. **irritation** *n* **irritable** *adj* easily irritated. **irritability** *n* **irritably** *adv* **irritant** *adj, n* (something) causing irritation. < Latin *irritare*.

is (z, s; *stressed* ɪz) SEE **BE**.

Islam (ˈɪzlɑːm) *n* **1** the Muslim religion, started by Muhammad. **2** all the people and countries that adhere to this religion. **Islamic** *adj* < Arabic *islām* submission (to God's will).

island (ˈaɪlənd) *n* **1** an area of land surrounded by water. **2** something like this in being isolated or surrounded: a traffic island. **islander** *n* an inhabitant of an island. < Old English *īgland*.

isle (aɪl) *n* an island, esp. a small one; used in some names: Isle of Man.

isobar (ˈaɪsəˌbɑː) *n* a line on a map connecting places with the same atmospheric pressure. < Greek *isos* equal + *baros* weight.

isolate (ˈaɪsəˌleɪt) *vb* **1** place apart from others. **2** keep (a person) separated from other people so that he or she cannot infect them. **3** (*chemistry*) separate (an element or compound) in pure form from another compound or mixture. **isolationism** *n* the policy that opposes participation by a country in international affairs. **isolationist** *n, adj* < Latin *insula* island.

isometrics (ˌaɪsəˈmɛtrɪks) *pl n* physical exercises involving muscular contractions for the purpose of increasing the strength of the muscles. < Greek *isos* equal + *metron* measure.

isosceles (aɪˈsɒsɪˌliːz) *adj* (of a triangle) having two sides of equal length. < Greek *isos* equal + *skelos* leg.

issue (ˈɪʃuː) *n* **1** the action of going or flowing out. **2** something issued, such as an edition of a magazine. **3** a result; outcome. **4** a matter that is disputed. **5** a topic, esp. one that is controversial. **6** offspring: He died without issue.
• *vb* **1** go, come, or flow out. **2** distribute or publish. **3** give or send out: to issue a warning. **4** supply officially. **5** emerge; result. < Latin *ex-* out + *ire* to go.

isthmus (ˈɪsməs) *n* a narrow strip of land connecting two larger areas of land. < Greek *isthmos.*

it (ɪt) *pron* **1** the thing or creature that is mentioned. **2** the person in question: 'Who is it?'—'It's Paul!' **3** used as the subject of a verb that describes the weather, time, or distance: It's raining; It's 6 o'clock; It's 3 miles from Rye. **4** used as a dummy subject or object: It's hard to find a good secretary; Gill made it clear that she disagreed.
• *n* (in children's games) the player who tries to catch others. < Old English *hit.* SEE PANEL.

italic (ɪˈtælɪk) *adj* (of printed letters) slanting upwards to the right. **italics** *pl n* italic printed letters. **italicize** *vb* print in italics. **italicization** *n* < Greek *italikos* of Italy.

itch (ɪtʃ) *n* **1** an irritating sensation on the skin. **2** a restless desire.
• *vb* **1** have or feel an itch. **2** have a restless desire. **itchy** *adj* < Old English *giccan* to itch.

item (ˈaɪtəm) *n* **1** one single thing or unit in a list, series, or number of things. **2** a single piece of news or information. **itemize** *vb* state the items involved; list. < Latin *ita* thus.

itinerant (ɪˈtɪnərənt, aɪˈtɪnərənt) *adj* travelling from place to place: an itinerant preacher. < Latin *iter* journey.

itinerary (aɪˈtɪnərərɪ) *n* the planned route of a journey. < SEE **ITINERANT.**

its (ɪts) *determiner* of or belonging to it. SEE PANEL AT **IT.**

itself (ɪtˈsɛlf) *pron* the form of it used reflexively or for emphasis: The cat is washing itself. **by itself 1** without help. **2** alone. **in itself** considered in its intrinsic qualities: The climb was not dangerous in itself.

ITV *abbrev* Independent Television.

IUD *abbrev* intra-uterine device.

ivory (ˈaɪvərɪ) *n* **1** the hard, creamy-white tissue that forms the tusks of elephants and walruses. **2** a creamy-white colour. **3** something made of ivory. < Latin *ebur* ivory.

ivy (ˈaɪvɪ) *n* an evergreen, woody, climbing plant with dense, shiny foliage and aerial roots. < Old English *īfig.*

---

it's or its?

The problem of whether to use the apostrophe or not is one that bothers a surprisingly large number of people. The rule, equally surprisingly, is very straightforward:

It's means either 'it is': *It's* going to rain. *It's* mine or 'it has': *It's* got a wet nose. *It's* stopped.

Its means 'of it': Have you seen *its* bone?

It occurs in a large number of idiomatic phrases, including the following. It is interesting to speculate what, if anything, it stands for.

ask for it
beat it
be past it
cut it out
don't mention it
easy does it
fix it
give it a try
grin and bear it
have got it badly
have got it made
have it in for someone
hit it off with someone
hop it
jump to it
knock it off
let's face it
live it up
not put it past someone
owe it to someone
pack it in
run for it
sleep on it
snap out of it
spit it out
step on it
sweat it out
take it or leave it
that does it
that's about it
this is it
to put it mildly
wait for it
watch it
you said it

J

jab (dʒæb) *vb* **jabbed; jabbing** poke or thrust roughly and sharply.
• *n* **1** a rough, sharp poke or thrust. **2** (*informal*) an injection. < alteration of *job* to strike.

jabber (ˈdʒæbə) *vb* speak quickly and unintelligibly.
• *n* jabbering talk. < like the sound.

jack (dʒæk) *n* **1** a portable device for exerting pressure or lifting a heavy object off the ground. **2** a playing-card ranking below a queen. **3** a small, white, target ball in the game of bowls. **4** also **jack plug** a plug-in device for making electrical contact.
• *vb* raise with a jack. < *Jack,* nickname for *John.*

jackal (ˈdʒækɔːl, ˈdʒækl̩) *n* a wild, flesh-eating mammal related to the dog, with pointed ears and a bushy tail. < Turkish *çakal,* from Persian *shagāl,* from Sanskrit *sṛgāla.*

jackass (ˈdʒækˌæs) *n* **1** a male donkey. **2** a stupid person; fool.

jackdaw (ˈdʒækˌdɔː) *n* a small crow with black plumage, noted for its thieving habits. < *jack* + probably Old English *dawe.*

jacket (ˈdʒækɪt) *n* **1** a short, outer garment, esp. one that is hip-length and has a front opening. **2** the skin of a baked potato. **3** an insulating cover for a boiler or hot-water tank. **4** a dust jacket. < from Middle French *jacquet,* from the name *Jacques* James.

jack-knife (ˈdʒækˌnaɪf) *n, pl* **jack-knives** a knife with a blade that folds back into a recess in the handle.
• *vb* (of an articulated vehicle) turn or rise and form a sharp angle with its trailer.

jackpot (ˈdʒækˌpɒt) *n* a large prize or accumulated stake that may be won in gambling. **hit the jackpot** win a jackpot; be very successful, esp. unexpectedly.

Jacuzzi (dʒæˈkuːzɪ) *n* (*Trademark*) a bath with underwater jets of water that massage the body.

jade (dʒeɪd) *n* **1** an extremely hard, semi-precious gem-stone, usually green or greenish-white, used for making ornaments. **2** the green colour of jade. < Spanish (*piedra de*) *ijada* (stone of) the colic.

jaded (ˈdʒeɪdɪd) *adj* tired by working too hard; worn out. < Middle English *jade* poor or worn-out horse.

jagged (ˈdʒægɪd) *adj* having sharp, projecting notches. **jaggedly** *adv* **jaggedness** *n* < Middle English *jaggen* to stab.

jaguar (ˈdʒægjʊə) *n* a large member of the cat family, with dark spots on a yellow coat, found in tropical America. < Portuguese, from Guarani *yaguara* and Tupi *jaguara.*

jail, gaol (dʒeɪl) *n* a prison; imprisonment.
• *vb* confine in jail. **jailbird, gaolbird** *n* a person who has been habitually kept in jail. **jailbreak, gaolbreak** *n* an escape from jail. **jailer, gaoler** *n* a person in charge of prisoners in a jail. < ultimately Latin *cavea* cage. SEE PANEL.

jalopy (dʒəˈlɒpɪ) *n* (*informal*) a dilapidated, old car or aeroplane. < origin unknown.

jam[1] (dʒæm) *vb* **jammed; jamming** **1** squeeze into a confined space. **2** make or become wedged or blocked so as not to move or work: The window has jammed. **3** block the passage of; crowd or congest. **4** apply suddenly and forcibly: He jammed on the brakes. **5** cause interference to (radio communications) by transmitting other signals on the same wavelength.
• *n* **1** a squeeze, crush, or blockage caused by jamming. **2** a crowded mass that prevents movement: a traffic jam. **3** (*informal*) a difficult situation. **jam-packed** *adj* tightly packed or crowded. < probably like the sound.

jam[2] *n* a preserve containing fruit that has been boiled with sugar to a thick consistency. **jammy** *adj* (*informal*) lucky. < probably JAM[1]. SEE PANEL.

jamb (dʒæm) *n* one of the vertical sides of the frame of a door or window. < Late Latin *gamba* leg.

jamboree (ˌdʒæmbəˈriː) *n* **1** a large, festive gathering; celebration. **2** a large

---

jail or **gaol?**

Either jail or gaol is acceptable. In American usage, however, only jail is found.

Some users of English find gaol awkward—it can be misprinted as goal. Moreover, the ga spelling is a very rare example of a soft *g* before *a* or *o*, seen also in mortgagor.

---

gathering of Scouts or Guides. < origin unknown.

jangle (ˈdʒæŋgḷ) *n* a harsh, unpleasant, metallic sound.
• *vb* **1** make or cause to make this sound. **2** irritate (the nerves) tensely. < Old French *jangler.*

janitor (ˈdʒænɪtə) *n* (*chiefly US*) a caretaker. < Latin: doorkeeper.

japanned (dʒəˈpænd) *adj* varnished with a hard, glossy, black lacquer. < *japan* such a lacquer, originally from Japan.

jar[1] (dʒɑː) *n* **1** a wide-mouthed, cylindrical container, made of glass or earthenware. **2** the contents of a jar; amount it contains. **3** (*informal*) a glass of beer or other alcoholic drink. < Arabic *jarrah* earthen container.

jar[2] *vb* **jarred; jarring 1** make or cause to make a harsh, discordant sound. **2** have an irritating, harsh, or unpleasant effect. **3** be out of harmony (with). **4** vibrate.
• *n* a jarring movement or effect. < probably like the sound.

jargon (dʒɑːgən) *n* **1** a specialized language of a particular subject or profession: legal jargon. **2** unintelligible or pretentious language. < Middle French.

jasmine (ˈdʒæzmɪn) *n* a shrub with yellow or white, fragrant flowers. < Persian *yāsamīn.*

jasper (ˈdʒæspə) *n* an opaque quartz, usually red or reddish-brown. < Greek *iaspis.*

jaundice (ˈdʒɔːndɪs) *n* **1** yellowing of the skin and whites of the eyes caused by the presence of bile pigments. **2** a state of prejudice, resentment, or jealousy. **jaundiced** *adj* < Latin *galbus* yellow.

jaunt (dʒɔːnt) *n* a short outing for pleasure.
• *vb* go on such an outing. < origin unknown.

jaunty (ˈdʒɔːntɪ) *adj* **1** self-confident and cheerful. **2** (of clothes) smart. **jauntily** *adv* **jauntiness** *n* < modified from French *gentil* genteel.

> **jam tomorrow**
>
> The expression jam tomorrow, referring to the promise of better living or working conditions in the future, comes from 'Through the Looking-Glass' by the English writer Lewis Carroll, 1832–98: The rule is, jam tomorrow and jam yesterday—but never jam today.

javelin (ˈdʒævlɪn) *n* a light spear; sport of throwing this as an athletic field event. < Middle French *javeline.*

jaw (dʒɔː) *n* **1** either of the two bony parts that form the framework of the mouth and hold the teeth. **2** either of the two parts of a machine or tool which grip something. **3** (*informal*) idle conversation; chat.
• *vb* (*informal*) talk idly; chat. **jawbone** *n* either of the bones of the jaw. < Middle English.

jay (dʒeɪ) *n* a crow with a brownish-pink body, black-and-white wings, and a black-and-white crest. < Late Latin *gaius.*

jaywalk (ˈdʒeɪˌwɔːk) *vb* cross or walk in a street recklessly, without regard for traffic. **jaywalker** *n* < *jay* foolish person + *walk.*

jazz (dʒæz) *n* **1** a form of music marked by improvisation and syncopated rhythm. **2** (*informal*) similar things that are not mentioned specifically. **3** (*informal*) pretentious talk.
• *vb* **jazz up** (*informal*) **1** play (a piece of music) in the style of jazz, esp. with a quicker, livelier tempo. **2** make brighter or more showy. **jazzy** *adj* **1** of or like jazz. **2** (*informal*) bright and showy. < origin unknown.

jealous (ˈdʒɛləs) *adj* **1** feeling or showing resentful suspicion of a rival. **2** watching and guarding. **jealously** *adv* **jealousy** *n* < Late Latin *zelus* zeal. SEE PANEL AT **ENVY**.

jeans (dʒiːnz) *pl n* close-fitting trousers for casual wear, esp. made of denim or corduroy. SEE PANEL AT **DENIM.**

jeep (dʒiːp) *n* a small, robust motor vehicle with four-wheel drive. < probably from the initials *G.P.,* for general-purpose (vehicle).

jeer (dʒɪə) *vb* laugh or scoff (at) in a rude, mocking way.
• *n* a jeering remark or shout. < origin unknown.

jell, gel (dʒɛl) *vb* **jelled; jelling** or **gelled; gelling 1** change into a jelly-like substance. **2** make or become more definite. < back formation from *jelly.*

jelly (ˈdʒɛlɪ) *n* **1** a soft but firm, fruit-flavoured sweet made with gelatine. **2** a kind of jam made from the juice of fruit boiled with sugar. **3** any substance like jelly in consistency. **jellied** *adj* set in a jelly: jellied eels, **jellyfish** *n* a free-swimming, invertebrate sea-animal with a jelly-like body and stinging tentacles. < Latin *gelare* to freeze.

jemmy (ˈdʒɛmɪ) *n* a short, steel crowbar used by burglars. < *Jemmy,* nickname for *James.*

jeopardize (ˈdʒɛpəˌdaɪz) *vb* put in or expose to danger; risk. **jeopardy** *n* < Old French *jeu parti* divided game.

jerk (dʒɜːk) *vb* **1** move with a sudden, uneven action. **2** throw, push, pull, or stop with a sudden, sharp action.
• *n* **1** a jerking movement. **2** (*slang*) a stupid person. **jerky** *adj* marked by jerking movements. **jerkily** *adv* **jerkiness** *n* < origin uncertain.

jerkin (ˈdʒɜːkɪn) *n* a sleeveless jacket. < origin unknown.

jerry-built (ˈdʒɛrɪˌbɪlt) *adj* built badly and with poor materials. < origin unknown.

jerry can (ˈdʒɛrɪ) a narrow. flat-sided container for carrying petrol or water, with a capacity of about 20 litres. < *Jerry,* German + *can.* SEE PANEL.

jersey (ˈdʒɜːzɪ) *n, pl* **jerseys 1** a knitted garment covering the upper part of the body. **2** a machine-knitted fabric used for making clothes. < *Jersey,* one of the Channel Islands.

jest (dʒɛst) *n* **1** a joke. **2** playfulness: in jest.
• *vb* speak or act playfully; joke. **jester** *n* < Latin *gerere* to carry out.

jet[1] (dʒɛt) *n* **1** a stream of liquid, gas, or flame forced through a narrow opening or nozzle; such an opening or nozzle. **2** a jet engine or aeroplane powered by a jet engine.
• *vb* **jetted; jetting** travel by jet aeroplane: He goes jetting round the world. **jet engine** an engine that propels or lifts by the discharge of a high-speed jet of gases, etc. < Latin *jacere* to throw.

jet[2] *n* **1** a hard, black mineral that can be polished and is used for ornaments, jewellery, etc. **2** an intense, black colour. < Greek *Gagas,* town in Asia Minor (Turkey).

> **jerry can**
>
> With the advent of industrialized warfare, the safety of fuel supplies became of critical importance. To support their tank regiments in Africa in the Second World War the Germans designed a metal fuel container which was far superior to the one used by the Allies. When the British forces came upon it, they copied the design, calling the new container a jerry can.

jetsam (ˈdʒɛtsəm) *n* goods thrown overboard to lighten a ship in distress, esp. those washed ashore. < alteration of *jettison.*

jettison (ˈdʒɛtɪsn̩) *vb* **1** throw away; abandon. **2** throw (goods) overboard to lighten a ship, etc., in distress. < Latin *jacere* to throw.

jetty (ˈdʒɛtɪ) *n* a pier, breakwater, or landing-stage. < Middle French *jetee* projecting part, something thrown out, from Latin *jacere* to throw.

jew (dʒuː) *n* a person descended from the ancient Israelites; person whose religion is Judaism. **Jewish** *adj* < ultimately Hebrew *Yĕhūdhāh* Judah.

jewel (ˈdʒuːəl) *n* **1** a precious stone. **2** an ornament containing one or more precious stones. **3** a person or thing that is very precious or highly regarded. **jewelled** *adj* fitted or decorated with a jewel or jewels. **jeweller** *n* a person who makes, sells, or repairs jewellery. **jewellery** *n* jewels, esp. for wearing as ornaments. < ultimately Latin *jocus* joke. SEE PANEL.

jib[1] (dʒɪb) *n* a triangular sail set forward from the mast. < origin unknown.

jib[2] *vb* **jibbed; jibbing 1** (of a horse) stop and refuse to go further. **2** balk (at); show reluctance to do something. < origin unknown.

jib[3] *n* the projecting arm of a crane. < probably *gibbet.*

jiffy (ˈdʒɪfɪ) *n* (*informal*) a moment: I'll be ready in a jiffy. < origin unknown.

jig (dʒɪg) *n* **1** a lively, jumping dance; music for this. **2** a device used to hold a piece of work and guide the tools working on it.
• *vb* **jigged; jigging 1** dance a jig. **2** make quick, jerky movements up and down. < probably Middle French *giguer* to dance, from *gigue* fiddle.

jiggered (ˈdʒɪgəd) *adj* (*old-fashioned informal*) blowed; damned: Well, I'll be jiggered! < probably euphemism for *buggered.*

> **jewellery** or **jewelry?**
>
> Either spelling is acceptable. The spelling jewellery is more common in British usage, while jewelry is the standard American spelling.

jiggery-pokery (ˌdʒɪgərɪˈpəʊkərɪ) *n* (*informal*) dishonest and secret dealings; trickery. < Scottish *joukery-pawkery.*

jigsaw (ˈdʒɪgˌsɔː) *n* **1** also **jigsaw puzzle** a picture mounted on a base and cut into irregular, interlocking pieces that have to be reassembled. **2** a mechanically driven fretsaw.

jilt (dʒɪlt) *vb* leave or reject (one's lover) unfeelingly and without previous warning. < name *Jill.*

jingle (ˈdʒɪŋgḷ) *vb* ring or cause to ring repeatedly with a light, metallic sound: His keys jingled.
• *n* **1** a jingling sound. **2** a short catchy song or rhyme: advertising jingles. **jingly** *adj* < like the sound.

jingoism (ˈdʒɪŋgəʊˌɪzəm) *n* an aggressive patriotism; chauvinism. < *by jingo,* refrain in 19th-century British patriotic song.

jinx (dʒɪŋks) *n* a person, thing, force, or curse that brings bad luck.
• *vb* put a jinx on. < Greek *jynx* bird used in black magic.

jitter (ˈdʒɪtə) *vb* be nervous or behave nervously.
• *n* **the jitters** (*infornal*) great nervousness. **jittery** *adj* < origin unknown.

jive (dʒaɪv) *n* a lively, jerky dance; music accompanying this.
• *vb* dance a jive. < origin unknown.

job (dʒɒb) *n* **1** a piece of work; task. **2** an occupation; paid position of employment. **3** a responsibility; duty. **4** (*informal*) an object of a type that is mentioned: His new car's a neat little job! **5** (*informal*) a difficult task: She's getting old so has a job getting upstairs. **6** (*informal*) a crime, esp. a robbery.
• *vb* **jobbed; jobbing** do piece-work. **jobber** *n* a stockjobber. **job centre** a government office in a town or city centre in which vacancies are displayed. **jobless** *adj* unemployed. < origin uncertain. SEE PANEL.

just the job

The word job features in a number of idiomatic expressions, including:

it's a good job something is fortunate, convenient: It's a good job you brought your umbrella, otherwise we'd have got soaked!
jobs for the boys the assurance of paid employment, profit, etc., for a favoured group, especially one's friends.
just the job exactly what is needed: That pen you lent me was just the job—it was just right for all the fine lettering I wanted to do.

Job is also used with bad or good in the sense of 'a state of affairs': I guess I'll just have to make the best of a bad job.

jockey (ˈdʒɒkɪ) *n, pl* **jockeys** a person who rides a horse, esp. a professional rider in horse-races.
• *vb* **1** gain an advantage by manoeuvring: jockeying for position. **2** force by crafty means. < *Jockey,* Scottish nickname for *John.*

jock-strap (ˈdʒɒkˌstræp) *n* a support for the genitals worn by male athletes. < *jock* penis + *strap.*

jocular (ˈdʒɒkjʊlə) *adj* marked by joking and humour: a jocular reply. **jocularity** *n* **jocularly** *adv* < Latin *joculus* little joke.

jodhpurs (ˈdʒɒdpəz) *pl n* riding-breeches that fit loosely around the hips and tightly from the thighs to the ankles. < *Jodhpur,* city in India.

jog (dʒɒg) *vb* **jogged; jogging 1** run at a slow, steady pace, esp. for exercise. **2** continue in a routine way: We're just jogging along nicely. **3** shake, push, or nudge slightly. **4** stimulate: It jogged his memory. **5** move up and down unsteadily. **6** (of a horse) run or ride at a slow, regular trot.
• *n* **1** a slight push or nudge. **2** a jogging movement. **jogger** *n* **jogtrot** *n* a slow, regular trot. < probably alteration of *shog* to shake, influenced by English dialect *jot* to jolt.

joggle (ˈdʒɒgḷ) *vb* shake slightly.
• *n* a joggling movement. < SEE **JOG**.

joie de vivre (ˌʒwɑː də ˈviːv) *n* (*French*) enjoyment of life.

join (dʒɔɪn) *vb* **1** come or bring together so as to form a connected unit. **2** come or bring into close relationship or association. **3** come into the company of: I'll join you for a coffee. **4** become a member of (a group, club, profession, etc.): They joined the union. **5** participate (in). **6 join up** enlist in one of the armed forces.
• *n* a place where two things are joined. < Latin *yungere* to yoke.

joiner (ˈdʒɔɪnə) *n* a person who makes or repairs wooden articles, esp. furniture. **joinery** *n* the work of a joiner.

joint (dʒɔɪnt) *n* **1** a place where two or more things or parts join. **2** a point of contact between two or more bones in an animal body. **3** a large piece of meat cut from a carcass, for cooking. **4** (*informal*) a disreputable place for gambling, drinking, etc. **5** (*slang*) a marijuana cigarette.

• *adj* **1** shared or owned by or belonging to two or more. **2** combined.
• *vb* **1** fit together. **2** divide (a carcass) into joints. **jointly** *adv* **jointness** *n* < SEE JOIN.

joist (dʒɔɪst) *n* a beam of timber or metal that supports a floor or ceiling. < ultimately Latin *jacēre* to lie.

joke (dʒəʊk) *n* **1** something, esp. a funny anecdote, said or done to arouse laughter. **2** a ridiculous person, thing, or circumstance. **3** something that is not serious: Losing your money and passport when you're abroad is no joke!
• *vb* make jokes. **jokingly** adv **joker** *n* **1** a person who jokes. **2** (*informal*) a person, esp. an unimportant or incompetent one. **3** an extra playing-card in a pack. < Latin *jocus.*

jolly (ˈdʒɒlɪ) *adj* **1** full of high spirits; merry; cheerful. **2** very pleasant. **3** (*euphemistic*) slightly drunk.
• *adv* (*informal*) very: jolly well.
• *vb* **jollied; jollying** (*informal*) put in good humour; make bright or cheerful. **jollity** *n* **jollification** *n* a merry festivity. < Old French *joli.*

jolt (dʒəʊlt) *vb* **1** move with a sudden, jerky action. **2** give a sudden push or blow to. **3** shock or surprise.
• *n* **1** a jolting movement. **2** a shock or surprise. < probably blend of obsolete *joll* to strike + *jot* to jerk.

joss-stick (ˈdʒɒsˌstɪk) *n* a thin stick of incense. < *joss,* figure of a Chinese god, from Pidgin English, ultimately from Latin *deus* god.

jostle (ˈdʒɒsl̩) *vb* **1** push or bump (a person) roughly, as in a crowd. **2** compete (with) in trying to reach an aim.
• *n* an act of jostling. < SEE JOUST.

jot (dʒɒt) *n* a little bit.
• *vb* **jotted; jotting** write down briefly or quickly. **jotter** *n* a small book or pad for writing notes. **jotting** *n* something jotted down. < Latin *iota* iota.

joule (dʒuːl) *n* a unit of work or energy. < James *Joule,* died 1889, English physicist.

journal (ˈdʒɜːnl̩) *n* **1** a magazine or periodical. **2** a record of current transactions. **journalese** *n* a superficial style of writing containing clichés, considered typical of some newspapers. **journalism** *n* **1** the profession of collecting, writing, and editing material for the mass media, esp. newspapers and magazines. **2** the material published in a newspaper, etc. **journalist** *n* **journalistic** *adj* < Middle French: daily, ultimately from Latin *dies* day. SEE PANEL.

journey (ˈdʒɜːnɪ) *n, pl* **journeys 1** a travelling from one place to another, esp. by land. **2** the distance or duration of this.
• *vb* make a journey. < Old French *journee* day's journey, ultimately from Latin *dies* day.

joust (dʒaʊst) *n* a fight between two knights on horseback with lances.
• *vb* fight in a joust. < Old French *juster,* ultimately from Latin *juxta* near.

jovial (ˈdʒəʊvɪəl) *adj* having or showing cheerful, lively humour. **joviality** *n* **jovially** *adv* < Late Latin *Jovialis* of Jupiter.

jowl (dʒaʊl) *n* **1** the jaw, esp. the lower jaw. **2** a cheek. < Old English *ceafl.*

joy (dʒɔɪ) *n* **1** a feeling or state of deep happiness or pleasure. **2** a source of delight. **joyful** *adj* causing, showing, or filled with joy. **joyfully** *adv* **joyfulness** *n* **joyless** *adj* without joy. **joyous** *adj* joyful. **joyously** *adv* < Latin *gaudēre* to rejoice.

JP *abbrev* Justice of the Peace.

jubilant (ˈdʒuːbɪlənt) *adj* feeling or showing great joy. **jubilation** *n* being jubilant. < Latin *jubilare* to rejoice.

jubilee (ˈdʒuːbɪˌliː) *n* a special anniversary, esp. 25th, 50th, or 60th, such as of the accession of a king or queen; celebration of this. < Hebrew *yōbhēl* ram's horn.

Judaism (ˈdʒuːdeɪˌɪzəm) *n* the religion of the Jews, based on the Old Testament and a belief in one supreme God.

judder (ˈdʒʌdə) *vb* shake jerkily.
• *n* a juddering movement. < probably alteration of *shudder.*

judge (dʒʌdʒ) *n* **1** a public official with authority to hear and pronounce judgment on cases in a law-court. **2** a

journal

A journal is a publication which appears usually once a month or once a quarter. Strictly speaking, however, it should appear every day. The name journal comes from the Middle French *journal* meaning 'daily', from the Latin *diurnalis,* which derives ultimately from *dies* or 'day'.

Interestingly, the French have avoided the misnomer: *le journal* continues to be used as the word for 'newspaper'.

person appointed to decide the winner in a contest. **3** a person who gives a critical opinion authoritatively: a great judge of wines.
• *vb* **1** hear and pronounce judgment on (a case) in a law-court. **2** act as a judge in (a contest). **3** form an opinion of by carefully considering the evidence. **4** estimate or evaluate. **judgment** *n* **1** judging; being judged. **2** a formal decision by a law-court. **3** an opinion, esp. an authoritative one. **4** the ability to judge wisely; discernment. **judgmental** *adj* < ultimately Latin *judex*. SEE PANEL.

judicial (dʒuːˈdɪʃəl) *adj* **1** of the administration of justice or law-courts: the judicial process. **2** of a judge. **3** ordered by a law-court. **judiciary** *n* the body of judges or system of law-courts in a country. < SEE **JUDGE.** SEE PANEL.

judicious (dʒuːˈdɪʃəs) *adj* having, showing, or coming from wise judgment. **judiciously** *adv* SEE PANEL AT **JUDICIAL.**

judo (ˈdʒuːdəʊ) *n* a form of Japanese, unarmed wrestling. < Japanese *jū* weakness + *dō* art.

jug (dʒʌg) *n* **1** a vessel for holding and pouring liquids, with a handle and a lip or spout. **2** also **jugful** the contents of this. **3** (*slang*) prison: in jug.
• *vb* **jugged; jugging 1** cook (hare) by stewing. **2** (*slang*) imprison. < perhaps *Jug*, nickname for *Joan*.

juggernaut (ˈdʒʌgəˌnɔːt) *n* **1** an irresistible, overwhelming force or object: the inexorable juggernaut of bureaucracy. **2** a very large, articulated lorry. SEE PANEL.

juggle (ˈdʒʌgl̩) *vb* **1** throw and catch (several objects) skilfully so that most are kept in the air at one time, esp. as an entertainment. **2** manipulate (figures, etc.), esp. in order to deceive. **3** keep (several activities) in progress at any one time. **juggler** *n* < ultimately Latin *jocus* joke.

jugular (ˈdʒʌgjʊlə) *adj* of the throat or neck. **jugular vein** a large vein of the neck that returns blood from the head to the heart. < Latin *jugulum* throat.

juice (dʒuːs) *n* **1** a liquid that occurs naturally or is secreted by an organ of the body: lemon juice; gastric juices. **2** (*informal*) electricity. **3** (*informal*) petrol for an engine. **juicy** *adj* **1** full of juice; succulent. **2** (*informal*) interesting, esp. scandalous; spicy. **juicily** *adv* **juiciness** *n* < Latin *jus*.

juke-box (ˈdʒuːkˌbɒks) *n* a record-player in a large case that automatically plays a selected record when a coin is inserted.

---

judicial or **judicious?**

These words are sometimes confused. Judicial means 'of or concerned with the administration of justice or law-courts; ordered by a law-court' as in the *judicial* process, *judicial* proceedings, *judicial* decisions.

Judicious means 'having, showing, or coming from wise judgment' as in a *judicious* comment, a *judicious* use of statistical surveys.

---

juggernaut

The original meaning of juggernaut is 'an overwhelming or irresistible destructive force'. This usage precedes its application to giant lorries by several centuries. The word entered English in the 17th century from the Hindi *Jagannāth* or 'Lord of the World', which is one of the titles of the Hindu god, Vishnu.

---

judgment or **judgement?**

In brief, either spelling is acceptable. Some users reserve judgment for legal contexts and use judgement in all other contexts. It may be more helpful, however, to adopt one spelling and to use that consistently.

The spelling judgement tends to be more common in Britain, although the trend is increasingly to use judgment, the more common American spelling.

Note that acknowledg(e)ment and abridg(e)ment should also be spelt in a way that is consistent with the spelling of judg(e)ment.

< Gullah *juke* bawdy + *box*.
jumble (ˈdʒʌmbl̩) *vb* mix in a confused, disordered way.
• *n* **1** a mass of things jumbled together. **2** articles for a jumble sale. **jumble sale** a sale of miscellaneous articles, esp. cheap and second-hand, usually to raise money for a charitable purpose. < origin uncertain.
jumbo (ˈdʒʌmbəʊ) *n, pl* **jumbos 1** a very large person or thing. **2** also **jumbo jet** a large, jet aeroplane that carries several hundred passengers. **3** a child's name for an elephant.
• *adj* very large. < the name of an elephant displayed by P.T. Barnum, from Gullah *jamba* elephant.
jump (dʒʌmp) *vb* **1** move oneself suddenly from the ground by using the muscles of the feet and legs. **2** move suddenly in surprise, shock, etc. **3** pass over or cause to pass over by jumping. **4** move quickly (into, out of, etc.): He jumped into the car and drove off. **5** increase suddenly: Inflation has jumped by 2% in one month. **6** pass (intervening matter or objects); skip. **7** leave (a track or rails) accidentally. **8** move or act before (a signal).
• *n* **1** a jumping movement. **2** a sudden movement caused by a shock or surprise. **3** a space, distance, or obstacle to be jumped or that has been jumped. **4** a sudden, sharp increase or change. **5** a break in continuity. **6** a stage: He was one jump ahead of his rivals. **jumper** *n* a person or animal that jumps. **jump-jet** *n* a jet aeroplane that can take off and land vertically. **jump-lead** *n* a thick electric cable for starting the engine of a motor vehicle with a flat battery, by connecting it to a second battery. **jumpy** *adj* very nervous. **the jumps** (*informal*) great nervousness. < origin uncertain.
SEE PANEL.

Jump to it!

Jump features in a number of expressions, many of them idiomatic including:

jump at to accept eagerly, with no hesitation: He jumped at the chance of a free trip to Africa.
jump down someone's throat to launch a sudden verbal attack on someone, especially in response to something he or she has just said.
jump on to criticize or challenge sharply.
jump the gun 1 to be too hasty in doing or saying something, especially in drawing a conclusion. **2** to make a false start in a race, by beginning before the starting-gun has been fired.
jump the queue 1 to move ahead of others in a queue. **2** to obtain something without waiting one's turn.
jump to conclusions to be too hasty in reaching a conclusion.
jump to it to move or start quickly: 'Jump to it! We're leaving in a few minutes!'

jumper (ˈdʒʌmpə) *n* a knitted garment for the upper part of the body. < obsolete *jump* loose jacket, perhaps from *jupe*, from Arabic *jubbah* long cloth coat.
junction (ˈdʒʌŋkʃən) *n* **1** a place where several roads or railway lines meet; place of meeting. **2** joining or being joined. < Latin *jungere* to join.
juncture (ˈdʒʌŋktʃə) *n* **1** a point in time. **2** a place of joining; connection.
jungle (ˈdʒʌŋgl̩) *n* **1** land overgrown with masses of vegetation, esp. in the tropics. **2** a confused, complex, and impenetrable mass: the jungle of tax regulations. **3** a scene of intense struggle or competition: the concrete jungle. < Hindi *jangal*.
junior (ˈdʒuːnɪə) *adj* **1** younger in age. **2** lower in rank; subordinate. **3** for younger children: a junior school. **4** (*US*) being the younger; used to distinguish a son with exactly the same name as his father: Chester K. Jensen, Junior.
• *n* **1** a junior person. **2** a person holding a subordinate rank or role: the office junior. < Latin: younger, from *juvenis* young.
juniper (ˈdʒuːnɪpə) *n* a coniferous tree or shrub with needle-like or scale-like leaves and purple, berry-like cones. < Latin *juniperus*.
junk¹ (dʒʌŋk) *n* **1** discarded articles; rubbish. **2** something of poor quality or low value. **3** (*slang*) narcotics, esp. heroin. **junkie** *n* (*slang*) a drug addict. **junk-shop** *n* a shop selling miscellaneous, cheap, second-hand goods. < Middle English *jonke*.
junk² *n* a sailing ship used in the Far East with a high poop, a flat bottom, and square sails. < Portuguese *junco*, from Javanese *jon*.
junta (ˈhʊntə, ˈdʒʊntə, ˈdʒʌntə) *n* a group of people who hold the power in a country, esp. after seizing it in a revolution. < Spanish: council, ultimately from Latin *jungere* to join.

jurisdiction (ˌdʒʊərɪsˈdɪkʃən) *n* **1** the right or authority to administer justice and to apply the laws. **2** the exercise of authority. **3** the limits or territory within which authority may be exercised. < Latin *juris,* from *jus* law + *dictio* declaration.

jurisprudence (ˌdʒʊərɪsˈpru:dn̩s) *n* the science or philosophy of law. < Late Latin *jurisprudentia.*

jury (ˈdʒʊərɪ) *n* **1** a group of people, usually 12, sworn to decide questions of fact in a court case according to the evidence presented. **2** a committee that judges the winner or winners in a competition. **juror** *n* a member of a jury. **juryman** fem. **jurywoman** *n* a juror.

just (dʒʌst) *adj* **1** fair or right: a just law. **2** fitting or proper; deserved: a just reward. **3** righteous: a just man. **4** well-founded: just cause to complain.
• *adv* **1** exactly: That's just what I said would happen. **2** simply; only: I can stay just for a few minutes. **3** at this or that very moment: He's only just got the job; I'm just coming! **4** at a small distance away: just round the corner. **5** (*informal*) absolutely: It's just terrific! **justly** *adv* **justness** *n* **just now 1** at this moment. **2** a moment ago. **just so 1** neatly arranged: Everything was just so. **2** used to express complete agreement. **just the same** nevertheless: Just the same, I wish you'd told us earlier. < Latin *jus* law.

justice (ˈdʒʌstɪs) *n* **1** the quality of being just; just treatment; fairness. **2** the administration of the law: a court of justice. **3** the title of a judge: Mr Justice Evans. < Latin *justus* just.

justify (ˈdʒʌstɪˌfaɪ) *vb* **justified; justifying 1** show to be right, just, or reasonable. **2** declare or show to be free from guilt. **3** space out (a line of printed text) so that it is level with a margin. **justification** *n* **justifiable** *adj* able to be justified. **justifiably** *adv* < Latin *justus* just.

jut (dʒʌt) *vb* **jutted; jutting** project. < probably JET[1].

jute (dʒu:t) *n* either of two Indian annual plants cultivated for their fibres, used in making sacks, rope, etc. < Hindi and Bengali *jūṭ.*

juvenile (ˈdʒu:vəˌnaɪl) *adj* **1** immature or childish. **2** for young people.
• *n* a young person. < Latin *juvenis* young person.

juxtapose (ˌdʒʌkstəˈpəʊz) *vb* put side by side. **juxtaposition** *n* < *juxtaposition,* from Latin *juxta* next to + *position.*

K

K *abbrev* **1** 1000. **2** (*computers*) 1024: 64K. < *k*ilo- 1000.
kale (keɪl) *n* a variety of cabbage grown for its large, edible leaves. < Old English *cāl*.
kaleidoscope (kəˈlaɪdəˌskəʊp) *n* a tube that contains loose chips of coloured glass between mirrors placed in such a way that changing, symmetrical patterns are produced as the instrument is turned. **kaleidoscopic** *adj* < Greek *kalos* beautiful + *eidos* form + English *-scope*, from Greek *skopein* to look at.
kangaroo (ˌkæŋgəˈruː) *n* the largest marsupial mammal, which leaps along on its long hind legs. < probably a native Australian language.
kaolin (ˈkeɪəlɪn) *n* a fine, white clay used esp. in ceramics. < *Kaoling*, hill in China where it was originally obtained.
kapok (ˈkeɪpɒk) *n* a mass of fine, silky hairs surrounding the seeds of the silk-cotton tree, used for stuffing mattresses, etc. < Malay.
kaput (kæˈpʊt) *adj* (*informal*) no longer working; broken; exhausted. < German *kaputt*, from French *être capot* to have made no tricks at the game of piquet.
karate (kəˈrɑːtɪ) *n* an oriental form of unarmed combat in which opponents use their hands, feet, elbows, etc., to deliver blows. < Japanese: empty hand.
karma (ˈkɑːmə) *n* the sum of all a person's actions, thought of in Hinduism and Buddhism as a moral force that determines that person's destiny in his or her next existence. < Sanskrit: work, action, effect.
kayak (ˈkaɪæk) *n* a small, light canoe made of a light frame covered with animal skins, as used by Eskimos; small canoe like this. < Eskimo *qajaq*.
kebab (kəˈbæb) *n* a dish consisting of small pieces of marinated meat cooked with onions, mushrooms, etc., on a skewer. < Arabic *kabāb*, from Turkish *kebap*.
kedgeree (ˌkɛdʒəˈriː) *n* a dish consisting of rice, cooked, flaked fish, and hard-boiled eggs. < Hindi *khicaṛī*, from Sanskrit *khiccā*.
keel (kiːl) *n* the main timber or piece of steel along the bottom of a ship or boat. • *vb* turn (over); collapse. **on an even keel** steady. < Old Norse *kjölr*.
keen (kiːn) *adj* **1** eager; enthusiastic: He's keen to start as soon as possible. **2 keen on** interested in; attracted to: keen on reading. **3** intense: keen interest. **4** with a sharp point or edge. **5** affecting one as if piercing: a keen wind. **6** (of prices) low, because competitive. **7** having a sensitive, astute perception: keen eyesight. **keenly** *adv* **keenness** *n* < Old English *cēne* brave.
keep (kiːp) *vb* **kept; keeping 1** remain or cause to remain in a state, position, etc., that is mentioned: keep quiet. **2** continue to possess. **3** manage; look after. **4** fulfil (a promise, etc.). **5** raise (livestock): They keep chickens. **6** provide for; support. **7** hold back; restrain: I kept her from telling you. **8** conceal (a secret); not disclose. **9** observe; celebrate. **10** remain in good condition; stay fresh. **11** watch over and defend. **12** maintain by making regular entries in: keep a diary. **13** delay; detain: What kept you? **14** save for future use; reserve. **15** continue, without interruption: Keep smiling!; keep on talking. **16** have (a commodity) regularly in stock for sale. **17** continue in a direction that is mentioned: Keep left.
• *n* **1** provision for the necessities of life, esp. food and shelter. **2** a fort or castle. **keeper** *n* a person in charge of something, such as a museum. **keeping** *n* **1** care; custody. **2** conformity or harmony: in keeping with his character. **keepsake** *n* something kept in memory of its giver. < Old English *cēpan*. SEE PANEL.
keg (kɛg) *n* a small barrel, esp. one made of metal and used for storing beer; beer from this. < Scandinavian.
ken (kɛn) *n* range of knowledge or sight: beyond my ken.
• *vb* (*Scottish*) know. < Old English *cennan*.
kennel (ˈkɛnl) *n* a shelter for a dog. • *vb* **kennelled; kennelling** put into a kennel. **kennels** *pl n* an establishment where dogs are bred, kept, etc. < Latin *canis* dog.
kept (kɛpt) SEE **KEEP**.
kerb (kɜːb) *n* the edging of stone, concrete, etc., along a pavement. **kerbstone** *n* one of the stones that make up a kerb. < alteration of *curb*.
kerchief (ˈkɜːtʃiːf) *n* a square piece of cloth used as a covering for the head or around the neck. < Old French *covrir* to cover + *chief* head.

kerfuffle (kə'fʌfl̩) *n* (*informal*) commotion or disorder; fuss. < Scottish *curfuffle.*

kernel ('kɜːnl̩) *n* **1** the edible seed of a nut or fruit in a shell or stone. **2** the part of a grain or seed in a hard husk. **3** the central, important, or essential part of something. < Old English *corn* seed.

kerosene ('kɛrəˌsiːn) *n* (*chiefly US*) paraffin. < Greek *kēros* wax + English *-ene.*

kestrel ('kɛstrəl) *n* a small falcon with a long tail, noted for its habit of hovering before diving on its prey. < Middle French *crecerelle,* from *crecelle* rattle, perhaps like its cry.

ketch (kɛtʃ) *n* a small, sailing vessel with two masts. < Middle English *cacchen* to hunt.

ketchup ('kɛtʃəp) *n* a thick sauce made with vinegar and seasonings, esp. one made from tomatoes flavoured with onions, etc. < Malay *kĕchap* fish-sauce.

kettle ('kɛtl̩) *n* a metal container with a lid, handle, and spout, used for boiling water. **kettledrum** *n* a large, basin-shaped drum. < Old Norse *ketill.*

key (kiː) *n* **1** a metal instrument shaped in such a way that it will turn the bolt of a lock. **2** an instrument that is turned to wind a clock, control a valve, etc. **3** a means of gaining access, control, etc. **4** one of a set of levers that operate a typewriter, etc., or are used in playing a musical instrument. **5** a system of related musical notes based on a particular note: the key of F major. **6** the general mood or style of something: in a restrained key. **7** something that is an essential part of an explanation or solution: The key to good teaching lies in communicating one's knowledge effectively. **8** a list of explanations of symbols, codes, etc. **9** the roughness of a surface that helps paint, plaster, etc., adhere to it. **10** a dry winged fruit of a tree such as an ash.
• *vb* conform or make appropriate.
• *adj* fundamental; most important: a key decision. **keyhole** *n* a hole in a lock into which a key is put. **keynote** *n* the fundamental, most important fact, principle, etc. **keystone** *n* the central, wedge-shaped stone at the top of an arch that locks the other stones in position. **key up** make excited, tense, etc. < Old English *cǣg.*

keyboard ('kiːˌbɔːd) *n* the set of keys on a piano, typewriter, typesetting-machine, etc.
• *vb* set (data, a text, etc.) using a keyboard, as for typesetting.

kg *abbrev* kilogram(s).

KGB *abbrev* (*Russian*) Komitet Gosudarstvennoi Bezopasnosti (Committee of State Security); Russian secret police.

khaki ('kɑːkɪ) *adj, n* a dull, yellowish-brown colour; (made of) a khaki-coloured, hard-wearing cloth used for military uniforms. < Hindi *khākī* dust-coloured, from Persian.

kHz *abbrev* kilohertz.

kibbutz (kɪ'bʊts) *n, pl* **kibbutzim** a

---

keep on

Keep features in a number of idiomatic expressions, including:

for keeps permanently: Do you really mean it's mine for keeps?

keep back to withhold.

keep down **1** to control the spread of: keep the weeds down. **2** not to vomit (food).

keep fit to exercise one's body in order to remain in a healthy condition. **keep-fit** *adj, n*

keep in to make (a child or pupil) stay at home, or at school, especially as a punishment.

keep in with to remain on friendly terms with (someone).

keep on **1** to continue: They kept on walking and eventually found a phone to ring for help. **2** to complain constantly: He keeps on at his son to get his hair cut. **3** to retain in employment.

keep one's hair on also **keep one's cool** not to lose one's temper.

keep the peace to obey the law and not cause trouble.

keep the wolf from the door to avoid hunger or starvation: We don't earn much, but at least we manage to keep the wolf from the door.

keep up **1** to continue or maintain. **2** to progress at the same pace, etc. **3** to maintain (a house, etc.) in good condition.

keep up with the Joneses to maintain the same material standards as one's wealthier neighbours. The expression comes from the title of a comic strip by Arthur R. Momand which was published in the New York 'Globe' from 1913 to the early 1940s. It derives from the artist's own attempts to keep up with his neighbours.

collective settlement in Israel. < Hebrew *qibbūs* gathering.

kick (kɪk) *vb* **1** strike, hit, or propel with the foot. **2** strike out with the feet, as in fighting. **3** score (a goal) by kicking. **4** (of a gun) recoil. **5** (*informal*) free oneself of (an addiction or habit).
• *n* **1** an act of kicking; blow with the foot. **2** (*informal*) a stimulating, pleasurable experience or effect; thrill.
kickback *n* a strong reaction. **kick off 1** start play in a game of football by kicking the ball. **2** (*informal*) begin proceedings. **kick-off** *n* kicking-off in football. **kick oneself** reproach oneself for an omission, etc. **kick out** force (someone) to leave; dismiss. **kick-start** *vb* start the engine of a motor cycle by jerking down a lever with one's foot. **kick-starter** *n* **kick up** create (a fuss, etc.). < Middle English *kiken*, perhaps from Scandinavian.

kid¹ (kɪd) *n* **1** the young of a goat or related animal; leather made from goatskin. **2** (*informal*) a child; young person. **kiddy** *n* (*informal*) a small child. < Middle English *kide*, from Scandinavian.

kid² *vb* **kidded; kidding 1** deceive; tease. **2** convince (oneself) that something improbable is true. **3** act or speak deceptively or for fun. < probably KID¹.

kidnap (ˈkɪdnæp) *vb* **kidnapped; kidnapping** seize and hold (a person), esp. for ransom. **kidnapper** *n* < from KID¹. + obsolete *nap* to steal.

kidney (ˈkɪdnɪ) *n, pl* **kidneys 1** one of two bean-shaped glands of excretion that also control the amount of salt and water in the blood. **2** the kidneys of certain animals eaten as food. **kidney bean** a French bean; seeds of this. < Middle English.

kill (kɪl) *vb* **1** cause the death of (a person or animal). **2** destroy the vitality of (a plant). **3** spoil the effect of; subdue. **4** defeat (a parliamentary bill, proposal, etc.).
• *n* **1** the act of killing. **2** the animals killed by a hunter. **killer** *n* **killjoy** *n* a person who spoils the pleasure of other people. < Middle English *killen*.

killing (ˈkɪlɪŋ) *adj* (*informal*) **1** very tiring. **2** very funny.
• *n* (*informal*) a sudden, great gain or profit. **killingly** *adv*

kiln (kɪln) *n* an oven for drying, burning, or baking things such as pottery, bricks, or grain. < Old English *cyln*, from Latin *culina* kitchen.

kilo (ˈkiːləʊ) *n, pl* **kilos** a kilogram.

kilo- *prefix* **1** 1000: kilometre. **2** (*computers*) 1024: kilobyte. < French, from Greek *chilioi*.

kilogram (ˈkɪləˌgræm) *n* the SI unit of mass; 1000 grams.

kilohertz (ˈkɪləˌhɜːts) *n* a unit of frequency equal to 1000 hertz.

kilometre (ˈkɪləˌmiːtə, kɪˈlɒmɪtə) *n* a distance of 1000 metres.

kilowatt (ˈkɪləˌwɒt) *n* the power of 1000 watts.

kilt (kɪlt) *n* a knee-length, pleated skirt, esp. made of tartan and worn as part of the dress of men of the Scottish Highlands. < Scandinavian.

kimono (kɪˈməʊnəʊ) *n, pl* **kimonos** a loose, outer garment with wide sleeves and a broad sash, traditionally worn by the Japanese. < Japanese: clothing.

kin (kɪn) *n* a person's relatives. < Old English *cyn*.

kind¹ (kaɪnd) *n* **1** a group with common features. **2** a recognizable member or example (of a group). **3** essential nature or quality. **in kind 1** in goods or natural produce, in contrast to money. **2** with the equivalent of what has been offered or received. **kind of** (*informal*) somewhat: It was kind of scaring. < Old English *cynd, gecynde*. SEE PANEL.

kind² *adj* friendly, generous, and helpful to other people. **kind-hearted** *adj* **kindness** *n* < Old English *gecynde*.

kindergarten (ˈkɪndəˌgɑːtn̩) *n* a school for very young children. < German: children's garden.

kindle (ˈkɪndl̩) *vb* **1** set alight; start to burn. **2** arouse or stimulate. **kindling** *n* material, such as dry wood, for lighting

different kinds of things

When kind of is followed by a plural noun, it is sometimes used with the plural these or those: *those kind of* people, *these kind of* oranges.

Careful users of English regard such usage as incorrect, however, preferring to use a singular noun with this or that or a different wording altogether: *that kind of* person, people *of that kind, this kind of* orange, oranges *of this kind*.

The same guidelines apply to sort of: some users prefer *that sort of* clock or clocks *of that sort* to *those sort of* clocks.

fires. < Old Norse *kynda*.

kindly (ˈkaɪndlɪ) *adj* kind in manner. • *adv* in a kind way. **kindliness** *n* **take kindly to** react favourably to; accept willingly.

kindred (ˈkɪndrɪd) *n* a person's relatives. • *adj* similar in nature, qualities, or interests: a kindred spirit. < Middle English, from *kin* + Old English *ræden* condition.

kinetic (kɪˈnɛtɪk) *adj* of, relating to, or caused by movement. **kinetic energy** energy possessed by a body because of its motion. < Greek *kinein* to move.

king (kɪŋ) *n* **1** a male sovereign who is the official ruler of an independent country. **2** a person, animal, or thing that is the best or most important of its kind. **3** a large species of animal: the king penguin. **4** the piece in chess that must be protected against check. **5** a playing-card with a stylized picture of a king and ranking next above a queen. **kingly** *adj* **kingfisher** *n* a fish-eating bird with a brightly coloured bill and plumage, often crested. **kingpin** *n* the most important person, thing, or feature. **kingship** *n* the position or authority of a king. **king-size** or **king-sized** *adj* larger or longer than the standard size. < Old English *cyning*.

kingdom (ˈkɪŋdəm) *n* **1** a territory ruled by a king or queen. **2** one of the three divisions of the natural world: the animal kingdom. **3** the reign or rule of God: the kingdom of heaven.

kink (kɪŋk) *n* **1** a sharp twist in a wire, hair, etc. **2** an eccentricity, esp. in sexual behaviour. • *vb* make or form kinks. **kinky** *adj* **1** marked by kinks. **2** (*informal*) eccentric or bizarre, esp. in sexual behaviour. < Dutch.

kiosk (ˈkiːɒsk) *n* **1** a small booth from which newspapers, cigarettes, sweets, etc., are sold. **2** a public telephone booth. < French *kiosque*, from Turkish *köşk* pavilion, from Persian *kūshk* portico.

kip (kɪp) *n* (*informal*) **1** a sleep. **2** a place to sleep. • *vb* **kipped; kipping** (*informal*) lie down to sleep; sleep. < perhaps Danish *kippe* tavern.

kipper (ˈkɪpə) *n* a fish, esp. a herring, that has been cleaned, salted, and smoked. • *vb* cure (herrings, etc.) by salting and smoking. < Old English *cypera*.

kirk (kɜːk) *n* (*chiefly Scottish*) a church. < Old Norse *kirkja*, from Old English *cirice*.

kirsch (kɪəʃ) *n* a dry, colourless brandy distilled from cherries. < German, short for *Kirschwasser* cherry water.

kiss (kɪs) *vb* **1** touch with the lips, to show affection or in a greeting. **2** express by kissing. **3** touch lightly. • *n* an act or instance of kissing. < Old English *cyssan*. SEE PANEL.

kit (kɪt) *n* **1** a set of tools, materials, etc.: a first-aid kit. **2** a set of parts ready to be assembled: a model aircraft kit. **3** a set of clothes and equipment, esp. for a particular activity or a traveller or soldier. • *vb* **kitted; kitting** equip with kit. **kitbag** *n* a bag for holding a soldier's or traveller's kit. < probably Middle Dutch *kitte* tankard.

kitchen (ˈkɪtʃɪn) *n* a room or part of a building where food is prepared and cooked. < Old English *cycene*, ultimately Latin *coquere* to cook.

kite (kaɪt) *n* **1** a light frame covered with a thin material, flown in the wind at the end of a long string. **2** a reddish-brown bird of the hawk family with long, narrow wings, a long tail, and a narrow bill. < Old English *cȳta*.

kith (kɪθ) *n* a person's acquaintances: kith and kin. < Old English *cȳthth*, from *cūth* known.

kitsch (kɪtʃ) *n* art, literature, or articles that show a lack of good taste. < German.

kitten (ˈkɪtn̩) *n* a young cat.

the kiss of life

Kiss features in a number of idiomatic expressions, including:

kiss of death an act that causes ruin: The decision to stop the government grant to the theatre is tantamount to a kiss of death.

kiss of life 1 mouth-to-mouth resuscitation. **2** an act that provides new energy, a stimulating influence, etc.: Plans to revitalize the area's economy were given the kiss of life in the Chancellor's statement.

kiss (something) better to kiss (a young child's wound or injury), as a pretended cure: 'Have you hurt your knee, darling? Come to mummy and let me kiss it better!'

• *vb* give birth to kittens. < Old Northern French *caton,* from cat.

kitty (ˈkɪtɪ) *n* **1** the pool of bets in certain gambling games. **2** a shared fund of money. < SEE **KIT.**

kiwi (ˈkiːwiː) *n* a nocturnal, flightless, New Zealand bird with a long bill, tiny wings, strong legs, and large claws. **Kiwi** *n* (*informal*) a New Zealander. < Maori, like its sound.

kleptomania (ˌklɛptəˈmeɪnɪə) *n* a strong, uncontrollable desire to steal things, esp. when not accompanied by an obvious motivation. **kleptomaniac** *n* < Greek *kleptein* to steal + Late Latin *mania.*

km *abbrev* kilometre(s).

knack (næk) *n* a special ability or skill that enables something, esp. something awkward or difficult, to be easily done. < Middle English *knak* sharp knock, like the sound.

knacker (ˈnækə) *n* a person who buys up old horses for slaughter. **knackered** *adj* (*informal*) exhausted. < probably English dialect *nacker* saddler, from Scandinavian.

knapsack (ˈnæpˌsæk) *n* a bag, made esp. of canvas or leather, strapped on the back and used by soldiers or hikers. < Low German *knappsack,* probably from *knappen* to bite + *sack* bag.

knave (neɪv) *n* **1** (*old-fashioned*) a dishonest man; rogue. **2** (in playing-cards) the jack. **knavery** *n* **knavish** *adj* < Old English *cnafa* boy. SEE PANEL AT **VILLAIN.**

knead (niːd) *vb* work and press (dough, etc.) into a mass by pressing and squeezing with the hands. < Old English *cnedan.*

knee (niː) *n* **1** the joint between the thigh and the lower part of the human leg; corresponding joint in animals. **2** the part of a garment that covers this. **3** the area between the knee and the thigh: Come and sit on my knee. **4** something shaped like a bent knee. **kneecap** *n* the bone that forms the front part of the knee joint; protective covering for this. **knee-deep** *adj* **1** also **knee-high** so deep as to reach the knees. **2** deeply involved: knee-deep in work. **knee-length** *adj* reaching to the knees. **knees-up** (*informal*) a boisterous party, esp. one with dancing. < Old English *cnēow.*

kneel (niːl) *vb* **knelt, kneeled; kneeling** rest or go down on the knee or knees, as in prayer or reverence. < Old English *cnēowlian.*

knell (nɛl) *n* the sound of a bell rung slowly at a funeral, death, etc. < Old English *cnyll.*

knelt (nɛlt) SEE **KNEEL.**

knew (njuː) SEE **KNOW.**

knickerbockers (ˈnɪkəˌbɒkəz) *pl n* short, baggy breeches gathered in at the knee. < Diedrich *Knickerbocker,* fictitious author of W. Irving's 'History of New York'.

knickers (ˈnɪkəz) *pl n* women's or girl's pants. < short for *knickerbockers.*

knick-knack (ˈnɪkˌnæk) *n* a small ornament. < SEE **KNACK.**

knife (naɪf) *n, pl* **knives 1** a cutting instrument with a sharp blade attached to a handle. **2** an instrument like this used as a weapon. **3** the cutting-blade of a machine.

• *vb* cut, stab, or kill with a knife. < Old English *cnīf.* SEE PANEL AT **SHELF.**

knight (naɪt) *n* **1** a man who has been given a non-hereditary rank in recognition of services or achievements, entitling him to use the title *Sir* before his name. **2** a chess piece usually in the form of a horse's head.

• *vb* make (a person) a knight. **knightly** *adv* **knighthood** *n* the rank of knight. < Old English *cniht.*

knit (nɪt) *vb* **knitted, knit; knitting 1** make (a garment, fabric, etc.) by looping yarn or thread together using two or more needles or a knitting-machine. **2** join closely or firmly; unite. **3** (of the brows) draw or be drawn together, as in frowning. **knitting** *n* work that has been or is being knitted. **knitwear** *n* knitted clothes. < Old English *cnyttan* tie in.

knob (nɒb) *n* **1** a rounded handle of a door, drawer, etc. **2** a rounded projection, as on a tree. **3** a small piece or lump: a knob of butter. **knobby** *adj* **knobbly** *adj* with small, round irregularities. < Middle English *knobbe.*

knock (nɒk) *vb* **1** strike with a sharp blow. **2** rap on a door, esp. to seek admittance. **3** drive, force, etc., by striking sharply: knock a nail into a wall. **4** make a sharp, thumping noise. **5** force into motion. **6** cause to collide with. **7** (*informal*) find fault with.

• *n* **1** a knocking blow or sound. **2** misfortune or bad luck; setback. **knocker** *n* a hinged, metal bar, etc., attached to a door and used for knocking. < Old English *cnocian.* SEE PANEL.

knoll (nəʊl) *n* a small, rounded hill; mound. < Old English *cnoll.*

knot (nɒt) *n* **1** an interlocking of one or more pieces of string, thread, etc., to

hold them together. **2** a bow of ribbon or braid tied as an ornament. **3** a small, closely knit group; cluster. **4** a protuberance in tissue. **5** a sense of tightness, as in the stomach muscles. **6** a speed of one nautical mile per hour.
• *vb* **knotted; knotting 1** tie or fasten with a knot. **2** unite closely. **knotty** *adj* very difficult to solve: a knotty problem. < Old English *cnotta*.

know (nəʊ) *vb* **knew; known; knowing 1** be aware of directly. **2** understand or grasp in one's mind. **3** recognize or identify (a person). **4** be well-informed about or familiar with. **5** be certain of. **6** have firmly in one's memory. **7** be able
to distinguish: Do you always know the difference between right and wrong? **8** experience: I've never known it be so hot. **know-how** *n* practical knowledge, skill, or experience. **knowing** *adj* **1** having knowledge; clever. **2** having secret knowledge. **knowingly** *adv* < Old English *cnāwan*. SEE PANEL.

knowledge (ˈnɒlɪdʒ) *n* **1** knowing. **2** everything that is known; body of information. **3** everything that a person knows. **knowledgeable** *adj* well-informed. **knowledgeably** *adv* < SEE KNOW.

known (nəʊn) SEE **KNOW**.

knuckle (ˈnʌkḷ) *n* **1** a finger-joint. **2** a cut of meat of the lowest leg joint of a pig, etc.
• *vb* **knuckle down** apply oneself seriously. **knuckle under** yield; submit. < Middle English *knokel*.

KO *abbrev* knock-out. **KO'ed** knocked out.

knock for six

Those who are not conversant with the lore of cricket will doubtless be stumped if asked to give the origin of knock for six. The phrase, meaning 'to inflict or suffer a devastating blow or defeat', properly refers to the inspired stroke of the bat which sends the ball flying over the boundary line without it once touching the ground. This feat scores six runs for the batsman and his side.

Nowadays the phrase is of virtually unbounded application: The shareholders were knocked for six by the news of the company's collapse.

Knock also features in the following expressions:

knock about 1 to treat roughly, as by punching, etc. **2** also **knock around** to travel or wander casually. **3** also **knock around** to be in a place, especially with no definite purpose.
knock back 1 to swallow (a drink). **2** to cost (someone) (a large amount of money): That car repair bill knocked us back over £200!
knock down 1 to hit with a vehicle and cause to fall. **2** to demolish. **3** to reduce (the price) of an article.
knock-down *adj* (of a price) very low; greatly reduced.
knock off 1 to stop work. **2** to deduct (an amount) from a price. **3** to steal. **4** to complete (a book, painting, etc.) quickly.
knock-on *adj* causing repercussions, especially similar changes, elsewhere: The reduction in tax will have a knock-on effect throughout the economy.
knock out 1 to render unconscious. **2** to shock or overwhelm greatly. **3** to eliminate from a competition.
knock-out *n* **1** also *adj* (of) a competition in which the loser in each successive round is eliminated. **2** a person or thing that is irresistible, very striking, etc.: His new girlfriend's a real knock-out!
knock spots off to be far better than; outshine.
knock up 1 to wake by ringing at the door, etc. **2** to make hastily. **3** to practise before a game of tennis, etc. **knock-up** *n*

you know

Know features in a number of expressions, many of them idiomatic, including:

in the know better informed in a particular sphere than other people.
know-all *n* a person who behaves as if he or she knows everything.
know-how *n* practical expertise or skill.
you know used to draw the attention of the listener to something: 'How can I get another job? I'm over 55, you know!' You know is also used as a marker of hesitant expression: 'I kind of wondered ... you know ... if you might like to come with me to the cinema.' This is often overused, so attracting criticism from many careful users of English.

kowtow

To kowtow to people means to behave with servile respect towards them. Kowtow comes from Mandarin Chinese *kòu* 'to strike' + *tóu* 'head'.

Originally, this respect was shown by kneeling before the person and touching the ground with one's forehead.

koala (kəʊˈɑːlə) *n* an Australian, tree-dwelling marsupial with thick, greyish fur, tufted ears, and long claws. < native Australian name.

kosher (ˈkəʊʃə) *adj* (of food) conforming to Jewish dietary laws. < Hebrew *kāshēr* fit.

kowtow (ˈkaʊtaʊ) *vb* behave with servile respect towards a person. SEE PANEL.

kudos (ˈkjuːdɒs) *n* glory and honour. < Greek *kydos.*

kung fu (ˌkʌŋ ˈfuː) *n* a Chinese form of combat, mainly for self-defence. < Chinese: martial art.

kW *abbrev* kilowatt(s).

L

l *abbrev* litre(s).

L *abbrev* learner driver.

lab (læb) *n* (*informal*) a laboratory.

label (ˈleɪbḷ) *n* **1** a piece of cloth, paper, etc., fixed on or near something to give information about it. **2** a phrase or term that describes something.
• *vb* **labelled; labelling 1** fix a label to. **2** describe or classify with or as if with a label. < Old French.

labial (ˈleɪbɪəl) *adj* of or relating to the lips. < Latin *labium* lip.

laboratory (ləˈbɒrətrɪ) *n* a place that is equipped for scientific experiments or research. < SEE **LABOUR**.

laborious (ləˈbɔːrɪəs) *adj* involving or marked by great effort. **laboriously** *adv* < SEE **LABOUR**.

labour (ˈleɪbə) *n* **1** physical or mental exertion. **2** a task. **3** the process or period of childbirth. **4** workers or working people seen as providing goods or services in an economy or as distinct from management. **5 Labour** the Labour Party.
• *vb* **1** exert oneself. **2** move with great effort. **3** be burdened by: labouring under a sense of grievance. **4** treat in excessive detail: to labour a point. **laboured** *adj* marked by great effort; not having free, easy expression. **labourer** *n* a person who does unskilled, manual work, esp. outdoors: a farm labourer. **Labour Party** a British political party organized to support and further the interests of organized workers. < Latin *labor* work.

labrador (ˈlæbrəˌdɔː) *n* also **Labrador retriever** a retriever dog with a smooth, black or golden coat. < *Labrador,* district of NE Canada.

laburnum (ləˈbɜːnəm) *n* an ornamental tree with smooth, olive-green or brown bark, and bright-yellow flowers that droop in clusters. < Latin.

labyrinth (ˈlæbərɪnθ) *n* **1** a network of paths, tunnels, and chambers, through which it is very hard to find one's way. **2** a complicated arrangement or state. < Greek *labyrinthos.*

lace (leɪs) *n* **1** fabric of silk, linen, etc., woven in ornamental openwork design. **2** a cord or string used to pull two edges of a garment or shoe together.
• *vb* **1** fasten with a lace or laces. **2** weave together. **3** decorate with lace. **4** add a dash of spirits to. < Old French *laz,* from Latin *laqueus* noose.

lacerate (ˈlæsəˌreɪt) *vb* **1** tear or cut roughly. **2** wound mentally or emotionally. **laceration** *n* < Latin *lacerare* to tear.

lachrymose (ˈlækrɪˌməʊs) *adj* tearful. < Latin *lacrimare* to weep.

lack (læk) *n* an insufficiency; state of insufficiency: He died from a lack of oxygen.
• *vb* **1** be deficient in; be short of. **2** be missing. < Middle Dutch *laken.*

lackadaisical (ˌlækəˈdeɪzɪkḷ) *adj* lacking vitality or enthusiasm. **lackadaisically** *adv* < *alack the day* expression of regret.

lackey (ˈlækɪ) *n, pl* **lackeys 1** a low-ranking male servant. **2** a servile follower. < Middle French *laquais.*

lack-lustre (ˈlækˌlʌstə) *adj* lacking brilliance or vitality.

laconic (ləˈkɒnɪk) *adj* using few words; terse. **laconically** *adv* < Greek *Lakōnikos* Spartan.

lacquer (ˈlækə) *n* a coloured, usually opaque varnish that is applied to a surface for protection and decoration.
• *vb* coat with lacquer. < Portuguese *laca* resinous substance, from Arabic, from Persian *lak.*

lacrosse (ləˈkrɒs) *n* a field game played with a ball and a long-handled racket which has a netted pocket for catching, carrying, or throwing the ball. < Canadian French *la crosse* the hooked stick.

lactation (lækˈteɪʃən) *n* the secretion of milk by a mammal. < Latin *lac* milk.

lacuna (ləˈkjuːnə) *n, pl* **lacunae** a gap or space. < Latin: pool, gap.

lad (læd) *n* **1** a boy or young man. **2** (*informal*) a fellow; chap. < Middle English *ladde.*

ladder (ˈlædə) *n* **1** a portable framework of two parallel lengths of wood, metal, etc., connected by rungs, for use in climbing up and down. **2** a vertical line of stitches that have become undone in a stocking, etc. **3** a series of ascending steps, esp. to a higher or more advanced position.
• *vb* (of stockings, etc.) develop a ladder. < Old English *hlǣder.*

laden (ˈleɪdṇ) *adj* weighed down. < past participle of *lade,* from Old English *hladan.*

la-di-da (ˌlɑːdɪˈdɑː) *adj* (*informal*) marked by an affectedly genteel manner or way of speaking. < like this style of speech.

lading (ˈleɪdɪŋ) *n* cargo. < SEE **LADEN.**

ladle (ˈleɪdl̩) *n* a spoon with a long handle and a deep bowl, used for serving or transferring liquids.
• *vb* transfer in a ladle. < Old English *hlædel.*

lady (ˈleɪdɪ) *n* **1** (*chiefly polite*) a woman: Ladies and gentlemen .... **2** a woman who is refined, etc.; woman of a high social position. **3** (*old-fashioned informal*) a wife. **4 Lady** used as a title for various women; female member of an order of knighthood. **ladybird** *n* a small, round beetle, commonly red with black spots. **ladylike** *adj* like a lady, esp. in behaviour; refined; suitable for a lady. **ladyship** *n* used as a title for a woman of the rank of Lady. SEE PANEL. SEE PANEL AT **WOMAN.**

lag[1] (læg) *vb* **lagged; lagging** fall or stay behind others in movement or progress.
• *n* lagging; delay; interval between two events. < perhaps Scandinavian.

lag[2] *vb* **lagged; lagging** cover (pipes, a tank, etc.) with lagging to reduce loss of heat. **lagging** *n* insulating material. < Scandinavian.

lager (ˈlɑːgə) *n* a light beer. < German *Lagerbier* beer for storing, from *Lager* storehouse + *Bier* beer.

lagoon (ləˈguːn) *n* a shallow body of water separated from a larger body of water by coral reefs, a sandbank, etc. < Latin *lacuna* pool.

laid (leɪd) SEE **LAY**[1]. **laid-back** *adj* relaxed: a laid-back approach to life.

lain (leɪn) SEE **LIE**[2].

lair (lɛə) *n* the place where a wild animal rests or lives. < Old English *leger.*

laissez-faire (ˌlɛseɪˈfɛə) *n* the policy of non-interference in the affairs of others. < French: let (people) do (as they wish).

laity (ˈleɪətɪ) *n* people not ordained as clergy. < SEE **LAY**[2].

lake (leɪk) *n* a body of water that is completely surrounded by land. < Latin *lacus.*

lamb (læm) *n* **1** the young of a sheep; flesh of this eaten as food. **2** a gentle, innocent person.
• *vb* give birth to a lamb. **lambskin** *n* the skin of a lamb or small sheep, still with the wool on; leather made from this skin. **lambswool** *n* soft, fine wool. < Old English.

lambaste (læmˈbeɪst) *vb* (*informal*) beat or criticize strongly. < perhaps Scandinavian *lam* to thrash + *baste* to beat.

lame (leɪm) *adj* **1** disabled in the legs or feet. **2** painful. **3** (of an excuse, etc.) weak; unconvincing.
• *vb* make lame. **lamely** *adv* **lameness** *n* **lame duck** (*informal*) an inefficient or ineffective person or thing. < Old English *lama.*

lamé (ˈlɑːmeɪ) *n* a fabric in which threads of silver or gold are interwoven. < French, ultimately from Latin *lamina* thin plate.

lament (ləˈmɛnt) *vb* feel or show great sorrow or regret (for); mourn.
• *n* **1** an expression of great sorrow. **2** a poem or song in which a death is lamented. **lamentation** *n* **lamentable** *adj* regrettable; deplorable. **lamentably** *adv* < Latin *lamentum* lament. SEE PANEL.

lady or **woman?**

Lady conveys a sense of nobility or gentility: it is used in titles, for example *Lady* Ponsonby, *Lady* Byron. As such, lady is used in polite address: 'Please show this *lady* to her seat.' '*Ladies* and gentlemen ...'. Woman is a more neutral word.

The difference between lady and woman is therefore reflected by the difference between lord (and gentleman) and man. Lord, like lady, is used in titles (*Lord* Dunsmore), gentleman is used in polite address, and man is the neutral word.

lamentable exceptions

Language learning would be much easier if there were no exceptions to the rule. Unfortunately this is seldom the case. Take for example the class of adjectives that are derived from verbs by the addition of -able or -ible. The meaning of such adjectives is usually 'able to be -ed', as in washable, ironable, scorchable, and repairable. But what about lamentable? A lamentable decision is not one that is 'able to be' but which 'ought to be' lamented. A different meaning again is found in admirable—an admirable attempt is not one that is 'able to be' or that 'ought to be' but which is 'worthy of being' admired. See also panel at **attach.**

laminate (ˈlæmɪˌneɪt) *vb* **1** press or separate into a thin sheet or thin sheets. **2** make by covering with thin layers, one upon the other; cover with these.
• *n* (ˈlæmɪnət, ˈlæmɪˌneɪt) a material made by laminating. < Latin *lamina* thin plate.

lamp (læmp) *n* **1** a device that gives light: a street lamp. **2** a device that produces radiation: a sun-lamp. **lamppost** *n* a post that supports a light which illuminates a public area, esp. a road. **lampshade** *n* a decorative shade placed round an electric light bulb to soften its glare. < Greek *lampein* to shine.

lampoon (læmˈpuːn) *n* a strong, satirical attack that ridicules a person, institution, etc.
• *vb* ridicule in a lampoon. < French *lampon,* perhaps from *lampons* let us drink, refrain in a drinking song.

lamprey (ˈlæmprɪ) *n* an eel-like vertebrate with a circular, sucking mouth for clinging to things. < Medieval Latin *lampreda.*

lance (lɑːns) *n* **1** a long weapon with a sharp head, used by horsemen. **2** a spear or harpoon for killing whales. **3** a lancet.
• *vb* pierce with a lancet. **lance-corporal** *n* a non-commissioned officer of the rank below a corporal. < Latin *lancea.*

lancet (ˈlɑːnsɪt) *n* **1** a pointed, surgical knife with two sharp edges, used to make small incisions. **2** a high, narrow, pointed arch or window. < SEE **LANCE**.

land (lænd) *n* **1** the solid part of the earth's surface not covered by water. **2** a country or region. **3** ground or soil: good farming land. **4** ground owned as property. **5** rural, agricultural regions. **6** a realm or domain.
• *vb* **1** arrive on land from a ship. **2** set (something) from a ship onto land. **3** bring or come down after a flight or jump. **4** bring to a place, state, etc., that is mentioned: You'll land up in jail if you carry on like this. **5** catch and bring in (a fish). **6** obtain: I've just landed a fantastic new job! **7** deliver (a blow). **8** present; lumber: You've landed us with the job of sorting out the mess. **landed** *adj* **1** owning land: the landed gentry. **2** consisting of land: a landed estate. **landfall** *n* the sighting of land after a journey by sea or air. **landlady** *n* **1** a woman who leases or rents rooms, land, etc., to others. **2** a woman who keeps an inn or boarding-house. **land-locked** *adj* surrounded or nearly surrounded by land. **landlord** *n* **1** a person who leases or rents rooms, land, etc., to others. **2** a person who keeps an inn or boarding-house. **landlubber** *n* a person who is unfamiliar with the sea and seamanship. **landmark** *n* **1** a conspicuous object or feature of a landscape. **2** an event marking a stage or a new development in something. **landowner** *n* a person who owns land. **landslide** *n* **1** also **landslip** a fast movement of earth, rock, etc., down a slope. **2** an overwhelming victory in an election. **see how the land lies** find out what the situation is like. < Old English.

landing (ˈlændɪŋ) *n* **1** the act of coming to land, esp. after a journey by sea or air. **2** the place where people and cargo may be landed from a ship. **3** a level area at the top of a flight of stairs or between flights of stairs. **landing-craft** *n* a naval vessel intended for putting troops and equipment ashore. **landing-gear** *n* the undercarriage of an aircraft. **landing-stage** *n* a platform used to land goods and passengers from a boat, etc. **landing-strip** *n* a runway without normal airport facilities.

landscape (ˈlændˌskeɪp) *n* **1** an area of scenery. **2** a picture of this.
• *vb* improve the natural features of (a garden, etc.). **landscape gardening** laying out gardens and grounds to make them more attractive. < Dutch *land* land + *-schap* -ship.

lane (leɪn) *n* **1** a narrow passage, road, or track. **2** a strip of road for a single line of traffic: Get in lane! **3** a designated route for ships or aircraft. **4** one of several parallel courses marked out for competitors in running or swimming: the inside lane. < Old English *lanu.*

language (ˈlæŋgwɪdʒ) *n* **1** words and their use by a particular people as a means of communication. **2** the faculty of human speech. **3** a means of communicating information by signs, symbols, etc. **4** a system of symbols, rules, etc., for use in programming a computer. **5** a particular style or way of wording: poetic language. **6** the specialized vocabulary of a particular group of people: scientific language. **language laboratory** a room equipped with tape-recorders, etc., where language skills are learnt. < Latin *lingua.*

languid (ˈlæŋgwɪd) *adj* lacking liveliness and vigour; weak. **languidly** *adv* < Latin *languēre* to languish.

languish (ˈlæŋgwɪʃ) *vb* **1** lose strength, energy, or intensity. **2** become dispirited. **3** suffer hardship. < SEE **LANGUID**.

languor (ˈlæŋgə) *n* **1** weariness or

laziness. **2** dreaminess or wistfulness. **languorous** *adj* < SEE **LANGUID**.

lank (læŋk) *adj* **1** straight and limp: lank hair. **2** thin and tall; gaunt. **lanky** *adj* ungracefully tall and thin. **lankiness** *n* < Old English *hlanc*.

lanolin (ˈkænəlɪn) *n* a purified wax extracted from wool, used as a base for creams, soaps, etc. < Latin *lana* wool + *oleum* oil + *-in*.

lantern (ˈlæntən) *n* a transparent case holding a light and protecting it against wind, etc., outdoors. < Greek *lampein* to shine.

lap[1] (læp) *n* **1** the upper surface of the thighs of a seated person. **2** the part of a garment covering this. < Old English *læppa*.

lap[2] *n* **1** one circuit of a racecourse, track, etc. **2** a stage or part of a journey. **3** an overlapping part; amount of overlap.
• *vb* **lapped; lapping 1** fold or wrap round. **2** overlap. **3** overtake (a competitor) in a race so as to be one or more circuits ahead. < probably **LAP**[1].

lap[3] *vb* **lapped; lapping 1** take in liquids with the tongue, as a cat does. **2** (of small waves) splash (against) gently. **lap up** take in eagerly. < Old English *lapian*.

lapel (ləˈpɛl) *n* a flap on the front of a coat or jacket, extending downwards from the collar. < SEE **LAP**[1].

lapidary (ˈlæpɪdərɪ) *adj* engraved on stone; of stones.
• *n* a person who cuts, shapes, and polishes precious stones. < Latin *lapis* stone.

lapse (læps) *n* **1** a slight error: a temporary lapse of memory. **2** the passage of a period of time. **3** a moral decline. **4** the ending of a legal right or privilege through failure to exercise it.
• *vb* **1** decline in condition, status, etc. **2** be discontinued, as through disuse. **3** slide gradually (into) a state. < Latin *lapsus*, from *labi* to glide, slip.

lapwing (ˈlæpˌwɪŋ) *n* a greenish-black bird with a long crest, broad, rounded wings, and a short tail; known for its call and acrobatic courtship flights; peewit. < Old English *hlēapewince*.

larceny (ˈlɑːsənɪ) *n* theft. < Latin *latro* robber.

larch (lɑːtʃ) *n* a tall, deciduous conifer that produces small, woody cones. < German *Lärche*, ultimately from Latin *larix*.

lard (lɑːd) *n* a soft, white, solid fat prepared from the fat of a pig and used in cooking.
• *vb* **1** prepare (meat, etc.) for cooking by covering with or inserting bacon, fat, etc. **2** cover with grease. **3** embellish (speech or writing). < Latin *lardum*.

larder (ˈlɑːdə) *n* a room or cupboard used to store food. < SEE **LARD**.

large (lɑːdʒ) *adj* **1** greater or bigger than average. **2** great in amount, scope, power, etc. **largeness** *n* **largish** *adj* **at large 1** not confined: The escaped prisoner is still at large. **2** as a whole: The public at large remained unaware of the danger. **by and large** generally speaking. **largely** *adv* to a great extent: The plan's failure was largely due to the extra costs incurred. **large-scale** *adj* **1** extensive; involving great numbers or amounts: a large-scale operation. **2** (of a map) showing a lot of detail. < Latin *largus*.

largess (lɑːˈdʒɛs) *n* generous giving; money, etc., given generously. < SEE **LARGE**.

lark[1] (lɑːk) *n* a slender, brown, long-winged singing bird, esp. a skylark. < Old English *lāwerce*.

lark[2] *vb* have fun; play about.
• *n* a playful adventure; harmless, amusing incident. < origin uncertain.

larva (ˈlɑːvə) *n, pl* **larvae** the immature form of many animals that hatches from the egg and is transformed into a different adult form. < Latin: ghost.

larynx (ˈlærɪŋks) *n* the organ at the front of the neck that contains the vocal cords. **laryngitis** *n* inflammation of the larynx. < Greek.

lasagne (ləˈzænjə) *n* **1** a baked dish of minced meat, sauce, and pasta in wide, flat sheets. **2** this type of pasta. < Italian *lasagna*, from Latin *lasanum* cooking-pot.

lascivious (ləˈsɪvɪəs) *adj* lustful. **lasciviously** *adv* **lasciviousness** *n* < Latin *lascivia* wantonness.

laser (ˈleɪzə) *n* a device that generates a beam of high-intensity, coherent, monochromatic light or other electromagnetic radiation. < *l*ight *a*mplification by *s*timulated *e*mission of *r*adiation. SEE PANEL AT **RADAR**.

lash[1] (læʃ) *n* **1** a blow with a whip, etc. **2** the flexible part of a whip. **3** an eyelash.
• *vb* **1** move suddenly and forcefully. **2** beat or strike forcefully. **3** attack physically or verbally. **4** rouse. **lashing** *n* a beating. **lashings** *pl n* (*informal*) a large amount (of). **lash out** strike out forcefully; be extravagant in spending money. < like the sound.

lash[2] *vb* fasten or secure with rope, etc. **lashing** *n* a rope, etc., used for fastening or securing. < ultimately Latin *laqueus* noose.

lass (læs) *n* a girl or young woman. < Middle English *las.*

lassitude (ˈlæsɪˌtjuːd) *n* a lack of energy; weariness. < Latin *lassus* weary.

lasso (læˈsuː) *n, pl* **lassos** a long rope with a running noose, used to catch horses and cattle.
• *vb* catch with a lasso. < Spanish *lazo,* from Latin *laqueus* noose.

last[1] (lɑːst) *adj* **1** being or coming after all others or at the end. **2** most recent: last year. **3** only remaining. **4** least suitable or likely.
• *adv* **1** after all others; at the end. **2** most recently.
• *n* a person or thing that is last; final part. **lastly** *adv* < Old English *latost,* from *læt* late. SEE PANEL.

last[2] *vb* **1** continue for a period of time. **2** remain in good, etc., condition. **3** be sufficient for the needs of. **lasting** *adj* continuing for a long time: a lasting friendship. < Old English *lǣstan.*

last[3] *n* a wooden or metal form shaped like a foot, used for making or repairing shoes. < Old English *lāst* footprint.

latch (lætʃ) *n* a fastener on a door, esp. one that consists of a small bar that falls into a notch.
• *vb* fasten with a latch. **latchkey** *n* a key to an outer door. **latch on to** (*informal*) attach oneself to; understand. < Old English *læccan.*

late (leɪt) *adj* **1** also *adv* coming, happening, arriving, etc., after the expected or usual time. **2** also *adv* far on in the day or night: It's getting late—we'd better go now. **3** far on in a period that is mentioned: in the late 1980s. **4** most recent: Some late news has just come in. **5** recently deceased: the late Professor Smith. **lateness** *n* **latecomer** *n* a person or thing that comes late. **lately** *adv* recently. **latest** *n* the most recent fashion or development. < Old English *læt.* SEE PANEL.

latent (leɪtn̩t) *adj* existing but not yet shown, active, or developed: his latent artistic abilities. < Latin *latēre* to lie hidden.

lateral (ˈlætərəl) *adj* of, on, or towards, the side.
• *n* a lateral part, branch, etc. **laterally** *adv* **lateral thinking** thinking that seeks to solve problems by means of unorthodox approaches. < Latin *latus* side.

latex (ˈleɪtɛks) *n* **1** a milky liquid produced by various plants, for example the rubber tree. **2** a synthetic product like this, used for example in adhesives. < Latin: liquid.

lath (lɑːθ) *n* a thin, narrow strip of wood, used as a support for plaster, etc. < Old English *lætt.*

lathe (leɪð) *n* a machine that shapes wood, metal, etc., by holding and turning it quickly against a cutting tool. < probably Scandinavian.

lather (ˈlɑːðə) *n* **1** foam or froth produced when soap or other detergent is mixed with water. **2** frothy sweat, esp. on horses.
• *vb* **1** cover with lather. **2** form a lather. **3** (*informal*) flog or beat. < Old English *lēathor.*

latitude (ˈlætɪˌtjuːd) *n* **1** the distance north or south of the equator, measured in degrees. **2** a region considered with respect to its latitude. **3** freedom of action; scope. **latitudinal** *adj* < Latin *latus* wide.

latrine (ləˈtriːn) *n* a toilet, esp. a small pit or trench, in a camp, barracks, etc. < Latin *lavere* to wash.

---

the last word

Last features in a number of expressions, many of them idiomatic, including:

at last at the end of a period of time; after waiting.
last-ditch *adj* undertaken as one last effort before surrendering or losing: a last-ditch attempt to save the threatened school.
last-minute *adj* undertaken urgently and quickly, immediately before an event: last-minute Christmas shopping.
last straw an additional burden which, when added to other difficulties, makes a situation unbearable. The expression comes from the saying it is the last straw that breaks the camel's back.
last thing just before going to bed at night.
last word **1** the most modern or fashionable example: This car is the last word in luxury. **2** the remark that ends an argument: We may disagree but the boss always has the last word.
on its last legs nearing the end of its usefulness; near death.

---

latter (ˈlætə) *adj* **1** nearer to the end: the latter half of the 20th century. **2** the second of two mentioned: the latter. **latter-day** *adj* modern; recent. **latterly** *adv* recently. < SEE **LATE**. SEE PANEL AT **FORMER**.

lattice (ˈlætɪs) *n* **1** an open framework of crossed, wooden or metal strips. **2** a structural network like this. < Middle French *lattis.*

laud (lɔːd) *vb* (*literary*) praise. **laudable** *adj* deserving praise. **laudably** *adv* < Latin *laus* praise.

Late train arrives on time!

Late is an example of an adjective which can change its meaning according to whether it precedes or follows the noun to which it applies. For example, the meaning of late in I think I'll take the late train is not the same as in the train was late. A late train may well arrive on time or, for that matter, even early.

A similar shift of meaning occurs when late is used in connection with people. Imagine the consternation when the non-fluent wife of a foreign VIP arrives unaccompanied at a reception and utters, 'my late husband' instead of, 'My husband is late'. The difference here between 'deceased' and 'arriving after the expected time' is a matter of the adjective's *attributive* (before the noun) or *predicative* (following the noun) position.

Late features in a number of idiomatic expressions, including:

better late than never it is better to arrive late than not at all.

late in the day at a later time than one that is suitable or might bring beneficial results: 'It's a bit late in the day to tell me that you don't want to go—I've already bought the tickets!'

of late recently: 'She's been looking very tired of late.'

laugh (lɑːf) *vb* **1** make the sounds and movements of the face that express amusement, ridicule, etc. **2** utter with or as if with a laugh. **3** make fun (of); sneer (at).
• *n* **1** the act or sound of laughing. **2** a cause of laughter. **laughable** *adj* causing laughter or derision; ridiculous. **laughing-gas** *n* nitrous oxide. **laughing-stock** *n* a person or thing that is ridiculed. **laugh off** treat or regard as if of no consequence. **laughter** *n* the sound or action of laughing. < Old English *hliehhan.*

launch¹ (lɔːntʃ) *vb* **1** propel with force; set (a missile) into motion: launch a rocket. **2** move (a vessel) into the water. **3** enter on (a course of action): launch a campaign. **4** involve (oneself) energetically (in). **5** start (a new company). **6** put (a new product) onto the market.
• *n* the act or process of launching something. **launching-pad** *n* a platform from which a rocket is launched. < Late Latin *lanceare* to use a lance.

launch² *n* a large motor boat. < Spanish *lancha.*

launder (ˈlɔːndə) *vb* wash and often also starch and iron (clothes). **launderette** *n* a self-service laundry. **laundry** *n* **1** a place where clothes, etc., are laundered. **2** clothes to be laundered. < ultimately Latin *lavare* to wash.

laureate (ˈlɔːrɪət, ˈlɒrɪət) *adj* **Poet Laureate** a poet appointed to write poems for important public occasions. < Latin *laureatus* crowned with laurel, from Latin *laurus* laurel.

laurel (ˈlɒrəl) *n* **1** an evergreen shrub or small tree with glossy leaves. **2** a crown of laurel given as a sign of victory or honour. < Latin *laurus.* SEE PANEL.

lava (ˈlɑːvə) *n* molten rock that is discharged from a volcano; such rock when cooled and solidified. < Italian, from Latin *lavare* to wash.

lavatory (ˈlævətrɪ) *n* a toilet. < Latin

rest on your laurels

The expression rest on one's laurels means 'to enjoy with satisfaction the fame, distinction, etc., that one has gained and not try to achieve more': Now is not the time to *rest on your laurels!* The expression look to one's laurels means 'to be careful to maintain one's favoured position by guarding against attempts by others to do better': If he wants to come first again in the race this year then he'd better *look to his laurels* and train harder. The laurel in these expressions derives from the wreaths of laurel with which the Greeks crowned poets and victors at the Pythian games.

lavare to wash.

lavender (ˈlævəndə) *n* a small shrub with narrow, aromatic, grey-green leaves and spikes of purple flowers which are dried and used in perfumes. < Medieval Latin *lavendula.*

lavish (ˈlævɪʃ) *adj* **1** giving or spending very generously. **2** very abundant.
• *vb* spend or give very generously. **lavishly** *adv* **lavishness** *n* < Latin *lavare* to wash.

law (lɔː) *n* **1** a rule that governs the relationship of one country to another, a state and its citizens, or one person and another; set of such rules. **2** the condition and controlling influence of such laws: law and order. **3** a rule of behaviour, conduct of a field of activity, or procedure. **4** the legal profession. **5** jurisprudence. **6 the law** (*informal*) the police. **7** a binding force: His word is law. **8** a general principle that describes a regular, natural occurrence: the laws of nature. **law-court** *n* a room or building in which legal cases are heard and judged. **lawful** *adj* allowed by law; rightful. **lawfully** *adv* **lawless** *adj* **1** not controlled by or based on law. **2** disobedient to the law. **lawlessly** *adv* **lawlessness** *n* **lawsuit** *n* a non-criminal case in a law-court. **lawyer** *n* a person who advises clients on legal matters or represents them in lawsuits. < Scandinavian. SEE PANEL.

lawn (lɔːn) *n* an area of mown grass, for example in a garden or park. **lawn-mower** *n* a machine for cutting the grass on lawns. **lawn tennis** tennis played on a grass court. < Middle French *lande* heath, from Celtic.

lax (læks) *adj* **1** not strict, firm, or rigid. **2** loose; slack. **laxly** *adv* **laxness** *n* < Latin *laxus* loose. SEE PANEL AT **RELAX.**

laxative (ˈlæksətɪv) *n* a medicine that stimulates the emptying of the bowels. < Latin *laxus* loose.

lay[1] (leɪ) *vb* **laid; laying 1** put or place in a horizontal position. **2** put or place in a particular position or state. **3** put in the proper position: lay a carpet. **4** arrange (a table) for eating a meal. **5** prepare (a fire) for lighting by putting fuel in the grate. **6** (of birds, esp. hens) produce one or more eggs. **7** make (a bet) with (a person). **8** place or assign: All the blame was laid on him. **9** formulate or establish. **10** present or put forward for consideration. **11** beat down. < Old English *lecgan.* SEE PANEL.

lay[2] *adj* **1** of or relating to people who are not clergymen: a Lay Reader. **2** non-professional: lay opinion. **layman** fem. **laywoman** *n* a lay person. < Greek *laos* people.

lay[3] SEE **LIE**[2].

layer (leɪə) *n* **1** a single thickness, coat, etc. **2** a laying hen. **3** a shoot or branch in propagation that takes root while still attached to the parent plant; plant developed in this way.
• *vb* **1** arrange in layers. **2** cut (hair) in layers. **3** take root or cause to take root as a layer.

laze (leɪz) *vb* **1** behave or rest lazily. **2** spend (time) idly. **lazy** *adj* **1** not wanting to work or be active. **2** not energetic; inactive. **lazily** *adv* **laziness** *n* **lazy-bones** *n* (*informal*) a lazy person. < *lazy:* origin uncertain.

lb *abbrev* pound(s) weight. < Latin *libra.*

lbw *abbrev* leg before wicket.

lead[1] (liːd) *vb* **led; leading 1** guide, esp. by going ahead. **2** live or pass: She leads a very busy life. **3** influence the actions, feelings, behaviour, etc., of. **4** be a route or channel for. **5** control, guide, or direct; have the main part in: Mac led the expedition. **6** be in the first position in: Which country leads the world in computer technology? **7** result in: The oil crisis led to price increases.
• *n* **1** a position in front of others. **2** example or guidance. **3** something that guides; clue. **4** the main role in a film, play, etc.; actor playing such a role. **5** a wire or other conductor that conveys electrical current. **6** a leash. **leader** *n* **1** a person or thing that leads, esp. a person with overall authority. **2** (in an orchestra) the principal first-violin player. **3** also **leading article** a newspaper editorial. **leadership** *n* being a leader; leaders considered as a group.

---

lawful or **legal?**

Lawful means 'allowed by law; rightful' and tends to refer to moral or religious 'laws': Is it *lawful* for Christians to bear arms? and to be used in fixed phrases such as one's *lawful wife,* be engaged in one's *lawful* business.

Legal is used more frequently than lawful and means 'of or concerned with law' (the *legal* profession, a *legal* adviser), 'established by law; allowed or requested by law' (a *legal* ruling, *legal* documents).

---

leading *adj* coming in first position; principal: He took a leading part in the founding of the organization. < Old English *lǣdan.* SEE PANEL.

lead² (lɛd) *n* **1** a heavy, soft, bluish-grey metal. **2** a thin stick of graphite in a pencil. **3** a lead weight on a line used to measure the depth of water. **leaden** *adj* **1** made of lead. **2** heavy and sluggish. **3** of a grey colour; gloomy. < Old English *lēad.*

leaf (li:f) *n, pl* **leaves 1** an outgrowth from the stem of a plant, usually green and flat. **2** the state of having foliage: in leaf. **3** a sheet of paper. **4** a thin sheet of metal. **5** a hinged section of a table or a section that can be inserted to extend it. • *vb* turn over the pages of a book, magazine, etc., quickly, looking only briefly at the contents: He leafed through some magazines while waiting to see the doctor. **leafless** *adj* having no leaves. **leaflet** *n* a single sheet of paper or loose-leaf pamphlet giving information, esp. for distribution. **leafy** *adj* **1** covered with leaves. **2** like a leaf or leaves. < Old English *lēaf.* SEE PANEL AT **SHELF.**

league¹ (li:g) *n* **1** an association of countries, groups, or people that have combined for a common purpose. **2** a group of sports clubs that compete against one another. **3** (*informal*) a group or class: They're not in the same league. • *vb* form a league. **in league** (**with**) allied or associated (with). < Latin *ligare* to bind.

league² *n* a unit of distance equal to about three miles (five kilometres).

a leading question

Lead features in a number of expressions, including:

lead on to encourage (someone) to believe something that is not true.
lead up the garden path to allow or encourage (someone) to believe something that is not true; deceive or mislead.
lead up to to precede: events leading up to the election.

A **leading question** is one that encourages a person to answer in a particular way. Careful users reserve leading question for this usage and object to its use in the sense of 'main, searching, or challenging question'.

lay or **lie?**

There are probably no two words more commonly confused than lay and lie. This is due to the two verbs being very similar in their parts.

Lay (laid, laying) is nearly always transitive. In other words, a person or thing has to lay *something: Lay* him down on the floor. She *laid* the table. They have *laid* themselves open to criticism. I've been *laying* bricks all morning. The exception to the rule involves the meaning 'to produce one or more eggs': The chickens have stopped *laying.*

Lie (lay, lain, lying), on the other hand, is never transitive: I must go and *lie* down. The cat *lay* curled up in front of the fire. Why has the money *lain* untouched all these years? She was *lying* in wait for him on his return.

It may surprise some that there is no such word as layed.

Lay features in a number of idiomatic expressions, including:

layabout *n* a lazy person.
lay bare to expose or reveal.
lay-by *n, pl* **lay-bys** a strip at the edge of a road where a driver may stop without causing a hazard.
lay down 1 to establish or state authoritatively (a law, rule, etc.). **2** to give up (office). **3** to store (wine) in a cellar, etc., while it matures.
lay into to attack.
lay it on to exaggerate, as in flattery.
lay low to weaken or destroy.
lay off 1 to discharge from work, esp. temporarily. **2** to stop or avoid (eating or drinking or annoying someone).
lay-off *n* a temporary discharge from work.
lay on to supply or organize: The firm is laying on a fantastic Christmas party this year!
lay open to expose or reveal.
lay out 1 to arrange according to a plan. **2** to spend (a lot of money). **3** to render unconscious or flat. **4** to prepare (a corpse) for a funeral.
layout *n* an arrangement of something, especially according to a plan.
lay up 1 to store or save. **2** to confine to bed or indoors: laid up for a week with the flu.

< ultimately Celtic.

leak (li:k) *n* **1** a hole or crack through which something, esp. a liquid or gas, enters or escapes: The boat sprang a leak. **2** a leaking; liquid, etc., that is leaked. **3** a loss of electrical charge through faulty insulation. **4** a disclosure of secret information.
• *vb* **1** (of a liquid, etc.) enter or escape through an opening. **2** (of a container) allow a liquid, etc., to enter or escape by a leak. **3** (of a secret) make or become known: The news of the cabinet reshuffle has been leaked to the press. **leakage** *n* leaking; something that enters or escapes by leaking. **leaky** *adj* leaking or tending to leak: a leaky roof. < Scandinavian.

lean[1] (li:n) *vb* **leant, leaned; leaning** **1** be or put in a slanting position. **2** rest (against or on) for support. **3** depend on for support and help. **4** incline, in opinion, etc. **5 lean on** (*informal*) put pressure on (someone) to do something, esp. by intimidation. **leaning** *n* a tendency: rebellious leanings. **lean-to** *n, pl* **lean-tos** a small building with a roof that rests on the side of a larger building. < Old English *hleonian*.

lean[2] *adj* **1** having little flesh or bulk. **2** (of meat) containing little or no fat. **3** insufficient; not abundant. **leanness** *n* < Old English *hlǣne*.

leap (li:p) *vb* **leapt, leaped; leaping** **1** jump or spring through the air. **2** accept eagerly: He leapt at the opportunity. **3** rise quickly: Inflation leapt from 3% to 20% in just six months!
• *n* an instance of leaping. < Old English *hlēapan*.

leap-frog (ˈli:pˌfrɒg) *n* a game in which one child leaps over another who is bending over.
• *vb* **leap-frogged; leap-frogging** **1** perform a leap-frog (over). **2** overtake in turn.

leapt (lɛpt, li:pt) SEE **LEAP**.

learn (lɛ:n) *vb* **learnt, learned; learning** **1** gain knowledge of or skill in. **2** memorize: Have you learnt your lines? **3** come to be able (to perform a skill). **4** become aware: I learnt later that he was one of the world's art experts. **learner** *n* **learned** *adj* **1** marked by or noted for erudition or scholarship: learned periodicals. **2** gained by learning. **learning** *n* knowledge or skill that has been gained by study, etc. < Old English *leornian*.

lease (li:s) *n* **1** a contract for the use of land or property, usually for a stated period and in return for payment. **2** a prospect of renewed health, vitality, or happiness: a new lease of life.
• *vb* **1** grant the use of by lease. **2** hold by lease. **leasehold** *n* **1** land or property held on a lease. **2** the right to use this. **leaseholder** *n* < Latin *laxare* to loosen.

leash (li:ʃ) *n* a strap, cord, etc., fixed to the collar of a dog to restrain it.
• *vb* hold (a dog) on a leash. < Old French *laissier* to loose.

least (li:st) *determiner, adj* **1** smallest in size, amount, quantity, etc. **2** slightest: not the least bit interested.
• *n* **the least** the smallest thing, amount, etc.: The least she'll accept is £10.
• *adv* to the smallest degree: She always arrives when you least expect it. **at least 1** at the minimum; not less than what is mentioned: He'll stay with us for at least a week. **2** this much is true, even if no more; if nothing else: At least it was cheap. **in the least** at all: This is not in the least a new idea. < Old English, superlative of *lǣssa* less.

leather (ˈlɛðə) *n* **1** animal skin prepared for use. **2** something made of leather.
• *vb* **1** cover with leather. **2** beat; thrash. **leathery** *adj* having the appearance or feel of leather; tough. < Old English *lether-*.

leave[1] (li:v) *vb* **left; leaving 1** go away (from). **2** stop living in, working for, etc.: When did you leave the firm? **3** allow or cause to remain: Who left the door open? **4** cause to be in a position or state that is mentioned: The accident left her blind, deaf, and dumb. **5** fail to use or include: He found he'd left his equipment at home. **6** abandon: He left his

---

leave it at that

Leave features in a number of idiomatic expressions, including:

leave it at that to do or say nothing further.
leave much to be desired to be below standard: Your behaviour over the last term leaves much to be desired.
leave off to stop: It hasn't left off raining all day.
leave out to omit; exclude.
leave well alone not to meddle with something that is satisfactory.
take French leave to be absent from one's work or duty without permission. The expression comes from the 18th-century custom of leaving a social gathering without saying goodbye to the host or hostess.
take one's leave to say goodbye and go away.

---

wife. **7** have remaining after one's death; be survived by: He leaves a widow and two children. **8** bequeath: She left £1 million to charity. **9** entrust or commit; deposit: You can leave your coat in the cloakroom. **10** permit to proceed without interference: I briefed her then left her to get on with it. **11** not eat or deal with: You mustn't leave your cabbage, Hugh! **12** have remaining: 2 from 6 leaves 4. < Old English *lǣfan.* SEE PANEL.

leave² *n* **1** permission to do something. **2** permission to be absent: All leave has been cancelled because of the emergency. < Old English *lēaf.* SEE PANEL AT **LEAVE¹**.

leaven (ˈlɛvn̩) *n* **1** a substance such as yeast that produces fermentation in a dough. **2** something that lightens or changes.
• *vb* **1** add leaven to. **2** lighten. < Latin *levare* to rise.

lecher (ˈlɛtʃə) *n* a man who pursues sexual pleasure to an excessive degree, esp. promiscuously. **lecherous** *adj* **lecherously** *adv* **lechery** *n* < Old French *lechier* to lick.

lectern (ˈlɛktən) *n* a reading desk, esp. one from which a Bible is read aloud in a church. < Latin *legere* to read.

lecture (ˈlɛktʃə) *n* **1** a formal talk given to an audience, esp. for instruction. **2** a long, serious reprimand.
• *vb* **1** give a lecture or series of lectures (to). **2** reprimand at length. **lecturer** *n* < Latin *legere* to read.

led (lɛd) SEE **LEAD¹**.

ledge (lɛdʒ) *n* a narrow, horizontal surface projecting from a wall, etc. < Middle English *legge.*

ledger (ˈlɛdʒə) *n* a book, etc., in which the accounts of a business are kept. **ledger line** (*music*) a short line added above or below the staff for a note that is too high or low to be shown on the staff. < Middle English *legger.*

lee (liː) *n* a sheltered part or side, esp. the side of a ship that is away from the wind. < Old English *hlēo.*

leech (liːtʃ) *n* **1** a carnivorous, aquatic, blood-sucking, worm-like animal. **2** a person who clings to another person in the hope of gaining advantage. < Old English *lǣce.*

leek (liːk) *n* a biennial plant with a slender, white bulb, a thick, edible stem, and long, broad leaves; cooked as a vegetable. < Old English *lēac.*

leer (lɪə) *vb* give a lustful, knowing, or sly look.
• *n* a leering look. < perhaps Old English *hlēor* cheek.

leeward (ˈliːwəd *nautical* ˈluːəd) *adj, adv* in the direction in which the wind is blowing.
• *n* the leeward side.

leeway (ˈliːˌweɪ) *n* **1** a margin of money, time, etc. **2** room for freedom of action or change.

left¹ (lɛft) SEE **LEAVE¹**. **left luggage** luggage temporarily deposited at a railway station, etc. **left-overs** *pl n* food that has not been eaten at a meal.

left² *adj, adv* on or towards the side of something or someone facing west when the front faces north.
• *n* **1** the left side or area. **2** the left hand; blow with this. **3 the Left** those with socialist or radical political views. **left-hand** *adj* **1** on the left. **2** left-handed. **left-handed** *adj* **1** also *adv* using the left hand usually or more easily than the right. **2** of, designed for, or operated with the left hand: left-handed scissors. **3** clumsy; awkward. **4** ambiguous. **leftist** *n, adj* (a supporter or member) of the Left. **left wing** the more socialist or radical part of a group or party. **left-wing** *adj* **left-winger** *n* < Old English: weak.

leg (lɛg) *n* **1** one of the lower limbs of an animal which supports the body and on which it stands or moves. **2** this part of an animal used as food. **3** either of the two lower limbs of the human body, from the hip to the foot; artificial replacement for this. **4** the part of a garment covering this. **5** one of the supports of a piece of furniture. **6** one of the stages of a journey. **7** a single stage, game, etc., in a competition. < Old Norse *leggr.* SEE PANEL.

legacy (ˈlɛgəsɪ) *n* **1** a gift to someone by a will, esp. money or property. **2** something passed on from a predecessor.

Show a leg!

Show a leg! meaning 'Get out of bed as quick as you like!' goes back to the days when women were allowed to sleep below decks on naval vessels. In the mornings the women, unlike the ratings, were allowed to lie in. This meant that before the bo'sun's mate could tip the occupant of a hammock onto the mess deck, it was first necessary to identify them as male or female. The summons to display a leg over the side of the hammock proved an expedient method of determining this.

< Latin *legatus* deputy.

legal (ˈliːgl̩) *adj* **1** of or concerned with law. **2** established by law. **3** allowed or required by law. **legality** *n* **legally** *adv* **legal aid** payments from public funds to people who cannot afford the cost of legal advice or proceedings. **legalism** *n* strict adherence to the law or a rule. **legalist** *n* **legalistic** *adj* **legalistically** *adv* **legalize** *vb* make legal. < Latin *lex* law. SEE PANEL AT **LAW**.

legation (lɪˈgeɪʃən) *n* a diplomatic mission; official residence of such a mission and its minister. < Latin *legatus* deputy, emissary.

legend (ˈlɛdʒənd) *n* **1** a story handed down from the past, esp. popularly thought to be historical. **2** such stories collectively. **3** a person much talked about in his or her own lifetime. **4** an inscription on a coin, etc. **legendary** *adj* **1** of or like a legend; described in a legend. **2** very famous; notorious. < Latin *legere* to read.

leggings (ˈlɛgɪŋz) *pl n* additional outer, protective covering for the lower part of each leg.

legible (ˈlɛdʒəbl̩) *adj* capable of being read or deciphered. **legibility** *n* **legibly** *adv* < Latin *legere* to read.

legion (ˈliːdʒən) *n* **1** the main unit of the ancient Roman army. **2** a multitude. • *adj* numerous. < Latin *legere* to choose.

legislate (ˈlɛdʒɪsˌleɪt) *vb* make or pass laws. **legislation** *n* legislating; laws so made. **legislative** *adj* having the authority to legislate: a legislative assembly. **legislator** *n* a person who makes laws. **legislature** *n* the body of people with the authority to legislate. < *legislator*: Latin *lex* law + *lator* proposer, from *latus*, from *ferre* to bring, propose.

legitimate (ləˈdʒɪtəmət) *adj* **1** reasonable or valid. **2** logical, justifiable, or genuine. **3** in accordance with laws or rules. **4** (of a child) born of parents who are married to each other. • *vb* (ləˈdʒɪtəˌmeɪt) also **legitimize** make legitimate. **legitimacy** *n* **legitimately** *adv* < Latin *lex* law.

leguminous (lɪˈgjuːmɪnəs) *adj* of or resembling a group of plants whose fruit is in the form of a pod. < ultimately Latin *legere* to pick (a crop).

leisure (ˈlɛʒə) *n* time free from work, in which one can do as one chooses; free time. **leisurely** *adv* **at leisure; at one's leisure** in one's free time; in an unhurried way. < ultimately Latin *licēre* to be allowed.

lemming (ˈlɛmɪŋ) *n* a rodent with long, thick fur found in northern regions of Asia, America, and Europe. < Norwegian.

lemon (ˈlɛmən) *n* **1** an oval fruit with a thick, yellow skin and acid-tasting pulp. **2** the tree or shrub that bears this. **3** a pale yellow colour. **4** (*informal*) a person or thing that is unsuccessful or worthless. **lemonade** *n* a drink made of lemon juice, water, and sugar, often effervescent. < ultimately Arabic *laymūn*. SEE PANEL.

lend (lɛnd) *vb* **lent; lending 1** let another person have or use (something) temporarily. **2** supply (money) temporarily in return for repayment and interest. **3** give or contribute; impart. **4** be suitable for. **lender** *n* < Old English *lǣn* loan. SEE PANEL AT **LOAN**.

length (lɛŋkθ, lɛŋθ) *n* **1** the measure of how long something is from one end to the other, esp. along its longest dimension. **2** a measured distance; piece of a certain length. **3** extent in space or time. **4** a unit of measure equivalent to the length of an animal, boat, etc., in a race: The winning horse won by six lengths. **5** the degree to which something is performed: She went to great lengths to explain all that the job would involve. **at length 1** finally. **2** in great detail. **3** for a long time. **lengthen** *vb* make or become longer. **lengthways, lengthwise** *adj, adv* in the direction of the length of something. **lengthy** *adj* of great, exceptional, or excessive length. **lengthily** *adv* < Old English *lengthu*.

lenient (ˈliːnɪənt) *adj* mild or merciful; not strict or severe. **lenience** *n* **leniently** *adv* < Latin *lenis* soft.

lens (lɛnz) *n* **1** a piece of glass or other transparent material with one or both

lemon and **lime**

Many of the words that are used for the names of colours have been taken from the names of things found in nature. As well as lemon and lime, fruits have provided a number of everyday colour terms including, for example, orange, apricot, aubergine, olive, tangerine, plum, and peach.

Flowers have also made a significant contribution to this area of the vocabulary. Without them we would be lacking names such as lavender, rose, lilac, primrose, and violet.

sides curved; used in an optical instrument. **2** the transparent part of the eye that focuses light rays on the retina. < Latin: *lentil,* from its shape.

lent (lɛnt) SEE **LEND.**

lentil (ˈlɛntl̩) *n* an annual herb, the pod of which produces small, round, green or reddish seeds which are rich in protein; such a seed. < Latin *lens.*

leopard (ˈlɛpəd) fem. **leopardess** *n* a large, slender, flesh-eating animal of the cat family, having a yellow coat with dark spots. < Greek *leōn* lion + *pardos* panther.

leotard (ˈlɪəˌtɑːd) *n* a close-fitting, one-piece garment worn by dancers, acrobats, etc. < Julius *Léotard,* died 1870, French acrobat.

leper (ˈlɛpə) *n* a person who suffers from leprosy. < Greek *lepros* scaly, from *lepein* to peel.

leprechaun (ˈlɛprəˌkɔːn) *n* a mischievous elf in Irish folklore. < Middle Irish *lū* small + *corpān* little body.

leprosy (ˈlɛprəsɪ) *n* a chronic, infectious disease marked by lumps appearing on the skin, wasting of muscles, and disfigurement. **leprous** *adj* < SEE **LEPER.**

lesbian (ˈlɛzbɪən) *n* a female homosexual. **lesbianism** *n* < Latin *lesbius,* from *Lesbos,* birthplace of Sappho, c. 600 BC, Greek poetess and reputed homosexual.

lesion (ˈliːʒən) *n* **1** a harmful change in the structure of an organ or tissue of the body, due to injury or disease. **2** an injury or wound. < Latin *laedere* to injure.

less (lɛs) *determiner, pron* **1** smaller in quantity, amount, size, etc.: less than £1000. **2** not so much: You should eat less butter.

• *adv* to a smaller degree: less important; less likely.

• *n* **the less** a smaller quantity, amount, etc.

• *prep* minus: £10000, less tax and other deductions. **lessen** *vb* make or become less. **lesser** *adj* not so great as the other. < Old English *lǣssa, lǣs.* SEE PANEL.

lessee (lɛˈsiː) *n* a person who holds property under a lease. < SEE **LEASE.**

lesson (ˈlɛsn̩) *n* **1** a period of instruction; class: a history lesson. **2** something from which useful knowledge has been gained; knowledge, etc., so learned; example. **3** a rebuke. **4** a part of the Bible read in church. < Latin *legere* to read.

lessor (ˈlɛsɔː, lɛˈsɔː) *n* a person who lets property under a lease. < SEE **LEASE.**

lest (lɛst) *conj* **1** in order that not: lest we forget. **2** (*formal*) that: He was afraid lest they found out. < Old English *thȳ lǣs the* by the less that.

let[1] (lɛt) *vb* **let; letting 1** allow; not prevent or forbid: I let him borrow my car. **2** cause to: Let it be known that I had nothing to do with the matter. **3** allow or cause to go, escape, etc.: He let the dogs loose. **4** allow the occupation of (a house, etc.) in return for rent: Flat to let. **5** used to introduce a request, proposal, command, assumption, or challenge: Let's go!; Let us pray; Let x equal 5; Just let him do his worst!

• *n* a period of letting a house, etc. < Old English *lætan* to permit. SEE PANEL.

let[2] *n* **1** (*formal*) an obstruction or impediment: without let or hindrance. **2** (in tennis, etc.) an obstruction, making it necessary for the ball to be served again. < Old English *lettan* to hinder.

lethal (ˈliːθəl) *adj* causing or capable of causing death: a lethal dose. **lethality** *n* **lethally** *adv* < Latin *letum* death.

lethargy (ˈlɛθədʒɪ) *n* lack of energy, vitality, or interest; slowness or dullness. **lethargic** *adj* **lethargically** *adv* < Greek *lēthē* forgetfulness + *argos* lazy.

letter (ˈlɛtə) *n* **1** any of the symbols that make up the alphabet. **2** a written message, esp. sent through the post. **3** *pl* scholarly learning, esp. in literature: a man of letters. **letter-bomb** *n* an explosive device concealed in a letter or package and sent through the post. **letter-box** *n* **1** a hole in a door through which letters are delivered. **2** a public post-box.

less or **fewer?**

These two words are often confused. Grammatically, less is the comparative of little, fewer the comparative of few. The rule is that less is used to show quantity, fewer to show number.

So less is used with nouns that cannot be preceded by a or an, such as money, rice, or courage: *less* money, *less* rice, *less* courage.

Fewer is used with nouns that can be preceded by a or an, such as book, orange, or visitor: *fewer* books, *fewer* oranges, *fewer* visitors. Problems arise when the use of less is extended to cover nouns that show number: *less* troops, *less* supplies. Careful users object to this usage.

letterhead *n* paper with the name, address, etc., of a person or company printed as a heading; such a heading. **the letter** the actual wording or exact literal meaning of a rule, law, agreement, etc., as distinct from the general meaning: the letter of the law. < Latin *littera*.

lettuce (ˈlɛtɪs) *n* a plant with large, edible leaves that are used esp. in salads; such leaves. < Latin *lac* milk, from its milky juice.

leukaemia (luːˈkiːmɪə) *n* a disease in which the blood contains an abnormally high number of white blood cells. < Greek *leukos* white + *aemia*, from *haima* blood.

level (ˈlɛvl̩) *n* **1** a horizontal line or plane. **2** a device for testing whether a surface is horizontal: a spirit-level. **3** a position of height relative to the ground. **4** an amount or degree: the level of alcohol in the blood. **5** a position or rank in a series: The problem is best dealt with at ministerial level. **6** an approximately flat area of land.
• *adj* **1** horizontal. **2** having a surface of equal height; having an equal height as something else. **3** on a level with. **4** at the same rank, position, etc., as another. **5** uniform; steady. **6** also **level-headed** well-balanced; even-tempered.
• *vb* **levelled; levelling 1** make or become level. **2** knock (buildings, etc.) to the ground; raze. **3** direct: Whatever criticism may be levelled at us, we are still right. **4** aim (a gun, etc.). **level crossing** the crossing of a railway line and road or two railway lines at the same level. **one's level best** the best one can do; one's utmost. **on the level** honest. < Latin *libra* balance, scales.

lever (ˈliːvə) *n* **1** a rigid bar that turns about a fixed point, used to raise something or exert a pressure. **2** a part used to control or adjust a machine. **3** a strategic means of achieving something.
• *vb* move, raise, or open with a lever. **leverage** *n* **1** the action or power of a lever. **2** strategic power to accomplish something; influence. < Latin *levare* to raise.

leveret (ˈlɛvərɪt) *n* a young hare. < Latin *lepus* hare.

leviathan (lɪˈvaɪəθən) *n* **1** (*Bible*) a sea monster. **2** something huge or powerful. < Hebrew *liwyāthān*.

levitate (ˈlɛvɪˌteɪt) *vb* rise or float or cause to rise or float in the air in defiance of gravity. **levitation** *n* < Latin *levis* light.

levity (ˈlɛvɪtɪ) *n* lack of seriousness in manner or behaviour; inappropriate frivolity. < Latin *levis* light.

levy (ˈlɛvɪ) *vb* **levied; levying** impose and collect (a tax, fine, etc.).
• *n* levying; payment levied: a betting levy. < Latin *levare* to raise.

lewd (luːd) *adj* marked by or intended to excite sexual desire; obscene. **lewdly** *adv* **lewdness** *n* < Old English *lǣwede* ignorant. SEE PANEL.

lexicon (ˈlɛksɪkən) *n* **1** a dictionary, esp. of Greek or Hebrew. **2** a vocabulary. **lexicography** *n* the art or process of compiling dictionaries. **lexicographer** *n* < Greek *lexis* word, from *legein* to speak.

liable (ˈlaɪəbl̩) *adj* **1** habitually likely (to). **2** subject (to): Offenders are liable to a fine of £100. **3** legally responsible. **liability** *n*

let slip

Let features in a number of expressions, many of them idiomatic, including:

let alone 1 far from: I haven't even seen the report, let alone read it. **2** also **leave alone; let be** not to interfere with (a person or thing).
let down 1 to disappoint. **let-down** *n* **2** to release the air from (a balloon, tyre, etc.). **3** to lengthen (a garment).
let go 1 to release from captivity; set free. **2** to release one's grip of; stop holding. **3** to allow (oneself) to express one's feelings without restraint. **4** not to discuss something further: I think we'd better let it go at that.
let in for to cause (someone) to be responsible for (hard work, problems, etc.).
let off 1 to cause to explode; fire (a gun). **2** to excuse from a duty or punishment.
let off steam to release energy or tense feelings: The children can run around in the garden to let off steam. The expression originally referred to releasing steam from an engine to reduce the pressure.
let on to reveal (a secret).
let out 1 to make (a garment) wider. **2** to reveal (a secret). **3** to release from (a duty, obligation, or confinement). **let-out** *n*
let slip 1 to reveal (a secret). **2** to fail to make the best use of (an opportunity).
let up to stop, lessen, or relax. **let-up** *n*

1 being liable. **2** (*informal*) a hindrance; disadvantage. **3** *pl* financial obligations; debts. < Latin *ligare* to bind. SEE PANEL.

liaise (lɪˈeɪz) *vb* communicate and keep in contact (with). **liaison** *n* **1** communication and co-operation between different groups: There is a need for closer liaison between schools and industry. **2** a secretive, illicit sexual relationship. < Latin *ligare* to bind.

liar (ˈlaɪə) *n* a person who tells lies.

libel (ˈlaɪbl̩) *n* **1** a false and derogatory statement that damages a person's reputation, made in a permanent form such as in a published work. **2** any defamatory or damaging statement or representation.
• *vb* **libelled; libelling** make or publish a libel about. **libellous** *adj* < Latin *liber* book. SEE PANEL AT **SLANDER**.

liberal (ˈlɪbrəl) *adj* **1** generous; abundant. **2** tolerant; broad-minded. **3** not strict or literal; free. **4** favouring moderate political reforms. **5** (of education) providing a general knowledge rather than professional or technical skills: liberal studies.
• *adj, n* **Liberal** (of) the Liberal Party or a member of this. **liberality** *n* **liberally** *adv* **liberalize** *vb* make or become liberal. **liberalization** *n* **Liberal Party** a British political party supporting liberal policies. < Latin *liber* free.

liberate (ˈlɪbəˌreɪt) *vb* **1** set free. **2** free (a country) from occupation by a foreign power. **liberation** *n* **liberator** *n* < SEE **LIBERAL**.

libertine (ˈlɪbəˌtiːn) *n* a person with loose morals. < SEE **LIBERAL**.

liberty (ˈlɪbətɪ) *n* **1** freedom from restraints or control. **2** the right to do as one wishes. **3** a right or privilege given by authority. **4** an impertinent breach of etiquette. < SEE **LIBERAL**.

libido (lɪˈbiːdəʊ) *n* sexual drive or instinct. < Latin: desire.

library (ˈlaɪbrərɪ) *n* **1** a room or building in which books are kept for reference or borrowing. **2** a collection of such books. **3** a similar collection of records, cassettes, films, videos, etc. **4** a set of books issued by a publisher as a series. **librarian** *n* a person who is in charge of or who works in a library. **librarianship** *n* < Latin *liber* book.

lice (laɪs) SEE **LOUSE**.

licence (ˈlaɪsəns) *n* **1** a formal or legal permit to do something specified. **2** permission to act; freedom. **3** disregard for rules of behaviour; irresponsible use of freedom. **4** a writer's or artist's disregard of conventions for the sake of effect: poetic licence. < Latin *licēre* to be permitted. SEE PANEL.

license (ˈlaɪsəns) *vb* **1** give official permission to or for. **2** grant a licence for (the sale of alcoholic drinks). **licensee** *n* a person who holds a licence, esp. for the sale of alcoholic drinks. SEE PANEL AT **LICENCE**.

licentiate (laɪˈsɛnʃɪət) *n* a person who holds a licence to practise a certain profession. < SEE **LICENCE**.

licentious (laɪˈsɛnʃəs) *adj* sexually unrestrained. **licentiousness** *n* < SEE **LICENCE**.

lichee (ˈlaɪtʃiː) SEE **LITCHI**.

lichen (ˈlaɪkən, ˈlɪtʃən) *n* any of a large group of plants consisting of an alga and a fungus that grow on tree-trunks, rocks, and soil. < Greek *leikhein* to lick.

lick (lɪk) *vb* **1** pass the tongue over. **2** bring into a condition that is mentioned by passing the tongue over: He

lewd

Something which is obscene or sexually suggestive in a coarse way might be described as lewd. This word comes from the Old English *lǣwede* meaning 'ignorant' or 'unlearned'. By the 14th century, however, the word had acquired the additional sense of 'coarse' or 'rude'. To understand this development one has to remember that the learned members of the population were thought to be the clergy, and so there was a natural association of the 'unlearned' with the 'unholy'.

liable to misuse

Many careful users of English avoid using liable to express a mere probability, preferring likely instead: It is *likely* (not liable) to rain. He is *likely* (not liable) to pass the exam.

In such usage, liable implies a habitual likelihood or the possibility or probability of being subject to something: Such comments are *liable* to be misunderstood. We are *liable* to be overheard if we stay here. He is *liable* to get angry at the least cause.

licked the plate clean. **3** (of a flame or wave) pass lightly over. **4** (*informal*) overcome; defeat.
• *n* **1** an act of licking. **2** a small amount (of paint, etc.). **3** (*informal*) speed or pace. **licking** *n* (*informal*) **1** a beating. **2** a defeat. < Old English *liccian*.
SEE PANEL.

lid (lɪd) *n* **1** a cover that is hinged or removable. **2** an eyelid. < Old English *hlid*.

lido (ˈliːdəʊ, ˈlaɪdəʊ) *n, pl* **lidos** a public, outdoor recreation area with a swimming-pool. < *Lido*, resort near Venice in Italy, from *litus* shore.

lie[1] (laɪ) *vb* **lied; lying 1** speak falsely, with intent to deceive. **2** be deceptive.
• *n* **1** a false statement, esp. one intended to deceive. **2** something that deceives. **lie-detector** *n* an instrument that measures blood pressure, respiration rate, etc., to try to determine whether a person is lying. < Old English *lēogan*.

lie[2] *vb* **lay**; **lain; lying 1** be or put one's body in a horizontal position; rest. **2** (of a thing) be in a flat or horizontal position on a surface. **3** be or remain in a state or position that is mentioned: The machinery is lying idle; The town lies to the east of the forest. **4** exist (in): The secret of good teaching lies in effective communication. **5** (of snow) remain on the ground without melting. **6** weigh (on): Responsibility lay heavily on her. **7** be buried: Here lies Clive Chapman.
• *n* the way or position in which something lies: the lie of the land. **lie down 1** have a short rest or sleep in or on a bed. **2** submit without protest. **lie-down** *n* **lie in** stay in bed late. **lie-in** *n* **lie in state** (of the body of a famous person) be placed in a public place of honour before burial. **lie low** remain in hiding. < Old English *licgan*. SEE PANEL AT **LAY**[1].

lieu (ljuː, luː) *n* **in lieu** instead (of): You don't get paid extra for working in the evenings but you can take time off in lieu. < Middle French: place, from Latin *locus*.

lieutenant (lɛfˈtɛnənt *Royal Navy* luːˈtɛnənt) *n* **1** an army officer next below a captain. **2** a navy officer next below a lieutenant commander. **3** an officer having the rank below the one mentioned: a lieutenant general. **4** a deputy. < Middle French: place-holding.
SEE PANEL AT **LOCUM.**

life (laɪf) *n, pl* **lives 1** the property of organisms that enables them to take in food, grow, etc., and that ends at death; state of having this property. **2** living things collectively: animal life. **3** a person's existence; aspect of existence: one's private life. **4** a biography: the life of Queen Victoria. **5** the period for which a person has been alive: I've lived in Bath all my life. **6** the remaining period of one's life: a life sentence. **7** business and social activity of the world: to see life. **8** liveliness: The children are full of life today! **9** a way of existence: city life. **10** a period of useful activity or operation: an expected life of 1000 hours. **lifebelt** *n* a buoyant belt used for keeping a person

---

licence or license?

Do you buy a licence or a license for your television? Like practice and practise, the question hinges on whether you need to use a verb or a noun. The verb form has an s: 'Do I have to license the car if I'm not using it?' The noun employs a c: 'Do I need a licence for the car if I'm not using it?'

Off-licence is so spelt as the proprietors have a licence (noun) to sell alcohol only if it is drunk off the premises. In other words they are licensed (verb) to sell alcohol on unlicensed (verb used as adjective) premises as long as it is drunk elsewhere, unlike the proprietor of the licensed (verb used as adjective) hotel.

In American English the tendency is to use -se for both parts of speech.

---

lick into shape

Lick features in a number of idiomatic expressions, including:

a lick and a promise a quick, superficial attempt to do something, especially to wash or clean something.
lick into shape to put into a proper, especially presentable, form: The sergeant-major is keen to lick the new recruits into shape as soon as possible. The expression derives from the ancient belief that a bear cub was born as a shapeless mass and that it was literally licked into shape by its parents.
lick one's lips to show enjoyment or eagerness. The expression comes from eating.
lick someone's boots to act in a servile way towards someone.

afloat in the water. **life-blood** *n* **1** the blood considered as essential to maintain life. **2** a vital force. **lifeboat** *n* **1** a shore-based boat used for rescuing people at sea. **2** one of a number of small boats carried on a ship for use in an emergency. **lifebuoy** *n* a device that keeps a person afloat. **life cycle** the series of stages through which an organism, etc., passes in its lifetime. **life-guard** *n* a person employed at a beach or pool to rescue swimmers in danger of drowning. **life-jacket** *n* a buoyant device designed to keep a person afloat. **lifeless** *adj* **1** without life; dead or inanimate. **2** without vitality or liveliness. **lifelessness** *n* **lifelike** *adj* accurately resembling or describing life. **lifeline** *n* **1** a rope for saving or preserving life, for example the one by which a diver is lowered or raised. **2** a sole means of contact or communication. **life-long** *adj* lasting through all one's life. **lifer** *n* (*informal*) a prisoner sentenced to life imprisonment. **life science** a science such as biology that deals with living organisms. **life-size** *adj* also **life-sized** of the same size as in real life. **life-style** *n* a person's way of life. **lifetime** *n* the length of time for which a person or other living thing exists. < Old English *līf*. SEE PANEL.

lift (lɪft) *vb* **1** raise or rise to a higher level. **2** end (a siege, blockade, etc.) by withdrawing forces. **3** revoke (a restriction, etc.). **4** (*informal*) plagiarize. **5** (*informal*) steal. **6** (of fog) disperse. • *n* **1** lifting; being lifted. **2** a device for transporting people or goods from one level to another in a building. **3** a ride as a passenger, esp. without payment: Can you give me a lift home? **4** a chair-lift or ski-lift. **lift-off** *n* the vertical movement of a rocket, etc., at its launching. < Old Norse *lypta*. SEE PANEL AT **ELEVATOR.**

ligament (ˈlɪgəmənt) *n* a strong, fibrous tissue that keeps two bones of a joint together. < Latin *ligare* to bind.

ligature (ˈlɪgətʃə) *n* **1** a thread used in tying in surgical operations. **2** printed letters that are joined, such as æ < SEE **LIGAMENT.**

light[1] (laɪt) *n* **1** the form of electromagnetic radiation to which the eye is sensitive. **2** brightness or illumination; amount of this. **3** a source of light, such as an electric lamp or candle. **4** a flame for lighting a cigarette, etc.: Have you got a light? **5** understanding; illumination; enlightenment. **6** a particular aspect or viewpoint: in the light of the latest developments, **7** information that explains something: Can you shed any light on the affair? • *vb* **lit, lighted; lighting 1** ignite or cause to ignite. **2** also **light up** illuminate or cause to illuminate. **3** also **light up** make or become bright or cheerful. **bring/come to light** make/become known. **lighten** *vb* **1** make or become brighter. **2** shed light on; illuminate. **lighter** *n* a device for lighting cigarettes, etc. **lighthouse** *n* a device, esp. a tower, equipped with a powerful light to warn or guide ships at sea. **lighting** *n* the apparatus for providing artificial light; such light. **lightship** *n* a moored ship equipped with a powerful light to warn or guide ships at sea. **light up 1** light a cigarette, etc. **2** switch on lights on vehicles at dusk. **light-year** *n* (*astronomy*) the distance light travels in one year, 9.46 million million kilometres. < Latin *lux*. SEE PANEL.

light[2] *adj* **1** having little weight. **2** less or less intense than usual. **3** easy, esp. because involving little physical work. **4** cheerful; free from worry: with a light heart. **5** not important; trivial: Stealing is no light matter! **6** not abundant. **7** (of sleep or a sleeper) easily disturbed. **8** soft; gentle:

That's life!

Life features in a number of idiomatic expressions, including:

a matter of life and death 1 an event or situation that determines whether someone will live or die. **2** something of the utmost importance.

for dear life as though one's life were in danger: The ladder gave way and he found himself hanging on for dear life.

for life for the rest of one's life: imprisoned for life.

for the life of one no matter how hard one tries: For the life of me, I can't remember her name.

not on your life most certainly not: 'Will you ever marry her?'—'Not on your life!'

that's life that's how things happen; used especially when having to accept something unpleasant.

a light touch. **9** lively; serving mainly to entertain; not serious: light reading, **10** easily digested: a light snack. **11** (of soil) crumbly. **12** (of an industry) producing small consumer goods.
• *adv* lightly; with little luggage: to travel light.
• *vb* **lit, lighted; lighting 1** alight; settle. **2** arrive at or find accidentally: We suddenly lit on this old manuscript. **lightly** *adv* **lightness** *n* **lighten** *vb* **1** make or become less in weight. **2** relieve of a worry, burden, etc. **3** make or become more cheerful. **light-fingered** *adj* **1** given to stealing. **2** nimble. **light-headed** *adj* dizzy; giddy. **light-hearted** *adj* cheerful. **lightweight** *n* **1** a person or thing below average weight. **2** also *adj* (a person) of little importance. < Old English *lēoht.*

lighter (ˈlaɪtə) *n* a large, flat-bottomed barge used to unload and load ships. < probably Middle Dutch *lichten* to unload.

lightning (ˈlaɪtnɪŋ) *n* an electrical discharge in the atmosphere between two clouds or between a cloud and the ground.
• *adj* very quick: at lightning speed. **lightning-conductor** *n* a metal, conducting rod fixed to the highest point of a building and connected to the earth that provides a safe path for the discharge of lightning. < SEE LIGHT[1].

light-year

Many scientific terms involve the adoption of words in common usage and their redefinition in a more restricted sense. For example, velocity and speed are fairly synonymous in non-scientific usage, but in physics their meanings are quite distinct.

Sometimes, however, the opposite process occurs. This is when a scientific term re-enters general usage with a meaning quite different from its scientific sense. For example, light-years ago is now widely used in everyday English to mean 'ages ago', but in astronomy the phrase is nonsensical. In this discipline a light-year is a unit of *distance*—the *distance* travelled by light in one year—not a unit of *time*. Similarly, the word quantum is commonly used to mean 'vast' or 'giant' as in a quantum leap ('Our latest communications centre represents a quantum leap in desk-top efficiency'). The scientific application of quantum jump or quantum leap, however, involves a phenomenon so small as to be barely detectable!

lights (laɪts) *pl n* the lungs of sheep, pigs, etc., used as food. < LIGHT[2], referring to their light weight.

like[1] (laɪk) *adj* similar; having characteristics of.
• *prep* **1** similar to; characteristic of: He's like his brother. **2** similarly to: He plays chess like a professional. **3** to the same degree as. **4** such as: Take a subject like history, for example .... **5** appearing to be: It looks like rain, **6** in the mood for: I feel like a sleep.
• *conj* **1** in the same way as: Do it like I do. **2** (*chiefly US*) as if.
• *n* one that is similar or equal: cats, dogs, and the like; I've met the likes of you before! **like-minded** *adj* agreeing in outlook, attitudes, etc. **liken** *vb* find similarities in; compare. **likeness** *n* resemblance; copy. **likewise** *adv* **1** similarly. **2** moreover. < Old English *gelīc.* SEE PANEL. SEE PANEL AT **SUCH.**

like[2] *vb* **1** find agreeable or enjoyable; be fond of: I like playing the piano. **2** wish (to do something): I'd like to go now. **3** regard or consider.
• *n* a favourable opinion, feeling, or taste: his likes and dislikes. **likable** *adj* pleasant. **liking** *n* fondness; taste. < Old English *līcian.*

likely (ˈlaɪklɪ) *adj* **1** probable: the likely result. **2** believable; plausible. **3** suitable.
• *adv* probably. **likeliness** *n* **likelihood** *n* probability. < Old Norse *glīkligr.* SEE PANEL.

lilac (ˈlaɪək) *n* **1** a shrub with heart-shaped leaves and dense clusters of white, purple, or pink, fragrant flowers. **2** also *adj* (of) a light purple colour.

telling it like it is

Careful users of English avoid using like as a conjunction to mean 'in the same way as' as in Do it *like* I do. He spoke French *like* he used to years ago. In such usage, as is used instead.

Like is also used as a conjunction to mean 'as if': You look *like* you've just woken up. He has no power but he acts *like* he has a lot. This usage is chiefly American and is regarded as very informal in British usage.

On whether to use like or such as to introduce examples, see panel at **such.**

< Persian *nīlak* bluish, from *nīl* blue.

lilt (lɪlt) *n* a regular, flowing rhythm, esp. in music.
• *vb* (of music) have a lilt. < Middle English *lulten.*

lily (ˈlɪlɪ) *n* a plant that grows from bulbs and has large, showy flowers. < Latin *lilium.*

limb (lɪm) *n* **1** an arm or leg on a human being or the analogous part on an animal. **2** any of the main branches of a tree. **out on a limb** isolated; without support from others. < Old English *lim.*

limber (ˈlɪmbə) *adj* (esp. of the body) able to bend or move with ease; flexible.
• *vb* **limber up** (esp. of athletes, etc.) loosen the muscles before a race, etc., by doing exercises. < origin uncertain.

limbo[1] (ˈlɪmbəʊ) *n, pl* **limbos** a state of neglect or uncertainty; intermediate state. **in limbo** unable to act because uncertain about future events. < Latin *limbus* border.

limbo[2] *n, pl* **limbos** a type of West Indian dance in which the dancer bends backwards to pass beneath a bar: a limbo dancer. < origin uncertain.

lime[1] (laɪm) *n* a white substance used to reduce the acid level of soils and in making cement; calcium oxide.
• *vb* treat with lime. **in the limelight** enjoying great popularity or attention.

limestone *n* a type of rock from which lime is obtained. < Old English *līm.*

lime[2] *n* a small, round citrus fruit, greenish-yellow and very bitter.
• *adj* having this colour or taste: lime juice. < Arabic *līm.* SEE PANEL AT **LEMON**.

lime[3] *n* one of a group of trees, with heart-shaped leaves and fragrant, pale yellow blossom. < Old English *lind.*

limerick (ˈlɪmərɪk) *n* a comic, often bawdy verse of five lines. SEE PANEL.

limey (ˈlaɪmɪ) *n* (*US slang*) an Englishman, esp. an English sailor.
• *adj* British. SEE PANEL.

limit (ˈlɪmɪt) *n* **1** the furthest point, maximum degree, amount, etc., that something reaches or is allowed to reach; boundary: a speed limit; Their generosity knows no limits. **2** (*informal*) a person or thing that is exasperating.
• *vb* impose a limit on: limit one's expenditure. **limitless** *adj* **limitation** *n* **1** limiting; being limited. **2** a flaw or weakness that restricts power or potential: We all have our limitations. **limited** *adj* restricted in degree, amount, etc.: limited powers; a limited liability company. **within limits** to a certain extent. < Latin *limes* boundary.

limousine (ˈlɪməˌziːn) *n* a large, luxuri-

---

a likely cause of error

Careful users of British English avoid using likely as in We'll *likely* meet you at the station. When used as an adverb, likely does not stand on its own but should be used with very, quite, more, or most: We'll *most likely* meet you at the station.

---

limey

In American English an Englishman is still sometimes referred to as a limey. This slang expression is an abbreviated form of *lime-juicer* and derives from the days when lime was served to British crews as a means of preventing scurvy. Initially it referred only to British sailors but in time the application widened to anyone of British nationality.

---

limerick and **limousine**

These two words appear to have nothing in common until we look at their origins. Limerick probably came into the language from *Limerick*, a city and county of Eire, where such rhyming was popular.

Limousine also derives from a place-name, the French province of *Limousine*. In France, in the early days of motoring, the word was used to describe a car with the first proper weather protection, either a closed body or a collapsible hood, since the original collapsible hoods resembled those worn by people in *Limousine*.

Words like limerick and limousine that begin life as place-names are known as *toponyms*. Other examples include:

jodhpurs from the Indian city of *Jodhpur*
manilla (as in manilla envelopes) from *Manila*, city in the Philippines
rugby (the game) from *Rugby* school

ous motor car, esp. one with a glass partition between chauffeur and passengers. SEE PANEL AT **LIMERICK**.

limp[1] (lɪmp) *vb* **1** walk unevenly because of injury or disability. **2** proceed with difficulty: The surviving destroyer limped into port. • *n* a limping movement: She walks with a limp. < Old English *lemphealt* lame.

limp[2] *adj* **1** not stiff or firm; floppy. **2** lacking strength or energy. **limply** *adv* **limpness** *n* < probably Scandinavian.

limpet (ˈlɪmpɪt) *n* a small shellfish with the shape of a flat cone that clings firmly to rocks. < ultimately Medieval Latin *lampreda*.

limpid (ˈlɪmpɪd) *adj* **1** (*often literary*) (esp. of liquids and eyes) clear or transparent: a limpid pool. **2** simple in style and therefore easy to understand. < ultimately Latin *limpidus* clear.

linchpin (ˈlɪntʃˌpɪn) *n* **1** a pin or rod that locks a wheel into position on an axle. **2** a person or thing depended upon as a vital factor: the linchpin of the organization. < Old English *lynis*.

linctus (ˈlɪŋktəs) *n* a syrupy liquid taken to relieve coughs and sore throats. < Latin *lingere* to lick.

linden (ˈlɪndən) *n* a lime tree. < Old English *lind*.

line[1] (laɪn) *n* **1** the mark made by a pen, pencil, etc., when drawn along a surface. **2** something resembling this: lines across the forehead. **3** a length of cord, rope, wire, etc.: telephone lines. **4** a row of similar things: a line of houses. **5** a row of words, etc., on a page. **6** (*informal*) a short letter: Do drop me a line. **7** a route or course: the Victoria Line. **8** a railway track. **9** an occupation or business: 'What line are you in?' **10** a system of ships, aircraft, etc., that regularly take a particular route; company that operates such a system. **11** a related series of people that follow one another chronologically; family: a long line of alcoholics. **12** a course of action, thought, or conduct: a line of enquiry. **13** a category of merchandise: one of the most popular lines in kitchen furniture. **14** a series of connected military field works: the front line. **15** the equator. • *vb* **1** mark with a line or lines. **2** place (oneself) or be placed in a line or queue: line up to be served. **3** align. **hard lines!** bad luck! **in line for** due or likely to receive: in line for a pay increase. **in line with** in accordance with. **liner** *n* a large passenger ship. **linesman** *n* an official who assists the referee in sports like football, rugby, etc. **line-up** *n* a group of people or things assembled for a particular purpose: a star-studded line-up. **on the line** at risk. < Middle English.

line[2] *vb* **1** cover the inside of (a garment, drawer, etc.) with a lining. **2** be the lining of: walls lined with Chinese paintings. **liner** *n* a replaceable or disposable lining: nappy liners. **lining** *n* (a layer of) material, esp. fabric or paper, fixed in position over the inner surface of something to protect it or make it look tidy. < Old English *līn*.

lineage (ˈlɪnɪɪdʒ) *n* line of descent; ancestry. **lineal** *adj* < Old French *ligne*.

linear (ˈlɪnɪə) *adj* **1** of or in lines: linear arrangement. **2** of length. **linearity** *n* **linearly** *adv* < Latin *linearis*.

linen (ˈlɪnɪn) *n* **1** a hard-wearing cloth made from flax. **2** clothing and household articles such as shirts, sheets, or tablecloths, made from linen, cotton, or a washable cloth. < Latin *linum* flax.

linger (ˈlɪŋgə) *vb* **1** delay departure, esp. because of reluctance to leave. **2** continue to live when close to dying: She can't linger on indefinitely. **3** go slowly; saunter. **lingerer** *n* **lingering** *adj* slow to end or disappear: a lingering death. **lingeringly** *adv* < Old English *lengan* to delay, lengthen.

lingerie (ˈlɒnʒərɪ) *n* women's underwear and nightclothes. < Latin *lineus* made of flax.

lingo (ˈlɪŋgəʊ) *n, pl* **lingoes** (*often humorous or derogatory*) **1** a foreign or unfamiliar language. **2** jargon. < Latin *lingua* tongue.

lingua franca (ˌlɪŋgwə ˈfræŋkə) *n, pl* **lingua francas, linguae francae** a language used between people of different mother tongues. < Italian: Frankish language.

linguist (ˈlɪŋgwɪst) *n* **1** a person who has studied and understands linguistics. **2** a person who knows foreign languages. **linguistic** *adj* of language or linguistics. **linguistics** *n* the scientific study of human language. < Latin *lingua* tongue.

liniment (ˈlɪnɪmənt) *n* an oily liquid that is rubbed into parts of the body to relieve pain or stiffness. < Latin *linere* to smear.

link (lɪŋk) *n* **1** one of the rings that form a chain. **2** a person or thing with a connecting function: the link between smoking and lung cancer. **3** a cuff-link. • *vb* connect or be connected. **linkage** *n* the act of linking; state or style of being linked. **linkman** *n* a person whose job is to provide continuity, esp. a television sports presenter. < Scandinavian.

lino (ˈlaɪnəʊ) *n. pl* **linos** linoleum. **linocut** *n* (a print made from) a design cut in relief on a piece of linoleum.

linoleum (lɪˈnəʊlɪəm) *n* a type of floor covering, common in bathrooms and kitchens, composed of a patterned, waterproof surface on a canvas backing. < Latin *linum* flax + *oleum* oil.

linseed (ˈlɪnˌsiːd) *n* the seed of the flax plant. **linseed oil** a yellow oil obtained from this seed, used in paint, printing ink, varnish, etc. < Old English *linsǣd,* from *līn* flax + *sǣd* seed.

lint (lɪnt) *n* **1** a soft, linen-based material, used for dressing wounds. **2** any shreds of yarn, fibre, etc. < probably Latin *linteus* made of linen.

lintel (ˈlɪntl̩) *n* a horizontal beam of wood, stone, etc., supporting the load over a door, window, or other opening. < Latin *limes* boundary.

lion (ˈlaɪən) fem. **lioness** *n* **1** a large, powerful, flesh-eating member of the cat family, the male having a shaggy mane. **2** an important, courageous, or celebrated person. **lion-hearted** *adj* very courageous. **lionize** *vb* treat (someone) as a celebrity. **lion's share** the largest or best part of something shared out. < Greek *leōn.* SEE PANEL.

lip (lɪp) *n* **1** either of the two fleshy edges of the mouth-opening. **2** the edge of a cup, jug, etc., esp. one designed for pouring. **3** (*informal*) verbal insolence. **lipped** *adj* having (a mentioned kind of) lips: tight-lipped. **lip-read** *vb* understand what a person is saying by watching his or her lips. **lip-service** *n* an insincere expression of admiration, approval, agreement, not supported by actions: mere lip-service. **lipstick** *n* (a stick of) cosmetic for colouring the lips. < probably Latin *labium.*

the lion's share

A person with a considerably larger share of something than anyone else is sometimes said to have the lion's share. This expression derives from Aesop's fable 'The Lion and His Fellow-Hunters'. In this fable the lion and several other animals go hunting. When it comes to dividing the spoils, the lion claims one quarter for being king of the beasts, one quarter for his superior courage, one quarter for his mate and cubs, 'and as for the fourth, let he who will dispute it with me'.

liquefy (ˈlɪkwɪˌfaɪ) *vb* **liquefied; liquefying** make or become liquid. **liquefaction** *n*

liqueur (lɪˈkjʊə) *n* **1** a strong, sweet, alcoholic drink, typically served after a dinner. **2** a hollow chocolate containing liqueur. < Old French *licour* liquid.

liquid (ˈlɪkwɪd) *n* **1** (any) matter such as water, oil, or paint, which flows freely but is not a gas. **2** *pl* drinks as opposed to solid foods.
• *adj* **1** having the form of a liquid: liquid chocolate. **2** (*often literary*) clear or transparent; limpid. **3** (of sounds) flowing smoothly, with pure notes. **4** easily convertible into money: liquid assets. **liquidity** *n* **liquidness** *n* **liquidize** *vb* change (esp. solid foods) into liquid or pulp. **liquidizer** *n* < Latin *liquidus,* from *liquēre* to be fluid.

liquidate (ˈlɪkwɪˌdeɪt) *vb* **1** pay (a debt). **2** terminate the operations of (a business), esp. because of bankruptcy, and share the remaining assets between creditors. **3** destroy, kill, or eliminate. **liquidation** *n* **liquidator** *n* **go into liquidation** (of a business) be closed down, esp. because of bankruptcy. < Late Latin *liquidare* to become liquid, from Latin *liquidus.*

liquor (ˈlɪkə) *n* **1** alcoholic drink. **2** the juice or liquid in which food has been cooked. < Latin *liquēre* to be fluid.

liquorice (ˈlɪkərɪs, ˈlɪkərɪʃ) *n* **1** a European leguminous shrub. **2** the dried root of this shrub, used in medicine and confectionery. **3** a black sweet with the flavour of liquorice. < Greek *glykyrrhiza,* from *glykys* sweet + *rhiza* root.

lisp (lɪsp) *n* a speech defect which causes s and z sounds to be pronounced like the th sounds in thing and this respectively.
• *vb* speak with a lisp. < Old English *wlyspian.*

list[1] (lɪst) *n* a series of names, figures, etc., usually written or printed one under the other: a shopping list.
• *vb* **1** make a list of. **2** include in a list. **listed building** a building officially recorded as being of architectural or historical importance. **list price** the retail price of goods as shown in a catalogue. < Italian *lista,* of Germanic origin.

list[2] *vb* (of a ship) lean over to one side.
• *n* a leaning position. < origin unknown.

listen (ˈlɪsn̩) *vb* **1** pay attention (to sound). **2** remain alert in order to hear something. **3** give a hearing (to an argument, complaint, or account): They agreed to listen to our side of the story. **listener** *n* **1** a person who listens attentively to what someone says: a good listener. **2** a person listening to the radio. **listen in** **1** listen to a radio broadcast. **2** listen to a private conversation; eavesdrop. < Old English *hlysnan.*

listless (ˈlɪstləs) *adj* lacking energy, interest, or enthusiasm: a listless look. **listlessly** *adv* **listlessness** *n* < Middle English *list* desire + *-les* -less.

lit (lɪt) SEE LIGHT[1].

litany (ˈlɪtənɪ) *n* a form of prayer consisting of a series of invocations, made by the clergy, each followed by a set response from the congregation. < Greek *litanos* entreating.

litchi (ˌlaɪˈtʃiː) *n* a Chinese tree grown for its edible fruit; its fruit. < Cantonese *lai chi.*

literacy (ˈlɪtərəsɪ) *n* the ability to read and write.

literal (ˈlɪtərəl) *adj* **1** of the primary meaning of a word or phrase; not figurative. **2** showing careful attention to the exact words used; word for word: a literal translation. **3** lacking imagination or interpretation: far too literal a rendering. • *n* a printing mistake. **literally** *adv* **literalness** *n* < Latin *littera* letter. SEE PANEL.

literary (ˈlɪtərərɪ) *adj* **1** of or concerned with literature: literary criticism. **2** fond of or knowledgeable about literature. **3** (of a word) formal in style.

literate (ˈlitərɪt) *adj* **1** able to read and write. **2** educated. • person who is literate. < Latin *litteratus* learned, from *litterae* letters.

literature (ˈlɪtərɪtʃə, ˈlɪtrɪtʃə) *n* **1** writings such as poems, plays, or novels, produced by an artistic imagination: language and literature. **2** printed matter, esp. on a particular subject: travel literature.

lithe (laɪð) *adj* able to bend and twist easily; supple. < ultimately Old English *līthe* gentle.

litigate (ˈlɪtɪˌgeɪt) *vb* **1** contest an action in a court of law. **2** carry on a lawsuit. **litigant** *n* a person involved in a lawsuit. **litigation** *n* legal proceedings; lawsuit. < Latin *litigare,* from *lis* lawsuit + *agere* to drive.

litmus (ˈlɪtməs) *n* a water-soluble dye obtained from certain lichens that is turned red by acids and blue by alkalis. **litmus paper** paper soaked in litmus solution that is used as a rough measure of acidity or alkalinity. < Scandinavian.

litre (ˈliːtə) *n* a metric unit of capacity used for measuring liquids; one cubic decimetre. < Medieval Latin *litra* measure, from Greek: weight.

litter (ˈlɪtə) *n* **1** untidy rubbish, esp. discarded wrappings or containers left in a public place. **2** straw, etc., used as a bed for an animal. **3** the offspring produced by an animal at one birth. • *vb* **1** strew with litter; scatter untidily. **2** give birth to a litter. < ultimately Latin *lectus* bed.

little (lɪtl̩) *determiner, pron* **less; least** **1** hardly any: He receives little help. **2** a small amount: Help yourself to a little. • *adj* **1** small in size, amount, etc., or short in duration: a little talk. **2** small relative to others of the same kind: a little elephant. **3** young: a little kitten. **4** of no special interest or importance. • *adv* **less; least** **1** in a small amount, to a small extent, etc.: We talked a little. **2** not at all: She little expected such a homecoming. • *n* a small amount, short duration, etc.: We saved a little of our money. **a little** rather, somewhat: a little tired. **little by little** by small amounts; gradually. < Old English *lȳtel.*

liturgy (ˈlɪtədʒɪ) *n* a fixed form of public worship used in a church. **liturgical** *adj* **liturgically** *adv* < Greek *leitourgos* minister.

live[1] (lɪv) *vb* **1** have life; be alive. **2** continue to be alive. **3** survive, last, or continue: The name will live on. **4** exist or spend one's time in a particular way: to live well. **5** have one's home; reside: living in Leeds. **6** support oneself: not enough money to live on. **7** feed oneself: to live on fruit. **8** enjoy a full life or rich experience: You haven't lived! **9** put into practice in daily life. **livable** *adj* able to be lived in or with. **lived-in**

literally

Careful users prefer not to use literally with an expression that is obviously metaphorical: He sat there, *literally glued to* the television. She was *literally swept off her feet* by his dazzling good looks. Such users prefer to use literally to show that an expression that is usually regarded as metaphorical is on this occasion to be considered at its face value, not metaphorically. So He *literally* died laughing means that he actually died.

adj (of a room) used frequently. < Old English *libban.* SEE PANEL.

live² (laɪv) *adj* **1** having life; not dead: live flowers. **2** having power, energy, etc.: live wires. **3** causing current interest: a live issue. **4** (*radio, television*) recorded and broadcast simultaneously: a live interview. **5** at which an audience or performers are present; not filmed or recorded: a live concert.

• *adv* (of a radio or television broadcast) recorded and broadcast simultaneously. < short for *alive.*

livelihood (ˈlaɪvlɪˌhʊd) *n* an occupation, employment, or means of supporting oneself. < Old English *līflād,* from *līf* life + *lād* course.

lively (ˈlaɪvlɪ) *adj* **1** full of energy, spirit, or vigour: a lively imagination. **2** full of action or incident: a lively morning. **liveliness** *n*

liven (ˈlaɪvn̩) *vb* make or become lively.

liver (ˈlɪvə) *n* **1** a large organ in the abdomen of vertebrates which cleans the blood, etc. **2** the liver of certain animals, used as food. **liverish** *adj* **1** suffering from a liver disorder. **2** irritable or peevish. < Old English *lifer.* SEE PANEL.

livery (ˈlɪvərɪ) *n* the identifying uniform or clothing worn by the male servants of an important household or by the members of a guild. **livery stable** a stable where horses may be boarded or hired. < ultimately Latin *liberare* to free.

livestock (ˈlaɪvˌstɒk) *n* animals such as cattle, sheep, or goats, that are kept for use or profit.

livid (ˈlɪvɪd) *adj* **1** extremely angry. **2** of a leaden or bluish-grey colour. < Latin *lividus,* from *livere* to be blue.

living (ˈlɪvɪŋ) *adj* **1** currently alive, existing, or in use: a living reminder. **2** true to life; exact: a living image of. **3** suited for living.

• *n* **1** being alive. **2** a means of supporting oneself. **3** a life-style. **living-room** *n* the room in a house that a family uses most. **living wage** a wage that is high enough to allow an acceptable standard of living.

lizard (ˈlɪzəd) *n* any of a group of reptiles with four legs, a long tail, and a dry scaly skin. < Latin *lacerta.*

llama (ˈlɑːmə) *n* a South American ruminant mammal of the camel family, valued for its wool and as a pack animal. < ultimately Quechua.

load (ləʊd) *n* **1** something (to be) carried or supported. **2** the maximum amount which a cart, etc., can carry. **3** anything burdensome or worrying: took a load off his mind. **4** (*informal*) a large quantity of. **5** the amount of power output (of a generator, etc.).

• *vb* **1** put (a load, goods, etc.) in or on: load a car. **2** encumber with something burdensome: Don't load me with your problems. **3** insert a bullet in (a gun), film in (a camera), disk in (a computer), etc. **4** add

---

live and let live

Live features in a number of idiomatic expressions, including:

live and let live not to interfere with the way other people run their lives; be tolerant.
live down to cause (something unpleasant or embarrassing in one's past) to be forgotten, esp. by one's present conduct.
live happily ever after the standard conclusion to a children's story, etc., expressing a future life of unbroken happiness: She married the prince and they lived happily ever after.
live in/out (of an employee) to have one's home where/away from where one works.
live it up to have a lively time at a party, etc., full of pleasure.
live through to undergo or experience (a crisis, period of tension, etc.).
live together also **live with** to live as husband and wife, though not legally married.
live up to to reach or match (a particular standard or expectation).
live with to tolerate or accept: Learning to live with the noise of the traffic wasn't easy.
you live and learn you learn through experience.

---

lily-livered

A person who displays a certain lack of courage is sometimes informally described as lily-livered or white-livered. The allusion is to the ancient superstition that a person's courage or cowardice was directly determined by the amount of blood in the liver. The paler the liver, the greater the coward.

an extra sum to an insurance premium. **loader** *n* **loaded** *adj* **1** biased or unfairly weighted; one-sided: loaded dice. **2** (*informal*) very wealthy. **load line** a line painted on the side of a ship to mark the highest safe water level; Plimsoll line. **loads** *pl n* lots: loads of money. < Old English *lād* course.

loaf[1] (ləʊf) *n, pl* **loaves** **1** a shaped mass of bread. **2** a shaped mass of food. **3** (*informal*) the head: Use your loaf! < Old English *hlāf*. SEE PANEL. SEE PANEL AT **SHELF.**

loaf[2] *vb* spend time idly; lounge or loiter. **loafer** *n* < perhaps German *Landläufer* vagabond.

loam (ləʊm) *n* rich, crumbly soil containing sand, clay, and decayed vegetable matter. < Old English *lām*.

loan (ləʊn) in **1** an act of lending. **2** something lent or borrowed. • *vb* lend.< Old Norse *lān*. SEE PANEL.

loath (ləʊθ) *adj* reluctant. < Old English *lāth*. SEE PANEL.

loathe (ləʊð) *vb* detest. **loathing** *n* a feeling of detestation. **loathsome** *adj* detestable. < SEE **LOATH.** SEE PANEL AT **LOATH.**

lob (lɒb) *vb* **lobbed; lobbing 1** cause (something, esp. a ball) to travel in a high arc. **2** cause (a ball) to travel above an opponent's head in tennis, badminton, etc. < probably Low German.

lobby (ˈlɒbɪ) *n* **1** a porch or hallway. **2** (in the House of Commons) one of two ante-rooms where MPs go to vote. **3** a group of people engaged in lobbying. • *vb* **lobbied; lobbying** try to influence legislation by communicating with a public official. **lobbyist** *n* < of Germanic origin.

lobe (ləʊb) *n* **1** the soft part of the ear closest to the jaw. **2** a curved projection. < Greek *lobos*.

lobster (ˈlɒbstə) *n* any of a group of large,

Use your loaf!

To use one's loaf is just one of the many informal expressions that owe their origin to Cockney rhyming slang. This is a type of slang in which a word is cryptically replaced by another word or phrase that rhymes with it. So one's wife becomes one's trouble and strife; one's feet, one's plates of meat.

Sometimes the intended word is twice removed from its slang equivalent. To use one's loaf is a reduced form of to use one's loaf of *bread* which in turn is a rhyme for to use one's *head*.

Other examples of rhyming slang include:

Adam and Eve 'believe'
apples and pears 'stairs'
Bath bun 'son'
country cousin 'dozen'
daisy roots 'boots'
dickory dock 'clock'
earwig 'twig' (to understand)
ginger (**ginger beer**) 'queer'
lord mayor 'swear'
Lucy Locket 'pocket'
mince pies 'eyes'
north and south 'mouth'
pig's ear 'beer'
Rosy (**Rosy Lea**) 'tea'
tea leaf 'thief'
titfer (**tit for tat**) 'hat'

loan or **lend?**

As a verb loan is common in America but in British English lend is generally preferred: He's *lent* (not loaned) his car to a friend. I've *lent* (not loaned) her my dictionary for the weekend.

In British English, however, loan is increasingly being used, especially for long-term or large financial loans: The family decided to *loan* some of its artistic treasures to the British Museum. The bank will consider *loaning* you £100,000 over 10 years.

loathe or **loath?**

Loathe is the verb: I *loathe* the mere thought of boiled cabbage! The derived words loathing and loathsome both contain an a.

The adjective, with the alternative spellings loath and loth (but never with a final e), means 'reluctant or unwilling': He was *loth* to destroy all the work he had so painstakingly built up over the years. I am *loath* to let a further six weeks pass by until a decision is made.

edible shellfish with four pairs of legs and two large claws; its flesh as food. < Old English *loppe* spider.

local (ˈləʊkl̩) *adj* **1** of a particular place or district: local news. **2** affecting a part, not the whole: a local anaesthetic.
• *n* **1** a local inhabitant. **2** (*informal*) a local public house. **local authority** the group of people responsible for administering local government. **local colour** description in a literary work that gives details of the idiosyncrasies of a place and its inhabitants. **local government** the government of a county or district by locally elected officials. **locality** *n* a particular position or situation. **localize** *vb* confine within an area. **locally** *adv* in the neighbourhood; nearby. < Latin *locus* place.

locale (ləʊˈkɑːl) *n* a scene or locality, esp. with regard to an action or event. < French *local.*

locate (ləʊˈkeɪt) *vb* **1** find by searching for: hard to locate. **2** establish in a particular place: We need to find a better place to locate the new theatre. **be located** be situated. **location** *n* **1** the place where something is situated; situation. **2** locating or being located. **on location** (of people making a film) in a place away from the film studio, where one or more scenes are being filmed. < SEE **LOCAL.**

loch (lɒk, lɒx) *n* (*Scottish*) a lake; arm of the sea. < Scottish Gaelic.

lock[1] (lɒk) *n* **1** a fastening device, usually operated by turning a key. **2** a mechanism for exploding the charge of a firearm. **3** an enclosure in a canal, etc., where the water level can be regulated. **4** a fastening together; interlocking. **5** the turning via a steering-wheel of a vehicle's front wheels; extent to which the front wheels of a vehicle may be turned: on full lock. **6** a wrestling hold.
• *vb* **1** operate a lock to fasten (something); be able to be fastened by means of a lock: Does the door lock? **2** secure (a building) by operating one or more locks. **3** shut in or out; make inaccessible: He likes to lock himself away in his study. **4** make or become fixed or immovable: My elbow keeps locking. **5** fix or become fixed together. **locker** *n* a small cupboard or compartment fitted with a lock. **lockjaw** *n* tetanus. **lock-keeper** *n* a person in charge of a lock on a canal, etc. **lock out** prevent workers from entering their place of work, esp. until they agree to something. **lock-out** *n* an instance of this. **locksmith** *n* a maker and repairer of locks. **lock, stock, and barrel** (*informal*) completely. **lock up 1** put in prison. **2** invest (money) in something that cannot easily be changed back into cash: His money is mostly locked up in property. **lock-up** *adj* able to be locked: a lock-up garage. < Old English *loc.*

lock[2] *n* a strand or curl of hair. **locks** *pl n* the hair of the head. < Old English *locc.*

locket (ˈlɒkɪt) *n* a small metal case for holding a memento, usually worn around the neck on a chain. < Middle Dutch *loke.*

locomotion (ˌləʊkəˈməʊʃən) *n* the act or power of moving from one place to another. < Latin *locus* place + English *motion.*

locomotive (ˌləʊkəˈməʊtɪv) *n* a power-driven engine for hauling carriages, wagons, etc.
• *adj* of locomotion.

locum (ˈləʊkəm) *n* a doctor or clergyman who substitutes for another in his absence. < short for Latin *locum tenens* one holding a place. SEE PANEL.

locust (ˈləʊkəst) *n* a winged insect that flies in great swarms and devastates crops and vegetation. < Latin *locusta.*

locution (ləʊˈkjuːʃən) *n* a word or expression. < Latin *loqui* to speak.

lode (ləʊd) *n* a vein of mineral deposit. **lodestar** *n* a star used in navigation. < Old English *lād* course.

lodge (lɒdʒ) *n* **1** a small house, usually at the gates of a private estate. **2** a porter's room. **3** the members or the meeting place of a branch of a secret society. **4** the den or lair of a wild animal. **5** a house in the country used in a particular season.
• *vb* **1** provide temporary accommodation for. **2** occupy temporarily; be a lodger. **3** fix or become fixed in a place. **4** formally present (a complaint, application, etc.). **lodger** *n* a person who pays for accommodation in

locum

A doctor who stands in for another during sickness or leave is commonly known as a locum. This is a shortened form of locum tenens, a Medieval Latin phrase meaning 'holding the place'.

The same source gave rise to the word lieutenant, which found its way into English via Middle French.

another's house. **lodging** *n* a place to live. **lodgings** *pl n* one or more rented rooms in a private house. < of Germanic origin.

loft (lɒft) *n* **1** the space under the roof of a house; attic. **2** an upper floor in a barn, warehouse, etc., used for storage. **3** a gallery in a church or hall.
• *vb* cause (something, esp. a ball) to travel in a high arc. < Old Norse *lopt* air.

lofty (ˈlɒftɪ) *adj* **1** impressively tall or high. **2** proud; haughty. **3** of high rank; noble. **loftily** *adv* **loftiness** *n*

log (lɒg) *n* **1** a length of unshaped timber. **2** an instrument for measuring a ship's speed. **3** a detailed record of the movements of a ship or aircraft. **4** a log-book.
• *vb* **logged; logging 1** cut (timber) into logs. **2** enter (details) in a log-book. **3** attain (a particular distance, speed, etc.), often as noted in a log-book. **log-book** *n* **1** a book in which a full record of a voyage is recorded. **2** a car owner's registration book. < probably Scandinavian.

loganberry (ˈləugənbərɪ) *n* a prickly raspberry hybrid; its dark-red, edible fruit. < J.H. *Logan*, died 1928, US lawyer + *berry*, SEE PANEL.

logarithm (ˈlɒgəˌrɪðəm) *n* an exponent that indicates the power to which a fixed number must be raised in order to produce a given number. **logarithmic** *adj* < ultimately Greek *logos* ratio + *arithmos* number.

loggerheads (ˈlɒgəˌhɛdz) *pl n* **at loggerheads** on bad terms; engaged in confrontation. < probably English dialect *logger* wooden block + *head*.

logic (ˈlɒdʒɪk) *n* **1** the science of the principles and methods of reasoning. **2** the system of reasoning used in a particular discipline. **3** correct reasoning: There's no logic in what he says. **4** a way of reasoning: false logic. **5** the cause and effect relationship of successive happenings: the logic of events. **logical** *adj* **1** in accordance with the principles of logic: a logical statement. **2** able to reason correctly: a logical mind. **3** (of an action or event) natural because in accordance with the law of cause and effect; to be expected: That she refused to attend was completely logical. **logicality** *n* **logically** *adv* **logistics** *pl n* the handling or organization of a complex operation. **logistic** *adj* **logistically** *adv* < Greek *logos* reason.

logo (ˈləugəu) *n, pl* **logos** a symbol or small drawing used by a company as its emblem.

loin (lɔɪn) *n* **1** the part of the body between the hip and the lower ribs. **2** a cut of meat comprising this part and the adjoining half of the vertebrae. < Latin *lumbus*.

loiter (ˈlɔɪtə) *vb* **1** stand about idly. **2** walk slowly with frequent stops; dawdle. < probably Middle Dutch *loteren* to waggle.

loll (lɒl) *vb* **1 lie**, lean, or slump lazily: lolling against the fence. **2** hang loosely; dangle. < Middle English *lollen*.

lollipop (ˈlɒlɪˌpɒp) *n* a large, flat, boiled sweet on the end of a stick. **lollipop man** or **lady** (*informal*) an official who carries a round warning sign on a stick and guides children across a road. < probably English dialect *lolly* tongue + *pop*.

lollop (ˈlɒləp) *vb* **1** flop about; lounge. **2** move with ungainly, loping bounds.

lolly (ˈlɒlɪ) *n* **1** (*informal*) a lollipop. **2** an ice lolly. **3** (*informal*) money. < short for *lollipop*.

lone (ləun) *adj* (*formal*) without anybody else present; solitary: a lone figure. **lonely** *adj* **1** unhappy because without a friend, company, etc. **2** (of a place) unfrequented; desolate: a lonely spot. **3** without companions or company. **loneliness** *n* **loner** *n* a person who avoids company. **lonesome** *adj* (*chiefly US*) lonely. < Middle English, short for *alone*.

long[1] (lɒŋ) *adj* **1** having relatively more than average length in space or time: a long walk. **2** having a specified length: two miles long. **3** seeming of greater length than usual: five long years behind bars. **4** (*informal*) having a great deal of a particular quality: not long on good looks.
• *adv* **1** for or during a long time: He hasn't been home long. **2** for a specified length of time: How long will it take? **3** a long time: long before the tragedy. **longhand** *n* ordinary handwriting (esp. as opposed to shorthand). **longship** *n* a long, open ship with oars and a sail, used esp. by the Vikings. **long-sighted** *adj* able to see

loganberry

Rubus ursinus loganobaccus is commonly known by the less forbidding name of loganberry. The latter derives from James H. *Logan*, 1841–1928, an American lawyer turned judge whose hobby was horticulture. Judge Logan developed the loganberry in 1881.

only distant things clearly. **long-standing** *adj* having existed for a long time: a long-standing arrangement. **long-suffering** *adj* enduring patiently for a long time. **long-term** *adj* of, for, or over a long period of time. **long-winded** *adj* tediously long. < Old English *lang.*
SEE PANEL.

long[2] *vb* feel a longing: longing for a hot bath. **longing** *n* a persistent desire or craving, esp. for something immediately unavailable. < Old English *langian.*

longitude (ˈlɒndʒɪˌtjuːd, ˈlɒŋgɪˌtjuːd) *n* the distance due east or west of Greenwich meridian, measured in degrees. **longitudinal** *adj* **1** of longitude. **2** extending lengthwise. < Latin *longus* long.

loo (luː) *n, pl* **loos** (*informal*) a toilet.

loofah (ˈluːfə) *n* the fibrous, dried pod of a type of gourd, used as a rough bath sponge. < Arabic *lūf.*

look (lʊk) *vb* **1** direct the eyes towards: Look at me. **2** seem to be; appear: She looks ill. **3** take care or heed: Look where you're going! **4** face in a certain direction: The house looks onto the main road. **5** direct one's thoughts or attention to: It's time to stop looking back. • *n* **1** a glance, gaze, etc.: an angry look. **2** appearance or expression: a look of innocence. **have a look 1** have sight of: Let's have a look. **2** search: Will you have a look for my new pen? **look after 1** take care of. **2** be responsible for. **look-alike** *n* a person or thing with a very close resemblance to another. **look at 1** examine or inspect: When did the dentist last look at your teeth? **2** consider (buying, accepting, etc.): I wouldn't even look at such a low offer. **look back** stop making progress: After his first novel was published, there was no looking back. **look down on** regard as inferior or unworthy. **look down one's nose at** regard with contempt. **look for** try to find. **look forward to** await eagerly or excitedly. **look here!** used to express indignation. **look in** pay (someone) a short casual visit. **look-in** *n* a chance to participate. **looking-glass** *n* a mirror. **look into** investigate. **look on** (merely) stand and watch. **looker-on** *n* a (mere) spectator. **look on** or **upon** consider to be: look upon someone as a friend. **look out** be careful; used as a warning or expression of annoyance. **look-out** *n* **1** a guard; place from which a watch is kept. **2** a prospect. **look out for** keep watching attentively for. **look over 1** do a tour of inspection around. **2** examine or scrutinize. **look through** read or scan. **look to** approach for help, support, etc.: She always looks to me for advice. **look up 1** search for (in a reference book, etc.). **2** improve: Things are starting to look up at last. **look up to** admire and respect. < Old English *lōcian.*

loom[1] (luːm) *n* an apparatus for weaving cloth. < Old English *gelōma* tool.

loom[2] *vb* come into view suddenly or in a threatening way; approach ominously. **loom large** be prominent. < origin unknown.

loony (ˈluːnɪ) *n* (*informal*) a lunatic. • *adj* (*informal*) crazy. < *lunatic.*

loop (luːp) *n* **1** the shape produced by a piece of string, rope, etc., that is curved round to touch or cross itself. **2** a length of string, rope, etc., that has this shape. • *vb* **1** form into one or more loops. **2** fasten or encircle with a loop. **loophole** *n* **1** a means of escaping or evading something, esp. an ambiguity or imprecise wording in a document. **2** a small opening in a wall, etc., through which a rifle may be fired. **loop the loop**

a long shot

Long features in a number of expressions, many of them idiomatic, including:

as or **so long as 1** for the length of time that. **2** provided that; on condition that.
before long in a short time; soon.
in the long run in the course of time.
long in the tooth rather old. The expression originally referred to horses.
long johns underpants with long legs that extend to the ankles.
long jump the athletic field event of jumping as far as possible from a running start.
long shot an attempt or effort that is unlikely to be successful: It's a long shot but it's worth trying.
no longer formerly but not any more.
not by a long chalk not by any means: You've not finished yet by a long chalk. The expression originally referred to the use of chalk to note the points scored in a game: a long chalk was a large number of points.
the long and the short of it the essential point; gist: The long and the short of it is that they've run out of money.

(of a pilot or aircraft) perform a vertical loop at the height of which the aircraft is upside down. < Middle English *loupe*.

loose (lu:s) *adj* **1** not fastened or fitting firmly or tightly: a loose connection. **2** not tethered, confined, etc.; free: loose animals. **3** not packaged, boxed, etc.: loose sweets. **4** imprecise or inexact; vague: a loose arrangement. **5** not compact or firmly packed: loose soil. **6** (of a woman) morally slack, esp. in sexual behaviour.
• *vb* **1** release (from confinement). **2** unfasten, untie, etc. **loosely** *adv* **looseness** *n* **at a loose end** having nothing to do to occupy oneself. **loose covers** removable covers for chairs, etc. **loose-leaf** *adj* (of an album, folder, etc.) allowing removal of pages. **on the loose** free or escaped from confinement. < Old Norse *lauss*.

loosen (ˈlu:sn̩) *vb* make or become less tight, taut, rigid, etc. **loosen up** exercise to relax the muscles; limber up.

loot (lu:t) *n* **1** valuables taken in war from the vanquished. **2** stolen money or valuables.
• *vb* plunder. < Hindi *lūt*.

lop (lɒp) *vb* **lopped; lopping 1** cut off (branches) from a tree. **2** remove or cut off in a rough or indifferent manner. < Middle English *loppe*.

lop-eared *adj* having long ears that hang down loosely.

lopsided (ˌlɒpˈsaɪdɪd) *adj* **1** leaning to one side. **2** with one side shorter, heavier, etc., than the other. **lopsidedly** *adv* **lopsidedness** *n*

loquacious (lɒˈkweɪʃəs) *adj* (*formal*) talkative. **loquaciously** *adj* **loquaciousness** *n* < Latin *loqui* to speak.

lord (lɔ:d) *n* **1** a monarch or ruler; master. **2** a nobleman. **3** the title of certain high ranking officials. (**House of**) **Lords** the upper assembly in Parliament. **lord it** act in a lordlike or superior manner: He's always trying to lord it over everyone. **lordly** *adj* **1** grand or lordlike; noble. **2** haughty. **lordship** *n* the rank or position of a lord. **Lordship** *n* the title applied to a lord. < Old English *hlāford*, from *hlāf* loaf + *weard* keeper.

lore (lɔ:) *n* a body of knowledge or traditions: bird lore. < Old English *lār*.

lorgnette (lɔ:ˈnjɛt) *n* spectacles or opera glasses on a long handle. < Old French *lorgne* squinting.

lorry (ˈlɒrɪ) *n* a large motor vehicle for transporting heavy or bulky goods. < perhaps English dialect *lurry* to pull.

lose (lu:z) *vb* **lost; losing 1** mislay: lose one's keys. **2** have no longer; be deprived of: lose one's father. **3** fail to keep or maintain: lose one's job. **4** fail to remain aware of: lose one's way. **5** fail to win (a contest, fight, etc.). **6** fail to get, make use of, benefit from, etc.: lose an opportunity. **7** allow to wander astray or disappear from view. **8** rid oneself of: lose weight. **9** (of a watch, clock, etc.) run slow. **10** (cause a person to) fail to follow or understand: 'You've lost me completely, I'm afraid.' **11** end up with less, in a worse position, etc.: We seem to have lost on the deal. **loser** *n* **lose one's head** fail to maintain one's self-control. **lose out** (*informal*) suffer loss or defeat: They're bound to lose out in the election. **losing battle** a struggle or situation in which defeat seems inevitable. < Old English *losian* to perish.

loss (lɒs) *n* **1** losing or being lost. **2** a person, thing, or amount that is lost. **3** damage, disadvantage, or suffering caused by losing. **4** a failure to win. **5** a decrease in amount, degree, or size. **at a loss** puzzled and uncertain about what to do. < Middle English *los*.

lost (lɒst) SEE **LOSE**. **lost cause** a cause for which defeat seems inevitable.

lot (lɒt) *n* **1** an item or group of items for sale at an auction. **2** a plot of land. **3** a person's share or fate. **4** one of a set of objects used in deciding something by chance: draw lots. **5** (the result of) this method of deciding something: chosen by lot. **a lot 1** a large number or amount: I didn't buy a lot. **2** much: a lot older. **3** frequently: She goes to the cinema a lot. **a lot of** or **lots of** a large number or amount: a lot of complaints. **the lot** the whole mass, group, quantity, etc.; all: She bought the lot. < Old English *hlot*.

lotion (ˈləʊʃən) *n* a liquid, medicinal or cosmetic preparation that is applied to the skin. < Latin *lotio* act of washing.

lottery (ˈlɒtəːɪ) *n* **1** a scheme for the distribution of prizes by lot. **2** an event or matter whose outcome is governed by chance. < Middle Dutch *lotcrije*.

lotto (ˈlɒtəʊ) *n* a game resembling bingo. < ultimately of Germanic origin.

lotus (ˈləʊtəs) *n* **1** tropical water-lily. **2** a fruit believed in Greek legend to cause dreamy contentment and forgetfulness when eaten. **lotus position** a position in meditation in which one sits upright with legs crossed. < Greek *lotos*.

loud (laʊd) *adj* **1** of high sound volume; noisy. **2** (of colours, etc.) unpleasantly striking; unrefined. **loudly** *adv* **loudness** *n* **loud hailer** a megaphone. **loudspeaker** *n* an apparatus that turns electrical impulses into sound waves. < Old English *hlūd.*

lounge (laʊndʒ) *n* **1** a domestic sitting-room. **2** a large room in a hotel, etc., that people sit in. **3** a waiting-room at an airport, etc.
• *vb* sit, stand, or move lazily. < origin unknown.

lour (laʊə) SEE LOWER².

louse (laʊs) *n* **1** *pl* **lice** a small, wingless insect, parasitic on warm-blooded animals. **2** *pl* **louses** (*informal*) a contemptible person. **lousy** *adj* **1** infested with lice. **2** (*informal*) unpleasant; incapable. **3** (*informal*) amply provided with. **louse up** spoil or make a mess of. < Old English *lūs.* SEE PANEL AT MONGOOSE.

lout (laʊt) *n* an ill-mannered (young) man. **loutish** *adj* < perhaps Old English *lūtan* to stoop.

louvre, louver (ˈluːvə) *n* any of a set of horizontal parallel slats (in a door or window) arranged so as to admit air but exclude light or rain. **louvred** or **louvered** *adj* < Old French *lovier.*

love (lʌv) *n* **1** strong or deep-seated affection; devotion. **2** a strong liking or interest: a love of motor cars. **3** a person who is loved. **4** a score of nil in tennis, etc. **5** (*informal*) a friendly or affectionate form of address.
• *vb* **1** feel deep-seated affection for. **2** have a great liking for. **lovable** *adj* having endearing qualities. **love affair** a romantic or sexual relationship, often temporary. **loveless** *adj* without love: a loveless marriage. **lovely** *adj* **1** attractive or beautiful. **2** (*informal*) pleasing or enjoyable; fine: lovely weather. **loveliness** *n* **lovemaking** *n* sexual activity or intercourse. **lover** *n* **1** a person in love. **2** a person engaged in a love affair. **3** a person who has a strong liking for something: music lovers. **4** *pl* two people having a love affair. **lovesick** *adj* languishing with love. **loving** *adj* feeling or showing love: a loving kiss. **lovingly** *adv* < Old English *lufu.* SEE PANEL.

> **thirty love**
>
> To do something for love is to do it without payment or 'for nothing'. It is in the latter sense that the word love is used in games such as tennis and badminton: a score of thirty love is a score of thirty to nothing. This usage derives from the phrase to play for love meaning 'to play without stakes'.

low¹ (ləʊ) *adj* **1** not high or tall: a low ceiling. **2** lying below the normal level: a low neckline. **3** not loud: a low whisper. **4** not shrill or high-pitched: lower octaves. **5** (of the sun) near the horizon. **6** of inferior rank or status; humble: of low birth. **7** lacking strength or vigour; dispirited: 'He's feeling a bit low'. **8** below normal in size, amount, value, etc.: low prices. **9** intended for slow speed: a low gear. **10** unfavourable; disapproving: a low opinion. **11** common or vulgar: keep low company. **12** (*informal*) contemptible: a low trick.
• *adv* **1** in, at, or to a low level, degree, or position: He loves flying low. **2** in a low tone.
• *n* **1** a low level: Production has reached an all-time low. **2** a region of low atmospheric pressure. **lowbrow** *adj, n* (a person) having no interest in the arts or intellectual things. **low-key** *adj* of low (emotional) intensity; subdued. **low tide** (the time of) the tide at its lowest level. < Old Norse *lāgr.*

low² *n* the deep, sustained sound made by cattle; moo.
• *vb* make this sound. < Old English *hlōwan.*

lower¹ (ˈləʊə) *adj* **1** less high in position, rank, or order. **2** of a less highly advanced evolutionary state: the lower organisms.
• *vb* **1** cause to descend; haul down: lower a flag. **2** reduce the height of: lower a wall. **3** reduce in amount, quality, intensity, value, etc.: lowered prices. **4** direct downwards: lower one's eyes. **lower-case** *adj* (of letters) small as opposed to capital.

lower² (laʊə) *vb* also **lour** frown or scowl. < Middle English *louren.*

lowland (ˈləʊlənd) *adj, n* (of or connected with) low, flat land.

lowly (ˈləʊlɪ) *adj* modest or humble. **lowliness** *n*

loyal (ˈlɔɪəl) *adj* unwavering in one's allegiance to a person, cause, country, etc. **loyally** *adv* **loyalty** *n* **loyalist** *n* a person who remains loyal to his or her king, government, etc., esp. in times of revolt. < Old French *loial.*

lozenge (ˈlɒzɪndʒ) *n* **1** a small, medicinal tablet that is dissolved in the mouth. **2** a diamond-shaped figure. < Old French.

LP *n* also **long player** a long playing gramophone record. < *l*ong *p*laying.

L-plate *n* a sign on a motor vehicle indicating that the person at the wheel is learning to drive. < learner + *plate.*

LSD *abbrev* lysergic acid diethylamide.

Ltd *abbrev* (of companies) Limited.

lubricate (ˈluːbrɪˌkeɪt) *vb* oil or grease (machinery) to assist smooth movement. **lubricant** *n* a lubricating substance such as oil. **lubrication** *n* **lubricator** *n* < Latin *lubricus* slippery.

lucid (ˈluːsɪd) *adj* **1** clearly expressed; easily understood: a lucid account. **2** sane: lucid moments. **lucidity** *n* **lucidly** *adv* < Latin *lucidus.*

luck (lʌk) *n* **1** good fortune: a bit of luck. **2** good or bad fortune; chance: leave it to luck. **luckless** *adj* **in luck** enjoying good fortune. **lucky** *adj* having, arising from, or considered to bring good luck; fortunate. **luckily** *adv* **lucky dip** a stall at a fair, bazaar, etc., where one pays to draw an unseen article from a receptacle. **out of luck** not enjoying good fortune. < Middle Dutch *luc.*

lucrative (ˈluːkrətɪv) *adj* producing a large profit. **lucratively** *adv* **lucrativeness** *n* < Latin *lucrari* to gain.

ludicrous (ˈluːdɪkrəs) *adj* laughable; ridiculous. **ludicrously** *adv* **ludicrousness** *n* < Latin *ludicrus* done in sport.

ludo (ˈluːdəʊ) *n* a children's board-game. < Latin *ludere* to play.

lug[1] (lʌg) *vb* **lugged; lugging** pull or haul along; carry with great effort. < probably Scandinavian.

lug[2] *n* a small projection by which something is located, connected, or supported. < Middle English (Scottish dialect) *lugge* ear.

luggage (ˈlʌgɪdʒ) *n* the filled suitcases, holdalls, etc., that a person takes on a journey. < probably *lug* + *-age.*

lugubrious (lʊˈguːbrɪəs) *adj* mournful; dismal. < Latin *lugubris.*

lukewarm (ˌluːkˈwɔːm) *adj* **1** moderately warm. **2** lacking enthusiasm. < Middle English *luke* tepid + *warm.*

lull (lʌl) *vb* **1** soothe, calm, or send to sleep. **2** cause to become less alert or vigilant.
• *n* a temporary pause in activity. < Middle English *lullen.*

lullaby (ˈlʌləˌbaɪ) *n* a slow, gentle song sung to lull a baby to sleep. < probably *lull* + goodbye.

lumbago (lʌmˈbeɪgəʊ) *n* rheumatism of the muscles and loins, often resulting from exposure to cold. < Latin *lumbus* lumbar.

lumbar (ˈlʌmbə) *adj* of or in the loins. < Latin *lumbus* lumbar.

lumber (ˈlʌmbə) *n* **1** unwanted household articles that are stored away. **2** (*US*) timber sawn into planks.
• *vb* **1** burden with something unwanted; saddle: We found ourselves lumbered with their dog. **2** clutter. **lumberjack** *n* a person whose job is to fell trees and log timber. < origin unknown.

luminary (ˈluːmɪnərɪ) *n* **1** a natural body that gives light, esp. the sun or moon. **2** a person of distinction; leader. < Middle English *luminarye.*

luminous (ˈluːmɪnəs) *adj* **1** giving out light. **2** glowing in the dark: a luminous clock. **luminosity** *n* < Latin *luminosus.*

lump[1] (lʌmp) *n* **1** a piece or mass of no particular size, shape, etc.: a lump of wood. **2** a swelling or bump.
• *vb* put or group together indiscriminately: We were all lumped together despite our different backgrounds. **lump sum** a sum of money that is paid at one time as opposed to in instalments. **lumpy** *adj* full of or covered in lumps. **lumpiness** *n* **the lump** the whole body of self-employed workers in the building trade. < Middle English.

lump[2] *vb* (*informal*) put up with: You'll just have to lump it.

lunar (ˈluːnə) *adj* of the moon. **lunar month** the interval between successive new moons. < Latin *luna* moon.

lunatic (ˈluːnətɪk) *n* **1** an insane person. **2** a person whose behaviour is wild or foolish.
• *adj* **1** insane; used for the care of the insane: a lunatic asylum. **2** wild or foolish. **lunacy** *n* < Latin *luna* moon. SEE PANEL.

lunatic and lupin

Very often the choice of a naming word reveals something about the identity of the name-giver. Such is the case with lunatic and lupin.

Our awareness has not always been as developed as it is today: until relatively recently in our history it was believed that a person's level of insanity fluctuated with the phases of the moon. This superstition is embodied in lunatic, which derives ultimately from *luna*, Latin for 'moon'.

Similarly, it was long believed that the lupin was a plant that ravenously exhausted the soil. This is again reflected in the choice of name, which is based upon the Latin *lupinus* 'wolfish'.

lunch (lʌntʃ) *n* **1** a meal usually taken in the middle of the day. **2** the food eaten at this meal.
• *vb* eat lunch. < probably short for *luncheon*.

luncheon (ˈlʌntʃən) *n* a formal lunch. **luncheon voucher** a voucher received as part of one's pay that can be exchanged for food at certain restaurants. < origin uncertain.

lung (lʌŋ) *n* one of the two breathing organs in the chest of an animal. < Old English *lungen*.

lunge (lʌndʒ) *n* a sudden thrust or forward motion.
• *vb* make a lunge. < French *allonger* to stretch out one's arm.

lupin (ˈlu:pɪn) *n* a garden plant with long spikes of flowers. < Latin *lupinus* wolfish. SEE PANEL AT **LUNATIC.**

lurch[1] (lɜ:tʃ) *n* a swaying or staggering movement to one side.
• *vb* move in this way. < origin uncertain.

lurch[2] *n* **leave in the lurch** SEE PANEL.

lure (lʊə) *n* **1** (the power of) something that attracts or entices. **2** a bait or decoy, esp. for catching fish.
• *vb* attract or entice. < Middle French *loire*. SEE PANEL.

lurid (ˈlʊərɪd) *adj* **1** vividly coloured; gaudy. **2** gruesomely vivid: lurid details. **luridly** *adv* **luridness** *n* < Latin *luridus* pale yellow.

lurk (lɜ:k) *vb* **1** secretly lie in wait, ready to attack. **2** move about stealthily or inconspicuously. **3** exist unobtrusively. < Middle English *lurken*.

luscious (ˈlʌʃəs) *adj* **1** pleasingly sweet in taste or smell. **2** voluptuous; seductive. **lusciously** *adv* **lusciousness** *n* < Middle English *lucius*.

left in the lurch

A person who is deserted while in a difficult or vulnerable position is sometimes said to be left in the lurch. This meaning of lurch derives from the French word *lourche* which was used both for the name of a game similar to backgammon and to describe the state of a player facing an overwhelming defeat in such a game. A closely related sense is used in cribbage, where it describes the position of a player who, by the end of the game, has still to complete one length of the board.

lush (lʌʃ) *adj* **1** (of grass, vegetation, etc.) growing profusely. **2** luxurious; sumptuous. **lushly** *adv* **lushness** *n* < Middle English *lusch* soft.

lust (lʌst) *n* **1** strong sexual desire. **2** a longing to have or enjoy something; craving: a lust for money.
• *vb* feel lust. **lustful** *adj* < Old English.

lustre (ˈlʌstə) *n* **1** the sheen of a smooth or shining surface. **2** glory; distinction. **lustreless** *adj* without lustre. **lustrous** *adj* shining evenly. < Old Italian *lustrare* to shine.

lusty (ˈlʌstɪ) *adj* vigorously healthy. **lustily** *adv* **lustiness** *n* < SEE **LUST.**

lute (lu:t) *n* a stringed musical instrument with a broad, fretted neck and large, pear-shaped body. < Middle French *lut*.

luxuriant (lʌgˈzjʊərɪənt) *adj* **1** growing profusely; lush. **2** highly ornate. **luxuriance** *n* **luxuriantly** *adv*

luxuriate (lʌgˈzjʊərɪˌeɪt) *vb* take sensual pleasure; revel: luxuriate in a hot bath.

luxury (ˈlʌkʃərɪ) *n* **1** something unnecessary but desirable that is expensive or hard to obtain: it's a pity that mangoes are a luxury in the UK. **2** indulgence in things that gratify the senses. **3** a style of living that is indulgent in this way. **luxurious** *adj* **1** furnished with luxuries: a luxurious holiday . **2** fond of luxury. **luxuriously** *adv* **luxuriousness** *n* < Latin *luxuria*.

LV *abbrev* luncheon voucher.

lychee (ˈlaɪˌtʃi:) SEE **LITCHI.**

lying (ˈlaɪɪŋ) SEE **LIE**[1]**, LIE**[2]**.**

lymph (lɪmf) *n* a pale fluid containing white blood-cells that supplies nutriment to the cells of the body before being returned to the blood. **lymphatic** *adj* < Latin *lympha* water.

lynch (lɪntʃ) *vb* (of a mob) to kill, esp. to hang, without trial. SEE PANEL.

lynx (lɪŋks) *n, pl* **lynxes, lynx** a wild cat of the Northern Hemisphere with a ruff

lure

Nowadays anything that serves to attract or entice may be described as a lure: It was the *lure* of the Dales that brought him back to Yorkshire. Originally this word was used in a much narrower sense, entering the language in the 14th century as a falconry term. It derives from the Middle French *loire*, the name of the lure used by a falconer to recall his bird.

> **Lynch law**
>
> The act whereby a person is seized and executed by a mob, usually by hanging, is sometimes referred to as a lynching. The word lynch is believed to derive from the name of William *Lynch,* a US citizen and self-appointed protector of public order who in the second half of the 18th century organized and headed a band of vigilantes in the southern state of Virginia. Their deeds gave rise to the phrase lynch law or 'mob justice'.

on each side of the face, long, usually tufted ears, and keen eyesight. **lynx-eyed** *adj* keen-sighted. < Greek.

lyre (laɪə) *n* a stringed musical instrument of the harp family, popular in ancient Greece. < Greek.

lyric (ˈlɪrɪk) *adj* **1** suitable for being sung to music. **2** (of poetry) expressing the writer's thoughts and feelings.
• *n* **1** a lyric poem. **2** an idea expressed in a song: catchy lyrics. **lyrical** *adj* **1** lyric. **2** full of praise or enthusiasm. < SEE LYRE.

M

m *abbrev* **1** metre(s). **2** mile(s).
MA *abbrev* Master of Arts.
mac (mæk) *n* (*informal*) a raincoat. < short for *mackintosh*.
macabre (məˈkɑːbrə) *adj* grim or gruesome. < Old French *danse macabre* dance of death.
macadam (məˈkædəm) *n* (a road surface made of) compacted layers of small crushed stones. **macadamize** *vb* surface a road with macadam. < John *McAdam*, died 1836, Scottish engineer.
macaroni (ˌmækəˈrəʊnɪ) *n, pl* **macaronis, macaronies** short tubes of pasta made from wheat flour, wider in diameter than spaghetti. < ultimately Italian dialect *maccarone*.
macaroon (ˌmækəˈruːn) *n* a small sweet cake or biscuit made of egg whites, sugar, and ground almond. < Italian dialect *maccarone* macaroni.
macaw (məˈkɔː) *n* a large, tropical American parrot with brilliant plumage and a long tail. < Portuguese *macau*.
mace[1] (meɪs) *n* a ceremonial staff held by or placed before an official as a symbol of authority. < Middle French.
mace[2] *n* a spice made from the dried outer covering of nutmeg. < Latin *macir* oriental spice, from Greek *makir*.
machete (məˈʃɛtɪ) *n* a large, broad-bladed knife used as a tool and weapon. <Spanish.
machiavellian (ˌmækɪəˈvɛlɪən) *adj* cunning, deceitful, or unscrupulous in the pursuit of a goal. < Niccolo *Machiavelli*, died 1527, Italian statesman.
machinate (ˈmækɪˌneɪt) *vb* scheme or plot, esp. to do harm. **machination** *n* **1** a cunning plot or strategy. **2** the act of plotting. < Latin *machina* contrivance.
machine (məˈʃiːn) *n* **1** an assembly of various, esp. moving parts that performs a certain function: sewing-machines. **2** a person or group that behaves like a machine. **3** a highly organized group or system.
• *vb* **1** shape, cut, or finish by using a machine. **2** use a machine, esp. a sewing-machine, to perform a certain operation. **machine-gun** *n, vb* (shoot at with) a mounted gun capable of continuous rapid fire. **machinery** *n* **1** machines. **2** the parts of a machine; mechanism. **3** an organized system for doing something. **machine tool** a power-driven tool for cutting and shaping metal, wood, etc. **machinist** *n* **1** a person who operates a machine. **2** a producer or repairer of machines. < Greek *mēchanē*, from *mēchos* means.
machismo (məˈkɪzməʊ, məˈtʃɪzməʊ) *n* a man's exaggerated sense and assertion of his masculinity, esp. the urge to display fearlessness and virility. **macho** *n, adj* (*informal*) (a man) exhibiting machismo. < Spanish *macho* male.
mackerel (ˈmækrəl) *n, pl* **mackerel, mackerels** any of a large group of edible sea-fish with oily, strong-tasting flesh and bands of dark-blue colour across its back. < Old French.
mackintosh (ˈmækɪnˌtɒʃ) *n* also **macintosh** a raincoat made of rubberized cloth. < Charles *Macintosh*, died 1843, Scottish chemist.
macramé (məˈkrɑːmɪ) *n* **1** a loose type of lacework made by knotting cords in patterns. **2** the art of making macramé < Arabic *migramah* embroidered veil.
mad (mæd) *adj* **madder; maddest** **1** mentally deranged; insane. **2** extremely foolish: a mad idea. **3** (*informal*) highly enthusiastic about: mad about football. **4** (*informal*) angry or annoyed: Is he still mad with you? **5** wild and disorderly; frenzied: a mad rush for the door. **6** (of a dog) suffering from rabies. **madly** *adv* **madness** *n* **madden** *vb* infuriate. **madhouse** *n* (*informal*) a scene of wild uproar. **madman** fem. **madwoman** *n* a mad person.
madam (ˈmædəm) *n* **1** a respectful way of addressing a woman, as used by shop assistants. **2** a conceited or precocious girl or young woman. < Old French *ma dame* my lady.
made (meɪd) SEE **MAKE.**
madonna (məˈdɒnə) *n* a picture or statue of the Virgin Mary. < Old Italian *ma donna* my lady.
madrigal (ˈmædrɪgḷ) *n* an unaccompanied song for several voices singing several melodies. < Italian *madrigale*.
maelstrom (ˈmeɪlstrəm) *n* a violent whirlpool. < Dutch *maalstroom*, from *malen* to grind + *strom* stream.
maestro (ˈmaɪstrəʊ) *n, pl* **maestri, maestros** **1** a celebrated musician, composer, conductor, or music teacher. **2** a master of any art. < Latin *magister*.

magazine (ˌmægəˈziːn) *n* **1** a weekly or monthly publication of large format, usually geared to a particular subject or readership. **2** a storehouse for guns, ammunition, etc. **3** a metal case holding cartridges before they are fed into the breech of a gun. **4** a similar storage device in a camera or slide projector. < Arabic *makhāzin,* from *makhzan* storehouse.

magenta (məˈdʒɛntə) *n* a deep purplish-red. < *Magenta,* town in Italy. SEE PANEL.

maggot (ˈmægət) *n* the larva of a fly. < Scandinavian.

magic (ˈmædʒɪk) *n* **1** the art that supposedly harnesses supernatural forces to influence normal events; sorcery. **2** the art of producing illusions, esp. by sleight of hand. **3** a mysterious, hypnotic, uplifting quality.
• *adj* **1** of or used in magic. **2** having supernatural qualities: a magic carpet. **3** (*informal*) used as an expression of approval. **magical** *adj* **magically** *adv* **magician** *n* **1** a person who practises magic. **2** a conjuror. < Iranian.

magistrate (ˈmædʒɪˌstreɪt) *n* a public official authorized to hear and judge cases in minor law-courts. **magisterial** *adj* **1** commanding, imperious, or dictatorial. **2** of or relating to a magistrate. < Latin *magister* master.

magnanimous (mægˈnænɪməs) *adj* showing great generosity and selflessness; big-hearted. **magnanimity** *n* **magnanimously** *adv* < Latin *magnus* great + *animus* spirit.

magnate (ˈmægneɪt) *n* a person of great wealth and influence, esp. in a particular business sphere: an oil magnate. < Latin *magnus* great.

magnesia (mægˈniːʃə, mægˈniːʒə) *n* a white, tasteless powder used in medicine as an antacid and laxative; magnesium oxide. < SEE **MAGNET.**

magnesium (mægˈniːzɪəm) *n* a light, silvery-white metal that burns with a very intense, white light.

magnet (ˈmægnɪt) *n* **1** any object that can attract certain other objects and that aligns itself north and south when suspended. **2** a person or thing that exerts a powerful attraction. **magnetic** *adj* **1** (capable of) having the properties of a magnet. **2** acting or produced by magnetism: a magnetic compass. **3** exerting a powerful attraction: a magnetic personality. **magnetic tape** a thin, plastic strip coated with iron oxide, used for recording or storing sound, video, etc., signals. **magnetism** *n* **1** the property of attraction displayed by magnets. **2** the scientific study of magnets. **3** the power to attract, esp. by virtue of strong personal charm: a magnetic personality. **magnetize** *vb* **1** provide with magnetic properties. **2** exert the attractive force of a magnet. **magnetization** *n* < Greek *magnes* stone of Magnesia, ancient city in Thessaly.

magneto (mægˈniːtəʊ) *n, pl* **magnetos** a small electric generator employing one or more magnets, esp. one that provides the spark in an ignition system. < short for *magneto*electric machine.

magnificent (mægˈnɪfɪsn̩t) *adj* **1** splendid, grand, or impressive. **2** of excellent quality. **magnificence** *n* **magnificently** *adv*

magnify (ˈmægnɪˌfaɪ) *vb* **magnified; magnifying 1** make (something) appear larger than in reality. **2** exaggerate the significance of (something). **magnification** *n* **1** magnifying. **2** the magnifying power of a lens, etc. **3** a magnified image. **magnifier** *n* **magnifying glass** an optical lens that magnifies. < Latin *magnificare* to make great, extol.

magnitude (ˈmægnɪˌtjuːd) *n* **1** size or extent. **2** level of importance. **3** the degree of brightness of a star. < Latin *magnus* great.

magnolia (mægˈnəʊlɪə) *n* any of a group of shrubs and trees with large, usually white or pink, wax-like flowers. < Pierre *Magnol,* died 1715, French botanist.

magnum (ˈmægnəm) *n* a wine bottle whose capacity is twice that of a normal bottle. < Latin *magnus* great.

magpie (ˈmægˌpaɪ) *n* **1** a bird of the crow family with black and white plumage, noted for its chattering and for collecting small, bright objects. **2** (*informal*) a

magenta

The colour that is roughly describable as a deep purplish-red is known as magenta. This word entered the language in the second half of the 19th century following the discovery of the dye from which magenta is produced. The dye was named after *Magenta,* a town in northern Italy, with an allusion to the notoriously bloody Battle of Magenta in 1859, when the Austrian army was defeated by French and Sardinian forces.

person who collects or hoards small objects. **3** (*informal*) a chatterbox. < *Mag,* short for *Margaret,* signifying a chatterbox + *pie.*

maharajah (ˌmɑːhəˈrɑːdʒə) *n* the title of an Indian prince, esp. the ruler of a former state. < Sanskrit *mahārāja,* from *mahat* great + *rājan* raja.

maharishi (ˌmɑːhəˈriːʃɪ) *n* a Hindu teacher and mystic. < Sanskrit *mahārṣi,* from *mahat* great + *ṛṣi* sage.

mah-jong (ˌmɑːˈdʒɒŋ) *n* a Chinese game for four people, played with 144 small tiles. < Chinese *má què* sparrows.

mahogany (məˈhɒgənɪ) *n* **1** any of a group of tropical trees with a hard, heavy, reddish-brown wood; its wood. **2** a reddish-brown colour. < origin unknown.

maid (meɪd) *n* **1** a female servant. **2** (*archaic*) an unmarried girl or woman; maiden. **maid of honour** an unmarried lady attending a queen or princess. **old maid** a spinster. < Middle English *maide,* short for *maiden.*

maiden (ˈmeɪdn̩) *n* **1** (*archaic*) an unmarried girl or woman; virgin. **2** also **maiden over** an over in cricket in which no runs are scored.
• *adj* **1** unmarried: maiden name. **2** first: maiden voyage. **3** (of a racehorse) not yet having won a prize. **maidenhood** *n* **maidenly** *adj* < Old English *mægden.* SEE PANEL.

mail[1] (meɪl) *n* **1** a system of sending, delivering, and collecting letters and parcels; post. **2** a batch of letters, etc.
• *vb* send by post. **mail order** buying goods by post. < of Germanic origin.

mail[2] *n* also **chain mail** flexible body armour made of links or small metal plates. < Latin *macula* mesh.

maim (meɪm) *vb* cripple, disfigure, or mutilate: maimed for life. < Old French *maynier.*

main (meɪn) *adj* principal or most important; major.
• *n* **1** the principal pipe or cable in a system distributing water, electricity, etc. **2** *pl* a distribution system for water, electricity, etc. **in the main** on the whole; mostly. **mainland** *n* the principal land mass of a country or continent, as opposed to adjacent islands. **mainly** *adv* for the most part; chiefly. **mainspring** *n* **1** the principal spring in a watch, clock, etc. **2** the primary motivating force. **mainstay** *n* the chief means of support. **mainstream** *n* the principal trend in style, thinking, etc. < Old English *mægen* strength.

maintain (meɪnˈteɪn) *vb* **1** keep in operation, existence, etc.; continue: maintain good relations. **2** keep in good order or repair. **3** provide financial support for. **4** assert or affirm (an opinion, etc.). **maintenance** *n* **1** maintaining; being maintained. **2** keeping (buildings, machinery; etc.) in good order or repair. **3** money given for financial support, esp. by a husband to a former wife. < Latin *manu tenēre* to hold in the hand.

maisonette (ˌmeɪzəˈnɛt) *n* a self-contained dwelling often on two floors of a large building. < Latin *mansio* dwelling-place.

maize (meɪz) *n* also **sweet corn 1** a tall, cereal grass with cobs tightly packed with large, yellow grains; its grain. **2** a yellow colour. < Taino *mahiz.*

majesty (ˈmædʒəstɪ) *n* **1** sovereign power. **2** used in addressing or mentioning a king or queen: Your Majesty. **3** impressive grandeur. **majestic** *adj* having great dignity or grandeur. **majestically** *adv* < Latin *majestas.*

major (ˈmeɪdʒə) *adj* **1** great or important: a major influence. **2** (of a musical scale or key) having notes separated by a

maiden means?

As dictionaries show, very many words in a language have more than one meaning: they are *polysemous*. A goal, for example, can be something that one finds at either end of a football pitch, a point scored each time the ball enters it, or on a more abstract level a general aim or purpose. How is it then that we can understand which meaning the user of a word intends? One major source of information that helps us decode correctly is the word's immediate context. Consider, for example, how the meaning of maiden is made clear in each of the following:

maiden voyage 'first'
maiden over 'no runs scored'
maiden name 'woman's family name before marriage'

The co-occurrence of voyage, over, or name tells us which of the meanings is intended.

whole tone, except for semitones between the third and fourth, and between the seventh and eighth.
• *n* **1** an officer ranking between a captain and a lieutenant colonel. **2** a principal subject of study at certain colleges and universities.
• *vb* (*US, Australian, NZ*) specialize (in a certain subject) at college or university.

majority *n* **1** the greater or greatest part or number: the majority of diseases. **2** the amount by which votes for the winning candidate exceed those for the runner-up. **3** the time or state of being of full **legal age**. < Latin, from *magnus* great. SEE PANEL.

make (meɪk) *vb* **made; making 1** create, construct, or produce: made in Hong Kong. **2** bring into existence; establish: make peace. **3** formulate in the mind: make a decision. **4** cause or force something to happen, be done, etc.: make someone wait. **5** cause to be or become: It made her ill. **6** earn, gain, or acquire: make a fortune. **7** compute or calculate: I make it five each. **8** amount to: That makes 19 altogether. **9** tidy or prepare for use: Are the beds made? **10** reach or arrive at; catch (a train,

the majority is... or the majority are...?

Whether you use a singular or plural verb with majority depends on the sense. When majority refers to the difference between two numbers, it is used with a singular verb: The winning candidate's majority *was* nearly 7000 votes.

When majority refers to the group that is more numerous, either a singular or plural verb is used. When the group is thought of as an entity, a singular verb is used: The majority *is* not always right. When the group is considered as a number of individuals, a plural is used: The vast majority *are* decent, hard-working people.

make it

Make features in a number of idiomatic expressions, including:

be made for to be perfectly suited to.
have it made to be certain of success.
have the makings of to have the necessary qualities for becoming.
make after to chase or pursue.
make away or **off** to leave or escape in a hurry.
make believe to pretend. **make-believe** *adj, n* (something) pretended or imaginary.
make do to manage or get by: You'll just have to make do without the car.
make for 1 to move towards. **2** to rush towards in order to attack: The dog made for him. **3** to help to bring something about: Communication makes for better understanding.
make good 1 to be successful in life. **2** to carry out: make good one's promise. **3** to repair.
make it to achieve one's goal; be successful.
make it up to to compensate or return a favour: Somehow I'll make it up to you.
make love to have sexual intercourse.
make much/little of to treat as important/unimportant.
make of to interpret, decipher, or understand from: What do you make of this letter?
make out 1 to complete (a cheque, form, etc.); write out. **2** to manage to see, read, or distinguish. **3** to understand the nature or motives of: I can't make her out.
make over to transfer ownership.
make room to provide a space (for).
make tracks to leave: It's time we were making tracks.
make up 1 to invent (a story or excuse). **2** to compose (a rhyme or tune). **3** to prepare (a mixture or an assortment): Shall I make up some more weedkiller? **4** to recover, repay, or replace. **5** to make a number, total, or amount complete: We need just one more to make up a full team. **6** to form or constitute. **7** to apply cosmetics, etc., to. **8** to become friendly again after a quarrel, etc.
make-up *n* **1** cosmetics. **2** the way in which the parts of something are put together; composition. **3** a person's physical, mental, or moral constitution.
make up to to try to gain the favour, affection, etc., of (someone) by subservience or flattery.
on the make seeking personal gain.

etc.): We only just made the station in time. **11** establish (a law, rule, etc.). **12** score or accumulate (points, runs, etc.): make a century. **13** perform, deliver, or execute: make a speech. **14** draw up officially: make a will. **15** provide or prove to be: She'll make him a good wife. **16** appoint: George was made spokesman. **17** be responsible for the success of: It was the wine that made the evening.
• *n* **1** origin of manufacture; brand: a foreign make. **2** the way something is made. **maker** *n* the person or company that makes something. < Old English *macian.* SEE PANEL.

makeshift (ˈmeɪkˌʃɪft) *adj, n* (serving as) a temporary substitute.

maladjustment (ˌmæləˈdʒʌstmənt) *n* a failure to adapt to or cope with one's personal circumstances. **maladjusted** *adj* showing this failure.

maladminister (ˌmælədˈmɪnɪstə) *vb* manage business or public affairs inefficiently or dishonestly. **maladministration** *n*

malady (ˈmælədɪ) *n* an illness or mental disorder. < Latin *male habitus* in bad condition.

malaise (mælˈeɪz) *n* a general feeling of uneasiness or vague discomfort. < French, from *mal-* bad + *aise* comfort.

malapropism (ˈmæləprɒpˌɪzəm) *n* an unintentional confusion of words that has a comical effect; instance of this. SEE PANEL.

malaria (məˈlɛərɪə) *n* a disease transmitted by the bite of mosquitos, causing recurrent attacks of fever. **malarial** *adj* < Italian *mala aria* bad air. SEE PANEL.

malcontent (ˈmælkənˌtɛnt) *adj, n* (a person who is) discontented, esp. with political circumstances, and inclined to rebel. < Old French.

male (meɪl) *adj* **1** of the sex that does not bear offspring or produce eggs. **2** (of a plant) with stamens but no ovary. **3** with a projection which fits into a corresponding female part.
• *n* a male animal or plant. < ultimately Latin *masculus.* SEE PANEL.

malevolent (məˈlɛvələnt) *adj* wishing harm to others; malicious. **malevolence** *n* **malevolently** *adv* < Latin *malevolens,* from *male* badly + *velle* to wish. SEE PANEL.

malformation (ˌmælfɔːˈmeɪʃən) *n* **1** the condition of being abnormal in form or shape. **2** a deformity. **malformed** *adj*

malfunction (ˌmælˈfʌŋkʃən) *vb* function imperfectly; fail to function.
• *n* an instance of this.

malice (ˈmælɪs) *n* a desire to do harm to others. **malicious** *adj* showing, feeling, or caused by ill will. **maliciously** *adv* **maliciousness** *n* < Latin *malus* bad. SEE PANEL.

malign (məˈlaɪn) *adj* 1 harmful in nature or effect. **2** showing ill will or hostility.
• *vb* speak ill of. **malignant** *adj* **1** (of a tumour, etc.) growing uncontrollably or resistant to treatment. **2** having or showing a desire to harm others; malevolent. **malignancy** *n* **malignantly** *adv* < Latin *malignus,* from *male* badly + *gignere* to beget. SEE PANEL

malapropisms

One way in which some people try to impress others is by using long words, or words that sometimes they don't really understand or know how to use correctly. In day-to-day life this can lead to rather strange-sounding utterances such as mental *facilities* instead of mental *faculties,* or under the *affluence* of alcohol instead of under the *influence.* Such instances of muddled usage are known as *malapropisms.*

English literature contains a vast gallery of comic characters who are remembered for their verbal misusage or tomfoolery. With the first performances of Richard Sheridan's 'The Rivals' in 1775 the type was finally immortalized in the ludicrously mal propos (out of place) utterances of Mrs Malaprop: 'Sure, if I *reprehend* anything in this world, it is the use of my *oracular* tongue, and a nice *derangement* of epitaphs'. It is from Mrs Malaprop with her verbal blunders that this muddled usage takes its name.

malaria

Nowadays it is widely known that malaria is caused by a parasite that is introduced into the blood by a certain type of mosquito. As the name of the disease testifies, this has not always been the case. Malaria is an Italian borrowing, from *mala aria* or 'bad air'. At the time when the disease was originally named, it was believed to be caused by the unwholesome air that characterized swampy districts.

AT **MALEVOLENT.**

malinger (mə'lɪŋgə) *vb* fake illness or incapacity in order to avoid work. **malingerer** *n* < French *malingre* sickly.

mallard ('mælɑːd) *n* a common wild duck, the male having a dark green head. < Middle French *mallart.*

malleable ('mælɪəbl̩) *adj* **1** able to be hammered, pressed, etc., into shape. **2** easily influenced. < Latin *malleus* hammer.

mallet ('mælɪt) *n* **1** a hammer, esp. one with a wooden head. **2** a similar object but with a longer handle, used in polo and croquet. < Latin *malleus* hammer.

malnutrition (ˌmælnjuː'trɪʃən) *n* faulty or insufficient nutrition.

malodorous (mæl'əʊdərəs) *adj* (*formal*) having an unpleasant smell; stinking.

malpractice (mæl'præktɪs) *n* (esp. of a professional person or organization) negligence or improper conduct.

malt (mɔːlt) *n* **1** germinated grain, usually barley, used in brewing and distilling. **2** an unblended whisky.
● *vb* make or become malt. **malty** *adj* < Old English *mealt.*

maltreat (mæl'triːt) *vb* treat badly or cruelly. **maltreatment** *n*

mamba ('mæmbə) *n* any of a group of poisonous African tree snakes, usually black or green. < Zulu *im-amba.*

mammal ('mæməl) *n* a member of the group of vertebrates that suckle their young. **mammalian** *adj* < Latin *mamma* breast.

mammary ('mæmərɪ) *adj* of or relating to the breast: mammary gland.

mammoth ('mæməθ) *n* any of a group of large, extinct elephants, having a hairy coat, a long tail, and long tusks.
● *adj* gigantic. < Russian *mamot.*
SEE PANEL.

man (mæn) *n, pl* **men 1** a human being. **2** an adult male human being. **3** any person or individual: Man overboard! **4** the human race; mankind. **5** a male employee or servant. **6** a manly person: Call yourself a man! **7** one of the pieces or tokens used in certain board-games, such as chess.
● *vb* **manned; manning** supply with enough men for operation, defence, etc., to be possible: man the guns. **manful** *adj* brave and resolute. **manfully** *adv* **manhandle** *vb* **1** move something by human force alone. **2** treat or handle roughly. **manhole** *n* a hole or opening, usually with a cover, through which access may be gained to a sewer, boiler, etc. **manhood** *n* **1** the state of being a man. **2** manly qualities. **man-hour** *n* a unit of work equal to that done by one person in one hour. **manhunt** *n* an extensive organized search for somebody, esp. a fugitive. **mankind** *n* the human race. **manly** *adj* having qualities such as strength and courage that are

---

male or masculine?

These two words are sometimes confused. Male refers to the sex of the animal or to a physical part of such an animal as in A colt is a young *male* horse.

Masculine means 'of men or the qualities thought typical of or suitable for men' as in She spoke in a deep, *masculine* voice. It is also used to refer to a gender of words in some languages: Der Tisch is a *masculine* noun in German (see also panel at **host**[1]).

---

malevolent or malignant?

Malevolent means 'wishing harm to others; showing a strong, harmful desire' as in a *malevolent* look, *malevolent* gods. Malignant can have this same meaning but tends to refer to an even more intense and determined desire: savage, *malignant* intentions.

Malignant, however, usually refers to a tumour that grows uncontrollably or is resistant to treatment and leads to death: a *malignant* growth.

---

malice aforethought

Malice aforethought or 'premeditated malice' is one of several legal phrases occurring in English as a result of the Norman conquest. It is a slightly anglicized equivalent of the original *malice prepense.* Phrases of similar origin include court martial and heir apparent. All of these phrases retain the French word order of an adjective following its noun.

associated with being a man. **manliness** *n* **man-made** *adj* made by man rather than by nature. **manned** *adj* having people on board: the first manned flight. **man-of-war** *n, pl* **men-of-war** a warship. **manpower** *n* **1** the number of people working on a particular job, or required or available for work. **2** the power supplied by human labour. **manslaughter** *n* the killing of a person unintentionally. **man to man** with frankness. **mantrap** *n* (formerly) a trap for catching people, esp. poachers. **the man in the street** any ordinary person, having representative opinions, attitudes, etc. **to a man** without exception. < Old English. SEE PANEL AT **MONGOOSE**.

manage (ˈmænɪdʒ) *vb* **1** be in charge of (a business, etc.). **2** supervise the training and business affairs of (a boxer, football team, etc.). **3** succeed in (doing something): How did he manage to pass? **4** succeed in coping: I don't know how she manages. **5** have enough room, time, etc., for: Can you manage another piece of toast? **6** have control over: She can't manage the children. **manageable** *adj* able to be managed. **management** *n* **1** a person or group that runs a business, etc. **2** the act or manner of managing. **3** the science or techniques of managing: a course in management. **manager** *n* **1** a person who runs a business, etc. **2** a person who supervises the training and business affairs of a boxer, football team, etc. **3** a person with a talent for managing. **managerial** *adj* **managing** *adj* having executive control: managing director. < Latin *manus* hand.

mammoth

Any large, long-tailed elephant of the Pleistocene epoch may be referred to as a mammoth. More common as an adjective for something of great size, this word came into English in the 18th century from the Russian *mamot*. This word is believed to be a derivative of *mamma*, the Tartar word for 'earth', which was inspired by the belief that the creature made burrows in the ground.

Words that have passed into English from Russian are very few in number. They include:

bolshevik
cosmonaut
intelligentsia
sputnik
vodka

mandarin (ˈmændərɪn) *n* **1** a small, sweet, orange, citrus fruit, like a tangerine. **2 Mandarin** the Chinese dialect upon which the official language is based. **3** a public official during the Chinese Empire; any high-ranking official. < Portuguese, ultimately from Sanskrit *mantrin* counsellor.

mandate (ˈmændeɪt) *n* an official authorization to perform a certain task or implement certain policies. **mandatory** *adj* compulsory. < Latin *mandatum*, from *mandare* to entrust.

mandolin (ˌmændəˈlɪn) *n* also **mandoline** a musical instrument rather like a lute with a rounded back and four pairs of strings. < ultimately Greek *pandoura* three-stringed lute.

mane (meɪn) *n* **1** the long hair on the back of the neck of a horse, lion, etc. **2** any long, thick hair. < Old English *manu*.

mange (meɪndʒ) *n* any of a group of skin disorders chiefly affecting domestic animals, caused by parasitic mites and characterized by sores and hair loss. **mangy** *adj* **1** suffering from mange. **2** (*informal*) shabby or squalid. < Middle French *mangene* itching, from *mangier* to eat.

manger (ˈmeɪndʒə) *n* a long, open box or trough from which cattle, etc., feed. < ultimately Latin *mandere* to chew.

mangle¹ (ˈmæŋgḷ) *n* (formerly) a machine with two rollers that squeeze water from wet laundry; wringer.
• *vb* pass (laundry) through a mangle. < ultimately Latin *manganum* war engine.

mangle² *vb* (esp. of bodies) disfigure or ruin, esp. by cutting or crushing. < ultimately Old French *maynier* to maim.

mango (ˈmæŋgəʊ) *n, pl* **mangoes**, **mangos** a tropical evergreen tree bearing a fruit with a large stone beneath succulent, yellow or orange flesh; its fruit. < Portuguese *manga*, from Tamil *mān-kāy*.

mangrove (ˈmæŋgrəʊv) *n* any of a group of tropical trees or shrubs growing in swamps or along shorelines, whose exposed, tangled roots tend to form dense thickets. < probably Portuguese *mangue*.

mania (ˈmeɪnɪə) *n* **1** great enthusiasm: a mania for football. **2** a mental disorder manifested in great excitement and sometimes violent behaviour. **maniac** *n* **1** a person with a mania. **2** (*informal*) any person whose behaviour is wild or irrational. **maniacal** *adj* < ultimately

Greek *mainesthai* to be mad.

manicure (ˈmænɪˌkjʊə) *n* **1** care of the hands and finger-nails, chiefly involving shaping of the nails and cuticles. **2** also **manicurist** *n* a person who gives manicures as a profession.
• *vb* give a manicure to. < ultimately Latin *manus* hand + *cura* care.

manifest (ˈmænɪˌfɛst) *adj* plain, obvious, or easily perceived: a manifest lie.
• *vb* show, reveal, or display clearly.
• *n* a customs document listing the passengers and cargo carried by a ship, aircraft, etc. **manifesto** *n, pl* **manifestos** a public declaration, esp. by a political party, of policies and intentions. < ultimately Latin *manifestus* hit by the hand.

manifold (ˈmænɪˌfəʊld) *adj* (*formal*) many and varied.
• *n* a pipe or chamber with a number of inlets and outlets, used to conduct or extract fluids or gases. < Old English *manigfeald*, from *manig* many + *-feald* -fold.

manikin (ˈmænɪkɪn) *n* **1** a tailor's dummy; mannequin. **2** a dwarf. < Dutch *mannekijn* little man, from Middle Dutch *man*.

manilla (məˈnɪlə) *n* also **manila** a strong, brown paper with a smooth finish used for wrapping and envelopes, made from Manila hemp. < *Manila*, city in the Philippines.

manipulate (məˈnɪpjʊˌleɪt) *vb* **1** handle, manage, or control skilfully. **2** control or influence, esp. in an artful and selfish way. **3** move (a bone or joint) into its proper position by manual pressure. **manipulation** *n* **manipulative** *adj* **manipulator** *n* < French *manipule* handful, from Latin *manipulus*.

mannequin (ˈmænɪkɪn) *n* **1** a fashion model. **2** a tailor's dummy. < SEE MANIKIN.

manner (ˈmænə) *n* **1** the way in which something happens or is done: in an orthodox manner. **2** a person's way of speaking and behaving: an offhand manner. **3** (*old-fashioned*) a type, sort; types. **mannered** *adj* **1** having a kind of manners that is mentioned: ill-mannered. **2** having affected ways of speaking or behaving. **mannerism** *n* a distinctive or idiosyncratic habit. **manners** *pl n* **1** a person's social conduct. **2** a type of social conduct of which society approves: She lacks manners. < ultimately Latin *manus* hand.

manoeuvre (məˈnuːvə) *n* **1** a carefully planned and controlled movement of troops, vehicles, etc.: on manoeuvres. **2** any clever or artful move or method.
• *vb* **1** move or guide something (into position, etc.) with care, artfulness, or skill. **2** perform one or more manoeuvres. < ultimately Latin *manu operare* to work by hand.

manor (ˈmænə) *n* **1** a large country house. **2** a landed estate. **3** also **manor house** the home of the lord of the manor. **4** (*informal*) a police district. **manorial** *adj* < ultimately Latin *manēre* to remain, dwell.

manse (mæns) *n* the home of a clergyman. < ultimately Latin *manēre* to remain, dwell.

mansion (ˈmænʃən) *n* a large, stately or imposing house, often with extensive grounds. **Mansions** (in names of buildings) a block of flats. < ultimately Latin *manēre* to remain, dwell.

mantel (ˈmæntl̩) *n* also **mantelpiece** an ornamental structure of wood, marble, etc., framing a fireplace, usually with a projecting shelf. **mantelpiece** *n* the projecting shelf of a mantel. < Middle French *mantel*.

mantis (ˈmæntɪs) *n, pl* **mantises**, **mantes** also **praying mantis** a carnivorous insect of mostly tropical regions that resembles a grasshopper and sits in a praying posture with front legs raised. < ultimately Greek: prophet.

mantle (ˈmæntl̩) *n* **1** a loose, sleeveless cloak. **2** something that covers, envelops, or conceals. **3** a fine, metal mesh which produces a bright light when placed over the flame of a gas or oil lamp.
• *vb* cover or conceal with or as if with a mantle. < ultimately Latin *mantellum*.

manual (ˈmænjʊəl) *adj* **1** of or concerning the hands. **2** done or operated by hand; requiring physical effort.
• *n* **1** a reference book providing instruction; handbook. **2** a keyboard, esp. on an organ, that is played by the hands. < ultimately Latin *manus* hand.

manufacture (ˌmænjʊˈfæktʃə) *vb* **1** produce (goods) on a large scale, esp. by using machinery. **2** invent or fabricate: manufacture an excuse.
• *n* the process of manufacturing. **manufacturer** *n* < ultimately Latin *manu factus* made by hand.

manure (məˈnjʊə) *n* any material used as a fertilizer, esp. animal excrement.
• *vb* apply manure to (the ground). < ultimately Latin *manu operare* to work by hand.

manuscript (ˈmænjʊˌskrɪpt) *n* **1** any document written by hand as opposed to typed or printed. **2** a text that is written or typed by an author. < Latin *manu scriptus* written by hand.

many (ˈmɛnɪ) *determiner, pron, n* **more; most** a large number: Many jobs were lost; not many; I don't think many of them will come.
• *adv* a lot: Many more letters arrived the next day. **a good many** rather a lot. **many a** a large number: Many a time I've thought of retiring. < Old English *manig.*

map (mæp) *n* a plan or representation of (part of) the surface area of a city, country, etc.; plan of the stars.
• *vb* **mapped; mapping 1** make a map of (an area). **2** make a detailed plan of something: map out a plan of attack. **put on the map** (*informal*) make famous or well-known. < ultimately Latin *mappa* cloth.

maple (ˈmeɪpl̩) *n* any of a group of trees or shrubs with star-shaped leaves, grown for ornament or timber; its wood. < Old English *mapul-.*

mar (mɑː) *vb* **marred; marring** spoil or detract from. < Old English *mierran* to obstruct.

marathon (ˈmærəθən) *n* **1** the longest race in athletics (about 42 km). **2** any long competition or test of endurance. SEE PANEL.

maraud (məˈrɔːd) *vb* raid in search of plunder. **marauder** *n* < French *marauder.*

marble (ˈmɑːbl̩) *n* **1** a form of hard limestone that can be cut and polished, used in sculpture and building. **2** a statue or other ornament made of marble. **3** a small ball of glass, metal, etc., used esp. in the game of marbles. **4** *pl* a children's game characterized by the attempt to strike an opponent's marble with one's own.
• *vb* give a veined or mottled appearance to. **marbled** *adj* having a veined or mottled appearance. < ultimately Greek *marmaros.*

march (mɑːtʃ) *vb* **1** walk with regular paces like a soldier. **2** make (a person or group) walk or march. **3** progress steadily: Time marches on.
• *n* **1** the act of marching. **2** the distance marched. **3** steady progression. **4** a musical composition written to accompany soldiers marching. **get one's marching orders** (*informal*) be dismissed, expelled, etc. < probably Germanic.

marchioness (ˌmɑːʃəˈnɛs) *n* **1** the wife or widow of a marquis. **2** a woman with the rank of marquis. < ultimately Medieval Latin *marca* border region.

mare (mɛə) *n* a mature female horse, zebra, etc. < ultimately Old English *mere.*

margarine (ˌmɑːdʒəˈriːn) *n* a substance used like butter, usually made from vegetable oils and skimmed milk. < ultimately Greek *margaron* pearl.

margin (ˈmɑːdʒɪn) *n* **1** a blank border between written text and the edge of the page. **2** any edge and the area adjacent to it; border. **3** a spare or extra amount: allow a margin for error. **4** (*commerce*) the difference between cost price and selling price. **marginal** *adj* **1** of or positioned in a margin. **2** very small in amount: marginal increases. **3** (*politics*) having only a small majority at an election; closely contested: a marginal seat. **marginally** *adv* < ultimately Latin *margo* border.

marguerite (ˌmɑːgəˈriːt) *n* any of a group of white, pink, or yellow daisy-like flowers. < ultimately Greek *margaron* pearl.

marigold (ˈmærɪˌgəʊld) *n* a popular garden plant with bright yellow or orange flowers. < Middle English *Mary* mother of Jesus + *gold.*

marijuana (ˌmærɪjʊˈɑːnə) *n* the dried leaves and flowers of the hemp plant, used as a hallucinogenic drug. < Mexican Spanish.

marina (məˈriːnə) *n* a harbour for yachts and pleasure boats. < ultimately Latin *marinus* marine.

marinate (ˈmærɪˌneɪt) *vb* also **marinade** soak (meat or fish) in a seasoned liquid before cooking. **marinade** *n* the liquid used for this. < Italian *marinare.*

marine (məˈriːn) *adj* of or connected with the sea or shipping.
• *n* a soldier trained to serve on land and at sea. **mariner** *n* (*old-fashioned*) a sailor or seaman. < ultimately Latin *mare* sea.

marionette (ˌmærɪəˈnɛt) *n* a puppet with jointed limbs that are operated by

marathon

A race that is run over a distance of 42.195 kilometres (26 miles and 385 yards) is called a marathon. This word derives from the legend of the Greek messenger who in 490 BC ran from *Marathon* to Athens to tell of the victory of the Greeks over the Persians. Having delivered the good news, the messenger reputedly collapsed and died.

strings. < ultimately Middle French *maryonete,* from *Marion* Mary + *-ette.*

marital (ˈmærɪtl̩) *adj* of or connected with marriage: marital problems. < Latin *maritus.*

maritime (ˈmærɪˌtaɪm) *adj* **1** of, near, or connected with the sea. **2** of or connected with seafaring or shipping: a maritime museum. < Latin *mare* sea.

marjoram (ˈmɑːdʒərəm) *n* a herb with fragrant leaves and small, purplish-white flowers, used in cooking. < Medieval Latin *majorana.*

mark (mɑːk) *n* **1** a stain, scratch, or other visible impression that alters or spoils the appearance of something: a dirty mark. **2** a lasting or permanent impression: Suffering had left its mark. **3** a distinguishing or recognizable feature: the mark of a good upbringing. **4** a token or indication: a mark of our gratitude. **5** a written or printed symbol: punctuation marks. **6** points awarded by a teacher, examiner, etc.; grade. **7** a target, standard, or norm: Her performance fell short of the mark.

• *vb* **1** make a mark on; become marked: Don't mark the table: I've just polished it. **2** put a recognizable sign on. **3** award points of merit to; grade. **4** (of team-games) keep close to (an opponent). **mark down** reduce the price of (an item). **marked** *adj* clearly noticeable; dramatic: a marked improvement. **markedly** *adv* (*formal*) noticeably. **marker** *n* **1** a person or thing that marks. **2** something that indicates a position or location. **3** a type of pen, esp. one with a thick point. **marking** *n* **1** a mark or marks. **2** the colouring of an animal's fur, skin, etc. **mark off** separate by a line or boundary. **mark out 1** select for special treatment; single out. **2** mark the boundaries of (a football pitch, etc.). **marksman** *n* a person who shoots well. **marksmanship** *n* **mark time 1** move the legs as if marching, but without advancing. **2** not move forward, esp. because waiting until a suitable time. **mark up 1** raise the price of. **2** fix or decide the selling price of. **3** prepare (a manuscript) for printing. **mark-up** *n* the amount added to the cost price of an item to make the selling price. < Old English *mearc.*

market (ˈmɑːkɪt) *n* **1** a gathering of people for the purpose of trade. **2** a building or public place where goods are bought and sold. **3** any group or organization involved in trade: the international money market. **4** any class of potential purchasers: the outsize market. **5** selling opportunities; demand: no market for second-hand shoes. **6** trade in a particular commodity.

• *vb* sell or trade in (a commodity). **in the market for** wanting to buy. **marketable** *adj* easy or fit to sell. **market-day** *n* the day in the week on which a particular market is held. **market garden** a garden or area of land on which fruit or vegetables are grown for sale. **market research** the systematic study of consumers' purchasing habits, preferences, etc., esp. to discover new selling opportunities. < ultimately Latin *merx* merchandise.

marmalade (ˈmɑːməˌleɪd) *n* a type of jam made from oranges or other citrus fruits. < Portuguese *marmelada* quince jam, ultimately from Greek *melimēlon,* from *meli* honey + *mēlon* apple. SEE PANEL.

marmot (ˈmɑːmət) *n* any of a group of small, burrowing rodents of the squirrel family. < French.

maroon¹ (məˈruːn) *adj, n* (having) a brownish-red colour. < French *marron* chestnut.

maroon² *vb* abandon ashore or in an isolated place: marooned on a desert island. < *Maroon,* a runaway Negro slave. SEE PANEL.

marquee (mɑːˈkiː) *n* a large tent used for outdoor parties, exhibitions, etc. < French *marquis.*

marquetry (ˈmɑːkɪtrɪ) *n* decorative inlay of wood, ivory, etc., chiefly used in furniture.< Middle French *marqueter* to inlay, from *marque* mark.

marquis (ˈmɑːkwɪs) *n* also **marquess** a nobleman next in rank below a duke. < Middle French *marchis,* from *marche* march.

marriage (ˈmærɪdʒ) *n* **1** the state of being husband and wife. **2** the ceremony at

marmalade

A preserve that is made from a citrus fruit, especially oranges, is called marmalade. This is one of the few words in the language of Portuguese descent. It comes from the Portuguese *marmelada* meaning 'quince jam', quince being the fruit from which marmalade was originally made.

Other words deriving from Portuguese include:

albino	**dodo**	**tank**
caste	**mandarin**	

which a man and woman become husband and wife. **3** any union or joint relationship: the marriage of beauty and intelligence. **marriageable** *adj* old enough or suitable for marriage. < Middle French *marier* to marry.

marrow (ˈmærəʊ) *n* **1** the soft, fatty substance in the central cavities of bones, in which blood cells are formed. **2** a large vegetable with a dark-green skin and creamy-white flesh that resembles a giant cucumber. < Old English *mearg.*

marrowfat (ˈmærəʊˌfæt) *n* any of a group of pea plants that have large seeds; seeds of such a plant.

marry (ˈmærɪ) *vb* **married; marrying** **1** make or become husband and wife. **2** take a husband or wife in marriage. **3** join or unite. < ultimately Latin *maritus* married.

marsh (mɑːʃ) *n* (an area of) low-lying, watery land; swamp. **marshy** *adj* **marshland** *n* marsh. < Old English *mersc.*

marshal (ˈmɑːʃəl) *n* **1** an officer of the highest rank. **2** an official responsible for organizing or overseeing ceremonies, parades, or other public events. **3** an official with secretarial duties who accompanies a circuit judge.
• *vb* **marshalled; marshalling** **1** lead or usher. **2** arrange in order. **3** assemble and organize. **marshalling yard** a railway yard where goods wagons are sorted and made up into trains. < of Germanic origin.

marshmallow (ˌmɑːʃˈmæləʊ) *n* a soft, spongy sweet, usually white or pink.

marsupial (mɑːˈsjuːpɪəl) *adv, n* (of) any of a group of mammals whose young are carried in the pouch of the female until properly developed. < New Latin *marsupium.*

martial (ˈmɑːʃəl) *adj* of or connected with war or the armed forces. **martial art** any oriental fighting method, such as karate or judo, that is practised as a sport. **martial law** rule of law maintained by a country's armed forces in the absence of civil law. < ultimately Latin *Mars.*

martin (ˈmɑːtɪn) *n* any of a group of birds of the swallow family. < origin uncertain.

martinet (ˌmɑːtɪˈnɛt) *n* a person who enforces the strictest discipline. < Jean *Martinet,* died 1672, French army officer. SEE PANEL.

martyr (ˈmɑːtə) *n* **1** a person who undergoes death or great suffering rather than forsake a belief, cause, etc. **2** any person who suffers or is a victim.
• *vb* torture or put to death as a martyr. **martyrdom** *n* < ultimately Greek *martys* witness.

marvel (ˈmɑːvəl) *vb* **marvelled; marvelling** be very surprised or astonished: We marvelled at his rapid recovery.
• *n* **1** something that causes great

maroon

To be left stranded in a desolate place such as a desert island is to be marooned. This word was originally the name applied in the 17th century to escaped Negro slaves and their descendants who established communities in the least accessible parts of the West Indies and Guiana. It derives via the American Spanish *cimarrón* meaning 'wild' or 'living on the mountain tops' from the Spanish *cima* or 'peak'.

martinet

A person who is known to be a very strict disciplinarian is sometimes referred to as a martinet: 'The new headmaster won't stand for any nonsense; he's a real *martinet.*' The word martinet comes from Jean *Martinet,* a French army officer in the reign of Louis XIV. It was Martinet who managed to introduce military discipline as we know it today into the French army. Under his influence the latter was transformed from an ill-disciplined rabble into an efficient and formidable fighting force. All this was accomplished only by the employment of a severe training system, one that included endless drilling and an amount of flogging unprecedented even by Greek or Roman standards.

Rather ironically, in 1672 Martinet was killed by his own men. The story has it that while leading an assault at the siege of Duisberg a certain over-enthusiasm caused him to enter his rear ranks' line of fire. Those familiar with the harshness of Martinet's training methods might be less ready to accept that the event was an accident.

surprise or astonishment. **2** (*informal*) used to express strong approval, delight, etc.: She's a real marvel. **marvellous** *adj* **1** of excellent quality, skill, etc.: a marvellous swimmer. **2** (*informal*) used to express strong approval, delight, etc. **marvellously** *adv* < ultimately Latin *mirari* to wonder.

marzipan (ˈmɑːzɪˌpæn) *n* a paste of ground almonds, sugar, and egg whites, chiefly used to coat fruit cakes and to make sweets. < ultimately Arabic *mawthabān* medieval coin.

mascara (mæˈskɑːrə) *n* a cosmetic used for darkening the eyelashes. < Italian *maschera* mask.

masculine (ˈmæskjʊlɪn) *adj* **1** of men or the qualities thought typical or suitable for men. **2** of a particular grammatical gender.
• *n* a masculine word, etc. **masculinity** *n* < ultimately Latin *mas* male. SEE PANEL AT **MALE**.

mash (mæʃ) *n* **1** any soft, pulpy mixture. **2** (*informal*) mashed potatoes. **3** animal feed made from bran, meal, etc., and water. **4** a mixture of malt and hot water, used in brewing.
• *vb* crush or beat into a mash. < Old English *māx*-.

mask (mɑːsk) *n* **1** a covering worn over (part of) the face, for protection or disguise. **2** something that disguises or conceals. **3** a sculpted or moulded replica of a face or head. **4** also **gasmask** a respirator. **5** the face or head of an animal, esp. of a fox.
• *vb* **1** cover with a mask. **2** disguise, conceal, or screen.

masochism (ˈmæsəˌkɪzəm) *n* a mental disorder which causes a person to find enjoyment or excitement in the experience of pain, humiliation, etc. **masochist** *n* **masochistic** *adj* < Leopold von Sacher *Masoch*, died 1895, Austrian novelist.

mason (ˈmeɪsn̩) *n* a person skilled in building with stone. **Mason** *n* a Freemason. **masonry** *n* stonework; trade of a mason. < of Germanic origin.

masquerade (ˌmæskəˈreɪd) *n* **1** a pretence or disguise. **2** a social function at which guests wear masks and costumes.
• *vb* **1** disguise oneself; dissemble. **2** attend a masquerade. < ultimately Old Italian *maschera*.

mass (mæs) *n* **1** a large quantity or number: a mass of tulips. **2** a large body of matter: a mass of ice. **3** the main part of a group; majority. **4** (*physics*) the amount of matter a body contains.
• *vb* gather or form into a mass. **mass meeting** one attended by a great number of people. **mass-produce** *vb* manufacture (goods) in great quantities. **the masses** *pl n* the common people. < ultimately Greek *maza*.

Mass (mæs) *n* **1** (esp. Roman Catholic) a religious ceremony celebrating the Eucharist. **2** a musical setting for the parts of the Eucharist that are sung. < ultimately Latin *mittere* to send.

massacre (ˈmæsəkə) *n* **1** the slaughter of a great number of people or animals. **2** (*informal*) an overwhelming defeat.
• *vb* **1** slaughter indiscriminately. **2** (*informal*) defeat overwhelmingly. < Middle French.

massage (ˈmæsɑːʒ, ˈmæsɑːdʒ) *n* rubbing and kneading of (parts of) the body to relieve stiffness, pain, etc.
• *vb* treat (the body) in this way. **masseur** fem. **masseuse** *n* a man or woman who does this for a living. < French *masser* to massage.

massive (ˈmæsɪv) *adj* **1** bulky, heavy, or solid: a massive tree-trunk. **2** unusually large: massive increases. **3** impressive or imposing. **massively** *adv* **massiveness** *n* < Middle French *masse* mass.

mast (mɑːst) *n* **1** a tall, upright spar that supports a ship's sail. **2** a tall, upright pole from which a flag is hung. **3** any tall, upright support. < Old English *mæst*.

master (ˈmɑːstə) *n* **1** a man in authority such as an owner or employer. **2** a person or abstract thing that has control or influence in a situation. **3** a male teacher. **4** a person with an academic degree next above a bachelor's. **5** a craftsman qualified to teach apprentices: master carpenter. **6** a world-class chess player. **7** a highly respected teacher or leader. **8** the commander of a merchant ship. **9** an original document, recording,

masterful or **masterly?**

These two words are sometimes confused, partly because they come from different meanings of master: 'a person in authority' and 'a craftsman'. These form the roots of masterful and masterly.

Masterful means 'domineering; authoritative': a *masterful* tone of voice. Masterly means 'showing great skill': a *masterly* display of horsemanship.

etc., as opposed to a copy. **10 Master** the title used for a boy or youth too young to be called Mister.
• *vb* **1** bring under control; overcome: master the difficulties involved. **2** acquire skill or proficiency in; gain an understanding of.
• *adj* main or principal: master bedroom. **masterful** *adj* domineering. **masterfully** *adv* **master-key** *n* a key which will open several different locks. **masterly** *adj* showing great skill. **masterpiece** *n* **1** an impressive work of art, piece of workmanship, etc. **2** a person's best piece of work. **master-stroke** *n* a masterly act or performance. **mastery** *n* **1** complete control (of a situation). **2** skill, proficiency, or understanding. < ultimately Latin *magister*. SEE PANEL.

mastermind (ˈmɑːstəˌmaɪnd) *vb* plan and direct (a complex operation).
• *n* a person of great intelligence or managerial skill.

masticate (ˈmæstɪˌkeɪt) *vb* chew; reduce to pulp. **mastication** *n* < ultimately Greek *mastichan* to gnash the teeth.

mastiff (ˈmæstɪf) *n* any of a group of large, stocky, short-haired dogs, used chiefly as guard dogs. < ultimately Latin *mansuetus* tame.

masturbate (ˈmæstəˌbeɪt) *vb* excite oneself or another person sexually by stimulating the genitals with the hand. **masturbation** *n* **masturbatory** *adj* < Latin *masturbari*.

mat (mæt) *n* **1** a piece of durable material used as a floor covering. **2** a flat, often decorative piece of wood, cork, etc., used chiefly to protect surfaces from stains, heat marks, etc.
• *vb* **matted; matting** make or become tangled. < ultimately Semitic.

matador (ˈmætədɔː) *n* a bullfighter who taunts the bull with a cape and eventually tries to kill it with a sword. < Spanish *matar* to kill.

match¹ (mætʃ) *n* a short, wooden stick with a specially prepared tip which ignites when dragged across a rough surface. **matchbox** *n* a small box for holding matches. **matchwood** *n* **1** wood suitable for matches. **2** small pieces or splinters of wood. < Middle French *meiche*.

match² *n* **1** a contest: a football match. **2** a person or thing that is equal to another in skill, strength, etc.: meet one's match. **3** a person or thing that is exactly like or goes well with another: a good match. **4** a marriage; prospective marriage partner.
• *vb* **1** set in competition or opposition. **2** equal in skill, strength, etc. **3** be similar or harmonious in colour, design, etc. **4** find or produce the exact counterpart of or equivalent to: You'll never match that marble exactly. **5** pair counterparts. **matchless** *adj* unequalled; peerless. **matchmaker** *n* a person who arranges or tries to arrange marriages. < ultimately Old English *mæcca*.

mate¹ (meɪt) *n* **1** the breeding partner of an animal. **2** (*informal*) a friend or companion; also used as a term of address between males. **3** a workman's assistant. **4** a fellow member: team-mate. **5** any merchant ship's officer ranking beneath the master.
• *vb* **1** come or bring together for breeding. **2** connect or join as a pair. < probably Middle Low German *māt*.

mate² *n*, *vb* (*chess*) checkmate.

material (məˈtɪərɪəl) *n* **1** the substance of which a thing is made. **2** cloth or fabric. **3** facts or data to be used in writing or composing something: material for a new book. **4** a person with qualities suitable for a particular role, occupation, etc.
• *adj* **1** of or connected with matter: the material world. **2** of physical (not spiritual) needs: His reasons for helping are purely material. **3** important; essential; relevant: material evidence. **materialism** *n* **1** the belief or theory that only physical things exist and that everything may be explained by physical laws. **2** concern with material rather than spiritual or intellectual well-being. **materialist** *n* a believer in materialism. **materialistic** *adj* **materialize** *vb* **1** give or adopt a bodily or visible form. **2** become a fact; come into effect. **materially** *adv* to a significant extent. < ultimately Latin *materia* matter.

maternal (məˈtɜːnḷ) *adj* **1** of or connected with a mother or motherhood. **2** related through the mother's side of the family: maternal aunt. **maternally** *adv* **maternity** *n* **1** motherhood. **2** of or connected with pregnancy: maternity ward < ultimately Latin *mater* mother.

matey (ˈmeɪtɪ) *adj* (*informal*) friendly or sociable. **matiness** *n*

mathematics (ˌmæθəˈmætɪks) *n* the science of number, quantity, and space. **mathematical** *adj* of, used in, or connected with mathematics. **mathematically** *adv* **mathematician** *n* a person skilled in mathematics. < ultimately Greek *manthanein* to learn.

maths (mæθs) *n* (*informal*) mathematics.

matinée (ˈmætɪˌneɪ) *n* an afternoon performance at a theatre, cinema, etc. **matinée coat** or **jacket** a jacket or short coat worn by a baby. < ultimately Latin *Matuta* goddess of morning.

matriarch (ˈmeɪtrɪˌɑːk) *n* a female head of a family or tribe. **matriarchal** *adj* **matriarchy** *n* a form of social organization in which the female is head of the family, and descent and inheritance are through the female line. < ultimately Latin *mater* mother.

matricide (ˈmætrɪˌsaɪd) *n* the killing by a person of his or her mother. < ultimately Latin *matricidium*.

matriculate (məˈtrɪkjʊˌleɪt) *vb* enter or admit to a university as a student. **matriculation** *n* < ultimately Latin *matrix* list.

matrimony (ˈmætrɪmənɪ) *n* marriage. **matrimonial** *adj* < Latin *matrimonium*.

matrix (ˈmeɪtrɪks) *n, pl* **matrixes, matrices 1** a substance, environment, etc., in which something originates. **2** a mould in which metal, etc., is cast. **3** the natural material in which for instance a gem or fossil lies embedded. **4** a regular array of mathematical quantities, etc. < Latin.

matron (ˈmeɪtrən) *n* **1** a dignified, rather elderly, married woman or widow. **2** a woman housekeeper in a school or other institution. **3** (formerly) a woman in charge of the nursing staff in a hospital. **matronly** *adj* < ultimately Latin *mater* mother.

matt (mæt) *adj* (of a surface) having a dull finish; not glossy. < French *mat*.

matter (ˈmætə) *n* **1** physical substance. **2** a particular substance or material: printed matter. **3** a focus of thought or attention; subject: money matters. **4** what is said in a book, speech, etc. (as opposed to how it is said); material: subject matter. **5** discharge from the body; pus.
• *vb* be of importance: It doesn't matter. **matter-of-fact** *adj* factual (as opposed to imaginative): a matter-of-fact account. **no matter 1** it is not important. **2** irrespective of. **the matter** the cause of worry, anxiety, etc.: What's the matter? < ultimately Latin *materia*.

matting (ˈmætɪŋ) *n* woven material used as a floor covering.

mattock (ˈmætək) *n* an agricultural tool resembling a pickaxe. < Old English *mattuc*.

mattress (ˈmætrɪs) *n* a fabric casing filled with foam rubber, springs, etc., used as (part of) a bed. < ultimately Arabic *maṭraḥ* place where something is thrown.

mature (məˈtjʊə) *adj* **1** fully grown or developed. **2** having the mental powers associated with an adult. **3** (of a wine) ready for consumption. **4** (of a bill) due for payment.
• *vb* come or bring to full development. **maturely** *adv* **maturation** *n* the process of maturing. **maturity** *n* the state of being mature. < Latin *maturus* ripe.

maudlin (ˈmɔːdlɪn) *adj* sentimental in a silly or tearful way. < Middle English *Maudelen* Mary Magdalene, typically depicted as a tearful penitent. SEE PANEL.

maul (mɔːl) *vb* injure by clawing or by rough handling. < ultimately Latin *malleus* hammer.

mausoleum (ˈmɔːsəˌlɪəm) *n* a grand or stately tomb. < Greek *mausōleion*, from *Mausolos*, died 353 BC, ruler of Caria in Asia Minor. SEE PANEL.

mauve (məʊv) *adj, n* pale-purple. < ultimately Latin *malva*.

mawkish (ˈmɔːkɪʃ) *adj* excessively sentimental; insipid. **mawkishly** *adv* **mawkishness** *n* < Middle English *mawke* maggot, from Old Norse *mathkr*.

maxim (ˈmæksɪm) *n* a general truth or widely accepted rule of conduct. < ultimately Latin *maximus* greatest.

maximum (ˈmæksɪməm) *n, pl* **maximums, maxima** the greatest possible number, amount, etc. **maximal** *adj* greatest possible. **maximize** *vb* increase to a maximum or as much as possible: maximize one's chances of success. **maximization** *n* < Latin.

may (meɪ) *auxiliary vb* **might 1** used to express possibility: She may come. **2** used to request or give permission: May I use your pen? **3** used to express a wish or

maudlin

A person or thing that displays insipid sentimentality is sometimes described as maudlin: If he's full of *maudlin* stories when he's sober, what's he like when he's drunk? This adjective comes from *Maudelen*, the Middle English name for (Mary) Magdalene, who is traditionally depicted with tearful red eyes.

The subsequent change in spelling which saw *Maudelen* become Magdalene had no affect upon maudlin at all.

Curiously, the names of Magdalen College, Oxford, and Magdalene College, Cambridge, underwent the spelling reform, but continued to be pronounced as if this had not occurred.

desire. < Old English *mæg.*

maybe (ˈmeɪˌbiː) *adv* perhaps. < Middle English.

mayday (ˈmeɪˌdeɪ) *n* the international radio signal of distress. < French *m'aider* help me.

mayhem (ˈmeɪhɛm) *n* violent or destructive action. < ultimately Old French *maynier* to maim.

mayonnaise (ˌmeɪəˈneɪz) *n* a creamy dressing made with egg yolks, oil, and vinegar, used chiefly on salads. < French.

mayor (mɛə) *n* the executive head of a city or borough. **mayoral** *adj* **mayoress** *n* **1** a female mayor. **2** the wife of a mayor or a woman performing the same ceremonial role. < ultimately Latin *major* greater.

maypole (ˈmeɪˌpəʊl) *n* a tall pole, garlanded with ribbons, around which people traditionally dance on May Day.

maze (meɪz) *n* **1** a complex network of hedge-lined paths, carefully designed to puzzle those who enter it. **2** something confusingly complicated. < probably Old English *masian* to confuse.

MC *abbrev* Master of Ceremonies.

MCC *abbrev* Marylebone Cricket Club.

me (mɪ; *stressed* miː) *pron* the object case of *I.*
• *n* in keeping with the personality of the speaker: That hat's not really me. < Old English *mē.*

mead (miːd) *n* an alcoholic drink of water, honey, malt, and yeast. < Old English *medu.*

meadow (ˈmɛdəʊ) *n* a field of grass. < Old English *mǣdwe.*

meagre (ˈmiːgə) *adj* **1** deficient in quantity or quality: meagre wages. **2** thin or lean. < ultimately Latin *macer* lean.

meal[1] (miːl) *n* **1** an occasion like breakfast or dinner when people eat. **2** the food that is had on one of these occasions. **make a meal of** (*informal*) perform (a task) with an unnecessary amount of effort. **mealtime** *n* a regular time when breakfast, dinner, etc., is eaten. < Old English *mǣl.*

meal[2] *n* a coarse powder made by crushing grain, used esp. for flour or animal food. < Old English *melu.*

mealy (ˈmiːlɪ) *adj* **1** dry and powdery. **2** containing meal. **mealy-mouthed** *adj* unwilling to speak in a frank way, esp. because of a desire not to offend.

mean[1] (miːn) *vb* **meant; meaning** **1** intend or have as a purpose: She means to look for another job. **2** design for a particular use, function, etc.: not meant for children. **3** intend to convey (a sense) or indicate (a person or thing): I don't mean that one; I mean this one. **4** (of words) have as an equivalent or paraphrase: What does rubella mean? **5** entail: The job means a lot of hard work. **6** have (a particular degree of) importance or significance: The medal means a lot to him. **7** be a sign of: Does this incident mean another political upheaval? **mean business** or **it** be in earnest. **mean well** have good intentions. < Old English *mǣnan.*

mean[2] *adj* **1** selfishly miserly; not generous: too mean to buy presents. **2** (of behaviour) spiteful or unkind: a mean trick. **3** poor in appearance or quality; lacking distinction: no mean feat. **meanly** *adv* **meanness** *n* < Old English *gemǣne.*

mean[3] *adj, n* (a point, number, or course) equally distant from two extremes. < ultimately Latin *medianus,* from *medius* middle.

meander (mɪˈændə) *vb* **1** (of a stream) follow a winding course. **2** wander here and there. < Greek *Maiandros,* winding river in Asia Minor.

meaning (ˈmiːnɪŋ) *n* **1** that which is (intended to be) conveyed: The meaning of the poem is uncertain. **2** value or significance.
• *adj* intended to be expressive; meaningful. **meaningful** *adj* full of significance. **meaningfully** *adv* **meaningless** *adj*

means (miːnz) *n* **1** the way by which a result is obtained: a means of saving money. **2** *pl* resources or income. **by all means**

---

mausoleum

A grand or imposing tomb such as that of Karl Marx in Highgate Cemetery, London, is known as a mausoleum. This comes ultimately from the Greek word for mausoleum, *mausōleion*, which was originally the name of the monumental tomb built in memory of Mausolus, king of Caria in the 4th century BC. The tomb was erected at Halicarnassus in 353 BC by order of Artemisia, the king's inconsolable widow.

The monument was among the seven wonders of the ancient world. It is believed to have been destroyed either by an earthquake in the Middle Ages or by the knights of St John.

---

certainly. **by no means** on no account. **means test** an official examination of a person's financial circumstances to assess his or her eligibilty for assistance.

meant (mɛnt) SEE **MEAN**[1].

meantime (ˈmiːnˌtaɪm) *adv* meanwhile.

meanwhile (ˈmiːnˌwaɪl) *adv* **1** during the intervening period. **2** at the same time.

measles (ˈmiːzəlz) *n* an infectious disease causing fever and red spots on the body. < Middle English *meseles.* SEE PANEL.

measly (miːzlɪ) *adj* (*informal*) contemptibly deficient in quantity or quality.

measure (ˈmɛʒə) *n* **1** the size, quantity, etc., of something. **2** a unit, standard, or system used in stating size, quantity, etc. **3** a device for determining size, quantity, etc. **4** extent or amount. **5** a step or action taken for a particular purpose; (proposed) law: take drastic measures. **6** the rhythm of a poem; time of a piece of music.
• *vb* **1** determine the size, quantity, etc., of. **2** (of things) be of (a certain length, size, etc.). **3** deal out a certain quantity of. **measurable** *adj* able to be measured. **measured** *adj* **1** regular in rhythm or movement. **2** carefully considered. **measurement** *n* **1** details as to length, size, etc. **2** measuring. **measure up** have qualities, skills, etc., of a required standard. < Latin *metiri.*

meat (miːt) *n* flesh of animals used as food. **meaty** *adj* **1** providing a lot of meat. **2** resembling meat. **3** (*informal*) having a substantial content. SEE PANEL.

mechanic (mɪˈkænɪk) *n* a skilled workman who uses, maintains, or repairs machines. **mechanical** *adj* of or connected with machines. **mechanically** *adv* **mechanics** *n* **1** the scientific study of motion and force. **2** the scientific study of machines. **3** *pl* mechanical details. **mechanism** *n* **1** a piece of machinery; way this works. **2** an action or process by which a result is obtained. **mechanize** *vb* use machines in or for. **mechanization** *n* < ultimately Greek *mēchanē* machine.

medal (ˈmɛdl̩) *n* a piece of metal like a

Do you mean **German measles?**

Since the majority of the technical terms used in medicine are borrowings or derivatives from Latin and Greek, it is not surprising that to most of us they are largely unintelligible. What are the meanings, for example, of chondromyxosarcoma, hyperprebetalipoproteinaemia or phacoanaphylaxis?
Common diseases and ailments, however, often have a nontechnical name existing alongside their technical one. *Rubella,* for example, is referred to by the layperson as German measles, while *pertussis* goes by the more familiar name of whooping-cough.
Other pairs of medical synonyms belonging to technical and nontechnical *registers* include:

alopecia—baldness
varicella—chicken-pox
pyrosis—heartburn
myopia—shortsightedness
variola—smallpox
rhinorrhea—runny nose

---

meat

Meat has not always meant what it means today. In the Authorized (King James) Version of the Bible, for instance, God says that to every bird and animal, 'I have given every green herb for meat' (Genesis 1:30). As illustrated here, meat was once a much more general term, meaning 'all food'. (What we understand by meat today was previously known as flesh.) Since the 17th century the word has undergone a contraction of meaning or *narrowing*.

Narrowing of meaning is by no means peculiar to meat. Starve once meant to die any manner of death, not just to die of hunger. The broader meaning was that used by Chaucer when he referred to Christ starving on the cross. Similarly, deer once meant any kind of animal and hound any breed of dog. Interestingly, in German these broad meanings have survived in the equivalent words Tier and Hund. For Shakespeare a duke was any leader, who could make a voyage as much by land as by sea.

Before the Norman Conquest one might find ox, pig, calf, and sheep on the menu, words which contracted in meaning when their 'meat' senses were taken over by the French words for beef, pork, veal, and mutton. (See also panel at **girl.**)

large coin, made to commemorate an event or to be given as an award. **medallist** *n* a person who wins a medal. < Old Italian *medaglia.*

medallion (mɪˈdæljən) *n* **1** a large medal. **2** a large, circular, ornamental design, panel, or relief. < Italian *medaglione.*

meddle (ˈmɛdl̩) *vb* **1** interfere in a person's affairs. **2** toy or tinker with. **meddlesome** *adj* in the habit of meddling. < Latin *miscēre* to mix.

media (ˈmiːdɪə) SEE **MEDIUM**. SEE PANEL.

medial (ˈmiːdɪəl) *adj* of or situated in the middle. **medially** *adv*

median (ˈmiːdɪən) *adj* of, situated in, or passing through the middle. < Latin *medius* middle.

mediate (ˈmiːdɪˌeɪt) *vb* act as a go-between, negotiator, or peacemaker. **mediation** *n* **mediator** *n* < Latin *medius* middle.

medic (ˈmɛdɪk) *n* (*informal*) a doctor or medical student.

medical (ˈmɛdɪkl̩) *adj* of or connected with the science of medicine, as distinct from surgery.
• *n* (*informal*) a medical examination. **medically** *adv* < Latin *medicus,* from *mederi* to heal.

medicament (məˈdɪkəmənt) *n* medicine.

medicate (ˈmɛdɪˌkeɪt) *vb* treat with a medicinal substance: medicated gauze. **medication** *n*

medicine (ˈmɛdɪsən, ˈmɛdsən) *n* **1** the scientific study of the prevention and cure of disease. **2** a substance used to treat a disease, esp. one taken by mouth. **medicinal** *adj* having the properties of a medicine. **medicinally** *adv* **medicine-man** *n* a witch-doctor or sorcerer. < Latin *medicus* physician.

medieval, mediaeval (ˌmɛdɪˈiːvl̩) *adj* of or like in the Middle Ages. < Latin *medius* middle + *aevum* age.

mediocre (ˌmiːdɪˈəʊkə) *adj* **1** of average quality, ability, etc.; indifferent. **2** second-rate. < Latin *mediocris* half-way up a mountain, from *medius* middle + *ocris* stony mountain.

meditate (ˈmɛdɪˌteɪt) *vb* **1** to empty the mind and focus upon one thing, especially as a mental or religious exercise. **2** think deeply (about). **meditation** *n* **meditative** *adj* **meditator** *n* < Latin *meditari.*

medium (ˈmiːdɪəm) *n, pl* **media,** except def. **4 mediums 1** a middle or intermediate state or degree: a happy medium. **2** a substance or agency in which something exists or through which it is transmitted; vehicle: Air is the medium that conveys sound. **3** a means for diffusing information to the public: advertising media. **4** a person who claims to be a go-between between the living and the spirits of the dead. **5** a mode of artistic expression.
• *adj* intermediate in amount, degree, etc.; average. < Latin *medius* middle. SEE PANEL AT **MEDIA**.

medley (ˈmɛdlɪ) *n* **1** a musical composition that strings together pieces of music from different sources. **2** a (confused) mixture or assortment. < Middle French *medler* to mix.

meek (miːk) *adj* patient and humble. < Scandinavian.

meet (miːt) *vb* **met; meeting 1** come face to face with. **2** be present to attend the arrival of: I'll meet you off the train. **3** come into contact: The ends don't meet. **4** undergo or experience: meet with an accident. **5** make the acquaintance of: I'd like you to meet her. **6** pay in full: meet the cost. **7** be in keeping with; satisfy: This should meet their requirements. **meeting** *n* **1** a coming together: a chance meeting. **2** a planned gathering of people for a particular purpose, esp. for discussion. **3** a race-meeting. < Old English *mētan.*

mega- *prefix* **1** great; huge: megalith. **2** one million: megahertz. < Greek *megas* large.

megahertz (ˈmɛgəˌhɜːts) *n* one million hertz.

megalith (ˈmɛgəlɪθ) *n* a huge stone forming part of a prehistoric monument. **megalithic** *adj*

megalomania (ˌmɛgələˈmeɪnɪə) *n* a mental disorder producing delusions of personal grandeur or an obsession for grandiose things. **megalomaniac** *n*

megaphone (ˈmɛgəˌfəʊn) *n* a hand-held funnel-shaped device used for directing or amplifying the voice.

melamine (ˈmɛləˌmiːn) *n* a resilient plastic material, commonly used to face

the media is... or the media are...?

The media—or the mass media—refer to channels of communication such as television, radio, and newspapers. Since media is a plural noun, careful users prefer to use a plural verb: The media *are* becoming increasingly important in modern life. The singular of media is medium: Television *is* a very powerful medium. See also panels at **criterion; data.**

kitchen furniture. < German *Melamin.*

melancholia (ˌmɛlənˈkəʊlɪə) *n* mental depression. **melancholic** *adj*

melancholy (ˈmɛlənkəlɪ) *n* **1** mental depression. **2** a mood of sad thoughtfulness.
• *adj* sad, depressed, or gloomy.
< Greek *melan* dark + *cholē* bile.

mêlée (ˈmɛleɪ) *n* a noisy brawl or struggle; riotous or confused crowd. < Old French *mesler* to mix.

mellifluous (məˈlɪflʊəs) *adj* sweet-sounding or smooth-flowing. **mellifluously** *adv* < Latin *mel* honey + *fluere* to flow.

mellow (ˈmɛləʊ) *adj* **1** mature or rich, but free from harshness: a mellow sound. **2** sympathetic or subdued, esp. on account of maturity.
• *vb* become mellow. < Middle English *melowe.*

melodrama (ˈmɛləˌdrɑːmə) *n* **1** a play, film, etc., of a crudely emotional or sensational style. **2** the dramatic genre embodied by such works. **3** a real-life situation comprising sensational events. **melodramatic** *adj* **melodramatically** *adv* < French *mélodrame,* from Greek *melos* song + French *drame* drama.

melody (ˈmɛlədɪ) *n* **1** pleasing sound arrangement. **2** a song or tune. **3** the main line or part in a harmonic composition. **melodic** *adj* of or creating melody. **melodious** *adj* full of melody. **melodiously** *adv* < Greek *melodia,* from *melos* song + *aeidein* to sing.

melon (ˈmɛlən) *n* any of a group of large, round fruits with an abundance of juicy flesh, usually served in moon-shaped slices as a starter. < Greek *mēlopepōn,* from *mēlon* apple + *pepōn* edible gourd.

melt (mɛlt) *vb* **1** make or become liquid by heating. **2** make or become soft; dissolve. **3** fade or disappear: The sound melted away. **4** make or become sympathetic or emotional. **5** blend or lose a distinct shape, outline, etc. **melt down** melt (metal objects) completely to reuse the raw material. **melting-point** *n* the temperature at which a solid melts. **melting-pot** *n* a place or situation where people or things are being mixed together, losing their original identity, form, etc. < Old English *meltan.*

member (ˈmɛmbə) *n* **1** a person belonging to a club, society, etc. **2** any part of the body. **3 Member** a Member of Parliament. **membership** *n* **1** being a member: terminate one's membership. **2** the total number of members: a large membership. < Latin *membrum.*

membrane (ˈmɛmbreɪn) *n* a thin, skin-like tissue, esp. in an animal or plant. **membranous** *adj* < Latin *membrana* skin.

memento (mɪˈmɛntəʊ) *n, pl* **mementoes, mementos** a souvenir. < Latin *meminisse* to remember.

memo (ˈmɛməʊ) *n, pl* **memos** (*informal*) a memorandum.

memoir (ˈmɛmwɑː) *n* **1** a biography, esp. of someone known personally by the writer. **2** *pl* an autobiography. < Latin *memoria* memory.

memory (ˈmɛmərɪ) *n* **1** the ability to remember or recall: a poor memory. **2** something recalled; mental image: memories of one's childhood. **3** the length of time going back into the past which the memory embraces: within living memory. **4** an electronic device in a computer, calculator, etc., where information is stored. **from memory** recalled without referring to notes, etc. **in memory of** in commemorative remembrance of. **memorable** *adj* worth remembering; notable: a memorable occasion. **memorandum** *n, pl* **memorandums, memoranda 1** an informal business communication. **2** a written record or statement. **memorial** *adj, n* (something) made or done in remembrance of an event or person: a memorial service. **memorize** *vb* learn by heart. < Latin *memor* mindful.

men (mɛn) SEE **MAN.**

menace (ˈmɛnɪs) *n* **1** a person or thing that habitually annoys or irritates: He's a real menace. **2** a threat or source of danger.
• *vb* threaten with harm, violence, etc. **menacingly** *adv* < Latin *minari* to threaten.

ménage (meɪˈnɑːʒ) *n* a household. < Latin *mansio* dwelling.

menagerie (mɪˈnædʒərɪ) *n* a collection of wild or exotic animals; place where these are kept or exhibited. < Middle French *menage* household.

mend (mɛnd) *vb* **1** restore to good condition or working order; repair. **2** improve or rectify: mend one's ways. **mending** *n* things to be mended, esp. clothes. **on the mend** (of the sick or injured) recovering. < Middle English *amenden.*

mendacity (mɛnˈdæsɪtɪ) *n* **1** (*informal*) the practice of being untruthful. **2** a falsehood. **mendacious** *adj* < Latin *mendax* lying.

mendicant (ˈmɛndɪkənt) *adj, n* (living as) a beggar. < Latin *mendicus* beggar.

menial (ˈmiːnɪəl) *adj* **1** of or connected with servants. **2** low and degrading.

3 uninteresting and undemanding: a menial task. < Latin *mansio* dwelling.

menopause (ˈmɛnəʊˌpɔːz) *n* the time in a woman's life when she finally stops menstruating. **menopausal** *adj* < French.

menstruate (ˈmɛnstrʊˌeɪt) *vb* (of non-pregnant women prior to menopause) discharge blood, etc., from the womb at approximately monthly intervals. **menstruation** *n* < Latin *mensis* month.

menswear (ˈmɛnzˌwɛə) *n* men's clothes for sale in shops.

mental (ˈmɛntl̩) *adj* **1** of or performed by the mind or intellect: mental arithmetic. **2** (*informal*) suffering from a disorder of the mind. **mentality** *n* **1** a person's degree of mental power or maturity. **2** a person's mental attitude. **mentally** *adv* < Latin *mens* mind.

menthol (ˈmɛnθɒl) *n* a substance extracted from peppermint oil or made synthetically, used for instance as a cooling agent, antiseptic, or flavouring: menthol cigarettes. **mentholated** *adj* < Latin *mentha* mint.

mention (ˈmɛnʃən) *vb* refer to or speak about briefly.
• *n* **1** mentioning: little mention of the cost. **2** a brief reference. < Latin *mens* mind. SEE PANEL.

mentor (ˈmɛntɔː) *n* a trusted adviser and helper. < *Mentor,* adviser of Telemachus in Homer's 'Odyssey'. SEE PANEL.

menu (ˈmɛnjuː) *n* **1** a list of dishes available in a restaurant. **2** (of computers) a list of options shown on a screen. < Latin *minutus* minute.

mercantile (ˈmɜːkənˌtaɪl) *adj* of or connected with merchants or trading. < Latin *mercari* to trade.

mercenary (ˈmɜːsɪnrɪ) *adj* **1** motivated purely by the attraction of being rewarded. **2** (of professional soldiers) hired to serve a foreign country.
• *n* a professional soldier serving a foreign country. < Latin *merces* wages.

merchandise (ˈmɜːtʃənˌdaɪz) *n* things that are bought and sold; goods for sale.
• *vb* buy and sell; trade. < Latin *mercari* to trade.

merchant (ˈmɜːtʃənt) *n* **1** a wholesaler. **2** (*Scottish and US*) a shopkeeper. **3** (*derogatory*) a person given to a certain activity: a speed merchant. **merchant bank** a firm of private bankers primarily handling foreign bills and guaranteeing new security issues. **merchant navy** the ships of a country that are used in trading. < Latin *mercari* to trade.

mercury (ˈmɜːkjʊrɪ) *n* a heavy, silver-coloured metal, usually in liquid form as found in thermometers. **mercurial** *adj* **1** lively; volatile: a mercurial temperament. **2** prone to sudden changes. **3** of, containing, or connected with mercury. < Latin *Mercurius* Mercury.

mercy (ˈmɜːsɪ) *n* **1** compassion or restraint shown to an offender. **2** a piece of good fortune: It was a mercy she saw the car

Don't mention it!

Don't mention it is used as a polite acknowledgment of thanks or of an apology: 'Thank you for a lovely evening!'—*'Don't mention it.* It was super to see you again!' Other expressions that are used in acknowledging thanks include:

Any time!	**Not at all!**
It's all right!	**That's all right!**
It was nothing!	**Think nothing of it!**
My pleasure!	**You're welcome!**

Although they perform the same function, these expressions are not all interchangeable. Some are appropriate in informal contexts, for example Any time!, some are appropriate in formal contexts, for example My pleasure!

mentor

A wise and trusted adviser is sometimes referred to as a mentor. This word derives from the Greek *Mentōr,* the name of Odysseus' loyal friend who was also the tutor of his son, Telemachus.

In Homer's 'Odyssey', Mentor is a relatively minor character. His identity and role are assumed by Athene, the goddess of wisdom, who accompanies Telemachus in his search for his father. The character of the friendly counsellor is more fully drawn by the French prelate and writer, Fenelon, 1651–1715, in 'Les Aventures de Télémaque' (1699).

in time. **merciful** *adj* showing mercy; compassionate. **mercifully** *adv* **merciless** *adj* showing no mercy. **mercilessly** *adv* **mercy killing** euthanasia. < Latin *merx* merchandise.

mere (mɪə) *adj* (surprisingly) nothing more or nothing else than what is specified; just: It took a mere six minutes. **merely** *adv* < Latin *merus* pure.

meretricious (ˌmɛrɪˈtrɪʃəs) *adj* **1** superficially attractive. **2** insincere. < Latin *meretrix* prostitute, from *merēre* to earn.

merge (mɜːdʒ) *vb* **1** unite or join to become a single body or entity: The companies are about to merge. **2** blend or cause to blend. **merger** *n* the combining of two businesses, etc., into one. < Latin *mergere* to plunge.

meridian (məˈrɪdɪən) *n* any of the imaginary lines joining the North and South Poles and cutting the equator at right angles. < Latin *meridies* noon, from *medius* mid + *dies* day.

meringue (məˈræŋ) *n* **1** a mixture of sugar and beaten egg whites, baked until crisp. **2** a small cake made of this mixture. < French.

merino (məˈrɪːnəʊ) *n, pl* **merinos** **1** a breed of sheep with fine, soft wool. **2** the yarn or fabric made from the wool of this sheep. < Spanish.

merit (ˈmɛrɪt) *n* **1** worth or degree of excellence: Appointments are made strictly on merit. **2** a praiseworthy quality or act; virtue. **3** *pl* intrinsic good or bad qualities; deserts: The proposal will be judged according to its merits.
• *vb* deserve. **meritorious** *adj* deserving reward; praiseworthy. < Latin *merēre* to deserve.

mermaid (ˈmɜːˌmeɪd) *n* a mythical sea-creature with the upper body of a woman and the tail of a fish. **merman** *n* a similar male creature. < Middle English *mermaide,* from *mere* sea + *maide* maid.

merry (ˈmɛrɪ) *adj* **1** cheerful, jolly, or in high spirits. **2** (*informal*) slightly intoxicated; tipsy. **merrily** *adv* **merriment** *n* **merry-go-round** *n* a fairground machine with model horses, etc., on a revolving circular platform. < Old English *myrge.*

mesh (mɛʃ) *n* **1** one of the regular gaps in netting: a fine mesh. **2** a net or net-like fabric.
• *vb* (of cogged wheels, etc.) engage or interlock. < probably Middle Dutch *maesche.*

mesmerize (ˈmɛzməˌraɪz) *vb* hypnotize or hold spellbound. < F.A. *Mesmer,* died 1815, Austrian physician.

mess (mɛs) *n* **1** (a person or thing in) a dirty or untidy state. **2** a confused or chaotic state of affairs. **3** a group, esp. of servicemen, that eats regularly together. **4** the place where such a group eats and relaxes: the officers' mess.
• *vb* **1** make dirty or untidy. **2** make a muddle or botch of something; spoil: mess up one's plans. **3** potter, meddle, or tinker: mess about with radios. **4** spend one's time lazily. **5** treat in a rough or inconsiderate way. **6** take one's meals (with one's fellow servicemen) in a mess. **make a mess of** botch or bungle. **messy** *adj* **1** dirty or untidy. **2** not easy to do, handle, or deal with; complicated: a messy job. **messily** *adv* < Latin *mittere* to send.

message (ˈmɛsɪdʒ) *n* **1** any communication from one person to another. **2** an idea, philosophy, etc., intended to inspire: a book with a message. **messenger** *n* a person who bears a message. < Latin *mittere* to send.

met (mɛt) SEE **MEET**.

metabolism (məˈtæbəˌlɪzəm) *n* the process by which food is converted into the substance of plants and animals, or is used to supply their energy. **metabolic** *adj* **metabolize** *vb* make or be made by metabolism. < Greek *meta-* change + *ballein* to throw.

metal (ˈmɛtḷ) *n* any of a group of mineral substances such as iron, copper, or silver, that are typically good conductors of heat and electricity.
• *adj* made of metal. **metallic** *adj* **1** of or like metal. **2** resembling the sound of metals striking together. < Greek *metallon.*

metallurgy (mɛˈtælədʒɪ) *n* the scientific study of the properties of metals, the extraction of metals from their ores, and their preparation for use. **metallurgic** or **metallurgical** *adj* **metallurgist** *n*

metamorphosis (ˌmɛtəˈmɔːfəsɪs) *n, pl* **metamorphoses** a complete or striking change in physical form or character; transformation. **metamorphose** *vb* experience or cause to experience metamorphosis. < Greek *meta-* change + *morphē* form.

metaphor (ˈmɛtəfə, ˈmɛtəfɔː) *n* (an instance of) a figure of speech in which a word or phrase is used suggestively to make an implicit comparison. **metaphorical** *adj* **metaphorically** *adv* **mixed metaphor** an incongruous combination of metaphors. < Greek

meta- change + *pherein* to bear.
SEE PANEL AT **GLUE**.

metaphysics (ˌmɛtəˈfɪzɪks) *n* a branch of philosophy that deals with the nature of existence, truth, and knowledge. **metaphysical** *adj* < Greek *ta meta ta physika* the things after the physical things, (from the position of Aristotle's treatise on the subject in his collected works).

mete (miːt) *vb* **mete out** allot or administer: mete out punishment. < Old English *metan*. SEE PANEL AT **EKE OUT**.

meteor (ˈmiːtɪə) *n* a body moving through space that becomes luminous as it enters the earth's atmosphere. **meteoric** *adj* **1** of or connected with meteors. **2** like a meteor in speed, sudden brilliance, etc. **meteorite** *n* a fragment of a meteor that has reached the earth's surface. < Greek *meta-* beyond + *aeirein* to raise.

meteorology (ˌmiːtɪəˈrɒlədʒɪ) *n* the scientific study of the atmosphere, esp. in order to forecast weather conditions. **meteorological** *adj* **meteorologist** *n* < Greek *meteōron* thing in the sky + *-logia* -logy, ultimately *lōgos* word.

meter[1] (ˈmiːtə) *n* an instrument that measures and records the amount of something that has been used.
• *vb* measure by means of a meter.
< ultimately Greek *metron* measure.
SEE PANEL.

meter[2] *n* (*US*) metre.

methane (ˈmiːθeɪn) *n* a colourless, odourless, flammable gas, used as a fuel.

method (ˈmɛθəd) *n* **1** a way of doing something; procedure. **2** systematic orderliness. **methodical** *adj* orderly in a systematic way. < Greek *methodos*, from *meta-* after + *hodos* way.

meths (mɛθs) *n* (*informal*) methylated spirits.

methylated spirits (ˈmɛθɪˌleɪtɪd) a form of alcohol, adulterated usually with methanol, used domestically as a fuel and solvent.

meticulous (məˈtɪkjʊləs) *adj* extremely careful and exact about details. **meticulously** *adv* **meticulousness** *n* < Latin *meticulosus* timid.

metre (ˈmiːtə) *n* **1** the SI unit of length. **2** a rhythmical pattern in poetry. **metrical** *adj* having a rhythmic pattern. < Latin *metrum*. SEE PANEL AT **METER**[1].

metric (ˈmɛtrɪk) *adj* **1** of or based on the metric system. **2** of poetic metre. **metricate** *vb* convert to a metric system. **metrication** *n* **metric system** a decimal measuring system, based on the metre, litre, and kilogram.

metronome (ˈmɛtrəˌnəʊm) *n* an instrument that marks tempo for a musician by means of an adjustable pendulum. < Greek *metron* measure + *nomos* law.

metropolis (məˈtrɒpəlɪs) *n* the chief city of a country, state, or region. **metropolitan** *adj* (typical) of a metropolis. < Greek *metropolis*, from *mētēr* mother + *polis* city.

mettle (ˈmɛtl̩) *n* strength of character; spirit. < SEE **METAL**.

mew (mjuː) *n* the typical cry of a cat; miaow.
• *vb* make this sound. < Middle English *mewen*, like the sound.

mews (mjuːz) *n, pl* **mews** a small row or square of what were formerly stables, now converted into living accommodation. < Latin *mutare* to change.
SEE PANEL.

mezzanine (ˈmɛzəˌniːn, ˈmɛtsəˌniːn) *n* an intermediate storey, usually between the ground and first floors of a building. < Latin *medianus* middle.

miaow (mɪˈaʊ, mjaʊ) mew.

mica (ˈmaɪkə) *n* any of a group of mineral substances that divide readily into thin layers; used chiefly for electrical

---

meter or **metre?**

The spelling of these two words is sometimes confused, partly no doubt because the American spelling of the measurement metre is meter.

A meter in British spelling is an instrument that measures and often records the amount of something that has been used as in an electricity *meter*, a speed*ometer*, a parking-*meter*.

A metre is the basic unit of metric measurement and is used for all units of length derived from it, for example milli*metre*, kilo*metre*.

Metre is also used to describe a rhythmical pattern in poetry, but note that in compounds describing such measures or units, the spelling is -meter penta*meter*. Note, too, that the spelling -meter is also used in such words as dia*meter*, para*meter*, and peri*meter*.

---

insulation. < Latin: crumb.
mice (maɪs) SEE **MOUSE**.
micro- *prefix* **1** small or minute: microwave. **2** one millionth of (a unit): microsecond. < Greek *mikros* small.
microbe (ˈmaɪkrəʊb) *n* a minute organism, esp. one causing disease or fermentation. < Greek *mikros* small + *bios* life.
microchip (ˈmaɪkrəʊˌtʃɪp) *n* a tiny wafer of silicon or germanium that is made so as to form a complex integrated electronic circuit.
microcomputer (ˈmaɪkrəʊkəmˌpjuːtə) *n* a small computer whose central processor is held in one or more silicon chips.
microcosm (ˈmaɪkrəʊˌkɒzəm) *n* a miniature representation, esp. of the world. < Greek *mikros kosmos* little world.
microdot (ˈmaɪkrəʊˌdɒt) *n* a photographic copy of printed matter reduced to the size of a pin-head.
microfiche (ˈmaɪkrəʊˌfiːʃ) *n, pl* **microfiche, microfiches** a sheet of microfilm the size of a postcard containing the greatly reduced images of pages of printed matter. < French, from *micro* + *fiche* slide.
microfilm (ˈmaɪkrəʊˌfɪlm) *n* a length of film on which printed matter is recorded in greatly reduced size.
• *vb* photograph with this film.
micro-organism (ˌmaɪkrəʊˈɔːgənɪzəm) *n* any organism that cannot be seen with the naked eye.
microphone (ˈmaɪkrəˌfəʊn) *n* an instrument that converts sound waves into electrical waves, used in recording, etc.

the mutable mews

An open courtyard or small street lined by buildings that were once used as stables is known as a mews. This word came into English in the 14th century as the name of the royal hawk-houses at Charing Cross in London. Demolished in 1537, these were then replaced by the royal stables. Through the process of *transference*, the new buildings took over the old name. Further extension of the meaning led to mews becoming the name of any row of stables with accommodation above.

Mews comes from the Old French *muer* 'to moult'. This derives, most appropriately, from the Latin *mutare* 'to change'.

microscope (ˈmaɪkrəˌskəʊp) *n* an optical instrument for making greatly magnified images of minute objects. **microscopic** *adj* **1** too small to be seen without a microscope. **2** very small.
microwave (ˈmaɪkrəʊˌweɪv) *n* **1** an electromagnetic wave of between 0.3 m and 0.001 m in wavelength. **2** a microwave oven. **microwave oven** an oven using such waves to heat food very rapidly.
mid (mɪd) *adj* in the middle of; middle: mid-September. **midday** *n* noon. **midnight** *n* twelve o'clock at night. **midsummer/midwinter** *n* the middle of the summer/winter. **midway** *adv* half-way. < Old English *midde*.
middle (ˈmɪdl̩) *adj* **1** equally distant from given extremes. **2** between the beginning and end. **3** intermediate.
• *n* **1** a middle point, part, etc.: the middle of the lake. **2** the waist. **middle age** the years between youth and old age. **middle-aged** *adj* **Middle Ages** about 500–1500 AD. **middle C** the note shown by the first ledger line below the treble staff and the first ledger line above the bass staff. **middle class** the section of society comprising mostly business and professional people, ranked between the upper and lower classes. **middleman** *n* a trader who handles goods at some stage after they leave the producer and before they reach the consumer. **middle-of-the-road** *adj* in keeping with the majority in opinions, attitudes, etc.; moderate. **middle school** (part of) a school for children aged between 8 or 9 and 12 or 13. < Old English.
middling (ˈmɪdlɪŋ) *adj, adv* moderately good or well. < Middle English *mydlyn*.
midge (mɪdʒ) *n* any small gnat or fly. < Old English *mycg*.
midget (ˈmɪdʒɪt) *n* **1** an abnormally small person; dwarf. **2** a thing that is unusually small of its kind.
• *adj* very small. < *midge* + *-et*.
midriff (ˈmɪdrɪf) *n* the part of the body between the chest and the waist; equivalent part of a garment. < Old English *midde* mid + *hrif* belly.
midshipman (ˈmɪdʃɪpmən) *n, pl* **midshipmen** a young man training to become a naval officer.
midst (mɪdst) *n* **in the midst of** in the middle of. < Middle English *amiddes*.
midwife (ˈmɪdˌwaɪf) *n, pl* **midwives** a woman trained to assist other women in childbirth. **midwifery** *n* the training, skill, or practice of a midwife. < Middle English *mid* with + *wif* woman.

mien (mi:n) *n* a person's manner, air, or bearing. < obsolete *demean.*
might[1] (maɪt) SEE **MAY.**
might[2] *n* (great) strength or power. < Old English *miht.*
mighty (ˈmaɪtɪ) *adj* **1** very strong or powerful. **2** very large; vast.
• *adv* (*informal*) very: He's mighty sure of himself. **mightily** *adv*
migraine (ˈmi:greɪn, ˈmaɪgreɪn) *n* a severe headache that tends to recur, sometimes with interference of vision. < Greek *hēmi-* hemi- + *kranion* cranium.
migrate (maɪˈgreɪt) *vb* **1** go from one country or region to settle in another. **2** (of animals) go periodically from one region or climate to another, esp. for feeding or breeding. **migration** *n* **migratory** *adj* < Latin *migrare.*
mike (maɪk) *n* (*informal*) a microphone.
mild (maɪld) *adj* **1** gentle in nature or behaviour. **2** moderate; not extreme or severe: a mild headache. **3** not strong in flavour. **mildly** *adv* **mildness** *n* < Old English *milde.*
mildew (ˈmɪldju:) *n* (a fungus producing) a thin, whitish coating on organic matter, plants, and things exposed to damp. < Old English *meledēaw.*
mile (maɪl) *n* **1** a unit of distance equal to 1760 yards (1.61 kilometres). **2** (*informal*) a great distance or amount: He missed by a mile. **3** a race extending over a mile. **mileage** *n* **1** distance in miles. **2** the number of miles a vehicle will travel on one measure of fuel. **3** the total number of miles a vehicle has travelled. **4** an allowance for travelling expenses at a fixed rate per mile. **5** (*informal*) advantage or benefit. **miler** *n* a person or horse that competes in one-mile races. **milestone** *n* **1** a large, roadside stone that shows the distance in miles to a particular place. **2** a significant event in life, history, etc. < Old English *mīl.*
milieu (ˈmi:ljɜ:) *n, pl* **milieus, milieux** an environment, setting, or surrounding. < French *mi-* mid + *lieu* place.
militant (ˈmɪlɪtənt) *adj* **1** engaged in warfare or combat. **2** vigorously or aggressively engaged in the support of a cause.
• *n* a militant person. **militancy** *n* < Latin *militare* to engage in warfare.
military (ˈmɪlɪtərɪ, ˈmɪlətrɪ) *adj* of or connected with soldiers or the armed forces. **militarism** *n* a policy that supports and depends upon military preparedness. **militarist** *n* **militaristic** *adj* **militate** *vb* have a strong influence or effect. **the military** the armed forces. < Latin *miles* soldier. SEE PANEL.
militia (mɪˈlɪʃə) *n* a body of citizens with military training who can serve as a supplementary force in an emergency. < Latin *miles* soldier.
milk (mɪlk) *n* **1** a whitish fluid secreted by glands in female mammals for feeding their young. **2** this fluid extracted from cows, goats, etc., for human consumption. **3** a milk-like liquid, as found in the coconut.
• *vb* **1** draw milk from the udder of (a cow, goat, etc.). **2** extract a liquid from (a tree, etc.). **3** (*informal*) extract as much as possible from (a person or situation): She proceeded to milk him for all he was worth. **4** extract or draw off something in small quantities; tap. **milker** *n* an animal that produces milk. **milk float** a small motor vehicle used for delivering milk. **milkmaid** *n* a girl or woman who milks cows. **milkman** *n, pl* **milkmen** a man who delivers milk. **milk shake** a cold drink made of milk and flavouring shaken or stirred until frothy. **milk tooth** a tooth of a young mammal, esp. of a child, that is replaced in later life. **milky** *adj* **1** of, containing, or made with milk. **2** resembling milk in appearance; cloudy. **milkiness** *n* **the Milky Way** a broad band of light in the sky at night comprising millions of stars, etc. < Old English *meolc.*
mill (mɪl) *n* **1** a building in which grain is ground into flour. **2** a factory containing machinery for producing cloth, paper,

---

militate or **mitigate?**

Mitigate is sometimes confused with militate.

Militate means 'to have a strong influence or effect'. It is usually followed by against; militate against means 'to work or serve as a reason against' as in The fact that he had a prison record *militated against* his chances of obtaining work. Several factors *militated against* the success of the project.

Mitigate means 'to make or become less harsh, intense, or severe', as in the government's attempts to *mitigate* the effects of the strike. Mitigating circumstances are circumstances that may partly excuse a crime and so lessen the blame to be attributed to an offender.

---

etc.: a cotton mill. **3** any machine for grinding, crushing, etc., into powder or pulp: a coffee mill.
• *vb* **1** grind, crush, etc., in a mill. **2** subject (cloth, metal, etc.) to an operation in a mill. **3** cut or shape by means of a rotary cutter. **4** cut regular grooves in the surface of (metal). **5** move about in a confused or agitated way. **miller** *n* a person who owns or runs a flour mill. **millstone** *n* **1** one of a pair of heavy stones used for grinding grain. **2** a serious hindrance. < Old English *mylen.*

millennium (mɪˈlɛnɪəm) *n, pl* **millennia, millenniums 1** a period of 1000 years. **2** a future time of great happiness for all; golden age. < New Latin, from Latin *mille* thousand + New Latin *-ennium* period of.

millepede (ˈmɪlɪˌpiːd) *n* an insect resembling a centipede, but with two pairs of legs on each segment of its body. < Latin *millepeda,* from *mille* thousand + *pes* foot.

millet (ˈmɪlɪt) *n* **1** a kind of cereal grass with small seeds. **2** the grain of this grass. < Latin *milium.*

milli- *prefix* one thousandth: milligram, millilitre, millimetre. < Latin *mille* thousand.

milliner (ˈmɪlɪnə) *n* a person who makes or sells women's hats. **millinery** *n* **1** the hats, etc., sold by a milliner. **2** a milliner's shop. < *Milan,* city in Italy. SEE PANEL.

million (ˈmɪljən) *determiner, pron* 1 000 000 in number.
• *n* **1** the number 1 000 000. **2** an enormous number: millions of spectators. **millionth** *determiner, pron, n* **millionaire** *n* a person who possesses a million or more pounds, dollars, etc.

< Latin *mille* thousand.

milometer (maɪˈlɒmɪtə) *n* an instrument that measures the number of miles a vehicle travels.

mime (maɪm) *n* (an instance of) acting with gestures and facial movements but without speaking, esp. to entertain.
• *vb* act in this way. < Greek *mimos* imitator.

mimic (ˈmɪmɪk) *vb* **mimicked; mimicking** imitate, esp. in order to entertain.
• *n* a person who is able to mimic skilfully. **mimicry** *n* < SEE **MIME**.

mimosa (mɪˈməʊzə) *n* any of a group of tropical trees, shrubs, or herbs, with globular heads of small, esp. yellow flowers. < Latin *mimus* mime.

minaret (ˌmɪnəˈrɛt) *n* a tall, slender tower of a mosque. < Arabic *minārah* lighthouse.

mince (mɪns) *vb* **1** cut into small pieces. **2** walk or speak in an affected way.
• *n* minced meat. **mincer** *n* **mincemeat** *n* a mixture of chopped apples, raisins, suet, etc., chiefly used as a filling for pies. **mince pie** a small pie containing mincemeat. **not mince matters** or **words** speak frankly. < Latin *minutia* smallness.

mind (maɪnd) *n* **1** the thing inside the head that provides a person with consciousness and intelligence. **2** thought or attention: My mind keeps wandering. **3** memory or recollection: bear something in mind. **4** intention or inclination: I had half a mind to walk out. **5** choice, preference, or opinion: change one's mind. **6** mood or disposition: peace of mind. **7** normal mental faculties: out of one's mind.
• *vb* **1** tend or take care of; look after. **2** have an objection to; dislike: Don't you mind her shouting at you? **3** feel concern about; care: I don't mind where we go. **4** be careful or cautious about; heed: Mind the step! **minded** *adj* having a (specified kind

milliner

A person who makes or sells women's hats is traditionally known as a milliner. This word dates from the 16th century when it had the slightly different form *Milaner,* meaning 'a trader in fancy goods from Milan'. Throughout its history the Italian city of Milan has been a celebrated trading and fashion centre. The origin of milliner testifies to its renown amongst the Elizabethans as a centre of women's finery.

Mind your p's and q's!

The expression to mind one's p's and q's means 'to take care not to give offence, especially by saying the wrong thing': 'You'd better *mind your p's and q's* if you don't want to upset him again'. The phrase is probably an allusion to the difficulty presented by these letters to a child who is learning to distinguish them.

of) mind or inclination: narrow-minded. **minder** *n* a person whose job is to look after someone or something: a child minder. **mindful** *adj* keeping in mind; heedful: remain mindful of the cost. **mindless** *adj* **1** stupid or unintelligent. **2** requiring no intelligence: a mindless activity. **mindlessly** *adv* **mindlessness** *n* < Old English *gemynd.* SEE PANEL.

mine[1] (maɪn) *possessive pron* (the one or ones) belonging to or associated with me. < Old English *mīn.*

mine[2] *n* **1** an excavation from which coal, ores, etc., are dug. **2** a plentiful source or store: a mine of information. **3** a metal case filled with high explosive designed to go off when disturbed by enemy vehicles, etc.
• *vb* **1** (try to) extract (coal, etc.) from (the ground) by excavation. **2** make a hole, tunnel, etc., by digging or boring. **3** plant explosives. **mining** *n* **minefield** *n* an area where explosives have been planted. **miner** *n* a person who works in a mine. **minesweeper** *n* a ship that clears away mines. < probably Celtic.

mineral (ˈmɪnərəl) *n* a natural substance not animal or vegetable, such as coal or gold.
• *adj* of or containing minerals. **mineralogy** *n* the study of minerals. **mineralogist** *n* **mineral water** water naturally or artificially impregnated with mineral salts or gases. < Medieval Latin *minera* ore.

minestrone (ˌmɪnɪˈstrəʊnɪ) *n* a thick Italian soup containing vegetables and pasta. < Italian *ministrare* to serve, from Latin *minister* servant.

mingle (ˈmɪŋgl̩) *vb* **1** blend or mix together. **2** go about among people; join in a crowd. < Old English *mengan.*

mingy (ˈmɪndʒɪ) *adj* (*informal*) mean; stingy. < probably *m*ean + st*ingy.*

mini (ˈmɪnɪ) *n* **1** a miniskirt. **2** something very small of its kind.
• *adj* very small; miniature. < *mini-.*

mini- *prefix* very small, short, etc.: minicomputer, miniskirt. < *miniature.*

miniature (ˈmɪnɪtʃə) *adj* made or represented on a reduced scale.
• *n* **1** a very small portrait. **2** a small-scale copy or model. < Latin *miniare* to colour with red lead. SEE PANEL.

minibus (ˈmɪnɪˌbʌs) *n* a small passenger vehicle with seats for up to approximately ten people.

minicab (ˈmɪnɪˌkæb) *n* a motor car which serves as a taxi but which may not ply for hire.

minicomputer (ˌmɪnɪkəmˈpjuːtə) *n* a small digital computer.

minim (ˈmɪnɪm) *n* a note in music lasting two crotchets or half a semibreve. < Latin *minimum* smallest.

minimum (ˈmɪnɪməm) *n, pl* **minima, minimums** the smallest possible amount, number, etc.
• *adj* the smallest or lowest possible or recorded: minimum temperatures. **minimal** *adj* the least possible: minimal fuss. **minimally** *adv* **minimize** *vb* **1** reduce to a minimum: minimize the risk. **2** represent as less than the true value, significance, etc.; belittle or play down. < Latin *minimus* smallest.

minion (ˈmɪnjən) *n* (*derogatory*) a servile assistant or attendant. < Middle French *mignon* darling.

miniskirt (ˈmɪnɪˌskɜːt) *n* a woman's skirt or dress with the hem-line several inches above the knee.

minister (ˈmɪnɪstə) *n* **1** a person entrusted with the management of a government department. **2** a government representative sent to a foreign country on diplomatic business. **3** a clergyman.
• *vb* provide help or service. **ministerial** *adj* **ministry** *n* **1** a government department presided over by a minister. **2** all the ministries forming a government; period of one government in office. **3** the office or duties of a clergyman. < Latin: servant.

mink (ˈmɪŋk) *n, pl* **mink, minks 1** a small slender animal of the stoat family, with partially webbed feet and highly valued fur. **2** the fur of this animal: a mink coat. **3** a garment made of this fur. < Middle English.

minnow (ˈmɪnəʊ) *n, pl* **minnow, minnows** a small freshwater fish of the carp family. < Middle English *menawe.*

minor (ˈmaɪnə) *adj* **1** less in size, degree, importance, etc.: minor difficulties. **2** (of a musical scale or key) having a semitone

miniature

A very small painting, especially a portrait, is known as a miniature. This is a 16th-century word which comes from the Italian *miniatura,* meaning the art of illuminating a manuscript. The Italian word derives from the Medieval Latin verb *miniare,* 'to colour with minium (red lead)', which comes from the noun *minium,* 'red lead'.

between the second and third, and fifth and sixth notes.
• *n* a person who is not legally of age. **minority** *n* **1** the smaller of two groups forming a body. **2** a small group of people with the same aims, interests, etc., that differ from those of the population as a whole. **3** the state of not being legally of age. < Latin.

minster (ˈmɪnstə) *n* a church that is or once was attached to a monastery. < Late Latin *monasterium* monastery.

minstrel (ˈmɪnstrəl) *n* **1** (formerly) a travelling writer and singer of songs. **2** any of a group of performers with blackened faces who present a programme of supposedly Negro songs, jokes, etc. < Latin *minister* servant.

mint¹ (mɪnt) *n* **1** a place where money is made. **2** a vast amount of money; fortune: He's made a mint from used cars.
• *vb* **1** make (coins) by stamping metal. **2** invent (a word, etc.).
• *adj* completely unspoilt; pristine: in mint condition. < ultimately Latin *moneta* money. SEE PANEL.

mint² *n* **1** any of a group of fragrant plants, including the peppermint and spearmint, used esp. for flavouring. **2** a sweet with this flavour. < Old English *minte*.

minuet (ˌmɪnjʊˈɛt) *n* (music for) a slow, graceful dance. < Old French *menu* small.

minus (ˈmaɪnəs) *prep* **1** with the subtraction of: six minus two is four. **2** without: left home minus his trousers.
• *adj* **1** below zero: minus thirty degrees. **2** having disadvantages or negative qualities.
• *n* a negative factor; disadvantage. < Latin *minor* smaller.

minuscule (ˈmɪnəˌskjuːl) *adj* extremely small. < Latin *minusculus* rather small.

minute¹ (mɪnɪt) *n* **1** one sixtieth of an hour. **2** a short time; moment: Wait a minute! **3** (of angles) one sixtieth of a degree. **4** a memorandum. **5** *pl* the official record of proceedings at a meeting. < Latin *minutus* small.

minute² (maɪˈnjuːt) *adj* **1** extremely small; tiny. **2** of little importance. **3** very detailed: a minute description. **minutely** *adv* < Latin *minutus* small.

minx (mɪŋks) *n* a cheeky or flirtatious girl. < origin unknown.

miracle (ˈmɪrəkl̩) *n* **1** an act or event that cannot be explained by any known natural law. **2** a remarkable example: a miracle of precision engineering. **miraculous** *adj* of or like a miracle. **miraculously** *adv* < Latin *mirari* to wonder at.

mirage (ˈmɪraːʒ) *n* **1** an optical illusion caused by atmospheric conditions. **2** any illusion. < Old French *mirer* to look at, from Latin *mirari*.

mire (maɪə) *n* **1** deep mud. **2** an area of waterlogged ground; bog. < Old Norse *mȳrr*.

mirror (ˈmɪrə) *n* a piece of glass or a polished surface that reflects images.
• *vb* reflect as a mirror does. < Old French *mirer* to look at, from Latin *mirari*.

mirth (mɜːθ) *n* laughter and amusement; merriment. **mirthful** *adj* < Old English *myrge* merry.

mis- *prefix* badly; wrongly: misbehave, misjudge. < Old English.

misadventure (ˌmɪsədˈvɛntʃə) *n* (an accident, event, etc., caused by) bad luck; misfortune.

misanthropist (mɪˈzænθrəˌpɪst) or **misanthrope** (ˈmɪzənˌθrəʊp) *n* a person who dislikes or distrusts mankind. **misanthropy** *n* dislike of mankind. **misanthropic** *adj* < Greek *misanthrōpos* hating mankind.

misapprehend (ˌmɪsæprɪˈhɛnd) *vb* misunderstand. **misapprehension** *n*

misappropriate (ˌmɪsəˈprəʊprɪˌeɪt) *vb* take dishonestly; embezzle. **misappropriation** *n*

misbehave (ˌmɪsbɪˈheɪv) *vb* behave badly. **misbehaviour** *n*

miscalculate (ˌmɪsˈkælkjʊˌleɪt) *vb* calculate wrongly. **miscalculation** *n*

miscarry (mɪsˈkærɪ) *vb* **1** have an undesired outcome; go wrong. **2** suffer a miscarriage of a foetus. **miscarriage** *n* **1** failure to achieve the desired outcome or proper result: a miscarriage of justice. **2** the expulsion of a foetus from the womb before it can live independently.

miscellaneous (ˌmɪsəˈleɪnɪəs) *adj* of various sorts or things: miscellaneous items.

> **mint**
>
> The place where money is coined is known as a mint. Mint derives ultimately from the Latin noun *moneta* meaning 'money' or 'mint'. This usage came about through the process of *transference*. The Romans coined their money in the temple of Juno *Moneta* (Juno 'the Admonisher') and it was by the epithet added to the goddess' name that the mint and its product came to be known.

miscellany *n* a collection of various things. < Latin *miscellus* mixed

mischance (mɪsˈtʃɑːns) *n* (a piece of) misfortune.

mischief (ˈmɪstʃɪf) *n* **1** (of children) foolish or playful conduct that adults often find irritating: always getting into mischief. **2** the playful desire to tease or provoke: eyes full of mischief. **3** harm, damage, or injury: did a lot of mischief. **mischievous** *adj* **1** engaged in or inclined to acts of mischief. **2** teasing or provocative. **3** harmful or malicious. **mischievously** *adv* < Old French *meschief* calamity.

misconceive (ˌmɪskənˈsiːv) *vb* interpret wrongly; misunderstand. **misconception** *n*

misconduct (mɪsˈkɒndʌkt) *n* improper behaviour; mismanagement.

misconstrue (ˌmɪskənˈstruː) *vb* under stand wrongly; misinterpret. **misconstruction** *n*

miscount (ˌmɪsˈkaʊnt) *vb* count wrongly. • *n* (ˈmɪsˌkaʊnt) a wrong count.

miscreant (ˈmɪskrɪənt) *n* a villain or scoundrel. < Middle French *mescreant*. from *mescroire* to disbelieve.

misdeal (ˌmɪsˈdiːl) *vb* **misdealt; misdealing** deal (playing cards) incorrectly. • *n* an instance of this.

misdeed (ˌmɪsˈdiːd) *n* a wrongful or unlawful deed; offence.

misdemeanour (ˌmɪsdɪˈmiːnə) *n* **1** a misdeed; transgression. **2** a minor crime.

miser (ˈmaɪzə) *n* a person who hoards money. **miserly** *adj* **miserliness** *n* < Latin *miser* miserable.

misery (ˈmɪzərɪ) *n* **1** a feeling of great unhappiness. **2** (a cause of) discomfort or suffering. **3** (*informal*) a grumpy person: Don't be such a misery. **miserable** *adj* **1** very unhappy. **2** (*informal*) grumpy or disagreeable. **3** causing misery: miserable weather. **4** of poor quality. **miserably** *adv* < Latin *miser* wretched, unfortunate.

misfire (ˌmɪsˈfaɪə) *vb* **1** (of an engine, etc.) fail to fire at the regular time. **2** (of a gun) fail to fire. **3** fail to have the intended effect or outcome; go wrong: The plan misfired badly.
• *n* (ˈmɪsˌfaɪə) a misfiring.

misfit (ˈmɪsˌfɪt) *n* **1** something that fits badly. **2** a person not adjusted to his or her environment or circumstances.

misfortune (mɪsˈfɔːtʃən) *n* (a piece of) bad luck.

misgiving (mɪsˈgɪvɪŋ) *n* a feeling of apprehension or distrust.

misguided (ˌmɪsˈgaɪdɪd) *adj* led by wrong ideas, principles, etc.; ill-advised. **misguidedly** *adv*

mishap (ˈmɪshæp) *n* an unfortunate accident. < Middle English, from *mis-* mis- + *hap* happening.

mishear (ˌmɪsˈhɪə) *vb* **misheard; mishearing** hear wrongly.

mishmash (ˈmɪʃˌmæʃ) *n* (*informal*) a confused mixture; hotchpotch. < Middle High German *mischmasch*.

misinform (ˌmɪsɪnˈfɔːm) *vb* give wrong information to. **misinformation** *n*

misinterpret (ˌmɪsɪnˈtɜːprɪt) *vb* understand or explain wrongly. **misinterpretation** *n*

mislay (mɪsˈleɪ) *vb* **mislaid; mislaying** lose something temporarily by forgetting where it was put.

mislead (mɪsˈliːd) *vb* **misled; misleading** give a wrong impression or understanding to. **misleading** *adj*

mismanage (ˌmɪsˈmænɪdʒ) *vb* manage badly or irresponsibly. **mismanagement** *n*

misnomer (ˌmɪsˈnəʊmə) *n* the wrong use of a name or designation. < Middle French *mesnommer* to misname.

misogynist (mɪˈsɒdʒɪnɪst) *n* a person who hates women. **misogynous** *adj* **misogyny** *n* < Greek *misogynēs*, from *mis-* hatred + *gynē* woman.

misplace (ˌmɪsˈpleɪs) *vb* **1** put in the wrong place, mislay. **2** direct (one's affection, confidence, etc.) to the wrong person or in the wrong direction. **3** use in an inappropriate situation: misplaced humour. **misplacement** *n*

misprint (ˌmɪsˈprɪnt) *vb* print wrongly. • *n* (ˈmɪsprɪnt) a printing error.

misquote (ˌmɪsˈkwəʊt) *vb* quote inaccurately. **misquotation** *n*

misread (ˌmɪsˈriːd) *vb* **misread; misreading** read or interpret incorrectly.

misrepresent (ˌmɪsrɛprɪˈzɛnt) *vb* represent in a false or misleading way. **misrepresentation** *n*

misrule (ˌmɪsˈruːl) *vb* govern incompetently or unjustly.
• *n* **1** incompetent or unjust government. **2** disorder.

miss[1] (mɪs) *vb* **1** fail to hit, catch, meet, etc. **2** fail to see, hear, understand, etc.: miss the point. **3** fail to do, attend, etc.: miss a lesson. **4** experience the absence of: We're missing our regular goalkeeper. **5** feel sad about the absence or loss of (a friend, pet, etc.): She still misses him. **6** omit: Miss out the next paragraph. **7** avoid or escape: I like to miss the Christmas rush. **8** (of an engine) misfire. • *n* failure to hit, catch, etc. **missing** *adj* absent or lost. **miss out** fail to enjoy, profit from, etc. < Old English *missan.*

miss[2] *n* **1** a girl or unmarried woman. **2 Miss** a title before the surname of a girl or unmarried woman: Miss Honey. < short for *mistress.*

misshape (ˌmɪsˈʃeɪp) *vb* shape badly; deform. **misshapen** *adj*

missile (ˈmɪsaɪl) *n* **1** a self-propelled weapon; rocket. **2** any object suitable for throwing or projecting at a target. < Latin *missilis* capable of being thrown.

mission (ˈmɪʃən) *n* **1** a group of envoys or missionaries sent to a foreign country. **2** the task or work of such a group; building used by such a group. **3** a special vocation: a sense of mission. **missionary** *n* a member of a religious mission. < ultimately Latin *mittere* to send.

missis, missus (ˈmɪsɪz) *n* **1** (*informal or humorous*) a wife. **2** (*informal*) used to address a woman. < *mistress.*

missive (ˈmɪsɪv) *n* (*formal or humorous*) a letter. < ultimately Latin *mittere* to send.

misspell (ˌmɪsˈspɛl) *vb* **misspelt; misspelling** spell incorrectly. **misspelling** *n* a spelling mistake.

misspend (ˌmɪsˈspɛnd) *vb* **misspent; misspending** spend wastefully or unwisely. **misspent** *adj* foolishly spent: a misspent youth.

mist (mɪst) *n* **1** water vapour suspended in the air. **2** a film of vapour on a window, etc.

• *vb* cover or become covered with mist. **misty** *adj* **1** obscured by or as if by mist. **2** indistinct. **mistily** *adv* **mistiness** *n* < Old English.

mistake (mɪˈsteɪk) *n* something done, believed, etc., incorrectly; error.

• *vb* **mistook; mistaken; mistaking** **1** misunderstand the meaning or intention of. **2** choose wrongly. **3** identify wrongly; confuse with another: You can't mistake him. **mistaken** *adj* **1** of the wrong opinion. **2** based on incorrect thinking. **mistakenly** *adv* < Old Norse *mistaka* to take by mistake.

mister (ˈmɪstə) *n* **1** (*informal*) used to address a man. **2 Mister** the full form of *Mr.* < *master.*

mistime (ˌmɪsˈtaɪm) *vb* do or say something at the wrong time.

mistletoe (ˈmɪsḷˌtəʊ) *n* a plant with wax-like, white berries that grows as a parasite on trees. < Old English *misteltān.*

mistook (mɪˈstʊk) SEE **MISTAKE**.

mistress (ˈmɪstrɪs) *n* **1** a woman in a position of power or authority, such as the head of a household. **2** a woman teacher. **3** a man's female lover. < ultimately Old French *maistre* master.

mistrust (ˌmɪsˈtrʌst) *vb* lack trust or confidence in.

• *n* lack of trust or confidence. **mistrustful** *adj* **mistrustfully** *adv*

misunderstand (ˌmɪsʌndəˈstænd) *vb* **misunderstood; misunderstanding** fail to understand; understand incorrectly. **misunderstanding** *n* **1** a failure to understand; a wrong interpretation. **2** a disagreement or argument.

misuse (ˌmɪsˈjuːz) *vb* **1** use incorrectly. **2** maltreat.

• *n* (ˌmɪsˈjuːs) **1** also **misusage** incorrect use. **2** maltreatment. SEE PANEL AT **ABUSE**.

mite (maɪt) *n* **1** any of a group of tiny, spider-like creatures that often infest animals and stored food. **2** (*informal*) a tiny amount. **3** (*informal*) a very small creature or object, esp. a small child. < Old English *mīte.*

mitigate (ˈmɪtɪˌgeɪt) *vb* make or become less harsh, severe, etc. **mitigation** *n* < Latin *mitigare* to soften. SEE PANEL AT **MILITARY**.

mitre (ˈmaɪtə) *n* **1** a tall head-dress worn by bishops and abbots. **2** a join of two pieces of wood or cloth made by tapering their ends so that when brought together they form a right angle.

• *vb* taper the end of (pieces of wood, etc.). < Latin *mitra* headband.

mitten (ˈmɪtən) *n* a kind of glove with a division for the thumb but not for the fingers. < Old French *mite.*

mix (mɪks) *vb* **1** put or stir (different things) together so that they combine. **2** prepare by doing this: mix a drink. **3** combine (one thing) with another or with a mass: mix in one pint of milk. **4** be able to be blended or combined successfully: Wine and beer don't mix. **5** (of a person) be sociable or gregarious: He doesn't like mixing. **6** cross-breed. **7** become involved.

• *n* a mixture; combination. **mixed** *adj* **1** comprising different items, types, etc.: mixed seeds. **2** comprising or involving people of different races, classes, sexes, etc.: a mixed school. **mixer** *n* **1** a device that mixes or blends (food, drinks, etc.). **2** a person with a mentioned degree of sociability: a good mixer. **mix up** **1** confuse the identity of: I keep mixing her up with somebody else. **2** make confused. **3** disarrange or disorder. **mix-up** *n* < ultimately Latin *miscere* to mix.

mixture (ˈmɪkstʃə) *n* **1** mixing or being mixed. **2** something produced by mixing. < Latin *mixtus.*

ml *abbrev* millilitre(s).

mm *abbrev* millimetre(s).

mnemonic (nɪˈmɒnɪk) *adj* helping or intended to help the memory.
• *n* an acronym, verse, or other memory aid. < Greek *mimnēskesthai* to remember.

moan (məʊn) *n* **1** a prolonged, mournful sound, often expressing pain or misery. **2** a complaint or grumble.
• *vb* **1** utter a moan when in pain, etc. **2** complain or grumble. **moaner** *n* < probably Old English *mān.* SEE PANEL.

moat (məʊt) *n* a water-filled ditch encircling a castle or other fortified place. < Middle French *motte* mound, embankment.

mob (mɒb) *n* **1** a violent or disorderly crowd. **2** the common people; populace. **3** a gang of criminals.
• *vb* **mobbed; mobbing** crowd round, esp. to attack or cheer. < Latin *mobile vulgus* fickle crowd. SEE PANEL.

moan and groan

It is sometimes thought that rhyme is found only in poetry. However, there are many rhyming phrases in everyday use, such as moan and groan, which indicate that the fondness for rhyme extends beyond verse. Other examples include:

eager beaver	**hocus-pocus**
fairly and squarely	**hoity toity**
hanky-panky	**make or break**
higgledy-piggledy	**silly billy**
highways and byways	**snug as a bug in a rug**
	super duper

mob

A disorderly or riotous crowd of people is known as a mob. This early 18th-century word is a reduction of the Latin phrase *mobile vulgus* or 'fickle crowd'. The reduced form has been used for so long that its Latin roots have been forgotten.

mobile (ˈməʊbaɪl) *adj* **1** able to move or be moved easily; movable. **2** (of facial features) changing quickly in expression.
• *n* a delicate structure suspended in mid-air with parts that are moved by currents of air. **mobile home** a large, permanent caravan used as a home. **mobility** *n* < Latin *mobilis,* from *movēre* to move.

mobilize (ˈməʊbɪˌlaɪz) *vb* **1** assemble and prepare for service or war. **2** assemble (resources, etc.) for a particular purpose; marshal. **mobilization** *n*

moccasin (ˈmɒkəsɪn) *n* **1** a soft, leather shoe without a heel, traditionally worn by North American Indians. **2** any shoe resembling this. < Algonquian.

mocha (ˈmɒkə) *n* **1** a kind of superior coffee. **2** a flavouring obtained from coffee and chocolate. < *Mocha,* town in Arabia.

mock (mɒk) *vb* **1** make fun of, esp. by mimicking. **2** treat with contempt; ridicule.
• *adj* sham or simulated: a mock battle. **mocking-bird** *n* a bird that imitates the calls of other birds. **mock-up** *n* a full-sized model of something. < Old French *moquier.*

mode (məʊd) *n* **1** the manner in which something is done. **2** the current fashion or style. **modish** *adj* fashionable. < Latin *modus.*

model (ˈmɒdl̩) *n* **1** a three-dimensional copy of something, usually smaller than the original. **2** a style of structure: the latest model. **3** a person or thing to be copied; pattern. **4** a person who poses for an artist. **5** a person whose job is to display clothes by parading in them in public; mannequin.
• *vb* **modelled; modelling 1** design or make something by following a pattern. **2** make a model of (in clay, etc.); shape (clay, etc.) into a model. **3** display (clothes) by parading in them. **4** work as a fashion model or artist's model.
• *adj* **1** designed or regarded as a pattern or example to be imitated; exemplary: model behaviour. **2** being a small replica of something: a model aeroplane. < Latin *modulus* small measure.

modem (ˈməʊdɛm) *n* an electronic device that converts computer data so that it can be sent by telephone to a second modem which reconverts it. < *mo*dulator + *dem*odulator.

moderate (ˈmɒdərət, ˈmɒdrət) *adj* **1** not extreme or violent: moderate opinions. **2** kept within reasonable limits: moderate

demands. **3** average or just less than average in amount, quality, etc.: moderate success. **moderately** *adv*
• *n* a person holding moderate views.
• *vb* (ˈmɒdəˌreɪt) make or become moderate. **moderation** *n* **in moderation** in moderate amounts. < Latin *moderare* to moderate.

modern (ˈmɒdn̩) *adj* **1** of the present time or of recent times. **2** currently used, in fashion, etc. **3** (of art forms) embodying new as opposed to traditional styles and techniques. **modernity** *n* **modernize** *vb* make or become modern; get up to date. **modernization** *n* < Latin *modus* mode.

modest (ˈmɒdɪst) *adj* **1** not vain or boastful: a modest disposition. **2** not very large, fine, etc.; moderate: a modest income. **3** (of a woman) observant of traditional proprieties in dress and behaviour. **modestly** *adv* **modesty** *n* < Latin *modestus* moderate.

modicum (ˈmɒdɪkəm) *n* a small amount. < Latin *modicus* moderate.

modify (ˈmɒdɪˌfaɪ) *vb* **modified; modifying 1** make changes or alterations to. **2** make less severe, violent, etc. **3** (*grammar*) limit the meaning of; qualify. **modification** *n* < Latin *modificare* to moderate.

modulate (ˈmɒdjʊˌleɪt) *vb* **1** vary the tone of: modulate one's voice. **2** adjust or regulate. **3** vary the amplitude, frequency, etc., of. **4** pass from one musical key to another. **modulation** *n* < Latin *modus* measure.

module (ˈmɒdjuːl) *n* **1** a standard or unit used in measuring. **2** a standardized or independent component: space module. **modular** *adj* < Latin *modus* measure.

modus operandi (ˌməʊdəs ɒpəˈrændiː) *n, pl* **modi operandi** a way of working or operating. < New Latin.

modus vivendi (ˌməʊdəs vɪˈvɛndiː) *n, pl* **modi vivendi** a practical compromise, esp. one that allows opposed parties to carry on. < New Latin: way of living.

mogul (ˈməʊgəl) *n* a very powerful or influential person, esp. in the world of business. < Persian *Mughul*, from Mongolian *Mongol*.

mohair (ˈməʊˌhɛə) *n* **1** the silky hair of the Angora goat; mixture of this hair with wool or cotton. **2** a fabric or yarn made from this. < ultimately Arabic *mukhayyar* choice.

moist (mɔɪst) *adj* slightly wet; damp. **moisten** *vb* make or become moist. **moisture** *n* liquid either absorbed by a substance or in the form of vapour or condensed on a surface in small drops. **moisturize** *vb* add moisture to (the skin, etc.). **moisturizer** *n* < Latin *mucidus* slimy.

molar (ˈməʊlə) *n* any of the broad teeth at the back of the jaw, used for chewing and grinding.
• *adj* of these teeth. < Latin *mola* millstone.

molasses (məˈlæsɪz) *n* the thick, brown syrup that drains from raw sugar during refining. < ultimately Latin *mel* honey.

mole[1] (məʊl) *n* a small, dark, permanent spot or protuberance on the human skin. < Old English *māl*.

mole[2] *n* **1** any of a group of small, burrowing mammals with soft, dark fur and very small eyes. **2** a person within an organization who passes secret information to an enemy or competitor. **molehill** *n* a mound of earth thrown up by a burrowing mole. < Middle English.

mole[3] *n* a breakwater or jetty. < Latin *moles* mass.

molecule (ˈmɒlɪˌkjuːl) *n* the smallest particle of a substance that still retains its chemical properties. **molecular** *adj* < Latin *moles* mass.

molest (məˈlɛst) *vb* cause (a person) annoyance, distress, or injury by pestering, touching, or attacking. **molestation** *n* < Latin *molestus* annoying.

mollify (ˈmɒlɪˌfaɪ) *vb* **mollified; mollifying** calm or pacify. < ultimately Latin *mollis* soft.

mollusc (ˈmɒləsk) *n* any of a group of invertebrates which have soft, unsegmented bodies, some with a shell, including snails and oysters, and some without, such as slugs. < Latin *molluscus* soft.

mollycoddle (ˈmɒlɪˌkɒdl̩) *vb* pamper.
• *n* a person who is mollycoddled. < *Molly*, girl's name + *coddle*.

molten (ˈməʊltən) *adj* made liquid by intense heat; melted. < Middle English *melten* to melt.

moment (ˈməʊmənt) *n* **1** a very brief length of time; instant: It won't take a moment! **2** a point of time: at any moment. **3** importance: of great moment. **at the moment** now. **in a moment** very soon. **momentary** *adj* lasting only a very short time; short-lived. **momentarily** *adv* **momentous** *adj* of great importance. **momentum** *n* the force of a moving body. < Latin *momentum*. SEE PANEL.

monarch (ˈmɒnək) *n* a person who reigns over a kingdom or empire; sovereign. **monarchical** *adj* **monarchist** *n* a person who supports monarchy. **monarchy** *n*

1 a system of government in which a monarch is the supreme ruler. **2** a country which has this system. < Greek *monarchos.*
monastery (ˈmɒnəstrɪ) *n* a building inhabited by a religious community, esp. of monks. **monastic** *adj* of or connected with monks. **monasticism** *n* the monastic life or system. < SEE **MONK.**
money (ˈmʌnɪ) *n, pl* **moneys, monies** **1** coins and banknotes used as a conventional means of payment. **2** a particular form of currency, such as the US dollar. **3** (a person with) lots of money; wealth. **monetarism** *n* the theory that the economy is best controlled by regulating the supply of money. **monetarist** *adj, n* **monetary** *adj* of or connected with money or currency: enormous monetary value. **moneybags** *n* (*derogatory humorous*) a wealthy person. **money box** a container used for personal savings, esp. by children. **moneyed** *adj* **1** having a lot of money. **2** consisting of, derived from, or characterized by money. **money-maker** or **money-spinner** *n* something that is highly profitable. < Latin *moneta.*
mongol (ˈmɒŋgl̩) *n* a person suffering from mongolism. **mongolism** *n* a congenital disorder in which a child is born with a broad, flattened skull, short stubby fingers, slanting eyes, and mental deficiency; Down's syndrome. < Mongolian *Mongol* Mongolian.
mongoose (ˈmɒŋˌguːs) *n, pl* **mongooses, mongeese** an agile, predatory, stoat-like animal that feeds mostly on snakes and rodents. < Marathi *mangūs.* SEE PANEL.
mongrel (ˈmʌŋgrəl) *n* a dog or other animal of mixed or unknown breeding. • *adj* of mixed breeding, origin, etc.

momentary or **momentous?**

These two words are sometimes confused, partly because they come from different meanings of the word moment.

Momentary, from moment 'a very short time', means 'lasting only a very short time': *momentary* hesitation, a *momentary* shudder.

Momentous, from moment 'importance', means 'of great importance': a *momentous* decision, *momentous* changes.

So: Her eyes met his in a *momentary* exchange, but for Ralph it was a momentous occasion.

< probably Middle English *mong* mixture.
monitor (ˈmɒnɪtə) *n* **1** person or instrument that observes, records, checks, etc., the operation of something. **2** a school pupil with special duties. **3** a type of television that allows a person to view the data entered in a computer or the picture received by a television camera.
• *vb* observe, record, check, etc., the operation of. < Latin *monēre* to warn.
monk (mʌŋk) *n* a member of a religious community of men living apart from the world under vows of poverty, chastity, and obedience. < ultimately Greek *monos* single.
monkey (ˈmʌŋkɪ) *n, pl* **monkeys** **1** a primate mammal closely related to man. **2** a mischievous person, esp. a child: You little monkey!
• *vb* **1** behave in a boisterous, silly, or mischievous way. **2** tamper or interfere with something; meddle. **monkey business** or **tricks** (*informal*) mischievous or underhand activity. **monkey nut** a peanut. **monkey wrench** a wrench

Beware of the mongoose!

A small group of nouns in English, mostly monosyllabic, form their plurals not by adding an s in the usual way but by a process known as *mutation.* This involves the changing of a vowel, so that foot becomes not foots but feet. Other members of this group include:

goose	**geese**
louse	**lice**
man	**men**
mouse	**mice**
tooth	**teeth**
woman	**women**

Compounds which incorporate these words form their plurals in the same way: forefoot—forefeet, dormouse—dormice, chairman—chairmen, etc. But beware of the word resembling one of these compounds but which is not! The goose in mongoose has no connection whatsoever with birds. Mongoose comes from *mangūs*, the Marathi name for the animal. So the plural of mongoose should therefore be mongooses, but by analogy with goose, mongeese is often used.

with adjustable jaws. < probably Low German.

mono (ˈmɒnəʊ) *adj, n* monophonic (sound).

monochrome (ˈmɒnəˌkrəʊm) *adj* black-and-white or in shades of a single colour.
• *n* a monochrome photograph, painting, etc.< Greek *monos* single + *chrōma* colour.

monocle (ˈmɒnəkl̩) *n* an eyeglass for one eye only. < Late Latin *monoculus*, from Latin *mon-* single + *oculus* eye.

monogamy (mɒˈnɒgəmɪ) *n* the system or state of being married to one person at a time. < Greek *mon-* single + *gamos* marriage.

monogram (ˈmɒnəˌgræm) *n* a design consisting of a person's initials or other letters that are combined or intertwined. < Greek *mon-* single + *gramma* letter.

monograph (ˈmɒnəˌgrɑːf) *n* a scholarly paper or treatise concerned with a single subject or area of research.

monolith (ˈmɒnəlɪθ) *n* a single, upright, massive block of stone. < Greek *mon-* single + *lithos* stone.

monologue (ˈmɒnəˌlɒg) *n* **1** a long speech by a single person, esp. in a play, novel, etc.; soliloquy. **2** a long speech by a single person that prevents conversation or is found boring. < ultimately Greek *mon-* single + *legein* to speak.

monophonic (ˌmɒnəʊˈfɒnɪk) *adj* (of sound reproduction) using only one channel between source and output.

monoplane (ˈmɒnəʊˌpleɪn) *n* an aircraft with a single wing on either side of the fuselage.

monopoly (məˈnɒpəlɪ) *n* **1** (a person or group with) exclusive possession or control of something: set out to break the monopoly. **2** the commodity or thing monopolized. **monopolist** *n* a person who has or favours a monopoly. **monopolize** *vb* gain exclusive possession or control of. < Greek *mono-* single + *pōlein* to sell.

monorail (ˈmɒnəʊˌreɪl) *n* a (railway) track consisting of a single rail.

monosyllable (ˈmɒnəˌsɪləbl̩) *n* a word of one syllable. **monosyllabic** *adj* < Greek *mon-* single + *syllabē* syllable.

monotheism (ˈmɒnəʊθiːˌɪzəm) *n* the belief that there is only one God. **monotheistic** *adj* < Greek *monos* one + *theos* god.

monotone (ˈmɒnəˌtəʊn) *n* an unvarying pitch when speaking, singing, etc. **monotonous** *adj* lacking variety and therefore tedious. **monotonously** *adv* **monotony** *n* tedious sameness or lack of variety. < Greek *mon-* single + *tonos* tone.

monsoon (mɒnˈsuːn) *n* **1** a seasonal wind of southern Asia. **2** the rainy season accompanying the south-west monsoon. < ultimately Arabic *mawsim* season.

monster (ˈmɒnstə) *n* **1** a large, ugly, imaginary creature that tends to terrify people. **2** an abnormally developed person, animal, or plant. **3** a wicked or inhuman person: Why does she live with such a monster? **4** a person or thing that is extremely large. **monstrosity** *n* **monstrous** *adj* **1** of or like a monster. **2** extremely large; enormous. **3** absurd, outrageous, or impossible. < Latin *monstrum*.

montage (mɒnˈtɑːʒ) *n* **1** a picture made up of (parts of) several other pictures or designs arranged for a particular effect. **2** the technique of creating such a picture or composition. **3** a method of film editing that juxtaposes or superimposes disconnected shots, often to indicate passage of time. < French *monter* to mount.

month (mʌnθ) *n* **1** one of the twelve parts into which the year is divided. **2** the interval between the same dates in successive months. < Old English *mōnath*. SEE PANEL.

monthly (ˈmʌnθlɪ) *adj, adv* (appearing, happening, etc.) once a month.
• *n* a monthly magazine, etc.

monument (ˈmɒnjʊmənt) *n* **1** a stone, structure, or sculpture that commemorates a person or event. **2** any lasting reminder of a person or event. **3** a structure or site of historical importance. **monumental** *adj* **1** of, like, or suitable for a monument. **2** of lasting value or importance; outstanding: a monumental achievement. **3** very great; enormous. < Latin *monumentum* memorial.

moo (muː) *n* the typical low sound of a cow.
• *vb* make this sound. < like the sound.

mood[1] (muːd) *n* **1** a state of mind or spirit: in a good mood. **2** the predominant feeling conveyed by a film, poem, song, etc. **3** a fit of temper or irritability: You're in a mood! **moody** *adj* subject to fits of irritability. < Old English *mōd*.

mood[2] *n* the grammatical form of a verb or its position in relation to its subject that indicates whether, for instance, a sentence is to be understood as a statement or question: the indicative mood. < *mode*.

moon (muːn) *n* **1** the earth's natural

satellite, seen by virtue of the light it reflects from the sun. **2** the moon when it is visible. **3** a satellite.
• *vb* wander or pass time listlessly. **moonbeam** *n* a ray of light from the moon. **moonlit** *adj* lit by the moon. **moonshine** *n* foolish talk or ideas; twaddle. **over the moon** (*informal*) delighted. < Old English *mōna*.

moonlight (ˈmuːnˌlaɪt) *n* light from the moon.
• *vb* do a second job, usually at night, in addition to a regular one. **moonlighter** *n*

moor[1] (mʊə, mɔː) *n* an expanse of open, uncultivated land, often covered with gorse or heather. **moorhen** *n* a small, common water-bird. < Old English *mōr*.

moor[2] *vb* secure (a boat, etc.) by means of a rope, cable, or anchor; (of a vessel) be secured in this way. **moorings** *pl n* **1** the ropes, cables, etc., used to secure a vessel. **2** the place where a vessel is moored. < Middle English *moren*.

moose (muːs) *n, pl* **moose 1** a large, North American member of the deer family with large, flattened antlers. **2** the European elk. < Algonquian.

moot (muːt) *adj* subject to argument or debate: a moot point.
• *vb* raise (a matter) for discussion. < Old English *gemōt*.

mop (mɒp) *n* **1** a floor-cleaning implement comprising a bundle of rags, yarn, or other absorbent material fixed to the end of a handle. **2** a similar, but much smaller implement: a dish mop. **3** a mass of thick, often untidy hair.
• *vb* **mopped; mopping** wipe with a mop. **mop up 1** complete a task by doing the few minor things that remain. **2** remove the last pockets of resistance after a battle. < Middle English *mappe*.

mope (məʊp) *vb* be listless and preoccupied with brooding. **moper** *n* < origin uncertain.

moped (ˈməʊpɛd) *n* a bicycle with a small petrol engine. < *mo*tor + *ped*al.
SEE PANEL.

moquette (mɒˈkɛt) *n* a fabric used for carpets and upholstery which has a thick, velvety pile. < French.

moraine (mɒˈreɪn) *n* a mass of earth and stones carried down and deposited by a glacier. < French.

moral (ˈmɒrəl) *adj* **1** of or concerned with the principles of good and bad or right and wrong behaviour: a moral question. **2** righteous or virtuous: a moral life. **3** intended to teach or project a conception of right behaviour: a moral book **4** based on an instinctive as opposed to legal or conventional sense of right and wrong: moral obligation. **5** capable of distinguishing right and wrong: moral

the month mystery

Upon examining the names of the months, a modern-day student of Latin might think that the Romans couldn't count. September October, November, and December derive from the Latin numerals *septem* (seven), *octo* (eight), *novem* (nine), and *decem* (ten). And yet everybody knows that September is the ninth month of the year, October is the tenth, November the eleventh, and December the twelfth! The solution to the mystery lies in the change undergone by the Roman calendar at around 700 BC. Before this there were only ten months in the year—the first being March—and so the names tallied with their numerical order. With the reformation of the calendar two new months were added—January and February. Had these been placed at the end of the year instead of at the beginning, the 'misnomers' could have been avoided!

mopeds and motels

Moped (*mo*tor + *ped*al cycle) and motel (*mo*tor + ho*tel*) are examples of ***blends***, or ***portmanteau words***: words that have been formed by the blending of two root words. This particular process of word formation is relatively rare and most of the words so produced (like lubritection and sexibition) tend to be short-lived. Other examples of *blends* that have more or less established themselves in the language include:

bit (*bi*nary + digi*t*)
brunch *US* (*br*eakfast + l*unch*)
electrocute (*electro* + exe*cute*)
heliport (*heli*copter + air*port*)
newscast (*news* + broad*cast*)
paratroops (*para*chute + *troops*)
smog (*sm*oke + f*og*)
transistor (*trans*fer + res*istor*)

awareness. **6** having a psychological as opposed to physical effect: a moral victory; moral support.
• *n* **1** a moral lesson: the moral of the story is ... **2** *pl* principles of (sexual) behaviour judged in terms of conventional standards. **morally** *adv* **moralist** *n* a person who is concerned with (teaching) moral standards. **morality** *n* **1** a particular moral code: Buddhist morality. **2** (degree of) conformity to conventional moral principles: question the morality of arms sales. **3** the quality of being moral. **moralize** *vb* make pronouncements about right and wrong conduct. < ultimately Latin *mos* custom.

morale (mɒˈrɑːl) *n* a person's or group's mental or moral condition, in terms of degree of hopefulness, enthusiasm, etc. < French *moral*.

morass (məˈræs) *n* a stretch of low, wet land; marsh. < Old French *maresc*.

moratorium (ˌmɒrəˈtɔːrɪəm) *n, pl* **moratoriums, moratoria** **1** legal authorization to delay payment of debts. **2** a temporary suspension of an activity. < ultimately Latin *mora* delay.

morbid (ˈmɔːbɪd) *adj* **1** (of the mind) unnaturally preoccupied with unpleasant things. **2** of, caused by, or connected with disease. **morbidity** or **morbidness** *n* **morbidly** *adv* < Latin *morbidus* diseased.

mordant (ˈmɔːdnt) *adj* caustic or sarcastic. < Middle French *mordre* to bite.

more (mɔː) *determiner, pron* **1** greater in number or quantity: There are more people than last year. **2** additional: Two more teas, please.
• *adv* **1** used for forming the comparative of many adjectives and adverbs: more intelligent; more often. **2** to or in a greater degree: I only wish I could help more. **3** again: once more.
• *n* **1** a greater or additional quantity, amount, etc. **2** additional ones. **more or less** roughly or approximately: It's more or less an hour's drive. **moreover** *adv* in addition (to this). < Old English *māra*.

morello (məˈrɛləʊ) *n, pl* **morellos** a bitter cherry, chiefly used in jams. < probably Medieval Latin *amarellum* cultivated cherry.

morgue (mɔːg) *n* a mortuary. < French.

moribund (ˈmɒrɪˌbʌnd) *adj* about to die; dying. < Latin *mori* to die.

morning (ˈmɔːnɪŋ) *n* **1** the early part of the day ending at noon or the midday meal. **2** the dawn. **3** (*literary*) the beginning. **in the morning** tomorrow morning. **morning after** the after-effects of over-indulgence; hangover. **morning dress** men's dress for formal, daytime occasions. **morning sickness** nausea and vomiting during the early months of pregnancy, esp. in the mornings. < Middle English.

moron (ˈmɔːrɒn) *n* **1** a person who is mentally deficient. **2** (*informal*) a very stupid person, **moronic** *adj* < Greek *mōros* stupid.

morose (məˈrəʊs) *adj* sullen and irritable. **morosely** *adv* **moroseness** *n* < Latin *morosus* capricious.

morphia (ˈmɔːfɪə) *n* morphine.

morphine (ˈmɔːfiːn) *n* a drug obtained from opium, used for relieving pain. < French, from *Morpheus*, in Greek myth, the god of sleep.

morsel (ˈmɔːsl̩) *n* a small piece or quantity, esp. of food: Just a morsel for me, please. < ultimately Latin *mordēre* to bite.

mortal (ˈmɔːtl̩) *adj* **1** destined to die: man's mortal condition. **2** causing death; fatal: a mortal injury. **3** lasting or continuing until death: mortal combat. **4** intense or severe.
• *n* a human being: a mere mortal. **mortality** *n* **1** being mortal. **2** great loss of life. **mortality rate** the death rate. < Latin *mors* death.

mortar (ˈmɔːtə) *n* **1** a building material made of lime and cement mixed with sand, water, etc. **2** a vessel in which substances are pounded with a pestle. **3** a short-barrelled cannon used for firing shells at high angles.
• *vb* make fast with mortar. **mortarboard** *n* a cap with a flat, square top worn as part of academic dress. < Latin *mortarium*.

mortgage (ˈmɔːgɪdʒ) *n* **1** a transfer of property as security for the payment of a debt on the understanding that the transfer is void once the debt is paid. **2** the amount of money borrowed or lent in such an arrangement.
• *vb* transfer the ownership of (a property) by a mortgage. **mortgagee** *n* a bank, building society, etc., to whom a property is mortgaged. **mortgager, mortgagor** *n* a person who mortgages his or her property. < Middle English *morgage*.

mortify (ˈmɔːtɪˌfaɪ) *vb* **mortified; mortifying** **1** subject to great humiliation. **2** humble or subdue, esp. by self-denial, strict religious discipline, etc. **mortification** *n* < ultimately Latin *mors* death.

mortise (ˈmɔːtɪs) *n* a hole made in a piece of wood to receive a protruding piece on another, so that the two pieces interlock firmly. **mortise lock** a lock that is fixed into a mortise at the edge of a door. < Middle French *mortaise*.

mortuary (ˈmɔːtʃʊərɪ) *n* a place where dead bodies are kept before burial or cremation. < Latin *mortuarius* of the dead.

mosaic (məʊˈzeɪɪk) *n* a decorative design or picture made by inlaying different-coloured pieces of material, esp. glass or stone. < ultimately Latin *Musa* muse.

moselle (məʊˈzɛl) *n* a dry, white wine made in the Moselle valley. < *Mosel*, river in Germany.

mosque (mɒsk) *n* a public place of worship for Muslims. < Arabic *masjid* temple.

mosquito (məˈskiːtəʊ) *n pl* **mosquitoes** a small, two-winged insect, the female of which sucks blood and sometimes transmits diseases. < Spanish, ultimately from Latin *musca* fly.

moss (mɒs) *n* one of a group of primitive, flowerless plants that grow densely on trees, rocks, bogs, etc. **mossy** *adj* like or covered in moss. < Old English *mōs* bog.

most (məʊst) *determiner, pron* the greatest in number or quantity.
• *n* the greatest number or amount.
• *adv* **1** used for forming the superlative of many adjectives and adverbs: the most intelligent boy in the class. **2** to the greatest degree or extent. **3** very: a most entertaining evening. **at most** or **at the most** as an upper limit. **for the most part** for the greatest part; usual. **make the most of** use or show to the best advantage. **mostly** *adv* for the greatest part; usually. < Old English *mǣst*.

MOT (ˌɛməʊˈtiː) *n* a compulsory, annual test of roadworthiness for motor vehicles of more than a certain age. < *M*inistry *o*f *T*ransport.

motel (məʊˈtɛl) *n* a roadside hotel for motorists, often with direct access from the accommodation to the parking space. < *mo*tor + ho*tel*. SEE PANEL AT **MOPED**.

moth (mɒθ) *n* **1** a night-flying insect like a butterfly but with a usually stouter body and duller colours. **2** one of these which lays its eggs in cloth or fabric for its larvae to feed on. **in moth-balls** stored or suspended indefinitely. **moth-ball** *n* a ball of pungent material to keep moths away from clothing. **moth-eaten** *adj* **1** partly eaten by moth larvae. **2** decrepit or antiquated. < Old English *moththe*.

mother (ˈmʌðə) *n* **1** a female parent. **2** (*archaic*) an elderly woman. **3** a woman who leads a female religious community: Mother Superior. **4** a source: Necessity is the mother of invention.
• *vb* care for in a motherly way. **motherhood** *n* **Mothering Sunday** the fourth Sunday in Lent, observed in honour of mothers. **mother-in-law** *n, pl* **mothers-in-law** the mother of one's husband or wife. **motherland** *n* one's native country. **motherless** *adj* not having a living mother. **motherly** *adj* like a mother; kind and caring. **motherliness** *n* **mother-of-pearl** *n* a hard, pearly substance which lines the inside of the shells of mussels, oysters, etc. **Mother's Day** Mothering Sunday. **mother tongue** one's native language. < Old English *mōdor*.

motif (məʊˈtiːf) *n* **1** a feature which recurs in works of art, literature, or music, establishing a theme. **2** a single or repeated shape, ornament, etc. < French.

motion (ˈməʊʃən) *n* **1** an act of moving or changing position. **2** the capacity or manner of movement. **3** a movement of the body; gesture. **4** a proposal formally discussed and debated at a meeting. **5** the emptying of the bowels.
• *vb* make a sign to someone to do something: He motioned me to sit down. **go through the motions** do something mechanically and without enthusiasm. **motionless** *adj* not moving. **motion picture** a film. < ultimately Latin *movēre* to move.

motive (ˈməʊtɪv) *n* an incentive to do something; reason.
• *adj* producing action; driving: motive power. **motivate** *vb* provide with an incentive; inspire. **motivated** *adj* stimulated to act positively. **motivation** *n* < Middle French *motif* moving.

motley (ˈmɒtlɪ) *adj* **1** made up of different elements. **2** multi-coloured. < perhaps Middle English *mot* speck.

motor (ˈməʊtə) *n* **1** a machine that causes motion in, for example, a boat or vehicle; power unit driving moving parts in, for example, an internal-combustion engine. **2** (*informal*) a motor car.
• *adj* **1** causing or giving motion: motor nerves. **2** powered or driven by a motor. **3** of or concerning motor vehicles: the motor trade.
• *vb* travel by motor vehicle; drive. **motor bike** a motor cycle. **motorcade** *n* motor vehicles in procession. **motor car** a usually four-wheeled motor vehicle for conveying a small number of people.

motor cycle a two-wheeled motor vehicle that carries the rider and sometimes one passenger astride the engine. **motor-cyclist** *n* the rider of a motor cycle. **motorist** *n* the driver of a motor car. **motorize** *vb* **1** equip with a motor. **2** supply (military units) with motor vehicles. **motor vehicle** a road vehicle with a motor engine. **motorway** *n* a major road built for fast traffic, controlled by special regulations. < Latin *movēre* to move.

mottled (ˈmɒtḷd) *adj* marked with streaks or blotches of different colours or shades. < probably back formation from *motley*.

motto (ˈmɒtəʊ) *n, pl* **mottoes** **1** a short phrase or sentence which expresses the guiding principle of a family, organization, etc. **2** a maxim or humorous saying printed on paper, esp. in a party cracker. < Italian, from Latin *muttire* to mutter.

mould[1] (məʊld) *n* **1** a hollow form, used to give something shape by pouring liquid metal, plastic, etc., into it and leaving it to set. **2** a fixed form, design, or pattern.

• *vb* **1** give form or shape to. **2** direct or influence the development of. **moulding** *n* a moulded article; decorative strip or outline on a cornice, etc. < Latin *modulus* small measure.

mould[2] *n* a growth of fine, furry fungi which forms on moist or decaying matter. **mouldy** *adj* **1** covered with mould. **2** stale or rotten. **3** (*slang*) boring; miserable. **mouldiness** *n* < Middle English *mowlde*.

mould[3] *n* a soft, loose soil rich in nutrients for plant growth: leaf-mould. < Old English *molde*.

moult (məʊlt) *vb* (of birds, animals, or insects) shed feathers, hair, or outer layers periodically. < ultimately Latin *mutare* to change.

mound (maʊnd) *n* **1** a mass of raised earth, stones, etc.; small hill. **2** a heap or pile. < origin unknown.

mount[1] (maʊnt) *n* a mountain or high hill, used in names as in Mount Everest. < ultimately Latin *mons*.

mount[2] *vb* **1** climb; ascend. **2** increase in amount, extent, or intensity. **3** get or set up on (a horse, bicycle, stand, etc.). **4** fix in position or to a support for display. **5** prepare and carry out: The allies mounted an offensive. **6** put in position for defence or observation.

• *n* **1** a horse for riding. **2** a support of backing material on which something is mounted.

mountain (ˈmaʊntɪn) *n* **1** a high projecting land-mass, esp. of over 1000 ft. **2** a large amount. **3** a surplus amount of a commodity: the butter mountain. **mountain ash** the rowan tree. **mountaineer** *n* someone who is skilled in climbing mountains. **mountaineering** *n* mountain-climbing for sport. **mountainous** *adj* **1** with many mountains. **2** enormous. < SEE **MOUNT**[1].

mourn (mɔːn) *vb* feel or express grief over a death or something which is past. **mourner** *n* **mournful** *adj* sad; grieving. **mournfully** *adv* **mournfulness** *n* **mourning** *n* **1** grief; sorrow. **2** the outward symbols of this, such as the wearing of black clothes. < Old English *murnan*.

mousaka (muːˈsɑːkə) *n* also **moussaka** a Greek dish of minced meat and aubergine or potato in layers usually with a cheese topping. < New Greek *mousakas*.

mouse (maʊs) *n, pl* **mice** **1** a small rodent with a pointed snout and a long, slender tail. **2** someone who is timid or shy. **mouser** *n* a mouse-hunting cat. **mousetrap** *n* **1** a trap for mice. **2** poor-quality cheese. **mousy** *adj* **1** timid or quiet. **2** (of hair) light greyish-brown. < Old English *mūs*. SEE PANEL. SEE PANEL AT **MONGOOSE**.

mousse (muːs) *n* a light, creamy dish, usually made with whipped egg-whites and set with gelatin. < French: froth.

moustache (məˈstɑːʃ) *n* the hair allowed

mouse

The language of very small children with all its 'peculiarities' like mouses and mices is highly revealing as to the way in which language is acquired. In its first stages the child's grammar is extremely simple, lacking all the many exceptions to rules that characterize adult grammar. Plurals, for example, are made simply by adding an s, z, or iz sound, as in cat cats, dog dogs, and horse horses. When the word mouse comes along, it is made to follow the same standard pattern: the plural becomes mouses. On the other hand, mice is not recognized as a plural form as irregular forms do not yet exist in the child's grammar, and so by analogy with face, race, etc., the form mice is pluralized as mices.

to grow on someone's upper lip. < ultimately Greek *mystax.*

mouth (maʊθ) *n* **1** the opening in an animal's body through which food passes. **2** (*informal*) cheek; insolence. **3** the opening of a container, cave, volcano, etc. **4** the area where a river flows into the sea.
• *vb* (maʊð) **1** form (words) soundlessly with the lips. **2** speak pompously or insincerely. **mouthful** *n* **1** an amount that fills the mouth; small amount of food. **2** a long word or phrase, esp. that is difficult to pronounce. **mouth-organ** *n* a small oblong wind instrument, played by blowing or sucking. **mouthpiece** *n* **1** the part of a musical instrument or device that comes into contact with the mouth. **2** someone or something that expresses the opinion of others. **mouthwash** *n* a medicated liquid for cleansing the mouth. < Old English *mūth.* SEE PANEL.

move (muːv) *vb* **1** change in location or position. **2** set or be in motion. **3** change (one's dwelling or place of business). **4** also **move on** proceed or progress. **5** (of the bowels) empty or be emptied. **6** give rise to an emotion or reaction in: The song moved me to tears. **7** motivate; drive. **8** change the position of (a piece) in chess. **9** propose formally at a debate or meeting. **10** live in a particular environment: move in the best circles. **11** take action.
• *n* **1** moving or being moved. **2** moving a piece in chess. **3** an action taken with a particular purpose. **get a move on** (*informal*) hurry up. **movable** *adj* able to be removed. **move in 1** occupy a new dwelling or job. **2** advance in order to capture or control. **movement** *n* **1** moving or being moved. **2** activity; action. **3** a trend; style. **4** a tendency in market prices. **5** moving parts, esp. of a clock or watch. **6** a combined effort to achieve a purpose: the Women's Liberation movement. **7** a division of an extended musical composition. **movie** *n* a cinema film. **moving** *adj* causing an emotional response. < Latin *movēre.*

mow (məʊ) *vb* **mowed; mowed, mown; mowing** cut down (esp. grass); cut grass from: mow the lawn. **mow down** kill or destroy in large quantities. **mower** *n* a person or a machine that mows. < Old English *māwan.*

MP *abbrev* Member of Parliament.

m.p.h. *abbrev* miles per hour.

Mr (ˈmɪstə) *n, pl* **Messrs** a courtesy title used before a man's surname or official address: Mr Chairman. < abbreviation of Middle English *maister* master.

Mrs (ˈmɪsɪz) *n, pl* **Mrs** a courtesy title used before a married woman's surname. < abbreviation of *mistress.*

Ms (məz, mɪz) *n* a courtesy title used before a woman's surname when marital status is irrelevant or unknown.

MS *abbrev, pl* **MSS** manuscript.

Mt *abbrev* Mount.

much (mʌtʃ) *determiner* great in extent or amount.
• *pron, n* **1** a large amount. **2** something remarkable or impressive: He isn't up to much; I didn't think much of that.
• *adv* **1** to a great extent. **2** nearly: much the same. **as much** the same amount. **much as** even though. **much of a muchness** almost the same. < Old English *mycel.* SEE PANEL.

muck (mʌk) *n* **1** farmyard dung. **2** filth; dirt. **3** (*informal*) mess; rubbish. **make a muck of** (*informal*) ruin; bungle. **muck about** or **around** (*informal*) mess around. **muck in** (*informal*) share a task or expenses. **muck out** remove manure from (an animal's quarters). **muck-raking** *n* searching out and exposing scandal. **muck up** (*informal*)

---

straight from the horse's mouth

Mouth features in a number of idiomatic expressions, including:

keep one's mouth shut to refrain from revealing a secret, expressing one's opinion, etc.

make one's mouth water to arouse one's desire for food. **mouth-watering** *adj*

open one's big mouth to reveal a secret: 'Of course you would have to go and open your big mouth about Madge's party! They weren't supposed to know!'

put words into someone's mouth to anticipate, especially wrongly, what someone is going to say; represent, especially falsely, what someone has said.

straight from the horse's mouth (of information) directly from the source; first-hand. The expression derives from the fact that the only reliable way of determining the age of a horse is to examine its incisors.

---

bungle. **mucky** *adj* covered with dirt or filth. < Old English *-moc*.

mucus (ˈmjuːkəs) *n* a sticky secretion that protects the inside of the nose and throat. **mucous** *adj* **mucous membrane** moist skin with mucus-secreting glands in the nose, throat, mouth, etc. < Latin.

mud (mʌd) *n* soft earth or clay that has been wet. **muddy** *adj* **1** filled or covered with mud. **2** (of colour) dull or unclear. **3** vague; confused. **muddiness** *n* **mud-flap** *n* a flap behind the wheel of a vehicle which stops mud being thrown up. **mud-flats** *pl n* an area of muddy ground left exposed at low tide. **mudguard** *n* a curved metal or plastic cover above the wheels of a cycle, motor cycle, etc., to reduce the amount of mud thrown up. **mud-slinging** *n* (*informal*) speaking maliciously of others. < Middle English *mudde*. SEE PANEL.

muddle (ˈmʌdl̩) *vb* **1** mix up; disarrange. **2** bewilder; confuse.
• *n* state of confusion or disorder. **muddler** *n* **muddle-headed** *adj* mentally vague or confused. **muddle on** or **along** carry on in a disorganized fashion. **muddle through** manage despite lack of organization. < perhaps Middle Dutch *modde* mud.

muesli (ˈmjuːzlɪ) *n* a food of mixed cereals, nuts, dried fruit, etc. < Old High German *mous* pulp.

muff[1] (mʌf) *n* an open tube of fur or cloth into which both hands are placed for warmth. < Medieval Latin *muffula* mitten.

muff[2] *vb* (*informal*) mismanage; blunder. < perhaps *muff*[1].

muffin (ˈmʌfɪn) *n* a light, round bun, usually eaten hot with butter. < probably Low German *muffen* cakes.

muffle (ˈmʌfl̩) *vb* **1** cover or wrap up, esp. for protection. **2** deaden (a sound) by wrapping or padding. **3** stifle; suppress: muffled laughter. **muffler** *n* **1** a warm, thick scarf. **2** something that deadens noise. < Middle English *muflen*.

mufti (ˈmʌftɪ) *n* ordinary clothes worn by one who normally wears uniform. < probably Arabic *muftī* Muslim jurist.

mug[1] (mʌg) *n* **1** a large, usually cylindrical drinking vessel; what it contains. **2** (*slang*) someone's face or mouth. **3** (*informal*) someone who is easily swindled.
• *vb* **mugged; mugging** attack and rob (someone), esp. in the street. **mugger** *n* **a mug's game** (*informal*) a profitless activity. < origin unknown.

mug[2] *vb* **mug up** (*informal*) study hard, esp. for an exam. < origin unknown.

muggins (ˈmʌgɪnz) *n* (*informal*) someone who is gullible; fool. < probably the name *Muggins*.

muggy (ˈmʌgɪ) *adj* (of weather) heavy, warm, and humid. **mugginess** *n* < English dialect *mug* drizzle.

mulatto (mjuːˈlætəʊ) *n, pl* **mulattos** someone with one Negro and one White parent. < Spanish, ultimately from Latin *mulus* mule. SEE PANEL.

mulberry (ˈmʌlbərɪ) *n* **1** one of a group of trees of the fig family bearing an edible,

---

much trouble

Much provides an example of a word whose grammatical behaviour is rather curious. Although it is used in negative sentences—'He doesn't earn *much* money'—and in interrogative sentences—'Does he earn *much* money?', it is never used in affirmative sentences: 'He earns *much* money' is ungrammatical. In contrast with lots of, a lot of, or a great deal of, which can be used in all three types of sentence, the grammatical potential of much is restricted. This is one of the many intricate rules of English that a native speaker acquires unconsciously as a child, but which trip up a foreign learner time and time again.

---

his name is mud

The expression his name is mud derives from the name of Samuel *Mudd,* 1833–83, a US country doctor. It was Dr Mudd's misfortune to treat the injured John Wilkes Booth following the latter's assassination of President Abraham Lincoln in 1865. Although the doctor knew nothing of the assassination at the time of treating Booth, he was charged with conspiracy, sentenced to life imprisonment, and spent the next 24 years in jail. Because of the association of Mudd with Lincoln's assassination, the name came to stand for the worst name that a person could be called.

purple or white fruit like a blackberry; this fruit. **2** a dull purple colour. < ultimately Greek *moron* mulberry + Middle English *berie* berry.

mulch (mʌltʃ) *n* a covering of compost, etc., spread over ground to protect plants or enrich the soil.
● *vb* spread mulch over. < perhaps English dialect *melch* soft.

mule[1] (mju:l) *n* the offspring of a horse and an ass, sterile and known for its obstinacy. **mulish** *adj* obstinate. **mulishly** *adv* **mulishness** *n* < Latin *mulus*. SEE PANEL AT **MULATTO**.

mule[2] *n* a backless slipper or shoe. < Latin *mulleus* magistrate's shoe.

mull[1] (mʌl) *vb* heat up, sweeten, and flavour (wine or beer) with spices. < origin unknown.

mull[2] *vb* **mull over** think about; contemplate. < Middle English *mullen*.

mullet (ˈmʌlɪt) *n* one of a family of long-bodied, edible fishes. < ultimately Greek *myllos*.

mulligatawny (ˌmʌlɪgəˈtɔ:nɪ) *n* a rich meat soup with a curry flavour. < Tamil *milaku* pepper + *taṇṇi* water.

mullion (ˈmʌlɪən) *n* a vertical strip between the panes of a window or the panels of a screen or door. < perhaps Middle French *moyen* middle.

multi- *prefix* many: multi-coloured. < Latin *multus* much, many.

multifarious (ˌmʌltɪˈfɛərɪəs) *adj* of numerous kinds; various. < Latin *multifarius*.

multilateral (ˌmʌltɪˈlætərəl) *adj* **1** involving two or more parties: multilateral disarmament. **2** with many sides.

multinational (ˌmʌltɪˈnæʃənl̩) *adj* (of a business or firm) with divisions in more than two countries.
● *n* a multinational company.

multiple (ˈmʌltɪpl̩) *adj* with more than one part or element.
● *n* a quantity that can be divided by a number without leaving a remainder. **multiple sclerosis** a progressive disease in which hardening patches of nerve tissue in the brain and spinal cord lead to paralysis. **multiple store** a chain store. < Latin *multi-* + *-plex* -fold.

multiplicity (ˌmʌltɪˈplɪsɪtɪ) *n* a great number or variety.

multiply (ˈmʌltɪˌplaɪ) *vb* **multiplied; multiplying 1** find the quantity resulting from adding a number to itself a specified number of times. **2** increase in number; accumulate. **multiplication** *n* **multiplication sign** the sign X, placed between quantities to be multiplied. **multiplication tables** ordered lists of the results of two numbers multiplied together. < Latin *multiplex* multiple.

multiracial (ˌmʌltɪˈreɪʃəl) *adj* comprising people of numerous races.

multi-storey (ˌmʌltɪˈstɔ:rɪ) *adj* having many storeys or levels: a multi-storey car-park.

multitude (ˈmʌltɪˌtju:d) *n* **1** a large number of people or things. **2 the multitude** the populace. **multitudinous** *adj* great in number. < Latin *multus* much.

mum[1] (mʌm) *adj* (*informal*) silent: keep mum; mum's the word. < probably like the sound made with closed lips.

mum[2] *n* (*informal*) mother. < short for *mummy*.

mumble (ˈmʌmbl̩) *vb* utter without clear articulation.
● *n* an indistinct utterance or sound. **mumbler** *n* < Middle English *momelen*, like the sound.

mumbo-jumbo (ˈmʌmbəʊˈdʒʌmbəʊ) *n* **1** meaningless ritual or superstition. **2** overcomplicated language or actions designed to obscure and confuse. <*Mumbo Jumbo*, tribal god worshipped in Africa.

mummer (ˈmʌmə) *n* a masked performer in a traditional mime or folk play. < Middle French *momer* to go masked.

mummy[1] (ˈmʌmɪ) *n* **1** a ritually embalmed and preserved body, esp. in ancient Egypt. **2** a dried-up body preserved by accidental conditions. **mummify** *vb* **mummified; mummifying 1** dry up and embalm (a body) to preserve it. **2** dry up; shrivel. < Persian *mūm* wax.

mummy[2] *n* (*informal*) mother. < alteration of baby language *mama*.

mumps (mʌmps) *n* a virus infection causing gross and painful swellings in the neck. < obsolete *mump* grimace.

munch (mʌntʃ) *vb* chew steadily while making a crunching sound. < Middle English *monchen*, probably like the sound.

mundane (mʌnˈdeɪn) *adj* **1** routine;

---

mulatto and **mule**

Unlike the donkey, the mule is a hybrid: the offspring of a mating between a male donkey (jackass) and a female horse (mare). This hybrid sense of mule is also present in the derived word mulatto 'a person with one White and one Negro parent'.

---

commonplace. **2** worldly; secular. < Latin *mundus* world.

municipal (mjuːˈnɪsɪpl̩) *adj* of a town, city, or borough, or its local government. **municipality** *n* a self-governing urban district. < Latin *munus* duty + *capere* to take.

munificent (mjuːˈnɪfɪsənt) *adj* generous; liberal. **munificence** *n* **munificently** *adv* < Latin *munus* gift.

munitions (mjuːˈnɪʃənz) *pl n* armaments and ammunition for military use. < Latin *munire* to fortify.

mural (ˈmjʊərəl) *adj* of or applied to a wall.
• *n* a painting made on a wall; fresco. < Latin *murus* wall.

murder (ˈmɜːdə) *n* **1** the crime of killing someone unlawfully with intent. **2** (*informal*) something unpleasant, difficult, or dangerous.
• *vb* **1** kill unlawfully with intent. **2** (*informal*) ruin; spoil. **3** (*informal*) defeat; thrash. **murderer** fem. **murderess** *n* **murderous** *adj* **1** capable of, guilty of, or intent on murder. **2** unpleasant, difficult, or dangerous. < Old English *morthor*.

murky (ˈmɜːkɪ) *adj* **1** gloomy; dark. **2** cloudy; foggy. **murkiness** *n* < Middle English *mirke* darkness.

murmur (ˈmɜːmə) *n* **1** a low, continuous, indistinct noise or utterance. **2** an abnormal sound made by the heart. **3** a subdued grumble or complaint.
• *vb* make a murmur; utter indistinctly. < Latin.

muscatel (ˌmʌskəˈtɛl) *n* a sweet wine made from muscat grapes. < Late Latin *muscus* musk.

muscle (ˈmʌsl̩) *n* **1** a tissue of elongated cells in an animal body which expand and contract to produce motion; organ consisting of this. **2** muscular strength. **3** (*informal*) forcefulness.
• *vb* **muscle in** force one's way in; impose oneself. **muscular** *adj* **1** of or concerning the muscles. **2** with well-developed muscles. **muscularity** *n* < Latin *musculus* small mouse.

muse (mjuːz) *vb* think over; contemplate. < Medieval Latin *musus* mouth of an animal.

museum (mjuːˈziːəm) *n* a place where objects of historical interest or value are displayed. **museum piece 1** an object suitable for display in a museum. **2** (*derogatory*) someone or something regarded as ridiculously old-fashioned. < ultimately Greek *Mousa* Muse.

mush (mʌʃ) *n* a soft, pulpy mass. **mushy** *adj* **1** pulpy. **2** cloying; sentimental. **mushiness** *n* < probably alteration of *mash*.

mushroom (ˈmʌʃruːm, ˈmʌʃrʊm) *n* a fungus, esp. edible, with a slender stalk and a cap-like top; something with this shape.
• *vb* **1** grow or multiply suddenly and rapidly. **2** take on the shape of a mushroom. < Late Latin *mussirio*.

music (ˈmjuːzɪk) *n* **1** the art of combining and arranging sounds and tones in sequences with unity and continuity. **2** a musical composition, or the written or printed score for this. **3** any pleasant sound. **music centre** a system of a record-player, radio, and tape-recorder in combination. **music-hall** *n* (a theatre formerly presenting) variety entertainment. **musician** *n* someone who composes or performs music, esp. professionally. < ultimately Greek *Mousa* Muse.

musical (ˈmjuːzɪkl̩) *adj* **1** of or like music; melodic. **2** interested or talented in music. **3** accompanied by or set to music.
• *n* a light, musical comedy in the theatre or on film. **musically** *adv* **musical box** a box with an apparatus that produces a tune mechanically when opened. **musical chairs** a game in which music is played as people walk round a number of chairs, always one fewer than the number of players, then each time the music stops there is a scramble for seats.

musk (mʌsk) *n* **1** a strong-smelling substance secreted by the male musk-deer, used in making perfumes; artificial substance like this. **2** one of a group of plants with a musky smell. **musky** *adj* **musk-deer** *n* a small, hornless deer found in Central Asia. **musk-rat** *n* a large, aquatic rodent found in North America, sometimes trapped for its fur. **musk-rose** *n* a rose with large, white flowers smelling of musk. < Sanskrit *muṣka* testicle. SEE PANEL.

musket (ˈmʌskɪt) *n* a heavy shoulder firearm with a long barrel, formerly used by the infantry. **musketeer** *n* a soldier armed with a musket. < Old Italian *moschetto* arrow, from Latin *musca* fly.

Muslim (ˈmʊzlɪm, ˈmʌzlɪm) *n* a follower of the religion of Islam.
• *adj* of or associated with Islam. < Arabic: one who surrenders (to God).

muslin (ˈmʌzlɪn) *n* a fine, plain, cotton cloth. < Arabic al-*Mawṣil*, Mosul, city in Iraq. SEE PANEL AT **TULLE**.

musquash (ˈmʌskwɒʃ) *n* the musk-rat or its pelt. < Algonquian.

mussel (ˈmʌsl̩) *n* a type of bivalve mollusc, of which the marine variety can be eaten. < Old English *muscelle*.

must (məs, məst; *stressed* mʌst) *auxiliary vb* **1** used to express obligation, compulsion, or necessity: You must do as ordered. **2** used to express certainty or supposition: He must have been delayed. **3** used to express resolution or insistence: You must come round to dinner.
• *n* a necessity; prerequisite. < Old English *mōtan*.

mustang (ˈmʌstæŋ) *n* a small, often wild horse found in the south-western USA. < Spanish *mestengo* stray.

mustard (ˈmʌstəd) *n* **1** a plant with yellow flowers and long, straight pods, grown for their pungent seeds. **2** a paste made from the ground seeds of this. **mustard gas** a poison gas that blisters the skin. < ultimately Latin *mustum* new.

muster (ˈmʌstə) *vb* **1** gather; assemble. **2** call up; summon: He mustered up his courage.
• *n* an assembled group; gathering. **pass muster** be acceptable; qualify. < ultimately Latin *monstrum* omen.

musty (ˈmʌstɪ) *adj* mouldy; stale. **mustiness** *n* < Middle French, alteration of *musc* musk.

mutate (mjuːˈteɪt) *vb* cause or undergo changes in form. **mutable** *adj* liable to alter. **mutant** *n* a living entity with a genetically altered form, **mutation** *n* alteration in form; mutant. < Latin *mutare* to change.

mute (mjuːt) *adj* **1** lacking the power of speech; dumb. **2** silent; speechless. **3** unexpressed: mute hatred. **4** (of a letter) unpronounced.
• *n* **1** someone who cannot speak. **2** a device fitted to a musical instrument to soften its tone. **mutely** *adv* **muteness** *n* < Latin *mutus*.

the musk mouse

The long history of musk tells us that its fragrance has been enjoyed for many centuries. The word came into Middle English from the Middle French *musc*. This in turn derived from the Late Latin *muscus* which was a descendant of the Greek *moschos*. The Greek form came from the Persian *mushk*, which had its roots in the Sanskrit *muska* 'a testicle'. This was a diminutive of *mus* 'a mouse'.

mutilate (ˈmjuːtɪˌleɪt) *vb* **1** maim; disfigure. **2** spoil or damage by removing an essential part of. **mutilation** *n* **mutilator** *n* < Latin *mutilus* mutilated.

mutiny (ˈmjuːtɪnɪ) *n* a revolt against lawful authority, esp. by seamen or soldiers against their officers.
• *vb* **mutinied; mutinying** be involved in a mutiny; revolt. **mutineer** *n* someone who mutinies. **mutinous** *adj* rebellious. **mutinously** *adv* < ultimately Latin *movēre* to move.

mutter (ˈmʌtə) *vb* **1** utter (words) indistinctly in a low tone. **2** grumble, esp. in a low voice.
• *n* muttered words or sounds. < Middle English *muteren*.

mutton (ˈmʌtn̩) *n* the flesh of a mature sheep, eaten as food. < Old French *moton* ram.

mutual (ˈmjuːtʃʊəl) *adj* **1** felt or directed each towards the other: mutual assistance. **2** with the same relationship towards each other: mutual enemies. **3** common to two or more parties: mutual interests. **mutually** *adv* < Latin *mutuus* borrowed, reciprocal.

muzzle (ˈmʌzl̩) *n* **1** the projecting jaws and nose of some animals such as dogs. **2** a strap or guard fitted over an animal's mouth to prevent it biting or eating. **3** the open end of a gun-barrel.
• *vb* **1** fit a muzzle on (an animal). **2** restrict the free expression of; suppress. < ultimately Medieval Latin *musus* mouth of an animal.

muzzy (ˈmʌzɪ) *adj* dazed; confused. **muzziness** *n* < perhaps *muddled* + *fuzzy*.

my (maɪ) *determiner* **1** of or belonging to me. **2** used in certain forms of address: my dear boy. **3** used in certain exclamations of surprise or disbelief: My God! My foot! **myself** *pron* the form of *I* and *me* used reflexively or for emphasis: I cut myself; I did it myself. **be myself** behave in a normal way: I'm not quite myself today. **by myself** **1** without help. **2** alone. < Old English *mīn*.

myopia (maɪˈəʊpɪə) *n* near-sightedness. **myopic** *adj* < Greek *myōps*.

myriad (ˈmɪrɪəd) *n* an infinitely large number. < Greek *myrioi* ten thousand.

myrrh (mɜː) *n* an aromatic gum resin, used in making incense, perfume, etc.

< Greek *myrrha,* of Semitic origin.
myrtle (ˈmɜːtl̩) *n* an evergreen shrub with sweet-smelling leaves. < Greek *myrtos.*
mystery (ˈmɪstərɪ) *n* **1** something that cannot be or has not been explained. **2** a puzzling or secretive quality. **3** a work of fiction dealing with the solving of a puzzling crime. **4** (in religion) a truth beyond the powers of human understanding. **mysterious** *adj* **mysteriously** *adv* **mystery tour** a pleasure trip to an unspecified destination. < ultimately Greek *myein* to be closed.
mystic (ˈmɪstɪk) *adj* **1** also **mystical** with symbolical or spiritual meaning or value. **2** of mystics or mysticism. **3** puzzling; enigmatic. **4** inspiring awe or wonder.
• *n* someone who seeks union with God through direct personal experience and self-surrender. **mysticism** *n* **1** the quality of being a mystic. **2** the occult or supernatural. **mystify** *vb* **mystified; mystifying** baffle; confuse. **mystification** *n* **mystique** *n* an atmosphere of mystery or power surrounding someone; charisma.
myth (mɪθ) *n* **1** a traditional story containing popular beliefs or explanations of events and practices; folk tale. **2** someone or something imaginary. **3** something believed but not backed up by fact. **mythical** *adj* **1** of or described in a myth. **2** made-up; imagined. **mythology** *n* **1** a body of myths, esp. of a particular culture: Greek mythology. **2** the study of myths. **mythological** *adj* **mythologist** *n* < Greek *mythos* tale.
myxomatosis (ˌmɪksəməˈtəʊsɪs) *n* an infectious virus disease of rabbits, usually fatal. < ultimately Greek *myxa* mucus + *-osis* abnormal condition.

N

N. *abbrev* north; northern.

nab (næb) *vb* **nabbed; nabbing** (*informal*) **1** arrest (someone committing a crime). **2** grab; snatch. < perhaps Scandinavian.

nadir (ˈneɪdɪə) *n* **1** the point in the sky directly opposite the zenith and vertically downwards from the observer. **2** the lowest or deepest point. < Arabic *nazīr* opposite.

nag[1] (næg) *n* (*informal*) a horse, esp. old or worn-out. < Middle English *nagge*.

nag[2] *vb* **nagged; nagging 1** scold or find fault with incessantly. **2** cause persistent discomfort or worry to. < probably Scandinavian.

nail (neɪl) *n* **1** a horny layer which covers the upper end of a finger or toe. **2** a small, thin, metal spike driven in by a hammer to fasten or join things together. • *vb* **1** attach or join (as if) with nails. **2** seize; arrest. **nail-brush** *n* a brush for cleaning the finger-nails. **nail-file** *n* a small, flat file for trimming the finger-nails. **nail polish** or **varnish** a quick-drying substance for colouring the finger-nails or making them shiny. < Old English *nægl*.

naïve (naɪˈiːv) *adj* showing inexperience or lack of sophistication. **naïvely** *adv* **naïvety** or **naïveté** *n* < ultimately Latin *nativus* native.

naked (ˈneɪkɪd) *adj* **1** unclothed; bare. **2** with no covering or decoration; exposed: a naked flame. **3** stark; plain: the naked truth. **nakedly** *adv* **nakedness** *n* **with the naked eye** unaided by an optical device. < Old English *nacod*. SEE PANEL.

namby-pamby (ˌnæmbɪˈpæmbɪ) *n, adj* (a person who is) marked by insipidly sentimental tendencies. SEE PANEL.

name (neɪm) *n* **1** a word or term by which someone or something is known or identified. **2** a reputation: She made a name for herself. **3** someone famous. • *vb* **1** give a name to; call. **2** specify the name or names of. **3** appoint; nominate. **4** mention or decide on: name the day. **name-dropping** *n* mentioning famous people as if one is familiar with them in order to impress. **nameless** *adj* **1** with an unknown or no name. **2** anonymous; unmentioned: someone who shall remain nameless. **3** too terrible to be mentioned: nameless terrors. **namely** *adv* that is to say. **namesake** *n* someone or something with the same name as another. **name-tape** *n* a small strip of cloth, etc., attached to a garment, with the name of the owner on it. < Old English *nama*. SEE PANEL.

nancy (ˈnænsɪ) *n* (*informal*) a

naked nude

One of the unspoken principles of language use is that the repetition of words or ideas should be avoided when nothing new is added. For this reason sentences like 'My cat is an animal.' 'The winner came first.' 'Her late husband is dead.' and 'He likes painting naked nudes.' are rarely if ever encountered. Statements of this type provide extreme examples of *tautology*, 'the needless repetition of a word or idea', from the Greek *taut-* 'the same' and *legein* 'to say'.

Tautologous utterances occur in everyday usage all too frequently. Some typical examples are: The scheme is the *brainchild* of Councillor George Metcalfe, *who thought of the idea.*' '*Possible* education shake-up *on the cards.*' 'Work is due to start *shortly in October.*' and 'The explanatory booklet comes *absolutely free* and *without charge.*' Only when such repetition deliberately serves the purpose of emphasis, as in the last example, can it be defended.

namby-pamby

A person with insipidly sentimental tendencies is sometimes referred to as a namby-pamby. This expression derives from the satirical nickname given to Ambrose Philips, 1674–1749, an English poet who pioneered a type of sentimental pastoral verse, which was widely proscribed as being mawkish and vapid. The nickname was coined by the dramatist Henry Carey following the publication of Philips' verses addressed to the children of Lord Carteret.

homosexual or effeminate boy or man. < from the female name *Nancy*.

nanny (ˈnænɪ) *n* **1** a nurse for children. **2** (*children's informal*) grandmother. **nanny-goat** *n* a female goat. < probably baby language.

nap¹ (næp) *n* a short sleep, esp. during the daytime.
• *vb* **napped; napping** have a nap. **catch someone napping** catch someone off guard. < Old English *hnappian*.

nap² *n* raised fibres on the surface of a fabric; pile. < Middle Dutch *noppe*.

nap³ *n* also **napoleon 1** a card-game similar to whist in which the number of tricks expected to be won is declared; declaration of this. **2** risking everything on one chance, esp. in horse-racing.
• *vb* **napped; napping** name a horse as likely to win a race. SEE PANEL.

---

a big name

Name features in a number of expressions, some of them idiomatic, including:

a big name a celebrity: big names in light entertainment.
call someone names to speak abusively to someone; jeer at or taunt.
the name of the game the main purpose: Making a profit is the name of the game.
what's in a name? the character or quality of something is more important than its name. The expression comes from Shakespeare's 'Romeo and Juliet', Act 2, Scene 1:

What's in a name? that which we call a
rose
By any other name would smell as sweet.

---

nap

The card-game similar to whist in which each player names the number of tricks that he or she will take is known as nap or napoleon. The name derives from *Napo*leon Bonaparte, 1769–1821, Emperor of the French from 1804–15. Why the game was named after him remains uncertain.

Napalm (ˈneɪpɑːm) *n* (*Trademark*) a thick liquid of gelled petrol and aluminium soaps, used in incendiary bombs.

nape (neɪp) *n* the back of the neck. < Middle English.

napkin (ˈnæpkɪn) *n* **1** a square piece of linen or paper used to protect clothing or wipe the lips and fingers at meals. **2** a nappy. < Latin *mappa* napkin.

nappy (ˈnæpɪ) *n* a piece of folded cloth or paper worn by babies to absorb or retain their excrement. < *napkin* + *-y*.

narcissus (nɑːˈsɪsəs) *n, pl* **narcissi** one of a group of bulb plants including the daffodil, of which the flowers have spreading segments around a crown. < Greek *narkissos*.

narcosis (nɑːˈkəʊsɪs) *n* stupor or unconsciousness caused by drugs or chemicals. **narcotic** *adj, n* (of) a pain-relieving drug such as heroin or morphine that deadens the senses and is usually addictive. < Greek *narkoun* to benumb.

nark (nɑːk) *n* (*slang*) **1** a police informer. **2** (*chiefly Australian*) someone or something that irritates.
• *vb* (*informal*) **1** irritate. **2** spy for the police. < probably Romany *nak* nose.

narrate (nəˈreɪt) vb recount; tell (a story). **narration** *n* **narrator** *n* **narrative** *adj, n* **1** (of or like) an account, report, or story. **2** (of) the art or technique of narrating. < ultimately Latin *gnarus* knowing.

narrow (ˈnærəʊ) *adj* **1** of little width compared to length. **2** limited in size or range. **3** small-minded; inflexible. **4** barely successful or enough: a narrow escape.
• *vb* make or become narrow or narrower. **narrowly** *adv* **narrowness** *n* **narrow boat** a canal boat usually less than 7 ft wide. **narrow-minded** *adj* bigoted; intolerant. < Old English *nearu*.

nasal (ˈneɪzl̩) *adj* **1** of the nose. **2** (of a sound) made through the nose with the mouth passage blocked. **nasally** *adv* < Latin *nasus* nose.

nasturtium (nəˈstɜːʃəm) *n* one of a group of trailing plants with leaves and bright, trumpet-shaped, spurred flowers, usually orange, yellow, or red. < Latin: a cress, perhaps from *nasus* nose + *torquēre* to twist, SEE PANEL.

nasty (ˈnɑːstɪ) *adj* **1** disagreeable; offensive. **2** mean; spiteful. **3** painful or serious: a nasty cut. **nastily** *adv* **nastiness** *n* **nasty piece of work** (*informal*) someone who is mean or disagreeable. < Middle English.

natal (ˈneɪtl̩) *adj* of or related to one's birth. < ultimately Latin *nasci* to be born.

nation (ˈneɪʃən) *n* a people who have a usually defined territory and government, and share a common language, ancestry, and culture.

national (ˈnæʃənl̩) *adj* of or concerning a nation as a whole.
• *n* a citizen of a particular nation. **nationally** *adv* **national anthem** a patriotic hymn or song adopted by a country. **nationalism** *n* loyalty or devotion to one's country, esp. setting it above all others. **nationalist** *n, adj* **nationalistic** *adj* **nationality** *n* national status or character; citizenship. **nationalize** *vb* cause (business firms, industry, etc.) to change control and ownership from private to government hands. **nationalization** *n* **national park** an area of special interest that is maintained in its natural state. **national service** a period of compulsory service in a country's armed forces. **nation-wide** *adj* covering the whole of a nation. < ultimately Latin *nasci* to be born.

native (ˈneɪtɪv) *adj* **1** built-in or inborn. **2** being born in a particular place; characteristic because of this: one's native tongue. **3** made, grown, or coming from a particular place.
• *n* **1** someone born in a particular place: a native of Scotland. **2** a local inhabitant, esp. non-European. < ultimately Latin *nasci* to be born.

nativity (nəˈtɪvɪtɪ) *n* **1** birth. **2 the Nativity** the birth of Jesus Christ; picture of the manger scene. **Nativity play** a play depicting the circumstances of the birth of Jesus. < Latin *nativus* birth.

NATO (ˈneɪtəʊ) *abbrev* North Atlantic Treaty Organization.

nasturtium

A foreign name can sometimes carry a certain attraction which is lost as soon as the meaning of the name becomes known. Such is the case with nasturtium. This is a Latin word that is thought to derive from *nasus* 'nose' and *torquēre* 'to twist'. In translation, then, the nasturtium is a 'nose-twister', so called after its pungent smell.

natter (ˈnætə) *n, vb* (*informal*) (a) chat; gossip. < probably like the sound.

natty (ˈnætɪ) *adj* stylish; smart. **nattily** *adv* < perhaps obsolete *net* neat.

natural (ˈnætʃərəl) *adj* **1** native; indigenous: natural resources. **2** occurring in accordance with nature: death from natural causes. **3** inborn: a natural talent. **4** expected; unsurprising: the natural course of events. **5** genuine; unaffected: a natural manner. **6** of or produced by nature; wild. **7** unaltered or unrefined: natural rice. **8** (of a musical note) not sharp or flat. **9** related by blood: her natural father.
• *n* **1** someone who seems fitted to something by nature. **2** (in music) a natural note. **naturally** *adv* **naturalness** *n* **natural childbirth** giving birth with no analgesics, but with breathing and relaxing exercises. **natural gas** gas found in the earth's crust, used as a fuel. **natural history** the science of studying animal and plant life. **naturalist** *n* an expert in natural history. **naturalize** *vb* **1** grant full citizenship to (someone born in a foreign country). **2** introduce (a word, custom, etc.) into common use. **3** establish (a plant) in a country where it is not indigenous. **4** make natural. **naturalization** *n* **natural selection** a process resulting in the survival of organisms best adapted to their environment. < Latin *natura* nature.

nature (ˈneɪtʃə) *n* **1** the external world and everything in it. **2** the essential features or qualities of something. **3** a class, kind, or type. **back to nature** returning to a pre-civilized state. **nature study** the study of plants and animals, esp. in schools. **nature trail** a planned walk in the countryside past natural objects of interest. **naturism** *n* practising nudity. **naturist** *n* < ultimately Latin *nasci* to be born.

naught (nɔːt) *n* (*archaic*) nothing; nought. < Old English *nā* no + *wiht* thing.

naughty (ˈnɔːtɪ) *adj* **1** misbehaving; disobedient. **2** slightly obscene; smutty. **naughtily** *adv* **naughtiness** *n* < *naught* + *-y*.

nausea (ˈnɔːzɪə) *n* **1** a state of wanting to vomit; queasiness. **2** repugnance; disgust. **nauseous** *adj* **nauseate** *vb* cause nausea to; repel. < ultimately Greek *nautēs* sailor.

nautical (ˈnɔːtɪkl̩) *adj* of seamen, ships, or navigation. **nautical mile** a unit of distance in sea and air navigation, about 6076 ft (1852 metres). < ultimately Greek *naus* ship.

naval (ˈneɪvl̩) *adj* of ships of war or a navy. < Latin *navis* ship.

nave (neɪv) *n* the main body of a church up to the chancel, without the transepts or aisles. < Latin *navis* ship.

navel (ˈneɪvl̩) *n* **1** a small depression in the middle of the abdomen where the umbilical cord was once attached. **2** a central point. < Old English *nafela.*

navigate (ˈnævɪˌɡeɪt) *vb* **1** sail on, over, or through (a river, sea, etc.). **2** steer or manage the course of (a vehicle, aircraft, or ship). **navigation** *n* **navigator** *n* **navigable** *adj* **1** (of a watercourse or ocean) suitable for sailing on or through. **2** (of ships) capable of being steered and sailed. < Latin *navis* ship + *agere* to drive.

navvy (ˈnævɪ) *n* a labourer, as employed in the digging of roads, railways, canals, etc. < alteration of *navigator* construction worker. SEE PANEL.

navy (ˈneɪvɪ) *n* **1** the warships of a country with their officers, crews, and associated organization. **2** navy blue. **navy blue** *n, adj* deep, dark blue. < Latin *navigare.*

NB *abbrev* (*Latin*) nota bene (note well).

NCO *abbrev* non-commissioned officer.

near (nɪə) *adv* **1** at or to a point not far away in space or time: The date of the exam is getting near. **2** closely; nearly.
• *prep* near to.
• *adj* **1** close in space, time, or degree: in the near future. **2** closely associated or related. **3** being the closer of two or the one on the left: the near-side wheel. **4** narrow; close: a near miss.
• *vb* come or go nearer. **nearness** *n* **nearby** *adj* close by. **near by** not far away. **nearly** *adv* **1** closely: nearly related. **2** just about; not quite. **near-sighted** *adj* short-sighted. **near thing** something which only just misses being a success, failure, disaster, etc. **not nearly** nowhere near. < Old English *nēah* nigh.

neat (niːt) *adj* **1** tidy and clean. **2** skilful; well-judged: a neat answer. **3** not mixed or diluted: neat gin. **neatly** *adv* **neatness** *n* **neaten** *vb* arrange; tidy. < ultimately Latin *nitēre* to shine.

nebula (ˈnɛbjʊlə) *n, pl* **nebulae 1** a body of rarefied gas or dust in space. **2** a galaxy. **nebulous** *adj* unformed; confused: nebulous reasons. < Latin: mist, cloud.

necessary (ˈnɛsəsərɪ) *adj* **1** needed to accomplish something; indispensable. **2** certain; inevitable: draw the necessary conclusions. **necessarily** *adv* **necessaries** *pl n* food, provisions, etc., which are necessary for living. **necessitate** *vb* make necessary or inevitable. **necessitous** *adj* poor; needy. **necessity** *n* **1** the condition of needing something; something needed. **2** fate; inevitability. **3** poverty; destitution. < ultimately Latin *ne-* not + *cedere* to withdraw.

neck (nɛk) *n* **1** the narrow part of the body which connects the head to the shoulders and chest. **2** the flesh of an animal neck as food. **3** the part of a garment covering the neck. **4** a narrow part of something: the neck of a guitar. **5** the length of a horse's head and neck as a measure of its lead in a race.

navvy

An unskilled labourer on a building site is sometimes informally referred to as a navvy. This word derives from *navigator* which was once the name for a labourer involved with excavation or earthworks, especially the digging of a *navigation* or 'canal'. The demanding nature of such work is witnessed in the expression to work like a navvy, meaning 'to work remarkably hard'.

neck and neck

Neck features in a number of idiomatic expressions, including:

a pain in the neck a person or thing that is constantly annoying: 'She's a real pain in the neck!'

break one's neck to make such a great effort that one virtually risks one's life, etc.: I nearly broke my neck trying to get here on time!

get it in the neck to receive a severe reprimand.

in this neck of the woods in this area: If ever you're down in this neck of the woods again, do drop in. The expression originally referred to a remote forest community in America.

neck and neck exactly level, especially in a race. The expression comes from horse-racing.

risk one's neck to risk losing one's own life, all one's possessions, etc.

• *vb* (*informal*) (of couples) kiss and caress passionately. **neckband** *n* a band around the neck of a garment. **necklace** *n* an ornamental chain of jewels, beads, etc., worn around the neck. **neckline** *n* the shape or position of the upper edge of a garment: a plunging neckline. **necktie** *n* a tie. < Old English *hnecca.* SEE PANEL.

necromancy (ˈnɛkrəˌmænsɪ) *n* **1** the art of communicating with the dead in order to predict or influence future events. **2** magic; witchcraft. **necromancer** *n* < Greek *nekr-* black + *manteia* divination.

nectar (ˈnɛktə) *n* **1** the drink of the gods in classical mythology. **2** a delicious drink. **3** a sweet liquid secreted by various plants and used by bees to make honey. < Greek *nektar.*

nectarine (ˈnɛktəriːn) *n* a variety of firm-bodied peach with a smooth skin. < obsolete *nectarine* like nectar.

née (neɪ) *adj* born; used to give the maiden name of a married woman: Mrs Thomson, née Jones. < French, ultimately from Latin *nasci* to be born.

need (niːd) *n* **1** a reason; something required: There's no need to wait. **2** something necessary for life or well-being. **3** poverty; destitution. **4** a state requiring help or relief: in dire need.
• *vb* **1** be in want of; require. **2** be obliged to; find it necessary to: Need I ask? **if need be** if required. **needful** *adj* required; essential. **needless** *adj* not required; unnecessary. **needlessly** *adv* **needs** *adv* necessarily: if needs must. **needy** *adj* poor; in want .< Old English *nēd.* SEE PANEL AT **DARE.**

needle (ˈniːdl̩) *n* **1** a small, thin, steel instrument, pointed at one end and with a hole for thread at the other, used for sewing. **2** any similar object without a hole: knitting-needle; pine needle. **3** a thin, pointed object like a needle in shape, such as a rocky pinnacle or an obelisk: Cleopatra's needle. **4** a pointer on a dial, as on a compass or gauge.
• *vb* provoke; irritate. **needlecraft** *n* the skill or practice of needlework. **needlewoman** *n* a woman skilled in needlework. **needlework** *n* embroidery or sewing. < Old English *nǣdl.*

nefarious (nɪˈfɛərɪəs) *adj* evil; wicked. **nefariously** *adv* < Latin *ne-* not + *fas* divine law.

negate (nɪˈgeɪt) *n* cancel out or refute. **negation** *n* < Latin *negare* to deny, say no.

negative (ˈnɛgətɪv) *adj* **1** indicating denial or refusal. **2** lacking positive features; pessimistic: a negative outlook. **3** (of numbers) minus; less than zero. **4** (of an electric charge) having electrons to excess. **5** (of photographic images) having the dark and light parts reversed, or colours replaced by complementary ones.
• *n* **1** a refusal, denial, or negation. **2** a negative photograph, from which prints are taken.
• *vb* **1** reject; veto. **2** contradict; disprove. **negatively** *adv*

neglect (nɪˈglɛkt) *vb* **1** disregard; ignore. **2** forget or omit to do something.
• *n* neglecting; being neglected. **neglectful** *adj* **negligence** *n* carelessness, forgetfulness. **negligent** *adj* **negligently** *adv* **negligible** *adj* trivial; insignificant. < ultimately Latin *nec-* not + *legere* to gather.

négligé (ˈnɛglɪˌʒeɪ) *n* a flimsy, decorative dressing-gown worn by a woman. < Latin *neglegere* to neglect.

negotiate (nɪˈgəʊʃɪˌeɪt) *vb* **1** discuss in order to reach a settlement or agreement. **2** (of cheques, bonds, etc.) turn into cash or equivalent value. **3** succeed in getting round, through, or over (an obstacle or difficulty). **negotiation** *n* **negotiator** *n* **negotiable** *adj* **1** able to be discussed: The salary is negotiable. **2** (of cheques) convertible; transferable. **3** able to be got round or through. < Latin *neg-* not + *otium* leisure.

Negro (ˈniːgrəʊ) *n, pl* **Negroes** a member of the black-skinned race of mankind, esp. of African descent. **Negroid** *adj* **Negress** *n* a female Negro. < Spanish or Portuguese, from Latin *niger* black.

neigh (neɪ) *vb, n* (utter) the prolonged, high-pitched cry of a horse. < Old English *hnǣgan.*

neighbour (ˈneɪbə) *n* **1** someone living near or next to another; something situated near another thing. **2** a fellow human: love thy neighbour. **neighbourhood** *n* **1** the immediate surroundings; district. **2** the people who live in this. **3** the area around a point: in the neighbourhood of £150. **neighbouring** *adj* nearby. **neighbourly** *adj* sociable; kind. **neighbourliness** *n* < Old English *nēahgebūr.*

neither (ˈnaɪðə, ˈniːðə) *determiner, pron* not one or the other of two: Neither of them speaks English.
• *adv, conj* **1** not either: He neither smoked nor drank. **2** nor; also not: She didn't go and neither did I. **be neither here nor there** be irrelevant or unimportant. < Old English *nā* not + *hwæther* which of

two. SEE PANEL.

nemesis (ˈnɛmɪsɪs) *n* a downfall; retribution. < ultimately Greek *nemein* to distribute.

neo- *prefix* new, recent, or modern in form. < Greek *neos* new.

neo-classical (ˌniːəʊˈklæsɪkḷ) *adj* based on or influenced by a classical style in art, literature, or music.

neolithic (ˌniːəˈlɪθɪk) *adj* of the later Stone Age.< Greek *neos* + *lithos* stone.

neologism (niːˈɒləˌdʒɪzəm) *n* a newly-coined word or expression. < Greek *neos* new + *logos* word.

neon (ˈniːɒn) *n* one of the inert gases, used in lighting because of its glow when electric current is passed through it. < Greek *neos* new.

nephew (ˈnɛfjuː) *n* the son of one's brother or sister. < Latin *nepos.*

nepotism (ˈnɛpəˌtɪzəm) *n* favouritism shown to relatives or close friends, esp. in appointing them to jobs.

nerve (nɜːv) *n* **1** a fibre or group of fibres in the body that transmit impulses and sensations to the brain. **2** determination; bravery: He lost his nerve. **3** (*informal*) cheek; impudence.
• *vb* fortify (oneself) with courage; brace (oneself). **get on someone's nerves** annoy someone. **nerve-centre** *n* a controlling centre. **nerveless** *adj* **1** lacking strength or energy. **2** cool and calm. **nerve-racking** *adj* stressful; tense. **nerves** *pl n* anxiety; apprehension. **nervous** *adj* **1** of or relating to nerves or the nervous system. **2** edgy; excitable. **3** uneasy; timid: nervous laughter. **nervously** *adv* **nervousness** *n* **nervous breakdown** a mental and emotional collapse. **nervous system** the brain, spinal cord, and nerve tissue in the body. **nervy** *adj* restless; on edge. < Latin *nervus.*

nest (nɛst) *n* **1** a structure made by a bird for laying its eggs and protecting its young. **2** a similar structure made by other creatures, such as ants, wasps, or mice. **3** somewhere to rest in or retreat to; den. **4** a set of objects designed to fit closely or one inside the other.
• *vb* make or live in a nest. **nest-egg** *n* an amount of money saved for the future. < Old English.

nestle (ˈnɛsḷ) *vb* **1** settle in or curl up comfortably. **2** lie in a sheltered position. **nestling** *n* a bird that is not yet old enough to leave the nest. < Old English *nest.*

net[1] (nɛt) *n* **1** an open-work fabric of rope, wire, etc., joined at regular intervals; mesh. **2** a device made of this, used for a specific purpose, such as dividing a tennis court or catching fish.
• *vb* **netted; netting 1** cover or surround with or as if with a net. **2** catch or trap with or as if with a net. **netball** *n* a team-game played on a hard court in which goals are scored by throwing a ball so that it falls through a horizontal ring on a high post. **netting** *n* netted fabric; mesh. **network** *n* **1** a system or pattern of lines that cross each other at regular intervals. **2** any interconnected system, chain, or group of people: a television network. < Old English *nett.*

net[2] *adj* **1** remaining after all deductions, such as taxes or outlays have been made: net profit. **2** final; conclusive: net result.
• *vb* **netted; netting** bring in or gain as a net profit. < Middle French: clean.

nether (ˈnɛðə) *adj* situated below or underground: the nether regions. **nethermost** *adj* < Old English *nither* down.

nettle (ˈnɛtḷ) *n* one of a group of common wild plants whose leaves are covered with stinging hairs; any plant like this.
• *vb* annoy; provoke. **nettle-rash** *n* red patches appearing on the skin like those made by nettle stings. < Old English *netel.*

neural (ˈnjʊərəl) *adj* of or affecting the nerves. **neuralgia** *n* sharp spasms of pain travelling along the course of a nerve, usually in the face or head. **neuralgic** *adj* < Greek neuron nerve.

neurology (njʊˈrɒlədʒɪ) *n* the study of the nervous system and its diseases. **neurological** *adj* **neurologist** *n*

neurosis (njʊˈrəʊsɪs) *n, pl* **neuroses** a nervous disorder characterized by phobias, obsessions, or depressions.

neither is ... or neither are ...?

The general rule is that the number of the verb depends on whether the immediately preceding noun is singular or plural: Neither my uncle nor my aunts *are* coming—aunts is plural and so the verb is plural. Neither my uncle nor my aunt *is* coming—aunt is singular, and so the verb is singular. In informal usage, however, a plural verb is often preferred: Neither my uncle nor my aunt *are* coming.

neurotic *adj, n* (someone) affected by or subject to neurosis. **neurotically** *adv* < New Latin *neuron* nerve + Greek *-osis* abnormal condition.

neuter (ˈnjuːtə) *adj* **1** (of nouns) neither masculine nor feminine. **2** lacking or having non-functional sexual parts.
• *n* **1** a word of neuter gender. **2** a neuter plant or animal; castrated animal.
• *vb* doctor; castrate. < ultimately Latin *ne-* not + *uter* which of two.

neutral (ˈnjuːtrəl) *adj* **1** not participating on either side in an argument, conflict, etc. **2** with no particular distinguishing parts; indifferent. **3** colourless; dull.
• *n* **1** a country or person that is neutral. **2** the position of the gear-stick when the gears are not engaged. **3** a neutral colour. **neutrality** *n* **neutrally** *adv* **neutralize** *vb* cancel the effect of with an opposite force or action. **neutralization** *n*

neutron (ˈnjuːtrɒn) *n* a particle without electric charge, present in the nuclei of all atoms except normal hydrogen. **neutron bomb** a nuclear bomb that produces high levels of radiation but relatively little blast. < probably *neutral*.

never (ˈnɛvə) *adv* **1** at no time; not ever. **2** under no conditions: That will never do.
• *interj* surely not: 'So I told him straight.' Never!' **never mind** don't worry about (something). **nevermore** *adv* never again. **nevertheless** even so; yet. **the never-never** *n* (*informal*) hire-purchase. < Old English *ne-* not + *ǣfre* ever.

new (njuː) *adj* **1** recently made or brought into existence. **2** recently discovered or recognized: the new liberalism. **3** having just recently become: the new boss. **4** unfamiliar; fresh: I'm new to this area. **5** changed; refreshed: She felt a new woman.
• *adv* newly; just: a new-born baby. **newcomer** *n* someone who has just arrived. **newfangled** *adj* (*derogatory*) modern and overcomplicated or gimmicky. **newly** *adv* just; recently: a newly-wed couple. **new moon** the phase of the moon when its dark side faces the earth. **new year** the first days of January. **New Year's Day** 1 January. **New Year's Eve** 31 December. < Old English *nīwe*.

news (njuːz) *n* **1** current events, esp. interesting or noteworthy; written or broadcast report of these. **2** interesting or previously unknown information: That's news to me. **newsagent** *n* a shopkeeper who sells newspapers and magazines. **newscast** *n* broadcast news. **newscaster** *n* **newsletter** *n* a printed circular letter containing matters of interest to members of a club or group. **newspaper** *n* **1** a paper published usually daily or weekly containing news, topical articles, advertisements, etc.; organization that publishes this. **2** the paper on which this is printed. **newsprint** *n* a type of cheap paper used for newspapers. **newsreel** *n* a cinema film giving an account of current events. **news-stand** *n* a street-stall for selling newspapers at. **newsvendor** *n* someone who sells newspapers, esp. in the street. **newsworthy** *adj* interesting enough to be reported as news. **newsy** *adj* full of news, esp. gossipy.

newt (njuːt) *n* a small type of salamander that lives on land or in water. < Middle English, incorrect division of *an ewte*. SEE PANEL AT **APRON.**

next (nɛkst) *adj* **1** following immediately in time or order. **2** being closest to something.
• *adv in* the time immediately following.
• *n* the next item, event, or person. **next best** second best. **next door** in the adjacent house or room. **next-door** *adj* **next of kin** one's closest relative. < Old English *nīehst.*

nexus (ˈnɛksəs) *n* a linked group or series. < Latin *nectere* to bind.

NHS *abbrev* National Health Service.

nib (nɪb) *n* the sharpened point of a pen, which comes into contact with the paper. < probably alteration of *neb* snout, tip.

nibble (ˈnɪbl̩) *vb* **1** eat in small bites, esp. carefully or gently. **2** show interest carefully and tentatively.
• *n* **1** a small bite. **2** a very small amount, esp. of food. **nibbler** *n* < origin unknown.

nice (naɪs) *adj* **1** agreeable; good or satisfactory. **2** friendly; likable. **3** fine; delicate: a nice point. **4** (*ironic*) bad; inappropriate: She's a nice one to talk! **niceness** *n* **nicety** *n* **1** exactness. **2** delicacy; subtlety. < ultimately Latin *nescire* not to know. SEE PANEL.

niche (nɪtʃ, niːʃ) *n* **1** a wall recess, esp. for a vase or ornament. **2** an appropriate place or job for someone. < ultimately Latin *nidus* nest. SEE PANEL.

nick (nɪk) *n* **1** a tiny cut or groove. **2** (*slang*) a prison or police station. **3** (*informal*) a state or condition: in good nick.
• *vb* **1** make a tiny cut or groove in. **2** (*slang*) steal. **3** (*slang*) arrest (a criminal). **in the nick of time** only just in time. < probably Middle English,

alteration of *nocke* nock, notch.

nickel (ˈnɪkl) *n* **1** a hard, silvery-white, metallic element, often used in alloys. **2** (*US*) a five-cent piece. **nickel silver** an alloy of copper, zinc, and nickel. < probably German *Kupfernickel* niccolite, from *kupfer* copper + *nickel* goblin.

nickname (ˈnɪkˌneɪm) *n* a name used instead of or as well as someone's proper name, often humorously.
● *vb* give (someone) a nickname. < Middle English *nekename,* incorrect division of *an ekename.* SEE PANEL.

nicotine (ˈnɪkəˌtiːn) *n* a poisonous drug found in tobacco. < Jean *Nicot,* died 1600, French diplomat. SEE PANEL.

niece (niːs) *n* the daughter of one's brother or sister. < Latin *neptis.*

niggardly (ˈnɪgədlɪ) *adj* miserly. < Scandinavian.

nigger (ˈnɪgə) *n* (*offensive*) a Negro; someone dark-skinned. **a nigger in the woodpile** a hidden snag. < ultimately Latin *niger* black.

niggle (ˈnɪgl) *vb* **1** fuss over trivia. **2** annoy slightly; bother; rankle. < origin unknown.

nigh (naɪ) *adv, prep* near; almost: It's nigh on ten years since she went. < Old English *nēah.*

night (naɪt) *n* **1** the period of darkness between sunset and sunrise. **2** an evening or night characterized by a special purpose. **make a night of it**

nice and warm

What exactly does the word nice mean in the expression 'I'm nice and warm'? Clearly the expression cannot be interpreted literally, i.e. 'I am nice and I am warm'.

Nice and warm is an example of something called *hendiadys.* This is a figure of speech, rarely encountered outside poetry, in which a single concept (for example 'comfortably warm') is expressed by two elements (nice, warm) that are joined by a conjunction (and). By being joined with and the two elements seem to be of equal status and independent of each other, although our understanding of the expression tells us that they are not.

There can be few words with roots longer or more twisted than the word nice. Now used to express general approval, nice can be traced back to the Latin *nescius,* 'ignorant', a meaning associated with disapproval. It wasn't until the 13th century that the word first appeared in English. Very soon the original Latin sense began to shift and by the 14th century it meant not 'ignorant' but 'silly', 'simple', or 'foolish'. Also, a secondary meaning emerged: a woman considered 'foolish' for letting her favours be won too readily was held to be 'wanton' or 'promiscuous'.

From this meaning there developed during the 15th century, for reasons unestablished, the sense 'coy' or 'shy'. By the time we reach the reign of Elizabeth I, 'coy' had come to mean 'fastidious', or 'subtle', the latter being a sense that we recognize today in phrases such as a nice point and a nice distinction. It wasn't until the 18th century, however, that the word assumed its primary modern application.

niche or nook?

These two words are sometimes confused.

A niche is a recess in a wall, as for a vase or other ornament. Niche is also used to refer to a position or activity that is highly suitable for someone or something: She's found her *niche* in life at last; a *niche* in the market for the new product.

A nook is a partly-hidden or sheltered place or corner. The word mostly occurs in the expression every nook and cranny, a cranny being a small crack or crevice: We searched *every nook and cranny* for the key.

nickname

A nickname is a name that is often used informally in place of a person's proper name: On account of his ruddy complexion, he got the *nickname* Beetroot. The word nickname derives from the Middle English *nekename.* Previous to this the form had been *ekename*—the initial *n* appeared as a result of people mistakenly hearing *an ekename* as *a nekename.* (See also panel at **apron.**) *Ekename* or 'additional name' was a simple compound of *eke* 'also' and *name* 'name'.

celebrate all or most of the night. **night and day** all the time. **night-cap** *n* **1** a soft, warm cap worn in bed. **2** a drink taken just before bedtime. **night-clothes** *pl n* garments worn in bed. **night-club** *n* a club open at night and usually providing entertainment, food, drink, etc. **nightdress, nightgown,** or **nightie** *n* a loose garment worn in bed by a woman or child. **nightfall** *n* dusk; twilight. **night-life** *n* entertainment or social life in the late evening. **night-light** *n* a faint light kept burning all night, esp. in a child's bedroom. **nightly** *adj, adv* (taking place) at night or every night. **nightmare** *n* **1** a frightening dream. **2** a terrible experience. **night-marish** *adj* **night safe** a receptacle where money, etc., can be deposited when the banks are closed. **nightshade** *n* one of a group of several, esp. poisonous plants. **nightshirt** *n* a long shirt worn in bed usually by a man or child. **night-watchman** *n* someone employed to watch over (a building) at night. < Old English *niht.* SEE PANEL.

nightingale (ˈnaɪtɪŋˌgeɪl) *n* a type of brown European thrush, noted for the sweet song of the male. < Old English *niht* night + *galan* to sing.

nil (nɪl) *n* zero; nothing. < Old Latin *ne-* not + *hilum* trifle.

nimble (ˈnɪmbl̩) *adj* **1** quick-moving; agile. **2** quick-witted. **nimbly** *adv* < Old English *niman* to take.

nincompoop (ˈnɪnkəmˌpuːp) *n* an idiot; simpleton. < origin unknown. SEE PANEL.

nine (naɪn) *determiner, pron* 9 in number.
• *n* the number 9. **dressed up to the nines** dressed elaborately or in special clothes. **nine days' wonder** a short-lived sensation. **ninepins** *n* skittles. < Old English *nigon.*

nineteen (ˌnaɪnˈtiːn) *determiner, pron* 19 in number.

night

The unpredictability of language is nicely illustrated in the following set of time expressions. A speaker wishing to refer to an event that occurred on the previous day could say: yesterday morning or yesterday lunchtime or yesterday afternoon or yesterday evening but *not* yesterday night. For some mysterious reason yesterday may be used with each of the nouns except night.

It would be quite reasonable to expect tomorrow to behave in the same way. However, it is unwise to look for too much logic and symmetry in language: tomorrow morning, tomorrow lunchtime, tomorrow afternoon, tomorrow evening, *and* tomorrow night are all acceptable.

nicotine

The name of the principal drug in tobacco, nicotine, owes its origin to Jean *Nicot,* 1530–1600, a French diplomat and scholar. Nicot became informed of the existence of tobacco in 1560 while serving in Lisbon as French ambassador to Portugal. Within no time at all the first cargo of New World tobacco was being unloaded in Paris, where it became very popular amongst fashionable society. In recognition of Nicot's services, the tobacco plant was called *herba nicotiana,* and for the next 150 years or so the words tobacco and nicotine were synonymous. It was only during the 19th century that the latter's meaning narrowed to its modern sense.

nincompoop

Nincompoop, 'a foolish or silly person', and skivvy 'a female domestic servant' are members of a large group of words whose origin finally remains a mystery. A characteristic of these 'mystery' words is that they tend to be informal. Others include:

ballyhoo	**peter out**	**scrap** (in the sense 'fight')
dingy	**phoney**	**scrawl**
fuzz (slang for 'police')	**pimp**	**scrawny**
G-string	**podgy**	**slog**
lush (a heavy drinker)	**pong**	**stash**
nicker (slang for '£1')	**quandary**	**turmoil**
	ricochet	
	scallywag	
	scoundrel	

• *n* the number 19. **nineteenth** *determiner, pron, n, adv* **talk nineteen to the dozen** talk fast and continually. < Old English *nigontēne.*

ninety (ˈnaɪntɪ) *determiner, pron* 90 in number.
• *n* the number 90. **ninetieth** *determiner, pron, n, adv* **nineties** *pl n* between 90 and 99 in years, numbers, or degrees of temperature. < Old English *nigontig.*

ninny (ˈnɪnɪ) *n* someone who is silly or stupid. < perhaps *an innocent.*

ninth (naɪnθ) *determiner, pron, adv* next after eighth.
• *n* **1** something that is ninth. **2** one of nine equal parts of a thing. **ninthly** *adv*

nip[1] (nɪp) *vb* **nipped; nipping 1** squeeze, pinch, or bite sharply; cut off in this way. **2** harm or numb with cold. **3** (*informal*) go; hurry: He's just nipped out.
• *n* **1** a squeeze, pinch, or bite. **2** a sharp chill in the air. **nipper** *n* **1** (*informal*) a child. **2** the large, pincer-like claw of a crab, lobster, etc. **nippers** *pl n* an instrument for gripping, pinching, or clipping. **nippy** *adj* **1** quick; agile. **2** sharply cold. < Middle English *nippen.*

nip[2] *vb, n* (take) a small drink or measure of spirits. < probably *nipperkin* small liquor container.

nipple (ˈnɪpl̩) *n* **1** the small protrusion of the mammary gland from which milk is secreted in a female mammal. **2** the artificial teat on a baby's feeding bottle. **3** something resembling a nipple, such as a device for oiling or greasing machine parts. < earlier *neble, nible* small nib.

nirvana (nɪəˈvɑːnə, nɜːˈvɑːnə) *n* (in Buddhism and Hinduism) the state of release from the cycle of reincarnation, reached by becoming free of all desire and sense of individuality. < Sanskrit *nirvāṇa* extinguishing, from *nis-* out + *vāti* it blows.

Nissen hut (ˈnɪsn̩) a prefabricated hut with an arched roof of corrugated iron and a cement floor. < Peter *Nissen,* died 1930, British mining engineer. SEE PANEL.

nit (nɪt) *n* **1** a parasitic insect such as a louse; its egg. **2** (*informal*) a fool. **nit-picking** *n* trivial criticism. < Old English *hnitu.*

nitrate (ˈnaɪtreɪt) *n* **1** an ester or salt of nitric acid. **2** sodium nitrate or potassium nitrate, used as a fertilizer.

nitric (ˈnaɪtrɪk) *adj* of or containing nitrogen. **nitric acid** a colourless, corrosive liquid, used esp. in making fertilizers and explosives. < ultimately Greek *nitron.*

nitrogen (ˈnaɪtrədʒən) *n* a gaseous element without smell or colour that constitutes about 78% of the atmosphere and is present in compounds in all living things. **nitrogenous** *adj*

nitro-glycerine (ˌnaɪtrəʊˈglɪsərɪn) *n* a highly explosive liquid used in making dynamite, and in medicine to dilate blood-vessels. < Greek *nitron* + *glykeros* sweet.

nitrous (ˈnaɪtrəs) *adj* of or containing nitrogen. **nitrous oxide** a gas used as a general anaesthetic; laughing-gas.

nitty-gritty (ˌnɪtɪˈgrɪtɪ) *n* (*informal*) the essence of a matter; basics. < origin unknown.

nitwit (ˈnɪtˌwɪt) *n* (*informal*) someone foolish or scatty. < probably German dialect *nit* not + English *wit.* SEE PANEL AT TWIT.

no (nəʊ) *determiner* **1** not any. **2** hardly any. **3** not a; quite other than a: He's no youngster.
• *adv* **1** used to deny, refuse, or disagree. **2** in no degree: no worse than before. **3** used to express incredulity or amazement.
• *n, pl* **noes** a vote or reply in the negative. **no one** not anyone; nobody. < Old English *ne* not + *ā* always. SEE PANEL.

No. or **no.** *abbrev* number.

nob[1] (nɒb) *n* (*informal*) someone's head. < probably alteration of *knob.*

nob[2] *n* (*informal*) someone wealthy or of high rank. < perhaps *nob*[1].

nobble (ˈnɒbl̩) *vb* **1** disable or weaken (esp. a racehorse) by drugging. **2** (*infor-*

Nissen hut

A prefabricated shelter with the shape of a giant oil drum that has been sliced down the middle and laid on its side is known as a Nissen hut. Originally used for military purposes, the hut takes its name from its designer, Lt. Col. Peter *Nissen*, 1871–1930, a British mining engineer.

In America the equivalent structure is known as a Quonset hut, after *Quonset* Point, Rhode Island, where they were first manufactured. Like the Nissen hut, this has a cement floor, while the main walls and roof are made of rounded corrugated iron sheeting.

mal) win over or get hold of dishonestly. < perhaps *nab*.

noble (ˈnəʊbḷ) *adj* **1** of high birth or rank; aristocratic. **2** worthy or honourable. **3** grand or imposing; excellent.
• *n* someone of high birth or rank. **nobleman** fem. **noblewoman** *n* **nobleness** *n* **nobly** *adv* **nobility** *n* **1** dignity, honour, or excellence. **2 the nobility** the aristocracy. < ultimately Latin *noscere* to know.

nobody (ˈnəʊbədɪ) *pron* not anybody.
• *n* someone of no importance or with no authority. **like nobody's business** with great intensity or enthusiasm.

nocturnal (nɒkˈtɜːnḷ) *adj* **1** of or happening in the night. **2** active in the night: nocturnal animals. **nocturne** *n* an artistic work dealing with night, esp. a dreamy piece of piano music. < ultimately Latin *nox* night.

nod (nɒd) *vb* **nodded; nodding 1** quickly move (the head) down then up again in greeting or to show agreement. **2** allow the head to fall forward through sleepiness. **3 nod off** (*informal*) fall asleep.
• *n* **1** a nodding movement. **2** a signal of agreement or approval: get the nod. **a nodding acquaintance** a slight knowledge of. < Middle English *nodden*.

node (nəʊd) *n* **1** a small bump or swelling. **2** a point on a plant stem where leaves or buds grow out. < Latin *nodus*.

nodule (ˈnɒdjuːl) *n* a small, rounded lump, knot, or node. **nodular** *adj* < Latin *nodulus* small node.

noggin (ˈnɒgɪn) *n* **1** a small measure of spirits, usually ¼ pint. **2** (*slang*) the head. < origin unknown.

noise (nɔɪz) *n* a sound or mixture of esp. unconnected, harsh, or unwanted sounds.
• *vb* make generally known: It was noised abroad. **noiseless** *adj* **noisy** *adj* loud, esp. unpleasantly. **noisiness** *n* < ultimately Latin *nausea* nausea.

nomad (ˈnəʊmæd) *n* **1** a member of a tribe that wanders, seeking pasture for its animals within a usually defined area. **2** someone who wanders aimlessly. **nomadic** *adj* < ultimately Greek *nemein* to pasture.

nom de plume (ˌnɒm də ˈpluːm) an author's pseudonym; pen-name. < French: name of pen.

nomenclature (nəʊˈmɛnklətʃə) *n* a system of terms or names, used in a particular art, science, or discipline. < Latin *nomen* name + *calare* to call.

nominal (ˈnɒmɪnḷ) *adj* **1** in name only; titular: a nominal head of State. **2** insignificant; token: a nominal charge. **nominally** *adv* **nominal value** face value. < Latin *nomen* name.

nominate (ˈnɒmɪˌneɪt) *vb* **1** recommend or propose (for a reward or appointment). **2** specify (a place, time, etc.). **nomination** *n* **nominator** *n* **nominee** *n* someone who is nominated.

non- *prefix* not: non-vocational. < Old Latin *ne*- not + *oinos* one.

non-aligned (ˌnɒnəˈlaɪnd) *adj* not aligned with any group of nations, esp. the superpowers. **non-alignment** *n*

nonchalant (ˈnɒnʃələnt) *adj* cool and casual; indifferent. **nonchalance** *n* **nonchalantly** *adv* < ultimately Latin *non*- + *calēre* to be warm.

non-combatant (nɒnˈkɒmbətənt) *n* **1** a civilian in wartime. **2** an army doctor, chaplain, etc., whose duties do not include fighting.

non-commissioned (ˌnɒnkəˈmɪʃənd) *adj* of officers in the armed forces not holding a commission.

non-committal (ˌnɒnkəˈmɪtḷ) *adj* not revealing any particular attitude or opinion.

non compos mentis (nɒn ˌkɒmpəs ˈmɛntɪs) of unsound mind. < Latin:

---

no way

No features in a number of expressions, many of them idiomatic, including:

no-ball *n* a delivery of the ball in cricket that is disallowed by the rules.
no-claims bonus a reduction in an insurance premium when no claims have been made in a given period.
no fear certainly not.
no-go *adj* (of a district) having access prohibited to certain groups: a no-go area.
no man's land 1 the area separating the lines of two opposing armies. **2** disputed or unowned land. **3** a condition or sphere of uncertainty and confusion; between two points: the uneasy no man's land between factual statements and personal opinions.
no way under no circumstances; not at all: 'After the way she's treated me, no way will I ever help her again!' replied Olivia.

---

not having control of one's mind.

non-conformist (ˌnɒnkən'fɔːmɪst) *n* **1** someone who is unconventional in behaviour or ideas. **2 Nonconformist** a member of a Protestant grouping that does not conform to the doctrines of the Church of England.

nondescript ('nɒndɪˌskrɪpt) *adj* with no outstanding features; unmemorable. • *n* someone or something that is unremarkable. < *non-* + Latin *describere* to describe.

none (nʌn) *pron* **1** not any. **2** no one; nobody. • *adv* not at all; to no extent: She's none too happy. **none other** no one else. **none the less** in spite of that. < Old English *ne* not + *ān* one. SEE PANEL.

nonentity (nɒ'nɛntɪtɪ) *n* someone or something of no importance.

non-event (ˌnɒnɪ'vɛnt) *n* an event that is expected to have significance but disappoints.

non-existent (ˌnɒnɪg'zɪstənt) *adj* not in existence. **non-existence** *n*

non-fiction (nɒn'fɪkʃən) *n* literature dealing with facts, events, etc., rather than imaginary narrative.

non-flammable (nɒn'flæməbl̩) *adj* not capable of catching fire.

non-intervention (ˌnɒnɪntə'vɛnʃən) *n* the policy of not joining in the disputes of others.

nonplussed (nɒn'plʌst) *adj* completely baffled or confused. < Latin *non plus* no further.

non-resident (nɒn'rɛzɪdənt) *n, adj* (someone) not living or staying in a specified place, esp. a hotel.

nonsense ('nɒnsəns) *n* foolish or meaningless talk, ideas, or conduct. • *interj* used to express strong disagreement. **nonsensical** *adj* **nonsensically** *adv*

non sequitur (ˌnɒn 'sɛkwɪtə) a statement or conclusion that does not logically follow from previous statements or evidence. < Latin: it does not follow.

non-smoker (nɒn'sməʊkə) *n* **1** someone who does not smoke. **2** a compartment in a train in which smoking is not allowed.

non-starter (ˌnɒn'stɑːtə) *n* **1** a horse that does not run in a race although it has been entered. **2** someone or something that is bound to fail or prove useless.

non-stick (ˌnɒn'stɪk) *adj* (of saucepans, etc.) coated with a substance that stops food sticking to it when cooking.

non-stop (ˌnɒn'stɒp) *adj* **1** (of aircraft, trains, buses, etc.) not stopping en route to an ultimate destination. **2** never-ending. • *adv* constantly.

non-U (nɒn'juː) *adj* not characteristic of the upper classes, esp. in speech or conduct.

noodles ('nuːdl̩z) *pl n* narrow strips of pasta often made with egg and eaten with soups, sauces, etc. < German *Nudel*.

nook (nʊk) *n* a partly-hidden or sheltered place or corner; alcove. < Middle English *nok*. SEE PANEL AT **NICHE**.

noon (nuːn) *n* 12 o'clock in the daytime; middle of the day. **noonday** *adj* < ultimately Latin *nonus* ninth.

noose (nuːs) *n* a loop of rope or cord secured by a slipknot that tightens when pulled. < Latin *nodus* knot.

nor (nə; *stressed* nɔː) *conj* also not: He neither knew nor cared. < Middle English *nother* neither.

norm (nɔːm) *n* **1** a standard or level of behaviour, achievement, etc., taken as a model. **2** an average level of performance, productivity, etc. **normal** *adj* **1** ordinary; usual. **2** mentally well-adjusted. **normality** *n* **normally** *adv* **normalize** *vb* make or become normal. **normalization** *n* < Latin *norma* carpenter's square.

north (nɔːθ) *n* the point or direction to the left of a person facing east. • *adj, adv* **1** in, towards, or facing the north. **2** (of the wind) from the north. **the north** often also **the North** land lying in or towards the north. **north-east** *n* the point or direction midway between north and east. **northerly** *adj* **1** in or towards the north. **2** (of the wind) from the north. **northern** *adj* of or in the north. **northerner** *n* a native or inhabitant of the north. **northernmost** *adj* furthest north. **North Pole** the northernmost point of the earth. **northward,**

none is ... or none are ...?

When none refers to a plural countable noun, it may be followed by a singular or plural verb, depending on the sense. When none means 'not one', it tends to be followed by a singular verb: I bought three different types of lock but none *was* suitable. When none means 'not any', it tends to be followed by a plural verb: I've tried all the telephones but none *are* working.

northwards *adj, adv* towards the north. **north-west** *n* the point or direction midway between north and west. < Old English.

Nos. or **nos.** *abbrev* numbers.

nose (nəʊz) *n* **1** the organ used for breathing and smelling in humans and animals, projecting from the middle front part of the head and including the nostrils. **2** the sense of smell. **3** anything resembling a nose in position, shape, or function, such as a spout or nozzle. **4** an instinct or skill for discovering things. • *vb* **1** search or discover (as if) by smell. **2** touch or rub with the nose; nuzzle. **3** also **nose into** pry; interfere in. **4** push forward cautiously. **nosebag** *n* a bag hung over a horse's head for it to feed from. **nosebleed** *n* bleeding from the nose. **nosedive** *n* **1** a steep, downward plunge of an aircraft with the nose first. **2** a sudden, drastic fall or drop. **nosey** *adj* (*informal*) overly curious. **nosily** *adv* **nosiness** *n* **Nosey Parker** (*informal*) someone who is excessively curious. < Old English *nosu*.
SEE PANEL.

nosh (nɒʃ) *vb, n* (*slang*) (eat) food. **nosh-up** *n* (*slang*) a meal, esp. a large one. < Yiddish.

nostalgia (nɒˈstældʒə) *n* a sentimental longing for or remembrance of things past. **nostalgic** *adj* **nostalgically** *adv* < Greek *nostos* return home + New Latin *-algia* pain.

nostril (ˈnɒstrɪl) *n* one of the two openings of the nose through which air is breathed. < Old English *nosu* nose + *thyrel* hole.

not (nɒt) *adv* **1** used to express the negation of a word or group of words. **2** used to show denial, negation, or refusal. **not at all** a polite response to thanks or apology. **not half 1** not nearly. **2** (*informal*) absolutely: 'Do you like it?'—'Not half!' < Middle English *naught* nothing.

notable (ˈnəʊtəbl̩) *adj* remarkable; distinguished. • *n* someone who is distinguished; celebrity. **notability** *n* **1** a celebrity. **2** being notable. **notably** *adv* particularly. < Latin *notare* to note.
SEE PANEL.

notation (nəʊˈteɪʃən) *n* particular marks, signs, symbols, etc., used to express quantities or elements in a specialized system, such as music or mathematics.

notch (nɒtʃ) *n* **1** a cut or indentation in a V-shape. **2** step; degree. • *vb* **1** make a notch in. **2 notch up** achieve; score. < Middle English *an otch*, from Middle French *oche*.
SEE PANEL.

note (nəʊt) *n* **1** a musical sound of definite pitch; written sign representing this. **2** a brief explanatory comment (on a passage in a book). **3** a short letter, message, or memorandum. **4** a banknote. **5** a brief summary of something, written down as a reminder. **6** a characteristic sign of attitude or feeling: a note of sarcasm. **7** attention; observation: Take note! **8** fame; eminence: people of note.

pay through the nose

The expression pay through the nose means 'to pay far too much': Why pay through the nose for expensive double glazing when you can try our reliable and inexpensive service? The expression is believed to derive from a poll tax levied upon the Irish by the Danes in the ninth century. Those unfortunates who failed to pay the tax had their noses slit.

notable or **noticeable?**

These two words are sometimes confused.

Notable means 'worthy of note; remarkable or distinguished': a *notable* example, a *notable* exception.

Noticeable means 'clear or obvious': The whining noise is most *noticeable* at high speeds; *noticeable* lines on his face.

notch

In Middle English the word for notch is believed to have been *otch*, a derivative of the Middle French word for 'notch': *oche*. Theory has it that the initial *n* appeared as a result of syllabic merging. In other words *an otch* was probably heard as *a notch*, and with the advent of printing it was the latter form that became established. See also panel at **apron.**

• *vb* **1** write down; record. **2** notice; observe. **notebook** *n* a book for recording notes or memoranda in. **notecase** *n* a wallet. **noted** *adj* renowned; famous. **notelets** *pl n* a set of small, folded cards for writing short messages on. **notepaper** *n* letter-writing paper. **noteworthy** *adj* worthy of notice; remarkable. < Latin *nota* mark.

nothing (ˈnʌθɪŋ) *pron* **1** not anything; no thing. **2** no part or amount: I want nothing to do with it.
• *n* **1** non-existence. **2** someone or something insignificant.
• *adv* in no degree; not all. **nothingness** *n* **for nothing 1** not costing anything; free. **2** without an end result or reward. **nothing doing** (*informal*) used to express failure or refusal. < Old English *nān* no + *thing*.

notice (ˈnəʊtɪs) *n* **1** information about current or future events. **2** a formal notification of the ending of an agreement or employment at a fixed time: He was given a month's notice. **3** regard; attention: It came to my notice. **4** a printed or written public announcement. **5** a printed review (of a play, performance, etc.).
• *vb* **1** comment or remark on. **2** become aware of. **at short notice** with little warning. **noticeable** *adj* clear; obvious. **noticeably** *adv* **notice-board** *n* a board for displaying printed announcements. **take notice** show interest in. < ultimately Latin *noscere* to know. SEE PANEL AT **NOTABLE.**

notify (ˈnəʊtɪˌfaɪ) *vb* **notified; notifying 1** advise; inform. **2** report; announce, esp. officially. **notification** *n* **notifiable** *adj* (of a disease) that must be reported to the health authorities. < Latin *notus* known.

notion (ˈnəʊʃən) *n* **1** a concept or impression. **2** a vague desire or whim. **3** *pl* (*chiefly US*) small articles used in sewing or haberdashery. **notional** *adj* theoretical; assumed. **notionally** *adv* < SEE **NOTICE.**

notorious (nəʊˈtɔːrɪəs) *adj* well-known, esp. in an unfavourable light; infamous. **notoriety** *n*

notwithstanding (ˌnɒtwɪðˈstændɪŋ) *prep* despite; although.
• *adv* yet; nevertheless. < Middle English *not* + *withstonden* to withstand.

nougat (ˈnuːgɑː) *n* a chewy, pink or white sweet containing nuts, dried fruit, etc. < ultimately Latin *nux* nut. SEE PANEL.

nought (nɔːt) *n* **1** the symbol 0. **2** nothing; naught.

noun (naʊn) *n* a word which refers to a person, place, or thing. < Latin *nomen* name.

nourish (ˈnʌrɪʃ) *vb* **1** sustain by feeding. **2** cultivate or entertain (a feeling). **nourishment** *n* < Latin *nutrire*.

nous (naʊs) *n* (*informal*) common sense. < Greek.

novel (ˈnɒvl̩) *n* an extended work of narrative fiction in prose.
• *adj* new and original; different. **novelette** *n* a short novel. **novelist** *n* someone who writes novels. **novelty** *n* **1** being novel; something with this quality. **2** a small, usually cheap ornament or gadget. < Latin *novus* new.

novice (ˈnɒvɪs) *n* **1** a beginner. **2** a probationer in a religious community. < Latin *novicius* new, inexperienced.

now (naʊ) *adv* **1** at the time of speaking or writing. **2** at once; immediately. **3** under the present circumstances. **4** very recently or very soon: She left just now. **5** used to introduce an explanation, point, or change of procedure.
• *conj* seeing that; since: Now we're all together.
• *n* **1** the present time. **2** a time referred to. **for now** until later. **nowadays** *adv* these days. **now and again** or **now and then** on occasion. < Old English *nū*.

nowhere (ˈnəʊwɛə) *adv* not anywhere. **come from nowhere** suddenly appear. **get nowhere** fail to progress or achieve anything.

nowt (naʊt) *n* (*Northern England informal*) nothing. < *naught*.

noxious (ˈnɒkʃəs) *adj* harmful to health or morality. < Latin *noxa* harm.

nozzle (ˈnɒzl̩) *n* a spout or similar projection used on a pipe, etc., to direct or regulate the flow of a liquid. < SEE **NOSE.**

nuance (ˈnjuːɑːns) *n* a subtle shade or distinction in meaning, colour, etc.

nutty nougat

According to the derivation of the word, nougat should always have nuts in it. The word came into English via French and Provençal from the Old Provençal word *nogat*. This in turn derived from *noga* 'a nut', which evolved from the Latin word for 'nut', *nux*.

< ultimately Latin *nubes* cloud.

nub (nʌb) *n* **1** a lump or knob. **2** the central point; core. < probably Low German *knubbe.*

nubile (ˈnjuːbaɪl) *adj* (of a girl) young and desirable; marriageable. < Latin *nubere* to marry.

nucleus (ˈnjuːklɪəs) n, *pl* **nuclei 1** the central part of something around which things gather; basis. **2** the positively-charged core of an atom. **nuclear** *adj* **1** of or being a nucleus. **2** using the nuclear energy of the atom. **nuclear energy** the energy released in a nuclear reaction, when atomic fission or fusion takes place. **nuclear physics** the branch of physics concerned with the behaviour and reactions of the nuclei of atoms. < Latin: kernel, small nut.

nude (njuːd) *adj* naked; unclothed. • *n* a naked human figure in a painting, sculpture, etc. **nudity** *n* **in the nude** naked. **nudism** *n* the belief that going around in the nude is good for the health. **nudist** *n* **nudist camp** a camp where people practise nudism. < Latin *nudus* naked.

nudge (nʌdʒ) *vb* **1** prod or push gently with the elbow, esp. to attract someone's attention. **2** push slowly or lightly. • *n* a nudging movement. < perhaps Scandinavian.

nugget (ˈnʌgɪt) *n* **1** a rough, solid lump of precious metal found naturally in the earth. **2** something small but of value: nuggets of wisdom. < perhaps English dialect *nug* lump.

nuisance (ˈnjuːsəns) *n* someone or something that troubles or irritates. < ultimately Latin *nocēre* to harm.

null (nʌl) *adj* **1** not (legally) valid: null and void. 2 worthless; ineffectual. **nullity** *n* **nullify** *vb* **nullified; nullifying** make null or ineffective; neutralize. **nullification** *n* < Latin *ne-* not + *ullus* any.

numb (nʌm) *adj* deprived of sensation or emotion, usually through cold or shock. • *vb* make numb; paralyse. **numbly** *adv* **numbness** *n* < Old English *niman* to take.

number (ˈnʌmbə) *n* **1** one of a set of symbols or figures used in counting or to designate; numeral. **2** a total amount. **3** a single issue of a published periodical. **4** a song or piece of music, esp. in a musical show. **5** a group of people. **6** (in grammar) the category distinguishing singular and plural. **7** an admired item, esp. a garment: a nice little number in silk. **8** something seen as advantageous: He's on to a good number. • *vb* **1** count; reckon. **2** designate by a number. **3** amount to; total. **number-plate** *n* the registration plate on a motor vehicle. < Latin *numerus.* SEE PANEL.

numeral (ˈnjuːmərəl) *n* a conventional symbol that represents a particular number; figure. **numerical** *adj* of or measured in numbers. **numerous** *adj* many; plentiful. < Latin *numerus.*

numerate (ˈnjuːmərət) *adj* understanding numbers and basic mathematics. **numeracy** *n* **numerator** *n* the number of a fraction written above the line, for example, 2 in $\frac{2}{3}$, showing how many parts of the denominator.

numismatics (ˌnjuːmɪzˈmætɪks) *n* the study or collecting of coins, paper money, medals, etc. **numismatist** *n* < ultimately Greek *nomisma* coin.

nun (nʌn) *n* a member of a religious order of women. **nunnery** *n* a convent where nuns live. < Late Latin *nonna.*

nuptial (ˈnʌpʃəl) *adj* of marriage or the wedding ceremony. **nuptials** *pl n* a wedding. < Latin *nubere* to marry.

nurse (nɜːs) *n* **1** someone skilled in looking after sick or injured people, or helping a doctor in this. **2** a woman employed to look after young children. • *vb* **1** tend (sick or injured people). **2** breast-feed; suckle. **3** handle carefully. **4** keep in mind; harbour: nurse a grudge. **nursemaid** *n* a young woman employed to look after young children. **nursery** *n* **1** a playroom for young

---

a number of people is ... or **a number of people are ...?**

In the sentence A number of people have asked the same question, the subject of the verb is people (modified by the phrase a number of). Since people is plural, the verb is plural.

The structure the number of ... behaves differently. In the sentence The number of deaths remains unchanged, the subject of the verb is number (modified by of deaths). Since number is singular, the verb is singular.

The rule of thumb is that *a* number of ... takes a plural verb, *the* number of ... takes a singular verb.

---

children. **2** a day nursery. **3** a place in which young plants are cultivated and often sold. **nurseryman** *n* one who owns or works in one of these. **nursery rhyme** a simple, traditional rhyme for children, sung or chanted. **nursery school** a school for children between the ages of 2 and 5. **nursery slopes** slopes suitable for beginners at a ski resort. **nursery stakes** a race for two-year-old horses. **nursing home** a private hospital for invalids. < ultimately Latin *nutricius* nourishing.

nurture (ˈnɜːtʃə) *vb* **1** cultivate; tend. **2** bring up; rear.
● *n* **1** food; nourishment. **2** training; development. < ultimately Latin *nutrire* to nourish.

nut (nʌt) *n* **1** a dry fruit or seed with a hard shell surrounding an edible kernel. **2** the kernel of this. **3** a usually hexagonal piece of metal with a central hole, made to be used with a bolt for fastening or tightening. **4** the ridge at the top of the neck of a guitar, violin, etc., over which the strings pass. **5** a small lump (of coal, etc.). **6** (*slang*) someone's head. **7** (*informal*) also **nut-case or nutter** someone who is mad or eccentric. **nut-brown** *adj, n* (of) the colour of ripe hazel-nuts. **nutcrackers** *pl n* an implement like pincers for cracking nuts open. **nuts** *adj* (*informal*) **1** mad; crazy. **2** intensely keen on: He's nuts about cricket. **nutshell** *n* the hard, outer covering of a nut. **in a nutshell** briefly. **nutty** *adj* **1** containing or tasting of nuts. **2** (*slang*) mad; crazy. < Old English *hnutu.*

nutmeg (ˈnʌtmɛg) *n* **1** a tropical tree that produces a fragrant seed. **2** the seed of this, ground and used as a spice. < Old Provençal *noz* nut + *muscat* musky.

nutrient (ˈnjuːtrɪənt) *n, adj* (something) providing nourishment. **nutriment** *n* a nutrient. **nutrition** *n* the process of taking in food; nourishing. **nutritional** *adj* **nutritious** *adj* beneficial; nourishing. **nutritive** *adj* concerning nutrition; nourishing. < Latin *nutrire* to nourish.

nuzzle (ˈnʌzl̩) *vb* **1** to rub or push gently with the nose. **2** snuggle; nestle. < SEE NOSE.

nylon (ˈnaɪlɒn) *n* **1** a tough, elastic, synthetic fibre. **2** *pl* stockings made from nylon. < originally a trademark.

nymph (nɪmf) *n* **1** (in mythology) a nature spirit in the form of a young female. **2** one of various types of immature insects looking like the adult, esp. a dragonfly larva. < Greek *nymphē.*

O

oaf (əʊf) *n* a clumsy idiot. **oafish** *adj* < Scandinavian.
oak (əʊk) *n* one of a group of trees of the beech family, with irregular, lobe-shaped leaves and producing acorns as fruit; its wood. **oaken** *adj* made of oak. < Old English *āc*.
OAP *abbrev* old-age pensioner.
oar (ɔː) *n* **1** a long pole with a broad blade at one end, used to propel and steer a boat. **2** an oarsman. **oarsman** *n* someone who rows. **oarsmanship** *n* rowing skill. **put** or **stick one's oar in** meddle; interfere. < Old English *ār*.
oasis (əʊˈeɪsɪs) *n, pl* **oases 1** a fertile area in a desert. **2** a refuge; sanctuary. < Greek.
oast (əʊst) *n* a kiln for hop-drying. **oast-house** *n* a building that contains this. < Old English *āst*.
oath (əʊθ) *n* **1** a solemn promise to do something or that one is telling the truth, calling upon God or something revered as a witness. **2** casual or disrespectful use of a sacred word; swear-word. **on** or **under oath** having made a solemn promise. < Old English *āth*.
oats (əʊts) *pl n* a tough cereal grass grown as a crop for food; its seed. **oatcake** *n* a thin cake or biscuit made of oatmeal. **oatmeal** *n* **1** meal made from oats, used in making porridge. **2** a greyish-yellow colour. **sow one's wild oats** live adventurously when young, before settling down. < Old English *āte*.
obdurate (ˈɒbdjʊrət) *adj* stubborn; inflexible. **obduracy** *n* < Latin *ob-* against + *durus* hard.
obedient (əˈbiːdɪənt) *adj* willing to do as one is ordered to; submissive. **obedience** *n* **obediently** *adv* < Latin *oboedire* to obey.
obelisk (ˈɒbəlɪsk) *n* a large, upright, tapering pillar, serving as a monument. < ultimately Greek *obelos* pointed pillar.
obese (əʊˈbiːs) *adj* very fat. **obesity** *n* < Latin *ob-* against + *edere* to eat.
obey (əˈbeɪ, əʊˈbeɪ) *vb* do as ordered or laid down by (a person, rule, etc.). < Latin *oboedire*.
obituary (əˈbɪtjʊərɪ) *n* a notice of someone's death, usually in a newspaper and with a short biography. < ultimately Latin *ob-* down + *ire* to go.
object[1] (ˈɒbdʒɪkt) *n* **1** a solid thing that can be felt or examined. **2** someone or something that arouses a reaction or emotion: an object of ridicule. **3** a goal or reason for doing something. **4** a noun, pronoun, etc., that is acted on by a verb or preposition. **5** something limiting or significant: money's no object. **object lesson** a practical demonstration of some principle. < ultimately Latin *ob-* in the way + *jacere* to throw.
object[2] (əbˈdʒɛkt) *vb* argue against or disapprove of. **objection** *n* **1** a reason given against something. **2** dislike; disapproval. **objectionable** *adj* offensive; unpleasant.
objective (əbˈdʒɛktɪv) *adj* **1** existing in the outside world, independent of someone's mind. **2** detached from personal feelings or beliefs; impartial. **3** (*grammar*) of the case that follows a verb or preposition.
● *n* something one is trying to achieve, seize, or get to; aim. **objectively** *adv*
objet d'art (ˌɒbʒeɪ ˈdɑː) *n, pl* **objets d'art** a small item of artistic value. < French: art object.
obligation (ˌɒblɪˈgeɪʃən) *n* **1** a debt owed in return for a favour or service: under an obligation. **2** something binding, such as an agreement or contract. **obligatory** *adj* necessary; compulsory. < ultimately Latin *offerre* to offer.
oblige (əˈblaɪdʒ) *vb* **1** require by law, custom, or circumstances. **2** do (someone) a favour; help. **be obliged to** be indebted to. **much obliged** thank you very much. **obliging** *adj* helpful; considerate. **obligingly** *adv*
oblique (əˈbliːk) *adj* **1** sloping. **2** evasive; indirect: an oblique answer. **obliquely** *adv* **oblique angle** an acute or obtuse angle. < Latin *obliquus*.
obliterate (əˈblɪtəˌreɪt) *vb* destroy completely; wipe out. **obliteration** *n* < Latin *ob-* in the way of + *littera* letter.
oblivion (əˈblɪvɪən) *n* **1** being forgotten or neglected. **2** being mentally unaware or blank. **oblivious** *adj* unconscious or regardless of. < perhaps Latin *ob-* in the way + *levis* smooth.
oblong (ˈɒblɒŋ) *adj, n* (being) a rectangle with adjacent sides unequal. < Latin *ob-* towards + *longus* long.
obnoxious (əbˈnɒkʃəs) *adj* offensive; disgusting. **obnoxiously** *adv* < Latin *ob-* exposed to + *noxa* harm.
oboe (ˈəʊbəʊ) *n* a double-reed, woodwind

instrument of treble pitch. **oboist** *n* < French *hautbois.*

obscene (əb'si:n) *adj* shockingly offensive or indecent. **obscenely** *adv* **obscenity** *n* **1** being obscene. **2** an obscene word or act. < Latin *obscaenus.*

obscure (əb'skjʊə) *adj* **1** shadowy; dim. **2** hard to understand; vague. **3** little-known: an obscure author.
• *vb* **1** hide; screen. **2** make unclear; blur. **obscurely** *adv* **obscurity** *n* < Latin *obscures.*

obsequious (əb'si:kwɪəs) *adj* nauseatingly submissive; grovelling. < Latin *ob-* towards + *sequi* to follow.

observe (ɒb'zɜ:v) *vb* **1** watch; take note of. **2** conform to; comply with (rules, etc.). **3** say; comment. **4** celebrate or commemorate (a festival, ceremony, etc.). **observable** *adj* **observer** *n* **observance** *n* **1** a customary practice or ritual; formality. **2** compliance with rules, etc. **observant** *adj* paying close attention; alert. **observantly** *adv* **observation** *n* **1** observing or being observed. **2** an opinion or comment uttered. **observatory** *n* a place where natural phenomena such as the weather or the night sky are observed scientifically. < Latin *ob-* towards + *servare* to keep.

obsess (əb'sɛs) *vb* be on the mind of constantly or abnormally. **obsessive** *adj* **obsessively** *adv* **obsession** *n* an intense preoccupation. < Latin *ob-* against + *sedēre* to sit.

obsolete ('ɒbsəˌli:t) *adj* no longer in use or practised; outdated. **obsolescent** *adj* becoming obsolete. **obsolescence** *n* < Latin *obsolescere* to become disused.

obstacle ('ɒbstəkl̩) *n* something that obstructs or hinders. **obstacle race** a race in which competitors are hindered by physical obstacles on the course. < Latin *ob-* in the way + *stare* to stand.

obstetrician (ˌɒbstə'trɪʃən) *n* a physician who specializes in childbirth. **obstetrics** *n* the branch of medicine dealing with this. **obstetric** or **obstetrical** *adj* < Latin *obstetrix* midwife, from *obstare* to stand against.

obstinate ('ɒbstɪnət) *adj* **1** holding firmly to an opinion or course of action; unyielding. **2** not easily got rid of; lingering: an obstinate headache. **obstinacy** *n* **obstinately** *adv* < Latin *obstinare* to persist in.

obstreperous (əb'strɛpərəs) *adj* noisy; wild. < Latin *ob-* against + *strepere* to make a noise.

obstruct (əb'strʌkt) *vb* **1** block or cut off (a road, path, etc.) by means of an obstacle. **2** interrupt or hinder the course of. **obstruction** *n* **obstructive** *adj* < Latin *ob-* against + *struere* to build.

obtain (əb'teɪn) *vb* **1** get hold of; acquire. **2** be customary; prevail. **obtainable** *adj* < Latin *ob-* in the way + *tenēre* to hold.

obtrude (əb'tru:d) *vb* push (oneself or one's ideas) on others, esp. in an unwelcome way. **obtrusion** *n* **obtrusive** *adj* **1** pushy; forward. **2** obvious; prominent. **obtrusively** *adv* < Latin *ob-* in the way + *trudere* to thrust.

obtuse (əb'tju:s) *adj* **1** blunt; rounded. **2** (of an angle) more than 90° and less than 180°. **3** dim-witted; slow. < Latin *ob-* against + *tundere* to beat.

obverse ('ɒbvɜ:s) *n* the face of a coin, medal, etc., that bears the main design. < Latin *ob-* towards + *vertere* to turn.

obviate ('ɒbvɪˌeɪt) *vb* do away with; render unnecessary. < SEE OBVIOUS.

obvious ('ɒbvɪəs) *adj* clearly seen or understood; unmistakable. **obviously** *adv* < Latin *ob-* in the way + *via* way.

occasion (ə'keɪʒən) *n* **1** the time at which something happens. **2** a suitable moment; opportunity. **3** a special event; celebration. **4** a reason or excuse.
• *vb* bring about. **occasional** *adj* **1** happening at irregular or infrequent intervals. **2** meant for special occasions. **occasionally** *adv* **on occasion** sometimes. < ultimately Latin *ob-* towards + *cadere* to fall.

Occident ('ɒksɪdənt) *n* the western world. **occidental** *adj* western. **Occidental** *n* someone who comes from the western world. < Latin *occidere* to go down.

occult (ɒ'kʌlt, 'ɒkʌlt) *adj* **1** concerning the magical or supernatural. **2** hidden from those without special understanding; secret. < Latin *occulere* to hide.

occupy ('ɒkjʊˌpaɪ) *vb* **occupied; occupying 1** stay or reside in (a dwelling). **2** take or keep possession of (a building, territory, etc.). **3** take up (space or time). **4** keep (someone) busy or absorbed. **5** hold or fill (a rank or office). **occupancy** *n* **occupant** or **occupier** *n* someone established in a dwelling, office, etc. **occupation** *n* **1** an activity that keeps one occupied, esp. one's job or profession. **2** the seizing and controlling of a country or territory, esp. by foreign armed forces. **3** residency; tenure. **occupational** *adj* of or caused by a particular occupation: occupational hazards. **occupational therapy** involvement in crafts, hobbies, etc., to help recovery from certain disorders of the body or mind. < Latin *occupare.*

occur (əˈkɜː) *vb* **occurred; occurring** **1** happen; arise. **2** be found; appear. **3** come to mind; suggest itself. **occurrence** *n* < Latin *ob-* in the way + *currere* to run.

ocean (ˈəʊʃən) *n* **1** the expanse of salt water that surrounds the land-masses of the earth. **2** one of the five great named stretches of sea: the Atlantic Ocean. **oceanic** *adj* **ocean-going** *adj* (of a ship) designed for travel on the ocean. **oceanography** *n* the science concerning the ocean and the life-forms within it. < ultimately Greek *Ōkeanos,* river believed to flow around the earth.

ochre (ˈəʊkə) *n* **1** a red or yellow mineral, usually iron ore, used as a pigment. **2** a yellowish-orange colour. < Greek *ōchros* yellow.

o'clock (əˈklɒk) *adv* **1** used in expressions of time: 12 o'clock. **2** used to indicate direction as if the observer is at the centre of a clock dial. < *of the clock.*

octagon (ˈɒktəˌgən) *n* an eight-sided polygon. **octagonal** *adj* < Greek *okta* eight + *gōnia* angle.

octane (ˈɒkteɪn) *n* a liquid hydrocarbon that occurs in petrol. **high octane** (of fuel) containing a large proportion of a form of octane, and therefore efficient. **octane number** a number showing the relative anti-knock properties of a petrol. < Greek *okta* eight.

octave (ˈɒktɪv) *n* **1** a series of eight notes as from one C to the C next above it. **2** the top or bottom note of this series, or the interval between them. < Latin *octo* eight.

octavo (ɒkˈteɪvəʊ) *n* the size of a page or book resulting from the folding of a sheet of paper into eight leaves. < Latin *octavus* eighth.

octet (ɒkˈtɛt) *n* eight instruments, voices, or performers; piece of music for these.

octogenarian (ˌɒktəʊdʒəˈnɛərɪən) *n* someone between 80 and 90 years old. < Latin *octoginta* eighty.

octopus (ˈɒktəpəs) *n* one of a group of sea-animals with eight tentacles each with two rows of suckers. < Greek *oktōpous.*

ocular (ˈɒkjʊlə) *adj* concerning the eyes. **oculist** *n* a specialist in eye defects or diseases. < Latin *oculus* eye.

odd (ɒd) *adj* **1** (of a number) not able to be divided exactly by two. **2** not matching: odd socks. **3** left over from a set or series. **4** casual; occasional: odd jobs. **5** more than a specified number or amount: 20-odd people. **6** strange; peculiar. **oddly** *adv* **oddball** *n* (*informal*) someone who is eccentric. **oddity** *n* **1** peculiarity. **2** someone or something strange or unusual. **odd man out** someone or something which differs from the rest of a group. **oddment** *n* a left-over; remnant. **odds** *pl n* **1** a likelihood; probability. **2** an expression of this as a ratio. **3** the ratio between the amount paid if a bet is successful and the amount bet. **4** advantage; superiority: He won against all odds. **5** disagreement: at odds. **odds and ends** miscellaneous items; oddments. < Old Norse: triangle, odd number.

ode (əʊd) *n* a lyric poem which usually celebrates an event or is addressed to someone, written in an elevated tone. < ultimately Greek *aidein* to sing.

odious (ˈəʊdɪəs) *adj* vile; hateful. **odiously** *adv* **odiousness** *n* < Latin *odium* hatred.

odour (ˈəʊdə) *n* a smell, esp. an unpleasant one. **odorous** *adj* **odourless** *adj* < Latin *odor.*

oesophagus (iːˈsɒfəgəs) *n* the tube leading from the back of the throat to the stomach. < ultimately Greek *oisein* to be going to carry + *phagein* to eat.

oestrogen (ˈiːstrədʒən) *n* a hormone that stimulates the growth of female sex characteristics. < Greek *oistros* frenzy + *-o-* + *-genēs* born.

of (əv; *stressed* ɒv) *prep* **1** used to show possession, relation, or origin. **2** consisting of or containing: a cup of tea. **3** concerning: the story of my life. **4** used to show separation or removal: cured of his cold. **5** directed towards; for: love of life. **6** with regard to: hard of hearing. **7** (*informal*) during: He went of an evening. < Old English.

off (ɒf) *adv* **1** away; from. **2** used to show separation or removal: He took his jacket off. **3** not engaged, connected, or in operation; cancelled. **4** used to show completion: finish it off. **5** off-stage: noises off. **6** (of food) beginning to decay. **7** provided: How are you off for supplies?

• *prep* **1** used to show separation or distance from: He fell off his bike. **2** no longer using, interested, or involved in: She's off her food. **3** used to show where something comes from: I got it off a friend. **4** near, connected, or adjacent to: just off the High Street.

• *adj* **1** not engaged, connected, or in operation: Is the radio off? **2** (of a vehicle, road, etc.) on the right-hand side. **3** decaying; rotten; sour. **4** (*cricket*) of

the side of the field to the right of the wicket-keeper. **5** unsatisfactory; disappointing: an off day.
• *n* **1** (*cricket*) the off-side. **2** the start of a journey, race, etc. **offhand** *adj* **1** without preparation. **2** abrupt in manner; curt. **offhanded** *adj* **offhandedly** *adv* **offshore** *adj* out at sea. **offside** *adj, adv* (of a football player) illegally in front of the ball, so not allowed to play it. < Old English. SEE PANEL.

offal (ˈɒfl) *n* the edible, internal parts of a butchered animal, such as the heart, liver, and kidneys. < Middle English *of* off + *fall*.

offend (əˈfɛnd) *vb* **1** cause displeasure or annoyance to. **2** also **offend against** break (a law, etc.). **offence** *n* an act of offending. < ultimately Latin *ob-* against + *-fendere* to strike.

offensive (əˈfɛnsɪv) *adj* **1** rude. **2** unpleasant; disgusting. **3** used in aggression: offensive weapons.
• *n* **1** an aggressive position or attitude: take the offensive. **2** a large-scale, military attack. **offensively** *adv* **offensiveness** *n*

offer (ˈɒfə) *vb* **1** present (something) to be considered, accepted, or rejected. **2** show willingness or intention; volunteer. **3** state what one will pay; bid. **4** make available; provide. **5** put up: He offered no resistance.
• *n* **1** an amount of money offered. **2** a declaration that one is prepared to undertake or pay something. **offering** *n* something offered, esp. as a contribution or religious sacrifice. **offertory** *n* **1** the offering of Communion bread and wine for consecration. **2** money collected at a church service. **on offer** for sale at a reduced price. < Latin *offerre*. SEE PANEL.

office (ˈɒfɪs) *n* **1** a room or building where business is carried out, or a particular service is provided: a lost-property office. **2** the staff working in this. **3 Office** a major government department: the Home Office. **4** a position of authority and responsibility, esp. public. **5** a set form of religious worship; ceremony. **6** a service or kindness: I got the job through his good offices. **office-block** *n* a large building built to contain business offices. **office-boy** fem. **office-girl** *n* a young person employed to run errands in an office. **office hours** hours of business. **officer** *n* **1** someone who holds a position of authority or responsibility. **2** someone who holds authority in the armed forces, esp. with a commission, or in the merchant navy. **3** a policeman. < ultimately Latin *opus* work + *facere* to do.

official (əˈfɪʃəl) *adj* **1** of an office or its related duties. **2** formal; ceremonial. **3** legitimate; authorized: an official statement.
• *n* someone who holds an office. **officially** *adv* **officiate** *vb* act as an official; supervise. SEE PANEL.

officious (əˈfɪʃəs) *adj* self-important;

off

It is not unusual to hear off of used instead of off, as in for example, 'The vase fell off *of* the table' or 'She pulled the button off *of* his shirt'. This use of of after off is considered nonstandard and is best avoided. Ironically, the reverse procedure happens with out of: the of is sometimes omitted, as in She ran out the house. This omission of of after out also constitutes nonstandard usage.

The word off features in a number of expressions:

off-beat *adj* unconventional.
off colour not well.
off-cut *n* a remnant of wood, carpet, etc.
off-day *n* a day when a person is not feeling, working, etc., well.
off-licence *n* a shop that is licensed to sell alcoholic drinks that are to be consumed off the premises.
off-load *vb* **1** to unload. **2** to relieve of (something burdensome).
off-peak *adj* relating to a time when a service or supply is used less than when demand is greatest: off-peak electricity.
off-putting *adj* disconcerting; repelling or hindering.
off-season *n* the time of reduced activity or business.
off-stage *adj, adv* **1** on a part of the stage that is not visible to the audience. **2** not in the public gaze.
off the record unofficially.
off-white *n, adj* (a) yellowish or greyish white.
on the off chance just in case (something is or was possible): We called in on the off chance of seeing you.

bossy. **officiously** *adv* SEE PANEL AT OFFICIAL.

offing (ˈɒfɪŋ) *n* **in the offing** likely to happen soon; imminent.

offset (ˌɒfˈsɛt) *vb* **offset; offsetting** make up for; balance out.
• *n* (ˈɒfˌsɛt) **1** an offshoot of a plant, family, or race. **2** a printing process in which an inked impression is transferred from a rubber surface to paper.

offshoot (ˈɒfˌʃuːt) *n* **1** a branch off the stem of a plant. **2** a by-product.

offspring (ˈɒfˌsprɪŋ) *n, pl* **offspring** children or the young of animals. < Old English *of* off + *springan* to spring.

often (ˈɒfn̩) *adv* **1** much of the time; frequently. **2** in many cases. < Old English *oft*.

ogle (ˈəʊɡl̩) *vb* look at (someone) with sexual interest. < Low German *oog* eye.

ogre (ˈəʊɡə) fem. **ogress** *n* **1** a hideous, man-eating giant in legends and folklore. **2** a cruel or terrifying person. < French.

ohm (əʊm) *n* a unit for measuring electrical resistance. SEE PANEL AT **VOLT**.

OHMS *abbrev* On His (or Her) Majesty's Service.

oil (ɔɪl) *n* **1** one of many smooth, greasy liquids that are insoluble in water. **2** petroleum; form of this used as a fuel. **3** oil-paint or a painting done with this.
• *vb* treat with oil; lubricate. **oilcan** *n* a can with a nozzle, designed to release a regulated flow of oil. **oilcloth** *n* a cloth treated with oil, used as a covering for shelves, tables, etc. **oil-colour** *n* also **oil-paint** paint made from powdered pigment and oil. **oilfield** *n* an area under the ground or sea where oil is found. **oil-fired** *adj* fuelled by oil. **oil-painting** *n* a picture painted in oil colours. **oilskin** *n* a cloth treated with oil to make it waterproof. **oilskins** *pl n* clothing made from this. **oil tanker** a large ship which carries petroleum in bulk. **oily** *adj* **1** of, like, covered with, or containing oil. **2** unpleasantly flattering. < ultimately Greek *elaia* olive.

ointment (ˈɔɪntmənt) *n* an oily paste applied to the skin to heal or soothe. < ultimately Latin *unguere* to anoint. SEE PANEL.

OK (ˌəʊˈkeɪ) *adv, adj* (*informal*) all right.
• *n* (*informal*) agreement; authorization.
• *vb* (*informal*) **OK'd; OK'ing** consent to; authorize. SEE PANEL.

okey-doke (ˈəʊkɪˌdəʊk) *adv* (*informal*) OK

old (əʊld) *adj* **1** advanced in years; aged. **2** having lived or existed for a specified time: five years old. **3** made a long time ago. **4** worn-out through age and use. **5** established; known for a long time: an old friend. **6** earlier; former. **7** experienced:

---

offer and **prefer**

Whether or not to double a final r before adding an -ed suffix to words like offer and prefer continues to be a major spelling problem. Why is it that offered does not double its r and yet preferred does? The answer has to do with sound. If the final syllable is stressed, as is the *fer* of prefer, then the final r is doubled: referred, deferred, interred, inferred. However, if the final syllable is not stressed, then there is no doubling of the r: delivered, considered, withered, watered.

---

official or **officious?**

These two words are sometimes confused.

The basic meaning of official is 'authorized': *official* sources, an *official* statement, an *official* welcome.

In contrast with this, officious is a pejorative term meaning 'self-important or bossy, especially in an interfering way': 'How *officious* can you get? From next week, we have to report to the manager every time we want to go to the loo!'

---

a fly in the ointment

The expression a fly in the ointment means 'a person or thing that spoils something that is otherwise pleasant or perfect': I enjoy my work at the office. The only fly in the ointment is the boss's secretary who tends to get on my nerves. The expression comes from the Authorized (King James) Version of the Bible, Ecclesiastes 10:1: Dead flies cause the ointment of the apothecary to send forth a stinking savour: so doth a little folly him that is in reputation for wisdom and honour.

an old hand. **8** used to emphasize or mention in a friendly manner: any old day; Good old John. **oldness** *n* **of old** of or from an earlier time. **old age** the period of someone's life from roughly 65 onwards.

OK?

Most people know that KO comes from *k*nock *o*ut: 'He was KO'ed in the third round.' But where does OK come from? There seem to be two main schools of thought. On the one hand, some suggest that it may stand for *o*rl *k*orrekt, (all correct). Others believe that its roots are to be found in Old *K*inderhook, (the birthplace and subsequent nickname of Martin Van Buren, Democratic candidate for the American presidency in 1840) and the O.K. Club, the political society formed to promote his campaign.

Whatever its origins, the word has become well established and now operates as no less than four different parts of speech: These are OK (adjective), They played OK for a change (adverb), The doctor gave him the OK (noun), and Her father refuses to OK the wedding (verb). In fact, OK is so firmly entrenched in English that an extended spelling has emerged, okay.

old-fashioned *adj* not in style; dated. **old man's beard** a trailing plant with white, fluffy hairs round its seeds. **old year** the year just ended or about to end. < Old English *eald.* SEE PANEL. SEE PANEL AT **ELDER**[1].

oleander (ˌəʊlɪˈændə) *n* a poisonous, evergreen, Mediterranean shrub with pink, white, or red flowers. < Medieval Latin.

olfactory (ɒlˈfæktərɪ) *adj* concerning smelling or the sense of smell. < Latin *olēre* to smell + *facere* to do.

oligarchy (ˈɒlɪˌɡɑːkɪ) *n* **1** government concentrated in the hands of a few people. **2** these people, or a country governed in this way. < Greek *oligos* few + *archein* to rule.

olive (ˈɒlɪv) *n* **1** an evergreen tree that bears a small, bitter, stone fruit from which olive oil is obtained. **2** the fruit of this. **3** a dull green colour. • *adj* **1** dull green. **2** (of the complexion) brownish-yellow. **olive-branch** *n* something offered in goodwill or conciliation. < Greek *elaia.*

ombudsman (ˈɒmbʊdzmən) *n, pl* **ombudsmen** an official appointed to investigate the complaints of individuals against public or government bodies. < Swedish, from Old Norse *umboth* commission + *mathr* man.

omelette (ˈɒmlɪt) *n* a mixture of beaten eggs cooked in a frying-pan, often served folded in half round a filling. < ultimately Latin *lamella* small,

old things

Old features in a number of expressions, many of them idiomatic, including:

old boy fem. **old girl 1** a former pupil at a school. **2** a person or animal regarded affectionately: 'Come on, old boy,' encouraged Jack, giving his dog a biscuit. This sense is also used in a disrespectful, mocking way: The old girl's always losing her keys!

old guard or **school** a group of people following principles, methods, etc., that are being or have been superseded: He was a craftsman of the old school—clean and thorough—not like some of the workers today. The expression old guard comes from *l'Ancienne Garde,* the name of the most experienced regiments of Napoleon's Imperial Guard.

old hand someone who is skilled and experienced: He's an old hand at mending zips.

old hat something that is commonly well-known or old-fashioned: I expect all this will be old hat to most of you, but I'll explain it for the sake of those who don't know it.

old lady a wife or mother.

old maid an elderly spinster.

old man 1 a male employer or manager; boss. **2** a husband or father.

old master a great painter of the 16th to early 18th centuries; painting of this period.

old-time *adj* of a former time: old-time dancing.

old wives' tale a belief handed down as traditional wisdom.

old woman 1 a very fussy person: He's a bit of an old woman. **2** a female employer or manager; boss. **3** a wife or mother.

thin plate.

omen (ˈəʊmən) *n* an event believed to signal something to happen in the future. < Latin.

ominous (ˈɒmɪnəs) *adj* sinister; threatening.

omit (əʊˈmɪt) *vb* **omitted; omitting** **1** leave out. **2** fail to do; overlook. **omission** *n* < Latin *ob-* towards + *mittere* to send.

omnibus (ˈɒmnɪˌbəs) *n* **1** a book containing a number of works, usually by one author. **2** (*formal*) a bus. < Latin *omnis* all.

omnipotent (ɒmˈnɪpətənt) *adj* having enormous or unlimited power. **omnipotence** *n* < Latin *omni-* + *potens* potent.

omniscient (ɒmˈnɪsɪənt) *adj* all-knowing. **omniscience** *n* < Latin *omni-* + *scientia* science.

omnivorous (ɒmˈnɪvərəs) *adj* **1** feeding on plants and animals. **2** eagerly absorbing, esp. reading material. < Latin *omnivorus*.

on (ɒn) *prep* **1** touching, supported by, covering, or attached to. **2** carried with: Have you got a cigarette on you? **3** very close to; towards: a house on the seafront. **4** during (esp. a day or date). **5** dealing with: a programme on gardening. **6** having as a basis or source: on good authority. **7** in a certain state, process, or manner: on the way; on strike. **8** by means of (esp. a mode of transport): on foot. **9** sustained by or regularly taking: on drugs. **10** at the time of or immediately after: shoot on sight.
• *adv* **1** so as to be in contact with, cover, or be supported by something. **2** forwards or ahead; further: time to move on. **3** continually; without interruption: He went on talking. **4** into operation; engaged or active: The lights came on.
• *adj* **1** taking place, performing, or broadcasting. **2** in operation; engaged or active: Is the television on? **3** (of odds) in favour: ten to one on. **4** (*cricket*) of the side of the field to the left of a right-handed batsman.
• *n* (*cricket*) the on side. **be on** (*informal*) be acceptable or ready for (something). **be** or **keep on at** (*informal*) nag. **be on to something** recognize the importance of something. **on and off** also **off and on** occasionally. **on and on** continually. **on-line** *adj* controlled directly by the central processor of a computer. < Old English *an, on*. SEE PANEL AT **ONTO**.

once (wʌns) *adv* **1** also *n* one time only. **2** in the past; formerly. **3** ever; at all.
• *conj* from the moment that. **at once** immediately; at the same time. **once and for all** for good; finally. **once in a while** very occasionally. **once-over** *n* (*informal*) a quick examination. **once upon a time** a long time ago. < Middle English *on* one.

oncoming (ˈɒnˌkʌmɪŋ) *adj* advancing; forthcoming.

one (wʌn) *determiner, pron* **1** 1 in number. **2** any at all.
• *pron* used to refer to people generally.
• *n* **1** the number 1. **2** an individual person or thing. **3** the first of a series, or a particular example of. **4** (*informal*) a blow: He gave him one. **5** (*informal*) a drink: Just a quick one. **6** (*informal*) a joke: Do you know the one about.... **one another** each other. **one day** at some future time. **one-man** *adj* performed or managed by one individual. **one-off** *adj, n* (made or carried out) as a single item, etc. **one-sided** *adj* biased; unfair. **one-time** *adj* former; ex-. **one-way** *adj* allowing movement or travel in one direction only. < Old English *ān*. SEE PANEL. SEE PANEL AT **EACH**.

onerous (ˈəʊnərəs) *adj* hard; demanding. < Latin *onus* burden.

oneself (wʌnˈsɛlf) *pron* **1** the form of *one* used reflexively or for emphasis: wash oneself. **2** one's normal self: not feeling oneself. **by oneself** **1** without help. **2** alone.

ongoing (ˈɒnˌgəʊɪŋ) *adj* in progress; developing.

onion (ˈʌnjən) *n* a plant of the lily family, cultivated for its strong-tasting bulb which is eaten as a vegetable. **oniony** *adj* **know one's onions** know one's subject thoroughly. < perhaps Latin *unus* one.

onlooker (ˈɒnˌlʊkə) *n* an observer; bystander.

only (ˈəʊnlɪ) *adj* **1** alone or exclusive in

---

one of those things

Which is correct: One of the problems *is* getting worse or One of the problems *are* getting worse? The first is correct: one is the 'head' of the phrase, and since this is singular, the verb is singular.

This is one of the problems that *perplexes* the experts or This is one of the problems that *perplex* the experts? The second is correct: the subject of perplex is not one, but problems, and since this is plural, the verb is plural.

---

type or class. **2** undoubtedly the best: the only way to travel.
• *adv* **1** merely; just. **2** exclusively. **3** no earlier than. **4** in the end: It'll only make you ill.
• *conj* however; but. **only too** very much. < Old English *ānlīc*.

onomatopoeia (ˌɒnəˌmætəˈpiːə) *n* the forming of words that suggest or imitate the thing or action they represent. **onomatopoeic** *adj* < Greek *onoma* name + *poiein* to make. SEE PANEL AT **BUZZ**.

onset (ˈɒnˌsɛt) *n* **1** a start. **2** an attack.

onslaught (ˈɒnˌslɔːt) *n* a fierce charge or attack. < alteration of Dutch *aanslag* striking.

onto (ˈɒntə; *stressed* ˈɒntʊ) also **on to** *prep* **1** to a position on. **2** having become aware of: The police were onto him. **3** (*informal*) in touch with about (something). SEE PANEL.

onus (ˈəʊnəs) *n* **1** blame. **2** responsibility, esp. to prove something. < Latin: burden.

onward (ˈɒnwəd) *adv, adj* forward; ahead. **onwards** *adv*

onyx (ˈɒnɪks) *n* a marble-like mineral with layers of different colours, often green and white or brown and white. < Greek: finger-nail.

oodles (ˈuːdl̩z) *pl n* (*informal*) a lot. < origin uncertain.

ooze[1] (uːz) *vb* **1** (of a liquid) flow out in a slow trickle. **2** give out a slow trickle of. **3** overflow with: She oozed vitality. < Old English *wōs* juice.

ooze[2] *n* a muddy deposit on a sea or river bed. < Old English *wāse* mire.

opal (ˈəʊpl̩) *n* a semi-transparent mineral of silica used as a gem-stone. **opalescent** *adj* reflecting a milky light. **opalescence** *n* < Sanskrit *upala* stone, jewel.

opaque (əʊˈpeɪk) *adj* **1** not reflecting light or allowing light through. **2** difficult to follow or understand. **opacity** *n* < Latin *opacus*.

---

onto or **on to?**

Onto may generally be written as either one word or two words: both onto and on to are correct. Sometimes, however, only on to may be used, as in He then drove *on to* Spain. In this sentence, on has its own meaning ('further') and to is a separate preposition. Another example is He went *on to* suggest some ways of solving the problem, where to is part of an infinitive structure.

OPEC (ˈəʊpɛk) *abbrev* Organization of Petroleum Exporting Countries.

open (ˈəʊpn̩) *adj* **1** having nothing which confines, encloses, obstructs, or seals. **2** generally available or accessible. **3** (of places of business) receiving customers or clients. **4** unresolved; undecided: The case is still open. **5** candid; forthright. **6** ready (to receive offers). **7** exposed to view. **8** spread out. **9** having many small spaces in: open texture. **10** (of a cheque) uncrossed.
• *n* **1 the open** outdoors. **2 Open** an open competition or tournament.
• *vb* **1** make or become open. **2** begin; launch. **3** give public access to, esp. with a ceremony. **4** make openings in. **5** also **open out** spread out. **openness** *n*
open-air *adj* taking place outdoors. **opencast** *adj* (of mining) worked from the surface of the earth. **open-ended** *adj* without specified limits. **opener** *n* **1** someone or something that opens. **2** a device for opening cans or bottles.

---

an open question

Open features in a number of expressions, including:

open-and-shut *adj* easily solved; clear-cut: an open-and-shut case.
open day a day on which a country house, institution, etc., is open to the public.
open-handed *adj* generous.
open letter a letter of protest, explanation, etc., addressed to one person, but published in a newspaper, etc.
open mind a mind that is receptive to new ideas: I prefer to keep an open mind on such issues. **open-minded** *adj*
open-plan *adj* without permanent dividing walls: an open-plan office.
open prison a prison with fewer security restrictions than a conventional prison, allowing prisoners more freedom of movement.
open question an undecided matter.
open secret something that is supposed to be a secret but is in fact widely known.
open verdict a verdict that does not state the cause of a person's death.
with open arms with a warm welcome; enthusiastically: The club received the new members with open arms.

---

opening *n* **1** a gap or space. **2** a start. **3** a chance; vacancy. **openly** *adv* candidly; publicly. **open up 1** begin firing. **2** become less shy; become more talkative. **3** (of a game or contest) make or become more interesting. **4** make more available or accessible. **open-work** *n* a work of strips of metal, fabric, etc., with spaces in between. < Old English. SEE PANEL.

opera (ˈɒpərə) *n* **1** a drama in which the dialogue is sung to an orchestral accompaniment. **2** the branch of the arts which deals with this. **operatic** *adj* **opera-glasses** *pl n* small binoculars used at an opera or theatre. **operetta** *n* a light opera, often humorous and romantic. < Italian, from Latin: work.

operate (ˈɒpəˌreɪt) *vb* **1** function or work or cause to function or work. **2** direct the attention of; handle. **3** perform surgery. **operable** *adj* able to be operated on, esp. surgically. **operating-theatre** *n* a room where surgical operations are performed, usually in a hospital. **operation** *n* **1** functioning or working; activity. **2** the manner in which something functions. **3** a process performed on the body by a surgeon. **4** a military action; its planning. **5** a business transaction. **operational** *adj* **1** of or involved in operations. **2** capable of functioning. **operator** *n* **1** someone who operates (a business, machinery, etc.). **2** someone who connects telephone lines at a switchboard or exchange. < Latin *opus* work.

operative (ˈɒpərətɪv) *adj* **1** functioning. **2** significant.
- *n* a worker, esp. in a factory.

ophthalmic (ɒfˈθælmɪk) *adj* of or concerning the eyes. < Greek *ophthalmos* eye.

opinion (əˈpɪnjən) *n* **1** a view or judgment formed without proof or certainty. **2** a generally held attitude: public opinion. **3** professional advice or judgment. **opinionated** *adj* holding opinions in a single-minded way. **opinion poll** an assessment of public opinion. < Latin *opinio.*

opium (ˈəʊpɪəm) *n* the dried juice of a type of poppy, smoked or chewed as a narcotic drug, or used as a sedative in medicine. < Greek *opion* little sap.

opponent (əˈpəʊnənt) *n* someone or a group of people taking an opposite side in a war, contest, etc.

opportune (ˈɒpəˌtjuːn) *adj* **1** fitting. **2** well-timed. **opportunely** *adv* **opportunism** *n* seizing the advantage, esp. without principles. **opportunist** *n* **opportunity** *n* a favourable circumstance; chance. < Latin *ob-* towards + *portus* harbour.

oppose (əˈpəʊz) *vb* **1** speak or fight against; resist. **2** set against or opposite, so as to contrast or compare. **as opposed to** as compared with.

opposite (ˈɒpəzɪt) *adj* **1** facing; corresponding. **2** contrary; other: the opposite sex.
- *n* an opposite person or thing.
- *adv* to or on an opposite side.
- *prep* corresponding to; facing. **one's opposite number** someone who works in a similar capacity to oneself in another organization. **opposition** *n* **1** hostility or resistance; those who resist. **2 the Opposition** the major political party opposing the one in office. **3** comparison; contrast. < Latin *ob-* against + *ponere* to place.

oppress (əˈprɛs) *vb* **1** rule in a cruel, unjust manner. **2** be a burden of worry on; depress. **oppression** *n* **oppressor** *n* **oppressive** *adj* **1** severe; overbearing. **2** depressing. **3** (of weather) heavy; stifling. **oppressively** *adv* **oppressiveness** *n* < Latin *ob-* against + *premere* to press.

opt (ɒpt) *vb* **opt for** decide on. **opt out** decide against involvement in. < Latin *optare.*

optic (ˈɒptɪk) *adj* of sight or the eyes. **optical** *adj* of or aiding sight. **optically** *adv* **optician** *n* someone who makes or sells spectacles or other aids to vision. **ophthalmic optician** someone who prescribes and supplies these. **optics** *n* the science of the nature and properties of light. < ultimately Greek *optos* visible.

optimism (ˈɒptɪˌmɪzəm) *n* an inclination to see the best in everything, or to expect the most favourable results. **optimist** *n* **optimistic** *adj* **optimistically** *adv* < Latin *optimus* best.

optimum (ˈɒptɪməm) *adj, n* (the) most advantageous; best.

option (ˈɒpʃən) *n* **1** the right or freedom to choose. **2** a choice; alternative. **3** the right to buy or sell at a specified price within certain time limits. **keep one's options open** avoid committing oneself. **optional** *adj* noncompulsory; left to the individual. **optionally** *adv* < Latin *optio* free choice.

opulent (ˈɒpjʊˌlənt) *adj* **1** rich; affluent. **2** lavish; plentiful. **opulence** *n* **opulently** *adv* < Latin *ops* wealth.

opus (ˈəʊpəs) *n, pl* **opera** a piece of

music by a particular composer, esp. numbered in order of issue. < Latin.

or (ə; *stressed* ɔː) *conj* **1** used to show that what follows is an alternative: kill or be killed. **2** and not; used after negatives: He doesn't smoke or drink. **3** used to explain further or equate: tolerate or put up with. **4** used to show a consequence: Don't, or you'll hurt yourself. < Old English *oththe.*

oracle (ˈɒrəkl̩) *n* **1** a place where a divinity is consulted for advice or prophecy, esp. in ancient Greece. **2** the often enigmatic reply given. **3** someone or something considered to give wise advice; this advice. **oracular** *adj* < ultimately Latin *orare* to speak.

oral (ˈɔːrəl, ˈɒrəl) *adj* **1** spoken; verbal. **2** relating to or taken through the mouth.
• *n* (*informal*) a spoken examination. **orally** *adv* < Latin *os* mouth.

orange (ˈɒrɪndʒ) *n* **1** a citrus tree that bears a round, juicy fruit with a yellowish-red rind; this fruit. **2** a reddish-yellow colour.
• *adj* reddish-yellow. **orangeade** *n* a gassy, soft drink flavoured with orange. < Sanskrit *nāraṅga* orange tree.

orang-utan (ɔːˌræŋuːˈtæn) *n* a large, tree-dwelling ape with long arms, found in Borneo and Sumatra. < Malay *orang* man + *hutan* forest. SEE PANEL.

oration (əˈreɪʃən) *n* a long, formal speech. **orator** *n* **1** someone who makes an oration. **2** someone skilled in making speeches. **oratorical** *adj* **oratorio** *n, pl* **oratorios** a long musical work, esp. on a religious theme. **oratory** *n* **1** the art of public speaking. **2** an eloquent style of speech. < Latin *orare* to plead, pray.

orang-utan

The human resemblance of the orang-utan is captured in its name. Orang-utan comes from the Malay *orang hutan,* 'man of the forest', from *orang* 'man' and *hutan* 'forest'.

Other Malay words that have entered English include:

amok, amuck from *amok*
bamboo from *bambu*
caddy from *kati* 'a unit of weight'
gingham from *genggang* 'checkered cloth'
gong
kampong
ketchup from *kĕchap* 'spiced fish-sauce'
paddy from *padi*
rattan from *rotan*
sago from *sagu*

orb (ɔːb) *n* **1** a globe; sphere. **2** a globe with a cross on top, as a symbol of royal power. < Latin *orbis* circle, disc, round surface.

orbit (ˈɔːbɪt) *n* **1** the circular path of one body or object round another, such as that of the earth round the sun. **2** a range of influence; scope.
• *vb* move in an orbit around. **orbital** *adj* **1** of an orbit. **2** (of a road) passing round a city. < Latin *orbita.*

orchard (ˈɔːtʃəd) *n* an area of land where fruit-trees are cultivated; these trees. < probably Latin *hortus* garden + Old English *geard* yard.

orchestra (ˈɔːkɪstrə) *n* **1** a large group of instrumental musicians. **2** the space in front of a stage in a theatre where these sit. **orchestral** *adj* **orchestrate** *vb* **1** compose and arrange (music) for an orchestra. **2** put together; co-ordinate. **orchestration** *n* < ultimately Greek *orcheisthai* to dance.

orchid (ˈɔːkɪd) *n* one of a group of plants with striking, usually three-petalled flowers. < New Latin *orchis* testicle.

ordain (ɔːˈdeɪn) *vb* **1** invest with priestly, etc., authority. **2** enact; decree. **3** predestine. < ultimately Latin *ordo* order.

ordeal (ɔːˈdiːl) *n* a trying experience. < Old English *ordāl.*

order (ɔːdə) *n* **1** a type; category. **2** the manner in which things are arranged or organized. **3** a regular or customary arrangement. **4** a functioning condition: in working order. **5** a social class. **6** a rule of law prevailing in a society. **7** a system of rules and regulations. **8** an authoritative command or instruction. **9** a request to supply goods; goods bought or sold. **10** a written instruction (to a bank, etc.) to pay money or carry out a similar transaction. **11** a religious organization. **12** a group of people who have had an award of honour or merit conferred on them; this award: Order of the Garter. **13** one of the classical styles in architecture.
• *vb* **1** arrange systematically. **2** instruct; command. **3** request (goods, food in a restaurant, etc.). **holy orders** the status of an ordained priest, etc. **in order to** or **that** so that. **made to order** made according to customer specifications. **on order** requested but not yet supplied. **order about** give commands to continually. < Latin *ordo.*

orderly (ˈɔːdəlɪ) *adj* **1** tidy. **2** disciplined.

• *n* **1** a soldier who attends an officer. **2** a hospital attendant. **orderliness** *n*

ordinal (ˈɔːdɪnl̩) *adj* **ordinal numbers** numbers which show the position of something in a sequence, such as first, second, third.

ordinance (ˈɔːdɪnəns) *n* a rule or decree made by authority. < Latin *ordinare* to put in order.

ordinary (ˈɔːdn̩rɪ) *adj* **1** usual; regular. **2** unremarkable; dull. **ordinarily** *adv* **Ordinary level** the lowest of the GCE examinations. < Latin *ordinarius*.

ordination (ˌɔːdɪˈneɪʃən) *n* the investing of a minister with holy orders.

ordnance (ˈɔːdnəns) *n* military supplies and munitions; government department concerned with this. **Ordnance Survey** an official survey of Great Britain and Ireland for which detailed maps are prepared. < Middle French *ordenance* arranging.

ore (ɔː) *n* a mineral in the earth's crust from which metal or other useful substances are extracted. < Old English *ār*.

organ (ˈɔːgən) *n* **1** a musical instrument with keys and pedals that, when depressed, cause air to flow through pipes and make sounds. **2** a part of the body of an animal or plant with a specific function. **3** a means of communication for a particular group, such as a periodical. **organic** *adj* **1** concerning the organs of the body. **2** of or formed from living organisms. **3** (of food) produced naturally, without chemicals. **4** integrated; systematic. **organically** *adv* **organic chemistry** chemistry concerned with carbon compounds, which are present in all living matter. **organism** *n* a living thing; body. **organist** *n* a musician who plays the organ. < Latin *organum* tool.

organize (ˈɔːgəˌnaɪz) *vb* **1** put together in a systematic way. **2** plan; arrange. **3** form an association of people. **organization** *n* **organizer** *n*

orgasm (ˈɔːgæzəm) *n* the most intense point reached during sexual excitement. < Greek *organ* to mature.

orgy (ˈɔːdʒɪ) *n* **1** a wild party characterized by excessive drinking and sexual activity. **2** an excess of or overindulgence in something. < Greek *orgia*. SEE PANEL AT **VILLAIN**.

Orient (ˈɒrɪənt) *n* the part of the world east of the Mediterranean. **oriental** *adj* **Oriental** *n* someone who comes from the Orient. < Latin *oriri* to rise.

orientate (ˈɔːrɪənˌteɪt) or **orient** (ˈɔːrɪˌɛnt) *vb* **1** adjust to a particular situation. **2** align or find the position of according to the compass points. **3 orientate oneself** familiarize oneself with new surroundings, etc. **orientation** *n* **orienteering** *n* the sport of finding one's way across country using a map and compass.

orifice (ˈɒrɪfɪs) *n* a vent or opening into a cavity. < Latin *os* mouth + *facere* to make.

origami (ˌɒrɪˈgɑːmɪ) *n* the art of folding paper into complex shapes. < Japanese.

origin (ˈɒrɪdʒɪn) *n* **1** the source or root of something. **2** family descent; lineage. **originate** *vb* come or bring into existence. **origination** *n* **originator** *n* < ultimately Latin *oriri* to rise.

original (əˈrɪdʒɪnəl) *adj* **1** earliest; first. **2** being the source of something imitated or translated. **3** novel; creative. • *n* the source of something from which copies or translations are made. **originally** *adv* **originality** *n* creativity. **original sin** the state of sin in which mankind is thought to have been since the fall of Adam.

ornament (ˈɔːnəmənt) *n* **1** something that adds decoration or enhances appearance. **2** someone that brings honour or distinction to something. • *vb* brighten; decorate. **ornamental** *adj* **ornamentation** *n* < Latin *ornare* to adorn.

ornate (ɔːˈneɪt) *adj* elaborately decorated.

ornithology (ˌɔːnɪˈθɒlədʒɪ) *n* the branch of zoology concerned with the study of birds. **ornithological** *adj* **ornithologist** *n* < Greek *ornis* bird + *logos* word.

orphan (ˈɔːfən) *n* a child, both of whose parents are dead. • *vb* cause to become an orphan. **orphanage** *n* an institution where orphans are looked after. < Greek *orphanos*.

orthodox (ˈɔːθəˌdɒks) *adj* conforming to accepted beliefs or practice, esp. in religion. **orthodoxy** *n* **Orthodox Church** the Eastern Christian Church, whose head is the Patriarch of Constantinople. < Greek *orthos* straight + *doxa* opinion.

orthography (ɔːˈθɒgrəfɪ) *n* correct spelling or the way something is spelled. **orthographic** or **orthographical** *adj* < Greek *orthos* + *graphein* to write.

orthopaedics (ˌɔːθəˈpiːdɪks) *n* the branch of surgery concerned with correcting or preventing bone or muscle deformities. **orthopaedic** *adj* **orthopaedist** *n* < Greek *orthos* + *pais* child.

oscillate (ˈɒsɪˌleɪt) *vb* **1** swing back and forth like a pendulum. **2** move between

extremes of feeling, belief, etc. **oscillation** *n* < Latin *oscillum* swing.
osprey (ˈɒspreɪ) *n, pl* **ospreys** a large, brown and white hawk which preys on fish. < Latin *ossifraga.*
ostensible (ɒˈstɛnsɪbl) *adj* apparent rather than real; professed. **ostensibly** *adv* < Latin *ostendere* to show.
ostentation (ˌɒstɛnˈteɪʃən) *n* an excessive display designed to impress; showing off. **ostentatious** *adj* **ostentatiously** *adv*
osteopath (ˈɒstɪəˌpæθ) *n* someone qualified to treat physical disorders by the manipulation of bones and muscles. **osteopathic** *adj* **osteopathy** *n* this system of treatment. < Greek *osteon* bone + *pathos* suffering.
ostracize (ˈɒstrəˌsaɪz) *vb* banish from a group; ignore. **ostracism** *n* < Greek *ostrakon* shell, tile, potsherd.
ostrich (ˈɒstrɪtʃ) *n* **1** a tall, swift-running, flightless bird found in Africa. **2** someone who refuses to face reality. < Latin *avis* bird + Greek *strouthos.*
other (ˈʌðə) *determiner* **1** being the remaining or additional one of two. **2** distinct; different.
● *pron* someone or something other.
● *adv* otherwise. **the other day** some days ago. **the other world** the spiritual world. < Old English *ōther.*
otherwise (ˈʌðəˌwaɪz) *adv* **1** differently. **2** or else; if not. **3** in other respects.
● *adj* of another kind.
otter (ˈɒtə) *n* a mammal with webbed feet, thick brown fur, and a flat tail, that lives in water and feeds on fish. < Old English *otor.*
ottoman (ˈɒtəmən) *n* a long, padded seat without back or arms, or a storage box with padding on top. < *Ottoman* Turk.
ought (ɔːt) *auxiliary vb* used to express moral obligation, probability, recommendation, or advisability. < Middle English *āgan* to owe. SEE PANEL.

> **didn't ought to** or **ought not to**?
>
> Careful users of British English avoid using didn't ought to, preferring ought not to. In speech this is commonly used in the contracted form oughtn't to: You oughtn't to have gone to town by yourself.
>
> For the use of didn't use to and used not to, see panel at **used.**

ounce (aʊns) *n* a measure of weight equal to one-sixteenth of a pound (about 28.35 grams). < ultimately Latin *unus* one.
our (aʊə) *determiner* of or belonging to us. **ours** *possessive pron* (the one or ones) belonging to or associated with us. **ourselves** *pron* the form of *we* and *us* used reflexively or for emphasis. **by ourselves 1** without help. **2** alone. < Old English *ūre.*
oust (aʊst) *vb* throw out; expel (from an office or position). < Latin *ob-* against + *stare* to stand.
out (aʊt) *adv, adj* **1** away from a place, esp. one's home or work; not inside or central. **2** clearly visible or revealed: The word is out. **3** old-fashioned or no longer in use. **4** exhausted; finished: worn out. **5** not possible or allowed. **6** (*cricket*) having finished one's batting innings. **7** in completed form: written out. **8** not in the normal place: left out. **9** in error: The bill is 50p out. **10** used to signal that the transmission is finished on a two-way radio. **11** unconscious.
● *prep* out of.
● *n* a way of escaping.
● *interj* get out. **be out to** have the intention of. **out-and-out** *adj* absolute; outright. **out of 1** away from. **2** without a supply of. **3** from among. **4** with as its origin: out of pity. **out-of-date** *adj* old-fashioned or no longer valid. **out of doors** outside in the open. **out of this world** extremely good. **out-patient** *n* someone who visits but does not stay in a hospital for treatment. **out-tray** *n* a tray holding papers, etc., that have been dealt with. **out with it** say what is on your mind. < Old English *ūt.*
out- *prefix* going beyond or forward: outlast.
outback (ˈaʊtˌbæk) *n* (*Australian*) the remote interior.
outbid (ˌaʊtˈbɪd) *vb* **outbid; outbidding** bid higher than.
outboard (ˈaʊtˌbɔːd) *adj, adv* away from or outside the hull of a ship, aircraft, etc. **outboard motor** a motor attached to the stern of a boat.
outbreak (ˈaʊtˌbreɪk) *n* a sudden eruption of war, anger, disease, etc.
outbuilding (ˈaʊtˌbɪldɪŋ) *n* a small building away from but related to a main building.
outburst (ˈaʊtˌbɜːst) *n* **1** a fit of emotion. **2** a sudden surge of growth or activity.
outcast (ˈaʊtˌkɑːst) *n* someone who has been rejected by society or a group of people.
outclass (ˌaʊtˈklɑːs) *vb* surpass; excel.

outcome (ˈaʊtˌkʌm) *n* a consequence; end result.
outcrop (ˈaʊtˌkrɒp) *n* **1** the part of a lower layer of a rock formation that projects above the surface. **2** an outbreak.
outcry (ˈaʊtˌkraɪ) *n* **1** a loud cry or commotion. **2** a public protest.
outdated (ˌaʊtˈdeɪtɪd) *adj* out of style.
outdistance (ˌaʊtˈdɪstəns) *vb* outrun (someone) in a race, etc.
outdo (ˌaʊtˈduː) *vb* **outdid; outdone; outdoing** exceed; surpass.
outdoor (ˌaʊtˈdɔː) *adj* **1** of or used outdoors. **2** liking life out of doors. **outdoors** *adv* in or to the open air.
outer (ˈaʊtə) *adj* further out; external. **outermost** *adj* furthest.
outfit (ˈaʊtˌfɪt) *n* **1** a complete set of equipment for a special purpose. **2** a set of clothes, esp. for a particular task or occasion. **3** (*informal*) a group or organization. **outfitter** *n* someone who supplies equipment or retails men's clothing.
outflank (ˌaʊtˈflæŋk) *vb* **1** go round or beyond the flank of (an enemy force). **2** gain the advantage over.
outgoing (ˈaʊtˌgəʊɪŋ) *adj* **1** leaving; retiring. **2** sociable; friendly. **outgoings** *pl n* costs; outlay.
outgrow (ˌaʊtˈgrəʊ) *vb* **outgrew; outgrown; outgrowing 1** grow more quickly than. **2** grow too old or too large for (clothes, habits, etc.).
outgrowth (ˈaʊtˌgrəʊθ) *n* **1** something growing out of something else. **2** a by-product; effect.
outhouse (ˈaʊtˌhaʊs) *n* a building which is separate from but related to a house.
outing (ˈaʊtɪŋ) *n* an excursion or trip made for pleasure.
outlandish (aʊtˈlændɪʃ) *adj* strange or exotic; bizarre. **outlandishness** *n*
outlast (ˌaʊtˈlɑːst) *vb* endure longer than.
outlaw (ˈaʊtˌlɔː) *n* a fugitive from justice.
• *vb* declare illegal.
outlay (ˈaʊtˌleɪ) *n* spending; costs.
outlet (ˈaʊtˌlɛt) *n* **1** a vent or exit, esp. for water, steam, etc. **2** a means of releasing one's feelings. **3** a shop, agency, etc., through which goods are marketed.
outline (ˈaʊtˌlaɪn) *n* **1** a line denoting the outer limits of something. **2** the main features; synopsis.
• *vb* draw in outline; summarize.
outlive (ˌaʊtˈlɪv) *vb* live longer than; survive.
outlook (ˈaʊtˌlʊk) *n* **1** a view from a particular place; vista. **2** a point of view; attitude. **3** future expectations.
outlying (ˈaʊtˌlaɪɪŋ) *adj* out-of-the-way; remote.
outmanoeuvre (ˌaʊtməˈnuːvə) *vb* get the better of by manoeuvring.
outmoded (ˌaʊtˈməʊdɪd) *adj* out of date; unfashionable.
outnumber (ˌaʊtˈnʌmbə) *vb* exceed in number.
outpost (ˈaʊtˌpəʊst) *n* **1** a detachment stationed at a distance from a main body of troops. **2** an outlying settlement.
output (ˈaʊtˌpʊt) *n* production; amount produced.
• *vb* produce; yield.
outrage (ˈaʊtˌreɪdʒ) *n* **1** an act that offends one's sense of decency. **2** an atrocity; violent act.
• *vb* affront; shock. **outrageous** *adj* **outrageously** *adv* < ultimately Latin *ultra* beyond.
outright (ˈaʊtˌraɪt) *adv* **1** absolutely. **2** at once.
• *adj* absolute; utter.
outrun (ˌaʊtˈrʌn) *vb* **outran; outrun; outrunning 1** run further or faster than. **2** surpass.
outsell (ˌaʊtˈsɛl) *vb* **outsold; outselling** sell more or be sold in greater numbers than.
outset (ˈaʊtˌsɛt) *n* the start; starting-point.
outshine (ˌaʊtˈʃaɪn) *vb* **outshone; outshining** be superior to or more splendid than.
outside (ˌaʊtˈsaɪd, ˈaʊtsaɪd) *n* the exterior, front, or surface.
• *adj* (ˈaʊtsaɪd) **1** of, on, near, or towards the outside; exterior. **2** maximum: That's my outside offer. **3** having an external source: an outside broadcast.
• *adv* (aʊtˈsaɪd) on, to, or at the outside.
• *prep* (ˌaʊtˈsaɪd) **1** to or on the outside of. **2** beyond; besides. **at the outside** at the most. **outsider** *n* **1** someone who does not belong to a particular group, organization, etc. **2** a horse or someone considered to have no chance in a race, etc.
outsize (ˈaʊtˌsaɪz) *adj* above normal size, esp. unusually.
outskirts (ˈaʊtˌskɜːts) *pl n* the outlying areas (of a town); suburbs.
outsmart (ˌaʊtˈsmɑːt) *vb* act more cleverly than.
outspoken (ˌaʊtˈspəʊkən) *adj* frank and blunt in speech.
outstanding (ˌaʊtˈstændɪŋ) *adj* **1** exceptional; distinguished. **2** unresolved or unpaid: outstanding debts. **3** notable; striking. **outstandingly** *adv*
outstay (ˌaʊtˈsteɪ) *vb* **1** overstay: He

outstayed his welcome. **2** have more stamina than.
outstretched (ˌaʊtˈstrɛtʃt) *adj* extended.
outstrip (ˌaʊtˈstrɪp) *vb* **outstripped; outstripping** get ahead of; surpass.
SEE PANEL.
outvote (ˌaʊtˈvəʊt) *vb* defeat by a larger number of votes.
outward (ˈaʊtwəd) *adj* **1** situated on or moving towards the outside. **2** outer; superficial: Outward appearances are deceiving. **outwardly** *adv* seemingly; superficially. **outwards** *adv* towards the outside.
outweigh (ˌaʊtˈweɪ) *vb* make up for or surpass in weight or importance.
outwit (ˌaʊtˈwɪt) *vb* **outwitted; outwitting** gain an advantage over through superior craftiness.
oval (ˈəʊvl̩) *n* a rounded, symmetrical shape like an egg.
• *adj* with this shape. < Latin *ovum* egg.
ovary (ˈəʊvərɪ) *n* **1** either of the two reproductive organs in female animals that produce eggs. **2** the hollow, basal region on a flowering plant that produces fruit. **ovarian** *adj*
ovation (əʊˈveɪʃən) *n* an enthusiastic expression of applause; loud cheers. < Latin *ovare* to exult.
oven (ˈʌvən) *n* a chamber in which food is heated or cooked. **ovenware** *n* heat-resistant serving dishes in which food can be cooked. < Old English *ofen.*
over (ˈəʊvə) *adv* **1** across and downwards from a brim or edge. **2** across a space in between. **3** downwards from an upright position: fall over. **4** so as to fold or reverse: turn over. **5** from one person, side, etc., to another: Hand it over. **6** extra; remaining. **7** so as to cover: It clouded over. **8** finished; past. **9** with repetition: over and over again. **10** used on a two-way radio to show that it is the other's turn to transmit. **11** in detail: Let's talk it over.

> **outstrip**
>
> Unless you know the meaning of outstrip ('to move faster than; to get ahead of'), you might be tempted to associate it with the activities of a striptease artiste: Belinda outstripped the other girls by taking two hours and ten minutes just to remove her gloves. The *strip* of outstrip, however, has nothing to do with the verb as we know it today. It derives from an obsolete word meaning 'to move fast'.

• *n* (*cricket*) a set of six deliveries by a bowler.
• *prep* **1** above; higher than. **2** above and across. **3** through; throughout: Look it over. **4** during the whole extent of: over the years. **5** more than. **6** by means of (a mode of communication): over the phone. **7** about; concerning. **8** while occupied with: over a glass of beer. **9** used to show advantage or preference: a lead over others. **over and above** far beyond. < Old English *ofer.*
over- *prefix* **1** above: overhang. **2** to excess: overflow.
overact (ˌəʊvərˈækt) *vb* perform in an exaggerated manner.
overall (ˈəʊvərɔːl) *n* a loose-fitting protective garment worn over one's normal clothes.
• *adj* (ˈəʊvərɔːl) **1** general; inclusive. **2** taking everything into account.
• *adv* (ˌəʊvəˈrɔːl) on the whole.
overarm (ˈəʊvəˌrɑːm) *adj, adv* with the arm raised over the shoulder and then brought down: to bowl overarm.
overawe (ˌəʊvərˈɔː) *vb* fill with awe.
overbalance (ˌəʊvəˈbæləns) *vb* lose or cause to lose balance.
overbearing (ˌəʊvəˈbɛərɪŋ) *adj* bossy; arrogant.
overblown (ˌəʊvəˈbləʊn) *adj* **1** (of a flower) past its prime of bloom. **2** pompous; inflated.
overboard (ˈəʊvəˌbɔːd) *adv* over the side of a boat and into the water. **go overboard** (*informal*) show excessive enthusiasm.
overcast (ˈəʊvəˌkɔːst) *adj* (of the sky) covered with cloud.
overcharge (ˌəʊvəˈtʃɑːdʒ) *vb* **1** charge too much money. **2** strain; overburden.
overcoat (ˈəʊvəˌkəʊt) *n* a warm, thick coat for wearing outdoors.
overcome (ˌəʊvəˈkʌm) *vb* **overcame; overcome; overcoming 1** defeat; subdue. **2** rise above; succeed in dealing with. **3** win.
overcrowd (ˌəʊvəˈkraʊd) *vb* pack too many people into.
overdo (ˌəʊvəˈduː) *vb* **overdid; overdone; overdoing 1** do or use (something) to excess. **2** exaggerate. **3** cook for too long.
overdose (ˈəʊvəˌdəʊs) *n* too large a dose of drugs, medicine, etc.
overdraw (ˌəʊvəˈdrɔː) *vb* **overdrew; overdrawn; overdrawing** take more money out of (a bank account) than one has in credit. **overdraft** *n* overdrawing; amount overdrawn.
overdrive (ˈəʊvəˌdraɪv) *n* a gear in a

motor vehicle with a higher ratio than the normal top gear.
overdue (ˌəʊvəˈdjuː) *adj* **1** owing; unpaid. **2** delayed; behind schedule.
overestimate (ˌəʊvərˈɛstɪˌmeɪt) *vb* put too high a value on; overrate.
overflow (ˌəʊvəˈfləʊ) *vb* flow over or beyond the limits or edge of.
• *n* (ˈəʊvəˌfləʊ) **1** overflowing or what overflows. **2** an outlet for surplus liquid.
overgrown (ˌəʊvəˈgrəʊn) *adj* **1** grown too large. **2** grown over with weeds, etc.
overhang (ˌəʊvəˈhæŋ) *vb* **overhung; overhanging** extend over; stick out.
• *n* (ˈəʊvəˌhæŋ) something overhanging, esp. an upper part of a building.
overhaul (ˌəʊvəˈhɔːl) *vb* **1** inspect and make any necessary repairs to. **2** overtake.
• *n* (ˈəʊvəˌhɔːl) an inspection and repair operation.
overhead (ˈəʊvəˌhɛd) *adj, adv* above the level of one's head. **overheads** *pl n* general business expenses such as rent, etc., not directly attributable to what is produced.
overhear (ˌəʊvəˈhɪə) *vb* **overheard; overhearing** hear without the knowledge or intention of the speaker.
overjoyed (ˌəʊvəˈdʒɔɪd) *adj* extremely delighted; euphoric.
overland (ˈəʊvəˌlænd) *adj, adv* by or across land, not sea or air.
overlap (ˌəʊvəˈlæp) *vb* **overlapped; overlapping 1** lie over or cover partly. **2** coincide partly.
• *n* (ˈəʊvəˌlæp) overlapping; amount which overlaps.
overlay (ˌəʊvəˈleɪ) *vb* **overlaid; overlaying** lay over or across; cover.
• *n* (ˈəʊvəˌleɪ) something laid over another thing; covering.
overleaf (ˈəʊvəˌliːf, ˌəʊvəˈliːf) *adv* on the other side of a page (in a book, etc.).
overload (ˌəʊvəˈləʊd) *vb* load to excess.
overlook (ˌəʊvəˈlʊk) *vb* **1** have as a view from above. **2** fail to notice; miss. **3** make allowances for; excuse.
overman (ˌəʊvəˈmæn) *vb* **overmanned; overmanning** have or supply too many workers for.
overnight (ˌəʊvəˈnaɪt) *adv* **1** throughout or during the night. **2** suddenly.
• *adj* (ˈəʊvəˌnaɪt) **1** during or for a night. **2** sudden: an overnight success.
overpay (ˌəʊvəˈpeɪ) *vb* **overpaid; overpaying** pay too much.
overplay (ˌəʊvəˈpleɪ) *vb* **1** exaggerate in performance or importance. **2** overestimate (one's potential): overplay one's hand.
overpower (ˌəʊvəˈpaʊə) *vb* defeat by greater force or numbers. **overpowering** *adj* intense; powerful.
overrate (ˌəʊvəˈreɪt) *vb* put too high a value on; overestimate.
overreach (ˌəʊvəˈriːtʃ) *vb* **overreach oneself** fail by trying to achieve too much.
over-react (ˌəʊvərɪˈækt) *vb* react more strongly than the occasion demands.
override (ˌəʊvəˈraɪd) *vb* **overrode; overridden; overriding 1** set aside or annul (an order) with or as if with superior authority. **2** prevail over; outweigh: overriding considerations. **3** neutralize the effect of (a mechanism). **overrider** *n* an upright attachment to a bumper on a motor vehicle to prevent it locking with bumpers on other vehicles.
overrule (ˌəʊvəˈruːl) *vb* set aside (an order, decision, etc.) by having superior authority.
overrun (ˌəʊvəˈrʌn) *vb* **overran; overrun; overrunning 1** invade and occupy. **2** swarm; infest. **3** go beyond (a time limit, etc.).
overseas (ˌəʊvəˈsiːz) *adj, adv* across the sea; abroad.
oversee (ˌəʊvəˈsiː) *vb* **oversaw; overseen; overseeing** supervise; manage. **overseer** *n*
overshadow (ˌəʊvəˈʃædəʊ) *vb* **1** cast a shadow or darkness over. **2** cause to appear insignificant by comparison; dominate.
overshoot (ˌəʊvəˈʃuːt) *vb* **overshot; overshooting** go beyond (a limit, target, etc.).
oversight (ˈəʊvəˌsaɪt) *n* **1** an error made through inattention. **2** direction; control.
oversimplify (ˌəʊvəˈsɪmplɪˌfaɪ) *vb* **oversimplified; oversimplifying** make something too simple, so as to cause error or distortion.
oversleep (ˌəʊvəˈsliːp) *vb* **overslept; oversleeping** sleep beyond the time intended.
overspend (ˌəʊvəˈspɛnd) *vb* **overspent; overspending** spend to excess.
overspill (ˈəʊvəˌspɪl) *n* an excess; overflow, esp. the surplus population that have moved away from a town.
overstaffed (ˌəʊvəˈstɑːft) *adj* having more staff than necessary.
overstate (ˌəʊvəˈsteɪt) *vb* exaggerate; overemphasize.
overstay (ˌəʊvəˈsteɪ) *vb* stay beyond the limits of; outstay.
overstep (ˌəʊvəˈstɛp) *vb* **overstepped; overstepping** exceed (a proper or certain limit).

overstrung (ˌəʊvəˈstrʌŋ) *adj* oversensitive.
overt (əʊˈvɜːt) *adj* open; undisguised. **overtly** *adv* < ultimately Latin *aperire* to open.
overtake (ˌəʊvəˈteɪk) *vb* **overtook; overtaken; overtaking 1** pass (someone or a motor vehicle) by moving faster. **2** catch up with. **3** happen suddenly to: Disaster overtook him.
overthrow (ˌəʊvəˈθrəʊ) *vb* **overthrew; overthrown; overthrowing** defeat; bring down, esp. by force.
• *n* (ˈəʊvəˌθrəʊ) **1** a defeat. **2** (*cricket*) the throwing of a ball too far by a fielder.
overtime (ˈəʊvəˌtaɪm) *adv* in excess of normal working hours.
• *n* time worked over normal hours; payment for this.
overtone (ˈəʊvəˌtəʊn) *n* an additional meaning, quality, or effect.
overture (ˈəʊvəˌtjʊə) *n* **1** an orchestral introduction to a ballet, opera, or other musical show. **2** an opening move; approach: making overtures. < ultimately Latin *apertura* opening.
overturn (ˌəʊvəˈtɜːn) *vb* turn over.
overweight (ˌəʊvəˈweɪt) *adj* weighing more than is proper, normal, or allowed.
overwhelm (ˌəʊvəˈwɛlm) *vb* **1** submerge; engulf. **2** overcome by force of numbers. **3** overcome with emotion. **overwhelming** *adj* < Middle English *over* + *whelmen* to turn over.
overwind (ˌəʊvəˈwaɪnd) *vb* **overwound; overwinding** wind (a watch, clock, etc.) beyond its limit.
overwork (ˌəʊvəˈwɜːk) *vb* **1** work to the point of exhaustion. **2** use to excess.
overwrought (ˌəʊvəˈrɔːt) *adj* overexcited; tense. < *overwork*.
ovoid (ˈəʊvɔɪd) *adj, n* (something) with the shape of an egg. < Latin *ovum* egg.
ovulate (ˈɒvjʊˌleɪt) *vb* produce or discharge eggs from an ovary. **ovulation** *n* **ovule** *n* a small structure within the ovary of a flower that develops into a seed when fertilized.
ovum (ˈəʊvəm) *n, pl* **ova** a female egg-cell that when fertilized can develop into a new individual. < Latin.
owe (əʊ) *vb* **1** be under an obligation to pay or pay back (money or a service). **2** have as a result of a particular cause: She owes her success to hard work. **owing** *adj* as yet unpaid. **owing to** because of. < Old English *āgan*. SEE PANEL AT **DUE**.
owl (aʊl) *n* a nocturnal bird of prey with a large head and eyes and a hooked bill. **owlish** *adj* < Old English *ūle*.
own (əʊn) *determiner, pron* of or belonging to oneself or itself; individual.
• *vb* **1** have; possess. **2** admit; acknowledge. **3** confess. **get one's own back** have revenge. **hold one's own** keep one's position when at a disadvantage or under attack. **on one's own** by oneself or one's own efforts. **own brand** goods for sale under the trademark of the retailer. **owner** *n* a person who owns something. **ownership** *n* **owner-driver** *n* someone who owns and drives a vehicle. **owner-occupier** *n* someone who owns and occupies a house. **own goal** a goal scored by a player against his or her own side in football, hockey, etc. **own up** admit guilt. < Old English *āgan*.
ox (ɒks) *n, pl* **oxen 1** a type of bovine mammal. **2** an adult castrated male of any domestic species of cattle. **oxtail** *n* the tail of an ox, used in making soups or stews. < Old English *oxa*. SEE PANEL.
oxide (ˈɒksaɪd) *n* a compound of oxygen with another element. **oxidation** *n* **oxidize** *vb* combine with oxygen. < French *oxygène* oxygen + *acide* acid.

oxen

Ox—oxen is one of just three nouns in English which have a plural form ending in -en. The other two are child—children and brother—brethren. Grammarians at one time believed that the -en of chicken was also a plural marker, making the word a fourth member of the group. However, as well as being a marker of plurality, the -en suffix operates diminutively as in maiden and kitten, and it is this function that is also found in chicken. A chicken was therefore once 'a little chicken', and not a plural form.

the world is my oyster

The expression the world is one's oyster means 'all the pleasures, opportunities, etc. that one wants are available to one': You're young and you've got lots of money—the world is your oyster. The expression comes from Shakespeare's 'The Merry Wives of Windsor', Act 2, Scene 2:

Why, then the world's mine oyster,
Which I with sword will open.

oxygen ('ɒksɪdʒən) *n* a gaseous element without smell, colour, or taste, needed for maintaining life in all plants and animals and that combines with hydrogen to form water. **oxygenate** *vb* combine, supply, or treat with oxygen. **oxygenation** *n* < ultimately Greek *oxys* acid, sharp.

oxymoron (ˌɒksɪ'mɔːrɒn) *n* the combining of words that are apparently contradictory. < Greek *oxys* sharp + *mōros* foolish. SEE PANEL AT **BITTER.**

oyster ('ɔɪstə) *n* a type of edible shellfish. < Greek *ostreon.* SEE PANEL.

oz. *abbrev* ounce(s).

P

p *abbrev* **1** penny; pence. **2** page.

pace (peɪs) *n* **1** the speed at which someone or something moves. **2** the speed at which something happens or is done. **3** a single step; distance covered in this. **4** a style of moving or activity: living at a fast pace.
• *vb* **1** walk at a slow, measured rate. **2** walk back and forth. **3** mark out by pacing. **4** set the pace for, esp. in a race. **keep pace** move at the same speed as. **pacemaker** *n* **1** someone or something that sets the pace for another. **2** an electrical apparatus that applies regular impulses to the heart to stimulate contractions. **put** (**someone**) **through his** or **her paces** test the ability of. < ultimately Latin *pandere* to spread.

pacific (pəˈsɪfɪk) *adj* peace-loving; calm. **pacifically** *adv* **pacifism** *n* a creed opposing war as a way of settling disputes. **pacifist** *n* **pacify** *vb* **pacified; pacifying 1** calm; appease. **2** restore to order; subdue. < ultimately Latin *pax* peace.

pack (pæk) *n* **1** a bundle of things tied together or wrapped up, carried esp. on the back. **2** a large amount: a pack of lies. **3** a container or wrapping for retailed goods. **4** a set of playing-cards. **5** a group of dogs, wolves, etc. **6** an organized band of people. **7** damp material applied to the body for soothing.
• *vb* **1** put into a container for storage or transporting. **2** crowd; fill. **3** press (something) tightly on, into, or round. **4** gather into a pack. **packer** *n* **pack-horse** *n* a horse used for carrying packs. **pack-ice** *n* large, compressed masses of ice floating in the sea. **packing-case** *n* a wooden crate, used for storing or transporting goods. **pack it in** (*informal*) stop doing something. **pack up** (*informal*) **1** stop (an activity). **2** stop functioning. < Middle English.

package (ˈpækɪdʒ) *n* **1** something wrapped or sealed; parcel. **2** a container or wrapper for packing things in. **3** a complete unit or combination. **package deal** an agreement made on the acceptance of all the elements or proposals involved. **package holiday** a holiday which includes transport, accommodation, etc., for one price.

packet (ˈpækɪt) *n* **1** a small parcel or pack. **2** (*informal*) a lot of money: It cost a packet. **3** a mail-boat on a fixed, regular route. < Anglo-French *pacquet* small pack.

pact (pækt) *n* an alliance or agreement. < Latin *pacisci* to agree.

pad (pæd) *n* **1** a flat, soft piece of material, used to cushion something, absorb liquid, shape clothing, or add bulk. **2** a guard worn to protect a part of the body in cricket, hockey, etc. **3** the fleshy underpart of the end of the finger, or of the toes of animals such as cats and dogs. **4** sheets of blank paper fastened together at one edge. **5** a launching area for helicopters or spacecraft. **6** (*slang*) a flat or lodgings.
• *vb* **padded; padding 1** apply pads or padding to. **2** also **pad out** expand on (speech or writing) unnecessarily. **3** walk with soft steps. < origin unknown.

paddle (ˈpædl̩) *n* **1** a short oar, used to steer a canoe, etc.; instrument shaped like this. **2** paddling.
• *vb* **1** propel with or as if with a paddle. **2** wade barefooted in shallow water. **paddle-wheel** *n* a power-driven wheel with paddles round its rim, which propels a boat. **paddling pool** a shallow pool for children to play in. < Middle English *padell*.

paddock (ˈpædək) *n* **1** a small, enclosed field, esp. for keeping horses. **2** an area at a race-track where motor cycles or cars are worked on before the race. < Old English *pearroc*.

paddy (ˈpædɪ) *n* **1** a rice-field. **2** unmilled or unharvested rice. < Malay *padi*.

padlock (ˈpædˌlɒk) *n* a detachable lock with a shackle that fastens by being passed through a link or staple.
• *vb* secure with a padlock. < Middle English *padlok*.

paediatrics (ˌpiːdɪˈætrɪks) *n* medicine concerned with the care of children and diseases affecting them. **paediatric** *adj* **paediatrician** *n* < ultimately Greek *pais* child.

pagan (ˈpeɪgən) *n, adj* (a) heathen. **paganism** *n* < ultimately Latin *pagus* village.

page[1] (peɪdʒ) *n* a leaf of paper in a book, magazine, etc.; one side of this. < Latin *pagina*.

page[2] *n* **1** a young boy employed to run errands, deliver messages, etc. **2** a young boy who attends people at formal

functions, esp. weddings.
• *vb* summon (someone) by calling out his or her name, esp. over a public-address system. < Italian *paggio*.

pageant (ˈpædʒənt) *n* a colourful, public show or parade in costume, esp. one showing historical scenes. **pageantry** *n* < ultimately Latin *pagina* page.

pagoda (pəˈgəʊdə) *n* a tower with many storeys usually built as a temple or memorial in Far Eastern countries. < Portuguese *pagode* temple.

paid (peɪd) SEE **PAY**. **paid-up** *adj* having made all payments required. **put paid to** put an end to.

pail (peɪl) *n* a bucket; its contents. < Old English *pægel*.

pain (peɪn) *n* **1** bodily suffering caused by injury or disease. **2** mental anguish. **3** a nuisance; bother. **4** *pl* care or trouble taken.
• *vb* cause suffering to. **a pain in the neck** (*informal*) a source of irritation; bother. **pained** *adj* hurt; unhappy. **painful** *adj* **1** causing or feeling pain. **2** hard; trying. **painfully** *adv* **painfulness** *n* **pain-killer** *n* a drug that lessens pain. **painless** *adj* pain-free; easy. **painlessly** *adv* **painlessness** *n* **painstaking** *adj* extremely careful or thorough. < ultimately Greek *poinē* penalty. SEE PANEL.

paint (peɪnt) *n* a liquid substance which is applied to a surface for colouring.
• *vb* **1** apply paint to. **2** make a picture by painting. **3** describe; tell vividly: She's not as black as she's painted. **4** apply (make-up) to the skin. **paintbox** *n* a box containing artist's paints. **paintbrush** *n* a brush used for painting with. **painter** *n* someone who paints. **painting** *n* a picture made in paints. **paint the town red** celebrate wildly. **paintwork** *n* painted surfaces. < ultimately Latin *pingere* to paint.

pair (pɛə) *n* **1** a set of two things that go together. **2** something made up of two connected, matching parts: a pair of shorts. **3** two animals kept together for breeding. **4** a couple who are in love, engaged, or married. **5** one of a matching pair of things. **6** two MPs from opposite parties who agree to abstain from voting on a specific issue.
• *vb* **1** put together in twos; match. **2** join with someone of the opposite sex, esp. in marriage. **pair off** form or cause to form pairs. < ultimately Latin *par* equal.

pal (pæl) *n* (*informal*) a friend.
• *vb* **palled; palling** also **pal up** make friends. **pally** *adj* friendly. < Romany, ultimately from Sanskrit *bhrātr*.

palace (ˈpælɪs) *n* **1** the official residence of a ruler, bishop, or archbishop. **2** a large, magnificent house or building. **palatial** *adj* < ultimately Latin *palatium*, the Palatine hill in Rome. SEE PANEL.

palate (ˈpælɪt) *n* **1** the roof of the mouth. **2** the sense of taste. **3** appreciation; relish. **palatable** *adj* agreeable to the taste or to the mind. < Latin *palatum*.

palaver (pəˈlɑːvə) *n* (*informal*) a tedious business; fuss. < Late Latin *parabola* parable.

pale[1] (peɪl) *adj* **1** (of colour) lacking intensity; whitish. **2** feeble; weak.
• *vb* become pale or paler. **palely** *adv* **paleness** *n* < ultimately Latin *pallēre* to be pale.

pale[2] *n* **1** an upright, wooden post, used in fencing. **2** a district or boundary. **beyond the pale** outside normal social

no ordinary pain

One of the interesting things about idioms and sayings is that they sometimes preserve words or meanings which have otherwise disappeared from the language. Take, for example, the idiom under pain of death. In this expression the word pain—ultimately from the Greek *poinē* 'penalty'—retains its old meaning of 'punishment'.

Another example of a 'fossilized' meaning is to be found in the exception proves the rule, where prove retains its original Latin meaning of 'test'—the exception *tests* the rule.

palace

The official residence of a monarch, archbishop, or similar dignitary is known as a palace. This comes via Old French from the Latin *palatium,* which in turn derives from *Palatium,* the Palatine Hill in Rome. It was on this hill that the Roman emperors had their residences built.

conventions; improper. < Latin *palus* stake.
palette (ˈpælɪt) *n* a thin, hand-held board used by artists for mixing colours. **palette knife** a blunt knife with a flexible steel blade, used by artists or in cooking. < ultimately Latin *pala* spade.
palindrome (ˈpælɪnˌdrəʊm) *n* a word, etc., that reads the same backwards as forwards. < Greek *palin* again + *dramein* to run.
pall (pɔːl) *n* **1** a heavy cloth spread over a coffin or tomb. **2** a dark, gloomy covering: a pall of black smoke.
• *vb* become dull or boring. **pallbearer** *n* someone who escorts or carries a coffin at a funeral. < ultimately Latin *pallium* cloak.
pallet[1] (ˈpælɪt) *n* **1** a mattress filled with straw. **2** a hard, makeshift bed. < ultimately Latin *palea* straw.
pallet[2] *n* a movable platform, used for lifting goods in storage, esp. by fork-lift truck. < Middle French *palette* small shovel.
palliative (ˈpælɪətɪv) *adj* calming; soothing.
• *n* something that relieves or soothes. < ultimately Latin *pallium* cloak.
pallid (ˈpælɪd) *adj* lacking colour, esp. in the face. **pallor** *n* < Latin *pallidus.*
palm (pɑːm) *n* **1** the inner part of the hand between the wrist and fingers; corresponding part on a glove. **2** a tropical or sub-tropical tree with a straight trunk, no branches, and a crown of large leaves; leaf of this. **3** a symbol of triumph or success.
• *vb* **1** hide in the hand. **2 palm off** get rid of (something useless) deceitfully. **palmist** *n* someone who professes to read someone's character or future by interpreting the lines on the palm of the hand. **palmistry** *n* < Latin *palma.*
palpable (ˈpælpəbl̩) *adj* **1** real; tangible. **2** apparent to the senses; obvious. **palpability** *n* **palpably** *adv* < Latin *palpare* to stroke.
palpitate (ˈpælpɪˌteɪt) *vb* **1** (of the heart) beat or throb rapidly. **2** quiver; tremble. **palpitation** *n* < Latin *palpare* to stroke.
palsy (ˈpɔːlzɪ) *n* uncontrollable tremors or paralysis in the body. **palsied** *adj* affected by this. < ultimately Latin *paralysis.*
paltry (ˈpɔːltrɪ) *adj* meagre; worthless. < obsolete: trash.
pamper (ˈpæmpə) *vb* treat with excessive care; indulge. < Middle English *pamperen.*
pamphlet (ˈpæmflɪt) *n* a small, printed leaflet with a paper cover dealing usually with information on a particular topic. < *Pamphilus,* popular 12th-century Latin love poem. SEE PANEL.
pan[1] (pæn) *n* **1** a round, shallow vessel with a long handle, used in cooking. **2** any similarly shaped article, or its contents. **3** the dish of a pair of scales. **4** a lavatory bowl.
• *vb* **panned; panning 1** wash (earth or gravel) in a pan while searching for gold. **2** (*informal*) criticize strongly. **pan out** turn out; develop or succeed. < Old English *panne.*
pan[2] *vb* **panned; panning** (of a camera) turn or rotate horizontally to follow a moving object or give a panoramic effect. < *panorama.*
pan- *prefix* all; every: Pan-American. < Greek *pas.*
panacea (ˌpænəˈsiːə) *n* a remedy for all troubles or ills; cure-all. < Greek *pan-* + *akos* remedy. SEE PANEL.

pamphlet

Very often a word ending in *-let* is a diminutive of its root. For example, a book*let* is 'a small book', a drop*let* is 'a small drop', and a flat*let* means 'a small flat'. All this looks very straightforward. However, not every word ending in *-let* is a diminutive. Take for example the word pamphlet. Pamphlet (Middle English *pamflet*) derives from the Old French *Pamphilet,* from Medieval Latin *Pamphilus.* This was the shortened name of a popular 12th-century love poem called *Pamphilus seu De Amore* 'Pamphilus or On Love'.

panacea

Panacea, 'a universal remedy' or 'cure-all', comes from the Greek word *panakeia,* from *pan-* 'all' and *akeisthai* 'to heal', from *akos* 'remedy'. In Greek mythology the meaning was personified in the form of Panacea, the daughter of Asclepius, the god of healing and medicine.

panache (pəˈnæʃ, pæˈnæʃ) *n* stylishness; dash. < Late Latin *pinnaculum* small wing.
panatella (ˌpænəˈtɛlə) *n* a long, thin cigar. < American Spanish: long, thin biscuit, from Latin *panis* bread.
SEE PANEL.
pancake (ˈpænˌkeɪk) *n* **1** a thin, flat cake of batter cooked on both sides, often with a filling. **2** a flat cake of make-up for the face.
panchromatic (ˌpænkrəʊˈmætɪk) *adj* (of photographic film) sensitive to all colours in the visible spectrum. < Greek *pan-* all + *chrōma* colour.
pancreas (ˈpæŋkrɪəs) *n* a gland situated behind the stomach that secretes a digestive fluid into the duodenum. **pancreatic** *adj* < Greek *pan-* + *kreas* flesh.
panda (ˈpændə) *n* **1** a large, rare, black-and-white, plant-eating mammal resembling a bear, found in south-west China. **2** an animal resembling the raccoon, found in the Himalayas. **panda car** a small police patrol car with doors and bodywork in different colours. < French, from Nepalese.
pandemonium (ˌpændɪˈməʊnɪəm) *n* chaos; tumult. < ultimately Greek *pan-* + *daimōn* evil spirit.
pander (ˈpændə) *vb* **pander to** satisfy or indulge (the desires and weaknesses of others).
• *n* a pimp. < Greek *Pandaros* mythical procurer. SEE PANEL.
p. & p. *abbrev* postage and packing.
pane (peɪn) *n* a sheet of glass framed in a door or window. < ultimately Latin *pannus* rag.
panegyric (ˌpænɪˈdʒɪrɪk) *n* formal or elaborate speech or writing praising someone or something. < Greek *pan-* + *agyris* assembly.
panel (ˈpænl̩) *n* **1** a separate, usually rectangular section of a surface such as a door or wall, or a section of the bodywork of a car. **2** a flat strip on which controls or dials are mounted (in a car, aircraft, etc.). **3** a distinct strip of fabric set in a garment. **4** a group of people chosen or meeting to discuss, decide, or investigate something. **5** a list of jurors summoned; jury.
• *vb* **panelled; panelling** furnish with panels. **panelling** *n* panels in a wall or door; wood used for this. **panellist** *n* a panel member. < ultimately Latin *pannus* cloth.
pang (pæŋ) *n* a sharp spasm of pain, mental distress, or hunger. < origin unknown.
panic (ˈpænɪk) *n* sudden, uncontrollable fear.
• *vb* **panicked; panicking** feel or cause

crumby panatellas

The name of the long, thin cigar known as a panatella comes from the American Spanish word *panetela.* This has nothing to do with tobacco but means 'a long, slim biscuit', and derives from the Italian *panatella* 'a small loaf'. The Italian word derives in turn from the Latin *panis* meaning 'bread'.

pander

To pander to a person's weaknesses or whims is to seek to gratify them, especially in order to win or retain favour: Even news programmes pander to our love of violence. The original meaning of the verb was 'to act as a procurer'. It derives ultimately from the name of *Pandaros,* Pandaras, the leader of the Lycians in the Trojan War. In their versions of 'Troilus and Cressida', Boccaccio, Chaucer, and later Shakespeare cast Pandarus as procurer and go-between.

panicky or panicy?

Words ending in -c add a k before certain suffixes: panic*k*ed, panic*k*y. The suffixes are -y and those that begin with e- or i-, such as -ed, -er, and -ing.

Other words ending in -c that add a k include:

frolic—frolicked, frolicking
mimic—mimicked
picnic—picnicker
traffic—(drug) trafficker

An exception is arc: arced, arcing, not arcked, arcking.

to feel panic. **panicky** *adj* **panic-stricken** *adj* alarmed; terrified. < Greek *panikos*, from *Pan*, rural god causing terror. SEE PANEL.

pannier (ˈpænɪə) *n* **1** a large basket, esp. one of a pair slung over a pack animal. **2** one of a pair of boxes fixed at the rear of a motor cycle or bicycle. < ultimately Latin *panis* bread.

panoply (ˌpænəplɪ) *n* a magnificent array; regalia. < Greek *pan-* + *hoplon* tool.

panorama (ˌpænəˈrɑːmə) *n* **1** a wide scenic view; picture or photograph of this. **2** an overall survey of a sequence of events. **panoramic** *adj* < Greek *pan-* + *horan* to see.

pansy (ˈpænzɪ) *n* **1** a garden plant of the violet family with velvety petals of white, yellow, or purple. **2** an effeminate or homosexual male. < ultimately Latin *pensare* to ponder. SEE PANEL.

pant (pænt) *vb* **1** breathe in short, quick bursts. **2** utter when or as if out of breath; gasp. **3** yearn for; crave. • *n* a panting breath; sound of this. < ultimately Greek *phantasia* imagination.

pantaloons (ˌpæntəˈluːnz) *pl n* (*humorous*) trousers; old style of these. < Old Italian *Pantalone*.

pantechnicon (pænˈtɛknɪkən) *n* a large van, used for household furniture removals. SEE PANEL.

panther (ˈpænθə) *n* a leopard, esp. of the black variety. < Greek *panthēr*.

panties (ˈpæntɪz) *pl n* short knickers worn by women or children.

pantihose (ˈpæntɪˌhəʊz) *n* tights for women.

pantomime (ˈpæntəˌmaɪm) *n* **1** a dramatic musical presentation of a fairy-tale, usually for children at Christmas-time. **2** bodily gestures and facial expressions conveying meaning; story conveyed like this. < Greek *pas* + Latin *mimus* mime.

pantry (ˈpæntrɪ) *n* a room or cupboard where food or dishes, cutlery, etc., are stored. < ultimately Latin *panis* bread.

pants (pænts) *pl n* **1** men's underpants. **2** knickers. **3** (*chiefly US*) trousers. < short for *pantaloons*.

pap (pæp) *n* **1** a soft, mushy food for invalids or infants. **2** trivia; rubbish. < Middle English.

papacy (ˈpeɪpəsɪ) *n* the office of pope; system of government of the Roman Catholic Church. **papal** *adj* of the papacy or the pope. < Late Latin *papa* pope.

paper (ˈpeɪpə) *n* **1** a substance made from pulped wood, rags, etc., used for writing or drawing on or wrapping things; piece of this. **2** wallpaper. **3** a newspaper. **4** a document: identification papers. **5** a formal, written composition. **6** a set of questions in an examination. • *vb* line or cover with paper, esp. wallpaper. **on paper** in writing; ideally. **paperback** *adj*, *n* (a book) bound in a paper cover. **paper-boy** fem. **paper-girl** *n* a young person who delivers newspapers. **paper-clip** *n* a clip made of wire loops for holding sheets of paper

pantechnicon

Pantechnicon is a Greek word meaning 'belonging to all the arts'. In view of this it seems a highly inappropriate name for a removal van. The explanation of how it came to be used in this way goes back to 1830 when a group of London businessmen used the word as the high-sounding name for a type of artwork supermarket that they had had built in Motcomb Street. The venture proved a disastrous flop and the building changed hands to become the property of a furniture removal and storage company. The name, however, was retained and was extended to the vehicles that entered and left the one-time arts centre.

pensive pansies

The name of the pansy is enough to set one thinking. The reason is that it comes into English via the French words *pense*, 'thought' and *penser*, 'to think', from the Latin *pensare* 'to ponder'. It is therefore closely related to pensive 'deeply or sadly thoughtful', which has the same root.

In recent years pansy has also come to be applied to people. It is used, however, not to refer to those of meditative or pensive habit; it is an informal, derogatory term for homosexual or effeminate men. Which raises the question, why pansy as opposed to daffodil or some other flower?

together. **paper-knife** *n* a knife for opening envelopes or slitting uncut pages. **paper money** banknotes. **paper over** explain away or hide (flaws or disagreements) to preserve an image of unity. **paper tiger** someone or something that looks dangerous but is actually powerless. **paperweight** *n* a small, heavy object used to hold down loose papers. **paperwork** *n* routine clerical or record-keeping work. < ultimately Greek *papyros* papyrus.

papier mâché (ˌpæpjeɪ ˈmæʃeɪ) *adj, n* (made of) paper pulped with glue, used for moulding into boxes, trays, ornaments, etc. < French: chewed paper.

paprika (ˈpæprɪkə, pæˈpriːkə) *n* a mild seasoning made from powdered, sweet red pepper. < ultimately Greek *peperi*.

par (pɑː) *n* **1** an average or standard level, amount, condition, etc.: par for the course. **2** the monetary value of stocks and shares, or of a unit of foreign currency in a unit of another country. **3** the number of strokes a good golfer needs for each hole. **on a par with** the same as. < Latin: equal.

parable (ˈpærəbl̩) *n* a short story which illustrates a moral or spiritual principle. < ultimately Greek *paraballein* to compare.

parabola (pəˈræbələ) *n* a curve like one described by an object thrown up and then falling down to earth. **parabolic** *adj* **1** of or like a parabola in form. **2** of or expressed by a parable. < New Latin.

parachute (ˈpærəˌʃuːt) *n* a device made of a light fabric for slowing down the fall of someone or something from a great height, esp. from an aircraft in flight.
• *vb* drop or descend by parachute. **parachutist** *n* < Old Italian *parare* to shield + French *chute* fall.

parade (pəˈreɪd) *n* **1** an ostentatious exhibition; display. **2** an ordered assembly of troops for ceremonial purposes; place where this is held. **3** a public procession. **4** a street of shops, etc.; promenade.
• *vb* **1** march or walk in procession. **2** exhibit; display. **3** assemble in formation. < French: preparation, from Spanish, ultimately from Latin *parare* to prepare.

paradigm (ˈpærəˌdaɪm) *n* a model or ideal; archetype. < Greek *paradeiknynai* to show.

paradise (ˈpærəˌdaɪs) *n* **1** a blissful place; heaven. **2** the garden of Eden. < Greek *paradeisos* enclosed park.

paradox (ˈpærəˌdɒks) *n* a statement that is apparently self-contradictory or ridiculous yet has truth in it. **paradoxical** *adj* **paradoxically** *adv* < Greek *para-* besides + *dokein* to seem.

paraffin (ˈpærəfɪn) *n* a distillation of petroleum, used as a fuel or solvent. **liquid paraffin** a colourless, tasteless form of this used as a laxative. **paraffin wax** solid paraffin. < Latin *parum* too little + *affinis* related.

paragon (ˈpærəgən) *n* a model of perfection; ideal. < ultimately Greek *parakonan* to sharpen, from *para-* + *akē* point.

paragraph (ˈpærəˌgrɑːf) *n* a section of a piece of writing which treats a single theme, usually indented at the beginning.
• *vb* organize in paragraphs. < Greek *para-* + *graphein* to write.

parallel (ˈpærəˌlɛl) *adj* **1** equidistant at every point and never meeting: parallel lines. **2** similar; corresponding.
• *n* **1** parallel line, surface, or curve, esp. a line of latitude on the earth's surface. **2** an exact likeness; counterpart. **3** a correspondence or comparison.
• *vb* **1** make parallel; equal. **2** compare. **parallelism** *n* **parallelogram** *n* a four-sided, geometric figure with opposite sides parallel and equal. < Greek *para-* beside + *allēlōn* of one another.

paralyse (ˈpærəˌlaɪz) *vb* **1** cause to lose the ability to move. **2** bring to a halt. **paralysis** *n* **paralytic** *adj* **1** also *n* (a person) affected by paralysis. **2** extremely drunk. < Greek *para-* + *lyein* to loosen.

parameter (pəˈræmɪtə) *n* **1** something constant in a specific case but variable in other cases. **2** a characteristic, esp. one that defines; limit, framework, or guideline. < Greek *para-* + *metron* measure.

paramilitary (ˌpærəˈmɪlɪtrɪ) *adj* organized on military lines but not part of the armed forces.
• *n* a member of a paramilitary force.

paramount (ˈpærəˌmaʊnt) *adj* of supreme importance; principal. < Latin *per* by + *a* to + *mont* mountain.

paranoia (ˌpærəˈnɔɪə) *n* **1** a disorder of the mind featuring delusions, esp. of persecution or grandeur. **2** excessive or abnormal suspicion or distrust of others. **paranoiac** or **paranoid** *n, adj* (someone) suffering from paranoia. < Greek *para-* + *nous* mind.

parapet (ˈpærəpɪt) *n* a wall or rampart protecting the edge of a platform, bridge, roof, etc. < ultimately Latin

parare to prepare + *pectus* chest.
paraphernalia (ˌpærəfəˈneɪlɪə) *n* personal items or articles of equipment; trappings. < Medieval Latin, from Greek *para-* + *pherein* to bear. SEE PANEL.
paraphrase (ˈpærəˌfreɪz) *vb* give the meaning of in another form; re-word. ● *n* a re-worded phrase or passage. < Greek *para-* + *phrazein* to point out.
paraplegia (ˌpærəˈpli:dʒə) *n* paralysis of the lower body. **paraplegic** *adj, n* < Greek *para-* + *plēssein* to strike.
parasite (ˈpærəˌsaɪt) *n* **1** an organism that depends on another for nourishment and survival. **2** someone who lives off others without returning anything; scrounger. **parasitic** *adj* < Greek *para-* + *silos* grain.
parasol (ˈpærəˌsɒl) *n* a lightweight umbrella, used as a sunshade. < Old Italian *parare* to shield + Latin *sol* sun. SEE PANEL AT **UMBRELLA**.
paratroops (ˈpærəˌtru:ps) *pl n* parachute troops. **paratrooper** *n*
parboil (ˈpɑ:ˌbɔɪl) *vb* boil (food) briefly so that it is partly cooked. < ultimately Latin *per* through + *bulla* bubble.
parcel (ˈpɑ:sl̩) *n* **1** something wrapped up; package. **2** a plot of land. **3** an amount of people or things with something in common; batch. ● *vb* **parcelled; parcelling 1** pack; wrap. **2 parcel out** divide into parts; share out. < ultimately Latin *particula* small part.
parch (pɑ:tʃ) *vb* make or become hot, dry, or thirsty. < Middle English *parchen*.
parchment (ˈpɑ:tʃmənt) *n* a material for writing on, prepared from animal skin; paper resembling this. < ultimately Greek *Pergamon* Pergamum, ancient city in Asia Minor.
pardon (ˈpɑ:dn̩) *n* **1** an instance of forgiving or excusing. **2** a cancellation of punishment; absolution. ● *vb* **1** absolve; acquit. **2** forgive; excuse. **pardonable** *adj* **pardonably** *adv* < Latin *per-* thoroughly + *donare* to give. SEE PANEL AT **BEG**.
pare (pɛə) *vb* **1** clip or trim (an edge); peel. **2** cut back or decrease gradually. **parings** *pl n* things pared off: apple parings. < Latin *parare* to prepare.
parent (ˈpɛərənt) *n* **1** a father or mother. **2** an animal or plant from which others come. **3** a source; origin. **parental** *adj* **parenthood** *n* **parentage** *n* family; ancestry. < Latin *parere* to give birth to.
parenthesis (pəˈrɛnθɪsɪs) *n, pl* **parentheses 1** a word or phrase inserted in a passage, which explains or amplifies but is grammatically unnecessary, and is usually marked off by brackets, commas, or dashes. **2** either of the punctuation marks (or), used for this; bracket. **in parenthesis** in brackets; aside. **parenthetic** or **parenthetical** *adj* **1** bracketed. **2** incidental; by the way. < Greek *para-* + *en* in + *tithenai* to place.
par excellence (ˌpɑ:r ˈɛksəlɒns) of the highest order; beyond comparison. < French: by excellence. SEE PANEL.
parish (ˈpærɪʃ) *n* **1** an area that is part of a diocese, served by esp. one church and one clergyman. **2** a rural area regarded as a unit of local government. **3** the

paraphernalia

The married women of ancient Greece and Rome would have been lost without their paraphernalia. The word derives from the Greek *parapherna* 'the personal belongings of a bride', from para—'beside' or 'excluded from' and *phernē* 'dowry'. Without her paraphernalia, then, which she was legally entitled to keep, a married woman wouldn't have had a thing she could call her own.

par excellence

Unlike phrases such as nom de plume ('pseudonym') or inter alia ('among other things'), par excellence (literally 'by excellence') is an example of one of the foreign expressions in common usage for which there is no adequate translation: 'Shakespeare is considered to be the English dramatist *par excellence*'. The meaning is not merely 'without equal' but has to do with 'incorporating the finest imaginable qualities of the group'. Other words and phrases which do not translate freely and which often provide le mot juste include:

ad nauseam	**nouveaux riches**
à la carte	**pièce de résistance**
au fait	**pied-à-terre**
bête noire	**status quo**
en masse	**table d'hôte**
fait accompli	**tour de force**
faux pas	

people of a parish. **parish council** a body that administrates a civil parish. **parishioner** *n* a member of a parish. **parish register** a book with records of the baptisms, marriages, and burials in a parish. < ultimately Greek *para-* beside + *oikos* house.

parity(ˈpærɪtɪ) *n* **1** equality; equivalence. **2** equivalence of a price in one country expressed in another. < Latin *par* equal.

park (pɑːk) *n* **1** an area of open land for public recreation. **2** an enclosed area of wood and grassland as part of a private estate. **3** a space where vehicles can be left.
• *vb* **1** position and leave (a vehicle) temporarily. **2** (*informal*) position temporarily. **parking-meter** *n* a coin-operated device which shows the time a vehicle may be left by it and the required payment. **parking-ticket** *n* a document left on an illegally-parked vehicle, giving notice of the fine which must be paid. < Old French *parc* enclosure.

parley (pɑːlɪ) *n, pl* **parleys** a talk, esp. between opposing sides in a dispute to discuss terms.
• *vb* negotiate, esp. with an enemy. < Late Latin *parabola* speech, parable.

parliament (ˈpɑːləmənt) *n* **1 Parliament** the supreme law-making body in the UK, comprising the House of Commons and the House of Lords. **2** the law-making body of a country. **parliamentary** *adj* **parliamentarian** *n* someone skilled in the rules and practice of a parliament. < Old French *parler* to speak.

parlour (ˈpɑːlə) *n* **1** a sitting-room in a private house. **2** a room in an inn, club, etc., for semi-private uses. **3** a place of business: beauty parlour. **4** a place where cows are milked. **parlour game** an indoor board-game, etc. < Old French *parler* to speak. SEE PANEL.

parochial (pəˈrəʊkɪəl) *adj* **1** of a church parish. **2** narrow in outlook; provincial. **parochialism** *n* < Latin *parochia* parish.

parody (ˈpærədɪ) *n* **1** an imitation of an artistic work, style, or someone's manner, done for comic effect. **2** a weak or badly-done imitation; travesty.
• *vb* **parodied; parodying** imitate humorously; make a parody of. < Greek para- + *aidein* to sing.

parole (pəˈrəʊl) *n* **1** someone's word of honour. **2** the release of a convict before expiry of sentence, on condition of good behaviour. **3** a promise made by a prisoner to fulfil certain conditions in return for lifting restrictions.
• *vb* free (a prisoner) on parole. < Late Latin *parabola* speech.

parquet (ˈpɑːkeɪ) *n* a floor of inlaid wooden blocks in a decorative pattern. < Middle French: small enclosure.

parrot (ˈpærət) *n* **1** a usually brightly-coloured, tropical bird with a short, hooked bill, often good at mimicry. **2** someone who mindlessly copies the words and actions of another. < Middle French *perroquet*.

parry (ˈpærɪ) *vb* **parried; parrying** **1** block or deflect (a weapon or blow). **2** evade (questions) cleverly.
• *n* an act of parrying. < ultimately Latin *parare* to prepare.

parse (pɑːz) *vb* describe (a word or phrase) in terms of parts of speech and grammatical relationship. < Latin *pars orationis* part of speech.

parsimonious (ˌpɑːsɪˈməʊnɪəs) *adj* extremely frugal; miserly. **parsimoniously** *adv* **parsimony** *n* < ultimately Latin *parcere* to spare.

parsley (ˈpɑːslɪ) *n* a plant of the carrot family, grown for its crinkled leaves, used in sauces, or for seasoning or garnishing food. < ultimately Greek *petros* rock + *selinon* parsley.

parsnip (ˈpɑːsnɪp) *n* a plant of the carrot family with a long, yellowish, tapering root, eaten as a vegetable; this root. < ultimately Latin *pastinum* two-pronged tool for digging.

parson (ˈpɑːsn̩) *n* a clergyman; vicar.

parlour talk

The modern-day 'sitting-room' or 'living-room' was formerly known as a parlour. It was here that guests and visitors were received and entertained. The name of the room derives from the Old French word *parleur,* meaning a reception-room in a monastery or convent. This room was named after its special advantage. *Parleur* derives from *parler* 'to speak' and it was in the parlour that social interactions were allowed.

Nowadays, the root meaning of parlour has virtually disappeared. The word is encountered most often in phrases such as funeral parlour, and beauty parlour, where it means 'a place equipped for conducting a specified business'.

parsonage *n* a house provided for a parson by the church. **parson's nose** the fatty end of the rump of a fowl when cooked. < Latin *persona.*

part (pɑ:t) *n* **1** a piece or fraction; each of several subdivisions of something. **2** a division of a literary work, radio or television serial, etc. **3** a line of music for a voice or instrument; score for this. **4** a character played by an actor in a play or film; words spoken by this. **5** a distinct piece of the body of a human, animal, or plant. **6** one of the pieces which make up a mechanism or other device: spare parts. **7** an essential element. **8** a side in a dispute or conflict. **9** a role; function or duty. **10** a territory: in foreign parts.
• *adv* partly.
• *vb* **1** come or cause to come apart; divide. **2** (of people) take leave of one another: They parted company. **3 part with** let go of; relinquish. **in good part** without becoming annoyed. **in part** partly. **part and parcel of** an essential part of. **part-exchange** *n* paying for something in goods and money. **parting** *n* **1** going; departure. **2** a line on the head where the hair is parted. **partly** *adv* in part. **part-time** *adj, adv* (working) less than the usual or normal working hours. **part-timer** *n* < Latin *pars.*
SEE PANEL.

partake (pɑ:ˈteɪk) *vb* **partook; partaken; partaking 1** share or participate (in). **2** receive or consume food. **partaker** *n* < back formation from *partaker,*

parts of speech

What is meant by the phrase parts of speech? Underlying the expression is the idea that each word in the language can be used only in certain slots in a sentence.

One way of illustrating this is with a sentence such as the following: She was holding a party to farewell some friends. In this sentence the word farewell has been put in a slot that it doesn't normally occupy. The person who wrote the sentence, a foreign learner, knew the meaning of farewell, but mistook its identity as a part of speech. Farewell is a part of speech known as a *noun;* the writer of the above sentence used it mistakenly as a *verb.*

alteration of *part taker.*

partial (ˈpɑ:ʃəl) *adj* **1** of a part; not total. **2** unfair; prejudiced. **3 partial to** keen on; fond of. **partiality** *n* **partially** *adv* < Latin *pars* part.

participate (pɑ:ˈtɪsɪˌpeɪt) *vb* join or take part in. **participant** *n* **participation** *n* < Latin *pars* part + *capere* to take.

participle (ˈpɑ:tɪsɪpl̩, pɑ:ˈtɪsɪpl̩) *n* a verbal form used in compound verb forms or as an adjective. **past participle** a verbal form such as danced or gone. **present participle** a verbal form such as dancing or going. < Latin *particeps.*

particle (ˈpɑ:tɪkl̩) *n* **1** a minute amount of matter, such as an atom or proton. **2** an extremely tiny amount. **3** a minor speech unit or affix. < Latin *particula* small part.

particular (pəˈtɪkjʊlə) *adj* **1** concerning a specific person or thing; individual. **2** special; unusual. **3** thorough; detailed. **4** choosy; hard to please: She's particular about her food.
• *n* a fact; detail. **in particular** especially; exactly. **particularity** *n* **particularly** *adv* **particularize** *vb* detail; itemize. < Latin *particula* small part.

partisan (ˌpˈ:tɪˈzæn, ˈpɑ:tɪˌzæn) *n* **1** a devoted follower of a cause, person, or party. **2** a guerrilla. **partisanship** *n* < Old Italian *partigiano.*

partition (pɑ:ˈtɪʃən) *n* **1** dividing; separation. **2** a part; portion. **3** something that divides, esp. a thin wall or screen in a room.
• *vb* **1** subdivide or separate into parts. **2** separate off by means of a dividing structure. < Latin *partire* to divide.

partner (ˈpɑ:tnə) *n* **1** someone involved equally with one or more people in an association, esp. a business firm. **2** one of a couple who dance together or play a game or sport on the same side. **3** a wife or husband; person with whom one has a sexual relationship.
• *vb* act as a partner to or put together as partners. **partnership** *n* < alteration of Anglo-French *parcener.*

partook (pɑ:ˈtʊk) SEE **PARTAKE.**

partridge (ˈpɑ:trɪdʒ) *n* one of a group of chiefly European game-birds with a stout body and brown feathers. < ultimately Greek *perdrix.*

party (ˈpɑ:tɪ) *n* **1** a social gathering, often held to celebrate something. **2** a group of people working or travelling together: a search party. **3** a group of people engaged in organized political activity. **4** someone concerned or participating in something: I won't be a party to deception.

5 (*humorous*) an individual. **party line 1** the fixed policies of a political party. **2** a telephone line shared by two subscribers. **party-wall** *n* a wall which divides and is common to two properties. < Old French *partir* to divide.

pass (pɑːs) *vb* **1** move onward or past; proceed. **2** cause to go through, across, over, or past. **3** go beyond; exceed. **4** give over; transfer. **5** go from the control of one group or person to another. **6** change from one state or quality to another. **7** happen; take place: It came to pass. **8** disappear: His anger passed. **9** cause to be officially approved, esp. by a legislative body. **10** be tolerated or permitted. **11** be accepted as adequate. **12** utter; pronounce: pass a comment. **13** be accepted as having reached a required standard in (an inspection or examination). **14** emit from the body: pass water. **15** (in a game) omit one's turn. • *n* **1** the passing of an examination. **2** written permission to move about freely or be absent from a post. **3** a movement of the hands along or over something. **4** (in a ball-game) transferring the ball from one player to a team-mate. **5** a usually bad state of affairs: It's come to a pretty pass. **6** a narrow gap in a range of mountains. **7** a sexually inviting gesture. **passable** *adj* **1** able to be passed. **2** adequate but not outstanding. **passbook** *n* a book which records customer transactions in a bank or building society account. **passer-by** *n* someone who is going past, esp. by chance. **passkey** *n* **1** a master key. **2** a key to a gate or door; latchkey. **password** *n* a chosen word or phrase that must be uttered before being let past a guard. < ultimately Latin *passus* step. SEE PANEL.

pass words

Pass features in a number of idiomatic expressions, including:

pass away to die: I was sorry to hear that your mother passed away last week. See also panel at **die**[1].

pass down to transfer to the next generation: The tradition has been passed down from father to son for centuries.

pass for or **as** to be accepted, especially mistakenly as: She's only 14 but passes easily for 18.

pass off 1 to cease or disappear gradually: The pain soon passed off. **2** to take place: The parade passed off smoothly. **3** to offer with intent to deceive: The police caught him passing off counterfeit banknotes.

pass out 1 to faint or lose consciousness. **2** to complete one's military training.

pass over to avoid or ignore: Let's pass over the matter of timing and think about the cost of the project.

pass up to reject, refuse, or ignore.

The expression **ships that pass in the night,** used of strangers who meet and converse briefly and then never see each other again, comes from the poem 'Tales of a Wayside Inn' by the US poet Henry Wadsworth Longfellow, 1807-82:

> Ships that pass in the night, and speak to each other in passing;
> Only a signal shown and a distant voice in the darkness.

passage (ˈpæsɪdʒ) *n* **1** the action of passing. **2** a way of entering or leaving; corridor or channel. **3** a right to pass or be conveyed as a passenger: She booked her passage. **4** a journey, esp. by sea or air. **5** a brief section of a work of music or literature. **6** also **passageway** a corridor.

passenger (ˈpæsɪndʒə) *n* **1** someone travelling in but not operating a vehicle, ship, or aircraft. **2** a team member who contributes little or nothing. < Old French *passer* to pass.

passing (ˈpɑːsɪŋ) *adj* **1** going past. **2** short-lived: a passing fancy. • *n* an end point; death.

passion (ˈpæʃən) *n* **1** intense feeling. **2** an angry outburst. **3** ardent sexual desire. **4** strong liking or fondness for something; object of this. **5 Passion** the sufferings of Christ between the Last Supper and the Crucifixion; musical setting of this. **passionate** *adj* **1** capable of or showing strong feeling. **2** very enthusiastic. **passionately** *adv* **passion-flower** *n* a tropical climbing-plant with showy flowers. **passion-fruit** *n* the edible fruit of some kinds of passion-flower. < ultimately Latin *pati* to suffer.

passive (ˈpæsɪv) *adj* **1** acted on by outside forces; not active. **2** unresisting; compliant. **3** inert. **4** also *n* (*grammar*) (of) a verb form that expresses an action that is done to the subject. **passively** *adv* **passiveness** or **passivity** *n* **passive resistance** resistance by non-violent non-cooperation. < Latin *passivus.* SEE PANEL.

passport (ˈpɑːspɔːt) *n* **1** an official document issued by a government as proof of the identity and nationality of the holder, and affording some protection when travelling abroad. **2** something which ensures entry or acceptance: a passport to success. < Middle French *passer* to pass + Latin *portus* port.

past (pɑːst) *adj* **1** that was or has been. **2** showing time that has gone; previous. • *n* **1** time that has gone; things that occurred then. **2** an earlier period of life, esp. kept secret: a woman with a past. • *prep* **1** beyond in space or time. **2** beyond the range or capacity of: I wouldn't put it past her. • *adv* so as to go beyond. **past it** (*informal*) too old or worn to be effective. **past master** an expert. < Middle English *passen* to pass.

pasta (ˈpæstə) *n* a flour-and-water dough often mixed with egg or oil then shaped and dried, as spaghetti or macaroni. < Italian, from Late Latin.

paste (peɪst) *n* **1** a soft, moist material; adhesive made from starch and water. **2** a sweet, doughy confection. **3** a preparation of ground meat, fish, etc., that is easily spread. **4** a hard, brilliant, glassy material used in making imitation gems.
• *vb* **1** stick or coat with paste. **2** (*informal*) punch or beat. < Late Latin *pasta* dough.

passive

Michael opened the book at the first page. Helen has added up the figures. In these sentences the action expressed by the verb (opened, added up) affects the object (the book, the figures). Sometimes, however, it is not the object but the subject of the sentence that is affected by the action: The book was opened at the first page. The figures have been added up. By changing a sentence around in this way one changes its *voice* from *active* to *passive.* One of the most common functions of the passive voice is to create a formally impersonal style: These sockets must be connected to an existing master socket. The All Risks Package has been increased to a premium of £20.00 a year. Further information may be obtained from your dealer.

pastel (ˈpæstḷ) *n* **1** a paste of mixed gum and powdered pigment; crayon made of this. **2** one of various pale or delicate colours. < Late Latin *pastellus* woad.

pasteurize (ˈpæstʃəˌraɪz) *vb* sterilize (milk) by heating briefly. **pasteurization** *n* < Louis *Pasteur*, died 1895, French chemist. SEE PANEL.

pastiche (pæˈstiːʃ) *n* a work of art, literature, or music that imitates the style of an earlier work, or is made up of borrowed elements. < Late Latin *pasta* dough.

pastille (ˈpæstɪl) *n* a small, flavoured lozenge for sucking or chewing. < Latin *pastillus* small loaf.

pastime (ˈpɑːsˌtaɪm) *n* something that helps pass the time pleasantly; game or hobby.

pastor (ˈpɑːstə) *n* a priest or clergyman looking after a congregation. **pastoral** *adj* **1** of a pastor, spiritual welfare, or guidance. **2** of shepherds or rural life, esp. in an idyllic sense. < ultimately Latin *pascere* to feed.

pastry (ˈpeɪstrɪ) *n* **1** a dough of flour and water, esp. baked as a covering or container for pies. **2** a cake made with pastry. < *paste.*

pasture (ˈpɑːstʃə) *n* grassland used for grazing cattle; plants or grass growing on this.
• *vb* put to graze or feed on pasture. < ultimately Latin *pascere* to feed.

pasty[1] (ˈpæstɪ) *n* a pastry filled with a sweet or savoury filling, baked without a container. < Middle French *paste* dough.

pasty[2] (ˈpeɪstɪ) *adj* **1** like paste; sticky. **2** looking pale and unhealthy: pasty-faced.

pat (pæt) *vb* **patted; patting 1** dab or tap softly with the open hand or a flat

pasteurize

To pasteurize a beverage such as milk or wine is to heat it so as to destroy any harmful micro-organisms it may contain. The process is named after the man who discovered it, Louis *Pasteur,* 1822-95, the French chemist and bacteriologist. The origin of pasteurize is nowadays obscured by its resemblance to pasture, the word which has shaped its pronunciation and which many mistakenly regard as its root.

surface, esp. to show reassurance or approval. **2** flatten, smooth, or mould by doing this.
• *n* **1** patting; sound of this. **2** a small lump of something soft, such as butter.
• *adj* **1** exactly right; suitable. **2** contrived; glib: a pat answer.
• *adv* **off pat** promptly or exactly memorized. **pat on the back** a word or gesture of praise or approval. < Middle English *patte*, probably like the sound.

patch (pætʃ) *n* **1** a piece of material used to cover or mend a hole. **2** plaster or padding applied to a wound, or a protective shield over an eye. **3** an area which differs from its surroundings in colour, texture, etc. **4** a plot of ground: vegetable patch. **5** a short period of time: going through a bad patch.
• *vb* **1** cover with or put on a patch or patches. **2** put together with patches. **not a patch on** (*informal*) nowhere near as good as. **patch up 1** mend or put together with patches. **2** put an end to a quarrel or differences. **patchwork** *n* needlework consisting of different pieces of cloth sewn together; something made like this: patchwork quilt. **patchy** *adj* **1** having or made up of patches. **2** of irregular quality; bitty. **patchily** *adv* **patchiness** *n* < perhaps Middle French *pieche* piece.

pâté (ˈpæteɪ) *n* a rich paste of spiced meat, fish, etc. < Old French: paste.

patent (ˈpeɪtn̩t) *adj* **1** unmistakable; obvious. **2** of or protected by a patent.
• *vb* secure a patent for. **patent leather** leather with a smooth, glossy surface.
• *n* (also ˈpætn̩t) **1 letters patent** an exclusive right granted by the government to make or sell an invention. **2** a patented invention. **Patent Office** the government office which issues patents. < ultimately Latin *patēre* to be open.

paternal (pəˈtɜːnl̩) *adj* **1** of or like a father. **2** related through one's father: paternal grandmother. **paternally** *adv* **paternalism** *n* a system of organizing or governing people like a father; seeing to needs but retaining authority. **paternalistic** *adj* **paternity** *n* **1** being a father. **2** descent from a father. < Latin *pater* father.

paternoster (ˌpætəˈnɒstə) *n* **1** the Lord's Prayer. **2** a type of continuous lift that passengers enter and leave while its platforms are moving. < Latin: our father.

path (pɑːθ) *n* **1** also **pathway** a track formed or made for the passage of animals or people on foot. **2** a route; direction. **3** a way of life; conduct. < Old English *pæth*.

pathetic (pəˈθɛtɪk) *adj* **1** evoking sorrow or pity. **2** pitifully inadequate; meagre. **pathetically** *adv* < ultimately Greek *paschein* to suffer.

pathology (pəˈθɒlədʒɪ) *n* **1** the study of bodily diseases. **2** the abnormalities in the body caused by disease. **pathological** *adj* **pathologist** *n* < ultimately Greek *pathos* suffering + *logos* word.

pathos (ˈpeiθɒs) *n* a quality that evokes sadness or compassion. < Greek: suffering.

patience (ˈpeɪʃəns) *n* **1** the capacity to tolerate hardship, irritation, inconvenience, etc., calmly and without complaint. **2** a card-game played by one person which involves arranging the cards into a pattern.

patient (ˈpeɪʃənt) *n* someone who undergoes or awaits medical treatment.
• *adj* having or showing patience. **patiently** *adv* < ultimately Latin *pati* to suffer.

patio (ˈpætɪˌəʊ) *n, pl* **patios** an enclosed courtyard or paved terrace beside a house. < Spanish.

patriarch (ˈpeɪtrɪˌɑːk) *n* **1** one of the biblical ancestors of mankind or the Hebrew race; male founder of any race, tribe, etc. **2** a high-ranking bishop or head of various Eastern Churches. **3** a very old or venerable man. **patriarchal** *adj* < Greek *patēr* father + *archēs* arch.

patrician (pəˈtrɪʃən) *n* a member of the nobility, esp. in ancient Rome.
• *adj* of high birth. < Latin *patres* senator, from *pater* father.

patricide (ˈpætrɪˌsaɪd) *n* the act of murdering one's own father. < Latin *pater* father + *caedere* to kill.

patrimony (ˈpætrɪmənɪ) *n* **1** an inheritance from one's father or ancestor. **2** the endowment or estate of a church. < Latin *patrimonium*.

patriot (ˈpeɪtrɪət, ˈpætrɪət) *n* someone who is totally devoted to his or her country. **patriotic** *adj* **patriotically** *adv* **patriotism** *n* < ultimately Greek *patēr* father.

patrol (pəˈtrəʊl) *vb* **patrolled; patrolling** go round or through (a particular area) regularly to observe or maintain security.
• *n* **1** patrolling. **2** people, ships, vehicles, etc., that are on patrol. **3** a subgroup of Scouts or Guides of between 6 and 8 members. < Middle French *patrouiller* to paddle.

patron (ˈpeɪtrən) fem. **patroness** *n* **1** someone who helps a cause or activity, using wealth or influence. **2** a regular customer. **patronage** *n* **1** the support of a patron. **2** the power to appoint to a position, esp. in government. **3** condescending behaviour. **patronize** *vb* **1** support as a patron. **2** visit regularly as a customer. **3** behave condescendingly towards. **patronizing** *adj* condescending. **patronizingly** *adv* **patron saint** a saint considered to be the protector of a particular person, group, activity, etc. < ultimately Latin *pater* father.

patronymic (ˌpætrəˈnɪmɪk) *adj, n* (a name) that is derived from the name of the father or a paternal ancestor. SEE PANEL.

patter[1] (ˈpætə) *vb* **1** beat or tap quickly and repeatedly. **2** run with light, quick steps; scurry.
• *n* a series of light, quick taps. < *pat.*

patter[2] *n* **1** glib, rapid-fire talk characteristic of a salesman or entertainer. **2** empty talk; chatter. < Middle English *patren,* from *paternoster.*

pattern (ˈpætn̩) *n* **1** a usually repeated ornamental design. **2** a model for imitation; example. **3** a design or set of instructions to be followed in making something. **4** a sample. **5** a chance or natural arrangement of things or events.
• *vb* make or decorate according to a pattern. < Medieval Latin *patronus.*

paucity (ˈpɔːsɪtɪ) *n* shortage; scarcity. < Latin *paucus* little.

paunch (pɔːntʃ) *n* **1** the belly. **2** a belly that protrudes. < Latin *pantex.*

pauper (ˈpɔːpə) *n* someone who is extremely poor. **pauperize** *vb* make poor or destitute. < Latin: poor.

pause (pɔːz) *n* a temporary stop or rest, esp. in speech or action.
• *vb* stop temporarily; hesitate. **give pause** cause to hesitate. < ultimately Greek *pauein* to stop.

pave (peɪv) *vb* cover (a road or path) with a hard layer of stone, concrete, etc. **pavement** *n* a paved surface for walking on, esp. at the side of the road. **pave the way** prepare the way; make easier. **paving-stone** *n* a stone slab, used in paving. < Latin *pavire* to strike.

pavilion (pəˈvɪljən) *n* **1** a sometimes temporary, light, ornamental building in a park or garden. **2** a permanent building on a sports ground, used by players and spectators. < ultimately Latin *papilio* butterfly.

paw (pɔː) *n* **1** the clawed foot of an animal. **2** (*humorous*) someone's hand.
• *vb* **1** hit with a paw. **2** scrape or hit (as if) with a hoof. **3** (*informal*) handle roughly or awkwardly. < Middle French *poue.*

pawn[1] (pɔːn) *n* **1** the smallest and least valuable chess-piece. **2** someone who is used to further another's purposes. < Medieval Latin *pedo* foot soldier. SEE PANEL.

pawn[2] *vb* leave (an article) as a security for money borrowed.
• *n* something left as security. **pawnbroker** *n* someone with a licence to lend money on the security of property left behind. **pawnshop** *n* a pawnbroker's shop. < alteration of Middle French *pan.*

---

patronymic

A name which indicates a person's ancestry is known as a *patronymic*. This word derives ultimately from the Greek *patronumikos,* a joining of *patēr* 'father' and *onyma* 'name'.

Such names are recognizable by the presence of an affix. Common examples include the -son of Peterson 'the son of Peter', the O' of O'Sullivan, and the Norman Fitz of Fitzgerald 'the son of Gerald' (from the Old French *fils*).

---

a mere pawn

A person who is referred to as a pawn is regarded as someone of no real importance who is manipulated by another. This figurative usage has entered the language from the game of chess, where the pawn is nominally the least powerful of all the pieces. Other words whose application was originally restricted to this game include:

checkmate a position of total defeat (from the situation in the game when a player is unable save his or her king from being directly attacked): If we can't raise the money by Thursday, it'll mean checkmate.

stalemate a situation in which neither of two parties can win (from the situation in the game when a player is unable to move without causing his or her king to be in a direct line of attack): The struggle ended in a stalemate.

pay (peɪ) *vb* **paid; paying 1** give (money) in return for goods or services; give (someone) money for this. **2** settle (a debt). **3** answer for; undergo: pay the penalty. **4** bring profit or benefit to: It'll pay you to keep quiet. **5** grant; present: He paid her compliments.
• *n* **1** payment or employment. **2** salary or wages. **payee** *n* **payer** *n* **payable** *adj* that can or must be paid. **pay back** punish or take revenge on. **pay-bed** *n* a hospital bed, for the use of which the patient, not the State, pays. **pay for** suffer or be punished for. **payload** *n* **1** the cargo or passengers carried by a vehicle, aircraft, etc., that bring in income. **2** the instruments, bombs, or explosives carried by an aircraft. **paymaster** *n* an official who pays wages or salaries. **payment** *n* **1** paying; something paid. **2** a reward or punishment. **pay off 1** pay in full and then dismiss. **2** have a favourable outcome: All the preparations really paid off. **3** (*informal*) bribe. **pay-off** *n* **1** a payment; retribution. **2** a climax, esp. one unexpected. **pay out** slacken and let out (a rope). **payroll** *n* a list of employees to be paid by a business firm. < ultimately Latin *pax* peace.

PAYE *abbrev* pay-as-you-earn.

PC *abbrev* police constable.

pea (pi:) *n* **1** a climbing plant that bears a round, edible, green seed; this seed. **2** one of various plants related to this: chick-pea; sweet pea. **pea-green** *adj, n* the colour of vegetable peas. **pea-shooter** *n* a toy tube from which peas or similar pellets are shot out by blowing. **peasouper** *n* (*informal*) a dense fog. < ultimately Greek *pison*. SEE PANEL.

peace (pɪ:s) *n* **1** an ending or absence of war; agreement to end hostilities. **2** public order: keeping the peace. **3** a state of calm and tranquillity. **4** a state of harmony or friendship between people. **peaceable** *adj* **1** friendly; inoffensive. **2** free of conflict. **peaceful** *adj* **1** peaceable. **2** of a state of peace. **peacefully** *adv* **peacefulness** *n* **peacemaker** *n* a mediator. **peace-offering** *n* a gesture or gift designed to reconcile or bring peace. < Latin *pax*.

peach (pi:tʃ) *n* **1** a round, juicy, stoned fruit with a thin, furry, reddish-yellow skin; tree bearing this. **2** (*informal*) someone or something of excellence, esp. an attractive young woman. **3** a pinkish-yellow colour.
• *adj* pinkish-yellow. **peachy** *adj* **peach Melba** a dish of peaches, ice-cream, and raspberry syrup. < ultimately Latin *persicus* Persian.

peacock (ˈpi:ˌkɒk) *n* the male peafowl, whose large, colourful tail-feathers can be spread upwards and out like a fan. **peacock blue** a brilliant greenish-blue. < Old English *pēa* peafowl + *cok* cock.

peahen (ˈpi:ˌhɛn) *n* the female peafowl.

peak (pi:k) *n* **1** the sharp, pointed top of a hill or mountain. **2** a hill or mountain; something with this shape. **3** a projecting part on the front edge of a cap. **4** the point of maximum strength, value, activity, etc.
• *vb* reach a maximum level. **peaked** *adj* with peaks. **peak hours** the hours of the heaviest traffic or consumption of electricity, etc. < perhaps *pike*.

peal (pi:l) *n* **1** a loud ringing of bells. **2** a set of bells tuned for ringing changes. **3** a loud, prolonged noise of laughter or thunder.
• *vb* give out or utter in peals. < Middle English, short for *appel* appeal.

peanut (ˈpi:ˌnʌt) *n* a plant grown for its pods containing one to three seeds that ripen underground; seed of this. **peanut butter** a paste made of ground, roasted peanuts. **peanuts** *pl n* (*informal*) a meagre amount, esp. of money.

pear (pɛə) *n* a tree of the rose family bearing a fleshy, rounded fruit that tapers towards the stalk; this fruit. < Latin *pirum*.

pearl (pɜ:l) *n* **1** a hard, round,

pea

In the 17th century the word for a pea was *pease*. This word sounded very much as if it were a regular plural form consisting of pea plus -s but in actual fact was no more a plural form than the nouns piece or sneeze are today. What mattered, however, was that users believed *pease* to be a plural. This assumption was sufficient to trigger the process of *back formation* (see also panel at **television**), whereby the 'singularized' form pea came into being.

Another word resulting from this process is tee, from the now obsolete *teaz*.

milky-white mass formed inside the shells of some oysters, used as a gem. **2** something with this shape. **3** someone or something valued as rare or precious.
• *adj* (of an electric-light bulb) made with opaque glass. < ultimately Latin *perna* sea-mussel.

peasant (ˈpɛzn̩t) *n* a farm-labourer or small landowner in some countries. **peasantry** *n* peasants. < ultimately Latin *pagus* district.

peat (piːt) *n* partly carbonized vegetable matter formed by decomposition by water in bogs, used as a fertilizer or as a domestic fuel for heating. **peaty** *adj* < Medieval Latin *peta*.

pebble (ˈpɛbl̩) *n* **1** a small, round stone worn smooth by the action of water. **2** a variety of rock crystal used in making certain lenses: pebble glasses. **pebble-dash** *n* a coating of mortar studded with pebbles used for surfacing an outside wall. **pebbly** *adj* < Old English *papolstān* pebblestone.

peck (pɛk) *vb* **1** pierce or tap repeatedly with a beak or pointed device. **2** make (a hole) by pecking. **3** kiss quickly and lightly.
• *n* **1** a tap or nip made by a beak. **2** a light, quick kiss. **keep one's pecker up** (*informal*) keep cheerful. **peckish** *adj* (*informal*) hungry. **pecking order** a ranking order; hierarchy. < alteration of Middle English *piken* to pierce.

pectoral (ˈpɛktərəl) *adj* of, on, or worn on the chest: pectoral muscles. < Latin *pectus* breast.

peculiar (pɪˈkjuːlɪə) *adj* **1** odd; extraordinary. **2** exclusive to a particular person, group, or thing. **3** distinctive; special. **peculiarity** *n* **peculiarly** *adv* < ultimately Latin *pecus* cattle.

pecuniary (pɪˈkjuːnɪərɪ) *adj* relating to or measured in money. < Latin *pecunia* money.

pedagogue (ˈpɛdəˌgɒg) *n* (*derogatory*) a pedantic teacher. **pedagogic** *adj* < ultimately Greek *paid-* children + *agein* to lead.

pedal (ˈpɛdl̩) *n* a lever pressed by the foot, which operates a mechanism in a vehicle, cycle, etc., or is used in some musical instruments.
• *vb* **pedalled; pedalling 1** work or operate by a pedal or pedals. **2** ride a bicycle. < Latin *pes* foot.

pedant (ˈpɛdn̩t) *n* someone who insists on unnecessary details and formalities. **pedantic** *adj* **pedantically** *adv* **pedantry** *n* < Italian *pedante*. SEE PANEL AT **VILLAIN**.

peddle (ˈpɛdl̩) *vb* trade as a pedlar. < back formation from *pedlar*.

pedestal (ˈpɛdəstl̩) *n* the base that supports a column, statue, etc. **put on a pedestal** hold (someone) in great esteem; idealize. < Old Italian *pie di stallo* foot of a stall.

pedestrian (pɪˈdɛstrɪən) *n* a person who goes on foot.
• *adj* **1** of walking; of or for pedestrians: pedestrian precinct. **2** dull; commonplace. **pedestrian crossing** a marked area where pedestrians crossing a street have priority over traffic. < ultimately Latin *pes* foot.

pedigree (ˈpɛdɪˌgriː) *n* an ancestral line, esp. a distinguished one.
• *adj* (of animals) recorded as having been bred from a pure strain. < Middle French *pie de grue* crane's foot.

pedlar (ˈpɛdlə) *n* someone who goes from place to place selling small items. < Middle English *ped* basket.

peek (piːk) *vb, n* (take) a quick look; peep. < Middle English *piken*.

peel (piːl) *n* the skin or rind of a fruit or vegetable.
• *vb* **1** pull or strip an outer layer from. **2** come off in strips or layers. **3** also **peel off** (*informal*) undress. **peelings** *pl n* strips of peeled skin or rind. **peel off** break or veer away from a group or formation. < ultimately Latin *pilus* hair.

peep (piːp) *vb* **1** look carefully through an opening or from a hidden place.

a peeping Tom

The phrase peeping Tom comes from the legend of Lady Godiva. Dating from the 11th century, the legend tells of how Lady Godiva's husband, the Lord of Coventry, imposed on the people of Coventry crippling tax demands. When besought by his wife to remove these, he finally agreed, but only on condition that she ride naked through the streets. This she did, but with fewer blushes than might be imagined: for the duration of her procession the townspeople tactfully stayed indoors and kept their shutters closed. The one exception was a tailor called Tom who couldn't resist having a peep and was struck blind as a consequence.

2 start to emerge or show partially. • *n* a quick or furtive look. **peep-hole** *n* a small hole for looking through. **peeping Tom** a man who spies furtively on someone undressing or on sexual activities. < Middle English *pepen*. SEE PANEL.

peer[1] (pɪə) *vb* look searchingly or curiously, esp. at something difficult to make out. < perhaps alteration of *appear*.

peer[2] *n* **1** a baron, viscount, earl, marquess, or duke of the British nobility. **2** someone equal to another in age, rank, or status: peer group. **peerage** *n* **1** the nobility. **2** the rank of a peer or peeress. **peeress** *n* a peer's wife or widow, or a female peer. **peerless** *adj* outstanding; beyond compare. < ultimately Latin *par* equal.

peeve (piːv) *vb* (*informal*) bother; irritate. **peeved** *adj* **peevish** *adj* bad-tempered. **peevishly** *adv* **peevishness** *n* < Middle English *pevish* foolish, spiteful.

peewit (ˈpiːwɪt) *n* a lapwing. < from its sound.

peg (pɛg) *n* **1** a small, usually cylindrical pin of wood, metal, or plastic, used for holding things down or together, or marking a position. **2** a wooden pin for adjusting the tension on violin strings, etc. **3** a clothes-peg. • *vb* **pegged; pegging 1** mark or fasten with a peg or pegs. **2** restrict: peg someone down. **3** limit; fix (prices or wages). **off the peg** (of clothes) ready-to-wear. **peg away** work at persistently. **peg-board** *n* a board with holes and pegs for storing or displaying items. **peg out** (*slang*) die. < Middle English *pegge*.

pejorative (pəˈdʒɒrətɪv) *adj* debasing; belittling. **pejoratively** *adv* < Latin *pejor* worse.

pelican (ˈpɛlɪkən) *n* a large, web-footed bird with a long bill containing a pouch for storing fish. **pelican crossing** a pedestrian crossing with a pedestrian-controlled system of traffic-lights. < Greek *pelekan*.

pellet (ˈpɛlɪt) *n* **1** a small, round, soft, compact mass. **2** a piece of small shot. < ultimately Latin *pila* ball.

pelmet (ˈpɛlmit) *n* an ornamental strip of board or fabric above a window, esp. to cover curtain fixtures. < ultimately Latin *palma* palm.

pelt[1] (pɛlt) *n* the skin of an animal with the hair or fur still attached. < Middle English.

pelt[2] *vb* **1** throw things at. **2** (of rain) fall hard and rapidly. **3** hurry; dash. **at full pelt** as fast as possible. < Middle English *pelten*.

pelvis (ˈpɛlvɪs) *n* the basin-shaped structure of bones formed by the pelvic girdle and adjoining spinal bones. **pelvic** *adj* < Latin: basin.

pen[1] (pɛn) *n* a small enclosed area for keeping sheep, cattle, etc. • *vb* **penned; penning** confine in a pen. < Old English *penn*.

pen[2] *n* an implement used for writing or drawing with ink. • *vb* **penned; penning** write (a letter, etc.). **penfriend** *n* a friend that one corresponds with but doesn't usually meet. **penknife** *n*, *pl* **penknives** a small pocket-knife. **pen-name** *n* the pseudonym of a writer. **pen-pushing** *n* routine clerical work. < ultimately Latin *penna* feather. SEE PANEL.

penal (ˈpiːnl̩) *adj* of or relating to punishment: penal system. **penalize** *vb* **1** impose a penalty on. **2** put at a disadvantage. **penalization** *n* **penalty** *n* **1** a legally imposed punishment. **2** a forfeit made for breaking a rule, contract, etc. **3** loss, disadvantage, or suffering resulting from an action. **4** a penalty kick. **penalty area** (*football*) the area in front of the goal from where a penalty kick is taken. **penalty box** (*ice hockey*) an area for players suspended from play for a time. **penalty kick** (*football*) a free kick at the goal awarded for an offence in the penalty area. < Latin *poena* punishment.

penance (ˈpɛnəns) *n* **1** something done to express repentance for sin. **2** in the Roman or Orthodox Church, a sacrament involving confession, absolution, and an act of penitence, directed by a

pens and **penknives**

Over the centuries a great number of books might never have been written had it not been for birds. This seems a strange assertion until it is remembered that not so very long ago writing was done by means of a feather. A reminder of this is in the name pen, which derives from the Latin word *penna*, 'a feather'. Another reminder is penknife, so called because it was originally used to shape the point of the feather into a nib.

priest. < Medieval Latin *poenitentia* penitence.

penchant (ˈpɒnʃɒn) *n* a strong inclination or fondness. < ultimately Latin *pendere* to weigh.

pencil (ˈpɛnsl̩) *n* a tube-shaped implement containing a thin strip of graphite, chalk, etc., used for writing or drawing; something with this shape.
• *vb* **pencilled; pencilling** write, draw, or mark with a pencil. < Latin *penicillus* little tail.

pendant (ˈpɛndənt) *n* an ornament that hangs from a piece of jewellery worn round the neck. < ultimately Latin *pondus* weight.

pendent (ˈpɛndənt) *adj* suspended or overhanging. < SEE **PENDANT**.

pending (ˈpɛndɪŋ) *adj* **1** not yet settled or decided. **2** forthcoming; imminent.
• *prep* until.

pendulous (ˈpɛndjʊləs) *adj* hanging loosely downward.

pendulum (ˈpɛndjʊləm) *n* a weight suspended from a fixed point so as to swing freely, used esp. in clockwork movements. < ultimately Latin *pendere* to weigh.

penetrate (ˈpɛnɪˌtreɪt) *vb* **1** pass through or into; pierce. **2** permeate; diffuse. **3** see through or into. **4** understand or be understood. **penetrable** *adj* **penetrability** *n* **penetrating** *adj* **1** keen; discerning: penetrating insight. **2** (of sound) loud and piercing. **penetrative** *adj* < Latin *penetrate*.

penguin (ˈpɛŋgwɪn) *n* a flightless sea-bird with short legs, found in Antarctic regions. < perhaps Welsh *pen gwyn* white head. SEE PANEL.

penicillin (ˌpɛnɪˈsɪlɪn) *n* a type of antibiotic obtained from mould. < Latin *penicillium* little brush.

peninsula (pəˈnɪnsjʊlə) *n* a piece of land which sticks out into or is almost completely surrounded by water. **peninsular** *adj* < Latin *paene* almost + *insula* island.

penis (ˈpiːnɪs) *n* the male organ of copulation and urination. < Latin: penis, tail.

penitent (ˈpɛnɪtənt) *n, adj* (someone) feeling or expressing sorrow for doing wrong. **penitence** *n* **penitently** *adv* **penitential** *adj* **penitentiary** *n* (*US*) a prison. < Latin *paenitēre* to be sorry.

pennant (ˈpɛnənt) *n* a flag which tapers to a point, used esp. on a ship for signalling. < alteration of *pendant*.

penny (ˈpɛnɪ) *n, pl* **pennies, pence 1** a bronze coin, 100 of which are worth £1. **2** a former bronze coin, 240 of which

the penny's dropped

Penny features in a number of idiomatic expressions, including:

cost a pretty penny to cost a lot of money.
penny farthing an early type of bicycle with a very large front wheel and a small rear one. The expression comes from the sizes of the former penny and farthing coins.
penny wise and pound foolish thrifty in small matters but wasteful in larger ones.
spend a penny to urinate or defecate. The expression comes from the former charge for using a public toilet.
ten or **two a penny** easily obtainable; commonplace.
the penny drops one suddenly understands: He couldn't work out what she was saying but then the penny finally dropped. The expression is an allusion to the dropping of a coin to operate a slot-machine.

penguin

Penguin, the word used to refer to the flightless sea-bird common in the Antarctic and cooler southern regions, is believed to derive from the Welsh *pen gwyn* or 'white head', from *pen* 'head' and *gwyn* 'white'. According to theory the name was originally applied by Welsh seamen not to the penguin but to the great auk, a flightless sea-bird of the northern hemisphere which is now extinct. When explorers eventually ventured south and came upon the penguin, a bird that closely resembled the great auk, they called it by the same name. Strictly speaking, however, this involves a misnomer as the head of the penguin is black.

For other words of Welsh origin, see panel at **corgi.**

were worth £1. **3** (*US informal*) a cent. **4** a small amount of money. **penniless** *adj* without money; poor. < Old English *penning, penig.* SEE PANEL.

pension[1] (ˈpɛnʃən) *n* a fixed income provided regularly by the State or a company to people who are past the age of retirement, widowed, or with certain disabilities.
• *vb* provide with a pension. **pensioner** *n* **pensionable** *adj* entitled or entitling to a pension. < ultimately Latin *pendere* to pay.

pension[2] (ˈpɒnsɪɒn) *n* **1** a small boarding-house on the Continent. **2** room and board. < French.

pensive (ˈpɛnsɪv) *adj* deep in serious thought; preoccupied. **pensively** *adv* **pensiveness** *n* < ultimately Latin *pendere* to weigh.

pent (pɛnt) *adj* **pent in** or **up** enclosed; confined. **pent-up** *adj* held back; suppressed. < obsolete *pend* to confine.

pentagon (ˈpɛntəˌgɒn) *n* **1** a five-sided geometric figure. **2 the Pentagon** a building in the USA that houses the US military establishment and Defense Department. **pentagonal** *adj* < Greek *penta-* five + *gōnia* angle. SEE PANEL.

pentameter (pɛnˈtæmɪtə) *n* a line of verse that has five metrical feet. < Greek *penta-* five + *metron* measure.

pentathlon (pɛnˈtæθlən) *n* an athletic competition consisting of five events which each contestant must take part in. < Greek *penta-* five + *athlon* contest.

penthouse (ˈpɛntˌhaʊs) *n* **1** a sloping roof on a shed, etc., attached to the wall of a building. **2** a dwelling built on the roof of a tall building. < probably ultimately Latin *appendix.*

penultimate (pɪˈnʌltɪmət) *adj* next to the last. **penultimately** *adv* < Latin *paene* almost + *ultimus* last.

peony (ˈpiːənɪ) *n* one of a group of plants with showy white, pink, or red flowers. < Greek *Paiōn* Paeon, physician of the gods. SEE PANEL.

people (ˈpiːpl̩) *pl n* **1** human beings in general. **2** a specified group of these: hill people. **3** the masses; ordinary folk. **4** relations or immediate family. **5** a body of persons sharing a common culture, ancestry, or language.
• *vb* populate; inhabit. < ultimately Latin *populus.*

pep (pɛp) *n* energy and liveliness.
• *vb* **pepped; pepping** also **pep up** enliven; stimulate. **pep pill** a tablet that contains a stimulant drug. **pep talk** a talk designed to liven up or raise the spirits of the hearers. < short for *pepper.*

pepper (ˈpɛpə) *n* **1** one of a group of tropical shrubs with berries that are dried and ground into a hot-tasting powder for sprinkling on food; this powder. **2** any of various plants with a red, green, or yellow fruit that is eaten as a vegetable; capsicum.
• *vb* **1** sprinkle pepper over. **2** sprinkle; dot: His essay was peppered with errors.

the Pentagon

The Pentagon refers to the five-sided building in Arlington, Virginia in the USA that houses the US military establishment and Defense Department. When it is observed that *The Pentagon* last night issued a detailed statement concerning the use of the new weapon, it is not the building that is being referred to, but the department housed in the building. This is an example of ***metonymy,*** where the name of an attribute of something is used instead of the name of the thing itself. (See also panel at **bottle.**)

Other examples of political metonymy include:

10 Downing Street or **Number 10** 'the British Prime Minister'
the Crown 'the monarchy'
the Kremlin 'the central government of the Soviet Union'
the White House 'the US President'
Westminster 'the British parliament'
Whitehall 'the British government and its central administration'

peony

The peony is typically a healthy and vigorous plant, which is only to be expected in view of its name. In Middle English this was *peonie,* which came into the language by way of French and Latin from the Greek word *paiōnia.* The peony was the flower of their god of healing, *Paiōn,* Paeon—a name meaning 'physician'—and for many centuries afterwards it was regarded as an emblem of good health.

3 shower or pelt with small objects. **pepper-and-salt** *adj* woven with dark and light thread in small flecks. **peppercorn** *n* the black berry of the pepper plant. **peppercorn rent** a very low or token rent. **peppermint** *n* **1** a type of mint producing an aromatic oil; this oil. **2** a sweet made with this. **peppery** *adj* **1** hot or spicy like pepper. **2** irritable. < Old English *pipor.*

per (pə; *stressed* pɜː) *prep* **1** according to: as per instructions. **2** for every: 30 miles per hour. **3** by means of; through. **per annum** for every year. **per capita** for every person. **per cent** for or in every hundred. < Latin: through.

perceive (pəˈsiːv) *vb* notice or see; realize. **perceptible** *adj* **perceptibility** *n* **perceptibly** *adv* **perception** *n* observation; understanding. **perceptive** *adj* observant or understanding. **perceptively** *adv* **perceptiveness** *n* < Latin *per* thoroughly + *capere* to take.

percentage (pəˈsɛntɪdʒ) *n* **1** a proportion expressed as per cent. **2** a proportion; share. < Latin *per* + *centum* hundred.

perch[1] (pɜːtʃ) *n* **1** a place where a bird rests, such as a branch or a bar in a cage. **2** a resting place for a person.
• *vb* put or settle on a perch. < Latin *pertica* pole.

perch[2] *n, pl* **perch, perches** a small, edible, spiny-finned, freshwater fish. < Greek *perkē.*

percolate (ˈpɜːkəˌleɪt) *vb* **1** filter through or permeate. **2** make (coffee) in a percolator. **percolator** *n* a coffee pot in which boiling water circulates repeatedly up a tube and down through a perforated drum containing ground coffee. < Latin *per-* through + *colare to* strain.

percussion (pəˈkʌʃən) *n* **1** the striking of an object, esp. a musical instrument. **2** the percussion instruments in a band or orchestra. **percussive** *adj* **percussion instrument** a musical instrument played by striking, such as a xylophone or drum. < Latin *per-* thoroughly + *quatere* to shake.

peremptory (pəˈrɛmptərɪ) *adj* **1** decisive; absolute. **2** bossy; authoritative. **peremptorily** *adv* < ultimately Latin *per-* completely + *emere* to take.

perennial (pəˈrɛnɪəl) *adj* **1** lasting or recurring over a long period; constant. **2** (of a plant) growing for several years.
• *n* a perennial plant. **perennially** *adv* < Latin *per-* throughout + *annus* year.

perfect (ˈpɜːfɪkt) *adj* **1** superb; flawless. **2** accurate; precise. **3** skilful; expert: Practice makes perfect. **4** absolute; complete: a perfect gentleman.
• *vb* (pəˈfɛkt) **1** realize in final form. **2** make perfect; improve. **perfection** *n* **perfectionist** *n* someone who accepts nothing less than perfection. **perfectionism** *n* **perfectly** *adv* **1** in a perfect manner. **2** absolutely. **to perfection** perfectly. < Latin *per-* through + *facere* to do.

perfidious (pəˈfɪdɪəs) *adj* disloyal; traitorous. **perfidy** *n* < Latin *per fidem decipere* to deceive by trust.

perforate (ˈpɜːfəˌreɪt) *vb* make a hole or rows of holes in; penetrate. **perforation** *n* < Latin *per-* through + *forare* to bore.

perforce (pəˈfɔːs) *adv* of necessity. < Middle French *par force* by force.

perform (pəˈfɔːm) *vb* **1** do; carry out (an action). **2** fulfil; comply with (a request). **3** function: The new car performs well. **4** act or play (music, etc.) in front of an audience. **performer** *n* **performance** *n* **1** performing; something performed. **2** one presentation of a play, concert, etc. **3** the manner in which something functions. **4** behaviour or activity, esp. bothersome. < Latin *per-* thoroughly + Old French *fournir* to provide.

perfume (ˈpɜːfjuːm) *n* **1** a sweet, pleasant scent. **2** a preparation of fragrant oils and essences from flowers, etc., used to make the body smell pleasant.
• *vb* (pəˈfjuːm) apply perfume to or fill with a sweet smell. **perfumery** *n* perfumes, their manufacture, or a place where they are sold. < Latin *per-* thoroughly + *fumare* to smoke.

perfunctory (pəˈfʌŋktərɪ) *adj* **1** done mechanically or superficially. **2** uninterested; inattentive. **perfunctorily** *adv* **perfunctoriness** *n* < Latin *per-* thoroughly + *fungi* to perform.

perhaps (pəˈhæps) *adv* possibly; maybe. < *per* + *hap* chance.

peril (ˈpɛrəl) *n* exposure to risk or danger; danger. **perilous** *adj* **perilously** *adv* < Latin *periculum.*

perimeter (pəˈrɪmɪtə) *n* the outer boundary of an area or enclosed plane figure; length of this. < Greek *peri-* round + *metron* measure.

period (ˈpɪərɪəd) *n* **1** an interval of time. **2** a specified time; epoch: the Elizabethan period. **3** a lesson in school; time it lasts. **4** an occurrence of menstruation. **5** the full stop at the end of a sentence.
• *adj* typical of a particular past age: period costume. **periodic** *adj* **1** recurring at fixed intervals; cyclic. **2** occasional. **periodical** *n* a journal or magazine,

usually published weekly, monthly, or quarterly. < Greek *peri-* round + *hodos* way.

peripatetic (ˌpɛrɪpəˈtɛtɪk) *adj* going from place to place: a peripatetic music teacher. < Greek *peripatein* to pace up and down.

peripheral (pəˈrɪfərəl) *adj* **1** of, on, or forming a periphery. **2** of minor importance.
• *n* device such as a VDU or floppy disk that provides input or output communication when connected to a computer.

periphery (pəˈrɪfərɪ) *n* **1** the outer limits of a surface or area. **2** the edge of a subject. < Greek *peri-* round + *pherein* to carry.

periphrasis (pəˈrɪfrəsɪs) *n, pl* **periphrases** a roundabout way of expressing something; circumlocution. **periphrastic** *adj* < Greek *peri-* round + *phrazein* to declare.

periscope (ˈpɛrɪˌskəʊp) *n* a device consisting of a tube, lenses, and mirrors for seeing objects not in the direct line of sight, used esp. on submarines. **periscopic** *adj* < Greek *peri-* round + *-skopion* instrument for viewing.

perish (ˈpɛrɪʃ) *vb* **1** be destroyed or killed, esp. suddenly and violently. **2** (of rubber, etc.) spoil; deteriorate. **3** weaken or numb with cold. **perishable** *adj* liable to rot or decay; short-lived. **perishables** *pl n* food that is perishable. **perisher** *n* (*slang*) someone irritating or troublesome. **perishing** *adj* **1** extremely cold. **2** damned. < Latin *per-* away + *ire* to go.

perjure (ˈpɜːdʒə) *vb* **perjure oneself** give false evidence in a court of law; violate an oath. **perjury** *n* **perjured** *adj* **1** having committed perjury. **2** involving perjury: perjured evidence. < Latin *per-* to destruction + *jurare* to swear. SEE PANEL.

perjure

A verb which takes as an object a pronoun ending in -self or -selves is called *a reflexive verb.* It is so called because the action it denotes is directed back upon the subject, as in she dressed herself; they enjoyed themselves. However, verbs such as dress and kick may be used non-reflexively as well: she dressed the child; they enjoyed the meal. There are in fact very few verbs which must always be used reflexively. An example is perjure. It is impossible to perjure anyone or anything but oneself.

perk[1] (pɜːk) *vb* **perk up** cheer up; recover energy. **perky** *adj* cheerful; spirited. **perkily** *adv* **perkiness** *n* < origin uncertain.

perk[2] *n* (*informal*) an incidental benefit or privilege, esp. in addition to one's normal salary or wages. < *perquisite.*

perm (pɜːm) *n* **1** a permanent wave. **2** a permutation in football pools.
• *vb* **1** give a permanent wave to. **2** make a permutation of.

permanent (ˈpɜːmənənt) *adj* enduring indefinitely; stable. **permanence** *n* **permanency** *n* **permanently** *adv* **permanent wave** a long-lasting wave fixed in the hair by chemicals. < Latin *per-* through + *manēre* to remain.

permeate (ˈpɜːmɪˌeɪt) *vb* fill or filter through every part of; diffuse. **permeation** *n* **permeable** *adj* that can be permeated, esp. by fluids. < Latin *per-* through + *maere* to pass.

permit (pəˈmɪt) *vb* **permitted; permitting** **1** give consent or authorization to. **2** make possible; allow.
• *n* (ˈpɜːmɪt) a written authorization to enter, act, or possess something; licence. **permission** *n* **permissible** *adj* allowable. **permissive** *adj* **1** allowing. **2** tolerant or liberal, esp. in social or sexual matters. < Latin *per-* through + *mittere* to send. SEE PANEL.

permutation (ˌpɜːmjʊˈteɪʃən) *n* **1** a change or variation in order, or an altered arrangement of things. **2** a fixed plan for selection of results in a football pools entry. < Latin *per-* + *mutare* to change.

pernicious (pəˈnɪʃəs) *adj* harmful; destructive. < Latin *per-* + *nex* death.

pernickety (pəˈnɪkɪtɪ) *adj* (*informal*) fussy; fastidious. < origin uncertain.

peroxide (pəˈrɒksaɪd) *n* a compound that contains a high proportion of oxygen. **hydrogen peroxide** a compound used as an antiseptic or to bleach the hair.
• *vb* bleach (hair) with hydrogen peroxide. < Latin *per-* throughout + *-oxide.*

perpendicular (ˌpɜːpɛnˈdɪkjʊlə) *adj* at right angles to the horizontal plane; upright.
• *n* a line or direction at right angles to the horizontal. **perpendicularity** *n* **perpendicularly** *adv* < Latin *per-* + *pendēre* to hang.

perpetrate (ˈpɜːpɪˌtreɪt) *vb* be responsible for or commit (an action).

perpetration *n* **perpetrator** *n* < Latin *per-* through + *patrare* to perform.
perpetual (pə'pɛtjʊəl) *adj* **1** never-ending; permanent. **2** occurring repeatedly; constant. **perpetually** *adv*
perpetuate *vb* maintain the existence of; continue. **perpetuation** *n* **perpetuity** *n* eternity. **in perpetuity** for ever. < Latin *per-* through + *petere* to go to.
perplex (pə'plɛks) *vb* **1** confuse; bewilder. **2** tangle; complicate. **perplexedly** *adv* **perplexity** *n* < Latin *per-* thoroughly + *plectere* to twine.
perquisite ('pɜːkwɪzɪt) *n* **1** something considered to be an exclusive right. **2** a perk. < Latin *per-* thoroughly + *quaerere* to seek.
persecute ('pɜːsɪˌkjuːt) *vb* **1** subject to oppression or ill-treatment, esp. because of race, religion, or political beliefs. **2** annoy; torment. **persecution** *n* **persecutor** *n* < Latin *per-* through + *sequi* to follow.
persevere (ˌpɜːsɪ'vɪə) *vb* keep going with determination, esp. in the face of hardship or difficulty. **perseverance** *n* < Latin *per-* through + *severus* severe.
persist (pə'sɪst) *vb* **1** carry on firmly or stubbornly. **2** remain in existence. **persistence** *n* **persistency** *n* **persistent** *adj* **persistently** *adv* < Latin *per-* + *sistere* to stand firm.
person ('pɜːsn̩) *n* **1** a human being. **2** a living human body. **3** one of the three modes of the Holy Trinity in the Christian faith. **4** (*grammar*) one of the three verb or pronoun forms referring to the subject as speaking, spoken to, or spoken about. **in person** present in physical form. **personable** *adj* attractive-looking. **personage** *n* a distinguished or important person. **personify** *vb* **1** represent as having human form or characteristics. **2** typify; incarnate: She is virtue personified. **personification** *n* **personnel** *n* **1** the body of employees in a firm or organization. **2** the department in an organization concerned with the appointment and welfare of staff. < Latin *persona* actor's mask.
persona (pɜː'səʊnə) *n, pl* **personae** **1** one's social personality. **2** *pl* the characters in a play, book, etc. < Latin.
persona grata (pɜːˌsəʊnə 'grɑːtə) an acceptable person. **persona non grata** an unacceptable person. < Latin.
personal ('pɜːsənl̩) *adj* **1** individual; private: my personal life. **2** of the person or the body: personal hygiene. **3** of or directed towards a particular individual: a personal favour. **4** done by an individual: a personal appearance. **5** commenting on an individual, esp. offensively: personal remarks. **6** existing as a person. **personal column** a newspaper column for private messages or advertisements, **personalize** *vb* **1** personify. **2** make personal; mark as an individual's personal property: personalized writing-paper. **personally** *adv* **1** in person. **2** as a person. **3** against oneself in an offensive way: He took it personally. **4** as far as oneself is concerned.

How do you pronounce **permit?**

One way in which the vocabulary of a language is extended is when a particular word, for instance one that has always been used as a noun, starts being used in a different way as well, say as a verb. The original word undergoes a process known as *conversion,* a doubling-up of grammatical function.

Permit is a member of a relatively small group of two-syllable verbs that have come to operate also as nouns: I refuse to *per*mit it (verb)—She needs a *per*mit to get in (noun). In the written language the conversion of verb to noun involves no changes at all to the original form: verb and noun are identical. However, in the spoken language the conversion often also involves a shift of stress from the second syllable to the first, and frequently a change or lengthening of the vowel of the first syllable. With permit for example the vowel of the verb form is much shorter than that of the noun.

The following list provides further examples of two-syllable words that have undergone conversion:

abstract	**escort**	**progress**
compound	**extract**	**protest**
conduct	**incline**	**rebel**
conflict	**increase**	**record**
contest	**insult**	**refund**
contrast	**misprint**	**reject**
convert	**pervert**	**survey**
convict	**present**	**suspect**
digest	**produce**	

personality (ˌpɜːsəˈnælɪtɪ) *n* **1** the character and temperament of an individual. **2** a distinguished individual; celebrity. **3** *pl* personal comments, esp. critical.

perspective (pəˈspɛktɪv) *n* **1** the technique of representing solid objects on a flat surface with respect to their relative position, distance, etc. **2** the appearance of visible objects in relationship to each other, as determined by the viewer. **3** a view; vista. **4** a way of looking at facts and situations; objective overview: get things in perspective. < Latin *per-* through + *specere* to look.

perspicuous (pəˈspɪkjʊəs) *adj* easily understood; clear. **perspicuity** *n* **perspicuously** *adv* < Latin *perspicuus.*

perspire (pəˈspaɪə) *vb* secrete a salty fluid from the sweat glands; sweat. **perspiration** *n* < Latin *per-* through + *spirare* to breathe.

persuade (pəˈsweɪd) *vb* influence to do or believe something by argument or reasoning. **persuasion** *n* **1** persuading; being persuaded. **2** the ability to persuade. **3** a firm belief or conviction, esp. religious. **4** a sort; faction. **persuasive** *adj* able or tending to persuade. **persuasively** *adv* **persuasiveness** *n* < Latin *per-* thoroughly + *suadēre* to urge.

pert (pɜːt) *adj* **1** bold; impudent. **2** trim; dashing. **pertly** *adv* **pertness** *n* < ultimately Latin *aperire* to open.

pertain (pəˈteɪn) *vb* **1** be appropriate to. **2** be part of; belong to. < Latin *per-* through + *tenēre* to hold.

pertinacious (ˌpɜːtɪˈneɪʃəs) *adj* clinging determinedly to an opinion or course of action; stubborn. **pertinaciously** *adv* **pertinacity** *n* < Latin *per-* through + *tenax* tenacious.

pertinent (ˈpɜːtɪnənt) *adj* relevant; applicable. **pertinence** *n* **pertinently** *adv*

perturb (pəˈtɜːb) *vb* cause unease or anxiety to; alarm. **perturbation** *n* < Latin *per-* + *turbare* to agitate.

peruse (pəˈruːz) *vb* read or examine in detail; study. **perusal** *n* < probably Latin *per-* thoroughly + Middle English *usen* to use.

pervade (pəˈveɪd) *vb* spread through every part of; diffuse. **pervasive** *adj* **pervasiveness** *n* < Latin *per-* through + *vadere* to go.

perverse (pəˈvɜːs) *adj* **1** deliberately opposing what is good, normal, or proper. **2** contrary; uncooperative. **perversely** *adv* **perverseness** *n* **perversity** *n* < Latin *per-* + *vertere* to turn.

pervert (pəˈvɜːt) *vb* **1** cause to turn from what is good or right: pervert the course of justice. **2** distort; misuse.
• *n* (ˈpɜːvɜːt) someone with perverted sexual instincts. **perversion** *n* **1** perverting; being perverted. **2** something perverted, esp. sexual behaviour.

pessimism (ˈpɛsɪˌmɪzəm) *n* an inclination to expect the worst; gloominess. **pessimist** *n* **pessimistic** *adj* **pessimistically** *adv* < Latin *pessimus* worst.

pest (pɛst) *n* **1** someone or something annoying; nuisance. **2** an animal or insect that causes disease or damage to crops, etc. **pester** *vb* annoy; nag. **pesticide** *n* a substance that destroys animal or insect pests. < Latin *pestis.*

pestilence (ˈpɛstɪləns) *n* an epidemic of a highly infectious disease.

pestle (ˈpɛsḷ) *n* a club-shaped implement, used for pounding substances in a mortar. < Latin *pistillum.*

pet (pɛt) *n* **1** a domesticated animal, kept as a companion or as an amusement. **2** someone treated with affection or favouritism: teacher's pet.
• *adj* **1** treated or kept as a pet. **2** favourite. **3** showing affection: a pet name.
• *vb* **petted; petting 1** treat kindly and affectionately. **2** fondle; caress. < Middle English *pety* small.

petal (ˈpɛtḷ) *n* any of the usually brightly-coloured leaves of a flower-head. < Greek *petalon.*

petard (pɪˈtɑːd) *n* **hoist with one's own petard** being the victim of one's own schemes or devices. SEE PANEL.

peter (ˈpiːtə) *vb* **peter out** gradually fade and cease. < origin unknown.

petite (pəˌtiːt) *adj* (of a woman) small and

hoist with one's own petard

To end up the victim of one's own schemes or devices is to be hoisted with one's own petard. Petard was originally the name of a large container for explosives. Once filled, it was raised into position against the wall or barricade to be breached. All too often, however, the explosive went off prematurely, in which case the engineer responsible for firing the petard did not live to tell the story.

Petard comes ultimately from the Latin *pedere,* 'to break wind'.

trimly built. < French: small.

petition (pəˈtɪʃən) *n* **1** an earnest appeal. **2** a formal, written request signed by a large number of people, appealing to an authority for action. **3** a formal, written application for judicial action in a court of law.
• *vb* address or give a petition to. **petitioner** *n* < ultimately Latin *petere* to seek.

petrify (ˈpɛtrɪˌfaɪ) *vb* **petrified; petrifying 1** convert into stone or a similar substance. **2** paralyse with fear; appal. **petrification** *n* SEE PANEL.

petro- (ˈpɛtrəʊ) *prefix* indicating petroleum or its products: petrochemical; petrodollar. < Greek *petros* stone or *petra* rock.

petrol (ˈpɛtrəl) *n* a flammable liquid hydrocarbon refined from petroleum, used as a fuel in internal-combustion engines. **petroleum** *n* an oily liquid found underground, refined for use as petrol, oil, etc. **petroleum jelly** a greasy mixture obtained from petroleum, used as a lubricant or basis for ointments. < Latin *petr-* rock + *oleum* oil. SEE PANEL AT **DIESEL**.

petticoat (ˈpɛtɪˌkəʊt) *n* an underskirt worn by a woman or girl. < Middle English *pety* small + *cote* coat. SEE PANEL.

petty (ˈpɛtɪ) *adj* **1** trivial; insignificant. **2** secondary; inferior. **3** spiteful; mean. **pettily** *adv* **pettiness** *n* **petty cash** cash kept by for small payments in an office, etc. **petty officer** a non-commissioned naval officer. **petty sessions** a magistrates' court. < Middle French *petit* small.

petulant (ˈpɛtjʊlənt) *adj* ill-tempered; impatient. **petulance** *n* **petulantly** *adv* < Latin *petulans*.

pew (pjuː) *n* **1** one of a row of long, bench-like seats for a church congregation. **2** (*informal*) a seat: take a pew. < Latin *podium* parapet.

pewter (ˈpjuːtə) *n* an alloy made with tin and other metals, esp. lead; vessel or utensil made of this. < Middle French *peutre*.

phallic (ˈfælɪk) *adj* of or representing an erect penis. < Greek *phallos* penis.

phantom (ˈfæntəm) *n* **1** a spectre; ghost. **2** something unreal or imagined. < Latin *phantasma*.

pharmacology (ˌfɑːməˈkɒlədʒɪ) *n* the branch of study connected with medicinal drugs and their effects. < ultimately Greek *pharmakon* drug.

pharmacy (ˈfɑːməsɪ) *n* **1** the preparation and dispensing of drugs and medicines. **2** a place where these are sold or dispensed; chemist. **pharmaceutical** *adj* engaged in or relating to pharmacy. **pharmacist** *n*

pharynx (ˈfærɪŋks) *n* the part of the alimentary canal between the mouth and the oesophagus. **pharyngitis** *n* inflammation of the pharynx. < Greek.

phase (feɪz) *n* **1** a period or stage in development. **2** one of the recurring shapes of the moon or a planet illuminated by the sun.
• *vb* conduct (an operation) in planned stages. **phase in/out** introduce/discontinue the use or practice of. < ultimately Greek *phainein* to show.

Ph.D. *abbrev* Doctor of Philosophy.

pheasant (ˈfɛzənt) *n* a game-bird with a long tail and brightly-coloured feathers. < ultimately *Phasis*, river in Asia.

phenomenon (fɪˈnɒmɪnən) *n, pl* **phenomena 1** an event, fact, or change that can be observed. **2** someone or something unusual or extraordinary. **phenomenal** *adj* **phenomenally** *adv* < ultimately Greek *phainein* to show.

phial (ˈfaɪəl) *n* a small, usually glass container for liquid medicine. < Greek *phialē*.

petrify

A person who is paralysed with fear is said to be petrified. Petrify comes via the French *pétrifier* from the Greek word *petra* or 'stone'. To be petrified, therefore, is literally 'to be turned into stone'.

petticoat

A woman's underskirt is sometimes referred to as a petticoat. Those who see in the word a symbol of femininity may be surprised to know that petticoats were originally worn not by women but by men. The word derives from the Middle English *petycote,* which was the name of a short tunic worn under a doublet or under chain mail. *Petycote,* a compound of *pety* 'small' and *cote* 'coat', meant literally 'small coat'.

philander (fɪˈlændə) *vb* (of a man) flirt; womanize. **philanderer** *n* < ultimately Greek *phil-* loving + *anēr* man.
philanthropy (fɪˈlænθrəpɪ) *n* love and generosity towards mankind; altruism. **philanthropic** *adj* **philanthropically** *adv* **philanthropist** *n* < Greek *phil-* loving + *anthrōpos* man.
philately (fɪˈlætəlɪ) *n* collecting stamps. **philatelic** *adj* **philatelist** *n* < Greek *phil-* loving + *ateleia* tax exemption.
philology (fɪˈlɒlədʒɪ) *n* the study of language. **philologist** *n* < Greek *phil-* + *logos* word.
philosophy (fɪˈlɒsəfɪ) *n* **1** the study of existence, knowledge, truth, and principles of moral conduct. **2** the principles of a particular school of thought. **3** any system of beliefs or aesthetic and moral values. **4** calmness in the face of difficulty. **philosopher** *n* **philosophical** *adj* **philosophically** *adv* **philosophize** *vb* **1** reason in a philosophical way. **2** moralize. < Greek *phil-* + *sophos* wise.
phlegm (flɛm) *n* thick mucus secreted into the nose, throat, and bronchial passages. **phlegmatic** *adj* **1** not easily agitated or excited. **2** indifferent or lethargic. **phlegmatically** *adv* < ultimately Greek *phlegein* to burn.
phobia (ˈfəʊbɪə) *n* a consuming fear of or aversion to something. **phobic** *adj* < Greek *phobos* fear.
phone (fəʊn) *n* **1** a telephone. **2** an earphone.
• *vb* also **phone up** call by telephone. **phone-in** *n* a broadcast programme in which viewers or listeners take part by telephone. < *telephone*.
phonetic (fəˈnɛtɪk) *adj* representing speech-sounds by symbols, each with a single value: phonetic alphabet. **phonetically** *adv* **phonetics** *n* the study and categorization of the sounds of speech. < Greek *phōnē* voice, sound.
phoney (ˈfəʊnɪ) *adj* (*slang*) fake or insincere.
• *n* (*slang*) someone or something phoney. < origin unknown.
phonograph (ˈfəʊnəˌgrɑːf) *n* **1** an early type of record-player using cylindrical recordings. **2** (*US or humorous*) a gramophone.
phosphate (ˈfɒsfeɪt) *n* a salt or ester of phosphoric acid; one of these used as a fertilizer.
phosphoresce (ˌfɒsfəˈrɛs) *vb* glow luminously without emitting noticeable heat. **phosphorescence** *n* **phosphorescent** *adj* < Greek *phōs* light + *pherein* to bring.
phosphorus (ˈfɒsfərəs) *n* a non-metallic element occurring in several forms, some of which are luminous and flammable, used in matches, pesticides, etc. **phosphoric** *adj* < Greek *phōsphoros* light-bearing.
photo (ˈfəʊtəʊ) *n, pl* **photos** (*informal*) a photograph. **photocopy** *vb, n* (make) a duplicate copy of by photography. **photocopier** *n* a machine for photocopying. **photoelectric** *adj* of or involving the electrical effects of the interaction of light with matter. **photoelectric cell** an electronic device activated by a beam of light. **photo finish** a race so close that the winner must be decided by examining a photograph of the finish. **photofit** *n* a system of reconstructing a facial likeness of, for example, a police suspect, by assembling photographs of various features. < *photograph*.
photogenic (ˌfəʊtəˈdʒɛnɪk) *adj* looking attractive in photographs; suitable for photography.
photograph (ˈfəʊtəˌgrɑːf) *n* an image formed on a sensitized surface by the action of light or other radiated energy.
• *vb* **1** take a photograph of. **2** appear a certain way when photographed: She photographs well. **photographer** *n* **photographic** *adj* **photographically** *adv* **photographic memory** a very accurate memory for precise details. **photography** *n* taking and printing photographs. < Greek *phōs* light + *graphein* to write.
photosynthesis (ˌfəʊtəʊˈsɪnθəsɪs) *n* the conversion by plants of carbon dioxide and water into carbohydrate in the presence of sunlight. < Greek *phōs* + *syntithenai* to put together.
phrase (freɪz) *n* **1** a group of grammatically related words that form a unit within a clause or sentence. **2** an idiom or inventive expression. **3** a manner of speaking or expressing oneself. **4** a short musical passage within a melody that forms a natural unit.
• *vb* **1** put into words; express. **2** divide (music) into melodic units. **phrasal** *adj* **phrase-book** *n* a book that contains words and phrases in a foreign language and their translation. **phraseology** *n* a choice of words or the way they are organized. < Greek *phrazein* to explain, tell.
phut (fʌt) *n* a dull sound like that of air escaping when something bursts. **go phut 1** make a noise like this. **2** break

down; fail. < like the sound.
physical (ˈfɪzɪkl̩) *adj* **1** of material things; subject to the laws of nature. **2** of the body: physical education. **3** of physics or natural science.
• *n* physical examination of the body. **physically** *adv* < Latin *physica* physics.
physician (fɪˈzɪʃən) *n* a doctor of medicine as distinct from surgery.
physics (ˈfɪzɪks) *n* the science that deals with matter and energy, with their properties and interactions. **physicist** *n* < ultimately Greek *physis* nature.
physiognomy (ˌfɪzɪˈɒnəmɪ) *n* someone's facial features and expressions; these as an indication of personality. < Greek *physis* nature + *gnōmōn* judge.
physiology (ˌfɪzɪˈɒlədʒɪ) *n* the branch of biology concerned with the functions of living matter; these functions. **physiological** *adj* **physiologist** *n* < Greek *physis* + *logos* word.
physiotherapy (ˌfɪzɪəʊˈθɛrəpɪ) *n* the treatment of an illness or injury by exercise, massage, etc. **physiotherapist** *n* < Greek *physis* + *therapia* therapy.
physique (fɪˈziːk) *n* someone's physical form and structure. < Greek *physikos* of nature.
piano (pɪˈænəʊ) *n, pl* **pianos** a musical instrument sounded by keys that, when pressed down, cause hammers to strike metal strings. **pianist** *n* SEE PANEL.
piazza (pɪˈætsə) *n* a public square, esp. in an Italian town. < Latin *platea* street.

pianoforte

Piano, the name of today's most popular domestic keyboard instrument, is a shortened, form of pianoforte. This word is a conflation of the Italian *piano e forte* or 'soft and loud', which comes from the phrase *gravecembalo col piano e forte* 'harpsichord with soft and loud'. This was the name given to the instrument produced in Florence by the Italian harpsichord maker Bartolommeo Cristofori at the beginning of the 18th century. For the first time the harpsichordist enjoyed direct control over the volume of the notes produced.

In musical notation piano and forte retain their Italian meaning.

pica (ˈpaɪkə) *n* **1** a unit for measuring printing type, about ⅙ of an inch (4.23 millimetres). **2** a typewriting size of 10 characters to the inch. < probably Medieval Latin: list of church rules.
picador (ˈpɪkəˌdɔː) *n* (*bullfighting*) a horseman with a lance to weaken the bull by prodding its neck and shoulder muscles. < Spanish *picar* to prick.
piccaninny (ˌpɪkəˈnɪnɪ) *n* a small Negro or Aboriginal child. < probably Portuguese *pequeno* small.
piccolo (ˈpɪkəˌləʊ) *n, pl* **piccolos** a small flute with a range an octave higher than the ordinary one. < Italian *piccolo flauto* small flute.
pick¹ (pɪk) *n* **1** also **pickaxe** an implement consisting of a curved iron bar with pointed ends on a heavy handle; used for breaking rocks or hard ground. **2** a plectrum. < Middle English *pik*.
pick² *vb* **1** choose or select. **2** make a hole in or penetrate with a sharp instrument. **3** gather (fruit, flowers, etc.) by plucking. **4** probe and remove small bits from: pick one's teeth. **5** nibble fussily or without hunger: pick at one's food. **6** pluck the strings of (a guitar, banjo, etc.). **7** loosen or pull apart (a weave). **8** provoke on purpose: pick a fight. **9** proceed slowly and carefully on foot: They picked their way through the debris.
• *n* **1** picking. **2** choosing; choice: take your pick. **3** the best: the pick of the bunch. **picker** *n* < Middle English *piken*. SEE PANEL.
picket (ˈpɪkɪt) *n* **1** a sharp stake or post driven into the ground as a marker, part of a fence, etc. **2** a small detachment of troops or sentries. **3** one or more strikers positioned outside a place of work to persuade others not to enter.
• *vb* **1** fence or enclose with pickets. **2** act as a picket during a strike. < Middle French *piquer* to prick.
pickle (ˈpɪkl̩) *n* **1** a solution of vinegar or brine for preserving food; food preserved in this. **2** (*informal*) a mess; trouble. **3** (*informal*) a naughty child.
• *vb* preserve in or treat with a pickle. < probably Middle Dutch *pekel*.
picnic (ˈpɪknɪk) *n* **1** an outing that includes an informal meal in the open air; food eaten at this. **2** (*informal*) something pleasant or easy to accomplish.
• *vb* **picnicked; picnicking** participate in a picnic. **picnickers** *n* < French *pique-nique*.
pictorial (pɪkˈtɔːrɪəl) *adj* **1** of (a) painting or drawing. **2** illustrated or expressed by

pictures. **3** evoking pictures; vivid.
• *n* a newspaper or magazine that is made up largely of pictures. **pictorially** *adv*

picture (ˈpɪktʃə) *n* **1** a representation or design made by painting, drawing, or photography. **2** a vivid description that evokes a mental image; this mental image. **3** someone or something attractive-looking: pretty as a picture. **4** a perfect example: He's the picture of health. **5** the image on a television screen. **6** a cinema film. **7** *pl* (*informal*) the cinema: We went to the pictures.
• *vb* **1** paint or draw a representation of; depict. **2** give a vivid description of. **3** imagine; visualize. **in the picture** informed about. **picturesque** *adj* **1** pleasant or charming to the eye; scenic. **2** (of language) vivid and descriptive. **picture window** a large, esp. single-pane window providing an attractive view. < ultimately Latin *pingere* to paint.

piddling (ˈpɪdlɪŋ) *adj* (*informal*) trivial; worthless. < origin unknown.

pidgin (ˈpɪdʒɪn) *n* a simplified language made up of elements of two or more others, used esp. for trading between people speaking different languages: pidgin English. SEE PANEL.

pie (paɪ) *n* a dish of meat, fish, fruit, etc., covered or encased by pastry and baked in a container. **pie in the sky** an unrealistic hope of something good in the future. < Middle English.

piebald (ˈpaɪˌbɔːld) *adj* (of a horse or other animal) with patches of different colours, esp. black and white. < Middle English *pie* magpie + *bald*.

piece (piːs) *n* **1** a distinct part of or a part broken from a whole. **2** one of a set, kind, or class. **3** a fixed size or quantity in which something is sold, or a fixed amount of work. **4** a composition of art, music, or literature. **5** a coin: a ten-pence piece. **6** (*derogatory*) a person, esp. a woman. **7** a movable object used in playing board-games, or a chessman superior to a pawn.
• *vb* also **piece together** assemble by joining parts. **a piece of cake** (*informal*) something very easy. **a piece of one's mind** a frank, severe scolding. **go to pieces** lose one's self-control, etc. **of a piece** consistent. **piecemeal** *adv* done one step at a time. **piece-work** *n* work paid for according to the quantity done. < Old French.

pièce de résistance (piːˌɛs də rɛˈzɪstɒns) **1** the main dish of a meal. **2** a masterwork; showpiece. < French:

not my pidgin or **pigeon?**

The word pidgin as in pidgin English is believed to derive from the attempt of Chinese traders to pronounce the word business. Hence the expression this is not my pidgin (this is not my business or responsibility). Nowadays, however, the form that is being used more and more in this usage is not pidgin but pigeon: It's not my pigeon—someone else can take care of it.'

pick and choose

Pick features in a number of idiomatic expressions, including:

pick and choose to select with great care and deliberation.
pick holes in to find fault with.
pick-me-up *n* **1** a stimulating drink; tonic to restore health, etc. **2** anything that stimulates or restores.
pick on to single out, especially for harassment or unpleasant tasks: Why do you always pick on me?
pick out 1 to choose or select. **2** to identify or recognize. **3** to play (a tune) note by note.
pick someone's brains to obtain ideas from a person for one's own use.
pick someone's pocket to steal from a person's pocket or bag. **pickpocket** *n*
pick up 1 to lift up; raise. **2** to take on board: pick up passengers. **3** to obtain or acquire: She picked up a working knowledge of German. **4** to get to know (a person of the opposite sex) casually, especially for sexual purposes. **5** to improve: After a slow start, business is now picking up. **6** to function normally again; accelerate or gain momentum. **7** to receive (radio signals). **8** to arrest. **9** to rescue.
pick-up *n* **1** a device that converts the vibrations of a stylus in a record groove into electrical signals. **2** a small, open truck.

piece of resistance.

pied-à-terre (pjeɪɑːˈtɛə, ˌpjeɪdɑːˈtɛə) *n*, *pl* **pieds-à-terre** a flat or lodging for secondary or occasional use. < French: foot on the ground.

pier (pɪə) *n* **1** a structure extending into the sea, used as a landing-stage, breakwater, or promenade. **2** an upright support for a structure such as a bridge or arch. **3** the part of a wall between any openings in it, such as windows or doors. < Medieval Latin *pera*.

pierce (pɪəs) *vb* **1** penetrate or make a hole in (something) with a sharp instrument. **2** force a way through or into. **3** move or affect emotionally. **piercing** *adj* **1** loud; shrill. **2** sharply cold; biting: a piercing wind. **3** keen; perceptive. **4** acute; intense: a piercing look. < Latin *per*-through + *tundere* to beat.

piety (ˈpaɪətɪ) *n* piousness; devoutness. < ultimately Latin *pius* dutiful.

piffle (ˈpɪfl̩) *n* (*informal*)rubbish; nonsense. **piffling** *adj* trivial; worthless. < probably like the sound.

pig (pɪg) *n* **1** a usually domesticated mammal with a stout body, short legs, and a long, blunt snout. **2** (*informal*) someone who is dirty, greedy, or selfish. **3** (*informal*) something difficult or disagreeable. **4** (*derogatory slang*) a policeman. **5** a shaped mass of metal, from a furnace: pig-iron.

• *vb* **pigged; pigging** live like a pig; eat in a greedy way: pig it. **buy a pig in a poke** buy something without seeing it or knowing about it before. **piggy** *adj* of or like a pig: piggy eyes. **piggy-back** *adj, n* (having) a ride on someone's back or shoulders. **piggy-bank** *n* a money box in the shape of a pig. **pig-headed** *adj* stubborn; self-willed. **piglet** *n* a young pig. **pigskin** *n* the skin of a pig; leather made from this. **pigsty** *n* **1** a partly-covered enclosure for pigs. **2** a place that is very dirty or untidy. **pigtail** *n* a long, tight plait of hair worn at the back of the head. < Middle English *pigge*. SEE PANEL.

pigeon (ˈpɪdʒən) *n* **1** a bird of the dove family, often adapted to living in urban areas. **2** (*informal*) someone's business or concern. **pigeon-hole** *n* **1** a compartment for letters or documents in a desk, cabinet, etc. **2** a category. **pigeonhole** *vb* **1** put off; defer. **2** label; classify. **pigeon-toed** *adj* having inward-pointing toes. < ultimately Latin *pipire* to chirp. SEE PANEL AT **PIDGIN**.

pigment (ˈpɪgmənt) *n* a colouring substance, esp. one occurring in plant or animal tissue.

• *vb* colour with a pigment. < Latin *pingere* to paint.

pike[1] (paɪk) *n* a long shaft of wood with a pointed steel head, formerly used as a weapon. < perhaps ultimately Latin *piccus* woodpecker.

pike[2] *n* a large, long-snouted, voracious, freshwater fish. < Middle English *pike* spike.

pilchard (ˈpɪltʃəd) *n* a small sea-fish of the herring family, common along the coasts of Europe. < origin unknown.

pile[1] (paɪl) *n* a column of steel, timber, reinforced concrete, etc., driven into the ground to support the weight of a structure such as a bridge or building. **pile-driver** *n* a machine that drives piles into the ground. < Old English *pīl*.

pile[2] *n* **1** a quantity of things gathered in a heap. **2** a heap of wood on which a corpse is burnt; funeral pyre. **3** (*informal*) a large amount. **4** (*informal*) a lot of money: He's made his pile. **5** a tall building or group of buildings. **6** a nuclear reactor.

• *vb* **1** gather or heap into a pile. **2** crowd or pack: They all piled on to the bus. **pile it on** (*informal*) exaggerate. **pile up 1** amass. **2** (of vehicles) be involved in a crash. **pile-up** *n* a multiple collision of motor vehicles. < Latin *pila* pillar.

pile[3] *n* the cut threads or loops on a fabric, giving it a raised surface. < probably

a pig in a poke

Whereas the English say to buy a pig in a poke, the French say 'to buy a cat in a bag' (acheter chat en poche) and so do the Germans (die Katze im Sack kaufen). In each instance the reference is to the age-old trick of trying to sell a cat for a sucking pig. The trickster would approach potential buyers in the market-place carrying a single piglet. This was claimed to be a sample of those that were tied up in bags. The deception was revealed only when the poke or 'bag' was opened, and the unhappy victim let the cat out of the bag.

ultimately Greek *pilos* felt cap.

piles (paɪlz) *pl n* haemorrhoids. < Latin *pila* ball.

pilfer (ˈpɪlfə) *vb* steal (articles of low value, or in small amounts). **pilferage** *n* **pilferer** *n* < Middle French *pelfre* booty.

pilgrim (ˈpɪlgrɪm) *n* someone who journeys to a shrine or holy place as an act of devotion. **pilgrimage** *n* < Latin *peregrinus* foreign, from *per* through + *ager* land.

pill (pɪl) *n* **1** a small, rounded mass of a medicinal substance for swallowing. **2 the pill** an oral contraceptive taken regularly over a monthly cycle: on the pill. **bitter pill** something disagreeable that must be endured. < Latin *pilula* small ball.

pillage (ˈpɪlɪdʒ) *vb, n* loot or plunder, esp. in war. < ultimately Latin *pilleus* felt cap.

pillar (ˈpɪlə) *n* **1** an upright column or other structure, used for support or decoration; something resembling this. **2** a chief supporter of something: a pillar of the community. **from pillar to post** from one place to another. **pillar-box** *n* a pillar-shaped public letter-box, usually painted red. < ultimately Latin *pila*. SEE PANEL.

pillbox (ˈpɪlˌbɒks) *n* **1** a usually small, shallow, round box for pills. **2** a woman's hat with this shape. **3** a small, low, concrete emplacement for guns.

pillion (ˈpɪljən) *n* a passenger-seat behind the driver of a motor cycle: ride pillion. < Gaelic *pillean*.

pillory (ˈpɪlərɪ) *n* a wooden frame with holes for the head and hands, formerly used for punishing offenders publicly. • *vb* **pilloried; pillorying 1** punish by placing in a pillory. **2** expose to public contempt or ridicule. < Old French *pilori*.

from pillar to post

The origin of this phrase has been traced back to the game of court tennis, the indoor precursor of lawn tennis. The original form of the expression was from post to pillar and it was used to refer to a particular type of volley in which the ball would strike first a post and then a pillar. As the phrase entered common usage, its technical application was forgotten and the sequence of post and pillar was reversed.

pillow (ˈpɪləʊ) *n* a cushion placed under the head for support, esp. in bed. • *vb* rest or support (as if) on a pillow. **pillowcase** or **pillowslip** *n* a cloth cover for a pillow. < Old English *pyle*.

pilot (ˈpaɪlət) *n* **1** someone who controls an aircraft in flight. **2** someone qualified to guide a ship in and out of a harbour or through certain waters. **3** a leader or guide. • *vb* **1** act as a pilot of (an aircraft or ship). **2** guide; lead. • *adj* trial; experimental: a pilot scheme. **pilot-light** *n* **1** a small jet of gas kept alight so as to ignite a burner when turned on. **2** an electric indicator light. **pilot officer** an RAF officer of the lowest commissioned rank, below a flying officer. < ultimately Greek *pēdon* oar.

pimp (pɪmp) *vb, n* (act as) a man who solicits for a prostitute or brothel. < origin unknown.

pimple (ˈpɪmpḷ) *n* a small, round skin inflammation. **pimply** *adj* < Middle English *pinple*.

pin (pɪn) *n* **1** a short piece of thin, stiff metal with a sharp point and blunt head, used for fastening papers or fabrics together: drawing-pin. **2** anything with this shape. **3** one of the wooden targets in a bowling game such as skittles. **4** a safety-pin, rolling-pin, or hairpin. **5** a peg. **6** (*golf*) the flagpole that marks a hole in the green. **7** *pl* (*informal*) someone's legs. • *vb* **pinned; pinning 1** secure with a pin or pins. **2** hold down; restrain: pinned against the wall. **3** attach; fasten: She pinned her hopes on the interview. **pinball** *n* a game played on a sloping table in which a ball is propelled at pins and targets to score points if they are hit. **pincushion** *n* a small pad for sticking pins in to keep them ready for use. < Old English *pinn*. SEE PANEL.

pinafore (ˈpɪnəˌfɔː) *n* an apron. **pinafore dress** a usually low-necked dress without sleeves, worn over a blouse. < *pin* + *afore*. SEE PANEL.

pince-nez (ˈpænsˌneɪ) *n* spectacles that are held in place only by a spring that clips on the nose. < French: pinch-nose.

pincers (ˈpɪnsəz) *pl n* **1** a tool with two short handles which press together pivoted jaws, used for gripping. **2** the claws of a lobster or similar shellfish. **pincer movement** the enveloping of an enemy position on two sides. < probably Middle French *pincier* to pinch.

pinch (pɪntʃ) *vb* **1** squeeze tightly between two surfaces, for example, the finger and thumb, esp. causing pain. **2** prune the top of (a plant) to cause more branches to grow. **3** stint; economize. **4** (*informal*) steal. **5** (*informal*) arrest.
• *n* **1** the action of pinching. **2** the amount of something that can be held between thumb and forefinger. **3** a critical or stressful time: feeling the pinch. **at a pinch** if really necessary. **with a pinch of salt** with reservations as to the truth of something. < Middle English *pinchen*.

pine[1] (paɪn) *n* one of a group of coniferous, evergreen trees with needle-shaped leaves and brown cones; its wood. < Latin *pinus*.

pine[2] *vb* **1** long for intensely; yearn. **2** weaken through grief or longing; languish. < ultimately Latin *poena* punishment.

pineapple (ˈpaɪnˌæpl̩) *n* a tropical plant bearing a large, oval fruit with a hard, segmented skin; this fruit. < Middle English *pin* pine + *appel* apple, fruit. SEE PANEL.

ping (pɪŋ) *vb, n* (make) a short, high-pitched, ringing sound. **pinger** *n*

Ping-Pong *n* (*Trademark*) table tennis. < like the sound.

pinion[1] (ˈpɪnjən) *n* a bird's wing, esp. the outer section with the flight feathers.
• *vb* **1** restrict the power of flight of (a bird) by clipping its wings. **2** restrain or immobilize (someone) by binding or holding the arms. < Middle French *pignon*.

pinion[2] *n* a cog-wheel designed to engage with a rack or larger gear wheel. < ultimately Latin *pecten* comb.

pink[1] (pɪŋk) *n* a pale shade of red.
• *adj* **1** pale red. **2** moderately left-wing in politics. **tickled pink** highly gratified or amused. < origin unknown.

pink[2] *n* **1 a** garden plant grown for its pink, white, or variegated flowers. **2** the

pin-money

Pin features in a number of expressions, many of them idiomatic, including:

pin down 1 to define or determine exactly. **2** to persuade (someone) to state his or her position, opinion, etc.: He's very difficult to pin down.
pinpoint *n* **1** the point of a pin. **2** something very small.
pinpoint *vb* to determine or locate precisely.
pins and needles a tingling sensation in a limb recovering from numbness.
pin-stripe *n* a very narrow stripe on a fabric; such fabric. **pin-striped** *adj*
pin-up *n* a photograph of an attractive or glamorous celebrity, for pinning on a wall; person in such a photograph.

Pin-money is a small amount of money, earned for example from doing odd jobs: 'You don't expect me to work for pin-money do you?' It was formerly a woman's allowance of money or money for her own personal use. There are a number of different explanations of the origin of this expression. Pin-money may originally have been money set aside for the purchase of pins, which—before they were mass-produced in the 19th century—were very expensive. Wives asked their husbands for pin-money on 1 January every year and then went to the market to buy as many as they could afford. Once pins became cheaper, women spent the allowance on other items but the expression pin-money persisted.

pinafore

A type of apron that protects the top half of the body as well as the lower part is known as a pinafore. Like the names of various other garments such as *over*coat and *under*skirt, pinafore contains a reference to the part of the body on which it is worn. It derives from *pin* and *afore,* a dialect form of 'before'.

pineapple

In Middle English pinappel was the name not of a tropical fruit but of a pinecone, the 'fruit' or 'apple' of the pine. By the 17th century, however, the resemblance of the tropical fruit to a pinecone had caused the name to be transferred.

best degree or condition. SEE PANEL.

pink[3] *vb* **1** cut a serrated edge on. **2** pierce slightly; prick. **pinking shears** a pair of dressmaker's scissors with serrated blades, used to cut a zigzag edge. < Middle English *pinken*.

pink[4] *vb* (of an internal-combustion engine) make a metallic, knocking sound. < like the sound.

pinnacle (ˈpɪnəkl̩) *n* **1** a decorative, pointed structure set on a buttress or tower. **2** a mountain peak. **3** the highest level or point: the pinnacle of her career. < ultimately Latin *pinna* wing.

pint (paɪnt) *n* **1** a measure of liquid capacity (in the UK 0.568 litre, USA 0.473 litre). **2** this amount of liquid, esp. beer or milk. < ultimately Latin *pingere* to paint.

pioneer (ˌpaɪəˈnɪə) *n* someone who settles or explores new territory, or opens up a new subject, method, or activity.
• *vb* act as a pioneer; open up or participate in the development of. < Old French *peon* foot soldier.

pious (ˈpaɪəs) *adj* **1** devout; spiritual. **2** falsely reverent; self-righteous. **piously** *adv* **piousness** *n* < Latin *pius*.

pip[1] (pɪp) *n* a small fruit seed in an orange, apple, lemon, etc. < short for *pippin*, from Old French *pepin*.

pip[2] *n* **1** a dot indicating a number on dice, dominoes, or playing-cards. **2** a star on the shoulder of a uniform, showing the rank of an army officer. **3** a brief, high-pitched tone, such as that broadcast as a time-signal. **pip at the post** defeat at the very last minute. < origin unknown.

pipe (paɪp) *n* **1** a tube for a gas or liquid to flow through. **2** a wind instrument consisting of a hollow tube; one of these as part of an organ or the bagpipes. **3** a device with a tubular stem and a small bowl at one end, used for smoking tobacco, etc.; amount of smoking material in this. **4** any tubular object or passage: windpipe.
• *vb* **1** convey by means of a pipe. **2** play (music) on a pipe, or summon by sounding this. **3** equip with pipes. **4** utter in a high, shrill voice. **5** trim (clothing) with piping. **6** force (cream or icing) through a nozzle, to make decorative shapes. **pipe down** (*informal*) stop talking. **pipe-dream** *n* a fanciful hope or scheme. **pipeline** *n* **1** a pipe that conveys liquids, esp. petroleum, over long distances. **2** a medium through which supplies or communications pass: There's a new book in the pipeline. **piper** *n* someone who plays the pipe or bagpipes. **pipe up** start speaking, singing, or playing the pipe. **piping** *n* **1** a length or system of pipes. **2** a strip of folded material like a pipe, used to decorate hems or seams. **3** a decorative line of icing piped on to a cake, etc. **piping hot** (of food or water) extremely hot. < Old English *pīpa*.

pipette (pɪˈpɛt) *n* a narrow, glass tube for measuring or transferring small amounts of liquids. < French: little pipe.

pipsqueak (ˈpɪpˌskwiːk) *n* (*informal*) someone small or insignificant; upstart.

piquant (ˈpiːkənt) *adj* **1** having an agreeably sharp taste. **2** mentally stimulating; agreeably so. **piquancy** *n* **piquantly** *adv* < Middle French *piquer* to prick.

pique (piːk) *vb* **1** cause resentment or hurt pride in. **2** mentally stimulate.
• *n* resentment; hurt pride: a fit of pique. < French *piquer* to prick.

piranha (pɪˈrɑːnə) *n* a ferocious freshwater fish found in tropical America, with strong jaws and teeth. < Portuguese, from Tupi.

pirate (ˈpaɪrət) *n* **1** someone who attacks and robs a ship at sea from another ship; ship used for this. **2** someone who broadcasts or reproduces copyright material without authorization.
• *vb* copy or broadcast without authorization. **piracy** *n* **piratical** *adj* < ultimately Greek *peiran* to attempt, attack.

pirouette (ˌpɪrʊˈɛt) *vb, n* (perform) a rapid spin of the body while balancing on the toe or ball of one foot, esp. in ballet. < French: spinning-top.

pistil (ˈpɪstɪl) *n* a carpel. < SEE **PESTLE**.

pistol (ˈpɪstl̩) *n* a small handgun. **pistol-grip** *n* the handle on a gun, tool, etc., shaped like a pistol stock. < Czech

pink

Contrary to popular belief, the garden plant known as the pink does not take its name from its colour, which can be either pink, white, red, or variegated. The pink is believed to be so called on account of the 'pinked' or serrated edge of its petals, which look as if they have been trimmed with a tailor's pinking shears.

pištal pipe.
piston (ˈpɪstən) *n* **1** a disc or cylinder that slides back and forth in a tube under pressure, esp. in an internal-combustion engine. **2** a sliding valve that alters the pitch of a note in a brass instrument such as the trumpet or cornet. < ultimately Latin *pinsere* to crush.
pit (pɪt) *n* **1** a hole in the ground or other surface. **2** a coal-mine. **3** the area between the stalls and the stage of a theatre: orchestra pit. **4** a dent or hollow in the skin; natural hollow in the body: the pit of the stomach. **5** an area beside a motor-racing track where racing-cars are refuelled or repaired during a race.
• *vb* **pitted; pitting 1** make dents or hollows in. **2** also **pit against** oppose; set against. **pit-head** *n* the top of a mine-shaft; area around this. < Old English *pytt.*
pitch¹ (pɪtʃ) *vb, n* (coat with) a dark, viscous substance obtained in distilling tars. **pitch-black** or **pitch-dark** *adj* absolutely black. < Latin *pix.*
pitch² *vb* **1** throw; hurl. **2** erect and fix in place: pitch a tent. **3** set at a particular level, degree, or quality. **4** (*music*) set in a particular key; sing or play (a note). **5** fall heavily downwards or forwards; incline downwards. **6** (of a ship or aircraft) plunge and rise alternately at each end. **7** (*cricket*) bowl (a ball) so that it hits the ground in front of the batsman.
• *n* **1** pitching; up-and-down movement. **2** a relative level or intensity: a high pitch of excitement. **3** the angle of a slope. **4** the highness or lowness of a musical note or sound. **5** a playing-field for soccer, rugby, hockey, etc. **6** an area where a street-trader takes up position. **7** persuasive, high-pressure sales talk. **pitched battle** an intensive battle fought from chosen positions. **pitch in** (*informal*) start working or contribute to a joint effort. **pitch into 1** pitch in. **2** attack physically or verbally. < Middle English *pichen.*
pitcher¹ (ˈpɪtʃə) *n* (*baseball*) the player who throws the ball to the batter.
pitcher² *n* a large, two-handled vessel or jug, usually earthenware, for holding and pouring liquids. **pitcher-plant** *n* a plant with leaves shaped like pitchers that contain a liquid which traps and digests insects. < ultimately Greek *bikos* earthen jug.
pitchfork (ˈpɪtʃˌfɔːk) *n* a two-pronged fork with a long handle, used in tossing hay.
• *vb* **1** toss or lift with a pitchfork. **2** thrust suddenly into an office or position.
pitfall (ˈpɪtˌfɔːl) *n* a hidden or unforeseen difficulty or danger.
pith (pɪθ) *n* **1** a spongy tissue in many plant-stems or between the flesh and rind of an orange, lemon, etc. **2** the essence or core. **pithy** *adj* **1** having much pith. **2** concise and meaningful. < Old English *pitha.*
pittance (ˈpɪtn̩s) *n* a small amount of money as an allowance or wages. < Latin *pietas* pity.
pituitary (pɪˈtjuːɪtərɪ) *n* also **pituitary gland** a small, ductless organ at the base of the brain that secretes hormones controlling growth and metabolism. < Latin *pituita* phlegm.
pity (ˈpɪtɪ) *n* **1** sorrow and sympathy for the unhappiness or suffering of another. **2** something unfortunate: It's a pity you can't come.
• *vb* **pitied; pitying** have or show sympathy for. **pitiable** *adj* arousing or worthy of pity or scorn. **pitiably** *adv* **pitiful** *adj* pitiable. **pitifully** *adv* **pitiless** *adj* without pity; merciless. < ultimately Latin *pius* pious.
pivot (ˈpɪvət) *n* a pin or shaft that supports something which turns; movement of this.
• *vb* turn or cause to turn on a pivot. **pivotal** *adj* **1** of a pivot. **2** central; crucial. < French.
pixie (ˈpɪksɪ) *n* a mischievous fairy or elf in folklore. < origin unknown.
pizza (ˈpiːtsə) *n* a round cake of dough baked with a topping of mixed tomatoes, cheese, herbs, etc. < Italian, ultimately from Latin *pix* pitch.
placard (ˈplækɑːd) *n* a notice for public display, often backed with stiff material.
• *vb* **1** post placards on. **2** give notice of by means of placards. < Middle French *plaquier* to plate.
placate (pləˈkeɪt) *vb* pacify; appease. **placatory** *adj* < Latin *placare* to please.
place (pleɪs) *n* **1** an indefinite area; environment. **2** a particular point on a surface. **3** a particular town, region, or building. **4** an open square or short street in a town or city. **5** a house or dwelling. **6** an available space or seat: set a place for dinner. **7** a job or appointment. **8** a leading position in a race or competition, esp. second or third. **9** an appropriate or designated moment, position, or rank: know one's place. **10** a point in a passage of writing, esp. where one has stopped reading temporarily. **11** the

relative position of a figure in a number, esp. after a decimal point. **12** a point in the development of an argument or explanation: In the first place, your information is wrong.
• *vb* **1** set in a particular position, state, or order. **2** find a home or employment for. **3** identify through memory: I couldn't quite place her. **4** make (a bet); give (an order) to a supplier. **be placed** finish first, second, or third in a race. **go places** (*informal*) achieve success. **in place** in a suitable or proper place. **in place of** instead of. **out of place** in an unsuitable or wrong place. **place-kick** *n* (*rugby*) a kick made when the ball is placed in a certain spot. **place-setting** *n* cutlery, dishes, etc., for one person at table. **put someone in his** or **her place** humble someone. **take place** happen; occur. < ultimately Greek *platys* broad. SEE PANEL.

placebo (plə'si:bəʊ) *n, pl* **placebos** an inactive substance given as a medicine to soothe a patient or as a control in the testing of, for example, a new drug; anything tending to humour or soothe another. < Latin *placēre* to please.

placenta (plə'sɛntə) *n* an organ that forms in most mammals during pregnancy and which provides nourishment for the foetus; afterbirth. < ultimately Greek *plax* flat object.

placid ('plæsɪd) *adj* calm and serene; even-tempered. **placidity** *n* **placidly** *adv* < Latin *placēre* to please.

plagiarize ('pleɪdʒəˌraɪz) *vb* take (ideas, words, etc.) from (another) and pass them off as one's own. **plagiarism** *n* < Latin *plagiarius* plunderer, kidnapper, literary thief.

plague (pleɪg) *n* **1** a highly contagious disease usually causing death, often transmitted by rats: bubonic plague. **2** a large-scale affliction or infestation: a plague of locusts. **3** an irritant; pest.
• *vb* bother; irritate. < Latin *plaga* blow.

plaice (pleɪs) *n, pl* **plaice** a kind of edible European flatfish with a brownish, oval body and red or orange spots. < Greek *platys* flat.

plaid (plæd) *n* **1** a rectangular piece of tartan worn over the left shoulder as part of Highland dress. **2** woollen cloth with a tartan pattern; this pattern. < Scottish Gaelic *plaide*.

plain (pleɪn) *adj* **1** simple in style; not decorative. **2** distinct; obvious. **3** frank; honest: plain words. **4** common; unaffected. **5** unattractive. **6** not complicated. **7** unmixed; pure: a plain whisky.
• *adv* **1** simply; obviously. **2** completely: It's plain idiotic.
• *n* **1** a flat expanse of land, esp. without trees. **2** a simple knitting stitch. **plainly** *adv* **plainness** *n* **plain clothes** civilian clothes rather than uniform, esp. for police. **plain flour** flour not containing a raising agent. **plain sailing** smooth progress without hindrance. **plain-spoken** *adj* direct in speech. < Latin

place-names

'What's in a name?' asked Juliet. When it comes to place-names, the answer is, 'A great deal'. Many of the combining elements that we find in place-names are traceable to Old English. Examples include:

-borough, -burgh, -bury Old English *burgh* 'fortified place' as in Salisbury
-ham Old English *hām* 'homestead or village' as in Durham
-ington Old English *ing* + *tun* 'the people of' as in Workington
-ley, -leigh Old English *lēah* 'glade or wood' as in Burnley
-pool, -pole Old English *pol* 'pool or stream' as in Liverpool
-ton, -tone Old English *tūn* 'homestead or village' as in Brighton
-wald, -wold Old English *wald* or *weald* 'forest' as in Coxwold
-worth, -worthy Old English *worþ* or *worþig* 'enclosure or homestead' as in Kenilworth

as plain as a pikestaff

Something that is completely clear or obvious may nowadays be described as being as plain as a pikestaff. Originally, however, this informal expression was applied to something that was 'simple' or 'unadorned'. The allusion is to the plain wooden staff or walking stick formerly used by foot travellers.

An earlier variant of the expression is plain as a packstaff, which refers to the equally simple staff on which a pedlar carried his pack.

planus flat. SEE PANEL. SEE PANEL AT **SHEER**[1].

plaintiff (ˈpleɪntɪf) *n* someone who brings a legal action in a civil court. < Middle French *plaintif.*

plaintive (ˈpleɪntɪv) *adj* sad; mournful. **plaintively** *adv* **plaintiveness** *n* < Middle French *plaint.*

plait (plæt) *vb* intertwine several strands of (hair, etc.) into one length.
• *n* a length of something plaited, esp. hair. < ultimately Latin *plicare* to fold.

plan (plæn) *n* **1** a drawing of a building, machine, etc., on a horizontal plane. **2** a map of a town or small area. **3** a scheme or method for proceeding or achieving something.
• *vb* **planned; planning 1** design. **2** prepare; think out. **3** intend; propose. **planner** *n* **planning** *n* making plans, esp. for the development of an area: town planning. < French, from Latin *planus* flat.

plane[1] (pleɪn) *n* one of a group of tall trees with lobe-shaped leaves. < Greek *platanos.*

plane[2] *n* **1** a level surface. **2** (*mathematics*) a surface in which a straight line joining two points lies completely on that surface. **3** a level of existence, development, or consciousness: on the spiritual plane. **4** an aeroplane.
• *adj* flat, level, or lying in a plane: a closed plane figure. < Latin *planus* level.

plane[3] *n* a tool with a sharp, metal blade set in a wooden or metal body, used for levelling or smoothing wooden surfaces.
• *vb* level or smooth off with a plane. < Latin *planare* to level.

planet (ˈplænɪt) *n* any of the nine celestial bodies, including the Earth, that revolve around the sun. **planetary** *adj* **planetarium** *n* a room with a domed roof onto which images of the night sky are projected. < ultimately Greek *planasthai* to wander.

plank (plæŋk) *n* **1** a long, thick piece of wood. **2** a policy in the programme of a political party.
• *vb* cover or lay with planks. < Latin *planca.*

plankton (ˈplæŋktən) *n* microscopic organisms that float in the sea or in fresh water. < Greek *planktos* drifting.

plant (plɑːnt) *n* **1** any living organism that grows with roots in the ground and lacks the power of movement or sensation. **2** a small variety of this, such as a flower or herb. **3** a factory or works; machinery or equipment. **4** (*informal*) something left to be discovered on purpose, esp. to incriminate someone.
• *vb* **1** set in the soil for growth. **2** put firmly in position: He planted his foot in the doorway. **3** found; establish. **4** place secretly in order to observe or incriminate. **plantation** *n* **1** an area of land where trees or plants are grown; these plants or trees. **2** a large estate, esp. in the tropics, where cash crops such as rubber, tea, or coffee are grown. **planter** *n* **1** the owner or manager of a plantation. **2** a container for ornamental plants. **3** a planting machine. < Latin *planta.*

plaque (plæk) *n* **1** a flat plate of ceramic, wood, metal, etc., to decorate or commemorate something. **2** a soft, filmy substance that forms on teeth and harbours bacteria. < Middle Dutch *placken* to patch.

plasma (ˈplæzmə) *n* the clear fluid part of blood in which cells and corpuscles are suspended. < Greek *plassein* to form.

plaster (ˈplɑːstə) *n* **1** a paste of mixed sand, lime, and water, used to coat ceilings, walls, etc. **2** also **sticking plaster** a strip of cloth or plastic for dressing a cut or wound. **3** a mould of plaster of Paris, used to immobilize a broken limb while mending; plaster cast.
• *vb* **1** coat with plaster. **2** smear thickly on: Her face was plastered with make-up. **3** cause to lie flat or stick to a surface: hair plastered down. **plasterer** *n* **plasterboard** *n* a board made with a plaster core, used to make or cover walls. **plastered** *adj* (*informal*) drunk. **plaster of Paris** a quick-setting, white paste of gypsum and water, used to make casts or moulds. < Greek *plassein* to form.

plastic (ˈplæstɪk) *n* one of many synthetic materials that can be moulded by heat into a permanent shape.
• *adj* **1** made of plastic. **2** capable of being formed or shaped. **3** of modelling or sculpture: the plastic arts. **4** artificial; synthetic. **plasticity** *n* **plastic surgery** the repair or restoration of external body tissue by skin grafting. < Greek *plassein* to form.

Plasticine (ˈplæstɪˌsiːn) *n* (*Trademark*) a soft material used for modelling, esp. by children.

plate (pleɪt) *n* **1** a usually round, shallow dish for serving or eating food from. **2** the amount of food on a plate, or one course in a meal. **3** a shallow dish for collecting money at a church service. **4** a smooth, flat, rigid piece of material such as metal or glass. **5** a thin coating of metal deposited on another by chemical action, etc. **6** a piece of glass coated with

light-sensitive material, for use in photography. **7** a flat piece of material bearing a design or inscription. **8** household utensils, cutlery, etc., coated with gold or silver. **9** a full-page illustration in a book, often on special paper. **10** a rigid layer of bone, horn, or scale forming part of the body of a plant or animal. **11** a device fitting in the mouth to hold artificial teeth or straighten existing ones; denture. **12** one of the huge, rigid segments making up the Earth's crust.
• *vb* **1** cover with metal plates: an armour-plated vehicle. **2** coat with a thin layer of metal, esp. gold, silver, or tin. **on a plate** (*informal*) so as to demand little effort. **on one's plate** (*informal*) requiring attention or action. **plateful** *n* **1** the amount a plate can hold. **2** a lot of work or business to attend to. **plate glass** strong, high-quality glass used in shop windows. < probably Greek *platys* broad.

plateau (ˈplætəʊ) *n, pl* **plateaus, plateaux 1** a relatively flat area of raised ground. **2** a state, period, or level of relative stability: Spiralling prices reached a plateau. < Middle French *plat* flat.

platen (ˈplætn̩) *n* **1** the roller on a typewriter. **2** the flat plate on a printing press that presses the type and paper together. < Middle French *plate.*

platform (ˈplætfɔːm) *n* **1** a raised floor used as a stage by speakers. **2** a raised area beside a railway line where passengers get on or off a train. **3** the floor area at the entrance or exit of a bus. **4** the declaration of principles and policies of a political party. < Middle French *plate-forme* flat form.

platinum (ˈplætɪnəm) *n* a greyish-white, precious, metallic element that does not corrode. **platinum blonde** someone with silvery-blonde hair, esp. bleached. < Spanish *platina* small silver.

platitude (ˈplætɪˌtjuːd) *n* a trite remark or cliché, delivered as if it were original. **platitudinous** *adj* < French *plat* flat.

platonic (pləˈtɒnɪk) *adj* **1** of a relationship between a man and woman involving affection but not sexual love. **2 Platonic** of Plato or his teachings. < *Plato,* died 349 BC, Greek philosopher.

platoon (pləˈtuːn) *n* a subdivision of a company in the armed forces. < French *pelote* little ball.

platter (ˈplætə) *n* **1** a large, oval dish for serving food, esp. meat. **2** (*chiefly US informal*) a gramophone record. < Middle French *plat* plate.

plausible (ˈplɔːzəbl̩) *adj* **1** seemingly reasonable or truthful: a plausible excuse. **2** (of a person) persuasive; smooth-tongued. **plausibility** *n* **plausibly** *adv* < Latin *plaudere* to applaud.

play (pleɪ) *vb* **1** engage in (a game,

playing the game

Play features in a number of expressions, many of them idiomatic, including:

play about or **around** to behave in a silly, irresponsible way.
play along to pretend to co-operate.
play at to do something in a casual or half-hearted manner.
play back to play (something recorded) on a tape-recorder, video-recorder, etc. **play-back** *n*
play by ear 1 to perform without a written musical score. **2** to deal with (a matter) step by step as it proceeds, rather than according to a set plan.
play down to make (something) appear less important or serious than it really is.
played out exhausted; worn out.
play for time to delay, especially in order to avoid defeat or loss.
play into someone's hands to do something that enables someone to gain an advantage over one.
play off 1 to determine the winner of a drawn competition by playing an extra match. **play-off** *n* **2** to set (someone) against (another person) for one's own advantage: We won the contract by playing off our rivals against each other.
play on to exploit: playing on her weakness.
play one's cards right to make judicious use of one's resources, especially to achieve one's desired aim.
play on words a pun.
play safe to avoid risks.
play the game 1 to act according to the rules. **2** to behave fairly and honourably.
play up 1 to give emphasis to: play up the important points. **2** to cause pain or anxiety to: His leg's playing him up again. **3** to behave in a mischievous manner; perform badly.
play up to to pretend to admire; try to endear oneself to.
play with to act or deal with, without serious intentions: just playing with the girl's affections.

sport, or other recreation); compete against (someone) in this. **2** occupy (a particular position) in a game. **3** deliver (a ball or a card) in a game. **4** perform (a dramatic role); act or behave in a particular way: play the fool. **5** perform (music or on a musical instrument); have the ability to do this: She plays guitar. **6** emit or cause to emit sound. **7** move lightly and intermittently: The lights played over her face. **8** cause (water or light) to discharge or fall on. **9** allow (a hooked fish) to tire itself by alternately reeling in and letting out the line.
• *n* **1** playing; course of action in a game. **2** games or activities undertaken esp. by children. **3** playing on words; punning. **4** operation; action: a new factor came into play. **5** a dramatic work performed on a stage. **6** freedom of movement: There's not enough play in the rope. **7** (in a game) the defined area of playing and position of the ball according to the rules: out of play. **player** *n* **play-acting** *n* **1** playing a role in a play. **2** overdramatizing; pretending. **playboy** *n* a man who lives for the pursuit of pleasure. **playfellow** *n* a playmate. **playful** *adj* **1** lively; spirited. **2** humorous; teasing. **playfully** *adv* **playfulness** *n* **playground** *n* **1** an area of land for children to play on. **2** a favourite place for amusement or recreation. **playgroup** *n* a supervised group of preschool children who play together. **playing-card** *n* one of a set of 52 rectangular pieces of card, marked on one side to indicate one of 13 ranks in one of four suits, used to play various games. **playing-field** *n* a field used to play outdoor games and sports. **playleader** *n* an adult who leads children's play in a play-group. **playmate** *n* a friend or partner in play. **play-pen** *n* a usually portable and collapsible enclosure for an infant to play in. **playroom** *n* a recreation room for children. **plaything** *n* a toy, or a person treated like one. **playtime** *n* a time designated for recreation, esp. at school. **playwright** *n* someone who writes plays; dramatist. < Old English *plega* movement, exercise. SEE PANEL.

plc *abbrev* public limited company.

plea (pliː) *n* **1** a formal allegation or declaration of guilt or innocence made in a court of law. **2** an earnest appeal or request: a plea for rescue. **3** a pretext or excuse. < ultimately Latin *placēre* to please.

plead (pliːd) *vb* **pleaded, pled; pleading** **1** make a plea in a court of law. **2** put forward (a case) in a court of law. **3** beg; implore. **4** offer as an excuse: plead ignorance. < Old French *plaid* plea.

pleasant (ˈplɛzn̩t) *adj* **1** agreeable; satisfying. **2** friendly; likable. **pleasantly** *adv* **pleasantness** *n* **pleasantry** *n* a good-natured or amusing remark, esp. made out of courtesy. < Middle French *plaisir* to please.

please (pliːz) *vb* **1** bring pleasure or satisfaction to; cause to feel glad. **2** like; desire: do as you please.
• *adv* used to express polite requests or acceptance: 'A drink?'—'Please!' **if you please 1** (*informal*) please. **2** used ironically to suggest that something is unfair. **pleased** *adj* glad; delighted. **please oneself** do as one likes. < ultimately Latin *placēre*.

pleasure (ˈplɛʒə) *n* **1** an enjoyable or satisfying sensation or emotion; something bringing this: It's a pleasure to see her. **2** wish; inclination: at her pleasure. **pleasurable** *adj* enjoyable. **pleasurably** *adv* **with pleasure** gladly.

pleat (pliːt) *vb, n* (make) a flat fold in cloth by doubling it over itself: pleated skirt. < Middle English *plete* plait.

plebeian (pləˈbiːən) *adj* **1** of the common people, esp. in ancient Rome. **2** vulgar; unrefined.
• *n* also **pleb** someone common or vulgar. < Latin *plebs* common people of ancient Rome.

plectrum (ˈplɛktrəm) *n* a small, thin piece of plastic, metal, bone, etc., used to pluck the strings of a musical instrument. < Greek *plēssein* to strike.

pled (plɛd) SEE PLEAD.

pledge (plɛdʒ) *n* **1** an item left as security for payment of a debt or fulfilment of an obligation. **2** a binding promise or an assurance. **3** a token or gesture: as a pledge of my good intention. **4** a toast.
• *vb* **1** leave (an item) as a security. **2** promise faithfully: pledge allegiance. **3** drink the health of; toast. < Late Latin *plebere* to pledge.

plenary (ˈpliːnərɪ) *adj* **1** absolute; unrestricted: plenary powers. **2** attended by all those involved: plenary session. < Latin *plenus* full.

plenty (ˈplɛntɪ) *n* a sufficient amount; abundance.
• *determiner* ample; enough: plenty of time. **plentiful** *adj* abundant. **plentifully** *adv* < ultimately Latin *plenus* full.

plethora (ˈplɛθərə) *n* an excess; surplus. < Greek *plēthein* to be full.

pleurisy (ˈplʊərɪsɪ) *n* a painful inflammation of the membrane surrounding the lungs and lining the thorax. < Greek *pleura* side.

pliable (ˈplaɪəbl̩) *adj* **1** easily bent; flexible. **2** docile; easily led. **pliability** *n* **pliably** *adv* < ultimately Latin *plicare* to fold.

pliant (ˈplaɪənt) *adj* pliable. **pliancy** *n* **pliantly** *adv*

pliers (ˈplaɪəz) *pl n* a tool for gripping, consisting of two arms on a pivot and long, often grooved jaws. SEE PANEL.

plight (plaɪt) *n* an unpleasant or serious predicament. < Old English *pliht*.

plimsoll (ˈplɪmsəl) *n* a canvas sports shoe with a rubber sole. < probably from Samuel *Plimsoll*, died 1898, English advocate of shipping reform. SEE PANEL.

plinth (plɪnθ) *n* a slab or block which serves as a base or support for a column, pedestal, etc. < Greek *plinthos*.

plod (plɒd) *vb* **plodded; plodding 1** walk with slow, heavy steps; trudge. **2** work in a slow, laborious way.
• *n* plodding. **plodder** *n* < like the sound.

plonk[1] (plɒŋk) *vb* drop, throw, or put down heavily. < like the sound.

plonk[2] *n* (*informal*) cheap or low-quality wine. < perhaps French *vin blanc* white wine. SEE PANEL.

plop (plɒp) *vb*, *n* (make) a sound like something dropping into water without splashing. < like the sound.

plot (plɒt) *n* **1** a small piece of land. **2** the story-line in a novel, film, or play. **3** an intrigue or conspiracy.
• *vb* **plotted; plotting 1** make a map or plan of; mark (a course) on this. **2** plan in secret; conspire. **3** construct (a story). < Old English.

plough (plaʊ) *n* **1** an implement drawn by a horse or tractor, used to cut and turn over earth in furrows in preparation for sowing. **2** any similar implement: snow-plough.
• *vb* **1** cut and turn (earth) with a plough. **2** plunge violently forwards: The car ploughed into the fence. **3** move laboriously; plod. **plough back** reinvest (profits) in a business or industry. **ploughman** *n*, *pl* **ploughmen** someone who ploughs; farm labourer. **ploughman's lunch** a meal of bread, cheese, etc., usually served with beer. **ploughshare** *n* the cutting edge of a plough. < Old English *plōh* measure of land.

plover (ˈplʌvə) *n* a type of wading-bird with a short beak and stout body. < ultimately Latin *pluvia* rain.

ploy (plɔɪ) *n* a tactic devised to give one an advantage; ruse. < probably *employ*.

pluck (plʌk) *vb* **1** pull off or out; pick; pluck flowers. **2** remove from by plucking, esp. bird's feathers. **3** pull at; snatch. **4** sound (the strings of a musical instrument) with the fingers or a plectrum.
• *n* **1** plucking; pulling. **2** nerve; courage. **3** an animal's liver, heart, and lungs, used as food. **pluck up courage** gather courage. **plucky** *adj* bold; courageous. **pluckily** *adv* < Old English *pluccian*.

pliers

Pliers is an example of a noun which is plural in form and which takes a plural verb and yet is typically used to refer to a single object. Other nouns belonging to this group include:

bellows	**pincers**	**shorts**
binoculars	**pyjamas**	**spectacles**
jeans	**scissors**	**tights**
pants	**shears**	**trousers**

These all share the property of being made in two equal parts which are joined together to form 'a pair'.

plimsoll

A rubber-soled, canvas gym shoe is sometimes referred to as a plimsoll. This name is thought to derive from the resemblance of the sole of the shoe to a Plimsoll line, a line painted on the hull of a ship indicating the maximum level to which it may legally be loaded in salt water. The Plimsoll line takes its name from Samuel *Plimsoll*, 1824–98, the English MP who advocated its adoption.

plonk

Wine of no particular distinction is often informally referred to as plonk. This term perhaps derives from the French *(vin) blanc* 'white (wine)', a name which enjoyed considerable popularity amongst servicemen during the First World War.

plug (plʌg) *n* **1** a device of wood, rubber, etc., used to fill or block a hole; stopper. **2** a device with metal pins, used to make an electrical connection by means of a socket; this socket. **3** a sparking-plug. **4** a pressed cake or twist of tobacco for chewing. **5** (*informal*) a favourable mention of a commercial product via radio, television, newspapers, etc.
• *vb* **plugged; plugging 1** block or fill with a plug. **2** (*slang*) shoot (someone) with a bullet. **3** (*informal*) commend or publicize constantly. **plug away** work hard at; slog. **plug in** make an electrical connection by fitting a plug in a socket. < Middle Dutch *plugge*.

plum (plʌm) *n* **1** a tree of the rose family that bears a fleshy, sweet fruit with an oval stone; this fruit. **2** a raisin used in cooking: plum pudding. **3** a purplish-red colour. **4** something superior or desirable: a plum job. < Old English *plūme*.

plumage (ˈplu:mɪdʒ) *n* a bird's covering of feathers. < Old French *plume* feather.

plumb (plʌm) *n* a lead weight tied to a cord, used to measure the depth of water or to indicate a vertical line.
• *adv* **1** vertically. **2** precisely. **3** (*US informal*) absolutely: plumb crazy.
• *vb* **1** measure or adjust to vertical with a plumb line. **2** go into; explore. **3** undergo; experience: plumbing the depths of despair. **4** supply with a system of drainage and waterpipes; install (something) as part of this. **plumber** *n* someone who fits or repairs plumbing. **plumbing** *n* a system of drains, cisterns, and water-pipes in a building. **plumb-line** *n* a line with a plumb at the end. < Latin *plumbum* lead.

plume (plu:m) *n* **1** a bird's feather, esp. showy and used for decoration; cluster of these worn as an ornament. **2** something resembling this, such as a trail of smoke or an animal's bushy tail. **plumed** *adj* < Latin *plums* small, downy feather.

plummet (ˈplʌmɪt) *n* a plumb-line or plumb.
• *vb* fall abruptly and steeply. < Old French *plomb* lead.

plump[1] (plʌmp) *adj* rounded; chubby.
• *vb* make or become plump: She plumped up the cushions. **plumpness** *n* < Middle Dutch: dull, blunt.

plump[2] *vb* drop suddenly or heavily; flop.
• *adv* heavily or abruptly. **plump for** decide on from several choices. < Middle English *plumpen*, like the sound.

plunder (ˈplʌndə) *vb* **1** steal forcibly, esp. in wartime; loot. **2** steal from (someone); rob.
• *n* robbing or looting; things taken in this way. **plunderer** *n* < Middle High German: household goods.

plunge (plʌndʒ) *vb* **1** force or go into or through quickly. **2** fall or dip abruptly. **3** dive or jump (as if) into water. **4** cause to enter a particular state: The room was plunged into darkness. **5** become or cause to become deeply occupied with: He plunged into his work. **6** (*informal*) gamble heavily and recklessly.
• *n* a dive or swim. **plunger** *n* **1** a machine part such as a piston that acts with a plunging movement. **2** a rubber suction cap on a handle, used to remove blockages from plumbing. **take the plunge** boldly decide on a difficult or dangerous course of action. < ultimately Latin *plumbum* lead.

plural (ˈplʊərəl) *adj* **1** involving or referring to more than one person, kind, or thing. **2** of a verb or noun form denoting this.
• *n* the plural form of a verb or noun. < Latin *plus* more.

plus (plʌs) *prep* **1** with the addition of. **2** and also; with.
• *adj* **1** additional. **2** positive. **3** more than indicated: He got a C plus in French.
• *n* **1** an additional or surplus amount. **2** a bonus; advantage. **plus-fours** *pl n* baggy trousers gathered in a band just below the knee, worn by golfers. < Latin: more. SEE PANEL.

plush (plʌʃ) *n* a kind of cloth with a cut pile, softer and less dense than velvet.
• *adj* **1** of or like plush. **2** plushy. **plushy** *adj* lavish; luxurious. **plushiness** *n* < Middle French *peluche*.

plutonium (plu:ˈtəʊnɪəm) *n* a radioactive element formed in atomic reactors, used as fuel for these and in nuclear weapons. < *Pluto*, the planet.

ply[1] (plaɪ) *n* **1** a layer, fold, or thickness of wood, cloth, yarn, etc. **2** one of the strands twisted to form rope, wool, or

plus fours

The baggy trousers formerly popular amongst golfers were known as plus fours. The name derived from the provision of a four-inch overhang below the knee-band, designed so as to provide the sportsman with unrestricted movement.

yarn. **3** plywood. **plywood** *n* a thin board of sheets of wood glued together with the grains arranged crosswise. < Latin *plicare* to fold.

ply² *vb* **plied; plying 1** use or manipulate (a tool or weapon). **2** carry on or work at: plying one's trade. **3** keep supplying with or subjecting to: She plied them with drinks. **4** perform or work steadily. **5** travel or go regularly. **6** (of a boatman or taxi-driver) wait for custom in a regular place: ply for hire. < Middle English *applien* to apply.

PM *abbrev* Prime Minister.

p.m. *abbrev*(*Latin*) post meridiem (after noon).

pneumatic (njʊˈmætɪk) *adj* containing or worked by compressed air: pneumatic tyre. **pneumatically** *adv* < ultimately Greek *pnein* to breathe.

pneumonia (njuːˈməʊnɪə) *n* inflammation of the lungs, forming liquid in the air sacs. < Greek *pneumōn* lung.

PO *abbrev* **1** Post Office. **2** postal order.

poach¹ (pəʊtʃ) *vb* cook (fish or eggs) in a gently simmering liquid. **poacher** *n* a pan with individual cups for putting eggs in over boiling water. < Old French *pochier* to enclose in a bag, from *poche* bag. SEE PANEL.

poach² *vb* **1** catch (fish or game) illegally while trespassing on private land. **2** intrude or trespass on another's property or rights. **poacher** *n* < Middle French *pocher.*

pock (pɒk) *n* a spot erupting on the face from smallpox, etc., or a scar left by this. **pock-marked** *adj* scarred or pitted. < Old English *pocc.*

pocket (ˈpɒkɪt) *n* **1** a small bag sewn into a garment for holding money or small items. **2** any pouch, bag, container, or compartment. **3** one's money supply; means: It's beyond my pocket. **4** one of the six openings at the corners and sides of a billiard-table, into which balls are hit. **5** a small isolated area or group: a pocket of resistance.
• *adj* small enough to fit in the pocket: pocket camera.
• *vb* **1** put in one's pocket. **2** take for oneself; steal. **3** hit (a ball) into a pocket on a billiard-table. **4** hold back; suppress: She pocketed her pride. **in/out of pocket** having gained/lost in a transaction. **pocket-book** *n* a small case for papers and money; notebook. **pocketful** *n* the amount a pocket can hold. **pocket-knife** *n* a knife with one or more folding blades, carried in the pocket. **pocket-money** *n* money for small expenses; regular allowance for children. < Old Northern French *pokete* small bag.

pod (pɒd) *n* a long fruit or seed-case, esp. of a bean or pea.
• *vb* **podded; podding 1** produce pods. **2** remove (peas) from a pod. < perhaps ultimately alteration of *cod* bag.

podgy (ˈpɒdʒɪ) *adj* short and stout; tubby. < origin unknown.

podium (ˈpəʊdɪəm) *n*, *pl* **podia 1** a small, raised platform. **2** a stone base or pedestal. < Latin.

poem (ˈpəʊɪm) *n* a verse composition, usually designed to evoke an imaginative response through its sound, rhythm, etc. **poet** fem. **poetess** *n* a person who writes poems. **poetic** *adj* **poetic justice** a fitting reward or punishment. **poetical** *adj* poetic. **poetically** *adv* **poetry** *n* **1** poems; art of writing these. **2** qualities of grace, beauty, etc. < ultimately Greek *poiein* to make.

poignant (ˈpɔɪnjənt) *adj* **1** intensely moving; distressing. **2** to the point; keen: poignant criticism. **poignancy** *n* **poignantly** *adv* < ultimately Latin *pungere* to sting.

point (pɔɪnt) *n* **1** a dot used in punctuation or to show a decimal place. **2** a spot, place, or moment in time. **3** the sharp end or tip of something. **4** a projecting piece of land. **5** a stage of development: the point of no return. **6** one of the directions referred to or marked on a compass. **7** a unit of counting or scoring in a game or contest. **8** an objective; purpose. **9** an individual aspect or detail. **10** a distinguishing characteristic or quality. **11** the essential feature in a discussion, joke, story, etc. **12** (*cricket*) the fielding position on the off side near the batsman. **13** a socket for an electric plug. **14** a device of moving rails for redirecting a train on to another line. **15** one of the

poached eggs

Eggs that have been cooked by simmering gently in water are described as poached. This application of poach stems from the Old French verb *pochier,* 'to enclose in a bag', from *poche* 'bag'. The allusion is to the way in which the yolk of a poached egg is enclosed by the white, as if it were enclosed in a bag.

two electrical contacts in the distributor of an internal-combustion engine.
• *vb* **1** direct or be directed in a specific direction: point a gun. **2** sharpen. **3** suggest; indicate: Everything points to his guilt. **4** replace old mortar in (brickwork) with new material. **beside the point** irrelevant; irrelevantly. **on the point of** on the verge of. **point-blank** *adj* **1** (of a shot) fired at close range. **2** also *adv* (made) in a blunt, direct way: She refused point-blank. **pointed** *adj* **1** with a point; sharp. **2** (of speech or behaviour) directed at a particular person or group. **pointedly** *adv* **pointer** *n* **1** a rod used for pointing at things on a blackboard, etc. **2** a needle or mark that points to figures on a scale or dial. **3** a type of large, strong gundog that points its muzzle towards game when it has the scent. **4** a suggestion; tip. **pointless** *adj* having no meaning or purpose. **pointlessly** *adv* **point of view** a way of considering something; opinion. **point out** draw attention to. **point-to-point** *n* a steeplechase, usually for amateurs. **point up** emphasize. **to the point** relevant; relevantly. < ultimately Latin *pungere* to prick.

poise (pɔɪz) *vb* **1** balance or cause to be balanced. **2** support or keep suspended.
• *n* **1** a state of balance. **2** a self-possessed or composed manner. **poised** *adj* **1** composed; confident. **2** ready; prepared: poised for action. < ultimately Latin *pendere* to weigh.

poison (ˈpɔɪzn̩) *n* **1** a substance that harms or kills a plant or animal. **2** anything harmful; corruption.
• *vb* **1** harm or kill with poison; add poison to. **2** turn (someone's mind) against; corrupt. **poisoner** *n* **poisonous** *adj* **poison-pen letter** a malicious or slanderous letter written anonymously. < ultimately Latin *potio* drink.

poke (pəʊk) *vb* **1** prod or thrust with the finger or an object. **2** thrust forward; project. **3** make a hole by poking. **4** stir up (a fire). **5** (*informal*) strike, esp. with the fist.
• *n* poking; jab or nudge. **poke fun at** mock; laugh at. **poke one's nose into** pry; snoop. **poker** *n* a metal rod, used to poke a fire. < Middle English *poken*.

poker (ˈpəʊkə) *n* a card-game in which bets are made on which player's hand of cards is of the highest value. **poker-face** *n* a face completely without expression. < French *poque* card-game similar to poker.

poky (ˈpəʊkɪ) *adj* tiny; cramped: a poky little room. < *poke*.

pole[1] (pəʊl) *n* a long, thin, round piece of wood, metal, etc.; rod.
• *vb* push with a pole. **pole-vault** *n* an athletic event consisting of a jump over a high crossbar, using a pole for leverage. **up the pole** (*slang*) **1** slightly crazy. **2** in error. < Latin *palus* stake.

pole[2] *n* **1** either of the ends of the axis of the earth or other body: North Pole; South Pole. **2** either of the terminals of an electric cell or battery. **3** either of the two areas in a magnet where magnetic flux is concentrated. **4** either of two opposing actions, principles, etc. **polar** *adj* **polar bear** a large white bear found in Arctic regions. **polarity** *n* the state of having poles. **polarize** *vb* **1** restrict vibrations of (light or electromagnetism) to a single plane or direction. **2** acquire or cause to acquire polarity. **3** make or become divided in opinion. **polarization** *n* **poles apart** differing widely. **pole-star** *n* a star in Ursa Minor, close to the North Pole in the sky. < Greek *polos* pivot.

polecat (ˈpəʊlˌkæt) *n* **1** a dark brown mammal related to the weasel that gives off an unpleasant smell. **2** (*US*) a skunk. < probably Middle French *pol* cock + Middle English *cat*.

polemic (pəˈlɛmɪk) *n* an aggressive attack on someone's beliefs or principles.
• *adj* also **polemical** contentious; controversial. < ultimately Greek *polemos* war.

police (pəˈliːs) *n* **1** the civil force of a State that is concerned with maintaining public order and enforcing the law; its members. **2** a similar civil force operating for a particular organization: military police.
• *vb* keep control of, esp. by means of police. **policeman** fem. **policewoman** *n* a member of a police force. **police-officer** *n* a policeman or policewoman. **police state** a nation in which repressive government control is usually enforced by political police. **police station** the headquarters of the local police force. < ultimately Greek *polis* city.

policy[1] (ˈpɒlɪsɪ) *n* a plan or course of action adopted, esp. by a political party or business firm. < Late Latin *politia*.

policy[2] *n* an insurance contract; document this is set out in. < ultimately Greek *apodeiknynai* to prove.

polio (ˈpəʊlɪəʊ) *n* poliomyelitis. **poliomyelitis** *n* a severe virus disease, causing paralysis and often deformity. < Greek *polios* grey + *myelos* marrow.

polish (ˈpɒlɪʃ) *vb* **1** make or become shiny and smooth by rubbing. **2** also **polish up** perfect; refine.
• *n* **1** polishing. **2** a smooth, shiny surface. **3** a substance used for polishing. **4** style; finesse. **polished** *adj* **polisher** *n* **polish off** get rid of; eat up. < Latin *polire.*

polite (pəˈlaɪt) *adj* **1** well-mannered; courteous. **2** socially proper; refined: polite society. **politely** *adv* **politeness** *n* < Latin *polire* to polish.

politic (ˈpɒlɪtɪk) *adj* **1** wise or prudent. **2** shrewd; scheming. **body politic** the State. < Greek *politēs* citizen.

political (pəˈlɪtɪkl̩) *adj* **1** of or involved in politics. **2** of government. **political asylum** protection in another country for political refugees. **political prisoner** someone imprisoned for his or her political beliefs.

politics (ˈpɒlɪtɪks) *n* **1** the science or art of government. **2** political affairs or activities. **3** activity concerned with gaining one's own ends, esp. acquiring power: company politics. **4** *pl* one's political sympathies. **politician** *n* someone involved in politics. < Greek *politikos* political.

polka (ˈpɒlkə) *n* a lively dance of Bohemian origin in double time. **polka dots** round, evenly-spaced spots on a fabric design. < Czech *půl* half.

poll (pəʊl) *n* **1** the casting, recording, or counting of votes at an election. **2** a place where voting takes place. **3** also **opinion poll** a survey of public opinion made by selecting people at random.
• *vb* **1** cast (a vote) in an election. **2** receive (votes). **3** cut short or remove the horns of (cattle). **4** trim the top of (a tree). **polling-booth** or **polling-station** *n* a place where votes are cast and recorded. **pollster** *n* someone who conducts a poll. < Middle Low German *polle* head.

pollen (ˈpɒlən) *n* the fine particles produced from the anther of a flower, the male gamete of which fertilizes a female ovule. **pollen count** a figure indicating the amount of pollen in the air. **pollinate** *vb* put pollen on the stigma of (a flower); fertilize like this. < Latin: fine flour.

pollute (pəˈluːt) *vb* **1** make dirty; contaminate, esp. with man-made waste. **2** corrupt; defile. **pollution** *n* **pollutant** *n* a substance that pollutes. < Latin *polluere.*

polo (ˈpəʊləʊ) *n* a game resembling hockey, played on horseback, using long-handled mallets and a wooden ball. **polo neck** a high, close-fitting collar that is folded over. < Balti: ball.

poltergeist (ˈpɒltəˌgaɪst) *n* a noisy, mischievous spirit believed to be responsible for mysterious physical disturbances, esp. in a building. < German *poltern* to be noisy + *Geist* Spirit. SEE PANEL.

poly- *prefix* much; many. < Greek *polys.*

polygamy (pəˈlɪgəmɪ) *n* the state or system of being married to more than one woman at the same time. **polygamist** *n* **polygamous** *adj* < Greek *poly-* + *-gamia* marriage.

polyglot (ˈpɒlɪˌglɒt) *adj* knowing or written in many languages; multilingual.
• *n* someone with a command of many languages. < Greek *poly-* + *glōtta* language.

polygon (ˈpɒlɪˌgɒn) *n* a closed plane figure with usually more than five sides. **polygonal** *adj* < Greek *poly-* + *gōnia* angle.

polymer (ˈpɒlɪmə) *n* a chemical compound with large molecules containing many repeated structural units. **polymerization** *n* < Greek *poly-* + *meros* part.

polystyrene (pɒlɪˈstaɪriːn) *n* a rigid polymer of the hydrocarbon styrene, used in packaging, etc.

polysyllabic (ˌpɒlɪsɪˈlæbɪk) *adj* (of words) having more than three syllables.

polytechnic (ˌpɒlɪˈtɛknɪk) *n* an educational institution offering courses in many subjects, often with a practical bias. < Greek *poly-* + *technē* art.

polythene (ˈpɒlɪˌθiːn) *n* a light, tough, plastic material, used in packaging, insulation, or moulded articles. < *polyethylene,* from Greek *poly-* + *aithein* to burn.

polyunsaturated (ˌpɒlɪʌnˈsætʃʊˌreɪtɪd)

> **poltergeist**
>
> A spirit that is believed to be responsible for unexplained noises, rearranging furniture, and other acts of mischief is known as a poltergeist. This is a borrowing from German, derived from *poltern* 'to be noisy' and *Geist* 'a ghost'. The spirit's notorious noisiness is also embraced in the French name *esprit frappeur* or 'the spirit that knocks'.

adj of a kind of animal or vegetable fat less likely to cause cholesterol to form in the blood, often used in margarine, etc.

pomander (pəʊˈmændə) *n* a mixture of sweet-scented substances in a bag or box, used to perfume clothes or linen in cupboards. < alteration of Middle French *pome d'ambre* apple of amber.

pomegranate (ˈpɒmɪˌgrænɪt) *n* a tree found in warm climates bearing a thick-skinned fruit with a reddish pulp containing many seeds; this fruit. < Middle French *pome grenate* seedy apple.

pommel (ˈpʌməl) *n* **1** a knob on the hilt of a sword or other weapon. **2** a projection at the front and top of a saddle. < Late Latin *pomum* apple.

pomp (pɒmp) *n* **1** a show of splendour; ceremonial. **2** a grandiose or ostentatious display. **pomposity** *n* **pompous** *adj* self-important; bombastic. **pompously** *adv* < Greek *pompē* sending.

poncho (ˈpɒntʃəʊ) *n, pl* **ponchos** a blanket-like cloak with a hole in the middle for the head. < American Spanish, from Araucanian *pontho* woollen material.

pond (pɒnd) *n* a small body of still water, often man-made. < alteration of *pounde* enclosure.

ponder (ˈpɒndə) *vb* weigh up mentally; think over. < Latin *pondus* weight.

ponderous (ˈpɒndərəs) *adj* **1** cumbersome; heavy. **2** dull or long-winded in style. **ponderously** *adv*

pong (pɒŋ) *vb, n* (*informal*) (emit) a bad smell; stink. < origin unknown.

pontificate (pɒnˈtɪfɪˌkeɪt) *vb* speak in a preaching or dogmatic manner. < ultimately Latin *pons* bridge + *facere* to make.

pontoon[1] (pɒnˈtuːn) *n* a type of flat-bottomed boat; one of these used in floating a temporary bridge. < Latin *pons* bridge.

pontoon[2] *n* a card-game in which the object is to acquire cards with a face value of not more than 21; score of 21 with two cards in this game. < probably alteration of French *vingt-et-un* 21.

pony (ˈpəʊnɪ) *n* a small breed of horse, esp. under 14.2 hands high. **pony-tail** *n* hair drawn back tightly and tied at the back of the head so that it hangs down. **pony-trekking** *n* the pastime of travelling on ponies in a group across country. < ultimately Latin *pullus* foal.

poodle (ˈpuːdl̩) *n* one of a breed of dogs with a thick curly coat, often clipped in a pattern. < German *Pudelhund*, from *pudeln* to splash + *Hund* dog. SEE PANEL.

pool[1] (puːl) *n* **1** a small, relatively deep body of still water, or a deep, still part in a stream. **2** a swimming-pool. **3** a shallow body of still liquid; puddle. < Old English *pōl*.

pool[2] *n* **1** a collective stake to which everyone contributes, esp. in gambling. **2** a game played on a billiard-table with 15 coloured and numbered balls. **3** any communal supply of facilities, commodities, services, etc.: car pool. **4** *pl* the football pools.
• *vb* contribute to a common fund or supply to be shared by all. < Old French *poul* cock.

poop (puːp) *n* the raised part at the stern of a ship, higher than the main deck. < Latin *puppis*.

poor (pʊə, pɔː) *adj* **1** lacking money or means. **2** meagre; insufficient: poor wages. **3** mediocre; substandard: poor workmanship. **4** (of land) barren or arid. **5** unlucky; pitiable: poor man! **6** modest; humble. **poorness** *n* **poor-spirited** *adj* lacking courage or confidence. < Latin *pauper*.

poorly (ˈpʊəlɪ, ˈpɔːlɪ) *adj* sick or ill.
• *adv* in a poor way.

pop[1] (pɒp) *n* **1** a light, sharp, explosive sound. **2** a flavoured fizzy drink.
• *vb* **popped; popping 1** make or cause to make a popping sound. **2** put or thrust suddenly: She popped a sweet in her mouth. **3** (*slang*) pawn. **4 pop in/out** enter/leave suddenly or quickly. **popcorn** *n* maize kernels heated to form a puffy mass. **pop-eyed** *adj* with eyes staring or bulging in amazement or horror. **popgun** *n* a toy gun that shoots a cork or pellet with a popping sound. **pop off** (*informal*) die. **pop the question** (*informal*) propose marriage.

poodle

A dog with a thick, curly coat which is often elaborately clipped is known as a poodle. This name comes from the German *Pudel*, which is a shortened form of *Pudelhund*. *Pudelhund* is a combination of *pudeln* 'to splash' and *Hund* 'dog'. Nowadays poodles are generally kept as pets. However, the name of the poodle is a reminder of the fact that it was once used as a gundog or water-dog—literally 'the dog that splashes'.

pop-up *adj* of a device that causes its contents to spring up: pop-up book; pop-up toaster. < Middle English *poppen,* like the sound.

pop² *adj* of a popular, modern style in music, culture, etc.
• *n* music, esp. commercially orientated, short, strongly rhythmic songs: pop group; pop festival. < *popular.*

pope (pəʊp) *n* the head of the Roman Catholic church; bishop of Rome. < ultimately Greek *pappas* father.

poplar (ˈpɒplə) *n* one of a group of slender, fast-growing trees of the willow family; its wood. < Latin *populus.*

poppet (ˈpɒpɪt) *n* (*informal*) an affectionate term for a loved child or person. < Middle English *popet* puppet.

poppy (ˈpɒpɪ) *n* one of several groups of plants with showy flowers and a milky sap. **poppycock** *n* (*informal*) nonsense; drivel. < alteration of Latin *papaver.*

populace (ˈpɒpjʊləs) *n* the public; masses. < Latin *populus* people.

popular (ˈpɒpjʊlə) *adj* **1** commonly liked or enjoyed. **2** of or for the public. **3** prevailing among the general public: popular unrest. **popularity** *n* **popularly** *adv* **popular front** an alliance of left-wing political parties. **popularize** *vb* **1** make generally known or available; make generally understandable. **2** cause to be generally liked. **popularization** *n* **popularizer** *n* **populate** *vb* occupy; inhabit. **population** *n* the inhabitants of a particular place. **populous** *adj* densely populated.

porcelain (ˈpɔːsəlɪn) *n* a type of high-quality ceramic; objects made from this. < ultimately Latin *porcellus* little pig.

porch (pɔːtʃ) *n* a roofed structure forming a covered entrance to the front of a house. < ultimately Latin *porta* gate.

porcupine (ˈpɔːkjʊˌpaɪn) *n* a large rodent whose body is covered with sharp, protective spines. < Latin *porcus* pig + *spina* spine.

pore¹ (pɔː) *n* one of the minute openings on the skin or a leaf, through which fluid is absorbed or emitted. < Greek *poros* passage, pore.

pore² *vb* **pore over** study (something) closely; reflect upon. < Middle English *pouren.*

pork (pɔːk) *n* the flesh of a pig as food. **porker** *n* a young pig, fattened for eating. < Latin *porcus* pig.

pornography (pɔːˈnɒgrəfɪ) *n* books, films, or pictures that show or describe erotic activity with the intention of arousing sexual excitement. **pornographer** *n* **pornographic** *adj* < Greek *pornē* prostitute + *graphein* to write.

porous (ˈpɔːrəs) *adj* **1** having pores or spaces. **2** able to absorb fluids. **porosity** *n*

porpoise (ˈpɔːpəs) *n* a blunt-snouted sea-mammal related to the whale. < Latin *porcus* pig + *piscis* fish.
SEE PANEL.

porridge (ˈpɒrɪdʒ) *n* **1** a food made by boiling oatmeal or other cereal in water or milk until it thickens. **2** (*slang*) time served in prison. < alteration of *pottage,* from *pot¹.*

port¹ (pɔːt) *n* **1** a town or city with a harbour where ships take on or unload passengers or cargo; this harbour. **2** any place where goods or people are allowed to pass in or out of a country: airport. < Latin *portus.*

port² *n* **1** an opening in a ship's side for loading or admitting air or light. **2** an opening in a machine by which fluid enters or leaves. **3** a porthole. **porthole** *n* a window-like opening in the side of a ship or aircraft, etc. < Latin *porta* gate.

port³ *vb, n* (turn to) the left-hand side of a ship or aircraft, when looking forwards. < origin uncertain.

port⁴ *n* a sweet, fortified wine made in Portugal. < *Oporto,* city in Portugal.
SEE PANEL AT **CHAMPAGNE.**

portable (ˈpɔːtəbl̩) *adj* that can be carried, moved about, or transferred easily.
• *n* a portable article. **portability** *n* < Latin *portare* to carry.

portal (ˈpɔːtl̩) *n* an entrance or door, esp. grand and imposing. < ultimately Latin *porta* gate.

portcullis (pɔːtˈkʌlɪs) *n* a strong grating of iron or wood that can be lowered to

porky porpoise

A small toothed whale with a torpedo-shaped body and a blunt snout is known as a porpoise. Of the creature's features it is the pig-like snout which lies behind the choice of name. Porpoise derives ultimately from the Medieval Latin *porcopiscis,* which combines the Latin *porcus* 'pig' and *piscis* 'fish'.

prevent entry to a castle or other fortification. < Middle French *porte coleïce* sliding door.

portend (pɔː'tɛnd) *vb* warn of; indicate. **portent** *n* a warning of things to come; omen. **portentous** *adj* **1** ominous. **2** amazing; awe-inspiring. < Latin *por-* forwards + *tendere* to stretch.

porter[1] ('pɔːtə) *n* a doorman or gatekeeper in a large building. < Latin *porta* gate.

porter[2] *n* a person employed to carry luggage at a hotel or railway station, etc. < Latin *portare* to carry.

portfolio (pɔːt'fəʊlɪəʊ) *n, pl* **portfolios** **1** a soft case or cover for holding papers, drawings, etc. **2** the office of a minister of State. **3** the securities held by one investor. **Minister without portfolio** a cabinet minister who is not in charge of any government department. < Latin *portare* to carry + *folium* leaf.

portico ('pɔːtɪkəʊ) *n, pl* **porticoes** a covered entrance or veranda, often supported on ornamental columns. < Latin *porticus.*

portion ('pɔːʃən) *n* **1** a fraction of something; bit. **2** an allotted part or share. **3** a helping of food. **4** one's fate or destiny.
• *vb* also **portion out** divide or share out in portions. < Latin *portio.*

portly ('pɔːtlɪ) *adj* plump; stout; corpulent. **portliness** *n* < *port* deportment, bearing.

portmanteau (pɔːt'mæntəʊ) *n* a traveller's trunk or case that opens into two equal compartments. **portmanteau word** a word derived from the combination of sounds and meanings of two words; blend. < Latin *portare* to carry + *mantellum* mantle. SEE PANEL AT **MOPED.**

portrait ('pɔːtrɪt, 'pɔːtreɪt) *n* **1** a drawing, picture, or photograph of someone. **2** a verbal description. **portray** *vb* **1** make a pictorial likeness of. **2** describe verbally. **3** act the role of (in a play). **portrayal** *n* < ultimately Latin *pro-* forth + *trahere* to draw.

pose (pəʊz) *vb* **1** place or be placed in a particular position to be painted or photographed, etc. **2** affect; show off. **3** pretend to be: posing as a VIP. **4** present for consideration: pose a question.
• *n* **1** a position assumed by someone. **2** a sham; pretence. **poser** *n* a problem or puzzle. **poseur** *n* someone who shows off. < ultimately Latin *pausa* pause.

posh (pɒʃ) *adj* (*informal*) **1** smart and elegant; luxurious. **2** upper-class: a posh accent. SEE PANEL.

position (pə'zɪʃən) *n* **1** the place occupied by someone or something. **2** a usual or proper place: in position. **3** a preferred or advantageous place: jockeying for position. **4** a relative situation or condition: I'm not in a position to do anything. **5** a job; post. **6** an arrangement of parts of the body: a kneeling position. **7** official or social status. **8** an opinion.
• *vb* put in a particular position. < Latin *ponere* to put.

positive ('pɒzɪtɪv) *adj* **1** expressing certainty; definite. **2** clearly expressed; explicit. **3** utter; absolute: It's a positive disgrace. **4** self-assured; confident: I'm positive she'll come. **5** helpful; beneficial: positive criticism. **6** greater in number than zero. **7** having specified qualities; real: a positive improvement. **8** (of a photograph) having the light and dark parts similar in tone to the subject. **9** (of an electric charge) characterized by a deficiency of electrons. **positively** *adv* **positiveness** *n* **positive discrimination** the policy of showing a deliberate bias in opportunity to underprivileged groups. < SEE **POSITION.**

posse ('pɒsɪ) *n* a body of men summoned to assist a law officer in maintaining order, esp. in North America. < Medieval Latin: power.

possess (pə'zɛs) *vb* **1** have or own as one's property; have. **2** take over; dominate: possessed by a demon. **possession** *n* possessing or being possessed;

posh

Posh, a colloquialism for 'grand' or 'upper-class', is believed to derive from the days when British passenger ships sailed regularly to and from India, at that time still part of the British Empire. To escape the direct glare of the sun, passengers endeavoured to book cabins that were on the shaded side of the ship on both outward and return voyages. This became known as travelling *p*ort *o*ut *s*tarboard *h*ome, of which posh is supposedly an acronym. The meaning of the word reflects the price of such cabins and the class of people who could afford them.

something possessed. **possessive** *adj* **1** of or showing possession in grammar, for example, Jane's; the man's. **2** wanting to control or dominate; jealous. **possessively** *adv* **possessiveness** *n* **take possession of** take on the ownership of; seize. < Latin *possidēre.*

possible (ˈpɒsɪbḷ) *adj* **1** capable of occurring, existing, or being achieved. **2** that may or may not happen.
• *n* **1** something possible. **2** someone that may be chosen; candidate: I agree, Smith is a possible for the job. **possibility** *n* **1** being possible; something possible. **2** promise; potential. **possibly** *adv* **1** maybe; perhaps. **2** used as an intensifier: Do all you possibly can. < ultimately Latin *posse* to be able.

post¹ (pəʊst) *n* **1** a long piece of metal, timber, etc., fixed vertically in the ground, esp. as a support or marker. **2** a pole marking the start or finish of a race: left at the post. **3** a goal-post.
• *vb* also **post up** fasten (a notice, etc.) to a board to publicize it; announce. **poster** *n* a large, sometimes decorative piece of paper or placard for public display or advertising. < Old English.

post² *n* **1** the place where a soldier or body of troops is stationed: frontier-post. **2** a developing settlement: trading-post. **3** paid employment; job.
• *vb* **1** station; position. **2** appoint to an office or command. **last post** a bugle call giving notice of the time to retire for the night. < Old Italian *porre* to place.

post³ *n* **1** the system for conveying letters, parcels, etc. **2** the letters conveyed; single collection or delivery of these.
• *vb* **1** convey by post. **2** (in book-keeping) enter in a ledger. **keep someone posted** keep informed. **postage** *n* the fee for sending something by post. **postage stamp** a small, printed piece of paper stuck on posted items as evidence that the charge for posting has been paid. **postal** *adj* of or conducted by post: postal vote. **postal order** an order for sending money by post. **post-box** *n* a box for posting letters in. **postcard** *n* a card for sending by post without an envelope. **postcode** *n* a combination of letters and numbers used in a postal address to assist sorting. **post-haste** *adv* as fast as possible. **postman** fem. **postwoman** *n* someone who collects or delivers letters, etc. **postmark** *vb, n* (mark with) an official mark showing the place and date of posting. **postmaster** fem. **postmistress** *n* a person who runs a local post office. **post office** a room or building where postal business is carried on. **Post Office** the national or government organization that runs a postal system. **post-office box** a private numbered place in a post office where letters are kept until called for. **post town** a town with a main Post Office branch, acting as a clearing-point. < Old Italian *posta,* from Latin *ponere* to put. SEE PANEL.

post- *prefix* after; subsequent to: post-war. < Latin.

post-date (pəʊstˈdeɪt) *vb* date (a document or cheque) with a date later than the actual one.

posterior (pɒˈstɪərɪə) *adj* **1** placed behind or to the rear. **2** following; subsequent.
• *n* the buttocks. < Latin *posterus* coming after.

posterity (pɒˈstɛrɪtɪ) *n* **1** the generations to come. **2** someone's descendants.

post-graduate (pəʊstˈgrædjʊət) *n, adj* (of or for) a student continuing higher studies after taking a first degree.

posthumous (ˈpɒstjʊməs) *adj* **1** received, following, or happening after someone's death: posthumous fame. **2** born after the death of a father. **posthumously** *adv* < alteration of Latin *postumus* the last.

postilion (pɒˈstɪljən) *n* a rider who guides a near-side horse pulling a coach, etc., esp. when there is no coach-driver. < Italian *posta* post.

post-mortem (ˌpəʊstˈmɔːtəm) *adv, adj* **1** after death. **2** after the event.
• *n* **1** an examination of a body to determine the cause of death; autopsy. **2** (*informal*) a detailed examination of a failed plan or event, esp. to find the cause of failure. < Latin: after death.

post-natal (ˌpəʊstˈneɪtḷ) *adj* happening or existing immediately after giving birth or being born.

postpone (pəʊsˈpəʊn) *vb* delay or defer (an event) until later. **postponement** *n* < Latin *post-* + *ponere* to place.

post-haste

The adverb post-haste means 'very quickly' or 'as quickly as possible'. This term derives from the days when mail was conveyed by teams of fresh horses and riders operating in relay systems along the major routes.

postscript (ˈpəʊstˌskrɪpt) *n* **1** a note or message at the end of a letter, book, etc. **2** a supplementary part. < Latin *post-* + *scribere* to write.

postulate (ˈpɒstjʊˌleɪt) *vb* take as true or given; presuppose.
• *n* (ˈpɒstjʊlət) something postulated. **postulation** *n* < Latin *postulare* to demand.

posture (ˈpɒstʃə) *n* the manner in which someone sits, stands, or walks; bearing.
• *vb* **1** assume a posture, esp. for effect. **2** affect; show off. **postural** *adj* **posturer** *n* < ultimately Latin *ponere* to place.

posy (ˈpəʊzɪ) *n* a small bunch of flowers; bouquet. < alteration of *poesy:* SEE POEM.

pot[1] (pɒt) *n* **1** a rounded vessel of earthenware, metal, etc., used esp. for cooking or serving liquid or solid food; its contents. **2** a large mug, esp. for beer. **3** the collected stakes in a gambling game, esp. poker. **4** a large quantity, esp. of money. **5** a shot in snooker or billiards in which the ball is hit into a pocket.
• *vb* **potted; potting 1** put in a pot. **2** pocket (a ball) in billiards or snooker. **3** shoot (an animal) esp. for food. **4** (*informal*) sit (a child) on a chamber-pot. **5** shorten; condense: a potted history. **go to pot** (*informal*) deteriorate. **pot-belly** *n* a protruding belly. **pot-hole** *n* **1** a deep, tubular hole in the ground or a cave. **2** a hole in a road surface. **pot-holing** *n* the exploration of systems of underground pot-holes. **pot plant** a plant grown in a flowerpot. **pot-shot** *n* a random shot or attempt. **potter** *n* someone who makes earthenware vessels or ornaments. **pottery** *n* **1** the craft or workshop of a potter. **2** objects made of fired clay. **take pot luck** accept whatever is available. < Old English *pott.* SEE PANEL.

pot[2] *n* (*slang*) marijuana; cannabis. < Mexican Spanish *potiguaya.*

potash (ˈpɒtæʃ) *n* one of various potassium salts, esp. potassium carbonate. < obsolete Dutch *potaschen.*

potassium (pəˈtæsɪəm) *n* a soft, light, silvery, metallic element, occurring widely combined in minerals. < *potash.*

potato (pəˈteɪtəʊ) *n, pl* **potatoes** a plant of the nightshade family, grown for its starchy, edible tubers; one of these tubers. < Taino *batata.*

potent (ˈpəʊtn̩t) *adj* **1** having a strong effect: a potent drug. **2** powerful; influential. **potency** *n* **potentate** *n* someone who wields power and authority. < Latin *potēre* to be powerful.

potential (pəˈtɛnʃəl) *adj* capable of being realized or used; possible or latent.
• *n* **1** a capacity or ability as yet unrealized. **2** also **potential difference** the difference in voltage between any two points in an electrical circuit. **potentiality** *n* **potentially** *adv* < Latin *potentia* power.

potion (ˈpəʊʃən) *n* a drink of mixed substances, taken as a medicine or drug. < ultimately Latin *potare* to drink.

pot-pourri (ˌpəʊˈpʊərɪ) *n* **1** a collection of dried petals, spices, herbs, etc., often kept in a jar for their fragrance. **2** a miscellany or medley, esp. of musical or literary items. < French: rotten pot. SEE PANEL.

potter (ˈpɒtə) *vb* occupy oneself in

pot-pourri

A mixture of dried herbs and flower petals kept in a jar or vase for their perfume is known as a pot-pourri. The meaning of this French borrowing is literally 'rotten pot' (the pot with the rotten flowers). The name is thus more suited to foul odours than sweet fragrances.

gone to pot

Something that has suffered considerable deterioration or decline might be informally described as having gone to pot: 'The business has really gone to pot since his father died.' The origin of this expression is uncertain. Some argue that it refers to the fate of an animal that is killed for meat and cooked in a pot. Others associate it with the ancient custom of putting a cremated person's ashes into a pot or urn. A third theory is that the reference is to the fate of stolen silver or gold, which is melted down in a pot to prevent its identification and recovery.

aimless but leisurely activity: potter about the house. **potterer** *n* < probably Old English *potian*.
potty[1] (ˈpɒtɪ) *adj* (*informal*) **1** silly; crazy. **2** petty; trivial. < probably *pot*[1].
potty[2] *n* (*informal*) a chamber-pot for a child's use.
pouch (pautʃ) *n* **1** a small, flexible bag or similar container: tobacco pouch. **2** a structure like this in some animals, esp. marsupials.
• *vb* **1** place (as if) in a pouch. **2** cause to resemble a pouch. < of Germanic origin.
pouffe (puːf) *n* a stuffed cushion to sit or rest the feet on. < French *pouf*, like the sound.
poultice (ˈpəʊltɪs) *vb, n* (apply) a soft, moist, heated mass, consisting of substances such as kaolin, mustard, etc., to sore or inflamed skin. < Latin *puls* porridge.
poultry (ˈpəʊltrɪ) *n* domesticated birds such as fowls, geese, and ducks, kept for their meat or eggs. < ultimately Latin *pullus* young of an animal.
pounce (pauns) *vb* **1** swoop down on and seize, esp. as prey. **2** attack suddenly; ambush.
• *n* pouncing. < Middle French *poinçon* pointed tool.
pound[1] (paund) *n* **1** a measure of weight (0.454 kilograms). **2** **pound sterling** the basic unit of money in the UK and certain other countries. **poundage** *n* **1** a charge per pound sterling. **2** a charge per pound of weight. **3** weight in pounds. < Old Norse *pund*.
pound[2] *vb* **1** hammer or crush by striking with repeated heavy blows. **2** run or move along with heavy steps: a policeman pounding his beat. **3** (of the heart) throb or beat heavily. < Old English *pūnian*.
pound[3] *n* an enclosure for holding stray animals or officially removed motor vehicles until claimed. < Old English *pund-* enclosure.
pour (pɔː) *vb* **1** flow or cause to flow in a stream. **2** serve (a drink) in this way. **3** move together continuously in large quantities; stream. **4** supply or be supplied freely and abundantly: money kept pouring in. **5** also **pour down** rain hard. **pourer** *n* < Middle English *pouren*.
pout (paut) *vb* **1** show that one is annoyed or sulking by pushing out (the lips). **2** (of lips) project outwards.
• *n* pouting. < Middle English *pouten*.
poverty (ˈpɒvətɪ) *n* **1** the state of lacking enough money, food, or possessions. **2** any shortage or scarcity. **poverty-stricken** *adj* extremely poor. **poverty trap** a situation in which a poor family's State benefits are reduced as their earned income rises, leaving them no better off. < ultimately Latin *pauper* poor.
POW *abbrev* prisoner of war.
powder (ˈpaudə) *n* **1** a mass of fine, loose, dry grains. **2** a preparation of this as a medicine or cosmetic. **3** gunpowder.
• *vb* **1** cover (as if) with powder; apply powder to. **2** reduce to powder; pulverize. **powdery** *adj* **powder blue** pale blue. **powdered** *adj* turned into powder. **powder-puff** *n* a small, soft or fluffy pad for applying powdered cosmetics to the skin. **powder-room** *n* a ladies' toilet in a public place, such as a hotel. < ultimately Latin *pulvis* dust.
power (ˈpauə) *n* **1** the capability to do something. **2** physical strength or force. **3** a position of control, influence, or authority: emergency powers. **4** a sovereign state, or any group with political authority. **5** a legal authority to act on someone's behalf; document conferring this: power of attorney. **6** (*mathematics*) the result arrived at when a quantity is multiplied by itself a specified number of times; number of times a quantity is multiplied by itself: three to the third power is 27. **7** a specific type of energy: nuclear power. **8** a source of energy, esp. electrical: power supply. **9** the rate at which mechanical work is performed: horse-power. **10** the capacity of a lens for magnification. **11** a large amount: It'll do you the power of good.
• *vb* give or supply power to. **powerful** *adj* strong; influential. **powerfully** *adv* **powerhouse** *n* **1** a power-station. **2** a strong or dynamic person, team, etc.

the powers that be

The heads of a government, major organization, etc., are sometimes referred to as the powers that be: No doubt *the powers that be* thought that we would work more efficiently if they reduced our grant. This expression comes from the Authorized (King James) Version of the Bible, Romans 13:1: Let every soul be subject unto the higher powers. For there is no power but of God: the powers that be are ordained of God.

powerless *adj* helpless or ineffective. **power point** a wall socket for connecting electrical appliances to the mains. **power politics** (esp. international) political activity based on the threat to use force. **power-station** *n* a building where electricity is generated. < ultimately Latin *potēre* to be powerful. SEE PANEL.

powwow (ˈpaʊˌwaʊ) *n* a meeting or talk. < Algonquian: medicine man.

pp *abbrev* pages.

p.p. *abbrev* (*Latin*) per procurationem (through the agency of; by proxy).

practice (ˈpræktɪs) *n* **1** the carrying out or application of something. **2** regular or repeated exercise to improve a skill; instance of this: out of practice. **3** a usual method; habit or custom. **4** a professional business, esp. law or medicine; performance of this. **practicable** *adj* capable of being done. **practicability** *n* **practical** *adj* **1** of or involving action or experience, esp. as opposed to theory. **2** virtual. **3** useful; serviceable. **4** (of people) skilled at doing or making things. **5** sensible; realistic. **practicality** *n* **practical joke** a trick played on someone to give amusement to others. **practically** *adv* **1** realistically. **2** nearly; almost. < Greek *praktikos*. SEE PANEL. SEE PANEL AT **PRACTISE**.

practise (ˈpræktɪs) *vb* **1** carry out; do: He practises what he preaches. **2** work at repeatedly to improve one's skill. **3** do (something) actively; observe: a practising Christian. **4** work at professionally: practise medicine. **practised** *adj* skilled; accomplished. **practitioner** *n* someone engaged in a profession, esp. law or medicine. SEE PANEL.

pragmatic (prægˈmætɪk) *adj* down-to-earth; realistic or practical. **pragmatically** *adv* **pragmatism** *n* < ultimately Greek *prassein* to do.

prairie (ˈprɛərɪ) *n* an extensive area of grassland with few trees, esp. in North America. < Latin *pratum* meadow.

praise (preɪz) *vb* **1** show approval of; commend. **2** honour or glorify (God). • *n* **1** expression of approval. **2** worship of God. **praiseworthy** *adj* fine; admirable. < ultimately Latin *pretium* price.

pram (præm) *n* a baby carriage with four wheels, pushed by someone walking. < alteration of *perambulator*, from Latin *per* through + *ambulare* to walk.

prance (prɑːns) *vb* **1** (of a horse) jump or spring eagerly from the hind legs. **2** dance or move about gaily. **3** swagger; show off. < Middle English *prauncen*.

prang (præŋ) *vb*, *n* (*slang*) (have) a crash in a vehicle or aircraft, causing damage. < like the sound.

prank (præŋk) *n* a trick; mischief. < origin uncertain.

prattle (ˈprætl̩) *vb* chatter in a foolish or childish way. • *n* childish talk. < Low German *pratelen*.

prawn (prɔːn) *n* one of various small, ten-legged, edible shellfish resembling a shrimp. < Middle English *prane*.

pray (preɪ) *vb* **1** say prayers (to God or other object of worship). **2** plead; implore. **3** (*old-fashioned*) please: pray sit down. **prayer** *n* **1** praying; something prayed for. **2** an earnest request or thanksgiving, esp. to God or other

practicable or **practical?**

Practicable means 'capable of being carried out or accomplished, especially without great difficulty': It is not *practicable* to relocate the firm outside London. The project is far too expensive to be *practicable*.

Practical means 'useful or serviceable; sensible or realistic': Of course a video would be very nice, but a new vacuum cleaner would be far more *practical;* a coat of a very *practical* design. Practical is often opposed to theoretical: the *practical* application of the teaching; the *practical* difficulties of implementing the proposals.

practise or **practice?**

Whether to use practice or practise is a question that causes some people difficulty.

For users of British English the choice between practice and practise is a grammatical one. Practice is a noun, and practise a verb: 'With a bit more practice, you'll be able to play it.' 'If you practise a bit more, you'll be able to play it.'

The same is true when the word is applied to doctors, lawyers, etc.: 'He went into practice three years ago.' 'He's been practising for three years.'

Users of American English tend to use the -ice spelling for both parts of speech.

object of worship. **3** a religious service: morning prayer. **4** a set form of words for praying. **prayer-book** *n* a book containing official forms of worship. **prayer mat** a small rug used by Muslims to kneel on when praying. < Latin *prex* request.

pre- *prefix* before; earlier than: predate; pre-war. < Latin *prae* before.

preach (priːtʃ) *vb* **1** give (a religious address or sermon): preach the gospel. **2** urge or advocate, esp. in a moralizing way. **preacher** *n* < Latin *prae-* + *dicare* to proclaim.

preamble (ˈpriːæmbl̩) *n* a preliminary or introductory statement, esp. to a law, constitution, etc. < Latin *prae-* + *ambulare* to walk.

precarious (prɪˈkɛərɪəs) *adj* uncertain; hazardous. **precariously** *adv* < Latin *precarius* obtained by entreaty.

precaution (prɪˈkɔːʃən) *n* **1** caution; forethought. **2** a measure taken to avoid possible risk; safeguard. **precautionary** *adj* < Latin *prae-* + *cavēre* to beware.

precede (prɪˈsiːd) *vb* be, go, come, or place before in time or order; preface. **precedence** *n* priority in importance; right to this: take precedence. **precedent** *n* something happening earlier that can be taken as an example to be followed, esp. in a court of law. < Latin *prae-* + *cedere* to go. SEE PANEL.

precept (ˈpriːsɛpt) *n* an order or principle, esp. taken as a moral guideline. < Latin *prae-* + *capere* to take.

precinct (ˈpriːsɪŋkt) *n* **1** an enclosure marked by a wall or other fixed boundary: cathedral precinct. **2** an area in a town where traffic may not enter: shopping precinct. **3** (*US*) an administrative district for the purposes of policing or elections. **4** *pl* an immediate surrounding area. < Latin *prae-* + *cingere* to gird.

precious (ˈprɛʃəs) *adj* **1** loved; adored. **2** valuable; expensive. **3** fastidious; affected. **4** used ironically to express worthlessness: A precious lot of good that is! **preciously** *adv* **preciousness** *n* **precious metal** gold, silver, or platinum. **precious stone** a highly valuable mineral, esp. cut and used in jewellery. < Latin *pretium* price.

precipice (ˈprɛsɪpɪs) *n* **1** a very steep or perpendicular rock face or overhang. **2** a situation full of risk. < Latin *prae-* + *caput* head.

precipitate (prɪˈsɪpɪˌteɪt) *vb* **1** bring about or happen suddenly or too soon: The petrol shortage precipitated a crisis. **2** throw down violently; fling. **3** cause (a substance) to separate from a solution in which it is suspended; be separated in this way. **4** (of vapour) condense and fall as rain, snow, hail, etc.
• *n* (prɪˈsɪpɪˌtət) a substance separated from a solution or suspension.
• *adj* (prɪˈsɪpɪtət) **1** showing frantic haste. **2** rash; ill-advised. **precipitately** *adv* **precipitation** *n* < Latin *praecipitare.*

precipitous (prɪˈsɪpɪtəs) *adj* **1** dangerously steep; sheer. **2** rash; hasty. **precipitously** *adv* **precipitousness** *n* < Latin *precipitiun* precipice.

précis (ˈpreɪsiː) *n, pl* **précis** a summary. < French: precise.

precise (prɪˈsaɪs) *adj* **1** exact; accurate. **2** strict in conforming to rules or conventions; careful. **precisely** *adv* **precision** *n* < Latin *prae-* + *caedere* to cut.

preclude (prɪˈkluːd) *vb* make impossible; prevent or exclude. < Latin *prae-* + *claudere* to close.

precocious (prɪˈkəʊʃəs) *adj* **1** very advanced in development. **2** (of a child)

---

precede or **proceed?**

These two words are sometimes confused.

Precede means 'to be, go, come, or place before in time or order': The final agreement was *preceded* by months of long negotiation. Please refer to the *preceding* pages for the survey.

Proceed means 'to continue, especially after stopping or pausing': Thereupon she *proceeded* to tell me her life story and 'to issue or arise from': The conflict *proceeded* from a misunderstanding.

---

precocious

A child who shows qualities normally associated with an older person is sometimes described as precocious: 'I've never encountered such a precocious little madam before!' This common application of the word to children involves an extension of its original meaning. Precocious comes from the Latin *praecox* or 'ripening early'. The latter sense is retained in botanical usage.

---

showing a high level of development much earlier than expected. **precociously** *adv* **precocity** *n* < Latin *prae-* + *coquere* to ripen. SEE PANEL.

preconceived (ˌpriːkənˈsiːvd) *adj* formed without previous knowledge or experience: preconceived ideas. **preconception** *n*

pre-condition (ˌpriːkənˈdɪʃən) *n* an essential condition; prerequisite.

precursor (prɪˈkɜːsə) *n* **1** someone or something that comes before or gives notice of another. **2** a forerunner; predecessor. < Latin *prae-* + *currere* to run.

predator (ˈprɛdətə) *n* **1** an animal that preys on others. **2** someone who exploits others. **predatory** *adj* < Latin *praedari* to prey.

predecessor (ˈpriːdɪˌsɛsə) *n* **1** the former occupant of an office, position, etc. **2** an ancestor. **3** anything that has been replaced by another. < Latin *prae-* + *decedere* to depart.

predestine (priːˈdɛstɪn) *vb* determine beforehand as if by fate; preordain. **predestination** *n* the doctrine that God has preordained all events, esp. the salvation of certain souls. < Latin *prae-* + *destinare* to determine.

predicament (prɪˈdɪkəmənt) *n* a puzzling, difficult, or embarrassing situation. < Latin *praedicare* to assert.

predicate (ˈprɛdɪkət) *n* the part of a clause or sentence that gives information about the subject, for example is blue in The sky is blue. **predicative** *adj* part of or occurring within a predicate: predicative adjective. **predicatively** *adv* < Latin *praedicatus.*

predict (prɪˈdɪkt) *vb* foretell; prophesy. **predictable** *adj* that can be foreseen. **predictability** *n* **predictably** *adv* < Latin *prae-* + *dicere* to say.

predilection (ˌpriːdɪˈlɛkʃən) *n* an inclination or preference. < Latin *prae-* + *diligere* to love.

predispose (ˌpriːdɪˈspəʊz) *vb* **1** affect or influence in advance. **2** make susceptible to: predisposed to worry. **predisposition** *n*

predominate (prɪˈdɒmɪˌneɪt) *vb* **1** have the advantage in number or level of intensity. **2** have controlling power; prevail. **predominance** *n* **predominant** *adj* superior in strength, number, or influence. **predominantly** *adv* < Medieval Latin *praedominari.*

pre-eminent (prɪˈɛmɪnənt) *adj* superior; unequalled. **pre-eminence** *n* **pre-eminently** *adv*

pre-empt (prɪˈɛmpt) *vb* obtain or seize before or to the exclusion of others; make useless like this. **pre-emption** *n* **pre-emptive** *adj* done to prevent an action planned by others: pre-emptive strike. < Latin *prae-* + *emere* to buy.

preen (priːn) *vb* (of a bird) clean and arrange (the feathers) with the beak. **preen oneself 1** dress up; groom oneself. **2** pride or congratulate oneself. < Middle English *preinen.*

prefabricate (priːˈfæbrɪˌkeɪt) *vb* manufacture parts (of a building) that can be assembled elsewhere. **prefabrication** *n* **prefab** *n* (*informal*) a prefabricated building.

preface (ˈprɛfɪs) *n* an introduction to a book or speech; foreword.
• *vb* **1** introduce with a preface. **2** introduce; precede. **prefatory** *adj* introductory. < Latin *prae-* + *fari* to say.

prefect (ˈpriːfɛkt) *n* **1** an older secondary school pupil, given some authority over younger pupils. **2** a chief official in a department of certain countries such as France, Italy, and Japan. < Latin *prae-* + *facere* to make.

prefer (prɪˈfɜː) *vb* **preferred; preferring 1** choose or value above something else; like better. **2** put (an accusation) before a court of law: prefer charges. **3** advance or promote (someone). **preferable** *adj* favourable. **preferably** *adv* as a matter of choice. **preference** *n* **1** preferring; something preferred. **2** special consideration. **3** priority in the settlement of a debt or obligation. **preferential** *adj* favoured; biased. < Latin *prae-* + *ferre* to carry. SEE PANEL. SEE PANEL AT **OFFER.**

prefix (ˈpriːfɪks) *n* an affix that goes in front of a word in order to modify its meaning. < Latin *prae-* + *fixus* fixed.

pregnant (ˈprɛgnənt) *adj* **1** carrying an

---

prefer to or **prefer than?**

Prefer is usually followed by to, not than: He prefers radio *to* television. I prefer cycling *to* driving.

Difficulties arise when a sentence contains an infinitive with to, since we cannot say: I prefer to ignore the matter to to discuss it. To overcome the difficulty, it is possible to use rather than followed by an infinitive without or with to: I prefer to ignore the matter *rather than* discuss it.

---

unborn or developing young in the womb. **2** meaningful; expressive: a pregnant silence. **3** full; fruitful. **pregnancy** *n* < Latin *praegnans.*

prehistoric (ˌpriːhɪˈstɒrɪk) *adj* **1** of times before written records of events were made. **2** (*informal*) very old-fashioned; antiquated. **prehistory** *n*

prejudge (priːˈdʒʌdʒ) *vb* form an opinion of prematurely or without full knowledge or information. < Latin *prae-* + *judicare* to judge.

prejudice (ˈprɛdʒʊdɪs) *n* **1** an idea or opinion formed without sufficient facts; bias. **2** unreasoned dislike, esp. to those of another race or kind: racial prejudice. **3** harm or disadvantage caused by disregard for one's rights, esp. legal.
• *vb* **1** cause (someone) to be biased. **2** cause harm or disadvantage to. **prejudiced** *adj* showing prejudice. **prejudicial** *adj* liable to harm someone's rights. **without prejudice** (*law*) without harming or taking away one's rights. < Latin *prae-* + *judicium* judgment.

prelate (ˈprɛlət) *n* a high-ranking clergyman such as a bishop. < Latin *prae-* + *latus,* from *ferre* to carry.

preliminary (prɪˈlɪmɪnərɪ) *adj* coming before something as an introduction; preparatory.
• *n* **1** a start; introduction. **2** a preliminary examination. < Latin *prae-* + *limen* threshold.

prelude (ˈprɛljuːd) *n* **1** something that introduces an action or event. **2** an introduction to a piece of music that states the theme; short piece of music like this, esp. for piano. < Latin *prae-* + *ludere* to play.

premature (ˌprɛməˈtjʊə) *adj* **1** done or happening before the expected or proper time; untimely. **2** (of a baby) born between three and 12 weeks before the time expected. **prematurely** *adv* < Latin *prae-* + *maturus* ripe.

premeditated (priːˈmɛdɪˌteɪtɪd) *adj* thought over and planned beforehand: premeditated murder. **premeditation** *n* < Latin *prae-* + *meditari* to meditate.

premier (ˈprɛmjə) *adj* first in rank, time, or importance; principal.
• *n* a prime minister. **premiership** *n* < Latin *primarius.*

première (ˈprɛmɪˌɛə) *n* the first showing or performance in public of a play, film, etc. < French *premier* first.

premises (ˈprɛmɪsɪz) *pl n* an area of land together with the buildings on it; building. < Latin *praemissa.*

premiss (ˈprɛmɪs) *n* also **premise** an assertion taken as grounds for an argument or reasoning; matter previously stated. < Latin *prae-* + *mittere* to send.

premium (ˈpriːmɪəm) *n* **1** a sum of money paid regularly to maintain an insurance policy. **2** a reward or bonus. **3** a high value or regard: put a premium on efficiency. **at a premium** valuable, esp. because difficult to obtain. **Premium Bond** a government bond earning no interest, put into a monthly draw for cash prizes. < Latin *prae-* + *emere* to buy.

premolar (priːˈməʊlə) *n* a tooth that grows between the molar and canine teeth.

premonition (ˌprɛməˈnɪʃən) *n* a feeling of something about to happen; forewarning. < Latin *prae-* + *monēre* to warn.

preoccupied (priːˈɒkjʊˌpaɪd) *adj* deep in thought to the extent that one is unaware of the outside world. **preoccupation** *n* **1** being preoccupied. **2** the matter engaging one's thoughts. < Latin *prae-* + *occupare* to occupy.

prep (prɛp) *n* **1** work done outside school; homework. **2** a period within school hours for this to be done. **prep school** a preparatory school. < *preparation.*

pre-pack (ˌpriːˈpæk) *vb* package (food, etc.) before distribution and selling.

prepare (prɪˈpɛə) *vb* **1** make or get ready in advance. **2** assemble or put together: prepared foods. **be prepared** be able and willing (to do something). **preparation** *n* **1** preparing or being prepared. **2** something done to make or get ready. **3** a prepared food, medicine, etc. **preparatory** *adj* **preparatorily** *adv* **preparatory school** a private school where pupils are prepared for public school in the UK, or college in the USA. < Latin *prae-* + *parare* to prepare.

preponderate (prɪˈpɒndəˌreɪt) *vb* be greater than in amount, power, importance, etc. **preponderance** *n* **preponderant** *adj* **preponderantly** *adv* < Latin *prae-* + *pondus* weight.

preposition (ˌprɛpəˈzɪʃən) *n* a word such as to, at or with used in combination with a noun or pronoun to indicate direction, time, manner, etc. **prepositional** *adj* < Latin *prae-* + *ponere* to put.

preposterous (prɪˈpɒstərəs) *adj* ridiculous; outrageous. < Latin *prae-* + *posterus* following.

prerequisite (priːˈrɛkwɪzɪt) *n, adj* (something) requiring fulfilment before something else can take place.

prerogative (prɪˈrɒgətɪv) *n* an exclusive

right or privilege belonging esp. to a person or group with a particular rank or status. < Latin *praerogativa* privilege, from *prae-* + *rogare* to ask.

presage (ˈprɛsɪdʒ) *n* a sign or intuition of some future event.
• *vb* (ˈprɛsɪdʒ, prɪˈseɪdʒ) **1** foreshadow; portend. **2** predict; forecast. < Latin *prae-* + *sagire* to perceive.

prescribe (prɪˈskraɪb) *vb* **1** set down as a rule or directive. **2** recommend or order the use of (a medicine or remedy). **prescription** *n* **1** prescribing. **2** a written instruction from a doctor for the preparation and use of a medicine; medicine prescribed. < Latin *praescribere* to write previously. SEE PANEL.

present[1] (ˈprɛznt) *adj* **1** that is now. **2** showing time that is now: the present tense. **3** in or at a specified place: She wasn't present at classes. **4** being considered or dealt with: the present matter.
• *n* the time that is now. **at present** now. **for the present** for the time being. **presence** *n* **1** being present or very near. **2** someone or something present, or felt to be so. **3** a distinctive bearing or charisma; someone having this. **presence of mind** the ability to remain level-headed in a crisis. **present-day** *adj* current; modern. **presently** *adv* **1** soon; before too long. **2** (*chiefly US and Scottish*) now. < Latin *prae-* + *esse* to be. SEE PANEL.

present[2] (prɪˈzɛnt) *vb* **1** introduce (someone), esp. to a person of higher rank. **2** offer as a gift, award, or for action: presented with the bill. **3** put on before the public; show: present a play. **4** give or endow formally. **5** point or aim (a weapon). **6** act the role of (in a play); behave as. **7** introduce (a programme) on radio or television.
• *n* (ˈprɛznt) a gift or offering. **presenter** *n* **presentable** *adj* acceptable; fit to be seen. **present arms** hold a firearm vertically in front of the body in salute. **presentation** *n* **1** presenting or being presented; manner of this. **2** something offered for consideration or action. **present oneself** appear; turn up. < Latin *praesens* present, now existing.

presentiment (prɪˈzɛntɪmənt) *n* a feeling of something about to happen; premonition. < Latin *prae-* + *sentire* to feel.

preserve (prɪˈzɜːv) *vb* **1** keep safe or unchanged; protect. **2** protect (food) from decomposition by treating. **3** maintain and protect (land or game) for private or sporting use.
• *n* **1** an area where game, fish, etc., are kept for private use. **2** fruit or jam preserved by cooking with sugar. **3** a special area of interest. **preservation** *n* **preserver** *n* **preservative** *n, adj* (a substance) that preserves, esp. against decay or decomposition. < Latin *prae-* + *servare* to keep safe.

preside (prɪˈzaɪd) *vb* be in authority or control; supervise. **presidency** *n* **president** *n* **1** someone who heads a meeting, club, council, etc. **2** someone who is elected as head of State in a republic. **presidential** *adj* < Latin *prae-* + *sedēre* to sit.

press (prɛs) *vb* **1** apply a steady force or weight against; move (something) like this. **2** smooth out by pressing; iron (clothes). **3** squeeze so as to alter in shape or extract the contents of: pressed fruit. **4** clasp in affection; embrace. **5** make (objects) by pressing, esp. in a form or mould: press records. **6** harass; oppress: hard-pressed. **7** force; compel. **8** insist on; urge: He pressed his point home. **9** plead; implore. **10** force one's way. **11** crowd together; throng. **12** also

prescribe or **proscribe?**

These two words are sometimes confused.
Prescribe means 'to set down as a rule': New directions may be *prescribed* in order to fulfil the safety requirements or 'to recommend the use of': The doctor *prescribed* a course of antibiotics.
Proscribe is a less common word and means 'to condemn or forbid; outlaw': the *proscribed* trade union, undesirable activities that have been *proscribed* by the government.

presently

Some careful users of English object to the use of presently to mean 'now', as in Sir Hugh Treasure, ex-university professor, *presently* chairman of the new broadcasting commission. Such users prefer to restrict the meaning of presently to 'soon; before too long': We'll come and join you *presently*.

press-gang (*archaic*) compel to join the army or navy.
• *n* **1** pressing; being pressed. **2** a crowd of people. **3** a machine or apparatus for shaping, flattening, or extracting liquid: wine-press. **4** a printing-press. **5** often **Press** newspapers and magazines collectively; people working for, or comments and reviews contained in these. **6** a cupboard, esp. for books or linen. **7** stress; urgency. **be pressed for** have hardly enough: pressed for time. **press conference** an interview for press and television reporters given by a public figure. **press cutting** an article or piece cut from a newspaper. **press-gang** *n* a group of people who force others to do something. **press-stud** *n* a metal clothes fastener of two parts joined together by pressing. **press-ups** *pl n* physical exercise performed by lying face down and raising and lowering the body with the arms. < ultimately Latin *premere*.

pressing (ˈprɛsɪŋ) *adj* **1** urgent; crucial. **2** earnest; persistent.
• *n* something made by pressing, such as a gramophone record or batch of these made at one time.

pressure (ˈprɛʃə) *n* **1** the steady application of force to something; this force. **2** atmospheric pressure. **3** influence or compulsion, esp. oppressive: put pressure on. **4** stress; demand: He works well under pressure.
• *vb* apply pressure to. **pressure-cooker** *n* an airtight saucepan for cooking things rapidly by steam under high pressure. **pressure group** an interest group trying to influence esp. government policy by organized effort. **pressurize** *vb* **1** attempt to force or compel. **2** keep (an enclosed area, such as the inside of an aircraft) at normal atmospheric pressure. **pressurization** *n*

prestige (prɛˈstiːʒ) *n* high standing or esteem by virtue of wealth, success, status, etc. **prestigious** *adj* < ultimately Latin *praestigiae* juggler's tricks.

presume (prɪˈzjuːm) *vb* **1** take as reasonably certain; suppose. **2** do without leave or justification; dare. **3** rely or depend on. **4** take advantage of: Don't presume on their hospitality. **presumable** *adj* that can be presumed. **presumably** *adv* **presumption** *n* **presumptive** *adj* **1** believed; expected. **2** probable; likely. **presumptuous** *adj* bold; impudent. **presumptuousness** *n* < Latin *prae-* + *sumere* to take.

presuppose (ˌpriːsəˈpəʊz) *vb* **1** take as given; assume. **2** need as an earlier condition; imply. **presupposition** *n*

pretend (prɪˈtɛnd) *vb* **1** create an appearance of (something), either in play or to deceive. **2** claim falsely. **3** present a claim to: pretend to the throne. **pretence** *n* **1** charade or deception. **2** a claim, esp. unsupported. **3** affectation; pretentiousness. **pretendedly** *adv* **pretender** *n* **1** someone who pretends. **2** someone who claims a title, throne, etc. **pretension** *n* **1** a claim, esp. unjustified. **2** pretentiousness. **pretentious** *adj* pompous; affected. **pretentiously** *adv* **pretentiousness** *n* < Latin *prae-* + *tendere* to stretch.

pretext (ˈpriːtɛkst) *n* a false reason given to conceal the true one; pretence. < Latin *prae-* + *texere* to weave.

pretty (ˈprɪtɪ) *adj* **1** attractive or appealing in a delicate way; charming. **2** (*ironic*) unfortunate: A pretty mess you're in!
• *adv* **1** (*informal*) quite; moderately: He felt pretty bad. **2** (*informal*) very: pretty nearly ready. **prettily** *adv* **prettiness** *n* **prettify** *vb* **prettified; prettifying** make pretty, esp. superficially. < Old English *prætt* trick.

pretzel (ˈprɛtsəl) *n* a crisp, glazed, and salted biscuit in the shape of a knot. < German, ultimately from Latin *bracchium* arm.

prevail (prɪˈveɪl) *vb* **1** gain mastery; triumph. **2** be current or occur widely: a prevailing custom. **3** predominate: prevailing winds. **4 prevail on** or **upon** influence or convince. **prevalent** *adj* widespread. **prevalence** *n* **prevalently** *adv* < Latin *prae-* + *valēre* to be strong.

prevaricate (prɪˈværɪˌkeɪt) *vb* speak or act in an evasive manner, as if to disguise the truth. **prevarication** *n* **prevaricator** *n* < Latin *praevaricari* to walk crookedly. SEE PANEL.

prevent (prɪˈvɛnt) *vb* **1** stop (something) from happening; avert. **2** stop (someone) (from) doing something. **prevention** *n* **preventable** *adj* that can be prevented. **preventative** *adj* preventive. **preventive** *adj, n* (something) that can prevent. **preventive detention** imprisonment for habitual criminals. < Latin *prae-* + *venire* to come.

preview (ˈpriːvjuː) *n* an advance viewing of a film, play, etc., before public presentation; brief sight.
• *vb* view in advance.

previous (ˈpriːvɪəs) *adj* **1** coming before in time or position; prior. **2** done or happening too soon; premature. **previously** *adv* < Latin *prae-* + *via* way.

prey (preɪ) *n* **1** an animal taken as food by

another. **2** someone or something that falls victim to a person, influence, fear, etc.

• *vb* **prey on 1** take or kill as prey. **2** disturb or distress: Fears preyed on his mind. **bird** or **beast of prey** a bird or animal that hunts and kills others for food. < Latin *praeda.*

price (praɪs) *n* **1** the cost in money, goods, or services for something bought or sold; value or worth. **2** the cost at which something is achieved. **3** the odds in gambling.

• *vb* **1** put a price on. **2** find out the price of. **a price on someone's head** a reward for capturing or killing someone. **at a price** at a high price. **priceless** *adj* **1** beyond pricing; invaluable. **2** extremely amusing or absurd. **pricey** *adj* (*informal*) dear; costly. < ultimately Latin *pretium.*

prick (prɪk) *vb* **1** make a small hole or mark in with a sharp instrument. **2** feel or cause to feel a sharp sensation by pricking. **3** feel or cause to feel slight sorrow or remorse: prick one's conscience. **4** mark or outline (a pattern) with dots made by pricking.

• *n* pricking; hole or sensation caused by this. **prick up one's ears 1** (of a dog) cause the ears to stand erect. **2** (of a person) suddenly pay keen attention. < Old English *prica.*

prickle (ˈprɪkl) *n* **1** a sharp, pointed needle on the bark or leaf of a plant. **2** a stinging or tingling sensation. **3** a spiny needle on a hedgehog, etc.

• *vb* feel or cause to feel a stinging or tingling sensation. **prickly** *adj* **1** covered with or full of prickles. **2** bad-tempered; touchy. **3** difficult: a prickly problem. **prickliness** *n* < Old English *pricle.*

prevaricator

Prevaricate—'to speak or answer in a deliberately evasive manner so as to deceive'—entered English in the 16th century from the Latin verb *praevaricari* 'to walk crookedly or in a zigzag'. Originally, this verb was applied to a farm worker who ploughed a crooked furrow. From the literal usage, however, there developed a metaphorical one and the word came to be used of a legal representative who, having made a secret pact with the opposite party, proceeded to betray his own client.

pride (praɪd) *n* **1** pleasure or satisfaction in some achievement, possession, or quality. **2** a source of pride, or the best in a group: his pride and joy. **3** an inordinately high opinion of oneself; conceit. **4** dignity; self-respect. **5** a group of lions.

• *vb* **pride oneself on** take pride in; be proud of. **pride of place** the first or most important position. < Old English *prūd* proud.

priest (pri:st) *n* **1** a clergyman ranking below a bishop and above a deacon in the Anglican and Roman Catholic Churches. **2** someone authorized to perform sacred rites in a non-Christian religion. **priesthood** *n* **priestess** *n* a female priest, esp. in a non-Christian religion. **priestly** *adj* of, like, or for a priest. < ultimately Greek *presbys* old man. SEE PANEL.

prig (prɪg) *n* (*derogatory*) an irritatingly self-righteous or formal person. **priggish** *adj* < origin uncertain.

prim (prɪm) *adj* **primmer; primmest 1** (*chiefly derogatory*) (esp. of a woman) having a noticeable concern for the niceties of behaviour or appearance. **2** prudish. **primly** *adv* **primness** *n* < origin uncertain.

prima ballerina (ˈpri:mə) the leading female dancer in a ballet company. < Italian: first ballerina.

primacy (ˈpraɪməsɪ) *n* **1** the office or rank of a primate. **2** pre-eminence.

prima donna (ˌpri:mə ˈdɒnə) **1** a leading female operatic singer. **2** (*informal*) a highly sensitive or temperamental person. < Italian: first lady.

prima facie (ˌpraɪmə ˈfeɪʃɪ) at first sight; on a first impression. < Latin *primus* first + *facies* face.

primary (ˈpraɪmərɪ) *adj* **1** chief or of most importance: primary causes. **2** being or connected with an initial stage: primary

priest

The word used by the ancient Greeks for 'an old man' was *presbys.* From this there developed *presbyteros* 'a priest or elder'. *Presbyteros* then gave rise to the Late Latin word for 'priest' *presbyter,* from which came the Old English *prēost.* By the time we come to Middle English *prēost* had become *preist,* from which finally evolved the modern-day form priest.

education. **3** basic or fundamental: primary meaning. **primarily** *adv* **primary colour** any one of a set of three bands of the spectrum, usually red, green, or blue, which can be combined to approximate all other colours. < Latin *primus* first.

primate (ˈpraɪmeɪt) *n* **1** a member of the order of mammals that includes man, apes, and monkeys. **2** an archbishop.

prime[1] (praɪm) *adj* **1** chief or most important; principal. **2** best or first-rate: prime beef. **prime minister** the chief minister in a government. **prime number** a number such as 3, 7, or 11 that can be exactly divided only by itself or 1. **primer** *n* a simple textbook used in teaching children. < ultimately Latin *primus* first.

prime[2] *vb* **1** prepare (something) so that it is ready for use: prime a gun. **2** prepare (a surface) for painting by coating it with primer. **3** provide with information; brief. **4** ply with food or drink, esp. liquor. **primer** *n* **1** a person or thing that primes. **2** a substance used for sealing or undercoating a surface before it is painted. < origin uncertain.

primeval (praɪˈmiːvl̩) *adj* of or connected with prehistoric times. **primevally** *adv* < Latin *primus* first + *aevum* age.

primitive (ˈprɪmɪtɪv) *adj* **1** of or at an early stage of development: primitive man. **2** crude or lacking sophistication: primitive weapons. **primitively** *adv* **primitiveness** *n* < ultimately Latin *primus* first.

primordial (praɪˈmɔːdɪəl) *adj* relating to the earliest times. < Latin *primordium* origin.

primrose (ˈprɪmˌrəʊz) *n* **1** any of a group of small plants with clusters of pale yellow flowers. **2** pale yellow. < ultimately Medieval Latin *prima rosa* first rose.

primula (ˈprɪmjʊlə) *n* any plant of the genus that includes the primrose, polyanthus, etc. < Medieval Latin *primula veris* little first one of the spring.

prince (prɪns) *n* **1** a male member of a royal family, esp. a son of a sovereign. **2** a ruler, esp. of a state. **3** a person of high standing in his or her field. **princely** *adj* **1** of a prince. **2** generous or lavish: a princely sum. **princess** *n* **1** a female member of a royal family, esp. a daughter of a sovereign. **2** the wife of a prince. < ultimately Latin *princeps* ruler.

principal (ˈprɪnsɪpl̩) *adj* chief or most important.
• *n* **1** the head of a school, college, etc. **2** a person who has overall authority. **3** a person who has a leading part or role, esp. in a theatrical production. **4** a person who employs another as an agent. **5** a sum of money on which interest is paid, esp. the amount of the loan itself. **principally** *adv* chiefly. < ultimately Latin *principalis*. SEE PANEL.

principality (ˌprɪnsɪˈpælɪtɪ) *n* a state or territory ruled by a prince.

principle (ˈprɪnsɪpl̩) *n* **1** a basic truth, law, or doctrine. **2** (any of the rules constituting) a person's code of behaviour: a man of principle. **3** a theory or law which underlies the working of a machine, instrument, etc. **in principle** in general (as opposed to in detail): In principle we have no objection. **on principle** because of the principles involved: She refuses to sign on principle. < ultimately Latin *principium* beginning. SEE PANEL AT PRINCIPAL.

print (prɪnt) *vb* **1** produce (lettering or illustrations) on (paper, etc.) by impressing it against an inked surface. **2** produce (books, magazines, etc.) in this way; publish. **3** stamp or impress. **4** write (something) without joining the letters. **5** produce (a photograph) from a negative or transparency.
• *n* **1** a mark or impression made by pressure. **2** printed lettering. **3** a photograph: Do you take prints or slides? **4** a printed reproduction of a portrait, design, etc. **5** fabric with a printed design. **printed circuit** an electronic circuit etched in a conducting material onto a flat insulating board. **printer** *n* **1** a person or company that prints books, etc. **2** a machine or device that prints. **printing-press** *n* a machine that produces printed copies of books, newspapers, etc. **print-out** *n* printed matter produced by a computer, etc.

principal or **principle?**

As these two words are pronounced in the same way, their spelling is sometimes confused. Only principal may be used as an adjective, meaning 'main; chief': the *principal* reason, the *principal* method. As a noun the same spelling refers to the head of an organization: the *principal* of a school.

A principle is a basic belief, truth, or guideline: The *principle* of forgiveness is clearly stated. Borrowing money is against his *principles*.

< ultimately Latin *premere* to press.

prior[1] (ˈpraɪə) *adj* **1** previously arranged: a prior engagement. **2** taking precedence; more important. **priority** *n* **1** (the right to take) precedence: The women and children were given priority. **2** something that must take precedence over other considerations: Our first priority is to avoid bankruptcy. **prior to** before. < Latin: previous.

prior[2] fem. **prioress** *n* the head of a priory. **priory** *n* a religious house in which a community of monks or nuns lives. < Late Latin: head.

prise (praɪz) *vb* **1** move, open, or dislodge by leverage. **2** extract with difficulty. < Old French *prendre* to take.

prism (ˈprɪzm̩) *n* **1** (*geometry*) a figure whose sides are usually parallelograms and whose two ends are parallel and alike in size and shape. **2** a transparent object of similar shape which disperses light into the colours of the rainbow. **prismatic** *adj* **1** of or like a prism. **2** (of colours) formed or dispersed (as if) by a prism. < ultimately Greek *priein* to saw.

prison (ˈprɪzn̩) *n* **1** a public building used for confining people convicted of crimes. **2** any place of confinement. **prisoner** *n* **1** a person kept in prison, captivity, or custody. **2** a person or thing that is not free to move, act, etc. **prisoner of war** a person captured during wartime. < ultimately Latin *prehendere* to seize. SEE PANEL.

prissy (ˈprɪsɪ) *adj* (*derogatory*) prim, esp. in an irritating or affected way. < probably *prim* + *sissy*.

pristine (ˈprɪstiːn) *adj* **1** undamaged and seemingly new; mint: in pristine condition. **2** belonging to an earlier period; original. < Latin *pristinus*.

private (ˈpraɪvɪt) *adj* **1** of or belonging to an individual person or group; not public: private property. **2** not intended for general circulation, view, use, etc.: Private and confidential. **3** not holding official or public office: a private detective. **4** (of a place) affording privacy; sequestered. **5** not run, sponsored, or financed by the government: private medicine.
• *n* a soldier of the lowest rank. **privately** *adv* **in private** without others being present, listening, watching, etc. **privacy** *n* the state of being private or secluded. **private enterprise** the management of business by individuals rather than by the state. **private means** income other than wages or salary, usually from investments, etc. **private member** an MP who does not hold a government appointment. **private parts** the genitals. **privatize** *vb* assign or return to private ownership. **privatization** *n* < ultimately Latin *privus*.

privation (praɪˈveɪʃən) *n* a lack of necessities; hardship. < ultimately Latin *privare* to deprive.

privet (ˈprɪvɪt) *n* a common evergreen shrub, widely used for hedges. < origin unknown.

privilege (ˈprɪvɪlɪdʒ) *n* **1** a special right or advantage granted to a particular person or group. **2** the practice of granting or receiving privileges. **privileged** *adj* having privileges. < ultimately Latin *privus* private + *lex* law.

privy (ˈprɪvɪ) *adj* **1** informed of something secret or private: He was privy to their intentions. **2** (*archaic*) secret or private.
• *n* (esp. in former times) an outside toilet. **privy council** a group of statesmen chosen as advisers by a monarch. **privy purse** an allowance granted by parliament for the private expenses of a monarch. < ultimately Latin *privatus*.

prize[1] (praɪz) *n* **1** a reward for an achievement, victory, success, etc. **2** something won in a competition or lottery. **3** something valuable or worth striving for. **4** something seized or captured, esp. in former times at sea.

prisoners in the larder?

The -er suffix (with its variant forms, -or, -ar, -yer, -ier, and -r) is one of the most productive in English. The most common function of -er is to indicate a person or thing that performs whatever is expressed by the root word, (either a noun or a verb). A farmer is therefore someone who farms, a thriller is a book or film that thrills, a photographer is someone who takes photographs, and a jailer is someone who looks after a jail. According to this pattern, a prisoner should be someone who looks after or puts people into a prison. But this is not its meaning. Whereas the -er noun is usually the 'doer' or 'performer' of the root word, with prisoner the opposite is true: the -er of prisoner indicates not the 'doer' but the 'receiver'. In this respect the word is very unusual.

There is in fact a small group of -er nouns in which the -er suffix has a similar 'receiver' meaning. These include words like cooker ('an apple that is cooked'), broiler ('a chicken that is broiled'), and other food items.

• *adj* **1** awarded or worthy of receiving a prize: a prize cauliflower. **2** given as a prize: prize money. **3** (*informal*) used to give emphasis; absolute: a prize idiot.
• *vb* value highly. **prize-fight** *n* a professional boxing contest. **prize-fighter** *n* < ultimately Latin *pretium* price.
prize[2] *vb* prise.
pro[1] (prəʊ) *n, pl* **pros** (*informal*) **1** a professional. **2** a prostitute.
pro[2] *adv, prep* in favour of (something). **pros and cons** arguments for and against something.
pro- *prefix* in favour or support of: pro-British. < Latin.
probable (ˈprɒbəbḷ) *adj* likely to happen or be true. **probably** *adv* **probability** *n* **1** being probable. **2** something probable. **3** the likelihood of something happening: Let's consider the probabilities. **in all probability** most probably. < Latin *probabilis*.
probate (ˈprəʊbeɪt) *n* **1** the official process of establishing that a will is valid. **2** an official copy of a will certified as valid. < ultimately Latin *probare* to examine.
probation (prəˈbeɪʃən) *n* **1** a trial period. **2** a system whereby certain offenders report regularly to an official instead of receiving a prison sentence. **probationary** *adj* **probationer** *n* **1** a person undergoing assessment during a probationary period. **2** an offender on probation. < SEE **PROBATE.**
probe (prəʊb) *n* **1** a slender instrument used for examining a wound or cavity. **2** a device or machine used for investigating a dangerous or inaccessible area: a space probe. **3** a close investigation.
• *vb* **1** examine (as if) with a probe. **2** investigate closely. < SEE **PROBATE.** SEE PANEL.
probity (ˈprəʊbɪtɪ) *n* honesty or integrity. < ultimately Latin *probus* honest.
problem (ˈprɒbləm) *n* **1** something difficult to understand, deal with, or resolve: The situation poses serious problems. **2** a question raised for consideration or to be solved: mathematical problems. **problematic** or **problematical** *adj* **1** not straightforward; puzzling. **2** doubtful or uncertain. < ultimately Greek *proballein* to throw forwards.
procedure (prəˈsiːdʒə) *n* an (established) method of doing something, considered esp. in terms of the sequence of stages. **procedural** *adj* < Middle French *proceder* to proceed.
proceed (prəˈsiːd) *vb* **1** continue, esp. after a pause or stop: proceed with one's journey. **2** begin and continue. **3** issue or arise from. **4** advance along a course or route. **proceedings** *pl n* **1** the things said and done on a particular occasion, esp. at a meeting of a society, club, etc. **2** legal action: divorce proceedings. **proceeds** *pl n* the money or profit obtained from a sale, public performance, etc.: The proceeds went to charity. SEE PANEL AT **PRECEDE.**
process (ˈprəʊsɛs) *n* **1** a method of making or manufacturing something, esp. one involving a series of operations. **2** a series of actions connected with change or development: chemical processes. **3** progress or proceeding: Learning to read is a slow process. **4** a lawsuit considered in terms of its entirety. **5** a projection or

probe the headlines

From its regular appearance in headlines such as Politician in Garden Party Probe Shock a foreign learner of English might be led to think that probe ('investigate') belongs to the common stock of English words. However, this is not the case. Outside the field of medicine, probe hardly ever occurs except in the language of newspaper headlines. Examples of other words which feature predominantly in this particular variety or *register* of English include:

blaze	(fire)
rap	(charge)
riddle	(mystery)
pit	(coal-mine)
aid	(help)
attack	(criticize)
quiz	(question)
pact	(agreement)
wed	(marry)
trek	(journey)
cut	(reduction)
hit	(affect)
key	(important)

Many of these words have the advantage of being smaller than their standard English equivalents and therefore help the headline writer to overcome the restriction of space. Others, such as blaze and attack, are chosen for their sensational, eye-catching quality. See also panel at **headline.**

outgrowth on a body or plant.
● *vb* **1** cause to undergo a process. **2** perform operations on. **processor** *n* < ultimately Latin *processus.*

procession (prəˈsɛʃən) *n* a number of people, vehicles, etc., advancing in a line, esp. for ceremonial purposes. **processional** *adj*

proclaim (prəˈkleɪm) *vb* **1** announce or make known, esp. publicly. **2** make manifest. **proclamation** *n* < ultimately Latin *proclamare.*

proclivity (prəˈklɪvɪtɪ) *n* a tendency or predisposition: He has a natural proclivity towards alcohol. < Latin *proclivis* sloping.

procrastinate (prəʊˈkræstɪˌneɪt, prəˈkræstɪˌneɪt) *vb* put off doing something without good reason; delay. **procrastination** *n* **procrastinator** *n* < Latin *procrastinare* to postpone until tomorrow.

procreate (ˈprəʊkrɪˌeɪt) *vb* produce offspring. **procreation** *n* **procreative** *adj* < Latin *procreare.*

proctor (ˈprɒktə) *n* a university official charged with maintaining student discipline, esp. at Oxford or Cambridge. < Middle English *procutour,* from *procuratour.*

procure (prəˈkjʊə) *vb* **1** obtain or acquire, esp. by particular care or effort. **2** provide (esp. a woman) to act as a prostitute. **procurement** *n* **procurer** *n* a person who procures, esp. women for prostitution. < ultimately Latin *procurare* to take care of.

prod (prɒd) *vb* **prodded; prodding** **1** poke or goad, esp. with a pointed object. **2** stimulate into action; urge.
● *n* **1** an act of prodding; poke. **2** something used for prodding. **3** an incitement to action; reminder. < origin uncertain.

prodigal (ˈprɒdɪgl̩) *adj* **1** recklessly wasteful or extravagant, esp. with money. **2** lavish.
● *n* a squanderer or spendthrift. **prodigality** *n* **prodigally** *adv* < Latin *prodigere* to squander. SEE PANEL.

prodigious (prəˈdɪdʒəs) *adj* **1** enormous. **2** wonderful or amazing. **prodigiously** *adv* **prodigiousness** *n* < SEE **PRODIGY.**

prodigy (ˈprɒdɪdʒɪ) *n* **1** a person with exceptional abilities, esp. a child. **2** a wonder; exceptional example. < Latin *prodigium.*

produce (prəˈdjuːs) *vb* **1** bring about; cause: Mechanization produced enormous unemployment. **2 bring into view:** From his inside pocket he produced a fat leather wallet. **3** bear or yield; create. **4** make or manufacture. **5** organize and present (a play, film, etc.).
● *n* (ˈprɒdjuːs) something produced, esp. farm products. **producer** *n* **1** a person or thing that produces: a major wheat producer. **2** a person who produces a play, etc. **product** *n* **1** something made or manufactured to be sold; commodity. **2** a person or thing brought about by a particular cause; result: The child is a product of parental neglect. **3** the result of multiplying two or more numbers, quantities, etc. **production** *n* **1** the act or process of producing something. **2** the amount produced: an increase in production. **3** a play, film, etc. **productive** *adj* **1** (capable of) producing plentifully; fertile. **2** giving good results; fruitful: a productive meeting. **3** resulting in. **productively** *adv* **productiveness** *n* **productivity** *n* productiveness, esp. considered in terms of efficiency. < ultimately Latin *producere.*

profane (prəˈfeɪn) *adj* **1** showing contempt or disrespect for what is holy. **2** blasphemous or irreverent: profane talk. **3** not meant or designed for religious use; secular.
● *vb* treat (something holy) with irreverence or contempt; debase. **profanely** *adv* **profanity** *n* < ultimately Latin *profanus.* SEE PANEL.

profess (prəˈfɛs) *vb* **1** state or declare openly. **2** state or declare falsely or insincerely; pretend. **3** confess one's faith in (a religion). **professed** *adj* < Latin *professus* openly declared.

profession (prəˈfɛʃən) *n* **1** an occupation requiring advanced learning. **2** the body of people engaged in such an occupation: the legal profession. **3** an open statement or declaration.

professional (prəˈfɛʃənl̩) *adj* **1** of or

---

the prodigal son

The expression the prodigal son alludes to the parable recorded in the Bible, in Luke 15:11–32. The actual expression does not, however, appear in the Bible text.

Similar expressions that have biblical allusions but do not actually appear in the Bible include:

a doubting Thomas—John 20:24–29
a good Samaritan—Luke 10:30–37
the writing on the wall—Daniel 5:5–29

---

connected with a profession. **2** having or displaying a high quality or standard: a very professional performance. **3** engaged in (a sport, etc.) as a full-time occupation. **4** engaged in by professionals: professional tennis.
• *n* a person who engages in a sport, etc., as a profession. **professionalism** *n* **professionally** *adv*

professor (prəˈfɛsə) *n* an academic of the highest rank in a university department. **professorial** *adj* **professorship** *n*

proffer (ˈprɒfə) *vb* (*formal*) offer; tender.
• *n* an offer. < Old French *poroffrir.*

proficient (prəˈfɪʃənt) *adj* skilled or competent. **proficiency** *n* **proficiently** *adv* < Latin *proficere* to accomplish.

profile (ˈprəʊfaɪl) *n* **1** (an outline of) a side view, esp. of a person's face. **2** a brief biographical article or account.
• *vb* produce a profile of. < Latin *pro-* before + *filum* thread.

profit (ˈprɒfɪt) *n* **1** a gain, advantage, or benefit. **2** money gained from a business transaction after the deduction of expenditure.
• *vb* **1** gain a profit (from). **2** benefit or be advantageous to. **profitable** *adj* yielding a profit. **profitability** *n* **profitably** *adv* < Latin *proficere* to gain advantage.

profiteer (ˌprɒfɪˈtɪə) *n* a person who makes excessive profits unethically.
• *vb* make excessive profits.

profligate (ˈprɒflɪgət) *adj* **1** recklessly wasteful or extravagant. **2** highly immoral or dissolute.
• *n* a profligate person. **profligacy** *n* < Latin *profligare* to strike down.

profound (prəˈfaʊnd) *adj* **1** deep, extreme, or intense: profound regret. **2** showing or arising from a deep level of understanding: a profound insight. **3** requiring effort to understand; puzzling. **profoundly** *adv* **profundity** *n* < Latin *profundus* deep.

profane

Profane is used to describe something that displays disrespect for what is considered holy, such as gambling in a church. It derives via Middle French from the Latin *profanus*. This word is a compound of *pro-* 'before' and *fanum* 'temple' and therefore has the literal meaning 'before or outside the temple'.

profuse (prəˈfjuːs) *adj* **1** abundant or plentiful. **2** poured forth freely or excessively: profuse thanks. **profusely** *adv* **profuseness** or **profusion** *n* < Latin *profundere* to pour forth.

progenitor (prəʊˈdʒɛnɪtə) *n* an ancestor or forefather. **progeny** *n* (*formal*) children or offspring. < ultimately Latin *progignere* to beget.

prognosis (prɒgˈnəʊsɪs) *n, pl* **prognoses** a forecast of the course of a disease. < ultimately Greek *progignōskein* to know before.

program (ˈprəʊgræm) *n* **1** a series of instructions for a computer. **2** (*US*) programme.
• *vb* **programmed; programming** supply (a computer) with a program. **programmer** *n*

programme (ˈprəʊgræm) *n* **1** a plan of action. **2** (a leaflet giving) a list of events, items, etc., to be presented in a performance. **3** the performance of these events, etc. **4** a radio or television broadcast. < ultimately Greek *prographein* to write before.

progress (ˈprəʊgrɛs) *n* **1** forward or onward movement; advance. **2** growth or improvement, esp. the development of civilization. **in progress** currently taking place.
• *vb* (prəˈgrɛs) **1** go forward or onward. **2** grow or improve. **progression** *n* **progressive** *adj* **1** advancing or developing steadily or in stages: progressive deterioration. **2** employing or favouring new methods: progressive attitudes. **3** (of a verb form) indicating continuation. **progressively** *adv* **progressiveness** *n* < Latin *progredi* to go forth.

prohibit (prəʊˈhɪbɪt) *vb* forbid, esp. officially. **prohibition** *n* **prohibitive** *adj* **1** prohibiting or restraining. **2** (of prices, etc.) so high as to preclude the purchase or hire of. **prohibitively** *adv* **prohibitiveness** *n* < Latin *prohibēre* to hold away.

project[1] (ˈprɒdʒɛkt) *n* **1** a plan or scheme, esp. one involving careful preparation and concerted effort. **2** a research exercise. < Middle French *pourjeter* to plan.

project[2] (prəˈdʒɛkt) *vb* **1** protrude; jut out. **2** throw outwards, forwards, or upwards. **3** cause (an image) to be cast on a surface. **4** cause (one's voice) to be heard at a distance. **5** transport (oneself) by means of the imagination into a particular situation. **6** present (oneself) or communicate (one's ideas) successfully. **7** plan or propose; devise. **8** attribute (one's own attitudes, ideas, etc.) to others. **projection** *n* **projectionist** *n* a person who operates a projector. **projector** *n* an apparatus for projecting films or slides onto a screen. < Latin *proicere* to throw forwards.

projectile (prəˈdʒɛktaɪl) *n* **1** an object that is hurled or fired, esp. a missile. **2** a self-propelling missile.

proletarian (ˌprəʊlɪˈtɛərɪən) *adj*, *n* (a member) of the proletariat. **proletariat** *n* the working class. SEE PANEL.

proliferate (prəˈlɪfəˌreɪt) *vb* grow, increase, or multiply rapidly. **proliferation** *n* < ultimately Latin *proles* progeny + *ferre* to bear.

prolific (prəˈlɪfɪk) *adj* producing in great quantity: a prolific writer. **prolifically** *adv* < ultimately Latin *proles* progeny.

prologue (ˈprəʊlɒg) *n* **1** the introduction of a play, poem, etc. **2** any introductory act, episode, etc. < ultimately Greek *prologos*.

prolong (prəˈlɒŋ) *vb* lengthen in time or space. **prolongation** *n* < ultimately Latin *prolongare*.

promenade (ˌprɒməˈnɑːd) *n* **1** a paved walkway, esp. along a seafront. **2** (*old-fashioned*) a walk or stroll.
• *vb* (*old-fashioned*) go or take for a promenade. **promenade concert** a concert at which some of the audience stand or can walk about. < ultimately Latin *prominare* to drive forwards. SEE PANEL.

prominent (ˈprɒmɪnənt) *adj* **1** jutting out; projecting: a prominent chin. **2** conspicuous: a prominent landmark. **3** distinguished or well-known: a prominent citizen. **prominence** *n* **prominently** *adv* < Latin *prominēre* to jut forwards.

promiscuous (prəˈmɪskjʊəs) *adj* having an unusually high number of casual sexual relationships. **promiscuously** *adv* **promiscuousness** or **promiscuity** *n* < Latin *promiscuus*.

promise (ˈprɒmɪs) *n* **1** a declaration guaranteeing that one will do or not do something. **2** a sign or indication that provides a reason to expect something: a promise of things to come. **3** a sign or indication that provides a reason to expect success, etc.: His work shows great promise.
• *vb* **1** make a promise to. **2** be a sign or indication providing a reason to expect something: It promises to be a lively afternoon. **promising** *adj* likely to result in success, etc. **promissory note** a formal, written promise to pay a certain sum of money to a certain person. < Latin *promittere*.

promontory (ˈprɒməntrɪ) *n* a piece of land that juts out, esp. into the sea; headland. < Latin *promunturium*.

promote (prəˈməʊt) *vb* **1** raise (a person) in rank, position, etc. **2** encourage, further, or put forward. **3** encourage the purchase of, esp. by publicizing or advertising. **promoter** *n* **promotion** *n* **1** promoting; being promoted. **2** a campaign or event aimed at promoting sales. **promotional** *adj* < Latin *promovēre* to move forwards.

prompt (prɒmpt) *adj* **1** acting, happening, etc., without delay: a prompt reply. **2** on time; punctual: She's always prompt.
• *adv* (of time) exactly: I'll be there at 4 o'clock prompt.
• *vb* **1** stir (a person) into performing a particular action; cause: What prompted you to start the business? **2** give rise to (a thought, feeling, etc.). **3** assist (an actor, etc.) by saying the words that come next.
• *n* the act or an instance of prompting. **prompter** *n* **promptly** *adv* **promptness** or **promptitude** *n* < Latin *promptus*.

promulgate (ˈprɒməlˌgeɪt) *vb* make generally known; proclaim. **promulga-**

proletariat

Proletariat was the name given by Karl Marx to the working class, those who earn a living by selling their labour. The word comes from the French *prolétariat,* from the Latin *proletarii.* The latter name reveals what those of higher standing considered to be the one social role for which the common people were qualified. It derives from *proles* or 'offspring': the single responsibility entrusted to the *proletarii* was boosting the population!

promenade concert

Promenade entered English in the 16th century from the French verb *promener* 'to take for a walk'. A promenade concert or 'prom', as it is informally known, is an orchestral concert with a difference—some members of the audience are not seated but are standing and, especially when the concert is held outdoors, may stroll about.

tion *n* < Latin *promulgare* to proclaim.

prone (prəʊn) *adj* **1** lying flat, esp. face downwards. **2** inclined or disposed to: prone to accidents. **proneness** *n* < Latin *pronus* tending.

prong (prɒŋ) *n* a slender, spiked projection, esp. one of several on a fork. **pronged** *adj* < Middle English *pronge* fork.

pronoun (ˈprəʊˌnaʊn) *n* a word used in place of a noun or noun phrase, or to refer to a discourse participant. **pronominal** *adj* **pronominally** *adv* < Latin *pro-* for + *nomen* name.

pronounce (prəˈnaʊns) *vb* **1** say or utter (a sound, word, etc.): How do you pronounce your name? **2** declare officially or formally: I now pronounce you man and wife. **3** declare as an opinion. **pronounced** *adj* noticeable or distinct: a pronounced dent. **pronouncement** *n* an official or formal declaration. **pronunciation** *n* the act or manner of pronouncing something. < ultimately Latin *pronuntiare*.

proof (pruːf) *n* **1** (any piece of) evidence that shows something to be true or factual. **2** a test or trial that shows whether something is true, as it should be, or as it is claimed to be: His integrity was put to the proof. **3** a measure of the strength of certain alcoholic drinks: 75% proof. **4** (*printing*) a trial impression, esp. to facilitate the correction of errors. **5** a trial print from a negative.
• *adj* able to resist or keep out: rain-proof. **proofreader** *n* a person whose job is to read and correct proofs. < Latin *probare* to prove.

prop[1] (prɒp) *n* **1** a support, used esp. for something heavy that is in danger of falling. **2** any source of support or strength.
• *vb* **propped; propping** support (as if) with a prop. < Middle Dutch *proppe* stopper.

prop[2] *n* any object used on a stage or as part of a film set, apart from the scenery. < stage *property*.

propaganda (ˌprɒpəˈgændə) *n* (the spreading of) ideas, doctrines, etc., that are intended to sway opinions or sympathies. **propagandist** *n* SEE PANEL.

propagate (ˈprɒpəˌgeɪt) *vb* **1** reproduce or multiply: Many plants can be propagated from seeds or cuttings. **2** spread or disseminate. **3** transmit. **propagation** *n* **propagator** *n* < Latin *propagare*.

propel (prəˈpɛl) *vb* **propelled; propelling** drive or thrust forward. **propellant** or **propellent** *n* something that propels, such as an explosive or compressed gas.

propeller *n* a rotating device comprising two or more blades that propel a ship, aircraft, etc. **propelling pencil** a pencil comprising a metal or plastic case that houses an adjustable lead. < Latin *propellere*.

propensity (prəˈpɛnsɪtɪ) *n* a tendency or inclination. < Latin *propendēre* to incline.

proper (ˈprɒpə) *adj* **1** appropriate or suitable: I don't have the proper tools for the job. **2** right or correct: She wishes she had learnt to play the proper way. **3** (*informal*) complete or thorough: He looked a proper fool. **4** in keeping with social norms: proper behaviour. **5** as strictly defined. **properly** *adv* **proper name** proper noun. **proper noun** the name of a particular person, place, or thing. < ultimately Latin *proprius* special.

property (ˈprɒpətɪ) *n* **1** something that is owned, esp. a piece of real estate. **2** a quality or characteristic: The gas has several important properties. **3** a stage prop. < ultimately Latin *proprius* own.

prophecy (ˈprɒfɪsɪ) *n* **1** a prediction, esp. one based upon mystical powers. **2** the power of predicting the future. **prophesy** *vb* **prophesied; prophesying** make a prophecy. **prophet** fem. **prophetess** *n* **1** a person who makes prophecies. **2** a spokesman for a cause, etc. **prophetic** *adj* having the nature of a prophecy: His words proved prophetic. **prophetically** *adv* < ultimately Greek

propaganda

Ideas and philosophies that are spread abroad for purposes of indoctrination are known as propaganda. This word dates back to the 17th century and the *Sacra Congregatio de Propaganda Fide,* ('Sacred Congregation for Propagating the Faith'). This was the title of the committee established by Pope Gregory XV in 1623 for the purpose of promoting and overseeing missionary activities. In conversation the name was to prove too much of a mouthful and it became shortened to 'the Propaganda'.

Although originally of a religious orientation, present-day propaganda commonly serves to further political interests and the word has acquired a derogatory connotation.

prophētēs prophet. SEE PANEL.
prophylactic (ˌprɒfɪˈlæktɪk) *adj*, *n* (a medicine, drug, etc.) having the property of protecting against disease. **prophylactically** *adj* < Greek *prophylassein* to keep guard before.
proportion (prəˈpɔːʃən) *n* **1** a part or percentage (of a total amount): Only a small proportion of the men failed to attend. **2** an equal part or share. **3** a ratio: The proportion of women to men was 5:1. **4** a balanced or correct ratio: The size of the door is out of proportion. **proportions** *pl n* size or dimension: a figure of huge proportions.
• *vb* make proportionate. **proportional** *adj* **1** in correct or corresponding proportion: proportional representation. **2** of or connected with proportion. **proportionally** *adv* **proportionate** *adj* in correct or corresponding proportion. **proportionately** *adv* < ultimately Latin *proportio*.
propose (prəˈpəʊz) *vb* **1** offer for consideration; suggest. **2** recommend or nominate for a post, vacancy, etc. **3** intend: He proposes to sack everybody. **4** make an offer of marriage. **5** offer as a toast in drinking. **proposal** *n* **1** an act of proposing. **2** something proposed. **3** an offer of marriage. < ultimately Latin *proponere*.
proposition (ˌprɒpəˈzɪʃən) *n* **1** a proposal or suggestion. **2** a statement or assertion, esp. one that is to be expanded upon, proven, etc. **3** a thing, matter, or situation: an entirely different proposition. **4** a proposal of sexual intercourse.
• *vb* make a proposition to, esp. to suggest sexual intercourse. **propositional** *adj*

prophecy or **prophesy?**

Prophecy is the noun; prophesy the verb: the gift of *prophecy;* Could anyone have *prophesied* the disaster?

Similar pairs of words with c and s spellings for the noun and verb in British English are:

noun	verb
advice	advise
device	devise
licence	license
practice	practise

For further discussion, see panels at **license; practise.**

propound (prəˈpaʊnd) *vb* (*formal*) offer for consideration. **propounder** *n* < ultimately Latin *proponere* to set forth.
proprietary (prəˈpraɪətərɪ, prəˈpraɪətrɪ) *adj* **1** manufactured and marketed by a particular firm, usually under a trade name: a proprietary brand. **2** of or belonging to a proprietor. **3** privately owned. < Latin *proprietas* property.
proprietor (prəˈpraɪətə) fem. **proprietress** (prəˈpraɪətrɪs) *n* an owner, esp. of a business. **proprietorship** *n*
propriety (prəˈpraɪətɪ) *n* **1** conformity to established standards of behaviour; decorum. **2** appropriateness or suitability. **proprieties** *pl n* the manners of polite society. < Middle French *proprieté* quality of a person or thing.
propulsion (prəˈpʌlʃən) *n* **1** the act or process of propelling. **2** something that propels. < Latin *propellere* to propel.
pro rata (ˌprəʊ ˈrɑːtə) *adj*, *adv* proportionate or proportionately: pro rata increase. < Latin: according to the rate.
prosaic (prəʊˈzeɪɪk) *adj* **1** dull or unimaginative. **2** having the qualities of prose. **prosaically** *adv* < Latin *prosa* prose.
proscribe (prəʊˈskraɪb) *vb* **1** condemn or forbid. **2** outlaw or exile. < Latin *proscribere*. SEE PANEL AT **PRESCRIBE.**
prose (prəʊz) *n* ordinary written or spoken language as opposed to verse. < Latin *prosa*.
prosecute (ˈprɒsɪˌkjuːt) *vb* **1** take legal action against. **2** continue, carry on, or pursue. **prosecutor** *n* **prosecution** *n* **1** the act of prosecuting. **2** the party which prosecutes another. < Latin *prosequi* to pursue.
prosody (ˈprɒsədɪ) *n* **1** the study of verse forms and poetic metre. **2** the patterns of stress and intonation with which a language is spoken. < ultimately Greek *prosōidia* song sung to music.
prospect (ˈprɒspɛkt) *n* **1** (*formal*) a view or outlook. **2** an anticipation of a future event: She doesn't relish the prospect of having to go out to work again. **3** a possibility: reasonable prospects of success. **4** a potential customer, candidate, etc. **prospects** *pl n* possibilities to advance or improve oneself: a job with no prospects.
• *vb* (prəˈspɛkt) explore in search of gold or other minerals. **prospector** *n* **prospective** *adj* expected or anticipated in the future: prospective customers. **prospectus** *n* a booklet or brochure describing a school, university, business

enterprise, etc. < Latin *prospectus*.

prosper (ˈprɒspə) *vb* flourish or thrive, esp. economically. **prosperity** *n* **prosperous** *adj* financially successful; wealthy. **prosperously** *adv* < ultimately Latin *prosperus* favourable.

prosthesis (ˈprɒsθɪsɪs) *n, pl* **prostheses** an artificial limb. < ultimately Greek: addition.

prostitute (ˈprɒstɪˌtjuːt) *n* a person, esp. a woman, who may be hired for sexual intercourse.
• *vb* **1** make a prostitute of. **2** put to an unworthy use. **prostitution** *n* < Latin *prostituere* to expose to prostitution.

prostrate (ˈprɒstreɪt) *adj* **1** lying flat, esp. face downwards. **2** weak or exhausted; overcome: prostrate with grief.
• *vb* (prɒˈstreɪt) **1** adopt or cast into a prostrate position. **2** adopt a position of humility or submission. **prostration** *n* < Latin *prosternere*.

protagonist (prəʊˈtægənɪst) *n* **1** the major character in a play, novel, etc. **2** a leading supporter of a cause. < Greek *prōtagōnistēs*.

protect (prəˈtɛkt) *vb* guard from danger, injury, etc. **protection** *n* **protector** *n* **protectionism** *n* an economic policy of protecting home industries, esp. by regulating imports. **protective** *adj* affording protection. **protectively** *adv* **protectorate** *n* a country that is protected and partly governed by another. < Latin *protegere*.

protégé fem. **protégée** (ˈprəʊtɪˌʒeɪ, ˈprɒtɪˌʒeɪ) *n* a person who is under the care or guidance of another. < French.

protein (ˈprəʊtiːn) *n* a nourishing substance found in the cells of all living organisms and which is an essential element of their diet. < ultimately Greek *prōtos* first.

protest (ˈprəʊtɛst) *n* a statement or demonstration of disapproval.
• *vb* (prəˈtɛst) **1** make a protest. **2** assert or declare, esp. when under accusation: He protested his innocence. **protestation** *n* a solemn declaration. **under protest** unwillingly. < ultimately Latin *protestari*.

protocol (ˈprəʊtəˌkɒl) *n* **1** correct or conventional procedure; etiquette. **2** an original draft of an agreement, esp. one forming the basis of a treaty. < Late Greek *prōtokollon* sheet glued to the front of a manuscript.

proton (ˈprəʊtɒn) *n* a particle with a positive electric charge. < Greek *prōtos* first.

prototype (ˈprəʊtəˌtaɪp) *n* the first model or example of something upon which later ones are based. < ultimately Greek *prōtotypos* archetypal.

protract (prəˈtrækt) *vb* cause to last longer; prolong. **protraction** *n* **protractor** *n* an instrument for measuring angles. < Latin *protrahere* to prolong.

protrude (prəˈtruːd) *vb* jut out from a surface; project. **protrusion** *n* < Latin *protrudere*.

protuberant (prəˈtjuːbərənt) *adj* swelling out; bulging. **protuberance** *n* < Latin *protuberare* to bulge out.

proud (praʊd) *adj* **1** feeling or displaying pleasure or self-satisfaction, esp. on account of one's achievements or possessions. **2** giving reason for this feeling: a proud moment. **3** having self-respect: They are far too proud to accept charity. **4** having an excessively high opinion of oneself; haughty. **5** majestic or impressive. **6** projecting slightly. **proudly** *adv* < Old English *prūd*.

prove (pruːv) *vb* **proved; proved, proven; proving 1** provide or be proof of. **2** turn out; be found to be: The rumour proved false. **3** (*law*) establish the genuineness of (a will). **4** (of dough) rise or cause to rise before baking. **proven** *adj* shown to be true or genuine: a woman of proven ability. < Latin *probare* to test.
SEE PANEL AT **PAIN.**

provenance (ˈprɒvənəns) *n* a source or origin. < Latin *provenire* to come forth.

proverb (ˈprɒvɜːb) *n* a short saying, usually containing a maxim or general truth. **proverbial** *adj* **1** of or like a proverb. **2** commonly cited or widely known. **proverbially** *adv* < Latin *proverbium*. SEE PANEL AT **COOK.**

provide (prəˈvaɪd) *vb* cause to have possession or use of something needed; supply. **provide against 1** take precautionary measures. **2** (of a law) forbid. **provide for 1** supply with the means of support: provide for one's family. **2** make suitable arrangements or plans for (something anticipated). **provider** *n* **provided** or **providing** *conj* on condition that. < Latin *providēre*.

providence (ˈprɒvɪdəns) *n* **1** being provident. **2** God, considered as the power determining human destiny; fate. **provident** *adj* (*old-fashioned*) providing for future needs, esp. by saving. **providently** *adv* **providential** *adj* happening (as if) by providence. **providentially** *adv* < Latin *providentia*.

province (ˈprɒvɪns) *n* **1** an administrative division of a country. **2** a sphere of knowledge, expertise, or authority. **3 the provinces** all the parts of a country outside the capital. **provincial** *adj* **1** of or connected with the provinces: All provincial services have been disrupted. **2** of a province: a provincial governor. **3** (*derogatory*) narrow-minded or unsophisticated: provincial attitudes. **provincialism** *n* < ultimately Latin *provincia.*

provision (prəˈvɪʒən) *n* **1** the act of providing or supplying. **2** plans or preparations in anticipation of something: The store has made provision for a very heavy demand. **3** a stipulation or condition, esp. in a contract, treaty, etc.
• *vb* supply with food. **provisional** *adj* arranged on a temporary or unconfirmed basis: a provisional acceptance. **provisionally** *adv* **provisions** *pl n* (a supply of) food and drink. < ultimately Latin *providēre* to see ahead.

proviso (prəˈvaɪzəʊ) *n, pl* **provisos, provisoes** (a clause stating) a condition or stipulation. < Medieval Latin *proviso quod* provided that.

provoke (prəˈvəʊk) *vb* **1** make angry or irritated. **2** stir (a person) into acting. **3** cause or stir up: The rumour provoked considerable speculation. **provocation** *n* **provocative** *adj* arousing or stimulating, esp. heated reaction or sexual desire: a provocative comment. **provocatively** *adv* < ultimately Latin *provocare.*

provost (ˈprɒvəst) *n* **1** the head of certain university colleges. **2** a church dignitary. **3** the chief magistrate of a Scottish burgh. < ultimately Latin *praeponere* to place at the head.

prow (praʊ) *n* the bow of a ship or boat. < Middle French *proue.*

prowess (praʊɪs) *n* (*formal*) outstanding skill or bravery. < Old French *proue* valiant.

prowl (praʊl) *vb* move about stealthily, esp. as a precursor to attacking, breaking into a house, etc.
• *n* the act of prowling: on the prowl. **prowler** *n* < Middle English *prollen.*

proximity (prɒkˈsɪmɪtɪ) *n* nearness; neighbourhood. < ultimately Latin *proximus* nearest.

proxy (ˈprɒksɪ) *n* **1** (a document giving someone) authority to act or vote for another. **2** a person who has been given this authority. < ultimately Latin *procuratio* procuration.

prude (pruːd) *n* a person who is excessively fastidious about moral proprieties, esp. in sexual matters. **prudish** *adj* **prudishly** *adv* **prudishness** *n* < Old French *prode femme* good woman. SEE PANEL.

prudent (ˈpruːdənt) *adj* wise, shrewd, or showing foresight. **prudence** *n* **prudently** *adv* < ultimately Latin *providēre* to provide.

prune[1] (pruːn) *n* a dried plum. < ultimately Greek *proumnon* plum.

prune[2] *vb* **1** trim (a shrub, tree, etc.) by cutting away dead or unwanted growth. **2** shorten or reduce (a manuscript, speech, etc.) by removing certain (unnecessary) parts. < Middle French *proignier.*

pry (praɪ) *vb* **pried; prying** survey or investigate the property or affairs of others in an over-inquisitive or intrusive way. < Middle English *prien.*

PS *abbrev* postscript.

psalm (sɑːm) *n* a sacred song, esp. one in the book of Psalms. SEE PANEL.

pseudo (ˈsjuːdəʊ, ˈsuːdəʊ) *adj* fake or false.

pseudo- *prefix* fake or false. < ultimately Greek *pseudēs.*

pseudonym (ˈsjuːdəˌnɪm, ˈsuːdəˌnɪm) *n* a false name used by an author. < ultimately Greek *pseudōnymos* having a false name.

psyche (ˈsaɪkɪ) *n* **1** the human soul or spirit. **2** the mind. < Greek *psychē.*

psychedelic (ˌsaɪkɪˈdɛlɪk) *adj* **1** (of drugs) causing hallucinations. **2** having effects like those produced by psychedelic drugs. < Greek *psychē* soul + *dēloun* to show.

psychiatry (saɪˈkaɪətrɪ) *n* the branch of medicine that deals with mental disorders. **psychiatric** *adj* **psychiatrist** *n*

psychic (ˈsaɪkɪk) *adj* also **psychical** **1** of the mind or soul. **2** of powers that seem to be beyond nature. **3** having or sensitive to these powers. **psychically** *adv* < Greek *psychē.*

psychoanalyse (ˌsaɪkəʊˈænəlaɪz) *vb*

prude

A person who affects or shows excessive modesty, especially with regard to sexual matters, is sometimes referred to as a prude. This is a direct borrowing from French. The French word derives from *prudefemme* meaning 'a good or respectable woman', from the Old French *prode femme.* According to its etymology, therefore, the word was originally a complimentary term, which in the course of its evolution acquired a pejorative sense.

treat by means of psychoanalysis. **psychoanalysis** *n* a method of treating mental disorders by encouraging patients to speak freely, thereby allowing repressed motives or other unconscious factors to come to light. **psychoanalyst** *n*

psychology (saɪˈkɒlədʒɪ) *n* the scientific study of the mind and mental processes. **psychologist** *n* **psychological** *adj* **1** of the mind and its processes. **2** of psychology. **psychologically** *adv*

psychopath (ˈsaɪkəʊˌpæθ) *n* a person with a severe personality disorder, esp. one with violent tendencies. **psychopathic** *adj*

psychosomatic (ˌsaɪkəʊsəˈmætɪk) *adj* (of an illness or bodily disorder) caused or influenced by mental or emotional factors. **psychosomatically** *adv*

psychotherapy (ˌsaɪkəʊˈθɛrəpɪ) *n* the treatment of mental disorders by psychological methods.

PT *abbrev* physical training.

PTO *abbrev* please turn over.

pub (pʌb) *n* (*informal*) a public house.

puberty (ˈpjuːbətɪ) *n* the stage in a person's life when sexual maturity develops. < Latin *puber* adult.

pubic (ˈpjuːbɪk) *adj* of or situated in the region of the sexual organs: pubic hair.

public (ˈpʌblɪk) *adj* **1** of, intended for, or connected with people as a whole; not private: a public library. **2** open or available to all people: a public meeting. **3** made known to all; not kept secret: The news has been made public. **4** widely known: a public figure. **5** working on behalf of the community: a public official.
• *n* all the members of (a section of) the community: the reading public. **in public** publicly. **public-address system** a system comprising a microphone, amplifier, and loudspeakers, used for addressing a large audience. **publican** *n* the keeper of a public house. **public house** a building where alcoholic drinks are sold for consumption on the premises. **publicity** *n* **1** public notice or attention. **2** the process of gaining public attention (for a product, etc.). **publicize** *vb* make widely known. **publicly** *adv* in front of people; openly. **public relations** the practice of inducing, developing, or maintaining the public's sympathetic attitude towards a person or organization. **public school** **1** an endowed independent secondary school, usually a single-sex boarding-school. **2** (*US and Scottish*) a secondary school run by a local authority. **public sector** the part of the economy comprising those industries and services owned and run by the state. **public-spirited** *adj* prepared to do things for the good of the community. < ultimately Latin *populus* the people.

publication (ˌpʌblɪˈkeɪʃən) *n* **1** the act of publishing. **2** something that is published.

publish (ˈpʌblɪʃ) *vb* **1** organize the printing of (a book, newspaper, etc.) that is then sold or distributed to the public. **2** make widely known. **3** proclaim publicly. **publisher** *n* < SEE PUBLIC.

puck (pʌk) *n* a hard, rubber disc used in ice hockey. < English dialect: to poke.

pucker (ˈpʌkə) *vb* make or become wrinkled or creased.
• *n* a wrinkle or crease. < origin uncertain.

pudding (ˈpʊdɪŋ) *n* **1** a cooked dessert made with flour, milk, eggs, etc. **2** the dessert course: 'What's for pudding?' asked David. **3** a savoury dish: steak and kidney pudding. **4** (*informal*) a small, roundish or podgy person. < Middle English.

puddle (ˈpʌdl̩) *n* a small temporary pool, esp. of rain-water. < Middle English *podel*.

puerile (ˈpjʊəraɪl) *adj* **1** (*derogatory*) befitting a child; childish: a puerile comment. **2** juvenile. **puerility** *n* < ultimately Latin *puer* boy.

puff (pʌf) *n* **1** a brief, light discharge of smoke, air, etc.; light gust (of wind). **2** a powder-puff. **3** a light, fluffy pastry.
• *vb* **1** expel (smoke, etc.) in a puff or puffs. **2** breathe hard; pant: puffing and blowing. **3** swell or inflate: Both the champion's eyes had puffed up by the third round. **puff pastry** light, flaky pastry. **puffy** *adj* swollen. **puffiness** *n* < Old English *pyffan*, like the sound.

puffin (ˈpʌfɪn) *n* any of a number of black-and-white sea-birds with a

---

psalm

Each of the 150 sacred songs collected in the book of Psalms is known as a psalm. This word dates back to pre-Christian days. It derives via the Old English *psealm* and the Late Latin *psalmus* from the Greek *psalmos* 'a song accompaniment' (literally 'the twanging of a harp'). The root of this is the verb *psailein* 'to pluck (a stringed instrument)'.

---

grooved, multi-coloured bill. < Middle English *pophyn.*

pugnacious (pʌgˈneɪʃəs) *adj* keen to fight; aggressive. **pugnaciously** *adv* **pugnacity** *n* < Latin *pugnare* to fight.

puke (pjuːk) *vb, n* (*slang*) (to) vomit. < probably like the sound.

pull (pʊl) *vb* **1** exert force on (something) to move it towards the source of the force: The car was pulling a small trailer. **2** damage or strain by pulling: pull a muscle. **3** remove, extract, or draw out by pulling: pull a tooth. **4** row (a boat): He pulled for the shore. **5** steer (a ball) in a certain direction by striking it in a certain way. **6** (of an engine) exert a (powerful) driving force: The old car doesn't pull very well on hills. **7** attract (customers, visitors, etc.) in large numbers: A circus always manages to pull the crowds. **8** bring out (a weapon) ready for use: One of the gang suddenly pulled a gun. **9** draw on (a pipe, cigarette, etc.).
• *n* **1** the act of pulling. **2** the force exerted by pulling: The rope wasn't strong enough to take the pull. **3** the power to influence or sway. **4** the power to attract customers, visitors, etc. **5** the act of drawing on a pipe, cigarette, etc. < Old English *pullian.* SEE PANEL.

pullet (ˈpʊlɪt) *n* a young hen. < Middle French *poulet* young fowl.

pulley (ˈpʊlɪ) *n* an apparatus comprising one or more wheels around the rim of which passes a rope, chain, or belt; used for hoisting or changing the direction of a force. < Middle English *pouley.*

pullover (ˈpʊləʊvə) *n* a knitted garment for the top half of the body that is put on by being pulled over the head; jumper.

pulmonary (ˈpʌlmənərɪ) *adj* of, affecting, or connected with the lungs. < Latin *pulmo* lung.

pulp (pʌlp) *n* **1** the soft, fleshy part of a fruit or vegetable or of any animal or vegetable matter. **2** the soft, sensitive tissue at the centre of a tooth. **3** any vegetable material that is reduced to a soft, moist mass for the making of paper. **4** any reading material that is mass-produced and of poor quality.
• *vb* reduce to pulp. **pulpy** *adj* **pulpiness** *n* < ultimately Latin *pulpa.*

pulpit (ˈpʊlpɪt) *n* a raised, enclosed platform in a church from which sermons are preached. < Latin *pulpitum* platform.

pulse¹ (pʌls) *n* **1** the rhythmic throbbing of the arteries caused by the contractions of the heart. **2** the number of such throbs within a certain length of time. **3** any steady, rhythmic throbbing. **4** a single beat or throb.
• *vb* also **pulsate** move rhythmically; throb or vibrate. < ultimately Latin *pellere* to beat.

pulse² *n* the seeds of plants such as peas, beans, and lentils which are used as food; plants themselves. < ultimately Latin *puls* porridge.

pulverize (ˈpʌlvəˌraɪz) *vb* **1** reduce or be reduced to powder. **2** defeat utterly; annihilate. **pulverizer** *n* < ultimately Latin *pulvis* powder.

puma (ˈpjuːmə) *n* a large American mammal of the cat family. < Spanish, from Quechua.

pumice (ˈpʌmɪs) *n* a light, porous volcanic rock, used for removing stains from the skin and for polishing. **pumicestone** *n* (a piece of) pumice. < ultimately Latin *pumex.*

pummel (ˈpʌməl) *vb* **pummelled; pummelling** strike repeatedly, esp. with the fists. < *pommel.*

pump¹ (pʌmp) *n* **1** a device for raising, transferring, or compressing a fluid or gas, esp. by suction or pressure. **2** the act of pumping.
• *vb* **1** operate a pump. **2** raise or transfer by means of a pump. **3** inflate by means of a pump: The tyre needs pumping up. **4** move (something) rapidly up and down as if operating a manual pump: pump someone's hand. **5** pour or force into a steady stream: He's tired of pumping his savings into the business. **6** question (a person) persistently: She pumped him for information. < probably Spanish *bomba,* like the sound.

pump² *n* **1** a low, light shoe used esp. by ballet dancers. **2** a plimsoll. < origin unknown.

pumpkin (ˈpʌmpkɪn) *n* a large, round, thick-skinned, yellowish-orange fruit, used as a vegetable. < ultimately Greek *pepōn* ripened.

pun (pʌn) *n* a humorous or witty use of a word which has two meanings, both of which are simultaneously evoked, or of two words which have the same or a similar sound.
• *vb* **punned; punning** make a pun. < possibly Italian *puntiglio* word-play. SEE PANELS AT **ROPE**; **TIP¹**.

punch¹ (pʌntʃ) *vb* **1** strike with the fist. **2** hit (a ball) with a short, sharp stroke.
• *n* **1** a blow with the fist. **2** (*informal*) force or impact: The headline needs a bit more punch. **punch-drunk** *adj* (as if) suffering from brain damage as the result of being repeatedly punched. **punch line** a sentence, etc., that provides the climax

to a joke or story. **punch-up** *n* (*informal*) a fist-fight; brawl. < origin uncertain.

punch[2] *n* **1** a tool used for making holes, embossing, or driving the head of a nail beneath a surface. **2** a device for making holes in sheets of paper, etc., so that they may be filed.
• *vb* make holes in, etc., with a punch. < ultimately Latin *pungere* to prick.

punch[3] *n* any drink made of wine or spirits mixed with fruit juice. SEE PANEL.

punctilious (pʌŋkˈtɪlɪəs) *adj* very strict or fastidious about correctness of details. **punctiliously** *adv* **punctiliousness** *n* < Italian *puntiglio* scruple.

punctual (ˈpʌŋktjʊəl) *adj* (in the habit of) arriving or doing something at the agreed time. **punctuality** *n* **punctually** *adv* < Latin *punctus* point.

punctuate (ˈpʌŋktjʊˌeɪt) *vb* **1** use or insert punctuation marks. **2** interrupt at intervals: The essay was punctuated by a series of grammatical howlers. **punctuation** *n* (the use of) punctuation marks. **punctuation mark** a mark such as a full stop or comma that is added to written material to facilitate comprehension. < Latin *punctuare*.

puncture (ˈpʌŋktʃə) *n* a small hole or perforation made by a sharp, pointed object or instrument, esp. one made accidentally in a tyre.
• *vb* **1** make a puncture in; become punctured. **2** deflate as if by puncturing: He went home nursing his punctured pride. < ultimately Latin *pungere* to prick. SEE PANEL AT **COMPUNCTION.**

pundit (ˈpʌndɪt) *n* an expert or authority. < Hindi *paṇḍit.*

pungent (ˈpʌndʒənt) *adj* **1** having a sharp smell or taste. **2** (of comments, etc.) biting or caustic; to the point. **pungency** *n* **pungently** *adv* < ultimately Latin *pungere* to sting.

punish (ˈpʌnɪʃ) *vb* **1** cause (someone) to suffer for a crime, misdeed, etc. **2** inflict a penalty for: Crimes of violence should be severely punished. **3** treat roughly.

---

pulling together

Pull features in a number of idiomatic expressions, including:

pull apart to criticize severely.
pull back to withdraw or cause to withdraw: The troops pulled back to a safer position.
pull down 1 to demolish (a building). **2** to cause to feel weak and depressed: A long spell of flu really pulls you down.
pull in 1 to earn as money or profit. **2** to take into custody. **3** to arrive: The train eventually pulled in an hour late. **4** to move towards the kerb or off the road.
pull-in *n* **1** a place where vehicles may pull in. **2** a roadside cafe.
pull off to complete or perform successfully.
pull oneself together to regain one's self-control: 'Pull yourself together and stop behaving like a baby!'
pull one's punches to criticize, scold, etc., with deliberate restraint.
pull one's socks up to make an effort to improve one's work, behaviour, etc.: You'd better pull your socks up soon, my boy, if you want to pass the exam.
pull one's weight to do one's fair share of work in a joint undertaking.
pull out 1 to depart: The train pulled out on time. **2** to move out of a line of traffic, especially in order to overtake. **3** to withdraw or cause to withdraw: The government wants to pull the troops out immediately.
pull out all the stops to do everything possible to achieve something: We're pulling out all the stops to meet the deadline. The expression originally referred to an organ: an organ will give its loudest, fullest sound when all the stops have been pulled out.
pull rank to make unfair use of one's authority.
pull someone's leg to try to deceive someone in a playful way. **leg-pull** *n*
pull the strings to use one's influence, especially secretly, to gain a personal advantage. The expression comes from the use of strings to control the movements of puppets.
pull the wool over someone's eyes to hide one's true intentions from someone; deceive or mislead.
pull through to come or bring successfully through a severe illness or difficulty.
pull together 1 to work as a team; co-operate: People always seem to pull together in a crisis. **2** to make better or more efficient, by organizing properly: We need someone to pull the whole project together.
pull up 1 to stop: The lorry's brakes screeched as it pulled up at the traffic-lights. **2** to reprimand.

punishable *adj* liable to be punished: a punishable offence. **punishment** *n* **1** punishing or being punished. **2** the penalty imposed on an offender or for an offence. **3** rough treatment. < ultimately Latin *punire.*

punitive (ˈpjuːnɪtiv) *adj* inflicting or involving punishment.

punk (pʌŋk) *n* **1** (*informal*) a ruffian or good-for-nothing. **2** a devotee of punk music and fashion. **3** punk music.
• *adj* of or connected with a movement among young people in Britain in the 1970s and 1980s, noted for the aggression of its music and the outrageousness of its fashions. < origin unknown.

punnet (ˈpʌnɪt) *n* a small basket in which soft fruit is sold. < origin unknown.

punt¹ (pʌnt) *n* a long, narrow, flat-bottomed boat that is propelled by means of a long pole.
• *vb* **1** travel or transport in a punt. **2** propel (a punt) by using a long pole. **punter** *n* < Latin *ponto.*

punt² *vb* gamble or speculate.
• *n* a gamble or bet. **punter** *n* < ultimately Latin *punctum* point.

puny (ˈpjuːnɪ) *adj* (*derogatory*) small and weak. **puniness** *n* < Middle French *puisné* born afterwards, from *puis* afterwards + *né* born. SEE PANEL.

pup (pʌp) *n* **1** a young dog. **2** the young of other animals such as the seal. < *puppy.*

pupa (ˈpjuːpə) *n, pl* **pupae, pupas** a chrysalis. **pupal** *adj* < Latin: girl.

pupil¹ (ˈpjuːpl) *n* a person who is given instruction by a teacher, esp. a schoolchild. < ultimately Latin *pupus* child.

pupil² *n* an opening in the centre of the iris through which light passes to the retina. < ultimately Latin *pupa* doll.

puppet (ˈpʌpɪt) *n* **1** a kind of doll or toy figure that fits over the hand. **2** a marionette. **3** a person who is manipulated by another. **puppeteer** *n* **puppetry** *n* < ultimately Latin *pupa* doll.

puppy (ˈpʌpɪ) *n* a young dog. **puppy fat** temporary plumpness in children and adolescents. < Middle English *popi,* from Middle French *poupée* doll.

purchase (ˈpɜːtʃɪs) *vb* buy.
• *n* **1** the act of buying. **2** something bought. **3** a firm hold or grip. **purchaser** *n* < Old French *purchacier* to try to obtain.

pure (pjʊə) *adj* **1** not mixed with any other substance: pure gold. **2** sheer: pure nonsense. **3** chaste or innocent. **4** theoretical (as opposed to practical): pure science. **purity** *n* **purely** *adv* **1** in a pure manner. **2** merely; simply: I ask the question purely out of interest. **3** wholly or entirely: The jobs are awarded purely according to qualifications. **purify** *vb* **purified; purifying** make pure. **purifier** *n* **purist** *n* a person who insists on purity or traditional notions of correctness, esp. in the field of language. < ultimately Latin *purus.* SEE PANEL AT SHEER¹.

purée (ˈpjʊəreɪ) *n* fruit or vegetables reduced to a thick, soft pulp: tomato purée.
• *vb* **puréed; puréeing** reduce to a purée. < SEE PURE.

purgative (ˈpɜːgətɪv) *n* a laxative.

purgatory (ˈpɜːgətərɪ) *n* **1** (according to Roman Catholic belief) a place or state after death in which the soul is purified. **2** a place or state of suffering. < Medieval Latin *purgatorium.*

purge (pɜːdʒ) *vb* **1** cause evacuation of (the bowels). **2** rid or free of (people or things) that are unwanted or undesirable. **3** atone for (a sin, crime, etc.).
• *n* an act of purging. < ultimately Latin *purgare.*

puritan (ˈpjʊərɪtən) *n* a person who is excessively fastidious about morals and

punch

The name of the popular party drink known as punch comes from the Hindi word *pā̃c* meaning 'five'. This in turn derives from the Sanskrit word for 'five': *pañca.* The name is a reference to the drink's original five ingredients: wine or spirit, water or milk, sugar, spice, and lemon juice.

puny

Someone or something that is weak, inferior, or undersized is sometimes described as puny: 'What a *puny* excuse!' Puny comes from the Middle French *puisné* meaning 'younger' or literally 'born afterwards', from *puis* 'afterwards' and *né* 'born'. This was one of the many legal expressions imposed upon the English by the Normans and survives to this day in the legal expression puisne (judge) or '(judge) of junior status'.

sensual enjoyment. **puritanical** *adj* **puritanically** *adv* SEE PANEL.

purl (pɜːl) *n vb* (knit in) a stitch in which the needle is put into the front of the stitch, producing a ridge towards the knitter. < obsolete *pirl* to twist.

purple (ˈpɜːpl̩) *n* a colour made by mixing red and blue.
• *adj* having this colour. < ultimately Greek *porphyra* purple fish. SEE PANEL.

purport (pɜːˈpɔːt) *vb* be intended to seem: This memo purports to be from head office.
• *n* (ˈpɜːpɔːt) the implied meaning of something; gist. **purportedly** *adv* < Old French *porporter* to convey.

purpose (ˈpɔːpəs) *n* **1** the reason for doing something. **2** the function performed by something: What's the purpose of this button? **3** determination. **on purpose** deliberately. **purpose-built** *adj* built to serve a particular purpose. **purposeful** *adj* **1** having a purpose: a purposeful look. **2** determined. **purposefully** *adv* **purposefulness** *n* **purposeless** *adj* without a purpose. **purposely** *adv* deliberately. < ultimately Latin *proponere* to propose.

purr (pɜː) *vb* **1** (of a cat) make a low, vibratory sound in the throat, esp. when content. **2** make a sound similar to this.
• *n* a purring sound. < like the sound.

purse (pɜːs) *n* **1** small bag for carrying money. **2** funds or finances. **3** prize money. **4** (*US*) a handbag.
• *vb* form (the lips) into a small, rounded shape. **hold the purse-strings** have control of expenditure. **purser** *n* an officer on a ship in charge of accounts. < ultimately Greek *byrsa*.

pursue (pəˈsjuː) *vb* **1** chase or follow in order to catch, capture, etc. **2** afflict or trouble constantly: He was pursued by a long criminal record. **3** proceed along: pursue a southerly course. **4** engage in or carry on: pursue one's studies. **pursuer** *n* **pursuance** *n* (*formal*) the act of performing or carrying out: The officers were killed while in pursuance of their duties. **pursuit** *n* **1** an act of pursuing. **2** an activity or occupation: leisure pursuits. < ultimately Latin *prosequi*.

purvey (pəˈveɪ) *vb* (*formal*) (of traders) provide or supply (esp. food and provisions). **purveyor** *n* < ultimately Latin *providēre* to provide.

pus (pʌs) *n* a thick, yellow, semi-fluid substance produced by inflammation. < Latin.

push (pʊʃ) *vb* **1** exert force on (something) to move it away from the source of the force; thrust. **2** force one's way: The gatecrashers pushed through the front door. **3** cause (something) to change as the result of pressure or force: The poor harvest has pushed up the price of cereals. **4** (*informal*) urge or pressurize: They pushed him into applying for university. **5** speak or act in support of: He's always pushing the idea that we should all use bicycles. **6** promote the use, adoption, etc., of by aggressive methods. **7** (*informal*) act vigorously or aggressively to promote one's own ends: You've got to push if you want to get on in this world. **8** exert (oneself): You'll never finish the job if you don't push yourself. **9** (*informal*) sell (drugs, etc.) illegally. **10** (*informal*) approach in years: She must be pushing 40.
• *n* **1** (the force applied in) an act of pushing. **2** a vigorous effort: One more push and we'll reach the summit. **3** a military offensive: The second push took them into enemy

puritan

A person who is excessively fastidious about morals and sensual enjoyment is sometimes referred to as a puritan. The word puritan comes ultimately from the Late Latin *puritas* meaning 'purity'. It entered the language as the name of the 16th- and 17th-century Protestant group, *the Puritans,* who wished to purify the Church of England of all elaborate ceremonies and procedures which it regarded as Catholic. The Puritans were of the opinion that Elizabeth I's reformation of the church had not gone far enough.

In time the name came to be applied to anyone who was excessively strict in matters of morals and religion.

purple

The colour that is produced by mixing red and blue is known as purple. This derives ultimately from the Greek word *porphyra,* the name of a purple shellfish which was used by the Greeks in making purple dye. In time the application of the word shifted from the shellfish to the dye and then later from the dye to the colour.

territory. **4** (*informal*) drive or determination: We need a spokesman with a bit more push. **push-bike** (*informal*) *n* a pedal bicycle. **push-button** *adj, n* (worked by pushing) a button or knob which operates an electrical switch. **push-chair** *n* a folding carriage on wheels for transporting a small child. **pusher** *n* **1** a child's utensil for pushing food onto a spoon. **2** (*slang*) a person who sells drugs illegally. **pushing** *adj* excessively self-assertive. **push-up** *n* a press-up. **pushy** *adj* (*informal*) pushing. < ultimately Latin *pellere* to drive. SEE PANEL.

pusillanimous (ˌpjuːsɪˈlænɪməs) *adj* (*formal*) cowardly. **pusillanimity** *n*

at a push

Push features in a number of idiomatic expressions, including:

at a push if made necessary by special circumstances: At a push, we might be able to finish the work by Wednesday.

give/get the push to dismiss/be dismissed from a job.

push about or around to treat in a rough, bullying, or officious manner.

push along to leave: 'It's getting late—I think we'd better be pushing along soon.'

push off to go away; leave: 'Push off, will you! I'm fed up with you bothering me!'

push one's luck to take excessive risks.

push-over *n* **1** something that is easily done. **2** a person who is easily defeated, persuaded, or charmed.

putting up with it

Put features in a large number of idiomatic expressions, including:

hard put finding it difficult (to do something): You'll be hard put to get there by 6 o'clock.

put about to circulate (a rumour, etc.).

put across or **over 1** to communicate effectively. **2** to deceive or trick someone: put it across someone.

put away 1 to eat or drink. **2** to confine in a prison or mental hospital.

put back to move to a later time; postpone: The meeting has been put back by a week.

put by to save for future use.

put down 1 to record in writing. **2** to have (an animal) destroyed. **3** to humiliate or snub. **put-down** *n* **4** to suppress or subdue (a riot, etc.).

put down as to form an opinion of: We put him down as a complete fool.

put down to to attribute to: The success of the garden festival was put down to the extensive publicity it received.

put forward 1 to move to an earlier time. **2** to suggest or recommend.

put in 1 to submit: put in an application. **2** to spend (time) working. **3** to install: have central heating put in.

put off 1 to postpone. **2** to distract, discourage, or repel.

put on 1 to present or stage (a play, etc.). **2** to gain (weight). **3** to feign or assume (a particular emotion, etc.): She's not ill—she's just putting it on.

put out 1 to extinguish (a fire). **2** to inconvenience. **3** to disconcert. **4** to dislocate (a joint). **5** to issue (information).

put through 1 to subject to: The new train has been put through rigorous safety tests. **2** to connect by telephone.

put up 1 to increase the price of. **2** to construct or build. **3** to lend (money); advance: The bank are willing to put up the money. **4** to offer (resistance, etc.): They didn't put up much of a fight. **5** to receive or provide accommodation (for).

put-up *adj* fraudulently contrived: a put-up job.

put upon to trouble (someone) unreasonably: I hope you don't feel I'm putting upon you by asking for your help.

put up to to entice (someone) to (do something wrong).

put up with to tolerate: I can't put up with such behaviour any longer!

< Late Latin *pusillanimis,* from *pusillus* very small + *animus* spirit.

puss (pʊs) *n* (*informal*) a cat. **pussy** *n* (*chiefly children's informal*) a cat. **pussyfoot** *vb* (*often derogatory*) move or behave in a cautious or timid way. **pussy willow** any of a group of willows with grey, silky catkins. < origin unknown.

pustule (ˈpʌstjuːl) *n* an inflamed pimple containing pus. < Latin *pustula.*

put (pʊt) *vb* **put; putting 1** move and place in a certain position. **2** cause to be (in a certain state): Not even the accountant could put the books straight. **3** cause to be occupied in a certain way: Her parents have put her to the piano. **4** cause to experience, suffer, or undergo: You're not putting me to any trouble. **5** estimate: I would put the cost at about 30 pounds a head. **6** submit or present (a proposal, etc.): Some of the questions the group put to him were not easy to answer. **7** express or phrase: If you're asking for money, be sure to put it tactfully. **8** translate: How do you put it in German? **9** invest (money, etc.) in, spend (time) on: He's put half his savings into the firm. **10** bet or stake: I doubled what I put on the horse. **11** (of ships, etc.) move along a certain course: I watched the little fleet put to sea. **12** imagine or picture: Put yourself in my place! **13** heave (a shot) as far as one can.
• *n* a heave of a shot. < Middle English *putten.* SEE PANEL.

putative (ˈpjuːtətɪv) *adj* (*formal*) supposed or reputed: the putative father of the child. **putatively** *adv* < ultimately Latin *putare* to think.

putrefy (ˈpjuːtrɪˈfaɪ) *vb* **putrefied; putrefying** become or cause to become rotten or decayed. **putrefaction** *n* < ultimately Latin *putrefacere.*

putrid (ˈpjuːtrɪd) *adj* **1** decomposing (and usually giving off a foul smell). **2** obnoxious or foul: a putrid smell. **3** (*informal*) of very inferior quality: a putrid attempt. < Latin *putris* rotten.

putt (pʌt) *vb* strike (a golf ball) lightly so that it rolls towards or into the hole.
• *n* a putting stroke. **putter** *n* a golf-club used for putting. **putting-green** *n* a smooth area around the hole where the grass is kept short to facilitate putting. < *put.*

putty (ˈpʌtɪ) *n* a dough-like material used for fixing glass in window frames and stopping holes, etc. < French *potée* potful.

puzzle (ˈpʌzl̩) *vb* **1** perplex or bewilder. **2** think long and hard about; ponder. **3** discover a solution to.
• *n* **1** a person or thing that is hard to fathom or understand. **2** a problem or game that is designed to test one's capacity to fathom: a crossword puzzle. **puzzlement** *n* **puzzler** *n* < origin unknown.

pygmy (ˈpɪgmɪ) *n* a very short person; dwarf. **Pygmy** *n* a member of one of the dwarf tribes of equatorial Africa. < ultimately Greek *pygmaios* dwarfish.

pyjamas (pəˈdʒɑːməz) *pl n* a loose, lightweight suit for sleeping in. < Hindi *pājāma.* SEE PANEL.

pylon (ˈpaɪlən) *n* a tall steel framework used esp. for supporting overhead power cables. < Greek *pylē* gate.

pyramid (ˈpɪrəmɪd) *n* **1** a solid shape with a square base and sloping triangular sides that form an apex. **2** something that has such a shape, esp. one of the tombs built by the ancient Egyptians. **pyramidal** *adj* < ultimately Greek *pyramis.*

pyre (paɪə) *n* a structure of wood on

pyjamas

Loose-fitting nightwear comprising a lightweight jacket and trousers are known as pyjamas. This word entered the language in the early 19th century from the Hindi *pājāma.* This was the name of a pair of loose, lightweight, ankle-length trousers fastened by a string which were worn in the East by members of either sex. Travellers from England were quick to recognize the nightwear potential of the garment on account of the comfort and freedom of movement it provided.

The Hindi name derives from the Persian *pā* 'leg' and *jāma* 'garment'.

Pyrrhic victory

A Pyrrhic victory is a victory that is gained only at the expense of unjustifiably heavy losses. The reference is to the costly victory of *Pyrrhus* (king of Epirus) over the Romans at Asculum in 279 BC. The losses sustained by Pyrrhus were so great that he is recorded as saying 'One more such victory and Pyrrhus is undone'.

mighty python

A snake that winds itself round its prey and then crushes it by constriction is known as a python. This genus includes amongst its members the largest snakes in the world, a fact that is reflected in its name. Dating from the 16th century, python derives from the Latin *Python,* a huge monstrous serpent (*Pythōn* in Greek mythology) which was killed by Apollo.

which a corpse is placed and burnt as part of a funeral rite. < ultimately Greek *pyr* fire.

pyrotechnics (ˌpaɪrəʊˈtɛknɪks) *pl n* (a display of) fireworks. **pyrotechnic** *adj* of or like fireworks; spectacular. < French *pyrotechnique,* from Greek *pyr* fire + *technē* art.

Pyrrhic victory (ˈpɪrɪk) a victory gained at too great a cost. SEE PANEL.

python (ˈpaɪθən) *n* a large, non-poisonous snake that kills its prey by crushing it. SEE PANEL.

Q

QC *abbrev* Queen's Counsel.
QED *abbrev* (*Latin*) quod erat demonstrandum (which was to be proved).
quack[1] (kwæk) *n* the sound made by a duck.
• *vb* (of a duck) make this sound. < like the sound.
quack[2] *n* (*derogatory*) a person who falsely claims to have medical skill. **quackery** *n* **quackish** *adj* < *quacksalver* charlatan, from Dutch.
quad (kwɒd) *n* **1** a quadrangle. **2** one of a set of quadruplets.
quadrangle (ˈkwɒdræŋgḷ) *n* **1** a four-sided open area surrounded by buildings, esp. in the grounds of a school or college. **2** a quadrilateral. **quadrangular** *adj* < ultimately Late Latin *quadriangulum* figure with four corners.
quadrant (ˈkwɒdrənt) *n* **1** a quarter of (the circumference of) a circle. **2** an instrument for measuring angles, used in astronomy, navigation, etc. < Latin *quadrans* fourth part.
quadraphonic (ˌkwɒdrəˈfɒnɪk) *adj* (able to reproduce sound that has been) recorded through four separate channels to give the effect of directional sound. **quadraphonics** *n*
quadrilateral (ˌkwɒdrɪˈlætərəl) *n* a figure with four straight sides.
• *adj* having four sides. < Latin *quadri-* four + *latus* side.
quadruped (ˈkwɒdrʊˌpɛd) *n* an animal with four feet.
• *adj* having four feet. < Latin *quadri-* four + *pes* foot.
quadruple (ˈkwɒdrʊpḷ, kwɒˈdruːpḷ) *vb* **1** make or become four times as great: The number of unemployed has quadrupled.
• *adj* **1** four times as much or as many. **2** having four members, units, etc.: a quadruple alliance. < ultimately Latin *quadri-* four + *-plus* multiplied by.
quadruplet (ˈkwɒdrʊplɪt, kwɒˈdruːplɪt) *n* one of four children born of the same mother at the same time. < *quadruple.*
quaff (kwɒf) *vb* (*literary*) drink in great gulps. < origin unknown.
quagmire (ˈkwægˌmaɪə, ˈkwɒgˌmaɪə) *n* **1** an area of soft, wet, muddy ground. **2** (*informal*) a difficult predicament. < *quag* marsh + *mire.*
quail[1] (kweɪl) *n, pl* **quails, quail** a game bird of the partridge family. < ultimately Medieval Latin *quaccula.*
quail[2] *vb* flinch or draw back in fear. < ultimately Latin *coagulare* to curdle.
quaint (kweɪnt) *adj* old-fashioned or unusual but attractive. **quaintly** *adv* **quaintness** *n* < ultimately Latin *cognitus* known.
quake (kweɪk) *vb* **1** (of people) shake or tremble, esp. with fear. **2** (of the ground) shake or vibrate.
• *n* **1** a quaking movement. **2** (*informal*) an earthquake. < Old English *cwacian.*
qualify (ˈkwɒlɪˌfaɪ) *vb* **qualified; qualifying 1** make, become, or be eligible or fit for: Knowledge alone doesn't qualify you to teach. **2** make or become eligible to enter a contest, sporting event, etc., esp. through surpassing others or attaining a certain level of proficiency: Only three of the ten runners in the heat can qualify for the final. **3** restrict or modify, esp. in meaning or application. **4** describe or characterize as. **5** (*grammar*) (of a word or phrase) restrict the sense of another word or phrase. **qualifier** *n* **qualification** *n* **1** the act of qualifying. **2** a restriction or modification: Their agreement is not without certain qualifications. **3** something that makes a person eligible or fit for something: She wants to improve her qualifications. < Medieval Latin *qualificare.*
quality (ˈkwɒlɪtɪ) *n* **1** a trait or characteristic: His paintings show several distinctive qualities. **2** a level of excellence: The price depends on the quality. **3** excellence: quality rather than quantity. **qualitative** *adj* of or connected with quality: a qualitative difference. < ultimately Latin *qualis* of what kind.
qualm (kwɑːm) *n* **1** a feeling of doubt or uncertainty: He has no qualms at all about taking on extra work. **2** a pang of conscience: Don't you have any qualms about spending all your wife's savings? < origin unknown.
quandary (ˈkwɒndrɪ) *n* a state of perplexity. < origin unknown.
quango (ˈkwæŋgəʊ) *n, pl* **quangos** an autonomous administrative body appointed but not controlled by the government. < *qu*asi-*a*utonomous *n*on-*g*overnmental *o*rganization.
quantify (ˈkwɒntɪˌfaɪ) *vb* **quantified; quantifying** express as an amount. **quantifiable** *adj* < Latin *quantus* how much.
quantity (ˈkwɒntɪtɪ) *n* **1** an amount or portion. **2** a large amount: We seldom have such a quantity of wine in the house. **quantitative**

adj of or connected with quantity. **quantity surveyor** a person who estimates the quantities and costs of building materials. < SEE **QUANTIFY.**

quantum (ˈkwɒntəm) *n, pl* **quanta** the smallest amount, esp. the smallest indivisible unit of energy. < Latin: how much.

quarantine (ˈkwɒrənˌtiːn) *n* (a period of) isolation imposed on people or animals for the sake of preventing the spread of contagious disease.
• *vb* place in quarantine. SEE PANEL.

quarrel (ˈkwɒrəl) *n* **1** an argument or heated disagreement. **2** a cause for complaint or bad feelings towards someone: I have no quarrel with him.
• *vb* **quarrelled; quarrelling 1** engage in a quarrel; argue. **2** disagree or find fault with: I'm not quarrelling with the decision. **quarrelsome** *adj* inclined to quarrel. < ultimately Latin *queri* to complain.

quarry[1] (ˈkwɒrɪ) *n* a large, open pit from which stone, sand, etc., has been or is being excavated.
• *vb* extract (stone, etc.) from a quarry. < ultimately Latin *quadrum* square.

quarry[2] *n* **1** a person or animal that is hunted or pursued, esp. the prey of a predator. **2** any object of a search or pursuit. < Middle English *querre* entrails offered to the hounds. SEE PANEL.

quart (kwɔːt) *n* a measure of liquid capacity (in the UK 1.136 litres, USA 0.946 litres). < ultimately Latin *quartus* fourth.

quarter (ˈkwɔːtə) *n* **1** one of four equal parts or corresponding parts into which something is divided: an hour and a quarter. **2** a quarter of an hour: a quarter to five. **3** one of the four three-month periods into which the year is divided: We pay for our gas by the quarter. **4** a measurement of weight (in the UK 12.7 kg, USA 11.34 kg). **5** (*US and Canada*) (a coin worth) 25 cents (a quarter of a dollar). **6** an area within a city or town; district: Montmartre is in the Latin quarter. **7** (*formal*) an unidentified person, group, or place, esp. considered as a source: Help soon arrived from all quarters. **8** a direction or point of the compass: In summer visitors descend on the resort from all quarters. **9** (*formal*) mercy or clemency: The opposition were shown no quarter by the home team. **10** a leg and the adjacent area of a four-legged animal. **11** one of the four stages of the moon's monthly cycle.
• *vb* **1** cut or divide into quarters. **2** reduce to one quarter of the original amount: We've managed to quarter the time it usually takes. **3** provide (a soldier, etc.) with lodgings; billet.
• *adj* being one of four equal or approximately equal parts, **quarter-final** *n* the second to last round before the final of a knock-out competition. **quarter-finalist** *n* **quarter-light** *n* a small, usually triangular side-window in a motor vehicle. **quarters** *pl n* lodgings or accommodation. < ultimately Latin *quartus* fourth.

quarterly (ˈkwɔːtəlɪ) *adj, adv* produced, happening, payable, etc., every three months: a quarterly bill.
• *n* a periodical that is published every three months.

quartermaster (ˈkwɔːtəˌmɑːstə) *n* **1** an army officer responsible for food, clothing, quartering, etc. **2** a naval officer with navigational and signalling duties.

quartet (kwɔːˈtɛt) *n* **1** (a musical composition for) a group of four different instruments or voices. **2** any group or set of four. < SEE **QUARTER.**

quarto (ˈkwɔːtəʊ) *n, pl* **quartos 1** (the size of) a sheet of paper produced by

quarantine

Quarantine is the name given to the isolation imposed on people, animals, and plants in order to prevent the spread of infectious disease. The length of the period of isolation varies according to the incubation period of the suspected disease. However, according to the etymology of the word, the isolation period should last 40 days. Quarantine comes from the Italian word *quarantina* 'a period of 40 days', which derives ultimately from the Latin word for 40 *quadraginta*.

quarry

An animal that is pursued by a hunter or predator is sometimes referred to as a quarry This is a development of the Middle English word *querre* meaning 'the entrails of a beast that were given to the hounds as a reward'. *Querre* comes from the Middle French *cuiree* or 'what is placed on the hide', from the Old French word for hide, *cuir*. The root is the Latin *cor* or 'heart'.

folding a standard-sized sheet twice and then cutting along the folds. **2** a book with pages of this size. < SEE **QUARTER.**

quartz (kwɔːts) *n* a very common hard mineral consisting of silicon dioxide, often in the form of hexagonal crystals. • *adj* worked by the vibrations of a special type of quartz crystal that has been prepared in a certain way. < German *Quarz.*

quash (kwɒʃ) *vb* **1** reject or nullify: The jury's verdict was later quashed. **2** suppress or subdue: The military were quick to quash the rebellion. < ultimately Latin *cassus* void.

quasi- (ˈkwɑːzɪ, ˈkweɪzaɪ) *prefix* in outward appearance only; to some extent but not wholly: a quasi-vegetarian diet. < Latin *quasi* as it were.

quaver (ˈkweɪvə) *vb* **1** shake or tremble. **2** say in a trembling voice. • *n* **1** a quavering sound. **2** a note in music lasting half as long as a crotchet. < Middle English *quaven* to tremble.

quay (kiː) *n* a landing place used for loading and unloading ships. **quayside** *n* an area being used as or adjacent to a quay. < ultimately of Celtic origin.

queasy (ˈkwiːzɪ) *adj* **1** feeling slightly nauseous. **2** reticent or squeamish. **queasiness** *n* < Middle English *coysy.*

queen (kwiːn) *n* **1** a female monarch, usually inheriting her position by right of succession. **2** the wife of a king. **3** a woman or thing regarded as being in some respect without equal. **4** the chess-piece with the most power, able to move in any direction over any number of vacant squares. **5** a playing-card showing the picture of a queen. **6** the only egg-laying female in a colony of bees, ants, etc. **7** (*slang derogatory*) an aging male homosexual. • *vb* (*chess*) (of a pawn) be converted to a queen after reaching the opponent's end of the board. **queen it** (*informal*) behave in an imperious manner. **queenly** *adj* of, resembling, or befitting a queen. **queenliness** *n* < Old English *cwēn.*

queer (kwɪə) *adj* **1** odd or unusual; eccentric. **2** suspicious or unsettling: queer goings-on. **3** (*informal*) slightly ill. **4** (*informal derogatory*) homosexual. • *n* (*informal derogatory*) a homosexual. **queerly** *adv* **queerness** *n* **in Queer Street** (*informal*) in (financial) difficulties. **queer someone's pitch** (*informal*) spoil someone's plans or chances of success. < perhaps German *quer* oblique. SEE PANEL.

quell (kwɛl) *vb* **1** calm or pacify: quell someone's fears. **2** subdue or suppress: quell a rebellion. < Old English *cwellan* to kill.

quench (kwɛntʃ) *vb* **1** drink and satisfy (one's thirst). **2** extinguish. < Old English *acwencan.*

querulous (ˈkwɛrʊləs, ˈkwɛrjʊləs) *adj* habitually complaining. **querulously** *adv* **querulousness** *n* < Latin *queri* to complain.

query (ˈkwɪərɪ) *n* **1** a question, esp. one arising from doubt. **2** a question mark. • *vb* **queried; querying 1** express doubt about the accuracy of. **2** (*literary*) ask. < Latin *quaerere* to ask.

quest (kwɛst) *n* a search or pursuit. • *vb* (*literary*) search for. < ultimately Latin *quaestus.*

question (ˈkwɛstʃən) *n* **1** a stretch of language, esp. a sentence, which requires an answer. **2** a problem set as (part of) a test, examination, etc. **3** a matter or issue: We have to consider the question of expenditure. **4** doubt or dispute: That we shall win is beyond question. • *vb* **1** put questions to: Police spent an hour questioning him. **2** express doubt about the accuracy of; query. **questioner** *n* **in question** under discussion or consideration. **out of the question** preposterous; unthinkable. **questionable** *adj* **1** open to doubt; uncertain. **2** morally dubious or suspect: I'd say that their motives are highly questionable. **questionably** *adv* **question mark** the punctuation mark ? used to indicate a question. **questionnaire** *n* list of questions used in data gathering. < ultimately Latin *quaerere* to ask.

queue (kjuː) *n* a line of people, vehicles, etc., waiting for something. • *vb* wait in a queue. < French: tail.

quibble (ˈkwɪbl̩) *n* a minor objection. • *vb* make minor objections; equivocate.

in Queer Street

To be in Queer Street is to be in a difficult situation, especially one of financial embarrassment: After investing heavily in tin, the market went dead and he ended up in Queer Street. The origin of this phrase, which dates from about the beginning of the 19th century, is uncertain. It is believed to derive from the tradesman's practice of putting a question mark or *query* alongside the names of those who were considered financially suspect.

< origin uncertain.

quiche (ki:ʃ) *n* a pastry shell with a savoury filling. < ultimately German *Kuchen* a cake.

quick (kwɪk) *adj* **1** done, happening, etc., in a short time: a quick lunch. **2** marked by speed or rapidity: a quick walker. speed. **4** (of temper) easily aroused.
• *adv* in a quick manner.
• *n* highly sensitive flesh, esp. that covered by the nails. **quickly** *adv* **quickness** *n* **quicken** *vb* **1** make or become quicker. **2** stimulate or become stimulated. **3** reach the stage in pregnancy when movement of the foetus can be felt. **quickie** *n* (*informal*) something done in a hurry. **quicklime** *n* lime. **quicksand** *n* a mass or area of loose, wet sand. **quicksilver** *n* mercury. **quickstep** *n* (a musical composition for) a type of fast ballroom dance. **quick-witted** *adj* quick in understanding; sharp. < Old English *cwic* alive. SEE PANEL.

quid (kwɪd) *n, pl* **quid** (*slang*) a pound sterling (£1). **quids in** (*slang*) in a position that shows a profit. < origin uncertain.

quid pro quo (ˌkwɪd prəʊ ˈkwəʊ) one thing in return for another. < Latin: something for something.

quiet (ˈkwaɪət) *adj* **1** making or marked by little or no noise: I wish they'd be quiet! **2** of low volume: She has a rather quiet voice. **3** with little movement or activity: Business has been very quiet this week. **4** with little disturbance; peaceful. **5** (of colours, designs, etc.) subdued. **6** not openly expressed: quiet gratitude.
• *n* absence of noise and activity; tranquillity: peace and quiet. **quietly** *adv* **quietness** *n* **on the quiet** without people knowing. **quieten** *vb* make or become quiet. < ultimately Latin *quietus*.

cut to the quick

A person who is cut to the quick is one whose feelings have been deeply hurt. The expression provides an illustration of the original meaning of quick, which comes from the Old English adjective *cwic* or 'alive'. A cut which penetrates the quick is one which goes through the skin and enters the painfully sensitive living flesh, as found beneath the nails.

quiff (kwɪf) *n* a lock of hair that stands up above the forehead. < origin unknown.

quill (kwɪl) *n* **1** a large wing or tail feather. **2** (formerly) a pen made from this. **3** one of the spines of a hedgehog, porcupine, etc. **4** the hollow stem of a feather. < Middle English *quil* hollow reed.

quilt (kwɪlt) *n* **1** a thick, padded bed-cover. **2** any bed-cover.
• *vb* pad and stitch like a quilt. < ultimately Latin *culcita* mattress.

quince (kwɪns) *n* **1** a hard, yellow, pear-like fruit widely used for making preserves. **2** the tree that bears this. < ultimately *kydōnia* Cydonia, ancient city in Crete.

quinine (ˈkwɪni:n) *n* a bitter-tasting drug that was formerly widely used in the treatment of malaria. < Spanish *quina* cinchona bark.

quintessence (kwɪnˈtɛsəns) *n* **1** a perfect example or representation of something. **2** the essence of something in a totally pure form. **quintessential** *adj* **quintessentially** *adv* < ultimately Medieval Latin *quinta essentia* the fifth essence.

quintet (kwɪnˈtɛt) *n* **1** (a musical composition for) a group of five different instruments or voices. **2** any group or set of five. < ultimately Latin *quintus* fifth.

quip (kwɪp) *n* a quick, witty, or sarcastic remark.
• *vb* **quipped; quipping** make a quip. < origin uncertain.

quire (kwaɪə) *n* 24 sheets of paper of the same size and quality. < ultimately Latin *quater* four times.

quirk (kwɜ:k) *n* **1** a peculiarity of behaviour or manner. **2** an unexpected happening; accident: a quirk of fate. **quirky** *adj* < origin unknown.

quit (kwɪt) *vb* **quit, quitted; quitting** **1** resign from or give up: quit one's job. **2** leave or depart from: They were ordered to quit the building. **3** cease doing something, often in defeat: He quit smoking a year ago. **quitter** *n* a person who gives up easily. < ultimately Latin *quietus* at rest.

quite (kwaɪt) *adv, determiner* **1** completely; entirely: I quite agree. **2** fairly; somewhat: quite expensive. **3** used emphatically, esp. in expressions of approval: That was quite a meal! **4** quite so. **quite a few** a fairly large number. **quite so** (*formal*) used to express total agreement with someone's previous assertion: 'He needs to work harder.'—'Quite so.' < Middle English quite quit.

quits (kwɪts) *adj* on even terms after an

quixotic

A person who is possessed by the impractical pursuit of lofty ideals is sometimes referred to as quixotic. This word derives from the name of Don *Quixote*, the hero of the novel 'Don Quixote de la Mancha' by the Spanish writer Miguel de Cervantes Saavedra, 1547–1616. Don Quixote is a gaunt country gentleman helplessly infatuated with the noble-minded ideals that he has come across in his reading of chivalric romances. His unflagging pursuit of them in the company of his double, the pot-bellied, down-to-earth Sancho Panza, produces a series of absurd, rough and tumble encounters with reality. See also panel at **wind[1].**

act of repayment or retaliation. **call it quits** agree that things are even or settled. < origin uncertain.

quiver[1] (ˈkwɪvə) *n* a narrow case for arrows. < Old French *cuivre.*

quiver[2] *vb* tremble or shake: quiver with fear.
• *n* a quivering sound or motion.
< Middle English *quiveren,* probably from *quiver* quick.

quixotic (kwɪkˈsɒtɪk) *adj* idealistic or chivalrous to an impractical degree. SEE PANEL.

quiz (kwɪz) *n, pl* **quizzes** a form of entertainment in which the knowledge of contestants is tested by a series of questions.
• *vb* **quizzed; quizzing** question closely. **quizzical** *adj* **1** showing puzzlement or non-comprehension. **2** gently mocking or teasing. < origin uncertain. SEE PANEL.

quoit (kɔɪt) *n* a ring of rubber, metal, etc., used in quoits. **quoits** *pl n* a game in which quoits are tossed to land on an upright peg. < Middle English *coite.*

quiz

The origin of the word quiz is uncertain. It is accredited by some sources to a Dublin theatre manager by the name of Daly. The latter reputedly bet a friend in 1780 that he would introduce a new word into the language within 24 hours. Once the wager was laid Daly proceeded to have the word painted and chalked up on every available wall in the city. The mystery word became animmediate talking-point. As a consequence, Daly won his bet and the language was said to have acquired a new word.

quorum (ˈkwɔːrəm) *n* the smallest number of people required to be present at a meeting before any business can be transacted. < ultimately Latin *qui* who.

quota (ˈkwəʊtə) *n* **1** a fixed share or proportion (of something) that is allotted to a person or group. **2** a numerical upper limit or ceiling: an import quota. < Latin *quota pars* how great a part.

quote (kwəʊt) *vb* **1** repeat or copy exactly (something that has been said or written). **2** cite as proof or as an example. **3** give an estimate of (the price of goods, labour, etc.). **4** state (the price of a commodity).
• *adv* a word used in speech to show that what follows is a quotation.
• *n* a quotation. **quotation** *n* **1** something quoted. **2** quoting; being quoted. **3** an estimate. **4** a statement of the price of a commodity. **quotation marks** single or double inverted commas (' ' or " ") used to indicate a quotation.
< ultimately Latin *quot* how many.

quotient (ˈkwəʊʃənt) *n* the result obtained when one number is divided by another. < Latin *quot* how many.

R

rabbi (ˈræbaɪ) *n* a Jewish spiritual leader. **rabbinical** *adj* of or connected with rabbis. < Hebrew *rabbi* my master, from *rabh* master + *-ī* my.

rabbit (ˈræbɪt) *n* **1** a long-eared, burrowing animal, often kept as a pet. **2** its fur. **3** its meat used as food.
• *vb* **1** hunt for rabbits. **2** (*informal*) talk in a rambling, inconsequential way. < origin uncertain. SEE PANEL.

rabble (ˈræbl̩) *n* **1** a disorderly crowd. **2** (*derogatory*) the common people. < Middle English *rabel* pack of animals.

rabid (ˈræbɪd, ˈreɪbɪd) *adj* **1** highly enthusiastic; fanatical: a rabid supporter. **2** suffering from rabies. **rabidly** *adv* < Latin *rabidus* mad, from *rabere* to rave.

rabies (ˈreɪbiːz) *n* a fatal infectious disease of the central nervous system, chiefly affecting dogs, but sometimes transmitted to man by the bite of an infected animal. < Latin: madness, from *rabere* to rave.

race[1] (reɪs) *n* **1** a contest of speed. **2** a competition or contest: The race for the championship is hotting up. **3** a rapid current of water. **4** a groove in which the balls of a ball-bearing roll around.
• *vb* **1** participate or compete with in a race. **2** run, drive, etc., at full speed: race after a bus. **3** work or cause to work, operate, move, etc., at top speed. **racer** *n* **racecourse** *n* **1** a broad grass track on which horse-races are run. **2** this track and its surroundings. **racehorse** *n* a horse bred for racing. **race-meeting** *n* a public event at which a series of horse-races or greyhound races are held. **the races** a race-meeting. < Old Norse *rās*.

race[2] *n* **1** a major division of mankind whose members share common characteristics. **2** a group of people sharing common ancestry. **3** a group of animals or plants with common characteristics. **racial** *adj* **1** characteristic of a particular race: racial features. **2** of or connected with relations between different races: racial prejudice. **racially** *adv* **racialism** also **racism** *n* **1** a belief in the superiority of one race over another. **2** prejudice against a person on the grounds of his or her race. **racialist** also **racist** *n* a person who believes in or practises racialism. < ultimately Old Italian *razza*.

rack (ræk) *n* **1** a framework or shelf-like structure for storing or displaying things on: a shoe rack. **2** (formerly) an instrument of torture on which a person's body was stretched. **3** a bar with teeth along one edge which engage with those on the outside of a wheel.
• *vb* cause to suffer (pain, torment, etc.): She was racked with uncertainty. **rack one's brains** think very hard.
• *n* **rack and ruin** a state of total ruin or collapse that is caused by neglect: The business has gone to rack and ruin. < probably Middle Dutch *rec* framework.

racket[1] (ˈrækɪt) also **racquet** *n* a bat with interlaced strings used in tennis, badminton, etc. **rackets** *pl* a game similar to squash. < ultimately Arabic *rāhah* palm of the hand. SEE PANEL.

racket[2] *n* **1** a commotion or din.

Welsh rabbit or rarebit?

The original name given to melted cheese on toast was Welsh rabbit. At the time when it was coined, this phrase contained a wry allusion to the fact that only the very wealthy could afford to eat game. Cheese on toast was humorously upheld as the poor man's equivalent.

In time the socio-economic significance of rabbit became lost. Under the influence of *folk etymology,* whereby an unfamiliar form slowly acquires the form of one that is more familiar, the variant Welsh rarebit came into circulation. The two phrases now exist side by side, although hoteliers and other caterers show a distinct preference for the latter.

---

racket

The instrument used for striking the ball in games such as tennis, badminton, and squash is known as a racket. This word derives via the Middle French *raquette* and Italian *racchetta* from the Arabic *rāhah* meaning 'palm of the hand'.

---

2 (*informal*) a dishonest or illegal means of making money: the drugs racket. **3** (*informal*) an occupation or means of livelihood: What sort of racket is he in? **racketeer** *n* a person who operates a dishonest business. **racketeering** *n* < probably like the sound.

raconteur (ˌrækɒnˈtɜː) *n* a person with skill in telling stories or anecdotes. < French.

racy (ˈreɪsɪ) *adj* **1** spirited or vigorous. **2** suggestive or risqué. **racily** *adv* **raciness** *n* < *race*².

radar (ˈreɪdɑː) *n* **1** a system used for detecting the location of an object by means of high-frequency radio waves. **2** a device that employs this system. SEE PANEL.

radial (ˈreɪdɪəl) *adj* spreading outwards from a central point.
● *n* **1** a radial line or part. **2** a radial-ply tyre. **radially** *adv* **radial-ply tyre** a pneumatic tyre whose ply cords run at right angles to the centre of tread. < SEE **RADIATE**.

radiant (ˈreɪdɪənt) *adj* **1** sending out rays of light. **2** emanating joy or happiness: a radiant smile. **3** (of heat, energy, etc.) emitted by radiation. **radiance** *n* **radiantly** *adv* < SEE **RADIATE.**

detecting **radar**

Long names consisting of several words are sometimes too much of a mouthful and consequently give rise to short forms. Such was the case with *ra*dio *d*etecting *a*nd *r*anging, nowadays simply radar. A short form like radar that combines the initial letters of the full form is known as an *acronym*.

Unlike radar, a large number of acronyms are pronounced as sequences of letters: FBI, UN, EEC, and COD are examples. Nobody, for instance, would say Do you want to pay *cod?* (rhyming with God). The pronunciation of COD is see oh dee. When pronounced as a sequence of letters, a word is obviously an acronym and continues to be recognized as such. When pronounced as a word, however, an acronym is less recognizable, and therefore like radar its origin tends to slip more quickly from memory. Laser (*l*ightwave *a*mplification by *s*timulated *e*mission of *r*adiation) and sonar (*so*und *na*vigation *r*anging) also belong to this group.

radiate (ˈreɪdɪˌeɪt) *vb* **1** spread outwards from a central point. **2** send out rays of (light, heat, etc.). **3** display or exude: She radiates health and contentment. **radiation** *n* **1** the act of radiating. **2** rays or particles that are radiated, esp. those deriving from radioactive sources. **radiator** *n* **1** an appliance that radiates heat. **2** an apparatus that cools an engine in a motor vehicle by means of water circulation. < ultimately Latin *radius* ray.

radical (ˈrædɪkl̩) *adj* **1** basic or fundamental: a radical fault. **2** thorough or drastic: radical changes. **3** favouring major social, political, or economic changes; extremist.
● *n* a person who holds radical views. **radicalism** *n* **radically** *adv* < Latin *radix* root.

radio (ˈreɪdɪəʊ) *n, pl* **radios 1** the sending of signals by means of electromagnetic radiation. **2** an apparatus for sending or receiving such signals; wireless. **3** sound broadcasting.
● *vb* send a signal by radio. **radiogram** *n* a piece of furniture housing a radio and record-player. < *radiotelegraphy*.

radioactivity (ˌreɪdɪəʊækˈtɪvɪtɪ) *n* the property possessed by uranium and certain other elements of having atoms which emit alpha and beta particles and gamma rays upon disintegration. **radioactive** *adj* **radioactively** *adv*

radiography (ˌreɪdɪˈɒgrəfɪ) *n* the production of X-ray or gamma-ray photographs. **radiographer** *n*

radiology (ˌreɪdɪˈɒlədʒɪ) *n* the study and use of X-rays and other forms of radiation, esp. for medical purposes. **radiologist** *n*

radiotherapy (ˌreɪdɪəʊˈθɛrəpɪ) *n* the treatment of cancer and allied diseases by the use of X-rays and other forms of radiation. **radiotherapist** *n*

radish (ˈrædɪʃ) *n* any of a group of plants with a hot-tasting, red-skinned root which is usually eaten raw in salads; its root. < ultimately Latin *radix* root.

radius (ˈreɪdɪəs) *n, pl* **radii, radiuses 1** a straight line reaching from the centre of a circle or sphere to its circumference or surface. **2** the length of such a line. **3** a circular area whose size is expressed in terms of its radius: Police quickly set up road blocks within a 10-mile radius. **4** the shorter of the two bones in the forearm. < Latin.

RAF *abbrev* Royal Air Force.

raffia (ˈræfɪə) *n* fibre from a type of palm-tree, used for making baskets, mats, etc. < Malagasy *rafia*.

raffle (ˈræfl̩) *n* a form of lottery, often a

means of raising money for charity.
• *vb* dispose of in a raffle. < Middle English: game played with dice.

raft (rɑːft) *n* a floating structure consisting of lengths of timber tied together in a row, used as a type of boat or platform. < Old Norse *raptr* rafter.

rafter (ˈrɑːftə) *n* one of the sloping timbers forming the framework of a roof. < Old English *ræfter.*

rag[1] (ræɡ) *n* **1** a piece of old or worn cloth, usually torn from a discarded garment. **2** rags considered collectively: You could always stuff it with rag. **3** (*derogatory*) a newspaper: the local rag. **ragged** *adj* **1** damaged or torn from use; tattered. **2** wearing tattered clothes. **3** faulty or unpolished: a ragged performance. **raggedly** *adv* **raggedness** *n* **rag-and-bone man** a dealer in discarded items, traditionally associated with a horse and cart. **rag-bag** *n* a miscellaneous assortment or collection. < ultimately Old Norse *rögg* shagginess.

rag[2] *n* a piece of ragtime music. < *ragtime.*

rag[3] *vb* **ragged; ragging** tease or play practical jokes on.
• *n* **1** a practical joke. **2** an annual event at a college or university, usually of about a week's duration, when students perform various stunts to raise money for charity. < origin unknown.

ragamuffin (ˈræɡəˌmʌfɪn) *n* (*old-fashioned*) a ragged and unkempt person, esp. a child. SEE PANEL.

rage (reɪdʒ) *n* **1** (an outburst of) violent anger. **2** a highly popular fashion; craze: Did you know that plastic hair has become all the rage?
• *vb* **1** show violent anger. **2** (of a storm, wind, etc.) continue violently. < ultimately Latin *rabere* to be mad.

raglan (ˈræɡlən) *adj* (of a sleeve) having diagonal seams that run from the underarm to the neck.
• *n* a coat with raglan sleeves. SEE PANEL.

ragout (ræˈɡuː, ˈræɡuː) *n* a meat and vegetable stew. < French *ragoût,* from *ragoûter* to revive the taste.

ragtime (ˈræɡˌtaɪm) *n* a style of jazz music with a syncopated rhythm, developed around 1900 by American Negroes. < probably *ragged* + *time.*

raid (reɪd) *n* **1** a sudden, short attack or incursion; foray. **2** an attack for the purpose of robbery: a bank raid. **3** a surprise descent by police.
• *vb* make a raid. **raider** *n* < Old English *rād.*

rail[1] (reɪl) *n* **1** a horizontal bar of timber, metal, etc., that runs along the top of vertical supports, as in fencing. **2** a horizontal bar on which things are hung: a clothes rail. **3** either of the two lengths of steel which form a railway track. **4** the railway: travel by rail.
• *vb* enclose with rails. < ultimately Latin *regere* to keep straight.

rail[2] *vb* (*formal*) complain bitterly about or utter abuse at. < ultimately Late Latin *ragere* to yell.

railing (ˈreɪlɪŋ) *n* (one of a series of vertical bars forming) a fence or barrier.

railroad (ˈreɪlˌrəʊd) *n* (*US*) a railway.
• *vb* **1** force or push through hastily, esp. without allowing time for consideration. **2** pressurize (a person) into hasty action; hustle.

railway (ˈreɪlˌweɪ) *n* **1** a track consisting of two parallel steel rails for vehicles with flanged wheels, esp. trains. **2** a system of transport that uses trains. **railwayman** *n*

rain (reɪn) *n* **1** drops of water which fall from clouds; shower of these. **2** (a period of) rainy weather. **3** rain-water. **4** a steady flow or stream; torrent.
• *vb* **1** (of rain) to fall. **2** (*formal*) fall or cause to fall like rain: Bombs rained down on the city day after day. **be rained off** be cancelled because of rain. **rainbow** *n* a multi-coloured arc formed in the sky when rain and sunshine occur

ragamuffin

A child who always looks ragged and unkempt is sometimes described as a ragamuffin. This word derives from *Ragamoffyn,* a demon in the poem 'The Vision of Piers the Plowman' by the 14th-century English poet, William Langland.

raglan

A type of sleeve that extends all the way up to the neck—thereby covering the shoulder—is known as a raglan. The term derives from Fitzroy James Henry Somerset, 1788–1855, otherwise known as Lord *Raglan*. In addition to being commander-in-chief of British forces during the Crimean War, Raglan was the first public figure to wear a coat with sleeves of this design.

simultaneously. **rain cats and dogs** rain very heavily. **raincoat** *n* a coat which affords protection against rain. **rainfall** *n* the total amount of rain falling on a particular area during a given period. **rain forest** a dense tropical forest with a heavy rainfall. **rain-water** *n* water that has come from clouds. **rainy** *adj* characterized by continuous rain or many outbreaks of rain. **save for a rainy day** save for a future period of need or hardship. < Old English *rēn.*

raise (reɪz) *vb* **1** move to a higher or upright position. **2** make the uppermost edge or point of (something) higher: I need to raise the wall another inch. **3** increase: They've raised the prices. **4** grow or breed: raise pigs. **5** bring up or rear: raise a family. **6** introduce or put forward for consideration: raise a question. **7** build or erect: raise a monument. **8** collect or gather: His job is to raise funds for charity. **9** cause or provoke: Not one of his jokes raised a laugh. **10** enliven or invigorate: You need a long holiday to raise your spirits.
• *n* (*chiefly US*) an increase in wages or salary; rise. **raise hell** also **raise Cain** (*informal*) **1** complain angrily and noisily. **2** make an uproar. < Old Norse *reisa.*

raisin (ˈreɪzn̩) *n* a dried grape. < ultimately Latin *racemus* cluster of grapes. SEE PANEL AT **CURRANT.**

raison d'être (ˌreɪzɒn ˈdɛtrə, ˌrɛzɒn ˈdɛtrə) *n* the reason for or justification for something's existence. < French.

raj (rɑːdʒ) *n* the period of British rule in India. **rajah** *n* **1** (formerly) an Indian ruler. **2** a Malay or Javanese prince. < Hindi *rāj.*

rake[1] (reɪk) *n* **1** a long-handled garden tool with a comb-like head for levelling soil, gathering leaves, etc. **2** any similar tool or implement.
• *vb* **1** level or gather with a rake. **2** examine (a room, container, etc.) in search of something. **3** direct or strike along the length of: The trenches were raked with machine-gun fire. **rake in** (*informal*) gain or earn (a lot of money). **rake-off** *n* (*informal*) a share of profits; commission. **rake up** seek out and bring to light: Where do these reporters go to rake up so many scandals? < Old English *racu.*

rake[2] *n* a backward slope or slant; degree of this.
• *vb* slope or cause to slope. < origin unknown.

rake[3] *n* a man of immoral character. < archaic *rakehell.*

rally (ˈrælɪ) *vb* **rallied; rallying 1** come or bring together for a common purpose or enterprise: Loyal supporters rallied round the party banner. **2** (esp. of troops) reassemble or regroup for renewed effort. **3** improve or recover strength after illness. **4** regain lost value: The dollar rallied briefly just before the close of trading.
• *n* **1** a mass meeting or demonstration. **2** a meeting at which a competition, etc., is held: a car rally. **3** a series of exchanges in tennis, badminton, etc., before a point is scored. **4** an act of rallying; recovery. < Old French *re-* again + *alier* to join, ally.

ram (ræm) *n* **1** an uncastrated male sheep. **2** a battering-ram. **3** any of various solid structures or devices used for battering or striking forcefully.
• *vb* **rammed; ramming 1** strike with a heavy blow. **2** force (something) down or in. **3** stuff or cram. **4** crash into (a vehicle), esp. in order to demobilize it. < Old English *ramm.*

ramble (ˈræmbl̩) *vb* **1** stroll or wander along a winding course. **2** speak in an incoherent or confused way.
• *n* a long, leisurely walk without a fixed route. **rambler** *n* **1** any of various climbing roses. **2** a person who takes country walks. < origin uncertain.

ramification (ˌræmɪfɪˈkeɪʃən) *n* **1** a consequence or effect. **2** a part of a complex system or network. < ultimately Latin *ramus* branch.

ramp (ræmp) *n* **1** a slope connecting two different levels. **2** a movable stairway used for entering or leaving an aircraft. < French *ramper* to crawl.

rampage (ræmˈpeɪdʒ, ˈræmpeɪdʒ) *vb* rush about excitedly and violently.
• *n* (ˈræmpeɪdʒ) excited and violent behaviour: on the rampage. < Scottish.

rampant (ˈræmpənt) *adj* **1** spreading freely without restraint: a rampant disease. **2** showing or known for extremism: a rampant feminist. **3** (*heraldry*) (of an animal) rearing up on the hind legs. < Middle French *ramper* to rear.

rampart (ˈræmpɑːt) *n* a broad embankment (and the wall which it supports), built in olden days as a fortification. < Middle French *remparer* to fortify.

ramrod (ˈræmˌrɒd) *n* (formerly) a rod used for ramming a charge down the barrel of a muzzle-loading gun.

ramshackle (ˈræmˌʃækl̩) *adj* (esp. of buildings) collapsing or in need of repair; rickety. < *ransack.*

ran (ræn) SEE **RUN.**

ranch (rɑːntʃ) *n* **1** large farm esp. in North America where cattle and other livestock are bred. **2** (*chiefly US*) a farm where a particular type of livestock or crop is bred or grown. **rancher** *n* < Mexican Spanish *rancho.*

rancid (ˈrænsɪd) *adj* (tasting or smelling) stale or rank. **rancidness** *n* < Latin *rancēre* to be rancid.

rancour (ˈræŋkə) *n* profound ill will or resentment. **rancorous** *adj* **rancorously** *adv* < SEE **RANCID.**

random (ˈrændəm) *adj* done or made without a plan or order; haphazard: a random selection.
• *n* **at random** haphazardly. **randomly** *adv* **randomness** *n* < Old French *randir* to gallop.

randy (ˈrændɪ) *adj* (*informal*) having a strong sexual appetite. **randily** *adv* **randiness** *n* < probably obsolete *rand* to rant.

rang (ræŋ) SEE **RING**[2]**.**

range (reɪndʒ) *n* **1** the extent to which something may vary or operate: a vocal range of three octaves. **2** a series of things in a line or row: a range of mountains. **3** the maximum distance over which something can travel or operate effectively: The gun has a range of 600 metres. **4** the distance between a missile and a target: at close range. **5** an area used for shooting-practice: a rifle range. **6** a vast, unfenced tract of land where cattle, etc., graze, esp. in North America. **7** an old-fashioned type of stove, often incorporated in a fireplace.
• *vb* **1** place or be situated in a row or other formation. **2** vary within specified limits: Their ages range from 3 to 5. **3** extend, stretch, or reach. **4** roam or wander without restraint. **range-finder** *n* a device for ascertaining the distance of an object or target: a range-finder camera. **ranger** *n* a warden who looks after a park or forest. < Old French *rengier* to range.

rank[1] (ræŋk) *n* **1** a row or line of people or things. **2** a place where taxis wait to be hired. **3** a position in a scale of importance or status: the rank of brigadier. **4** a high position or status: people of rank. **the ranks** the rank and file.
• *vb* **1** assign or have a particular rank or status: He ranks as one of the world's greatest entertainers. **2** arrange in a rank or other formation. **the rank and file** the main body of a group or organization as opposed to those in charge. < Middle French *renc.*

rank[2] *adj* **1** (having a smell or flavour which is) highly offensive. **2** (of a garden, etc.) covered or carpeted with: a garden rank with weeds. **3** complete or total; utter: a rank outsider. **4** unmistakable; out-and-out: rank disobedience. **rankly** *adv* **rankness** *n* < Old English *ranc* overbearing.

rankle (ˈræŋkl̩) *vb* cause to feel lasting annoyance or resentment. < Middle English *ranclen* to fester.

ransack (ˈrænsæk) *vb* **1** search through with a thoroughness that results in upheaval. **2** pillage or plunder. < Old Norse *rannsaka.*

ransom (ˈrænsəm) *n* **1** the amount of money demanded by extortionists for the release of a captive. **2** the release of a captive in exchange for such a sum.
• *vb* **1** release or obtain the release of (a captive) upon receiving or paying a ransom. **2** hold to ransom. **hold to ransom** demand a ransom for the release of a captive. < ultimately Latin *redimere* to redeem.

rant (rænt) *vb* talk in a loud and dramatic or hysterical way. **ranter** *n* **rantingly** *adv* < obsolete Dutch *ranten.*

rap (ræp) *n* **1** (the sound of) a sharp, light blow. **2** (*informal*) blame or punishment: I'm not going to take the rap.
• *vb* **rapped; rapping 1** strike with a sharp, light blow. **2** reprimand or criticize sharply. **3** utter sharply. < Middle English *rappe.*

rapacious (rəˈpeɪʃəs) *adj* (*formal*) greedy or grasping. **rapaciously** *adv* **rapaciousness** *n* **rapacity** *n* < Latin *rapere* to seize.

rape[1] (reɪp) *n* **1** the unlawful act of forcing a person to have sexual intercourse. **2** (*formal*) the act of despoiling.
• *vb* **1** commit rape on. **2** despoil or treat improperly. **rapist** *n* < Latin *rapere* to take by force.

rape[2] *n* a plant grown as feed for livestock and for the oil derived from its seeds. < Latin *rapum.*

rapid (ˈræpɪd) *adj* **1** moving or happening with speed. **2** happening or done within a short period: a rapid rise to fame. **rapidity** *n* **rapidly** *adv* **rapids** *pl n* a part of a river where the current accelerates dramatically. < Latin *rapidus.*

rapier (ˈreɪpɪə) *n* a double-edged sword with a narrow blade. < Middle French (*espee*) *rapiere.*

rapport (ræˈpɔː) *n* (a feeling of) mutual and harmonious understanding. < French *rapporter* to bring back.

rapt (ræpt) *adj* **1** deeply engrossed or absorbed: a rapt expression. **2** enraptured. < Latin *rapere* to seize.

rapture (ˈræptʃə) *n* great delight; ecstasy.

in raptures feeling or expressing great delight. **rapturous** *adj* expressing great delight or enthusiasm: a rapturous reception. **rapturously** *adv* < Latin *raptus*.

rare[1] (rɛə) *adj* **1** seldom occurring or encountered. **2** lacking density; thin: a rare atmosphere. **3** marked by unusual excellence. **rarely** *adv* **rareness** *n* **rarity** *n* **1** something which is rare. **2** the state of being rare. < Latin *rarus*. SEE PANEL.

rare[2] *adj* (of meat) lightly cooked, with the inside still reddish. < Old English *hrēre* boiled lightly.

rarefied (ˈrɛrɪˌfaɪd) also **rarified** *adj* **1** (of air, atmosphere, etc.) lacking density; thin. **2** lofty or exalted. < *rarefy*, from Latin *rarus* rare + *facere* to make.

raring (ˈrɛərɪŋ) *adj* bursting with eagerness: raring to go. < English dialect *rare* to rear.

rascal (ˈrɑːskl̩) *n* **1** a roguish or dishonest person. **2** a mischievous person, esp. a child. **rascally** *adj, adv* < Middle English *rascaile* rabble.

rash[1] (ræʃ) *n* an eruption of spots or reddish patches on the skin. < obsolete French *rache* scurf.

rash[2] *adj* acting with or resulting from undue haste and lack of forethought. **rashly** *adv* **rashness** *n* < Middle English *rasch* quick.

rasher (ˈræʃə) *n* a thin slice of bacon or ham. < origin uncertain.

rasp (rɑːsp) *n* **1** a coarse file. **2** a harsh, grating sound.

• *vb* **1** scrape with or as if with a rasp. **2** make a harsh, grating sound. **3** utter in a rasping voice. **4** grate upon or irritate. **raspingly** *adv* < Middle English *raspen*.

raspberry (ˈrɑːzbərɪ) *n* **1** a shrub that bears edible, purplish-red berries; its fruit. **2** a purplish-red colour. **3** a rude noise made with the tongue and lips. SEE PANEL.

rat (ræt) *n* **1** a rodent resembling a large mouse. **2** (*informal*) a contemptible person.

• *vb* **ratted; ratting 1** betray or desert one's colleagues, etc. **2** hunt rats. **rat race** a tiring, unending struggle to deal with the pressures of urban life. < Old English *ræt*.

ratchet (ˈrætʃɪt) *n* a device consisting of a wheel with teeth set at a slant and spaced to accommodate a sliding bolt which allows the wheel to move in one direction only. < French *rochet*.

rate (reɪt) *n* **1** a quantity or amount stated in relation to some unit or standard of measurement: at the rate of 20 litres per second. **2** a charge or payment made on a per unit basis. **3** a tax imposed by a local authority to provide revenue for local public services.

• *vb* **1** estimate the value or quality of; consider. **2** assign or be assigned (a particular rank or status). **3** deserve or warrant. **4** set a rate (on a property). **at any rate** in any case; anyway. **rateable** or **ratable** *adj* (of a property) liable to rates. **ratepayer** *n* a person who pays rates. < ultimately Latin (*pro*) *rata* (*parte*) according to a fixed proportion.

rather (ˈrɑːðə) *adv, determiner* **1** slightly; somewhat: It's got rather dark in here. **2** preferably: I'd rather not let her know. **3** to be more exact: He teaches—or rather he tries to teach. < Old English *hrathor*.

ratify (ˈrætɪˌfaɪ) *vb* **ratified; ratifying** confirm or approve officially. **ratification** *n* < ultimately Latin *reri* to think.

rating (ˈreɪtɪŋ) *n* **1** a place on a particular

rarely

Some people believe that there are only two words in English that can be used to make a clause negative—not and never. However, a number of other adverbs have negative force, including rarely, hardly, scarcely, seldom, and barely. This can be easily demonstrated.

Whether a clause is negative or not can be discovered grammatically through the some/any test. In a negative clause we always have to use any, not some: I don't have *any* money (not I don't have *some* money). Like not and never, all of the adverbs mentioned above take any: I rarely have *any* money. She seldom does *any* work. There was barely or scarcely *any*thing to eat. They hardly ate *any*thing. This behaviour shows that each of the adverbs contains the meaning 'not'.

raspberry

Raspberry, the name given to a number of brambles which bear soft, edible, purplish-red berries, is a derivative of the English dialect term for 'raspberry'—*rasp*. Etymologically, therefore, raspberry means 'a raspberry berry'.

scale, esp. one of popularity: The last programme got a very low rating. **2** a non-commissioned sailor.

ratio (ˈreɪʃɪˌəʊ) *n, pl* **ratios** the numerical relationship between one number or amount and another. < Latin: computation.

ration (ˈræʃən) *n* a fixed amount or share of something allowed to one person.
• *vb* **1** limit (a person) to a fixed amount. **2** restrict the supply of. < SEE **RATIO.**

rational (ˈræʃənl) *adj* **1** based on or in accordance with reason or logic: a rational decision. **2** able to use reason; thinking. **3** sane or sensible. **rationality** *n* **rationally** *adv* **rationale** *n* an underlying reason or motive for something: Let me explain the rationale behind the proposal. **rationalize** *vb* **1** make rational, logical, or consistent. **2** invent a rational basis for (an action or state of affairs) in order to justify it: They'll never rationalize the use of the nuclear bomb. **3** make (a business, industry, etc.) more efficient by streamlining its organization. **rationalization** *n* < Latin *ratio* reason.

rattle (ˈrætl̩) *vb* **1** make or cause to make a rapid series of short, sharp sounds. **2** move with a rattling sound: The tea trolley rattled along the corridor. **3** utter in rapid succession: She rattled off a long list of names. **4** (*informal*) annoy or irritate.
• *n* **1** a rattling sound. **2** a toy or other device for producing a rattling sound. **rattlesnake** *n* any of a group of poisonous American snakes with a tail structure that can produce a rattling sound. **rattling** *adj* brisk or vigorous: a rattling pace. < Middle English *ratelen.*

ratty (ˈrætɪ) *adj* (*informal*) irritable. < *rat* + *-y.*

raucous (ˈrɔːkəs) *adj* loud and harsh: a raucous laugh. **raucously** *adv* **raucousness** *n* < Latin *raucus* hoarse.

ravage (ˈrævɪdʒ) *vb* (*formal*) cause great damage or injury to; devastate.
• *n* **ravages** havoc, ruin, or devastation. < Middle French *ravir* to ravish.

rave (reɪv) *vb* **1** talk in a wildly incoherent way. **2** talk with wild enthusiasm.
• *n* (*informal*) **1** a highly favourable review of a book, film, etc. **2** a wild or lively event. **rave-up** *n* (*informal*) a wild or lively party. **ravings** *pl n* (*derogatory*) wildly incoherent talk. < Middle English raven.

ravel (ˈrævl̩) *vb* **ravelled; ravelling** **1** make or become tangled. **2** fray or disentangle.
• *n* a tangle. < Dutch *rafelen.*

raven (ˈreɪvən) *n* a large, black bird of the crow family with glossy plumage.
• *adj* glossy black. < Old English *hræfn.*

ravenous (ˈrævənəs) *adj* **1** very hungry. **2** insatiable. **ravenously** *adv* **ravenousness** *n* < Latin *rapina* plunder.

ravine (rəˈviːn) *n* a long, narrow valley bounded by mountains. < French.

ravish (ˈrævɪʃ) *vb* **1** rape or violate. **2** fill with joy or delight. **ravishing** *adj* (esp. of a woman) very beautiful. < ultimately Latin *rapere* to seize.

raw (rɔː) *adj* **1** not cooked. **2** not prepared, treated, processed, etc.: raw sugar. **3** with the outer layer of skin removed; sore and sensitive. **4** lacking experience and know-how: a raw recruit. **5** (esp. of alcohol) not mixed or blended. **6** in a crude, unpolished, or unfinished state. **7** (of weather) cold and wet. **rawly** *adv* **rawness** *n* **in the raw** **1** in a crude or natural state: life in the raw. **2** naked. **raw deal** unfair treatment. < Old English *hrēaw.*

ray¹ (reɪ) *n* **1** a narrow line representing a beam of light; one of a number of lines which radiate from a central point. **2** a trace or slight indication: a ray of hope. < Middle French rai.

ray² *n* any of a group of large, flat fish. < Middle French *raie.*

raze (reɪz) *vb* destroy completely by levelling to the ground. < Middle French *raser.*

razor (ˈreɪzə) *n* any of various cutting instruments, chiefly used for shaving unwanted hair. < Old French *raseor.*

RC *abbrev* Roman Catholic.

re (riː) *prep* with regard to. < Latin *res* thing.

re- *prefix* **1** again: reprint; reappear. **2** back or backwards: rebound. < ultimately Latin.

reach (riːtʃ) *vb* **1** arrive at or get to: When does the train reach Paris? **2** stretch out in order to grasp or touch: She reached for the book. **3** grasp or touch by reaching: She couldn't reach the book. **4** spread or extend to: The epidemic soon reached the surrounding villages. **5** communicate with: You can reach me by telephone. **6** sail in a direction that is at right angles to the wind.
• *n* **1** the act of reaching. **2** the distance or area that a person or thing reaches or can reach: The alarm bell was just out of reach. **3** a distance that can be travelled easily: They want to move to within reach of the school. **4** the range of a person's mental powers: Algebra is completely beyond his reach. **5** the length of a river between two curves. **6** a continuous expanse: vast reaches of desert. < Old English *rǣcan.*

react (rɪˈækt) *vb* act or behave in a way that is a response to something. **reaction** *n* **1** an act or instance of reacting. **2** a chemical change resulting from the combination of two or more substances. **3** a physical or mental change, esp. to an undesirable condition: With this drug you're bound to suffer a reaction. **4** a force that is equal in strength but working in the opposite direction to some other force. **5** a conservative tendency (esp. of a political group). **reactionary** *adj, n* (a person) opposed to change. **reactor** *n* an apparatus for the production of nuclear energy. < New Latin *reagere.*

read (riːd) *vb* **read** (rɛd); **reading 1** (be able to) receive the meaning of (written material). **2** say (written material) aloud. **3** get to know by reading. **4** take an academic course in: She's reading for a degree in physics. **5** read the works of (a particular author, period, etc.): You've never read Shakespeare! **6** have (a particular wording). **7** (of something written) yield (a particular impression) upon being read: The chapter reads very well. **8** indicate (a particular measurement); register: The thermometer reads 35 degrees Celsius. **9** understand or interpret the meaning or significance of: I read it that they would prefer us not to interfere. **10** (esp. of a computer) decode the information on a tape, etc.
• *n* **1** a period spent reading: Have a good read. **2** written material considered in terms of the pleasure, interest, etc., it affords: It's an absolutely nail-biting read. **readable** *adj* **1** legible or decipherable. **2** easy or interesting to read. **reader** *n* **1** a person who reads, esp. one who regularly purchases a particular newspaper or magazine. **2** a senior lecturer at certain universities. **3** a textbook, esp. one used in foreign-language learning. **readership** *n* the readers of a particular newspaper or magazine considered collectively. **reading** *n* **1** the act of reading. **2** the manner in which something is read or interpreted: The essay showed a highly sensitive reading of the novel. **3** something to read: Remember to take some reading into hospital with you. **4** the figure or amount registered by a measuring instrument. **read-out** *n* information retrieved from storage in a computer system, esp. a printed sheet or a screen display. **take something as read** accept something as obviously true, likely, etc. < Old English *rǣdan.*

readjust (riːəˈdʒʌst) *vb* **1** adjust (something) again. **2** adapt oneself to new circumstances: Some ex-prisoners find it hard to readjust. **readjustment** *n*

ready (ˈrɛdɪ) *adj* **1** prepared for immediate action or use: The runners are now ready for the off. **2** willing: We are now ready to accept your offer. **3** liable to do something: I feel just about ready to drop. **4** quick: a ready wit. **5** eager: too ready to find fault. **6** conveniently available or to hand: a ready market. **readiness** *n* **at the ready** prepared for immediate use or action. **readily** *adv* **1** willingly. **2** without difficulty: readily available. **ready-made** *adj* **1** made in standard sizes for immediate purchase; off the peg. **2** conveniently available: a ready-made solution. **3** lacking originality; hackneyed. **ready money** coins and banknotes. **ready reckoner** a book of tables providing the answers to everyday business calculations. < Middle English *redy.*

real (ˈrɪəl) *adj* **1** having perceivable existence: How does religion relate to the real world? **2** natural or genuine: real leather. **3** true or actual: What is her real reason for resigning? **4** complete or utter; used to intensify: He's a real comedian. **5** (of income, etc.) measured or regarded in terms of purchasing power as opposed to nominal value. **real estate** buildings and land considered as property. **realism** *n* **1** an acceptance of things as they are without any need to romanticize or idealize them. **2** a style of art and literature which embodies this attitude and represents things as they are in reality. **realist** *adj, n* **realistic** *adj* **realistically** *adv* **reality** *n* **1** the state of being real: I'm not questioning the reality of the danger. **2** something real: His dream suddenly became a reality. **3** the real world as opposed to an imaginary one: You can't escape from reality. **really** *adv* **1** in actual fact: We really came just to watch. **2** very; used to intensify: a really interesting book. **3** used in an exclamatory way to express surprise, disbelief, indignation, etc.: 'Well, really! I've never been so insulted!' **real tennis** an early form of tennis played in a walled, indoor court. < ultimately Latin *res* thing. SEE PANEL AT **SHEER**[1].

realize (ˈrɪəˌlaɪz) *vb* **1** understand or appreciate: Do you realize what you've done? **2** turn into a fact or reality: realize one's ambition. **3** convert (property, etc.) into money: realize one's assets. **4** yield (a particular price) upon sale. **realization** *n* < French *réaliser,* from Middle French *realiser.*

realm (rɛlm) *n* **1** (*formal*) a kingdom. **2** a sphere, field, or area: the realm of photography. < ultimately Latin *regimen* rule.

ream (riːm) *n* a quantity of paper, esp. 480 or 500 sheets. **reams** *pl n* (*informal*) a lot (of written material). < ultimately Arabic *rizmah* bundle.

reap (riːp) *vb* **1** cut and harvest (a crop or grain). **2** receive or gain, esp. as a consequence of something: Under the new policy the workers have reaped enormous benefits. **reaper** *n* < Old English *reopan*.

rear[1] (rɪə) *n* **1** the back part of something. **2** the area at or adjoining the back of something: There's a factory to the rear of the house. **3** (*informal euphemistic*) the buttocks.
• *adj* situated in or at the rear: The rear seat lifts out. **rearguard** *n* a detachment of soldiers whose duty is to protect the rear of the main body. **rearmost** *adj* furthest back. **rearward** *adj, adv* towards the rear. **rearwards** *adv* < origin uncertain.

rear[2] *vb* **1** feed and care for (a child or young animal) until fully grown. **2** (of a horse) rise up on the hind legs. **3** build or erect. **4** lift into an upright position. < Old English *rǣran*.

rearm (riːˈɑːm) *vb* arm again, esp. with new, improved weapons. **rearmament** *n*

reason (ˈriːzn̩) *n* **1** a cause or motive. **2** an explanation or justification. **3** the power to think logically. **4** sanity. **5** good sense or sound judgment.
• *vb* **1** use the power to think logically to reach a conclusion. **2** try to persuade by the use of logical arguments. **reasonable** *adj* **1** rational or sensible: a reasonable man. **2** based upon or in accord with good sense or sound judgment: reasonable behaviour. **3** not excessive; fair: a reasonable price. **reasonableness** *n* **reasonably** *adv* < ultimately Latin *ratio* reason. SEE PANEL.

reassure (ˌrɪəˈʃʊs) *vb* **1** restore confidence to. **2** assure again: I reassured him that he would be receiving help. **reassurance** *n*

> **the reason is because ...**
>
> The reason for the cutbacks *is because* the government has reduced our grant. Careful users avoid the reason ... is because ... and the reason why ..., considering them to be tautological. The reason ... is that ... is preferred instead: The reason for the cutbacks *is that* the government has reduced our grant.

rebate (ˈriːbeɪt) *n* a reduction, discount, or refund: a tax rebate. < Old French *rabattre* to beat down again.

rebel (rɪˈbɛl) *vb* **rebelled; rebelling** **1** oppose or resist a power or authority. **2** take up arms against a government, etc.
• *n* (ˈrɛbl̩) a person who rebels. **rebellion** *n* an act of rebelling, esp. in the form of armed resistance. **rebellious** *adj* (*formal*) rebelling or likely to rebel. **rebelliously** *adv* < ultimately Latin *rebellis*, from *re-* + *bellum* war.

rebirth (ˌriːˈbɜːθ) *n* **1** a new or second birth. **2** a revival or renaissance.

rebound (rɪˈbaʊnd) *vb* **1** spring or bounce back, esp. upon impact with something. **2** have an adverse effect upon the perpetrator; misfire.
• *n* (ˈriːbaʊnd) an act or instance of rebounding. **on the rebound** while in an unstable state following some misfortune: She married him on the rebound. < Middle French *rebondir*.

rebuff (rɪˈbʌf) *vb* (*formal*) reject or refuse in a cold or contemptuous way.
• *n* an act or instance of rebuffing. < Middle French *rebufer*, from Old Italian *ribuffare* to reprimand.

rebuke (rɪˈbjuːk) *vb* (*formal*) reprimand or criticize.
• *n* a reprimand. < Old Northern French *rebuker*.

rebut (rɪˈbʌt) *vb* **rebutted; rebutting** (*formal*) prove (a statement, etc.) to be false. **rebuttal** *n* < Old French *reboter*, from *re-* + *boter* to butt.

recalcitrant (rɪˈkælsɪˌtrənt) *adj* (*formal*) stubbornly defiant of authority; uncontrollable. **recalcitrance** *n* < ultimately Latin *re-* + *calcitrare* to kick.

recall (rɪˈkɔːl) *vb* **1** bring back to mind; remember. **2** order (someone) to return.
• *n* **1** the power to retrieve something from one's memory. **2** a summons to return.

recant (rɪˈkænt) *vb* (*formal*) formally renounce or withdraw (one's former belief or statement). **recantation** *n* < Latin *re-* + *cantare* to sing.

recap (ˈriːˌkæp) *vb* **recapped; recapping** (*informal*) recapitulate.

recapitulate (ˌriːkəˈpɪtjʊˌleɪt) *vb* repeat or summarize the main points of. **recapitulation** *n* < Late Latin *recapitulare*.

recapture (riːkæptʃə) *vb* **1** capture again. **2** experience or cause others to experience again.
• *n* the act of recapturing.

recast (ˌriːˈkɑːst) *vb* **recast; recasting**

1 cast again. **2** provide with a different form; refashion.
recede (rɪˈsiːd) *vb* **1** move back or away. **2** slope or slant backwards. **3** become less: Hopes of finding the lost boy are receding. < Latin *recedere* to go back.
receipt (rɪˈsiːt) *n* **1** a written acknowledgment that something has been paid or received. **2** something received: Receipts to date total £900. **3** the act of receiving. • *vb* issue a receipt for; mark as paid. < ultimately Latin *recipere* to receive.
receive (rɪˈsiːv) *vb* **1** accept or come into possession of (something sent, paid, etc.). **2** experience or suffer: Both drivers received serious injuries. **3** be a container for; hold. **4** take the force or weight of. **5** (*formal*) accept or admit as a guest or member. **6** welcome on arrival. **7** be the player in tennis, badminton, etc., who has to return service. **8** (of a radio, etc.) convert electromagnetic signals into sound. **9** accept stolen goods. **receiver** *n* **1** a radio, telephone, or other device which converts an electromagnetic signal into sound. **2** the part of a telephone that is lifted from the cradle or hook. **3** an official appointed to take charge of a bankrupt business, etc. **4** a person who accepts stolen goods. < ultimately Latin *re-* + *capere* to take. SEE PANEL.
recent (ˈriːsənt) *adj* **1** happening, done, or introduced not long ago. **2** of the time just before the present. **recently** *adv* < Latin *recens*.
receptacle (rɪˈsɛptəkl̩) *n* a holder or container. < ultimately Latin *recipere* to receive.
reception (rɪˈsɛpʃən) *n* **1** receiving or being received. **2** the manner in which something is received; response: a cool reception. **3** a formal gathering or party to welcome guests: a wedding reception. **4** the receiving of broadcast signals; their quality. **5** a place where a person registers his or her arrival, esp. in a hotel or on business premises. **receptionist** *n* < ultimately Latin *recipere* to receive.
receptive (rɪˈsɛptɪv) *adj* open to new ideas, suggestions, etc. **receptively** *adv* **receptiveness** *n*
recess (rɪˈsɛs, ˈriːsɛs) *n* **1** a part of a wall that is set back from the rest of it. **2** an interval between periods of work, esp. for relaxation: the summer recess. • *vb* (rɪˈsɛs) make or place in a recess. < Latin *recedere* to recede.
recession (rɪˈsɛʃən) *n* **1** the act of receding; withdrawal. **2** a decline in economic activity.
recipe (ˈrɛsɪpɪ) *n* **1** a set of instructions for preparing and cooking a dish. **2** a formula: a recipe for success. < Latin *recipere* to take. SEE PANEL.
recipient (rɪˈsɪpɪənt) *n* a person who receives something. < Latin *recipere* to receive.
reciprocal (rɪˈsɪprəkl̩) *adj* **1** given and received in turn; mutual: reciprocal admiration. **2** given or done in return. < Latin *reciprocus* alternating.
reciprocate (rɪˈsɪprəˌkeɪt) *vb* **1** give or do in return: reciprocate someone's hospitality. **2** give and receive mutually. **3** move

receive

The correct order of the letters i and e in words like receive has deceived generations of writers and continues to do so. As a spelling aid, there is the rule of thumb 'i before e except after c'. Those with an eye for exceptions to the rule are quick to seize upon them. Spellings of the seize type can be embraced by the same rule, however, if it is remembered that the s of seize represents exactly the same sound as the c of receive. Nor are words like weight exceptions if the rule of thumb is given in full: 'i before e except after c' applies to those spellings where the ei represents the long vowel sound of, say, sheep. However, even the extended rule of thumb is not completely watertight. As with all rules connected with language, it would be very weird if there were no exceptions at all.

recipe

In cookery a list of ingredients and directions for making something is known as a recipe. This word is a 14th-century borrowing of the Latin imperative *recipe*, 'take', from the verb *recipere* 'to take'. The imperative form originally featured not in cookery books but at the top of medical prescriptions, where it meant 'Take the following:'. Although nowadays associated more with the preparation of food than drugs, the medical use of Recipe (symbolized by ℞) continues to this day.

forwards and backwards alternately. **reciprocation** *n*

recite (rɪˈsaɪt) *vb* **1** repeat from memory or read aloud, esp. before an audience. **2** give a detailed account of. **recital** *n* **1** a musical performance; concert. **2** a detailed account. **3** the act of reciting. **recitation** *n* **1** the act of reciting, esp. a poetry reading. **2** something recited. < Latin *recitare* to cite again.

reckless (ˈrɛkləs) *adj* marked by an undue lack of care or caution: reckless driving. **recklessly** *adv* **recklessness** *n* < archaic *reck,* from Old English *reccan* to care + *-less.*

reckon (ˈrɛkən) *vb* **1** (*informal*) used to express an opinion, suggestion, etc.: I reckon you should wait a while. **2** anticipate or rely on: We were reckoning on a better attendance. **3** count or calculate. **4** consider or regard: He's reckoned to be one of the best surgeons in the country. **day of reckoning** the time in the future when one's sins, misdeeds, etc., have to be atoned for. **reckon with** deal with or answer to: One more noise and you'll have the headmaster to reckon with. **to be reckoned with** to be taken seriously: a force to be reckoned with. < Old English *(ge)recenian* to narrate.

reclaim (rɪˈkleɪm) *vb* **1** regain possession of. **2** obtain (something useful) from a waste product. **3** recover (land) for human use or habitation, esp. by draining or banking up. **reclamation** *n* < ultimately Latin *reclamare* to shout.

recline (rɪˈklaɪn) *vb* **1** put one's body into a horizontal or resting position. **2** rest or lean. < Latin *reclinare.*

recluse (rɪˈkluːs) *n* a person who lives a solitary life. < Late Latin *recludere* to shut up.

recognize (ˈrɛkəgˌnaɪz) *vb* **1** identify as being a person or thing that one has encountered previously: I recognized her face immediately. **2** realize or accept the reality of: He recognized that he had to work hard. **3** acknowledge or accept the validity of: The court refused to recognize the claim. **4** show appreciative acknowledgment of (something) by rewarding, honouring, etc.: The hospital committee recognized his contribution by naming the new wing after him. **recognition** *n* the act of recognizing; state or fact of being recognized. **recognizable** *adj* **recognizably** *adv* < Latin *recognoscere.*

recoil (rɪˈkɔɪl) *vb* **1** (esp. of a gun on firing) jump or spring back. **2** shrink or withdraw from, esp. in fear or horror. **3** rebound.
• *n* (ˈriːkɔɪl, rɪˈkɔɪl) the act of recoiling. < Old French *reculer,* from *re-* + *cul* backside.

recollect (ˌrɛkəˈlɛkt) *vb* remember or recall. **recollection** *n* < ultimately Latin *recolligere* to gather again.

recommend (ˌrɛkəˈmɛnd) *vb* **1** advise or suggest: The doctor recommended a long holiday. **2** declare (a person or thing) to be good or suitable for a particular purpose: Can you recommend anyone for the job? **3** cause to be considered suitable or acceptable: The design has several new safety features to recommend it. **recommendation** *n* < ultimately Latin *re-* + *commendare* to commend. SEE PANEL.

recompense (ˈrɛkəmˌpɛns) *vb* repay, reward, or compensate.
• *n* repayment or compensation. < ultimately Latin *re-* + *compensare* to compensate.

reconcile (ˈrɛkənˌsaɪl) *vb* **1** cause to be on friendly terms again. **2** settle or resolve. **3** cause to accept (an unpleasant fact or situation): Her parents finally became reconciled to the idea of her marrying him. **4** make consistent or bring into harmony. **reconcillation** *n* **reconcillatory** *adj* < Latin *reconciliare,* from *re-* + *conciliare* to conciliate.

recondite (ˈrɛkənˌdaɪt, rɪˈkɒndaɪt) *adj*

recommend

In the sense of 'advise' or 'suggest', the verb recommend shows a considerable amount of grammatical elasticity, commonly operating in four patterns. These are:

recommend something 'I'd recommend a walk along the Seine.'
recommend (that) someone do something 'I'd recommend (that) you take a walk along the Seine.'
recommend someone to do something 'I'd recommend you to take a walk along the Seine.'
recommend doing something 'I'd recommend taking a walk along the Seine.'

The various grammatical arrangements in which a word operates together make up its *syntax* (ultimately from the Greek verb *syntassein* 'to arrange together'). For the foreign learner, mastering a word's syntactic behaviour can sometimes be more troublesome than learning its meaning, as recommend shows.

involving or dealing with a subject which is profound or obscure. < Latin *recondere* to conceal.

recondition (ˌriːkənˈdɪʃən) *vb* restore to working order, esp. by replacing worn or damaged parts; overhaul.

reconnaissance (rɪˈkɒnɪsəns) *n* (*military*) an exploration or survey of an area for intelligence purposes. < French: recognition.

reconnoitre (ˌrɛkəˈnɔɪtə) *vb* make a reconnaissance (of). < obsolete French *reconnoître* to recognize.

reconstruct (ˌriːkənˈstrʌkt) *vb* **1** construct or create again. **2** re-create (an event, esp. a crime) on the basis of available evidence. **reconstruction** *n*

record (ˈrɛkɔːd) *n* **1** a written account: She kept a careful record of her expenses. **2** a flat disc on which sound is recorded; the sound itself. **3** a body of facts that are known about someone or something: The company has a poor safety record. **4** a criminal past. **5** the best or most extraordinary performance to date, esp. in a field of sport: The relay team set a new world record. • *vb* (rɪˈkɔːd) **1** set down in writing or some other permanent form. **2** contain an account of: The novel records the experiences of a Victorian chamber-maid. **3** register or indicate: The device records the slightest vibration. **4** put (sound, etc.) onto a disc or tape for reproduction purposes. **off the record** not for publication; confidentially. **on record** in writing or some other permanent form: He wanted his objections to be put on record. **record-player** *n* a machine for playing records; gramophone. < ultimately Latin *recordari* to remember.

recorder (rɪˈkɔːdə) *n* **1** a person or thing that records. **2** a magistrate in certain courts. **3** any of a group of wind instruments of the flute family.

recount (rɪˈkaʊnt) *vb* relate in detail. Middle French *reconter*.

recoup (rɪˈkuːp) *vb* **1** regain or recover. **2** pay back or compensate. **recoupable** *adj* < French *recouper* to cut back.

recourse (rɪˈkɔːs) *n* a source of help. **have recourse to** turn or resort to, esp. when in a difficult situation. < ultimately Latin *recurrere* to run back.

recover (rɪˈkʌvə) *vb* **1** (of a person) return to a healthy or normal condition: He is now recovering in hospital. **2** return to a former position of strength: The dollar is steadily recovering. **3** get back or regain: None of the stolen goods were recovered. **4** obtain, esp. by legal action: recover damages. **recovery** *n* **recover oneself** regain one's poise or balance. < ultimately Latin *recuperare*. SEE PANEL.

recreation (ˌrɛkrɪˈeɪʃən) *n* **1** a pastime or other pleasurable activity. **2** the relaxation or diversion provided by this. **recreational** *adj* < ultimately Latin *recreare* to refresh.

recrimination (rɪˌkrɪmɪˈneɪʃən) *n* a counter accusation. **recriminatory** *adj* < ultimately Latin *re-* + *criminari* to accuse.

recruit (rɪˈkruːt) *n* a new member of a group, society, etc., esp. a newly enlisted member of the armed forces. • *vb* **1** enlist (recruits or new members). **2** enlist as a recruit. **recruitment** *n* < ultimately Latin *recrescere* to grow up again.

rectangle (ˈrɛktæŋgḷ) *n* a parallelogram with four right angles. **rectangular** *adj* < Medieval Latin *rectangulus* having a right angle.

rectify (ˈrɛktɪˌfaɪ) *vb* **rectified; rectifying** **1** correct or remedy. **2** purify, esp. by distillation. **3** convert (alternating current) to direct current. **rectification** *n* < ultimately Latin *rectus* right.

rectitude (ˈrɛktɪˌtjuːd) *n* (*formal*) correctness of thought or conduct;

re-cover or **recover?**

The prefix re- is followed by a hyphen before a word-stem that begins with an e, such as re-elect, re-enact, re-establish, re-entry. It may be followed by a hyphen before stems beginning with other vowels, although this is becoming less common: reorganize, reappear, reassure.

Sometimes, however, it is necessary to use a hyphen to avoid two words being confused, such as re-cover ('to put a new cover on') and recover ('to return to normal health'). Similar examples are:

re-count 'to count again'—recount 'to relate in detail'

re-creation 'a new creation'—recreation 'relaxation'

re-present 'to present again'—represent 'to be a sign of'

re-sort 'to sort again'—resort 'to turn to'

integrity. < ultimately Latin *rectus* right.

rector (ˈrɛktə) *n* **1** a clergyman in charge of a parish. **2** the head of any of certain colleges and universities. **rectory** *n* the house or residence of a rector. < Latin: director.

rectum (ˈrɛktəm) *n* the lower end of the large intestine that terminates at the anus. < Latin *rectum* (*intestinum*) straight (intestine).

recuperate (rɪˈkjuːpəˌreɪt, rɪˈkuːpəreɪt) *vb* **1** regain one's health, strength, etc. **2** regain (a loss). **recuperation** *n* **recuperative** *adj* < Latin *recuperare.*

recur (rɪˈkɜː) *vb* **recurred; recurring** happen or appear again, esp. after an interval: The problem keeps recurring. **recurrence** *n* **recurrent** *adj* < Latin *recurrere* to run back.

recycle (riːˈsaɪkl̩) *vb* convert (waste) into usable material.

red (rɛd) *adj* **redder; reddest 1** of the colour of a ripe tomato. **2** (of the face) flushed. **3** bloodshot; enflamed: tired red eyes. **4** (of the hair) of a shade between orange and russet. **5** Communist; Soviet. **6** leftist or revolutionary.
• *n* **1** red colour. **2** something that has a red colour: dressed in red. **3** a Communist. **4** a leftist or revolutionary. **reddish** *adj* **redness** *n* **red-blooded** *adj* (*informal*) virile or vigorous. **redbrick** *adj* of or denoting a British university founded after 1800. **redden** *vb* make or become red. **red ensign** the flag of the merchant navy. **red-handed** *adj, adv* in the act of committing a crime. **redhead** *n* a person with red hair. **red-hot** *adj* **1** glowing with heat. **2** extremely hot. **3** eager or enthusiastic. **4** ardent or passionate. **5** very new or recent; sensational: red-hot news. < Old English *rēad.* SEE PANEL.

redeem (rɪˈdiːm) *vb* **1** recover possession of by payment. **2** pay off (a loan, debt, etc.). **3** exchange (coupons, etc.) for cash or goods. **4** free or rescue by payment. **5** compensate or make amends for. **6** (*religion*) deliver from sin and its consequences. **redeemable** *adj* **redemption** *n* < ultimately Latin *redimere.*

redeploy (ˌriːdɪˈplɔɪ) *vb* transfer (troops, workers, etc.) to a new position or task. **redeployment** *n*

redolent (ˈrɛdələnt) *adj* (*formal*) **1** smelling strongly (of). **2** evocative or reminiscent. **redolence** *n* < ultimately Latin *redolēre* to emit an odour.

redoubtable (rɪˈdaʊtəbl̩) *adj* (*formal*) formidable or awe-inspiring, esp. as an adversary. < Middle French *redonter* to dread.

redress (rɪˈdrɛs) *vb* **1** rectify or compensate for. **2** make even or equal: redress the balance of power.
• *n* compensation or reparation. < ultimately Old French *redrecier.*

reduce (rɪˈdjuːs) *vb* **1** make or become smaller in size, number, etc. **2** lower in status, rank, or value. **3** make or become slimmer; lose weight. **4** bring into a specified state or condition: She was reduced to accepting charity. **5** break down by crushing, pounding, etc. **reducible** *adj* **reduction** *n* **1** reducing or being reduced. **2** the amount something is reduced: a £2 reduction. < ultimately Latin *reducere* to lead back.

redundant (rɪdˈʌndənt) *adj* **1** superfluous or unnecessary. **2** (of workers) no longer needed. **redundancy** *n* **redundantly** *adv* < Latin *redundare* to overflow.

reduplicate (rɪˈdjuːplɪˌkeɪt) *vb* **1** make or become double. **2** repeat or be repeated; reiterate. **reduplication** *n*

reed (riːd) *n* **1** any of various tall, grass-like plants that grow in marshy areas. **2** the slender, hollow stem of such a plant. **3** a vibrating device in wind instruments such as the oboe, clarinet,

in the red

Colour terms, in particular red and black, feature regularly in idiomatic usage. In fact, you could list them until you were blue in the face. Below is a list containing some of the expressions:

- a white lie
- a white elephant
- in the pink
- rose-coloured spectacles
- see red
- paint the town red
- catch somebody red-handed
- a red-letter day
- red tape
- a scarlet woman
- out of the blue
- blue murder
- a bolt from the blue
- somebody's blue-eyed boy
- a blue fit
- once in a blue moon
- green with envy
- have green fingers
- browned off
- grey matter
- black and blue
- (in) black and white
- a black look
- a black spot
- the black sheep (of the family)
- a black day
- a black mark

or organ. **reedy** *adj* **1** full of or covered with reeds. **2** (of a sound) having a high, thin tone. < Old English *hrēod.*

reef (ri:f) *n* a ridge of rock, coral, etc., which breaks or comes close to the surface of the sea. < Dutch *rif.*

reek (ri:k) *n* a strong, unpleasant smell.
• *vb* **1** smell strongly: His breath always reeks of whisky. **2** be highly suggestive of (something undesirable). < Old English *rēc* smoke.

reel[1] (ri:l) *n* **1** a cylindrical device on which something is wound; spool: She wound the tape onto an empty reel. **2** this device and what is wound on it.
• *vb* **1** draw or pull towards one by means of a reel. **2** wind on or off a reel. **3** walk or step unsteadily; stagger. **4** go round and round; whirl: My mind was reeling. **reel off** utter (a number of things) in rapid succession. < Old English *hiēol.*

reel[2] *n* **1** a lively Scottish dance. **2** music composed for such a dance. < origin uncertain.

refectory (rɪˈfɛktərɪ) *n* a dining hall in a college, school, etc. < Latin *refectus.*

refer (rɪˈfɜː) *vb* **referred; referring** **1** mention or speak about: Why do you always refer to him as a failure? **2** direct to a source of assistance, information, etc.: She's been referred to an eye specialist. **3** turn to or consult: During the lecture he kept referring to his notes. **4** relate or apply to; concern. **5** ascribe or attribute to. **referable** *adj* **referral** *n* < Latin *referre.* SEE PANEL.

referee (ˌrɛfəˈriː) *n* **1** an official who enforces the rules of certain sports such as football and boxing. **2** a person to whom disputes are referred. **3** a person who provides a testimony as to someone's character, aptitude, etc.
• *vb* **refereed; refereeing** act as a referee (in).

refer back?

You should *refer back* to what I said earlier. They *returned back* home early. I see that Bob's been *re-elected* chairman *again*. They may *revert back* to the old methods soon. All these sentences are normally considered unacceptable. The prefix re- means 'back' and 'again', and so refer back, return back, re-elect again, revert back are tautological. They are, however, sometimes used for emphasis.

reference (ˈrɛfərəns) *n* **1** the act or an instance of referring to or mentioning something. **2** a written testimony as to someone's character, aptitude, etc. **3** a direction in a book, article, etc., to a source of further information. **4** a book, passage, etc., that is cited. **5** an authoritative source of information. **reference book** a book such as a dictionary or encyclopaedia that is periodically consulted for information. **terms of reference** (a precise statement of) the responsibilities and duties of an investigating body, committee, etc.

referendum (ˌrɛfəˈrɛndəm) *n, pl* **referendums, referenda** **1** the submitting of an issue or measure to the votes of the electorate. **2** a vote on such an issue. < Latin *referre* to refer.

refill (riːˈfɪl) *vb* fill again.
• *n* (ˈriːfɪl) **1** a replacement for used contents. **2** a second or subsequent filling.

refine (rɪˈfaɪn) *vb* **1** remove impurities from. **2** make more elegant, tasteful, etc. **refiner** *n* **refinement** *n* **1** refining or being refined. **2** delicacy of manners or behaviour. **3** a device or feature added as an improvement. **refinery** *n* a factory where a substance is refined: a sugar refinery.

refit (riːˈfɪt) *vb* **refitted; refitting** renovate or renew the fittings of.
• *n* (ˈriːfɪt) the act or an instance of refitting.

reflate (riːˈfleɪt) *vb* adopt a policy of reflation in. **reflation** *n* a controlled increase in the money supply in order to increase economic activity. **reflationary** *adj* < back formation from *reflation,* from *re-* + *-flation,* as in *inflation.*

reflect (rɪˈflɛkt) *vb* **1** throw back (light, heat, etc.). **2** (of a mirror, etc.) show an image of. **3** make manifest: The price increase reflects an increase in demand. **4** project a particular image or reputation upon: The boy's rudeness reflects badly on his upbringing. **5** think carefully; ponder. **reflector** *n* **reflection, reflexion** *n* **1** reflecting or being reflected. **2** something reflected; image. **3** contemplation or consideration; idea, suggestion, etc., resulting from this. **reflective** *adj* **1** reflecting. **2** thoughtful. < Latin *reflectere* to bend back.

reflex (ˈriːflɛks) *n* an automatic or instinctive response to a stimulus.
• *adj* occurring automatically or instinctively: a reflex action. **reflexes** *pl n* the

power of responding automatically: test a person's reflexes. < Latin *reflectere* to reflect.

reflexive (rɪˈflɛksɪv) *adj* (*grammar*) **1** denoting a class of pronouns ending in *-self* or *-selves.* **2** denoting a class of verbs which are always used with such pronouns. < Latin *reflexus.* SEE PANEL AT **PERJURE.**

reform (rɪˈfɔːm) *vb* change or be changed for the better, esp. by the correction of previous faults, abuses, etc.
• *n* reforming or being reformed. **reformation** *n* **reformer** *n* **the Reformation** the 16th-century religious movement which resulted in the establishment of Protestant churches. **reformatory** *n* an institution for the reforming of young offenders. < ultimately Latin *reformare.*

refract (rɪˈfrækt) *vb* bend or deflect (a ray of light, etc.). **refraction** *n* **refractive** *adj* **refractor** *n* < Latin *refringere.*

refrain[1] (rɪˈfreɪn) *vb* keep oneself (from doing something); forbear. < ultimately Latin *refrenare* to check with a bridle.

refrain[2] *n* **1** the lines of a song or poem which are repeated regularly, esp. after each verse. **2** the musical accompaniment for this. < ultimately Latin *refringere* to check.

refresh (rɪˈfrɛʃ) *vb* revive or renew the freshness of, esp. by resting, nourishing, etc. **refreshing** *adj* **refresh a person's memory** assist the memory by reminding or providing a stimulus. **refresher** *n* something that refreshes. **refresher course** a course of instruction intended to bring participants up to date with recent developments. **refreshment** *n* **1** refreshing or being refreshed. **2** something that refreshes, esp. food and drink. **refreshments** *pl n* snacks and drinks.

refrigerate (rɪˈfrɪdʒəˌreɪt) *vb* make or keep cold, esp. so as to preserve. **refrigeration** *n* **refrigerator** *n* < Latin *refrigerare.*

refuge (ˈrɛfjuːdʒ) *n* **1** shelter or protection from pursuit, danger, persecution, etc. **2** a place which provides this. **refugee** *n* a person who has fled his or her country in search of refuge. < ultimately Latin *refugere* to escape.

refund (rɪˈfʌnd) *vb* return (the money) someone has paid; reimburse.
• *n* (ˈriːfʌnd) **1** the act of refunding. **2** money refunded. < ultimately Latin *refuadere* to pour back.

refurbish (riːˈfɜːbɪʃ) *vb* renovate or restore. **refurbishment** *n* < *re-* + Middle French *forbir* to polish.

refuse[1] (rɪˈfjuz) *vb* **1** say one is unwilling to accept or do something. **2** (of a horse) be unwilling to jump (a fence, etc.). **refusal** *n* < ultimately Latin *refundere* to pour back.

refuse[2] (ˈrɛfjuːs) *n* waste material; rubbish. < Middle French *refus* rejection. SEE PANEL.

refute (rɪˈfjuːt) *vb* prove (a statement, etc.) is wrong. **refutable** *adj* **refutably** *adv* **refutation** *n* < Latin *refutare.* SEE PANEL.

regain (rɪˈgeɪn) *vb* **1** get (something) back again; recover: regain possession. **2** (*formal*) reach again.

regal (ˈriːgl) *adj* **1** of or suitable for a king or queen. **2** stately or splendid. **regality** *n* **regally** *adv* < Latin *regalis.*

regale (rɪˈgeɪl) *vb* (*formal*) **1** entertain or amuse. **2** entertain with food and drink; feast. < French *régaler.*

regalia (rɪˈgeɪlɪə) *pl n* **1** the insignia or emblems of office, esp. of a monarch. **2** ceremonial clothes. < Latin *regalis.*

regard (rɪˈgɑːd) *vb* **1** look steadily or attentively at; observe. **2** consider to be: She regards the matter as unimportant. **3** have a particular opinion of: His work is highly regarded. **4** concern or relate to. **5** take notice of; heed.
• *n* **1** a steady gaze. **2** heed or attention: Pay no regard to her. **3** respect or esteem: Her staff have a high regard for her. **regarding** *prep* also **as regards** with reference to; concerning. **regardless** *adv* despite

refuse collector

One area of the vocabulary that has undergone considerable transformation involves the use of euphemisms for the names of certain occupations. For example, a 'dustman' usually goes by the name of refuse collector, a 'bookmaker' has become a turf accountant, and a 'charwoman', previously elevated to 'charlady', now answers only to the name of domestic help. In each instance the occupation is of a relatively low social status; significantly, the occupational titles of doctors, dentists, and accountants remain unchanged. The name changes are attempts to verbally upgrade each type of work in the hope that a shift in social attitudes will follow.

everything. **regards** *pl n* friendly greetings. < Middle French *regarder* to look at.

regatta (rɪˈgætə) *n* a meeting at which a series of yacht or boat races are held. < Italian. SEE PANEL.

regenerate (rɪˈdʒɛnəˌreɪt) *vb* **1** give or receive new life. **2** reform morally. **regeneration** n **regenerative** *adj* < Latin *regenerare.*

regent (ˈriːdʒənt) *n* a person appointed to govern a kingdom when the sovereign is too young, too ill, etc., to rule. **regency** *n* the office or rule of a regent or regents. < ultimately Latin *regere* to rule.

regime, régime (reɪˈʒiːm) *n* a system of government. < ultimately Latin *regimen.*

regiment (ˈrɛdʒɪmənt) *n* **1** a military unit. **2** a large number or array. • *vb* (ˈrɛdʒɪˌmɛnt) subject to strict discipline, organization, or control. **regimentation** *n* < ultimately Latin *regere* to rule.

region (ˈriːdʒən) *n* **1** an area, part, or district. **2** an administrative division. **regional** *adj* **regionally** *adv* < ultimately Latin *regere* to rule.

register (ˈrɛdʒɪstə) *n* **1** a list or record. **2** a book containing such lists. **3** a mechanical device which keeps a list or record: a cash register. **4** the range of a person's voice or of a musical instrument. **5** (*linguistics*) a variety of language used in a particular situation: a technical register. • *vb* **1** enter or cause to be entered in a register: register a death. **2** show (a reading) on a scale, dial, etc. **3** note or record. **4** enrol or give one's name upon arrival. **5** secure special postal protection for (a letter or parcel) by paying extra postage. **6** show (a feeling, etc.) by means of facial expression or gesture: Her face registered disbelief. **register office** a registry office. **registration** *n* registering or being registered. **registration number** a series of letters and numbers by which a motor vehicle is identified. < ultimately Latin *regerere* to transcribe.

registrar (ˌrɛdʒɪˈstrɑː) *n* **1** an official responsible for keeping registers or records. **2** a hospital doctor next below the rank of a consultant. < ultimately Medieval Latin *registrare* to register.

registry (ˈrɛdʒɪstrɪ) *n* **1** registration. **2** a place where registers or records are kept. **registry office** a place where births, deaths, and marriages are recorded, and where civil marriages take place.

regress (rɪˈgrɛs) *vb* return to an earlier or less advanced state. **regression** *n* **regressive** *adj* < Latin *regredi* to go back.

regret (rɪˈgrɛt) *n* a feeling of sorrow often combined with longing, repentance, or disappointment. • *vb* **regretted; regretting** feel regret about. **regretful** *adj* feeling regret. **regretfully** *adv* **regrettable** *adj* to be regretted. **regrettably** *adv* < Middle French *regreter.*

regular (ˈrɛgjʊlə) *adj* **1** normal or usual: We stock all the regular sizes . **2** occurring, acting, etc., at fixed intervals or in a uniform manner: regular visits. **3** occurring, acting, etc., frequently or on each occasion: a regular attender. **4** not varying or fluctuating: a regular pace. **5** symmetrical in design, structure, etc.: a regular pattern. **6** made, done, etc., according to a standard method or principle: regular procedure. **7** permanent: the regular army. **8** (*grammar*) denoting a verb, noun, etc., that has normal inflections. **9** (*informal*) complete or absolute. • *n* **1** (*informal*) a regular customer, etc. **2** a member of the regular armed forces. **regularity** *n* **regularly** *adv* **regularize** *vb* **1** make regular. **2** make lawful or correct. **regularlzation** *n* < ultimately Latin *regula* rule.

refute or **deny?**

Refute is sometimes confused with deny, but there is an important difference between them. Whereas deny means 'to assert to be untrue' and 'to reject as untrue', refute means 'to prove conclusively that something is untrue or wrong'. The distinction is evident in a sentence such as Since the directors could not *refute* the allegations of mismanagement, all they could do was *deny* them.

regatta

Regatta, 'a meeting at which a series of rowing or sailing races take place', derives from the Venetian dialect *regata* meaning 'gondola race', literally 'a striving for mastery'. The original regattas were contests between Venetian gondoliers.

regulate (ˈrɛgjʊˌleɪt) *vb* **1** control by means of rules, restrictions, etc. **2** adjust (a machine, etc.) so that it works according to one's requirements. **regulator** *n* < SEE **REGULAR.**
regulation (ˌrɛgjʊˈleɪʃən) *n* **1** regulating or being regulated. **2** a rule or restriction: safety regulations.
regurgitate (rɪˈgɜːdʒɪˌteɪt) *vb* **1** bring back (food) into the mouth after it has been swallowed. **2** pour back. **regurgitation** *n* < Medieval Latin *regurgitare.*
rehabilitate (ˌriːəˈbɪlɪˌteɪt) *vb* **1** restore to a state of good or improved health, condition, or behaviour: Attempts to rehabilitate the offenders proved useless. **2** reinstate. **rehabilitation** *n* < Medieval Latin *rehabilitare.*
rehash (riːˈhæʃ) *vb* (*derogatory*) use again in another guise without any substantial changes or improvement. • *n* (ˈriːhæʃ) something that has been rehashed.
rehearse (rɪˈhɜːs) *vb* **1** practise (a play, concert, etc.) before performing before an audience. **2** train (performers) by this means. **3** utter or recount. **rehearsal** *n* **1** rehearsing. **2** a session when a play, concert, etc., is rehearsed. < Middle French *rehercier* to harrow again.
rehouse (ˌriːˈhaʊz) *vb* provide with new or alternative accommodation.
reign (reɪn) *n* **1** (the period of) a monarch's rule; sovereignty. **2** any dominating power or influence: the reign of fear.
• *vb* **1** hold the office of a monarch. **2** be supreme or prevalent. < ultimately Latin *rex* king.
reimburse (ˌriːɪmˈbɜːs) *vb* repay or refund. **reimbursement** *n* < *re-* + obsolete *imburse,* from Medieval Latin *imbursare* to put in a moneybag.
rein (reɪn) *n* **1** a long strap attached to a bridle by which a horse, etc., is guided. **2** a similar device for controlling the movement of a young child. **3** a means or position of control.
• *vb* **1** check or control by means of reins. **2** control or restrain. **give free rein to** impose no restraints on. **keep a tight rein on** impose multiple restraints on. < ultimately Latin *retinēre* to restrain.
reincarnate (riːɪnˈkɑːneɪt) *vb* bring back after death into another body.
• *adj* (ˌriːɪnˈkɑːnət) reincarnated. **reincarnation** *n*
reindeer (ˈreɪndɪə) *n, pl* **reindeer, reindeers** a deer of northern regions with large antlers. SEE PANEL.
reinforce (ˌriːɪnˈfɔːs) *vb* make stronger by adding more support. **reinforcement** *n* **reinforcements** *pl n* additional troops, ships, etc., sent to strengthen a combat unit.
reinstate (ˌriːɪnˈsteɪt) *vb* restore to a previous state or position. **reinstatement** *n*
reiterate (riːˈɪtəˌreɪt) *vb* say or do again or repeatedly. **reiteration** *n* < Latin *reiterare* to repeat.
reject (rɪˈdʒɛkt) *vb* **1** refuse to accept, use, believe, etc. **2** (of an organism) fail to accept: It is possible that the grafted tissue may be rejected. **3** throw away or discard.
• *n* (ˈriːdʒɛkt) something which is rejected, esp. because imperfect. **rejection** *n* < Latin *reicere.*
rejoice (rɪˈdʒɔɪs) *vb* (*formal*) feel or express joy. < Middle French *rejoir.*
rejoin[1] (riːˈdʒɔɪn) *vb* **1** join again; reunite. **2** come into the company of again.
rejoin[2] (rɪˈdʒɔɪn) *vb* (*formal*) say sharply in reply to; retort. **rejoinder** *n* something said in reply; retort. < Middle French *rejoindre.*
rejuvenate (rɪˈdʒuːvəˌneɪt) *vb* cause to feel youthful again. **rejuvenation** *n* < *re-* + Latin *juvenis* young.
relapse (rɪˈlæps) *vb* fall or slip back into a previous or worse condition.
• *n* relapsing. < Latin *relabi* to slide back.
relate (rɪˈleɪt) *vb* **1** give an account of; narrate. **2** connect or be connected with: It is thought that the two accidents may be related. **relationship** *n* **related** *adj* **1** connected, linked, or associated. **2** connected by kinship or marriage. **relation** *n* **1** a connection or association. **2** a relative. **3** narrating or being narrated. **relations** *pl n* dealings, interaction, or communication: diplomatic relations. < Latin *referre* to carry back.

reindeer

The word reindeer is sometimes regarded as a compound of rein and deer. Reindeer, however, has no connection with rein. It comes from the Old Norse word for 'reindeer' *hreinn,* to which was added the Middle English *deer.* Etymologically, therefore, the name reindeer means 'a reindeer deer'.

relative (ˈrɛlətɪv) *adj* **1** considered in relation or comparison with something else: relative luxury. **2** relevant or related. **3** (*grammar*) referring to a preceding noun or clause: relative pronouns.
• *n* a person who is related to another by kinship or marriage. **relatively** *adv* **relativeness** *n* **relativity** *n*

relax (rɪˈlæks) *vb* **1** make or become looser or less tense. **2** make or become less strict or severe. **3** become free of care or worry. **relaxant** *n* **relaxation** *n* < Latin *relaxare* to loosen. SEE PANEL.

relay (ˈriːleɪ) *n* **1** a body of workers who relieve those on an earlier shift, etc. **2** a fresh team of horses. **3** a relay race. **4** a relayed message. **5** an electrical device in which a change in current in one circuit triggers a switch in a second circuit.
• *vb* (rɪˈleɪ) **1** convey or pass along by relays. **2** provide with relays. **relay race** a race in which each runner in turn covers part of the total distance. < Middle French *relaier.*

release (rɪˈliːs) *vb* **1** free from captivity, imprisonment, etc. **2** free from obligation, suffering, or oppression. **3** move (a device which prevents a mechanism from moving or being operated): release a safety catch. **4** stop holding or grasping: He released the cup and it fell to the ground. **5** issue or put into circulation: release a film. **6** make or be made widely known. **7** give up or relinquish (a right, etc.).
• *n* **1** releasing or being released. **2** a catch, lever, etc., which prevents a mechanism from moving or being operated. **3** something made widely known or released to the public: a press release. < ultimately Latin *relaxare* to relax.

relegate (ˈrɛlɪˌgeɪt) *vb* **1** transfer to a less prestigious or prominent position; demote. **2** transfer (a football club) to a lower division. **relegation** *n* < Latin *relegare* to send away.

relent (rɪˈlɛnt) *vb* become less harsh, severe, etc.; yield. **relentless** *adj* unrelenting. **relentlessly** *adv* **relentlessness** *n* < *re-* + Latin *lenrare* to bend.

relevant (ˈrɛlɪvənt) *adj* having a bearing on the matter under discussion. **relevance** *n* < Latin *relevare* to raise up.

reliable (rɪˈlaɪəbl) *adj* able to be relied on; dependable. **reliability** *n* **reliably** *adv*

reliance (rɪˈlaɪəns) *n* **1** the act or state of relying on. **2** confidence or dependence. **reliant** *adj*

relic (ˈrɛlɪk) *n* **1** something which has survived from an earlier age. **2** an object that is revered because of its association with a saint or martyr, esp. skeletal remains. < ultimately Latin *relinquere* to leave behind.

relief (rɪˈliːf) *n* **1** a lessening or removal of pain, anxiety, boredom, etc. **2** aid such as food and medical supplies given to those in special need: famine relief. **3** a worker who takes over from another so that the latter may rest, etc. **4** a method of carving, etc., in which the design stands proud of its background. **5** a carving, etc., done in this way. **6** a bold impression resulting from contrast. **relief map** a map which shows topographical features, esp. by means of shading and contours. < SEE **RELIEVE.**

relieve (rɪˈliːv) *vb* **1** bring or give relief to. **2** bring aid or assistance to. **3** (of a worker) take over from (another). **4** dismiss from a job, etc.: be relieved of one's duties. **5** give relief to by taking from: Can I relieve you of one of those cases? **relieve oneself** (*euphemistic*) urinate or defecate. < ultimately Latin *relevare.*

religion (rɪˈlɪdʒən) *n* **1** belief in or worship of a god. **2** a particular system of belief or worship. **3** something whose control or influence is likened to that of a religion: Golf is his religion. **religious** *adj* **1** of or connected with religion. **2** abiding by the rules and practices of a religion. **3** conscientious. **religiously** *adv* < Latin *religio.*

relax and **lax**

Despite their similarity of form, it is not always realized that lax and relax are etymologically related. Both words derive ultimately from the Latin adjective *laxus* meaning 'loose' or 'slack'.

Lax entered English in the 14th century, at which time it was used only of the bowels. Over the centuries, however, its meaning has broadened considerably. Laxative appeared in the language at about the same time. Unlike lax, however, it has retained its narrow application.

Relax did not appear in the language until a century later.

relinquish (rɪˈlɪŋkwɪʃ) *vb* **1** surrender or give up; abandon. **2** let go or release. **relinquishment** *n* < ultimately Latin *relinquere* to leave behind.

relish (ˈrɛlɪʃ) *n* **1** great enjoyment, appreciation, or delight. **2** a savoury sauce added to plain food to add flavour. **3** a pleasing or appetizing taste or quality.
• *vb* enjoy or savour. < Old French *relaisser* to leave behind. SEE PANEL.

reluctant (rɪˈlʌktənt) *adj* disinclined to do something; unwilling. **reluctance** *n* **reluctantly** *adv* < Latin *reluctari* to struggle against.

rely (rɪˈlaɪ) *vb* **relied; relying 1** have confidence in; trust: Henry is a man you can rely on. **2** be dependent: They rely on my help. < ultimately Latin *religare* to tie back.

remain (rɪˈmeɪn) *vb* **1** be left, not used, not done, etc.: Several questions remain to be answered. **2** stay in the same place: Remain where you are. **3** continue to be: He remains on the critical list. **remains** *pl n* **1** that which survives or is left over: The remains of the dinner went in the dustbin. **2** a corpse. < ultimately Latin *ramanēre.*

remainder (rɪˈmeɪndə) *n* **1** the people or things that remain after others have gone or been taken away, etc. **2** the number that remains after subtraction or division. **3** a book sold by a publisher at a reduced price.
• *vb* dispose of (books) at a reduced price.

remand (rɪˈmɑːnd) *vb* return (a prisoner) into custody.
• *n* remanding or being remanded. **on remand** having been remanded. **remand home** or **centre** (formerly) a centre where young offenders are held. < ultimately Latin *re-* + *mandare* to order.

remark (rɪˈmɑːk) *vb* **1** say or comment, esp. in a casual way. **2** notice or observe.
• *n* **1** a written or spoken comment or utterance. **2** notice: worthy of remark. **remarkable** *adj* extraordinary or noteworthy. **remarkably** *adv* < French *remarquer.*

remedy (ˈrɛmədɪ) *n* **1** something which cures or relieves: a remedy for headache. **2** something which corrects or counteracts: a remedy for hooliganism.
• *vb* **remedied; remedying** serve as a remedy for. **remedial** *adj* intended as or providing a remedy for something. < ultimately Latin *remedium.*

remember (rɪˈmɛmbə) *vb* **1** retain in one's mind. **2** bring to mind; recall. **3** convey greetings from: Remember me to your parents. **4** give money or a gift to, esp. in a will. **remembrance** *n* **1** remembering or being remembered. **2** a person's memory of something. **3** something which serves to remind someone of a person or thing. < ultimately Latin *memor* mindful.

remind (rɪˈmaɪnd) *vb* cause to remember. **reminder** *n*

reminisce (ˌrɛmɪˈnɪs) *vb* think or talk nostalgically about past experiences. **reminiscence** *n* **1** reminiscing. **2** a recollection or memorable experience. **3** an account of past experiences. **reminiscent** *adj* **1** inspiring memories (of). **2** inclined to reminisce. < Latin *reminisci* to remember.

remiss (rɪˈmɪs) *adj* (*formal*) negligent or neglectful. < Latin *remittere* to send back.

remission (rɪˈmɪʃən) *n* **1** a lessening or weakening in force, intensity, etc. **2** a reduction of the length of a prison sentence. **3** the act of excusing or releasing from an obligation. **4** forgiveness of sins. < SEE **REMIT.**

remit (rɪˈmɪt) *vb* **remitted; remitting** (*formal*) **1** make or become less intense. **2** send (money, etc.) to a person or place. **3** refer or send to for consideration. **4** excuse or release from (an obligation). **5** cancel or refrain from enforcing. **6** forgive or pardon. **remittance** *n* **1** the sending of money, esp. in payment for something. **2** the money sent. < Latin *remittere* to send back.

remnant (ˈrɛmnənt) *n* a small remaining part or quantity. < ultimately Latin *remanēre* to remain.

remonstrate (ˈrɛmənˌstreɪt) *vb* (*formal*) utter or argue in protest. **remonstrance** *n* < Medieval Latin *remonstrare* to show.

remorse (rɪˈmɔːs) *n* deep regret for one's misdeeds. **remorseful** *adj* **remorsefully** *adv* **remorseless** *adj* without pity; relentless. **remorselessly** *adv* < ultimately Latin *remordēre* to bite

relish

A sauce or other savoury substance that is added to a meal is sometimes referred to by the name relish. Those who are familiar with the lingering quality of garlic- or onion-based relishes will not be surprised to learn that this word derives from the Old French verb *relaisser* 'to leave behind'.

again. SEE PANEL.

remote (rɪˈməʊt) *adj* **1** distant in time or place. **2** secluded: a remote backwater. **3** not closely related: a remote cousin. **4** slight or small: a remote possibility. **remotely** *adv* **remoteness** *n* **remote control** control from a distance, esp. by means of radio waves or electricity. < Latin *remotus*.

remove (rɪˈmu:v) *vb* **1** take off, away, etc.: We removed the legs to get it up the stairs. **2** take off (clothing). **3** get rid of or erase: remove a stain. **4** sack or dismiss: The president has been removed from office. **5** (*formal*) move to a new location or residence.
• *n* a step or degree: several removes from the truth. **remover** *n* **removal** *n* **1** removing or being removed. **2** the transfer of belongings, etc., to a new residence. **removed** *adj* separated to a specified extent in distance or relationship: a cousin twice removed. < ultimately Latin *removēre*.

remunerate (rɪˈmju:nəˌreɪt) *vb* pay or recompense. **remuneration** *n* **remunerative** *adj* profitable. < Latin *remunerare* to recompense.

renal (ˈri:nl̩) *adj* of or situated near the kidneys. < Latin *renes* kidneys.

rend (rɛnd) *vb* **rent; rending** tear. < Old English *rendan*.

render (ˈrɛndə) *vb* **1** cause to become: be rendered speechless. **2** submit or present: render an account. **3** give or provide: for services rendered. **4** give a performance of. **5** depict or represent. **6** translate. **7** melt down. **8** coat (the surface of a wall) with rendering. **rendering** *n* **1** a performance. **2** a material composed chiefly of sand and cement used to coat external walls. **rendition** *n* a performance or interpretation. < Middle French *rendre* to give back.

rendezvous (ˈrɒndɪˌvu:, ˈrɒndeɪˌvu:) *n, pl* **rendezvous 1** an arranged meeting. **2** a place where people arrange to meet.
• *vb* meet at an arranged place.
< Middle French, from *rendez vous* present yourselves.

renegade (ˈrɛnɪˌgeɪd) *n* (*derogatory*) a person who deserts a cause, group, etc., for another. < Spanish *renegado*, from Medieval Latin *renegare* to deny.
SEE PANEL.

renege (rɪˈneɪg) *vb* go back on one's word or promise, **reneger** *n* < Medieval Latin *renegare*.

renew (rɪˈnju:) *vb* **1** make new or fresh again: renewed vitality. **2** replace with new or fresh supplies: The stylus needs renewing. **3** begin again: renew a friendship. **4** cause to continue for a further period; extend: renew a subscription. **renewal** *n*

renounce (rɪˈnaʊns) *vb* **1** give up (a claim, etc.). **2** repudiate or disown. **renouncement** *n* < ultimately Latin *renuntiare*.

renovate (ˈrɛnəˌveɪt) *vb* restore to good condition. **renovation** *n* **renovator** *n* < Latin *renovare*.

renown (rɪˈnaʊn) *n* fame or acclaim. **renowned** *adj* famous or celebrated. < Middle French *renon*.

rent[1] (rɛnt) *n* a payment made at regular intervals for the use of something.
• *vb* obtain or give the use of something upon payment of rent: rent a flat. **rental** *n* money paid as rent. < Old French *rente* revenue.

rent[2] SEE **REND**.
• *n* a tear or split.

renunciation (rɪˌnʌnsɪˈeɪʃən) *n* the act or an instance of renouncing.

rep[1] (rɛp) *n* (*informal*) a representative, esp. one promoting sales.

rep[2] *n* (*informal*) repertory.

the bite of remorse

A person's feeling of profound regret for something that he or she has done or said is commonly referred to as remorse. The pain that is central to this emotion is poignantly conveyed in the origin of the word. Remorse derives ultimately from the Latin verb *remordēre*, 'to bite again'.

renegade

Renegade, a name that is nowadays loosely applied to any person who abandons a cause or movement and goes over to the other side, was originally used of someone who abandoned his or her religion for a different one. The word derives via the Spanish *renegado* from the Medieval Latin *renegare* 'to deny', a compound of the Latin *re-* 'again' and *negare* 'to deny'. The same root provides the verb renege, 'to go back on a promise'.

repair[1] (rɪˈpɛə) *vb* **1** restore to good or usable condition. **2** heal or mend (a division, etc.); remedy. **3** make amends for.
• *n* **1** the act or process of repairing something. **2** a part or place that has been repaired. **repairer** *n* < Latin *reparare.*

repair[2] *vb* (*archaic*) go or take oneself (somewhere). < Late Latin *repatriare* to return to one's own country.

reparation (ˌrɛpəˈreɪʃən) *n* the act of making amends. **reparations** *pl n* compensation for war damage that is payable by a defeated nation. < ultimately Latin *reparere* to repair.

repartee (ˌrɛpɑːˈtiː) *n* **1** quick, witty retorts. **2** skill in making such replies. < French *repartie.*

repatriate (riːˈpætrɪˌeɪt, riːˈpeɪtrɪˌeɪt) *vb* send or bring (someone) back to his or her own country. **repatriation** *n* < Latin *re-* + *patria* fatherland.

repay (rɪˈpeɪ) *vb* **repaid; repaying 1** pay back. **2** do or give in return: repay a kindness. **repayment** *n*

repeal (rɪˈpiːl) *vb* cancel or revoke (a law); rescind.
• *n* the act of repealing. < ultimately Old French *repeler.*

repeat (rɪˈpiːt) *vb* **1** say, do, or experience again: Could you repeat the address, please? **2** say aloud: Repeat each sentence after me. **3** tell to someone: She asked me not to repeat what I'd heard to the newspapers. **4** (of food) be tasted again as the effect of belching.
• *n* **1** the act of repeating. **2** something repeated, esp. a radio or television broadcast. **repeatedly** *adv* again and again. **repetition** *n* **1** repeating or being repeated. **2** something repeated. **repetitious** *adj* repetitive. **repetitiously** *adv* **repetitiousness** *n* **repetitive** *adj* marked by needless repetition. **repetitively** *adv* **repetitiveness** *n* < ultimately Latin *repetere,* from *re-* + *petere* to seek.

repel (rɪˈpɛl) *vb* **repelled; repelling 1** drive back or away; repulse. **2** refuse to accept; reject. **3** resist penetration by a liquid, etc. **4** cause a feeling of disgust in. < Latin *repellere.*

repellent (rɪˈpɛlənt) *adj* **1** repulsive or disgusting. **2** unable to be penetrated by a liquid, etc.: water-repellent.
• *n* something that repels, esp. a substance that repels insects.

repent (rɪˈpɛnt) *vb* **1** feel regret or remorse about a misdeed. **2** turn from sin. **repentance** *n* **repentant** *adj* < Old French *repentir.*

repercussion (ˌriːpəˈkʌʃən) *n* **1** the indirect effect of an action or event, esp. one that is far-reaching. **2** a recoil or rebound. **3** an echo. < Latin *repercussio.*

repertoire (ˈrɛpəˌtwɑː) *n* a list or stock of songs, plays, compositions, etc., that a person or group is prepared to perform. < French *répertoire.*

repertory (ˈrɛpətrɪ) *n* **1** a repertoire. **2** a theatre or theatrical company which stages several different plays during a season. < Late Latin *repertorium* storehouse.

replace (rɪˈpleɪs) *vb* **1** put back in place. **2** take the place of: Nothing can replace good health. **3** put a new person or thing in the place of: All the damaged books will have to be replaced. **replacement** *n*

replay (ˈriːˌpleɪ) *n* **1** a match or contest that is held again, esp. because of a previous tie. **2** the showing of a videotape, etc.: an action replay.
• *vb* (ˌriːˈpleɪ) play again.

replenish (rɪˈplɛnɪʃ) *vb* (*formal*) fill again. **replenishment** *n* < Middle French *replenir* to fill.

replete (rɪˈpliːt) *adj* (*formal*) well filled, esp. with food. **repletion** *n* < ultimately Latin *replēre* to fill.

replica (ˈrɛplɪkə) *n* an exact copy or reproduction; facsimile. < Italian: repetition, from *replicare* to repeat.

reply (rɪˈplaɪ) *vb* **replied; replying** do or say something in response.
• *n* something said or done in response. < ultimately Latin *replicare.*

report (rɪˈpɔːt) *vb* **1** give a detailed account of (what has been said, done, or observed). **2** give an account of the findings of (an investigation, etc.). **3** complain about, esp. to a superior or official: The boy was reported for disobedience. **4** be responsible (to). **5** go or present oneself (somewhere); esp. to announce one's arrival: Upon arrival all guests should report to the reception.
• *n* **1** a detailed account of something said, done, or observed. **2** a detailed statement as to the performance of a pupil, employee, etc.: a school report. **3** general talk; gossip. **4** (of a gun, etc.) an explosive sound. **reportage** *n* **1** the reporting of news. **2** the typical style of a news report. **3** something written in this style. **reportedly** *adv* according to reports; supposedly. **reporter** *n* a person whose job is to gather and write news stories; journalist. < ultimately Latin *reportare.*

repose (rɪˈpəʊz) *n* **1** rest or relaxation.

2 peace; calm.
• *vb* **1** lie restfully or dead. **2** lay at rest. < Middle French *reposer.*
repository (rɪˈpɒzɪtrɪ) *n* a place where things are stored or deposited. < Latin *repositorium.*
repossess (ˌriːpəˈzɛs) *vb* regain or resume possession of. **repossession** *n*
reprehend (ˌrɛprɪˈhɛnd) *vb* criticize, censure, or rebuke. **reprehensible** *adj* warranting rebuke or censure. **reprehensibly** *adv* < Latin *reprehendere.*
represent (ˌrɛprɪˈzɛnt) *vb* **1** act or speak on behalf of. **2** portray or depict. **3** serve as a sign or symbol of; stand for. **4** claim or declare to be, often falsely: He represented himself as a sales executive. **5** be a typical example of: Her statement by no means represents the general feeling. **6** be the product or outcome of: These four pages represent a lot of tedious research. **representation** *n* < ultimately Latin *repraesentare.*
representative (ˌrɛprɪˈzɛntətɪv) *adj* **1** typical; characteristic. **2** serving to represent. **3** based upon or made up of elected representatives: representative government.
• *n* **1** a typical example or specimen. **2** a person elected or delegated to act or speak on behalf of another or others. **representatively** *adv* **representativeness** *n* **House of Representatives** the lower house of Congress in the USA and certain other countries.
repress (rɪˈprɛs) *vb* check or hold back. **repression** *n* **repressive** *adj* **repressively** *adv* < Latin *reprimere.*
reprieve (rɪˈpriːv) *n* **1** a postponement or cancellation of punishment. **2** a temporary relief (from something unpleasant).
• *vb* give a reprieve to. < origin uncertain.
reprimand (ˈrɛprɪˌmɑːnd) *n* a severe rebuke or censure.
• *vb* give a reprimand to. < ultimately Latin *reprimere* to check.
reprisal (rɪˈpraɪzl̩) *n* an act of retaliation. < Middle French *reprisaille.*
reproach (rɪˈprəʊtʃ) *vb* blame or express disappointment with (a person), esp. to arouse feelings of shame or remorse.
• *n* **1** an act or instance of reproaching. **2** something that incurs censure or discredit. **reproachful** *adj* **reproachfully** *adv* < Old French *reprochier.*
reprobate (ˈrɛprəˌbeɪt) *n* an unprincipled or dissolute person.
• *adj* dissolute or depraved.
• *vb* disapprove strongly of; condemn. **reprobation** *n* < Late Latin *reprobare.*
reproduce (ˌriːprəˈdjuːs) *vb* **1** produce young, offspring, etc. **2** produce a copy or replica of; imitate. **3** produce again; re-create. **4** translate into sound. **reproduction** *n* **1** reproducing or being reproduced. **2** a copy or replica. **reproductive** *adj*
reproof (rɪˈpruːf) *n* a reprimand or censure. **reprove** *vb* reprimand or censure. < ultimately Old French *reprover.*
reptile (ˈrɛptaɪl) *n* a snake, lizard, or other member of the class of cold-blooded, air-breathing vertebrate animals. **reptilian** *adj* < ultimately Latin *repere* to creep.
republic (rɪˈpʌblɪk) *n* **1** a state or form of government in which the supreme power is held by the electorate or their representatives. **2** a country in which the head of state is not a monarch but a president. < ultimately Latin *respublica,* from *res* affair, thing + *publicus* public.
republican (rɪˈpʌblɪkən) *adj* of, like, or in favour of a republic.
• *n* a person who favours republican government. **Republican** *adj, n* (a member) of the US Republican party.
repudiate (rɪˈpjuːdɪˌeɪt) *vb* reject, deny, or disclaim. **repudiation** *n* < Latin *repudiare.*
repugnant (rɪˈpʌgnənt) *adj* repulsive. **repugnance** *n* **repugnantly** *adv* < Latin *repugnare* to fight against.
repulse (rɪˈpʌls) *vb* **1** drive back (an attack); repel. **2** rebuff. **repulsion** *n* **repulsive** *adj* causing extreme aversion; repellent. **repulsively** *adv* **repulsiveness** *n* < Latin *repellere* to repel.
reputation (ˌrɛpjʊˈteɪʃən) *n* **1** people's overall opinion or estimation of a person, etc.: The new dentist has an excellent reputation. **2** a good or bad reputation: Her new boyfriend has got a bit of a reputation. **reputable** *adj* having a good reputation; well thought of. **repute** *n* fame or favourable reputation: a man of repute. **reputed** *adj* according to what is generally believed. **reputedly** *adv* < Latin *reputare* to think over.
request (rɪˈkwɛst) *n* **1** the act of asking (someone) for something or asking (someone) to do something. **2** something asked for.
• *vb* make a request. < Middle French *requeste.*
requiem (ˈrɛkwɪˌɛm, ˈrɛkwɪəm) *n* **1** a Mass for the dead. **2** a musical setting for this. < Latin *requies* rest.
require (rɪˈkwaɪə) *vb* **1** need. **2** demand or oblige: All pupils are required to wear grey

socks. **3** (*formal*) wish to have or be served with. **requirement** *n* < ultimately Latin *requirere*.

requisite (ˈrɛkwɪzɪt) *adj* required or necessary; essential.
• *n* an essential requirement. < SEE REQUIRE.

requisition (ˌrɛkwɪˈzɪʃən) *n* a formal demand, application, or request.
• *vb* demand, etc., by means of a requisition. < ultimately Latin *requisitio* searching.

rescind (rɪˈsɪnd) *vb* repeal, cancel, or withdraw. **rescission** *n* < Latin *rescindere*.

rescue (ˈrɛskjuː) *vb* save or free from danger, confinement, etc.
• *n* rescuing or being rescued. **rescuer** *n* < ultimately Latin *excutere*, from *ex-* + *quatere* to shake.

research (rɪˈsɜːtʃ) *n* careful or systematic study, esp. to learn new facts or information.
• *vb* conduct research into. **researcher** *n* < Middle French *recherchier* to investigate.

resemble (rɪˈzɛmbl̩) *vb* be or look like. **resemblance** *n* < Middle French *resembler*.

resent (rɪˈzɛnt) *vb* feel indignant or bitter about: I resent being called lazy. **resentful** *adj* **resentfully** *adv* **resentfulness** *n* **resentment** *n* < French *ressentir*.

reserve (rɪˈzɜːv) *vb* **1** save or set aside for later use. **2** set aside or have set aside for the use of a particular person: It's always wise to reserve a seat. **3** defer or postpone: reserve judgment.
• *n* **1** a supply reserved for later use; stock. **2** an auxiliary military force that is called upon in an emergency. **3** a member of such a force. **4** a member of a team who stands by as a substitute. **5** a tract of land set aside for a particular purpose: a wildlife reserve. **6** restraint or reticence in the way one speaks or conducts oneself. **7** a price below which something is not to be sold. **8** the act of reserving or state of being reserved: There's still plenty of food in reserve. **reservation** *n* **1** reserving or being reserved. **2** a limitation or qualification: We accepted the proposal without reservation. **3** a booking: hotel reservations. **4** a tract of land set aside for occupation by a particular group or tribe: Indian reservations. **reserved** *adj* (of a person) showing restraint in outward manner. **reservist** *n* a member of a military reserve. < ultimately Latin *reservare*.

reservoir (ˈrɛzəˌvwɑː) *n* **1** a natural or man-made lake used for the storage of water. **2** any container for a liquid. **3** a supply or store. < French *réservoir*.

reside (rɪˈzaɪd) *vb* **1** live or have one's home (in a particular place). **2** belong to or be vested in. < ultimately Latin *residēre* to sit back.

residence (ˈrɛzɪdəns) *n* **1** a place where a person resides. **2** a large house: a stately residence. **3** the act or state of residing: take up residence. **in residence** living in a particular place, esp. to perform a duty or pursue studies.

resident (ˈrɛzɪdənt) *adj* **1** living in a place. **2** employed as a member of the permanent staff.
• *n* **1** a person who lives in a particular place. **2** a hotel guest who stays overnight. **residential** *adj* **1** containing or set aside for private houses as opposed to shops or factories: a residential area. **2** entailing or connected with residence: a residential post.

residue (ˈrɛzɪˌdjuː) *n* what remains or is left over; remainder. **residual** *adj* remaining or left over. < ultimately Latin *residēre* to remain.

resign (rɪˈzaɪn) *vb* give up (a job or position). **resigned** *adj* having a frame of mind which accepts (something undesirable) as inevitable. **resignedly** *adv* **resign oneself to** accept (something undesirable) as inevitable. < ultimately Latin *resignare* to unseal.

resignation (ˌrɛzɪgˈneɪʃən) *n* **1** the act or an instance of resigning. **2** written notification of resigning. **3** the quality of being resigned.

resilient (rɪˈzɪlɪənt) *adj* **1** able to spring back to a former shape; elastic. **2** able to recover from setbacks. **resilience** *n* **resiliently** *adv* < Latin *resilire* to jump back.

resin (ˈrɛzɪn) *n* **1** a sticky, non-flammable, plant secretion used in making varnish, ink, plastic, etc. **2** a synthetic substitute for this. < ultimately Greek *rhētinē* pine resin.

resist (rɪˈzɪst) *vb* **1** oppose or fight against. **2** refrain from accepting or doing (something): He finds a good cigar hard to resist. **3** be unaffected or unharmed by: The wood is treated to resist heat. **resistance** *n* **1** the act or an instance of resisting. **2** the power to resist: Oranges will help you build up your resistance. **3** an opposing force or influence: wind resistance. **4** the opposition provided by a substance to the flow of electricity passing through it; measure of this. **5** an underground organization whose purpose is to sabotage occupying enemy forces. **resistant** *adj* resisting or able to resist: water-resistant. **resistive** *adj* resistant. **resistor** *n* an electrical component providing resistance to the flow of electricity passing through it. < ultimately Latin *resistere.*

resolute (ˈrɛzəˌluːt) *adj* showing firm determination. **resolutely** *adv* **resoluteness** *n* < SEE **RESOLVE.**

resolution (ˌrɛzəˈluːʃən) *n* **1** firm determination. **2** a firm decision; pledge: New Year resolutions. **3** a formal statement of a proposal or decision: The resolution was carried by six votes to five. **4** the act of resolving (a problem, etc.). **5** the act of separating something into its parts or constituents.

resolve (rɪˈzɒlv) *vb* **1** decide firmly. **2** (of a committee, etc.) pass a resolution. **3** solve, settle, or deal with (a problem, issue, etc.). **4** separate into parts or constituents.
• *n* **1** firm determination. **2** a firm decision. **resolved** *adj* resolute. < Latin *re-* + *solvere* to loosen.

resonant (ˈrɛzənənt) *adj* **1** continuing to sound; echoing. **2** (of walls, etc.) causing a voice, etc., to resound. **3** (of a voice, etc.) resounding. **resonance** *n* < SEE **RESOUND.**

resort (rɪˈzɔːt) *vb* **1** turn to or have recourse to: resort to improved methods. **2** go or visit, esp. frequently or regularly.
• *n* **1** a person or thing resorted to. **2** a place visited regularly by many people, esp. a holiday centre: a seaside resort. **3** recourse. < Middle French *resortir.*

resound (rɪˈzaʊnd) *vb* **1** fill (a place) with deep or echoing sound. **2** become filled with sound. **resounding** *adj* notable or emphatic: a resounding success. < ultimately Latin *re-* + *sonare* to sound.

resource (rɪˈzɔːs) *n* **1** an available means of support or assistance. **2** a reserve stock or supply: natural resources. **3** cleverness or ingenuity, esp. in handling problems. **resourceful** *adj* skilful in handling problems or devising strategies. < ultimately Latin *resurgere* to rise again.

respect (rɪˈspɛkt) *n* **1** esteem or high regard. **2** thoughtfulness or consideration. **3** connection or reference: With respect to your last comment, I have to disagree. **4** a detail or aspect.
• *vb* **1** show or feel respect for. **2** acknowledge as proper, inviolable, etc.: We respect your right to differ on this issue. **3** show consideration for. **respectable** *adj* **1** having a socially acceptable character, appearance, etc.; decent: The collar and tie made him look a bit more respectable. **2** of an acceptable standard, size, etc. **respectability** *n* **respectably** *adv* **respectful** *adj* having or showing respect. **respectfully** *adv* **respecting** *prep* with regard to; concerning. **respective** *adj* (of two or more people or things) relating to each as a separate entity: My husband and I like to visit our respective parents at least once a year. **respectively** *adv* in the same order as previously mentioned: Arthur and Mary received first prize and third prize respectively. **respects** *pl n* polite greetings: Send them my respects. < Latin *respicere* to look back. SEE PANEL.

respire (rɪˈspaɪə) *vb* (*formal*) breathe. **respiration** *n* breathing. **respirator** *n* **1** a filtering device worn over the nose and mouth to prevent the breathing of harmful dust or gases. **2** a device used for providing artificial respiration. **respiratory** *adj* of or connected with respiration. < Latin *respirare.*

respite (ˈrɛspɪt, ˈrɛspaɪt) *n* **1** a pause or interval providing relief. **2** a period of temporary delay. < ultimately Latin *respectus* looking back.

resplendent (rɪˈsplɛndənt) *adj* having a brilliant or splendid appearance. **resplendently** *adv* < Latin *resplendēre* to shine back.

respond (rɪˈspɒnd) *vb* **1** answer or reply. **2** react in response to a stimulus. **3** react favourably in response to: Most people respond to kindness. **respondent** *n* a person against whom a lawsuit is brought, esp. a defendant in a divorce case. **response** *n* **1** the act of responding. **2** an answer, reply, or reaction. < ultimately Latin *respondēre.*

responsible (rɪˈspɒnsəbl̩) *adj* **1** having a duty or obligation to see that something is done, taken care of, etc.; liable or answerable. **2** involving important duties: a responsible job. **3** being the cause or perpetrator of something: The teacher

respectively

The conference was addressed by Mr E.A. Carter and Dr R. Beecham, on behalf of the polytechnic and university lecturers *respectively.* Respectively is used to state a linear correspondence between the individual items in two series. In the above sentence it clarifies that Mr Carter spoke for the polytechnic lecturers and Dr Beecham for the university lecturers.

wants to interview the boy responsible for the graffiti. **4** trustworthy or sensible. **5** capable of rational behaviour: A child of five can hardly be considered responsible. **responsibleness** *n* **responsibly** *adv* **responsibility** *n* **1** the state of being responsible. **2** a person or thing that one is responsible for. < SEE **RESPOND.**

responsive (rɪˈspɒnsɪv) *adj* **1** quick to react or respond; sensitive: a responsive pupil. **2** reacting in a favourable way. **3** done or made as a response. **responsively** *adv* **responsiveness** *n*

rest[1] (rɛst) *vb* **1** stop working, exercising, moving, etc., in order to regain energy. **2** allow (a person, etc.) to do this: Sit down and rest your legs. **3** be lying or sitting down, esp. to relax or regain energy. **4** be at ease: I won't rest until I catch the culprit. **5** place on, against, etc., for support: Rest your head on my shoulder. **6** depend or be based: The outcome rests on nothing but the team's fitness. **7** be no longer investigated, discussed, etc.: I suggest we let the matter rest. **8** (of a gaze, look, etc.) be directed: Her eyes rested on the fairy at the top of the tree.
• *n* **1** freedom from work or activity; period of this. **2** sleep or repose. **3** the state of not moving: The kite finally came to rest against a tree. **4** something serving as a support: a headrest. **5** (*music*) a silence between notes; sign for this. **restful** *adj* **1** providing rest. **2** quiet or peaceful. **restfully** *adv* **restfulness** *n* **restless** *adj* **1** not affording rest or sleep: a restless night. **2** unable to stay still; fidgety. < Old English. SEE PANEL.

rest[2] *n* **the rest** all the others; remainder.
• *vb* continue to be; remain: Rest assured that we will do our best. < ultimately Latin *restare* to stand back.

restaurant (ˈrɛstrã, ˈrɛstrənt) *n* a place where a person can buy a meal and eat it while sitting down. < French.

restitution (ˌrɛstɪˈtjuːʃən) *n* **1** the returning of something to its rightful owner. **2** compensation for loss, damage, or injury. < ultimately Latin *restituere* to restore.

restive (ˈrɛstɪv) *adj* **1** restless or fidgety. **2** showing signs of impatience. **restively** *adv* **restiveness** *n* < Middle French *rester* to remain.

restore (rɪˈstɔː) *vb* **1** give back or return. **2** return (something) to its original condition. **3** bring back to good health or a normal condition. **4** bring back into use; reinstate. **restoration** *n* **restorer** *n* **restorative** *adj* restoring to a healthy or normal condition. < ultimately Latin *instaurare* to renew.

restrain (rɪˌstreɪn) *vb* prevent from moving or doing something. **restrained** *adj* showing restraint. **restraint** *n* **1** restraining; being restrained. **2** something which restrains. **3** moderation in manner or expression: The news coverage of the disaster showed remarkable restraint. < ultimately Latin *restringere.*

restrict (rɪˈstrɪkt) *vb* keep within certain limits; regulate. **restriction** *n* **restrictive** *adj* restricting. < Latin *restringere.*

result (rɪˈzʌlt) *n* **1** an outcome or effect. **2** the answer to a calculation. **3** the outcome of a contest or sporting event.
• *vb* **1** arise or occur as a result. **2** have a specified outcome: The brief encounter resulted in a lasting friendship. **resultant** *adj* following or coming about as a result. < ultimately Latin *resultare* to rebound.

resume (rɪˈzjuːm) *vb* **1** begin again after an interval or interruption; recommence. **2** (*formal*) take or occupy again: resume one's seat. **resumption** *n* < ultimately Latin *resumere.*

résumé (rɛzjʊˌmeɪ, reɪˈzjuːmeɪ) *n* a short summary. < French.

resurgence (rɪˈsɜːdʒəns) *n* a revival or rising again into activity. **resurgent** *adj* < Latin *resurgere* to rise again.

resurrect (ˌrɛzəˈrɛkt) *vb* **1** bring back from the dead. **2** bring back into use. **resurrection** *n* < ultimately Latin *resurgere* to rise again.

resuscitate (rɪˈsʌsɪˌteɪt) *vb* bring back to consciousness; revive. **resuscitation** *n* **resuscitator** *n* a machine used for resuscitating. < Latin *resuscitare.*

retail (ˈriːteɪl) *n* the sale of goods to the general public.
• *vb* sell or be sold to the general public.
• *adj, adv* of or connected with such trade. **retailer** *n* < Middle French *retaillier* to cut back.

retain (rɪˈteɪn) *vb* **1** continue to have, keep, use, etc.: She retained the championship. **2** continue to keep in the memory. **3** hire or engage, esp. by paying a fee in advance. **4** hold or keep something in

The Traveller's Rest

The use of the noun rest in inn signs such as 'The Traveller's Rest' is a reminder of its earlier meaning. Rest derives from the Old English *rest* or *ræst* meaning 'a resting place for the night' or 'bed'.

place: a retaining wall. **retainer** *n* a fee paid to retain a professional person's services. < ultimately Latin *retinēre* to hold back.

retaliate (rɪˈtælɪˌeɪt) *vb* reciprocate an injury or unkindness. **retaliation** *n* **retaliatory** *adj* < Late Latin *retaliare.*

retard (rɪˈtɑːd) *vb* delay or slow down. **retardation** *n* **retarded** *adj* slower than average in intellectual development. < Latin *retardare.*

retch (rɛtʃ) *vb* make an involuntary but usually ineffectual attempt to vomit. < Old English *hrǣcan* to spit.

retention (rɪˈtɛnʃən) *n* **1** retaining or being retained. **2** the power to retain. < SEE **RETAIN.**

retentive (rɪˈtɛntɪv) *adj* able to retain: a retentive memory.

reticent (ˈrɛtɪsənt) *adj* reluctant or unwilling to say or reveal something. **reticence** *n* **reticently** *adv* < Latin *reticēre* to keep silent.

retina (ˈrɛtɪnə) *n, pl* **retinas** the sensory membrane at the back of the eye which sends messages to the brain via the optic nerve. < Medieval Latin.

retinue (ˈrɛtɪˌnjuː) *n* a group of attendants accompanying an important person. < Middle French *retenir* to retain.

retire (rɪˈtaɪə) *vb* **1** give up one's occupation for ever, esp. because of age; cause an employee to do this. **2** go to bed. **3** (*formal*) go or withdraw (to a quieter place): May I suggest we all retire to the lounge. **4** (*cricket*) end an innings undefeated. **retirement** *n* **retiring** *adj* shy or reserved. < Middle French *retirer.*

retort[1] (rɪˈtɔːt) *vb* utter (something) sharply in reply.
• *n* a sharp or witty reply. < Latin *retorquēre* to twist back.

retort[2] *n* **1** a glass vessel with a long, downward-sloping neck, used for distilling. **2** a vessel used for heating coal or ores in the production of gas or steel. < Middle French *retorte.*

retouch (riːˈtʌtʃ) *vb* make minor alterations to (a photograph, etc.).

retrace (riːˈtreɪs) *vb* **1** go back over: retrace one's footsteps. **2** recall or form a mental picture of (a previous experience).

retract (rɪˈtrækt) *vb* **1** draw or be drawn in. **2** withdraw (a statement, etc.); recant. **retraction** *n* < Latin *retrahere.*

retread (ˈriːˌtrɛd) *n* a restored tyre whose original worn tread has been replaced by a new one.

retreat (rɪˈtriːt) *vb* **1** move back; withdraw. **2** go away for shelter or refuge.
• *n* **1** the act of retreating. **2** a bugle call to retreat or retire. **3** a refuge or sanctuary. **4** a period of rest, prayer, or meditation. < ultimately Latin *retrahere* to withdraw.

retrench (rɪˈtrɛntʃ) *vb* cut back or reduce. **retrenchment** *n* < Middle French *retrenchier.*

retribution (ˌrɛtrɪˈbjuːʃən) *n* deserved punishment. **retributive** *adj* relating to or involving retribution. < ultimately Latin *retribuere* to pay back.

retrieve (rɪˈtriːv) *vb* **1** regain possession of. **2** bring back or recover: The information can easily be retrieved. **3** rescue or restore: An apology was sufficient to retrieve the situation. **4** (of a dog) find and bring in (killed game, etc.). **retrievable** *adj* **retrieval** *n* retrieving or being retrieved. **retriever** *n* a dog commonly used for retrieving game. < Middle French *retrouver* to find again.

retroactive (ˌrɛtrəʊˈæktɪv) *adj* affecting the past (as well as the present and future): retroactive laws. < ultimately Latin *retro-* back + *agere* to drive.

retrograde (ˈrɛtrəˌɡreɪd) *adj* **1** moving backwards. **2** reverting to or tending towards a worse or less advanced state. < SEE **RETROGRESS.**

retrogress (ˌrɛtrəˈɡrɛs) *vb* revert to a worse state; deteriorate. **retrogression** *n* **retrogressive** *adj* < *Latin retrogradi,* from *retro-* + *gradi* to go.

retrospect (ˈrɛtrəˌspɛkt) *n* a survey of past events. **in retrospect** (considering a past event) with hindsight. **retrospective** *adj* **1** (of a law, etc.) affecting the past (as well as the present and future). **2** surveying or looking back on the past. **retrospectively** *adv* < Latin *retro-* + *specere* to look.

return (rɪˈtɜːn) *vb* **1** come or go back. **2** send, give, or take back. **3** resume: Can we now return to the question of funding? **4** repay: return a compliment. **5** (of a jury) reach (a verdict). **6** reply or retort. **7** state formally or officially. **8** elect (a candidate), esp. as an MP.
• *n* **1** the act of returning. **2** the profit or proceeds of a transaction. **3** a formal statement: a tax return. **4** a return ticket. **5** a return match.
• *adj* **1** (of a match, contest, etc.) taking place for the second time: The return leg ended in a 1-1 draw. **2** enabling or connected with return: a return ticket. **returning-officer** *n* an official who presides over an election and declares the result. < ultimately Old French *retourner*, from *re-* + *tourner* to turn.

reunion (riːˈjuːnɪən) *n* **1** a gathering of people for social purposes after a long period of separation: an annual reunion. **2** reuniting or being reunited. **reunite** *vb* unite again after separation.

rev (rɛv) *n* a revolution of an engine.
• *vb* **revved; revving 1** increase the speed of revolution of (an engine). **2** (of an engine) run at an increased speed. < *revolution.*

Rev., Revd *abbrev* Reverend.

reveal (rɪˈviːl) *vb* **1** disclose, divulge, or make known. **2** expose to view; uncover. < ultimately Latin *revelare* to uncover.

reveille (rɪˈvælɪ) *n* a signal to get up in the morning, esp. a bugle call for rousing soldiers. < French *réveiller* to awaken.

revel (ˈrɛvl̩) *vb* **revelled; revelling 1 revel in** take great delight or satisfaction in. **2** take part in wild or lively merrymaking. **reveller** *n* **revelry** *n* wild or lively merrymaking. **revels** *pl n* revelry. < ultimately Latin *rebellare* to rebel.

revelation (ˌrɛvəˈleɪʃən) *n* **1** the act of revealing. **2** something revealed, esp. a sudden, surprising disclosure. **3 Revelation** the last book of the New Testament. < SEE **REVEAL.**

revenge (rɪˈvɛndʒ) *n* **1** an act done in retaliation for a wrong or injury that one has suffered. **2** a desire to perform such an act. **3** a return match considered as an opportunity to make up for a previous defeat.
• *vb* take revenge; avenge. **revengeful** *adj* < Middle French *revengier.*

revenue (ˈrɛvəˌnjuː) *n* income, esp. that which a government receives from taxation. < ultimately Latin *revenire* to return.

reverberate (rɪˈvɜːbəˌreɪt) *vb* echo repeatedly; resound. **reverberation** *n* < Latin *reverberare* to strike back.

revere (rɪˈvɪə) *vb* regard with awe and respect. < Latin *revereri.*

reverence (ˈrɛvərəns) *n* a feeling of profound awe and respect. **Reverence** *n* a title sometimes used for a Roman Catholic priest.
• *vb* treat or regard with reverence. **reverend** *adj* **1** revered. **2 the Reverend** a title of respect for a clergyman. **reverent** *adj* feeling or expressing reverence. **reverently** *adv*

reverie (ˈrɛvərɪ) *n* **1** a day-dream. **2** the state of day-dreaming or being lost in thought. < French *rêverie,* from Middle French *resver* to be delirious.

reverse (rɪˈvɜːs) *adj* **1** opposite or contrary in order, position, nature, etc. **2** effecting backward motion: a reverse gear.
• *vb* **1** move or drive backwards or in the opposite direction: Now try reversing the car round the corner. **2** change the order or direction of: reverse the items on an agenda. **3** revoke or annul (a decision, etc.). **4** turn inside out or upside down. **5** change completely in nature or character: reverse a defeat.
• *n* **1** the opposite of something. **2** the back of a coin, medal, etc. **3** a gear that effects backward motion. **4** a misfortune; reversal. **reversible** *adj* **reversal** *n* **1** the act of reversing. **2** a misfortune: a series of reversals. **reverse the charges** have the recipient of a telephone call pay for it. < ultimately Latin *revertere* to turn back.

reversion (rɪˈvɜːʃən) *n* the act of reverting.

revert (rɪˈvɜːt) *vb* **1** return to a former state, condition, or practice, esp. one that is undesirable. **2** resume a previous topic. **3** (*law*) (of property) return to the former owner. < Middle French *revertir.*

review (rɪˈvjuː) *n* **1** a general survey: a comprehensive review of current research. **2** a short, critical report, esp. of a new book, film, play, etc. **3** (the section of) a magazine or journal devoted to such reports. **4** a second or additional examination: The schedule requires further review. **5** an inspection of troops, etc.
• *vb* **1** give, write, or present a review of. **2** re-examine. **3** hold a review of (troops, etc.). **reviewer** *n* < Middle French *revue,* from *revoir* to look over.

revile (rɪˈvaɪl) *vb* subject to verbal abuse. < Middle French *reviler* to despise.

revise (rɪˈvaɪz) *vb* **1** re-examine and change or amend: revise one's opinions. **2** study (notes, etc.) in preparation for an examination. **revision** *n* **1** the act of revising. **2** a revised version. < ultimately Latin *revidēre* to see again.

revive (rɪˈvaɪv) *vb* **1** return to life or consciousness. **2** become or cause to become popular or fashionable again. **revival** *n* **1** reviving or being revived. **2** something that has been reintroduced. **3** a reawakening of religious interest or faith; campaign designed to promote this. **revivalism** *n* the spirit characterizing religious revivals. **revivalist** *n* < Latin *revivere.*

revoke (rɪˈvəʊk) *vb* **1** withdraw, cancel, or annul (a will, etc.), **2** fail to follow suit in a card-game when able to do so.
• *n* the act or an instance of revoking in

a card-game. < ultimately Latin *revocare.*

revolt (rɪˈvəʊlt) *vb* **1** rise up in rebellion. **2** cause feelings of disgust in: Some of the habits she'd picked up in prison quite revolted him.
• *n* the act of rising against or defying authority. **revolting** *adj* < Old Italian *rivoltare* to overthrow.

revolution (ˌrɛvəˈluːʃən) *n* **1** the overthrow of a political system or regime. **2** a drastic change. **3** the act or process of rotating. **4** a single rotation. **revolutionize** *vb* change drastically or completely. < SEE **REVOLVE.**

revolutionary (ˌrɛvəˈluːʃənərɪ) *adj* **1** connected with political revolution: revolutionary activities. **2** involving or bringing about drastic changes; totally new and different.
• *n* a person who supports or is engaged in revolution.

revolve (rɪˈvɒlv) *vb* **1** turn or cause to turn upon an axis; rotate. **2** move along a circular path around a central point. **revolver** *n* a pistol with a revolving cylinder that allows several shots to be fired without reloading. < ultimately Latin *revolvere* to roll back, from *re-* + *volvere* to roll.

revue (rɪˈvjuː) *n* a light-hearted, theatrical entertainment usually comprising a number of songs and satirical sketches. < SEE **REVIEW.**

revulsion (rɪˈvʌlʃən) *n* **1** a feeling of profound loathing or disgust. **2** a sudden change of feeling, opinion, etc. < ultimately Latin *revellere* to pull away.

reward (rɪˈwɔːd) *n* **1** something offered or given for some service or achievement. **2** payment or recompense.
• *vb* **1** give a reward to. **2** recompense. **rewarding** *adj* satisfying or fulfilling. < of Germanic origin.

rhapsody (ˈræpsədɪ) *n* **1** a highly emotional musical composition with an irregular structure. **2** rapturous delight or ecstatic enthusiasm. **3** an expression of this. < ultimately Greek *rhaptein* to stitch together.

rhetoric (ˈrɛtərɪk) *n* **1** the art of using words persuasively or impressively. **2** (*derogatory*) language which has an excess of ornament and a lack of substance. **rhetorical** *adj* **1** of or connected with rhetoric. **2** (of language) affected or insincere. **rhetorical question** an utterance with the form of a question but without an interrogative function. < ultimately Greek *eirein* to speak.

rheumatism (ˈruːməˌtɪzəm) *n* any of various diseases causing pain in the joints or muscles. **rheumatic** *adj* caused by, connected with, or suffering from rheumatism. **rheumatoid** *adj* of or resembling rheumatism. < ultimately Greek *rheuma* stream, flow.

rhino (ˈraɪnəʊ) *n, pl* **rhinos, rhino** (*informal*) a rhinoceros.

rhinoceros (raɪˈnɒsərəs) *n, pl* **rhinoceroses, rhinoceros** any of a family of African or Asian mammals with a massive body, very thick skin, and either one or two horns on the snout. SEE PANEL.

rhododendron (ˌrəʊdəˈdɛndrən) *n* any of a group of evergreen shrubs and trees, usually with abundant clusters of trumpet- or bell-shaped flowers. < ultimately Greek *rhodon* rose + *dendron* tree.

rhombus (ˈrɒmbəs) *n* a geometric figure with the shape of a diamond. **rhomboid** *adj*) shaped like a rhombus. < ultimately Greek *rhombos.*

rhubarb (ˈruːbɑːb) *n* **1** a garden plant with long, thick, red or pink stalks that are cooked and eaten as a dessert; stalks used as food. **2** (*informal*) nonsense. < Middle French *reubarbe,* from Medieval Latin *reubarbarum.*

rhyme (raɪm) *n* **1** sound correspondence in (the final syllable of) words, esp. those ending lines of verse. **2** a word which rhymes with another. **3** rhyming verse; instance of this.
• *vb* **1** compose rhymes or rhyming verse. **2** form a rhyme. **rhyme or reason** sense or logic. **rhyming slang** slang in which a word is substituted by a word or phrase that rhymes with it. < Old French, probably from Latin *rhythmus* rhythm. SEE PANEL AT **LOAF**[1].

rhythm (ˈrɪðəm) *n* **1** the pattern produced by recurring sound prominences in music or speech. **2** a characteristic or recognizable pattern. **3** movement or a

---

rhinoceros

Rhinoceros came into English via Latin in the 13th century from the Greek word *rhinokerōs,* from *rhis* 'nose' and *keras* 'horn'. The same Greek word for nose provides the combining form rhino-, which is found in a number of medical terms such as rhinology 'the study of the nose', rhinoplasty 'plastic surgery of the nose', and rhinorrhoea 'an abnormally runny nose'.

---

sense of movement communicated by a regular recurrence of emphases. **4** any recurrent pattern. **rhythmic** *adj* **rhythmical** *adj* **rhythmically** *adv* < ultimately Greek *rhythmos,* from *rhein* to flow. SEE PANEL.

rib (rɪb) *n* **1** one of the slender, curved bones which form a framework around the heart and lungs. **2** a cut of meat including one or more ribs. **3** any structural part resembling a rib. **4** one of several curved bands forming part of the moulding on a vaulted ceiling. **5** a vertical, raised band in knitted or woven material.
• *vb* **ribbed**; **ribbing** (*informal*) tease. **ribbed** *adj* having raised or projecting bands. **rib-cage** *n* the framework of ribs around the heart and lungs. < Old English.

ribald (ˈrɪbl̩d, ˈraɪbɔːld) *adj* expressing or characterized by coarse or obscene humour. **ribaldry** *n* < Old French *ribauld* wanton.

ribbon (ˈrɪbn̩) *n* **1** a long, narrow strip of brightly-coloured fabric used for decoration or for tying. **2** a piece of ribbon of special pattern worn as a military decoration. **3** a long, narrow strip of material that carries the ink for a typewriter or printer. **4** anything resembling or likened to a ribbon. **in ribbons** ragged or shredded. < Middle French *riban.*

rice (raɪs) *n* **1** a kind of grass that grows on wet ground in warm climates and whose grains provide an important source of food. **2** the grains used as food. < ultimately of Oriental origin. SEE PANEL.

rich (rɪtʃ) *adj* **1** having a lot of money; wealthy. **2** having a great deal of something: The country is rich in natural resources. **3** of splendid or highly ornate appearance: a rich tapestry. **4** (of food) having a high fat, sugar, etc., content. **5** (of fuel mixtures) having a high proportion of petrol, etc. **6** producing abundantly; fertile: rich soil. **7** prolific; luxuriant: a rich crop. **8** (of a colour, sound, smell, or taste) deep or intense, esp. in a satisfying way. **9** (*informal*) ironic or amusing. **richness** *n* **riches** *pl n* wealth. **richly** *adv* **1** in a rich manner: richly dressed. **2** fully or thoroughly: richly deserved reward. < Old English *rīce.*

rick[1] (rɪk) *n* a stack of hay or straw. < Old English *hrēac.*

rick[2] *vb* strain or wrench: rick one's neck. < origin uncertain.

rickets (ˈrɪkɪts) *n* a deficiency disease in young children caused by lack of vitamin D which causes softening and deformity of the bones. < origin unknown.

rickety (ˈrɪkɪtɪ) *adj* **1** shaky or tottering. **2** resembling or suffering from rickets. < *rickets.*

rickshaw (ˈrɪkʃɔː) *n* a small, two-wheeled, cart-like vehicle that is pulled by one or more people and is used in the

rhythm

Rhythm is one of a number of words in the language whose spelling does not include an a,e,i,o, or u—the five letters that are used to indicate vowel sounds. Other words of this type include pygmy, nymph, lynch, gypsy, tryst, and hymn, where the y represents a short vowel, and try, sly, and fry where it represents a diphthong.

Conversely, there are words such as audio, eerie, and queue which contain a disproportionately high number of vowel letters.

rice

The word rice has a very long history. It first appeared in English in the 13th century as *rys,* developed from the Old French *ris.* The Old French name came from *riso,* the Old Italian word, which in turn derived from the Greek *oryza*. How the Greeks came by the word is unknown. However, as one would expect, the word is ultimately of Oriental origin.

rickshaw

The two-wheeled carriage pulled by one or occasionally two men that is used in various parts of Asia is called a rickshaw. The word derives from the Japanese *jinrikisha,* literally 'manpower vehicle', from *jin* 'man', *riki* 'power', and *sha* 'vehicle'. The reduced form that we use today (without the *jin*) is something of a misnomer—the rickshaw is hardly a 'power vehicle'!

Far East. < Japanese *jinrikisha,* from *jin* man + *riki* power + *sha* vehicle. SEE PANEL.

ricochet (ˈrɪkəˌʃeɪ) *vb* (of a bullet or missile) rebound at an angle from a surface.
• *n* a rebound of this kind. < French.

rid (rɪd) *vb* **rid; ridding** free (someone or oneself) from an unwanted person or thing: I wish they'd rid me of the responsibility. **get rid of 1** remove. **2** cause to go away. **3** disencumber oneself of; sell. **good riddance** used to express one's relief that a person or thing has gone. < Old Norse *rythja* to clear.

ridden (ˈrɪdn̩) SEE **RIDE.**
• *adj* afflicted or overwhelmed by: a guilt-ridden conscience.

riddle[1] (ˈrɪdl̩) *n* **1** a verbal puzzle, usually humorous. **2** anything puzzling. < Old English *rædelse.*

riddle[2] *n* a coarse sieve.
• *vb* **1** sift with a riddle. **2** make full of holes: riddled with bullets. **3** spread through pervasively: riddled with decay. < Old English *hriddel.*

ride (raɪd) *vb* **rode; ridden; riding 1** sit on a horse, bicycle, etc., and control its movements. **2** use a means of transport or conveyance: Shall we ride or walk? **3** be carried or conveyed by. **4** be supported or sustained by. **5** float or appear to float, esp. with a bobbing motion: ride at anchor. **6** continue without objection or interference: let things ride. **7** sway away from a blow to soften its impact.
• *n* **1** a trip on horseback, in a car, etc.: go for a ride. **2** a path or track used for riding. **3** a device at a fairground on which people ride for excitement or pleasure. **4** a vehicle or horse considered in terms of the comfort, control, etc., it affords: a rough ride. **ride out** survive (a difficult situation). **rider** *n* **1** a person who rides a horse, bicycle, etc. **2** a clause or condition added to a document as a qualification. **riderless** *adj* **ride up** (of a garment) work upwards out of its proper position. **take someone for a ride** (*informal*) deceive someone. < Old English *rīdan.*

ridge (rɪdʒ) *n* **1** a long, narrow, raised strip of land, esp. a range of hills. **2** a line where two upward-sloping sides meet. **3** any long, narrow, raised strip. **ridged** *adj* < Old English *hrycg.*

ridicule (ˈrɪdɪˌkjuːl) *n* the act of ridiculing; derision.
• *vb* make fun of; deride. **ridiculous** *adj* **1** warranting derision. **2** preposterous; unthinkable. < ultimately Latin *rīdēre* to laugh.

rife (raɪf) *adj* **1** very common; widespread. **2** abounding (in); rampant. < Old English *rȳfe.*

riff-raff (ˈrɪfˌræf) *n* (*derogatory*) rabble. < Middle French *rif et raf,* from *rifler* to plunder + *raffe* sweeping.

rifle[1] (ˈraɪfl̩) *n* **1** a gun with a long barrel cut with spiral grooves and effective over a long range. **2** *pl* a military unit equipped with rifles.
• *vb* cut spiral grooves into. < French *rifler* to file.

rifle[2] *vb* search and loot; plunder. < French *rifler* to plunder.

rift (rɪft) *n* **1** a split or crack, esp. in the earth. **2** an estrangement between two parties. **rift-valley** *n* a valley formed by land subsidence between two or more faults. < Scandinavian.

rig[1] (rɪg) *vb* **rigged; rigging 1** provide with clothes or equipment. **2** fit out (a ship) with rigging. **3** build or set up hastily or in a makeshift way.
• *n* **1** the arrangement of a ship's masts, spars, and ropes. **2** machinery or equipment for a special purpose, esp. drilling: an oil rig. **rigging** *n* the ropes and chains that hold and move the masts, spars, and sails on a ship. **rig-out** *n* (*informal*) an outfit of clothing. < Middle English *riggen.*

rig[2] *vb* manipulate dishonestly: Prices were rigged. < origin unknown.

right (raɪt) *adj* **1** morally correct; just: Taxing the poor is not right. **2** correct or true: a right answer. **3** normal, proper, or sound: in one's right mind. **4** appropriate: She has the gift of saying the right thing at the right time. **5** (*informal*) used emphatically: You've made a right mess of it! **6** on the side of something or someone facing east when the front faces north.
• *n* **1** what is morally correct or just: A child must learn the difference between right and wrong. **2** something to which a person is entitled or has a just claim: I know my rights. **3** the right side or area. **4** the right hand; blow with this. **5 the Right** those with conservative political views.
• *vb* **1** return to a correct, usually upright position: Luckily the boat righted itself. **2** correct or rectify: The electrical fault soon righted itself. **3** avenge: right a wrong.
• *adv* **1** correctly: to guess right. **2** on or towards the side of something facing east when its front faces north. **3** directly or straight: I went right into his office and demanded an explanation. **4** precisely; exactly: She came in right at the most awkward moment. **5 all** the way: The lift goes right to the top.

6 (*informal*) without delay; immediately: I'll be right back. **rightness** *n* **right angle** an angle of 90°. **right-angled** *adj* **right away** immediately. **rightful** *adj* in accordance with what is morally or legally correct: the rightful owner. **rightfully** *adv* **right-hand** *adj* **1** on the right. **2** right-handed. **right-handed** *adj* **1** also *adv* using the right hand usually or more easily than the left. **2** of, designed for, or operated with the right hand. **rightly** *adv* **1** in a morally correct way. **2** correctly: She rightly assumed that they needed her help. **3** really: I don't rightly know. **right of way** **1** the right to proceed while other vehicles wait. **2** the right to cross another's land; path used for this. **right wing** the more conservative part of a group or party. **right-wing** *adj* **right-winger** *n* < Old English *riht*. SEE PANEL AT **SHEER[1]**.

righteous (ˈraɪtʃəs) *adj* **1** acting in accordance with what is morally good; virtuous. **2** resulting from justifiable anger: righteous indignation. **righteously** *adv* **righteousness** *n* < Old English *rihtwīs*, from *riht* right + *wīs* wise.

rigid (ˈrɪdʒɪd) *adj* **1** not flexible or pliable; stiff. **2** strict: rigid laws. **rigidity** *n* **rigidly** *adv* < ultimately Latin *rigēre* to be stiff.

rigmarole (ˈrɪgməˌrəʊl) *n* (*derogatory*) any long or complicated procedure. < obsolete *ragman roll* list.

rigour (ˈrɪgə) *n* **1** strictness or severity. **2** (of weather, etc.) harsh conditions: the rigours of a Siberian winter. **rigorous** *adj* **1** very strict. **2** exercising scrupulous attention to detail and precision. **3** harsh or severe. < SEE **RIGID.**

rile (raɪl) *vb* annoy or irritate. < *roil* to disturb.

rill (rɪl) *n* (*literary*) a small stream. < Low German *rille*.

rim (rɪm) *n* the outer edge of a curved or circular object such as a saucer or wheel. **rimless** *adj* (of spectacles) without a rim. **rimmed** *adj* having a rim or rims of a specified type: red-rimmed eyes. < Old English *rima*.

rind (raɪnd) *n* a hard, outer skin or layer, as found on fruit, cheese, or bacon. < Old English.

ring[1] (rɪŋ) *n* **1** a small, circular band of metal worn on the finger as an ornament or as a sign of marriage or engagement, usually made of precious metal. **2** a circular band of wood or metal used for keeping things together or in shape: a key-ring. **3** anything which resembles or is likened to a ring: a ring of spectators. **4** an enclosed area for circus performers. **5** a raised, enclosed platform for boxers or wrestlers. **6** a group of people working as a team or gang, often clandestinely or for dishonest purposes: a vice ring. • *vb* **1** encircle. **2** put a small, metal band around the leg of a bird to identify it. **ring-finger** *n* the finger next to the little finger, usually of the left hand, on which a wedding-ring is worn. **ringleader** *n* the leader of a gang. **ringlet** *n* a long, spiral curl. **ringmaster** *n* the person who presides over a circus performance. **ring road** a road that encircles a town or town centre whose purpose is to relieve congestion. **ringside** *n* **1** the area immediately adjoining a boxing ring. **2** a place close to the scene of an event which affords a clear view. < Old English *hring*. SEE PANEL.

ring[2] *vb* **rang; rung; ringing 1** (of a bell) sound; cause this to happen. **2** make a noise like a bell. **3** be filled with sound. **4** telephone. **5** ring a bell for a particular purpose, esp. as a summons or signal. **6** make a loud, resonant sound: Two shots rang out. **7** (of ears) be filled with a continuous humming sound. • *n* **1** an act or instance of ringing a bell. **2** the sound that a bell makes when it rings. **3** a sound suggestive of something: a ring of truth. **ring a bell** come or bring to the memory. **ring off** end a telephone conversation by replacing the receiver. **ring up 1** telephone. **2** record (an amount) on a cash register. < Old English *hringan*.

rink (rɪŋk) *n* a smooth expanse of ice for ice-skating; smooth floor for roller-skating; building containing either of these. < Middle French *renc* place.

rinse (rɪns) *vb* **1** wash lightly. **2** remove soap from by immersing in clean water. • *n* **1** rinsing. **2** a solution used for temporarily tinting the hair. < Middle French *rincer*.

riot (ˈraɪət) *n* **1** a wild, violent disturbance by a large number of people. **2** a dazzling

ringleader

A person who leads others in a riot or undesirable activity is sometimes referred to as a ringleader. This name originally applied to the leader of a coven of witches, ring being a reference to the ring dances supposedly performed on witches' sabbaths.

display: a riot of colour.
• *vb* take part in a riot. **rioter** *n* **riotous** *adj* **1** disorderly; wild. **2** characterized by lack of restraint: riotous laughter. **run riot 1** act in a wild, unruly way. **2** (of plants) grow or spread prolifically. < Old French: dispute, debate, quarrel.
SEE PANEL.

rip (rɪp) *vb* **ripped; ripping 1** tear or be torn. **2** remove violently. **3** (*informal*) rush along.
• *n* a tear. **let rip** (*informal*) act or speak with a sudden release of violence or energy. **rip-cord** *n* a cord for opening a parachute. **rip off** (*informal*) **1** steal. **2** cheat or exploit. **rip-off** *n* (*informal*) a case of being cheated or exploited. **rip-roaring** *adj* wild or unrestrained: a rip-roaring success. < probably Flemish *rippen.*

RIP *abbrev* (*Latin*) requiescat (requiescant) in pace (may he or she (or they) rest in peace).

ripe (raɪp) *adj* **1** (of fruit, grain, etc.) ready to be gathered in or eaten. **2** (of cheese) matured. **3** advanced: a ripe old age. **4** right or ready: the time is ripe. **ripeness** *n* **ripen** *vb* make or become ripe. < Old English *rīpe.*

riposte (rɪˈpɒst) *n* a quick, sharp reply; retort. < ultimately Latin *respondēre* to respond.

ripple (ˈrɪpl̩) *n* **1** a small wave. **2** something resembling or likened to this: a ripple of laughter.
• *vb* form or cause to form ripples. < origin uncertain.

rise (raɪz) *vb* **rose; risen; rising 1** increase in height, degree, extent, etc.: Prices keep rising. **2** move, go, or extend upwards. **3** get out of bed. **4** assume an upright position; stand up. **5** (of the sun) appear on the horizon at day-break. **6** rebel. **7** achieve a higher rank or status. **8** (of the wind) begin to blow; increase in strength. **9** (of a river) begin. **10** be built or erected. **11** (of a meeting) end a session. **12** return to life: rise from the dead.
• *n* **1** the act or an instance of rising. **2** an increase in height, degree, extent, etc. **3** an increase in salary or wages. **4** an upward slope; incline: a steep rise. **5** an elevated area; hill. **6** the beginning or origin of something. **7** the height of a step. **give rise to** cause or bring about. **riser** *n* the vertical part between the treads of a staircase. **rising** *n* a revolt or insurrection. < Old English *rīsan.*

read the riot act

Nowadays to read the riot act to someone means to give him or her a severe reprimand. The allusion is to the Riot Act of 1715. This proclaimed that within one hour of having the act read to them by a magistrate, those who were committing a riot (being a crowd of 12 or more) had to disperse. Should they fail to disperse, they were breaking the law.

risk (rɪsk) *n* **1** the possibility of incurring loss, injury, or harm. **2** a source of risk, esp. a person or thing that is insured.
• *vb* **1** expose to risk or danger: The climbers risked their lives with every step. **2** take a chance on. **risky** *adj* full of risk. **riskily** *adv* **riskiness** *n* < French *risque,* from Italian *risco.*

risotto (rɪˈzɒtəʊ) *n, pl* **risottos** an Italian dish of rice cooked in meat stock and served with tomatoes, cheese, etc. < Italian, from *riso* rice.

risqué (ˈrɪskeɪ) *adj* slightly improper or indecent; daring. < SEE **RISK.**

rissole (ˈrɪsəʊl) *n* a small ball of fried minced food, especially meat mixed with potato. < Middle French *roissole.*

rite (raɪt) *n* a ritual. < Latin *ritus.*

ritual (ˈrɪtjʊəl) *n* **1** a formal or prescribed act or series of acts used in a religious or solemn ceremony. **2** any regular or customary procedure.
• *adj* of or performed as a ritual. **ritualistic** *adj* **ritually** *adv*

rival (ˈraɪvl̩) *n* **1** a person or group that competes against another. **2** a person or group of comparable quality; equal.
• *vb* **rivalled; rivalling 1** be in competition with. **2** be comparable to or the equal of. **rivalry** *n* < ultimately Latin *rivus* stream. SEE PANEL.

river (ˈrɪvə) *n* **1** a large, natural stream of water flowing across country. **2** any flow of great volume. < ultimately Latin *ripa* bank.

rivet (ˈrɪvɪt) *n* a metal pin used as a fastening device.
• *vb* fasten with a rivet. **riveted** *adj* unable to move; held fast. **riveting** *adj* engrossing. < Middle French *river* to fix.

rivulet (ˈrɪvjʊlət) *n* a small stream. < Italian *rivoletto,* from Latin *rivus* stream.

roach (rəʊtʃ) *n* a small, freshwater fish of the carp family. < Middle French *roche.*

road (rəʊd) *n* **1** a stretch of ground with a prepared surface along which vehicles travel. **2** a route or way: the road to success. **one for the road** (*informal*) a last alcoholic drink before setting out. **on the road** travelling, esp. on business. **road-block** *n* a barricade set up across a road by the army or police. **road-hog** *n* an inconsiderate driver. **roadside** *n* the strip of ground running alongside a road. **roadway** *n* a road. **road-works** *pl n* (the site of) repairs to a road. **roadworthy** *adj* (of a vehicle) fit to be driven on a road. **roadworthiness** *n* < Old English *rād.*

roam (rəʊm) *vb* **1** wander aimlessly. **2** wander unhindered.
• *n* a wander. < Middle English *romen.*

roar (rɔː) *vb* **1** (of a lion, etc.) utter a long, deep cry. **2** make a sound like a lion. **3** utter (something) in a loud, often angry voice.
• *n* **1** the sound produced by roaring. **2** a prolonged loud noise; din. < Old English *rārian.*

roaring (ˈrɔːrɪŋ) *adj* brisk: a roaring trade.
• *adv* (*informal*) extremely: roaring drunk.

roast (rəʊst) *vb* **1** cook (meat, etc.) by exposing to dry heat. **2** brown or dry by exposure to heat. **3** undergo roasting.
• *n* joint of meat for roasting; roast meat. **roasting** *adj* uncomfortably hot. < of Germanic origin.

rob (rɒb) *vb* **robbed; robbing 1** steal from. **2** deprive of. **robber** *n* **robbery** *n* < of Germanic origin.

robe (rəʊb) *n* a long, loose gown, esp. one signifying office.
• *vb* put (a robe, etc.) on. < of Germanic origin.

robin (ˈrɒbɪn) *n* a small, brownish bird of the thrush family with a distinctive orange breast and throat. < Middle English *robin redbrest,* from *Robin,* nickname for *Robert.*

robot (ˈrəʊbɒt) *n* **1** a machine popular in science fiction with humanoid resemblances and abilities. **2** a machine which is programmed to perform certain tasks automatically. **3** a person who acts like a machine. **robotic** *adj* **robotics** *pl n* (the study of) the application of robots, esp. in industry. < Czech, from *robota* work. SEE PANEL.

robust (rəʊˈbʌst) *adj* **1** strong, healthy, or vigorous. **2** sturdily built. **3** (of a sport, etc.) suitable for those of strong constitution. **robustly** *adv* **robustness** *n* < Latin *robur* oak.

rock[1] (rɒk) *n* **1** the solid part of the earth's crust. **2** a large stone; boulder. **3** a hard sweet in the shape of a cylindrical stick. **on the rocks** (*informal*) **1** undergoing collapse or destruction. **2** (of an alcoholic drink) with ice. **rock bottom** the lowest level. **rock-bottom** *adj* very low: rock-bottom prices. **rockery** *n* a rock-garden. **rock-garden** *n* a garden featuring large rocks, often stocked with alpine plants. **rock-plant** *n* a plant that grows on or among rocks. **rock salmon** a trade name for dogfish. **rocky** *adj* **1** covered in rocks. **2** of or like rock. < Old Northern French *roque.*

rock[2] *vb* **1** sway or cause to sway back and forth. **2** shake violently: The explosion rocked the building. **3** cause to reel; shock.
• *n* **1** rocking. **2** also **rock music** any of

rival

A person who competes with another for the same prize or object is sometimes referred to as a rival. This word derives via Middle French from the Latin *rivalis,* literally 'one who uses the same stream as another', from *rivus* 'a stream'. In view of the value of the water supply at stake, the right to use a stream frequently served as a serious source of contention. Moreover, a stream sometimes marked the boundary of one's land. Thus a 'neighbour', the broad meaning of *rivalis,* could easily become an 'adversary'. By the time the word entered English in the 16th century it carried both meanings, but in the course of time it was the latter that prevailed.

robot

An automated machine which can perform one or more tasks traditionally done by a human being is known as a robot. This is one of the very few words in the language deriving from Czech. It comes from the Czech word *robota* meaning 'work' and entered English as a result of the popularity of a play called 'R.U.R.' (Rossum's Universal Robots) by Karel Čapek. Written in 1920, the play received its first English performance in London in 1923.

Other words that come from Czech include howitzer, pistol, and polka.

various types of modern music derived from rock 'n' roll. **rocker** *n* **1** a rocking-chair. **2** one of the curved timbers on which a cradle or rocking-chair is mounted. **3** any of various devices that work with a rocking motion. **4** a member of a group of young British people in the 1960s, characterized by a fondness for leather jackets and motor cycles. **rocking-chair** *n* a chair mounted on rockers. **rocking-horse** *n* a toy horse mounted on rockers or springs. **rock 'n' roll** also **rock and roll 1** a variety of pop music originating in the 1950s, characterized by a strong beat and the repetition of simple phrases. **2** a dance performed to such music. **rock the boat** (*informal*) do something that causes disorder or turmoil. **rocky** *adj* unsteady. < Old English *roccian.*

rocket ('rɒkɪt) *n* **1** a self-propelling device commonly used for launching space-vehicles. **2** a space vehicle that is propelled by such a device. **3** a cylindrical firework on a long stick that rises into the air when ignited. **4** (*informal*) a severe reprimand.
• *vb* **1** move with the speed of a rocket. **2** increase rapidly: Prices have rocketed in recent months. < of Germanic origin.

rod (rɒd) *n* **1** a straight, slender pole or bar. **2** a fishing-rod. < Old English *rodd.*

rode (rəʊd) SEE **RIDE.**

rodent ('rəʊdn̩t) *n* any of a number of mammals with teeth designed for gnawing, such as rats, mice, and squirrels. < Latin *rodere* to gnaw. SEE PANEL AT **ERODE.**

rodeo ('rəʊdɪˌəʊ) *n, pl* **rodeos 1** an outdoor entertainment comprising a series of competitions exhibiting the various skills of a cowboy. **2** a cattle round-up. < ultimately Latin *rota* wheel.

roe[1] (rəʊ) *n* **1** also **hard roe** the egg-filled ovary of a female fish. **2** also **soft roe** the sperm-filled testis of a male fish. < Middle English *roof.*

roe[2] *n, pl* **roes, roe** a roe deer. **roe deer** a small deer noted for its grace and agility. < Old English *rā.*

rogue (rəʊg) *n* **1** a dishonest person; scoundrel. **2** a playfully mischievous person, esp. a child. **roguery** *n* **rogues' gallery** a collection of photographs of criminals. **roguish** *adj* mischievous. **roguishly** *adv* < origin uncertain.

role (rəʊl) *n* also **rôle 1** an actor's part. **2** the function of someone or something: a crucial rote. < French *rôle.*

roll (rəʊl) *vb* **1** move or cause to move by turning over and over while in contact with a surface: The ball rolled right into the hole. **2** (of something on wheels, rollers, etc.) move; cause this to happen: He released the handbrake and the car rolled backwards. **3** assume or give a cylindrical or spherical shape: The cat had rolled up in front of the fire. **4** cover with something by rolling: Roll the fish in breadcrumbs. **5** wrap: I rolled her in a blanket. **6** flatten by means of a roller, rolling-pin, etc. **7** rock or sway from side to side, esp. while going or walking along. **8** move (one's eyes) in a circle. **9** move steadily. **10** (esp. of thunder) make a long, continuous, reverberating sound. **11** utter or sound with a succession of taps: roll one's r's.
• *n* **1** a cylinder formed by something that has been rolled up: a roll of toilet-paper. **2** a swell or rounded mass: rolls of fat. **3** a small cake of bread. **4** a list or register: the electoral roll. **5** the act or an instance of rolling. **roll-call** *n* the calling of a list of names to check attendance. **roller** *n* **1** a small wheel or cylinder on which something can be rolled along. **2** a heavy, cylindrical device used for crushing or flattening: a garden roller. **3** a cylindrical device used for spreading paint. **4** a cylinder on which something is wound: hair rollers. **5** a long, powerful wave advancing towards the shore. **roller-coaster** *n* an entertainment in an amusement park comprising a railway

roll on Friday

Roll features in a number of expressions, many of them idiomatic, including:

roll in 1 to arrive in large quantities: Donations for the new hospital equipment rolled in steadily. **2** to arrive casually. **3** to have a lot of money: The Jacksons are really rolling in it!

roll on used to express a wish that a time that is mentioned would come quickly: Roll on Christmas!

roll-on, roll-off designed for vehicles to be driven on to and off: a roll-on, roll-off ferry.

roll up to come or arrive: Sue eventually rolled up in a posh new sports car.

with sharp curves and steep inclines. **roller-skate** *n* a boot with usually four small wheels fixed to the sole. **roller-skating** *n* **rolling-pin** *n* a cylindrical device used for flattening dough. **rolling-stock** *n* railway engines, carriages, wagons, etc. **roll-top desk** a writing desk with a sliding, flexible cover. < ultimately Latin *rota* wheel. SEE PANEL.

rollick (ˈrɒlɪk) *vb* behave in a boisterous or carefree manner. < perhaps *romp* + *frolic*.

roman (ˈrəʊmən) *adj* (of lettering) in plain, upright type. **Roman numerals** a system of numerals based on that of ancient Rome in which numbers are represented by letters. < ultimately Latin *Roma* Rome.

romance (rəˈmæns, ˈrəʊmæns) *n* **1** tender feelings arising from the sexual attraction of two people. **2** a love affair. **3** a love story. **4** (*literary*) a narrative dealing with imaginary characters in a remote setting. **5** literature of this kind. **6** something without a basis in fact.
• *vb* invent fictions; exaggerate. **romantic** *adj* **1** of, evoking, or given to romance: a romantic atmosphere. **2** dealing with romance: a romantic novel. **3** characterized by or given to the impractical or unrealistic: silly, romantic notions. **romantically** *adv* **romanticize** *vb* treat or regard romantically; have romantic ideas. < ultimately Latin *Romanus* Roman.

romp (rɒmp) *vb* play in a boisterous, carefree manner.
• *n* a spell of romping. **rompers** *pl n* a one-piece garment for a baby. **romp home** (*informal*) win easily. < *ramp*, from Old French *ramper* to crawl.

roof (ru:f) *n, pl* **roofs, rooves 1** the cover of a building. **2** something with a similar function to this, such as the top of a car.
• *vb* cover with or serve as a roof. **have a roof over one's head** have somewhere to live. **hit the roof** (*informal*) become very angry. **raise the roof 1** make a great din. **2** complain or protest loudly. **roof-garden** *n* a garden situated on a flat roof. **roof-rack** *n* a luggage rack fixed to the roof of a car, etc. < Old English *hrōf*. SEE PANEL AT **SHELF.**

rook[1] (rʊk) *n* a large, black crow with a raucous voice.
• *vb* (*informal*) cheat or swindle. < Old English *hrōc*.

rook[2] *n* also **castle** either of two pieces in a set of chessmen which can move backwards, forwards, or sideways over any number of vacant squares. < ultimately Arabic *rukhkh*.

room (ru:m, rʊm) *n* **1** any of a number of compartments into which a house or building is divided by walls. **2** any area or space which could be occupied by someone or something. **3** opportunity or scope: room for improvement. **room-divider** *n* a piece of furniture which serves to divide a room into separate areas. **roomful** *n* the number or amount that fills a room: a roomful of furniture. **room-mate** *n* a person with whom one shares a room used as living quarters. **room service** the service in a hotel whereby a guest can have food or drinks brought to his or her room. **roomy** *adj* having plenty of room; spacious. < Old English *rūm*. SEE PANEL.

roost (ru:st) *n* a place where a bird roosts; perch.
• *vb* (of birds) settle for rest or sleep. **come home to roost** (*informal*) have unfavourable repercussions. **rooster** *n* (*chiefly US*) a farmyard cock. **rule the roost** (*informal*) be in charge. < Old English *hrōst*.

root[1] (ru:t) *n* **1** the part of a plant which holds it in the soil and which absorbs moisture and nourishment. **2** an edible root. **3** the embedded part of a hair, tooth, etc. **4** something likened to a root: My roots are still in Wales where I grew up. **5** the source, cause, or fundamental part of something: the root of all evil. **6** (*grammar*) the part of a word that remains after all affixes have been removed.

no room to swing a cat

Cramped conditions often trigger the complaint that there is no room to swing a cat. The origin of this expression is uncertain. Some sources suggest that it was the invention of frustrated sea captains—the cat in question being the cat-o'-nine-tails, the instrument used for scourging wayward sailors. However, the expression no room to swing a cat predates the first recorded mention of the cat-o'-nine-tails by several decades.

An alternative theory identifies cat with a sailor's *cot* or 'hammock'.

• *vb* **1** take root or cause to take root. **2** fix or anchor: We all stood rooted to the spot. **rootless** *adj* **be rooted in** have as a cause or source. **root crop** a plant with roots that are grown for food. **rooted** *adj* firmly established: rooted in tradition. **take root** (of a plant) send down roots into the soil. < Old English *rōt*.

root² *vb* **1** (of a pig, etc.) dig with the snout. **2** search or rummage. **root for** (*chiefly US*) voice one's support for (a contestant, etc.). **root out 1** discover by searching or digging out. **2** remove or get rid of; eliminate. < Old English *wrōtan*.

rope (rəʊp) *n* **1** a strong, thick cord made of strands twisted together. **2** a number of objects strung together in a row: a rope of pearls.

• *vb* **1** fasten or bind with a rope. **2** catch with a rope: rope a horse. **3** enclose or separate with a rope. **know** or **learn the ropes** (*informal*) know or learn the correct procedures. **rope in** (*informal*) persuade (a reluctant party) to join or take part in. **rope-ladder** *n* a ladder made of rope. **ropy** *adj* (*informal*) **1** of poor quality. **2** in poor health. < Old English *rāp*. SEE PANEL.

rosary (ˈrəʊzərɪ) *n* **1** a series of prayers in the Roman Catholic Church. **2** the beads used for keeping count of these prayers as they are recited. < ultimately Latin *rosa* rose.

rose¹ (rəʊz) *n* **1** any of a vast group of garden shrubs with thorny stems and usually showy, fragrant flowers. **2** the flower of such a shrub. **3** a deep pink colour. **4** a perforated device fitted to a watering-can or shower which causes water to fall in a spray.

• *adj* deep pink. **rosebud** *n* the bud of a rose. **rosewood** *n* any of various tropical trees with hard, dark wood used in making fine furniture. < ultimately Latin *rosa*.

rose² SEE **RISE.**

rosé (ˈrəʊzeɪ) *n* a light, pink wine. < French: pink.

rosemary (ˈrəʊzmərɪ) *n* an aromatic evergreen shrub used as a herb. < Latin *rosmarinus*, from *ros* dew + *marinus* of the sea.

rosette (rəʊˈzɛt) *n* **1** an arrangement of ribbons in the shape of a rose, worn often as a badge or trophy. **2** a rose-shaped carving. < SEE **ROSE¹.**

roster (ˈrɒstə) *n* a list or register showing when each member of a group is to be on duty and the duty involved. < Dutch *rooster* grating.

rostrum (ˈrɒstrəm) *n, pl* **rostrums, rostra** a platform for public speaking. < Latin: beak, ship's prow.

rosy (ˈrəʊzɪ) *adj* **1** pink: rosy cheeks. **2** promising or hopeful: a rosy future. **rosily** *adv* **rosiness** *n*

rot (rɒt) *vb* **rotted; rotting 1** decay or cause to decay. **2** disintegrate. **3** perish or degenerate.

• *n* **1** decay. **2** (*informal*) nonsense; rubbish: What a lot of rot! **rotten** *adj* **1** in a state of decay; putrid. **2** disintegrating. **3** morally corrupt. **4** (*informal*) of poor quality: a rotten performance. **5** contemptible. **rotter** *n* (*informal*) a contemptible person. < Old English *rotian*.

rota (ˈrəʊtə) *n* a list showing a fixed sequence of rotation: a cooking rota. < Latin: wheel.

rotary (ˈrəʊtərɪ) *adj* **1** turning; revolving. **2** of or characterized by rotation. < ultimately Latin *rota* wheel.

rotate (rəʊˈteɪt) *vb* **1** turn or cause to turn about an axis. **2** alternate in sequence. **rotation** *n* **1** the act of rotating. **2** a single cycle of rotation. < SEE **ROTARY.**

rote (rəʊt) *n* **by rote** in a purely mechanical or parrot-like fashion: learn something by rote. < Middle English.

rope

The *pun* is often referred to as the lowest form of wit. This particular figure of speech refers to a play on the different senses of a word (or on two words or parts of words similar in sound) for humorous effect: 'I'm going to take a course in tree diseases.'—'Oh, really! Which *branch* will you be specializing in?' Here the play exploits the ambiguity of branch, 'the limb of a tree' and branch, 'division of a discipline'. The pun figures largely in children's riddles or 'teasers', such as: 'What's black and white and *read* all over?'—'A newspaper', where read is heard as red. Not all puns, however, are deliberate concoctions; many occur naturally in everyday conversation: 'They asked me to take part in the tug of war,'—'Did you?'—'No. I didn't want to get *roped* in.'

rotund (rəʊˈtʌnd) *adj* plump or rounded. < SEE **ROUND.**

rotunda (rəʊˈtʌndə) *n* a round building, usually covered by a dome. < SEE **ROUND.**

rouge (ruːʒ) *n* **1** a red cosmetic, esp. for colouring the cheeks. **2** a red powder used in polishing glass, metal, etc. < French, ultimately from Latin *rubeus* reddish.

rough (rʌf) *adj* **1** irregular or uneven: rough terrain. **2** not smooth; coarse: a rough skin. **3** lacking tenderness, gentleness, or politeness: Don't play with them if they're too rough. **4** violent or turbulent: rough seas. **5** done or arrived at hastily and without attention to detail: a rough sketch. **6** approximate: a rough estimate. **7** difficult or unpleasant: a rough time.
• *adv* roughly.
• *n* **1** a person who behaves in a rough way; ruffian. **2** ground that is uneven or covered with high grass, esp. at the sides of a fairway on a golf-course. **3** hardship or adversity. **4** a preliminary piece of artwork.
• *vb* roughen. **roughly** *adv* **roughness** *n* **roughen** *vb* make or become rough. **rough out** sketch or shape roughly. < Old English *rūh.* SEE PANEL.

roughage (ˈrʌfɪdʒ) *n* coarse, indigestible food constituents that give bulk to the diet and thereby stimulate the action of the intestines.

roughshod (ˈrʌfˌʃɒd) *adj* **ride roughshod over** treat inconsiderately. SEE PANEL.

roulette (ruːˈlɛt) *n* a gambling game in which players bet on the compartment that a ball will enter when dropped into a revolving wheel. < French: small wheel, ultimately Latin *rota* wheel.

round (raʊnd) *adj* **1** having the shape of a curve, circle, or sphere. **2** plump or rotund. **3** denoting a journey which finishes where it began: a round trip. **4** (of numbers) full or complete: a round dozen.
• *n* **1** something round. **2** a single complete slice of bread. **3** (of a tradesman) a regular route along which deliveries, etc., are made: a milk round. **4** a recurring series: the latest round of wage settlements. **5** a number of drinks served at one time to each of the members of a group. **6** a complete circuit of a golf-course. **7** one of the periods into which a boxing or wrestling bout is divided. **8** one of the stages in a tournament: City were knocked out in the first round. **9** (of guns) a single shot or discharge. **10** a bullet. **11** a song for three or four voices which sing the same tune but start in succession. **12** a general outburst: a round of applause.
• *prep* **1** on all sides of; encircling: The wall went right round the house. **2** in a circle about: She had a pink scarf wrapped round her neck. **3** on or to the further side of: He disappeared round the corner. **4** to all parts of; over: The parents wish to be shown round the school.
• *adv* **1** in a circle or curve: I like to watch the

riding roughshod

To ride roughshod over someone is to treat a person harshly or in an inconsiderate way. The allusion is to the blacksmith's practice of leaving nail heads protruding slightly from a horse's shoe as a prevention against slipping. Further, the shoes fitted to horses that were to go into battle had sharp projections for inflicting maximum injury upon those who fell in their path. In each case, the horse was referred to as roughshod.

roughing it

Rough features in a number of expressions, many of them idiomatic, including:

rough-and-ready *adj* crude and makeshift: a rough-and-ready solution.

rough and tumble disorderly struggling in life or work: the rough and tumble of family life. The expression originally referred to a form of boxing in which the usual rules did not apply.

rough diamond a good-natured person who lacks social graces.

rough it to accept uncomfortable conditions: If you're willing to rough it, you could always sleep in the basement.

take the rough with the smooth to accept the disadvantages of a situation as well as its advantages: I guess growing up is all about learning to take the rough with the smooth.

hands go round. **2** so as to face in a different direction: Turn round and sit up straight! **3** to someone's house, etc.: I promised to go round and see him tonight. **4** to each person present: Pass the sweets round.
• *vb* **1** make or become round: round one's lips. **2** travel or move round: round a bend. **3** encircle. **4** make into a round number. < ultimately Latin *rotundus*. SEE PANEL.

roundabout (ˈraʊndəˌbaʊt) *n* **1** a merry-go-round. **2** a major road junction in the form of a hub from which the various roads radiate.
• *adj* indirect or circuitous.

rounders (ˈraʊndəz) *n* a ball-game resembling baseball.

roundsman (ˈraʊndzmən) *n, pl* **roundsmen** a milkman or other tradesperson with a regular round.

rouse (raʊz) *vb* **1** wake up. **2** stir, excite, or provoke: rouse interest. **rousing** *adj* exciting or stirring: a rousing speech. < Middle English *rousen*.

rout[1] (raʊt) *n* (a disorderly retreat following) an overwhelming defeat.
• *vb* defeat decisively. < Middle French *route* defeat.

rout[2] *vb* **1** find by rummaging. **2** drive or force out. < SEE **ROOT**[2].

route (ruːt) *n* **1** the course along which a person chooses to travel to reach a destination. **2** a regularly travelled way: a bus route.
• *vb* send by a selected route. **route march** a long march made by troops, esp. during training. < Old French *rute*.

routine (ruːˈtiːn) *n* **1** a customary method of procedure. **2** a fixed sequence of dance steps.
• *adj* **1** ordinary or commonplace. **2** in accordance with customary procedure. **routinely** *adv* < French.

rove (rəʊv) *vb* (*literary*) roam or wander. < Scandinavian.

row[1] (rəʊ) *n* **1** a number of people or things arranged in a line. **2** a line of seats in a cinema, theatre, etc. < Middle English *rawe*.

row[2] *vb* **1** propel (a boat) by means of oars. **2** transport in a rowing-boat. **rowing-boat** also **row-boat** *n* a boat propelled by rowing. < Old English *rōwan*.

row[3] (raʊ) *n* **1** (*informal*) a din. **2** a quarrel or dispute.
• *vb* quarrel. < origin unknown.

rowan (ˈrəʊən) *n* a tree of the rose family that bears clusters of bright red berries. < Scandinavian.

rowdy (ˈraʊdɪ) *adj* noisy and disorderly.
• *n* a rowdy person. **rowdily** *adv* **rowdiness** *n* **rowdyism** *n* < origin uncertain.

rowlock (ˈrɒlək) *n* a U-shaped device on the side of a rowing-boat that holds an oar in place. < probably *oarlock*.

royal (ˈrɔɪəl) *adj* **1** of or in the service of a monarch: the royal household. **2** suitable for a monarch; magnificent: a royal welcome.
• *n* (*informal*) a member of a royal family. **royally** *adv* **royal blue** deep, vivid blue. **royalist** *n* a person who favours the monarchy. **royalty** *n* **1** the state of being royal. **2** one or more members of a royal family: in the presence of royalty. **3** any quality characteristic of a monarch. **4** a percentage of the revenue from the sale of a book, record, etc., which is paid to the writer or performer. < ultimately Latin *rex* king.

RSVP *abbrev* (*French*) répondez s'il vous plaît (please reply).

Rt. Hon. *abbrev* Right Honourable.

rub (rʌb) *vb* **rubbed; rubbing 1** move (something) backwards and forwards over (a surface) while applying pressure. **2** clean or polish by rubbing. **3** chafe: There was a red mark on her heel where the shoe had been rubbing.

---

in the round

Round features in a number of idiomatic expressions, including:

do the rounds to make a series of customary social or professional calls: We'll be doing the rounds as usual over the Christmas holiday, seeing all our old friends again.
in the round 1 with the audience seated around a central stage: a theatre in the round. **2** (of a sculpture) capable of being viewed from all sides; not attached to a background.
round about approximately.
round off to conclude in a suitable way; make complete.
round on to attack; reprimand unexpectedly and suddenly.
round-the-clock *adj* continuous; constant; day-and-night: The police have mounted a round-the-clock guard on the witnesses.
round up to gather or collect. **round-up** *n*

● *n* **1** a spell of rubbing. **2** an obstacle, difficulty, or impediment. < Middle English *rubben.* SEE PANEL.

rubber[1] (ˈrʌbə) *n* **1** an elastic substance obtained from the white, coagulated juice of a tropical tree or made synthetically. **2** a small piece of this used for erasing pencil or ink marks. **rubbery** *adj* **rubberize** *vb* coat or treat with rubber. **rubber stamp** a device used for making imprints. **rubber-stamp** *vb* approve or endorse, esp. without due consideration. < *rub* + *-er.*

rubber[2] *n* (*bridge, whist, etc.*) a match of three games. < origin unknown.

rubbish (ˈrʌbɪʃ) *n* **1** waste matter. **2** something that is worthless or of very poor quality. **3** nonsense. **rubbishy** *adj* < Middle English *robys.*

rubble (ˈrʌbl̩) *n* fragments of brick, stone, or masonry. < Middle English *robyl.*

rubric (ˈru:brɪk) *n* words set apart from the body of a text which form a heading, explanatory note, or direction. < Middle English *rubrike* red lettering.

ruby (ˈru:bɪ) *n* **1** a deep red, precious stone. **2** a deep red colour.
● *adj* deep red. **ruby wedding** the 40th anniversary of a wedding. < ultimately Latin *rubeus* reddish.

ruck (rʌk) *n* a crease or wrinkle.
● *vb* crease or wrinkle. < Scandinavian.

rucksack (ˈrʌkˌsæk) *n* a bag with shoulder straps and supported on the back by walkers, climbers, etc. < German, from *Rücken* back + *Sack* bag.

ruction (ˈrʌkʃən) *n* an uproar; commotion. < origin uncertain.

rudder (ˈrʌdə) *n* **1** a vertical blade hinged to the stern of a ship, used for steering. **2** a similar device attached to the fin of an aircraft. < Old English *rōther* paddle.

ruddy (ˈrʌdɪ) *adj* **1** red or reddish. **2** having a healthy, reddish colour: a ruddy complexion. **3** also *adv* (*slang*) bloody; chiefly used emphatically. **ruddily** *adv* **ruddiness** *n* < Old English *rudu* redness.

rude (ru:d) *adj* **1** impolite or discourteous. **2** vulgar or obscene: rude gestures. **3** crude or primitive. **4** sudden or abrupt: a rude awakening. **rudely** *adv* **rudeness** *n* < ultimately Latin *rudis.*

rudiment (ˈru:dɪmənt) *n* a basic principle or skill: the rudiments of physics. **rudimentary** *adj* basic or elementary. < Latin *rudimentum* beginning, from *rudis* raw, rude.

rue (ru:) *vb* regret: He'll live to rue the day he ignored his father's advice. **rueful** *adj* **1** sorry or regretful. **2** inspiring pity. **ruefully** *adv* < Old English *hrēowan.*

ruff (rʌf) *n* **1** a broad, pleated collar worn round the neck by men and women in the 16th and 17th centuries. **2** a projecting band of feathers or hair round the neck of a bird or animal. < probably back formation from *ruffle.*

ruffian (ˈrʌfɪən) *n* a thug or hoodlum. < Middle French *rufian,* from Italian, ultimately of Germanic origin.

ruffle (ˈrʌfl̩) *vb* **1** make or become wrinkled, uneven, or irregular. **2** make or become annoyed or irritated; vex.
● *n* a ruff or frill. < Middle English *ruffelen.*

rug (rʌg) *n* **1** a thick, heavy floor-mat. **2** a thick blanket often used when travelling. < Scandinavian.

rugby (ˈrʌgbɪ) *n* a form of football played with an oval ball which may be bandied as well as kicked. **rugger** *n* (*informal*)

there's the rub

Rub features in a number of idiomatic expressions, including:

rub along to manage to remain on friendly terms.

rub it in to keep talking about something that someone does not want to be reminded of: 'There's no need to rub it in!'

rub off to have an influence by example: 'Let's hope that some of Ian's politeness rubs off onto John.'

rub out to erase.

rub shoulders with to associate with: The ideal candidate will be someone who has rubbed shoulders with the long-term unemployed for several years.

rub (up) the wrong way to arouse the anger of; irritate or annoy.

The expression **there's the rub** meaning 'that is where the difficulty is' comes from Shakespeare's 'Hamlet', Act 3, Scene 1:

To die, to sleep;
To sleep: perchance to dream: ay, there's the rub;
For in that sleep of death what dreams may come.

rugby. < *Rugby* School, in Warwickshire.

rugged (ˈrʌgɪd) *adj* **1** having an uneven surface or outline. **2** craggy or wrinkled: a rugged face. **3** sturdy or tough: of rugged build. **ruggedly** *adv* **ruggedness** *n* < Scandinavian.

ruin (ˈruːɪn) *n* **1** the state of being collapsed or decayed. **2** a destroyed or collapsed building, etc.: The temple is now a ruin. **3** loss of all wealth, power, prospects, etc.: The company faces ruin. **4** a cause of this: Gambling proved to be his ruin.
• *vb* **1** reduce to a state of ruin; destroy. **2** spoil, injure, or damage, esp. beyond repair, remedy, etc.: Smoking can ruin one's health. **ruination** *n* **ruinous** *adj* **1** likely to bring ruin. **2** in ruins; dilapidated. **ruinously** *adv* < ultimately Latin *ruina*.

rule (ruːl) *n* **1** a principle of behaviour or conduct; regulation: school rules. **2** a customary procedure: The rule was to arrive early and leave early. **3** government, authority, or control: under foreign rule. **4** a ruler used for measuring or drawing straight lines.
• *vb* **1** govern or control. **2** give an official decision or judgment. **3** draw (a straight line) using a ruler. **as a rule** usually. **rule of thumb** a rough guiding principle. **rule out** exclude or dismiss: We can't rule out the possibility of someone objecting. **ruler** *n* **1** a person who rules. **2** a straight, narrow length of wood, plastic, or metal, used for measuring and drawing straight lines. **ruling** *n* an official decision or judgment. < ultimately Latin *regere* to lead straight. SEE PANEL.

rum[1] (rʌm) *n* an alcoholic spirit made from molasses or sugar-cane. < origin unknown.

rum[2] *adj* (*informal*) queer, odd, or strange. < perhaps Romany *rom* man.

rumble (ˈrʌmbl̩) *vb* **1** make a deep, prolonged, rolling sound like thunder. **2** move or utter with this sound: The cart rumbled across the courtyard. **3** (*informal*) discover or disclose (an act of deception, etc.).
• *n* a rumbling sound. < Middle English *rumblen*.

ruminate (ˈruːmɪˌneɪt) *vb* **1** chew the cud. **2** meditate or ponder. **rumination** *n* **ruminant** *adj*, *n* (of) an animal that chews the cud. < Latin *ruminari*.

rummage (ˈrʌmɪdʒ) *vb* search for something haphazardly or by disarranging things.
• *n* a search of this kind. < probably of Germanic origin.

rummy (ˈrʌmɪ) *n* a card-game in which players try to collect runs or sets. < origin uncertain.

rumour (ˈruːmə) *n* **1** information passed around by word of mouth, the truth of which is uncertain. **2** gossip or hearsay. **be rumoured** (of a rumour) be passed around by word of mouth. < ultimately Latin *rumor*.

rump (rʌmp) *n* **1** the buttocks or hindquarters. **2** a cut of meat from this area. < Scandinavian.

rumple (ˈrʌmpl̩) *vb* make or become creased, wrinkled, or untidy.
• *n* a crease or wrinkle. < Dutch *rompelen*.

rumpus (ˈrʌmpəs) *n* a noisy commotion; uproar. < origin unknown.

run (rʌn) *vb* **ran; run; running 1** (of a person or animal) move quickly. **2** cover (a distance) by running: I ran two miles this morning. **3** move on or as if on wheels, castors, or runners. **4** (of water) flow. **5** (of a machine) operate or function: Leave the engine running in case the battery is flat. **6** (of a film or tape) be shown or played. **7** manage or control: Who runs the company? **8** participate in a race, contest, election, etc. **9** (of buses, trains, etc.) travel back and forth: How often do the trains run? **10** convey (someone) in a car, etc.: 'Don't worry! I'll run you home.' **11** continue to be valid or in force; last: The licence runs for twelve months. **12** (of a film, theatrical presentation, etc.) be shown to the public: The play ran for twelve weeks. **13** own and use (a car, etc.). **14** (of wet paint, varnish, etc.) form sags. **15** (of a colour, dye, etc.) spread or mingle: The ink has run. **16** move or direct: She ran her fingers lightly over the strings. **17** extend or reach: A six-foot wall ran right round the building. **18** discharge (tears, mucus, etc.): Onions make my eyes run. **19** (of a stocking, etc.) ladder. **20** enter or cause to enter a certain state: The battery has run dry. **21** recur: Artistic talent runs in the family.
• *n* **1** the act or a spell of running: go for a run. **2** a trip or excursion; drive. **3** the

> **rule of thumb**
>
> The phrase rule of thumb means 'a rough guideline or way of assessing something': 'As a rule of thumb, the more expensive the material, the longer it will last.' The allusion is to the former practice of using the thumb as a rough-and-ready measuring instrument.

length of time that a play, etc., is performed to the public: a record-breaking run of eighty-three weeks. **4** a ladder (in a stocking, etc.). **5** heavy demand for something: a run on the bank. **6** an uninterrupted series or sequence: a run of bad luck. **7** a point scored in cricket or baseball. **8** a pen or enclosure: a chicken run. **9** a course, route, or track: a ski-run. **10** a school of salmon going up river to spawn. < Old English *runnen*.
SEE PANEL.

runaway ('rʌnəˌweɪ) *n* a person who has escaped or run away; fugitive.
• *adj* **1** escaped or fugitive. **2** out of control: a runaway lorry. **3** won easily; decisive: a runaway victory.

rung[1] (rʌŋ) *n* **1** one of the cross-pieces of a ladder. **2** a cross-piece between the legs of a chair, etc. **3** a level in a scale or hierarchy: After six years with the firm he's still on the bottom rung. < Old English *hrung*.

rung[2] SEE **RING[2]**.

runner ('rʌnə) *n* **1** a person or horse, etc., that takes part in a race. **2** a messenger. **3** a slender stem that grows along the ground and takes root. **4** a part or fixture along which something moves or slides: The drawers of the filing cabinet are on runners. **5** a part on which a sledge, etc., slides. **6** a long, narrow strip of carpet. **7** a long, narrow table-cloth. **8** a player who runs

runner-up

Runner-up is rather an unusual word. Most nouns with this structure are derived from a two-part verb. Thus a washer-up is a person who washes up and a show-off is a person who shows off. A runner-up, however, is not a person who runs up but one who comes second.

on the run

Run features in a number of idiomatic expressions, including:

on the run 1 running away from authority, to avoid capture. **2** in haste; unable to stop, especially because on the way to somewhere: Sorry, I can't stop. I'm on the run.

runabout *n* a small motor car; light motor boat or plane.

run across to meet unexpectedly: I ran across old Fred in town today.

run after to pursue; seek the affections of.

run away 1 to leave or go away by running. **2** to escape from someone's control.

run away with 1 to elope with (someone). **2** to win easily. **3** to take control of: His feelings ran away with him. **4** to steal and escape with.

run down 1 to lose or cause to lose power, etc. **2** to decline or cause to decline. **3** to criticize. **4** to knock down: He was run down by a lorry.

run-down *adj* **1** in a state of disrepair. **2** in poor health; exhausted.

run-down *n* a summary or analysis.

run in 1 to prepare (a new engine) for ordinary use: Cars don't need to be run in these days. **2** to arrest (someone).

run into 1 to meet by chance. **2** to collide with.

run off 1 to make (copies) on a machine: I'll run off 30 copies of the report. **2** to run away.

run-of-the-mill *adj* ordinary; commonplace: everyday, run-of-the-mill matters. The expression originally referred to material such as sawn timber that was produced by a mill and was not graded for quality.

run on 1 to continue. **2** to talk constantly.

run out 1 to become used or consumed: Time is running out! **2** to have used one's supply. **3** to expire: My licence runs out next month. **4** to dismiss (a batsman) in cricket while he is running between the wickets.

run over 1 to knock down with a motor vehicle. **2** to repeat or review: Let's just run over the last scene again.

run rings round to perform far better than; defeat easily: Last year we won 7–0 but I'm not sure whether we'll run rings round them this year.

run through to repeat or review.

run up 1 to raise (a flag, etc.). **2** to make quickly by sewing. **3** to incur (a large bill, etc.). **4** to gather speed in an approach to give momentum in jumping, throwing, etc.

run-up *n* **1** the period leading to an event: the run-up to the election. **2** the gathering of speed in an approach, to give momentum in jumping, throwing, etc.

in place of an injured batsman in cricket. **runner bean** also **scarlet runner** a climbing bean plant; its long, edible pod containing large, red and black seeds. **runner-up** *n* a contestant who finishes in second place. SEE PANEL.

running (ˈrʌnɪŋ) SEE **RUN.**
• *adj* **1** (of water) flowing. **2** (of water) flowing from taps: Each chalet has hot and cold running water. **3** performed while running: a running kick. **4** performed simultaneously with an event: a running commentary.
• *adv* in uninterrupted succession: three days running. **in/out of the running** with/without a good chance or winning, etc. **make the running** set the pace.

runny (ˈrʌnɪ) *adj* **1** in a liquid or semi-liquid state. **2** discharging (a fluid): a runny nose.

runt (rʌnt) *n* **1** an undersized animal, esp. the smallest of a litter. **2** (*derogatory*) a puny person; used as a term of abuse. < origin unknown. SEE PANEL.

runway (ˈrʌnˌweɪ) *n* a strip of ground on an airfield used for landing and taking off.

rupture (ˈrʌptʃə) *n* **1** a breach, esp. of friendly or normal relations. **2** the act of breaking or bursting. **3** the state of being broken or burst. **4** a hernia.
• *vb* **1** burst or break: rupture a blood-vessel. **2** undergo a breach of relations. **3** cause (oneself) to have a rupture. < Latin *rumpere* to break.

rural (ˈrʊərəl) *adj* of the countryside or country people. < ultimately Latin *rus* open land. SEE PANEL.

ruse (ruːz) *n* a clever trick or ploy. < ultimately Middle French *ruser* to deceive.

rush[1] (rʌʃ) *n* any of various marsh plants with slender, hollow stems, used for making mats, baskets, etc. < Old English *risc*.

rush[2] *vb* **1** move or cause to move hastily: She rushed into the room. **2** act or cause to act hastily. **3** do or convey (something) hastily: rush a meal. **4** charge or run at, esp. in a surprise attack: Two of the prisoners tried to rush the guard.
• *n* **1** a sudden quick or forceful movement: He made a rush for the door. **2** a hurry: be in a rush. **3** a period of great activity: There is always a rush just before Christmas. **4** a sudden demand for something.
• *adj* requiring or characterized by haste or urgency. **rush-hour** *n* a period in the day when traffic is heaviest. < Middle French *ruser* to repel, from Latin *recusare* to refuse.

rusk (rʌsk) *n* a kind of light, dry biscuit, often given to babies when teething. < Spanish or Portuguese *rosca* twisted bread roll.

russet (ˈrʌsɪt) *adj* reddish-brown.
• *n* **1** a reddish-brown colour. **2** an eating apple with a mellow, reddish-brown skin. < Latin *russus* red.

rust (rʌst) *n* **1** a reddish-brown coating that forms on iron and other metals when exposed to air and moisture. **2** a reddish-brown colour. **3** (a fungus causing) any of various plant diseases characterized by reddish-brown spots on the leaves and stems.
• *vb* **1** affect or be affected with rust. **2** degenerate or deteriorate, esp. through lack of use. **rust-proof** *adj* **rusty** *adj* **1** affected with rust. **2** of the colour of rust. **3** impaired through advanced age or lack of use: My German's getting a bit rusty nowadays. **rustiness** *n* < Old English *rūst*.

rustic (ˈrʌstɪk) *adj* **1** rural. **2** having the rough simplicity associated with country life. **3** crude, unrefined, or uncouth. **4** made of rough timber: a rustic seat

What a big runt!

According to its common usage, a runt is the smallest or puniest member of a litter, especially the most undersized piglet in a litter of pigs. In other words, smallness or stuntedness is a core component of the word's basic meaning. However, as pigeon fanciers know, runt has another, less familiar meaning, in which the idea not of smallness but of largeness is central. A runt is also 'a *large* pigeon, originally bred for eating'. It is unusual for a word to have meanings so much at variance with one another.

rural or rustic?

Both rural and rustic refer to the country.

Rural means 'of the countryside or country people': *rural* scenery, *rural* areas, *rural* population.

Rustic has connotations of rough simplicity: The bridge over the stream has a certain *rustic* charm. When applied to people it means 'crude or unrefined': *rustic* manners.

• *n* a country person, esp. a simple, unsophisticated one. **rusticity** *n* < ultimately Latin *rus* the country. SEE PANEL AT **RURAL.**

rustle (ˈrʌsl̩) *vb* **1** make or cause to make a sound like dry leaves being crumpled. **2** (*chiefly US*) steal (cattle or horses).
• *n* a rustling sound. **rustler** *n* **rustle up** (*informal*) make or produce hastily. < Middle English *rustelen*, like the sound.

rut¹ (rʌt) *n* **1** a narrow track or furrow made in soft ground, esp. one made by a wheel. **2** a narrow, tedious way of life: get into a rut. < origin uncertain.

rut² *n* **1** the annual state of sexual excitement of certain male animals. **2** the period when this occurs.
• *vb* **rutted; rutting** (of certain male animals) be in a period of sexual excitement. < ultimately Latin *rugire* to roar.

ruthless (ˈruːθləs) *adj* having or showing no pity or compassion. **ruthlessly** *adv* **ruthlessness** *n* < archaic *ruth* compassion, from Middle English *ruen* to rue. SEE PANEL.

rye (raɪ) *n* **1** a kind of grass widely grown for grain. **2** the grain of this grass used for making flour and as food for cattle. **3** a kind of whisky made from rye. < Old English *ryge*.

ruthless

Harmless, childless, powerless, etc., are examples of adjectives derived from noun stems by the addition of *-less*. Ruthless, 'without compassion or mercy', is also a member of this group. However, whereas the noun stems continue to flourish in other cases (harm, child, power, etc.), the noun which forms the base of ruthless has disappeared. The lost stem is *ruth,* meaning 'compassion', which comes ultimately from Middle English *ruen* 'to rue'.

The same stem also provided ruthful, 'full of compassion or sorrow'. This has likewise fallen from usage, leaving ruthless and its own derivatives (ruthlessly, ruthlessness) the sole surviving members of the family.

S

S. *abbrev* south; southern.
's SEE PANEL.
sabbath (ˈsæbəθ) *n* **1** the last day of the week (Friday evening to Saturday evening) observed by Jews as a day of rest and worship. **2** the first day of the week (Sunday) observed by Christians as a day of rest and worship. < ultimately Greek *shabbāth* rest.
sabbatical (səˈbætɪkl̩) *adj* **1** of or like the sabbath. **2** of or constituting a sabbatical: a sabbatical year.
• *n* a period of leave granted usually every seventh year to a university or similar teacher. < ultimately Greek *sabbaton.*
sable (ˈseɪbl̩) *n* **1** a small, ferret-like animal valued for its dark-brown fur. **2** its fur.
• *adj* black; dark. < of Slavonic origin.
sabotage (ˈsæbəˌtɑːʒ) *n* **1** the deliberate destruction of machinery, installations, or resources by enemy agents, dissatisfied employees, etc., esp. for purposes of disruption or obstruction. **2** subversion.
• *vb* **1** commit sabotage on. **2** subvert. **saboteur** *n* a person who commits sabotage. < French, from *saboter* to spoil through clumsiness.
sabre (ˈseɪbə) *n* a cavalry sword with a curved blade. < of Slavonic origin.
sac (sæk) *n* a bag-like part in an animal or plant, often containing fluid. < ultimately Latin *saccus* bag.
saccharin (ˈsækərɪn) *n* a very sweet substance used as a substitute for sugar, esp. by diabetics and slimmers. < Greek *sakcharon* sugar.
sachet (ˈsæʃeɪ) *n* **1** a small, sealed packet containing shampoo, sugar, etc. **2** a small bag containing a perfumed substance for laying amongst clothes, etc. < SEE **SAC**.
sack[1] (sæk) *n* **1** a large, strong, rectangular bag used for coal, potatoes, etc. **2** the amount held by a sack: a sack of turnips. **3 the sack** (*informal*) dismissal from employment.
• *vb* **1** put into sacks. **2** (*informal*) dismiss from employment. **sackful** *n*

's or **s'?**

When used to denote possession, the apostrophe is frequently put in the wrong place. Confusion can be avoided if it is remembered that its position before or after an s directly affects the number of the noun to which it is adjoined. For example, the lady who writes my husbands' children instead of my husband's children labels herself as a bigamist. The apostrophe is placed before the s if the reference is to a singular noun, and after the s if the reference is plural: my son's school (one son, one school); my sons' school (two or more sons, one school); my sons' schools (two or more sons, two or more schools).

Another common mistake is the use of the apostrophe with the pronouns yours, hers, its, ours, and theirs. These are possessive in their own right and are never used with an apostrophe: Is this ours or theirs? On the difference between it's and its, see panel at it.

sack and **sackcloth**

A person who is dismissed from employment is informally said **to get the sack.** The origin of this phrase remains something of a mystery. The most common suggestion is that, having been dismissed by his employer, a workman piled his tools back into the same bag or sack which he had originally used to bring them in.

An alternative theory is that the sack in question is a short form of sackcloth. This is suggested on the basis that upon dismissal an employee looks less than cheerful and proceeds to go around, as it were, 'in sackcloth and ashes'.

The expression **sackcloth and ashes** alludes to the Hebrew custom of wearing garments of sackcloth and scattering ashes over the head and body as a means of humbling oneself, especially in times of mourning or penitence. The phrase is used in its literal sense in both the Old and New Testaments.

sackcloth *n* material used for making sacks. **sackcloth and ashes** a spirit or display of sorrow or grief. **sacking** *n* sackcloth. **sack-race** *n* a race in which each contestant has his or her legs inside a sack and moves by jumping. < Old English *sacc.* SEE PANEL.

sack² *vb* plunder (a city, etc.).
• *n* the plundering of a captured city, etc. < Old Italian *sacco* plunder, bag.

sacrament (ˈsækrəmənt) *n* **1** any Christian rite regarded as especially sacred, esp. baptism and the Eucharist. **2** the consecrated elements of the Eucharist, esp. the bread. **sacramental** *adj* < ultimately Latin *sacrare* to consecrate.

sacred (ˈseɪkrɪd) *adj* **1** of, associated with, or dedicated to a god. **2** connected with religion; not secular: sacred music. **3** to be treated or regarded with great respect or reverence; sacrosanct. **4** dedicated (to); used chiefly on gravestones: sacred to the memory of a loving husband. **sacredly** *adv* **sacredness** *n* **sacred cow** someone or something that is revered by a group to such an extent that criticism is not tolerated. < ultimately Latin *sacer* holy. SEE PANEL.

sacrifice (ˈsækrɪˌfaɪs) *n* **1** the offering of something to a deity in order to win favour. **2** the giving up of something valued for the sake of something else. **3** the thing offered or given up in this way.
• *vb* offer or give up as a sacrifice. **sacrificial** *adj* < ultimately Latin *sacrificium,* from *sacer* holy + *facere* to make.

sacrilege (ˈsækrɪlɪdʒ) *n* a violation of something considered sacred. **sacrilegious** *adj* **sacrilegiously** *adv* **sacrilegiousness** *n* < ultimately Latin *sacer* holy + *legere* to take.

sacrosanct (ˈsækrəʊˌsæŋkt) *adj* so sacred as to be inviolable. < Latin *sacer* holy + *sancirc* to hallow.

sad (sæd) *adj* **sadder; saddest 1** feeling, showing, or causing unhappiness. **2** regrettable: It's sad that the couple split up. **3** inadequate or inferior: a sad attempt. **sadly** *adv* **sadness** *n* **sadden** *vb* make sad. < Old English *sæd* sated.

saddle (ˈsædl̩) *n* **1** a leather seat tied to the back of a horse, etc. **2** a seat on a bicycle, tractor, etc. **3** anything resembling a saddle in shape, position, or function. **4** a ridge between two peaks. **5** a joint of cut meat comprising both loins.
• *vb* **1** put a saddle on (an animal). **2** burden or encumber. **in the saddle** in control. **saddle-bag** *n* **1** either of a pair of attached bags which are slung over the back of a horse, etc., and hang down on each side behind the saddle. **2** a bag fixed behind the saddle of a bicycle, or one of a pair hanging alongside the rear wheel of a motor cycle. **saddler** *n* a person who makes, repairs, or deals in saddles and other equipment for horses. **saddlery** *n* a shop or business run by a saddler. < Old English *sadol.*

sadism (ˈseɪdɪzəm) *n* **1** delight in inflicting or watching the infliction of pain. **2** a sexual perversion based upon this. **sadist** *n* **sadistic** *adj* **sadistically** *adv* < Marquis de *Sade,* died 1814, French writer.

s.a.e. *abbrev* stamped addressed envelope.

safari (səˈfɑːrɪ) *n* **1** a hunting expedition, esp. in Africa. **2** the people and equipment that go on the expedition. **safari park** an area of land reserved for wild animals. < Arabic *safara* to travel.

safe (seɪf) *adj* **1** free from risk or danger: Is it safe to light the gas now? **2** without harm or injury: The hostages were returned safe and in good spirits. **3** providing protection or security: Put the money in a safe place.
• *adv* safely.
• *n* **1** a room, cupboard, box, etc., designed for the secure storage of valuables. **2** a cupboard with one or more mesh sides, used for keeping meat, etc., from insects. **safely** *adv* **safeness** *n* **safe conduct** (an official document providing) safe passage through an area, esp. in time of war. **safe deposit** a room or building with facilities for the secure storage of valuables. < ultimately Latin *salvus.*

safeguard (ˈseɪfˌgɑːd) *n* any measure that provides protection.
• *vb* protect.

a sacred cow

A person or thing that is granted total immunity from criticism or interference is sometimes called a sacred cow: Sociologists and psychiatrists have turned the handling of young offenders into yet another *sacred cow.* The phrase contains an allusion to the Hindu veneration of the animal, which dictates that it may not be killed for food.

safety (ˈseɪftɪ) *n* the state of being safe. **safety-belt** *n* **1** a belt that is fastened to an immovable object and prevents the wearer from falling. **2** a seat-belt. **safety-catch** *n* a device that prevents a mechanism from being operated accidentally, esp. on a gun. **safety net** a net that is slung beneath trapeze artistes, etc., to catch them if they fall. **safety-pin** *n* a clasp-like pin whose point is covered by a guard. **safety razor** *n* a razor fitted with a guard to prevent the risk of a deep cut. **safety-valve** *n* **1** a valve that opens automatically upon excessive pressure, etc. **2** an outlet for releasing pent-up emotion, etc., in a harmless way. < ultimately Old French *sauveté*, from *sauve* safe.

saffron (ˈsæfrən) *n* **1** the dried orange stigmas of a kind of crocus, used for colouring and flavouring food. **2** yellowish-orange. < ultimately Arabic *za'farān*.

sag (sæg) *vb* **sagged; sagging 1** sink or droop, esp. due to fatigue or pressure. **2** hang unevenly. **3** lose firmness or vigour; weaken.
• *n* a part that sags. < Middle English *saggen*.

saga (ˈsɑːgə) *n* a long, detailed story or account. < Old Norse.

sagacious (səˈgeɪʃəs) *adj* (*formal*) showing wisdom or sound judgment. **sagaciously** *adv* **sagacity** *n* < Latin *sagax*.

sage[1] (seɪdʒ) *n* **1** a plant of the mint family with greyish-green leaves, used in cooking for flavouring. **2** the leaves used in cooking. < ultimately Latin *salvus* healthy. SEE PANEL.

sage[2] *adj* (*literary*) profoundly wise.
• *n* a man renowned for his profound wisdom and teachings. **sagely** *adv* < ultimately Latin *sapere* to be wise.

sago (ˈseɪgəʊ) *n, pl* **sagos** a starchy cereal used esp. for puddings. < Malay *sagu* sago palm.

said (sɛd) SEE **SAY.**

sage

The name of the sage plant comes into English via the French word *sauge* from the Latin *salvus* meaning 'intact', 'healthy', or 'well'. The name reflects its reputed healing powers as a medicinal herb.

sail (seɪl) *n* **1** a piece of canvas or other strong fabric held by means of rigging so as to catch the wind and propel a ship or boat. **2** something which has the shape, position, or function of a sail: the sails of a windmill. **3** a voyage by ship.
• *vb* **1** (of a boat or ship) travel on the water. **2** (of people) travel by ship. **3** start on a voyage: When does the ship sail? **4** direct or navigate (a ship). **5** move or proceed smoothly or effortlessly, or in a stately manner. **sailcloth** *n* **1** a strong canvas used for sails. **2** a lightweight canvas used for clothing. **sailing-ship** *n* a ship driven by sails. **sailor** *n* member of a ship's crew, esp. one belonging to a navy. < Old English *segl*.

saint (sənt; *stressed* seɪnt) *n* **1** a person who is officially recognized after death as worthy of veneration. **2 Saint** the title of such a person: Saint Joan of Arc. **3** (*informal*) a person who shows great patience, tolerance, selflessness, etc. **sainthood** *n* **saintly** *adj* **saintliness** *n* **St Vitus's dance** a nervous disease characterized by involuntary contraction of the muscles. < ultimately Latin *sancire* to hallow.

sake (seɪk) *n* **1** benefit or interest: Do it for my sake. **2** purpose or motive: She accepted the invitation purely for the sake of keeping the peace. **for God's, goodness, heaven's,** or **pity's sake** used as an exclamation of protest, impatience, etc. < Old English *sacu* lawsuit.

salad (ˈsæləd) *n* **1** lettuce, tomato, celery, etc., served often with dressing as a side-dish. **2** such vegetables served with meat, egg, cheese, etc., as a main course. **3** a cold dish of one or more chopped or sliced foods served with a dressing: potato salad. < ultimately Latin

salad

Salad has been relished as a dish for many centuries. In Middle English the word was *salade*, a loan-word from Middle French which in turn derived from the Old Provençal *salada*. This came from the verb *salar* 'to season with salt', ultimately from the Latin word for salt, *sal*.

Other words with the same root include:

salami	**saline**	**sauce**
salary	**salt**	

sal salt. SEE PANEL.
salami (sə'lɑːmɪ) *n* a type of strongly-seasoned sausage. < Italian, from *salare* to salt, from Latin *sal* salt.
salary ('sælərɪ) *n* payment made to an employee, usually calculated on an annual basis and paid monthly. **salaried** *adj* receiving a salary. SEE PANEL.
sale (seɪl) *n* **1** the act of selling or being sold: The sale of the shares raised £1.5 million. **2** an instance of this: The assistants get commission for each of their sales. **3** an event at which goods are offered for purchase. **4** an offer of goods at reduced prices for a limited period: the winter sales. **for** or **on sale** offered for purchase. **saleable** *adj* fit to be sold; capable of being sold. **saleroom** *n* a room in which goods are displayed for sale, esp. prior to an auction. **salesman** fem. **saleswoman** *n* a salesperson. **salesmanship** *n* the art of persuading someone to purchase something. **salesperson** *n* a man or woman employed to sell something. **sales talk** (*often derogatory*) persuasive talk used by a salesperson to a prospective customer. < Old English *sala*, from Old Norse.
salient ('seɪlɪənt) *adj* **1** jutting out or protruding. **2** conspicuous or striking: a salient feature. **salience** *n* **saliently** *adv* < Latin *salire* to leap.
saline ('seɪlaɪn) *adj* consisting of, containing, or resembling salt; salty. • *n* a saline solution. < Latin *salinus*, from *sal* salt.
saliva (sə'laɪvə) *n* the clear, slightly acid fluid secreted by glands in the mouth. **salivary** *adj* of or producing saliva: salivary glands. **salivate** *vb* produce saliva, esp. excessively. **salivation** *n* < Latin.
sallow ('sæləʊ) *adj* of an unhealthy, yellowish colour: a sallow complexion. **sallowness** *n* < Old English *salu*.
sally ('sælɪ) *n* **1** the act of rushing forward, esp. in attack. **2** a short excursion. **3** a quick or witty remark. • *vb* **sallied; sallying** rush out in attack. **sally forth** set out (on a journey). < ultimately Latin *salire* to leap.
salmon ('sæmən) *n, pl* **salmon 1** a large, powerful fish with orange-pink flesh, highly valued for food and game. **2** its flesh used as food. **3** orange-pink. < ultimately Latin *salmo*. SEE PANEL.
salon ('sælɒn) *n* **1** an elegant reception room in a large, grand house. **2** (formerly) a fashionable gathering of famous people at the home of a wealthy person or dignitary. **3** the business premises of a hairdresser, beauty specialist, etc. < French.
saloon (sə'luːn) *n* **1** a car of standard design. **2** a public room on a ship. **3** a saloon bar. **4** (*US*) an establishment where alcoholic drinks are bought and consumed. **saloon bar** a room in a public house which is relatively well-furnished and where drinks are usually more expensive. < French *salon*, from Italian *sala* hall, of Germanic origin.
salt (sɔːlt) *n* **1** very common, white, crystalline solid used mostly for preserving and flavouring food; sodium

salary

Salary, 'the monthly sum received by an employee for his or her services', derives from the Latin word *salarium*, the part of a Roman soldier's pay that he was given for the purchase of salt (Latin *sal*). This provides an explanation of the expression not worth one's salt. A worker who is not worth his salt is one who doesn't deserve the salary he receives.

salmon and salmonella

Those fond of eating salmon will be heartened to know that this highly valued fish has no direct link with the genus of bacteria known as salmonella. Salmonella, a cause of typhoid, gastroenteritis, and food poisoning, takes its name from Dr Daniel E. *Salmon*, an American veterinary surgeon, 1850–1914, who first isolated the bacterium in the late 19th century.

the salt of the earth

The expression the salt of the earth means 'people who are known for their kindness and warmth of human feeling': Old George is *the salt of the earth*. He'd give you his last penny if you needed it. The expression comes from the Authorized (King James) Version of the Bible, Matthew 5:13: Ye are the salt of the earth: but if the salt have lost its savour, wherewith shall it be salted?

chloride. **2** a chemical compound formed by the action of an acid on a metal. **3** *pl* any of a group of salt-like substances, chiefly used as a laxative. **4** *pl* smelling-salts.

• *adj* **1** tasting of salt; salty. **2** preserved or treated with salt.

• *vb* **1** season, preserve, or treat with salt. **2** add piquancy or interest to. **salt away** or **down** store or save. **salt-cellar** *n* a container for salt used at mealtimes. **salt-marsh** *n* an area of flat land frequently flooded by seawater. **salt-pan** *n* a hollow by the sea in which salt is deposited by the evaporation of seawater. **salty** *adj* containing or tasting of salt. **take (something) with a grain** or **pinch of salt** (*informal*) adopt a sceptical attitude towards something. < Old English *sealt.* SEE PANEL. SEE PANEL AT SALARY.

SALT *abbrev* Strategic Arms Limitation Talks.

saltpetre (ˌsɔːltˈpiːtə) *n* a substance used in making gunpowder and preserving meat; potassium nitrate. < ultimately Medieval Latin *sal petrae* salt of the rock.

salubrious (səˈluːbrɪəs) *adj* (*formal*) conducive to good health. **salubriously** *adv* **salubriousness** *n* **salubrity** *n* < Latin *salubris.*

salutary (ˈsæljʊtərɪ) *adj* **1** causing or intended to cause improvement. **2** having a beneficial effect. < ultimately Latin *salus* health.

salutation (ˌsæljʊˈteɪʃən) *n* a word, expression, or gesture that serves as a greeting.

salute (səˈluːt) *vb* **1** greet or acknowledge with an expression or gesture of respect. **2** (of military personnel) make a formal gesture of respect, esp. by raising the right arm. **3** express praise or admiration for.

• *n* an act of saluting. < ultimately Latin *salus* greeting.

salvage (ˈsælvɪdʒ) *n* **1** the act of saving a ship or its cargo from being lost. **2** the act of saving any property from loss or destruction. **3** property that is saved in this way.

• *vb* save from loss or destruction. < Middle French *salver* to save.

salvation (sælˈveɪʃən) *n* **1** (*religion*) the freeing of the soul from the power and effects of sin. **2** the freeing from danger, ruin, or destruction. < ultimately Late Latin *salvare* to save.

salve (sælv) *n* **1** an ointment that soothes or heals. **2** anything that heals, alleviates, or soothes.

• *vb* soothe or ease with or as if with a salve: salve one's conscience. < Old English *sealf.*

salver (ˈsælvə) *n* a small, ornamental tray, often made of silver. < ultimately Late Latin *salvare* to save. SEE PANEL.

salvo (ˈsælvəʊ) *n, pl* **salvos, salvoes** **1** the simultaneous discharge of a number of guns. **2** concentrated fire, as in a battle. **3** a sudden outburst. < ultimately Latin *salvus* safe.

same (seɪm) *adj* **1** similar or identical: They all wore the same clothes. **2** unchanged: The house had the same musty smell as when I first visited it. **3** being the one previously mentioned.

• *adv* in the same manner.

• *pron* **1** the same thing or person: I would have done the same. **2** the thing previously mentioned. **sameness** *n* **all** or **just the same** despite that. < Old Norse *samr.*

samovar (ˈsæməˌvɑː) *n* a metal urn for heating water, used esp. in Russia for making tea. < Russian *samo-* self + *varit'* to boil.

sampan (ˈsæmpæn) *n* a small, flat-bottomed boat used in the Far East. < Chinese *sān pǎn,* from *sān* three + *pǎn* plank.

sample (ˈsɑːmpl̩) *n* a part that is (intended to be) representative of the whole: Send me a sample of your work.

• *vb* take a sample of (something), esp. for testing purposes. **sampler** *n* **1** a person or thing that takes samples. **2** a piece of cloth embroidered so as to display a person's skill in needlework. < ultimately Latin *exemplum* example.

samurai (ˈsæmʊˌraɪ) *n, pl* **samurai** **1** (formerly) a member of the warrior caste in Japan. **2** this caste. < Japanese.

salver

A salver is a fine ornamental tray nowadays used chiefly for serving drinks and refreshments, especially on formal occasions. Salver is a modification of the French word *salve,* which comes from the Spanish *salva.* This was a tray of similar design as that used today from which the king's food-taster sampled food to detect poison. *Salvar,* the verb from which *salva* derived, meant both 'to sample food in order to detect poison' and also 'to save'.

sanatorium (ˌsænəˈtɔːrɪəm) *n, pl* **sanatoriums, sanatoria** an establishment for the care of convalescents and the chronically ill. < Late Latin *sanatus* curative.

sanctify (ˈsæŋktɪˌfaɪ) *vb* **sanctified; sanctifying** make holy or sacred. **sanctification** *n* **sanctity** *n* holiness or sacredness. < ultimately Latin *sanctus* sacred.

sanctimonious (ˌsæŋktɪˈməʊnɪəs) *adj* pretending to be religious or holy. **sanctimoniously** *adv* **sanctimoniousness** *n* < ultimately Latin *sanctus* sacred.

sanction (ˈsæŋkʃən) *n* **1** official permission or approval. **2** a coercive measure used as a way of making a foreign government or regime abide by an international law or code of conduct. • *vb* give official permission or approval to. < ultimately Latin *sancire* to make holy.

sanctuary (ˈsæŋktjʊərɪ) *n* **1** a holy or consecrated place. **2** the most sacred part of a religious building, esp. that surrounding the altar. **3** a refuge for wildlife. **4** (any place providing) refuge or protection. < ultimately Latin *sanctus* sacred.

sand (sænd) *n* **1** very fine particles produced by the action of the sea on rock. **2** an expanse of sand; beach. • *vb* **1** make smooth by means of sandpaper. **2** sprinkle with sand. **sander** *n* **sandbag** *n* a bag filled with sand that is used to make a defensive wall against enemy fire, flood-water, etc. **sand-blast** *vb* clean by means of a jet of sand propelled by compressed steam or air. **sand-castle** *n* a model of a castle made by a child on the sea-shore. **sandpaper** *n* paper that is coated on one side with sand and is used as an abrasive. **sand-pit** *n* a hollow or enclosure partly filled with sand for children to play in. **sandstone** *n* sedimentary rock formed of consolidated sand. **sandstorm** *n* a storm of wind that carries along clouds of sand, esp. in a desert. **sandy** *adj* **1** covered with or containing sand. **2** resembling sand in colour or texture; reddish-yellow. < Old English.

sandal (ˈsændl̩) *n* a type of light, airy shoe consisting of a sole held to the foot by means of straps or thongs. < ultimately Greek *sandalon*.

sandalwood (ˈsændl̩ˌwʊd) *n* a hard, fragrant, light-coloured wood of a tropical tree, used chiefly in carving and cabinetwork. < of Dravidian origin.

sandwich (ˈsænwɪdʒ, sænwɪtʃ) *n* **1** two slices of bread, usually buttered, with a filling between them. **2** anything resembling or likened to a sandwich. • *vb* insert or squeeze (a person or thing) between two others: My car was sandwiched between a bus and a lorry. **sandwich-board** *n* either of two notice-boards worn at the front and back of a person's body and supported by straps passing over the shoulders, used esp. for advertising. **sandwich course** a course of instruction organized so that periods spent at college or university alternate with periods of practical work with a company. **sandwich-man** *n* a man who wears sandwich-boards. SEE PANEL.

sane (seɪn) *adj* **1** having a sound mind; not mad. **2** produced by rational thinking: a sane decision. **sanely** *adv* **saneness** *n* < Latin *sanus*.

sang (sæŋ) SEE **SING**.

sanguine (ˈsæŋgwɪn) *adj* **1** (*formal*) hopeful or optimistic. **2** having a healthy red colour; ruddy: a sanguine complexion. < ultimately Latin *sanguis* blood.

sanitary (ˈsænɪtərɪ) *adj* **1** clean and free from germs; hygienic. **2** promoting or concerning good health. **sanitary towel** an absorbent pad worn during

the noble sandwich

Sandwich, the name given to two slices of bread with a filling between them, comes from John Montagu, the fourth Earl of *Sandwich,* 1718–92. This is nowadays fairly common knowledge. What is less well known, however, is the reason why the sandwich was named after him.

It might well be assumed that Lord Sandwich must have had some special interest in food, or at least in the retailing of what have come to be known as 'fast foods'. This was not the case, however. Montagu's first love was gambling, to the extent that instead of leaving the gaming table to eat, he would have food brought to him. In this way the card-game could continue uninterrupted. Invariably, the snack would consist of a slice of beef between two slices of bread. Far from inventing the sandwich, then, Montagu merely brought the phenomenon to the public eye.

menstruation. **sanitation** *n* measures for protecting and promoting good health. < ultimately Latin *sanitas*.

sanity (ˈsænɪtɪ) *n* the state of being sane.

sank (sæŋk) SEE **SINK.**

Santa Claus (ˈsæntə ˌklɔːz) Father Christmas. SEE PANEL.

sap (sæp) *n* **1** a watery solution that circulates in plants and trees, carrying food, chemical matter, etc. **2** (any vital source of) energy or vigour.
• *vb* **sapped; sapping** drain or weaken: sap one's strength. **sapling** *n* a young tree. < Old English *sæp*.

sapphire (ˈsæfaɪə) *n* **1** a transparent, deep-blue, precious stone. **2** a deep-blue colour.
• *adj* deep-blue. < ultimately Sanskrit *śanipriya* beloved of Saturn, from *Śani* Saturn + *priya* dear.

sarcasm (ˈsɑːkæzəm) *n* (the use of) mocking or taunting language, often full of irony. **sarcastic** *adj* **sarcastically** *adv* < ultimately Greek *sarkazein* to tear the flesh.

sardine (sɑːˈdiːn) *n* a young pilchard or similar small fish, often preserved and canned. < ultimately Latin *sardina*.

sardonic (sɑːˈdɒnɪk) *adj* humorous in a grim, sarcastic, or cynical way. **sardonically** *adv* < ultimately Greek *sardonios*. SEE PANEL.

sari (ˈsɑːrɪ) *n* the traditional main garment of Hindu women, consisting of a long length of cloth draped around the body. < Hindi *sāṛī*.

sarong (səˈrɒŋ) *n* a skirt-like garment worn by men and women in a number of tropical countries. < Malay: sheath.

sash[1] (sæʃ) *n* a band of usually brightly-coloured cloth worn round the waist or over one shoulder, either for ornament or as a sign of rank. < Arabic *shāsh* muslin.

sash[2] *n* **1** a frame that holds the pane or panes of a window or door. **2** either of two such frames, complete with panes, that slide up and down and form a sash-window. **sash-cord** *n* a strong cord used for attaching a window sash to a counterbalance. **sash-window** *n* a window consisting of two glazed sashes which slide up and down. < probably French *châssis* chassis.

sat (sæt) SEE **SIT.**

Satan (ˈseɪtn̩) *n* the Devil. **satanic** *adj* **1** wicked or evil; fiendish. **2** of Satan. **satanism** *n* the worship of the Devil. < ultimately Hebrew *śāṭān* opponent.

satchel (ˈsætʃəl) *n* a small bag fitted with a shoulder strap, used by schoolchildren. < ultimately Latin *saccus* bag.

satellite (ˈsætəˌlaɪt) *n* **1** a heavenly body that orbits another of larger size. **2** a man-made object that orbits a heavenly body. **3** a country, region, or community that is dependent on or controlled by another. < ultimately Latin *satelles* attendant.

satiate (ˈseɪʃɪˌeɪt) *vb* satisfy to excess. **satiation** *n* **satiety** *n* the state of being satiated. < ultimately Latin *satis* enough.

satin (ˈsætɪn) *n* a silk fabric with a glossy surface. < ultimately Arabic *Zaytūn* Qingjiang, seaport in China. SEE PANEL AT **TULLE.**

satire (ˈsætaɪə) *n* **1** wit and irony used for purposes of censuring, exposing, or ridiculing. **2** a novel, play, etc., in which satire is predominant. **3** such works considered collectively. **satirical** *adj* **satirically** *adv* **satirist** *n* **satirize** *vb* attack or censure by means of satire. < ultimately Latin *satur* sated.

satisfy (ˈsætɪsˌfaɪ) *vb* **satisfied; satisfying 1** make content by fulfilling needs or

Where does Santa come from?

Santa Claus comes from the Dutch word *Sinterklaas,* which in turn is a shortened form of *Sint Nikolaas,* (Saint Nicholas). St Nicholas' day was originally celebrated on 6 December. In some European countries, including Germany, the Netherlands, and Belgium, this continues to be the day when the patron saint of children makes his rounds. However, in other countries Christian influence shifted the date of St Nicholas' round to Christmas Eve. Hence the name Father Christmas.

sardonic laughter

A smile or laughter that is scornful or derisive is sometimes described as sardonic. This word derives ultimately from the Greek *herba sardonia* or 'herb of Sardis' (now Sardinia). This herb was reputedly so bitter that it caused the facial muscles of those who tasted it to convulse into what appeared to be a grimace of disdain.

demands: When it comes to hygiene, Dr Cook is a hard man to satisfy. **2** convince: I'm not satisfied he's telling the truth. **3** put an end to. **4** meet the requirements of. **5** repay. **satisfaction** *n* **1** the act of satisfying or state of being satisfied. **2** reparation for an insult, loss, or injury. **3** something that fulfils or gratifies. **satisfactory** *adj* satisfying needs or requirements. **satisfactorily** *adv* < ultimately Latin *satisfacere.*

satsuma (sæt'suːmə) *n* a kind of seedless mandarin. < *Satsuma,* a former province of Japan.

saturate ('sætʃəˌreɪt) *vb* **1** soak thoroughly. **2** fill or permeate with something to the point where no more can be absorbed: The market for used cars is completely saturated. **saturation** *n* < ultimately Latin *satur* sated.

satyr ('sætə) *n* **1** a woodland deity in Greek mythology, usually characterized as half human and half goat. **2** a lecherous man. < ultimately Greek *satyros.*

sauce (sɔːs) *n* **1** a liquid or semiliquid preparation served with food, esp. to add flavour. **2** (*informal*) cheek or impudence. **saucy** *adj* **1** impudent. **2** (*informal*) sexually provocative in an amusing way. **saucily** *adv* **sauciness** *n* < ultimately Latin *sal* salt.

saucepan ('sɔːspən) *n* a round, deep, metal cooking-pot, usually having a lid and handle.

saucer ('sɔːsə) *n* **1** a small, circular, shallow dish on which a cup stands. **2** the amount that a saucer holds: a saucer of milk. **3** something resembling or likened to a saucer. < Middle French *sausse* sauce.

sauna ('sɔːnə) *n* (a room or building equipped for) a Finnish form of steam bath, in which steam is produced by throwing water on hot stones. < Finnish.

saunter ('sɔːntə) *vb* walk in a casual or leisurely way.
• *n* a casual or leisurely walk. < origin uncertain.

sausage ('sɒsɪdʒ) *n* a thin, edible tube filled with a mixture of minced fat, cereal, meat, and seasoning. **sausagemeat** *n* this mixture. **sausage roll** a small roll of pastry filled with sausagemeat. < ultimately Latin *salsus* salted.

savage ('sævɪdʒ) *adj* **1** barbarous or uncivilized. **2** not domesticated; wild. **3** vicious or fierce: a savage attack.
• *n* **1** a member of a society considered to be primitive. **2** a vicious person or animal.
• *vb* (of a wild animal) bite or claw fiercely in an attack; maul. **savagely** *adv* **savageness** *n* **savagery** *n* < ultimately Latin *silva* forest.

savanna (sə'vænə) *n* also **savannah** an expanse of open grassland with scattered trees, esp. in tropical Africa. < Spanish *zavana,* from Taino *zabana.*

save (seɪv) *vb* **1** remove from danger or harm; rescue. **2** put (esp. money) aside for future use. **3** avoid wasting (something): He turned the lights off to save the battery. **4** make unnecessary: Sending it by post will save me a trip. **5** prevent an opponent from scoring, winning, etc. **6** (*religion*) release from sin.
• *n* an action that prevents an opponent from scoring.
• *prep* except (for).
• *conj* were it not. **saver** *n* **saving** *prep* except. **saving grace** a redeeming feature or quality. **savings** *pl n* money put aside for future use. < ultimately Latin *salvus* safe.

saviour ('seɪvjə) *n* a person who delivers people from harm or danger. **Saviour** *n* Jesus Christ regarded as the saviour of mankind from sin. < ultimately Late Latin *salvare* to save.

savoir-faire ('sævwɑːˌfɛə) *n* the capacity of knowing the right thing to do in any situation. < French: knowing how to do.

savour ('seɪvə) *n* **1** the taste or smell of something. **2** a stimulating quality.
• *vb* **1** have a certain taste, smell, or quality. **2** taste or smell (something) with enjoyment. **3** relish or enjoy: He savoured the news with visible delight. < ultimately Latin *sapor.*

savoury ('seɪvərɪ) *adj* **1** having a salty or spicy taste (as opposed to sweet). **2** having an appetizing taste or smell. **3** respectable.
• *n* a savoury dish. **savouriness** *n*

saw[1] (sɔː) SEE **SEE**[1].

saw[2] *n* a tool with a sharp-toothed blade or disc, used for cutting hard material such as wood.
• *vb* **sawed; sawn; sawing 1** cut or shape with a saw. **2** make back and forth movements as though using a saw. **sawdust** *n* fine particles of wood produced in sawing. **sawmill** *n* a factory where timber is sawn into planks. < Old English *sagu.*

sawn (sɔːn) SEE **SAW**[2]. **sawn-off** *adj* (of a gun) having part of the barrel sawn off.

saxifrage ('sæksɪˌfrɪdʒ) *n* any of a large group of rock-plants, often with tufted leaves. < ultimately Latin *saxum* rock

\+ *frangere* to break.

saxophone (ˈsæksəˌfəʊn) *n* any of a group of woodwind instruments with a curved metal body, finger keys, and a single reed. **saxophonist** *n* < Adolphe *Sax*, died 1894, Belgian musical-instrument maker + *-phone*. SEE PANEL.

say (seɪ) *vb* **said; saying 1** express in spoken words; utter. **2** state or declare: The notice said that the road was to be closed for repairs. **3** state positively. **4** accept (something) as a possibility or for the sake of argument. **5** give an opinion or estimate as to: I can't say when I'm likely to see her again. **6** recite or repeat.
• *n* the right or opportunity to exert one's influence: I was given very little say in the matter. **saying** *n* a well-known phrase; maxim. < Old English *secgan*. SEE PANEL.

scab (skæb) *n* **1** a crust that forms over a wound as it heals. **2** (*derogatory*) a blackleg. **3** any of various plant diseases. **scabby** *adj* < Scandinavian.

scabbard (ˈskæbəd) *n* a sheath for the blade of a sword, bayonet, etc. < Anglo-French *escaubers*.

scabies (ˈskeɪbiːz) *n* a contagious skin disease caused by a mite, characterized by itching. < Latin *scabere* to scratch, scrape.

scabious (ˈskeɪbɪəs) *n* any of a group of herbaceous plants with dense clusters of blue, red, or whitish flowers. < Medieval Latin *scabiosa herba* scabies plant. SEE PANEL.

scaffold (ˈskæfəld, ˈskæfəʊld) *n* **1** a raised platform on which a criminal, etc., is executed. **2** scaffolding. < Old Northern French *escafaut*.

scaffolding (ˈskæfəldɪŋ) *n* **1** a temporary

saxophone and **sousaphone**

Inventions are frequently named after their inventors and musical instruments are no exception. The saxophone takes its name from Antoine (known as Adolphe) *Sax*, 1814–94, a Belgian maker of musical instruments who patented his invention in 1846. Some half a century later in 1899 appeared the sousaphone, the brain-child of John Philip *Sousa*, 1854–1932, a US composer and bandmaster.

that is to say

That is to say is such a common expression that its rather unusual structure tends to go unnoticed. The construction is French, the phrase being a word for word translation of *C'est'à dire*. Other idiomatic expressions which are literal translations of French prototypes include It goes without saying from *Cela va sans dire*, in evidence from *en évidence*, that's life from *c'est la vie*, as for me from *quant à moi*, and according to me from *selon moi*.

The word say occurs in a number of idiomatic expressions, including:

have one's say to express one's views or opinions fully.

I'll say yes indeed; used as a strong form of agreement: 'Will she want to go and see the Princess?'—'I'll say she will!'

(**just**) **say the word** just state your wishes, request, etc., and they will be immediately fulfilled: 'Just say the word and we'll come!'

say one's piece to state one's opinion, protest, etc., formally.

say-so *n* **1** an assertion made without proof. **2** the right to decide something: on whose say-so?

say something to say a few words; make a short speech: 'Come on, George, say something—everyone's expecting it of you.'

say when to state when an action should stop, especially pouring a drink: 'Say when!'—'Right, that's enough, thank you!'

to say nothing of and also; and more importantly: Adding further insulation to the building would take another three months, to say nothing of the additional money involved.

to say the least without exaggerating: To be alone in a foreign country, with no money, and not knowing a soul, is, to say the least, rather disconcerting.

you can say that again used to express emphatic agreement with what has just been said: 'It's raining outside!'—'You can say that again! I got drenched just bringing in the milk!'

structure of poles, planks, etc., used by workmen when erecting or repairing a building. **2** the poles, planks, etc., used in such a structure.

scald (skɔːld) *vb* **1** burn or injure with hot liquid or steam. **2** subject to boiling water, esp. to sterilize. **3** heat (milk) almost to boiling-point.
• *n* an injury to the skin from scalding. < Latin *ex-* + *calda* warm water, from *calidus* warm.

scale[1] (skeɪl) *n* **1** one of the thin, hard plates that overlap to form a protective covering for many fishes and reptiles. **2** something like this on a leaf or plant. **3** a flake of dead skin. **4** a coating that forms on the inside of a kettle or boiler by the continual passage of hard water.
• *vb* **1** remove scale or scales from. **2** come off in scales or flakes. **3** cover or become covered with a hard layer or coating. **scaly** *adj* with a layer of scales or scale. < of Germanic origin.

scale[2] *n* **1** one of the two pans of a balance. **2** *pl* balance pans; instrument for weighing. **tip the scales** be a decisive influence. < Old Norse *skāl*.

scale[3] *n* **1** a graduated series of marks, units, degrees, etc., used for measuring. **2** a graduated table or system: salary scale. **3** a group of musical notes at fixed intervals, ascending or descending in order. **4** the proportion of something in relation to a model or drawing of it; marked line showing this proportion. **5** a relative size or degree: He entertains on a grand scale.
• *vb* **1** climb. **2** modify or regulate according to a particular rate or ratio. < Latin *scala* ladder.

scallop (ˈskɒləp) *n* **1** a shellfish with a shell of two fan-shaped halves. **2** one of these halves used to bake or serve food in. **3** one of a series of curves forming a decorative border, esp. on cloth.
• *vb* **1** bake in a scallop-shell or similar dish. **2** decorate (a border) with scallops. **scalloping** *n* < of Germanic origin.

scallywag (ˈskælɪˌwæg) *n* (*informal*) someone that is mischievous; scamp. < origin unknown.

scalp (skælp) *n* **1** the skin of the part of the head usually covered by hair. **2** this skin with the hair, formerly taken from an enemy as a trophy, esp. by North American Indians.
• *vb* cut or tear the scalp from. < Scandinavian.

scalpel (ˈskælpl̩) *n* a knife with a short, thin blade, used by surgeons. < Latin *scalpere* to carve.

scamp (skæmp) *n* a mischievous child or person; rascal. < obsolete *scamp* to rob on the highway.

scamper (ˈskæmpə) *vb* run about playfully; scuttle.
• *n* scampering. < ultimately Latin *ex-* + *campus* field.

scampi (ˈskæmpɪ) *pl n* large prawns, often eaten cooked in batter. < Italian *scampo* European lobster.

scan (skæn) *vb* **scanned; scanning** **1** examine intently and in detail. **2** read or look through quickly and casually. **3** analyse (verse) so as to show metre and rhythm. **4** (of verse) conform to a rhythmical or metrical pattern. **5** search (an area) by sweeping a radar or sonar beam over it. **6** resolve (an image) by moving an electron beam across a screen, esp. for television broadcasting.
• *n* scanning. **scanner** *n* a device for systematic monitoring: radar scanner. < Latin *scandere* to climb.

scandal (ˈskændl̩) *n* **1** shame or discredit brought about by someone's conduct. **2** something shameful or outrageous. **3** malicious gossip or rumour. **scandalize** *vb* shock; appal, esp. by improper behaviour. **scandalmonger** *n* someone who spreads scandal or gossip. **scandalous** *adj* **1** shameful; outrageous. **2** containing scandal; defamatory. **scandalously** *adv* < Greek *skandalon* trap.

scant (skænt) *adj* hardly sufficient; minimal: The problem has received only scant attention by the media. **scanty** *adj* scant; meagre, esp. in coverage. **scantily** *adv* **scantiness** *n* < Old Norse *skammr* short.

scapegoat (ˈskeɪpˌgəʊt) *n* someone or something made to carry the blame for the faults of others. SEE PANEL.

scar (skɑː) *n* **1** a mark left on skin tissue after an injury has healed. **2** a mark left

scabious

In the Middle Ages, plants were often valued less for their beauty than for their reputed medicinal properties. Those regarded as having a healing function were sometimes allotted the name of the disease or ailment that they were supposed to cure. Such was the sad fate of the scabious, which was once considered a remedy for *scabies* or 'the itch'.

on a plant from where a leaf has fallen. **3** any mark left by wear or damage. **4** a lasting emotional injury.
• *vb* **scarred; scarring 1** form or mark with a scar or scars. **2** cause lasting grief to. < ultimately Greek *eschara* scab.

scarce (skɛəs) *adj* **1** not enough to meet a demand. **2** uncommon; rare. **make oneself scarce** (*informal*) go away, esp. quickly. **scarcely** *adv* **1** hardly; only just. **2** not at all; by no means. **scarcity** *n* shortage; deficiency. < ultimately Latin *excerpere* to pluck out. SEE PANEL AT **HARDLY.**

scare (skɛə) *vb* **1** make or become frightened suddenly. **2 scare off** or **away** drive away by frightening.
• *n* **1** a sudden fright. **2** a state of general fear or panic: bomb scare. **scarecrow** *n* **1** a human-like figure dressed in old clothes, fixed in a field to frighten birds away from crops. **2** someone who is very thin or untidy. **scaremonger** *n* someone who spreads fright or panic unnecessarily. **scaremongering** *n* **scary** *adj* **1** alarming. **2** easily alarmed; timid. < Old Norse *skjarr* timid.

scarf (skɑːf) *n, pl* **scarves** a square or long, narrow piece of cloth worn round the neck, shoulders, or head for warmth or as an ornament. < Old Northern French *escarpe* sash.

scarify (ˈskɛərɪˌfaɪ) *vb* **scarified; scarifying 1** make small cuts in (skin or other tissue) esp. surgically. **2** break up and loosen (soil, road surfaces, etc.). < Greek *skariphasthai* to sketch.

scarlet (ˈskɑːlət) *adj* of a vivid red colour.
• *n* the colour of scarlet; clothing of this colour. **scarlet fever** an infectious fever causing a red rash and inflammation in the mouth, nose, and throat. **scarlet runner** a runner bean. **scarlet woman** (*old-fashioned*) a prostitute. < Persian *saqalāt* scarlet cloth.

scarp (skɑːp) *n* a steep slope, esp. formed by erosion or faulting; escarpment. < Italian *scarpa.*

scarper (ˈskɑːpə) *vb* (*slang*) run away. < perhaps Italian *scappare* to escape.

scathing (ˈskeɪðɪŋ) *adj* severely critical; harsh: scathing remarks. < Old Norse *skathi* harm.

scatter (ˈskætə) *vb* **1** distribute or throw about in all directions. **2** disperse or diffuse (beams of light, radiation, etc.) at random. **3** separate and move in all directions: The enemy scattered.
• *n* **1** scattering. **2** a small amount of something scattered; extent of this. **scatter-brain** *n* someone who is incapable of concentrating. **scatter-brained** *adj* < Middle English *scateren.*

scatty (ˈskætɪ) *adj* (*informal*) scatter-brained.

scavenge (ˈskævɪndʒ) *vb* **1** (of animals) hunt for decaying flesh to eat. **2** salvage (any usable material) from refuse or discarded things. **scavenger** *n* < Old Northern French *escauwage* inspection.

SCE *abbrev* Scottish Certificate of Education.

scenario (sɪˈnɑːrɪˌəʊ) *n, pl* **scenarios 1** an outline of a film or play. **2** a screenplay or play script with details of scenes, etc. **3** an imagined or projected course of future events. < ultimately Latin *scaena* stage. SEE PANEL.

scene (siːn) *n* **1** a continuous sequence of action in a film or play; division of an act. **2** a situation or incident considered in this way. **3** a stage set or scenery. **4** a place where something happens,

scenario

He outlined the various scenarios in which the government would call out the troops. In this sentence, scenario is used to mean 'an imagined or projected course of future events'. Some careful users of English prefer not to use the word in this way, reserving it to mean 'an outline of a film or play'.

scapegoat

A person who is made to bear the blame for others is called a scapegoat. The coining of this word, a blend of *escape* and *goat,* is ascribed to the English Protestant reformer, William Tyndale, c. 1494–1536, best known for his translation of the Bible. Scapegoat was a mistaken translation of the Hebrew word *'azāzēl* (probably the name of a demon), which was confused with *'ēz 'ōzēl* 'the goat that escapes'.

In Jewish tradition a scapegoat is a goat that is symbolically loaded with the sins of the Israelites and then sent into the wilderness.

whether real or imaginary: the scene of the crime. **5** a show of unrestrained feeling or temper: make a scene. **6** a view; landscape. **7** (*informal*) an area of interest: the music scene; not my scene. **behind the scenes** out of sight of public view. **scenery** *n* **1** the props and painted backdrops on a theatre stage that represent the place of action. **2** a landscape; attractive features of this. **scene-shifter** *n* someone who moves theatre scenery about the stage. **scenic** *adj* picturesque; striking. **scenically** *adv* < ultimately Greek *skēnē* tent, stage.

scent (sɛnt) *n* **1** a characteristic smell, esp. agreeable. **2** a smell left by an animal along the area it passes over, perceived by other animals. **3** the sense of smell of an animal. **4** a perfume.
• *vb* **1** detect by smelling. **2** sense; suspect. **3** fill with a pleasant smell; perfume. **scented** *adj* < Latin *sentire* to perceive.

sceptic (ˈskɛptɪk) *n* someone who doubts accepted, esp. religious beliefs or principles. **scepticism** *n* **sceptical** *adj* inclined to doubt or question. **sceptically** *adv* < ultimately Greek *skeptesthai* to consider.

sceptre (ˈsɛptə) *n* a ceremonial staff carried by a sovereign as a symbol of authority. < Greek *skēptron.*

schedule (ˈʃɛdjuːl) *n* **1** a plan showing the procedure and times for something to be carried out. **2** a timetable.
• *vb* plan or put on a schedule; fix a certain time for (something). **on schedule** at the arranged time. < Late Latin *schedula* slip of paper.

scheme (skiːm) *n* **1** a programme of action; plan. **2** a crafty or secret plan. **3** an ordered arrangement of elements or parts: colour scheme.
• *vb* **1** make plans; devise. **2** plot; conspire. **schemer** *n* **schematic** *adj* of or in the form of a scheme, diagram, etc. **schematically** *adv* < ultimately Greek *schēma* form.

schism (ˈsɪzəm, ˈskɪzm̩) *n* a separation into opposed groups through differences of opinion or belief, esp. in a religious body. **schismatic** *n, adj* (someone) that creates or is involved in a schism. < ultimately Greek *schizein* to split.

schizoid (ˈskɪtsɔɪd) *n, adj* (someone) that tends towards or suffers from schizophrenia. **schizophrenia** *n* a disorder of the mind characterized by personality disintegration, unpredictable behaviour patterns, and delusions. **schizophrenic** *n, adj*

scholar (ˈskɒlə) *n* **1** someone who attends school. **2** someone who is very learned or academic. **3** someone who holds a scholarship. **scholarly** *adj* **scholarship** *n* **1** advanced knowledge of a particular subject. **2** academic work; learning. **3** a grant of money for someone's education. **scholastic** *adj* of schools or scholars. < Latin *schola* school.

school¹ (skuːl) *n* a group of fish, whales, etc., that swim together; shoal. < Middle Dutch *schole.*

school² *n* **1** an institution where children are taught; its buildings, pupils, or staff. **2** the time during which instruction is carried out in this. **3** the process of education at a school. **4** a university department concerned with one area of study. **5** a body of artists, philosophers, etc., sharing a common influence or doctrine. **6** people with similar thoughts or opinions: a school of thought. **7** experience or activity that instructs.
• *vb* discipline; instruct. **schoolboy** fem. **schoolgirl** *n* a child attending school. **schooling** *n* instruction in school. **school-leaver** *n* someone leaving school for ever. **schoolmaster** fem. **schoolmistress** *n* a teacher in a school. **schoolroom** *n* a room for teaching children in. **schoolteacher** *n* a person who teaches in a school. < ultimately Greek *scholē* leisure, school.

schooner (ˈskuːnə) *n* **1** type of sailing-ship with two or more masts. **2** a large glass used esp. for a measure of sherry or port. < origin unknown.

sciatica (saɪˈætɪkə) *n* intense pain in the hip and back of the thigh caused by pressure on the sciatic nerve. **sciatic** *adj* **sciatic nerve** one of two large nerves in the body extending from the pelvis down the back of the thigh. < ultimately Greek *ischion* hip joint.

science (ˈsaɪəns) *n* **1** an area of knowledge that is studied systematically, esp. one dealing with the properties of substances, living things, or the physical universe, for example, biology and chemistry. **2** a systematically learnt skill. **scientific** *adj* **scientifically** *adv* **science fiction** fiction often set in the future that deals mainly with the effect of scientific advances or discoveries on individuals or society. **scientist** *n* someone who studies or is expert in any of the sciences, esp. the natural ones. < ultimately Latin *scire* to know.
SEE PANEL.

scintillate (ˈsɪntɪˌleɪt) *vb* **1** give off

sparks; sparkle. **2** be stimulating or brilliant: scintillating conversation. **scintillation** *n* < Latin *scintilla* spark.

scissors (ˈsɪzəz) *pl n an* implement used for cutting, that has two crossed blades on a pivot with handles for the thumb and finger of one hand. < ultimately Latin *caedere* to cut.

sclerosis (skləˈrəʊsɪs) *n* a diseased condition in which usually soft tissue hardens abnormally. < Greek *sklēros* hard.

scoff[1] (skɒf) *vb* laugh at with contempt; ridicule. **scoffer** *n* < probably Scandinavian.

scoff[2] *vb* (*informal*) eat rapidly and greedily. < origin uncertain.

scold (skəʊld) *vb* reprimand or rebuke (esp. a child).
• *n* (*old-fashioned*) a woman who constantly finds fault. < probably Scandinavian.

scone (skɒn, skəʊn) *n* a small, light cake of dough, batter, etc., baked quickly and usually eaten buttered. < perhaps Dutch *schoonbrood* fine bread.

scoop (sku:p) *n* **1** an implement with a round bowl and a long handle, used for taking up liquids, ice-cream, etc. **2** an implement used as a shovel for lifting and moving sand, coal, grain, etc. **3** a scooping action. **4** the amount held in a scoop. **5** a piece of news reported in one newspaper in advance of all the others.
• *vb* **1** take up or out (as if) with a scoop. **2** hollow or dig out. **3** report (news) before or to the exclusion of rival newspapers. < Middle Dutch *schope*.

scoot (sku:t) *vb* (*informal*) go suddenly and quickly; dash. < probably Scandinavian.

scooter (ˈsku:tə) *n* **1** a toy vehicle for a child with a narrow footboard and a wheel at each end. **2** also **motor scooter** a type of light motor cycle with small wheels, a front shield, and an enclosed engine. **scooterist** *n*

scope (skəʊp) *n* **1** a range of treatment, influence, etc. **2** freedom of opportunity for thought or action: There's scope for improvement. < Greek *skopos* target.

scorch (skɔ:tʃ) *vb* **1** burn so as to discolour or cause pain. **2** (*informal*) travel extremely fast.
• *n* a mark caused by scorching.
scorcher *n* (*informal*) a very hot day.
scorching *adj* (*informal*) very hot.
< probably Scandinavian.

score (skɔ:) *n* **1** a record of the number of points made by either team or player in a game, competition, etc.; total number of points obtained in this. **2** a mark or notch made by a sharp instrument. **3** a motive; reason. **4** a grudge; grievance: settle old scores. **5** twenty, or a set of twenty things. **6** very many. **7** a musical composition printed or written down in musical notation.
• *vb* **1** gain (points) in a game or competition; keep a record of these. **2** have as a value in a game or competition: a try scores four points. **3** achieve; gain. **4** cut a mark or notch into. **5** write or arrange (music) for specific voices or instruments. **6** write the music for (a film or play). **7** also **score off** gain an advantage over (someone). **8** also **score out** cancel with a line or notch. **scorer** *n* **know the score** know the true or relevant facts. **score-board** *n* a large board for showing the score in a game or competition. < Old Norse *skor* notch, tally, twenty.

scorn (skɔ:n) *vb, n* (show) open contempt or derision; expression of this: His ideas were laughed to scorn. **scornful** *adj* **scornfully** *adv* **scornfulness** *n* < of Germanic origin.

scorpion (ˈskɔ:pɪən) *n* a small animal of the spider family with a long body, claws like those of a lobster, and a venomous

---

science

The language of science is framed upon the vocabularies of Latin and Greek. Indeed the word science is itself of classical origin, deriving ultimately from the Latin verb *scire* 'to know'. The same root is found in words such as conscience and omniscience.

Another derivative that is worthy of mention, albeit it has long since disappeared from usage, is unscience. This was used by Chaucer with the sense 'false knowledge' or 'error'.

While science dates from the 14th century, scientist is of far more recent vintage. It was coined along with physicist by the 19th-century English philosopher William Whewell, in whose 'Philosophy of Inductive Sciences' (1840) both words first appeared.

sting at the tip of its tail. < Greek *skorpios.*

scotch (skɒtʃ) *vb* stamp out; put an end to: scotch rumours. < Middle English *scocchen.*

scot-free (ˌskɒtˈfriː) *adj* without punishment, damage, or injury. SEE PANEL.

scoundrel (ˈskaʊndrəl) *n* someone who is dishonest or worthless. < origin unknown.

scour[1] (skaʊə) *vb* **1** rub hard in order to clean. **2** clear or dig out (as if) by the force of a powerful current of water. **3** remove dirt or impurities from; purge.
• *n* scouring. **scourer** *n* < Middle English *scouren.*

scour[2] *vb* move rapidly over (an area of land), esp. searching thoroughly for something. < probably Scandinavian.

scourge (skɜːdʒ) *n* **1** a whip used for punishment or torture. **2** a cause of affliction or suffering.
• *vb* **1** flog; whip. **2** afflict; torment. < ultimately Latin *ex-* + *corrigia* whip.

scout (skaʊt) *n* **1** someone sent out to gain information, esp. for military purposes; ship or aircraft that does this. **2 Scout** a member of a worldwide movement of boys and young men that teaches character, responsibility, and good citizenship.
• *vb* explore or search for information. < ultimately Latin *auscultare* to listen.

scowl (skaʊl) *vb, n* (make) an angry frown. < probably Scandinavian.

scrabble (ˈskræbl̩) *vb* grope for or scratch about with the hands and feet, esp. in a frantic search for something. < Dutch *schrabbelen.*

scraggy (ˈskrægɪ) *adj* lanky and lean. < perhaps of Celtic origin.

scram (skræm) *vb* **scrammed; scramming** (*informal*) go away immediately. < short for *scramble.*

> **scot-free**
>
> A person who escapes without paying any penalty or suffering any loss is sometimes said to get off scot-free: 'Just because it's your first offence, don't expect to get off *scot-free.*' The scot in question is a 13th-century word of Germanic origin meaning 'payment' or 'tax'. There is no connection with Scots or Scotland.

scramble (ˈskræmbl̩) *vb* **1** move or climb hurriedly, esp. using the hands and feet. **2** do something eagerly and hurriedly. **3** (of an aircraft or its crew) take off rapidly in response to an enemy alert. **4** throw together; jumble. **5** cook (eggs) by stirring in a pan while cooking. **6** put (a message, etc.) into an unintelligible form, to be received by someone with a special receiver to decode it.
• *n* **1** a walk or race over rough ground. **2** a motor-cycle rally over rough ground. **3** an emergency take-off by aircraft. **scrambler** *n* an electronic device that makes speech in a telephone conversation unintelligible, then restores it at the receiving end. < perhaps alteration of *scrabble.*

scrap[1] (skræp) *n* **1** a small bit or fragment. **2** waste material, esp. from a manufacturing process: scrap metal. **3** *pl* small pieces of food left over from a meal.
• *vb* **scrapped; scrapping 1** turn into scrap for reprocessing. **2** throw away; abandon. **scrap-book** *n* a book of blank pages for sticking in newspaper cuttings, photographs, postcards, etc. **scrappy** *adj* made up of bits thrown together; disjointed. < Old Norse *skrap.*

scrap[2] *n* (*informal*) a minor fight or argument.
• *vb* **scrapped; scrapping** fight; argue. < origin unknown.

scrape (skreɪp) *vb* **1** move (an object with a rough or sharp edge) across (something), esp. in order to clean or smooth; remove (a layer) like this. **2** damage or injure by scraping. **3** make a harsh, grating sound. **4** gather up with difficulty: He scraped up enough money to go abroad.
• *n* **1** the sound or action of scraping. **2** a mark or wound made by scraping. **3** an awkward situation; predicament. **scraper** *n* **bow and scrape** behave in an excessively humble way. **scrape through** pass (a test) or escape from (a difficult situation) by a narrow margin. **scrapings** *pl n* fragments scraped from something. **scraping the barrel** using something inferior as a last resort. < Old Norse *skrapa.*

scratch (skrætʃ) *vb* **1** mark or tear (a surface) with something sharp. **2** scrape with the finger-nails; do this to relieve itching. **3** make a scraping sound. **4** achieve or obtain with difficulty: scratch a living. **5** erase by drawing a line through. **6** withdraw (an entry) from a race, competition, etc.

• *n* **1** a mark or slight injury made by scratching. **2** scratching, or the sound of this. **3** the starting-line in a race.
• *adj* **1** gathered hastily: a scratch team. **2** (*sport*) without a handicap: scratch golfer. **scratchy** *adj* **1** (of a drawing) looking as if made up of scratches. **2** making a scratching noise. **3** irritable. **4** itchy. **start from scratch** start from the very beginning. **up to scratch** (*informal*) up to standard. < probably of Germanic origin. SEE PANEL.

scrawl (skrɔːl) *vb, n* (write in) awkward, careless handwriting. < origin unknown.

scrawny (ˈskrɔːnɪ) *adj* lean; skinny. < origin unknown.

scream (skriːm) *vb* **1** utter a long, piercing cry of pain, fright, or excitement. **2** produce a piercing, high-pitched sound: screaming wind. **3** be conspicuous; startle: screaming colours
• *n* **1** a screaming sound or cry. **2** (*informal*) someone or something highly amusing. **screamingly** *adv* extremely: screamingly funny. < Middle English *scremen*.

scree (skriː) *n* a mass of loose stones and rocks on a mountain side. < Scandinavian.

screech (skriːtʃ) *vb, n* (make) a shrill, piercing sound like screaming; shriek. **screech-owl** *n* an owl with a high, shrill cry. < Middle English *scrichen*.

screed (skriːd) *n* **1** a tediously long, dull piece of writing. **2** a strip of plaster, wood, etc., that serves as a guide to the correct thickness of a coat of material to be laid on. **3** a layer of cement, mortar, etc., laid on a floor to give a smooth finish. < Old English *scrēade*.

screen (skriːn) *n* **1** a light, movable frame used to partition, stop a draught, or for decoration. **2** anything that protects, shelters, or conceals. **3** a meshed frame put over a window to keep out insects. **4** a sieve. **5** a surface onto which television or cinema images are projected.
• *vb* **1** protect, shelter, or hide. **2** sort; sift through a screen. **3** check (someone) to assess his or her suitability for a post or task. **4** check for disease or hidden weapons. **5** broadcast (a television programme); show (a film). **screenplay** *n* a film script. **screen-printing** *n* also **silk screen-printing** a printing process in which ink or dye passes through part of a piece of prepared fabric. **screen test** a test of an actor or actress for a part in a film. < probably Middle Dutch *scherm*.

screw (skruː) *n* **1** a tapering metal rod with a spiral ridge round its length, used to hold things together by driving into a body by rotation; this action. **2** anything resembling this, used to apply pressure or tighten. **3** the propeller of a ship or boat. **4** (*slang*) a prison warder. **5** (*vulgar*) an instance of sexual intercourse.
• *vb* **1** fasten, tighten, or adjust with a screw. **2** twist or turn; contort: She screwed up her face in disgust. **3** (*slang*) put pressure on; extort: He screwed them for every penny. **4** (*vulgar*) have sexual intercourse with. **have a screw loose** (*informal*) be slightly crazy. **put the screws on** (*slang*) put pressure on. **screwball** *n, adj* (*US slang*) (someone who is) crazy. **screwdriver** *n* a device for turning screws. **screwy** *adj* (*informal*) absurd; crazy. < ultimately Latin *scrofa* sow.

scribble (ˈskrɪbl̩) *vb* **1** write or draw in a hasty or careless way. **2** make meaningless or illegible marks.
• *n* something scribbled. **scribbler** *n* < Latin *scribere* to write.

scribe (skraɪb) *n* **1** someone who made handwritten copies of documents before printing was invented. **2** a professional scholar and teacher of Jewish religious law in ancient Israel. **3** (*humorous*) an author or journalist. < Latin *scribere* to write.

scrimmage (ˈskrɪmɪdʒ) *n* a rough or confused struggle. < alteration of *skirmish*.

script (skrɪpt) *n* **1** handwriting; any style or system of this: Arabic script. **2** a written text, esp. of a play, film, etc. **3** the written answers of an examination candidate.

not up to scratch

Someone or something that is below standard or unsatisfactory is sometimes informally referred to as not up to scratch. The expression derives from the early days of prize-fighting. In contrast with modern boxing procedure, a round in a prize-fight ended with the knock-down of one of the combatants. There followed an interval of 30 seconds, after which each fighter had to make his way unaided to a mark which had been scratched in the centre of the ring. The one who failed to 'come up to scratch' was declared the loser.

• *vb* prepare a script. < Latin *scribere* to write.

scripture (ˈskrɪptʃə) *n* sacred writings, esp. of the Jewish or Christian faiths. **scriptural** *adj*

scroll (skrəʊl) *n* **1** a document of paper or parchment in a roll. **2** a decorative carving or design in the form of a scroll. < of Germanic origin.

scrooge (skruːdʒ) *n* (*informal*) a mean or miserly person. SEE PANEL.

scrotum (ˈskrəʊtəm) *n* the pouch of loose skin enclosing the testicles in most male mammals. < Latin.

scrounge (skraʊndʒ) *vb* (*informal*) beg; cadge. **scrounger** *n* < alteration of English dialect *scrunge* to steal. SEE PANEL.

scrub[1] (skrʌb) *n* vegetation consisting of bushes and stunted trees; semi-arid land covered with this. < Middle English, alteration of *shrobbe* shrub.

scrub[2] *vb* **scrubbed; scrubbing 1** rub with a stiff, wet brush or something similar in order to clean. **2** (*informal*) get rid of; cancel: scrub one's plans.
• *n* the act or instance of scrubbing. **scrub up** (of a surgeon) scrub the hands and arms thoroughly before an operation. < Scandinavian.

scruff[1] (skrʌf) *n* the back of the neck. < origin uncertain.

scruff[2] *n* someone who is dirty or untidy in appearance. **scruffy** *adj* messy; untidy. **scruffily** *adv* **scruffiness** *n* < alteration of *scurf*.

scrum (skrʌm) *n* (*rugby*) a play in which the forwards of the opposing teams bunch together to try to pass the ball back to their team-mates. < short for *scrummage*, from *scrimmage*.

scrumptious (ˈskrʌmpʃəs) *adj* (*informal*) very tasty; delicious. < probably alteration of *sumptuous*.

scruple (ˈskruːpl̩) *vb, n* (experience) hesitation in acting because of moral considerations or principles. **scrupulous** *adj* **1** painstakingly precise. **2** honest; principled. **scrupulously** *adv* **scrupulousness** *n* < Latin *scrupulus* small, sharp stone.

scrutinize (ˈskruːtɪˌnaɪz) *vb* inspect carefully. **scrutiny** *n* < Latin *scrutari* to search.

scuba (ˈskuːbə) *n* an aqualung. < initials of *s*elf-*c*ontained *u*nderwater *b*reathing *a*pparatus. SEE PANEL.

scud (skʌd) *vb* **scudded; scudding** move or sweep along quickly. < probably Scandinavian.

scuffle (ˈskʌfl̩) *vb, n* (take part in) a usually brief, disorderly fight or struggle. < probably Scandinavian.

scull (skʌl) *n* **1** either of a pair of short-handled oars used by a single rower.

scrooge

A person who is regarded as mean or miserly is sometimes informally referred to as a scrooge. This word borrows the name of Ebenezer *Scrooge,* a character in Charles Dickens' 'A Christinas Carol' (1843).

scrounge

A person who acquires or seeks to acquire something by wheedling or cajoling is commonly termed a scrounger. The verb to scrounge is believed to derive from the English dialect word *scrunge* meaning 'to steal'. Other words that the standard language has inherited from British dialects include:

clutch (nest of eggs)	**raid**
gruesome	**skewer**

scuba

Very often the form of a word provides a good clue as to its origin. For example, a noun ending in *us* such as terminus or bonus very likely derives from Latin, while one ending in *ette* such as cigarette or marionette almost certainly derives from French. However, the word scuba shows how easy it is to be misled.

In view of its final *a,* it would be quite reasonable to suspect that scuba comes from Latin, as do nouns such as retina, tibia, data, and formula. On the other hand, the *sk* sound at the beginning of the word sounds Scandinavian, in the manner of scalp, scurf, and scorch. Scuba, however, is in fact an acronym comprising the first letters of *s*elf-*c*ontained *u*nderwater *b*reathing *a*pparatus.

2 an oar at the stern of a boat, worked to and fro.
• *vb* propel (a boat) with a scull or sculls. < Middle English *sculle*.

scullery (ˈskʌlərɪ) *n* a room for washing dishes, preparing vegetables, etc. < ultimately Latin *scutella* bowl.

sculpture (ˈskʌlptʃə) *n* **1** the art of carving wood, stone, metal, etc., into artistic objects. **2** an object made in this way.
• *vb* **1** portray in a sculpture. **2** form or shape a sculpture by carving (wood or stone) or casting (metal). **sculptural** *adj* **sculpt** *vb* sculpture. **sculptor** *n* < ultimately Latin *sculpere* to carve.

scum (skʌm) *n* **1** impurities collecting on the surface of a liquid. **2** someone or a group of people considered to be low-class or worthless: scum of the earth. **scummy** *adj* < Middle Dutch *schum*.

scupper[1] (ˈskʌpə) *n* an opening in the side of a ship to drain water from the deck. < origin uncertain.

scupper[2] *vb* put an end to; wreck. < origin unknown.

scurf (skɜːf) *n* **1** dry skin flaking off, esp. from the scalp. **2** any dry matter flaking off from a surface. < Scandinavian.

scurrilous (ˈskʌrɪləs) *adj* **1** coarse; insulting. **2** obscenely humorous. **scurrility** *n* **scurrilously** *adv* < Latin *scurra* buffoon.

scurry (ˈskʌrɪ) *vb* **scurried; scurrying** move or run quickly, esp. with short, quick steps.
• *n* **1** scurrying. **2** a crisp, whirling movement like that of snow falling. < short for *hurry-scurry*.

scurvy (ˈskɜːvɪ) *n* a disease caused by lack of vitamin C, causing bleeding under the skin, loose teeth, and soft gums. < *scurf*.

scuttle[1] (ˈskʌtl̩) *n* a bucket or box for keeping coal in inside a house. < Latin *scutella* bowl.

scuttle[2] *vb* hurry; bustle.
• *n* scuttling. < probably *scud* + shu*ttle*.

scythe (saɪð) *n* an implement with a long, curving blade set at an angle to a handle, used for cutting long grass, etc.
• *vb* cut with a scythe. < Old English *sīthe*.

SDP *abbrev* Social Democratic Party.

sea (siː) *n* **1** the body of salt water covering most of the earth's surface. **2** any section of this, usually named. **3** a large inland body of fresh or salt water. **4** the motion or waves of the sea: heavy seas. **5** something likened to the sea in its limitlessness: a sea of faces. **at sea 1** on the sea, esp. on a boat. **2** confused; puzzled. **by sea** conveyed by boat. **sea anemone** a tube-shaped sea-animal with a cluster of tentacles like a flower-head. **sea-bird** *n* a bird that frequents the open sea. **seafarer** *n* a sailor. **seafaring** *n, adj* (concerning) working or travelling at sea. **seafood** *n* edible fish, shellfish, etc., found in the sea. **seafront** *n* the part of a coastal town facing the sea. **sea-green** *n, adj* green with a bluish tinge. **seagull** *n* a gull. **sea-horse** *n* one of a group of small fishes with a horse-like head and neck. **sea-kale** *n* a fleshy plant of the mustard family, whose shoots can be eaten as a vegetable. **sea-legs** *pl n* the ability to keep one's balance and resist seasickness on a moving boat. **sea-level** *n* the level of the surface of the sea midway between low and high tide. **sea-lion** *n* one of a group of large Pacific seals. **seaman** *n, pl* **seamen 1** a sailor in the navy ranking below an officer. **2** someone skilled in seafaring. **seaplane** *n* an aircraft designed to be able to take off from and land on water. **seaport** *n* a town or port on a coast. **seascape** *n* a view of the sea, or a picture showing this. **sea shell** the shell of a marine animal, esp. a mollusc. **sea-shore** *n* the land next to the sea. **seasick** *adj* feeling nausea from the motion of a ship. **seasickness** *n* **seaside** *n* a coast; beach or holiday resort on this. **sea-urchin** *n* a round-shelled, marine animal covered with sharp spines. **seaweed** *n* any of various plants growing in or close to the sea. **seaworthy** *adj* (of a ship) suitable for voyages at sea. < Old English *sǣ*.

seal[1] (siːl) *n* a sea-mammal with limbs modified as flippers for swimming, found usually in cold regions. **sealing** *n* seal-hunting. **sealskin** *n* the skin or fur of a seal, treated and used for clothing. < Old English *seolh*.

seal[2] *n* **1** an impression of a word or symbol, esp. on wax, made on a document to show that it is genuine; object used to make this. **2** something such as a strip of wax or plastic that closes tightly and must be broken to give access to the contents of a document, container, etc. **3** a decorative stamp, often sold to help a charity. **4** anything that gives security or confirmation: a seal of approval.
• *vb* **1** fasten a seal to; secure or confirm by this. **2** close tightly with a seal to prevent access or leaking. **3** cover with a protective substance. **4** stick down (an

envelope). **5** determine once and for all: Her fate was sealed. **sealant** *n* a substance for coating (wood) with a protective layer or waterproofing. **sealing-wax** *n* a resinous substance that softens when heated, used for sealing letters and documents. **seal off** close securely so as to prevent passage. **seal-ring** *n* a signet ring. < ultimately Latin *signum.*

seam (siːm) *n* **1** a line, groove, or ridge formed where two edges meet, esp. of wood, or fabric joined by stitching. **2** a line left by a wound; scar or wrinkle. **3** a layer of coal, mineral ore, etc.
• *vb* **1** join (as if) by sewing. **2** mark with a seam or scar. **seamstress** *n* a woman who sews for a living. **seamy** *adj* squalid; unpleasant: the seamy side of life. < Old English *sēam.* SEE PANEL.

séance (ˈseɪɒns) *n* a meeting at which spiritualists attempt to contact the dead. < French, from Latin *sedēre* to sit.

sear (sɪə) *vb* burn or scorch (a surface); brand. < Old English *sēar* dry.

search (sɜːtʃ) *vb* **1** look through or over (someone's body or clothes, or a place) in order to find something. **2** examine closely: search one's heart.
• *n* searching. **searcher** *n* **searching** *adj* intent; penetrating: a searching look. **searchlight** *n* a movable, outdoor light with a powerful beam; this beam. **search-party** *n* a group of people organized to search for someone lost or missing. **search-warrant** *n* a document authorizing the searching of a premises for weapons, stolen goods, etc. < ultimately Latin *circus* circle.

season (ˈsiːzn̩) *n* **1** one of the four periods into which a year is divided. **2** a period of distinctive weather or temperature: wet season. **3** a time of year associated with particular activities or events: the mating season; holiday season.
• *vb* **1** give more flavour to (food) by adding salt, pepper, etc. **2** treat or expose (wood) gradually to prepare for use. **3** train or toughen by experience: a seasoned campaigner. **in season 1** (of food) readily available and in the best condition for eating. **2** (of an animal) on heat. **3** (of game) available for hunting or catching. **4** (of advice) timely: a word in season. **out of season** not in season. **seasonable** *adj* **1** befitting the season. **2** opportune; well-timed. **seasonably** *adv* **seasonal** *adj* of or varying according to the season. **seasoning** *n* a spice or condiment used to flavour food. **season-ticket** *n* a ticket allowing unlimited journeys over one route or attendance at events over a given period. < ultimately Latin *serere* to sow.

seat (siːt) *n* **1** a piece of furniture made for sitting on, such as a chair or stool; part of this that one sits on. **2** a place to sit requiring a ticket, as on a train or in a theatre. **3** the buttocks, or the part of a garment covering these: trouser seat. **4** something forming the base of an object, or a part on which an object rests. **5** a central location for authority or a particular activity: the seat of government; seat of learning. **6** membership of a body, or the right to this: parliamentary seat. **7** a large country mansion: the family seat. **8** the way someone sits on horseback.
• *vb* **1** cause to sit. **2** provide seats for: The stadium seats 100 000 people. **3** fit (machinery) on or with a seat. **be seated** sit down. **seat-belt** *n* a strap keeping someone secure in the seat of an aircraft, vehicle, etc. **seated** *adj* **1** sitting. **2** (of a garment) wearing through in the seat. **seating** *n* places; accommodation. < Old Norse *sæti.*

secateurs (ˈsɛkətɜːz, ˌsɛkəˈtɜːz) *pl n* a pair of shears for pruning, used with one hand. < Latin *secare* to cut.

secede (sɪˈsiːd) *vb* withdraw formally from an organization or alliance. **secession** *n* seceding. < Latin *se* without + *cedere* to go.

seclude (sɪˈkluːd) *vb* keep (someone) from contact with others. **secluded** *adj* sheltered; isolated. **seclusion** *n* < Latin *se-* apart + *claudere* to close.

second[1] (ˈsɛkənd) *determiner, pron, adv* next after first.
• *n* **1** something that comes next after first in time, position, order, or precedence. **2** someone who helps or stands in for another, esp. a boxer's assistant. **3** a slightly flawed article, as in a shop. **4** the second level of an honours degree. **5** the second gear of a motor vehicle. **6** a 60th

the seamy side

The less pleasant aspect of something is occasionally referred to as its seamy side. This use of the adjective seamy is a simple metaphoric extension of its use as a noun. Just as, say, a knitted jumper has a right side and a wrong side (with rough, unsightly seams) so many things have a less attractive side which, like the seams on the wrong side of a jumper, remain hidden and therefore unseen.

part of a minute of time or measure of an angle. **7** (*informal*) a moment: Hold on a second.
• *vb* **1** assist or encourage. **2** endorse or express formal support for (a motion): Who will second that motion? **seconder** *n* **secondly** *adv* **second-best** *adj* of lower quality. **second class 1** of a level or standard of accommodation, treatment, etc., lower than first class. **2** (of letters) of a delivery service that has less priority than first-class. **second-class** *adj* **second in command** someone second in rank to an official or officer in charge. **seconds** *pl n* a second helping of a meal. < ultimately Latin *sequi* to follow. SEE PANEL.

second[2] (sɪˈkɒnd) *vb* to transfer (an official, teacher, etc.) to another department or organization temporarily. **secondment** *n* < French *en second* in second rank.

secondary (ˈsɛkəndərɪ) *adj* **1** second in rank, importance, or position. **2** deriving from an original or primary source. **secondarily** *adv* **secondary colour** a colour resulting when two primary colours are mixed. **secondary school** a school between a primary school and a college, etc., of higher education.

secret (ˈsiːkrɪt) *adj* **1** kept hidden from the view or knowledge of others. **2** conducted secretly: secret negotiations.
• *n* **1** something kept concealed or unexplained; mystery. **2** a means of achieving something: the secret of a long life. **secretly** *adv* **in secret** secretly. **secrecy** *n* **1** being secret. **2** keeping secrets. **secret agent** a spy. **secretive** *adj* reserved; uncommunicative. **secretively** *adv* **secretiveness** *n* **secret police** a political police force operating in secret. **Secret Service** a government department responsible for spying activities. **secret society** a society that keeps its activities secret from non-members. < Latin *se-* apart + *cernere* to sift, separate.

secretary (ˈsɛkrətərɪ) *n* **1** someone employed to handle correspondence, filing, and other routine work, esp. in an office. **2** an officer of an organization in charge of its records and correspondence. **3** an officer of state that superintends a government department under a minister. **secretarial** *adj* **secretariat** *n* **1** a government administrative department. **2** the clerical staff of a large organization. **secretary-bird** *n* a long-legged African bird of prey with a crest of long feathers, feeding mainly on reptiles. **Secretary-General** *n* a principal administrative official. **Secretary of State** the head of one of several specified government departments. < Medieval Latin *secretarius*.

secrete (sɪˈkriːt) *vb* **1** put in a hidden place. **2** produce and emit (a substance) in the body. **secretion** *n* **secretory** *adj* < Latin *secernere* to separate: SEE SECRET.

sect (sɛkt) *n* **1** a group of people who differ in esp. religious beliefs from a main body. **2** a group of people with common interests; faction. **sectarian** *adj* **1** of a sect. **2** limited in scope; narrow-minded. < ultimately Latin *sequi* to follow.

section (ˈsɛkʃən) *n* **1** a part cut off or separated from a main body. **2** a distinct part or portion. **3** surgical cutting: caesarean section. **4** a cross-section.
• *vb* cut or divide into sections. **sectional** *adj* **1** made up of sections. **2** limited to a particular place or group. < Latin *secare* to cut.

sector (ˈsɛktə) *n* **1** a part of an area divided for the purpose of military operations. **2** a part of a field of activity, esp. business and trade: the private sector. **3** part of a circle bounded by two radii and the part of the circumference between them. < Latin: cutter.

secular (ˈsɛkjʊlə) *adj* **1** concerned with worldly and not spiritual matters. **2** not related to or concerned with religion.

second thoughts

Second features in a number of expressions, many of them idiomatic, including:

second childhood a period in old age when a person feels, thinks, etc., like a child.

second-hand *adj* **1** also *adv* not purchased as a new item: a second-hand car. **2** not from an original source: second-hand information.

second-hand *adv* also **at second hand** gained indirectly.

second nature a habit or ability that is instinctive.

second thoughts further thoughts that lead to a revised decision or opinion: I didn't think I'd go but then I had second thoughts.

< Latin *saecularis* temporal.
secure (sɪˈkjʊə) *adj* **1** safe; protected. **2** certain; dependable.
● *vb* **1** make safe or secure; fasten. **2** obtain; acquire. **3** guarantee; assure. **securely** *adv* < Latin *se-* without + *cura* care.
security (sɪˈkjʊərətɪ) *n* **1** being secure; something that secures. **2** protection or measures taken against sabotage, espionage, etc., in a country or organization; department concerned with this. **3** something pledged to guarantee a payment or the fulfilment of an obligation. **4** a certificate of ownership of stocks, bonds, or shares.
sedan (sɪˈdæn) *n* **1** a sedan-chair. **2** (*US*) a saloon car. **sedan-chair** *n* an enclosed chair, used esp. in the 17th and 18th centuries, carried on poles by two bearers. < origin uncertain.
sedate[1] (sɪˈdeɪt) *adj* calm and composed in manner or pace. **sedately** *adv* **sedateness** *n* < Latin *sedare* to calm.
sedate[2] *vb* administer a sedative to. **sedation** *n* a calm state, induced by a sedative. **sedative** *n, adj* (a medicine or influence) that reduces nervousness or agitation.
sedentary (ˈsɛdn̩trɪ) *adj* spending or requiring much time sitting: a sedentary occupation. < Latin *sedēre* to sit.
sediment (ˈsɛdɪmənt) *n* **1** particles of matter that settle at the bottom of a liquid. **2** solid matter such as sand or mud deposited by wind or water. **sedimentary** *adj* < Latin *sedēre* to sit.
sedition (sɪˈdɪʃən) *n* incitement to defy the authority of the State. **seditious** *adj* < Latin *se-* apart + *ire* to go.
seduce (sɪˈdjuːs) *vb* **1** persuade (someone) to betray or disobey, esp. with tempting promises. **2** persuade (someone) to have sexual intercourse. **seducer** *n* **seduction** *n* **seductive** *adj* alluring; inviting. **seductively** *adv* **seductiveness** *n* < Latin *se-* apart + *ducere* to lead.
see[1] (siː) *vb* **saw; seen; seeing 1** perceive with the eyes. **2** perceive mentally; comprehend. **3** imagine; regard: I can't see him as a leader. **4** undergo; experience: This jacket has seen better days. **5** watch; observe: see a film. **6** consider; reflect: Let me see... **7** find out; determine: I'll see it he's in. **8** make sure: See you get here by nine. **9** grant an interview to: The doctor will see you now. **10** visit; call on: see the dentist. **11** escort; accompany: He saw her home. **12** read; refer to: See page 34. **13** keep company or go out with on a relatively frequent basis: She's seeing a new man. **seeing that** in view of the fact; since. < Old English *sēon*. SEE PANEL.
see[2] *n* the office of a bishop; diocese. < Latin *sedes* seat.
seed (siːd) *n, pl* **seed, seeds 1** the mature, fertilized ovule of a plant that produces a new plant when germinated. **2** grains of plants kept for sowing. **3** semen or milt. **4** (*archaic*) descendants; progeny. **5** the origin or germ of anything: seeds of discontent. **6** a seeded player in a sports tournament: the number one seed at Wimbledon.
● *vb* **1** sow seeds in; produce seeds. **2** treat (a cloud) with solid particles so as to cause condensation that produces rain

seeing things

See features in a number of idiomatic expressions, including:

see about to attend to: I must see about the garden fence—it needs repairing
see eye to eye with to agree fully with (someone).
see off 1 to accompany (someone) to a station, airport, etc., and say goodbye to him or her: We saw them off at the airport. **2** to chase away; beat back.
see out 1 to last until the end of: We've enough fuel to see out the winter. **2** to accompany (someone) to the door, exit, etc., and say goodbye to him or her.
see red to become very angry: She sees red every time I mention my ex-girlfriend's name.
see the light to realize one's mistakes, etc., and follow a different course of action; undergo conversion.
see things to experience hallucinations or illusions.
see through 1 to help (someone) endure or survive a difficult time. **2** to perceive the real meaning, intentions, etc., of; not be deceived by: We saw through his tricks at once! **3** to tackle (something), bringing it to a successful conclusion: He stayed to see the project through.
see-through *adj* transparent.
see to to attend to.

or snow. **3** take out seeds from (a fruit). **4** schedule (superior players) in a tournament so that they do not meet in early rounds. **go** or **run to seed 1** (of a plant) develop seed. **2** go to waste; degenerate. **seed-bed** *n* fine soil in which seeds are sown. **seed-cake** *n* a sweet cake containing esp. caraway seeds. **seedless** *adj* not having seeds. **seedling** *n* a young plant growing from a seed. **seed-pearl** *n* a small, often flawed pearl. **seed-potato** *n* a potato kept for planting. **seedsman** *n, pl* **seedsmen** someone who sows or deals in seeds. **seedy** *adj* **1** containing seeds. **2** shabby; squalid: a seedy area. **3** (*informal*) unwell; poorly. < Old English *sǣd.*

seek (siːk) *vb* **sought; seeking 1** look or search for; pursue. **2** aspire to; attempt: seek fame. **3** ask for; request: seek advice. **seek out** search very hard for. < Old English *sēcan.*

seem (siːm) *vb* look as if; appear to be. **seeming** *adj* apparent or illusory. < Scandinavian.

seemly (ˈsiːmlɪ) *adj* proper or fitting; in good taste. < Old Norse *sœmr* becoming.

seen (siːn) SEE **SEE**[1].

seep (siːp) *vb* ooze or leak through small openings. **seepage** *n* < Old English *sipian.*

see-saw (ˈsiːˌsɔː) *n* **1** a plank balanced in the middle for someone to sit at each end, pushing alternately with the feet so that they rise and fall with the plank, esp. used as a game for children. **2** any frequently repeated up-and-down or back-and-forth movement.
• *vb* **1** play see-saw or have this movement. **2** alternate; vacillate. < probably *saw*[2].

seethe (siːð) *vb* **1** be extremely agitated: seething with anger. **2** bubble or churn as if boiling. < Old English *sēothan.*

segment (ˈsɛgmənt) *n* a piece of something separated, cut, or marked off. **segmented** *adj* < Latin *secare* to cut.

segregate (ˈsɛgrɪˌgeɪt) *vb* **1** set apart; isolate. **2** separate (different groups of people), esp. according to race. **segregation** *n* **segregationist** *n* < Latin *se-* apart + *grex* herd.

seismic (ˈsaɪzmɪk) *adj* of or caused by earthquakes or artificially produced vibrations in the earth. **seismograph** *n* an instrument used for measuring and recording vibrations in the earth. < Greek *seiein* to shake.

seize (siːz) *vb* **1** take hold of eagerly or by force; grab. **2** take possession of by force, esp. with legal authority. **3** affect suddenly and dramatically: seized by fear. **4** also **seize up** (of a machine or moving parts within it) become stuck or jammed through pressure, heat, or friction. **seize on** lay hold of eagerly to make use of: She seized on the plan. **seizure** *n* **1** seizing or being seized. **2** a sudden attack of a recurrent disease, for example, epilepsy. < of Germanic origin.

seldom (ˈsɛldəm) *adv* rarely; infrequently. < Old English *seldan.*

select (sɪˈlɛkt) *vb* choose according to preference; pick out.
• *adj* **1** chosen for value or quality. **2** (of a club or society) fastidious in its choice of members; exclusive. **select committee** a temporary committee appointed to look into one special matter. **selection** *n* **1** selecting or being selected. **2** a range of things to be chosen from. **selective** *adj* carefully chosen or choosing. **selectively** *adv* **selectivity** *n* **selector** *n* **1** someone or something that chooses. **2** someone who picks members for a sports team. **3** a switching device that connects an electrical circuit with another in an automatic telephone system. < Latin *se-* without + *legere* to choose.

self (sɛlf) *n, pl* **selves 1** the body and mind of an individual. **2** someone's character, or an aspect of this: back to her old self. **3** one's own interest, advantage, or welfare: She always puts self first. **4** (*humorous*) myself, yourself, etc.: seats for self and friend.
• *adj* the same throughout, esp. in colour or material. < Old English.

self- (sɛlf) *prefix* of, by, to, for, or in oneself or itself. **self-addressed** *adj* (of an envelope) for a reply addressed to oneself. **self-assertive** *adj* confident or opinionated. **self-assurance** *n* confidence in oneself. **self-assured** *adj* **self-catering** *adj* supplied with accommodation and cooking facilities but not meals, esp. on holiday. **self-centred** *adj* concerned mostly with oneself; egotistical. **self-confidence** *n* faith in one's own abilities. **self-confident** *adj* **self-conscious** *adj* ill at ease because of being observed or noticed by others. **self-consciousness** *n* **self-contained** *adj* **1** complete in itself. **2** keeping one's thoughts and feelings to oneself; reserved. **self-control** *n* the ability to control one's impulses and emotions. **self-controlled** *adj* **self-defeating** *adj* frustrating its own success. **self-defence** *n* defending or justifying oneself; legal right to do this. **self-denial** *n* limitation of one's desires; unselfishness. **self-employed** *adj* working for oneself. **self-evident** *adj* needing no further proof; obvious. **self-explanatory** *adj* easily understood without explanation. **self-governing** *adj* (of a nation) controlling its own political affairs. **self-government** *n* **self-help** *n* helping oneself without reliance on others. **self-important** *adj* pompous; conceited. **self-importance** *n* **self-indulgence** *n* unrestrained gratification of one's desires or whims. **self-indulgent** *adj* **self-interest** *n* one's own advantage or welfare. **self-made** *adj* having become successful through one's own efforts: a self-made man. **self-pity** *n* dwelling on one's own sorrows. **self-portrait** *n* an artist's portrait of himself or herself or a writer's description of his or her life. **self-possessed** *adj* calm and composed. **self-preservation** *n* the instinct to protect oneself from harm or injury. **self-raising flour** prepared flour containing a raising agent. **self-reliant** *adj* capable; independent. **self-respect** *n* a sense of one's own dignity and worth. **self-righteous** *adj* smugly sure of one's righteousness; sanctimonious. **self-sacrifice** *n* denial of one's own wishes for the sake or benefit of others. **self-sacrificing** *adj* **self-satisfaction** *n* smugness; complacency. **self-satisfied** *adj* **self-seeking** *adj* seeking only to further one's own interests. **self-service** *adj* serving oneself (in a restaurant or supermarket) and paying at the cashier's desk. **self-styled** *adj* named by oneself, esp. without justification. **self-sufficient** *adj* able to maintain itself or oneself without outside help. **self-supporting** *adj* **1** self-sufficient, esp. as regards finances. **2** able to support its own weight: a self-supporting wall. **self-taught** *adj* having learnt by oneself without formal lessons. **self-willed** *adj* stubborn; obstinate. **self-winding** *adj* (of a watch or clock) winding itself automatically.

selfish (ˈsɛlfɪʃ) *adj* acting only in one's own interests and not caring about others. **selfishly** *adv* **selfishness** *n* SEE PANEL.

selfless (ˈsɛlfləs) *adj* self-sacrificing; unselfish.

selfsame (ˈsɛlfˌseɪm) *adj* exactly the same.

sell (sɛl) *vb* **sold; selling 1** exchange (property, goods, etc.) for money. **2** deal in (goods, property, etc.). **3** promote the sales of: Advertising sells products. **4** be in demand: His new record is selling well. **5** persuade (someone) to accept, believe, or desire (something): He sold her the idea. **6** cheat; deceive.
• *n* **1** the manner in which something is sold: hard sell. **2** (*informal*) a hoax or deception. **sell down the river** betray. **seller** *n* **1** someone who sells. **2** something that is sold: a good seller. **sell off** sell at reduced prices to clear. **sell out 1** sell all of one's stock. **2** betray. **sell-out** *n* **1** a commercial success, esp. a show or contest for which all seats have been sold. **2** a betrayal. **sell up** sell one's house or business; sell (the assets) of a debtor to repay his or her creditors. < Old English *sellan*. SEE PANEL AT **SOLD.**

Sellotape (ˈsɛləˌteɪp) *n* (*Trademark*) a usually transparent, adhesive tape of cellulose or plastic.
• *vb* stick or fix with Sellotape.

semantic (sɪˈmæntɪk) *adj* of meaning in language. **semantically** *adv* **semantics** *n* the branch of linguistics dealing with meaning and its relationship to the signs and symbols that represent it. < ultimately Greek *sēma* sign.

semaphore (ˈsɛməˌfɔː) *n* **1** a system of signalling by holding a flag in each hand and moving the arms to denote different letters of the alphabet. **2** an apparatus that gives visual signals, esp. on railways.
• *vb* signal or inform by means of semaphore. < Greek *sēma* sign + *pherein* to carry.

semblance (ˈsɛmbləns) *n* **1** an outward and often illusory show: some semblance of order. **2** a likeness; resemblance. < Old French *sembler* to seem.

semen (ˈsiːmən) *n* a whitish fluid

> **selfish**
>
> Selfish is an example of a word ending in the suffix -ish, meaning 'having the character of'. Words in this sense often have pejorative connotations: bookish, childish, snobbish, amateurish.
>
> Other meanings of the suffix -ish are:
>
> **1** of or belonging to a nation, region, etc.: Swedish, Cornish, English.
> **2** somewhat or rather: greenish, baldish.
> **3** having the approximate age of: fiftyish.
> **4** at the approximate time of: sevenish.

produced in the male reproductive glands. < Latin: seed.

semester (sɪˈmɛstə) *n* an academic course or term lasting half a year, esp. in Germany or the USA. < Latin *sex* six + *mensis* month.

semi (ˈsɛmɪ) *n* (*informal*) a semi-detached house.

semi- (ˈsɛmɪ) *prefix* half or partially. **semi-basement** *n* a storey in a building that is partially below ground level. **semicircle** *n* a half-circle; something with this shape. **semicircular** *adj* **semicolon** *n* the punctuation mark ; used mainly to denote breaks in a sentence when there is no conjunction. **semi-conductor** *n* a substance such as silicon that has electrical conducting properties between those of a conductor and an insulator. **semi-detached** *adj* being one of a pair of dwellings joined into one building by a common wall. **semifinal** *n* the last round before the final of a knock-out competition. **semifinalist** *n* **semi-precious** *adj* (of a gem-stone) of a lower value than a precious stone. **semi-skilled** *adj* partly skilled, but not enough to perform skilled work. **semitone** *n* a musical interval that is half of a tone. < Latin.

seminal (ˈsɛmɪnəl) *adj* **1** of semen or seed. **2** formative; influential: a seminal work of art. < Latin *semen* seed.

seminar (ˈsɛmɪˌnɑː) *n* a class of students, etc., for informal discussion or exchanging information. < Latin *seminarium* seminary.

seminary (ˈsɛmɪnərɪ) *n* an institution for training priests, rabbis, etc. < Latin *semen* seed.

semolina (ˌsɛməˈliːnə) *n* hard grains left after wheat has been milled, used in making milk puddings and pasta. < ultimately Latin *simila* finest wheat flour.

senate (ˈsɛnɪt) *n* **1** the supreme council of ancient Rome. **2 Senate** the upper house of the legislatures of the USA, Canada, and certain other countries. **3** the governing body of some universities. **senator** *n* < Latin *senatus* council of elders, from *senex* old man.

send (sɛnd) *vb* **sent; sending 1** cause to be conveyed by a means of communication: send a letter. **2** bring to a particular condition: It sent him crazy. **3** pass on (a message or request) for delivery. **4** direct; request: send out for groceries. **5** cause to move or go in a particular direction: The blow sent him backwards. **sender** *n* **send down** expel from a university. **send for** order to be brought. **send-off** *n* an enthusiastic demonstration at a person's departure, etc. **send up** (*informal*) ridicule, esp. by imitating. **send-up** *n* < Old English *sendan*. SEE PANEL.

senile (ˈsiːnaɪl) *adj* showing mental and physical weakness because of old age. **senility** *n* < Latin *senex* old man.

senior (ˈsiːnjə) *adj* **1** elder. **2** higher in status or rank.
• *n* **1** someone older or higher in rank or status than another. **2** an older pupil at a secondary school. **seniority** *n* **senior citizen** someone elderly or retired. < Latin *senex* old.

sensation (sɛnˈseɪʃən) *n* **1** mental awareness or feeling produced by stimulation of a sense-organ; ability to feel this. **2** a wave of excitement or interest; something that provokes this. **sensational** *adj* **1** arousing intense interest or excitement. **2** (*informal*) excellent; impressive. **sensationally** *adv* **sensationalism** *n* the use of a style of presentation (of news, etc.), designed to arouse strong emotions. **sensationalist** *n* < Late Latin *sensus* sense.

sense (sɛns) *n* **1** the meaning conveyed or intended by a word, phrase, passage,

---

send to Coventry

To send someone to Coventry is to refuse to speak to him or her or break off all social contact. According to one school of thought the phrase dates back to the English Civil War and the days when Royalist prisoners were sent to Coventry, where they would find somewhat less than chatty Parliamentary sympathizers. Another theory has it that the people of Coventry once held soldiers in such contempt that any woman found in one's company was immediately ostracized. This meant that any soldier transferred to Coventry could expect social alienation.

Depriving an offender of social contact was formerly a common practice amongst army officers. Judging one of their brethren to be guilty of some impropriety, they would conduct themselves about the mess as if he were absent. Anyone who talked to or answered the person who had been sent to Coventry usually suffered the same fate.

---

etc. **2** any of the powers of sight, hearing, touch, sense, or smell by which a living being perceives the external world. **3** the ability to make sound judgments: good sense. **4** the capacity to be aware of or appreciate an idea or feeling: a sense of humour. **5** a purpose; point: What's the sense of doing that?
• *vb* **1** be or become aware of. **2** perceive by the senses. **3** (of a machine) detect automatically. **come to one's senses** **1** recover consciousness. **2** stop behaving stupidly. **make sense** be reasonable or sensible. **make sense of** find meaning in. **senseless** *adj* **1** foolish; mindless. **2** unconscious. **senselessness** *n* **sense-organ** *n* one of the structures in the body such as the ear or eye through which the external world is perceived. **senses** *pl n* sanity: She's taken leave of her senses. < Latin *sentire* to feel.

sensibility (ˌsɛnsɪˈbɪlɪtɪ) *n* the capacity to feel or respond to emotion; mental awareness.

sensible (ˈsɛnsɪbl̩) *adj* **1** having or showing sound reason. **2** having the ability to perceive; sensitive. **sensibly** *adv*

sensitive (ˈsɛnsɪtɪv) *adj* **1** having the power to sense. **2** easily affected by outside conditions or stimuli. **3** touchy; easily offended. **4** showing delicacy and consideration for the feelings of others. **5** (of a topic) requiring delicate treatment. **sensitively** *adv* **sensitivity** *n* **sensitive plant** mimosa or another plant with leaves that droop or fold when touched. **sensitize** *vb* make sensitive, esp. excessively. **sensitization** *n*

sensor (ˈsɛnsə) *n* a device in which stimuli such as heat, light, or sound trigger a response, esp. to measure, or operate a control.

sensory (ˈsɛnsərɪ) *adj* of sensation or the senses.

sensual (ˈsɛnsjʊəl) *adj* **1** pleasing to the body; physical. **2** tending to indulge in the delights of the senses; having this appearance. **sensuality** *n* **sensually** *adv* **sensuous** *adj* pleasurable to the senses; producing rich impressions. **sensuously** *adv* < ultimately Latin *sentire* to feel. SEE PANEL.

> **sensual** or **sensuous?**
>
> These two words are sometimes confused. Sensual means 'giving pleasure to one's body rather than the mind or spirit': indulge in *sensual* pleasures. Sensuous is used in describing appreciations of colour, sound, warmth, etc.: *sensuous* art.

sent (sɛnt) SEE **SEND**.

sentence (ˈsɛntəns) *n* **1** a self-contained expression of thought in a group of words, usually containing a verb and beginning with a capital letter when written. **2** a judgment pronounced in a court of law specifying a punishment for a convicted criminal.
• *vb* impose a sentence on in a court of law. < Latin *sentire* to feel.

sententious (sɛnˈtɛnʃəs) *adj* **1** terse; pointed. **2** pompous; moralizing. **sententiously** *adv* **sententiousness** *n* < Latin *sententia* sentence.

sentient (ˈsɛnʃn̩t, ˈsɛntɪənt) *adj* capable of feeling things with the senses; conscious: sentient beings.

sentiment (ˈsɛntɪmənt) *n* **1** a thought or opinion. **2** delicate or sensitive feeling; emotion. **3** an excessively romantic or nostalgic feeling. **sentimental** *adj* **1** having or showing delicate or tender feelings, esp. excessively. **2** marked by emotions rather than reason. **sentimentality** *n* **sentimentally** *adv*

sentinel (ˈsɛntɪnl̩) *n* someone or something that keeps watch, such as a sentry. < Latin *sentire* to perceive.

sentry (ˈsɛntrɪ) *n* a soldier that keeps guard at a door or other entrance. **sentry-box** *n* a usually wooden shelter for a standing sentry. **sentry-go** *n* sentry duty. < perhaps obsolete *centrinel* sentinel.

separate (ˈsɛpərət) *adj* **1** not attached or connected to anything else. **2** individual; distinct.
• *vb* (ˈsɛpəˌreɪt) **1** put or keep apart; detach. **2** lie between: The Channel separates England and France. **3** go different ways; diverge. **4** (of a married couple) cease to live together. **separately** *adv* **separation** *n* **separable** *adj* that can be separated. **separates** *pl n* items of clothing that can be worn together in various combinations. **separatism** *n* a belief or movement in favour of separating, esp. from a larger political unit. **separatist** *n* **separator** *n* a machine that separates liquids of different consistency, such as cream and milk. < Latin *separare* to separate.

sepia (ˈsiːpɪə) *n* **1** a brown pigment obtained from the inky secretion of the cuttlefish, used in making drawings. **2** a

rich, brownish-red colour.
• *adj* **1** of sepia colour. **2** made in sepia: a sepia print. < Greek *sēpia* cuttlefish.

septic (ˈsɛptɪk) *adj* infected with spreading, harmful bacteria. **septic tank** a tank in which bacteria disintegrates solid sewage that flows into it. < Greek *sēpein* to make rotten.

sepulchre (ˈsɛpəlkə) *n* a burial vault; tomb. **sepulchral** *adj* **1** of a burial or tomb. **2** gloomy; mournful. **3** (of a voice) deep and sonorous: sepulchral tones. < Latin *sepelire* to bury.

sequel (ˈsiːkwəl) *n* **1** a result; outcome. **2** a play, film, or novel that continues the narrative begun in an earlier one. < Latin *sequi* to follow.

sequence (ˈsiːkwəns) *n* **1** an orderly arrangement; progression. **2** a successive order of things. **3** a distinct section of a film, play, piece of music, etc. **sequential** *adj* **1** ordered in a sequence. **2** following as a result. **sequentially** *adv*

sequester (sɪˈkwɛstə) *vb* **1** set apart; seclude. **2** appropriate; confiscate. < Latin: trustee.

sequestrate (ˈsiːkwəstreɪt) *vb* confiscate; sequester. **sequestration** *n* < SEE **SEQUESTER.**

sequin (ˈsiːkwɪn) *n* a small, decorative disc of metal, plastic, etc., worn esp. on clothing. **sequinned** *adj* < French, from Italian, ultimately from Arabic *sikkah* die, coin.

seraph (ˈsɛrəf) *n, pl* **seraphim** one of the higher order of angels. **seraphic** *adj* angelic. < Hebrew *śĕrāphīm.*

serenade (ˌsɛrəˈneɪd) *n* **1** a piece of music played or sung, esp. to a woman in the evening. **2** a musical composition with several movements, similar to a suite.
• *vb* perform a serenade for. < Latin *serenus* calm.

serendipity (ˌsɛrənˈdɪpɪtɪ) *n* the faculty of making pleasant discoveries by chance. SEE PANEL.

serene (səˈriːn) *adj* **1** (of weather) calm; fine. **2** relaxed; peaceful. **serenely** *adv* **serenity** *n* < Latin *serenus.*

serf (sɜːf) *n* a labourer that worked for and was owned by a landowner on his estate in feudal times. **serfdom** *n* < Latin *servus* slave, serf.

sergeant (ˈsɑːdʒənt) *n* **1** a non-commissioned officer in the army ranking above a corporal and below a staff sergeant. **2** a police officer ranking above a constable and below an inspector. **sergeant-major** *n* a warrant-officer in a branch of the armed forces. < Latin *servire* to serve.

serial (ˈsɪərɪəl) *n* a novel, play, etc., presented or published in regular instalments.
• *adj* of or relating to a series. **serialize** *vb* make a serial out of. **serialization** *n* **serial number** a number distinguishing one item in a series. < Latin *series* series.

series (ˈsɪərɪz, ˈsɪəriːz) *n, pl* **series** **1** a number of similar or related things or events following one another in ordered succession. **2** a set of coins or stamps of a particular country and period. < Latin *serere* to join together.

serious (ˈsɪərɪəs) *adj* **1** thoughtful and unsmiling; solemn. **2** earnest; sincere: a serious offer. **3** important; crucial. **4** causing great concern; alarming: a serious injury. **seriously** *adv* **seriousness** *n* < Latin *serius.*

sermon (ˈsɜːmən) *n* a religious or moral talk given esp. by a clergyman as part of a religious service. **sermonize** *vb* talk or advise in a moralizing way. < Latin *sermo* speech.

serpent (ˈsɜːpənt) *n* (*literary*) a large snake. **serpentine** *adj* of or like a snake in shape or movement; twisting. < Latin *serpere* to creep.

serrated (sɛˈreɪtɪd) *adj* having a line of notches or teeth like a saw. **serration** *n* < Latin *serra* saw.

serum (ˈsɪərəm) *n, pl* **sera, serums** **1** the watery part of blood remaining after clotting: blood serum. **2** blood serum that contains certain antibodies. < Latin: whey.

servant (ˈsɜːvn̩t) *n* someone employed to work for another, esp. performing household duties. < Latin *servire* to serve.

serve (sɜːv) *vb* **1** help or work for; act as

serendipity

The faculty of making lucky finds is known as serendipity. This word was coined by the English man of letters Horace Walpole, 1717–97, best known for his Gothic novel 'The Castle of Otranto' (1765).

Walpole's inspiration for the coinage came from the Persian fairy tale 'The Three Princes of Serendip', whose heroes were graced with the faculty. *Serendip* is the ancient name for Sri Lanka.

a servant (to). **2** attend (customers) in a restaurant, shop, etc.; supply (guests) with (food and drink). **3** be of use or function as. **4** spend time as a member of the armed forces: serve in the navy. **5** spend or pass (time): serve a prison sentence; serve an apprenticeship. **6** supply with (something required): The town is served by frequent buses. **7** be sufficient or adequate for; suit: It will serve my purpose. **8** (*tennis*) put (the ball) into play. **9** treat in a specified way: She was badly served. **10** present (someone) with (a legal writ). **server** *n* **serve someone right** used to express satisfaction at seeing someone get something unpleasant but deserved. **serve up** offer up; supply. < ultimately Latin *servus* slave.

service (ˈsɜːvɪs) *n* **1** help; assistance: Can I be of service? **2** the occupation and status of a domestic servant. **3** work done for or employment with another. **4** a public or government department and its staff: Civil Service. **5** any branch of the armed forces. **6** an organized system for supplying some public demand: bus service; telephone service. **7** a ceremony of public worship: the marriage service. **8** the provision and maintenance of goods by a dealer. **9** the delivering of a legal writ to someone named in it. **10** (*tennis*) serving the ball. **11** a complete set of dishes, plates, etc., for use at table. **12** a periodical overhaul of a vehicle, machine, or appliance. **13** (of male animals) mating.
• *vb* **1** overhaul; maintain. **2** provide with a service. **serviceable** *adj* **1** that can be used. **2** durable; hard-wearing. **serviceably** *adv* **service area** an area beside a motorway where petrol and refreshments can be obtained. **service charge** a charge added to a bill in a restaurant, etc., for service. **service flat** a flat in which services such as cleaning are inclusive in the rent. **service industry** an industry providing services such as insurance or transport rather than goods. **serviceman** fem. **servicewoman** *n* a person serving in the armed forces. **service road** a narrow road providing access to shops, buildings, etc., but not to through traffic. **service station** a petrol station.

serviette (ˌsɜːvɪˈɛt) *n* a table napkin. < Middle French *servir* to serve.

servile (ˈsɜːvaɪl) *adj* **1** excessively humble; obsequious. **2** of or befitting a servant; menial. **servility** *n*

servitude (ˈsɜːvɪˌtjuːd) *n* lack of freedom; bondage.

servo- (ˈsɜːvəʊ) *prefix* power-assisted: servomotor. < Latin *servus* slave, servant.

sesame (ˈsɛsəmɪ) *n* a tropical Asian plant with small seeds used as a food or source of oil; these seeds. < Greek *sēsamē*.

session (ˈsɛʃən) *n* **1** a meeting or meetings for discussion or transaction of business. **2** a period of time devoted to a specified activity: recording session. **3** a time in which school classes are held; academic year. < ultimately Latin *sedēre* to sit.

set (sɛt) *vb* **set; setting 1** put or place in a particular position. **2** apply: set fire to. **3** put in readiness for use: set the table; set a

setting out

Set features in a number of idiomatic expressions, including:

set about 1 to begin (doing something). **2** to attack with blows or words.
set back 1 to hinder or delay progress.
setback *n* **2** to cost (someone) (a large amount of money): It set them back over £1000.
set in to begin and last for a long time; become established: You'll need a warmer coat now that the cold weather has set in.
set off 1 also **set out** to begin a journey. **2** to cause to begin: It set her off crying. **3** to cause to explode. **4** to improve the appearance of, by providing a contrast. **5** to trigger: set off an alarm.
set out 1 to make known or organize clearly; arrange. **2** to start work, intending to achieve a particular aim: He set out just to mend the gutter but ended up by replacing it all.
set sail to begin a voyage.
set store by to consider reliable or important.
set to 1 to begin to do something with determination. **2** to begin arguing or fighting.
set-to *n*
set up 1 to assemble and prepare for use. **2** to establish (an investigation, business, etc.). **3** to provide (with) the money required to open a business; provide with adequate supplies: He gave his son the capital needed to set him up. **4** to cause or produce: set up a reaction. **5** to restore to health. **6** to cause to be blamed or accused; frame: I've been set up!
set-up *n* an arrangement or organization.

trap. **4** present in a specified place or time: a story set in Victorian times. **5** provide a melody or arrangement for: set to music. **6** adjust (an alarm, the hands of a clock, etc.) to a desired position. **7** put (a broken bone) in a fixed position in order to heal. **8** make or become hard or rigid: set concrete. **9** fix (hair) in a desired style when wet. **10** establish; decide: set a date for the wedding. **11** prescribe or assign (a task): set an exam. **12** put in a particular state: set free. **13** (of the sun) sink below the horizon. **14** (of clothes) hang in a particular way when worn. **15** have a certain direction: a course set to the north. **16** arrange (jewels) in a particular way; put in a framework. **17** grind in order to sharpen: set a blade.
• *n* **1** a number of similar or related people or things that form a unit. **2** a series of games forming a subdivision of a match in tennis, etc. **3** a television or radio receiver. **4** the manner in which something is arranged or placed. **5** scenery, props, etc., used as background in a play or film. **6** an arrangement of the hair in a particular style. **7** a direction of movement. **8** a young plant or shoot for planting. **9** a session of music, esp. rock or jazz; music played at this. **be set on** be firmly decided. **set square** a triangular drawing instrument, with one right angle. **setter** *n* **1** someone or something that sets: typesetter. **2** a type of long-haired dog trained to stand rigid when scenting game. **setting** *n* **1** the time, manner, place, or direction in which something is set. **2** a musical accompaniment. **3** cutlery, plates, etc., for a single place at table. **4** the metal mounting of a gem. < Old English *settan.* SEE PANEL.

sett (sɛt) *n* also **set 1** a badger's burrow. **2** a block of wood or stone used for paving. < *set.*

settee (sɛˈtiː) *n* a long, usually upholstered seat with a back and often arms for seating two or more people; sofa. < alteration of *settle[1]*.

settle[1] (ˈsɛtl̩) *n* a wooden seat for more than two people with a back and arms, and often a box-like space under the seat, used for storage. < Old English *setl.*

settle[2] *vb* **1** put or be put in a fixed or comfortable position. **2** put in order; arrange as desired: settle one's affairs. **3** set up home; occupy or colonize. **4** bring or come to rest after descending: The snow settled. **5** make or become calm or stable: settle to work. **6** pay off (a bill, debt, etc.). **7** confirm or decide conclusively. **8** become established in a job, life-style, etc. **settle down 1** calm down. **2** apply oneself with concentration. **3** take up a routine way of life or a permanent job, esp. after marriage. **settlement** *n* **1** settling or being settled. **2** an agreement, esp. financial or to resolve differences. **3** an estate or amount legally bestowed on someone. **4** a newly colonized or occupied place. **settler** *n* an immigrant or colonist. **settle up** pay an amount owed. < Old English *setl* seat.

seven (ˈsɛvn̩) *determiner, pron* 7 in number.
• *n* the number 7. < Old English *seofon.*

seventeen (ˌsɛvn̩ˈtiːn) *determiner, pron* 17 in number.
• *n* the number 17. **seventeenth** *determiner, pron, n, adv* < Old English *seofontēne.*

seventh (ˈsɛvn̩θ) *determiner, pron, adv* next after sixth.
• *n* **1** something that is seventh. **2** one of seven equal parts of a thing. **seventhly** *adv* **seventh heaven** euphoria; bliss.

seventy (ˈsɛvn̩tɪ) *determiner, pron* 70 in number.
• *n* the number 70. **seventieth** *determiner, pron, n, adv* **seventies** *pl n* the numbers, range of temperatures, ages, or dates in a century from 70–79. < Old English *seofontig.*

sever (ˈsɛvə) *vb* **1** break off; put an end to: sever diplomatic relations. **2** cut off; separate. **severance** *n* severing or being severed. **severance pay** a sum of money paid to an employee in compensation for loss of employment. < ultimately Latin *separare.*

several (ˈsɛvrəl) *determiner* **1** a few; some. **2** various; different: We went our several ways.
• *pron* a few things or people. < Latin *separare* to separate.

severe (sɪˈvɪə) *adj* **1** harsh or strict in character. **2** plain; austere, esp. in dress. **3** intense; extreme: severe weather conditions. **4** demanding; arduous: a severe trial. **severely** *adv* **severity** *n* < Latin *severus.*

sew (səʊ) *vb* **sewed; sewn, sewed; sewing 1** attach or fasten by passing a needle and thread through repeatedly. **2** close or attach by sewing. **3** make or mend (a garment) by sewing. **sewing-machine** *n* a machine for sewing and stitching material. < Old English *sīwian.*

sewage (ˈsuːɪdʒ) *n* liquid waste, esp. excrement, carried away in drains or sewers from houses, factories, etc., to be disposed of. **sewage-farm** *n* a place for treating sewage to use as manure. **sewage-works** *pl n* a place where sewage is treated so that it can be discharged safely into the sea or a river. **sewer** *n* an underground pipe used to carry off sewage via drains. **sewerage** *n* a system of sewers; sewage. < ultimately Latin *ex-* + *aqua* water.

sewn (səʊn) SEE **SEW.**

sex (sɛks) *n* **1** either of the two main categories of living things as regards reproductive functions; male or female. **2** physical desires or reproduction as a topic; sexual impulses. **3** sexual intercourse.
• *vb* determine the sex of. **sex act** sexual intercourse. **sex appeal** attractiveness to the opposite sex. **sexed** *adj* having sexual impulses or characteristics to a specified degree: highly sexed. **sexism** *n* **1** discrimination on the basis of sex, esp. against women. **2** believing that sex determines roles and abilities in society. **sexist** *adj, n* **sexless** *adj* lacking sexuality or sexual characteristics. **sexlessly** *adv* **sexpot** *n* (*slang*) someone who makes a show of being sexually attractive. **sexual** *adj* of sex. **sexuality** *n* **sexually** *adv* **sexual intercourse** the insertion of the penis into the vagina, for the purpose of reproduction or pleasure; copulation. **sexy** *adj* sexually arousing or attractive. < Latin *sexus.*

sexagenarian (ˌsɛksədʒəˈnɛərɪən) *n* someone between 60 and 69 years old. < Latin *sexaginta* sixty.

sextant (ˈsɛkstənt) *n* an instrument for measuring the angular distance of a heavenly body above the horizon, to find out one's position; used in navigation or surveying. < ultimately Latin *sextans* one sixth.

sextet (sɛksˈtɛt) *n* a group of six voices or instruments; musical composition for this.

sexton (ˈsɛkstən) *n* a church official who looks after a churchyard and church property. < Medieval Latin *sacristanus.*

shabby (ˈʃæbɪ) *adj* **1** run-down and neglected; tatty. **2** mean; contemptible: a shabby thing to do. **shabbily** *adv* **shabbiness** *n* < obsolete *shab* scab, scoundrel.

shack (ʃæk) *n* a small, roughly-built hut.
• *vb* **shack up** (*slang*) live with someone, esp. a lover. < perhaps English dialect *shackly* rickety.

shackle (ˈʃækḷ) *n* **1** a metal ring put round an ankle or wrist to restrain a prisoner. **2** anything that restricts freedom.
• *vb* **1** confine with shackles. **2** restrict; limit. < Old English *sceacul.*

shade (ʃeɪd) *n* **1** partial darkness in an area where something blocks rays of light. **2** a place sheltered from the light and heat of the sun. **3** something that shields or gives protection from direct light: lampshade. **4** a darker area in a painting, drawing, etc. **5** a colour or hue. **6** a slight difference or amount: a shade more milk please. **7** (*literary*) a ghost.
• *vb* **1** cover with a shade; shelter or screen. **2** make darker. **3** darken parts of (a drawing) to give the effect of varying light and shade. **4** change gradually by a small amount. **put in the shade** cause to appear inferior by comparison. **shades** *pl n* **1** the darkness as night falls. **2** (*US informal*) sunglasses. **3** suggestions or reminders of something. **shady** *adj* **1** affording shade. **2** sheltered from the sun. **3** dubious; suspect: shady deals. **shadiness** *n* < Old English *sceadu.*

shadow (ˈʃædəʊ) *n* **1** a dark image cast by something that blocks rays of light. **2** darkness; shade. **3** a trace; hint: beyond all shadow of doubt. **4** a remnant; vestige: a mere shadow of his former self. **5** someone who follows or accompanies another closely. **6** gloom: His death cast a shadow over everything.
• *vb* **1** shade; cast a shadow over. **2** follow and watch (someone) closely or secretly. **shadower** *n* **shadow-boxing** *n* boxing with an imaginary opponent, esp. as a form of training. **Shadow Cabinet** members of the Opposition Party who would be ministers if their party were in power. **shadowy** *adj* **1** dark; full of shadows. **2** vague; imaginary. < Old English *sceadu* shade.

shaft (ʃɑːft) *n* **1** a spear, lance, or similar weapon; long handle of this. **2** a beam or ray, esp. of light. **3** something like a missile aimed at someone: shafts of sarcasm. **4** any long rod or pole serving as a handle for something, such as a hammer, golf-club, etc. **5** a rotating rod that transmits power or motion. **6** one of two wooden bars for harnessing a horse to a vehicle. **7** a vertical or sloping passage or opening, esp. man-made: lift-shaft; mine-shaft. < Old English *sceaft.*

shag (ʃæg) *n* **1** a matted tangle of hair or fibre. **2** coarse tobacco. **shaggy** *adj* **1** having long, matted hair or fibre.

2 rough or untidy: shaggy hair. **shagginess** *n* **shaggy-dog story** a long, funny story with a pointless or anticlimactic conclusion. < Old English *sceacga.*

shake (ʃeɪk) *vb* **shook; shaken; shaking** **1** move up and down or to and fro in a rapid, jerky manner. **2** wave; flourish. **3** dislodge or eject by shaking: He shook the dust off his shoes. **4** disturb the calm of; upset. **5** shake hands. **6** weaken; undermine: Her faith was shaken. **7** sway; tremble.
• *n* **1** shaking or being shaken; this movement. **2** a shock or vibration. **3** a milk shake. **4** a moment: I'll be there in two shakes. **no great shakes** (*informal*) not very good. **shake down** become used to new conditions, etc. **shake hands** clasp right hands in greeting, farewell, or agreement. **shake off** get rid of: I can't shake off this cold. **shake one's head** move one's head from side to side to show refusal, disapproval, denial, etc. **shaker** *n* a container used to mix ingredients or sprinkle: salt shaker. **shake up** reorganize, esp. to make more efficient. **shake-up** *n* **shaky** *adj* **1** unsteady; wobbly. **2** dubious; unreliable. **shakily** *adv* < Old English *sceacan.* SEE PANEL AT **SWAP.**

shale (ʃeɪl) *n* a dark, finely-laminated rock made by compressed layers of clay. < Old English *scealu.*

shall (ʃəl; *stressed* ʃæl) *auxiliary vb* **should** **1** used with *I* and *we* to express the future. **2** used to express obligation, firm intention, or determination: He shall go. **3** used to express an offer, request, etc. < Old English *sceal.*

shallot (ʃəˈlɒt) *n* a plant resembling an onion that grows in clusters of bulbs, used often for pickling and seasoning. < alteration of Old French *eschaloigne.*

shallow (ˈʃæləʊ) *adj* **1** not deep. **2** lacking depth of thought or feeling; superficial.
• *n* a shallow part of a body of water.
• *vb* make or become shallow. **shallowly** *adv* **shallowness** *n* < Middle English *schalowe.*

sham (ʃæm) *n* **1** a pretence of sincerity; hypocrisy. **2** an imitation; counterfeit. **3** someone who shams.
• *adj* fake; imitation.
• *vb* **shammed; shamming** pretend; feign: sham illness. **shammer** *n* < perhaps alteration of *shame.*

shambles (ˈʃæmbl̩z) *n* a scene or state of great confusion, slaughter, or destruction. SEE PANEL.

shame (ʃeɪm) *n* **1** a feeling of mental pain resulting from awareness of one's guilt or shortcomings; susceptibility to this. **2** disgrace; humiliation. **3** something to be regretted; disappointment.
• *vb* **1** cause to feel shame. **2** compel by arousing feelings of guilt. **shamefaced** *adj* showing shame; ashamed. **shameful** *adj* causing feelings of shame; disgraceful. **shamefully** *adv* **shameless** *adj* showing no sense of shame; brazen or immodest. **shamelessly** *adv* < Old English *scamu.*

shampoo (ʃæmˈpuː) *n* **1** a liquid substance used for washing and lathering hair. **2** a liquid for cleaning carpets, upholstery, etc. **3** shampooing, esp. at a hairdresser's.
• *vb* clean with a shampoo. < Hindi *cā̃pnā* to shampoo.

shamrock (ˈʃæmˌrɒk) *n* one of a group of plants like clover with a stem bearing three leaves, used as a national emblem by Ireland. < Irish Gaelic *seamrōg.*

shandy (ˈʃændɪ) *n* a drink of mixed beer and lemonade or ginger beer. < origin unknown.

shanghai (ʃæŋˈhaɪ) *vb* trick or compel (someone) to do something or go somewhere. SEE PANEL.

shank (ʃæŋk) *n* **1** the part of the leg between the knee and the ankle. **2** the meat from this part of an animal. **3** the long, narrow stem of something, for example, a spoon, handle, key, or nail. **4** the part of an object attached to something else, such as the end of a drill bit, or the ring or stem at the back of some buttons. < Old English *scanca.*

shanty[1] (ˈʃæntɪ) *n* a crudely-built shelter;

a right shambles!

A state or scene of utter confusion and disorder is sometimes referred to as a shambles: 'We've only just moved into the house so we're still in a bit of a shambles.' The word shambles derives ultimately from the Old English word *scamul* or *sceamul* meaning 'a stool' or 'table'. By the Middle Ages it had come to refer to a table or stall on which a butcher displayed meat for sale. This explains the popularity of The Shambles as a street name. A street so called was once the location of a meat market or row of butchers' stalls. In those days the rear of the butcher's stall served as an impromptu slaughterhouse, hence the use of shambles in this sense. Furthermore, the scene of such goings-on was typically one of chaotic disorder—in other words a right shambles.

shack. **shanty-town** *n* part of a town that is full of shanties. < ultimately Latin *cantherius* trellis.

shanty² *n* a traditional song sung by sailors in rhythm with their work. < alteration of French *chanter* to sing.

shape (ʃeɪp) *n* **1** the visible outline of an object or someone's body. **2** an assumed form; guise: a devil in human shape. **3** an organized form: The idea look shape. **4** a state; condition: in good shape. **5** a mould or pattern.
• *vb* **1** make or form, esp. in a particular shape. **2** develop in a certain way: It's shaping up well. **3** plan or modify (a course of action, an idea, etc.). **shaper** *n* **shapeless** *adj* **1** having no definite form. **2** lacking a pleasing or regular shape. **shapely** *adj* well-proportioned; attractively formed. < Old English *scieppan*.

share (ʃɛə) *n* **1** a part of something belonging to, given to, or contributed to by an individual. **2** a large or full part: She's had her share of bad luck. **3** one of the equal parts the capital or stock of a business company is divided into, usually represented by a certificate.
• *vb* **1** also **share out** divide into portions; give away a portion. **2** have part of, use, or experience jointly with others. **sharer** *n* **go shares** share equally. **share-cropper** *n* (*US*) a tenant farmer, esp. one who pays over a part of his crop as rent to the landowner. **shareholder** *n* someone that has shares in a business company. < Old English *scearu*.

shark¹ (ʃɑːk) *n* one of a group of large marine fish, often predatory and ferocious. < origin unknown. SEE PANEL.

shark² *n* someone who extorts money from or exploits others. < probably ultimately German *Schurke* scoundrel. SEE PANEL AT **SHARK¹**.

sharp (ʃɑːp) *adj* **1** that can cut or pierce, esp. with a fine edge or point. **2** sudden; abrupt: a sharp rise in unemployment. **3** keenly perceptive or attentive: sharp ears. **4** clear; well-defined: sharp focus. **5** severe; acute: a sharp pain. **6** sly; crafty: sharp practice. **7** loud; intense. **8** fiery; irritable: a sharp temper. **9** acutely affecting the senses, esp. taste or smell. **10** brisk; vigorous: a sharp pace. **11** (of a musical note) higher in pitch by a semitone.
• *adv* **1** precisely on time: 9 o'clock sharp. **2** abruptly. **3** higher than the correct musical pitch.
• *n* **1** (*music*) a note higher by one semitone than the natural, shown by the sign #. **2** (*informal*) a swindler. **sharpish** *adj* **sharply** *adv* **sharpen** *vb* make or become sharp. **sharpener** *n* **sharp-eyed** *adj* quick to notice things. **sharpshooter** *n* a marksman. < Old English *scearp*. SEE PANEL AT **ACUTE**.

shatter (ˈʃætə) *vb* **1** burst or break into pieces, esp. by sudden force; destroy.

shanghai

To be shanghaied into doing something means to be tricked, cajoled, or forced into doing it against one's will: Last December I was *shanghaied* into dressing up as Father Christmas. The original application of this word was to the press-ganging of unwary seamen for enforced service on an outward bound ship. During the last century voyages to the Orient and such places as *Shanghai* (China's major commercial port) were far from popular and forceful methods were often called upon to obtain a full crew.

Watch out for sharks!

A person who grows rich through the unscrupulous exploitation of others is often referred to as a shark. This is one of a number of creatures whose names are used derogatorily of human beings. In some cases, as with cow, the name is simply a general term of abuse and does not hinge upon any particular characteristic of the creature in question. Other cases involve a transfer of some distinctive quality or behaviour pattern perceived in the original owner. For example, the application of shark to people invokes the fish's predatory habit: both swindler and shark prey upon their fellows, often with a ferocious appetite. Other examples include:

ass (stupid)
beaver (busy, hard-working)
elephant (large, clumsy)
fox (cunning, sly)
monkey (mischievous)
pig (greedy)
squirrel (given to hoarding)
vixen (ferocious)

2 affect or upset greatly: We were shattered by the news. **3** cause to be extremely tired. < Middle English *schateren*.

shave (ʃeɪv) *vb* **1** cut off (hair) on the face, etc., close to the skin with a razor. **2** cut thin layers or slices from (wood, etc.). **3** pass very close to; graze or brush against in passing. **4** reduce (prices or costs) slightly.
• *n* the removal of hair from the face by shaving. **close shave** (*informal*) a narrow escape. **shaven** *adj* shaved. **shaver** *n* **1** an electric razor. **2** (*informal*) a boy; youngster. **shaving-brush** *n* a brush used to lather the skin before shaving. **shaving-cream** *n* cream applied to the face before shaving. **shavings** *pl n* thin strips shaved from something: wood shavings. < Old English *scafan*.

shawl (ʃɔːl) *n* a large piece of often decorative fabric used to cover the head and shoulders or wrapped around a baby. < Persian *shāl*.

she (ʃɪ; *stressed* ʃiː) *pron* **1** the female person or animal mentioned. **2** a car, ship, aircraft, or nation personified as female.
• *n* a female animal or human: she-wolf. < probably alteration of Old English *hēo* she. SEE PANEL AT **HE**.

sheaf (ʃiːf) *n, pl* **sheaves 1** a bundle of cut stalks and ears of cereal crops tied together. **2** a collection of objects tied or laid together: a sheaf of papers. < Old English *scēaf*.

shear (ʃɪə) *vb* **sheared; shorn, sheared; shearing 1** clip or cut off (hair, wool, etc.), esp. with shears. **2** divest or deprive of: shorn of his power. **3** also **shear off** fracture or distort because of force being applied.
• *n* a force that causes layers or parts of a body to slide over each other. **shears** *pl n* an instrument for clipping or cutting, resembling a large pair of scissors, and operated with both hands. < Old English *scieran*.

sheath (ʃiːθ) *n* **1** a case or covering for a blade or tool; any similar covering or structure. **2** a close-fitting dress with a tapering skirt. **3** a contraceptive cover for the penis; condom. **sheathe** *vb* **1** put away in a sheath. **2** cover or encase (as if) with a sheath. **sheath-knife** *n* a knife with a fixed blade carried in a sheath. < Old English *scēath*.

shed[1] (ʃɛd) *n* a small, single-storeyed building used for storage, keeping livestock, or as a workshop. < probably Middle English *shade* shade.

shed[2] *vb* **shed; shedding 1** allow to flow: shed tears; shed blood. **2** cast off (a natural covering): shed hair; shed leaves. **3** repel: Duck feathers shed water. **4** take off (clothes). **shed light on** make more clear. < Old English *scēadan* to separate.

sheen (ʃiːn) *n* a shine; lustre. **sheeny** *adj* < Old English *scīene*.

sheep (ʃiːp) *n, pl* **sheep** a domesticated animal feeding mainly on grass, kept in flocks for its meat and thick coat or fleece. **sheep-dip** *n* a liquid preparation for dipping sheep in to clean their fleece and kill parasites. **sheep-dog** *n* a dog trained to tend, herd, and guard sheep. **sheep-farmer** *n* one that keeps sheep. **sheep-fold** *n* an enclosure for sheep. **sheepish** *adj* embarrassed; ashamed. **sheepishly** *adv* **sheepishness** *n* **sheepshank** *n* a knot made in a rope to shorten it. **sheepskin** *n* the skin of a sheep used to make clothing, bags, etc. < Old English *scēap*. SEE PANEL AT **SHIP**.

sheer[1] (ʃɪə) *adj* **1** pure or utter; used emphatically: sheer nonsense. **2** very steep: a sheer drop. **3** (of fabrics) very thin or transparent.
• *adv* straight up or straight down. < Old Norse *skærr* pure. SEE PANEL.

sheer[2] *vb* turn or swerve from a course; change direction. < origin uncertain.

sheet (ʃiːt) *n* **1** a large, rectangular piece of cotton, nylon, etc., used in pairs as inner bedclothes. **2** a thin, rectangular piece of any material: a sheet of glass. **3** a rectangular piece of paper, esp. one used in writing or printing. **4** a broad surface: a sheet of water. **sheeting** *n* fabric for making sheets. **sheet lightning** lightning that appears as a broad sheet of light. **sheet music** loose sheets of music not bound into a book.< Old English *scȳte*.

sheikh (ʃeɪk) *n* an Arab chief or religious leader. **sheikhdom** *n* < Arabic *shaykh*.

shelf (ʃɛlf) *n, pl* **shelves 1** a thin, flat, long, narrow board fastened horizontally to the wall, in a cupboard, etc., to display or store things on. **2** something resembling this; ledge. **on the shelf** no longer of use or sought after; esp. of an unmarried woman thought to be past the age of marriage. **shelf-life** *n* the length of time a food item, etc., will keep without deteriorating. < probably Old English *scylfe*. SEE PANEL.

shell (ʃɛl) *n* **1** the hard casing of an egg, nut, etc. **2** the hard exterior of a tortoise, crab, snail, etc. **3** something resembling or likened to a shell : The house was reduced to a mere shell. **4** the material of which a shell is formed: made of shell. **5** a metal case

containing explosives. **6** a light, narrow, rowing boat, used for racing.
• *vb* **1** remove from the shell: shelled peas. **2** bombard with explosives. **come out of one's shell** becomes less shy and more gregarious. **shellfish** *n* a water creature with a shell, esp. one used as human food such as a crab or cockle. **shell out** (*informal*) pay out (money) reluctantly. **shell-shock** *n* nervous exhaustion or breakdown due to prolonged exposure to battle. < Old English *sciell.*

shellac (ˈʃɛlæk) *n* a resin used in varnish.
• *vb* **shellacked; shellacking** varnish with shellac. < *shell* + *lac,* translation of French *laque en écailles* lac in thin plates.

shelter (ˈʃɛltə) *n* **1** something that provides cover or protection: a bus shelter. **2** refuge or protection: seek shelter.
• *vb* **1** provide with security, protection, refuge, etc.: shelter an orphan. **2** take shelter. < origin uncertain.

shelve (ʃɛlv) *vb* **1** arrange or store on a shelf. **2** equip with shelves. **3** put aside (for later consideration); reject. **4** dismiss from service. **5** slope gradually. **shelving** *n* material for making shelves; shelves. < *shelf.*

shepherd (ˈʃɛpəd) fem. **shepherdess** *n* a person who tends sheep.
• *vb* guide or watch over. < Old English *scēaphyrde,* from *scēap* sheep + *hierde* herdsman.

sherbet (ˈʃɜːbət) *n* **1** a sweet powder eaten as a sweet or added to water to make a fizzy drink. **2** a water-ice; sorbet. < Arabic *sharbah.*

sheriff (ˈʃɛrɪf) *n* **1** (*US*) the chief official responsible for law enforcement in a county. **2** the chief executive officer of the Crown in counties in England and Wales, with mostly ceremonial duties. **3** the chief judge of a Scottish county or district. **sheriffdom** *n* < Old English *scīr* shire + *gerēfa* local official.

shelfs or shelves?

Most of us who acquire English as our mother tongue rarely appreciate the learning difficulties it presents to others. Think how English words ending in an f sound like shelf form their plurals. In many cases the f sound changes to a v sound and a z sound is added: knife—knives, leaf—leaves, loaf—loaves, shelf—shelves. The plural formation seems regular and straightforward. But now think of words like cliff, proof, and safe. In these cases the plural is formed differently, by adding an s sound. For the foreign learner, life suddenly starts getting difficult!

However, the picture is not yet complete. There is a third group, which includes words like dwarf, hoof, and roof. Words in this group have two plural forms: dwarfs, dwarves: hoofs, hooves; roofs, rooves. Handkerchief with its alternative forms handkerchiefs and handkerchieves also belongs to this group, although sadly for the foreign learner chief does not, simply adding an s sound.

sheer

The most common meaning of sheer as in, for example, sheer stupidity, is not easy to define. The same is true of utter as in, say, utter rubbish, and of pure as in pure nonsense. The same type of problem is faced when trying to define very in a very beautiful tree. With such words it may be more appropriate to talk about 'effect' than about 'meaning': the effect of sheer is to intensify the meaning that follows.

The difference between adjectives like sheer, utter, and pure and most other adjectives like, say, beautiful is also seen in the way they occur with other words. Most adjectives can occur either before or after a noun: a beautiful tree—the tree is beautiful. However, sheer, utter, and pure are not transposable like this; they must come in front of the word they qualify.

For reasons such as this they are seen as belonging to a subdivision of the adjective class, whose members are known as *intensifiers*. Other members of this very small group include:

simple the *simple* answer is 'no'
real a *real* help
true a *true* genius
right a *right* idiot
total a *total* disaster
plain the *plain* truth

sherry (ˈʃɛrɪ) *n* a fortified wine, originally from southern Spain. < *Xeres,* now Jerez, city in Spain. SEE PANEL. SEE PANEL AT **CHAMPAGNE.**

shibboleth (ˈʃɪbəˌlɛθ) *n* **1** a catchword, slogan, or pet phrase. **2** a custom or practice that distinguishes members of a particular group. < Hebrew *shibbōleth* stream. SEE PANEL.

shield (ʃiːld) *n* **1** a broad plate of defensive armour carried on the arm. **2** something that provides defence or protection. **3** a representation of a shield that serves as an identifying emblem. **4** a trophy in the form of a small, usually triangular shield.
• *vb* protect, shield, or save from detection. < Old English *scield.*

shift (ʃɪft) *vb* **1** move or cause to move from one place to another: trying to shift the wardrobe. **2** transfer: shift one's office. **3** change in form, direction, etc.: The wind has shifted. **4** manage or be responsible; get by: You'll just have to shift for yourself. **5** (*informal*) move quickly: 'Come on! Shift!'
• *n* **1** shifting or being shifted. **2** a group of workers that alternates with other groups; period worked by such a group: the night shift. **3** a scheme, expedient, or subterfuge. **4** a slip or loose dress. **shiftless** *adj* lacking resourcefulness; lazy. **shiftlessly** *adv* **shiftlessness** *n* **shifty** *adj* evasive or untrustworthy: a shifty character. **shiftily** *adv* **shiftiness** *n* < Old English *sciftan.*

shilling (ˈʃɪlɪŋ) *n* a former British coin; 5p. < Old English *scilling.*

shimmer (ˈʃɪmə) *vb* shine with a soft, wavering light; glimmer.
• *n* a shimmering light or effect. < Old English *scimerian.*

shin (ʃɪn) *n* **1** the front part of the leg below the knee. **2** the lower foreleg, esp. as a cut of beef.
• *vb* **shinned; shinning** climb (a pole, tree, etc.) by gripping with the hands or arms and legs and hauling oneself up. < Old English *scinu.*

shine (ʃaɪn) *vb* **shone**, except def. **5 shined; shining 1** emit or reflect light; cause this to happen: The sun shone all morning. **2** direct the light of (a torch, etc.): Shine the light over here a minute. **3** be outstanding; excel: a shining example. **4** (of a face or expression) look radiant. **5** polish.
• *n* **1** sheen or lustre. **2** radiance. **come rain or shine** whatever the weather; whatever may happen. **shiner** (*informal*) a black eye. **shiny** *adj* having a gloss or sheen: a shiny apple. **take a shine to** (*informal*) take a liking to. < Old English *scīnan.*

shingle (ˈʃɪŋgl̩) *n* **1** coarse gravel, esp. that found on beaches. **2** an area covered in shingle. < probably Scandinavian.

shingles (ˈʃɪŋgl̩z) *n* a viral disease characterized by inflammation and blisters along the path of the affected nerve, and often severe pain. < Latin *cingulum* girdle.

ship (ʃɪp) *n* **1** a large seagoing vessel. **2** (*informal*) an aircraft, airship, or spaceship.
• *vb* **shipped; shipping 1** put or receive on board a ship for conveyance. **2** transport. **3** (*informal*) send away: They've shipped the children off to their grandmother's. **4** take into a boat, ship, etc.: The dug-out was shipping water at a dangerous rate. **shipboard** *adj* happening, used, or intended for use on board a ship. **shipbuilder** *n* a person or company that designs or builds ships. **shipbuilding** *n* **shipload** *n* the maximum amount or quantity that a ship will carry. **shipmate** *n* a fellow sailor; fellow passenger on a

A sherry is it?

The derivation of sherry is rather unusual. The original form of the word was *sherris,* an approximation of Xeres (now Jerez) in southern Spain, where the drink was first produced. Sherris, however, was mistakenly taken to be a plural form. On the basis of this misassumption, a singular equivalent, sherry, came into being, eventually replacing the original name.

shibboleth not sibboleth!

Shibboleth is a word of biblical origin. In Judges 12:4–6 we read that correct pronunciation of the word was used by Jephthah as a type of acid test. Being a bit of a phonetician, Jephthah knew that the Ephraimites, unlike his own Gileadites, were unable to make a sh sound properly. Accordingly, his strategy for distinguishing members of the two groups was to make individuals say the word. Anybody who said sibboleth instead of shibboleth was killed.

ship. **shipment** *n* **1** a collection of goods that are shipped at one time; consignment. **2** shipping or being shipped. **shipowner** *n* a person who owns or has shares in one or more ships. **shipper** *n* a person or company that transports goods by ship. **shipping** *n* **1** ships, esp. those in one port or belonging to one country. **2** transportation of goods by ship. **shipshape** *adj* neat and tidy. **shipwreck** *n* **1** a wrecked ship. **2** destruction or loss of a ship. **3** an irrevocable collapse; ruin. **shipwrecked** *adj* **1** having suffered a shipwreck. **2** ruined. **shipwright** *n* a craftsman with one of the skills required in shipbuilding. **shipyard** *n* a place where ships are built, maintained, and repaired. < Old English *scip*. SEE PANEL.

shire (ʃaɪə) *n* **1** a county. **2** a shire horse. **shire horse** a large, heavy, British cart-horse. < Old English *scīr*.

shirk (ʃɜːk) *vb* evade (a duty, task, etc., for which one is responsible). **shirker** *n* < origin unknown.

shirt (ʃɜːt) *n* a light garment, esp. for a boy or man, that in colder weather or climates is worn under a jumper or jacket and on top of a vest. **shirty** *adj* (*informal*) bad-tempered or argumentative. < Old English *scyrte*.

shiver[1] (ˈʃɪvə) *vb* tremble, esp. when very cold or feverish.
• *n* a shivering movement. **shivery** *adj* < Middle English *shiveren*. SEE PANEL.

shiver[2] *n* any of the fragments that result from something shattering.
• *vb* break into shivers. < Middle English. SEE PANEL AT **SHIVER[1]**.

shoal[1] (ʃəʊl) *n* a large group, esp. of fish. < Old English *scolu*.

shoal[2] *n* a shallow; underwater sandbank.
• *vb* make or become shallow. < Old English *sceald* shallow.

shock[1] (ʃɒk) *n* **1** a sudden, traumatic disturbance of a person's mind or emotions: suffer a shock. **2** a state of weakness or depression caused by this: left in a state of shock. **3** a sudden, violent shaking or impact: The shock was felt almost two miles away. **4** an electric shock.
• *vb* **1** cause a feeling of great surprise, horror, or disgust in. **2** give an electric shock to. **3** produce a state of severe weakness in. **shock absorber** a device that absorbs shocks to a vehicle, machine, etc. **shocker** *n* **1** something that horrifies or causes offence, esp. a sensational film, novel, etc. **2** (*informal*)

---

ship or **sheep?**

To lose or spoil the ship for a ha'porth of tar means 'to risk losing a great deal for the sake of a little further expenditure': 'You'd be wise to invest in a case for that new camera of yours. There's no point in losing the ship for a ha'porth of tar!'

This expression is in fact of rustic derivation. The original saying was to lose the *sheep* for a ha'porth of tar, and arose from the use of tar as a treatment for sores.

Which **shiver?**

Words like shiver 'to tremble with cold, etc'. and shiver 'a fragment of broken glass, etc'. are known as *homonyms*. These are words which differ in meaning and origin but whose spelling and pronunciation are identical. Other examples of homonyms include:

alight 'to leave a vehicle'
alight 'burning'
ball 'sphere'
ball 'large gathering for dancing'
bank 'sloping ground'
bank 'institution for keeping money'
bank 'row of switches, etc.'
blow 'to cause air to move'
blow 'powerful stroke with the fist'
case 'example or instance'
case 'container'
cleave 'to split by cutting'
cleave 'to stick fast or adhere'
fast 'quick(ly)'
fast 'to abstain from food'
rest 'to repose'
rest 'remainder'
saw past tense of see
saw 'cutting-tool'
spit 'to eject saliva'
spit 'pointed rod used in roasting meat'
stole past tense of steal
stole 'vestment'
till 'until'
till 'to work (the land)'
till 'a cash register'

a person that shocks, esp. a habitually mischievous child. **shocking** *adj* **1** causing a feeling of indignation or disgust. **2** very bad: shocking weather. **shockingly** *adv* **shockproof** *adj* able to absorb shocks without damage: a shockproof watch. **shock therapy** or **treatment** treatment of certain mental conditions by inducing a coma or convulsions either by drugs or by subjecting the brain to an electric current. **shock wave** a wave of increased atmospheric pressure caused by an explosion or by something travelling at supersonic speed. < of Germanic origin.

shock² *n* a bushy mass, esp. of hair on the head. < origin uncertain.

shod (ʃɒd) SEE **SHOE.**

shoddy (ˈʃɒdɪ) *adj* **1** of poor quality or workmanship. **2** shameful; shabby. **shoddily** *adv* **shoddiness** *n* < origin unknown.

shoe (ʃuː) *n* **1** a protective covering for a person's foot. **2** something resembling a shoe. **3** a horseshoe. **4** the part of a brake that presses on the (drum of the) wheel.
• *vb* **shod, shoed; shoeing** fit (a horse) with a shoe or shoes. **shoehorn** *n* a curved device for easing the heel into the back of a shoe. **shoelace** *n* a cord or lace for fastening a shoe. **shoemaker** *n* a person whose job is to make or repair shoes; cobbler. **shoestring** *adj, n* (*informal*) (consisting of or operating on) a small amount of money: a shoestring budget. **shoe-tree** *n* a device inserted in a shoe or boot that helps it to keep its shape. < Old English *scōh*. SEE PANEL.

shone (ʃɒn) SEE **SHINE.**

shook (ʃʊk) SEE **SHAKE.**

shoot (ʃuːt) *vb* **shot; shooting 1** hit or kill with a bullet, arrow, etc. **2** fire (a gun, etc.): Someone is shooting. **3** use a gun, etc., skilfully: Neither of them can shoot. **4** hunt with a gun,etc.: go shooting. **5** (of a gun, etc.) propel a missile: How far does it shoot? **6** propel or thrust violently: shot the keys into the back of the drawer. **7** be expelled or emitted violently; spurt: Water suddenly shot out over everybody. **8** move very quickly; dart: The animal shot past me. **9** (of a plant, etc.) show buds or shoots; sprout. **10** photograph; film. **11** engage or release by sliding, esp. the bolt of a door. **12** kick or drive (a ball, etc.) at an opponent's goal in an attempt to score. **13** pass quickly by, over, or along: shoot the rapids.
• *n* **1** a young growth on a plant, etc.; bud. **2** a shooting expedition. **3** an area where game is hunted. **shooter** *n* **shooting brake** (*US*) an estate car. **shooting gallery** an enclosed, indoor area equipped with targets, chiefly used for shooting practice. **shooting star** a meteor. **shooting stick** a walking-stick with a small folding seat at one end. < Old English *scēotan*.

Sh..., you know **shoe**

The vast majority of English words beginning with sh- are derived from Old English words beginning with *sc*-. For example, today's ship was yesterday's *scip*, shoe was once *scōh*, and shop formerly *sceoppa*.

An approximation of the way in which the sc- sound was pronounced can be achieved by trying to say the sound represented by sh while pushing the middle of the tongue upwards towards the roof of the mouth.

shop (ʃɒp) *n* **1** a building or room where goods or services are sold to the public. **2** a workshop.
• *vb* **shopped; shopping 1** visit a shop or shops, esp. to buy something. **2** (*informal*) inform on, esp. to the police. **shopper** *n* **shop around** visit several shops in search of the best bargain. **shop assistant** a person who serves in a shop. **shop-floor** *n* **1** the workers at a factory as opposed to the management. **2** the area in a factory, etc., where the machines or workbenches are located. **shopkeeper** *n* a person who owns or runs a shop. **shop-lifter** *n* a person who steals goods from a shop. **shopping** *n* the goods purchased on a visit to one or more shops. **shopping centre** a concentrated group of shops, restaurants, etc. < Old English *sceoppa* booth.

shore¹ (ʃɔː) *n* the land adjoining the sea or any other large expanse of water. < probably Old English *scor*.

shore² *vb* **1** support (a wall, etc.) with a large piece of timber; brace. **2** give esp. financial support to. < Middle English *shoren*.

shorn (ʃɔːn) SEE **SHEAR.**

short (ʃɔːt) *adj* **1** less long or less tall than average: short sleeves. **2** brief in time: a short performance. **3** seeming to pass quickly: a few short hours. **4** not great in distance: a short drive. **5** (of the memory, etc.) not powerful. **6** insufficient or lacking enough; not supplied in sufficient quantity: short of money. **7** curt; abrupt: You didn't have to be so short with her. **8** not reaching the required distance, standard, or amount. **9** being a nickname or abbreviated form: short for Margaret. **10** (of vowel sounds) relatively brief. **11** crisp and crumbly: short pastry. **12** easily provoked: a short temper. **13** (of drinks) alcoholic; concentrated. • *n* **1** a small alcoholic drink. **2** a short circuit. **shortage** *n* a lack of something; deficiency. **shortbread** *n* a thick, rich biscuit. **shortcake** *n* shortbread.

for short

Short features in a number of idiomatic expressions, including:

be caught or **taken short** to need suddenly to urinate or defecate.
for short as a shortened form: Her full name is Beverley but most people call her Bev for short.
in the short run over the course of a short period of time; in the near future.
make short work of to deal with very quickly.
run short of to have little or few of (something) remaining: We're running a bit short of sugar.
sell (someone) short 1 to cheat (someone), as by selling less than an agreed quantity. **2** to make little of the merits of (oneself or another person).
short cut a route or method that takes less time than the usual one.
short list a reduced list of candidates from whom a final choice will be made.
short-list *vb* to place on a short list.
short of 1 with the exception of: Short of murdering someone, he's prepared to do just about anything. **2** without; lacking: short of friends.

To give someone or something short shrift is used nowadays in the figurative sense of dealing with someone or something in an impatiently curt or dismissive way: 'If that salesman knocks here again, I'll give him *short shrift.* You mark my word.' Originally, the expression applied only to someone who was about to be publicly executed. To grant such a person short shrift was to allow him or her a few minutes to make a confession of sins and to receive absolution.

short-change *vb* give less than the correct amount of change to, sometimes intentionally. **short circuit** the (accidental) joining of two points on an electrical circuit so that the current flows directly between them. **short-circuit** *vb* **1** bypass. **2** cause a short circuit in. **shortcoming** *n* a failing or deficiency. **shorten** *vb* make or become shorter. **shortfall** *n* a deficit. **shorthand** *n* a method of writing very quickly by means of symbols and abbreviations. **short-handed** *adj* insufficiently staffed or without enough helpers. **short-lived** *adj* lasting only a short time. **shortly** *adv* **1** in a short time; soon: coming shortly to this cinema. **2** in a few words. **3** curtly or abruptly. **shorts** *pl n* trousers with legs that reach no lower than the knees. **short-sighted** *adj* **1** able to see only close things clearly; myopic. **2** lacking foresight. **short-sleeved** *adj* having sleeves that reach no lower than the elbow. **short-tempered** *adj* easy to make angry. **short-term** *adj* of, for, or over a short period of time. **short time** reduced working hours, esp. as a result of lack of work. **shorty** *adj, n* (*informal*) (a person or garment that is) shorter than average. < Old English *scort.* SEE PANEL.

shot (ʃɒt) SEE **SHOOT.**
• *n* **1** the act of firing of a gun, etc. **2** the sound of this: We heard two shots. **3** an aimed propelling of a bullet, etc.: The first shot hit the wall behind him. **4** anything calculatedly thrown or propelled: The shot landed at his feet. **5** an attempt to hit a target or drive (a ball, etc.) into a goal: an unlucky shot. **6** a person considered in terms of his or her shooting skill: a poor shot. **7** *pl* **shot** a single projectile for a gun or cannon. **8** lead pellets for firing from a shotgun. **9** a very heavy, metal ball thrown as a sport. **10** an attempt to do something; experimental trial: I thought I'd have a shot at trying to mend it myself. **11** a hypodermic injection. **12** a photograph; scene or episode filmed by a cine-camera. **13** a

Parthian shot

A hostile retort or gesture made while departing, leaving its recipient no time to reply, is known as a parting or Parthian shot. The allusion is to the tactic practised by archers of ancient Parthia. While retreating, or feigning flight, these warriors would turn and discharge a shower of arrows at their pursuers.

single photographic exposure: How many shots do we have left? **shotgun** *n* a gun used for firing a charge of small lead pellets at close range. < Old English *scot.* SEE PANEL.

should (ʃəd; *stressed* ʃʊd) *auxiliary vb* SEE **SHALL. 1** ought to; used to express obligation or give advice: You should take more exercise. **2** used to express predicted likelihood: He should be here by tonight. **3** used to express contingency: Should you see her, tell her to call me. **4** used to mitigate a statement: I should expect that they'll ask you to do it again. < Old English *sceolde.* SEE PANEL.

shoulder (ˈʃəʊldə) *n* **1** the part of a body where the arm or a corresponding limb joins the trunk. **2** the corresponding part in a garment. **3** the shoulder of an animal as a cut of meat. **4** a projection resembling the shoulder.
• *vb* **1** push with the shoulder. **2** take or carry on the shoulder: Shoulder arms! **3** accept the burden of or responsibility for: shoulder the blame. **shoulder-bag** *n* a bag with a long strap that is hung over the shoulder. **shoulder-blade** *n* either of the two flat, triangular bones at the top of the back. **shoulder to shoulder** side by side. < Old English *sculdor.*

shout (ʃaʊt) *n* a loud cry.
• *vb* **1** make a loud cry; utter (a name, etc.) in a loud voice. **2** speak in a very loud voice, esp. when angry. **shout down** drown the words of by shouting; silence. < Middle English *shouten.*

shove (ʃʌv) *n* a violent push.
• *vb* **1** push violently. **2** push with sustained effort. **3** (*informal*) place or put: Shove it back in the box. **shove off 1** move a boat away from the shore by pushing. **2** (*informal*) go away; leave. < Old English *scūfan.*

shovel (ˈʃʌvḷ) *n* **1** a tool for scooping up loose material. **2** a shovelful.
• *vb* **shovelled; shovelling 1** clear or shift (snow, etc.) with a shovel. **2** lift indelicately as if using a shovel. < Old English *scofl.*

show (ʃəʊ) *vb* **showed ; shown, showed; showing 1** cause or allow to be seen or noticed: That colour shows the dirt. **2** display or exhibit: show one's holiday photographs. **3** explain or demonstrate: She showed me how to do it. **4** prove or make evident: The experiment shows that the drug can be lethal. **5** guide or conduct; usher: Show them in. **6** indicate or register: The petrol gauge showed empty. **7** be visible: Don't worry. The hole doesn't show. **8** treat in a certain way: They showed us a lot of kindness as children. **9** reveal by one's actions or behaviour: He showed himself to be very patient. **10** present or stage at a cinema, theatre, etc.; be presented or staged.
• *n* **1** a display or exhibition. **2** a competitive exhibition: a flower show. **3** a public entertainment or spectacle. **4** an insincere display; pretence: These gestures of friendship are just show! **5** a trace or sign: a show of respect. **6** ostentation: The family has never gone in for show. **show business** the theatrical profession; entertainment industry. **showcase** *n* a case, cabinet, etc., with a glass or transparent top, used esp. in a museum for displaying valuable or precious items. **showdown** *n* the culminating episode of a protracted struggle, conflict, etc. **showgirl** *n* a young woman who dances or sings in or adds decoration to a theatrical production. **showing** *n* a display of evidence; performance: On today's showing, he's bound to win. **showjumping** *n* the competitive sport of riding a horse at speed over a course with fences or obstacles. **showman** *n* **1** a person who presents or organizes theatrical productions, etc. **2** a person with a flair for entertaining or dramatic presentation. **showmanship** *n* **show off 1** display proudly. **2** behave in a way that is designed to attract attention or admiration: I wish you'd stop showing off! **show-off** *n* a person who behaves in this way. **showpiece** *n* a prized example or specimen that is used for exhibition. **showroom** *n* a room where samples of goods for sale are displayed. **show up**

---

should or **would?**

☐ conditional. Either should or would is used in the first person: I *would* tell her if I were you. We *should* be very pleased to fulfil your order once payment is received. Would is used in the second and third persons: You *would* lend me the money if I needed it, *wouldn't* you? If we had more time life *would* be so much easier.

☐ should—not would—is used to mean 'ought to': You *should* get more exercise, you know.

☐ would—not should—is used to describe past habits: In his later years, he *would* have a short sleep after lunch. Would is also used in polite requests: *Would* you prefer tea or coffee? *Would* you close the window, please?

---

1 embarrass by behaving badly. **2** (*informal*) arrive; be present: I don't think she's going to show up. **3** make or be clearly visible: It needs a dark background to show it up. **showy** *adj* **1** gaudy; ostentatious. **2** making an attractive display. **showily** *adv* **showiness** *n* < Old English *scēawian*. SEE PANEL.

shower (ʃaʊə) *n* **1** a brief fall of rain, snow, etc. **2** a sudden hail, gush, or fall of: a shower of tears. **3** a device that sprays water on a person's body; structure in a bathroom that encloses this. **4** (*informal*) used to show contempt or mock-contempt for a group of people.
• *vb* **1** pour down in a shower. **2** take a shower. **3** cause to fall or be received in a shower: shower confetti. **showery** *adj*

---

show off and **show-off**

One highly productive way in which the vocabulary has expanded in recent years has been the change of a two-part verb into a corresponding noun. Show off, 'to behave in a way that is designed to attract attention or admiration', has provided us with a show-off, 'a person who behaves in this way'. Other examples of nouns derived from two-part verbs include:

back-up	**knock-out**	**set-to**
blackout	**knock-up**	**set-up**
breakdown	**lay-off**	**shake-up**
break-in	**layout**	**shut-down**
build-up	**let-down**	**slip-up**
cast-off	**let-up**	**sort-out**
check-in	**lie-in**	**splash-down**
check-out	**lift-off**	**stand-by**
come-back	**line-up**	**stand-in**
cover-up	**look-out**	**stopover**
cutback	**make-up**	**stowaway**
drop-out	**mark-up**	**take-off**
flashback	**mess-up**	**take-over**
follow-up	**mix-up**	**tip-off**
getaway	**pay-off**	**top-up**
get-up	**phone-in**	**turn-out**
give-away	**pick-up**	**turnover**
go-ahead	**pile-up**	**walk-out**
grown-up	**print-out**	**work-out**
hand-out	**rig-out**	**write-off**
hand-over	**rip-off**	
hang-out	**sell-out**	
hold-up	**send-up**	
kick-off	**setback**	

---

showerproof *adj* (of a garment) treated so as to prevent light rain from penetrating. < Old English *scūr*.

shown (ʃəʊn) SEE **SHOW.**

shrank (ʃræŋk) SEE **SHRINK.**

shrapnel (ˈʃræpnəl) *n* **1** an artillery shell filled with bullets or fragments of metal and a charge that explodes before impact, scattering the projectiles. **2** one or more of the projectiles scattered upon explosion. SEE PANEL.

shred (ʃrɛd) *n* **1** a narrow piece that is torn or cut from something. **2** a very small amount.
• *vb* **shredded; shredding** tear or cut into shreds. **shredder** *n* < Old English *scrēade*.

shrew (ʃruː) *n* **1** a small, mouse-like animal. **2** a woman who nags habitually. **shrewish** *adj* ill-tempered. **shrewishly** *adv* **shrewishness** *n* < Old English *scrēawa*. SEE PANEL AT **GIRL.**

shrewd (ʃruːd) *adj* having or resulting from sound judgment and worldly wisdom; astute. **shrewdly** *adv* **shrewdness** *n* < Middle English *shrewed* wicked. SEE PANEL.

shriek (ʃriːk) *n* a shrill cry; scream.
• *vb* utter or emit with a shriek. < probably Middle English *shriken*.

shrill (ʃrɪl) *adj* very high-pitched; piercing: a shrill whistle.
• *vb* utter or emit with a shrill sound. **shrillness** *n* **shrilly** *adv* < Middle English *shrillen*.

shrimp (ʃrɪmp) *n* **1** a small, slender,

---

shrapnel

Shrapnel was originally the surname of Lieutenant General Henry Shrapnel, 1761–1842, a British army officer and inventor of the explosive device that was named after him. Other *eponyms* that derive from the inventors of guns and explosive devices include:

colt from Colonel Samuel Colt, 1814–62, US inventor of the repeating pistol.
derringer from Henry Deringer, 1786–1869, US gunsmith and inventor of the pocket pistol. The word derringer acquired its extra r from a pirate manufacturer who, seeing the potential of Deringer's invention, copied it and marketed it under the slightly altered name so as to avoid patent laws.

edible shellfish. **2** (*derogatory humorous*) a very small or puny person. < Middle English *shrimpe*.

shrine (ʃraɪn) *n* **1** an altar, temple, or other place that is considered sacred. **2** a tomb, esp. of a saint. < Old English *scrīn*.

shrink (ʃrɪŋk) *vb* **shrank, shrunk; shrunk, shrunken; shrinking 1** make or become smaller, esp. by exposure to heat or moisture. **2** make or become smaller. **3** withdraw or recoil. **4** cower or quail.
• *n* (*informal*) a psychiatrist. **shrinkage** *n* **1** shrinking. **2** the amount by which something shrinks: Leave an extra inch to allow for shrinkage. **shrink-wrap** *vb* **shrink-wrapped; shrink-wrapping** wrap (an object) in clear, plastic film that is then heated so that it clings tightly. < Old English *scrincan*.

shrivel (ˈʃrɪvl̩) *vb* **shrivelled; shrivelling** contract into wrinkles, esp. with exposure to heat or cold; wrinkle up. < probably Scandinavian.

shroud (ʃraʊd) *n* **1** a sheet wrapped around a body before burial. **2** something that covers or conceals. **3** any of the ropes or cables that support the mast of a ship.
• *vb* **1** wrap in a shroud. **2** cover or conceal: shrouded in secrecy. < Old English *scrūd*.

shrub (ʃrʌb) *n* a perennial plant, smaller than a tree, usually with several woody stems. **shrubby** *adj* **shrubbery** *n* an area planted with shrubs. < Old English *scrybb* brushwood.

shrug (ʃrʌg) *vb* **shrugged; shrugging** raise and drop the shoulders, esp. to express indifference, doubt, etc.
• *n* the act of doing this. **shrug off** dismiss as unimportant; brush aside: shrug off a criticism. < Middle English *schruggen*.

shrewd

Nowadays, to refer to someone as shrewd ('having lots of good sense and worldly wisdom') is to speak approvingly. This, however, has not always been the case. For while some words undergo *deterioration* over the course of time (see panel at **villain**), there are words that undergo the reverse procedure, *amelioration*. This means that they lose their original negative or neutral meaning and acquire a positive one. Shrewd provides a good example of this process, as in Middle English it meant 'wicked'.

shrunk (ʃrʌŋk) SEE **SHRINK**. **shrunken** SEE **SHRINK**.

shudder (ˈʃʌdə) *vb* shake or tremble violently.
• *n* a violent shake or tremble. < Middle English *shoddren*.

shuffle (ˈʃʌfl̩) *vb* **1** mix up or jumble. **2** mix up to rearrange the order of (playing-cards). **3** walk lazily or clumsily without lifting the feet clear of the ground. **4** move or shift from place to place. **5** dance slowly with a sliding step.
• *n* **1** the act of mixing up or rearranging. **2** a lazy or clumsy gait. **3** a slow, sliding dance step. < probably Low German *schüffeln*.

shun (ʃʌn) *vb* **shunned; shunning** avoid deliberately: shun publicity. < Old English *scunian*.

shunt (ʃʌnt) *vb* **1** (of trains) switch from one track to another, esp. to a side track. **2** divert along an alternative course.
• *n* shunting; being shunted. **shunter** *n* < origin uncertain.

shut (ʃʌt) *vb* **shut; shutting 1** close (a door, window, etc.). **2** move or be moved into a closed position: The lid shut with a bang. **3** prevent access to or escape from: Has someone shut the dog out? **4** close (a book, penknife, etc.) by bringing the movable parts together. **5** trap accidentally: shut one's finger in the door. **6** (of shops) cease or cause to cease trading: When does the supermarket shut? **shut down** stop or cause to stop operating, either temporarily or permanently: The factory's been forced to shut down. **shut-down** *n* **shut-eye** *n* (*informal*) sleep. **shut off** (of a gas supply, water supply, etc.) stop or cause to stop operating. **shut up** *vb* (*informal*) stop or cause to stop talking or making a noise. < Old English *scyttan*.

shutter (ˈʃʌtə) *n* **1** a movable outside cover for a window. **2** a device in a camera that opens and closes the lens opening.

shuttle (ˈʃʌtl̩) *vb* move or travel to and fro.
• *n* **1** a weaving instrument used for passing the horizontal threads between the vertical threads. **2** the equivalent part in a sewing-machine. **3** a vehicle used in a shuttle service. **4** a shuttlecock. **shuttle service** a transport service in which a vehicle goes to and fro regularly over a particular route. < Middle English *shittle*.

shuttlecock (ˈʃʌtl̩ˌkɒk) *n* the cone-shaped, usually feathered projectile used in badminton. < *shuttle* + *cock*.

shy[1] (ʃaɪ) *adj* **shier, shyer; shiest, shyest 1** (of a person) lacking confidence when in company; withdrawing. **2** easily startled; timid: The robin was less shy than the other birds. **3** cautious about; wary of: shy of lending money to friends.
• *vb* **shied; shying** (of a horse) suddenly give a start through fright. **shyly** *adv* **shyness** *n* < Old English *scēoh*.

shy[2] *vb* **shied; shying** (*old-fashioned*) throw or fling.
• *n* (*old-fashioned*) a throw. < of Germanic origin.

SI *abbrev*. Système International (d'Unités); an international system of metric units.

Siamese (ˌsaɪəˈmiːz) *adj, n* Thai. **Siamese cat** a short-haired, blue-eyed cat with a slender body and a long, tapering tail. **Siamese twin** either of two congenitally joined twins. SEE PANEL.

sibilant (ˈsɪbɪlənt) *adj* having or containing a hissing sound.
• *n* a sibilant speech sound. **sibilance** *n* **sibilantly** *adv* < Latin *sibilare* to hiss.

sibling (ˈsɪblɪŋ) *n* a brother or sister. < Old English: relative.

sic (sɪk) *adv* spelt, written, etc., exactly in this way; used after a printed word or passage to show that it is in fact correct. < Latin: thus.

sick (sɪk) *adj* **1** physically or mentally ill. **2** connected with illness or ill people: a sick ward. **3** nauseated: feel sick. **4** (*informal*) disgusted, bored, or fed up with: I'm sick of their complaints. **5** (*informal*) having a liking for black humour and the macabre; having a basis in black humour: a sick joke. **6** (*informal*) downcast; disgruntled. **sicken** *vb* **1** make or become ill. **2** (*informal*) make or become tired or disgusted: What sickens me is the way they never thank you. **sickening** *adj* disgusting or repugnant. **sickly** *adj* **1** regularly ill. **2** unhealthy in appearance. **3** not encouraging good health: a sickly climate. **4** causing repugnance, distaste, or a feeling of nausea: a sickly grin. **sickness** *n* **1** illness. **2** a disease. **3** nausea. < Old English *sēoc*.

sickle (ˈsɪkl̩) *n* a tool comprising a curved, metal blade on a short handle, used for cutting grass, corn, etc. < Old English *sicol*.

side (saɪd) *n* **1** an inner or outer surface, esp. one that is not the top or bottom: the sides of a cupboard. **2** either of the two surfaces of a page, record, or other flat object. **3** the right or left part of an object or body. **4** a district or area in relation to a point of reference: the south side of the city. **5** one of the lines that form the border of a figure: A square has 4 sides. **6** a place away from a central point or line: put something to one side. **7** a position considered to be opposite to another: on the other side of town. **8** an aspect of something: several sides to the problem. **9** either of two opposing teams or groups. **10** a line of descent: on one's father's side.
• *adj* at or on the side: a side door.
• *vb* support in a dispute or argument: I can't understand why she always sides with the management. **get on the right side of** win the approval or sympathy of. **get on the wrong side of** incur the disapproval or hostility of. **on the side** as a secret or subsidiary activity, esp. one that is outside the law. **sideboard** *n* a piece of dining-room furniture with drawers and shelves for storing china, etc. **sideboards** *pl n* sideburns. **sideburns** *pl n* the hair that grows down the sides of a man's face in front of the ears. **side by side** close together. **side-car** *n* a passenger compartment that attaches to the side of a motor cycle. **side-effect** *n* a secondary effect, usually undesirable: The drug is not without side-effects. **sidelight** *n* **1** light coming from one side. **2** incidental or supplementary information. **3** a light at the side of a vehicle. **4** a light at either side of a ship that is underway at night. **sideline** *n* **1** something done as a secondary activity to a main occupation. **2** a line of goods sold alongside a main line. **3** either of the two lines that mark the side boundaries of a pitch or field of play. **4** a non-participatory role or position. **sidelong** *adj* directed to one side: a sidelong glance. **side-saddle** *adv, n* (sitting on) a saddle for a woman rider with long skirts whose legs are not astride but on the same side of the horse.

Siamese twins

Two babies that are born joined together at some point are referred to as Siamese twins. The name derives from Chang and Eng Bunker, 1811–74, who were born in Maklong, *Siam* (now Thailand). Chang and Eng were the first conjoined twins to receive world-wide publicity.

side-step *vb* **side-stepped; side-stepping 1** avoid by stepping to one side. **2** evade (a responsibility, issue, etc.). **side street** a minor street leading off or to the side of a main one. **sidetrack** *vb* distract or divert from the main issue or purpose. **sidewalk** *n* (*US*) pavement. **sideways** *adv, adj* **1** to or from one side. **2** with one side facing the front. < Old English *sīde*. SEE PANEL.

siding (ˈsaɪdɪŋ) *n* a length of railway track branching off a main line, used for shunting.

sidle (ˈsaɪdl̩) *vb* approach or advance in a furtive manner. < probably back formation from *sideling* sideways.

siege (siːdʒ) *n* the surrounding of a fortified place by troops, police, etc., to force a surrender. < ultimately Latin *sedēre* to sit.

sienna (sɪˈɛnə) *n* a type of earth containing iron oxides that is used as a pigment either in its untreated form or after burning; colour of this substance. < Italian *terra di Siena* earth of Siena, city in Italy.

sierra (sɪˈɛərə) *n* a long range of mountains whose peaks form a jagged outline. < Latin serra saw.

siesta (sɪˈɛstə) *n* a rest or nap after the midday meal. < Latin *sexta* (*hora*) noon.

sieve (sɪv) *n* a round utensil with a bottom of wire mesh, used for separating the finer particles of a substance from the coarser, or liquid from solid matter.
• *vb* feed through a sieve. < Old English *sife*.

sift (sɪft) *vb* **1** sieve. **2** sprinkle lightly from a sieve or similar utensil. **3** examine carefully one by one: sift through the papers in search of a clue. < Old English *siftan*.

sigh (saɪ) *n* a long, audible breath, usually indicating relief, boredom, etc.
• *vb* **1** give a sigh. **2** (esp. of wind) make a sound resembling this. **3** yearn or long (for). **4** utter with sighs. < Old English *sīcan*.

sight (saɪt) *n* **1** the faculty of seeing. **2** the act or an instance of seeing. **3** the range or field of a person's vision: within sight of home. **4** something seen or enjoyable to see: Wild daffodils make a beautiful sight. **5** (*informal*) something considered to be odd in appearance or unsightly: She looked a real sight! **6** a device or instrument on a gun, telescope, etc., that assists aiming or alignment.
• *vb* **1** get a glimpse or view of: sight land. **2** aim or view by means of the sight on a gun, telescope, etc. **a sight** (*informal*) a lot: It'll look a sight better for a coat of paint. **at** or **on sight** as soon as seen: He's to be arrested on sight. **in sight 1** visible. **2** close at hand: The end of their worries was in sight. **lower one's sights** be more moderate in one's ambitions, ideals, etc. **sight-read** *vb* **sight-read; sight-reading** play or sing from a piece of written music without previous practice. **sight-screen** *n* a large, white, movable screen that helps a batsman to see a cricket ball. **sight-seeing** *n* the visiting of places of interest, esp. as a tourist. **sightseer** *n* < Old English *gesiht*.

sign (saɪn) *n* **1** a symbol: a sign of success. **2** a gesture: She made a sign for him to go away. **3** a signboard, poster, or similar notice displayed in a public place. **4** a trace or indication: signs of rain. **5** a conventional symbol in mathematics, etc.: a minus sign. **6** any of the twelve divisions of the zodiac.
• *vb* **1** write one's signature on. **2** communicate by means of a gesture. **3** sign on. **sign away** or **over** formally give up or transfer (one's rights, property, etc.) by signing a document. **signboard** *n* a board carrying a sign or notice. **sign in** record one's arrival by writing one's name and the time, esp. at a place of employment. **sign off 1** end a letter. **2** mark the end of a programme or transmission, esp. by playing a particular piece of music. **3** stop work for the day. **4** (of a doctor) sign a piece of paper

sideburns

Many of us no doubt suspect that the side in sideburns has some connection with the side of the face, where sideburns grow, but this is not so.

Sideburns is a very unusual type of transformed *eponym*. (See panel at **galvanize**.) The word is traceable to Ambrose Everett Burnside, 1824–81, a general who fought for the Union in the American Civil War. From the general's shaving habits came burnsides, the style of beard that comprised full side whiskers which joined the moustache. In time the side whiskers became less extensive, and more strangely, the two halves of the word became transposed.

to say that (a person) is not well enough to work. **sign on 1** engage or be engaged by signing a contract, etc.: City is just about to sign a new goalkeeper. **2** register as unemployed. **3** mark the beginning of a programme or transmission, esp. by playing a particular piece of music. **sign out** record one's departure by writing one's name and the time, esp. at a place of employment. **signpost** *n* **1** a post supporting one or more signs that indicate a place, direction, distance, etc. **2** an indication, token, or clue. < Latin *signum*.

signal (ˈsɪgnl̩) *n* **1** a sign or gesture: Wait for the signal to start. **2** a sign that triggers a reaction: The minister's arrival was the signal for us to stand. **3** a conventional sign used to give notice or warning: traffic signals. **4** a variable parameter containing and conveying information in an electronic system.
• *vb* **signalled; signalling 1** communicate by means of one or more signals. **2** make one or more signals.
• *adj* (*formal*) notable or conspicuous: a signal success. **signaller** *n* **signally** *adv* **signal-box** *n* a railway building operating the signals in its area. **signalize** *vb* make noteworthy. < SEE **SIGN.**

signatory (ˈsɪgnətrɪ) *n* a person who signs a document jointly with other parties. < Latin *signare* to sign.

signature (ˈsɪgnətʃə) *n* **1** a person's name or initials as written by that person. **2** a distinguishing or characteristic mark or sign. **3** the act of signing one's name. **4** a sign in music used to indicate key or tempo. **signature tune** a tune used habitually to introduce and identify a particular programme or performer. < Latin *signare* to sign.

signet (ˈsɪgnɪt) *n* a person's seal. **signet ring** a finger ring engraved with a signet or seal. < Middle French *signe* seal.

signify (ˈsɪgnɪˌfaɪ) *vb* **1** mean or convey: What does their silence signify? **2** make known by one or more signs: signify one's indifference. **3** matter: What does it signify if they refuse the offer? **significance** *n* **1** meaning: We don't understand its significance. **2** importance: Don't underestimate the significance of their approval. **significant** *adj* **1** having a (special) meaning: a significant smile. **2** important or notable: a significant victory. **significantly** *adv* **signification** *n* meaning. < Latin *significare*.

Sikh (siːk) *n, adj* (an adherent) of a monotheistic religion of India. **Sikhism** *n* < Hindi: disciple.

silage (ˈsaɪlɪdʒ) *n* green fodder stored and fermented in a silo for use as cattle feed. < short for *ensilage*.

silence (ˈsaɪləns) *n* **1** the state of being silent; stillness. **2** avoidance of speaking or making a noise: Silence in the classroom! **3** failure to mention something in particular.
• *vb* make silent. **silencer** *n* a device that reduces the noise made by a vehicle's exhaust, a gun, etc. **silent** *adj* **1** free from sound or noise. **2** not speaking or making a noise. **3** without mention of something in particular: The opposition remains silent on the issue. **silently** *adv* **silent majority** a majority who do not express or assert their opinions. < Latin *silens*.

silhouette (ˌsɪluːˈɛt) *n* **1** a drawing of the profile of a person or object that is filled in usually with solid black; similar profile drawing that is cut out of black paper and mounted on a light background. **2** a profile as it appears against a lighter background.
• *vb* cause to appear in silhouette. < Etienne de *Silhouette*, died 1767, French politician.

silica (ˈsɪlɪkə) *n* a hard, white mineral found esp. in quartz, used in the manufacture of glass, ceramics, etc. < Latin *silex* quartz.

silicon (ˈsɪlɪkən) *n* a non-metallic element that is very abundant in the earth's crust. < SEE **SILICA.**

silk (sɪlk) *n* **1** a fine, strong, soft fibre produced by a silkworm for its cocoon. **2** the thread or cloth made from this. **silken** *adj* **1** made of silk. **2** resembling silk. **silkworm** *n* a caterpillar (from the larva of a Chinese moth) that feeds on the leaves of the mulberry tree and produces silk fibre for its cocoon. **silky** *adj* resembling silk. < Old English *seolc*.

sill (sɪl) *n* a length of wood, metal, or stone that runs along the bottom of a window, door, etc. < Old English *syll*.

silly (ˈsɪlɪ) *adj* **1** lacking common sense; foolish: a silly decision. **2** frivolous; playful: Children do like to be silly. **3** stunned; senseless.
• *n* a silly person. **sillily** *adv* **silliness** *n* < Old English *sǣl* happiness. SEE PANEL.

silo (ˈsaɪləʊ) *n, pl* **silos 1** a pit or tower-like structure for making and storing silage. **2** an underground launching-pad for a guided missile. < perhaps of Celtic origin.

silt (sɪlt) *n* an earth-like sediment deposited by a river, lake, etc.
• *vb* block or become blocked with silt. < probably Scandinavian.

silver (ˈsɪlvə) *n* **1** a soft, greyish-white, precious metal that is used for jewellery, cutlery, etc. **2** coins made of this metal or of an alloy that resembles it. **3** silverware. **4** the greyish-white colour of this metal. **5** a medal (of silver) awarded to the runner-up in a contest or race.
• *adj* **1** made of, containing, or plated with silver. **2** resembling silver in colour, sheen, etc. **3** the 25th anniversary of: silver wedding.
• *vb* **1** coat or plate with silver or silver-like substance. **2** become the colour of silver. **silver birch** the common birch, characterized by its white bark. **silver-fish** *n* a small, wingless insect with a body like a fish, found in damp places. **silver foil** or **paper** tin foil. **silver lining** something that provides consolation or hope, esp. following adversity. **silverside** *n* a cut of beef from the haunch. **silversmith** *n* a person whose job is making things with silver. **silverware** *n* cutlery, candlesticks, etc., made of silver or something resembling silver. **silvery** *adj* **1** having the colour or sheen of silver. **2** having a soft but clear ringing sound: a silvery voice. < Old English *seolfor*.

similar (ˈsɪmɪlə) *adj* **1** like or resembling. **2** roughly equal in amount, value, etc.: a similar price. **similarity** *n* **similarly** *adv* < Latin *similis*.

simile (ˈsɪmɪlɪ) *n* a figure of speech which draws an explicit comparison. < SEE **SIMILAR**.

simmer (ˈsɪmə) *vb* **1** boil gently. **2** be just in control of some suppressed emotion: simmer with anger. **simmer down** become calm or calmer. < origin uncertain.

simper (ˈsɪmpə) *vb* smile in an affected way.
• *n* an affected smile. **simperer** n **simperingly** *adv* < probably Dutch *simper* affected.

simple (ˈsɪmpl̩) *adj* **1** not difficult to do or understand: a simple question. **2** not showy or ornate; plain: a simple dress. **3** not complex or subdivided: a simple machine. **4** pure; mere: the simple truth. **5** of humble rank or low status: of simple birth. **6** naïve and easily cheated: You're just too simple for words. **7** feeble-minded: He's always been a bit simple. **simply** *adv* **simple interest** interest paid only on the original amount. **simpleton** *n* a person lacking common sense. **simplicity** *n* the state or quality of being simple. **simplify** *vb* **simplified; simplifying** make simple or more simple. < Latin *simplex* plain. SEE PANEL AT **SHEER**[1].

simulate (ˈsɪmjʊˌleɪt) *vb* **1** reproduce the conditions or circumstances of: simulate a telephone conversation. **2** pretend to have, feel, etc.: simulate illness. **3** have the appearance of; imitate. **simulator** *n* **simulated** *adj* made so as to have the appearance of; artificial: simulated leather. **simulation** *n* < Latin *simulare* to copy.

simultaneous (ˌsɪməlˈteɪnɪəs) *adj* occurring or operating at the same time. **simultaneity** *n* **simultaneously** *adv* < Latin *simul* at the same time.

sin (sɪn) *n* **1** a transgression of a religious or moral law: free of sin. **2** an offence; misdeed. **3** something considered to be wasteful, unjust, or undesirable.
• *vb* **sinned; sinning** commit a sin. **sinful** *adj* wrong or wicked. **sinfully** *adv* **sinfulness** *n* **sinner** *n* < Old English *synn*.

since (sɪns) *conj* **1** seeing that; as: Since you're going out, would you mind posting this letter? **2** from a previous time until now: Since I've been living in London, I've made a lot of friends. **3** at some time after a previous time and before now: Since agreeing to come, they've changed their minds.
• *adv* **1** from a previous time until now: I saw her last Tuesday but I haven't seen her since. **2** at some time after a previous time and before now: They have since decided to look elsewhere. **3** ago: The decision was made long since.
• *prep* **1** from a previous time until now: They've been working since I arrived. **2** at some

silly

Silly has not always been a term of disparagement. On the contrary, the origin of the word is believed to be the Old English *sǣlig*, meaning 'happy' or 'blessed'. By the 15th century the primary sense had changed to 'innocent'. This soon gathered strong negative connotations, resulting in the new meanings, 'naïve' or 'simple'. The degeneration of the word has continued over the years, culminating in today's meaning of 'foolish'.

Interestingly, the Old High German equivalent, sālig 'happy', has for some reason avoided such decline; *selig*, its Modern German descendant, means 'blessed'.

time after a previous time and before now: Since Thursday there has been a change of plan. **3** from the time of (the invention, etc., of something): It's the best thing we've produced since sliced bread. < Old English *siththan*, from *sith* since + *thæt* that.

sincere (sɪnˈsɪə) *adj* free from deceit or pretence; genuine: sincere intentions. **sincerely** *adv* **sincerity** *n* < Latin *sincerus*.

sine (saɪn) *n* (of a right-angled triangle) the ratio of the length of a side opposite an acute angle to the hypotenuse. < Latin *sinus* curve.

sinecure (ˈsaɪnɪˌkjʊə) *n* a well-paid, official position involving little work. < Medieval Latin (*beneficium*) *sine cura* (benefice) without cure of souls.

sinew (ˈsɪnjuː) *n* a tough cord that joins muscle to bone; tendon. **sinewy** *adj* **1** having sinews; muscular. **2** (of meat) tough and stringy. < Old English *seono*.

sing (sɪŋ) *vb* **sang; sung; singing** **1** make musical sounds with the voice. **2** perform (a song). **3** perform songs as an occupation. **4** make a buzzing or whistling sound: The arrow sang past his ear. **5** proclaim enthusiastically: sing someone's praises. **6** celebrate or tell a story about in song or verse. **singer** *n* **sing out** (*informal*) shout or call: Sing out if you want anything. < Old English *singan*. SEE PANEL.

singe (sɪndʒ) *vb* **1** burn the surface of; scorch. **2** burn the ends of: singed hair. • *n* a superficial burn. < Old English *sengan*.

single (ˈsɪŋgl̩) *adj* **1** one only; often used emphatically: She couldn't give me a single example. **2** designed or suitable for one person only: a single bed. **3** unmarried. **4** not accompanied; solitary: There were just two single survivors. **5** individual: Every single person was questioned. **6** (of a ticket) valid for an outward journey only. **7** composed of one part or unit; composed of the normal number of: a single whisky. • *n* **1** one person or thing. **2** a room in a hotel, etc., for one person. **3** a ticket for an outward journey only. **4** a short gramophone record. **singly** *adv* **single-action** *adj* (of a gun, camera, etc.) needing to be cocked again before firing. **single-breasted** *adj* (of a garment) having a centre fastening with little overlap and just one row of buttons. **single-decker** *n* a bus with only one deck. **single figures** any number below 10. **single file** a line of people or things arranged one behind the other. **single-handed** *adj* without help from anybody. **single-minded** *adj* having just one goal, cause, or purpose. **single out** select deliberately from others. **single parent** a parent without a partner. **singles** *pl n* a game with just one player on each side. < Latin *singulus* one only.

singlet (ˈsɪŋglɪt) *n* **1** a vest. **2** a sleeveless or short-sleeved garment, worn esp. by athletes. < *single*.

singsong (ˈsɪŋˌsɒŋ) *adj* having a monotonous rising and falling of tone. • *n* an informal session of group singing.

singular (ˈsɪŋgjʊlə) *n* the form of a word when it refers to one person or thing. • *adj* **1** of this form: 'Man' takes a singular verb. **2** (*formal*) extraordinary; exceptional: a man of singular ability. **singularity** *n* **singularly** *adv* < Latin *singulus* only one.

sinister (ˈsɪnɪstə) *adj* threatening or suggestive of harm, evil, or misfortune; treacherous: sinister motives. < Latin *sinister* on the left-hand side, unlucky. SEE PANEL.

sink (sɪŋk) *vb* **sank; sunk; sinking** **1** go down in level. **2** fall slowly: He sank to his knees. **3** go or cause to go beneath the surface of a liquid: This ship will never sink! **4** drill or dig a hole or channel for: sink a cable. **5** invest (capital). **6** hit (a ball) into a hole or pocket. **7** slowly fail in health or strength. **8** penetrate or cause to penetrate: It sank its teeth into his leg. **9** seep: The pool of water quickly sank into the soil. **10** become depressed or hollow: His cheeks seem to have sunk. **11** look miserable:

sing

Some speakers of English might object if they were told that they spoke through their noses. However, to a degree this is true of everyone. The English sound system includes three sounds which are produced by air being expelled through the nose. These comprise the *m* sound in words like moth and come, the *n* sound in words like no and bin, and the *ng* sound in words like sing and longing.

Anyone who disbelieves this should try to pronounce any of the above words while pinching the nose between thumb and forefinger.

Her face sank at the news.

• *n* a permanent basin, usually connected to a water supply and drainage system in a kitchen. **sinker** *n* a weight used to sink a fishing-line, etc. **sink in** be understood : The sentence took a long time to sink in. **sinking-fund** *n* a fund that is set up to repay a long-term debt when it falls due. < Old English *sincan.*

sinuous (ˈsɪnjʊəs) *adj* curving in and out. **sinuously** *adv* < SEE **SINUS.**

sinus (ˈsaɪnəs) *n* a cavity in a bone of the skull that connects with the nostrils: blocked sinuses. **sinusitis** *n* inflammation of this cavity. < Latin *sinus* curve.

sip (sɪp) *vb* **sipped; sipping** drink (esp. a hot drink) very slowly by taking small mouthfuls.

• *n* **1** a small mouthful of liquid. **2** an act of sipping. < Middle English *sippen.*

siphon, syphon (ˈsaɪfn̩) *n* **1** a bent tube through which a liquid can be transferred by means of atmospheric pressure from one container to a lower one. **2** a bottle from which aerated water may be forced by means of gas pressure.

• *vb* **1** draw off by means of a siphon. **2** draw off or remove from a larger source, often illicitly. < Greek *siphōn.*

sir (sə; *stressed* sɜː) *n* a polite way of addressing a man: Can I help you, sir? **Sir** *n* a title prefixed to the name of a knight or baronet. < *sire.*

sire (saɪə) *n* **1** the male parent of an animal, esp. a horse or dog. **2** (in former times) a respectful way of addressing a king.

• *vb* (of a horse, dog, etc.) be the sire of. < ultimately Latin *senex* old man.

siren (ˈsaɪərən) *n* **1** a device that produces a very loud, high-pitched noise, esp. as a warning or distress signal. **2** a dangerously seductive or alluring woman. < Greek *seirēn.*

sirloin (ˈsɜːˌlɔɪn) *n* a cut of beef from the upper part of the loin. < Middle French *surlonge,* from *sur* over + *loigne* loin. SEE PANEL.

sissy (ˈsɪsɪ) *n* **1** (*derogatory*) an effeminate boy or man. **2** a cowardly person. < *sis,* short for *sister.*

sister (ˈsɪstə) *n* **1** a daughter of the same parents as another child. **2** a senior nurse, esp. one in charge of a hospital ward. **3** a female who has a bond or tie with another, esp. a fellow member of a group. **4** a member of any of several religious orders of women; nun.

• *adj* closely similar in design, function, etc.: a sister school. **sisterly** *adv* **sisterhood** *n* **1** a group or order of women formed for religious, charitable, etc., purposes. **2** the state of being a sister. **sister-in-law** *n, pl* **sisters-in-law** the sister of one's husband or wife; wife of one's brother. < Old English *sweoster.*

sit (sɪt) *vb* **sat; sitting 1** rest or cause to rest on the buttocks or hindquarters. **2** lie, rest, or be positioned: The lamp sat right in the middle of the table. **3** (of birds) perch. **4** enter as a candidate for (an examination). **5** pose for an artist. **6** (of a bird) cover eggs with the body in order to hatch them. **7** (of Parliament, law-courts, committees, etc.) be in session. **8** (of a garment) fit or hang (in a certain way). **9** remain unused or inactive: The computer's still sitting in the cupboard. **10** keep watch over a baby, invalid, etc. **sit back** relax and do nothing, esp. after working hard or when there is the opportunity to help. **sit by** observe without taking action. **sit in 1** occupy (a part of) a building as a

sinister

Something which threatens evil or harm is often described as sinister. To Roman literati, from whose writings we took the word, sinister meant 'on the left-hand side' or 'inauspicious'. These two meanings went hand in hand. According to Greek tradition, unfavourable omens would always appear on the left of a north-facing soothsayer, while favourable ones would appear on his right. Although these directions were disputed by Roman augurs, the men of letters followed the Greek line on the issue.

sirloin

A cut of beef from the upper part of the hind loin is known as sirloin. This name derives from the Middle French *surlonge,* from *sur* 'over' and *loigne* 'loin'.

The change from sur to sir was reputedly the outcome of a number of reports about the word's origin. In each account a British monarch is said to have been so impressed with the quality of the cut in question that, with a mock-heroic gesture, he invested it with a knighthood, pronouncing Arise, *Sir Loin.*

protest. **2** act as a substitute: The chairman is ill, so I'll be sitting in for him. **sit-in** *n* **sit in on** attend (a meeting, course, etc.) without taking an active part in it. **sit on 1** delay taking action on. **2** serve as an official member of (a committee, etc.). **3** repress or subdue, esp. for being rude or unruly. **sit out 1** not dance to a piece of music. **2** stay until the end of a play, recital, etc., esp. with reluctance. **sit up 1** not go to bed. **2** become alert and pay attention. < Old English *sittan.* SEE PANEL.

sitar (sɪˈtɑː) *n* an Indian lute with a long neck and movable frets. < Hindi *sitār.*

site (saɪt) *n* **1** the area of ground on which something stood, stands, or will stand. **2** an area of ground used for a particular activity: a caravan site. **3** location.
• *vb* provide with a site or location. < Latin *sinere* to be placed.

sitter (ˈsɪtə) *n* **1** a baby-sitter. **2** a person sitting for a portrait artist. **3** a hen sitting on its eggs.

sitting (ˈsɪtɪŋ) *n* **1** a period of being seated or in session. **2** the serving of an entire meal in a canteen, refectory, etc. **sitting duck** (*informal*) an easy target or helpless victim. **sitting-room** *n* a living-room. **sitting tenant** a tenant in occupation of rented accommodation when there is a change of owner.

situate (ˈsɪtjʊˌeɪt) *vb* provide with a location.
• *adj* (*formal*) situated; located. **situated** *adj* having a particular position or location: The new offices are situated right in the city centre. **situation** *n* **1** position or location. **2** a set of circumstances: What would you do in my situation? **3** a job. < Latin *situs.*

six (sɪks) *determiner, pron* 6 in number.
• *n* the number 6. **at sixes and sevens** in confusion or disorder. < Old English *siex.* SEE PANEL.

sixteen (ˌsɪkˈstiːn) *determiner, pron* 16 in number.
• *n the number* 16. **sixteenth** *determiner, pron, n, adv* < Old English *sixtȳne.*

sixth (sɪksθ) *determiner, pron, adv* next after fifth.
• *n* **1** one of six equal parts. **2** something that is sixth. **sixthly** *adv* **sixth form** the most senior form in a secondary school. **sixth sense** a means of perception in addition to the five basic senses; intuition.

sixty (ˈsɪkstɪ) *determiner, pron* 60 in number.
• *n* the number 60. **sixtieth** *determiner, pron, n, adv* **sixties** *pl n* the years, numbers, degrees, etc., between 60 and 69. < Old English *siextig.*

size[1] (saɪz) *n* **1** measurements or dimensions. **2** any of a series of categories graduated according to measurement: What size do you take?
• *vb* grade or group according to size. **sizable** *adj* fairly large. **size up** (*informal*) form an opinion or judgment of. < Old French *sise.*

size[2] *n* a glue-like solution used for sealing walls, etc.
• *vb* treat with size. < SEE SIZE[1].

sizzle (ˈsɪzl̩) *vb* **1** make a hissing sound like fat that is frying. **2** (*informal*) be very hot. < Middle English *sissen.*

skate[1] (skeɪt) *n* a boot fitted with a metal

sit-in

A sit-in is the occupation by a group of demonstrators of part of a building or other public place as a protest. The suffix -in has been adopted in the names of other public gatherings, for example: love-in, sing-in, teach-in, work-in.

at sixes and sevens

Idioms like at sixes and sevens which contain a number comprise a surprisingly large group; in fact, it could be said that they are practically ten a penny. Other examples of this group include:

dressed to the nines
put two and two together
one over the eight
kill two birds with one stone
the 64 thousand dollar question
two's company, three's a crowd
be six of one and half a dozen of the other
talk nineteen to the dozen
knock (someone or something) for six
look after number one
ten to one
at the eleventh hour
as thick as two short planks
nine times out of ten
thanks a million

runner or small wheels for gliding over ice or a flat surface.
• *vb* move or perform on skates. **skater** *n* **skateboard** *n* a board fitted with small wheels for gliding over smooth surfaces. **skateboarder** *n* **skate over** avoid dealing with; treat lightly. < Dutch *schaats.*

skate[2] *n, pl* **skate** or **skates** any of a group of flat, edible rays. < Old Norse *skata.*

skein (skeɪn) *n* a loose coil of yarn, thread, etc. < Middle French *escaigne.*

skeleton (ˈskɛlɪtən) *n* **1** the bone framework of the head and body of an animal. **2** any supporting framework. **3** (*informal*) a very thin person or animal. **4** a basic outline. **skeletal** *adj* **skeleton key** a key which will open several different locks. < Greek *skeletos* dried up.

sketch (skɛtʃ) *n* **1** a hastily composed drawing or painting. **2** a brief account or rough outline. **3** a short theatrical episode forming part of a revue.
• *vb* make a sketch or sketches (of). **sketch-book** *n* a pad of paper used for sketching. **sketchy** *adj* superficial or incomplete; without detail: a sketchy account. **sketchily** *adv* **sketchiness** *n* < Dutch *schets,* from Italian *schizzare* to splash. SEE PANEL.

skew (skjuː) *adj* having an oblique direction or position.
• *vb* take or cause to take an oblique direction; twist. **on the skew** askew. < Middle English *skewen.*

skewbald (ˈskjuːˌbɔːld) *adj* having patches of white and another colour.
• *n* a horse with this marking. < *skewed* + *bald.*

skewer (ˈskjʊə) *n* a long pin for keeping meat together during roasting, etc.
• *vb* to pierce with a skewer or similar object. < English dialect *skiver.*

ski (skiː) *n* one of a pair of long, narrow strips of wood, metal, etc. attached to the feet for gliding over snow.
• *vb* move or travel on skis. **skier** *n* **ski-lift** *n* a powered towing or lifting device used for transporting skiers up a slope. < Old Norse *skīth.*

skid (skɪd) *vb* **skidded; skidding** (of a vehicle) slide uncontrollably due to loss of traction, esp. on ice.
• *n* **1** the act of skidding. **2** a runner forming part of the landing-gear of an aircraft. **3** a device placed against or under a wheel to prevent it from turning. **4** a log or timber for lifting, supporting, or moving heavy objects. **skid-pan** *n* a slippery surface on which drivers learn how to control skidding. **skid row** (*US*) a district frequented by vagrants and alcoholics. < perhaps Scandinavian.

skiff (skɪf) *n* a small, light boat for rowing or sculling. < of Germanic origin.

skill (skɪl) *n* ability to do something well. **skilful** *adj* having or showing great skill. **skilfully** *adv* **skilled** *adj* **1** having skill or training: a skilled worker. **2** of, for, or requiring workers with skill or training: a skilled job. < Old Norse *skil* distinction.

skim (skɪm) *vb* **skimmed; skimming** **1** remove from the top of a liquid. **2** glide or pass lightly across a surface. **3** read quickly for the main points only. **skim** or **skimmed milk** milk with the cream removed by skimming. < Middle English *skimmen.*

skimp (skɪmp) *vb* use or supply sparingly; work hastily and carelessly. **skimpy** *adj* inadequate or insufficient; scanty. **skimpily** *adv* **skimpiness** *n* < origin uncertain.

skin (skɪn) *n* **1** the thin tissue that forms the outer covering of a human or animal body. **2** the outermost layer of a vegetable, fruit, etc.: a banana skin. **3** a person's complexion. **4** any film or layer formed on a surface. **5** an animal skin, esp. one that has been removed from the body. **6** a container for water, wine, etc., made from animal skin.
• *vb* **skinned; skinning** **1** strip the skin from. **2** cover or become covered with new skin. **3** (*informal*) strip of money. **skin-deep** *adj* slight or superficial. **skin-diver** *n* a person who practises skin-diving. **skin-diving** *n* swimming under water with flippers, a mask, and breathing apparatus. **skinflint** *n* (*informal*) a miser. **skinhead** *n* a youth with

sketch

A rough preliminary drawing is known as a sketch. This word came into English in the 17th century from the Dutch *schets.*

In the 16th and 17th centuries the influence of the Low Countries upon European art was profound. Linguistic evidence of this lies in a small group of Dutch-derived fine-art terms which were borrowed at that time. In addition to sketch these include easel, etch, landscape, and manikin (originally an anatomical model used in art and medical instruction).

close cropped hair and distinctive clothes. **skinny** *adj* very thin. **skin-tight** *adj* (of a garment) very close fitting. Old Norse *skinn.* SEE PANEL.

skint (skɪnt) *adj* (*informal*) penniless. *skinned.*

skip[1] (skɪp) *vb* **skipped; skipping** **1** move with light leaps and bounds. **2** jump in time with the turns of a skipping-rope. **3** pass quickly from one point to another. **4** not bother to deal with; omit: You can skip the introductions. **5** (*informal*) leave hastily or secretly. • *n* a light leap or bound. **skipping-rope** *n* a length of rope that is rotated and jumped over either in play or for exercise. < Middle English *skippen.*

skip[2] *n* **1** a large, metal container for rubble, etc. **2** a cage or bucket for raising and lowering men or materials, esp. in a mine. < *skep,* from Old Norse *skeppa* bushel.

skipper (ˈskɪpə) *n* a captain. • *vb* be captain of. < Middle Dutch *schipper.*

skirmish (ˈskɜːmɪʃ) *n* a minor engagement in war. • *vb* take part in a skirmish. < of Germanic origin.

skirt (skɜːt) *n* **1** (a part of) a girl's or woman's garment that hangs from the waist down. **2** a cut of beef taken from the lower flank. **3** (*informal*) a teenage girl or young woman. **4** the flap round the base of a hovercraft. • *vb* **1** go or be situated along the border of. **2** bypass or avoid: I managed to skirt the subject. **skirting board** the wooden board that runs along the bottom of an inside wall. < Old Norse *skyrta* shirt.

skit (skɪt) *n* a brief, dramatic sketch containing humorous or satirical mimicry. < origin unknown.

skittish (ˈskɪtɪʃ) *adj* **1** frivolous; irresponsible. **2** easily frightened; nervous: a skittish horse. **skittishly** *adv* **skittishness** *n* < Middle English.

skittle (ˈskɪtl̩) *n* one of several wooden pins used in skittles. **skittles** *n* a game in which wooden pins are stood up in a group in order to be bowled over. < origin unknown.

skive (skaɪv) *vb* (*informal*) shirk one's duties. **skive off** (*informal*) absent oneself in order to avoid a duty. **skiver** *n* < Scandinavian.

skivvy (ˈskɪvɪ) *n* (*derogatory*) a female domestic servant. < origin unknown.

skulduggery (skʌlˈdʌgərɪ) *n* unscrupulous behaviour; trickery. < origin unknown.

skulk (skʌlk) *vb* move stealthily; lurk. < Scandinavian.

skull (skʌl) *n* **1** the bone framework of the head of an animal. **2** (*derogatory*) the brain. **skull and crossbones** a representation of the human skull above two crossed bones, used as a warning of great danger. **skull-cap** *n* a small, close fitting cap with no peak. < Scandinavian.

skunk (skʌŋk) *n* **1** an American mammal related to the weasel, capable of forcibly ejecting a foul-smelling secretion. **2** (*informal*) a contemptible person. < Algonquian.

sky (skaɪ) *n* **1** the upper atmosphere; firmament. **2** weather: a clear sky. **3** heaven. • *vb* **skied; skying** hit (a ball) high into the air. **sky-blue** *adj, n* (having) the light blue colour of a clear sky. **sky-diving** *n* the sport of jumping from an aircraft and dropping a long way before opening a parachute. **sky-diver** *n* **sky-high** *adj, adv* very high: Prices have rocketed sky-high. **skylight** *n* a window set into a roof, ceiling, etc. **skyscraper** *n* a very tall multi-storey building. < Old Norse *ský.*

skin

When used in the context of fruit and vegetables, skin and peel have virtually the same meaning: 'an outer covering'. And yet although we say banana skin, we do not say banana peel. On the other hand, although we say orange peel, we do not say orange skin. This shows that in English, as in all other languages, there are silent rules governing the range of words with which any particular word may occur. These are known as the rules of *collocation.* On account of these rules we find that even words with compatible meanings, like banana and peel, are not always allowed to go together. Other examples include:

strong coffee (not powerful coffee)
tall women (not high women)
bacon *rind* (not bacon skin)
great difficulty (not large difficulty)

skylark (ˈskaɪˌlɑːk) *n* a lark noted for its song and soaring flight habit.
• *vb* play about boisterously or mischievously; frolic.

slab (slæb) *n* a broad, flat piece of stone, chocolate, etc. < Middle English *slabbe*.

slack[1] (slæk) *adj* **1** not tight or taut; loose. **2** careless; negligent. **3** sluggish or slow; listless: a pretty slack pace. **4** not busy or active: Business has been a bit slack recently.
• *n* the slack part of anything: Wind in the slack.
• *vb* **1** slacken. **2** be lazy or negligent. **slacken** *vb* make or become slack. **slacker** *n* **slackly** *adv* **slackness** *n* **slacks** *pl n* trousers for casual or sports wear. < Old English *sleac*.

slack[2] *n* the dust and small pieces that remain after coal is screened. < Middle English *sleck*.

slag (slæg) *n* the waste remaining after the smelting of ores and the removal of metal from them. < Middle Low German *slagge*.

slain (sleɪn) SEE **SLAY**.

slalom (ˈslɑːləm) *n* a race in and out of a series of obstacles, either on skis or in a canoe. < Norwegian: sloping track.

slam (slæm) *vb* **slammed; slamming** **1** shut forcefully and noisily. **2** put down or strike against violently and noisily. **3** (*informal*) criticize severely.
• *n* a slamming noise made on impact. < probably Scandinavian.

slander (ˈslɑːndə) *n* a false statement that tends to injure a person's reputation.
• *vb* utter a slanderous statement about. **slanderous** *adj* containing slander. **slanderously** *adv* **slanderousness** *n* < Old French *esclandre*. SEE PANEL.

slang (slæŋ) *n* **1** words and phrases restricted to very informal usage. **2** words and phrases indicative of group membership; jargon.
• *vb* attack with abusive language. **slangy** *adj* **slanging-match** *n* a protracted exchange of abusive language. < origin unknown.

slant (slɑːnt) *vb* **1** slope or lean at an angle. **2** present from a biased point of view: The story had been slanted to show him in a favourable light.
• *n* **1** a sloping line, direction, etc. **2** the point of view determining the way something is presented. < Scandinavian.

slap (slæp) *vb* **slapped; slapping** **1** strike with the open hand. **2** put down, on, or against violently or carelessly: slap the paint on the wall.
• *n* a sharp blow, esp. with the open hand.
• *adv* (*informal*) directly: He ran slap into the arms of a policeman. **slapdash** *adj, adv* lacking care and attention to detail. **slap-happy** *adj* careless, carefree, or irresponsible. **slapstick** *n* comedy that exploits horseplay and simple practical jokes. **slap-up** *adj* (*informal*) lavish or extravagant; first-class: a slap-up meal. < Low German *slapp*.

slash (slæʃ) *vb* **1** cut with violent, sweeping strokes, esp. with a knife, sword, etc. **2** cut a slit in. **3** reduce (prices, etc.) considerably.
• *n* **1** a long slit or cut. **2** a sweeping stroke or blow. < possibly Middle French *esclachier* to break.

slat (slæt) *n* one of a series of narrow strips of wood, plastic, etc., as used in a blind, louvre door, etc. < Old French *esclater* to splinter.

slate (sleɪt) *n* **1** a dense, smooth rock that splits easily into thin layers. **2** a roofing tile made of slate. **3** a writing tablet, usually made of slate.
• *vb* **1** roof with slate. **2** (*informal*) criticize severely. < Middle French *esclat* splinter.

slaughter (ˈslɔːtə) *n* **1** the butchering of animals for food. **2** ruthless destruction of lives. **3** (*informal*) an ignominious defeat.
• *vb* **1** butcher (animals) for food. **2** kill ruthlessly. **3** (*informal*) defeat ignominiously. **slaughterer** *n* **slaughterhouses** *n* a place where animals are butchered. < Scandinavian.

slave (sleɪv) *n* **1** a person who is the property of another. **2** a person who works very hard for another. **3** a person unable to resist an influence or appeal: be a slave to one's work. **4** a mechanism that is triggered or controlled by another mechanism.

slander or **libel?**

Both slander and libel refer to defamatory statements. The difference is that slander refers to spoken statements, libel to written statements. To remember the difference, it may help to pair libel with library (associated with written language) and slander with slang (associated with spoken language).

• *vb* work very hard. **slave-driver** *n* a person who forces another to work very hard. **slavery** *n* **1** the condition of being a slave. **2** the custom of owning slaves. **3** very hard work; drudgery. **slavish** *adj* **1** excessively submissive; servile. **2** showing no freedom of choice or judgment. **slavishly** *adv* **slavishness** *n* < Medieval Latin *Sclavus* Slav.
SEE PANEL.

slaver (ˈslævə) *vb* have saliva running from the mouth; slobber. < Scandinavian.

slay (sleɪ) *vb* **slew; slain; slaying** kill, esp. ruthlessly. **slayer** *n* < Old English *slēan.*

sleazy (ˈsliːzɪ) *adj* (*informal*) shabby or dirty; squalid. **sleaziness** *n* < origin unknown.

sledge[1] (slɛdʒ) *n* **1** a vehicle on two runners that is pulled by reindeer, dogs, etc., over snow and ice. **2** a toboggan.
• *vb* ride or transport on a sledge.
< Dutch dialect *sleedse.*

sledge[2] *n* a sledge-hammer. < Old English *slecg.*

sledge-hammer (ˈslɛdʒˌhæmə) *n* a large, heavy hammer with a long handle, used with both hands.

sleek (sliːk) *adj* **1** (of hair, fur, etc.) smooth and glossy. **2** well-fed or well-groomed; prosperous-looking. **3** suave or stylish.
• *vb* make smooth and glossy. **sleekly** *adv* **sleekness** *n* < Middle English *sliken.*

sleep (sliːp) *n* **1** the regularly recurring, natural condition of unconsciousness. **2** a period spent sleeping: Have a good sleep. **3** a period of dormancy or hibernation. **4** (*literary*) death.
• *vb* **slept; sleeping 1** be asleep. **2** be dormant or inactive. **3** provide sleeping accommodation for: The cottage sleeps four. **4** pass (time) sleeping. **5** (*literary*) be dead. **sleep around** be sexually promiscuous. **sleeper** *n* **1** a person or animal that sleeps (in a particular manner): a heavy sleeper. **2** a sleeping-car. **3** one of the beams that support railway lines. **4** a ring worn in a pierced ear to prevent the hole from closing. **sleep in** sleep until later than usual. **sleeping-bag** *n* a large, warm bag for sleeping in, esp. when camping. **sleeping-car** *n* a railway carriage equipped with sleeping berths. **sleeping partner** a person who invests money in something but takes no active part in running it. **sleeping-pill** *n* a pill that induces sleep. **sleepless** *adj* unable to sleep; without sleep: a sleepless night. **sleeplessly** *adv* **sleeplessness** *n* **sleep off** get rid of (something unpleasant) by sleeping. **sleep on** consider (a matter) before making a decision: I'll sleep on it and let you know tomorrow. **sleep together** have sexual relations. **sleepwalk** *vb* walk about while asleep. **sleepwalker** *n* **sleepwalking** *n* **sleep with** have sexual relations with. **sleepy** *adj* **1** ready or desiring to sleep. **2** quiet and inactive: a sleepy village. **sleepily** *adv* **sleepiness** *n* **sleepyhead** *n* (*humorous*) a sleepy person. < Old English *slæp.*

slave

The Medieval Latin name for a Slav was *Sclavus*. However, in the Middle Ages a large number of Slavonic peoples in central Europe were conquered and held in bondage. The name *Sclavus* thereby acquired the extended meaning of 'slave'.

Sclave entered English in the 13th century via the Old French *esclave*.

sleet (sliːt) *n* a mixture of rain and snow or rain and hail.
• *vb* (of sleet) fall. < Middle English *slete.*

sleeve (sliːv) *n* **1** the part of a garment covering the arm. **2** (of machines) a tubular part that fits over another part. **3** the cover of a gramophone record. **4** anything that serves as a protective cover. **-sleeved** *adj* **sleeveless** *adj* without sleeves. < Old English *slīefe.*

sleigh (sleɪ) *n* a sledge.
• *vb* ride in a sleigh. < Dutch *slede.*

sleight (slaɪt) *n* **sleight of hand** dexterity in using the hands to perform conjuring tricks, etc. < Old Norse *slægr* sly.

slender (ˈslɛndə) *adj* **1** thin, slim, or narrow: a slender figure. **2** slight or scanty. **slenderly** *adv* **slenderness** *n* < Middle English *slendre.*

slept (slɛpt) SEE **SLEEP.**

sleuth (sluːθ) *n* (*informal*) a detective. < ultimately Old Norse *sloth* track, trail.

slew[1] (sluː) SEE **SLAY.**

slew[2] *vb* turn or swing in a certain direction. < origin unknown.

slice (slaɪs) *n* **1** a thin, flat piece cut from something. **2** (*informal*) a share or portion: a slice of the takings. **3** a kitchen utensil with a broad, flat blade for lifting bacon, fish, etc. **4** a stroke or shot in

golf, tennis, etc., which causes the ball to swerve away from the intended direction.
• *vb* **1** cut into slices. **2** cut (a slice) from a larger piece. **3** cut cleanly and easily: The blade sliced off the top of his finger. **4** hit (a ball) with a slice. **slicer** *n* < of Germanic origin.

slick (slɪk) *adj* **1** excessively suave, polished, or clever. **2** faultlessly arranged or executed; deft: a slick performance.
• *n* a slippery area, esp. an expanse of oil floating on the sea.
• *vb* make sleek or smooth. **slickly** *adv* **slickness** *n* < Middle English *sliken.*

slide (slaɪd) *vb* **slid; sliding 1** move or cause to move in continuous contact with a smooth surface: slide down the banisters. **2** move or go slyly or unobtrusively: He slid the money into his pocket. **3** gradually fall or lapse.
• *n* **1** the act of sliding. **2** a sloping apparatus for children to slide down; chute. **3** a transparency. **4** a small piece of glass on which something is placed for examination under a microscope. **5** a sliding part of a machine, musical instrument, etc. **6** a hair-slide. **slide-rule** *n* a device for making rapid calculations by means of logarithmic scales. **sliding scale** a scale which may be varied in response to fluctuations in some external factor. < Old English *slīdan.*

slight (slaɪt) *adj* **1** small in amount or extent: a slight difference. **2** slender or delicately built.
• *vb* speak badly of (a person); show insufficient attention or courtesy.
• *n* a snub, insult, or affront. **slighting** *adj* disparaging. **slightly** *adv* **slightness** *n* < Old Norse *slēttr* smooth.

slim (slɪm) *adj* **slimmer; slimmest 1** of slender build. **2** small or scanty: a slim chance.
• *vb* **slimmed; slimming** try to make oneself slimmer by dieting, etc. **slimmer** *n* a person who slims. **slimly** *adv* **slimness** *n* < Middle Dutch *slimp* crooked.

slime (slaɪm) *n* **1** liquid mud. **2** any thick, slightly sticky fluid. **slimy** *adj* < Old English *slīm.*

sling (slɪŋ) *n* **1** a looped bandage passed around the neck to support an injured arm. **2** a strap, chain, etc., used for holding a heavy object being lifted, carried, etc. **3** a short strap with a string at either end, used for hurling stones.
• *vb* **slung; slinging 1** (*informal*) throw; fling. **2** hurl with a sling. **3** lift or suspend with a sling. < probably Old Norse *slyngva.*

slink (slɪŋk) *vb* **slunk; slinking 1** move stealthily or shamefacedly. **2** move in a sensual or provocative way. **slinky** *adj* **1** (*informal*) having a suave or provocative style. **2** having a slinking movement. < Old English *slincan* to creep.

slip[1] (slɪp) *vb* **slipped; slipping 1** lose one's footing or balance: She slipped and fell. **2** slide, escape, or fall from (one's grasp or from a secure position): The pen slipped. **3** go quietly and without drawing attention: She slipped out of the room. **4** get quickly into or out of an item of clothing: She slipped into her dress. **5** move smoothly: The yacht slipped through the waves. **6** put or be put with a quick, smooth movement: She slipped a coin into his pocket. **7** escape: It slipped my memory. **8** pass unnoticed or undone: He prefers to let it slip.
• *n* **1** a mistake; blunder: a slip in the calculations. **2** the act of slipping. **3** a woman's one-piece, sleeveless undergarment; petticoat. **4** a slipway. **5** a fieldsman in cricket. **slip in** introduce deftly into a conversation: I notice she managed to slip in the news of their engagement. **slipknot** *n* a knot that slips along the rope or line around which it is made. **slip-on** *adj* (of a garment) easy to put on or take off. **slipper** *n* a loose, light, low shoe for wearing in the house. **slippery** *adj* **1** having a surface that causes slipping or sliding. **2** untrustworthy; shifty: a slippery character. **slip-road** *n* a road that leaves or enters a motorway. **slipshod** *adj* careless; slovenly. **slipstream** *n* **1** a path of reduced air pressure immediately behind a rapidly moving vehicle. **2** a stream of air or water forced backward by a propeller. **slip up** make a mistake or blunder. **slip-up** *n* **slipway** *n* a ramp leading into the water, used for building and launching ships. < Middle English *slippen.*

slip[2] *n* **1** a small, printed form or paper. **2** a long, narrow strip of material. **3** a plant cutting used for grafting or planting. **4** a young, slender person: a mere slip of a girl. < Middle English *slippe.*

slip[3] *n* a liquid containing water and fine clay, used for coating pottery. < Old English *slypa* paste.

slit (slɪt) *n* a long, narrow cut or opening.
• *vb* **slit; slitting 1** make a slit in. **2** cut into narrow pieces. < Middle English *slitten.*

slither (ˈslɪðə) *vb* glide along unsteadily or like a snake. **slithery** *adj* < Old English *slīdan* to slide.

sliver (ˈslɪvə) *n* a splinter of glass, wood, etc. < Old English *-slīfan* to slice off.
slob (slɒb) *n* (*derogatory*) an uncouth person. **slobbish** *adj* < Irish *slab* mud.
slobber (ˈslɒbə) *vb* have saliva dribbling from the mouth; slaver. **slobber over** behave mawkishly towards. < Middle English *sloberen.*
slog (slɒg) *vb* **slogged; slogging 1** work hard. **2** walk or travel with laborious slowness; trudge. **3** hit hard.
• *n* **1** laboriously hard work: She finds homework a real slog. **2** a hefty blow. < origin unknown.
slogan (ˈsləʊgən) *n* a word or phrase associated by usage with a political party, commercial product, etc. < Scottish Gaelic *sluagh-ghairm* army cry.
sloop (slu:p) *n* a sailing vessel rigged fore-and-aft, with one mast. < Dutch *sloep.*
slop (slɒp) *vb* **slopped; slopping 1** spill over or cause to spill over the edge of a container. **2** serve, ladle, or pour (soup, etc.) carelessly.
• *n* **1** drink or liquid food that is thin and tasteless. **2** slopped liquid. **slops** *pl n* waste food that is fed to pigs and other animals; swill. **sloppy** *adj* **1** careless or slovenly. **2** (of a liquid) easily splashed. **3** mawkish. **sloppily** *adv* **sloppiness** *n* < probably Old English *sloppe* dung.
slope (sləʊp) *vb* **1** lie or cause to lie on a slant or incline. **2** follow a sloping path or course. **3** go stealthily. < Middle English *slope* obliquely.
slosh (slɒʃ) *vb* (*informal*) **1** pour, ladle, etc., in a clumsy way. **2** hit or strike: Do it again and I'll slosh you! **3** splash or move about vigorously in a liquid.
• *n* (*informal*) **1** the splash of liquid. **2** a hefty blow. **sloshed** *adj* (*informal*) drunk. < probably *slop* + *slush.*
slot (slɒt) *n* **1** a narrow groove or opening into which something fits. **2** a narrow opening through which something is pushed: Put another coin in the slot. **3** a (regular) position in a system or timetable.
• *vb* **slotted; slotting 1** put into a slot: Slot your money in. **2** be assembled by means of slots: I like the way the cabinet slots together. **3** make one or more slots in. **slot-machine** *n* a machine that is activated by pushing a coin or token into a slot. < origin unknown.
sloth (sləʊθ) *n* **1** laziness. **2** an animal of tropical America related to the armadillo, known for its slow movement. **slothful** *adj* lazy. **slothfully** *adv* **slothfulness** *n* < Middle English *slouthe.*
slouch (slaʊtʃ) *n* a lazy, drooping posture.
• *vb* stand, sit, walk, etc., with a slouch. < origin unknown.
slovenly (ˈslʌvənlɪ) *adj* careless and untidy in work, appearance, habits, etc. **slovenliness** *n* < perhaps Flemish *sloef* dirty.
slow (sləʊ) *adj* **1** less quick than average. **2** (of clocks, etc.) showing a time that is earlier than the actual time. **3** less quick to learn than average; dull. **4** lacking liveliness or interest; sluggish: Business is always slow on Mondays. **5** taking more than the usual time: a slow train. **6** having a design or qualities that do not allow quick progression: a slow, three-year course. **7** (of an oven) having a lower temperature. **8** (of photographic film) relatively less sensitive to light.
• *vb* reduce or cause to reduce in speed: The train slowed down.
• *adv* slowly. **slowly** *adv* **slowness** *n* **slowcoach** *n* (*informal*) a person who acts or thinks slowly. **slow motion** a filming technique whose visual effect is to make actions unnaturally slow. < Old English *slāw.*
sludge (slʌdʒ) *n* a thick mud or mud-like substance. < probably *slush.*
slug[1] (slʌg) *n* a small, slimy mollusc resembling a snail without a shell, regarded as a garden pest. < Scandinavian.
slug[2] *vb* **slugged; slugging** (*chiefly US informal*) strike hard, esp. with the fist.
• *n* a hard blow. < origin uncertain.
sluggish (ˈslʌgɪʃ) *adj* **1** slow in movement, flow, etc.: a sluggish stream. **2** lacking energy or liveliness: a sluggish feeling. **3** exhibiting a below normal response to treatment or stimulation. **sluggishly** *adv* **sluggishness** *n* < SEE SLUG[1].
sluice (slu:s) *n* **1** a channel or stream that carries away surplus water. **2** a gate or valve that controls the flow of this. **3** a long, inclined trough.
• *vb* **1** draw off through a sluice. **2** wash or rinse thoroughly with a flow of water. < Latin *excludere* to exclude.
slum (slʌm) *n* **1** a squalid house, flat, etc. **2** a squalid, run-down area of a city.
• *vb* **slummed; slumming** (*informal*) live in squalor. < origin unknown.
slumber (ˈslʌmbə) *vb* (*literary*) sleep.
• *n* (*literary*) sleep. < Old English *slūma.*
slump (slʌmp) *vb* **1** (of prices, etc.) fall dramatically. **2** (of people) flop down in a heap.
• *n* a sustained fall or decline.

< probably Scandinavian.
slung (slʌŋ) SEE **SLING.**
slunk (slʌŋk) SEE **SLINK.**
slur (slɜː) *vb* **slurred; slurring 1** run (words, sounds, musical notes, etc.) together so that they cannot be separately distinguished. **2** disparage.
• *n* **1** the act of slurring. **2** (a curved line indicating) the smooth and flowing performance of successive notes. **3** a disparaging remark. **4** a stain on one's reputation. **slur over** pass over without due mention or treatment. < probably Middle Low German.
slurp (slɜːp) *vb* make a noisy, sucking sound when drinking or eating.
• *n* this sound. < Dutch *slurpen.*
slush (slʌʃ) *n* **1** a mixture of melting snow, ice, and dirt. **2** (*informal*) sentimental talk or writing. **slushy** *adj* **slush fund** a secret fund for bribing officials, etc. < perhaps Scandinavian.
slut (slʌt) *n* a slovenly or promiscuous woman. **sluttish** *adj* **sluttishly** *adv* **sluttishness** *n* < Middle English *slutte.* SEE PANEL.
sly (slaɪ) *adj* **1** cunning and secretive: a sly manner. **2** roguish; mischievous: a sly smile. **slyly** *adv* **slyness** *n* **on the sly** secretly. < Old Norse *slǣgr* clever.

sluts and **slugs**

Generally, the pairing of a word and the thing or concept it stands for is purely arbitrary. Words that are *onomatopoeic* provide one major exception to this rule (see panel at **buzz**). Further, some speech sounds also have a symbolic meaning. In an experiment conducted by the US psychologist, Wolfgang Köhler (1887–1967), subjects were asked to assign the words takete and maluma to either of two geometric figures. One of the figures comprised a number of acute angles; the other flowing curves. The results of the experiment showed conclusively that takete was the name of something rather prickly, while maluma was the name of something smooth and rounded.

In English there are groups of words that seem to support Köhler's findings. Words like sleazy, slime, slovenly, sloppy, slut, sly, slug, and slush seem appropriate names for the things they represent. The reason for this, it is suggested, lies in the initial sl sound combination, which has associations with something wet and slippery or otherwise unpleasant.

smack[1] (smæk) *n* **1** a sharp slap or blow. **2** a noisy opening of the lips. **3** (*informal*) a loud kiss.
• *vb* slap or strike smartly.
• *adv* (*informal*) directly: The ball fell smack in the middle of the pond. < Middle Low German or Middle Dutch *smacken.*
smack[2] *n* a slight trace, suggestion, or flavour.
• *vb* have a slight trace, suggestion, or flavour. < Old English *smæc.*
smack[3] *n* a small inshore fishing vessel. < Low German *smack* or Dutch *smak.*
small (smɔːl) *adj* **1** less great or big than average: a small elephant. **2** little in amount, value, quantity, etc.: a small deposit. **3** young or immature: small children. **4** of minor importance: a small complaint. **5** operating on a minor scale: a small business. **6** petty: a small mind. **7** humble or humiliated: make someone feel small. **8** lower-case: small letters.
• *adv* into small pieces; in a small way.
• *n* a small part, esp. the narrowest part of the back. **smallness** *n* **small arms** firearms that are held in the hand when fired. **small change** coins of low value. **smallholder** *n* the owner or tenant of a smallholding. **smallholding** *n* a small farm. **small hours** the hours immediately after midnight. **small-minded** *adj* **1** limited in interests or outlook. **2** selfish; petty. **smallpox** *n* a contagious viral disease producing a rash which often leaves pock-marks. **small print** things written in small type at the bottom of an official document, esp. restrictive clauses. **smalls** *pl n* (*humorous*) underwear. **small-scale** *adj* **1** small in scope or operation. **2** (of a map) showing little detail. **small talk** casual conversation; chit-chat. **small-time** *adj* operating on a minor scale: a small-time thief. < Old English *smæl.* SEE PANEL AT **BIG.**
smarm (smɑːm) *vb* smear (hair-cream, make-up, etc.) profusely. **smarmy** *adj* excessively flattering or suave. **smarminess** *n* < origin unknown.
smart (smɑːt) *adj* **1** neat and tidy; stylish. **2** clever; intelligent: a smart pupil. **3** brisk or lively: a smart pace. **4** shrewd: a smart businessman. **5** stinging or sharp.
• *vb* **1** cause or feel a stinging pain. **2** feel mental distress.
• *n* **1** a stinging pain. **2** mental distress. **smartly** *adv* **smartness** *n* **smarten** *vb* make or become smart or smarter;

spruce : smarten oneself up for an interview. **smart aleck** (*informal*) a know-all. < Old English *smeortan.*

smash (smæʃ) *vb* **1** break or be broken into pieces: Who smashed the vase? **2** strike or cause to strike with great force; crash: The car smashed into a tree. **3** wreck or ruin; collapse: He's smashed his new car up. **4** hit (a ball, etc.) downwards with great force in tennis, etc. **5** defeat, overthrow, or destroy.
• *n* **1** the act or sound of smashing: It hit the floor with a smash. **2** a collision. **3** ruin; collapse. **4** a smash hit. **smash-and-grab** *adj, n* (a robbery) performed by breaking a shop-window and snatching valuables on display. **smasher** *n* (*informal*) an excellent or very attractive person or thing. **smashing** *adj* (*informal*) excellent. **smash hit** (*informal*) something outstandingly successful. < probably *smack* + *mash.*

smattering (ˈsmætərɪŋ) *n* a minimal or superficial knowledge: a smattering of German. < Middle English *smateren.*

smear (smɪə) *vb* **1** spread with oil, grease, etc.: Something keeps smearing the windscreen. **2** try to damage the reputation of.
• *n* **1** a mark made by smearing. **2** an attempt to damage a name or reputation. **3** material smeared on a slide for examination under a microscope. **smeary** *adj* < Old English *smeoru* grease.

smell (smɛl) *n* **1** the faculty of perceiving through the nose's sense organs. **2** something that is perceived by this faculty: the smell of the sea. **3** something perceived as unpleasant by this faculty; stink. **4** the act of smelling: Let's have a smell.
• *vb* **smelt, smelled; smelling 1** (try to) perceive the smell of. **2** emit (a particular kind of) smell: These flowers don't smell. **3** emit an unpleasant smell; stink. **smelling-salts** *pl n* a preparation which is sniffed to cure faintness, a headache, etc. **smelly** *adj* having an unpleasant smell. < Middle English *smellen.*

smelt[1] (smɛlt) SEE **SMELL.**

smelt[2] *vb* **1** melt (ore) to separate the metal it contains. **2** separate (metal) by smelting. **smelter** *n* < Dutch or Low German *smelten.*

smile (smaɪl) *n* a change of facial expression to express happiness, pleasure, etc., in which the corners of the mouth curve upwards.
• *vb* **1** give a smile; express by smiling. **2** look upon approvingly or sympathetically; favour. **smilingly** *adv* < Middle English *smilen.*

smirch (smɜːtʃ) *vb* **1** soil or stain. **2** bring discredit upon.
• *n* a smear; discredit. < Middle English *smorchen.*

smirk (smɜːk) *n* an affected or self-satisfied smile.
• *vb* give a smirk. < Old English *smearcian.*

smith (smɪθ) *n* a person who works with metal; blacksmith. < Old English. SEE PANEL AT **COOPER.**

smithereens (ˌsmɪðəˈriːnz) *pl n* (*informal*) tiny fragments: smashed to smithereens. < Irish Gaelic *smidirīn.*

smithy (ˈsmɪðɪ) *n* **1** a blacksmith. **2** the workshop of a smith.

smitten (ˈsmɪtn̩) *adj* **1** severely affected by (a disease, etc.). **2** in love: She seems to be fairly smitten with him. < *smite,* from Old English *smītan.*

smock (smɒk) *n* a long, loose garment resembling a shirt, worn over clothes. < Old English *smoc.*

smog (smɒg) *n* a mixture of fog, smoke, and fumes. **smoggy** *adj* < *smoke* + *fog.*

smoke (sməʊk) *n* **1** the visible gas produced by burning something containing carbon. **2** fumes, clouds, etc., resembling smoke. **3** (*informal*) the act of smoking a cigarette, etc. **4** (*informal*) a cigarette or cigar.
• *vb* **1** inhale and exhale the fumes of (a burning cigarette, etc.). **2** give off smoke or something like smoke. **3** cure and flavour (meat, fish, etc.) by drying in smoke. **4** (of a fire) send smoke out into the room instead of up the chimney. **5** colour or darken with smoke. **smokeless** *adj* **1** (of fuels) producing little or no smoke when burnt. **2** in which the production of smoke is illegal: a smokeless zone. **smoke out** drive out (from a concealed or defensive position) by means of smoke. **smoker** *n* **1** a person who smokes. **2** a compartment on a train, etc., in which smoking is allowed. **smokescreen** *n* **1** a dense wall of smoke used to conceal military activity. **2** anything which serves to conceal or disguise activities. **smoky** *adj* **1** emitting smoke profusely: a smoky chimney. **2** filled with smoke: a smoky room. **3** suggestive of smoke in taste, smell, or colour. < Old English *smoca.*

smooth (smuːð) *adj* **1** not rough or uneven. **2** not jarring or jolting: a smooth ride. **3** bland or mild: a smooth whisky. **4** without lumps: a smooth paste. **5** (*informal*) suave; glib; ingratiating:

smooth sales talk.
● *vb* **1** make or become smooth: smooth out the creases. **2** remove or cover up (dangers, difficulties, etc.). **smoothly** *adv* **smoothness** *n* < Old English *smōth*.

smother (ˈsmʌðə) *vb* **1** stifle or suffocate. **2** put out or subdue (a fire) by heaping ash, etc., on. **3** cover thickly or profusely; plaster: smothered in grease. **4** suppress or restrain. < Old English *smorian*.

smoulder (ˈsməʊldə) *vb* **1** burn and smoke slowly without flames. **2** burn inwardly with anger, etc.: Her eyes smouldered with jealousy. **3** (*literary*) exist in a suppressed state: His anger continued to smoulder. < Middle English *smolder*.

smudge (smʌdʒ) *n* a dirty or blurred mark made by erasing, touching wet ink, etc.
● *vb* **1** make or become blurred or smeared: The ink has smudged. **2** make a smudge on. < Middle English *smogen*.

smug (smʌg) *adj* **smugger; smuggest** highly self-satisfied. **smugly** *adv* **smugness** *n* < Middle Low German *smucken* to dress.

smuggle (ˈsmʌgl̩) *vb* **1** convey secretly: The books were smuggled out of the library. **2** import or export illegally. **smuggler** *n* < Low German *smuggeln* and Dutch *smokkelen*.

smut (smʌt) *n* **1** a particle of soot or dirt; black smudge made by this. **2** bawdy or indecent language, jokes, etc. **3** a fungal disease affecting plants. **smutty** *adj* < Middle English *smotten*.

snack (snæk) *n* a quick meal, often taken between regular meals. **snack-bar** *n* a place where snacks are sold and sometimes eaten. < probably Middle Dutch *snacken* to bite.

snag (snæg) *n* **1** an unexpected problem or difficulty. **2** a sharp or jagged projection. **3** a pull or slight tear in a fabric that has caught on a snag.
● *vb* **snagged; snagging** catch or tear on a snag. < Scandinavian.

snail (sneɪl) *n* a small, slow-moving mollusc with a shell into which it can withdraw. **at a snail's pace** very slowly. < Old English *snægl*.

snake (sneɪk) *n* **1** any of a group of legless, long-bodied reptiles. **2** a treacherous or untrustworthy person.
● *vb* move with a winding motion like a snake. **snakes and ladders** a board-game for children. < Old English *snaca*.

snap (snæp) *vb* **snapped; snapping** **1** make or cause to make a cracking sound: She snapped her fingers. **2** break suddenly, often with a cracking sound: The pen snapped into two. **3** shut or cause to shut with a cracking sound: Its jaws snapped shut. **4** utter with sudden anger or irritation. **5** (of a dog) bite or try to bite: The corgi snapped at his heels. **6** buy, accept, or get with great haste: snap up the bargains. **7** take a snapshot of.
● *n* **1** the act or sound of snapping. **2** a snapshot. **3** a clip, clasp, or other fastener that closes with a snapping sound. **4** a sudden bite or attempt to bite. **5** a thin, crisp biscuit. **6** a sudden spell of cold weather. **7** a card-game.
● *adj* done or made spontaneously or with little thought and preparation: a snap decision.
● *adv* with a snapping sound. **snappy** *adj* **1** lively; vigorous. **2** suave; stylish. **3** irritable or short-tempered. **snappily** *adv* **snappiness** *n* **snappish** *adj* inclined to be short-tempered with people. **snapshot** *n* a photograph taken informally by an amateur. < Dutch or Low German *snappen*.

snare (snɛə) *n* **1** a device for trapping animals and birds. **2** anything which traps or entangles. **3** any of the strings stretched across a drum to increase reverberation. **4** a snare drum.
● *vb* trap in a snare. **snare drum** a small drum with one or more snares. < Old Norse *snara*.

snarl[1] (snɑ:l) *vb* **1** growl with bared teeth. **2** utter angrily or bad-temperedly.
● *n* the act or sound of snarling. < of Germanic origin.

snarl[2] *vb* **snarl up** cause to become entangled, confused, etc., and stop working.
● *n* a tangle. **snarl-up** *n* **1** a traffic jam. **2** any instance of breakdown or disorder. < Middle English *snarle*.

snatch (snætʃ) *vb* **1** grasp or try to grasp (something) with a sudden movement of the arm; grab: It's rude to snatch. **2** take eagerly: snatch an hour's sleep.
● *n* **1** the act of snatching. **2** a fragment of a song, conversation, etc. **3** a brief period. < Middle English *snacchen* to seize.

sneak (sni:k) *vb* **1** go, move, or convey in a furtive manner: She sneaked out without waking anybody. **2** do or perform in a furtive manner: I saw him sneak a glance at her. **3** tell tales on.
● *n* a tell-tale. **sneaking** *adj* perceived intuitively: a sneaking suspicion. **sneaky** *adj* **sneakily** *adv* **sneakiness** *n* < Old English *snīcan* to creep.

sneer (snɪə) *vb* **1** raise the top lip on one side in an expression of scorn. **2** show contempt by such an expression or by verbal derision.
• *n* an expression of scorn or contempt. < origin uncertain.

sneeze (sni:z) *n* a sudden, violent, involuntary expulsion of air through the nose and mouth.
• *vb* give a sneeze. **not to be sneezed at** not to be dismissed or treated lightly. < Old English *fnēosan.*

snick (snɪk) *n* **1** a small cut or groove. **2** a light, glancing blow or stroke.
• *vb* **1** make a snick in. **2** strike with a snick. < probably Scandinavian.

snide (snaɪd) *adj* covertly disparaging: snide remarks. < origin unknown.

sniff (snɪf) *vb* **1** draw air audibly up the nose. **2** smell by sniffing.
• *n* the act or sound of sniffing. **sniff at** dismiss or treat something too lightly: Their offer is not to be sniffed at. **sniff out** detect: sniff out trouble. < Middle English *sniffen.*

sniffle (ˈsnɪfḷ) *vb* sniff repeatedly.
• *n* the act or sound of sniffling. **sniffler** *n* < *sniff.*

snigger (ˈsnɪgə) *vb* laugh quietly and derisively.
• *vb* give a snigger. < *snicker,* like the sound.

snip (snɪp) *vb* **snipped; snipping** cut deftly with scissors or shears.
• *n* **1** the act or sound of snipping. **2** a small piece snipped off; small cut. **3** (*informal*) a bargain. **snippet** *n* **1** a very small piece snipped off. **2** a fragment of news, gossip, etc. < probably Low German or Dutch *snippen.*

snipe (snaɪp) *n* a long-billed wading-bird, valued as game.
• *vb* **1** fire shots from a concealed position. **2** make critical or disparaging remarks. **sniper** *n* < Scandinavian.

snivel (ˈsnɪvḷ) *vb* **snivelled; snivelling** **1** weep and sniff simultaneously. **2** complain in a whining way.
• *n* the act or sound of snivelling. **sniveller** *n* < Old English *snyflan.*

snob (snɒb) *n* a person who scorns (the values and habits of) those people that he or she regards as socially inferior. **snobbery** *n* **snobbish** *adj* of or like a snob. **snobbishly** *adv* **snobbishness** *n* < English dialect: shoemaker.

snooker (ˈsnu:kə) *n* **1** a game played on a billiard table with fifteen red balls, six balls of other colours, and a white cue ball. **2** a shot that leaves one's opponent unable to shoot directly at the target ball.
• *vb* make this shot. **snookered** *adj* (*informal*) in a difficult position; defeated. < origin unknown.

snoop (snu:p) *vb* pry into others' affairs.
• *n* an act of snooping. **snooper** *n* < Dutch *snoepen* to eat on the sly.

snooty (ˈsnu:tɪ) *adj* **1** (*informal*) aloof or haughty. **2** snobbish. **snootily** *adv* **snootiness** *n* < obsolete *snoot:* nose.

snooze (snu:z) *n* (*informal*) a short sleep; nap.
• *vb* take a snooze. < origin unknown.

snore (snɔ:) *n* a grunting sound made while sleeping.
• *vb* make this sound. **snorer** *n* < Middle English *snoren.*

snorkel (ˈsnɔ:kḷ) *n* a bent tube that allows a person to breathe while face down in water.
• *vb* swim with this device. < German *Schnorchel.*

snort (snɔ:t) *n* a rough, hoarse sound made by expelling air forcibly through the nose, esp. to show disgust, etc.
• *vb* make a snort. < Middle English *snorten.*

snout (snaʊt) *n* **1** the long, projecting nose (and mouth) of an animal, esp. of a pig. **2** (*humorous*) a person's nose. < Middle English *snute.*

snow (snəʊ) *n* **1** crystals of ice that fall from the sky in small, white flakes. **2** snow that has fallen and formed a white layer.
• *vb* (of snow) fall. **snowbound** *adj* prevented from leaving a place by heavy falls of snow; snowed in. **snowdrift** *n* a bank of snow heaped up by the wind. **snowdrop** *n* a plant of the daffodil family with a small, white flower blooming in early spring. **snowed in** confined to a place by heavy falls of snow. **snowed under** overwhelmed with a mass of letters, work, etc. **snowfall** *n* the amount of snow that falls at one time. **snowflake** *n* a flake of snow. **snowman** *n* a heap of compacted snow made to resemble a human figure. **snow-plough** *n* a vehicle used for clearing snow from roads, runways, etc. **snow-shoe** *n* a device shaped like a tennis racket that is attached to the foot to allow a person to walk on deep snow without sinking. **snowstorm** *n* a storm in which snow falls. **snow-white** *adj* pure white. **snowy** *adj* **1** covered with or characterized by snow. **2** snow-white. < Old English *snāw.*

snowball (ˈsnəʊˌbɔ:l) *n* a round mass of compacted snow, thrown in fun.
• *vb* **1** throw or pelt with snowballs. **2** develop, increase, or expand at a fast

pace: Demand for the product has snowballed.

snub[1] (snʌb) *vb* **snubbed; snubbing** treat with contempt, esp. by ignoring; insult.
• *n* an instance of this. < Scandinavian.

snub[2] *adj* (of the nose) short and stubby. < Old Norse *snubba* to scold.

snuff[1] (snʌf) *n* powdered tobacco for inhaling or sniffing into the nostrils. **snuffbox** *n* a small container for snuff. < Dutch *snuf.*

snuff[2] *vb* extinguish (a candle) by smothering or pinching the flame. **snuff it** (*humorous*) die. < Middle English *snoffe.*

snuffle (ˈsnʌfl̩) *vb* breathe noisily through the nose, esp. when it is partly blocked.
• *n* the act or sound of snuffling. < Low German or Dutch *snuffelen.*

snug (snʌg) *adj* **snugger; snuggest 1** (of garments) close-fitting. **2** providing a warm, comfortable, and relaxed environment: a snug little room. **snugly** *adv* **snugness** *n* < perhaps Scandinavian.

snuggle (ˈsnʌgl̩) *vb* nestle comfortably. < *snug.*

so (səʊ) *adv* **1** to such an extent (that): It was so hot I had to take my jumper off. **2** very; extremely: She's so stupid! **3** in the state or manner mentioned or suggested; often used to avoid repeating a previous word, etc.: 'Do you really think so?' **4** also; too: Helen likes the theatre and so do I. **5** to this amount, extent, etc., usually accompanied by a gesture: I've been looking after this plant since it was so high.
• *conj* **1** in order (that): I invited Janet so you could meet her. **2** therefore: I was late so I took a taxi.
• *adj* factual; true: What he claimed was not so. **and so on** and continuing in a similar way. **just so** done, arranged, etc., in a particular way: He likes his coffee to be just so. **or so** approximately: Some sixty or so visitors were turned away. **quite so** (*formal*) used to express agreement. **so-and-so** *n* **1** a person whose name has been forgotten. **2** (*euphemistic*) a despicable person. **so as** in order (that): I left early so as I wouldn't be late. **so-called** *adj* going (perhaps undeservedly) by the name of: Some of these so-called teachers don't know the meaning of education. **so long** (*informal*) goodbye for now. **so much for** used to express scorn for someone or something: So much for paper cups! I'll never get these stains off. **so-so** *adj, adv* (*informal*) not particularly good or bad, well or badly, etc. < Old English *swā.*

soak (səʊk) *vb* **1** lie in a liquid; steep: Try soaking it in milk. **2** drench or saturate: I forgot the umbrella and got soaked. **3** suck up and absorb: Soak it up with a sponge.
• *n* the act or process of soaking. < Old English *socian.*

soap (səʊp) *n* a substance used with water to remove dirt.
• *vb* apply soap to. **soap-flakes** *pl n* soap in the form of small flakes for washing clothes, etc. **soap opera** a highly sentimental or melodramatic radio or television drama. **soapsuds** *pl n* lather or froth produced by soap. **soapy** *adj* **1** resembling soap. **2** covered with or full of soap. **soapiness** *n* < Old English *sāpe.* SEE PANEL.

soar (sɔː) *vb* **1** rise into the air. **2** rise quickly and dramatically: Prices soared. **3** (of a glider, etc.) glide on currents of air. < Middle French *essorer.*

sob (sɒb) *n* a heave of the chest while weeping.
• *vb* **sobbed; sobbing 1** give a sob. **2** utter with a sob. **sob story** (*informal*) a story, account, etc., that is intended to arouse sympathy for the speaker. < Middle English *sobben.*

sober (ˈsəʊbə) *adj* **1** not drunk. **2** serious and subdued in mood, character, etc. **3** rational; well-balanced: a sober decision. **4** subdued in colour, design, etc. **soberly** *adv* **sober up** become sober or less drunk. **sobriety** *n* the state of being sober. < Latin *sobrius.*

soccer (ˈsɒkə) *n* a form of football played with a round ball which may be kicked; only the goalkeepers may touch the ball with the hands. < *association football.*

sociable (ˈsəʊʃəbl̩) *adj* **1** fond of the company of others; friendly. **2** (of an occasion) affording the opportunity for companionship. **sociability** or **sociableness** *n* **sociably** *adv* < Latin *sociare* to associate. SEE PANEL AT **SOCIAL.**

social (ˈsəʊʃəl) *adj* **1** living or preferring

> **soap opera**
>
> A serialized, sentimental drama broadcast on radio or television is commonly known as a soap opera. This genre came into being in the United States with the dawning of commercial television. Its derogatory title is a reminder of the fact that the original sponsors of soap operas were manufacturers of soap.

to live in a community; gregarious. **2** of or concerning the welfare, habits, and relationships of people living in a society: social identity. **3** of or promoting companionship: a social club. **4** of or concerning the structure or organization of a society: social divisions. **5** of or concerning the upper classes.
• *n* a social gathering. **socially** *adv* **social democracy** a movement that favours a gradual and democratic change to socialism. **socialism** *n* a theory of social organization based on government ownership and management. **socialite** *n* a person who is socially active or prominent. < Latin *socius* companion. SEE PANEL.

society (sə'saɪətɪ) *n* **1** a social community; organization of this: British society. **2** a group of people with common interests who hold regular gatherings: a photographic society. **3** the upper classes. **4** company; companionship.

sociology (ˌsəʊsɪ'ɒlədʒɪ) *n* the scientific study of human beings living together in social communities. **sociological** *adj* **sociologist** *n* < French *sociologie*, from *socio-* + *-logie* -logy.

sock[1] (sɒk) *n* **1** a cloth covering for the foot, reaching no higher than the knee. **2** a loose sole put inside a shoe for a better fit. < Latin *soccus* light shoe. SEE PANEL.

social or **sociable?**

These two words are sometimes confused. Social has a number of meanings: 'living or preferring to live in a community': Man is a *social* being, 'concerned with the effects, etc., of living in a society': one's *social* identity, and 'of or promoting companionship': the miners' *social* club.

Sociable is used mostly of people and means 'fond of the company of others; friendly', so a sociable person is someone who enjoys going to parties, etc., and meeting other people. Sociable is also used to describe gatherings that provide a good opportunity for people to get to know one another: a *sociable* occasion.

The difference between the two words is seen in a sentence such as: He went along to the *social* club but didn't find the people there very *sociable*.

sock[2] *vb* (*informal*) strike (a person) with the fist; punch.
• *n* a punch. < probably Scandinavian.

socket ('sɒkɪt) *n* **1** a device that receives an electric plug or bulb. **2** any hollow thing, place, or device into which something else fits: the eye socket. < of Celtic origin.

soda ('səʊdə) *n* **1** a powdery compound of sodium, used for washing, baking, making glass, etc. **2** soda-water. **soda-water** *n* a beverage of water charged with carbon dioxide. < Medieval Latin *sodanum* barilla, plant from which sodium carbonate was obtained.

sodden ('sɒdn̩) *adj* saturated. < Middle English *sethen* to seethe.

sodium ('səʊdɪəm) *n* a soft, silver-white,

Pull your socks up!

Everyday conversation is full of idioms that, like pull one's socks up, ('to make an effort to improve one's behaviour'), feature a garment or part of a garment. Below is a list of some of the more common examples; it starts with head apparel and works down to footwear:

keep something under one's hat
a hat trick
old hat
eat one's hat
keep one's hat on
pass the hat round
take one's hat off to
cap it all
cut one's coat according to one's cloth
hot under the collar
lose one's shirt
have something up one's sleeve
off the cuff
fit like a glove
hand in glove
get something under one's belt
(who) wears the trousers
be caught with one's trousers down
have ants in one's pants
get one's knickers in a twist
put a sock in it
be in someone's shoes
bet one's boots
get the boot
too big for one's boots

metallic element that occurs as the chloride in sea-water and is chemically highly reactive. < New Latin, from English *soda*.

sodomy (ˈsɒdəmɪ) *n* anal intercourse. < Late Latin *Sodoma* Sodom, city of ancient Palestine.

sofa (ˈsəʊfə) *n* a long, upholstered seat for usually two or three people, with a back and arms at either end. < Arabic *ṣuffah*.

soft (sɒft) *adj* **1** not hard; yielding: a soft cushion. **2** easily worked, shaped, spread, etc.: soft margarine. **3** of fine or delicate material: soft leather. **4** (of sounds) not loud; gentle: a soft voice. **5** (of colours, light, etc.) not glaring or brilliant; subdued. **6** (*informal*) emotionally susceptible; tender-hearted. **7** without force; gentle: a soft breeze. **8** (of water) conducive to the lathering of soap. **9** (of a line or outline) slightly blurred; not sharp: soft focus.
• *adv* in a soft or gentle manner; softly. **softly** *adv* **softness** *n* **soft-boil** *vb* boil (an egg) until the white solidifies but the yolk remains liquid. **soft drink** a non-alcoholic drink, usually made from soda-water. **soft drugs** drugs that are not likely to cause addiction. **soften** *vb* make or become soft or less hard. **soft fruit** fruits such as strawberries and blackberries that are small and stoneless. **soft furnishings** curtains, carpets, rugs, etc. **soft-hearted** *adj* compassionate. **softie** *n* (*informal*) a person who is soft-hearted. **soft option** a less troublesome or difficult alternative. **soft-pedal** *vb* **soft-pedalled; soft-pedalling** try to minimize the significance or obviousness of. **soft sell** the use of subtle persuasion rather than heavy pressure. **soft-soap** *vb* (*informal*) try to persuade or influence by flattering. **soft spot** an emotional weakness. **software** *n* **1** computer programs. **2** films, transparencies, tapes, etc., as opposed to the machines which show or play them. **softwood** *n* the wood of a coniferous tree. < Old English *sōfte*.

soggy (ˈsɒgɪ) *adj* **1** saturated; waterlogged. **2** moist and heavy: soggy bread. **sogginess** *n* < English dialect *sog* to soak.

soil[1] (sɔɪl) *n* **1** the loose surface material of the earth in which plants grow. **2** land or territory: on French soil. < Latin *solium* seat.

soil[2] *vb* make or become dirty. < Old French: pigsty.

soirée (ˈswɑːreɪ) *n* an evening party or social gathering, usually at a private house. < French.

sojourn (ˈsɒdʒɜːn) *n* (*formal*) a temporary stay.
• *vb* make a temporary stay. < Old French *sojorner*.

solace (ˈsɒlɪs) *n* (a source of) consolation or comfort. < Latin *solari* to relieve, console.

solar (ˈsəʊlə) *adj* **1** of or derived from the sun: solar energy. **2** measured by the sun: solar time. **solar heating** heating powered by solar energy. **solar plexus 1** the network of nerves behind the stomach. **2** the pit of the stomach. **solar system** a sun and its planets, moons, comets, etc. < Latin *sol* sun.

sold (səʊld) SEE SELL. **sold on** (*informal*) highly enthusiastic about. SEE PANEL.

solder (ˈsɒldə) *n* an alloy used when melted to join or mend metallic surfaces.
• *vb* join or mend with solder. **soldering-iron** *n* a tool used for melting and applying solder. < Latin *solidus* solid.

soldier (ˈsəʊldʒə) *n* a member of an army, esp. an enlisted man as opposed to a commissioned officer.
• *vb* serve as a soldier. **soldierly** *adj*

sold down the river

People who complain of being sold down the river feel that they have somehow been cheated or betrayed. The expression derives from the days of the American slave trade and was used of slaves who, after the tobacco belt was exhausted, were shipped down the Mississippi River to the cotton and sugar plantations in the deep South. This often involved a severing of all ties, including the disbanding of family units, and, at the end of the journey, a notoriously cruel new master.

soldier

The word soldier derives ultimately from the Late Latin noun *solidus*, the name of a gold coin. This strongly suggests that the first fighting men to be referred to as soldiers were hirelings or mercenaries, men who were paid for their services. See also panel at **free.**

soldier on continue or persevere in spite of difficulties. < Old French *soulde* pay. SEE PANEL.
sole[1] (səʊl) *n* **1** the under surface of the foot. **2** the bottom of a shoe, boot, etc.
• *vb* provide (a shoe, etc.) with a sole or new sole. < Latin *solea* sandal.
sole[2] *n, pl* **sole, soles** any of a group of flatfish used as food. < Latin *solea* sole, from the shape of the fish.
sole[3] *adj* **1** being the only one: the sole survivor. **2** exclusive to one person or group: They enjoy sole use of the court. **solely** *adv* < ultimately Latin *solus*.
solecism (ˈsɒlɪˌsɪzəm) *n* **1** a mistake in speech or writing. **2** a breach of etiquette. < Greek *soloikos* speaking incorrectly. SEE PANEL.
solemn (ˈsɒləm) *adj* **1** serious and sombre; glum: a solemn look. **2** formal or ceremonious: a solemn vow. **3** impressive; awesome: a solemn occasion. **solemnity** *n* **solemnly** *adv* **solemnize** *vb* **1** celebrate solemnly. **2** formally unite (a couple) in marriage. **solemnization** *n* < Latin *sollemnis*.
solicit (səˈlɪsɪt) *vb* **1** entreat or appeal to. **2** seek to obtain by urgent requests: solicit votes. **3** (of a prostitute) lure or proposition. **solicitation** *n* < Latin *sollicitare* to disturb.
solicitor (səˈlɪsɪtə) *n* a lawyer who advises clients, represents them in lower courts, prepares cases for barristers, etc.
solicitous (səˈlɪsɪtəs) *adj* (*formal*) **1** anxious and concerned. **2** eager; willing.
solid (ˈsɒlɪd) *adj* **1** not hollow: a solid lump of rubber. **2** neither liquid nor gaseous. **3** all of one material: solid gold. **4** without a break or interruption: a solid line. **5** of rigid structure; firm: The wall seems pretty solid. **6** having a firm or sound basis: a solid argument. **7** united as a group; unanimous: solid support.
• *n* **1** a solid substance or body. **2** a body or figure with three dimensions.
• *adv* in or into a solid state: The icing had set solid. **solidity** *n* **solidly** *adv* **solidarity** *n* unity amongst a group of people. **solidify** *vb* make or become solid. **solid-state** *adj* making use of transistors rather than valves. < Latin *solidus*.
soliloquy (səˈlɪləkwɪ) *n* a speech made by a person to himself, esp. a dramatic monologue by an actor or actress. **soliloquize** *vb* utter a soliloquy. < Latin *solus* alone + *loqui* to speak.
solitaire (ˈsɒlɪˌtɛə) *n* **1** a single diamond set alone. **2** a game for one person involving the rule-governed removal of pieces from a board. **3** (*US*) the card-game of patience. < SEE **SOLITARY.**
solitary (ˈsɒlɪtrɪ) *adj* **1** alone; unaccompanied: solitary confinement. **2** preferring to be alone: a solitary character. **3** single; sole: a solitary example. **4** lonely and secluded; unfrequented: a solitary cottage.
• *n* a recluse. **solitarily** *adv* **solitariness** *n* **solitude** *n* **1** being alone; seclusion. **2** a lonely place. < Latin *solitarius*.
solo (ˈsəʊləʊ) *n, pl* **solos 1** a composition played or sung by just one person. **2** any performance given by just one person. **3** a flight by one person alone in an aircraft.
• *adj, adv* unaccompanied; alone. **soloist** *n* < Latin *solus* alone.
solstice (ˈsɒlstɪs) *n* either of the two times in the year when the sun is furthest away from the equator. < Latin *sol* sun + *sistere* to come to a stop.
soluble (ˈsɒljʊbl) *adj* **1** able to be dissolved in water: soluble aspirin. **2** able to be solved. **solubility** *n* < Latin *solvere* to dissolve.
solution (səˈluːʃən) *n* **1** the act or process of solving a problem. **2** an answer to a problem. **3** the act or process of mixing a substance with a liquid. **4** a liquid in which something has been dissolved; mixture.
solve (sɒlv) *vb* **1** find the answer to (a problem). **2** find the solution to (a difficulty, mystery, etc.). < SEE **SOLUBLE.**
solvent (ˈsɒlvənt) *adj* **1** able to pay all one's debts. **2** able to dissolve another substance.
• *n* a liquid used for dissolving something. **solvency** *n* the condition of being solvent. < Latin *solvere* to free.
sombre (ˈsɒmbə) *adj* **1** dark and gloomy. **2** serious or grave; melancholy: a sombre mood. **sombrely** *adv* < French.
some (səm; *stressed* sʌm) *determiner* **1** used to indicate an unfixed or

solecism

A mistake or inaccuracy in speech or writing is sometimes referred to as a solecism. This word derives via the Latin *solecismus* and Greek *soloikos* ('speaking incorrectly') from *Soloi*, the name of an Athenian colony in ancient Cilicia, where a highly corrupt form of Greek was spoken.

uncertain amount or quantity: some eggs. **2** used to indicate a certain, unspecified person or thing. **3** used to indicate that one has been impressed by what the following noun refers to: That was some fight! **4** approximately: He earns some £90 a week. **5** a fairly considerable amount or quantity: It happened some years ago.
• *pron* **1** used to indicate an unfixed or uncertain amount or quantity: Would you like some? **2** used to indicate a certain, unspecified person or thing: Not all men like football. Some do and some don't. < Old English *sum*. SEE PANEL AT **SOMETIME.**

somebody (ˈsʌmbədɪ) *pron* an unknown or unspecified person.
• *n* a person of importance: He thinks he's a real somebody.

somehow (ˈsʌmˌhaʊ) *adv* **1** in some unspecified manner. **2** by some means or another.

someone (ˈsʌmˌwʌn) *pron*, *n* somebody.

somersault (ˈsʌməˌsɔːlt) *n* a movement in which a person rolls forward head over heels.
• *vb* do a somersault. < Middle French *sombresaut*.

something (ˈsʌmˌθɪŋ) *pron* an unknown or unspecified thing.
• *n* a thing that is impressive: That new car is really something!

sometime (ˈsʌmˌtaɪm) *adj* former; late: the sometime chairman.
• *adv* at some unspecified point of time. SEE PANEL.

sometimes (ˈsʌmˌtaɪmz) *adv* occasionally.

somewhat (ˈsʌmˌwɒt) *adv* to some extent; rather: somewhat boring.

somewhere (ˈsʌmˌwɛə) *adv* at or in or to an unknown or unspecified place.

somnambulism (sɒmˈnæmbjʊˌlɪzəm) *n* walking while asleep. **somnambulist** *n* < Latin *somnus* sleep + *ambulare* to walk. SEE PANEL.

son (sʌn) *n* **1** a male child, offspring, or descendant. **2** a person deriving from or closely associated with a certain country, institution, background, etc. **3** (*informal*) a familiar way of addressing a boy

sometime or some time?

When the meaning is 'former; late', as in Max Wolff, *sometime* chairman of the Anglo-German Society, sometime is written as one word. When the meaning is 'at some unspecified point of time', either sometime or some time may be used: I hope we'll meet again *sometime*. The hotel was built *some time* in the 1930s.

Following a preposition such as for or at, some time is written as two words: I've been worried about her for *some time*.

Sometimes is always written as one word.

somnambulism

Somnambulism, the medical or technical name for 'sleep-walking', derives from two Latin words—*somnus* meaning 'sleep' and *ambulare 'to walk'*.

In medical usage a large number of words derive from *somnus,* including somnambule or somnambulist 'a sleep-walker', somnifacient '(an agent) causing sleep', somniferous or somnific 'producing sleep', somniloquence or somniloquism 'habitual talking in one's sleep', somniloquist 'a person who talks habitually in his or her sleep', somnipathy 'any disorder of sleep', somnocinematograph 'an apparatus for recording movements made while asleep', somnolence 'sleepiness or unnatural drowsiness', somnolism 'a state of hypnotic trance', and somnolentia 'incomplete sleep'. Words such as these are unfamiliar to non-specialists because they belong to the technical language of medicine or medical *register*.

In everyday usage *somnus* derivatives are far fewer. The only one that can be regarded as common is insomnia 'the inability to fall or remain asleep'. Those who suffer with this complaint might do well to keep by the bed a full-length medical dictionary. Such a tome can have a surprisingly somniferous effect.

son of a gun

This was originally a term of abuse, meaning 'the bastard son of a soldier or sailor'. It derives from the time when women were allowed to live on naval ships and bore children of unknown or unacknowledged paternity. In time the phrase not only lost its derogatory sense but gained a positive one, functioning as a way of addressing a man in a friendly way: 'Well if it isn't Harry, you old son of a gun! Long time no see!'

or young man. **son-in-law** *n*, *pl* **sons-in-law** the husband of one's daughter. < Old English *sunu*. SEE PANEL.

sonar (ˈsəʊnɑː) *n* a device that uses reflected sound waves for detecting the presence and location of things under water. < *so*und *na*vigation *r*anging. SEE PANEL AT **RADAR.**

sonata (səˈnɑːtə) *n* a musical composition, usually in three or four movements, for one or two instruments. < Italian *sonare* to sound.

song (sɒŋ) *n* **1** a short, musical composition with words for singing. **2** the act or art of singing. **3** the musical sound of certain birds. **4** poetry; verse. **for a song** (*informal*) for a very low price. **songbird** *n* a bird that produces musical sounds. **songster** *n* **1** a singer. **2** a songbird. < Old English *sang*.

sonic (ˈsɒnɪk) *adj* **1** of, connected with, or producing sound waves. **2** having a speed equal to that of sound in air. **sonic boom** a sound like an explosion made by the shock wave of an aircraft travelling at supersonic speed. < Latin *sonus* sound.

sonnet (ˈsɒnɪt) *n* a poem of 14 lines having any of several rhyme schemes. < Italian *sonetto*.

soon (suːn) *adv* **1** in a short time; before long. **2** early: It's too soon to know. **3** promptly: as soon as possible. **sooner** *adv* rather; preferably: I'd sooner walk than beg for a lift. **as soon as** readily or willingly: I would as soon stay in as go out. **sooner or later** eventually. < Old English *sōna*. SEE PANEL AT **HARDLY.**

soot (sʊt) *n* the black, powdery substance formed when something burns and which sticks to the sides of a chimney.
• *vb* cover with soot. **sooty** *adj* **1** covered with soot. **2** resembling soot, esp. in colour. < Old English *sōt*.

soothe (suːð) *vb* **1** calm, comfort, or pacify. **2** ease or relieve (pain, etc.). **soothing** *adj* **soothingly** *adv* < Old English *sōth* true.

soothsayer (ˈsuːθˌseɪə) *n* a person who predicts the future; prophet. < Old English *soth* truth.

sop (sɒp) *vb* **sopped; sopping** absorb (liquid) like a sponge. **sopping** *adj* saturated: sopping wet. < Old English *sopp*.

sophisticated (səˈfɪstɪˌkeɪtɪd) *adj* **1** (of people) having refined or urbane tastes and habits. **2** (of things) favoured by sophisticated people; high-class: a sophisticated restaurant. **3** elaborate or complicated. **4** having a good deal of knowledge and experience; worldly-wise: She's very sophisticated for a child of her age. **sophistication** *n* < Medieval Latin *sophisticare* to complicate.

sophistry (ˈsɒfɪstrɪ) *n* deceptively subtle reasoning. < Greek *sophistēs* wise man.

soporific (ˌsɒpəˈrɪfɪk) *adj* **1** causing sleep. **2** sleepy or lethargic.
• *n* a drug or other substance that causes sleep. < Latin *sopor* sleep.

soprano (səˈprɑːnəʊ) *n, pl* **sopranos** **1** the highest singing voice, esp. of a woman or boy. **2** a singer with such a voice. **3** a part written for such a voice. **4** the highest part of a harmony. **5** either of the two instruments that are highest in a family of instruments. < Latin *supra* above.

sorbet (ˈsɔːbɪt, ˈsɔːbeɪ) *n* a frozen dessert of water, sugar, and flavouring. < Middle French: fruit drink.

sorcery (ˈsɔːsərɪ) *n* magic; witchcraft. **sorcerer** *n* < Old French *sorcier* sorcerer.

sordid (ˈsɔːdɪd) *adj* **1** dirty; squalid. **2** mercenary; base: sordid motives. **sordidly** *adv* **sordidness** *n* < Latin *sordes* dirt.

sore (sɔː) *adj* **1** causing pain; painfully sensitive: a sore elbow. **2** experiencing pain: Do you still feel sore? **3** causing worry, irritation, or annoyance: a sore point. **4** urgent; desperate: in sore need. **5** (*informal*) angry; annoyed.
• *n* **1** a sore area on a body. **2** a source of irritation or distress. **soreness** *n* **sorely** *adv* very; extremely: sorely tempted. < Old English *sār*.

sorrow (ˈsɒrəʊ) *n* **1** sadness or distress caused esp. by loss, bereavement, etc. **2** a cause of this. **3** deep regret.
• *vb* feel or express sorrow. **sorrowful** *adj* feeling or expressing sorrow: a sorrowful look. **sorrowfully** *adv* < Old English *sorg*.

sorry (ˈsɒrɪ) *adj* **1** feeling regret, sadness, or sympathy; used often as an apology. **2** inspiring pity or contempt; wretched: a sorry sight. < Old English *sār* sore.

sort (sɔːt) *n* **1** a group with similar characteristics; kind. **2** a recognizable member or example (of a group): It's a sort of vegetable. **3** (*informal*) a person considered in terms of character or nature: a good sort.
• *vb* separate into groups according to sort, quality, destination, etc. **sorter** *n* **of sorts** or **of a sort** not a true or typical member of the group: She's a singer of sorts. **out of sorts** (*informal*) somewhat ill or depressed. **sort of** (*informal*) somewhat. **sort out 1** select and remove; sort

into groups. **2** resolve (an argument, etc.): You'll just have to sort out your differences **3** organize: son out one's office. **4** (*informal*) attack verbally or physically. **sort-out** *n* < Middle French *sorte.* SEE PANEL AT KIND[1].

sortie (ˈsɔːtɪ) *n* **1** an assault by troops begun from a besieged or defensive place. **2** a flight or attack by an aircraft on a military operation. **3** a trip into hostile or unknown territory. < Middle French *sortir* to go out.

SOS (ˌɛs əʊ ˈɛs) *n* an internationally recognized distress signal, used esp. by ships and aircraft.

soufflé (ˈsuːfleɪ) *n* a light, spongy dish made with stiffly beaten egg-whites. < French *souffler* to puff up.

sought (sɔːt) SEE SEEK. **sought-after** *adj* in great demand.

soul (səʊl) *n* **1** something in humans considered by some to be immortal and the centre of spiritual being. **2** the emotional or moral nature of humans that is considered by some to separate them from other animals. **3** the essential part: the soul of the party. **4** (*informal*) a personification or paradigm: the soul of honesty. **5** (*informal*) a person: I didn't see a soul. **6** powerful feelings conveyed by American Negro performers. **7** the music that conveys these feelings. **soul-destroying** *adj* intensely depressing or dispiriting. **soulful** *adj* full of or expressing deep feeling. **soulfully** *adv* **soulfulness** *n* **soulless** *adj* **1** lacking sensitivity or warmth of feeling. **2** bleak or uninteresting. **soul mate** a person who shares a strong bond or affinity with another. **soul-searching** *n* scrutiny of one's conscience, motives, etc. < Old English *sāwol.*

sound[1] (saʊnd) *n* **1** everything perceived by the ear; noise. **2** a particular impression produced by an instance of this: the sound of glass breaking. **3** a speech sound. **4** the overall impression or underlying significance of something: I don't like the sound of that. **5** the distance within which a particular sound may be heard; earshot: within the sound of Bow Bells. **6** a recognizable or characteristic musical style: the Mersey sound. **7** quality of sound; volume: Turn the sound up.

• *vb* **1** produce or cause to produce a sound: The bell sounds on the hour. **2** give a particular impression to the ear: It sounds like a fox. **3** cause a particular overall impression to be received: It sounds like she could do with a holiday. **4** order or signal by a sound or sounds: sound a retreat. **5** pronounce or articulate: sound one's h's. **6** examine the condition of by causing to produce sounds. **sound barrier** the drag experienced by an aircraft, etc., as it nears the speed of sound. **sound effects** background sounds that are added to a play, film, etc., esp. to enhance authenticity of context. **sound off** (*derogatory*) express one's opinions in a loud and forceful manner. **sound out** try to discover (a person's opinions, plans, etc.) in a cautious or secretive way. **sound-track** *n* a narrow strip running along the edge of a cine-film for recording sound; sound recorded. < Latin *sonus.*

sound[2] *adj* **1** in good health or condition; undamaged. **2** free from error; logical: sound reasoning. **3** showing good judgment: a sound decision. **4** solid, firm, or secure: The ceiling is fairly sound. **5** thorough; severe: a sound beating.

• *adv* fully: sound asleep. **soundly** *adv* **soundness** *n* < Old English *gesund.*

sound[3] *vb* **1** measure the depth of (the sea, etc.). **2** probe, explore, or examine.

• *n* a probe. **sounder** *n* < Middle French *sonder.*

sound[4] *n* a strait or inlet. < Old English *sund* narrow sea.

soundproof (ˈsaʊndˌpruːf) *adj* unable to be penetrated by sound.

• *vb* make soundproof.

soup (suːp) *n* a liquid food traditionally made by boiling meat, fish, or vegetables, etc., in water.

• *vb* (*informal*) improve the performance of (an engine). **in the soup** (*informal*) in trouble or difficulty. < French *soupe.*

soupçon (ˈsuːpsɒn) *n* a very small amount; trace. < French: suspicion.

sour (saʊə) *adj* **1** having an acid or vinegary taste: sour plums. **2** having this taste because stale, rancid, etc.: sour milk. **3** morose, bad-tempered, or disagreeable. **4** (of soil) excessively acid.

• *vb* make or become sour. **sourly** *adv* **sourness** *n* **soured cream** cream deliberately made sour by the adding of bacteria. < Old English *sūr.* SEE PANEL.

source (sɔːs) *n* **1** the place from which something originates or is obtained: the source of the leak. **2** a means of supply: a source of income. **3** a person, book, etc., that supplies information. **4** the starting-point of a stream. < Old French *sourdre* to rise.

souse (saʊs) *vb* **1** steep in pickle or marinade. **2** plunge into liquid; drench. < Middle French *souce* pickling

solution.
south (saʊθ) *n* the point or direction to the left of someone facing west.
• *adj, adv* **1** in, towards, or facing the south. **2** (of the wind) from the south. **the south** often also **the South** land lying in or towards the south. **south-east** *n* the point or direction midway between south and east. **southerly** *adj* **1** in or towards the south. **2** (of the wind) from the south. **southern** *adj* of or in the south. **southerner** *n* a native or inhabitant of the south. **southernmost** *adj* furthest south. **South Pole** the southernmost point of the earth. **southward, southwards** *adj, adv* towards the south. **south-west** *n* the point or direction midway between south and west. < Old English *sūth.*
souvenir (ˌsuːvəˈnɪə) *n* something that serves as a reminder, esp. of a place visited; memento. < Middle French: to remember.
sou'wester (ˌsaʊˈwɛstə) *n* a waterproof hat with a broad flap at the back, worn chiefly by seamen.

sour grapes

Sour grapes is an informal expression used to describe the bitterness a person feels when pretending not to like or want something because it cannot be had or done by himself or herself: 'If you ask me it's a case of *sour grapes.* It's not that she doesn't like your new flat—it's that she wishes she'd had the sense to buy it herself.'

The phrase is an allusion to Aesop's fable of 'The Fox and the Grapes'. The story tells of how a fox, when faced with the impossibility of reaching some grapes that were hanging too high overhead, disparaged them as sour.

spa

A town or resort that is developed around a mineral spring is known as a spa. This word comes from *Spa,* a town in south-east Belgium, whose celebrated springs have attracted visitors since the 14th century.

sovereign (ˈsɒvrɪn) *n* **1** the supreme ruler of a country. **2** (formerly) a British gold coin worth one pound.
• *adj* **1** supreme in power or authority. **2** having independent authority: sovereign states. **3** excellent; highly effective. **sovereignty** *n* < Old French *soverain.*
sow[1] (səʊ) *vb* **sowed; sown, sowed; sowing 1** scatter or plant with seed. **2** implant or introduce: sow suspicions. **sower** *n* < Old English *sāwan.*
sow[2] (saʊ) *n* a female, adult pig. < Old English *sugu.*
sown (səʊn) SEE **sow**[1].
spa (spɑː) *n* a mineral spring; resort developed around such a spring. < *Spa,* watering-place in Belgium. SEE PANEL.
space (speɪs) *n* **1** the boundless expanse in which all things exist and move. **2** a measurable portion of this: office space. **3** an empty or unoccupied place or area: Is there a space to sit down? **4** a period of time: within the space of five minutes. **5** also **outer space** the area beyond the earth's atmosphere.
• *vb* arrange with spaces between: The letters should be uniformly spaced. **spacecraft** *n* a vehicle for travelling in outer space. **spaced-out** *adj* (*informal*) in a dazed, drugged, or stupefied condition. **spaceman** *n* a person who travels in outer space. **spaceship** *n* a spacecraft. **space shuttle** a reusable spacecraft. **space station** a manned, artificial satellite intended as a base for operations in outer space. **spacious** *adj* having lots of room; roomy. **spaciously** *adv* **spaciousness** *n* < Old French *espace.*
spade[1] (speɪd) *n* a tool for digging and lifting soil, etc. **spadeful** *n* < Old English *spadu.*
spade[2] *n* a black figure resembling an inverted heart on a playing-card; playing-card of the suit (**spades**) marked with these. < ultimately Greek *spathē* blade.
spaghetti (spəˈgɛtɪ) *n* pasta in the form of long, thin strings, smaller in diameter than macaroni. < Italian.
span (spæn) *n* **1** the space or distance from end to end or between two points. **2** the distance from the tip of the thumb to the tip of the little finger when the fingers are fully spread. **3** a part of a bridge between two adjacent supports; length of this. **4** a limited extent of time.
• *vb* **spanned; spanning 1** extend across. **2** extend across by spreading the fingers fully. < Old English *spann.*
spangle (ˈspæŋgḷ) *n* one of many very

small, glittering discs, used chiefly for dress ornamentation; sequin.
• *vb* adorn with spangles. < Middle English *spang* tiny object.

spaniel (ˈspænjəl) *n* any of a group of dogs with large, drooping ears, short legs, and long hair. < Middle French *espaigneul* Spanish (dog).

spank (spæŋk) *vb* slap the buttocks of. **spanking** *adj* vigorous; brisk.
• *n* the act of spanking. < probably like the sound.

spanner (ˈspænə) *n* a tool for gripping or turning a nut. < German *spannen* to stretch. SEE PANEL.

spar¹ (spɑː) *n* a mast, boom, or other strong pole on a vessel. < Middle English *sparre*.

spar² *vb* **sparred; sparring 1** (of a boxer) train or practise boxing skills, esp. with a sparring partner. **2** argue; wrangle. **sparring partner** a boxer employed to give another practice as part of training < origin uncertain.

spare (spɛə) *vb* **1** manage to give, afford, or do without: Can you spare a moment? **2** refrain from killing, punishing, etc.; show mercy to: The women and children were spared. **3** exempt or release from: Spare me the ordeal. **4** refrain from using: Spare the rod and spoil the child.
• *adj* **1** in excess; surplus: a spare chair. **2** for use as a replacement; in reserve: a spare part. **3** scanty; frugal. **4** (of a person) thin; lean.
• *n* spare part. **sparely** *adv* **spareness** *n* **not spare oneself** exert oneself fully. **spare-rib** *n* a cut of pork from the lower ribs with most of the meat removed. **spare tyre** (*informal*) a roll of fat around the waist. **sparing** *adj* **1** not wasteful; thrifty. **2** meagre; frugal. **sparingly** *adv* < Old English *sparian*.

spark (spɑːk) *n* **1** a fiery particle produced by something burning or by two metallic surfaces striking each other. **2** a flash of light accompanying a sudden discharge of electricity. **3** a germ, trace, or hint: a spark of enthusiasm.
• *vb* **1** produce a spark or sparks. **2** kindle, trigger, or precipitate: The announcement sparked off a series of protests. **spark-plug** or **sparking-plug** *n* a device that produces a spark in the cylinder of an internal-combustion engine, igniting the mixture. < Old English *spearca*.

sparkle (ˈspɑːkl̩) *vb* **1** gleam with flashes of light. **2** (of wine) effervesce. **3** show wit or vivacity.
• *n* sparkling. **sparkler** *n* **1** a type of firework that throws out sparks. **2** (*informal*) a gem. **sparkling wine** wine that is effervescent. < Middle English *sparken* to spark.

sparrow (ˈspærəʊ) *n* any of a group of small, brownish songbirds related to the finch. **sparrow-hawk** *n* a small hawk. < Old English *spearwa*.

sparse (spɑːs) *adj* thinly scattered; not dense. **sparsely** *adv* **sparseness** *n* **sparsity** *n* < Latin *spargere* to scatter.

spartan (ˈspɑːtn̩) *adj* severely simple or austere; rigorously strict: spartan surroundings. < *Sparta*, city in ancient Greece. SEE PANEL.

spasm (ˈspæzəm) *n* **1** an involuntary contraction of a muscle. **2** any sudden short effort or spell of activity: He works in spasms. **spasmodic** *adj* **1** occurring in sudden, brief spells. **2** of or characterized

---

spartan

Something which is severely simple and far removed from comfort or luxury may be described as spartan: In those days we existed on the spartan diet of bread and cheese. The adjective *spartan* derives from the Latin name of the ancient Greek city of *Sparta*. Sparta was renowned for the austerity of its government and the discipline of its formidable army.

---

spanner

A tool that is used for tightening and loosening nuts is known as a spanner. This word entered the language in the 17th century from the German noun *Spanner* which then signified 'an instrument for winding springs', from *spannen* 'to stretch'.

Surprisingly few German words have found their way into English. In addition to spanner these include:

blitz	**poltergeist**
dachshund	**quartz**
hinterland	**snorkel**
kindergarten	**swindler**
plunder	**zinc**

by spasm. **spasmodically** *adv* < Greek *spasmos*.

spastic (ˈspæstɪk) *adj* **1** suffering from spastic paralysis; physically disabled. **2** of, affected by, or characterized by spasm: spastic paralysis. **3** (*informal*) ineffectual; incompetent.
• *n* a spastic person. **2** (*informal*) an incapable or ineffectual person; used chiefly by children. **spastically** *adv* < SEE **SPASM.**

spat (spæt) SEE **SPIT.**

spate (speɪt) *n* **1** a sudden rush or outpouring: a spate of anger. **2** a large number or amount: a spate of enquiries. **in spate** (of a river) unusually high and fast flowing. < Middle English.

spatial (ˈspeɪʃəl) *adj* of, existing in, or connected with space. **spatially** *adv* < Latin *spatium* space.

spatter (ˈspætə) *vb* **1** sprinkle or splash with liquid: spattered with mud. **2** shower or rain down; spurt.
• *n* spattering. < probably like the sound.

spatula (ˈspætjʊlə) *n* a knife-like instrument with a broad, blunt, flexible blade. < Latin *spatha* flat wooden instrument.

spawn (spɔːn) *n* **1** the eggs of fish, frogs, oysters, etc. **2** (*often derogatory*) any offspring, esp. when numerous. **3** the thread-like substance from which mushrooms and other fungi grow.
• *vb* **1** produce or deposit spawn. **2** engender or give rise to. < Old French *espandre* to spread out, shed, spill.

spay (speɪ) *vb* remove the ovaries of (a female animal). < Old French *espee* sword.

speak (spiːk) *vb* **spoke; spoken; speaking 1** utter or pronounce (words); talk. **2** have a conversation with; converse: Can I speak to you for a minute? **3** express or give voice to (an opinion, feeling, etc.): Why don't you speak the truth! **4** address or lecture a gathering. **5** know how to communicate orally in: Does he speak Italian? **6** engage in friendly conversation (with someone): She always stops to speak. **7** be indicative of: Her tired face spoke of another sleepless night. **8** communicate as if in words: The figures speak for themselves. **speaker** *n* **1** a person who speaks, esp. to a meeting or gathering. **2** a loudspeaker. **3** the presiding officer at a legislative or deliberative assembly. **the Speaker** the speaker at the House of Commons. < Old English *sprecan*. SEE PANEL.

spear (spɪə) *n* **1** a weapon with a long shaft and a sharp point, for thrusting, hurling, etc. **2** a young shoot of grass, asparagus, etc.
• *vb* strike or pierce with or as if with a spear. < Old English *spere*.

spearhead (ˈspɪəˌhɛd) *n* **1** the pointed head of a spear. **2** the leading force in a movement, attack, crusade, etc.
• *vb* be the spearhead of.

spearmint (ˈspɪəˌmɪnt) *n* a common, purple-flowered mint used for flavouring.

spec (spɛk) *n* **on spec** (*informal*) as a risk or gamble. < short for *speculation*.

special (ˌspɛʃəl) *adj* **1** of a distinguished or prominent kind: a very special beer. **2** individual; unique: This is my own special recipe. **3** not everyday, common, or ordinary: a special occasion. **4** exceptional in amount, intensity, etc.: She takes a special pride in her baking.
• *n* something that is special. **specially** *adv* **special constable** a part-time auxiliary policeman. **specialism** *n* an area of knowledge or expertise in which a person is an expert. **specialist** *n* a person who has a specialism. **speciality** *n* **1** something that is specialized in: Fast, reliable repairs are our speciality. **2** a distinctive mark or feature. **3** a special interest or aptitude. **specialize** *vb* **1** study to become a specialist. **2** concentrate one's efforts on a particular activity, product, service, etc. **3** (*biology*) adapt to a particular environment or for a particular purpose. **specialization** *n* **special**

speaking out

Speak occurs in a number of idiomatic expressions, including:

on speaking terms on friendly terms.
so to speak as it were: Language is, so to speak, a mirror of society.
speak for oneself to give one's opinion oneself.
speak one's mind to express one's views frankly.
speak out to express one's opinions freely or forcefully.
speak to to reprimand or rebuke: It's time someone spoke to that child.
speak up to speak more loudly; speak out: Can you speak up—we can't hear you.
to speak of worth mentioning: There was nothing of interest to speak of.

licence a licence allowing marriage to take place at a time or place other than those usually authorized by law. < Latin *specialis*. SEE PANEL.

species (ˈspiːʃiːz) *n, pl* **species 1** a sort or kind. **2** a group of plants or animals whose members share basic characteristics. < Latin.

specific (spəˈsɪfɪk) *adj* **1** exact, definite, or particular: a specific purpose. **2** factually precise: Try to be more specific. • *n* something that is specific, esp. the remedy for a particular disease. **specifically** *adv* **specific gravity** the ratio of the density of a substance to that of water.

specification (ˌspɛsɪfɪˈkeɪʃən) *n* **1** the act of specifying. **2** a set of details or detailed instructions.

specify (ˈspɛsɪˌfaɪ) *vb* **specified; specifying 1** mention, state, or refer to specifically. **2** include in a specification. < Old French *specifier*.

specimen (ˈspɛsɪmən) *n* **1** a typical or representative part, item, or member; sample: rock specimens. **2** a urine sample. **3** (*chiefly derogatory*) a person: a strange specimen. < Latin *specere* to look at.

specious (ˈspiːʃəs) *adj* **1** seeming to be correct, logical, or genuine, but not really so: specious arguments. **2** deceptively attractive. **speciously** *adv* **speciousness** *n* < Latin *speciosus* plausible.

speck (spɛk) *n* **1** a small spot or blemish. **2** a small particle: specks of dust. < Old English *specca*.

> **specially** or **especially?**
>
> These two words are sometimes confused.
>
> Specially means 'for a particular purpose': a car *specially* designed for handicapped people; *specially* trained workers.
>
> Especially is used in all other instances: People often find it difficult to occupy themselves and this is *especially* ('particularly') true of the old and unemployed. We have many visitors here, *especially* ('particularly') in the summer. Many employees find the technical details *especially* ('particularly') hard to understand. Young people *especially* ('in particular') need to feel loved.
>
> The difference between the words is evident in a sentence such as: We're *especially* grateful, because they came here *specially* to help us.

speckle (ˈspɛkl̩) *n* a small spot or speck. • *vb* mark with speckles.

specs (spɛks) *pl n* (*informal*) spectacles.

spectacle (ˈspɛktəkl̩) *n* **1** something observed or displayed, esp. an impressive public pageant or entertainment. **2** (*informal*) a bizarre or ridiculous sight. **spectacles** *pl n* a pair of lenses held in a frame and worn in front of the eyes to correct vision. < Latin *spectare* to watch.

spectacular (spɛkˈtækjʊlə) *adj* striking or impressive; sensational. • *n* a lavishly produced film, show, pageant, etc. **spectacularly** *adv* < Latin *spectaculum*.

spectator (spɛkˈteɪtə) *n* **1** a person who attends a sports event, display, etc., in order to watch: a football spectator. **2** a person who watches or observes; onlooker. < Latin *spectare* to watch.

spectral (ˈspɛktrəl) *adj* **1** of, like, or connected with a spectre; ghostly. **2** of, produced by, or connected with a spectrum.

spectre (ˈspɛktə) *n* **1** a ghost or apparition. **2** an unpleasant foreboding: the spectre of slavery. < Latin *specere* to look at.

spectrum (ˈspektrəm) *n, pl* **spectra 1** the graduated series of bands produced when light or sound is broken up into its constituent wavelengths. **2** a range or spread. < Latin: appearance.

speculate (ˈspɛkjʊˌleɪt) *vb* **1** ponder; meditate. **2** form ideas or opinions on the basis of few facts or flimsy evidence; conjecture. **3** engage in a risky business; deal in the hope of making a large gain. **speculation** *n* **speculative** *adj* **speculator** *n* < Latin *specula* watchtower.

sped (spɛd) SEE **SPEED**.

speech (spiːtʃ) *n* **1** the faculty of speaking. **2** the act or manner of speaking. **3** conversation; talk. **4** a public talk or address. **5** a language, dialect, or individual manner of speaking. **speech day** an annual ceremonial day at a school when prizes are awarded, speeches are made, etc. **speechless** *adj* unable to speak, esp. because of shock or great emotion. **speechlessly** *adv* < Old English *spǣc*.

speed (spiːd) *n* **1** the rate at which a vehicle, runner, etc., moves; rate at which a machine operates. **2** swiftness; rapidity. **3** a measure of the sensitivity of photographic film, paper, etc., to light. **4** a measure of the ability of a lens to admit light. **5** (*informal*) an

amphetamine drug.
• *vb* **sped; speeding 1** move or operate quickly: A white sports car sped past in the outside lane. **2** drive at an illegally fast speed: fined for speeding. **3** pass quickly: The days on the beach sped by. **4** cause to move or advance quickly: This medicine should speed your recovery. **5** cause to grow or develop quickly: A little bone meal will speed them along. **at speed** quickly. **speedboat** *n* a small, fast motor boat. **speedometer** *n* a device that indicates the speed of a vehicle (and the distance travelled). **speed up** move, operate, work, etc., faster; cause this to happen. **speed-up** *n* **speedway** *n* **1** an oval race-track for motor cycles. **2** the sport of motor cycle racing. **speedy** *adj* **1** fast; swift: a speedy little car. **2** done or happening soon; without delay: a speedy recovery. **speedily** *adv* **speediness** *n* < Old English *spēd.*

spell[1] (spɛl) *vb* **spelt, spelled; spelling 1** name or write the letters of (a word) in the conventionally accepted way. **2** (of letters) form or signify: 'P-i-g spells pig.' **3** mean or amount to: The slightest exposure to heat could spell disaster. **speller** *n* **spell out 1** spell aloud. **2** state or explain clearly and explicitly. < Old French *espeller.*

spell[2] *n* **1** a period of time, usually fairly brief: cold spells. **2** a period spent doing a particular job or activity; tour of duty.
• *vb* relieve (a person) temporarily. < Old English *spelian* to take the place of.

spell[3] *n* **1** words that make up a supposedly magic formula. **2** a state of enchantment. **3** power or influence; fascination. **spellbound** *adj* entranced; fascinated. < Old English.

spend (spɛnd) *vb* **spent; spending 1** pay out (money, etc.): I spent £30 today. **2** use up (time, etc.): Don't spend more than an hour on the job. **3** pass (time, etc.): We intend to spend the weekend in London. **4** (of storms, anger, etc.) wear out; exhaust. **spender** *n* **spendthrift** *n* a person who spends money wastefully or extravagantly. < Old English *spendan.*

spent (spɛnt) SEE **SPEND.**
• *adj* used up; exhausted: a spent match.

sperm (spɜːm) *n* **1** a male reproductive cell. **2** semen. **sperm whale** a large, toothed whale from which a waxy oil is obtained. < ultimately Greek *sperma* seed.

spew (spjuː) *vb* **1** vomit. **2** discharge or eject; be discharged or ejected. < Old English *spīwan.*

sphere (sfɪə) *n* **1** a perfectly round ball or globe. **2** something that resembles this. **3** a field or area: Which sphere of chemistry interests you most? **4** a range of social experience; social circle: They move in different spheres. **spherical** *adj* shaped like a sphere. **spheroid** *n* a figure resembling a sphere. < ultimately Greek *sphaira* ball.

sphinx (sfɪŋks) *n, pl* **sphinxes 1** any of a number of stone statues built by the ancient Egyptians, having the body of a lion and a human head. **2** a mysterious or enigmatic person. < Greek *sphingein* to pull tight. SEE PANEL.

spice (spaɪs) *n* **1** any of various substances such as nutmeg or cinnamon which have a strong taste or smell and are used for flavouring food; these substances collectively. **2** something that adds interest, excitement, or relish.
• *vb* **1** flavour with spice. **2** add interest, excitement, or relish to: The story needs spicing up a bit. **spicy** *adj* **1** of, like, or flavoured with spice. **2** sexually sensational; risqué. < Old French *espice.*

spick (spɪk) *adj* **spick and span** perfectly clean and tidy. SEE PANEL.

spider (ˈspaɪdə) *n* a wingless, insect-like animal with eight legs that spins webs in which to catch its prey. **spidery** *adj* < Old English *spīthra.*

spiel (ʃpiːl) *n* (*informal*) glib talk, usually intended to persuade. < German *spielen* to play.

spike[1] (spaɪk) *n* **1** a sharply pointed projection: Be careful not to tear your trousers on the spikes. **2** any of the metal projections on the bottom of a running shoe. **3** a

the Sphinx

Sphinx was originally an ancient Greek word derived from *sphingein* 'to pull tight or strangle'. According to Greek myth, the Sphinx or 'Strangler' was a monster with the head of a woman and the body of a lion that lay in wait outside the gate at Thebes. Travellers who wished to pass it had first to answer its riddle: 'What animal with just one voice has first four feet, then two feet, then three?' Those who failed to produce the answer were killed.

Oedipus, nobody's fool, produced the correct answer which was man, who first crawls on all fours, then walks on two feet, but in old age requires the support of a stick. Upon hearing this answer the Sphinx hurled herself from the walls of Thebes' citadel.

very large nail.
• *vb* **1** pierce or injure with a spike. **2** put an end to; thwart: spike one's chances. **3** (*informal*) add alcohol to (a drink). **spiky** *adj* **spikes** *pl n* running shoes. < Middle English *spyk*.

spike[2] *n* **1** an ear of grain. **2** an elongated cluster of flowers. < Middle English *spik* head of grain.

spill[1] (spɪl) *vb* **spilt, spilled; spilling** **1** cause or allow to fall or run over the edge of a container: Be careful not to spill the coffee. **2** fall or go with a rush: Onions spilled out of the sack. **3** (*informal*) disclose or reveal: spill the news. **4** cause to fall: The horse spilled her at the first fence. **spill blood** cause blood to be shed. **spill over 1** overflow. **2** spread beyond certain limits. **spill the beans** (*informal*) disclose something indiscreetly.
• *n* spilling or being spilt. **spillage** *n* the amount spilt. < Old English *spillan* to destroy.

spill[2] *n* a taper used for lighting a candle, pipe, etc. < of Germanic origin.

spin (spɪn) *vb* **spun; spinning 1** draw out and twist into threads. **2** (of a spider etc.) form the threads of (a web, etc.). **3** rotate or revolve: The dancer kept spinning round. **4** have the dizzy sensation produced by spinning: I wish my head would stop spinning. **5** compose and narrate (a story)
• *n* **1** a rotating movement. **2** a short journey in a vehicle: go for a spin. **3** a state of confusion: His head is still in a spin. **4** (of an aircraft) a continuously revolving descent. **spin-drier** or **spin-dryer** *n* a machine that dries clothes, etc., by spinning them very quickly in a perforated drum. **spin-dry** *vb* **spin-dried; spin-drying** dry (clothes, etc.) in a spin-drier. **spinning-wheel** *n* a household device for spinning thread or yarn, in which a single spindle is driven by a wheel. **spin-off** *n* an unintended benefit. **spin out** make (something) last as long as possible. < Old English *spinnan*.

spinach (ˈspɪnɪdʒ, ˈspɪnɪtʃ) *n* **1** a plant with dark-green, edible leaves. **2** the leaves of this plant, boiled as a vegetable. < Persian.

spindle (ˈspɪndḷ) *n* **1** a slender rod on which thread is wound in spinning. **2** any slender pin or rod that serves as a shaft or axis. **spindly** *adj* tall and thin; long and thin. < Old English *spinel*.

spine (spaɪn) *n* **1** the backbone. **2** a sharp, spiky projection on a cactus, hedgehog, etc. **3** the part of a book where the pages are held, usually bearing the book's name. **spine-chiller** *n* a film, story, etc., that is designed to cause fear or terror. **spine-chilling** *adj* **spineless** *adj* lacking courage or resolution. < Old French *espine*.

spinet (spɪˈnɛt, ˈspɪnɪt) *n* a small harpsichord. < Italian *spinetta,* probably from G. *Spinetti,* 16th-century Italian maker of musical instruments.

spinnaker (ˈspɪnəkə *nautical* ˈspæŋkə) *n* a very large, triangular sail used on a racing yacht when running before the wind. < origin unknown.

spinney (ˈspɪnɪ) *n* a small wood; thicket. < Middle French *espinaye* thorny thicket.

spinster (ˈspɪnstə) *n* an unmarried woman, esp. one who seems unlikely or too old to marry. **spinsterhood** *n* **spinsterish** *adj* < Middle English *spinnestere* woman engaged in spinning. SEE PANEL.

spiral (ˈspaɪərəl) *adj* **1** winding round a central point at an ever-increasing distance, in the manner of a watch-spring. **2** winding round a central point while continuously changing plane, in the manner of a bed-spring.
• *n* **1** a spiral figure, form, or object. **2** a continuously accelerating increase or decrease: a wage spiral.
• *vb* **spiralled; spiralling** move or cause to move in a spiral course; take a spiral form. **spirally** *adv* < Medieval Latin *spiralis*.

spire (spaɪə) *n* a slender structure tapering to a point like a cone, esp. that on top of a church tower. < Old English *spīr*.

spick and span

Something that is spotlessly clean and very tidy is sometimes described as spick and span. This idiom derives ultimately from the Old Norse *spānnȳr* meaning 'absolutely new'. *Spick,* meaning a 'spike' or 'nail', was added in the 16th century at which time *span new* became spick-and-span-new. This addition both reinforced the idea of newness and provided the phrase with alliterative balance.

The notion of 'absolute newness' remained central to the expression until the mid-18th century.

spirit (ˈspɪrɪt) *n* **1** the soul. **2** a ghost, fairy, etc.: haunted by evil spirits. **3** a person's mind, will, resolve, etc.: The spirit is willing but the flesh is weak. **4** enthusiasm or vivacity: The whole performance displayed a lack of spirit. **5** courage or valour: She showed amazing spirit before the operation. **6** mood or disposition: a spirit of disillusionment. **7** loyalty; allegiance: team spirit. **8** real intention or meaning: the spirit of the law. **9** a highly alcoholic drink; short. **10** a distilled solution.
• *vb* lead or carry away secretly or mysteriously. **spirited** *adj* **1** having vitality or courage: put up a spirited fight. **2** having a particular mood or disposition: high-spirited. **spiritedly** *adv* **spiritedness** *n* **spiritless** *adj* lacking enthusiasm or vitality. **spirit-level** *n* a device that indicates whether a surface is level or not. **spirits** *pl n* **1** a person's feelings or emotions: We did our best to lift his spirits. **2** alcoholic drinks; shorts. < Latin *spiritus* breath.

spiritual (ˈspɪrɪtʃʊəl) *adj* **1** of or connected with the soul; not worldly or material: spiritual needs. **2** of or connected with religion; ecclesiastical. **3** of or connected with supernatural beings.
• *n* a religious song originating amongst Negroes in the southern states of America. **spirituality** *n* **spiritually** *adv* **spiritualism** *n* also **spiritism** the belief that the spirits of the dead can communicate with the living; rites and dealings based upon this. **spiritualist** *n, adj* < SEE **SPIRIT.**

spit[1] (spɪt) *vb* **spat, spit; spitting 1** eject saliva from the mouth. **2** eject forcibly from the mouth: He spat the pieces of cork out. **3** utter angrily. **4** (of rain) fall lightly. **5** make a noise as if spitting. **6** display anger, hostility, etc.
• *n* **1** saliva. **2** the act of spitting. **spit it out** (*informal*) used often impatiently as a command to someone to say what he or she is thinking. **spitting image** an exact likeness. < Old English *spittan.*

spit[2] *n* **1** a thin, pointed, metal rod pushed through meat to hold and turn it during roasting. **2** a long, narrow strip of land that runs out into the sea, etc. < Old English *spitu.*

spite (spaɪt) *n* a malicious urge to hurt, humiliate, etc.
• *vb* hurt, humiliate, etc., out of spite. **spiteful** *adj* **spitefully** *adv* **spitefulness** *n* **in spite of** despite. < Middle English, short for *despite.*

spittle (ˈspɪtl̩) *n* saliva, esp. that which is spat out. < Old English *spǣtl.*

spittoon (spɪˈtuːn) *n* a receptacle for spit.

spiv (spɪv) *n* (*derogatory*) an individual who makes a living from sharp practice or underhand dealings. < back formation from English dialect *spiving* smart.

splash (splæʃ) *vb* **1** wet, soil, or scatter with drops of water, paint, etc.: You'll splash the ceiling if you're not careful. **2** cause drops of water, paint, etc., to fly around: He loves to splash in the bath. **3** (of rain, etc.) fall or descend in drops: Heavy rain splashed against the windscreen. **4** move or advance with splashing: He splashed his way through the puddles. **5** display prominently: The news was splashed across the front page. **6** daub with: She splashed paint all over the walls.
• *n* **1** the act or sound of splashing. **2** a mark or stain caused by splashing. **3** a drop or quantity of liquid that has been splashed. **4** a patch or small area: a splash of colour. **5** a sensational or striking impression: His aim is to make a big splash. **6** a small amount, esp. of a liquid: a splash of milk. **splashy** *adj* **splash-down** *n* the landing of a spacecraft in the sea. < *plash,* probably like the sound.

splatter (ˈsplætə) *vb* fall noisily in heavy drops; splash.
• *n* the act or sound of splattering; splash. < probably *splash* + *spatter.*

splay (spleɪ) *vb* spread out; extend.
• *adj* spread out or turned outwards. < Middle English *splayen.*

spleen (spliːn) *n* a large organ situated close to the stomach which produces

spinster

An elderly woman who has never married is commonly known as a spinster. This word is a development of the Middle English *spinnestere,* that is, 'a person, especially a woman, engaged in spinning', from the Old English *spinnan* 'to spin' and the agent suffix *-estere* '-ster'. When the word entered the language in the 14th century it applied to anyone in the household whose main occupation was spinning. It so happened that these members were typically female and unmarried. By the 17th century these two semantic features had taken over the meaning of the word.

lymph cells and breaks down the blood corpuscles. < Middle French *esplen.*

splendid (ˈsplɛndɪd) *adj* **1** very enjoyable: a splendid afternoon in the countryside. **2** excellent; admirable: a splendid attempt. **3** having grandeur or magnificence: a splendid tiara studded with jewels. **splendidly** *adv* **splendidness** *n* **splendour** *n* the state or quality of being splendid. < Latin *splendēre* to shine.

splice (splaɪs) *vb* **1** join (the ends of two ropes) by weaving the strands together. **2** join (two pieces of film, etc.) by overlapping the ends.
• *n* a join made by splicing. **get spliced** (*informal*) marry. < probably Middle Dutch *splissen.*

splint (splɪnt) *n* a length of rigid material bound usually to a broken or fractured limb to prevent it from moving.
• *vb* secure and support with a splint. < Middle Low German *splinte.*

splinter (ˈsplɪntə) *n* a thin, sharp piece of material that has split off lengthwise from a larger piece.
• *adj* that has broken away from a larger body: a splinter group.
• *vb* split into splinters. < SEE **SPLINT.**

split (splɪt) *vb* **split; splitting 1** break or divide, esp, lengthwise. **2** divide or separate into parts or (hostile) groups: How shall we split the money? **3** rip, burst, or come apart: split one's sides laughing. **4** (*informal*) reveal a person's secret, etc.; inform on. **5** (*informal*) leave.
• *n* **1** splitting or being split. **2** a tear, crack, etc., caused by splitting. **3** a division: a split in the party. **4** (*informal*) a share or portion: a split of the loot. **5** a sweet dish of fruit, esp. a banana split lengthwise, and ice-cream, etc. **split infinitive** an infinitive which has a word coming between to and the verb, as in to clearly see. **split-level** *adj* **1** having one or more floors that do not coincide with the main storey levels. **2** (of a cooker) having the oven and burners or hotplates separated so that each is at a convenient working height. **split personality** schizophrenia. **split pin** a sturdy metal pin that is split at one end or made of a strip of metal folded double, which is used as a fastening device. **split second** a fraction of a second. **split-second** *adj* **1** involving or done with the greatest precision: split-second timing. **2** done or made in an extremely short time: a split-second decision. **splitting** *adj* (of a headache) severe. **split up** (of a married couple, etc.) separate. **the splits** a gymnastic exercise in which one sinks to a sitting position with the legs out straight and at right angles to the body. < Dutch *splitten.* SEE PANEL AT **TO.**

splutter (ˈsplʌtə) *vb* **1** speak indistinctly or with spitting sounds; make such a noise. **2** eject food particles or saliva noisily from the mouth, esp. when laughing or choking.
• *n* the act or sound of spluttering. < probably *sputter.*

spoil (spɔɪl) *vb* **spoilt, spoiled; spoiling 1** damage or destroy the value, beauty, usefulness, etc., of: Try not to spoil your new shoes. **2** become unfit for use; go bad: The tomatoes have spoilt. **3** harm the character of (a person, esp. a young child) by complying excessively with his or her desires. **be spoiling for** be eager for: spoiling for a fight. **spoils** *pl* profit or reward; plunder: the spoils of war. **spoilsport** *n* a person who spoils the enjoyment of others. < Middle French *espoillier.*

spoke[1] (spəʊk) SEE **SPEAK.**

spoke[2] *n* **1** one of the thick wires or rods that run from the hub of a wheel to the rim. **2** any similar radial member, such as one of the struts of an umbrella. **3** a rung of a ladder. < Old English *spāca.*

spoken (ˈspəʊkən) SEE **SPEAK. spoken for** unavailable because already sold or promised to another person.

spokesman (ˈspəʊksmən) fem. **spokeswoman** *n* a person who speaks on behalf of another person or group.

sponge (spʌndʒ) *n* **1** an aquatic animal with a highly porous body. **2** the skeleton of this animal, used chiefly for washing or padding; something man-made that resembles this. **3** a sponge-cake. **4** the act of washing with a sponge.
• *vb* **1** wipe or wash with a sponge. **2** live or eat at another person's expense: sponge on people. **sponge-bag** *n* a waterproof bag for toiletries. **sponge-cake** *n* a light, airy cake made with sugar, flour, and eggs. **sponger** *n* a person who sponges on others. **spongy** *adj* soft, springy, or absorbent like a sponge. < ultimately Greek *spongia.*

sponsor (ˈspɒnsə) *n* **1** a person or organization that promotes or provides the funds for a project or activity. **2** a person who assumes responsibility for some other person or thing; surety. **3** a godparent. **4** a person who proposes something.
• *vb* act as a sponsor. **sponsorship** *n* < Latin *spondēre* to promise. SEE PANEL AT **SPOUSE.**

spontaneous (spɒnˈteɪnɪəs) *adj* done, said, or produced naturally and without external pressure; impulsive: spontaneous laughter. **spontaneous combustion** the igniting of a combustible mass as a result of the heat produced within itself. **spontaneously** *adv* **spontaneousness** or **spontaneity** *n* < Latin *sponte* voluntarily.

spoof (spu:f) *n* (*informal*) light-hearted satire or parody. < *Spoof,* game invented by A. Roberts, died 1933, English comedian.

spook (spu:k) *n* (*informal*) a ghost. **spooky** *adj* suggestive of ghosts; eerie. < Dutch.

spool (spu:l) *n* a reel or cylinder on which film, wire, yarn, etc., is wound. < of Germanic origin.

spoon (spu:n) *n* **1** an implement comprising a round or oval, shallow bowl on a handle, used chiefly for preparing and serving food, or for conveying soup, custard, etc., to the mouth. **2** a spoonful. • *vb* convey with a spoon. **spoon-feed** *vb* **spoon-fed; spoon-feeding 1** feed with a spoon. **2** assist (a person) in a way that saves him or her from having to act or think independently. **spoonful** *n, pl* **spoonfuls** the amount a spoon holds. < Old English *spōn* splinter.

spoonerism (ˈspu:nəˌrɪzəm) *n* the unintentional transposition of the initial sounds of two or more words. SEE PANEL.

sporadic (spəˈrædɪk) *adj* occurring or appearing irregularly: sporadic bursts of gunfire. **sporadically** *adv* < Medieval Latin *sporadicus.*

spore (spɔ:) *n* any of the minute reproductive cells produced by plants such as fungi and ferns, and by some plant-like animals. **sporiferous** *adj* < Greek *speirein* to sow.

sporran (ˈspɒrən) *n* a large pouch worn hanging in front of the kilt as part of Highland costume. < Scottish Gaelic *sporan* purse.

sport (spɔ:t) *n* **1** any game or competition involving physical activity organized for the enjoyment or exercise of the participants or for the pleasure of the spectators. **2** these games and competitions viewed as a whole: He loves sport. **3** any of various indoor and outdoor pastimes, such as hunting, fishing, etc. **4** fun or mockery: make sport of someone's efforts. **5** (*informal*) a person considered in terms of his or her sportsmanlike qualities: a good sport. • *vb* **1** wear or have on view: sport a new tie. **2** play; frolic. **sporting** *adj* **1** sportsmanlike. **2** interested in or connected with sport. **3** with reasonable prospects of success: a sporting chance. **sportingly** *adv* **sportive** *adj* playful; frolicsome. **sportively** *adv* **sports** *adj* of, suitable for, or connected with sport: a sports hall. **sports car** a fast, low car, usually for just two people. **sports jacket** a man's jacket designed for casual wear. **sportsman** fem. **sportswoman** *n* **1** a person who engages in sport. **2** a sportsmanlike person. **sportsmanlike** *adj* in accordance with fair, honourable, or magnanimous conduct. **sportsmanship** *n* sportsmanlike conduct. **sportswear** *n* clothing designed for sporting activity or casual wear. **sporty** *adj* **1** stylish; dashing. **2** having talent or interest in sport. < Middle English *sporten* to divert.

spot (spɒt) *n* **1** a round or roundish mark of a different colour to the rest of a surface: a red tie with black spots. **2** a mark or blemish: The rain dried up but left spots on the windscreen. **3** a pimple: break out in spots. **4** (*informal*) a small amount: a spot of milk. **5** a drop: spots of rain. **6** a place or location: a nice quiet spot for a picnic. **7** a spotlight. • *vb* **spotted; spotting 1** mark with one or more spots: spotted with ink. **2** catch sight

spoonerisms

Children love to play games and language lends itself readily to their fun-making. A timeless source of amusement is the transposing of initial sounds in words, as in chish and fips (fish and chips) and mad and dum (dad and mum). The more ludicrous the effect of these so-called *spoonerisms,* the better.

The term *spoonerism* derives from the Rev. William A. Spooner, 1844–1930, who was Dean and Warden of New College, Oxford. Spooner's *spoonerisms,* however, were not produced deliberately but accidentally as a result of absent-mindedness and nervous exhaustion. Amongst the best-known examples attributed to him are: 'We all know what it is to have a half-warmed fish within us.' (half-formed wish) 'Yes, indeed; the Lord is a shoving leopard.' 'Kinquering kongs their titles take.' 'Excuse me, but I think you are occupewing my pie.' 'I have never before addressed so many tons of soil.'

Sometimes the same term is applied to a similar slip of the tongue: the transposing of whole words. How embarrassing to have to confess to a hole full of socks or to having let the bag out of the cat!

of; notice: I spotted him getting into a taxi. **3** detect by close scrutiny: Can you spot the deliberate mistakes? **4** identify and record the details of: train-spotting. **spot check** an inspection made randomly and without warning. **spotless** *adj* perfectly clean. **spotlessly** *adv* **spot-on** *adj* (*informal*) perfectly accurate or appropriate. **spotter** *n* a person or thing that spots: a talent spotter. **spotty** *adj* **1** covered with spots or pimples. **2** irregular or uneven; patchy: spotty attendance. < Middle English.

spotlight ('spɒtˌlaɪt) *n* a light with a powerful, narrow beam.
• *vb* **spotlit, spotlighted; spotlighting** **1** illuminate with a spotlight. **2** draw attention to.

spouse (spaʊs) *n* a person's husband or wife. < ultimately Latin *spondēre* to betroth. SEE PANEL.

spout (spaʊt) *n* **1** a projecting pipe or tube, esp. for pouring liquid. **2** a jet of liquid.
• *vb* **1** eject or be ejected in a jet: Oil spouted from the crack in the tank. **2** speak in a prolific or tiresome way. < Middle English *spouten*. SEE PANEL.

sprain (spreɪn) *vb* injure (a joint, muscle, etc.) by violent twisting or wrenching.
• *n* an injury caused by this. < origin unknown.

sprang (spræŋ) SEE **SPRING.**

sprawl (sprɔːl) *vb* **1** lie or sit with limbs spread out inelegantly. **2** extend irregularly or in an untidy way.
• *n* a sprawling position, mass, or extent. < Old English *sprēawlian*.

spray[1] (spreɪ) *vb* **1** disperse (water or some other liquid) in a mist or fine drops. **2** wet, moisten, or coat by spraying.
• *n* **1** water or other liquid that is sprayed: Try not to breathe in the spray. **2** a device used for spraying. **sprayer** *n* **spray-gun** *n* a gun-shaped device that sprays liquids by means of compressed air. < Middle Dutch *sprayen*.

spray[2] *n* **1** a single, slender branch with its leaves, flowers, etc. **2** a decorative arrangement of flowers having a similar form. < Middle English.

spread (sprɛd) *vb* **spread; spreading** **1** hold out or unfold: spread one's fingers. **2** extend further: The epidemic began to spread. **3** apply or be applied in a layer or coating: The butter won't spread. **4** distribute over a period of time or among various persons: spread the payments over two years.
• *n* **1** spreading; being spread. **2** the extent in space or time of spreading; range: a two-mile spread. **3** something to be spread on bread: cheese spread. **4** (*informal*) a lavish meal; feast. **5** something in a magazine, newspaper, etc., occupying a large area: a two-page spread. **spread-eagle** *vb* cause (a person) to lie with arms and legs stretched out, esp. by a blow or attack. **spread-eagled** *adj* < Old English *sprǣdan*.

spree (spriː) *n* a bout of unrestrained indulgence: a spending spree. < perhaps Scottish *spreath* cattle raid. SEE PANEL.

sprig (sprɪg) *n* **1** a small shoot or twig. **2** an ornament with this form. **3** a small, headless nail. < Middle English *sprigge*.

sprightly ('spraɪtlɪ) *adj* lively; brisk. < obsolete *sprite* + *-ly*.

spring (sprɪŋ) *vb* **sprang; sprung; springing** **1** rise or move quickly and suddenly: spring to one's feet. **2** grow or appear quickly and suddenly: New buildings are springing up all over the city. **3** pour

spouse

The formal or legal word for a marriage partner is spouse. This word comes via Old French from the Latin *sponsus* 'a betrothed man' and *sponsa* 'a betrothed woman'. Both of these forms derive from the verb *spondēre* 'to promise solemnly; betroth'. A spouse is therefore literally 'the person to whom someone is solemnly promised'.

The same Latin root provides the word sponsor, in one of its senses 'a person who pledges to take responsibility for another'.

up the spout

From round about the beginning of the 18th century an article that had gone up the spout had been taken to the pawnbroker's. This usage derived from the *spout*, the name of the hoist inside a pawnbroker's shop which carried a pledge to the storeroom above. This literal meaning was swallowed up as application of the phrase broadened and it acquired its modern, metaphorical sense of 'in a hopeless condition; ruined'.

forth suddenly and copiously: Tears sprang from her eyes. **4** arise or result: Her anxiety springs from a lack of trust. **5** make or become warped or split: sprung floorboards. **6** operate or cause to operate suddenly: spring a trap. **7** develop: spring a leak. **8** disclose or make known suddenly: spring the news. **9** (*informal*) engineer the escape of.
• *n* **1** the act of springing; leap. **2** any of several mechanical devices that return to their original shape when an external force is removed, such as a coil of heavy wire in a mattress. **3** elasticity or resilience: The seats have lost their spring. **4** the season of the year between winter and summer. **5** a natural outflow of water or oil. **6** a source or origin. **spring balance** a device that measures weight by the pull exerted on a coiled spring. **springboard** *n* a springy board used by gymnasts and divers for gaining extra height. **spring-clean** *vb* give (a house) a thorough cleaning, usually in the spring. **spring-cleaning** *n* **spring onion** an onion with a small, white bulb and long, green shoots, usually eaten raw in salads. **spring tide** a tide which has the greatest rise and fall of water occurring at new and full moon. **springtime** *n* the season of spring. **springy** *adj* having bounce, elasticity, or resilience. **springiness** *n* < Old English *springan*.

sprinkle (ˈsprɪŋkl̩) *vb* scatter (drops of liquid, etc.) lightly over something.
• *n* a sprinkling. **sprinkler** *n* a device for sprinkling or spraying, esp. water. **sprinkling** *n* a small quantity or amount: a sprinkling of pepper. < Middle English *sprinclen*.

sprint (sprɪnt) *vb* run at full speed.
• *n* **1** a run at full speed; burst of speed. **2** a short-distance race. **sprinter** *n* < Scandinavian.

> **spree**
>
> A bout of unrestrained indulgence is sometimes referred to as a spree. Nowadays this word is used mostly in association with spending or drinking. Occasionally, however, it is used of criminals such as thieves or housebreakers: Burglars had a real *spree* over the holiday weekend with reports of more than 200 break-ins. The latter usage recalls the origin of the word. Spree is believed to derive from the Scottish *spreath* meaning 'cattle raid'.

sprocket (ˈsprɒkɪt) *n* one of a series of teeth shaped to interlock with the links of a chain. < origin unknown.

sprout (spraʊt) *vb* **1** push out new leaves, shoots, etc. **2** begin to grow or develop; germinate.
• *n* **1** the shoot of a plant. **2** a Brussels sprout. < Old English *sprūtan*.

spruce[1] (spru:s) *adj* neat and smart.
• *vb* smarten: spruce oneself up. **sprucely** *adv* **spruceness** *n* < perhaps *Spruce leather* leather imported from Prussia.

spruce[2] *n* any of a group of evergreen trees of the pine family; its wood. < short for *Spruce fir*, from obsolete *Spruce* Prussia.

sprung (sprʌŋ) SEE **SPRING**.
• *adj* fitted with springs.

spry (spraɪ) *adj* nimble; active. **spryly** *adv* **spryness** *n* < origin uncertain.

spun (spʌn) SEE **SPIN**. **spun silk** yarn or fabric made from waste silk.

spur (spɜ:) *n* **1** a pointed device attached to the heel of a horseman for urging on a horse. **2** a stimulus or incentive. **3** a spur-like projection on the back of the leg of a cock. **4** a ridge projecting sideways from a mountain or mountain range. **5** a minor branch of a road or railway track. **6** a short or undeveloped branch of a tree.
• *vb* **spurred; spurring 1** urge (a horse) on with spurs. **2** urge on, incite, or inspire. **on the spur of the moment** on impulse; spontaneously. < Old English *spura*.

spurious (ˈspjʊərɪəs) *adj* not genuine or real; false. **spuriously** *adv* **spuriousness** *n* < Latin *spurius* of illegitimate birth.

spurn (spɜ:n) *vb* reject scornfully: She spurned our invitation. < Old English *spurnan*.

spurt (spɜ:t) *vb* gush or cause to gush out in a jet: Blood spurted from the wound.
• *n* **1** a sudden gush or outpouring: a spurt of jealousy. **2** a burst of increased effort or activity. < origin uncertain.

spy (spaɪ) *n* a person employed by a government or institution to try to obtain secret information about a rival country or institution.
• *vb* **spied; spying 1** see or catch sight of. **2** observe secretly: He was caught spying on her. **3** act as a spy. < Old French *espier*.

squabble (ˈskwɒbl̩) *vb* quarrel noisily like children about something trivial.
• *n* a trivial argument. < probably

Scandinavian.
squad (skwɒd) *n* **1** a small group of people engaged in some common activity or effort; team: a football squad. **2** the smallest military unit. < Middle French *esquade.*
squadron (ˈskwɒdrən) *n* **1** the basic unit of the RAF usually comprising between 10 and 18 aircraft. **2** a cavalry unit comprising two or more troops. **3** a naval unit assigned to a particular mission. **squadron leader** an RAF officer next in rank below wing commander. < Italian *squadrone* soldiers drawn up in square formation.
squalid (ˈskwɒlɪd) *adj* **1** dirty and unpleasant, esp. because of poverty and neglect. **2** degraded; base. **squalidly** *adv* **squalor** *n* < Latin *squalidus.*
squall[1] (skwɔːl) *n* **1** a sudden violent wind, often with rain or snow. **2** a commotion. < probably Scandinavian.
squall[2] *vb* scream or cry out raucously. **squaller** *n* < Scandinavian.
squander (ˈskwɒndə) *vb* spend extravagantly or wastefully. **squanderer** *n* < origin unknown.
square (skwɛə) *n* **1** a geometric figure with four equal sides and four right angles. **2** something shaped like this. **3** an open area with four sides, usually bordered by streets and buildings: Cadogan Square. **4** the product of a number multiplied by itself: The square of 9 is 81. **5** an instrument with at least one right angle, used for testing or drawing right angles: a T-square. **6** (*informal*) a person who is considered old-fashioned or conservative in ideas, taste, etc.
• *adj* **1** having the shape of a square. **2** right-angled: a square corner. **3** having the same measurement on all four sides: two metres square. **4** of a unit used in the measuring of an area: two square metres. **5** sturdy; stocky: a square frame. **6** properly adjusted, arranged, or sorted out. **7** honest, just, or straightforward: a square answer. **8** even, balanced, or settled: all square at half-time. **9** (*informal*) old-fashioned or conservative in ideas, taste, etc.
• *adv* **1** directly; squarely: look someone square in the face. **2** fronting on to. **3** at right angles.
• *vb* **1** make into a square or similar shape. **2** mark off into squares. **3** position so as to be level or form approximate right angles: square one's shoulders. **4** multiply a number by itself. **5** settle (an account); pay (a bill): You pay for now and we'll square up later. **6** conform or agree; make consistent: I'm unable to square her story with the police report. **squarely** *adv* **squareness** *n* **square dance** a dance in which 4 couples form a square. **square root** a number that multiplied by itself makes a given number: The square root of 81 is 9. **square up to 1** stand as if ready to fight. **2** prepare oneself to deal with (a difficult situation). < ultimately Latin *quadrare* to make square. SEE PANEL AT **CIRCLE.**
squash[1] (skwɒʃ) *vb* **1** crush or press into a pulp; flatten. **2** force or squeeze into a small space: We all managed to squash in. **3** put down or suppress: squash a rebellion. **4** reduce to silence.
• *n* **1** the act or sound of squashing; state of being squashed or crowded together: It was a bit of a squash but they all got in. **2** something squashed. **3** a still drink made from fruit juice and water. **4** also **squash rackets** a game for two people played with rackets and a small ball on a closed court. **squashy** *adj* easily squashed; soft. < Old French *esquasser.*
squash[2] *n, pl* **squash, squashes** any of a group of plants of the cucumber family; its fruit, used as a vegetable. < Amerindian *askútasquash* green vegetable eaten green.
squat (skwɒt) *vb* **squatted; squatting** **1** sit on one's heels; crouch. **2** (of an animal) crouch close to the ground. **3** enter and live in unoccupied property without the right to do so. **4** settle on public land without legal entitlement.
• *n* **1** the act of squatting. **2** a squatting position.
• *adj* short and stout; dumpy. **squatter** *n* a person who squats in unoccupied property or on public land. < Middle French *esquatir.*
squaw (skwɔː) *n* a North American Indian woman. < Algonquian.
squawk (skwɔːk) *n* a loud, harsh cry, like that of a frightened bird.
• *vb* **1** utter a squawk. **2** (*informal*) complain or protest noisily. < probably *squall* + *squeak.*
squeak (skwiːk) *n* a short, shrill cry or sound.
• *vb* make a squeak. **narrow squeak** (*informal*) a narrow escape. **squeaky** *adj* making squeaks. **squeakily** *adv* **squeakiness** *n* < Middle English *squeken.*
squeal (skwiːl) *n* a prolonged, shrill cry.
• *vb* **1** utter a squeal. **2** (*informal*) turn informer. < Middle English *squelen.*
squeamish (ˈskwiːmɪʃ) *adj* **1** easily shocked or nauseated by the sight of

blood, violence, etc. **2** excessively scrupulous about principles, behaviour, etc. **squeamishly** *adv* **squeamishness** *n* < Middle English *squaymisch*.

squeeze (skwi:z) *vb* **1** exert pressure on, esp. from opposite sides: She squeezed his hand affectionately. **2** extract by pressing: squeeze juice from a lemon. **3** force into, through, etc.: He squeezed into the crowded compartment. **4** (*informal*) harass or pressurize: squeeze someone for money.
● *n* **1** the act of squeezing or being squeezed; instance of this: He gave her an affectionate squeeze. **2** a small amount: a squeeze of lemon. **3** the state of being squeezed: They all got in the telephone box, but it was a very tight squeeze. **4** a time of financial restriction. **squeezer** *n* a device for extracting juice from fruit. < Old English *cwȳsan*.

squelch (skwɛltʃ) *n* the sound of semi-liquid material being pressed down and sucked up, such as when walking through thick, wet mud.
● *vb* make this sound. **squelchy** *adj* < like the sound.

squib (skwɪb) *n* a small firework which hisses and then explodes. **damp squib** something that is expected to impress, etc., but which fails to do so. < origin unknown.

squid (skwɪd) *n, pl* **squids, squid** a sea-animal with ten arms and a long body. < origin unknown.

squiggle (ˈskwɪɡl̩) *n, vb* (draw) a short, curly or twisting line. **squiggly** *adj* < *squirm* + *wriggle*.

squint (skwɪnt) *vb* **1** look at something with the eyes partly closed: squinting into the sun. **2** be cross-eyed.
● *n* **1** a disorder of the eye muscles which causes the eyes to look in different directions. **2** the act or an instance of squinting. **squintingly** *adv* < short for *asquint*.

squire (skwaɪə) *n* **1** a country gentleman, esp. the principal local landowner. **2** (*informal*) sir. < Old French *esquier*.

squirm (skwɜːm) *vb* **1** wriggle or twist about. **2** feel uneasy with embarrassment.
● *n* a squirming movement. < origin uncertain.

squirrel (ˈskwɪrəl) *n* a small, tree-climbing rodent with a long, bushy tail and strong hind legs; its fur. < Middle French *esquireul*. SEE PANEL.

squirt (skwɜːt) *vb* send out (liquid) in a jet or (of a liquid) be sent out in a jet.
● *n* **1** a jet of liquid. **2** (*derogatory*) a small or insignificant person. < Middle English *squirten*.

SRN *abbrev* State Registered Nurse.

St *abbrev* **1** Street. **2** Saint.

stab (stæb) *vb* **stabbed; stabbing** **1** pierce or wound with or as if with a knife, etc. **2** thrust (a knife, etc.) into; try to do this.
● *n* **1** the act or an instance of stabbing. **2** a wound made by stabbing. **3** a painful feeling: a stab of jealousy. < Middle English *stabbe* stab wound.

stable¹ (ˈsteɪbl̩) *adj* **1** firm or rigid: The table legs aren't very stable. **2** constant or unfluctuating: Prices remained stable. **stability** *n* **stably** *adv* **stabilize** *vb* make or become stable. **stabilization** *n* **stabilizer** *n* **1** a device for keeping a ship steady in rough seas. **2** either of a pair of additional rear wheels which keep a child's bicycle upright. < ultimately Latin *stare* to stand.

stable² *n* **1** a building in which horses are kept. **2** all the racehorses or racing-cars owned by one establishment; racing establishment. **3** a group, collection, or organization: They all come from the same stable.
● *vb* put or keep in a stable. < Old French *estable* cowshed.

stack (stæk) *n* **1** a large pile of hay, straw, etc. **2** an orderly pile or heap: a stack of books. **3** (*informal*) a great amount or quantity: stacks of work. **4** a chimney-stack. **5** a part of a library where books are stored on compactly spaced shelves. **6** a number of aircraft at different altitudes, each waiting its turn to land.
● *vb* **1** pile or arrange in a stack. **2** arrange unfairly, esp. for cheating: The cards were stacked against him. **3** (of aircraft) fly in a stack while waiting to land; cause (aircraft) to wait like this. < Old Norse *stakkr*.

squirrel

Perhaps the most distinguishing feature of the squirrel is its bushy tail. It was certainly this feature which caught the eye of the ancients when they provided the creature with a name. Squirrel comes via the French *esquireul* and the Latin *sciurus* from the Greek *skiouros*. This is a blend of *skia* 'shadow' and *oura* 'tail'. Evidently the Greeks believed that the squirrel or 'shadow tail' used its rear appendage as a parasol.

stadium (ˈsteɪdɪəm) *n, pl* **stadiums, stadia** a sports ground surrounded by tiers of seats for spectators. < Greek *stadion.*

staff (stɑːf) *n, pl* defs. **1–2 staffs,** defs. **3–4 staffs, staves 1** all the people who work under another or run an establishment; personnel. **2** a group of officers assisting a commanding officer. **3** a rod, pole, or stick. **4** the five horizontal lines on which music is written.
• *vb* equip with employees. < Old English *stæf.* SEE PANEL AT **STAVE.**

stag (stæg) *n* a fully-grown male deer.
• *adj* for men only: a stag party. < Old English *stagga.*

stage (steɪdʒ) *n* **1** a platform or area on which plays, etc., are performed before an audience. **2** a raised platform, esp. at the front of a hall. **3** the scene of any significant action or event. **4** one step or episode in a series: The project is still in its early stages. **5** a stopping-place on a route; distance between such stops. **6** a powered section of a space-rocket, jettisoned when its fuel is spent.
• *vb* **1** present (a play, etc.) on a stage. **2** organize and conduct: stage an exhibition. **stage-coach** *n* an enclosed, horse-drawn carriage, formerly used to carry passengers, mail, etc., over a certain route. **stage fright** nervousness caused by (the thought of) being in front of an audience. **the stage** the acting profession; the theatre. < Old French *estage.*

stagger (ˈstægə) *vb* **1** walk unsteadily as if about to fall. **2** shock, overwhelm, or astonish: We were staggered by the news. **3** arrange in alternating periods or positions: staggered holidays.
• *n* a staggering movement. **staggering** *adj* astonishing; overwhelming: The response was staggering. < Old Norse *staka* to push.

stagnant (ˈstægnənt) *adj* **1** (of water, etc.) not flowing; foul. **2** inactive; lifeless. **stagnate** *vb* **1** be or become stagnant. **2** stop developing through lack of incentive, opportunity, etc. **stagnation** *n* < Latin *stagnum* pool of standing water.

staid (steɪd) *adj* sober and sedate. < obsolete past participle of *stay¹.*

stain (steɪn) *vb* **1** mark, soil, or discolour; leave such a mark, etc., on: That ink will stain the carpet. **2** smear or blemish: stain a person's reputation. **3** change (the colour of wood, etc.) to a new colour.
• *n* **1** a mark caused by staining. **2** a smear: The trial left a stain on his character. **3** a liquid dye used for staining. **stained glass** glass coloured or stained for use in church windows, etc. **stainless** *adj* free from stains or blemish: a stainless record. **stainless steel** a type of steel which contains chromium and is highly resistant to corrosion. < ultimately Latin *tingere* to tinge.

stair (stɛə) *n* one of a series of fixed indoor steps leading from one level to another. **staircase** *n* a flight of stairs, usually fitted with a handrail. **stairs** *pl n* a staircase. < Old English *stǣger.*

stake (steɪk) *n* **1** a length of pointed wood, metal, etc., driven into the ground as a support or marker. **2** the post to which a person was bound for execution by burning. **3** a sum of money or some valuable wagered on the outcome of a race, contest, etc. **4** an investment or involvement.
• *vb* **1** support or secure with one or more stakes. **2** mark the position or boundary of by means of one or more stakes. **3** wager (money, etc.). **at stake** at risk. < Old English *staca.*

stalactite (ˈstæləkˌtaɪt) *n* a mass of calcium carbonate hanging like an icicle from the roof of a cave. < Greek *stalaktos* dripping. SEE PANEL.

stalagmite (ˈstæləgˌmaɪt) *n* a tapering pillar of calcium carbonate on the floor of a cave. < Greek *stalagmos* dripping. SEE PANEL AT **STALACTITE.**

stale (steɪl) *adj* **1** lacking freshness: stale bread. **2** not funny or interesting because previously heard: stale jokes. **3** no longer able to work, perform, etc., well because of too much exertion or practice. **stalely** *adv* **staleness** *n* < origin uncertain.

stalemate (ˈsteɪlˌmeɪt) *n* **1** a position in chess in which a player can move only his or her king but not without putting it into check. **2** any deadlock.
• *vb* bring into a position of stalemate.

stalactite or **stalagmite?**

These two words are sometimes confused. Which one hangs from the roof of a cave, and which one points upwards from the floor?

The one that hangs from the roof is a stalactite (think of *c* for ceiling). The one that points upwards from the floor is a stalagmite (think of *g* for ground).

< obsolete *stale,* from Old French *estal* stall + (*check*)*mate.*

stalk[1] (stɔːk) *n* **1** the stem of a plant, flower, leaf, fruit, etc. **2** any long, slender supporting structure. < Middle English *stalke.*

stalk[2] *vb* **1** pursue or approach (a prey) stealthily. **2** walk in a stiff or haughty manner. **stalker** *n* < Old English *bestealcian.*

stall (stɔːl) *n* **1** a bench, stand, etc., on which articles are displayed for sale. **2** a small booth from which business is conducted. **3** a compartment in a stable or cowshed. **4** a seat in the chancel of a church; pew. **5** one of the seats on the ground floor of an auditorium.
• *vb* **1** cause an engine to stop unintentionally; (of an engine) stop suddenly. **2** (of an aircraft) plummet because of insufficient speed; cause this to happen. **3** use delaying tactics: stall for time. **4** put or keep (an animal) in a stall. < Old English *steall.*

stallion (ˈstæljən) *n* an uncastrated male horse. < Middle French *estalon.*

stalwart (ˈstɔːlwət) *adj* **1** (*literary*) strong and sturdy; robust. **2** staunch: stalwart supporters.
• *n* a stalwart person. < Old English *stǣlwierthe* serviceable.

stamen (ˈsteɪmɛn) *n* the male part of a flower made up of a filament and an anther. < Latin: thread.

stamina (ˈstæmɪnə) *n* the strength required for prolonged physical effort. < Latin *stamen* thread of life spun out by the Fates; energy.

stammer (ˈstæmə) *vb* speak with involuntary hesitations or repetitions; stutter.
• *n* a stammering speech tendency. **stammerer** *n* < Old English *stamerian.*

stamp (stæmp) *vb* **1** bring (one's foot) down heavily on the ground, like an angry child. **2** strike with the bottom of the foot: stamp a fire out. **3** walk noisily with heavy steps: He stamped out of the room. **4** impress with a mark or design. **5** attach a postage stamp to: stamp an envelope. **6** provide with a distinguishing characteristic: stamped as a traitor.
• *n* **1** the act or sound of stamping. **2** a device used for impressing a mark or design upon something; mark or design made by this. **3** a postage stamp. **4** a distinguishing mark or characteristic: the stamp of truth. **stamp duty** a tax on certain legal documents. **stamping-ground** *n* (*informal*) a place regularly visited by a person or animal. **stamp out** put down or suppress (a rebellion, etc.). < Middle English *stampen.*

stampede (stæmˈpiːd) *n* a wild, headlong rush by a herd of horses, cattle, or other large group, esp. due to panic.
• *vb* rush headlong or cause to rush headlong in a stampede. < American Spanish *estampida* crash.

stance (stɑːns, stæns) *n* **1** a way of standing or positioning the body, as when about to make a stroke in golf, cricket, etc.: an unorthodox stance. **2** an attitude or standpoint: He adopted a firm stance on the issue. < Latin *stare* to stand.

stanch (stɑːntʃ) *vb* stop or check the flow of (blood, tears, etc.); staunch. < Middle French *estancher.* SEE PANEL.

stand (stænd) *vb* **stood; standing** **1** adopt or remain in an upright position: We all stood up as she came in. **2** put upright in a particular place: She stood the umbrella in the corner. **3** be in a particular place: The cottage stood at the bottom of the hill. **4** remain motionless: The taxi stood thirty minutes in the traffic jam. **5** remain unchanged, valid, or in a particular condition: The temperature still stood at 45°. **6** offer oneself for election or a particular position: He has agreed to stand for chairman. **7** endure, tolerate, or put up with: She can't stand red cabbage. **8** undergo: stand trial. **9** pay for (a meal, etc.) for someone.
• *n* **1** an act, manner, or place of standing: The policeman took his stand in front of the door. **2** a standpoint or opinion: She took a firm stand on capital punishment. **3** an effort to resist an attack: We must make a firm stand against these proposals. **4** a bench or trestle table where goods are displayed. **5** a small booth or kiosk; stall. **6** a pedestal, rack, or other object for holding or supporting something: Put the vase back on its stand. **7** a raised structure with tiers of seats for spectators beside a football pitch, racecourse, etc. **8** a place where

stanch or **staunch?**

These words are sometimes confused. In the meaning 'to stop or check the flow of', either stanch or staunch may be used, though stanch is old-fashioned: *stanch* the flow of blood; *staunch* one's tears. However, in the meaning 'firm or loyal', only staunch is possible: a *staunch* ally, a *staunch* union supporter.

vehicles wait: a taxi stand. **stand-pipe** *n* a vertical pipe leading directly from a water-main, chiefly used as a hydrant or emergency water supply. **standpoint** *n* a point of view. **standstill** *n* a prolonged halt or stoppage: The traffic came to a standstill. < Old English *standan.* SEE PANEL.

standard (ˈstændəd) *n* **1** a level of quality, achievement, etc., which serves as a basis for evaluation or example to be aimed at: Standards must be maintained. **2** an official or recognized standard: His marks are well below standard. **3** an official or established unit of measurement: The metre is the international standard of length. **4** an image, figure, or symbol, esp. on a flag, adopted by a country as an emblem. **5** a flag or banner. **6** an upright support. **7** a shrub that grows on an upright stem. • *adj* **1** accepted as standard or usual: standard lengths. **2** basic or without extras: a standard model. **3** widely recognized as the best, most authoritative, etc.: a standard text. **standardize** *vb* make (something) conform to a standard. **standardization** *n* **standard lamp** a lamp mounted on a tall pillar that stands on the floor. **standard of living** the level of comfort and material wealth enjoyed by an individual or group. < Middle French *estandard.*

standing (ˈstændɪŋ) *adj* **1** permanent or continuing indefinitely. **2** not yet cut or harvested: standing corn. **3** (of water) not flowing; stagnant. **4** (of a jump) performed without a run-up. **5** done while

taking a stand

Stand features in a number of idiomatic expressions, including:

as things stand considering the present state of affairs.
it stands to reason it is natural or logical; used to add rhetorical force: If the government lowers taxes, then it stands to reason that we'll be better off.
stand a chance to have the possibility of success: He doesn't stand a chance of passing the exam.
stand by 1 to watch or observe without taking part or interfering: I couldn't stand by and watch the child being beaten. **2** to wait, ready for when needed: The men are standing by for further orders. **3** to remain loyal to: His wife has always stood by him. **4** to keep to (a promise, agreement, etc.): I stand by my word.
stand-by *n* a person or thing available when needed.
stand down 1 to leave the witness box in a court of law: The witness may now stand down. **2** to withdraw or resign: It's time I stood down as president and let a younger man have a go.
stand for 1 to tolerate or put up with: She won't stand for any nonsense. **2** to mean, signify, or represent: What does GB stand for?
stand in to deputize or substitute (for): Henry has agreed to stand in for George while he's away. **stand-in** *n*
stand off to sack or dismiss: Another 50 men are to be stood off.
stand-offish *adj* aloof or reserved.
stand on ceremony to be very formal in one's behaviour.
stand on one's own two feet to be independent.
stand out to be noticeable or conspicuous: One of the girls stood out as being particularly talented.
stand out against to persist in one's opposition to: The miners stood out against further pit closures.
stand out for to persist in one's demand for: The union stood out for a 12 per cent increase.
stand over to supervise closely: He never does his homework unless I stand over him.
stand to to be prepared for action: The regiment was told to stand to.
stand up 1 to withstand scrutiny or investigation: Their account of what happened will never stand up in court. **2** to fail to keep an appointment to see (a boyfriend, etc.): That's the third time he's stood her up.
stand up and be counted to declare one's position, opinion, etc., openly and fearlessly.
stand up for to defend against criticism or attack: Not even his mother will stand up for him.
stand up to 1 to withstand pressure, damage, etc., without collapsing or breaking: The chair won't stand up to that sort of treatment. **2** to confront or resist defiantly: I'm surprised she dared stand up to him.

standing: a standing ovation.
• *n* **1** status or position: of high standing in the community. **2** length of past duration: an acquaintance of long standing.

stank (stæŋk) SEE **STINK.**

stanza (ˈstænzə) *n* a verse of poetry. < Italian.

staple[1] (ˈsteɪpl̩) *n* **1** a U-shaped piece of metal used to hold something in place. **2** a small piece of thin wire with ends bent at right angles which can be pushed through sheets of paper, etc., and clinched so as to hold them together.
• *vb* secure by means of a staple. **stapler** *n* < Old English *stapol* post.

staple[2] *adj* principal, chief, or standard: a staple food.
• *n* a staple food or commodity. < Middle Dutch *stapel* warehouse.

star (stɑː) *n* **1** a heavenly body that is seen as a point of light in the night sky. **2** (*astronomy*) a large gaseous body, like the sun, which radiates energy. **3** (*astrology*) a planet which is supposed to influence a person's life. **4** a figure or object with radiating points. **5** a famous, brilliant, or highly talented person.
• *vb* **starred; starring 1** mark with a star or asterisk. **2** perform a leading role in: star in a West End musical. **3** feature: The new production stars several well-known personalities.
• *adj* **1** principal or chief: the star attraction. **2** famous, brilliant, etc.: a star pupil. **stardom** *n* being a star or famous person. **starfish** *n* a star-shaped sea-animal. **stargaze** *vb* **1** observe or study the stars. **2** day-dream. **stargazing** *n* **starlight** *n* light from the stars. **starlit** *adj* illuminated by starlight: a starlit night. **starry** *adj* **1** of or connected with stars. **2** illuminated by or shining like stars. **starry-eyed** *adj* given to romantic dreams; unrealistic. < Old English *steorra.* SEE PANEL.

starboard (ˈstɑːˌbəd) *n* the right-hand side of a ship or aircraft when looking towards the front.
• *vb* turn to the right. < Old English *stēorbord.* SEE PANEL.

starch (stɑːtʃ) *n* **1** a common carbohydrate that is an important foodstuff, yielding glucose when digested. **2** a preparation derived from this, used for stiffening clothes. **3** formality or stiffness of manner. **starchy** *adj* **starchiness** *n* < Middle English *sterchen.*

stare (steə) *vb* look at with a fixed gaze: It's rude to stare.
• *n* a fixed gaze. < Old English *starian.*

stark (stɑːk) *adj* **1** barren or desolate; severely bare or simple: cold, stark surroundings. **2** sheer, utter, or complete: stark stupidity. **3** blunt: a stark description.
• *adv* completely: stark raving mad. **starkly** *adv* **starkness** *n* < Old English *stearc.* SEE PANEL.

starling (ˈstɑːlɪŋ) *n* any of a group of common, greenish-black birds that lives

four-star petrol

We say four-*star* petrol, not four-*stars* petrol. Why? The general rule in English is that when a noun is used as an adjective in front of another noun, it is usually singular. So when horses race, they run in a *horse*-race, not a *horses*-race. A brush for teeth is a *tooth*brush, not a *teeth*brush. Tickets are sold at a *ticket*-office, not a *tickets*-office.

This rule holds even with some nouns that are always plural: we say *pyjama* top, not *pyjamas* top; a *trouser* leg, not a *trousers* leg. Phrases containing numbers greater than one also become singular when used as adjectives: four *stars*—but four-*star* petrol; three *years*—but a three-*year*-old toddler.

starboard

The starboard side of a ship takes its name from the Old English word *st ēorbord.* This is a compound of *st ēor* meaning 'steering oar' and *bord* or 'side'. The reference is to the manner in which ships were formerly steered, which was by means of an oar held over the right-hand side.

stark-naked

Stark-naked ('completely naked') has evolved from the Middle English *stert naked* literally 'tail-naked'. The root of the expression is the Old English word *steort* meaning 'tail' or 'rump'.

in large flocks and makes a chattering sound. < Old English *stærlinc.*

start (stɑːt) *vb* **1** begin or cause to begin: start a journey. **2** begin to operate; set into operation: The car won't start. **3** come or bring into existence; establish or found: start a company. **4** make a sudden, involuntary movement, esp. because shocked or startled. **5** spring up or gush out violently: He started from his seat and stormed to the door. **6** take part in the beginning of a contest or race. **7** leave: When do you start for India?
• *n* **1** the beginning of something: the start of a film. **2** the place where something begins. **3** an advantage; lead or handicap: They gave him a five-point start. **4** a sudden, involuntary movement: give a start. **start back** begin a return journey. **starter** *n* **1** a person or thing that starts, esp. a horse or competitor about to run in a race. **2** the first course of a meal. **3** a person who signals the start of a race. **starting-gate** *n* a line of stalls which open simultaneously at the start of a horse-race. **starting price** the latest odds offered at the start of a race. **start off** or **out** begin a journey: We started off at 3 pm and arrived just after 5. **start out** begin (an activity, etc.) with a particular intention. **start up** begin a career, business, etc.: He's thinking of starting up as a private detective. < Middle English *sterten.*

startle (ˈstɑːtl̩) *vb* shock or frighten by surprising: I'm sorry. Did I startle you? < Middle English *stertlen.*

starve (stɑːv) *vb* **1** die or suffer because of hunger; cause this to happen. **2** deprive of something needed: starved of affection. **3** coerce by starving: They were starved into surrender. **starvation** *n* **starving** *adj* (*informal*) very hungry. < Old English *steorfan* to die.

stash (stæʃ) *vb* (*informal*) store or hide away. < origin unknown.

stately home

A stately home is a large country house, especially one that is open to the public. The expression was coined by the British poet Felicia Dorothea Hemans, 1793–1835, in the poem 'The Homes of England':

The stately homes of England,
How beautiful they stand!
Amidst their tall ancestral trees,
O'er all the pleasant land.

state (steɪt) *n* **1** a condition of being: a state of anxiety. **2** an anxious or agitated condition: She got into a real state. **3** the civil government or administration of a country; its operations: affairs of state. **4** often **State** a country considered as a political power; its territory. **5** often **State** a self-governing division of a federation: the southern states of America. **6** regal dignity or grandeur.
• *vb* **1** express or assert. **2** fix or preset. **stateless** *adj* without citizenship. **stately** *adj* imposing, dignified, or majestic. **stateliness** *n* **statement** *n* **1** the act of stating. **2** something stated. **3** a written report of money paid, received, etc. **stateroom** *n* **1** a private cabin on a passenger ship. **2** a large room in a palace, etc., used for formal occasions. **statesman** *n* a person adept at handling affairs of state. **statesmanship** *n* < ultimately Latin *stare* to stand. SEE PANEL.

static (ˈstætɪk) *adj* **1** not moving or changing; inactive. **2** acting or exerting force by weight alone: static pressure.
• *n* electricity which is stationary in a body, often caused by friction. < Greek *statikos* causing to stand.

station (ˈsteɪʃən) *n* **1** a regular stopping place for trains, coaches, or buses; buildings, etc., at such a place. **2** the local headquarters of a public service; establishment equipped for a particular job: a police station. **3** (*formal*) the place where a person or thing stands or is assigned to remain for a length of time: remain at one's station. **4** social rank or standing: He had ideas way above his station. **5** a radio or television channel.
• *vb* put (a person, troops, etc.) at or in a particular place: His regiment is now stationed overseas. **station-master** *n* an official in charge of a railway station. < ultimately Latin *stare* to stand.

stationary (ˈsteɪʃənərɪ) *adj* **1** not moving or movable: The vehicle remained stationary. **2** unchanging in condition. < SEE **STATION.** SEE PANEL.

stationery (ˈsteɪʃənərɪ) *n* writing paper, envelopes, ink, etc. **stationer** *n* a person who sells stationery. < Medieval Latin *statio* shop. SEE PANEL AT **STATIONARY.**

statistics (stəˈtɪstɪks) *n* **1** the science of collecting, analysing, and interpreting quantitative data. **2** a collection of such data. **statistic** *n* an item of quantitative data. **statistical** *adj* **statistically** *adv* **statistician** *n* an expert in statistics. < German *Statistik* study of political facts.

statue (ˈstætjuː) *n* a sculptured, cast, or moulded likeness of a person, animal, etc. **statuesque** *adj* like a statue in stillness, dignity, etc. **statuette** *n* a small statue. < ultimately Latin *statuere* to set up.

stature (ˈstætʃə) *n* **1** the natural height of a person. **2** status gained by growth, ability, or achievement: a man of considerable stature in the medical world. < ultimately Latin *stare* to stand.

status (ˈsteɪtəs) *n* **1** a person's or group's rank or standing in relation to others. **2** high rank or standing. **status quo** the existing state of things: They're bent on preserving the status quo. **status symbol** a possession or activity considered to be an indication of wealth or high social standing. < Latin: posture.

statute (ˈstætjuːt) *n* **1** a written law of a country. **2** a rule of an institution, esp. one made when it was founded. **statutory** *adj* fixed, done, or required by statute. < ultimately Latin *statuere* to set up.

staunch (stɔːntʃ) *adj* unwaveringly firm or loyal: a staunch supporter. **staunchly** *adv* **staunchness** *n* < Middle French *estanche.* SEE PANEL AT **STANCH.**

stave (steɪv) *n* **1** one of a number of curved strips of wood arranged lengthwise to make the side of a barrel. **2** a staff in music.

• *vb* **stove, staved; staving** crush or break inwards; be crushed or holed. **stave off** prevent or ward off: stave off hunger. < back formation from *staves,* plural of staff. SEE PANEL.

stay[1] (steɪ) *vb* **1** remain in a place or condition: stay in bed. **2** reside at temporarily as a guest or visitor; lodge: stay at a hotel. **3** stop, suspend, or delay. **4** endure or withstand: He'll never be able to stay the course. **5** satisfy (an appetite, etc.) temporarily: stay one's hunger with a sandwich. **6** (*archaic*) pause or wait.

• *n* **1** a period of residing; stop: a short stay. **2** a postponement: a stay of execution. **staying-power** *n* endurance; stamina. **stay put** remain in one's place. < ultimately Latin *stare* to stand.

stay[2] *n* **1** a rope or wire used to support a ship's mast. **2** a brace or support. **stays** *pl n* (*archaic*) a corset stiffened with bones. < of Germanic origin.

STD *abbrev* subscriber trunk dialling.

stead (stɛd) *n* **in a person's** or **thing's stead** instead of someone or something. **stand in good stead** be of great benefit: Your qualifications should stand you in good stead. < Old English *stede* place.

steadfast (ˈstɛdˌfɑːst) *adj* firm and unwavering: a steadfast refusal. **steadfastly** *adv* **steadfastness** *n*

steady (ˈstɛdɪ) *adj* **1** stable or firm; not shaking: a steady hand. **2** regular or uniform: a steady temperature. **3** constant; dependable: a steady supporter. **4** not easily disturbed or upset: steady nerves.

• *adv* steadily.

• *vb* **steadied; steadying** make, keep,

stationary or **stationery?**

The spellings stationary and stationery are often confused, as the two words have the same pronunciation. Stationary means 'not moving': *stationary* vehicles. Stationery is the name given to writing materials.

One way of remembering which is which is to think of the person that sells stationery—a station*er*. Like bak*er*, greengroc*er*, etc., this name ends in -er. To spell the name of the merchandise, just add a y.

stave off

The word staff ('stick') has two plural forms—staffs and staves. By a process known as *back formation* staves produced stave, 'a stick or strip of wood'. Stave off, however, means 'to forestall'. How did the phrase acquire this meaning?

A form of entertainment popular in the 17th century was bull-baiting, a spectacle comprising the baiting of a bull by a pack of dogs. Once down, the bull would soon be dispatched by the dogs. However, at such times its owner often intervened to save it, not on humanitarian grounds but simply to save the source of his livelihood. The dogs would be driven off with a stick, or staved off. This act meant that the death of the bull would be forestalled or temporarily averted and this was the meaning that the phrase gradually assumed.

or become steady. **steadily** *adv* **steadiness** *n* **steady-state theory** a theory in cosmology that the universe has always existed in a steady state, that it had no beginning and will have no end. < *stead* + *-y*.

steak (steɪk) *n* **1** a thick slice of meat (esp. beef) or fish, which is grilled, fried, etc. **2** minced meat shaped and prepared like a steak. < Old Norse *steik*.

steal (sti:l) *vb* **stole; stolen; stealing** **1** take (another's property) unlawfully or without permission. **2** move stealthily: He stole quietly past the guard. **3** get by using surprise or stealth: She stole a look at him. < Old English *stelan*.

stealth (stɛlθ) *n* the act or trait of proceeding furtively or in a cunningly unnoticeable way. **stealthy** *adj* showing or performed with stealth. **stealthily** *adv* **stealthiness** *n* < Middle English *stelthe*.

steam (sti:m) *n* **1** the vapour or gas into which water changes when heated to boiling-point. **2** (*informal*) energy or power: let off steam.
• *vb* **1** emit steam or vapour. **2** cook by steam: steamed fish. **3** move by means of steam power: The ship steamed out of the harbour. **steamboat** *n* a boat driven by steam power. **steamed up** (*informal*) angry or excited. **steam-engine** *n* an engine worked by steam power. **steamer** *n* **1** a steamship. **2** a container for cooking things by steam. **steam iron** an electric iron which releases steam onto clothes, etc., to make them easier to iron. **steamroller** *n* a vehicle with massive rollers for levelling road surfaces, etc. **steamship** *n* a ship driven by steam. **steam up** cover or become covered with steam: The windows have steamed up again. **steamy** *adj* covered with or full of steam. < Old English *stēam*.

steed (sti:d) *n* (*literary*) a horse. < Old English *stēda*.

steel (sti:l) *n* **1** any of a group of very hard alloys of iron and carbon, used for making tools, cutlery, etc. **2** a rod of steel for sharpening knives.
• *vb* make hard, unfeeling, or determined: She steeled her heart towards him. **steel band** a West Indian band whose instruments are usually made from empty oil-drums. **steel wool** a mass of steel fibres used for cleaning or polishing. **steely** *adj* of or like steel in colour, hardness, etc. < Old English *stēle*.

steep[1] (sti:p) *adj* **1** rising or falling with a sharp slope: a steep hill. **2** (*informal*) (of a price) excessively high. **3** (*informal*) excessively demanding or exacting. **steeply** *adv* **steepness** *n* **steepen** *vb* make or become steep or steeper. < Old English *stēap*.

steep[2] *vb* soak thoroughly: cherries steeped in cognac. **steeped in** filled or imbued with: buildings steeped in history. < Middle English *stepen*.

steeple (ˈsti:pl̩) *n* (a tower with) a tall spire on a church. **steeplechase** *n* a horse-race run across country or over a course of obstacles. **steeplejack** *n* a man who climbs tall chimneys, steeples, etc., as part of his work. < Old English *stēpel* tower. SEE PANEL.

steer[1] (stɪə) *vb* **1** guide (a vehicle, etc.) along a course. **2** (of a vehicle, etc.) be able to be steered. **3** guide or direct: She steered her daughter through the exams. **steerer** *n* **steerage** *n* **1** steering. **2** the cheapest passenger accommodation on a ship. **steer clear of** avoid or stay away from. **steering** *n* the mechanism used for guiding a car, boat, etc. **steering-wheel** *n* a wheel used for controlling this mechanism. < Old English *stīeran*.

steer[2] *n* a bullock. < Old English *stēor*.

stem[1] (stɛm) *n* **1** the main trunk of a tree, shrub, or plant. **2** the slender part of a

steeplechase

Steeplechase, the name of a race that is run across country or over a course of obstacles, is believed to derive from a party of fox-hunters who one day decided as a frolic to race in a direct line to a nearby steeple. This event is said to have taken place in County Cork, Ireland, at the beginning of the 19th century.

from stem to stern

One of the many nautical expressions that have entered idiomatic usage is from stem to stern meaning 'throughout' or 'from front to back'. As can be guessed from the opposition of the word to stern or 'rear of a ship', stem refers to the bow or front part. Technically, it is the main timber or structure at the bow of a vessel to which the sides are fixed.

plant from which a leaf, flower, or fruit grows. **3** something resembling a stem: the stem of a wineglass. **4** the main part of a word to which endings are attached. **5** the forwardmost end of a vessel. **stem from** arise or originate from. < Old English *stefn.* SEE PANEL.

stem² *vb* **stemmed; stemming** stop or curb (a stream or flow): How can we stem the flood of complaints? < Old Norse *stemma.*

stench (stɛntʃ) *n* a stink. < Old English *stenc.*

stencil (ˈstɛnsḷ) *n* **1** a thin sheet of metal or card into which a design has been cut, which is laid on a surface and painted over, etc., to reproduce the design. **2** a design reproduced in this way. **3** a piece of waxed paper into which words have been cut by a typewriter.
• *vb* **stencilled; stencilling** produce or paint, etc., by using a stencil. < Middle English *stanselen* to decorate with bright colours.

stenographer (stəˈnɒgrəfə) *n* a person skilled in shorthand. **stenography** *n* the art of writing in shorthand. < Greek *stenos* narrow + *graphein* to write.

step (stɛp) *vb* **stepped; stepping 1** move by raising the foot and setting it down again in a new position, or by moving each foot alternately as in walking: step onto a train. **2** set the foot down (on): step on a snail. **3** measure by taking even paces.
• *n* **1** a flat, level surface for the foot in ascending or descending; stair: Mind the step! **2** a movement made by raising the foot and setting it down in a new position; advance: a step forward for mankind. **3** the distance covered by this; stride. **4** the sound or visual impression made by a step: There were steps outside the door. **5** a sequence of movements forming a dance pattern. **6** a stage in a series of stages: What's the next step? **7** a manner of walking; gait. **8** a short distance: The chemist's is just a short step from the supermarket. **in step** with each foot moving in time to a piece of music or in harmony with the foot movements of a partner or group. **out of step** not in step. **step by step** one stage at a time; gradually. **step down** resign. **step in** intervene: If the government doesn't step in, there'll be no trains on Monday. **step-in** *adj* (of shoes and clothes) without fastenings. **step-ladder** *n* a light, portable set of steps with a hinged support. **step on it** (*informal*) hurry. **step out** walk faster. **stepping-stone** *n* **1** one of several large stones placed at regular intervals across a stream, etc., to form a path. **2** a means of advancing or progressing. **steps** *pl* n a step-ladder. **step up** increase: step up production. **take steps** adopt certain measures. **watch one's step** be careful; often used as a warning. < Old English *stæpe.*

step- *prefix* related by remarriage. **stepbrother** *n* a son of one's step-parent by a previous marriage. **step child** *n* a child born of a spouse's previous marriage. **stepdaughter** *n* a daughter born of a spouse's previous marriage. **stepfather** *n* the husband of one's mother by remarriage. **stepmother** *n* the wife of one's father by remarriage. **step-parent** *n* the husband or wife of one's parent by remarriage. **stepsister** *n* a daughter of one's step-parent by a previous marriage. **stepson** *n* a son born of a spouse's previous marriage. < Old English *stēop-.*

steppe (stɛp) *n* a vast stretch of dry, treeless grassland, esp. in SE Europe and Asia. < Russian *step* lowland.

stereo (ˈstɛrɪəʊ) *n, pl* **stereos 1** stereophonic sound. **2** a record-player or other system that gives stereophonic sound. < short for *stereophonic.*

stereophonic (ˌstɛrɪəˈfɒnɪk) *adj* (of sound reproduction) using two different channels for recording and reproduction so as to give a spatial effect. < ultimately Greek *stereos* solid + *phōnos* sounding.

stereotype (ˈstɛrɪəˌtaɪp) *n* a person or thing considered to be in all ways representative of a particular type.
• *vb* make a stereotype of. **stereotyped** *adj* lacking originality; hackneyed. < French *stéréotype.*

sterile (ˈstɛraɪl) *n* **1** unable to reproduce; infertile. **2** unproductive: sterile years of research. **3** free from germs. **sterility** *n* **sterilize** *vb* make sterile. **sterilization** *n* **sterilizer** *n* < Latin *sterilis.*

sterling (ˈstɜːlɪŋ) *n* British money.
• *adj* **1** of or calculated in British money. **2** (of silver) of a standard degree of purity. **3** first-class; admirable: sterling qualities. < Middle English: silver penny. SEE PANEL.

stern¹ (stɜːn) *adj* harsh, strict, or severe: a stern disposition. **sternly** *adv* **sternness** *n* < Old English *styrne.*

stern² *n* the rear end of a ship or boat. < Middle English: rudder. SEE PANEL AT STEM¹.

stet (stɛt) *vb* **stetted; stetting** let it be kept or keep in its original form; written by the side of a word or passage that has been marked for deletion or alteration. < Latin *stare* to stand.

stethoscope (ˈstɛθəˌskəʊp) *n* a medical

instrument used for listening to sounds produced in the body, esp. in the chest. < French *stéthoscope,* from Greek *stēthos* chest + French *-scope.*

stetson (ˈstɛtsn̩) *n* a man's hat with a broad brim and a high crown. < John *Stetson,* died 1906, US hatmaker.

stevedore (ˈstiːvəˌdɔː) *n* a person whose work is to load and unload ships; docker. < Spanish *estibador,* from *estibar* to pack.

stew (stjuː) *vb* **1** cook by simmering for a long time in a closed vessel. **2** (*informal*) worry; fret.

• *n* **1** a dish, usually with meat, prepared by stewing. **2** a state of nervous anxiety or agitation. **stew in one's own juice** (*informal*) suffer the consequences of one's own actions. < Middle English *stu* cauldron.

steward (ˈstjʊəd) *n* **1** a man who waits on and attends to passengers on a ship, aircraft, etc. **2** a person who officiates at a race-meeting, fête, etc. **3** a person who organizes the supply of food and drink to a club, college, etc., and manages the eating arrangements. **4** a person employed to manage an estate. **stewardess** *n* a female steward, esp. one on an aircraft or ship. < Old English *stigweard,* from *stig* hall + *weard* ward.

stick[1] (stɪk) *n* **1** a long, narrow piece of wood. **2** something resembling this: a stick of rhubarb. **3** a walking-stick. **4** an implement used for propelling the ball in hockey, etc. **5** *pl* (*informal*) pieces of (furniture). **6** (*informal*) criticism: Her new novel has received a lot of stick. **old stick** a person of a type that is specified: He's a pretty decent old stick. **stick-insect** *n* any of a group of insects with twig-like bodies. < Old English *sticca.*

stick[2] *vb* **stuck; sticking 1** pierce with or as if with a pointed instrument; stab. **2** thrust so as to or as if to pierce. **3** (*informal*) place or put in a particular position: Don't stick your fingers in your mouth. **4** attach or be attached by or as if by glue, suction, etc. **5** remain in the same place for a long time: The name stuck in my memory for years to come. **6** become jammed or wedged: One of the keys on the piano has stuck. **7** (*informal*) tolerate or put up with: She can't stick her mother-in-law. **8** (of a charge or accusation) be shown to be valid. **stick at** (*informal*) persist in one's efforts: Stick at the essay and you'll have finished it by Monday. **stick by** continue to support: Her husband has always stuck by her. **sticker** *n* an adhesive label. **sticking-point** *n* something which causes a halt or impasse. **stick-in-the-mud** *n* a person who is against change, new ideas, etc. **stick it out** (*informal*) endure (something unpleasant) to the end. **stick one's neck out** (*informal*) expose oneself knowingly to danger, criticism, etc. **stick out** protrude or be conspicuous: Her teeth stick out. **stick out for** (*informal*) persist in a demand for. **stick to 1** not change (a plan, decision, etc.); not break (a promise, oath, etc.): We'll stick to the original schedule. **2** not stray from (a particular topic, etc.): stick to the point. **stick up** (*informal*) rob. **stick-up** *n* **stick up for** speak or act in defence of: You must stick up for your rights. **stick with** stay close or loyal to: He stuck with the Labour party all his life. **sticky** *adj* **1** covered with a gluey substance; adhesive. **2** (of weather) humid; muggy. **3** awkward; problematic: a sticky situation. **stickily** *adv* **stickiness** *n* < Old English *stician.*

stickleback (ˈstɪklˌbæk) *n* any of a group of small, freshwater fish with sharp spines on its back. < Middle English *stykylbak,* from Old English *sticel* goad + Middle English *bak* back.

stickler (ˈstɪklə) *n* a person who rigidly insists upon something: a stickler for punctuality. < Middle English *stightlen* to strive.

stiff (stɪf) *adj* **1** not pliant or flexible; rigid: stiff cardboard. **2** moving or moved with pain or difficulty: a stiff joint. **3** not flowing easily; thick: a stiff paste. **4** difficult: a stiff test. **5** strong; potent: a stiff drink. **6** formal or reserved; unrelaxed: a stiff atmosphere. **7** lacking grace or flow of movement: a stiff curtsy. **8** harsh, severe, or steep: stiff penalties. **9** brisk or forceful: a stiff breeze. **10** keenly fought or disputed; arduous: a stiff match.

• *adv* in a stiff manner.

• *n* (*informal*) a corpse. **stiffly** *adv* **stiffness** *n* **stiffen** *vb* make or become

sterling

Why is British currency commonly referred to as sterling? The answer would seem to be that sterling derives from the Old English word *steorling,* a compound of *steorra* 'a star' and the diminutive suffix *-ling.* The reference is to the small star that was stamped on a number of early Norman pennies.

stiff. **stiffener** *n* **stiffening** *n* **stiff-necked** *adj* obstinate; haughty. < Old English *stīf.*

stifle (ˈstaɪfl̩) *vb* **1** prevent or be prevented from breathing; suffocate. **2** suppress or hold back: stifle a yawn. **stifling** *adj* so hot, humid, etc., that breathing is difficult. < Middle English *stuflen.*

stigma (ˈstɪgmə) *n* **1** (a mark of) shame or disgrace. **2** (*botany*) the part of the pistil of a flower which receives the pollen. **stigmata** *pl n* the marks on certain people believed by some to resemble the wounds received by Christ at the crucifixion. **stigmatize** *vb* describe disparagingly. < Latin: mark, from Greek *stizein* to tattoo.

stile (staɪl) *n* a step or arrangement of steps for getting over a fence or wall, esp. on farmland. < Old English *stigel.*

stiletto (stɪˈlɛtəʊ) *n, pl* **stilettos** a dagger with a slender, tapering blade. **stiletto heel** a high heel on a woman's shoe which tapers to a narrow tip. < Italian *stilo* dagger.

still[1] (stɪl) *adj* **1** motionless; inactive: The wheels were completely still. **2** free from noise and activity; tranquil: a still, summer day. **3** (of drinks) without effervescence.
• *n* **1** (*literary*) quiet calmness: in the still of the evening. **2** a photograph taken from a cinema film.
• *vb* (*literary*) make or become still.
• *adv* **1** quietly or without moving: Sit still! **2** continuing then or in the present as before: They still ask me for money. **3** nevertheless; in spite of that. **4** in a greater degree, amount, etc.; even: Still colder weather is on its way. **stillness** *n* **still birth** a birth in which the infant is born dead. **stillborn** *adj* dead at birth. **still life** a painting or picture showing inanimate objects, such as a bowl of fruit. < Old English *stille.*

still[2] *n* a distilling apparatus, esp. for making spirits. < Middle English *stillen* to distil.

stilt (stɪlt) *n* **1** one of a pair of tall poles, each with a small platform for the foot, enabling the user to walk high above the ground. **2** one of a number of heavy poles or posts used to keep a building above ground or water level. < Middle English *stilte.*

stilted (ˈstɪltɪd) *adj* (*derogatory*) unnaturally formal or elevated; pompous.

stimulant (ˈstɪmjʊlənt) *n* something which stimulates, esp. a drug.
• *adj* stimulating.

stimulate (ˈstɪmjʊˌleɪt) *vb* rouse; make more active. **stimulation** n **stimulative** *adj* **stimulator** *n* < Latin *stimulus* goad.

stimulus (ˈstɪmjʊləs) *n, pl* **stimuli** **1** something that stimulates; incentive. **2** something that causes a reaction or response.

sting (stɪŋ) *n* **1** the organ of certain insects, plants, etc., used for wounding or injecting poison. **2** the act of stinging; wound caused by this or the pain of such a wound. **3** any sharp pain: She felt a sting of jealousy.
• *vb* **stung; stinging 1** (be able to) inflict a sting. **2** feel or cause to feel sharp pain. **3** stimulate; provoke. **4** (*informal*) cheat by overcharging. **stingray** *n* any of a group of rays with one or more large, sharp spines in the tail. < Old English *stingan.*

stingy (ˈstɪndʒɪ) *adj* (*informal*) **1** mean or miserly. **2** small or meagre, esp. because given without generosity. **stingily** *adv* **stinginess** *n* < origin uncertain.

stink (stɪŋk) *n* **1** a strong, offensive smell. **2** (*informal*) a fuss; commotion.
• *vb* **stank, stunk; stunk; stinking 1** emit a strong, offensive smell. **2** (*informal*) be very unpleasant or offensive: The whole business stinks. **stinker** *n* (*informal*) **1** an obnoxious person. **2** something unpleasant or very difficult to do: This crossword puzzle is a real stinker. < Old English *stincan.*

stinking (ˈstɪŋkɪŋ) *adj* (*informal*) very unpleasant: a stinking headache.
• *adv* (*informal*) extremely: stinking rich.

stint (stɪnt) *vb* restrict to a meagre amount or allowance.
• *n* **1** a fixed amount or period of work: I've done my stint of cleaning for today. **2** restraint or limit. < Old English *styntan* to blunt.

stipend (ˈstaɪpɛnd) *n* a fixed sum paid periodically as a salary, esp. that paid to a clergyman. **stipendiary** *adj* of or receiving a stipend. < ultimately Latin *stips* gift + *pendere* to weigh.

stipple (ˈstɪpl̩) *vb* **1** engrave, paint, draw, etc., with dots or dabs as opposed to lines or strokes. **2** roughen the surface of wet cement, plaster, etc. < Dutch *stippelen* to dot.

stipulate (ˈstɪpjʊˌleɪt) *vb* state, specify, or insist upon, often as a necessary condition of an agreement. **stipulation** *n* < Latin *stipulari.*

stir (stɜː) *vb* **stirred; stirring 1** move or cause to move, esp. gently or slightly: Not a leaf stirred. **2** mix or agitate by circular movements with a spoon: stir one's tea. **3** rouse or be roused: stir to action.
• *n* **1** the act of stirring. **2** a fuss or

commotion: The scandal caused quite a stir. **stirring** *adj* stimulating, inspiring, or exhilarating. < Old English *styrian.*

stirrup (ˈstɪrəp) *n* a loop-like support for a rider's foot, usually metal, which hangs down from the saddle. < Old English *stigrāp.* SEE PANEL.

stitch (stɪtʃ) *n* **1** a single, complete movement of a threaded needle in and out of fabric or skin tissue; product of this movement. **2** a single, complete movement of a knitting-needle, crochet hook, etc.; product of this movement: cast on 98 stitches. **3** a particular way of making a stitch; type of stitch so made: blanket stitch. **4** a sudden, sharp pain in the side: develop a stitch. **5** (*informal*) a single item of clothing: without a stitch on.
• *vb* join or adorn with stitches; sew. **in stitches** (*informal*) laughing uncontrollably. < Old English *stice.*

stoat (stəʊt) *n* a small mammal related to the weasel, with a brown fur coat and a black-tipped tail. < Middle English *stote.*

stock (stɒk) *n* **1** a supply of something available for use: a stock of paper. **2** the total supply of goods kept by a retailer, etc. **3** a person's line of descent; ancestry: of Irish stock. **4** farm animals; livestock. **5** (*commerce*) money lent to a government at a fixed rate of interest. **6** (*commerce*) the capital of a business company, raised through investors buying shares. **7** a plant which provides cuttings or onto which a graft is made. **8** the liquid in which bones, meat, vegetables, etc., have been simmered, used to make soups, sauces, etc. **9** a common, garden plant with bright, fragrant, single or double flowers. **10** the handle, frame, or supporting structure of a rifle, whip, plough, etc. **11** a scarf or cravat, worn esp. as part of riding dress.
• *adj* **1** kept regularly in stock; standard: a stock item. **2** commonplace; unoriginal.
• *vb* **1** keep in stock: We don't stock children's shoes. **2** provide with stock, livestock, etc.: She's been stocking the shelves with jam and marmalade. **in stock** currently available in a shop, etc. **out of stock** sold out. **stockbreeder** *n* a person who breeds livestock. **stockbreeding** *n* **stockbroker** *n* a person who buys and sells stocks and shares on behalf of clients. **stock-car** *n* an old car, usually modified for speed or protection, used in races where bumping is allowed. **stock exchange** a place where stocks and shares are bought and sold. **stockholder** *n* a person who owns stock. **stock-in-trade** *n* all the tools, equipment, accoutrements, etc., entailed by a particular trade or profession. **stockist** *n* a retailer, etc., stocking certain goods. **stockjobber** *n* a member of the stock exchange who deals only with brokers or other stockjobbers and not with the public. **stock market** a stock exchange; transactions which take place there. **stock-room** *n* a room in which stock is stored. **stocks** *pl n* **1** a heavy, wooden structure with holes for the ankles (and wrists) in which a criminal used to be locked as a punishment. **2** the wooden framework which supports a ship during its construction. **stock-still** *adj* completely motionless. **stock-taking** *n* the listing of all the stock in a shop, warehouse, etc., usually done once a year. **stock up** collect a stock or supply of something: She's stocking up in case there's a shortage. **stockyard** *n* an enclosure with pens where livestock is kept before slaughter, shipment, etc. < Old English *stocc* block of wood.

> **stirrup**
>
> The word stirrup is literally 'the rope to mount or climb up by'. It comes from the Old English word *stīgrāp,* which is a compound of the Old High German word *stīgan* 'to go or climb up' and the Old English *rāp* or 'rope'.

stockade (stɒˈkeɪd) *n* a wall of upright stakes, used as a fortification. < Spanish *estacada,* from *estaca* stake.

stocking (ˈstɒkɪŋ) *n* a close-fitting garment for the foot and leg of a woman, usually made of nylon. < obsolete *stock* leg-covering.

stockpile (ˈstɒkˌpaɪl) *n* an accumulated stock of goods or materials, kept in reserve.
• *vb* acquire a stockpile of.

stocky (ˈstɒkɪ) *adj* (of a person) solidly built; thickset. **stockiness** *n*

stodgy (ˈstɒdʒɪ) *n* **1** (of food) heavy and filling. **2** dull; uninteresting. **stodgily** *adv* **stodginess** *n* **stodge** *n* stodgy food. < origin unknown.

stoic (ˈstəʊɪk) *n* a person with stoical qualities.
• *adj* stoical. **stoical** *adj* showing few or no signs of feeling pain, distress, or pleasure. **stoically** *adv* < Greek

stōïkos, from *stoa*, porch in Athens where Zeno taught. SEE PANEL.

stoke (stəʊk) *vb* fuel and tend (a fire, furnace, etc.). **stoker** *n* < Dutch *stoken*.

stole[1] (stəʊl) *n* **1** a long, widish strip of fur or other material worn by women around the shoulders, esp. on formal occasions. **2** a long strip of silk or silk-like material worn by certain clergymen. < Greek *stolē* robe.

stole[2] SEE **STEAL. stolen** SEE **STEAL.**

stolid (ˈstɒlɪd) *adj* feeling or showing little or no emotion; impassive. **stolidity** *n* **stolidly** *adv* < Latin *stolidus* dull.

stomach (ˈstʌmək) *n* **1** the bag-like organ into which food passes after being swallowed. **2** the abdomen: a punch in the stomach. **3** appetite for food. **4** desire or inclination: no stomach for quarrels.
• *vb* (*informal*) endure or tolerate: I can't stomach people who show off like that. **stomach-pump** *n* a small suction pump used for removing the contents of the stomach via a long tube that passes down the oesophagus. < ultimately Greek *stomachos*, from *stoma* mouth.

stomp (stɒmp) *vb* walk with heavy steps, esp. in anger. < *stamp.*

stone (stəʊn) *n* **1** a small piece of rock. **2** the material of which rocks are composed: a house built of stone. **3** a piece of this shaped for a particular purpose: a gravestone. **4** a gem. **5** the hard covering round the seed of certain fruits such as the plum or cherry. **6** a small, hard mass formed in the kidney, gall-bladder, etc. **7** *pl* **stone, stones** a measure of weight (6.35 kilograms).
• *adj* made of stone.
• *vb* **1** remove the stone from (a plum, cherry, etc.). **2** throw stones at, esp. as a form of punishment or execution. **leave no stone unturned** try every possible means. **stoned** *adj* (*informal*) drunk. **stonemason** *n* a person who dresses, carves, or builds in stone. **stone's throw** (*informal*) a short distance: She doesn't live more than a stone's throw from here. **stonewall** *vb* use disarming, defensive tactics; obstruct. **stonework** *n* the parts of a building, etc., made of stone. **stony** *adj* **1** full of stones. **2** resembling stone, esp. in hardness. **3** insensitive, expressionless, or lifeless. **stony-broke** *adj* (*informal*) lacking even the slightest funds; broke. < Old English *stān*. SEE PANEL.

stone- *prefix* totally; completely: stone-deaf.

stood (stʊd) SEE **STAND.**

stooge (stuːdʒ) *n* **1** the minor partner in a comedy duo whose job is to feed lines to the principal comedian; butt. **2** (*informal*) a person who is completely subservient to another. **3** (*informal*) a spy or informer.
• *vb* act as a stooge. < origin unknown.

stool (stuːl) *n* **1** a movable, single seat without arms or a back. **2** a footstool or raised cushion for kneeling on. **3** a discharge from the bowels. **stool-**

stoic

A person who undergoes suffering and reversals of fortune calmly and without flinching may be described as being of stoic character. This word derives ultimately from the Greek word *stoa* or 'portico'. The reference is to the portico in the market-place in ancient Athens where the philosopher Zeno held class.

Zeno was the founder of Stoicism, a school of philosophy which included amongst its tenets the repression of passion and emotion.

leave no stone unturned

To leave no stone unturned is one of a vast number of stock phrases and expressions that are used every day in an automatic and indiscriminate way: 'We shall *leave no stone unturned* in our efforts to bring the guilty parties to justice' ('We shall try every possible means to bring the guilty parties to justice'). Such overworked phrases are referred to as *clichés*. Cliché is a French loan-word whose literal meaning is 'a (printer's) stereotype plate', from the verb *clicher* 'to stereotype'. Figuratively, the word is applied in a derogative way to all those expressions that have acquired a ring of staleness through overuse. Other examples include: much of a muchness, last but not least, neither rhyme nor reason, through thick and thin, explore every avenue, get down to brass tacks, all of which tend to sound to all intents and purposes, as old as the hills.

pigeon *n* (*informal*) a decoy, esp. one acting as a police informer. < Old English *stōl.* SEE PANEL.

stoop (stu:p) *vb* **1** bend forwards from the waist. **2** humiliate or lower oneself; condescend: He'll never stoop to stealing.
● *n* a stooping posture: walk with a stoop.
< Old English *stūpian.*

stop (stɒp) *vb* **stopped; stopping**
1 become completely still and not move any more; cause to do this: Will you stop the car and let me out? **2** interrupt a journey: Where shall we stop for lunch? **3** cease or cause to cease doing something: When are you going to stop smoking? **4** cause (an activity) to end sooner than was planned: The game was stopped because of crowd trouble. **5** visit someone or something, usually for a short time, when on the way to another place: I can stop by at the bank on the way home. **6** remain somewhere for a while instead of leaving or going on: 'Won't you stop to tea?' **7** stay in a place as a guest, visitor, etc.: I prefer to stop at the Hilton nowadays. **8** prevent (someone) from doing something; prevent (something) from happening: You couldn't stop me from going if I wanted to. **9** take action to prevent (something) from being sent, paid, or supplied, or from reaching the person or place it is going to: Don't forget to stop the newspapers. **10** deduct (a sum of money) from a person's wages, salary, etc.: I was stopped £70 tax last week. **11** cause (blood or other liquid) not to flow any more; suppress. **12** fill or cover (a hole or opening): What can we use to stop all the cracks? **13** block the inside of (a pipe): Something's stopping up the sink. **14** defeat (an opponent) in a boxing contest before the fight is planned to end: The challenger was stopped in the third round.

> **stool pigeon**
>
> Nowadays a police informer is sometimes referred to informally as a stool pigeon. This name was originally applied to the now extinct North American passenger pigeon. In the 19th century this bird was used extensively as a live decoy to attract other passenger pigeons to within range of the hunter's gun. The name stool pigeon came into being probably on account of the fact that the bird was often attached by means of a long string to the hunter's small, portable stool.

15 cover (a hole) or press down (a string) on a musical instrument: Stop the first string at the third fret.
● *n* **1** the act of stopping; pause. **2** the state of being stopped: They brought the plane to a stop. **3** a place where passengers may get on or off a bus, train, etc. **4** a punctuation mark, esp. a full stop. **5** a device for preventing something from moving or from moving beyond a certain point: a door-stop. **6** a device or means by which the pitch of a flute or other musical instrument is varied; knob on an organ which controls a set of pipes. **7** an aperture setting on a camera, enlarger, etc. **8** one of the speech sounds made by completely blocking the passage of air from the lungs and then suddenly releasing it. **stopcock** *n* a valve which regulates the flow of liquid or gas along a pipe; tap which controls this. **stop down** reduce the size of a lens aperture. **stopgap** *n* someone or something that fills a particular need temporarily, esp. because of an emergency, shortage, etc. **stop off** make a temporary halt in a journey: I stopped off in London to attend a conference. **stop over** make a temporary halt in a journey, esp. by plane, usually for sightseeing or business purposes: We intend stopping over in Delhi for two nights. **stopover** *n* **stoppage** *n* **1** the act of stopping or discontinuing. **2** an interruption of an event or activity: industrial stoppages. **3** an amount of money that is taken from a person's salary: After stoppages I'm left with just £400. **4** a place inside a tube, pipe, etc., which has become blocked; obstruction. **stopper** *n* **1** something which fits into and seals an opening, esp. that of a bottle. **2** a material used to fill holes and cracks in walls, woodwork, etc. **stopping** *n* a filling in a tooth. **stop-press** *n* items of news received after the printing of a newspaper has started and which are added at the last moment; column where these are printed. **stop-watch** *n* a watch that can be stopped and started instantly, chiefly used for timing races, etc. < Old English *-stoppian.* SEE PANEL.

store (stɔ:) *vb* **1** collect and keep for future use. **2** put somewhere for keeping: You could always store it in the attic. **3** supply with a store of something; stock.
● *n* **1** an available supply or quantity of something, usually accumulated over time. **2** a large amount or quantity. **3** a shop, esp. a large, multi-storey one. **4** a storehouse, storeroom, etc. **lay, put,**

or **set great store by** highly value or esteem. **storage** *n* **1** storing or safekeeping of goods, information, etc. **2** the space available or used for this. **3** a charge made for storing. **storage heater** an electric heater which accumulates energy during off-peak periods. **storehouse** *n* **1** a building where things are stored. **2** (*informal*) a rich source of something. **storeroom** *n* a room where things are stored. < Old French *estorer* to restore.

storey (ˈstɒrɪ) *n* (the rooms occupying) a floor or level of a building. < Medieval Latin *historia* picture.

stork (stɔːk) *n* a large, wading bird with long legs, neck, and bill. < Old English *storc.*

storm (stɔːm) *n* **1** a bout of violent weather characterized by thunder and lightning and high winds, often accompanied by rain, snow, etc. **2** a heavy fall or violent outbreak: a storm of abuse.
• *vb* **1** rain, snow, blow, etc., violently; rage. **2** move or stride violently, usually because of anger: She stormed into the room. **3** capture by an all-out attack: They stormed the fortress. **storm in a teacup** great commotion over something trivial. **stormy** *adj* **1** affected by or full of storms. **2** violent: a stormy wind. **3** full of angry or violent outbursts: a stormy meeting. **stormily** *adv* **storminess** *n* **take by storm** capture by an all-out attack. < Old English.

story[1] (ˈstɔːrɪ) *n* **1** an account of one or more events, either true or imaginary; narrative. **2** the plot of a novel, film, etc. **3** (the material of) a journalist's account of an event. **4** (*euphemistic*) a lie. **a tall story** a story told as if it were true but which is obviously not true. < SEE HISTORY.

story[2] SEE STOREY.

stout (staʊt) *adj* **1** (*chiefly euphemistic*) (of a person) thickset or fattish. **2** sturdy, thick, or solid. **3** (*literary*) brave and resolute.
• *n* a strong, dark beer, flavoured with roasted malt or barley. **stoutly** *adv* **stoutness** *n* < Old French *estout.*

stove[1] (stəʊv) *n* **1** an apparatus used for cooking; cooker. **2** a heating apparatus. < Old English *stofa* bathroom.

stove[2] SEE STAVE.

stow (stəʊ) *vb* pack away or place somewhere for storage. **stow away** hide oneself on a ship, aircraft, etc., before its departure to avoid paying the fare. **stowaway** *n* < Old English *stōw* place.

straddle (ˈstrædl̩) *vb* **1** stand or sit with one leg or support on either side of: straddle a horse. **2** stand or sit with the legs wide apart. < *stride.*

strafe (streɪf) *vb* fire upon (troops, etc.) from the air, esp. with a machine-gun.
• *n* the act or an instance of strafing. < German *strafen* to punish.

straggle (ˈstrægl̩) *vb* **1** grow or spread in a sparse, untidy, or irregular manner. **2** lag behind or stray from the main body. **straggler** *n* **straggly** *adj* < Middle English *straglen.*

straight (streɪt) *adj* **1** (following a path which is) neither curved nor crooked: a straight line. **2** correctly, symmetrically, or tidily arranged: Your tie isn't straight. **3** correct: get one's facts straight. **4** in uninterrupted succession: four straight knock-outs. **5** honest, frank, or upright: a straight answer. **6** unmodified; undiluted: a straight whisky. **7** (of a play, actor, etc.) serious. **8** (*informal*) conventional in behaviour, opinions, etc. **9** (*informal*) heterosexual.
• *adv* **1** in a straight line; along a direct route. **2** immediately; directly: He went straight home to bed. **3** in a level or symmetrical position: You haven't hung it straight. **4** frankly; candidly: She told him straight that she didn't intend to wait.
• *n* a straight part of something, esp. of

stop what?

A number of verbs can be followed either by a full infinitive or by the -ing form of a verb (*gerund*). For example, it is possible to say either She likes to *go* to the theatre or She likes *going* to the theatre. With verbs of this type, such as begin, continue, hate, intend, and prefer, the choice of pattern often has little if any effect on meaning: She *hates to be* kept waiting and She *hates being* kept waiting are essentially synonymous. In some cases, however, changing the pattern in which a verb appears involves changing its meaning completely. Compare, for instance, the different meanings of stop in He stopped *to help* her ('he paused in order to help her') and He stopped *helping* her ('he didn't help her any more').

Learners of English sometimes fail to associate a particular meaning with its appropriate pattern. This can produce rather amusing utterances: 'I stopped to cheat when I saw the teacher looking at me.' 'Try to add a little salt.'

a racecourse: They're now into the final straight. **straightness** *n* **go straight** (*informal*) lead an honest life. **straight away** immediately. **straighten** *vb* make or become straight. **straight fight** a contest between just two parties, esp. in an election. **straightforward** *adj* **1** simple; uncomplicated: a straightforward little job. **2** frank and honest: a straightforward disposition. **straightforwardly** *adv* **straightforwardness** *n* **straight off** immediately. **straight out** (*informal*) frankly; candidly. < Middle English *strecchen* to stretch.

strain[1] (streɪn) *vb* **1** draw or be drawn taut. **2** exert to the utmost extent: She strained her ears to hear who it was. **3** injure or damage by excessive effort or stretching: strain a muscle. **4** filter or remove by filtering: strain the tea.

• *n* **1** the act or an instance of straining. **2** the damage or injury incurred by excessive effort. **3** a force which is exerted: The rope will never take the strain. **4** an excessive demand on one's physical or mental energy: He's finding the monthly repayments a real strain. **5** exhaustion or anxiety caused by this. **6** a part of a melody or tune. **7** a manner of speaking or writing. **strained** *adj* not natural, spontaneous, or relaxed. **strainer** *n* a kitchen utensil for straining. < ultimately Latin *stringere* to draw tight.

strain[2] *n* **1** a line of descent. **2** (*biology*) a distinctive group of plants, animals, etc., within a species. **3** a trait or trace. < Old English *strēon*.

strait (streɪt) *n* **1** a narrow channel connecting two expanses of water: the straits of Gibraltar. **2** *pl* a difficult situation: in dire straits.

• *adj* (*archaic*) restricted; narrow. **straitened** *adj* **in straitened circumstances** short of money. **strait-jacket** *n* a jacket-like harness which deprives a (violent) person of arm movement. **strait-laced** *adj* puritanical; prudish. < Latin *strictus*.

strand[1] (strænd) *n* **1** one of the threads which are twisted together to form string, rope, yarn, etc. **2** something twisted or plaited like a rope: a strand of pearls. **3** a long, wispy lock of hair. < Middle English *strond*.

strand[2] *n* (*literary*) a shore.

• *vb* **1** run or cause to run aground. **2** leave in a helpless or difficult situation: They left her stranded without even her fare home. < Old English.

strange (streɪndʒ) *adj* **1** not known, seen, etc., previously; unfamiliar: It's unusual to see a strange face in the village. **2** unusual; odd: It's a bit strange that he hasn't written to you. **strangely** *adv* **strangeness** *n* **stranger** *n* **1** a person one doesn't know: We were complete strangers before the party. **2** a person who is new to a place. **3** a person unacquainted with something: a stranger to German wine. < Old French *estrange*, from Latin *extraneus* external.

strangle (ˈstræŋgḷ) *vb* **1** kill by throttling. **2** restrict or impede the free growth, expression, or development of. **strangler** *n* **stranglehold** *n* **1** a neck hold which can strangle. **2** a tight grip or control which restricts free movement, development, etc. < ultimately Greek *strangalē* halter.

strangulate (ˈstræŋgjʊˌleɪt) *vb* constrict (a vein, length of intestine, etc.) so that nothing can pass through it: a strangulated hernia. **strangulation** *n* < SEE **STRANGLE**.

strap (stræp) *n* **1** a strip of leather, cloth, or other flexible material for fastening, holding in position, etc. **2** a loop of leather, etc., hung from the roof of a carriage, by which a standing passenger can steady himself or herself.

• *vb* **strapped; strapping 1** secure, bind, or hold together by means of one or more straps. **2** beat with a leather strap. **strapless** *adj* (of a garment) without straps. **strapping** *adj* (*informal*) tall and robust. < Old English *strop*.

stratagem (ˈstrætɪdʒəm) *n* a cunning or deceptive scheme, method, or plan. < Greek *stratēgein* to be a general.

strategy (ˈstrætɪdʒɪ) *n* the art of (successfully) planning or managing a campaign or operation. **strategic** or **strategical** *adj* of or connected with strategy: a strategic withdrawal. **strategically** *adv* **strategic weapons** weapons intended to strike an enemy's home territory rather than be used in battle. **strategist** *n* an expert in strategy. < Greek *stratēgia* generalship.

stratosphere (ˈstrætəˌsfɪə) *n* an upper layer of the atmosphere from approximately 20 to 50 kilometres above the earth's surface, where the temperature is relatively constant. < New Latin *stratum* + *-o-* + French *sphère* sphere.

stratum (ˈstrɒːtəm) *n, pl* **strata 1** one of a series of horizontal layers, esp. of the earth's crust. **2** any layer, level, or class: social strata. **stratify** *vb* **stratified; stratifying** form or arrange in layers or levels. **stratification** *n* < ultimately Latin *sternere* to spread out.

straw (strɔː) *n* **1** the stalks of grain after

the grain has been removed, used chiefly for animal bedding; single piece of this. **2** a narrow tube of plastic, waxed paper, etc., used for sucking up liquids. **3** (*informal*) a thing of no value or importance: I couldn't give a straw. **strawberry** *n* a plant bearing a soft, juicy, sweet, red fruit; this fruit. < Old English *strēaw.*

stray (streɪ) *vb* wander from a group, course, or subject.
• *adj* **1** having strayed; lost: a stray cat. **2** randomly occurring; occasional.
• *n* a domestic animal which has strayed. < Middle French *estraier.*

streak (stri:k) *n* **1** a line, band, or mark of a different colour, texture, etc., from its background. **2** a trait or trace: a streak of jealousy. **3** a consecutive series; spell: a winning streak.
• *vb* **1** mark with one or more streaks. **2** move swiftly. **3** run naked through a public place. **streaker** *n* **streaky** *adj* < Old English *strica.*

stream (stri:m) *n* **1** a small river; brook. **2** a flowing body of water or other liquid. **3** any steady flow: a stream of people. **4** a group of pupils of the same ability. **5** drift or direction: the stream of opinion.
• *vb* **1** flow or move in a stream: Spectators streamed out of the gates. **2** emit liquid in a continuous stream: Onions always make my eyes stream. **3** float freely: hair streaming in the wind. **4** divide into levels of ability: Her headmaster doesn't believe in streaming. **streamer** *n* **1** a long, narrow flag; pennant. **2** a long, paper ribbon used as a party decoration. **streamline** *vb* **1** provide with a shape which offers minimal resistance to air or water. **2** make more efficient, esp. by simplifying. **streamlined** *adj* < Old English *strēam.*

street (stri:t) *n* a road in a town or village, usually lined with houses, shops, etc. **on the street** homeless. **on the streets** living by working as a prostitute. **streets ahead of** (*informal*) far superior to; well in advance of: When it comes to selling cars, the Japanese are streets ahead. **streetwalker** *n* a prostitute. **up one's street** (*informal*) in keeping with one's abilities, interests, or preferences. < Old English *strǣt.*

strength (strɛŋθ) *n* **1** the quality of being strong: You don't need strength if you have the right tools. **2** the capacity to resist or sustain pressure or attack: The strength of the rope is crucial. **3** an asset or forte: Her strength is her ability to read his mind. **4** the total number of people in a group, contingent, etc.: Due to absenteeism, the department is well below strength. **from strength to strength** with ever increasing success, progress, etc. **in strength** in large numbers. **on the strength of** on the basis of. **strengthen** *vb* make or become stronger. < Old English *strengthu.*

strenuous (ˈstrɛnjʊəs) *adj* **1** requiring considerable effort. **2** vigorous; energetic. **strenuously** *adv* **strenuousness** *n* < Latin *strenuus.*

stress (strɛs) *n* **1** nervous anxiety or tension: be under stress. **2** the force pressing on or acting within something: The stress was simply too much for the girder. **3** special weight or importance: You should lay stress on the need to be punctual. **4** the emphasis put on a word or syllable.
• *vb* **1** give importance to: The urgency of the matter cannot be stressed enough. **2** emphasize (a word or syllable). **stressful** *adj* **stressfully** *adv* < Middle English *stresse.*

stretch (strɛtʃ) *vb* **1** make or become longer or wider by pulling: If you stretch the elastic too much it will break. **2** extend fully: She stretched the finished sleeve out on the carpet. **3** distort or become distorted by stretching or being stretched: Once you've stretched it, you won't be able to wear it. **4** extend continuously from a point or between two points: The mountain range stretched far into the distance. **5** extend the arms, legs, and trunk while tightening the muscles. **6** make demands on (a person's abilities): She is not being stretched enough in her new job. **7** strain: These feeble excuses are enough to stretch anyone's patience.
• *n* **1** stretching or being stretched. **2** the capacity for being stretched: It will lose its stretch if you keep washing it. **3** a continuous extent or expanse: a beautiful stretch of unspoilt countryside. **4** a continuous period of time: a stretch of five years. **5** (*informal*) a term of imprisonment. **at a stretch** **1** without a pause or interruption. **2** by making a special effort: At a stretch, the car could be ready for collection by Thursday. **at full stretch** with all one's strength, resources, etc., in full use. **stretcher** *n* **1** a length of canvas fixed between two poles, used for carrying a sick or injured person in an emergency. **2** a wooden frame over which a piece of canvas, etc., is stretched and held taut. **stretch one's legs** (*informal*) go for a walk, esp. for exercise. **stretch out** extend or straighten: She stretched out a hand for the child to hold. < Old English *streccan.*

strew (stru:) *vb* **strewed; strewn, strewed; strewing** scatter or cover by scattering: There was litter strewn all over the floor. < Old English *strewian.*

stricken (ˈstrɪkən) *adj* afflicted, overwhelmed, or affected by: stricken with grief. < *strike.*

strict (strɪkt) *adj* **1** stern and demanding obedience. **2** rigorous or severe: strict discipline. **3** exact or precise: the strict meaning of the word. **4** complete; absolute: in strict confidence. **strictly** *adv* **strictness** *n* < Latin *stringere* to draw tight.

stricture (ˈstrɪktʃə) *n* **1** a hostile or critical remark. **2** (*medicine*) an unnatural constriction of an internal duct or vessel. < SEE **STRICT.**

stride (straɪd) *vb* **strode; stridden; striding 1** walk or run with long steps. **2** stand astride.
• *n* **1** (the length of) a single, long step. **2** a manner of walking; gait. **3** advance or progress: He's been making rapid strides over the last term. **get into one's stride** attain an efficient work habit or steady rate of progress. **take in one's stride** do or react to without great difficulty or getting upset. < Old English *strīdan.*

strident (ˈstraɪdn̩t) *adj* harsh or shrill: a strident voice. < Latin *stridēre* to make a grating noise.

strife (straɪf) *n* conflict; discord. < Old French *estrif.*

strike (straɪk) *vb* **struck; striking 1** hit or give a blow to; inflict (a blow): She struck him as hard as she could. **2** come into collision with: The car struck a tree. **3** attack or afflict suddenly: The killer has struck again. **4** cause suddenly to become, as if by a blow; render: be struck blind. **5** fill with a sudden feeling: The threat struck terror into their hearts. **6** cause to ignite: strike a match. **7** produce (a flame) by striking: strike a light. **8** produce (a sound, note, etc.) by moving, pressing, or striking; indicate by sounding: The clock struck ten. **9** produce a particular effect or impact on: How does his new wife strike you? **10** occur suddenly to the mind: It struck me that I won't be needing your help after all. **11** discover or reach, esp. by drilling: They've struck oil again in the North Sea. **12** set off or proceed in a particular direction: They struck off across the fields. **13** root or take root. **14** produce (a coin, medallion, etc.) by stamping; mint. **15** stop work because of a grievance: They're bound to strike if you stop their overtime. **16** make or arrive at, esp. after negotiation: strike a bargain. **17** lower or take down: strike a flag. **18** assume dramatically: strike a pose. **19** remove or delete: Strike the last remark from the records.
• *n* **1** the act or an instance of striking. **2** a refusal by employees to work because of a grievance. **3** an attack. **4** a sudden discovery of oil, gold, etc. **strike at** attempt to hit with a blow. **strike off** remove (a person's name) from (a professional register) because of misconduct. **strike on** or **upon** discover: They've struck on a new way of preventing gum disease. **strike out 1** start on a new venture: He's decided to strike out on his own. **2** set out: She struck out for the shore. **striker** *n* **1** a person on strike. **2** a player whose job is to attack the opponent's goal. **3** a person or thing that strikes. **strike up 1** (of an orchestra, musician, etc.) begin to play. **2** commence: strike up a friendship. **striking** *adj* causing a strong impression; attractive: a striking cream and brown swim-suit. < Old English *strīcan.*

string (strɪŋ) *n* **1** (a length of) narrow cord made of fibres twisted together, chiefly used for fastening. **2** something resembling string, esp. the tough fibre of a bean. **3** a number of objects threaded together: a string of pearls. **4** a length of taut catgut or wire on a musical instrument. **5** *pl* instruments which employ such strings. **6** one of the lengths of catgut, nylon, etc., which are interlaced to form the head of a racket. **7** a series of things coming one after the other: a string of questions. **8** a condition or obligation: Make sure there are no strings attached.
• *vb* **strung; stringing 1** fasten with string. **2** provide with strings: Where did you get your racket strung? **3** thread: I haven't got the patience for stringing beads. **4** remove the tough fibres from (beans). **string along** (*informal*) **1** deceive, esp. by giving false hopes; lead on. **2** accompany: Do you mind if I string along? **3** co-operate. **stringed** *adj* (of instruments) having strings. **string out 1** spread out or be spread out in a line. **2** prolong. **string quartet** a quartet of stringed instruments. **string together** combine (words, phrases, etc.) meaningfully. **string up 1** hang: Pretty little lights were strung up all over the room. **2** (*informal*) kill by hanging. **stringy** *adj* **1** like string. **2** (of beans, etc.) containing tough fibre. **stringiness** *n* < Old English *streng.*

stringent (ˈstrɪndʒənt) *adj* strict or rigorous: stringent laws. **stringency** *n* **stringently** *adv* < Latin *stringere* to draw tight.

strip[1] (strɪp) *vb* **stripped; stripping 1** remove the covering from: I always strip the walls before repapering. **2** remove (clothes) from; undress: We were told to strip to the waist. **3** remove the contents of; empty: The

bailiffs came in and stripped the house. **4** dismantle: The engine will have to be stripped down. **5** deprive or divest of: He was stripped of his title. **6** pull away or tear: Try not to strip the thread. **7** perform a striptease.
• *n* (*informal*) a striptease. **strip club** a place where striptease is performed. **stripper** *n* **1** a machine or solvent which removes paint, varnish, etc. **2** a striptease performer. **striptease** *n* a form of erotic entertainment in which a person, esp. a woman, gradually undresses to music. < Old English *-strīpan*.

strip[2] *n* a long, narrow piece: Instead of a proper bandage we used a strip of material. **strip cartoon** a story told through a series of drawings, with the words of characters shown in balloons coming out of their mouths. **strip lighting** lighting in the form of long, fluorescent tubes. < Middle Dutch *strīpe* stripe.

stripe (straɪp) *n* **1** a long, narrow band of a different colour, texture, etc., from its background. **2** a chevron worn on a sleeve to indicate rank. **striped** *adj* having stripes. < Middle Dutch *strīpe*.

strive (straɪv) *vb* **strove; striven; striving 1** make a great effort. **2** struggle or contend. < Old French *estriver*.

stroboscope (ˈstrəʊbəˌskəʊp) *n* an instrument producing an intense, flashing light which under certain conditions can cause something moving to appear stationary. **stroboscopic** *adj* < Greek *strobos* whirling + *-scope*.

strode (strəʊd) SEE **STRIDE**.

stroke[1] (strəʊk) *vb* pass the hand gently or caressingly along: stroke the cat.
• *n* the act of giving one or more strokes. < Old English *strācian*.

stroke[2] *n* **1** the act of striking; blow: a few strokes of the whip. **2** a single, continuous movement: It could break a child's arm with a single stroke of its wings. **3** a striking of the ball in tennis, cricket, etc. **4** an action or effort: a stroke of genius. **5** a chance occurrence: a stroke of good fortune. **6** the person rowing nearest the stern of a racing-boat. **7** a mark or line made by a single movement of a pen, paintbrush, etc. **8** the sound of a clock striking. **9** a sudden disorder in a part of the brain which can result in paralysis.
• *vb* (of an oarsman) act as stroke. < Middle English.

stroll (strəʊl) *vb* walk in a leisurely way.
• *n* a leisurely walk: go for a stroll. **stroller** *n* < probably German dialect *strollen*.

strong (strɒŋ) *adj* **1** having power: I'm not strong enough to lift it. **2** having the capacity to resist external or internal forces; not fragile: a strong rope. **3** powerful, weighty, or significant: The bill met with strong opposition. **4** violent: a strong wind. **5** sharp or distinct: a strong contrast. **6** competent or capable: She's always been strong in languages. **7** concentrated; highly alcoholic: a strong mixture of vodka and lemonade. **8** pungent: a strong smell. **9** having a certain number: The regiment is 500 strong. **10** (*informal*) objectionable; unacceptable: It's a bit strong inviting the wife and not the husband. **11** (of language) offensive. **12** (of verbs) undergoing a vowel change in the past tense and past participle as opposed to adding a suffix.
• *adv* in a strong manner: Even at 78, she's still going strong. **strong-arm** *adj* involving physical force or aggression: strong-arm tactics. **strong-box** *n* a reinforced metal box for keeping valuables. **strong-minded** *adj* having a determined mind or will. **strong point** a special aptitude or forte: Listening is not exactly her strong point. **strong-room** *n* a reinforced room in which valuables are stored. < Old English *strang*.

strove (strəʊv) SEE **STRIVE**.

struck (strʌk) SEE **STRIKE**. **struck on** (*informal*) impressed by: I can't really say I'm struck on the way he treats her.

structure (ˈstrʌktʃə) *n* **1** the way in which the parts of something are organized or arranged: the structure of the brain. **2** something formed or built of many parts; building. **3** a supporting framework: Despite its shabby appearance, its structure is still sound.
• *vb* provide with a structure; arrange. **structural** *adj* **structurally** *adv* < ultimately Latin *struere* to build.

struggle (ˈstrʌgl̩) *vb* **1** make violent movements, esp. when fighting or trying to free oneself. **2** make great efforts; exert oneself: struggling to work out how a computer works. **3** proceed with great difficulty: struggle through the undergrowth.
• *n* **1** great effort or exertion. **2** a conflict; fight. < Middle English *struglen*.

strum (strʌm) *vb* **strummed; strumming** sound the strings of (a guitar, etc.) by brushing a plectrum or thumb lightly across them. < like the sound.

strung (strʌŋ) SEE **STRING**. **strung up** (*informal*) nervously agitated; tense.

strut (strʌt) *n* **1** a length of wood, metal, etc., which is designed to strengthen or brace the framework into which it is inserted. **2** a strutting walk.
• *vb* **strutted; strutting** walk in a proud or pompous way. < Old English *strūtian* to stand rigid.

strychnine (ˈstrɪkniːn) *n* a white, highly poisonous substance in crystalline form, used in small doses as a stimulant. < ultimately Greek *strykhnos* nightshade.

stub (stʌb) *n* **1** a short stump: a pencil stub. **2** the counterfoil of a cheque which remains in the cheque-book.
• *vb* **stubbed; stubbing** strike against something hard: stub one's toe. **stubby** *adj* short and thick: stubby fingers. **stub out** extinguish (a cigarette, etc.) by pressing against a hard surface. < Old English *stybb*.

stubble (ˈstʌbl̩) *n* **1** the stalks of cereal grasses which remain in the ground after a harvest. **2** a short growth of beard or hair which resembles this. **stubbly** *adj* < ultimately Latin *stupula* stalk.

stubborn (ˈstʌbn̩) *adj* persistently unbending; obstinate. **stubbornly** *adv* **stubbornness** *n*

stucco (ˈstʌkəʊ) *n, pl* **stuccos, stuccoes** plaster or cement used for coating walls or for producing decorations from architectural moulds. < Italian.

stuck (stʌk) SEE **STICK**.
• *adj* **1** held fast and unable to move: The drawer's stuck. **2** baffled: If you get stuck, the solution is at the foot of the page. **stuck-up** *adj* (*informal*) haughty, conceited, or snobbish. **stuck with** (*informal*) unable to get rid of.

stud[1] (stʌd) *n* **1** a number of animals, esp. horses, kept for breeding. **2** a male animal, esp. a horse, kept for breeding. **3** (*humorous*) a man who is known for his sexual prowess. < Old English *stōd*.

stud[2] *n* **1** a type of fastener used instead of a button. **2** a nail, pin, rivet, etc., with a large head, esp. one which projects from the sole of a football boot, cricket boot, etc., providing better grip. < Old English *studu*.

student (ˈstjuːdn̩t) *n* **1** a person who studies at a college, university, etc. **2** any person who studies. < Latin *studēre* to study.

studio (ˈstjuːdɪˌəʊ) *n, pl* **studios 1** the place where an artist, photographer, etc., works. **2** (a part of) a building where cinema films are made; film production company. **3** a room in which radio or television programmes are recorded or from which they are broadcast. < Italian: study. SEE PANEL.

studious (ˈstjuːdɪəs) *adj* **1** having a regular habit of reading or studying: a studious pupil. **2** involving or connected with study. **3** painstaking: studious avoidance. **studiously** *adv* **studiousness** *n* < Latin *studiōsus* devoted to.

study (ˈstʌdɪ) *vb* **studied; studying 1** attempt to acquire knowledge of (a subject), esp. by reading: She's studying Greek literature. **2** examine closely: He sat studying the script for some time. **3** show consideration to: They study nobody but themselves.
• *n* **1** the process of studying. **2** (the pursuit of) a branch of knowledge: the study of electronics. **3** a room used for studying, reading, etc. **4** (a report resulting from) a careful examination of a subject: Her study shows that the drug can have harmful effects. **5** a musical, literary, or other artistic composition intended as an exercise or preliminary interpretation; étude. < Latin *studium*.

stuff (stʌf) *n* **1** any indeterminate material or substance: She spread some stuff on it to stop it blistering. **2** personal belongings: He packed his stuff and went. **3** materials, tools, equipment, etc., entailed by an activity: You'll never afford all the stuff you need to take up golf. **4** the material from which something is made; fabric: the stuff that champions are made of. **5** (*informal*) subject matter: know one's stuff. **6** (*informal*) rubbish; trash.
• *vb* **1** fill by packing tightly; cram. **2** plug, block, or stop up: We stuffed the hole up with newspaper. **3** fill with padding; pack: stuffed cushions. **4** fill (poultry, vegetables, etc.) with savoury stuffing. **5** (*informal*) eat greedily; gorge. **6** fill the skin of (an

studio

Studio is one of the words which have come into English from Italian. Other words of Italian derivation include:

balcony	**fresco**	**ruffian**
ballot	**gazette**	**sequin**
bandit	**grotto**	**sonnet**
bravo	**influenza**	**spaghetti**
bust	**lava**	**squadron**
cameo	**macaroni**	**stanza**
canto	**malaria**	**stiletto**
caricature	**manifesto**	**stucco**
carnival	**motto**	**terracotta**
cartoon	**opera**	**umbrella**
charlatan	**parapet**	**virtuoso**
concert	**pedantry**	**vista**
ditto	**piano**	**volcano**
domino	**regatta**	

animal) with material so that it can be mounted for display. **7** (*informal*) force; shove: She stuffed it through the letter-box. **8** (*informal*) dispose of (something) in an indeterminate way: If you don't like their offer, tell them to stuff it. **stuffing** *n* **1** the padding used to fill cushions, etc. **2** a savoury mixture used for stuffing poultry, vegetables, etc. **stuffy** *adj* **1** lacking fresh air or ventilation: a stuffy room. **2** dull or uninteresting: stuffy, old books. **3** (of a nose) blocked. **4** (*informal*) prim and proper; strait-laced. **stuffily** *adv* **stuffiness** *n* < Old French *estoffer* to equip.

stultify ('stʌltɪˌfaɪ) *vb* **stultified; stultifying** make futile, ineffective, or absurd. **stultification** *n* < Latin *stultus* foolish.

stumble ('stʌmbl̩) *vb* **1** trip when walking, running, etc. **2** walk unsteadily: The old man stumbled along the corridor. **3** speak, act, or perform clumsily or with a lot of mistakes: stumble through a lecture. **4** discover or meet by chance: I stumbled upon it in the Grand Bazaar. **stumbler** *n* **stumblingly** *adv* **stumbling-block** *n* an obstacle; difficulty: Don't let lack of funds act as a stumbling-block. < Middle English *stumblen*.

stump (stʌmp) *n* **1** the part of a tree which remains in the ground after the tree has been felled. **2** something resembling this, for example the remaining part of a severed limb or broken tooth. **3** one of the three upright pieces of wood which form a wicket in cricket.

• *vb* **1** (*informal*) baffle; bewilder: I refuse to be stumped by a simple crossword puzzle. **2** walk clumsily or noisily. **3** (of a wicket-keeper) dismiss (a batsman) by breaking the wicket with the ball while he is out of his crease. **stumpy** *adj* short and thick. **stumpiness** *n* < Middle English *stumpe*.

stun (stʌn) *vb* **stunned; stunning** **1** knock dizzy or senseless. **2** overcome with shock, strong emotion, etc.: We were all stunned by the news of the assassination. **stunning** *adj* strikingly attractive. **stunningly** *adv* < Middle English *stunen*.

stung (stʌŋ) SEE **STING**.

stunk (stʌŋk) SEE **STINK**.

stunt[1] (stʌnt) *vb* hinder the (natural) growth or development of. < English dialect: foolish.

stunt[2] *n* a dangerous, unusual, or difficult feat done for publicity or as a thrilling entertainment. **stunt man** a man who earns a living by performing stunts, esp. as a substitute for an actor in dangerous scenes. < origin uncertain.

stupefy ('stju:pɪˌfaɪ) *vb* **stupefied; stupefying** **1** make groggy or senseless; bewilder. **2** astonish; amaze. **stupefaction** *n* < Latin *stupēre* to be astonished.

stupendous (stju:'pɛndəs) *adj* **1** of tremendous size, height, etc. **2** astonishing; astounding. **stupendously** *adv* **stupendousness** *n* < Latin *stupēre* to be astonished.

stupid ('stju:pɪd) *adj* **1** slow to learn or understand: a stupid child. **2** lacking common sense; unthinking: That was a stupid thing to do. **3** uninteresting; unrewarding: a stupid job. **4** dazed or unconscious: knock someone stupid. **stupidity** *n* **stupidly** *adv* < Latin *stupēre* to be astonished. SEE PANEL.

stupor ('stju:pə) *n* a drowsy, dazed, or almost unconscious condition brought on by drugs, alcohol, etc. < Latin

He's not stupid!

When we say that so-and-so is not stupid, we usually mean that, far from being literally 'not stupid', he or she is quite the opposite, namely 'clever' or 'astute'. Similarly, not bad rarely means what it says it means—more typically it is used in the sense 'good' or even 'very good': 'What did you think of her new film?—'Not bad! What I really liked was the dialogue.'

This use of a negative before a word to express its opposite is known as *litotes,* ultimately from the Greek *litos* or 'simple'. A well-known example is the understatement by Queen Victoria: We are not amused!

stupor or **torpor?**

These two words are sometimes confused. A stupor is a drowsy, dazed, or almost unconscious condition that is brought on by drugs, alcohol, etc.: a drunken *stupor.* Torpor, a less common word, is an inactive state or suspension of physical activity, for example of a hibernating animal. Torpor can also suggest a sluggish, lethargic state.

stupēre to be astonished. SEE PANEL.

sturdy (ˈstɜːdɪ) *adj* **1** strongly built; robust: a sturdy piece of furniture. **2** healthy, strong, and vigorous: a sturdy child. **sturdily** *adv* **sturdiness** *n* < Old French *estourdi* stunned.

sturgeon (ˈstɜːdʒən) *n, pl* **sturgeon** any of a group of large, shark-like fish valued as food and as a source of caviar. < Old French *estourjon.*

stutter (ˈstʌtə) *vb* stammer.
• *n* a stammer. < Middle English *stutten.*

sty[1] (staɪ) *n* a pigsty. < Old English *stig.*

sty[2] also **stye** *n, pl* **sties, styes** an inflamed swelling, like a small boil, on the edge of the eyelid. < Middle English *styanye,* from Old English *stīgend* rising + *ye* eye.

style (staɪl) *n* **1** the manner in which something is done: a style of speaking. **2** a shape or design: Do you like the latest shoe styles? **3** elegance: a dress with a lot of style. **4** a distinctive manner of doing something: It's not Hilary's style to go by bus. **5** (*biology*) a slender extension of a plant ovary which supports the stigma.
• *vb* design, shape, or provide with a style: I like the way that the sleeves have been styled. **in style 1** elegantly: live in style. **2** without stinting or counting the expense: She prefers to do things in style. **stylish** *adj* fashionable; elegant. **stylishly** *adv* **stylishness** *n* **stylist** *n* **1** a person who designs or creates styles: a hair stylist. **2** a person, esp. a writer, who cultivates a good style. **stylistic** *adj* of or connected with style, esp. that of a literary or artistic work. **stylistically** *adv* **stylize** *vb* give a conventional style to. < Latin *stilus* style of writing.

stylus (ˈstaɪləs) *n, pl* **styli, styluses** a needle-like device which follows the grooves of a gramophone record and sends the resulting signals to the cartridge. < Latin *stilus* writing implement.

suave (swɑːv) *adj* polite and agreeable in a sophisticated way, sometimes excessively. < Middle French: sweet.

sub (sʌb) *n* (*informal*) **1** a submarine. **2** a substitute. **3** a small loan. **4** a subscription.

sub- *prefix* **1** under; below. **2** subordinate. < Latin.

subaqua (ˌsʌbˈækwə) *adj* of underwater sports or recreations.

subconscious (ˌsʌbˈkɒnʃəs) *adj* **1** of or connected with mental activities operating below the threshold of consciousness. **2** not (fully) conscious.
• *n* the subconscious mind or its activities. **subconsciously** *adv*

subcontinent (ˌsʌbˈkɒntɪnənt) *n* a vast land-mass within a continent.

subcontract (ˌsʌbˈkɒntrækt) *n* a secondary contract between a party to a main contract and a third party who is brought in to do (part of) the work, etc., of the main contract.
• *vb* (ˌsʌbkənˈtrækt) **1** hire an outside party to fulfil (part of) one's contract. **2** let out or take on (work) on a subcontract basis.

subdivide (ˌsʌbdɪˈvaɪd) *vb* divide into smaller parts or groups. **subdivision** *n* < Late Latin *subdividere.*

subdue (səbˈdjuː) *vb* **1** conquer, overcome, or bring under control. **2** make less harsh or intense. **subdued** *adj* < Middle French *soduire* to seduce.

subheading (ˈsʌbˌhɛdɪŋ) *n* **1** a heading given to a section of a chapter, article, etc. **2** a subordinate extension of a main heading or headline.

subject (ˈsʌbdʒɪkt) *n* **1** the person or thing that is being discussed, described, etc.; topic. **2** a person who owes allegiance to a ruler or government. **3** a branch of study or learning. **4** a person or thing that is the focus of an experiment, study, work of art, etc. **5** the word or phrase in a clause or sentence about which something is said.
• *adj* **1** politically dependent: a subject nation. **2** exposed or liable to: subject to subsidence. **3** dependent upon: Subject to your approval, I shall arrange a meeting for Friday.
• *vb* (səbˈdʒɛkt) **1** bring under control; conquer: Both of the neighbouring states have been subjected to his rule. **2** cause to undergo or experience: He's been subjected to a lot of pressure just recently. **subjection** *n* **subjective** *adj* **1** existing in or created by one's own mind as opposed to actually existing in the world outside it. **2** determined by one's individual outlook, prejudices, etc.; personal: Try to be less subjective in your opinions. **subjectively** *adv* **subjectivity** *n* < ultimately Latin *subicere* to subject.

subjugate (ˈsʌbdʒʊˌgeɪt) *vb* subdue, conquer, or bring under control. **subjugation** *n* < Latin *subjugare.*

subjunctive (səbˈdʒʌŋktɪv) *adj* (*grammar*) of a mood that is used when what is being said contains a contingency, possibility, wish, etc., as opposed to a statement of fact.
• *n* a subjunctive form. < Latin *subjungere* to append.

sublet (ˌsʌbˈlɛt) *vb* **sublet; subletting** let

(property that one is oneself renting).

sublimate (ˈsʌblɪˌmeɪt) *vb* redirect the energy of (an instinctive feeling or impulse) into a socially acceptable form. **sublimation** *n* < Medieval Latin *sublimare*.

sublime (səˈblaɪm) *adj* **1** of the most noble, lofty, or exalted kind. **2** awe-inspiring (in degree, intensity, etc.). **sublimely** *adv* **sublimity** *n* < Latin *sublimis* lofty.

subliminal (sʌbˈlɪmɪnl̩) *adj* directed at or perceived by the subconscious part of the mind: subliminal advertising. < *sub-* + Latin *limen* threshold.

submarine (ˈsʌbməˌriːn, ˌsʌbməˈriːn) *n* a vessel which is designed to travel under water, esp. one armed with torpedoes, missiles, etc.
• *adj* (ˌsʌbməˈriːn) living, existing, or intended to be used under water, esp. under the sea: submarine plants.

submerge (səbˈmɜːdʒ) *vb* **1** place under water. **2** go or dive under water. **3** cover with or as if with water; overwhelm. **submergence** *n* **submersion** *n* < Latin *submergere*.

submit (səbˈmɪt) *vb* **submitted; submitting 1** yield to the will or authority of another. **2** subject or let oneself be subjected to something. **3** present for consideration: All applications should be submitted before the end of the month. **4** put forward as an opinion. **submission** *n* **submissive** *adj* willing to submit or obey. **submissively** *adv* **submissiveness** *n* < Latin *submittere*.

subnormal (sʌbˈnɔːməl) *adj* **1** below average or less than normal. **2** having less than average intelligence. **subnormality** *n* **subnormally** *adv*

subordinate (səˈbɔːdɪnət) *adj* **1** of a lower or inferior status, class, or rank. **2** subject to the authority of another.
• *vb* (səˈbɔːdɪˌneɪt) **1** reduce in status, class, or rank. **2** make subservient; subdue. **subordination** *n* < Latin *subordinare*.

subpoena (səbˈpiːnə, səˈpiːnə) *n* a writ commanding a person to appear in court.
• *vb* serve with a subpoena. < Latin *sub poena* under penalty.

subscribe (səbˈskraɪb) *vb* **1** give or donate (money), esp. to a charity or other cause. **2** (undertake to) pay for something, usually regularly or in advance, esp. a series of issues of a publication. **3** sign (one's name), esp. to indicate approval. **4** express agreement or approval: I certainly don't subscribe to further lay-offs. **subscriber** *n* a person who subscribes, esp. one who rents a telephone. **subscriber trunk dialling** a system of dialling trunk calls oneself instead of having the operator obtain the number. **subscription** *n* **1** the act of subscribing. **2** a sum of money subscribed. **3** a membership fee. < Latin *subscribere* to write beneath.

subsection (ˌsʌbˈsɛkʃən) *n* a section within a larger section.

subsequent (ˈsʌbsɪkwənt) *adj* coming after or later; following: Subsequent meetings were rather more successful. **subsequently** *adv* < Latin *subsequi* to follow closely.

subservient (səbˈsɜːvɪənt) *adj* **1** meekly submissive; servile. **2** subordinate. **subservience** *n* **subserviently** *adv* < Latin *subservire* to be subservient.

subside (səbˈsaɪd) *vb* **1** (of land, houses, etc.) sink to a lower level. **2** sink lower, to the bottom, or to the normal level: The flood water subsided. **3** become subdued or less intense: We'll have to wait for these winds to subside. **subsidence** *n* < Latin *subsidere* to settle down.

subsidiary (səbˈsɪdɪərɪ) *adj* **1** of secondary importance. **2** serving or contributing to something larger, more important, etc.
• *n* a subsidiary person or thing, esp. a company which is owned by another. < Latin *subsidium* reserve troops.

subsidy (ˈsʌbsɪdɪ) *n* **1** a grant of money, esp. one paid by a government to an industry suffering financial difficulty. **2** government funds used to keep down the price of something. **subsidize** *vb* support with a subsidy. < Latin *subsidium* reserve troops.

subsist (səbˈsɪst) *vb* **1** continue to exist or stay alive. **2** have the bare necessities to stay alive. **subsistence** *n* **1** (a means of) subsisting. **2** the bare minimum necessary to stay or keep alive. < Late Latin *subsistere* to exist.

subsoil (ˈsʌbˌsɔɪl) *n* the layer of soil underneath the topsoil.

subsonic (ˌsʌbˈsɒnɪk) *adj* (flying or moving at) less than the speed of sound. **subsonically** *adv*

substance (ˈsʌbstəns) *n* **1** material or matter: a thick, sticky substance like glue. **2** a particular type of this. **3** the essential or basic part of something: I agree with the substance of what was said but object to certain details. **4** sturdiness, solidity, or body: The argument is without substance. **5** material wealth: a man of substance. < Latin *substare* to stand under.

substandard (ˌsʌbˈstændəd) *adj* below

the normal or prescribed standard.
substantial (səbˈstænʃəl) *adj* **1** of considerable size, importance, etc.: a substantial difference. **2** sufficiently satisfying: a substantial meat. **3** sturdy, strong, or solidly built. **4** having wealth or property. **5** real, actual, or true. **6** essential: in substantial agreement. **substantially** *adv* < ultimately Latin *substantia.*
substantiate (səbˈstænʃɪˌeɪt) *vb* support (a claim, assertion, etc.) with proof or evidence; verify. **substantiation** *n*
substitute (ˈsʌbstɪˌtjuːt) *n* a person or thing that serves in place of another. • *vb* use or serve as a substitute. **substitution** *n* < Latin *substituere* to put in place of.
subsume (səbˈsjuːm) *vb* incorporate within a group or category. < Latin *subsumere.*
subterfuge (ˈsʌbtəˌfjuːdʒ) *n* a sly or underhand strategy; trick. < Latin *subterfugere* to escape.
subterranean (ˌsʌbtəˈreɪnɪən) *adj* underground. < Latin *subterraneus,* from *sub* under + *terra* earth.
subtitle (ˈsʌbˌtaɪtl̩) *n* **1** a subordinate title, often serving to explain the main title. **2** a translation of foreign speech appearing at the bottom of a cinema or television screen.
subtle (ˈsʌtl̩) *adj* **1** hardly noticeable or detectable: subtle differences. **2** cunning or crafty: By subtle means he got her to agree. **3** having keen powers of perception: a subtle intelligence. **subtlety** *n* **subtly** *adv* < Latin *subtilis* finely woven.
subtract (səbˈtrækt) *vb* deduct or take away, esp. (one sum or number) from (another). **subtraction** *n* < Latin *subtrahere* to draw away from beneath.
suburb (ˈsʌbɜːb) *n* **1** a residential area on or near the outskirts of a city. **2** an area outside the central part of a city. **suburban** *adj* **1** of or connected with a suburb. **2** (*derogatory*) unadventurous in attitudes, tastes, interests, etc. **suburbia** *n* (*derogatory*) the suburbs of a city. < Latin *suburbium,* from *sub-* near + *urbs* city. SEE PANEL.

> **suburb**
>
> A residential district on the outskirts of a city or large town is known as a suburb. This word entered English as long ago as the 14th century from the Latin *suburbium,* a compound of *sub-* 'close to' and *urbs* 'a city'.

subvert (səbˈvɜːt) *vb* undermine the power or authority of; overthrow. **subversion** *n* **subversive** *adj* tending or attempting to subvert: subversive elements. < Latin *subvertere* to overturn.
subway (ˈsʌbˌweɪ) *n* **1** an underground passage, esp. one for pedestrians to cross a road in safety by walking under it. **2** (*US*) an underground railway.
succeed (səkˈsiːd) *vb* **1** achieve an aim or purpose. **2** follow as a successor; inherit sovereignty by doing this: He will one day succeed his father as head of the company. **3** (*formal*) follow or come after: The winter was succeeded by a glorious spring. **successor** *n* **success** *n* **1** the attainment of a goal or purpose: I tried to get him to sign, but without success. **2** the attainment of material wealth. **3** a person or thing that succeeds. **successful** *adj* having or achieving success. **successfully** *adv* **succession** *n* **1** a number of people or things following one after another; series: a succession of angry complaints. **2** the right or act of succeeding to a throne or position. **3** the line of people with this right: Who is next in succession? **in succession** one after another. **successive** *adj* following one after another in an unbroken sequence: nine successive wins. **successively** *adv* < Latin *succedere.*
succinct (səkˈsɪŋkt) *adj* expressed clearly and concisely. **succinctly** *adv* **succinctness** *n* < Latin *succingere* to gird from below.
succour (ˈsʌkə) *n* (*literary*) help or relief provided in time of need. • *vb* give such help. < Latin *succerrere* to run to help.
succulent (ˈsʌkjʊlənt) *adj* **1** full of juice. **2** (of a plant) having thick, fleshy leaves or stems which are full of moisture. • *n* a succulent plant. **succulence** *n* **succulently** *adv* < Latin *sucus* juice.
succumb (səˈkʌm) *vb* **1** yield or give in: succumb to temptation. **2** (*euphemistic*) die. < Latin *succumbere.*
such (sʌtʃ) *determiner* **1** of the same kind as that mentioned; similar: pens, pencils, and other such implements; I can't understand such a person committing a crime like this. **2** of the same intensity as that mentioned; used for emphasis: I've got such a terrible headache. **3** used to introduce a number of examples: We enjoyed such delicacies as salmon and caviar. **4** of sufficient intensity to produce a particular effect: He gave the door such a slam that the glass broke. • *pron* **1** (*formal*) those people: Such as no

longer need to be here may leave. **2** used to refer to some action, event, or circumstances previously mentioned: Such was the effect he had on her. **3** people or things of a similar type: We still need more pens, files, memo pads, and such. **suchlike** *pron* a similar person or thing. < Old English *swilc.* SEE PANEL.

suck (sʌk) *vb* **1** draw (esp. a liquid) into the mouth by using the lips. **2** keep (a sweet, etc.) in the mouth while dissolving. **3** draw in or absorb: Working in the garden seems to suck all his energy.
● *n* the sound or process of sucking. **sucker** *n* **1** a person or thing that sucks. **2** a device or part of an animal's body that can cling to a surface. **3** a shoot coming up from the roots or buried stem of a tree or shrub. **4** (*informal*) a person who is easily deceived. **suck in** (*informal*) deceive. **sucking-pig** *n* a young pig that is not yet weaned. **suck up to** (*informal*) flatter or toady to. < Old English *sūcan.*

suckle (ˈsʌkl̩) *vb* feed or take milk at the breast or udder. **suckling** *n* a young animal that is not yet weaned. < probably back formation from *suckling,* from *suck* + *-ling.*

sucrose (ˈsjuːkrəʊz) *n* the natural sugar obtained from sugar-cane or sugar-beet and which occurs in most plants. < French *sucre* sugar.

suction (ˈsʌkʃən) *n* **1** sucking. **2** the act or process of drawing liquid, etc., into a space by creating a partial or complete vacuum in it. < Latin *sugere* to suck.

sudden (ˈsʌdn̩) *adj* done, happening, or occurring unexpectedly or hastily. **suddenly** *adv* **suddenness** *n* **all of a sudden** suddenly. < Latin *subitus.*

suds (sʌdz) *pl n* soapsuds.

sue (sjuː) *vb* **sued; suing 1** bring legal action against: sue for damages. **2** petition or solicit: sue for peace. < ultimately Latin *sequi* to follow.

suede (sweɪd) *n* leather with the flesh side rubbed into a soft nap. < French (*gants de*) *Suède* Swedish (gloves). SEE PANEL.

suet (ˈsuːɪt) *n* hard fat obtained from round the kidneys and loins of sheep and cattle, often used in cooking. **suety** *adj* < ultimately Latin *sebum.*

suffer (ˈsʌfə) *vb* **1** experience or endure (pain, misery, etc.): I don't like to witness him suffering. **2** experience, sustain, or be subjected to: The government is likely to suffer a terrible defeat. **3** be neglected: You must try not to let your work suffer. **4** (*formal*) tolerate or put up with: He doesn't suffer fools gladly. **sufferance** *n* **on sufferance** (*formal*) tolerated but not welcome: He's only here on sufferance. **sufferer** *n* **suffering** *n* < ultimately Latin *sufferre,* from *sub-* up + *ferre* to bear.

suffice (səˈfaɪs) *vb* be enough (to meet a need): Half a dozen should suffice. **sufficient** *adj* enough. **sufficiency** *n* **sufficiently** *adv* < ultimately Latin *sufficere.*

suffix (ˈsʌfɪks) *n* one or more letters added to the end of a word to make a related word. < Latin *suffigere* to fasten underneath.

suffocate (ˈsʌfəˌkeɪt) *vb* **1** kill by depriving of oxygen; be killed in this way. **2** cause or experience discomfort through lack of air: I find this room suffocating. **suffocation** *n* < Latin *suffocare.*

suffrage (ˈsʌfrɪdʒ) *n* the right to vote; franchise. **suffragette** *n* a woman who fought for suffrage for women, esp. in the early 20th century. < Latin *suffragium* vote.

suffuse (səˈfjuːz) *vb* spread over or through. < Latin *suffendere* to pour beneath.

sugar (ˈʃʊgə) *n* a sweet, granular substance derived from sucrose, which is white when fully refined and is used mostly as a sweetener.

like or **such as?**

Would you use like or such as in:
He makes cages for dangerous animals_____ lions and tigers? Careful users prefer to use such as, arguing that like is potentially ambiguous, as it is used to introduce both examples and comparisons.

General usage, however, tends to ignore this preference and like is commonly accepted.

suede

Speakers of French and viewers of the Eurovision Song Contest will know that (La) Suède is the French word for Sweden. The English word suede is derived from this, being a 19th-century short-form of the French phrase gants de Suède, 'gloves made in Sweden'.

• *vb* sweeten or coat with sugar. **sugar-beet** *n* a beet from whose root sugar is obtained. **sugar-cane** *n* a tall, stout grass grown in tropical regions as a source of sugar. **sugary** *adj* **1** containing or resembling sugar. **2** unpleasantly sweet. SEE PANEL.

suggest (səˈdʒɛst) *vb* **1** put forward (an idea, etc.) for consideration; propose. **2** hint or intimate: Are you suggesting that I'm too old for the job? **3** call to mind; indicate: His sudden use of bright colours suggests a new optimism. **suggestible** *adj* easily influenced by suggestion. **suggestibility** *n* **suggestion** *n* **1** the act of suggesting. **2** something suggested. **3** a trace or hint: a suggestion of boredom. **suggestive** *adj* **1** conveying a suggestion, esp. of something indecent or improper: suggestive remarks. **2** giving an impression of; evocative. < Latin *suggerere*.

suicide (ˈsuːɪˌsaɪd) *n* **1** the act of killing oneself deliberately. **2** a person who does this. **3** ruination of one's own interests or prospects. **suicidal** *adj* **1** of or connected with suicide: suicidal tendencies. **2** having a desire to commit suicide. **3** harmful to one's own interests or prospects. < Latin *sui* of oneself + *caedere* to kill.

suit (suːt) *n* **1** two or more pieces of clothing, usually of the same cloth, designed to be worn together, esp. a jacket and trousers or skirt. **2** clothing for a particular purpose: a play suit. **3** one of the four sets of playing-cards: hearts, clubs, diamonds, or spades. **4** a lawsuit. **5** (*formal*) a petition or appeal; act of wooing.
• *vb* **1** be convenient, acceptable, or appropriate: Would a meeting in London suit you? **2** have an enhancing or becoming effect: Pink doesn't suit you. **3** adapt or accommodate. **suitable** *adj* suiting a particular need, occasion, etc.: I'm afraid that she really isn't suitable for the job. **suitability** *n* **suitably** *adv* **suit oneself** do, decide, etc., as one pleases. **suitor** *n* a person courting a woman with the desire to marry her. < Old French *sieute* set of things.

suitcase (ˈsuːtˌkeɪs) *n* a rectangular travelling case for carrying clothes, etc.

suite (swiːt) *n* **1** a group of things forming a set, esp. rooms, furniture, or musical pieces. **2** a group of attendants; retinue. < SEE SUIT.

sulk (sʌlk) *vb* be silent and unsociable because in a bad mood.
• *n* a fit of sulking. **sulky** *adj* **sulkily** *adv* **sulkiness** *n* < back formation from *sulky*, probably from obsolete *sulke* sluggish.

sullen (ˈsʌlən) *adj* **1** (of people) sulky or morose. **2** (of things) gloomy or dismal: a sullen day. **sullenly** *adv* **sullenness** *n* < Middle English *solain*.

sully (ˈsʌlɪ) *vb* **sullied; sullying** stain, blemish, or tarnish: sully one's reputation. < probably Middle French *soiller* to soil.

sulphate (ˈsʌlfeɪt) *n* a salt of sulphuric acid. < Latin *sulphur*.

sulphur (ˈsʌlfə) *n* a yellow, non-metallic element which burns with a blue flame and gives off a choking smell. **sulphuric** *adj* of or containing sulphur. **sulphuric acid** a strong, corrosive, oily acid. **sulphurous** *adj* of, like, or containing sulphur. < Latin *sulphur*.

sultan (ˈsʌltən) *n* the sovereign of a Muslim country or state. **sultanate** *n* a country or state ruled by a sultan. < Arabic *sulṭān*.

sultana (sʌlˈtɑːnə) *n* **1** a seedless raisin. **2** the wife, mother, sister, or daughter of a sultan. < Italian, feminine of *sultano* sultan.

sultry (ˈsʌltrɪ) *adj* **1** unpleasantly hot and humid; close. **2** sensual. **sultriness** *n* < obsolete *sulter* to swelter.

sum (sʌm) *n* **1** an amount (of money). **2** a total. **3** the result obtained by adding numbers together: The sum of 9 and 12 is 21. **4** a simple arithmetical problem. **sum up 1** make a summary of. **2** form or express an appraisal or opinion of: She summed him up at a glance. < ultimately Latin *summus* highest.

summary (ˈsʌmərɪ) *n* a concise statement of the main points or details of something.
• *adj* **1** brief or concise. **2** done or happening without delay or attention to

---

sugar

The fact that sugar has existed for a long time is seen in the length of its etymology. The modern form comes from the Middle English word *sucre,* a borrowing from Middle French. This was derived from the Medieval Latin term *zuccherum,* coming from the Old Italian form *zucchero. Zucchero* was taken from the Arabic word *sukkar,* which passed into Arabic from the Persian equivalent *shakar.* This in turn was derived from the Sanskrit *śarkarā.*

---

detail: a summary execution. **summarily** *adv* **summarize** *vb* be or make a summary of. < Latin *summa* sum.

summer (ˈsʌmə) *n* the warmest season of the year, between spring and autumn. **summer-house** *n* a small, simple building in a garden, providing shade in summer. **summer school** a course of tuition held during the summer vacation. **summer time** a time system operated during the summer months that is one hour ahead of the time as calculated according to the sun. **summer-time** *n* the summer season. **summery** *adj* like or suitable for summer. < Old English *sumor.*

summit (ˈsʌmɪt) *n* **1** the highest point of something, esp. a mountain. **2** a meeting of high-level officials, esp. heads of governments. < ultimately Latin *summus* highest.

summon (ˈsʌmən) *vb* **1** call upon (a person) to come: I was immediately summoned to his office. **2** command to appear in court. **3** convene. **4** gather together; muster. < Latin *summonēre* to remind in a discreet way. SEE PANEL.

summons (ˈsʌmənz) *n* **1** an official order to appear or attend. **2** an official document ordering a person to appear in court.
• *vb* serve with a summons. < Old French *somondre.* SEE PANEL AT **SUMMON.**

sumptuous (ˈsʌmptjʊəs) *adj* splendid, luxurious, or costly. **sumptuously** *adv* **sumptuousness** *n* < Latin *sumptus.*

sun (sʌn) *n* **1** the star around which the earth travels and which gives it light and heat. **2** the light or heat from this. **3** any star emitting its own light.
• *vb* **sunned; sunning** expose (oneself) to the sun: George is sunning himself out on the lawn. **sunbathe** *vb* lie or sit exposing one's body to the sun. **sunbeam** *n* a ray of sunlight. **sun-blind** *n* a blind or awning that gives shade or protection from the sun. **sunburn** *n* a sore inflammation of the skin caused by exposure to the sun. **sunburnt** *adj* **sundial** *n* an instrument which tells the time of day by means of the shadow cast by an upright rod or plate onto a calibrated base. **sundown** *n* sunset. **sunflower** *n* a tall, sturdy plant with large flowers consisting of a circular band of yellow petals around a dark centre, often grown for its oil-bearing seeds. **sun-glasses** *pl n* spectacles with tinted lenses which protect the eyes from bright sunlight. **sun-lamp** *n* an electric lamp emitting ultraviolet light, used for tanning the skin. **sunlight** *n* light from the sun. **sunlit** *adj* lit by the sun. **sunny** *adj* **1** having a lot of sunshine; bright. **2** cheerful. **sunrise** *n* (the time of) the rising of the sun. **sun-roof** *n* a sliding or removable panel in the roof of a car. **sunset** *n* **1** (the time of) the setting of the sun. **2** the sky in the west filled with a golden orange glow when the sun is setting. **sunshade** *n* something that affords protection from the sun's rays, such as a parasol or awning. **sunshine** *n* rays of the sun which reach the earth uninterrupted by cloud. **sunspot** *n* **1** a dark patch observed on the surface of the sun. **2** (*informal*) a holiday resort with a sunny climate. **sunstroke** *n* illness caused by over-exposure to the sun. **sun-tan** *n* a browning of the skin by exposure to the sun. **sun-tanned** *adj* browned by the sun. **sun-trap** *n* a sheltered place which gets hot in the sun. **under the sun** (*informal*) anywhere: It's one of the best restaurants under the sun. < Old English *sunne.*

sundae (ˈsʌndeɪ) *n* an ice-cream served with fruit, nuts, syrup, etc. < origin uncertain.

sundry (ˈsʌndrɪ) *adj* various; miscellaneous. **all and sundry** (*informal*) everybody. **sundries** *pl n* various small items. < Old English *syndrig.*

sung (sʌŋ) SEE **SING.**

sunk (sʌŋk) SEE **SINK. sunken** *adj* lying, constructed, or positioned below the level of the ground or surrounding area: a sunken garden.

super (ˈsuːpə) *adj* (*informal*) excellent; superb.
• *interj* (*informal*) used to express strong approval, enthusiasm, etc.
• *n* (*informal*) a (police) superintendent. < Latin: above.

super- *prefix* **1** over, outside, or beyond: superscript. **2** of greater size, extent, etc.,

summon or **summons?**

To express the meaning 'to serve with a legal summons', either summon or summons may be used, although summons is more common: He was *summonsed* to appear before the judge at 9 o'clock the next day.

Summon is used in other senses: She was *summoned* to the headmaster's office. He *summoned* all his strength.

than usual: superstore. **3** exceeding a standard or norm; extra: superfine flour. < Latin: above.

superannuate (ˌsuːpərˈænjʊˌeɪt) *vb* **1** retire (an employee) on a pension because of age. **2** discard as obsolete. **superannuation** *n* a pension paid to an employee following retirement; employee's contributions to this, paid regularly during employment. < Latin *superannuari* to be too old.

superb (suːˈpɜːb) *adj* magnificent; outstanding: a superb example of early Venetian art. **superbly** *adv* **superbness** *n* < Latin *superbus.*

supercilious (ˌsuːpəˈsɪlɪəs) *adj* having a haughty and disdainful air or manner: a supercilious look. **superciliously** *adv* **superciliousness** *n* < Latin super*cilium* eyebrow.

superficial (ˌsuːpəˈfɪʃəl) *adj* **1** on or restricted to the surface: a superficial wound. **2** not deep or thorough; slight: superficial knowledge. **3** shallow or insincere: Her friendship is all superficial. **superficiality** *n* **superficially** *adv* < Late Latin *superficialis.*

superfluous (suːˈpɜːflʊəs) *adj* more than is needed. **superfluously** *adv* **superfluity** *n* an amount, supply, or thing that is superfluous; excess. < Latin *superfluers* to overflow.

superhuman (ˌsuːpəˈhjuːmən) *adj* **1** exceeding human norms: superhuman strength. **2** having powers and abilities beyond those of a human being; divine.

superimpose (ˌsuːpərɪmˈpəʊz) *vb* lay or place on lop of something else. **superimposition** *n*

superintend (ˌsuːpərɪnˈtɛnd) *vb* supervise or direct. **superintendent** *n* **1** a supervisor. **2** a police officer next above the rank of inspector. < Late Latin *superintendere.*

superior (suːˈpɪərɪə) *adj* **1** higher in rank, importance, quality, etc.: A superior officer should be saluted. **2** of better quality: superior goods. **3** conceited; supercilious: She gave me a superior look.
• *n* **1** a person superior to another in rank, etc. **2** the head of a community of nuns, monks, etc. **superiority** *n* < Latin *superus* upper.

superlative (suːˈpɜːlətɪv) *adj* **1** of the highest degree or quality: She perfumed with the same superlative skill. **2** (of an adjective or adverb) expressing the highest degree of comparison.
• *n* an adjective or adverb in a superlative form. **superlatively** *adv* < Late Latin *superlativus.*

superman (ˈsuːpəˌmæn) fem. **superwoman** *n* a person with superhuman powers. SEE PANEL.

supermarket (ˈsuːpəˌmɑːkɪt) *n* a large self-service shop which sells groceries and household goods.

supernatural (ˌsuːpəˈnætʃərəl) *adj* of or connected with phenomena beyond the bounds of nature. **supernaturally** *adv*

superpower (ˈsuːpəˌpaʊə) *n* one of the world's most powerful nations.

superscript (ˈsuːpəˌskrɪpt) *adj, n* (a number, letter, or symbol) written or printed above another. **superscription** *n* one or more words written on the surface of or outside something. < Latin *superscriptus.*

supersede (ˌsuːpəˈsiːd) *vb* replace, supplant, or take the place of: The Mk II has been superseded by the Mk III. < Latin *supersedēre* to sit above.

supersonic (ˌsuːpəˈsɒnɪk) *adj* (flying or moving at) more than the speed of sound: supersonic aircraft. **supersonically** *adv*

superstition (ˌsuːpəˈstɪʃən) *n* **1** irrational belief in (and fear of) phenomena beyond the bounds of nature: The book is about witchcraft, magic, and superstition. **2** a notion, practice, or ritual deriving from this belief: There is an old superstition that to cross on the stairs is unlucky. **superstitious** *adj* **superstitiously** *adv* < Latin *superstare* to stand over.

superstore (ˈsuːpəˌstɔː) *n* a large supermarket.

superstructure (ˈsuːpəˌstrʌktʃə) *n* the part of a structure which rests on something else, such as the part of a

superman

The term superman was invented not in the comic strip but by the German philosopher, Friedrich Wilhelm Nietzsche, 1844-1900, one of the major influences on 20th-century thinking. The original label, *Übermensch,* was coined by Nietzsche for an idealized human being of outstanding intellectual prowess and moral integrity. The English translation, superman, came into common parlance after its inclusion by George Bernard Shaw in the title of his play, 'Man and Superman'.

Since the beginning of the 20th century the term has spawned a host of analogous compounds, from superwoman to supermouse.

ship above the deck or the part of a building above the foundations.

supertanker (ˈsuːpəˌtæŋkə) *n* a very large tanker.

supervise (ˈsuːpəˌvaɪz) *vb* direct or be in charge of (work, workers, etc.). **supervision** *n* **supervisory** *adj* **supervisor** *n* a person who supervises. < Latin *supervidēre.*

supine (ˈsuːpaɪn) *adj* **1** lying flat on the back. **2** lazy or lethargic. **supinely** *adv* < Latin *supinus.*

supper (ˈsʌpə) *n* **1** an evening meal. **2** a late evening snack. < Old French *souper* to sup.

supplant (səˈplɑːnt) *vb* oust or take the place of: The old government has been supplanted by a military dictatorship. < ultimately Latin *supplantare* to trip up.

supple (ˈsʌpl̩) *adj* able to bend easily; flexible: supple joints. **supplely** *adv* **suppleness** *n* < ultimately Latin *supplex* bowed.

supplement (ˈsʌplɪmənt) *n* **1** something added, esp. to make good a shortage or deficiency. **2** an extra, self-contained part of a newspaper or magazine: a colour supplement.
• *vb* (ˈsʌplɪˌmɛnt) provide or be a supplement to. **supplementary** *adj* < Latin *supplēre* to fill up, supply.
SEE PANEL.

supply (səˈplaɪ) *vb* **supplied; supplying** **1** provide (with) or make available: Who supplies the money for the rent? **2** fill or satisfy: supply a need.
• *n* **1** the act of supplying. **2** an amount or quantity that is needed or supplied. **3** the amount of goods and services available on the market: supply and demand. **4** *pl* stores, stocks, or provisions. < Latin *supplēre.*

support (səˈpɔːt) *vb* **1** hold in position, esp. by bearing the weight of: The shelf needs something else to support it. **2** add strength to: There are no facts to support the theory. **3** give (financial) help, backing, or approval to: support a cause. **4** be a fan of: Which team do you support? **5** provide with life's necessities: He has a wife and four children to support. **6** enable to continue: Without water, life cannot be supported. **7** (*formal old-fashioned*) bear or tolerate.
• *n* **1** supporting; being supported. **2** a person or thing that supports. **supporter** *n* a fan or follower: a City supporter. **supportive** *adj* providing support or encouragement: Helen is always very supportive when you're up against it. < Latin *supportare* to carry.

suppose (səˈpəʊz) *vb* **1** be inclined to think: I suppose we ought to wait for him. **2** assume to be true for the sake of argument: Suppose you won the pools. What would you do with the money? **3** used to make a suggestion or proposal: Suppose we try again later. **4** presuppose. **be supposed to 1** be meant or expected to: You're supposed to be helping your father in the garden. **2** be said to: He's supposed to have been married twice already. **supposed** *adj* according to what is generally said or believed: He is the supposed murderer of no fewer than eight victims. **supposedly** *adv* **supposition** *n* **1** the act of supposing or hypothesizing. **2** a hypothesis or theory. < Latin *supponere* to substitute.

suppository (səˈpɒzɪtərɪ) *n* a solid, wax-like piece of medicated substance designed for insertion into the rectum or vagina and which melts at body temperature. < Latin *supponere* to put under.

suppress (səˈprɛs) *vb* **1** quell or put down by the use of power or force: suppress a rebellion. **2** prevent from being seen, revealed, or published: suppress the truth. **suppression** *n* **suppressive** *adj* **suppressor** *n* **1** a person or thing that suppresses. **2** a device that suppresses radio interference. < Latin *supprimere.*

supra- *prefix* over, above, or greater than. < Latin.

supreme (suːˈpriːm) *adj* **1** highest in rank or authority. **2** highest in degree, intensity, or quality: an act of supreme courage. **supremacy** *n* **supremely** *adv* < Latin *superus* upper.

---

supplement or **complement?**

These two words are sometimes confused.

Supplement signifies an addition which makes good a shortage or deficiency: She has to work to *supplement* her husband's income. *Supplements* to the tax guide are published annually.

Complement, on the other hand, refers to something added as an accompaniment which provides a sense of rounded fullness: Home and school should *complement* each other in the education of a child. Practical work is included as a *complement* to theoretical instruction.

On the difference between complement and compliment, see panel at **complement.**

---

surcharge (ˈsɜːˌtʃɑːdʒ) *n* **1** an extra charge: guaranteed against surcharges. **2** a mark printed over a postage stamp changing its value or adding an extra charge.
• *vb* **1** make an extra charge. **2** print a surcharge on. < Middle French *surchargier*.

sure (ʃʊə, ʃɔː) *adj* **1** free from doubt or uncertainty; confident: Are you sure you want to buy it? **2** bound or certain: She is sure to invite you. **3** true beyond any doubt: One thing is sure: she likes you. **4** proven to be effective; reliable: a sure cure for headaches.
• *adv* (*informal*) of course; certainly. **sureness** *n* **make sure** make certain: Make sure the door is properly locked. **sure-footed** *adj* unlikely to stumble or fall. **surely** *adv* **1** used to indicate that what is said is considered true or highly probable: Surely you don't need yet another fast car? **2** without doubt. **to be sure** admittedly. < Latin *securus* secure. SEE PANEL.

surety (ˈʃʊərɪtɪ) *n* **1** a guarantee; security. **2** a person who makes himself responsible for another person's payment of a debt, appearance in court, etc. < Latin *securitas* security.

surf (sɜːf) *n* the white foam made by waves breaking. **surf-board** *n* a long, narrow board that floats on water and is used in surf-riding. **surfer** *n* a person who goes surf-riding. **surfing** *n* surf-riding. **surf-riding** *n* the sport of balancing on a board while being swept along by a wave. < origin unknown.

surface (ˈsɜːfɪs) *n* **1** the external part of something which is visible and has texture: a rough surface. **2** the topmost layer of something: The patio could do with a new surface. **3** a boundary of a liquid or body of matter, esp. the top boundary: The fish swim just beneath the surface. **4** the external appearance or superficial aspect of someone or something: On the surface he seems quite a nice chap.
• *vb* **1** give a new surface to. **2** rise to the surface. **surface mail** mail sent other than by airmail. < French.

surfeit (ˈsɜːfɪt) *n* (a feeling of discomfort or nausea resulting from having) an excess of something, esp. food and drink.
• *vb* fill to excess. < Middle French *surfaire* to overdo.

surge (sɜːdʒ) *vb* **1** sweep forward (as if) in waves. **2** (of current, voltage, etc.) rise suddenly; swell.
• *n* a wave-like movement; increase: Police tried to control the surge of the crowd. < Latin *surgere* to rise.

surgeon (ˈsɜːdʒən) *n* a medical practitioner who specializes in surgery. **surgery** *n* **1** the treatment of injuries, diseases, etc., by operative measures. **2** the place where or hours during which a doctor or dentist treats patients. **3** the place where or occasion when an MP or other professional person is available for consultation. **surgical** *adj* **surgically** *adv* **surgical spirit** a mixture of mostly methylated spirits used as a disinfectant, cleansing agent, etc. SEE PANEL.

surly (ˈsɜːlɪ) *adj* morose or bad-tempered. **surlily** *adv* **surliness** *n* < Middle English *sirly* imperious.

surmise (səˈmaɪz) *n* a guess, inference, or conjecture.
• *vb* conjecture. < Middle French *surmettre* to accuse.

surmount (səˈmaʊnt) *vb* overcome or cope successfully with (a difficulty, obstacle, etc.). **be surmounted by** have on top: The tower is surmounted by a tall steeple.

sure—the hidden care

Looking into the history of words can reveal some surprising connections. For example, the forms of sure and care are so different that it is hard to imagine how they might be related. However, sure comes from the Middle French word *sur,* and *sur* was the easy-to-pronounce Middle French adaptation of the Latin *securus* meaning 'secure'. *Securus,* in turn, was a compound of *se* 'without' and *cura* meaning 'care'.

surgery

Surgeons are noted for their skill in using their hands. This manual dexterity is seen in the word's etymology. *Surgery* is the modern form of the Middle English *surgerie,* which passed into English from the Old French word *cirurgie.* Like many French words, this was derived from Latin (*chirurgia*), which in turn was developed from the Greek word *cheirourgia.* A Greek surgeon was a cheirourgos, a person skilled in cheirourgos, 'working with the hand', a compound of *cheir,* 'hand', and *ergon,* 'work'.

surmountable *adj* < Middle French *surmonter.*
surname (ˈsɜːˌneɪm) *n* a person's family name. **surnamed** *adj* having a particular surname.
surpass (səˈpɑːs) *vb* be better than or superior to; excel: Her performance today surpasses all previous attempts at the record. **surpassing** *adj* greatly exceeding others. **surpassingly** *adv* < Middle French *surpasser.*
surplice (sɜːplɪs) *n* a loose, white over-garment with full sleeves worn by clergymen, choristers, etc. < Old French *surplis.*
surplus (ˈsɜːpləs) *n* **1** an amount in excess of what is used or required: surplus of grain. **2** the amount by which assets exceed liabilities, or by which revenue exceeds expenditure.
• *adj* in excess of: Half the delivery is surplus to our needs. < Middle French.
surprise (səˈpraɪz) *n* **1** (the feeling caused by) something which one is not expecting: News of his resignation came as quite a surprise. **2** the strategy of catching a person unawares: The success of the attack is based on surprise.
• *vb* **1** cause to feel surprise. **2** approach, attack, etc., without warning. **3** jolt or startle (a person) into action. **surprised** *adj* **surprising** *adj* causing surprise: A surprising number of the candidates failed. **surprisingly** *adv* < Middle French *surprendre.*
surrender (səˈrɛndə) *vb* **1** hand over to the power or control of someone or something else. **2** give (oneself) up; yield: They preferred to die fighting than surrender. **3** let (oneself) be overwhelmed by a feeling, emotion, etc. **4** cancel (an insurance policy) voluntarily in return for a certain repayment.
• *n* surrendering; being surrendered. < Middle French *surrendre,* from *sur-* over + *rendre* to give back.
surreptitious (ˌsʌrəpˈtɪʃəs) *adj* secret or stealthy: a surreptitious glance. **surreptitiously** *adv* **surreptitiousness** *n* < Latin *surripere* to steal.
surrogate (ˈsʌrəgət, ˈsʌrəgeɪt) *n* a deputy or substitute. < Latin *surrogare* to substitute.
surround (səˈraʊnd) *vb* **1** enclose on all sides: The stadium is surrounded by a high wall. **2** cause to be enclosed on all sides: The fort was completely surrounded, making escape impossible. **surroundings** *pl n* all the things which form an environment: natural surroundings. < Middle French *suronder* to overflow.
surveillance (sɜːˈveɪtəns) *n* careful observation of someone or something, esp. a suspected criminal: under close surveillance. < French *surveiller* to watch over.
survey (səˈveɪ, ˈsɜːveɪ) *vb* **1** have an overall view of: From the top of the hill you could survey the surrounding countryside. **2** examine closely or in detail. **3** measure and plot the form, extent, position, etc., of (an area of land). **4** inspect and report on the condition and value of (a property, etc.).
• *n* (ˈsɜːveɪ) **1** surveying; being surveyed. **2** a report, plan, or description arising from this. **surveyor** *n* a person whose job is to survey buildings or land. < Middle French *surveeir* to look over.
survive (səˈvaɪv) *vb* **1** manage to live through (a disaster, etc.): Few families survived the epidemic. **2** continue to live or exist: The ritual survives to this day. **survival** *n* **1** the act or state of survival. **2** a person or thing that has survived from earlier times. **survivor** *n* a person who survives a disaster, etc. < Middle French *survivre* to outlive.
susceptible (səˈsɛptəbl̩) *adj* **1** liable to be affected by: He's very susceptible to colds. **2** easily affected emotionally. **3** capable of undergoing something. **susceptibility** *n* **susceptibilities** *pl n* a person's (sensitive) feelings. < Latin *suscipere* to take up.
suspect (səˈspɛkt) *vb* **1** consider likely or probable. **2** have suspicions about; distrust: I suspect her motives for inviting us. **3** believe (a person) to be guilty, esp. of a crime.
• *n* (ˈsʌspɛkt) a person who is suspected of a crime, etc.
• *adj* (ˈsʌspɛkt) to be viewed with suspicion. **suspicion** *n* **1** suspecting; being suspected. **2** a feeling that something is likely: My suspicion is he will ask her to marry him. **3** a hint or slight trace: the smallest suspicion of garlic. **suspicious** *adj* feeling or arousing suspicion. **suspiciously** *adv* < Latin *suspicere.*
suspend (səˈspɛnd) *vb* **1** hang: The balloons were suspended on long strings from the ceiling. **2** keep from falling or sinking. **3** postpone or withhold: suspend judgment. **4** stop or discontinue temporarily: Further trading has been suspended until Thursday. **5** remove temporarily from office or duty. **suspender** *n* a strip of elastic with a fastener for holding up a stocking, usually hung from a suspender belt. **suspender belt** a belt or girdle with two pairs of suspenders. **suspense** *n* a state of excitement or anxious waiting. **suspension** *n*

1 suspending; being suspended. **2** the system of springs, etc., which supports the frame of a vehicle on its axles. **3** a mixture of a liquid with solid particles which disperse but do not dissolve. **suspension bridge** a bridge whose roadway is suspended by steel cables. < Old French *suspendre* to hang up.

sustain (sə'steɪn) *vb* **1** support or bear (the weight of). **2** suffer or undergo: He sustained serious injuries in the crash. **3** provide with sustenance; provide for. **4** provide with energy, strength, etc.: The memory of his family sustained him. **5** keep (something) going; maintain. **6** allow as valid; uphold: The objection was sustained. **7** endure or withstand. **sustenance** *n* **1** the act of sustaining. **2** food considered as a means of sustaining life; nourishment. < Old French *sustenir*, from Latin *sustinēre*.

suture ('suːtʃə) *n* (*medicine*) **1** a surgical stitch or series of stitches used to close a wound. **2** the closing of a wound by stitching. **3** the jagged line where the bones of the cranium join.
• *vb* close (a wound) with sutures. < ultimately Latin *suere* to sew.

swab (swɒb) *n* (*medicine*) **1** a wad of gauze or other absorbent material used for cleansing, drying, applying medication, or taking specimens. **2** a specimen taken with a swab.
• *vb* **swabbed; swabbing** clean with a swab. < probably Middle Dutch *swabbe* mop.

swag (swæg) *n* **1** (*humorous*) loot. **2** (*chiefly Australian*) a bundle or roll of personal belongings. < origin uncertain.

swagger ('swægə) *vb* walk or behave in a pompous or self-important way.
• *n* a swaggering walk. **swaggeringly** *adv* < origin uncertain.

swallow[1] ('swɒləʊ) *vb* **1** send (food, etc.) down the throat into the stomach by using the muscles in the throat; operate the throat muscles as if doing this. **2** engulf or consume completely: The electricity bill swallowed up his wages. **3** (*informal*) believe or accept too easily: He'll swallow any old excuse. **4** hold back or suppress: swallow one's tears.
• *n* **1** the act of swallowing. **2** an amount swallowed in a single act of swallowing; mouthful. < Old English *swelgan*.

swallow[2] *n* any of a group of small, migratory, insect-eating birds with long wings and a forked tail, noted for their graceful flight. < Old English *swealwe*.

swam (swæm) SEE **SWIM**.

swamp (swɒmp) *n* (an area of) wet, permanently waterlogged land.
• *vb* **1** flood or fill with water: A huge wave swamped the deck. **2** overwhelm as if by swamping: The office has been swamped with applications for the job. **swampy** *adj* < probably Middle Dutch *somp*.

swan (swɒn) *n* a large, white, long-necked water-bird, noted for its graceful movement through water.
• *vb* **swanned; swanning** (*informal*) go or travel in a leisurely way. < Old English.

swank (swæŋk) *vb* (*derogatory*) behave or talk in a pretentious or boastful way; show off.
• *n* (a person given to) swanking. **swanky** *adj* < perhaps Middle High German *swanken* to sway.

swap, swop (swɒp) *vb* **swapped; swapping** or **swopped; swopping** exchange (one thing) for another.
• *n* **1** the act of swapping. **2** something swapped. < Middle English *swappen* to strike. SEE PANEL.

swarm[1] (swɔːm) *n* a great number of insects or other small creatures moving together as a single mass, esp. honey-bees leaving a hive with a queen bee to form a new colony. **2** a crowd or throng: swarms of tourists.
• *vb* **1** move together in great numbers. **2** (of bees) leave a hive in a swarm. **3** teem or be crowded with: The whole market was swarming with bargain hunters. < Old English *swearm*.

swarm[2] *vb* **swarm up** climb up, esp. by gripping with one's arms and legs. < origin unknown.

swarthy ('swɔːðɪ) *adj* having a dark complexion. **swarthiness** *n* < Old English *sweart*.

swastika ('swɒstɪkə) *n* an ancient

swap and **shake**

Swap, 'to exchange one thing for another', comes from the Middle English word swappen, 'to strike'. This refers to the old custom in which the parties involved in a swap or other form of negotiation would slap each other's hand as a sign that the deal or agreement was sealed. A reminder of the practice is found in the phrase to strike a bargain. Nowadays, the practice of striking hands has generally been superseded by the handshake: by shaking on the terms of an agreement, you pledge to abide by them.

symbol in the form of a cross with the ends of the arms bent at right angles, adopted by the Nazi party. < Sanskrit *svastika*, from *svasti* prosperity. SEE PANEL.

swat (swɒt) *vb* **swatted; swatting** hit or kill (esp. a fly) with a sharp blow.
• *n* a sharp blow. **swatter** *n* < English dialect *squat*.

swath (swɒθ) *n* **1** the space or path cut by a single sweep of a scythe or single passage of a mowing machine. **2** a line of cut grass or grain. **3** a long, broad strip. < Old English *swæth*.

swathe (sweɪð) *vb* wrap in or as if in bandages. < Old English *swathian*.

sway (sweɪ) *vb* **1** swing or cause to swing gently from side to side or to one side: The tall trees swayed in the wind. **2** influence or win over: It was his hatred of nuclear arms that swayed the voters. **3** waver or fluctuate in one's opinion, attitude, etc.
• *n* **1** swaying; being swayed. **2** influence or power: Parents have a lot of sway in the running of the school. < probably Scandinavian.

swear (swɛə) *vb* **swore; sworn; swearing 1** state, assert as true, or promise on oath. **2** (*informal*) assert or promise emphatically: She swore she hadn't been anywhere near the fridge. **3** cause to promise or take an oath: sworn to secrecy. **4** use profane or obscene language; curse. **swearer** *n* **swear by** place great confidence in. **swear in** admit (a person) formally to office by administering an oath. **swear to** assert without doubt or reservation: It looks like the same girl, but I couldn't swear to it. **swear-word** *n* a word used in swearing or cursing. < Old English *swerian*.

sweat (swɛt) *n* **1** moisture exuded by the body, esp. when hot, through the pores; perspiration. **2** moisture that forms in drops on a surface. **3** a state or spell of sweating: He broke into a cold sweat. **4** (*informal*) a state of extreme anxiety. **5** (*informal*) hard work.
• *vb* **1** exude sweat; perspire. **2** be in a state of extreme anxiety. **3** (*informal*) work hard: I've been sweating away at it all day. **sweater** *n* a jumper or pullover. **sweat it out** (*informal*) endure (a difficult situation) to the very end. **sweat-shirt** *n* a loose-sleeved, heavy cotton pullover. **sweat-shop** *n* a factory, workshop, etc., where people work for long hours, often in poor or unhealthy conditions, for low wages. **sweaty** *adj* causing or covered with sweat. < Old English *swāt*.

swede (swi:d) *n* a type of large, yellow turnip. < *Sweden*.

sweep (swi:p) *vb* **swept; sweeping 1** clean, remove, or clear away by or as if by brushing. **2** move or remove (someone or something) as if by a brushing movement: A giant wave swept him overboard. **3** go quickly or gracefully; sail: A car swept past him. **4** pass quickly over or through: Her gaze swept the horizon. **5** extend continuously or in a curve: The hills swept right down to the shoreline. **6** touch lightly while moving quickly over: Her fingers swept lightly over the strings.
• *n* **1** the act of sweeping: The carpet needs a good sweep. **2** a sweeping movement. **3** an unbroken line, curve, or stretch: the sweep of the coastline. **4** the range or extent of a sweeping movement. **5** a chimney-sweep. **6** a sweepstake. **sweeper** *n* **1** a person or thing that sweeps. **2** a member of a football team who, except for the goalkeeper, provides a last line of defence. **sweeping** *adj* **1** of great scope or significance: sweeping changes. **2** without qualification or reservation: a sweeping statement. **sweepingly** *adv* **sweepings** *pl n* dust, rubbish, etc., collected by sweeping. **sweepstake** *n* **1** a race or contest in which all the money wagered is paid to those with winning tickets. **2** this system of gambling. < Middle English *swepen*. SEE PANEL.

sweet (swi:t) *adj* **1** having the taste of sugar or something similar. **2** having a fresh or pleasing taste: sweet and tender. **3** (of smells) fragrant. **4** (of sounds) pleasant to hear; melodious. **5** pretty or charming: What a sweet little puppy! **6** kind or gentle: a sweet disposition.
• *n* **1** a small piece of confectionery such as a toffee or chocolate, usually contain-

swastika

Following its adoption by Hitler as the emblem of the Nazi party, the swastika has enjoyed little popularity. However, the symbol existed long before the days of Hitlerism, being embraced as a symbol by various cultures all over the world. The word swastika comes from the Sanskrit word *svastika,* whose root is *svasti* meaning 'prosperity' or 'welfare'. In those days the swastika was regarded not as a symbol of war and anti-Semitism, but as a sign that would bring good luck and charm away evil spirits.

ing a lot of sugar. **2** a dessert. **3** (*informal*) a sweetheart; chiefly used as a term of address. **sweetly** *adv* **sweetness** *n* **sweet-and-sour** *adj* seasoned with a sauce containing sugar and vinegar or lemon juice. **sweet corn** (the grains of) a kind of maize. **sweeten** *vb* make or become sweet or more sweet. **sweetener** *n* **sweetening** *n* **sweetheart** *n* a darling; lover. **sweetie** *n* (*informal*) **1** a sweet. **2** a sweetheart. **sweetmeat** *n* a sweetened delicacy. **sweet pea** a climbing garden plant with slender stems and fragrant flowers of various bright colours. **sweet potato** (the large edible root of) a tropical climbing plant; yam. **sweet-william** *n* a garden plant with small, fragrant flowers which form in dense clusters. < Old English *swēte*. SEE PANEL.

swell (swɛl) *vb* **swelled; swollen, swelled; swelling 1** expand or puff up: Her ankles always swell up in the hot weather. **2** make or become greater in size, number, intensity, etc.
• *n* **1** the up and down movement of a stretch of sea. **2** an increase in volume. **3** a device in an organ which controls volume. **4** (*informal*) a fashionable or distinguished person.
• *adj* (*chiefly US*) excellent; stylish. **swelling** *n* **1** a swollen part of the body. **2** the act of swelling or state of being swollen. < Old English *swellan*.

swelter (ˈswɛltə) *vb* suffer from oppressive heat. **sweltering** *adj* (*informal*) oppressively hot. < Old English *sweltan* to die.

swept (swɛpt) SEE **SWEEP**.

swerve (swɜːv) *vb* turn or cause to turn abruptly from a straight course.
• *n* a swerving course or movement. < Old English *sweorfan* to scour.

swift (swɪft) *adj* **1** quick or rapid. **2** prompt: A swift reply would be appreciated.
• *n* any of a group of small, insect-eating birds noted for their long wings and darting flight. **swiftly** *adv* **swiftness** *n* < Old English.

swig (swɪg) *vb* **swigged; swigging** (*informal*) drink in long draughts, esp. from a bottle; gulp.
• *n* a gulp. < origin unknown.

swill (swɪl) *vb* **1** flow or cause to flow around. **2** wash or rinse. **3** (*derogatory*) drink greedily.
• *n* **1** a rinse: Give it a swill in warm water. **2** a mixture of waste food and water or milk that is fed to pigs. < Old English *swillan*.

sweep the board

A person who sweeps the board wins just about everything there is to win. This is one of a number of idiomatic expressions whose origin is to be found in card-games and gambling (see also panel at **chip**). Others include:

ace used informally to express strong approval: I think their new number one is really ace!
within an ace of very close to: He came within an ace of winning.
lay (or **put**) **one's cards on the table** to be frank or open: Let me lay my cards on the table. I've no experience but I'm willing to learn.
play one's cards right to handle things expediently: Play your cards right at the interview and you're bound to get the job.
load the dice to make circumstances unfavourable or prejudicial: With Stanley in goal the dice are loaded against us. He can't see further than ten yards.
no dice! used informally to express a refusal to co-operate.
a trick (**or two**) **up one's sleeve** a secret plan, strategy, etc., kept in reserve for later use: Don't be too confident. The opposition are bound to have a trick or two up their sleeve.
play one's trump-card to use one's most powerful argument, resource, weapon, etc., which has been kept in reserve: The prosecution waited until the last day of the trial before playing their trump-card.

sweet

Terms of endearment tend to fall into groups. A major group has as its core meaning the idea of 'sweetness'. As well as sugar, it includes sweet, sweetie, sweetheart, and, chiefly used in America, honey. The latter has a cognate in the Northern English dialect term hinny, which should not be confused with hinny, 'the sterile offspring of a male horse and female donkey'.

swim (swɪm) *vb* **swam; swum; swimming 1** move through water by means of bodily movements. **2** cross or cover (a river, distance, etc.) by swimming: swim the Channel. **3** be immersed in or flooded with: The bathroom floor was swimming in water. **4** (*informal*) overcome difficulties; survive: sink or swim. **5** have a dizzy sensation: My head is swimming.
• *n* **1** an act or period of swimming. **2** the main current of events or affairs: stay in the swim. **swimming-bath** *n* a swimming-pool, usually indoors. **swimming-pool** *n* an artificial pool for swimming in. **swim-suit** *n* also **swimming-costume** a garment worn for swimming. < Old English *swimman.*

swindle (ˈswɪndl̩) *vb* cheat (a person) out of something; defraud.
• *n* an act or instance of swindling; fraud. **swindler** *n* < German *Schwindler* giddy person.

swine (swaɪn) *n* **1** (*informal*) a detestable person or troublesome thing. **2** *pl n* (*archaic*) pigs. **swinish** *adj* detestable. < Old English *swīn.*

swing (swɪŋ) *vb* **swung; swinging 1** move or cause to move in one or more sweeping curves. **2** turn in a sudden curve: The car swung into the drive. **3** hang or be hung so as to move freely back and forth. **4** walk or run with a relaxed, steady, rhythmical movement. **5** shift from one mood, opinion, etc., to another. **6** influence decisively. **7** (*informal*) manage or manipulate successfully: swing a deal. **8** (*informal*) be hanged. **9** attempt to strike, esp. with a sweeping movement: She swung at him but missed. **10** (*informal*) be trendy.
• *n* **1** a swinging movement: Many a golfer could improve his swing. **2** the range through which something swings: a narrow swing to the SDP. **3** a suspended seat for a child to swing backwards and forwards on. **4** a lively rhythm or gait. **swing-door** *n* a door which pushes open in either direction, usually fitted with a return spring. **swinger** *n* (*informal*) a person who is considered trendy, **swing-wing** *adj* (of an aircraft) having wings whose angle can be adjusted to suit flying speed. < Old English *swingan.*

swingeing (ˈswɪndʒɪŋ) *adj* drastic: swingeing cuts. < Old English *swengan* to punish.

swipe (swaɪp) *vb* (*informal*) **1** hit with a sweeping blow. **2** steal.
• *n* (*informal*) a sweeping blow. < probably *sweep.*

swirl (swɜːl) *vb* move or cause to move with a whirling motion.
• *n* a whirling mass or motion; eddy. < probably Dutch *zwirrelen.*

swish[1] (swɪʃ) *vb* move with a rustling or whistling sound.
• *n* a swishing sound or movement. < like the sound.

swish[2] *adj* fashionable or stylish. < origin unknown.

switch (swɪtʃ) *n* **1** any device used for operating an electric circuit. **2** a device used for directing a train or engine from one track to another. **3** a slender, flexible whip or rod. **4** a tress of false hair. **5** a shift or change.
• *vb* **1** turn (on) or (off) by means of a switch. **2** direct (a train or engine) to another track. **3** shift, change, or divert: switch to a different subject. **4** exchange: Can we switch places? I can't see. **5** swing or whisk, esp. from side to side: The cat sat switching its tail. **switchboard** *n* a panel with switches used for connecting and disconnecting telephone lines or operating other electric circuits. < perhaps Middle Dutch *swijch* twig.

swivel (ˈswɪvl̩) *n* a link or pivot connecting two parts which allows one of them to move freely and independently of the other: a swivel chair.
• *vb* **swivelled; swivelling** turn on or as if on a swivel. < Old English *swīfan* to turn.

swizz, swiz (swɪz) *n* (*informal*) a swindle. < origin uncertain.

swollen (ˈswəʊln̩) SEE **SWELL.**

swoon (swuːn) *n, vb* (a) faint. < Old English *geswogen* unconscious.

swoop (swuːp) *vb* descend swiftly, esp. in attack.
• *n* a swooping movement. < Old English *swāpan.*

swop (swɒp) SEE **SWAP.**

sword (sɔːd) *n* a weapon with a long blade usually with a sharp point and one or two cutting edges. **sword-dance** *n* a dance performed while brandishing or dancing over and around swords. **swordfish** *n* a very large sea-fish with a long, sword-like, upper jaw. < Old English *sweord.*

swore (swɔː) SEE **SWEAR.**

sworn (swɔːn) SEE **SWEAR.**
• *adj* pledged by or as if by an oath: sworn enemies.

swot (swɒt) *vb* study hard, esp. for an examination.
• *n* **1** also **swotter** a person who studies hard. **2** hard study. < *sweat.*

swum (swʌm) SEE **SWIM.**

swung (swʌŋ) SEE **SWING.**

sycamore (ˈsɪkəmɔː) *n* a large tree of the maple family. < Middle French *sicamor.*

sycophant (ˈsɪkəfənt) *n* a person who tries to win favour by using flattery. **sycophancy** *n* sycophantic *adj* < Greek *sykophantēs* informer.

syllable (ˈsɪləbl̩) *n* a small word or part of a word which contains a vowel or vowel-like sound and is uttered as an uninterrupted unit. **syllabic** *adj* of, in, or connected with syllables. **syllabically** *adv* < Middle French *sillabe,* from Latin *syllaba.*

syllabus (ˈsɪləbəs) *n, pl* **syllabuses** a programme or outline of a course of study. < Latin *sillybus* parchment label.

syllogism (ˈsɪləˌdʒɪzəm) *n* a form of deductive reasoning by which a conclusion is reached on the basis of two premises. **syllogistic** *adj* < Greek *syllogismos.*

symbol (ˈsɪmbl̩) *n* **1** something which is used as a conventional means of representing something else: The dove is a symbol of peace. **2** a conventional sign such as a letter or arrow used in printing or writing. **symbolic, symbolical** *adj* **symbolically** *adv* **symbolism** *n* the use of symbols to represent or express things. **symbolize** *vb* **1** be a symbol of. **2** represent by means of a symbol. < Latin *symbolum.*

symmetry (ˈsɪmɪtrɪ) *n* **1** an exact balance or correspondence of parts on either side of a point or axis. **2** a pleasing harmony of form. **symmetrical** *adj* possessing or connected with symmetry. **symmetrically** *adv* < Latin *symmetria.*

sympathy (ˈsɪmpəθɪ) *n* **1** the capacity to share another person's feelings. **2** a feeling of pity or compassion for someone who is suffering or unfortunate. **3** the tendency of two people to think or feel alike. **sympathetic** *adj* **1** feeling or arising from sympathy. **2** likable or congenial. **3** favourably disposed (towards something). **sympathetically** *adv* **sympathize** *vb* feel or express sympathy. **sympathizer** *n* < Latin *sympathia.*

symphony (ˈsɪmfənɪ) *n* a long, musical composition for a full orchestra, usually in four movements. **symphonic** *adj* **symphony orchestra** a large orchestra capable of playing symphonies. < Latin *symphonia* concord.

symposium (sɪmˈpəʊzɪəm) *n, pl* **symposiums, symposia** a conference or meeting at which specialists present papers on a particular topic. SEE PANEL.

symptom (ˈsɪmptəm) *n* **1** any observable indication of the presence, nature, or location of a disease. **2** a sign or indication. **symptomatic** *adj* being or serving as a symptom of. **symptomatically** *adv* < ultimately Greek *sympiptein* to happen.

synagogue (ˈsɪnəˌgɒg) *n* (a building used for worship by) a Jewish congregation. < ultimately Greek *synagein* to bring together.

synchronous (ˈsɪŋkrənəs) *adj* occurring or operating at the same time or speed. **synchronously** *adv* **synchronize** *vb* **1** occur or cause to occur at the same time or speed. **2** cause to show the same time: synchronize watches. **3** cause (a film and its sound-track) to run in harmony. **synchronization** *n* **synchronizer** *n* < ultimately Greek *syn-* with + *chronos* time.

syndicate (ˈsɪndɪkət) *n* **1** an association of individuals or firms that combine for a particular purpose, esp. to undertake a commercial venture. **2** an agency which sells (articles, photographs, etc.) to a number of newspapers, etc., for simultaneous publication.
• *vb* (ˈsɪndɪˌkeɪt) **1** combine into or manage as a syndicate. **2** sell (articles, photographs, etc.) to a syndicate. **syndication** *n* < French *syndicat.*

syndrome (ˈsɪndrəʊm) *n* **1** a group of medical symptoms which regularly occur together and are characteristic of a particular condition. **2** any group of symptoms. < Greek *syn-* with + *dramein* to run.

synecdoche (sɪnˈɛkdəkɪ) *n* a figure of speech in which a part or attribute is used to refer to the whole of something.

A dry symposium?

A symposium is a conference or meeting at which a number of scholars or specialists give short addresses on a particular subject. The word that refers to this highly formal occasion has rather amusing roots. It came into English by way of Latin from the Greek word *symposion* 'a drinking party', from *sympinein* meaning 'to drink together'. Nowadays, it is commonly thought that symposiums tend to be pretty dry affairs.

or vice versa. < Greek *syn-* + *ekdochē* interpretation. SEE PANEL AT **HAND.**

synod (ˈsɪnəd) *n* a church council or advisory body. < ultimately Greek *syn-* with + *hodos* journey.

synonym (ˈsɪnənɪm) *n* a word or phrase with a very similar meaning to another word or phrase in the same language. **synonymous** *adj* similar in meaning. **synonymously** *adv* **synonymy** *n* **1** the study of synonyms. **2** the quality of being synonymous. < Middle English *sinonyme,* from Latin *synonymum.*

synopsis (sɪˈnɒpsɪs) *n, pl* **synopses** a brief summary or outline. **synoptic** *adj* of or serving as a synopsis. < Late Latin, from Greek.

syntax (ˈsɪntæks) *n* (the aspect of grammar dealing with) the ways in which words, phrases, and clauses combine to form larger units. **syntactic** *adj* **syntactically** *adv* < ultimately Greek *syntassein* to arrange together. SEE PANEL AT **RECOMMEND.**

synthesis (ˈsɪnθɪsɪs) *n, pl* **syntheses** the combining of parts or elements to form a whole. **synthesize** *vb* make by synthesis. **synthetic** *adj* **1** made artificially as opposed to produced naturally; man-made. **2** produced by synthesis. **synthetically** *adv* < Greek *syn-* together + *tithenai* to put.

syphilis (ˈsɪfɪlɪs) *n* a serious, contagious disease, usually venereal. **syphilitic** *adj* SEE PANEL.

syphon (ˈsaɪfən) SEE **SIPHON.**

syringe (sɪˈrɪndʒ) *n* a device used for injecting or withdrawing fluids, esp. into or from the body.
• *vb* irrigate by means of a syringe.
< ultimately Greek *syrinx* pipe.

syrup (ˈsɪrəp) *n* a thick, sweet liquid, esp. one made from sugar dissolved in water. **syrupy** *adj* < ultimately Arabic *sharāb.*

system (ˈsɪstəm) *n* **1** a combination of things or ideas that work together or form a whole: the digestive system. **2** the body considered in terms of its organs: Walking is good for the system. **3** a scheme, method, or procedure: They've discovered a system for recycling newspapers. **4** a rational or organized basis or framework: I can't see any system behind the marking scheme. **5** a method of classification: the metric system. **6 the System** (*informal*) a country's social, economic, and political institutions considered as a single, repressive power. **systematic** *adj* **systematically** *adv* **systematize** *vb* arrange into or according to a system. **systematization** *n* < Late Latin *systema.*

syphilis

The names of most diseases are of Latin or Greek derivation. Syphilis is a notable exception. It comes from the name of the principal character in the 16th-century poem Syphilis (sive Morbus Gallicus) 'Syphilis (or the French disease)', written by Giralamo Fracastoro, an Italian poet and physician. The poem, which appeared in English translation in 1686, tells of the adventures of Syphilis, a shepherd, who fell victim to the disease that was named after him.

T

tab (tæb) *n* **1** a small flap, tag, loop, etc., by which something may be draped, suspended, or identified: Each pupil has to have tabs sewn into his clothing. **2** (*chiefly US*) a bill, esp. for drinks or a meal.
• *vb* **tabbed; tabbing** provide with tabs. **keep tabs on** or **a tab on** (*informal*) keep under close surveillance. < origin uncertain.

tabby (ˈtæbɪ) *n* a domestic cat, esp. one with dark stripes. < *tabby*, striped silk, from French *tabis*.

tabernacle (ˈtæbəˌnækḷ) *n* **1** the sacred tent that according to the Bible was used by the Israelites during their wanderings from Egypt. **2** a receptacle in which consecrated bread and wine are kept in certain churches. **3** any place of worship that is not called a church. < ultimately Latin *taberna* hut.

table (ˈteɪbḷ) *n* **1** a piece of furniture with a flat top mounted on one or more legs. **2** the food placed on a table at a mealtime. **3** an orderly arrangement of figures or data, usually in columns: a conversion table.
• *vb* submit (a proposal, motion, etc.) for discussion. **table-cloth** *n* a cloth for covering a table, esp. at a mealtime. **table d'hôte** a restaurant meal offering little or no choice of dishes and served at a fixed price. **table-linen** *n* the tablecloth, serviettes, etc., used on a table at a mealtime. **table-mat** *n* a mat used for protecting the surface of a table from hot dishes, etc. **tablespoon** *n* **1** a large spoon used for serving food. **2** a tablespoonful. **tablespoonful** *n* the amount held by a tablespoon. **table tennis** a game resembling tennis that is played on a tabletop. < ultimately Latin *tabula a* writing tablet. SEE PANEL.

tableau (ˈtæbləʊ) *n, pl* **tableaux 1** a scene or event represented by a group of silent, motionless actors, etc. **2** any striking picture or scene. < French.

tablet (ˈtæblɪt) *n* **1** any small, round, solid mass containing medicine and taken orally; pill. **2** any small, compressed slab or block of something: a tablet of soap. **3** a slab or plaque of stone, etc., usually mounted on a wall and bearing an inscription. < Middle French *tablete*.

tabloid (ˈtæblɔɪd) *n* a newspaper that has a relatively small page size and lots of photographic material. < *Tabloid*, trademark for a medicine in tablet form.

taboo, tabu (təˈbuː) *n, pl* **taboos, tabus** a prohibition on doing or saying something, usually arising from religious belief, superstition, or social custom.
• *adj* banned or forbidden by religious or social custom.
• *vb* set apart as taboo. < Tongan *tabu*.

tabular (ˈtæbjʊlə) *adj* arranged in the form of a table, column, or list. **tabulate** *vb* arrange in columns. **tabulation** *n* **tabulator** *n* **1** a person or thing that tabulates. **2** a device on a typewriter that is used for arranging data in columns. < Latin *tabula* board.

tachograph (ˈtækəˌgrɑːf) *n* a device that records automatically the speed and travel duration of the vehicle in which it is fitted. < Greek *tachos* speed + English *-graph*.

tacit (ˈtæsɪt) *adj* implied or understood but not actually stated: a tacit agreement. **tacitly** *adv* < Latin *tacēre* to be silent.

taciturn (ˈtæsɪˌtɜːn) *adj* not given to conversation or talking. **taciturnity** *n* < SEE **TACIT**.

tack[1] (tæk) *n* **1** a short, sharp-pointed nail with a broad, flat head. **2** a long, loose stitch used to hold fabric temporarily in position. **3** a rope used for holding the corner of certain sails in position; corner

turn the tables

To turn the tables on someone is to reverse a person's situation so that it is suddenly disadvantageous. There are two schools of thought as to the origin of the expression. On the one hand it is believed to derive from the days when table tops were reversible. One side would be kept clean and polished for eating and entertaining while the other side served as a work surface. To give someone the opposite of a warm welcome, one simply turned the work surface uppermost.

A simpler theory ascribes the expression to the old practice of reversing a chess-board so that an opponent's position was entirely changed.

which is secured by this. **4** a course, direction, or line of action. **5** a movement diagonally against the wind in sailing.
• *vb* **1** fasten with one or more tacks. **2** sew with tacks. **3** sail a zigzag course. **tack on** (*informal*) add as a supplement. < Middle English *tak*.

tack² *n* all the equipment used for riding a horse, such as a saddle, bridle, etc. < *tackle*.

tackle (ˈtækl̩) *n* **1** an arrangement of ropes and pulleys for lifting heavy weights. **2** equipment for a sport or activity: fishing tackle. **3** the act of tackling. **4** the rigging of a ship.
• *vb* **1** attempt to deal with: tackle a problem. **2** grapple with or take hold of, esp. in the attempt to stop, restrain, or overcome. **3** intercept and (try to) take the ball from (an opposing player) in football, hockey, etc. **tackler** *n* < Middle English *takel*.

tacky (ˈtækɪ) *adj* (of newly applied paint, glue, etc.) slightly sticky. **tackiness** *n* < SEE TACK¹.

tact (tækt) *n* skill in handling people or situations without causing offence. **tactful** *adj* **tactfully** *adv* **tactless** *adj* lacking in tact. **tactlessly** *adv* **tactlessness** *n* < ultimately Latin *tangere* to touch.

tactic (ˈtæktɪk) *n* a plan or strategy for achieving an objective. **tactical** *adj* **1** of or connected with tactics or skilful planning: a tactical advantage. **2** of or intended to achieve small-scale objectives. **tactically** *adv* **tactician** *n* a person skilled in using tactics. **tactics** *n* **1** the art of manoeuvring forces in a battle or conflict. **2** *pl* any skilful or cunning strategy for achieving an objective. < ultimately Greek *tassein* to arrange.

tadpole (ˈtædˌpəʊl) *n* the larva of a frog, toad, etc. < Middle English *taddepol*, from *tode* toad + *polle* head.

tag¹ (tæg) *n* **1** a label: a price tag. **2** a common saying or quotation. **3** the hard binding at the end of a shoelace, etc.
• *vb* **tagged; tagging 1** attach a tag to. **2** label, brand, or classify. **3** add or attach to. **tag along** (*informal*) accompany or go along with a person or group. < Middle English *tagge*.

tag² *n* a children's chasing game. < origin unknown.

tail (teɪl) *n* **1** the movable growth which extends from the rear of an animal's body. **2** something which resembles this: The kite had a long tail of yellow ribbon. **3** the rearmost or concluding part of something: the tail of a queue. **4** *chiefly pl* the reverse side of a coin: 'Heads or tails?' **5** (*informal*) a person whose job is to follow and observe someone.
• *vb* **1** (*informal*) shadow or follow closely. **2** remove the stalk or tail of. **tail-back** *n* a long line of traffic in a queue, usually caused by an obstruction. **tail-board** *n* a hinged or removable board at the back of a lorry or cart. **tailcoat** *n* a man's formal evening coat, divided at the back into two tails. **tail-end** *n* the rearmost or concluding part of something: 'Don't expect the tail-end to score many runs.' **tail-gate** *n* a door at the rear of an estate car. **tail off** gradually decrease or diminish: Demand has tailed off. **tailplane** *n* the horizontal parts of an aircraft's tail. **tails** *pl n* **1** a tailcoat. **2** formal evening dress for men. < Old English *tægel*.

tailor (ˈteɪlə) *n* a person whose job is to make clothes, esp. for men.
• *vb* **1** make or adjust (a garment): The jacket has been tailored to fit tightly round the waist. **2** make, adjust, or adapt for a particular purpose. **tailor-made** *adj* **1** made by a tailor. **2** perfectly suited for the purpose: She's tailor-made for the job. < Old French *taillier* to cut.

taint (teɪnt) *n* a trace of something that contaminates, spoils, or corrupts.
• *vb* affect with a taint. < Middle French *teindre* to dye.

take (teɪk) *vb* **took; taken; taking** **1** seize, hold, or grasp: Take these books a minute while I open the door. **2** gain control or possession of; capture: They took 120 prisoners. **3** borrow, use, or remove without permission: Someone has taken my umbrella. **4** have a particular capacity; hold: The engine takes about ten litres of oil. **5** carry or convey to another place: I think I'll take the table into the garden. **6** perform (a particular action): to take a stroll. **7** get, buy, obtain, etc.: We've started taking a morning newspaper. **8** accept: Make them a good offer and I'm sure they'll take it. **9** require: It takes a lot of courage to resign after all these years. **10** use as a means of transport: She took the bus into town. **11** consider: I took him to be much older than he really was. **12** record: take a photograph. **13** be successfully applied, planted, or transplanted; be effectively injected: The paint won't take on a greasy surface. **14** subtract. **15** assume: Am I to take it that you don't want it after all? **16** eat or drink; consume: Take two tablets four times a day. **17** react to in a particular way: She's taken the news very badly. **18** feel or experience: take pride in one's work. **19** go along or into: Take the second turning on the left.

• *n* **1** proceeds or takings: How much was today's take? **2** the amount of something caught or taken. **3** a period of uninterrupted recording or filming: The scene needed nine takes before they got it right. **taker** *n* a person who takes, accepts, or buys something: Even though the tickets were free there were no takers. **taking** *adj* attractive; captivating. **takings** *pl n* the money a shop obtains from its sales. < Old English *tacan.* SEE PANEL.

talc (tælk) **1** a soft mineral that feels like soap, used in making paints, ceramics, and talcum powder. **2** talcum powder. < Middle French: mica, ultimately from Arabic *ṭalq.*

talcum (ˈtælkəm) *n* talc. **talcum powder** a fine, usually perfumed powder made from talc, used to make the skin feel dry and smooth. < Medieval Latin *talcum* mica, from *talk.*

tale (teɪl) *n* **1** a story or narrative. **2** a report or account. **3** an untrue assertion that is meant to deceive. **4** a piece of malicious gossip. < Old English *talu.* SEE PANEL.

talent (ˈtælənt) *n* **1** a special ability or aptitude: a talent for painting. **2** people who have such ability or aptitude. **3** (*slang*) women considered in terms of their

---

taking it in

Take features in a large number of idiomatic expressions, including:

take account of to include in one's considerations; make allowances for.
take after to resemble: He takes after his father.
take as read to accept as true and self-evident.
take away to subtract.
take-away *adj, n* (a shop selling food) to be consumed elsewhere.
take back 1 to withdraw (a comment). **2** to cause (someone) to recall (a distant happening or experience).
take down 1 to write down: Take down this letter, please, Miss Jones. **2** to dismantle.
take down a peg or two to make (a conceited person) humble. The expression probably derives from 18th-century British navy jargon. Then, a ship's flag was raised and lowered by pegs; the higher the peg, the higher the honour. To take a flag down a peg meant that the honour bestowed was lessened.
take for granted 1 to assume as true. **2** to be so used to (a person or thing) that one no longer appreciates his, her, or its true value.
take hold 1 to grasp or grip. **2** to become established.
take-home pay the amount of a person's wages or salary that remains after tax, etc., has been deducted.
take in 1 to understand or absorb. **2** to include or encompass. **3** to provide accommodation for. **4** to make (a garment) smaller. **5** to deceive or cheat.
take it out of to exhaust (someone).
take it out on to get rid of one's anger, frustration, etc., by becoming angry, etc., with (another person): You may have had a difficult day at work, but you don't have to take it out on me.
take it upon oneself to accept responsibility for doing something, often in a presumptuous manner.
take off 1 to remove. **2** to rise up into the air. **3** to become very popular. **4** (of sales, etc.) to increase rapidly. **5** to imitate humorously.
take-off *n* **1** the act of launching into the air. **2** a humorous imitation.
take on 1 to accept: take on more work. **2** to engage (an employee). **3** to acquire (a new meaning, etc.). **4** to accept as an opponent.
take on board to accept, adopt, or apply: Thanks, John, for the suggestion. We'll certainly be taking it on board.
take one's time not to hurry; be slow or careful.
take out 1 to take to a place for recreation or exercise. **2** to obtain (an insurance policy, etc.).
take over to gain control of (a business, etc.).
take-over *n*
take part to participate.
take stock 1 to list all the stock in a shop, warehouse, etc. **2** to consider one's position, resources, etc., carefully.
take to 1 to develop a liking for. **2** to adopt as a habit.
take up 1 to adopt as a hobby, etc.: take up tennis. **2** to occupy (time or space). **3** to resume or return to: take up the story where we left off. **4** to shorten (a garment). **5** to adopt or accept. **6** to discuss further with (a speaker, etc.). **7** to raise (an issue, etc.) for discussion.

sexual attractiveness. **talented** *adj* having talent. **talent scout** a person whose job is to spot and recruit people with a particular talent. < ultimately Greek *talanton* unit of weight or money.

talisman (ˈtælɪzmən) *n, pl* **talismans** an object that is supposed to have magical powers and act like a charm. < Greek *telein* to perform a rite. SEE PANEL.

talk (tɔːk) *vb* **1** use speech; speak: Stop talking and sit up straight! **2** gossip: People will start talking if we let her win all the prizes. **3** utter: He talks a lot of nonsense. **4** make (something) the subject of discussion; discuss: Let's talk business. **5** give a lecture: Tomorrow I'll be talking about convection and radiation. **6** reveal information: We have ways of making you talk! **7** persuade or bring round: He talked her into marrying him. **8** use (a particular language) for communicating: Do you talk German?
• *n* **1** a conversation or discussion. **2** an informal lecture or presentation. **3** gossip. **4** empty speech that is not followed up by action: Don't take any notice of him. He's all talk! **5** a person or thing that is talked about: She's the talk of the town.

and thereby hangs a tale ...

And thereby hangs a tale means 'there is an interesting or surprising story connected with what has just been mentioned'. This expression, with its word-play on tale ('tail') features in several of Shakespeare's plays, including 'As You Like It', Act 2, Scene 7:

And so, from hour to hour, we ripe and ripe,
And then from hour to hour, we rot and rot:
And thereby hangs a tale.

talisman

Judging by appearances, it would seem as if talisman 'a protective charm' belonged to the group of compound nouns postman, milkman, midshipman, etc., which form their plurals by a change of vowel (postmen, milkmen, midshipmen). Talisman, however, is not a compound of talis and man. It comes from the Greek word *telesma* meaning 'mystery' or 'ritual'. This explains why its plural form is not talismen but talismans.

talkative *adj* given to talking a lot. < Middle English *talken.* SEE PANEL.

tall (tɔːl) *adj* **1** of above average height. **2** of a certain height: He's over six feet tall. **3** extremely difficult to perform or fulfil: a tall order. **tallness** *n* **tallboy** *n* a tall chest of drawers. **tall story** a story that is hard to believe. < Middle English.

tallow (ˈtæləʊ) *n* animal fat used for making soap, candles, etc. < Middle English *talgh.*

tally (ˈtælɪ) *n* a record or account of figures, esp. of expenditure: Keep a tally of how much you spend.
• *vb* **tallied; tallying** agree or correspond: The two lots of evidence simply don't tally. < ultimately Latin *talea* twig.

talon (ˈtælən) *n* a sharp claw, esp. of a bird of prey. < ultimately Latin *talus* ankle.

tambourine (ˌtæmbəˈriːn) *n* a shallow, one-sided drum with metallic discs around the edge, held in the hand and played by shaking or striking. < Middle French *tambourin.*

tame (teɪm) *adj* **1** (of animals) used to living or being with human beings; domesticated. **2** not wild or dangerous; docile. **3** dull or uninspiring.
• *vb* make gentle, domesticated, or

Now you're talking!

Talk features in a number of idiomatic expressions, including:

money talks having money means that one can exert an influence.

now you're talking what you are suggesting appeals to me; used as an expression of agreement.

talk about this is a very good/bad example of; used to express annoyance, surprise, etc.: Talk about saving money, when you go and spend £100 on new clothes!

talk down 1 to silence (a speaker) by talking loudly. **2** to give instructions to (a pilot) to guide the landing of an aircraft. **3** to speak in a condescending manner (to).

talk over to discuss (a problem, etc.) fully: OK, we'll talk the whole thing over later.

talk shop to discuss matters concerned with one's job, etc., when this may be thought inappropriate or anti-social.

talk through one's hat to talk nonsense.

talk to to reprimand or scold. **talking-to** *n*

submissive. **tamely** *adv* **tameness** *n* **tamer** *n* a person who tames and trains wild animals. < Old English *tam.*

tamper (ˈtæmpə) *vb* **tamper with** **1** meddle or interfere with (something) without permission or in a way likely to cause damage. **2** use bribery or other improper tactics upon: The witnesses have obviously been tampered with. < Middle French *temprer* to meddle.

tampon (ˈtæmpɒn) *n* **1** a plug of absorbent material placed in the vagina to absorb blood during menstruation. **2** any similar plug used in medicine to absorb secretions or restrain haemorrhages. < French.

tan (tæn) *vb* **tanned; tanning 1** turn (animal hide) into leather, esp. by treating it with tannin. **2** make or turn brown by exposure to sun. **3** (*informal*) beat or thrash: I'll tan your hide if you do that again!

• *n* **1** light, yellowish brown. **2** the brown colour of skin that has been exposed to sun.

• *adj* of the colour tan. **tanner** *n* **1** a person who tans hides. **2** (*informal*) (formerly) a sixpenny coin. **tannery** *n* a place where hides are tanned. < Middle English *tannen.*

tandem (ˈtændəm) *n* a long bicycle with seats and pedals for two people sitting one behind the other.

• *adv* one behind the other. < Latin: at length.

tang (tæŋ) *n* a strong, distinctive taste, flavour, or smell. **tangy** *adj* < Scandinavian.

tangent (ˈtændʒənt) *n* a straight line that touches the edge of a curve but does not cut it. **go off at a tangent** change suddenly from one subject, etc., to a completely different one. < ultimately Latin *tangere* to touch.

tangerine (ˌtændʒəˈriːn) *n* a variety of orange with a loose skin that peels easily; its colour. < French *Tanger* Tangier, port in Morocco.

tangible (ˈtændʒɪbl̩) *adj* **1** real or actual: tangible evidence. **2** able to be perceived, esp. by touch: There is a tangible difference in the quality of the two materials. **tangibility** or **tangibleness** *n* **tangibly** *adv* < ultimately Latin *tangere* to touch.

tangle (ˈtæŋgl̩) *vb* make or become tangled. **tangled** *adj* **1** twisted together in an untidy or knotted mass. **2** in a confused or disordered state.

• *n* a tangled mass or state. < probably Scandinavian.

tango (ˈtæŋgəʊ) *n, pl* **tangos** (music written for) a ballroom dance of Latin-American origin.

• *vb* dance the tango. < American Spanish.

tank (tæŋk) *n* **1** a large container for liquids or gases: a hot-water tank. **2** a heavily armoured military vehicle armed with a powerful gun and moving on caterpillar tracks. **tanked up** *adj* (*informal*) full of alcoholic drinks. **tanker** *n* a ship, aircraft, lorry, or other vehicle designed to carry liquid in bulk. **tankful** *n* the amount that a tank will hold. **tank up** fill the tank of (a vehicle) with fuel. < Portuguese *tanque,* from *estancar* to stop the flow of.

tankard (ˈtæŋkəd) *n* a single-handled drinking vessel, usually of pewter or silver and sometimes with a hinged lid. < Middle English.

tannin (ˈtænɪn) *n* any of a number of complex chemicals found esp. in leaves and tree bark, used commonly in the making of leather and ink. **tannic** *adj* of tannin. **tannic acid** tannin. < French, from *tanner* to tan.

Tannoy (ˈtænɔɪ) *n* (*Trademark*) a type of public-address system.

tantalize (ˈtæntəˌlaɪz) *vb* tease or torment by, or as if by, keeping something that is desired just out of reach: Stop tantalizing the child with that teddy-bear and give it to her. **tantalizing** *adj* SEE PANEL.

tantamount (ˈtæntəˌmaʊnt) *adj* equivalent in effect, value, significance, etc.:

tantalize

To suspend a meaty bone deliberately just out of a hungry dog's reach is to tantalize it. This word, meaning 'to torment by exposing to something desired and then withholding it', comes from Greek mythology. *Tantalus,* the King of Phrygia, was a son of Zeus. As a punishment for divulging to mortals the secrets of the gods, he was condemned to stand immersed up to the chin in a river in Hades. Whenever he stooped to drink, the water receded. As if this were not punishment enough, fruit-laden branches hung overhead, but whenever he reached out the fruit would elude his grasp.

His refusal was tantamount to an insult. < ultimately Anglo-French *tant amunter* to amount to as much.

tantrum (ˈtæntrəm) *n* a violent fit of bad temper: The child is bound to throw a tantrum if it doesn't get its own way. < origin unknown.

tap[1] (tæp) *n* **1** a device for controlling the flow of liquid or gas from a pipe, barrel, cylinder, etc. **2** a plug for a cask, barrel, etc. **3** a device for cutting a female screw-thread.
• *vb* **tapped; tapping 1** fit with a tap. **2** draw off by means of a tap. **3** draw upon: They are always trying to tap our resources. **4** (*informal*) get money from. **5** secretly connect a listening-device to (a telephone line, etc.) in order to listen in: The phone's been tapped. **6** cut a female screw-thread in, by means of a tap. **on tap 1** readily available. **2** (of beer, etc.) on draught. **taproom** *n* a bar, esp. in a public house. < Old English *tæppa*.

tap[2] *vb* **tapped; tapping 1** knock or strike gently: Try tapping on the window. **2** strike gently with: Stop tapping your foot on the ground!
• *n* **1** a quick, gentle blow. **2** the sound this makes. **tap-dance** *vb, n* (perform) a dance on a hard surface wearing shoes fitted with metal clips so that rhythmic tapping sounds are audible. **tap-dancer** *n* < Middle French *taper*.

tape (teɪp) *n* **1** a long, narrow strip of fabric, used esp. for binding. **2** a long, narrow strip of paper, cellulose, etc., usually supplied in a roll: adhesive tape. **3** magnetic tape. **4** a tape-recording. **5** a tape-measure. **6** the string or ribbon that forms the finishing line of a race.
• *vb* **1** fasten or bind with tape. **2** record on magnetic tape. **tape deck** a device used for making and playing back recordings on magnetic tape. **tape-measure** *n* a length of tape or thin metal showing units of length and used for measuring. **tape-recorder** *n* an apparatus for recording sounds on magnetic tape and playing them back. **tape-recording** *n* a recording made on magnetic tape. **tapeworm** *n* a tape-like worm that lives as a parasite in the intestines of man and other animals. < Old English *tæppe*. SEE PANEL.

taper (ˈteɪpə) *n* **1** a slender candle. **2** a gradual decrease of thickness.
• *vb* **1** reduce or decrease gradually in thickness: The end of the stick tapered off to a sharp point. **2** gradually diminish or cease. < Old English *tapor*.

tapestry (ˈtæpəstrɪ) *n* a heavy cloth bearing a pictorial design, often used as a wall-hanging. < ultimately Greek *tapēs* carpet.

tapioca (ˌtæpɪˈəʊkə) *n* a granular substance obtained from cassava, used for making puddings. < ultimately Tupi *typyóca*.

tappet (ˈtæpɪt) *n* a projecting part of a machine, engine, etc., which moves or is moved by some other part. < *tap*[2].

tar (tɑː) *n* **1** a thick, black, sticky substance obtained from wood, coal, etc., used commonly in roadmaking. **2** a similar substance present in cigarette smoke, etc.: low tar cigarettes.
• *vb* **tarred; tarring** coat with tar. **tarred with the same brush** having the same faults as someone else. < Old English *teoru*.

tarantula (təˈræntjʊlə) *n, pl* **tarantulas, tarantulae 1** a large, black, hairy spider of Southern Europe. **2** any of various large, hairy spiders. < ultimately Old Italian *tarantola*, from *Taranto*, port in south Italy. SEE PANEL.

red tape

Excessively formal or bureaucratic methods of procedure are sometimes impatiently referred to as red tape: 'All these forms to fill in? What a lot of *red tape* just to get a licence!' This idiomatic phrase, believed to have originated with Charles Dickens, alludes to the former British practice of using red tape to bind legal and official documents together.

tarantula

The venomous spider known as the tarantula occurs in various parts of the world. However, the true tarantula—the so-called 'wolf spider'—is European. It takes its name ultimately from the south Italian port of *Taranto* where it was commonly found.

The bite of the tarantula was popularly believed to cause a disease by the name of tarantism, a type of dancing mania, for which dancing was thought to be a cure. The frenzied dancing of the spider's victim came to be known as the tarantella. This name was later borrowed for a fast, whirling folk dance of southern Italy.

tardy (ˈtɑːdɪ) *adj* (*often formal or literary*) slow or late. **tardily** *adv* **tardiness** *n* < ultimately Latin *tardus.*

target (ˈtɑːgɪt) *n* **1** an object or defined area which is aimed at in shooting practice, archery, etc. **2** an object or defined area at which bombs, shells, etc., are directed in wartime. **3** a goal or objective: Our target is to halve the deficit by the end of the year. **4** an object of criticism, scorn, etc. < Middle French *targette.*

tariff (ˈtærɪf) *n* **1** a list of prices, charges, or rates. **2** a duty or list of duties to be paid on goods entering or leaving a country. < Italian *tariffa,* from Arabic *ta'rīf* notification.

Tarmac (ˈtɑːmæk) *n* (*Trademark*) material used for surfacing roads, etc., comprising a mixture of tar and small pieces of broken stone; asphalt. **tarmac** *n* a runway, road, or other area surfaced with this.

tarn (tɑːn) *n* a small mountain lake. < Scandinavian.

tarnish (ˈtɑːnɪʃ) *vb* **1** make or become dull and without lustre, esp. by oxidation: The trouble with silver is it tarnishes easily. **2** spoil, stain, or blemish: a tarnished reputation.
• *n* a film which gives metal surfaces a dull, stained appearance. < Middle French *ternir.*

tarot (ˈtærəʊ) *n* any of a pack of 78 pictorial playing-cards used for fortune-telling. < ultimately Italian *tarocchi.*

tarpaulin (tɑːˈpɔːlɪn) *n* (a sheet of) heavy, waterproof canvas. < probably *tar* + *pall* + *-ing.*

tarry (ˈtærɪ) *vb* **tarried; tarrying** (*literary or archaic*) be slow or late in going or acting; linger. < Middle English *tarien.*

tart¹ (tɑːt) *n* **1** a pie or shell of pastry with a sweet filling. **2** (*slang*) a prostitute or woman who is likened to one. **tart up** (*often derogatory*) dress or decorate in a hurried, gaudy, or tasteless way: The old cars had obviously been tarted up to impress the customers. < Middle French *tarte.*

tart² *adj* **1** having a sharp or acid taste. **2** severe or caustic: a tart reply. **tartish** *adj* **tartishly** *adv* **tartly** *adv* **tartness** *n* < Old English *teart.*

tartan (ˈtɑːtn̩) *n* **1** any of a number of coloured patterns formed by lines or stripes that cross each other at right angles, esp. one distinctive of a Highland clan. **2** cloth that is woven with such a pattern. < probably Middle French *tiretaine* cloth of mixed fibres.

tartar¹ (ˈtɑːtə) *n* **1** a substance consisting mostly of calcium which forms a hard deposit on the teeth. **2** a reddish crust or sediment deposited inside wine casks by the juice of grapes. < Medieval Latin *tartarum.*

tartar² *n* (*informal*) a fearsome or severely exacting person. < *Tartar.* SEE PANEL.

task (tɑːsk) *n* **1** a piece of work, esp. something unpleasant: The worst task was having to clean the oven. **2** a duty: Having to identify the bodies was not a pleasant task. **task force** a unit formed to undertake a particular mission, esp. a military one. **taskmaster** *n* a person who assigns tasks: a hard taskmaster. < ultimately Latin *taxare* to tax.

tassel (ˈtæsl̩) *n* a bunch of dangling cords or threads, used as an ornament. **tasselled** *adj* < ultimately Latin *taxillus* small die.

taste (teɪst) *vb* **1** distinguish or recognize the flavour of: I can taste garlic in the soup. **2** test the flavour or quality of (something) by taking a little into the mouth: Taste this and tell me if it's burnt. **3** have a particular flavour or quality that is discovered by tasting: These crisps don't taste fresh. **4** experience: Once you've tasted success, there'll be no stopping you!
• *n* **1** the sense by which flavours are distinguished. **2** the flavour or quality of something that is perceived by this sense: What an unusual taste this cheese has! **3** the act of tasting; small quantity that is tasted: Have a taste for luck! **4** an experience of something: It was my first taste of Italy. **5** a

tartar

A person who is considered to be a particularly fearsome and difficult character is sometimes referred to as a tartar: The new Prime Minister is certainly sorting the country out, but he's a bit of a *tartar*! The word tartar derives from the *Tatars,* the Asiatic tribes who were amongst those who in the 13th century helped give Genghis Khan his formidable reputation.

The spelling of Tartar, often tartar, includes an r which by all rights shouldn't really be there. During their sweep across Asia and Eastern Europe the Tatar hordes proved so fierce that many saw in their ravages a fulfilment of Revelation, chapter 9. It seemed as if they had emerged from hell or 'the bottomless pit', otherwise known as Tartarus.

liking or preference: I've always had a taste for old things. **6** the ability to appreciate what is aesthetically excellent, socially appropriate, etc.: If you ask me, painting your whole house pink and orange shows very little taste. **tastebud** *n* any of the many small, sensory organs on the tongue which provide the sensation of taste. **tasteful** *adj* showing or conforming to good taste. **tastefully** *adv* **tastefulness** *n* **tasteless** *adj* **1** lacking flavour. **2** showing poor taste: a tasteless and uncalled-for remark. **tastelessly** *adv* **tastelessness** *n* **taster** *n* a person whose job is to assess the quality of food or drink by tasting it: a wine-taster. **tasty** *adj* having a pleasant flavour: a tasty meal. **tastily** *adv* **tastiness** *n* < ultimately Latin *tangere* to touch. SEE PANEL.

tattered (ˈtætəd) *adj* old and ragged.

tatters (ˈtætəz) *pl n* old, ragged pieces, esp. of clothing or material. < ultimately Scandinavian.

tattoo¹ (tæˈtuː) *n, pl* **tattoos 1** an evening drum or bugle call signalling soldiers to return to their quarters. **2** an outdoor military display. **3** a drumming sound. < Dutch *taptoe,* from *tap toe!* taps shut! SEE PANEL.

tattoo² *vb* make (a pattern of) indelible marks on the skin; mark (a part of the body) in this way.
• *n, pl* **tattoos** a pattern that has been tattooed. **tattooer** *n* **tattooist** *n* < Tahitian *tatau.*

tatty (ˈtætɪ) *adj* (*informal*) shabby or tattered. < origin uncertain.

taught (tɔːt) SEE **TEACH.**

taunt (tɔːnt) *vb* tease or jeer at in a provocative way.
• *n* a taunting remark. < origin uncertain.

taut (tɔːt) *adj* stretched or pulled tight: Keep the rope as taut as you can. **tautly** *adv* **tautness** *n* < Middle English *tought.*

tautology (tɔːˈtɒlədʒɪ) *n* (an instance of) unwanted repetition. **tautological** *adj* **tautologically** *adv* **tautologous** *adj* **tautologously** *adv* SEE PANEL AT **NAKED.**

tavern (ˈtævən) *n* (*literary or archaic*) an inn or public house. < ultimately Latin *taberna* hut.

tawdry (ˈtɔːdrɪ) *adj* cheap and gaudy. **tawdrily** *adv* **tawdriness** *n* SEE PANEL.

tawny (ˈtɔːnɪ) *adj* brownish-orange. < Middle French *tanner* to tan.

tax (tæks) *n* **1** a charge levied by a government on income, goods, or property. **2** something that makes heavy demands on: a tax on one's energy.
• *vb* **1** levy a tax on; require (someone) to pay tax: Are they still thinking of taxing books? **2** drain or make heavy demands on: Your mother really knows how to tax my patience! **3** pay the tax on: He can't even afford to tax the car. **4** charge or accuse. **taxation** *n* **after tax** net. **before tax** gross. **tax-free** *adj* exempt from tax. **taxpayer** *n* a person who pays or is liable to pay tax. < ultimately Latin *tangere* to touch.
taxi (ˈtæksɪ) *n, pl* **taxis, taxies** a car that is hired with its driver, esp. for short journeys.
• *vb* **taxied; taxiing**, **taxying 1** (of an aircraft) move slowly along the ground. **2** ride in a taxi. **taxi-cab** *n* a taxi. < short for *taximeter cab.*

taxidermy (ˈtæksɪˌdɜːmɪ) *n* the art of preserving, stuffing, and mounting animal skins so that they look lifelike. **taxidermist** *n* < Greek *taxis* arrangement + *derma* skin.

taxonomy (tækˈsɒnəmɪ) *n* **1** the classification of living things. **2** the science of

taste

The word taste is rather interesting in that in one of its senses it contains, as it were, an in-built adjective. The identity of this is revealed in a phrase such as a lack of taste. A person who is said to display a lack of taste does not of course display a lack of taste, which is impossible, but a lack of *good* taste. Similarly, the adjective tasteless, as in a tasteless joke, does not mean 'lacking taste' but 'lacking *good* taste'.

tattoo

To sound a tattoo is to beat a drum or sound a bugle as a signal for soldiers to return to their quarters for the night. The word tattoo derives ultimately from the Dutch phrase *tap toe!* meaning 'taps shut!' It is not that Dutch soldiers were so struck on hygiene that they had to be summoned nightly from the local baths. Rather, the signal was directed at the local tavern keepers who by its sounding were obliged to stem the flow of ale.

classification. **taxonomist** *n* < French *taxonomie*, from Greek *taxis* arrangement + *-nomia*, from *nemein* to distribute.

tea (tiː) *n* **1** an evergreen shrub grown in China, India, Sri Lanka, and other parts of Asia. **2** the dried, processed leaves of this shrub. **3** a drink made by steeping these in boiling water. **4** any similar drink: herbal tea. **5** a light meal taken in the late afternoon. **tea-bag** *n* a small, porous bag containing approximately one teaspoonful of tea-leaves. **tea-break** *n* a short interruption of work for the sake of resting and drinking tea, coffee, etc. **teacake** *n* a currant bun, usually served toasted. **tea-chest** *n* a large, wooden box in which tea is exported; also used for packing things in when moving house. **tea-cloth** *n* a tea-towel. **tea-cosy** *n* an insulating cover for a teapot. **teacup** *n* a cup in which tea is served. **teacupful** *n* the amount held by a teacup. **tea-leaf** *n* a fragment of a processed leaf of the tea shrub. **teapot** *n* a pot with a lid, handle, and spout used for making and pouring tea. **tea-room** *n* a restaurant where tea, coffee, cakes, etc., are served. **tea service** a tea-set. **tea-set** *n* the teapot, cups, saucers, etc., used in preparing and serving tea. **teaspoon** *n* **1** a small spoon. **2** a teaspoonful. **teaspoonful** *n* the amount held by a teaspoon. **tea-towel** *n* a cloth used for drying washed dishes, cutlery, etc. < Chinese (Amoy) *t'e*.

teach (tiːtʃ) *vb* **taught; teaching** **1** impart knowledge to (someone) or of (a subject): He teaches twelve-year-olds. **2** do this for a living: Does your wife teach too? **3** train: She taught her dog to walk on two legs. **4** advocate (a practice or principle) in the hope that it will be adopted; preach: Their leaders teach patience and forgiveness. **5** cause to learn or understand: His years overseas taught him that there was more to life than the kitchen sink. **teacher** *n* a person who teaches for a living, esp. at a school. **teach-in** *n* an informal conference with visiting speakers, usually held at a university, college, etc. **teaching** *n* **1** the profession of a teacher. **2** a principle or practice that is taught: the teachings of Buddha. < Old English *tǣcan*.

teak (tiːk) *n* (a large, evergreen, Asian tree with) hard, yellowish-brown wood that is used for making furniture. < Portuguese *teca*, from Malayalam *tēkka*.

team (tiːm) *n* **1** a group of people forming one of the sides in a game or contest: a football team. **2** a number of people or animals organized to work together. • *vb* **team up** combine in or as if in a team: The two women teamed up and opened a hair salon. **team spirit** willingness to give priority to the objectives of one's team or group. **team-work** *n* mutual co-operation. < Old English *tēam* offspring.

tear[1] (tɪə) *n* one of the drops of salty liquid that lubricate the eye and which are shed during times of grief, etc. **in tears** weeping: I found her in tears. **tear-drop** *n* a tear. **tearful** *adj* shedding, about to shed, or accompanied by tears: a tearful goodbye. **tear-gas** *n* any substance which causes the eyes to be blinded with floods of tears. **tear-jerker** *n* a sentimental story, film, etc., that is intended to provoke tears or sadness. < Old English *tēar*.

tear[2] (tɛə) *vb* **tore; torn; tearing 1** pull violently apart or into pieces: She tore the letter up. **2** seize or remove violently: He tore

tawdry

In earlier days an event at Ely not to be missed was St Audrey's Fair. This was held annually on 17 October in commemoration of the birthday of *St Audrey.* This was the Old French name given to *Etheldreda,* the 7th-century Queen of Northumbria who left her husband and fled to Mercia. Numbering amongst Etheldreda's many good deeds was the founding of an abbey at Ely, for which the people of the city made her their patron saint.

The fair by which they honoured their benefactress was originally noted for its jewellery and fine silk scarves. These came to be known as *St Audrey's laces.* In time, however, the quality scarves were superseded by cheap, gaudy imitations, since when tawdry—from (S)*t Audrey*('s laces)—has become a pejorative term applied to things that are cheap and tasteless.

At a time when new words and phrases were passed on orally, it was very easy for a final consonant to be mistakenly attached to a following word. The resultant initial t continues to obscure the word's origin, as does the modern-day regularization of the word's spelling by the dropping of the e.

the book from my grasp. **3** make (a hole or opening in) by tearing: Its claws tore holes in his sleeve. **4** be easily torn: The advantage of this fabric is it won't tear. **5** rush or hurry. **tearaway** *n* (*informal*) a wild or reckless young person. < Old English *teran*.

tease (ti:z) *vb* **1** annoy or irritate by constantly provoking: 'Stop teasing the cat!' **2** make fun of in a playful manner: Don't worry. I'm only teasing.' **3** raise the nap on (cloth). **4** disentangle by carding or combing. **teaser** *n* **1** a difficult problem. **2** a person who enjoys teasing. < Old English *tǣsan*.

teat (ti:t) *n* **1** a nipple. **2** something resembling this, esp. the rubber mouthpiece of a baby's feeding bottle. < of Germanic origin.

technical (ˈtɛknɪkḷ) *adj* **1** of or connected with industrial or applied sciences: a technical college. **2** of a particular subject: technical terms. **3** containing many specialist terms: The book is far too technical for beginners. **4** as defined by a particular law or rule: McGuire suffered a technical knock-out in the second round. **5** of or displaying technique. **technically** *adv* **technicality** *n* **1** a technical term, detail, etc., esp. a minor point made significant through strict interpretation or application of a law or rule: disqualified on a technicality. **2** the state of being technical. **technician** *n* **1** an expert in the practical aspects of a particular technical field. **2** a highly skilled, scientific or industrial worker. < Greek *technikos* skilful. SEE PANEL.

technique (tɛkˈni:k) *n* **1** a particular method of doing something, esp. in an art, science, or profession. **2** a body of (established) technical methods: The painting showed a complete lack of technique. < Greek *technikos* skilful.

technology (tɛkˈnɒlədʒɪ) *n* **1** (the study of) the practical applications of science to industry and commerce. **2** the sum total of the knowledge and skills available to a society. **technological** *adj* **technologically** *adv* **technologist** *n* an expert in technology. < Greek *technologia* systematic treatment, from *technē* art + *logos* word. SEE PANEL AT TECHNICAL.

teddy-bear (ˈtɛdɪˌbɛə) *n* a stuffed toy bear. SEE PANEL.

tedious (ˈti:dɪəs) *adj* tiresome or boring, esp. because of length: a tedious speech. **tediously** *adv* **tediousness** *n* **tedium** *n* tediousness. < Latin *taedium*, from *taedēre* to weary.

tee (ti:) *n* **1** a cleared, level area from which a golfer strikes the ball at the beginning of each hole. **2** a small peg or mound of sand on which a golf ball is placed at the beginning of each hole. • *vb* **teed; teeing** place (a golf ball) on a tee. **tee off 1** strike the ball from the tee. **2** (*informal*) begin. < back formation from obsolete *teaz*.

teem[1] (ti:m) *vb* **1** be full of: The river is teeming with salmon. **2** be present in large quantities. < Old English *tīman*.

teddy-bear

The teddy-bear, the most popular cuddly toy yet to enter the nursery, is an American import. It takes its name from Theodore (*'Teddy'*) Roosevelt, 1858–1919, the 26th President of the United States. Following a longstanding American tradition, Roosevelt was rather partial to the hunting of bears. In the course of one of his hunting expeditions the off-duty president apparently stumbled upon a young bear cub. Obviously unimpressed by the animal's trophy potential, he spared its life. The press were quick to lay hands on the story and it also featured in a number of cartoons. Not long afterwards, born of opportunism, the first generation of teddy-bears found their way into children's hearts.

technical or technological?

It is not always easy to distinguish these words. Technical means 'in the strict, formal interpretation': a *technical* advantage, and 'having or concerned with specialized, practical knowledge, especially of a mechanical or scientific subject': *technical* skills, *technical* training, a *technical* college. This second meaning overlaps with the meaning of technological: 'associated with the application of science to industry and commerce': *technological* advances brought about by space-research programmes; western countries' *technological* progress.

teem[2] *vb* (of rain, water, etc.) fall in a torrent; pour. < Old Norse *tæma.*

teens (ti:nz) *pl n* the years 13 to 19 in a person's lifetime. **teenage** *adj* of or being people in their teens. **teenaged** *adj* teenage. **teenager** *n* a person in his or her teens. < *-teen.*

teeny (ˈti:nɪ) *adj* (*informal*) tiny. **teeny-weeny** *adj* (*informal*) very tiny. < *tiny.* SEE PANEL.

tee-shirt (ˈti:ˌʃɜ:t) *n* a T-shirt.

teeter (ˈti:tə) *vb* stand or move unsteadily as if about to fall. < Middle English *titeren* to totter.

teeth (ti:θ) SEE TOOTH.

teethe (ti:ð) *vb* develop teeth. **teething** *n* **teething troubles** minor, temporary problems arising during something's initial stages. < back formation from *teething.*

teetotal (ti:ˈtəʊtl̩) *adj* abstaining completely from alcoholic drinks. **teetotaller** *n* SEE PANEL.

telecommunications (ˌtɛlɪkəˌmju:nɪˈkeɪʃənz) *pl n* the (science or means of) sending of messages by cable, telegraph, telephone, etc.

telegram (ˈtɛlɪˌgræm) *n* a message sent by telegraph and delivered in a written form.

telegraph (ˈtɛlɪˌgrɑ:f) *n* an apparatus or system for transmitting messages, esp. by sending electrical impulses along a wire.
• *vb* send (a message) or communicate by telegraph. **telegrapher** *n* a telegraph operator. **telegraphic** *adj* **1** of the telegraph. **2** void of unnecessary words. **telegraphist** *n* a telegrapher. **telegraphy** *n* the use or operation of a telegraphic apparatus or system. < ultimately Greek *tēle-* far off + *graphein* to write.

telekinesis (ˌtɛlɪkɪˈni:sɪs) *n* the movement of objects without physical means. < ultimately Greek *tēle-* far off + *kinēsis* motion.

telepathy (tɪˈlɛpəθɪ) *n* communication between minds without the use of writing, speaking, or any other known method. **telepathic** *adj* **telepathist** *n*

telephone (ˈtɛlɪˌfəʊn) *n* **1** an electrical device for speaking and listening to someone at a distance. **2** the communication system that uses this.
• *vb* **1** (attempt to) speak to (someone) by telephone. **2** send (a message) by telephone. **telephonic** *adj* **telephony** *n* **telephone box** a booth housing a public telephone. **telephone directory** a book listing the telephone numbers of subscribers. **telephonist** *n* a person who operates a telephone switchboard. < ultimately Greek *tēle-* far off + *-phōnē* sound.

telephoto (ˈtɛlɪˌfəʊtəʊ) *adj* of or being a type of lens which produces a large image of a distant object: a telephoto lens.

teleprinter (ˈtɛlɪˌprɪntə) *n* a device resembling a typewriter used for sending and receiving messages by telegraph.

telescope (ˈtɛlɪˌskəʊp) *n* an optical instrument with the shape of a long tube that is used for viewing distant objects.
• *vb* **1** slide one part within another in the manner of a telescope. **2** make or become condensed, compressed, or

a teeny sound

Generally, speech sounds do not have a meaning unless grouped into recognizable words or parts of words. (See panel at **buzz.**) Some sounds, however, seem to be symbolic of the meaning that they represent. Vowels made with the tongue in a high position and towards the front of the mouth, such as the ee sound in teeny, wee, and weeny provide an example. In various languages as well as English, this sound is sometimes equated with the sense of 'smallness'.

teetotal

To abstain completely from alcoholic drinks is to be teetotal. The origin of this word has been traced to a certain Richard Turner of Preston in Lancashire. However, there are two somewhat differing schools of thought as to how it was coined. Turner, it seems, was a strong advocate of total abstinence from alcohol and in 1833 he was airing his views at a public meeting. One theory has it that the poor fellow was plagued by a stutter and that teetotal evolved from a mimicking of the way in which he called for *'t-t-t-total* abstinence'. The more widely accepted explanation casts Turner as a more controlled speaker who, to give maximum emphasis to the word total, spelt out its first letter. His call was for *tee* (for) *total* abstinence.

shorter. **telescopic** *adj* **1** of, connected with, or being a telescope. **2** consisting of parts which can be slid one within another. < Greek *tēleskopos,* from *tēle-* far off + *skopos* watcher.

teletext (ˈtɛlɪˌtɛkst) *n* a computerized service providing pages of information on the screens of suitably adapted television sets. < Greek *tēle-* tele- + English *text.*

television (ˈtɛlɪˌvɪʒən) *n* **1** an electronic system of transmitting and reproducing sound-accompanied images. **2** also **television set** an electronic apparatus for receiving these. **3** television considered as a medium of communication: The headmaster is all for television in the classroom. **televise** *vb* transmit by television. < *tele-* + *vision.* SEE PANEL.

telex (ˈtɛlɛks) *n* **1** a system of sending and receiving messages by means of teleprinters. **2** a teleprinter used in this system. **3** a message sent or received by telex. • *vb* communicate (something or with someone) by means of this system. < *tel*eprinter + *ex*change.

tell (tɛl) *vb* **told; telling 1** inform: Can you tell me where the station is? **2** relate or narrate: She told me the whole story. **3** order or command: The children were told to keep quiet. **4** utter: He's always telling lies. **5** distinguish or discriminate: I can't tell the difference. **6** decide or ascertain: How can one tell which machine will last longer? **7** disclose a secret: 'Dad told me not to tell.' **8** be significant or decisive: What will tell in the long run is if the team starts winning. **9** (*informal*) used to give emphasis: She simply refuses to eat, I tell you. **teller** *n* **1** a person who relates; narrator: a story-teller. **2** a person who counts. **3** a bank cashier. **telling** *adj* having a marked effect: a telling argument. **tellingly** *adv* < Old English *tellan.* SEE PANEL.

tell-tale (ˈtɛlˌteɪl) *n* **1** a person who tells tales. **2** a monitoring device. • *adj* that provides a clue or suggestion about something; revealing: There was a certain tell-tale look on his face.

temerity (tɪˈmɛrɪtɪ) *n* cheek or audacity. < ultimately Latin *temere* at random.

temp (tɛmp) *n* (*informal*) a person employed on a temporary basis. • *vb* (*informal*) work on this basis. < short for *temporary.*

temper (ˈtɛmpə) *n* **1** a disposition or state of mind: an even temper. **2** a tendency to become wild or violent when angry: He has a terrible temper. **3** a state of anger: Don't get in a temper. **4** composure, esp. despite provocation: keep one's temper. **5** the state of a metal or other substance with regard to certain qualities. • *vb* **1** bring (steel, etc.) to the desired degree of hardness. **2** bring (clay, etc.) to a desired state by adding liquid and mixing. **3** moderate or make less severe: justice tempered with mercy. **tempered** *adj* < Old English *temprian.*

temperament (ˈtɛmpərəmənt) *n* a

Television came first!

Most new words are formed by adding a word or word segment to an existing word. From *cook,* for example, we get cookbook and cookery. However, this is not always the case. Sometimes the reverse process of 'subtracting' occurs, which goes by the name of *back formation.* Peddle, for example, derives from *peddler,* edit from *editor,* teethe from *teething,* and televise from *television.* In the past many cases of back formation have arisen as a result of false assumptions about a word's composition. For example, a noun ending in -er or -or outwardly seems to be composed of an existing verb and an agentive or 'doer' suffix. Peddler and editor were mistakenly viewed in this way as derivatives of peddle and edit, which then came into use even though before this false analysis they had never existed.

You're telling me!

Tell features in a number of idiomatic expressions, including:

tell off to reprimand or scold (someone).
tell on 1 to reveal the activities of (someone) to another person; inform on: Don't tell on me! **2** to have an adverse effect on: All this anxiety about Jim is beginning to tell on her.
tell tales to make certain facts known, especially in order to get someone into trouble; inform on someone.
tell the time to say what time it is by looking at a clock, etc.
you're telling me used to show emphatic agreement: 'It seems to have turned a lot colder today.'—'You're telling me!'

person's nature or disposition: a nervous temperament. **temperamental** *adj* **1** prone to sudden changes of mood. **2** of, in, or resulting from a person's temperament. **temperamentally** *adv* < ultimately Latin *temperare* to mix.

temperance (ˈtɛmpərəns) *n* **1** moderation or self-restraint, esp. in eating, drinking, etc. **2** total abstinence from alcoholic drinks. < ultimately Latin *temperare* to regulate.

temperate (ˈtɛmpərət) *adj* **1** moderate or mild: a temperate climate. **2** having a temperate climate: temperate zones. **3** displaying temperance. **temperately** *adv* **temperateness** *n* < SEE TEMPERANCE.

temperature (ˈtɛmprətʃə, ˈtɛmpərətʃə) *n* **1** the level of heat in a body, object, fluid, etc., esp. as measured by a thermometer. **2** an abnormally high level of body heat: He's in bed with a temperature. < SEE TEMPERANCE.

tempest (ˈtɛmpɪst) *n* a violent storm with strong winds. **tempestuous** *adj* **1** stormy. **2** violently emotional: a tempestuous debate. **tempestuously** *adv* **tempestuousness** *n* < Latin *tempus* time.

template, templet (ˈtɛmplɪt) *n* a pattern or gauge of wood, metal, etc., used as a guide in cutting or shaping. < origin uncertain.

temple[1] (ˈtɛmpl̩) *n* a building used for worship of a deity or deities. < Old English *tempel.*

temple[2] *n* either of the two flat areas on either side of the forehead. < ultimately Latin *tempora* temples.

tempo (ˈtɛmpəʊ) *n, pl* **tempos, tempi** speed or pace, esp. the speed at which a piece of music is played. < Italian, from Latin *tempus* time.

temporal (ˈtɛmpərəl) *adj* **1** of earthly or secular as opposed to spiritual affairs. **2** of or connected with time or tense. **temporally** *adv* < ultimately Latin *tempus* time.

temporary (ˈtɛmprərɪ, ˈtɛmpərərɪ) *adj* of limited duration.
• *n* a temp. **temporarily** *adv* **temporariness** *n* < SEE TEMPORAL.

temporize (ˈtɛmpəˌraɪz) *vb* **1** be vague or act evasively in order to gain time. **2** compromise temporarily. **temporization** *n* **temporizer** *n* < SEE TEMPORAL.

tempt (tɛmpt) *vb* **1** entice or try to persuade, esp. to do something unwise: His boss tempted him to stay with offers of promotion. **2** attract or allure: The smell of the curry tempted us inside. **3** provoke or put to the test: You'd be silly to tempt fate. **temptation** *n* **1** tempting or being tempted. **2** something that tempts. **tempter** fem. **temptress** *n* **tempting** *adj* attractive or alluring: a tempting offer. < ultimately Latin *temptare.*

ten (tɛn) *determiner, pron* 10 in number.
• *n* the number 10. **tenfold** *adj, adv* ten times as much or as many. **tenner** *n* (*informal*) a ten-pound note. < Old English *tīen.*

tenable (ˈtɛnəbl̩) *adj* **1** (of a theory, stance, etc.) able to be defended. **2** (of an office, position, etc.) able to be held: The post is tenable for two years. **tenability** or **tenableness** *n* **tenably** *adv* < ultimately Latin *tenēre* to hold.

tenacious (tɪˈneɪʃəs) *adj* **1** maintaining a firm hold: a tenacious grasp of first principles. **2** obstinate or stubborn. **3** retentive: a tenacious memory. **4** sticking or clinging firmly to something. **tenaciously** *adv* **tenaciousness** *n* **tenacity** *n* < SEE TENABLE.

tenant (ˈtɛnənt) *n* **1** a person who rents property or land from a landlord. **2** an occupant. **tenancy** *n* **tenantry** *n* tenants considered collectively. < Middle French *tenir* to hold.

tench (tɛntʃ) *n* a freshwater fish of the carp family. < ultimately Late Latin *tinca.*

tend[1] (tɛnd) *vb* take care of; look after. < Middle English *attenden.*

tend[2] *vb* **1** be inclined to; have a tendency: I tend to agree with you. **2** move, proceed, drift, etc., in a certain direction: Building societies are tending towards higher interest rates. **tendency** *n* **1** an inclination or predisposition. **2** a drift or trend. < ultimately Latin *tendere* to stretch.

tendentious (tɛnˈdɛnʃəs) *adj* (*often derogatory*) marked by an intentional slant or bias. **tendentiously** *adv* **tendentiousness** *n* < *tendency.*

tender[1] (ˈtɛndə) *adj* **1** not tough or hard; easily cut or chewed. **2** susceptible to damage or influences; delicate. **3** painful to touch; sensitive. **4** gentle or affectionate: a tender smile. **tenderly** *adv* **tenderness** *n* **tenderfoot** *n* a novice or newcomer. **tenderize** *vb* make more tender. **tenderizer** *n* < ultimately Latin *tener.*

tender[2] *vb* **1** offer formally for acceptance: tender one's resignation. **2** make a tender.
• *n* a formal offer to supply goods or do a job of work at a stated price. **legal tender** currency that may legally be offered in payment and that has to be accepted. < Middle French *tendre* to offer.

tender[3] *n* **1** a person who looks after something: a bartender. **2** a small boat or ship which carries provisions, freight, mail, etc., to a larger one. **3** a vehicle attached to the rear of a locomotive, carrying fuel and water. < *tend*[1] + *-er*.

tendon (ˈtɛndən) *n* a tough cord of tissue connecting a muscle to a bone, etc. < Latin *tendere* to stretch.

tendril (ˈtɛndrɪl) *n* a slender, coiling filament by which a plant attaches itself to a support. < origin uncertain.

tenement (ˈtɛnəmənt) *n* **1** a large building divided into flats. **2** a rented flat or room. **3** land or property rented by a tenant. < ultimately Latin *tenēre* to hold.

tenet (ˈtɛnɪt) *n* a firm belief or principle, esp. one held by the members of a group. < SEE **TENEMENT.**

tennis (ˈtɛnɪs) *n* **1** also **lawn tennis** a ball-game for two or four people played on an enclosed court divided by a net over which a ball is hit back and forth. **2** real tennis. < probably Anglo-French *tenetz!* receive!, from *tenir* to hold. SEE PANEL.

tenon (ˈtɛnən) *n* the shaped end of a piece of wood that fits into a mortise in another piece. < Old French *tenir* to hold.

tenor (ˈtɛnə) *n* **1** (a man with) a singing voice between alto and baritone; part that is written for such a voice. **2** a musical instrument whose range of pitch is slightly lower than alto. **3** the general meaning of something. **4** a course, direction, or drift. < ultimately Latin *tenēre* to hold.

tenpin bowling an indoor game similar to ninepins in which a heavy ball is rolled at 10 skittles.

tense[1] (tɛns) *n* (any of) a set of verb forms expressing time distinctions. < ultimately Latin *tempus* time.

tense[2] *adj* **1** tightly stretched; taut. **2** displaying or causing nervous tension: She's always tense before an examination.
● *vb* make or become tense. **tensely** *adv* **tenseness** *n* **tensile** *adj* **1** able to be stretched. **2** of or connected with tension. **tension** *n* **1** (the degree of) stretching or being stretched: Many players like to increase the tension of their racket strings. **2** nervous strain or mental pressure: Too much tension isn't good for you. **3** a situation of strained relations: increased tension in the Middle East. **4** voltage; electrical potential: high-tension cables. < ultimately Latin *tendere* to stretch.

tent (tɛnt) *n* a light, collapsible shelter used esp. for camping. < SEE **TENSE**[2].

tentacle (ˈtɛntəkl̩) *n* a long, arm-like projection used by a snail, octopus, etc., for feeling or grasping. < Latin *tentare* to touch.

tentative (ˈtɛntətɪv) *adj* **1** not permanent or definite; provisional: a tentative arrangement. **2** made, put forward, etc., guardedly or hesitantly and without conviction: a tentative suggestion. **tentatively** *adv* **tentativeness** *n* < SEE **TENTACLE.**

tenterhook (ˈtɛntəˌhʊk) *n* one of many small, sharp hooks used for attaching cloth to a drying and stretching frame during its manufacture. **on tenterhooks** in a state of anxious suspense. SEE PANEL.

tenth (tɛnθ) *determiner, pron, adv* next after ninth.
● *n* **1** one of ten equal parts. **2** something that is tenth. **tenthly** *adv* < Old English *tēotha.*

tennis

Few games could seem more typically English in character than tennis. Originally, however, tennis was not an English game at all—its prototype was played in ancient Greece. The version of the game that finally arrived in Britain came from France, as the name tennis reveals. This is believed to derive from the Anglo-French *tenetz*, an imperative form of *tenir* 'to hold or receive', which was shouted out by the server before each service. The closest translation of this in modern English would be something like 'Catch hold of this!'

on tenterhooks

Someone in a state of anxious suspense is said to be on tenterhooks. The phrase derives from a process formerly used in the manufacture of cloth, whereby newly made material was dried and stretched on long tenterframes. The cloth was attached to these frames by means of small, sharp hooks known as *tenterhooks*. To be on tenterhooks, therefore, is literally 'to be stretched', which is also the underlying meaning of on the rack.

tenuous (ˈtɛnjʊəs) *adj* **1** thin or delicate: a tenuous silk thread. **2** weak or flimsy: a tenuous grasp of realities. **tenuously** *adv* **tenuousness or tenuity** *n* < Latin *tenuis*.

tenure (ˈtɛnjə) *n* **1** the holding of land, property, or office; right to do this: They can't sack you once you've been given tenure. **2** the period during which an office is held. < ultimately Latin *tenēre* to hold.

tepee (ˈtiːpiː) *n* a wigwam. < Dakota *tipi*, from *ti* to dwell + *pi* to use for.

tepid (ˈtɛpɪd) *adj* (of water, etc.) moderately warm; lukewarm. **tepidly** *adv* **tepidness** or **tepidity** *n* < Latin *tepēre* to be moderately warm.

term (tɜːm) *n* **1** the period during which something lasts: a term of office. **2** the end or completion of this. **3** one of the periods of the year when instruction is given at schools, universities, etc., or when law-courts are in session. **4** a word or phrase with a specific meaning.
• *vb* refer to by means of a particular word or phrase. **terms** *pl n* **1** the conditions of an agreement, contract, etc.: The union leaders are seeking better terms. **2** fixed rates or charges. **3** a relationship between people: on good terms. **4** language considered in terms of the user's attitude: She spoke in rather angry terms. **come to terms** reach an acceptance or understanding. **in terms of** with regard to. < ultimately Latin *terminus* end.

terminal (ˈtɜːmɪnḷ) *adj* **1** of, connected with, or occurring at the end of something. **2** (undergoing the stage) ending in or leading to death: a terminal disease.
• *n* **1** a building at an airport used for passengers who are arriving or departing. **2** a building in a city where airline passengers may gather for transportation to an airport. **3** a terminus. **4** a device on a piece of electrical equipment by means of which power leaves or enters. **5** an instrument through which a user can communicate with a computer. **6** a terminating point or part. **terminally** *adv* **terminate** *vb* bring or come to an end. **termination** *n* **terminus** *n* an end or finishing point, esp. either of the ends of a bus route, railway line, etc. < Latin *terminus* end.

terminology (ˌtɜːmɪˈnɒlədʒɪ) *n* the technical words and phrases used in a particular discipline, profession, etc. **terminological** *adj* **terminologically** *adv* < SEE **TERM.**

termite (ˈtɜːmaɪt) *n* a tropical, wood-eating insect; white ant. < Latin *tarmes* woodworm.

tern (tɜːn) *n* a sea-bird resembling a gull, mostly white with a black cap and often with a forked tail. < Scandinavian.

terrace (ˈtɛrɪs) *n* **1** (one of several) level banks cut into a hillside like large steps to facilitate its cultivation. **2** the tiers of steps around a sports ground on which spectators stand. **3** a row of identical houses connected to each other by means of party walls; street in which these houses are situated. **4** a paved area adjoining a building, often forming part of a garden.
• *vb* make into a terrace. **terrace-house** *n* a house forming part of a terrace. < ultimately Latin *terra* earth.

terracotta (ˌtɛrəˈkɒtə) *n* **1** (statuettes, vases, etc., made from) a reddish-brown clay. **2** reddish-brown. < Italian *terra cotta* baked earth.

terra firma (ˌtɛrə ˈfɜːmə) dry land or solid ground. < New Latin: solid land.

terrain (ˈtɛreɪn) *n* a tract of land considered in terms of its physical features. < ultimately Latin *terra* earth.

terrapin (ˈtɛrəpɪn) *n* any of several edible, North American, freshwater reptiles resembling the tortoise. < Algonquian.

terrestrial (təˈrɛstrɪəl) *adj* **1** of the earth or land. **2** living on land as opposed to in water, etc. **3** worldly or mundane.
• *n* an inhabitant of the earth. **terrestrially** *adv* < SEE **TERRAIN.**

terrible (ˈtɛrəbḷ) *adj* **1** (*informal*) of very poor quality; very bad: terrible spelling. **2** (*informal*) extraordinarily great, intense, etc.: There's a terrible lot of work to do. **3** (*informal*) used to express strong disapproval; appalling: Can you hear that terrible noise? **4** causing distress or anguish: The surviving victims were a terrible sight. **terribly** *adv* < ultimately Latin *terrēre* to

a terrible liar

The words awful and terrible have a lot in common. Though originally meaning 'inspiring awe' or 'causing fear', their original force has been lost over the centuries and they are now commonly used either as terms of disapproval—an *awful* singer; she dresses *terribly*—or to express a high degree—'That's *awfully* kind of you.' 'I really am most *terribly* sorry.' This can lead to ambiguities. For example, does the man who is said to be 'a *terrible* liar' lie very badly or prolifically?

frighten. SEE PANEL.

terrier (ˈtɛrɪə) *n* (a member of) any of several breeds of small dog: a fox-terrier. < French (*chien*) *terrier* earth dog, ultimately from Latin *terra* earth. SEE PANEL.

terrific (təˈrɪfɪk) *adj* (*informal*) **1** used to express strong approval; excellent: a terrific meal. **2** extraordinarily great, intense, etc.: a terrific bang. **terrifically** *adv* < SEE **TERRIBLE.**

terrify (ˈtɛrɪˌfaɪ) *vb* **terrified; terrifying** fill with terror. **terrified** *adj* **terrifyingly** *adv* < Latin *terrificare.*

territory (ˈtɛrɪˌtərɪ) *n* **1** a region, district, or stretch of land, esp. one dominated by a particular animal or assigned to a particular person or group. **2** land belonging to or under the control of a ruler, state, etc. **3** a part of a country or state with less autonomy than other parts. **4** a protectorate. **5** an area of interest, knowledge, etc. **territorial** *adj* of or belonging to land or territory: territorial rights. **territorial waters** the sea within a certain distance of a country's shores, over which it has jurisdiction. < Latin *territorium* land round a town.

terror (ˈtɛrə) *n* **1** great fear. **2** a person or thing that terrifies. **3** (*informal*) a great nuisance; esp. a child: a little terror. **terrorism** *n* the use of violence and intimidation, esp. for political purposes. **terrorist** *n, adj* **terrorize** *vb* **1** fill with terror. **2** coerce by means of violence or intimidation. **terrorization** *n* **terror-stricken** *adj* overcome by great fear. < ultimately Latin *terrēre* to frighten.

terse (tɜːs) *adj* brief or concise; curt: a terse statement. **tersely** *adv* **terseness** *n* < Latin *tergēre* to wipe off.

tertiary (ˈtɜːʃərɪ) *adj* **1** third in rank, order, etc. **2** of higher education. < Latin *tertiarius* of or containing a third.

test (tɛst) *n* **1** a critical examination, analysis, or evaluation. **2** a means of doing this, such as a set of questions or an analytical procedure. **3** a test match. • *vb* **1** subject to a test: test one's strength. **2** try out: I won't know if it's the right racket until I've tested it. **tester** *n* **test case** a lawsuit or case whose outcome is likely to be used as a precedent. **test drive** a drive in a car for the sake of judging its performance. **test-drive** *vb* take a test drive in. **test match** one of a series of international matches, esp. in cricket. **test pilot** a pilot whose job is to test the performance and tolerance of newly designed aircraft. **test-tube** *n* a narrow, glass tube with one end closed, used in science laboratories. < ultimately Latin *testum* earthen pot.

testament (ˈtɛstəmənt) *n* **1** a will. **2** a proof or tribute: The hospital he founded stands as a testament to his boundless generosity. **Testament** *n* either of the two main divisions of the Bible: the New Testament. < ultimately Latin *testis* witness.

testate (ˈtɛsteɪt) *adj* having made a valid will. **testator** fem. **testatrix** *n* a person who has made a will. < Latin *testari* to make a will.

testicle (ˈtɛstɪkl̩) *n* either of the two sperm-producing, male, reproductive glands. < Latin *testiculus,* from *testis.*

testify (ˈtɛstɪˌfaɪ) *vb* **testified; testifying** **1** give evidence. **2** serve as evidence of. **3** state under oath. < ultimately Latin *testis* witness.

testimonial (ˌtɛstɪˈməʊnɪəl) **1** a written statement that testifies to a person's ability, character, etc.; reference. **2** something done for or given to a person as a token of appreciation for his or her services. • *adj* of or connected with a testimony or testimonial: a testimonial match. < SEE **TESTIFY.**

testimony (ˈtɛstɪmənɪ) *n* **1** a statement or declaration, esp. one made under oath. **2** strong evidence: The endless hours spent training are a testimony of his will to win. < SEE **TESTIFY.**

testis (ˈtɛstɪs) *n, pl* **testes** a testicle. < SEE **TESTICLE.**

testy (ˈtɛstɪ) *adj* irritable or impatient. **testily** *adv* **testiness** *n* < ultimately Old French *teste* head.

tetanus (ˈtɛtənəs) *n* also **lockjaw** a disease of the nervous system caused by the contamination of a wound and

---

terrier

Any of a number of small dogs which dig into the burrow of their prey is known as a terrier. But why? The answer is that terrier derives via the French *chien terrier* ('earth dog') from the Latin word for 'earth' *terra.*

Other words with 'earth' associations for which *terra* provides the root include: terrain, terrestrial, subterranean, (dis)inter, terrace, tureen (an earthen pan), territory, terra firma, and terracotta (baked earth).

---

resulting in the stiffening of certain muscles. < ultimately Greek *tetanos* rigid.

tetchy (ˈtɛtʃɪ) *adj* peevish or easily offended; touchy. < origin uncertain.

tête-à-tête (ˌtɛtɑːˈtɛt) *n* a private conversation between two people.
• *adj, adv* (in) private. < French: head to head.

tether (ˈtɛðə) *n* a rope or chain that restricts the movement of an animal to within a certain range.
• *vb* restrain with (or as if with) a tether.
at the end of one's tether having reached the limit of one's endurance.
< probably Scandinavian. SEE PANEL.

text (tɛkst) *n* **1** the writing in a book, brochure, etc., as opposed to the illustrations: The article contains very little text. **2** the main written matter of a book, etc., as distinct from notes and comments. **3** the actual or original wording of something written. **4** a short extract used as the basis of a sermon, talk, etc. **5** a written work that is prescribed for study: a set text. **6** a series of sentences forming a cohesive passage. **textbook** *n* a book used in the study of a subject. **textual** *adj* of, occurring in, or based on a text. **textually** *adv* < ultimately Latin *texere* to weave.

textile (ˈtɛkstaɪl) *n* **1** a woven or knitted cloth. **2** any yarn, fibre, etc., used in making cloth. < SEE **TEXT**.

texture (ˈtɛkstʃə) *n* **1** the feel of something when it is touched. **2** the structure and appearance of a fabric. **3** the distinctive character or quality of something: The style of her latest book has a very different texture. **textural** *adj* **texturally** *adv* **textured** *adj* < SEE **TEXT**.

Thalidomide (θəˈlɪdəˌmaɪd) *n* a sedative drug that was withdrawn after many women who took it during pregnancy gave birth to deformed children.
< ph*thal*ic acid + *-id-* + *-o-* + *imide*.

than (ðən; *stressed* ðæn) *conj, prep* used in making comparisons: Henry likes her more than I do. < Old English *thanne*.

thank (θæŋk) *vb* **1** express gratitude to. **2** (*informal*) hold responsible: You only have yourself to thank. **thankful** *adj* grateful or relieved: He was thankful that it was all over. **thankfully** *adv* **thankfulness** *n* **thankless** *adj* not likely to win thanks or be appreciated: a thankless task. **thanklessly** *adv* **thanklessness** *n* **thanksgiving** *n* the act of giving thanks, esp. in a prayer to God. **Thanksgiving** *n* also **Thanksgiving Day** a public holiday for expressing gratitude to God that falls on the fourth Thursday of November in the USA and on the second Monday of October in Canada. < Old English *thancian*. SEE PANEL.

that (ðət; *stressed* ðæt) *pron, pl* **those** **1** the thing or idea just mentioned: After that he found he could sleep better. **2** used to refer to something whose identity is understood from the context: Look at that! **3** used contrastively with *this* to distinguish one reference from another: Do you like this one or that? **4** used to introduce a defining relative clause: Is this the man that you met in Vienna?
• *determiner, pl* **those** **1** used before a noun that has previously been mentioned or is understood from the context: I don't care for that new manager at all. **2** used contrastively with *this* to distinguish one reference from another: Do you

at the end of one's tether

At the end of one's tether is an expression that is used of a person who has reached the limit of his or her endurance and is in desperate straits. Interpreted literally, the reference is to an animal which has used up the slack of the tether or rope that holds it and is unable to advance further. However, the word tether has often in the past been used as a metaphor for the hangman's rope. This usage has no doubt added to the intensity of the desperation which at the end of one's tether nowadays conveys.

many thanks

The word thank features in a number of idiomatic expressions, including:

have someone to thank (**for something**) to attribute the responsibility (for a success or failure) to someone: You'll only have yourself to thank if you go and catch a cold.

thank heavens or **goodness** an expression of gratitude or relief: Thank heavens she's home safely. I was worried sick about her!

thanks to on account of; because of the influence, effect, etc., of: Thanks to Smithson's efficiency, not a single file has ever gone missing.

like this book or that one?
• *conj* used to introduce a dependent clause: I do hope that you'll be able to make it.
• *adv* of the extent indicated or previously mentioned: It couldn't have been that big! < Old English *thæt.* SEE PANEL.

thatch (θætʃ) *n* **1** straw, rushes, or other plant material used as a roof-covering. **2** (*often humorous*) the hair on a person's head.
• *vb* cover (a roof) with thatch. **thatcher** *n* < Old English *theccan* to cover.

the house that Jack built or **the house which Jack built?**

Sarah gave John all the chocolates *which* she didn't want. Sarah gave John all the chocolates, *which* were far too rich for her. In the first sentence, which she didn't want is called an *identifying* (or *defining*) *relative clause,* because it identifies which chocolates Sarah gave John (those that she didn't want). In the second sentence which were far too rich for her is called a *non-identifying* (or non-defining) *relative clause,* because, as the name indicates, it does not identify the chocolates; it simply provides additional information about them.

The basic rules on the use of that, which, who, and whom are:

☐ that, which, who, and whom are used in identifying clauses: Is this the book *that* (or *which*) George lent you? The woman *that* (or *who*) came to dinner was her cousin. He's a man *that* (or *whom*) people find they can talk to easily.

☐ which, who, and whom, but *not* that are used in non-identifying clauses: I passed him a £10 note, *which* he immediately put in his wallet. The president, *who* was deposed last year, now resides in London. She appeared more interested in Lady Banbury's husband, *whom* she was regarding with faint amusement.

Note that an identifying clause is not preceded by a comma: The house that my aunt left me in her will has been valued at £100,000. A non-identifying clause is, on the other hand, always preceded by a comma, and, unless it concludes the sentence, is also followed by a comma: Leeds, which is 200 miles north of London, is an interesting city. Then we went to Leeds, which is 200 miles north of London.

thaw (θɔː) *vb* **1** make or become unfrozen; melt. **2** (of weather) become warm enough to melt ice and snow. **3** become less distant or formal in manner.
• *n* a spell of warmer weather that causes ice and snow to thaw. < Old English *thawian.*

the (ðə, ðɪ; *stressed* ðiː) *determiner* **1** used before a noun that has been previously mentioned: The man sat down and lit a cigarette. **2** used before a noun which is specified in the words that follow it: Tell the woman at the desk. **3** used before a singular noun for generic reference: The bee is such a busy little creature. **4** used before certain nouns to show that they are unique: the Houses of Parliament.
• *adv* **1** to that extent: the sooner, the better. **2** beyond all others. < Old English *thē.* SEE PANEL.

theatre (ˈθɪətə) *n* **1** a place where plays, operas, etc., are publicly performed. **2** a large room with tiers of seats where lectures, etc., are given. **3** a scene where important events take place: the theatre of war. **4** an operating-theatre. **5** drama considered as an art medium. **6** the world of actors, playwrights, performing companies, etc. **theatrical** *adj* **1** of or designed for the theatre. **2** exaggerated or artificial. **theatrically** *adv* **theatricals** *pl n* dramatic performances: amateur theatricals. < ultimately Greek *thea* seeing.

The busiest little word!

A language's total stock of words may be divided into two groups, with one as vast as the other is small. In the major group are the many thousands of *content* words—words such as dog, run, garden, see, and cat which, broadly speaking, allow us to name and describe things. The minor group contains the *function* words. These are words like the, and, into, because, of, it, and a which, together with the grammar, provide the means by which *content* words may be arranged in sentences: *The* dog ran *into the* garden *because it* saw *a* cat.

Excluding technical terms, the English language runs to some half a million words. Of these less than a thousand belong to the *function* group and therefore have to work overtime. In order of popularity, the three words most frequently used in written English are the, of, and and.

theft (θɛft) *n* the act of stealing. < Old English *thīefth.*
their (ðɛə) *determiner* **1** of or belonging to them. **2** his, her, or its. **theirs** *possessive pron, pl* **theirs 1** (the one or ones) belonging to or associated with them. **2** his or hers. < Old Norse *theirra.*
them (ðəm; *stressed* ðɛm) *pron* the objective case of *they:* Why not invite them over? **themselves** *pron* the form of *they* and *them* used reflexively or for emphasis: They treated themselves. **be themselves** behave in a normal way. **by themselves 1** without help. **2** alone. < Old English *thǣm.*
theme (θiːm) *n* **1** a topic or central idea, esp. in an essay, lecture, novel, etc, **2** the main melody of a musical composition. < ultimately Greek *tithenai* to place.
then (ðɛn) *adv* **1** at that time: I knew then that the game was up. **2** next in sequence or order; after that: She then left the office. **3** in that case: If he hasn't eaten anything, then he can't be hungry. **4** in addition; besides: And then don't forget there is the heating to pay for.
• *adj* existing, operating, or in office at that time: the then acting Vice-Chancellor.
• *n* that time: from then on. < Old English *thænne.*
thence (ðɛns) *adv* (*chiefly formal*) **1** from that place. **2** for that reason; from that premise. **thenceforth** *adv* (*chiefly formal*) from that time or point on. **thenceforward** *adv* thenceforth. < Old English *thanon.*
theodolite (θɪˈɒdəˌlaɪt) *n* an instrument for measuring horizontal and vertical angles, used in surveying. < New Latin *theodelitus.*
theology (θɪˈɒlədʒɪ) *n* **1** the study of the divine, esp. through the development and doctrines of a particular religion. **2** a branch of this study. **theological** *adj* **theologically** *adv* **theologian** *n* a specialist in theology. < ultimately Greek *theos* god + *logos* word.
theorem (ˈθɪərəm) *n* a proposition or formula that can be shown to be true by reasoning, esp. in mathematics. < ultimately Greek *thea* act of seeing.
theory (ˈθɪərɪ) *n* **1** a logically related set of ideas or propositions used to explain something: the Copernican theory. **2** (the study of) the ideas and principles on which a particular subject is based: The course includes both theory and practice. **3** a belief or conjecture: My theory is that they want us to drop our price. **in theory** in terms of abstract reasoning: The idea sounds good in theory, but I wonder how it will work in practice. **theoretical** *adj* **1** based on or relating to theory. **2** having a basis in theory as opposed to reality or experience: The difference is purely theoretical. **theoretically** *adv* **theorist** *n* a person who theorizes. **theorize** *vb* **1** form a theory or theories. **2** speculate or conjecture. < ultimately Greek *theōrein.*
therapy (ˈθɛrəpɪ) *n* the treatment of physical or mental disorders, esp. without the use of drugs or surgery. **therapeutic** *adj* healing or curative. **therapeutically** *adv* **therapeutics** *n* the science and art of healing or curing. **therapist** *n* a specialist in a branch of therapy. < ultimately Greek *therapeuein.*
there (ðɛə) *adv* **1** in, at, or to that place: Stay there! **2** at a particular point: I'll stop there and read you some more tomorrow. **3** used as the dummy subject of a verb, esp. to make a sentence grammatically complete or so that content words can be appropriately positioned: There was a great alsatian standing in the doorway.
• *adj* used emphatically when indicating: I'd like that one there!
• *interj* used to express satisfaction or annoyance: There, at long last it's ready to fly! **thereabouts** *adv* **1** somewhere near there. **2** in the region of: It must be 7 o'clock or thereabouts. **thereafter** *adv* after that. **thereby** *adv* **1** by that means. **2** in connection with which: thereby hangs a tale. **therefore** *adv* for that reason. **therein** *adv* (*formal*) in that place, matter, respect, etc.: Therein lies the solution. **thereof** *adv* (*formal*) of that or of it. **thereto** *adv*

there is ... or there are ...?

The basic rule is that a verb should agree in number with its subject: if the subject is grammatically singular, a singular verb is used: There *is* a cat in the garden. If the subject is plural, a plural verb is used: There *are* two cats in the garden.

A singular verb is also used where the subject is thought of as singular, even though it is grammatically plural:

☐ **when referring to a single entity:** There *is* £10 extra to pay.

☐ **when two or more nouns are considered as a single entity:** There is roast beef and Yorkshire pudding for dinner.

(*formal*) to that or to it. **thereupon** *adv* **1** immediately after that; as a consequence of that. **2** (*formal*) on that matter. < Old English *thǣr.* SEE PANEL. SEE PANEL AT **HERE.**

therm (θɜːm) *n* a unit of heat equal to 100 000 British thermal units.

thermal (ˈθɜːməl) *adj* **1** of or connected with heat. **2** designed to insulate the body: thermal underwear.
• *n* a rising current of warm air.
< Greek *thermē* heat.

thermodynamics (ˌθɜːməʊdaɪˈnæmɪks) *n* the branch of physics dealing with how different forms of energy are related, esp. with how one form is converted to another. **thermodynamic** *adj* **thermodynamically** *adv*

thermometer (θəˈmɒmɪtə) *n* an instrument used for measuring temperature. < ultimately Greek *thermē* heat + *metron* measure.

Thermos (ˈθɜːməs) *n* (*Trademark*) a type of vacuum flask.

thermostat (ˈθɜːməˌstæt) *n* a device that regulates the temperature of something by automatically terminating or restoring the heating or cooling source. **thermostatic** *adj* **thermostatically** *adv*

thesaurus (θɪˈsɔːrəs) *n, pl* **thesauri, thesauruses 1** a reference book containing groups of words of similar meaning arranged in a systematic way. **2** a dictionary of words drawn from a specific field or discipline. < ultimately Greek *thēsauros* treasure.

these (ðiːz) SEE **THIS.**

thesis (θiːsɪs) *n, pl* **theses 1** a proposition or theory put forward and supported by argument. **2** a long essay or dissertation, esp. one submitted for or as part of a university degree. < ultimately Greek *tithenai* to put down.

they (ðeɪ) *pron* **1** the people, things, or group mentioned. **2** people in general: They say every cloud has a silver lining. **3** the authorities: Are they really going to restore the death penalty? **4** he or she: If anyone knows the answer will they tell me? < Old Norse *their.* SEE PANEL. SEE PANEL AT **HE.**

thick (θɪk) *adj* **1** not thin or slender: a thick slice of cake. **2** made of thick material: a thick blanket. **3** of a specified thickness: The pile of the carpet was an inch thick. **4** closely grouped or packed; dense: a thick head of hair. **5** densely coated with; full of: The ground was thick with snow. **6** having a syrupy consistency; viscous: thick soup. **7** pronounced or noticeable: a thick accent. **8** (*informal*) stupid. **9** (*informal*) on intimate terms; friendly. **10** (*informal*) unreasonable; uncalled for: I'd say that being shot at while on holiday is a bit thick.
• *adv* thickly.
• *n* **1** the most active or intense part: Right in the thick of the debate the microphones stopped working. **2** the thicker part of something. **thickly** *adv* **thickness** *n* **thicken** *vb* make or become thick or thicker. **thickening** *n* an additive used to thicken. **thick-headed** *adj* stupid. **thickset** *adj* **1** heavily built; stocky. **2** placed or growing close together. **thick-skinned** *adj* not easily hurt by criticism, etc. < Old English *thicce.*

thicket (ˈθɪkɪt) *n* a group of shrubs and trees growing close together. < Old English *thiccet,* from *thicce* thick.

thief (θiːf) *n, pl* **thieves** a person who steals. **thievery** *n* **thievish** *adj* **thieve** *vb* steal. < Old English *thēof.*

thigh (θaɪ) *n* the part of the leg between the knee and the hip. < Old English *theōh.*

thimble (ˈθɪmbl̩) *n* a small, protective cap worn on the end of the finger in sewing. **thimbleful** *n* (of a liquid) a very small quantity. < ultimately Old English *thūma* thumb.

thin (θɪn) *adj* **thinner; thinnest 1** of little

---

they

A *pronoun* is commonly defined as a word which acts as a substitute for a noun or noun phrase (a group of words with the grammatical function of a noun). In practical terms, this means that a pronoun allows a speaker or writer to avoid unwanted repetition. Without this facility, sentences would be cluttered with redundant content words and decoding would take considerably longer: 'The chairman told the members of the committee that if the members of the committee needed more time, the chairman was willing to give the members of the committee more time.' (The chairman told the members of the committee that if *they* needed more time, he was willing to give *it* to *them.*)

On whether to use they or he or he or she in such sentences as Anyone can learn a foreign language if ______want(s) to, see panel at **he.**

---

distance between opposite surfaces; narrow. **2** made of thin material. **3** slightly built; slender. **4** loosely grouped or spaced; sparse: a thin population. **5** lacking density, intensity, substance, etc.: thin colours. **6** having a watery consistency. **7** (*informal*) poor or feeble: That's a pretty thin excuse!
• *adv* thinly.
• *vb* **thinned; thinning** make or become thin or thinner: She wants her hair thinning. **thinly** *adv* **thinness** *n* **thinner** *n* a liquid used for thinning paint, varnish, etc. < Old English *thynne*. SEE PANEL.

thing (θɪŋ) *n* **1** an object as opposed to something with life. **2** an event, business, or affair: What a terrible thing to happen! **3** something done or said: You shouldn't say such things. **4** something which cannot readily be named: Isn't life a wonderful thing? **5** (*often derogatory*) a creature: That thing behind the counter wouldn't give me my money back. **things** *pl n* **1** possessions: Get your things together. **2** tools or equipment: The plumber's arrived without his things. **3** matters or circumstances: Things are getting worse. < Old English. SEE PANEL.

thingumajig (ˈθɪŋəməˌdʒɪg) *n* also **thingummy, thingumabob** (*informal*) a person or thing that cannot readily be named. < *thing*.

think (θɪŋk) *vb* **thought; thinking 1** form ideas in the mind: Be quiet, will you. I'm trying to think. **2** have as an opinion, judgment, or belief: Arthur still thinks the earth is flat. **3** consider: She's thinking of selling the house. **4** remember or recall: Try to think where you left it. **5** conjure up (a picture in the mind): Just think how happy she will be if you accept. **6** anticipate or expect: We didn't think the weather would be this bad!
• *n* (*informal*) the act of thinking: Have a think about it. **thinker** *n* **thinking** *n* an opinion or view: What's your thinking on the matter? < Old English *thencan*. SEE PANEL.

third (θɜːd) *determiner, pron, adv* next after second.
• *n* **1** something that is third. **2** one of three equal parts of a thing. **3** the third gear of a motor vehicle. **4** the third level of an honours degree. **thirdly** *adv* **third degree** questioning by means of torture. **third party** a person other than the principals in a case, transaction, etc. **third-rate** *adj* of extremely poor quality. **Third World** the world's underdeveloped nations, esp. those of Africa, Asia, and Latin America. < Old English *thridda*. SEE PANEL.

thirst (θɜːst) *n* **1** the feeling that accom-

through thick and thin

Thin features in a number of idiomatic expressions, including:

as thin as a rake very thin: He looks as thin as a rake after his illness.
the thin end of the wedge the seemingly insignificant precursor of something far more drastic: The speaker warned that cuts in student grants were just the thin end of the wedge.
thin out to make or become less dense or crowded: The crowds gradually thinned out. Overcrowded seedlings should be thinned out.
through thick and thin through both good and bad times: He stuck by her through thick and thin.

just the thing

Thing features in a number of idiomatic expressions, including:
do one's own thing to pursue one's own interests, desires, etc.: They've started the youth club so that the teenagers can do their own thing.
for one thing used to introduce the first of a number of reasons for something: 'Why can't I go out tonight?'—'For one thing, you've been out every evening this week and for another, you're supposed to be revising for your exams.
have a thing about to be obsessed or preoccupied by: No wonder he's got a thing about brushing your teeth after every meal! He is a dentist, after all!
just the thing exactly what is needed: I've got just the thing for a cold—a nice hot lemon drink.
the thing is ... the most important point is: It sounds a great idea, but the thing is I've got no money.
too much of a good thing an unwelcome excess of something pleasant or beneficial: I don't mind staying a day or two over Christmas but staying to see the New Year in might be too much of a good thing.

panies a desire to drink. **2** a strong desire: a thirst for books.
• *vb* **1** feel thirsty. **2** experience a strong desire. **thirsty** *adj* **1** feeling thirst. **2** requiring or consuming a lot of liquid. **3** (*informal*) causing thirst: thirsty weather. **thirstily** *adv* **thirstiness** *n* < Old English *thurst.*

thirteen (ˌθɜːˈtiːn) *determiner, pron, n* the number 13. **thirteenth** *determiner, pron, adv, n* < Old English *thrēotīne.*

thirty (ˈθɜːtɪ) *determiner, n, pron* the number 30. **thirtieth** *determiner, pron, adv, n* **thirties** *pl n* the years, degrees, etc., between 30 and 39: She's in her late thirties. < Old English *thrītig.*

this (ðɪs) *pron, pl* **these 1** the thing or idea just mentioned: This meant he was able to retire. **2** used to refer to something whose identity is understood from the context: Have you seen this? **3** used contrastively with *that* to distinguish one reference from another, esp. to indicate the nearer or more prominent of two items: You can have either this or that.
• *determiner, pl* **these 1** used to refer to a person or thing that is nearby or that has just been mentioned. **2** used contrastively with *that* to distinguish one reference from another, esp. to indicate the nearer or more prominent of two items: Do you like this book or that one?
• *adv* of the extent indicated or obvious from the context: I didn't know it could take this long. < Old English *thes.*

thistle (ˈθɪsl̩) *n* any of a number of wild, prickly plants, usually with a purple flower. < Old English *thistel.*

thong (θɒŋ) *n* a narrow strip of leather or other material, chiefly used for fastening. < Old English *thwong.*

thorax (ˈθɔːræks) *n, pl* **thoraxes, thoraces 1** the part of the body between the neck and abdomen. **2** the chest cavity containing the heart, lungs, etc.

You don't think?

The usual function of not is to negate a verb or phrase which immediately follows it, as in 'My wife doesn't snore' or 'My wife doesn't snore as much as yours'. In a sentence like 'He doesn't think' the function of not remains the same: it negates the following verb, think, (with a somewhat disparaging effect). However, in sentences where think is followed by a clause, such as 'He doesn't think she likes goldfish', the function of not changes dramatically. Although not precedes think, it is not think that is negated. What the sentence means is 'He thinks she does *not* like goldfish'. In sentences like 'He doesn't think she likes goldfish' we find that not is transposed from its logical position. Negation of this type also occurs with other verbs including imagine, suppose, believe, reckon, and guess.

Think features in a number of idiomatic expressions, including:

not think of to refuse to consider: 'I wouldn't think of letting you pay for the meal!'
put on one's thinking-cap to ponder a problem: If plan B fails, we'll all have to put our thinking caps on!'
think again to reconsider one's decision or point of view.
think aloud to express one's thoughts out loud.
think better of to reconsider and decide to abandon (a plan, etc.).
think much of to have a high opinion of.
think nothing of to consider to be unremarkable.
think nothing of it! there is no need to thank me.
think out or **through** to consider carefully.
think over to ponder for a period of time.
think-tank *n* a group of people who give expert advice and new ideas.
think twice to pause and reflect, before taking a decision.
to think that just imagine; how surprising: 'To think that he arrived in this country without a penny to his name—and look at him now!'

third

The ability of language to change is illustrated in the way that sounds or letters in a word sometimes get switched around. In Old English, for example, *thir*d was *thri*dda, similar to the modern German dritte. Similarly, a was*p* went by the name of wæ*ps* before the last two sounds changed places. Such switching is known as *metathesis,* from the Greek word metatithenai, 'to transpose' or 'change places'.

< ultimately Greek *thōrax*.

thorn (θɔːn) *n* **1** a short, sharply-pointed projection on a plant. **2** a shrub or small tree which has thorns. **a thorn in the flesh** a source of constant annoyance or irritation. **thorny** *adj* **1** having thorns. **2** difficult or hard to deal with. < Old English.

thorough (ˈθʌrə) *adj* **1** (of a person) leaving not the slightest thing undone; careful: a thorough worker. **2** done carefully: They made a thorough job of it. **thoroughness** *n* **thoroughbred** *adj, n* (a horse, etc.) of pure stock or with a long pedigree. **thoroughfare** *n* a road, street, or public way: no thoroughfare. **thoroughgoing** *adj* very thorough. **thoroughly** *adv* **1** in a thorough way. **2** absolutely; totally: We were all thoroughly disgusted. < Old English *thuruh*.

those (ðəʊz) SEE **THAT.**

though (ðəʊ) *conj* despite the fact that; although.
• *adv* however. < Scandinavian.

thought[1] (θɔːt) SEE **THINK.**

thought[2] *n* **1** the act or process of thinking. **2** an idea: a sudden thought. **3** consideration: The decision requires a lot more thought. **4** the power of thinking. **5** the ideas of a particular group or period. **6** intention: We had no thought of accepting. **thoughtful** *adj* **1** showing consideration for others: a kind and thoughtful person. **2** showing careful thinking: a thoughtful piece of writing. **3** absorbed in thought: a thoughtful look. **thoughtfully** *adv* **thoughtfulness** *n*

A thousand apologies!

When a person says 'I burst my sides laughing', we don't reply, 'Oh, I am sorry. Which hospital were you taken to?' Within our speech community it is usual to use exaggerations like burst one's sides laughing for the sake of emphasis. This type of exaggeration, more obvious in a phrase like a thousand apologies is called *hyperbole*.

Hyperbole is one of our most common figures of speech, so common in fact that many examples in everyday use have completely lost their rhetorical impact and we tend not to notice them: The meal cost a *fortune* but there was *tons* of food and it took *years* to eat. Neither of us had eaten so much *for ages!*

thoughtless *adj* without forethought or concern for others. **thoughtlessly** *adv* **thoughtlessness** *n* < Old English *thōht*.

thousand (ˈθaʊzənd) *determiner, pron, n, pl* **thousands, thousand 1** the number 1000. **2** a vast number: thousands of applications. **thousandth** *determiner, n, pron, adv* < Old English *thūsend*. SEE PANEL.

thrash (θræʃ) *vb* **1** give repeated blows to, esp. as a punishment. **2** defeat easily. **3** swing, strike, or move violently: The fish wouldn't stop thrashing about. **thrashing** *n* a beating or defeat. **thrash out** discuss thoroughly; resolve or produce by such discussion. < *thresh*. SEE PANEL.

thread (θrɛd) *n* **1** a strand of cotton, wool, etc. **2** something resembling this in length and fineness. **3** the projecting spiral of a screw. **4** the line of reasoning that makes the parts of a talk, paragraph, etc., coherent.
• *vb* **1** pass a thread through (something, esp. the eye of a needle). **2** pass (a tape, film, etc.) into or through something. **3** cut a thread on (a screw), in (a nut, etc.). **4** make (one's way) through or along: She threaded her way through the narrow corridors. **threader** *n* **threadbare** *adj* **1** (of material) having lost its nap through wear. **2** hackneyed. < Old English *thrǣd*.

threat (θrɛt) *n* **1** an expression of intention to injure, punish, etc. **2** a sign of something undesirable or dangerous: a threat of rain. **3** a person, thing, or idea regarded as a source of danger. **threaten** *vb* **1** make a threat or threats against. **2** be a threat to. **3** be a sign or warning of. **4** seem likely to happen. < Old English *thrēat*.

thrash or thresh?

These two words are sometimes confused. Thrash means 'to give repeated blows to': to *thrash* a child and 'to defeat': to *thrash* the opposing team. Thrash is also used in the idiom thrash out 'to discuss thoroughly': They *thrashed out* all the problems involved.

Thresh means 'to beat (the stalks of cereal plants) to extract the grain': The corn is being *threshed*. The spelling thrash is occasionally used for this sense.

three (θriː) *determiner, pron* 3 in number.
• *n* the number 3. **three-dimensional** *adj* **1** having three dimensions. **2** having or appearing to have the dimension of depth. **threefold** *adj, adv* three times as much or as many: a threefold increase. **three-ply** *adj* consisting of three layers or three strands. **three-quarter** *adj* being three quarters of the full length. **the three R's** the fundamental skills of reading, (w)riting, and (a)rithmetic. **threescore** *adj, n* sixty. **threesome** *n* a group of three. < Old English *thrīe.*

thresh (θrɛʃ) *vb* beat (the stalks of cereal plants) to extract the grain; thrash. < Old English *threscan.* SEE PANEL AT THRASH.

threshold (ˈθrɛʃəʊld, ˈθrɛʃhəʊld) *n* **1** a piece of timber, stone, etc., forming the bottom of a doorway. **2** a doorway or entrance. **3** the point at which something begins: on the threshold of a new technological era. **4** the lowest level at which a stimulus can be perceived: a low pain threshold. < Old English *threscwald.*

threw (θruː) SEE THROW.

thrice (θraɪs) *adv* (*archaic*) three times. < Old English *thriga.*

thrift (θrɪft) *n* careful management of resources, esp. money. **thrifty** *adj* practising or embodying thrift. **thriftily** *adv* **thriftiness** *n* < ultimately Old Norse *thrīfask* to thrive.

thrill (θrɪl) *n* (something causing) a sudden feeling of pleasurable excitement.
• *vb* feel or cause to feel a thrill. **thriller** *n* a novel, film, etc., which produces thrills. < ultimately Old English *thurh* through.

thrive (θraɪv) *vb* **thrived, throve; thrived, thriven; thriving 1** grow or develop healthily and vigorously. **2** flourish or prosper; do well. < probably Old Norse *thrīfa* to grasp.

throat (θrəʊt) *n* **1** the front of the neck. **2** the passage in the neck through which food passes. **3** something resembling this. **throaty** *adj* uttered low in the throat; hoarse. **throatily** *adv* < Old English *throte.*

throb (θrɒb) *vb* **throbbed; throbbing 1** beat or pulsate rhythmically, esp. with unusual intensity. **2** pulsate with rhythmic surges of pain.
• *n* a beat or pulse. < probably like the sound.

throes (θrəʊz) *pl n* spasms or convulsions: death throes. **in the throes of** in the process of; struggling to: We're still in the throes of decorating the lounge. < Old English *thrag* time.

thrombosis (θrɒmˈbəʊsɪs) *n, pl* **thromboses** the formation of a clot in a blood-vessel. < ultimately Greek *thrombos* clot.

throne (θrəʊn) *n* **1** the ceremonial chair of a sovereign or bishop. **2** sovereignty. < ultimately Greek *thronos.*

throng (θrɒŋ) *n* a great number of people crowded together.
• *vb* **1** (of people) gather in great numbers. **2** come, go, etc., in a throng. < Old English *thrang.*

throttle (ˈθrɒtl̩) *n* a valve controlling the flow of fuel, etc., to an engine.
• *vb* **1** kill or injure by squeezing the throat. **2** reduce the speed of (an engine) by obstructing the flow of fuel. < Middle English *throte* throat.

through (θruː) *prep* **1** in one side or end and out the other: The train takes two minutes to get through the tunnel. **2** from one side or end to the other. **3** from the beginning to the end of: I slept through the entire performance. **4** on account of; due to: They lost the match through a lack of determination. **5** by means or by way of: She found the job through an agency. **6** between or among the parts of: look through the newspaper for the weather forecast.
• *adv* **1** from one side or end to the other: See if you can squeeze through. **2** from beginning to end; all the way: She slept the whole night through.
• *adj* **1** allowing a continuous journey, esp. without changing trains, etc.: a through train. **2** (of traffic) travelling through a place. **3** finished: I'm through with you! **through and through** in all respects; completely. **throughput** *n* the amount of material put through a process. < Old English *thurh.*

throughout (θruːˈaʊt) *prep* **1** in or to every part of: throughout the countryside. **2** during the whole of: throughout the afternoon.
• *adv* in every part: The house has been painted throughout.

throve (θrəʊv) SEE THRIVE.

throw (θrəʊ) *vb* **threw; thrown; throwing 1** send through the air with force, esp. by a violent movement of the arm. **2** cause to fall to the ground: The jockey was thrown at the first fence. **3** hurl or fling violently: He threw himself to the ground. **4** put abruptly or violently into a certain position, condition, situation, etc.: We were all thrown into confusion. **5** put on or take off hurriedly or casually. **6** make on a potter's wheel. **7** (*informal*) puzzle or disconcert: The question completely threw me.

8 (*informal*) lose deliberately: He was accused of throwing the fight. **9** operate (a switch or lever).

throwing in

Throw features in a number of idiomatic expressions, including:

throw a party to hold a party.
throw away to discard.
throw-away *adj* expressed or done in a casual or nonchalant way: a throw-away remark.
throw-back *n* a person, animal, etc., exhibiting the characteristics of an earlier type.
throw in 1 to include as part of what is being sold. **2** to add (a comment): He's famous for throwing in suggestions that upset everything. **3** to give up or resign from (one's job).
throw in the sponge or **towel** to admit defeat. This idiom comes from the manner in which defeat is conceded in boxing.
throw off 1 to get rid of: I just don't seem to be able to throw off this cold. **2** to succeed in becoming free of: He threw off his pursuers.
throw oneself into to involve oneself vigorously and enthusiastically in: She's certainly thrown herself into her new job.
throw oneself on to entrust oneself utterly to (someone's mercy, etc.).
throw one's weight about or **around** to use one's authority or influence aggressively; act in an overbearing manner.
throw out 1 to discard. **2** to expel. **3** to reject: The committee threw out the proposal. **4** to offer for discussion: The chairman threw out a few provocative ideas for the meeting to talk about. **5** to cause to be inaccurate: The sudden change in the price of oil threw out all their calculations. **6** to disconcert.
throw out the baby with the bathwater to discard something essential and important when getting rid of something unwanted.
throw over to jilt.
throw the book at to bring charges against (someone), especially in an attempt to inflict maximum punishment.
throw together 1 to cause to meet: Fate threw them together in the war. **2** to make or compose in a rough, hurried manner.
throw up 1 to vomit. **2** to build quickly. **3** to give rise to.

• *n* **1** the act of throwing. **2** the distance something is thrown. **thrower** *n* < Old English *thrāwan* to turn. SEE PANEL.

thrush[1] (θrʌʃ) *n* any of a family of songbirds, often with a spotted breast. < Old English *thrysce*.

thrush[2] *n* an infection of the mucous membranes, esp. in the mouth or vagina. < probably Scandinavian.

thrust (θrʌst) *vb* **thrust; thrusting** **1** push forcibly. **2** stab or pierce. • *n* **1** sudden, violent push or lunge. **2** an attack. < Old Norse *thrȳsta*. SEE PANEL.

thud (θʌd) *n* a dull sound caused by something heavy striking or falling onto a hard surface. • *vb* **thudded; thudding** strike or fall with a thud. < Old English *thyddan*.

thug (θʌg) *n* a violent ruffian or criminal.

thrust and parry

Thrust and parry is an idiomatic expression for the patterns of attack and defence or question and answer often encountered in an argument or other confrontation: The audience found the lively *thrust and parry* of the debate difficult to follow. Thrust and parry derives from fencing. In fencing a thrust or sudden forward attacking stroke is met by a parry, a defensive stroke which attempts to turn it aside.

thug

Today's thugs seem relatively harmless when compared with the original holders of the title. Thug came into English in the 19th century from the Hindi *thag*. This name—literally 'thief'—was applied to members of a fanatical religious order in India, comprising worshippers of the Hindu goddess Kali. These devotees practised *thuggee,* the robbery, murder, and burial of travellers performed according to religious ritual. The sect was proscribed and suppressed by the British and well before the end of the 19th century had virtually disappeared.

< Hindi, ultimately from Sanskrit *sthaga* rogue. SEE PANEL.

thumb (θʌm) *n* **1** the short, thick finger set at an angle from the other four. **2** the part of a glove that covers this.
• *vb* **1** turn (pages) with the thumb. **2** soil or wear by thumbing. **thumb-nail** *adj* brief or concise: a thumb-nail sketch. **thumbscrew** *n* **1** (formerly) an instrument of torture for squeezing the thumb. **2** a screw which can be turned by the thumb and forefinger. < Old English *thūma*. SEE PANEL.

thump (θʌmp) *vb* strike, esp. with a dull, heavy sound.
• *n* (the sound made by) a heavy blow. **thumping** *adv* (*informal*) whopping: a thumping great lie. < like the sound.

thunder (ˈθʌndə) *n* **1** the loud noise following a flash of lightning. **2** any similar sound.
• *vb* **1** sound with thunder: It's still thundering. **2** make a sound like thunder, esp. while moving: Lorries thunder past all day. **3** utter loudly and violently. **thundery** *adj* **thunderbolt** *n* **1** a flash of lightning accompanied by thunder. **2** something startling. **thunderclap** *n* a clap of thunder. **thunderous** *adj* like thunder: thunderous applause. **thunderstorm** *n* a storm accompanied by (lightning and) thunder. **thunderstruck** *adj* dumbfounded. < Old English *thunor*. SEE PANEL.

thus (ðʌs) *adv* **1** in this or that manner; in the way indicated. **2** consequently. **thus far** up to now or to this point. < Old English.

thwart (θwɔːt) *vb* prevent (something) from being accomplished; prevent from accomplishing something. < ultimately Old Norse *thverr* transverse.

thyme (taɪm) *n* a small shrub grown for its fragrant leaves and flowers, which are dried and used as a herb in cooking. < Greek *thymon*, from *thyein* to make a burnt offering.

thyroid (ˈθaɪrɔɪd) *adj* of the thyroid gland. **thyroid gland** a large gland in front of the windpipe, secreting hormones that control metabolism and body growth. < ultimately Greek *thyreos* door-shaped shield.

tiara (tɪˈɑːrə) *n* **1** a woman's decorative, usually jewelled, semicircular headband worn on ceremonial occasions. **2** the triple crown worn by the pope. < Latin, from Greek.

tibia (ˈtɪbɪə) *n* the inner, larger of the two bones of the lower part of the leg; shin-bone. < Latin.

tic (tɪk) *n* a spasmodic twitching of certain muscles, esp. of the face. < French.

tick[1] (tɪk) *n* **1** a regularly repeated, light, clicking sound, esp. that of a clock or watch. **2** a mark ✓ esp. used to show

all thumbs

Thumb features in a number of idiomatic expressions, including:

be all thumbs to handle things in a clumsy, awkward manner.
thumb a lift to hitch-hike.
twiddle one's thumbs to do nothing: Don't imagine I'm sitting here all day just twiddling my thumbs while you're at the office!
under someone's thumb completely under a person's control.

To give something the **thumbs up** is to give it one's approval: 'The plan to extend the runway has been given the thumbs up.'
Conversely, to give something the **thumbs down** is to refuse or express one's disapproval of it: The proposal involved exorbitant expenditure and it was given the thumbs down. Both phrases allude to practices used in ancient Rome. When a gladiator had been overcome in combat, spectators would show their desire for his life to be spared by making a thumbs up sign. Vanquished gladiators who were less popular with the crowd received the thumbs down.

steal someone's thunder

When we steal someone's thunder we undermine the anticipated impact of something that he or she is about to say or do. The expression is traceable to a certain John Dennis, 1657–1734, a critic and dramatist who introduced a backstage device for producing thunder effects. While Dennis's play in which the invention was first used was a flop, the thunder sheet proved a great success and theatres were quick to adopt it. This led Dennis to complain that, even though they were uninspired by his plays, they were keen to steal his thunder!

that an item on a list is correct or has been checked, included, etc. **3** (*informal*) a moment: I'll be with you in just a tick! • *vb* **1** (of a clock, etc.) make a series of ticks. **2** place a tick beside (an item). **3** motivate and cause to behave in a particular way: I've never been able to work out what makes her tick. **ticker** *n* (*informal*) **1** a watch. **2** the heart. **tick off 1** reprimand. **2** mark with a tick. **tick over 1** (of an engine) idle. **2** (of activities) run in a steady, routine way. **tick-tock** *n* the ticking of a clock. < Middle English *tek*.

tick[2] *n* any of various small, blood-sucking, parasitic creatures. < Middle English *tyke*.

tick[3] *n* (*informal*) credit: We bought the furniture on tick. < short for *ticket*.

ticket (ˈtɪkɪt) *n* **1** a piece of esp. printed paper, cardboard, etc., showing that the holder has certain rights such as travel on a train or bus, a seat in a theatre, or the use of particular services. **2** an official notification of a traffic offence: a parking ticket. **3** a label or tag: a price ticket **4** (*chiefly US*) a list of candidates for nomination or election. < Middle French *estiquet*, from Middle Dutch *steken* to stick.

tickle (ˈtɪkl̩) *vb* **1** touch or stroke lightly so as to cause laughter, twitching, etc. **2** have a tingling sensation. **3** delight or amuse.
• *n* the act or sensation of tickling. **tickled pink** (*informal*) extremely pleased or amused. **ticklish** *adj* **1** sensitive to tickling. **2** requiring careful handling. **ticklishness** *n* < Middle English *tikelen*.

tiddler (ˈtɪdlə) *n* (*informal*) **1** a small fish such as a minnow that children try to catch. **2** an exceptionally small child or thing. < probably *tiddly*, alteration of *little*.

tiddly (ˈtɪdlɪ) *adj* (*informal*) **1** very small. **2** slightly drunk. < origin unknown.

tiddly-winks (ˈtɪdlɪˌwɪŋks) *n* a game in which players try to flick small, plastic discs into a small container. < probably *tiddly* little.

tide (taɪd) *n* **1** the regular rise and fall of the level of the sea, caused by the gravitational attraction between the earth, sun, and moon. **2** the current of water resulting from this: The tide is going out. **3** a general, widespread movement; something that fluctuates: the rising tide of materialism. **tidal** *adj* of, caused by, or having tides. **tidal wave 1** a huge, destructive wave, esp. one caused by an earthquake. **2** an unexpected, overwhelming, and usually widespread movement or reaction. **tide-mark** *n* **1** a mark left by the highest point of a tide. **2** (*informal*) a mark on the skin showing the limit of washing; mark on a bath showing the level of water. **tide over** help (a person) through a temporary period of difficulty. < Old English *tīd*.

tidings (ˈtaɪdɪŋz) *pl n* (*literary*) news. < Old English *tīdung*.

tidy (ˈtaɪdɪ) *adj* **1** neat and orderly. **2** methodical: a tidy mind. **3** (*informal*) substantial: a tidy sum of money.
• *vb* **tidied; tidying** make (things) tidy.
• *n* a container for odds and ends: a sink tidy. **tidily** *adv* **tidiness** *n* < Middle English: timely, from *tide* time.

tie (taɪ) *vb* **tied; tying 1** attach or fasten with string, cord, etc.; unite. **2** arrange (ribbon, a necktie, etc.) to make (a knot or bow). **3** make (an equal score). **4** restrict or restrain.
• *n* **1** a string, cord, ribbon, etc., used in tying something. **2** a long, narrow piece of material worn round the neck and tied in a knot at the front; necktie. **3** something that unites or restricts; bond or hindrance: family ties. **4** a match between two or a group of competitors: a cup tie. **5** a contest that ends with equal scores between two or more competitors; such equality of scoring. **tie-breaker** *n* a means of choosing a winner from the competitors with equal scores. **tie-clip** *n* an ornamental clip used to hold a tie in place. **tied** *adj* **1** (of a public house) obliged to sell the beer, etc., of the brewery that owns or rents it. **2** owned by an employer and rented to an employee: a tied cottage. **tie-dyeing** *n* a method of producing dyed textiles by tying parts of the fabric together so that they will not absorb the dye. **tie in** link or co-ordinate; be or make compatible; correspond. **tie-pin** *n* a decorative pin used to hold a tie in place. **tie up 1** attach or fasten, with a cord, etc. **2** be compatible; fit together. **3** be or keep busy. **4** invest (money), so that it is unavailable for other purposes. < Old English *tēag*.

tier (tɪə) *n* one of a set of rows, ranks, or levels placed one above the other: a three-tier system of government.
• *vb* arrange in tiers. < Middle French *tire* rank.

tiff (tɪf) *n* a petty quarrel. < origin unknown.

tiger (ˈtaɪgə) *n* a large animal of the cat family with a tawny yellow coat with black stripes. **tigress** *n* a female tiger.

< Greek *tigris,* ultimately of Iranian origin.

tight (taɪt) *adj* **1** fully stretched; taut. **2** close-fitting: tight jeans. **3** difficult to move or undo: a tight knot. **4** fixed in place; firm. **5** with items packed closely together in space or time: a tight schedule. **6** of close or compact structure so as to prevent the passage of water, air, etc.: watertight. **7** difficult: in a tight situation. **8** not yielding; strict. **9** (of money) scarce relative to demand. **10** also **tight-fisted** (*informal*) miserly or mean; stingy. **11** (*informal*) drunk.
• *adv* **1** tightly. **2** soundly: Sleep tight! **tightly** *adv* **tightness** *n* **tighten** *vb* make or become tighter. **tighten up** make regulations, etc., stricter; enforce regulations, etc., more strictly. **tight-lipped** *adj* **1** silent. **2** with the lips held together in anger, etc. **tightrope** *n* a rope or wire on which acrobats perform. **tights** *pl n* a close-fitting, one-piece garment worn over the feet, legs, and lower part of the body. < probably alteration of *thight,* of Scandinavian origin.

tile (taɪl) *n* **1** a thin slab of fired clay used to cover roofs, walls, etc. **2** a thin piece of linoleum, cork, etc., used to cover floors or walls: carpet tiles.
• *vb* cover with tiles. < Old English *tigele.*

till[1] (tɪl) *conj, prep* until. < Old English *til.*

till[2] *vb* work (land) for the raising of crops, by ploughing, etc. < Old English *tilian.*

till[3] *n* **1** a cash register. **2** a container for money in a shop, etc. < Anglo-French *tylle.*

tiller (ˈtɪlə) *n* a bar or handle used to turn the rudder of a boat. < Middle French *telier* beam of a loom, ultimately from Latin *tela* web.

tilt (tɪlt) *vb* **1** slope or cause to slope. **2** attack with a lance in jousting.
• *n* tilting; slope. **at full tilt** at full speed or force. < Middle English *tilten.* SEE PANEL.

timber (ˈtɪmbə) *n* wood, esp. sawn and used for carpentry or woodwork.
• *vb* provide with timbers. **timbered** *adj* having walls with a timber framework. < Old English.

timbre (ˈtɪmbə, ˈtæmbə) *n* the distinctive quality in the sound of a particular musical instrument or voice. < Old French: drum, ultimately from Greek *tympanon.*

time (taɪm) *n* **1** the concept that measures the duration of events and intervals between them; continuous passage of existence. **2** *pl* a period of time marked by particular events, conditions, or experiences: in Victorian times. **3** a period or point of time available or suitable for something: dinner time. **4** an occasion: He was ill the last time I saw him. **5** a point of time expressed in hours and minutes of the day: The time is now 1 o'clock. **6** an experience: Have a good time! **7** measured time spent at work, etc.: a full-time job. **8** one of the standard systems for reckoning time: Greenwich Mean Time. **9** the point of time when something must take place or end: 'Time, gentlemen, please!' **10** *pl* the circumstances or conditions of a period: Times are difficult. **11** (*informal*) a period of imprisonment. **12** tempo; rhythm or metre.
• *vb* **1** arrange the time of; set a time for. **2** measure the time of.
• *adj* **1** of or recording time: a time-clock; time-sheet. **2** able to be set to operate automatically at a particular moment: a time bomb; time-switch. **time-and-motion** *adj* concerned with measuring the efficiency of industrial working methods. **time-consuming** *adj* occupying a lot of time. **time-honoured** *adj* sanctioned by custom: a time-honoured tradition. **timekeeper** *n* **1** a person who records time. **2** a person thought of in respect of punctuality: a good timekeeper. **time-lag** *n* an interval of time between two related events. **timeless** *adj* **1** not affected or

at full tilt

A person or thing that moves along at full speed in a rather reckless or abandoned fashion may be said to be going at full tilt: The runaway lorry came down the hill *at full tilt.* The phrase harks back to days of tilting or jousting and the wielding of the long lance. The further a lance was lowered or 'tilted' from the vertical, the greater the strain on the knight holding it. Therefore it was only when the combatants were virtually on top of each other that the lance was fully lowered or held at full tilt, at which time each knight's mount was going at full gallop.

For the origin of the expression tilt at windmills, see panel at **wind**[1].

changed by time. **2** not limited to a particular time. **3** eternal. **timely** *adj, adv* at an appropriate or opportune time. **timeliness** *n* **timepiece** *n* an instrument that measures time; clock or watch. **timer** *n* a device for measuring time. **times** *prep* multiplied by: 3 times 6 is 18. **time-sharing** *n* **1** simultaneous access to a computer by several users. **2** an arrangement in which many people share the cost of a holiday home by buying shares of the lease, so that each can spend a proportionate amount of time there each year. **time-signal** *n* an indication of the exact time, as on radio or television. **time zone** a geographical region in which a common standard time is used. **timing** *n* the choosing of the best moment to do something; judgment in this. < Old English *tīma.* SEE PANEL.

time and time again

Time features in a number of idiomatic expressions, including:

about time used to express relief when something that is long overdue finally happens: Look, here's the bus—and about time too!
at the same time despite this; nevertheless: But at the same time, it is not certain whether the meeting will in fact take place.
at times now and again.
do time to be in prison as a punishment.
for the time being for the present time, temporarily: He'll have to work in Jack's old office for the time being.
from time to time occasionally; at intervals.
half the time 1 often: I don't know where he is half the time. **2** in a much shorter time than expected.
have no time for to have a low opinion of: I've got no time for such tomfoolery.
in no time very quickly.
in time 1 not too late. **2** eventually: We'll succeed in time.
on time punctual; punctually.
the time of one's life a very enjoyable period; great fun.
time and (**time**) **again** repeatedly: very frequently: I've told him time and time again not to suck his thumb, but he still does it.

timetable (ˈtaɪmˌteɪbl̩) *n* **1** a list showing the times of departure and arrival of public transport vehicles. **2** a list showing an order of events, esp. school lessons; schedule.
• *vb* arrange in a timetable.

timid (ˈtɪmɪd) *adj* lacking courage or boldness; easily frightened. **timidity** *n* **timidly** *adv* < Latin *timēre* to fear.

timorous (ˈtɪmərəs) *adj* timid; hesitating because of fear. **timorously** *adv* **timorousness** *n* < Latin *timēre* to fear.

timpani (ˈtɪmpənɪ) *pl n* a set of kettledrums, **timpanist** *n* < Italian: kettledrums, ultimately Greek *tympanon* drum.

tin (tɪn) *n* **1** a silvery-white metal. **2** a container or sheet made of tin plate, esp. a sealed container in which food is preserved.
• *vb* **tinned; tinning 1** cover with tin. **2** preserve in a tin. **tin foil** a paper-thin sheet of tin, aluminium, or tin alloy. **tin god** (*informal*) a domineering, self-important person. **tin hat** (*informal*) a soldier's metal helmet. **tinny** *adj* **1** of or like tin. **2** having the appearance, smell, etc., of tin. **3** (esp. of metal objects) not solid or long-lasting. **4** having a light, high, metallic sound. **tin plate** sheet iron or steel that is coated with tin. **tin-plated** *adj* coated with tin plate. **tinpot** *adj* (*informal*) worthless. < Old English.

tincture (ˈtɪŋktʃə) *n* **1** a slight trace. **2** a solution of a drug in alcohol, for medicinal use.
• *vb* tinge. < SEE **TINGE.**

tinder (ˈtɪndə) *n* any dry substance that catches fire easily, used in lighting a fire. < Old English *tynder.*

ting (tɪŋ) *n* a high, metallic, ringing sound.
• *vb* make a ting. < like the sound.

tinge (tɪndʒ) *vb* **1** colour slightly. **2** add a slight trace to: suspicion tinged with jealousy.
• *n* a slight tint, trace, or colouring. < Latin *tingere.*

tingle (ˈtɪŋgl̩) *vb* feel a stinging or prickling sensation, as from cold, exhilaration, etc.
• *n* a tingling sensation. < alteration of *tinklen* to tinkle.

tinker (ˈtɪŋkə) *n* a travelling mender of household utensils.
• *vb* alter, mend, or work at something in a clumsy or aimless way. < Middle English *tinkere.*

tinkle (ˈtɪŋkl̩) *n* **1** a series of short, light, high, ringing sounds. **2** (*informal*) a telephone call.

• vb make or cause to make a tinkle. < Middle English *tinken,* like the sound.

tinsel (ˈtɪnsəl) *n* **1** a strip or thread of foil, etc., used to give a glittering effect in decoration. **2** something that produces a cheap, superficial, showy effect. **tinselled** *adj* < Middle French *estincelle* spark.

tint (tɪnt) *n* **1** a colour or shade of colour. **2** a delicate or pale colour.
• vb apply a tint to; colour. < ultimately Latin *tingere* to tinge.

tiny (ˈtaɪnɪ) *adj* very small. < Middle English *tine.*

tip[1] (tɪp) *n* **1** the extreme, esp. pointed, end of something. **2** a small piece serving as an end.
• *vb* **tipped; tipping** provide with a tip. **on the tip of one's tongue** about to be uttered or remembered. < Middle English. SEE PANEL.

tip[2] *vb* **tipped; tipping 1** tilt or cause to tilt, esp. so as to overturn. **2** deposit or discharge by tilting; dump (rubbish).
• *n* **1** the act of tipping. **2** a place for tipping something; dump. **tip-up** *adj* (of seats) able to be turned upwards. < Middle English *tipen.*

tip[3] *vb* **tipped; tipping** strike or touch lightly.
• *n* a light blow. < Middle English *tippe* light blow.

tip[4] *n* **1** a sum of money given as an appreciation of a service performed. **2** a piece of useful information; hint. **3** a piece of inside information in betting or investing.
• *vb* **tipped; tipping 1** give a sum of money to, as an appreciation of a service performed. **2** name as a likely winner, etc. **tip off** warn or inform of a crime, etc. **tip-off** *n* **tipster** *n* a person who gives tips for horse-races, etc. < probably TIP[3]. SEE PANEL AT TIP[1].

tipple (ˈtɪpl̩) *vb* (*informal*) drink (spirits, wine, etc.) habitually and in small amounts.
• *n* (*informal*) an alcoholic drink. < back formation from obsolete *tippler* seller of drink.

tipsy (ˈtɪpsɪ) *adj* slightly drunk. < SEE TIP[2].

tiptoe (ˈtɪpˌtəʊ) *vb* **1** walk with the heels off the ground. **2** walk silently or stealthily.
• *n* the tip of a toe.
• *adv* on tiptoe. **on tiptoe 1** on one's tiptoes. **2** eager with anticipation.

tiptop (ˌtɪpˈtɒp) *adj, adv* in the best, most excellent, etc., condition.

tirade (taɪˈreɪd, tɪˈreɪd) *n* a long, angry speech or denunciation. < French, from Old Italian *tirare* to draw.

tire (taɪə) *vb* **1** make or become tired. **2** reduce the patience of. **tired** *adj* **1** feeling the need for rest or sleep; weary. **2** discontented, bored, and impatient. **3** not fresh; trite. **tireless** *adj* not tiring easily; indefatigable. **tirelessly** *adv* **tiresome** *adj* tedious and irritating. < Old English *tēorian.*

tissue (ˈtɪʃuː, ˈtɪsjuː) *n* **1** (*anatomy*) a mass of cells and surrounding material that perform a particular function: muscle tissue. **2** a paper handkerchief. **3** a fine, gauzy, woven cloth. **tissue-paper** *n* very thin, soft paper used for wrapping and protecting goods. < ultimately Latin *texere* to weave.

tit[1] (tɪt) *n* any of various small, insect-eating songbirds. < short for *titmouse,* the bird, from Middle English *tit-* small object + Middle English *mose* titmouse.

tit[2] *n* **tit for tat** an equivalent given in

tip

Exploitation of the ambiguity of language has over the centuries provided one of the richest sources of humour. This exploitation takes various forms. At the word level it is found in the *pun*, a play on two of the meanings of a word: 'Our asparagus is very expensive but at least it includes the *tip*.'—or on two words which sound alike: 'I'm not really a mourner—I'm only here for the *bier*.'

Beyond the word level there are a number of grammatical structures which simultaneously trigger two (or sometimes even three) interpretations. Take, for example, a sentence like 'John loves his wife—and so do I.' This could be interpreted either as 'I love my wife' or 'I love John's wife'. A different type of structural ambiguity is illustrated by 'Sarah likes fascinating men' meaning either 'Sarah likes men who are fascinating' or 'Sarah likes to fascinate men'.

Beyond the sentence one finds that the sequencing of sentences can also produce ambiguity, as in the well-worn: Large Alsatian for sale. Eats anything. Very fond of children. When the last two sentences are switched round, the ambiguity is lost.

retaliation. < alteration of *tip for tap*. SEE PANEL.

titanic (taɪˈtænɪk) *adj* huge. < Greek *titanikos* of the *Titans*, Greek mythological giants.

titbit (ˈtɪtˌbɪt) *n* **1** a small, tasty piece of food. **2** a very interesting piece of information, scandal, etc. < perhaps *tit-*: SEE TIT[1] + *bit*.

tithe (taɪð) *n* one-tenth part of an income, produce, etc., allotted to religious or charitable purposes.
• *vb* pay a tithe (of). < Old English *teogotha* tenth.

titillate (ˈtɪtɪˌleɪt) *vb* excite or arouse pleasantly. **titillation** *n* < Latin *titillare*.

titivate (ˈtɪtɪˌveɪt) *vb* (*informal*) smarten up. **titivation** *n* < perhaps *tidy*.

title (ˈtaɪtḷ) *n* **1** the name of a book, poem, etc. **2** a book, etc., with a particular title: We publish 1000 titles every year. **3** a word such as Doctor or Mr used to show the rank, office, etc., of a person. **4** a word showing nobility such as Duke or Count. **5** a document giving proof of legal ownership; such ownership. **6** a designation as champion: the world heavyweight title.
• *vb* give a title to. **titled** *adj* (esp. of nobility) having a title. **title-deed** *n* a deed or document that gives evidence of a person's ownership of property. **title-page** *n* the page of a book that gives the title, author, publisher, and date of publication. **title-role** *n* the role of the character in a play, etc., with the same name as the title of the production. < ultimately Latin *titulus*.

titter (ˈtɪtə) *vb* **1** snigger; giggle. **2** express by tittering.
• *n* a tittering. < like the sound.

tittle-tattle (ˈtɪtḷˌtætḷ) *n, vb* gossip. < *tattle* to gossip, from Middle Dutch *tatelen*.

titular (ˈtɪtjʊlə) *adj* **1** in title or name only; nominal: the titular head of state. **2** of or relating to a title. < SEE **TITLE**.

tizzy (ˈtɪzɪ) *n* (*informal*) a state of confusion or nervous excitement. < origin unknown.

to (tə, tʊ; *stressed* tuː) *prep* **1** in the direction of; towards: travel to London. **2** as far as; until: from March to May. **3** against; onto: dancing cheek to cheek. **4** (*grammar*) used to show an indirect object: She gave the book to me. **5** used to show a comparison or relationship: They won by 6 goals to 3. **6** before the hour of: It's five to six. **7** into a condition of: his rise to fame. **8** concerning: What do you say to the idea? **9** according to: to the best of my knowledge. **10** accompanied by: sing to the guitar. **11** in honour of: Let's drink to the Queen. **12** (*grammar*) used before the infinitive of a verb: to go.

tit for tat

An act of retaliation is sometimes referred to as a case of *tit for tat*: Michael wouldn't let Brian use his computer, so Brian stopped lending Michael his car. It was *tit for tat*. The phrase tit for tat is a development of the 16th-century *tip for tap*, from *tip* 'blow' and *tap*. In other words, its literal meaning is 'blow for blow'.

to boldly go or to go boldly?

A number of careful users of English continue to avoid what are called *split infinitives*.

What is a split infinitive? An infinitive is the base form of a verb, such as have, go, enjoy. It is the form of a verb a person looks up in a dictionary. An infinitive is often preceded by to: to have, to go, to enjoy (known as *full infinitives*). A split infinitive occurs when an adverb comes between to and the verb as in: to really enjoy, to boldly go.

Split infinitives are best avoided in formal varieties of English, unless such avoidance leads to ambiguity or awkwardness.

□ **ambiguity.** In the sentence He failed to entirely convince me, the intended meaning ('I remained in the end not fully convinced') has been clearly expressed only by splitting the infinitive (to entirely convince). When the latter is avoided, either by He failed entirely to convince me or by He failed to convince me entirely, the sentences that result are ambiguous. In addition to the intended meaning, each sentence could be interpreted 'He completely failed to convince me'.

□ **awkwardness.** In the sentence You don't expect me to actually believe you, the natural rhythm of English is preserved only by splitting the infinitive (to actually believe). When the latter is avoided—You don't expect me actually to believe you—the result is a sentence that sounds rather awkward and foreign.

• *adv* **1** (of a door or window) to a closed or almost closed position. **2** back into consciousness: He was knocked out and came to half an hour later. **3** into a state of activity: set to. **to and fro** forwards and backwards. < Old English *tō*. SEE PANEL.

toad (təʊd) *n* a tailless, leaping amphibian that is related to the frog, but lives more on land and has a drier, rough, warty skin. **toadstool** *n* a fungus, esp. inedible and poisonous, with a slender stalk and a cap-like top. < Old English *tāde*.

toady (ˈtəʊdɪ) *n* a person who flatters and behaves in a servile way in order to gain favour.
• *vb* **toadied; toadying** behave as a toady. < *toadeater*. SEE PANEL.

toast (təʊst) *vb* **1** make (bread, etc.) crisp, hot, and brown by placing before a fire, etc. **2** warm thoroughly. **3** drink or propose a drink to the success, happiness, etc., of.
• *n* **1** a slice of toasted bread. **2** a proposal to a group of people to drink to a person or thing; words of loyalty, best wishes, etc., spoken before drinking. **3** the person, thing, etc., honoured by such an act. **toaster** *n* an electrical appliance for toasting bread. **toastmaster** *n* a person who proposes toasts, introduces speakers, etc., at a formal dinner. < ultimately Latin *torrēre* to dry. SEE PANEL.

tobacco (təˌbækəʊ) *n* **1** a plant grown for its leaves, which are used to make cigarettes, cigars, etc. **2** the leaves of this plant, esp. when prepared for smoking. **tobacconist** *n* a person who sells cigarettes, cigars, etc. < Spanish *tabaco*.

-to-be (təˈbiː) *adj* about to be; future: a mother-to-be.

toboggan (təˈbɒgən) *n* a long, low platform on steel runners, often curved at the front, used for sliding along on snow or ice.
• *vb* ride on a toboggan. **tobogganing** *n* the recreation or sport of riding on a toboggan. < Canadian French *tobogan*, from Algonquian.

today (təˈdeɪ) *n* **1** this present day. **2** this present time or age.
• *adv* **1** on this present day. **2** at this present time. < Old English *tō dæge*.

toddle (ˈtɒdl̩) *vb* **1** walk with short, unsteady steps, as a young child. **2** (*informal*) go slowly; walk or depart. **toddler** *n* a young child. < origin unknown.

toddy (ˈtɒdɪ) *n* a drink of spirits mixed with hot water, sugar, and spices. < Hindi *tārī* juice of a palm-tree.

to-do (təˈduː) *n, pl* **to-dos** (*informal*) a commotion or fuss.

toe (təʊ) *n* **1** one of the five parts extending from the end of the foot. **2** the front of something worn on the foot; something like a toe.
• *vb* **1** touch, kick, etc., with the toes. **2** provide with a toe; repair the toe of. **be on one's toes** be alert. **toe-cap** *n* a strong covering that reinforces the toe of a boot or shoe. **toe-hold** *n* a slight foothold. **toe the line** conform strictly to regulations or conventions. < Old English *tā*. SEE PANEL.

toff (tɒf) *n* (*informal*) an upper-class, superior, well-dressed person. < perhaps alteration of *tuft* titled undergraduate.

toffee (ˈtɒfɪ) *n* a kind of sweet made by boiling sugar, water, and butter. **can't do something for toffee** (*informal*) cannot do something at all: He can't sing for toffee! **toffee-apple** *n* a toffee-coated apple on a stick. **toffee-nosed** *adj* (*informal*) snobbish. < alteration of

toady

A person who goes to unnecessary lengths to ingratiate himself or herself is known as a sycophant or toady. This word is a 19th-century shortening of *toadeater,* the name given to a mountebank's servile assistant. In order to dupe the public into buying his master's wares, the stooge would appear to swallow a toad, in those days considered to be highly poisonous. The antidote was then administered and its curative power dramatically proved.

toast

The words used when calling upon company to drink to a person or thing form what is commonly known as a toast. This curious use of toast derives ultimately from the former practice of adding a piece of spiced toast to a glass or tankard so as to improve the flavour of the drink. Gradually it came to be used for the drink itself.

From **head** to **toe**

A surprisingly large number of idioms mention a part of the body. Below is a list of some examples; it starts at the head and works down to the toes:

make head or tail of something
hold one's head high
keep a cool head
lose one's head
head over heels
(have a) big head
head and shoulders above
by a hair's breadth
a slap in the face
have a red face
raise one's eyebrows
see eye to eye
be up to one's eyes in something
be all ears
pay through the nose
live from hand to mouth
hold one's tongue
armed to the teeth
grit one's teeth
neck and neck
jump down someone's throat
put someone's back up
send shivers down the spine
a pat on the back
give someone the cold shoulder
twist somebody's arm
cost an arm and a leg
get something off one's chest
heart to heart
a heart of gold
have no stomach for something
contemplate one's navel
have someone's guts for garters
keep one's hand in
get one's fingers burnt
keep one's finger on the pulse
not lift a finger
a rap on the knuckles
under someone's thumb
a rule of thumb
pull someone's leg
not have a leg to stand on
take to one's heels
put one's foot down
My foot!
vote with one's feet
toe the line

taffy, origin unknown.

tog[1] (tɒg) *n* **togs** (*informal*) clothes. • *vb* **togged; togging** dress. < short for obsolete *togeman* coat.

tog[2] *n* a unit used in measuring thermal insulation. < probably TOG[1].

toga (ˈtəʊgə) *n* a loose, outer garment worn by citizens of ancient Rome. < Latin.

together (təˈgɛðə) *adv* **1** in or into one group, place, etc. **2** in or into contact. **3** in or into relationship, agreement, or co-operation: work together. **4** at the same time; simultaneously: We started school together. **5** to or with each other. **6** considered collectively. **7** without interruption. **togetherness** *n* the feeling of belonging closely together. **together with** with the addition of. < Old English *togædere*.

toggle (ˈtɒgl̩) *n* a piece such as a peg or rod attached to the end of or to a loop in a rope, chain, etc., to act as a fastening, prevent slipping, etc. < origin unknown.

toil (tɔɪl) *n* long, hard, exhausting work. • *vb* **1** work hard and long. **2** move slowly with great effort. **toiler** *n* **toilsome** *adj* involving toil; laborious. < ultimately Latin *tudiculare* to crush. SEE PANEL.

toilet (ˈtɔɪlət) *n* **1** a fixture for receiving and disposing of urine and faeces; room containing this. **2** the process of dressing and grooming oneself. **toilet-paper** *n* thin, absorbent paper for cleaning oneself after defecation or urination. **toiletries** *pl n* articles used in washing and grooming. **toilet-roll** *n* a roll of toilet-paper. **toilet-training** *n* the training of a child to control his or her urination and defecation and to use a

toil

Fatiguing work that seems to go on and on is sometimes referred to as toil. This word has a long and rather curious history. It comes into English from the Anglo-French *toyl,* which is a development of the Old French *toeil* meaning 'battle' or 'confusion', from the verb *toeillier* 'to stir' or 'to confuse'. *Toeillier* in turn derives from the Latin *tudiculare,* 'to crush', which comes from the noun *tudicula,* 'a machine for crushing olives'. The root of *tudicula* is *tudes,* 'a hammer'.

toilet. **toilet water** scented water, applied to the skin. < Middle French *toile* cloth.

token (ˈtəʊkən) *n* **1** a sign or mark of something. **2** a disc used as a substitute for a coin, used in slot-machines, etc. **3** a voucher that can be used to pay for goods of a specified value: book token. **4** a keepsake.
• *adj* done or given as a token, but only slight; in appearance only: a token payment **by the same token** following logically from what has been said. < Old English *tācen.*

told (təʊld) SEE **TELL.**

tolerate (ˈtɒləˌreɪt) *vb* **1** allow or permit. **2** bear or endure; put up with. **3** acknowledge and respect (the beliefs, habits, etc., of a person) without hindrance or contradiction. **toleration** *n* **tolerable** *adj* **1** able to be tolerated. **2** moderately good. **tolerably** *adv* **tolerance** *n* **1** respect for the beliefs or habits of a person, esp. where they are different from one's own; toleration. **2** a permitted variation from a standard measurement, etc. **tolerant** *adj* showing tolerance; forbearing. **tolerantly** *adv* < Latin *tolerare* to endure.

toll¹ (təʊl) *vb* ring or cause to ring slowly and regularly, as for a death or funeral.
• *n* the stroke of a tolling bell. < Middle English *tollen.*

toll² (təʊl, tɒl) *n* **1** an amount of tax levied for the use of certain roads, bridges, tunnels, etc., or for a service. **2** the loss or damage caused esp. by a disaster: the death toll in the earthquake. **toll-gate** *n* a gate across a road at which a toll is taken. < Old English.

tom (tɒm) *n* a male animal, esp. a cat. **tom-cat** *n* a male cat. < *Tom,* nickname for *Thomas.*

tomahawk (ˈtɒməˌhɔːk) *n* a light axe used as a weapon by North American Indians. < Virginian Algonquian *tomahack.*

tomato (təˈmɑːtəʊ) *n, pl* **tomatoes** a plant grown for its fleshy, red fruit; this fruit eaten as a vegetable. < Spanish, from Nahuatl *tomatl.*

tomb (tuːm) *n* a grave, vault, or chamber in which a dead body is buried. **tombstone** *n* a gravestone. < ultimately Greek *tymbos.*

tombola (tɒmˈbəʊlə) *n* a lottery in which people buy numbered tickets, some of which entitle them to a prize. < Italian *tombolare* to tumble.

tomboy (ˈtɒmˌbɔɪ) *n* a girl who behaves or plays in a way thought typical of a boy, esp. one who enjoys rough, outdoor activities.

tome (təʊm) *n* a large book, esp. a heavy one. < ultimately Greek *tomos* section, slice.

tomfoolery (ˌtɒmˈfuːlərɪ) *n* foolish behaviour; nonsense.

tomorrow (təˈmɒrəʊ) *adv, n* **1** (on) the day after today. **2** (in) the future. < Old English *tō morgen.*

tom-tom (ˈtɒmˌtɒm) *n* a small-headed drum beaten with the hands. < Hindi *ṭamṭam.*

ton (tʌn) *n* **1** also **long ton** a measure of weight equal to 2240 pounds (1016.05 kilograms). **2** also **short ton** (*US*) a measure of weight equal to 2000 pounds (907.18 kilograms). **3** also **metric ton** SEE **TONNE. 4** a unit of volume in shipping. **5** (*informal*) a great quantity: tons of space. **6** (*slang*) a speed or score of 100: doing a ton down the motorway. < SEE **TUN.**

tone (təʊn) *n* **1** a vocal or musical sound or its quality. **2** a quality of colour. **3** a way of expression: the enthusiastic tone of the letter. **4** a general, prevailing mood or character. **5** a musical interval made up of two semitones. **6** the pitch of a syllable. **7** the general effect of colour, shade, etc., in a picture.
• *vb* **1** give a particular tone to. **2** take on a tone; harmonize. **toner** *n* **tone-deaf** *adj* unable to distinguish accurately differences in musical pitch. **tone down** make less bright, strident, etc. **toneless** *adj* not expressive. < ultimately Greek *tonos* stretching.

tongs (tɒŋz) *pl n* an instrument consisting of two arms joined at one end, used for grasping or lifting things. < Old English *tang.*

tongue (tʌŋ) *n* **1** a muscular organ in the mouth, used in tasting, swallowing, etc., and also speaking in human beings. **2** the tongue of an ox, etc., used as food. **3** a spoken language: His mother tongue is French. **4** the power of speech: She seems to have lost her tongue. **5** a manner of speaking: a sharp tongue. **6** something like a tongue in shape or function such as a narrow, projecting strip of land or a leather flap in a shoe. **tongued** *adj* having a tongue of a kind that is mentioned: smooth-tongued. **tongue-in-cheek** *adv* ironically. **tongue-tied** *adj* not able to speak freely, because of shyness or embarrassment. **tongue-twister** *n* a word or phrase that is difficult to say because of many similar consonant sounds, such as She sells sea shells on the sea-shore. < Old English *tunge.*

tonic (ˈtɒnɪk) *n* **1** a drug, medicine, etc., that improves bodily health. **2** something that restores, refreshes, or stimulates. **3** also **tonic water** a carbonated water containing quinine, often served mixed with gin, etc. < SEE **TONE.**

tonight (tə'naɪt) *adv, n* (on or during) the present or coming evening or night. < Old English *tō niht.*

tonnage ('tʌnɪdʒ) *n* **1** the total weight of all the ships belonging to a particular country. **2** the carrying-capacity of a ship, expressed in tons. < Old French *tonne* tun.

tonne (tʌn) *n* also **metric ton** a measure of weight equal to 1000 kilograms. < French.

tonsil ('tɒnsəl) *n* one of a pair of small masses of tissue that lie one on each side at the back of the mouth. **tonsillitis** *n* inflammation of the tonsils. < Latin *tonsillae* tonsils.

tonsure ('tɒnʃə) *n* **1** the shaving of a man's head when he becomes a priest or monk. **2** the part of the head shaved in this way. < Latin *tondēre* to shear.

too (tu:) *adv* **1** more than enough; excessively: too quickly. **2** also; as well: Can my sister come too? **3** (*chiefly US informal*) indeed; so. < Old English *tō.*

took (tʊk) SEE **TAKE.**

tool (tu:l) *n* **1** an implement used, esp. held in the hand, to carry out some mechanical work: garden tools. **2** a simple machine. **3** something useful or necessary in an occupation, profession, or pursuit: the tools of his trade. **4** a person manipulated by another.
• *vb* **1** equip with tools. **2** shape with a tool. < Old English *tōl.*

toot (tu:t) *n* a short blast, hoot, etc.
• *vb* make or cause to make a toot. < probably like the sound.

tooth (tu:θ) *n,* pl **teeth** **1** one of the hard, bony structures in the jaws, used for biting and chewing food. **2** a tooth-like projection, for example on a saw or comb. **3** a liking for a particular kind of food: a sweet tooth. **4** *pl* effective means of enforcement. **toothache** *n* pain in or around a tooth. **toothbrush** *n* a brush for cleaning the teeth. **toothed** *adj* having teeth, esp. of a kind that is mentioned: sharp-toothed. **toothless** *adj* having no teeth. **toothpaste** *n* a paste for cleaning the teeth. **toothpick** *n* a small, pointed instrument for removing particles of food from between the teeth. **toothy** *adj* having or showing prominent teeth. < Old English *tōth.* SEE PANEL. SEE PANEL AT **MONGOOSE.**

tootle ('tu:tl) *vb* **1** toot gently or repeatedly. **2** (*informal*) move in a leisurely way. < SEE **TOOT.**

top[1] (tɒp) *n* **1** the highest part or point of something. **2** the upper surface. **3** the highest place or rank in order of importance: top of the class. **4** the greatest degree or pitch: shrieking at the top of her voice. **5** a lid, cap, or stopper. **6** something that forms the upper part of something: the top of the milk. **7** a garment worn on the upper part of the body.
• *adj* **1** of or at the top. **2** leading; best: one of the country's top bands.
• *vb* **topped; topping 1** provide with a top; serve as a top for. **2** reach or exceed the top of: Inflation has topped the 10% mark. **3** be at the top of: Richard Unwin topped the poll with 82% of the votes cast. **4** remove the top of (a plant, etc.). **top coat** an overcoat. **top hat** a man's tall, stiff, black or grey hat, worn on formal occasions. **top-heavy** *adj* unsteady because overbalanced at the top. **topless** *adj* **1** leaving the breasts exposed. **2** (of a woman) wearing a garment that exposes the breasts. **topmost** *adj* highest. **topside** *n* a lean, boneless cut of beef from the thigh. **topsoil** *n* the surface layer of soil. < Old

old in the tooth

Old in the tooth is used to describe someone or something that is getting old or out of date. As horse lovers will be aware, the phrase derives from the custom of telling the age of the animal by studying the marks in its teeth. After a certain age these distinguishing marks gradually disappear, whereupon the horse is said to be old in the tooth.

Tooth and its plural teeth feature in a number of other idiomatic expressions, including:

armed to the teeth fully equipped with guns, etc.; fully supplied with things that are necessary for a particular task.
by the skin of one's teeth narrowly: He escaped death by the skin of his teeth. This phrase comes from the Bible, Job 19:20.
fiight tooth and nail to fight forcefully and with all available resources: Local parents are fiighting tooth and nail to make sure that the school is not closed.
get one's teeth into to deal with or tackle with great concentration and in a determined manner.
sweet tooth a liking for sweet foods.

English. SEE PANEL.
top[2] *n* a toy that spins on its pointed end. **sleep like a top** sleep very soundly. < Old English. SEE PANEL.
topiary (ˈtəʊpɪərɪ) *n* the art of trimming and training shrubs and trees into ornamental shapes. < ultimately Greek *topos* place.
topic (ˈtɒpɪk) *n* a subject for discussion or thought. **topical** *adj* **1** of current interest: topical issues. **2** arranged by topics: a topical concordance. **topicality** *n* **topically** *adv* < ultimately Greek *topos* place.
topography (təˈpɒgrəfɪ) *n* a description of the features of the land surface of an area, such as hills, rivers, and roads. **topographical** *adj* < ultimately Greek *topos* place + *graphein* to write.
topple (ˈtɒpl̩) *vb* **1** tip over or cause to tip over. **2** overthrow (a person, government, etc.) from power. < SEE **TOP**[1].
topsy-turvy (ˌtɒpsɪˈtɜːvɪ) *adj, adv* **1** in great confusion. **2** upside-down. < probably *tops:* SEE **TOP**[1] + obsolete *terve* to turn upside down.
tor (tɔː) *n* a high rock or rocky hill. < Old English *torr.*
torch (tɔːtʃ) *n* **1** a small, portable electric lamp powered by a battery or batteries. **2** a burning stick of resinous wood or other combustible material, used to give light. < Old French *torche* bundle of twisted straw.
tore (tɔː) SEE **TEAR**[2].
toreador (ˈtɒrɪəˌdɔː) *n* a bullfighter. < Spanish, from Latin *taurus* bull.
torment (tɔːˈmɛnt) *vb* subject to great pain or anguish.
• *n* (ˈtɔːmɛnt) great pain or anguish; something causing this. **tormentor** *n* < ultimately Latin *torquēre* to twist.
torn (tɔːn) SEE **TEAR**[2].
tornado (tɔːˈneɪdəʊ) *n, pl* **tornadoes** a violently rotating column of air that is accompanied by a funnel-shaped cloud, advances in a narrow path, and causes great destruction on land. < probably modified from Spanish *tronada* thunderstorm, from Latin *tonare* to thunder.
torpedo (tɔːˈpiːdəʊ) *n, pl* **torpedoes** a self-propelled, cigar-shaped, guided underwater explosive missile.
• *vb* **1** attack or destroy with a torpedo. **2** (*informal*) destroy or wreck suddenly. < Latin: numbness, from *torpēre* to be stiff. SEE PANEL.
torpid (ˈtɔːpɪd) *adj* sluggish or inactive; slow or dull. **torpor** *n* a torpid condition. < Latin *torpēre* to be stiff. SEE PANEL AT **STUPOR.**
torque (tɔːk) *n* a force that causes or tends

on top of

Top features in a number of idiomatic expressions, including:

off the top of one's head without thinking or working something out carefully: Off the top of my head, I think it would cost something like half a million pounds.
on top of 1 in addition to. **2** in control of: stay on top of one's job.
on top of the world extremely happy.
top out to put the highest section on (a building), so completing its basic structure.
top secret extremely confidential.
top up 1 to make up the full amount of (a liquid) in (a container). **2** to increase (an amount of money). **top-up** *n*

sleep like a top

A person who sleeps very soundly is sometimes said to sleep like a top. When a wheel reaches a certain speed of revolution it appears to be motionless. The same effect is produced by a top that reaches a certain rate of gyration. It is from this (apparent) state of motionlessness that the expression derives.

torpedo

A self-propelled underwater projectile is known as a torpedo. This name was taken from the *torpedo ray,* also known as the electric ray or crampfish, which for purposes of defence and food capture uses electric discharges to induce numbness.

Torpedo derives ultimately from the Latin *torpēre* meaning 'to be stiff or numb', which was coined in ancient times to describe the paralysing effect of the electric ray's sting. *Torpēre* is also the root of torpor and torpid.

to cause rotation. < Latin *torquēre* to twist.

torrent (ˈtɒrənt) *n* **1** a great, violent stream, esp. of water. **2** a violent flow: a torrent of insults. **torrential** *adj* like a torrent. < ultimately Latin *torrēre* to burn.

torrid (ˈtɒrɪd) *adj* **1** subjected to intense heat, esp. of the sun. **2** emitting intense heat. **3** ardent and passionate. **torridly** *adv* < Latin *torrēre* to burn.

torso (ˈtɔːsəʊ) *n, pl* **torsos** **1** the trunk of the human body; representation of this. **2** something considered incomplete or mutilated. < Italian: stalk, from Latin *thyrsus* stem.

tortoise (ˈtɔːtəs) *n* a slow-moving reptile with a protective, dome-shaped shell and tough, scaly legs. **tortoiseshell** *adj, n* (of the colour of) the hard, mottled, yellowish-brown shell of certain turtles, used in making decorative articles. < Middle French *tortue.*

tortuous (ˈtɔːtjʊəs) *adj* **1** having many twists and turns; winding. **2** complex and involved; intricate. **3** (of a policy, etc.) devious; indirect. **tortuously** *adv* < ultimately Latin *torquēre* to twist.

torture (ˈtɔːtʃə) *n* **1** the infliction of intense pain, esp. as a punishment or means of coercion. **2** great physical or mental anguish; cause of this.
• *vb* **1** inflict torture on. **2** subject to great physical or mental anguish. **3** distort from its original or proper form. **torturer** *n* < ultimately Latin *torquēre* to twist.

toss (tɒs) *vb* **1** throw (to). **2** move about unevenly and quickly: tossing and turning all night. **3** mix lightly: vegetables tossed in butter. **4** spin (a coin) in the air to decide an issue; decide an issue in this way: Let's toss to see who starts. **5** jerk upwards: He tossed his head impatiently.
• *n* **1** a tossing action or movement. **2** a tossing of a coin. **3** a fall from a horse. **toss off** produce quickly and without much thought. **toss up** toss a coin. **toss-up** *n* < probably of Scandinavian origin.

tot[1] (tɒt) *n* **1** a young child: tiny tots. **2** a small amount of alcoholic drink. < origin uncertain.

tot[2] *vb* **totted; totting** add (up); total. **totting-up** *n* the addition of separate convictions for driving offences to cause disqualification. < SEE **TOTAL.**

total (ˈtəʊtl̩) *adj* **1** making up the whole: the total number of students. **2** complete: total surrender.
• *n* the whole; result of addition.
• *vb* **totalled; totalling** **1** calculate the total of. **2** amount to. **totally** *adv* **totality** *n* **1** a total amount or number. **2** wholeness. < ultimately Latin *totus* entire, whole. SEE PANEL AT **SHEER**[1].

totalitarian (təʊˌtælɪˈtɛərɪən) *adj* of a political system in which one party strictly controls all thought and action and opposition is suppressed. < *total* + *-itarian,* as in *authoritarian.*

totem (ˈtəʊtəm) *n* a natural object adopted as the emblem of a family or clan; representation of this. **totem-pole** *n* a pole carved or painted with a series of totems. < Ojibwa *ototeman* his totem.

totter (ˈtɒtə) *vb* **1** move unsteadily. **2** rock or become unstable as if about to collapse.
• *n* a tottering movement. **tottery** *adj* < Middle English *toteren.*

toucan (ˈtuːkən) *n* a forest-dwelling, fruit-eating bird with a large, brightly coloured beak. < French, from Portuguese *tucano,* from Tupi.

touch (tʌtʃ) *vb* **1** put one's hand, finger, etc., on (something) so as to feel. **2** bring or come into contact with (something). **3** press or strike lightly. **4** harm or interfere with. **5** handle: We won't touch stolen goods. **6** eat or drink a little of: He hasn't even touched his lunch. **7** come up to; reach: The speedometer touched 90. **8** compare with; equal in quality. **9** affect or concern; relate to. **10** arouse sympathy, thankfulness, etc., in; move. **11** give a slight tint or expression to; tinge. **12** (*slang*) persuade to give or

touch and go

Touch features in a number of idiomatic expressions, including:

touch and go very uncertain; in the balance: It's touch and go whether he'll live or not.
touch down (of an aircraft, etc.) to land on the ground. **touchdown** *n*
touch off **1** to cause to occur; trigger: The arrest touched off a riot. **2** to cause to explode.
touch on to mention briefly.
touch up **1** to improve the appearance of (something), by painting small areas or making small alterations. **2** to make physical advances to; molest sexually.
touch wood used to express a hope for fortune or good luck, usually said while touching something made of wood. The American equivalent is knock on wood.

lend money.
● *n* **1** the sense or faculty of feeling. **2** the act or fact of touching. **3** a light tap or stroke. **4** the sensation felt through touch: a velvety touch. **5** a mark or impression made by touching. **6** a detail in a task or artistic work: finishing touches. **7** a trace or tinge: a touch of humour. **8** a slight attack: a touch of flu. **9** a special skill or quality, as in performing. **10** a relationship of contact or communication: We've lost touch with him. **11** the area outside the touch-lines. **12** (*slang*) the act of obtaining money from a person; person who can be easily persuaded to give or lend money: a soft touch. **touched** *adj* **1** emotionally moved, with sympathy, thankfulness, etc. **2** (*informal*) slightly mad. **touch-line** *n* either of the lines that mark the longer sides of the playing area in rugby and soccer. **touch-paper** *n* paper impregnated with a substance that burns slowly, used for lighting fireworks. **touchstone** *n* **1** a black or grey, flint-like stone formerly used to test the purity of gold and silver. **2** a standard or criterion by which something is judged. **touch-typing** *n* typewriting without looking at the keys. **touchy** *adj* very sensitive and easily offended. < Old French *tuchier*. SEE PANEL.

touché (ˈtuːʃeɪ, tuːˈʃeɪ) *interj* used to acknowledge that one's opponent has made a hit in fencing or a valid point in a discussion. < French: touched.

tough (tʌf) *adj* **1** difficult to bend, twist, tear, etc. **2** difficult to chew or cut: This meat is very tough. **3** unyielding and determined. **4** able to endure hardship. **5** very difficult. **6** severe; intense: tough competition. **7** aggressive and violent in behaviour. **8** (*informal*) unfortunate: tough luck.
● *n* a person who is aggressive and violent. **toughly** *adv* **toughness** *n* **toughen** *vb* make or become tough. < Old English *tōh*.

toupee (ˈtuːpeɪ) *n* a wig or hair-piece that covers a bald spot. < French, of Germanic origin.

tour (tʊə) *n* **1** a planned journey that includes several visits, esp. to places of interest. **2** a series of professional engagements in different places: a concert tour. **3** a walk or trip round a place in order to see it: a tour of the grounds.
● *vb* make a tour of. < Old French *tourn* lathe, turn.

tour de force (ˌtʊə də ˈfɔːs) a great feat of skill, strength, etc. < French.

tourist (ˈtʊərɪst) *n* a person who travels or tours for pleasure.
● *adj* **1** of or for tourists. **2** of the lowest class of accommodation: tourist class. **tourism** *n* tourist travel, esp. as a business.

tournament (ˈtʊənəmənt, ˈtɔːnəmənt) *n* a series of games or matches for a championship. < Old French *torneiement*.

tourniquet (ˈtʊənɪˌkeɪ, ˈtɔːnɪˌkeɪ) *n* a device or bandage drawn tightly round a limb to check bleeding. < French *tourner* to turn, from Old French.

tousle (ˈtaʊzl) *vb* tangle or ruffle (hair, etc.). < Middle English *touselen*.

tout (taʊt) *vb* **1** solicit (customers, business, etc.). **2** spy out information on (racehorses, etc.).
● *n* a person who touts. < Middle English *tuten* to peer.

tow (təʊ) *vb* pull along behind, esp. with a rope or cable.
● *n* towing; being towed. **in tow** being towed; in one's charge. **on tow** being towed. **tow-bar** *n* a rigid, metal bar used for towing vehicles, esp. attached to a car. **tow-path** *n* a path beside a canal, used by people or animals towing boats. < Old English *togian*.

towards (təˈwɔːdz) *prep* also **toward 1** in the direction of: travelling towards Wales. **2** near; not long before: towards the end of the year. **3** in relation to: What are your feelings towards her? **4** as a contribution to: towards the cost of a new car. < Old English *tōweardes*.

towel (ˈtaʊəl) *n* a piece of absorbent cloth or paper for drying or wiping something after washing.
● *vb* **towelled; towelling** dry or wipe with a towel. **throw in the towel** give up. **towelling** *n* fabric for making towels. < Old French *toaille*, of Germanic origin.

tower (ˈtaʊə) *n* a tall, usually square or circular structure, which stands by itself or forms part of a larger structure.
● *vb* be or rise to a great height. **tower block** a very tall block of flats or offices. **towering** *adj* **1** very high. **2** intense. **tower of strength** a person who gives strong, reliable support and help. < ultimately Greek *tyrsis*.

town (taʊn) *n* **1** a densely populated area, larger than a village but smaller than a city. **2** the inhabitants of a town. **3** a nearby town or city. **go to town** act enthusiastically and lavishly. **town clerk** (formerly) the chief administrative officer of a town. **town hall** the chief administrative building of a town. **town**

house a terraced house in a town with two or three storeys. **town planning** the designing of towns and cities to provide satisfactory living and working environments. **townscape** *n* a general view of a town. **townsfolk** *pl n* townspeople. **township** *n* (in South Africa) an urban area for non-Whites. **townspeople** *pl n* the inhabitants of a town. < Old English *tūn* village, town.

toxic (ˈtɒksɪk) *adj* **1** of or caused by poison. **2** poisonous. **toxicity** *n* **toxicology** *n* the scientific study of poisons. **toxicological** *adj* **toxicologist** *n* **toxin** *n* a poison produced by a living organism. SEE PANEL.

toy (tɔɪ) *n* **1** a thing for a child to play with. **2** something intended for amusement, not serious or practical use: executive toys.
• *adj* **1** serving as a toy. **2** (of an animal) of a tiny breed or variety.
• *vb* **toy with** deal with or think about something without seriousness : They toyed with the idea of emigrating. < Middle English *toye* dalliance.

trace (treɪs) *n* **1** a mark, track, etc., left behind by something. **2** a sign of something that existed or took place. **3** a slight amount or indication: no trace of blood.
• *vb* **1** follow the course or development of. **2** follow by noticing marks, tracks, and other signs. **3** copy (a drawing, map, etc.) by following the lines, etc., visible through a piece of paper placed over it. **4** sketch. **5** write with great care. **tracery** *n* decorative open-work in stone, esp. in a church window. **tracing** *n* something traced. **tracing-paper** *n* transparent paper for making tracings. < ultimately Latin *trahere* to drag.

trachea (trəˈkiːə) *n* the windpipe. < Greek *tracheia* (*arteria*) rough (artery).

toxic

Something that is poisonous is often referred to as toxic, as in toxic fumes or toxic chemicals. Toxic comes from the Latin word *toxicum* 'poison'. This derives from the Greek word *toxikon,* meaning 'poison used on the heads of arrows', from *toxon,* 'arrow'.

Toxon also provides the root of toxophily or 'archery', which is not to be confused with toxicology, 'the study of poisons'.

track (træk) *n* **1** a mark or marks left by something moving. **2** a path or rough road. **3** a prepared course for racing. **4** the parallel lines of a railway. **5** a rail along which something such as a curtain may be pulled. **6** the state of being aware of facts, developments, etc.: It's difficult to keep track of events. **7** a course of action or procedure: on the wrong track. **8** a section on a gramophone record. **9** the path on a magnetic tape along which information from a single channel is recorded.
• *vb* follow the tracks or trail of. **tracker** *n* **track events** athletic events, esp. running, that take place on the track. **track record** a record of past achievements. **track suit** a warm, loose-fitting suit worn by an athlete, etc., during training. < Middle French *trac.*

tract[1] (trækt) *n* **1** a large area of land. **2** a system of parts or organs of the body that has a particular function. < Latin *trahere* to pull, draw.

tract[2] *n* a pamphlet, esp. one on a religious subject. < ultimately Latin *tractare* to draw out, handle.

tractable (ˈtræktəbl̩) *adj* easily controlled or handled. **tractability** *n* < Latin *tractare* to handle.

traction (ˈtrækʃən) *n* **1** pulling or being pulled. **2** force exerted in pulling; power used in pulling. **3** the power of a moving object such as a tyre to grip a surface without slipping. **4** the continuous pull exerted on a bone using a special device, in treating a fracture, etc. < Latin *trahere* to pull.

tractor (ˈtræktə) *n* a powerful, four-wheeled vehicle used for pulling farm machinery. < SEE **TRACTION.**

trade (treɪd) *n* **1** the business of buying and selling goods or exchanging goods for goods. **2** a business of a particular kind: the textile trade. **3** the business in which one works. **4** an occupation needing manual or mechanical skills. **5** the people working in a particular trade.
• *vb* **1** buy and sell (goods); engage in trade. **2** give (one thing) in exchange for another in trading. **trader** *n* **trade gap** the amount by which a country's imports exceed its exports. **trade in** give (a used article) as partial payment for something. **trade-in** *n* **trademark** *n* the distinctive name, emblem, etc., of a manufacturer's or trader's goods. **trade on** take advantage of; exploit. **tradesman** *n, pl* **tradesmen 1** a man who works in a trade; shop-keeper. **2** a skilled worker. **trade union** also **trades**

union an organization of employees formed to advance its members' interests. **trade-unionist** *n* a member of a trade union. **trade wind** a mainly easterly wind that blows in the tropics. **trading estate** an area designed for occupation by industrial and commercial firms. **trading-stamp** *n* a stamp of a certain value given by a retailer to a customer, redeemable in quantities for certain goods or cash. < Middle English: track, course.

tradition (trəˈdɪʃən) *n* **1** the handing down of beliefs, customs, etc., from one generation to another, esp. when not in writing. **2** a belief, custom, etc., handed down in this way. **3** an established belief or procedure. **4** cultural heritage in beliefs, procedures, etc. **traditional** *adj* **traditionally** *adv* **traditionalist** *n* a person who upholds traditional beliefs, etc. < ultimately Latin *traditio* handing-down.

traffic (ˈtræfɪk) *n* **1** the flow of vehicles, ships, etc., along a route; such vehicles. **2** the business of trading, esp. in illegal or forbidden goods.
• *vb* **trafficked; trafficking** trade, esp. in illegal or forbidden goods: drug trafficking. **traffic-lights** *pl n* automatically operated coloured lights for controlling traffic at junctions, etc. **traffic warden** an official who assists police in controlling road traffic in a town, esp. the parking of vehicles. < ultimately Old Italian *trafficare* to trade.

tragedy (ˈtrædʒədɪ) *n* **1** an event that causes great sadness; disaster or calamity. **2** a drama or form of drama describing the fall, esp. the death, of the main character. **tragic** *adj* **1** of or to do with tragedy. **2** disastrous. **tragically** *adv* < ultimately Greek *tragōidia*.

trail (treɪl) *vb* **1** drag or be dragged behind one. **2** hang loosely; grow along the ground. **3** move wearily; lag behind. **4** follow the tracks of. **5** flow in a thin stream. **6** grow gradually weaker: His voice trailed away.
• *n* **1** a mark, track, etc., left by something that has passed: a trail of havoc. **2** a track or marked path: a nature trail. **3** something that trails. **trail-blazer** *n* a pioneer. **trailer** *n* **1** a wheeled vehicle designed to be towed by a vehicle. **2** (*US*) a caravan. **3** an extract or a series of extracts from a film, shown in advance to advertise it. < ultimately Latin *trahere* to drag.

train (treɪn) *n* **1** a line of linked carriages or wagons with or without a railway engine. **2** a line of moving people, vehicles, or animals. **3** a group of followers; retinue. **4** a linked series of ideas or actions: a train of events. **5** a part of a gown that trails on the ground behind the wearer.
• *vb* **1** teach or be taught by instruction and practice so as to make or become skilled. **2** make or become physically fit by exercise, etc. **3** teach and accustom (an animal) to obey commands, etc. **4** guide the growth of (a plant) by pruning, etc. **5** aim (a gun, etc.) at an object or goal. **trainee** *n* a person who is being trained for a job, etc. **trainer** *n* **1** a person who trains athletes. **2** a person who trains racehorses. **training** *n* **1** the bringing of a person, etc., to a desired standard of proficiency. **2** the condition of being trained, esp. physically fit: out of training. < Latin *trahere* to draw.

traipse (treɪps) *vb* (*informal*) walk heavily and steadily: We spent the whole afternoon traipsing round the shops. < origin unknown.

trait (treɪt, treɪ) *n* a distinctive characteristic. < Middle French: pulling, ultimately from Latin *trahere* to pull.

traitor (ˈtreɪtə) *n* a person who acts disloyally or who commits treason. **traitorous** *adj* < ultimately Latin *tradere* to hand over, betray.

trajectory (trəˈdʒɛktərɪ) *n* the curved path of something moving through air or space, such as that of a missile. < Latin *trans-*, *tra-* across + *jacere* to throw.

tram (træm) *n* a passenger vehicle that runs on rails set in the road. < English dialect: shaft of a cart, probably from Low German *traam* beam.

trammel (ˈtræməl) *n* often **trammels** something that hinders movement.
• *vb* **trammelled; trammelling** hinder movement. < Middle French *tremail* three-mesh net, from Latin *tres* three + *macula* mesh.

tramp (træmp) *vb* **1** walk heavily. **2** travel about on foot.
• *n* **1** a person who travels about on foot, living by begging or doing casual work; vagrant. **2** the sound of heavy footsteps. **3** a long, tiring walk. **4** a cargo vessel that works an irregular route. **5** (*informal*) a promiscuous woman. < Middle English *trampen*.

trample (ˈtræmpl̩) *vb* **1** tread roughly so as to crush, bruise, etc.; crush or bruise in this way. **2** act in a rough, insensitive, or destructive way so as to hurt or encroach upon (someone's feelings, rights, etc.). < SEE **TRAMP**.

trampoline (ˈtræmpəˌliːn) *n* a sheet of strong canvas, etc., supported by springs in a frame, used for jumping and tumbling on. < Italian *trampolino*, of Germanic origin.

trance (trɑːns) *n* **1** a sleep-like condition, for example that induced by hypnosis. **2** a dreamy condition in which a person is deeply absorbed in thought. < ultimately Latin *transire* to pass away.

tranquil (ˈtræŋkwɪl) *adj* calm, peaceful, and undisturbed. **tranquillity** *n* **tranquilly** *adv* **tranquillize** *vb* make tranquil; relieve the anxiety of and make calm by the use of drugs. **tranquillizer** *n* a drug that tranquillizes. < Latin *tranquillus.*

transact (trænˈzækt) *vb* conduct or perform; carry out (business). **transactor** *n* **transaction** *n* transacting; business transacted. **transactions** *pl n* the published record of the proceedings of a society, etc. < Latin *trans-* across + *agere* to do.

transatlantic (ˌtrænzətˈlæntɪk) *adj* **1** crossing or reaching across the Atlantic ocean. **2** of, on, or from the other side of the Atlantic.

transcend (trænˈsɛnd) *vb* **1** go beyond the limits of. **2** surpass or excel. **transcendent** *adj* going beyond the limits of normal, human experience. **transcendental** *adj* **1** transcendent. **2** supernatural; visionary. **3** abstract; obscure. < Latin *trans-* beyond + *scandere* to climb.

transcontinental (ˌtrænzkɒntɪˈnɛntl̩) *adj* crossing or reaching across a continent.

transcribe (trænˈskraɪb) *vb* **1** copy in written form: transcribe shorthand. **2** arrange (a piece of music) for a different musical instrument. **3** transfer (sound, etc.) for later reproduction: transcribe a record onto tape. **transcriber** *n* **transcription** *n* **transcript** *n* a written or printed copy. < Latin *trans-* over + *scribere* to write.

transept (ˈtrænsɛpt) *n* the part in a cross-shaped church at right angles to the nave; either arm of this. < Latin *trans-* across + *septum* enclosure.

transfer (trænsˈfɜː) *vb* **transferred; transferring 1** convey or move from one place, person, etc., to another. **2** make over the ownership of (a property, business, etc.) to. **3** move (a design, etc.) from one surface to another by contact. **4** (of a professional footballer, etc.) move or be moved to another club. • *n* (ˈtrænsfɜː) **1** transferring or being transferred. **2** a design transferred by contact from one surface to another. **3** the passing of a right of ownership from one person, etc., to another; document transferring such a right. **transferable** *adj* **transference** *n* < Latin *trans-* across + *ferre* to carry.

transfigure (trænsˈfɪgə) *vb* make a significant change in the appearance of. **transfiguration** *n* **the Transfiguration** the change in the appearance of Jesus on the mountain. < Latin *trans-* across + *figura* appearance.

transfix (trænsˈfɪks) *vb* **1** render motionless, with fear, surprise, etc. **2** pierce with a pointed weapon. < Latin *trans-* through + *figere* to thrust in.

transform (trænsˈfɔːm) *vb* **1** make a great change in the appearance, structure, function, etc., of. **2** become transformed. **transformation** *n* **transformer** *n* a device that converts alternating current from one voltage to another. < Latin *trans-* over + *forma* form.

transfuse (trænsˈfjuːz) *vb* **1** spread into, through, or across. **2** transfer (blood, etc.) into a blood-vessel. **transfusion** *n* < Latin *trans-* across + *fundere* to pour.

transgress (trænzˈgrɛs) *vb* **1** break (a law, etc.); go beyond (a limit). **2** sin. **transgression** *n* **transgressor** *n* < Latin *trans-* over + *gradi* to step.

transient (ˈtrænzɪənt) *adj* passing; short-lived. **transience** *n* < Latin *trans-* across + *ire* to go.

transistor (trænˈzɪstə) *n* **1** a semiconductor of three sections, having a voltage amplifying effect, and smaller and less fragile than its predecessor the valve. **2** also **transistor radio** a portable radio set powered by transistors. **transistorize** *vb* equip or construct with transistors. < *trans*fer + re*sistor.*

transit (ˈtrænzɪt) *n* the passage or conveyance of goods or people. **transit camp** a camp for temporary accommodation of soldiers, refugees, etc. < Latin *transire* to go across.

transition (trænˈzɪʃən) *n* the passage or development from one stage, state, etc., to another. **transitional** *adj* < SEE TRANSIT.

transitive (ˈtrænsɪtɪv) *adj* (of a verb) having a direct object. **transitively** *adv* < SEE **TRANSIT.** SEE PANEL AT **BRING.**

transitory (ˈtrænsɪtərɪ) *adj* existing or lasting for only a short time. < SEE TRANSIENT.

translate (trænzˈleɪt) *vb* **1** express in another language. **2** express in different, esp. simpler words. **3** be able to be translated: His poems don't translate well.

4 interpret. **5** change or transform: translate ideas into reality. **translation** *n* **translator** *n* **translatable** *adj* able to be translated. < SEE **TRANSFER.**

transliterate (trænzˈlɪtəˌreɪt) *vb* represent in the letters of a different alphabet. **transliteration** *n* < *trans-* across + Latin *littera* letter.

translucent (trænzˈluːsn̩t) *adj* allowing the passage of light, but not transparent. **translucence** *n* < Latin *trans-* through + *lucēre* to shine. SEE PANEL AT **TRANSPARENT.**

transmit (trænzˈmɪt) *vb* **transmitted; transmitting 1** transfer from one person or place to another. **2** pass on (a disease). **3** send out (a signal) by radio waves, etc. **4** cause (a light, force, etc.) to pass through a medium; act as a medium for. **transmissible** *adj* able to be transmitted. **transmission** *n* **1** transmitting or being transmitted. **2** something transmitted; broadcast. **3** the part of a motor vehicle by which power is transmitted to the axle. **transmitter** *n* an apparatus that transmits electric, radio, etc., signals. < Latin *trans-* over + *mittere* to send.

transmute (trænzˈmjuːt) *vb* change in form, character, or substance. **transmutation** *n* < Latin *trans-* over + *mutare* to change.

transom (ˈtrænsəm) *n* a piece that is set across something in a structure, such as the beam across a window or over the top of a door. < probably Latin *transtrum* cross-beam.

transparent (trænsˈpærənt) *adj* **1** allowing the passage of light so that a clear image of an object is formed. **2** open; frank; not showing deceit: transparent intentions. **3** easily understood. **transparently** *adv* **transparency** *n* **1** being transparent. **2** a photograph on a film, usually mounted in a frame and projected onto a screen; slide. < Latin *trans-* through + *parēre* to appear. SEE PANEL.

transpire (trænˈspaɪə) *vb* **1** happen or occur; take place. **2** become known. **3** give off (water vapour, etc.) from a surface. **transpiration** *n* < Latin *trans-* through + *spirare* to breathe. SEE PANEL.

transplant (trænsˈplɑːnt) *vb* **1** remove from one place and put, plant, or establish in another place. **2** transfer (living tissue or an organ) from one person or part of the body to another. • *n* (ˈtrænsˌplɑːnt) transplanting; something transplanted: a heart transplant. < Latin *trans-* across + *plantare* to plant.

transport (trænˈspɔːt) *vb* **1** move or convey from one place to another. **2** deport to a penal settlement. **3** affect in an emotionally intense way. • *n* (ˈtrænˌspɔːt) **1** the transporting of goods or people. **2** a means of transporting goods or people; ship, aeroplane, lorry, etc. **3** a strong, esp. pleasant emotion: transports of delight. **transportable** *adj* **transportation** *n* **transporter** *n* **transport café** a roadside café that caters mainly for long-distance lorry drivers. < Latin *trans-* over + *portare* to carry.

transpose (trænˈspəʊz) *vb* **1** change from one position, place, etc., to another. **2** put (music) in a different key. **transposition** *n* < Latin *trans-* across + *ponere* to place.

transverse (trænzˈvɜːs) *adj* lying, situated, or being across; crosswise.

transparent or **translucent?**

Something is transparent if light rays pass through it without being scattered. A plain glass window is transparent, as a clear image of what is on the other side of the window is given.

Something that scatters the light rays as they pass through it is translucent. Examples of translucent material are waxed paper and frosted glass—these allow the passage of light but objects cannot be seen clearly through them.

transpire

Some careful users of English object to the use of transpire to mean 'to happen or occur; take place' as in We will never find out what transpired at the meeting. Transpire is reserved for the meaning 'to become known': As a result of police enquiries, it transpired that the company had been falsifying its accounts for several years. However, the use of transpire in the first sense is nowadays becoming increasingly common.

transversely *adv* < SEE **TRAVERSE.**
transvestite (trænzˈvɛstaɪt) *n* a person who wears clothes that are usually associated with the opposite sex, esp. to gain sexual pleasure. **transvestism** *n* < Latin *trans-* over + *vestire* to clothe.
trap (træp) *n* **1** a device that catches and holds animals. **2** a device, plan, or trick to catch a person unawares. **3** a device that prevents the escape of gas, unpleasant smells, etc. **4** a light, two-wheeled carriage: pony and trap. **5** (*slang*) the mouth: Shut your trap!
• *vb* **trapped; trapping** catch or hold in a trap. **trapdoor** *n* a door that covers an opening in a floor or ceiling. **trapper** *n* a person who traps animals, esp. for their skins. < Old English *treppe.*
trapeze (trəˈpiːz) *n* a short, horizontal bar suspended between two ropes that is used as a swing by acrobats and gymnasts. < SEE **TRAPEZIUM.**
trapezium (trəˈpiːzɪəm) *n* a quadrilateral with only two sides parallel. < Greek *trapeza* table, from *tra-* four + *peza* foot.
trappings (ˈtræpɪŋz) *pl n* outward, esp. decorative trimmings or accessories. < Middle English *trappe* cloth.
trash (træʃ) *n* **1** something that is worthless or inferior; rubbish or nonsense. **2** worthless people. **trashy** *adj* < origin uncertain.
trauma (ˈtrɔːmə) *n* **1** a powerful, mental or emotional shock that has disordering effects on a person: the trauma of divorce. **2** a wound or injury. **traumatic** *adj* < Greek: wound.
travel (ˈtrævl̩) *vb* **travelled; travelling** **1** make a journey (through or over). **2** go or move from one place or point to another: Light waves travel in straight lines. **3** cover (a distance) in travelling: We travelled over 300 miles today. **4** go from place to place as a sales representative. **5** move along on a rail, runner, etc.: The sliding doors don't travel easily. **6** (*informal*) move at a high speed.
• *n* **1** travelling, esp. to distant places: space travel. **2** the movement of a piece of machinery. **travel agency** or **bureau** an agency that books flights, hotel accommodation, package holidays, etc., as a service for travellers. **travel agent** a person working in a travel agency. **travelled** *adj* having travelled widely. **traveller** *n* **1** a person who travels. **2** a travelling sales representative: a commercial traveller. **traveller's cheque** a cheque for a fixed sum that is bought from a bank, etc., to be cashed abroad in foreign currency. **travelogue** *n* a film, illustrated lecture, etc., on a distant, esp. exotic place. < Old French *travaillier* to work, toil.
traverse (ˈtrævɜːs) *vb* go, reach, or lie across.
• *n* **1** something that crosses or lies across. **2** a path or way across or over. **3** a zigzag course. < Latin *trans-* over + *vertere* to turn.
travesty (ˈtrævəstɪ) *n* an absurd, grotesque, or distorted imitation: a travesty of justice.
• *vb* **travestied; travestying** make a travesty of. < Latin *trans-* over + *vestire* to dress.
trawler (ˈtrɔːlə) *n* a boat that is equipped for catching fish by towing nets along the bottom of the sea. < probably Middle Dutch *traghelen* to drag.
tray (treɪ) *n* **1** a thin, flat object with a low rim used esp. for carrying or holding small articles. **2** a shallow, open receptacle for papers, etc., in an office: an in-tray. < Old English *trēg.*
treacherous (ˈtrɛtʃərəs) *adj* **1** marked by treachery. **2** unreliable, dangerous, and deceptive. **treacherously** *adv* **treachery** *n* a betrayal of loyalty or trust. < Old French *trechier* to deceive.
treacle (ˈtriːkl̩) *n* a dark, thick, viscous syrup produced when sugar is refined. **treacly** *adj* < Greek *thēriakē* remedy for a poisonous bite. SEE PANEL.

treacle

The thick, dark syrup that is produced in sugar refining is known as treacle. In Middle English the meaning of the word was very different. *Triacle* was a medicinal compound used primarily as an antidote to poison. This meaning reflects the use of the syrup in olden days as a base for medicinal matter, which thereby became more palatable. In time the name came to be used just for the syrup.

Triacle has a long and curious history, deriving via Middle French and Latin from the Greek *thēriakē*, 'an antidote against a poisonous bite'. *Thēriakē* comes ultimately from *thēr*, 'a wild animal'. The latter shift of meaning reflects the belief of the ancients that the best antidote for a toxic bite was a preparation containing the flesh of the animal that had done the biting.

tread (trɛd) *vb* **trod; trodden; treading** **1** set one's foot or walk (on, along, etc.). **2** crush or press with the feet. **3** repress or subdue as if by trampling. **4** form (a path, trail, etc.) by treading.
• *n* **1** the manner or sound of treading. **2** the part of a wheel or tyre that touches the ground. **3** the upper surface of a step. < Old English *tredan*. SEE PANEL.

treason (ˈtriːzn̩) *n* the offence of violating allegiance to one's country or ruler. **treasonable** *adj* of or being treason. < SEE **TRAITOR.**

treasure (ˈtrɛʒə) *n* **1** wealth or riches; hoard of these. **2** a very valuable object. **3** a highly valued person.
• *vb* value highly; keep as precious. **treasure-hunt** *n* a game in which players try to find what has been hidden. **treasurer** *n* a person in charge of funds of a society, etc. **treasure trove** any money, gold, bullion, etc., that is of unknown ownership. **the Treasury** the government department that is responsible for a country's finance. < ultimately Greek *thēsauros*.

treat (triːt) *vb* **1** act towards in a way that is mentioned: They treated him as one of the family. **2** consider or deal with in a way that is mentioned: The subject is treated in great detail. **3** give medical, surgical, etc., care to. **4** provide (esp. another person) with food, entertainment, etc., at one's own expense. **5** subject to a process, to bring about a change.
• *n* **1** an entertainment that is given free of charge. **2** a source of great pleasure, esp. when unexpected. **treatment** *n* **1** the act, method, etc., of treating. **2** medical, etc., treatment. < ultimately Latin *tractare* to manage, from *trahere* to draw.

treading on air

Tread features in a number of idiomatic expressions, including:

tread on air to be very happy.
tread on someone's toes to infringe on someone's area of responsibility; act insensitively towards someone; offend and upset.
tread water 1 to stay afloat in an upright position by using one's legs as if walking. **2** to maintain one's present position, not bothering or not able to make progress.

treatise (ˈtriːtɪs, ˈtriːtɪz) *n* a formal, written work, esp. one that treats a subject systematically. < Old French *traitier* to treat.

treaty (ˈtriːtɪ) *n* a formal agreement between two or more countries: a peace treaty. < SEE **TREAT.**

treble (ˈtrɛbl̩) *adj* **1** threefold. **2** of or relating to a high-pitched voice or musical instrument.
• *n* **1** a high-pitched voice; person, esp. a boy, with this. **2** something treble in value, amount, etc.
• *vb* make or become three times the amount, size, etc.: The population of the city has trebled in the last 20 years. **trebly** *adv* < Latin *triplus*. SEE PANEL.

tree (triː) *n* **1** a tall, perennial, woody plant with a trunk and branches that rise some distance above the ground. **2** a diagram with many branches from a single stem: a family tree. **3** a shoe-tree. < Old English *trēow*.

trek (trɛk) *n* a long, esp. difficult journey.
• *vb* **trekked; trekking** make a trek. < Middle Dutch *trekken* to draw, travel.

trellis (ˈtrɛlɪs) *n* an open framework of crossing wooden or metal strips, esp. used to support climbing plants. < ultimately Latin *tri-* three + *licium* thread.

tremble (ˈtrɛmbl̩) *vb* **1** shake or vibrate, esp. involuntarily, as with cold or fear; quiver. **2** feel great anxiety or fear.
• *n* a trembling movement. < Latin *tremere*.

tremendous (trɪˈmɛndəs) *adj* **1** great; immense: a tremendous difference. **2** (*informal*) excellent. **tremendously** *adv* < SEE **TREMBLE.**

tremolo (ˈtrɛməˌləʊ) *n, pl* **tremolos** a trembling effect in music or singing. < Italian: SEE **TREMBLE.**

tremor (ˈtrɛmə) *n* **1** a trembling from weakness, illness, fear, etc. **2** a slight shaking or trembling movement: an earth tremor. < SEE **TREMBLE.**

treble or triple?

Careful users distinguish triple and treble. Triple is used to mean 'consisting of three parts': a *triple* somersault, a *triple* crown, a *triple* alliance. Treble is used to mean 'three times as great': The additional sum will be calculated at *treble* the normal amount.

tremulous (ˈtrɛmjʊləs) *adj* **1** trembling or quivering. **2** timid. **tremulously** *adv* < SEE **TREMBLE.**

trench (trɛntʃ) *n* a deep, narrow ditch dug in the ground, esp. one used in military defence. **trench coat** a belted raincoat in a military style. < Middle French *trenchier* to cut.

trenchant (ˈtrɛntʃənt) *adj* **1** penetrating and sharp: trenchant criticism. **2** strong and effective. < SEE **TRENCH.**

trend (trɛnd) *n* a general tendency or movement: contemporary trends in fashion. **trend-setter** *n* a person who starts new trends, esp. in fashion. **trendy** *adj, n* (*informal*) (a person who is) very fashionable. **trendily** *adv* **trendiness** *n* < Old English *trendan* to turn.

trepidation (ˌtrɛpɪˈdeɪʃən) *n* nervous anxiety and fear. < Latin *trepidare* to be alarmed.

trespass (ˈtrɛspəs) *vb* **1** go on a person's land or property unlawfully. **2** intrude unreasonably (on). **3** (*old-fashioned*) sin.
• *n* **1** the act of trespassing. **2** (*old-fashioned*) a sin. **trespasser** *n* < Old French *tres-* across + *passer* to pass.

tress (trɛs) *n* a lock or plait of hair. < Old French *trece.*

trestle (ˈtrɛsl̩) *n* **1** a frame consisting of a horizontal beam attached at each end to a pair of spreading legs. **2** a braced framework for a bridge. < ultimately Latin *transtrum* transom.

triad (ˈtraɪæd) *n* a group of three. < ultimately Greek *treis* three.

trial (ˈtraɪəl) *n* **1** an examination in a law-court and determination of an accused person's guilt or innocence. **2** the testing of usefulness, quality, etc.: ten days' free trial. **3** a test of endurance; hardship; source of discontent, etc. **4** a preliminary match to assess players' abilities. **5** a test of a person's ability to handle a vehicle over rough ground. **6** a test of the skills of an animal: sheep-dog trials.
• *adj* of a trial, test, or experiment: a trial run. **on trial** undergoing a trial; being tested or examined. **trial and error** the process of experimenting repeatedly until the right result, etc., is found. < Anglo-French *trier* to try.

triangle (ˈtraɪˌæŋgl̩) *n* **1** a geometric figure with three sides and three angles. **2** something shaped like this, esp. a percussion instrument consisting of a metal bar bent into this shape and struck with a metal rod. **triangular** *adj* **1** having the form or shape of a triangle. **2** involving or between three groups, people, etc. < Latin *tri-* three + *angulus* angle. SEE PANEL AT **CIRCLE.**

tribe (traɪb) *n* a social group descended from the same ancestor; preliterate or nomadic people ruled by one or more chiefs. **tribal** *adj* of a tribe or tribes. **tribesman** *n, pl* **tribesmen** a member of a tribe. < Latin *tribus* division of the Roman people.

tribulation (ˌtrɪbjʊˈleɪʃən) *n* great suffering or distress; cause of this. < Latin *tribulare* to afflict.

tribunal (traɪˈbjuːnl̩) *n* a board of officials appointed to settle disputes of a particular kind or arbitrate on an issue: a rent tribunal < Latin *tribunus* tribune, probably from *tribus* tribe.

tributary (ˈtrɪbjʊtərɪ) *n* a stream or river that flows into a larger one.
• *adj* flowing in this way. < SEE **TRIBUTE.**

tribute (ˈtrɪbjuːt) *n* **1** something given, said, or done that shows thankfulness, respect, or admiration. **2** a sign of the value or effectiveness of. < Latin *tribuere* to grant, allot.

trice (traɪs) *n* a moment: in a trice. < Middle English *trise* pull, tug.

trick (trɪk) *n* **1** a cunning or deceitful action meant to deceive or cheat someone. **2** a mischievous action: The children are up to their tricks again. **3** a deceptive, skilful feat performed for entertainment: conjuring tricks. **4** a skilful act: teach a dog to do tricks. **5** an illusion or deception: a trick of light. **6** a habit or mannerism. **7** the cards played in one round of a card-game.
• *adj* of or involving tricks.
• *vb* mislead, deceive, or persuade by a trick. **trickery** *n* the use of tricks in deception. **trickster** *n* a person who tricks. **tricky** *adj* **1** involving difficulties; requiring care and skill in handling: a tricky manoeuvre. **2** marked by tricks. **trickiness** *n* < Old French *trichier* to cheat. SEE PANEL.

trickle (ˈtrɪkl̩) *vb* **1** flow in drops or a slow, thin stream. **2** move or go slowly or gradually.
• *n* a trickling flow or movement. < perhaps like the sound.

tricycle (ˈtraɪsɪkl̩) *n* a three-wheeled cycle, esp. one driven by pedals.

tried (traɪd) SEE **TRY.**

triennial (traɪˈɛnɪəl) *adj* **1** lasting three years. **2** occurring every three years. **triennium** *n, pl* **trienniums** a period of three years. < Latin *tri-* three + *annus* year.

trier (ˈtraɪə) *n* a person who tries hard.

trifle (ˈtraɪfl̩) *n* **1** a small amount, esp. of

money: It will cost a mere trifle. **2** a dessert made with sponge-cake soaked in wine, etc., and covered with jelly, custard, and cream.
• *vb* **1** act carelessly or frivolously. **2 trifle with** treat casually and without seriousness. **trifler** *n* **a trifle** a little; rather: looking a trifle startled. **trifling** *adj* not significant; trivial. < Old French *trufler* to cheat.

trigger (ˈtrɪgə) *n* a device such as a lever that releases the firing mechanism of a gun.
• *vb* **1** release or fire by a trigger. **2** also **trigger off** cause (an event, reaction, etc.). **trigger-happy** *adj* apt to use firearms irresponsibly or to act impulsively and belligerently. < Middle Dutch *trecken* to pull.

trigonometry (ˌtrɪgəˈnɒmətrɪ) *n* the branch of mathematics that deals with the relationships between the sides and angles of triangles. < ultimately Greek *trigōnon* triangle.

trilby (ˈtrɪlbɪ) *n* a man's soft, felt hat with an indented crown. < *Trilby*, novel by George du Maurier, died 1896, British writer. SEE PANEL.

trill (trɪl) *n* **1** (*music*) the rapid alternation of two notes that are a tone or semitone apart. **2** a bird's shrill warble.
• *vb* sound or sing with a trill. < Italian, probably from Middle Dutch *trillen* to vibrate.

trillion (ˈtrɪljən) *n* **1** (in the UK) one million million million. **2** (in the USA) one million million. **3** an indefinitely large number. < French, from *tri-* three + *-illion*, as in *million*.

trilogy (ˈtrɪlədʒɪ) *n* a group of three related literary, etc., works. < Greek *tri-* three + *logos* word.

trim (trɪm) *adj* **trimmer; trimmest** neat and orderly; clean-cut.
• *vb* **1** make trim, esp. by clipping. **2** cut or clip to a desired size or shape. **3** decorate with colourful materials, etc.
• *n* **1** a condition, esp. a good one. **2** physical fitness. **3** the trimming of hair by clipping or cutting. **4** a trimming on a dress, piece of furniture, etc. **5** one's clothes or general appearance. **trimly** *adv* **trimness** *n* **trimming** *n* **1** an additional, ornamental item on a dress, piece of furniture, etc. **2** *pl* pieces that are cut off. **3** *pl* ornaments or garnishes: roast turkey with all the trimmings. < Old English *trymman* to strengthen.

trinket (ˈtrɪŋkɪt) *n* a small, decorative article or item of cheap jewellery. < perhaps Old Northern French *trenquet*.

trio (ˈtriːəʊ) *n, pl* **trios 1** a group of three instruments, singers, or players; musical composition for this. **2** a group of three. < Italian, ultimately from Latin *tri-* three.

trip (trɪp) *n* **1** a journey or excursion. **2** (*slang*) the experience that follows the taking of a drug, esp. LSD. **3** a light, short step. **4** a device for tripping a mechanism.
• *vb* **tripped; tripping 1** also **trip up** stumble or fall; cause to do this. **2** move with light, short steps. **3** also **trip up** make a mistake; cause to do this. **4** flow smoothly and easily. **5** activate or operate (a mechanism), as by releasing a

do the trick

Trick features in a number of idiomatic expressions, including:

do the trick to achieve what is desired: This extra strong glue should do the trick nicely.
never miss a trick to remain constantly alert to everything, especially matters that will bring personal gain. The expression derives from card-games.
the whole bag of tricks all the items, methods, etc., that are required for an activity.
trick or treat used as a threat by children in the chiefly American custom of calling on houses at Hallowe'en, asking for small gifts and threatening to play tricks on people who refuse.

trilby

A soft, felt hat with a brim and the crown indented lengthwise is known as a trilby. The name of the hat derives from *'Trilby'*, a novel by the writer and caricaturist, George du Maurier, 1834–96, grandfather of Daphne du Maurier. The hat was first worn in a London stage production of the novel in 1895.

In the United States the trilby goes by the name of fedora. Rather curiously, this name is also of literary origin. It comes from *'Fédora'*, a play written in 1882 by the French dramatist, Victorien Sardou, 1831–1908.

catch. **tripper** *n* a person who goes on a pleasure trip: day-trippers. **trip-wire** *n* a hidden wire just above the ground that actuates a trap, explosive, warning device, etc., when tripped over. < Middle French *triper,* of Germanic origin.

tripartite (traɪˈpɑːtaɪt) *adj* composed of three parts.

tripe (traɪp) *n* **1** part of the stomach of an ox, etc., used as food. **2** (*informal*) something worthless; nonsense. < Old French.

triple (ˈtrɪpl) *adj* **1** consisting of three parts: a triple somersault. **2** three times as great or as many. **3** (of musical time) marked by three beats in each bar.
• *vb* make or become three times as great or as many. **triply** *adv* < Latin *triplus.* SEE PANEL AT **TREBLE.**

triplet (ˈtrɪplɪt) *n* **1** one of three children or animals born at one birth. **2** a set of three things. < *triple* + *-et,* as in *doublet.*

triplicate (ˈtrɪplɪkət) *adj* made up of three parts; being a triplicate; threefold.
• *vb* (ˈtrɪplɪˌkeɪt) make or be three identical copies of.
• *n* (ˈtrɪplɪkət) one of three things that are alike, esp. one of three identical copies. < Latin *triplex* threefold.

tripod (ˈtraɪpɒd) *n* a three-legged stand, as for a camera. < Greek *tri-* three + *pous* foot.

trite (traɪt) *adj* hackneyed; common and dull. < Latin *terere* to rub.

triumph (ˈtraɪəmf) *n* **1** a great success, achievement, or victory. **2** the fact of being successful or victorious. **3** the feeling of exultation and joy at a success, etc.
• *vb* **1** win a victory (over) or be successful; overcome. **2** rejoice over a success, etc. **triumphal** *adj* **triumphant** *adj* **1** successful or victorious; conquering. **2** rejoicing in a success, etc. **triumphantly** *adv* < Latin *triumphus.* SEE PANEL.

triumvirate (traɪˈʌmvɪrət) *n* a ruling group of three officials. < Latin *trium virum* of three men.

trivet (ˈtrɪvɪt) *n* a low, metal stand on which cooking vessels are placed. < Latin *tri-* three + *pes* foot.

trivia (ˈtrɪvɪə) *pl n* unimportant matters. **trivial** *adj* unimportant; ordinary. **triviality** *n* **trivially** *adv* < Latin *tri-* three + *via* road. SEE PANEL.

trod (trɒd) SEE **TREAD. trodden** SEE **TREAD.**

troll (trəʊl) *n* a dwarf or giant of Scandinavian folklore who lives in caves or mountains. < Old Norse.

trolley (ˈtrɒlɪ) *n, pl* **trolleys 1** a basket-like cart used to carry goods in a supermarket. **2** a small cart used to transport luggage at a railway station, etc. **3** a small table on castors or wheels used to convey food or small articles. **trolley-bus** *n* a bus powered by electricity from an overhead wire. < probably Middle English *trollen* to roll.

trombone (trɒmˈbəʊn) *n* a brass musical instrument that consists of a long tube with a movable slide for changing the pitch. < Italian *tromba* trumpet, of Germanic origin.

troop (truːp) *n* **1** a group of people or things. **2** a military unit, for example of cavalry. **3** a unit of Scouts or Guides. **4** *pl* the armed forces.
• *vb* move, esp. as a large group.

triumphal or triumphant?

These two words are sometimes confused.

Triumphal is the less common word and means 'associated with the celebration of a triumph'. It is used to describe events: a *triumphal* procession.

Triumphant means 'successful or victorious; rejoicing in a success'. It is used to describe people, their behaviour, or appearance: a *triumphant* army, a *triumphant* expression on his face.

trivial

A matter or detail which is of little importance might be described as trivial. This word derives via the Latin adjective *trivialis* from *trivium* or 'a three-forked crossroads', a compound of *tri* 'three' and *via* 'a road'. This was considered to be a typical spot where people would stop to engage in small talk or trivia.

Another word of the same origin is trivium. This was the name used in the Middle Ages for the arts of grammar, rhetoric, and logic, which together constituted the lower division of the seven liberal arts. The higher division or quadrivium comprised arithmetic, geometry, astronomy, and music.

trooper *n* a soldier in a cavalry regiment. < Middle French *troupe*, of Germanic origin. SEE PANEL.

trophy (ˈtrəʊfɪ) *n* **1** an object, such as a silver cup, that is awarded as a prize in a sports contest, etc. **2** something gained in a war, etc., and kept as a memorial of victory. < Greek *tropaion*, ultimately *trepein* to turn.

tropic (ˈtrɒpɪk) *n* **1** the parallel of latitude about 23½° north of the equator, the tropic of Cancer, or the same latitude south of it, the tropic of Capricorn. **2 the tropics** the region between the tropics of Cancer and Capricorn. **tropical** *adj* of, like, or relating to the tropics. < ultimately Greek *tropē* turn.

trot (trɒt) *n* **1** a gait of a horse, faster than a walk but slower than a canter. **2** a steady, brisk, walking pace.
• *vb* **trotted; trotting** go or cause to go at a trot. **on the trot** (*informal*) one after the other. **trot out** (*informal*) produce in a casual, predictable manner: He trotted out all the usual excuses. < Middle French *troter* to trot, of Germanic origin.

trotter (ˈtrɒtə) *n* **1** a horse trained for trotting-races, in which horses trot, pulling light vehicles. **2** an animal's foot used as food: pigs' trotters.

trouble (ˈtrʌbl̩) *n* **1** difficulty, misfortune, or distress; cause of this. **2** effort or bother: It's no trouble at all. **3** nuisance or inconvenience. **4** a disease or illness: stomach trouble. **5** a malfunction: engine trouble; teething troubles. **6** public disturbance or unrest. **7** a state of being pregnant while unmarried: He's got some girl into trouble.
• *vb* **1** cause trouble to; worry, upset, or inconvenience. **2** make an effort: Don't trouble to come. **3** make (waters) turbulent or rough. **trouble-maker** *n* a person who causes trouble. **trouble-shooter** *n* a person who can find and repair faults in machinery, or who acts as a mediator to settle disputes. **troublesome** *adj* causing trouble or annoyance. **trouble-spot** *n* a place where trouble recurs.

troop or **troupe?**

As these two words are pronounced in the same way, they are sometimes confused. A troop is a military unit: *troops* of soldiers or a unit of Scouts or Guides: a Scout *troop*. A troupe is a group of actors or performers: a *troupe* of acrobats.

< ultimately Latin *turbidus* turbid.

trough (trɒf) *n* **1** a long, narrow, open container, esp. for holding water or food for animals. **2** a channel for water. **3** a depression between waves, ridges, etc. **4** an elongated area of low atmospheric pressure. **5** a low point in the level of economic activity. < Old English *trog*.

trounce (traʊns) *vb* beat; thrash. < origin unknown.

troupe (truːp) *n* a company of actors, acrobats, etc. < SEE **TROOP.** SEE PANEL AT **TROOP.**

trousers (ˈtraʊzəz) *pl n* a two-legged garment reaching from the waist, esp. to the ankles. **trouser-suit** *n* a woman's suit of jacket and trousers. **wear the trousers** (*informal*) be the dominant partner, esp. in a marriage. < Scottish Gaelic *triubhas*.

trousseau (ˈtruːsəʊ) *n* a bride's outfit of clothes, linen, etc. < Old French *trousse* bundle.

trout (traʊt) *n, pl* **trout** any of several food and game fish mostly found in fresh water. < ultimately Greek *trōktēs* gnawer, sharp-toothed fish.

trowel (ˈtraʊəl) *n* **1** a small hand tool with a flat, metal blade, used for spreading mortar, etc. **2** a small garden tool with a curved blade used for lifting plants, etc. < ultimately Latin *trua* ladle.

truant (ˈtruːənt) *n* a child who stays away from school without permission.
• *adj* of or being a truant. **truancy** *n* **play truant** stay away as a truant. < Old French: vagabond, probably of Celtic origin.

truce (truːs) *n* an agreement to cease hostilities, esp. temporarily. < Old English *trēow* faith, fidelity.

truck[1] (trʌk) *n* **1** an open railway wagon for carrying goods. **2** (*chiefly US*) a lorry. **3** a cart for transporting heavy articles. < probably ultimately Greek *trochos* wheel.

truck[2] *n* **have no truck with** (*informal*) not be willing to deal with. < Old French *troquer* to barter.

truculent (ˈtrʌkjʊlənt) *adj* fierce, defiant, and aggressive. < Latin *trux* fierce.

trudge (trʌdʒ) *vb* walk heavily or laboriously. < origin unknown.

true (truː) *adj* **1** in accordance with fact or reality. **2** real or genuine; not false: true love. **3** accurate or exact: a true copy. **4** faithful or loyal: a true friend. **5** determined according to the earth's axis, not the magnetic poles: true north. **6** accurately formed, placed, or balanced.
• *adv* truly.

• *n* accurate alignment: out of true. **trueness** *n* **true-blue** *adj* staunchly loyal; Conservative in politics. **true-to-life** *adj* realistic. **truism** *n* a self-evident truth. **truly** *adv* **1** truthfully, sincerely, or genuinely. **2** indeed. **3** properly. < Old English *trēowe* faithful. SEE PANEL AT SHEER[1].

truffle (ˈtrʌfl̩) *n* **1** a fleshy, edible, rounded fungus that grows underground. **2** a rich, soft sweet flavoured with chocolate or rum. < ultimately Latin *tuber*.

trump (trʌmp) *n* **1** also **trump-card** a playing-card of a suit that ranks higher than others. **2** this suit; trumps.
• *vb* take (a trick, etc.) with a trump. < alteration of *triumph*. SEE PANEL.

trumpet (ˈtrʌmpɪt) *n* **1** a valved, brass musical instrument consisting of a narrow tube and a flaring bell. **2** something shaped like this.
• *vb* **1** blow a trumpet; sound like a trumpet. **2** proclaim with or as if with a trumpet. **trumpeter** *n* a person who plays the trumpet. < Old French *trompe*.

truncate (trʌŋˈkeɪt) *vb* shorten by cutting off a part. < Latin *truncus* trunk.

truncheon (ˈtrʌntʃən) *n* a short, thick stick carried esp. by the police. < Latin *truncus* trunk.

trundle (ˈtrʌndl̩) *vb* move heavily along on wheels. < Old English *trendel* wheel, disc.

trunk (trʌŋk) *n* **1** the main stem of a tree. **2** the human body excluding the head and limbs. **3** a large, strong box for transporting or storing clothes, etc. **4** (*US*) the boot of a car. **5** the long, flexible snout of an elephant. **trunk-call** *n* a long-distance, inland telephone call. **trunk-road** *n* a main road, esp. one for heavy vehicles. **trunks** *pl n* a man's swimming-costume or short underpants. < Latin *truncus*. SEE PANEL AT BONNET.

truss (trʌs) *vb* **1** tie or bind (up). **2** bind the wings, etc., of (a fowl) before cooking. **3** support with a truss.
• *n* **1** a rigid framework of beams, etc., used to support a structure such as a roof or bridge. **2** a bundle of hay, straw, etc. **3** a device worn to support a hernia. **4** a cluster of flowers or fruits. < Old French *trousser*.

trust (trʌst) *n* **1** firm belief in the reliability, character, etc., of a person or thing. **2** confident expectation. **3** the duties of a person in a responsible position. **4** care or custody. **5** formal responsibility for the property of another: hold money in trust. **6** an association of companies formed to monopolize a market: anti-trust laws.
• *vb* **1** have confidence (in); depend. **2** put in the care of; entrust. **3** expect or hope confidently. **trustee** *n* **1** a person who holds and administers property in trust for another. **2** one of a group of people administering the affairs of a company or institution. **trustful** *adj* having confidence in others. **trustfully** *adv* **trustworthy** *adj* worthy of being trusted; dependable. **trustworthiness** *n* **trusty** *adj* trustworthy. < Scandinavian.

truth (tru:θ) *n* **1** the quality of being true; reality or honesty. **2** something that is true; established fact. **truthful** *adj* **1** telling the truth; honest. **2** accurate. **truthfully** *adv* **truthfulness** *n* < Old English *trēowth*.

try (traɪ) *vb* **tried; trying 1** make an attempt (at). **2** investigate or test the condition, potential, etc., of, esp. for a particular purpose. **3** be a strain or stress on; afflict or vex: try someone's patience. **4** examine and determine (a case, etc.) in a law-court; conduct a trial of.
• *n* **1** an attempt. **2** (*rugby*) a score made by touching the ball down behind the opponent's goal-line. **trying** *adj* annoying or irritating. **try on 1** put on (a garment) to see whether it fits or suits one. **2** (*informal*) attempt to deceive. **try one's hand** attempt for the first time. **try one's luck** attempt something, hoping for success. < Old French *trier* to sift.

turning up trumps

Trump features in a number of idiomatic expressions, including:

play one's trump-card to use one's strongest argument: The defence waited until the last day of the hearing to play their trump-card.

trump up to concoct (a false accusation, etc.): trumped-up charges.

turn or **come up trumps** to behave in a helpful, generous way, especially when unexpected: When I was made redundant, my friends really turned up trumps—they even paid for the children's Christmas presents!

tsar (zɑː) *n* the title of the former rulers of Russia. < ultimately Latin *Caesar.*
T-shirt (ˈtiːˌʃɜːt) *n* a collarless, short-sleeved, upper garment for casual wear. < its shape like a *T.*
T-square (ˈtiːˌskwɛə) *n* a ruler with a short cross-piece at one end, used to draw horizontal lines, etc. < its shape like a *T.*
tub (tʌb) *n* **1** an open, flat-bottomed, usually round container used, for example, for washing. **2** a small, round, usually plastic container for ice-cream, margarine, etc. < Middle Dutch *tubbe.*
tuba (ˈtjuːbə) *n* a large, valved, low-pitched, brass musical instrument with a conical tube. < Latin: trumpet.
tubby (ˈtʌbɪ) *adj* short and fat. **tubbiness** *n*
tube (tjuːb) *n* **1** a long, hollow cylinder, used esp. for conveying liquids. **2** a small, cylindrical container of soft metal or plastic with a screw top, for holding pastes, etc., ready for use: a tube of toothpaste. **3** (*informal*) an underground railway system, esp. the one in London. **tubing** *n* a length of tube; tubes. **tubular** *adj* of or having the form of tubes; fitted with tubes or tube-shaped pieces. < Latin *tubus.*
tuber (ˈtjuːbə) *n* a short, thick, fleshy part of an underground stem, as of a potato. **tuberous** *adj* < Latin: lump.
tuberculosis (tjʊˌbɜːkjʊˈləʊsɪs) *n* an infectious disease marked by the formation of abnormal swellings on the body. < New Latin, from Latin *tuber* lump + Greek *-osis* abnormal condition.
TUC *abbrev* Trades Union Congress.
tuck (tʌk) *vb* **1** fold or push into a snug, esp. hidden place. **2** push the loose ends of into a confining space. **3** put a tuck or tucks in (a garment). **4** cover snugly in bed: The children are all tucked up.
• *n* **1** a fold stitched into a garment to shorten it or as a decoration. **2** (*informal*) food, esp. sweets. **tuck in** or **into** (*informal*) eat (food) heartily. **tuck-in** *n* (*informal*) a hearty meal. **tuck-shop** *n* a shop selling sweets, etc., to schoolchildren. < Old English *tūcian* to torment.
tuft (tʌft) *n* a bunch of hairs, grass, feathers, etc., growing or tied closely together. < perhaps Middle French *tufe.*
tug (tʌg) *vb* **tugged; tugging** pull hard (at).
• *n* **1** a hard pull. **2** also **tugboat** a small, powerful boat for towing ships, etc. **tug of war** a contest in which two teams pull on opposite ends of a rope to try to drag each other across a central line. < Middle English *tuggen.*
tuition (tjuːˈɪʃən) *n* instruction; teaching. < ultimately Latin *tueri* to watch over.
tulip (ˈtjuːlɪp) *n* a plant grown from a bulb with a large, bell-shaped flower and bluish-green leaves. < Turkish *tülbend* turban.
tulle (tjuːl) *n* a fine, silky net fabric, used for veils and dresses. SEE PANEL.
tumble (ˈtʌmbl̩) *vb* **1** fall or cause to fall helplessly or awkwardly. **2** roll over and over. **3** perform acrobatic tricks. **4** move in a hurried, careless way. **5** fall suddenly in value: Shares tumbled on the stock market yesterday. **6** disorder.
• *n* **1** a tumbling fall. **2** a confused state or heap. **tumbledown** *adj* dilapidated. **tumble-drier** *n* a machine with a rotating, heated drum, used to dry washing. **tumble to** (*informal*) realize suddenly. < Old English *tumbian.*
tumbler (ˈtʌmblə) *n* **1** a drinking-glass without a handle or stem. **2** an acrobat.
tumour (ˈtjuːmə) *n* an abnormal mass of tissue growing in or on the body. < Latin *tumēre* to swell.
tumult (ˈtjuːmʌlt) *n* **1** a commotion or riot; uproar. **2** a state of intense, esp. mental agitation. **tumultuous** *adj* < Latin *tumultus.*
tun (tʌn) *n* a large cask, esp. for wine.

tulle

It often happens that the name of a fabric derives from the country, city, or region where it originated. For example, tulle, the net-like material used for veils, is named after the French city of *Tulle,* whereas the silk referred to as shantung is so called after Shandong, a province in NE China. Other examples include:
astrakhan made from or resembling the tightly curled fleece of young lambs from *Astrakhan* in the Soviet Union
calico from *Calicut* in India from where the cotton cloth was first imported
cashmere from the *Kashmir* goat in India
damask from *Damascus*
lisle from *Lisle* (now Lille), a city in northern France
muslin from *Mosul,* a city in Iraq
satin from *Qingjiang,* a seaport in China

< Old English *tunne*.

tuna (ˈtjuːnə) *n* also **tuna-fish** a food and game fish; flesh of this tinned and used as food. < alteration of Spanish *atún*, ultimately from Greek *thynnos*.

tundra (ˈtʌndrə) *n* a vast, level, treeless area of arctic regions, with a permanently frozen subsoil. < Russian.

tune (tjuːn) *n* **1** a succession of musical notes; melody. **2** correct musical pitch: in tune.

• *vb* **1** put (a musical instrument) into a standard, correct pitch. **2** adjust (a radio receiver) to receive a particular station or programme. **3** adjust (an engine) to give the best performance. **tuner** *n* **tuneful** *adj* having a pleasing tune; melodious. **tunefully** *adv* **tunefulness** *n* **tuneless** *adj* not tuneful. **tunelessly** *adv* **tuning-fork** *n* a two-pronged, metal device that gives a note of a particular pitch when struck. < SEE **TONE.** SEE PANEL.

tungsten (ˈtʌŋstən) *n* a hard, heavy, grey metal with a high melting-point, used for different electrical purposes and in many hard alloys. < Swedish *tung* heavy + *sten* stone. SEE PANEL.

tunic (ˈtjuːnɪk) *n* **1** a close-fitting jacket worn as part of a uniform. **2** a loose, hip-length or knee-length garment. < Latin *tunica*.

tunnel (ˈtʌnḷ) *n* a man-made, underground passage, esp. one for trains or cars through a hill or under a river, etc.

• *vb* **tunnelled; tunnelling** dig a tunnel (through or under). < Medieval Latin *tonna* barrel, of Celtic origin.

turban (ˈtɜːbən) *n* **1** a head-covering worn esp. by Muslims and Sikhs, made of a long cloth wound round a cap or the head. **2** a woman's hat like this. < Turkish *tülbend*, from Persian *dulband*.

turbid (ˈtɜːbɪd) *adj* **1** muddy or cloudy; opaque. **2** confused. **turbidity** *n* **turbidly** *adv* < Latin *turba* crowd.

turbine (ˈtɜːbaɪn) *n* a machine in which a moving liquid or gas causes the blades of a rotor to turn. < Latin *turbo* whirlwind.

turbot (ˈtɜːbət) *n* a large, flat sea-fish highly valued as food. < Old French *tourbot*.

turbulent (ˈtɜːbjʊlənt) *adj* **1** causing disturbance and violence; agitated: a turbulent crowd. **2** marked by intense, irregular motion: turbulent waters. **turbulence** *n* **turbulently** *adv* < Latin *turba* crowd.

tureen (tjʊˈriːn, təˈriːn) *n* a dish with a cover, from which soup, etc., is served at the table. < ultimately Latin *terra* earth.

turf (tɜːf) *n, pl* **turfs, turves 1** a layer of earth containing a thick growth of short grass and its roots; piece of this cut from the ground. **2** peat. **3 the turf** horse-racing; track for horse-racing.

• *vb* lay with turf. **turf accountant** a bookmaker. **turf out** (*informal*) dismiss with force; eject. < Old English.

turgid (ˈtɜːdʒɪd) *adj* **1** (of writing) pompous; bombastic. **2** swollen and congested. **turgidity** *n* **turgidly** *adv* < Latin *turgēre* to swell.

turkey (ˈtɜːkɪ) *n, pl* **turkeys, turkey** a large bird farmed for its meat. **turkey-cock** *n* a male turkey. < ultimately *Turkey*, country in west Asia and south-east Europe. SEE PANEL.

tungsten

Tungsten has the highest melting-point of all metals. Moreover, it is so hard that it is commonly used in the steel alloy from which cutting tools are made. Neither of these qualities, however, is reflected in the etymology of the word. Tungsten is a Swedish compound of *tung* 'heavy' and *sten* 'stone'.

to the tune of

Tune features in a number of idiomatic expressions, including:

change one's tune to think or act in a way that is very different from the way one has thought or acted in the past: He'll soon change his tune when he hears how much each one will cost.

in/out of tune (**with**) fitting/not fitting in well (with); agreeing/disagreeing with: Old Jack's ideas are completely out of tune with our modern methods, I'm afraid.

to the tune of to the total amount of (a sum of money): The government is willing to back the scheme to the tune of £1 million.

turmeric (ˈtɜːmərɪk) *n* a herb grown for its underground stems that are boiled, dried, ground, and used as a spice and as a yellow dye; these stems. < Medieval Latin *terra merita* deserving earth.
turmoil (ˈtɜːmɔɪl) *n* a state of disorder or agitation. < origin unknown.
turn (tɜːn) *vb* **1** move or cause to move around an axis. **2** change or cause to change the position or direction of. **3** go or pass round: turn the corner. **4** change or become changed in appearance, nature, etc. **5** pass (a time or age): He has just turned 40. **6** direct or be directed: Our thoughts turn to him in his bereavement. **7** go (to) for help. **8** (of the stomach) make or become nauseated. **9** cause to go: The horse was turned into the field. **10** make or become sour. **11** (of leaves) change colour, as in autumn. **12** shape in a lathe.
• *n* **1** a turning movement. **2** turning or being turned. **3** a change of direction or course: No right turns. **4** an opportunity, place, etc., in succession or rotation: It's your turn now. **5** a deed or service of a kind that is mentioned: One good turn deserves another. **6** a tendency or disposition: a philosophical turn of mind. **7** a change: a sudden turn of events. **8** a spell or attack of illness; brief, nervous shock: It gave me quite a turn. **9** a short performance in an entertainment, etc. **10** a point of change in time: at the turn of the century. **11** a style of expression: a peculiar turn of phrase. **turncoat** *n* a person who betrays the principles of a

turkey

The large, meaty bird that forms the centre-piece of many Christmas dinners is known as a turkey. This name, however, is a complete misnomer. The African guinea-fowl was the original recipient of the name turkey, so called on account of the fact that *Turkey* was the gate through which it entered Europe. Later, when a bird resembling the guinea-fowl was discovered in America, the name was simply transferred.

at every turn

Turn features in a number of expressions, many of them idiomatic, including:

at every turn everywhere one goes; constantly: He encountered bureaucratic problems at every turn.
done to a turn cooked to perfection.
turn against to make or become hostile to.
turn away to refuse to admit; send away.
turn down 1 to refuse or reject: His planning application was turned down. **2** to reduce the volume, intensity, etc., of (sound, heat, etc.).
turn in 1 to deliver (to the police, etc.); inform on. **2** to submit (a piece of work). **3** to go to bed.
turn off 1 to stop the supply or operation of. **2** to cause to dislike or lose interest in.
turn on 1 to start the supply or operation of. **2** to excite emotionally or sexually: That music really turns her on. **3** to depend on: The success of the project turns solely on his contribution. **4** to attack.
turn one's back on to reject or abandon.
turn out 1 to turn off (a light etc.). **2** to prove to be: Everything turned out well in the end. The telephone call turned out to be a hoax. **3** to dress or equip: She wanted to be well turned out for Wimbledon. **4** to arrive or appear: A crowd of several hundred people turned out to welcome the royal couple.
turn-out *n* **5** to produce. **6** to expel. **7** to empty: He turned out his pockets.
turn over 1 to transfer or deliver. **2** to consider carefully. **3** to rob (a place).
turnover *n* **1** a small pastry case filled with fruit, jam, etc.: apple turnovers. **2** the total sales revenue of a business in a given period.
turn over a new leaf to abandon one's former bad way of life, and change for the better. The expression alludes to starting to write on a fresh page of a book.
turn-round *adj, n* (of) the time taken to complete a process, such as unloading and reloading a ship or fulfilling an order.
turn tail to turn round and run away.
turn the corner to pass a critical stage and be set on a more favourable course: I think we've turned the corner—at last sales have started to pick up.
turn turtle to capsize.
turn up 1 to arrive or appear. **2** to arise; be found. **3** to increase the volume, intensity, etc., of (sound, heat, etc.). **4** to discover.
turn-up for the book an unexpected event.

cause; traitor. **turner** *n* a person who works with a lathe. **turning** *n* a road, etc., that branches off a main route. **turning-point** *n* a point at which a significant change takes place. **turnpike** *n* **1** (*US*) an important road on which a toll is payable. **2** (*archaic*) a toll-gate. **turnstile** *n* a gate with metal arms that turn to allow one person at a time to pass. **turntable** *n* a circular, rotating platform, esp. one on which a gramophone record is played. < ultimately Greek *tornos* lathe. SEE PANEL.

turnip (ˈtɜːnɪp) *n* a plant grown for its white, fleshy root that is used as a vegetable; this root. < perhaps *turn*, from its rounded shape + *nepe*, from Latin *napus* turnip.

turpentine (ˈtɜːpənˌtaɪn) *n* an oily liquid obtained from pine trees and used as a solvent and paint thinner. **turps** *n* (*informal*) turpentine. < ultimately *terebinthos* tree yielding turpentine.

turpitude (ˈtɜːpɪˌtjuːd) *n* wickedness or depravity. < Latin *turpis* vile.

turquoise (ˈtɜːkwɔɪz) *n* **1** an opaque, greenish-blue mineral used as a gem. **2** also *adj* (a) light greenish-blue. < Old French *turqueise* Turkish.

turret (ˈtʌrɪt) *n* **1** a small tower, esp. at the corner of a building. **2** a low, armoured, usually rotating structure on warships, aircraft, etc., in which guns are mounted. **turreted** *adj* < Old French *tor* tower.

turtle (ˈtɜːtl̩) *n* an aquatic reptile with broad, paddle-like flippers. **turtle-neck** *n* a high, close-fitting neck on a sweater. < ultimately Greek *tartarouchos* of Tartarus, the underworld.

turtle-dove (ˈtɜːtl̩ˌdʌv) *n* a small, slender dove noted for its mournful coos. < ultimately Latin *turtur*, like the sound.

tusk (tʌsk) *n* one of a pair of long, pointed teeth that project from the mouth of an elephant, walrus, etc. < Old English *tūx*.

tussle (ˈtʌsl̩) *vb, n* (take part in) a struggle or scuffle. < Middle English *tusen* to pull.

tussock (ˈtʌsək) *n* a tuft of grass. < origin unknown.

tutelage (ˈtjuːtɪlɪdʒ) *n* **1** guardianship. **2** teaching. < Latin *tueri* to watch over.

tutor (ˈtjuːtə) *n* **1** a private teacher. **2** a university teacher who teaches students individually or in small groups, or one responsible for the welfare of students.
• *vb* act as a tutor to. < Latin *tueri* to watch over.

tutorial (tjuːˈtɔːrɪəl) *n* a class given by a tutor to a small group of students or an individual student.
• *adj* of or relating to a tutor.

tutu (ˈtuːtuː) *n* a short, stiff, projecting skirt worn by a ballet dancer. < alteration of French baby language *cucu* backside, ultimately from Latin *culus* the buttocks. SEE PANEL.

tuxedo (tʌkˈsiːdəʊ) *n, pl* **tuxedos** (*US*) a dinner-jacket. < *Tuxedo* Park, fashionable club in New York. SEE PANEL.

TV *abbrev* television.

twaddle (ˈtwɒdl̩) *n* rubbish; nonsense. < probably alteration of English dialect *twattle* idle talk.

twang (twæŋ) *n* **1** a sharp, vibrating sound as of a tense wire when plucked. **2** nasal intonation in speech.
• *vb* **1** make or cause to make a twang. **2** speak or sound with a twang. < like the sound.

tweak (twiːk) *vb* pinch with a twisting movement.
• *n* such a pinch. < Old English *twiccian*.

tutu

The short, stiff skirt of projecting gauze frills worn by a ballerina is known as a tutu. This word is a borrowing from French but has no connection with the pronoun for 'you'—*tu*. Tutu derives from *cucu*, the nursery word for 'backside' equivalent to the British English 'botty'. *Cucu* derives in turn from *cul*, 'backside', from the Latin *culus*. So the name of the skirt is a wry allusion to its length.

tuxedo

In American English a dinner-jacket is known as a tuxedo. This name derives from the *Tuxedo* Park Country Club near Tuxedo Lake in New York State. It was here that the jacket made its American début in 1886, reputedly on the shoulders of Griswold Lorillard who had acquired the garment on a previous trip to London.

Tuxedo derives from *P'tuksit*, the name given to the region around Tuxedo Lake by its previous Indian inhabitants. This means 'the one with a round foot' or 'wolf'.

tweed (twiːd) *n* **1** a kind of woollen fabric with a roughened surface. **2** *pl* clothes, esp. a suit made of this cloth. < alteration of Scottish *tweel* twill. SEE PANEL.

tweet (twiːt) *vb, n* (a) chirp. **tweeter** *n* a small loudspeaker for reproducing high-frequency sounds. < like the sound.

tweezers (ˈtwiːzəz) *pl n* small pincers used for handling or picking up very small things. < French *étui* case.

twelve (twɛlv) *determiner, n, pron* the number 12. **twelfth** *determiner, n, pron, adv* < Old English *twelf.*

twenty (ˈtwɛntɪ) *determiner, n, pron* the number 20. **twentieth** *determiner, n, pron, adv* **twenties** *pl n* the numbers, range of temperatures, ages, or dates in a century from 20–29. < Old English *twēntig.*

twice (twaɪs) *adv, determiner* two times. < Old English *twiga.*

twiddle (ˈtwɪdḷ) *vb* twirl or play with lightly.
• *n* a twist or turn. **twiddle one's thumbs** spend time in an idle way. < origin uncertain.

twig[1] (twɪg) *n* a small shoot from a branch or stem. < Old English *twigge.*

twig[2] *vb* **twigged; twigging** (*informal*) understand or realize (something): Hasn't he twigged yet? < perhaps Scottish Gaelic: I understand.

twilight (ˈtwaɪˌlaɪt) *n* the soft, dim light between sunset and night; period of this. < Old English *twi-* half + *light.*

tweed and **twill**

Once a word enters a dictionary it is very difficult to imagine that it could once have had any other form than the one that is shown. Even spellings originally based upon false assumptions acquire an immediate air of authority. Tweed is a case in point. This word, meaning 'a rough woollen fabric made in twill weaves', was originally *tweel,* the Scottish word for twill. However, when in 1826 a consignment of the cloth was sent from Scotland down to London, the label on it was read not as *tweel* but as tweed. This misreading, influenced by the knowledge that the cloth had come from the banks of the Tweed, gave the fabric the name by which it would thereafter be known.

twill (twɪl) *n* a fabric woven to give the appearance of diagonal lines. < Old English *twilic* having a double thread. SEE PANEL AT **TWEED.**

twin (twɪn) *n* **1** one of the two children or animals born at one birth. **2** one of two people or things that are alike or related.
• *adj* **1** being a twin. **2** made up of two similar or related things. **3** (of a town) having official associations with a town in another country.
• *vb* **twinned; twinning** pair or be paired together. < Old English *twinn.*

twine (twaɪn) *n* strong thread, string, etc., made of strands twisted together.
• *vb* twist, wind, or coil. < Old English *twīn.*

twinge (twɪndʒ) *n* a sudden, sharp pain or pang. < Old English *twengan* to pinch.

twinkle (ˈtwɪŋkḷ) *vb* **1** shine in a flickering manner. **2** (of the eyes) sparkle brightly.
• *n* **1** a twinkling light or look. **2** also **twinkling** a moment. < Old English *twinclian.*

twirl (twɜːl) *vb* rotate or twist quickly.
• *n* a twirling movement. < perhaps *tw*ist + wh*irl.*

twist (twɪst) *vb* **1** wind (strands, etc.) around each other. **2** wind (rope, etc.) around an object. **3** bend or wrench from its normal space. **4** distort the meaning of. **5** turn or bend round. **6** (of a road, etc.) wind; meander.
• *n* **1** something formed by twisting. **2** a knot. **3** a turn or bend. **4** a coil. **5** an unexpected action or development. **6** an eccentric tendency: a curious twist of character. **7** a dance marked by gyrations of the hips. **twist someone's arm** (*informal*) persuade someone. < Old English.

twit (twɪt) *n* (*informal*) a foolish or silly person. SEE PANEL.

twitch (twɪtʃ) *vb* move or pull with a sudden, light, jerky action.
• *n* a twitching movement. < Middle English *twicchen.*

twitter (ˈtwɪtə) *vb* **1** (of birds) make a series of high, chirping sounds. **2** talk quickly, in a nervous or excited way.
• *n* a twittering sound. < Middle English *twiteren.*

two (tuː) *determiner, n, pron* the number 2. **two-dimensional** *adj* having two dimensions. **two-edged** *adj* **1** having two cutting-edges. **2** having two interpretations. **two-faced** *adj* hypocritical. **twofold** *adj, adv* two times as much or as many. **two-piece** *adj, n* (a suit, swimming-costume, etc.) consisting of two matching pieces. **two-ply** *adj* consisting of two strands, thicknesses, etc. **twosome** *n* a group of two people or things. **two-time** *vb* (*informal*) deceive; be unfaithful to. **two-way** *adj* **1** moving or allowing movement in opposite directions: two-way traffic. **2** designed for transmitting and receiving: a two-way radio. **3** concerned with mutual responsibilities: a two-way relationship. **4** involving two ways or participants. < Old English *twā*. SEE PANEL.

tycoon (taɪˈkuːn) *n* a rich and powerful businessman. < Chinese *dà* great + *chǐ* ruler.

type (taɪp) *n* **1** a group, class, etc., with common characteristics. **2** one that is typical or representative of a group. **3** (*informal*) a person of a kind that is mentioned. **4** one of a collection of blocks with a raised letter, figure, etc., used in printing; collection, size, or style of these.
• *vb* write with or use a typewriter. **typecast** *vb* **typecast; typecasting** cast (an actor) repeatedly in the same kind of role. **typescript** *n* a typed manuscript. **typeset** *vb* **typeset; typesetting** set in type. **typewriter** *n* a machine with a keyboard for reproducing letters, figures, etc., like printed ones. **typical** *adj* showing the main characteristics (of). **typically** *adv* **typify** *vb* **typified; typifying** be typical of; symbolize. **typist** *n* a person who types, esp. as an occupation. **typography** *n* **1** the art or practice of arranging type for printing. **2** the appearance or style of type for printing. **typographical** *adj* < ultimately Greek *typtein* to strike.

typhoid (ˈtaɪfɔɪd) *n* an infectious disease marked by fever, headache, and intestinal inflammation; esp. caused by drinking infected water. < Greek *typhos* fever.

typhoon (taɪˈfuːn) *n* a tropical cyclone or hurricane. < Chinese, ultimately Greek *typhōn* whirlwind.

tyrannosaur (tɪˈrænəˌsɔː) or **tyrannosaurus** (tɪˌrænəˈsɔːrəs) *n* a large, flesh-eating dinosaur that walked on its hind legs. < Greek *tyrannos* tyrant + *sauros* lizard.

tyrant (ˈtaɪrənt) *n* a person who exercises authority or rules cruelly or oppressively. **tyrannical** *adj* like a tyrant or tyranny. **tyrannically** *adv* **tyrannize** *vb* rule as a tyrant. **tyranny** *n* **1** the rule, authority, etc., of a tyrant. **2** oppressive, cruel, and unjust government or exercise of power. **tyrannous** *adj* < ultimately Greek *tyrannos*.

tyre (taɪə) *n* a rubber covering, esp. an inflated, rubber tube, around the rim of a wheel, to absorb shocks. < Middle English *tire*, probably ultimately short for *attire*.

twits and nitwits

At first glance it might be thought that twit is simply a short form of nitwit. However, this is not the case.

Nitwit, on the one hand, is thought to be a compound of the German dialect word *nit* meaning 'not' and the English word *wit* 'intelligence', as in native wit. A nitwit is therefore 'a person without intelligence'.

Twit, on the other hand, is considered to derive from the verb to twit, meaning 'to tease or taunt', ultimately from the Old English word *ætwītan* 'to reproach'. Used as a noun, twit was first applied to a person given to twitting or 'teasing', schoolboyish behaviour that was obviously not relished by the more serious-minded. Gradually the sense widened and the term is now applied informally to any silly person.

It would seem, then, that twits and nitwits have much less in common than one would imagine.

two and two

Two features in several expressions, including:

put two and two together to draw the obvious conclusion. Note that to put two and two together and make five means 'to draw a reasonable but wrong conclusion': He saw Ray and Sarah talking closely to each other, put two and two together and made five.

two and two make four something is straightforward and self-evident.

two heads are better than one a proverb advising the benefit of consultation or discussion with someone else.

two's company, three's a crowd used when two people, especially a courting couple, want to be alone, without the company of a third person.

U

U *adj* characteristic of the upper classes, esp. in speech or conduct.

ubiquitous (juːˈbɪkwɪtəs) *adj* being everywhere at the same time. **ubiquity** *n* < Latin *ubique* everywhere.

U-boat (ˈjuːˌbəʊt) *n* a German submarine. < German *Untersee* undersea + *Boot* boat. SEE PANEL.

udder (ˈʌdə) *n* a bag-like, milk-secreting gland of cows, sheep, etc., with two or more teats. < Old English *ūder*.

UFO (sometimes ˈjuːfəʊ) *abbrev* unidentified flying object.

ugly (ˈʌglɪ) *adj* **1** unpleasant to look at: an ugly face. **2** morally objectionable. **3** threatening. **4** bad-tempered. **ugliness** *n* < Old Norse *uggr* fear. SEE PANEL.

UHF *abbrev* ultrahigh frequency.

UK *abbrev* United Kingdom.

ukulele (ˌjuːkəˈleɪlɪ) *n* a small, four-stringed guitar. < Hawaiian: jumping flea.

ulcer (ˈʌlsə) *n* an open sore on the skin or mucous membrane. **ulcerous** *adj* **ulcerate** *vb* make or become affected with an ulcer. **ulceration** *n* < Latin *ulcus*.

ulna (ˈʌlnə) *n* the bone on the inner side of the forearm, extending from elbow to wrist. **ulnar** *adj* **ulnar nerve** a nerve extending along the inner side of the arm and coming close to the surface at the elbow. < Latin: elbow.

ulterior (ʌlˈtɪərɪə) *adj* beyond what is revealed: ulterior motives. < Latin: further, more distant.

ultimate (ˈʌltɪmət) *adj* **1** last or final. **2** basic or fundamental.
• *n* something ultimate. **ultimately** *adv* < Latin *ulter* distant.

ultimatum (ˌʌltɪˈmeɪtəm) *n, pl* **ultimatums, ultimata** a final proposal or demand, the rejection of which will end negotiations or relations and lead to the use of force, etc. < SEE **ULTIMATE.**

ultramarine (ˌʌltrəməˈriːn) *adj, n* deep-blue.

ultrasonic (ˌʌltrəˈsɒnɪk) *adj* (of a sound wave or vibration) having a frequency beyond the range of normal human hearing. < Latin *ultra-* beyond + *sonus* sound. SEE PANEL.

ultraviolet (ˌʌltrəˈvaɪələt) *adj* **1** (of radiation) having a wavelength between that of the violet end of the spectrum and x-rays. **2** of, using, or producing this radiation: an ultraviolet lamp.

umber (ˈʌmbə) *n* a natural brown mineral used as a pigment. < Latin *umbra* shade.

umbilical (ʌmˈbɪlɪkl̩, ˌʌmbɪˈlaɪkl̩) *adj* of or near the navel. **umbilical cord** the

ugly duckling

The expression ugly duckling, meaning 'a person or thing, initially unattractive or unpromising, that becomes beautiful, successful, etc.' comes from the story 'The Ugly Duckling', by the Danish writer Hans Christian Andersen, 1805–75.

U-boat

The letter U is sometimes used to form the first part of a compound noun, as in U-turn and U-bend. In these words the U is used iconically to mean 'having the shape of a U', just as the T in T-junction means 'having the shape of a T'. U-boat, however, does not belong to this group. It is a direct borrowing of the German *U-boot,* in which the U stands for *Untersee* or 'undersea' and *Boot* means 'boat'.

ultra-

The prefix ultra-, originally from Latin, means 'beyond', 'extreme or extremely'. It features in a number of words, including:

ultra-cautious
ultra-conservative
ultra-fashionable
ultraheat-treated (UHT: UHT milk)
ultrahigh frequency (UHF)
ultra-left
ultra-modern

long, flexible, tubular structure that connects a foetus to the placenta in the womb. < Latin *umbilicus.*

umbra (ˈʌmbrə) *n, pl* **umbrae** the area in a shadow from which light is totally cut off, esp. in an eclipse. < Latin.

umbrage (ˈʌmbrɪdʒ) *n* **take umbrage** (**at**) be offended (by). < ultimately Latin *umbra* shade.

umbrella (ʌmˈbrɛlə) *n* **1** a portable protection against the weather, esp. rain, consisting of stretched fabric mounted onto a collapsible frame of ribs that radiate from a central rod. **2** something that gives protection or includes a range of different elements. < Italian *ombrella;* SEE **UMBRA.** SEE PANEL.

umpire (ˈʌmpaɪə) *n* **1** a referee in sports such as cricket. **2** a person who has the authority to settle disputes.
• *vb* act as an umpire in. < Middle English *noumpere,* from Middle French *nomper* not one of a pair. SEE PANEL AT **APRON.**

umpteen (ˌʌmpˈtiːn) *determiner, pron* (*informal*) very many. **umpteenth** *determiner, n* < *umpty* great deal + *-teen,* as in *thirteen,* etc.

UN *abbrev* United Nations. SEE PANEL.

un- *prefix* SEE PANEL.

unable (ʌnˈeɪbl̩) *adj* lacking the power, authority, etc., (to do something).

unaccountable (ˌʌnəˈkaʊntəbl̩) *adj* **1** not able to be explained; strange. **2** not responsible. **unaccountably** *adv*

unadopted (ˌʌnəˈdɒptɪd) *adj* (of a road) not maintained by a local authority.

unadulterated (ˌʌnəˈdʌltəˌreɪtɪd) *adj* pure.

unanimous (juːˈnænɪməs) *adj* in agreement; based on complete agreement: a unanimous decision. **unanimity** *n* **unanimously** *adv* < Latin *unus* one + *animus* mind.

unanswerable (ʌnˈɑːnsərəbl̩) *adj* incapable of being refuted.

unassailable (ˌʌnəˈseɪləbl̩) *adj* able to withstand attack: an unassailable position.

unassuming (ˌʌnəˈsjuːmɪŋ) *adj* modest; not arrogant.

unattended (ˌʌnəˈtɛndɪd) *adj* **1** (of a vehicle) having no person in charge of it. **2** not looked after. **3** unaccompanied; alone.

unavoidable (ˌʌnəˈvɔɪdəbl̩) *adj* unable to be avoided; inevitable. **unavoidably** *adv*

unaware (ˌʌnəˈwɛə) *adj* not aware. **unawares** *adv* without noticing; unexpectedly.

unbalanced (ʌnˈbælənst) *adj* **1** not balanced. **2** mentally disordered or deranged.

unbecoming (ˌʌnbɪˈkʌmɪŋ) *adj* **1** not suitable, esp. because unattractive.

umbrella and **parasol**

These two words would appear to have no more in common than rain and sun, and yet they have. The umbrella comes from the East, where it served as a sign of rank while protecting emperors and dignitaries from the sun's rays. It was also much favoured by the ladies of Rome, who wished to preserve the fairness of their complexions.

Umbrella originates, in fact, from (the Latin word umbra 'shade', and to provide shade was the umbrella's purpose. And this of course is the purpose of the parasol, an Italian borrowing that combines the Latin *para-* 'protection against' and *sol* 'the sun'.

UN

UN is the abbreviation for United Nations. This is a reduced form of UNO or United Nations Organization, a name which is still used in some parts of the world. Both titles refer to the alliance of nations, formally set up in 1945, which together stood in opposition against the Axis powers in the Second World War.

According to the US journalist and critic H.L. Mencken, the name United Nations was coined by President Franklin Roosevelt who thought of it one morning in bed at the time of Churchill's visit to Washington in December 1941. The aim of the organization is to promote world peace and encourage international co-operation.

un-words

The list below includes many of the more common words formed with the prefix un-. The meanings of these words can be understood as 'not' added to the meaning of the base word: uncomfortable, unselfish, or a reversal of the action indicated by the verb: unbolt, unbutton.

unabashed
unabridged
unacceptable
unaccompanied
unaccustomed
unaffected
unafraid
unaided
unambiguous
unambitious
unapproachable
unarmed
unashamed
unasked
unattainable
unattractive
unauthorized
unavailable
unbearable
unbeatable
unbeaten
unbend
unbiased
unbidden
unblock
unbolt
unbreakable
unbridled
unbusinesslike
unbutton
unceasing
unchanging
uncharacteristic
uncharitable
unchecked
uncivil
unclaimed
unclassified
unclouded
uncomfortable
uncommitted
uncommunicative
uncomplicated
uncomplimentary
uncompromising
unconcerned
unconfirmed
uncongenial
unconnected
unconstitutional
uncontrollable
unconventional
unconvincing
uncooked
uncooperative
uncritical
uncross
uncultivated
uncultured
undamaged
undated
undaunted
undecided
undefined
undemocratic
undeserved
undetected
undeterred
undeveloped
undignified
undiminished
undisciplined
undisclosed
undisguised
undismayed
undisputed
undistinguished
undivided
undramatic
undrinkable
unearned
uneatable
uneconomic
uneducated
unemotional
unemployable
unending
unenviable
unethical
uneventful
unexciting
unexpired
unexplained
unexploded
unexplored
unexpurgated
unfaithful
unfamiliar
unfashionable
unfasten
unfavourable
unfermented
unfertilized
unfinished
unforeseen
unforgettable
unforgivable
unforgiving
unformed
unfreeze
unfriendly
unfulfilled
unfurnished
ungovernable
ungrateful
unharmed
unhealthy
unheated
unheeded
unhelpful
unhook
unhurried
unhurt
unhygienic
unidentified
unimaginable
unimaginative
unimportant
unimpressed
uninformed
uninhabited
uninhibited
uninitiated
uninjured
uninspired
uninsured
unintelligible
unintentional
uninteresting
uninterrupted
uninvited
unjust
unjustifiable
unkind
unleavened
unlimited
unlined
unload
unlucky
unmanageable
unmarked
unmarried
unmerited
unmoved
unmusical
unnamed
unnatural
unnavigable
unobservant
unobserved
unobtainable
unobtrusive
unofficial
unopen
unopposed
unorthodox
unpaid
unpalatable
unpardonable
unpatriotic
unplanned
unpleasant
unpopular
unpredictable
unprepared
unpretentious
unpriced
unprintable
unproductive
unprofessional
unprofitable
unpromising
unprompted
unpronounceable
unprotected
unprovoked
unpublished
unpunished
unquestioning
unreadable
unreal
unrealistic
unreality
unrealized
unrecognizable
unrecognized
unrecorded
unregistered

unrelated
unreliability
unreliable
unrelieved
unrepeatable
unrepresentative
unresolved
unrestrained
unrestricted
unreturned
unrewarding
unripe
unsafe
unsalaried
unsalted
unsatisfactory
unsatisfied
unsatisfying
unscheduled
unscientific
unscripted
unselfish
unsentimental
unserviceable
unshakable
unshaven
unshockable
unsigned
unsimplified
unskilled
unsliced
unsmiling
unsmoked
unsold
unsolicited
unsolved
unsophisticated
unsound
unspecified
unspectacular
unspoilt
unspoken
unsportsmanlike
unsteady
unsterilized
unstoppable
unstressed
unsuccessful
unsuitable
unsuited
unsupervised
unsupported
unsure
unsurpassed
unsuspecting
unswayed
unsweetened
unswept
unswerving
unsympathetic
unsystematic
untamed
untapped
untarnished
untenable
untested
untidy
untiring
untraceable
untrained
untreated
untried
untrue
untrustworthy
untruthful
unusable
unused
unvarying
unverified
unwanted
unwary
unwashed
unwavering
unwelcome
unwell
unwholesome
unwise
unworkable
unworldly
unworn
unworthy
unyielding

2 not proper: behaviour unbecoming to a duke.

unbeknown (ˌʌnbɪˈnəʊn) *adv* without the knowledge (of): unbeknown to him.

unbelievable (ˌʌnbɪˈliːvəbl̩) *adj* unable to be believed; astonishing; incredible. **unbelievably** *adv*

unbeliever (ˌʌnbɪˈliːvə) *n* a person who does not believe, esp. in a particular religion.

unborn (ʌnˈbɔːn) *adj* not yet born.

unbosom (ʌnˈbʊzəm) *vb* disclose the thoughts or feelings of (oneself).

unbounded (ʌnˈbaʊndɪd) *adj* without limits: unbounded joy.

unbroken (ʌnˈbrəʊkən) *adj* **1** complete. **2** uninterrupted; continuous. **3** (of horses, etc.) not tamed. **4** (of a record) not improved on.

uncalled-for (ʌnˈkɔːldˌfɔː) *adj* unnecessary and out of place; impertinent.

uncanny (ʌnˈkænɪ) *adj* **1** mysterious. **2** beyond the normal; extraordinary: He has an uncanny knack of always being right.

unceremonious (ˌʌnsɛrɪˈməʊnɪəs) *adj* without ceremony; abrupt; rude. **unceremoniously** *adv*

uncertain (ʌnˈsɜːtn̩) *adj* **1** not known certainly. **2** not sure. **3** not to be relied on. **4** changeable. **uncertainly** *adv* **uncertainty** *n* **in no uncertain terms** speaking plainly and forcefully.

uncle (ˈʌŋkl̩) *n* **1** a brother of one's father or mother. **2** the husband of one's aunt. **3** an affectionate term for a man who is a close friend of a child or his or her parents. < Latin *avunculus.*

uncommon (ʌnˈkɒmən) *adj* not usual; remarkable. **uncommonly** *adv*

unconditional (ˌʌnkənˈdɪʃənl̩) *adj* without conditions; unqualified or absolute: unconditional surrender. **unconditionally** *adv*

unconscious (ʌnˈkɒnʃəs) *n* **1** not conscious or aware. **2** not marked by, spoken, or done with conscious intention.
• *n* the unconscious mind or its activities. **unconsciously** *adv* **unconsciousness** *n*

uncouth (ʌnˈkuːθ) *adj* lacking good manners; awkward. < Old English *uncūth,* from *un-* not + *cūth* known, familiar. SEE PANEL AT **INADVERTENT.**

uncover (ʌnˈkʌvə) *vb* **1** remove the cover from. **2** reveal or disclose.

unction (ˈʌŋkʃən) *n* anointing with oil, as a religious rite. **unctuous** *adj* marked by a smug, smooth pretence. < Latin *unguere* to anoint.

undeniable (ˌʌndɪˈnaɪəbl̩) *adj* obviously true. **undeniably** *adv*

under (ˈʌndə) *prep* **1** in, at, or to a lower place than; beneath the surface of. **2** lower in authority, value, etc., than: under £100. **3** because of; during; in: under certain conditions. **4** subject to or during the rule or influence of: A lot of progress has been made under the present government. **5** in the process of: under repair. **6** according to: under section 23 of the act. **7** in the designation of: file it under 'Miscellaneous'. **8** bound by: under oath. **9** (of land) planted with. **10** propelled by: under sail. **11** using a pseudonym, etc.: under the name of Cliff Richard.
• *adv* **1** in or to a lower or subordinate position. **2** in or into a state of unconsciousness. **3** in or to a lower number, rank, etc.: Children of 5 and under travel free.
• *adj* lying beneath. **under-age** *adj* below the legal age. **under way** in motion; in progress. < Old English.

underarm (ˈʌndərˌɑːm) *adj, adv* **1** below the arm. **2** thrown, bowled, or served with the hand brought forwards and upwards from below the level of the shoulder.

undercarriage (ˈʌndəˌkærɪdʒ) *n* the part of an aircraft containing the wheels, etc., that supports its weight on the ground, used in taking off and landing.

underclothes (ˈʌndəˌkləʊðz) *pl n* underwear.

undercoat (ˈʌndəˌkəʊt) *n* a layer of paint applied before a final coat; paint for this.
• *vb* apply an undercoat to.

undercover (ˌʌndəˈkʌvə) *adj* **1** done secretly. **2** engaged in spying: an undercover agent.

undercurrent (ˈʌndəˌkʌrənt) *n* **1** a current below a surface or another current. **2** an underlying, hidden influence, opinion, etc.: undercurrents of rebellion.

undercut (ˌʌndəˈkʌt) *vb* **undercut; undercutting** **1** offer at a lower price than. **2** cut away the part below.

underdeveloped (ˌʌndədɪˈvɛləpt) *adj* **1** not having reached its full economic potential: underdeveloped nations. **2** (of a film) not developed sufficiently.

underdog (ˈʌndəˌdɒg) *n* **1** a person, team, etc., that is expected to lose in a competition. **2** a person in an inferior, disadvantaged position.

underdone (ˌʌndəˈdʌn) *adj* not cooked sufficiently.

underestimate (ˌʌndərˈɛstɪˌmeɪt) *vb* make too low an estimate of. **underestimation** *n*

underexpose (ˌʌndərɪkˈspəʊz) *vb* expose for too short a time. **underexposure** *n*

underfelt (ˈʌndəˌfɛlt) *n* a thick felt for laying under a carpet.

underfoot (ˌʌndəˈfʊt) *adv* on the ground; under one's feet: rather wet underfoot; trample underfoot.

undergo (ˌʌndəˈgəʊ) *vb* **underwent; undergone; undergoing** experience or be subjected to: All applicants are required to undergo a medical examination.

undergraduate (ˌʌndəˈgrædjʊət) *n* a student at a university or college who is studying for a first degree.

underground (ˌʌndəˈgraʊnd) *adv* **1** under the surface of the earth. **2** in secret; into hiding or secrecy.
• *adj* (ˈʌndəˌgraʊnd) **1** occurring, growing, working, etc., under the surface of the earth. **2** secret: underground operations. **3** operated by a radical or avant-garde group: an underground movement.
• *n* (ˈʌndəˌgraʊnd) **1** an underground railway. **2** an underground organization. SEE PANEL.

undergrowth (ˈʌndəˌgrəʊθ) *n* bushes, bracken, etc., growing beneath large trees in a wood or forest.

underhand (ˈʌndəˌhænd) *adj* also **underhanded** sly; deceitful.

underlay (ˌʌndəˈleɪ) *vb* **underlaid; underlaying** place or lay (something) under or beneath.
• *n* (ˈʌndəˌleɪ) rubber or felt material laid under a carpet.

underlie (ˌʌndəˈlaɪ) *vb* **underlay; underlain; underlying** **1** lie or exist underneath, esp. in a hidden position: his underlying motives. **2** be the basis of.

underline (ˌʌndəˈlaɪn) *vb* **1** draw a line under. **2** emphasize; reinforce or stress.

underling (ˈʌndəlɪŋ) *n* a subordinate.

undermine (ˌʌndəˈmaɪn) *vb* **1** tunnel under. **2** weaken by wearing away the supports of. **3** weaken gradually or insidiously (confidence, authority, etc.).

underneath (ˌʌndəˈniːθ) *adv, prep* under

under-

The prefix under- has a number of meanings:

1 below or beneath: underfloor, underground, undermentioned, undernamed.
2 of lesser importance or rank; subordinate: under-secretary, undermanager.
3 insufficiently: underachieve, undernourished, undermanned, underpaid.

the surface of (something).
• *n* the bottom surface of something.
< Old English *under* + *neothan* below.

underpants (ˈʌndəˌpænts) *pl n* men's pants.

underpass (ˈʌndəˌpɑːs) *n* a passage for a road under another road or railway.

underpin (ˌʌndəˈpɪn) *vb* **underpinned; underpinning** strengthen from beneath; support.

underprivileged (ˌʌndəˈprɪvɪlɪdʒd) *adj* deprived of some of the basic rights of society: underprivileged children.

underrate (ˌʌndəˈreɪt) *vb* underestimate.

underscore (ˌʌndəˈskɔː) *vb* underline.

underseal (ˈʌndəˌsiːl) *n* a coating of a material such as bitumen applied to the undersurface of a vehicle to retard corrosion.
• *vb* apply underseal to.

under-secretary (ˌʌndəˈsɛkrətrɪ) *n* any of various Civil Servants or high officials in a government department.

undersell (ˌʌndəˈsɛl) *vb* **undersold; underselling** sell at a lower price than.

underside (ˈʌndəˌsaɪd) *n* the lower side or surface underneath.

undersigned (ˈʌndəˌsaɪnd) *n* **the undersigned** the person or the people who have signed at the bottom of a document: We, the undersigned, do hereby declare ....

undersized (ˌʌndəˈsaɪzd) *adj* of less than the usual size.

underskirt (ˈʌndəˌskɜːt) *n* a garment worn under a skirt; petticoat.

understand (ˌʌndəˈstænd) *vb* **understood; understanding 1** grasp the meaning of or know (something) thoroughly. **2** gather; believe or assume: I understand you've got a new job. **3** interpret. **4** supply (a word, etc.) mentally. **5** have a sympathetic rapport with: He understands children so well! **6** show sympathy, acceptance, etc.: They'll understand if we explain why we're late. **understandable** *adj* able to be understood. **understandably** *adv*
< Old English *understandan.*

understanding (ˌʌndəˈstændɪŋ) *n* **1** power of understanding; comprehension: reach a deeper understanding of human nature. **2** something that comes from understanding; opinion or conclusion. **3** sympathy towards the feelings and opinions of others. **4** harmony; harmonious relationship. **5** an informal agreement: It was just an understanding between us.
• *adj* sympathetic or tolerant; kindly. **on the understanding that** having agreed that.

understate (ˌʌndəˈsteɪt) *vb* represent as less than in reality; express in restrained terms, esp. for effect. **understatement** *n*

understood (ˌʌndəˈstʊd) SEE **UNDERSTAND.**

understudy (ˈʌndəˌstʌdɪ) *n* a person who is ready to take the part of another, as in a play, or the duties of another.
• *vb* **understudied; understudying** act as an understudy for.

undertake (ˌʌndəˈteɪk) *vb* **undertook; undertaken; undertaking 1** take upon oneself; agree to do. **2** guarantee or promise. **undertaker** *n* a person whose business is to prepare the dead for burial or cremation and to make arrangements for funerals. **undertaking** *n* **1** something undertaken; task or enterprise. **2** a promise or guarantee.

undertone (ˈʌndəˌtəʊn) *n* **1** a low, subdued tone or utterance. **2** an undercurrent of feeling: ominous undertones. **3** a subdued colour.

undertook (ˌʌndəˈtʊk) SEE **UNDERTAKE.**

undertow (ˈʌndəˌtəʊ) *n* a current below the surface of the sea, flowing in a different direction from the surface current.

undervalue (ˌʌndəˈvæljuː) *vb* put too low a value on.

underwater (ˌʌndəˈwɔːtə) *adj, adv* (being, used, or done) beneath the surface of the water.

underwear (ˈʌndəˌwɛə) *n* clothing worn next to the skin, under other garments.

underweight (ˌʌndəˈweɪt) *adj* weighing less than normal, average, or desired.

underwent (ˌʌndəˈwɛnt) SEE **UNDERGO.**

underworld (ˈʌndəˌwɜːld) *n* **1** the criminal members of society. **2** (in mythology) the abode of the dead, below the earth's surface.

underwrite (ˈʌndəˌraɪt) *vb* **underwrote; underwritten; underwriting 1** sign and assume liability for (loss or damage); sign (an insurance policy), assuming such liability. **2** agree to pay the cost of; finance. **underwriter** *n* SEE PANEL.

undesirable (ˌʌndɪˈzaɪrəbl̩) *adj, n* (a person or thing that is) unwanted, objectionable, or disliked.

undid (ʌnˈdɪd) SEE **UNDO.**

undies (ˈʌndɪz) *pl n* (*informal*) women's underwear.

undiscriminating (ˌʌndɪˈskrɪmɪˌneɪtɪŋ) *adj* not bothering to distinguish between different things, esp. good and bad. SEE PANEL AT **INDISCRIMINATE.**

undo (ʌnˈduː) *vb* **undid; undone; undoing 1** unfasten, untie, etc.; open or loosen. **2** cancel the effect of; reverse. **3** cause the downfall or ruin of. **undoing** *n* ruin or downfall; cause of this. **undone** *adj* not completed.

undoubted (ʌnˈdaʊtɪd) *adj* not doubted or disputed; certain. **undoubtedly** *adv*
undreamed (ʌnˈdriːmd) or **undreamt** (ʌnˈdrɛmt) *adj* not conceived (of).
undress (ʌnˈdrɛs) *vb* remove the clothes of; take off one's clothes.
• *n* **1** a state of having few or no clothes on. **2** ordinary or informal dress, as opposed to uniform.
undue (ʌnˈdjuː) *adj* excessive; improper: undue haste. **unduly** *adv*
undulate (ˈʌndjʊˌleɪt) *vb* have a wavy form or appearance. **undulation** *n*
< Latin *unda* wave.
undying (ʌnˈdaɪɪŋ) *adj* never-ending; eternal.
unearth (ʌnˈɜːθ) *vb* **1** dig up. **2** reveal or disclose; make known.
unearthly (ʌnˈɜːθlɪ) *adj* **1** not earthly. **2** mysterious or supernatural; eerie. **3** (*informal*) unreasonable; ridiculous: the unearthly hour of 5 o'clock.
uneasy (ʌnˈiːzɪ) *adj* **1** uncomfortable or awkward. **2** anxious or worried. **3** disturbing; precarious. **uneasily** *adv* **uneasiness** *n*
unemployed (ˌʌnɪmˈplɔɪd) *adj* **1** not having a paid job: the unemployed. **2** not being used. **unemployment** *n*
unequal (ʌnˈiːkwəl) *adj* **1** not equal in measurement, quality, status, etc. **2** not well matched. **3** not uniform in quality. **4** not able to meet the requirements of: prove unequal to the task.
unequivocal (ˌʌnɪˈkwɪvəkl̩) *adj* not ambiguous; clear. **unequivocally** *adv*
unerring (ʌnˈɜːrɪŋ) *adj* accurate; faultless. **unerringly** *adv*
UNESCO (juːˈnɛskəʊ) *abbrev* United Nations Educational, Scientific, and Cultural Organization.
uneven (ʌnˈiːvən) *adj* **1** not level or smooth. **2** varying in quality. **3** not well matched. **unevenly** *adv* **unevenness** *n*
unexceptionable (ˌʌnɪkˈsɛpʃənəbl̩) *adj* that cannot be objected to. **unexceptionably** *adv* SEE PANEL.
unexceptional (ˌʌnɪkˈsɛpʃənl̩) *adj* usual; ordinary. SEE PANEL AT **UNEXCEPTIONABLE.**
unexpected (ˌʌnɪkˈspɛktɪd) *adj* not expected; surprising. **unexpectedly** *adv* **unexpectedness** *n*
unfailing (ʌnˈfeɪlɪŋ) *adj* sure or inexhaustible; constant.
unfair (ʌnˈfɛə) *adj* not fair or just; dishonest or unethical. **unfairly** *adv*
unfeeling (ʌnˈfiːlɪŋ) *adj* unsympathetic; callous.
unfit (ʌnˈfɪt) *adj* **1** unsuitable. **2** not capable. **3** in a poor physical or mental condition.
unflappable (ʌnˈflæpəbl̩) *adj* remaining calm, esp. in a crisis; not easily excited or upset. SEE PANEL.
unfold (ʌnˈfəʊld) *vb* **1** open; spread out. **2** reveal or be revealed gradually.
unfortunate (ʌnˈfɔːtjʊnət) *adj* **1** bringing or resulting in misfortune. **2** unsuitable; regrettable: unfortunate comments.
• *n* an unfortunate person. **unfortunately** *adv*
unfounded (ʌnˈfaʊndɪd) *adj* not based on fact.
unfrock (ʌnˈfrɒk) *vb* deprive of the rank of priest.
unfurl (ʌnˈfɜːl) *vb* spread out; unroll.
< *un-* + *furl*, from Old Northern French *ferlier* to roll tightly.
ungainly (ʌnˈgeɪnlɪ) *adj* lacking grace; clumsy or awkward. **ungainliness** *n*
unget-at-able (ˌʌngɛtˈætəbl̩) *adj* inaccessible.
ungodly (ʌnˈgɒdlɪ) *adj* **1** not giving due reverence to God; not religious. **2** wicked; sinful. **3** (*informal*) outrageous.
unguarded (ʌnˈgɑːdɪd) *adj* **1** not protected; vulnerable. **2** marked by a lack of thought or prudence: in an unguarded moment.

---

underwriter

A person who puts his signature to an insurance policy and thereby assumes liability in the event of loss or damage is known as an underwriter. This name means literally what it says it means. An underwriter is the party who 'writes' his name 'under' the text of a policy.

Similarly, endorse is literally to put (one's name) on the back (of something). It derives ultimately from the Old French *endosser*, from *en-* 'put onto' and *dos* 'back'.

---

unexceptionable or **unexceptional?**

These two words are sometimes confused.

Something is unexceptional if it is usual or ordinary: *unexceptional* behaviour.

Unexceptionable is a less common word and refers to something that cannot be objected or taken exception to: I found the talk fairly *unexceptionable*.

---

unguent (ˈʌŋgwənt) *n* an ointment. < Latin *unguere* to anoint.
unhappy (ʌnˈhæpɪ) *adj* **1** not happy; sad or unfortunate. **2** inappropriate. **unhappily** *adv* **unhappiness** *n*
unheard (ʌnˈhɜːd) *adj* not heard. **unheard of** *adj* not previously known; unprecedented.
unhinge (ʌnˈhɪndʒ) *vb* **1** remove (a door, etc.) from its hinges. **2** make mentally unbalanced.
unholy (ʌnˈhəʊlɪ) *adj* **1** not holy. **2** wicked or immoral. **3** (*informal*) outrageous: an unholy din.
unhoped-for (ʌnˈhəʊptˌfɔː) *adj* not expected.
unhorse (ʌnˈhɔːs) *vb* throw from a horse.
UNICEF (ˈjuːnɪˌsɛf) *abbrev* United Nations Children's Fund. < *U*nited *N*ations *I*nternational *C*hildren's *E*mergency *F*und, its former name.
unicorn (ˈjuːnɪˌkɔːn) *n* a mythical animal resembling a white horse with a long, straight horn projecting from its forehead. < ultimately Latin *uni-* one + *cornu* horn.
uniform (ˈjuːnɪˌfɔːm) *n* clothing of a design that identifies the wearer as a member of a particular group. • *adj* unchanging in appearance, degree, etc.; regular or alike. **uniformity** *n* **uniformly** *adv* < Latin *uni-* one + *forma* shape.
unify (ˈjuːnɪˌfaɪ) *vb* **unified; unifying** make into a single unit. **unification** *n* < Latin *uni-* one + *facere* to make.
unilateral (ˌjuːnɪˈlætərəl) *adj* undertaken by or affecting one side only: unilateral disarmament. **unilaterally** *adv* **unilateralism** *n* the advocacy of unilateral action, esp. disarmament. **unilateralist** *n*
unimpeachable (ˌʌnɪmˈpiːtʃəbl̩) *adj* not questionable regarding honesty, etc.; utterly trustworthy; irreproachable.
uninterested (ʌnˈɪntrəstɪd) *adj* having no interest or concern; bored or indifferent. SEE PANEL AT **DISINTERESTED.**
union (ˈjuːnɪən) *n* **1** uniting; being united. **2** the formation of a group, esp. a political one, as from several countries or states. **3** a uniting in marriage; sexual intercourse. **4** a trade union. **5** an association of students at a college or university for students' interests, recreation, etc.; building used by such an association: the Student Union. **unionist** *n* **1** a member of a trade union; supporter of trade unions. **2 Unionist** an advocate of the Unionist party of Northern Ireland that supports union with Britain. **unionize** *vb* cause to join or form a trade union. **unionization** *n* **Union Jack** the national flag of the United Kingdom. < Latin *unus* one.
unique (juːˈniːk) *adj* being the only one of its kind. **uniquely** *adv* **uniqueness** *n* < Latin *unus* one. SEE PANEL.
unisex (ˈjuːnɪˌsɛks) *adj* of or relating to a style for people of both sexes; dealing in products, etc., for people of both sexes: a unisex hair-style.
unison (ˈjuːnɪsn̩) *n* **1** identity of musical pitch. **2** agreement or harmony: act in unison. < Latin *uni-* one + *sonus* sound.
unit (ˈjuːnɪt) *n* **1** a single person, thing, or group, esp. in calculations or as part of a whole: the unit price. **2** a quantity that is chosen as a standard measurement: metric and imperial units. **3** a part or group that has a specific function in something complex: a power unit; the Spinal Injuries unit. **4** a subdivision of a large military formation.

that unique word

Careful users of English avoid using words such as very, more, or rather with unique, pointing out that something is either unique or it isn't.

unflappable

A person who remains cool and calm no matter what the circumstances may be said to be unflappable. The root of this word is the verb *flap*, 'to panic or get into a fluster', from the way a bird flaps its wings when agitated or excited. This word and its noun equivalent are restricted to informal usage, as in 'She got herself into a right flap'. Unflappable, however, is not marked as informal, perhaps on account of the fact that it entered the language largely as an epithet for the imperturbable Harold Macmillan, British prime minister from 1957–63.

unitary *adj* **1** of a unit or units. **2** whole. < SEE **UNITE.**
unite (juːˈnaɪt) *vb* **1** make or become one; join. **2** act together. **unity** *n* **1** the state of being one or united. **2** something complete in itself. **3** harmony; agreement. < Latin *unus* one.
universal (ˌjuːnɪˈvɜːsl̩) *adj* **1** of, affecting, or including all: trying to reach universal agreement. **2** existing or occurring everywhere. **universally** *adv* < Latin *universum* universe.
universe (ˈjuːnɪvɜːs) *n* **1** all known or existing things, including the earth, sun, and all heavenly bodies. **2** all human beings; world. < Latin *universum* whole world, from *uni-* one + *vertere* to turn.
university (ˌjuːnɪˈvɜːsɪtɪ) *n* an educational institution that provides teaching and facilities for research and is authorized to confer degrees. < Medieval Latin *universitas* group of scholars, ultimately from Latin: whole, universe.
unkempt (ʌnˈkɛmpt) *adj* untidy or dishevelled: unkempt hair. < *un-* + *kempt*, from Old English *cemban* to comb. SEE PANEL AT **INADVERTENT.**
unknown (ʌnˈnəʊn) *adj* not known. • *n* an unknown person or thing: The third candidate is a complete unknown.
unladen (ˌʌnˈleɪdn̩) *adj* not laden. **unladen weight** the weight of a lorry, etc., when not loaded with goods.
unlearn (ʌnˈlɜːn) *vb* discard consciously from one's knowledge or memory.
unleash (ʌnˈliːʃ) *vb* set free from a leash or other restraint.
unless (ʌnˈlɛs) *conj* if ... not; except when: I never work unless I have to. < Middle English *on* on + *lesse* less.
unlike (ʌnˈlaɪk) *adj* not alike; different. • *prep* **1** different or differently from. **2** not characteristic of. **unlikely** *adj* **1** improbable; not expected. **2** not likely to succeed.
unlock (ʌnˈlɒk) *vb* **1** release the lock of; open. **2** disclose or reveal.
unlooked-for (ʌnˈlʊktˌfɔː) *adj* unexpected.
unman (ʌnˈmæn) *vb* **unmanned; unmanning** weaken the courage, strength, etc., of. **unmanned** *adj* operated without a crew: an unmanned spaceship.
unmask (ʌnˈmɑːsk) *vb* **1** remove the mask from. **2** reveal the true character of.
unmentionable (ʌnˈmɛnʃənəbl̩) *adj* not fit to be mentioned. **unmentionables** *pl n* (*humorous*) underwear.
unmistakable (ʌnmɪˈsteɪkəbl̩) *adj* clear and obvious. **unmistakably** *adv*
unmitigated (ʌnˈmɪtɪgeɪtɪd) *adj* absolute; severe; intense: an unmitigated disaster.
unnecessary (ʌnˈnɛsəsərɪ) *adj* not necessary. **unnecessarily** *adv*
unnerve (ʌnˈnɜːv) *vb* cause to lose courage, confidence, etc.
unnumbered (ʌnˈnʌmbəd) *adj* **1** countless; innumerable. **2** not marked with a number.
UNO *abbrev* United Nations Organization.
unpack (ʌnˈpæk) *vb* remove the contents of; remove from a container, etc.
unparalleled (ʌnˈpærəˌlɛld) *adj* having no equal; unique.
unparliamentary (ˌʌnpɑːləˈmɛntərɪ) *adj* contrary to parliamentary practice.
unpick (ʌnˈpɪk) *vb* undo (the stitches) in (a piece of sewing).
unplaced (ʌnˈpleɪst) *adj* not placed among the first three in a competition, esp. a horse-race.
unplug (ʌnˈplʌg) *vb* **unplugged; unplugging 1** disconnect by removing the plug from a socket: unplug the TV. **2** remove a plug from.
unprecedented (ʌnˈprɛsɪˌdɛntɪd) *adj* having no precedent; unparalleled; original or new.
unprincipled (ʌnˈprɪnsɪpl̩d) *adj* having no moral principles; unscrupulous.
unqualified (ʌnˈkwɒlɪˌfaɪd) *adj* **1** lacking the necessary qualifications. **2** not modified or restricted; absolute or outright: an unqualified success.
unquestionable (ʌnˈkwɛstʃənəbl̩) *adj* not able to be questioned; indisputable; certain. **unquestionably** *adv*
unquote (ʌnˈkwəʊt) *adv* used when speaking to show the end of a quotation.
unravel (ʌnˈrævl̩) *vb* **unravelled; unravelling 1** disentangle; undo. **2** solve or explain (something complex).
unreasonable (ʌnˈriːzənəbl̩) *adj* **1** not reasonable in one's attitudes, actions, etc. **2** excessive; immoderate. **unreasonably** *adv*
unrelenting (ʌnrɪˈlɛntɪŋ) *adj* not yielding in strength, determination, etc.
unremitting (ʌnriˈmɪtɪŋ) *adj* constant or persistent.
unrequited (ʌnrɪˈkwaɪtɪd) *adj* not reciprocated or returned: unrequited love. < *un-* + *requite* to make a suitable return to, from *re-* back + obsolete *quite* to discharge.
unreserved (ʌnrɪˈzɜːvd) *adj* **1** without reservation; entire. **2** open and frank. **unreservedly** *adv*
unrest (ʌnˈrɛst) *n* trouble or agitation.

unrivalled (ʌnˈraɪvl̩d) *adj* having no equal; matchless: a man of unrivalled experience.
unroll (ʌnˈrəʊl) *vb* open out or unwind; become opened or unwound.
unruffled (ʌnˈrʌfl̩d) *adj* calm; still.
unruly (ʌnˈruːlɪ) *adj* difficult to control or discipline; impetuous. violent, or headstrong. **unruliness** *n*
unsaid (ʌnˈsɛd) *adj* not said or spoken.
unsavoury (ʌnˈseɪvərɪ) *adj* disagreeable; morally offensive.
unscathed (ʌnˈskeɪðd) *adj* not injured at all.
unscramble (ʌnˈskræmbl̩) *vb* **1** restore from a confused, untidy state; separate into individual parts. **2** restore (a scrambled message) to intelligible form.
unscrew (ʌnˈskruː) *vb* **1** remove a screw from (an object). **2** remove (a screw-lid) by turning anticlockwise.
unscrupulous (ʌnˈskruːpjʊləs) *adj* having no moral scruples; unprincipled. **unscrupulously** *adv*
unseat (ʌnˈsiːt) *vb* **1** throw from a seat, saddle, etc. **2** remove from political office.
unseemly (ʌnˈsiːmlɪ) *adj* improper or vulgar.
unseen (ʌnˈsiːn) *adj* **1** not seen; invisible. **2** (of a passage of writing) to be translated without previous preparation.
• *n* an unseen translation.
unsettle (ʌnˈsɛtl̩) *vb* **1** move from a fixed or settled state. **2** disturb or agitate. **unsettled** *adj* not settled; changeable: unsettled weather.
unsightly (ʌnˈsaɪtlɪ) *adj* not pleasing to the eye; ugly.
unsociable (ʌnˈsəʊʃəbl̩) *adj* not enjoying the company of others.
unsocial (ʌnˈsəʊʃəl) *adj* **1** not social. **2** failing outside the normal working day: unsocial hours.
unspeakable (ʌnˈspiːkəbl̩) *adj* **1** not capable of description in words. **2** indescribably bad or evil: unspeakable treacheries.
unstable (ʌnˈsteɪbl̩) *adj* **1** not stable or fixed. **2** marked by a tendency to show sudden emotional or mental changes.
unstuck (ʌnˈstʌk) *adj* free from being stuck. **come unstuck** (*informal*) fail; go wrong.
unthinkable (ʌnˈθɪŋkəbl̩) *adj* too improbable or unacceptable to be considered; impossible or incredible.
unthinking (ʌnˈθɪŋkɪŋ) *adj* thoughtless; inconsiderate.
unthought-of (ʌnˈθɔːtɔv) *adj* not expected or imagined.
until (ʌnˈtɪl, ənˈtɪl) *conj* up to the time that.
• *prep* **1** up to the time of. **2** up to as far as. < Middle English *untill.*
untimely (ʌnˈtaɪmlɪ) *adj* **1** happening before the natural or normal time: his untimely death. **2** happening, said, etc., at an unsuitable time.
unto (ˈʌntuː) *prep* (*archaic*) to. < Middle English.
untold (ʌnˈtəʊld) *adj* **1** too great to be described; too many to be counted: untold suffering. **2** not told.
untouchable (ʌnˈtʌtʃəbl̩) *adj* not able or permitted to be touched or reached.
• *n* a member of the lowest Hindu caste in India.
untoward (ˌʌntəˈwɔːd) *adj* unfortunate or improper.
unusual (ʌnˈjuːʒʊəl) *adj* not common; remarkable, different, or exceptional. **unusually** *adv*
unutterable (ʌnˈʌtərəbl̩) *adj* too great or intense to be expressed in words; absolute. **unutterably** *adv*
unveil (ʌnˈveɪl) *vb* **1** remove a veil or other covering (from). **2** make known publicly; disclose or reveal.
unwarranted (ʌnˈwɒrəntɪd) *adj* not justified or authorized: unwarranted interference.
unwieldy (ʌnˈwiːldɪ) *adj* difficult and awkward to move or handle because of its shape, weight, etc. **unwieldiness** *n*
unwilling (ʌnˈwɪlɪŋ) *adj* not willing; reluctant. **unwillingly** *adv* **unwillingness** *n*
unwind (ʌnˈwaɪnd) *vb* **unwound; unwinding 1** draw out or become drawn out. **2** become less tense; relax.
unwitting (ʌnˈwɪtɪŋ) *adj* **1** not knowing or aware. **2** not intentional. **unwittingly** *adv* < Old English *un-* + *witting,* from *witan* to know. SEE PANEL AT **INADVERTENT.**
unwonted (ʌnˈwəʊntɪd) *adj* unusual.
unwound (ʌnˈwaʊnd) SEE **UNWIND.**
unwrap (ʌnˈræp) *vb* **unwrapped; unwrapping** remove the wrapping from.
unwritten (ʌnˈrɪtn̩) *adj* **1** not written, esp. formally: an unwritten law. **2** not containing writing.
unzip (ʌnˈzɪp) *vb* **unzipped; unzipping** open with a zip.
up (ʌp) *adv* **1** towards, to, at, or in a higher position, condition, or level. **2** in or into an upright or raised position. **3** off the ground or other surface. **4** towards a more important place or centre: go up to London. **5** in a particular area of a country, esp. towards the

north. **6** out of the stomach through the mouth: Baby's brought up her food again. **7** as far as: up to now. **8** used with verbs to show intensity or completion of an activity: Eat up all your cabbage. **9** into a compact or secure state: tie up a parcel.
• *prep* **1** upwards through, along, etc. **2** at the top of.
• *adj* **1** moving or directed upwards. **2** travelling towards a large place or centre: the up train. **3** finished: Time's up. **4** knowledgeable: She's well up in biology. **5** ahead of an opponent: two goals up at half-time. **6** ready: Dinner's up! **7** (*informal*) wrong: What's up?
• *vb* **upped; upping 1** do something suddenly and as a surprise: He upped and left his wife and children. **2** raise or increase: up the price. < Old English *upp*. SEE PANEL.

upbraid (ʌpˈbreɪd) *vb* reprove severely. < Old English *ūpbregdan*.

upbringing (ˈʌpˌbrɪŋɪŋ) *n* the training and education of a child.

update (ʌpˈdeɪt) *vb* bring up to date.

up-end (ʌpˈɛnd) *vb* set on end.

upgrade (ʌpˈgreɪd) *vb* raise to a higher grade, position, or quality.

upheaval (ʌpˈhiːvl̩) *n* an extreme change or violent disturbance.

uphill (ˌʌpˈhɪl) *adv* in a direction sloping upwards.
• *adj* **1** sloping upwards. **2** difficult: an uphill task.

uphold (ʌpˈhəʊld) *vb* **upheld; upholding** maintain or support, esp. against opposition or challenge.

upholster (ʌpˈhəʊlstə) *vb* provide with a soft covering, padding, and springs. **upholsterer** *n* **upholstery** *n* the materials used in upholstering furniture. < Middle English *upholdester* dealer in small furniture.

upkeep (ˈʌpˌkiːp) *n* keeping something in a good condition; cost of this.

upland (ˈʌplənd) *adj, n* (of or connected with) high land.

uplift (ʌpˈlɪft) *vb* **1** raise. **2** raise morally, spiritually, etc.
• *n* (ˈʌpˌlɪft) **1** being raised. **2** a morally, spiritually, etc., improving influence.

upon (əˈpɒn) *prep* on.

upper (ˈʌpə) *adj* **1** higher in position, rank, or order. **2** farther inland or north.
• *n* the part of a shoe or boot above the sole. **upper-case** *adj* (of letters) capital, not small. **upper crust** (*informal*) the highest social class. **upper hand** dominance; advantage: gain the upper hand. **uppermost** *adj, adv* at or in the highest or most prominent position: uppermost in his mind.

uppish (ˈʌpɪʃ) *adj* also **uppity** (*informal*) arrogant, supercilious, or snobbish.

upright (ˈʌpˌraɪt) *adj* **1** also *adv* in a vertical or erect position. **2** honest or honourable. **3** having the main part or frame mounted vertically: an upright piano.
• *n* **1** something such as a post that stands upright. **2** an upright piano.

uprising (ˈʌpˌraɪzɪŋ) *n* a rebellion or revolt.

uproar (ˈʌpˌrɔː) *n* a noisy, confused

on the up-and-up

Up features in a number of idiomatic expressions, including:

on the up-and-up on a steadily improving and successful course.
up against 1 in contact with. **2** confronting.
up against it facing great difficulties.
up-and-coming *adj* becoming increasingly successful: up-and-coming young businessmen.
up-and-over *adj* (of a door) opened by being raised and moved or slid into a horizontal position.
up front 1 in advance: I suppose you'll want some money up front. **2** in front.
up in the air undecided; unsettled: The whole project is up in the air at the moment.
up-market *adj* of superior quality.
ups and downs times of alternately good and bad fortune, spirits, etc.
up to 1 as far as: The water came up to their waists. **2** as many as: selling up to 1 million bottles a year. **3** used to indicate an activity, especially something mischievous or suspicious: What are the children getting up to? **4** capable of: I don't feel up to chairing the meeting this evening. **5** depending on; being the responsibility of: I'd like to give you the job, but it's not up to me.
up-to-date *adj* **1** modern; most recent. **2** including the latest information, requirements, etc.
up to one's eyes, etc. (virtually) overwhelmed with work. A number of words may be substituted for eyes such as ears and neck.

disturbance; commotion. **uproarious** *adj* **1** noisy; tumultuous. **2** extremely funny. **uproariously** *adv* < Middle Dutch *op* up + *roer* movement.

uproot (ʌpˈruːt) *vb* **1** remove by pulling up by the roots. **2** displace.

upset (ʌpˈsɛt) *vb* **upset; upsetting** **1** overturn or become overturned. **2** disturb or distress, emotionally, mentally, or physically. **3** confuse.
• *n* (ˈʌpsɛt) upsetting or being upset: a stomach upset.

upshot (ˈʌpˌʃɒt) *n* the final result; outcome. < originally the final shot in an archery match.

upside down **1** with the upper and lower parts reversed. **2** in confusion. **upside-down** *adj*

upstage (ˌʌpˈsteɪdʒ) *adj* **1** also *adv* at or of the back of the stage. **2** haughty; proud.
• *vb* divert attention from (someone else) for oneself.

upstairs (ˌʌpˈstɛəz) *adv* on or to a higher floor; up the stairs.
• *adj* located on an upper floor.

upstanding (ʌpˈstændɪŋ) *adj* **1** of good character; honourable. **2** strong and healthy. **3** standing up; erect.

upstart (ˈʌpstɑːt) *n* **1** a person who has risen suddenly, esp. to a powerful position. **2** an arrogant person.

upstream (ˌʌpˈstriːm) *adj, adv* in the direction from which a stream flows.

upsurge (ˈʌpˌsɜːdʒ) *n* a sudden rise.

uptake (ˈʌpˌteɪk) *n* **1** taking up. **2** (*informal*) understanding: quick on the uptake.

uptight (ʌpˈtaɪt) *adj* (*informal*) **1** nervous or tense. **2** annoyed.

upturn (ʌpˈtɜːn) *vb* turn up or over.
• *n* (ˈʌpˌtɜːn) an upward turn; improvement.

upward (ˈʌpwəd) *adj* moving towards a higher level or state.
• *adv* also **upwards** towards a higher level, etc.

uranium (jʊˈreɪnɪəm) *n* a heavy, silvery-white, radioactive, metallic element used as a fuel in nuclear reactors.
< New Latin, from the planet *Uranus*.

urban (ˈɜːbn̩) *adj* of, like, or relating to a city or town. **urbanize** *vb* provide with a more urban character. **urbanization** *n*
< Latin *urbs* city. SEE PANEL.

urbane (ɜːˈbeɪn) *adj* marked by polite and elegant sophistication; smooth and suave. < SEE **URBAN**. SEE PANEL AT **URBAN**.

urchin (ˈɜːtʃɪn) *n* **1** a mischievous, young, usually scruffy boy. **2** a sea-urchin. < Latin *ericius* hedgehog.

urge (ɜːdʒ) *vb* **1** demand very strongly; try persistently to persuade; plead. **2** drive or force onwards.
• *n* a strong, inner drive; impulse.
< Latin *urgēre*.

urgent (ˈɜːdʒənt) *adj* **1** requiring immediate attention or action: an urgent need for adequate housing. **2** showing that something is urgent. **urgency** *n* **urgently** *adv*

urine (ˈjʊərɪn) *n* waste liquid formed by the kidney and discharged from the body. **urinal** *n* a receptacle used by men for urination; room, building, etc., containing this. **urinary** *adj* of urine or the organs concerned with urine. **urinate** *vb* discharge urine. **urination** *n*
< Latin *urina*.

urn (ɜːn) *n* **1** a large, metal container with a tap, used for making, holding, and serving tea, coffee, etc. **2** a decorative vase, esp. with a base, used for preserving the ashes of a cremated person.
< Latin *urna*.

us (əs; *stressed* ʌs) *pron* **1** the objective case of *we*. **2** we. **3** (*not standard*) me: Give us a kiss!

US *abbrev* United States. **USA** *abbrev* United States of America.

use (juːz) *vb* **1** put into service or action. **2** exercise; apply: Use your common sense! **3** consume: use up petrol. **4** exploit: I feel I'm just being used. **5** treat in a way that is mentioned.
• *n* (juːs) **1** using; being used: make good use of one's money. **2** the ability or right to use something. **3** a way of using something; practical purpose. **user** *n* **usable** *adj* able to be used. **usage** *n* **1** a common, established way in which words, etc., are used. **2** a way of treating

---

urban or **urbane?**

These two words are sometimes confused.

Urban means 'of, like, or relating to a city or town': *urban* areas, *urban* renewal.

Urbane means 'marked by polite and elegant sophistication; smooth and suave': He spoke in a soft, *urbane* voice.

Urbane does in fact come from urban: an urbane person was one who showed characteristics associated with someone who lived in a city.

A similar relationship exists between human and humane: humane refers to the behaviour and attitudes associated with being human.

---

or handling. **useful** *adj* **1** having practical applications. **2** highly satisfactory; commendable. **3** helpful. **usefully** *adv* **usefulness** *n* **useless** *adj* **1** having no practical applications. **2** (*informal*) weak, poor, or inept. **3** futile or hopeless. **uselessly** *adv* **uselessness** *n* < ultimately Latin *uti.*

used (ju:zd) *adj* **1** second-hand: used cars. **2** (ju:st) accustomed: He's not used to working with other people.
● *vb* (ju:st) used to show a former habit or condition: I used to smoke heavily.
SEE PANEL.

usher (ˈʌʃə) fem. **usherette** *n* an official who shows people to their seats in a theatre, etc.
● *vb* **1** lead in a polite way. **2** introduce: usher in a new era. < Latin *ostium* door.

USSR *abbrev* Union of Soviet Socialist Republics.

usual (ˈju:ʒʊəl) *adj* in accordance with what is normal, customary, or habitual. **usually** *adv* **as usual** in the usual way. < SEE **USE.**

usurer (ˈju:ʒərə) *n* a person who lends money at an exorbitant rate of interest. **usury** *n* the lending of money at an exorbitant rate of interest; such a rate of interest. < SEE **USE.**

usurp (ju:ˈzɜ:p) *vb* seize wrongfully or by force. **usurpation** *n* **usurper** *n* < Latin *usurpare* to take into use.

utensil (ju:ˈtɛnsəl) *n* an implement or container: cooking utensils. < Latin *utensilis* useful.

uterus (ˈju:tərəs) *n* the womb. **uterine** *adj* of the womb. < Latin.

utility (ju:ˈtɪlɪtɪ) *n* **1** usefulness; something useful. **2** a service that supplies the public with something such as gas or water: public utilities.
● *adj* also **utilitarian** of practical use, rather than beautiful in appearance. **utility room** a room in a house used for general purposes such as washing or storage. **utilize** *vb* put to a practical use. **utilization** *n* < Latin *utilis* useful.

utmost (ˈʌtˌməʊst) or **uttermost** (ˈʌtəməʊst) *adj* greatest; farthest; extreme: a matter of the utmost importance.
● *n* the greatest degree, etc. **do one's utmost** do one's best.

utopia (ju:ˈtəʊpɪə) any perfect, imaginary place or situation. **utopian** *adj* < *Utopia,* title of a book by Sir Thomas More, died 1535, English statesman.
SEE PANEL.

---

used not to or **did not use to?**

Users of English sometimes have difficulty with the negative and interrogative forms of used to. These can be formed in two ways:

□ **negatives:** used not to and did not use to. Used not to is found in more formal varieties of English: The company *used not to* accept late applications. The contraction of used not to is usedn't to. Did not use to and its contracted form didn't use to are more informal: The other teachers *didn't use to* complain about my spelling.

Careful speakers avoid the alternative spellings of the contractions: usen't to (instead of usedn't to) and didn't used to (instead of didn't use to), but these are found in informal styles.

□ **interrogatives:** used A to and did A use to. Used A to is more formal: *Used there to* be a church on that corner? The awkwardness of this construction, however, causes the majority of users to employ alternative phrasing: Was there once a church on that corner? Did A use to is more informal: *Did there use* to be a church on that corner?

---

utopia

A place which enjoys a perfect political and social system is referred to as a utopia. This was originally the title of a book written in Latin by the English statesman and scholar, Sir Thomas More, 1478–1535. In his *'Utopia'* (1516) he describes an imaginary island of the same name where everything—politics, laws, morals, individual rights—is perfect.

According to the title of the book, such places exist only in the imagination—translated literally, utopia means 'nowhere'. It derives from the Greek words *ou* 'no' and *topos* 'place'. Today the adjective utopian means 'visionary' or 'impractical'.

utter[1] (ˈʌtə) *adj* absolute; complete: utter chaos. **utterly** *adv* < Old English *ūt* out. SEE PANEL AT **SHEER**[1].

utter[2] *vb* express with the voice. **utterance** *n* < Middle Low German *ūtern* to speak, sell.

U-turn (ˈjuːˌtɜːn) *n* **1** a turn made by a vehicle without reversing so as to return in the direction from which it has come. **2** a complete reversal, esp. of policy.

uvula (ˈjuːvjʊlə) *n* the flap of tissue that hangs down above the back of the tongue. < Medieval Latin: little grape.

V

vac (væk) *n* (*informal*) a vacation.
vacant (ˈveɪkənt) *adj* **1** not occupied. **2** marked by a lack of thought or intelligence; not having an expression: vacant faces. **vacantly** *adv* **vacancy** *n* **1** the state of being vacant; emptiness. **2** a vacant post or office of employment. **3** vacant accommodation: Sorry—no vacancies. **vacate** *vb* make vacant; cease to occupy. < ultimately Latin *vacare* to be empty.
vacation (vəˈkeɪʃən) *n* **1** an interval between the terms of a university, etc. **2** (*US*) a holiday. **3** vacating. < SEE VACANT.
vaccinate (ˈvæksɪˌneɪt) *vb* inoculate with a vaccine to produce an active immunity to a particular disease. **vaccination** *n*
vaccine (ˈvæksiːn) *n* a preparation of dead or modified micro-organisms designed to protect the body from a particular disease by stimulating the production of antibodies. < ultimately Latin *vacca* cow. SEE PANEL.
vacillate (ˈvæsɪˌleɪt) *vb* waver between different opinions or alternatives; hesitate. **vacillation** *n* < Latin *vacillare* to sway.
vacuous (ˈvækjʊəs) *adj* **1** empty. **2** expressionless and stupid; inane. **vacuity** *n* vacuousness; something vacuous. < Latin *vacuus* empty.
vacuum (ˈvækjʊəm) *n, pl* **vacuums, vacua 1** an area of space that contains no matter. **2** an area of space from which the air has been removed, esp. pumped out. **3** a state of isolation or emptiness. • *vb* clean with a vacuum cleaner. **vacuum cleaner** an electrical appliance that removes dust, dirt, etc., esp. from carpets, by suction. **vacuum flask** a flask with a vacuum between its double glass walls, used for keeping liquids hot or cold. **vacuum-packed** *adj* sealed in a wrapping from which most of the air has been removed. **vacuum pump** a pump for producing a vacuum. < Latin *vacuus* empty.
vagabond (ˈvægəˌbɒnd) *n* a wanderer or tramp. < ultimately Latin *vagari* to wander.
vagary (ˈveɪgərɪ) *n* an erratic, whimsical, or odd action or notion. < probably Latin *vagari* to wander.
vagina (vəˈdʒaɪnə) *n* the passage leading from the vulva to the womb in women and other female mammals. **vaginal** *adj* < Latin: sheath.
vagrant (ˈveɪgrənt) *n* a tramp. • *adj* wandering; random. **vagrancy** *n* < probably Old French *wacrer* to wander, of Germanic origin.
vague (veɪg) *adj* **1** not clearly expressed, defined, or perceived; indistinct or obscure. **2** not expressing one's thoughts clearly. **vaguely** *adv* **vagueness** *n* < Latin *vagus* wandering.
vain (veɪn) *adj* **1** excessively proud of one's appearance, achievement, etc. **2** worthless or futile: vain hopes of success. **vainly** *adv* **in vain** without gaining the desired result. < ultimately Latin *vanus* empty.
valance (ˈvæləns) *n* a short piece of drapery hung round the edge of a bed, canopy, shelf, etc. < perhaps *Valence*, town in France.
vale (veɪl) *n* (*literary*) a valley. < Latin *vallis*.
valediction (ˌvælɪˈdɪkʃən) *n* saying goodbye; words used in this. **valedictory** *adj* expressing goodbye: a valedictory speech. < Latin *vale* farewell + *dicere* to say.
valentine (ˈvælənˌtaɪn) *n* **1** a card sent anonymously to one's sweetheart on

---

vaccine

The word vaccine came into the language following the publication in 1798 of *'Variolæ vaccinæ'*, a medical treatise by the British physician Edward Jenner, 1749–1823. Variolæ vaccinæ was the New Latin name for 'cowpox', derived from the Latin *vacca* 'a cow'.

In his treatise Jenner demonstrated how the cowpox virus could be used as a vaccine to produce in humans antibodies against smallpox. Those who had been inoculated with the cowpox virus were said to have been vaccinated or to have undergone vaccination.

---

14 February to express one's affection. **2** the person to whom such a card is sent. < St *Valentine*. SEE PANEL.

valet (ˈvæleɪ) *n* **1** a man's personal servant who takes care of clothes, etc. **2** an employee, in for example a hotel, with similar responsibilities. < Old French *vaslet* page, from Medieval Latin *vassus* servant.

valiant (ˈvælɪənt) *adj* marked by bravery or courage. **valiantly** *adv* < ultimately Latin *valēre* to be strong.

valid (ˈvælɪd) *adj* **1** having legal force. **2** sound or justifiable; logical: valid reasons. **validity** *n* **validate** *vb* make valid; confirm or authenticate. **validation** *n* < SEE VALIANT.

valley (ˈvælɪ) *n, pl* **valleys 1** an elongated depression in the earth's surface, esp. with a river at its base. **2** a region drained by a river. < Latin *vallis*.

valour (ˈvælə) *n* bravery, esp. in fighting. < Latin *valēre* to be strong.

valuable (ˈvæljʊəbl̩) *adj* **1** of great monetary value. **2** very useful; helpful. • *n* a personal possession that is worth a lot of money.

value (ˈvæljuː) *n* **1** the amount of money, etc., considered to be a fair equivalent of something to be sold or exchanged; worth: The value of the house is £100 000. **2** the quality of being desirable or useful. **3** a relative quantity, magnitude, or importance attributed to something. **4** the relative duration of a musical note. **5** *pl* social, esp. moral standards. • *vb* **1** estimate the value of. **2** place an assessment of worth on. **3** think highly of; esteem. **valuer** *n* **valuation** *n* **1** a formal estimate of the worth of something such as property. **2** an assessment of worth, merit, or character. **value-added tax** an indirect tax calculated according to the value added to a product at each stage of production. **valueless** *adj* worthless. < Latin *valēre* to be worth, be strong.

valve (vælv) *n* **1** a device that controls the flow of a liquid or gas in a pipe. **2** an electronic device consisting of a set of electrodes in an evacuated glass container that allows the current to pass in one direction only. **3** a fold of membrane, esp. in the heart or a vein, that allows the passage of fluid in one direction only. **4** a device that changes the length of the tube on a brass musical instrument. < Latin *valva* folding door.

vampire (ˈvæmpaɪə) *n* a corpse believed to rise from its grave at night and suck the blood of living people. < German *Vampir*, of Slavonic origin.

van (væn) *n* **1** a covered motor vehicle for transporting goods, furniture, etc. **2** an enclosed railway goods wagon: a guard's van. < short for *caravan*.

vandal (ˈvændl̩) *n* a person who deliberately destroys or damages property. **vandalism** *n* **vandalize** *vb* destroy or damage (property, etc.) as a vandal. SEE PANEL.

vane (veɪn) *n* **1** a weather-vane. **2** a flat blade that is moved around an axis by air, water, etc., as on a windmill or turbine. < Old English *fana*.

vanguard (ˈvænˌgɑːd) *n* **1** the front, advancing part of an army. **2** the foremost part of a movement. < Old

valentine

A greeting card sent anonymously to a person on 14 February as a sign of affection is known as a valentine. This word derives from either of two Christian martyrs of the 3rd century AD called *St Valentine*. One was an Italian bishop and the other an Italian priest. Neither, however, was noted for the amorous practices which are nowadays associated with them. St Valentine's Day traditions date back to the pagan feast of Lupercalia in ancient Rome, held on 15 February in honour of the god Pan. This happily coincided with the day on which birds were supposed to choose their mates. Rather than abolish the feast, the early Christian church gave it a new name.

vandal

A person who wilfully causes damage to public or private property is known as a vandal. The word comes from the Latin *Vandalii* or 'Vandals', the name given to the Germanic tribe that during the first five centuries AD migrated south from Scandinavia and the southern shores of the Baltic, reaching as far as North Africa. The Vandals left behind them a trail of devastation, culminating in 455 AD with the sacking of Rome.

French *avant-* fore + *garde* guard.

vanilla (vəˈnɪlə) *n* **1** a flavouring prepared from the long pods of a type of tropical climbing orchid. **2** this orchid. < Spanish *vainilla,* ultimately Latin *vagina* sheath.

vanish (ˈvænɪʃ) *vb* **1** pass from sight suddenly or quickly. **2** cease to exist. < ultimately Latin *e-* out + *vanescere* to vanish.

vanity (ˈvænɪtɪ) *n* **1** excessive pride in one's appearance, achievements, etc. **2** the quality of being worthless or futile. **3** something vain. **vanity case** a small hand case used by women to carry cosmetics, etc. < ultimately Latin *vanus* empty.

vanquish (ˈvæŋkwɪʃ) *vb* defeat or overcome; conquer. < ultimately Latin *vincere.*

vantage (ˈvɑːntɪdʒ) *n* a position that gives an advantageous, commanding view: a vantage point. < SEE ADVANTAGE.

vapid (ˈvæpɪd) *adj* **1** having no taste or flavour. **2** uninteresting; dull. < Latin *vapidus.*

vapour (ˈveɪpə) *n* **1** particles of fog, smoke, etc., floating in the air. **2** the gaseous form of a substance that is normally a liquid: water vapour. **vaporous** *adj* **vaporize** *vb* convert or be converted into vapour. **vaporization** *n* **vaporizer** *n* < Latin *vapor.*

variable (ˈvɛərɪəbl̩) *adj* liable to change. • *n* something variable. **variability** *n* < SEE VARY.

variant (ˈvɛərɪənt) *adj* different or alternative: variant spellings. • *n* something that is variant. < SEE VARY.

varicoloured (ˈvɛərɪˌkʌləd) *adj* having various colours.

varicose (ˈværɪˌkəʊs) *adj* (of veins) swollen and tortuous, as a result of the valves in the veins not functioning properly. < Latin *varix* enlarged vein.

variegated (ˈvɛərɪˌgeɪtɪd) *adj* having patches, spots, etc., of different colours.

variety (vəˈraɪətɪ) *n* **1** the state of having different forms. **2** one of the different forms of something; sort: varieties of tulip. **3** a number of different kinds of thing: a wide variety of ways. **4** a form of entertainment consisting of several separate performances of different items such as singing, dancing, and comedy acts. < Latin *varietas.* SEE PANEL.

varnish (ˈvɑːnɪʃ) *n* a resinous solution that dries to form a hard, shiny, transparent coating on wood, etc. • *vb* cover with varnish. < Medieval Latin *veronix* resin.

vary (ˈvɛərɪ) *vb* **varied; varying 1** be different; fluctuate or change: Prices vary from shop to shop. **2** make or become different. **variance** *n* **1** the state or an instance of being divergent; discrepancy. **2** the state of disagreeing. at variance. **variation** *n* **1** varying or being varied. **2** an instance of varying; extent to which something varies. **3** the repetition of a musical theme with changes in rhythm, harmony, etc. **varied** *adj* **1** having many different forms. **2** full of variety. **various** *adj* **1** of several different kinds. **2** several. **variously** *adv* < Latin *variare,* from *varius* various, changing.

vascular (ˈvæskjʊlə) *adj* of, containing, or consisting of vessels that conduct liquids, esp. blood or sap, in an organism. < ultimately Latin *vas* vessel.

vase (vɑːz) *n* an open, usually tall container, used esp. for holding cut flowers. < Latin *vas* vessel.

vasectomy (væˈsɛktəmɪ) *n* the removal of part of the duct that conveys sperm from the testicle. < Latin *vas* vessel, duct + *-ectomy,* from Greek *ektemnein* to cut.

Vaseline (ˈvæsəˌliːn) *n* (*Trademark*) a type of petroleum jelly.

vassal (ˈvæsl̩) *n* **1** a person in the feudal system who held property from a lord in return for military service and homage. **2** a person in a subordinate position. < Medieval Latin *vassus* servant, of Celtic origin.

vast (vɑːst) *adj* very great in extent, size, etc.: the vast majority of people. **vastly** *adv* **vastness** *n* < Latin *vastus.*

vat (væt) *n* a large container for holding liquids. < Old English *fæt.*

VAT (sometimes væt) *abbrev* value-added tax.

vaudeville (ˈvɔːdəvɪl, ˈvəʊdəvɪl) *n*

Variety is the spice of life

The expression Variety is the spice of life means that it is the variety of experience that makes life interesting. The expression comes originally from the poem 'The Task' by the British poet William Cowper, 1731–1800:

Variety's the very spice of life,
That gives it all its flavour.

variety entertainment. < French *Vau-de-Vire* district in Normandy, France. SEE PANEL.

vault[1] (vɔːlt) *n* **1** an arched roof. **2** an underground room for storage; cellar. **3** a strong-room for the safe storage of valuables: locked up in the bank vault. **4** a burial chamber. **vaulted** *adj* < probably Latin *volvere* to roll.

vault[2] *vb* leap (over), esp. using one's hands or a pole for leverage.
• *n* an act of vaulting. < Latin *volvere* to roll.

vaunt (vɔːnt) *vb* display or describe in a showy, boastful way. < ultimately Latin *vanus* vain.

VCR *abbrev* video-cassette recorder.

VD *abbrev* venereal disease.

VDU *abbrev* visual display unit.

veal (viːl) *n* calf's flesh as food. < Old French *veel,* from Latin *vitulus* calf.

vector (ˈvɛktə) *n* **1** (*mathematics*) a quantity that has both magnitude and direction. **2** an organism, esp. an insect, that transmits a disease; carrier. < Latin: carrier, from *vehere* to carry.

veer (vɪə) *vb* **1** change direction, position, or course. **2** (of the wind) move clockwise. < Middle French *virer,* probably of Celtic origin.

vegetable (ˈvɛdʒtəbl̩) *n* **1** a plant with a part that is used as food, such as the potato or cabbage; this part of the plant. **2** a person with severely impaired mental faculties. **vegetarian** *n* a person who eats no meat. < ultimately Latin *vegēre* to excite.

vegetate (ˈvɛdʒɪˌteɪt) *vb* lead a dull, undemanding life. **vegetation** *n* **1** plant life, esp. of a particular area. **2** vegetating.

vehement (ˈviːəmənt) *adj* showing or expressing strong feeling. **vehemence** *n* **vehemently** *adv* < Latin *vehemens.*

vehicle (ˈviːəkl̩) *n* **1** a conveyance for carrying passengers or goods, esp. one fitted with wheels. **2** a means for the expression and communication of something. **vehicular** *adj* < Latin *vehere* to carry.

veil (veɪl) *n* **1** a piece of light fabric worn by women, esp. to conceal or obscure the face and head. **2** something that conceals or obscures like a veil: a veil of silence.
• *vb* cover with or as if with a veil: veiled threats. < ultimately Latin *velum* cloth.

vein (veɪn) *n* **1** a thin-walled vessel that carries blood from the tissues to the heart. **2** a small strand of tissue on a leaf. **3** a layer of ore, coal, etc., esp. in a rock opening or between rock strata. **4** a streak of a different colour, as in marble. **5** a distinctive quality; mood or manner: to continue in a lighter vein. **veined** *adj* < Latin *vena.*

vellum (ˈvɛləm) *n* **1** a fine parchment, usually prepared from the skin of a calf. **2** a strong, smooth writing-paper. < SEE VEAL.

velocity (vəˈlɒsɪtɪ) *n* speed in a certain direction. < Latin *velox* quick.

velvet (ˈvɛlvɪt) *n* a fabric of silk, cotton, etc., with a soft, thick, short pile. **velvety** *adj* < Latin *villus* shaggy hair.

vend (vɛnd) *vb* sell. **vending-machine** *n* a coin-operated machine that automatically dispenses small consumer articles. **vendor** *n* a person who sells something. < Latin *vendere* to sell.

vendetta (vɛnˈdɛtə) *n* a private feud, esp. one in which the relatives of a murdered person take vengeance by killing the murderer or a member of his or her family. < Italian, from Latin *vindicare* to vindicate.

veneer (vɪˈnɪə) *n* **1** a thin layer of fine wood, etc., used to cover a surface. **2** a superficial appearance.
• *vb* cover with a veneer. < Old French *fournir* to furnish, complete.

venerate (ˈvɛnəˌreɪt) *vb* regard with deep respect; revere. **veneration** *n* **venerator** *n* **venerable** *adj* worthy of respect or reverence because of age or associations. < Latin *venus* love.

venereal (vɪˈnɪərɪəl) *adj* **1** of a disease such as gonorrhoea or syphilis that is spread mainly by sexual intercourse: venereal disease. **2** relating to sexual love or intercourse. < Latin *venus* sexual love.

vengeance (ˈvɛndʒəns) *n* punishment inflicted in retaliation for hurt or harm done. **vengeful** *adj* seeking vengeance. **vengefully** *adv* **with a vengeance** to an

vaudeville

The French loan-word vaudeville comes from the Middle French *vaudevire,* meaning 'a popular satirical song'. This is a shortened form of *chanson du vau-de-Vire* 'a song of the valley of Vire', Vire being a district in Normandy where such songs were originally composed.

extreme degree. < SEE **VINDICATE.**
venison (ˈvɛnɪsən) *n* the flesh of a deer as food. < Latin *venari* to hunt.
venom (ˈvɛnəm) *n* **1** poison secreted by certain snakes, insects, etc., and transmitted to a victim by a bite or sting. **2** malevolence; spite. **venomous** *adj* **1** secreting venom. **2** full of ill will; malevolent or spiteful. < ultimately Latin *venenum* poison.
vent[1] (vɛnt) *n* an opening that allows fumes, liquids, etc., to pass or escape. • *vb* **1** provide with a vent. **2** give expression to: vent one's anger. **give vent to** express; release. < Latin *ventus* wind.
vent[2] *n* a slit in a garment, as at the back of a jacket. < Latin *findere* to split.
ventilate (ˈvɛntɪˌleɪt) *vb* **1** cause fresh air to circulate freely in. **2** expose to public examination and discussion. **ventilation** *n* **ventilator** *n* < Latin *ventus* wind.
ventricle (ˈvɛntrɪkl) *n* a small cavity in an organ of the body, esp. in the heart or brain. < Latin *venter* belly.
ventriloquism (vɛnˈtrɪləˌkwɪzəm) *n* the art of producing vocal sounds in such a way that they appear to come from another source. **ventriloquist** *n* < Latin *venter* belly + *loqui* to speak. SEE PANEL.
venture (ˈvɛntʃə) *n* a risky undertaking. • *vb* **1** risk. **2** express at the risk of criticism, etc.: May I venture to suggest an alternative plan? **3** move forward in spite of risks; dare to do or go. **venturesome** *adj* daring. < SEE **ADVENTURE.**
venue (ˈvɛnjuː) *n* the place where an event, meeting, etc., takes place. < ultimately Latin *venire* to come.
veracious (vəˈreɪʃəs) *adj* **1** truthful. **2** true. **veraciously** *adv* **veracity** *n* < Latin *verus* true.
veranda, verandah (vəˈrændə) *n* an open roofed gallery attached to the outside of a building. < Portuguese *varanda* and Spanish *baranda* balcony, ultimately from Hindi *varaṇḍā*.

---

ventriloquism

The art of producing speech sounds that seem to be made by something other than the vocal organs is known as ventriloquism. Of Latin origin, this word is a combination of *venter* 'belly' and *loqui* 'to speak'. According to popular theory, the source of the sound was the ventriloquist's belly.

---

verb (vɜːb) *n* a word that expresses an action, existence, or occurrence such as eat, be, or happen. **verbal** *adj* **1** of or in words. **2** spoken not written: a verbal contract. **3** of a verb. **verbally** *adv* **verbalize** *vb* express in words. **verbatim** *adj, adv* in the exact words. < Latin *verbum* word.
verbiage (ˈvɜːbɪɪdʒ) *n* the excessive use of words; verbosity.
verbose (vɜːˈbəʊs) *adj* using or having more words than are needed. **verbosely** *adv* **verbosity** *n*
verdant (ˈvɜːdn̩t) *adj* green; covered with green vegetation. < ultimately Latin *virēre* to be green.
verdict (ˈvɜːdɪkt) *n* **1** the decision reached by a jury. **2** a judgment, opinion, or decision. < ultimately Latin *verus* true + *dicere* to say.
verge (vɜːdʒ) *n* **1** an edge, margin, or limit. **2** a grassy strip of land at the edge of a road, flower bed, etc. **3** the point beyond which something will take place; brink: on the verge of a nervous breakdown. • *vb* **verge on** be near to. < Latin *virga* rod.
verger (ˈvɜːdʒə) *n* a church official who is a caretaker or attendant. < Latin *virga* rod.
verify (ˈvɛrɪˌfaɪ) *vb* **verified; verifying** prove to be true; check the correctness of; confirm. **verification** *n* **verifier** *n* < Latin *verus* true + *facere* to make.
verisimilitude (ˌvɛrɪsɪˈmɪlɪtjuːd) *n* the appearance or semblance of being true or real. < Latin *veri similis* like the truth.
veritable (ˈvɛrɪtəbl̩) *adj* truly being what is named.
vermicelli (ˌvɜːmɪˈtʃɛlɪ, ˌvɜːmɪˈsɛlɪ) *n* pasta in the form of long threads. < Italian: little worms.
vermilion (vɜːˈmɪljən) *adj, n* brilliant-red. < ultimately *vermiculus* little worm.
vermin (ˈvɜːmɪn) *n* **1** small animals or insects that are considered objectionable or harmful. **2** a very unpleasant person. **verminous** *adj* < Latin *vermen* worm.
vermouth (ˈvɜːməθ, vɜːˈmuːθ) *n* a fortified wine flavoured with aromatic herbs. < ultimately German *Wermut* wormwood.
vernacular (vəˈnækjʊlə) *n* the commonly spoken language of a country or region. • *adj* expressed in the vernacular. < Latin *verna* household slave.
versatile (ˈvɜːsəˌtaɪl) *adj* **1** capable of

being used in many different ways. **2** able to do many different things. < Latin *vertere* to turn.

verse (vɜːs) *n* **1** a line of metrical writing; group of lines in a poem, song, etc. **2** poetry in contrast to prose. **3** one of the parts into which chapters of the Bible are divided. **versed** *adj* having a thorough knowledge (of); skilled (in): well-versed in French literature. < Latin *vertere* to turn.

version (ˈvɜːʃən, ˈvɜːʒən) *n* **1** an account or description from a particular point of view. **2** a translation, esp. of the Bible. **3** an adaptation or variant form: the film version of the play. < Latin *vertere* to turn.

versus (ˈvɜːsəs) *prep* against; in contrast to. < Latin *vertere* to turn.

vertebra (ˈvɜːtɪbrə) *n, pl* **vertebrae** one of a series of small bones that form the backbone. **vertebral** *adj* < Latin: joint, from *vertere* to turn.

vertebrate (ˈvɜːtɪbrət,ˈvɜːtɪbreɪt) *adj* (of an animal) having a backbone.
• *n* a vertebrate animal.

vertex (ˈvɜːtɛks) *n, pl* **vertices 1** the highest point. **2** the point of a triangle, pyramid, cone, etc. < Latin: whirlpool, from *vertere* to turn.

vertical (ˈvɜːtɪkl̩) *adj* at right angles to the horizontal; moving or reaching in this way: vertical take-off. **vertically** *adv* < SEE **VERTEX.**

vertigo (ˈvɜːtɪˌgəʊ) *n* a sensation of dizziness and loss of balance. < Latin *vertere* to turn.

verve (vɜːv) *n* energetic enthusiasm, as in performing an artistic work. < French, from Latin *verba* words.

very (ˈvɛrɪ) *adv* **1** to a high degree; extremely: very good. **2** used for emphasis: that very same day.
• *adj* **1** actual: caught in the very act. **2** exactly or precisely; used for emphasis: You're the very person I'm looking for! **3** mere: The very thought terrifies me! < Latin *verus* true.

vessel (ˈvɛsl̩) *n* **1** a hollow structure that travels on water, designed to carry people or goods. **2** a hollow container, esp. used for holding liquids. **3** a tube-like structure in the body for conveying a liquid, esp. blood. < ultimately Latin *vas* vase.

vest (vɛst) *n* **1** an undergarment for the upper part of the body. **2** (*chiefly US*) a waistcoat.
• *vb* give (rights, etc.) (to): the power vested in the presidency. **vested interest** an established right or privilege enjoyed by a person or group. < ultimately Latin *vestire* to clothe.

vestibule (ˈvɛstɪˌbjuːl) *n* a small entrance hall; lobby. < Latin *vestibulum.*

vestige (ˈvɛstɪdʒ) *n* a trace left by something. **vestigial** *adj* < Latin *vestigium* track.

vestment (ˈvɛstmənt) *n* a garment or robe, esp. one of ceremony or worn by clergy at a religious service. < ultimately Latin *vestire* to clothe.

vestry (ˈvɛstrɪ) *n* a room in a church where vestments, etc., are kept and where some religious meetings are held. < ultimately Latin *vestire* to clothe.

vet (vɛt) *n* a veterinary surgeon.
• *vb* **vetted; vetting** examine, check, or assess thoroughly. < SEE **VETERINARY.**

veteran (ˈvɛtərən) *n* a person with long experience, as of military service.
• *adj* experienced: a veteran supporter of disarmament. **veteran car** an old motor car, esp. one built before 1916. < Latin *vetus* old.

veterinary (ˈvɛtənrɪ, ˈvɛtən̩rɪ) *adj* of or concerned with the health and medical treatment of farm and domestic animals. **veterinary surgeon** a person skilled in treating farm and domestic animals. < Latin *veterinae* beasts of burden.

veto (ˈviːtəʊ) *n, pl* **vetoes 1** an authoritative prohibition or rejection. **2** the authority to prohibit or reject something, such as legislation.
• *vb* forbid; prevent from being enacted by veto. < Latin: I forbid, from *vetare* to forbid.

vex (vɛks) *vb* **1** irritate, annoy, or distress. **2** puzzle or worry. **vexation** *n* **1** vexing; being vexed. **2** something causing this. **vexatious** *adj* causing vexation. **vexed question** a much-discussed problem to which no satisfactory solution has been found. < ultimately Latin *vexare* to agitate, jolt.

VHF *abbrev* very high frequency.

via (ˈvaɪə) *prep* by way of; by means of. < Latin *via* way.

viable (ˈvaɪəbl̩) *adj* **1** capable of independent growth or existence: a viable foetus. **2** practicable: a viable scheme. **viability** *n* < Latin *vita* life. SEE PANEL.

viaduct (ˈvaɪəˌdʌkt) *n* a long bridge, usually supported by arches, that carries a road or railway across a deep valley. < Latin *via* way + English *-duct,* as in aqueduct, from *ducere* to lead.

vibes (vaɪbz) *pl n* (*informal*) **1** a vibraphone. **2** a feeling or atmosphere that is sensed.

vibrant (ˈvaɪbrənt) *adj* **1** showing or marked by vibration; pulsating or resonant. **2** marked by great energy or activity.

vibraphone (ˈvaɪbrəˌfəʊn) *n* a type of xylophone that has metal bars and electrically operated fans which produce a characteristic vibrating effect. < Latin *vibrare* to vibrate + English *-phone*, from Greek *-phōnos* sounding.

vibrate (vaɪˈbreɪt) *vb* **1** move backwards and forwards rapidly. **2** resonate or resound. **vibratory** *adj* **vibration** *n* vibrating. **vibrations** *pl n* a feeling or atmosphere that is sensed. **vibrator** *n* a device that produces a vibrating action, esp. used in massage. < Latin *vibrare*.

vicar (ˈvɪkə) *n* a clergyman who is the priest of a parish. **vicarage** *n* the house of a vicar. < Latin *vicarius* deputy: SEE VICARIOUS.

vicarious (vaɪˈkɛərɪəs, vɪˈkɛərɪəs) *adj* **1** endured or undergone by one person as a substitute for another: vicarious punishment. **2** experienced by imagining the feelings, etc., of another person: vicarious pleasures. **vicariously** *adv* < Latin *vicis* interchange.

vice[1] (vaɪs) *n* **1** immoral behaviour; wickedness; form of this. **2** sexual immorality; prostitution. **3** a minor fault or habit. < ultimately Latin *vitium*.

vice[2] *n* an instrument, usually fixed to a work-bench. with two jaws that close to hold something firmly. < Latin *vitis* vine.

vice- *prefix* next in rank below; deputy; acting for: vice-president. < Latin *vicis* change.

viceroy (ˈvaɪsrɔɪ) *n* a person who governs a colony, province, etc., ruling as the representative of the sovereign. < French, from *vice-*, from Latin *vicis* interchange + *roy* king, from Latin *rex*.

vice versa (ˌvaɪsə ˈvɜːsə) *adv* with the order reversed; the other way round. < Latin.

viable

Some careful users of English object to the use of viable to mean 'practicable; capable of working successfully': a viable scheme, a viable proposition. Viable is reserved by such users for the meaning 'capable of independent growth or existence': a viable foetus. General usage, however, tends to ignore this preference and the use of viable in the sense of 'practicable' is commonly accepted.

vicinity (vɪˈsɪnɪtɪ) *n* a surrounding or nearby area. < ultimately Latin *vicus* village.

vicious (ˈvɪʃəs) *adj* **1** marked by or done with cruelty or brutality: vicious attacks on old ladies. **2** malicious or spiteful: vicious gossip. **3** (of animals) ferocious; dangerous. **4** very fierce; severe. **viciously** *adv* **viciousness** *n* < ultimately Latin *vitium* defect.

vicissitude (vɪˈsɪsɪˌtjuːd) *n* a change in the circumstances or conditions of life. < Latin *vicis* change.

victim (ˈvɪktɪm) *n* **1** a person or thing that suffers injury or harm: victims of the hijack. **2** a person who is tricked. **victimize** *vb* make a victim of; choose to suffer mistreatment. **victimization** *n* < Latin *victima*.

victory (ˈvɪktərɪ) *n* **1** winning in a battle or contest. **2** success or mastery in a struggle against an obstacle or problem. **victor** *n* a person, country, etc., that has won a battle or contest. **victorious** *adj* having won a victory; triumphant. < Latin *vincere* to conquer.

victuals (ˈvɪtl̩z) *n* food; provisions. < Latin *victus* sustenance.

video (ˈvɪdɪəʊ) *adj* of or relating to television, esp. the transmission, reception, or reproduction of its visual image.
• *n* also **video-cassette recorder; video-recorder** an apparatus for recording and replaying television broadcasts.
• *vb* videotape. **videotape** *vb, n* (record (television pictures and sound) onto) magnetic tape. < Latin *vidēre* to see; based on *audio*.

vie (vaɪ) *vb* **vied; vying** contend for superiority. < probably ultimately Latin *invitare* to invite.

view (vjuː) *n* **1** the act of seeing or observing. **2** range of vision: The ship came into view. **3** a scene that can be observed from a particular point: glorious views of the mountains. **4** also **point of view; viewpoint** a way of considering something; opinion: a frank exchange of views. **5** an opportunity to see and inspect something: a private view.
• *vb* **1** watch or see. **2** inspect: We viewed the house, but decided not to buy it. **3** consider. **4** watch television. **in view of** considering. **on view** exhibited for public inspection. **viewdata** *n* a system in which television sets are linked to a central computer by telephone lines and computerized information is selected and displayed. **viewer** *n* **1** a person who views something. **2** a person who

watches television. **3** an optical device used to view photographic slides. **viewfinder** *n* a device on a camera that enables the user to see the area to be included in the picture. **with a view to** with the intention or hope of. < ultimately Latin *vidēre* to see.

vigil (ˈvɪdʒɪl) *n* a staying awake to guard or pray, sometimes before a religious festival. **vigilant** *adj* alert, esp. looking out for danger. **vigilance** *n* **vigilantly** *adv* **vigilante** *n* one of a self-appointed group of citizens who try to prevent crime and disorder, esp. where the normal legal processes are considered unsatisfactory. < Latin: alert.

vignette (vɪˈnjɛt) *n* **1** an illustration or photograph with undefined edges that fade into the background. **2** a short descriptive sketch. < French: little vine.

vigour (ˈvɪgə) *n* **1** active physical or mental strength or energy. **2** forcefulness of action, movement, or effect. **3** strong, healthy growth in plants. **vigorous** *adj* full of or performed with vigour. **vigorously** *adv* **vigorousness** *n* < ultimately Latin *vigēre* to be lively.

vile (vaɪl) *adj* **1** extremely wicked; shameful. **2** disgusting to the senses: a vile smell. **3** (*informal*) very bad. **vilely** *adv* **vileness** *n* **vilify** *vb* **vilified; vilifying** say evil things about; malign or defame. **vilification** *n* < ultimately Latin *vilis* cheap, base.

villa (ˈvɪlə) *n* **1** a country house, esp. a large one. **2** a suburban house. **3** a house at the seaside that is rented to holiday-makers. < Latin: country estate.

village (ˈvɪlɪdʒ) *n* a group of houses in a country area, smaller than a town and usually having a church. **villager** *n* an inhabitant of a village. < SEE VILLA.

villain (ˈvɪlən) *n* **1** an evil person; scoundrel or criminal. **2** an evil character in a story, play, etc. **villainy** *n* **villainous** *adj* wicked; evil: villainous deeds. **villainously** *adv* < Medieval Latin *villanus* worker on a country estate. SEE PANEL.

vinaigrette (ˌvɪnɪˈgrɛt, ˌvɪneɪˈgrɛt) *n* **1** a small decorative bottle for holding smelling-salts, etc. **2** a salad dressing of oil, vinegar, and seasoning. < French *vinaigre* vinegar.

vindicate (ˈvɪndɪˌkeɪt) *vb* **1** clear from guilt; exonerate or justify. **2** defend or uphold. **vindication** *n* **vindicator** *n* < Latin *vindex* claimant.

vindictive (vɪnˈdɪktɪv) *adj* spiteful or vengeful. **vindictively** *adv* **vindictiveness** *n* < SEE VINDICATE.

vine (vaɪn) *n* any of various climbing or trailing plants, esp. the grapevine. **vineyard** *n* a plantation of grapevines. < ultimately Latin *vinum* wine.

vinegar (ˈvɪnɪgə) *n* an acid-tasting liquid made from fermentation of wine, beer, etc., used mostly for flavouring and preserving. **vinegary** *adj* < Old French *vin* wine + *aigre* sour, keen.

vintage (ˈvɪntɪdʒ) *n* **1** the yield of grapes for making wine. **2** wine, esp. of a type, region, or year that is mentioned. **3** the period of origin: of Edwardian vintage. • *adj* **1** (of wine) of a very good year. **2** of continuing interest and importance; classic: the vintage years of radio comedy. **3** of the best and most representative: The film is vintage Bogart. **vintage car** a car built between 1917 and 1930. < Latin *vinum* wine + *demere* to remove.

viol (ˈvaɪəl) *n* one of a group of string instruments, with six strings, frets, and a flat back, which is held between the knees when played. < Middle French *viole*.

viola (vɪˈəʊlə) *n* a string instrument slightly larger than a violin and lower in pitch. < Italian.

violate (ˈvaɪəˌleɪt) *vb* **1** infringe (a law, agreement, etc.). **2** treat (a sacred place) with disrespect. **3** interrupt or disturb. **4** rape. **violation** *n* **violator** *n* < Latin *violare*.

violent (ˈvaɪələnt) *adj* **1** marked by great force or intensity: violent opposition. **2** using

---

villain

To refer to people as villains has not always been to speak disapprovingly of them. In Medieval Latin *villanus*, from which villain derives, simply meant 'a worker on a country estate' and in feudal England a *villein* was simply 'a serf'. Other formerly neutral or positive words which have acquired a negative or derogatory value during the course of time include:

knave formerly 'a boy or servant' (compare German Knabe)
pedant formerly 'a teacher'
crafty formerly 'skilled as a craftsman'
imp formerly a name conveying dignity and honour and used of royal offspring
orgy formerly 'a religious ceremony'

physical force in a way that presents a danger or causes injury to others: The patient became violent. **3** not natural; caused by force: a violent death. **violently** *adv* **violence** *n* being violent; violent behaviour. < Latin *violentus.*

violet (ˈvaɪələt) *n* **1** a plant with fragrant, bluish-purple flowers. **2** also *adj* bluish-purple. < Latin *viola.*

violin (ˌvaɪəˈlɪn) *n* a string instrument with four strings and no frets, played with a bow. **violinist** *n* a person who plays the violin. < Italian *violino* little viola: SEE **VIOLA.**

VIP *abbrev* very important person.

viper (ˈvaɪpə) *n* an adder or related snake. < Latin *vipera.*

virgin (ˈvɜːdʒɪn) *n* a person, esp. a woman, who has not had sexual intercourse.
• *adj* **1** also **virginal** being a virgin; of or like a virgin; modest. **2** free from impurities; undefiled. **3** not used or exploited; untouched: virgin territory. **virginity** *n* < Latin *virgo.*

virginals (ˈvɜːdʒɪnl̩z) *pl n* a keyboard instrument of the 16th and 17th centuries; simplest form of the harpsichord. < probably Latin *virginalis* of a virgin.

virile (ˈvɪraɪl) *adj* **1** having the characteristics of an adult male. **2** strong; vigorous. **3** (of a male) able to copulate. **virility** *n* < Latin *vir* man.

virology (vaɪˈrɒlədʒɪ) *n* the branch of science that studies viruses. **virologist** *n* < *virus* + *-logy,* ultimately from Greek *logos* word.

virtual (ˈvɜːtʃʊəl) *adj* with the effect or nature, but not the name or form of. **virtually** *adv* nearly. < SEE **VIRTUE.**

virtue (ˈvɜːtjuː, ˈvɜːtʃuː) *n* **1** moral excellence; goodness; form of this. **2** a beneficial quality; advantage. **3** chastity, esp. in a woman. **by virtue of** on account of; because of. < Latin *virtus* manliness, strength.

virtuoso (ˌvɜːtjʊˈəʊzəʊ) *n, pl* **virtuosos, virtuosi** a person who excels in the technique of doing something, esp. performing music. **virtuosity** *n* < Italian, from Late Latin *virtuosus* virtuous.

virtuous (ˈvɜːtjʊəs) *adj* **1** marked by virtue; morally good. **2** chaste. **virtuously** *adv* **virtuousness** *n*

virulent (ˈvɪrʊlənt) *adj* **1** (of a disease) severe and developing rapidly. **2** very poisonous; deadly. **3** very bitter, hostile, and spiteful. **virulence** *n* **virulently** *adv* < Latin *virus* poison.

virus (ˈvaɪrəs) *n* **1** a minute agent of a disease that can reproduce inside a living cell; cause of a wide range of diseases. **2** (*informal*) a disease caused by a virus. **3** a corrupt, poisoning influence. < Latin: poisonous liquid.

visa (ˈviːzə) *n* an endorsement in a passport, authorized by officials of a country, showing that the bearer may enter that country. < ultimately Latin *vidēre* to see.

visage (ˈvɪzɪdʒ) *n* (*literary*) a face; countenance. < Old French, ultimately Latin *vidēre* to see.

vis-à-vis (ˌviːzɑːˈviː) *prep* **1** in relation to. **2** opposite. < French: face to face.

viscera (ˈvɪsərə) *pl n* the internal organs of the body. < Latin: entrails.

viscount (ˈvaɪkaʊnt) fem. **viscountess** *n* a member of the nobility ranking below an earl and above a baron. < Medieval Latin *vicecomes,* from Late Latin *vice-* deputy + *comes* count.

viscous (ˈvɪskəs) *adj* (of a liquid) thick and sticky, not flowing easily. **viscosity** *n* < Latin *viscum* bird-lime, sticky substance.

visible (ˈvɪzɪbl̩) *adj* able to be seen or perceived. **visibly** *adv* **visibility** *n* **1** being visible. **2** clearness or range of vision: poor visibility. < ultimately Latin *vidēre* to see. SEE PANEL.

vision (ˈvɪʒən) *n* **1** the act or power of seeing; sight. **2** something seen in a dream, trance, etc.; strong mental image. **3** the power of imaginative foresight, discernment, and wisdom: leaders with vision. < Latin *vidēre* to see.

visionary (ˈvɪʒənərɪ) *adj* **1** marked by vision. **2** imaginary; unrealistic. **3** given to having visions.
• *n* a person with visionary ideas or plans.

visit (ˈvɪzɪt) *vb* **1** go or come to see for social or business reasons; call on. **2** stay with temporarily as a guest; stay in (a place) temporarily.

viper

Strictly speaking, the name viper is a misnomer. It derives ultimately from the Latin *vipera,* from *vivus* 'alive' and *parere* 'to bear'. This reveals the belief that the viper is viviparous—that it bears living young—whereas in actual fact the young are still enclosed in an egg-like membrane at the time of birth, out of which they immediately hatch.

• *n* an act of visiting; temporary stay; call. **visitation** *n* **1** an official visit. **2** a visit by a supernatural being. **visitor** *n* **1** a person who makes a visit; caller. **2** a migratory bird that is present in an area only for a short time. < ultimately Latin *vidēre* to see.

visor (ˈvaɪzə) *n* **1** the hinged part of a helmet that is lowered to protect the face. **2** the projecting part on the front of a cap. **3** a movable shade at the top of a car's windscreen. < Old French *vis* face.

vista (ˈvistə) *n* **1** a view, esp. one seen through a long, narrow avenue of trees, etc. **2** a wide-reaching mental view, for example of a series of events. < Italian: view, ultimately from Latin *vidēre* to see.

visual (ˈviʒuəl, ˈvɪzjuəl) *adj* **1** of or used in seeing. **2** performed or received by sight. **visually** *adv* **visual aids** pictures, films, charts, etc., used as aids to teaching. **visual display unit** a device consisting of a cathode-ray tube used for displaying information held in a computer. **visualize** *vb* form a mental image of. **visualization** *n* < ultimately Latin *vidēre* to see.

vital (ˈvaɪtl̩) *adj* **1** essential to life; concerned with life. **2** essential or extremely important. **3** full of vitality. **vitally** *adv* **vitality** *n* life and vigour; power to live or endure. **vitalize** *vb* put life and vigour into. **vitalization** *n* **vital statistics** the measurements of a woman's bust, waist, and hips. < ultimately Latin *vita* life.

vitamin (ˈvɪtəmɪn, ˈvaɪtəmɪn) *n* an organic compound that is essential in small amounts for the normal life and growth of most animals. < Latin *vita* life. SEE PANEL.

vitiate (ˈvɪʃɪˌeɪt) *vb* make ineffective or imperfect. **vitiation** *n* < Latin *vitium* fault.

vitreous (ˈvɪtrɪəs) *adj* of, like, or containing glass. < Latin *vitrum* glass.

vitrify (ˈvɪtrɪˌfaɪ) *vb* **vitrified; vitrifying** change into glass or a substance like glass. **vitrification** *n* < Latin *vitrum* glass.

viva (ˈvaɪvə) *n* a viva voce examination.

vivacious (vɪˈveɪʃəs) *adj* lively and animated. **vivaciously** *adv* **vivacity** *n* < Latin *vivax* lively.

viva voce (ˌvaɪvə ˈvəutʃɪ) *n, adv* (an examination conducted) orally. < Latin: with the living voice.

vivid (ˈvɪvɪd) *adj* **1** (of colours) very bright; intense. **2** producing clear, mental images: vivid details. **3** full of vigour and life: a vivid imagination. **vividly** *adv* **vividness** *n* < Latin *vivere* to live.

vivisection (ˌvɪvɪˈsɛkʃən) *n* the use of live animals for surgical operations or other experiments. < Latin *vivus* living + English *section*, as in dis*section*.

vixen (ˈvɪksən) *n* a female fox. < Old English *fyxe*.

viz. *abbrev* videlicet (namely). SEE PANEL.

V-neck (ˈviːˌnɛk) *adj, n* (a garment, esp. a pullover) with a V-shaped neckline.

vocabulary (vəuˈkæbjulərɪ, vəˈkæbjulərɪ) *n* **1** a list of words, esp. arranged alphabetically and defined or translated. **2** the words used by a language, individual, or in a particular book, area of knowledge, etc. < ultimately Latin *vocare* to call.

vocal (ˈvəukl̩) *adj* **1** of, for, or produced

vitamin

The word vitamin is a misnomer. Originally spelt with a final *e*, *vitamine* was the brainchild of the US biochemist Casimir Funk, 1884–1967, who coined it in 1912 by conflating the Latin *vita* 'life' and *amine* (an organic compound containing nitrogen). The coinage was based on the theory that vitamins contained amines. When this was later found to be untrue, the final e was dropped.

visibly

Most users of English would refrain from producing sentences such as He seemed emotionally unhappy or The doctor said verbally that she had no need to worry. Each of these sentences contains an adverb (emotionally and verbally) which is completely redundant. However, this type of tautology is an everyday event in current journalistic English. In particular, the adverbs visibly and noticeably tend to be used in an unnecessary way with verbs such as look and appear: She looked visibly shaken by the outburst and The princess appeared noticeably distressed.

by the voice. **2** marked by forceful expression, **vocally** *adv* **vocal cords** either of the two pairs of folds of tissue in the larynx that vibrate to produce sound. **vocalist** *n* a singer. **vocalize** *vb* utter. < Latin *vox* voice.

vocation (vəʊˈkeɪʃən) *n* **1** the work, career, etc., which a person believes himself or herself to be called to. **2** a call to follow a particular career, esp. a religious one. **3** a particular trade or profession. **vocational** *adj* of or relating to training in skills needed in a particular trade or career. < ultimately Latin *vocare* to call.

vociferous (vəˈsɪfərəs, vəʊˈsɪfərəs) *adj* expressing one's views very strongly and insistently. **vociferously** *adv* < Latin *vox* voice + *ferre* to bear.

vodka (ˈvɒdkə) a colourless, alcoholic spirit distilled from potatoes, grain, etc. < Russian, from *voda* water.

vogue (vəʊɡ) *n* **1** the current fashion: Long dresses are in vogue this year. **2** popular acceptance. < French: rowing, fashion, ultimately from Old Italian *vogare* to row.

voice (vɔɪs) *n* **1** sounds made in the larynx and produced through the mouth, esp. by human beings in speaking or singing. **2** the ability to make such sounds, as with regard to singing; range of such sounds made by a particular person. **3** a sound like a vocal utterance: the voice of conscience. **4** a medium of expression: The newspaper sees itself as the voice of the people. **5** expression of an opinion; right to express an opinion; opinion. **6** a form of a verb showing whether it is active or passive.
• *vb* express in words. **voice-over** *n* the voice of an unseen narrator in a film, television programme or advertisement, etc. < Latin *vox* voice. SEE PANEL AT PASSIVE.

void (vɔɪd) *adj* **1** empty or vacant. **2** not legally valid: null and void. **3** useless.
• *n* an empty space; feeling of emptiness. < ultimately Latin *vacuus* empty.

volatile (ˈvɒləˌtaɪl) *adj* **1** (of a liquid such as petrol) evaporating quickly. **2** likely to change, esp. quickly; lively. **volatility** *n* < Latin *volare* to fly.

vol-au-vent (ˈvɒləʊˌvã) *n* a light, round puff-pastry case with a savoury filling. < French: flight in the wind.

volcano (vɒlˈkeɪnəʊ) *n, pl* **volcanoes** an opening in the earth's crust from which steam, lava, gases, and rocks are forced out. **volcanic** *adj* of, marked by, or produced by volcanoes. SEE PANEL.

vole (vəʊl) *n* a small rodent with a short tail and a blunt nose. < short for *vole-mouse,* from *vole-*, of Scandinavian origin + *mouse.*

volition (vəˈlɪʃən) *n* the act or power of making a choice or decision. < ultimately Latin *velle* to wish.

volley (ˈvɒlɪ) *n* **1** the discharge of a number of missiles at the same time; flight of such missiles. **2** a burst of many things at the same time or in close succession. **3** a return or striking of a ball before it touches the ground.
• *vb* **1** discharge or be discharged in a volley. **2** return or strike (a ball) before it touches the ground. **volleyball** *n* a game for two teams of six players in which a ball is volleyed by hand over a net. < ultimately Latin *volare* to fly.

volt (vəʊlt) *n* the SI unit of potential, equal to the potential difference between two points on a conductor carrying a current of one ampere when the power dissipated between these two points is one watt. **voltage** *n* potential difference expressed in volts. < Alessandro *Volta,* died 1827, Italian physicist. SEE PANEL.

voluble (ˈvɒljʊbḷ) *adj* marked by easy,

viz.

The abbreviation viz. or 'namely' comes from the Latin *videlicet* meaning 'one is permitted to see'. The final z is a corruption of the numeral *3* which was used by monks in the Middle Ages as a shorthand method of denoting a contraction.

Viz. is normally encountered only in its written form. When read aloud it is usually replaced by namely or that is to say.

volcano

An opening in the earth's crust out of which molten matter issues from the depths below is known as a volcano. This word derives via the Italian *vulcano* from the Latin *Volcanus* or 'Vulcan', the Roman god of fire and metal-working. Vulcanize, 'to treat (rubber) so as to improve its properties', comes from the same mythological source.

ready, or quick speech; talkative or fluent. **volubility** *n* **volubly** *adv* < ultimately Latin *volvere* to roll.

volume (ˈvɒljuːm) *n* **1** a book, esp. one of a series. **2** a series of issues of a magazine or periodical, esp. for one year. **3** the amount of space taken up by an object in three dimensions; cubic capacity. **4** a large mass; amount. **5** the degree of loudness of sound. **voluminous** *adj* **1** having great volume. **2** (of a garment) large and full. < ultimately Latin *volvere* to roll.

voluntary (ˈvɒləntərɪ, ˈvɒləntrɪ) *adj* **1** acting, performed, given, etc., of one's own free will. **2** working or performed without compulsion and without payment: voluntary work. **3** supported by voluntary action: voluntary welfare organizations. **4** controlled by the will. • *n* an esp. organ solo played at a church service. **voluntarily** *adv* < Latin *voluntas* will, from *velle* to wish.

volunteer (ˌvɒlənˈtɪə) *n* **1** a person who offers to do something of his or her own free will. **2** a person who enlists for military service voluntarily. • *vb* offer (oneself or one's help, etc.) voluntarily; perform voluntarily. < SEE VOLUNTARY.

voluptuous (vəˈlʌptjʊəs) *adj* **1** full of, producing, or suggesting pleasure to the senses. **2** (of a woman) sexually attractive, esp. because of a shapely figure. **voluptuousness** *n* < Latin *voluptas* pleasure.

volt

Volt, ohm, and ampere are three common electrical terms which derive from the surnames of distinguished physicists. The unit of electric potential known as the volt takes its name from the Italian professor, Count Alessandro *Volta,* 1745–1827. The unit of electrical resistance, the ohm. is so called in honour of the German professor, Georg Simon *Ohm,* 1787–1854. Finally, the unit of current known as the ampere or amp immortalizes the work of the French professor, André Marie *Ampère,* 1775–1836.

To this list must be added the name of the Scottish engineer, James *Watt,* 1736–1819, whose surname was adopted for the standard unit of electrical power.

vomit (ˈvɒmɪt) *vb* eject (matter from the stomach) through the mouth; be sick. • *n* vomited matter. < Latin *vomere.*

voodoo (ˈvuːduː) *n* a set of magical cults of West African origin, including trances induced by spirit possession. < Louisiana French *voudou,* of African origin.

voracious (vəˈreɪʃəs) *adj* **1** greedy or gluttonous. **2** extremely eager: a voracious reader. **voraciously** *adv* **voracity** *n* < Latin *vorare* to devour.

vortex (ˈvɔːtɛks) *n* a whirling mass of water, air, etc., such as a whirlpool, hurricane, or cyclone. < Latin: whirlpool.

vote (vəʊt) *n* **1** the expression, esp. formally, of a choice or opinion; right to make such an expression. **2** a choice or opinion that is expressed, esp. formally. **3** the set of votes given or to be given. • *vb* **1** express a choice or opinion in a vote. **2** (*informal*) declare generally; judge. **3** (*informal*) suggest. **voter** *n* **vote down** defeat or reject in a vote. **vote with one's feet** declare one's opposition or disagreement by leaving or not attending a meeting, etc. < Latin *votum* vow.

vouch (vaʊtʃ) *vb* **1** give an assurance, guarantee, etc. (for). **2** provide evidence (for). **voucher** *n* **1** a document that serves as evidence of a transaction; receipt for money paid: a petty-cash voucher. **2** a printed card that serves as a substitute for cash and can be exchanged for certain goods or services: a gift voucher; luncheon voucher. < ultimately Latin *vocare* to call.

vouchsafe (ˌvaʊtʃˈseɪf) *vb* (*formal*) grant in a gracious or condescending manner. < Middle English *vouchen safe* vouch as safe.

vow (vaʊ) *n* a solemn promise or undertaking, as one made before God. • *vb* make a vow; promise solemnly or decide firmly. < Latin *vovēre* to vow.

vowel (ˈvaʊəl) *n* a speech-sound made without obstruction in the vocal tract; letter or letters representing such a sound, such as a, e, or i < Latin *vocalis,* from *vox* voice.

voyage (ˈvɔɪɪdʒ) *n* a long journey, esp. by sea or into space. • *vb* make a voyage. **voyager** *n* < ultimately Latin *via* way.

voyeur (vwaɪˈɜː) *n* a person who gains sexual pleasure from watching the sexual activities of others. < French: one who sees.

vulcanize (ˈvʌlkəˌnaɪz) *vb* treat (natural

rubber, etc.) chemically to increase its elasticity, hardness, etc. **vulcanization** *n* SEE PANEL AT **VOLCANO.**

vulgar (ˈvʌlgə) *adj* **1** marked by a lack of good taste. **2** showy; pretentious. **3** indecent or obscene. **4** of the common people. **vulgarity** *n* **vulgarly** *adv* **vulgarism** *n* **1** a word or phrase that is used chiefly by uneducated people. **2** a coarse or obscene word or phrase. **vulgarize** *vb* **1** popularize. **2** make vulgar; debase. **vulgarization** *n* < Latin *vulgus* common people.

vulnerable (vʌlnərəbl̩) *adj* **1** able to be wounded. **2** exposed to danger, attack, etc. **vulnerability** *n* < Latin *vulnus* wound.

vulture (ˈvʌltʃə) *n* a large bird of prey with broad wings that eats the flesh of dead animals. < Latin *vultur.*

vulva (ˈvʌlvə) *n* the external parts of the female genital organs. < Latin: womb.

W

W. *abbrev* **1** west; western. **2** watt; watts.
wad (wɒd) *n* **1** a small, soft, compact mass. **2** a collection or roll of banknotes, documents, etc. **wadding** *n* soft, fibrous material used for stuffing or padding. < origin unknown.
waddle (ˈwɒdl̩) *vb* walk with short steps, swaying slightly from side to side.
• *n* a waddling walk. < SEE **WADE.**
wade (weɪd) *vb* **1** walk through water, mud, etc. **2** proceed slowly and with difficulty: wade through a mass of correspondence. **3** attack vigorously. **wader** *n* also **wading-bird** a long-legged water-bird that wades in shallow water looking for food. **waders** *pl n* long, waterproof boots. < Old English *wadan.*
wafer (ˈweɪfə) *n* a thin, crisp, light biscuit. < Old Northern French *waufre*, of Germanic origin.
waffle[1] (ˈwɒfl̩) *n* (*informal*) vague, wordy talk or writing.
• *vb* (*informal*) express in waffle. < obsolete *woff* to yelp.
waffle[2] *n* a crisp cake of batter with indentations on each side. < Middle Dutch *wafel.*
waft (wɒft) *vb* carry or move or be carried or moved lightly and easily through the air or water.
• *n* something that is wafted, esp. a scent. < Middle Dutch *wachten* to guard.
wag (wæg) *vb* **wagged; wagging** move from side to side or up and down.
• *n* an act of wagging. < Old English *wagian* to shake.
wage (weɪdʒ) *n* often **wages** regular payment for work done, esp. manual work, or on an hourly or weekly basis.
• *vb* engage in (war). < Old Northern French *wagier* to pledge, of Germanic origin.
wager (ˈweɪdʒə) *n, vb* (a) bet. < Old Northern French *wagier* to pledge.
waggle (ˈwægl̩) *n, vb* (a) wag. < SEE **WAG.**
wagon, waggon (ˈwægən) *n* **1** a four-wheeled vehicle for transporting heavy loads. **2** an open railway goods truck. **3** a trolley for carrying food, etc. **wagoner, waggoner** *n* the driver of a wagon. < Middle Dutch *wagen.*
waif (weɪf) *n* a homeless, helpless person, esp. a child. < Scandinavian.
wail (weɪl) *vb* **1** utter a sad, long, high cry; lament. **2** complain.
• *n* a wailing cry, sound, or utterance. < Scandinavian.
wainscot (ˈweɪnskət) *n* also **wainscoting** the wooden lining or panelling on the wall of a room. < Middle Dutch *wagenschot.*
waist (weɪst) *n* the narrow part of the body between the chest and the hips; part of a garment covering this. **waistband** *n* a band on trousers or a skirt that fits round the waist. **waistcoat** *n* a man's sleeveless, waist-length garment that fastens down the front, worn esp. under the jacket of a suit. **waistline** *n* **1** a line round the body at the waist. **2** the part of a garment worn at, above, or below this line. < Middle English *wast.*
wait (weɪt) *vb* **1** remain in place in expectation (of) and readiness (for). **2** delay in expectation of. **3** serve at meals: wait at table.
• *n* an act or period of waiting. **waiter** fem. **waitress** *n* a person employed to serve food, etc., esp. in a restaurant. **waiting-list** *n* a list of people waiting for something such as a house or job to become available. **waiting-room** *n* a room for people who are waiting, for example for a train or to see a doctor or dentist. **wait on 1** serve with food, etc., in a restaurant. **2** look after the needs and wants of. < Old Northern French *waitier.*
waive (weɪv) *vb* refrain from insisting on or enforcing (a right, demand, etc.); forgo. **waiver** *n* the relinquishment of a

waive, waiver, or **waver?**

These words are sometimes confused.

Waive means 'to refrain from insisting on or enforcing' as in *waive* one's rights, *waive* one's demands.

Waver means 'to become unsteady; hesitate between alternatives': His determination *wavered;* to *waver* between accepting and refusing an offer.

Waver should not be confused with waiver 'the relinquishment of a right': The *waiver* of the claim meant that the land was his and his alone.

claim or right; document stating this. < Old Northern French *weyver,* from *waif* abandoned. SEE PANEL.

wake[1] (weɪk) *vb* **woke; woken; waking** also **wake up** emerge or rouse from sleep.
• *n* **1** a watch or vigil held by a corpse before burial. **2** an annual holiday in industrial areas in northern England: wakes week. **wakeful** *adj* not sleeping; awake. **waken** *vb* wake. **wake up** (**to**) make or become aware (of): He finally woke up to his responsibilities. < Old English *wacian.*

wake[2] *n* the track left by something moving: in the wake of the hurricane. < Scandinavian.

walk (wɔːk) *vb* **1** move on foot at a moderate pace with at least one foot always on the ground. **2** travel or go (over) on foot. **3** cause (a dog, etc.) to walk, as for exercise. **4** escort or lead by walking: I'll walk you home.
• *n* **1** a journey on foot, esp. for pleasure or exercise. **2** a manner of walking. **3** the distance walked. **4** a route or place for walking. **5** a route regularly covered by a postman, policeman, etc. **6** the slowest pace of a horse, in which at least two feet are always on the ground. **walker** *n* **1** a person who walks. **2** a framework that supports a baby who is learning to walk or a cripple who needs help with walking. **walkie-talkie** *n* a compact, portable radio transmitter and receiver. **walking-stick** *n* a stick used as a support in walking. **walkway** *n* a passage or platform for walking. < Old English *wealcan.* SEE PANEL.

wall (wɔːl) *n* **1** a solid, vertical structure, as of brick, concrete, etc., that supports, encloses, divides, or retains. **2** something like this in form or function. **3** the material layer around a space or hollow structure.
• *vb* protect, surround, or divide with or as if with a wall. **drive or send up the wall** (*informal*) infuriate: You children are really driving me up the wall! **go to the wall** become bankrupt; fail. **wallflower** *n* **1** a plant with narrow leaves and clusters of fragrant yellow, orange, or red flowers. **2** (*informal*) a person who fails to get partners at a dance, etc. **wallpaper** *n* decorative paper for pasting onto the interior walls of a room. **wall-to-wall** *adj* (of carpets) covering the whole floor of a room. < Old English *weall.*

wallaby (ˈwɒləbɪ) *n* a kind of small kangaroo. < *wolabā,* native Australian name.

wallet (ˈwɒlɪt) *n* a small, flat folding case with compartments for banknotes, credit cards, stamps, etc. < Middle English *walet.*

wallop (ˈwɒləp) *vb* (*informal*) strike hard; thrash or beat.
• *n* **1** (*informal*) a hard blow. **2** (*slang*) beer; alcohol generally. **walloping** *adj* (*informal*) great; big. < Old Northern French *waloper* to gallop.

wallow (ˈwɒləʊ) *vb* **1** roll about in mud, water, etc. **2** indulge oneself excessively (in); revel (in): wallowing in self-pity.
• *n* an act of wallowing; place where animals wallow. < Old English *wealwian* to roll.

walnut (ˈwɔːlnʌt) *n* **1** a nut with a wrinkled seed enclosed in a wrinkled, pale-brown shell. **2** the tree bearing this nut. **3** the richly grained wood of this tree, used in making furniture, etc. < Old English *wealhhnutu* foreign nut.

walrus (ˈwɔːlrəs) *n* a large sea-mammal of northern seas with a tough, heavy skin and a pair of long, ivory tusks. < Dutch, of Scandinavian origin.

waltz (wɔːls) *n* a ballroom dance in triple time; music for this.
• *vb* **1** dance a waltz (with). **2** (*informal*) move lightly and easily. **waltzer** *n*

walking

Walk features in a number of idiomatic expressions, including:

walkabout *n* an informal walk among a crowd by a famous person, head of state, member of the royal family, etc.
walk away or **off with** to win (a prize, competition, etc.) very easily.
walking dictionary, encyclopaedia, etc. a person with extensive knowledge of words, facts, etc.
walk into 1 to obtain (a job, position, etc.) very easily. **2** to enter (a trap, etc.), unwittingly.
walk of life one's profession, rank, or social background.
walk out 1 to go on strike suddenly.
walk-out *n* **2** to leave suddenly and angrily.
walk out on to leave or abandon: Would you walk out on a friend who was in trouble?
walk over to defeat thoroughly; treat in a domineering, overpowering way.
walk-over *n* an easy victory.

< Old High German *walzan* to roll.

wan (wɒn) *adj* **wanner; wannest 1** pale, esp. because of poor health; weak. **2** (of a smile or light) faint or slight. **wanly** *adv* **wanness** *n* < Old English *wann* dark.

wand (wɒnd) *n* a slender rod, esp. one used by conjurors or magicians: a magic wand. < Old Norse *vöndr.*

wander (ˈwɒndə) *vb* **1** travel or go about aimlessly: wander round the garden. **2** (of a river, etc.) follow a winding path; meander. **3** stray from a way, course, etc. **4** (of thoughts) stray or digress.
• *n* an act of wandering. **wanderer** *n* **wanderlust** *n* a strong desire to travel. < Old English *wandrian.*

wane (weɪn) *vb* **1** (of the moon) show a gradually decreasing area of illumination. **2** (of light, etc.) grow dim or weak. **3** decline in power, influence, etc. **on the wane** waning. < Old English *wanian.*

wangle (ˈwæŋgḷ) *vb* (*informal*) use trickery, manipulation, etc., to obtain or arrange: They wangled a free ticket.
• *n* (*informal*) an act of wangling. < perhaps *waggle.*

want (wɒnt) *vb* **1** desire or wish for: I want to be alone. **2** require or need: His hair wants cutting. **3** suffer from the lack of. **4** (*informal*) ought: You want to be more careful!
• *n* **1** a desire for something. **2** something wanted; need. **3** the lack of something: for want of a better word. **4** the lack of the necessities of life: living in want. **wanted** *adj* sought by the police for questioning. **wanting** *adj* not reaching the required standard; deficient. < Old Norse *vanta.*

wanton (ˈwɒntən) *adj* **1** uncontrolled and irresponsible; wilful. **2** immoral; licentious. < Old English *wan* lacking + *tēon* to bring up, train.

war (wɔː) *n* **1** armed strife, esp. between countries. **2** a major conflict or struggle: the war against famine.
• *vb* **warred; warring** engage in war. **in the wars** having signs of injury. **on the war-path** angry and preparing for a conflict. **war-cry** *n* **1** a rallying cry in battle. **2** a slogan used to encourage support. **warfare** *n* fighting or war; form of this: nuclear warfare. **warhead** *n* the part of a missile containing the explosive. **warlike** *adj* **1** of or associated with war. **2** prepared for war. **3** hostile. **war of nerves** a conflict in which one tries to destroy the opponent's morale by psychological means. **warship** *n* an armed ship for use in war. < of Germanic origin.

warble (ˈwɔːbḷ) *vb* sing or sound with a gentle trilling, as a bird.
• *n* a warbling sound. **warbler** *n* any of several small songbirds with a slender bill and thick plumage. < Old Northern French *werbler,* of Germanic origin.

ward (wɔːd) *n* **1** a room or division in a hospital: the men's surgical ward. **2** a division of a town, city, etc., for administrative or electoral purposes. **3** a person, esp. a child, placed under the protection of a guardian or law-court: a ward of court.
• *vb* **ward off** turn aside or fend off; avert. **warden** *n* a person responsible for something; official with certain responsibilities to supervise or enforce laws: traffic warden. **warder** fem. **wardress** *n* an officer in charge of prisoners in a jail. **wardrobe** *n* **1** a large cupboard, with shelves, a rail, etc., for keeping clothes. **2** a collection or store of clothes. **3** the collection of costumes of a theatrical company. **wardroom** *n* the mess-room for officers, except the captain, on a warship. < Old English *weard* watching.

ware (wɛə) *n* **1** articles of a kind that is mentioned: enamel ware. **2** pottery or porcelain of a kind that is mentioned. **warehouse** *n* a place where goods are stored. **wares** *pl n* articles for sale. < Old English *waru.*

warm (wɔːm) *adj* **1** having or marked by a moderate heat; not cold or cool. **2** (of clothes, blankets, etc.) keeping the body adequately warm. **3** enthusiastic; cordial: a warm welcome. **4** friendly and affectionate: a warm personality. **5** (of colours) suggesting warmth; esp. yellow, orange, or red. **6** (of a scent in hunting) recently made; strong and fresh. **7** (esp. in children's games) near to finding the object or guessing the solution.
• *vb* also **warm up** make or become warm or warmer. **warmly** *adv* **warmness** *n* **warm-blooded** *adj* maintaining a fairly constant high body temperature. **warm-hearted** *adj* having an affectionate, friendly disposition. **warmth** *n* the quality of being warm. **warm to** become enthusiastic about or well-disposed to. **warm up 1** reheat (cooked food). **2** prepare the body for strenuous physical exertion by doing exercises. **3** make or become more interesting or lively: The match warmed up in the second half. < Old English *wearm.*

warn (wɔːn) *vb* **1** give (someone) advance notice that something dangerous, unpleasant, etc., may happen. **2** advise or notify. **3** order to go away: He warned them off the property. **warning** *n* an act of warning; something that warns. < Old English *wearnian.*

warp (wɔːp) *vb* **1** bend or twist out of shape. **2** pervert or distort: a warped sense of humour.

• *n* **1** a warped state or condition. **2** the yarns extending lengthways in a loom, to be crossed by the weft. < Old English *wearp* throw.

warrant (ˈwɒrənt) *n* **1** something that gives authority; authorization: a search warrant. **2** a document authorizing the holder to receive particular services, etc.: a travel warrant. **3** a ground or reason; justification.

• *vb* **1** serve as a warrant for; justify or authorize: This case warrants special intervention. **2** declare certainly; assure or guarantee. **warrantee** *n* a person to whom a warranty is made. **warrant-officer** *n* an officer in any of certain armed services ranking between a commissioned and non-commissioned officer. **warrantor** *n* a person who provides a warranty. **warranty** *n* a written guarantee given by a seller to a buyer. < Old Northern French *warant,* variant of Old French *guarant.*

warren (ˈwɒrən) *n* **1** an area of ground containing a number of connecting burrows in which rabbits live and breed. **2** a building or area that is crowded or has many narrow passages. < Old Northern French *warenne.*

warrior (ˈwɒrɪə) *n* a person engaged or experienced in war. < Old Northern French *werreier* to wage war.

wart (wɔːt) *n* **1** a small, firm, roundish, abnormal elevation of the skin. **2** a similar growth on a plant. < Old English *wearte.* SEE PANEL.

wary (ˈwɛərɪ) *adj* cautious and watchful, esp. concerning possible dangers, etc. **warily** *adv* **wariness** *n* < Old English *wær.*

was (wəz; *stressed* wɒz) SEE **BE.** SEE PANEL AT **IF.**

wash (wɒʃ) *vb* **1** cleanse with water or other liquid. **2** wash oneself or one's hands, face, etc.; wash clothes. **3** (of clothes) undergo washing without being damaged. **4** (of water) flow past, over, etc. **5** pass water over, etc.; sweep by the force of flowing water: The body was washed ashore. **6** (*informal*) be considered valid: His excuses won't wash.

• *n* **1** washing or being washed; act of this. **2** clothes, etc., to be washed. **3** a place where something can be washed: a car wash. **4** the rushing movement of waves. **5** a thin coat of paint. **washable** *adj* capable of being washed without being damaged. **wash-basin** *n* a basin for washing one's hands and face. **washer** *n* **1** a washing-machine. **2** a thin, flat ring of metal, rubber, etc., used to make a seal in a tap, etc., or to spread the load under a tightened bolt or nut. **washing** *n* articles, esp. clothes, to be washed or that have just been washed. **washing-machine** *n* a machine for washing clothes, etc. **washy** *adj* faded or pale; weak. < Old English *wascan.* SEE PANEL.

wasp (wɒsp) *n* a stinging insect related to the bee, with a black-and-yellow striped body. **waspish** *adj* easily annoyed; bad-tempered. **waspishly** *adv* < Old English *wæsp, wæps.* SEE PANEL AT **THIRD.**

waste (weɪst) *vb* **1** use or spend carelessly, inefficiently, or without gain: waste time. **2** not take advantage of: waste an opportunity. **3** make or become gradually weaker: waste away.

• *n* **1** an act of wasting: a waste of money. **2** waste material; waste food. **3** an expanse of waste land.

• *adj* **1** rejected or left over because no longer needed: waste paper; waste products. **2** used to carry off waste: a waste pipe. **3** (of land) barren or devastated; desolate; not productive. **waster** *n* **lay waste** devastate. **wastage** *n* **1** loss, esp. due to

warts and all

The expression warts and all is used in descriptions to mean 'with none of its imperfections omitted' as in: a warts-and-all account of life in our inner cities. The expression derives from the instruction by the English statesman Oliver Cromwell to his painter Sir Peter Lely, recorded in Horace Walpole's 'Anecdotes of Painting'. Cromwell wanted Lely to paint a true likeness of him, with all his prominent warts: 'Mr Lely, I desire you would use all your skill to paint my picture truly like me, and not flatter me at all; but remark all these roughnesses, pimples, warts, and everything as you see me, otherwise I will never pay a farthing for it.'

decay, leaking, etc.; process of wasting. **2** the loss of employees through retirement or leaving: natural wastage. **wasteful** *adj* marked by waste. **wastefully** *adv* **wastefulness** *n* **wasteland** *n* an area of waste land. **waste-paper basket** a container for household, office, etc., items that are no longer needed, esp. waste paper. < ultimately Latin *vastare* to lay waste.

wastrel (ˈweɪstrəl) *n* a worthless person. < SEE **WASTE.**

watch (wɒtʃ) *vb* **1** look at, esp. with close attention. **2** wait with alertness (for). **3** guard or look after closely. **4** be careful about.
• *n* **1** a small, portable device that indicates the time, usually worn on the wrist. **2** the act of watching. **3** a period of keeping guard; sailor's period of duty on deck, usually four hours. **on the watch** alert. **watch-dog** *n* **1** a dog trained to guard property. **2** a person or group that seeks to prevent inefficiency, dishonest practices, etc. **watchful** *adj* watching closely. **watchfully** *adv* **watchfulness** *n* **watchmaker** *n* a person who makes or repairs watches. **watchman** *n, pl* **watchmen** a person employed to look after a building, etc., at night. **watch one's step** take care not to fall; behave or talk with care. **watch out** be careful. **watch-tower** *n* a tower on which a guard keeps watch. **watchword** *n* a word or phrase used as a slogan. < Old English *wæccan.*

water (ˈwɔːtə) *n* **1** a liquid without colour, odour, or taste, that is a compound of oxygen and hydrogen. **2** a body or stretch of water or sea. **3** the supply of water for domestic and industrial use. **4** the level of the tide that is mentioned: at high water. **5** the surface of the water: swimming under water. **6** a liquid containing or like water: toilet water; soda-water.
• *vb* **1** sprinkle with water. **2** supply with water. **3** also **water down** dilute; make less forceful or effective. **4** secrete tears or saliva: His eyes were watering. **water-bird** *n* an aquatic bird that swims or wades in water. **water-biscuit** *n* an unsweetened biscuit made with flour and water. **water-butt** *n* a large barrel used to catch rain-water. **water-cannon** *n* a device for shooting a powerful jet of water, used to disperse crowds, etc. **water-closet** *n* a toilet. **water-colour** *n* **1** a pigment that is mixed with water and used as a paint by artists. **2** a picture

wash

The verb wash is usually transitive: She washed the jumper. He's washing the car. Go and wash your face. Sometimes, however, it is used intransitively as in this material washes well. In this sentence it is evident that the subject and verb have a rather unusual relationship. Although this material occupies the subject slot in the sentence, it is not the subject of wash but the object. The true subject is understood. Verbs which may be used in this way are known as *ergatives.* Other examples include:

The dress *irons* badly.
The door won't *open.*
I hope this chicken *cooks* better than the last one.
The joint *carves* like a dream.
The bonnet *shut* with a bang.
Light colours *mark* easily.
That pen doesn't *write.*
The lid won't *close.*
Some soft fruits don't *freeze* well.

The word wash features in a number of idiomatic expressions, including:

come out in the wash to become apparent in the end.
washed-out *adj* **1** faded. **2** pale; exhausted.
wash one's dirty linen in public to reveal and discuss one's private faults, scandals, quarrels, etc., publicly.
wash one's hands of to disclaim responsibility for. The expression alludes to the action of Pontius Pilate in the Bible, Matthew 27:24, symbolizing his dissociation from the responsibility for the death of Jesus. The Authorized (King James) Version reads:
When Pilate saw that he could prevail nothing ... he took water, and washed his hands before the multitude, saying, I am innocent of the blood of this just person.
wash out to make (a game, etc.) impossible, because of rain. **wash-out** *n*
wash-out *n* a complete failure.
wash up to wash (dishes, cutlery, etc.) after use. **washing-up** *n*

painted with this. **watercourse** *n* a stream, river, or canal; channel of this. **watercress** *n* a plant of streams or clear ponds, grown for its young shoots that are used in salads. **waterfall** *n* a steep fall of water of a river or stream. **waterfowl** *pl n* water-birds. **waterfront** *n* also **waterside** the part of a town adjoining a harbour, lake, etc. **water-hole** *n* a natural hollow in the surface of the ground, in which water collects. **water-ice** *n* a frozen dessert of water, sugar, and flavouring. **watering-can** *n* a container with a long spout, for watering plants. **watering-place** *n* **1** a place where animals go to drink water. **2** a spa or seaside resort. **water-jump** *n* an obstacle such as a ditch or channel, for example in a steeplechase. **water-lily** *n* a freshwater plant with round, floating leaves and large, showy flowers. **water-logged** *adj* filled, saturated, or soaked with water. **watermark** *n* a manufacturer's distinctive design impressed on paper, visible when the paper is held to the light. **water-melon** *n* a large, round fruit with a shiny, dark-green skin, juicy, red flesh, and many seeds. **water-mill** *n* a mill worked by a water-wheel. **water-pistol** *n* a toy pistol that shoots a jet of water. **water polo** a ball game played in water by two teams of seven swimmers. **water-power** *n* power obtained from moving, esp. falling water. **watershed** *n* **1** a line of high ground between two different river systems. **2** a significant dividing-line. **water-skiing** *n* a sport in which a person skims across water on skis, towed by a speedboat. **water-softener** *n* a device for softening hard water. **water-table** *n* the level below which the ground is saturated with water. **watertight** *adj* **1** not allowing the passage of water in or out. **2** impossible to disprove; having no loopholes. **3** isolated from other influences: watertight divisions. **water-tower** *n* a raised tank used for storing water, which provides the necessary steady pressure for its distribution. **waterway** *n* a navigable channel. **water-wheel** *n* a wheel that is turned by a flow of water, used to drive machinery. **water-wings** *pl n* a pair of air-filled floats worn by a person learning to swim. **waterworks** *n* **1** an establishment that stores, pumps, etc., water to an area. **2** (*informal*) the urinary system: How are the waterworks? **3** (*informal*) tears: turn on the waterworks. **watery** *adj* **1** of, like, or containing water. **2** made weak or thin by too much water. **3** secreting water: watery eyes. **4** pale. < Old English *wæter*. SEE PANEL.

a lot of water

Water features in a number of idiomatic expressions, including:

a lot of water has passed under the bridge a lot has happened since a particular event.
hold water (of a theory, etc.) to be sound or valid.
in or **into hot water** in or into trouble: They'll get into hot water if they're caught.
like water off a duck's back not having any effect. The expression derives from the fact that the feathers on a duck's back are oily, and so water flows straight off them.
make one's mouth water to arouse one's desire for food. **mouth-watering** *adj*
pour or **throw cold water on** to discourage.

waterproof (ˈwɔːtəˌpruːf) *adj* unable to be penetrated by water.
• *n* a waterproof garment.
• *vb* make waterproof.

watt (wɒt) *n* the SI unit of electric power equal to one joule per second. **wattage** *n* an amount of power expressed in watts. < James *Watt*, died 1819, Scottish engineer. SEE PANEL AT **VOLT**.

wattle (ˈwɒtl̩) *n* a structure of rods interwoven with twigs, branches, etc., used in building: wattle and daub. < Old English *watul*.

wave (weɪv) *vb* **1** move or cause to move backwards and forwards or from side to side; sway: wave a stick in the air. **2** move the hand from side to side in greeting, farewell, etc. **3** signal or express in this way: wave goodbye. **4** have or cause to have a curving form.
• *n* **1** one of a series of moving ridges of water on the surface of the sea. **2** a form or appearance with curves. **3** a sweep of the hand or an object held in the hand. **4** a spell of a particular kind of weather: a heat wave. **5** a surging movement or feeling: a wave of optimism. **6** (*physics*) a periodic disturbance in a medium or space in which light, sound, etc., is transferred. **wave aside** refuse to consider; dismiss. **waveband** *n* a range of radio frequencies. **wave down** signal (the driver of a car, etc.) to stop, by waving one's hand. **wavelength** *n*

(*physics*) the distance between corresponding points of a wave. **wavy** *adj* having waves or curves like waves. < Old English *wafian*.

waver (ˈweɪvə) *vb* **1** become unsteady; sway. **2** hesitate between two alternatives. **3** (of light) flicker. **waverer** *n* < Middle English *waveren*. SEE PANEL AT **WAIVE**.

wax[1] (wæks) *n* **1** a smooth substance with a low melting-point; used in making polishes, candles, etc.: beeswax. **2** a yellow, waxy secretion from the ear. • *vb* treat or coat with wax. **waxen** *adj* made of wax; pale or smooth like wax. **waxwork** *n* an effigy modelled in wax, esp. of a person. **waxy** *adj* made of or like wax. **waxiness** *n* < Old English *weax*.

wax[2] *vb* **1** (of the moon) show a gradually increasing area of illumination. **2** increase in power, influence, etc. **3** become: wax lyrical. < Old English *weaxan*.

way (weɪ) *n* **1** a manner or method: a way of life; the right way to do something. **2** a road or route: on the way to the station. **3** an opening: the way in. **4** a direction: Come this way! **5** room for movement: get in someone's way. **6** a course leading towards a particular aim: a way out of the difficulty. **7** a distance to be travelled: There's still a long way to go. **8** a respect or regard: We'll help in every possible way. **9** a person's desired course of action: get one's own way. **10** an advance made by an action that is mentioned: forcing his way through the undergrowth. **11** a custom: the ways of the world. **12** the area in which one lives: Call in when you're down our way again. **13** a condition: Our finances are in a bad way. **wayfarer** *n* a traveller, esp. on foot. **waylay** *vb* **waylaid; waylaying** **1** approach and speak to. **2** attack in an ambush. **wayside** *n* the side of a road; land by this. < Old English *weg*. SEE PANEL.

wayward (ˈweɪwəd) *adj* wanting one's own desires in a determined way; unpredictable. **waywardness** *n* < alteration of Middle English *awayward* turned away.

WC *abbrev* water-closet.

we (wɪ; *stressed* wiː) *pron* the person who is speaking or writing and one or more others. < Old English *wē*. SEE PANEL.

w/e *abbrev* week ending.

weak (wiːk) *adj* **1** not strong physically. **2** not able to resist external or internal forces; easily bent or broken; fragile.

by the way

Way features in a number of idiomatic expressions, including:

by the way incidentally: By the way, have you heard from Peter recently?

by way of as a kind or form of: by way of illustration.

in a way to some extent: I suppose in a way you're right.

in the way causing an obstruction to someone's path or line of vision; hindering: Do you mind moving? You're in the way.

in the way of as regards: a little less in the way of rain.

no way under no circumstances; not at all: 'Can you help me?'—'No way!'

on the way about to happen; coming: more price rises on the way.

way back long ago: It happened way back.

way-out *adj* very unconventional: way-out hair-styles.

We are not amused

Many people are familiar with the use of the so-called *royal* we, meaning 'I', as in Queen Victoria's 'We are not amused' (see also panel at **amuse**). There are, however, other uses of we that generally pass unnoticed:

□ **the editorial** we, used in formal writing or speech to refer to a company, organization, etc., or when it is thought that I would draw too much attention to the speaker or writer: We are not prepared to enter upon an agreement which would not be legally binding. As we showed in chapter 2 ....

□ **the use of** we **to mean 'you'**, especially to children or people who are ill: 'We don't want to hurt ourselves, do we?' 'How are we today?' This use can have overtones of condescension.

3 lacking determination or skill: a weak team. **4** lacking in firm, convincing facts: a weak argument. **5** lacking in moral strength; not able to resist temptation or persuasion: a weak will. **6** lacking full strength or flavour; diluted: weak tea. **7** easily upset: a weak stomach. **8** (of verbs) adding a suffix in the past tense and past participle as opposed to undergoing a vowel change. **weaken** *vb* make or become weaker. **weak-kneed** *adj* not strong morally; submitting readily to intimidation, etc. **weakling** *n* a person or animal of weak physical or moral strength. **weakly** *adj, adv* (in a way that is) weak. **weak-minded** *adj* lacking a determined mind or will; feeble-minded. **weakness** *n* **1** the state of being weak. **2** a defect or fault. **3** a special fondness: a weakness for walnut whirls. < Old Norse *veikr*.

weal (wiːl) *n* a raised mark on the flesh caused by a blow. < Old English *walu*.

wealth (wɛlθ) *n* **1** the state of being rich. **2** a large amount of money or other valuable possessions. **3** an abundance: a wealth of factual information. **wealthy** *adj* rich. **wealthily** *adv* **wealthiness** *n* < Old English *wela*.

wean (wiːn) *vb* **1** accustom (a baby or other young mammal) to take food other than its mother's milk. **2** cause (a person) to give up something one disapproves of. < Old English *wenian* to accustom.

weapon (ˈwɛpən) *n* **1** an object used in fighting used to inflict harm. **2** a means, action, etc., used to achieve one's objective in a conflict: the weapon of propaganda. **weaponry** *n* weapons. < Old English *wǣpen*.

wear (wɛə) *vb* **wore; worn; wearing** **1** have on the body, as clothing or ornament. **2** have (a particular expression) on the face. **3** damage or diminish or become damaged or diminished, as by constant use or friction. **4** last; endure use: The curtains are wearing well. **5** pass slowly: The evening wore on. **6** (*informal*) find acceptable; tolerate.
• *n* **1** wearing or being worn. **2** clothing: men's wear. **3** ability to endure use: It's still got a lot of wear left in it. **4** minor damage caused by ordinary use. **wearer** *n* < Old English *werian*. SEE PANEL.

weary (ˈwɪərɪ) *adj* **1** tired or exhausted; showing tiredness. **2** no longer able to tolerate or enjoy: weary of life. **3** tiring.
• *vb* **wearied; wearying** make or become weary. **wearily** *adv* **weariness** *n* **wearisome** *adj* causing weariness. < Old English *wērig*.

weasel (ˈwiːzl̩) *n* a small, short-legged, flesh-eating mammal with reddish-brown fur. < Old English *weosule*.

wearing out

Wear features in a number of idiomatic expressions, including:

wear a different hat to occupy a different role. Sometimes a particular role is mentioned: wearing his legal hat.

wear down to weaken by constant pressure: wear down the opposition.

wear off to become less intense: Gradually the effects of the drug wore off.

wear one's heart on one's sleeve to allow one's innermost feelings to be known to all. For the origin of this expression, see panel at **heart.**

wear out **1** to make or become unusable through constant wear, handling, etc. **2** to exhaust.

wear the trousers to be the dominant partner in a marriage.

wear thin to be ineffective, weak, or unconvincing: His constant excuses are beginning to wear a bit thin.

weatherwise

The suffix -wise has two meanings:

1 in the manner, direction, or position of: He stretched it out lengthwise. Turn it clockwise.

2 in respect of: Weatherwise, it will be dry and sunny tomorrow. Performancewise, the car is excellent.

Careful users of English consider the indiscriminate use of the second meaning unacceptable, preferring to rephrase the sentences, for example As far as the weather is concerned, it will be dry and sunny tomorrow or simply The weather will be dry and sunny tomorrow.

weather (ˈwɛðə) *n* the atmospheric conditions at a particular place and time, esp. with regard to sunshine, rainfall, and wind.
• *adj* windward: on the weather side. **make heavy weather of** perform (a task) with greater effort than it really needs. **under the weather** not well; depressed. **weather-beaten** *adj* worn or toughened by exposure to weather. **weathercock** *n* a weather-vane in the shape of a cockerel. **weatherman** *n, pl* **weathermen** a meteorologist, esp. one who broadcasts a weather forecast. **weatherproof** *adj* able to be exposed to weather without being damaged. **weather-vane** *n* a movable pointer, mounted in a high place, that turns to show the direction from which the wind is blowing. < Old English *weder.* SEE PANEL.

weave (wi:v) *vb* **wove, weaved; woven, weaved; weaving 1** make (a fabric) by joining threads crosswise. **2** form (threads) into a fabric in this way. **3** make (a basket, etc.) by intertwining straw, etc. **4** (of spiders, etc.) spin (a web). **5** form by combining different elements: weave a plot. **6** move from side to side: weaving in and out of the line of cars.
• *n* a pattern or style of weaving. **weaver** *n* **get weaving** (*informal*) start to do something vigorously. < Old English *wefan.*

web (wɛb) *n* **1** the network of fine threads made by a spider, etc. **2** an intricate structure. **3** a membrane joining the toes of some water-birds, etc. **webbed** *adj* **webbing** *n* strong fabric that is woven in strips and used for straps, upholstery, etc. **web-footed** *adj* having webbed feet. < Old English *webb.*

wed (wɛd) *vb* **wed, wedded; wedding 1** marry. **2** unite. **wedded to** committed to; unable to give up: wedded to old ideas. **wedding** *n* a marriage ceremony and festivities. **wedding-breakfast** *n* a celebration meal following a marriage ceremony. **wedding-ring** *n* a ring given by one marriage partner to the other during the marriage ceremony and worn after that time to indicate married status. **wedlock** *n* the state of being married. < Old English *weddian.*

wedge (wɛdʒ) *n* **1** a block of wood, metal, etc., tapering to a thin edge, used esp. to split wood or stop movement. **2** something shaped like this: a wedge of cheese. **3** something used to cause a separation.
• *vb* **1** fasten with a wedge. **2** force apart with a wedge. **3** pack in tightly. < Old English *wecg.*

wee (wi:) *adj* very small. < Old English *wǣg* weight.

weed (wi:d) *n* **1** a wild plant growing where it is not wanted in a garden or other cultivated area. **2** (*slang*) marijuana. **3** (*informal*) a weak or thin person.
• *vb* **1** remove weeds (from). **2** remove something inferior or unwanted: weed out the unsuitable candidates. **weed-killer** *n* a substance, esp. a chemical, used to destroy weeds. **weedy** *adj* **1** full of weeds. **2** weak and thin. < Old English *wēod.*

week (wi:k) *n* **1** a period of seven days, esp. from a Sunday to a Saturday. **2** the working days during such a period. **3** the hours or days worked in this period: a 35-hour week. **4** a week after or before (a day that is mentioned): on Monday week. **weekday** *n* a day except Sunday, or except Saturday and Sunday. **weekend** *n* the end of the week; period from Friday night or Saturday morning to Sunday night. **weeknight** *n* a night on any day of the week except Saturday or Sunday. < Old English *wicu.* SEE PANEL.

weekly (ˈwi:klɪ) *adj* happening, published, or calculated by the week.
• *adv* once a week; every week.
• *n* a weekly newspaper or magazine.

weeny (ˈwi:nɪ) *adj* (*informal*) tiny. < *wee* + tiny.

weep (wi:p) *vb* **wept; weeping 1** shed (tears). **2** give off (a fluid) slowly; ooze.

le weekend

To underestimate the number of French words and phrases that are commonly used in modern English would be to commit a faux pas (see panel at **par excellence**). However, a considerable number of English words are also used in French. Some examples of *franglais* include:

le camping	**le pop**
le cow-boy	**le ready-to-wear**
le drugstore	**le snack-bar**
le hamburger	**le snob**
le hit-parade	**le sport**
le marketing	**le taxi**
le non-sens	**le weekend**
le parking	**le western**
le pickpocket	

• *n* a spell of weeping. **weeping** *adj* (of a tree) having slender, drooping branches: a weeping willow. **weepy** *adj* inclined to weep; tearful. < Old English *wēpan.*

weevil (ˈwiːvəl) *n* any of various kinds of small beetle with a long snout, many of which are pests to crops and grain. < Old English *wifel.*

weft (wɛft) *n* the yarns extending across a fabric through the lengthways warp. < Old English.

weigh (weɪ) *vb* **1** measure the weight of. **2** have a certain weight. **3** measure a certain quantity, esp. on scales: weigh out 150 grams of sugar. **4** also **weigh up** consider carefully. **5** have importance; count: the evidence weighing against him. **6** be burdensome: The responsibilities weighed heavily on him. **weighbridge** *n* a weighing-machine for vehicles and their loads. < Old English *wegan.*

weight (weɪt) *n* **1** a measure of the heaviness of an object, person, etc. **2** the force of gravity on a mass. **3** a system of units for measuring weight: weights and measures. **4** a quantity that weighs a certain amount. **5** a heavy object, as used to hold something down: the weights of a clock. **6** a heavy load. **7** a burden: That's a weight off my mind. **8** importance or influence: His opinions don't carry much weight.
• *vb* **1** attach a weight to. **2** oppress with a burden. **3** arrange so as to form a bias. **weighting** *n* an additional amount of money paid on top of wages, usually to allow for the higher cost of living in a particular area: London weighting. **weightless** *adj* having little or no weight, as in space. **weightlessness** *n* **weight-lifting** *n* the sport of lifting heavy weights. **weight-lifter** *n* **weighty** *adj* **1** heavy. **2** burdensome. **3** important, serious, or influential. **weightily** *adv* < Old English *wiht.*

weir (wɪə) *n* **1** a small dam built across a river to raise the level of the water or to control its flow. **2** a barrier in a stream, etc., to catch fish. < Old English *wer.*

weird (wɪəd) *adj* strange or bizarre; odd. **weirdly** *adv* **weirdness** *n* < Old English *wyrd.*

welcome (ˈwɛlkəm) *adj* **1** received with gladness. **2** freely permitted: You're welcome to use our facilities.
• *interj* used to express a friendly greeting to a person who has arrived.
• *vb* **1** greet, esp. in a friendly way. **2** receive with pleasure.
• *n* an act or expression of welcoming. < Old English *wilcuma* welcome guest.

weld (wɛld) *vb* **1** fuse or join (pieces of metal), as by melting or hammering the parts together. **2** produce by such a process. **3** able to be welded. **4** join to form a whole. **welder** *n* < obsolete *well,* from Middle English *wellen.*

welfare (ˈwɛlˌfɛə) *n* **1** good health, happiness, and prosperity; well-being. **2** also **welfare work** organized efforts to improve the welfare of the poor, disabled, etc. **welfare state** a country that operates a system in which the government operates the social services to ensure the welfare of its citizens; such a system. < Middle English *wel faren* fare well.

well[1] (wɛl) *adv* **better; best 1** in a good, desirable, or satisfactory way. **2** favour-

Well, well!

☐ Well **as an adverb.** The adverb well often teams up with other parts of speech, especially past participles, to form compound adjectives. Examples include well-behaved, well-informed, and well-spoken, to name just a few of those that are more well known. Used *attributively,* that is *before* the nouns they modify, these combinations are normally hyphenated: 'It is a well-known book.' 'He is a well-mannered child.' However, when the same combinations are used *predicatively,* that is *after* the noun they modify, the hyphen tends to drop out: 'The book is well known.' 'The child is well mannered.'

The adverbs better, best, ill, worse, and worst exhibit similar behaviour: 'It was certainly an ill-advised move' but The move was certainly ill advised.'

☐ Well **as an adjective.** By far the largest group of adjectives are like pretty: they can occur both before a noun (a *pretty* girl) and after a verb like be or look (the girl is *pretty*). A small number of adjectives, however, are like asleep: they do not occur before a noun (we can't say an *asleep* child).

Well is basically of the asleep type: we can say, 'He's *well*' but we can't say a *well* man. What is strange about this word, however, is that it *does* occur before a noun when preceded by not or a similar negative: 'He is not a *well* man.'

ably: They spoke well of her. **3** thoroughly: Dry it well. **4** far; quite: He is well over six feet tall. **5** probably: It may well be the reason.
• *adj* **1** in good health. **2** satisfactory; acceptable. **3** advisable: It's as well to take a raincoat.
• *interj* used to express surprise, indignation, etc., or when pausing. **well-advised** *adj* marked by good sense. **well-being** *n* the state of being happy, healthy, and prosperous. **well-born** *adj* born of a respected or noble family. **well-bred** *adj* marked by good breeding; refined. **well-connected** *adj* having good, useful contacts. **well-disposed** *adj* kindly or sympathetic. **well-done** *adj* cooked thoroughly. **well-groomed** *adj* well-dressed, neat, and clean. **well-heeled** *adj* (*informal*) wealthy. **well-known** *adj* known to many; famous. **well-meaning** *adj* marked by good intentions, but often having unfortunate results. **wellnigh** *adv* almost. **well-off** *adj* **1** in a comfortable or good situation: You don't know when you're well off! **2** wealthy. **well-oiled** *adj* (*informal*) drunk. **well-preserved** *adj* (of an old person) still looking young. **well-read** *adj* having read widely. **well-spoken** *adj* speaking in a clear, polite, and correct way. **well-to-do** *adj* wealthy. **well-tried** *adj* tested thoroughly and found reliable. **well-versed** *adj* knowing thoroughly. **well-wisher** *n* a person who wishes another well. **well-worn** *adj* **1** worn by much use. **2** (of a phrase) used excessively; hackneyed. < Old English *wel.* SEE PANEL.

well[2] *n* **1** a hole or shaft dug into the earth to reach a supply of water, oil, gas, etc. **2** a natural pool. **3** an open, vertical space through the floors of a building: a stair well. **4** a hole, space, etc., used to contain a liquid: an ink-well. **5** a deep enclosed space in a building. **6** a source.
• *vb* rise; flow. < Old English *welle.*

wellington (ˈwɛlɪŋtən) *n* also **wellington boot** a waterproof boot of rubber, etc., that reaches nearly to the knee. < Arthur Wellesley, 1st Duke of *Wellington,* died 1852, British soldier and statesman.

welsh (wɛlʃ) *vb* **1** cheat by failing to pay a debt, etc. **2** not keep one's promise. < origin uncertain.

welt (wɛlt) *n* **1** a strip of material such as leather joining the sole and upper of a shoe. **2** a seam or edge of a garment for decoration or strengthening. **3** a raised mark on the skin from a heavy blow. < Middle English *welte.*

wench (wɛntʃ) *n* (*old-fashioned or chiefly humorous*) a young woman or girl. < Old English *wencel.*

wend (wɛnd) *vb* **wend one's way** go; proceed. < Old English *wendan.*

went (wɛnt) SEE **GO.**

wept (wɛpt) SEE **WEEP.**

were (wə; *stressed* wɜː) SEE **BE.** SEE PANEL AT **IF.**

werewolf (ˈwɪəˌwʊlf, ˈwɛəˌwʊlf) *n, pl* **werewolves** a person who supposedly changes into a wolf at night. < Old English *werwulf.*

west (wɛst) *n* the point or direction to the left of a person facing north; general direction of sunset.
• *adj, adv* **1** towards, in, or from the west. **2** (of the wind) from the west. **the west** often also **the West** land lying in or towards the west. **the West 1** Europe and America in contrast with Oriental countries. **2** the non-Communist countries of Europe and America in contrast with the Communist countries of the East. **westerly** *adj* **1** in or towards the west. **2** (of the wind) from the west. **westerner** *n* a native or inhabitant of the west. **westernize** *vb* influence or be influenced with qualities, ideas, etc., associated with the West. **westernization** *n* **westernmost** *adj* furthest west. **westward, westwards** *adj, adv* towards the west. < Old English.

western (ˈwɛstən) *adj* of or in the west.
• *n* a film, novel, etc., about cowboys, etc., in the western USA, esp. in the time of early development.

wet (wɛt) *adj* **wetter; wettest 1** covered, moistened, or soaked with a liquid, esp. water. **2** rainy. **3** not yet dry: wet paint. **4** allowing the sale of alcohol. **5** (*informal*) feeble and weak.
• *vb* **wet, wetted; wetting 1** make wet. **2** urinate.
• *n* **1** moisture. **2** wet weather. **3** (*informal*) a feeble and weak person. **wetly** *adv* **wetness** *n* **wet behind the ears** (*informal*) immature; inexperienced. **wet blanket** a person who dampens the enthusiasm or enjoyment of others. **wet suit** a porous, close-fitting, rubber suit worn by a skin-diver. < Old English *wǣt.*

wether (ˈwɛðə) *n* a castrated male sheep. < Old English.

whack (wæk) *vb* strike with a heavy, resounding blow.
• *n* **1** a heavy, resounding blow. **2** (*informal*) an attempt. **whacked** *adj* (*informal*) exhausted. **whacking** *adj, adv* (*informal*) very great. < probably

like the sound.

whale (weɪl) *n* any of several very large sea-mammals, some of which are hunted for oil, flesh, etc. **whalebone** *n* the horny material that hangs from the upper jaw of some kinds of whale; formerly used as a stiffener in corsets, etc. **a whale of a time** (*informal*) a very enjoyable time. **whaler** *n* a person or ship engaged in whaling. **whaling** *n* hunting whales. < Old English *hwæl.* SEE PANEL.

wharf (wɔːf) *n, pl* **wharves, wharfs** a platform built along or out from the shore, where ships dock and load or unload. < Old English *hwearf.*

what (wət; *stressed* wɒt) *determiner, pron* **1** used in questions to ask about the identity, character, etc., of a person or thing: What's the weather like? **2** that or the one which: He knows what he wants. **3** how surprising or remarkable: What a coincidence! **4** used to ask for something to be repeated because it has not been properly heard or understood.
• *adv* to what extent.
• *interj* used as an expression of surprise. **whatever** *determiner, pron* **1** any or anything at all that. **2** no matter what. **whatsoever** *determiner, pron* whatever. < Old English *hwæt.* SEE PANEL.

wheat (wiːt) *n* **1** a cereal grass from whose grain flour is made. **2** such grain, used for bread, pasta, etc. < Old English *hwǣte.*

wheedle (ˈwiːdl̩) *vb* influence or persuade by flattery, coaxing, etc.; obtain in this way. < origin unknown.

wheel (wiːl) *n* **1** a circular frame or disc that turns on an axle. **2** something like a wheel in shape or movement: a potter's wheel. **3** a turning movement. **4** *pl* the controlling forces: the wheels of government. **5** *pl* (*informal*) a car.
• *vb* **1** turn on an axis; rotate or revolve. **2** push or pull on wheels. **3** change direction and face the other way. **4** supply with a wheel or wheels. **at the wheel** steering a vehicle or vessel; in charge. **wheelbarrow** *n* an open container for transporting small loads, used mostly by gardeners and on building sites. **wheelbase** *n* the distance between a vehicle's front and rear axles. **wheelchair** *n* a chair for invalids which is mounted on large wheels that can be turned by the user. **wheeling and**

a whale of a time

A whale of a time is one of the many idiomatic expressions that include the name of an animal or bird. Others include:

a cock-and-bull story
separate the sheep from the goats
smell a rat
run with the fox and hunt with the hounds
give someone the bird
a bear with a sore head
parrot-fashion
like water off a duck's back
the lion's share
as the crow flies
a wild goose chase
no room to swing a cat
a dog's life
talk turkey
one swallow does not make a summer
have kittens
get someone's goat
like a cat on hot bricks
be the cat's whiskers
be going to the dogs

knowing what's what

What features in a number of idiomatic expressions, including:

know what's what to have a thorough knowledge of something: He certainly knows what's what when it comes to selling computers.
what d'you call him, her, or **it** also **what's-his, her,** or **its name** a person or thing whose name you cannot recall.
what for 1 for what purpose or reason: What's this lever for? **2** a severe reprimand; scolding: He gave him what for.
what have you other similar things: nails, bolts, and what have you.
what is more moreover; more importantly.
what it takes the qualities required to do something successfully: He's really got what it takes to manage the team well.
what with as a result of (certain circumstances): What with the children being ill and Jim being away on business, I just haven't got round to ringing her up.

dealing intense, shrewd, and sometimes unscrupulous scheming in an attempt to gain a commercial or political advantage. < Old English *hwēol.*

wheeze (wi:z) *vb* breathe with a whistling, breathy sound.
• *n* **1** the sound of wheezing. **2** (*informal*) a cunning trick or plan. **wheezy** *adj* < probably of Scandinavian origin.

whelk (wɛlk) *n* any of several large sea snails. < Old English *weoloc.*

whelp (wɛlp) *n* any of the young of certain animals, esp. a dog; pup.
• *vb* give birth to young ones. < Old English *hwelp.*

when (wɛn) *adv* **1** at what time. **2** at which: at the time when we met.
• *conj* **1** at the time at which. **2** if. **3** considering; since.
• *pron* what or which time. **say when** state when an action should stop, esp. pouring a drink. < Old English *hwanne.*

whence (wɛns) *adv, conj* (*archaic or formal*) from where; from what place, source, etc. < Old English *hwanon.*

whenever (wɛnˈɛvə) *adv* at any such time; when.
• *conj* at whatever time. SEE PANEL AT **EVER.**

where (wɛə) *adv* **1** at, to, or in what place. **2** at or to which: locations where an outside aerial is needed.
• *conj* **1** at, to, or in the place at which. **2** in a situation or regard in which.
• *pron* what place. **whereas** *conj* but in contrast. **whereby** *conj* by which. **wherein** *adv, conj* in what; in which. **whereupon** *adv, conj* after which. **wherewithal** *n* resources, esp. money. < Old English *hwǣr.*

whereabouts (ˈwɛərəˌbaʊts) *adv, conj* in what general area.
• *n* the general location of a person or thing.

wherever (wɛərˈɛvə) *adv* anywhere at all; where.
• *conj* at, to, or in whatever place. SEE PANEL AT **EVER.**

whet (wɛt) *vb* **whetted; whetting** **1** sharpen by rubbing against a stone, etc. **2** stimulate: whet one's appetite. < Old English *hwettan.*

whether (ˈwɛðə) *conj* used to introduce an alternative possibility or a choice between two alternatives. < Old English *hwæther.* SEE PANEL.

whetstone (ˈwɛtˌstəʊn) *n* a stone for sharpening tools.

whey (weɪ) *n* the watery part of sour milk that separates from the curds. < Old English *hwæg.*

which (wɪtʃ) *determiner, pron* **1** what (person or thing). **2** being the one or ones that. **3** being the thing or animal referred to: The book, which will be published in May, is a revision of an earlier edition. **4** and that: He speaks German, which is very useful for his job. **whichever** *determiner, pron* **1** being one of a set that. **2** which. **3** no matter which. < Old English *hwilc.* SEE PANELS AT **EVER; THAT.**

whiff (wɪf) *n* a light puff of air, wind, or odour. < like the sound.

while (waɪl) *n* **1** a period of time, esp. a short time. **2** the time and trouble involved: worth one's while.
• *conj* also **whilst** **1** during the time

---

whether or **whether or not?**

Careful users of English avoid using whether or not when only one possibility is being considered: I'm not sure whether or not I'll have time. I wondered whether he could help me or not. In such cases, just whether is used: I'm not sure whether I'll have time. I wondered whether he could help me. Whether or not is reserved for the consideration of two possibilities: We will pay them whether or not we actually stay there.

---

while

On 18 August 1967 the 'Daily Telegraph' reported, somewhat amusingly, that the Ministry of Transport had decided to change the wording on new level-crossing warning notices. Apparently, the original sign read Stop while lights are flashing. For speakers of standard English this was perfectly unambiguous ('remain stationary for as long as the lights are flashing'). In Yorkshire dialect, however, while also meant (and continues to mean) 'until', as in Wait here while I come back. For the many speakers who used while in this way, the original wording was highly ambiguous and might have had lethal consequences.

that. **2** whereas; although.
• *vb* **while away** spend (time) in a leisurely, usually pleasant manner.
< Old English *hwīl.* SEE PANEL.

whim (wɪm) *n* a sudden, passing, often irrational idea, desire, or impulse.
< short for *whim-wham,* of unknown origin.

whimper (ˈwɪmpə) *vb* cry or utter with a low, whining sound.
• *n* a whimpering sound. < like the sound.

whimsy (ˈwɪmzɪ) *n* **1** a fanciful, esp. slightly odd, idea. **2** fanciful humour. **whimsical** *adj* marked by whims; playful or fanciful. **whimsicality** *n* **whimsically** *adv* < SEE **WHIM.**

whine (waɪn) *vb* **1** make or utter in a long, high-pitched cry, esp. showing suffering. **2** complain feebly.
• *n* a whining sound or complaint. **whiner** *n* **whiny** *adj* < Old English *hwīnan.*

whip (wɪp) *n* **1** an instrument consisting of a rod with a lash attached to one end, used for striking or flogging. **2** an official of a political party responsible for discipline and obtaining the attendance and votes of members on a particular occasion; instruction to vote issued by such a person: a three-line whip. **3** a dessert made by whipping a mixture of cream and fruit flavouring.
• *vb* **whipped; whipping 1** hit or urge on with or as if with a whip. **2** mark, pull, etc., suddenly and quickly. **3** beat (eggs, cream, etc.) into a frothy mixture. **4** (*informal*) steal. **have the whip hand** be in a powerful, controlling position. **whiplash** *n* the lash of a whip. **whippy** *adj* bending or springing back easily. **whip-round** *n* an informal appeal for money from a group of people. **whip up** arouse; incite: whip up support. < Middle English *whippen.*

whipper-snapper (ˈwɪpəˌsnæpə) *n* an insignificant, impertinent, esp. young person. < probably alteration of *snippersnapper.*

whippet (ˈwɪpɪt) *n* a breed of dog related to the greyhound, used for racing, etc. < origin uncertain.

whirl (wɜːl) *vb* **1** spin or swing round and round or cause to do this. **2** follow a curving or circling course. **3** become confused or dizzy; reel. **4** move or go quickly.
• *n* **1** a whirling movement; something having a form like this. **2** a confused state; turmoil. **3** bustling activity. **4** (*informal*) an attempt: We'll give it a whirl. **whirlpool** *n* a very strong, circular current of water, esp. drawing floating objects into its centre. **whirlwind** *n* **1** a small current of air revolving quickly around a central point. **2** also *adj* (of) something like this, esp. in a fast movement: a whirlwind romance. < Old Norse *hvirfla.*

whirr (wɜː) *vb* make a constant buzzing or vibrating sound like that of a motor turning quickly.
• *n* a whirring sound. < probably of Scandinavian origin.

whisk (wɪsk) *n* **1** a whisking motion. **2** an instrument for whisking food.
• *vb* **1** move quickly and lightly. **2** brush lightly from a surface. **3** beat (eggs, cream, etc.) into a froth. < Old Norse *visk* wisp.

whisker (ˈwɪskə) *n* **1** one of the long hairs growing near the mouth of a cat, etc. **2** *pl* (*informal*) a moustache. **3** (*informal*) a very small amount, distance, or margin: He won by a whisker. < SEE **WHISK.**

whiskey (ˈwɪskɪ) *n* whisky made in Ireland or the USA.

whisky (ˈwɪskɪ) *n* a spirit distilled from malted barley or other grain. < Irish Gaelic *uisce beathadh* water of life.

whisper (ˈwɪspə) *vb* **1** speak or utter softly, esp. not vibrating the vocal cords. **2** utter or suggest privately or secretly. **3** make a rustling sound: the leaves whispering in the breeze.
• *n* **1** a whispering sound or comment. **2** a rumour. **3** a trace or hint. **whisperer** *n* < Old English *hwisprian.*

whist (wɪst) *n* a card-game for two pairs of partners, in which the aim is to win the highest number of tricks. **whist drive** a series of games of whist, with a periodic change of partners. < perhaps alteration of *whisk.*

whistle (ˈwɪsl̩) *n* **1** a device for making a shrill sound when air, steam, etc., is

a whistle-stop tour

In American English a whistle-stop is a small station at which a train does not stop unless it is signalled to do so. By association, it also came to mean a small community. The phrase whistle-stop tour came into being to denote a politician's breathless tour of these communities, especially in the days before an election, when very often he would deliver his speech from the back of the train.

forced through a small opening or against a sharp edge. **2** a shrill sound produced by such a device or by whistling; sound like this.
• *vb* **1** make a shrill sound by forcing breath through puckered lips or blowing a whistle. **2** signal, call, etc., by whistling or blowing a whistle. **3** produce or express by whistling. **whistler** *n* **whistle for** ask for (money, etc.), esp. in vain. **whistle-stop** *adj* consisting of brief appearances in different places, as during an election campaign: a whistle-stop tour. < Old English *hwistle.* SEE PANEL.

whit (wɪt) *n* the smallest possible part. < Old English *wiht* creature.

white (waɪt) *adj* **1** of the colour of newly fallen snow. **2** pale, as from fear, illness, etc. **3** (of coffee) served with milk or cream. **4 White** having a light-coloured skin.
• *n* **1** a white colour. **2** white clothing. **3** the clear part round the yolk of an egg that turns white when cooked. **4 White** a White person. **whitely** *adv* **whiteness** *n* **whitebait** *n, pl* **whitebait** the young of herrings, etc., used as food. **white Christmas** a Christmas accompanied by snow. **white-collar worker** a worker who is engaged in professional or business employment as distinct from manual work. **whiten** *vb* make or become white. **white lie** a harmless lie, told for example to avoid hurting someone's feelings. **White Paper** a government report setting out official policy. < Old English *hwit.* SEE PANEL.

whitewash (ˈwaɪtˌwɒʃ) *n* **1** a mixture of lime, washed and ground chalk, water, etc., used for painting walls or other surfaces. **2** a hiding of faults or mistakes, esp. to clear someone from blame.
• *vb* **1** paint with whitewash. **2** hide or gloss over.

whiting (ˈwaɪtɪŋ) *n, pl* **whiting** a food fish related to cod. < Old English *hwītling.*

whittle (ˈwɪtl̩) *vb* **1** cut off thin slices from the surface of (wood). **2** reduce or destroy gradually. < Old English *thwītan* to cut.

whiz (wɪz) *vb* **whizzed; whizzing 1** make a loud, buzzing sound. **2** move quickly.
• *n* a whizzing sound. **whiz-kid** *n* (*informal*) an exceptionally clever or successful, young person. < like the sound.

who (hʊ; *stressed* hʊː) *pron* **1** what person or people. **2** the one or ones. **whoever** *pron* anyone who; no matter who. < Old English *hwā.* SEE PANEL. SEE PANELS AT **EVER; THAT.**

whole (həʊl) *adj* **1** containing all its parts; complete. **2** not broken, damaged, etc. **3** healthy; sound.
• *n* **1** a complete amount with all its parts. **2** a complete, complex system. **on the whole** generally speaking. **whole-hearted** *adj* with no hesitation; with full sincerity. **whole-heartedly** *adv* **wholemeal** *adj* made with whole wheat kernels. **wholesome** *adj* beneficial for health or physical, moral, etc., welfare. **wholesomeness** *n* **wholly** *adv* completely. < Old English *hwā.*

wholesale (ˈhəʊlˌseɪl) *n* the selling of goods in relatively large quantities, esp. for further sale by a retailer.

who or whom?

Who is often used instead of whom in spoken English, especially in questions: *Who* are you looking for? He's a man *who* people find they can talk to easily.

Whom is used in more formal, usually written styles: Would you kindly advise us to *whom* we should address our complaints? Whom must be used immediately after a preposition: For *whom* was the report intended? though *Who* was the report intended for? is acceptable in informal English.

white elephant

A white elephant is something that is costly but unwanted and useless: The council spent millions on the new theatre, but it turned out to be something of a *white elephant.* The expression refers to the former tradition in Thailand where white or albino elephants were so rare that when captured they became the property of the king. He was the only one who could ride or use such an animal. When the king was displeased with one of his courtiers, he would bestow upon him a white elephant. The distressingly high cost of the animal's upkeep and the fact that it could not be put to work gave rise to the present meaning.

• *adj, adv* **1** of or relating to wholesale. **2** on a large scale; extensive: wholesale slaughter.
• *vb* sell wholesale. **wholesaler** *n*
whom (hu:m) *pron* the objective case of *who.* < Old English *hwām.* SEE PANELS AT **THAT; WHO.**
whoop (hu:p) *vb* utter a loud cry, esp. of excitement or enthusiasm.
• *n* such a cry. **whooping-cough** *n* a respiratory infection of children marked by coughing fits that end in a whoop. **whoop it up** (*informal*) have a noisy, exuberant time. < like the sound.
whopper (ˈwɒpə) *n* (*informal*) **1** something that is unusually large. **2** a big lie. **whopping** *adj* (*informal*) extremely large. < ultimately Middle English *wappen* to pull violently.
whore (hɔ:) *n* a prostitute.< Old English *hōre.*
whorl (wɜ:l) *n* **1** (*botany*) a circle of similar parts growing round something such as the stem of a plant. **2** something shaped like a coil. **3** a complete circle formed by the ridges of a fingerprint. < Middle English *wharle,* pulley part of a spindle in a spinning-machine.
whose (hu:z) *determiner, pron* **1** of or belonging to whom. **2** of whom; of which. < Middle English *whos.*
why (waɪ) *adv* for what reason, cause, etc.
• *conj* the reason or cause for which.
• *interj* used to express surprise. **why not** used to make a suggestion: Why not look it up now? **whys and wherefores** reasons, causes, or explanations. < Old English *hwȳ.*
wick (wɪk) *n* a cord of loosely woven fibres in a candle, etc., that burns as the wax melts. **get on someone's wick** (*informal*) annoy someone. < Old English *wēoce.*
wicked (ˈwɪkɪd) *adj* **1** morally bad; evil or immoral. **2** mischievous: a wicked smile. **3** severe; unpleasant. **wickedly** *adv* **wickedness** *n* < alteration of Middle English *wicke* evil.
wicker (ˈwɪkə) *n* thin, flexible twigs, canes, reeds, etc., woven together. **wickerwork** *n* furniture, baskets, etc., made of wicker. < Scandinavian.
wicket (ˈwɪkɪt) *n* **1** (*cricket*) one of two sets of three stumps with two bails, at which the batsman stands; area between these; batsman's turn at batting. **2** also **wicket-gate** a small gate or door, esp. part of a larger one. **wicket-keeper** *n* the fielder in cricket who stands behind the batsman's wicket. < Old Northern French *wiket.*
wide (waɪd) *adj* **1** extending a long way from one side to the other. **2** measuring in width: three metres wide. **3** covering much; having a great range: a wide variation. **4** fully-opened: wide eyes.
• *adv* **1** widely; to a great extent. **2** missing a target. **widely** *adv* **wideness** *n* **wide awake** completely awake; very alert. **wide-eyed** *adj* surprised; innocent. **widen** *vb* make or become wider. **widespread** *adj* widely distributed; prevalent or extensive. < Old English *wīd.*
widow (ˈwɪdəʊ) *n* a woman whose husband has died, esp. one who has not remarried. **widowed** *adj* made a widow. **widower** *n* a man whose wife has died, esp. one who has not remarried. < Old English *wuduwe.*
width (wɪtθ, wɪdθ) *n* **1** the distance measured from side to side. **2** wideness. **3** a measured piece of woven material. **widthways, widthwise** *adj, adv* in the direction of the width of something.
wield (wi:ld) *vb* **1** hold and use (a tool, weapon, etc.). **2** exercise (authority, etc.). < Old English *wieldan.*
wife (waɪf) *n, pl* **wives** a married woman, in relation to her husband. < Old English *wīf.*
wig (wɪg) *n* a covering of natural or artificial hair, worn on the head. < short for *periwig,* altered from Middle French

a short wig

One of the minor ways in which new words enter the language is by *shortening,* also known as *clipping.* For example, photograph has given us photo, and omnibus has given us bus. Similarly, people now go to a pub rather than a public house; babies fall not out of perambulators but out of prams; and how many women ask for a perm rather than a permanent wave? Parts of words and phrases are being lopped off all the time as we look for verbal short cuts. In the 17th century the word periwig, like photograph and public house today, was considered to be rather too much of a mouthful. Nowadays it is only the shortened form that survives.

There are three ways in which words become shortened. An initial element may be lost as in wig, or a final element as in pram. Alternatively, there are words like flu (influenza) that undergo attack at both ends.

perruque, from Old Italian *parrucca* head of hair. SEE PANEL.

wiggle (ˈwɪgḷ) *vb* move or cause to move from side to side, esp. jerkily.
• *n* a wiggling movement. < Middle Dutch *wiggelen.*

wigwam (ˈwɪgˌwæm) *n* a hut having a framework of poles covered with bark, rushes, or skins, as formerly used by North American Indians. < Abnaki and Massachuset *wīkwām.*

wild (waɪld) *adj* **1** living in a natural state; not tame. **2** growing in a natural state; not cultivated. **3** uncivilized; savage. **4** lacking restraint or control. **5** stormy: a wild night. **6** full of intense feeling, such as anger or enthusiasm. **7** random: a wild guess. **8** fantastic or unreasonable; extravagant or rash.
• *adv* in a wild manner.
• *n* a wild, desolate, or uncivilized area: out in the wilds. **wildly** *adv* **wildness** *n* **like wildfire** very quickly. **run wild** grow or behave in an unrestrained way. **sow** (**one's**) **wild oats** lead a reckless, self-indulgent life while young. **wildcat** *adj* **1** financially risky; unsound. **2** (of a strike) spontaneous and undertaken without formal union approval. **wildfowl** *n* a game bird. **wild-goose chase** a useless search or undertaking. **wildlife** *n* wild animals. < Old English *wilde.*

wilderness (ˈwɪldənɪs) *n* a wild, desolate, or uncultivated area. < Old English *wilddēoren* of wild beasts.

wile (waɪl) *n* a deceitful trick. **wily** *adj* sly or crafty. < origin uncertain.

wilful (ˈwɪlfʊl) *adj* **1** done intentionally: wilful damage. **2** stubborn and self-willed. **wilfully** *adv* **wilfulness** *n*

will[1] (wɪl) *auxiliary vb* **would 1** used for future reference. **2** used to express a willingness or firm intention. **3** used in requests or orders: Will you come this way, please? **4** used to describe repeated, habitual, or characteristic behaviour or actions: Sometimes she will just sit in her room for hours. **5** used to express ability, capacity, etc.: The hall will seat 400. **6** used to express an assumption: Was that the doorbell? It'll be for you.
• *vb* wish or desire: Do what you will. < Old English *wyllan.*

will[2] *n* **1** the mental faculty by which one controls one's actions, wishes, etc. **2** a choice, desire, or purpose. **3** determination. **4** an attitude towards others. **5** a written statement of a person's wishes concerning the disposal of his or her property after death.
• *vb* **1** exercise the will; control or compel by this. **2** determine or decree. **3** bequeath by a will. **at will** as one wishes. **will-power** *n* determination; firmness of will; self-control. < Old English *willa.*

willing (ˈwɪlɪŋ) *adj* **1** inclined or ready (to). **2** undertaken or given readily.
• *n* willingness. **willingly** *adv* **willingness** *n*

willow (ˈwɪləʊ) *n* **1** any of a large group of trees or shrubs that bear catkins, for example the weeping willow, with slender, drooping branches. **2** the wood from such a tree or shrub. **willow-pattern** *n* china with an oriental design of a willow-tree, river, and bridge, traditionally in blue and white. **willowy** *adj* **1** full of willow-trees. **2** graceful and slender. < Old English *welig.*

willy-nilly (ˌwɪlɪˈnɪlɪ) *adv* haphazardly. < *will I, nill I;* archaic *nill* to refuse.

wilt (wɪlt) *vb* **1** (of a plant) lose freshness and droop. **2** cause to do this. **3** lose strength or courage. < Middle English *welken.*

win (wɪn) *vb* **won; winning 1** gain a victory; finish first in a contest, etc. **2** gain in a battle, contest, etc. **3** gain as a result of an effort, etc. **4** gain the favour of, esp. by persuasion: He soon won them round to his way of thinking.
• *n* a victory or success in a contest, etc. **winner** *n* **1** a person, etc., who wins. **2** (*informal*) something that is successful or is expected to be successful. **win through** succeed after a long period of difficulties. < Old English *winnan.*

wince (wɪns) *vb* draw back suddenly, as from pain, embarrassment, etc.
• *n* a wincing movement. < of Germanic origin.

winch (wɪntʃ) *n* **1** a machine for hoisting or pulling by means of a drum, around which a cable is wound. **2** a crank or handle that gives motion to a machine.
• *vb* hoist or pull with a winch. < Old English *wince.*

wind[1] (wɪnd) *n* **1** the movement of air, either naturally, as over the earth's surface, or artificially, as by a fan. **2** a force or trend: the winds of change. **3** air breathed; ability to breathe. **4** gas in the stomach or intestines. **5** musical wind instruments. **6** (*informal*) idle or boastful talk. **windbag** *n* (*informal*) a person who talks a lot. **wind-break** *n* a fence, etc., that gives protection from the full force of the wind. **wind-cheater** *n* a wind-proof jacket. **windfall** *n* **1** an apple or other fruit blown off a tree by the wind. **2** a piece of unexpected good fortune, esp. money gained. **wind instrument** a musical instrument, such as the oboe, sounded by air, esp. the player's breath. **windmill** *n* a mill with a set of vanes that are turned by the wind to produce power. **windpipe** *n* the tube by which air passes from the larynx to the bronchi. **windscreen** *n* the glass that forms a window, esp. at the front of a motor vehicle. **wind-sock** *n* a truncated canvas cone open at both ends, mounted and flown esp. at an airport to show the wind direction. **windsurfing** *n* the sport of sailing with a flat, buoyant board, fitted with a sail. **wind-swept** *adj* exposed to the wind. **windward** *adj, adv, n* (in or moving to) the direction from which the wind is blowing. **windy** *adv* **1** with much wind; exposed to great winds. **2** verbose. **3** (*informal*) frightened. < Old English. SEE PANEL.

wind[2] (waɪnd) *vb* **wound; winding** **1** coil. **2** go in a curving course. **3** surround by encircling something. **4** turn or cause to turn. **5** also **wind up** tighten the spring of (a clock, etc.). **6** pull or hoist by turning a handle, etc. **7** make (one's way) by a curving course. • *n* a turn or coil. **winder** *n* **wind down** bring to an end gradually; become more relaxed. **wind up 1** bring or come to an end. **2** end (a business) by liquidation. **3** make (someone) excited. < Old English *windan.*

windlass (ˈwɪndləs) *n* a machine for hoisting or pulling things by means of a rope or chain that is wound round a drum. < probably Old Norse *vinda* to wind + *āss* pole.

window (ˈwɪndəʊ) *n* **1** an opening, esp. in the wall of a building, that admits light and air, usually set in a framework of glass and designed to open and close. **2** the glass in a window. **3** an opening like a window, such as the transparent panel in an envelope that shows an address. **window-box** *n* a long, narrow box for plants, fixed outside a window. **window-dressing** *n* **1** the displaying of goods in a shop window. **2** a presentation that gives a superficially attractive appearance to something. **window-shopping** *n* looking at displays in shop windows without intending to make purchases. < Old Norse *vindr* wind + *auga* eye.

wine (waɪn) *n* **1** an alcoholic drink made from fermented grape-juice. **2** an alcoholic drink made from other fruits or plants. **wine and dine** entertain with or drink wine at a meal. < Old English *wīn.*

wing (wɪŋ) *n* **1** one of a pair of organs used in flight by a bird, insect, etc. **2** one of the main projecting, supporting surfaces of an aeroplane. **3** a part of a building, esp. extending from the main part: the east wing. **4** the area at either side of the stage of a theatre that is not visible to the audience: in the wings. **5** the part of the body of a car above a wheel. **6** a projecting side-piece at the top of a high-backed armchair. **7** a section of a political party with particular views: right-wing. **8** an end of a military formation; flank. **9** either of the attacking players or positions in a game such as football or

the wind

Wind features in a number of idiomatic expressions, including:

get wind of to find out about, especially by hearing of as a rumour: The police got wind of the plan to rob the bank. The expression referred originally to the smell of an animal carried by the wind.
in the wind about to happen.
like the wind very fast.
put the wind up to frighten (a person).
sail close to the wind to act in such a way that accepted principles, rules of behaviour, etc., are nearly broken.
see which way the wind is blowing to see what other people are thinking or planning or what is likely to happen, before reaching a decision.
take the wind out of someone's sails to reduce someone's self-confidence or self-importance. The expression derives from one ship sailing close to another on the windward side, so preventing the wind from catching the other's sails.
The expression **tilt at windmills** means 'to attack an imaginary enemy, in the belief that it is real'. The expression comes from the novel 'Don Quixote de la Mancha' by the Spanish writer Miguel de Cervantes Saavedra, 1547–1616. Don Quixote travels through the countryside attacking windmills in the belief that they are giants.

hockey on either side of the centre position.
● *vb* **1** make (one's way) with or as if with wings; fly. **2** wound, esp. in the wing. **under one's wing** in one's protection or care. **wing commander** an officer in the RAF below a group captain and above a squadron leader. **winged** *adj* having wings. **winger** *n* a player in football, hockey, etc., occupying a position on the wing. **wing-nut** *n* a nut with projections that enable it to be tightened by hand. < Scandinavian.

wink (wɪŋk) *vb* **1** close and open one's eye deliberately, esp. as a signal. **2** shine intermittently. **3 wink at** pretend not to notice (a wrong action).
● *n* **1** an act of winking. **2** a brief period of sleep: I didn't sleep a wink all night. **winker** *n* a small, flashing light on a motor vehicle that shows an intended change of direction. < Old English *wincian.*

winkle (ˈwɪŋkḷ) *n* an edible marine snail. **winkle out** extract or discover. **winkle-pickers** *pl n* shoes with long pointed toes. < short for *periwinkle,* origin uncertain.

winning (ˈwɪnɪŋ) SEE **WIN.**
● *adj* charming or attractive. **winnings** *pl n* money, etc., won, esp. in gambling.

winnow (ˈwɪnəʊ) *vb* **1** separate (chaff) from (grain) by a current of air. **2** remove (something unwanted); sift. < Old English *windwian.*

winsome (ˈwɪnsəm) *adj* having an attractive, engaging appearance or manner. < Old English *wynsum.*

winter (ˈwɪntə) *n* the coldest season of the year, between autumn and spring.
● *vb* spend the winter. **winter sports** open-air sports on snow or ice, such as skiing. **wintry** *adj* **1** of or like winter; cold. **2** without cheer; bleak. < Old English.

wipe (waɪp) *vb* **1** clean or dry (a surface) by rubbing; rub (a cloth, etc.) over a surface. **2** remove by or as if by rubbing. **3** apply (a substance such as grease) to a surface.
● *n* the act of wiping. **wipe out** destroy completely; cancel. **wiper** *n* **1** something used in wiping. **2** a rubber strip that is moved mechanically across a windscreen to clean it. < Old English *wīpian.*

wire (waɪə) *n* **1** a slender, usually flexible rod of metal. **2** a piece of this used for conducting electric current. **3** a framework made of wire. **4** a telegram: send a wire.
● *vb* **1** provide or connect with wires. **2** install a system of wires for conducting electricity in (a building). **get one's wires crossed** (*informal*) misunderstand. **wireless** *n* (*old-fashioned*) a radio. **wire wool** a mass of fine wire used to scour kitchen utensils, etc. **wiring** *n* a system of wires for conducting electricity in a building. **wiry** *adj* **1** like wire. **2** thin but strong. **wiriness** *n* < Old English *wīr.*

wise (waɪz) *adj* **1** having wisdom. **2** well-informed: be none the wiser. **3** (*informal*) aware: I've got wise to his little tricks. **4** prudent; sensible: It'd not be wise to rush things. **wisely** *adv* **wisdom** *n* understanding and discernment, esp. as a result of learning and experience. **wisdom tooth** one of the four molar teeth that are the last to emerge. **wise guy** (*informal*) a know-all. < Old English *wīs.*

wish (wɪʃ) *vb* **1** have or express a desire or aim. **2** express a hope about another person's well-being; bid: I wish you well; He didn't even wish us good morning.
● *n* **1** an act or instance of wishing; object of this. **2** an expressed desire, esp. for another person's well-being; greeting: She sends her best wishes. **wishbone** *n* the forked bone in front of the breastbone of a bird. **wishful** *adj* having or marked by a wish. **wishful thinking** convincing oneself that one's wishes accord with reality, esp. when they do not. **wish on** want (a person or thing) to become the responsibility of someone else. < Old English *wȳscan.*

wishy-washy (ˈwɪʃɪˌwɒʃɪ) *adj* (*informal*) weak in strength, character, colour, etc. < SEE **WASH.**

wisp (wɪsp) *n* **1** a small bundle of something: wisps of grass. **2** a thin streak of smoke, etc. **3** something frail or delicate. **wispy** *adj* < Middle English.

wistful (ˈwɪstfʊl) *adj* full of pensive yearning. **wistfully** *adv* **wistfulness** *n* < perhaps obsolete *wistly* attentive, intently.

wit[1] (wɪt) *n* **1** the ability to associate different words, etc., in an ingenious way that informs or entertains; instance of this. **2** a witty person. **3** often **wits** the ability to reason and act, esp. quickly: have one's wits about one; no time to collect one's wits. **4** often **wits** mental soundness: scared out of her wits; at one's wits' end. **witted** *adj* having wit of a kind or degree that is mentioned: half-witted; quick-witted. **witticism** *n* a witty remark. **wittingly** *adv* intentionally. **witty** *adj* full of wit. **wittily** *adv* **wittiness** *n* < Old English.

wit[2] *adv* **to wit** that is to say. < archaic *wit*

to know, from Old English *witan*.

witch (wɪtʃ) *n* **1** a person, esp. a woman, who practises witchcraft. **2** an ugly woman. **witchcraft** *n* (the exercise of) magical power, esp. with the aid of evil spirits. **witch-doctor** *n* a person in a primitive tribe who seeks to cure sickness by magical power. **witch-hunt** *n* the seeking, discrediting, and harassing of individuals with dissenting or unpopular views. < Old English *wicca*.

witch-hazel (ˈwɪtʃˌheɪzl̩) *n* **1** a shrub with small, attractive, yellow flowers; source of a soothing lotion made from its bark and leaves. **2** this lotion. < Old English *wice*.

with (wɪð) *prep* **1** by means of: open it with a coin. **2** against: arguing with you. **3** in the company of: He came with us. **4** on one's person: I haven't got any money with me. **5** marked by: a man with a quiet disposition. **6** used to show a cause or reason: shivering with cold. **7** in proportion or relation to: The length varies with the temperature. **8** in spite of: With all his faults, he's still a good friend. **9** working for: He's been with the company all his life. **10** in the care of: You can leave the baby with me. **11** at the same time as: get up with the lark. **12** in the same direction as: with the wind. **13** by the addition of: fill the bottle with water. **14** used to express agreement or support: We're with you all the way. **15** used to express understanding: Are you with me? **with it** (*informal*) **1** modern; fashionable. **2** understanding what is happening. < Old English.

withdraw (wɪðˈdrɔː) *vb* **withdrew; withdrawn; withdrawing 1** remove; take back. **2** move back; retreat. **3** remove (money) from a bank, etc. **4** retract (a statement). **5** remove oneself socially or emotionally. **withdrawal** *n* **1** withdrawing. **2** the cessation of taking drugs, esp. with unpleasant side-effects. **withdrawn** *adj* socially and emotionally detached. < Middle English *with* from + *draw*.

wither (ˈwɪðə) *vb* **1** make or become dry and shrivelled. **2** lose or cause to lose vitality and freshness. **3** overwhelm, esp. with a scornful look. < Middle English *widren*.

withers (ˈwɪðəz) *pl n* the ridge between the shoulder-blades of a horse, etc. < Old English *wither* against.

withhold (wɪðˈhəʊld) *vb* **withheld; withholding 1** hold or keep back. **2** refrain from allowing or giving: withhold permission. < Middle English *withholden*.

within (wɪˈðɪn) *prep* **1** inside; enclosed by. **2** not more than: within a week. **3** not beyond the range, etc., of: within sight. < Old English *withinnan*.

without (wɪˈðaʊt) *prep* **1** not having; not accompanied by. **2** not doing or feeling: speak without looking at one's notes.
• *adv* **1** with something lacking: manage without. **2** (*old-fashioned*) outside. < Old English *witbūtan*.

withstand (wɪðˈstænd) *vb* **withstood; withstanding** resist or endure successfully. < Old English *withstandan*.

witness (ˈwɪtnɪs) *n* **1** a person who sees or hears something. **2** a person who gives evidence in a law-court. **3** a person asked to be present at a particular event in order to testify to its occurrence, as by signing his or her name. **4** evidence; sign or testimony.
• *vb* **1** be a witness at or of. **2** sign (a document) as a witness. **witness-box** *n* an enclosure in which a witness gives evidence in a law-court. < Old English *witnes*.

wizard (ˈwɪzəd) *n* **1** a magician; male witch. **2** (*informal*) a person who is very skilled in a field that is mentioned: an electronics wizard.
• *adj* (*old-fashioned informal*) excellent. **wizardry** *n* < Middle English *wysard*.

wizened (ˈwɪzənd) *adj* wrinkled and shrivelled, esp. with age. < Old English *wisnian* to make or become wizened.

wobble (ˈwɒbl̩) *vb* **1** rock from side to side; move unsteadily. **2** (of the voice) tremble.
• *n* a wobbling movement or sound. **wobbly** *adj* < probably Low German *wabbeln*.

wodge (wɒdʒ) *n* a chunk or lump. < alteration of wedge.

woe (wəʊ) *n* **1** sorrow or suffering. **2** misfortune.
• *interj* an expression of sorrow, suffering, regret, etc. **woebegone** *adj* looking sad. **woeful** *adj* **1** marked by or expressing sorrow. **2** deplorable. **woefully** *adv* < Old English *wā*.

wok (wɒk) *n* a large, bowl-shaped Chinese cooking utensil. < Cantonese.

woke (waʊk) SEE **WAKE**[1]. **woken** SEE **WAKE**[1].

wold (wəʊld) *n* an area of esp. high open country. < Old English *weald* forest.

wolf (wʊlf) *n, pl* **wolves 1** a large, flesh-eating, wild dog that often hunts in a pack. **2** a fierce or greedy person.
• *vb* eat (food) greedily. < Old English *wulf*.

woman (ˈwʊmən) *n, pl* **women 1** an adult female human being. **2** women in general. **3** (*informal*) a charwoman. **womanhood** *n* **1** the state of being a woman. **2** womanly qualities. **womanish** *adj* not suitable for a man; effeminate. **womanize** *vb* seek the company of women, esp. for sexual purposes. **womanizer** *n* **womanly** *adj* having qualities that are associated with being a woman. **womanliness** *n* **women's liberation** a movement directed towards achieving rights and opportunities for women equal to those of men. < Old English *wīfman*. SEE PANEL. SEE PANELS AT **LADY; MONGOOSE.**

womb (wu:m) *n* the hollow, muscular organ of female mammals in which a foetus develops; uterus. < Old English *wamb*.

won (wʌn) SEE **WIN.**

wonder (ˈwʌndə) *n* **1** the feeling of surprise, amazement, and sometimes awe, at something strange, miraculous, etc. **2** something causing such a feeling; marvel.
• *vb* **1** feel wonder or surprise. **2** be curious about; desire to know: I wonder if I should have told him. **do** or **work wonders** have an extraordinarily successful effect. **no wonder** not surprising: It's no wonder you're feeling ill—you've eaten ten bars of chocolate! **wonderful** *adj* causing a feeling of wonder; extremely good. **wonderfully** *adv* **wonderland** *n* a place full of wonderful things. **wonderment** *n* a feeling of wonder. < Old English *wundor*.

wonky (ˈwɒŋkɪ) *adj* (*informal*) shaky; liable to break down. < ultimately Old English *wancol*.

woman and **lady**

Both woman and lady have their roots in Old English. Woman derives ultimately from *wīfman*, a compound of *wīf* meaning 'adult female' and *man* 'a human being'. This in time became *wimman* which in turn gradually became woman, although the initial vowel sound of the earlier form was retained. The change from *wīfman* also left *wīf* free to become wife as it is used today.

Lady, on the other hand, comes from *hlǣfdīge*, from *hlāf* meaning 'bread' and *dǣge* 'kneader'. 'Bread-kneader' was the title used for the female head of the household. Unlike woman the term lady has always carried a sense of rank. (See also panel at **lady.**)

wont (wəʊnt) *adj* accustomed (to do something).
• *n* a usual practice. < Old English *wunian* to be accustomed to.

woo (wu:) *vb* **1** try to win the affection and commitment in marriage of (a woman). **2** seek after, esp. zealously. **wooer** *n* < Old English *wōgian*.

wood (wʊd) *n* **1** the hard, fibrous tissue of the stems and branches of trees and shrubs. **2** this used for fuel, building, etc. **3** also **woods** an area of land covered with trees and undergrowth, usually smaller than a forest. **4** a golf-club with a wooden head. **not see the wood for the trees** be so preoccupied with details that one is unable to see a general view. **out of the wood** escaped from difficulties or dangers. **woodcut** *n* a block of wood engraved with a design; print made from this. **wooded** *adj* covered with trees. **wooden** *adj* **1** made of wood. **2** awkward and stiff. **woodenly** *adv* **wooden spoon** a booby prize. **woodland** *n* land covered with trees and shrubs. **woodpecker** *n* a bird with bright, multicoloured plumage and a strong bill that taps through bark to find insects. **woodwind** *n* wind orchestral instruments that were originally made of wood but now are often made of metal, such as the oboe and flute. **woodwork** *n* **1** the craft of making things from wood. **2** things made from wood, such as the doors and window-frames in a house. **woodworm** *n* the larva of a kind of beetle that bores in dead wood; condition caused by this. **woody** *adj* **1** of or like wood. **2** covered with woods. < Old English *widu*.

woof[1] (wu:f) *n* weft. < alteration of Old English *ōwef*.

woof[2] (wʊf) *vb, n* (make) the low, gruff barking sound of a dog. **woofer** *n* a loudspeaker for reproducing low-frequency sounds. < like the sound. SEE PANEL.

wool (wʊl) *n* **1** the fine, soft, curly hair from the fleeces of sheep, etc. **2** yarn spun from this; garment or fabric made from such yarn. **3** a fibrous mass. **woollen** *adj* made of wool; concerned with the production, sale, etc., of wool. **woollens** *pl n* woollen garments. < Old English *wull*.

woolly (ˈwʊlɪ) *adj* **1** of or like wool; covered with wool. **2** vague: woolly thinking.
• *n* (*informal*) a woollen jumper or cardigan. **woolliness** *n*

word (wɜ:d) *n* **1** a unit of speech sounds

or letters that conveys meaning; one of the basic elements of language. **2** something that is expressed; remark or short talk: Can I have a word with you? **3** information or news; message: He sent word he would be late. **4** an order or command. **5** a promise or assurance: I give you my word. **6** *pl* a quarrel: have words with someone.

• *vb* express in words. **wording** *n* the manner of expression in words. **wordless** *adj* silent. **word-perfect** *adj* memorized perfectly. **word processor** a computerized typewriter and visual display unit that stores and organizes words in the required way, used esp. in business to produce letters, reports, etc. **wordy** *adj* having too many words. **wordily** *adv* **wordiness** *n* < Old English. SEE PANEL.

wore (wɔː) SEE **WEAR.**

work (wɜːk) *n* **1** activity performed by effort; such effort. **2** an activity that is one's usual job; employment. **3** something produced by work; materials needed in this: needlework. **4** an artistic composition. **5** *pl* a place where an industrial activity is undertaken; factory. **6** *pl* the interior, operative parts of a machine.

• *vb* **1** perform an activity; exert effort in this. **2** be employed. **3** function or operate or cause to function or operate: The radio doesn't work. **4** bring into a certain condition: He worked his hands free. **5** produce the desired effect: I hope your idea will work! **6** move or cause to move slowly, with effort. **7** finance with one's labour: work one's way through college. **8** undertake a task in (an area); cover. **9** cause to labour or toil: He works his staff hard. **10** cultivate (land). **11** shape or manipulate; fashion. **workable** *adj* able to be worked; practicable. **workaday** *adj* everyday; ordinary. **workaholic** *n* (*informal*) a person addicted to working. **work-basket** *n* a basket for sewing materials and implements. **worker** *n* **1** a person who works: clerical workers. **2** a sterile female bee, etc. **work-force** *n* the total number of workers in a factory, etc., or available for work in a country. **workman** *n, pl* **workmen** a manual worker. **workmanlike** *adj* characteristic or worthy of a good workman; hard-working or well-made. **workmanship** *n* **1** the skill of a workman. **2** the quality of a product. **work of art** a fine picture, sculpture, etc. **work-sheet** *n* a piece of paper on which work is recorded. **workshop** *n* **1** a room or building in

woof, woof!

Presumably, dogs all over the world produce fairly similar sounds. However, the words used in different languages to report these sounds have rather less in common. For example, in English dogs go woof, woof!, whereas in French the bark is rendered as oua, oua! (pronounced 'waa waa'). The German equivalent, wau wau! ('wow wow'), is similar to the French, although there is a variant form wuff wuff!

There will obviously be some similarity amongst a group of words that imitate one of nature's sounds, but they will never be identical as each word has developed in a particular sound system and no two systems are the same.

in a word

Word features in a number of idiomatic expressions, including:

by word of mouth in spoken, not written words.
eat one's words to have to admit that what one said was wrong.
from the word go from the very beginning: The whole thing was doomed from the word go.
have a word with someone to speak to someone, for example in order to give advice or make an enquiry: 'Can I have a word with you a moment? It's about Patrick.'
have words (with someone) to reprimand (someone); quarrel (with someone): Poor David looks upset. I think the boss has been having words with him again.
in a word very briefly.
not in so many words not explicitly; often used as an indirect way of saying no: 'But did they actually invite you to the party?'—'Well, no, not in so many words.'
word for word in the same words; exactly. **word-for-word** *adj*
words fail me I cannot express how I feel; I'm flabbergasted; used especially when one is overcome by surprise, embarrassment, etc.

which manual or manufacturing work is performed. **2** a type of informal class for a small group of people: a drama workshop. **workshy** *adj* disinclined to work. < Old English *weorc*. SEE PANEL.

working (ˈwɜːkɪŋ) *adj* **1** operating; performing. **2** spent at work: the working day. **3** sufficiently adequate to be useful or to allow work to be done: a working knowledge of Spanish. **4** provisional: a working hypothesis.

• *n* **1** a part of a mine or other excavation. **2** the operating of something; way something works. **working class** the class of people who work esp. in manual or industrial jobs and are paid wages. **working party** a committee appointed to investigate and report on a particular problem.

world (wɜːld) *n* **1** the earth, with all its inhabitants and countries. **2** the whole universe. **3** a planet or star, esp. one that has life on it. **4** the human race. **5** a division of the world or period in the world's history: the western world; the ancient world. **6** a particular group of people and their interests; particular area of interest: the literary world; the computer world. **7** a group of living beings: the insect world. **8** human society; fashionable society. **9** the affairs of material, secular existence as distinct from spiritual or religious existence: fighting against the world, the flesh, and the devil. **10** the environment of a person's life; sphere: the world of Charles Dickens; living in a world of misery and darkness. **11** a great amount: A holiday will do him a world of good.

• *adj* **1** of or relating to the whole world. **2** extending throughout the whole world: world-famous. **worldling** *n* a worldly person. **worldly** *adj* **1** of or concerned with material and secular not spiritual and religious matters. **2** devoted to pleasure-seeking and material gain. **worldliness** *n* **worldly-wise** *adj* having

the works

Work features in a number of idiomatic expressions, including:

give the works 1 to treat lavishly; provide with all one possibly can: We'll give the visitors the works: the usual trip round St Paul's Cathedral, the Tower, and so on, and an evening at the theatre. **2** to subject to intense punishment, abuse, etc.: And remember if you tell anyone, we'll give you the full works.

work in 1 to insert gradually. **2** to include, especially slyly: He always manages to work in an element of humour.

work off to get rid of by physical activity: He worked off his extra weight by playing tennis.

work on to use one's influence on: If you leave me to work on Madge, I think I can get her to change her mind.

work out 1 to calculate or be calculated. **2** to devise or plan. **3** to have a result that is mentioned: It all worked out well in the end.

work-out *n* a set of physical exercises.

work over 1 to consider in detail. **2** to give a systematic beating to.

work to rule to follow strictly the requirements of one's job, in order to reduce the rate of working, as a form of industrial protest.

work-to-rule *n*

work up to develop gradually; arouse or excite: work up an appetite.

in the world

World features in a number of idiomatic expressions, including:

it's a small world used when one meets someone whom one knows, completely unexpectedly, especially in an unfamiliar place: 'Harriet—what on earth are you doing here? I thought you were still in York!'—'Well, well, well, it's a small world, isn't it, Jane?'

out of this world wonderful; superb.

the best of both worlds all the benefits of two different ways of life, without their disadvantages.

think the world of to have a very high opinion of: You know I've always thought the world of you, Derek.

worlds apart very dissimilar or different: We're good friends although our political views are worlds apart.

a shrewd understanding of human affairs. **world war** a war engaged in by many major countries. **world-weary** *adj* bored with life. **world-wide** *adj* extending throughout the whole world. < Old English *weorold.* SEE PANEL.

worm (wɜːm) *n* **1** a small, elongated, soft-bodied, invertebrate animal. **2** a contemptible person. **3** *pl* a disease caused by parasitic worms in the intestines.

• *vb* **1** proceed in a slow, winding manner. **2** free from intestinal worms. **3** extract from someone in a devious manner. **worm-eaten** *adj* eaten into by worms; old and worn or decayed. < Old English *wyrm.*

wormwood (ˈwɜːmˌwʊd) *n* **1** an aromatic herb that yields a bitter, dark-green oil. **2** a bitter experience. < alteration of Old English *wermōd.*

worn (wɔːn) SEE **WEAR. worn-out** *adj* **1** worn or used until shabby or useless. **2** exhausted.

worry (ˈwʌrɪ) *vb* **worried; worrying** **1** make or be anxious or troubled. **2** disturb or bother. **3** tear or shake with the teeth.

• *n* **1** a state of worrying; anxiety. **2** something causing this. **worrisome** *adj* causing worry. **worry beads** a string of beads played with to relieve tension. < Old English *wyrgan* to strangle.

worse (wɜːs) *adj* SEE **BAD. 1** less good; of a more unpleasant, unfavourable, or evil kind. **2** in poorer health.

• *adv* in a worse manner.

• *n* something worse. **worsen** *vb* make or become worse. < Old English *wiersa.*

worship (ˈwɜːʃɪp) *n* **1** reverence or devotion to a deity; act of this. **2** adoration of a person or thing. **3** a title of respect for some officials such as mayors or magistrates: Your Worship.

• *vb* **worshipped; worshipping** **1** honour or give reverence to (a deity). **2** participate in an act or service of worship. **3** adore; idolize. **worshipper** *n* **worshipful** *adj* **1** marked by reverence or adoration. **2** a title of respect for certain people. < Old English *weorthscipe* worthiness.

worst (wɜːst) *adj* SEE **BAD.** least good; of the most unpleasant, unfavourable, or evil kind.

• *n* **1** the worst part or condition; person or thing that is worst. **2** the greatest harm.

• *adv* in the worst manner.

• *vb* defeat or overcome. **at worst** in the worst circumstances. **if the worst comes to the worst** if the worst happens. < Old English *wierresta.*

worsted (ˈwʊstɪd) *n* a type of woollen yarn used to make fine, smooth fabrics; such a fabric. < *Worstead,* Norfolk, England.

worth (wɜːθ) *prep* **1** having a value of; having property or wealth to the value of. **2** deserving of: The plan is worth considering.

• *n* **1** value; equivalent of something specified: The thieves stole £200 000 worth of jewellery. **2** merit. **worthless** *adj* **1** without value. **2** useless. **worthlessness** *n* **worthwhile** *adj* worth the time or effort taken. < Old English *weorth.*

worthy (ˈwɜːðɪ) *adj* **1** deserving: worthy of closer examination. **2** having worth or value. **3** honourable.

• *n* a worthy person. **worthily** *adv* **worthiness** *n*

would (wəd; *stressed* wʊd) *auxiliary vb* SEE **WILL**^{1}. **1** used in reported speech or writing: He said he would be here by 3 o'clock. **2** used to express a conditional statement, question, polite request, or suggestion: If we had more money, life would be easier; Would you like a cup of tea? **3** used to express a willingness or intention: If only he would listen! **4** used to describe past habits and characteristics: He would have a nap after lunch. **5** used to express a characteristic, annoying tendency: You would be the one to lose your gloves! **6 would rather** used to express a preference: I'd rather come later. **would-be** *adj* wanting, pretending, or intending to be: would-be leaders. < Old English *wolde.* SEE PANEL AT **SHOULD.**

wound^1 (wuːnd) *n* **1** an injury to the body in which the skin or other tissue is broken, torn, etc., esp. caused by a weapon. **2** hurt to a person's honour, feelings, etc.

• *vb* cause a wound to. < Old English *wund.*

wound^2 (waʊnd) SEE **WIND**^{2}.

wove (wəʊv) SEE **WEAVE. woven** SEE **WEAVE.**

wrack (ræk) *n* seaweed, etc., floating on the sea or thrown up on the shore. < Middle English *wrak* wreckage.

wraith (reɪθ) *n* the apparition of a person, seen esp. before his or her death. < origin uncertain.

wrangle (ˈræŋgl̩) *vb* argue or quarrel.

• *n* an argument or quarrel: a long and bitter, legal wrangle. < Middle English *wranglen.*

wrap (ræp) *vb* **wrapped; wrapping** **1** enclose (something) with paper, etc. **2** fold (a covering such as a scarf) round (a person or thing). **3** hide or envelop: a valley wrapped in mist.

• *n* a shawl, garment, etc., wrapped round a person. **under wraps** secret. **wrapper** *n* a cover of paper, etc., wrapped round something. **wrapping** *n* the material used to wrap something: tissue wrappings. **wrap up 1** protect oneself with warm clothes. **2** enclose in wrapping. **3** (*informal*) settle; conclude. **4** absorb: wrapped up in his own troubles. **5** (*slang*) be silent. < Middle English *wrappen.*

wrath (rɒθ) *n* **1** angry indignation. **2** divine punishment. **wrathful** *adj* **wrathfully** *adv* < Old English *wrāth.*

wreak (riːk) *vb* inflict (vengeance); cause (havoc). < Old English *wrecan.*

wreath (riːθ) *n* **1** a ring of flowers, leaves, etc., as a mark of honour or respect. **2** a coil-shaped form: wreaths of smoke. < Old English *writha.*

wreathe (riːð) *vb* **1** shape or twist into a wreath. **2** encircle or decorate with or as if with a wreath. **3** move in a coiling or twisting line. < SEE **WREATH.**

wreck (rɛk) *n* **1** a shipwreck. **2** wrecking or being wrecked; destruction or ruin. **3** the remains of something after it has been damaged. **4** a person in very poor health: a nervous wreck.
• *vb* **1** damage or become damaged severely. **2** cause to be shipwrecked. **wrecker** *n* **wreckage** *n* the remains of something after it has been wrecked. < Scandinavian.

wren (rɛn) *n* a small, brown bird with a short, cocked tail. < Old English *wrenna.*

wrench (rɛntʃ) *vb* **1** pull or twist sharply. **2** injure by a sharp pulling or twisting movement.
• *n* **1** a sharp pull or twist. **2** intense emotional pain, as at a parting. **3** a spanner, esp. one with adjustable jaws. < Old English *wrencan.*

wrest (rɛst) *vb* **1** pull away sharply, esp. with a twisting motion. **2** obtain with great effort. < Old English *wrǣstan.*

wrestle (ˈrɛsl̩) *vb* **1** engage an opponent in wrestling. **2** struggle to deal (with): wrestling with the controls.
• *n* the action of wrestling. **wrestling** *n* the sport of unarmed hand-to-hand combat in which two people try to throw and hold each other to the ground. < Old English *wræstlian.*

wretch (rɛtʃ) *n* **1** a very unfortunate or sad person. **2** a contemptible person. **wretched** *adj* **1** very sad. **2** inadequate; very bad. **3** causing annoyance; confounded. **wretchedly** *adv* **wretchedness** *n* < Old English *wrecca.*

wriggle (ˈrɪɡl̩) *vb* **1** move in short twists and turns. **2** remove oneself, esp. by subtle or clever means: wriggle out of an awkward situation.
• *n* a wriggling movement. < Middle English *wriggeln.*

wring (rɪŋ) *vb* **wrung; wringing** **1** squeeze, twist, etc., esp. so as to force out water; force out (water) in this way. **2** twist (clasped hands), as a sign of great distress, despair, etc. **3** shake (someone's hand) very strongly, as in greeting. **4** twist so as to break. **5** extort or obtain with force or great difficulty.
• *n* a wringing movement or action. **wringer** *n* a mangle. < Old English *wringan.*

wrinkle (ˈrɪŋkl̩) *n* a slight ridge or furrow in a smooth surface, esp. one produced by age.
• *vb* form wrinkles. < probably ultimately Old English *gewrinclian* to wind.

wrist (rɪst) *n* **1** the joint between the hand and the forearm. **2** the part of a garment covering this. **wrist-watch** *n* a watch worn round the wrist. < Old English.

writ (rɪt) *n* **1** a legal document ordering or forbidding something. **2** (*archaic*) writing: holy writ. < Old English.

write (raɪt) *vb* **wrote; written; writing** **1** form (letters or other symbols) on a surface, esp. with a pen or pencil. **2** spell (a word, etc.) in writing. **3** compose (a poem, etc.); be an author. **4** fill in (a cheque, etc.). **5** write the alphabet, words, etc.: to learn to write. **6** write a letter: Will you write to me? **7** display signs or evidence of: Guilt was written all over his face. **write down** express in written form. **write off** cancel; acknowledge the loss of. **write-off** *n* something written off or lost; something damaged beyond repair:

write

Compared with the number of vocabulary differences that exist between British and American English, the grammatical differences are relatively few. However, that they do exist is illustrated by write.

In American English I wrote the school and I wrote John are both perfectly acceptable. In other words, American usage of write no longer requires the preposition to before an indirect object.

The car was a complete write-off. **write out** express in a full, written form. **writer** *n* a person who writes as an occupation; person who writes in a way that is mentioned. **writer's cramp** painful, muscular spasms in the hand or fingers, caused by writing for too long. **write up** **1** write in a full or finished form: I'll write up the notes later. **2** write full entries in (a diary). **3** write an account of. **4** praise in writing. **write-up** *n* a written account; review. **writing** *n* **1** handwriting. **2** *pl* the written work. **3** the art, style, or occupation of writing. **writing-paper** *n* paper for writing letters on, esp. in ink. < Old English *wrītan* to scratch. SEE PANEL.

writhe (raɪð) *vb* **1** twist (the body or part of the body), as in pain. **2** move along with a twisting action. **3** suffer greatly. < Old English *wrīthan* to twist.

written (ˈrɪtn̩) SEE **WRITE.**

wrong (rɒŋ) *adj* **1** not true, correct, or proper; mistaken. **2** (of behaviour) morally bad: Stealing is wrong. **3** unsatisfactory; not operating normally: Something's wrong with the radio. **4** undesirable: on the wrong side of 40.
• *adv* in a wrong condition or way; incorrectly or improperly.
• *n* **1** something wrong, esp. an unjust or immoral action. **2** the state of being wrong: in the wrong.
•*vb* **1** do a wrong to. **2** misrepresent. **wrongly** *adv* **wrongness** *n* **get someone wrong** (*informal*) misunderstand. **wrongdoer** *n* a person who acts against laws or accepted morals. **wrongdoing** *n* **wrongful** *adj* unjust or harmful; unlawful. **wrongfully** *adv* < Old English *wrang* injustice.

wrote (rəʊt) SEE **WRITE.**

wrought (rɔːt) *adj* **1** (*chiefly old-fashioned*) worked; brought about. **2** formed or fashioned. **3** (of metals) shaped by hammering. **wrought iron** iron that contains very little carbon and can be beaten or rolled into the desired shape. < past participle of Old English *wyrcan* to work.

wrung (rʌŋ) SEE **WRING.**

wry (raɪ) *adj* **1** twisted; made by twisting the features. **2** (of humour) dry and ironic. **wryly** *adv* **wryness** *n* < Old English *wrigian* to turn.

X

xenophobia (ˌzɛnəˈfəʊbɪə) *n* hatred or fear of foreigners. < Greek *xenos* stranger + *-phobia,* from *phobos* fear.
Xerox (ˈzɛrɒks) *n* (*Trademark*) a photocopy made using a dry printing process.
• *vb* produce a Xerox in this way; photocopy. < Greek *xēros* dry.
Xmas (ˈɛksməs, ˈkrɪsməs) *n* (*informal*) Christmas. SEE PANEL.
X-ray (ˈɛksreɪ) *n* **1** electromagnetic radiation with a wavelength between that of ultraviolet and gamma radiation, able to penetrate solids. **2** an examination or photograph made by means of X-rays.
• *vb* examine, photograph, or treat with X-rays. < German *X-Strahlen,* coined by W.C. Röntgen, died 1923, German physicist.
xylophone (ˈzaɪləˌfəʊn) *n* a musical instrument consisting of a series of wooden bars graduated in length that are played with two sticks. < Greek *xylon* wood + *-phōnē* sound.

Xmas

We all know that Xmas means 'Christmas', but where does the X come from? The answer is the X was originally the Greek letter *chi,* written exactly after the manner of the Roman X but sounding like the Roman letters *kh.* X was thus the initial letter in the Greek spelling of Christ and was used as an abbreviation for the word.

Y

yacht (jɒt) *n* a small sailing-boat or powered vessel, esp. used for pleasure cruising or racing. **yachting** *n* pleasure cruising or racing in a yacht. **yachtsman** *n, pl* **yachtsmen** a person who owns or sails a yacht. < obsolete Dutch *jaght.*

yak (jæk) *n* a shaggy-haired, wild ox of central Asia. < Tibetan *gyak.*

yam (jæm) *n* a tropical climbing plant grown for its edible, starchy tubers; such a tuber; sweet potato. < Portuguese *inhame.*

yank (jæŋk) *vb* pull with a short, sharp movement; tug.
• *n* such a movement. < origin unknown.

yap (jæp) *vb* **yapped; yapping 1** make a sharp, shrill bark. **2** (*informal*) talk in an annoying way; jabber.
• *n* a sharp, shrill bark. < like the sound.

yard[1] (jɑːd) *n* **1** a unit of length equal to three feet (0.9144 metre). **2** a long beam on a mast to support and spread a sail. **yardage** *n* length measured in yards. **yard-arm** *n* either end of a yard supporting a sail. **yardstick** *n* **1** a graduated stick one yard long. **2** a standard of comparison. < Old English *gierd* rod, twig.

yard[2] *n* a piece of enclosed ground, esp. one next to or surrounding a building or used for a particular purpose that is mentioned: a builder's yard. < Old English *geard.*

yarn (jɑːn) *n* **1** a long, continuous, spun thread of wool, cotton, etc., prepared and used in making cloth or rope. **2** (*informal*) a tale, esp. one that is improbable, invented, or exaggerated. < Old English *gearn.*

yarrow (ˈjærəʊ) *n* a fragrant plant with feathery leaves and small, white flowers. < Old English *gearwe.*

yashmak (ˈjæʃmæk) *n* a veil covering all the face, except the eyes, worn by Muslim women. < Arabic.

yawn (jɔːn) *vb* **1** open the mouth wide and breathe in, as when tired or bored. **2** have a wide opening; gape. **3** express in a yawn.
• *n* **1** an act of yawning. **2** (*informal*) something boring. < Old English *ginian.*

yd(s) *abbrev* yard(s).

ye (jiː) SEE PANEL.

year (jɪə) *n* **1** the time taken by the earth to complete one revolution round the sun, about 365¼ days. **2** the period from 1 January to 31 December. **3** any period of twelve consecutive months. **4** a period of about a year during which a school, college, etc., is in session: the academic year. **5** a group of students in a school, college, etc., who are admitted and taught together: first-year students. **6** *pl* age; old age: He looks young for his years. **year-book** *n* a book published annually containing details of events, statistics, etc. **yearling** *n* an animal one year old. **yearly** *adj* **1** also *adv* (occurring once) every year. **2** calculated by the year. < Old English *gēar.*

yearn (jɜːn) *vb* be filled with a deep longing. < Old English *giernan.*

yeast (jiːst) *n* a fungus that ferments carbohydrates and is used in baking, brewing, etc. < Old English *giest.*

yell (jɛl) *vb* give a loud cry or shout.
• *n* a loud cry or shout. < Old English *giellan.*

yellow (ˈjɛləʊ) *adj* **1** of the colour of butter. **2** (*informal*) cowardly.
• *n* **1** a yellow colour. **2** something that is yellow; yellow material or clothes: dressed all in yellow.
• *vb* make or become yellow. **yellowness** *n* **yellow fever** an acute, tropical,

ye

A name used on a sign is sometimes given an air of antiquity by being preceded by the word ye, as in Ye Olde Teashoppe. The word is usually pronounced like the *ye* in yeast. Underlying this practice, however, is a misunderstanding.

In medieval texts, the was often represented by just two letters. This was possible on account of the use of the runic letter thorn (*þ*), which was the equivalent of today's *th.*

In later generations this unfamiliar character was often transcribed mistakenly as *y* on account of the similarity of form. Therefore when people say Ye Olde Teashoppe, they are strictly speaking perpetuating a centuries-old blunder.

infectious disease transmitted by a certain kind of mosquito. **yellow line** a yellow line painted along the edge of a road to show parking restrictions. **Yellow Pages** (*Trademark*) a directory of business addresses and telephone numbers listed alphabetically according to the type of business or service. < Old English *geolu*.

yelp (jɛlp) *n, vb* (give) a short, sharp cry or bark. < Old English *gielpan* to boast.

yen (jɛn) *n* a longing. < Cantonese *yǎn* craving, addiction.

yeoman (ˈjəʊmən) *n, pl* **yeomen** a farmer who cultivates his own land. **yeoman of the guard** a member of the ceremonial bodyguard of the English monarch. **yeoman service** long, faithful service. < perhaps Middle English *yong man* young man.

yes (jɛs) *adv* **1** used to show agreement, approval, affirmation, etc. **2** used to show one's attentiveness, presence, etc.: 'Waiter!'–'Yes, sir?'
• *n* the word or reply *yes*; affirmative. **yes-man** *n, pl* **yes-men** (*informal*) a person who always agrees with his superior; sycophant. < Old English *gēse*. SEE PANEL.

yesterday (ˈjɛstəˌdeɪ) *n* **1** the day before today. **2** recent time.
• *adv* on the day before today. < Old English *giestran* yesterday + *dæg* day.

yet (jɛt) *adv* **1** up to this or that moment; now; then: The play has not yet been performed in Britain. **2** in the future: We may yet win. **3** still; even: yet more difficult. **4** in addition: yet another warning. **5** nevertheless: young, yet mature.
• *conj* nevertheless. < Old English *gīet*.

yeti (ˈjɛtɪ) *n* the abominable snowman; large man-like creature believed to live high in the Himalayas. < Tibetan.

yew (juː) *n* an evergreen tree with dark-green, needle-like leaves and red, berry-like fruits; wood of this tree. < Old English *īw*.

yield (jiːld) *vb* **1** produce as fruit, results, etc. **2** surrender; give way or concede. **3** render what is appropriate or needed. **4** give way under pressure.
• *n* the amount yielded. < Old English *gieldan*.

yob (jɒb) *n* an aggressive, loutish youth. < back slang for *boy*.

yodel (ˈjəʊdl̩) *vb* **yodelled; yodelling** sing with sudden changes between the natural voice and a falsetto.
• *n* a yodelling cry or effect. **yodeller** *n* < German *jodeln*.

yoga (ˈjəʊgə) *n* **1** a Hindu philosophy designed to achieve spiritual union with the Supreme Being, freeing the self from body, mind, and will. **2** mental and physical exercises to reach tranquillity and insight. < Sanskrit: yoking.

yoghurt, yogurt (ˈjɒgət) *n* a semi-solid food prepared from milk fermented by certain bacteria, often with sweetening or flavouring added. < Turkish *yoğurt*.

yoke (jəʊk) *n* **1** a wooden frame fastened across the necks of two draught animals. **2** a frame fitted over a person's shoulders for carrying a bucket, etc., on each end. **3** an oppression or burden: the yoke of slavery.
• *vb* **1** harness (a draught animal) to (something) by means of a yoke. **2** unite. < Old English *geoc*.

yokel (ˈjəʊkl̩) *n* a simple or gullible country person. < perhaps English dialect *yokel* green woodpecker.

yolk (jəʊk) *n* the round, yellow part of an egg, surrounded by the white. < Old English *geolu* yellow.

yonder (ˈjɒndə) *determiner, adv* situated at a distance; over there. < Old English *geond*.

you (jʊ; *stressed* juː) *pron* **1** the person or people being addressed. **2** referring to people generally; one.
• *n* something suitable for you: That suit really isn't you. < Old English *ēow*. SEE PANEL.

young (jʌŋ) *adj* **1** being in an early period

yes-men

A subordinate who always agrees with his superior, no matter whether he really agrees or not, is informally referred to as a yes-man. This phrase first appeared in print in 1913 in a cartoon by the American sports cartoonist Thomas Aloysius Dorgan, 1877–1929, better known as TAD. The yes-men depicted in the cartoon are assistants to a newspaper editor and are shown to be busy sycophantically admiring the freshly printed sheets of a first edition.

To T.A. Dorgan we also owe the expression hot dog.

of life or growth. **2** having characteristics such as liveliness associated with young people. **3** not advanced in time: The night is young.
• *n* **1** young people. **2** young animals. **with young** (of animals) pregnant. **youngster** *n* a young person; child. < Old English *geong.* SEE PANEL.

your (jə; *stressed* jɔː, jʊə) *determiner* **1** of or belonging to you. **2** used in some titles: Your Majesty. **yours** *possessive pron* **1** (the one or ones) belonging to or associated with you. **2** used in conventional phrases at the ending of letters: Yours sincerely. **yourself** *pron, pl* **yourselves** the form of *you* used reflexively and for emphasis. **be yourself** behave in a normal way. **by yourself 1** without help. **2** alone. < Old English *ēower.* SEE PANEL.

youth (juːθ) *n* **1** the time between childhood and adulthood; adolescence. **2** a young man; young people. **3** the state of being young. **youthful** *adj* **1** of or characteristic of young people: youthful enthusiasm. **2** young; looking young. **youthfully** *adv* **youthfulness** *n* **youth hostel** a lodging place providing cheap accommodation, esp. for young people and hikers. < Old English *geogoth.*

yo-yo (ˈjəʊjəʊ) *n, pl* **yo-yos** a toy consisting of a reel that may be spun up and down on a string. < *Yo-yo,*

you

Although the personal pronoun system we use today retains a certain complexity, it is nevertheless considerably simpler than its Old English prototype. For example, the Old English second person pronoun grouping had no fewer than 18 different forms. The number was high because a different set was used depending upon whether the speaker was referring to one person (*þū*), two people (*git*), or more than two people (gē).

Also, each set contained four case distinctions in the manner of the present-day I, me, my, me. All that survives of this grouping today is the single form you. This derives from ēow, the accusative and dative form of *gē*.

How young are you?

One of the interesting things about pairs of antonyms like young and old, big and small, and short and tall is that one member of the pair tends to have a neutral or unmarked function. The unmarked term is the one that is always used in such questions as, 'How *old* is he?' Even when referring to a new baby we would never say, 'How *young* is he?' because young is the marked member of the pair. Like old, big and tall are also unmarked. We would think it very strange indeed if someone asked, 'How small is your new house?' or 'How short is your husband?'

yours

Yours faithfully, yours sincerely, and yours truly are conventional ways of ending a letter before signing it. Usage varies, but generally Yours faithfully is used in formal letters that begin Dear Sir(s) or Dear Madam. Yours sincerely is used in formal letters that begin with a person's surname: Dear Mr Duckworth. Yours truly is occasionally used as an alternative.

yule

Nowadays it is a pre-Christmas custom to bring an evergreen tree into the house as a centre-piece of the Christmas decorations. In earlier days the equivalent custom was to bring home on Christmas Eve a great log known as a yule log, which was laid across the hearth and burnt during the course of the Christmas festivities.

The word yule derives from the Old English *geōl.* This was a midwinter feast lasting 12 days which was held (after the winter solstice) in celebration of the nights becoming shorter.

originally a trademark.
yucca (ˈjʌkə) *n* a type of plant with stiff, sword-shaped leaves and a cluster of white flowers. < Spanish *yuca*.

yule (juːl) *n* (*chiefly archaic*) Christmas. **yule log** a large log formerly laid as the foundation of a fire on Christmas Eve. < Old English *geōl*. SEE PANEL.

Z

zany (ˈzeɪnɪ) *adj* ridiculous in a fantastic or crazy way. SEE PANEL.

zeal (ziːl) *n* great eagerness or enthusiasm. **zealot** *n* a zealous person; fanatic. **zealous** *adj* full of zeal. **zealously** *adv* SEE PANEL.

zebra (ˈzɛbrə, ˈziːbrə) *n* an African wild animal of the horse family with black and white stripes over part or all of the body. **zebra crossing** a pedestrian crossing where the road is marked with alternate black and white stripes. < Spanish *cebra*.

zenith (ˈzɛnɪθ) *n* **1** the point in the sky directly above an observer. **2** the highest point. < ultimately Arabic *samt arrās* path above the head.

zero (ˈzɪərəʊ) *n, pl* **zeros 1** the symbol 0; nought. **2** nothing; lowest point. **3** the point marked 0 on a graduated scale, esp. the point from which measurements begin.
• *vb* adjust (an instrument, etc.) to zero. **zero hour** the time set for the beginning of an attack, etc.; critical moment. **zero in on 1** adjust (a weapon) to concentrate its firing on (a target): zero in on the enemy's headquarters. **2** concentrate one's efforts or attention on. **zero-rated** *adj* (of goods or services) on which the buyer pays no value-added tax. < ultimately Arabic *ṣifr* empty. SEE PANEL AT **ALGEBRA**.

zest (zɛst) *n* **1** keen enjoyment. **2** a stimulating or exciting quality. **3** the peel or skin of an orange or lemon, used as a flavouring. **zestful** *adj* **zestfully** *adv* < French *zeste* orange peel.

zigzag (ˈzɪgzæg) *n* a course or pattern that is marked by sharp turns in alternate directions.
• *adj, adv* forming a zigzag.
• *vb* **zigzagged; zigzagging** move in a zigzag course. < French.

zinc (zɪŋk) *n* a bluish-white metal, used in alloys. < German *Zink*.

zip (zɪp) *n* **1** also **zip-fastener** a fastening device consisting of two strips of material with projections that interlock by means of a sliding tab. **2** a short, sharp, zipping sound. **3** (*informal*) liveliness; vigour.
• *vb* **zipped; zipping 1** also **zip up** fasten by means of a zip. **2** move with a zip; move at a great speed. **zippy** *adj* (*informal*) lively; vigorous. < like the sound.

zither (ˈzɪðə) *n* a musical instrument having 30–40 strings stretched over a shallow, resonating box, played by plucking. < ultimately Greek *kithara*.

zodiac (ˈzəʊdɪæk) *n* **1** a zone in the sky containing the paths of the sun, moon, and most of the major planets, divided into twelve equal parts: the signs of the zodiac. **2** a diagram of these signs. **zodiacal** *adj* < ultimately Greek *zōion* animal.

zealot

Religious fanatics are sometimes referred to somewhat disparagingly as zealots. The original zealots were members of an extreme Jewish sect founded in the early years of the 1st century AD. They were bitterly opposed to all aspects of Roman rule in Palestine and were a major force in the Jewish revolt against Rome in 66 AD. After being besieged at Masada for almost two years and on the eve of being overrun, the Zealots ended their stand by committing mass suicide.

zany

Something that is humorous in an amusingly ridiculous or fantastic way may be referred to as zany. This word entered the language in the 16th century from the Italian *zanni,* a buffoom in the 'commedia dell'arte' (comedy of art) whose role was to mimic one of the other performers. The name given to the buffoon figure was also the nickname in Venetian and Lombardic dialect for *Giovanni* or 'John', which was one of the traditional names for a clown.

The commedia dell'arte also gave rise to the figures of Harlequin and Pantaloon who survive in pantomime to this day.

zombie (ˈzɒmbɪ) *n* **1** (in voodoo) a corpse that has been brought back to life by a supernatural spirit. **2** (*informal*) a person who seems lifeless, without an active mind or will. < of African origin.

zone (zəʊn) *n* an area marked by a particular feature or used for a particular purpose: a smokeless zone.
● *vb* **1** arrange or divide into zones. **2** assign to a particular zone. **zonal** *adj* < ultimately Greek *zōnē*.

zoo (zuː) *n, pl* **zoos** a place where animals are kept, esp. for study and exhibition to the public. **zoology** *n* the scientific study of animals. **zoological** *adj* **zoologist** *n* **zoological gardens** a zoo. < short for *zoological gardens*, ultimately from Greek *zōion* animal.

zoom (zuːm) *vb* **1** move quickly, esp. with a humming or buzzing sound. **2** rise quickly. **3** change the size of an image by adjusting a zoom lens. **zoom lens** a lens system in which the size of the image can be changed quickly, while keeping the subject in focus. < like the sound.